# Jazz Records

## 1897-1942

4th Revised and Enlarged Edition

### VOLUME 2
### Abe Lyman to Bob Zurke

Index of Song Titles ∗ Index of Artists

## Brian Rust

ARLINGTON HOUSE·PUBLISHERS
NEW ROCHELLE, NEW YORK

Manufactured in the United States of America
P 10 9 8 7 6 5 4 3 2 1

Library of Congress Cataloging in Publication Data

Rust, Brian A    L    1922–
    Jazz records, 1897–1942.

    Includes indexes.
    1. Jazz music—Discography.    I. Title.
ML156.4.J3R9   1978       016.7899'12       78–1693
ISBN 0–87000–404–2

ABE LYMAN AND HIS CALIFORNIA ORCHESTRA : Abe Lyman dir. Ered Ferguson-Horace Smith-t/
Orlando "Slim" Martin-Warren Smith-tb/Al Baker-Jim Welton-cl-as/Horace "Zip" Keyes-
cl-ts/Harry Podalsky-Dave Herman-vn/Ted Dale-p-a/Teddy Powell-bj-g/Ed Landry-sb/
Gary Gillis-d.                      New York, May 12, 1933.

| B-13327-A | Weary Blues | Br 6637 |
|---|---|---|
| B-13328-A | The New St. Louis Blues | - |

New York, January 24, 1934.

| B-14683-A | Jimmy Had A Nickel - v3 | Br 6756, 01726 |
|---|---|---|

## AL LYNCH AND HIS ORCHESTRA

Al Lynch-v dir. 2t/tb/2as/ts/vn/p/bj-g/bb/d.
New York, July 6, 1927.

| 7380- | Sing Me A Baby Song - vAL | Ban 6025, Dom 3996, Re 8355 |
|---|---|---|
| 7381-3 | What Do We Do On A Dew-Dew-Dewy Day ? | Ban 6026, Dom 3992, 21303, |
| | - vAL&ch | Re 8352, Apex 8642, LS 24111, |
| | | Mic 22188, St 10271, EBW 4720 |
| 7382-1-3 | You Don't Like It - Not Much - vAL | Ban 6027, Dom 3997, 21316, |

NOTE:- Banners as SHERIDAN ENTERTAINERS; Domino   PA 36658, Per 14839, P-325,
and Regal as LUCKY TEN ENTERTAINERS; Pathe       Re 8354, Apex 8645, LS 24121,
Actuelle 36658 and Perfect 14839 as NEWPORT      Mic 22198, St 10271, Imp 1863
DANCE ORCHESTRA; Perfect P-325 as RAYNER'S DANCE ORCHESTRA; Edison Bell Winner 4720
as GAIETY DANCE ORCHESTRA; Imperial 1863 as MARKEL'S SOCIETY FAVOURITES.

New York, September 30, 1927.

| 7536- | Washington And Lee Swing - v3 | Ban 6102, Bwy 1105, Or 1046 |
|---|---|---|

NOTE:- Oriole as DIXIE JAZZ BAND.

New York, March 7, 1928.

| 7828-3 | Put Your Loving Arms Around Me - vAL | Ban 7109, Chg 616 |
|---|---|---|

Other records by this band may be equally interesting as "hot" dance music. (See THE
AMERICAN DANCE BAND DISCOGRAPHY, 1917-1942).

## GLEN LYTE'S ORCHESTRA

The following title is known to feature good solos; there may be others like it.

2t/tb/as-f/as/ts/p/g/bb/d.          Grafton, Wis., c. May, 1931.

| L-930-5 | When I Take My Sugar To Tea - v2 | Bwy 1459, EBW 5319 |
|---|---|---|

NOTE:- Edison Bell Winner 5319 as PARAMOUNT RHYTHM BOYS.

## JIMMY LYTELL

Clarinet solos, acc. by Frank Signorelli-p/Eddie Lang-bj-g.
New York, c. November 20, 1926.

| 107225 | Old Folks Shuffle | PA 36568, Per 14749 |
|---|---|---|
| 107226 | Red House Blues | - - |

C added; ? Dick McDonough-bj-g replaces Lang.
New York, c. January 10, 1927.

| 107334-C | Messin' Around | PA 36584, Per 14765 |
|---|---|---|
| 107335-B | Coney Island Washboard | - - |

C omitted.                          New York, c. March 13, 1927.

| 107420-C | Alexander's Ragtime Band | PA 36607, Per 14788 |
|---|---|---|
| 107421-A | Pardon The Glove | - - |

New York, June, 1927.

| 107613-1 | Zulu Wail | PA 36665, 11488, Per 14846 |
|---|---|---|
| 107614-1 | Fakir's Rhythm | - - - |

Clarinet solos, acc. by Frank Signorelli-p/? Dick McDonough-bj-g.
                                    New York, c. October 24, 1927.

107861-1   Headin' For Harlem                    PA 36717, 11534, Per 14898
107862-2   Sugar                                  -          -        -

                                    New York, c. December, 1927.

           Why Be Blue ?                          PA 36741, Per 14922
           Stockholm Stomp                         -          -

Harry Reser-bj replaces previous bj-g.  New York, February, 1928.

108056     Missouri Squabble                      PA 36775, 11557, Per 14956
108057     Davenport Blues                         -          -        -

                                    New York, June, 1928.

108221     Sweet Emmalina (Emmaline*)             PA 36824, 11567*, Per 15005
108222     Yellow Dog Blues                        -          -        -

NOTE:- At least three takes of each of matrices 108056 and 108057 are known to have
   been issued on the labels shown, and it is likely that this is true of some of the
   others.

## HARRY MACDONALD'S ORCHESTRA

Harold Macdonald-d dir. 2c/tb/2cl-ss-as/cl-ss-ts/vn/p/bj/bb/Benny Davis-v.
                                    New York, August 27, 1926.

36136-4   Who Could Be More Wonderful Than You ?   Vic 20149, HMV EA-144
             - vBD
36137-2   My Pal Jerry                                  -            -

## BABY MACK

Vocal, acc. by Louis Armstrong-c/Richard M. Jones-p.
                                    Chicago, February 23, 1926.

9512-A   You've Got To Go Home On Time            OK 8313
9513-A   What Kind O' Man Is You ?                 -

See also Sam Robinson.

## BILLY AND MARY MACK

Vocal duets, acc. by Punch Miller-c/Edgar Brown-p.
                                    New Orleans, January 22, 1925.

8892-A   Black But Sweet, Oh God !                OK 8195
8897-B   My Heart-Breakin' Gal
NOTE:- Matrix 8893 is by John Tobin's Midnight Serenaders; 8895/6 are by Anthony
Parenti and his Famous Melody Boys, both q.v.; 8894 is untraced.

Acc. by Clarence Williams' Trio : Tb/Clarence Williams-p/? Buddy Christian-bj; Mary
Mack only*.                         New York, c. January 11, 1926.

73906-B  *Oh ! Me Oh ! My Blues                   OK 8339
73907-A   You've Got To Quit Your Low Down Ways   OK 8274
73908-B   Fetch It When You Come                   -
73909-B  *How Could My Good Man Turn His Back On  OK 8296
             Me Now ?
73911-B   You Don't Want Much                      -
NOTE:- Matrix 73910 is untraced.

MARY AND MACK : Vocal duets acc. by ? Albert Ammons-p.
                                    Chicago, December 22, 1936.

01898-1   You Gotta Quit Your Low Down Ways       BB B-6894
01899-1   Black                                   BB B-7908

MARY AND MACK : Vocal duets, acc. by p/sb.
                              Chicago, January 13, 1937.

C-1741-1-2  You Know You Wasn't Raised That Way    Voc rejected
C-1742-1-2  You Don't Want Much                      -

MARY MACK : Vocal, acc. by the State Street Swingers : Probably :- Herb Morand-t/
   Arnett Nelson-cl/"Black Bob"-p/sb/d.    Chicago, January 26, 1937.

C-1770-1-2  You Drink Too Much                     Voc 03462
C-1771-1  Don't Tear My Clothes No. 2                -      Jay 12
   NOTE:- Jay 12 as VICTORIA SPIVEY WITH LEE COLLINS AND THE STATE STREET SWINGERS.

   Acc. by ? Aletha Dickerson-p/? Big Bill Broonzy-g/sb.
                              Aurora, Ill., May 4, 1937.

07622-1  Stingaree Man                             BB B-8131
07623-1  Every Night                               BB B-7097
07624-1  Get Going                                   -
07625-1  I Vouch For My Man                         BB B-8131

## CHARLES E.  MACK

This member of the "Two Black Crows" black-face cross-talk team of Moran and Mack
   recorded a monologue accompanied by C. Luckeyth "Lucky" Roberts-p.
                              New York, December 22, 1927.

98411-3  Our Child                                 Col 50061-D, 02619

## IDA MAY MACK

Vocal, acc. by K. D. Johnson-p.        Memphis, August 29, 1928.

45438-1  Wrong Doin' Daddy                         Vic V-38532
45439-1-2  Sunday Mornin' Blues                    Rejected
45442-2  Elm Street Blues                          Vic V-38030
45443-1-2  Country Spaces                          Rejected

                              Memphis, August 30, 1928.

45446-1  Mr. Moore Blues                           Vic 21690
45447-1  When You Lose Your Daddy                    -
45450-2  Mr. Forty-Nine Blues                      Vic V-38532
45451-1  Goodbye Rider                             Vic V-38030

NOTE:- Intervening matrices in the above sessions are by Bessie Tucker, q.v.

## MARY  MACK

See Billy and Mary Mack.

## MACK  AND MITCHELL

See Billie Wilson, Silvertone 3544.

## MADAME TUSSAUD'S DANCE ORCHESTRA

Stanley Barnett-ts dir. Billy Farrell-t/Abe Walters-tb/Harry Constable-cl-as/Laurie
   Bookin-as/Jack Dent-p/Albert Harris g/Al Foreman-sb/Claude Dawson-d/Phyllis Robins-
   v.                              London, June 22, 1933.

EB-18-    Rocking In Rhythm                        EBW 5572, Astra D-111, Cam 2003,
   NOTE:- Super as GREAT DANCE ORCHESTRA.         Imp 155193, Oly D-2228,SB 25359,
                                                  Sondor P-248, Super B-7035,
                                                  Triumph 583

Stanley Barnett-ts dir. Billy Farrell-t/Abe Walters-tb/Harry Constable-cl-as/Laurie
  Bookin-as/Jack Dent-p/Albert Harris-g/Al Foreman-sb/Claude Dawson-d/Phyllis Robins-
  v.                                     London, July 14, 1933.

| | | |
|---|---|---|
| EB-1021-1-2 | Jazz Cocktail | EBW rejected |
| EB-1022-1-2 | My Bluebird's Singing The Blues - vPR | - |

London, July 21, 1933.

| | | |
|---|---|---|
| EB-1021-3 | Jazz Cocktail | EBW 5580, Astra D-111, Imp 155194, |
| | NOTE:- Sondor as ORCHESTRE DE DANSE. | SB 25371, Sondor P-249,Triumph 583 |

London, July 25, 1933.

| | | |
|---|---|---|
| EB-1022-3 | My Bluebird's Singing The Blues - vPR | EBW 5580, Sondor P-250 |

London, August 8, 1933.

| | | |
|---|---|---|
| EB-1047-2 | Stevedore Stomp | EBW 5590, Astra D-106, Imp 155194, Sondor P-250, Triumph 571 |
| EB-1048-2 | Roll Up The Carpet - v | EBW 5590 |

London, September 19, 1933.

| | | |
|---|---|---|
| EB-1059-2 | Lightning | EBW 5597 |

London, October 12, 1933.

| | | |
|---|---|---|
| EB-1073-2 | Wild Goose Chase | EBW 5609, Astra D-106, Imp 155193, SB 25359, Super B-7035,Triumph 571 |
| EB-1074-2 | Sophisticated Lady - v | EBW 5609 |

London, November 17, 1933.

| | | |
|---|---|---|
| EB-1088- | Echoes Of The Jungle | EBW 5617, Disclair K-1769 |
| EB-1089- | Old Man Blues - v | -       - |

NOTE:- Astra, Imperial, Silver Bell and Triumph issues as simply DANSORKEST, TANZ-
  ORCHESTER or DANCE ORCHESTRA. This band made other Edison Bell Winner records
  during the latter part of 1933 and early in 1934, some of which may feature short
  solos by the above musicians (whose performances of Duke Ellington and other
  "advanced" scores are truly remarkable, considering their location and date), but
  it is not felt that they call for detailed listing here.

## SHERRY MAGEE AND HIS DIXIELANDERS

Herman Drewes-t/William Drewes-tb/Gus Fetterer-cl/Sherry Magee-cl-as/Henry Schnier-ts
/Harry Ford-p/Arnold Fishkind-sb/Fred J. Bauer-d.
                                 New York, November 27, 1939.

| | | |
|---|---|---|
| 25690-1 | Shake It And Break It | Voc 5281, Decatur 511 |
| 25691-1 | Satanic Blues | Voc/OK 5436, Decatur 518 |
| 25692-1 | Tin Roof Blues | Voc 5281, Decatur 511 |
| 25693-1 | Bluin' The Blues | Voc/OK 5436, Decatur 518 |

## MAGEE STRING BAND

Esau McGhee or Magee-vn/Alcide "Slow Drag" Pavageau-sb, others unknown.
                             New Orleans, December 15, 1928.

| | | |
|---|---|---|
| 147650-1 | Mister Johnson, Turn Me Loose | Col rejected |
| 147651-1 | Mustard And Onions | - |

## IVOR MAIRANTS

See the Geraldo Swing Septet, and Albert Harris.

Pseudonym for the following items listed in this book :-

Banner 0596/Cameo 0196/Jewel 5852/Oriole 1852  I've Seen My Baby (Adrian Schubert and
    his Salon Orchestra)
Banner 0851/Cameo 0451/Jewel 6098/Oriole 2098/Regal 10157/Romeo 1465  You're Simply
    Delish (Jack Teagarden and his Orchestra)
Broadway/Puritan 11282  Bebe (Original Indiana Five)
Cameo 0139  I'm Following You (Adrian Schubert and his Salon Orchestra)
Embassy E-100  Never Swat A Fly (All Star Californians)
        E-101  I'm Proud Of You (All Star Californians)
Madison 6036  That Wicked Stomp (Grey Gull Studio Band)
Oriole 928  Magnolia (California Ramblers)
       933  Zulu Wail (California Ramblers)
       980  Both sides by the California Ramblers
Pathe Actuelle 020883/Perfect 14076  Both sides by Nathan Glantz and his Orchestra
               036295  Charleston Baby Of Mine (Nathan Glantz and his Orchestra)
               37004/Perfect 15185  Am I Blue ? (Irving Mills Orchestra)
Perfect 14391  Both sides by the Original Memphis Five
Puretone 11311  Both sides by the Midway Gardens Orchestra
Silvertone 2584  Angry ( even Missing Links)

## MAJOR AND HIS ORCHESTRA

2t/tb/cl-as/as/ts/p/bj/bb/d.              Hollywood, c. October, 1924.

| 186 | Blue Evening Blues | Hwd 1028 |
| 187 | Hottest Man In Town | - |

## MATTY MALNECK AND HIS ORCHESTRA

Matty Malneck-vn dir. Manny Klein-t/Bobby van Eps-p/Marshall Fisher-g/Merwin Fischel-
    sb/Joseph Quintell-harp/Ralph Hansell-d. This is the personnel for the last session
    listed; it may apply to the first three also.
                                          Los Angeles, July 8, 1938.

DLA-1309-A  St. Louis Blues                Dec 2182, Y-5596

                                          Los Angeles, August 21, 1938.

DLA-1431-   Humoresque (Dvorak)            Dec 2182
DLA-1432-A  By The Waters Of Minnetonka    Dec 2616, Br SA-1692
DLA-1433-   On The Trail                   Rejected
DLA-1434-A  Hearts And Flowers             Dec 2060
DLA-1435-A  Sing, You Sinners              -

  Martha Mears-v.                          Los Angeles, March 22, 1939.

DLA-1735-A  Lazy Rhapsody - vMM            Dec 2616, Y-5596, Br SA-1692

  Cl/f/pac added.                          Los Angeles, May 24, 1939.

LA-1389-A  Londonderry Air                 Br 8413, Col DB-5071
LA-1890-   Souvenir (Drdla)               Br 8396, Col DO-1998
LA-1891-A  Listen To The Mocking Bird      Br 8413, Col DB-5071
LA-1892-   Flight Of The Bumble Bee        Br 8396, Col DO-1998

  Cl/f/pac omitted.                        Los Angeles, August 17, 1939.

LA-1966-A  Park Avenue Fantasy            Col 35212
LA-1967-A  Carnival Of Venice             Col 35299, DO-2378
LA-1968-A  Then I Wrote The Minuet In G   Col 35212, DO-2052
LA-1969-A  William Tell Overture          Col 35299, DO-2378

Further Columbia records by this group are of even less interest than the foregoing.

## MANDEL SISTERS

Pseudonym on Supertone for the Sunshine Boys (Joe and Dan Mooney) (!) (q.v.)

See the Rhythm Masters.

## MANHATTAN DANCE MAKERS

Ben Selvin directed this studio organization recording for Harmony between 1925 and
   1928.  Several of them feature short solos by Earl Oliver-t and Larry Abbott-cl-as
   amongst others (see THE AMERICAN DANCE BAND DISCOGRAPHY, 1917-1942).

## MANHATTAN IMPERIAL ORCHESTRA

Pseudonym on Puritan/Triangle 11251 (WET YO' THUMB) for (Fletcher) Henderson's Dance
   Players, q.v., and others on these and associated labels, but of no known jazz
   interest.

## MANHATTAN  MUSICIANS

Pseudonym on National Music Lovers for the following items listed in this book :-

1099  I Can't Get The One I Want (Fletcher Henderson and his Orchestra)
1127  So That's The Kind Of A Girl You Are (Ben Selvin and his Orchestra)

## MANHATTAN SERENADERS

Pseudonym on Duophone D-4025 and D-4033 for Ben Bernie and his Hotel Roosevelt Orchestra, q.v., and on Paramount 20669 for the Castle Farms Serenaders, q.v.

## MANHATTAN  SYNCOPATORS

See the Grey Gull studio bands.

## MANLEY BROTHERS' ORCHESTRA

Pseudonym on Broadway 1352 for the Dorsey Brothers' Orchestra, q.v.

## ESTELLE MANN

Pseudonym on Broadway for Edmonia Henderson, q.v.

## SAM  MANNING

Sam Manning, a pioneer calypso artist, made a few sides with interesting accompaniments, as follows.

SAM MANNING AND HIS COLE JAZZ ORCHESTRA : ? Bob Fuller-as/? Porter Grainger-p/bj/sb/d/
   Sam Manning-v.                        New York, September 21, 1925.

| | | |
|---|---|---|
| 141020-1 | Let Go My Hand - vSM | Col 14110-D |
| 141021-1 | Bungo - vSM | - |
| 141022-1 | Mabel, Open Your Door - vSM | Col 2300-X |
| 141023-2 | Lignum Vitae (Long Life) | - |

SAM MANNING AND HIS BLUE HOT SYNCOPATORS : C/as/p/bj/Sam Manning-v.
                                        New York, c. March 1, 1926.

| | | |
|---|---|---|
| 74031- | Keep Your Hands Off That | OK 8302 |
| 74032- | Go, I've Got Somebody Sweeter Than You | - |

## WINGY MANONE

MANNONE'S SAN SUE STRUTTERS (sic) : Wingy Manone-c/Jerry Bump-tb/? Johnny Dodds-cl/
   George Harper-cl-as/Paul Freed-p/Lennie Esterdahl-bj/? Min Leibrook-bb/Earl McDowell
   d.                                   Chicago, November, 1925.

| | | |
|---|---|---|
| 9500-A | Mother Me, Tennessee | OK rejected |
| | Desdemona | - |
| | Golden Leaf Rag | - |
| | San Sue Strut | - |
| | Tiger Rag | - |

JOE MANNONE'S HARMONY KINGS : Wingy Manone-c-v/Hal Jordy-cl-as/Bob Sacks-ts/Johnny
   Miller-p/Steve Brou-g/Arnold Loyacano-sb/John Ryan-d/Earl Warner-v.
                                         New Orleans, April 11, 1927.

143949-2  Sadness Will Be Gladness - vEW         Col 14282-D
143950-2  Cat's Head                             -
143951-2  Up The Country Blues - vWM             Col 1044-D, HJCA 611
143952-2  Ringside Stomp - vWM                   -            -

WINGY MANNONE AND HIS ORCHESTRA : Wingy Manone-c/Jack Teagarden-tb/Sidney Arodin-cl/
   Terry Shand-p/Benny Pottle-sb/Tommy de Rose-d.
                                         New York, December 2, 1927.

E-6819/20 There'll Come A Time                   Voc rejected
E-6821/2  Toot, Toot, Toot                       -

JOE "WINGY" MANNONE AND HIS CLUB ROYALE ORCHESTRA : Wingy Manone-c-v/Wade Foster-cl/
   Bud Freeman-ts/Jack Gardner-p/Gene Krupa-d.
                                         Chicago, September 4, 1928.

C-2292-   Downright Disgusted - vWM              Voc 15728
C-2293-   Fare Thee Well - vWM                   -

   Wingy Manone-c-v/Frank Teschmacher-cl/George Snurpus-ts/Art Hodes-p/Ray Biondi-g/
   Augie Schellange-d.                   Chicago, December 17, 1928.

C-2682-B  Trying To Stop My Crying - vWM         Voc 15797, HRS 3, Br 80064
C-2683-   Isn't There A Little Love ? - vWM       -         HRS 13, Decatur 510

BARBECUE JOE AND HIS HOT DOGS : Wingy Manone-c-v/George Walters-cl/Joe Dunn-ts/May-
   nard Spencer-p/Dash Burkis-d.         Richmond, Ind., August 28, 1930.

16949, -A-B  Tin Roof Blues                      Rejected
16950-C   Shake That Thing - vWM                 Ch 16192, 40054, Dec 7366,Br 02504
16951     Tar Paper Stomp (Wingy's Stomp)        Ch 16153, 40005, Spr 2818,
                                                 Dec 7425, F-7807
16952     Up The Country - vWM                   Rejected

   Miff Frink-tb/bj/Orville Haynes-bb added; Bob Price-Ed Camden-t added*.
                                         Richmond, Ind., September 19, 1930.

17058     Up The Country Blues - vWM             Gnt 7320, Ch 16127, 40054,
                                                 Dec 7366, Sav 500, Br 03520
17059-E   Tin Roof Blues                         Ch 16153, 40005, Spr 2818,
                                                 Dec 7425, F-7807
17060     Weary Blues - vWM                      Gnt 7320, Ch 16127, 40055,
                                                 Dec 7415, Sav 500
17061     *Big Butter And Egg Man - vWM          Ch 16192, Ch 40055, Dec 7415,
                                                 Br 03520
NOTE:- Superior 2818 as SPEED WILLIAMS' ORCHESTRA; Brunswick 03520, Champion 16153,
40055, Decca F-7807 as WINGY MANNONE AND HIS ORCHESTRA; Savoy 500 as NEW ORLEANS
RHYTHM KINGS (!)

WINGY MANNONE AND HIS ORCHESTRA : Wingy Manone-t-v/Matty Matlock-cl/Eddie Miller-ts/
   Gil Bowers-p/Nappy Lamare-g-v/Harry Goodman-sb/Ray Bauduc-d.
                                         New York, May 2, 1934.

B-15150-A No Calling Card - vWM-NL               Br 6911, 01818, A-500462
B-15151-A Strange Blues - vWM-NL                 As above, plus Par R-2875, DPE-75,
                                                 PZ-11025, Col DS-1965
B-15152-A Send Me                                Br 6940, 02007, A-9739, A-500463,
                                                 Par R-2875, DPE-75, PZ-11025,
                                                 Col DS-1965
B-15153-A Walkin' The Streets - vWM              Br 6940, 02055, A-500463,
                                                 Voc/OK 4464

WINGY MANNONE AND HIS ORCHESTRA : Wingy Manone-t-compere*/Dicky Wells-tb/Artie Shaw-
cl/Bud Freeman-ts/Jelly-Roll Morton or Teddy Wilson-p/Frank Victor-g/John Kirby-sb/
Kaiser Marshall-d.                        New York, August 15, 1934.

B-15629-A-B  Easy Like - pTW              Rejected
B-15630-A-B  In The Slot - pTW               -
B-15631-B  *Never Had No Lovin' - pJRM    SE 5011-S
B-15632-A  I'm Alone Without You - pJRM      -


Wingy Manone-t/Santo Pecora-tb/Sidney Arodin-cl/Terry Shand-p/? Nappy Lamare-g/
Benny Pottle-sb/Bob White-d.              New York, October 3, 1934.

16086-1  Royal Garden Blues               OK 41570, HJCA HC-78
16087-2  Just One Girl                    OK 41569, Col 35685, Decatur 509
16088-1  She's Crying For Me                 -            -              -
16089-1  Zero                             OK 41570, HJCA HC-78


Wingy Manone-t-v/Matty Matlock-cl/Eddie Miller-cl-ts/Gil Bowers-p/Nappy Lamare-g-v/
Harry Goodman-sb/Ray Bauduc-d.            New York, January 15, 1935.

16571-1  The Blues Have Got Me - vWM       Ban 33356, Mt M-13323, Or 3098,
                                           Per 16081, Ro 2472, Voc S-17,
                                           Imp 6032, 18009, 35010
16572-1  Nickel In The Slot - spWM-NL      OK 41573, Voc 3171, Par R-2126,
                                           A-6301, PZ-11151, HJCA HC-122
16573-1  Breeze - vWM                      Ban 33356, Mt M-13323, Or 3098,
                                           Per 16081, Ro 2472, Voc S-17,
                                           Imp 17499, 18009, 35010
16574-1  Swing, Brother, Swing - vWM       OK 41573, Voc 3171, Par R-2126,
                                           A-6301, HJCA HC-122
NOTE:- Imperial 18009 and Vocalion S-17 as HARLEM HOT SHOTS.


                                          New York, February 20, 1935.

16798-1  March Winds And April Showers - vWM-NL   Ban 33366, Mt M-13333, Or 3103,
                                           Per 16085, Ro 2477, Voc S-3,
                                           Imp 17041, 17499, 35002, Kr 307
16799-1  (Oh Susannah) Dust Off That Old Pianna   Ban 33386, Mt M-13353, Or 3116,
         - vWM                             Per 16095, Ro 2490, Rex 8475,
                                           Imp 6054, Kr 255
16800-1  Love Is Just Around The Corner - vWM     Ban 33366, Mt M-13333, Or 3103,
                                           Ro 2477, Per 16085, Rex 8475,
                                           Imp 6054, Kr 255
16801-1  House Rent Party Day - vWM-NL     Ban 33386, Mt M-13353, Or 3116,
                                           Per 16095, Ro 2490, Kr 307
NOTE:- All issues from the above session as HARLEM HOT SHOTS  except Imperial 35002
(credited to BENNY GOODMAN AND HIS MODERNISTS HARLEM HOT SHOTS (!)


                                          New York, March 8, 1935.

17005-1  The Isle Of Capri (Capri, What You Done   Voc 2913, 4464, Br RL-254*,
         To Me*) - vWM                     A-9999, A-86002
17006-1  I Believe In Miracles - vWM       Voc 2913, Pan 25748, Br A-999,
                                           A-86002
17007-1  Fare Thee Well, Annabelle (Fare Thee      Voc 2914, Br A-9997, A-86000*
         Well, Annabel*) - vWM-NL
17008-1  On The Good Ship Lollipop - vWM-NL         - Br RL-254 -      -


                                          New York, April 8, 1935.

17257-2  About A Quarter To Nine           Voc 2934, Br 02064
17258-2  You're An Angel                   Voc 2933
17259-2  I'm In Love All Over Again            -
17260-2  Let's Spill The Beans             Voc 2934


                                          New York, May 27, 1935.

17638-1  Every Little Moment - vWM         Voc 2963, Br 02064, A-86032
17639-1  Black Coffee - vWM                   -      Br 02055     -
17640-1  Sweet And Slow - vWM              Voc 2972
17641-1  Lulu's Back In Town - vWM

WINGY MANNONE AND HIS ORCHESTRA : Wingy Manone-t-v/Matty Matlock-cl/Bud Freeman-ts/
   Gil Bowers-p/Carmen Mastren-g/Sid Weiss-sb/Ray Bauduc-d.
                                          New York, July 5, 1935.

```
17782-1  Let's Swing It - vWM                 Voc 2990, Br A-86034
17783-1  A Little Door, A Little Lock, A Little  Voc 2989, Br 02073, A-9879,A-86035
            Key - vWM
17784-2  Love And Kisses - vWM                 -                      -
17785-1  Rhythm Is Our Business - vWM          Voc 2990, Br 02073, A-9879,A-86034
```

   Tony Zimmers-ts replaces Freeman.        New York, August 27, 1935.

```
18020-1-2-3  A Smile Will Go A Long, Long Way-vWM Rejected
18021-1  From The Top Of Your Head - vWM       Voc 3023, Br A-9878, A-86039
18022-1  Takes Two To Make A Bargain - vWM     -           -         -
```

                                          New York, September 13, 1935.

```
18020-4  A Smile Will Go A Long, Long Way - vWM   Voc 3058, Br A-86053
18083-1  I'm Gonna Sit Right Down And Write    -           -
            Myself A Letter - vWM
```

   Wingy Manone-t-v/Jack Teagarden-tb-v/Joe Marsala-cl/Horace Diaz-p/Carmen Mastren-g/
   Sid Weiss-sb/Sam Weiss-d/Johnny Mercer-v.
                                          New York, October 8, 1935.

```
18133-1  Every Now And Then - vWM              Voc 3071, Br A-86058
18134-1  I've Got A Feelin' You're Foolin'-vWM-JT Voc 3070, Br 5033
18135-1  You Are My Lucky Star - vWM           -           -
18136-2  I've Got A Note - vWM-JT-JM           Voc 3071, Br A-86058
```

                                          New York, October 17, 1935.

```
18136-3  I've Got A Note - vWM-JM              Voc 3071
```

   Wingy Manone-t-v/Joe Marsala-cl/Gil Bowers-p/Carmen Mastren-g/Sid Weiss-sb/Ray
   Bauduc-d.                               New York, December 18, 1935.

```
18403-1  I'm Shooting High - vWM               Voc 3134
18404-1  The Music Goes 'Round And Around - vWM  -       Br 5034, A-86059
18405-1  You Let Me Down - vWM                 Voc 3135
18406-1  I've Got My Fingers Crossed - vWM     -
```

   George Brunies-tb added.                New York, January 28, 1936.

```
18596-1  (If I Had) Rhythm In My Nursery Rhymes  Voc 3158
            - vWM
18597-1  Old Man Mose - vWM                    Voc 3159, Br 02196, A-9989,
                                               A-81025, A-86060
18598-1  The Broken Record - vWM               Voc 3158
18599-1  Please Believe Me - vWM               Voc 3159, Br A-9989, A-86060
```

   Wingy Manone-t-v/Ward Silloway-tb/Joe Marsala-cl/Eddie Miller-ts/Gil Bowers-p/
   Nappy Lamare-g-v/Artie Shapiro-sb/Ray Bauduc-d.
                                          New York, March 10, 1936.

```
18795-1  Shoe-Shine Boy - vWM                  Voc 3192, Br 5046, A-9990, A-86061
18796-1  West Wind - vWM                       -         -       -        -
18797-1  Is It True What They Say About Dixie ?  Voc 3191, Br 5045
18798-1  Goody-Goody - vWM                     -         Br 02196, 5034, A-81025
```

   Silloway omitted; Matty Matlock-cl-ts added; Miller db cl; Conrad Lanoue-p replaces
   Bowers.                                 New York, April 9, 1936.

```
101197-1  You Started Me Dreaming - vWM        BB B-6359, MW M-4883, HMV B-8451
101198-1  Tormented - vWM                      -         -         -
101199-1  Dallas Blues - vWM                   BB B-6375, MW M-4884
101300-1  It's No Fun - vWM                    BB B-6360
101301-1  Rhythm Saved The World - vWM         -
101302-1  Swingin' At The Hickory House   vWM-NL  BB B-6375, MW M-4884
```

WINGY MANONE AND HIS ORCHESTRA : Wingy Manone-t-v/Joe Marsala-cl/Tommy Mace-as/
  Eddie Miller-ts/Conrad Lanoue-p/Carmen Mastren-g/Artie Shapiro-sb/Sam Weiss-d.
                              New York, May 8, 1936.

| | | |
|---|---|---|
| 101573-1 | Basin Street Blues - vWM | BB B-6411, RZ MR-2301 |
| 101574-1 | Hesitation Blues - vWM | BB B-6394, MW M-4992 |
| 101575-1 | Sing Me A Swing Song - vWM | -       - |
| 101576-1 | Isn't Love The Strangest Thing ? - vWM | BB B-6393, MW M-4991 |
| 101577-1 | Every Once In A While - vWM | -       - |
| 101578-1 | Panama | BB B-6411 |

Wingy Manone-t-v/Mike Viggiano-cl/Tommy Mace-as/James Lamare-cl-ts/Conrad Lanoue-p
/Jack LeMaire-g/Artie Shapiro-sb/Abby Fisher-d.
                            New York, July 1, 1936.

| | | |
|---|---|---|
| 102374-1 | River Man - vWM | BB B-6483 |
| 102375-1 | Summer Holiday - vWM | BB B-6473 |
| 102376-1 | No Regrets - vWM | - |
| 102377-1 | Afterglow - vWM | BB B-6483, RZ MR-2301 |
| 102378-1 | I Just Made Up With That Old Girl Of Mine - vWM | BB B-6472 |
| 102379-1 | You're Not The Kind - vWM | - |

Al Mastren-tb added; Joe Marsala-cl-as replaces Mace; Sam Weiss-d replaces Fisher;
Sally Sharon-v.                 New York, August 20, 1936.

| | | |
|---|---|---|
| 0216-1 | It Can Happen To You - vWM | BB B-6536 |
| 0217-1 | It's The Gypsy In Me - vWM | BB B-6549 |
| 0218-1 | Cottage By The Moon - vWM | BB B-6536 |
| 0219-1 | And They Said It Wouldn't Last - vWM | BB B-6549 |
| 0220-1 | Fancy Meeting You - vWM | BB B-6537, RZ MR-2364 |
| 0221-1 | A Good Man Is Hard To Find - vWM-SS | - |

NOTE:- The reverse of Regal Zonophone MR-2364, though credited to Wingy Manone and
his Orchestra, is in fact by a hillbilly group of no jazz interest whatever.

Mastren omitted; George Wettling-d replaces Weiss.
                          New York, October 1, 1936.

| | | |
|---|---|---|
| 0551-1 | In The Groove - vWM | BB B-6616 |
| 0552-1 | Let Me Call You Sweetheart - vWM | BB B-6618 |
| 0553-1 | Easy Like - vWM | - |
| 0554-1 | I Can't Pretend - vWM | BB B-6606 |
| 0555-1 | Floatin' Down To Cotton Town - vWM | BB B-6605 |
| 0556-1 | A Fine Romance - vWM | BB B-6606 |

Wingy Manone-t-v/George Brunies-tb/Matty Matlock-cl/Joe Marsala-ts/Conrad Lanoue-p/
Jack LeMaire-g/Artie Shapiro-sb/Danny Alvin-d.
                          New York, February 4, 1937.

| | | |
|---|---|---|
| 04565-1 | Formal Night In Harlem - vWM | BB B-6816, RZ MR-2438 |
| 04566-1 | Sweet Lorraine - vWM | - |
| 04567-1 | Boo-Hoo - vWM | BB B-6806, RZ MR-2414 |
| 04568-1 | You Showed Me The Way - vWM | BB B-6804 |
| 04569-1-2 | I Can't Lose That Longing For You-vWM | - |
| 04570-1 | Oh, Say ! Can You Swing ? - vWM | BB B-6806, RZ MR-2438 |

Wingy Manone-t-v/Al Mastren-tb/Joe Marsala-cl-as/Babe Russin-ts/Conrad Lanoue-p/
Jack LeMaire-g-v/Artie Shapiro-sb/Danny Alvin-d.
                          New York, May 25, 1937.

| | | |
|---|---|---|
| 010246-1 | The Image Of You - vWM | BB B-7003 |
| 010247-1 | Don't Ever Change - vWM | BB B-7002 |
| 010248-1 | Life Without You - vWM | BB B-7003 |
| 010249-1 | You're Precious To Me - vWM | BB B-7002 |
| 010250-1 | It Must Be Religion - vWM-JL | BB B-7014 |
| 010251-1 | The Prisoner's Song - vWM | - |

WINGY MANONE  AND HIS ORCHESTRA : Wingy Manone-t-v/Joe Marsala-cl-as/Babe Russin-ts/
Conrad Lanoue-p/Jack LeMaire-g/Artie Shapiro-sb/Danny Alvin-d.
                              New York, September 28, 1937.

| | | |
|---|---|---|
| 013880-1 | I Ain't Got Nobody - vWM | BB B-7198, HMV B-9493, JK-2432 |
| 013881-1 | I've Got My Heart Set On You - vWM | BB B-7214, RZ MR-2659 |
| 013882-1 | Everything You Said Came True - vWM | BB B-7197 |
| 013883-1 | Getting Some Fun Out Of Life - vWM | -             RZ MR-2640 |
| 013884-1 | Jazz Me Blues - vWM | BB B-7198 |
| 013885-1 | Laugh Your Way Through Life - vWM | BB B-7214, RZ MR-2659 |

Wingy Manone-t-v/Joe Marsala-cl-as/Doc Rando-as/Bud Freeman-ts/Conrad Lanoue-p/
Clayton Duerr-g/unknown negro sb/Danny Alvin-d.
                              New York, January 12, 1938.

| | | |
|---|---|---|
| 018321-1 | Annie Laurie - vWM | BB B-7389, RZ MR-2732 |
| 018322-1 | Loch Lomond - vWM | -              - |
| 018323-1 | Down Stream - vWM | BB B-7391 |
| 018324-1 | Where's The Waiter ? - vWM | - |
| 018325-1 | My Mariuccia Take A Steamboat - vWM | BB B-7395 |
| 018326-1 | In The Land Of Yamo Yamo - vWM | -        RZ MR-2850 |

Wingy Manone-t-v/Brad Gowans-vtb/Al Kavich-cl-as/Wilder Chase-p/Bobby Bennett-g/Sid
Jacobs-sb/Danny Alvin-d.          New York, May 23, 1938.

| | | |
|---|---|---|
| 023415-1 | Heart Of Mine - vWM | BB B-7622 |
| 023416-1 | Let's Break The Good News - vWM | BB B-7633, RZ MR-2850 |
| 023417-1 | Martha - vWM | BB B-7621, MW M-7516, RZ MR-2812 |
| 023418-1 | Mannone Blues - vWM | BB B-7633, HMV B-9376 |
| 023419-1 | The Flat Foot Floogie - vWM | BB B-7621, MW M-7516, RZ MR-2812 |
| 023420-1 | Little Joe From Chicago - vWM | BB B-7622 |

Wingy Manone-t-v/Buster Bailey-cl/Chu Berry-ts/Conrad Lanoue-p/Zeb Julian-g/Jules
Cassard-sb/Cozy Cole-d.          New York, April 26, 1939.

| | | |
|---|---|---|
| 036534-1 | Downright Disgusted Blues - vWM | BB B-10296, MW M-8353 |
| 036535-1 | Corrine Corrini (Where've You Been So | BB B-10266, HMV B-9352*, EA-3344, |
| | Long ?) (Corinne Corinna*) - vWM | MW M-8355 |
| 036536-1 | I'm A Real Kinda Papa (Lookin' For A | BB B-10266, MW M-8355       - |
| | Real Kinda Girl) - vWM | |
| 036537-1 | Jumpy Nerves | BB B-10289, MW M-8354, HMV B-9352, |
| | | EA-3747 |
| 036538-1 | Casey Jones (The Brave Engineer) - vWM | -     - HMV B-9360, EA-3280 |
| 036539-1 | Boogie Woogie - vWM | BB B-10296, MW M-8353, HMV B-9493, |
| | | JK-2432 |

Danny Barker-g replaces Julian.      New York, June 19, 1939.

| | | |
|---|---|---|
| 037729-1 | Royal Garden Blues | BB B-10331, MW M-8352, HMV B-9376 |
| 037730-1 | Beale Street Blues - vWM | BB B-10401, MW M-8351, HMV B-9155 |
| 037731-1 | In The Barrel - vWM-? | BB B-10331, MW M-8352, |
| | | HMV B-9360, EA-3613 |
| 037732-1 | Farewell Blues | BB B-10401, MW M-8351 |
| 037733-1 | Fare Thee, My Baby, Fare-Thee-Well - vWM | BB B-10432, MW M-8350 |
| 037734-1 | Limehouse Blues | -         -      HMV EA-2751 |

Wingy Manone-t-v/Buck Scott-tb/Gus Fetterer-cl/Chu Berry-ts/Ernie Hughes-p/Zeb
Julian-g/Sid Jacobs-sb/Cozy Cole-d.    New York, September 6, 1939.

| | | |
|---|---|---|
| 041971-1 | Blue Lou | BB B-10749 |
| 041972-1 | Sudan | BB B-10560, HMV EA-2751 |
| 041973-1 | How Long Blues - vWM&ch | BB B-10749 |
| 041974-1 | When The Saints Go Marching In - vWM | BB B-10560 |
| 041975-1 | My Honey's Lovin' Arms - vWM | BB 30-0801, HMV B-9313, JO-114 |
| 041976-1 | When My Sugar Walks Down The Street-vWM | -        -      - |

WINGY MANONE  AND HIS ORCHESTRA : Wingy Manone-t-v/Buck Scott-tb-v/Phil Olivella-cl/
    Conrad Lanoue-p/Zeb Julian-g/Sid Jacobs-sb/Danny Alvin-d.
                                        New York, January 15, 1940.

| | | |
|---|---|---|
| 045934-1 | She's Crying For Me | BB B-10773, HMV EA-3747, Vic 29871 |
| 045935-1 | South With The Boarder - vWM-BS&ch | BB B-10604, HMV B-9155 |
| 045936-1 | The Mosquito Song (Where Do The | BB B-10773, HMV EA-3280 |
|          | Mosquitoes Go In The Winter Time ?)-vWM-BS | |
| 045937-1 | Put On Your Old Grey Bonnet - vWM | BB B-10604 |

    Wingy Manone-t-v Babe Bowman-tb-v/Bill Covey-cl-as/Stan Wrightsman-p/Russell Soule-
    g/Bill Jones-sb/Dick Cornell-d.       Hollywood, August 6, 1940.

| | | |
|---|---|---|
| 049980-1 | Rhythm On The River - vWM | BB B-10844, HMV EA-2632, Twin FT-8996 |
| 049981-1 | Ain't It A Shame About Mame ? - vWM | BB B-10844        - |
| 049982-1 | Dinner For The Duchess - vWM | BB B-10909 |
| 049983-1 | When I Get You Alone Tonight - vWM-BS | - |

    Wingy Manone-t-v/Marty Marsala-t*/George Brunies-tb/Joe Marsala-cl/Mel Powell-p/
    Carmen Mastren-g/Al Morgan-sb/Zutty Singleton-d.
                                        New York, March 19, 1941.

| | | |
|---|---|---|
| 062858-1 | *Ochi Chornya - vWM | BB B-11298, HMV EA-3613, Vic 29916 |
| 062859-1 | *Mama's Gone, Goodbye - vWM&ch | BB B-11107, BRS 1000 |
| 062860-1 | *The Boogie Beat'll Getcha - vWM | BB B-11298, Vic 29916 |
| 062861-1 | Stop The War (The Cats Are Killin' | BB B-11107, BRS 1000 |
|          | Themselves) - vWM | |

WINGY MANONE-EDDIE MARR : Vocal duets, acc. by Wingy Manone-t/King Jackson-tb/Archie
    Rosati-cl/Stan Wrightsman-p/Lim Lynch-sb/Dick Cornell-d.
                                        Los Angeles, August 26, 1941.

| | | |
|---|---|---|
| DLA-2693-A | Jam And Jive - Part 1 | Dec 18325 |
| DLA-2694-A | Jam And Jive - Part 2 | - |
| DLA-2695-A | Jam And Jive - Part 3 | Dec 18326 |
| DLA-2696-A | Jam And Jive - Part 4 | - |
| DLA-2697-A | Jam And Jive - Part 5 | Dec 18327 |
| DLA-2698-A | Jam And Jive - Part 6 | - |

## ANDY MANSFIELD AND  HIS BAND

See the Cotton Pickers.

## MAPLE CITY FOUR

Despite the appearance in the Vocalion Race series of records by this group, which
    consisted of ocarina, piano, banjo and washboard and various corny effects, this
    is a white country-style quartet of no jazz interest whatever.  It recorded in
    Chicago on April 13, 1933; its members were Al Rice, Pat Peterson, Fritz Meissner
    and Art Janes.

## EDDIE MAPP

Harmonica solo (see also Guy Lumpkin).   Long Island City, c. May, 1929.

| | | |
|---|---|---|
| 466-A | Riding The Blues | QRS R-7078 |

## FATE MARABLE'S SOCIETY SYNCOPATORS

Fate Marable (mis-spelt MORABLE on the labels)-p dir. Sidney Desvignes-Amos White-t/
    Harvey Lankford-tb/Norman Mason-Bert Bailey-cl-as/Walter Thomas-ts-bar/Willie
    Foster-bj-g/Henry Kimball-bb/Zutty Singleton-d.
                                        New Orleans, c. March 16, 1924.

| | | |
|---|---|---|
| 8564-A | Frankie And Johnny | OK 40113 |
| 8565-A | Pianoflage | - |

Norman J. Thiess dir. Harry Thompson-t/Boyce Cullen-tb/Art Landry-cl-as-vn/Mrs.Norman
J. Thiess-p/Eddie Landry-bj/Howard Emerson-d.
New York, c. February 13, 1922.

| | | |
|---|---|---|
| 7767, -A | Bootblack Blues | Con 3059, St 9218 |
| 7768, -A | You've Had Your Day | Gnt 4843    — |

New York, c. April 18, 1922.

| | | |
|---|---|---|
| 7858, -A | Oh, Sing-a-Loo | Gnt 4871, St 9249 |
| 7859, -A-B | Rosy Posy | —      — |

## PAUL MARES AND HIS FRIARS SOCIETY ORCHESTRA

Paul Mares-t/Santo Pecora-tb/Omer Simeon-cl/Boyce Brown-as/Jess Stacy-p/Marvin Saxbe-
g/Pat Pattison-sb/George Wettling-d.    Chicago, January 7, 1935.

| | | |
|---|---|---|
| C-870-1-2 | Nagasaki | OK rejected |
| C-871-1-2 | Reincarnation | — |
| C-872-1-2 | Maple Leaf Rag | — |
| C-873-1-2 | The Land Of Dreams | — |

Chicago, January 26, 1935.

| | | |
|---|---|---|
| C-870-C | Nagasaki | OK 41574, Col 35880 |
| C-871-C | Reincarnation | OK 41575, Col 35686, DO-2568, |
| | | Decatur 503 |
| C-872-C | Maple Leaf Rag | OK 41574    —      — |
| C-873-C | The Land Of Dreams | OK 41575, Col 35880, Decatur 503 |

## THE MARIGOLD ENTERTAINERS

Oscar Westlund dir. unknown band; Art White-v.
Minneapolis, January, 1929.

| | | |
|---|---|---|
| TMP-30- | Jealous - vAW | Voc 15800 |
| TMP-31- | When My Sugar Walks Down The Street | — |

## THE MARINERS

Vocal trio, acc. by Eddie Lang-g, with Frank Signorelli-p/Red McKenzie-comb*.
New York, May 26, 1930.

| | |
|---|---|
| 404045-A-B-C | Down The River Of Golden Dreams (w)  OK rejected |
| 404046-A-B-C | *Happy Feet                          — |

New York, June 11, 1930.

| | |
|---|---|
| 404045-F | Down The River Of Golden Dreams (w) | OK 41433, Par R-730, A-3080, |
| | Od A-221280 |
| 404046-D | *Happy Feet | As above except Par A-3080 |

Acc. by Frank Signorelli-p/Eddie Lang-g.
New York, August 29, 1930.

| | | |
|---|---|---|
| 404388-C | (Just A Little Dance) Mam'selle | OK 41449 |
| 404389-C | I Don't Mind Walkin' In The Rain | —       Par R-787, Ar 4637 |
| | NOTE:- Ariel 4637 as VOCAL TRIO. | |

## MIKE MARKEL

Mike Markel was a popular dance-band ledder in New York supper-clubs in the inter-
war era; as might be expected, very few of the considerable number of records his
bands made are of interest as jazz, but the following are exceptions, and there
may be others similar.

MARKELS ORCHESTRA (sic) : Mike Markel-p dir. Hymie Farberman-Marty Berger-t/Fred
Schilling-tb/as/bsx/Eddie Davis-vn/Frank Gravito-bj/bb/d.
New York, March 23, 1922.

| | |
|---|---|
| 70560-B | Lonesome Mama Blues                          OK 4580, 4807, Od 03205 |

MARKELS ORCHESTRA (sic) : Mike Markel-p dir. 2t/tb/2cl-ss-as/ts or Cm/bsx/vn/bj/bb/d.
                                      New York, c. January 21, 1924.

  72282-A  31st Street Blues                        OK 40045

MIKE MARKEL'S ORCHESTRA : Mike Markel-p dir. 2t/tb/Phil Cole-cl-ss-as/cl-ss-as-bsx/cl
   ts/sometimes vn/bj/d/Al Bernard-v.    New York, February 8, 1926.

E-17880/3  Flamin' Mamie - vAB                       Br 3091*

MARKEL AND HIS DANCE ORCHESTRA : Same.   New York, February 23, 1926.

141712-4  Black Horse Stomp                          Col 617-D

MIKE MARKEL'S ORCHESTRA : Same.          New York, April 29, 1926.

E-18942/4  Lulu Belle                                Br 3189*
E-18945    Just A Little Dance                         -

                                         New York, late May, 1926.

  74175-A  Deep Henderson                       OK 40625, Starck 504, Par E-5638,
                                                Od 03391
  74176-B  Who'd Be Blue ?                      As above, except Od 03391

  Ray Stilwell-v (and tb ?)             New York, September 15, 1926.

  80113-B  For My Sweetheart - vRS               OK 40686, Par E-5715

The name MARKEL'S SOCIETY FAVOURITES was used on Imperial 1863 (YOU DON'T LIKE IT -
   NOT MUCH) for Al Lynch and his Orchestra, q.v.

## MARKS AND HIS FIVE OH-MY'S

See Mendello and his Five Gee-Gees.

## GERALD MARKS AND HIS ORCHESTRA

Gerald Marks was a well-known mid-West bandleader during the late 1920s, who made
   thirteen sides for Columbia, of which the following is known to be of some interest
   as "hot" dance music.

Gerald Marks dir. 2t/tb/2cl-as/cl-ts/vn/Nelson Bitterman-p-v/bj/bb/d.
                                      Chicago, March 19, 1928.

145812-3  If I Can't Have You (I Want To Be       Col 1432-D
            Lonesome - I Want To Be Blue) - vNB

## MARLBOROUGH (MELODY) SYNCOPATORS

The following item issued under this name is of some jazz interest; see also the New
   Orleans Blue Nine.

Earl Oliver and another-t/Sam Lewis-tb/? Larry Abbott and another-cl-as/cl-ts/p/bj/bb
   /d.                                  New York, c. July, 1925.

  3694    Footloose                                Clover 1610

## MARLBOROUGH  ORCHESTRA

Pseudonym on Grafton for the following items listed in this book :-

9167  Mamie (Five Birmingham Babies)
9212  Let's Grow Old Together (Mike Speciale and his Orchestra)
9219  My Carmenita (California Ramblers)

## EARL/RUDY MARLOW AND HIS ORCHESTRA

Pseudonym on Harmony and associated labels for Fred Rich and his Orchestra, q.v., and
   on Parlophone PNY-34184 for Phil Dannenberg and his Orchestra, q.v.

JOE MARSALA'S CHICAGOANS : Marty Marsala-t/Joe Marsala-cl/Ray Biondi-vn/Joe Bushkin-p
/Adele Girard-harp/Eddie Condon-g/Artie Shapiro-sb/Danny Alvin-d.
New York, April 21, 1937.

| M-412-1 | Wolverine Blues | Vri 565 |
|---|---|---|
| M-413-1 | Chimes Blues | Epic LN-24029 (LP) |
| M-414-2 | Jazz Me Blues | Vri 565 |
| M-415-1-2 | Clarinet Marmalade | Rejected |

Jack LeMaire-g-v replaces Condon; Buddy Rich-d replaces Alvin.
New York, March 16, 1938.

| M-779-1 | Mighty Like The Blues | Voc 4168 |
|---|---|---|
| M-780-1 | Woo-Woo - vJL | Voc 4116 |
| M-781-1 | Hot String Beans | Voc 4168 |
| M-782-1 | Jim Jam Stomp | Voc 4116 |

JOE MARSALA AND HIS DELTA FOUR : Bill Coleman-t-v/Joe Marsala-cl/Pete Brown-as/Carmen
Mastren-g/Gene Traxler-sb/Dell St. John-v.
New York, April 4, 1940.

| R-2796-2 | Wandering Man Blues - vDSJ | Gnl 1717 |
|---|---|---|
| R-2797-3 | Salty Mama Blues - vBC | - |
| R-2798-2 | Three O'Clock Jump - vDSJ | Gnl 3001, Com 1524 |
| R-2799-2 | Reunion In Harlem | - - |

JOE MARSALA AND HIS ORCHESTRA : Marty Marsala-t/Joe Marsala-cl/Ben Glassman-as/John
Smith-ts/Dave Bowman-p/Adele Girard-harp/Carmen Mastren-g/Jack Kelleher-sb/Shelly
Manne-d.                                  New York, March 21, 1941.

| 68854-A | Bull's Eye | Dec 3715, M-30212 |
|---|---|---|
| 68855-A | Lower Register | Dec 3764, Br 03245 |
| 68856-A | I Know That You Know | - - |
| 68857-A | Slow Down | Dec 3715, M-30212 |

Instrumentation and personnel unknown.  New York, October 29, 1941.

| 69877-A | Thou Swell | Dec rejected |
|---|---|---|
| 69878-A | Moanin' Low | - |

JOE MARSALA AND HIS CHOSEN SEVEN : Max Kaminsky-t/George Brunies-tb/Joe Marsala-cl-as
/Dick Cary-p/Carmen Mastren-g/Haig Stephens-sb/Zutty Singleton-d.
New York, July 6, 1942.

| 71001-A | Chimes Blues | Dec 27074 |
|---|---|---|
| 71002-A-B | Sweet Mama (Papa's Getting Mad) | - |
| 71003-A | Walkin' The Dog | Dec 27075, Od 286186 |
| 71004-A | Lazy Daddy | - - |

NOTE:- Matrix 71002 was reallocated on July 16, 1942 to a non-jazz commercial dance
recording by Johnny Long and his Orchestra - yet both this and Decca 27074 bear the
same matrix number !  See also Leonard Feather.

## GILBERT MARSH AND HIS ORCHESTRA

Pseudonym on Parlophone PNY- series for Miff Mole and his Little Molers, q.v.

## TED MARSHALL AND HIS ORCHESTRA

Pseudonym on Champion 15006 for Bailey's Lucky Seven, q.v., and other bands of no
jazz interest.

## MARTIN AND ROBERT

Alfred Martin-g/Robert Cooksey-h-v.      New York, March 21, 1927.

| E-22052 | Dollar Blues | Br 7007 |
|---|---|---|
| E-22059 | Hock My Shoes | - |

New York, September 1, 1927.

| E-6415 | South Street Blues | Voc 1127 |
|---|---|---|
| E-6418 | Maxwell And Peoria Blues | - |

Pseudonym on Australian Grand Pree 18530, 18531, 18551, 18596 and 18622 for Sam Lanin
   and his Orchestra, q.v., and on 18330 (WHEN MY SUGAR WALKS DOWN THE STREET) for
   Hazay Natzy and his Westchester Dance Orchestra (or Hotel Biltmore Orchestra), q.v.

## BOBBY MARTIN AND HIS ALL-STAR ORCHESTRA

Bobby Martin-t-v dir. Bill Coleman-Jack Butler-t/Billy Burns-tb/Glyn Paque-as-v/
   Ernest Purce-as/Johnny Russell-cl-ts-v/Ram Ramirez-p/Johnny Mitchell or Bobby McRae
   g/Ernest Hill-sb/Kaiser Marshall-d.      Hilversum, April, 1938.

             Crazy Rhythm                              Br A-81578, Pol 25857
             Let's Dance (At The Make-Believe Ballroom)  -            -
             - vBM-GP-JR

## BRAM MARTIN'S BORDERLINERS

Bert Hagerty-t/Benny Brownwick-cl/Les Williams-ts/Tommy Benton-p/Bert Fleet-g/Joe
   Lowborough-sb/Sid Plummer-d/Gene Crowley-v.
                                            London, March 9, 1937.

CA-16279-1  Squeeze Me - vGC                        Col FB-1679
CA-16280-1-2  Arkansas Blues - vGC                  Rejected
CA-16281-1-2  Candy Lips - vGC                         -
CA-16282-1  West End Blues - vGC                    Col FB-1679

## CLIFF MARTIN AND HIS ORCHESTRA

See the ARC-Brunswick studio bands.

## DAISY MARTIN

Vocal, acc. by the Five Jazz Bell-Hops : Probably :- Gus Aiken-t/Jake Frazier-tb/
   Garvin Bushell-cl-as/Dude Finlay-p/bj.  New York, March-April, 1921.

   7466-A   Royal Garden Blues                       Gnt 4712, St 9115
   7467     Spread Yo' Stuff                             -         -

   Acc. by her Jazz Bell Hops : Probably as above, with bb instead of d.
                                            New York, c. April 15, 1921.

   7854-A   Play 'Em For Mama Sing 'Em For Me       OK 8001
   7855-B   I Won't Be Back 'Till You Change Your Ways  -

                                            New York, c, early July, 1921.

   70012-B  Won't Someone Help Me Find My Lovin' Man OK 8008
   70013-B  Everybody's Man Is My Man                   -

   Acc. by the Tampa Blue Jazz Band : Jules :evy, Jr.-c/? Ephraim Hannaford-tb/Joseph
   (Joe) Samuels-cl-bsx/Larry Briers-p/d.  New York, c. August 1, 1921.

   70066-B  How Long ? How Long ? (Absent Blues)     OK 8009

                                            New York, c. August 2, 1921.

   70070-B  I Didn't Start In To Love You (Until     OK 8009
               You Stopped Loving Me)

The next two titles almost certainly belong to the above two sessions.

             Honolulu Lou                            OK 8010
             Sweet Daddy                                -

                                            New York, c. August 10, 1921.

   70087-C  Nightmare Blues                          OK 8013
   70088-B  Keep On Goin'                               -

Acc. by the Tampa Blue Jazz Band : Jules Levy, Jr.-c/? Ephraim Hannaford-tb/Joseph
(Joe) Samuels-cl-bsx/Larry Briers-p/d/Clarence Williams-v.
                                   New York, c. December 5, 1921.

70352-A  Brown Skin (Who You For ?) - vCW          OK 8027
70353-B  If You Don't Want Me Please Don't Dog Me   -
         'Round

Acc. by her Royal Tigers : T/tb/cl/p/d. It has been suggested that these are either
the Original Memphis Five or the New Orleans Jazz Band, both q.v., but nothing has
so far been discovered in support of these.
                                   New York, c. August 2, 1923.

5237-1  Feelin' Blue                            Ban 1262, Re 9548
5238-1  What You Was You Used To Be (But You Ain't   -        -
        No More)

## DOLLY MARTIN

Vocal, acc. by ? Ike Rodgers-tb/vn/? Henry Brown-p.
                                   Chicago, August 24, 1934.

C-9349-A  All Men Blues                          Dec 7080

## FATTY MARTIN'S ORCHESTRA

Fatty Martin-p dir. Earl Church and another-t/Lee Cheatham-tb/Cm-as/cl-ss-as-bsx/
Billy Bacon-cl-ts/Earl McMann-bj/Pops Graham-bb/J. B. "Jelly" Zeller-d.
                                   Houston, March 19, 1925.

32111-1  End O' Main                            Vic 19700
32112-3  Jimtown Blues                          -

## FREDDIE MARTIN AND HIS ORCHESTRA

As this was a "sweet society" dance orchestra that enjoyed great popularity during
the 1930s and 1940s it is not surprising that very few of its many records are of
interest as jazz; these are known exceptions.

Freddie Martin-cl-ts dir. Bunny Berigan-t/Elmer Rehmus-tb/Elmer Feldkamp-cl-as-v/Joe
Poretta-Jack Condon-cl-as/Al Wagner-Ross Dickson-Bennie Eaton-vn/Terry Shand-p-a/
Bobby van Eps-2nd p (when used)/Vincent Pirro-pac (when used)/George van Eps-g/
George Green-sb/Eddie Schaff-d.    New York, March 20, 1933.

13141-1  What Have We Got To Lose ? (Hi-Ho     Ban 32719, Mt M-12648, Or 2668,
         Lack-a-day) - vEF                     Per 15746, Ro 2041, Imp 2860
NOTE:- Imperial 2860 as BOB CAUSER AND HIS ORCHESTRA.

                                   New York, April 11, 1933.

152392-2  Look What I've Got - vEF ?           Col 2769-D, CB-627
NOTE:- Both these issues as HOTEL BOSSERT ORCHESTRA.

Helen Rowland-v.                   New York, May 11, 1933.

13316-1  I've Got To Sing A Torch Song - vHR   Pan 25548
13317-1  I've Got To Sing A Torch Song - vHR   Ban 32767, Mt M-12696, Or 2700,
                                               Per 15771, Ro 2073, Voc 15888,
                                               Rex 8018
13318-1  Remember My Forgotten Man - vHR       Pan 25548
13319-1  Remember My Forgotten Man - vHR       Ban 32767, Mt M-12696, Or 2700,
                                               Per 15771, Ro 2073, Voc 15891,
                                               Rex 8005
NOTE:- Vocalion 15888 as ROY CARROLL AND HIS BEACH CLUB ORCHESTRA; 15891 as BUNNY
BERIGAN AND HIS ORCHESTRA; Panachord 25548 as ALLEN BURNS AND HIS ORCHESTRA; all
others as ED LOYD (LLOYD on Rex 8005 and 8018) AND HIS BAND.

This was probably a studio band; nothing is known of its personnel, but the following
is said to feature good t/cl/as/Cavan O'Connor-v.

London, c. November, 1930.

P-149-A  Two Of Everything - vCO'C                Phonycord P-102

## JOHN MARTIN AND HIS ORCHESTRA

Pseudonym on Broadway for Eubie Blake and his Orchestra, q.v.

## SARA MARTIN

Vocal, acc. by Clarence Williams-p.      New York, c. October 17, 1922.

70935-D  Sugar Blues                              OK 8041

New York, c. November 3, 1922.

70990-B  Achin' Hearted Blues                     OK 8041

Acc. by her Brown-Skin Syncopators : Arthur Whetsel-t/Claude Hopkins-p/Elmer
Snowden-bj.                     New York, November 18, 1922.

80678-1-2  I Loved You Once But You Stayed Away   Col rejected
               Too Long
80679-1-2  'Tain't Nobody's Biz-ness If I Do          -

Acc. by Fats Waller (as T. Waller)-p.   New York, c. December 1, 1922.

71068-C  'Tain't Nobody's Bus'ness If I Do     OK 8043
71069-B  You Got Ev'rything A Sweet Mama Needs     -
             But Me

Same acc., as Thomas Waller.         New York, c. December 14, 1922.

71105-B  Mama's Got The Blues                  OK 8045
71106-B  Last Go Round Blues                       -

Acc. by Clarence Williams-p.         New York, c. April 6, 1923.

71390-B  Keeps On A-Rainin' (Papa, He Can't    OK 8060
             Make No Time)
71391-A-B  Joe Turner Blues                    OK 8058

Shelton Brooks-speech (and p acc. ?) where shown.*
                         New York, c. April 9, 1923.

71398-B  Michigan Water Blues                  OK 8060
71399-B  If Your Man Is Like My Man (I Sympathize OK 8063
             With You)
71400-B  *I Got What It Takes To Bring You Back  OK 8062
71401-B  *Original Blues                           -

Acc. by W. C. Handy's Orchestra : W. C. Handy dir. probably Rick Gray-c/Sylvester
Bevard-tb/as/ts/Charlie Hillman-p/bj/Archie Walls-bb/d.
                         New York, c. April 21, 1923.

71431-A  Come Home Papa Blues                  OK 8061
71432-C  It Takes A Long Time To Get 'Em But       -
             You Can Lose 'Em Overnight
71433-A  Laughin' Cryin' Blues                 OK 8064

Acc. by Clarence Williams-p.         New York, c. April 27, 1923.

71449-A  Cruel Backbitin' Blues                OK 8053
71450-B  Leave My Sweet Daddy Alone            OK 8065

Vocal duet with Clarence Williams, acc. by ? Clarence Johnson-p.
                         New York, c. April 30, 1923.

71455-A-B  Monkey Man Blues                    OK 8067

Vocal duet with Eva Taylor, acc. by Tom Morris-c/Clarence Williams-p.
                                    New York, c. May 4, 1923.

71465-A  Yodeling Blues                           OK 8067

Vocal, acc. by Clarence Williams-p.      New York, c. June 15, 1923.

71629-A  Where Can That Somebody Be               OK 4904
71630-A  Just Thinkin' Blues                       OK 8084
71631-B  If You Don't Like It, Leave               OK 8078
71632-B  Nobody In Town Can Bake Sweet Jelly Roll    -
         Like Mine

Vocal duets with Eva Taylor, acc. by Tom Morris-c/Clarence Williams-p.
                                    New York, c. June 20, 1923.

71640-B  That Free And Easy Papa O' Mine          OK 8082
71641-B  Hesitation Blues                          -

Vocal, acc. by Clarence Williams-p.      New York, c. June 27, 1923.

71653-B  Tired O' Waitin' Blues                   OK 8084
71654-B  You Just Can't Have No One Man By        OK 8083
         Yourself
71655-B  Goin' Down To The Levee                  OK 4904
71656-B  Ye Shall Reap Just What You Sow          OK 8083

                                    New York, c. July 6, 1923.

71669-B  New Orleans Hop Scop Blues               OK 8085
71670-B  Uncle Sam Blues                           -

                                    New York, c. July 25, 1923.

71696-B  Sweet Man Was The Cause Of It All        OK 8088
71697-B  Sympathizing Blues                        -

                                    New York, c. July 27, 1923.

71701-B  Mistreated Mama Blues                    OK 8086
71702-B  Runnin' 'Round With The Blues             -

Acc. by Clarence Williams' Blue Five : Tom Morris-c/John Mayfield-tb/Sidney Bechet-
ss/Clarence Williams-p/Buddy Christian-bj.
                                    New York, c. August 1, 1923.

71711-B  Blind Man Blues                          OK 8090
71712-B  Atlanta Blues                             -

Acc. by ? Porter Grainger-p.             New York, c. August 3, 1923.

71715-B  My Good Man's Blues (Mahalia's Blues)    OK 8087
71716-B  Jelly's Blues                             -
71717-B  Troubled Blues                           OK 8093
71718-B  I'm Satisfied                             -

                                    New York, c. August 6, 1923.

71736-B  Blue Gum Blues                           OK 8097
71738-A  Slow Down Sweet Papa Mama's Catching Up   -
         On You
NOTE:- Matrix 71737 is untraced.

Acc. by Clarence Williams' Harmonizing Four : Tom Morris-c/Sidney Bechet-ss/Clarence
Williams-p/Buddy Christian-bj.          New York, October 11, 1923.

71961-B  Graveyard Dream Blues                    OK 8099, Par E-5235
71962-B  A Green Gal Can't Catch On Blues           -          -

Acc. by Sylvester Weaver-g.              New York, October 31, 1923.

71980-A  Longing For Daddy Blues                OK 8117
71981-A  I've Got To Go And Leave My Daddy Behind    -

Vocal duets with Clarence Williams, acc. by Fats Waller-p.
                                         New York, November 1, 1923.

71984-B  I'm Cert'ny Gonna See 'Bout That        OK 8108
71985-B  Squabbling Blues                             -

Vocal, acc. by Sylvester Weaver-g (or bj*).
                                         New York, November 2, 1923.

71998-A  Roamin' Blues                          OK 8104
71999-B  Good-Bye Blues                         OK 8117

                                         Atlanta, March 19, 1924.

8582-A  *Everybody's Got The Blues              OK 8136
8583-A  *My Man Blues                                -
8584-B  Pleading Blues                          OK 8161
8585-B  Every Woman Needs A Man                 OK 8146

                                         Atlanta, c. March 21, 1924.

8595-B  Got To Leave My Home Blues              OK 8146
8596-B  Poor Me Blues                           OK 8226

Acc. by Clarence Williams-p.             New York, May 29, 1924.

72586-B  If I Don't Find My Brown I Won't Be    OK 8161
           Back At All
72587-A  Too Late Now To Get Your Baby Back     OK 8154

Acc. by Clarence Williams' Harmonizers : Tom Morris-c/Charlie Irvis-tb/? Ernest
Elliott-cl/Clarence Williams-p/Buddy Christian-bj (some authorities say no bj used).
                                         New York, June 4, 1924.

72592-B  He's Never Gonna Throw Me Down         OK 8154

Acc. by her Jug Band : Clifford Hayes-vn/Cal Smith bj/Earl McDonald-jug; no v on
sides marked ** (labelled SARA MARTIN'S JUG BAND).
                                         New York, c. September 16, 1924.

72324-B**Blue Devil Blues                       OK 8188
72825-B  Jug Band Blues                         OK 8166

                                         New York, c. September 19, 1924.

72831-B**Jug Band Blues                         OK 8188
72832-B  Don't You Quit Me Daddy                OK 8166
72833-B  I Got The Crying Blues                 OK 8176
72834-B  I Ain't Got No Man                     OK 8211

                                         New York, c. September 22, 1924.

72835-B  Blues, Please Go Away                  OK 8176
72836-B  Come Back Daddy And Ease My Aching Heart OK 8231
72837-B  I'm Gonna Be A Lovin' Old Soul         OK 8211
72838-B  Papa, Papa Blues                       OK 8231

Acc. by Lemuel Fowler-p.                 New York, September 24, 1924.

72846-B  What Kinda Man Is You ?                OK 8191
72847-B  Some Blues (No Name Blues)             OK 8226

Acc.  by Clarence Williams-p.            New York, c. September 26, 1924.

72853-B  Old Fashioned Sara Blues                OK 8249
72854-B  Sobbin' Hearted Blues                   OK 8172
72855-B  I'd Rather Be Blue Than Green           OK 8191
72856-B  Cage Of Apes                            OK 8172

Acc. by Clarence Williams' Blue Five : C/tb/as/Clarence Williams-p/Buddy Christian-
bj.                                      New York, c. September 29, 1924.

72857-B  Things Done Got Too Thick               OK 8203
72858-A-B  Eagle Rock Me, Papa                   -

Acc. by Sylvester Weaver-g/Charles Washington-bj, with E. L. Coleman-vn*.
                                         St. Louis, March-April, 1925.

9023-A  Can't Find Nobody To Do Like My Old      OK 8214
          Daddy Do
9024-A  I'm Sorry Blues                          OK 8249
9025-A  Daddy, Ease This Pain Of Mine            OK 8237
9029-A  *Strange Lovin' Blues                    OK 8214
9030-A  *I Can Always Tell When A Man Is Treatin'  OK 8237
          Me Cool
NOTE:- Matrix 9026 is untraced; 9027 by the above accompanists (see INSTRUMENTAL
TRIO, page 803), and 9028 is by E. L. Coleman, q.v.

Acc. by, June Clarke-c/Jimmy Harrison-tb/Clarence Williams-p.
                                         New York, c. November 16, 1925.

73753-B  Down At The Razor Ball                  OK 8283
73754-A  Mournful Blues                          OK 8427
73755-B  Georgia Stockade Blues                  -

Acc. by Bubber Miley-c/Robert Cooksey-h/? Phil Worde-p.
                                         New York, c. November 17, 1925.

73759-B  Forget Me Not Blues                     OK 8292
73760-A  Nobody Knows And Nobody Cares Blues     OK 8304
73761-B  Give Me Just A Little Of Your Time      -

Acc. by Clarence Williams' Blue Five : —— Thomas-c/? Charlie Irvis-tb/as/Clarence
Williams-p-v/? Buddy Christian-bj.       New York, November 23, 1925.

73773-B  I'm Gonna Hoodoo You - vCW              OK 8270
73774-B  Your Going Ain't Giving Me The Blues    -
73775-B  What More Can A Monkey Woman Do ?       OK 8283

Acc. by Harry's Happy Four : Harry Cooper-Louis Metcalf-c/Earres Prince-p/Bernard
Addison-bj.                              New York, November 24, 1925.

73778-B  Some Of These Mornings                  OK 8292
73779-B  Yes, Sir, That's My Baby                OK 8262
73780-B  Alabamy Bound                           -

Acc. by Eddie Heywood-p.                 New York, March 24, 1926.

74062-A  You Don't Want Me Honey                 OK 8354
74063-A  That Dance Called Messin' Around        OK 8308
74064-A  The Last Time                           -
74065-A  Don't Never Figure                      OK 8354

Acc. by Clarence Williams' Blue Five : C/tb/as/Clarence Williams-p/bj/? Cyrus St.
Clair-bb.                                New York, March 24, 1926.

74066-B  What's The Matter Now ?                 OK 8336
74067-B  I Want Every Bit Of It, I Don't Like It  -
          Second Hand

Acc. by Clarence Williams' Blue Five : ? Bubber Miley-c/tb/Otto Hardwick or Don
Redman-as/Clarence Williams-p/bj/? Cyrus St. Clair-bb.
                                        New York, March 25, 1926.

| | | |
|---|---|---|
| 74072-A | Brother Ben | OK 8325 |
| 74073-A | The Prisoner's Blues | OK 8442 |
| 74074-B | Careless Man Blues | OK 8325 |
| 74075-A | How Could I Be Blue ? | OK 8442 |

Acc. by Richard M. Jones' Jazz Wizards : ? Shirley Clay-c/Artie Starks-cl-as/?
Barney Bigard-ts/Richard M. Jones-p/Cliff Jones-d.
                                        Chicago, June 14, 1926.

| | | |
|---|---|---|
| 9708-A | Late Last Night | OK 8374 |
| 9709-A | Some Sweet Day | - |

Acc. by Clarence Williams-p.          New York, September 5, 1926.

| | | |
|---|---|---|
| 74335-B | A Glass Of Beer, A Hot Dog And You | OK 8394 |
| 74336-B | Look Out, Mr. Jazz | - |
| 74337-B | Numbers On The Brain | OK 8412 |
| 74338-B | Shipwrecked Blues | - |

MARTIN-WEAVER-WITHERS : Sara Martin-Sylvester Weaver-Hayes B. Withers-v trio, acc. by
   Sylvester Weaver-g.                 New York, April 6, 1927.

| | | |
|---|---|---|
| 80700-A | Where Shall I Be ? | OK 8661 |
| 80701-A-B | I'm Going To Wait On The Lord | Rejected |
| 80702-A-B | There's Plenty Of Room 'Way In The Kingdom- | |
| 80703-A | I Am Happy In Jesus | OK 8661 |

SALLY ROBERTS : Sara Martin-v, acc. by Sylvester Weaver-g.
                                        New York, April 7, 1927.

| | | |
|---|---|---|
| 80704-A | Gonna Ramble Blues (Roamin' Blues) | OK 8485 |
| 80705-B | Teasing Brown Blues (Mama's Got The Blues) | - |

Vocal, acc. by Clarence Williams' Blue Five : Charlie Irvis-tb/Benny Waters-cl/
   Arville Harris-as/Clarence Williams-p/Cyrus St. Clair-bb.
                                        New York, April 9, 1927.

| | | |
|---|---|---|
| 80712-B | Cushion Foot Stomp | OK 8461, Par R-3506 |
| 80713-B | Take Your Black Bottom Outside (Stop | -      -* |
| | That Black Bottom Dance*) | |

NOTE:- Parlophone R-3506 as MARGARET JOHNSON WITH CLARENCE WILLIAMS' DIXIELAND
ORCHESTRA.

Acc. by Sylvester Weaver-g.           New York, August 30, 1927.

| | | |
|---|---|---|
| 81292-A | Loving Is What I Crave | OK 8513 |
| 81293-B | Useless Blues | OK 8500 |
| 81294-B | Black Hearse Blues | - |
| 81295-B | Orn'ry Blues | OK 8513 |

NOTE:- OKeh 8500 as SALLY ROBERTS.

Acc. by Clarence Williams and his Orchestra : Ed Allen-King Oliver-c/Ed Cuffee-tb/
   Arville Harris-cl/Clarence Williams-p/Cyrus St. Clair-bb.
                                        Long Island City, c. November, 1928.

| | | |
|---|---|---|
| 276-A | Hole In The Wall | QRS R-7035 |
| 277-B | Don't Turn Your Back On Me | - |

Allen omitted; unknown tb replaces Cuffee.
                                        Long Island City, c. November, 1928.

| | | |
|---|---|---|
| 278 (and -A ?) | Death Sting Me Blues | QRS R-7042,Pm 12841,14025,JC L-105 |

Harris omitted.
                                        Long Island City, December, 1928.

| | | |
|---|---|---|
| 305-A | Mean Tight Mama | QRS R-7043 |
| 306 | Mistreating Man Blues | QRS R-7042, Pm 12841 |
| 307-A | Kitchen Man Blues | QRS R-7043 |

Mis-spelling on Paramount and associated labels for Jelly-Roll Morton, q.v.

## FRANK MARVIN

Frank Marvin made hundreds of records for almost every label during the late 1920s
   and early 1930s, but apart from the following, those under his own name are not of
   any interest as jazz, even for their accompaniments.

Vocal, acc. by own g/Mike Mosiello-t.     New York, c. January 15, 1930.

E-31876-   Frankie And Johnny (You'll Miss Me     Br 400, 01135
              In The Days To Come)

   Acc. by ? Manny Klein-t/Tommy Dorsey-tb/Jimmy Dorsey-cl-as/p/Dick McDonough-g/Joe
   Tarto-sb.                                New York, October, 1930.

E-33831/2  My Baby Just Cares For Me              Br 4949, 01052
E-34833-   You're Simply Delish                   -         -

## JOHNNY   MARVIN

This Texan artist made hundreds of sides for Victor, Columbia, the ARC group and (as
   Honey Duke and his Uke) for Harmony and Gennett between 1925 and 1933, of which the
   following have interesting jazz accompaniments, or which have no vocals.

Guitar duets with William Carola.       New York, December 2, 1926.

36991-3  Twelfth Street Rag (Euday L. Bowman)   Vic 20386

                                        New York, December 6, 1926.

37103-4  Memphis Blues                          Vic 20386

Vocal, acc. by Andy Sannella-cl-stg/Frank Banta-p/own u.
                                    New York, April 22, 1927.

38487-3  There's Everything Nice About You      Vic 20612, HMV B-2517, EA-189

Vocal duet with Aileen Stanley, acc. by Jimmy Lytell-cl/Frank Banta-p/? Andy Sannella
   g/own u.                              New York, May 25, 1927.

38781-3  Red Lips, Kiss My Blues Away           Vic 20714, HMV B-2519, EA-212,
                                                El EG-648

Vocal, acc. by Jimmy Lytell-cl/Frank Banta-p/Andy Sannella-stg/own stg-u; the files
   indicate a vn on the second side, but what is heard is a high-pitched cymbal. The
   first side was directed by Leonard Joy, the second by Nat Shilkret, and the rather
   bizarre "scat" vocal effect on the second side is by Marvin himself.
                                    New York, June 7, 1927.

39224-3  Magnolia (Mix The Lot-What Have You Got) Vic 20731, HMV B-2554, EA-215
39225-3  Ain't That A Grand And Glorious Feeling ?   -      HMV B-2529    -

   Acc. by Jimmy Lytell-cl/? Frank Banta-p/Charlie Magnante-pac/own stg-u.
                                    New York, July 27, 1927.

39909-2  It's A Million To One You're In Love    Vic 20832, HMV B-2591, EA-245
39910-2  I'm Afraid You Sing That Song To Somebody Else -      -        -

   Acc. by Mike Mosiello-t/Andy Sannella-cl/Frank Banta-p/own u.
                                    New York, August 24, 1927.

39109-1  Marvelous                              Vic 20893, HMV B-2636, EA-238
39110-3  It All Belongs To Me                     -       HMV B-2643, EA-251

   Acc. by c/Benny Goodman-cl-as/? Lou Raderman-vn/Frank Banta-p/Andy Sannella-g-stg/
   own u.                                New York, April 18, 1928.

43578-1  Angel - cl                             Vic 21376, HMV B-2789, EA-361
43579-3  My Pet - as                            Vic 21435, HMV B-2812, EA-369

Acc. by ? Benny Goodman-cl/Lou Raderman-vn/Abe Borodkin-vc/? Frank Banta-p/? Andy
Sannella-g.                              New York, April 19, 1928.

43654-2-3  I Still Love You                      Vic 21435, HMV B-2812
43655-3  Sweetheart O' Mine                      Vic 21376, HMV EA-361

Acc. by Mike Mosiello-t/Andy Sannella-cl-as/Lou Raderman-vn (except where marked *)
/Frank Banta-p/own g.                    New York, May 2, 1928.

43695-4  Think Of Me Thinking Of You             Vic 21427, HMV B-2786, EA-370
43696-3  *Oh ! You Have No Idea                   Vic 21509, HMV EA-428
43697-2  Golden Gate                             Vic 21427, HMV B-2786, EA-370

                                         New York, August 8, 1928.

46672-3  Old Man Sunshine Little Boy Bluebird    Vic 21609, HMV B-2872, EA-423
46673-2  If You Don't Love Me                     -          -        EA-427

Acc. by ? Manny Klein-t/? Alfie Evans-cl/Joe Venuti-vn/? Arthur Schutt-p/? Tony
Colucci-g.                               New York, August 21, 1928.

46925-1  Crazy Rhythm                            Vic 21650
46926-3  Heartbroken And Lonely                   -        HMV EA-482

Acc. by Mike Mosiello-t/Andy Sannella-cl-as/Louis Martin-as/Joe Ginsberg-ts/Lou
Raderman-vn/Frank Banta-p/Charlie Magnante-pac/Dick Cherwin-sb.
                                         New York, November 7, 1928.

48130-3  There's A Rainbow 'Round My Shoulder    Vic 21780, HMV B-2926, EA-465

Acc. by Mike Mosiello-t/Andy Sannella-cl-as/Lou Raderman-Murray Kellner-Benny
Posner-vn/Abe Borodkin-vc/Frank Banta-p/Dick Cherwin-sb/Joe Green-d.
                                         New York, April 11, 1929.

51615-3  Down Among The Sugar Cane               Vic 21959, HMV B-3077, EA-564

Earl Oliver-t possibly replaces Mosiello; Posner and Borodkin omitted; ? own g.
                                         New York, August 3, 1929.

55644-3  Little By Little                        Vic 22070, HMV B-3185

Acc. by t/cl/p/g.                        New York, March 2, 1932.

152112-1  Seven Come Eleven                      Col 15750-D, Re G-21498

Acc. by Manny Klein-t/Jimmy Dorsey-cl/Harry Hoffman-Matt Malneck-vn/Fulton McGrath-
p/Eddie Lang-g/Artie Bernstein-sb/Chauncey Morehouse or Larry Gomar-d-vib.
                                         New York, January 25, 1933.

12982-1  I'm Playing With Fire                   Mt M-12610, Pan 25471

## MARYLAND DANCE ORCHESTRA

Pseudonym on Coliseum for the following items listed in this book :-

1675  Savannah (The Ambassadors)
1690  Any Way The Wind Blows (Bar Harbor Society Orchestra)
1717  Cuddle Up A Little Closer (The Ambassadors)
1723  Words (Fletcher Henderson and his Orchestra)
1724  Oh ! How I Love My Darling (The Ambassadors)
1734  How I Love That Girl (Ben Bernie and his Hotel Roosevelt Orchestra)
1788  Sweet Georgia Brown (Ben Bernie and his Hotel Roosevelt Orchestra)
1789  Steppin' In Society (Ben Selvin and his Orchestra)
1824  Let's Wander Away (Ben Selvin and his Orchestra)
1828  Breezin' Along (To Georgia) (Ben Selvin and his Orchestra)
1867  That's All There Is (Jeffries and his Rialto Orchestra)
1870  Shanghai Honeymoon (Bob Deikman and his Orchestra)
1878  Sweet Child (Bailey's Lucky Seven)
1880  I Want Somebody To Cheer Me Up (Bailey's Lucky Seven)
1884  The Roses Brought Me You (Bailey's Lucky Seven)
    (cont. on page 1017)

1894  Dinah (Bailey's Lucky Seven)
1906  Both sides by the Vagabonds
1909  Goodnight (I'll See You In The Morning) (The Southerners)
1912  After I Say I'm Sorry (Bailey's Lucky Seven)
1921  I'd Climb The Highest Mountain (The Vagabonds)
1953  St. Louis Hop (Joe Candullo and his Everglades Orchestra)
1971  Don't Take That Black Bottom Away (Fred Rich and his Times Square Orchestra)
2039  What Do I Care What Somebody Said ? (Harry Pollock's Maurice Club Blue Diamonds)

## ALBERT MASON'S ORCHESTRA

Pseudonym on Parlophone PNY-34069 for Smith Ballew's Orchestra; on PNY-34104, 34105,
   34115 and 34174 for Sam Lanin's Famous Players; and on PNY-34185 and 34187 for Fred
   Rich and his Orchestra, q.v. in each case.

## BILLY MASON AND HIS ORCHESTRA

Duncan Whyte-t/David Shand-cl-as/Buddy Featherstonhaugh-ts/Billy Mason-p/Alan
   Ferguson-g/Bill Busby-sb/George Elrick-d.
                                        London, February 25, 1935.

TB-1719-1  It Had To Be You                    Dec rejected
TB-1720-1  St. Louis Blues                     -

                                   London, May 7, 1935.

TB-1788-1  Paradise                            Dec F-5773
TB-1789-2  If You Knew Susie                   Dec F-5564, Ch 40035
TB-1790-2  Don't Be Angry                      -          -
TB-1791-2  My Mammy                            Dec F-5773

See also Valaida.

## CHARLES MASON AND HIS MELODY BOYS

Pseudonym on Clarite for Joe Candullo and his Everglades Orchestra, q.v.

## JERRY MASON'S CALIFORNIANS

Pseudonym on Harmony 1242-H and 1260-H for the Travelers (see the Dorsey Brothers'
   Orchestra), and on Harmony 965-H for Ben Selvin and his Orchestra, q.v.  Others
   issued under this name are not known to be of great - or even any - interest as
   "hot" dance music.

## MASON-DIXON ORCHESTRA

Charlie Margulis-Harry Goldfield-Andy Secrest-t/Bill Rank-tb/Izzy Friedman-cl-as/
   Frank Trumbauer-Cm/Charles Strickfaden-as-bar/Min Leibrook-bsx/Lennie Hayton-p/
   Snoozer Quinn-g/George Marsh-d.        New York, May 15, 1929.

148537-3  What A Day !                         Col 1861-D
148538-4  Alabamy Snow                         -

## MASON-DIXON SEVEN ORCHESTRA

Art Weems-c/Ted Weems-tb/Norman Nugent-cl-as/Nelson Maple-p/Fuzzy Knight-d/Dillon Ober
   marimba, possibly others.              New York, May 19, 1922.

80355-1-2-3  I'm Just Wild About Harry        Col rejected

## MASSELTOP KAPELLE

See Original Excentric Band.

## PETE MASSEY'S ALL-BLACK BAND

Pseudonym on Guardsman for the Tennessee Tooters, q.v., except for the following :-

7012  Throw-Down Blues (The Ambassadors)
7014  Memphis Bound (Fletcher Henderson and his Orchestra)
7017  When You Do What You Do (Fletcher Henderson and his Orchestra)

Pseudonym on National Music Lovers Records for the following items listed in this
  book :-

1037  You Know You Belong To Somebody Else (California Ramblers)
1133  Then I'll Be Happy (Fletcher Henderson and his Orchestra)
1178  Baby Face (The Buffalodians)

## THE MASTER PLAYERS

See Nathan Glantz and his Orchestra (Apex 8242 and 8272).

## FRANKIE MASTERS AND HIS ORCHESTRA

The following titles made by this band for Victor in 1928 are known to be of interest
  as "hot" dance music; so far, none of the Vocalion-OKeh issues of 1939-1942 have
  been reported so.

Leroy Shield dir. S. J. Stocco and another-t/tb/2cl-as/Frank Wagner-cl-ts/vn/p/bj-g/
  bb/d/Frankie Masters-v.                    Chicago, July 5, 1928.

    46061-2  My Darling - vFM                      Vic 21565

                                        Chicago, July 17, 1928.

    46418-3  Is It Gonna Be Long ? (Till You Belong   Vic 21602
             To Me) - vFM

## MINNIE MATHES

Vocal, acc. by ? Buster Bennett-as/md/Willie Bee James-g/Ransom Knowling-sb.
                                        Chicago, September 19, 1938.

C-2335-1  Ball Game Blues                          Voc 04431
C-2336-1  Please Come Home Daddy Blues              -
C-2337-1-2  Winding Daddy Come On                  Rejected
C-2338-1-2  Chicago Men Blues                       -

## EMMET MATHEWS

See Emmett Matthews.

## CHARLES MATSON

Charles Matson was a negro pianist and arranger who was very active in New York in
  the mid-1920s.  Apart from various blues accompaniments, he recorded as director of
  Ted Claire's Snappy Bits Band, q.v., and the following.  The Edisons have been
  ascribed to Freddie Keppard on the one hand and the Benson Orchestra of Chicago on
  the other, but the performances do not bear the slightest resemblance to anything
  recorded by either artist, and the true identities of the personnel remain unknown.

CHAS. A. MATSON'S CREOLE SERENADERS : Charles Matson-p-a dir. c/tb/cl-as/as/ts/bj/bb/
  d.                                     New York, July 30, 1923.

    9104    'Tain't Nobody's Business If I Do      Ed 51222
    9105    I Just Want A Daddy (I Can Call My Own)  Ed 51224

MATSON'S LUCKY SEVEN : Charles Matson-p-a dir. 2c/? John Mayfield-tb/? Ernest Elliott
  cl-as/? Sam Speed-bj.                  New York, January, 1924.

    1654-1-3  Lawdy Lawdy Blues                    Pm 20306, Cx 40306, Pur 11306
    1655-1-2  Jail House Blues                      -            -          -

## EMMETT MATTHEWS

EMMET MATHEWS : Vocal, acc. by Cassino Simpson-p, with Laura Rucker-v.*
                                        Grafton, Wis., c. May, 1931.

    L-903-3  *Upside Down                          Pm 13087
    L-905-2  St. James' Infirmary                   -

Emmett Matthews-as-v dir. Herman Autrey-t/Fred Robinson-tb/Rudy Powell-cl-as/Hank
    Duncan-p/Gene Fields-g/Charles Turner-sb/Slick Jones-d.
                                        New York, April 10, 1936.

| | | |
|---|---|---|
| 18995-1 | You Can't Pull The Wool Over My Eyes-vEM Voc 3228 | |
| 18996-1 | I'll Stand By - vEM | Voc 3226 |
| 13997-1 | There's Always A Happy Ending - vEM | - |
| 18998-1 | Take A Good Look At Mine - vEM | Voc 3228 |

    Robinson omitted; Powell db bar; Gene Sedric-cl-ts added.
                                        New York, September 8, 1936.

| | | |
|---|---|---|
| 19826- | You Came To My Rescue - vEM | Voc 3332 |
| 19827- | Bojangles Of Harlem - vEM | Voc 3317 |
| 19828- | The Way You Look Tonight - vEM | - |
| 19829- | Night In Manhattan - vEM | Voc 3332 |

## GEORGE MATTHEWS AND THE CAROLINA NIGHT HAWKS

2c/tb/2as/ts/vn/p/bj/bb/d.                  New York, June 16, 1927.

GEX-678-B  Oh Miss Hannah !                  Gnt 6183, Ch 15305, GS 40111
    NOTE:- Champion 15305 as KING PORTER AND HIS ORCHESTRA (!)

## MAE MATTHEWS

Johnnie Mae Matthews-girl v, acc. by ? W. E. Burton-p.
                                        Richmond, Ind., March 23, 1928.

| | | |
|---|---|---|
| 13607 | Dirty Woman Blues | Gnt 6438 |
| 13608 | Satisfied Blues | Gnt 6439, Ch 15490, Spr 387 |

    NOTE:- Champion 15490 as MAXINE HARRIS.

## MAURICE MELODY MAKERS

Pseudonym on Scala 768 (AFTER I SAY I'M SORRY) for Vailey's Lucky Seven, q.v.

## MAXSA'S NEW YORK ORCHESTRA

Pseudonym on Maxsa 1512 (IT HAD TO BE YOU) for the New Orleans Jazz Band, q.v.

## TINY MAYBERRY

Vocal, acc. by Charlie Shavers or Jonah Jones-t/? Buster Bailey-cl/? Lil Armstrong-p/
    sb/? Sid Catlett-d.                  New York, July 20, 1938.

| | | |
|---|---|---|
| 64325-A | I Got A Feeling For You | Dec 7593 |
| 64326-A | Someday, Someday | Dec 7496 |
| 64327-C | Oh That Nasty Man | - |
| 64328-A | Mailman Blues | Dec 7593 |
| 64329-A | Mayberry Blues | Dec 7520 |
| 64330-B | Evil Hearted Woman | - |

## ETHEL MAYES

Pseudonym on Harmograph for Monette Moore, q.v.

## MAYFAIR DANCE ORCHESTRA

The Gramophone Company's "house" orchestra made hundreds of sides for HMV between
    1912 and 1921, the undermentioned being of curio interest. The personnel included
    only 2c and 2tb, but collectively it was as follows.

George W. Byng dir. Charles Smith-Frank Kettlewell-Henry Godard-c/Jesse Stamp- ——
    Atherley- —— Mayhew- —— Godard-tb/Robert McKenzie-Frank Hughes- —— Leonard-cl
    /Arthur Foreman-o/Edwin Hinchcliffe-bsn/Gilbert Barton-pic/W. E. Gordon Walker-f-a/
    Jean Bobbe and another-vn/Pietro Nifosi-vc/E. W. Rushforth or Charles "Wag" Abbey-d.
                                        Hayes, Middlesex, April 1, 1919.

HO-4809ae  Balloons And Kisses - Jazz One-Step     HMV B-1027

George W. Byng dir. same personnel as shown at the foot of page 1019.
                                    Hayes, Middlesex, October 16, 1919.

HO-4011af  Fidgety Feet - aWEGW                    HMV C-924

## MAYFIELD DANCE ORCHESTRA

Pseudonym on Coliseum for the following items listed in this book :-

1659  Shine (Jeffries and his Rialto Orchestra)
1729  Too Tired (The Ambassadors)
1729  Mandy (Ben Bernie and his Hotel Roosevelt Orchestra)
1745  Why Couldn't It Be Poor Little Me ? (Ben Bernie and his Hotel Roosevelt Orch.)
1834  Charleston Mad (Jeffries and his Rialto Orchestra)
1869  That Certain Party (The Southerners)
1882  What Did I Tell Ya ? (Kerr's Famous Players)
1885  Too Too (Jeffries and his Rialto Orchestra)
1886  Old Fashioned Love (The Ambassadors)
1911  Mysterioys Eyes (Jack Stillman's Orchestra)
1915  Then I'll Be Happy (Bailey's Lucky Seven)
1922  That's Why I Love You (Joe Candullo and his Everglades Orchestra)
1927  Kantinka (Joe Candullo and his Everglades Orchestra)
1927  Horses (Barney Zeeman's Kentucky Cardinals)
1939  Me Too (Harry Bidgood and his Orchestra)
1950  Both sides by the Vagabonds
1961  Cry Baby (Joe Candullo and his Everglades Orchestra)
1967  In A Little Garden (Joe Candullo and his Everglades Orchestra)

## MAYFLOWER SERENADERS

Pseudonym on Pathe Actuelle 10846 for Harl Smith and his Orchestra, q.v.

## NORRIDGE MAYHAMS

BLUE CHIP NORRIDGE MAYHAMS AND HIS BLUE BOYS : Probably similar to the second session.
                                    New York, November 27, 1936.

20337-1-2  Sloppy Drunk Woman                      ARC rejected

NORRIDGE MAYHAMS AND HIS BARBECUE BOYS : Ts/p/g/sb/d/Johnny Tunsill-v.
                                    New York, December 11, 1936.

20337-   Sloppy Drunk Woman - vJT              Voc 03498, ARC 7-05-63
20391-1  Wrap Your Troubles In Dreams - vJT    Voc 03465, ARC 7-04-74
20392-1  Ash Haulin' Blues - vJT               Voc 03429
20393-1  Enuff To Run You - vJT                     -
20394-1  If I Had My Way - vJT                 Voc 03465, ARC 7-04-74
20395-   'Tain't No Use - vJT                  Voc 03498, ARC 7-05-63

## TED MAYS AND  HIS BAND

T/as/p/bj-g/d/Claytie Polk-v.          San Antonio, September 18, 1937.

014310-1  Gee, It Must Be Love - vCP              BB B-7193
014311-1  Married Man Blues - vCP                 BB B-7237
014312-1  Take It On Home To Grandma - vCP        BB B-7206
014313-1  I Want Some - vCP                           -
014314-1  My Cabin Of Dreams - vCP                BB B-7193
014315-1  You Don't Mean Me No Good - vCP         BB B-7237

## McALPIN  ORCHESTRA

Pseudonym on Pathe Actuelle 36866 and 36870 (Perfect ;5047 and 15051) for the California Ramblers, q.v.

## THE  McALPINEERS

Pseudonym on Edison for the California Ramblers, q.v.

Piano solo.                          Richmond, Ind., June 27, 1928.

  13935    Maple Leaf Rag (Scott Joplin)          Gnt 20335

## GEORGE McCLENNON

GEORGE McCLENNON'S JAZZ DAVILS : Probably :- Tom Morris-c/Charlie Irvis-tb/George
  McClennon-cl/Bob Fuller-as/Clarence Williams-p/Buddy Christian-bj/d.
                                         New York, May 9, 1924.

  72512-B  Box Of Blues                         OK 8143, Od 03180
  72513-B  Dark Alley Blues                        -         -

    ?2c/probably :- John Lindsay-tb/George McClennon-cl/as/Clarence Williams-p/Buddy
    Christian-bj/d.                       New York, c. May 14, 1924.

  72524-B  New Orleans Wiggle                     OK 8150, Od 03221
  72525-B  Michigan Water Blues                      -

Clarinet solos, acc. by Eddie Heywood-p.  New York, c. May 2, 1925.

  73343-B  Cut Throat Blues                       OK 8314
  73344-B  Larkin Street Blues                       -       Par R-3256

GEORGE McCLENNON'S JAZZ DAVILS : C/tb/George McClennon-cl-v/as/? Eddie Heywood-p/bj/
    d.                                   New York, May 7, 1925.

  73359-   Home Alone Blues - vGM                 OK 8236
  73360-   Anybody Here Want To Try My Cabbage ?-vGM   -

                                         New York, June 11, 1925.

  73425-D  Everybody But Me - vGM                 OK 8337
  73426-C  Bologny                                   -

                                         New York, c. June 18, 1926.

  74177-A  Stolen Kisses - vGM                    OK 8329
  74178-A  While You're Sneakin' Out - vGM           -

    Bb added; d omitted.               New York, August, 1926.

  74320-B  Pig Foot Blues                         OK 8397

GEORGE McCLENNON'S JAZZ BAND : As last.   New York, September 29, 1926.

  74377-B  Cotton Club Stomp                      OK 8397

The following titles probably belong one each to the last two sessions.

          Disaster                               OK 8406
          Narrow Escape                             -

## CLYDE  McCOY

Despite interesting titles among the sides made by the famous "wa-wa" trumpet-player,
  only the following seem to come within the scope of this book.

CLYDE McCOY AND HIS DRAKE HOTEL ORCHESTRA : Clyde McCoy-t-mel dir. W. L. Waller-t/
  Tommy Miller-tb/Bud Prentiss-John Cameron-cl-as/Bobby Blair-ts/Eddie Lowth-vn/
  Johnny Petrone-p/Freddy Taylor-bj-g/Stan McCoy-bb-sb/Mel Wilke-d.
                                         Chicago, August 22, 1933.

152477-2  Nobody's Sweetheart                    Col 2808-D
152480-2  Tear It Down - v                       Col 2909-D, Mt M-13409, Per 16124

CLYDE McCOY AND HIS ORCHESTRA : Probably very similar to the personnel shown on page
   1021.                                    Chicago, July 5, 1935.

| | | |
|---|---|---|
| C-90073-A | Rose Room | Ch 40102 |
| C-90074-A | Maple Leaf Rag (Scott Joplin) | Dec 681, Rex 9902 |
| C-90075-A | Oh Baby | Ch 40102 |
| C-90076-A | After You've Gone | Ch 40108, Rex 9375 |
| C-90077-A | Some Of These Days | – |
| C-90078-A | Farewell Blues | Rex 9933 |

   NOTE:- Champion 40102 and 40108 as BILLY CLYDE AND HIS ORCHESTRA.

## VIOLA McCOY

Vocal, acc. by Porter Grainger-p.          New York, c. March 7, 1923.

| | | |
|---|---|---|
| 8267 | Whoa, Tillie ! Take Your Time | Rejected |
| 8268, -A | If You Want To Keep Your Daddy Home | Gnt 5108, St 9374 |
| 8269 | Laughin' Cryin' Blues | –        – |

                                           New York, March 27, 1923.

| | | |
|---|---|---|
| 80912-3 | Laughin' Cryin' Blues | Col A-3867 |
| 80913-1 | Strut Long Papa | – |

   NOTE:- This issue as AMANDA BROWN.

                                           New York, April 11, 1923.

| | | |
|---|---|---|
| 8328, -A | Midnight Blues (A Wee Hour Chant) | Gnt 5128 |
| 8329-B | Triflin' Blues (Daddy Don't You Trifle On Me) – | |

Acc. by Bob Ricketts' Band : Possibly : Tom Morris-c/Charlie Irvis-tb/Ernest
Elliott-cl/Bob Fuller-as/Bob Ricketts-p/Buddy Christian or Elmer Snowden-bj.
                                           New York, April 26, 1923.

| | | |
|---|---|---|
| 8355, -A | Tired O' Waitin' Blues | Gnt 5151 |
| 8356, -A | Gulf Coast Blues | – |

Acc. by Porter Grainger-p.                 New York, April 27, 1923.

| | | |
|---|---|---|
| 80990-3 | Triflin' Blues | Col A-3901 |
| 80991-3 | Chirpin' The Blues | – |

   NOTE:- This issue as AMANDA BROWN.

Acc. by Bob Ricketts-p.                     New York, May 16, 1923.

| | | |
|---|---|---|
| 8370 | Just Thinkin' (A Blues) | Gnt 5162, St 9405 |
| 8371 | Chirpin' The Blues | –        – |

Acc. by Porter Grainger-p, with own k.   New York, May 24, 1923.

| | | |
|---|---|---|
| 81033-3 | Tired O' Waitin' Blues | Col A-3921 |
| 81034-3 | Michigan Water Blues - kVM | – |

   NOTE:- This issue as AMANDA BROWN.

                                           New York, June 5, 1923.

| | | |
|---|---|---|
| 8389-A | Long Lost Mama | Gnt 5175 |
| 8390 | Wish I Had You (And I'm Gonna Get You Blues) | – |

                                           New York, June 27, 1923.

| | | |
|---|---|---|
| 11655 | Sad And Lonely Blues | Voc 14632, Sil 3005 |
| 11656/7 | Just Thinkin' (Blues) | –        – |
| 11659 | Bleeding Hearted Blues | Voc 14633, Sil 3006 |
| 11661 | If You Want To Keep Your Daddy Home | –        – |

                                           New York, August 7, 1923.

| | | |
|---|---|---|
| 11805 | 'Tain't No Tellin' What The Blues Will<br>Make You Do | Voc 14653 |
| 11806 | Bama Bound Blues | – |

Acc. by Porter Grainger-p.        New York, September 27, 1923.

| 12029 | Mistreatin' Daddy | Voc 14689 |
| 12032 | Wish I Had You (And I'm Gonna Get You Blues) - | |

Acc. by Fletcher Henderson-p.       New York, c. October, 1923.

| | Don't Mean You No Good Blues | Ajax 17010 |
| | Lonesome Daddy Blues | - |

New York, c. February 1, 1924.

| 105114 | I've Got The World In A Jug | PA 032035, 10693, Per 12114 |
| 105115 | Do Right Blues | -       -      - |

NOTE:- Pathe Actuelle 032035 and Perfect 12114 as AMANDA BROWN.

Acc. by Fletcher Henderson's Jazz Five : Elmer Chambers-c/Teddy Nixon-tb/Don Redman cl/Fletcher Henderson-p/Charlie Dixon-bj.
New York, February 13, 1924.

| 12516/7 | Do Right Blues | Br rejected |
| 12518/9 | Ev'ry Day Blues | - |

New York, March 11, 1924.

| 12689/91 | If Your Good Man Quits You, Don't Wear | Br 2591 |
| | No Black | |
| 12692/3 | I Ain't Gonna Marry, Ain't Gonna Settle Down- | |

Acc. by Edgar Dowell-p, with ? Robert Cooksey-h/Elmer Snowden-bj*.
New York, April 14, 1924.

| 13007 | *West Indies Blues | Voc 14801, Gmn 7003 |
| 13012 | It Makes No Difference Now | -     Gmn 7002 |

NOTE:- Guardsman 7002 and 7003 as DAISY CLIFF.

Acc. by Charles Dixon-g.       New York, c. April 17, 1924.

| 5482-2 | Mama's Gone, Goodbye | Ban 1357, Dom 361, Or 264, Re 9653 |
| 5483-1-2 | You Don't Know My Mind | Ban 1371, Dom 363, Or 265, Re 9667 |

NOTE:- Domino 361 and 363 as BESSIE WILLIAMS acc. by MELVILLE AMES; Oriole 264 and 265 as CLARA WHITE acc. by HARRY SIMS.

Acc. by Fletcher Henderson-p.      New York, c. April 18, 1924.

| 5484-1-2 | Buzzin' Around | Ban 1357, Dom 363, Or 264, Re 9653 |
| 5490-1 | I Don't Know And I Don't Care Blues | ᴰᵒᵐ 364 |

NOTE:- Domino 363 and 364 as BESSIE WILLIAMS acc. by EMMETT TAYLOR; Oriole 264 as CLARA WHITE acc. by SAM HILL. It is possible that matrix 5484 was made at the same session as 5482 and 5483; it is very likely that 5490 is not from eithersession.

Acc. by Fletcher Henderson's Jazz Five : Probably as for February 13, 1924.
New York, April 22, 1924.

| 12946/7 | I Don't Want Nobody That Don't Want Me | Br rejected |
| 12948/9 | It Makes No Difference Now | - |

Acc. by Edgar Dowell-p, with own k and Elmer Snowden-bj as shown.
New York, May 2, 1924.

| 13147 | I Don't Want Nobody That Don't Want Me-k | Voc 14818 |
| 13150 | Mama, Mama (Don't Love Her Papa No More) | - |
| | Stop It, Joe - k/bj | Rejected |

Acc. by Fletcher Henderson-p.      New York, c. May 20, 1924.

| 5509-2 | How Come You Do Me Like You Do ? | Ban 1371, Dom 362, Or 265, Re 9667 |

NOTE:- Domino 362 as BESSIE WILLIAMS, acc. by EMMETT TAYLOR; Oriole 265 as CLARA WHITE, acc. by SAM HILL.

Acc. by Fletcher Henderson-p.                    New York, c. June 30, 1924.

5544-1-2  Clearing House Blues                   Ban 1394, Dom 364, Or 263, Re 9690
NOTE:- Domino 364 as BESSIE WILLIAMS, acc. by EMMETT TAYLOR; Oriole 263 as CLARA
WHITE, acc. by SAM HILL.

Vocal duets with Billy Higgins, acc. by ? Bubber Miley-c/? Arthur Ray-p.
                                New York, October, 1924.

13805     Keep On Going                          Voc 14912, Sil 3019
13806     Get Yourself A Monkey Man And Make Him        -              -
            Strut His Stuff

Acc. by the Choo Choo Jazzers : Bob Fuller-cl/Louis Hooper-p.
                                New York, c. October, 1924.

31696     I Don't Want Nobody (That Don't Want Me)  Ajax 17069
31699     Keep On Going                            -

Acc. by the Kansas City Five : ? Bubber Miley-c/Jake Frazier-tb/Bob Fuller-cl/
Arthur Ray or Louis Hooper-p/Elmer Snowden-bj/own k.
                                New York, November 21, 1924.

9860      Memphis Bound                          Ed 51478

Acc. by the Dixie Trio : Bob Fuller-cl/vn/? Louis Hooper-p.
                                New York, c. December, 1925.

          South Street Blues                     Voc 1002, 15268, Or 1002
          Charleston Blues                         -        -        -
NOTE:- This issue is labelled as accompanied by cornet, clarinet and piano.  It is
said that copies exist of Oriole 1002 that are not by Viola McCoy, but this is most
improbable.

Acc. by Rex Stewart-c/vn/p, not vn/vc/p as labelled.
                                New York, January 6, 1926.

E-2043/5  Stomp Your Blues Away                  Voc 15245
E-2046/8  Shake That Thing                         -

Acc. by Louis Metcalf-c/Cliff Jackson-p. New York, c. November 29, 1926.

2219-C  I'm Savin' It All For You                Cam 1066, Ro 302, Vri 5033
2220-B  Papa, If You Can't Do Better               -         -
          (I'll Let A Better Man Move In)
NOTE:- Variety 5033 as GLADYS JOHNSON.

                                New York, c. December 28, 1926.

2261-C  "Git" Goin'                              Cam 1097, Lin 2612, Ro 374
2262-B  Someday You'll Come Back To Me             -         -         - Vri 5048
NOTE:- Lincoln 2612 as SUSAN WILLIAMS; Variety 5048 as GLADYS JOHNSON.

Acc. by Rex Stewart-c/Louis Hooper-p.    New York, c. March 1, 1927.

2364-A-C  Slow Up Papa                           Cam 1144, Ro 375, Vri 5048
2365-A-B  Fortune Teller Blues                     -         -
NOTE:- Cameo 1144 as FANNIE JOHNSON; Variety 5048 as GLADYS JOHNSON.

Acc. by ? Horace Holmes-c/cl/Cliff Jackson-p.
                                New York, c. May 2, 1927.

2447-C  Black Snake Blues                        Cam 1158, Ro 385, Vri 5085
2448-B  Soul And Body (He Belongs To Me)           -         -        -
NOTE:- Cameo 1158 as FANNIE JOHNSON; Variety 5085 as GLADYS JOHNSON.

Acc. by ? Horace Holmes-c/Louis Hooper-p.New York, c. June 7, 1927.

2495-B  Back Water Blues                         Cam 1189, Lin 2651, Ro 416
2496-A  Mama Is Waitin' For You                    -         -        -
NOTE:- Lincoln 2651 as SUSAN WILLIAMS; Romeo 416 as FANNIE JOHNSON.

Acc. by Bob Fuller-cl/Louis Hooper-p.    New York, c. August 26, 1927.

2584-C  Dyin' Crap-Shooter's Blues            Cam 1225, Lin 2690, Ro 453
2585-A  Gay-Catin' Daddy                         -           -        -
NOTE:- Lincoln 2690 as SUSAN WILLIAMS; Romeo 453 as FANNIE JOHNSON.

Acc. by the California Ramblers : Chelsea Quealey-t/Al Philburn-tb/Pete Pumiglio-cl
/Sam Ruby-ts/Spencer Clark-bsx/Jack Russin-p/Tommy Felline-bj/Herb Weil-d.
                                          New York, November 3, 1927.

        I Wish I Could Shimmy Like My Sister Kate Cam rejected
        A Good Man Is Hard To Find                    -
        I Ain't Got Nobody                            -
NOTE:- Only two of these scheduled titles were actually recorded, but which these
were is not known.

Acc. by c/p.                              New York, January 11, 1929.

147772-3  I Want A Good Man (And I Want Him Bad)   Col 14395-D
147773-1  If You Really Love Your Baby                -

NOTE:- On some of the above records, t is artist is described as VIOLET McCOY.

## WILLIAM  McCOY

Harmonica ("mouth harp") solos, with speech.
                                          Dallas, December 6, 1927.

145334-2  Mama Blues                            Col 14302-D, 15269-D
145335-1  Train Imitations and The Fox Chase       -           -

Acc. by ? Sam Harris-g.                   Dallas, December 7, 1928.

147593-2  Just It                               Col 14393-D
147594-1  How Long Baby                            -

Jesse Hooker-cl added*.                   Dallas, December 8, 1928.

147610-1-2  *Out Of Doors Blues                 Col 14453-D
147611-1  Central Tracks Blues                     -

## RANDOLPH McCURTAIN'S  COLLEGE RAMBLERS

C/tb/cl-as/cl-ts/vn/p/bj/bb/d.            Dallas, October, 1925.

9366-A  Sweet Girl Mary                        OKeh Ramblers' Record 1
9368-A  Low Down Brown                            -
NOTE:- Matrix 9367 is untraced.

## HATTIE McDANIELS

Vocal, acc. by Phram and Utterbach (—— Phram-p/Sam Utterbach-c).
                                          Kansas City, c. June, 1926.

2-X  Quittin' My Man Today                     Merritt 2202
3-X  Brown-Skin Baby Doll                        -

Acc. by Lovie Austin's Serenaders : C/Preston Jackson-tb/Darnell Howard-as/Lovie
Austin-p/Johnny St. Cyr-bj.               Chicago, November 17, 1926.

9899-A  I Wish I Had Somebody                   OK 8434
9900-A  Boo Hoo Blues                             -
NOTE:- This issue as HATTIE McDANIEL.

Acc. Richard M. Jones' Jazz Wizards : Probably :- Shirley Clay-c/Artie Starks-cl-as
/Richard M. Jones-p/Johnny St. Cyr-bj, and others.
                                          Chicago, May 7, 1927.

80845-A-B  Wonderful Dream                      OK rejected
80846-A  Lonely Heart                             -

Acc. by Richard M. Jones' Jazz Wizards : (?) Shirley Clay-c/Artie Starks-cl-as/
Richard M. Jones-p/Johnny St. Cyr-bj.    Chicago, May 10, 1927.

| | | |
|---|---|---|
| 80852-A-B | Sam Henry Blues | OK rejected |
| 80853-A-B | Poor Boy Blues | - |

Acc. by Tiny Parham-p.                    Chicago, December 14, 1927.

| | | |
|---|---|---|
| 82061-A | I Thought I'd Do It | OK 8569 |
| 82062-B | Just One Sorrowing Heart | - |
| 82063-A-B | Sam Henry Blues | Rejected |
| 82064-A-B | Destroyin' Blues | - |

Vocal duets with "Dentist" Jackson (? Papa Charlie Jackson-g)/?.Lovie Austin-p.
                              Chicago, c. March, 1929.

| | | |
|---|---|---|
| 21203-2 | Dentist Chair Blues - Part 1 | Pm 12751 |
| 21204-2 | Dentist Chair Blues - Part 2 | - |

Vocal, acc. by Vance Dixon-cl/? Kline Tyndall-p, not c/p as shown on the labels.
                              Chicago, c. March, 1929.

| | | |
|---|---|---|
| 21224-2 | That New Love Maker Of Mine | Pm 12790 (also allocated to issue |
| 21225-2 | Any Kind Of A Man Would Be Better Than You  - | by Charlie Spand) |

## EARL McDONALD'S ORIGINAL LOUISVILLE JUG BAND

Lucien Brown-as/Cal Smith-bj/Benny Calvin-md/Earl McDonald-jug-v/v quartet (most
probably the band).                    Atlanta, March 30, 1927.

| | | |
|---|---|---|
| 143805-2 | She's In The Graveyard Now - vEM | Col 14255-D |
| 143806-2 | Casey Bill - vEM | Col 14371-D |
| 143807-2 | Louisville Special | Col 14226-D |
| 143808-2-3 | Rocking Chair Blues - vEM | - |
| 143809-2 | Mama's Little Sunny Boy | Col 14371-D |
| 143810-1 | She Won't Quit But She'll Slow Down | Col 14255-D |
| 143811-2 | Under The Chicken Tree - vEM&4 | Col 14206-D |
| 143812-2 | Melody March Call | - |

## HELEN McDONALD

Vocal, acc. by Lemuel Fowler-p.        New York, c. July 4, 1923.

| | | |
|---|---|---|
| 8431-B | Squawkin' The Blues | Gnt 5193 |
| 8432-B | You Got Ev'rything A Sweet Mama Needs (But Me)- | |

## TEE McDONALD

Girl singer, acc. by Henry Brown-p.    Chicago, August 24, 1934.

| | | |
|---|---|---|
| C-9350- | Beef Man Blues | Dec 7018 |

## DICK McDONOUGH

DICK McDONOUGH AND HIS ORCHESTRA : Dick McDonough-g dir. unknown instrumentation and
personnel.                        New York, March 13, 1929.

| | | |
|---|---|---|
| 401711-A | Broadway Rose | OK rejected |

Guitar solos.                         New York, November 22, 1934.

| | | |
|---|---|---|
| TO-1481/TO-1482 | Unknown titles | "Tests for John Hammond" |
| TO-1483-1 | Honeysuckle Rose | CBS AL-33567 (LP) |

DICK McDONOUGH AND HIS ORCHESTRA : ? Yank Lawson and another-t/tb/Toots Mondello-cl-
as/Babe Russin or Larry Binyon-cl-ts/Claude Thornhill-p/Dick McDonough-g/Mort
Stuhlmaker or Artie Bernstein-sb/? Cozy Cole-d/Chick Bullock-Dorothy Dreslin-v.
                              New York, June 4, 1936.

| | | |
|---|---|---|
| 19373-1 | Take My Heart - vCB | ARC 6-08-07, Rex 8834, Kr 4222 |
| 19374-2 | Stars In My Eyes (w) - vDD | -        Lucky S-71 |
| 19375-1 | The Scene Changes - vCB | ARC 6-08-08, Cq 8678, Cr 235 |
| 19376-1 | On The Beach At Bali-Bali - vCB | - Rex 8807  -      Kr 4223, |
| | | Lucky 60509 |

NOTE:- 9" Crown 235 as BUDDY BARNETT AND HIS MUSIC.

Bunny Berigan-t/Artie Shaw-cl/Larry Binyon-cl-ts/Adrian Rollini-bsx/Claude Thornhill-
p/Dick McDonough-g/sb/Chauncey Morehouse-d/Buddy Clark—v/possibly others.
New York, June 23, 1936.

| 19466-1 | Summer Holiday - vBC | ARC 6-09-07 | | |
| 19467-1 | I'm Grateful To You - vBC | - | | |
| 19468-1 | Dear Old Southland - vBC | ARC 6-09-08, Voc C-0012, Imp 6094 | | |
| 19469-1 | 'Way Down Yonder In New Orleans - vBC | - | - | - |

Bunny Berigan-t/Lloyd Turner-tb/Toots Mondello-cl-as/Larry Binyon-cl-ts/Adrian
Rollini-bsx-vib/Manny Prager-p/Dick McDonough-g/Paul Prince-sb/Cozy Cole-d/Buddy
Clark-v.                                     New York, August 4, 1936.

| 19649-1 | Dardanella | ARC 7-02-04, Voc C-0004, S-174, Imp 18018 |
| 19650-1 | It Ain't Right - vBC | ARC 6-11-02, Voc C-0003 |
| 19651-1 | Between The Devil And The Deep Blue Sea | ARC 7-02-04, Voc C-0004, S-174, Imp 6050 |
| 19652-1 | In A Sentimental Mood | ARC 6-11-02, Voc C-0003, Imp 18018 |

Rollini omitted.                              New York, August 5, 1936.

| 19663-1 | When The Moon Hangs High - vBC | ARC 6-11-04 | |
| 19664-1 | Midnight Blue - vBC | - | Cq 8724 |
| 19665-1 | South Sea Island Magic - vBC | ARC 6-11-01, Cq 8750, Rex 8890 | |
| 19666-1 | Afterglow - vBC | - | - | - |

Bunny Berigan and another-t/Jack Lacey-tb/? Toots Mondello-cl-as/Babe Russin-ts/
Claude Thornhill-p/Dick McDonough-g/Paul Prince-sb/Cozy Cole-d/Larry Stewart-Chick
Bullock-v.                                   New York, September 17, 1936.

| 19891-1 | I'm One Step Ahead Of My Shadow - vCB | ARC 6-12-02 |
| 19892-1 | Now Or Never - vCB | |
| 19893-1 | Love, What Are You Doing To My Heart-vLS | ARC 6-12-03 |
| 19894-1 | You're Giving Me A Song And A Dance - vLS | - |

Stan King-d replaces Cole.                    New York, November 3, 1936.

| 20183-1 | With Thee I Swing - vCB | ARC 7-01-07, Cq 8761 |
| 20184-1 | Tea On The Terrace - vCB | ARC 7-01-11 |
| 20185-1 | I'm In A Dancing Mood - vCB | ARC 7-01-07, Cq 8761 |
| 20186-1 | There's Frost On The Moon - vCB | ARC 7-01-11, Cq 8775 |

Manny Klein or Sterling Bose-t believed present (one of these may be the unknown
2nd t above); Art Gentry-v.          New York, January 5, 1937.

| 20479-2 | He Ain't Got Rhythm - vCB | ARC 7-03-11 |
| 20480-1 | The Girl On The Police Gazette - vCB | - |
| 20481-1 | I Can't Lose That Longing For You - vAG | ARC 7-03-12, Rex 9045 |
| 20482-2 | The Goona Goo - vAG | - |

Mondello definite; Charlie Barnet, Art Drelinger and Freddy Fellensby have all been
suggested as replacement for Russin-ts; Barry McKinley-v; Carl Kress-g may also be
present (see Note below).            New York, February 16, 1937.

| 20686-2 | The Mood That I'm In - vBM | ARC 7-05-02 |
| 20687-2 | All God's Chillun Got Rhythm - vBM | ARC 7-06-14 |

NOTE:- ARC 7-06-14 as DICK McDONOUGH-CARL KRESS ORCHESTRA.

Sam Shapiro-Russ Case-t/Jerry Colonna-tb/Milt Yaner-Joe Marsala-cl-as/Babe Russin-ts/
Claude Thornhill-p/Dick McDonough-g/Artie Bernstein-sb/Cozy Cole-d/Barry McKinley-v.
New York, March 19, 1937.

| 20844-1 | I've Got Beginner's Luck - vBM | ARC 7-05-18 |
| 20845-2 | I'm Never Blue Where The Grass Is Green - vBM | ARC 7-06-03 |
| 20846-1 | Shall We Dance ? - vBM | ARC 7-05-18 |
| 20847-1 | Spring Cleaning (Getting Ready For Love) - vBM | ARC 7-06-03 |

Manny Klein-Charlie Margulis or Johnny McGhee-t/Jack Jenney-tb/Toots Mondello-Johnny
   Ingram-as/Larry Binyon-ts/Claude Thornhill-p/Dick McDonough-g/Artie Bernstein-sb/
   Billy Gussak-d/Barry McKinley-v.          New York, May 18, 1937.

| 21163- | Don't Ever Change - vBM | ARC 7-07-16 | |
| 21164- | Two Hearts Are Dancing - vBM | - | |
| 21165-1 | And Then They Called It Love - vBM | ARC 7-07-07 | |
| 21166-1 | You're Looking For Romance - vBM | - | |

   Cliff Weston-t-v replaces both previous t; remainder probably as above.
                                            New York, July 15, 1937.

| 21393-2 | Public Melody No. 1 - vCW | ARC 7-09-08 | |
| 21394-1 | My Cabin Of Dreams - vBM | - | Cq 8908 |
| 21395-2 | Love Is On The Air Tonight - vBM | ARC 7-10-04, | Cq 8907 |
| 21396-1 | Have You Got Any Castles, Baby ? - vBM | - | - |

   Bunny Berigan-t replaces Weston; Howard Phillips-v.
                                            New York, September 2, 1937.

| 21607- | You And I Know - vHP | ARC 7-11-11, Cq 8903 | |
| 21608- | An Old Flame Never Dies - vHP | - | |
| 21609-1 | The Big Apple - vHP | ARC 7-11-02 | |
| 21610-1 | That Old Feeling - vHP | - | Cq 8903 |

See also Carl Kress.

## EDWIN J. McENELLY'S ORCHESTRA

The following sides by this commercial dance orchestra are of mild jazz interest.

Edwin J. McEnelly-vn dir. Waino Kauppi and another-c/Homer Greene-tb/2cl-as/cl-ts/
   Frankie Carle-p/bj/bb/d.          New York, November 2, 1925.

33837-4  Spanish Shawl                      Vic 19851, HMV B-2273, EA-16

   W. C. Kihulein-tb/Frederick L. Wade-v (and 2nd p ?) added.
                                            New York, April 1, 1927.

38188-5  My Sunday Girl - vFLW              Vic 20589

## BOB McGOWAN AND HIS ORCHESTRA

This side features good t/tb/cl; McGowan Trio-v.
                                            Richmond, Ind., November 28, 1928.

   14483    Me And The Man In The Moon - vM3        Gnt 6709, Ch 15637
   NOTE:- Champion 15637 as ROY MERRITT AND HIS ORCHESTRA.

## LETHER McGRAW

Vocal, acc. by Sam Price's Fly Cats : Charlie Shavers-t/Buster Bailey-cl/Sam Price-p/
   ? Wellman Braud-sb/? O'Neil Spencer-d. New York, March 24, 1939.

   65267-A  Do Your Duty                    Dec 7580, Voc S-238
   65268-A  Low Down Dirty Groundhog        -          -
   NOTE:- This singer is a girl, billed as "The Ghost of Bessie Smith" (!)

## JIMMY McHUGH'S BOSTONIANS

Manny Klein-t/Sunny Clapp-tb/Fud Livingston and another-cl/Jack Pettis-cl-ts/vn/p/bj/
   bb/d/Al Shayne-Tommy Weir-v.          New York, September 25, 1928.

| 147061-2 | Girl Of My Dreams (w) - vTW | Har 743-H |
| 147062-3 | I Don't Care - vAS | Har 763-H |
| 147063-1 | When Love Comes Stealing (w) - vTW | Har 743-H |

Jimmy McPartland-Al Harris-c/Jack Teagarden-tb/Benny Goodman-cl/Gil Rodin-as/Larry
Binyon-ts/Eddie Bergman-vn (first two sides only)/Vic Breidis-p/Dick Morgan-bj/
Harry Goodman-bb/Ben Pollack-d/Claude Reese (? Sonny Clapp pseudonym)-v.
New York, November 27, 1928.

| | | |
|---|---|---|
| 147495-2 | Baby - vCR | Har 795-H |
| 147496-2 | Remember I Love You - vCR | Har 899-H |
| 147497-2 | The Whoopee Stomp | Har 836-H |

NOTE:- Harmony 899-H as SUNNY CLAPP AND HIS BAND O' SUNSHINE.

Irving Kaufman (as MARVIN YOUNG or JIM ANDREWS as shown)-v.
New York, January 9, 1929.

| | | |
|---|---|---|
| 147759-2 | Futuristic Rhythm - v"MY" | Har 836-H |
| 147760-2 | Let's Sit And Talk About You - v"JA" | Har 823-H |
| 147761-3 | In A Great Big Way - v"JA" | - |

## ARTHUR (ART) McKAY

ARTHUR McKAY : Vocal, acc. by ? Ike Rodgers-tb/Henry Brown-p, possibly others.
Chicago, August 24, 1934.

| | | |
|---|---|---|
| C-9344- | Central Limited Blues | Dec 7068 |
| C-9345- | Heavy Stuff Blues | - |

ART McKAY : Vocal, acc. by Odell Rand-cl/Roosevelt Sykes-p/sb.
Chicago, April 30, 1937.

| | | |
|---|---|---|
| 91216-A | She Squeezed My Lemon | Dec 7364 |
| 91217-A | Somebody's Been Ridin' My Black Gal | - |

## MARION McKAY AND HIS ORCHESTRA

The following title by this orchestra has a solo by Leroy Morris, once thought to be
by Bix Beiderbecke. Other titles by this band on Gennett are of no known interest.

Marion McKay-bj dir. Ambrose Barringer-t/Leroy Morris-c-ss-as/Doc Marshall-tb/Ernie
McKay-cl-bcl-ss-as/Russell Mock-as/Henry Lange-p/Ed Johns-bb/Al Anderson-d.
Richmond, Ind , December 17, 1924.

| | | |
|---|---|---|
| 12109 | Doo Wacka Doo | Gnt 5615, 3045, Ch 15011, |
| | | Cx 40408 |

NOTE:- Champion 15011 as BILL WILLIAMS AND HIS GANG; Claxtonola as THE DREAMLAND
HARMONISTS.

## RED McKENZIE

McKENZIE'S CANDY KIDS : Red McKenzie-comb/Dick Slevin-k/Jack Bland-bj/Eddie Lang-g.
New York, December 12, 1924.

| | | |
|---|---|---|
| 14470; 288 | When My Sugar Walks Down The Street | Voc 14977, Sil 3054, Gmn 7013 |
| 14472; 290 | Panama | - - Bel 825 - |

NOTE:- Silvertone 3054 as THE DANCING STEVEDORES; Beltona 825 as SOUTHERN STATES
DANCE ORCHESTRA; Guardsman 7013 as ORIGINAL BLACK BAND.

Vocal, acc. by Eddie Lang-g.                New York, December 13, 1924.

| | | |
|---|---|---|
| 14474 | Nobody Knows What A Red Head Mama Can Do | Br rejected |
| 14475/6 | My Syncopated Melody Man | - |

McKENZIE'S CANDY KIDS : **As before,** but Harry Reser-bj replaces Bland.
New York, January 27, 1925.

| | | |
|---|---|---|
| 334 | Best Black | Voc 14978, Sil 3056, Gmn 7011 |
| 336 | Stretch It, Boy | - - - |

NOTE:- Silvertone 3056 as THE DANCING STEVEDORES; Guardsman 7011 as COLORADO CANDY
KIDS.

McKENZIE'S CANDY KIDS : Red McKenzie-comb/Dick Slevin-k/Jack Bland-bj/Eddie Lang-g.
New York, August 7, 1925.

1068    The Morning After Blues              Voc 15088, Lev A-103
1070/1  Happy Children Blues                 -
NOTE:- Levaphone A-103 as THE KANDY KIDS.

New York, September 1, 1925.

E-16302/4  Hot Honey                         Br rejected
E-16305/7  If You Never Come Back            -

New York, October 29, 1925.

E-1642/4; E-16792/4  Hot Honey              Voc 15166
E-1645 ; E-16795    If You Never Come Back   -        Aco G-16033
NOTE:- Aco G-16033 as OHIO NOVELTY BAND.

Joe Humby-g replaces Lang; Red McKenzie-v.
New York, March 7, 1927.

E-4679; E-21684  What Do I Care What Somebody   Voc 15539, Br 3484*, 02507,
                 Said ? - vRM                    A-418, A-81005
E-4682; E-21687  Nervous Puppies                As above, excdpt Br 02507
NOTE:- All Brunswick issues as MOUND CITY BLUE BLOWERS.

RED McKENZIE AND HIS MUSIC BOX : Red McKenzie-comb-v/Joe Venuti-vn/Eddie Lang-g.
New York, June 21, 1927.

81037-B  There'll Be Some Changes Made - vRM    OK 40893, Par R-3382, A-2359,
                                                Od 165194, A-189120
81038-C  My Syncopated Melody Man - vRM         As above

Eddie Condon-bj added.                 New York, May 28, 1928.

400720-A  My Baby Came Home - vRM        OK 41071, Par R-184, Od A-189193
400721-A  From Monday On - vRM           CBS CL-2229, BPG-62546 (LP)
400721-B  From Monday On - vRM           OK 41071, Par R-184, Od A-189193

McKENZIE'S MOUND CITY BLUE BLOWERS : Red McKenzie-comb-v/Benny Goodman-cl-as/Bud
Freeman-Coleman Hawkins-ts (both on 10194-3 only)/Fats Waller-p/Eddie Condon-bj/Joe
Billings-percussion.              New York, October 30, 1930.

10194-3  Girls Like You Were Meant For Boys Like   IAJRC 1 (LP)
         Me
10195-1  Arkansas Blues - vRM                       CBS D-77 (LP)

Vocal, acc. by small orchestra (the file card of the fourth session specifies 6 men,
without saying who they were or what they played), but of little jazz interest; the
sessions are included here for completeness' sake.
New York, October 15, 1931.

151843-3  Time On My Hands (You In My Arms)     Col 2556-D
151844-2  Just Friends                         -

New York, December 14, 1931.

152044-1  I Found You                          Col 2537-D
152045-3  I'm Sorry, Dear                      -

New York, February 10, 1932.

152108-1  There's Something In Your Eyes       Col 2620-D
152109-3  Can't We Talk It Over ?              -

New York, April 12, 1932.

152171-1  Lovable                              Col 2645-D
152172-1  Dream Sweetheart                     -

Acc. by ? Sterling Bose-t/Tommy Dorsey-tb/Jimmy Dorsey-cl/as/? Fulton McGrath or
Joe Meresco-p/Dick McDonough-g/? Artie Bernstein-sb/Larry Gomar or Adrian Rollini-
d-vib.                                      New York, September 1, 1933.

| | | |
|---|---|---|
| 13933-1 | It's The Talk Of The Town | Voc 2534, Pan 25599 |
| 13934-1 | This Time It's Love | —        — |

RED McKENZIE AND HIS ORCHESTRA : Jack Teagarden-Tommy Dorsey-tb/Pee Wee Russell-cl/
Bud Freeman-ts/Fulton McGrath-p/Casper Reardon-harp/Eddie Condon-g/Art Miller-sb/
Red Norvo-x/Red McKenzie-v.                 New York, December 28, 1933.

| | | |
|---|---|---|
| 14497-A | Whispering - vRM | Voc rejected |
| 14498-A-B | Delta Bound - vRM | — |
| 14499-A-B | Mean To Me - vRM | — |

RED McKENZIE WITH THE SPIRITS OF RHYTHM : Vocal, acc. by p/Leo Watson-Wilbur and/or
Douglas Daniels-Teddy Bunn-g/Wilson Myers-sb/Virgil Scoggins-d.
                                            New York, September 11, 1934.

| | | |
|---|---|---|
| 38633-A | 'Way Down Yonder In New Orleans | Dec 186, Br 01997 |
| 38634-A | I've Got The World On A String | Dec 302    — |
| 38635 | From Monday On | Dec 186, Br 01891 |
| 38636 | As Long As I Live | Dec 302    — |

Vocal, acc. by t/2-3 vn/p/g/sb.             New York, October 5, 1934.

| | | |
|---|---|---|
| 38799 | It's All Forgotten Now | Dec 243 |
| 38804 | What's The Use Of Getting Used To You ? | |

NOTE:- Matrices 38800/3 inclusive are by Louis Katzman's Castillians, who may have
supplied the non-jazz accompaniment to the above two titles.

RED McKENZIE AND HIS RHYTHM KINGS : Eddie Farley-t/Mike Riley-tb/Slats Long-cl-ts/
Conrad Lanoue-p/Eddie Condon-g/George Yorke-sb/Johnny Powell-d/Red McKenzie-comb-v.
                                            New York, July 12, 1935.

| | | |
|---|---|---|
| 39721-A | Murder In The Moonlight (It's Love In | Dec 507, Br 02088 |
| | The First Degree) - vRM | |
| 39721-B | Murder In The Moonlight - vRM | — |

New York, July 15, 1935.

| | | |
|---|---|---|
| 39722-A | Let's Swing It - vRM | Dec 507 |

New York, August 2, 1935.

| | | |
|---|---|---|
| 39805-A | Double Trouble - vRM | Dec 521, Br 02088 |
| 39805-B | Double Trouble - vRM | — |

New York, August 5, 1935.

| | | |
|---|---|---|
| 39807-A | That's What You Think - vRM | Dec 521, Br 02157 |
| 39807-B-C | That's What You Think - vRM | — |

New York, October 22, 1935.

| | | |
|---|---|---|
| 60096-A | Georgia Rockin' Chair - vRM | Dec 609, Y-5050, Br 02105 |
| 60097-B-C | Monday In Manhattan - vRM | Dec 587 |
| 60098-A-D | Every Now And Then - vRM | —       —        — |
| 60099-A | Wouldn't I Be A Wonder ? - vRM | Dec 609 |

Bunny Berigan-t/Forrest Crawford-cl/Babe Russin-ts/Frank Signorelli-p/Carmen
Mastren-g/Sid Weiss-sb/Stan King-d/Red McKenzie-comb-v.
                                            New York, January 20, 1936.

| | | |
|---|---|---|
| 60365-A | Sing An Old Fashioned Song (To A Young | Dec 667, Br 02181 |
| | Sophisticated Lady) - vRM | |
| 60368-A | I'm Building Up To An Awful Letdown - vRM | —   Y-5091, Br 02167 |

RED McKENZIE AND HIS RHYTHM KINGS : Bunny Berigan-t/? Al Philburn-tb/Forrest Crawford
  cl/Babe Russin-ts/Frank Signorelli-p/Carmen Mastren-g/Sid Weiss-sb/Stan King-d/Red
  McKenzie-comb-v.                        New York, February 5, 1936.

| | | |
|---|---|---|
| 60444-A | Don't Count Your Kisses (Before You're Kissed) - vRM | Dec 721, Br 02157 |
| 60445-A | When Love Has Gone - vRM | Dec 734, Br 02167 |
| 60446-A | I Don't Know Your Name (But You're Beautiful) - vRM | Dec 721, Br 02181 |
| 60447-B | Moon Rose - vRM | Dec 734 |

    Paul Ricci-cl replaces Crawford.       New York, April 3, 1936.

| | | |
|---|---|---|
| 60977-A | I Can't Get Started With You - vRM | Dec 790 |
| 60978-A | I Can Pull A Rabbit Out Of My Hat - vRM | — |

Vocal, acc. by Dave Wade-t/Pete Pumiglio-cl/Dave Harris-ts/Raymond Scott-p/g/Lou
  Shoobe-sb/Johnny Williams-d.           New York, February 26, 1937.

| | | |
|---|---|---|
| M-136-2 | Sweet Lorraine | Vri 520 |
| M-137-2 | Wanted | — |

  Acc. by Bunny Berigan-t/? Sid Stoneburn-cl-as/? Fulton McGrath-p/? Dick McDonough-g
  /George Hnida-sb/? Al Sidell-d/Adrian Rollini-vib.
                                          New York, March 17, 1937.

| | | |
|---|---|---|
| M-271-1 | I Cried For You | Vri 589 |
| M-272-2 | The Trouble With Me Is You | — |

RED McKENZIE AND HIS ORCHESTRA : Bobby Hackett-c/Vernon Brown-tb/Slats Long-cl/Babe
  Russin-ts/Fulton McGrath-p/Dave Barbour-g/Artie Shapiro-sb/Stan King-d/Red McKenzie
  comb-v.                                 New York, November 16, 1937.

| | | |
|---|---|---|
| 22033-1 | Farewell, My Love - vRM | ARC 8-01-13, Voc 3875, Cq 8966 |
| 22034-1 | You're Out Of This World - vRM | ARC 8-02-04, Voc 3898 |
| 22035-1 | Sail Along, Silvery Moon - vRM | ARC 8-01-13, Voc 3875 |
| 22036-2 | Georgianna - vRM | ARC 8-02-04, Voc 3898 |

See also the Mound City Blue Blowers; sides issued on Parlophone and associated labels
  as RED McKENZIE'S CELESTIAL BEINGS will be found in the chapter on the Mound City
  Blue Blowers, as that is the name under which they were recorded and issued by OKeh.

## McKENZIE AND CONDON'S CHICAGOANS

Jimmy McPartland-c/Frank Teschmacher-cl/Bud Freeman-ts/Joe Sullivan-p/Eddie Condon-bj/
  Jim Lannigan-bb-sb/Gene Krupa-d.        Chicago, December 8, 1927.

| | | |
|---|---|---|
| 82030-A | Sugar | OK 41011, Col 35951, UHCA 9, Par R-2379, A-2483, A-7410,B-71154, DP-211, 85363, Od 165321, 193161, A-189189 |
| 82031-B | China Boy | OK 41011, Col 35951, UHCA 10, Par R-1033, A-2483, A-7517,B-27609, B-71174, TT-9083, 85363, Od 165321, 193161, A-189189, A-286046,B-35628 |

  Mezz Mezzrow reportedly plays cymbals.  Chicago, December 16, 1927.

| | | |
|---|---|---|
| 82082-B | Nobody's Sweetheart | OK 40971, Col 35952, UHCA 11, Par R-643, A-7517, B-27609,B-71174, TT-9083, 85378, Od A-189113, A-286014 |
| 82083-A | Liza | OK 40971, Col 35952, UHCA 12, Par R-2379, A-7410, A-71154,DP-211, 85377, Od A-189113 |

  NOTE:- UHCA 9 and 10, and 11 and 12 are coupled.

McKENZIE AND CONDON'S BOYS : Muggsy Spanier-c/Frank Teschmacher-cl/Mezz Mezzrow-ts/
Joe Sullivan-p/Eddie Condon-bj/Gene Krupa-d.
                                        Chicago, March 27, 1928.

| | | |
|---|---|---|
| C-1808/9 | Jazz Me Blues | Voc rejected |
| C-1810/1 | Singin' The Blues | - |

## RAY McKINLEY'S JAZZ BAND

George Thow-t/Joe Yukl-tb/Skeets Herfurt-cl/Joe Sullivan-p/Jim Taft-sb/Ray McKinley-
d.                                      Los Angeles, March 31, 1936.

| | | |
|---|---|---|
| DLA-328-A | Love In The First Degree | Dec 1019, 27072, Y-5959, Br 02374 |
| DLA-329-A | New Orleans Parade | - 3685 -    -       - |
| DLA-330-A | Shack In The Back (Smack In The Back*) | Dec 1020, 27073, Br 02403* |
| DLA-330-B | Shack In The Back | Dec Y-5894 |
| DLA-331-A | Fingerwave | Dec 1020, 27073, Y-5894, Br 02403 |

See also Will Bradley.

## McKINNEY'S COTTON PICKERS

Don Redman-cl-as-bar-v-a dir. John Nesbitt-t-a/Langston Curl-t/Claude Jones-tb/Milton
Senior-cl-as/George Thomas-cl-ts-v/Prince Robinson-cl-ts/Todd Rhodes-p-cel/Dave
Wilborn-bj-g-v/Ralph Escudero-bb/Cuba Austin-d-vib/Jean Napier-v.
                                        Chicago, July 11, 1928.

| | | |
|---|---|---|
| 46092-1-2 | Sweet Sue - Just You | Rejected |
| 46093-2 | Four Or Five Times - vDR-GT-DW/aDR | Vic 21583 |
| 46094-2 | Put It There (Shag Nasty) | Vic V-38025, BB B-5145, Sr S-3226 |
| 46095-2 | Crying And Sighing - aJN | Vic V-38000, HMV B-4892, B-6287, AE-4227, EA-1200, JK-2826 |
| 46096-2 | Milenberg Joys - aDR | Vic 21611, BB B-10954, HMV B-9228, EA-3606, JK-2812 |
| 46096-3 | Milenberg Joys - aDR | X LVA-3031, Vic RA-5314, Swaggie JCS-33758 (all LPs) |

                                        Chicago, July 12, 1928.

| | | |
|---|---|---|
| 46098-2 | Cherry - vJN/aDR | Vic 21730, BB B-5145, B-6304, Sr S-3226, HMV R-14061 |
| 46098-3 | Cherry - vJN/aDR | Vic 21730, 24938, 40-0114, 62-0082 |
| 46099-1 | Stop Kidding (Neckbones And Sauerkraut) - aJN | X LVA-3031, Vic RA-5314, Swaggie JCS-33758 (all LPs) |
| 46400-2 | Nobody's Sweetheart - vGT/aDR or JN | Vic V-38000, BB B-5728, HMV B-4892 |
| 46401-2 | Some Sweet Day | Vic 21730, HMV R-14061 |
| 46402-3 | Shim-Me-Sha-Wabble - aJN | Vic 21611, 40-0114, 62-0082, HMV B-9228, EA-467, EA-3606, JK-2812 |

NOTE:- Victor V-38000 credits 46095-2 with a
vocal, but not the reverse (46400-2).

Jimmy Dudley or Joe Moxley-cl-as replaces Senior.
                                        Chicago, November 23, 1928.

| | | |
|---|---|---|
| 48619-2 | It's Tight Like That - vGT-DW | Vic V-38013, BB B-6304 |
| 48620-3 | There's A Rainbow 'Round My Shoulder - vDW | - |

                                        New York, April 8, 1929.

| | | |
|---|---|---|
| 51084-2 | It's A Precious Little Thing Called Love | Vic V-38051 |
| 51085-2 | Save It, Pretty Mama - v-aDR | Vic V-38061, BB B-7695, HMV R-14269 |
| 51086-2 | I've Found A New Baby - vGT | -      -      - |
| 51087-1 | Will You, Won't You Be My Babe ? - aJN | Vic 22932, HMV B-4914 |

Claude Jones-Cuba Austin-v.             New York, April 9, 1929.

| | | |
|---|---|---|
| 51204-1 | Beedle-Um-Bum - vCJ-DR-GT-DW/aDR | Vic V-38052, BB B-6595 |
| 51205-1 | Do Something | Vic V-38051 |
| 51206-2 | Sellin' That Stuff - vGT-CA/aDR | Vic V-38052, BB B-6595 |
| 51207-1-2 | It Feels So Good - vDR | Rejected |

Don Redman-cl-as-bar-v-a dir. Joe Smith-Sidney de Paris-Leonard Davis-t/Claude Jones-
    tb/Benny Carter-cl-as/Coleman Hawkins-Theodore McCord-cl-ts/Fats Waller-p-cel/Dave
    Wilborn-bj/Billy Taylor-bb/Kaiser Marshall-d/John Nesbitt-a.
                              New York, November 5, 1929.

| | | |
|---|---|---|
| 57064-2 | Plain Dirt - aJN | Vic V-38097, 40-0115, 62-0083, BB B-11590, HMV B-4990, K-6950 |
| 57065-1 | Gee, Ain't I Good To You ? - v-aDR | Vic V-38097, J-5208, BB B-5205, B-10249, B-11590, HMV B-4967, JK-2155, K-6950, Sr S-3286 |

                              New York, November 6, 1929.

| | | |
|---|---|---|
| 57066-2 | I'd Love It | Vic V-38133, 62-0059, BB B-10706, HMV B-4967, JK-2474 |
| 57067-1 | The Way I Feel Today - v-aDR | Vic V-38102, 760-0001, BB B-10232, HMV B-4901, B-6204, JK-2166 |
| 57068-2 | Miss Hannah - vDR | Vic V-38102, 760-0001, BB B-10232, HMV B-4901, B-6215, JK-2166, El EG-2614 |

                              New York, November 7, 1929.

| | | |
|---|---|---|
| 57139-3 | Peggy | Vic V-38133, 62-0059, BB B-10706 |
| 57140-2 | Wnerever There's A Will, Baby - vDR | Vic 22736, BB B-10249, HMV BD-135, JK-2155 |
| 57141-3 | Wherever There's A Will, Baby - vDR | Vic RA-5314 |

Don Redman-cl-as-bar-v-a dir. Joe Smith-c/John Nesbitt-t-a/Langston Curl-t/Ed Cuffee
    tb/Benny Carter-cl-as/George Thomas-cl-as-ts-v/Prince Robinson-cl-ts/Todd Rhodes-p
    cel/Dave Wilborn-bj-g-v/Billy Taylor-bb/Cuba Austin-d/Frank Marvin-v.
                              New York, January 31, 1930.

| | | |
|---|---|---|
| 58543-2 | I'll Make Fun For You - vGT | Vic V-38142, HMV B-4907 |
| 58544-1 | Words Can't Express The Way I Feel - vGT | Vic V-38112, J-5208, BB B-5205, B-5647, Sr S-3286 |
| 58544-2 | Words Can't Express The Way I Feel - vGT | Vic LPM-10020, 430721 (LP) |
| 58545-2 | If I Could Be With You One Hour Tonight - vGT | Vic V-38118, BB B-5905, HMV B-6168, X-3998 |
| 58547-1 | Then Someone's In Love (w) - vFM | Vic V-38142 |

                              New York, February 3, 1930.

| | | |
|---|---|---|
| 58546-1 | Honeysuckle Rose - vDW | Vic LPM-10020, 430721 (LPs) |
| 58546-2 | Honeysuckle Rose - vDW | Pirate MPC-518 (LP) |
| 59140-1 | Zonky - vDW | Vic V-38118, 40-0115, 62-0083, BB B-5728 |
| 59141-2 | Travelin' All Alone - vGT/aJN | Vic V-38112, BB B-5647 |

James P. Johnson-p replaces Rhodes.     Camden, N. J., July 28, 1930.

| | | |
|---|---|---|
| 64002-2 | Just A Shade Corn - vDW | Vic 23012, HMV B-4931, K-6262 |
| 64003-3 | Baby, Won't You Please Come Home ? - vGT | Vic 22511, 40-0116, 62-0084 |

                              Camden, N. J., July 29, 1930.

| | | |
|---|---|---|
| 64004-2 | Okay, Baby - vGT | Vic 23000, HMV B-4837 |
| 64005-2 | Blues Sure Have Got Me - vDR | Vic 40-0116, 62-0084 |

NOTE:- The American (green label) issue of 40-0116 is dubbed both sides; the
Canadian (purple label) is dubbed on neither. This may be true of all the 40-
reissues.

                              Camden, N. J., July 30, 1930.

| | | |
|---|---|---|
| 64006-3 | Hullabaloo - vDW | Vic 22511, HMV JF-24 |
| 64007-3 | I Want A Little Girl - vGT | Vic 23000 |
| 64007-4 | I Want A Little Girl - vGT | -     BB B-5905, B-10954 |

Don Redman-cl-as-bar-v-a dir. Joe Smith-c/John Nesbitt-Langston Curl-t/Ed Cuffee-tb/
  Benny Carter-cl-as/George Thomas-cl-as-ts-v/Prince Robinson-cl-ts/James P. Johnson-p
  /Dave Wilborn-bj-v/Billy Taylor-bb/Cuba Austin-d.
                              Camden, N. J., July 31, 1930.

64008-2  Cotton Picker's Scat - vGT&ch          Vic 23012, HMV B-4931, K-6262

  Rex Stewart-c replaces Nesbitt; Edward Inge-cl-as-a replaces Thomas; Todd Rhodes-p-
  cel replaces Johnson.              New York, November 3, 1930.

64605-1  Talk To Me - vDR               Vic 22640, HMV B-4870, B-6087,
                                          R-14588
64605-2  Talk To Me - vDR               Pirate MPC-518 (LP)
64606-1  Rocky Road - vDR               Vic 22932, 40-0117, 62-0085,
                                          HMV B-4914, B-6286, EA-1098,
                                          JK-2838

                              New York, November 4, 1930.

64607-2  Laughing At Life - vBC          Vic 23020
64608-1  Never Swat A Fly - vBC            - 40-0117, 62-0085, HMV JF-24

  George Bias-v.                  New York, November 5, 1930.

63195-2  I Want Your Love - vDW          Vic 22683
63196-2  Hello ! - vDW                   Vic 23031, HMV B-4945, B-6335
64609-2  After All, You're All I'm After - vGB   Vic 23024, HMV B-6262
64610-2  I Miss A Little Miss - vGB        -
NOTE:- The gap in the matrix numbers is accounted for by the last pair of sides
having been recorded in a different studio from the first pair, on the same day.

  Buddy Lee-t replaces Smith; Quentin Jackson-tb-v added; Don Redman speaks*; Lois
  Deppe-v.                    Camden, N. J., December 17, 1930.

64055-2  To Whom It May Concern - vLD       Vic 23035
64056-2  *You're Driving Me Crazy - vDW/aEI  Vic 23031, HMV B-6286, JK-2838

                              Camden, N. J., December 18, 1930.

64058-2  Come A Little Closer - vQJ        Vic 23035

  Donald King-v.                 Camden, N. J., February 12, 1931.

67934-2  It's A Lonesome Old Town (When You're   Vic 22628
           Not Around) - vLD
67935-1  She's My Secret Passion - vDK        -

Benny Carter-cl-as dir. Rex Stewart-c/Buddy Lee-Adolphus "Doc" Cheatham-t/Ed Cuffee-tb
  /Quentin Jackson-tb-v/Joe Moxley-Hilton Jefferson-cl-as/Prince Robinson-cl-ts/Todd
  Rhodes-p-cel/Dave Wilborn-bj-g/Billy Taylor-bb/Cuba Austin-d.
                              Camden, N. J., September 8, 1931.

68300-1  Do You Believe In Love At Sight ? - vQJ   Vic 430272 (LP)
68300-2  Do You Believe In Love At Sight ? - vQJ   Vic 22811, HMV B-4880
70495-1  Wrap Your Troubles In Dreams (And Dream   -
           Your Troubles Away) - vQJ

                         NINA MAE  McKINNEY

See Garland Wilson.

                         SADIE McKINNEY

Vocal, acc. by Charley Williamson-c/James Alston-p.
                              Memphis, February 24, 1927.

37945-1  Rock Away                    Vic 20565
37946-1  Brownskin Flapper               -

Instrumentation and personnel unknown; the only title known to have been made by this
band is the following, and tests of both takes were sent to Joe McKown at the New
Lincoln Theatre, Danville, Illinois, on October 17, 1925.

                                           Richmond, Ind., October 8, 1925.

12362, -A  Mah Jongg Blues                            Gnt rejected

## McLAUGHLIN'S MELODIANS

Jack McLaughlin-vn dir. probably :- Henry Krompart-Frank Davis-t/Norman Booth-tb/Bill
    Wullen-Ivan Beaty-cl-ss-as/Jules Pillar or Piller-cl-ss-ts/Harold Arlen-Dick
    George-p/Charles Panico-bj-g/Hal Raub-bb/Harold Tapson-d.
                                           New York, c. August 19, 1926.

107056    Someone Is Losin' Susan                PA 36518, 11215, Per 14699
107057    I Never Knew What The Moonlight Could Do PA 36517, Per 14698
107058    Broken-Hearted Sue                      PA 36524, Per 14705
107059    Play, Gypsies, Dance, Gypsies           PA 36515, Per 14696
    NOTE:- Pathe Actuelle 11215 as THE BUFFALODIANS (q.v. for further titles by this
    band).

## CONNIE  McLEAN

CONNIE McLEAN'S RHYTHM BOYS : Connie McLean-cl-ss-as-v dir. Chubby Wright-t-v/Ray
    Durant-p/Ludvick Brown-g-v/Alfred Hill-sb/Alex Miller-d-v.
                                           New York, April 24, 1936.

61067-A   When The Breath Bids The Body Goodbye   Dec 7189
             - vCM ?
61068-A   Sissy Man Blues - vCM ?                 Dec 7176
61069-A   I Can't Use That Thing - vCM ?          Dec 7175
61070-A   You Done Lost Your Good Thing Now - vCM? Dec 7189
61071-A   Rockin' My Troubles                     Dec 7175
61072-A-B Shylock Blues                           Dec 7176

CONNIE McLEAN AND HIS RHYTHM ORCHESTRA : As above.
                                           New York, July 7, 1936.

102343-1  High-Falutin' Stomp - vAM               BB B-6482
102344-1  All I Want In This World Is You - vCM-AM  -
102345-1  How Can You Face Me ? - vCW             BB B-6485
102346-1  Without A Shadow Of A Doubt - vAM       BB B-6474
102347-1  Sing, Sing, Sing - vAM                    -           RZ MR-2214
102348-1  Breeze, Ray, Breeze - vLB               BB B-6485

## McMURRAY'S CALIFORNIA THUMPERS

Phil Napoleon-Jules Levy, Jr.-t/? Miff Mole-tb/Loring McMurray-as/Frank Signorelli-p/
    ? John Cali-bj.                        New York, c. June 8, 1922.

7922-A  Haunting Blues                              Gnt 4904, R-T 7045, St 9260
7923-A  Just Because You're You, That's Why I Love You -   - Apex 466 -
NOTE:- Rich-Tone 7045 as DIXIE BOYS.

                                           New York, c. September 4, 1922.

8016, -A  Oogie Oogie Wa Wa                         Gnt 4943, Apex 464, St 9292
8020-B  Blue                                          -           -

## JIMMY McPARTLAND

JIMMY McPARTLAND'S SQUIRRELS : Jimmy McPartland-c/Joe Harris-tb/Rosy McHargue-cl/Dick
    Clark-ts/Jack Gardner-p/Dick McPartland-g/Country Washburn-sb/George Wettling-d.
                                           Chicago, April 24, 1936.

90697-A  Eccentric                              HRS 1004, Dec 3363, 18445,
                                                Od 286225
90698-A  Original Dixieland One-Step            HRS 1004, Dec 18441, Y-5985,
                                                Br 03486, Od 286226

JIMMY McPARTLAND'S SQUIRRELS : Jimmy McPartland-c/Joe Harris-tb/Rosy McHargue-cl/Dick
   Clark-ts/Jack Gardner-p/Dick McPartland-g/Country Washburn-bb/George Wettling-d.
                              Chicago, April 25, 1936.

| | | |
|---|---|---|
| 90699-A | I'm All Bound 'Round With The | HRS 1003, Dec 18441, BM-30861,Y-5985, |
| | Mason-Dixon Line | Br 03486, Od 286226 |
| 90700-A | Panama | HRS 1003, Dec 3363, 3522, 18445, |
| | | BM-30861, Od 286225 |

    NOTE:- Decca 3363, 18441, 18445 and Y-5985 as JIMMY McPARTLAND AND HIS ORCHESTRA.

JIMMY McPARTLAND AND HIS ORCHESTRA : Jimmy McPartland-c/Bud Jacobson-cl/Boyce Brown-
   as/Floyd Bean-p/Dick McPartland-g/Jim Lannigan-sb/Hank Isaacs-d.
                              Chicago, October 11, 1939.

| | | |
|---|---|---|
| 91832-A | Jazz Me Blues | Dec 18042, Y-6095, Br 03057,A-82610, |
| | | Od 286125 |
| 91833-A | China Boy | As above, but Dec Y-5636, not Y-6095 |
| 91834-A | The World Is Waiting For The Sunrise | Dec 18043, Br 03058, Od 286126 |
| 91835-A | Sugar | - Y-6095 - - |

## LINDSAY McPHAIL

Piano solos, included as being the composer's own versions of a title long accepted
   as a jazz standard.            New York, c. August, 1921.

        San                             Oly 15122

        San                             PA 020623

McPHAIL'S JAZZ ORCHESTRA OF CHICAGO : Lindsay McPhail-p dir. c/tb/cl/d.
                              New York, c. August, 1921.

        Zowie !                         Oly 15123

## OZIE McPHERSON

Vocal, acc. by Lovie Austin's Serenaders : Bob Shoffner-c/Jimmy O'Bryant-cl/Lovie
   Austin-p/W. E. Burton-d.           Chicago, c. November, 1925.

| | | |
|---|---|---|
| 11005-2 | You Gotta Know How | Pm 12327, Sil 3522 |
| 11006-2 | Outside Of That He's All Right With Me | - - |

    NOTE:- Silvertone 3522 as EVA WOODS.

    Unknown c replaces Shoffner; Kid Ory-tb added.
                              Chicago, c. January, 1926.

| | | |
|---|---|---|
| 2422-1-2 ? | Down To The Bottom Where I Stay | Rejected |
| 2423-1 | Standing On The Corner Blues | Pm 12350, Sil 3557 |
| 2425-2 | He's My Man | - - |

    NOTE:- Silvertone 3557 as EVA WOODS.  Matrix 2424 is untraced.

Acc. by Fletcher Henderson and his Orchestra : Joe Smith-c/Charlie Green-tb/Buster
Bailey-cl/? Coleman Hawkins-bsx/Fletcher Henderson-p/Charlie Dixon-bj. (The band is
not identified on Paramount 12355).  Chicago, mid-February, 1926.

| | | |
|---|---|---|
| 2422-4 | Down To The Bottom Where I Stay | Pm 12362 |
| 2453-4 | I Want My Loving | - |
| 2455-3 | Nobody Rolls Their Jelly Roll Like | Pm 12355 |
| | Mine | |
| 2456-3 | I'm So Blue Since My Sweetie Went Away | - |

NOTE:- Paramount 12362 as OZIE (DAYBREAK) MACPHERSON.  Matrix 2454 is untraced.

## JAY McSHANN

JAY McSHANN COMBO : Jay McShann-p dir. Orville Minor-Bernard Anderson-t/Bud Gould-tb-
   vn/Charlie Parker-as/William J. Scott-ts/Gene Ramey-sb/Gus Johnson-d.
                              Radio KFBI, Wichita, Kansas, Nov. 30, 1940.

        I've Found A New Baby              Pol 236525 (LP)

JAY McSHANN COMBO : Jay McShann-p dir. Orville Minor-Bernard Anderson-t/Bud Gould-tb-
   vn/Charlie Parker-as,/Bob Mabane-ts/Gene Ramey-sb/Gus Johnson-d.
                                    Radio KFBI, Wichita, Kansas, Dec, 2, 1940.

               Coquette                          Pol 236525 (LP)
               Moten Stomp                              -

JAY McSHANN AND HIS ORCHESTRA : Jay McShann-p dir. Harold Bruce-Orville Minor-Bernard
   Anderson-t/Joe Baird-tb/Charlie Parker-as-a/John Jackson-as/Bob Mabane-Harry
   Ferguson-ts/Gene Ramey-sb/Gus Johnson-d/Walter Brown-v/William J. Scott-a; JAY
   McSHANN-p, acc. by Ramey and Johnson only (where marked *).
                                    Dallas, April 30, 1941.

   93730-A  Swingmatism - aWJS                  Dec 8570
   93731-A  Hootie Blues - vWB/aCP              Dec 8559
   93732-A  Dexter Blues - aWJS                 Dec 8583, Br 03401, A-82647
   93733-A  *Vine Street Boogie                 Dec 8570, 60666, BM-30817
   93734-A  *Confessin' The Blues - vWB         Dec 8559, 48008
   93735-A  *Hold 'Em Hootie                    Dec 8583, 60666, BM-30817,
   NOTE:- Decca 48008 as WALTER BROWN.          Br A-82647

JAY McSHANN QUARTET : Jay McShann-p/Leonard Enois-g/Gene Ramey-sb/Gus Johnson-d/
   Walter Brown-v, with Orville Minor-t/Charlie Parker-as added**.
                                    Chicago, November 18, 1941.

   93809-A**One Woman's Man - vWB               Dec 8607
   93810-A  'Fore Day Rider - vWB               Dec 8635
   93811-B  So You Won't Jump                   Dec 8607
   93812-A  New Confessin' The Blues (Confessin' Dec 8595, 48008*
               The Blues, Part 2*)                     -
   93813-A  Red River Blues - vWB
   93814-A  Baby Heart Blues - vWB              Dec 8623
   93815-A  Cryin' Won't Make Me Stay - vWB            -
   93816-A  Hootie's Ignorant Oil - vWB         Dec 8635

JAY McSHANN AND HIS ORCHESTRA : Jay McShann-p dir. Bob Merrill-Orville Minor-Bernard
   Anderson-t/Joe Baird-Lawrence Anderson-tb/Charlie Parker-John Jackson-as/Bob Mabane
   Fred Culliver-ts/Leonard Enois-g/Gene Ramey-sb/Harold West-d/Al Hibbeler-Walter
   Brown-v/Archie Hall-a.           New York, July 2, 1942.

   70993-A  Lonely Boy Blues - vWB              Dec 4387
   70994-A  Get Me On Your Mind - vAH           Dec 4418
   70995-A  The Jumpin' Blues - vWB                    -
   70996-A  Sepian Bounce - aAH                 Dec 4387

                              HENRY  MELLAND

This artist's real name is Neville Melland, under which the HMV session is entered in
   the recording book.

                                    London, late January, 1928.
Piano solos.

   E-1714    Fourth's Fever                     Par R-3495
   E-1716    Missing Every Note
   E-1717-1-2 Don't Name It                     Rejected
   NOTE:- Matrix E-1715 was never issued, and the file card gives no information as to
what or by whom it might have been played.

                              Small Queen's Hall, London, March 21, 1928.

   Bb-12855-1  Discord Rag (Neville Melland)    HMV rejected
   Bb-12856-1  Fascination Blonde                     -

                              THE  MELODIANS

Sid Phillips-cl-as-bar dir. Harry Phillips-t/Sid Kruger-tb/Jean Paques-p/Ralph
   Phillips-bj/Joe Badis-d.         London, early January, 1928.

   11389-    Wistful And Blue                   EBW 4800
   11390-    Sugar                                    -
   11391-1   Hold Everything                    EBW 4814
   11392-1   Bogey Man                                -

See the Washboard Rhythm Kings.

## "MELODY MAKER" COMPETITION BAND

George Chisholm-tb-a dir. Dave Wilkins-Kenny Baker-Tommy McQuater-t/Woolf Phillips-tb
/Harry Parry-cl/Harry Hayes-as/George Evans-Aubrey Franks-Reg Dare-ts/George
Shearing-p/Joe D$_e$niz-g/Tommy Bromley-sb/Jock Cummings-d.
                                                    London, May 31, 1942.

DR-6847-1  Red Duster Rag                          Dec F-8176
    NOTE:- The reverse of this record is by a similar group directed by Bert Ambrose.
    It has no pretensions to being anything but a good arrangement, excellently played,
    of a commercial dance tune of the period.

## THE MELODY MASTERS

Pseudonym on Australian Regal Zonophone G-23533 (DUST) for Jan Savitt and his Orches-
    tra, and on G-23642 and G-23661 for Artie Shaw and his Orchestra, both q.v., and
    for other bands of no jazz interest, on the same label.

## THE MELODY SHEIKS

Pseudonym on OKeh 40303 (WHY COULDN'T IT BE POOR LITTLE ME ?) for the Arkansas
    Travelers, q.v., and for a similar Sam Lanin group on the same label, the following
    being of interest for their solo work and arrangements.

Sam Lanin dir. Red Nichols-Vic d'Ippolito-t/Herb Winfield-tb/Clarence Heidke-Alfie
    Evans-cl-ss-as/George Slater-cl-ts/Bill Krenz-p/Tony Colucci-bj/Joe Tarto-bb/Vic
    Berton-d.                                       New York, January 15, 1925.

73106-A  Tokio Blues                               OK 40279, Par E-5357

? Hymie Farberman-t replaces d'Ippolito. New York, c. February 11, 1925.

73165-C  Sob Sister Sadie                          OK 40326
73166-C  Cheatin' On Me                            -

    Possibly other changes (cf. Sam Lanin's Orchestra of the period).
                                                    New York, January 21, 1926.

73947-B  What Can I Say After I Say I'm Sorry ?    OK 40550, Par E-5579

SAM LANIN'S MELODY SHEIKS : Very similar; Paul Hagan-v.
                                                    New York, December 24, 1926.

80265-B  Tell Me Tonight - vPH                     OK 40744, Par E-5770, A-2148,
                                                    Ar 4208
80266-B  Idolizing - vPH                           As above, except Ar 4208
    NOTE:- Ariel 4208 as ARIEL DANCE ORCHESTRA.

## MELOTO DANCE ORCHESTRA

Pseudonym on Meloto S-1187 (THE SHEIK) for the California Ramblers, q.v., and for
    other items of no known interest on the same label.

## THE MELOTONE BOYS

Pseudonym on Melotone and Panachord for the Sunshine Boys, q.v.

## MELROSE DIXIELAND THUMPERS

Probably :- Natty Dominique-c/Johnny Dodds-cl/Frank or Walter Melrose-p/Baby Dodds or
    Jimmy Bertrand-wb.                              Chicago, c. February 24, 1927.

12600    Dixieland Stomp                           Gnt rejected

                                                    Chicago, c. February 26, 1927.

12611    Goo Goo Blues                             Gnt rejected
12612, -A  Sweetness                               -
12613    47th Street Stomp                         -
12614    Cootie Stomp                              -

Piano solos, acc. by Tommy Taylor-d.      Richmond, Ind., February 12, 1929.

| 14803 | Pass The Jug | Gnt 6774 |
| 14804 | Jelly Roll Stomp | - |

KANSAS CITY FRANK : As above.        Chicago, March 8, 1929.

| C-3078-A | Jelly Roll Stomp | Br 7062, <u>80031</u> |
| C-3079- | Pass The Jug | -     <u>-</u> |

BROADWAY RASTUS : As above.         Chicago, c. March, 1929.

| 21227-1 | Rock My Soul | Pm 12764 |
| 21228-2 | Whoopee Stomp | - |

NOTE:- Alternative takes of both the above titles are included on Paramount LP CJS-103.

KANSAS CITY FRANK AND HIS FOOTWARMERS : Herb Morand-c/Joe Wiggins-as/Frank Melrose-p/
? Charles Melrose-pac/Tommy Taylor-d-sw.
                           Chicago, c. November, 1929.

| 21469-1 | Wailing Blues | Pm 12898, Bwy 1355 |
| 21470-1-2 | St. James Infirmary Blues | -      - |

NOTE:- Broadway 1355 as HARRY'S RECKLESS FIVE.

Piano solos.                          New York, April 9, 1930.

| 9602-3 | Market Street Jive | <u>Pm CJS-103</u> (LP) |

New York, April 10, 1930.

| 9608-2 | Piano Breakdown | <u>Pm CJS-103</u> (LP) |
| 9609-1 | Whoopee Stomp | |

New York, April 11, 1930.

| 9620-1 | Distant Moan | <u>Pm CJS-103</u> (LP) |

## JAMES MELTON

The following sides by James Melton, once the "hot" alto sax soloist with Francis
Craig's orchestra (q.v.) who became an opera singer via dance band and popular
vocal records and films, are of interest for the accompaniments.

Vocal, acc. by Benny Goodman-cl/3vn/p/sb. New York, December 6, 1929.

| 149446-6 | The Shepherd's Serenade | Col 2084-D, DO-46 |
| 149695-3 | There Will Never Be Another Mary | Col 2065-D, 01875 |
| 149696-3 | The Sacred Flame | Col 2084-D, Re G-20766 |

NOTE:- Matrix 149446-6 is a re-make of a master originally made on November 19,
1929. Benny Goodman is not in evidence on 149445-3 from this session, which was
issued, and thus it is likely he took no part in it at all.

## ALICE MELVIN

Vocal, acc. by George Isador-tb/James Brown-p.
                               Memphis, November 17, 1930.

| 62958-1-2 | Lonesome Woman Blues | Vic rejected |
| 62959-1-2 | Trouble Blues | - |
| 62960-1-2 | Kind Friend Blues | - |
| 62961-1-2 | Treated You Kind | - |

## MEMPHIS BELL-HOPS

Pseudonym on Challenge for the following items listed in this book :-

| 134 | Li'l Farina (Duke Ellington and his Orchestra) |
| 134 | Ya Gotta Know How To Love (Fess Williams and his Orchestra) |
| 135 | Both sides by Duke Ellington and his Orchestra |

Pseudonym on Silvertone for Jelly James and his Fewsicians, q.v.

## MEMPHIS FIVE

See Original Memphis Five.

## MEMPHIS  HOT  SHOTS

Pseudonym on Harmony 1368-H, Clarion 5381-C and Velvet Tone 2445-V for Clarence
  Williams' Jazz Kings, q.v., and on Harmony 1377-H, Clarion 5391-C and Velvet Tone
  2455-V for Duke Ellington and his Orchestra, q.v.

## MEMPHIS  JAZZERS

Most records issued on Grey Gull, Radiex, Van Dyke and associated labels under this
  name are of commercial dance music, sometimes featuring good solos; details of the
  more outstanding titles will be found under the heading GREY GULL STUDIO BANDS. The
  following session, however, is quite exceptional.

Mike Mosiello-t/Andy Sannella-cl-as/as/? Porter Grainger (composer of all four titles
  recorded at this session)-p/unknown negro v.
                                         New York, November, 1929.

| | | |
|---|---|---|
| 3741-A  Don't Know And Don't Care | GG 1797, Rx 966 | |
| 3742-B  Ev'rybody Dance - v | GG 1816, VD 81816, Tem R-10 | |
| 3743-B  Miss Golden Brown | GG/Rx/Spm 1805, VD 71805 - | |
| 3744-A-B  In Harlem's Araby | GG/Rx/Spm 1804, Rx 931, VD 71804, | |
| | Met 1258, Pic 494, Bm 1024, | |
| | JC L-59, Tem R-27 | |

NOTE:- Grey Gull 1797 and 1816 as THE JAZZOPATORS; Van Dyke 71804 and 71805 as THE
DIXIE DEVILS; 71816 as THE WHITE WAY PLAYERS; Metropole 1258 as BOHEMIAN DANCE
BAND; Piccadilly as THE WHITE STAR SYNCOPATORS; Biltmore 1024 as KING OLIVER'S
DIXIE DEVILS; Jazz Collector L-59 and both Tempo issues as KING OLIVER'S MEMPHIS
JAZZERS.  When the latter reissues appeared at the end of 1949, many collectors,
myself included, were firmly of the opinion that King Oliver was the trumpet man
on the session, and even now, I still think of it as the nearest approach to King
Oliver's playing I have ever heard from another musician.  See also Clarence
Williams.

## MEMPHIS JUG BAND

Will Shade-h-g-v/Ben Ramey-k/Will Weldon-g-v/Charlie Polk-jug-v.
                                         Memphis, February 24, 1927.

| | | |
|---|---|---|
| 37941-1-3  Sun Brimmers - hWS/vWW | Vic 20552 | |
| 37941-2  Sun Brimmers - hWS/vWW | X LVA-3009 (LP) | |
| 37942-1  Stingy Woman - hWS/vWW | - | |
| 37942-2  Stingy Woman - hWS/vWW | Vic 20552 | |
| 37943-2  Memphis Jug - gWS/vWS-WW-CP | Vic 20576 | |
| 37944-1  Newport News - g-vWS | X LVA-3009 (LP) | |
| 37944-2  Newport News - g-vWS | Vic 20576 | |

Ben Ramey-v/"Shaky Walter"-h where noted; rest as above.
                                         Chicago, June 9, 1927.

| | | |
|---|---|---|
| 38657-1  Sometimes I Think I Love You - hSW/g-vWS | Vic 20809 | |
| 38658-1  Sunshine Blues - hSW/gWS/vWW | Vic 20781 | |
| 38659-1  Memphis Boy - g-vWS/vBR-WW | Vic 20809 | |
| 38660-2  I'm Looking For The Bully Of The Town | Vic 20781 | |
|   - g-vWS/vBR-WW | | |

Polk omitted; Vol Stevens-bj-md-g-v/Jennie Clayton-v added.
                                         Atlanta, October 19, 1927.

| | | |
|---|---|---|
| 40312-1  I Packed My Suitcase, Started To The | Vic 21412 | |
|   Train - g-vWS/mdVS/vJC | | |
| 40313-2  State Of Tennessee Blues-g-vWS/mdVS/vJC | Vic 21185 | |
| 40314-2  Bob Lee Junior Blues - gWS/mdVS/vJC | Vic 21412 | |
| 40315-1  Kansas City Blues - h-vWS/gVS/vBR-WW | Vic 21185, BB B-5430, RZ MR-2331 | |

Will Shade-h-g-v/Ben Ramey-k-v/Vol Stevens-bj-md-g-v/Will Weldon-g-v/Charlie Polk-jug
  (except where marked*).                    Atlanta, October 20, 1927.

40320-1 *Beale Street Mess Around - hWS/g-vVS      Vic 21066
40321-1  I'll See You In The Spring, When The        -
         Birds Begin To Sing - g-vVS

   Ramey omitted.                            Memphis, February 1, 1928.

41817-2-3  Snitchin' Gambler Blues - mdVS/v ?     Vic 21524
41813-2  Evergreen Money Blues - g-vWS/mdVS       Vic 21657

   Ramey returns.                            Memphis, February 13, 1928.

41888-2  Coal Oil Blues - hWS/g-vVS              Vic 21278
41889-2  Papa Long Blues - hWS/g-vVS              -
41890-2  Peaches In The Springtime - mdVS/vBR-WW  Vic 21657
41891-2  She Stays Out All Night Long-mdVS/g-vWS  Vic 21524

   Charlie Burse-g-v replaces Weldon; Jab Jones-jug-v; unknown h where shown; no jug*.
                                             Memphis, September 11, 1928.

47008-1-2  Lindberg Hop (Overseas Stomp)         Vic 21740
           - gWS/mdVS/vJJ
47009-1  Sugar Pudding -'hWS/mdVS/v3              -
47010-2 *A Black Woman Is Like A Black Snake     Vic V-38015
           - g-vWS/h/vCB
47011-1  On The Road Again - g-vWS/h/vCB          -

                                             Memphis, September 17, 1928.

47036-2  Whitewash Station Blues - hWS/mdVS/v5   Vic V-38504
47037-2  Stealin', Stealin' - hWS/gVS/v5          -
47038-2  Jug Band Waltz - hWS/gVS                Vic V-38537
47039-2  Mississippi River Waltz - hWS/gVS        -

Will Shade-Charlie Burse-g/Ben Ramey-k/Milton Robie-vn/Jab Jones-jug; the v duet may
  be by Ramey and Burse, with Shade making the trio.
                                             Memphis, September 17, 1929.

55529-1  I Can't Stand It - v2                   Vic V-38551
55530-2  What's The Matter ? - v3                 -

   Vocals by the Jug Band (cf. files).    Memphis, September 27, 1929.

55598-1  Feed Your Friend With A Long-Handled    Vic V-38578
         Spoon - vMJB
55599-1  I Can Beat You Plenty (That Hand You     Vic V-38586
         Tried To Deal Me) - vMJB

Will Shade-h-g-v/Ben Ramey-k-v/Charlie Nickerson-p/Charlie Burse-Teewee Blackman-g/
  Jab Jones-jug/Hattie Hart and two differently constituted trios, possibly including
  Burse and Jones-v; instrumentation of each side shown after title.
                                             Memphis, October 3, 1929.

56343-3  Taking Your Place - k/2g/jug/vWS       Vic 23347
56344-2  Tired Of You Driving Me - h/k/2g/jug/vBR Vic V-38586

                                             Memphis, October 4, 1929.

56345-2  Memphis Yo Yo Blues - h/2g/jug/vHH     Vic V-38558
56346-1-2  K. C. Moan - h/k/2g/jug/vWS-3         -          BB B-5430, RZ MR-2331
56347-2  I Whipped My Woman With A Singletree    Vic V-38578, BB B-5040, Sr S-3137
           - h/k/p/g/v3

Ben Ramey-k/? Vol Stevens-bj/Charlie Burse-md/Will Shade-g/Hambone Lewis-jug/Charlie
  Nickerson-v.                               Memphis, May 12, 1930.

59917-2  Everybody's Talking About Sadie Green   Vic V-38599
           - vCN

Ben Ramey-k-v/Will Shade-Vol Stevens-g-v/Hambone Lewis-jug/Hattie Hart-v.
Memphis, May 17, 1930.

| | | |
|---|---|---|
| 59932-2 | Oh Ambulance Man - vHH-WS | Vic V-38605, BB B-5040, Sr S-3137 |
| 59933-2 | Cocaine Habit Blues - vHH-BR-WS | Vic V-38620 |

Ben Ramey-k/Milton Robie-vn/Charlie Nickerson-p-v/Will Shade-g-v/Charlie Burse-md-g/
Hambone Lewis-jug/individual instrumentation shown after each title.
Memphis, May 21, 1930.

| | | |
|---|---|---|
| 59961-2 | Jim Strainer Blues - k/p/g-vWS/jug | Vic 23421 |
| 59962-2 | Cave Man Blues - vn/2g/jug/vCN | Vic V-38605 |
| 59963-1 | Fourth Street Mess Around-k/md/gWS/jug/ - vCN | Vic 23251 |
| 59964-2 | It Won't Act Right - k/2g/jug/vCN ? | Vic V-38620 |

Will Shade-h/Charlie Burse-g/"Memphis Minnie" McCoy-g-v/Hambone Lewis-jug.
Memphis, May 26, 1930.

| | | |
|---|---|---|
| 59993-2 | Bumble Bee Blues - vMM | Vic V-38599 |
| 59994-2 | Meningitis Blues - vMM | Vic 23421 |

Ben Ramey-k/Will Shade-g-v/Charlie Burse-g/Hambone Lewis-jug/Hattie Hart-? Vol Stevens
Charlie Nickerson-v.                    Memphis, May 29, 1930.

| | | |
|---|---|---|
| 62541-2 | Aunt Caroline Dyer Blues - vVS ? | Vic 23347 |
| 62542-2 | Stonewall Blues - vVS ? | BB B-5675 |

Memphis, June 5, 1930.

| | | |
|---|---|---|
| 62581-2 | Spider's Nest Blues - vHH-WS | Vic 23319 |
| 62582-2 | Papa's Got Your Bath Water On - vHH-WS | Vic 23251 |
| 62583-1 | Going Back To Memphis - vCN&ch | Vic 23310 |

NOTE:- Victor 23310 as CHARLIE NICKERSON; 23319 as CAROLINA PEANUT BOYS.

Will Shade-h/Vol Stevens-md/Charlie Burse-g-? v/Jab Jones-jug/Charlie Nickerson-v.
Memphis, November 21, 1930.

| | | |
|---|---|---|
| 62990-2 | He's In The Jailhouse Now - vCN-? CB | Vic 23256 |

NOTE:- This issue as MEMPHIS SHEIKS.

Ben Ramey-k added**; Stevens db g.     Memphis, November 26, 1930.

| | | |
|---|---|---|
| 64731-2** | Got A Letter From My Darlin' - v? CN/h/k/g/jug | Vic 23267 |
| 64732-2** | Round And Round - h/k/md/jug/vCN | Vic 23256 |
| 64733-2 | You May Leave But This Will Bring You Back - h/md/g/jug/vCN | Vic 23267 |

NOTE:- Victor 23256 as MEMPHIS SHEIKS; 23267 as CAROLINA PEANUT BOYS.

Memphis, November 28, 1930.

| | | |
|---|---|---|
| 64740-2 | Move That Thing - h/md/g/jug/vCN | Vic 23274 |
| 64741-2 | You Got Me Rollin' - h/md/g/jug/vCN | - |

NOTE:- This issue as CAROLINA PEANUT BOYS.

Will Shade-h-g-v/Charlie Pierce-vn/Jab Jones-p-jug/Charlie Burse-md-g-v/Robert Burse-d
/individual instrumentation shown after each title.
Chicago, November 6, 1934.

| | | |
|---|---|---|
| C-780-2 | Mary Anna Cut Off - h-vWS/vn/p/gCB/d | OK 8960 |
| C-781-1 | My Love Is Cold - vn/p/g/d/vCB | OK 8963, Voc 03081 |
| C-782-2 | Jazzbo Stomp - h/vn/gCB/jug/d | OK 8955, Bm 1101 |
| C-783-2 | Gator Wobble - h-gWS/vn/p/md/d | OK 8958, WS 102 |
| C-784-1-2 | Poor Jab's Blues (instruments unknown) | Rejected |
| C-785-2 | Tear It Down, Bed Slats And All - g-vWS/ vn/g/jug/d | OK 8956, Voc 03182 |

Will Shade-h-g-v/Charlie Pierce-vn/Jab Jones-p-jug/Charlie Burse-md-g-v/Robert Burse-
   d/individual instrumentation shown after each title.
                                        Chicago, November 7, 1934.

C-792-1  Boodie Bum Bum - gWS/vn/g-vCB/jug/d      OK 8956, Voc 03182
C-793-1  Take Your Fingers Off It - vn/g-vCB/jug/ Voc 03175
         d/vWS
C-794-1  Little Green Slippers-vn/g-vWS-CB/jug/d   OK 8966, Voc 03050
C-795-1  Fishin' In The Dark - vn/g-vWS-CB/jug/d   Voc 03175
C-796-1  Bottle It Up And Go-vn/g-vWS/md-vCB/jug/  OK 8959, Voc 03080
         d
C-797-1  Insane Crazy Blues - vn/g-vWS/g/jug/d         -          -
C-798-1  I Got Good Potatoes-vn/h or gWS/g-vCB/    Rejected
         jug/d
C-799-1  What's The Matter With The Well ?             -
         - vn/h or gWS/g-vCB/jug/d
C-800-1  She Done Sold It Out - vn/g/-vWS-CB/jug/  OK 8963, Voc 03081
         d
   NOTE:- OKeh 8959 and Vocalion 03080 as CHARLIE BURSE WITH MEMPHIS JUG BAND.

                                        Chicago, November 8, 1934.

C-803-2  Memphis Shakedown - vn/2g/jug/d          OK 8960
C-804-1  Gonna Cut It Tonight (inst. unknown)     Rejected
C-805-1  Rukus Juice And Chittlin'-vn/2g/jug/d    OK 8955, Bm 1101
C-806-1  My Business Ain't Right - vn/g/md/jug/d  OK 8958, WS 102
C-807-1  Jug Band Quartette - vn/g-vWS-CB/jug/d   OK 8966, Voc 03050

### MEMPHIS  MELODY BOYS

Pseudonym for the following items listed in this book :-

Buddy 8005  Washboard Blues (Hitch's Happy Harmonists)
     8005  Creole (Ross Reynolds' Palais Gardens Orchestra)
Challenge 143  I'd Rather Be Alone (Barney Zeeman's Kentucky Cardinals)
Superior 2503  I've Got Somebody Now (Black Diamond Orchestra)

### MEMPHIS  MELODY MAKERS

Pseudonym on Australian Embassy E-152 for the Carolina Club Orchestra (see Hal Kemp).

### MEMPHIS MELODY MEN

Pseudonym on Superior for Ted Smith and his Orchestra, q.v.

### MEMPHIS  NIGHT HAWKS

C (except where otherwise noted)/Roy Palmer-tb (except where otherwise noted)/
   Darnell Howard-cl-as-vn/cl-ts/Bob Hudson and or W. E. Burton-p/bj/Jimmy Bertrand-d-
   wb/v duet.                           New York, March 29, 1932.

11612-2  Georgia Grind - vnDH              Ban 32434, Or 8136, Per 0205,
                                           Ro 5136, BRS 15, HJCA HC-71
11613-1-2  Slow Drag Blues                 Rejected
11614-1-2  Baby, If You Can't Do Better         -
11615-1  Shanghai Honeymoon - v2           Voc 2593
11616-1-2  Beedle-Um-Bum - v2 ?            Rejected

                                        New York, March 30, 1932.

11618-2  Biscuit Roller - vnDH (cl not DH)  Voc 1744, HJCA HC-74
11619-1  Rukus Juice Shuffle               Ban 32434, Or 8136, Per 0205,
                                           Ro 5136
11620-1; 19995*  Dirty Dozen's Cousins - v2  Per 0246, ARC 7-01-63*, BRS 17,
                                           HJCA HC-72
11621-1; 20000*  Nancy Jane                As above
11622-2  Jockey Stomp                      Ban 32760, Mt M-12689, Or 8229,
                                           Per 0240, Ro 5229, Voc 1736,
                                           BRS 16, HJCA HC-70, JD 009
11623-1  Wild Man Stomp no c or tb         Voc 2593, HJCA HC-73

C (unless otherwise noted)/Roy Palmer-tb/Darnell Howard-cl-as-vn/cl-ts/Bob Hudson and
/or W. E. Burton-p/bj/Jimmy Bertrand-d-wb/v.
                                    New York, March 31, 1932.

11627-2  Come On In, Baby                       Voc 1744, HJCA HC-74
11628-2  Stomp That Thing - v                   Ban 32760, Mt M-12689, Or 8229,
                                                Per 0240, Ro 5229, BRS 15,
                                                HJCA HC-71
11629-1  Endurance Stomp                        Or 8137, Per 0260, Ro 5137,
                                                BRS 16, HJCA HC-70

                                    New York, April 1, 1932.

11633-1  Sweet Feet - no c                      Voc 1736, HJCA HC-73, JD 009
11634-1-2  Weary Way Blues                      Rejected

NOTE:- All issues except Vocalions as ALABAMA RASCALS; BRS 15 and 16 as ROY PALMER'S
  ALABAMA RASCALS; HJCA HC-70, 71 and 72 as ROY PALMER AND THE MEMPHIS NIGHT HAWKS;
  HC-73 and 74 as DARNELL HOWARD AND THE MEMPHIS NIGHT HAWKS.

## MEMPHIS PICKANINNY BAND

Small brass band with percussion.     New York, c. June, 1917.

66402     Some Jazz Blues                       P 20236, Crescent 10031, Emp 5531
  NOTE:- Crescent as ALABAMA JAZZ BAND; Empire 5531 as EMPIRE BAND.

## MEMPHIS SHEIKS

Pseudonym on Victor for the Memphis Jug Band, q.v.

## MEMPHIS STOMPERS

Snooks Friedman-d dir. James Migliore or Estes Monasco-c/Ken Herlin-tb/Elly Bellare-
  cl-as/Rupe Biggadike-p/Bob Cooke-bj.     Memphis, February 4, 1928.

41840-1  Memphis Stomp                          Vic 21641
41841-2  Hold It Still                          Vic 21270

                                    Memphis, February 11, 1928.

41882-2  Kansas City Blues                      Vic 21270
41883-1  Goofer Feathers Blues                  Vic 21641

  Walter (Wally) Ashby-cl-as-bar added; pac (probably by someone db)*.
                                    Memphis, September 6, 1928.

45486-2  Yea Alabama                            Vic 21709
45487-3  Washington And Lee Swing               -
45488-1-2-3 *Hot Dog                            Rejected
45489-1-2  Standing In The Rain                 -

  Migliore and Monasco present; Al Muller-cl-ts/Chuck Jordan-sb added.
                                    Camden, N. J., July 2, 1929.

49446-1  Stompin' Away                          Vic 23371
49447-2  Gettin' The Bird                       -

NOTE:- See also Snooks and his Memphis Ramblers.  The name MEMPHIS STOMPERS was also
  a pseudonym on Electradisk for Dave (Nelson)'s Harlem Highlights (see Nelson).

## THE MEMPHIS STRUTTERS

Pseudonym on Champion 15415 for the Triangle Harmony Boys, q.v.

Toots Mendello-c/Glenn Miller-tb/Fud Livingston-cl/Arthur Schutt-p/? Carl Kress-g/Vic
    Berton-d/Jack Kaufman (as DICK HOLMES or RAY COVERT)-v.
                                        New York, July 3, 1928.

| | | |
|---|---|---|
| 8071- | Dancing Eyes | ARC rejected |
| 8072- | A Mad Mean Mama | - |
| 8073- | You Can Have Him If You Want Him | - |

                                        New York, August 15, 1928.

| | | |
|---|---|---|
| 8148-1 | Cool Papa (You'd Better Warm Up) - vJK | Ban 6206, Or 1371 |
| 8149-1 | Sunday Afternoon - vJK | Ban 7248, Or 1387 |
| 8150-1 | High Hattin' Hattie - vJK | Ban 6213, Or 1363 |

                                        New York, October 16, 1928.

| | | |
|---|---|---|
| 8260-1 | Easy | Ban 7246, Bwy 1213, Or 1368, Pm 20754 |
| 8261-1 | Dixie Drag (Blue Bottom) | Cr 81020 |
| 8261-2 | Dixie Drag (Blue Bottom) | Ban 6214, Je 5446, Or 1396, Apex 8877 |
| 8262-2 | Baby's Coming Back - vJK | Ban 6205, Chg 919, Dom 31020, |

NOTE:- All Banner issues as MENDELLO'S DANCE      Je 5405, Or 1360, Apex 8863,
ORCHESTRA; Challenge 919, Jewel 5405 and 5406     LS 24368, Mic 22368, St 10416
and all Oriole issues as DIXIE JAZZ BAND; Broadway 1213 and Paramount 20754 as
MARKS AND HIS FIVE OH MY'S, ROY CLARK-v; Crown 81020 as PIERROT SYNCOPATORS; Microphone 22368 as JENKINS' BLACK ACES.

## FELIX MENDELSSOHN AND HIS HAWAIIAN SERENADERS

Although the vast majority of the many records made by the late Felix Mendelssohn are
    of not the slightest interest as jazz, the following are truly exceptional.

Felix Mendelssohn dir. Roland Peachey-stg/Fred Day-Jimmy Mack or Jack Llewellyn-2g/
    Harry Brooker-p/Fred Mortledge-sb/Harry Jimmick-tom-tom/Ernie Mack-d/Gaby Rogers-
    vib.                                London, July 12, 1940.

| | | |
|---|---|---|
| CA-18066-1 | Japanese Sandman | Col FB-2525, RZ G-25113, Par MP-30 |
| CA-18067-1 | Tiger Rag | Col FB-2494, Od 028758, Par PZ-7152, RZ G-24365 |
| CA-18068-1 | Lady Be Good | Col FB-2525, RZ G-25113, Par MP-30 PZ-7151 |
| CA-18069-1 | Goodbye Blues | Col FB-2494, RZ G-24365 |

                                        London, October 28, 1940.

| | | |
|---|---|---|
| CA-18194-1 | In The Mood | Col FB-2667 |
| CA-18195-1 | I Got Rhythm | - |

## THE MEN FROM MINTON'S

Hot Lips Page-Victor Coulson and another-t/Rudy Williams-as/Don Byas-ts/Alan "Pee Wee"
    Tinney-p/Charlie Christian-elg/Ebenezer Paul-sb/Taps Miller or unknown*-d.
                                        Monroe's Uptown House, New York, 1941.

| | |
|---|---|
| Guy's Got To Go/*On With Charlie C/*Up | Esoteric ESJ-4, ES-548, |
| On Teddy's Hill | Counterpoint CPT-548 (LPs) |

## JOHNNY MERCER

Vocal, acc. by Victor Young dir. Sterling Bose-t/Jack Teagarden-tb/Fulton McGrath-p/
    Dick McDonough-g/Hank Wayland-sb.      New York, August 24, 1934.

| | | |
|---|---|---|
| 38417-A | Lord, I Give You My Children | Dec 142 |
| 38418-A-B | If I Could Only Read Your Mind | Rejected |
| 38419-A | The Bathtub Ran Over Again | Dec 142 |

The following sides by this commercial dance band are of some interest as "hot" dance
music; the name was used on OKeh 40912 for Frankie Trumbauer and his Orchestra, q.v.
and on OKeh 41079 (TOO BUSY) for Sam Lanin and his Famous Players, q.v.

Benny Meroff-as dir. Phil Grossi-Joe Harris-t/Norman Hendrickson-tb/Pete Ross-as/
Harold White-ts/Gene Gory-Marcel Klauberg-vn/Bill Hughes-p/Hyman Milrod-bb/Al DeVito
d.                                         Camden, N. J., August 8, 1925.

33412-1-2  Eccentric                              Vic rejected

Benny Meroff-v dir. Wild Bill Davison-Rosie Rusciolelli-Joe Rullo-t/Al Marineau-Joe
Quartell-tb/Lenny Cohen-Tony Ciccone-as/Arnold Pritikin-ts-a/Al Nillson-p/Sid
Pritikin-g/Fritz Ciccone-bb and/or George Physter-sb/Benny Metz-d/Roy Cole-vn if
used.                                       Chicago, December 9, 1928.

402202-C  Smiling Skies - vBM                    OK 41171, Od A-189238
402203-C  Me And The Man In The Moon - vBM       -          -   Par R-316, A-2723
NOTE:- Parlophone A-2723 also appeared in Australia with the upper part of the label
covered by a sticker bearing the name Capitol !

Al King-Larry Powell-Meyer Druzinsky-t/Vernon Brown-Jack Marshall-tb/Jimmy Lord-cl-as/
Don Ellis-cl-as-bar/Irving Barnett-ts/Bill Gollan-p/Marty Ross-g/Phil Stevens-sb/
Johnny Perrin-d.                            New York, June 13, 1935.

CO-17597-1  Cowboy In Manhattan                  Col 3072-D
CO-17598-1  Aristocrat Of Harlem                 Col 3065-D
CO-17599-1  Yankee In Havana                     Col 3072-D, Par R-2448
CO-17600-1  The Pleasure Was All Mine !          Col 3065-D

## MERRIE'S DANCE QUINTET

Pseudonym on Aco G-15218 (LOOSE FEET) for the Original Memphis Five, q.v.

## ROY MERRITT AND HIS ORCHESTRA

Pseudonym on Champion for Bob McGowan and his Orchestra, q.v.

## CYRIL MERRIVALE AND HIS ORCHESTRA

Pseudonym on American Parlophone for Arthur Schutt and his Orchestra, q.v.

## THE MERRY MAKERS

Pseudonym on Australian Bon Marche 148 for the Buffalodians, q.v.

## MERTON ORCHESTRA

Pseudonym on Parlophone E-6391 (I'LL BE BLUE, JUST THINKING OF YOU) for Fred Rich and
his Orchestra, q.v., and for other,non-jazz bands on the same label.

## JIMMY MESSINI/MESENE

See Nat Gonella.

## JOHNNY MESSNER AND HIS MUSIC BOX BAND

The following sides by this commercial dance band are of some interest as jazz.

Johnny Messner-cl-as-v dir. Charles Cerborra-Shanty Diamant-Shorty Skipper-t/Huff
Allen-tb/Will Cottrell-George Ward-as-ts/Paul Kuhlthan-p/Russell Moss-g/Al Dell-sb/
Dick Cornell-d/Jeanne d'Arcy-v.            New York, March, 1940.

S-1412-1  Ooh ! What You Said - vJM-JD           Var 8219

Probably somewhat different personnel.     New York, May 20, 1941.

69218-    Mobile Flag Stop (Catching The 8.02 Local)Dec 3816

                                          New York, September 19, 1941.

69759-A  A Clarinet In A Haunted House           Dec 4040

<u>SARA MESSON</u>

Pseudonym on Oriole 325 for Clementine Smith, q.v.

<u>METOMKIN INN ORCHESTRA</u>

Pseudonym on Champion 15458 for Hogan Hancock and his Orchestra, q.v.

<u>THE METRO FIVE</u>

Paul Fenoulhet-t-tb/Cyril Rusby-as-bar/Archie Griffiths-p/Ronnie Rae-bj/Bob Purcell-
  d-v. (These two titles are coupled).     London, c. 1927.

| | | |
|---|---|---|
| Grey Eyes - vBP | | Br R-44 |
| Metro Blues | | Br T-45 |

<u>METRONOME ALL-STAR BANDS</u>

METRONOME ALL STAR BAND : Charlie Spivak-Harry James-Ziggy Elman-t/Jack Teagarden-
Jack Jenney-tb/Benny Goodman-cl/Toots Mondello-Benny Carter-as/Eddie Miller-Charlie
Barnet-ts/Jess Stacy-p/Charlie Christian-elg/Bob Haggart-sb/Gene Krupa-d/Fletcher
Henderson-a, or METRONOME ALL STAR NINE : Same, without Spivak, Elman, Jenney,
Mondello and Barnet, marked *.        New York, February 7, 1940.

26489-A  King Porter Stomp                  Col 36389, 291180, DO-2107, M-233,
                                            Par R-2746, B-7102, PZ-11172,
                                            V-Disc 894
26490-A *All-Star Strut                     As above, plus Col AS-10009, but
NOTE:- V-Disc 879 as BANDLEADER STARS.      V-Disc 879

Harry James-Ziggy Elman-Cootie Williams-t/Tommy Dorsey-J. C. Higginbotham-tb/Benny
Goodman-cl/Toots Mondello-Benny Carter-as/Coleman Hawkins-Tex Beneke-ts/Count Basie-
p/Charlie Christian-elg/Artie Bernstein-sb/Buddy Rich-d.
                                            New York, January 16, 1941.

060331-1  Bugle Call Rag                    Vic 27314, 27-0036, 1AC-0069,
                                            HMV B-9195, EA-3004
060332-1  One O'Clock Jump                  As above plus Vic A-1337

Harry James-Cootie Williams-Roy Eldridge-t/J. C. Higginbotham-Lou McGarity-tb/Benny
Goodman-cl/Toots Mondello-Benny Carter-as/Vido Musso-Tex Beneke-ts/Count Basie-p/
Freddy Green-g/Doc Goldberg-sb/Gene Krupa-d.
                                            New York, December 31, 1941.

32079-1  Royal Flush                        Col 36499, C-601, DO-2481,
                                            DS-1598, 20317, Par R-2967
32079-2  Royal Flush                        CBS CL-2528, Har HL-7044 (LPs)
32080-1  Dear Old Southland

METRONOME ALL-STAR LEADERS : Cootie Williams-t/J. C. Higginbotham-tb/Benny Goodman-cl
  /Benny Carter-as/Charlie Barnet-ts/Count Basie-p/Alvino Rey-g/John Kirby-sb/Gene
  Krupa-d.                          New York, January 16, 1942.

32261-1  I Got Rhythm                       Col C-601, DO-2481
32261-2  I Got Rhythm                       Col 36499, DS-1598, 20317,
                                            Par R-2967

See also All Star Band.

<u>METROPOLITAN  BAND</u>

Pseudonym on HMV C-600, C-603, C-819 and S-8752 for the Victor Military Band, q.v.

<u>METROPOLITAN DANCE ORCHESTRA</u>

Pseudonym on Domino 31002 for Ted Wallace and his Orchestra, q.v.

<u>METROPOLITAN DANCE PLAYERS</u>

Pseudonym on Globe, Grey Gull, Nadsco and Radiex for the following items listed in
  this book :-

1283  In Harlem's Araby (Leroy Smith's Orch.)  1298  I'm Wild (Grey Gull studio band)

This name was used for the first studio recording orchestra in the history of sound-recording, at any rate on disc.  It first appeared on Emile Berliner's discs in the late 1890s, continued on Eldridge R. Johnson's Improved Gram-O-Phone records, and on the earliest Victor records.  All kinds of music, mostly of a light nature, was recorded, until the summer of 1904, when an attempt at a stablized personnel brought about the formation of the Victor Orchestra, q.v.  The following are of interest as ragtime, played at the time of its first era of popularity; the instrumentation does not seem to have varied much from session to session, though doubtless the musicians did.  It consisted basically of 2c/tb/cl/f/pic/vn/p/bb/d, with perhaps ah/th/bh on occasion.                                    ? New York, c. early 1897.

| 1470 | Coon Town Capers (A New Negro Oddity) | Ber 1470 |
| 1472 | Georgia Camp Meeting ("Another lively | Ber 1472 |
|      | new one" - Berliner catalogue, September, 1897) | |

New York, January 18, 1900.

| 0893 | Smoky Mokes (Abe Holzmann) | Ber 0893 |
| 0894 | A Bunch O' Blackberries (Abe Holzmann) | Ber 0894 |

New York, January 26, 1900.

| 0911 | Who Dat Say Chicken In Dis Crowd ? | Ber 0911 |
|      | (Will Marion Cook) | |

New York, September 28, 1900.

| 251-1-2 | A Bunch O' Blackberries (Abe Holzmann) | Vic 251 |
| 271-1-2 | Smoky Mokes (Abe Holzmann) | Vic 271 |

NOTE:- Two further takes of matrix 251 were made on each of the following dates :- December 1, 1900; March 26 and April 14, 1902.  A third take of matrix 271 was made on September 29, 1900.  All appear to have been used for issue.

New York, September 29, 1900.

| 289-1 | Who Dat Say Chicken In Dis Crowd ? | Vic 289 |
|       | (Will Marion Cook) | |

New York, June 13, 1901.

| 872-1 | Rag Time Society (composer unknown) | Vic 872 |

New York, October 16, 1901.

1023-1  Creole Belles (J  Bodewalt Lampe)        Vic 1023
NOTE:- Matrices 1023-2-3-4 were made on October 18, 1901; -5 on November 14, 1901; -6-7 on November 15, 1901; -8 on November 22, 1901; -9-10 on March 27, 1902; -11-12 on April 1, 1902 - and apparently all were used for issue.

## MEYER'S  DANCE  ORCHESTRA

seudonym on English Perfect for the following items listed in this book :-

-315  Souvenirs (California Ramblers, copies bearing matrix number 107913 only)
-315  Side By Side (Sam Lanin and his Orchestra)
-359  Without You, Sweetheart (Van and his Half Moon Orchestra)
-379  After My Laughter Came Tears (Lou Gold and his Orchestra)

he name was also used on Australian Grand Pree 18331, 18458, 18485 and 18539 for the California Ramblers, q.v., and on English Perfect for the following very interesting performance, not issued on any other label, apparently.

ed Nichols-t/? Jimmy Lytell-cl/? Fred Morrow-as/Arthur Schutt-p/Dick McDonough-bj/Vic Berton-d.                                    New York, c. October 10, 1927.

)7330    Everybody Loves My Girl                Per P-378

Vocal, acc. by the Original Memphis Five : Phil Napoleon-t/Charlie Panelli-tb/Jimmy
Lytell-cl/Frank Signorelli-p/Jack Roth-d.
                                          New York, October 19, 1922.

69905    That Da Da Strain                      PA 020870, Per 12031, Dav 5067
69906    'Tain't Nobody's Biz-ness If I Do         -           -         -

  Ray Kitchingman-bj added.              New York, December 4, 1922.

69958    Evil Minded Blues                      PA 020877, Per 12038
69959    Last Go Round Blues                      -           -

## HAZEL  MEYERS

Vocal, acc. by Porter Grainger-p.       New York, c. September, 1923.

         Love Ain't Blind No More              Ajax 17007
         Wish I Had You (And I'm Gonna Get You Blues)  -
NOTE:- The copy of this record examined bore no matrix numbers.

  Acc. by Leslie A. Hutchinson ("Hutch")-p.
                                          New York, October 1, 1923.

12048    Graveyard Dream Blues                  Voc 14688, Sil 3011
12051    Low Down Papa (Treat Sweet Mama Kind)    -           -

  Acc. by Joe Smith-c/Fletcher Henderson-p.
                                          New York, October 30, 1923.

12208/9  He's Never Gonna Throw Me Down         Voc 14709
12211/2  Awful Moanin' Blues                      -

  Acc. by Porter Grainger-p.            New York, c. November, 1923.

31015-1  Tired O' Waitin' Blues                 Ajax 17013
31016-1  He's My Man, Your Man (Somebody Else's Too)  -

  Acc. by Joe Smith-c/Fletcher Henderson-p.
                                          New York, November 30, 1923.

12377    Mason-Dixon Blues                      Voc 14725
12379    Chicago Bound Blues                      -

  Acc. unknown.                         New York, c. December, 1923.

         Bleeding Hearted Blues                 Bell P-255
         Down Hearted Blues                       -

  Acc. by Ernest Elliott-cl-as/Porter Grainger-p.
                                          New York, c. January, 1924.

31502    Mississippi Blues - cl                 Ajax 17019
31504    The Man Ain't Born Who Can Treat Me Like  -
           You Do - as

  Acc. by Porter Grainger-p.             New York, March, 1924.

5457-2   'Tain't A Doggone Thing But The Blues   Ban 1358, Dom 362, Hg 925, Re 9654
5458-2   Plug Ugly (The Worst Lookin' Man In Town)  -      Dom 361      -         -
NOTE:- Domino 361 and 362 as MAE HARRIS acc. by CLARENCE NELSON.

  Acc. by Henderson and his Jazzy Cornetist (sic): Howard Scott-c/Fletcher Henderson-
p.                                        New York, April, 1924.

31555    Heart Breakin' Joe                     Ajax 17026
31558    Don't Mess With Me                       -

Acc. by Elmer Chambers-c/Don Redman-cl/Fletcher Henderson-p.
                              New York, April, 1924.

| 42592-1 | Don't Know And Don't Care Blues | Em 10748 |
| 42593-1 | I'm Gonna Tear Your Playhouse Down | - |

Acc. by Howard Scott-c/Fletcher Henderson-p.
                              New York, c. May 19, 1924.

| 105326 | Pipe Dream Blues | PA 032053, Per 12132, Hg 967 |
| 105327 | Black Star Line | -          -        - |

Acc. by her Sawin' Trio : Bubber Miley-c/Bob Fuller-cl/Louis Hooper-p/? Elmer
Snowden-bj, or Hooper and ? Snowden only*.
                              New York, c. June, 1924.

| 31571 | Papa Don't Ask Mama Where She Was | Ajax 17039 |
| 31574 | I'm Every Man's Mama | Ajax 17040 |
| 31575 | *You Better Build Love's Fire (Or Your Sweet Mama's Gone) | - |

Acc. by the Choo Choo Jazzers : Bob Fuller-cl/Louis Hooper-p, with Bubber Miley-
c**.                          New York, c. July, 1924.

| 31597 | **War Horse Mama | Ajax 17047 |
| 31599 | **Cold Weather Papa | - |
| 31602 | Hateful Blues | Ajax 17048 |
| 31603 | Frankie Blues | - |

Acc. by Louis Metcalf-c/Louis Hooper-p.
                              New York, c. August, 1924.

| 31622 | He Used To Be Mine (But You Can Have Him Now) | Ajax 17082 |
| 31624 | Lost My Sweetie Blues | Ajax 17077 |

Acc. by Fats Waller-p.        New York, August 5, 1924.

| 13467 | Maybe Someday | Voc 14861, Sil 3012 |
| 13469 | When Your Troubles Are Just Like Mine | -         - |

Acc. by the Choo Choo Jazzers : Bob Fuller-cl/p or Bubber Miley-c/Louis Hooper-p.
                              New York, c. August, 1924.

| 31630 | You'll Never Have No Luck By Quittin' Me - cl/p | Ajax 17054 |
| 31631 | Lonesome For That Man Of Mine - c/p | - |

Acc. by Starks' Hot Five : Shirley Clay-c/Preston Jackson-tb/Artie Starks-cl-as/
Cassino Simpson-p/Johnny St. Cyr-bj.  Chicago, June 21, 1926.

| 9766-A | Blackville After Dark | OK 8364 |
| 9767-A | Heartbreaking Blues | - |

## KEN MEYERS

Pseudonym on Regal 8183 for Ken "Goof" Moyer, q.v.

## VIC MEYERS AND HIS ORCHESTRA

This West Coast-based commercial dance band made a number of sides for Brunswick,
Columbia and Cameo, the following being unusually interesting as jazz.

Vic Meyers dir. Billy Stewart-Bill Zimmerman-c/Jim Taft-tb/Art Kenton-cl-as-a/Cecil
Harnack-as/Bob Gordon-ts-bsx/Al Newman-p/bj/"Chief"-bb/Bob Goodwin-d.
                              Los Angeles, August 21, 1923.

| 11229 | Mean, Mean Mama | Br 2501* |
| 11233 | Shake It And Break It | - |

Vic Meyers dir. Billy Stewart-Bill Zimmerman-c/Jim Taft-tb/Art Kenton-cl-as-a/Cecil
Harnack-as/Bob Gordon-ts-bsx/Al Newman-p/bj/"Chief"-bb/Bob Goodwin-d.
Los Angeles, May 7, 1924.

| A-20/22 | Weary Blues | Br 2664 |
| A-23/25 | Tell Me What To Do | Br 2733* |
| A-36/38 | Beets And Turnips | Br 2664 |

Los Angeles, May 8, 1924.

| A-41/3 | Springtime Rag | Br 2630 |

Los Angeles, May 13, 1924.

| A-78/79 | Mean Looks | Br 2733* |
| A-80/82 | Helen Gone | Br 2630 |

Vic Meyers-d dir. Frank McMuir-c-vn/Bill Zimmerman-c/Jim Taft-tb/Art Kenton-cl-as-a/
E. E. Elliott, Sr.-cl-as-bb/Bob Gordon-cl-ts/Earl Gibson-p-a/Harry Reser-bj.
New York, November 28, 1924.

| 14324/6) Nay, Dearie, Nay | Voc 15056, Bel 882, Clm 1835, |
| 900/2) | Lev A-102 |

NOTE:- Beltona 882 as PALM BEACH PLAYERS; Coliseum 1835 as COLISEUM DANCE ORCHES-
TRA; Levaphone A-102 as DIXIE PLANTATION ORCHESTRA.

New York, December 1, 1924.

| 14362/4) Three O'Clock Blues | Voc 15056, Lev A-102 |
| 903/5) | |

NOTE:- Levaphone A-102 as DIXIE PLANTATION ORCHESTRA.

## MEZZ MEZZROW

MEZZ MEZZROW AND HIS ORCHESTRA : Max Kaminsky-Freddy Goodman-Ben Gusick-t/Floyd
O'Brien-tb/Mezz Mezzrow-cl-as-a/Benny Carter-t-as-v-a/Johnny Russell-ts/Teddy
Wilson-p/Clayton "Sunshine" Duerr-g/Pops Foster-sb/Jack Maisel-d.
New York, November 6, 1933.

| B-14272-A | Free Love - aBC | Br 7551, A-9527, A-500369 |
| B-14273-A | Dissonance - aMM | - 02509 -　　　　　- Par R-2881, |
| | | PZ-11006, Col 291564, Pol 580008 |
| B-14274-A | Swinging With Mezz - aMM-FO'B | Br 6778, 01762, A-500370, |
| | | Par R-2881, PZ-11006, Col 291564, |
| | | Pol 5800008 |
| B-14275-A | Love, You're Not The One For Me - vBC | Br 6778, 01762, A-500370 |

Max Kaminsky-Reunald Jones-Chelsea Quealey-t/Floyd O'Brien-tb-a/Mezz Mezzrow-cl-
as-a/Benny Carter-as/Bud Freeman-ts/Willie "The Lion" Smith-p/John Kirby-sb/Chick
Webb-d/Alex Hill-a.　　　　　　　New York, May 7, 1934.

| 82392-1 | Old Fashioned Love - aAH | Vic 25202, 62-0056, BB B-10251, |
| | | HMV B-8408, JF-9, K-7690, SG-245 |
| 82393-1 | Apologies - aMM | Vic 25019, JA-1277, BB B-10250, |
| | | HMV B-8403, JF-9, K-7049, SG-244 |
| 82394-1 | Sendin' The Vipers - aMM | Vic 25019, JA-1277, BB B-10250, |
| | | HMV B-8403, JF-5, K-7049, SG-244 |
| 82395-1 | 35th And Calumet - aFO'B | Vic 25202, BB B-10251, HMV B-8408, |
| | | JF-5, K-7690, SG-245 |

MEZZ MEZZROW AND HIS SWING BAND : Frank Newton-t/Mezz Mezzrow-cl/Bud Freeman-ts/
Willie "The Lion" Smith-p-v/Albert Casey-g/Wellman Braud-sb/George Stafford-d/
Lucille Stewart-v.　　　　　　　New York, March 12, 1936.

| 99772-1 | A Melody From The Sky - vLS | BB B-6320,　MW M-4998, HMV GW-1338, |
| | | K-7753 |
| 99773-1 | Lost | As above except HMV GW-1338 |
| 99774-1 | Mutiny In The Parlor | (BB B-6319, Vic A-1291, MW M-4999, |
| 99775-1 | The Panic Is On | (RZ MR-2440, HMV GW-1336, K-7771, |
| | | (X-4844, HJCA HC-121 |
| 99776-1/99777-1 | I'se A Muggin'-Pts.1-2-vWS&ch | BB B-6321, MW M-4997 |

NOTE:- Regal Zonophone MR-2440 as BROADWAY SWING STARS.

MEZZ MEZZROW AND HIS ORCHESTRA : Sy Oliver-t/J. C. Higginbotham-tb/Mezz Mezzrow-cl-a
/Happy Caldwell-ts/Sonny White-p/Bernard Addison-g/Pops Foster-sb/Jimmy Crawford-d
/Larry Clinton-Edgar Sampson-a.        New York, June 14, 1937.

| | | |
|---|---|---|
| 010569-1 | Blues In Disguise - aMM-ES | Vic 25636, A-1368, HMV B-8656, K-8028 |
| 010570-1 | That's How I Feel Today - aES | As above |
| 010571-1 | Hot Club Stomp - aES | Vic 25612, A-1259, HMV B-8646, JK-2065, K-8100 |
| 010572-1 | The Swing Session's Called To Order-aLC | As above |

Tommy Ladnier-Sidney de Paris-t/Mezz Mezzrow-cl/James P. Johnson-p/Teddy Bunn-g/
Elmer James-sb/Zutty Singleton-d.        New York, November 21, 1938.

| | | |
|---|---|---|
| 028988-1 | Revolutionary Blues | BB B-10088, HMV B-9470, EA-3333, HN-2953, JK-2174, SG-350,Swing 78 |
| 028989-1 | Comin' On With The Come On - Part 1 | BB B-10085, HMV B-9468, EA-2336, SG-353, Swing 47 |
| 028990-1 | Comin' On With The Come On - Part 2 | As above |
| 028991-1 | Swingin' For Mezz (Careless Love) | Rejected |
| 028991-2 | Swingin' For Mezz (no t or p used) | - |

MEZZROW-LADNIER QUINTET : Tommy Ladnier-t/Mezz Mezzrow-cl/Teddy Bunn-g-v/Pops Foster
sb/Manzie Johnson-d.        New York, December 19, 1938.

| | | |
|---|---|---|
| 030450-1 | Royal Garden Blues | BB B-10087, HMV B-9416, EA-2597, SG-354, Swing 57 |
| 030450-2 | Royal Garden Blues | X LVA-3027, Vic RA-5324, HMV DLP-1110 (LPs) |
| 030451-1 | Everybody Loves My Baby | BB B-10090, HMV B-9447, HN-2943, SG-355, Swing 209 |
| 030451-2 | Everybody Loves My Baby | X LVA-3027, Vic RA-5324, HMV DLP-1110 (LPs) |
| 030452-1 | I Ain't Gonna Give Nobody None O' This Jelly-Roll | BB B-10090, HMV B-9447, HN-2943, SG-355, Swing 209 |
| 030452-2 | I Ain't Gonna Give Nobody None O' This Jelly-Roll | X LVA-3027, Vic RA-5324, HMV DLP-1110 (LPs) |
| 030453-1 | If You See Me Comin' - vTB | BB B-10087, HMV B-9416, EA-2597, SG-354, Swing 57 |
| 030453-2 | If You See Me Comin' - vTB | X LVA-3027, Vic RA-5324, HMV DLP-1110 (LPs) |
| 030454-1 | Gettin' Together | As above |
| 030454-2 | Gettin' Together | BB B-10088, HMV B-9470, HN-2953, JK-2174, SG-350, Swing 78 |

## MIAMI BEACH BAND

Pseudonym on Swedish Grand 707 for the Washboard Serenaders, q.v.

## MIAMI  JAZZ BAND

Pseudonym on Oriole for the following items listed in this book :-

253  Dixie Flyer Sam (New Orleans Jazz Band)
551  Spanish Shawl (Ben Selvin and his Orchestra)
552  Who ? (Ben Selvin and his Orchestra)

## MIAMI  LUCKY SEVEN

T/tb/cl-as/cl-ts/p/bj/d, from the Casino Gardens, Indianapolis.
                              Richmond, Ind., March 21, 1922.

11077, -A-B-C  Granny (You're My Mammy's Mammy)  Gnt rejected
11078, -A-B-C  I Wonder Blues                    -
11079    Teasin'                                 -

                              Richmond, Ind., April 3, 1922.

11086-C  I Wonder Blues                Gnt Special (un-numbered)
11087-C  Teasin'                       -

T/tb/cl-as/cl-ts/vn/p/bj/ob/d. (It is believed that the vn is played by one of the other members of the band).                     Richmond, Ind., May 29, 1924.

11891    Red Hot Mama                        Gnt 5473
11892-B  Heart-Broken Rose                   -

                                             Richmond, Ind., November 3, 1924.

12063-A  Blackin' Blues                       Gnt 5585
12064    Boll Weevil Blues                    -

                                             Richmond, Ind., September 28, 1925.

12353, -A-B  I Want To See A Little More Of What  Gnt rejected
             I Saw In Arkansas
12354, -A  Everybody Stomp                    -

                                             Richmond, Ind., October 13, 1925.

12371, -A  Fallin' Down                       Gnt 3165, Ch 15039
12372-A  Ida, I Do                            Gnt 3174
NOTE:- Champion as MOON ALLEN'S ORCHESTRA.

                                             Richmond, Ind., November 9, 1925.

12403-A  Slippery Elm                         Gnt 3174
12404, -A-B  Static                           Rejected

                                             Richmond, Ind., January 19, 1928.

13383    So Tired                             Chg 757

## MIAMI  MELODISTS

Pseudonym on Perfect 14638 for the California Ramblers, q.v.

## MIAMI ROYAL PALM ORCHESTRA

Pseudonym on Cameo 8236, Lincoln 2884, Romeo 659 and Dominion A-9 (GET OUT AND GET UNDER THE MOON) for Sam Lanin and his Orchestra, q.v.

## MIAMI  SOCIETY ORCHESTRA

Pseudonym for the following items listed in this book :-

Challenge 963  Before The Rain (Carolina Collegians - see Hal Kemp)
Oriole 1479  Dream Train (Devine's Wisconsin Roof Orchestra)

## ERNEST "MIKE" MICHALL AND HIS NEW ORLEANS BOYS

Ernest "Mike" Michall-cl/Sterling Payne-as/Archie Anderson-vn/Troy Snapp-p/Ferman Tupp-d.                          Chicago, c. July 19, 1927.

12932-B  Embarrassment Blues (Sidewalk Blues*)    Gnt 6393, BP 8046*, Ch 15491,
NOTE:- Gennett 6393 as KING BRADY'S CLARINET       Chg 372
BAND; Black Patti 8046 as ERNEST MICHALL (CLARINET BAND).

                                             Chicago, c.  July 24, 1927.

12945    Lazybone Blues (Toledano Street Blues*)  Gnt 6393, BP 8046*, Ch 15455,
         (Dry Bones**)                             Pm 12783**
NOTE:- Gennett 6393 as KING BRADY'S CLARINET BAND; Paramount 12783 as JOE'S HOT BABIES.

## MICHIGAN MELODY MAKERS

Pseudonym on Pennington for Leroy Smith and his Orchestra, q.v.

## MICKEY'S NIGHT BIRDS

Pseudonym on Mayfair G-2007 (HELLO ! BEAUTIFUL) for Will Osborne's Orchestra, q.v.

Red Nichols-t dir. Mickey Bloom-Tommy Thunen-t/Glenn Miller-tb/2as/Fud Livingston-cl
 ts/? Henry Whiteman or Maurice Goffin-vn/? Rube Bloom-p/? Joe Tarto-bb/Gene Krupa-
 d/Red McKenzie-v.                        New York, September 13, 1929.

149002-3  Swanee Shuffle - vRM                  Col 1981-D, A-8332
149003-2  I Gotta Have You - vRM                  - CB-14,  A-8347

## THE  MIDNIGHT BROADCASTERS

Pseudonym on Duophone D-4020 and D-4046 for Meyer Davis and his Orchestra, q.v.

## THE MIDNIGHT MERRYMAKERS

Harry Bidgood-p-a dir. Ernie Abbey-? another-t/Ted Heath-tb/George Gibson-cl-as/Fred
 Gilmore-cl-ts/Ramon Newton-vn-v/Len Shevill-bj/Barney Singleton-bb/Wag Abbey-d.
                                  London, late November, 1927.

 Z-279    I'm Going Back To HIMAZAS - vRN           Bcst 182

Other titles under this name may feature occasional brief solos, but the above is
 more than usually interesting, despite the unpromising comedy material.

## THE MIDNIGHT MINSTRELS

Pseudonym on Regal and Regal Zonophone for the folloeing items listed in this book:-

MR-403  Pardon Me, Pretty Baby (Fred Rich and his Orchestra)
MR-499  I Don't Know Why (Benny Goodman and his Orchestra)
MR-1025 Roll Up The Carpets (Billy Cotton and his Band)

## THE MIDNIGHT REVELLERS

Pseudonym on Australian Regal for the following items listed in this book :-

G-20602  If I Had My Way (Merle Johnston and his Ceco Couriers)
G-21577  Let's Have A Party (Joe Haymes and his Orchestra)

## THE  MIDNIGHT ROUNDERS

Jimmy Blythe-p/William Lyle-sb/Jimmy Bertrand-wb.
                                  Chicago, August 21, 1928.

C-2254-A-B  Bull Fiddle Rag                    Voc rejected
C-2255-A-B  Barrell House Baker (sic)               -

Jimmy Blythe-p/Bill Johnson-sb/W. E. Burton-wb-v.
                                  Chicago, October 9, 1928.

C-2421-B  Shake Your Shimmy - vWEB          Voc 1218, Spt S-2234, Creole 20
C-2422-A  Bull Fiddle Rag                   Voc 1237

## MIDNIGHT  SERENADERS

Harry Tropper-bb-sb dir. Andy Pedulla-Bill Mach-t/Frank Lhotak-tb/Eddie Obermiller-
 cl/Stanley Norris-as/Art Cope-cl-ts-vn/Benny Sans-p/bj/Tony Monico-d.
                                  Chicago, July, 1928.

20765-2  When Sweet Susie Goes Stepping By      Pm 20657, Bwy 1216

                                  Chicago, August, 1928.

20789-1  Tin Roof Blues                        Pm 20657, Bwy 1216

Also a pseudonym on Paramount 20571 and Broadway 1129 for two waltzes by Fred Rich
 and his Orchestra.

## THE  MIDNIGHT STOMPERS

Pseudonym on Edison Bell Winner 4874 for Devine's Wisconsin Roof Orchestra, q.v.

Pseudonym on Canadian Domino 21316 for the California Ramblers, q.v.

## THE MIDWAY DANCE ORCHESTRA

Elmer Schoebel-p-a dir. Murphy Steinberg and another-c/Jesse Barnes-tb/Art Kassel-Roy
Kramer-cl/Lou Black-bj/Steve Brown-bb-sb/Bobby de Lys-d.
Chicago, October 18, 1923.

| | | |
|---|---|---|
| 81311-1 | Lots O' Mama | Col 33-D |
| 81312-2 | The Black Sheep Blues | - |
| 81313-1 | Cotton Pickers' Ball | Col 51-D, Re G-8148 |

NOTE:- Regal G-8148 as CORONA DANCE ORCHESTRA.

Chicago, c. October 19, 1923.

| | | |
|---|---|---|
| 1532-1 | Black Sheep Blues | Pm 20272, Cx 40272, Hg 863, VJR 9, Adisco (un-numbered) |
| 1533-1-2 | Lots O' Mama | Pm 20273, Cx 40273, Hg 864, Pur 11273, Pt/Tri 11311 |
| 1534-1 | Sobbin' Blues | As above |

NOTE:- All issues from this session as MIDWAY GARDEN ORCHESTRA.

Phil Wing-cl replaces Kassel.          Chicago, December 5, 1923.

| | | |
|---|---|---|
| 81383-2 | Buddy's Habits (sic) | Col 51-D |

## EDDIE MILES AND HIS FLORENTINE CLUB ORCHESTRA

C/tb/cl-as/ts/p/bj/bb/d/Sol Bearman-Wallace Chambers-v.
Birmingham, Ala., c. July 12, 1927.

| | | |
|---|---|---|
| GEX-727-B | One O'Clock Baby - vWC | Gnt 6200, Ch 15326, Sil 5109 |
| GEX-728, -A-B | At Sundown - vWC | Rejected |

Birmingham, Ala., c. July 20, 1927.

| | | |
|---|---|---|
| GEX-746-B | At Sundown - vSB | Gnt 6200, 6106, Ch 15322 |
| GEX-747, -A-B | No Wonder I'm Happy - vSB | Rejected |

NOTE:- Gennett 6106 is an Australian issue.

Birmingham, Ala., August 1, 1927.

| | | |
|---|---|---|
| GEX-764, -A-B | Cornfed | Gnt rejected |

Birmingham, Ala., c. August 15, 1927.

| | | |
|---|---|---|
| GEX-829-A | Give Me A Night In June - vSB | Gnt 6247 |
| GEX-830-A | Is It Possible ? - vSB | -     Ch 15345, Sil 5108 |

NOTE:- All Champion issues as GREEN PARROT INN ORCHESTRA.

## JOSIE MILES

Vocal, acc. by Q. Roscoe Snowden-p.     Long Island City, c. August, 1922.

| | |
|---|---|
| Please Don't Tickle Me Babe | BS 14121, Pm 12156 |

Acc. by Fletcher Henderson-p.     Long Island City, c. August, 1922.

| | |
|---|---|
| When You're Crazy Over Daddy | BS 14121, Pm 12156 |

Acc. by Joe Smith-c/? George Brashear-tb/? Clarence Robinson-cl/Fletcher Henderson
p/? Ralph Escudero-bb.          Long Island City, c. September, 1922.

| | | |
|---|---|---|
| 424-2 | If You Want To Keep Your Daddy Home | BS 14130, Pm 12157 |
| 425-1 | You're Fooling With The Wrong Gal Now | -     - |

Acc. by t/tb/cl/p.          Long Island City, c. November, 1922.

| | | |
|---|---|---|
| 461-2 | When I Dream Of Old Tennessee Blues | BS 14133, Pm 12158 |
| 463-1 | I Don't Want You (If You Don't Want Me) | -     - |

Acc. by t/tb/cl/p.                          Long Island City, c. January, 1923.

```
476    Low Down 'Bama Blues            BS 14139, Pm 12160
484-2  Love Me In Your Old Time Way    -           -         Oly 1515
       Four O'Clock Blues              BS 14136, Pm 12159    -
       How I've Got Dem Twilight Blues  -           -
```
NOTE:- Olympic 1515 as PEARL HARRIS.

Acc. by Stanley Miller-p.                    New York, September 15, 1923.

```
8522-A  Baby's Got The Blues            Gnt 5261
8523-A  Kansas City Man Blues           -
```

                                             New York, October 26, 1923.

```
8572-A  He's Never Gonna Throw Me Down  Gnt 5292, St 9475
8573-A  Graveyard Dream Blues           -
```

Acc. by Fletcher Henderson-p.                New York, November 24, 1923.

```
8607-A  He Went Away And Left Me Blues  Gnt 5307
8608-A  I Want My Sweet Daddy Now       -
```

                                             New York, December 12, 1923.

```
8661-A  He's My Man, Your Man (Somebody Else's  Gnt 5339, Sil 4051
           Too)
8662-A  Awful Moanin' Blues                     -           -
```

Acc. by Joe Smith-c/Fletcher Henderson-p.
                                             New York, January 19, 1924.

```
8708-A  War Horse Mama                  Gnt 5359, Sil 4048
8709-A  You Don't Know My Mind Blues    -           -
```

Smith omitted.                               New York, February 8, 1924.

```
8760    31st Street Blues               Gnt 5391, Sil 4043
8761-A  Pipe Dream Blues                -           -
```

Acc. by the Choo Choo Jazzers : Louis Metcalf-c or ? Bob Fuller-cl/Cliff Jackson-p.
                                             New York, c. September, 1924.

```
31641   Lovin' Henry Blues - c          Ajax 17057
31644   Freight Train Blues - cl        -
```

Acc. by Bubber Miley-c/Arthur Ray-p.   New York, September 15, 1924.

```
9707    Sweet Man Joe                   Ed 51476 (never issued ?)
```

Acc. by the Kansas City Five : Bubber Miley or Johnny Dunn-c/Jake Frazier-tb/Bob
Fuller-cl/Louis Hooper or Arthur Ray-p/? Elmer Snowden-bj.
                                             New York, October 2, 1924.

```
9761    Temper'mental Papa              Ed 51477
9762    Sweet Man Joe                   Ed 51476 (never issued ?)
```

Acc. by the Choo Choo Jazzers : Louis Metcalf-c/Cliff Jackson-p/Elmer Snowden-bj.
                                             New York, c. October, 1924.

```
31679   Flora's Weary Blues             Ajax 17070

31690   Believe Me, Hot Mama            Ajax 17066
```

Acc. by the Choo Choo Jazzers : ? Bubber Miley-c/Jake Frazier-tb/Bob Fuller-cl/
Charlie Pryme or Louis Hooper-p/Elmer Snowden-bj.
                                             New York, c. October, 1924.

```
31703   Won't Someone Help Me Find My Lovin' Man Ajax 17076, PA 032124
31705   South Bound Blues                        Ajax 17070
        Sweet Man Joe                            Ajax 17076
```

Vocal duets with Billy Higgins, acc. by the Choo Choo Jazzers : Bubber Miley-c/Bob
    Fuller-cl*/? Louis Hooper-p.                New York, c. November, 1924.

31725    *I'm Done, Done, Done With You          Ajax 17080
31727    A To Z Blues                            -

    Instrumentation uncertain.               New York, c. November, 1924.

31733    Satisfied                              Ajax 17083
31735    Picnic Time                             -

Vocal, acc. by the Kansas City Five : Bubber Miley or Johnny Dunn-c/Jake Frazier-tb/
    Bob Fuller-cl/Louis Hooper or Arthur Ray-p/? Elmer Snowden-bj.
                                               New York, November 21, 1924.

9862    Mad Mama's Blues                        Ed 51477

Vocal duets with Billy Higgins (as JAZZ CASPER), acc. by Bubber Miley or Louis Met-
    calf-c/Louis Hooper-p/Elmer Snowden-bj. New York, c. November 22, 1924.

5741-1-2  Let's Agree To Disagree              Ban 1499, Dom 3469, Re 9796

Vocal, acc. by the Choo Choo Jazzers : Bob Fuller-cl/Louis Hooper-p, with Elmer
    Snowden-bj**.                             New York, c. December, 1924.

31743    Cross Word Papa (You Sure Do Puzzle Me) Ajax 17087
31745   **I'm A Cabaret Nightingale            Ajax 17090
31749    There'll Be Some Changes Made          Ajax 17087

    Acc. by unknown (white ?) bj.           New York, c. January, 1925.

31769    De Clouds Are Gwine To Roll Away       Ajax 17092
31771    It Ain't Gonna Rain No Mo'              -

    Acc. by Bob Fuller-cl-as/? Ernest Elliott-as-ts/Louis Hooper-p/Billy Higgins-v (as
    JAZZ CASPER)/Joe Davis-v effects, all as shown.
                                               New York, c. January 26, 1925.

5327-1-2  Bitter Feelin' Blues - asBF/ts       Ban 1498, Dom 3468,Or 353,Re 9797
5828-2   Thunderstorm Blues - clBF/vJD          -      -      -      -
5829-2   It's The Last Time I'll Be A Pastime   Ban 1499, Dom 3469, Re 9796
            For You - vBH/as/asBF
NOTE:- Oriole 353 as CAROLINE LEE.

    Acc. by Bubber Miley or Tom Morris-c/Louis Hooper-p, with ? Jake Frazier-tb or Bob
    Fuller-cl as shown.                       New York, c. February 18, 1925.

5861-2   Ghost Walkin' Blues - cl               Ban 1516, Dom 3485, Re/Fos 9810
5862-2   Can't Be Trusted Blues - tb            -      -      -
NOTE:- Fossey's is an Australian store label stuck on American Regal pressings.

    Acc. by the Choo Choo Jazzers : Rex Stewart-c/Jake Frazier-tb/Louis Hooper-p.
                                               New York, c. February, 1925.

31801    Give Me Just A Little Bit Of Love      Ajax 17134
31805    At The Cake Walk Steppers' Ball        Ajax 17127

    Acc. by Bob Fuller-? Ernest Elliott-as/Louis Hooper-p.
                                               New York, c. March 17, 1925.

5910-1   Low Down Daddy Blues                   Ban 1534, Dom 3504, Em 10874,
                                               Re 9831, Sil 2542
NOTE:- Emerson 10874 as JOSIE MILLS; Silvertone 2542 as MAZIE GREEN.
       Subsequent records by this artist are as JOSEPHINE MILES, sometimes with
       the prefix MISSIONARY; in all cases they are of gospel material, as might
       be expected, and of no jazz interest (see BLUES AND GOSPEL RECORDS).

Vocal, acc. by t/cl/as/vn/p/whistler.    New York, c. February 24, 1922.

70496-B  Muscle Shoals Blues                        OK 8031
70497-B  She Walked Right Up And Took My Man Away    -

                                    New York, c. March 11, 1922.

70534-B  Virginia Blues                             OK 8032
70535-B  State Street Blues                          -

Acc. by orchestra (probably the white OKeh house band directed by either Milo Rega
or Fred Hager, possibly Justin Ring).  New York, c. August 17, 1922.

70783-B  Wicked Blues                               OK 8037
70784-B  He May Be Your Man, But He Comes To See     -
         Me Sometimes

                                    New York, c. September 27, 1922.

70866-C  Lonesome Monday Morning Blues              OK 8039
70867-A  Please Don't Tickle Me Babe                 -

                                    New York, c. October 18, 1922.

70936-B  Hot Lips                                   OK 8040
70937-B  Take It, 'Cause It's All Yours              -

Acc. by Ricketts' Stars : T/tb/cl/as/Bob Ricketts-p/bb.
                                    New York, January, 1923.

71249-B  The Yellow Dog Blues                       OK 8052
71250-B  The Black Bottom Blues                     OK 8050
71251-A  He Used To Be Your Man But He's My Man     OK 8048
         Now

71254-B  Sweet Smellin' Mama (Poro Blues)            -
71255-B  The Trixie Blues                           OK 8049
NOTE:- Matrices 71252/3 are untraced.  The above five titles probably represent
the work of two sessions.

Acc. by her Creole Jazz Hounds : T/tb/cl/p/ob/d.
                                    New York, c. January, 1923.

42319-1-2  Four O'Clock Blues                       Em 10586
42320-2    Aggravatin' Papa                          -

42337-1-2  Tell Me Gypsy                            Em 10603
42338-1-2  You've Got To Come And See Mama           -
           Every Night (sic)

Acc. by Clarence Johnson-p.          New York, c. February, 1923.

42364-2  Your Time Now                              Em 10613
42365-2  Haitian Blues                               -

                                    New York, April 24, 1923.

         Tishomingo Blues                           Vic test (un-numbered)

                                    New York, April 26, 1923.

80986-2  Sweet Smellin' Mama (Poro Blues)           Col A-3897
80987-3  Haitian Blues (Wild Weepin' Moan)           -

                                    New York, May 23, 1923.

28025-3  You're Always Messin' 'Round With My       Vic 19083, HMV B-1703
         Man
NOTE:- Some copies of Victor 19083 show the accompanist as Clarence Williams; on
HMV B-1703 he is anonymous.

Acc. by Clarence Johnson-p.              New York, May 24, 1923.

81029-1  Family Trouble Blues                    Col A-3920
81030-2  Triflin' Man                            -

                                         New York, June 18, 1923.

10858    My Pillow And Me                        Br 2462*
10864    Black Man (Be On Yo' Way)               -
10868/70 Low Down Papa                           Rejected
10874/6  She Walked Right Up And Took My Man Away -
NOTE:- Many of the missing matrix numbers in the above sequence are by Edna Hicks,
q.v.  The remainder are unissued takes of the above two issued titles.

                                         New York, July 19, 1923.

28297-2  Keep Yourself Together Sweet Papa       Vic 19158
         (Mama's Got Her Eyes On You)
28298-4  Cotton Belt Blues                       Vic 19124

Acc. by Louis Metcalf-c/Louis Hooper-p. New York, March 18, 1927.

80644-B  Slow Up Papa                            OK 8456
80645-A  Grievin' Mama Blues                     -

Acc. by cl/p.                            New York, October 12, 1927.

7554-1  Mean Old Bed Bug Blues                   Ban 6117, Cq 7128, Dom 4055,
                                                 Je 5138, Or 1059, Re 8434
7555-1-2  You Can't Have It Unless I Give It     Ban 6117, Cq 7082, Dom 4085,
          To You                                 Je 5138, Or 1118, Re 8473
NOTE:- Jewel 5138 and Oriole 1059, 1118 as MANDY SMITH.

Acc. by Clarence Johnson-p.              New York, November 13, 1927.

7610-3  When You Get Tired Of Your New Sweetie   Ban 6162, Cq 7084, Dom 4099,
                                                 Je 5188, Or 1118, Re 8493
7611-   Police Blues                             Cq 7082, Dom 4085, Re 8473
7612-2  Don't Let Your Love Come Down            Ban 7025, Je 5207, Or 1147
NOTE:- Jewel 5188, 5207 and  Oriole 1118, 1147 as MANDY SMITH.

Acc. by Porter Grainger-p.               New York, January 4, 1928.

7708-2  Shootin' Star Blues                      Ban 7025, Dom 4112, Je 5207,
                                                 Or 1170, Re 8512
7709-2  Lonesome Ghost Blues                     Ban 7048, Dom 4112, Je 5230,
                                                 Or 1147, Re 8512
7710-2  If You Can't Control Your Man            Ban 7048, Cq 7084, Dom 4099,
                                                 Je 5230, Or 1170, Br 8493
NOTE:- Jewel 5207, 5230 and Oriole 1147 and 170 as MANDY SMITH.

Acc. by Bob Fuller-cl/Louis Hooper-p.   New York, February 29, 1928.

7820-2  Nobody Shows What My Baby Shows          Ban 7075, Je 5254, Or 1197
7821-1-2  Second-Hand Daddy                      - Cq 7185 - Dom 4126, Re 8530
7822- -3  A Good Man Is Hard To Find             -              - Or 1197 -
NOTE:- Jewel 5254 and Oriole 1197 as MANDY SMITH.

Bj added.                                New York, May 2, 1928.

7953-2  Shake It Down                            Ban 7128, Je 5309, Or 1249
7954-1  Banjo Papa (Stop Pickin' On Me)                   Dom 4152    - Re 8572
7955-2-3  Your Worries Ain't Like Mine           -          - Je 5309 -
NOTE:- Jewel 5309 and Oriole 1249 as MANDY SMITH.

Acc. by King Oliver-c/Albert Socarras-as-f/Clarence Williams-p.
                                         New York, June 12, 1928.

146430-1-2-3  You're Such A Cruel Papa To Me - fAS Col rejected
146431-1-2-3  My Dif'rent Kind O' Man - asAS          -

Acc. by King Oliver-c/Albert Socarras-as-f/Clarence Williams-p.
                                    New York, June 30, 1928.

146430-6  You're Such A Cruel Papa To Me - fAS     Col 14335-D
146431-4  My Dif'rent Kind O' Man - asAS           —

Acc. by Jelly-Roll Morton-p.        New York, December 11, 1929.

57761-2  I Hate A Man Like You              Vic V-38571, Bm 1023
57762-2  Don't Tell Me Nothin' 'Bout My Man    —          —

Acc. by Harry Brooks-p.             New York, January 27, 1930.

59122-2  My Man O' War                      Vic 23281, BB B-5064. B-6152,
                                            Sr S-3149
59123-2  Electrician Blues                  Vic 23298    —       - Sr S-3149
59124-1  Good Time Papa                     Vic 23306, V-38607
59125-1-2  You Ain't Had No Blues           Rejected

Acc. by Porter Grainger-p/Teddy Bunn-g/Pops Foster-sb.
                                    New York, February 27, 1930.

58676-1  The Man I Got Ain't The Man I Want   Vic 23281
58677-1 or -2  Yellow Dog Gal Blues          Camden CDN-147 (LP)
58578-2  Too Slow Blues                      Vic 23298
58579-1  Done Throwed The Key Away           Vic 23306
NOTE:- Victor 23298 was never issued.

Acc. by the Melrose Stompers : T/cl-as/cl-ts/p/g/sb/d; Lizzie Miles does not sing
on the side marked *.               Chicago, October 7, 1939.

WC-2773-A  *Mellow Rhythm                    Voc 05260
WC-2774-A  He's My Man                       —
WC-2775-A  That's All Right Daddy            Voc 06165, Cq 9357
WC-2776-A  Hold Me, Parson                   Voc 05325
WC-2777-A  Keep Knockin' No. 2 (But You Can't Come Voc 05125, Cq 9357
            In)
WC-2778-A  Stranger Blues                    Voc 05392
WC-2779-A  Twenty Grand Blues                —
WC-2780-A  He's Red Hot To Me                Voc 05325

## BUBBER MILEY AND HIS MILEAGE MAKERS

Bubber Miley-Ward Pinkett and another-t/Wilbur de Paris-tb/Hilton Jefferson and
  another-cl-as/Happy Caldwell-ts/Earl Frazier-p-cel/Bernard Addison and another-bj-
  g/Bill Benford-bb/Tommy Benford-d/Frank Marvin-v.
                                    New York, May 16, 1930.

62232-3  I Lost My Gal From Memphis - vFM    Vic V-38138
62233-3  Without You, Emaline - vFM          —

Buster Bailey-cl-as replaces (or may be identified as) the unknown; unknown sb
replaces Benford; George Bias-v.    New York, July 3, 1930.

63108-2  Black Maria - vGB                   Vic V-38146, 760-0006
63109-2  Chinnin' And Chattin' With May - vGB   —          —

As for May 16, 1930, without the unknown cl-as; Addison plays bj and g; Edith
Wilson-v replaces Marvin.           New York, September 11, 1930.

63645-1-2-3  Loving You The Way I Do - vEW   Vic rejected
63646-1-2-3  The Penalty Of Love - vEW       —

                                    New York, September 17, 1930.

63645-6  Loving You The Way I Do - vEW       Vic 23010
63646-5  The Penalty Of Love - vEW           —

## ALLEN MILLER AND HIS MODERN MEN OF RHYTHM

Pseudonym on Hit 7035 for Rex Irving and the Boys, q.v.

Pseudonym on Cameo 1168 and Romeo 396 for the Original Indiana Five, q.v.

## EMMETT MILLER

Vocal, acc. unknown.                    New York, October 25, 1924.

72936-   Anytime                        OK 40239

New York, November 7, 1924.

72960-   The Pickaninnies' Paradise     OK 40239

Ashville, N. C., September 1, 1925.

```
9324-   You're Just The Girl For Me         OK 40545
9325-   Big Bad Bill Is Sweet William Now   OK 40465
9326-   Lovesick Blues                      -
9327-   I Never Had The Blues               OK 40545
```

Acc. by his Georgia Crackers : Leo McConville-t/Tommy Dorsey-tb/Jimmy Dorsey-cl-as /Arthur Schutt-p/Eddie Lang-g/Stan King-d, "assisted by Dan Fitch" where noted.
New York, June 12, 1928.

```
400781-A  God's River Blues                   OK 41438, Par R-198
400782-C  I Ain't Got Nobody (And Nobody Cares OK 41062, Od 165494
            For Me)
400783-B  Lovesick Blues - DF                 -          -        Par R-198
400784-A  The Lion Tamers - DF                OK 41205
```
NOTE:- Parlophone R-198 as EMMETT MILLER assisted by THE UNIVERSITY FIVE.

Manny Klein-t may replace McConville on some, if not all the next four sessions; there appears to be a second as on these.
New York, August 9, 1928.

```
401060-A  Anytime                             OK 41095, Od 165415
401061-3  St. Louis Blues                        - Par R-2270 -
```

New York, September 14, 1928.

```
401116-C  Take Your Tomorrow                  OK 41135, Par R-314
401117-C  Dusky Stevedore                        -         -
```
NOTE:- Parlophone R-314 as EMMETT MILLER accompanied by MIFF MOLE'S MOLERS.

Charles Chiles-v added where shown.     New York, January 8, 1929.

```
401509-A  I Ain't Gonna Give Nobody None O' This  OK 41280, Par R-2163, Od 165812
            Jelly Roll
401510-B  (I Got A Woman Crazy For Me)        OK 41182
            She's Funny That Way
401511-C  You Lose - vCC                      OK 41205, Par R-1155
```
NOTE:- Parlophone R-1155 as SAM AND BILL; reverse by different artists, under the same pseudonym, but of no interest as jazz.

Joe Tarto-sb added.                     New York, January 19, 1929.

```
401546-B  Right Or Wrong                      OK 41280, Od 165812
401547-C  That's The Good Old Sunny South     OK 41438
401548-C  You're The Cream In My Coffee       OK 41182
```

As for June 12, 1928, plus Joe Tarto-sb; Phil Pavey-v where shown.
New York, September 5, 1929.

```
402932-A  Lovin' Sam (The Sheik Of Alabam')   OK 41305, Od ONY-41305,Par R-2270
402933-A  Big Bad Bill Is Sweet William Now      -         -
402934-B  The Ghost Of The St. Louis Blues - vPP  OK 41342, Par PNY-34013, R-1138,
                                                Od 238013, A-286056
```
NOTE:- Some copies of Odeon A-286056 are pressed from matrix 402534 (see Louis Armstrong !)

Acc. by his Georgia Crackers : Tommy Dorsey-t/Jack Teagarden-tb/Jimmy Dorsey-cl-as
/Arthur Schutt-p/Eddie Lang-g/Joe Tarto-sb/Gene Krupa-d.
                                   New York, September 12, 1929.

| 402948-C | Sweet Mama (Papa's Getting Mad) | OK 41342, Par PNY-34013,Od 238013 |
| 402949-C | The Pickaninnies' Paradise | OK 41377 |
| 402950-C | The Blues Singer (From Alabam') | -        Par R-1115, Od A-286054 |

Similar instrumentation, but entirely different personnel, with Gene Cobb-v.
                                   New York, September 1, 1936.

| 0277-1 | I Ain't Got Nobody - vGC | BB B-6550 |
| 0278-1 | The Gypsy - vGC | BB B-6577 |
| 0279-1 | Anytime - vGC | - |
| 0280-1 | Right Or Wrong | BB B-6550 |

## GLENN MILLER AND HIS ORCHESTRA

The records made by Glenn Miller under his own name prior to September, 1938, when
he began his long series of Bluebird and Victor recordings, are generally of some
interest as jazz. These are listed below; the whole Glenn Miller story on record
is given in minutely documented detail in MOONLIGHT SERENADE by John Flower
(Arlington House, 1972).

Smith Ballew-v dir. Charlie Spivak-Bunny Berigan-t/Jack Jenney-Glenn Miller-tb/
Johnny Mince-cl-as/Eddie Miller-ts/Harry Bluestone-Wladimir Selinsky-vn/Harry
Waller-vl/Bill Schumann-vc/Claude Thornhill-p/Larry Hall-g/Delmar Kaplan-sb/Ray
Bauduc-d; Jenney and strings omitted*.  New York, April 25, 1935.

| 17379-1 | A Blues Serenade - vSB | Col 3051-D, Bm 1022 |
| 17380-1 | Moonlight On The Ganges - vSB | -        - |
| 17381-1 | In A Little Spanish Town - aGM | Col 3058-D,35881,FB-1150,Bm 1045 |
| 17382-1 | *Solo Hop - aGM | -         -         -        - |

Glenn Miller-tb-a dir. Charlie Spivak-Manny Klein-t/Sterling Bose-t-v/Jesse Ralph-
Harry Rodgers-tb/George Siravo-Hal McIntyre-cl-as/Jerry Jerome-Carl Biesacker-cl-
ts/Howard Smith-p/Dick McDonough-g/Ted Kotsoftis-sb/George Simon-d/Doris Kerr-The
Tune Twisters (including Jack Lathrop)-v/Hal McIntyre-a.
                                   New York, March 22, 1937.

| 62058-A | Peg O' My Heart - aGM | Dec 1342, 25075, 10113, M-32538, |
|         |                       | Br 03807, A-82414 |
| 62059-A | Wistful And Blue - vDK | Dec 1284, Br A-82574 |
| 62060-A | How Am I To Know ? - vDK/aGM | Dec 1239, Br 02831 |
| 62061-A | Anytime, Anyday, Anywhere - vSB-TT | Dec 1284 |
| 62062-A | Moonlight Bay - vO/aGM | Dec 1239, 25075, M-32538, |
|         |                        | Br 02831, 03807, A-82414 |
| 62063-A | I'm Sitting On Top Of The World - aHM | Dec 1342, 10113, Br A-82574 |

Carl Biesacker-a.           New York, June 9, 1937.

| B-21234-3 | I Got Rhythm - aGM | Br 7915, Cq 9488, Voc/OK 5051, |
|           |                    | Col DB-3416, DYC-154, Lucky LX-5, |
|           |                    | Ph B-21542-H, Bm 1046 |
| B-21235-1 | Sleepy Time Gal - aGM | Br 7923, Voc/OK 5051, Col DB-3416 |
|           |                       | DYC-154, M-164, Voc S-127, |
|           |                       | Ph B-21543-H, Pol 6002 |
| B-21236-1 | Community Swing - aGM | Br 7923, Voc S-127 - |
| B-21240-1 | Time On My Hands (You In My Arms)-aCB | Br 7915, Lucky LX-5, Ph B-21542-H |
|           |                                       | Bm 1046 |

Glenn Miller-tb-a-speech dir. Pee Wee Erwin-Bob Price-Ardell Garrett-t/Jesse Ralph-
Bud Smith-tb/Irving Fazola-cl-as/Hal McIntyre-Tony Viola-as/Jerry Jerome-ts/Carl
Biesacker-ts-a/J. C. McGregor-p-speech/Carmen Mastren-g/Rowland Bundock-sb/Doc
Carney-d/Kathleen Lane-v.        New York, November 29, 1937.

| B-22079-1 | My Fine Feathered Friend - vKL/aCB | Br 8034, A-81468, RZ G-23387 |
| B-22080-1 | Humoresque | Br 8062, Cq 9488, Voc/OK 4449, |
|           |            | Pol 6001 |
| B-22081-1 | Doin' The Jive - vKL/spGM-JCM/aGM | Br 8062, Cq 9489, Voc/OK 5131, |
|           |                                   | Pol 6001 |
| B-22082-1 | Silhouetted In The Moonlight - vKL/aGM | Br 8034, A-81468 |

NOTE:- Regal Zonophone G-23387 as CASINO ROYAL ORCHESTRA.

Glenn Miller-tb-a dir. Pee Wee Erwin-Bob Price-Ardell Garrett-t/Jesse Ralph-Bud
   Smith-tb/Irving Fazola-cl-as/Hal McIntyre-Tony Viola-as/Jerry Jerome-ts/Carl
   Biesacker-ts-a/J. C. McGregor-p/Carmen Mastren-g/Rowland Bundock-sb/Doc Carney-d/
   Kathleen Lane-v.                        New York, December 13, 1937.

| | | |
|---|---|---|
| B-22135-1 | Every Day's A Holiday - vKL/aCB | Br 8041, A-81457, Bm 1047 |
| B-22136-1 | Sweet Stranger - vKL/aGM | - - - |

Glenn Miller-tb-a dir. Johnny Austin-Bob Price-Gasparre Rebito-t/Brad Jenney-Al
   Mastren-tb/Hal McIntyre-Wilbur Schwartz-cl-as/Stanley Aronson-as-bar/Tex Beneke-
   Sol Kane-ts/J. C. McGregor-p/Rowland Bundock-sb/Bob Spangler-d/Gail Reese-Ray
   Eberle-v.                             New York, May 23, 1938.

| | | |
|---|---|---|
| B-22972-1 | Don't Wake Up My Heart - vRE | Br 8152, RZ G-23612, Bm 1048 |
| B-22973-1 | Why'd Ya Make Me Fall In Love ? - vGR | -    RZ G-23502 |
| B-22974-1 | Sold American - vO/aGM | Br 8173, A-81677, Voc/OK 4449, Col DO-2783, Ph B-21543-H, Bm 1108 |
| B-22975-1 | Dipper Mouth Blues - vO/aGM | Br 8173, A-81677, Cq 9489, Voc/OK 5131, Col DO-2783, Bm 1108 |

   NOTE:- Regal Zonophone G-23512 as CASINO ROYAL ORCHESTRA.

## JACK MILLER

This light vocalist made a number of records for Harmony in the late 1920s, of which
   the following are reportedly of jazz interest for their accompaniments.

Vocal, acc. by the New England Yankees (a Ben Selvin orchestra probably including
   Manny Klein and/or Bob Effros-t/Tommy Dorsey-tb/Larry Abbott-Merle Johnston-cl-as/
   Hymie Wolfson or Joe Dubin-ts/Irving Brodsky-p/Tony Colucci-bj-g/Jack Hansen or
   Hank Stern-bb/Stan King-d.            New York, February 11, 1929.

147953-3  (When I'm Walkin' With My Sweetness)    Har 881-H
          Down Among The Sugar Cane

   Acc. by the New Englanders : Probably similar.
                                   New York, June 24, 1929.

148751-2  Singin' In The Rain                Har 953-H, SR 1039-P

   Acc. by the New Englanders : Includes Manny Klein-t/Adrian Rollini-bsx.
                                   New York, March 1, 1930.

150047-2  The Moon Is Low                    Har 1125-H, SR 2021-P

## JIM MILLER

Jim Miller was a popular American singing comedian during the late 1920s. He made a
   considerable number of records, mostly for Victor, on which he was usually teamed
   with Charlie Farrell. The following are of interest as jazz for their accompaniments.

Vocal duets with Charlie Farrell, acc. by Lennie Hayton-p/Carl Kress-g, with Red
   Nichols-Bob Ashford-t/Vic Berton-d*.   New York, January 11, 1928.

41537-3  The Grass Grows Greener ('Way Down Home)Vic 21209, Zon EE-100
41538-3  *Tin Pan Parade                        - HMV B-2717 -

                          New York, April 19, 1928.

43585-3  What Do You Say ?                    Vic 21390, HMV EA-380
43586-1-2-3  I'm Wingin' Home                 Rejected

   Acc. by Mike Mosiello-t/Andy Sannella-cl-as/Lou Raderman-vn/Milt Rettenberg or
   Frank Banta-p/? Carl Kress-g.         New York, January 29, 1929.

49695-1  Happy Humming Bird                   Vic 21887

Vocal duets with Charlie Farrell, acc. by Mike Mosiello-t/Andy Sannella-cl-as/Lou
    Raderman or Murray Kellner-vn/Frank Banta-p/Carl Kress-g/Al Armer-sb.
                                    New York, July 29, 1929.

55165-3  Lovable And Sweet                          Vic 22078, HMV B-3133, EA-618
55166-3  Where The Sweet Forget-Me-Nots Remember      -                    -

## JOHNNIE MILLER'S NEW ORLEANS FROLICKERS

Sharkey Bonano-c/Sidney Arodin-cl/Hal Jordy-as/Johnnie Miller-p/Steve Brou-bj/Chink
    Martin-bb/Leo Adde-d.                     New Orleans, April 25, 1928.

146192-1  Everybody's Got Somebody To Love Them    Rejected
146193-3  Panama                                    Col 1546-D, Gothic 510, HJCA HC-86
146194-2  Dipper Mouth Blues                          -            -          -

## KID PUNCH MILLER TRIO

Punch Miller-c/ —— Harris-p/Cliff Jones-d.
                                    Chicago, January 28, 1941.

        Shine                                   Pm CJS-102 (LP)
        Harris Blues - vCJ                        -
        Chinatown, My Chinatown                   -
        High Society                              -

## LILLIAN MILLER

Vocal, acc. by Hersal Thomas-p.       Chicago, March 4, 1926.

9570-A  Kitchen Blues                           OK 8381

    Acc. by George W. Thomas-p-v/Charlie Hill-g (and possibly a 2nd g*).
                                    Richmond, Ind., c. May 3, 1928.

13713-A  Harbor Blues - vGT                      Gnt 6518, Spt 9282
13714-A  You Just Can't Keep A Good Woman Down   Gnt 6486, Ch 15510
13716-B  Butcher Shop Blues                        -       Ch 15529, Spt 9282
13717    Hammond Blues                           Rejected
13718-A  *Dead Drunk Blues - vGT                 Gnt 6518, Ch 15550
    NOTE:- Matrix 13715 is by Charlie Hill (see BLUES AND GOSPEL RECORDS, 1902-1942).
    Champion 15510, 15529 and 15550 as HELEN HARRIS; Supertone 9282 as BESSIE THOMAS.

## LUELLA MILLER

Vocal, acc. by ? James Johnson-p/Lonnie Johnson-vn-g.
                                    New York, c. August 25, 1926.

E-3628   Dago Hill Blues - vn                    Voc 1044, Br A-166
E-3629   Pretty Man Blues - g                      -        -

                                    New York, January 23, 1927.

E-4438/9  Twelve O'Clock Blues - vn              Voc 1080
E-4440/1  Down In The Alley - g                    -
E-4442/3  Rattle Snake Groan - vn                Voc 1081
E-4444/5  Dreaming Of You Blues - g                -

    Lonnie Johnson also plays bj where shown; ? Dewey Jackson-c added*.
                                    St. Louis, April-May, 1927.

E-5081/2  Carrier Pigeon Blues - vn/g            Voc 1102
E-5083/4  Peeping At The Rising Sun Blues - bj     -
E-5086    *Triflin' Man Blues - g                Voc 1103
E-5089    *Jackson's Blues - g                     -
E-5091    *Through And Through Blues - bj        Voc 1104
E-5092    Smiling Rose Blues - vn/g                -
E-5095    North Wind Blues - bj/g                Voc 1105
E-5096    East St. Louis Blues - bj/g              -
    NOTE:- Vocalion 1105 as LUELLA MILLER AND HER DAGO HILL STRUTTERS.

Acc. by ? Elmore Booker-p.          Chicago, c. October 28, 1927.

E-6751    Muddy Stream Blues          Voc 1147
E-6754    Tornado Groan          -

         Chicago, late November, 1927.

E-6812/3   Tombstone Blues          Voc 1151
E-6814    Walnut Street Blues          -

Md/g added.          Chicago, July 30, 1928.

C-2165-   'Frisco Blues          Voc 1202
C-2166-   Brick House Blues          -

Acc. by ? Lil Hardaway's Orchestra (q.v.) or ? Lil Hardaway-p.
         Chicago, August 1, 1928.

C-2174-   Chicago Blues - 0          Voc 1234
C-2175-   Wee Wee Daddy Blues - p          -

## RAY MILLER

Ray Miller was a prominent bandleader during the 1920s, recording extensively for many labels, particularly OKeh, Vocalion, Columbia and Brunswick. The following are known or are reported to be of some interest as jazz, and certainly the personnels suggest there may be others like them, despite unpromising titles.

RAY MILLER'S BLACK AND WHITE MELODY BOYS : Ray Miller-d dir. Earl Oliver-t/Tom Brown tb/Jim Welton-as/Billy Fazioli-p/Gus Lazaro-bj.
         New York, May, 1920.

7429-B   Rose Of Spain          OK 4119

         New York, c. July 16, 1920.

6172    Can You Tell ?          Voc 14106
6173    Rose Of Spain          -

         New York, c. July-August, 1920.

     Rose Of Spain          P 22427, 1347
     Can You Tell ?          -      -

         New York, c. September, 1920.

7328-A   Rose Of Spain          Gnt 9075, Gmn 1087
NOTE:- Guardsman 1087 as VIRGINIA VARSITY BOYS.

         New York, January-February, 1921.

7751-B   Beale Street Blues          OK 4274, 4709

         New York, March, 1921.

     Sandman Blues          OK 4304

2nd t/Bernard Daly-cl-as/Phil Saxe-cl-ts/Mike Cirina-vn/Louis Epstein-bb-bsx added (the drummer may not be Ray Miller).    New York, January 31, 1922.

80168-1   Doo Dah Blues          Col A-3563

RAY MILLER AND HIS ORCHESTRA : Ray Miller dir. Joe Brooco-t/Andy Sindelar-tb/Bernard Daly-cl-as/Phil Saxe-cl-ts/Harry Archer-vn/Billy Fazioli-p/Ralph Golati-bj/Louis Epstein-bb/Ward Archer-d.      New York, June 1, 1923.

80933-9   Blue Hoosier Blues          Col A-3926, Re G-8096
NOTE:- Regal G-8096 as REGAL NOVELTY ORCHESTRA.

RAY MILLER AND HIS ORCHESTRA : Ray Miller dir. Earl Oliver-Ray Lodwig-t/Andy Sindelar
  tb/Bernard Daly-Andy Sannella-cl-as/Phil Saxe-cl-ts/Harry Archer-Don Yates-vn/Harry
  Perrella-Tom Satterfield-p/Ralph Golati-Frank di Prima-bj/Louis Cassagne-bb-sb/Ward
  Archer-d.                             New York, December 20, 1923.

12146/9  Lovey Came Back                        Br 2547

                                       New York, January 5, 1924.

12233/6  I'm Goin' South                        Br 2546

                                       New York, January 29, 1924.

12409/12 Mindin' My Bus'ness                     Br 2564*

                                       New York, February 19, 1924.

12559/61 Nine O'Clock Sal                        Br 2573*

                                       New York, March 8, 1924.

12660    You Can Take Me Away From Dixie       Br 2607
           (But You Can't Take Dixie Away From Me)

                                       New York, March 28, 1924.

12751    Come On, Red ! (You Red Hot Devil Man)   Br 2606*

Charles Rocco-Roy Johnston-t replace Oliver and Lodwig; Miff Mole-tb added; Frank
Trumbauer-Cm replaces Saxe; Harry Archer and Golati omitted.
                                       New York, April 23, 1924.

12964    Lots O' Mama                           Br 2613*

                                       New York, June 3, 1924.

13205    Mama's Gone, Goodbye                    Br 2632

                                       New York, July 10, 1924.

13494/7  I Can't Get The One I Want (Those I Get  Br 2643
           I Don't Want)

                                       New York, August 5, 1924.

13677/9  Red Hot Mama                           Br 2681*

Larry Abbott-cl-as replaces Daly; Billy Richards-ts added; Rube Bloom-p replaces
Perrella.                             New York, September 27, 1924.

13856/9  Doodle-Doo-Doo                         Br 2724*

                                       New York, October 13, 1924.

13926    Me And The Boy Friend                  Br 2753

                                       New York, December 16, 1924.

14497/9  Nobody Knows What A Red Head Mama Can Do Br 2778*

                                       New York, January 7, 1925.

14588/91 Tessie (Stop Teasing Me)               Br 2830

                                       New York, February 5, 1925.

14814/7  That's My Girl                         Br 2823

RAY MILLER AND HIS ORCHESTRA : Ray Miller dir. Charles Rocco-Roy Johnston-t/Miff Mole
   Andy Sindelar-tb/Larry Abbott-Andy Sannella-cl-as/Frank Trumbauer-Cm/Billy Richards
   ts/Don Yates-vn/Rube Bloom-Tom Satterfield-p/Frank di Prima-bj/Louis Cassagne-bb-sb
   /Ward Archer-d.                              New York, February 27, 1925.

15007/10 We're Back Together Again              Br 2847

                                                New York, March 16, 1925.

15131     Red Hot Henry Brown                   Br 2855*

                                                New York, April 11, 1925.

15513     Phoebe Snow                           Br 2898*

Volly de Faut-cl-as replaces Sannella; Carl Orech-ts replaces Richards; Trumbauer
   omitted.                                     New York, August 19, 1925.

E-16174/6 Ya ! Ya ! Alma                        Br 2935*

Ray Miller dir. Charlie Margulis-Bob Howard-t/Andy Sindelar-Mike Durso-tb/Volly de
   Faut-cl-as/Fred Crissey-as/Karl Spaeth-ts/Herman Kaplan-vn/Bill Krenz-Joe Breiten-
   bach-p/Happy Masefield-bb-sb/Tony Briglia-d.
                                                New York, November 24, 1925.

E-16950/2 Spanish Shawl                         Br 2989

                                                New York, March 9, 1926.

E-18319   Stomp Your Stuff                      Br 3132*
E-13325   I Want You To Want Me To Want You     Br 3133*

                                                New York, September 13, 1926.

E-20198   Mercy Percy                           Br 3328*

RAY MILLER AND HIS HOTEL GIBSON ORCHESTRA : Ray Miller-v dir. Bob Jones-Doug Wellmon
   t/Ted Skiles-tb/Roland Chastain-cl-as/Frank Wagner-ts-vn/Karl Milles-vn-v/Coonie
   Conrad-Andy Mansfield-p/Mort Clavner-bj-v/Cookie Trantham-bb-sb-v/Sam Bird-d.
                                                Chicago, October 2, 1927.

C-1150    I Ain't Got Nobody - vRM              Br 3677, 3716
C-1153    Weary Blues                              -      -
C-1156    Blue Baby - vRM-MC-CT                 Br 3676*
C-1160    Yep ! 'Long About June - vRM-MC-CT       -

                                                ? Chicago, c. February 1, 1928.

E-7101    Is She My Girl Friend ?               Br 3829, 3731
E-7105    I Wish I Could Shimmy Like My Sister Kate  -     -
E-7107    Sorry                                 Br 3828, 3749
E-7111    My Honey's Lovin' Arms                   -      -

RAY MILLER AND HIS ORCHESTRA : Ray Miller dir. Max Connett-Lloyd Wallen-t/Jules
   Fasthoff-tb/Jim Cannon-cl-as/Maurice Morse-as/Lyle Smith-ts/Paul Lyman-vn/Art
   Gronwall-p-a/Al Carsella-pac/Leon Kaplan-bj-g/Jules Cassard-bb-sb/Bill Paley-d/
   Harry Maxfield-v.                            Chicago, September 21, 1928.

C-2333-   Anything You Say - vHM                Br 4077, 3892

Muggsy Spanier-c added; Dick Teela-v.  Chicago, December 31, 1928.

C-2739-   Who Wouldn't Be Jealous Of You ? - vDT  Br 4131, 3920

                                                Chicago, January 3, 1929.

C-2743-   That's A Plenty                       Br 4224, 3947
C-2744-   Angry - vBN                              -      -

"Sunny Meadows" Program B (matrices XC-2751/6) recorded January 5, 1929; no titles
   known.

RAY MILLER AND HIS ORCHESTRA : Ray Miller dir. Muggsy Spanier-c/Max Connett-Lloyd
    Wallen-t/Jules Fasthoff-tb/Jim Cannon-cl-as/Maurice Morse-as/Lyle Smith-ts/Paul
    Lyman-vn/Art Gronwall-p-a/Leon Kaplan-bj-g/Jules Cassard-bb-sb/Bill Paley-d/Bob
    Nolan-Mary Lou Williams-v.              Chicago, January 12, 1929.

XC-2785-   Angry                              Sunny Meadows Program C
XC-2786-   Crazy Rhythm                           -
    NOTE:- XC-2787/90 also part of this program; no titles known.

                                      Chicago, January 18, 1929.
XC-2826-   You're The Cream In My Coffee/I Ain't   Sunny Meadows Program D
               Got Nobody - vMLW
    NOTE:- XC-2825 and 2827/30 also part of this program; no titles known.

                                      Chicago, January 24, 1929.
C-2858-    Mississippi, Here I Am - vBN           Br 4194

                                      Chicago, January 25, 1929.
XC-2862-   I'll Never Ask For More/He, She And Me  Sunny Meadows Program E
               - vMLW
XC-2866-   Tell Me Who                            -
    NOTE:- XC-2861 and 2863/5 also part of this program; no titles known.

                                      Chicago, January 28, 1929.
XC-2878-   What A Girl ! What A Night !          Sunny Meadows Program F
XC-2879-   Dream House/How About Me ? - vMLW       -
XC-2880-   Sweetheart Of All My Dreams             -
XC-2881-   In My Garden Of Memories                -
XC-2882-   Some Of These Days-vMLW/Me And The Man In The Moon     -
XC-2883-   Tiger Rag                               -

    Different personnel; Dusty Roads-v.    Chicago, December 21, 1929.

C-5040-    Harlem Madness - vDR                 Br 4692, 1096 (French)
C-5041-    Ain't You, Baby ? - vDR                -      -

RAY MILLER AND HIS BAND on Australian Sterling denotes the Varsity Eight, q. v.

                            SODARISA  MILLER

Vocal, acc. by Jimmy Blythe-p.        Chicago, c. August, 1924.
    9026 ?  Hot Springs Water Blues           Pm 12231
    9027-1-2  Who'll Drive My Blues Away ?       -     Sil 3519

    Jimmy O'Bryant-cl added*.         Chicago, c. November, 1924.
    9074-2-4 *Broadway Daddy Blues (Uptown Daddy*)  Pm 12261, Sil 3539, 3566*
    9075-1-2  Down By The River Blues (Riverside    Pm 12243, Sil 3568*
                Blues*)
    9078-1  Don't Dog Me 'Round (Doggin' Blues*)     -        -*
    NOTE:- Paramount 12261 as SODARISSA MILLER.  Matrices 9076/7 are untraced.

                                      Chicago, c. December, 1924.
    10016-2  Confession Blues (Confessin' Blues)   Pm 12261, Sil 3538*, 3566
    10017-2  Nobody Knows                          Pm 12293, Sil 3518, 3573

                                      Chicago, April, 1925.
    2092-1-2  Sunshine Special (Outside Man Blues)  Pm 12276, Sil 3538
    2093-2  Be Yourself                             -      Sil 3540
    Acc. by Clarence Johnson-p.       Chicago, May, 1925.
    2141-2  Fightin' Blues (Scrappin' Blues)      Pm 12293, Sil 3573*
    Acc. by Jimmy Blythe-p.           Chicago, c. August, 1925.

    2225-1  Midnight Special                      Pm 12306, Sil 3540
    2227-1  Reckless Don't Care Mama Blues          -      Sil 3539
    NOTE:- Matrix 2226 is untraced.  The above eight Silvertones are labelled thus:-
    3518, 3519, 3538, 3539, 3540 - VIE COLLINS; 3566, 3568, 3573 - AMY WARD.

    Acc. by Cicero Thomas-c/? George W. Thomas-p.
                                      Chicago, December 8, 1926.

37212-1  Lonesome Room Blues                     Vic 20404
37213-2  I Keeps My Kitchen Clean                  -

Lucky Millinder-v dir. William Scott-Archie Johnson-Nelson Bryant-t/George Stevenson
   Donald Cole-Eli Robinson-tb/Billy Bowen-George James-as/Buster Bailey-cl-ts/
   Stafford Simon-ts/Ernest Purce-bar/Bill Doggett-p/Trevor Bacon-Sister Rosetta
   Tharpe-g-v/Abe Bolar-sb/Panama Francis-d.
New York, June 27, 1941.

| | | |
|---|---|---|
| 69437-A | Trouble In Mind - vSRT | Dec 4041, 48053, Br 03295, |
| | | V-Disc 129 |
| 69438-A | Slide, Mr. Trombone - vTB | Dec 3956 |
| 69439-A | Ride, Red, Ride - vLM | Dec 4146 |
| 69440-A | Rock, Daniel - vSRT | Dec 3956 |
| 69441-A | That's All - vSRT | Rejected |

Floyd Brady-Edward Morant-tb replace Cole and Robinson; Ted Barnett-as replaces
Bowen; Bailey omitted.
New York, September 5, 1941.

| | | |
|---|---|---|
| 69706-A | Big Fat Mama - vTB | Dec 4041, 48053, Br 03295 |
| 69707-A | Shout, Sister, Shout - vSRT | Dec 18386, 48057 |
| 69708-A | Apollo Jump | Dec 18529, Br 03519 |
| 69709-A | Rock Me - vSRT | Dec 18353 |

Lucky Millinder-v dir. Freddy Webster-Archie Johnson-Nelson Bryant-t/Edward Morant-
   George Stevenson-Sandy Williams-tb/George James-Ted Barnett-as/Stafford Simon-ts/
   Ernest Purce-bar/Bill Doggett-p/Sterling Marlowe-g/George Duvivier-sb/Panama
   Francis-d/Trevor Bacon-Sister Rosetta Tharpe-v.
New York, November 6, 1941.

| | | |
|---|---|---|
| 69908-A | Hey Huss' - vTB-O | Dec 4146 |
| 69909-A | Let Me Off Uptown - vTB | Dec 4099 |
| 69910-A | That's All - vSRT | Dec 18496, 48057, V-Disc 129 |
| 69911-A | How About That Mess ? | Dec 4099 |

Joe Britton-tb replaces Williams; Billy Bowen-as replaces Barnett; Clyde Hart-p
replaces Doggett; Trevor Bacon-g-v replaces Marlowe.
New York, February 18, 1942.

| | | |
|---|---|---|
| 70344-A | Fightin' Doug MacArthur - vTB-O | Dec 4261 |
| 70345-A | I Want A Tall Skinny Papa - vSRT | Dec 18386 |
| 70346-A | We're Gonna Have To Slap The Dirty | Dec 4261 |
| | Little Jap - vTB-O | |
| 70347-A | Savoy - vTB-O | Dec 18353 |

Leroy Millinder dir. William Scott-Dizzy Gillespie-Nelson Bryant-t/George Stevenson-
   Joe Britton-tb/Billy Bowen-as/Tab Smith-as-a/Stafford Simon-Dave Young-ts/Ernest
   Purce-bar/Bill Doggett-p/Trevor Bacon-g-v/Nick Fenton-sb/Panama Francis-d.
New York, July 29, 1942.

| | | |
|---|---|---|
| 71243-A | Are You Ready ? - vTB&ch | Dec 18529, Br 03519 |
| 71244-A | Mason Flyer - aTS | **Br 03406** |
| 71245-A | **When The Lights Go On Again - vTB** | Dec 18496 |
| 71246-A | Little John Special | Br 03406, A-87505 |

See also Mills Blue Rhythm Band.

THE MILLION-AIRS

Arthur Lally-cl-as-bar dir. Jack Jackson-Andy Richardson-t/Ben Oakley-tb/Peter Rush-
   as-vn/Harry Berly-ts-vl-oc/Pat Dodd-p Bob Martin-g/Jim Bellamy or Tiny Stock-sb/
   Bill Harty-d.
London, January 17, 1931.

| | | |
|---|---|---|
| GB-2520-1 | Bessie Couldn't Help It - v-v3 | Dec F-2210 |

London, January 31, 1931.

| | | |
|---|---|---|
| GB-2608-3 | Choo Choo - v3 | Dec F-2241 |

Other records by this studio band may have short "hot" solos.

MILLS MUSIC MASTERS : Wardell Jones-Shelton Hemphill-Ed Anderson-t/Harry White-Henry
  Hicks-tb/Crawford Wethington-cl-as-bar/Ted McCord-Castor McCord-cl-ts/Edgar Hayes-
  p-a/Benny James-bj/Hayes Alvis-sb/Willie Lynch-d/Charlie Lawman-v.
                                        New York, January 21, 1931.

E-35948-    They Satisfy - vCL                    Mt M-12091, Pan P-12091
E-35949-    Please Don't Talk About Me When I'm Gone-vCL -          -          Emb E-129
  NOTE:- Embassy E-129 as THE BROADWAY ORCHESTRA.

MILLS BLUE RHYTHM BAND : As above, but Dick Robertson-v.
                                        New York, March 30, 1931.

E-35985-B   Straddle The Fence - vDR               Voc 1646, Br 02002, A-9734
E-35986-    Levee Low Down - vDR                       -
E-35987-A   Moanin' (House Hop*)                   Br 6156, 02004, A-9736, A-500192,
                                                   Pan 25047*, Pol 580014
    NOTE:- Vocalion 1646 and Brunswick 02002 as THE CHOCOLATE DANDIES; Panachord 25047
  as EARL JACKSON'S MUSICAL CHAMPIONS.

BLUE RHYTHM BOYS : As above, but Charlie Holmes-cl-as replaces Wethington; George
  Morton-v/Nat Leslie-a.                 New York, April 28, 1931.

E-36665-    Minnie The Moocher - vGM              Mt M-12164, Per 15753,
                                                  Polk P-9004, Br A-500166
E-36666-    Blue Rhythm - aNL                     Br 6143, 01177, 4777, A-9137,
                                                  602092, Dec M-30379
E-36667-    Blue Flame                            As above
E-36668-A   Red Devil (Diablo Rojo*)              Ban 32733, Mt M-12164, M-12662,
    NOTE:- Melotone M-12662 as DUKE WILSON AND HIS   MS-16072*, Or 2677, Per 15753,
  TEN BLACK BERRIES; MS-16072 as EARL JACKSON Y      Polk P-9004, Ro 2050, Br 01226,
  SUS CHAMPIONS; all other issues from matrix        A-500166
  E-36668-A as EARL JACKSON AND HIS MUSICAL CHAMPIONS.

BLUE RIBBON BOYS : As above; Wardell Jones-Chick Bullock-v.
                                        New York, May 1, 1931.

  10589-2-3  Star Dust - vCB                      Ban 32166, Cq 7865, Or 2265,
                                                  Per 15468, Re 10342, Ro 1631,
                                                  Royale 391133
  10590-2-3  Poor Minnie The Moocher - vCB        As above
  10600-1-2-3  Blue Rhythm - aNL                  Rejected
  10601-1-3  Black And Tan Fantasy               Ban 32199, Cq 7866, Or 2284,
    NOTE:- Oriole 2265 as BLUE RIBBONS BOYS, 2284  Per 15481, Ro 1651, Br A-500461,
  as HARLEM HOT SHOTS; Perfect 15468 and 15481 as  Stg 291153
  EARL JACKSON AND HIS MUSICAL CHAMPIONS.

    Alvis plays bb*.                     New York, May 12, 1931.

  10625-2-3-4  Sugar Blues - vGM                  Ban 32199, Cq 7866, Or 2284,
                                                  Per 15481, Ro 1651, Br A-500461
  10626-3  *Low Down On The Bayou - aNL           Ban 32240, Or 2318, Per 15505,
                                                  Ro 1690, Cr 91184, Dec F-2728,
                                                  Br A-500459
  10627-1  I Can't Get Along Without My Baby - vGM  Rejected
  10628-2  Futuristic Jungleism - vGM             Ban 32240, Or 2318, Per 15505,
    NOTE:- Oriole 2284 and Perfect 15481 as HARLEM  Ro 1690, Cr 91184, Dec F-2728,
  HOT SHOTS; Perfect 15505 and Crown 91184 as       Br A-500459
  BILLY BANKS AND HIS BLUE RHYTHM BAND; Decca F-2728 as EARL JACKSON AND HIS ORCH.

MILLS BLUE RHYTHM BAND : As above; Bob Stephens-dir.
                                        New York, June 18, 1931.

  69963-1  Moanin' - vGM                          Vic 22800, HMV EA-1078
  69964-1  Blue Rhythm - aNL                      Rejected
  69965-1  I Can't Get Along Without My Baby - vGM    -

    Benny Carter-a.                      New York, June 26, 1931.

  69978-1  Heebie Jeebies - vWJ/aBC               Vic 22763, HMV B-4881, B-6290
  69979-1  Tiger Rag                              Rejected
  69980-1  Minnie The Moocher - vGM-CB&ch         Vic 22763, HMV B-4371, B-6087,
                                                  EA-1098, R-14668
  69981-1  Radio Rhythm                           Rejected

Wardell Jones-Shelton Hemphill-Ed Anderson-t/Harry White-tb-a/Henry Hicks-tb /Charlie
    Holmes-cl-as/Ted McCord-Castor McCord-cl-ts/Edgar Hayes-p-a/Benny James-bj-g/Hayes
    Alvis-bb-sb/Willie Lynch-d/Nat Leslie-a. New York, July 30, 1931.

| | | |
|---|---|---|
| E-36992- | Savage Rhythm | Br 6229, 01227, A-500152 |
| E-36993- | I'm Sorry I Made You Blue | - |
| E-36994- | Every Time I Look At You | Br 6199, 01206, A-9185, A-500151 |
| E-36995-A | Snake Hips | -      -      -      - |

    NOTE:- Brunswick 01206 (as BLUE RHYTHM BAND) has no vocals, despite the labels.

BARON LEE AND THE BLUE RHYTHM BAND : Baron Lee dir. same personnel, except that
    Crawford Wethington-as-bar and Joe Garland-cl-ts-bar replace the McCord brothers,
    and O'Neil Spencer-d-v replaces Lynch.   New York, February 25, 1932.

| | | |
|---|---|---|
| 11360-1 | The Scat Song | Or 2464, Per 15605 |
| 11361- | Trickeration | Rejected |
| 11362- | Trickeration - vO'NS | - |
| 11363-1 | Heat Waves - aNL | Ban 32444, Mt M-12366, Or 2469, Per 15606, Ro 1842, Br 01325, A-500217, A-500460, Kr 21201 |
| 11364-1 | Doin' The Shake - aHW | Ban 32493, Per 15634, Voc C-0002 Imp 6026 |

    NOTE:- Kristall 21201 as BILLY BANKS AND HIS BLUE RHYTHM BOYS.


                                    New York, April 5, 1932.

11651-A  The Scat Song - vO'NS                Ban 32445, Mt M-12366, Or 2464,
    NOTE:- Decca F-3434 as THE BLUE RACKETEERS.    Per 15605, Dec F-3434

    Billy Banks-v.                    New York, April 28, 1932.

11751-1  Cabin In The Cotton - vBB            Ban 32445, Mt M-12381, Or 2464,
                                               Per 15605
11752-1  Minnie The Moocher's Wedding Day - vBB  Ban 32444, Or 2469, Per 15606,
                                               Ro 1842, Kr 21201
    NOTE:- Kristall 21201 as BILLY BANKS AND HIS BLUE RHYTHM BOYS.


                                    New York, May 2, 1932.

11751-   Cabin In The Cotton - vBB            Rejected ?
11767-1  The Growl                            Ban 32465, Mt M-12381, Per 15621
                                               Ro 1862, Br 01325, A-500193


                                    New York, May 7, 1932.

11752-   Minnie The Moocher's Wedding Day - vBB   Rejected ?
11788-1  Mighty Sweet - vBB                   Ban 32465, Per 15621, Ro 1862


                                    New York, May 12, 1932.

11823-1  Rhythm Spasm - aHW                   Mt M-12418, Per 15629, Ro 1874,
                                               Br 01401, A-500193
11824-1  Swanee Lullaby - vBB                 Rejected
11825-1  White Lightning - aHW                Mt M-12414, Per 15629, Ro 1874,
                                               Br 01463, A-500192
11826-1  Wild Waves - aHW                     Ban 32493, Mt M-12414, Per 15634
                                               Br 01463
11826-2  Wild Waves - aHW                     Jazz Panorama LP-3

George Washington-tb replaces White; Gene Mikell-cl-as replaces Holmes.
                                    New York, August 17, 1932.

12181-1  Sentimental Gentleman From Georgia - vBB  Ban 32531, Cq 8030, Mt M-12480,
                                               Or 2535, Per 15652, Br 01365
12182-1  You Gave Me Everything But Love - vBB    Ban 32531, Cq 8030, Mt M-12464,
                                               Or 2535, Per 15652
12203-1  Old Yazoo - vBB                      Mt M-12480, Per 15676, Br 01401,
                                               Kr 21200
12204-2  Reefer Man - vBB                     Mt M-12464, Per 15676, Kr 21200
    NOTE:- Kristall 21200 as BARON LEE AND HIS BLUE RHYTHM BOYS.

Baron Lee dir. Wardell Jones-Shelton Hemphill-Ed Anderson-t/George Washington-Henry
Hicks-tb/Crawford Wethington-as-bar/Gene Mikell-cl-as/Joe Garland-cl-ts-bar-a/Edgar
Hayes-p-a/Benny James-bj-g/Hayes Alvis-bb-sb/O'Neil Spencer-d/Benny Carter-a.
New York, September 23, 1932.

| | | |
|---|---|---|
| 12356- | Maniacs' Ball | Rejected |
| 12357-1 | Jazz Cocktail - aBC | Ban 32608, Mt M-12515, Per 15696, |
| | | Br 02077, A-9939,A-500461,Kr 31212 |
| 12358-1 | Smoke Rings | Ban 32608, 32806, Dom 128, |

NOTE:- Banner 32806, Domino 128, Melotone      Mt M-12515, M-12739, Per 15696,
M-12739, Perfect 15789 and Romeo 2095 as EARL    15789, Ro 3095, Voc 15892,Kr 31212
HARLAN AND HIS ORCHESTRA; Vocalion 15892 as DUKE WILLIAMS AND HIS ORCHESTRA.

THE BLUE RHYTHM BAND : As above, plus Eddie Mallory-t.
New York, March 1, 1933.

| | | |
|---|---|---|
| 265074-3 | Ridin' In Rhythm - aJG | Col CB-734, DO-1226 |
| 265075-2 | Weary Traveller - aEH | Par R-2366 |
| 265076-2 | Buddy's Wednesday Outing | Col CB-734, DO-1226 |

New York, August 31, 1933.

| | | |
|---|---|---|
| 13929-1 | Harlem After Midnight - aJG | Voc S-6, Imp 6048, 17038, 35000 |
| 13930-1 | Jazz Martini - aJG | Mt M-12793, Per 15822, Br 01742, |
| | | A-500376, Kr 31210 |
| 13931-1 | Feelin' Gay | As above |
| 13932- | Out Of A Dream | Rejected |

MILLS BLUE RHYTHM BAND : As for March 1, 1933.
New York, October 5, 1933.

| | | |
|---|---|---|
| 78093-1 | Break It Down | Vic 24482, HMV B-4983, BD-103 |
| 78094-1 | Kokey Joe | - - |
| 78095-1 | Love's Serenade | Vic 24442, HMV B-6487 |
| 78096-1 | Harlem After Midnight | - HMV B-8433 |

Lucky Millinder-dir replaces Lee; Adelaide Hall-v.
New York, December 4, 1933.

| | | |
|---|---|---|
| 78827-1-2 | Drop Me Off In Harlem - vAH | Vic rejected |
| 78828-1-2-3 | Reaching For The Cotton Moon - vAH | - |
| 78829-1-2 | Love Is The Thing | - |

J. C. Higginbotham-tb replaces Hicks.   Chicago, February 20, 1934.

| | | |
|---|---|---|
| 80278-1 | The Stuff Is Here (And It's Mellow) | BB B-5688 |
| 80279-1 | The Growl | - Vic JA-1294 |

Henry Allen-t replaces Anderson; Lawrence Lucie-g replaces James; Elmer James-sb
replaces Alvis; George Washington-Alex Hill-a/Chuck Richards-v.
New York, October 4, 1934.

| | | |
|---|---|---|
| CO-16035-A | Swingin' In E flat - aGW | Col 3038-D, Par R-2381 |
| CO-16036-A | Let's Have A Jubilee - aAH | Col 2963-D |
| CO-16037-A | Out Of A Dream - vCR | - |

New York, December 5, 1934.

| | | |
|---|---|---|
| CO-16271-1 | African Lullaby | Col 3038-D |
| CO-16272-1 | Solitude - vCR | Col 2994-D |
| CO-16273-1 | Dancing Dogs | Col 3044-D |

New York, December 11, 1934.

| | | |
|---|---|---|
| 16465-1 | Love's Serenade - vCR | Voc 2867, Br 01983, A-500545 |
| CO-16466-1 | Keep The Rhythm Going | Col 2994-D |
| 16467-1 | Like A Bolt From The Blue - vCR | Voc 2867, Br 01983, A-500545 |

NOTE:- Vocalion 2867, Brunswick 01983 and A-500545 as CHUCK RICHARDS.

Lucky Millinder-v dir. Wardell **Jones-Shelton** Hemphill-t/Henry Allen-t-v/George
Washington-tb-v/J. C. Higginbotham-tb/Gene Mikell-Crawford Wethington-cl-as/Joe
Garland-cl-ts-bar-a/Edgar Hayes-p-a/Lawrence Lucie-g/Elmer James-sb/O'Neil Spencer
d/Alex Hill-Will Hudson-a.                    New York, January 25, 1935.

| | | |
|---|---|---|
| CO-16700-1 | Back Beats - aAH | Col 3020-D, FB-1065, Voc 4769 |
| CO-16701-1 | Spitfire | - - - |
| CO-16702-1 | Brown Sugar Mine - vCR | Col 3044-D, Par R-2366 |

New York, July 2, 1935.

| | | |
|---|---|---|
| CO-17759-1 | Ride, Red, Ride - vLM/aWH | Col 3087-D, DO-1467, MC-3140, |
| | | MZ-255, OK 6119, Par R-2145 |
| CO-17760-1 | Harlem Heat - aWH | Col 3071-D, Par R-2392 |
| CO-17761-1 | Once To Every Heart - vCR | Br 7534 |

New York, July 9, 1935.

| | | |
|---|---|---|
| CO-17796-1 | Congo Caravan | Col 3087-D, DO-1467, MC-3140, |
| | | MZ-255, OK 6119, Par R-2145 |
| CO-17797-1 | There's Rhythm In Harlem | Col 3071-D |
| CO-17798-1 | Tallahassee | Br 7534 |

New York, August 1, 1935.

| | | |
|---|---|---|
| CO-17922-1 | Waiting In The Garden - vCR | Col 3083-D |
| CO-17923-1 | Dinah Lou - vCR | - |
| CO-17924-1 | Cotton - vCR | Col 3078-D, FB-1153 |
| CO-17925-1 | Truckin' - vHA | - - |

Tab Smith-as-a replaces Mikell.        New York, December 20, 1935.

| | | |
|---|---|---|
| CO-18419-2 | Blue Mood | JP LP-3 |
| CO-18420-2 | E flat Stride | JA 10 (LP) |
| CO-18421-1 | Broken Dreams Of You - vCR | Col 3111-D |
| CO-18422-1 | Yes ! Yes ! - vLM&ch | - MC-3069 |

New York, January 21, 1936.

| | | |
|---|---|---|
| CO-18547-2 | Shoe Shine Boy - vCR | JP LP-3 |
| CO-18548-2 | Midnight Ramble | - |

New York, May 20, 1936.

| | | |
|---|---|---|
| CO-19296-1 | Red Rhytam - vLM | Col 3135-D |
| CO-19297-1 | Everything Is Still Okay - vCR | Col 3134-D |
| CO-19298-1 | Jes' Natch'ully Lazy - vCR-GW | - |
| CO-19299-1 | St. Louis Wiggle Rhythm | Col 3135-D, DB/MC-5024 |

NOTE:- Columbia DB/MC-5024 as LUCKY MILLINDER WITH MILLS BLUE RHYTHM BAND.

New York, August 11, 1936.

| | | |
|---|---|---|
| CO-19685-1 | Merry-Go-Round | Col 3147-D |
| CO-19686-1 | Until The Real Thing Comes Along - vCR | - |
| CO-19687-1-2 | In A Sentimental Mood - vCR | Col 3148-D |
| CO-19688-1 | Carry Me Back To Green Pastures - vCR | - |

Billy Kyle-p-a replaces Hayes; Hayes Alvis-sb replaces James.
                                    New York, October 15, 1936.

| | | |
|---|---|---|
| CO-20073-1 | Balloonacy | Col 3156-D, DO-1680, Par R-2392 |
| CO-20074-1 | Barrel House - aTS | - - DB/MC-5026 |
| CO-20075-1 | The Moon Is Grinning At Me - vCR | Col 3157-D |
| CO-20076-2 | Showboat Shuffle | - Par R-2381 |

NOTE:- Columbia DB/MC-5026 as LUCKY MILLINDER WITH MILLS BLUE RHYTHM BAND.

New York, November 20, 1936.

| | | |
|---|---|---|
| CO-20294-1 | Big John's Special | Col 3162-D, Par R-2337 |
| CO-20295-1 | Mr. Ghost Goes To Town | Col 3158-D, DB/MC-5026, DO-1710 |
| CO-20296-1 | Callin' Your Bluff - aBK | Col 3162-D, DO-1676, Par R-2337 |
| CO-20297-1 | Algiers Stomp | Col 3158-D, DO-1710 |

Lucky Millinder dir. Charlie Shavers-Carl Warwick-Harry Edison-t/Sandy Watson-Wilbur
  de Paris-tb/Tab Smith-as/Eddie Williams-Ronald Haynes-Harold Arnold-ts/Billy Kyle-p
  /Danny Barker-g/John Williams-sb/Lester Nichols-d-vib/Chappie Willet-a.
                                      New York, February 11, 1937.

| | | |
|---|---|---|
| M-1-2 | Blue Rhythm Fantasy - aCW | Vri 503, Voc 3808 |
| M-2-1 | Prelude To A Stomp - aCW | Vri 546, Voc 3817 |
| M-3-2 | Rhythm Jam - aCW | - - |
| M-4-1 | Jungle Madness - aCW | Vri 503, Voc 3808 |

Alfred Cobbs-tb replaces Watson; Ben Williams-cl-ts replaces Haynes; Chuck Richards
  v.                                  New York, April 28, 1937.

| | | |
|---|---|---|
| M-429-1 | The Lucky Swing | Vri 604 |
| M-430-1-2 | Please Pity My Heart - vCR | Rejected |
| M-431-1 | Let's Get Together - vibLN | Vri 604 |
| M-432-1-2 | Since I've Heard It From You - vCR | Rejected |

Unknown girl v; Eli Robinson-a.        New York, July 1, 1937.

| | | |
|---|---|---|
| M-545-1 | Jammin' For The Jack-Pot - aER | Vri 634 |
| M-546-1 | The Image Of You - v | Vri 604 |
| M-547-1 | When Irish Eyes Are Smiling | Vri 624 |
| M-548-1 | Camp Meeting Jamboree | - |

NOTE:- Many of the above issues as LUCKY MILLINDER WITH MILLS BLUE RHYTHM BAND.

## THE MILLS BROTHERS

This most famous of Negro male quartets began recording for Gennett in 1929, but in
    1931 their first Brunswick records brought them world fame for their uncanny vocal
    impressions of brass and reed instruments, accompanied - as the earlier labels
    stressed - by only one guitar.  A complete account of their records within the date
    limits of this book will be found in THE COMPLETE ENTERTAINMENT DISCOGRAPHY,  as it
    is felt that theirs was a novelty vaudeville act rather than a jazz band, but the
    following is accompanied by something more ambitious than one guitar !

Vocal quartet (John, Herbert, Harry and Donald Mills), acc. by Duke Ellington and his
    Orchestra : Duke Ellington-p dir. Arthur Whetsel-Cootie Williams-Freddy Jenkins-t/
    Joe Nanton-Lawrence Brown-tb/Juan Tizol-vtb/Barney Bigard-cl-ts/Johnny Hodges-ss-as
    /Otto Hardwick-as-bsx/Harry Carney-cl-as-bar/Fred Guy-bj-g/Wellman Braud-sb/Sonny
    Greer-d.                          New York, December 22, 1932.

B-12781-A  Diga Diga Doo                        Br 6519, 01520, A-9396, A-82230,
                                                A-500258, 4835, Dec M-30355,
                                                Col DO-1129, Lucky 60012

## MILLS  CAVALCADE  ORCHESTRA

George Brunies-tb dir. Florence Dieman-Elvira Rohl-t/Norman Conley-Althea Conley-tb/
    Jules Harrison-Marie Carpenter-as/Evelyn Pennak-Herbie Haymer-ts/Henrietta Borchard
    Rudy Berson-Sid Sidney-vn/Gladys Mosier-p/Jessie Moore-sb/Frank Carlson-d.
                                      New York, June 11, 1935.

| | | |
|---|---|---|
| CO-17587-1 | Lovely Liza Lee | Col 3066-D, Par F-219 |
| CO-17588-1-2 | Out Of A Dream | Rejected |
| CO-17589-1 | Rhythm Lullaby | Col 3066-D, Par F-219 |
| CO-17590-1-2 | A Heart Like The Ocean | Rejected |

## FLOYD MILLS AND  HIS MARYLANDERS

Floyd Mills-tb dir. probably :- Hugh Parks-Bob Alexy-t/Art Laney-Les Brown-cl-as/
    Howard Shaffer-cl-ts/Lloyd Mills-p/Paul Bankert-bj/Jack Jones-bb/Charles Bowers-d.
                                      Richmond, Ind., June 26, 1929.

| | | |
|---|---|---|
| 15276-B | Hard Luck | Gnt 6909, Ch 16423, Spt 9447, |
| | | Spr 2829 |
| 15277-A | Chicago Rhythm | - - |
| 15277-B | Chicago Rhythm | Gnt 6909, Ch 15759    - |

NOTE:- Champion 15759 and 16423 as RED OWENS AND HIS GANG; Superior 2829 as GEORGE
DREW AND HIS ORCHESTRA; Supertone 9447 as THE HOTTENTOTS.

Irving Mills was an important impresario, bandleader, vocalist and composer during
the inter-war years, and arranged countless recording sessions for many labels in
New York during that time.  Of these, a considerable number are of great interest
as jazz, as follows.

THE HOTSY TOTSY GANG : Jimmy McPartland-c/Fud Livingston-cl-ts/Jack Pettis-Cm-ts/
Dudley Fosdick-mel/Vic Breidis-p-cel/? Perry Botkin-bj-u/Eddie Lang-g/Harry Goodman
bb/Ben Pollack-d/Elizabeth Welch-v.     New York, July 27, 1928.

E-27901-A  Doin' The New Low Down - vEW           Br 4014
E-27901-G  Doin' The New Low Down                 Br A-7850
E-27902-A  Diga Diga Doo - vEW&ch                 Br 4014
E-27902-G  Diga Diga Doo                          Br A-7850
E-27903-A-B  Don't Mess Around With Me            Br 4044, 3878, A-7901


Jimmy McPartland-Al Harris-t/Jack Teagarden-tb/Benny Goodman-cl-ss-as/Gil Rodin-cl-
as/Larry Binyon-ts/? Irving Mills-vn (definitely v as MILTON IRVING)/Vic Breidis-p/
Dick Morgan-bj/Harry Goodman-bb/Ben Pollack-d-v (as JIM BRACKEN).
                                        New York, October 16, 1928.

E-28356-A-B  Dardanella - vBP                     Voc 15763
E-28357-A-B  I Couldn't If I Wanted To - vIM      Br 4112
E-28358-A-B  Since You Went Away - vIM            Br 4122, A-8064
NOTE:- Vocalion 15763 as THE WHOOPEE MAKERS.

MILLS' MERRY MAKERS : ? Harry Reser-bj dir. Tommy Gott-Hymie Farberman-t/Sam Lewis-tb
/Larry Abbott-cl-as/Norman Yorke-ts/Bill Wirges-p/Joe Tarto-bb/Tom Stacks-d-v.
                                        New York, c. October 19, 1928.

E-28367-B  Here's That Party Now In Person - vTS   Duo D-4042
E-28369-A  Dusky Stevedore - vTS                   Duo D-4046

2t/tb/2cl-as/cl-ts/p/bj/bb/d/v.         New York, c. November 8, 1928.

3454-B    I Found My Sunshine In The Rain - v    Cam 9020, Lin 3049, Ro 824
3455-A    Stardust                              Cam 9012, Lin 3041, Ro 816
108499    Stardust                              PA 36903, Per 15084
3456-     Oh, Boy ! It's A Pleasure - v         Cam 9007, Lin 3036, Ro 811
NOTE:- All issues from matrices 3454 and 3456 as THE LUMBERJACKS; 3455 as THE
DETROITERS; Pathe Actuelle 36903 and Perfect 15084 as GOODY'S GOOD TIMERS (the
latter also credit the non-existent vocal to GOODY GOODWIN, a pseudonym for Irving
Mills !)

GOODY'S GOOD TIMERS : Manny Klein or Jimmy McPartland-t/Jack Teagarden-tb/? Benny
Goodman-Jimmy Dorsey-cl-as/ts/? Irving Mills-vn-certainly v as ERWIN MAGEE on Pathe
Actuelle, GOODY GOODWIN on Perfect), but no vn at all on 3502/108486-1-2)/? Frank
Signorelli-p/bj/bb/Ray Bauduc-d.        New York, c. November 16, 1928.

108485-1-2  'Cause I'm In Love - vIM             PA 36924, Per 15105
3503        'Cause I'm In Love - vIM             Cam 9004, Lin 3033, Ro 808
108486-1-2  Diga Diga Doo - vIM                  PA 36902, X-6279, Per 15083
3502        Diga Diga Doo - vIM                  Cam 9004, Lin 3033, Ro 808
NOTE:- Cameo 9004, Lincoln 3033 and Romeo 808 as DIXIE DAISIES.

MILLS' MUSICAL CLOWNS : Jimmy McPartland-Al Harris-t/Jack Teagarden-tb-speech/Benny
Goodman-cl-as/Gil Rodin-as/Larry Binyon-ts/Vic Breidis-p/Dick Morgan-bj/Harry
Goodman-bb/Ben Pollack-d.               New York, c. November 23, 1928.

3514-A    Whoopee Stomp                         Cam 9030, Lin 3059, Ro 834
108513-1  Whoopee Stomp                         PA 36915, Per 15096, Shrdlu 7051
3561      Baby                                  Cam 9034, Lin 3063, Ro 838
108514-2  Baby                                  PA 36930, Per 15111
3562      Bugle Call Rag - spJT                 Cam 9035, Lin 3064, Ro 839
108515-2  Bugle Call Rag - spJT                 PA 36945, Per 15126, Voc S-12,
                                                Imp 6002, 10-221, Shrdlu 7051
NOTE:- Late pressings of Perfect 15126, and all copies of Vocalion S-12, and both
Imperials, show -3 in the wax, but they are all dubbings of -2. All issues from
matrix 3514-A as THE LUMBERJACKS; from 3561 and 3562 as DIXIE DAISIES; Pathe
Actuelle 36945 and Perfect 15126 as THE WHOOPEE MAKERS; Vocalion S-12, Imperial
6002 and 10-221 and Shrdlu 7051 as BENNY GOODMAN'S WHOOPEE MAKERS WITH JACK TEA-
GARDEN.

Jimmy McPartland-t/Jack Teagarden-tb/Benny Goodman-cl-as/Gil Rodin-as/Larry Binyon-ts
/Nic Breidis-p/Dick McPartland-bj-g/Harry Goodman-bb/Ray Bauduc-d/v. (Label names
as shown after each title).              New York, c. December 23, 1928.

3579-B  Blue Little You - v (The Lumberjacks)    Cam 9041, Lin 3070, Ro 845
3580-B  Japanese Dream - v (The Dixie Daisies)   Cam 9043, Lin 3072, Ro 847
3581-C  Hungry For Love - v (The Caroliners)     Cam 9042, Lin 3071, Ro 846

Same instrumentation, but probably entirely different personnel, although Benny
Goodman remains on cl-as (and f on 3590-A-B-C,?).
                                         New York, c. December 26, 1928.

3588-B-C  Let Me Be Alone With You-v (L'jacks)   Cam 9045, Lin 3074, Ro 849
3589-C  June - v (The Caroliners)                Cam 9046, Lin 3075, Ro 850
3590-A-B-C  I'm Just Wondering Who (Dixie Daisies)Cam 9047, Lin 3076, Ro 851
        I'm Just Wondering Who (Ted Vincent's O.) Worth 7048

MILLS' MUSICAL CLOWNS : As for c. December 23, 1928, but Rodin omitted from 3591/
108567-1; Dick Morgan-bj-g-v replaces McPartland; Mildred Roselle-v; Breidis db
cel on several titles.                   New York, c. December 27, 1928.

108565-1-3  Futuristic Rhythm - vMR          PA 36944, Per 15125
108566-1  Out Where The Blues Begin - vMR       -          -
108567-1  Railroad Man - vDM                 PA 36930, Per 15111
3591      Railroad Man - vDM                 Cam 9048, Lin 3077, Ro 852
NOTE:- Cameo 9048, Lincoln 3077 and Romeo 852 as THE COTTON PICKERS.

THE WHOOPEE MAKERS : Bill Moore-Phil Hart-t/Paul Weigan-tb/Jack Pettis-cl-as-Cm/
? Jimmy Dorsey-cl-as/Matt Malneck-vn/Al Goering-p/Clay Bryson-bj/Merrill Kline-bb/
Dillon Ober-d.                           New York, January 10, 1929.

E-28948-  Rush Inn Blues                       Voc 15769
E-28949-  Freshman Hop                          -
E-29050-  I've Never Been Loved                Voc 15768

THE HOTSY TOTSY GANG : As for c. December 27, 1928, plus Al Harris-t (he may have
been present on all the first three sessions on this page, but is not audible on
matrix 3591/108567-1); Smith Ballew-v.   New York, January 14, 1929.

E-29064-A-B  Futuristic Rhythm - vSB&ch        Br 4200, A-8149
E-29065-A-B  Out Where The Blues Begin - vSB    -         -
NOTE:- Non-vocal takes appear to have been made of both these titles, but the ones
used for German issue are the same as the American, with vocals.

Same personnel as the Hotsy Totsy Gang above, but v unknown.
                                         New York, c. January 15, 1929.

3620-B  I Wonder Where Mary Is Tonight ? - v    Cam 9087, Lin 3114, Ro 889
3621-C  There's Something New 'Bout The Old     Cam 9085, Lin 3112, Ro 887
        Moon Tonight - v
3622-C  Mexicali Moon - v                       Cam 9072, Lin 3101, Ro 876
NOTE:- All issues from matrix 3620-B as THE CAROLINERS; from 3621-C as DIXIE
DAISIES, and from 3622-C as SOCIETY NIGHT CLUB ORCHESTRA.

Jimmy McPartland-t/Glenn Miller-tb/Benny Goodman-cl-as/Larry Binyon-ts/Nic Breidis-p
/Dick Morgan-bj-v (as ICKY MORGAN on Banner, Bernardo and Domino, TOM HOWARD on
Challenge and Oriole)/Harry Goodman-bb/Ray Bauduc-d.
                                         New York, January 18, 1929.

8476-1-2  Tiger Rag                        Rejected
8477-2  Shirt Tail Stomp                   Dom 4274, Re 8726, Apex 8950
8478-2-3  Icky Blues - vDM                 Ban 6323, Bernardo 3001, Chg 958,
NOTE:- Domino 4274, 4278, Regal 8723, 8726 and   Cq 7303, Dom 4278, Je 5547,
Apex 8950 as JIMMY BRACKEN'S TOE TICKLERS;       Or 1515, Re 8723
Banner 6323, Bernardo 3001 and Conqueror 7303 as KENTUCKY GRASSHOPPERS; Challenge
958, Jewel 5547 and Oriole 1515 as DIXIE JAZZ BAND.

Jimmy McPartland-c/? Al Harris-t/Jack Teagarden-tb-v/Benny Goodman-cl/Larry Binyon-ts/Vic Breidis-p/Dick Morgan-bj/Harry Goodman-bb/Ray Bauduc-d.
                              New York, February 11, 1929.

| | | |
|---|---|---|
| 8541-1-2 | It's Tight Like That - vJT | Ban 6295, Dom 4274, Je 5520, Or 1483, Re 8726, Apex 8950, Cr 81092, Mic 22455 |
| 8542-1-2 | Four Or Five Times | Ban 6295, Bernardo 3001, Cq 7303, Dom 4278, Je 5520, Or 1483, Re 8723, Apex 8936 |
| 8543-1-2 | Makin' Friends - vJT | Rejected |

NOTE:- Banner 6295 as KENTUCKY GRASSHOPPERS; Bernardo 3001, Conqueror 7303, Domino 4274, 4278, Apex 8936 and 8950 as JIMMY BRACKEN'S TOE TICKLERS; Jewel 5520 and Oriole 1483 as LOU CONNOR'S COLLEGIANS; Crown 81092 as SOUTHERN NIGHT HAWKS; Microphone 22455 as FRANK ARNOLD'S ORCHESTRA.

MILLS' MUSICAL CLOWNS : Bill Moore-Phil Hart-t/Paul Weigan-tb/Benny Goodman-cl/Jack Pettis-Cm/Al Goering-p/Clay Bryson-bj/Merrill Kline-bb/Dillon Ober-d.
                              New York, c. February 14, 1929.

| | | |
|---|---|---|
| 108645-2 | Freshman Hop | PA 37054, Per 15235 |
| 9103-2 | Freshman Hop | Ban 0508, Cam 0108, Ro 1125 |
| 108646-2 | Sweetest Melody | PA 36955, Per X-6277, Per 15136 |
| 108647-2 | Bag O' Blues | PA 37054, Per 15235 |

NOTE:- All issues from matrix 9103-2 as TEN BLACK DIAMONDS; from 108645-2 and 108647-2 as TEN FRESHMEN; Pathe Actuelle X-6277 as JACK PETTIS AND HIS ORCHESTRA.

THE LUMBERJACKS : 2t/tb/2cl-as/cl-ts/p/bj/bb/d/v.
                              New York, c. February 21, 1929.

| | | |
|---|---|---|
| 3682-A | I've Never Been Loved By Anyone Like You | Cam 9084, Lin 3111, Ro 886 |
| | - v | |

2t/Tommy Dorsey-tb/Jimmy Dorsey and another-cl-as/ts/p/bj/bb/d/Irving Kaufman-v.
                              New York, c. March 8, 1929.

| | | |
|---|---|---|
| 3698-A; 108684-1 | The Sorority Stomp - vIK | Cam 9098, Lin 3125, PA 37042, Per 15223, Ro 900, 976 |

NOTE:- Cameo 9098, Lincoln 3125 and Romeo 900 as VARSITY EIGHT; Pathe Actuelle 37042 and Perfect 15223 as THE WHOOPEE MAKERS; Romeo 976 as TEN BLACK BERRIES.

As for February 11, 1929 above, without Harris (?), plus Gil Rodin-as.
                              New York, March 15, 1929.

| | | |
|---|---|---|
| 8477-5 | Shirt Tail Stomp | Ban 6355, Dom 4274, Je 5577, Or 1544, Re 8726, Apex 8950 |
| 8541-4 | It's Tight Like That - vJT | Ban 6295, Dom 4274, Je 5520, Or 1483, Re 8726, Apex 8950, Cr 81092, Mic 22455 |
| 8542-3 | Four Or Five Times - vDM | Ban 6295, Bernardo 3001, Cq 7303, Dom 4278, Je 5520, Or 1483, Re 8723, Apex 8936 |

NOTE:- Banner 6295 and 6355 as KENTUCKY GRASS-HOPPERS; Bernardo 3001, Conqueror 7303, Domino 4274, 4278, Regal 8723, 8726, Apex 8936 and 8950 as JIMMY BRACKEN'S TOE-TICKLERS; Jewel 5520 and Oriole 1483 as LOU CONNOR'S COLLEGIANS; Jewel 5577 and Oriole 1544 as TED WHITE'S COLLEGIANS; Crown 81092 as SOUTHERN NIGHT HAWKS; Microphone 22455 as FRANK ARNOLD'S ORCHESTRA.

PAUL MILLS AND HIS MERRY MAKERS : As last above, possibly with Tommy Thunen-t added; Scrappy Lambert-v.          New York, c. April 3, 1929.

| | | |
|---|---|---|
| 3760-C | Little Rose Covered Shack - vSL | Cam 9126, Lin 3153, Ro 928 |

As last above, but Jimmy Dorsey-cl-as replaces Goodman; Harry Goodman db sb; Jack Kaufman-v.          New York, April 4, 1929.

| | | |
|---|---|---|
| 8476-3 | Tiger Rag | Ban 6355, 0839, Cam 9195, 0439, Chg 822, Dom 4322, Je 5577, 6089, Lin 3222, Or 1544, 2089, Re 8768, 10145, Ro 997, 1453 |
| 108864-3 | Tiger Rag | PA 37013, Per 15194 |

(cont. on page 1079)

Jimmy McPartland-c/Tommy Thunen ?-t/Jack Teagarden-tb-v/Jimmy Dorsey-cl-as/Gil Rodin-
as/Larry Binyon-ts/Vic Breidis-p/Dick Morgan-bj-g/Harry Goodman-bb-sb/Ray Bauduc-d.
                                  New York, April 4, 1929 (cont.)

8543-4  Makin' Friends - vJT              Ban 6360, Chg 999, Col 36010,
                                          M-673, Dom 4322, Je 5569, Or 1537,
                                          Re 8768
8657-1  Sweet Liza - vJK                  Ban 6358, Je 5575, Or 1540
NOTE:- Banner 6355, 6358 and 6360 as KENTUCKY GRASSHOPPERS;  Banner 0839, Cameo
0439, Jewel 6089, Oriole 2089, Regal 10145 and Romeo 1453 as TEN BLACK BERRIES;
Cameo 9195, Lincoln 3222 and Romeo 997 as THE COTTON PICKERS; Domino 4322 and Regal
8768 as JIMMY BRACKEN'S TOE TICKLERS; Challenge 822, Jewel 5577 and Oriole 1544 as
TED WHITE'S COLLEGIANS; Columbia 36010 and M-673 as JACK TEAGARDEN AND THE WHOOPEE
MAKERS; Pathe Actuelle 37013 and Perfect 15194 as THE WHOOPEE MAKERS; Challenge 999
Jewel 5569, 5575, Oriole 1537 and 1540 as DIXIE JAZZ BAND.  Some copies of Perfect
15126, labelled ST. LOUIS BLUES (see Sam Lanin (Broadway Broadcasters) play TIGER
RAG from the above session.

Benny Goodman-cl-as replaces Dorsey; Irving Kaufman-v.
                                  New York, c. April 5, 1929.

3766-C   Dirty Dog - vJT                  Cam 9174, Lin 3201, Ro 976
108775   Dirty Dog - vJT                  PA 37042, Per 15223, UHCA 40
3767-B- Would You Be Happy ? - vIK        Cam 9147, Lin 3174, Ro 949
3768-A  Eyes Of Blue, You're My Waterloo - vIK    Cam 9142, Lin 3169, Ro 944
NOTE:- All issues from matrix 3766-C as THE COTTON PICKERS; from 3767-B as THE
LUMBERJACKS; from 3768-A as DIXIE DAISIES; Pathe Actuelle 37042 and Perfect 15223
as THE WHOOPEE MAKERS; UHCA 40 as JACK TEAGARDEN AND THE WHOOPEE MAKERS.

MILLS' MUSICAL CLOWNS : 2t/tb/2cl-as/cl-ts/p/bj/bb/d/Billy Murray-Walter Scanlan-v.
                                  New York, c. April 6, 1929.

108727-4  I Used To Love Her In The Moonlight    PA 36974, Per 15155
3831      (But She's In The Limelight Now)-vBM-WS Cam 9182, Lin 3209, Ro 984
3832      In A Great Big Way - v            Cam 9170, Lin 3197, Ro 972
NOTE:- All issues from matrix 3831 as IRVING MILLS AND HIS ORCHESTRA; and from 3832
as MILLS' MERRY MAKERS.

Irving Kaufman-v.                         New York, c. April 8, 1929.

108734-2  Wipin' The Pan - vIK            PA 36974, Per 15155

Personnel probably similar to that of June 6, 1929 below.
                                  New York, May 17, 1929.

8761-(1-2-3 ?)  After You've Gone          ARC rejected
8762-(1-2-3 ?)  Twelfth Street Rag         -
8763-(1-2-3 ?)  It's So Good - vJT         -

IRVING MILLS AND HIS MODERNISTS : Irving Mills-v dir. Bill Moore and another-t/Tommy
Dorsey-tb/Tony Parenti and another-cl-as/Jack Pettis and another-ts/Nat Brušiloff-
? Nicky Gerlach-another (3rd) vn/Lennie Hayton or Jack Cornell-p/? Carl Kress-g/sb/
? Dillon Ober-d.                  New York, May 23, 1929.

53435-3  At The Prom - vIM                Vic V-38105, HMV B-4893, B-6204
53436-1-2  Just Goofy - vIM               Rejected

IRVING MILLS AND HIS HOTSY TOTSY GANG : Irving Mills-? vn-? v dir. Bill Moore-t/Tommy
Dorsey-tb/Jimmy Dorsey-cl-as/Jack Cornell-pac/Al Goering-p/Clay Bryson-bj/Merrill
Kline-bb/Dillon Ober-d.           New York, May 24, 1929.


E-29946-   What A Night ! - v             Br 4998, A-8831
E-29947-A  St. Louis Blues                Ban 32701, Mt M-12051, M-12632,
                                          Or 2654, Per 15738, Polk P-9031,
                                          Ro 2027, Voc 15860
E-29948-   I Wonder What My Gal Is Doin'  Rejected
  NOTE:- All issues from matrix E-29947-A as LOUISIANA RHYTHM MAKERS, except Melotone
M-12632, Polk P-9031 and Vocalion 15860, all as JACK WYNN'S DALLAS DANDIES.

2t/tb/2cl-as/cl-ts/p/bj/bb/d/Billy Murray-v.
                                          New York, c. May 31, 1929.

108829-2  Am I Blue ? - vBM              PA 37004, Per 15135
   3917   Am I Blue ? - vBM              Cam 9204, Lin 3231, Ro 1006,
                                         Ang 3153, Plaza 6033
   NOTE:- Pathe Actuelle 37004 and Perfect 15135 as MAJESTIC DANCE ORCHESTRA; Cameo
   9204, Lincoln 3231 and Romeo 1006 as THE DETROITERS; Australian Angelus 3153 as
   VINCENT RICHARDS AND HIS ORCHESTRA; Australian Plaza 6033 as PLAZA DANCE BAND.

MILLS' MERRY MAKERS : Irving Mills-?vn-v dir. t/Tommy Dorsey-tb/? Tony Parenti-cl-as
   /Larry Abbott-cl-as-comb/cl-ts/p/bj/bb/d.
                                          New York, c. June 5, 1929.

   3900-C  The Junior-Senior Prom. - vIM   Cam 9206, Lin 3233, Ro 1008
   3902-B  It Took A Lot Of Blue - vIM     Cam 9204, Lin 3231, Ro 1006
   NOTE:- All issues from matrix 3902-B as DIXIE DAISIES.  Matrix 3901 is untraced.

Jimmy McPartland-c/? Tommy Gott-t/Jack Teagarden-t-tb-v/Jimmy Dorsey-Gil Rodin-cl-as
   /Bud Freeman-Pee Wee Russell-cl-ts/Vic Breidis-p/Dick Morgan-bj-v/Harry Goodman-bb
   /Ray Bauduc-d/Jack Kaufman-v.          New York, June 6, 1929.

8761-5-6  After You've Gone - vJK         Ban 6441, Cq 7389, Dom 4381,
                                          Je 5648, Or 1624, Re 8826
8762-6    Twelfth Street Rag - vDM        Ban 6441, Cq 7382, Dom 4369,
                                          Je 5648, Or 1624, Re 8813
108931-6  Twelfth Street Rag - vDM        PA 37036, Per 15217
8763-5    It's So Good - t-vJT            Ban 6483, Cq 7382, Dom 4369,
                                          Je 5685, Or 1668, Re 8813
108930-5  It's So Good - t-vJT            PA 37036, Per 15217, UHCA 39
   NOTE:- All issues from matrices 8761-5-6 and 8762-6 as JIMMY BRACKEN'S TOE
   TICKLERS, except Jewel 5648 and Oriole 1624 (as DIXIE JAZZ BAND; this applies to
   Jewel 5685 and Oriole 1668 also); all other issues besides the latter from matrix
   8763-5 as GIL RODIN'S BOYS; Pathe Actuelle 37036 and Perfect 15217 as THE WHOOPEE
   MAKERS; UHCA 39 as JACK TEAGARDEN AND THE WHOOPEE MAKERS.

As for c. June 5, 1929.                  New York, c. June 14, 1929.

   3912   Hot Heels                      Cam 9207, Lin 3234, Ro 1009
   3913   Dance Your Blues Away          Cam 9208, Lin 3235, Ro 1010
   NOTE:- All issues from matrix 3912 as THE COTTON PICKERS, and from 3913 as VARSITY
   EIGHT.

IRVING MILLS AND HIS ORCHESTRA : Irving Mills dir. similar group to that of c. June
   5, 1929; Al Shayne (as ROY STEWART)-v. New York, July, 1929.

108910-2  Moanin' Low - vAS             PA 37027, Per 15208
8894-1-3  Moanin' Low - vAS             Ban 6472, Dom 4385, Je 5677,
                                        Or 1663, Re 8832, Cr 81143
   3980   Moanin' Low - vAS             Cam 9203, Lin 3230, Ro 1005
          Milwaukee Walk                 -        -       -
   NOTE:- Jewel 5677 and Oriole 1663 as DIXIE JAZZ BAND; Crown 81143 as SOUTHERN
   NIGHT HAWKS; Cameo 9203, Lincoln 3230 and Romeo 1005 as MILLS' MERRY MAKERS.

IRVING MILLS AND HIS HOTSY TOTSY GANG : Manny Klein-Phil Napoleon-t/Miff Mole-tb/
   Arnold Brilhart-cl-as/Larry Binyon-ts/p/g/Joe Tarto-bb/Chauncey Morehouse-d/Lilian
   Morton-v.                             New York, July 31, 1929.

E-30420-   Some Fun                     Br 4498, 1037 (French), A-8465
E-30421/2  Can't We Get Together ? - vLM  Br 4482
E-30423-   Sweet Savannah Sue - vLM       -

   Similar personnel, acc. Bill Robinson-tap dancing.
                                          New York, September 4, 1929.

E-30526-   Ain't Misbehavin'            Br 4535, 7706, 01112, A-8500, 5048
E-30527-   Doin' The New Low Down         -      -      -       -      -

IRVING MILLS AND HIS HOTSY TOTSY GANG : Manny Klein-Leo McConville-t/Miff Mole-tb/
    Jimmy Dorsey-Arnold Brilhart-cl-as/Pee Wee Russell-cl-ts/Hoagy Carmichael-p-cel-v/
    Joe Tarto-bb/Chauncey Morehouse-d-vib.  New York, c. September 20, 1929.

E-30958-    Harvey - vHC                      Br 4559
E-30959-    Harvey                            Rejected ?
E-30960-    March Of The Hoodlums             Br 4559
E-30961-    Star Dust                         Br 4587

    Tommy Dorsey-tb replaces Mole; Russell omitted; the vn and arranger is allegedly
    Matt Malneck, but he was at that time in California with Paul Whiteman's Orchestra,
    filming KING OF JAZZ.  The man here may be Irving Mills himself.
                                              New York, November 7, 1929.

E-31315-    Manhattan Rag                     Br 4641, A-8645
E-31316-    What Kind Of Man Is You ?         -        -
E-31317-    My Little Honey And Me            Br 4674, A-8594, 3009 (Argentine)

    Manny Klein-Bill Moore-t/Tommy Dorsey-tb/Jimmy Dorsey-cl-as/Babe Russin-ts/Jack
    Cornell-pac/Hoagy Carmichael-p-cel-v/Joe Tarto-bb-sb/Gene Krupa-d.
                                              New York, January 6, 1930.

E-31757-    High And Dry - vHC                Br 4920, 01023
E-31758-    High And Dry                      Br A-8883
E-31759-    Barbaric                          Br 4920, 01023, A-8883
E-31760-    South Breeze                      Rejected

MILLS' MERRY MAKERS : Ruby Weinstein-t/Charlie Teagarden-t-v/Jack Teagarden-tb-v/Gil
    Rodin-Matty Matlock-cl-as/Larry Binyon-ts/Eddie Bergman-Al Beller-vn/Vic Breidis-p
    /Dick Morgan-bj/Harry Goodman-bb-sb/Ray Bauduc-d. Both the Teagarden brothers are
    described as BUDDY EDWARDS on the labels.
                                              New York, January 31, 1930.

149950-1-2-3  What Did I Do To Be So Black And   Rejected
                Blue ? - vJT
149953-1   St. James' Infirmary - vCT          Har 1104-H
149954-2   When You're Smiling - vJT           Har 1099-H
149955-2   Farewell Blues                      VT 7121-V
149955-3   Farewell Blues                      IAJRC 2 (LP)
    NOTE:- Matrices 149951/2 are piano duets by James P. Johnson and Clarence Williams,
    recorded on the same day.

IRVING MILLS AND HIS HOTSY TOTSY GANG : Irving Mills-? vn dir. Manny Klein-Bill Moore
    t/Tommy Dorsey-tb/Benny Goodman-cl-as/Jack Pettis-ts/Al Goering-p/Dick McDonough-g/
    Harry Goodman-sb/Gene Krupa-d.       New York, March 21, 1930.

E-32401-    I Wonder What My Gal Is Doin' ?   Br 4998, A-8831
E-32402-    Crazy 'Bout My Gal                Br 4838, 03297, A-500147
E-32403-    Railroad Man                      -       -       -

    Irving Mills dir. Bix Beiderbecke-c/Ray Lodwig-t/Jack Teagarden-tb/Benny Goodman-cl
    /ts/Min Leibrook-bsx/Joe Venuti-Matt Malneck-vn/Frank Signorelli-p/Gene Krupa-d/
    Dick Robertson-v.                    New York, June 6, 1930.

E-32948-A  Loved One                          Voc 15860, Br X-15860, Mt M-12051,
                                                Polk P-9031
E-32948-B  Loved One                                              -
E-32949-A  Deep Harlem                        Br 4983, 02821, A-500091
E-32950-B  Strut, Miss Lizzie - vDR           -       -       -
    NOTE:- Vocalion 15860, Melotone M-12051 and Polk P-9031 as JACK WINN'S DALLAS
    DANDIES.  Brunswick X-15860 was pressed for export only.

## JOSIE MILLS

Nis-spelling of Josie Miles (q.v.) on Emerson 10874.

## LILLIAN MILLS

Pseudonym on Gennett for Lillian Miller, q.v.

## MAUDE MILLS

Vocal, acc. unknown.                                New York, c. April, 1923.

        Tired Of Waiting Blues                    Em 10624
        Triflin' Blues                            -

                            New York, c. February, 1927.

        Somebody's Been Loving My Baby            PA 7526, Per 126
        I've Got The Joogie Blues                 -        -
NOTE:- Both these issues as MAUDIE MILLS.

Acc. by Fats Waller-p.                             New York, early June, 1927.

7295-1  I've Got The Joogie Blues               Ban 6043,Dom 4022,Or 976,Re 8391
        Black Snake Blues                         -     Dom 4006   -    Re 8371
        Anything That Happens Just Pleases Me   Ban 6019,Dom 3987,Or 949,Re 8348
        My Old Daddy's Got A Brand New Way To Love  -        -        -     -
NOTE:- Oriole 949 and 976 as MAY CRANE.

Acc. by "novelty" group (sic), including p, with Jack Jones-v where shown.
                            New York, June 21, 1927.

7348-   Golden Brown Blues - vJJ                  ARC rejected
7349-   Hard Headed Mama - vJJ                    -
7350-   Black Snake Blues                         -

Acc. by p, with Jack Jones-v.                      New York, July 22, 1927.

7348-   Golden Brown Blues - vJJ                  Ban 6067, Dom 4006, Re 8371
7349-5  Hard Headed Mama - vJJ                    -     Dom 4022, Re 8391
NOTE:- Some issues as FRANKIE AND JONES.

## MILLS' MERRY MAKERS/MILLS' MUSICAL CLOWNS

See Irving Mills.

## MILLS' MUSIC MASTERS

See Mills Blue Rhythm Band.

## PAUL MILLS' MERRY-MAKERS

See Irving Mills.

## PECK MILLS AND HIS ORCHESTRA

Peck Mills-p dir. unknown instrumentation and personnel.
                            New York, September 28, 1925.

        Deep Elm (You Tell 'Em I'm Blue)          Vic test (un-numbered)
        Papa De Da Da                             -

## MILLS  SWINGPHONIC ORCHESTRA

Charlie Spivak-Manny Weinstock-t/Paul Ricci-cl/Larry Binyon-as/Babe Russin-ts/Frank-
lyn Marks-p/Carl Kress-g/Artie Bernstein-sb/Sam Weiss-d.
                            New York, April 6, 1937.

M-364-1 Lullaby To A Lamp Post                   Mas 119
M-365-1 At A Cuban Cabaret                        -
M-366-1 Merry Widow On A Spree                    Mas 126
M-367-1 Dear, Dear, What Can The Matter Be ?      -

## MILLS' TEN BLACK BERRIES

Pseudonym on Velvet Tone and associated labels for Duke Ellington and his Orchestra,
    q.v.

## VIOLET MILLS

Pseudonym on Domino for Julia Moody, q.v.

Matt Malneck-vn dir. white orchestra (t/tb/2as/ts/5vn/p/g/bb/d) and featuring Duke
   Ellington and his Cotton Club Orchestra : -Bubber Miley-Arthur Whetsel-t/Freddy
   Jenkins-t-fh/Joe Nanton-tb/Barney Bigard-cl-ts/Johnny Hodges-ss-as/Harry Carney-
   cl-as-bar/Duke Ellington-p-a/Fred Guy-bj/Wellman Braud-sb/Sonny Greer-d-v/girl v.
                                         New York, December 20, 1928.

| | | |
|---|---|---|
| 49007-1 | St. Louis Blues - v | JA 21 (LP) |
| 49007-2 | St. Louis Blues - v | Vic 35962 |
| 49008-1-2 | Gems from BLACKBIRDS OF 1928 - vSG | Rejected |
| 49008-3 | Gems from BLACKBIRDS OF 1928 | - |

Matt Malneck-vn dir. 3t/Tommy Dorsey-tb/2as/ts/4vn/p/g/2bb/d// female and 6 male (4
   of them negro) voices, with unknown girl soloist.
                                         New York, February 1, 1929.

| | | |
|---|---|---|
| 49008-5 | Gems from BLACKBIRDS OF 1928 | Vic 35962, HMV EB-44 |
| 49008-6 | Gems from BLACKBIRDS Of 1928 | JA 21 (LP) |

## MIMOSA DANCE ORCHESTRA

See Ronnie Munro.

## IRENE MIMS

Vocal, acc. by Clarence Williams-p.      New York, March 26, 1928.

400173-A-B  Hop Head Blues                      OK rejected

                                         New York, c. March 30, 1928.

| | | |
|---|---|---|
| E-7263 | Dirty Blues | Voc 1183 |
| E-7265 | Close Fit Blues | - |

## JACK MIRANDA AND HIS MEANDERERS

Norman Payne-t/Jack Miranda-cl/Buddy Featherstonhaugh-ts/Felix King or Pat Dodd-p as
   shown/Eddie Freeman-g/Al Burke-sb/Ronnie Gubertini-d.
                                         London, December 5, 1935.

| | | |
|---|---|---|
| CE-7345-1 | Bread And Jam - pFK | Par R-2149, A-6363 |
| CE-7346-3 | Ida, Sweet As Apple Cider - pPD | -      - |

## MISS FRANKIE

Pseudonym on Banner, Domino and Regal for Jane Howard, q.v.

## THE MISSISSIPPI COONS

Pseudonym on Homochord H-220 for the Novelty Five, q.v. (See Harry Yerkes).

## MISSISSIPPI JAZZ KINGS

Pseudonym on Australian Regal G-21480 for the Mound City Blue Blowers (GEORGIA ON MY
   MIND) and the Original Memphis Five (MY HONEY'S LOVIN' ARMS), both q.v.

## MISSISSIPPI MAULERS

Leo McConville-Bill Moore-t/Tommy Dorsey-tb/Dudley Fosdick-mel/Fud Livingston-cl-ts/
   Joe Venuti-vn/Frank Signorelli-p/Eddie Lang-g/Joe Tarto-bb Stan King-d/Roy Evans-v.
                                         New York, July 20, 1928.

| | | |
|---|---|---|
| 146754-1 | Doin' The New Low Down - vRE | Rejected |
| 146755-3 | My Angeline - vRE | Col 1545-D |
| 146756-2 | Don't Mess Around With Me - vRE | - |

## MISSISSIPPI TRIO

See the Novelty Blue Boys and the Wabash Trio.

Pseudonym on Connorized for Eliza Christmas Lee, q.v.

## THE MISSOURIANS

Lockwood Lewis-v dir. R. Q. Dickerson-Lammar Wright-t/De Priest Wheeler-tb/William
   Thornton Blue-George Scott-cl-as/Andrew Brown-cl-ts/Earres Prince-p/Morris White-
   bj/Jimmy Smith-bb/Leroy Maxey-d.          New York, June 3, 1929.

| | | |
|---|---|---|
| 53802-2 | Market Street Stomp | Vic V-38067, HMV JF-16, R-14270 |
| 53803-2 | Ozark Mountain Blues | Vic V-38071, HMV JF-19, R-14293 |
| 53804-2 | You'll Cry For Me, But I'll Be Gone - vLL | - |
| 53805-1 | Missouri Moan | Vic V-38067, HMV JF-16, JF-19, R-14270 |

New York, August 1, 1929.

| | | |
|---|---|---|
| 53971-2 | I've Got Someone | Vic V-38103, 1AC-0136, HMV R-14399 |
| 53972-2 | "400" Hop | Vic V-38084 |
| 53973-3 | Vine Street Drag | Vic V-38103, 1AC-0136, HMV AE-4365, R-14399 |
| 53974-2 | Scotty Blues | Vic V-38084, BB B-6084 |

Walter Thomas-cl-ts-bar replaces Brown.
                                     New York, February 17, 1930.

| | | |
|---|---|---|
| 59173-2 | Two Hundred Squabble | Vic V-38145, HMV JF-21, Alb 22958 |
| 59174-2 | Swingin' Dem Cats | -     - |
| 59175-1 | Stoppin' The Traffic | Vic V-38120, 760-0002 |
| 59176-1 | Prohibition Blues | X LVA-3020 (LP) |
| 59176-2 | Prohibition Blues | Vic V-38120, 760-0002 |

## MISSOURI DANCE ORCHESTRA

Pseudonym on Banner 1621 and Domino 3592 (STOMP OFF, LET'S GO) for Sam Lanin and his
   Orchestra, q.v.

## MISSOURI JAZZ BAND/MISSOURI JAZZ HOUNDS

Pseudonym for the following items listed in this book :-

Apex/Leonora 693  Meditation (Original Memphis Five)
Banner 1399  San (Six Black Diamonds - see Nathan Glantz)
       1409  Any Way The Wind Blows (Six Black Diamonds - see Sam Lanin)
       1457  Where's My Sweetie Hiding ? (Sam Lanin and his Orchestra) (also Domino
                428, Regal 9753 and Imperial 1396)
       1564  Save Your Sorrow For Tomorrow (Sam Lanin and his Orchestra) (also
                Domino 3539)
       1634  Angry (Seven Missing Links) (also Domino 3605 and Imperial 1541)
       1728  I've Got Those Charleston Blues (Six Black Diamonds - may be Sam Lanin
                or Adrian Schubert) (also Domino 3696)
       1846  Sadie Green, The Vamp Of New Orleans (Adrian Schubert and his Salon
                Orchestra) (also Domino 3814, 21231 and Apex 8561)
       1964  South Wind (The Rambling Ragadors - see Lou Gold) (also Domino 3935,
                Paramount 20512 and Maxsa 1622)
       7106  Know Nothing Blues (Six Jelly Beans)
       7135  Try To Smile (Ten Jacks of Diamonds) (also Challenge 638)
       7140  Straight Back Home (Six Jelly Beans)
       7157  Puttin' On The Dog (Six Jelly Beans)                              )900)
       7160  If I Can Ba-Ba-Baby You (Billy James and his Orchestra) (also Challenge
Conqueror 7110  Ready For The River (Devine's Wisconsin Roof Orchestra) (also Domino
                4184 and Regal 8615)
          7487  The Man From The South (Adrian Schubert and his Salon Orchestra)
Domino 3507  Ah-Ha ! (California Ramblers)
       3610  I'm Sitting On Top Of The World (Sam Lanin and his Orchestra)
       3632  My Charleston Dancing Man (Six Black Diamonds - see Nathan Glantz)
       4011  Tiger Rag (California Ramblers)
Oriole 518  Fallin' Down (California Ramblers)
       521  When A Blonde Makes Up Her Mind To Do You Good (Lou Gold and his Orch.)
       528  Then I'll Be Happy (Fletcher Henderson and his Orchestra)
       536  Sleepy-Time Gal (Fletcher Henderson and his Orchestra)
  (cont. on page 1085)

Pseudonym for the following items listed in this book (cont.)

Perfect 15273  Both sides by Adrian Schubert and his Salon Orchestra(also Regal 8942)
        15283  Sing, You Sinners (Adrian Schubert and his Salon Orch.)(also Perfect
Regal 9470  Nothin' But (Joseph Samuels' Jazz Band)                          )15283)
        9504  Long-Lost Mama (Six Black Diamonds - see Joseph Samuels)
        9514  Bugle Call Rag (Joseph Samuels and his Orchestra)
Supertone S-2172  Both sides by Ozzie Nelson and his Orchestra
          S-2173  Both sides by Noble Sissle and his Orchestra

## EDDIE MITCHELL AND HIS ORCHESTRA

C/tb/cl/as/ts/vn/pac/p/bj/bb/d.          Richmond, Ind., December 12, 1924.

| | | |
|---|---|---|
| 12098-A | Pleasure Mad | Gnt 5612 |
| 12099, -A-B | Helen Gone | Rejected |
| 12100 | Pickin' 'Em Up And Layin' 'Em Down | Gnt 5612 |

## MITCHELL'S  JAZZ KINGS

Louis Mitchell-d dir. Cricket Smith-t/Frank Withers-tb/James Shaw-as/ts/Joe Meyers-p/
Walter Kildaire-bj/Dan Parrish-bb-sb.    Paris, c. January, 1922.

| | | |
|---|---|---|
| 5890 | Ain't We Gol Fun ? (sic) | P 6542 |
| 5891 | Oh Me ! Oh My ! | -          PA 7017 |
| 5892 | Une femme qui passe | P 6544 |
| 5893 | J'en ai marre | -          PA 7017, 7023, 15108 |
| 5894 | Hep | P 6543 |
| 5895 | Sally, Won't You Please Come Back ? | - |

NOTE:- Pathe Actuelle 15108 as CASINO DANCE ORCHESTRA; 7017 is anonymous.

Paris, c. February, 1922.

| | | |
|---|---|---|
| 5926 | The Sheik Of Araby | P 6550 |
| 5927 | Now And Then | - |
| 5928 | Spooning | P 6549 |
| 5929 | When Happiness Begins | - |

Paris, c. May, 1922.

| | | |
|---|---|---|
| 6062 | Ça, c'est une chose | P 6557, 5715, PA 15114, Sal 100504 |
| 6064 | Machinalement | -          5714 |
| 6068 | Si j'avais su | P 6556, 5715, Sal 100505 |
| 6069 | Dans la vie, faut pas s'en faire | P 6555, 5716, PA 15115, Sal 100507 |
| 6070 | Non, non, jamais les hommes | -          5714, PA 15124 |
| 6071 | Je m' donne | P 6556, 5716, PA 15115, Sal 100505 |
| 6074 | Dans la vie, faut pas s'en faire | P 6555 |
| 6075 | Indecision - "Big Or Small Hat ?" | P 6554 |
| 6076 | Camomille | - |
| 6077 | Hooch - An Indian Idol (? Idyll) | P 6558 |
| 6080 | Ten Little Fingers And Ten Little Toes | - |

NOTE:- Pathe Actuelle 15114, 15115 and 15124 as CASINO DANCE ORCHESTRA.

Paris, c. July, 1922.

| | | |
|---|---|---|
| 6114 | Cutie | P 6564 |
| 6116 | Lovable Eyes | P 6565, Sal 100506 |
| 6117 | I'm Just Wild About Harry | - |
| 6118 | Oh Gee ! Oh Gosh ! | P 6564 |
| 6121 | The Montmartre Rag | P 6566 |
| 6122 | Wabash Blues | -          Sal 100506 |

Paris, c. September-October, 1922.

| | | |
|---|---|---|
| 6161 | Ty-Tee | P 6573 |
| 6162 | Jimmy (I Love But You) | P 6574 |
| 6165 | Everybody Step | - |
| 6166 | Say It With Music | P 6575, Sal 100502 |
| 6167 | Some Sunny Day | - |
| 6168 | All That I Need Is You | P 6572, Sal 100501 |
| 6169 | Stumbling | - |
| 6170 | Bimini Bay | P 6573, Sal 100501 |

Louis Mitchell-d dir. Cricket Smith-t/Frank Withers-tb/James Shaw-as-sw*/ts/Ralph
  "Shrimp" Jones-vn/Joe Meyers-p/Walter Kildaire-bj/Dan Parrish-bb-sb.
                                        Paris, c. September-October, 1922.

| | | |
|---|---|---|
| 6188 | Send Back My Honeyman | P 6578 |
| 6189 | Angel Child | P 6576 |
| 6190 | Dancing Fool | - |
| 6191 | Do It Again | P 6577 |
| 6194 | April Showers | - |
| | Turkish Ideals | P 6578 |

                                        Paris, c. April, 1923.

| | | |
|---|---|---|
| 6674 | Japanese Lanterns Blues | P 6598 |
| 6675 | Chicago | - |
| 6692 | Who Cares ? | P 6599 |
| 6709 | Sing 'Em Blues | - |
| | By The Sapphire Sea | P 6597 |
| | Ji-Ji-Boo | - |

                                        Paris, c. July, 1923.

| | | |
|---|---|---|
| 6923 | Si vous n'aimez pas ça | P 6607, Sal 100503 |
| 6924 | C'est Paris          ' | -            - |
| 6929 | Carolina In The Morning | P 6608 |
| 6931 | Toot-Toot-Tootsie (Goo'bye) | - |
| 6932 | Tomorrow (I'll Be In My Dixie Home) | P 6606 |
| 6933 | *Blue | - |

NOTE:- M. Robert Goffin, in his book LA NOUVELLE HISTOIRE DU JAZZ, refers to four
  titles made by this band (BRIGHT EYES, PEACHES, WHEN BUDDHA SMILES and YADA - this
  is presumably intended to be JA DA), but so far, no trace can be found of any other
  details.  In the same book there is a reference to recording of Jean Cocteau reading his poem LE COQ ET L'ARLEQUIN on two sides of an otherwise unidentified record,
  accompanied by "Orchestre Dan Parrish."  It should be pointed out that there is
  very little jazz to be heard on most of the above records, and they are listed more
  for the historical than for the musical interest.

## MOBILE JAZZERS

Pseudonym on Claxtonola for the Windy City Jazzers, q.v.

## MOBILE MELODY MAKERS

Pseudonym on Radiex 1225 (A LITTLE BIT OF JAZZ) for the Jazeliers, q.v.

## THE MODERNISTS

Pseudonym on Banner 33192, Conqueror 8526, Melotone M-13159, Oriole 2990, Perfect
  16002 and Romeo 2364 for Benny Goodman and his Orchestra, q.v.

## MIFF MOLE'S  (LITTLE) MOLERS

Red Nichols-t/Miff Mole-tb/Arthur Schutt-p/Dick McDonough-bj-g/Vic Berton-d.
                                        New York, January 26, 1927.

| | | |
|---|---|---|
| 80338-A | Alexander's Ragtime Band | OK 40758, Col 36280, C-6179, Par R-3320, A-2155, Od 165090, 193042 |
| 80339-A | Some Sweet Day | OK 40758, Par R-3320, R-2506, A-2155, Od 193042 |
| 80340-A | Hurricane | OK 40848, Par R-3362, Od 193053, A-189176 |

NOTE:- Some copies of Parlophone R-2506, labelled SOME SWEET DAY in accordance
  with the catalogue entry, play ALEXANDER'S RAGTIME BAND.  The absence of any matrix
  numbers, merely the OKeh catalogue number suffixed A or B, doubtless accounts for
  this.

Red Nichols-t/Miff Mole-tb/Jimmy Dorsey-cl-as/Arthur Schutt-p/Dick McDonough-bj-g/Joe
   Tarto-bb/Ray Bauduc-d.                    New York, March 7, 1927.

80501-B  Davenport Blues                     OK 40848, Par R-3362, Od 193053,
                                             A-189176
80502-A  The Darktown Strutters' Ball        OK 40784, Voc 3041, Par R-3326,
                                             A-2188, A-4903, Od 193008, 194865
80503-B  A Hot Time In The Old Town Tonight  As above except Par A-2188 and
                                             Od 194865
   NOTE:- The dubbing of Vocalion 3041 omits the spoken introduction, starting with
   the cymbal crash immediately following it.  The matrix numbers on both sides of
   this issue are false.

Red Nichols-t/Miff Mole-tb/Pee Wee Russell-cl/Fud Livingston-cl-ts/Adrian Rollini-bsx
   /Arthur Schutt-p/Dick McDonough-bj/Eddie Lang-g/Vic Berton-d.
                                             New York, August 30, 1927.

81296-B  Imagination                         OK 40890, Col 35687, Par R-3420,
                                             R-2286, A-7618, Od 165192,
                                             193092, A-189145
81297-B  Feelin' No Pain                     OK 40890, Col 35687, Voc 3074,
                                             Par R-3420, R-2269, A-7600,
                                             Od 165192, 193092, A-189145,
                                             028536
81298-B  Original Dixieland One-Step         OK 40932, Col 36010, Br 8243,
                                             Par R-3530, Od 165276, A-189106

                         New York, September 1, 1927.

81413-B  My Gal Sal                          OK 40932, Par R-3530, Od 165276,
                                             A-189106
81414-B  Honolulu Blues                      OK 40984, Br 8243, Par R-3441,
                                             Od 165328, 193171, A-189122
81415-C  The New Twister                     OK 40984, Voc 3074, Par R-3441,
                                             Od 165328, 193171, A-189122

Red Nichols-t/Miff Mole-tb/Frank Teschmacher-cl/Joe Sullivan-p/Eddie Condon-bj/Gene
   Krupa-d.                                  New York, July 6, 1928.

400849-C  One Step To Heaven (Windy City Stomp*)  HRS 15*, Col 35953
400850-A  Shim-Me-Sha-Wabble                 OK 41445, Cl 5474-C, Har 1427-H,
   NOTE:- Clarion 5474-C, Harmony 1427-H and Velvet  VT 2534-V, UHCA 23, Col 35953,
   Tone 2534-V as TENNESSEE MUSIC MEN.       Par R-2506, Od 238185, 279713

Red Nichols-Leo McConville-t/Miff Mole-tb/Dudley Fosdick-mel/Fud Livingston-cl-ts/
   Arthur Schutt-p/Carl Kress-g/Joe Tarto-bb/Stan King-d.
                                             New York, July 27, 1928.

400895-B  Crazy Rhythm                       OK 41098, Par R-230, Od 165412,
                                             193237, A-189188
400896-A  You Took Advantage Of Me           OK 41098, Par R-1157, Od 165412,
                                             193237, A-189188, A-286057
   NOTE:- Parlophone R-230 as SAM LANIN'S FAMOUS PLAYERS AND SINGERS, despite there
   being no vocalist !

Phil Napoleon-Manny Klein-t/Miff Mole-tb/Fud Livingston-cl-ts/Arthur Schutt-p/Joe
   Tarto-bb/Stan King-d.                     New York, November 26, 1928.

401394-B  You're The Cream In My Coffee      OK 41153, Od ONY-41153, 195546,
                                             182493, 193279, A-189209, 0126,
                                             Par E-4593, R-368, 22230
401395-B  Wild Oat Joe                       OK 41153, Od ONY-41153, 165546,
                                             182493, 193279, 028536,
                                             Par R-2328, 22230
   NOTE:- Odeon ONY-41153 as EDDIE GORDON'S BAND; Parlophone E-4593 as COMEDY DANCE
   ORCHESTRA.

Leo McConville-Manny Klein-t/Miff Mole-tb/Jimmy Dorsey-cl-as/Arthur Schutt-p/Eddie
   Lang-g/Stan King-d.                    New York, April 19, 1929.

| | | |
|---|---|---|
| 401815-C | I've Got A Feeling I'm Falling | OK 41232, Par PNY-41232, R-421, R-2355, A-2976, Od 279695, A-189260 |
| 401816-A | That's A Plenty | - |
| 401816-B | That's A Plenty | OK 41232, Par PNY-41232, R-421, R-2336, A-2964 |
| 401816-C | That's A Plenty | Od A-189260 |

   NOTE:- Parlophone PNY-41232 as JOE CURRAN AND HIS ORCHESTRA.  401816-A has been
reported as issued on Parlophone R-421, R-2336 and Odeon A-286090; it was included
on the LP Parlophone PMC-7126.

Phil Napoleon-t replaces Klein; Tommy Felline-g replaces Lang.
                                          New York, July 12, 1929.

| | | |
|---|---|---|
| 402529-C | Birmingham Bertha | OK 41273, Od ONY-41273, 165788, 193378, A-189275, A-189307, A-221170, Par R-432, A-3046 |
| 402530-C | Moanin' Low | OK 41273, Od ONY-41273, 193378, |
| | NOTE:- Odeon ONY-41273 as EDDIE GORDON'S BAND. | A-2324, A-189275, A-189307, A-221170, A-286028,Par R-849,22525 |

Phil Napoleon t/Miff Mole-tb/Jimmy Dorsey-cl-as/Babe Russin-ts/Arthur Schutt-p/Dick
   McDonough-g/Stan King-d.               New York, September 24, 1929.

| | | |
|---|---|---|
| 402986-B | You Made Me Love You | Par R-647, Od 193622, A-286015 |
| 402987-C | After You've Gone | OK 41445, UHCA 24, Par R-1063, A-3339, Od 193622,238185, A-286049 |

Adrian Rollini-bsx added; Lennie Hayton-p replaces Schutt; Carl Kress-g replaces
   McDonough; Scrappy Lambert-v.          New York, February 6, 1930.

| | | |
|---|---|---|
| 403740-A | Navy Blues - vSL | OK 41371, Od ONY-36045, 193500, 279684, A-286018, Par PNY-34040, R-701, A-2986 |
| 403741-B | Lucky Little Devil - vSL | OK 41371, Od ONY-36045, 279684, Par PNY-34041, R-702, A-2986 |
| 490036-A | Navy Blues | Od ONY-36043, Par PNY-34038 |
| 490036-B | Navy Blues | Par PMC-7126 (LP) |
| 490037-A | Lucky Little Devil | Od ONY-36043, Par PNY-34039 |
| 490037-B | Lucky Little Devil | Par PMC-7126 (LP) |

   NOTE:- Parlophone PNY-34038, 34039, 34040 and 34041 as GILBERT MARSH AND HIS
ORCHESTRA.

Harry James-Gordon Griffin-Tony Tortomas-t/Miff Mole-Glenn Miller-Vincent Grande-tb/
   Paul Ricci-cl/Toots Mondello-as/Frank Signorelli-p/Carl Kress-g/Sid Weiss-sb/Sam
   Weiss-d/Midge Williams-Chick Bullock-v. New York, February 17, 1937.

| | | |
|---|---|---|
| 20690-1 | On A Little Bamboo Bridge - vCB | Br 7842 |
| 20691-1 | How Could You ? - vMW | -        Voc S-87 |
| 20692-1 | I Can't Break The Habit Of You - vMW | Voc 3468    - |
| 20693-1 | Love And Learn - vCB | - |

## TOOTS MONDELLO

TOOTS MONDELLO AND HIS ORCHESTRA : Toots Mondello-as dir. 2t/2tb/? 2as/? 2ts/p/g/sb/
   Gene Krupa-d/Barry McKinley-v.         New York, November 19, 1937.

| | | |
|---|---|---|
| B-22051-2 | Let That Be A Lesson To You - vBM | Br 8031, A-81467, RZ G-23388 |
| B-22052-1 | Thanks For The Memory - vBM | -        - |
| B-22053-1 | You're In Love With Love - vBM | Br 8061 |
| B-22054-1 | Naughty, Naughty (I'm Surprised At You)-vBM- | |

   NOTE:- Regal Zonophone G-23388 as CASINO ROYAL ORCHESTRA.

      It is very probable that at least some of the personnel of the next session
(see page 1089) also took part in the above.

TOOTS MONDELLO AND HIS ORCHESTRA : Toots Mondello-as dir. Charlie Margulis-Russ Case
t/Will Bradley-Jack Jenney-tb/Arnold Brilhart-Eric White-as/Henry Wade-Hank Ross-
cl-ts/Claude Thornhill-p/Larry Hall-g/Delmar Kaplan-sb/Sam Weiss-d/Franklyn Marks-
a/Barry McKinley-v.                              New York, February 26, 1938.

| | | |
|---|---|---|
| B-22475- | Let Me Day Dream - vBM | Br 8094, A-81553 |
| B-22476- | I Love You Just Because - vBM | - - |
| B-22477-1-2 | At Sundown | Br 8105, Voc S-151 |
| B-22478-1 | I'll See You In My Dreams | - - |

Ziggy Elman-t/Toots Mondello-Noni Bernardi-as/Jerry Jerome-Arthur Rollini-ts/Claude
Thornhill-p/Carl Kress-g/Joe Swarzman-sb/Al Kendis-d.
                                                 New York, November, 1939.

| | | |
|---|---|---|
| US-1098-1 | St. Louis Gal | Var 8118 |
| US-1099-2 | Louisiana | - |
| US-1100-1 | Sweet Lorraine | Var 8110 |
| US-1101-1 | Beyond The Moon | - |

Alto saxophone solos, acc. by Claude Thornhill-p/Nick Fatool-d.
                                                 New York, December 18, 1939.

| | | |
|---|---|---|
| US-1177-1 | Here's Your Change | Royale 1817 |
| US-1178-1 | Sunset Lullaby | Royale 1823 |
| US-1179-1 | Shades Of Jade | - |
| US-1180-2 | Burnin' Sticks | Royale 1817 |

## GEORGE MONKHOUSE AND HIS CAMBRIDGE UNIVERSITY QUINQUAGINTA RAMBLERS

George Monkhouse-bj-g dir. John d'Arcy Hildyard-Dick Battle-t/Jack Donaldson-cl-as/
L. H. Kettridge-as/Maurice Allom-ts/Ben Edwards-p/Bud Williams-bb/F. Childs-v.
                                                 London, c. December 17, 1929.

| | | |
|---|---|---|
| E-2991-1 | So The Bluebirds And The Blackbirds Got Together | Par R-561 |
| E-2992-2 | Birmingham Bertha - v | Par R-560 |
| E-2993-2 | Stamp Your Feet - v | - |

                                                 London, March 12, 1930.

| | | |
|---|---|---|
| E-3139-2 | Singapore Sorrows | Par R-656 |
| E-3140-1 | Avalon | - |
| E-3141-2 | Crying All Day | Par R-657 |

## MONTEREY DANCE BAND

Pseudonym on Duophone for the following items listed in this book :-

B-5110  Jimtown Blues (The Tennessee Tooters)
B-5136  Roll 'Em, Girls (The Southerners)
B-5136  I Ain't Got Nobody (The Tennessee Tooters)

## J. NEAL MONTGOMERY AND HIS ORCHESTRA

J. Neal Montgomery-p dir. Henry Mason-Karl Burns-t/tb/George Derrigotte- —— Puckett
cl-as/ —— Brown-cl-ts/bj-g/Jesse Wilcox-bb/Ted Gillum-d/v.
                                                 Atlanta, March 14, 1929.

| | | |
|---|---|---|
| 402313-B | Atlanta Low Down | OK 8682 |
| 02314-B-C | Auburn Avenue Stomp - v | - |

## JULIA MOODY

Vocal, acc. by Joe Smith's Jazz Band : Joe Smith-c/? George Brashear-tb/? Clarence
Robinson-cl/Fletcher Henderson-p/? Ralph Escudero-bb.
                                                 Long Island City, c. July-August, 1922.

| | |
|---|---|
| The Cootie Crawl | BS 14122, Pm 12153 |
| Ja Da Blues | - - |

Acc. by c/tb/cl/vn/p/bb.          Long Island City, c. September, 1922.

429-1  Good Man Sam                    BS 14144, Pm 12155

Acc. by t/tb/cl/as/vn/p.          Long Island City, c. January, 1923.

499-2  Laughin' Cryin' Blues          BS 14140, Pm 12154
500-1  Starvin' For Love                 —··          —
       Scandal Blues                   BS 14150
NOTE:- Black Swan 14150 was announced in THE TALKING MACHINE WORLD as including
SCANDAL BLUES by Julia Moody, but all known copies are by Mary Straine, q.v. There
is always the possibility of a printer's error, but more probably the Julia Moody
title was announced to the trade, and changed at the last moment for some reason
which will never be known now.

Acc. by Bubber Miley-c or Jake Frazier-tb as noted/Bob Fuller-cl/Louis Hooper-p.
                          New York, c. October 29, 1924.

5693-3  Worried Blues - tb            Ban 1468, Dom 437, Re 9765
5694-2  Mad Mama's Blues - c          Ban 1451, Dom 438, Or 298, Re 9749
NOTE:- Domino 437 and 438 as VIOLET MILLS; Oriole 298 as EDITH VAUGHAN.

Acc. by Bubber Miley-c/Louis Hooper-p/Elmer Snowden-bj.
                          New York, c. November 3, 1924.

5700-1  Broken Busted Can't Be Trusted Blues   Ban 1468, Dom 437, Or 311, Re 9765
5701-1  Don't Forget, You'll Regret           Ban 1467, Dom 438, Re 9764
NOTE:- Domino 437 and 438 as VIOLET MILLS; Oriole 311 as EDITH VAUGHAN.

Acc. by Percy Glascoe-cl/Edgar Dowell-p.
                          New York, July 10, 1925.

140756-2  Strivin' Blues               Col 14087-D
140757-3  Last Night Blues                  —

Acc. by her Dixie Wobblers (Col 14121-D) or Edgar Dowell's Chicago Waddlers (Col
14103-D) : Robert Starr-c/Teddy Nixon-tb/Edgar Dowell-p/James Thomas-bj.
                          New York, September 18, 1925.

140957-2  That Chicago Wiggle          Col 14121-D
140958-1  Midnight Dan                 Col 14103-D
140959-1  Police Blues                     —
140960-2  He'll Do You Wrong           Col 14121-D

### HENRY MOON AND GEORGE THOMAS

Pseudonym on Herwin for Henry Johnson's Boys, q.v.

### ETTA MOONEY

Vocal, acc. by ? Johnny Dunn-c/tb/cl/p/bb.
                          Long Island City, c. June, 1922.

       Early Every Morn (I Want Some Lovin')  BS 14118, Pm 12151
       Lonesome Monday Morning Blues             —          —

                          New York, c. December, 1922.

469-1  Cootie For Your Tootie         BS 14134, Pm 12152
470-   Harmony Blues                      —          —
       Throw It In The Creek (Don't Want Your  BS 14129
          Lovin' No More)
NOTE:- Black Swan 14129, according to THE TALKING MACHINE WORLD, was scheduled to
include THROW IT IN THE CREEK and COOTIE FOR YOUR TOOTIE, but the former title
never appeared, and the latter was issued and coupled as shown.  Black Swan 14129
as issued is by Lena Wilson, q.v.

C/tb/? George James-cl-as/ts/? J. C. Johnson-p/bj.
                                        New York, August, 1929.

3606-A  Alabama Shuffle                  GG 1775, VD 71775, Px 4, VJR 19
3607-A  Memphis Stomp                    GG 1786, VD 71786
3608-A-B  Baby Knows How (Someone To Love Me*)  GG 1767, Mad 802*, Rx 952,VD 71767
NOTE:- Madison 802 is anonymous; Radiex 952, Van Dyke 71767, 71775 and 71786 as
FIVE HOT CHOCOLATES; Paradox 4 and VJR 19 as NEW ORLEANS STOMPERS.

## MOONLIGHT SERENADERS

The following title issued under this name is of considerable jazz interest; it may
  be by a Fred Hall group, q.v.

2c/tb/cl/cl-as/p/bj/d.                   New York, c. July, 1925.

3839-2  Hot Stuff Blues                  Bell 383

## ALICE MOORE

The following titles by this blues artist are included here for their accompaniments;
  all her later sides are accompanied in the country blues idiom (see BLUES AND
  GOSPEL RECORDS, 1902-1942).

Vocal, acc. by Ike Rodgers-tb/Henry Brown-p-v.
                                        Richmond, Ind., August 16, 1929.

15447   Black And Evil Blues            Pm 12819, 14031, 106, Bwy 5092
15448   Prison Blues (County Farm Blues) Pm 12868, Cen 3022, Poydras MC-66
15449-A My Man Blues                    -          -         -
15452   Broadway Street Woman Blues     Pm 12819, 14031, 106, Bwy 5092
NOTE:- Matrices 15450/1 are piano solos by Henry Brown, q.v.

                                        Grafton, Wis., c. February, 1930.

L-164-1 Have Mercy Blues               Pm 12973
L-165-3 Cold Iron Walls                 -
L-166-2 Loving Heart Blues             Pm 12947
L-167-2 Serving Time Blues              -
L-170-2 Lonesome Dream Blues           Pm 13107
L-171-2 Kid Man Blues - vHB/no tb       -
NOTE:- Matrices L-168/9 are untraced.

Ike Rodgers prob. db vn*.               Chicago, August 18, 1934.

C-9317-A Black Evil Blues               Dec 7028
C-9318   *Riverside Blues               -

                                        Chicago, August 24, 1934.

C-9333-A Lonesome Woman Blues           Dec 7056
C-9334-A Trouble Blues                  -

## ARAH "BABY" MOORE

Vocal, acc. by Charley Williamson-c/James Alston-p, with as*.
                                        Memphis, February 25, 1927.

37952-2 Everybody Has The Blues Sometime  Vic 20553
37953-3 *Drop Down Blues                 -

## BILL MOORE'S SYNCOPATORS

Bill Moore-t/tb/as/? Dudley Fosdick-mel/vn/p/bj/g/sb/d/Paul Hagan-v.
                                        New York, June 26, 1929.

53584-1-2-3 Birmingham Bertha - vPH     Vic rejected
53585-1-2-3 Am I Blue ? - vPH            -

GERRY  MOORE

Piano solos.                              London, September 26, 1935.

CE-7169-1  Truckin'                          Par F-297, Od OF-5035
CE-7170-1  Send Me                              -           -

                                          London, March 3, 1936.

CE-7501-1  Gerry Building                      Par R-2223, A-6525
CE-7502-1  May Write Blues                      -           -

                                          London, October 5, 1936.

CE-7858-1  Stealin' Apples                      Par F-602, Od OF-5301

GERRY MOORE AND HIS CHICAGO BRETHREN : Johnny Claes-t/George Chisholm-tb/Jimmy
    Williams-cl/Reg Dare-ts/Gerry Moore-p/Jim Reid-sb/Ben Edwards-d.
                                          London, February 22, 1937.

TB-2853-1  Oh ! Lady, Be Good                  Dec F-6347
TB-2854-1  Honeysuckle Rose                      -

Piano solos, acc. by George Senior-sb/Ben Edwards-d.
                                          London, January 3, 1938.

CE-8834-1  Wabash Blues                        Par F-1014, A-6903
CE-8835-1  Rosetta                              -        A-6968

NOTE:- Gerry Moore made a number of other piano solos for Parlophone under the super-
    vision of Victor Silvester.  As a result, they were admirable for dancing, but the
    jazz enthusiast is unlikely to find anything of interest either in the contents or
    the manner of their presentation.

                     GRANT MOORE AND HIS NEW ORLEANS BLACK DEVILS

Grant Moore-cl-as dir. Robert Russell-Sylvester Friel-t/Thomas Howard-tb/Earl Keith-
    cl-as/Willard Brown-ts/J. Norman Ebron-p/Harold Robbins-bj-g/Lawrence Williams-bb/
    Harold Flood-d.                       Chicago, May 6, 1931.

VO-161-   Mama Don't Allow No Music Playing In   Voc 1622
              Here - v
VO-162-A  Original Dixieland One-Step             -

                             MONETTE  MOORE

Vocal, acc. by Clarence Johnson-p. (An advertisement for this record in THE CHICAGO
    DEFENDER for March 17, 1923, states that Clarence Williams is the accompanist).
                                          New York, c. January, 1923.

A-987-    Sugar Blues                          Pm 12015, Hg 781
A-988-    Best Friend Blues                      - 12034  -

Acc. by Clarence Jones-p.                  New York, January, 1923.

5047-     I Just Want A Daddy                  Pm 12028
5048-     Come Home Papa Blues                   -

Acc. by Clarence Williams-p according to the labels, but aural evidence does not
suggest this (? Clarence Jones).          New York, January, 1923.

5052-     Gulf Coast Blues                     Pm 12030, Hg 2544
5053-     Down Hearted Blues                     -
NOTE:- Harmograph 2544 as ETHEL HAYES.

Acc. by Clarence Jones and the Paramount Trio : Tommy Ladnier-c/Jimmy O'Bryant-cl/
    Clarence Jones-p.                     Chicago, June, 1923.

1431-1-2  I'll Go To My Grave With The Blues   Pm 12046
          I'm Going To My Grave With The Blues   Hg 842

Acc. by Clarence Jones-p.                    Chicago, June, 1923.

1441-1-2  Goin' Down To The Levee              Pm 12046, Hg 842
NOTE:- Harmograph 842 as ETHEL HAYES.

Acc. by Naomi Carew-p.                       Chicago, c. August, 1923.

1489-3  Treated Wrong Blues                    Pm 12067
1490-4  Muddy Water Blues                       -

Acc. by Wyatt Houston-vn/James Cassino (? pseudonym for Cassino Simpson)-p.
                                             Chicago, c. April, 1924.

8074-2  Rocking Chair Blues                    Pm 12210, Sil 3542

Acc. by Jimmy Blythe-p.                       Chicago, c. April, 1924.

8077-1-2-3  Friendless Blues                   Pm 12210, Sil 3542
NOTE:- Silvertone 3542 as GRACE WHITE.  Matrices 8075/6 are by Anna Lee Chisholm,
q.v.

Acc. by John Montagu-p.                       New York, September 3, 1924.

13641    Texas Man Blues                       Voc 14903

Rex Stewart-c added.                          New York, September 15, 1924.

13692    I Wanna Jazz Some More - cRS          Voc 14903

Rudy Powell-cl added.                         New York, September 25, 1924.

13767    I'm A Heart-Broken Mama - cRS         Voc 14911, Sil 3018
13768    Death Letter Blues - cRS/clRP          -            -

The following Ajax sessions were all made and issued under the pseudonym SUSIE SMITH,
except Ajax 17124 which is credited correctly to MONETTE MOORE.

Acc. by the Choo Choo Jazzers : Bubber Miley-c/Jake Frazier-tb/Louis Hooper-p, with
effects by Joe Davis*.                        New York, c. October, 1924.

31692    Work House Blues                      Ajax 17064
31694/5 *House Rent Blues                       -

Acc. by Bubber Miley-c/Jake Frazier-tb/Bob Fuller-cl/own !k/Louis Hooper-p, as
shown after each title.                       New York, c. November, 1924.

31706    Bullet Wound Blues - c/tb/p           Ajax 17075
31718    Graveyard Bound Blues - cl/k/p          -
31721    Salt Water Blues - tb/cl/p            Ajax 17073
31722    Rainy Weather Blues - tb/cl/p           -
31729    The Bye Bye Blues - c/tb/p            Ajax 17079
31730    Weeping Willow Blues - c/tb/p           -

Acc. by the Choo Choo Jazzers : Bob Fuller-cl/Louis Hooper-p.
                                             New York, c. December, 1924.

31737    Meat Man Pete                         Ajax 17081, PA 032124

Jake Frazier-tb added.                        New York, c. December, 1924.

31747    Nobody Knows The Way I Feel Dis Mornin'  Ajax 17086, PA 032122, Per 12201
31751    Sore Bunion Blues                        Ajax 17089
31753    Put Me In The Alley Blues
NOTE:- Ajax 17086 does not refer to the Choo Choo Jazzers on the label.  Pathe
Actuelle 032122, 032124 and Perfect 12201 as NELLIE POTTER.

Vocal duets with Billy Higgins, acc. by the Choo Choo Jazzers : Rex Stewart-c/Louis
   Hooper-p.                              New York, c. January, 1925.

31773   How Can I Miss You ?               Ajax 17095
31775   You Ain't Nothin' To Me            -

Vocal, acc. by the Choo Choo Jazzers : Jake Frazier-tb/Bob Fuller-cl/Louis Hooper-p.
                                          New York, c. January, 1925.

31777   How Can I Miss You ?               Ajax 17093
31779   Scandal Blues                      -
31785   Crepe Hanger Blues                 Ajax 17134

   Acc. by the Texas Trio : Instrumentation and personnel unknown for the first two
   sides; Bob Fuller-h/Louis Hooper-p/Elmer Snowden-bj on the third.
                                          New York, c. February, 1925.

        All Alone                          Ajax 17124
        Memphis Blues                      -
31809   Texas Special Blues                Ajax 17127

   Acc. by the Choo Choo Jazzers : Bubber Miley-c/Bob Fuller-as/Elmer Snowden-ts/Louis
   Hooper-p as shown.                     New York, c. March, 1925.

31847   Undertaker's Blues - c/p           Ajax 17132
31848   Black Sheep Blues - as/ts/p        -

   Acc. by Rex Stewart-c/Louis Hooper-p.   New York, October 19, 1925.

141153-3  Take It Easy                     Col 14105-D
141154-3  Get It Fixed                     -

   Acc. by Rex Stewart-c/Ernest Elliott-cl/? Phil Worde-p.
                                          New York, November 9, 1926.

36916-2   If You Don't Like Potatoes       Vic 20356
36917-2   Somebody's Been Lovin' My Baby   -

   Bcl/f added.                           New York, January 26, 1927.

37572-2   Moaning Sinner Blues             Vic 20484
37573-1   Hard Hearted Papa                Vic LPV-534, RD-7840
37573-2   Hard Hearted Papa                Vic 20484

   Acc. by her Swing Shop Boys : T/? Sammy Price-p/g/sb/d.
                                          New York, February 19, 1936.

60520-B   Rhythm For Sale (Swing Shop Swing)   Dec 7161, Voc S-200
60521-A   Two Old Maids In A Folding Bed       -            -

## SAM MOORE

Octochorda solos, acc. by Frank Banta-p.   New York, July, 1921.

7534-A  Laughing Rag (Sam Moore-Harry Skinner)   Gnt 4747

   Unacc.                                 New York, c. July 29, 1921.

70054-E  Chain Gang Blues                  OK 4412
70055-C  Laughing Rag (Sam Moore-Harry Skinner)   -

   Acc. by Horace Davis-harp g (? zither).  New York, c. August 10, 1921.

70085-C  Wang-Wang Blues                   OK/Apex 4423
70086-E  Tuck Me To Sleep In My Old 'Tucky Home   -

                                          New York, August 24, 1921.

25543-1  Laughing Rag (Sam Moore-Harry Skinner)   Vic 18849, HMV B-1406
Other records by this artist are of no jazz interest.

Pseudonym on Harmony 1197-H for Sam Lanin and his Orchestra, q.v.

## CHAUNCEY MOREHOUSE

CHAUNCEY MOREHOUSE AND HIS SWING SIX : Charlie Spivak-t/George Brunies-tb/Jimmy
  Lytell-cl/Claude Thornhill-p/Artie Bernstein-sb/Chauncey Morehouse-d-vib.
                              New York, June 1, 1937.

| | | |
|---|---|---|
| M-512-2 | My Gal Sal | Vri 638 |
| M-513-2 | Blues In B flat | Vri 608 |
| M-514-1 | On The Alamo | – |

CHAUNCEY MOREHOUSE AND HIS ORCHESTRA : Chauncey Morehouse-d dir. Toots Camarata-Ralph
  Muzzillo-Chelsea Quealey-t/Andy Russo-Larry Altpeter-tb/Milt Yaner-Slats Long-as/
  Carl Biesacker-Tony Zimmers-ts/Fulton McGrath-p/Jack LeMaire-g/Felix Giobbe-sb/Stan
  King-d.                        New York, March 17, 1938.

| | | |
|---|---|---|
| M-783-1 | Plastered In Paris | Br 8122 |
| M-784-1 | Ku-Li-A | Br 8142 |
| M-785-1 | Mazi-Pani (No Work, No Pay) | Br 8122 |
| M-786-1 | Oriental Nocturne | Br 8142 |

## FRED MORGAN'S  BANJO RHYTHMICS

Fred Morgan-bj-v dir. t/tb/ts/p/sb/d.    London, October 26, 1937.

| | | |
|---|---|---|
| CE-8669-1 | Ha ! Ha ! – vFM | Par F-953 |
| CE-8670-1 | Shake Yo' Feet – vFM | – |

## HELEN MORGAN

The following titles by this famous musical comedy star have interesting accompaniments; her other records are of no known interest.

Vocal, acc. by Henry Levine-t/cl-as/cl-ts/p.
                              London, July, 1927.

| | | |
|---|---|---|
| R-181 | Lazy Weather | Br 113 |
| | Nothing But | Br 122 |

## RAY MORGAN'S  HOTEL LINCOLN BAND

Pseudonym on Australian Gracelon 4031 for Sam Lanin and his Orchestra, q.v.

## RUSS MORGAN AND  HIS ORCHESTRA

Russ Morgan-tb dir. Russ Case-Phil Capicotta-Harry Gluck-t/Will Bradley-Charlie
  Butterfield-tb/Toots Mondello-Sid Trucker-cl-as/Arthur Rollini-Paul Ricci-ts/Joe
  Venuti-Nick Pisani-Tony Alongi-vn/Claude Thornhill-p/Jimmy Lewis-g/Charlie Barber-
  sb/Chauncey Morehouse-d-vib.            New York, May 3, 1935.

| | | |
|---|---|---|
| CO-17459-1 | Phantom Fantasie | Col 3067-D |
| CO-17460-2 | Tidal Wave | Col 3050-D, FB-1098, DO-1365 |
| CO-17461-1 | Sliphorn Sam | Col 3067-D |
| CO-17462-1 | Midnight Oil | Col 3050-D, FB-1098 |

See also Chick Bullock; other records by this band are of little or no jazz interest.

## SAM MORGAN'S JAZZ BAND

Sam Morgan-c-v/Ike Morgan-c/Jim Robinson-tb/Earl Fouche-as/Andrew Morgan-cl-ts/Tink
  Baptiste-p/Johnny Davis-bj/Sidney Brown-sb/Nolan Williams-d.
                              New Orleans, April 14, 1927.

| | | |
|---|---|---|
| 143975-1 | Steppin' On The Gas | Col 14258-D,BR 5,JCl 521,VJR SP-5 |
| 143976-2 | Everybody's Talking About Sammy – vSM | Col 14213-D, TpI 535 |
| 143977-2 | Mobile Stomp | Col 14258-D,BR 5,JCl 521,VJR SP-6 |
| 143978-2 | Sing On | Col 14213-D, 14539-D, BR 3, |
| | | Jay 14, JCl 540 |

Sam Morgan-c-v/Ike Morgan-c/Jim Robinson-tb/Earl Fouche-as/Andrew Morgan-cl-ts-v/O.C.
  Blancher-p/Johnny Davis-bj/Sidney Brown-sb-v/Roy Evans-d.
                            New Orleans, October 22, 1927.

```
145000-2  Short Dress Gal - vSM&ch            Col 14351-D,BR 4,JC1 520,VJR SP-4
145001-2  Bogalousa Strut                        -       -       -     VJR SP-3
145002-1  Down By The Riverside - vSM-AM-SB&ch Col 14267-D, Tpl 535
145003-1  Over In The Glory Land                 - 14539-D, BR 3, Jay 14, JC1 540
```
    NOTE:- Jazz Classics 520 as JIM ROBINSON WITH SAM MORGAN'S JAZZ BAND; 540 as JIM
ROBINSON'S JAZZ BAND. Temple 535 is re-titled I AIN'T GONNA STUDY WAR NO MORE.

## ALICE MORLEY

The following record by this musical comedy star of the late 1920s is of interest as
  jazz in view of the remarkable accompaniment !

Vocal, acc. by Leslie A. Hutchinson ("Hutch")-p.
                            London, c. September, 1927.

```
          I Ain't That Kind Of A Baby          Br 126
          It Takes A Good Woman (To Keep A Good   -
            Man At Home)
```

## THOMAS MORRIS

THOMAS MORRIS PAST JAZZ MASTERS : Tom Morris-Bubber Miley-c/Charlie Irvis-tb/ts/p/bj/
  d.                               New York, February, 1923.

```
71306-A  E flat Blues No. 2 (Memphis, Tennessee)  OK 8055
71307-B  Original Charleston Strut                   -
```

  D omitted.                        New York, April, 1923.

```
71531-C  Lonesome Journey Blues                   OK 4867
71532-B  When The Jazz Band Starts To Play           -
```

                           New York, May, 1923.

```
71582-B  Just Blues, That's All                   OK 8075, LAR A-4157
71583-C  Bull Blues (E flat No. 1 Blues)             -          -
```

  ? Ernest Elliott-cl/bb added.       New York, August 7, 1923.

```
71739-B  Those Blues                              OK 4940
71740-B  Beaucoupe de Jazz (sic) (Lots Of Jazz)      -
```

THOMAS MORRIS AND HIS SEVEN HOT BABIES : Tom Morris-Rex Stewart-c/Geechie Fields-tb/
  as/Ernest Elliott-cl-ts-bar/Mike Jackson-p-v/? Lee Blair-bj/? Bill Benford-bb.
                              New York, July 13, 1926.

```
35762-3  Lazy Drag                                Vic 20483
35763-3  Jackass Blues                            Vic 20179
35764-2  Charleston Stampede                      Vic 20180
```

  Jabbo Smith-c replaces Stewart; Elliott plays as, Happy Caldwell-ts replacing the
  unknown; unknown bj.         New York, August 17, 1926.

```
36047-3  Georgia Grind - vMJ                      Vic 20180, WS 103
36048-2  Ham Gravy                                Vic 20179
```
    NOTE:- Wax Shop 103 as THOMAS MORRIS AND HIS NEW ORLEANS BLUE SEVEN.

THOMAS MORRIS AND HIS ORCHESTRA : Tom Morris-c-speech/Charlie Irvis-tb-speech/Bob
  Fuller-cl/Mike Jackson-p.       New York, August 27, 1926.

```
36071-2  Who's Dis Heah Stranger ? - spTM-CI      Vic 20316
```

THOMAS MORRIS AND HIS SEVEN HOT BABIES : Tom Morris-c/Joe Nanton-tb/Ernest Elliott-cl-
    ts/Mike Jackson or Phil Worde-p/Buddy Christian-bj/Wellman Braud-sb/d.
                                        New York, November 12, 1926.

36925-2  Blues From The Everglades            Vic 20331
36926-3  P. D. Q. Blues                       -

    Bob Fuller-cl-as replaces Elliott.    New York, November 24, 1926.

36962-3  The Mess                             Vic 20364
36963-2  The Chinch                           Vic 20483

See also Fats Waller; New Orleans Blue Five.

### VICTOR MORRIS AND  HIS ORCHESTRA

Pseudonym on Australian Gracelon 4001 for Sam Lanin and his Orchestra, q.v.

### MORRISON'S  JAZZ ORCHESTRA

The following records are included in view of their historical significance, which on
    the evidence provided by the only title issued, is greater than their jazz value.

George Morrison-vn dir. Leo Davis-t/Ed Carwell-tb/Jimmy Lunceford-as-vn/Cuthbert Byrd
    as/Ed Kelly-ts/Desdemona Davis, Mary E. Kirk or Jesse Andrews-p/Lee Morrison-bj/
    Eugene Montgomery-d.              New York, March 26, 1920.

49780-1-2-3  Pip-Pip, Toot-Toot, Goodbye-ee     Col rejected

                                     New York, April 2, 1920.

79097-1-2-3  Royal Garden Blues                Rejected
79098-3  I Know Why (Intro. My Cuban Dreams)   Col A-2945

                                     Camden, N. J., April 13, 1920.

        Royal Garden Blues                   Vic test (un-numbered)
        Jean                                 -

### LEE MORSE AND HER  BLUE GRASS BOYS

The following titles by this well-known white cabaret artist have interesting jazz-
    styled accompaniments in which extended solo or ensemble passages can be heard; as
    a rule, the late Lee Morse either provided her own ukulele-kazoo accompaniment, or
    gave little chance for her supporting musicians to establish themselves.

Vocal, acc. by own k and probably :- Hymie Farberman-t/Sam Lewis-tb/Larry Abbott-cl/
    Max Terr-p/bj.                   New York, c. August 12, 1925.

106192   Sweet Man                           PA 025157, Per 11591
         Only This Time I'll Be True         PA 025156, Per 11590
         What-Cha-Call-'Em Blues             -         -

                                     New York, c. August 28, 1925.

106224   Oh, Boy ! What A Girl               PA 025158, 11004, Per 11592
106225   Want A Little Lovin'                PA 025161, Per 11595
106226   I Love You So                       PA 025158, 11003, Per 11592

                                     New York, c. December 7, 1925.

106459-B  I Love My Baby (My Baby Loves Me)  PA 025168, 11005, Per 11602

                                     New York, c. December 9, 1925.

106466-A  The Deep Wide Ocean Blues          PA 025168, 11303, Per 11602

Vocal, acc. by Earl Oliver-t/Sam Lewis-tb/Larry Abbott-cl/Jimmy Johnston-bsx/Max Terr
    or Bill Wirges-p/? Harry Reser-bj.      New York, c. April 20, 1926.

106813     Could I ? I Certainly Could          PA 025182, 11176, Per 11616

                                         New York, c. June 1, 1926.

106894     Hoodle-Dee-Doo-Dee-Doo-Doo          PA 025187, 11176, Per 11621

                                         New York, c. August 4, 1926.

107033     He's Still My Baby                   PA      , 11247, Per

    Lee Morse does not appear on this session; John Ryan is the vocalist with a band
    described on most labels LEE MORSE'S BLUE GRASS BOYS (Pathe Actuelle 11273 and
    11397 as THE BLUE GRASS BOYS).  The personnel seems to be as above, but Red Nichols
    t replaces Oliver, and Miff Mole-tb may replace Lewis.
                                         New York, c. October 8, 1926.

107135     Ev'rything's Peaches (For Peaches And Me)PA 36546, Per 14727
107136     Bolshevik - vJR                      PA 36541, 11273,Per 14722,GP 18644
107137     Look Up And Smile - vJR              PA 36545, Per 14726
107138     Tuck In Kentucky (And Smile) - vJR   PA 36556, 11397, Per 14737
    NOTE:- Australian Grand Pree 18644 as TAMPICO JAZZ BAND.

Vocal, acc. by the same group as last, with Sam Lewis-tb certain, plus Tom Stacks-d.
                                         New York, c. November 9, 1926.

107199     The Little White House             PA 25201, 11410, Per 11635
107200     Ain't That Too Bad ?               PA 25205, 11434, Per 11639
107201     With All My Heart                  PA 25202       Per 11636
107202     The Jersey Walk                       -      11410,        -

    Acc. by Phil Napoleon-t/Tommy Dorsey-tb/Jimmy Dorsey-cl/Frank Signorelli-p/Stan
    King-d.                              New York, July 24, 1929.

148847-1  Sweetness                           Col 1922-D, DB-161

    Acc. by Tommy Dorsey-t/Charlie Butterfield-tb/Jimmy Dorsey-cl/Adrian Rollini-bsx/
    Frank Signorelli-p/Carl Kress-g/own k.  New York, February 27, 1930.

150032-3  'Tain't No Sin                       Col 2136-D, DB-140, A-8736

    Rollini omitted; ? Arthur Schutt-harmonium added or replaces Signorelli.
                                         New York, March 27, 1930.

150139-2  Sing, You Sinners                    Col 2124-D, DB-161

    Acc. by ? Tommy Dorsey-t/Jimmy Dorsey-cl/? Frank Signorelli-p/Eddie Lang-g/d.
                                         New York, October 31, 1930.

150924-1  Wasting My Love On You               Col 2333-D, DB-370, Re G-20971
150925-3  Loving You The Way I Do                 -        DB-413

    Acc. by t/tb/p/g/d.                  New York, November 26, 1930.

150987-3  He's My Secret Passion               Col 2348-D, Re G-20971

    Acc. by Manny Klein-t/Tommy Dorsey-tb/Benny Goodman-cl/Rube Bloom-p/Eddie Lang-g.
                                         New York, February 20, 1931.

151334-3  Walkin' My Baby Back Home            Col 2417-D
151335-3  I've Got Five Dollars                   -

    Irving Brodsky-p replaces Bloom.     New York, July 8, 1931.

151670-1  It's The Girl !                      Col 2497-D
151671-3  I'm An Unemployed Sweetheart            -

Piano duet with Abe Frankel, acc. by d.    New York, c. September, 1917.

66667    Jazzin' Around                          PA 20430

## BENNY MORTON AND HIS ORCHESTRA

Henry Allen-t-v/Benny Morton-tb/Edward Inge-cl-as/Jerry Blake-cl-as-v-a/Ted McRae-ts/
Don Kirkpatrick-p/Bobby Johnson-g/Billy Taylor-sb-a/Manzie Johnson-d.
New York, February 23, 1934.

152717-2  Get Goin' - v-aJB                  Col 2902-D, CB-746, DO-1214
152718-1  Fare Thee Well To Harlem - vJB        -           -         -
152719-1  Taylor Made - aBT                  Col 2924-D
152720-1-2 The Gold Digger's Song (sic) - vHA    -         36011 (-1)

## JELLY-ROLL   MORTON

JELLY-ROLL MARTON AND HIS ORCHESTRA (spelt thus on all issues except Tempo R-7) :
  ? Bernie Young-c/tb/Wilson Townes-cl/Charles Harris-as/Jelly-Roll Morton-p/Jasper
  Taylor-woodblocks.                       Chicago, June, 1923.

1434-1   Big Foot Ham                       Pm 12050
1434-2   Big Foot Ham                          -         14007, Cen 3004,
                                            JC L-11, AF A-053
1435-2   Muddy Water Blues                  Pm 12050, 14007, 20251, Fam 3245,
                                            Hg 834, Nat 12251, Pur 11251,
                                            Cen 3004, JC L-11, Tem R-7,
                                            AF A-08, VJR 10

Piano solos.                               Richmond, Ind., July 17, 1923.

11537    King Portor - A Stomp (sic)        Gnt 5289, JC L-121, Tem R-47
11538    New Orleans (Blues) Joys (sic)     Gnt 5486, Sil 4041, BRS 3
11538-A  New Orleans (Blues) Joys (sic)        -         Bm 1070, HJCA HC-55,
NOTE:- XX 13 as GOOD OLD JELLY.             JC L-132, Tem R-5, AF A-09, XX 13

Richmond, Ind., July 18, 1923.

11544    Grandpa's Spells                   Gnt 5218, Bm 1069, HJCA HC-54,
                                            JC L-37, Tem R-50, XX 16
11545    Kansas City Stomp                  As above
11546    Wolverine Blues                    Gnt 5289, JC L-121, Tem R-47
11547    The Pearls (A Stomp)               Gnt 5323, XX 2, JD 004
NOTE:- XX (KANSAS CITY STOMP) is anonymous; GRANDPA'S SPELLS as JELLY.

JELLY-ROLL MORTON'S JAZZ BAND : Natty Dominique-c/Zue Robertson-tb/Horace Eubanks-cl/
  Jelly-Roll Morton-p/? W. E. Burton-d.    Chicago, c. October 30, 1923.

8498-A   Someday, Sweetheart                OK 8105, Bm 1058, HJCA HC-4
8499-A   London Blues                          -          -         - AF A-042

JELLY-ROLL MORTON'S STEAMBOAT FOUR : "Memphis"-comb/Jack Russell-k/Boyd Senter-cl/
  Jelly-Roll Morton-p.                     Chicago, April, 1924.

8065     Mr. Jelly Roll (sic)               Cvl 11397
8065-2   Mr. Jelly Lord                     Pm 20332, Bwy/Mit/Pur/Tri 11397,
                                            Pur 11232, SD 109, JC L-96

JELLY-ROLL MORTON'S STOMPS KINGS or JAZZ KIDS : "Memphis"-comb/Russell Senter-k/Boyd
  Senter-k-bj. This personnel, supplied by Mr. Boyd Senter, proves to be the only
  one bearing Jelly-Roll Morton's name in which he took no audible part !
Chicago, April, 1924.

8066-1   Steady Roll                        Pm 20332, Bwy/Cvl/Mit/Pur/Tri
                                            11397, SD 109, JC L-96
8066-2   Steady Roll                        Pm 20332, Pur 11332

Piano solos.                              Chicago, c. April, 1924.

8071    Thirty-Fifth Street Blues (sic)    Pm/Pur 12216, SD 101, JD 021, XX 8
8072    Mamanita                            -              -       -       -
NOTE:- Steiner-Davis 101 reverses the matrix numbers on the labels.  XX 8 as SLAP
RAGS LEFTON WHITE, PIANO BY FERDINAND BOULE DE SUIF MORTON.


                                          Richmond, Ind., June 9, 1924.

11907-A  Tia Juana (Tee Wana)             Gnt 5632, 3043, Sil 4048, Bm 1003,
                                          JRS AA-110, JC L-5, Tem R-49
11908-A  Shreveport Stomps                Gnt 5590, Bm 1073, HJCA HC-64,
                                          JRS AA-120, JC L-80, Tem R-48
11909, -A Froggie Moore (Frog-I-More)     Rejected
11910-A  Mamamita (sic)                   Gnt 5632, 3043, Sil 4028, Bm 1003,
                                          JRS AA-110, JC L-5, Tem R-49
11911-A  Jelly-Roll Blues                 Gnt 5552, Sil 4038, Bm 1072,
                                          HJCA HC-57, JC L-50
11912-A  Big Foot Ham                     As above, plus AF A-053
11913-A  Bucktown Blues (Bucktown Stomp*) Gnt 5515, Buddy 8015, Sil 4040,
                                          Bm 1071, HJCA HC-56, JC L-71,
                                          Tem R-32, XX 11,* JRS AA-122
11914    Tom Cat Blues                    As above
11915-A  Stratford Hunch                  Gnt 5590, Sil 4036, Bm 1073,
                                          HJCA HC-64, JRS AA-120, JC L-80,
                                          Tem R-48
11916    Milenberg Joys                   Rejected
11917    Perfect Rag                      Gnt 5486, Sil 4041, Bm 1070, BRS 3
                                          HJCA HC-55, Tem R-5, XX-13, AF A-09
NOTE:- XX 11 as JELLY; XX as TREMENDOUS OLD JELLY.


                                          Chicago, late June, 1924.

534     Froggie Moore (Frog-I-More)       Pm 14032, SD 103, JD 004, XX 8
535     London Blues                      Rialto (un-numbered), Ses 3,
NOTE:- XX 8 as SLAP RAGS LEFTON WHITE.    JC L-7, AF A-042
The issues from matrix 534 were dubbed from a test pressing in the possession of
Mr. John Steiner of Milwaukee, to whom I am grateful for the opportunity of
inspecting it by eye and ear.  The Riverside-London LP alleging to include the
Gennett recording of FROGGIE MOORE (see matrix 11909 above) in fact merely uses an
edited version of the above matrix 534.

JELLY-ROLL MORTON'S KINGS OF JAZZ : Lee Collins-c/Roy Palmer-tb/"Balls" Ball-cl/Alex
Poole-as/Jelly-Roll Morton-p.            Chicago, c. September, 1924.

635     Fish Tail Blues                   Auto 606, Ses 2, JC L-25, Tem R-19
636     High Society                      -         -        -         -
638     Weary Blues                       Auto 607, Ses 4 (never issued)
639     Tiger Rag                         -         -
NOTE:- Matrix 637 is untraced.

JELLY-ROLL MORTON'S JAZZ TRIO : Volly de Faut-cl/W. E. Burton-k/Jelly-Roll Morton-p.
                                          Chicago, c. May, 1925.

791     My Gal                            Auto 623, Reissue 8, JC L-65
792     Wolverine Blues                   -         -          -
NOTE:- The second side is credited to VOLTAIRE DE FAUT.

JELLY-ROLL MORTON'S INCOMPARABLES : Jelly-Roll Morton-p dir. Ray Bowling/tb/as/ts/bj/
Clay Jefferson-d.  This is Jelly-Roll Morton's touring band, and probably the only
example of a recording by a regular Morton organization, as distinct from a studio
group.                                   Richmond, Ind., February 23, 1926.

12466, -A Milenberg Joys                  Rejected
12467    Mr. Jelly Lord                   Gnt 3259, Buddy 8004, Ch 15105
NOTE:- The Gennett files for December 1, 1925 list for matrix 12440 a test recording of MILENBERG JOYS by an un-named artist, with the mysterious note "Re Re." This
almost certainly means a subsequent re-recording of the title by the same artist,
who is probably Jelly-Roll Morton, with a band including Punch Miller and Edwin
Swayzee on cornets.  Buddy 8004 as NEW ORLEANS RHYTHM KINGS.

Piano solos.                        Chicago, April 20, 1926.

C-160; E-2863  The Pearls                          Voc 1020, Or 1007, Br 80067,
                                                   03564, Col MZ-354, Dec MG-3564
C-163; E-2866  Sweetheart O' Mine                  Voc 1019, V-1019, Br 80068,
                                                   JSo AA-584
C-164; E-2867  Fat Meat And Greens                 As above
C-166; E-2869  King Porter Stomp                   Voc 1020, Or 1007, Br 80067,
                                                   03564, Col DZ-354, Dec MG-3564

JELLY-ROLL MORTON'S RED HOT PEPPERS : Jelly-Roll Morton-p-v-speech dir. George
  Mitchell-c/Kid Ory-tb/Omer Simeon-cl/Johnny St. Cyr-bj/John Lindsay-sb/Andrew
  Hilaire-d.                        Chicago, September 15, 1926.

36239-2  Black Bottom Stomp                        Vic 20221, BB B-10253, HMV B-5164,
                                                   B-10048, AE-1753, HN-2885, JK-2712,
                                                   K-5010, R-7475, SG-459, El EG-7812,
                                                   Bm 1063, HJCA HC-45
36240-2  Smoke-House Blues (Beale Street Blues*)   Vic 20296, BB B-8372, HMV B-10645,
                                                   EA-4005*, JK-2759, El EG-7775,
                                                   Bm 1055, BRS 8, HJCA HC-48, NOM M11
36241-1  The Chant                                 HJCA HC-45
36241-3  The Chant                                 Vic 20221, BB B-10253, HMV B-5164,
                                                   B-10456, AE-1753, HN-3172, JK-2759,
                                                   SG-459, El EG-383, EG-7774, Bm 1063

NOTE:- Late pressings of Bluebird B-10253 are from dubbed masters (single-ring
eccentric run-off), and Victor 20221 is known to exist coupling THE CHANT with a
side from Victor 19921 by the Brox Sisters.

Barney Bigard-Darnell Howard-cl/Marty Bloom-effects added; the files quote a second
c, but this may refer to the klaxon horn used on the first side.  Simeon is the
only cl heard on the third title.      Chicago, September 21, 1926.

36283-2  Sidewalk Blues - spJRM-JSC               X LX-3018, Vic 730605, 731059(LPs)
36283-3  Sidewalk Blues - spJRM-JSC               Vic 20252, 40-0118, HMV B-5212,
                                                   B-10270, EA-3785, HN-3016, JK-2755
                                                   El EG-7773
36284-1  Dead Man Blues - spJRM-JSC               Vic 20252, 40-0118, HMV B-10270,
                                                   EA-3785, HN-3016, JK-2755,
                                                   El EG-7774
36284-2  Dead Man Blues - spJRM-JSC               Vic 20252
36285-3  Steamboat Stomp - spJRM-JSC              Vic 20296, BB B-8372, HMV B-9979,
NOTE:- Some copies of Victor 40-0118 are          HMV HN-2884, JF-56, JK-2686,
pressed from dubbed masters.                       SG-295, El EG-7545, Bm 1065,
                                                   BRS 8, HJCA HC-48, NOM M-II

As for September 15, 1926, plus Clarence Black-Wright Smith (or Darnell Howard,
according to Mr. Howard himself)-vn*; Simeon db bcl*; St. Cyr db g.
                                   Chicago, December 16, 1926.

37254-2  *Someday Sweetheart                       Vic 20405
37254-3  *Someday Sweetheart                       BRS 1001
37255-2  Grandpa's Spells                          BB B-10254, HMV B-10048, HN-2885,
                                                   JK-2712, El EG-7812, Homart JC-54
37255-3  Grandpa's Spells                          Vic 20431, Bm 1066, BRS 9,
                                                   HJCA HC-49
37256-1  Original Jelly-Roll Blues                 BB B-10255, HMV EA-3632
37256-2  Original Jelly-Roll Blues                 Vic 20405, A-1465, HMV B-9848,
                                                   ALS-5018, DA-4986, HN-2933,
                                                   JK-2666, K-8741, El EG-7907,
                                                   BRS 12, HJCA HC-47
37257-3  Doctor Jazz - vJRM                        Vic 20415, A-1465, BB B-10255,
                                                   HMV B-9848, ALS-5018, DA-4986,
                                                   EA-3632, HN-2933, JK-2767, K-8741,
                                                   El EG-7907, Bm 1011, BRS 12,
                                                   HJCA HC-47
37258-1  Cannon Ball Blues                         BB B-10254, Vic A-1368, HMV B-9979,
                                                   HN-2884, JK-2686, SG-295, El EG-7545
                                                   Bm 1066, BRS 9, HJCA HC-49,
                                                   Homart JC-54
37258-2  Cannon Ball Blues                         Vic 20431

JELLY-ROLL MORTON'S RED HOT PEPPERS : Jelly-Roll Morton-p dir. George Mitchell-c/
Gerald Reeves-tb/Johnny Dodds-cl/Stump Evans-as/Bud Scott-g/Quinn Wilson-bb/Baby
Dodds-d/Lew LeMar-effects.             Chicago, June 4, 1927.

| | | |
|---|---|---|
| 38627-2 | Hyena Stomp - eLL | Vic 20772, Bm 1059, HJCA HC-11 |
| 38627-3 | Hyena Stomp - eLL | HMV JK-2760 |
| 38628-1 | Billy Goat Stomp - eLL | Vic 20772, Bm 1059, HJCA HC-11 |
| 38628-3 | Billy Goat Stomp - eLL | HMV JK-2760 |
| 38629-1 | Wild Man Blues | BB B-10256, HMV B-10645, JK-2761, El EG-7772, BRS 4, JCl 506 |
| 38630-2 | Jungle Blues | As above, but HMV B-10683 |
| 38630-3 | Jungle Blues | Vic 21345 |

Dodds Brothers and Morton only*.        Chicago, June 10, 1927.

| | | |
|---|---|---|
| 38661-1 | Beale Street Blues | Vic 20948, BB B-10252, HMV B-10341, EA-4005, HN-3078, JK-2599, SG-493, VSG-11, Bm 1077, HJCA HC-88, NOM M-12, Record Shack 2 |
| 38661-2 | Beale Street Blues (all microgrooves) | X LVA-3028, Vic RD-27113, 741040 |
| 38662-2 | The Pearls | Vic 20948 |
| 38662-3 | The Pearls | —     BB B-10252, HMV B-10341, EA-4005, HN-3078, JK-2599, SG-493, VSG 11, Bm 1077, HJCA HC-88, NOM M-12, Record Shack 2 |
| 38663-1 | *Wolverine Blues | Vic 21064, BB B-10258, HMV B-10173, HN-2997, JK-2233, SG-400, Bm 1075, Trad T-594 |
| 38663-2 | *Wolverine Blues (all microgrooves) | X LVA-3028, Vic RD-27184, 741040 |
| 38664-1 | *Mr. Jelly Lord | Vic 21064, BB B-10258, HMV B-10328, |
| | NOTE:- Victor 21064 as JELLY-ROLL MORTON - | HN-3073, JK-2233, SG-474, |
| | Piano solo with Clarinet and Traps; other | El EG-7864, Bm 1075, Trad T-594 |
| | issues as JELLY-ROLL MORTON TRIO. | |

Jelly Roll Morton-p-v dir. Ward Pinkett-t/Geechie Fields-tb/Omer Simeon-cl/Lee
Blair-bj/Bill Benford-bb/Tommy Benford-d; instrumentation of trio and quartet
sides shown after titles.             New York, June 11, 1928.

| | | |
|---|---|---|
| 45619-2 | Georgia Swing | Vic V-38024, BB B-5109, B-8515, Sr S-3192, HMV B-9221, DA-4987, EA-3419, HN-2944, JF-10, JK-2666, JK-2680, K-8742, SG-308, Bm 1062, HJCA HC-44 |
| 45620-3 | Kansas City Stomps | Vic V-38010, BB B-5109, B-7757, Sr S-3192, HMV B-10151, DA-4987, HN-2984, JK-2736, K-8742, SG-41, Bm 1068, HJCA HC-51 |
| 45621-3 | Shoe Shiner's Drag | Vic 21658, BB B-5707, B-7725, HMV B-10151. EA-468, HN-2984, JK-2758, R-14054, Bm 1067, HJCA HC-50 |
| 45622-2 | Boogaboo | Vic V-38010, BB B-6031, B-7725, HMV B-10173, HN-2997, JK-2736, Bm 1067, HJCA HC-50 |
| 45623-1 | Shreveport - cl/p/d | Vic 21658 |
| 45623-2 | Shreveport - cl/p/d | — BB B-5707, B-7710, HMV B-9220, EA-468, EA-3158, JK-2710, R-14054, JCl 501 |
| 45624-1 | Mournful Serenade - tb/cl/p/d | Vic V-38024 |
| 45624-2 | Mournful Serenade - tb/cl/p/d | — BB B-6601, B-8515, HMV B-9221, HN-2944, JK-2680, SG-308, Bm 1062, HJCA HC-44 |
| 45625-1-2 | Honey Babe - t/p/d/vJRM | Rejected |
| 45626-1-2 | Sidewalk Blues | — |
| | NOTE:- Some reissues of matrix 45624-2 as JELLY ROLL MORTON'S QUARTET. | |

JELLY-ROLL MORTON AND HIS ORCHESTRA : Jelly-Roll Morton-p dir. Ed Anderson-Edwin
Swayzee-t/William Cato-tb/Russell Procope-cl/Paul Barnes-ss/Joe Garland-ts/Lee
Blair-g/Bass Moore-bb/Manzie Johnson-d. New York, December 6, 1928.

| | | |
|---|---|---|
| 48433-1-2 | Everybody Loves My Honey Now | Rejected |
| 48434-1 | Red Hot Pepper | Vic V-38055, 40-0119, BB B-6601, HMV JK-2737 |
| 48435-3 | Deep Creek | Vic V-38055, 40-0119, BB B-5333, Sr S-3414, HMV B-9220, EA-3158, JF-10, JK-2710 |
| 48436-1-2 | You Oughta See My Gal | Rejected |

NOTE:- Some copies of Victor 40-0119 are pressed from dubbed masters on both sides.

Piano solos.                               Camden, N. J., July 8, 1929.

| | | |
|---|---|---|
| 49448-2 | Pep | Vic V-38627, BB B-10257, HMV B-10619, JK-2201, BRS 1010, HJCA 609 |
| 49449-1 | Seattle Hunch | Vic V-38527 |
| 49449-2 | Seattle Hunch | Vic 27565, HMV JK-2762,El EG-7776 |
| 49450-2 | Frances (Fat Frances*) | Vic V-38627, BB B-10257, HMV B-10619, JK-2201*, BRS 1010, HJCA 609 |
| 49451-1 | Freakish | Vic 27565, HMV JK-2762,El EG-7776 |
| 49451-2 | Freakish | Vic V-38527 |

JELLY-ROLL MORTON AND HIS ORCHESTRA (.....RED HOT PEPPERS on Victor V-38075) : Jelly-
Roll Morton-solo p dir. Red Rossiter-Barclay S. "Horsecollar" Draper or Walter
Briscoe-2t/Charlie Irvis-tb/George Baquet-cl/Paul Barnes-ss/Joe Thomas-as/Walter
Thomas-ts/Rod Rodriguez-ensemble p/Barney Alexander-bj/Harry Prather-bb/William
Laws-d.                                    Camden, N. J., July 9, 1929.

| | | |
|---|---|---|
| 49452-1 | Burnin' The Iceberg | Vic 741054 (LP) |
| 49452-2 | Burnin' The Iceberg | Vic V-38075, 40-0120, HMV B-10762 EA-3730, JK-2738, R-14329 |
| 49453-1 | Courthouse Bump | Vic 741054 (LP) |
| 49453-2 | Courthouse Bump | Vic V-38093 |
| 49454-1 | Pretty Lil | Vic 741054 (LP) |
| 49454-2 | Pretty Lil | Vic V-38078, 40-0120, HMV EA-3730 JK-2738, SG-53 |

Camden, N. J., July 10, 1929.

| | | |
|---|---|---|
| 49455-1 | Sweet Aneta Mine (sic) | Vic V-38093, HMV R-14433 |
| 49455-2 | Sweet Aneta Mine (sic) | Vic LPV-524, RD-7807, 730599(LPs) |
| 49456-1 | New Orleans Bump (Monrovia) | Vic V-38078, BB B-7757, HMV JK-2737, BRS 1001, JC1 501 |
| 49456-2 | New Orleans Bump (Monrovia) | Vic LPV-546 (LP) |

Camden, N. J., July 12, 1929.

| | | |
|---|---|---|
| 49457-1 | Down My Way | Vic V-38113 |
| 49458-2 | Try Me Out | - |
| 49459-2 | Tank Town Bump | Vic V-38075, HMV B-10456, JF-56, JK-2758, R-14329, El EG-7771 |

JELLY-ROLL MORTON AND HIS RED HOT PEPPERS : Jelly-Roll Morton-p dir. Henry Allen-t/
J. C. Higginbotham-tb/Albert Nicholas-cl/Will Johnson-g/Pops Foster-sb/Paul
Barbarin-d.                                New York, November 13, 1929.

| | | |
|---|---|---|
| 57080-1 | Sweet Peter | Vic 23402, Bm 1061, HJCA HC-34 |
| 57080-2 | Sweet Peter | HMV JK-2860 |
| 57081-1 | Jersey Joe | Vic 23402, HMV JK-2862 |
| 57081-2 | Jersey Joe | Bm 1061, HJCA HC-34 |
| 57082-1 | Mississippi Mildred | Vic 23424, HMV JK-2862 |
| 57082-2 | Mississippi Mildred | Bm 1060, HJCA HC-35 |
| 57083-1 | Mint Julep | Vic 23334 |

JELLY-ROLL MORTON TRIO : Barney Bigard-cl/Jelly-Roll Morton-p/Zutty Singleton-d.
New York, December 17, 1929.

| | | |
|---|---|---|
| 57784-1 | Smilin' The Blues Away | Vic V-38108, BB B-10194, HMV JK-2186, BRS 1011, HJCA 609 |
| 57785-1 | Turtle Twist | As above |
| 57786-1 | My Little Dixie Home | Vic V-38601,HMV JK-2861,HJCA HC-15 |
| 57787-2 | That's Like It Ought To Be | -      -      - |

JELLY-ROLL MORTON AND HIS RED HOT PEPPERS : Jelly-Roll Morton-p dir. Ward Pinkett and
another-t/Wilbur de Paris-tb/Ernie Bullock or Jerry Blake-cl-bcl/Bernard Addison-g/
Billy Taylor-bb/Cozy Cole-d.    New York, March 5, 1930.

| | | |
|---|---|---|
| 59504-1 | Each Day | Vic 23351, HJCA HC-33 |
| 59505-2 | If Someone Would Only Love Me - bcl | Vic 23321, HMV JK-2860, Tpl 525 |
| 59506-1 | That'll Never Do | Vic 23019, HMV B-4836, HJCA HC-76 |
| 59507-2 | I'm Looking For A Little Bluebird | Vic 23004 |

NOTE:- A special pressing, bearing a yellow Victor label and the same performance
of EACH DAY on each side was made for use in cinemas and theatres.

Jelly-Roll Morton-p dir. Ward Pinkett-Bubber Miley-t/Wilbur de Paris-tb/Lorenzo Tio
Jr.-cl/bj/Bernard Addison-g/Bill Benford-bb/Tommy Benford-d.
New York, March 19, 1930.

| | | |
|---|---|---|
| 59532-2 | Little Lawrence | Vic V-38135, 40-0121, HMV EA-3680, JK-2756, SG-53 |
| 59533-1 | Harmony Blues | Vic V-38135, HMV B-10683, ALS-5059, El EG-7773 |

NOTE:- The latter title was scheduled for issue on Bluebird B-11594, but it never
appeared in this form.

Ernie Bullock or Jerry Blake-cl-bcl replaces Tio.
New York, March 20, 1930.

| | | |
|---|---|---|
| 59643-1 | Fussy Mabel | Vic V-38125, 760-0003, HMV B-10762 |
| 59644-1 | Ponchatrain | -   40-0121   -   HMV EA-3680 El EG-7775 |

NOTE:- The first title was scheduled for issue on Bluebird B-11593, but it never
appeared in this form.

Jelly-Roll Morton-p dir. Ward Pinkett and another-t/Geechie Fields-tb/Happy Cald-
well-cl/Joe Thomas-as/Walter Thomas-cl-bar/Lee Blair-bj/Billy Taylor-bb/Cozy Cole-
d.    New York, June 2, 1930.

| | | |
|---|---|---|
| 62182-1 | Oil Well | Vic 23321, Tpl 525 |
| 62183-1 | Load Of Coal (Load Of Cole) | Vic 23429 |
| 62183-2 | Load Of Coal (Load Of Cole) | Bm 1060, HJCA HC-35 |
| 62184-2 | Crazy Chords | Vic 23307, HMV B-4898, Bm 1074, HJCA HC-68 |
| 62185-1 | Primrose Stomp | Vic 23424, HMV JK-2877 |

NOTE:- Victor 23307 and HMV B-4898 as JELLY-ROLL MORTON AND HIS ORCHESTRA.

Jelly-Roll Morton-p dir. Ward Pinkett-t/Geechie Fields-tb/Albert Nicholas-cl/Howard
Hill-g/Pete Biggs-bb/Tommy Benford-d.   New York, July 14, 1930.

| | | |
|---|---|---|
| 62339-1 | Low Gravy | Vic 23334, BB B-8302, HMV JK-2763, SG-457, Bm 1068, BRS 10,HJCA HC-51 |
| 62340-1 | Strokin' Away | HJCA HC-33 |
| 62340-2 | Strokin' Away | Vic 23351, BB B-8302, HMV JK-2763, SG-457 |
| 62341-1 | Blue Blood Blues | Vic 22681, A-1335, BB B-8201, HMV EA-3419, JK-2859, R-14645, Bm 1064, BRS 11, HJCA HC-46 |
| 62342-1 | Mushmouth Shuffle | Vic 23004, BB B-8201, HMV B-10328, HN-3073, JK-2796, SG-474, El EG-7864, Bm 1064, BRS 11, HJCA HC-46 |

JELLY-ROLL MORTON AND HIS RED HOT PEPPERS : Jelly-Roll Morton-p dir. Ward Pinkett-t/
   Geechie Fields-tb/? Eddie Scarpa-cl/Bernard Addison-g/Billy Taylor-bb/Bill Beason-d.
                              New York, October 9, 1930.

64313-1  Gambling Jack                         Vic 23307, HMV JK-2859, Bm 1074,
                                               HJCA HC-68
64314-1  Fickle Fay Creep                      Vic 23019, HMV B-4837, HJCA HC-76
   NOTE:- Victor 23307 as JELLY-ROLL MORTON AND HIS ORCHESTRA.

Interviews with Alan Lomax, acc. by own p, with illustrative songs -v and p solos*.
                              Washington, D. C., May 21-July, 1938.

| 1638 | Alabama Bound - v | Cir 67-68 |
| 1639 | *King Porter Stomp/You Can Have It - v | Cir 23-24 |
| 1640 | Ancestry and Early Life | Cir 5-6 |
| 1641 | Tiger Rag - Quadrille and metamorphosis | Cir 1 |
|      | *Tiger Rag/*Panama | Cir 2 |
| 1642 | Ragtime: Sammy Davis and Tony Jackson/ | Cir 47 |
|      | Pretty Baby - v | |
| 1643 | *The Naked Dance/Sporting Life In New | Cir 85 |
|      | Orleans | |
|      | Honky-Tonk Blues - v | Cir 87-88 |
| 1644 | New Orleans Sporting Houses/Levee Man | Cir 84-83 |
|      | Blues - v | |
|      | Aaron Harris | Cir 33-34 |
| 1645 | Aaron Harris Was A Bad, Bad Man - v | Cir 34 |
|      | Aaron Harris, Madame Papa Loos, Sheep- | Cir 34-35 |
|      | Eye and Robert Charles | |
| 1646 | Robert Charles's Story | Cir 35-36 |
|      | Game Kid Blues - v | Cir 51 |
| 1647 | Game Kid and Buddy Carter | Cir 52 |
|      | New Orleans funeral customs and food | Cir 12 |
| 1648 | New Orleans funeral customs and origins | Cir 14-15-16 |
|      | of jazz | |
| 1649 | The beginnings of jazz | Cir 16-17 |
| 1650 | Styles of playing : *Kansas City Stomps | Cir 18-19-20 |
| 1651 | Breaks and riffs; Swing and jazz | - - - |
| 1652 | Bill Johnson; early bands and leaders | Cir 64 |
|      | If You Was Whiskey And I Was A Duck - v | Cir 89 |
| 1653 | My Gal Sal - v | Cir 72 |
|      | *Maple Leaf Rag | Cir 22 |
| 1654 | St. Louis piano style : *Maple Leaf Rag | Cir 21-22 |
| 1655 | Low-Down Blues - v | Cir 57, 87-88 |
| 1656 | The Winin' Boy - v | Cir 90 |
| 1657 | The Animule Ball-v/Improvised scat song-v | Cir 9-10 |
| 1658 | Early Blues/Buddy Bolden/Buddy Bolden's | Cir 77-78 |
|      | Blues - v | |
| 1659 | Mr. Jelly Lord - v | Cir 3 |
|      | Jelly-Roll Blues - v/Origin of the name | Cir 4 |
| 1660 | Jelly-Roll Blues - v | - '74 |
|      | New Orleans Honky-Tonks | Cir 84 |
| 1661 | New Orleans tough characters; The Skin | Cir 37-40 |
|      | Game | |
| 1662 | See See Rider - v | Cir 12-13 |
| 1663 | New Orleans clubs, street parades, fights | Cir 75-76 |
| 1664 | Early experiences and travels with Jack | Cir 61-64 |
| 1665 | the Bear; saloons and pianists of Beale Street and Memphis | |
| 1666 | Bad Sam and Benny Frenchy | Cir 63-64 |
| 1667 | Make Me A Pallet On The Floor - v | Rejected |
| 1668 | Swinging the operas; early memories | Cir 66-67 |
| 1669 | The Dirty Dozens-v/The Murder Ballad-v | Rejected/Cir 59 |
| 1670 | Now Let Me Tell You-v/You Got My Man | - |
| 1671 | They Brought That Gal To The Prison Gates-v | - |
|      | Gal, When I'm Through You'll Think I'm A Man-v- | |
| 1672 | Ask My Sister, Please Don't Be Like Me-v | - |
|      | Goodbye To The World, I Know I'm Goin'-v | - |

NOTE:- Parts of matrices 1669/1672 are included in Circle 59, the remainder being
omitted as the lyrics are frankly pornographic. (Cont on page 1106).

Interviews with Alan Lomax, acc. by own p, with illustrative songs -v and p solos*.
(cont.)                                Washington, D. C., May 21-July, 1938.

```
1673    *Fickle Fay Creep/*Jungle Blues          Cir 32-46
1674    *King Porter Stomp/*Sweet Peter           Cir 73-69
1675    *Hyena Stomp/*Wolverine Blues             Cir 8-55
1676    *Wolverine Blues/*State And Madison       Cir 56-70
1677    *The Pearls                               Cir 41-42
1678    *Bert Williams/*Freakish                  Cir 45-71
1679    *Pep/The Georgia Skin Game                Cir 43-39-40
1680    The Georgia Skin Game/Card-Players' Rag - v      - -
1681    Indian songs at the Mardi Gras            Cir 82
        New Orleans Blues - v                     Cir 27
1682    Jazz and Blues/*La Paloma as a blues      Cir 28
1683    Creepy Feeling (with explanation)         Cir 29-30
1684    *Mama 'Nita                               Cir 25
        C'est 'n aut' can-can, pays donc - v/     Cir 81
        If You Don't Shake, Don't Get No Cake - v
1685    *Spanish Swat/Ain't Misbehavin' - v       Cir 26-44
1686    I Hate A Man Like You - v/Michigan Water  Cir 86-58
        Blues - v
1687    The Winin' Boy - v                        Cir 60
1688    Mamie Desdoumes' Blues - v                Cir 49
        Albert Carroll :*Crazy Chords Rag         Cir 50
        Buddy Bertrand :*Boogie Woogie            -
2487/9  New Orleans Street Bands                  Cir 79-82
 ?      *The Crave                                Cir 31
```
NOTE:- All the above Circle records were dubbed from original acetates made in the
Coolidge Auditorium in Washington's Library of Congress. They have since been re-
mastered twice and issued on sets of LPs.

JELLY-ROLL MORTON : Dick Bird-t/Teddy Smith-as/Jelly-Roll Morton-p-or (solos as
shown)/g/sb/d.                         Baltimore, c. August, 1938.

```
        The Pearls - p                   Swaggie JCS-116, S-1213 (LPs)
        King Porter Stomp - p            Rejected
        Organ Interlude - or             Swaggie JCS-116 (LP)
        Honeysuckle Rose                 -
        Melancholy Baby (sic)            -
```

G/sb/d omitted; Morton-v.                 Baltimore, c. August, 1938.

```
        I Would Do Anything For You      Swaggie S-1213 (LP)
        I Ain't Got Nobody - vJRM        -
        My Melancholy Baby - vJRM        -
        Honeysuckle Rose                 -
```

Teddy Smith-as/Jelly-Roll Morton-p.       Baltimore, c. August, 1938.

```
        After You've Gone                Swaggie JCS-116 (LP)
        Trees                            -
        Tiger Rag                        Swaggie S-1213 (LP)
        Blues                            -
```

Piano solos, with own v where shown.     Washington, D. C., December, 1938.

```
MLB-145  Finger Buster              JM 12, BSt 185, Vogue GV-2256
MLB-146  Creepy Feeling             -       -        -
MLB-147  Winin' Boy Blues - vJRM    JM 11, BSt 170, Vogue GV-2255
MLB-149  Honky Tonk Music           -       -        -
```
NOTE;- Matrix MLB-148 is untraced. These four sides are apparently dubbed from
acetates made privately; careful listening on suitably adjusted "hi-fi" equipment
reveals the slightest suggestion of original surface noise.

JELLY-ROLL MORTON'S NEW ORLEANS JAZZMEN : Jelly-Roll Morton-p-v dir. Sidney de Paris-
    t/Claude Jones-tb-preaching/Albert Nicholad-cl/Sidney Bechet-ss/Happy Caldwell-ts/
    Lawrence Lucie-g/Wellman Braud-sb/Zutty Singleton-d-preaching.
                                     New York, September 14, 1939.

| | | |
|---|---|---|
| 041456-1 | Oh, Didn't He Ramble ? - prCJ | BB B-10429, MW M-8406, HMV B-9217, EA-3151, JK-2017, <u>HJCA HC-95,</u> Jazz Time MS-109 |
| 041456-2 | Oh, Didn't He Ramble ? - prZS | <u>Vic LPV-559, 730605</u> (LPs) |
| 041457-1 | High Society | BB B-10434, MW M-8405, HMV B-9216, EA-3094, JK-2018, <u>HJCA HC-94,</u> Jazz Time MS-110 |
| 041458-1 | I Thought I Heard Buddy Bolden Say-vJRM | As above |
| 041459-1 | Winin' Boy Blues - vJRM | Vic 730605 (LP) |
| 041459-2 | Winin' Boy Blues - vJRM | BB B-10429, MW M-8406, HMV B-9217, EA-3151, JK-2017, <u>HJCA HC-85,</u> Jazz Time MS-109 |

        Fred Robinson-tb replaces Jones; Bechet omitted.
                                     New York, September 28, 1939.

| | | |
|---|---|---|
| 041360-1 | Climax Rag (James Scott) | MW M-8404 |
| 041360-2 | Climax Rag (James Scott) | BB B-10442, HMV B-9219, EA-3315, JK-2019, Jazz Time MS-111 |
| 041361-1 | Don't You Leave Me Here - vJRM | BB B-10450, MW M-8403, HMV B-9218, EA-2607, JK-2020, Jazz Time MS-112 |
| 041361-2 | Don't You Leave Me Here - vJRM | <u>Vic LPV-559, 730605</u> (LPs) |
| 041362-1 | West End Blues | - |
| 041362-2 | West End Blues | BB B-10442, MW M-8404, HMV B-9219, EA-3315, JK-2019, Jazz Time MS-111 |
| 041363-1 | Ballin' The Jack - vJRM | BB B-10450, MW M-8403, HMV B-9218, EA-2607, JK-2020, Jazz Time MS-112 |

Piano solos, with own v where shown.    New York, December 14, 1939.

| | | |
|---|---|---|
| R-2560 | Sporting House Rag | Rejected |
| R-2561 | Original Rags (Scott Joplin) | Gnl 4001, Com 587, <u>Vogue V-2122,</u> JS 695 |
| R-2562 | The Crave | Gnl 4003, Com 589, <u>Vogue V-2067,</u> JS 794 |
| R-2563 | The Naked Dance | Rejected |
| R-2564 | Mister Joe | Gnl 4004, Com 590, <u>Vogue V-2121,</u> JS 791 |
| R-2565 | King Porter Stomp | Gnl 4005, Com 591, <u>Vogue V-2123</u> |
| R-2566 | Winin' Boy Blues - vJRM | Gnl 4004, Com 590, <u>Vogue V-2121,</u> JS 791 |
| R-2567 | The Animule Ball - vJRM | Rejected |

                                     New York, December 16, 1939.

| | | |
|---|---|---|
| R-2570 | Buddy Bolden's Blues - vJRM | Gnl 4003, Com 589, <u>Vogue V-2067,</u> JS 794 |
| R-2571 | The Naked Dance | Gnl 4002, Com 588, <u>Vogue V-2120</u> |
| R-2572 | Don't You Leave Me Here - vJRM | Gnl 4005, Com 591, <u>Vogue V-2123</u> |
| R-2573 | Mamie's Blues - vJRM | Gnl 4001, Com 587, <u>Vogue V-2122,</u> JS 695 |
| R-2574 | Michigan Water Blues - vJRM | Rejected |

                                     New York, December 18, 1939.

| | | |
|---|---|---|
| R-2579 | Michigan Water Blues - vJRM | Gnl 4002, Com 588, <u>Vogue V-2120</u> |

JELLY-ROLL MORTON'S SEVEN : Jelly-Roll Morton-p-v dir. Henry Allen-t/Joe Britton-tb/
    Albert Nicholas-cl/Eddie Williams-as/Wellman Braud-sb/Zutty Singleton-d.
                                     New York, January 4, 1940.

| | | |
|---|---|---|
| R-2582 | Sweet Substitute - vJRM | Gnl 1703, Com 631, <u>Vogue V-2066,</u> JS 799 |
| R-2583 | Panama | As above |
| R-2584 | Good Old New York - vJRM | Gnl 1704, Com 632, JS 697 |
| R-2585 | Big Lip Blues - vJRM | -     -     - |

THE MORTON SIX : Jelly-Roll Morton-p-v dir. Henry Allen-t/Albert Nicholas-cl/Eddie
   Williams-as/Wellman Braud-sb/Zutty Singleton-d.
                                          New York, January 23, 1940.

| R-2621 | Why ? - vJRM | Gnl 1706, Com 636 |
| R-2622 | Get The Bucket - vJRM | - Com 634, JS 804 |
| R-2623 | If You Knew - vJRM | Gnl 1707, Com 636 |
| R-2624 | Shake It - vJRM | - Com 634, JS 804 |

THE MORTON SEVEN : As above, plus Claude Jones-tb.
                                          New York, January 30, 1940.

| R-2632 | Dirty, Dirty, Dirty - vJRM | Gnl 1711, Com 633, JS 807 |
| R-2633 | Swinging The Elks | - - - |
| R-2634 | Mama's Got A Baby - vJRM | Gnl 1710, Com 635 |
| R-2635 | My Home Is In A Southern Town - vJRM | - - |

Piano solos, acc. by the house band of the radio show NBC CHAMBER MUSIC SOCIETY OF
   LOWER BASIN STREET (Henry Levine-t/Jack Epstein-tb/Alfie Evans-cl/Rudolph Adler-ts/
   Tony Colucci-g/Harry Patent-sb/Nat Levine-d) or by Nat Levine-d only as shown. On
   this occasion, almost a year to the day before his death in Los Angeles, Jelly-Roll
   Morton was the featured guest-artist.   New York, July 14, 1940.

            Winin' Boy Blues (both microgrooves)   Pirate MPC-502, Swaggie S-1213
            King Porter Stomp - p/d only            -

## TOM MORTON

TOMMY MORTON'S GRANGERS : Tom Morton-d dir. Tony Tortomas-Sammy Castin-t/Pete
   Pellizzi or Mike Fucillo-tb/Nick Vitalo and another-cl-as/ts/vn/Harry Ford-p/Tony
   Colucci-bj/John Ryan-v.          New York, c. November 1, 1926.

| 107183 | How Could Red Riding Hood ? - vJR | PA 36544, 11275,Per 14725,Gra 9259 |
| 107184 | When I Kissed You I Kissed The Blues Goodbye - vJR | PA 36549, Per 14730 |
| 107185 | Baby Mine - vJR | PA 36548, Per 14729 |

TOM MORTON'S ORCH., featuring ORIGINAL INDIANA FIVE : Similar to the above; Irving
   Kaufman (as GEORGE KAY)-v.        New York, May 21, 1929.

| 148606-1 | Anything To Hold Your Baby - vIK | Har 930-H |
| 148607-3 | Birmingham Bertha - vIK | - |
| 148608-1 | Broadway Baby Dolls - vIK | Har 937-H |

## CURTIS MOSBY AND HIS  DIXIELAND BLUE BLOWERS

Curtis Mosby-d dir. James Porter-t/Ashford Hardee-tb/Charles Hite-Leo Davis-cl-as/
   Bumps Myers-ts/Attwell Rose-vn/Henry Starr-p-v/Thomas Valentine-bj/ —— Perkins-bb.
                                          Los Angeles, October 14, 1927.

| 144761-2 | Weary Stomp | Col 1191-D |
| 144762-3 | Whoop 'Em Up Blues | Col 1192-D |
| 144763-1-3 | In My Dreams (I'm Jealous Of You)-vHS | Col 1191-D |
| 144764-1 | Tiger Stomp | Col 1192-D |

Curtis Mosby-d dir. James Porter-t/Ashford Hardee-tb/Charlie Lawrence-Les Hite-cl-as/
   Bumps Myers-ts/? Andy Iona (Aiona)-vn-stg/Walter Johnson-p/Freddy Vaughan-bj/bb.
                                          Los Angeles, March 28, 1928.

| 145924-2 | Blue Blowers Blues | Col 1442-D |
| 145925-2 | Hardee Stomp | - |

   Country Allen-tb replaces Hardee.    Los Angeles, January 21, 1929.

| 147817-3 | Between You And Me (And The Deep Blue Sea) - v | Col 40001-D |
| 147818-3 | Louisiana Bo Bo | - |
| 147819-1 | Dearie | Rejected |
| 147824-1 | Don't Make Sweet Mama Mad | - |

NOTE:- Matrices 147820/1 are by Andy Aiona's Novelty Four, q.v.

Pseudonym on Supertone 9686 for Syd Valentine and his Patent Leather Kids, q.v.

## MIKE MOSIELLO AND HIS RADIO STARS

See the Grey Gull studio bands.

## JOSEPH MOSKOWITZ

Cembalom solos, acc. by Eddie King-p.    Camden, N. J., February 4, 1916.

17117-2  Operatic Rag (Julius Lenzberg)           Vic 17978
17118-1  Panama Pacific Drag (Leo Edwards)         -

Other titles by this artist are of Greek, Roumanian and Turkish folk music.

## SNUB MOSLEY AND HIS BAND

Bob Carroll-t/Snub Mosley-slide s-v/Willard Brown-as/Lloyd Phillips-p/Vernon King-sb/
A. G. Godley-d/Gordon Magey-v.          New York, March 11, 1940.

67288-A  Swinging With Mose - vSM                 Dec 7728
67289-A  Ol' Man River - vSM                      Dec 7768
67290-A  The Man With The Funny Little Horn-vSM    Dec 7728
67291-A  I'm Just A Substitute For Love - vGM      Dec 7768

Courtney Williams-t/Snub Mosley-slide s-tb-v,as shown/Don Stovall-as/Hank Duncan-p/
John Brown-sb/A. G. Godley-d/The Tampa Boys-v.
New York, October 21, 1941.

69842-A  Swampland - vSM&ch/sSM        Dec 8636, Coral 65020
69843-A  Snub's Blues - tbSM             -            -          Br 03449
69844-A  Sing A Little Ditty - s-vSM   Dec 8586
69845-B  Hey Man, Hey Man ! - vTB        -

Henry Smith-as-a replaces Stovall; Joe Smith-d replaces Godley; Hazel Diaz-v.
New York, February 11, 1942.

70306-A  'Deed I Do - vHD              Dec 8626
70307-A  Case Of The Blues - vHD        -
70308-A  Blues At High Noon - aHS     Dec 8614, Br 03462
70309-A  Between You And The Devil - vSM  -

## BENNIE MOTEN'S KANSAS CITY ORCHESTRA

Bennie Moten-p dir. Lammar Wright-c/Thamon Hayes-tb/Woody Walder-cl-ts-k effect/Sam
Tall-bj/Willie Hall-d.          St. Louis, September, 1923.

8459-A  Elephant's Wobble              OK 8100, Tpl 532
8460-A  Crawdad Blues                    -         -

Harry Cooper-c/Harlan Leonard-cl-as added. (Matrix 8773 is untraced).
St. Louis, c. November 29, 1924.

8769-B  South                          OK 8194
8770-A  Vine Street Blues                -
8771-A  Tulsa Blues                    OK 8184
8772-A  Goofy Dust                       -        WS 109
8774-A  Baby Dear                      OK 8213

LaForest Dent-bj replaces Tall; Vernon Page-bb added; William Little, Jr.-v.
Kansas City, c. May 14, 1925.

9118-A  She's Sweeter Than Sugar - vWL  OK 8255
9119-A  South Street Blues                -
9120-A  Sister Honky Tonk              OK 8277
9121-A  As I Like It                   OK 8213
9123-A  Things Seem So Blue To Me      OK 8242
9124-A  18th Street Strut                -
9125-A  Kater Street Rag               OK 8277, Par R-3256
NOTE:- Matrix 9122 is untraced.

Bennie Moten-p dir. Lammar Wright-c/Thamon Hayes-tb/Harlan Leonard-cl-as/LaForest
  Dent-as-bar/Woody Walder-cl-ts/Sam Tall-bj/Vernon Page-bb/Willie McWashington-d.
                                            Chicago, December 13, 1926.

| | | |
|---|---|---|
| 37232-1 | Thick Lip Stomp | Vic 20406, HMV B-5302 |
| 37232-2 | Thick Lip Stomp | HMV DLP-1057, Vic 741056 (LPs) |
| 37233-1 | Harmony Blues | Vic 20406, HMV B-5302 |
| 37233-2 | Harmony Blues | HMV DLP-1057, Vic 741056 (LPs) |
| 37234-1 | Kansas City Shuffle | Vic 20485, WS 109 |
| 37235-2 | Yazoo Blues | - |
| 37236-1 | White Lightnin' Blues | Vic 20811 |

                                            Chicago, December 14, 1926.

| | | |
|---|---|---|
| 37237-1 | Muscle Shoals Blues | Vic 20811 |
| 37238-1 | Midnight Mama | Vic 20422 |
| 37239-2 | Missouri Wobble | - |

Bennie Moten-p dir. Ed Lewis-Paul Webster-c/Thamon Hayes-tb-v/Harlan Leonard-cl-ss-as
  /Jack Washington-cl-as-bar/Woody Walder-cl-ts/LaForest Dent-as-ts-v/Leroy Berry-bj/
  Vernon Page-bb/Willie McWashington-d.   Chicago, June 11, 1927.

| | | |
|---|---|---|
| 38667-3 | Sugar | Vic 20855, X-16189, HMV B-5430 |
| 38668-4 | Dear Heart | - |
| 38669-2 | The New Tulsa Blues | Vic 21584 |
| 38670-3 | Baby Dear - vTH-LD | Vic 20946 |
| 38671-1 | 12th Street Rag | - |
| 38671-2 | 12th Street Rag | X LX-3025, Vic 741056 (LPs) |

NOTE:- Victor X-16189 is anonymous.
                                            Chicago, June 12, 1927.

| | | |
|---|---|---|
| 38672-3 | Pass Out Lightly (There Ain't Nothin'<br>    To It) | Vic 21199 |
| 38673-1 | Ding-Dong Blues - v3 | HMV DLP-1057, Vic 741056 (LPs) |
| 38673-2 | Ding-Dong Blues - v3 | Vic 21199 |
| 38673-3 | Ding-Dong Blues - v3 | Vic LPM-10122 (LP) |
| 38674-3 | Moten Stomp | Vic 20955, BB B-6204 |

NOTE:- Despite the label of PASS OUT LIGHTLY, there is no vocal on this side.

Booker Washington-c replaces Webster; Dent omitted; James Taylor-v.
                                            Camden, N. J., September 6, 1928.

| | | |
|---|---|---|
| 42924-1 | Justrite | Vic 21739 |
| 42924-2 | Justrite | X LX-3025 (LP) |
| 42925-1-2 | It's Hard To Laugh Or Smile - vJT | Rejected |
| 42926-3 | Slow Motion | Vic V-38012 |
| 42927-1 | Tough Breaks | Vic V-38037, BB B-6638 |

  Moten and Lewis speak*.                  Camden, N. J., September 7, 1928.

| | | |
|---|---|---|
| 42925-3-4 | It's Hard To Laugh Or Smile | Vic V-38037, BB B-6431, B-8228,<br>  HMV R-14294, El EG-1284 |
| 42928-2 | Sad Man Blues - vJT | Vic V-38048 |
| 42929-1 | Kansas City Breakdown | Vic 21693, HMV JF-17 |
| 42930-1 | Trouble In Mind | Vic 21739 |
| 42931-2 | Hot Water Blues | Vic V-38012, BB B-7938, HMV JF-17 |
| 42932-1-2 | When Life Seems So Blue - vJT | Rejected |
| 42933-1 | *Get Low-Down Blues | Vic 21693 |
| 42934-1 | She's No Trouble (Sweetheart) | Vic V-38021, 24893, A-1046 |
| 42935-1 | South | -        -       - |

NOTE:- Copies of Victor 24893 can be found on which both sides are pressed from
dubbed masters, others where only SOUTH is dubbed, and rarely where both sides are
pressed from original masters.  SOUTH also appeared as a dubbing on both sides of
Victor 44-0004.

Bennie Moten-p dir. Ed Lewis-Booker Washington-c/Thamon Hayes-tb/Harlan Leonard-cl-ss
   as/Jack Washington-cl-as-bar/Woody Walder-cl-ts/Ira "Buster" Moten-pac-2nd p/Leroy
   Berry-bj/Vernon Page-bb/Willie McWashington-d/Bob Clemmons-v.
                                              Chicago, July 16, 1929.

55420-1  Terrific Stomp                        Vic V-38081, BB B-6304
55421-3  Let's Get It                          Vic V-38072
55422-2  Kansas City Squabble                  Vic V-38091

                                              Chicago, July 17, 1929.

55423-1  Rite Tite                             Vic V-38104
55424-2  Moten's Blues                         Vic V-38072, BB B-7938
55425-1  That's What I'm Talking About         Vic V-38081
55426-1  That Certain Motion                   Vic V-38104
55427-1-2  It Won't Be Long - vBC              Rejected
55427-3  It Won't Be Long                      Vic V-38123

Instrumentation as shown individually.  Chicago, July 18, 1929.

42932-4  When Life Seems So Blue - all but pac  Vic V-38132
55428-2  Loose Like A Goose - clWW/2p/d         Vic V-38123
55429-1  Just Say It's Me-c/JW/WW/2p/bj/bb/d    Vic V-38132
55430-1  Now Goofy Dust - Rag (sic) - full band Vic V-38091, HMV R-14374
55431-1-2  Michigan Rag - 2p                    Rejected
NOTE:- Victor V-38123 as BUSTER MOTEN-BENNIE MOTEN.

Eddie Durham-tb-g-a added; Count Basie-p replaces Bennie Moten, who now directs
   without playing.                          Chicago, October 23, 1929.

57301-1  Rumba Negro (Spanish Stomp)           Vic 23037, HMV B-4845
57302-2  The Jones Law Blues                   Vic 23357
57303-1  Band Box Shuffle                      Vic 23007, BB B-6710
57304-3  Small Black                           Vic 23342
57305-2  Every Day Blues (Yo Yo Blues)         Vic V-38144, 1AC-0442

Willie McWashington-v.                       Chicago, October 24, 1929.

57312-3  Boot It                               Vic V-38144, 1AC-0442
57313-3  Mary Lee                              Vic V-38114, BB B-6638
57314-2  Rit-Dit-Ray - vWM                     Vic 23342
57315-1  New Vine Street Blues                 Vic LPV-514 (LP)
57315-2  New Vine Street Blues                 Vic 23007, BB B-6710
57316-2  Sweetheart Of Yesterday               Vic V-38114, BB B-6851

Oran "Hot Lips" Page-t added; Jimmy Rushing-v.
                                              Kansas City, October 27, 1930.

62909-1  Won't You Be My Baby ? - vJR          Vic LPV-514 (LP)
62909-2  Won't You Be My Baby ? - vJR          Vic 23028, BB B-6711

                                              Kansas City, October 28, 1930.

62910-2  I Wish I Could Be Blue                Vic 22734
62911-2  Oh ! Eddie                            Vic 22958, HMV B-4986
62912-1  That Too, Do - vJR                    Vic LPM-10023 (LP)
62912-2  That Too, Do - vJR                    Vic 22793, HMV B-4912
62913-1  Mack's Rhythm                         Vic LPM-10023 (LP)
62914-1  You Made Me Happy                     Pirate MPC-521 (LP)
62915-1  Here Comes Marjorie                   Vic 23391
62916-1  The Count                                -    BB B-6719

                                              Kansas City, October 29, 1930.

62921-1  Liza Lee - vJR                        Vic 23023, Zon EE-285

Bennie Moten dir. Ed Lewis-Booker Washington-Hot Lips Page-t/Thamon Hayes-tb/Eddie
Durham-tb-g-a/Harlan Leonard-cl-ss-as/Jack Washington-cl-as-bar/Woody Walder-cl-ts/
Count Basie-p-v/Buster Moten-pac/Leroy Berry-bj/Vernon Page-bb/Willie McWashington-
d/Jimmy Rushing-v.                          Kansas City, October 30, 1930.

| | | |
|---|---|---|
| 62922-2 | Get Goin' (Get Ready To Love) - vJR | Vic 23023, Zon EE-285 |
| 62923-1 | Professor Hot Stuff | Vic 23429 |
| 62924-2 | When I'm Alone - vJR | Vic 22734 |
| 62925-2 | New Moten Stomp | Vic 23030, BB B-6709 |
| 62926-2 | As Long As I Love You (Jeannette) - vJR | Vic 22660, HMV B-4912 |

                                            Kansas City, October 31, 1930.

| | | |
|---|---|---|
| 62927-1 | Somebody Stole My Gal - vCB | Vic 23028, BB B-5481, B-6709, MW M-4894, HMV B-4844 |
| 62928-1 | Now That I Need You - vJR | BB B-6711 |
| 62929-2 | Bouncin' Round | Vic 23030 |
| 62930-1 | Break A Day Schuffle (sic) | Rejected |

                                            New York, April 15, 1931.

| | | |
|---|---|---|
| 53012-2 | Ya Got Love - vJR | Vic 22680, HMV B-4889 |
| 68900-2 | I Wanna Be Around My Baby All The Time - vJR | - |

Bennie Moten dir. Hot Lips Page-Joe Keyes-Dee Stewart-t/Dan Minor-tb/Eddie Durham-tb-
g-a/Eddie Barefield-cl-as/Jack Washington-as-bar/Ben Webster-ts/Count Basie-p/Leroy
Berry-g/Walter Page-sb/Willie McWashington-d/Jimmy Rushing-Josephine Garrison-The
Sterling Russell Trio (Sterling Russell-Hamilton Stewart-Clifton Armstrong)-v; Hot
Lips Page-Barefield-Basie-Durham-g-Walter Page/Willie McWashington only*.
                                            Camden, N. J., December 13, 1932.

| | | |
|---|---|---|
| 74846-1 | Toby | Vic 23384, DC-17, BB B-6032, B-10259, HMV B-4986, B-6426 |
| 74847-1 | Moten Swing | Vic 23384  BB B-6032, B-10259, HMV B-6377 |
| 74848-1 | The Blue Room (Curatito de Dichas*) | Vic 24381, 32212*, BB B-5585, HMV B-4990 |
| 74849-1 | Imagination - vSR3 | Vic 23378, BB B-5078, Sr S-3159 |
| 74850-1 | New Orleans - vJR | Vic 24216, 28160, BB B-6218, B-10955 |
| 74851-1 | The Only Girl I Ever Loved - vSR3 | Vic 23378, BB B-5078, Sr S-3159 |
| 74852-1 | Milenberg Joys (Estrambotico*) | Vic 24381, 32212*, BB B-5585, HMV B-4953 |
| 74853-1 | Lafayette | Vic 24216, 28160, BB B-10955, HMV B-4953, B-6390 |
| 74854-1 | Prince Of Wails | Vic 23393, A-1294, BB B-6851 |
| 74855-1 | *Two Times - vJG | - |

NOTE:- Victor 32212 as DON BENJAMIN Y SU ORQUESTA DE JAZZ PURO (!)

## MOULIN ROUGE ORCHESTRA

Pseudonym on Banner 1492 and Regal 9784 for Ben Selvin and his Orchestra, q.v.

## MOUND CITY  BLUE BLOWERS

Red McKenzie-comb/Dick Slevin-k/Jack Bland-bj.
                                            Chicago, February 23, 1924.

| | | |
|---|---|---|
| 77-CH | Arkansaw Blues (sic) | Br 2581* |
| 80-CH | Blue Blues | - |

Frank Trumbauer-Cm added.                   Chicago, March 13, 1924.

| | | |
|---|---|---|
| 103/105-CH | Red Hot ! | Br rejected |

                                            Chicago, March 14, 1924.

| | | |
|---|---|---|
| 112-CH | San | Br 2602* |
| 114-CH | Red Hot ! | - |

Red McKenzie-comb/Dick Slevin-k/Jack Bland-bj.
                              New York, July 9, 1924.

13491/3  Barb Wire Blues                  Br 2648*

                              New York, July 10, 1924.

13501/3  You Ain't Got Nothin' I Want     Br 2648*

    Eddie Lang-g added.       New York, December 10, 1924.

14438    Tiger Rag                         Br 2804*
14440    Deep Second Street Blues          -

                              New York, February 4, 1925.

14806/7  Play Me Slow                      Br rejected

                              New York, February 9, 1925.

14872/4  Gettin' Told                      Br 2849*
14875/6  Play Me Slow                      -

                              New York, March 24, 1925.

  596/8; 15775  Wigwam Blues               Br 2908*

                              New York, March 25, 1925.

  611/2; 15778  Blues in F                 Br 2908*
NOTE:- These two titles were originally recorded for Vocalion, and were allocated
their Brunswick matrix numbers on May 24, 1925 while the band was in London.  It
has been suggested that they were recorded there, but this is not so.

Red McKenzie-comb-v/Bruce Yantis-vn*/Eddie Condon-bj-v/Jack Bland-g-v/Gene Krupa-d-v.
                              New York, August 19, 1929.

148895-3 *Indiana - vRM                    Col 1946-D
148896-2 Firehouse Blues - vEC-JB-GK       -

Red McKenzie-comb-v/Jack Teagarden-tb-v/Eddie Condon-bj-v/Jack Bland-g-v/Pops Foster-
    sb/Josh Billings-d.       New York, September 25, 1929.

56151-1  Tailspin Blues - vRM-JT-EC-JB     Vic V-38087, BB B-6456, B-10209,
                                           HMV B-6252, BD-5758, EA-3040,
                                           JK-2877, K-6951
56152-3  Never Had A Reason To Believe In You-vRM  Vic V-38087, BB B-6270, B-10209,
                                           HMV BD-187, K-6951
NOTE:- Bluebird B-10209 as RED McKENZIE AND THE MOUND CITY BLUE BLOWERS.

Red McKenzie-comb/Glenn Miller-tb/Pee Wee Russell-cl/Coleman Hawkins-ts/Eddie Condon-
    bj/Jack Bland-g/Pops Foster-sb/Gene Krupa-d.
                              New York, November 14, 1929.

57145-3  Hello, Lola                       Vic V-38100, 62-0058, BB B-6270,
                                           B-10037, HMV B-6168, B-8952,
                                           EA-2963, JK-2260, JO-149, K-6501,
                                           K-8525, El EG-7729
57146-3  One Hour                          Vic V-38100, 62-0058, BB B-6456,
                                           B-10037, HMV B-6150, B-8952,
                                           EA-2963, JK-2260, JO-149, K-6501,
                                           K-8525, El EG-7729
NOTE:- Bluebird B-10037, HMV B-8952 and JO-149 as RED McKENZIE AND THE MOUND CITY
BLUE BLOWERS.

Red McKenzie-comb-v/Muggsy Spanier-c/Jimmy Dorsey-cl-as/Coleman Hawkins-ts/Jack
  Russin-p/Eddie Condon-bj/Jack Bland-g/Al Morgan-sb/Josh Billings-d/2nd v (? Eddie
  Condon).                                New York, June 30, 1931.

404966-C  Georgia On My Mind - vRM              OK 41515, Cl 5389-C, Har 1375-H,
                                                VT 2453-V, UHCA 51, Par R-1071,
                                                85104, Od A-286051, 031813,
                                                Re G-21480
404967-B  I Can't Believe That You're In Love   OK 41515, Cl 5389-C, Har 1375-H,
          With Me - vRM                          VT 2453-V, UHCA 52, Par R-1003,
                                                A-3339, 85104, Od A-286044,OR-1003
404994-A  The Darktown Strutters' Ball - vRM    OK 41526, Col 5392-C, Har 1378-H,
                                                VT 2456-V, Col 36281, C-6180,
                                                Par R-1044, 85184, A-3282,B-71213,
                                                Od A-286048, B-35638, 031813
404995-A  You Rascal, You - vRM-? EC             OK 41526, Cl 5392-C, Lar 1378-H,
                                                VT 2456-V, Col DB-5007, Par 85184,
                                                A-3282
NOTE:- UHCA 51/52 and Columbia 36281, C-6180 and DB-5007 as RED McKENZIE AND THE
MOUND CITY BLUE BLOWERS; all Harmony, Clarion and Velvet Tone issues as TENNESSEE
MUSIC MEN; all Parlophones (except A-3339, correctly labelled) and Odeons as RED
McKENZIE AND THE CELESTIAL BEINGS; Australian Regal G-21480 as MISSISSIPPI JAZZ
KINGS.  Only the OKehs bear the correct artist credit and matrix numbers as shown;
all the others have a 351000 series matrix number.  Despite the gap in the OKeh
numbering, these four sides were all made on the same day.

Red McKenzie-comb-v/Bunny Berigan-t/Al Philburn-tb/Eddie Miller-cl-ts/Gil Bowers-p/
 Nappy Lamare-g/Harry Goodman-sb/Ray Bauduc-d.
                                        New York, May 9, 1935.

17515-1  What's The Reason (I'm Not Pleasin' You) Voc 2957, Br 02061, A-86046
         - vRM
17516-1  She's A Latin From Manhattan - vRM     -            -           -
17517-1  You've Been Takin' Lessons - vRM       Voc 2973, Br A-500562
17518-1  Indiana - vRM                          -            -

Red McKenzie-comb/Yank Lawson-t/Eddie Miller-cl-ts/Nappy Lamare-g-v/Bob Haggart-sb/
  Ray Bauduc-d.                         New York, November 8, 1935.

60137-A  Red Sails In The Sunset - vNL          Ch 40060, MW 5001
60138-A  I'm Sittin' High On A Hill Top - vNL   Ch 40059, MW 5000
60139-A-B  On Treasure Island - vNL             Ch 40060, MW 5001
60140-A  Thanks A Million - vNL                 Ch 40059, MW 5000

  Pete Peterson-sb replaces Haggart.    New York, December 12, 1935.

60219-A  Eeney Meeney Miney Mo - vNL            Ch 40073, Pan 25842
60220-A  A Little Bit Independent - vNL         -
60221-A  I'm Shootin' High - vNL                Ch 40076
60222-A  I've Got My Fingers Crossed - vNL      -          Pan 25842
60223-A  High Society (High Society Blues*)     Ch 40103, Dec 1274*, F-7808,
                                                Y-6096, Br 80157
60224-A  Muskrat Ramble                         As above
NOTE:- Panachord 25842 as LEN HERMAN AND HIS ORCHESTRA.

Red McKenzie-comb/Bunny Berigan-t/Forrest Crawford-cl-ts/Dave Barbour-g/Mort Stuhl-
  maker-sb/Dave Tough-d/v trio.         New York, January 3, 1936.

60295-A  The Broken Record - v3                 Pan 25841
60295-B  The Broken Record - v3                 Ch 40081, MW 5022
60296-A  The Music Goes 'Round And Around - v3  -          -
NOTE:- Panachord 25841 as LEN HERMAN AND HIS ORCHESTRA.

Red McKenzie-comb/Bunny Berigan-t/Forrest Crawford-cl-ts/Eddie Condon-Carmen Mastreng/Sid Weiss-sb/Stan King-d/Spooky Dickenson-v.
                                     New York, January 8, 1936.

60311-A  I'm Gonna Sit Right Down And Write Myself Ch 40082, Pan 25841, Dec Y-5115
           A Letter - vSD
60312-A  Mama Don't Allow It - vSD            Ch 40091, Dec F-5905
60313-A  (If I Had) Rhythm In My Nursery Rhymes-vSDCh 40082    -      Y-5115
60314-A-B  I Hope Gabriel Likes My Music - vSD   Ch 40091
NOTE:- Panachord 25841 as LEN HERMAN AND HIS ORCHESTRA.

Red McKenzie-w where shown/Bunny Berigan-t/Al Philburn-tb/Sid Trucker-cl-as/Frank
   Signorelli-p/Dave Barbour-g/Pete Peterson-sb/Dave Tough-d/Billy Wilson (as BILLY
   HILL on Decca F-5926)-v.            New York, February 17, 1936.

60481-A  You Hit The Spot - vBW            Ch 40098, Dec F-5926, Pan 25847
60482-A  Spreadin' Rhythm Around - vBW         -
60483-A  Saddle Your Blues To A Wild Mustang-vBW  Ch 40099    -      Pan 25846
60484-A-B  Wah-Hoo ! - vBW                  -    Dec F-5949, Pol 15299
60485-A  I'm Gonna Clap My Hands - vBW/wRM     Ch 40103    -
NOTE:- Panachord 25846 and 25847 as LEN HERMAN AND HIS ORCHESTRA.

See also Red McKenzie.

## THE  MOUNTAINEERS SERENADERS

Pseudonym on Parlophone E-6310 (MONA) for Sam Lanin and his Famous Players, q.v.

## KEN "GOOF" MOYER

Clarinet-bass clarinet-alto saxophone-mellophone solos in turn, acc. by Phil Oliwitz-
   vn/Fred Rich-p-cel/Ray Bauduc-d.      New York, c. July 7, 1926.

106977   Mellophone Stomp               PA 36511, 11280, Per 14692
106978   Idol Of My Eyes                PA 36528    -    Per 14709

KEN MOYER'S NOVELTY TRIO : As above; Oliwitz or Bauduc db k where shown; Rich-p only.
                                     New York, c. October 1, 1926.

6857-3   Stampede                  Ban 1872,Dom 3841,Or 762,Re 8183
6858-3   The Arkansas Mule           -        -        -
NOTE:- Oriole 762 as DIXIE JAZZ BAND; Regal 8183 as KEN MEYERS.

                                     New York, c. November 19, 1926.

6948 ?   Echoes Of Oklahoma          Ban 1891, Dom 3861, Re 8203
6949 ?   Mellophone Stomp             -        -        -

## MAE MUFF

Pseudonym on Varsity for Mae Glover, q.v.

## GUS MULCAY

Harmonica solo, acc. by Eddie King-p.    New York, February 18, 1926.

        Farewell Blues                Vic test (un-numbered)

   Acc. by Irving Sherman-p.          New York, June 18, 1926.


142316-1  St. Louis Blues              Har 408-H
142317-1  Farewell Blues                -

Other records by this artist are of little or no interest as jazz, being more in the
   nature of "novelty" and hillbilly items.

JIMMY MUNDY AND HIS SWING CLUB SEVEN : Walter Fuller-t-v/Trummy Young-tb/Omer Simeon-
cl-as/Jimmy Mundy-ts-a/Billy Kyle-p/Dick Palmer-g/Quinn Wilson-sb/Chick Webb-d.
New York, March 3, 1937.

| | | |
|---|---|---|
| M-159-1 | I Surrender, Dear - vWF | Vri 598 |
| M-160-1 | Ain't Misbehavin' - vWF | - |

JIMMY MUNDY AND HIS ORCHESTRA : Jimmy Mundy-a dir. Frank Galbreath-Bobby Moore-Leroy
Hill-t/Ed Johnson-Ed McConnell-Norman Greene-tb/Ted Barnett-Skippy Williams-as, one
db bsx/Al Gibson-Jimmy Hamilton-cl-ts/Bill Doggett-p/Connie Wainwright-g/Jack
Jarvis-sb/Shadow Wilson-d/Madeleine Greene-v.
New York, December 19, 1939.

| | | |
|---|---|---|
| US-1181-1 | Sunday Special | Var 8148 |
| US-1182-1 | Little Old Lady From Baltimore - vMG&ch | Var 8136 |
| US-1183-1 | All Aboard | Var 8148 |
| US-1184-1 | A Lover Is Blue - vMG | Var 8136 |

## RONNIE MUNRO

Although none of the following interesting dance records was issued under Ronnie
Munro's name, they were all made under his direction.

MIMOSA DANCE ORCHESTRA : Ronnie Munro-p dir. ? Max Goldberg and another-t/Lew Davis-
tb/Ben Davis-cl-as/Arthur Lally-as-bar/Buddy Featherstonhaugh-cl-ts/bj/bb/Max Bacon
d.                                    London, June 15, 1927.

| | | |
|---|---|---|
| E-460-2 | Black Bottom | Mimosa P-137 (6-inch) |

ROOF GARDEN ORCHESTRA : Same instrumentation, plus vn; Perley Breed-cl-as-bar replaces Lally, others unknown; Maurice Elwin-v.
London, April, 1928.

| | | |
|---|---|---|
| E-1862-2 | Nebraska - vME | Par R-102, A-2508 |

London, c. June 14, 1928.

| | | |
|---|---|---|
| E-1969-2 | Singapore Sorrows | Par R-159 |

COMEDY DANCE ORCHESTRA : Probably similar; Leslie Sarony-v.
London, August, 1928.

| | | |
|---|---|---|
| E-2052-2 | I Left My Sugar Standing In The Rain-vLS | Par E-4579 |
| E-2054-2 | Ammoniated Tincture Of Quinine - vLS | - |
| E-2055-2 | How Long Has This Been Going On ? - vLS | Par E-6076 |

## LYLE "SPUD" MURPHY AND HIS ORCHESTRA

Spud Murphy-cl-as-a dir. Nate Kazebier-Joe Meyer-Oliver Suderman-t/Al Sherman-Joe
Harris-tb/Bill DePew-cl/Earl Boyle-as/Dick Petit-Bill Covey-ts/Chuck Edwards-p/Al
Costi-g/Woody Bushell-sb/Mack Halladay-d.
Los Angeles, April 21, 1938.

| | | |
|---|---|---|
| DLA-1264-A | Quaker City Jazz | Dec 2040 |
| DLA-1265-A | Cherokee | - |
| DLA-1266-A | Trans-Continental | Dec 1853, Voc S-203 |
| DLA-1267-A | Ecstacy | Dec 2109, Y-5337, Voc S-213 |
| DLA-1268-A | Dancing With A Debutante | -         -         - |
| DLA-1269-A | My Little Girl | Dec 1853, Voc S-203 |

Spud Murphy-cl-as-a dir. John Lincoln-Stanley Wilson-Sid Feldstein-t/Gus Mayhew-Cappy
Crouse-tb/Ted Duane-Pete Brendel-as/Carl Biesacker-ts/Clyde Rogers-ts-v/Mark Hyams-
p/Michael Storme-sb/Harry Fulterman-d/Lucy Ann Matthews-v.
New York, February 14, 1939.

| | | |
|---|---|---|
| 033720-1 | Hold Out For Love | BB B-10157 |
| 033721-1 | Blame It On My Last Affair - vLAM | BB B-10151 |
| 033722-1 | Just A Phrase | BB B-10157 |
| 033723-1 | It's Easy To Blame The Weather - vCR | BB B-10151 |

Spud Murphy dir. Frank Beraidi-Stanley Wilson-Frank Wysochanski-t/Bill Heathcock-Bill
    Abel-tb/Ted Duane-Pete Brendel-as/Charles Brosen-Clyde Rogers-ts/Mark Hyams-p/Ken
    Binford-g/Michael Storme-sb/Ed O'Hara-d. New York, December 4, 1939.

| | | |
|---|---|---|
| 043949-1 | Dance Of The Doinks | BB B-10539 |
| 043950-1 | Pinetop Breakaway | BB B-10875, RZ G-24549 |
| 043951-1 | Sand Dune | -        - |
| 043952-1 | Booly Ja-Ja (Jungle Dance) | BB B-10539 |

## MURRAY'S MELODY MAKERS

Usually a pseudonym on Edison Bell Winner for the company's "house" band, directed by
    Harry Hudson, q.v., this name was also applied to Ernie Golden and his Orchestra
    (q.v.) playing MAKIN' WHOOPEE (EBW 4961).

## MURRAY'S RAGTIME TRIO/BANJO QUARTET

MURRAY'S RAGTIME TRIO : Bill Blanche-bj/Dave Comer-p/Harry Robbins, Sr.-d, acc. by
    the Mayfair Orchestra : James Sale dir. 2t/2tb/cl/f/pic/2vn/bb, members of the
    London Palladium Orchestra of the period.
                                            Hayes, Middlesex, April 8, 1915.

| | | |
|---|---|---|
| HO-743ac | Hors d'oeuvres (Dave Comer) | HMV C-399 |
| HO-744ac | Beets And Turnips (Cliff Hess-Fred Ahlert) | - |

MURRAY'S RAGTIME BANJO QUARTET : As above, plus Joe Wilbur-bj, acc. by the Bohemian
    Band (apparently t/tb/f/vn/bb).          London, c. April, 1915.

| | | |
|---|---|---|
| 4729-2 | Hors d'oeuvres (Dave Comer) | EBW 2871 |
| 4730-1 | Beets And Turnips (Cliff Hess-Fred Ahlert) | - |

## MURRAY'S SAVOY QUARTET

This title is the only one by this unit without a vocal, and the only one likely to
    be of interest to the student of ragtime. See also Comer and Blanche; Murray's
    Ragtime Trio, and the Savoy Quartet.

Joe Wilbur-Bill Blanche-bj/Dave Comer-p/Harry Robbins, Sr.-d.
                                            London, November 13, 1915.

| | | |
|---|---|---|
| 19672e | Hide And Seek (Dave Comer) | HMV B-575 |

## BILLY MURRAY

Billy Murray's recording career began in 1903 and continued almost unbroken until
    1942. Although he was a light comedian and in no sense a jazz artist, on the
    following sides he was accompanied by musicians who were.

Vocal, acc. by the Seven Blue Babies : T/tb/cl/p/bj/bb/d.
                                            New York, October 5, 1928.

| | | |
|---|---|---|
| 18786; N-484 | Doin' The Raccoon | Rejected |
| 18787 | Ho-Ho-Ho-Hogan | Ed 52448 |
| N-485 | Ho-Ho-Ho-Hogan | Rejected |

Acc. by the Seven Blue Babies : Angie Rattiner-t/Carl Loffler-tb/Carl Orech-cl-as/
    Chauncey Gray-p/Tommy Felline-bj-g/Stan King-d.
                                            New York, November 8, 1928.

| | | |
|---|---|---|
| 18857 | Doin' The Raccoon | Ed 52448 |
| N-555 | Doin' The Raccoon | Rejected |
| 18858 | Don't Do That To The Poor Puss Cat | Ed 52454 |
| N-556 | Don't Do That To The Poor Puss Cat | Rejected |

Acc. by the Merry Melody Men : As above, plus Al Duffy-vn, but Miff Mole-tb re-
    places Loffler.          New York, January 5, 1929.

| | | |
|---|---|---|
| 18987; N-678 | A Gay Caballero | Ed rejected |
| 18988; N-679 | Ever Since The Movies Learned To Talk | - |

Acc. by the Merry Melody Men : Angie Rattiner-t/Miff Mole-tb/Carl Orech-cl-as/Al
Duffy-vn/Chauncey Gray-p/Tommy Felline-bj-g/Stan King-d.
                                        New York, January 22, 1929.

| 18987 | A Gay Caballero | Ed 52518 |
| N-678 | A Gay Caballero | Rejected |
| 13988 | Ever Since The Movies Learned To Talk | Ed 52518 |
| N-679 | Ever Since The Movies Learned To Talk | Rejected |

## GLADYS MURRAY

Pseudonym on Banner and Regal for Clementine Smith, q.v.

## JAMES MURRAY'S COLORED SYNCOPATED HARMONY KINGS

James Murray dir. Oscar Howard-t/Aaron Thompson-tb/Bernardin S. Brown-as/Billy Taylor
Elmer W. Harrell-vn/Walter R. Johnson-p/Clark Goodly-sb/Harry Nickens-d.
                                        New York, c. April, 1921.

| 1252-B | What Could Be Sweeter, Dear ? | Murray (un-numbered) |
| 1253-A | Cheer Up, Kentucky | - |

## JIMMY MURRAY AND HIS MUSIC MASTERS

Pseudonym on Arcadia 2043 for Fred Rich and his Orchestra, q.v.

## JOE MURRAY

Piano solo.                             Richmond, Ind., October 24, 1921.

| 11031 | Tenth Interval Rag (? Herman Ruby) | Gnt rejected |

## MUSE NOVELTY SEXTET

Pseudonym on Muse for the Varsity Eight, q.v.

## THE MUSICAL AVOLOS

This was a British music-hall act specializing in xylophone duets, but the following
show that they not only featured stringed instruments, but were well aware of the
existence of original ragtime under that name during the closing years of the
Victorian era and the nineteenth century.

Guitar and mandolin duet.               London, May 4, 1899.

| 2059 | March from Rice's Ragtime Opera | Ber 7350 |

## THE MUSICAL COMRADES

Pseudonym for the following items listed in this book :-

Muse 416  Wop Blues (Johnny Johnson and his Orchestra)
     491  Knock At The Door (Varsity Eight)
     498  I Can't Find A Name Sweet Enough For You (Varsity Eight)
Tremont 0515  Copenhagen (Varsity Eight)
     0544  If You Knew Susie (Varsity Eight)

## THE MUSICAL MANIACS

Irving Fazola-cl/Lloyd Reiner-g/Manny Stein-sb/Lou Singer-d/Bud Johnson-v.
                                        New York, July 26, 1937.

| 21432- | Down By The Old Mill Stream | Voc 3691 |
| 21433-1 | Pagan Love Song - vBJ | Voc 3655 |
| 21434- | Am I Blue ? | Voc 3691 |
| 21435-1 | Somebody Stole My Gal | Voc 3655, S-135 |

Freddy Jenkins-Louis Metcalf-t/Henry Hicks-tb/Clarence Grimes-Charlie Holmes-cl-ss-
   as/Cliff Jackson-p-cymbal/Elmer Snowden-bj/Bud Hicks-bb/scat v.
                                          New York, January 30, 1929.

147899-3  Happy Rhythm                          Col 14406-D
147900-3  Honeycomb Harmony                     -

## MUSICAL TRIO

See the Novelty Blue Boys.

## THE MUSICAL VOYAGERS

Pseudonym on Parlophone PNY-34152 and PNY-34153 for the Travelers (see the Dorsey
   Brothers' Orchestra).

## THE  MUSIC MASTERS

See Jay Whidden.

## MUSTANG BAND OF  SOUTHERN METHODIST UNIVERSITY

Tom Johnson dir. Garner Clark-t/others.  Los Angeles, January 2, 1936.

DLA-291-   Limehouse Blues                      Dec 706
DLA-292-   Peruna (S. M. U. Song)               Dec 705
DLA-293-   Eeney, Meeney, Miney, Mo             Dec 706
DLA-294-   Tiger Rag                            Rejected
DLA-295-   Sugar Blues                          -
DLA-296-   St. Louis Blues                      -
DLA-297-   College Medley                       Dec 705

## VICK MYERS' ATLANTA MELODY ARTISTS

2c/tb/cl-ss/as/ts/vn/Taylor Flannigan-p/bj/bb/d/Billy Meyers-v/Lambdin Kay, of
   Station WSB Atlanta, comperes*.         Atlanta, January 10, 1925.

 8853-A  Blue Eyed Sally                        OK 40281
 8854-A  If You Don't Want Me, Stop Doggin' Me 'Round-

                                          Atlanta, April 14, 1925.

 9050-B  Oh ! That Sweet In Suite 16 - vBM      OK 40386

                                          Atlanta, April 15, 1925.

 9059-A  Sweet Man Blues                        OK 40386
 9060-A  *Mamie                                 OK 40364
 9061-A  *Flag That Train (To Alabam')          -

                                          Atlanta, July 5-6, 1925.

 9220-A  Save Your Sorrow                       OK 40434, Od 03309, 5672
 9226-A  Nantucket Nan                          -        -        -

                                          Atlanta, March 16, 1926.

 9630-A  I'd Rather Be Alone - vBM              OK 40614

Other titles by Vic Myers' Music (Columbia, 1929) are of no interest, being waltzes.

## THE  MYSTERY ORCHESTRA

Red McKenzie-tin can-v/? Dick Slevin-tin can/bj/Jack Bland-g/Josh Billings-suitcase.
   (The tin-cans are probably kazoos).   Chicago, February 23, 1929.

50517-1-2  Arkansas Blues - vRM                 Vic rejected
50518-1-2  Never Had A Reason To Believe In You    -

Gregoire Nakchounian-cl-as dir. Martin Helsmuorte-c/Julian Testaert-tb/Albert
Deveydt-cl-ts-bsx/Jean (John) Paques-p/Erwin Steinbacher-bj/Eugene t'Sas-d/some-
times vn and k added/v.                Berlin, December, 1926.

| 890-D | Brotherly Love - v | Vox H-10268-E |
| 892-D | Schreeveport Stomp (sic) | Vox H-10269-E |

Berlin, January, 1927.

| 919-D | She Was Just A Sailor's Sweetheart | Vox H-10270-E |
| 920-D | Wa Wa Wa | - |
| 921-D | Katinka | Vox H-10269-E |
| 922-D | Krazy Kapers (GN-as/JP-p only) | Vox H-10271-E |
| 924-D | Sugar Baby - v | Vox H-10268-E |

## MABEL NANCE

Pseudonym on Silvertone for Thelma La Vizzo, q.v.

## PHIL NAPOLEON

PHIL NAPOLEON AND HIS ORCHESTRA : Phil Napoleon-t dir. Warren Hookway and/or Reece
Henry-t/Dave Harman-tb/Carroll Thorne-Carl Irish-cl-ss-as/Frank Ward-cl-ss-ts/Harry
Hoffman-vn/Steve Kretzmer-p/Dave Skine-bj/Edward Stern-bb/Eddie Schaaf-d.
                                   New York, December 23, 1926.

| 11394 | Go, Joe, Go | Ed 51908 |
| 11395 | Tiger Rag | - |

Phil Napoleon-t dir. Warren Hookway or John Azevedo-t/Ted Raph-tb/Carroll Thorne-
Carl Irish-cl-ss-as/Frank Ward-cl-ss-ts/Frank Vigneau-p/Dave Skine-bj/Al Kunze-bb/
Charlie Jondro-d/Jack Kaufman-v.     New York, February 7, 1927.

| 37744-1-2-3 | Tiger Rag | Rejected |
| 37745-2 | Clarinet Marmalade | Vic 20647 |

New York, February 24, 1927.

| 11539 | It Made You Happy When You Made Me Cry | Ed 51960, Amb 5309 |
|  | - vJK |  |
| 11540 | The Cat | Ed 51962 |

New York, March 22, 1927.

| 11594 | Rubber Heels | Ed 52021 |
| 11595 | Clarinet Marmalade | - |

2nd tb added; Billy Murray-v.        New York, March 31, 1927.

| 38313-1 | Take Your Finger Out Of Your Mouth-vBM | Vic 20605, HMV B-5331, EA-198 |
| 38314-2 | Go, Joe, Go | -    - |

One of the saxes db f; J. Donald Parker-v.
                                   New York, April 6, 1927.

| 11628 | Mary Dear, I Miss You Most Of All - vJDP | Ed 51996 |
| 11629 | La Lo La | Ed 51997 |
| 11630 | Underneath The Weeping Willow | Ed 51996 |

New York, November 12, 1927.

| 18027 | Moon Of Japan | Rejected |
| 18028 | Five Pennies | Ed 52147 |

NAPOLEON'S EMPERORS : Phil Napoleon-t/Tommy Dorsey-tb/Jimmy Dorsey-cl-as/Joe Venuti-
vn/Frank Signorelli-p/Eddie Lang-g/Joe Tarto-sb/Stan King-d.
                                   New York, May 14, 1929.

| 53615-3 | Mean To Me | Vic V-38057, BB B-6574, B-7101 |
| 53616-2 | My Kinda Love | -    -    - |

NAPOLEON'S EMPERORS : Phil Napoleon-t/Tommy Dorsey-tb/Jimmy Dorsey-cl-as/Joe Venuti-vn
/Frank Signorelli-p/Eddie Lang-g/Joe Tarto-bb/Ted Napoleon-d.
New York, May 23, 1929.

```
53506-2  Gettin' Hot (Waterloo)                  Vic 23039, HMV B-4890
53507-2  Anything (Thunder In My Dreams*)        Vic V-38069, BB B-7039*,HMV B-4955
53508-1-2  You Can't Cheat A Cheater               -                  - BD-120
NOTE:- Victor 23039 and HMV B-4890 as JOE VENUTI AND HIS ORCHESTRA.
```

PHIL NAPOLEON AND HIS ORCHESTRA : Phil Napoleon-t dir. Jesse Ralph-tb/Carl Orech and
another-as/John Sadola-ts/Carl Biesacker-cl-ts/Mac Sanfield-Walter Scott-Mac Ceppos-
vn/Al Ulin-p/g/stg/Harry Cohn-sb/d/Val Bolton-Lola Bard-v.
New York, March 31, 1937.

```
M-341-1-2  All God's Chillun Got Rhythm          Vri rejected
M-342-1-2  Solitary Soul - vLB                        -
M-343-1-2  Blue Venetian Waters - vVB                 -
M-344-1-2  Music Makin' Man                           -
```

Phil Napoleon-t dir. Ford Leary-tb-v/2as/ts/3vn/p/g/sb/d/Ruth Denning-v.
New York, September 14, 1937.

```
M-628-1-2  Love Me (As I Love You) - vRD         Vri 656, Voc 3792
M-629-1  That's A Plenty                         Vri 669, Voc 3800
M-630-2-3  Blue Bayou - vFL                      Vri 656, Voc 3792
M-631-1  Swing Patrol                            Vri 669, Voc 3800
NOTE:- Variety 656 and Vocalion 3792 as PHIL NAPOLEON AND HIS WHISPERING RHYTHM;
Variety 669 and Vocalion 3800 as PHIL NAPOLEON AND HIS EMPERORS OF RHYTHM.
```

Three sides on Pathe Actuelle and Perfect (matrices 107266/8) by Phil Napoleon and his
Orchestra are by the same band as the first Edison session, but offer nothing to
interest a jazz enthusiast.

## WILLIAM NAPPI AND  HIS ORCHESTRA

William Nappi-t dir. t/tb/2cl-as/cl-ts/p/bj/bb/d.
Atlanta, April 22, 1926.

```
142090-2  If You Just Knew                       Col 1262-D
142091-1-2  No 'Count Blues                      Rejected
```

Atlanta, April 4, 1927.

```
143881-2  I'll Dream Of You                      Col 1042-D
143882-3  Look Me Over                                -
```

## SAM NASH AND HIS ORCHESTRA

Pseudonym on American Parlophone for Ben Selvin and his Orchestra, q.v. for titles of
jazz interest; also for Phil Dannenberg and his Orchestra on Parlophone PNY-34187,
q.v.

## NASHVILLE  JAZZERS

Tom Morris-c/Bob Fuller-cl/as/? Mike Jackson-p/bj.
New York, c. 1927.

```
102-A-B  St. Louis Blues                  VD/Mad 5001, 50001, VD 7023,MF 102
NOTE:- The matrix number shown here is probably false, but all copies inspected show
only this.
```

## NATIONAL MUSIC LOVERS DANCE ORCHESTRA

Pseudonym on National Music Lovers Records for the following items listed in this
book :-

```
1097  Charley, My Boy (Fletcher Henderson and his Orchestra)
1123  I Miss My Swiss (California Ramblers)
1134  I'm Sitting On Top Of The World (Sam Lanin and his Orchestra)
1152  Steppin' Along (The Hotsey-Totsey Boys)
1186  Brown Pepper (correct title BROWN SUGAR) (Original Indiana Five)
```

Of the considerable number made by this once-famous American dance band leader, only
the following is of jazz interest.

HOTEL BILTMORE ORCHESTRA : Hazay Natzy dir. t/tb/cl/as/ts/p/bj/bb/d.
                                          New York, c. February 2, 1925.

105834    When My Sugar Walks Down The Street      PA 036206, Per 14387, Hra 9115,
          (All The Little Birdies Go "Tweet Tweet Tweet")    I-S 7150
NOTE:- Perfect 14387 as WESTCHESTER DANCE ORCHESTRA; Grafton 9115 as BAR HARBOUR
ORCHESTRA; Ideal Scala 7150 as ASTORIA ORCHESTRA.

## KING NAWAHI'S  HAWAIIANS

Most of the records issued under this name are of no jazz interest, but the following
are exceptional.

Benny Nawahi-stg/Harry Volpe-James Ferraro-g.
                                          New York, December 20, 1929.

149608-2  Hawaiian Capers                          Col 2076-D, DB-225

                                          New York, January 30, 1930.

149945-2  Tickling The Strings                     Col 2138-D, DB-225, Re G-20762

## OLIVER  NAYLOR

NAYLOR'S SEVEN ACES : Oliver Naylor-p dir. Edward "Pinky" Gerbrecht-c/Charles Hartman-
tb/Bill Creger-cl-as/Newton Richardson-ts/Jules Bauduc-bj/Louis Darrough-d.
                                          New York, c. February 1, 1924.

8740, -A  High Society                             Gnt 5392, St 9517, Ch 15038
8741-A  Oh, Johnny ! Please Don't - Mom-Ma !       Gnt 5386      -
8742-A  Ringleberg Blues                           Gnt 5393

                                          New York, c. February 4, 1924.

8743-A  Hugo (I Go Where You Go)                   Gnt 5375, St 9548
8744-A  She Wouldn't Do (What I Asked Her To)      Gnt 5376, St 9523
8745-A  I've Got A Cross-Eyed Papa (But He Looks      -            -
        Straight To Me)

                                          New York, c. February 5, 1924.

8746-A  You                                        Gnt 5375, St 9524
8747-A  31st Street Blues                          Gnt 5392
8748-A  Ain't That Hateful ?                       Gnt 5393, St 9518

                                          New York, c. February 8, 1924.

8758-A  Twilight Rose                              Gnt 5432, St 9524
8759-A  So I Took The Fifty Thousand Dollars       Gnt 5386, St 9518
NOTE:- Champion 15038 as SUNSET DANCE ORCHESTRA.  THE PHONOGRAPH AND TALKING
MACHINE WEEKLY for February 27, 1924 reports that Naylor's Seven Aces also made the
following titles about this date :- COME ON, RED/WHY DID I KISS THAT GIRL ?/IN THE
EVENING/MY SWEETIE'S SWEETER THAN THAT.  Whether this is a piece of bad reportage,
or whether these four titles were in fact recorded for some rival firm whose files
have long since been destroyed, is anyone's guess; they were not made for Gennett.

One of the reeds db bcl; Jack Kaufman-v.
                                          New York, c. May 20, 1924.

8884-A  Driftwood                                  Gnt 5470, St 9557
8885    Say, Say, Sadie - vJK                         -            -

──── White-bb added.                      New York, January 3, 1925.

9261    Susquehanna Home                            Gnt 5638

NAYLOR'S SEVEN ACES : Oliver Naylor-p dir. Edward "Pinky" Gerbrecht-c/Charles Hartman
   tb/Bill Creger-cl-as/Newton Richardson-ts/Jules Bauduc-bj/ —— White-bb/Louis
Darrough-d.                              New York, c. January 6, 1925.

   9268-A  You And I                          Gnt 5643
   9269-A  Take Me                            Gnt 5638
   9270-A  Bye Bye Baby                       Gnt 5643

OLIVER NAYLOR'S ORCHESTRA : As above.     New York, January 7, 1925.

          Sand (sic - probably SAN)          Vic test (un-numbered)

   Bill   Perry-a  dir. Edward "Pinky" Gerbrecht-c/Pete Beilman-tb/Jerry Richel-cl-as/
Jack Howard-as/Lester "Gilly" Bouchon-cl-ts/Oliver Naylor-Bob Zurke-p/Jules Bauduc-
bj/Carl Hansen-bb/Louis Darrough-d.     Camden, N. J., May 1, 1925.

   32565-3  Sweet Georgia Brown              Vic 19688, HMV B-2078

                                         Camden, N. J., May 14, 1925.

   32703-2  Slowin' Down Blues              HMV B-2079
   32704-1-2-3-4  I'm Goin' Back To My Mammy's  Rejected
            Cabin Door

Subsequent records (on OKeh, in 1929) by Oliver Naylor's Orchestra are both waltzes.

## NBC CHAMBER MUSIC SOCIETY  OF LOWER BASIN STREET

See Sidney Bechet, Paul Laval, Henry Levine and Jelly-Roll Morton.

## NOBBY NEALE AND AL LYONS

Nobby Neale-cl/Al Lyons ("The Boy With The Steinway On His Stomach," vide labels !)-
   pac.                                 Chicago, July, 1929.

   21327-3  Come From It                    Pm 12775
   21328-1  Go To It                        -

## NEGER-JAZZ-ORCHESTER

Presumably a negro - and hence American ? - group; instrumentation and personnel
   unknown.                             Berlin, October, 1924.

          Nothin' But                        Vox 01637
          Runnin' Wild                       -

## ARNETT NELSON AND HIS HOT FOUR

Arnett Nelson-cl/Black Bob-p/? Will Weldon ("Casey Bill")-g-v/Big Bill Broonzy-g/?
   Bill Settles-sb.                     Chicago, October 8, 1936.

   C-1535-1  Oh ! Red                       ARC 6-12-69, Cq 8765
   C-1536-2  You Waited Too Long            -           -

## CHUCK NELSON AND  HIS BOYS

Pseudonym on Champion for Zach Whyte and his Orchestra, q.v.

## DAVE  NELSON

DAVE NELSON AND THE KING'S MEN : Dave Nelson-t-v dir. Melvin Herbert-Harry Brown-t/
   Wilbur de Paris-tb/Buster Bailey-Glyn Paque-cl-as/Charles Frazier-ts/Wayman Carver-
   ts-f/Sam Allen-p/Arthur Taylor-bj-g/Simon Marrero-bb/Gerald Hobson-d.
                                         New York, January 14, 1931.

   64849-2  I Ain't Got Nobody - vDN        Vic 22639, BB 1849, B-5029,
                                            MW M-4893, Sr S-3115
   64850-2  When Day Is Done - vDN          Vic 22639
   64851-2  Some Of These Days - vDN        Vic 23039, BB 1849, B-5029,
                                            MW M-4894, Sr S-3115, HMV B-4853

DAVE'S HARLEM HIGHLIGHTS : Dave Nelson-t-v dir. Clarence Brereton and either Melvin
  Herbert or Harry Brown-t/Wilbur de Paris-tb/Buster Bailey-Glyn Paque-cl-as/Charles
  Frazier-ts/Wayman Carver-ts-f/Sam Allen-p/Danny Barker-bj/Simon Marrero-bb/Gerald
  Hobson-d.                                  New York, June 9, 1931.

| | | |
|---|---|---|
| 69905-1 | Somebody Stole My Gal - vDN | TT C-1587, Eld 1930, MW M-4894 |
| 69906-1 | Rockin' Chair - vDN | TT C-1576 |
| 69907-2 | Loveless Love - vDN | TT C-1577 |
| 69908-2 | St. Louis Blues - vDN | TT C-1588, Eld 1931, Aur 36-134 |

  NOTE:- Electradisk 1930 as MEMPHIS STOMPERS; 1931 as HARLEM HOT SHOTS.

## JEWELL NELSON

Vocal, acc. by Leroy Williams-c/p/g.      Dallas, December 8, 1928.

| | | |
|---|---|---|
| 147614-2 | Jet Black Snake Blues | Col 14390-D |
| 147615-2 | Beating Me Blues | - |

## OZZIE NELSON AND HIS ORCHESTRA

Most of the records made by this well-known American dance orchestra are of little or
no interest as jazz, but the following are exceptions.

Ozzie Nelson-v dir. Charlie Spivak-t/Jack Teagarden-tb/Charlie  Bubeck-Donald Wright-
  cl-as/Bill Nelson-cl-ts/Sid Brokaw and another-vn/Harry Murphy-p/Sandy Wolf-g/Fred
  Whiteside-sb/Joe Bohan-d.                 New York, February 16, 1931.

| | | |
|---|---|---|
| E-36081-A | Do I Really Deserve It From You ?-vON | Br 6060, Spt S-2172 |
| E-36082-A | Dream A Little Dream Of Me - vON | -          - |

  NOTE:- Supertone S-2172 as MISSOURI JAZZ BAND.

Ozzie Nelson-v dir. Harry Johnson-Holly Humphreys-Bo Ashford-t/Elmer Smithers-Abe
  Lincoln-tb/Charlie Bubeck-Bill Stone-cl-as/Bill Nelson-cl-ts/Sid Brokaw-vn/Harry
  Murphy-Chauncey Gray-p/Sandy Wolf-g/Fred Whiteside-sb/Joe Bohan-d/Harriet Hilliard-
  v.                                        New York, February 5, 1934.

| | | |
|---|---|---|
| 14772-1 | What's Good For The Goose (Is Good For The Gander) - vON-HH | Voc 2642, EBW W-98, RZ G-22126 |

  NOTE:- Edison Bell Winner W-98 as OWEN FALLON AND HIS CALIFORNIANS.

                                            New York, June 23, 1935.

| | | |
|---|---|---|
| B-17726-1 | Tiger Rag | Br 7523, A-9868 |

                                            New York, April 6, 1936.

| | | |
|---|---|---|
| B-18944-1 | Streamline Strut | Br 7651, RZ G-22891 |
| B-18945- | Doing The Prom | Br 7659, RZ G-22899 |
| B-18946- | Stomping At The Savoy | -          - |
| B-18947-1 | Is It True What They Say About Dixie ? - vON | Br 7651, RZ G-22891 |

Lincoln omitted; Irving Gellers-p replaces Gray.
                                            New York, March 12, 1937.

| | | | |
|---|---|---|---|
| 06637-1 | Whoa Babe | BB B-6875, HMV BD-5228 | |
| 06638-1 | Poor Robinson Crusoe - vON | -          - | El EG-6252 |

Buddy Rice-ts added.                        New York, May 3, 1937.

| | | |
|---|---|---|
| 010111-1 | Satan Takes A Holiday (Spookie Takes A Holiday*) | BB B-6965, HMV BD-5240* |
| 010112-1 | Peckin' | BB B-6974          - |
| 010113-1 | The Jelly-Fish | - |

                                            Hollywood, November 2, 1937.

| | | |
|---|---|---|
| 09775-1 | Queen Isabella | BB B-7256 |

Ozzie Nelson dir. Harry Johnson-Holly Humphreys-Bo Ashford-t/Elmer Smithers-tb/
   Charlie Bubeck-Bill Stone-cl-as/Bill Nelson-cl-ts/Sid Brokaw-vn/Harry Murphy-
   Irving Gellers-p/Sandy Wolf-g/Fred Whiteside-sb/Joe Bohan-d.
                                         Hollywood, March 5, 1938.

| | | |
|---|---|---|
| 019041-1 | The Black Cat | BB B-7502 |
| 019042-1 | Don't Be That Way | - |

                                         Hollywood, April 6, 1938.

| | | |
|---|---|---|
| 019194-1 | The Sheik Of Araby | BB B-7517 |

                                         New York, July 18, 1938.

| | | |
|---|---|---|
| 024054-1 | Maple Leaf Rag (Scott Joplin) | BB B-7726, MW M-7527 |
| 024055-1 | Yes Suh ! | -                -  |

                                         New York, September 7, 1938.

| | | |
|---|---|---|
| 027002-1 | Stompin' At The Stadium | BB B-7814, RZ G-24033 |

NOTE:- Regal Zonophone G-24033 as THE RHYTHM KINGS.

### NELSON'S ORCHESTRA

Pseudonym on Australian Dahlmont for Joe Candullo and his Everglades Orchestra, q.v.

### NELSON'S PARAMOUNT SERENADERS

Don Nelson-c/cl/J. Norman Ebron-p.        Chicago, c. June, 1927.

| | | |
|---|---|---|
| 4560-2 | Phillips Street Stomp | Pm 12494 |
| 4561-1 | Nelson Blues | - |

D. C. NELSON'S PARAMOUNT SERENADERS : Same.
                                         Chicago, c. September, 1927.

| | | |
|---|---|---|
| 20031-1 | New Orleans Breakdown | Pm 12543 |
| 20032- | Coo Coo Stomp | - |

### TOM NEVILL

Pseudonym on Coliseum for Irving Kaufman-v.

### NEW DIXIE DEMONS

This wa  a comedy pseudo-hillbilly group, recording for Decca during the later 1930s,
   and at least some sessions used Jimmy Lytell-cl/Perry Botkin-g/George Yorke or
   Ward Lay-sb/Ray McKinley-d/Frank Novak-effects/Dan Hornsby-v, but neither the
   material nor its presentation, however diverting it may be, is likely to interest
   the jazz collector.

### NEW FRIENDS OF RHYTHM

The following titles by this group are included solely because of the presence of
   Buster Bailey; those on which he does not appear are of purely "novelty" arrangements of popular classics - usually with "clever" titles - for a string orchestra
   with rhythm.

Buster Bailey-cl/Sylvan Shulman-Harry Glickman-vn/Louis Kievman-vl/Alan Shulman-vc/
   Tony Colucci-g/Laura Newell-harp/Harry Patent-sb.
                                         New York, May 24, 1940.

| | | |
|---|---|---|
| 050856-1 | Heavy Traffic On Canal Street | Vic 26647, 27927 |
| 050857-1 | Coo, Dinny, Coo | Vic 27412, 27929 |
| 050858-2 | The Mood In Question | Vic 26647 |

Pseudonym on Guardsman for the following items listed in this book :-

1180  Georgia Rose (California Ramblers)
1182  The Sheik (California Ramblers)
1306  Apple Sauce (Gene Fosdick's Hoosiers)
1316  Four O'Clock Blues (Original Memphis Five)
1318  Aggravatin' Papa (Original Memphis Five)
1327  Peggy Dear (Gene Fosdick's Hoosiers)
1328  Who's Sorry Now ? (Ben Bernie and his Hotel Roosevelt Orchestra)
1376  Both sides by Fletcher Henderson and his Orchestra
1379  Ivy (The Southland Six)
1392  Henpecked Blues (Ben Bernie and his Hotel Roosevelt Orchestra)
1419  Sittin' In A Corner (Broadway Syncopators)
1425  House Of David Blues (Broadway Syncopators)
1478  Both sides by Fletcher Henderson and his Orchestra
1505  Cotton Pickers' Ball (Fletcher Henderson and his Orchestra)
1613  Pleasure Mad (The Ambassadors)
1634  Susquehanna Home (Ben Selvin and his Orchestra)
1669  Cuddle Up A Little Closer (The Ambassadors)
1685  Oh ! How I Love My Darling (The Ambassadors)
1685  How I Love That Girl (Ben Bernie and his Hotel Roosevelt Orchestra)
1700  Prince Of Wails (The Tennessee Tooters)
1701  Why Couldn't It Be Poor Little Me ? (Ben Bernie and his Hotel Roosevelt Orch.)
1701  I Ain't Got Nobody To Love (The Tennessee Tooters)
1873  That's All There Is (Jeffries and his Rialto Orchestra)
1873  Then I'll Be Happy (Bailey's Lucky Seven)
1892  Sweet Child (Bailey's Lucky Seven)
1894  The Kiss I Can't Forget (Bailey's Lucky Seven)
1896  Both sides by Bailey's Lucky Seven
1914  What Did I Tell Ya ? (Kerr's Famous Players)
1918  Wimmin - Aah ! (Fess Williams' Royal Flush Orchestra)
2008  Don't Be Angry With Me (Joe Candullo's Everglades Orchestra)

## THE  NEW LYRES

Alf Bowes-t-mel/ts/Oscar Grasso-vn/Ernest Wilson-p/George Senior-sb/Jack Simpson-d.
                              London, February 10, 1938.

CE-8938-1  Doctor Rhythm                    Par F-1219, A-7013, Od OF-5783
CE-8939-1  Bull It In C                         -          -        -

## RUBY NEWMAN AND  HIS ORCHESTRA

The following sides are known exceptions to the general rule that records by this
  dance band are of no jazz interest.

Ruby Newman-vn dir. Jack Lacey-Felix Giardina-tb/Alfie Evans-Sid Stoneburn-cl-as/
  Larry Binyon-cl-ts/Rudolph Adler-bar/Sam Liner-p/Dick McDonough-g/Sam Shopnick-sb/
  Al Lepin-d/Barry McKinley-v.              New York, August 31, 1936.

  083-1  Sing, Baby, Sing - vBM                Vic 25401, HMV EA-1803
  085-1  Make-Believe Ballroom - vBM           -

## NEW MAYFAIR  DANCE ORCHESTRA

The following sides from the large number recorded by the Gramophone Company's house
  orchestra are of considerable interest as "hot" dance records.

Carroll Gibbons-p dir. Sylvester Ahola-Max Goldberg-t/tb/Jack Miranda-cl-as/Laurie
  Payne-cl-as-bar/Johnny Helfer-cl-ts/Eric Siday-Reg. Pursglove-Jean Pougnet-vn/Bert
  Thomas-bj/? Tiny Stock-bb/Rudy Starita-d-vib.
                              Hayes, Middlesex, February 6, 1929.

Bb-15660-6  I'm Crazy Over You               HMV B-5603

  Unknown t replaces Ahola; unknown cl-as replaces Miranda; Eddie Brandt-Phil Arnold-
  Les Allen-v.                  Hayes, Middlesex, February 14, 1929.

Bb-15775-3  What A Wonderful Wedding That Will Be   HMV B-5601
            - vEB-PA-LA

Carroll Gibbons-p dir. Norman Payne and another-t/Lew Davis-tb/Jack Miranda-cl-as/
   Laurie Payne-cl-as-bar-hfp/Johnny Helfer-cl-ts/Eric Siday-Reg. Pursglove-Jean
   Pougnet and 3 others-vn/Bert Thomas-bj/? Tiny Stock-bb/Rudy Starita-d-vib.
                                          Hayes, Middlesex, March 20, 1929.

Bb-16160-4  Deep Hollow                   HMV B-5632

Ray Noble dir. Sylvester Ahola-George Ratcliffe-t/Jock Fleming-tb/Harry Hines-cl-as/
   Laurie Payne-cl-as-bar/Johnny Helfer-cl-as-ts/Eric Siday-Reg. Pursglove-Jean Pougnet
   and another-vn/Harry Jacobson-p/Ray Noble-cel/Bert Thomas-bj/? Spike Hughes-sb/Bill
   Harty-d/Rudy Starita-vib.              Small Queen's Hall, London, October 7,1929.

Bb-17268-6  Teardrops                     HMV B-5716
Bb-18014-2  Copper Blues (Intro. Dancing Shoes)   HMV B-5717
Bb-18016-1  Terribly Fond Of You (Intro. Dance Away   -
            Your Blues)

   Max Goldberg-? Bill Shakespeare-t replace Ahola and Ratcliffe; unknown 4th sax replaces unknown 4th vn; apparently 3rd p replaces sb according to the HMV files.
                                          Hayes, Middlesex, October 31, 1929.

Bb-17748-2  So The Bluebirds And The Blackbirds   HMV B-5732
            Got Together

   Starita omitted; sb added; Jacobson only p.
                                          Small Queen's Hall, London, Nov. 7, 1929.

Bb-18134-2  Every Now And Then            HMV B-5740
Bb-18136-2  Baby, You've Got The Right Idea   -

Ray Noble dir. Norman Payne-t/Laurie Payne-cl-as-bar/Eric Siday-Reg. Pursglove-Jean
   Pougnet-vn/Bert Thomas-g/Spike Hughes-sb/Bill Harty-d. Despite the label, there is
   no vocal on this title.               Small Queen's Hall, London, Feb. 20, 1930.

Bb-18869-2  Every Day Away From You       HMV B-5800

Ray Noble dir. Max Goldberg and 2 other t/? Jock Fleming-tb/? Harry Hines-cl-as/
   Laurie Payne-cl-as-bar/? Leon Goossens-ts/5 vn including Eric Siday-Reg. Pursglove-
   Jean Pougnet/Harry Jacobson-p/Bert Thomas-bj/Spike Hughes-sb/Bill Harty-d/Rudy
   Starita-vib (and chimes and tymps ?)/W. Vernon-v.
                                          Small Queen's Hall, London, April 11, 1930.

Bb-19238-2  You've Got To Be Modernistic - vWV   HMV B-5819
Bb-19239-2  Crazy Feet - vWV             -

   2 unknown vn omitted; only 2 t used; Harry Berly-ts-oc replaces (or may even be) the
   previous ts.                          Small Queen's Hall, London, April 28, 1930.

Bb-19276-2  Harmony Heaven - vWV          HMV B-5827

Ray Noble dir. Max Goldberg-Bill Shakespeare-? Norman Payne-t/Jock Fleming-tb/Harry
   Hines-cl-as/Laurie Payne-cl-as-bar/George Smith-ts/Eric Siday-vn/Harry Jacobson-p/
   Spike Hughes-sb/Bill Harty-d/Jack Plant-v.
                                          Small Queen's Hall, Lndon, Sept. 16, 1930.

Bb-20207-2  I've Got A Feeling - vJP      HMV B-5893

   Reg. Pursglove-Jean Pougnet-vn/vc/? Ray Noble-cel added.
                                          Small Queen's Hall, London, Oct. 20, 1930.

Bb-20318-2  Just Imagine - vJP            HMV B-5918

Ray Noble dir. Max Goldberg-Bill Shakespeare-Jack Jackson-t/Tony Thorpe-tb/Laurie
   Payne-cl-as-bar/Bob Wise-George Smith-ts/Eric Siday-Reg. Pursglove-Jean Pougnet-vn/
   Harry Jacobson-p/Bert Thomas-g/Jack Evetts-sb/Bill Harty-d/Al Bowlly-v. (The third
   title is part of a triple-track record.) Small Queen's Hall, London, Feb. 19, 1931.

OB-369-3  Makin' Wickey-Wackey Down In Waikiki-vAB  HMV B-5989
OB-370-3  Shout For Happiness - vAB      HMV B-5984
OB-375-4  Puzzle Record - Part 2 (Sweet Jennie Lee) HMV B-3775, Vic 22745, Zon EE-246
NOTE:- All issues from matrix OB-375-4 as NOVELTY ORCHESTRA.

Ray Noble dir. Max Goldberg-Bill Shakespeare-t/Tony Thorpe-tb/Harry Hines-cl-as/Laurie
   Payne-cl-as-bar/? George Smith-ts/Hugo Rignold-probably Reg. Leopold-Nobby Clarke-vn
   /Harry Jacobson-p/Bert Thomas-g/Jack Evetts-sb/Bill Harty-d/Jack Plant-v.
                                        Small Queen's Hall, London, May 14, 1931.

OB-889-2   Come And Have A Cuddle On The Common - vJP HMV B-6019

   Probably as above, plus 1 tb (the files show 2 bass tb !); Al Bowlly-v.
                                        London, October 31, 1931.

OB-1778-1  This Is The Day Of Days - vAB            HMV B-6091

                        NEW MAYFAIR  NOVELTY ORCHESTRA

Max Goldberg-t/Laurie Payne-cl-bar/Ray Noble-Harry Jacobson-p/Bert Thomas-g/Al Bowlly-
   v.                                   Small Queen's Hall, London, Nov. 14, 1931.

OB-2231-2  Twentieth Century Blues - vAB            HMV B-4001, K-6979, El EG-2930,
                                                    Vic 24090

                        NEW ORLEANS  BLACK BIRDS

Phil Napoleon-t/Miff Mole-tb/Jimmy Dorsey-cl-as/Matt Malneck-vn/Frank Signorelli-p/
   Dick McDonough-g/Joe Tarto-bb/Ted Napoleon-d.
                                        New York, December 11, 1928.

   49248-1-2  Red Head                              Vic V-38027, BB B-6611
   49249-2  Playing The Blues                       -        BB B-7881

NOTE:- Two other titles were issued under this name on Victor V-38026 and the same
   Bluebirds as above.  As they were made at a session directed by Jack Pettis, details
   are shown under his name.

                        NEW ORLEANS  BLUE FIVE

Tom Morris-c/Joe Nanton-tb/Bob Fuller-cl-ss/Mike Jackson-p/Buddy Christian-g/Helen
   Baxter-Tom Morris-Joe Nanton-dialogue*.  New York, November 2, 1926.

   36895-1  My Baby Doesn't Squawk - clBF          Vic 20364
   36896-1  *The King Of The Zulus - clBF          Vic 20316, WS 103
   36897-1  South Rampart Street Blues - ssBF      Vic 20653
   NOTE:- Wax Shop 103 as THOMAS MORRIS AND HIS NEW ORLEANS BLUE SEVEN.

                        NEW ORLEANS  BLUE NINE

2t/tb/as/ts/vn/p/bj/bb/d (probably a negro band).
                                        New York, c. April, 1921.

   A-104-1  Hard Time Blues                         Pm 12003, Globe/Rx 7018
   A-105-2  John Henry Blues                        -        GG/Nadsco/Rx 1263
   NOTE:- Paramount as HARLEM HARMONY KINGS.

Earl Oliver-? Harry Gluck-t/Sam Lewis-tb/2cl-as/cl-ts/Ben Selvin-vn/p/bj/bb/d.
                                        New York, c. January, 1924.

   3190-A  Stale Bread Blues                        GG/Rx 1214, Or 204
           Limehouse Blues                          -
   NOTE:- Oriole 204 as GULF COAST SPASM BAND.

                                        New York, c. January, 1925.

   3620-A  Yellow Dog Blues                         GG/Rx 1282, Clover 1581

                                        New York, c. February-March, 1925.

   3657-A-B  Always Got The Blues                   GG/Globe/Rx/Spm 1290, Ebs 1069,
                                                    Mad 1604, Hom B-1900
   NOTE:- Clover 1581 as MARLBOROUGH MELODY SYNCOPATORS; Everybody's as SUNKIST
   SERENADERS; Madison 1604 as THE DIXIE TROUBADOURS.

Pseudonym on Varsity 6029 for Zach Whyte's Chocolate Beau Brummls, q.v.

## NEW ORLEANS BOOTBLACKS

George Mitchell-c/Kid Ory-tb/Johnny Dodds-cl/Joe Clark-as/Lil Armstrong-p/Johnny St.
  Cyr-bj.                              Chicago, July 14, 1926.

| | | |
|---|---|---|
| 142436-1 | Mixed Salad | Col 14465-D, Bm 1085, HJCA HC-31, VJR 2 |
| 142437-3 | I Can't Say | As above |
| 142438-1 | Flat Foot | Col 14337-D, DB-3422, BF-618, CQ-2780, DCH-250, DZ-883, Bm 1083, HJCA HC-26, VJR 1 |
| 142439-1 | Mad Dog | As above, but Col DCH-112 |

## NEW ORLEANS  FEETWARMERS

Tommy Ladnier-t/Dan Minor-tb/Sidney Bechet-cl-ss/James P. Johnson-p/Walter Page-sb/
  Joe Jones-d.                         Carnegie Hall, New York, Dec. 23, 1938.

        Weary Blues (all microgroove issues)   Van 8523, TR 35-064, Fon TFL-5187
        I Wish I Could Shimmy Like My Sister Kate    -         -          -

See also Sidney Bechet, and Fats Waller (HMV JK-2475).

## NEW ORLEANS FIVE

Pseudonym on Romeo 370 for the Original Indiana Five, q.v.

## NEW ORLEANS  JAZZ BAND

Harry Gluck-t/Mike Martini-tb/Sidney Arodin-cl/Wilder Chase-p/Tommy de Rose-d.
                              New York, c. February 12, 1924.

| | | |
|---|---|---|
| 5422-1 | Tin Roof Blues | Ban 1318, Re 9615, Poydras 27 |

                              New York, c. February, 1924.

| | | |
|---|---|---|
| 10030-1 | Mindin' My Bus'ness | Dom 306 |
| 10031-2 | Lots O' Mama | Dom 308 |
| 10032 | Hula Lou | Dom 306 |

NOTE:- All the above three issues as DIXIE JAZZ HOUNDS.

                              New York, c. March, 1924.

| | | |
|---|---|---|
| 10058-2 | Waitin' Around | Dom 329 |
| 10059-2 | 31st Street Blues | Dom 328 |
| 10060-2 | My Papa Doesn't Two-Time No Time | Dom 335, Cvl/Pt/Tri 11383, Apex 8250 |

                              New York, c. April, 1924.

| | | |
|---|---|---|
| 10083-1-2 | Limehouse Blues | Dom 338, Pen 1383 |
| 10084-1 | It Had To Be You | Dom 335  - Cvl/Pt/Tri 11383, Fed 5405, Sil 2405, Max 1512 |
| 10085-1-2 | Down Where The South Begins | Dom 338, Bwy/Pt/Tri 11382 |

Dave Skine or Dick Maffei-bj added.   New York, c. September 10, 1924.

| | | |
|---|---|---|
| 5623-3 | Dixie Flyer Sam | Ban 1428, Dom 401,Or 253, Re 9725 |
| 5624-1-2 | I'm Gonna Get Acquainted In A Quaint Old-Fashioned Town | -    Dom 389    - |
| 5625-1 | How Could You Leave Me Now ? | Dom 387, Or 271, Apex 8270, Poydras 27 |

NOTE:- Banner 1428, Regal 9725 as SIX BLACK DIAMONDS; Broadway/Triangle 11382 as
GOLDEN GATE ORCHESTRA; Carnival/Puretone/Triangle 11383 and Pennington 1393 as
SCHUBERT'S METROPOLITAN ORCHESTRA; Domino 328 and 329 as DIXIE JAZZ HOUNDS; Maxsa
1512 as MAXSA'S NEW YORK ORCHESTRA; Oriole 253 as MIAMI JAZZ BAND; Oriole 271 as
DIXIE JAZZ BAND.

Harry Gluck-t/Mike Martini-tb/Sidney Arodin-cl/Wilder Chase-p/Dave Skine or Dick
   Maffei-bj/Tommy de Rose-d.              New York, c. October 23, 1924.

```
5677-1-2-3  Honey, Don't You Shake Me Down    Or 291
5678-2  Alabamy Stay-At-Home                  Dom 403, Or 272
5679 1  My Lovey Lee                          Or 269
5680-1  Copenhagen                            Ban 1445, Dom 416, Or 291, Re 9739
5680-2  Copenhagen                            Apex 8272
```
NOTE:- Domino 416 as RIALTO DANCE ORCHESTRA; Oriole 269 and 291 as DIXIE JAZZ BAND;
Oriole 272 as ORIOLE DANCE ORCHESTRA.

Herman Drewes-t/Ted Raph-tb/Brad Gowans-cl/Tony Franchini-p/Dick Maffei-bj/Tommy de
   Rose-d-ldr.                              New York, May 6, 1925.

```
6006-1  Some Of These Days          Ban 1544, Dom 3509, Or 413, Re 9839
6006-2  Some Of These Days          Apex 8359, Leo 10019
6007-1-2  My Sweet Louise           Ban 1556, Dom 3524, Em 10868,
                                    Re 9852, Sil 2498, Poydras 63
```
NOTE:- Emerson 10868 as PENNSYLVANIA SYNCOPATORS; Oriole 413 as DIXIE JAZZ BAND;
Silvertone 2498 as LANIN'S ROSELAND ORCHESTRA.

                                    New York, June 12, 1925.

```
6046-2  Right Or Wrong             Or 445
6047-1  Red Hot Henry Brown        Or 464, Apex 8398
6047-2  Red Hot Henry Brown        Beeda 112
```
NOTE:- Oriole 445 and 464 as DIXIE JAZZ BAND.

                                    New York, October 8, 1925.

```
6216-1  The Camel Walk            Apex 8429, Dom 21107, St 10094
6216-2-3  The Camel Walk          Ban 1618, Dom 3590, Re 9923,
                                  Mic 22056
6218-1  Melancholy Lou            Apex 8411, Dom 21091, Mic 22043,
                                  St 10078
6218-2  Melancholy Lou            Ban 1624, Dom 3594, Or 497,
                                  Re 9920, Poydras 63
```
NOTE:- Oriole 497 as SIX BLACK DIAMONDS.
        The name NEW OR EANS JAZZ BAND was itself a pseudonym for the following
        items listed in this book :-

Banner 6049  Tiger Rag (Five Birmingham Babies)
Domino 3439  Hot Sax (Booker's Jazz Band)

See also the Original New Orleans Jazz Band.

## NEW ORLEANS   JAZZ TRIO

Bob Fuller-cl/Louis Hooper-p/Elmer Snowden-bj.
                                    New York, June 18, 1926.

```
X-186, -A  Dancin' The Blues              Gnt rejected
X-187, -A  Desert Blues                        -
```

## NEW ORLEANS   LUCKY SEVEN

Pseudonym on OKeh 8544 and Australian Columbia DO-2245 for Bix Beiderbecke and his
   Gang, q.v.

## NEW ORLEANS OWLS

Benjie White-cl-as dir. Bill Padron-c/Lester Smith-ts/Mose Farrar-p/Rene Gelpi-bj-g/
   Dan LeBlanc-bb/Earl Crumb-d.          New Orleans, September 24, 1925.

```
140992-2  Stomp Off, Let's Go         Col 489-D
140993-2  Oh Me ! Oh My !                  -
140994-2  The Owls' Hoot              Col 605-D
140995-1-2  Zero                      Rejected
```

Benjie White-cl-as dir. Bill Padron-c/Frank Netto-tb/Pinky Vidacovich-cl-as/Lester
   Smith-ts/Mose Farrar-p/Rene Gelpi-bj-g/Dan LeBlanc-bb/Earl Crumb-d.
                                                New Orleans, April 14, 1926.

| 142018-1-2 | Spaghetti | Rejected |
| 142019-3 | Piccadilly | Col 1158-D |
| 142020-2 | Tampeekoe | Col 688-D |
| 142021-2 | Dynamite | Col 1045-D |
| 142022-1 | Pretty Baby | - |
| 142023-2 | West End Romp | Col 688-D |

   Sigfre Christensen-p replaces Farrar.  Atlanta, November 8, 1926.

| 143110-2 | Blowin' Off Steam | Col 823-D |
| 143111-1 | Boneyard Shuffle | Rejected |
| 143112-2 | White Ghost Shivers | Col 862-D |
| 143113-2 | The Nightmare | Col 943-D, 4452 |
| 143114-2 | Brotherly Love | Col 823-D |
| 143115-2 | Eccentric | Col 943-D, 4452 |

                                                New Orleans, April 15, 1927.

| 143979-1 | So Long, Joe | Rejected |
| 143980-1 | Killing Time | - |
| 143981-1 | That's A Plenty | Col 1547-D |
| 143982-1 | Meat On The Table | Col 1158-D |

   Red Bowman-c-v added; Nappy Lamare-bj-v replaces Gelpi.
                                                New Orleans, October 26, 1927.

| 145022-2 | The New Twister | Col 1547-D |
| 145023-2 | Goose Pimples | Col 1261-D |
| 145024-2 | Throwin' The Horns - vRB-NL | - |

### NEW ORLEANS PEPSTERS

Pseudonym on Van Dyke for the following items listed in this book :-

77038  Close Fit Blues (Clarence Williams unit)
81836  The Harlem Stomp Down (Levee Syncopators)

### NEW ORLEANS RAMBLERS

Bob Haring dir. Sterling Bose-Charlie Spivak-t/Jack Teagarden-tb-v/Jimmy Dorsey-cl-
   as/Gil Rodin-as/Eddie Miller-ts/Al Beller-vn/Gil Bowers-p/Nappy Lamare-g/Harry
   Goodman-sb/Ray Bauduc-d/The Cotton Pockers-v quartet/Ben Pollack-v.
                                                New York, February 18, 1931.

| E-36104- | That's The Kind Of Man For Me - vJT | Mt M-12230, Decatur 508 |
| E-36105- | I'm One Of God's Children (Who Hasn't | Mt M-12133       -       |
|          | Got Wings) - vJT |  |
| E-36106- | No Wonder I'm Blue - vBP | - |
| E-36107-A-B | There's Rhythm In The River - vCP | Rejected |

### NEW ORLEANS RHYTHM KINGS

FRIARS SOCIETY ORCHESTRA, Direction - Husk O'Hara (sic) : Elmer Schoebel-p-a dir.
   Paul Mares-c/George Brunies-tb/Leon Rappolo-cl/Jack Pettis-Cm-ts/Lou Black-bj/
   Steve Brown-sb/Frank Snyder-d.  Richmond, Ind., August 29, 1922.

| 11178-B | Eccentric | Gnt 5009, Br 02211 |
| 11179-C | Farewell Blues | Gnt 4966       -       St 9303 |
| 11180-A | Discontented Blues | Gnt 4967, St 9304 |
| 11181-B | Bugle Call Blues | -        -  Br 02213, Tpl 538 |

                                                Richmond, Ind., August 30, 1922.

| 11182-B | Panama | Gnt 4968,St 9313,Br 02212,Tpl 550 |
| 11183-C | Tiger Rag | -        -        -        - |
| 11184 | Livery Stable Blues | Pm 14028 |
| 11185 | Oriental | Gnt 4966, St 9303, EBW 3868, |
|  |  | Wp 3044 |

NOTE:- Edison Bell Winner 3868 and Westport 3044 as REGENT ORCHESTRA.

Paul Mares-c/George Brunies-tb/Leon Roppolo-cl/Mel Stitzel-p/Ben Pollack-d; according
to the Gennett labels the band was "Formerly Friars Society Orchestra."
                              Richmond, Ind., March 12, 1923.

| | | |
|---|---|---|
| 11352 | Sweet Lovin' Man | Gnt 5104, Tpl 534 |
| 11352-A | Sweet Lovin' Man | -      Br 02210 |
| 11353 | That's A Plenty | Gnt 5105, UHCA 88 |
| 11353-A | That's A Plenty | -      Br 02208, Tpl 521 |
| 11353-B | That's A Plenty | |
| 11354, -B | Shimmeshawabble (sic) | Gnt 5106, BRS 1004, JCl 503, |
| | | VJR 24, JC L-27 |
| 11355-B | Weary Blues | Gnt 5102, Buddy 8003, Gothic 509, |
| | | Tpl 549, Poydras MJC-12, Tem R-2 |

                              Richmond, Ind., March 13, 1923.

| | | |
|---|---|---|
| 11356 | Da Da Strain | Gnt 5106 |
| 11357-A-B | Wolverine Blues | Gnt 5102, Gothic 509, Tpl 549, |
| | | Tem R-2 |
| 11358-B | Maple Leaf Rag (Scott Joplin) | Gnt 5104, UHCA 45,Tpl 534,Br 02209 |
| 11359 | Tin Roof Blues | Gnt 5105, UHCA 87, Tpl 521 |
| 11359-A | Tin Roof Blues | -      Buddy 8001, Br 02208 |
| 11359-B | Tin Roof Blues | -      -      St 9435 |

Paul Mares-c/George Brunies-tb/Leon Roppolo-cl/Jack Pettis-Cm/Glenn Scoville-as-ts/
Don Murray-cl-ts/Jelly-Roll Morton or Kyle Pierce-p (as shown)/Bob Gillette-bj/
Chink Martin-bb/Ben Pollack-d.     Richmond, Ind., July 17, 1923.

| | | |
|---|---|---|
| 11535-A | Sobbin' Blues - pJRM | Gnt 5219, Buddy 8003, Tpl 551 |
| 11536-A | Marguerite - pKP | Gnt 5217 |
| 11539 | Angry - pKP | Gnt 5219, Tpl 551, JC L-27 |
| 11539-A | Angry - pKP | -      Buddy 8002 |
| 11540 | Clarinet Marmalade - pJRM | Gnt 5220, Buddy 8004, VJR 15 |
| 11540-A | Clarinet Marmalade - pJRM | -      Tpl 520, Br 02209 |
| 11541-A | Mr. Jelly Lord - pJRM | -      - Buddy 8004, VJR 15 |
| NOTE:- Matrices 11537/8 are piano solos by Jelly-Roll Morton, q.v. | | |

                              Richmond, Ind., July 18, 1923.

| | | |
|---|---|---|
| 11550 | London Blues - pJRM | Gnt 5221, Tpl 533, Br 02210 |
| 11551 | Milenberg Joys - pJRM | Gnt 3076, Buddy 8002 |
| 11551-A | Milenberg Joys - pJRM | Gnt 5217 |
| 11551-C | Milenberg Joys - pJRM | -      3076, BRS 1004, JCl 503, |
| | | VJR 4, Tem R-3, JC L-113 |
| 11552-A | Mad ('Cause You Treat Me This Way)-pKP | Gnt 5221, Tpl 533 |

ORIGINAL NEW ORLEANS RHYTHM KINGS : Paul Mares-c/Santo Pecora-tb/Leon Roppolo-cl/
Charlie Cordella-ts/Glyn Lea "Red" Long-p/Bill Eastwood-bj/Chink Martin-bb/Leo
Adde-d.                        New Orleans, January 23, 1925.

| | | |
|---|---|---|
| 8902-A | Baby | OK 40422 |
| 8903-B | I Never Knew What A Gal Could Do | -      HRS 6 |
| 8904-A | She's Crying For Me Blues | OK 40327, Par R-3254, Col DB-3470, |
| | | Od 03279, 5584, BRS 18, Tpl 556, |
| | | Plato 116 |
| 8905-A | Golden Leaf Strut | As above |

NEW ORLEANS RHYTHM KINGS : As last above, but Charlie Cordella-cl replaces Roppolo,
and there is no ts.            New Orleans, March 26, 1925.

| | | |
|---|---|---|
| 32125-1 | She's Cryin' For Me | BB B-10956 |
| 32125-4 | She's Cryin' For Me | Vic 19645, 28206 |
| 32126-1 | Everybody Loves Somebody Blues (But | -      - |
| | Nobody Loves Me) | |
| 32126-2 | Everybody Loves Somebody Blues (But | BB B-10956 |
| | Nobody Loves Me) | |

Wingy Manone-t/George Brunies-tb/Sidney Arodin-cl/Terry Shand-p/Benny Pottle-sb/Bob
  White-d.                              New York, September 12, 1934.

38608-A  San Antonio Shout                    Dec 161, 336419, M-39002,
                                              Br 02040, Od 284150
38609-A  Tin Roof Blues                       Dec 161, 3523, Br 01910
38610-A  Panama                               Dec 162, 3945    -       Br 80145
38611-A  Jazz It Blues (The Jazz Me Blues*)    - 336419*, M-39002*   - 02040*
                                              Od 284150

                                    New York, September 26, 1934.

38734-A  Bluin' The Blues                     Dec 464, Br 02337
38735-A  Ostrich Walk                         Dec 229, Br 80119, 01988, A-9767
38736-A  Original Dixieland One-Step           -      -       -       -
38737-A  Sensation                            Dec 464, Br 02337

Muggsy Spanier-c/George Brunies-tb/Eddie Miller-cl/Terry Shand-p/Benny Pottle-sb/Gene
  Krupa-d/Red McKenzie-v.                New York, February 20, 1935.

39378-A  Baby Brown - vRM                     Dec 401, Br 03447
39378-B  Baby Brown                            -
39379-A  No Lovers Allowed - vRM               -    Br 02510
39380-A  (Oh ! Susanna) Dust Off That Old Piano  Dec 388, Br 02008
          - vRM
39380-B  (Oh ! Susanna) Dust Off That Old Piano - vRM -
39381-A  Since We Fell Out Of Love - vRM       -      -

NOTE:- Savoy 500 (by Wingy Manone, q.v.) is credited to the New Orleans Rhythm Kings.

### NEW ORLEANS SEVEN  ORCHESTRA

Pseudonym on Elite 5032 for the Varsity Seven, q.v.

### NEW ORLEANS STOMPERS

Pseudonym on Paradox 4 and VJR for the Moonlight Revelers (ALABAMA SHUFFLE) and Jelly
  James and his Fewsicians (GEORGIA BO BO), both q.v.

### NEW ORLEANS  STRUTTERS

Pseudonym on Champion 15398 for Frank Bunch and his Fuzzy Wuzzies, q.v.

### NEW ORLEANS TRIO

Despite its name, this was often a quartet from the Original Capitol Orchestra, q.v.,
  but not of any jazz interest.

### NEW ORLEANS  WANDERERS

George Mitchell-c/Kid Ory-tb/Johnny Dodds-cl/Joe Clark-as except on 142426-1/Lil
  Armstrong-p/Johnny St. Cyr-bj-speech.   Chicago, July 13, 1926.

142426-1  Perdido Street Blues                Col 698-D, DB-2860, BF-417,
                                              CQ-2239, DZ-789, GN-5086,
                                              GNS-5092, M-199, SE 5008-S,
                                              UHCA 15, Tpl 540
142427-2  Gate Mouth                          As above, but UHCA 16
142428-3  Too Tight - spJSC                   Col 735-D, DB-2920, CQ-2240,
                                              DW-5080, DZ-813, GNS-5093,
                                              Bm 1084, HJCA HC-30, VJR 20
142429-2  Papa Dip                            As above
  NOTE:- UHCA 15 and 16 are coupled.

### NEW ORLEANS  WILD CATS

See Eddie Edinborough and his New Orleans Wild Cats.

NEWPORT DANCE ORCHESTRA

Pseudonym on Pathe Actuelle 36658 and Perfect 14839 for Al Lynch and his Orchestra, q.v.

## NEWPORT SOCIETY ORCHESTRA

This was usually a pseudonym on various makes for Ben Selvin and his Orchestra, and on Broadway, Paramount and Puritan it often masked the identity of Fred Rich and his Orchestra, but without referring to anything likely to interest the jazz or "hot" dance band collector.

## NEWPORT SYNCOPATORS

Pseudonym on Van Dyke for Cliff Jackson and his Krazy Kats, q.v.

## NEW PRINCE'S TORONTO BAND

Between October, 1924 and February 25, 1926, this Canadian band was resid nt in London, and recorded over fifty sides for Columbia. The following is a good example of "hot" dance music of the time.

Hal Swain-as-ts-v dir. Alfie Noakes-t/Bill Hall-tb/Les Allen-as-v/Frank Walsh-p/Dave Caplan-bj/Ron Garrison-bb/Ken Kenny-d. London, November 5, 1925.

WA-2561-3  Paddlin' Madelin' Home - vHS-LA          Col 3824

## NEW SYNCO JAZZ BAND

See Synco Jazz Band.

## FRANK NEWTON

FRANK NEWTON AND HIS UPTOWN SERENADERS : Frank Newton-t-a/Edmond Hall-cl/Pete Brown-as/Cecil Scott-ts/Don Frye-p/John Smith-g/Richard Fullbright-sb/Cozy Cole-d/ Clarence Palmer-v.                      New York, March 5, 1937.

| | | |
|---|---|---|
| M-173-1-2 | You're The One - vCP | Rejected |
| M-174-1 | You Showed Me The Way - vCP | Vri 518, Voc 3811, Col DS-1703, MZ-335, Swing 324 |
| M-175-1 | Please Don't Talk About Me When I'm Gone | As above, except Col DS-1703 |
| M-176-1 | Who's Sorry Now ? | JA 9 (LP) |
| M-176-2 | Who's Sorry Now ? | Vri 647, Voc 3839, Col MZ-530 |

Russell Procope-as added; Hall db bar, Scott cl; Slim Gaillard-v.
New York, April 15, 1937.

| | | |
|---|---|---|
| M-402-2 | I Found A New Baby | Vri 571 |
| M-403-2 | The Brittwood Stomp (I'm A Ding Dong Daddy) | - |
| M-404-2 | There's No Two Ways About It - vSG | Vri 550 |
| M-405-2 | 'Cause My Baby Says It's So - vSG | - |

Frank Newton-t-v/Edmond Hall-cl/Pete Brown-as-v/Gene Johnson-as/Cecil Scott-ts/Don Frye-p/Frank Rice-g/John Kirby-sb/O'Neil Spencer-d/Leon LaFell-v.

New York, July 13, 1937.

| | | |
|---|---|---|
| M-558-1 | Easy Living - vLL | Vri 616, Voc 3777, Col DS-1703 |
| M-559-1 | The Onyx Hop - vFN-PB&ch | Vri 647, Voc 3839 |
| M-560-2 | Where Or When - vLL | Vri 616, Voc 3777 |

FRANKIE NEWTON AND ORCHESTRA : Frank Newton-t/Mezz Mezzrow-cl/Pete Brown-as/James P. Johnson-p/Albert Casey-g/John Kirby-sb/Cozy Cole-d.
New York, January 13, 1939.

| | | |
|---|---|---|
| 031460- | Rosetta | BB B-10176, Swing 53 |
| 031461- | Minor Jive | BB B-10186    -    HMV EA-2671 |
| 031462- | The World Is Waiting For The Sunrise | BB B-10176, Swing 198 |
| 031463- | Who ? | BB B-10216, HMV B-8927, Swing 68 |
| 031464- | The Blues My Baby Gave To Me | -    Swing 198 |
| 031465- | Rompin' | BB B-10186, HMV B-8927, B-9154, EA-2671, Swing 68 |

FRANK NEWTON QUINTET : Frank Newton-t/Albert Ammons-p/Teddy Bunn-g/Johnny Williams-
    sb/Sidney Catlett-d.                    New York, April 7, 1939.

GM-512-B  Daybreak Blues                           BN 501

FRANK NEWTON AND HIS CAFE SOCIETY ORCHESTRA : Frank Newton-t/Tab Smith-ss-as/Stanley
    Payne-as/Kenneth Hollon-ts/Kenny Kersey-p/Ulysses Livingston-g/Johnny Williams-sb/
    Eddie Dougherty-d.                      New York, April 12, 1939.

    24365-A  Tab's Blues                    Voc 4821, Par R-2708, Br A-82183,
                                            Od A-2379, A-272262
    24366-A  Jitters                        Voc 4851
    24367-A  Frankie's Jump                 Voc 4821, Par R-2708, Br A-82183,
                                            Od A-2379, A-272262
    24368-A-B  Jam Fever                    Voc 4851

FRANK NEWTON QUINTET : Frank Newton-t/Meade Lux Lewis-p/Teddy Bunn-g/Johnny Williams
    sb/Sidney Catlett-d.                    New York, June 8, 1939.

GM-531    After Hour Blues                          BN 14

FRANK NEWTON AND HIS CAFE SOCIETY ORCHESTRA : Probably as for April 12, 1939, plus
    tb.                                     New York, August 15, 1939.

    25203-1  Vamp                           Voc 5410
    25204-1  Parallel Fifths                       -

## RAMON NEWTON

Also known as Cyril Newton, the leader, violinist and vocalist of the original Savoy
    Havana Band made some solo sides for HMV, accompanied by a small group that played
    quite interesting music.  The following are known or reported to be in this cate-
    gory, despite the titles.

Vocal, acc. by Syncopated Quartet : Probably :- Jimmy Wornell-t/Van Phillips-cl-as/
    Billy Mayerl-p/Dave Thomas-bj.          Hayes, Middlesex, October 8, 1925.

Bb-6887-1  Where Is That Girl Who Was Stolen      HMV B-2156
              From Me ?
Bb-6890-1  Chick, Chick, Chicken                         -

                                            Hayes, Middlesex, December 2, 1925.

Bb-7439-2  If You Knew Susie (Like I Know Susie)  HMV B-2241
Bb-7440-1  I'm An Airman                                 -

                                            Hayes, Middlesex, February 17, 1926.

Bb-7915-1  Brown Eyes, Why Are You Blue ?        HMV B-2285

## THE  NEWTOWN PIPPINS

The following titles credited thus are reportedly of jazz interest.

T/tb/2as/ts/p/bj/bb/d/Elmer Russell-v.      New York, March 8, 1928.

GEX-1119-A  Caroline - vER                   Gnt 6741, Bell 598, Ch 15498,
                                             Spr 2512
GEX-1120    Isabella (Tell Your Fella) - vER Gnt 6413, Bell 592, Ch 15456,
                                             Spr 2545
GEX-1121    Green River Blues - vER          Bell 591, Ch 15459
GEX-1122    Oh ! Daisy - vER                 Bell 589, Spr 2532
    NOTE:- Bell 589, 591, 592 and 598 as KIRBY'S KINGS OF JAZZ; Champion 15456, 15458
    and 15459 as CHUCK KING AND HIS KENTUCKIANS; Superior 2512, 2532 and 2545 as EMIL
    RUCKER AND HIS BOYS.

Pseudonym on Coliseum for the following items listed in this book :-

1489  Georgia Rose (California Ramblers)
1489  Stop ! Rest Awhile (Yerkes S.S. Flotilla Orchestra)
1507  The Sheik (California Ramblers)
1600  Runnin' Wild (The Southland Six)
1621  Sittin' In A Corner (Broadway Syncopators)

## NEW YORK DANCE ORCHESTRA

Pseudonym on Guardsman for the following item listed in this book :-

1312  Loose Feet (Original Memphis Five)

## THE  NEW YORKERS

Pseudonym on Victor and HMV for Gene Kardos and his Orchestra, q.v., on Brunswick
   6164 for the Dorsey Brothers' Orchestra, q.v., and on Australian Ångelus for the
   following items listed in this book :-

3008  Is She My Girl Friend ? (Varsity Eight)
3082  Makin' Whoopee (Ernie Golden and his Orchestra)

The following sides issued under this name have never been more closely identified.
   They are said to feature good t/tb/ts/vn/p amongst others.
                                      New York, c. January, 1930.

   2024-3  Kickin' A Hole In The Sky - v            QRS Q-1027, Gds 208

                                      New York, c. March, 1930.

       Let Me Sing - And I'm Happy - v             QRS Q-1053

                                      New York, c. May, 1930.

   2378-2  Fireworks                               QRS Q-1053

See also the Boswell Sisters.

## NEW YORKERS  TANZORCHESTER

George Carhart-bj-g dir. Evelyn Bazell-t/Eddie Norman-tb/Danny Polo-cl-as/Andy Fors-
   ter-ts/Jack O'Brien-p/Dave Tough-d/Al Bowlly-v.
                                      Berlin, September 28, 1927.

M-19450    Hoosier Sweetheart                Hom 4-2420
M-19451    Sunny Disposish - vAB             -
   NOTE:- This issue as GEORGE CARHART'S NEW YORKERS JAZZ ORCHESTER.

   Unknown v.                        Berlin, October, 1927.

MO-1078    It All Belongs To Me - v          Tri-Ergon TE-5108
MO-1079    A Siren Dream - v                 Tri-Ergon TE-5109
           Music And Moonlight - v                -
           My Sunday Girl - v                Tri-Ergon TE-5108
           I'm Living On Love - v3           Tri-Ergon TE-5110
           There's A Cradle In Caroline - v      -

                                      Berlin, November, 1927.

MO-1163    Ostrich Walk                      Tri-Ergon TE-5134
MO-1164    Pretty Girl                       Tri-Ergon TE-5135
MO-1165    By The Waterfall                  Tri-Ergon TE-5134
MO-1166    The Song Is Ended (w)             Tri-Ergon TE-5135
MO-1167    Clarinet Marmalade                Tri-Ergon TE-5136
MO-1168    Smile                             Tri-Ergon TE-5137
MO-1169    One More Night                    Tri-Ergon TE-5136
MO-1170    It's A Million To One You're In Love   Tri-Ergon TE-5137

Pseudonym on Mayfair for Joe Venuti (q.v.) and Eddie Lang's All-Star Orchestra.

## NEW YORK SYNCOPATORS

Pseudonym for the following items listed in this book :-

Broadcast W-529    I Want To Meander In The Meadow (Fred Rich and his Orchestra)
Odeon ONY-36148    It's A Great Life (Sam Lanin's Famous Players)
      ONY-36149/Parlophone R-823    When Kentucky Bids The World "Good Morning" (Sam
                        Lanin's Famous Players)
      ONY-36152    Both sides by Sam Lanin's Famous Players
      ONY-36157    I'll Be Blue, Just Thinking Of You (Fred Rich and his Orchestra)
      ONY-36158    I Got Rhythm (Fred Rich and his Orchestra)
      ONY-36165    Both sides by Fred Rich and his Orchestra
      ONY-36189    I'm So In Love With You (Duke Ellington and his Orchestra)
      ONY-36190    I Can't Realise You Love Me (Duke Elington and his Orchestra)
      ONY-36194    Both sides by Fred Rich and his Orchestra
      ONY-36208    Just A Crazy Song (Sam Lanin's Famous Players)
OKeh 40757/Parlophone E-5769    Both sides by Ted Wallace and his Orchestra
      40860    Both sides by Ted Wallace and his Orchestra
      40965    Both sides by Ted Wallace and his Orchestra
      41003    Both sides by Sam Lanin's Famous Players
      41202    Both sides by the Goofus Five and their Orchestra
      41264    The One That I Love Loves Me (Sam Lanin's Famous Players)
Parlophone A-2462    Mary (Ted Wallace and his Orchestra)
          R-857    Cheerful Little Earful (Fred Rich and his Orchestra)
          R-874/A-3147    The Little Things In Life (Fred Rich and his Orchestra)

## THE NICHOLAS BROTHERS

Vocal duets with tap-dancing, acc. by George Scott Wood-p dir. t/tb/Freddy Gardner-
    cl/Joe Young or George Elliott-g/? George Senior-sb/? Max Abrams-d.
                            London, September 15, 1936.

OEA-4052-1    Keep A Twinkle In Your Eye            HMV BD-373
OEA-4053-1    Your Heart And Mine                  -

    Acc. by Bobby Hackett-Ralph Muzzillo-t/Al Philburn-tb/Don Watt-cl/Frank Signorelli-
    p/Dave Barbour-g/Haig Stephens-sb/Stan King-d.
                            New York, December 6, 1937.

62858-A    Wrap Your Cares In Rhythm And Dance    Dec 1604, Br 02588
62859-A    They Say He Ought To Dance             -         -

## NICK NICHOLS AND HIS ORCHESTRA

Jack Cox and another-t/tb/2as/ts/p/bj/bb/d.
                            Camden, N. J., January 22, 1929.

267    She Belongs To Me                    Vic test
269    The World Is Waiting For The Sunrise  -

                            New York, November, 1929.

3700-A    Breakin' A Leg (Jazz Me Blues)        GG 1820

## RAY NICHOLS AND HIS FOUR TOWERS ORCHESTRA

The following titles by this commercial dance orchestra are of some interest as jazz
    or "hot" dance music; strangely, the name was used as a pseudonym for Fletcher
    Henderson and his Connie's Inn Orchestra, q.v., on Bluebird B-5904 (SUGAR FOOT
    STOMP).

Ray Nichols-t dir. t/tb/2as/ts/p/g/sb/d/Al Graf-Billie Hibberd-v.
                            New York, April 1, 1935.

89399-1    Who's Sorry Now ?                    BB B-5902
89500-1    Rosetta - vAG                        -

                            New York, June 27, 1935.

92530-1    Black Coffee - vBH                   BB B-6013

RED AND MIFF'S STOMPERS : Red Nichols-t/Miff Mole-tb/Jimmy Dorsey-cl-as/Alfie Evans-
    as/Arthur Schutt-p/Joe Tarto-bb/Vic Berton-d.
                                                New York, October 13, 1926.

11245    Alabama Stomp                          Ed 51854, <u>SD 106</u>
11246    Stampede                               -          -    -

                                                New York, November 10, 1926.

11291    Hurricane                              Ed 51878, <u>SD 105</u>
11292    Black Bottom Stomp                     -          -    -

RED NICHOLS AND HIS FIVE PENNIES : Red Nichols-t/Jimmy Dorsey-cl-as/Arthur Schutt-p/
    Eddie Lang-g/Vic Berton-d.                  New York, December 8, 1926.

E-4178; E-20992   Washboard Blues               Voc 15498, Br 40602
E-4179; E-20993   Washboard Blues               Br 3407*, 6814, 80072, 01801,
                                                A-222, Voc 1069
E-4180; E-20994   That's No Bargain             Br 3407*, 40608
E-4181; E-20995   That's No Bargain             -       6814, 80072, 01801,
                                                A-222, Voc 1069, 15498

    Miff Mole-tb added.                         New York, December 20, 1926.

E-21594; E-4263   Buddy's Habits                Br 3477*, 6815, 80071, 01802,
                                                A-358, Voc 1076, 15573
E-21597; E-4260   Boneyard Shuffle              As above

                                                New York, January 12, 1927.

E-4382; E-22981   Alabama Stomp                 Br 3550*, 6817, 01804, A-456
E-4383; E-22982   Alabama Stomp                 Voc 15566
E-4384; E-22983   Alabama Stomp                 Br 3550
E-4385: E-22984   Hurricane                     -*  6817, 01804, A-456, Voc 15566
E-4386/7; E-22985/6  Hurricane                  -

RED AND MIFF'S STOMPERS : As last Five Pennies session above, but Tony Colucci-bj
    replaces Lang.                              New York, February 11, 1927.

37768-2  Delirium                               Vic 20778
37768-3  Delirium                               JA 21 (LP)
37769-2  Davenport Blues                        Vic 20778
37769-3  Davenport Blues                        JA 21 (LP)

RED NICHOLS AND HIS FIVE PENNIES : Red Nichols-t Miff Mole-tb/Jimmy Dorsey-cl-as/Joe
    Venuti-vn/Arthur Schutt-p/Eddie Lang-g/Vic Berton-d.
                                                New York, March 3, 1927.

E-21718; E-4643   Bugle Call Rag                Br 3490, 3510, 6816, 01803,
                                                A-7556, Voc 15536
E-21721; E-4640   Back Beats                    As above

    Venuti probably omitted.                    New York, May 18, 1927.

E-5143/5  Alabama Stomp                         Voc rejected
E-5146/8  Hurricane                             -

    Adrian Rollini-bsx added.                   New York, June 20, 1927.

E-23665; E-6302   Cornfed                       Br 3597*, 6818, Voc 15602
E-23666           Cornfed                       -       01805, A-7543
E-23668           Five Pennies                  Br 3855, 3819, 6821, 01851,
                                                4844 (Canadian), Col DO-1354
    NOTE:- Some copies of Brunswick 4844 play MY GAL SAL (matrix E-26751, q.v.) though
    labelled FIVE PENNIES.

                                                New York, June 25, 1927.

E-23755; E-6300   Mean Dog Blues                Br 3597*, 6818, 01805, A-7543,
                                                Voc 15602

RED NICHOLS AND HIS FIVE PENNIES : Red Nichols-t, plus Leo McConville-Manny Klein-t*/
Miff Mole-tb/Pee Wee Russell-cl/Fud Livingston-ts-a/Adrian Rollini-bsx-gfs/Lennie
Hayton-p-cel-a/Dick McDonough-g/Vic Berton-d.
                              New York, August 15, 1927.

| | | |
|---|---|---|
| E-24224 | *Riverboat Shuffle - aFL | Br 3627 |
| E-24225 | *Riverboat Shuffle - aFL | - 3698,6820,01306,A-7601,A-500400 |
| E-24228 | *Eccentric - aFL | As above, plus Gol DO-1354 |
| E-24230 | Ida, Sweet As Apple Cider - aLH | Br 3626 |
| E-24232 | Ida, Sweet As Apple Cider - aLH | -* 6819, 80069, 01536, |
| | | A-7559, A-500401, Coral 91015, |
| | | Mt M-12443, Per 15648, Voc 4654, |
| | | 15622 |
| E-24235 | Feelin' No Pain - aFL | As above |

NOTE:- Melotone M-12443 and Perfect 15648 as THE RED HEADS.

RED AND MIFF'S STOMPERS : Red Nichols-t/Miff Mole-tb/Pee Wee Russell-Fud Livingston-
cl-ts-a/Lennie Hayton-p/Carl Kress-g/Jack Hansen-bb/Vic Berton-d.
                              New York, October 12, 1927.

| | | |
|---|---|---|
| 40168-1 | Slippin' Around | Vic 21397 |
| 40169-2 | Feeling No Pain | Vic 21183 |

RED NICHOLS' STOMPERS : Red Nichols-Bob Ashford- (or Bo Ashford)-t/Bill Rank-another-
tb/Max Farley-as/Frank Trumbauer-Cm/Pee Wee Russell-cl-ts/Adrian Rollini-bsx/Arthur
Schutt-or Lennie Hayton-p/Carl Kress-g/Jack Hansen-bb/Chauncey Morehouse-d/Jim
Miller-Charlie Farrell-v.     New York, October 26, 1927.

| | | |
|---|---|---|
| 40512-1 | Sugar - vJM-CF | Vic 21056, HMV B-5433, AM-1211 |
| 40513-1 | Make My Cot Where The Cot-Cot-Cotton Grows | - - - |
| | - vJM-CF | |

RED NICHOLS AND HIS FIVE PENNIES : Red Nichols-t/Miff Mole-tb/Dudley Fosdick-mel/Fud
Livingston-Pee Wee Russell-cl-ts/Lennie Hayton-p-cel/Carl Kress-g/Vic Berton-d.
                              New York, February 25, 1928.

| | | |
|---|---|---|
| E-7168; E-26749 | Nobody's Sweetheart | Br 3854, 3801, 6681, 80070, 01569, |
| | | 4867 (Italian), A-7707, A-500402, |
| | | Ban 32550, Or 2555, Per 15688 |
| E-7170/1; E-26751/2 | My Gal Sal | Rejected |

NOTE:- Oriole 2555 as THE RED HEADS; and see note under June 20, 1927 session.

                              New York, February 27, 1928.

| | | |
|---|---|---|
| E-26693 | Avalon | Br 3854, 3801, 6681, 80070, 01569, |
| | | 4867 (Italian), A-7707, A-500402, |
| | | Ban 32550, Or 2555, Per 15688 |
| E-26695 | Japanese Sandman | Br 3855, 3819, 6821, 01851, 4844 |
| E-26696 | Japanese Sandman | - |

NOTE:- Brunswick 4844 is a Canadian issue.  Oriole 2555 as THE RED HEADS.

Red Nichols-Leo McConville-Manny Klein-t/Miff Mole-tb/Dudley Fosdiok-mel/Fud
Livingston-cl-ts/Murray Kellner-vn/Arthur Schutt-p/Carl Kress-g/Art Miller-sb/Vic
Berton-d/Scrappy Lambert-v.   New York, March 2, 1928.

| | | |
|---|---|---|
| XE-26772 | Poor Butterfly - vSL | Br 20062 |
| XE-26773 | Poor Butterfly - vSL | - 20066 |
| XE-26774 | Poor Butterfly | Br A-5044 |
| XE-26775 | Can't Yo' Hear Me Calling, Caroline ? | Br 20062, 20066 |
| | - vSL | |
| XE-26776 | Can't Yo' Hear Me Calling, Caroline ? | Br A-5044 |

Jimmy Dorsey-cl-as added.     New York, May 29, 1928.

| | | |
|---|---|---|
| -27605- | Panama | Br 3961, 03499, UHCA 20, |
| | | Dec BM-1197 |
| -27606-A | There'll Come A Time | Br 3955, 3850, 6822, A-7849, |
| | | A-9932 |

RED NICHOLS AND HIS FIVE PENNIES : Red Nichols-Leo McConville-Manny Klein-t/Miff Mole
  tb/Dudley Fosdick-mel/Fud Livingston-cl-ts/Murray Kellner-vn/Arthur Schutt-p/Eddie
  Lang-g/Art Miller-sb/Vic Berton-d/Scrappy Lambert-v.
                                    New York, May 31, 1928.

| | | |
|---|---|---|
| XE-27621- | Dear Old Southland - vSL | Br 20070, 20075, 0125 |
| XE-27621-G | Dear Old Southland | Br A-5081 |
| XE-27622- | Limehouse Blues - vSL | Br 20070, 20075, 0125 |
| XE-27622-G | Limehouse Blues | Br A-5081 |

  Klein and Lang omitted (and McConville also from E-27624); Joe Venuti-vn replaces
  Kellner,                          New York, May 31, 1928.

E-27623-A  Whispering                       Br 3955, 3850, 6822, 01852, A-7849,
                                              A-9932
E-27624-   I Can't Give You Anything But Love   Voc 15710
  NOTE:- Vocalion 15710 as LOUISIANA RHYTHM KINGS.

  Mannie Klein-t returns; Carl Kress-g added; Chauncey Morehouse-d-vib replaces
  Berton.                           New York, June 1, 1928.

E-27625-   Margie                           Br 3961, 03499, UHCA 19,
                                              Dec BM-1197
E-27626-A  Imagination                      Br 3989, 3871, 6823, 01855
E-27627-   Original Dixieland One-Step      -       -       -       -

RED NICHOLS AND HIS ORCHESTRA : Red Nichols-Leo McConville-t/Miff Mole-tb/Dudley
  Fosdick-mel/Fud Livingston-cl-ts/Arthur Schutt-p/Carl Kress-g/Chauncey Morehouse-
  d-vib-v.                          New York, June 21, 1928.

45814-2-3  Harlem Twist - vCM              Vic 21560
45815-2  Five Pennies                        -       HMV EA-467
  NOTE:- Red Nichols himself requested that 45814-3 be used after 45814-2 had been
  issued.

RED NICHOLS AND HIS FIVE PENNIES : Red Nichols-Manny Klein-t/Miff Mole-tb/Dudley
  Fosdick-mel/Fud Livingston-cl/Jimmy Dorsey-as/Arthur Schutt-p/Carl Kress-g/Vic
  Berton-d.                         New York, October 2, 1928.

E-28326-A  A Pretty Girl Is Like A Melody   Br 4456, 6826, 01854, 1033, A-8337
E-28327-   I Must Have That Man             Rejected

  Benny Goodman-cl-as replaces Livingston and Dorsey; Chauncey Morehouse-d replaces
  Berton.                           New York, February 1, 1929.

E-29209-   I Never Knew                     Br 4243, 3931, 02356
E-29210-   Who's Sorry Now ?                -       -       -

  As for October 2, 1928, but Benny Goodman-cl-as replaces Dorsey; Lennie Hayton-p-
  cel replaces Schutt.              New York, February 5, 1929.

E-29222-   Chinatown, My Chinatown          Br 4363, 5019, 6825, 01856, 1029,
                                              A-8298, A-500403
E-29223-   On The Alamo                     Rejected

  As for October 2, 1928, plus Adrian Rollini-bsx.
                                    New York, February 16, 1929.

E-29294-   Alice Blue Gown                  Br 4456, 1033
E-29294-   Alice Blue Gown                  Br 6826, 01854, A-8337
E-29295-A  Allah's Holiday                  Br 4286, 3960, 01853, 1002, A-8264
E-29295-B  Allah's Holiday                  Br 6824
E-29296-   Roses Of Picardy                 Br 4286, 3960, 6824, 01853, 1002,
                                              A-8264

THE CAPTIVATORS, DIRECTION OF RED NICHOLS : Red Nichols-t dir. Manny Klein-t/Glenn
Miller-tb/Alfie Evans-Pete Pumiglio-cl-as/Jimmy Crossan-cl-ts/Arthur Schutt (and
another ?)-p/Carl Kress-bj-g/Art Miller-sb/Chick Condon-d/Scrappy Lambert-v.
New York, March 20, 1929.

| | | |
|---|---|---|
| E-29507- | I'm Marching Home To You - vSL | Br 4308, 3991 |
| E-29507-G | I'm Marching Home To You | Br A-8257 |
| E-29508- | Building A Nest For Mary - vSL | Br 4321, 5014, 1019 |
| E-29508-G | Building A Nest For Mary | Br A-8258 |
| E-29509- | I Used To Love Her In The Moonlight | Br 4308, 3991 |
| | (But She's In The Limelight Now) - vSL | |
| E-29509-G | I Used To Love Her In The Moonlight | Br A-8257 |
| | (But She's In The Limelight Now) | |

NOTE:- Brunswick 3991 and 5014 as RED NICHOLS AND HIS CAPTIVATORS; 1019 as
ORCHESTRE THE CAPTIVATORS DIRECTION RED NICHOLS.

RED NICHOLS AND HIS FIVE PENNIES : Red Nichols-Leo McConville-Manny Klein-t/Glenn
Miller-tb-a/Jack Teagarden-? Bill Trone or Herb Taylor-tb/Benny Goodman-cl-as-bar/
as/Babe Russin-ts/Arthur Schutt-p/Carl Kress-g/Art Miller-sb/Gene Krupa-d/Scrappy
Lambert-v.                            New York, April 18, 1929.

| | | |
|---|---|---|
| E-29708-A | Indiana - aGM | Br 4373, 6718, 01591, A-9206, |
| | | A-500404m Voc 4599, Col DO-1236 |
| E-29708-B | Indiana - aGM | Br 80006 |
| E-29709-A | Dinah | Br 4373, 6718, 80006, 01591, |
| | | A-9206, A-500404, Voc 4599, |
| | | Lucky S-28 |
| E-29710-A | On The Alamo - vSL | Br 4363, 5019 |
| E-29710-B | On The Alamo | Br 6825, 01856, 1029, A-8298, |
| | | A-500403 |

Red Nichols-Leo McConville-Manny Klein-t/Jack Teagarden-tb-v/Glenn Miller-tb-a/
Bill Trone-tb/Jimmy Dorsey-cl-as/Alfie Evans-Arnold Brilhart-cl-as-bsn-f-o/Larry
Binyon-ts-f-o/Murray Kellner-Joe Raymond-Lou Raderman-Henry Whiteman-vn/Lucien
Schmidt-vc/Arthur Schutt-p-a/Carl Kress-g/Joe Tarto-bb/Vic Berton-d/Scrappy
Lambert-v.                            New York, May 20, 1929.

| | | |
|---|---|---|
| XE-29957-A | Sally, Won't You Come Back ? - vJT-SL | Br 20092, 0101 |
| CE-29957-G | Sally, Won't You Come Back ? | Rejected |

Tommy Thunen-t replaces McConville; Herb Taylor-tb-a replaces Trone; Jimmy Crossan
ts-bsn-f-o replaces Evans; Art Miller-sb added; Red Nichols-a.  All three titles
were made without vocals, but were rejected.
New York, June 7, 1929.

| | | |
|---|---|---|
| XE-29994-A | It Had To Be You - aAS/vSL | Br 20092, 0101 |
| XE-29995-A | I'll See You In My Dreams - aGM/vSL | Br 20091 |
| XE-29996-A | Some Of These Days - aRN-HT/vJT-SL | - |

Red Nichols-Manny Klein-Tommy Thunen-t/Jack Teagarden-Glenn Miller-? Herb Taylor-
tb/Pee Wee Russell-cl/Bud Freeman-ts/Joe Sullivan-p/Tommy Felline-bj/Art Miller-sb
/Dave Tough-d/Red McKenzie-v.         New York, June 12, 1929.

| | | |
|---|---|---|
| E-30056-A | Who Cares ? - vRM | Br 4778, 6831 |
| E-30056-G | Who Cares ? | Rejected |
| E-30057-A | Rose Of Washington Square | Br 4778, 6831, 01204, 4730 (Can.) |
| | | A-500200 |

Red Nichols-Tommy Thunen-John Egan-t/Jack Teagarden-Glenn Miller-Herb Taylor-tb/
Jimmy Dorsey-Pee Wee Russell-cl/Fud Livingston-ts-a/Henry Whiteman-Maurice Goffin-
vn/Irving Brodsky-p/Tommy Felline-bj/Jack Hansen-ab/George Beebe-d/Scrappy Lambert
Red McKenzie-v.                       New York, August 20, 1929.

| | | |
|---|---|---|
| E-30502-A | I May Be Wrong, But I Think You're | Br 4500, 6753 |
| | Wonderful - vSL | |
| E-30502-B | I May Be Wrong, But I Think Uou're | -      -   4891 (Canadian), |
| | Wonderful - vSL | A-8493 |
| E-30503-G | I May Be Wtong, But I Think You're | Br A-9520 |
| | Wonderful | |
| E-30504-A | The New Yorkers - vRM | Br 4500, A-8493 |
| E-30505-G | The New Yorkers | Br A-9520 |

RED NICHOLS AND HIS FIVE PENNIES : Red Nichols-Tommy Thunen-John Egan-t/Jack Teagarden-Glenn Miller-Herb Taylor-tb/Jimmy Dorsey-Pee Wee Russell-cl/Fud Livingston-
ts-a/Irving Brodsky-p/Tommy Felline-bj/Jack Hansen-bb/George Beebe-d/Scrappy
Lambert-v.                          New York, August 27, 1929.

| | | |
|---|---|---|
| E-30712-A-B | They Didn't Believe Me - vSL | Br 4651, 6827 |
| E-30713-G | They Didn't Believe Me | Br A-8655 |
| XE-30714-A-B | They Didn't Believe Me | Radio Broadcast 29 |
| XE-30715-A-B | I May Be Wrong, But I Think You're | Radio Broadcast 30 |
| XE-30716-A-B | The New Yorkers      )Wonderful) | Radio Broadcast 31 |
| XE-30717-A-B | On The Alamo | Radio Broadcast 32 |
| XE-30718-A-B | That's A Plenty | Radio Broadcast 33 |

Henry Whiteman-Maurice Goffin-vn/Dick Robertson-v added.
                                   New York, September 6, 1929.

| | | |
|---|---|---|
| E-30531-A-B | Wait For The Happy Ending - vSL/aFL | Br 4510, 1043 |
| E-30532-G | Wait For The Happy Ending | Rejected |
| E-30533-A-B | Can't We Be Friends ? - vDR | Br 4510, 6827, 1043 |
| E-30534-G | Can't We Be Friends ? | Rejected |

Red Nichols-Mickey Bloom-Tommy Thunen-t/Jack Teagarden-Glenn Miller-Bill Trone-tb/
Benny Goodman-cl/Jimmy Dorsey-cl-as/Rube Bloom p/Tommy Felline-bj/Joe Tarto-bb/
Dave Tough-d/Scrappy Lambert-v.      New York, September 9, 1929.

| | | |
|---|---|---|
| E-30538-A | Nobody Knows (And Nobody Seems To Care) - vSL | Br 4790, 6832, 02505 |
| E-30539-G | Nobody Knows (And Nobody Seems To Care) | Br A-8744 |
| E-30540-A | Smiles - vSL | Br 4790, 6832 |
| E-30541-G | Smiles | Br A-8744 |
| E-30542-A-B | Say It With Music - vSL | Rejected |
| E-30543-G | Say It With Music | - |

Teagarden and Goodman omitted; Herb Taylor-tb replaces Trone; Brunswick 4591 as
THE CAPTIVATORS, DIRECTION OF RED NICHOLS.
                                   New York, October 22, 1929.

| | | |
|---|---|---|
| E-31266- | Get Happy - vSL | Br 4591 |
| E-31267-G | Get Happy | Br A-8615 |
| E-31268- | Somebody To Love Me - vSL | Br 4591 |
| E-31269-G | Somebody To Love Me | Br A-8615 |
| E-31270- | Say It With Music - vSL | Br 4651 |
| E-31271-G | Say It With Music | Br A-8655 |

Red Nichols-Ruby Weinstein-Charlie Teagarden-t/Tommy Dorsey-Glenn Miller-tb/Jimmy
Dorsey-cl-as/Sid Stoneburn-as/Babe Russin-Larry Binyon-ts/Jack Russin-p/Treg Brown
bj/Gene Krupa-d/v.                   New York, January 17, 1930.

| | | |
|---|---|---|
| E-31882-B | Strike Up The Band - v | Br 4695, 6753 |
| E-31883-G | Strike Up The Band | Br A-8659 |
| E-31884- | Soon - v | Br 4695 |
| E-31885-G | Soon | Br A-8659 |

Teagarden, Miller, Stoneburn, Binyon omitted; Adrian Rollini-bsx added.
                                   New York, January 24, 1930.

| | | |
|---|---|---|
| E-31903- | Sometimes I'm Happy | Br 4701, 6828, A-8673 |
| E-31904- | Hallelujah ! | -     -     - |

Red Nichols-Tommy Thunen-Manny Klein-t/Jack Teagarden-tb-v/Glenn Miller-tb/Jimmy
Dorsey-cl-as/Babe Russin-ts/Adrian Rollini-bsx/Jack Russin-p/Weston Vaughan-g/Jack
Hansen-bb/Gene Krupa-d.              New York, February 3, 1930.

| | | |
|---|---|---|
| E-31923-A | I'm Just Wild About Harry | Br 4839, 6833, 01121, A-500405 |
| E-31924-A | After You've Gone - vJT | -     -     01104     - |

                                   New York, February 14, 1930.

| | | |
|---|---|---|
| E-32040-A | I Want To Be Happy | Br 4724, 6830, 80007, 01032, A-8832, 3005 (Argentine) |
| E-32041-A | Tea For Two | As above |

RED NICHOLS AND HIS FIVE PENNIES : Red Nichols-Ruby Weinstein-Charlie Teagarden-t/
    Jack Teagarden-Glenn Miller-tb/Benny Goodman-cl/Sid Stoneburn-as/Babe Russin-ts/Joe
    Sullivan-p/Treg Brown-bj/Art Miller-sb/Gene Krupa-d.
                                        New York, July 2, 1930.

E-33304-A  Peg O' My Heart                    Br 4877, 6835, 01019, A-8962,
                                              Dec BM-1166
E-33304-B  Peg O' My Heart                    Br 80004
E-33305-A  Sweet Georgia Brown                Br 4944, 6841, 01048, A-8997
E-33306-A  China Boy                          Br 4877, 6835, 01019, 80004,
                                              A-8962, Dec BM-1166, F-49014
E-33307-A-B  Chong (He Come From Hongkong)    Rejected

    Jack Teagarden-Treg Brown-v.             New York, July 3, 1930.

E-33333-A  The Sheik Of Araby - vJT-TB        Br 4885, 6836, 80005, 01104,
                                              A-8866, A-500403
E-33334-A  Shim-Me-Sha-Wabble                 Br 4885, 6836, 01204, A-8866,
                                              A-500200
E-33334-B  Shim-Me-Sha-Wabble                 Br 80005

    Weinstein, Stoneburn, Brown and Art Miller omitted; Bud Freeman-ts replaces Russin;
    Adrian Rollini-bsx-x added.              New York, August 27, 1930.

E-34109-  Carolina In The Morning             Br 4925, 6839, 01062
E-34110-  How Come You Do Me Like You Do ?    Rejected
E-34111-  Who ?                               Br 4925, 6839, 01062
E-34112-  By The Shalimar                     Br 4944, 6841, 01048, A-8997

    Red Nichols-Ruby Weinstein-Charlie Teagarden-t/Jack Teagarden-tb-v/Glenn Miller-
    George Stoll-tb/Benny Goodman-cl/Sid Stoneburn-as/Larry Binyon-ts-f/Jack Russin-p/
    Art Miller-sb/Gene Krupa-d/The Foursome (Marshall Smith-Ray Johnson-Del Porter-
    Dwight Snyder)-v.                        New York, September 26, 1930.

E-34626-A  On Revival Day - Part 1 - vJT-F    Br 6026, 6843, 01087, A-9008
E-34627-A  On Revival Day - Part 1 - vJT-F    Rejected ?
E-34628-A  On Revival Day - Part 2 - vJT-F    Br 6026, 6843, 01087, A-9008

    Jack Teagarden and Stoll omitted; Ed Bergman-Wladimir Selinsky-vn/Treg Brown-bj/
    Dick Robertson-v.                        New York, October 23, 1930.

E-34958-  Embraceable You - vDR               Br 4957, 6842, A-8963
E-34959-  I Got Rhythm - vDR                    - 4872, 6711 -          01300
E-34960-  A Girl Friend Of A Boy Friend Of Mine   Mt M-12005
          - vDR
E-34961-  Sweet Jennie Lee - vDR                - Pan 25001, P-12005, Emb E-125
    NOTE:- Melotone M-12005, Panachord P-12005 and 25001 as THE CAPTIVATORS; Embassy
    E-125 as BLUEY SCHAEFFER'S ORCHESTRA.

    Jack Teagarden-tb added; Harold Arlen-Eddy Thomas-v.
                                        New York, November 6, 1930.

E-35214-A  Linda - vHA                        Br 4982, 6844, A-9003
E-35215-A  Yours And Mine - vET                 -      -      -

RED AND HIS BIG TEN : Red Nichols-Ruby Weinstein-t/Glenn Miller-tb/Benny Goodman-cl/
    Sid Stoneburn-as/Babe Russin-ts/Roy Bargy-p/Carl Kress-g/Art Miller-sb/Gene Krupa-
    d/Dick Robertson-v.                      New York, November 18, 1930.

64623-1  That's Where The South Begins - vDR    Vic 23026
64624-3  I'm Tickled Pink With A Blue-Eyed Baby-vDR  -    HMV B-5977

RED NICHOLS AND HIS FIVE PENNIES : Red Nichols-Charlie Teagarden-t/Wingy Manone-t-v/
    Glenn Miller-tb/Jimmy Dorsey-cl-as/Babe Russin-ts/Joe Sullivan-p/Art Miller-sb/
    Gene Krupa-d.                            New York, December 1, 1930.

-35618-A  My Honey's Lovin' Arms -            Br 6012, 01121, A-9005
-35619-A  Rockin' Chair - vWM                   -    01852    -

RED NICHOLS AND HIS FIVE PENNIES : Red Nichols-Ruby Weinstein-Charlie Teagarden-t/
   Wingy Manone-t-v/Glenn Miller-tb/Benny Goodman-cl-bar/Babe Russin-ts/Jack Russin-p/
   Art Miller-sb/Gene Krupa-d/Harold Arlen-v.
                                          New York, December 10, 1930.

E-35733-A  Bugaboo - vWM                       Br 6058, 01120, A-9024, Mt M-12495
                                               Or 2574, Per 15684, Ro 1120
E-35734-A  Corrinne Corrina - vWM              As above
E-35735-A  How Come You Do Me Like You Do ? - vHA  Br 6149, 01180, A-9099
   NOTE:- All issues other than the Brunswicks as THE RED HEADS.

   Red Nichols-Ruby Weinstein-t/Glenn Miller-tb/Benny Goodman-cl/Gil Rodin-as/Eddie
   Miller-ts/p/Nappy Lamare-g/Harry Goodman-sb/Ray Bauduc-d/Scrappy Lambert-Dick
   Robertson-v.                           New York, December 12, 1930.

E-35738-B  Blue Again - vDR                    Br 6014, 01082, 4764, A-9002,
                                               Spt S-2167
E-35739-B  When Kentucky Bids The World "Good  As above, plus Pan P-11988
              Morning" - vDR
E-35740-   What Good Am I Without You ? - vSL  Mt M-12049, Pan 25015, P-12049,
                                               Mf G-2003
E-35741-   We're Friends Again - vSL           Mt M-12049                    -
   NOTE:- Melotone M-12049 and Panachord 25015 as THE CAPTIVATORS; Panachord P-11998
   as HAGAN'S HOTEL RITZ ORCHESTRA; Mayfair G-2003 as CLUB ALBANY ORCHESTRA; Supertone
   S-2167 as BLUE DIAMOND ORCHESTRA.

RED AND HIS BIG TEN : Red Nichols-Ruby Weinstein-t/Glenn Miller-tb/Benny Goodman-cl/
   Sid Stoneburn-as/Babe Russin-ts/Roy Bargy-p/Carl Kress-g/Art Miller-sb/Gene Krupa-
   d/Paul Small (as JOHNNY DAVIS on HMV)-v.
                                          New York, January 5, 1931.

67760-1  At Last I'm Happy - vPS               Vic 23033, HMV R-14590
67761-1  If You Haven't Got A Girl - vPS           -    Zon EE-252

RED NICHOLS AND HIS FIVE PENNIES : Red Nichols-Ruby Weinstein-Charlie Teagarden-t/
   Jack Teagarden-tb-v/Glenn Miller-tb/Benny Goodman-cl/Sid Stoneburn-as/Larry Binyon
   ts/Ed Bergman-Wladimir Selinsky-vn/Jack Russin-p/Treg Brown-bj/Art Miller-sb/Gene
   Krupa-d/Harold Arlen-v.                 New York, January 16, 1931.

E-35167-A  You Said It - vHA                   Br 6029, 6842, A-9007
E-35168-A  Sweet And Hot - vHA                    - 6711, 4872 - 01300,
                                               Col DO-1236
E-35169-A-B  Keep A Song In Your Soul - vJT   Rejected
   NOTE:- Brunswick 6711 as RED NICHOLS AND HIS ORCHESTRA.

   Glenn Miller, Brown, Bergman and Selinsky all omitted; three Cuban drummers and
   Paul Small-v added.                    New York, January 23, 1931.

E-35954-A  The Peanut Vendor - vPS             Br 6035, 01076, A-9000,Spt S-2186
E-35955-A  Sweet Rosita - vPS                     -      -       -      -

   As for January 16, 1931, without Brown. New York, February 19, 1931.

E-36108-A  Things I Never Knew Till Now - vHA  Br 6068, A-9032
E-36109-A  Teardrops And Kisses - vHA          Br 6070, A-9046, Spt S-2191
E-36110-A  Were You Sincere ? - vHA               -      -       -      -
E-36111-A  Keep A Song In Your Soul - vJT      Br 6068, 6845, 6069, A-9032
   NOTE:- Supertone S-2186 and S-2191 as SUPERTONE DANCE ORCHESTRA.  Brunswick 6069
   is an Australian issue.

   As for January 16, 1931, but George Stoll-tb replaces Teagarden; Fulton McGrath-p
   replaces Russin; Brown plays g; Smith Ballew-v.
                                          New York, April 24, 1931.

E-36728-B  It's The Darndest Thing - vSB       Br 6191, 01275
E-36729-A  Singin' The Blues - vSB                - 6845 -
E-36730-A  Love Is Like That (What Can You Do ?)  Br 6118, A-9055, 6098 (Austral-
              - vSB                            ian)

RED NICHOLS AND HIS FIVE PENNIES : Red Nichols-t with probably similar personnel to
   the foregoing or the undermentioned; Paul Small-v.
                                        New York, May 11, 1931.

E-36757-A-B  Faithfully Yours - vPS              Br rejected

   Red Nichols-Charlie Teagarden-t/Glenn Miller-tb/Jimmy Dorsey-cl-as/Babe Russin-ts/
   Jack Russin-p/Perry Botkin-g/Art Miller-sb/Ray McKinley-d-v/Red McKenzie-v.
                                        New York, May 26, 1931.

E-36830-A  Just A Crazy Song (Hi-Hi-Hi)          Br 6133, 01163, A-9090
E-36831-A  You Rascal, You - vRM                 -          -        -
E-36832-A  Moan, You Moaners - vRayM             Br 6149, 01180, A-9099

   Red Nichols-Ruby Weinstein-Charlie Teagarden-t/Glenn Miller-George Stoll-tb/Jimmy
   Dorsey-cl-as/Sid Stoneburn-as/Larry Binyon-ts-f/Ed Bergman-Wladimir Selinsky-vn/
   Paul Mertz-p-a/Treg Brown-g/Art Miller-sb/Gene Krupa-d/Smith Ballew-v. (Brunswick
   6138 as LORING NICHOLS AND HIS ORCH.)   New York, June 11, 1931.

E-36855-A  Slow But Sure - vSB                   Br 6138, A-9094
E-36856-A  Little Girl - vSB                     -       -
E-36857-A  How The Time Can Fly - vSB            Br 6164, A-9140

   As for May 26, 1931 without Teagarden.  New York, June 24, 1931.

E-36877-A  How Long Blues - vRM                  Br 6160, 01213, A-9117
E-36878-A  Fan It - vRM                          -          -        -

   Red Nichols-t/Jimmy Dorsey-cl-as/Joe Venuti-vn/Fulton McGrath-p/Eddie Lang-g/Vic
   Berton-d.                            New York, September 16, 1931.

E-37204-A  Oh ! Peter (You're So Nice)           Br 6198, 01233, A-9170
E-37205-B  Honolulu Blues                        -          -        -

   Red Nichols-Don Moore-t/Johnny Davis-t-v/Will Bradley-tb/Jimmy Dorsey-cl-as/Russ
   Lyon-Babe Russin-ts/Fulton McGrath-p/Tony Starr-bj/Artie Bernstein-sb/Victor Engle
   d.                                   New York, October 2, 1931.

E-37233-A  Get Cannibal - vJD                    Br 6219, 01281, 4875, A-9192
E-37234-A  Junk Man Blues - vJD                  -      01225   -        -

Moore and Lyon omitted; Jack Russin-p replaces McGrath.
                                        New York, December 2, 1931.

E-37436-A  Slow And Easy - vJD                   Br 6767, 01312
E-37437-A  Waiting For The Evening Mail - vJD       - 4896  -

   As for September 16, 1931, but Arthur Schutt-p replaces McGrath.
                                        New York, December 2, 1931.

E-37438-A  Yaaka Hula Hickey Dula                Br 6234, 01262, A-9199
E-37439-A  Haunting Blues                        -          -        -

   As for E-37436/7, but Starr omitted; Dick Robertson-v.
                                        New York, December 15, 1931.

E-37462-A-B  Twenty-One Years - vDR              Br 6241, 01293, A-9203
E-37463-A  My Sweetie Went Away                  -          -        -
NOTE:- Matrix E-37463-A on Brunswick 01293 is dubbed.

   Red Nichols-Johnny Davis-t/Will Bradley-tb/Jimmy Dorsey-cl-as/Babe Russin-ts/Larry
   Binyon-ts-f/Harry Hoffman-vn/Jack Russin-p/Dick McDonough-g/Artie Bernstein-sb/
   Stan King-d/Connie Boswell-Sid Garry-Art Jarrett-v.
                                        New York, February 15, 1932.

X-11282-A-B  New Orleans Medley - Part 1 - vSG   Rejected
X-11283-A  New Orleans Medley - Part 2 - CB-AJ   Br 20110, 0118

RED NICHOLS AND HIS FIVE PENNIES : Red Nichols-t/Jimmy Dorsey-cl-as/Babe Russin-ts/
    Fulton McGrath-p/Dick McDonough-g/Artie Bernstein-sb/Victor Engle-d.
                                          New York, February 18, 1932.

B-11314-A  Clarinet Marmalade                  Br 6266, 01301, A-500176,
                                               Par R-2598, B-71157
B-11315-A  Sweet Sue - Just You                As above
B-11315-B  Sweet Sue - Just You                ARC F-152 ("for theatre use only")

    Red Nichols-Johnny Davis-t/Tommy Dorsey-tb/Jimmy Dorsey-cl-as/Babe Russin-ts/Larry
    Binyon-ts-f/Joe Venuti-vn/Jack Russin-p/Dick McDonough-g/Artie Bernstein-sb/Stan
    King-d/The Boswell Sisters-Sid Garry-Art Jarrett-v.
                                          New York, March 10, 1932.

BX-11427-A  New Orleans Medley - Part 1-vBS-SG-AJ Br 20110, 0118
BX-11432-A  California Medley - Part 1 -vBS-SG-AJ Br 20107, 0108, A-5112

    Chick Bullock-v added.                New York, March 26, 1932.

BX-11569-A  California Medley - Part 2 -vBS-CB-SG Br 20107, 0108, A-5112

    As for February 18, 1932, but Jack Russin-p replaces McGrath; Dick Robertson-v.
                                          New York, May 19, 1932.

B-11868-A  Goin' To Town                        Br 6312, A-9269
B-11869-A  Goofus - vDR                          -      -
B-11870-A  Our Home Town Mountain Band-Pt. 1-vDR Br 6348, 01343, A-9267
B-11871-A  Our Home Town Mountain Band-Pt. 2-vDR  -      -      -

RED NICHOLS AND HIS ORCHESTRA : Red Nichols-t-v dir. Ernie Mathias t-v/Frank Sacco-
    Snub Pollard-t'/Alex Palocsay-tb/Ted Klein-Joe Catalyne-cl-as/Fred Morrow-cl-as-ts
    /Charlie Roddick-p/Tony Sacco-g-v/Bill Lower-sb/Victor Engle-d.
                                          Chicago, November 28, 1932

C-8823-    Wail Of The Winds                    Rejected
C-8824-    Three Little Words - vEM              -
C-8825-1   Love, Nuts And Noodles (Bring 'Em Back Br 6451, A-9372, 4808
           Alive) - vEM
C-8826-1   Everybody Loves My Baby - vRN        Br 6461, 01441, A-9367
C-8827-1   I'm Sorry I Made You Cry - vTS        -      -
C-8828-    Do You Ever Think Of Me ? - vTS      Rejected
C-8829-1   Sugar (That Sugar Baby O' Mine) - vEM Br 6534

                                          Chicago, November 29, 1932.

C-8830-1   Heat Waves                           Br 7451, A-9372
C-8831-1   Dinah Lou - vEM                      Br 6534, 01441
C-8832-1   Waiting For The Evening Mail - vEM   Rejected

RED NICHOLS AND HIS WORLD-FAMOUS PENNIES : Red Nichols-t dir. Ray McCosh-George
    Schmidt-t/Buck Weaver or Buford Trevor-tb/Gilbert Schweser-Howard Jenkins-as/Don
    Purviance-ts/Manny Strand-p/King Harvey-g-v/Bill Lower-sb/Paul Collins-d/The
    Soncopators-v.                        Chicago, June 18, 1934.

80631-1  The Prize Waltz - vKH               BB B-5549, RZ MR-1390
80632-1  Shine - vS                          BB B-5553, MW M-4885, HMV JF-22
80633-1  Rollin' Home - vKH-S                BB B-5548, RZ MR-1365
80634-1  I'm Hummin', I'm Whistlin', I'm Singin' BB B-5552
         - vS
80635-1  Jungle Fever - vS                   BB B-5547
80636-1  Let Me Call You Mine (w) - vS       BB B-5549
80637-1  Straight From The Shoulder - vKH    BB B-5552
80638-1  Rockin' In Rhythm                   BB B-5547
80639-1  The Very Thought Of You - vKH       BB B-5548
80640-1  Silver Threads Among The Gold (r)   BB B-5583, Vic JR-11, RZ MR-1961
80641-1  Old White's Whiskers - vS            -      -      HMV EA-1475
80642-1  Runnin' Wild - vS                   BB B-5553, MW M-4885   - JF-22

RED NICHOLS AND HIS ORCHESTRA : Red Nichols-t dir. Ray McCosh-George Schmidt-t/Buck
   Weaver-Buford Trevor-tb/Gilbert Schweser-Howard Jenkins-as/Don Purviance-ts/Manny
   Strand-p/King Harvey-g-v/Bill Lower-bb-sb/Paul Collins-d/The Songcopators-v.
                                    New York, September 18, 1934.

| | | |
|---|---|---|
| B-15930-A | Three Little Words - vS | Br 7460, Dec F-5540 |
| B-15931-A | Harlem (Harlem's Heaven To Me) - vKH-S | - - |
| B-15932-A | When You And I Were Young, Maggie | Br 7358 |
| B-15933-A | Dardanella | - |
| B-15934-A | Dream Of A Doll | Rejected |
| B-15935-A | Redhead, Redhead, Gingerbread Head | - |
| B-15936-A | Hilly Billy Willy - vS | - |
| B-15937-A | It's Not A Secret Any More - vS | - |

Red Nichols-t dir. George Kennedy-Barney Zudecoff-t/Leo Moran-Frank Perry-tb/
   Murray Williams-Carl Swift-cl-as/Don Purviance-John Harrell-ts/Manny Strand-p/Tony
   Colicchio-g/Mort Stuhlmaker-sb/Paul Collins-d/Russell Cromwell-The Three Songies-
   v.                               New York, March 14, 1937.

| | | |
|---|---|---|
| M-244-1 | Wake Up And Live - vRC | Vri 524 |
| M-245-1 | They All Laughed - v3S | Vri 502 |
| M-246-1 | Never In A Million Years - vRC | Vri 524 |
| M-247-1 | Let's Call The Whole Thing Off - v3S | Vri 502 |
| M-248-1 | Troublesome Trumpet - v3S | Vri 545  Voc 3816 |

                                    New York, March 15, 1937.

| | | |
|---|---|---|
| M-253-1-2 | Night Ride | Rejected |
| M-254-2 | Humoresque (Dvorak) | Vri 595, Voc 3827 |
| M-255-1 | Cream Puff | Vri 655, Voc 3833 |
| M-256-1 | Love's Old Sweet Song | Vri 545, Voc 3816 |
| M-257-1 | 'O sole mio | Vri 595, Voc 3827 |
| M-258-1 | Twilight In Turkey | Vri 655, Voc 3833 |
| M-259-1-2 | L'amour, toujours l'amour | Rejected |

Red Nichols-t dir. Don Stevens-J. Douglas Wood-t/Martin Croy-Robert Gebhart-tb/
   Harry Yolonsky-Ray Schultz-cl-as/Bobby Jones-Billy Shepard-cl-ts/Billy Maxted-p-a
   /Tony Colucci-g/Jack Fay-sb/Victor Engle-d/Marion Redding-Bill Darnell-v.
                                    New York, March 12, 1939.

| | | |
|---|---|---|
| 032955-1 | The Hour Of Parting | BB B-10190, HMV EA-2548 |
| 032956-1 | Our Love - vBD | BB B-10179 |
| 032957-1 | You're So Desirable - vBD | -       HMV EA-2412 |
| 032958-1 | The King Kong | BB B-10190, HMV EA-2548 |
| 032959-1 | I Never Knew Heaven Could Speak - vBD | BB B-10200, MW M-7964 |
| 032960-1 | Tears From My Inkwell - vBD | -       -       HMV EA-2408 |

                                    New York, June 21, 1939.

| | | |
|---|---|---|
| 037665-1 | Sassin' The Boss | BB B-10328 |
| 037666-1 | Poor Loulie Jean - vBD | - |
| 037667-1 | Davenport Blues | BB B-10408, MW M-8347, HMV B-9028 X-6823 |
| 037668-1 | Wail Of The Winds (Theme Song of Red Nichols) | As above |
| 037669-1 | Coquette | Rejected |
| 037670-1 | Hot Lips | BB B-10360, HMV B-8980 |

                                    New York, June 26, 1939.

| | | |
|---|---|---|
| 037682-1 | I'll Get By | Rejected |
| 037683-1 | The Parade Of The Pennies | BB B-10360, HMV B-8980 |
| 037684-1 | It's 'Way Past My Dreaming Time - vBD | BB B-10332, MW M-8348 |
| 037685-1 | Address Unknown - vMR | -       - |
| 037686-1 | Love Me Or Leave Me | Rejected |

RED NICHOLS AND HIS ORCHESTRA : Red Nichols-t dir. Don.Stevens-J. Douglas Wood-t/
    Slim Wilbur-Martin Croy-tb/Conn Humphreys-as/Billy Jones-Billy Shepard-cl-ts/
    Billy Maxted-p-a/Mike Bryan-g/Jack Fay-sb/Harry Jaeger-d/Bill Darnell-v
                                        New York, October 2, 1939.

042772-2  Poor Butterfly - vO/aBM            BB B-10522, HMV B-9038
042773-2  A Pretty Girl Is Like A Melody - aBM    -              -
042774-1  I Live Again - vBD                 BB B-10451, HMV EA-2851
042775-1  You're The Greatest Discovery (Since 1492)-vBD -

RED NICHOLS AND HIS FIVE PENNIES : Red Nichols-t-v-w/Bobby Jones-cl-as/Billy Shepard
    cl-ts/Mike Bryan-g/Jack Fay-sb/Harry Jaeger-d-v.
                                        New York, October 6, 1939.

041717-1  My Melancholy Baby               BB B-10593
041718-1  Robins And Roses - vRN-HJ         -
041719-1  Let Me Dream - vRN               BB B-10683
041720-1  She Shall Have Music              -

RED NICHOLS AND HIS ORCHESTRA : Red Nichols-t dir. J. Douglas Wood-Hilton Brockman-t/
    Al Mastren-Jack Knaus-tb/Conn Humphreys-Bobby Jones-Ray Schultz-cl-as/Heinie Beau-
    cl-ts/Billy Maxted-p-a/Merritt Lamb-g/Frank Ray (? Jack Fay)-sb/Harry Jaeger-d-v.
                                        New York, June 11, 1940.

26918-A  Overnight Hop                    OK 5648
26919-A  Lowland Blues - vHJ              OK 5676, Par R-2777
26920-A  Meet Miss Eight Beat             OK 5648
26921-A  Beat Me Daddy (Eight To A Bar) - vHJ   OK 5676, Par R-2777

See also Van's Collegians, whose JIG WALK was ascribed to Red Nichols and his Orchestra on Pathe Actuelle 11134.

In August, 1930, a Red Nichols organization made some Brunswick records for radio
    transmission; matrix XE-33549 is CALL OF THE FREAKS, and XE-34058 contains BALLIN'
    THE JACK and WALKIN' THE DOG, but no other details are known at present.

## NIGHT CLUB KINGS

Ray Noble-harpophone-a dir. Sylvester Ahola-t/Danny Polo-cl/bar/vn/Arthur Young-p/
    Pat O'Malley-g-v/Bill Harty-d.         Small Queen's Hall, London, Jan. 21, 1930.

Bb-18577-2  In The Moonlight - vPO'M        HMV B-5776
Bb-18578-1  Someone - vPO'M                  -

Ray Noble-cel-a dir. Norman Payne-t/Jock Fleming-tb/Harry Hines-cl-as/Laurie Payne-
    bar/Spike Hughes-sb/Bill Harty-d/Al Bowlly-v.
                                        Hayes, Middlesex, July 17, 1930.

Bb-19913-1-2-3  Allah's Holiday - vAB        HMV rejected
Bb-19914-1-2-3  Whispering - vAB              -
Bb-19915-1-2    Give Me Back My Heart - vAB   -

    Jack Plant-v replaces Bowlly.          Hayes, Middlesex, October 3, 1930.

Bb-19913-4  Allah's Holiday - vJP            HMV B-5913
Bb-19914-5  Whispering - vJP                  -

A further recording by a straight dance band directed by Ray Noble and issued as by
    the Night Club Kings on HMV accompanying the late Raie da Costa at the piano is
    of no jazz interest.

## NIGHT CLUB ORCHESTRA

On Vocalion and Harmony, this name denotes a Harry Reser band, and may do so on the
    following, although some sources claim the presence of Leo McConville-t and Jimmy
    Dorsey-cl-as.                         New York, November, 1928.

E-28625-B  Oh ! You Have No Idea - v       Duo D-4018

Pseudonym on Silvertone 3549 for Blythe's Sinful Five, q.v.

## TOM NILES AND HIS ORCHESTRA

Pseudonym on American Parlophone for Tommy Bohn's Penn-Sirens, q.v.

## NIXON'S ROYAL FLUSH ORCHESTRA

Pseudonym on Bell 595 for the Black Diamond Orchestra, q.v.

## RAY NOBLE AND HIS ORCHESTRA

Ray Noble, as director of the Gramophone Company's "house" band in London and Hayes,
   Middlesex, between July, 1929 and August, 1934, made hundreds of first-class dance
   records, of which the following are of interest as jazz. His subsequent American
   recordings for Victor, Brunswick and Columbia are by a regular band, and those that
   fall into the same category are included here also.

Ray Noble-a dir. Max Goldberg-Bill Shakespeare-t/Tony Thorpe-? Joe Ferrie-tb/probable
   sax team :- Ernie Ritte-cl-as-bar/Bob Wise-cl-as/Reg Pink-Harry Carter or Harry
   Berly-ts (2 of these)/Eugene Pini-Nobby Knight-Adolph Zimbler-vn/Harry Jacobson-p/
   Bert Thomas-g/Jack Evetts or Tiny Winters-sb/Bill Harty-d/Al Bowlly-v.
                                             London, December 17, 1932.

OB-4358-3  Brighter Than The Sun - vAB              HMV B-6302, Vic 24314

   Nat Gonella-t replaces Shakespeare; Harry Berly-vl (Pink and Carter probably the
   2 ts used).                               London, February 7, 1933.

OB-6435-2  Love Tales - vAB                         HMV B-6319, Vic 24278

                                             London, February 20, 1933.

OB-6442-3  What A Perfect Combination              HMV B-6321

                                             London, March 16, 1933.

OB-6479-1  Stay On The Right Side Of The Road-vAB  HMV B-6331, EA-1440, Vic 24375

Ray Noble-a dir. Max Goldberg-Nat Gonella-t/Lew Davis-tb/Freddy Gardner-cl-as-bar/
   cl-as/Harry Berly-ts-vl/Harry Jacobson-p/Bert Thomas-g/Tiny Winters-sb/Bill Harty-
   d.                                        London, October 4, 1933.

B-5119-1  Tiger Rag                                 HMV B-6425, Vic 24577
B-5120-1  Japanese Sandman                          -           -

   Ernie Ritte-cl-as-bar replaces unknown (or may even be identified as such); 2nd
   ts (db cl)/Al Bowlly-v added; Monia Liter-p replaces Jacobson.
                                             London, December 20, 1933.

B-5835-2  You Ought To See Sally On Sunday - vAB   HMV B-6440, Vic 24575

   2nd tb added; Berly db vl (but 4th sax may be someone else); 2vn added also.
                                             London, February 1, 1934.

B-4770-1-2  Who Walks In When I Walk Out ? - vAB   HMV B-6453, Vic 24571

Ray Noble-a dir. Max Goldberg-? Nat Gonella-t/Lew Davis-? Tony Thorpe or Joe Ferrie-
   tb/Freddy Gardner-? Ernie Ritte-cl-as-bar/Reg. Pink-? Harry Carter-cl-ts/2vn/Harry
   Berly-vl/Monia Liter-p/Bert Thomas-g/Tiny Winters-sb/Bill Harty-d/Al Bowlly-v.
                                             London, July 11, 1934.

B-7442-1  All I Do Is Dream Of You - vAB            HMV B-6508

Other records of jazz interest by Ray Noble, made anonymously as by the New Mayfair
   Dance Orchestra, will be found under that heading.

Ray Noble dir. Pee Wee Erwin-Charlie Spivak-t/Glenn Miller-tb-a/Will Bradley-tb/.
  Johnny Mince-Jim Cannon-Milt Yaner-cl-as/Bud Freeman-ts/Nick Pisani-Fritz Prospero-
  Dan d'Andrea-vn/Claude Thornhill-p-a/George van Eps-g/Delmar Kaplan-sb/Bill Harty-d
  /Al Bowlly-The Freshmen-v.          New York, February 9, 1935.

87498-1  Down By The River - vAB            Vic 24879, HMV BD-140, EA-1512

                                    Camden, N. J., May 10, 1935.

88965-1-2  'Way Down Yonder In New Orleans     Rejected
88966-1  Chinatown, My Chinatown              Vic LPV-536, LSA-3067 (LPs)

                                    New York, June 8, 1935.

92230-1  Let's Swing It - vF               Vic 25070, HMV BD-5186, EA-1547,
                                           JF-49

                                    New York, June 10, 1935.

88965-4  'Way Down Yonder In New Orleans     Vic 25082, HMV BD-5004, EA-1547,
                                           El EG-3571
88966-4  Chinatown, My Chinatown            Vic 25070, HMV BD-5186, JF-49,
                                           El EG-3571
92232-1  St. Louis Blues - vAB              Vic 25082, HMV BD-5004

  No vn used on this date.          New York, October 9, 1935.

95190-1  Bugle Call Rag                  Vic 25223, HMV BD-5197, EA-1642
95191-1  Dinah                             -          -          -

Ray Noble dir. Charli  Spivak-t/Sterling Bose-t-v/Glenn Miller-tb-a/Alex Polascay-tb
  /Johnny Mince-Mike Doty-Milt Yaner-cl-as/John van Eps-cl-ts/Nick Pisani-Fritz
  Prospero-Dan d'Andrea-vn/Frank Vigneau-p/George van Eps-g/Delmar Kaplan-sb/Bill
  Harty-d/Al Bowlly-v.          New York, May 25, 1936.

101864-1  Big Chief De Sota - vAB-SB        Vic 25346, HMV BD-5095,El EG-3853

Ray Noble dir. Jim Davison-George Connell-Frank Barnard-t/George Guerette-Jack Madden
  tb/Herb Mason-cl-bcl-as-f/Vern Kahanen-as/Ted Davison-Howard Campbell-cl-ts/Cliff
  Timms-Cliff Cadman-Jack Neilson-vn/Johnny Burt-p/Red McGarvey-g/Joe Niosi-sb/Bill
  Harty-d/Reefe McGarvey-tympani.     Los Angeles, February 3, 1938.

LA-1577-A  Crazy Rhythm                 Br 8098, Col FB-2022

                                    Los Angeles, March 20, 1938.

LA-1601-A  Alexander's Ragtime Band     Br 8180, A-81682, Col FB-2044

                                    New York, October 11, 1938.

B-23574-1  By The Waters Of Minnetonka     Br 8247, A-81806, Col 36116,
                                           FB-2102, DO-1902
B-23575-1  Cherokee                        As above

Ray Noble dir. Don Anderson-Bob Goodrich-Harry Johnson-t/Earle Hagen-Carl Loffler-tb/
  Jack Chaney-Don Bonnee-cl-as/Jack Dumont-Bud Smith-Jacques Marx-ts/Frank Leithner-p
  /George van Eps-g/Manny Stein-sb/Bill Harty-d.
                                    Los Angeles, September 29, 1939.

LA-2007-A  Comanche War Dance           Col 35258, FB-2622
LA-2008-A  Iroquois                       -          -

                                    Los Angeles, January 19, 1940.

LA-2120-A  Seminole                     Col 35557, C-36
LA-2121-A  Sioux Sue                    Col 35850

                                    Chicago, August 8, 1940.

WC-3250-B  From Oakland To Burbank      Col 35708, FB-2568
WC-3251-A  Harlem Nocturne                -          -

Pseudonym on Victor V-38556 for Irene Scruggs, q.v.

## JIMMIE NOONE

JIMMIE NOONE'S APEX CLUB ORCHESTRA : Jimmie Noone-cl-v dir. Joe Poston-cl-as-v/Earl
Hines-p/Bud Scott-bj-g/Johnny Wells-d. Chicago, May 16, 1928.

| | | |
|---|---|---|
| C-1937-C; E-7355 | I Know That You Know | Voc 1184, Br 80024, JSo AA-587 |
| C-1938-C; E-7356 | Sweet Sue - Just You | -          - |
| C-1939-B; E-7357 | Four Or Five Times - vJN-JP | Voc 1185, V-1026, Mt M-12543, |
| | | Br 80025, A-500320 |
| C-1939-C; E-7357 | Four Or Five Times - vJN-JP | Voc 1135, Spt S-2228 |
| C-1940-B; E-7358 | Every Evening (I Miss You) | -     Mt M-12543, Br 80025 |
| C-1940-C; E-7358 | Every Evening (I Miss You) | - |

NOTE:- The original cream-and-black label Vocalion 1185 uses take C on both sides;
the later gold label uses takes B and C; Brunswick 80025, though marked -C, is in
fact pressed from a dubbing of C-1940-B.

Chicago, June 14, 1928.

| | | |
|---|---|---|
| C-2015- ; E-7402 | Ready For The River - vJN-JP | Voc 1188, JSo AA-527 |
| C-2016- ; E-7403 | Forevermore - | -       - |

Lawson Buford-bb added.          Chicago, July 23, 1928.

| | | |
|---|---|---|
| C-2111- | Apex Blues | Voc rejected |
| C-2112- | Oh, Sister ! Ain't That Hot ? | - |
| C-2113- | Blues My Naughty Sweetie Gives To Me | - |

Chicago, July 24, 1928.

| | | |
|---|---|---|
| C-2121- | Sweet Lorraine | Voc rejected |
| C-2122- | King Joe | - |
| C-2123- | A Monday Date | - |

Chicago, August 23, 1928.

| | | |
|---|---|---|
| C-2258-B | Apex Blues | Voc 1207, Br 80023, JSo AA-581 |
| C-2259-C | A Monday Date (My Monday Date*) | Voc 1229, V-1026*, Br 80026, |
| | | UHCA 41, JSo AA-582 |
| C-2260-C | Blues My Naughty Sweetie Gives To Me | Voc 1215    -    - |

Chicago, August 25, 1928.

| | | |
|---|---|---|
| C-2266-A-B-C | Oh, Sister ! Ain't That Hot ? | Voc 1215, AF A-030 |
| C-2267- | King Joe | Voc 1229, HRS 13, Decatur 515, |
| | | AF A-024 |
| C-2268-A | Sweet Lorraine | Voc 1207, Br A-500320 |
| C-2268-B | Sweet Lorraine | Br 80023 |

Jimmie Noone-cl-v dir. Joe Poston-cl-as-v/Alex Hill-p/Junie Cobb-bj-g-v/Bill
Newton-bb/Johnny Wells-d.          Chicago, December 6, 1928.

| | | |
|---|---|---|
| C-2639-A-B | I Must Have That Man | Rejected |
| C-2640-A-B | Some Rainy Day | Voc 1240 |
| C-2641-A-B | Baby | Rejected |

George Mitchell-c/? Fayette Williams-tb added.
Chicago, December 27, 1928.

| | | |
|---|---|---|
| C-2710-A | It's Tight Like That - vJN-JP-JC | Voc 1238, JSo AA-522, NOM M-10 |
| C-2710-B | It's Tight Like That - vJN-JP-JC | - V-1007, Dec MG-36265, MU-31024 |
| C-2711-A | Let's Sow A Wild Oat - vJN-JP | -       JSo AA-522 |
| C-2711-B | Let's Sow A Wild Oat - vJN-JP | - |
| C-2712- | She's Funny That Way - vJC | Voc 1240 |

JIMMIE NOONE'S APEX CLUB ORCHESTRA : Jimmie Noone-cl-v dir. Joe Poston-cl-as-v/Alex
   Hill-p/Junie Cobb-bj-g/Bill Newton-bb/Johnny Wells-d.
                                             Chicago, February 26, 1929.

C-3005-   St. Louis Blues                    Swaggie JCS-33787 (LP)
C-3006-   Chicago Rhythm                      Voc 1267, AF A-024

                                             Chicago, March 2, 1929.

C-3031-   I Got A Misery                      Voc 1267, AF A-030

                                             Chicago, April 27, 1929.

C-3378-   Wake Up, Chillun, Wake Up - vJN-JP  Voc 1272, Spt S-2254
C-3379-   Love Me Or Leave Me - vJN-JP          -          -

   Zinky Cohn-p replaces Hill; Newton omitted.
                                             Chicago, June 21, 1929.

C-3683-   Anything You Want                   Voc 15823

                                             Chicago, June 24, 1929.

C-3710-   Someone's Falling In Love           Voc rejected
C-3711-   Serenading The Moon                   -

   Bill Newton-bb returns; George Mitchell-c/? Fayette Williams-tb added*; May Alix-v.
                                             Chicago, July 11, 1929.

C-3844-   Birmingham Bertha - vMA             Voc 1296
C-3845-   Am I Blue ? - vMA                     -
C-3848-A *My Daddy Rocks Me (With One Steady Roll) Voc 2779, V-1007, Br 7096,
          - vMA                              A-500196, Dec MG-36265, MU-31024,
                                             BRS 1008
C-3849-A *Apex Blues                         Voc 2779, Br 7096, A-500196,
                                             BRS 1008
   NOTE:- Brunswick 7096 as CLUB AMBASSADORS ORCHESTRA.

                                             Chicago, July 18, 1929.

C-3898-   Ain't Misbehavin' - vMA             Voc 15819
C-3899-   That Rhythm Man - vMA               Voc 15823
C-3900-   Off Time                            Voc 15819

   Mitchell and Williams omitted.    Chicago, September 24, 1929.

C-4397-   S'posin'                            Voc 1415
C-4398-   True Blue Lou                         -

                                             Chicago, September 26, 1929.

C-4617-   Through (How Can You Say We're Through ?)Voc 1416
C-4618-   Satisfied                             -

   Helen Savage-v.                    Chicago, October 15, 1929.

C-4647-   I'm Doin' What I'm Doin' For Love   Voc 1436
C-4648-   He's A Good Man To Have Around - vHS   -

                                             Chicago, October 21, 1929.

C-4687-   My Melancholy Baby                  Br 7124, 1086
C-4688-   After You've Gone - vHS               -         -
   NOTE:- Brunswick 7124 as THE SAVANNAH SYNCOPATORS.

   Elmo Tanner-v.                     Chicago, October 25, 1929.

C-4692-   Love Me - vET                       Voc rejected
C-4693-   Love Me                               -
C-4694-   Love - vET                            -
C-4695-   Song Of The Sands                     -

JIMMIE NOONE'S APEX CLUB ORCHESTRA : Jimmie Noone-cl-v dir. Joe Poston-cl-as/Zinky
  Cohn-p/Junie Cobb-bj-g/Bill Newton-bb/Johnny Wells-d/Elmo Tanner-v.
                                       Chicago, November 19, 1929.

C-4725-B  Love - vET                              Voc 1439
C-4726-B  Love Me - vET                              -
  NOTE:- This issue as JIMMIE'S BLUE MELODY BOYS.

                                       Chicago, November 26, 1929.

C-4748-   Zonky - vET                             Voc rejected
C-4749-   Singin' River - vET                        -
C-4750-   Zonky - vET ?                               -
C-4751-   I'll Still Go On Wanting You - vET          -

  Wilbur Gorham-bj-g replaces Cobb.    Chicago, February 3, 1930.

C-5358-   El Rado Scuffle                         Voc 1490
C-5359-   Deep Trouble                               -

                                       Chicago, February 6, 1930.

C-5370-   Cryin' For The Carolines - vET          Voc 1466
C-5371-   Have A Little Faith In Me - vET            -

                                       Chicago, February 18, 1930.

C-5521½   Should I ? - v                          Voc 1471
C-5522-   I'm Following You - v                      -

  Eddie Pollack-cl-as-bar-v replaces Poston; Georgia White-v added.
                                       Chicago, May 16, 1930.

C-5754-   When You're Smiling - vGW               Voc 1497
C-5755-   I Lost My Gal From Memphis                 -

                                       Chicago, May 28, 1930.

C-5766-   On Revival Day - vET                    Voc 1506, Spt S-2233
C-5767-   I'm Drifting Back To Dreamland             -           -

                                       Chicago, July 1, 1930.

C-5900-   Virginia Lee - v                        Voc 1518
C-5901-   So Sweet                                   -
C-5903-A  San                                     Swaggie JCS-33786 (LP)
C-5903-B  San                                     AH 84 (LP)
  NOTE:- Matrix C-5902 is untraced.

                                       Chicago, July 29, 1930.

C-5950-A  You Rascal, You - vJN-EP                Voc 1584
C-5951-A  Bring It On Home To Grandma - vEP          -

                                       Chicago, August 23, 1930.

C-6107-   Little White Lies - vEP                 Voc 1531
C-6108-   Moonlight On The Colorado - vEP            -

  May Alix-v.                          Chicago, October 30, 1930.

C-6465-   Something To Remember You By - vMA      Voc 1554
C-6466-   Three Little Words                         -

  Mildred Bailey-v.                    Chicago, January 12, 1931.

C-7300-   He's Not Worth Your Tears - vMB         Voc 1580
C-7301-   Trav'lin' All Alone - vMB                  -

JIMMIE NOONE AND HIS ORCHESTRA : Jimmie Noone-cl dir. Eddie Pollack-as-bar-v/Earl
    Hines-p/John Henley-g/Quinn Wilson-sb/Benny Washington-d/Art Jarrett-v.
                                        Chicago, July 27, 1931.

C-7913-   I Need Lovin' - vAJ                   Br 6174, 01234, A-9134
C-7914-   It's You - vAJ                        Br 6192, A-9135
C-7915-   River, Stay 'Way From My Door - vAJ      -          -
C-7916-   When It's Sleepy Time Down South - vAJ   Br 6174, 01234, A-9134

    Zinky Cohn-p replaces Hines.         Chicago, December 15, 1933.

C-686-1   Dixie Lee - vEP                       Voc 2620, Dec F-3904, EBW W-99,
                                                JSo AA-524
C-687-1   Inka Dinka Doo - vEP                  Voc 2619      -
C-688-1   Delta Bound                           Voc 2620, JSo AA-524
C-689-1   Like Me A Little Bit Less - vEP       Voc 2619
    NOTE:- Edison Bell Winner W-99 as SLEEPY HALL AND HIS COLLEGIANS.

    Jimmy Cobb-t added; John Lindsay-sb replaces Wilson.
                                        Chicago, November 23, 1934.

C-858-A   A Porter's Love Song                  Voc 2888, Br A-500513
C-859-A   I'd Do Anything For You               Voc 2862      -
C-860-A   Shine                                 Voc 2888, Br A-500514
C-861-A   Liza                                  Voc 2862      -

                                        Chicago, February 21, 1935.

C-903-B   Soon (There'll Just Be Two Of Us)     Voc 2907, Pan 25720
C-904-A   Lullaby Of Broadway                   Voc 2908, Pan 25749
C-905-A   Lookie, Lookie, Lookie, Here Comes Cookie   -   Pan 25763
C-906-A   It's Easy To Remember                  Voc 2907, Pan 25720

JIMMIE NOONE AND HIS NEW ORLEANS BAND (....ORCHESTRA on Decca 18439 and 18440) : Guy
    Kelly-t-v/Preston Jackson-tb/Jimmie Noone-cl/Frances Whitby-ts/Gideon Honore-p/
    Israel Crosby-sb/Tubby Hall-d.       Chicago, January 15, 1936.

90575-A   He's The Different Type Of Guy        Par R-2303, PZ-11115, Dec 18439,
                                                60379, M-30859, Od 286228, OR-2303
90576-A   'Way Down Yonder In New Orleans       Par R-2281, A-7296, Dec 18440,
                                                60380, Od 286229, A-2329
90577-A   The Blues Jumped A Rabbit - vGK       Par R-2303, A-6739, PZ-11115,
                                                Dec 18439, 60379, M-30859,
                                                Od 286228, OR-2303
90578-A   Sweet Georgia Brown                   Par R-2281, A-7296, Dec 18440,
                                                60380, Od 286229, A-2329

JIMMIE NOONE AND HIS ORCHESTRA : Charlie Shavers-t/Jimmie Noone-cl/Pete Brown-as/
    Frank Smith-p/Teddy Bunn-g/Wellman Braud-sb/O'Neil Spencer-d-v/Teddy Simmons-v.
                                        New York, December 1, 1937.

62830-A   Sweet Lorraine - vO'NS                Dec 7553, Voc S-216
62831-A   I Know That You Know                  Dec 1584, 3863, 60457, 60524,
                                                Voc S-216
62832-A   Bump It (The Bumps) (Apex Blues)      Dec 1584, 3519, 60336, M-30398,
                                                Voc S-209, Br 03303
62833-A   Four Or Five Times - vO'NS&ch         Dec 1621, 60336, M-30398,
                                                Voc S-209, Br 03303
62834-A   Hell In My Heart - vTS                Dec 7553
62835-B   Call Me Darling, Call Me Sweetheart,  Dec 1730, Od 286359
            Call Me Dear - vO'NS
62836-A   I'm Walkin' This Town - vO'NS            -          -
62837-A   Japansy - vO'NS                       Dec 1621
    NOTE:- Some copies of Brunswick 03303 use a dubbed master from 62832-A.

    Natty Dominique-c/Preston Jackson-tb/Jimmie Noone-cl/Richard M. Jones-p/Lonnie
    Johnson-g/John Lindsay-sb/Tubby Hall-d.Chicago, June 5, 1940.

93030-A   New Orleans Hop Scop Blues            Dec 18095, 25104, 60335, M-30315,
                                                Br 03169, A-82725
93031-A   Keystone Blues                        As above

JIMMIE NOONE TRIO : Jimmie Noone-cl/Gideon Honore-p/Henry Fort (despite the labels)-
    sb/Ed Thompson-v.                         Chicago, December 11, 1940.

| 053725-1 | Moody Melody - vET | BB B-8609 |
| 053726-1 | Then You're Drunk - vET | BB B-8649 |
| 053727-1 | I'm Going Home - vET | - |
| 053728-1 | They Got My Number Now - vET | BB B-8609 |

JIMMIE NOONE QUARTET : Jimmie Noone-cl/Frank Smith-p/John Frazier-sb/Wallace Bishop-
    d.                                  Yes Yes Club, Chicago, July 17, 1941.

| Sweet Lorraine (both LPs) | Swaggie S-1210, Forsgate WOP-69-0 |
| A Porter's Love Song | -          - |
| Blues For Roy | -          - |
| Goodbye, Don't Cry | -          - |
| Lady, Be Good | -          - |
| Memories Of You | -          - |
| Honeysuckle Rose | -          - |
| Body And Soul | Swaggie S-1226 (LP) |

## CECIL AND LESLIE NORMAN

The following titles made under the direction of these well-known brothers feature
good "hot" solos, and the use of the pseudonym NORMAN SISSEL AND HIS RHYTHM
TWISTERS on some suggested to some collectors years ago that Noble Sissle and his
Orchestra who were in London at the time, had taken part in them. The labels bear
the names shown in parentheses after the catalog numbers : SPB - Savoy Plaza Band;
CC - Connecticut Collegians from the Edgewood Inn, Greenwich, Connecticut; NS -
Norman Sissel and his Rhythm Twisters. All recorded in Sessions House, Clerkenwell
Road.

Cecil Norman-p-a dir. Sylvester Ahola and Max Goldberg or Bill Shakespeare-t/Ben
    Oakley-tb/Bill Rogers-Les Norman-cl-as/ ---- Cohen or ---- Leon-ts/vn/Emile Grim-
    shaw-bj-g/ ---- Stanley-bb/Ronnie Gubertini-d/Cavan O'Connor-unknown girl-v.
                                    London, October 8, 1929.

| 100-X | Louise - vCO'C | Worldecho A-1001, Duo D-4048 (SPB) |

London, October 9, 1929.

| 107 | Honey - vCO'C | Worldecho A-1002 (SPB) |

London, October 10, 1929.

| 113 | I've Got A Feeling I'm Falling - vCO'C | Worldecho A-1010 (NS) |
| 114 | This Is Heaven - vCO'C | Worldecho A-1004 (CC) |
| 115 | I'm In Seventh Heaven - vCO'C | Worldecho A-1010 (NS) |

London, October 25, 1929.

| 127 | In An Old-World Garden - vCO'C | Worldecho A-1011 (SPB) |
| 129 | Come On, Baby - vCO'C | Worldecho A-1008 (NS) |

London, November 1, 1929.

| 142 | Ain't Misbehavin' - vCO'C | Worldecho A-1017 (SPB) |

London, November 7, 1929.

| 153 | Maryland - vg | Worldecho A-1021 (CC) |
| 154-X | Birmingham Bertha - vg | Worldecho A-1020 (CC) |

London, November 20, 1929.

| 176-X | Shady Lady - vCO'C | Worldecho A-1041 (NS) |

London, November 22, 1929.

| 180-X | Welcome Home - vg | Worldecho A-1020 (CC) |
| 184-Y | If I Had A Talking Picture Of You-vCO'C | Worldecho A-1036 (SPB) |

# BEN NORSINGLE

Vocal, acc. by Don Albert-t/Charlie Dixon-tb-bb*/Allen Van-p/John Henry Braggs-g.
Dallas, c. October 28, 1928.

| | | |
|---|---|---|
| DAL-700-A | Black Cat Blues | Br 7043 |
| DAL-701-A | Motherless Blues | - |
| DAL-702-A | Red River Bottom Blues | Br 7041 |
| DAL-703-A | *Rover's Blues | - |

## HATTIE NORTH

Pseudonym on Vocalion for Edith North Johnson, q.v.

## JACK NORTH AND HIS BAND/JACK NORTH'S ORCHESTRA

Pseudonym on Panachord for Dick Robertson and his Orchestra, q.v.

## NORTHWEST MELODY BOYS

Pseudonym on Champion for Walter Anderson's Golden Pheasant Hoodlums, q.v.

## RED NORVO

Xylophone or marimba solos, acc. by Jimmy Dorsey-cl/Fulton McGrath-p/Dick McDonough-g
/Artie Bernstein-sb.                       New York, April 8, 1933.

| | | |
|---|---|---|
| B-13205-A | Knockin' On Wood | Br 6562, 01568, A-9419, RZ G-22242 |
| B-13206-A | Hole In The Wall | -       -        -      - |

Acc. by Benny Goodman-bcl/Dick McDonough-g/Artie Bernstein-sb.
New York, November 21, 1933.

| | | |
|---|---|---|
| B-14361-A | In A Mist | Br 6906,8236,01686,A-9528,A-500368 |
| B-14362-A | Dance Of The Octopus | -      -      -      -      - |

RED NORVO AND HIS SWING SEPTET : Jack Jenney-tb/Artie Shaw-cl/Charlie Barnet-ts/Teddy
Wilson-p/Bobby Johnson-g/Hank Wayland-sb/Billy Gussak-d/Red Norvo-x.
New York, September 26, 1934.

| | | |
|---|---|---|
| CO-16021-A | Old Fashioned Love | Col 3059-D, 35688, DB/MC-5012 |
| CO-16022-A | I Surrender, Dear | Col 2977-D   -       - |

New York, October 4, 1934.

| | | |
|---|---|---|
| CO-16033-A | Tomboy | Col 2977-D, MC-3031, Par R-2110 |
| CO-16034-A | The Night Is Blue | Col 3026-D, Par R-2088 |

RED NORVO AND HIS SWING OCTET : Bunny Berigan-t/Jack Jenney-tb/Johnny Mince-cl/Chu
Berry-ts/Teddy Wilson-p/George van Eps-g/Artie Bernstein-sb/Gene Krupa-d/Red Norvo-
x.                                    New York, January 25, 1935.

| | | |
|---|---|---|
| CO-16703-2 | Honeysuckle Rose | Col 3059-D, MC-3020, Par R-2117, A-6269 |
| CO-16709-1 | With All My Heart And Soul | Col 3026-D, MC-3031, Par R-2110 |
| CO-16710-1 | Bughouse | Col 3079-D, 36158, Br 8208, Par R-2241 |
| CO-16711-1 | Blues in E flat | As above, plus Par A-6739 |

RED NORVO AND HIS ORCHESTRA : Stew Pletcher-t/Eddie Sauter-mel-a/Donald McCook-cl/
Herbie Haymer-ts/Dave Barbour-g/Pete Peterson-sb/Bob White-d/Red Norvo-x/v trio.
New York, January 6, 1936.

| | | |
|---|---|---|
| 60300-A | Gramercy Square | Dec 691 |
| 60301-A | Polly Wolly Doodle - v3 | Dec 670, F-7806, Y-5071 |

New York, January 8, 1936.

| | | |
|---|---|---|
| 60315-A | Decca Stomp | Dec 691, 3527, F-5923, Br A-9968, A-505043 |
| 60318-A | The Wedding Of Jack And Jill - v3 | Dec 670, F-5923, Y-5071, Br A-9968, A-505043 |

NOTE:- Decca 3527 as KENNETH "RED" NORVO AND HIS SWING SEXTETTE.

KEN KENNY AND HIS ORCHESTRA (first four sides) or LEN HERMAN AND HIS ORCHESTRA (last
  two) : Stew Pletcher-t/Eddie Sauter-mel-a/Donald McCook-cl/Herbie Haymer-ts/Dave
  Barbour-g/Pete Peterson-sb/Maurice Purtill-d/Red Norvo-x/v.
                                       New York, February 26, 1936.

| | | |
|---|---|---|
| 60589-A | You Started Me Dreaming - v | Ch 40107, Pan 25860 |
| 60590- | Misty Islands Of The Highlands - v | Ch 40101 |
| 60591-A | What's The Name Of That Song ? - v | Ch 40107 |
| 60592- | Let Yourself Go - v | Ch 40100 |
| 60593-A | Life Begins When You're In Love - v | Ch 40101, Pan 25846 |
| 60594-A | If You Love Me - v | Ch 40100, Pan 25847 |

RED NORVO AND HIS SWING SEXTETTE : As above, without Sauter, but with Howard Smith-p.
                                       New York, March 16, 1936.

| | | |
|---|---|---|
| 60898-A | I Got Rhythm | Dec 779, Br 02255 |
| 60899-A | Oh ! Lady, Be Good | - 3884 - |

RED NORVO AND HIS ORCHESTRA : Red Norvo-x dir. Bill Hyland-Stew Pletcher-Eddie
  Meyers-t/Leo Moran-tb/Slats Long-cl-as/Frank Simeone-as/Herbie Haymer-ts/Joe Liss-
  p/Dave Barbour-g/Pete Peterson-sb/Maurice Purtill-d/Mildred Bailey-v/Eddie Sauter-
  a.                                   New York, August 26, 1936.

| | | |
|---|---|---|
| B-19749-1 | It All Begins And Ends With You - vMB/aES | Br 7732, A-81063, A-500676, Voc S-36, RZ G-22974 |
| B-19750-1 | A Porter's Love Song To A Chambermaid - vMB/aES | Br 7744, A-500691, 5081, Voc S-32, Lucky S-23 |
| B-19751-1 | I Know That You Know - aES | As above |
| B-19752-1 | Picture Me Without You - vMB | Br 7732, A-81063, A-500676, Voc S-36, RZ G-22974 |

  Al Mastren-tb replaces Moran; Hank d'Amico-cl replaces Long; Lou Hirst-v.
                                       New York, October 19, 1936.

| | | |
|---|---|---|
| B-20092-1 | It Can Happen To You - vMB | Br 7761, A-81105, Voc S-43 |
| B-20093-1 | Now That Summer Is Gone - vMB | Br 7767 |
| B-20094- | It's Love I'm After - vMB | Rejected |
| B-20095-1 | Peter Piper - vMB | Br 7767 |
| B-20096- | When Is A Kiss Not A Kiss ? - vLH | Br 7761, A-81105 |

  Eddie Sauter-t-a replaces Meyers.        Chicago, January 8, 1937.

| | | |
|---|---|---|
| C-1733-2 | A Thousand Dreams Of You - vMB | Br 7815, A-500709, Voc S-59 |
| C-1734-2 | Smoke Dreams - vMB/aES | -      -      - RZ G-23078 |
| C-1735-2 | Slummin' On Park Avenue - vMB | Br 7813, A-500707, Voc S-102, RZ G-23094 |
| C-1736-1 | I've Got My Love To Keep Me Warm - vMB | CBS C3L-22, BPG-62099 (LPs) |
| C-1736-2 | I've Got My Love To Keep Me Warm - vMB | Br 7813, A-500707, Voc S-102, RZ G-23094 |

  Charles Lamphere-as added.               Chicago, March 22, 1937.

| | | |
|---|---|---|
| C-1853-1 | Remember - aES | Br 7896, Voc S-91 |
| C-1854-2 | Liza | Br 7868, Voc S-85 |
| C-1855-1 | I Would Do Anything For You | -     Voc S-84 |
| C-1856-1 | Jiving The Jeep | Br 7896, Voc S-91 |

  Red Norvo-x dir. Louis Mucci-George Wendt-Stew Pletcher-t/Al Mastren-tb/Charles
  Lamphere-Hank d'Amico-cl-as/Len Goldstein-as/Herbie Haymer-ts/Bill Miller-p/Red
  McGarvey-g/Pete Peterson-sb/Maurice Purtill-d/Mildred Bailey-v.
                                       New York, July 9, 1937.

| | | |
|---|---|---|
| B-21374- | Everyone's Wrong But Me - vMB | Br 7928 |
| B-21375- | Posin' | - |
| B-21376-2 | The Morning After - vMB | Br 7932, Voc S-108 |
| B-21377-2 | Do You Ever Think Of Me ? | -     - |

                                       Los Angeles, September 22, 1937.

| | | |
|---|---|---|
| LA-1440-A | Tears In My Heart - vMB | Br 7970, Voc S-132 |
| LA-1441-A | Worried Over You | -     - |
| LA-1442-B | Clap Hands, Here Comes Charlie | Br 7975, Voc S-121 |
| LA-1443-A | Russian Lullaby | -     - |

RED NORVO AND HIS ORCHESTRA : Red Norvo-x dir. Jimmy Blake-Zeke Zarchy-Barney
    Zudecoff-t/Al Mastren-Wes Hein-tb/Hank d'Amico-cl/Len Goldstein-as/Charles Lamphere
    as-ts/Jerry Jerome-ts/Bill Miller-p/Alan Hanlon-g/Pete Peterson-sb/George Wettling-
    d/Mildred Bailey-v.                        New York, January 21, 1938.

B-22322-1  Always And Always - vMB              Br 8069, A-81572, Voc S-156,
                                                RZ G-23414
B-22323-1  I Was Doing All Right - vMB          Br 8068, A-81484
B-22324-2  It's Wonderful - vMB                 Br 8069, A-81572
B-22325-1  Love Is Here To Stay - vMB           Br 8068, A-81484
    NOTE:- Regal Zonophone G-23414 as CASINO ROYAL ORCHESTRA.


    Mastren omitted; Terry Allen-v.            New York, February 10, 1938.

B-22405-1  A Serenade To The Stars - vTA        Br 8085, A-81526, A-81773,A-500731
B-22406-2  More Than Ever - vMB                   -        -       Voc S-142
B-22407-2  The Week-End Of A Private Secretary-vMB Br 8088                -
B-22408-1  Please Be Kind - vMB                   -      Voc S-156


                                           New York, February 23, 1938.

B-22457-1  Jeannine                             Br 8103, A-81561, Voc S-143
B-22458-1  Tea Time                               -        -        -
B-22459-1  How Can You Forget ? - vTA           Br 8089, A-81530
B-22460-2  There's A Boy In Harlem - vMB         -        -


                                           New York, April 19, 1938.

B-22753-1-2  I Kiss Your Hand, Madame           Rejected
B-22754-1  Says My Heart - vMB                  Br 8135, Par R-2552, Col CQ-1420
  22755-1-2  I Let A Song Go Out Of My Heart - vMB Voc 4083, Cq 9046, Par R-2568,
                                                Od A-2358
B-22756-1-2  Hot Foot                           Rejected
    NOTE:- All issues from matrix 22755 as MILDRED BAILEY AND HER ORCHESTRA.

                                           New York, April 21, 1938.

  22767-1  Moonshine Over Kentucky - vMB        Voc 4109
  22768-1  Rock It For Me - vMB                 Voc 4083, Par R-2568
B-22769-1-2  After Dinner Speech - vMB          Br 8171, A-81675
  22770-1  If You Were In My Place - vMB        Voc 4109
    NOTE:- Vocalion 4083 and 4109, and Parlophone R-2568 as MILDRED BAILEY AND HER
ORCHESTRA.

    Red Norvo-x dir. Jack Owens-Jack Palmer-Barney Zudecoff-t/Andy Russo-Al George-tb/
    Hank d'Amico-cl/Frank Simeone-as/Maurice Kogan-George Berg-ts/Bill Miller-p/Alan
    Hanlon-g/Pete Peterson-sb/George Wettling-d/Mildred Bailey-v.
                                           New York, May 2, 1938.

B-22840-2  Day Dreamin' (All Night Long) - vMB   Br 8145, A-81649
B-22841-2  A Cigarette And A Silhouette - vMB    Br 8171, A-81675
B-22842-2  (I've Been) Savin' Myself For You - vMB Br 8145, A-81649
B-22843-1  You Leave Me Breathless - vMB         Br 8135, Par R-2552, Col CQ-1420


                                           New York, June 30, 1938.

B-23182-2  Put Your Heart In A Song - vMB       Br 8182, A-81684
B-23183-1  Wigwammin' - vMB                     Br 8194
B-23184-1  The Sunny Side Of Things - vMB       Br 8182, A-81684
B-23185-1  How Can I Thank You ? - vMB          Br 8194



                                           New York, July 26, 1938.

B-23293-2  Garden Of The Moon - vMB             Br 8202
B-23294-1  Just You, Just Me                    Br 8240, Par R-2607, Od A-2361

RED NORVO AND HIS ORCHESTRA : Red Norvo-x dir. Jack Owens-Jack Palmer-Barney Zudecoff
t/Andy Russo-Al George-tb/Hank d'Amico-cl/Frank Simeone-as/Maurice Kogan-George
Berg-ts/Bill Miller-p/Alan Hanlon-g/Pete Peterson-sb/George Wettling-d/Mildred
Bailey-Terry Allen-v.          New York, July 28, 1938.

| | | |
|---|---|---|
| 23299-1 | Now It Can Be Told - vMB | Voc 4282 |
| B-23300-1-2 | Jump Jump's Here - vMB | Br 8202 |
| 23301-1 | I Haven't Changed A Thing - vMB | Voc 4282 |
| 23302-2 | Love Is Where You Find It - vMB | Voc 4345, Cq 9106, Par R-2633, Br A-81935 |
| 23303-2 | I Used To Be Color Blind - vMB | Voc 4345, Cq 9106, Par R-2610 |

NOTE:- All issues except Brunswick 8202 as MILDRED BAILEY AND HER ORCHESTRA.

New York, September 12, 1938.

| | | |
|---|---|---|
| B-23454- | This Is Madness - vMB | Br 8230 |
| B-23455- | Who Blew Out The Flame ? - vMB | - |
| B-23456-1 | You're A Sweet Little Headache - vTA | Br 8227, A-81839, Par F-1370 |
| B-23457-1 | I Have Eyes - vTA | -          -          - |

Charlie Shavers-t/Buster Bailey-cl/Russell Procope-as/Billy Kyle-p/John Kirby-sb/
O'Neil Spencer-d/Red Norvo-x/Mildred Bailey-The Three Ickeys-v.
New York, September 29, 1938.

| | | |
|---|---|---|
| 23516-1 | St. Louis Blues - vMB (all LPs) | CBS CL-1861, C3L-22, BPG-62099 |
| 23516-3 | St. Louis Blues - vMB | Voc 4801, Cq 9217, Par R-2685, Br A-81907, A-82177, Od A-2386, A-272261 |
| B-23517-2 | You Must Have Been A Beautiful Baby-v3I | Br 8240, Par R-2607, Od A-2361 |
| B-23518- | Nuances By Norvo | Rejected |
| 23519-1 | Have You Forgotten So Soon ? - vMB | Voc 4432 |

NOTE:- All issues except those from matrix B-23517-2 as MILDRED BAILEY AND HER
ORCHESTRA.

As for July 28, 1938 above, but Billy Kyle-p replaces Miller on the first title.
New York, December 8, 1938.

| | | |
|---|---|---|
| B-23809-2 | Undecided | Br 8288, A-81955 |
| 23810-1 | They Say - vMB | Voc 4548, Par R-2633, Br A-81935, A-500760 |
| 23811-2 | Blame It On My Last Affair - vMB | Voc 4632, Par R-2659, Br A-82002, Od A-2358 |
| 23812-1 | I Go For That - vMB | Voc 4548, Br A-81935, A-500760 |
| 23813- | Funny Little Snowman - vMB | Rejected |
| B-23814-1-2 | Thanks For Everything - vTA | Br 8288, A-81955 |

NOTE:- All except Brunswick 8288 and A-81935 as MILDRED BAILEY AND HER ORCHESTRA.

Red Norvo-x dir. Steve Lipkins and another-t/Les Burness-as/Stuart MacKay-as or
George Berg-ts/Stew Anderson-ts/Len Goldstein-as-ts/Bill Miller-p/Alan Hanlon-g/
Pete Peterson-sb/Buddy Christian-d/Mildred Bailey-Terry Allen-v.
New York, February 8, 1939.

| | | |
|---|---|---|
| 24091- | I Get Along Without You Very Well - vTA | Voc 4648, Cq 9177, Br A-82009 |
| 24092- | Kiss Me With Your Eyes - vTA | -          - |
| 24093-2 | Cuckoo In The Clock - vMB | Voc 4698, Cq 9186, Br A-82150 |

New York, February 27, 1939.

| | | |
|---|---|---|
| 24173-1 | We'll Never Know - vTA | Voc 4698, Br A-82150 |
| 24174-1 | Toadie Toddle | Voc 4738, Par R-2706 |
| 24175- | Rehearsin' For A Nervous Breakdown | Voc 4833, Br A-82141 |
| 24176-2 | You're So Desirable - vTA | Voc 4785, Br A-82175 |
| 24177-1 | There'll Never Be Another You - vMB | Voc 4738, Par R-2706 |

New York, April 6, 1939.

| | | |
|---|---|---|
| 24342-C | I Can Read Between The Lines - vTA | Voc 4818 |
| 24343-A | Blue Evening - vTA | Voc 4833, Col DO-2037, Br A-82141 |
| 24344-D | Yours For A Song - vTA | Voc 4818 |
| 24345-C | Three Little Fishies (Itty Bitty Poo) - vMB | Voc 4785, Cq 9174, Br A-82175 |

RED NORVO AND HIS ORCHESTRA : Red Norvo-x dir. Steve Lipkins and another-t/Les
Burness-as/Stuart MacKay-as or George Berg-ts/Stew Anderson-ts/Len Goldstein-as-
ts/Bill Miller-p/Alan Hanlon-g/Pete Peterson-sb/Buddy Christian-d/Terry Allen-v.
                              New York, June 21, 1939.

| | | |
|---|---|---|
| 24801-4 | Some Like It Hot | Voc 5009 |
| 24802-1 | In The Middle Of A Dream - vTA | Voc 4953 |
| 24803-1 | My Love For You - vTA | - |
| 24804-4 | Have Mercy | Voc 5009 |

Red Norvo-x dir. Jimmy Salko-Jack Kim-Bob Kennedy-t/Moe Nole-Ed Bert-Leo Connors-
tb/Freddy Artzburger-Sal Dottore-as/Mickey Folus-Sammy Spumberg-Jimmy Gemus-ts/Bob
Kitsis-p/Freddy Sharp-g/Joe Kauchek-sb/Frank Vesely-d/Mildred Bailey-v.
                              New York, March 5, 1942.

| | | |
|---|---|---|
| 32564-2 | Jersey Bounce | Col 36557 |
| 32565-1-2 | Arthur Murray Taught Me Dancing In A Hurry - vMB | - |
| 32566- | I'll Be Around - vMB | Rejected |
| 32567- | My Little Cousin - vMB | - |

## EVAN NOVAK

Pseudonym on Australian Summit 134 for Roy Evans, q.v.

## NOVELTY BLUE BOYS

Andy Sannella-cl-as-v/Frank Banta-p/Fred van Eps-bj.
                              New York, c. May, 1927.

2507-A-B  St. Louis Blues                    GG 1464, GG/Rx 7023, Mad 1904,
                                             Pic 490
NOTE:- Grey Gull 1464 and Radiex 7023 as DIXIE TRIO; Madison 1904 as INSTRUMENTAL
TRIO; Piccadilly as MISSISSIPPI TRIO.

                              New York, c. June, 1927.

2586-A  John Henry Blues - vAS              GG 1465, GG/Rx 7023, Mad 1920
2587-   Mississippi Mud Blues               GG 1464, 7029
NOTE:- Grey Gull 1464 as DIXIE TRIO; 7029 is anonymous; Madison 1920 as MUSICAL
TRIO.

Vn added.                     New York, c. July, 1927.

2646-B  Beale Street Blues - vAS            GG/Rx 1479, GG 7024, Mad 1920.
NOTE:- Grey Gull/Radiex 1479 as WABASH TRIO; Madison 1920 as MUSICAL TRIO.

Vn omitted.                   New York, c. August, 1927.

2688-A  Hard Times Blues                    GG/Rx 7025, VD 77025
2689-A  Yellow Dog Blues                    - 1485  -        Mad 1921
NOTE:- Grey Gull 7025 as WABASH TRIO; Madison 1921 as SOUTHERN TRIO; Van Dyke
77025 as MISSISSIPPI TRIO.

Vn replaces van Eps.          New York, c. November, 1927.

2812-B  Deep River Blues - vAS              GG/Rx 1506, 7026, Mad 1927
NOTE:- Grey Gull 1506 as ARTISTIC TRIO; Madison 1927 is anonymous.

                              New York, c. January, 1928.

2910-A-B  Loveless Love                     GG 1522, GG/Rx 7026, Mad 1921,
                                            Rx 1527
NOTE:- Grey Gull 1522 is anonymous; Madison 1921 as SOUTHERN TRIO.

## NOVELTY FIVE

See Harry Yerkes.

See Billy Arnold.

NOVELTY   ORCHESTRA

See the New Mayfair Dance Orchestra, February 19, 1931.

SAM NOWLIN

Piano solos.                              Richmond, Ind., October 8, 1934.

19721    So What                          Ch 16828, 40012
19722    Change                              -        -
19723    Riff                             Rejected

OLLY   OAKLEY

The following titles from the enormous number made for many labels by James Sharpe
(alias Olly Oakley) between 1902 and 1930 are known to be of interest as ragtime.

Banjo solos, acc. by Landon Ronald-p.     London, March 12, 1903.
3274-R  Whistling Rufus (Kerry Mills)        G&T GC-6374, HMV B-138
NOTE:- This title was re-made on January 9, 1923 (matrix Bb-2359) with orchestra
directed by George W. Byng, and issued under the same (double-sided) number B-138.

Acc. by Madame Adami-p.                    London, March 6, 1913.
Ab-16373e  The College Rag (W. Hunter)        Zon 1060

JIMMIE   O'BRYANT

Clarinet solos, acc. by Jimmy Blythe-p/Jasper Taylor-wb.
                                          Chicago, c. November, 1924.
677      Red Hot Mama                      Pm 12246
679      Drunk Man's Strut                    -       12568, Bwy 1337
NOTE:- Broadway 1337 as JIMMY BRYANT.  Matrix 678 is untraced.

(JIMMIE) O'BRYANT'S (FAMOUS ORIGINAL) WASHBOARD BAND : As above; Ruth Coleman-v.
                                          Chicago, c. February, 1925.
10036-2  Washboard (Washboard Blues*)      Pm 12265, 12288*, Poydras 18
10037-1-2  Brand New Charleston - vRC         -

                                          Chicago, c. March, 1925.

758-1    Skoodlum Blues                    Pm 12260, Sil 3549
759-1    Midnight Strutters                   -       Sil 3548
NOTE:- Silvertone 3548 and 3549 as THE WASHBOARD WONDERS.

                                          Chicago, April, 1925.

2088-1   Georgia Breakdown (Snooping Blues*)  Pm 12277, Sil 3572*, VJR 18, XX 4
NOTE:- Silvertone 3572 as THE HOT DOGS; XX 4 as CRACKER JACK'S CORRUGATED CHARAC-
TERS.
                                          Chicago, c. May, 1925.
10079-2  Blue Eyed Sally                   Pm 12288

10086-2  Three J Blues                     Pm 12294
10087-2  Steppin' On The Gas                 -

Bob Shoffner-c added*.                    Chicago, c. June, 1925.

2146-1-2 *Hot-Hot-Hottentot               Pm 20400, Pur 11400
2147-2   *Alabamy Bound                       -        -
2148-1-2  Clarinet Getaway                 Pm 12287, Poydras 26
2149-1-2  Back Alley Rub                      -        -
NOTE:- Puritan 11400 as BOB WHITE'S DIXIE TRIO.

                                          Chicago, c. July, 1925.

2194-1 *The Joys (Slow Motion Special)     Pm 12297
2195-1-2 *Everybody Pile                   Pm 12312
2196-2 *Charleston Fever                      -
2197-1-2  Switch It, Miss Mitchell         Pm 12297

(JIMMIE/JIMMY) O'BRYANT'S FAMOUS ORIGINAL WASHBOARD BAND : Jimmie O'Bryant-cl/Jimmy
Blythe-p/Jasper Taylor-wb.               Chicago, c. August, 1925.

2233-1-2  Down To The Bricks              Pm 12308, Poydras 65
2234-2  I Found A Good Man After All       -              -

W. E. Burton-bj or wb as shown replaces Taylor.
                                        Chicago, c. November, 1925.

2322-1-2  Milenberg Joys - wb             Pm 12321
2323-1  Sugar Babe - bj                    -

Burton plays wb throughout.             Chicago, c. December, 1925.

911-1-2  Thirty-Eight And Two (It Must Be Forty)Pm 12329
912-1-2  Please Don't Break 'Em Down      -
913-1-2  Chicago Skiffle                  Pm 12339
914-2  My Man Rocks Me                     -

                                        Chicago, c. January, 1926.

2435-1-2  Shake That Thing                Pm 12346, Sil 3548
NOTE:- Silvertone 3548 as THE WASHBOARD WONDERS.

## ODEON  SYNCOPATORS

See the OKeh Syncopators.

## HUSK  O'HARE

HUSK O'HARE'S SUPER ORCHESTRA OF CHICAGO : Husk O'Hare dir. t/tb/cl-as/ts/2vn/p/bj/bb
/d.                                     Richmond, Ind., March 9, 1922.

11062, -A  Koo-Kee-Koo                    Rejected
11063, -A  Cry Baby Blues                 -
11064, -A  Da-Da-Da My Darling            -
11065-A-B  Boo Hoo Hoo                    Gnt 4850, St 9237

                                        Richmond, Ind., March 10, 1922.

11066-A-B  Tiger Rag                      Gnt 4850, Cdl 512, St 9237
11067-B  Russian Love Song                St 9252
11068    San                             Gnt 5009, Br 02213, Tpl 538

The following session was originally believed to have been directed by Sam Lanin,
but while this now seems open to doubt, the performances do not appear to have been
made by the same band as the above, they are of only very marginal interest as jazz
and are included here for completeness' sake. The instrumentation is the same or
similar.                                New York, July 14, 1922.

7972, -A-B  Clover Blossom Blues          Gnt 4921, St 9276
7973-A-B  Night                           -              -

Pac added; probably directed by Joseph Samuels-vn (and cl ?) as Gennett 4997 is
credited to JOE SAMUELS AND HIS MASTER PLAYERS.
                                        New York, October 19, 1922.

8075-A-B  You Gave Me Your Heart          Gnt 4983, Cdl 541, St 9313
8076    All Muddled Up                    Gnt 4997, Apex 453, St 9312
8077-A-B-C  Swanee Smiles                 Gnt 4983        -

HUSK O'HARE'S WOLVERINES : Jim Awad-c/Turk Savage-c-v/Pete Havlicheck-tb/Gus Lingo-
Art Cox-cl-ss-as/Harold Send-cl-ts/Tom Giblin-p/Dick Kettering-bj/Mal Woolin-bb/Al
Silverman-d.                            Chicago, January 10, 1928.

C-1423; E-6870  Milenberg Joys - vTS      Voc 15646
C-1425; E-6872  My Daddy Rocks Me - vTS   -

Pseudonym on Aco for the following items listed in this book :-

G-15163  Burning Sands (The Broadway Syncopators)
6-15177  Without You (The Broadway Syncopators)
G-15177  One Night In June (Gene Fosdick's Hoosiers)
G-15178  Starlight Bay (The Broadway Syncopators)
G-15221  Who's Sorry Now ? (Ben Bernie's Hotel Roosevelt Orchestra)
G-15221  Peggy Dear (Gene Fosdick's Hoosiers)
G-15237  Apple Sauce (Gene Fosdick's Hoosiers)

## OHIO  JAZZ ORCHESTRA

Harl Smith-d dir. Joe Rose-c/Barney Russell-tb/Henry Nathan-cl-as-vn/Fred Morrow-as/
    Bill Haid-p/Evert Davidson-bj.          Berlin, c. July, 1924.

> My Pickwick (? Mr. Pickwick)          Vox 8079
> A Shingled Hearth                       -

## OHIO  NOVELTY BAND

Pseudonym on Aco for the following items listed in this book :-

G-15237  Runnin' Wild (The Southland Six)
G-15567  Doodle Doo Doo (Ben Bernie and his Hotel Roosevelt Orchestra)
G-15584  I'm Satisfied (Ben Bernie and his Hotel Roosevelt Orchestra)
G-15651  A New Kind Of Man (Fletcher Henderson and his Orchestra)
G-15710  Why Couldn't It Be Poor Little Me ? (Ben Bernie and his Hotel Roosevelt O.)
G-15732  No One (Ben Bernie and his Hotel Roosevelt Orchestra)
G-15750  Sweet Georgia Brown (Ben Bernie and his Hotel Roosevelt Orchestra)
G-16033  If You Never Come Back (McKenzie's Candy Kids)
G-16082  Mandy (Ben Bernie and his Hotel Roosevelt Orchestra)
G-16120  Both sides by the Vagabonds
G016142  Don't Take That Black Bottom Away (Fred Rich's Times Square Orchestra)

## O. K. RHYTHM KINGS

Pseudonym on English Parlophone for the Casa Loma Orchestra, q.v.

## OKEH MELODIANS

Pseudonym on OKeh for Sam Lanin and his Famous Players, q.v.

## OKEH MELODY  STARS

2c/tb/cl-as/ts/p/bj/Clarence Todd-v.      New York, August 23, 1926.

74310-B  Look Out, Mr. Jazz                OK 8382
74311-B  A Glass Of Beer, A Hot Dog And You   -

## OKEH SYNCOPATORS

The following titles by this OKeh "house" band are known or are reported to be of
    some interest as jazz, and research may produce further examples in this category.

Harry Reser-bj dir. Earl Oliver-Hymie Farberman-t/Sam Lewis-tb/Larry Abbott-cl-as/
    cl-bcl-ss-as/Norman Yorke-ts/Bill Wirges-p/Joe Tarto-bb/Tom Stacks-d.
                            New York, c. March 3, 1924.

72383-B  Nobody's Sweetheart                OK 40072, Par E-5229
    NOTE:- Parlophone E-5229 as PARLOPHONE SYNCOPATORS.

                            New York, late April, 1924.

72489-B  Savannah (The Georgianna Blues)        OK 40100, Par E-5244, Od 03155
    NOTE:- Parlophone E-5244 as PARLOPHONE SYNCOPATORS; Odeon 03155 as ODEON SYNCO-
    PATORS.

Probably Justin Ring dir. Tommy Gott-? Hymie Farberman-t/Sam Lewis-tb/? Larry Abbott-
Sammy Feinsmith-cl-ss-as/? Norman Yorke-ts/p/bj/Joe Tarto-bb/d/Earl Rickard-v.
                                            New York, February 4, 1925.

73150-B  Birmingham Papa (Your Memphis Mamma's     OK 40316
         Comin' To Town) - vER
73151-B  It's All The Same To Me - vER                 -

Harry Raderman-tb dir. 2t/2cl-ss-as/cl-ts/p/bj/bb/d.
                                            New York, October 25, 1925.

73736-   Everybody's Doin' The Charleston     OK 40493, Par E-5537
73737-   Footloose                               -          -
NOTE:- Parlophone E-5537 as PARLOPHONE SYNCOPATORS.

                                            New York, c. February 20, 1926.

74019-B  Jig Walk                                  OK 40614

See also Harry Raderman.

## OLD GOLD  SERENADERS

Instrumentation and personnel unknown.     Richmond, Ind., January 16, 1928.

13362    Jazz Me Blues                             Gnt rejected

## OLD SOUTHERN DANCE ORCHESTRA

Pseudonym on Guardsman for the following items listed in this book :-

1830  Breezin' Along (Ben Selvin and his Orchestra)
1833  I Had A Sweet Mama (The Tennessee Tooters)
1864  Mother Me, Tennessee (Ben Bernie and his Hotel Roosevelt Orchestra)
1968  My Carmenita (Joe Candullo and his Everglades Orchestra)
1976  Both sides by Joe Candullo and his Everglades Orchestra
1991  Katinka (Joe Candullo and his Everglades Orchestra)
2000  Don't Take That Black Bottom Away (Fred Rich and his Times Square Orchestra)

## OLD SOUTHERN  JUG BAND

Theodore Boone-c/Clifford Hayes-vn/Cal Smith-Curtis Hayes-bj/Earl McDonald-jug.
                                New York, November 24, 1924.

14359    Hatchet Head Blues              Voc 14958, Sil 3061, Gmn 7010
14361    Blues, Just Blues, That's All        -          -        -
NOTE:- Guardsman 7010 as CAROLINA JUG BAND.

## THE OLD VIRGINIANS

Pseudonym on Aco for the following items listed in this book :-

G-15515  Savannah (The Georgianna Blues) (The Ambassadors)
G-15535  Pleasure Mad (The Ambassadors)
G-15625  Oh ! How I Love My Darling (The Ambassadors)

## ANNA  OLIVER

See Young's Creole Jazz Band.

## BARRIE  OLIVER

Vocal, acc. by Sylvester Ahola-t/Danny Polo-cl/Arthur Lally-as/Claude Ivy-p/? Alan
Ferguson-g.                        London, December 10, 1929.

MB-754-1-2-3  Let's Amalgamate             Rejected
MB-755-2  Ev'ry Day Away From You          Dec F-1606
MB-756-1-2-3  I May Be Wrong, But I Think You're   Rejected
         Wonderful
MB-757-3  'Tain't No Sin                   Dec F-1606

Acc. by Sylvester Ahola-t/Danny Polo-cl-as/Claude Ivy-p/Alan Ferguson-g/Spike
Hughes-sb.                         London, March 3, 1930.

| MB-1015-2 | Moanin' For You | Dec F-1722 |
| MB-1016-2 | I Have To Have You | - |
| MB-1017-2 | I'm On A Diet Of Love | Dec F-1682 |
| MB-1018-1 | Mona | - |

Other records by this American cabaret artist are of no known interest as jazz.

## EARL OLIVER'S JAZZ BABIES

See Harry Reser.  This band has nothing whatever to do with King Oliver !

## KING  OLIVER

KING OLIVER'S CREOLE JAZZ BAND : King Oliver-Louis Armstrong-c/Honore Dutrey-tb/
Johnny Dodds-cl/Lil Hardin-p/Bill Johnson-bj-v break/Baby Dodds-d.
Richmond, Ind., April 6, 1923.**

| 11383-B | Just Gone | Gnt 5133, Br 02202, Pol 51387, VJR 12, HJCA 610 |
| 11384-B | Canal Street Blues | Gnt 5133, Br 02200, Dec MG-36271, UHCA 67, JI 1 |
| 11385-C | Mandy Lee Blues | Gnt 5134, Br 02201, UHCA 69, JI. 2, Pol 1570 |
| 11386-C | I'm Going Away To Wear You Off My Mind | Gnt 5134, Br 02201, HJCA 610, VJR 12, Pol 1570 |
| 11387-A | Chimes Blues | Gnt 5135, UHCA 68, JI 1, JC L-3, Tem R-6, AF A-03, Sto KB-I03 |
| 11388 | Weather Bird Rag | Gnt 5132, Br 02202, UHCA 75,  JI 5 |
| 11389-B | Dipper Mouth Blues (Sugar Foot Stomp*)-vBJ --3076*,Br 02200, Dec MG-36271, JI 10, UHCA 77, BRS 2 |
| 11390-B | Froggie Moore | Gnt 5135, UHCA 70, JI 2, JC L-3, Tem R-6, AF A-06, Sto KB-I03, XX 3 |
| 11391 | Snake Rag | Gnt 5184, UHCA 76, JI 5, JC L-4, Tem R-7, AF A-03, Sto KB-I04, XX 3 |

NOTE:- XX 3 as GORGON GRUNDY'S EXPLODING MYTHS.

KING OLIVER'S JAZZ BAND : As above, but Bud Scott-bj-v break replaces Johnson; Baby
Dodds or Louis Armstrong db sw*.        Chicago, June 22, 1923.

| 8391-A | Snake Rag - vBS | OK 4933, SE 5016-S, Ph P-23577-H, VJR 6, JSo AA-516 |
| 8392-B | Sweet. Lovin' Man | OK 4906, LAR A-4175, Bm 1053, HJCA HC-8, AF A-039, JSo AA-501 |
| 8393-B | High Society Rag | OK 4933, HRS 12, SE 5016-S, Col S-10001, Ph P-23577-H, VJR 6, AF A-026, JSo AA-516 |
| 8394-B | *Sobbin' Blues | OK 4906, LAR A-4175, Ph P-42004-H, Bm 1053, HJCA HC-8, 610, AF A-039, JSo AA-501 |

Chicago, June 23, 1923.

| 8401-A | Where Did You Stay Last Night ? | OK 4918, Bm 1055, BRS 2, HJCA HC-25, VJR 22, 42, AF A-026, JSo AA-540 |
| 8402-A | Dipper Mouth Blues - vBS | OK 4918, Br 8223, Ph P-42004-H, HRS 4, Bm 1055, BRS 2, HJCA HC-25, AF A-028 |
| 8403-A | Jazzin' Babies' Blues | OK 4975, Bm 1051, HJCA HC-26, AF A-026 |

** The date frequently given in past works of reference and on LP sleeves is March
31, 1923, but this was due originally to a misinterpretation of the entry in the
Gennett numerical ledger, where this date is given at the head of the column, not
against the King Oliver session, which is undated.  The recording cards for each
title show it as April 6, 1923, however, which must be accepted as correct.

KING OLIVER AND HIS CREOLE JAZZ BAND : King Oliver-Louis Armstrong-c/Honore Dutrey-tb
  /Johnny Dodds-cl/Stump Evans-Cm/Lil Hardin-p/Johnny St  Cyr-bj/Baby Dodds-d.
                                    Richmond, Ind., October 5, 1923.

| | | |
|---|---|---|
| 11632, -A-B-C | When You Leave Me Alone To Pine | Rejected |
| 11633-B | Alligator Hop (Alligator Flop) | Gnt 5274, Cen 3008, JC L-15, |
| | | Tem R-4, AF A-07 |
| 11634-C | That Sweet Something, Dear | Gnt 5276 (never issued) |
| 11635-A | Zulus Ball | Gnt 5275, Bm 1028, Tem R-29 |
| 11636-B | Working Man's Blues | - - - |
| 11637, -A-B-C | Someday Sweetheart | Rejected |
| 11638 | Krooked Blues | Gnt 5274, Cen 3008, JC L-115, |
| | | Tem R-4, AF A-06 |
| 11639-B | If You Want My Heart (You Got To 'Low It, Babe) | Gnt 5276 (never issued) |

KING OLIVER'S JAZZ BAND : King Oliver-Louis Armstrong-c/? Ed Atkins-tb/Buster Bailey
  or Jimmie Noone-cl/Lil Hardin-p/Johnny St. Cyr-bj/Baby Dodds-d.
                                    Chicago, October 15, 1923.

| | | |
|---|---|---|
| 81300-3 | Chattanooga Stomp | Col 13003-D, DF /DZ-3079, LF-225, |
| | | Bm 1057, HJCA HC-63, VJM II |
| 81301-1-2-3 | Junk Man Blues | Rejected |
| 81302-1-2-3 | London (Cafe) Blues | - |

                                    Chicago, October 16, 1923.

| | | |
|---|---|---|
| 81302-5 | London (Cafe) Blues | Col 14003-D, Ph B-23573-H, |
| | | Bm 1054, HJCA HC-17, VJR 26 |
| 81303-2 | Camp Meeting Blues | As above |
| 81304-2 | New Orleans Stomp | Col 13003-D, DF /DZ-3079, LF-225, |
| | | Bm 1057, HJCA HC-63, VJR II |

King Oliver-Louis Armstrong-c/Honore Dutrey-tb/Johnny Dodds-cl/Charlie Jackson-bsx-
bb/Lil Hardin-p/Johnny St. Cyr-bj/Baby Dodds-d.  Louis Armstrong almost certainly
db sw where marked *.                Chicago, c. October 25, 1923.

| | | |
|---|---|---|
| 8475-B | *Buddy's Habit | OK 40000, Bm 1056, HJCA HC-37, |
| | | AF A-000, JSo AA-540 |
| 8476-B | Tears | OK 40000, HRS 12, Bm 1056, |
| | | HJCA HC-37, BRS 10 (never issued), |
| | | AF A-000, JSo AA-540 |
| 8477-B | I Ain't Gonna Tell Nobody | OK 8148, Od 03198, Bm 1049, |
| | | HJCA HC-1, AF A-033 |
| 8478-A | Room Rent Blues | As above |

                                    Chicago, c. October 26, 1923.

| | | |
|---|---|---|
| 8484-A | Riverside Blues | OK 40034, Od 03197, Bm 1052, |
| | | HJCA HC-7 |
| 8485-A | Sweet Baby Doll | OK 8235, Bm 1050, HJCA HC-2, |
| | | AF A-034, JRS AA-117, ViJazz V-7 |
| 8486-B | Working Man Blues | OK 40034, Od 03197, Bm 1052, |
| | | HJCA HC-7 |
| 8487-A | Mabel's Dream | OK 8235, Bm 1050, HJCA HC-2, |
| | | AF A-034, JRS AA-117, ViJazz V-7 |

St. Cyr omitted.                     Chicago, c. December 24, 1923.

| | | |
|---|---|---|
| 1622-1 | Mabel's Dream | Pm 20292, 14014, Cx 40292, |
| | | Pur 11292, Sig 905, SD 100, |
| | | Br 03575, Dec 60279 |
| 1622-2 | Mabel's Dream | Pm 20292,Pur 11292,Hg 890, VJR 27 |
| 1623-1 | The Southern Stomps | Pm 12088, Jazz 5008 (never issued) |
| 1623-2 | The Southern Stomps | - 14015, Cen 3011, JC L-4, |
| | | AF A-07, GzI 1014 |
| 1624-2 | Riverside Blues | Pm 20292, 14014, Cx 40292, Hg 890, |
| | | Pur 11292, Sig 905, SD 100,VJR 27, |
| | | Br 03575, Dec 60279, Jazz 5008 |

Cornet solos, acc. by Jelly-Roll Morton-p.
Chicago, c. December, 1924.

| | | |
|---|---|---|
| 685 | King Porter | Auto 617, <u>Ses 1</u>, <u>JC L-56</u> |
| 687 | Tom Cat | -         -      - |

NOTE:- Matrix 686 is untraced.

KING OLIVER'S JAZZ BAND : King Oliver-Bob Shoffner-c/Kid Ory-tb/Albert Nicholas-Billy
Paige-cl-ss-as/Barney Bigard-cl-ss-ts/Luis Russell-p/Bud Scott-bj/Bert Cobb-bb/Paul
Barbarin-d/Richard M. Jones-v.          Chicago, March 11, 1926.

E-2632     Too Bad - vRMJ                      Voc 1007, V-1009, Br 80082,
                                               Dec 31027, <u>MG-36267</u>
E-2633     Too Bad - vRMJ                      <u>Voc 1007</u>, <u>Br A-181</u>
E-2634     Snag It - vRMJ                       - 15503 - A-250,80039,JSo AA538
NOTE:- All issues except Vocalion 1007 and Brunswick A-181 as KING <u>OLIVER AND HIS</u>
DIXIE SYNCOPATORS, or some slight variant of this.

KING OLIVER AND HIS DIXIE SYNCOPATORS : As above.
Chicago, April 21, 1926.

C-195; E-2892; E-19679  Deep Henderson         Voc 1014, 15394, Br 3245, 5-1014,
                                               A-151, <u>JSo AA-537</u>

Georgia Taylor-v.                       Chicago, April 23, 1926.

C-226; E-2914; E-19676  Jackass Blues - vGT    Voc 1014, 15394, Br 3245, 3281,
                                               5-1014, A-151, HJCA 610,<u>JSo AA-537</u>
NOTE:- Brunswick 3245 and 3281 as THE SAVANNAH SYNCOPATORS.

Chicago, May 29, 1926.

C-370; E-3179; E-20503  Sugar Foot Stomp       Voc 1033, 15503, Br 3361*, 80081,
                                               A-178, A-226, A-250, <u>UHCA 42</u>,
                                               JSo AA-538
C-372; E-3181; E-20637  Wa Wa Wa               Voc 1033, V-1004, Br 3373*,
                                               A-178, <u>A-217</u>, <u>JSo AA-521</u>
C-373/4; E-3182/3       Hobo's Prayer          Rejected

Darnell Howard-cl-as replaces Paige; Stump Evans-ss added.
Chicago, July 23, 1926.

        E-3553  Someday, Sweetheart            Rejected
        E-3554  Messin' Around                  -
C-533; E-3556  Tack Annie                      Voc 1049

Nicholas omitted; Evans plays cl-as; Johnny Dodds-cl added*.
Chicago, September 17, 1926.

C-657; E-3843; E-20252; E-20639 *Someday,      Voc 1059, 15493, V-1004, Br 3373*,
                                Sweetheart     80082, A-179, A-217, A-81002,
                                               <u>Mt M-12064</u>, Polk P-9034,
                                               Pan 25035, JSo AA-521
C-659; E-3845; E-20254  Dead Man Blues         Voc 1059, <u>15493</u>, Br A-179,
                                               A-81002, JSo AA-539
C-661; E-3847; E-20256  New Wang-Wang Blues    Voc 1049
C-662; E-3848; E-20257; E-20591  Snag It       Br 3361*, A-226, <u>JSo AA-538</u>
C-663; E-3849; E-20258; E-20592  Snag It (Snag It No.2*)-     80081*
NOTE:- Brunswick 3361 and 3373 as THE SAVANNAH SYNCOPATORS; <u>Melotone M-12064</u>, Polk
P-9034 and Panachord 25035 as JACK WYNN'S DALLAS DANDIES.

King Oliver-Tick Gray-c/Kid Ory-tb/Omer Simeon-cl-ss-as/Paul Barnes-cl-as/Barney
Bigard-cl-ts/Luis Russell-p/Junie Cobb-bj/Lawson Buford-bb/Paul Barbarin-d.
Chicago, April 22, 1927.

C-800/2; E-5172/4; E-22729/31  Doctor Jazz     Voc 1113
C-804; E-5176; E-22733; E-26317 Showboat Shuffle  Voc 1114, Br 3998, A-7871,
                                               Aur A-22002, JSo AA-525
C-807; E-5179; E-22736; E-26315 Every Tub      As above, but <u>Aur A-22001</u>
C-809; E-5168; E-22738  Willie The Weeper      Voc 1112, Br 80079, <u>JSo AA-577</u>
NOTE:- Aurora A-22001 and A-22002 as AURORA ARISTOCRATS.

KING OLIVER AND HIS DIXIE SYNCOPATORS : King Oliver-Tick Gray-c/Kid Ory-tb/Omer
   Simeon-cl-ss-as/Paul Barnes-cl-as/Barney Bigard-cl-ts/Luis Russell-p/Junie Cobb-bj
   /Lawson Buford-bb/Paul Barbarin-d.     Chicago, April 27, 1927.

C-835; E-5170  Black Snake Blues                Voc 1112, V-1009, Br 80079,
                                                Dec 31027, JSo AA-577

King Oliver-?/ Henry Allen-c/? Jimmy Archey-tb/Omer Simeon-cl-as/Paul Barnes-as/2
   other s/Luis Russell-p/Willie Foster-bj/Lawson Buford-bb/d.
                                   New York, July 8, 1927.

E-6209; E-23880  Aunt Jemima                    Voc 1113

Unidentified 9-piece band; Benny Waters-a (and cl-ts ?)
                                   New York, October 13, 1927.

E-6655/7  Sobbin' Blues                         Voc rejected
E-6658/60 Tin Roof Blues                        -

                                   New York, October 14, 1927.

E-6667/8  Aunt Hagar's Blues - aBW              Voc rejected
E-6669/70 Farewell Blues                        -

King Oliver-c dir. Jimmy Archey-tb/Paul Barnes-ss-as/Barney Bigard-cl-ts/? Benny
   Waters-cl-ts-a/p/bj/bb/Paul Barbarin-d.
                                   New York, November 18, 1927.

E-6806; E-25352  Farewell Blues                 Voc 1152, Br 3741, 3727, A-7577,
                                                A-81255, Or 2573, Per 15685,
                                                JSo AA-511
E-6808/9          Tin Roof Blues                Rejected
E-6811; E-25355  Sobbin' Blues                  Voc 1152, Br 3741, 3727, A-7577,
   NOTE:- Oriole 2573 and Perfect 15685 as THE    A-81255, Or 2573, Per 15685,
   DIXIE SYNCOPATORS; Aurora A-22008 as HERMAN     Aur A-22008, HJCA 610, JSo AA-511
   BLACK AND HIS ORCHESTRA.

Unidentified 10-piece band, possibly similar to the last above, perhaps including
   Johnny Hodges-cl-ss-as.            New York, February 25, 1928.

E-7172/3  Tin Roof Blues                        Voc rejected
E-7174/5  Aunt Hagar's Blues - aBW              -

                                   New York, March 3, 1928.

E-7184/5  Who Threw That Rug ?                  Voc rejected
E-7186/7  Crab House Blues                      -

Clarence Williams-p-v dir. King Oliver-c/Jimmy Archey-tb/Ernest Elliott-cl-as/
   Arville Harris-cl-as-ts/Leroy Harris-bj/Cyrus St. Clair-bb.
                                   New York, June 11, 1928.

E-7388-A; E-27684-A    Tin Roof Blues           Voc 1189, V-1024, Dec MG-36266,
                                                Creole 11, JSo AA-539
E-7389-A; E-27685-A    West End Blues           As above
E-7390-A/B; E-27686-A/B  Sweet Emmalina - vCW   Voc 1190
E-7391-A/B; E-27687-A/B  Lazy Mama              -

King Oliver-Ed Anderson-c/Ed Cuffee-tb/Omer Simeon-cl/Arville Harris-as/Leroy
   Tibbs-p/Leroy Harris-bj/Cyrus St. Clair-bb/Andy Pendleton-Willie Jackson-v.
                                   New York, August 13, 1928.

E-28055-A or -B  Got Everything (Don't Want     Br 4028
                 Anything But You) - vAP-WJ
E-28055-G  Got Everything                       Br A-7890
E-28056-A or -B  Four Or Five Times - vAP-WJ    Br 4028
E-28056-G  Four Or Five Times                   Br A-7890

KING OLIVER AND HIS DIXIE SYNCOPATORS : King Oliver-Ed Anderson-c/J. C. Higginbotham-
  tb/Omer Simeon-cl-as/Barney Bigard-cl-ts/Luis Russell-p/Will Johnson-bj/Bass Moore-
  bb/Paul Barbarin-d/Benny Waters-a.     New York, September 10, 1928.

E-28185-A or -B  Speakeasy Blues                     Voc 1225, Spt S-2236, Br 80080,
                                                     JSo AA-578
E-28186-A or -B  Aunt Hagar's Blues - aBW            As above

                              New York, September 12, 1928.

E-28203-A or -B  I'm Watching The Clock              Br 4469, Voc V-1033, JSo AA-529
E-28204-A-B  Janitor Sam                             Rejected

  Louis Metcalf-t replaces Anderson; Charlie Holmes-cl-ss-as replaces Simeon; ? Teddy
  Hill-ts replaces Bigard.     New York, November 14, 1928.

E-28757-A or -B  Slow And Steady                     Br 4469, Voc V-1033, JSo AA-529

KING OLIVER AND HIS ORCHESTRA : King Oliver dir. Louis Metcalf-c/J. C. Higginbotham-
  tb/Charlie Holmes-cl-ss-as/Teddy Hill or Greely Walton-cl-ts/Luis Russell-p/Will
  Johnson-bj-g/Bass Moore-bb/Paul Barbarin-d/Walter Pichon-v.
                              New York, January 16, 1929.

49649-1-2  Freakish Light Blues                      Rejected
49650-2    West End Blues                            Vic V-38034, HMV R-14189
49651-1    I've Got That Thing - vWP                 X LX-3018, Vic RA-5317 (LPs)
49651-2    I've Got That Thing - vWP                 Vic V-38521

                              New York, February 1, 1929.

48332-1-2-3  Easy Goin'                              Rejected
48333-1    Call Of The Freaks                        Vic 741055, Historic HLP-33 (LPs)
48333-2    Call Of The Freaks                        Vic V-38039, BB B-6546, B-7705,
                                                     HMV EA-2989, JF-36, R-14188
48334-1    The Trumpet's Prayer                      As above, except BB B-6546
49649-3    Freakish Light Blues                      X LX-3018, Vic RA-5317 (LPs)
49649-4    Freakish Light Blues                      Vic V-38521

KING OLIVER'S ORCHESTRA : King Oliver dir. ? Punch Miller-c/William Franklin or Fred
  Robinson-tb/Omer Simeon and another-cl-as/? Cecil Irwin-cl-ts/Cassino Simpson-p/bj
  /Lawson Buford or Quinn Wilson-bb/Wallace Bishop-d.
                              Chicago, February 25, 1929.

50523-1  Can I Tell You ?                             X LX-3018, EVA-12, Vic RA-5317,
                                                     HMV 7EG-8091
50523-2  Can I Tell You ?                             Vic V-38049
50524-1-2  Uncle Ned's Stomp                         Rejected
50525-2  My Good Man Sam                             Vic V-38049
50526-1-2  I Can't Be Worried Blues                  Rejected

KING OLIVER AND HIS ORCHESTRA : George Rogers dir. King Oliver-Dave Nelson-t/Jimmy
  Archey-tb/Bobby Holmes-cl-as/Glyn Paque-as/? Charles Frazier-ts/Don Frye-p/Walter
  Jones or Arthur Taylor-bj/Clinton Walker-bb/Edmund Jones-d.
                              New York, October 8, 1929.

56756-1  What You Want Me To Do ?                     Vic V-38090, BB B-7242,HMV R-14424
56757-2  Sweet Like This                             Vic V-38101, 1A-1426
56758-2  Too Late                                    Vic V-38090, BB B-7442,HMV R-14424

  Loren L. Watson dir. King Oliver-t/Dave Nelson-t-v/tb/? Glyn Paque-cl-as/Hilton
  Jefferson-as/? Charles Frazier-ts/James P. Johnson-p/Arthur Taylor-bj/Clinton
  Walker-bb/Edmund Jones-d.     New York, November 6, 1929.

57527-1  I'm Lonesome, Sweetheart - vDN              Vic 23029
57528-1  I Want You Just Myself                      Vic V-38101, HMV R-14433
57529-1  I Can't Stop Loving You                     Vic 23029, HMV B-4844

KING OLIVER AND HIS ORCHESTRA : King Oliver-Dave Nelson-t/Jimmy Archey-tb/Glyn Paque
  ? Hilton Jefferson-as/ts/Don Frye-p/Arthur Taylor-bj/g/Roy Smeck-h-stg as noted/
  ? Clinton Walker-bb/Edmund Jones-d.    New York, December 30, 1929.

58338-1 Everybody Does It In Hawaii - stg      Vic V-38109
58339-2-3 Frankie And Johnny - h               -
58340-1 New Orleans Shout                      Vic 23388

  Bobby Holmes-cl-as/Walter Wheeler-ts replace the unknown or uncertain reedmen;
  ? Henry Duncan-p replaces Frye.    New York, January 15, 1930.

58338-4 Everybody Does It In Hawaii - stg      Vic V-38109
58339-4 Frankie And Johnny                     -
NOTE:- Despite the label, there is no h on matrix 58339-4.

  Carroll Dickerson-vn dir. King Oliver-Henry Allen-Bubber Miley-t/Jimmy Archey-tb/
  Bobby Holmes-cl-as/Glyn Paque and another-as/ts/Don Frye-p/Arthur Taylor-bj/Jean
  Stultz-g/Clinton Walker-bb/Frank Marvin (as SONNY WOODS on HMV K-6153)-v.
                                      New York, January 28, 1930.

58527-3 St. James Infirmary - vFM              Vic 22298, BB B-5466, HMV K-6153
58528-2 When You're Smiling (The Whole World   -            -
          Smiles With You) - vFW

  Carroll Dickerson dir. King Oliver-Dave Nelson-t/Jimmy Archey-tb/Bobby Holmes-cl/
  Hilton Jefferson-Glyn Paque-cl-as/? Henry Duncan-p/Arthur Taylor-bj/Clinton Walker
  bb/Fred Moore-d.                    New York, March 18, 1930.

59525-1 I Must Have It                          Vic V-38124, 62-0061
59526-2 Rhythm Club Stomp (Curwiship Glide)    Vic V-38137, 760-0004
59527-1 You're Just My Type                     Vic V-38124, 62-0061

  Henry Allen-t added; Walter Wheeler-ts replaces Holmes; Norman Lester-p replaces
  Duncan; Dave Nelson-a.              New York, April 10, 1930.

59747-2 Edna                                   Vic V-38137, 760-0004
59748-2 Boogie Woogie - aDN                    Vic V-38134, BB B-6778,
                                               HMV JK-2783, El EG-7808
59749-1 Mule Face Blues                        As above

  Carroll Dickerson dir. King Oliver-Dave Nelson-t/Jimmy Archey-tb/Bobby Holmes-cl-
  as/Glyn Paque-as/Charles Frazier-ts/Eric Franker-p/Arthur Taylor-bj/Clinton Walker
  bb/Fred Moore-d.                    New York, May 22, 1930.

62236-2 Struggle Buggy                         Vic 23001, HMV B-4930
62237-1 Don't You Think I Love You ?           -            -
62238-2 Olga                                   Vic 22681, A-1281, HMV B-4870

  King Oliver-t dir. Henry Allen and another-t/Jimmy Archey-tb/Hilton Jefferson-Glyn
  Paque-as/Charles Frazier-ts/Henry Duncan-p/Arthur Taylor-bj/Arthur Nipton-bb/Fred
  Moore-d.                            New York, September 10, 1930.

63639-2 Shake It And Break It                  Vic 23009, BB B-10707
63640-1 Stingaree Blues                        -            -

  Dave Nelson-t replaces (or may even be) the unknown; g replaces bj; rest almost
  certainly as above; George Bias-v.    New York, September 12, 1930.

63134-3 What's The Use Of Living Without Love ? Vic 23011
          - vGB
63135-1-3 You Were Only Passing Time With Me - vGB  -

  Allen and Bias omitted; rest as above. Camden, N. J., September 19, 1930.

64013-1 Nelson Stomp (all LPs)                 Vic LPV-529, 741055, Pirate MPC-500
64013-2 Nelson Stomp                           Vic 23388, 24926
64013-3 Nelson Stomp (all LPs)                 Vic LPM-10017, 430709, 741055
64014-1 Stealing Love                          -            -            -
64014-2 Stealing Love                          El EG-7853

KING OLIVER AND HIS ORCHESTRA : King Oliver-Dave Nelson-Bill Dillard-t/Ward Pinkett-
    t-v/Jimmy Archey-tb/Buster Bailey-cl/Henry Jones-as/Bingie Madison-ts-v/Fred
    Skerritt-bar-v/Gene Rodgers-p/Goldie Lucas-g-v/Richard Fullbright-bb/Bill Beason-d.
                                    New York, January 9, 1931.

E-35910-B  Papa De Da Da - vBM-FS-GL            Br 6053, A-9029
E-35911-A  Who's Blue ?                          Br 6046, A-9065
E-35912-A  Stop Crying - vWP                     Br 6053, 01105, A-9029
    NOTE:- Brunswick 6046 as THE SAVANNAH SYNCOPATORS.

    King Oliver and 2 others-t/tb/? Bobby Holmes and another-cl-as/ts/p/bj/bb/d.
                                    New York, February 18, 1931.

E-36101-A-B  Where That Ol' Man River Flows      Rejected
E-36102-A  Sugar Blues                           Br 6065
E-36103-A  I'm Crazy 'Bout My Baby               -

    King Oliver-t/Ward Pinkett-t-v/Jimmy Archey-tb/Fred Skerritt-as-v/Henry Jones-as/
    Bingie Madison-ts-v/Gene Rodgers-p/Goldie Lucas-bj-g-v/Richard Fullbright-bb-sb/
    Bill Beason-d.                  New York, April 15, 1931.

E-36474-A  Loveless Love - vBM-FS-GL             Voc 1610
E-36625-A  One More Time - vBM-FS-GL             -
E-36626-A  When I Take My Sugar To Tea - vWP     Voc 1617
    NOTE:- Both the above Vocalions as CHOCOLATE DANDIES.
           IN HARLEM'S ARABY, by the Memphis Jazzers, q.v., was issued on Biltmore 1024
           as KING OLIVER AND HIS DIXIE DEVILS; and on Jazz Collector L-59 and Tempo
           R-10 as KING OLIVER'S MEMPHIS JAZZERS.
           VJR 25 is credited to KING OLIVER AND CLARENCE WILLIAMS' BOYS, and Creole 6
           KING OLIVER WITH CLARENCE WILLIAMS' JUG BAND.  See Clarence Williams for
           correct details of both these issues.

                        GEORGE OLSEN AND HIS MUSIC

The following titles by this band, one of the most popular in America between 1923
    and 1934, are known to contain points of interest as jazz; others sometimes have
    short "hot" solos in the last chorus.

George Olsen-c dir. Red Nichols-t/Floyd Rice-t-mel-as/Chuck Campbell-tb/George Henkel
    ss-as-f/Buck Yoder-cl-as/Dave Phennig-ts-vn/Eddie Kilfeather-p-a/Billy Priest-bj-as
    /Jack Hansen-bb.                New York, May 16, 1924.

30115-3  He's The Hottest Man In Town           Vic 19375
30116-1-2-3  Sally Lou                           Rejected

                    New York, June 5, 1924.

30116-4  Sally Lou                               Vic 19374
30165-4  A New Kind Of Man                       Vic 19375, HMV B-1890

                    New York, June 26, 1924.

30326-1-2-3  Beale Street Blues                  Rejected
30327-2  You'll Never Get To Heaven With Those   Vic 19405, HMV B-1880, Zon 3787
           Eyes

Billy Murray-v.                    New York, July 25, 1924.

30326-5  Beale Street Blues                      Vic 19457
30622-2  My Papa Doesn't Two-Time No Time - vBM  Vic 19419

    Donald Lindley-t replaces Nichols; Milton Neul-cl-ts-vn replaces Phennig; Yoder
    omitted; Leslie Sheriff-bj replaces Priest.
                                    New York, January 29, 1925.

31787-4  Nobody Knows What A Red-Head Mama       Vic 19580
           Can Do

George Olsen-d dir. Floyd Rice-Donald Lindley-t/Chuck Campbell-tb/George Henkel-ss-
   as-f/Milton Neul-cl-ts-vn/Eddie Kilfeather-p-a/Leslie Sheriff-bj/Jack Hansen-bb.
                                          New York, February 20, 1925.

31989-1-2-3-4  Those Panama Mamas (Are Ruining    Rejected
               Me
31990-2  Why Couldn't It Be Poor Little Me ?      Vic 19573

                                          New York, March 4, 1925.

31989-5-6-7-8  Those Panama Mamas (Are Ruining    Rejected
               Me)
32050-3  Everybody Loves My Baby (But My Baby     Vic 19610, Zon 3853
         Don't Love Nobody But Me)

   Lou Raderman-vn added.             New York, March 24, 1925.

31989-9  Those Panama Mamas (Are Ruining Me)      Vic 19633

George Olsen-d dir. Floyd Rice-Bob Borger-t/Jack Fulton-tb/Fran Frey-as-v/Milton
   Neul-cl-ts/Eddie Kilfeather-p/Bob Rice-bj-g-v/Jack Hansen-bb.
                                          New York, August 21, 1925.

33338-3  Hot Aire                                 Vic 19761

                                          New York, November 17, 1925.

33881-1  A Little Bit Bad - vFF                   Vic 19852, HMV B-5050

   Edward Joyce-cl-as added.          New York, February 5, 1926.

34602-1  Too Bad                                  Vic 20024

## OLE OLSEN AND HIS ORCHESTRA

Charlie Margulis-Henry Levine-t/Ole Olsen-tb/Alfie Evans-as-bar/Arnold Brilhart-
   William McGill-cl-as-ts/Irving Brodsky-p/Floyd Campbell-bj/David Dappeer-bb/Stan
   King-d/John Ryan-v.                   New York, c. July 9, 1926.

106983    Sadie Green (The Vamp Of New Orleans)   PA 36488, Per 14669
          - vJR
106984    Take Your Time - vJR                    PA 36510, Per 14691
106985    Snag It                                 PA 36488, Per 14669

## JACK O'NEIL AND HIS ORCHESTRA

Pseudonym on Champion 15072 for Jack Stillman and his Orchestra, q.v.

## WALKER O'NEILL

Piano solos.                          Hayes, Middlesex, March 24, 1924.

Bb-4407-1  Scale It Down                          HMV B-1806
Bb-4408-1  Dustin' The Keys                        —

                                      London, c. April, 1924.

LO-0504   Dustin' The Keys                        Hom H-675
LO-0505   Scale It Down                            —

## D. ONIVAS AND HIS ORCHESTRA

This refers to Pathe musical director Domenico Savino, whose name was used on Pathe
   Actuelle 036196 for the Kansas City Five, q.v., and many other Pathe records which
   were actually made under his direction, without producing any recordings known to
   be of interest to the jazz enthusiast.

Pseudonym on Chantal for the following items listed in this book :-

934  Dinah (Bailey's Lucky Seven)
1334  Hot Lips (California Ramblers)
1339  Burning Sands (The Broadway Syncopators)

## ORCHESTRE  ERNEST HARE

Pseudonym on Salabert 297 (DESDEMONA) for the California Ramblers, q.v.

## ORCHESTRE JAZZ BAND  DU GRAMOPHONE

Pseudonym on Disque Gramophone (French HMV) for Earl Fuller's Jazz Band (K-576 and
K-577) and the Original Dixieland Jazz Band (K-578 and K-579), both q.v.

## ORCHESTRE THE PLAYBOYS

Probably an American band consisting of t/tb/cl/ts-vn/p/bb/d/v quartet.
Paris, c. July, 1927.

| 8257 | Ain't She Sweet ? - v4 | P 6996 |
| 8258 | Shanghai Dream Man | - |

## ORCHESTRE  POLLARD'S SIX

Harry Pollard-d dir. probably :- Arthur Briggs-t/John Forrester-tb/Roscoe Burnett-cl-
as/p/bj/bb, possibly others.        Paris, c. July, 1923.

| 6944 | I'm Just Wild About Harry | P 6614 |
| 6945 | You've Got To See Mama Ev'ry Night | - |

## ORCHESTRE  SCRAP-IRON JAZZERINOS

The name under which the Scrap Iron Jazz Band, q.v., appeared on Disque Gramophone.

## ORCHESTRE SYNCOPATED SIX

Gordon Stretton-d dir. 2t/tb/cl/as/ts/p/bj. (The jazz content of these sides is not
exceptional).                        Paris, c. July, 1923.

| 6934 | 'Way Down Yonder In New Orleans - v | P 6611 | |
| 6935 | C'est Paris - v | P 6609 | PA 15179 |
| 6936 | La-Haut | - | |
| 6937 | Lovin' Sam (The Sheik Of Alabam') - v | P 6611 | |
| 6938 | Fate | P 6610 | |
| 6939 | Tu verras Montmartre | - | |
| | Si vous n'aimez pas ça (If You Don't Like It) | P     | , PA 15179 |

NOTE:- Pathe Actuelle 15179 as THE SYNCOPATED SIX.

## L'ORCHESTRE  DU THEATRE DAUNOU

Jef de Murel dir. Leon Ferreri-t-tb-vn/Paul Jean-Jean-as/Michel Emer-p/Django
Reinhardt-g/Max Elloy-d and others.      Paris, March 14, 1933.

| OPG-640-2 | Ah ! Le Beguine | HMV K-6861 |
| OPG-641-2 | Si j'aime Suzy | - |

## ORESTE AND HIS  QUEENSLAND ORCHESTRA

Oreste-p dir. Jack Davis-t-v/t/tb/2cl-ss-as/cl-ts/bj/Joe Tarto-bb-a/d.
New York, March 24, 1927.

| 11604 | Coronado Nights - vJD | Ed 51988 | |

Arthur Fields-Jack Kaufman-v.        New York, July 29, 1927.

| 11823 | Eyeful Of You - vAF | Ed 52087 | |
| 11825 | Side By Side - vJK | - | Amb 5402 |

Oreste-p dir. 2t/tb/2cl-ss-as/cl-ts/p/bj/bb/d/"Happy Jack"-v.
                              New York, December 9, 1927.

18095    I'm Walkin' On Air - v"HJ"              Ed 52167

Bert Dixon-v.                        New York, March 26, 1928.

18336    Lila - vBD                             Ed 52273

The Rollickers-v quartet.            New York, May 17, 1929.

19199    Me And The Clock (Tick-i-ty Tock And    Ed 52592
N-903      You) - vR                             Ed .14009

There may well be other Edison records by this band of comparable "hot" dance music
   quality.

### ORIGINAL  ALABAMA DOMINOES

Instrumentation and personnel unknown, apart from Sol Bearman-v.
                              Birmingham, Ala., c. July 14, 1927.

GEX-731, -A-B  I Ain't That Kind Of A Baby - vSB   Gnt rejected
GEX-732, -A-B  Memphis Sprawler                       -
GEX-733, -A-B  Tomatoes                               -
GEX-734, -A-B  Meet Me In The Moonlight              -
GEX-735, -A-B  Lighthouse Blues                       -

### ORIGINAL ATLANTA FOOTWARMERS

Jack Cathcart t-as/tb/Ray Chestnut or Hunt Grant-cl/p/d.
                              Richmond, Ind., January 10, 1928.

13345    Hot Licks (That's A Plenty)            Bell 585

### ORIGINAL BLACK AND GOLDS

Instrumentation and personnel unknown.   New York, January 15, 1927.

GEX-458, -A-B  Someday, Sweetheart               Gnt rejected
GEX-459, -A-B  Tiger Rag                            -
GEX-460, -A   Stockholm Stomp                       -

### ORIGINAL  BLACK BAND

Pseudonym on Guardsman for the following items listed in this book :-

7000, 7001, 7005, 7006  Both sides of each by Fletcher Henderson and his Orchestra
7007  Savannah (The Georgianna Blues) (The Ambassadors)
7007  A New Kind Of Man (Fletcher Henderson and his Orchestra)
7012  The Throw-Down Blues (The Ambassadors)
7012  Jacksonville Gal (The Tennessee Tooters)
7013  Both sides by McKenzie's Candy Kids

### ORIGINAL CAPITOL ORCHESTRA

I. V. "Bud" Sheppard-p dir. Vic Sells-c/Billy Trittle-tb/George Byron Webb-as/Tracy
   Mumma-cl-as/Les Russick-bj/d.        Hayes, Middlesex, March 16, 1923.

Yy-2711-1-2  Runnin' Wild                       Zon rejected
Yy-2712-1-2  Black Man Blues                       -

                              Hayes, Middlesex, April 23, 1923.

Yy-2868-2  Chicago                        Zon 2342
Yy-2869-2  Romany Love                    Zon 2341
Yy-2870-2  Russian Rose                   Zon 2342
Yy-2871-1  Rose Of The Rio Grande         Zon 2341, Ar 655, 2329
   NOTE:- Ariel 655 as ARIEL DANCE ORCHESTRA; 2329 is anonymous.

I. V. "Bud" Sheppard-p dir. Vic Sells-c/Billy Trittle-tb/George Byron Webb-as/Tracey
   Mumma-cl-as/Les Russick-bj/d.          Hayes, Middlesex, May 22, 1923.

| | | |
|---|---|---|
| Yy-3005-1 | The Lady Of The Evening | Zon 2369 |
| Yy-3006-2 | Apple Sauce | Zon 2355 |
| Yy-3007-2 | I Wish I Could Shimmy Like My Sister Kate | - |
| Yy-3008-2 | Wonderland Of Dreams (w) | Zon 2369 |

Hayes, Middlesex, October 29, 1923.

| | | |
|---|---|---|
| Yy-3730-2 | Barney Google | Zon 2398 |
| Yy-3731-2 | Will You Always Love Me ? | - |
| Yy-3732-1 | The Cat's Whiskers | Zon 2399 |
| Yy-3733-2 | Why Worry Blues | -        Ar 319 |

NOTE:- Ariel 319 is anonymous.

Hayes, Middlesex, November 23, 1923.

| | | |
|---|---|---|
| Yy-3884-1 | House Of David Blues | Zon 2411 |
| Yy-3885-3 | Bye-Bye | - |
| Yy-3886-1-2 | Foolish Child | Rejected |

Hayes, Middlesex, December 14, 1923.

| | | |
|---|---|---|
| Yy-3970-1 | Blue Hoosier Blues | Zon 2426 |
| Yy-3971-1 | Broadway Blues | Zon 2427 |
| Yy-3972-1-2 | Felix Kept On Walking | Zon 2426, Ar 662 |
| Yy-3973-2 | Last Night On The Back Porch | Zon 2427, Ar 333 |

NOTE:- Ariel 333 and 662 as ARIEL DANCE ORCHESTRA.

Hayes, Middlesex, January 21, 1924.

| | | |
|---|---|---|
| Yy-4111-1-2 | Susannah's Squeaking Shoes | Rejected |
| Yy-4112-2 | When It's Night Time In Italy | Zon 2437, Ar 649 |
| Yy-4113-1 | There's A Bungalow That's Waiting | - |
| Yy-4114-2 | Tiger Rag | Zon 2447 |

NOTE:- Ariel 649 as ARIEL DANCE ORCHESTRA.

Hayes, Middlesex, February 18, 1924.

| | | |
|---|---|---|
| Yy-4211-2 | Mama Loves Papa | Zon 2436 |
| Yy-4212-2 | In A Tent | Zon 2447 |
| Yy-4213-1 | Gigolette | Zon 2436, Ar 655 |

NOTE:- Ariel 655 as ARIEL DANCE ORCHESTRA.

It should be noted that not all of the Original Capitol Orchestra's records are of
equal interest as jazz, but the best of them are musically and historically very
satisfactory, especially as they represent the only Mississippi riverboat band to
play and record in England during the years covered by this book.

## ORIGINAL CRESCENT CITY JAZZERS

Sterling Bose-c/Avery Loposer-tb/Cliff Holman-cl-as/Eddie Powers-ts/Johnny Riddick-p/
   Slim Hall-bj/Felix Guarino-d.          New Orleans, March 17, 1924.

| | | |
|---|---|---|
| 8566-A | Sensation Rag | OK 40101, Od 03202 |
| 8567-A | Christine | -        - |

## ORIGINAL DIXIELAND JAZZ BAND

Nick LaRocca-c dir. Eddie Edwards-tb/Larry Shields-cl/Henry Ragas-p/Tony Sbarbaro-d.
                              New York, January 30, 1917.

| | | |
|---|---|---|
| 77086-3-4 | Darktown Strutters' Ball | Col A-2297, 2903, S-10001 |
| 77087-2-3 | Indiana | -        - |

New York, February 26, 1917.

| | | |
|---|---|---|
| 19331-1 | Livery Stable Blues | Vic 18255, Bm 1110 |
| 19332-3 | Dixie Jass Band One-Step (Intro. That | -        Bm 1109 |

Teasin' Rag) (Some copies labelled DIXIELAND JASS BAND ONE-STEP)

Nick LaRocca-c dir. Eddie Edwards-tb/Larry Shields-cl/Henry Ragas-p/Tony Sbarbaro-d.
New York, July 29, 1917.

|  |  |  |
|---|---|---|
| | Indiana | AV rejected |
| | Ostrich Walk | - |

New York, August 17, 1917.

|  |  |  |
|---|---|---|
| | Barnyard Blues | AV 1205, JC L-53 |
| | Ostrich Walk | AV 1206, JC L-72 |
| | Tiger Rag | -          Br 02500 |
| | There It Goes Again | Rejected |

New York, September 3, 1917.

| A-247 | At The Jass Band Ball | AV 1205, JC L-53 |
|---|---|---|

New York, November 9, 1917.

|  |  |  |
|---|---|---|
| | Look At 'Em Doing'It Now | AV rejected |
| | That Loving Baby Of Mine | - |

New York, November 21, 1917.

| A-435 | Look At 'Em Doing It Now | AV 1242, JC L-72 |
|---|---|---|

New York, November 24, 1917.

| A-444 | Oriental Jazz | AV 12097 |
|---|---|---|
| | Reisenweber Rag | AV 1242, Br 02500 |

New York, March 18, 1918.

| 21583-1 | At The Jazz Band Ball | Vic 18457, HMV B-1021, AE-724, K-578, R-8323 |
|---|---|---|
| 21584-3 | Ostrich Walk | As above, plus HMV B-8485 |

NOTE:- HMV K-578 as ORCHESTRE JAZZ BAND DU GRAMOPHONE.

New York, March 25, 1918.

| 21700-2 | Skeleton Jangle | Vic 18472, Bm 1112 |
|---|---|---|
| 21701-3 | Tiger Rag | -        25908, HMV B-8466, El EG-7793, Bm 1111 |

The band sings where noted.           New York, June 25, 1918.

| 22041-3 | Bluin' The Blues | Vic 18483, HMV B-1022, B-8485, AE-725, K-579, R-8353, Bm 1114 |
|---|---|---|
| 22042-2 | Fidgety Feet (War Cloud) | Vic 18564 |
| 22043-1-2-3 | Mournin' Blues | Rejected |
| 22044-2 | Sensation Rag | Vic 18483, HMV B-1022, AE-725, K-579, R-8353 |
| | Sweet Mama (Papa's Getting Mad)-vODJB | Vic test (un-numbered) |

New York, July 17, 1918.

| 22043-4 | Mournin' Blues | Vic 18513 |
|---|---|---|
| 22066-2 | Clarinet Marmalade Blues | -        HMV B-8500, Bm 1113 |
| 22067-3 | Lazy Daddy | Vic 18564, Zon 3221 |

Emile Christian-tb replaces Edwards.    New York, December 3, 1918.

| 22337-1-2-3-4 | 'Lasses Candy (Belgian Doll) | Vic rejected |
|---|---|---|
| 22338-1-2-3-4 | Satanic Blues | - |

J. Russel Robinson-p replaces Ragas.    London, April 16, 1919.

| 76418-3 | Barnyard Blues | Col 735 |
|---|---|---|
| 76419-3 | At The Jazz Band Ball | - |

Nick LaRocca-c dir. Emile Christian-tb/Larry Shields-cl/J. Russel Robinson-p/Tony
  Sbarbaro-d.                          London, May 12, 1919.

76458-3  Ostrich Walk                          Col 736
76459-3  Sensation Rag                          -

                                       London, May 19, 1919.

76467-1  Look At 'Em Doing It                   Col 748
76468-3  Tiger Rag                              -

                                       London, August 13, 1919.

76566-2  Satanic Blues                          Col 759
76567-1-2  'Lasses Candy                        -

  Billy Jones-p replaces Robinson.     London, January 8, 1920.

76751-1  My Baby's Arms                         Col 805
76752-2  Tell Me                                Col 804
76753-2  I've Got My Captain Working For Me Now  Col 815

                                       London, January 10, 1920.

76754-2  I'm Forever Blowing Bubbles (w)        Col 805
76755-1-2  Mammy O' Mine                        Col 804
76756-2  I've Lost My Heart In Dixieland        Col 815

                                       London, May 14, 1920.

74103-1  Sphinx                                 Col 824
74104-2  Alice Blue Gown (w)                    -
74105-2  Soudan                                 Col 829

Nick LaRocca-c dir. Eddie Edwards-tb/Larry Shields-cl/Benny Krueger-as/J. Russel
  Robinson-p/Tony Sbarbaro-d.          New York, September 13, 1920.

         Sphinx                        Vic test (un-numbered)
         Tell Me, Little Gypsy         -
         Singin' The Blues             -

                                       New York, November 24, 1920.

24580-1-2-3  In The Dusk               Vic rejected
24581-1-2-3-4  Margie                  -

  Krueger omitted*.                    New York, December 1, 1920.

22337-5 *'Lasses Candy                 Rejected
22338-5-6 *Satanic Blues               -
24581-5  Margie (Intro. Singin' The Blues)  Vic 18717, HMV B-1199, K-914,
                                            R-8527, Zon 3296

                                       New York, December 4, 1920.

24580-4-5-6  In The Dusk               Rejected
24590-5  Palesteena                    Vic 18717, HMV B-1199, K-914,
                                            R-8527, Zon 3296

Clifford Cairns-Eddie King and members of the band-v where noted; Nick LaRocca
announces at the end of this side.     New York, December 30, 1920.

24809-2  Broadway Rose (Intro. Dolly, I Love You) Vic 18722, HMV B-1216, R-8815,
                                                   Zon 3305
24810-2  Sweet Mamma (Papa's Getting Mad) (Intro. As above
         Strut, Miss Lizzie) - vCC-EK-ODJB

Nick LaRocca-c dir. Eddie Edwards-tb/Larry Shields-cl/Benny Krueger-as/J. Russel
   Robinson-p/Tony Sbarbaro-d.              New York, January 28, 1921.

24825-3  Home Again Blues (Intro. Lindy)          Vic 18729, HMV B-1227, R-8817
24826-3  Crazy Blues (Intro. It's Right Here For        -
         You, If You Don't Get It - 'Tain't No Fault Of Mine)


   Frank Signorelli-p replaces Robinson; Lavinia Turner-Al Bernard-v.
                                          New York, May 3, 1921.

25072-1-2-3  Jazz Me Blues - vLT          Rejected
25072-5  Jazz Me Blues                    Vic 18772, 25908, HMV B-1257,
                                          B-8466, HN-3102, El EG-7793
25073-1-2-3-4  St. Louis Blues            Rejected


                                 New York, May 25, 1921.

25411-1-2-3  Satanic Blues - vAB          Rejected
25412-2  St. Louis Blues - vAB            Vic 18772
25413-4  Royal Garden Blues - vAB         Vic 18798, HMV B-8500, AE-131


                                 New York, June 7, 1921.

25432-5  Dangerous Blues - vAB                Vic 18798, HMV AE-131


                                 New York, December 1, 1921.

25836-3  Bow Wow Blues (My Mama Treats Me Like   Vic 18850
         A Dog)


Nick LaRocca-c dir. Eddie Edwards-tb/Artie Seaberg-cl/Don Parker-ss/Henry Vanicelli-
   p/Tony Sbarbaro-d.              New York, c. November 23, 1922.

71043-A-B-C  Some Of These Days           Rejected
71044-B  Toddlin' Blues                   OK 4738, Od 312926, Par E-5116


                                 New York, January 3, 1923.

71043-F  Some Of These Days               OK 4738, Od 312926


                                 New York, c. April 20, 1923.

71429-B  Tiger Rag                        OK 4841
71430-B  Barnyard Blues (Livery Stable Blues)    -


Phil Capicotta-t/Russ Morgan-tb-v/Sid Trucker-cl/Terry Shand-p-v/Larry Hall-sb/Tony
   Sbarbaro-d-k.
                                 New York, October 9, 1935.

18145-1  I'm Sittin' High On A Hill-Top - vTS   Voc 3084, Par DP-185, B-71158
18146-1  You Stayed Away Too Long - vTS         Voc 3099
18147-1  I Live For Love - vRM                  Voc 3084, Par DP-185, B-71158
18148-1  Slipping Through My Fingers - vTS      Voc 3099

NICK LAROCCA AND THE ORIGINAL DIXIELAND BAND : Nick LaRocca-c* dir. Earle Ison-
George Walters-George Johnson-t/Charles Harris-Alex Palocsay-tb/Larry Shields-cl/
Joe Hunkler-Buddy Saffer-as/George Dessinger-ts/J. Russel Robinson-p-v/Chris
Fletcher-g-v/Boyd Bennett-sb/Tony Sbarbaro-d.
                                    New York, September 2, 1936.

| | | |
|---|---|---|
| 0301-1 | Bluin' The Blues | Vic 25403, HMV GW-1650, K-7780 |
| 0302-1 | Tiger Rag | - - - X-4808 |
| 0303-1 | Ostrich Walk | Vic 25460 |
| 0304-1 | Original Dixieland One-Step | Rejected |
| 0305-1 | *Clarinet Marmalade | Vic 25411 |
| 0306-1 | Satanic Blues | Rejected |

                                    New York, September 25, 1936.

| | | |
|---|---|---|
| 0489-1 | Toddlin' Blues | Vic 25460 |
| 0490-1 | Did You Mean It ? - vCF | Vic 25420 |
| 0491-1 | Who Loves You ? - vCF | - |
| 0492-1 | Old Joe Blade - vJRR | Vic 26039 |
| 0493-1 | Your Ideas Are My Ideas - vCF | Rejected |
| 0494-1 | Fidgety Feet | Vic 25668 |

ORIGINAL DIXIELAND FIVE : Nick LaRocca-c dir. Eddie Edwards-tb/Larry Shields-cl/J.
Russel Robinson-p/Tony Sbarbaro-d.     New York, September 25, 1936.

| | | |
|---|---|---|
| 0495-1 | Clarinet Marmalade | Rejected |
| 0496-1 | Bluin' The Blues | - |
| 0497-1 | Tiger Rag | - |
| 0498-1 | Skeleton Jangle | Vic 25524, HMV B-8642, Bm 1112 |

                                    New York, November 10, 1936.

| | | |
|---|---|---|
| 0495-2 | Clarinet Marmalade | Vic 25525, Bm 1113 |
| 0496-2 | Bluin' The Blues | - Bm 1114 |
| 0497-2 | Tiger Rag | Vic 25524, HMV B-8642, Bm 1111 |
| 02488-1 | Barnyard Blues | Vic 25502, HMV B-8648, Bm 1110 |
| 02489-1 | Original Dixieland One-Step | - - JK-2637, Bm 1109 |

ORIGINAL DIXIELAND JAZZ BAND : Eddie Edwards dir. Sharkey Bonano-t/Buck Scott-tb/
Larry Shields-cl/Frank Signorelli-p/Artie Shapiro-sb/Tony Sbarbaro-d/Lola Bard-v.
                                    New York, February 18, 1938.

| | | |
|---|---|---|
| 019681-1 | Drop A Nickel In The Slot - vLB | BB B-7454 |
| 019682-1 | Please Be Kind - vLB | BB B-7442 |
| 019683-1 | Jezebel - vLB | BB B-7454 |
| 019684-1 | OoooOH Boom ! - vLB&ch | BB B-7442 |
| 019685-1 | In My Little Red Book - vLB | BB B-7444 |
| 019686-1 | Goodnight, Sweet Dreams, Goodnight-vLB | - |

NOTE:- Arto 9140 and associated labels were issued as by the Original Dixieland Jazz
Band, but both sides are in fact by the Original Memphis Five, q.v.

## ORIGINAL DIXIE RAG PICKERS

See the Grey Gull studio bands, and the Original Indiana Five (GG/Mit/Rx 1332).

## ORIGINAL EXCENTRIC BAND

This was probably part of an American military band stationed in Germany after World
War I. It was directed by F. Groundzell, and appears to have consisted of 2c/tb/
cl/bb/d.
                                    Berlin, December, 1919.

| | | |
|---|---|---|
| 15983 | Indianola | Hom B-557 |
| 15984 | Tiger Rag | - |
| | | |
| 15993 | O You Drummer (sic) | Hom 15993 |
| 15994 | All Aboard For Dixie Land (sic) | Hom 15994 |

NOTE:- Homochord B-557 as MASSELTOP KAPELLE. The last two sides are coupled.

Herman Drewes-c/William Drewes-tb/Larry Hart or Harry Dukes-cl/Ernest Borbee-p/Fred
   Bauer-d.                          Long Island City, c. April, 1923.

         Down Among The Sleepy Hills Of          Oly 1434
            Ten-Ten-Tennessee
         Oh, Sister ! Ain't That Hot ?           Oly 1445
         Wild Papa                                  -      Pt 11284
NOTE:- Puretone 11284 as BROADWAY MELODY MAKERS.

   Arthur Hall-v.                         Long Island City, c. July, 1923.

         Maggie ! - "Yes Ma'am ?" - vAH         Oly/Maj 1519, BS 2127, Pur 11252
         Yes ! We Have No Bananas - vAH             -         -         -
NOTE:- Black Swan 2127 as HOWARD LEWIS, WITH ORCHESTRA ACC.

                        ORIGINAL  INDIANA FIVE

Newman Fier-p dir. Johnny Sylvester-t/Vincent Grande-tb/Johnny Costello-cl/Tom Morton
   d.                                Long Island City, c. April, 1923.

         Louisville Lou                          Oly 1439
         Slow Poke                                  -
NOTE:- This issue as ORIGINAL INDIANA SYNCOPATORS.

   ? Nick Vitalo-cl-as/? Tony Colucci-bj added.
                                     Long Island City, c. May, 1923.

         Two-Time Dan                            Oly/Maj 1443, Pwy/Pt/Tri 11284
         When You Walked Out (Someone Else Walked Right In)-
         Bebe                                    Oly/Maj 1444, Pur 11282
         Beside A Babbling Brook                    -
NOTE:- Puretone and Triangle 11284 as BROADWAY MELODY MAKERS; Puritan 11282 as
MAJESTIC DANCE ORCHESTRA.

Johnny Sylvester-t dir. Charlie Panelli-tb/Nick Vitalo-cl-as/Harry Ford-p/? Tony
   Colucci-bj/Tom Morton-d.          New York, c. September 7, 1923.

70297    Stavin' Change (The Meanest Man In      PA 021070, Per 14173, Poydras 19
            New Orleans)
70298    Mean, Mean Mama                            -          -          -

                                     New York, c. November 6, 1923.

70397    Tin Roof Blues                          PA 036019, Per 14200
70398    St. Louis Gal                              -         -

                                     New York, January, 1924.

105053   Jubilee Blues                           PA 036044, Per 14225
105054   Back O' Town Blues                         -         -

   James Christie-t replaces Sylvester; Morton assumes leadership.
                                     New York, c. May 1, 1925.

9503     Everything Is Hotsy-Totsy Now           Gnt 3060
9504     Seminola                                   -
9505     Sweet Georgia Brown                     Gnt 3059, Ch 15015
NOTE:- Champion 15015 as THE BIRMINGHAM FIVE.

                                     New York, c. June 19, 1925.

9618-A   Cuckoo                                  Gnt 3083
9619-A   Say, Arabella                              -
9620-A   Two Tired Eyes                          Gnt 3093
                                     New York, c. July 14, 1925.

9666-A   Croonin' A Tune                         Gnt 3106
9667-B   Red Hot Henry Brown                     Gnt 3112, Ch 15008
9668-A   Indiana Stomp                              -         -
NOTE:- Champion 15008 as THE BIRMINGHAM FIVE.

Tom Morton-d-v dir. James Christie-t/Charlie Panelli-tb/Nick Vitalo-cl-as/Harry Ford-p/
Tony Colucci-bj (some sessions only).  New York, c. August 13, 1925.

9684-A  Oh ! Boy, What A Girl                Gnt 3121, Ch 15018, Sil 4003
NOTE:- Champion 15018 as THE BIRMINGHAM FIVE.

                                    New York, c. August 19, 1925.

9697   Loud Speakin' Papa - vTM              Rejected
9698-A  Pretty Puppy                          Gnt 3153

Pete Pellizzi-tb replaces Panelli.    New York, c. September 2, 1925.

73586-B  Oh ! Boy, What A Girl               OK 40456
73587-B  Indiana Stomp                        -

                                    New York, c. September 21, 1925.

9738   Siberia                               Gnt 3150, Ch 15028
9739-B  I'm Goin' Out If Lizzie Comes In      Gnt 3148, Sil 4002
9740-B  That's All There Is (There Ain't No   Gnt 3150
         More)
NOTE:- Champion 15028 as THE BIRMINGHAM FIVE.

                                    New York, c. October 8, 1925.

9763-A  I'm Gonna Hang Around My Sugar        Gnt 3166, Ch 15046
9764-A  Melancholy Lou                        Gnt 3165, Ch 15049
9765, -A  Fallin' Down                        Rejected
NOTE:- Champion 15046 and 15049 as THE BIRMINGHAM FIVE.

                                    New York, October 13, 1925.

141103-2  Everybody Stomp                     Har 47-H
141104-2  I'm Gonna Hang Around My Sugar       -

                                    New York, October 27, 1925.

141201-3  Everybody's Doin' The Charleston Now   Har 58-H

                                    New York, c. November 6, 1925.

9812-A  No Man's Mama                         Gnt 3183, Ch 15047
9813   Everybody's Doin' The Charleston Now  Gnt 3182, Ch 15050
9814-A  Everybody Stomp                       Gnt 3181
NOTE:- Champion 15047 and 15050 as THE BIRMINGHAM FIVE.

                                    New York, c. December 5, 1925.

9879, -A  'Tain't Cold                        Rejected
9880-A  Pensacola                             Gnt 3218
9881-A  Fallen Arches                         Gnt 3230

                                    New York, January 13, 1926.

41489-1  I'd Rather Be Alone                  Har 101-H, Poydras 8
41490-2  Running After You                    Har 134-H
41491-1  Pensacola                            Har 101-H

                                    New York, January 14, 1926.

06537   I'd Rather Be Alone                   PA 36377, Per 14558
06538   Lo-Nah                                PA 36379, Per 14560

Dale Wimbrow (as PETER DALE)-v.     New York, March 18, 1926.

        Hard-To-Get Gertie - vDW             Vic test (un-numbered)
        Shake That Thing                      -

Tom Morton-d-k-v dir. James Christie-t/Pete Pellizzi-tb/Nick Vitalo-cl-as/Harry Ford-
   p.                                    New York, c. March 19, 1926.

106726    Sittin' Around                      PA 36420, Per 14601
106727    Hard-To-Get Gertie                  PA 36428, Per 14609
106728    Too Bad                             PA 36420, Per 14601, Sal 335

                                   New York, c. March 30, 1926.

 1896-B  Pensacola                            Cam 924, Lin 2499
 1897-C  Hard-To-Get Gertie                     -           -

                                   New York, April 7, 1926.

 74092-B  Hard-To-Get Gertie - vTM            OK 40599
 74093-B  Pensacola                              -        Od FF-1129

                                   New York, April 9, 1926.

141942-2-3  Hangin' Around                    Har 267-H
141943-2-3  Florida Low-Down                    -
141944-2-3  So Is Your Old Lady               Har 179-H, Re G-8714
   NOTE:- Regal G-8714 as CORONA DANCE ORCHESTRA.

                                   New York, c. April, 1926.

 3829    My Own Blues                         GG/Mit/Rx 1332, Dandy 5154
   NOTE:- Grey Gull/Mitchell/Radiex 1332 as ORIGINAL DIXIE RAG PICKERS; Dandy 5154 as
ORIGINAL TAMPA FIVE.

                                   New York, May 18, 1926.

142219-2  Spanish Mama                        Har 217-H
142220-3  I'd Leave Ten Men Like Yours To Love   Har 245-H
             One Man Like Mine
142221-3  Deep Henderson                      Har 217-H

   Tony Tortomas-t replaces Christie.    New York, October, 1926.

 3973    Jackass Blues                        Em 3069  Bell 445
 3974    Gettin' The Blues                    Em 3070      -
 3975    Can You Picture That ?               Em 3069

 3988    My Baby Knows How                    Em 3079, Bell 456
 3989    Heebie Jeebies                          -           Dandy 5248
 3990-1  Cow Bell Blues                       Em 3079, NML 1191
   NOTE:- Some of the above Emersons as INDIANA FIVE; Dandy 5248 as ORIGINAL TAMPA
FIVE; Bell 445 and 456 as RED HOT SYNCOPATORS.

                                   New York, November, 1926.

 31022-1  Brown Sugar (Brown Pepper*)         Em 3088, Bell 463, NML 1186*
 31023    There Ain't No "Maybe" In My Baby's Eyes    -           -
   NOTE:- National Music Lovers as NATIONAL MUSIC LOVERS DANCE ORCHESTRA.

   Tony Pace-v; Tony Colucci-bj some some sides.
                                   New York, December 24, 1926.

142997-2  Delilah - vTP                       Har 327-H
142998-3  Stockholm Stomp                     Har 387-H
142999-2  The Chant                              -

   Bsx added.                       New Yirk, January, 1927.

 7017-1-2  Indiana Shuffle                    Ban 1931, Dom 3901, Or 819,Re 8248
 7018-2  The Crawl                            Chg 628, Je 5002, Or 829
 7019-1-2  Coffee Pot Blues                   Ban 1931, Dom 3901, Or 828,Re 8248
   NOTE:- Challenge 628, Jewel 5002 and Oriole 828, 829 as DIXIE JAZZ BAND.

Tom Morton-d-k-v dir. Tony Tortomas-t/Pete Pellizzi-tb/Nick Vitalo-cl-as/Harry Ford-p /Tony Colucci-bj (some sessions only). New York, c. January, 1927.

| | | |
|---|---|---|
| 31073-2 | Memphis Blues | Em 3131 |
| 31074-1-2 | Thrown Down Blues (sic) | Em 3119, Bell 490 |
| 31075-1-2 | St. Louis Blues | - - |

NOTE:- The reverse of Emerson 3131 (HOT STUFF) is not by the Original Indiana Five, although labelled so; it is most probably by a Fred Hall band (q.v.)

New York, c. March, 1927.

31110-2  Low-Down Sawed-Off Blues          Bell 547

As-ts added.                    New York, April, 1927.

2407-D  Some Of These Days - vTM          Cam 1138, Ro 371
2408-C  Memphis Blues                      -      -
NOTE:- Romeo 371 as NEW ORLEANS FIVE.

Bsx added.                      New York, May, 1927.

7289-2  Some Of These Days - vTM          Ban 6006, Dom 3971, 21298, Or 927,
                                          Re 8337, Sil 21506, Apex 8640,
                                          LS 24118, Mic 22195, St 10267
7290-2  Sugar - vTM                       Ban 6008, Or 926
7291-2  Struttin' Jerry                   Ban 6023, Dom 3997, Je 5067,
                                          Or 977, Re 8354, Sil 21509
NOTE:- Jewel 5067, Oriole 926, 927 and 977 as DIXIE JAZZ BAND, Vocal Chorus by FRANK MARSHALL; Silvertone 21506 and 21509 as GOLDEN GATE ORCHESTRA; Lucky Strike 24118 as THE BLUE RAMBLERS.

Joe Tarto-bb replaces bsx.      New York, May, 1927.

2475-A  Stompin' Fool                     Cam 1168, Ro 396, Vri 5078
2476-A  Indiana Mud                        -      -
NOTE:  Romeo 396 as EDDIE MILLER'S DANCE ORCHESTRA; Variety 5078 as CAL SMITH AND HIS ORCHESTRA.

Bsx replaces Tarto.             New York, May 26, 1927.

44226-3  Play It Red                       Har 432-H
44227-3  Struttin' Jerry                   Har 459-H
44228-3  One Sweet Letter From You - vTM   Har 432-H

Bsx omitted.                    New York, July 19, 1927.

7392-2-3  My Melancholy Baby - vTM        Ban 6032, 7027, Bell 547, Chg 566,
                                          Dom 3995, 4104, Je 5071, 5214,
                                          Or 963, 1156, Re 8356, 8498,
                                          Sil 21511, Voe XA-18059
7393-2  The Lighthouse Blues              Ban 6028, Dom 3998, Or 956, Re 8368
7395-2  Rarin' To Go                      Ban 6031, Or 960
NOTE:- Jewel 5071, Oriole 956, 960 and 963 as DIXIE JAZZ BAND; Jewel 5214, Oriole 1156 as LOU CONNOR AND HIS COLLEGIATES, Vocal Chorus by FRANK MARSHALL.

New York, September 28, 1927.

44805-2  Someday, Sweetheart - vTM         Har 501-H
44806-3  I'm Coming, Virginia              -
44807-3  Clementine (From New Orleans)     Har 510-H

New York, January 13, 1928.

45526-3  What Can A Poor Fellow Do ?       Har 632-H
45527-3  Junk Man's Dream                  -
45528-1-2  Rarin' To Go                    Rejected

Tom Morton-d-v dir. Tony Tortomas-t/Pete Pellizzi-tb/Nick Vitalo-cl-as/Harry Ford-p.
                                        New York, c.February 16, 1928.

| | | |
|---|---|---|
| 2895-A-C | Nobody's Sweetheart - vTM | Cam 8154, Lin 2808, Ro 577, Elec 5031 |
| 2896-B-C | Where Will I Be ? - vTM | As above, except Elec 5031 |

NOTE:- Electron 5031 as FRANK DOYLE'S MARIGOLD ORCHESTRA.

                                        New York, February 17, 1928.

| | | |
|---|---|---|
| 7790-3 | Where Will I Be ? - vTM | Ban 7057, Chg 591, Or 1171, Apex 8890 |
| 7791-3 | Moten Stomp | Ban 7084, Cq 7143, Dom 4165, Je 5263, Or 1172, Re 8592 |
| 7800-2-3 | Somebody's Making A Fuss Over Somebody - vTM | Ban 7137, Or 1275, Apex 8809, Dom 21462, St k0382 |

NOTE:- Challenge 591, Jewel 5263 as DIXIE JAZZ BAND; Oriole 1171, 1172 and 1275 as
LOU CONNOR AND HIS COLLEGIATES; Domino 21462 as FIVE ORIGINAL SYNCOPATORS.

See also Tom Morton.

## ORIGINAL INDIANA SYNCOPATORS

See the Original Indiana Five's first records.

## ORIGINAL JAZZ HOUNDS

Thornton G. Brown-c/Jake Frazier-tb/Bob Fuller-cl-as/Ernest Elliott-cl-ts/Mike
    Jackson-p/Sam Speed-bj/Perry Bradford-v.
                                        New York, July 14, 1925.

| | | |
|---|---|---|
| 140760-1 | 'Fo' Day Blues | Col 14086-D |
| 140761-2 | 1620 To 1865 (Uncle Eph's Dream) | - |

                                        New York, August 11, 1925.

| | | |
|---|---|---|
| 140840-2 | I Ain't Gonna Play No Second Fiddle-vPB | Col 14094-D |
| 140841-3 | Slow Down - vPB | - |

                                        New York, August 12, 1925.

| | | |
|---|---|---|
| 140846-2 | Cannon Ball Blues | Col 14124-D |
| 140847-3 | Vamping Lucy Long | - |

Louis Metcalf-c/Jake Frazier-tb/Bob Fuller-cl/James P. Johnson-p/bj/? Harry Hull-bb/
    d-chimes/Perry Bradford-v.        New York, March 15, 1927.

| | | |
|---|---|---|
| 143657-2 | All That I Had Is Gone - vPB | Col 14207-D |
| 143658-3 | Lucy Long - vPB | - |

## ORIGINAL  LOUISIANA FIVE

Al King-c dir. Fred Zumwalt-tb/Joe Garcia or Duke Smith-cl/Jack Dunn-p/Anton Lada-d.
                                        New York, August, 1924.

| | | |
|---|---|---|
| 1869-2 | San | Lyra/Pur/Tri 11413 |
| 1870-2 | The Hoodoo Man | - |
| 11012-B | Louisiana Toddle | Cdl/Emb/Pur/Ross/Tri 11417 |
| 11013-B | Too Tired | - |

## ORIGINAL  MEMPHIS FIVE

Phil Napoleon-t/Miff Mole-tb/Jimmy Lytell-cl/Frank Signorelli-p/Jack Roth-d.
                                        New York, April, 1922.

| | | | |
|---|---|---|---|
| 20139-2 | Gypsy Blues | Arto 9140, | Bell P-140 |
| 20140-3 | My Honey's Lovin' Arms | - | - |

NOTE:- These issues as ORIGINAL DIXIELAND JAZZ BAND (!)

Phil Napoleon-t/Miff Mole-tb/Jimmy Lytell-cl/Loring McMurray-as-ts/Frank Signorelli-p
/Jack Roth-d.                          New York, May 10, 1922.

  1057-1-2  Lonesome Mama Blues                 Pm 20131, Ban 1068, Bwy/Pur/Tri
                                                11129, Fam 3125, Pur 11131,Re 9301
  1058-1-2  Those Longing For You Blues         As above

McMurray omitted.                      New York, May 11, 1922.

            Cuddle Up Blues                     Arto 9149, Bell P-149
            Lonesome Mama Blues                   -            -

Loring McMurray-as-ts returns.         New York, c. June 10, 1922.

  1075-1-2  Deedle-Deedle-Dum                   Pm 20139, Ban 1082, Chat/Pur 11138
                                                Cx 40139, Fam 3132, Re 9325
  1076-1-2-3  Buzz Mirandy                      Pm 20139, Ban 1082, Bwy/Pur/Tri
                                                11137, Cx 40139, Fam 3132, Re 9325

McMurray omitted.                      New York, June 14, 1922.

20170-3  I Wish I Could Shimmie Like My Sister  Arto 9153, Bell P-153, Globe 7153,
         Kate (sic)                             Nord 3013
         Pacific Coast Blues                    As above

                                       New York, c. June 20, 1922.

  1090-1-2  Don't Pan Me When I'm Gone          Pm 20142, Ban 1062, Bwy 11141,
                                                Fam 3136, Pur/Tri 11142
  1091-1-2-3  I'm Going Away To Wear You Off    Pm 20142, Ban 1062, Bwy/Pur/Tri
            My Mind                             11141, Fam 3136, Pur 11142

                                       New York, August, 1922.

  1168-1-2-3  Struttin' At The Strutters' Ball  Pm 20161, Ban 1110, Bwy/Tri 11165,
                                                Fam 3155, GG 1140, Pur 11161,
                                                Re 9363
  1169-1-2-3  I Wish I Could Shimmy Like My     Pm 20161, Ban 1104, Bwy/Pur/Tri
            Sister Kate                         11166, Em 10552, Fam 3155,GG 1140,
                                                Pur 11161, Re 9365

                                       New York, August 28, 1922.

23024-2  Chicago                                Arto 9168, Bell P-168
23025-2  Got To Cool My Doggies Now               -            -

Manny Klein-t replaces Napoleon.       New York, September 11, 1922.

69846  I Wish I Could Shimmy Like My Sister     PA 020825, Per 14051
       Kate
69847  Got To Cool My Doggies Now                 -            -

Phil Napoleon-t replaces Klein.        New York, September 27, 1922.

23043-2  Indigo Blues                           Arto 9177, Bell P-177, Globe 7177
23044-3  That Da Da Strain                        -            -            -

                                       New York, October 2, 1922.

69879  Ji-Ji-Boo                                PA 020842, 10470, P 1671,
                                                Per 14061, Dav 5055
69880  You Can Have Him, I Don't Want Him,      As above, but PA 10476*
       Didn't Love Him Anyhow Blues (You Can Have Him, Blues*)

Anna Meyers-v.                         New York, October 19, 1922.

69904  Stop Your Kiddin'                        PA 020855,10470,Per 14067,Dav 5057
69905  That Da Da Strain - vAM                  PA 020870, Per 12031, Dav 5067
69906  'Tain't Nobody's Biz-ness If I Do - vAM    -            -            -
69907  He May Be Your Man, But He Comes To See  PA 020855, 10476, Per 14067,
       Me Sometimes                             Dav 5057

Phil Napoleon-t/Charlie Panelli-tb/Jimmy Lytell-cl/Frank Signorelli-p/Jack Roth-d.
                              New York, October 27, 1922.

| | | |
|---|---|---|
| 25009-1 | The Wicked Dirty Fives | Arto 9185, Bell P-185, Globe 7185 |
| 25010-3 | Stop Your Kiddin' | -          -          - |

                              New York, November 6, 1922.

| | | |
|---|---|---|
| 10215 | That Barking Dog, Woof ! Woof ! | Voc 14461, Hom H-391 |
| 10218 | Stop Your Kidding | -          - |

                              New York, November, 1922.

| | | |
|---|---|---|
| 1220-1-2 | Bees Knees | Ban 1132, Em 10558, GG 1138, |
| | | Re 9395, Curry's 152, Imp 1142 |
| 1221-2-3 | Stop Your Kiddin' | Ban 1132, Em 10557, GG 1137, |
| | | Re 9395 |

NOTE:- Grey Gull 1137 and 1138 as BOSTONIAN SYNCOPATORS; Curry's 152 as CASTLE JAZZ
BAND.  Matrix 1221-2 also appeared on an un-numbered Jewel label, pasted over that
of Grey Gull 1137.

                              New York, c. November, 1922.

| | |
|---|---|
| Great White Way Blues | Arto 9192, Bell P-192 |
| Railroad Man | -          - |

Ray Kitchingman-bj/Anna Meyers-v added. New York, December 4, 1922.

| | | |
|---|---|---|
| 69956 | Railroad Man | PA 020888, 10505, Per 14081 |
| 69957 | Great White Way Blues | -          -          - |
| 69958 | Evil Minded Blues - vAM | PA 020877, Per 12038 |
| 69959 | Last Go Round Blues - vAM | -          - |

Kitchingman omitted.          New York, December, 1922.

| | | |
|---|---|---|
| 1265-1-2-3 | Four O'Clock Blues | Pm 20192, Bwy/Pur/Tri 11209, |
| | | Cx 40192, Fam 3186, GG 1153, |
| | | GG/Globe/Nadsco/Rx 7013, Hg 775, |
| | | Nat 12192, Pur 11192 |
| 1266-1-2 | Haunting Blues | Pm 20192, Bwy/Pur/Tri 11209, |
| | | Cx 40192, Fam 3186, Nat 12192, |
| | | Pur 11192 |
| 5024-2-3 | Loose Feet | Ban 1143, Re 9407 |
| 5025-1-2-3 | Runnin' Wild | -          -      Imp 1186 |
| | Hot 'n' Cold | Arto 9199, Bell P-199 |
| | Whoa, Tillie ! Take Your Time | -          - |

                              New York, January 11, 1923.

| | | |
|---|---|---|
| 69996 | Ivy | PA 020900, Per 14090 |
| 69997 | Aunt Hager's Blues (sic) | -          - |
| 69998 | Four O'Clock Blues | PA 020893, Per 14087 |

                              New York, late January, 1923.

| | | |
|---|---|---|
| 10746 | Loose Feet | Voc 14527, Aco G-15218, Gra 9013, |
| | | Gmn 1312, Sc 615 |
| 10749 | Aggravatin' Papa | Voc 14506, Gmn 1318 |
| 10750 | The Great White Way Blues | Voc 14527 |
| 10752 | Four O'Clock Blues | Voc 14506, Gmn 1316, Sc 641 |

NOTE:- Aco G-15218 as MERRIE'S DANCE QUINTET; Guardsman 1312 as NEW YORK DANCE
ORCHESTRA; 1316 and 1318 as NEW JERSEY DANCE ORCHESTRA; Grafton 9013 as GAVIN'S
GRAFTON BAND; Scala 615 as VORZANGER'S BAND; 641 as ASTORIA ORCHESTRA.

Phil Napoleon-t/Charlie Panelli-tb/Jimmy Lytell-cl/Frank Signorelli-p/Jack Roth-d.
New York, February 7, 1923.

| 70047 | Farewell Blues | PA 020920, P 1713, Per 14104 |
| 70048 | That Eccentric Rag | PA 020921, Per 14105 |
| 70049 | Sweet Lovin' Mama | -        - |

New York, February 12, 1923.

Papa Blues                            Arto 9204, Bell P-204
Sweet Mama, Please Come Back To Me     -          -

New York, c. February 22, 1923.

| 5090-1 | Papa Blues | Ban 1178, Re 9455 |
| 5091-1 | Great White Way Blues | -        - |

New York, February 28, 1923.

Farewell Blues                        Arto 9210, Bell P-210, Globe 7210
Harmony Blues                          -          -           -

George White-v.                       New York, March 12, 1923.

| 70081 | I Never Miss The Sunshine - vGW | PA 020939, 10546,P 1742, Per 14121 |
| 70082 | That Red-Head Gal - vGW | -        -       -        - |
| 70083 | Papa Blues | PA 020977, Per 14129 |

New York, March 22, 1923.

27669-4  Snakes Hips                  Vic 19052, HMV B-1663,AM-71,K-2159
27670-1  Who's Sorry Now ?            -          -        -     -
NOTE:- All issues of the above two titles as MEMPHIS FIVE, apart from some copies
of Victor 19052, one side of which often appears as ORIGINAL MEMPHIS FIVE.

New York, March 29, 1923.

26031-2  If Your Man Is Like My Man   Bell P-216, Globe 7216
         (I Sympathize With You)
         Laughin' Cryin' Blues         -          -

New York, c. March 30, 1923.

| 5128-1-3 | Shufflin' Mose | Ban 1193, Re 9476, Apex 8040 |
| 5129-1-2 | Memphis Glide | -        -       Apex 8056 |

New York, April 20, 1923.

| 70145 | Keep It Under Your Hat | PA 020977, Per 14129 |
| 70146 | Henpecked Blues | Rejected |
| 70147 | Papa, Better Watch Your Step | -- |

New York, May 2, 1923.

| 70156 | Henpecked Blues | PA 020995, Per 14138 |
| 70157 | Memphis Glide | PA 020981, Per 14132 |
| 70158 | Papa, Better Watch Your Step | PA 020996, Per 14138 |

New York, May 23, 1923.

I Ain't Never Had Nobody Crazy Over Me  Bell P-228
You've Got To See Mama Ev'ry Night       -

Ray Kitchingman-bj added.             New York, May 25, 1923.

81035-1-2-3-4  Yes ! We Have No Bananas     Rejected
81036-2  Pickles                            Col A-3924

Phil Napoleon-t/Charlie Panelli-tb/Jimmy Lytell-cl/Frank Signorelli-p/Jack Roth-d.
                                    New York, June 20, 1923.

| 70233 | Sad News Blues | PA 021026, Per 14150 |
| 70234 | Shufflin' Mose | -          - |
| 70235 | Struttin' Jim | PA 021031, Per 14155 |

                                    New York, July 16, 1923.

| 9077 | Great White Way Blues | Ed 51204 |
| 9078 | Shufflin' Mose | - |

                                    New York, c. September 6, 1923.

| 5267-1-2-3 That Teasin' Squeezin' Man O' Mine | Ban 1254, GG/Rx 1188, GG/Globe/ |
| | | Nadsco/Rx 7013, Or 127, 241, |
| | | Re 9543 |
| 5268-1-2 Sad News Blues | Ban 1254, Globe 7011, GG/Rx 1184, |
| NOTE:- Oriole 241 as DIXIE JAZZ BAND. | Re 9543, Apex 8109 |

                                    New York, September 22, 1923.

| 9173 | The Jelly-Roll Blues | Ed 51246 |
| 9174 | A Bunch Of Blues | - |

Ray Kitchingman-bj/Billy Jones-v added. New York, September 27, 1923.

| 81242-2 Walk, Jenny, Walk - vBJ | Col 7-D |
| 81243-2 Last Night On The Back Porch - vBJ | -     Re G-8121 |
| NOTE:- Regal G-8121 as CORONA DANCE ORCHESTRA. | |

Miff Mole-tb replaces Panelli; no bj.  New York, October 4, 1923.

| 28717-3 I've Got A Song For Sale (That My | Vic 19170 |
|          Sweetie Turned Down) | |
| 28718-1 Tin Roof Blues | - |

                                    New York, c. October 25, 1923.

| 5314-2-3 House Of David Blues | Ban 1282, Re 9573, Apex 8132, |
| | Imp 1249 |
| 5315-1-2 Oh, Sister ! Ain't That Hot ? | Ban 1282, Bell P-257, Re 9573, |
| NOTE:- Curry's 166 as CURRY'S DANCE ORCHESTRA. | Apex 8132, Curry's 166, Imp 1274 |

                                    New York, November 6, 1923.

| 28911-1-2-3-4   Treat 'Em Rough | Vic rejected |

                                    New York, November 20, 1923.

| 9253 | Back O' Town Blues | Ed rejected |
| 9254 | St. Louis Gal | - |

As/? John Cali-bj added.          New York, c. December 1, 1923.

| 1583-2-3 St. Louis Gal (St. Louis Blues*) | Pm 20281, Cx 40281, Globe 7011, |
| | GG 1190, Pur*/Pt/Tri 11330 |
| 1584-1-3 Back O' Town Blues | As above, but GG 1192 |
| NOTE:- Grey Gull 1190 and 1192 as BROADWAY SEVEN; Puretone/Triangle 11330 as | |
| 'FRISCO SYNCOPATORS. | |

As and bj omitted.                New York, December 4, 1923.

| 81379-4 More - vBJ | Col 37-D |
| 81380-2 She Wouldn't Do What I Asked Her To - vBJ | - |
| 81393-1 St. Louis Gal | Col 50-D |
| 81394-2 Shuffin' Mose | - |

Phil Napoleon-t/Miff Mole-tb/Jimmy Lytell-cl/Frank Signorelli-p/Jack Roth-d.
                              New York, c. December 7, 1923.

    5357-1-2  Steppin' Out                      Ban 1296, Bell P-262, Re 9583,
                                                USA 262, Apex 8155, Imp 1310
    5358-1-3  Your Mama's Gonna Slow You Down    Ban 1296, Bell P-262, Re 9583

                              New York, c. December 10, 1923.

     752-B  Sweet Papa Joe                       Cam 478, Lin 2190, Tre 436
     753-B  Hootin' De Hoot                      Cam 481, Lin 2222, Tre 471
    NOTE:- Lincoln 2190 as BEALE STREET SERENADERS; Tremont as FRANK BAKER'S GROUP.

                              New York, c. December 20, 1923.

    5370-1-2-3  Lovey Came Back                  Ban 1292, Re 9588, Apex 8153

                              New York, c. December 27, 1923.

105036      Just Hot !                           PA 036061, 10662, Per 14242
105037      That Teasin' Squeezin' Man O' Mine   PA 036043  - Per 14224,Ajax 17038
105038      Snuggle Up A Bit                        -          -          -
    NOTE:- Ajax 17038 as CHOO CHOO JAZZERS.

                              New York, c. December 28, 1923.

    5377-2  Dancin' Dan                          Ban 1292, Re 9583, Apex 8168
    5378-1-2-3  That Bran' New Gal O' Mine       Ban 1309, Re 9601, Apex 8149

                              New York, c. January 2, 1924.

    5381-1-2-3  Shake Your Feet                  Ban 1309, Re 9601, Imp 1278

                              New York, January, 1924.

42548-1  Lots O' Mama                            Em 10725
42549-1-2  Mindin' My Bus'ness                      -        GG 1200, Or 173
42550-1  I've Got A Cross-Eyed Papa              Em 10723

    Charlie Panelli-tb replaces Mole; Billy Jones-v.
                              New York, January 25, 1924.

81500-1  Why Should I Weep About One Sweetie ?   Col 74-D, Re G-8159
81501-1  Since Ma Is Playing Mah Jongg - vBJ         -          -
    NOTE:- Regal G-8158 as CORONA DANCE ORCHESTRA.

                              New York, c. February 21, 1924.

    5432-2  Maybe She'll Write Me, She'll 'Phone Me  Ban 1322, Re 9615, Imp 1301,
    NOTE:- Curry's 179 as CASTLE JAZZ BAND.      Curry's 179

                              New York, February-March, 1924.

42567-1-2  Sioux City Sue                        Em 10740, Bwy/Lyra/Mit/Pen/Pur/
                                                 Res/Tri 11359
42568-1-2  My Papa Doesn't Two-Time No Time      Em 10740, Bwy/Cvl/Lyra/Mit/Pen/
                                                 Pur/Pt/Res/Tri 11359, GG/Nadsco/
                                                 Rx/VD 1206, Aus A-85
42569-2  31st Street Blues                       Em 10741, Aus A-143
    NOTE:- Mitchell 11359 as PASTERNACKI'S ORCHESTRA; Resona 11359 as FRISCO SYNCO-
    PATORS; Austra    A-85 and A-143 are anonymous.
                              New York, c. March 4, 1924.

    5443-1-2  Forgetful Blues                    Ban 1346, Re 9643
    5444-1-2  31st Street Blues                  Ban 1336, Re 9628

                              New York, c. March 11, 1924.

105196      Sioux City Sue                       PA 036072, 10718, Per 14253
105197      Forgetful Blues                      PA 036089, Per 14270
105198      Blue Grass Blues                     PA 036072, 10718, Per 14253

Phil Napoleon-t/Charlie Panelli-tb/Jimmy Lytell-cl/Frank Signorelli-p/Jack Roth-d.
New York, c. May 7, 1924.

| | | |
|---|---|---|
| 105305 | I Never Care 'Bout Tomorrow As Long As I'm Happy Today | PA 036096, P 1021, Per 14276 |
| 105306 | Shine | PA 036095, 10584,P 1081,Per 14275 |
| 105307 | Oh Baby (Don't Say No - Say Maybe) | PA 036096   -     -    Per 14276, Hom C-648 |

NOTE:- Homochord C-648 as ELDON'S DANCE ORCHESTRA.

New York, c. May 29, 1924.

| | | |
|---|---|---|
| 5516-1-2 | Big Boy | Ban 1360, Dom 345, Re 9656, Apex 8205 |
| 5517-1-2 | A Man Never Knows When A Woman's Gonna Change Her Mind | Ban 1375, Re 9670 |
| 5518-1-2 | Sioux City Sue | Ban 1373, Re 9672, Apex 8232 |

NOTE:- Domino as JOSEPH SAMUELS AND HIS BAND.

New York, June 4, 1924.

| | | |
|---|---|---|
| 81804-3 | It Ain't Gonna Rain No Mo' | Col 155-D, Re G-8230 |
| 81805-2 | Red Hot Mama | -      Re G-8258 |

NOTE:- Regal G-8230 and G-8258 as CORONA DANCE ORCHESTRA.

New York, June, 1924.

| | | |
|---|---|---|
| 42687-2 | You Know Me, Alabam' | Em 10783, Bwy/Pur/Tri 11400 |
| 42688-1 | Wait'll You See My Gal | Em 10782, Aus A-122 |
| 42689-1-2 | Red Hot Mama | - Or 228 - Bwy/Pur/Tri 11400, Rx 1226, Res 75400, Sil 2400 |

NOTE:- Resona 75400 and Silvertone 2400 as GOTHAM CLUB ORCHESTRA; Austral A-122 is anonymous.

New York, c. July 21, 1924.

| | | |
|---|---|---|
| 105477 | Superstitious Blues | PA 036117, Per 14298, Hg 951 |
| 105478 | Africa | ± 10752 --Hom C-718 - <u>Poydras 8</u> |
| 105479 | I'm Going Back To Those Who Won't Go Back On Me | PA 036134, Per 14315 |

NOTE:- Homochord C-718 as ELDON'S DANCE ORCHESTRA.

James A. Griffiths (as JOE GRIFFITH)-v. New York, July 25, 1924.

| | | |
|---|---|---|
| 81885-4 | The Grass Is Always Greener (In The Other Fellow's Yard) - vJG | Col 186-D |
| 81886-3 | Sioux City Sue - vJG | - |

New York, c. September 11, 1924.

| | | |
|---|---|---|
| 105548 | How Come You Do Me Like You Do ? | PA 036141, Per 14322 |
| 105549 | The Meanest Blues | PA 036142, Per 14323, Hg 975 |
| 105550 | Somebody Stole My Gal | PA 036141, Per 14322 |

New York, October 1, 1924.

| | | |
|---|---|---|
| 30876-5 | How Come You Do Me Like You Do ? | Vic 19480 |
| 30877-2 | Meanest Blues | - |

New York, c. October 14, 1924.

| | | |
|---|---|---|
| 105608 | Evening | PA 036151, 10989, Per 14332 |
| 105609 | Mama's Boy | PA 036168, Per 14349, Hg 992 |
| 105610 | Choo Choo (Gotta Hurry Home) | PA 036151, 10989,P 6759, Per 14332 |

Phil Napoleon-t/Charlie Panelli-tb/Jimmy Lytell-cl/Frank Signorelli-p/Jack Roth-d.
New York, October, 1924.

| | | |
|---|---|---|
| 42790-1 | No-One Knows What It's All About | Em 10815, Bwy/Tri 11445, Clover 1527, Globe/Rx 1246, Sil 2426 |
| 42791-2 | The Meanest Blues | Em 10815, Bwy/Tri 11445, Clover 1527, GG 1247, Sil 2426, Gra 9074, Acme 2101 |
| 42792-1 | Take Me | Em 10820, Ebs 1015, Globe/GG/Rx 1247, Res 75428 |

NOTE:- Grafton 9074 as BAR HARBOUR SOCIETY ORCHESTRA; Resona 75428 as THE CAROLIN-
IANS; Silvertone 2426 as THE SOUTHERN SYNCOPATORS.

New York, December 4, 1924.

| | | |
|---|---|---|
| 140163-3 | Mobile Blues | Col 260-D |
| 140164-4 | How Come You Do Me Like You Do ? | - |

Trixie Smith-v.                        New York, January, 1925.

| | | |
|---|---|---|
| 1995-4-6 | Everybody Loves My Baby (But My Baby Don't Love Nobody But Me) - vTS | Pm 12249, Max 1526 |
| 1996-6-7 | How Come You Do Me Like You Do ? - vTS | - Max 1536 |

NOTE:- While some copies of Paramount 12249 are credited to TRIXIE'S DOWN HOME
SYNCOPATORS, others, and the Maxsa issues, are labelled FLETCHER HENDERSON AND HIS
ORCHESTRA, q.v.  The Henderson band may have made the first few takes of each side,
but all known issues are by the Original Memphis Five.

New York, February 4, 1925.

| | | |
|---|---|---|
| 31912-1-2 | When My Sugar Walks Down The Street | Rejected |
| 31913-1 | Throw Down Blues | Vic 19594, Zon 3873 |

New York, c. February 6, 1925.

| | | |
|---|---|---|
| 105838-A | Thaïs : Meditation (Massenet) | PA 036208, Per 14389, Apex/Leo 693 |
| 105839 | Why Couldn't It Be Poor Little Me ? | PA 036210, Per 14391 |
| 105840 | One Of These Days | -            - |

NOTE:- Perfect 14391 as MAJESTIC DANCE ORCHESTRA; Apex/Leonora 693 as MISSOURI JAZZ
HOUNDS.

New York, February 10, 1925.

| | | |
|---|---|---|
| 140337-3 | Doo Wacka Doo | Col 308-D |
| 140338-2 | Nobody Knows What A Red-Head Mama Can Do | - Re G-8378 |

NOTE:- Regal G-8378 as CORONA DANCE ORCHESTRA.

New York, February 12, 1925.

| | | |
|---|---|---|
| 31941-4 | Sob Sister Sadie | Vic 19594, Zon 3873 |

Phil Napoleon db bb*; Miff Mole-tb replaces Panelli.
New York, September 17, 1925.

| | | |
|---|---|---|
| 33388-2 | *Bass Ale Blues | Vic 19805 |
| 33389-4 | Military Mike | - |

New York, September 25, 1925.

| | | |
|---|---|---|
| 141050-2 | Indiana Stomp | Col 480-D |
| 141051-1-2 | Throw Down Blues | Rejected |

New York, October 7, 1925.

| | | |
|---|---|---|
| 141051-4 | Throw Down Blues | Col 480-D |
| 33546-1-2-3-4-5 | Lookin' For The Blues | Vic rejected |

Phil Napoleon-t/Miff Mole-tb/Jimmy Lytell-cl/Frank Signorelli-p/Jack Roth-d.
                                    New York, October 22, 1925.

33546-6-7-8  Lookin' For The Blues          Vic rejected
33803-1-2-3-4  Loud-Speakin' Papa           -

                                    New York, October 26, 1925.

141193-3  Jacksonville Gal                  Col 502-D
141194-2  'Tain't Cold                      -

                                    New York, November 24, 1925.

33894-1-2-3-4  Washboard Blues              Vic rejected

                                    New York, c. November 28, 1925.

106436    Jacksonville Gal        PA 36358, Per 14539, Sal 246
106437    Nobody's Rose                  -  11138  -
106438    Throw Down Blues        PA 36384, P 6855,Per 14565,Sal 278

Red Nichols-t/Miff Mole-tb/? Alfie Evans-cl/Frank Signorelli-p/Ray Bauduc-d.
                                    New York, January 21, 1926.

E-17613    Chinese Blues                    Br 3039*

                                    New York, January 23, 1926.

E-2202/5; E-17656/9  'Tain't Cold           Br 3039*
E-2206/8    Chinese Blues                   Voc 15234
E-2209/11   Bass Ale Blues                  -
   NOTE:- Vocalion 15234 as THE HOTTENTOTS.

  As for October 22, 1925 above.    New York, February 16, 1926.

  34623-1-2-3-4-5  Bell Hoppin' Blues        Vic rejected

                                    New York, c. March 1, 1926.

106676    Bass Ale Blues          PA 36413, Per 14594
106677    Indiana Stomp           PA 36422, 11097, Per 14603
106678    Military Mike           PA 36413    -    Per 14594

  2nd p added** (? Roth db p).     New York, April 16, 1926.

35324-2  Static Strut             Vic LPV-557, RD-8000 (LPs)
35324-5  Static Strut             Vic 20039, HMV K-5346
35325-3**Tampeekoe                   -      HMV R-4811

  Ray Bauduc-d replaces Roth.      New York, c. November 26, 1926.

107239 ?  Missouri Squabble       Rejected
107240    The Chant               PA 36565, 11295, Per 14746
107241    One Sweet Letter From You   -      -      -
107242    Go, Joe, Go             PA 36576, Per 14757

                                    New York, December 28, 1926.

37188-2  A Blues Serenade         Vic 430744 (LP)
37189-2  Off To Buffalo           -
37190-1-2-3  Tiger Rag            Rejected

Red Nichols-t/Miff Mole-tb/George Bohn-cl-as/Frank Signorelli-p/Ray Bauduc-d/Annette
  Hanshaw-v.                       New York, c. April 14, 1927.

107486    Play It, Red            PA 11471
107487    Wistful And Blue - vAH  PA 36623, 11421, Per 14804
107488    What Do I Care What Somebody Said ? - vAH  -    -      -
107489    Nothin' - vAH           PA 11471

Phil Napoleon-t/Miff Mole-tb/George Bohn-cl/Lennie Hayton-p/Ray Bauduc-d
New York, August 16, 1927.

| | | |
|---|---|---|
| E-6537; E-24241 | Lovey Lee | Br 3713 (British only), Pan 25008 |
| E-6538; E-24242 | Lovey Lee | Br 3630, Mt M-12008, Polk P-9023, Voc 15623 |
| E-6539; E-24251 | How Come You Do Me Like You Do ? | Br 3713 (British only), Pan 25008 |
| E-6540; E-24252 | How Come You Do Me Like You Do ? | Br 3630, Mt M-12008, Polk P-9023, Voc 15623 |

NOTE:- The allocation of takes on the above session is possibly more haphazard
than is shown; it is likely that the takes known to have been used for British
issues may also have been used in the U.S.A. on at least one of the labels noted.
Melotone M-12008, Panachord 25008 and (in Australia only) Brunswick 3630 as JACK
WINN'S DALLAS DANDIES.

Probably as above.                        New York, March 19, 1928.

| | | |
|---|---|---|
| E-7204/5 | A Blues Serenade | Voc rejected |
| E-7206/7 | Denver Stomp | - |

Phil Napoleon-t/Tommy Dorsey-tb/Jimmy Dorsey-cl-as/Frank Signorelli-p/? Stan King-d/
Scrappy Lambert-v.                        New York, June 13, 1928.

| | | |
|---|---|---|
| E-7367- | I'm More Than Satisfied - vSL | Voc 15712 |
| E-7368- | My Angeline | - |
| E-7369- | Fireworks | Voc 15761 |

? Joe Tarto-sb added; Dick Robertson-v. New York, April 5, 1929.

| | | |
|---|---|---|
| E-29579- | Memphis Blues - vDR | Voc 15805 |
| E-29580- | Beale Street Blues - vDR | - |
| E-29581- | Kansas City Kitty - vDR | Voc 15810 |

Ted Napoleon-d replaces (or may even be) the previous drummer.
New York, November 24, 1931.

| | | |
|---|---|---|
| 151887-2 | Jazz Me Blues | Col 2588-D, 36064, DC-143, MC-3027 Par R-1399, A-3478 |
| 151888-2 | St. Louis Gal | Col 2577-D |
| 151889-2 | Anything | Col 2588-D, 36064, Par R-1297 |
| 151890-2 | My Honey's Lovin' Arms | Col 2577-D, DC-143, Re G-21480 |

NOTE:- Parlophone A-3478 as T.N.T. RHYTHM BOYS; Regal G-21480 as MISSISSIPPI JAZZ
KINGS.

The name of the Original Memphis Five was also used on Apex 8343 (THOSE PANAMA MAMAS)
for the Six Black Diamonds, q.v.

ORIGINAL MEMPHIS MELODY BOYS

Elmer Schoebel-p-a dir. Murphy Steinberg-c/Santo Pecora-tb/Charlie Bezimek-Roy Kramer
cl-as/Art Kassel-cl-ts/Otto Barberino-vn where marked * only/Lou Black-bj/Steve
Brown-bb/ ——— Schoebel (young relative of Elmer Schoebel)-d/Billy Meyers-v.
Richmond, Ind., April 2, 1923.

| | | |
|---|---|---|
| 11377-B | There's No Gal Like My Gal | Gnt 5157 |
| 11378-A | *Wonderful Dream | Gnt 5123, Cdl 562 |
| 11379-A | Blue Grass Blues | Gnt 5157 |
| 11380-A | Made A Monkey Out Of Me - vBM | Gnt 5123, 3097, Ch 15005 |

CHICAGO BLUES DANCE ORCHESTRA : As above. Chicago, May 30, 1923.

| | | |
|---|---|---|
| 81043-2 | Blue Grass Blues | Col A-3923, Re G-8096 |
| 81044-2 | House Of David Blues | - |

NOTE:- Regal G-8096 as REGAL NOVELTY ORCHESTRA.

Chicago, May 31, 1923.

| | | |
|---|---|---|
| 81049-1-2-3 | Eccentric Rag (J. Russel Robinson) | Col rejected |
| 81050-1-2-3 | Step, Daddy | - |

C/tb/cl-bar/as/p/bj/d/Guy Williams-v.      Chicago, c. February, 1925.

732    Owl Strut (Midnight Ramblers Stomp)      Auto (un-numbered)
733    Bowling Green (Midnight Ramblers Blues)-vGW -

## ORIGINAL NEW ORLEANS JAZZ BAND

NEW ORLEANS JAZZ BAND : Jimmy Durante-p dir. Frank Christian-c/Frank Lhotak-tb/
    Achille Baquet-cl/Arnold Loyacano-d.    New York, c. November, 1918.

477-B  Ole Miss                           OK 1156
478-B  Ja Da (Intro. You'll Find Old Dixieland  OK 1155
           In France)

ORIGINAL NEW ORLEANS JAZZ BAND : Same.    New York, January, 1919.

6026   He's Had No Lovin' For A Long, Long Time Gnt 4508
6027   Ja-Da (Intro. You'll Find Old Dixieland    -
           In France)

Unknown tb replaces Lhotak.              New York, c. March, 1919.

6091, -A  Ja-Da (Intro. You'll Find Old        Gnt 4508, Ristic 2
              Dixieland In France)
6092-A  He's Had No Lovin' For A Long, Long Time    -          -

NOTE:- The late Arnold Loyacano recalled that this band made some sides for Emerson
    while he was the drummer with it, between September, 1918 and December 30, 1919.
    No trace of these has ever been found, so evidently they were never issued.

## ORIGINAL  NEW ORLEANS RHYTHM KINGS

See the New Orleans Rhythm Kings.

## ORIGINAL PENNSYLVANIA SERENADERS

See Whitey Kaufman.

## ORIGINAL  ST. LOUIS CRACKERJACKS

Chick Finney-p dir. Elmer King-Levi Madison-George Smith-t/Robert "Buster" Scott-tb/
    Walter Martin-Freddy Martin-as/Ernest Franklin-ts/William Bede Baskerville-g/Kermit
    Haynes-sb/Nicholas Haywood-d/Austin Wright-v.
                                        Chicago, October 16, 1936.

90925-A  Crackerjack Stomp               Dec 7236
90926-A  Echo In The Dark                Dec 7248
90927-A  Blue Thinking Of You - vAW      Dec 7236
90928-A  Fussin'                         Dec 7248
90929-B  Good Old Bosom Bread            Dec 7235
90930-A  Swing Jackson                       -
90931-A  Chasing The Blues Away          Dec 7265
90932-A  Lonesome Moments - vAW              -

## ORIGINAL  TAMPA FIVE

Pseudonym on Dandy for the Original Indiana Five, q.v.

## ORIGINAL TUXEDO JAZZ ORCHESTRA

See Oscar Celestin.

## ORIGINAL WASHBOARD BEATERS

Pseudonym on Parlophone R-3381, R-3383 and R-2305 for Clarence Williams' Washboard
    Five, q.v., and on Parlophone R-3492 and R-113 for Louis Armstrong and his Hot
    Seven, q.v.

Dick Voynow-p dir. Jimmy McPartland-c/Mike Durso-tb/Maurie Bercov-cl-as/g/Basil DuPre
sb/Vic Moore-d.                              Chicago, October 12, 1927.

| | | |
|---|---|---|
| C-1290 | Royal Garden Blues | Br 3708, 4000, A-7616, A-7852, |
| | | A-81001, Voc 15635, CMS 101 |
| C-1292 | Shim-Me-Sha-Wabble | Br 3707, 3856, Voc 15634, CMS 102 |
| C-1303 | A Good Man Is Hard To Find | Br 3708, 4000, A-7616, A-7852, |
| | | A-81001, Voc 15635, CMS 100 |
| C-1306 | The New Twister | Br 3707, 3856, Voc 15634, CMS 102 |

NOTE:- Brunswick 3708 was never issued as such.

Unknown c replaces McPartland; unknown ts/pac added, v where shown.
Chicago, May 24, 1928.

| | | |
|---|---|---|
| C-1971- ; E-7353 | Limehouse Blues | Voc 15708, CMS 101 |
| C-1972- ; E-7354 | Dear Old Southland - v | -          CMS 100 |

2t/tb/2cl-as/ts/vn/p/Sid Pritikan-bj/bb/d-vib/Frank Sylvano-Harry Maxfield-v.
Chicago, October 15, 1928.

| | | |
|---|---|---|
| C-2441- | Sonny Boy - vHM | Voc rejected |
| C-2442- | There's A Rainbow 'Round My Shoulder - vHM | - |

Chicago, December 14, 1928.

| | | |
|---|---|---|
| C-2670- | Sweethearts On Parade - vFS | Voc 15751 |
| C-2671-A | I'll Get By (As Long As I Have You) - vFS | - |

Chicago, December 31, 1928.

| | | |
|---|---|---|
| C-2737- | There's A Rainbow 'Round My Shoulder-vHM | Voc 15732 |
| C-2738- | Sonny Boy - vHM | - |

Chicago, January 29, 1929.

| | | |
|---|---|---|
| C-2885- | I'll Never Ask For More - vFS | Voc 15768 |
| C-2886- | If I Had You - vFS | Voc 15766 |
| C-2887- | I Faw Down And Go 'Boom !' - vFS | - |

Other titles issued as by the Original Wolverines were directed by Fred Hamm, q.v.

## ORIGINAL YELLOW JACKETS

Aubrey Yancey-t-v/Earl Watkins-t/Monroe Fingers-Clifton Jones-as/William Pate-ts/
Durant Allen-p/Jesse Saville-g/Wiley Fuller-sb/Theodore Saville-d/Fats Smith-v.
Hot Springs, Ark., March 5, 1937.

| | | |
|---|---|---|
| HS-22- | Swingin' At The Chat 'n' Chew | Voc 03549 |
| HS-23- | Yellowjackets Get Together | - |
| HS-24- | Sleeping And Dreaming Of You - vFS | Rejected |
| HS-25- | Cross Street Swing | Voc 03591 |
| HS-26- | Blue Drag - vAY | - |
| HS-27- | Business After Midnight | Voc 03504, ARC 7-05-71 |
| HS-28- | The Hour Of Parting - vAY | -          - |
| HS-29- | My Blue Heaven - vFS | Rejected |

## ORIOLE DANCE ORCHESTRA

Pseudonym on Oriole for the following items listed in this book :-

374  Those Panama Mamas (Six Black Diamonds) 1542  I Get The Blues When It Rains
482  Silver Head (California Ramblers)               (Fred Rich and his Orchestra)

## ORIOLE ORCHESTRA

See Russo and Fiorito's Oriole Orchestra.

## ORIOLE SALON ORCHESTRA

Pseudonym on Australian Angelus 3334, 3345 and Lyric 3345 for Eubie Blake and his
Orchestra, q.v.

## THE ORIOLE SERENADERS

Pseudonym on Champion 15271 for Fred Rich and his Times Square Orchestra, q.v.

## ORK. PICCADILLI W LONDYNIE

Pseudonym on Usiba 245 for the Carolina Club Orchestra (see Hal Kemp).

## NICHOLAS ORLANDO'S ORCHESTRA

The following is the only title by this band likely to interest jazz collectors, as
it features good t/vn/g.  The vocalist is Jack Kaufman (as WALTER NEFF).
New York, c. September 9, 1927.

1077733    Dawning - vJK                    PA 36689  11503, Per 14870,  P-342
    NOTE:- Perfect P-342 as RAYNER'S DANCE ORCHESTRA.

## THE ORLEANIANS

Sharkey Bonano-c/probably :- Sidney Arodin-cl/Hal Jordy-as bar/Freddy Newman-p/Joe
    Cupero-g/Luther Lamar-bb/Honk Hazel-d-mel.
New Orleans, December 16, 1928.

147652-1-2-3  Banana Peel                    Col rejected
147653-1-2    Baby                           -

## ORPHEUM MELODY MASTERS

Pseudonym on Bell for the following items listed in this book :-

P-291  You'll Never Get To Heaven With Those Eyes (Sam Lanin and his Orchestra)
P-298  San (Nathan Glantz and his Orchestra)

## ORPHEUS DANCE BAND

This name was given to the Zonophone "house" dance band when the Arcadians Dance
    Orchestra name was dropped in 1930.  The following is known to be an excellent
    "hot" dance record, and there may well be others similar.

John Firman dir. Max Goldberg and another-t/2cl-as/? Joe Crossman-ts/Bert Read-p/
    Joe Brannelly-bj/Billy Bell or George Gibbs-bb/Rudy Starita or Harry Robbins-d/
    Charles W. Saxby-or.                    Kingsway Hall, London, February, 1931.

OY-442-2  Sweet Jennie Lee                    Zon 5841

## ORQUESTA  LOS DEAVELADOS

See Sam Lanin (Broadway Broadcasters).

## HAROLD ORTLI AND HIS OHIO STATE COLLEGIANS

T/tb/cl-as/as-ts-bsx/p/bj/bb/d/Clarence Buck-v (he may be the bj or d).
Cleveland, February, 1925.

8942-B  I Couldn't Get To It (In Time) - vCB    OK 40332
8943-A  My Daddy Rocks Me (With One Steady Roll)-vCB-

## KID  ORY

See Spikes' Seven Pods of Pepper.

## GEORGE OSBORN  AND HIS ORCHESTRA

Phil Burdick-Phil Bibbs-t/Hal Runyon-tb/Bill Burdick-cl/George Rice-Jack Moroni-as-ts
    /Emery Graneer-vn/Rollie Altmeyer-p/Larry Arndt-bj/Eli Barnett-d/Don Guthrie-x.
Lowry Hotel, St. Paul, c. June 18, 1927.

12868    Brainstorm                        Gnt 6215, Ch 15323
    NOTE:- Champion 15323 as FRANK HENDERSON AND HIS ORCHESTRA.
        Other titles by this band are of no interest as jazz.

The following titles by this famous popular vocalist and his orchestra contain points
of interest as jazz; there may be others among the considerable output between 1929
and 1939.

Will Osborne-v dir. probably :- George McGhee-and another-t/tb/Jack Stacey-and
another-cl-as/cl-ts/3vn/Frank Froeba-p/g/sb/d.
New York, February 10, 1931.

E-36044-   Hello ! Beautiful - vWO               Mt M-12099, Pan 25030, P-12098,
                                                 Mf G-2007
    NOTE:- Mayfair G-2007 as MICKEY'S NIGHT BIRDS.

Will Osborne-v dir. John Dillard-Tom Murphy-Estes Monasco-t/Yank Lawson-tb/Frank
Salto-Harold Lawson-cl-as/Tony Castellano-cl-ts/Joe Denton-cl-ts-bar/Bruce Yantis-
Jack Small-Elliott Russell-Gerald Bittick-vn/Simon Einhorn-p/George Odell-g/
Alfonso del Aquila-sb/Bill Gussak-d.   New York, August 22, 1935.

CO-17995-1  That's What You Think - vWO           Col 3080-D, FB-1235

## OSCAR'S CHICAGO SWINGERS

T/as/? John Oscar-p/sb/d/Sam Theard-v.    Chicago, May 5, 1936.

90711-A  New Rubbing On The Darned Old Thing-vST  Dec 7186
90712-A  I Wonder Who's Boogiein' My Woogie - vST    -

Odell Rand-cl/? John Oscar-p/? Kokomo Arnold and another-g/d/Sam Theard-v.
Chicago, July 9, 1936.

90796-B  Try Some Of That - vST                  Dec 7201
90797-B  My Gal's Been Foolin' Me - vST             -

## VESS L. OSSMAN

Sylvester Louis Ossman was one of the greatest American banjoists of all time. His
recording activities were prolific from 1897 until 1916, and his are the oldest
items included in this book, for they are of great interest as examples of ragtime
actually recorded during the two decades of its popularity, which coincided with
Vess Ossman's recording career so exactly.

Banjo solos, acc. by Fred Gaisberg-p.    New York, October 9, 1897.

        Ragtime Medley                          Ber 467
        Gayest Manhattan                        Ber 472

   Acc. by unknown p.                     New York, c. 1899-1900.

   3830   Ragtime Medley (Intro. All Coons Look   Col 3830
            Alike To Me (Ernest Hogan)/Oh ! Mr. Johnson)
   3856   Eli Green's Cake-Walk (Sadie Koninsky)  Col 3856
   3858   Smoky Mokes (Abe Holzmann)              Col 3858
   3861   A Bunch Of Rags (Vess L. Ossman)        Col 3861
   3862   The Honolulu Cake-Walk                  Col 3862

OSSMAN-DUDLEY TRIO : Vess Ossman-bj/ —— Dudley-md/Roy Butin-harp g.
New York, c. 1900.

85109   Panama Rag (Will H. Tyers)              Col 85109
   NOTE:- The above six Columbia cylinders were all available in Great Britain until
   1905.

Banjo solos, acc. by p.                   New York, c. 1900.

        A Coon Band Contest (Arthur Pryor)      Zon 9181

New York, January 8, 1900.

   0863   Sounds From Africa                      Ber 0863
   0865   Happy-Go-Lucky                          Ber 0865
   0867   An Ethiopian Mardi Gras (Maurice Levy)  Ber 0867

Banjo solos, acc. by Landon Ronald-p.    London, May 18, 1900.

| 4469 | Smoky Mokes (Abe Holzmann) | Ber 6311 |
| 4470 | A Ragtime Skedaddle (George Rosey) | Ber 6307 |
| 4478 | Whistling Rufus (Kerry Mills) | Ber 6306 |

London, May 25, 1900.

| 648 | Cotton Blossoms (M. H. Hall) | Ber 6319 |

Acc. by C. H. H. Booth-p.             New York, July 19, 1900.

| 149-1-2 | Whistling Rufus (Kerry Mills) | Vic 149 |
| 150-1-2 | An Ethiopian Mardi Gras (Maurice Levy) | Vic 150 |
| 153-1-2 | A Bunch Of Rags (Vess L. Ossman) | Vic 153 |
| 154-1-2 | A Coon Band Contest (Arthur Pryor) | Vic 154 |

New York, November 1, 1900.

| 149-3 | Whistling Rufus (Kerry Mills) | Vic 149 |
| 150-3 | An Ethiopian Mardi Gras (Maurice Levy) | Vic 150 |
| 153-1-2 | A Bunch Of Rags (Vess L. Ossman) | Vic 153 |
| 154-3-14 | A Coon Band Contest (Arthur Pryor) | Vic 154 |

New York, January 21, 1901.

| 150-4 | An Ethiopian Mardi Gras (Maurice Levy) | Vic 150 |
| 3042-1 | A Coon Band Contest (Arthur Pryor) | Vic 3042 |
| 3043-1 | An Ethiopian Mardi Gras (Maurice Levy) | Vic 3043 |
| 3050-1 | A Bunch Of Rags (Vess L. Ossman) | Vic 3050 |

New York, May 16, 1901.

| 808-1 | Hunky Dory (Abe Holzmann) | Vic 808 |
| 811-1 | Rusty Rags (Vess L. Ossman) | Vic 811 |
| 3363-1 | Hunky Dory (Abe Holzmann) | Vic 3363 |
| 3367-1 | Rusty Rags (Vess L. Ossman) | Vic 3367 |

Acc. by unknown p.                    New York, c. June, 1901.

| 290- | Hunky Dory (Abe Holzmann) | Col 290 |

New York, c. November, 1901.

| 461- | A Coon Band Contest (Arthur Pryor) | Col 461, 31412 (cylinder) |
| 464- | Hot Corn | Col 464 |
| 465-3 | Creole Belles (J. Bodewalt Lampe) | Col 465 |
| 469- | Rusty Rags Medley (Vess L. Ossman) | Col 469 |

Acc. by C. H. H. Booth-p.            New York, February 27, 1902.

| 1291-1-2 | Creole Belles (J. Bodewalt Lampe) | Vic 1291 |
| 3050-2-3 | A Bunch Of Rags (Vess L. Ossman) | Vic 3050 |

Acc. by unknown p.                    New York, c. April, 1902.

| 723-1 | Whistling Rufus (Kerry Mills) | Col 723 |

NOTE:- Matrix 723-4, issued anonymously on Columbia A-229, was probably recorded in 1905.

Acc. by C. H. H. Booth-p.             New York, April 11, 1902.

| 153-5-6 | A Bunch Of Rags (Vess L. Ossman) | Vic 153 |
| 1291-3 | Creole Belles (J. Bodewalt Lampe) | Vic 1291 |

New York, October 7, 1902.

| 1291-4 | Creole Belles (J. Bodewalt Lampe) | Vic 1291 |

Banjo solos, acc. by C. H. H. Booth-p.      New York, October 8, 1902.

  1660-1  Harmony Moze                              Vic 1660
  1664-1  Old Plunk's New Coon Medley (V.L.Ossman) Vic 1664

Acc. by Landon Ronald-p.                     London, May 13, 1903.

        Smoky Mokes (Abe Holzmann)            G&T 06257 (12-inch)
  3663-R  Hiawatha (Neil Moret)                G&T GC-6387
  3666-R  Smoky Mokes (Abe Holzmann)           G&T GC-6399

                                             London, May 16, 1903.

  3709-R  Harmony Moze                         G&T GC-6388

Acc. by unknown p.                           New York, c. August, 1903.

  1540-   Hiawatha (Neil Moret)                Col 1540, 32256 (cylinder)

Acc. by C. H. H. Booth-p.                    New York, October 23, 1903.

  578-1  Peaceful Henry (E. H. Kelly)          Vic
NOTE:- This title was recorded in one take of each of three sizes - 7, 10 and 12-
inch - but none of them appears to have been issued.

                                             New York, November 5, 1903.

  629-1  A Coon Band Contest (Arthur Pryor)    Vic 154
  631-1  An Ethiopian Mardi Gras (Maurice Levy) Vic 150
  632-1  Keep Off The Grass (Harry von Tilzer)  Vic 2616, 16266

Acc. by unknown p.                           New York, c. November, 1903.

  8576    Keep Off The Grass (Harry von Tilzer) Ed 8576 (cylinder)
  8618    Razzle Dazzle                        Ed 8618 (cylinder)

                                             New York, c. April, 1904.

  8726    St. Louis Rag (Tom Turpin)           Ed 8726 (cylinder)

Acc. by Columbia Orchestra (q.v. for probable personnel).
                                             New York, c. December, 1905.

  3360-3  The Buffalo Rag (Tom Turpin)         Col/Oxford 3360, Col A-218,
                                             Lakeside 70230

OSSMAN-DUDLEY TRIO : Vess L. Ossman-bj/ —— Dudley-md/Roy Butin-harp g.
                                             New York, January 24, 1906.

  3033-3  Dixie Girl (J. Bodewalt Lampe)       Vic 4679, 16667
  3037-2  St. Louis Tickle (Barney - Seymore)  Vic 4624, 16092
  3038-1  Koontown Koffee-Klatsch (J. P. Greenberg)Vic 4659

Banjo solos, acc. by the Victor Orchestra, q.v., or unknown p.*
                                             New York, January 26, 1906.

  3049-1 *The Buffalo Rag (Tom Turpin)         Vic 16779
  3049-3  The Buffalo Rag (Tom Turpin)         Vic 4628
  3050-1  St. Louis Tickle (Barney - Seymore)  Rejected
  3053-1  Cannon Ball Rag (Joseph Northup)     -

Acc. unknown.                                New York, c. May, 1906.

  9317    St. Louis Tickle (Barney - Seymore)  Ed 9317 (cylinder)

OSSMAN-DUDLEY TRIO : As for January 24, 1906.
                                             New York, c. July, 1906.

  3476-5  Koontown Koffee-Klatsch (J. P. Greenberg)Col 3476, A-218, 32984 (cylinder)

Banjo solos, acc. by p.                    New York, c. 1906-1907,

    7070    Smoky Mokes (Abe Holzmann)            Imp 45221
    7071    Whistling Rufus (Kerry Mills)         Imp 45222

    8264    Creole Belles (J. Bodewalt Lampe)     Imp 44826 (February, 1907)

    8974    The Smiler Rag (Percy Wenrich)        Imp 45484
    NOTE:- The date in brackets is the month of issue in the U. K.

    5372    St. Louis Tickle (Barney - Seymore)   Leader 200, Pelican P-18
  030810    St. Louis Rag (Tom Turpin)            Od 030810, Leader 201
  030814    Any Rags (Allen)                      Od 030814        -
  030815    Dixie Girl (J. Bodewalt Lampe)        Od 030815 (coupled with 030814)
    NOTE:- The above four titles are 10¾-inch records, and are announced.

OSSMAN-DUDLEY TRIO : Vess L. Ossman-bj/ —— Dudley-md/Roy Butin-harp g.
                                New York, c. January, 1907.

    3591-1  Chicken Chowder (Giblin)              Col 3591, A-220

Banjo solos, acc. by the Victor Orchestra, q.v.
                                New York, February 4, 1907.

    4238-1-2-3  Panama Rag (Will H. Tyers)        Vic rejected

                                New York, February 5, 1907.

    4238-4-5  Panama Rag (Will H. Tyers)          Rejected
    4239-1  Florida Rag (Lowry)                   Vic 5058

Acc. by Columbia Orchestra, q.v.    New York, c. March, 1907.

    3626-1  Maple Leaf Rag (Scott Joplin)         Col 3626, A-228

Acc. by ? Charles A. Prince-p.      New York, c. April, 1907.

    3644-1  Florida Rag (Lowry)                   Col 3644, A-224, 33147 (cylinder)

Acc. unknown.                       New York, c. May, 1907.

    9713    Florida Rag (Lowry)                   Ed 9713 (cylinder)

            Maple Leaf Rag (Scott Joplin)         Imp 45600 (April, 1908)
    NOTE:- The date in brackets is that of the month of issue in the U. K.

                                New York, c. November, 1907.

    9765    The Smiler Rag (Percy Wenrich)        Ed 9765 (cylinder)

Acc. by Theodore Morse-p.           New York, October 5, 1908.

    6504-1  Persian Lamb Rag (Winchester)         Vic 16127
    6508-1  A Bunch Of Rags (Vess L. Ossman)      Vic 153, 16667

                                New York, March 2, 1909.

    6844-1-2  White Wash Man (Jean Schwartz)      Rejected
    6848-1-2  The Buffalo Rag (Tom Turpin)        Vic 4628, 16779, HMV GC2-6251,
                                                  Zon 3931

                                New York, April 7, 1909.

    6848-3  The Buffalo Rag (Tom Turpin)          Vic rejected

Acc. by Columbia Orchestra, q.v.    New York, c. December, 1909.

    4268-4  Moose March                           Col A-787, 1366, Re G-6199

Banjo solos, acc. unknown.                    New York, c. April, 1910.

| 1002  | Persian Lamb Rag (Winchester) | Ed 1002 (cylinder)  |
| 10383 | Moose March                   | Ed 10383 (cylinder) |

Acc. by the Columbia Orchestra, q.v.   New York, September, 1910.

| 4919-1 | St. Louis Tickle (Barney - Seymore) | Col A-937, 1663, Re G-6200 |

New York, December 6, 1910.

| 569       | The Smiler Rag (Percy Wenrich) | LW 569 (5-inch)            |
| 19149-1-3 | The Smiler Rag (Percy Wenrich) | Col A-972, 1663, Re G-6200 |

Orch. acc.                                    New York, April 24, 1916.

| 4680 | Keep Off The Grass (Harry von Tilzer) | Ed 50377 |

NOTE:- Many of the single-sided Columbia records were also issued on Climax and Manhattan, in each case bearing the Columbia matrix-catalog number; the double-sided
A- series also appeared under the A- number on Harmony and Standard discs, with
large spindle-holes. The Victor 3000 series are all ten-inch records; the three-
and four-figure numbers prior to 1905 are of seven- and ten-inch discs alike. Prior
to 1901, records described as Victor bear the Improved Gram-O-Phone label of the
Consolidated Talking Machine Company of Philadelphia, the immediate forerunner of
the Victor Talking Machine Company of Camden, N. J.

## OSTEND'S KURSAAL'S ORCHESTRA

Pseudonym on Maxsa 1523 for the California Ramblers, q.v.

## GLEN OSWALD'S SERENADERS

Examination of the records issued of this band shows that only one is likely to be of
interest to the jazz enthusiast; one other, not issued, may have been similarly so.

Glen Oswald-vn dir. Claude Burch-Al Harris-t/Marty King-tb/George Smith-Del Porter-cl
ss-as/Abe Maule or Moll-cl-ts/Wayne Allen-p/Zebe Mann-bj/Tom Curtis-bb/Bill Weber-
d.                                            Los Angeles, March 3, 1925.

| PB-101-2 | Bucktown Blues | Vic 19733 |

Pete Olds-cl-ss-as replaces Smith; Peck Holten-p replaces Allen.
                                    Los Angeles, September 4, 1925.

| PBVE-136-1-2-3-4 | Everybody Stomp | Vic rejected |

## RED OWENS AND HIS GANG

Pseudonym on Champion for Floyd Mills and his Marylanders, q.v.

## WILLIE "SCARECROW" OWENS

THE SCARE CROW : Billy McOwens-v acc. by Gene Hill's Chicago Rhythm Boys : Punch
Miller-c/? George James-as/p/bj/d.   Richmond, Ind., May 15, 1930.

| 16607, -A | Scare Crow Blues      | Rejected                      |
| 16609-A   | Traveling Blues       | Gnt 7209, Ch 16036, Var 6046  |
| 16610-A   | Easy Creeping Mama    | Gnt 7229, Ch 16014, Var 6024  |
| 16612-A   | Want Your Ashes Hauled | Gnt 7209      -     Var 6041  |

NOTE:- Varsity 6024 as THE SCARCE CROW.

Acc. by the Harmony Boys : Probably as above, without d and probably without James.
                                    Richmond, Ind., May 17, 1930.

| 16622-A | Shake My Tree                        | Gnt 7229, Ch 16036, Var 6024 |
| 16623-A | The Scare Crow Ball                   | Gnt 7275                     |
| 16624, -A | I'm Going To Show You My Black Bottom | Rejected                  |
| 16625   | Everybody Wants To See My Black Bottom |      -                     |

NOTE:- Varsity 6024 as THE SCARCE CROW. Other records by this artist have no
particular interest as jazz as regards the accompaniments.

Pseudonym on American Parlophone for Carl Webster's Yale Collegians, q.v.

## HAROLD OXLEY AND HIS POST LODGE ORCHESTRA

The following title from five issued by OKeh and Pathe in 1924 by this band is of some interest as a "hot" dance record.

Harold Oxley-vn dir. 2t/tb/2cl-ss-as/cl-ts/p/bj/bb/d; the personnel included Archie Snead and Charlie Storm, both arrangers, but their instruments are not known.
                                        New York, c. August 5, 1924.

72729-B  I Don't Know Why                    OK 40180, Par E-5324

## FRED OZARK'S JUG BLOWERS

Probably Ed Smalle-Vernon Dalhart-Cliff Edwards-k, acc. by either or both of the latter two on bj and u.          New York, c. May 9, 1924.

105310    Bringing Home The Bacon            PA 036091, Per 14282
105313    Savannah (The Georgianna Blues)        -              -

## PACIFIC COAST PLAYERS

2t/tb/2as/ts/p/bj/bb/d.                 New York, c. April, 1926.

3818-A   Jazzing Around                        Rx 1326

## JACK PADBURY AND HIS COSMO CLUB SIX

Jack Padbury-cl-as-bar dir. Bert Hargest-t/Phil Silverston-vn/Tommy Hinsby-p/Pasquale Troise-bj-g/Charlie Knapp-d.      London, February 14, 1929.

12196-2   Today's A Sunny Day For Me          EBW 4915
12197-1   Two Weeks' Notice                      -
88702-2   Today's A Sunny Day For Me          EBR 941
88703-1   Two Weeks' Notice                      -

                                        London, March 6, 1929.

88729-1   Hot Bricks                          EBR rejected
88730-1   Deep Hollow                            -

                                        London, May 31, 1929.

88729-2-3  Hot Bricks                         EBR rejected

Cecil Smith-tb added.                   London, c. January 31, 1930.

12592-2   Cosmoitis                           EBW 4982
12593-1   Alabama Mama                           -
88914-1   Praying For Rain                    EBR 1254
88915-1   My Kinda Love                          -

Les Allen-v.                            London, December 3, 1930.

WAR-439-1-2  Just A Little Closer-- vLA        Re rejected
WAR-440-1-2  Sing (A Happy Little Thing) - vLA    -

Other recordings by this band, including those accompanying Vivien Lambelet on Piccadilly, are of no interest as jazz.

## JOSE PADILLA ORCHESTRA

Jose Padilla was the Spanish composer of such successful dance novelties as PAREE (CA C'EST PARIS), VALENCIA, EL RELICARIO and LA VIOLETERA, but the above style, used on Canadian Domino 21531, denoted the American bandleader Joe Candullo, q.v., and his Everglades Orchestra.

Billy Page-cl-as dir. Clarence Dolsey-Rex Stewart-c/Henry Robinson-tb/Harrison
   Jackson-? cl-as/Fred Washington-? cl-ts/Danny Wilson-p/Elmer Turner-bj/Frank Holden
   bb/Robert Dews-d/Floyd Fitch-unknown instrument.
                                        New York, May 23, 1924.

72559 ?  Chicago Gouge                        OK rejected
72560 ?  Burning Kisses                            -
NOTE:- These titles are shown in THE PITTSBURGH COURIER for May 24, 1924 as having
been made (or to be made) for OKeh "on Friday." There were no records made on May
30, so the date shown must be correct. The matrix numbers fit this, but which one
applies to which title obviously cannot be determined in the absence of recording
ledgers or test pressings.

## HOT LIPS PAGE

HOT LIPS PAGE AND HIS BAND : Hot Lips Page-t-v/Ben Smith-cl-as/Sam Simmons-ts/Jimmy
   Reynolds-p/Connie Wainwright-g/Wellman Braud-sb/Alfred Taylor-d.
                                        New York, March 10, 1938.

63393-A  Good Old Bosom Bread - vHLP           Dec 7451, Voc S-206
63394-A  He's Pulling His Whiskers                   -          -
63395-B  Down On The Levee (Levee Lullaby) - vHLP Dec 7433, Voc S-197
63396-A  Old Man Ben - vHLP                          -          -

   Hot Lips Page-t-v dir. Eddie Mullens-Bobby Moore-t/George Stevenson-tb/Harry White
   tb-a/Ulysses Scott-as/Ben Smith-cl-as/Benny Waters-Ernie Powell-ts/Jimmy Reynolds-
   p/Connie Wainwright-g/Abe Bolar-sb/Alfred Taylor-d.
                                        New York, April 27, 1938.

022923-1  Jumpin'                               BB B-7583, HMV B-9369, JK-2821
022924-1  Feelin' High And Happy - vHLP         BB B-7569
022925-1  At Your Beck And Call - vHLP          -
022926-1  Rock It For Me - vHLP                 BB B-7567, HMV B-9369, JK-2821
022927-1  Skull Duggery - aHW                   BB B-7583
022928-1  I Let A Song Go Out Of My Heart       BB B-7567, RZ MR-2811

   Dave Page-t replaces Mullens; Ben Williams-as-ts replaces Scott; Delores Payne-Ben
   Bowers-v.                             New York, June 24, 1938.

023732-1  If I Were You - vDP                   BB B-7684
023733-1  (A Sky Of Blue, With You) And So Forth BB B-7680
            - vDP
023734-1  The Pied Piper - vHLP                 BB B-7682
023735-1  Small Fry - vHLP                      BB B-7684, RZ MR-2880
023736-1  I'm Gonna Lock My Heart And Throw Away BB B-7682
            The Key - vHLP
023737-1  Will You Remember Tonight Tomorrow ?-vBB BB B-7680

   Hot Lips Page-t-v/Buster Smith-cl-as/Jimmy Powell-as/Sam Davis-ts/Jimmy Reynolds-p/
   Abe Bolar-sb/Ed McConney-d/Romayne Jackson-The Harlem Highlanders-v.
                                        New York, January 23, 1940.

67091-A  I Would Do Anything For You - vHLP      Dec 7699
67092-A  I Ain't Got Nobody - vHH                Dec 7714
67093-A  A Porter's Love Song To A Chambermaid   Dec 7757
            - vRJ
67094-A  Gone With The Gin                       Dec 7714, Br 03480
67099-A  Walk It To Me (Call Of The Wild*)       Dec 7757          -*
67100-A  I Won't Be Here Long - vHLP             Dec 7699

   Hot Lips Page-t/Eddie Barefield-cl-as/Don Stovall-as/Don Byas-ts/Pete Johnson-p/
   John Collins-g/Abe Bolar-sb/A. G. Godley-d.
                                        New York, November 11, 1940.

68334-A  Lafayette                              Dec 18124, Br A-82727, 88013
68335-A  South                                       -          -        -

ORAN "HOT LIPS" PAGE AND HIS BAND : Hot Lips Page-t/Eddie Barefield-cl-as/Don Stovall
as/Don Byas-ts/Pete Johnson-p/John Collins-g/Abe Bolar-sb/A. G. Godley-d/Bea Morton
v.                                     New York, December 3, 1940.

| 68435-A | Harlem Rhumbain' The Blues | Dec 8531 |
| 68436-A | No Matter Where You Are (When Evening Draws Her Curtain) - vBM | - |

HOT LIPS PAGE TRIO : Hot Lips Page-t-mel-v/Leonard Feather-p/Teddy Bunn-g-v/Ernest
Hill-bb-sb.                             New York, December 10, 1940.

| 058149-1 | Thirsty Mama Blues - vHLP | BB B-8981 |
| 058150-1 | Just Another Woman - vHLP | BB B-8660, HMV B-9261 |
| 058151-1 | My Fightin' Gal - vHLP | - |
| 058152-1 | Evil Man's Blues - vTB | BB B-8634 |
| 058153-1 | Do It If You Wanna | - |

## WALTER PAGE'S BLUE DEVILS

Walter Page-bb-sb dir. James Simpson-Hot Lips Page-t/Dan Minor-tb/Buster Smith-cl-as/
Ted Manning-as/Reuben Roddy-ts/Charlie Washington-p/Reuben Lynch or Thomas Owens-g/
Alvin Burroughs-d/Jimmy Rushing-v.     Kansas City, November 10, 1929.

| KC-612- | Blue Devil Blues - vJR/bb | Voc 1463 |
| KC-613- | Squabblin' - sb | - |

## JEWEL  PAIGE

See Joe Brown for the sides issued as Jewel Paige and her Brown Brownies.

## PALACE DANCE ORCHESTRA

Pseudonym on Broadway 1349 (I'M FOLLOWING YOU) for Adrian Schubert and his Orchestra,
q.v.

## PALACE GARDEN  ORCHESTRA

Pseudonym on Pathe Actuelle and Perfect for the California Ramblers, q.v.

## PALACE TRIO  AND ORCHESTRA

Most records by the Palace Trio, with or without the augmentation of "orchestra," are
of little or no jazz interest, despite the pianist on many of them being J. Russel
Robinson, but the following is rather different.

Rudy Wiedoeft-as dir. c/tb/cl/Harry Akst-p/Mario Perry-pac.
                                       New York, c. February, 1921.

| | Strut, Miss Lizzie | Oly 15101 |
| | Spread Yo' Stuff | - |

## PALAIS DE DANSE  ORCHESTRA

Pseudonym on Parlophone E-4605 for the Casa Loma Orchestra, q.v.

## LA PALINA BROADCASTERS

Pseudonym on Banner and associated labels for Fred Rich and his Orchestra, q.v.

## PALLEDO ORCHESTRA OF ST. LOUIS

2t/tb/2cl-as/cl-ts/? vn/p/bj/bb/d.      St. Louis, c. October 26, 1925.

| 9405-B | Close Your Eyes | OK 40521 |
| 9406-B | What-Cha-Call-'Em Blues | - |

Pseudonym on Guardsman for the following items listed in this book :-

1641  Hard-Hearted Hannah (Jeffries and his Rialto Orchestra)
1684  Too Tired (The Ambassadors)
1696  Mandy (Ben Bernie and his Hotel Roosevelt Orchestra)

## CHARLIE PALLOY

CHARLIE PALLOY AND HIS ORCHESTRA : Charlie Palloy-g-v dir. 2t/tb/2as/ts/p/bb/d.
New York, September-October, 1932.

   1879-1  It Don't Mean A Thing (If It Ain't Got    Cr 3392
              That Swing) - vCP

Vocal, acc. by own g/p.                   New York, September-October, 1932.

   1884-2  How Deep Is The Ocean ? (How High Is    Cr 3395, Bcst B-113
              The Sky ?)
   1887-2  Let's Put Out The Lights (And Go To Sleep)  -          -

CHARLIE PALLOY AND HIS ORCHESTRA : As before, but cl-as replaces previous saxes, and
   sb replaces bb.                        New York, c. October, 1932.

   1907-1  What A Perfect Combination - vCP        Cr 3410, Imp 2845

Other Crown records by this artist may reward investigation.

## PALM BEACH PLAYERS

Pseudonym on Beltona for the following items listed in this book :-

101  The Sheik (California Ramblers)
403  Old Fashioned Love (The Ambassadors)
427  Stuttering (California Ramblers)
849  Suite 16 (Ben Selvin and his Orchestra)
882  Nay, Dearie, Nay (Vic Meyers and his Orchestra)
1256 Song Of The Wanderer (Johnny Sylvester and his Orchestra)

## PALM BEACH SERENADERS

Pseudonym on Canadian Domino 21328 (SOMEDAY, SWEETHEART) for the California Ramblers,
   q.v.

## BEE PALMER

Although this cabaret artist is well-known to jazz connoisseurs for her having in her
   accompanying band at one time such luminaries as Emmett Hardy-c and Leon Roppolo-cl,
   not one of the four test records she made (for Victor in 1925 and Columbia in 1929)
   appears to contain anything of jazz interest, despite the fact that the Columbias
   were made under the nominal direction of Paul Whiteman, and allegedly, but by no
   means audibly, include Bix Beiderbecke-c.

## GLADYS PALMER

Vocal, acc. by own p and probably :- Eddie Farley-t/Mike Riley-tb/Slats Long-cl/
   Arthur Ens-g/George Yorke-sb/Vic Engle-d.
New York, August 6, 1935.

39819-A  I'm Livin' In A Great Big Way          Dec 7106, Br 02089
39820-A  In The Middle Of A Kiss                   -       -
39821-A  Get Behind Me, Satan                   Dec 7107, Br 02134

New York, August 7, 1935.

39825-A  Trees                                  Dec 7107, Br 02134

New York, August 9, 1935.

39845-   My Special Man Is Back In Town         Dec rejected

See the Memphis Night Hawks.

## PALMETTO NIGHT CLUB ORCHESTRA

Pseudonym on Champion 15308 for the Baby Aristocrats Band, q.v.

## PALOOKA WASHBOARD BAND

Herb Morand-t-v (where marked *)/Odell Rand-cl/Horace Malcolm-p/Joe McCoy or Charlie
    McCoy-g/sb/wb/Joe McCoy-v.　　　　　　　　Chicago, October 27, 1937.

```
91301-A  We Gonna Move - vJM                     Dec 7378
91302-A  Back Door - vJM                          -
91303-A  You Done Tore Your Pants With Me - vJM  Dec 7398
91304-A  *Save Me Some - vHM                      -
```

## PANACHORD BOYS

Pseudonym on Australian Panachord P-12103 for the Sunshine Boys, q.v.

## PAN-AMERICAN DANCE ORCHESTRA

Pseudonym on Victor 24041 for Gene Kardos and his Orchestra, q.v.

## LOUIS PANICO AND HIS ORCHESTRA

Louis Panico-t dir. Don Jones-tb/Maurie Bercov-cl/Putty Nettles-as/p/g/Andy Panico-
    bb/Bobby Christian-d/v.　　　　　　　　Chicago, c. February 10, 1930.

```
C-5379-C  Wabash Blues                     Br 4736, A-8710, ARC 35-10-27,
                                           Voc 2849
C-5380-C  Oh Doctor - v                    As above
```

Louis Panico-t dir. t/tb/cl-as/as/ts/p/g/sb/d/Jean Fay-v.
　　　　　　　　　　　　　　　　Chicago, September 7, 1934.

```
C-9420-A  Why Don't You Practice What You Preach ? Rejected
            - vJF
C-9421-   Wabash Blues                     Dec 159
C-9422-   Someday, Sweetheart               -
C-9423-A  Don't Let Your Love Go Wrong     Dec 230, Br 01888
```

　　　　　　　　　　　　　　　　Chicago, September 24, 1934.

```
C-9512-A  Why Don't You Practice What You Preach ? Dec 230, Br 01888
```
    NOTE:- The label of Brunswick 01888 shows the matrix number as C-9420, and Jean Fay
    as vocalist, but in the wax the correct matrix number is shown, and there is no
    vocal.

## PAPALIA AND HIS ORCHESTRA

Russ Papalia-tb dir. c/cl/Eddie Powers-ts/p/bj/bb/d.
　　　　　　　　　　　　　　　New Orleans, January 23, 1925.

```
8898-A  Cross-Word Mama You're Puzzling Me    OK 40347
8899-A  Sometime When You're Alone             -
```

## JEAN PAQUES

Piano solos.　　　　　　　　　　　London, c. January 5, 1928.

```
11394-1  Flapperette                     EBW rejected
11395-1-2  Hot Piano                      -
88007-1  Flapperette                     EBR 804
88008-1  Hot Piano                        -
```

　　　　　　　　　　　　　　　　London, July 6, 1929.

```
12368-2  Pianotes                        EBW 4932
12369-2  Crooked Notes                    -
```

Pseudonym on Conqueror 7459 (I'M FOLLOWING YOU) for Adrian Schubert and his Orchestra
q.v.

## JOE PARADISE AND HIS MUSIC

Laurie Bookin-vn/Phil Green-p-cel/Albert Harris-Freddy Watson-George Elliott-g/Don
Stuteley-sb/Marjorie Stedeford-v.        London, September 24, 1935.

CE-7165-1  Limehouse Blues                     Par F-288, A-6294, Od OF-5027,
                                               Grand 708
CE-7166-1  Solitude - vMS                      As above, except Grand 708
CE-7167-1  Lady Be Good                        Par F-327, A-6327, Od OF-5059
CE-7168-1  Sweet Sue - Just You                  -        -        -

    Joe Young-g replaces Watson; George Senior-sb replaces Stuteley.
                                London, November 29, 1935.

CE-7319-1  Twelfth Street Rag                  Par F-356,A-6362,0d OF-5079,025695
CE-7320-2  Love's Serenade - vMS                 -        -       -       -
CE-7321-1  Moonglow - vMS                      Par F-406,A-6420,0d OF-5120,025755
CE-7322-1  Whispering                            -        -       -       -

Laurie Bookin-Martin Smuts-as-vn/Albert Pike-ts-vl/Phil Green-harpsichord/Joe Young-g
/George Senior-sb/Marjorie Stedeford-Stan Patchett-v.
                                London, December 5, 1935.

CE-7341-1  Memories Of You - vMS               Par F-380, Od OF-5093
CE-7342-1  West End Blues                      Par F-427, A-6434, Od OF-5139
CE-7343-1  Body And Soul - vMS                   -        -        -
CE-7344-1  Squareface - vSP                    Par F-380, Od OF-5093

                                London, February 10, 1936.

CE-7458-1  Stars In The Making - Part 1        Par rejected
CE-7459-1  Stars In The Making - Part 2          -

                                London, July 16, 1936.

CE-7733-1  I Ain't Got Nobody                  Par F-580, Od OF-5279
CE-7734-1  I've Got The World On A String      Par F-533, A-6574, Od OF-5235,
                                               Dec 1066
CE-7735-1  Georgia On My Mind - vMS            Par F-580, Od OF-5279
CE-7736-1  Mood Indigo                         Par F-533, A-6574, Od OF-5235,
                                               Dec 1066, Grand 708
    NOTE:- Grand 708 as HOLLYWOOD SERENADERS.

## THE  PARAMOUNTEERS

Pseudonym on Special Records (Publix, etc.) 1065-P for the California Ramblers, q.v.,
and on 2002-P for The Georgians, q.v., and other sides of no jazz interest.

## PARAMOUNT  PICKERS

Johnny Dodds-cl/? Jimmy Blythe or Tiny Parham-p/? Junie Cobb-g-v.
                                Chicago, c. February, 1929.

21184-1  Steal Away                           Pm 12779, Bwy 5069, Her 93015,
                                              Cen 3010, Amp R-105, JD 002
21185-1-2  Salty Dog                          Pm 12779, Bwy 5069, Her 93015
    NOTE:- Broadway 5069 as BROADWAY PICKERS; Herwin 93015 as HERWIN HOT SHOTS; Century
    3010 as JOHNNY DODDS.

## PARAMOUNT  RHYTHM BOYS

Pseudonym on Edison Bell Winner for various American and British bands, of which the
following is listed in this book :-

5319  When I Take My Sugar To Tea (Glen Lyte's Orchestra)

(SING, YOU SINNERS, EBW 5135, also credited thus, is of moderate interest also).

ANTHONY PARENTI AND HIS FAMOUS MELODY BOYS : Tony Parenti-cl-as-bar dir. Henry Knecht
    c/Charles Hartman-tb/Tony Papalia-ts/Vic Lubowski-p/Mike Holloway-bj/Mario Finazzo-
    bb/George Triay-d.                          New Orleans, January 22, 1925.

    8895-A  That's A Plenty                     OK 40308, Od FF-1070
    8896-A  Cabaret Echoes                        -        Par R-3262


    Albert Brunies-c added.                     New Orleans, March 23, 1925.

    32115-5  Dizzy Lizzy                             Vic 19697
    32116-2  French Market Blues                     -


                                                New Orleans, March 24, 1925.

    32117-3  La Vida Medley (Intro. Ida/Gypsy Love  Vic 19698
             Song)
    32118-3  Be Yourself                             -
    32119-1  12th Street Blues                       Vic 19647
    32120-3  Creole Blues                            -

PARENTI'S LIBERTY SYNCOPATORS (LA VEEDA DANCE ORCHESTRA on Columbia 1549-D) : As for
    the Victor sessions, but Leon Prima-c replaces Brunies.
                                                New Orleans, September 23, 1925.

    140987-1  Strut Yo' Stuff                        Col 1549-D
    140988-1  Midnight Papa                          Col 545-D
    140989-2  I Need Some Lovin'                     Col 1549-D
    140990-1  Cabaret Echoes                         Col 545-D

    2nd as added ?                              New Orleans, April 12, 1926.

    142000-2  Up Jumped The Devil                    Col 836-D
    142001-1-2  Cafe Capers                          Rejected
    142002-1-2  Up And At 'Em                        -
    142003-1  Weary Blues                            Col 1264-D
    142004-1-2  New Crazy Blues                      Col 836-D
    142005-1  African Echoes                         Col 1264-D

TONY PARENTI'S NEW ORLEANIANS : John Hyman (Johnny Wiggs)-c/Charles Hartman-tb/Tony
    Parenti-cl-as/Buzzy Williams-p/Jack Brian-g-v/Monk Hazel-d-v.
                                                New Orleans, April 27, 1928.

    146221-2  In The Dungeon - vMH                   Col 1548-D
    146222-1  When You And I Were Pals - vJB


    Leon Prima-c replaces Hyman; Hal Jordy-as-bar/sb added.
                                                New Orleans, December, 1928.

    NO-753-A  Gumbo                                  Br 4184
    NO-754-A  You Made Me Like It, Baby              -

Clarinet solos, acc. by Vic Breidis-p.   New York, May 10, 1929.

    8743-1-2-3  St. Louis Blues                      ARC rejected
    8744-1-2-3  Old Man Rhythm                       -


                                                New York, June 28, 1929.

    8743-4-5  St. Louis Blues                        Rejected
    8744-5  Old Man Rhythm                           Ban 0580, Cam 0180, Je 5836,
                                                     Or 1836, Ro 1199


                              TINY  PARHAM

PARHAM'S BLACK PATTI BAND : Tiny Parham-p dir. ? Doc Cheatham-? Homer Hobson-t/tb/
    2as/ss-ts/? vn/oj/bb/d/Bob Butler-v.   St. Paul, c. June 28, 1927.

    12901-A  Um-Ta-Da-Da-Da - vBB&ch                BP 8038

TINY PARHAM AND HIS "FORTY" FIVE : Claude Alexander or Ray Hobson-c/Kid Ory-tb/
    Charles Johnson-cl-as/Tiny Parham-p/Charlie Jackson-bj-v.
                                    Chicago, December, 1927.

20206-4  Jim Jackson's Kansas City Blues - vCJ    Pm 12586, Cen 3005
20207-3  A Little Bit Closer                         -          -

TINY PARHAM AND HIS MUSICIANS : Tiny Parham-p-cel dir. Punch Miller-c/Charles Lawson-
    tb/Charles Johnson-cl-as/Charlie Jackson-bj/Quinn Wilson-bb/Ernie Marrero-d-wb.
                                    Chicago, July 2, 1928.

46037-1  The Head Hunter's Dream (An African      X LVA-3039, Vic RA-5313 (LPs),
           Fantasy)                               HMV 7EG-8210 (EP)
46037-2  The Head Hunter's Dream (An African      Vic 21553
           Fantasy)
46038-1  Stuttering Blues                         Vic V-38009, BB B-8130, WS 101
46038-2  Stuttering Blues                         X LVA-3039, Vic RA-5313 (LPs),
                                                  HMV 7EG-8210 (EP)
46039-1  Clarice                                  Vic 21659
46040-1  Snake Eyes                               -
46040-2  Snake Eyes                               X LVA-3039, Vic RA-5313 (LPs),
                                                  HMV 7EG-8210 (EP)
46041-2  Cuckoo Blues                             Vic 21553
46042-1  Jogo Rhythm                              Vic V-38009, BB B-8130, WS 101
46042-2  Jogo Rhythm                              X LVA-3039, Vic RA-5313 (LPs),
                                                  HMV 7EG-8210 (EP)

Ray Hobson-c replaces Miller; Elliott Washington-vn added; Mike McKendrick-bj replaces Jackson.                     Chicago, February 1, 1929.

48844-2  Voodoo                                   Vic V-38054
48845-1  Skag-a-Lag                               X LVA-3039, Vic RA-5313 (LPs)
48845-2  Skag-a-Lag                               Vic V-38054
48846-1  Stompin' On Down                         X LVA-3039, Vic RA-5313 (LPs)
48846-2  Stompin' On Down                         Vic V-38060
48847-1  Blue Melody Blues                        JA 21 (LP)
48847-2  Blue Melody Blues                        Vic V-38047

                                    Chicago, February 2, 1929.

48848-2  Tiny's Stomp (Oriental Blues)            Vic V-38060
48849-1  Subway Sobs                              Vic V-38041, BB B-6031
48850-2  That Kind Of Love                        Vic V-38047
48851-2  Blue Island Blues                        Vic V-38041, BB B- 005, B-10044,
                                                  Sr S-3414

                                    Chicago, July 22, 1929.

55460-2  Jungle Crawl                             Vic V-38082, BB B-5146, Sr S-3227,
                                                  Creole 13
55461-2  Lucky "3-6-9"                            Vic V-38082, Creole 13
55462-2  Echo Blues                               Vic V-38076
55463-1  Washboard Wiggles                        -          BB B-6570, Jay 11

Punch Miller-c replaces Hobson; unknown cl-as-ts replaces Johnson.
                                    Chicago, October 25, 1929.

57333-2  Pigs' Feet And Slaw                      Vic 23410
57334-2  Bombay                                   Vic 23426
57335-2  Fat Man Blues                            Vic V-38126, 1AC-0126, Jay 11
57336-3  Golden Lily                              Vic 23426
57337-3  Steel String Blues                       Vic 23410
57338-2  Sud Buster's Dream                       Vic 22778, HMV B-6150, K-6568,
                                                  Creole 18
                                    Chicago, December 3, 1929.

57216-1  Dixieland Doin's                         Vic V-38111, 1AC-0126, Creole 14
57217-2  Cathedral Blues                          -                      -
57218-1-2  Cheerful Blues                         Rejected
57219-2  Black Cat Moan                           Vic V-38126, BB B-5146, B-6570,
                                                  Sr S-3227

TINY PARHAM AND HIS MUSICIANS : Tiny Parham-p dir. ? Ray Hobson-c/Ike Covington-tb/
   Charles Johnson-cl-as/same cl-as-ts as on October 25 and December 3, 1929/Mike
   McKendrick-bj-g (and w, as MAURICE HENDRICKS ?)/Milt Hinton-bb/Ernie Marrero-d/
   Tommy Brookins-v.                        Chicago, November 4, 1930.

| | | |
|---|---|---|
| 62931-2 | Doin' The Jug-Jug | Vic 23027, HMV B-4839 |
| 62932-1 | Rock Bottom | Vic 22842 |
| 62933-1 | Down Yonder | Pirate MPC-505 (LP) |
| 62934-1 | Blue Moon Blues | Vic 23027 |
| 62935-1 | Squeeze Me | Pirate MPC-521 (LP) |
| 62936-1 | Back To The Jungle | Pirate MPC-505 (LP) |
| 62937-1 | Nervous Tension | JA 21 (LP) |
| 62937-2 | Nervous Tension | Vic 23386 |
| 62938-2 | Memphis Mamie | - |

  NOTE:- A limited edition of Victor 23386, both sides dubbed, was made available
  in 1964.

                                        Chicago, November 11, 1930.

| | | |
|---|---|---|
| 62951-1 | Now That I've Found You - wMH | Vic 22778 |
| 62952-2 | My Dreams - vTB | Vic 23432 |
| 62953-2 | After All I've Done For You - vTB | - |

TINY PARHAM'S FOUR ACES : Darnell Howard-cl-as/Tiny Parham-p-elo/John Henley-g/Bob
   Slaughter-d/Sam Theard-v.               Chicago, June 4, 1940.

| | | |
|---|---|---|
| 93027-A | Frogtown Blues - vST | Dec 7780 |
| 93028-A | Moving Day | Dec 7801 |
| 93029-A | Spo-De-O-Dee - vST | Dec 7780 |

See also Johnny Dodds.

## PARK CENTRAL ORCHESTRA

See Bert Lown.

## DON PARKER

The following titles from the considerable number recorded by Don Parker's various
  bands in New York and London between 1922 and 1926 are known to be of some jazz
  interest.

PARKER'S WESTERN MELODY BOYS : Don Parker-ss-as dir. Vic d'Ippolito-t/George Crozier-
   tb/as/2p/bj/bb/d.                        New York, c. March 8, 1923.

| | | |
|---|---|---|
| 70078 | Snakes Hips | PA 020934, 10487, P 1713, |

  NOTE:- Ideal-Scala 7017 as ASTORIA ORCHESTRA.    Per 14116, I-S 7017

                                        New York, c. June 21, 1923.

| | | |
|---|---|---|
| 70239 | Wild Papa | PA 021031, Per 14155 |

DON PARKER AND HIS ORCHESTRA : Probably as above.
                                        New York, c. October 3, 1923.

| | | |
|---|---|---|
| 70355 | Learn To Do The Strut | PA 36002, Per 14183 |

  NOTE:- Pathe Actuelle 036002 as DON PARKER AND HIS STRAND ROOF ORCHESTRA.

DON PARKER AND HIS BAND AT THE PICCADILLY HOTEL, LONDON : Don Parker-ss-as dir. Stan
   Goslin-t/Jock Fleming-tb/Eddie Lee-as/Henry Timms-ts/Norman Cole-vn/p/bj/bb/d.
                                        London, c. May, 1926.

| | |
|---|---|
| Static Strut | Voc X-9810 |

Don Barrigo-as-ts added.                 London, c. September, 1926.

| | |
|---|---|
| Deep Henderson | Voc X-9880 |

PARKER'S WESTERN MELODY BOYS was also a pseudonym on Pathe Actuelle 10410 (BEES
  KNEES) for the California Ramblers, q.v.

Pseudonym on OKeh for Ben Selvin and his Orchestra, q.v.

## PARK INN GOOD TIMERS

Pseudonym on Duophone D-4018 for "Kenn" Sisson and his Orchestra, q.v.

## PARLOPHONE MELODIANS

Pseudonym on Parlophone E-5854 (AIN'T THAT A GRAND AND GLORIOUS FEELING ?) for the
  Goofus Five, q.v.

## PARLOPHONE SYNCOPATORS

Pseudonym on Parlophone E-4578 (MISS ANNABELLE LEE) for Justin Ring and his OKeh
  Orchestra, q.v., and as a rule for the OKeh Syncopators, q.v.

## HARRY PARRY'S RADIO RHYTHM CLUB SEXTET

Although this group began its career in 1941, the music it played and the dates of
  the majority of its records place it in Jorgen Grunnet Jepsen's book JAZZ RECORDS,
  1942-1962, q.v.

## PASTERNACKI'S ORCHESTRA

Pseudonym on Mitchell 11359 for the Original Memphis Five, q.v.

## PATRICK ET SON ORCHESTRE

Guy Paquinet-tb dir. Gaston Lapeyronnie-Alphonse Cox-Noel Chiboust-t/Pierre Deck-
  Rene Weiss-tb/Andre Ekyan-Andy Foster-Charles Lisee-as/Alix Combelle-ts/Jean
  Chabaud-p/Django Reinhardt-g/Louis Pecqueux-sb/Maurice Chaillou-d-v/Roger Chomer-
  vib/v trio.                           Paris, November, 1934.

| | | |
|---|---|---|
| CPT-1701-1 | Black Panther Stomp | PA PA-467 |
| CPT-1702-1 | I Saw Stars - vMC | PA PA-468 |
| CPT-1703-1 | Okay, Toots - v3 | PA PA-466 |
| CPT-1704-1 | When My Ship Comes In - vMC | - |
| CPT-1705-1 | My Carolina Hideaway | PA PA-467 |
| | From Now On | PA PA-468 |

Alex Renard-t replaces Cox; Mairice Cizeron-as replaces Lisee; Joseph Reinhardt-g
  added; Hildegarde-v.                  Paris, March 4, 1935.

| | | | |
|---|---|---|---|
| CPT-1841- | Hands Across The Table | PA PA-530 | |
| CPT-1842- | We Were So Young | - | Od 194323 |
| CPT-1843-1 | From You | PA PA-537 | |
| CPT-1844- | Darling, je vous aime beaucoup - vH | PA PA-538 | |

Stephane Grappelly-Michel Warlop-Sylvio Schmidt-vn added.
                                        Paris, March 8, 1935.

| | | |
|---|---|---|
| CPT-1857-1 | Miss Otis Regrets (She's Unable To Lunch Today) | PA PA-537 |
| CPT-1858- | Waltzing With A Dream - vH | PA PA-538 |

Max Blanc-Charles Lisee-as replace Foster; Coco Kiehn-as-ts replaces Combelle; Guy
  Pacquinet-v; all vn omitted.          Paris, June 17, 1935.

| | | |
|---|---|---|
| CPT-2142- | You And The Night And The Music - vMC | PA PA-667 |
| CPT-2143-1 | I Get A Kick Out Of You - vMC | PA PA-669 |
| CPT-2144-1 | Seagulls | PA PA-668 |
| CPT-2145-1 | Anything Goes | PA PA-669 |
| CPT-2146- | Easter Parade - vGP | PA PA-667 |
| CPT-2147-1 | I'm Gonna Wash My Hands Of You - vGP | PA PA-668 |

The following sides by this white vaudeville artist have jazz-inflected accompaniments; see also The Virginians.

Vocal, acc. by t/tb/cl/as/p/bj/d.          New York, June, 1923.

11642    Oh, Sister ! Ain't That Hot ?          Voc 14623, Aco G-15289
NOTE:- Aco G-15289 as SADIE PETERS.

Acc. by the Ambassadors : Willie Creager-d dir. Jack Axelrod-Manny Klein-t/Harry
de Paola-tb/Sammy Feinsmith-Maurice Pierce-cl-as/Ted Green-ts/Joe Meresco-p/John
Cali-bj/Alex Goldfarb-bb.                    New York, August, 1924.

13513    Doodle Doo Doo                          Voc 14866

13538    No-One Knows What It's All About        Voc 14886, X-9518

                                          New York, September, 1924.

13674    That's Georgia                          Voc 14886, X-9518

## BOB PATTERSON AND HIS  VENETIAN GARDEN ORCHESTRA

Instrumentation and personnel unknown.    New York, July 26, 1926.

142472-1-2-3  I'm Leaving You                  Col rejected
142473-1-2-3  Minor Gaff                        -

## LILA PATTERSON

Pseudonym on Broadway for Ma Rainey, q.v.

## PAUL'S NOVELTY ORCHESTRA

Pseudonym on Australian Lyric 3370 for Lawrence Welk and his Orchestra, q.v.

## PHIL PAVEY

Vocal, acc. by p (probably Spencer Williams, composer of all four titles) and bj*
(probably his own).                        New York, February 15, 1929.

401613-A  Arizona Blues                        OK 45355
401614-A  Prairie Blues                        OK 45308, Par E-6207
401615-A  Utah Mormon Blues                    OK 45355
401616-A *Broncho Bustin' Blues                OK 45308, Par E-6207

## PAVILION ORCHESTRA

Pseudonym on Scala for the following items listed in this book :-

677  Sittin' In A Corner (The Broadway Syncopators)
731  Both sides by the Ambassadors
763  I Love My Baby (Bailey's Lucky Seven)
810  Don't Take That Black Bottom Away (Fred Rich and his Times Square Orchestra)

## PAVILION PLAYERS

Pseudonym for the following items listed in this book :-

Edison Bell Velvet Face 1054  Both sides by Bailey's Lucky Seven
Edison Bell Winner 3796  Nobody Lied (Bailey's Lucky Seven)
                   3797  Both sides by Bailey's Lucky Seven
                   3811  Sweet Indiana Home (Bailey's Lucky Seven)
                   3862/Portland 9003  Both sides by Bailey's Lucky Seven
                   3864/Westport 2070  'Way Down Yonder In New Orleans (Bailey's
                   3977  Linger Awhile (Bailey's Lucky Seven)          )Lucky Seven)
                   3977  Somebody's Wrong (Porter's Blue Devils)
                   3996  Both sides by Bailey's Lucky Seven
                   4174  I Want To Be Happy (The Vagabonds)
                   4198  Oh ! Mabel (Bailey's Lucky Seven)

This dance orchestra made sixteen sides for Gennett between 1923 and 1928, of which
   the following are known or believed to be of interest as jazz.

C/tb/Ray Putnam-cl-as/as/ts/p/bj/bb/d; one Schloemer may have been a member of the
   band, but it is not known what instrument he and Art Payne himself played.
                                          Richmond, Ind., December 15, 1924.

  12101-A  Oh Maud                            Gnt 5631, Ch 15036
  12102-B  You Can't Make A Woman Change Her Mind     -      Ch 15037
  NOTE:- Champion 15036 and 15037 as SOUTH SHORE MELODY BOYS.

Charles Lucik-t/tb/Dick Francis-cl-as/as/ts/p/bj/bb/Doug Williamson-d-v.
                                          Richmond, Ind., November 13, 1927.

  GEX-937, -A  The Lighthouse Blues               Gnt rejected
  GEX-938, -A  Ain't No Use Tryin' To High-Tone Me - vDW -

                                          Richmond, Ind., October 12, 1928.

  14329      Igloo Stomp                         Gnt 6644
  14330      Take Your Tomorrow                     -

                                          Richmond, Ind., December 3, 1928.

  14500-A  Blue Night - vDW                    Gnt 6694, Ch 15639, Spt 9334
  14501-A  Jo-Anne - vDW                          -      Ch 15638    -
  NOTE:- Champion 15638 and 15639 as SOUTH SHORE MELODY BOYS; Supertone 9334 as ART
  KAHN AND HIS ORCHESTRA. This session is dated December 2, 1928 in THE AMERICAN
  DANCE BAND DISCOGRAPHY, due to mis-reading the handwriting in the Gennett files.

## GUILFORD (PEACHTREE) PAYNE

Vocal, acc. by Eddie Heywood-p-v.      Chicago, c. October 25, 1923.

  8482-A  You Don't Worry My Mind              OK 8103
  8483-A  Peachtree Man Blues - vEH               -

## JACK PAYNE

The following records from among the hundreds recorded by the late Jack Payne are
   known to be of great interest as first-class big-band jazz of the period. Others
   may merit inclusion also.

JACK PAYNE AND HIS B.B.C. DANCE ORCHESTRA : Jack Payne-v dir. Frank Wilson-Harry
   Mills-t/Jesse Fuller-tb-bsx/Dave Roberts-cl-as-bar/Bob Easson-Bill Taylor-cl-ts-vn
   /Bob Busby-p-v/George Rives-bj/Julius Nussbaum-bb/Bob Manning-d-v/Ray Noble-a.
                                          London, October 2, 1928.

  WA-7919-2  Out Of The Dawn - vJP              Col 5074
  WA-7922-2  Sweet Sue - vJP-BB-BM                 -

                                          London, October 19, 1928.

  WA-8011-1  Hot And Heavy                      Col 5205
  WA-8012-1  Hot Bricks                            -
  WA-8013-1  Down By The Old Front Gate - vJP-BB-BM  Col 5118

                                          London, December 13, 1928.

  WA-8217-2  My Little Fella And Me - vJP       Col 5247
  WA-8218-1  Nobody's Fault But Your Own - vJP     -

                                          London, April 16, 1929.

  WA-8861-1  Haven't I ? - vJP-BB-BM            Col 5451
  WA-8874-1  Look In Her Eyes - vJP                -

JACK PAYNE AND HIS B.B.C. DANCE ORCHESTRA : Jack Payne-v dir. Frank Wilson-Harry
Mills-t/Jesse Fuller-tb-bsx/Dave Roberts-cl-as-bar/Frank Johnston-cl-as-o/Bob
Easson-Bill Taylor-cl-ts-vn/Herbert Powell-vn-vl/Bill Clark-Les Thomas-vn/Bob
Busby-p-v/George Rives-bj/Julius Nussbaum-bb/Bob Manning-d-v.
                                        London, June 3, 1929.

WA-9081-2  Do Something - vJP-BB-BM              Col 5417
WA-9083-2  I Wanna Go Places And Do Things       Col 5420

   Tommy Smith-t added.                 London, March 1, 1930.

WA-10020-3  Happy Days Are Here Again - vJP-BB   Col CB-9, DO-25
WA-10066-4  She's My Slip Of A Girl              Col CB-17
WA-10130-2  The Man From The South - vJP         Col CB-28
WA-10131-1  Blondy - vJP                          -

                                        London, June 18, 1930.

WA-10481-2  Here Comes Emily Brown - vJP         Col CB-98, Re G-20788
   NOTE:- Regal G-20788 as STELLAR DANCE BAND.

                                        London, August 25, 1930.

WA-10604-2  Under The Sweetheart Tree - vJP      Col CB-131

   Val Rosing-v.                        London, October 15, 1930.

WA-10775-1  If I Could Be With You One Hour Tonight Col CB-155
                - vVR

                                        London, February 10, 1931.

CA-11190-2  Choo Choo                            Col CB-228, DO-357

   Jack Payne-v dir. Jack Jackson-Tommy Smith-t/Jesse Fuller-Ben Oakley-tb/Dave
   Roberts-cl-ss-as-bar/Frank Johnston-clas-o/Bill Taylor-Bob Easson-cl-ts-vn/Eric
   Siday-vn/Herbert Powell-vl/Bob Busby-p-v/Billy Scott-Coomber-g-v/Bert Groves-bb-
   sb/Bob Manning-d-x-vib-v.            London, March 11, 1931.

CA-11325-2  Walking In The Sun - vBSC            Col CB-248

   Tommy Anderson-t replaces Smith.     London, August 7, 1931.

CA-11855-1  Ain't That The Way It Goes ? - vBSC  Col CB-327

                                        London, August 28, 1931.

CA-11912-2  I Like A Little Girl Like That - vJP   Col CB-370, Re G-21252
   NOTE:- Regal G-21252 as THE RHYTHMIC TROUBADOURS.

JACK PAYNE AND HIS BAND : As above, plus E. O. Pogson-cl-as-bar-f-o; Roberts plays
   ts, as Taylor leaves; Reg Leopold-vn / Billy Thorburn-2nd p/Dick Escott-sb added;
   Steve Gauna-bj-g replaces Scott-Coomber, now only v; Charlie Asplin-bb replaces
   Groves.                              London, c. March 10, 1932.

6014-1  Hot Coffee - vBSC                        Imp 2677, Kr 4060, 21090,
                                                 Summit 225

                                        London, c. March 11, 1932.

6029-1  Now's The Time To Fall In Love-vJP-BB-BM  Imp 2664, Summit 190

                                        London, October, 1932.

6252-3  How'm I Doin' (Hey-Hey) - vJP-BB-BM       Imp 2783, Kr 4084

JACK PAYNE AND HIS BAND : Jack Payne-v dir. Bert Bullimore-John Robertson-Sidney
Fearn-t/Jesse Fuller-Jack Jones-tb/Stan Osborne-as-pac/Sid Millward-cl-as-o/Phil
Trix-Dave Stephenson-as/Con Lamprecht-ts-a/Herbert Powell-Sid Williams-Bob Easson-
Jimmy Dunlop-vn/Billy Thorburn-p/Curt Smith-g/Charlie Asplin-bb/Bert Groves-sb/
Jack Simpson-d-x.                            London, late February, 1934.

F-696-2  Lazy Rhythm                         Rex 8179, 9339, Kr 182, 21231

                               London, March, 1934.

F-731-2  Tiger Rag - aCL                     Rex 8179, 9339, Kr 182, 21231

Garland Wilson-p featured, next title.  London, April, 1935.

F-1281-2  My Dance - vBSC                    Rex 8483, Kr 4165

Dave Shand-cl-as-bar-o replaces Millward and Trix; Bert Witham-p replaces Thorburn
Ronnie Genarder-bj-g replaces Smith; Asplin omitted; Joe Wyndham-d replaces Simpson.                                         London, September, 1936.

F-1979-1  Everybody Dance - vBSC             Rex 8874, Kr 21501, Imp 6023

## EDDIE PEABODY

This famous American vaudeville artist recorded on many labels in New York and
London during a career lasting nearly half a century. The following are of some
interest as jazz.

Violin and banjo solos, acc. by cl/p.    New York, October 14, 1925.

6239-2  Beale Street Blues                   Ban 1646, Dom 3617, Re 9952
6240-3  St. Louis Blues                        -         -        -

EDDIE PEABODY AND HIS BAND : Eddie Peabody-bj-vn dir. 2t/tb/2cl-as/ts/p/bb/d.
                                         New York, October 22, 1925.

6251-3  Along Came Love                      Ban 1654, Dom 3625, Re 9962

                               New York, November 12, 1925.

6294-3   Whoopee !                           Ban 1643, Dom 3615, Re 9944
6295-1-3 Clap Hands ! (Here Comes Charley !)-v  As above, plus Or 537, Apex 8434,
NOTE:-  Oriole 537 as THE TRICKY TEN; Imperial  Dom 21108, Mic 22056, Leo/St
1555 as NEW ORLEANS DANCE ORCHESTRA.            10093, Imp 1555

Violin and banjo solos, acc. by cl/p.    New York, November 21, 1925.

6303-1  Charleston Mad                       Ban 1665, Dom 3635, Re 9971
6304-2  Sweet Man                              -         -        -

Banjo solo, acc. p.                      New York, October, 1929.

4163-   St. Louis Blues                      Cam 9317, Lin 3344, Ang 3171

## LES PEABODY AND HIS MEMPHIS RAMBLERS

See the ARC-Brunswick studio bands.

## DAVID PEARSON

Vocal, acc. by   Henry Mason-c/? J. Neal Montgomery-p.
                                         Atlanta, March 21, 1929.

402397-A  Friendless Blues                   OK 8847

## WILLIAM PEARSON

Piano solo.                              Chicago, c. February 25, 1927.

12609, -A  Strange Woman's Dream             Gnt rejected

BILL PEARSON : Vocal, acc. by ? own p.      Chicago, January 8, 1929.

C-2749-   Good Stuff                                Br 7053
C-2750-   Detroit Blues                             -

## THE  PEBBLES

Baxter White-Alphonsus Egee-g-u duets, with own v*; one voice sings, the other hums,
and someone taps something occasionally.
                                            Chicago, late June, 1926.

          *Pebble Blues                            Voc 1042
          *Can't Sleep Blues                       -

                                            Chicago, June 7, 1927.

38643-1   Who's You Tellin' ?                      Vic 21429
38644-2   I Mean, It's Just Too Bad                -

                                            Chicago, June 8, 1927.

38655-2   Hot Pebble Blues                         Vic 20774
38656-2   Deep Henderson                           -

## SANTO PECORA AND  HIS BACK ROOM BOYS

Shorty Sherock-t/Santo Pecora-tb/Meyer Weinberg-cl/Stan Wrightsman-p/Frank Frederico
g/Thurman Teague-sb/Riley Scott-d-v.      Hollywood, April 22, 1937.

MH-1005-1-2  Doodle Bug                            Rejected
MH-1006-1  Magnolia Blues - vRS                    Col 36159, Par R-3050, B-71159
MH-1007-1  I Never Knew What A Gal Could Do        -          -          -
MH-1008-1-2  Never Had A Reason                    Rejected

## SIR ROBERT PEEL (BART.) AND HIS BAND

The following title is the only one by this British dance band so far reported as
being of any interest as jazz.

Sir Robert Peel dir. 2t/tb/2as/ts/vn/p/bj/bb/d/Cavan O'Connor-v.
                                            London, c. July, 1930.

S-801-1  Happy Feet - vCO'C                        Sterno 433

## ROBERT PEEPLES

Vocal, acc. by Henry Brown-p.              Grafton, Wis., c. February, 1930.

L-182-1   Wicked Devil's Blues                     Pm 12995
L-183-1   Fat Greasy Baby                          -

Acc. by ? Wesley Wallace-p.                Grafton, Wis., c. February, 1930.

L-190-1   Dying Baby Blues                         Pm 13033
L-191-2   Mama's Boy                               -

## THE PEERLESS ORCHESTRA

This was one of the names given by the Gramophone Company in London to its studio
orchestra when providing light popular and dance music on Zonophone between 1910
and 1920.  Amid the enormous output, there were recorded these excellent examples
of ragtime.

Eli Hudson dir. probably :- Charles Smith-Frank Kettlewell-Henry Godard-c/Jesse Stamp
---- Atherley- ---- Mayhew- ---- Godard-tb/Robert Mackenzie-Frank Hughes- ----
Leonard-cl/Gilbert Barton-W. E. Gordon-Walker-f-pic/Arthur Foreman-o/Edwin Hinch-
cliffe-bsn/Jean Bobbe and another-vn/Pietro Nifosi-vc/Charles "Wag" Abbey and/or
E. W. Rushforth-d-x-chimes etc. (This is a collective personnel; the usual strength
of the orchestra was 2c/2tb/cl (or 2cl)/bsn/f/o/pic/2vn/vc/bb/d.

Eli Hudson dir. 2c/2tb/cl or 2cl/bsn/f/o/pic/2vn/vc/bb/d (see page 1216).
London, July 2, 1912.

Ak-15282e  Red Pepper Rag Time (sic) (Henry Lodge) Zon 905

London, November 13, 1912.

Y-15984e   Powder Rag (Raymond Birch)              Zon 1016

  Peter Bernard-v effects.           London, December 3, 1912.

Y-16113/4e Everybody Two-Step (Wallie Herzer)       Zon 1000
Y-16115e   The Bacchanal Rag (Louis A. Hirsch)      Zon 998
Y-16116e   Tickled To Death (Charles Hunter) - vPB Zon 997
Y-16117e   Dynamite Rag (J. Russel Robinson) - vPB Zon 999
Y-16118e   The Wedding Glide (Louis A. Hirsch)      Zon 998
Y-16119e   Red Rose Rag (Percy Wenrich)             Zon 999

London, February 15, 1913.

Y-16298e   That Lovin' Rag (Bennie Adler)           Zon 1049
Y-16300e   Fiddlesticks Rag (Al. B. Correy)         -

This name was also a pseudonym on Perfect 14370 for the California Ramblers, q.v.

## PELHAM INN SOCIETY ORCHESTRA

Pseudonym on Domino 4133 and Regal 8534 for Devine's Wisconsin Roof Orchestra, q.v.

## ANDY PENDLETON

Vocal, acc. by Clarence Williams-p.     New York, June 26, 1928.

400826-C  Sweet Emmaline                 OK 8625
400827-C  Dreaming The Hours Away         -

  Acc. by Leroy Tibbs-p.           New York, February 10, 1933.

75073-1  He's A Son Of The South          Vic 23389
75074-1  Thinking Of You                  -

## TWIN-SIX GUITAR   JACK PENEWELL

Guitar solos.                    Chicago, c. November, 1924.

  674   Penewell Blues                  Auto 608
  682   Hen House Blues                  -

## ANN PENN

This pioneer broadcasting comedienne and impersonator was usually accompanied by a
  pianist on her records, but the following has a "hot" instrumental support.

Vocal, acc. by Sylvester Ahola-t/Johnny Helfer-cl-ts/? Eric Siday-vn/Carroll Gibbons
  p/g/sb.                        Hayes, Middlesex, May 14, 1929.

Bb-16491-3  A Precious Little Thing Called Love    HMV B-3086

## PENNINGTON ORCHESTRA

Pseudonym on Pennington 1384 (I CAN'T GET THE ONE I WANT) for Fletcher Henderson and
  his Orchestra, q.v.

## THE PENNSYLVANIA SYNCOPATORS

Pseudonym on Emerson for the following items listed in this book :-

10773  I Can't Get The One I Want (Fletcher Henderson and his Orchestra)
10868  My Sweet Louise (New Orleans Jazz Band)

This name was also used extensively by German Homokord for all kinds of bands, both German and American, the following being of unusual interest :-

Bob Fuller-cl/Louis Hooper-p/Elmer Snowden-bj.
                                          New York, c. June, 1926.

| 3904-1 | Dancin' The Blues | NML 1156 |
| 3905-1 | Desert Blues | NML 1155, Hom 4-2204 |

NOTE:- NML 1155 and 1156 as NATIONAL MUSIC LOVERS' SYNCOPATORS.

## ALBERTA PERKINS

Vocal duets with Billy Higgins (as JAZZ CASPER on all except Ajax 17125), acc. by Bubber Miley-c/Louis Hooper-p/Elmer Snowden-bj/? Joe Davis-chimes*.
                                          New York, c. October 30, 1924.

| 5695-1-2-3 | *Who Calls You Sweet Mama Now ? | Ban 1467, Dom 438, Hg 983, Re 9764 |
| 5696-1-2 | Sweet Mandy | Ban 1451, Dom 424    -    Re 9749 |

NOTE:- Banner 1451 and 1467 as LOUELLA JONES; Domino 424 and 436 as LUCILLE JOHN-SON; Regal 9749 as BILLY HIGGINS-LOUELLA JONES; 9764 as NETTIE POTTER only.

Acc. by the Choo Choo Jazzers : Jake Frazier-tb or Bob Fuller-cl/Elmer Snowden-bj (all as shown)/? Louis Hooper-p.        New York, c. March, 1925.

| 31820 | Levee Blues - tb/p | Ajax 17125 |
| 31823 | I'm Tired Of Begging You To Treat Me Right    - |
|       | - cl/p/bj |

## DOLLY PERKINS

Vocal, acc. by probably Porter Grainger or Bob Ricketts-p or harmonium/? Lincoln Conaway-g.                          New York, c. April, 1924.

| 42644-2 | My Doggone Lazy Man - p | Em 10761 |
| 42645-1 | 'Tain't A Doggone Thing But The Blues    - |
|         | - harmonium |

## GERTRUDE PERKINS

Vocal, acc. by Willie Tyson-p/g/Octave Gaspard-bb.
                                          Dallas, December 6, 1927.

| 145340-1 | No Easy Rider Blues | Col 14313-D |
| 145341-2 | Gold Daddy Blues    - |

## RED PERKINS AND HIS DIXIE RAMBLERS

Frank S. "Red" Perkins-t-v dir.   Joe Drake-t-as-a/Andre Oglesby-tb/Jesse Simmons-tb-a/Howard Fields-p/Charles Watkins-bj-g/Eugene Friels-t-bb/Harry Rooks-d/v trio.
                                          Richmond, Ind., May 5, 1931.

| 17727-A | Hard Times Stomp | Ch 16288, 40044, Spr 2693 |
| 17728-A | My Baby Knows How - vFSP | Ch 16661, Var 5092 |

NOTE:- Varsity 5092 as RED'S DIXIE RAMBLERS.

                                          Richmond, Ind., May 6, 1931.

| 17729-A | Old Man Blues - v3 | Ch 16439, 40044, Spr 2693 |
| 17730 | Minor Blues | Ch 16288 |

NOTE:- Superior 2693 as SAM BROWNE AND HIS ORCHESTRA.  Matrix 17730 was dubbed on matrix 17738 as a test, but the result was not used.

## SLIM PERKINS

See Bob Fuller.

Vocal, acc. by the Quintette of the Hot Club of France : Stephane Grappelly-vn/
Django Reinhardt Joseph Reinhardt-g/Sigismund Beck-sb.
Paris, January 5, 1938.

CL-6502-1   Les salades de l'Oncle François        Col DF-2344
CL-6503-1   Ric et Pussy                    ,         -

## HARRY PERRITT AND HIS ORCHESTRA

The late Harry Perritt was a well-known theatre orchestra conductor during the years
between the wars, and his recording activities were generally confined to directing the accompaniments for members of the casts for whom he conducted in the
theatre. The following pair of sides, however, show a closer affinity to jazz of
the early swing era, and are dedicated to Jack Buchanan, with whom Harry Perritt
was working at the time, and who arranged the recording.

Harry Perritt dir. Tommy Band and another-t/tb/Leslie Norman-as/as/ts/Gil Port-bsx/
Claude Ivy-p/Len Fillis-g/sb/Len Hunt-d, and possibly others.
London, December 18, 1934.

CA-14829-1   J. B. Blues                     Col FB-1076, DW-4297
CA-14830-1   Buchanan Stomp                       -          -        RZ G-22794

## PERRY AND HIS STOMP BAND

Pseudonym on Black Patti for Henry Johnson's Boys, q.v.

## PERRY'S HOT DOGS

? Tommy Gott-t/Miff Mole-tb/Alfie Evans or Ross Gorman-cl-as-bar/Arthur Schutt-p/bj/
? David Grupp-d/Arthur Fields (as HARRY CRANE on Oriole)-v.
New York, September 25, 1925.

6157-2-3   Show Me The Way To Go Home - vAF      Ban 1615, Dom 3589, 21087, Or 494
                                                Re 9917, Apex 8408, Mic 22032,
                                                Paling's 19008, St 10064
6199-1-3   Has Been Blues                       Ban 1641, Dom 3614, Or 530,
                                                Re 9945
6200-1   There Ain't No Flies On Auntie - vAF   Ban 1615, Dom 3589, Or 499,
                                                Re 9917
NOTE:- Oriole 494, 499 and 530 as DIXIE JAZZ BAND; Apex 8408 as PERRY'S RHYTHM
KINGS.
? Donald Lindley-t replaces Gott.       New York, October 15, 1925.

6228-1-2-3   Tweedle-Dee, Tweedle-Doo - vAF     Ban 1617, Dom 3585, Re 9919,
                                                Apex 8426, St 10089
6241-2   Hot Aire                               Or 517
NOTE:- Apex 8426 and Starr 10089 as PERRY'S RHYTHM KINGS.

Earl Oliver-t/Miff Mole-tb/Alfie Evans or Ross Gorman-cl-as-bar/Arthur Schutt-p/bj/
Arthur Fields-v.                        New York, November 10, 1925.

6284-2-3   Steppin' Fool - vAF                  Ban 1656, Dom 3633, Re 9965
6285-1   I'm Gonna Hang Around My Sugar - vAF   Ban 1641, Dom 3614, Re 9945
6286-1   Charlestonette                         Apex 8419, Dom 21096, Leo/Mic
                                                22048, St 10080
NOTE:- Banner 1656 and Domino 3633 as SIX BLACK DIAMONDS; all issues from matrix
6286-1 as PERRY'S RHYTHM KINGS.

Tommy Gott-t replaces Oliver; no bj.    New York, c. January 22, 1926.

6409-1-3   Say Mister Have You Met Rosie's Sister Ban 1714, Dom 3680, Or 590,
         - vAF                                  Re 8022, Apex 8458, St 10113
6411-2-3   Flamin' Mamie (Flamin' Manie*) - vAF  Ban 1692, Dom 3664, Re 8006,
                                                Apex 8450, Leo/St 10112*
NOTE:- Oriole 590 as DIXIE JAZZ BAND; Regal 8006 and 8022 as SIX BLACK DIAMONDS;
all Canadian issues as PERRY'S RHYTHM KINGS. Matrix 6410 is untraced.

This name was also used on Regal 8007 (GIVE ME JUST A LITTLE BIT OF YOUR LOVE, by Nathan Glantz and his Orchestra), but it is of very little interest as jazz. The following are all labelled DIXIE JAZZ BAND, but it is probable they are by a band similar to that listed on page 1219.

New York, c. May, 1926.

| | | |
|---|---|---|
| On The Puppy's Tail | Or 605 | |
| I'm Gonna Tear Your Playhouse Down | Or 619 | |
| Junk Bucket Blues | Or 625 | |

## KATHRYN PERRY

Vocal, acc. by Earl Hines-p.                    Chicago, July 27, 1926.

142502-1-2  Mandy                                    Col rejected
142503-1-2  Sadie Green (The Vamp Of New Orleans)    –

## PERRY'S ORCHESTRA

? Donald Lindley-t/Miff Mole-tb/Alfie Evans or Ross Gorman-cl as-bar/Arthur Schutt-p/bj/? David Grupp-d/Arthur Hall-v.    New York, December, 1925.

2366-1  That Certain Party - vAH            Pm 20431, Pur 11431, Max 1554, Us 1016
2367-1  Headin' For Louisville             As above, but Max 1559
2368-3  Smile A Little Bit                 Pm     , Max 1563
NOTE:- Maxsa 1554, 1559 and 1563 as THE BLUE KITTENS; Usiba 1016 as LONDYNSKIEJ-PICCADILLY-JAZZ.

## PERRY'S RHYTHM KINGS

The name used on Canadian Apex and associated labels for Perry's Hot Dogs, q.v.

## SAM PERRY'S RUBE BAND

Pseudonym on Supertone 9039 for Ezra Buzzington's Rustic Revelers, q.v.

## WILL PERRY AND HIS ORCHESTRA

Pseudonym on Parlophone for the following items listed in this book :-

E-6016  Both sides by Sol Wagner and his Orchestra
E-6035  Both sides by Fred Hall's Sugar Babies
E-6036  Look In The Mirror (Fred Hall's Sugar Babies)
E-6037  Both sides by Fred Hall's Sugar Babies
E-6130  How Could Anything So Good Be Bad ? (Arnold Frank and his Orchestra)
E-6148  Both sides by Sam Lanin's Famous Players
E-6150  Let's Do It (Let's Fall In Love) (Arthur Rosebery and his Orchestra)
E-6179  I'll Never Ask For More (Dorsey Brothers' Orchestra)
E-6197  Breakaway (The Travelers - see the Dorsey Brothers' Orchestra)
E-6208  Louise (Frankie Trumbauer and his Orchestra)
E-6284  'Tain't No Sin (Fred Hall's Sugar Babies)
E-6320  Stein Song (Ted Wallace and his Orchestra)
E-6340  I Love You So Much (Smith Ballew and his Orchestra)
E-6349  Can I Help It ? (Ben Selvin and his Orchestra)

## PETE AND REPEAT

? —— Fugitte and ? —— Bruns-v duets, acc. by p.
                                    Chicago, January 14, 1929.

C-2793-  Toodle-Oodle-Oo                    Br 7104
C-2794-  Hymn-Singing Bill                  Br 7055

Acc. by c/as/p/g.                    Richmond, Ind., June 20, 1930.

16775, -A  I Lost My Gal From Memphis      Gnt rejected
16776, -A-B  Worryin' Over You             –

Acc. by p/g.                            Richmond, Ind., August 6, 1930.

16890    Unknown title                              Gnt rejected

## JACK PETERS' DANCE ORCHESTRA

Pseudonym on Swedish Grand for Joe Daniels and his Hot Shots, q.v.

## MATT PETERS' ORCHESTRA

Pseudonym on Mayfair G-2195 for the ARC-Brunswick studio band, q.v.

## SADIE PETERS

Pseudonym on Aco G-15289 for Isabella Patricola, q.v.

## TEDDY PETERS

Female vocal, acc. by King Oliver-Bob Shoffner-c/? Billy Page-as/Luis Russell-p/Bud
   Scott-bj, or ? Johnny Dodds-cl/p.*        Chicago, March 11, 1926.

        Georgia Man                       Voc 1006, Jay 1
        *What A Man !                          -        -

## H.  PETERSON

Piano solo.                             London, July 9, 1929.

   717    Classic Rag (Le Chiffon Classique*)      Victory 234, 271*, Crystalate
                                                    FC-1054
   NOTE:- Victory 234 as MISS HOLSOM; 271 as HERBERT RICHARDS.

## LE  PETIT MIRSHA

Vocal, acc. by Michel Warlop et son Orchestre : 2t/2as/ts/Alec Siniavine-p/Django
   Reinhardt-g/sb/d, or Siniavine and Reinhardt only, as noted.
                                        Paris, February 5, 1935.

OLA-300-1  Maman ne vends pas la maison              Rejected
OLA-301-1  Petit homme, c'est l'heure de faire dodo     -
OLA-302-1  Vieni, Vieni - pAS/gDR                    HMV K-7464

   D omitted; one t omitted*.           Paris, February 22, 1935.

OLA-330-2  Maman ne vends pas la maison              HMV K-7464
OLA-331-1  *Petit homme, c'est l'heur' de fair' dodo HMV K-7437

## ERN PETTIFER

Clarinet solos, acc. by Jack Dent-p/Sam Gelsley-g.
                                        London, June 11, 1936.

CE-7686-1  Somebody's Wrong                          Par F-517, A-6523, Od OF-5219
CE-7687-1  Memphis Blues                                 -        -           -

## LEOLA B. PETTIGREW

See Leola B. Wilson, whose maiden name this was.

## JACK  PETTIS

JACK PETTIS AND HIS BAND : Bill Moore-c/tb/as/Jack Pettis-Cm-ts/Joe Venuti-vn/Al
   Goering-p/Eddie Lang-g/bb/? Dillon Ober-d.
                                        New York, c. December 16, 1926.

   6996-3  He's The Last Word                        Ban 1911, Dom 3882, Or 799,
                                                     Re 8225, Apex 8573
   6997-2-3  St. Louis Shuffle                       Ban 1908, Dom 3884    -   Re 8221
   6998-2  Stockholm Stomp                           Ban 1907, Dom 3883, Or 804,
   NOTE:- Oriole 799, 804 as DIXIE JAZZ BAND;        Re 8229, Sil 2860
Silvertone 2860 as GOTHAM CLUB ORCHESTRA; Apex 8573 as AL GOERING'S ORCHESTRA.

JACK PETTIS AND HIS BAND : Bill Moore-c/tb/as/Jack Pettis-Cm-ts/Joe Venuti-vn/Al
Goering-p/Eddie Lang-g/bb/? Dillon Ober-d/Scrappy Lambert-Billy Hillpot-v.
                                        New York, c. January 7, 1927.

7040-1-2  It All Depends On You - vSL-BH        Ban 1927, Bwy 1058, Dom 3897,
                                                Pm 20500, Pur 11500, Imp 1773,
                                                BM 204
7041-2  Muddy Water - vSL                       Ban 1927, Dom 3897, Or 829,
                                                Re 8243, Imp 1774
7043-2  I Gotta Get Myself Somebody To Love -   Ban 1929, Bwy 1055, Dom 3895,
        vSL-BH                                  Pm 20497, Pur 11497, Re 8244
NOTE:- Broadway 1055 and 1058, Paramount 20497 and 20500, Puritan 11497 and 11500
as THE BADGERS, vocal chorus by HARRY WOODS; Oriole 829 as BILLY JAMES AND HIS
ORCHESTRA; Imperial 1773 as BOSTON SOCIETY ORCHESTRA; Bon Marche 204 as GEORGE
ROSE SOCIETY ORCHESTRA.

2nd t added.                                    New York, c. February 11, 1927

7105-2  I'm Back In Love Again - vSL-BH         Ban 1940, Bwy 1064, Dom 3916,
                                                21258, Re 8267, Apex 8626,
                                                Leo 10258, LS 24110, Mic 22167
7106-3  That's My Hap-Hap-Happiness - vSL-BH    Ban 1942, Dom 3914, Re 8263
7107-2  Ain't She Sweet ? - vSL-BH                  - Or 846 - Imp 1742 - Savana 1599
NOTE:- Broadway 1064 as THE TUNE MAKERS; Oriole 846 as YANKEE TEN ORCHESTRA (Vocal
Chorus, HOLTON AND CROSS); Savana 1599 as SAVANA SERENADERS; Apex 8626 and Leonora
10258 as AL GOERING AND HIS ORCHESTRA. The reverse of Imperial 1742 is erroneously
credited to Jack Pettis and his Band.

Venuti omitted; Dick McDonough-bj replaces Lang.
                                        New York, December 22, 1927.

7669-3  Candied Sweets                          Ban 7004, Cq 7013, Dom 4080,
                                                Je 5192, Or 1131, Re 8463
7689-2  Once Over Lightly                       Ban 7001, Chg 561, Dom 4094,
                                                Je 5196, Or 1127, Re 8483
7690-3  Steppin' It Off                         Ban 7005, Chg 564, Dom 4094,
                                                Je 5199, Or 1123, Re 8483
NOTE:- Banner 7001, 7004 and 7005 as AL GOERING'S DANCE ORCHESTRA; Jewel 5192, 5196
and 5199, Oriole 1123, 1127 and 1131 as DIXIE JAZZ BAND.

JACK PETTIS AND HIS PETS : Bill Moore-Don Bryan-t/? Paul Weigan-tb/Don Murray-cl/Jack
Pettis-cl-Cm-ts/bsx/Al Goering-p/Clay Bryson-bj*/Eddie Lang-g/Dillon Ober-d.
                                        New York, June 20, 1928.

E-7394-  Dry Martini                            Voc 15703
E-7395-  *Hot Heels                                 -
E-7396-  Broadway Stomp                         Voc 15761

Tb omitted; Nicky Gerlach-vn added.     New York, July 3, 1928.

45672-3  Spanish Dream                          Vic 21559
45673-2  A Bag O' Blues                         Vic 21793, HMV R-14060, Zon EE-138
45674-1  Doin' The New Low Down                 Vic 21559

Bill Moore-Manny Klein-t/Tommy Dorsey-? Paul Weigan-tb/Len Kavash and another-cl-as
/Jack Pettis-Cm-ts/ts/Al Goering-p/? Carl Kress - g/Merrill Kline-bb-sb/Dillon Ober
d-x/Eugene Ramey-Erwin McGee-Irving Mills-v.
                                        New York, November 6, 1928.

48126-1  Nobody's Sweetheart - vER              Historical HLP-33 (LP)
48127-2  Freshman Hop - vEM                     Vic 21793, HMV R-14060, Zon EE-138
48128-2  Honolulu Blues - vEM                   Vic V-38026, BB B-7881
48129-2  Baby - vIM                                 -          BB B-6611
NOTE:- Victor V-38026, Bluebird B-6611 and B-7881 as NEW ORLEANS BLACKBIRDS. It is
thought that Eugene Ramey and Erwin McGee may be two of the unidentified members of
the personnel; although Irving Mills was also known as Erwin Magee on Pathe, there
seem to be two different voices on the above session, identified in the original
recording files as "McGee" and "Irving Mills."

JACK PETTIS AND HIS ORCHESTRA : Bill Moore-Donald Bryan-t/Jack Teagarden-tb/Benny
    Goodman-cl-as/Jack Pettis-Cm/Al Goering-p/Dick McDonough-bj-g/Merrill Kline-bb/
    Dillon Ober-d.                            New York, February 8, 1929.

| | | |
|---|---|---|
| 401594-B | Freshman Hop | OK 41411, Par PNY-34076, |
| | | Od 238288, 031814 |
| 401595-D | Sweetest Melody | OK 41411, Par R-673, Od A-2317, |
| | | A-286016, 238288 |
| 401596-B | Bag O' Blues | OK 41410, Par PNY-34076,Od 031814 |

    NOTE:- Parlophone PNY-34076 as JACK BINNEY AND HIS ORCHESTRA.

JACK PETTIS AND HIS PETS : Bill Moore-?.Donald Bryan-t/Glenn Miller-tb/Benny Goodman
    Tony Parenti-cl-as/Jack Pettis-Cm-ts/Matt Malneck-vn/Lennie Hayton-Al Goering-p-
    cel/Dick McDonough-g/Harry Goodman-sb/Dillon Ober-d.
                                              New York, May 9, 1929.

| | | |
|---|---|---|
| 51691-1-2-3 | Companionate Blues | Rejected |
| 51692-1-2-3 | Campus Crawl | - |
| 51693-1-2-3 | Wild And Woolly Willie | - |
| 51694-2 | Bugle Call Blues | Vic V-38105, HMV B-4893, B-6288 |

JACK PETTIS AND HIS ORCHESTRA : Shorty Sherock-t/Jack Pettis-cl-ts/Al Goering-p and
    others, included mainly for completeness.
                                              Hollywood, April 21, 1937.

| | | |
|---|---|---|
| MH-1001- | Going Harlem In Havana | Rejected |
| MH-1002- | Oh Yeah | - |
| MH-1003- | Hawaiian Heat Wave | Vri 558 |
| MH-1004- | Swing Session In Siberia | - |

## BENNY PEYTON'S JAZZ KINGS

Benny Peyton-d dir. Sidney Bechet-cl-ss/Fred Coxito-as/George Smith-vn/Pierre de
    Caillaux-p/Henry Sapiro-bj.            London, January-February, 1920.

| | |
|---|---|
| High Society | Col rejected |
| Tiger Rag | - |

## ROY PEYTON

Piano solos, acc. by Harald Jaang-d.        Oslo, summer, 1938.

| | | |
|---|---|---|
| RP-02 | Lullaby Of The Leaves | Rex EB-384 |
| RP-03 | Tiger Rag | - |
| RP-05 | St. Louis Blues | Rex EB-385 |
| RP-06 | Dinah/My Blue Heaven/Whispering | - |

## THE PHILADELPHIA MELODIANS

Pseudonym on Parlophone for the following items listed in this book :-

R-671  When You're Smiling (Louis Armstrong and his Orchestra)
R-883  Three Little Words (Duke Ellington and his Orchestra)

## PHILLIPS' LOUISVILLE JUG BAND

George "Hooks" Tilford-Cm/Philip Cann ("Cane Phillips")-f/George Williams-g-v/Carl
    "Jug" Reeves-jug-v.                      Chicago, August, 1930.

| | | |
|---|---|---|
| C-5994-A | Soldier Boy Blues | Br 7207, Voc 02784 |
| C-5995-A | That's A Lovely Thing For You | -          - |
| C-5996- | Sing, You Sinners - v | Br 7194 |
| C-5997- | Tiger Rag | - |

                                              Chicago, c. November 10, 1930.

| | | |
|---|---|---|
| C-6173-A | Smackin' The Sax | Br 7187, 01265, A-500092 |
| C-6174-A | That's Your Last | -        -        - |

EDGAR JACKSON PRESENTS SID PHILLIPS AND HIS RHYTHM : Max Goldberg-t-mel/Lew Davis-tb/
   Sid Phillips-cl-as/Billy Amstell-ts/Bert Barnes-p/George Elliott-g/Ralph Phillips-
   sb/Max Bacon-d/Jack Cooper-v.          London, February, 1936.

| | | |
|---|---|---|
| F-1728-2 | Eeny, Meeny, Miney, Mo - vJC | Rex 8742, Imp 6020, 17032, Kr 329, 21355 |
| F-1729-2 | Woe Is Me - vJC | As above except Imp 6020 |
| F-1730-2 | Sweet Sue, Just You | Rex 8863, Voc 3391, Imp 6034, Kr 386, 21503 |
| F-1731-2 | My Sweetie Went Away | As above |

SIDNEY PHILLIPS AND HIS ORCHESTRA : Max Goldberg-Paul Fenoulhet-t/Ted Heath-George
   Rowe-Eric Tann-tb/Ernie Ritte-cl-as/Dave Shand-George Evans-as-bar/Joe Crossman-ts/
   Monia Liter-p/George Elliott-g/George Gibbs-sb/Jock Jacobson-d.
                                         London, July 29, 1937.

| | | |
|---|---|---|
| OCB-341-1 | Comin' Through The Rye | Vri 654, Voc 3841 |
| OCB-342-1 | Annie Laurie | -            - |

                                         London, September 9, 1937.

| | | |
|---|---|---|
| OCB-367-1 | Amoresque | Rejected |
| OCB-368-1 | Message From Mars | Voc 3934 |
| OCB-369-2 | Swing Patrol | - |
| OCB-370-1 | Palais de Danse | Col 35312 |

   Charlie Margulis-Sam Shapiro-Angue Rattiner-t/Larry Altpeter-Jack Lacey-Chuck
   Campbell-tb/Jimmy Lytell-cl-as/Toots Mondello-Eddie Powell-as/Paul Ricci-cl-ts/
   Gil Bowers-p/Chick Reeves-g/Lou Shoobe-ab/Rollo Laylan-d.
                                         New York, January 21, 1938.

| | | |
|---|---|---|
| M-736-1-2 | Dinner And Dance | Br 8187 |
| M-737-1 | An Amazon Goes A-Wooing | - |
| M-738- | Champagne Cocktail | Br 8113 |

   Sid Phillips-cl-as-a dir. Max Goldberg-Tommy McQuater-Paul Fenoulhet-t/Ted Heath-
   Lew Davis-George Chisholm-tb/Harry Hayes-Joe Jeannette-as/Joe Crossman-Billy
   Amstell-ts/Bert Barnes-p/? George Elliott-g/George Gibbs-sb/Maurice Burman-d.
                                         London, November 15, 1938.

| | | |
|---|---|---|
| CTP-8097-1 | Blue Romance            . | Col 35312 |
| CTP-8098-1 | Voodoo | Br 8332 |
| CTP-8100-1 | Hullabaloo | - |

                                         London, December, 1938.

| | | |
|---|---|---|
| CTP-8134-1 | Music For You | Br 8384 |
| CTP-8135-1 | Plain Jane | Br 8403 |
| CTP-8137-1 | Wedding Of A Sophisticated Dutch Doll | Br 8384 |
| CTP-8138-1 | Mr. Reynard's Nightmare | Br 8403 |

   NOTE:- Mr. Harold Flakser suggests that the missing matrices CTP-8099 and CTP-8136
   are probably CORONATION SCOT and SWING BAND, both of which are believed to have
   been recorded about this date.

SID PHILLIPS TRIO : Sid Phillips-cl/Bert Barnes-p/Maurice Burman-d/The Greene Sisters
   and an unidentified male v.            London, February 2, 1940.

| | | |
|---|---|---|
| CE-10311-1 | Yodel In Swing - vGS-m | Par F-1661 |
| CE-10312-1 | Give Out - vGS | - |

                                         London, February 29, 1940.

| | | |
|---|---|---|
| CE-10332-3 | Anything Goes | Par F-1683 |
| CE-10333-1 | Plain Jane | - |
| CE-10360-1 | Music For All | Par F-1699 |
| CE-10361-1 | Who's Sorry Now ? | Par F-1731 |
| CE-10363-3 | In The Mood - vGS | Par F-1699 |

SID PHILLIPS TRIO : Sid Phillips-cl/George Shearing-p/Barry Wicks-d.
London, May 6, 1940.

| CE-10461-2 | Amoresque | Par F-1731 |
|---|---|---|
| CE-10471-1 | I Got Rhythm | Par F-1803 |
| CE-10472-2 | I Never Knew | - |

SID PHILLIPS QUINTET : Max Goldberg-t/Sid Phillips-cl/Rex Owen-ts/Bert Barnes-p/Max Abrams-d/The Greene Sisters-v trio.    London, November 27, 1940.

| DR-5122-1 | Six Lessons From Madame LaZonga - vGS | Dec F-7672 |
|---|---|---|
| DR-5123-1 | Tuxedo Junction | - |
| DR-5124-1-2 | 'Deed I Do | Rejected |
| DR-5125-2 | Strut, Miss Lizzie | Dec F-7758 |

London, December 20, 1940.

| DR-5185-1 | Pennsylvania 6-5000 | Dec F-7696 |
|---|---|---|
| DR-5186-1 | Southern Fried | - |
| DR-5187-1 | Wabash Blues | Dec F-7758 |
| DR-5188-1 | Mia Mia | Dec F-7845 |

London, January 14, 1941.

| DR-5242-1 | Yankee Doodle Blues | Dec F-8147 |
|---|---|---|
| DR-5243-1 | Hawaiian War Chant - vGS | Dec F-7723 |
| DR-5244-1 | Ridin' High - vGS | - |
| DR-5245-2 | Serenata | Dec F-7845 |

Leslie Hutchinson-t/Sid Phillips-cl/Arthur Birkby-ts/Yorke de Sousa-p/Max Abrams-d.
London, May 6, 1941.

| DR-5681-1 | Royal Garden Blues | Dec F-7972 |
|---|---|---|
| DR-5682-1 | Man About Town | - |
| DR-5683-1 | If You Hadn't Gone Away | Dec F-7888 |
| DR-5684-1 | Hot Time In The Old Town Tonight | - |

Woolf Phillips-tb replaces Birkby.    London, September 12, 1941.

| DR-6231-1 | Runnin' Wild | Dec F-8147 |
|---|---|---|
| DR-6232-1 | Copenhagen | Dec F-9446 |
| DR-6233-1-2 | You've Got To See Mama Ev'ry Night | Rejected |
| DR-6234-1-2 | Stratton Street Strut | - |

London, November 27, 1941.

| DR-6233-3 | You've Got To See Mama Ev'ry Night | Rejected |
|---|---|---|
| DR-6496-1-2 | St. Louis Blues | - |
| DR-6497-1-2 | Gin For Joan | - |
| DR-6498-1 | Darktown Strutters' Ball | Dec F-9446 |

## STAN PHILLIPS AND HIS ORCHESTRA

Pseudonym on Mayfair G-2164 (TOO MANY TEARS) for the ARC-Brunswick studio band, q.v.

## PICCADILLY DANCE BAND

Pseudonym on Piccadilly 184 (LOUISIANA) and 192 (HEAVEN FOR TWO) for Allan Selby and his Frascatians, q.v., and the following sides hitherto not otherwise identifiable (though of some interest as jazz).

T/tb/as/ts/p/bj/bb/d.                    London, c. October 9, 1928.

| 1276-2 | From Saturday Night Till Monday Morning | Pic 192 |
|---|---|---|
| 1277-2 | 'Cause I Feel Low Down | Pic 185 |

2t/Miff Mole-tb/? Andy Sannella-cl-as/ts/Charlie Magnante-pac/p/bj/bb/d/Irving Kaufman-v.                    New York, c. May, 1930.

| 4070-A | Dancing With Tears In My Eyes - vIK | Pic 605 |
|---|---|---|

There were two groups of this name in the late 1920s. One was directed by Mel Morris (recording for Edison in New York), the other a studio band directed by Al Starita for Columbia in London. The former feature an excellent but unidentified trumpet on several sides; the latter sometimes offer solos by star musicians, as follows.

Al Starita-cl-as dir. Sylvester Ahola and another-t/Ben Oakley-tb/Perley Breed-cl-as bar/George Smith-as-ts/Eddie Lee-vn when used/Sid Bright-p/Joe Brannelly-bj-g/Alf Field-bb/Bill Harty-d/Eddie Collis-v.    London, April 20, 1928.

| | | |
|---|---|---|
| WA-7274-1 | Kiss And Make Up - vEC | Col 4907 |
| WA-7275-1 | Yummy Yummy Yum - vEC | - |
| WA-7276-2 | I Want To Be Alone With Mary Brown-vEC | Col 4886, Re G-20272 |

NOTE:- Regal G-20272 as STELLAR DANCE BAND.

London, May 30, 1928.

| | | |
|---|---|---|
| WA-7425-2 | Do The Sugar Step | Col 4930 |
| WA-7427-1 | I'm Afraid Of You - vEC | Col 4931 |

NOTE:- Matrices WA-7424 and WA-7426 are by the same band, but are waltzes.

London, June 15, 1928.

WA-7510-1   Since I Met Mary Jane - vEC      Col 5003
NOTE:- The band accompanied Sophie Tucker on this session, but no jazz resulted.

Eddie Gross-Bart-v.       London, September 14, 1928.

WA-7813-1   Didn't I Tell You ? - vEGB      Col 5023

Unknown t replaces Ahola, possibly Norman Payne.
London, November 9, 1928.

| | | |
|---|---|---|
| WA-8080-2 | Heaven For Two - vEGB | Col 5156 |
| WA-8081-1 | From Monday On - vEGB | - |

London, August 23, 1929.

| | | |
|---|---|---|
| WA-9388-2 | Kansas City Kitty - vEC | Col 5539 |
| WA-9389-2 | You Wouldn't Fool Me, Would You ? - vEC | Col 5551 |

## PICCADILLY REVELS BAND

The following titles by this British dance band are of outstanding interest as jazz. There are probably others among the considerable number made about the same date that have short solos by the same musicians.

Ray Starita-cl-ts-v dir. Freddy Pitt-Andy Richardson-t/Bill Hall-tb/Ernie Smith-cl-as-o/Phil Cardew-cl-as/Eric Siday-vn/Donald Thorne-p/Jack Hill-bj-g/Clem Lawton-bb /Rudy Starita-d-x.      London, January 20, 1927.

WA-4726-1-2   Brown Sugar       Col 4249

London, May 24, 1927.

WA-5535-1   Back Beats       Col 4415

London, June 30, 1927.

WA-5805-1   When Erastus Plays His Old Kazoo - vRS   Col 4475

Vocal trio (including Ray Starita ?)     London, October 6, 1927.

| | | |
|---|---|---|
| WA-6358-1-2 | Buffalo Rhythm | Rejected |
| WA-6359-2 | Just The Same - v3 | Col 4603 |
| WA-6363-2 | Go, Joe, Go | Col 4610 |

London, October 20, 1927.

WA-6358-3   Buffalo Rhythm       Col 4610

Ray Starita-cl-ts-v dir. Freddy Pitt-Andy Richardson-t/Bill Hall-tb/Ernie Smith-cl-
   as-o/Phil Cardew-cl-as/Eric Siday-vn/Donald Thorne-p/Jack Hill-bj-g/Clem Lawton-bb
   /Rudy Starita-d-x/v trio.                    London, October 28, 1927.

| | | |
|---|---|---|
| WA-6453-1 | Deep River Blues - vRS | Col 4641 |
| WA-6455-1 | Banana Skin Stomp | Rejected |

London, December 5, 1927.

| | | |
|---|---|---|
| WA-6568-3 | Is She My Girl Friend ? - v3 | Col 4640 |

## WALTER PICHON

Vocal, acc. by Henry Allen-t/own p/Teddy Bunn-g.
                         New York, September 16, 1929.

| | | |
|---|---|---|
| 55843-2 | Doggin' That Thing | Vic V-38544, BB B-6329 |
| 55344-1 | Yo Yo | - - |

## THE PICKENS SISTERS

These famous singing sisters from Georgia are included on the strength of the small
   instrumental groups accompanying them on most of their records. They also made a
   couple of sides with Paul Whiteman, but these are of no jazz interest.

Helen, Jane and Marla Pickens-v trio, acc. by cl-as/p/g/sb.
                         New York, February 16, 1932.

| | | |
|---|---|---|
| 71860-1 | Was That The Human Thing To Do ? | Vic 22929, HMV B-4176, Zon EE-313 |
| 71861-1 | Goodnight, Moon | - - - |

New York, March 21, 1932.

| | | |
|---|---|---|
| 71977-1 | Too Many Tears | Vic 22965, HMV B-4191, Zon EE-319 |
| 71978-1 | Somebody Loves You | - - - |

Acc. by cl/p/g.                    New York, April 6, 1932.

| | | |
|---|---|---|
| 72241-1 | Dream Sweetheart | Vic 22975, HMV B-4212, Zon EE-333 |
| 72242-1 | Lawd, You Made The Night Too Long | - - - |

Sb added.                    New York, May 17, 1932.

| | | |
|---|---|---|
| 72593-1 | San | Vic 24025, HMV B-4250, Zon EE-339 |
| 72594-1 | Sweet Georgia Brown | - - - |

Acc. by t/cl/p/g, with sb*.         New York, July 26, 1932.

| | | |
|---|---|---|
| 73122-1 | *The Darktown Strutters' Ball | Vic 24355, HMV EA-1279 |
| 73123-1 | China Boy | - - |

Acc. by cl/p/g/sb.                New York, November 2, 1932.

| | | |
|---|---|---|
| 73905-1 | Back In The Old Sunday School | Vic 24180, Zon EE-380 |
| 73906-1 | Sentimental Gentleman From Georgia | Vic 24190 |
| 73907-1 | When Mother Played The Organ (And Daddy | Vic 24180, Zon EE-380 |
| | Sang A Hymn) | |

Acc. by Nat Finston dir. t/cl/2vn/p/g/sb.
                         Hollywood, October 25, 1933.

| | | |
|---|---|---|
| 68591-1 | Many Moons Ago | Vic 24471, HMV EA-1366 |
| 68592-1 | You're Such A Comfort To Me | Rejected |
| 68593-2 | May I ? | Vic 24625, HMV EA-1364 |
| 68594-1 | Good Morning, Glory | Rejected |

Acc. by p/g.                    Hollywood, November 1, 1933.

| | | |
|---|---|---|
| 68604-3 | Did You Ever See A Dream Walking ? | Vic 24468, HMV EA-1298 |

Acc. by Nat Finston dir. t/cl/2vn/p/g/sb.
                                    Hollywood, November 8, 1933.

68592-2  You're Such A Comfort To Me          Vic 24471, HMV B-8108, El EG-2990
68594-2  Good Morning, Glory                   Vic 24468    - EA-I298     -

Acc. by c/cl/as/p/g/sb.              New York, May 4, 1934.

82373-1  The Beat O' My Heart                  Vic 24625
82374-1  Riptide                               Vic 24630, HMV EA-1364
82375-1  Little Man, You've Had A Busy Day        -       HMV EA-1366

THE PICKENS SISTERS AND THEIR ORCHESTRA : 3t/3cl/o/p/g/harp/sb/d/The Pickens Sisters
  v trio.                             New York, October 11, 1934.

84466-1  Be Still, My Heart                    Vic 24751, HMV EA-1466
84467-1  Happiness Ahead                          - HMV BD-116 -
84468-1  The Thief Of Bagdad                   Vic 24753
84469-1  Love Is Just Around The Corner        Vic 24815, HMV EA-1464

### PICKETT-PARHAM  APOLLO SYNCOPATORS

B. T. Wingfield-c/Charles Lawson-tb/Junie Cobb-cl-ss-as/Leroy Pickett-vn/Tiny Parham-
   p/Jimmy Bertrand-d.                 Chicago, c. December, 1926.

4053-1  Alexander, Where's That Band ?         Pm 12441
4054-1  Mojo Strut                                -

### PIEDMONT DANCE ORCHESTRA

Pseudonym on Pathe Actuelle 036123 and Perfect 14304 for Sam Lanin and his Orchestra,
q.v.

### THE  PIED PIPERS

Eight men and one girl-v, acc. by Charlie Margulis-Ricky Traettino-t/Wes Hein-George
   Plumstead-tb/Benny Lagasse-as/Ned Yeagley-ts/Gil Bowers-p/Bill Barford-g/Felix
   Giobbe-sb/Maurice Purtill-d.        New York, June 6, 1939.

037190-1  In A Little Spanish Town            Vic 26364
037191-1  Polly Wolly Doodle All The Day      Vic 26320, HMV EA-2826
037192-1  Sugar Foot Stomp                       -          -
037193-1  What Is This Thing Called Love ?    Vic 26364

### CHARLES PIERCE AND HIS ORCHESTRA

Muggsy Spanier-Dick Feige-c/Frank Teschmacher-cl-as/Charles Pierce-as/Ralph Rudder-ts
   /Dan Lipscomb-p/Stuart Branch-bj/Johnny Mueller-bb-sb/Paul Kettler-d.
                                       Chicago, c. February, 1928.

20399-1  Bull Frog Blues                       Pm 12619, UHCA 2
20400-3  China Boy                                -       UHCA I

Charles Altier-c replaces Spanier and Feige; Maurie Bercov-cl replaces Teschmacher.
                                       Chicago, c. March, 1928.

20469-3  Jazz Me Blues                         Pm 12640, UHCA 71, Br 02502,
                                               Dec M-30356
20470-4  Sister Kate                           Pm 12640, UHCA 72, Col 35950,
                                               Tem R-35

As for c. February, 1928, plus Jack Read-tb, without Feige.
                                       Chicago, c. April, 1928.

20469-5  Jazz Me Blues                         Pm 12640
20470-7  Sister Kate                              -
20534-2  Nobody's Sweetheart                   Pm 20616, 14028, Bwy 1174,
                                               Col 35950, Tem R-35
NOTE:- Columbia 35950 bears an exact recording date on each label, but this can be
safely disregarded as quite inaccurate.  Columbia DB-3180 was never issued.

Kyle Pierce-p.                           Richmond, Ind., July 18, 1923.

11548   I Forgave You                         Gnt rejected
11549   St. Louis Blues                           -

## PIERROT SYNCOPATORS

Pseudonym on Canadian Ctown for the following items listed in this book :-

81020  Dixie Drag (Mendello's Five Gee-Gees)
81161  Piccolo Pete (Fred Rich and his Orchestra)

## MURRAY PILCER AND HIS JAZZ BAND

Murray Pilcer-d dir. Jack Rimmer-t/Stanley Jones-tb/Arthur Coombes-cl-as/Sam DeWolf-
bsn/Louis DeJong-vn/Van Ruth-p/Norton Greenop-bj/William Fowler-sb.
                                          London, January, 1919.

5960-2  The Wild Wild Women                    EBW 3288
5961-1  K-K-K-Katy (6/8 One-Step) - v              -
5962-2  I'm All Bound 'Round With The          EBW 3292
        Mason-Dixon Line
5963-1  That Moaning Trombone                      -
NOTE:- It should be pointed out that the above titles owe their inclusion solely
to the fact that they appear to be the first ever issued in the U.K. by a "jazz"
band (so-called). At least they demonstrate how little the jazz idiom was under-
stood in England before the coming of the Original Dixieland Jazz Band to London,
and how far jazz and dance music have advanced since then !

## PINKIE'S BIRMINGHAM FIVE

Edward "Pinkie" Gerbrecht-c/Pete Beilman-tb/Lester "Gilly" Bouchon-cl/? Bob Zurke-p/
? Jules Bauduc-bj-g.                      New York, c. December 2, 1925.

9869-A  Headin' For Louisville               Gnt 3208, Gmn 1880, Sc 761
9870-A  Carolina Stomp                           -   Gmn 1879
NOTE:- Guardsman 1879 as CABARET DANCE ORCHESTRA; 1880 as DICKSON'S DANCE BAND;
Scala 761 as D'ARCY'S CABARET COMBINATION.

## PIRON'S NEW ORLEANS ORCHESTRA

Armand J. Piron-vn-v dir. Peter Bocage-t/John Lindsay-tb/Lorenzo Tio, Jr.-cl-ts/
Louis Warnecke-as/Steve Lewis-p/Charles Bocage-bj-v/Bob Ysaguirre-bb/Louis
Cottrell-d.                              New York, November 24, 1923.

        Mama's Gone, Goodbye               Vic test (un-numbered)
        New Orleans Wiggle                      -

                                         New York, c. December 3, 1923.

72132-B  Bouncing Around                      OK 40021, Od 03204
72133-D  Kiss Me Sweet - vAJP-CB                 -        -

                                         New York, December 11, 1923.

29121-3  New Orleans Wiggle                   Vic 19233
29122-2  Mama's Gone, Goodbye                    -

                                         New York, December 21, 1923.

81435-3  Sud Bustin' Blues                    Col 14007-D
81436-2  West Indies Blues                       -

                                         New York, January 8, 1924.

29190-3  Do-Doodle-Oom                        Vic 19255
29191-2  West Indies Blues                       -

Armand J. Piron-vn dir. Peter Bocage-t/John Lindsay-tb/Lorenzo Tio, Jr.-cl-ts/Louis
Warnecke-as/Steve Lewis-p/Charles Bocage-bj/Bob Ysaguirre-bb/Louis Cottrell-d.
                                      New York, January 23, 1924.

29347-1-2-3  Purple Rose Of Cairo                Vic rejected

                                      New York, February 7, 1924.

29347-4-5  Purple Rose Of Cairo                  Vic rejected
29386-1  Day By Day                              -

                                      New York, February 15, 1924.

81569-1-3  Ghost Of The Blues                    Col 99-D
81570-3  Bright Star Blues                       -

                                      New York, c. February 18, 1924.

72320-B  Lou'siana Swing                         OK 40189, Od 03132
72322-B  Sittin' On The Curbstone Blues          -          -

                                      New York, February 21, 1924.

29386-2-3-4-5  Day By Day                        Vic rejected
29536-1-2-3-4  Kiss Me Sweet                     -

Lindsay omitted; unknown cl replaces Tio.
                                      New Orleans, March 25, 1925.

32121-3  Red Man Blues                           Vic 19646
32122-3  Do Just As I Say                        -

## PLANTATION DANCE/JAZZ  ORCHESTRA

This Emerson studio band made many titles between 1919 and 1921, of which these are
of interest as jazz, albeit mildly so.

Harry Raderman-tb dir. t/Bennie Krueger-as/2vn/p/sb/d, sometimes with bj and/or bb.
                                      New York, c. March, 1920.

41027-6  Railroad Blues                          Em 10157

                                      New York, c. December 8, 1920.

21682-2  Home Again Blues                        Med 771 (7")
41561-2  Home Again Blues                        Em 10328, 10420, Re 996
NOTE:- Regal 996 as REGAL JAZZ SYNCOPATORS.

                                      New York, c. March 30, 1921.

41719-3  Church Street Sobbin' Blues             Em 10368

                                      New York, December, 1921.

Bow Wow Blues                          Em 10507

## THE PLANTATION ORCHESTRA

Ralph "Shrimp" Jones-vn dir. Johnny Dunn-Pike Davis-t/Calvin Jones-tb/Rudolph Dunbar-
Nelson Kincaid-cl-as/Alonzo Williams-ts/George Smith vn/George Rickson-p/Maceo
Jefferson-bj/Bill Benford-bb/Jesse Baltimore-d.
                                      London, December 1, 1926.

WA-4519-2  Silver Rose                           Col 4185
WA-4543-1  Arabella's Wedding Day                Col 4238
WA-4544-1  Smiling Joe                           Col 4185
WA-4545-1  For Baby And Me                       Col 4238

See Harry Reser,

## PLANTATION SERENADERS

Pseudonym on Champion 15386 for Alex Jackson's Plantation Orchestra, q.v.

## THE PLAZA BAND

Pseudonym on Edison Bell Winner for the following items listed in this book :-

```
4765  Both sides by Harry Hudson's Melody Men
4798  Swing On The Gait (Harry Hudson's Melody Men)
4821  Both sides by Harry Hudson's Melody Men
4880  Blue Grass (Bill Haid's Cubs)
4924  She's Funny That Way (Ted Wallace and his Orchestra)
```

## PLAZA DANCE BAND

Pseudonym for the following items listed in this book :-

```
Plaza 6033  Am I Blue ? (Irving Mills and his Orchestra)
      P-161 Road House Shuffle (Oscar Rabin and his Romany Band)
      P-175 The Golden King Shuffle (Oscar Rabin and his Romany Band)
Starr 702   Get Out And Get Under The Moon (Sam Lanin and his Orchestra)
      707   Out Of The Dawn (California Ramblers)
```

## STEW PLETCHER

PLETCHER'S ELI PROM TROTTERS : Stew Pletcher-t-v-a dir. Seelye Vidal-Bob Stanley-t/
  tb/Louis Rapp-cl-as/Bob Bruce-cl-as-a/as/Al Thompson-ts/Sidney Fine-p/Neil Water-
  man-g/Alan Lutz-bb-sb/ ——— Pearlman-d. Long Island City, c. May, 1930.

```
2374-1  I Like To Do Things For You - v-aSP      QRS Q-1055
2375-2  That's Where You're Wrong - aBB            -
```

STEW PLETCHER AND HIS ORCHESTRA : Stew Pletcher-t-v dir. Donald McCook-cl/Herbie
  Haymer-ts/Roger Ramirez-p/Dave Barbour-g/Pete Peterson-sb/Maurice Purtill-d/Red
  Norvo-x.                                    New York, March 27, 1936.

```
101132-1  The Touch Of Your Lips - vSP       BB B-6345, Vic JR-62, HMV B-8452
101133-1  Will I Ever Know ? - vSP           BB B-6344
101134-1  I Don't Want To Make History - vSP   -
101135-1  I Hope Gabriel Likes My Music - vSP  BB B-6345, Vic JR-62
101136-1  You - vSP                          BB B-6343
101137-1  You Never Looked So Beautiful - vSP  -       RZ MR-2173
   NOTE:- Regal Zonophone MR-2173 as BROADWAY RHYTHM KINGS.
```

## PLYMOUTH DANCE ORCHESTRA

Pseudonym on Tremont 0540 (THE FLAPPER WIFE) for Lou Gold and his Orchestra, q.v.

## THE PODS OF PEPPER

See Ikey Robinson.

## BEN POLLACK

BEN POLLACK AND HIS CALIFORNIANS : Ben Pollack-d-v dir. Harry Greenberg-Al Harris-c/
  Glenn Miller-tb/Benny Goodman-cl/Gil Rodin-as/Fud Livingston-ts/Wayne Allen-p/John
  Kurzenknabe-bj/Harry Goodman-bb/Frank Sylvano-v.
                                         Chicago, September 14, 1926.

```
36237-1-2-3  I'd Love To Call You My Sweetheart  Vic rejected
             - vFS
36238-1-2-3  Sunday - vBP                            -
```

    Victor Young-Al Beller-vn added, also Earl Baker-c*; Joey Ray-v.
                                         Chicago, December 9, 1926.

```
37218-3    When I First Met Mary - vJR        Vic 20394
37219-1-2-3-4 *'Deed I Do - vBP               Rejected
```

BEN POLLACK AND HIS CALIFORNIANS : Ben Pollack-d-v dir. Earl Baker-Harry Greenberg-
   Al Harris-c/Glenn Miller-tb/Benny Goodman-cl/Gil Rodin-as/Fud Livingston-ts/Victor
   Young-Al Beller-vn*/Wayne Allen-p/John Kurzenknabe-bj/Harry Goodman-bb/Ilomay
   Bailey-Dorothy Williams-Hannah Williams-v.
                                              Chicago, December 17, 1926.

   37219-6 **Deed I Do - vBP                        Vic 20408, HMV B-5281, R-4819
   37260-3 *You're The One For Me - vIB             Vic 20461
   37261-2 He's The Last Word - vDW-HW              Vic 20425, HMV EA-156
   37261-3 He's The Last Word - vDW-HW              X LX-3003, EVAA-3003 (LP)

   Baker omitted; Vic Breidis-p replaces Allen; Lou Kessler-bj replaces Kurzenknabe..
                                              Chicago, June 24, 1927.

   39058-1-2-3-4-5 *That's What I Think Of You-vBP  Vic rejected
   39059-1-2-3-4-5 *Who Is Your Who ? - vBP             -

                                              Chicago, July 7, 1927.

   39090-1-2-3 *Honey Do - vBP                      Vic rejected
   39091-1-2-3-4-5  I Ain't That Kind Of A Baby - vBP  -

BEN POLLACK AND HIS ORCHESTRA : Ben Pollack-d-v dir. Jimmy McPartland-Frank Quartell-
   Al Harris-c/Glenn Miller-tb/Benny Goodman-cl-as (and t where shown)/Gil Rodin-as/
   Larry Binyon-ts-f/Vic Breidis-p/Dick Morgan-bj/Harry Goodman-bb/v trio (probably
   including Morgan and Pollack).        Chicago, December 7, 1927.

   41342-2  Waitin' For Katie - tBG/v3              Vic 21184
   41342-3  Waitin' For Katie - tBG/v3              X LX-3003, EVAA-3003 (LP)
   41343-1  Memphis Blues                               -          -
   41343-2  Memphis Blues                           Vic 21184
   41344-1  California Medley                        Rejected

BEN POLLACK AND HIS CALIFORNIANS : As last above, but Quartell omitted; Bud Freeman-
   ts replaces Binyon; Al Beller-Ed Bergman-vn added; Franklyn Baur-v.
                                              New York, April 6, 1928.

   43540-2-3  Singapore Sorrows - vBP (part only)   X LX-3003, EVAB-3003 (LP)
   43540-4  Singapore Sorrows - vBP                     -          -
   43541-1  Sweet Sue - Just You - vFB              Rejected

                                              New York, April 26, 1928.

   43540-6  Singapore Sorrows - vBP                 Vic 21437
   43541-5  Sweet Sue - Just You - vFB                  -

BEN POLLACK AND HIS PARK CENTRAL ORCHESTRA : Ben Pollack-d-v dir. Jimmy McPartland-Al
   Harris-c/Jack Teagarden-tb/Benny Goodman-cl-as/Gil Rodin-as/Larry Binyon-cl-ts-f/Al
   Beller-Ed Bergman-vn/Bill Schumann-vc/Vic Breidis-p/Dick Morgan-bj/Harry Goodman-bb
   /Franklyn Baur-v.                     New York, October 1, 1928.

   47576-1-2-3  You've Gone - vFB                   Rejected
   47577-2  Forever (w) - vFB                       Vic 21716, HMV B-5587, EA-456

   Belle Mann-v.                              New York, October 15, 1928.

   47742-1  Buy, Buy For Baby (Or Baby Will Bye-Bye Vic 21743, HMV B-5596
              You) - vBM
   47742-3  Buy, Buy For Baby (Or Baby Will Bye-Bye X LX-3003, EVAA-3003 (LP)
              You) - vBM
   47743-1  She's One Sweet Show Girl - vBM         Vic 21743, HMV B-5596

   Dick Robertson-Gene Austin-v.              New York, December 3, 1928.

   49220-3  Then Came The Dawn - vDR               Vic 21827, Zon EE-144
   49221-2  Sentimental Baby - vGA                     -          -          HMV R-14070

BEN POLLACK AND HIS PARK CENTRAL ORCHESTRA : Ben Pollack-v dir. Jimmy McPartland-Al
   Harris-c/Jack Teagarden-tb/Benny Goodman-cl-as/Gil Rodin-as/Larry Binyon-cl-ts-f/
   Al Beller-Ed Bergman-vn/Bill Schumann-vc/Vic Breidis-p/Dick Morgan-bj/Harry Good-
   man-bb/Ray Bauduc-d/Scrappy Lambert (as BURT LORIN)-v.
                                New York, December 24, 1928.

48286-1-2-3  Let's Sit And Talk About You - vSL   Rejected
48287-2  Futuristic Rhythm - vBP            Vic 21858, HMV R-14136

LOUISVILLE RHYTHM KINGS : As above, without Beller and Schumann; Smith Ballew-v.
                                New York, January 16, 1929.

401535-A  Let's Sit And Talk About You - vSB     OK 41189, Od 165642, A-189242,
                                       Par B-12755, B-25440

BEN'S BAD BOYS : Ben Pollack-v comments dir. Jimmy McPartland-c/Glenn Miller-tb/
   Benny Goodman-cl/Vic Breidis-p/Dick Morgan-bj/Harry Goodman-bb/Ray Buduc-d.
                               New York, January 22, 1929.

49673-2  Wang-Wang Blues                 Vic 21971
49674-2  Yellow Dog Blues - vBP           -
49675-1  Shirt Tail Stomp                Camden CAL-446 (LP)

BEN POLLACK AND HIS PARK CENTRAL ORCHESTRA : As for December 24, 1928 above.
                               New York, January 24, 1929.

48286-4  Let's Sit And Talk About You - vSL   Vic 21858
48302-1  Sally Of My Dreams - vSL         Vic 21857, HMV EA-530

LOUISVILLE RHYTHM KINGS : As for January 16, 1929, without Bergman; v trio (Ballew,
   Morgan and Pollack ?)           New York, January 25, 1929.

401558-A  Shout Hallelujah ! 'Cause I'm Home - vSB Par R-340, A-2822, 22305,
                                  Od A- 21129
401559-A  In A Great Big Way - v3        OK 41189, Od 165642, A-189242,
                                    Par B-12755
   NOTE:- Parlophone A-2822 as BEN POLLACK'S ORCHESTRA; Parlophone R-340 as BENNIE'S
LOUISVILLE RHYTHM KINGS; Odeon A-221129 as ROOF GARDEN ORCHESTRA.

BEN POLLACK AND HIS PARK CENTRAL ORCHESTRA : As for December 24, 1928 above, but
   Ruby Weinstein-t replaces Harris; Smith Ballew (as CHARLES ROBERTS)-v.
                               New York, March 1, 1929.

50905-2  Louise - vSB                     Vic 21941, HMV EA-543, X-3168
50906-3  Wait 'Til You See "Ma Cherie" - vSB   -        - R-14182 -

                               New York, March 5, 1929.

50912-2  My Kinda Love (One Way To Paradise)-vSB Vic 21944
50912-3  My Kinda Love (One Way To Paradise)-vSB Vic LPV-528, RD-7826, 731088 (LP)
50913-2  On With The Dance ! - vBP         Vic 21944

                               New York, May 27, 1929.

53517-3  I'd Like To Be A Gypsy - vSL      Vic 22252
53518-1-2-3  Finding The Long Way Home - vSL  Rejected

                                New York, July 25, 1929.

53947-2  In The Hush Of The Night - vSL    Vic 22071, HMV R-14236
53948-2  Won'tcha ? - vSL                 -
53949-2  Bashful Baby - vSL            X LX-3003, EVAB-3003 (LP)
53949-3  Bashful Baby - vSL            Vic 22074, HMV R-14234, El EG-1867

Murphy Steinberg-t replaces McPartland. New York, August 15, 1929.

53989-2  Where The Sweet Forget-Me-Nots Remember Vic 22106, HMV R-14253
      - vSL
53990-3  Song Of The Blues - vSL         Vic 22147, HMV R-14294
53991-2  True Blue Lou - vSL           Vic 22089, HMV EA-610, R-14287

BEN POLLACK AND HIS PARK CENTRAL ORCHESTRA : Ben Pollack-v dir. Jimmy McPartland-Ruby
Weinstein-t/Jack Teagarden-tb/Benny Goodman-cl-as/Gil Rodin-as/Larry Binyon-cl-ts-f
/Ed Bergman-Al Beller-vn/Bill Schumann-vc/Vic Breidis-p/Dick Morgan-bj/Harry Good-
man-bb/Ray Bauduc-d/Scrappy Lambert (as BURT LORIN)-Smith Ballew (as CHARLES
ROBERTS)-v.                                     New York, August 22, 1929.

56105-3  Sweetheart, We Need Each Other - vSL        Vic 22101, HMV B-5729, EA-646,
                                                     El EG-1760
56106-2  You're Always In My Arms (w) - vSL          As above

Snub Pollard-t replaces McPartland; Joe Catalyne-cl-as replaces Goodman.
                                                New York, September 27, 1929.

56721-3  You've Made Me Happy Today - vSB            Vic 22158
56722-3  From Now On - vSB                           -

Charlie Teagarden-t replaces Pollard; Matty Matlock-cl-as replaces Catalyne.
                                                New York, November 29, 1929.

57637-3  Keep Your Undershirt On - vSL              Vic 22267, HMV R-14379
57638-1-2-3  Reaching For The Moon - vSL            Rejected

BEN POLLACK'S ORCHESTRA : As last above.  New York, mid-January, 1930.

1026-D  I'm Following You - vBP                     HoW 1026
1027-C  Cryin' For The Carolines - vBP              HoW 1027

BEN POLLACK AND HIS ORCHESTRA : Ben Pollack-v dir. ? Charlie Spivak-Charlie Teagarden
t/Jack Teagarden-tb-v (as ROLAND LANCE)/Gil Rodin-Matty Matlock-cl-as/Babe Russin-
ts/Al Beller-vn/Bill Schumann-vc/Vic Breidis-p/Dick Morgan-bj/Harry Goodman-bb/Ray
Bauduc-d/v trio including Pollack, who is re-named PHIL BENNETT as vocalist on Bwy.
                                                New York, June 23, 1930.

9818-1-2-3  Rollin' Down The River - vBP            Ban 0752, Bwy 1391, Cam 0352,
                                                    Cq 7579, Dom 4591, Je 6002,
                                                    Or 2002, Per 15328, Re 10057,
                                                    Ro 1366, Imp 2338, Voc 790
9819-2-3-4  If I Could Be With You (One Hour        Ban 0747, Bwy 1409, Cam 0347,
            Tonight) - vJT                           Cq 7576, Chg 770, Cr 81416,
                                                    Dom 4588, Je 5998, Or 1998,
                                                    Per 15325, Re 10054, Ro 1363,
                                                    CMS/UHCA 103, Voc 749
9820-1-2-3  There's A Wah Wah Girl In               Ban 0750, Cam 0350, Cq 7576,
            Agua Caliente - v3                       Dom 4588, Je 6000, Or 2000,
                                                    Per 15325, Re 10055, Ro 1364,
                                                    Sterling 281408
NOTE:- Broadway 1391 as PHIL BENNETT AND HIS ORCHESTRA; 1409 as THE BADGERS; CMS/
UHCA 103 as JACK TEAGARDEN WITH BEN POLLACK'S ORCHESTRA.  Some copies of the latter
were pressed using Part 2 of Cliff Edwards' STACK O' LEE BLUES instead of the Ben
Pollack title.

Ben Pollack-v dir. Charlie Spivak-Sterling Bose-t/Jack Teagarden-tb-v/Benny Goodman
Gil Rodin-cl-as/Eddie Miller-cl-ts/Al Beller-vn/Gil Bowers-p/Nappy Lamare-g/Harry
Goodman-bb-sb/Ray Bauduc-d/Eddie Gale (both he and Ben Pollack as TED BANCROFT)-v.
                                                New York, January 21, 1931.

10378-2  Sing-Song Girl (Little Yella Cinderella) Ban 32074, Cq 7772, Je 6193,
         - vBP                                      Or 2193, Per 15424, Re 10250,
                                                    Ro 1561, Apex 41213, Mt 91066
10379-3  (When You Fall In Love) Fall In Love       As above, except Apex and Mt
         With Me - vEG
10380-2-3  You Didn't Have To Tell Me (I Knew It    Ban 32101, Cq 7763, Je 6208,
           All The Time) - vJT                       Or 2208, Per 15428, Re 10266,
                                                    Ro 1573, CMS/UHCA 103, Lyric 3375,
                                                    Voc 821
NOTE:- CMS/UHCA 103 as JACK TEAGARDEN WITH BEN POLLACK'S ORCHESTRA.

BEN POLLACK AND HIS ORCHESTRA : Ben Pollack-v dir. Charlie Spivak-Sterling Bose-t/
    Jack Teagarden-tb-v/Benny Goodman-Gil Rodin-cl-as/Eddie Miller-cl-ts/Al Beller-vn/
    Gil Bowers-p/Nappy Lamare-g/Harry Goodman-bb-sb/Ray Bauduc-d.
                                            New York, February 12, 1931.

10416-1-2  I've Got Five Dollars - vBP          Rejected ?
10417-1-2  Sweet And Hot - vBP                     -
10418-1  I'm A Ding Dong Daddy (From Dumas) - vBP Ban 32105, Je 6214, Or 2214,
                                                    Per 15432, Re 10267, Ro 1577
10418-2  I'm A Ding Dong Daddy (From Dumas)      Cr 91077 (Canadian)
           - vBP-JT
10422-1-2-3  Beale Street Blues - vJT            Rejected ?

Sammy Prager-p replaces Bowers; Nappy Lamare-v.
                                            New York, March 2, 1931.

10416-5  I've Got Five Dollars - vBP             Ban 32104, Cq 7684, Je 6213,
                                                    Or 2213, Per 15431, Re 10273,
                                                    Ro 1576
10417-4  Sweet And Hot - vBP-JT-NL               Epic SN-6044 (LP)
10417-5  Sweet And Hot - vBP-JT-NL               Ban 32104, Cq 7684, Je 6213,
                                                    Or 2213, Per 15431, Re 10273,
                                                    Ro 1576
10422-4-5  Beale Street Blues - vJT              Ban 32463, Or 2488, Per 15617,
                                                    Ro 1858, Mt/Royal 91358
NOTE:- All issues of the last title as DUKE WILSON AND HIS TEN BLACK BERRIES.
Matrices 10416 and 10417 were re-made for a third time on March 18, 1931, but by
a band under the direction of Ed Kirkeby, producing nothing of jazz interest,
but issued on the same labels under the same catalog numbers.

As for February 12, 1931, but Matty Matlock-cl-as replaces Goodman; Jerry Johnson-
sb replaces Goodman; Ralph Copsey-tb-v/Ray Cohen-vn/Doris Robbins-v added.
                                            Chicago, March 19, 1933.

75409-1  Linger A Little Longer In The Twilight  Vic 24284
           - vDR
75410-1-2-3  I Bring A Song - vRC                Rejected
75411-1-2  Low Down Upon The Harlem River - vJT    -
75412-2  Two Tickets To Georgia - vNL            Vic 24284

Ben Pollack-v dir. Yank Lawson-Charlie Spivak-Shirley Clay-t/Joe Harris-Benny
Morton-tb/Matty Matlock-cl/Deane Kincaide-Gil Rodin-as/Eddie Miller-ts/Al Beller-
Ray Cohen-vn/Gil Bowers-p/Nappy Lamare-g-v/Harry Goodman-sb/Ray Bauduc-d/Doris
Robbins-v.                                  New York, December 28, 1933.

152662-2  Got The Jitters - vNL                  Col 2870-D
152663-1  Deep Jungle                            Col 2879-D, DB-5036
152664-1  Swing Out                                 -
152665-1  I'm Full Of The Devil - vBP            Col 2870-D, CQ-1385

Clay and Morton omitted; Stew Pletcher-t replaces Lawson; Joe Harris-v.
                                            New York, January 23, 1934.

152692-1-2  I Wanna Be Loved - vDR               Rejected
152693-1  My Little Grass Shack In Kealakekua,   Col 2886-D, Par A-3832
           Hawaii - vBP-NL-DR
152694-1  Goin' To Heaven On A Mule - vJH           -       Par R-1800, RZ G-22083

Yank Lawson-t replaces Pletcher.         New York, February 23, 1934.

152721-2  Dancing In The Moonlight - vBP         Col 2901-D, RZ MR-1298, RZ G-22027
152722-2  The Voodoo (r)                         Col 2906-D, RZ MR-1305
152723-2  Ole Mammy Ain't Gonna Sing No More-vJH Col 2901-D, RZ MR-1298, Par A-3879
152724-2  Here Goes - vJH                        Col 2905-D
152725-2  The Beat O' My Heart - vDR                -       RZ MR-1305, G-22147
152726-2  Alone On The Range - vJH               Col 2910-D
NOTE:- Regal Zonophone G-22027 as THE BROADWAY BANDITS.

BEN POLLACK AND HIS ORCHESTRA : Ben Pollack-v dir. Yank Lawson-Charlie Spivak-t/Joe
    Harris-tb-v/Matty Matlock-cl/Deane Kincaide-Gil Rodin-as/Eddie Miller-ts/Al Beller
    Ray Cohen-vn/Gil Bowers-p/Nappy Lamare-g/Harry Goodman-sb/Ray Bauduc-d/Doris
    Robbins-v.                              New York, May 29, 1934.

| | | |
|---|---|---|
| 152755-1 | Night On The Desert - vJH | Col 2929-D |
| 152756-2 | Sleepy Head - vJH | -      DQ-1014 |
| 152757-2 | Freckle Face, You're Beautiful - vBP | Col 2931-D, RZ G-22156 |
| 152758-2 | I've Got A Warm Spot For You - vDR | - |

    Ben Pollack-d*-v dir. Harry James-Shorty Sherock-Charlie Spivak-t/Bruce Squires-
    Glenn Miller-tb/Irving Fazola-cl/Opie Cates-as/Dave Matthews-ts-a/Ray Cohen-vn/
    Freddy Slack-p/Frank Frederico-g/Joe Price-stg where shown/Thurman Teague-sb'/Sammy
    Taylor-d unless marked */Carol Mackay-Lois Still-v.
                                            New York, September 15, 1936.

| | | |
|---|---|---|
| B-19879-1 | *I'm One Step Ahead Of My Shadow - vLS | Br 7751, Voc 509 |
| B-19880-1 | *Thru' The Courtesy Of Love - vBP | Br 7747, RZ G-22965 |
| B-19881-1 | I Couldn't Be Mad At You - vCM | Br 7751 |
| B-19882-1 | Song Of The Islands - stg | Br 7764, Col 36325 |

NOTE:- Regal Zonophone G-22965 as THE CASINO ROYAL ORCHESTRA.

THE DEAN AND HIS KIDS : James (also v)-Squires-Fazola-Matthews-Slack-Frederico-
    Teague-Pollack (first two sides); the full band as above on the others, with Jim
    Hardy-v.                                New York, September 16, 1936.

| | | |
|---|---|---|
| 19887-1 | Spreadin' Knowledge Around | Voc 3342, S-55 |
| 19888-1 | Zoom Zoom Zoom - vHJ | - |
| B-19889-2 | Jimtown Blues | Br 7764, Col 36325, Voc S-113 |
| B-19890-1 | Now Or Never-- vJH | Br 7747 |

NOTE:- Brunswick 7747 and 7764 as BEN POLLACK AND HIS ORCHESTRA.

BEN POLLACK AND HIS ORCHESTRA : As for September 15, 1936 above.
                                            Hollywood, December 18, 1936.

| | | |
|---|---|---|
| B-4372-B | In A Sentimental Mood | Vri 556, Voc 3819 |
| B-4373-B | Deep Elm | Vri 504, Voc 3769 |
| B-4374-B | Peckin' - vBP&ch | Vri 556, Voc 3819 |
| B-4375-A | The Moon Is Grinning At Me - vBP | Vri 504, Voc 3769 |

    Ben Pollack-dir. Ray Woods-Joe Meyer-Muggsy Spanier-t/Joe Yukl-tb/Ben Kanter-Bud
    Carlton-cl-as/Artie Quenzer-Mort Friedman-ts/Al Beller-vn/Bob Laine-p/Garry McAdams
    g/Francis Palmer-sb/Graham Stevenson-d/Frances Hunt-v.
                                            Los Angeles, August 26, 1937.

| | | |
|---|---|---|
| DLA-852-B | Song Of The Islands - vFH | Dec 1424 |
| DLA-852-E | Song Of The Islands | - |
| DLA-855-A | I'm Yours For The Asking - vFH | - |

NOTE:- Matrices DLA-853/4 are by Connie Boswell, q.v., acc. by the orchestra.

                        Los Angeles, August 31, 1937.

| | | |
|---|---|---|
| DLA-866-A | Have You Ever Been In Heaven ? - vFH | Dec 1476, Pan 25976 |
| DLA-868-A | If You Ever Should Leave - vFH | Dec 1435 |
| DLA-869-B | Mama, I Wanna Make Rhythm - vFH | Dec 1476, X-1457, Pan 25976 |
| DLA-870-A | I'm Dependable (You Can Count On Me)- | Dec 1435 |
|           | - vFH | |

NOTE:- Matrix DLA-867 is by Connie Boswell, q.v., acc. by the orchestra.

BEN POLLACK AND HIS PICK-A-RIB BOYS : Muggsy Spanier-t/Ted Vesley-tb/Ben Kanter-cl/
    King Guion-ts/Bob Laine-p/Garry McAdams-g/Francis Palmer-sb/Ben Pollack-d/Peggy
    Mann-v.                                 Los Angeles, September 11, 1937.

| | | |
|---|---|---|
| DLA-910-A | Boogie Woogie | Dec 1517, Br 80148 |
| DLA-911-A | California, Here I Come | -         - |
| DLA-912-A | My Wild Irish Rose | Dec 1458, 3686, Br 80121 |
| DLA-913-A | Alice Blue Gown | Dec 1546, 3526, M-30107- Br 02557 |
| DLA-914-A | Cuddle Up A Little Closer - vPM | -         Br 80149 |
| DLA-915-A | Can't You Hear Me Calling, Caroline?-vPM | Dec 1458 |

BEN POLLACK AND HIS PICK-A-RIB BOYS : Muggsy Spanier-t/Ted Vesley-tb/Ben Kanter-cl/
Happy Lawson-ts/Bob Laine-p/Garry Adams-g/Francis Palmer-sb/Ben Pollack-d/Peggy
Mann-v.                                    Los Angeles, September 21, 1937.

DLA-945-A  If It's The Last Thing I Do - vPM        Dec 1465, M-30093, Br 02538
DLA-946-A  I'm In My Glory - vPM                    Dec 1488
DLA-947-A  You Made Me Love You - vPM               Dec 1465, M-30093, Br 80149,
                                                    02538, A-81261, A-81501
DLA-948-A  The Snake-Charmer                        Dec 1488, M-30107, Br 02557,80156

    Clyde Hurley-t/Joe Yukl-tb/Ben Kanter-cl/Happy Lawson-ts/Charles LaVere-p/Bob
    Hemphill-g/Slim Jim Taft-sb/Ben Pollack-d/Paula Gayle-v.
                                               Los Angeles, April 9, 1938.

DLA-1201-A  Morocco                                 Dec 1851, 80156
DLA-1204-A  Nobody's Gonna Take You From Me - vPG        -
NOTE:- Matrices DLA-1202/3 are by Connie Boswell, q.v., acc. by the band.

BEN POLLACK AND HIS ORCHESTRA : Ben Pollack dir. Don Anderson-Bob Goodrich-Andy
Secrest-t/Joe Yukl-tb/Opie Cates-Bud Carlton-as/Mort Friedman-Alan Harding-ts/Al
Beller-vn/Bob Laine-p/Bob Hemphill-g/Slim Jim Taft-sb/Graham Stevenson-d/Paula
Gayle-v.                                   Los Angeles, April 18, 1938.

DLA-1231-A  You'll Be Reminded Of Me - vPG          Dec 1815
DLA-1232-A  After You've Gone                        Dec 2057, Voc S-212
DLA-1233-A  There's Rain In My Eyes - vPG           Dec 1815, Pan 26001
DLA-1234-A  Everybody's Doin' It - vPG              Dec 1891, X-1606, Od 284392
DLA-1235-A  This Is The Life/The International Rag-vPG -        -            -
DLA-1236-A  Looking At The World Through Rose- ..o Dec 2057, Voc S-212
            Colored Glasses

    Ben Pollack-dir. Don Anderson-George Thow-Clyde Hurley-t/Earle Hagen-tb/Opie Cates
    Peyton Legare-as/Mort Friedman-George Hill-ts/Al Beller-vn/Bob Laine-p/Carroll
    Thompson-g/Jim Lynch-sb/Graham Stevenson-d/Paula Gayle-v.
                                               Los Angeles, August 4, 1938.

DLA-1360-A  Meet The Beat Of My Heart - vPG         Dec 2005
DLA-1361-A  Sing A Song Of Sixpence - vPG           Dec 2006
DLA-1362-A  What Are You Doing Tonight ? - vPG      Dec 2005
DLA-1363-A  Naturally - vPG                          Dec 2012
DLA-1364-A  So Unexpectedly - vPG                        -
DLA-1365-A  As Long As I Live - vPG                 Dec 2006

NOTE:- Australian Clifford 5250 (SWEETHEART TRAIL) is credited to Ben Pollack's Orch-
    estra, but it is in fact by Sam Lanin's Orchestra, and of no special interest.

## JIMMIE POLLACK'S ORCHESTRA

Pseudonym on Canadian Domino 181156 (SWEETNESS) for Fred Rich and his Orchestra, q.v.

## HARRY POLLOCK'S MAURICE CLUB DIAMONDS

The following sides by this band are of considerable interest as "hot" dance music,
and there is a likelihood of others, equally so, among the others.

Harry Pollock-vn dir. 2t/tb/cl-ss-as/cl-as/cl-ts/p/bj/bb/d/Hal Yates-v.
                                     New York, September 2, 1926.

X-256    Alabama Stomp                          Gnt 3377, Ch 15140
NOTE:- Champion 15140 as ALABAMA SERENADERS.

                                     New York, January 10, 1927.

GEX-446    There Ain't No "Maybe" In My Baby's    Gnt 6026, Ch 15213, Chg 236, 239,
           Eyes - vHY                             355, Sil 5029, Voc B-217, XA-18003
NOTE:- Champion 15213 as ALABAMA SERENADERS; Challenge 236, 239, 355 as FENWICK'S
DANCE ORCHESTRA; Vocalion B-217 as THE HARLEQUINADERS; XA-18003 as FRED GODFREY'S
JAZZ KNIGHTS.

Harry Pollock-vn dir. 2t/tb/cl-ss-as/cl-as/cl-ts/p/bj/bb/d/Joe O'Callihan-Al Shayne-v.                               New York, February 10, 1927.

| | | |
|---|---|---|
| GEX-526 | Underneath The Weeping Willow - vJO'C | Gnt 6069, Ch 15238, Voc X-10015 |
| GEX-527-A | I'm Gonna Meet My Sweetie Now - vAS | Gnt 6067, Ch 15229 |
| GEX-528 | You Can't Cry Over My Shoulder - vAS | - Ch 15228, Sil 5027, Spr 254 |

NOTE:- Champion 15228, 15229 as THE ALABAMA RED JACKETS; 15238 as THE ALABAMA SERENADERS; Vocalion X-10015 as THE RIVERSIDE DANCE BAND.

New York, March 28, 1927.

GEX-559    What Do I Care What Somebody Said ?-vAS Gnt 6083, Ch 15239, Sil 5049,
                                                Clm 2039, Gmn 2075, Voc B-**207**,
                                                Aco GA-20002

NOTE:- Champion 15239 as THE ALABAMA SERENADERS; Coliseum 2039 as MARYLAND DANCE ORCHESTRA; Guardsman 2075 as CABARET DANCE ORCHESTRA; Vocalion B-207 as THE HARLEQUINADERS; Aco GA-20002 as DAN HOWARD'S MELODY MAKERS.

## DANNY POLO AND HIS SWING STARS

Tommy McQuater-t/Danny Polo-cl/Sid Raymond-as*/Eddie Macauley-p/Eddie Freeman-g/Dick Ball-sb/Dudley Barber-d, or Polo and Macauley only**.
                                    London, October 1, 1937.

| | | |
|---|---|---|
| DTB-3248-1 | Stratton Street Strut | Dec F-6518, Y-5207 |
| DTB-3249-1 | More Than Somewhat | - - 1718 |
| DTB-3250-1 | *Blue Murder | Dec F-6550 - 3863, Lon 378 |
| DTB-3251-2 | *That's A Plenty | - |
| DTB-3252-2 | **Money For Jam | Dec F-6578 |
| DTB-3253-1 | **Mr. Polo Takes A Solo | |
| DTB-3254-1-2 | Home, Sweet Home | Rejected |

George Chisholm-tb added; Norman Brown-g replaces Freeman.
                                    London, January 11, 1938.

| | | |
|---|---|---|
| DTB-3483-2 | Jazz Me Blues | Dec F-6615, Y-5257 |
| DTB-3484-1 | Don't Try Your Jive On Me | Dec F-6604, Y-5216, Lon 378 |
| DTB-3485-1 | Mozeltov | - - |
| DTB-3486-1 | If You Were The Only Girl In The World | Dec F-6615, Y-5257 |

Philippe Brun-t/Danny Polo-cl/Alix Combelle-ts/Garland Wilson or Una Mae Carlisle-p/ Oscar Aleman-g/Louis Vola-sb/Jerry Mengo-d, or Polo, Wilson and Mengo only (where shown as 3).                      Paris, January 30, 1939.

| | | |
|---|---|---|
| 4859½hpp | You Made Me Love You - 3 | Dec F-7039, 59002 |
| 4860½hpp | Montmartre Moan - 3 | - - |
| 4861hpp | Doing The Gorgonzola - pGW | Dec F-6989, Br A-82071 |
| 4862hpp | Montparnasse Jump - pUMC | - - |
| 4863hpp | China Boy - pUMC | Dec F-7126, 59001 |
| 4864₂hpp | Polo-Naise - pGW | - - |

## THE PONCE SISTERS

Ethel and Dorothea Ponce-v, acc. by t/Joe Venuti-vn/? Frank Signorelli-p/Eddie Lang-g.                                 New York, December 16, 1932.

| | | |
|---|---|---|
| 265015-3 | Fit As A Fiddle | Col DB-1051 |
| 265016-1-2 | Contented | Rejected |
| 265017-2 | So At Last It's Come To This | Col DB-1051 |
| 265018-2 | A Million Dreams | Col DB-1073 |

## BOB POPE AND HIS ORCHESTRA

Bob Pope-v with unknown instrumentation and personnel other than Joan Lee and The Creole Sisters-v.                          New York, September 20, 1940.

| | | |
|---|---|---|
| 68132- | When You Got To Go You Got To Go-vBP&ch | Dec 8509 |
| 68133-A | That's All I Ask Of You - vJL | Dec 8519 |
| 68134- | I Want My Lagniappe - vBP-CS | Rejected |
| 68135- | Stop Teasing Me - vBP-CS | Dec 8509 |

BOB POPE AND HIS HOTEL CHARLOTTE ORCHESTRA : Bob Pope-t-v dir. t/tb/2as/ts/p/g/sb/d/
   Nolan Canova-Dixie Lee Sothern-v.     Charlotte, N. C., February 13, 1936.

| | | |
|---|---|---|
| 94695-1 | West Wind - vNC | BB B-6283, Vic JR-54, RZ MR-2081 |
| 94696-1 | The Bug | BB B-6300, RZ MR-2125 |
| 94697-1 | Early Bird - vBP | BB B-6283, Vic JR-54 |

Charlotte, N. C., February 16, 1936.

| | | |
|---|---|---|
| 99153-1 | Green Fields And Bluebirds - vNC | BB B-6286 |
| 99154-1 | Saddle Your Blues To A Wild Mustang-vNC | BB B-6284, RZ MR-2078 |
| 99155-1 | Moon Rose - vBP | - |
| 99156-1 | Breakin' In A Pair Of Shoes - vDLS | BB B-6285 |
| 99157-1 | Wah-Hoo ! - vDLS-BP-?NC | RZ MR-2080 |
| 99158-1 | Shoe-Shine Boy - vDLS | BB B-6286 |
| 99159-1 | That Lovely Night In Budapest - vNC | BB B-6299 |
| 99160-1 | That Never-To-Be-Forgotten Night - vNC | - |
| 99161-1 | Stop That Dog (He's Goin' Mad) - vDLS | BB B-6300 |

Charlotte, N. C., June 21, 1936.

| | | |
|---|---|---|
| 102749-1 | There's A Small Hotel - vNC | BB B-6453, Vic JR-54 |
| 102750-1 | Take My Heart - vNC | BB B-6454, Vic JR-64, RZ MR-2194 |
| 102751-1 | On Your Toes | BB B-6453, Vic JR-74, RZ MR-2320 |
| 102752-1 | Big Chief De Sota - vBP | BB B-6452 |
| 102763-1 | These Foolish Things Remind Me Of You-vNC | - |
| 102764-1 | Let's Get Hot And Truck - vNC | BB B-6471 |
| 102765-1 | Let's Sing Again - vNC | BB B-6454, Vic JR-64, RZ MR-2194 |
| 102766-1 | Madhouse | BB B-6508 |
| 102767-1 | On The Alamo - vNC | BB B-6502 |
| 102768-1 | When My Baby Smiles At Me - vNC | - |
| 102769-1 | Swamp Fire | BB B-6471 |

BOB POPE AND HIS ORCHESTRA : Bob Pope-t-v dir. t/tb/2as/ts/p/g/sb/Johnny Blowers-d-v/
   Nolan Canova-v.     Birmingham, Ala., April 11, 1937.

| | | |
|---|---|---|
| B-117- | When My Dream Boat Comes Home | ARC 7-07-12 |
| B-118-2 | Blue Skies | ARC 7-06-16 |
| B-119-1 | Marie | ARC 8-02-06 |
| B-120-2 | Rockin' Chair - vBP-JB | - |
| B-121-1 | I'll Always Be In Love With You | ARC 7-07-05 |
| B-122-1 | Whoa Babe ! - vBP | - |
| B-123-1-2 | I've Found A New Baby | Rejected |
| B-124-1 | The First Time I Saw You - vNC | ARC 7-06-16 |
| B-125-1-2 | Temptation | Rejected |
| B-126-1-2 | Estrellita | - |
| B-127-1-2 | Remember | - |
| B-128-1 | Nero | ARC 7-08-15 |
| B-129-1 | Washington Squabble | - |
| B-130- | Always | ARC 7-07-12 |

## PORTER'S BLUE DEVILS

Chicago band of t/tb/cl/p/bj/d.     New York, c. July 10, 1923.

| | | |
|---|---|---|
| 8454, -A | "E flat" Blues (sic) | Gnt 5210 |
| 8455-A | Original Charleston Strut | -    Apex 388, St 9425 |

Unknown as/ts/bb added; Ernest Hare-v. New York, c. September 5, 1923.

| | | |
|---|---|---|
| 8500, -A | Mama Goes Where Papa Goes - vEH | Gnt 5251, St 9442 |
| 8501-A-B | Steamboat Sal | Gnt 5249   - |
| 8502-A | Somebody's Wrong | Gnt 5251, EBW 3977 |

NOTE:- Edison Bell Winner 3977 as PAVILION PLAYERS.

New York, c. October 15, 1923.

| | | |
|---|---|---|
| 8559, -A-B | Walk, Jenny, Walk | Gnt 5282, St 9470 |
| 8560, -A | Mama Loves Papa (Papa Loves Mama) | Gnt 5281   - |
| 8561-A | Hot Dawg ! | Gnt 5282, St 9477 |

Chicago band of t/tb/cl/as/ts/p/bj/bb/d/Jack Kaufman-v.
                                        New York, c. November 12, 1923.

8600, -A  When It's Night Time In Italy - vJK     Gnt 5305,EBW 3964,Apex 405,St 9466
8601-A  I'm Sittin' Pretty In A Pretty Little City  -           -        -
NOTE:- Edison Bell Winner 3964 as REGENT ORCHESTRA.

### DICK PORTER AND  HIS ORCHESTRA

Jonah Jones-t/Joe Marsala-cl/Dick Porter-p-v/Eddie Condon-g/Ernest Myers-sb/George
  Wettling-d.                          New York, October 7, 1936.

20009-1  Sweet Thing - vDP                        Voc 3355
20010-1  (I'd Like To See Grandpa)                  -
         Swingin' To A Swing Tune - vDP
20011-1-2  Every Little Doggie Has His Day - vDP  Rejected
20012-1-2  Oh ! You Rogue (You Stole My Heart) - vDP  -

Jonah Jones-t/Edgar Sampson-as/Clyde Hart×p/Bobby Bennett-g/John Kirby-sb/Cozy Cole-
  d/Dick Porter-v.                      New York, February 16, 1937.

20682-2  Swing, Boy, Swing - vDP                  Voc 3478
20683-1  May I Have The Next Romance With You ?   Voc 3469
         - vDP
20684-2  There's No Two Ways About It - vDP          -
20685-1  Poor Robinson Crusoe - vDP               Voc 3478

### FLOSSIE PORTER

Pseudonym on Champion for Caroline Johnson, q.v.

### JOHN PORTER'S HARMONY TROUPE

Pseudonym on Australian Bon Marche for the following items listed in this book :-

188  'Deed I Do (Al Lentz and his Orchestra)
189  It Made You Happy When You Made Me Cry (Joe Candullo's Everglades Orchestra)
209  South Wind (Lou Gold and his Orchestra)

### KING PORTER AND  HIS ORCHESTRA

Pseudonym on Champion for George Matthews and the Carolina Night Hawks, q.v.

### SONNY PORTER

Willie Jackson (presumably New Orleans Willie Jackson, q.v.)-v, acc. by Eddie Lang-g
  /J. C. Johnson-p.                     New York, October 5, 1928.

147108-3  How Long - How Long Blues               Col 14366-D
147109-3  Deck Hand Blues                           -

### PORT OF HARLEM JAZZMEN

Frank Newton-t/J. C. Higginbotham-tb/Albert Ammons-p/Teddy Bunn-g/Johnny Williams-sb
  /Sidney Catlett-d.                    New York, April 7, 1939.

GM-515-A  Port Of Harlem Blues                    BN 14
GM-516-2  Mighty Blues                            BN 3
GM-517-1  Rocking The Blues                         -

### PORT OF HARLEM SEVEN

Frank Newton-t/J. C. Higginbotham-tb/Sidney Bechet-cl-ss/Meade Lux Lewis-p/Teddy
  Bunn-g/Johnny Williams-sb/Sidney Catlett-d.
                                        New York, June 8, 1939.

GM-532-X  Blues For Tommy                         BN 7, JS 545
GM-536-II Pounding Heart Blues                    BN 6

Vocal, acc. by Bubber Miley or Louis Metcalf-c/Louis Hooper-p, and either ? Jake
Frazier-tb or Bob Fuller-cl.              New York, c. December 15, 1924.

5786-1  A Good Man Is Hard To Find - tb        Ban 1483, Dom 3452,Or 325,Re 9782
5787-1  Blind Man Blues - cl                    Ban 1484, Dom 3453, Re 9781
NOTE:- Domino 3452 and 3453 as SALLY DALE; Oriole 325 as MAMIE ROMER.  The name
NETTIE POTTER is also used on Pathe Actuelle and Perfect as a pseudonym for Monette
Moore, and on Regal for Alberta Perkins, both q.v.

## ART POWELL'S ORCHESTRA

Pseudonym on Australian Golden Tongue for Lou Gold and his Orchestra, q.v.

## DICK POWELL

Before becoming a most popular film actor and playing straight roles on television,
Dick Powell was the banjoist and vocalist with Charlie Davis and his Orchestra,q.v.
The following sides made under his own name are of jazz interest for their accom-
paniments.

Vocal, acc. by cl/p.                  ? Indianapolis, c. January, 1928.

        Beautiful                          Voc 15647
        Is She My Girl Friend ? (How-de-ow-dow)      -

Acc. by Pee Wee Erwin-t/Elmer Rehmus-tb/Elmer Feldkamp-cl-as/Freddy Martin-cl-ts/
Terry Shand or Bobby van Eps-p/George van Eps-g/George Green-sb/Eddie Schaff-d, and
possibly others.                     New York, May 23, 1933.

13386-1  The Gold Diggers' Song (We're In The    Per 12919, Bcst 3339
           Money)
13387-1  Pettin' In The Park                     Per 12920       -
13389-1  I've Got To Sing A Torch Song                  Bsct 3340
NOTE:- Matrix 13388 is a waltz sung by Dick Powell.

Acc. by Victor Arden dir. Manny Klein-t/Tommy Dorsey-tb/cl-as/as/ts/Joe Venuti-vn/p
? Carl Kress-g/sb/d.                  New York, June 21, 1935.

B-17723-2  Lulu's Back In Town                  Br 7469, A-9951, Dec F-5694,
                                               Col DO-1426

## ELEANOR POWELL

See Tommy Dorsey.

## HERVY POWELL

Pseudonym on Australian Panachord for Seger Ellis, q.v.

## POWELL'S JAZZ MONARCHS

Jimmy Powell-cl-as-ts dir. t/George Lightfoot-as-ts/Isaac Jefferson-p/William Calloway
bj-v/Floyd Casey-d.                  St. Louis, May 14, 1926.

9682-A  Chauffeur's Shuffle                     OK 8333
9683-A  Laughing Blues - vWC                          -

## LOUIS POWELL

Vocal, acc. by the Jazz Wizards : Richard M. Jones-p/? George Barnes-elg/d.
                                     Chicago, March 23, 1938.

C-2155-1  Sissy                                 Voc 04040
C-2156-1  Mushmouth Blues                             -

Billy Butterfield-t/Lou McGarity-tb/Benny Goodman (as "SHOELESS" JOHN JACKSON)-cl/
George Berg-ts/Mel Powell-p/Al Morgan-sb/Kansas Fields-d.
                                        New York, c. February, 1942.

| | | |
|---|---|---|
| 76986-A | When Did You Leave Heaven ? | Com 543, 7531 |
| 76987-A | The World Is Waiting For The Sunrise | Com 544 |
| 76988-A | Blue Skies | Com 543, 7531 |
| 76989-A | Mood At Twilight | Com 544 |

### TEDDY POWELL AND HIS ORCHESTRA

Teddy Powell-a dir. George Esposito-Irving Goodman-Jerry Neary-t/Sam Genuso-Pete
Skinner-tb/George Koenig-as/Gus Bivona-cl-as/Don Lodice-Pete Mondello-ts/Milton
Raskin-p/Ben Heller-g/Felix Giobbe-sb/Charlie French-d/Jimmy Blair-Ruth Gaylor-v/
Ben Homer-Fred Norman-a.             New York, October 6, 1939.

| | | |
|---|---|---|
| 66733-A | In A Persian Market | Dec 2906, Br 03120 |
| 66734-A | Teddy's Boogie Woogie | Dec 2806, Br 02904 |
| 66735-A | March Of The Toys | Dec 2906    - |
| 66736-A | Jamaica Jam | Dec 2806, Br 80123, 03120, 03155 |

New York, November 13, 1939.

| | | |
|---|---|---|
| 66867-A | Pussy In The Corner - aBH | Dec 2941, Br 02955 |
| 66868-A | Flea On A Spree - aBH | Dec 2985, Br 02960 |
| 66869-A | Some Day - aBH | Dec 2941, Br 02935 |
| 66870-A | The Sphinx - aBH | Dec 2985, Br 02960 |

Joe Bauer-t replaces Goodman; John Grassi-tb replaces Genuso; Mascagni Ruffo-as
replaces Koenig; Tom Morgan-g replaces Heller.
                                        New York, February 1, 1940.

| | | |
|---|---|---|
| 67135-A | The One I Love (Belongs To Somebody Else) - vRG | Dec 3034 |
| 67136-A | I Get The Blues When It Rains - vJB |    - |
| 67137-A | Am I Blue ? - vRG | Dec 3094 |
| 67138-A | Ridin' The Subways |    -    Br 03155 |

Dick Fisher-g replaces Morgan; Ray Conniff-a.
                                        New York, May 20, 1940.

| | | |
|---|---|---|
| 67777-A | Please Take A Letter, Miss Brown - vJB | Dec 3218 |
| 67778-B | Feather Merchant's Ball - aRC | Dec 3234, Br 03123 |
| 67779-A | Outside Of That, I Love You - vRG | Dec 3218 |
| 67780-A | Teddy Bear Boogie - aTP | Dec 3234, 3383, Br 80123, 03123 |

Teddy Powell dir. Tom d'Agostino-Howard Gaffney-James Morreale-t/John Grassi-Tom Reo
John O'Rourke-tb/Gene Zanoni-as/Phil Olivella-cl-as/Harry Davis-Lenny Hartman-ts/
Buddy Weed-p-a/Dick Fisher-g/Tony Frederici-sb/Bill Schulza-d/Jimmy Blair-Ruth
Gaylor-v/Bob Mersey-a.               New York, December 4, 1940.

| | | |
|---|---|---|
| 058304-1 | It All Comes Back To Me Now - vRG | BB B-11000 |
| 058305-1 | It's Sad But True - vJB | BB B-10974, HMV EA-2788 |
| 058306-1 or -2 | I Can't Rub You Out Of My Eyes-vRG&4 | - |
| 058307-2 | Sunset At Sea - vJB | BB B-11000 |

Tony Aless-p replaces Weed; Turk van Lake-g replaces Fisher; Louis Fromm-d
replaces Schulza.                    New York, January 9, 1941.

| | | |
|---|---|---|
| 058790-1 | Slap-Happy Lassie - vRG | BB B-11039 |
| 058791-1 | All Night Long - vRG | - |
| 058792-1 | Taking A Chance On Love - vRG | BB B-11016 |
| 058793-1 | Here's My Heart - vRG/aBM | - |

Jesse Ray Heatn-tb replaces Reo.     New York, January 29, 1941.

| | | |
|---|---|---|
| 060399-1 | Boogin' On The Downbeat - aBM | BB B-11176 |
| 060600-1 | Bluebird Boogie Woogie - aBM | BB B-11082 |
| 060601-2 | That Old Gang Of Mine - vRG | - |
| 060602-1 | Time On My Hands - vRG | BB B-11176 |

Teddy Powell-a dir. Tom d'Agostino-Howard Gaffney-James Morreale-t/John Grassi-Bill
  Westfall-John O'Rourke-tb/Gene Zanoni-as/Phil Olivella-cl-as/Harry Davis-Lenny
  Hartman-ts/Tony Aless-p/Turk van Lake-g/Tony Frederici-sb/Louis Fromm-d/Ruth
  Gaylor-v/Bob Mersey-a.          New York, February 26, 1941.

| | | |
|---|---|---|
| 062709-1 | The Wise Old Owl - vRG | BB B-11089 |
| 062710-1 | Two Hearts That Pass In The Night - vRG | - |
| 062711-1 | Straight Eight Boogie - aBM | BB B-11092, RZ MR-3629, MR-20333 |
| 062712-1 | Talking To The Wind - vRG | - |

Harry Garey-tb replaces Grassi; Joe di Maggio-cl-as replaces Olivella; Mickey
Folus-ts replaces Hartman; Bobby Domenick-g replaces van Lake.
                              New York, March 24, 1941.

| | | |
|---|---|---|
| 062771-1 | Friendly Tavern - vRG&ch | BB B-11113 |
| 062772-1 | Blue Danube - aTP | BB B-11132 |
| 062773-1 | A Rendezvous In Rio (Un Momento) - vRG | - |
| 062774-1 | The Things I Love - vRG | BB B-11113 |

George Esposito-t added,          New York, April 23, 1941.

| | | |
|---|---|---|
| 063807-1 | I Went Out Of My Way - vRG | BB B-11152, RZ G-24616 |
| 063808-1 | Ode To Spring - aBM | - RZ MR-3629 - MR-20333 |
| 063809-1 | All I Need - vRG | BB B-11201 |
| 063810-2 | Sans Culottes - aBM | - RZ MR-3598 |

Bob Person-t replaces Morreale and Esposito; Dave Matthews-a.
                              New York, June 24, 1941.

| | | |
|---|---|---|
| 066137-1 | I See A Million People (But All I Can See Is You) - vRG | BB B-11232, RZ G-24726 |
| 066138-1 | Jim - vRG | BB B-11213 |
| 066139-1 | Jungle Boogie - aBM | BB B-11232 |
| 066140-1 | In Pinetop's Footsteps - aBM | BB B-11276, RZ MR-3598 |
| 066141-1 | Steady Teddy - aDM | BB B-11213 |

Mickey Cielo-t replaces Person; Joe Ortolano-tb replaces Westfall; Phil Olivella-
cl-as replaces di Maggio; Lester Merkin-ts replaces Folus; Dick Judge-v added.
                              New York, July 18, 1941.

| | | |
|---|---|---|
| 066961-1 | I Used To Love You (But It's All Over Now) - vRG | Rejected |
| 066962-1 | I'd Love You Again - VDJ | BB B-11248 |
| 066963-1 | Mickey - vRG | BB B-11276 |
| 066964-2 | Yes Indeed ! - vRG&ch | BB B-11248 |
| 066965-1 | Amour - vDJ | Rejected |

Teddy Powell dir. Tom d'Agostino-Harvey Streiner-Mickey Cielo-t/Harry Garey-Joe
  Ortolano-John O'Rourke-tb/Gene Zanoni-as/Joe di Maggio-cl-as/Harry Davis-Tino
  Isgrow-ts/Tony Aless-p/Barry Galbraith-g/Wilbur Hoffman-sb/Louis Fromm-d/Ruth
  Gaylor-Dick Judge-v.          New York, September 11, 1941.

| | | |
|---|---|---|
| 066961-2 | I Used To Love You (But It's All Over Now) - vRG | BB B-11270 |
| 067785-1 | Honey - vRG | - |
| 067786-1 | Make Love To Me - vRG | BB B-11300 |
| 067787-1 | The Birth Of The Blues - vRG | - |
| 067788-1 | I Love You Best Of All - vRG | BB B-11373 |

Roy Hammerslag-Ronnie Perry-ts replace Davis and Isgrow; Zeb Julian-g replaces
Galbraith; Ovid "Biddy" Bastien-sb replaces Hoffman.
                              New York, October 15, 1941.

| | | |
|---|---|---|
| 071490-1 | Hereafter | BB B-11358 |
| 071491-1 | When Your Old Wedding Ring Was New - v4 | BB B-11338 |
| 071492-1 | You're Not The Kind - vRG | BB B-11358 |
| 071493-1 | Sweethearts Or Strangers - vDJ | BB B-11338 |

Teddy Powell dir. Tom d'Agostino-Harvey Streiner-George Esposito-t/Harry Garey-Joe
Ortolano-John O'Rourke-tb/Gene Zanoni-as/Phil Olivella-cl-as/Roy Hammerslag-Ronnie
Perry-ts/Tony Aless-p/Zeb Julian-g/Ovid "Biddy" Bastien-sb/Louis Fromm-d/Peggy
Mann-Dick Judge-v.            New York, November 4, 1941.

| | | |
|---|---|---|
| 068074-1 | Serenade To A Maid (A Bronx Serenade)vO | BB B-11373 |
| 068075-1-2 | Hoe Down - vPM | BB B-11380 |
| 068076-1 | How About You - vPM | - |
| 068077-1 | How Do You Do Without Me ? - vPM-DJ | BB B-11427 |
| 068078-1 | Kickin' The Conga Around - vPM | BB B-11412 |

Sid Winnick-t replaces Esposito.      New York, December 16, 1941.

| | | |
|---|---|---|
| 068482-1 | Goodbye Mama (I'm Off To Yokohama) | BB B-11412 |
| | - vDJ-PM&ch | |
| 068483-1 | Would It Make Any Difference To You ? | Rejected |
| | - vPM | |
| 068484-1-2 | All Through The Night - vPM | BB B-11427, RZ G-24875 |
| 068485-1 | I Ain't Tellin' | Rejected |

Teddy Powell dir. Irving Goodman-Jack Hansen-Dick Mains-t/Harry Garey-Jack Satter-
field-John O'Rourke-tb/George Bohn-as/Hal Tenny on-cl-as/Roy Hammerslag-Ronnie
Perry-ts/Chuck Gentry-bar/Tony Aless-p/Zeb Julian-g/Ed Cunningham-sb/Louis Fromm-
d/Peggy Mann-Tommy Taylor-v.      New York, March 10, 1942.

| | | |
|---|---|---|
| 073420-1 | All Those Wonderful Years - vPM | BB B-11499 |
| 073421-1 | 'Tain't No Good (Like A Nickel Made | BB B-11516 |
| | Of Wood) - vPM-TT | |
| 073422-1 | If You Are But A Dream | - |
| 073423-1 | There Won't Be A Shortage Of Love-vPM | BB B-11499 |

John Austin-t replaces Goodman; Irving Fazola-cl-as replaces Tennyson; Larry
Molinelli-bar replaces Gentry.      New York, April 30, 1942.

| | | |
|---|---|---|
| 073856-1 | Somebody's Thinking Of You Tonight-vPM | BB B-11520 |
| 073857-1 | Got The Moon In My Pocket - vTT | - |

Leo Cecchi-tb replaces Satterfield; Nick Caiazza-Pete Mondello-ts replace Perry
and Hammerslag; Carmen Mastren-g replaces Julian.
            New York, June 12, 1942.

| | | |
|---|---|---|
| 075086-1 | Be Careful, It's My Heart - vTT | BB B-11554 |
| 075087-1 | Midsummer Matinee - vPM | - |
| 075088-1 | Love Is A Song - vPM | BB B-11556 |
| 075089-1 | Tapestry In Blue - vPM | - |

Teddy Powell dir. George Esposito-Jack Hansen-Dick Mains-t/Harry Garey-Leo Cecchi-
John O'Rourke-tb/George Bohn-as/Irving Fazola-cl-as/Roy Hammerslag-Ronnie Perry-
ts/Marty Berman-bar/Tony Aless-p/Carmen Mastren-g/Ed Cunningham-sb/Louis Fromm-d/
Peggy Mann-Tommy Taylor-v.      New York, July 17, 1942.

| | | |
|---|---|---|
| 075564-1 | There Will Never Be Another You - vPM | BB B-11568 |
| 075565-1 | Let's Get Lost - vPM | BB 30-0809 |
| 075566-1 | A Boy In Khaki - A Girl In Lace - vTT | BB B-11568 |
| 075567-1 | "Murder," He Says - vPM&ch | BB 30-0809 |

New York, July 24, 1942.

| | | |
|---|---|---|
| 075575-1 | Helpless - vPM | BB B-11575 |
| 075576-1 | Sweet Georgia Brown | Rejected |
| 075577-1 | Blue Sentimental Mood - vPM | - |
| 075578-1 | (As Long As You're Not In Love With | BB B-11575 |
| | Anyone Else) Why Don't You Fall In Love With Me ? - vPM | |

## TOMMY POWELL AND HIS HI-DE-HO BOYS

Instrumentation and personnel unknown.    Chicago, October 4, 1936.

| | | |
|---|---|---|
| 90919- | Hi-De-Ho Swing | Dec 7231 |
| 90920- | That Cat Is High | - |

Instrumentation and personnel unknown.    Chicago, November 18, 1936.

| | | |
|---|---|---|
| 90988- | Just About The Time | Dec 7255 |
| 90989- | Got The Blues For Harlem | - |

## WALTER POWELL AND HIS ORCHESTRA

Walter Powell-tb dir. unknown group including Joe Devoe-cl-as.
New York, December 16, 1938.

| | | |
|---|---|---|
| M-943-1-2 | Mint Julep | Rejected |
| M-944-1-2 | Listen To The Mocking Bird | - |
| M-945-1 | Devil's Holiday | Voc 4612 |
| M-946-2 | Definition Of Swing | - |

## JULIA/JULIUS POWERS

Pseudonym on Harmograph for Ida Cox, q.v.

## OLLIE POWERS

Vocal, acc. by Clarence M. Jones-p.      Chicago, June, 1923.

| | | |
|---|---|---|
| 1449-1-2 | Pensacola Joe | Pm 12047, Hg 841 |
| 1450 | That Old Gang Of Mine | -          - |

NOTE:- Harmograph 841 as HOWARD SIMMS, piano acc. by CLARENCE WRIGHT.

OLLIE POWERS' HARMONY SYNCOPATORS : Ollie Powers-d dir. Alex Calamese-Tommy Ladnier-c/Eddie Vincent-tb/Jimmie Noone-cl/Horace Diemer-as/Glover Compton-p/John Basley-bj/William "Bass" Moore-bb.      Chicago, September, 1923.

| | | |
|---|---|---|
| 1502-1 | Play That Thing | Cx 40263, Pur 11263 |
| 1502-3 | Play That Thing | -Pm 20263 - Hg 851,AM 7,Gzl 1039 |
| 1502-4 | Play That Thing | Pm 12059, UHCA 79, JI 6,Jazz 5003 |
| | | AFG 7, Sto KB-IOI |
| 1505-5 | Play That Thing | Pm 12059, Hg 874 |
| 1505-6 | Play That Thing | - |

NOTE:- Harmograph 851 as OLLIE POWERS' ORCHESTRA; 874 as CLARENCE YOUNG'S HARMONY SYNCOPATORS,

Vocal, acc. by Bernie Young-c/Preston Jackson-tb/Stump Evans-cl-Cm/Cassino Simpson-p/Mike McKendrick-bj/Eddie Temple-d.     Chicago, October, 1923.

| | | |
|---|---|---|
| 1538-1-2 | Jazzbo Jenkins | Pm 12059, Hg 874 |

NOTE:- Harmograph 874 as CLARENCE YOUNG.

Acc. by Shelton Brooks-p/Raymond Mayo-bj.
New York, January 14, 1925.

| | | |
|---|---|---|
| 140247-1 | After All These Years | Col rejected |
| 140248-2 | A Fool And A Butterfly | - |

## ANDY PREER AND THE COTTON CLUB ORCHESTRA

Andy Preer dir. R. Q. Dickerson-Lammar Wright-t/De Priest Wheeler-tb/Davey Jones-George Scott-cl-as/Andrew Brown-cl-ts/Earres Prince-p/Charley Stamps-bj/Jimmy Smith-bb/Leroy Maxey-d.      New York, February 3, 1927.

| | | |
|---|---|---|
| GEX-513, -A-C | I've Found A New Baby | Gnt 6056, Ch 15227, 40112, |
| | | KP K-102, Voc B-219 |

NOTE:- Champion 15227 as THE DIXIE BOYS.

## EVELYN PREER

This artist, whose real surname was Peer, made a number of records of popular songs for the Banner group, and for Victor, between the summers of 1926 and 1927. About half of them are of no interest as jazz either for their material, its present-ation or its accompaniment, but the remainder are very different and are included here.

Vocal, acc. by Tom Morris-c/Bob Fuller-cl/Mike Jackson-p.
                                    New York, September 7, 1926.

  36099-3  Make Me Know It                        Vic 20306

  Acc. by c/tb/cl/vn/p/bj/d.          New York, c. September 8, 1926.

  6810-2  Lucky Day                   Ban 1848, Dom 3821, Re 8159
  6811-2  The Birth Of The Blues           - BM 216 -          - Imp 1777
  NOTE:- Banner 1848, Domino 3821 and Regal 8159 as HOTSY JARVIS AND HER GANG;
  Imperial 1777 as RADIO RED; Bon Marche 216 as SINCLAIR FRANKS.

  Acc. by c/2as/vn/p/bj/bb/d.          New York, October 14, 1926.

  36823-2  It Takes A Good Woman To Keep A Good Man Vic 20306
           At Home

  Acc. by her Gang : Red Nichols-t/Miff Mole-tb/Alfie Evans or Dick Johnson-cl-as/
  ? Peter de Rose or Rube Bloom-p/own k.  New York, c. November 23, 1926.

  6954-6  Sunday                        Ban 1895, Dom 3864, Or 807,
                                        Re 8208, Imp 1788, Apex 8579
  6955-6  Cock-a-Doodle, I'm Off My Noodle   Ban 1895, Dom 3864, Re 8208
          (My Baby's Back)
  NOTE:- Oriole 807 and Apex 8579 as HOTSY JARVIS; Imperial 1788 as RADIO RED. The
  reverse of the latter, also as RADIO RED, is by another artist and of no interest.

  Acc. by Duke Ellington and his Orchestra : Duke Ellington-p dir. Bubber Miley-c/
  cl-as/Otto Hardwick-as-vn/Sonny Greer-d.New York, January 10, 1927.

  37527-1-2-3  Make Me Love You                   Rejected
  37528-1  If You Can't Hold The Man You Love     Tax LP-9 (LP)
  37528-3  If You Can't Hold The Man You Love     Vic 731043 (LP)

EVELYN THOMPSON : Vocal, acc. by c/cl/p.  New York, c. April 1, 1927.

  E-4786   Looking For The Sunshine - Walking     Voc 15548
           Around In The Rain

                                    New York, May, 1927.

  E-4941   One Sweet Letter From You              Voc 15548

                      PREMIER   DANCE ORCHESTRA

Pseudonym on Beltona 771 and 885 for Jeffries and his Rialto Orchestra, q.v.

                      THE PRESIDENT   ORCHESTRA

Pseudonym on Scala 529 (GEORGIA ROSE) for the California Ramblers, q.v.

                            SAM PRICE

SAMMY PRICE AND HIS FOUR QUARTERS : T/Bert Johnson-tb/Sam Price-p/bj.
                                    Dallas, October, 1929.

  DAL-464-  Blue Rhythm Stomp                     Br 7136

SAM PRICE AND HIS TEXAS BLUSICIANS : Joe Brown-Ed Mullens-t/Don Stovall-as/Ray Hill-
  ts/Sam Price-p-v/Duke Jones-sb/Wilbert Kirk-d.
                                    New York, March 13, 1940.

  67304-A  Fetch It To Me                         Dec 7781
  67305-A  Cow Cow Blues                          Dec 7732
  67306-A  Sweepin' The Blues Away                Dec 7781, 48011
  67307-A  Swing Out In The Groove - vSP          Dec 7732

                                    New York, September 26, 1940.

  68149-A  How 'Bout That Mess                    Dec 8505, Br 03453
  68150-A  Oh Red - vSP                              -
  68151-A  Oh Lawdy Mama - vSP                    Dec 7811
  68152-A  The Dirty Dozens - vSP                    -       48011

Lem Johnson-cl-v/Sam Price-p-v/sb/d-wb.　New York, December 6, 1940.

| | | |
|---|---|---|
| 68457-A | Thinking - vSP | Dec 8515 |
| 68458-A | Queen Street Blues - vLJ | Dec 7820 |
| 68459-A | Jumpin' The Boogie | Dec 8515 |
| 68460-A | Louise Louise - vLJ | Dec 7820 |

NOTE:- Decca 7820 as LEM JOHNSON AND HIS WASHBOARD BAND.

Shad Collins-Bill Johnson-t/Don Stovall-as/Lester Young-ts/Sam Price-p-v/Duke Jones-sb/Harold West-d/Yack Taylor-Spo-De-O Sam (presumably Sam Price)-v.
New York, April 3, 1941.

| | | |
|---|---|---|
| 68920-A | The Goon Drag (Gone Wid De Goon) | Dec 8547 |
| 68921-A | Things 'Bout Coming My Way - vYT | Dec 8557 |
| 68922-A | Lead Me Daddy Straight To The Bar-vS-S | Dec 8649 |
| 68923-A | Just Jivin' Around | Dec 8557 |

Sam Price-p-v/g/d unless marked */Yack Taylor-v.
New York, April 8, 1941.

| | | |
|---|---|---|
| 68951- | My Mellow Man - vYT | Dec 7836 |
| 68952- | Knockin' Myself Out - vYT | - |
| 68953-A | *You're Gonna Go Your Way And I'm Gonna Go Mine - vYT | Dec 7850 |
| 68954-A | I Lost Love (When I Lost You) - vSP | Dec 8547 |

NOTE:- Decca 7836 and 7850 as YACK TAYLOR.

Chester Boone-t/Floyd Brady-tb/Don Stovall-as/Skippy Williams-ts/Sam Price-p-v/
Ernest Hill-sb/Herb Cowens-d.　New York, June 13, 1941.

| | | |
|---|---|---|
| 69365-A | Do You Dig My Jive ? - vch | Dec 8575 |
| 69366-A | I Know How To Do It - vSP&ch | Dec 8566 |
| 69367-A | Valetta - vSP | - |
| 69368- | Boogie Woogie Moan | Dec 8575 |

Emmett Berry-t/Ray Hogan-tb/Fess Williams-cl-as/Don Stovall-as/Sam Price-p/Billy
Taylor-sb/J. C. Heard-d/Ruby Smith-Jack Meredith-v.
New York, December 10, 1941.

| | | |
|---|---|---|
| 70029-A | Why Don't You Love Me Any More ? - vRS | Dec 8609 |
| 70030-A | Harlem Gin Blues - vRS | - |
| 70031-A-B | My Name Is Jim - vJM | Rejected |
| 70032-B | Match Box Blues - vJM | Dec 8624 |

Herman Autrey-t/David Young-ts/Sam Price-p/William Lewis-g/Vernon King-sb/O'Neil
Spencer-d/Mabel Robinson-v.　New York, January 20, 1942.

| | | |
|---|---|---|
| 70187-A | Me And My Chauffeur - vMR | Dec 8601 |
| 70188-A | I've Got Too Many Blues - vMR | - |
| 70189-A | It's All Right, Jack | Dec 8649 |
| 70190-A | Blow, Katy, Blow | Dec 8624 |

Instrumentation and personnel unknown.　New York, July 25, 1942.

| | | |
|---|---|---|
| 71195-A | Teed Up | Dec 8642 |
| 71196-A | Frantic | - |

## VIC PRICE AND HIS ORCHESTRA

The following title from fifteen issued under this name on Gennett during 1928 is of
some interest as "hot" dance music, and there may be others like it.

Leo McConville and another-t/tb/Larry Abbott-cl-as/as/ts/p/bj/bb/d/Arthur Fields-v.
New York, April 5, 1928.

| | | |
|---|---|---|
| GEX-1184-A | I'm More Than Satisfied - vAF | Gnt 6440, Bell 605, Ch 15494, Her 8059, Spr 376 |

NOTE:- Champion 15494 as THE DIXIE RAMBLERS; Herwin 8059 as SHERMAN SUN-DODGERS.

LOUIS PRIMA AND HIS NEW ORLEANS GANG : Louis Prima-t-v/George Brunies-tb/Sidney
  Arodin-cl/Claude Thornhill-p/George van Eps-g/Artie Shapiro-sb/Stan King-d.
                                    New York, September 27, 1934.

B-16023-A  That's Where The South Begins - vLP    Br 7524, A-500515
B-16024-A  Jamaica Shout                               -      - Bm 1104, Dec F-5459
B-16025-A  Long About Midnight - vLP               Br 7335, A-500516
B-16026-A  Star Dust - vLP                             -      -    Pol 580009

  Benny Pottle-sb replaces Shapiro.         New York, October 30, 1934.

B-16150-A-B  Sing It 'Way Low Down - vLP           Br rejected

  Brunies speaks*.                          New York, November 1, 1934.

B-16150-D  Sing It 'Way Low Down - vLP            Dec F-5777, Br A-500540 ?
B-16286-B  *Let's Have A Jubilee - vLP            Dec F-5499   -
B-16288-A  I Still Want You - vLP                 Br 7320, A-500542, 4968, Bm 1104
B-16289-A  (Looks Like I'm) Breakin' The Ice-vLP    -      -      - Dec F-5459
  NOTE:- Biltmore 1104 as GEORGE BRUNIES AND HIS NEW ORLEANS GANG.  Matrix 16287 was
  not used.

                              New York, November 30, 1934.

B-16150-E  Sing It 'Way Low Down - vLP            Br 7394, A-500540 ?
B-16286-C  *Let's Have A Jubilee - vLP               -      -    4988

  Eddie Miller-cl-ts replaces Arodin; Nappy Lamare-g replaces van Eps.
                              New York, December 26, 1934.

B-16540-A  House Rent Party Day - vLP             Br 7376, A-500541
B-16541-A  It's The Rhythm In Me - vLP            Br 7471, A-500543, Dec F-5528
B-16542-A  *Worry Blues - vLP                        -      -
B-16543-A  Bright Eyes - vLP                      Br 7376, A-500541,4988,Dec F-5499

  Louis Prima-t-v/Larry Altpeter-tb/Eddie Miller-cl-ts/Frank Pinero-p/Garry McAdams-
  g/Jack Ryan-sb/Ray Bauduc-d.              New York, April 3, 1935.

B-17239-1  Put On An Old Pair Of Shoes - vLP      Br 7419, 5000, Dec F-5621
B-17240-1  Sugar Is Sweet And So Are You - vLP    Br 7431
B-17241-1  I'm Livin' In A Great Big Way - vLP    Br 7419
B-17242-1  Swing Me With Rhythm - vLP             Br 7431, 02077, A-9939, Lucky S-2

  Altpeter omitted; Pee Wee Russell-cl replaces Miller; Sam Weiss-d replaces Bauduc.
                              New York, May 17, 1935.

B-17612-1  The Lady In Red - vLP                  Br 7448, A-500575
B-17613-1  Chinatown, My Chinatown - vLP          Br 7456, A-500561, Dec F-5626
B-17614-1  Chasing Shadows - vLP                  Br 7448, A-500575, Dec F-5621
B-17615-1  Basin Street Blues - vLP               Br 7456, A-500561, Dec F-5626,
                                                  Pol 580009

                              New York, June 27, 1935.

B-17739-1  In A Little Gypsy Tea Room - vLP       Br 7479, Lucky S-26
B-17740-1-2  Let's Swing It - vLP                    -

                              New York, July 2, 1935.

B-17762-1  Plain Old Me - vLP                     Br 7499
B-17763-1-2  How'm I Doin' ? (Hey-Hey) - vLP      Br 7531, A-9869, Dec F-5692
B-17764-1  Weather Man - vLP                      Br 7499, Dec F-5777
B-17765-1  Solitude - vLP                         Br 7531, A-9869, Dec F-5692

                              New York, September 14, 1935.

B-17762-2  Plain Old Me - vLP                     Br 7499 ?
  NOTE:- B-17762 may be merely a dubbing of matrix B-17762-1.

LOUIS PRIMA AND HIS NEW ORLEANS GANG : Louis Prima-t-v/Pee Wee Russell-cl/Frank
Pinero-p/Garry McAdams-g/Jack Ryan-sb.  Los Angeles, November 30, 1935.

| | | |
|---|---|---|
| LA-1078-B | Sweet Sue - vLP | Br 7596, A-9975, Dec F-5911 |
| LA-1079-B | I'm Shooting High - vLP | Br 7586, RZ G-22696 |
| LA-1080-B | I Love You Truly - vLP | Br 7596, A-9975, Dec F-5911 |
| LA-1081-A-B | I've Got My Fingers Crossed - vLP | Br 7586, RZ G-22696 |

Joe Catalyne-ts/George Pemberty-d added.
                                  Los Angeles, February 28, 1936.

| | | |
|---|---|---|
| LA-1101-A | It's Been So Long - vLP | Br 7628 |
| LA-1102-A | At The Darktown Strutters' Ball - vLP | Br 7657, Dec F-6001 |
| LA-1103-A | Dinah - vLP | Br 7666, A-81011, 5065, Dec F-6001, Col CQ-1432 |
| LA-1104-A | Lazy River - vLP | Br 7666, A-81011 |
| LA-1105-A | Alice Blue Gown - vLP | Br 7657 |
| LA-1106-A | Sing, Sing, Sing - vLP | Br 7628, 5030 |

Gene Lafreniere-Denny Donaldson-t/Bill Atkinson-tb/George Moore-Peyton Legare-as
added to last personnel.         Los Angeles, May 17, 1936.

| | | |
|---|---|---|
| LA-1111-A | Let's Get Together And Swing - vLP | Br 7740, 5065, Col CQ-1432, Lucky S-23 |
| LA-1112-A | Cross Patch - vLP | Br 7680 |
| LA-1113-A | Swing Me A Lullaby - vLP | - |
| LA-1114-A | The Stars Know (I'm In Love With You) - vLP | Br 7740 |
| LA-1115-A | Confessin' - vLP | Br 7709 |
| LA-1116-A | Let's Have Fun - vLP | - |

Louis Prima-t-v/Red Bolmar-t/Julian Laine-tb/Meyer Weinberg-cl/Sal Franzella-Hal
Jordy-as/Joe Catalyne-ts/Frank Pinero-p/Garry McAdams-g/Jack Ryan-sb/George
Pemberty-d.                      Chicago, November 16, 1936.

| | | |
|---|---|---|
| C-1675-1 | Mr. Ghost Goes To Town | Voc 3388 |
| C-1676-1 | Pennies From Heaven - vLP | Voc 3376, Br A-81100 |
| C-1677-1 | The Goose Hangs High | Voc 3388 |
| C-1678-1 | What Will Santa Claus Say ? - vLP | Voc 3376, Br A-81100 |

Louis Prima-t-v/Meyer Weinberg-cl/George Moore-as/Joe Catalyne-ts/Frank Pinero-p/
Garry McAdams-g/Sherman Masinter-sb/Oscar Bradley-d.
                                  Los Angeles, March 20, 1937.

| | | |
|---|---|---|
| LA-1308-A | Fifty-Second Street - vLP | Voc 3509, Br A-81215 |
| LA-1309-A | The Love Bug Will Bite You - vLP | - - |
| LA-1310-A | I Just Can't Believe You're Gone - vLP | Voc 3921, S-177 |
| LA-1311-A | Rhythm On The Radio - vLP | - - |

                                  Los Angeles, July 7, 1937.

| | | |
|---|---|---|
| LA-1376-A | Danger, Love At Work - vLP | Voc 3628 |
| LA-1377-A | Afraid To Dream - vLP | - |
| LA-1378-A | You Can't Have Everything - vLP | Voc 3657 |
| LA-1379-A | Tin Roof Blues | - |

Moore and Catalyne omitted; Frank Frederico-g replaces McAdams; George Hirsch-d
replaces Bradley.                New York, January 17, 1938.

| | | |
|---|---|---|
| 63166-A | Now They Call It Swing - vLP | Dec 1674, Voc S-192 |
| 63167-A | Yes, There Ain't No Moonlight (So What) - vLP | Dec 1618  - |
| 63168-A | Rosalie - vLP | - |
| 63169-A | Where Have We Met Before ? - vLP | Dec 1674 |

                                  New York, May 16, 1938.

| | | |
|---|---|---|
| 63783-A | Why Should I Pretend ? - vLP | Dec 1953, Voc S-208 |
| 63784-A | Doin' The Serpentine - vLP | - - |
| 63785-A | You Call It Madness (But I Call It Love) - vLP | Dec 1871, Rex 9927 (as LOUIS PRIMA AND HIS BAND) |
| 63786-A | Nothing's Too Good For You - vLP | - |

LOUIS PRIMA AND HIS NEW ORLEANS GANG : Louis Prima-t-v/Meyer Weinberg-cl/Frank
   Pinero-p/Frank Frederico-g/Sherman Masinter-sb/John Castaing-d.
                                   Los Angeles, December 12, 1938.

DLA-1637-A  Show Me The Way To Go Home - vLP        Dec 2242, Rex 9927
DLA-1638-A  Exactly Like You - vLP                  Dec 2279
DLA-1639-A  Jitterbugs On Parade                    Dec 2242
DLA-1640-A  Now And Then - vLP                      Dec 2279
   NOTE:- Rex 9927 as LOUIS PRIMA AND HIS BAND.

                                   New York, July 12, 1939.

65952-A  A Good Man Is Hard To Find - vLP       Dec 2660
65953-A  If I Could Be With You One Hour Tonight-vLP  -
65954-A  Of Thee I Sing - vLP                    Dec 2749
65955-A  Sweet And Low Down - vLP                     -

LOUIS PRIMA AND HIS GLEEBY RHYTHM ORCHESTRA : Louis Prima-t-v dir. Sonny Berman-t/tb
   /2as/ts/p/Frank Frederico-g-v/sb/Jack Powers-d-v/Lily Ann Carol-v/Edgar Battle-a.
                                   New York, c. January 5, 1940.

US-1256-1  To You, Sweetheart, Aloha             Var 8170
US-1257-1  Say "Si Si" - vLP                          -
US-1258-1  Sing-a-Spell (Musical Spelling Bee)-vO  Var 8166
US-1259-1  Gleeby Rhythm Is Born - vLP                -

                                   New York, March-April, 1940.

US-1502-1  Dance With A Dolly (With A Hole In Her  Var 8245
              Stocking) - vLP-LAC-FF
US-1503-1  Daydreams Come True At Night - vLAC    Var 8247
US-1504-1  Look Out - aEB                         Var 8245
US-1505-1  Percy, Have Mercy - vLP-LAC&ch         Var 8247

LOUIS PRIMA AND HIS ORCHESTRA : Probably similar.
                                   New York, September 15, 1941.

31315-1-2  Jersey Bounce                         Rejected
31316-1-2  I'm Sorry I Made You Cry - vLP             -
31317-1  Tica-Tee, Tica-Ta - vLAC-LP             OK 6520
31318-1  Forgive Me - vLP                            -

See also Dave Rose.

                       ALBERTA PRIME

Vocal, acc. by Duke Ellington-p, with Sonny Greer-v.
                                   New York, c. November, 1924.

T-2001-1  It's Gonna Be A Cold, Cold Winter       B-D T-1007
             (So Get Another Place To Stay)
T-2002-2  Parlor Social De Luxe - vSG                 -

                  PRINCE'S BAND/ ORCHESTRA

Charles A. Prince was the Musical Director of Columbia Records in New York in the
   first two decades of the century.  Records made under his direction amount to many
   hundreds, but the following are of considerable interest as contemporary accounts
   of ragtime music.  The personnel is collective and approximate.

Charles A. Prince dir. Bohumir Kryl-Vincent C. Buono- ——— Haines-c/Leo Zimmerman-tb
   /Thomas Hughes-cl/Marshall P. Lufsky-f/Charles d'Almaine-Walter Biedermann-vn/ah/
   th/bb/Edward F. Rubsam-Howard Kopp-d-chimes etc.
                                   New York, c. August, 1903.

1556-  Dixie Girl (J. Bodewalt Lampe)            Col 1556

                                   New York, c. July, 1905.

3249-  St. Louis Tickle (Barney - Seymore)       Col 3249

Charles A. Prince dir. Bohumir Kryl-Vincent C. Buono-c/Leo Zimmerman-tb/Thomas Hughes
cl/Marshall P. Lufsky-f/Charles d'Almaine-Walter Biedermann-vn/ah/th/bb/Edward F.
Rubsam-Howard Kopp-d-chimes etc.        New York, c. September, 1909.

4117-1  Black And White Rag (George Botsford)    Col A-711

New York, c. May, 1910.

4535-1  Temptation Rag (Henry Lodge)             Col A-854, 1623, Re G-6129

4552-2  I'm Alabama Bound (Robert Hoffman)       Col A-901, 1662, Phoenix 0148

4586-1-2  Porcupine Rag (Charles L. Johnson)        -        1610, Re G-6172
NOTE:- Columbia 1623 and Regal G-6129 as KING'S MILITARY BAND; Columbia 1662 as
CASINO ORCHESTRA; Regal G-6172 as REGAL MILITARY BAND; Phornix 0148 as BURLINGTON
ORCHESTRA.

New York, December 27, 1910.

19172-2  Tickled To Death (Charles Hunter)       Col A-972

New York, May 6, 1911.

19337-1  High Society (Porter Steele)            Col A-1038

New York, June 7, 1911.

19397-1  Red Pepper - A Spicy Rag (Henry Lodge)  Col A-1031, 1910, Re G-6133

New York, November 4, 1911.

19652-1  Ramshackle Rag (Ted Snyder)             Col A-1107, 1910, Re G-6133
NOTE:- Columbia 1910 and Regal G-6133 as KING'S MILITARY BAND.

New York, February 12, 1912.

19758-1  Black Diamond Rag (Henry Lodge)         Col A-1140, 2011, Re G-6134

New York, March 30, 1912.

19838-2  Cabaret Rag (Harry A. Tierney)          Col A-1164, 2011, Re G-6134
NOTE:- Columbia 2011 and Regal G-6134 as KING'S MILITARY BAND.

New York, January 13, 1913.

38550-2  Another Rag (A Raggy Rag) (Theo. Morse) Col A-1292

New York, July 30, 1913.

38971-2  Chicago Tickle                          Re G-6845
NOTE:- This issue as REGAL MILITARY BAND.

New York, September 10, 1913.

39010-1-2-3  The Barbary Rag (Charles A. Prince) Col rejected

New York, October 6, 1913.

39010-5  The Barbary Rag (Charles A. Prince)     Re G-6727
NOTE:- This issue as KING'S MILITARY BAND.

New York, December 16, 1913.

39148-1-2  Ragamuffin Rag (Will T. Pierson)      Col rejected

New York, July 7, 1914.

36995-   That's A Plenty                         Col A-5582

Charles A. Prince dir. Bohumir Kryl-Vincent C. Buono-c/Leo Zimmerman-tb/Thomas Hughes
  cl/Marshall P. Lufsky-f/Charles d'Almaine-Walter Biedermann-vn/ah/th/bb/Edward F.
  Rubsam-Howard Kopp-d-chimes etc.       New York, July 24, 1914.

37010-    Memphis Blues                         Col A-5591

                                          New York, October 21, 1915.

37439-2  The Hesitating Blues                   Col A-5772

                                          New York, December 18, 1915.

37476-3  St. Louis Blues                        Col A-5772

### PRINCE BUDDA  AND HIS BOYS

Prince Budda-vib/p/g/sb/Heyward Jackson-Frankie Jaxon-v.
                                          New York, July 22, 1937.

62438-A  In My Miz - vHJ                 Dec 7363
62439-B  When A Woman Gets The Blues - vFJ      -

### PRINCETON TRIANGLE CLUB  JAZZ BAND

Clem Wells-t/Avery Sherry-cl-as/Kinney Ellis-ss-Cm-as/Dave Danforth-vn/Herb Sanford-
  p/Ed Botsford-bj-g/Kirk Gilmore-d.     New York, May 5, 1924.

91472-1  Sea Of Dreams                         Col 31-P
91473-1  Ships That Pass In The Night          Col 30-P

                                          New York, May 13, 1924.

91475-2  Join The Navy                         Col 30-P
91476-2  Pirate Gold                           Col 31-P

  Frank Orvis-t-cl-ts-pac added; Arnold Tietig-vn replaces Danforth; J. D. Evans-bj
  replaces Botsford.             Camden, N. J., October 29, 1924.

         June Night                       Vic test (un-numbered)
         Sweet Little You                      -

                                          New York, December 3, 1924.

170020-2  I'll Build An Igloo For You          Col 59-P
170021-2  My White Rose                        -

                                          New York, December 22, 1924.

170024-1  Indian Moon                          Col 63-P
170025-1  Broke Again                          -

  Theron Green-tb/John Berkshire-ts/Bill Green-2nd p/Squirrel Ashcraft-pac/Larry
  Braman-bb added; Randy Hall-as replaces Ellis; Bill Priestley-bj-g replaces Evans;
  Sanford db x.                  New York, March 27, 1926.

170205-1  Where Love Is King                   Col 84-P
170206-1  Twilight                             -
170207-2  Pretty Please                        Col 85-P
170208-2  Gondola Maid                         -

Clem Wells-Dick Turner-t/Avery Sherry-cl-as/Bill Thomas-Tom Wood-as/Jim Rodgers-bsx/
  Herb Sanford-p/Squirrel Ashcraft-pac/Bill Priestley-g/Don Mills-d.
                                          New York, April 30, 1927.

170273-2  Rhythmic Refrain                     Col 100-P
170274-2  Melody Moon                          -

Bill Priestly-c-g/Brainerd Kremer-cl-as/Philip Nash-Jack Howe-ts/Squirrel Ashcraft-
pac/DeFord Swann-p/Doug MacNamara-bj/Palmer Lathrop-bb-sb/Bob Bole-d.
New York, March 31, 1928.

| | | |
|---|---|---|
| 170299-1 | You Know Who | Col 114-P |
| 170300-1 | Everybody And You | - |
| 170301-2 | China Boy | Col 115-P |
| 170302-2 | That's A Plenty | - |

NOTE:- Columbia 115-P as EQUINOX ORCHESTRA OF PRINCETON, NEW JERSEY.

## HELEN PROCTOR

Vocal acc. by probably :- Henry Allen-t/Buster Bailey-cl/Lil Armstrong-p/Ulysses
Livingston-g/Wellman Braud-sb/Sidney Catlett or O'Neil Spencer-d.
New York, October 13, 1939.

| | | |
|---|---|---|
| 66764-A | Cheatin' On Me | Dec 7666 |
| 66765-A | Let's Call It A Day | Dec 7703 |
| 66766-A | Take Me Along With You | - |
| 66767-A | Blues At Midnight | Dec 7666 |

## CLARENCE PROFIT TRIO

Clarence Profit-p/Billy Moore-g/Ben Brown-sb.
New York, February 15, 1939.

| | | |
|---|---|---|
| B-24122-1 | Don't Leave Me | Epic LN-24028, SN-6042, Col 33SX-1506 (LPs) |
| B-24123-1 | There'll Be Some Changes Made | Br 8341 |
| B-24124-1 | I Got Rhythm | Epic LN-24028, SN-6042, Col 33SX-1506 (LPs) |
| B-24125-1-2 | Down Home | Rejected |
| B-24126-1-2 | Tropical Nights | - |
| B-24127-2 | Tea For Two | Br 8341 |

New York, November 29, 1939.

| | | |
|---|---|---|
| 26308-A | Body And Soul | Col 35378 |
| 26309-A | The Blues | Rejected |

New York, January 5, 1940.

| | | |
|---|---|---|
| 26308-B | Body And Soul | Col 35378 |
| 26396-A | I Didn't Know What Time It Was | - |

Jimmy Shirley-g replaces Moore.          New York, September 11, 1940.

| | | |
|---|---|---|
| 68079-A | Dark Eyes | Dec 8527 |
| 68080-A | Times Square Blues | Dec 8503 |
| 68081-A | Hot And Bothered | - |
| 68082-A | Azure | Dec 8527 |

## ARTHUR PRYOR'S BAND

This famous American concert band was formed in 1903 when Arthur Pryor, first trombone and assistant conductor of Sousa's Band, relinquished this position.   Late
that year, the band began recording for Victor - in competition with his erstwhile
employer ! - and according to Rudi Blesh in THEY ALL PLAYED RAGTIME (Alfred Knopf,
New York, 1950; Sidgwick and Jackson, London, 1958, p. 151), "Arthur Pryor.....
formed a band that played with far more syncopation than any other brass band,"
and in deference to that statement, the following obviously interesting titles
from the enormous number made between 1903 and 1926 are included here.  The
personnel shown is known to be correct for records made in 1910 and for a year or
two earlier, and probably holds good for all the titles listed.  Matrix numbers
prefixed A/B- refer to sides made in both 7- and 10-inch sizes, using the same
catalog ' number; E- prefix denotes 8-inch size, again using the same number.

Arthur Pryor-tb dir. Emil Keneke-Bert Brown- —— Smith-c/ —— Stoll- —— Rose-tb/
Louis H. Christie-A. Levy-cl/John Kiburz-f/ah/th/ —— Leone-bh/Simon Mantia-bb/d;
probably others augmenting from time to time.
                                        New York, November 24, 1903.

A/B-746-1  **Mr.** Black Man (Arthur Pryor) - v        Vic 2557
C-746-1    Mr. Black Man (Arthur Pryor) - v        Rejected ?

                                        New York, December 7, 1903.

A/B-793-1  A Coon Band Contest (Arthur Pryor)      Vic 4069

                                        New York, December 8, 1903.

A/B-746-2-3  Mr. Black Man (Arthur Pryor) - v      Vic 2557
C-746-2      Mr. Black Man (Arthur Pryor) - v      Vic 31169

                                        New York, December 14, 1903.

A/B-819-1  Cotton Blossoms (Milton H. Hall)        Vic rejected

                                        New York, December 16, 1903.

 B-835-1  Creole Belles (J. Bodewalt Lampe)        Vic rejected

                                        New York, March 23, 1904.

B-1154-1  The St. Louis Rag (Tom Turpin)           Vic 2783

                                        New York, April 21, 1904.

 B-1250-1-2  A Southern Belle (Eugene)             Vic 2825

                                        New York, April 26, 1904.

A-793-2; B-793-2-3-4  A Coon Band Contest (Pryor)  Vic 4069

                                        New York, October 17, 1905.

C-2818-1-2-3  Razzazza Mazzazza (Arthur Pryor)     Vic 35040

                                        New York, October 18, 1905.

B-2818-4  Razzazza Mazzazza (Arthur Pryor)         Vic 4525, 16816

                                        New York, March 26, 1906.

 B-793-6  A Coon Band Contest (Arthur Pryor)       Vic 4069, 16079

                                        New York, April 19, 1906.

E-1154-1-2  The St. Louis Rag (Tom Turpin)         Vic 2783

                                        New York, May 23, 1906.

B-1250-5  A Southern Belle (Eugene)                Vic 2825, 16155

                                        New York, May 24, 1906.

E-2818-1  Razzazza Mazzazza (Arthur Pryor)         Vic 4525

 (All 10- or 12-inch from this point).   New York, September 12, 1907.

 4800-1  The King Of Rags (A Two-Step Oddity)     Vic 5301, 16821, 62610
            (Swisher)

                                        New York, September 19, 1907.

 4820-2  Darkies' Spring Song (Egbert van Alstyne) Vic 5395

Arthur Pryor-tb dir. Emil Keneke-Bert Brown- —— Smith-c/ —— Stoll- —— Rose-tb/
Louis H. Christie-A. Levy-cl/John Kiburz-f/ah/th/ —— Leone-bh/Simon Mantia-bb/d;
probably others augmenting from time to time.

New York, September 16, 1908.

6412-3  Artful Artie (Arthur Pryor) - v              Vic 16021

New York, September 17, 1908.

 746-5  Mr. Black Man (Arthur Pryor) - v              Vic 2557
6419-2  That Rag (Browne)                             Vic 16043

New York, September 21, 1908.

6429-2  Southern Beauties Rag (Charles L. Johnson)Vic 16073, 62460

New York, September 22, 1908.

6438-2  Georgia Sunset - Cake-Walk (J. B. Lampe)  Vic 5607, 16796

New York, February 8, 1909.

6784-2  Dill Pickles Rag (Charles L. Johnson)      Vic 16482

New York, February 10, 1909.

6790-1-2  Frozen Bill Cake-Walk (Arthur Pryor)     Vic 5684, 17223

New York, February 11, 1909.

4820-3  Darkies' Spring Song (Egbert van Alstyne) Vic 5395, 16670, HMV GC2-421

New York, March 30, 1909.

6940-1-2  White Wash Man (Jean Schwartz)             Vic 16306

New York, March 31, 1909.

6951-2  Pickles And Peppers (Shepherd)             Vic 5713, HMV B-503

New York, May 7, 1909.

7057-1  Sweetmeats - Ragtime March (Percy Wenrich)Vic 5733, 16818, HMV B-245

New York, December 7, 1909.

8427-1-2  The African 400 (An Educated Rag)        Vic 16444, HMV B-503
          (Roberts)

New York, December 8, 1909.

8434-1  Tobasco - A Rag Waltz (Charles L. Johnson)Vic 35098

New York, June 7, 1910.

 746-6  Mr. Black Man (Arthur Pryor) - v           Vic 16668, HMV GC2-446
9060-2  Temptation Rag (Henry Lodge)               Vic 16511, HMV GC2-483, C-56
NOTE:- HMV C-56 is a 10-inch Indian issue.

New York, September 20, 1910.

9466-1  Grizzly Bear Rag (George Botsford)          Vic 5802

New York, September 21, 1910.

9471-1-2  Wild Cherry Rag (sic) (Ted Snyder)       Vic rejected

New York, January 5, 1911.

9760-2  A Rhinewine Rag (Henneberg)                 Vic 16834

Arthur Pryor-tb dir. Emil Keneke-Bert Brown- —— Smith-c/ —— Stoll- —— Rose-tb/
Louis H. Christie-A. Levy-cl/John Kiburz-f/ah/th/ —— Leone-bh/Simon Mantia-bb/d;
probably others augmenting from time to time.
New York, May 8, 1911.

10296-3  Canhanibalmo Rag (Arthur Pryor)          Vic.16883, HMV GC3-1,B-241,C-141
NOTE:- HMV C-141 is a 10-inch Indian issue.

New York, April 8, 1912.

11853-1  Grizzly Bear Turkey Trot (George Botsford)Vic 17111, HMV GC3-11, B-241,
NOTE:  HMV C-186 is a 10-inch Indian issue.       C-186

New York, April 12, 1912.

11864-2  Red Rose Rag (Percy Wenrich)             Vic 17138

New York, September 3, 1912.

9760-4  A Rhinewine Rag (Henneberg)               Vic 16834

Arthur Pryor-tb dir. Emil Keneke-Theodore Levy-c/Frank Schrader-tb/Louis H. Christie
A. Levy-cl/Clement Barone-f/J. Fuchs-Otto Winkler-H. Reitzel-ah-th-bh/Herman
Conrad-bb/William H. Reitz-d.      New York, June 10, 1914.

793-7  A Coon Band Contest (Arthur Pryor)         Vic 16079

Arthur Pryor-tb dir. similar instrumentation, but no personnel details known.
New York, September 16, 1924.

6438-3  Georgia Sunset - Cake-Walk (J. B. Lampe)  Vic 16796

## MARTHA PRYOR

The following sides by this white vaudeville artist have interesting accompaniments.

Vocal, acc. by c/tb/as/p/bj/bb/d.        New York, c. June, 1923.

485-E  Louisville Lou (The Vampin' Lady)          Cam 359

Acc. by the Golden Gate Orchestra (not the California Ramblers in this case) :
t/tb/as/ts/vn/p/bj.                      New York, March, 1924.

1724-3  Lazy                                      Bwy 11378, Pen 1378

## PURPLE PIRATES ORCHESTRA

Collegiate orchestra of Williams College : c/tb/cl-as/ts-bsx/p/bj/d.
New York, c. May, 1926.

2527-2  Tiger Rag                                 W (un-numbered; Pm recording)
2528-2  China Boy                                 —

## JACK PURVIS

Trumpet solos, acc. by John Scott Trotter-p/Gene Kintzle-g/Paul Weston-sb/Joe Dale-d.
New York, December 17, 1929.

403522-B  Copyin' Louis (Opus B)                  OK 41404
403523-A  Mental Strain At Dawn                   —       Par R-673, A-3642,
                                                  Od A-2317, A-286016

JACK PURVIS AND HIS ORCHESTRA : Jack Purvis-t-v/J. C. Higginbotham-tb-v/Coleman
Hawkins-ts/Adrian Rollini-bsx/Frank Froeba-p/Will Johnson-g-v/Charles Kegley-d.
New York, April 4, 1930.

403891-A  Dismal Dan                              OK 8808, Par R-1449, Od A-286069
403892-A  Poor Richard - vJP-JCH-WJ               OK 8782, Par R-992, A-7631,
                                                  Od A-286042
403893-B  Down Georgia Way                        OK 8782, Par R-698, Od A-286017

JACK PURVIS AND HIS ORCHESTRA : Jack Purvis-t/J. C. Higginbotham-tb-v/Greely Walton-
ts/Adrian Rollini-bsx/Frank Froeba-p/Will Johnson-g/Charles Kegley-d.
                                       New York, May 1, 1930.

| | | |
|---|---|---|
| 403992-B | What's The Use Of Cryin', Baby ? | Od ONY-36093, A-286080, Par PNY-34084, R-1669 |
| 403993-A | When You're Feelin' Blue | Od ONY-36093, A-2321, A-286034, Par PNY-34085, R-890 |
| 403994-A | Be Bo Bo - vJCH | OK 8808, Par R-1252, Od A-286063 |

NOTE:- Parlophone PNY-34084 and PNY-34085 as JOHN AYRES' ORCHESTRA.

## QUAGLINO'S QUARTET

See Brian Lawrence.

## SIS QUANDER

Vocal, acc. by Louis Hooper-p.             New York, May, 1927.

| | | |
|---|---|---|
| 107543 | Black Snake Blues | PA 7530, Per 130 |
| 107544 | Soul And Body (He Belongs To Me) | - - |
| | Mama Is Waiting For You | PA 7528, Per 128 |
| | Mine's Just As Good As Yours | - - |

## FRANKIE QUARTELL

FRANKIE QUARTELL AND HIS MELODY BOYS : Frankie Quartell-t/Louis Sha..tel-tb/Al Hyatt-
cl/Maurice Morris-as/Dave Sholden-ts/Johnny Petrone-p/Earl Wright-bj/Jules Cassard
bb/Danny Alvin-d.                      Chicago, December 5, 1924.

| | | |
|---|---|---|
| 8788-A | Heart-Broken Strain | OK 40257, Od 03166 |
| 8790-A | Prince Of Wails | OK 40258, Par E-5323 |

NOTE:- Matrix 8789 is untraced.

FRANKIE QUARTELL AND HIS LITTLE CLUB ORCHESTRA : Frankie Quartell-t/tb/Rod Cless-cl-
as/as-bsx/ts/p/pac - this may be Quartell himself, in which case the t is someone
else/g/bb/d/Ted Gilmore-v.             New Orleans, December, 1928.

| | | |
|---|---|---|
| NO-751-A | Pining - vTG | Br 4183, A-8138 |
| NO-752-A | Sweet Baby - vTG | - - |

## QUEEN CITY BLOWERS

Pseudonym on Champion for Richard Hitter's Blue Knights, q.v.

## QUEEN CITY BOYS

Pseudonym on Champion 15015 for Tom Griselle and his Orchestra, q.v.

## "QUEEN'S" DANCE ORCHESTRA

See Jack Hylton.

## DAN QUINN

The following title by this pioneer recording artist, whose career began in the mid-
1890s on wax cylinders and Berliner discs, is of interest as it has since become a
jazz standard.

Vocal, acc. by C. H. H. Booth-p.           New York, March 14, 1902.

| | | |
|---|---|---|
| 1327-1-2 | O Didn't He Ramble (sic) | Vic 1327 |

New York, July 11, 1902.

| | | |
|---|---|---|
| 1327-3 | O Didn't He Ramble | Vic 1327 |

New York, April 4, 1904.

| | | |
|---|---|---|
| 1181-1-2 | O Didn't He Ramble | Vic 1327 |

Edward "Snoozer" Quinn was an itinerant guitarist who was a member of Paul Whiteman's Orchestra between October, 1928 and May, 1929. He made very few records of any kind on which to base the claim made for him that he was superior to Eddie Lang, these being accompaniments to country-style singer Jimmy Davis for Victor in 1931, and some adequate and sporadic appearances with the Whiteman orchestra. He made the following solos, but unless test pressings are found, we shall never know how good or otherwise they may have been.

Guitar solos.                              San Antonio, May 21, 1928.

| | | |
|---|---|---|
| 42345-1-2 | Snoozer's Blues | Vic rejected |
| 42346-1-2-3 | Tiger Rag | - |
| 42347-1-2 | That'll Get It | - |
| 42348-1-2-3 | Rambling Blues | - |

## QUINTETTE OF THE HOT CLUB OF FRANCE

Stephane Grappelly-vn/Django Reinhardt-Roger Chaput-Joseph Reinhardt-g/Louis Vola-sb.
Paris, December, 1934.

| | | |
|---|---|---|
| P-77161 | Dinah | Ul AP-1422, B-14286, 11018, Or LV-100, LB-1000, Tel A-1959, Sup B-22642, Joe Davis 8004, DA-17-7, Royale 1753, Var 8377, Od 286044 |
| P-77162 | Tiger Rag | Ul AP-1423, B-14287, 11019, Or LV-101, LB-1001, Tel A-1959, Joe Davis 8003, DA-17-5, Royale 1753, Var 8380 |
| P-77163 | Lady Be Good | Ul AP-1422, B-14286, 11018, Or LV-100, LB-1000, Sup B-22642, Joe Davis 8003, Royale 1754, Var 8376 |
| P-77164 | I Saw Stars | Ul AP-1423, B-14287, 11019, Or LV-101, LB-1000 |

NOTE:- All the above as DJANGO REINHARDT ET LE QUINTETTE DU HOT CLUB DE FRANCE AVEC STEPHANE GRAPPELLY. This applies to all issues from the following session.

Jerry Mengo-v.                             Paris, March, 1935.

| | | |
|---|---|---|
| P-77240 | Lily Belle May June - vJM | Ul AP-1444, Dec F-6531, 23004, Br A-81304, Pol A-197 (Japanese) |
| P-77241 | Sweet Sue, Just You - vJM | Ul AP-1444, Or LV-104, LB-1004, Royale 1780 |
| P-77242 | Confessin' | Ul AP-1443, B-14289, Or LV-102, LB-1002, Sup B-22639, Joe Davis 8005, Royale 1788 |
| P-77243 | The Continental | Ul AP-1443, B-14288, Or LV-102, LB-1002 |

Paris, April, 1935.

| | | |
|---|---|---|
| P-77351 | Blue Drag | Ul AP-1479, B-14290, 11752, Or LV-103, LB-1003, Tel A-1958 |
| P-77352 | Swanee River | As above, plus Joe Davis DA-17-1, Royale 1785 and Var 8378 |
| P-77353 | Ton Doux Sourire (The Sunshine Of Your Smile) | Ul AP-1484, 14288, Or LV-104, LB-1004, Joe Davis DA-17-2, Royale 1807, Var 8380 |
| P-77354 | Ultrafox (Ultra Sox*) (Ultraphone Rhythm**) | Ul AP-1484, 14289**, Sup B-22639, Dec F-6150, 23003, Y-5205, Pol A-197 (Japanese), Joe Davis DA-17-3*, Royale 1785, Var 8376 |

NOTE:- All issues as for the first session above except Decca F-6150 (as STEPHANE GRAPPELLY AND HIS HOT FOUR).

Arthur Briggs-Alphonse Cox-Pierre Allier-t/Eugene d'Hellemmes-tb/Stephane Grappelly-
vn/Django Reinhardt-Roger Chaput-Joseph Reinhardt-g/Louis Vola-sb.
Paris, July, 1935.

| | | |
|---|---|---|
| P-77434 | Avalon | Ul AP-1512, Dec F-6077, 23002, |
| | | Y-5204, Br A-81074, Royale 1780, |
| | | Var 8379, Pol A-142 (Japanese) |
| P-77435 | Smoke Rings | Ul AP-1512, Dec F-6531, Br A-81304 |
| NOTE:- Decca F-6077, F-6531 as STEPHANE | | Joe Davis 8005, Royale 1788, |
| GRAPPELLY AND HIS HOT FOUR. | | Var 8379 |

All brass omitted; Pierre Feret-g replaces Chaput.
Paris, July, 1935.

| | | |
|---|---|---|
| P-77440 | Clouds | Ul AP-1511, Dec F-6406, 23002, |
| | | Y-5178, Br A-81187, Tel A-1960, |
| | | Pol A-142 (Japanese) |
| P-77441 | Believe It, Beloved | Ul AP-1511, Dec F-6406, Y-5178, |
| | | Br A-81187, Tel A-1960, Pol 624076 |

NOTE:- Decca F-6406 as STEPHABE GRAPPELLY AND HIS HOT FOUR; all others as DJANGO
REINHARDT ET LE QUINTETTE DU HOT CLUB DE FRANCE AVEC STEPHANE GRAPPELLY. Polydor
624076 is a Norwegian issue.

Paris, September, 1935.

| | | |
|---|---|---|
| P-77537 | Chasing Shadows | Ul AP-1547, Dec F-6002, Y-5120, |
| | | Br A-82106, Royale 1798 |
| P-77538 | I've Had My Moments | Ul AP-1547, Dec F-6150, Y-5205, |
| | | Br A-81206, Joe Davis DA-17-4, |
| | | Royale 1798, Var 8377 |
| P-77539 | Some Of These Days | Ul AP-1548, Dec F-6002, 23004, |
| | | Y-5120, Pol A-230 (Japanese) |
| P-77540 | Djangology | Ul AP-1548, Dec F-6077, 23003, |
| | | Y-5204, Br A-81047, Pol A-230(Jap) |

NOTE;- Decca F-6002, F-6150 and Y-5120 as STEPHANE GRAPPELLY AND HIS HOT FOUR; all
others as for the July, 1935 session immediately above.

Lucien Simoens-sb replaces Vola; Freddy Taylor-v.
Paris, May 4, 1936.

| | | |
|---|---|---|
| OLA-1057-1 | I'se A Muggin' - vFT | HMV K-7704, Vic JA-874 |
| OLA-1058-1 | I Can't Give You Anything But Love | HMV K-7706, B-8463, El EG-3717, |
| | - vFT | Vic 40-0122,68-0684,A-1204,JA-856 |
| OLA-1059-1 | Oriental Shuffle | HMV K-7704, B-8479, AM-4737, |
| | | El EG-3776, Vic 26506, JA-874 |
| OLA-1060-1 | After You've Gone - vFT | HMV K-7707, B-8479, AM-4737,N-4469 |
| | | El EG-3776, Vic 25511, JA-910 |
| OLA-1061-1 | Are You In The Mood ? | HMV K-7707, Vic 26506  - |
| OLA-1062-1 | Limehouse Blues | HMV K-7706, B-8463, El EG-3717, |
| | | Vic 25511, 68-0684, A-1204, JA-856 |

Louis Vola-sb replaces Simoens.    Paris, October 15, 1936.

| | | |
|---|---|---|
| OLA-1290-1 | Nagasaki - vFT | HMV K-7843, B-8518, El EG-3882, |
| | | Vic 25558, JA-1012, JA-1078 |
| OLA-1291-1 | Swing Guitars | HMV K-7898, B-8532, Vic 25601, |
| | | JA-1119 |
| OLA-1292-1 | Georgia On My Mind - vFT | HMV K-7790   - Vic 26578, JA-1119 |
| OLA-1293-1 | Shine - vFT | - B-8534, AL-2366, |
| | | El EG-3918, Vic 25558, 20-2760, |
| | | JA-1012, JA-1078 |
| OLA-1294-1 | In The Still Of The Night   . | HMV K-7898, B-8534, A-12366, |
| | | El EG-3918, Vic 26578, A-1277, |
| | | JA-1363 |
| OLA-1295-1 | Sweet Chorus | HMV K-7843, B-8518, El EG-3882, |
| | | Vic 40-0122 |

Stephane Grappelly-vn/Django Reinhardt-Marcel Bianchi-Pierre Feret-g/Louis Vola-sb.
Paris, April 21, 1937.

| | | |
|---|---|---|
| OLA-1702-1 | Exactly Like You | HMV B-8629, AL-2436, GW-1509, GY-333, JK-2332, El EG-6178, Vic 26733 |
| OLA-1703-1 | Charleston | Swing 2 |
| OLA-1704-1 | You're Driving Me Crazy | HMV K-8396, B-8606, AL-2404, GY-432, JK-2048, JO-16, El EG-6088 Vic 26733 |
| OLA-1705-1 | Tears | HMV B-8718 |
| OLA-1706-1 | Solitude | HMV B-8669, Vic 40-0124 |

Paris, April 22, 1937.

| | | |
|---|---|---|
| OLA-1712-1 | Runnin' Wild | HMV B-8614, HN-2495, El EG-6561, Vic 40-0124 |
| OLA-1713-1 | Chicago | Swing 2 |
| OLA-1714-1 | Liebestraum No. 3 (Liszt) | HMV B-8737, AL-2492, Vic A-1277, JA-1363 |
| OLA-1715-1 | Miss Annabelle Lee | HMV B-8614, HN-2495, El EG-6561, Vic 40-0125 |
| OLA-1716-1 | A Little Love, A Little Kiss | HMV B-8598 |
| OLA-1717-1 | Mystery Pacific | HMV K-8396, B-8606, AL-2404, GY-432, JK-2048, JO-15, El EG-6088 Vic 40-0125 |
| OLA-1718-1 | In A Sentimental Mood | HMV B-8629, AL-2436, GW-1509, GY-333, JK-2332, El EG-6178 |

Paris, April 27, 1937.

OLA-1737-1   The Sheik Of Araby          HMV B-8737, AL-2492
    NOTE:- Two other titles from this session are violin solos by Stephane Grappelly,
    accompanied by Django Reinhardt-g, and two more are unaccompanied solos by Django
    Reinhardt (both q.v.)


Stephane Grappelly-vn/Django Reinhardt-Joseph Reinhardt-Eugene Vees-g/Louis Vola-sb.
Paris, November 25, 1937.

| | | |
|---|---|---|
| OLA-1987- | Bricktop | Rejected |
| OLA-1988- | Speevy | - |
| OLA-1989- | Cavalerie | - |
| OLA-1990-1 | Minor Swing | Swing 23, HMV SG-367, Vic 26218 |
| OLA-1991-1 | Viper's Dream | -       -       - |


Michel Warlop-vn added.          Paris, December 7, 1937.

| | | |
|---|---|---|
| OLA-1995-1 | Swinging With Django | Swing 40, Vic 27272 |
| OLA-1996-1 | Paramount Stomp | -       - |


Philippe Brun-Gus Deloof-Andre Cornille-t/Guy Paquinet-Josse Breyere-tb/Maurice
Cizeron-f added for the first side, on which P. Bartel- ——— Swetschin-Michel
Warlop-vn replace Grappelly; Brun, Deloof, Cornille, Paquinet and Breyere also
added on X2LA-1997-2 to the Quintette personnel for November 25, 1937; this alone
is present on OLA-1998-1.          Paris, December 14, 1937.

| | | |
|---|---|---|
| X2LA-1996-1 | Bolero (Maurice Ravel) | HMV L-1046, Vic JB-215 |
| X2LA-1997-2 | Mabel | -       - |
| OLA-1998-1 | My Serenade | Swing 77 |

Stephane Grappelly-vn/Django Reinhardt-Roger Chaput-Eugene Vees-g/Louis Vola-sb;
  Reinhardt and Vola speak in French.*     London, January 31, 1938.

| | | |
|---|---|---|
| DTB-3523-1 | Honeysuckle Rose | Dec F-6639, 538 (It.), 23066, Br A-81503, A-505269, Od 284393, Pol A-315 (Japanese) |
| DTB-3524-1 | Sweet Georgia Brown | Dec F-6675, F-9045, F-9428, Y-5227 542 (It.), 23065, Br A-81603, A-505270, Od 284393, Pol 624076 |
| DTB-3525-1 | Night And Day | Dec F-6616, F-8068, Y-5212, 23067, Br A-81436, A-82559, A-505271, Od 284357, Pol 624076 |
| DTB-3526-2 | *My Sweet | Dec F-6769, F-9428, 573 (It.), 89045, Br A-81685, A-505270 |
| DTB-3527-1 | Souvenirs | Dec F-6639, 538 (It.), 23065, Br A-505269, Pol A-315 (Japanese) |
| DTB-3528-1 | Daphne | Dec F-6769, 573 (It.), 23152, Br A-81685, Od 284357 |
| DTB-3529-1 | Black And White | Dec F-6675, Y-5227, 542 (It.), 23067, Br A-81603, SA-1610 |
| DTB-3530-1 | Stompin' At Decca | Dec F-6616, F-8086, Y-5212, 23066, Br A-81436, A-82559 |

NOTE:- All Decca F- issues other than those in the 6000 series are Continental.

Roger Grasset-sb replaces Vola.          Paris, June 14, 1938.

| | | |
|---|---|---|
| 4209hpp | Billet Doux | Dec F-7568 |
| 4209½hpp | Billet Doux | -          23263, Od 286192 |
| 4210hpp | Swing From Paris | Dec F-6899, Y-5348  -  Br A-505276 |
| 4211hpp | Them There Eyes | - 573 (It.) - 23262 - |
| 4212hpp | Three Little Words | Dec F-6875, Y-5270, 572 (It.), 23264, 333016, Br A-81901,A-505277 Od 284778 |
| 4213hpp | Appel Indirect (Appel Direct*) (Direct Appeal**) | Dec F-6875*, Y-5270, 572 (It.), 23261**, 333016, Br A-81901, A-505277, Od 284778, 286044 |

London, August 30, 1938.

| | | |
|---|---|---|
| DR-2878-1 | The Flat Foot Floogie | Dec F-6776, 9433, Br A-81692, A-505267 |
| DR-2879-1 | Lambeth Walk | Dec F-6776  -   23077 - |
| DR-2880-1 | Why Shouldn't I Care ? | - |

Stephane Grappelly-vn/Django Reinhardt-Joseph Reinhardt-Pierre Feret-g/Emmanuel
  Soudieux-sb.                           Paris, March 21, 1939.

| | | |
|---|---|---|
| 4967hpp | Hungaria | Dec F-7198, Y-5580, 615 (It.) (?) |
| 4967½hpp | Hungaria | -          -        (?) |
| 4968hpp | Jeepers Creepers | Dec F-7027, 587 (It.), Br A-82082, A-505275, Col R-14124 |
| 4968½hpp | Jeepers Creepers | Dec F-7027 |
| 4969½hpp | Swing 39 | - -587 (It.), 23262, Br A-82082, A-82135, A-505275, Col R-14124 |
| 4970hpp | Japanese Sandman | Dec F-7133, Y-5450, 606 (It.), 23263, Fonit 606 |
| 4971hpp | I Wonder Where My Baby Is Tonight ? | Dec F-7100, Y-5408, 23152 |
| 4971½hpp | I Wonder Where My Baby Is Tonight ? | - 597 (It.)       - Od 283286, D-284563, D-286347 |

Paris, March 22, 1939.

| | | |
|---|---|---|
| 4972hpp, 4972½hpp | Tea For Two | Rejected |
| 4973hpp | My Melancholy Baby | Dec 23261 |
| 4974hpp | Time On My Hands | Dec F-7100 |
| 4974½hpp | Time On My Hands | - 59019, 597 (It.), 333016, Y-5408, Br A-505273, Od 238286, D-284363, D-286347 |
| 4975hpp | Twelfth Year | Dec 59023, F-7133, 606 (It.),23264 Y-5450, Br A-505272, Fonit 606 |
| 4975½hpp | Twelfth Year | Dec F-7133 |
| 4976hpp | Hungaria | Rejected |

Stephane Grappelly-vn/Django Reinhardt-Joseph Reinhardt-Pierre Feret-g/Emmanuel
   Soudieux-sb.                          Paris, May 17, 1939.

| 5080hpp | My Melancholy Baby | Dec F-7198, Y-5580, 615 (It.), |
| | | Col R-14231, Fonit 615 |
| 5081hpp | Japanese Sandman | Dec 59006, Br A-505274,Pol 580017 |
| 5082hpp | Tea For Two | - F-7568 - Od 284773     - |
| 5083hpp | I Wonder Where My Baby Is Tonight ? | Dec 59019, Br A-505273 |
| 5084hpp | Hungaria | Dec 59023, Br A-505272 |

   Eugene Vees-g replaces Joseph Reinhardt.
                                         Paris, June 30, 1939.

| OPG-1719-1 | Stockholm | Swing 128 |
| OPG-1720-1 | Younger Generation | Swing 77 |

   Joseph Reinhardt-g replaces Feret; Beryl Davis-v.
                                         London, August 25, 1939.

| DR-3861-1 | Undecided - vBD | Dec F-7140, 59018, 616 (It.), |
| | | Br A-505268, A-505271, Od 284997, |
| | | PA 20172 (Chinese) |
| DR-3862-2 | H. C. Q. Strut | Dec F-7390, 59045, 616 (It.), |
| | | Br A-505267, Col R-14231,Od 284997 |
| DR-3863-1 | Don't Worry 'Bout Me - vBD | Dec F-7140, 59018, Br A-505268, |
| | | PA 20172 (Chinese) |
| DR-3864-1 | The Man I Love | Dec F-7390, 59045 |

Hubert Rostaing -cl-ts/Django Reinhardt-Joseph Reinhardt-g/Francis Lucas-sb/Pierre
   Fouad-d/Josette Dayde-v.              Paris, October 1, 1940.

| OSW-127-1 | Nuages | Rejected |
| OSW-128-1 | Rythme Futur | Swing 83 |
| OSW-129-1 | Begin The Beguine | Rejected |
| OSW-130-1 | Blues | Swing 83 |
| OSW-131-1 | Cou-Cou - vJD | Rejected |
| OSW-132-1 | Indecision - tsHR | - |

   Alix Combelle-cl-ts added*; Tony Rovira-sb replaces Lucas. (All following as DJANGO
   REINHARDT ET LE QUINTETTE DU H. C. F.)   Paris, December 13, 1940.

| OSW-145-1 | *Swing 41 - clAC | Swing 95 |
| OSW-146-1 | *Nuages - clAC | Swing 88, PA PG-532, PI-1041, |
| | | PN-44126 |
| OSW-147-1 | *Pour vous (Exactly Like You) - cl-tsAC | Swing 118 |
| OSW-148-1 | Fantaisie sur une dance norvegienne | HMV FELP-236 (LP) |
| OSW-149-1 | Vendredi 13 | Swing 123 |
| OSW-150-1 | Liebesfreud | HMV FELP-236 (LP) |
| OSW-151-1 | Mabel | Swing 137 |
| OSW-152-1 | Petits Mensonges | Swing 103 |
| OSW-153-1 | Les Yeux Noirs | Swing 88, PA PG-532, PI-1041 |
| OSW-154-1 | Sweet Sue | Swing 118 |

                                         Paris, December 17, 1940.

| OSW-145-2 | Swing 41 | Rejected |
| OSW-155-1 | *Swing de Paris - clAC | Swing 176 |
| OSW-156-1 | *Oiseaux des Iles - cl-tsAC | Swing 103 |
| OSW-157-1 | *All Of Me - tsAC | Swing 218 |

Hubert Rostaing-cl/Django Reinhardt-Eugene Vees-g/Emmanuel Soudieux-sb/Pierre Fouad-
   d.                                    Paris, September 11, 1941.

| OSW-227-1 | Dinette | Swing 146 |
| OSW-228-1 | Crepuscule | Swing 123 |
| OSW-229-1 | Swing 42 | Swing 137 |

   Andre Jourdan-d replaces Fouad.       Paris, March 31, 1942.

| OSW-265-1 | Belleville | Swing 162 |
| OSW-266-1 | Lentement, Mademoiselle | Swing 146 |

Vocal group, acc. by Barney Bigard and his Orchestra : Duke Ellington-p dir. Rex
   Stewart-c/Juan Tizol-vtb/Barney Bigard-cl/Harry Carney-bar/Fred Guy-g/Billy Taylor
   sb/Sonny Greer-d.                              New York, June 8, 1939.

WM-1034-A  Utt-Da-Zay (The Tailor Song)               Voc 4928
WM-1035-A  Chew-Chew-Chew (Your Bubble Gum)           -

   Acc. by Buck Ram's Orchestra : Buck Clayton-t/George Koenig-cl/Clark Galehouse-ts/
   Les Burness-p/Walter Page-sb/Joe Jones-d; Burness, Page and Jones only*.
                                                 New York, September 5, 1939.

WM-1076-A  Sly Mongoose                               Voc 5509
WM-1077-A  *Fool That I Am                            Voc/OK 5172
WM-1078-A  When My Sugar Walks Down The Street         -

   Acc. by probably :- Joe Thomas-t/Benny Carter-as/Coleman Hawkins-ts/Eddie Heywood-
   p/Hayes Alvis-sb/Keg Purnell-d, or Eddie Heywood-p only**.
                                                 New York, February 2, 1940.

WM-1130-A  Honey Bunny Boo                            Voc 5596
WM-1131-A  The Five Little Quints                     Voc 5409
WM-1132-A  Harmony In Harlem                          Voc 5596
WM-1133-A  Midnight Jamboree                          Voc 5409
WM-1134-A**Heaven Will Protect The Working Girl       Voc 5509

## Q. R. S. BOYS

Robert Cloud-ts/Walter Pichon-p/Benny Nawahi-stg.
                                   Long Island City, c. February, 1929.

   336-A  Dad Blame Blues                             QRS R-7067
   337-A  Black Boy Blues                             -
   338    Wiggle Yo' Toes                             QRS R-7062
   339    I've Seen My Baby (And It Won't Be Long Now) -

## OSCAR RABIN AND HIS ROMANY BAND

Oscar Rabin-bsx-vn dir. Hamish Christie-t-tb/Nat Gonella-t-v/tb/Johnny Swinfen-
   Raymond Doughty-cl-as/Sid Burn-cl-ts/Alf Kaplan-p/Harry Davis-bj-g/bb/Cecil Walden
   d.                                            London, September 7, 1933.

S-3202_  Two Tickets To Georgia - vNG&ch          Sterno 1251, 4-in-1 64
S-3203   Roll Up The Carpet - vNG&ch                 -            -
                                   London, October 12, 1933.

S-3304; L-1264  Road House Shuffle  (The Golden    Plaza P-161, P-175*, P-234*,
         King Shuffle*)                             Lewis L-28*, Peacock PS-232*
NOTE:-  Plaza P-161, P-175 as PLAZA DANCE BAND; P-234 as WILLIE FREEMAN AND HIS
DANCE ORCHESTRA; Lewis L-28 as BILL FINDLAY'S DANCE BAND; Peacock PS-232 as PETER
ROMNEY'S DANCE BAND.
                                   London, January 18, 1934.

S-3505; L-1441  High Steppers (Rough And Tumble*)  Plaza P-208, P-265*
S-3506; L-1442  Violet Ray Blues                   Plaza P-209
NOTE:- Plaza P-208 and P-209 as WILLIE FREEMAN AND HIS DANCE ORCHESTRA; P-265 as
TWELVE CRACKER JACKS.
                                   London, August 22, 1934.

S-3941; L-1836  Hot And Strong                     Plaza P-318
S-3942; L-1837  Singing A Song - v                 Plaza P-304
NOTE:- Plaza P-304 as BEN FIELDS AND HIS ORCHESTRA; P-318 as AL GOLD AND HIS BAND.
    Other titles by this dance band may feature good solos occasionally.

## HARRY RADERMAN

The following titles from the vast recorded output of this trombonist are of some
interest as "hot" dance music.

RADERMAN'S ROYSTERERS : Harry Raderman-tb dir. Jules Berkman-another-t/? Larry Abbott
    another-cl-ss-as/ts/p/bj/bb/d.               New York, August 26, 1925.

140866-1  Want A Little Lovin'                     Har 25-H, Re G-8517
    NOTE:- Regal G-8517 as CORONA DANCE ORCHESTRA.

THE RED HOTTERS (Harry Raderman, Director) : Harry Raderman-tb dir. Jules Berkman
and another-t/? Bobby Davis-cl-ss-as/cl-as/cl-ts/p/bj/bb/d.
                                        New York, c. January 8, 1926.

73914-B  What Did I Tell Ya ?                    OK 40543, Par E-5563

                                        New York, June 22, 1926.

74182-A  Just A Little Dance                     OK 40642, Par E-5636
74183-A-B  Black Bottom                          OK 40641, Par E-5711, Od 03387
74184-A  I'd Climb The Highest Mountain          OK 40642, Par E-5636
NOTE:- OKeh 40641 as OKEH SYNCOPATORS; Parlophone E-5711 as PARLOPHONE SYNCO-
PATORS; Odeon 03387 as ODEON SYNCOPATORS.

There may be other titles by the above groups and others under Harry Raderman's
name containing solos of interest as jazz.

## LOU RADERMAN AND HIS  PELHAM HEATH INN ORCHESTRA

Lou Raderman dir. Manny Klein and another-t/tb/cl-ss-as/as/ts/p/bj/bb/d/Irving Kauf-
man-Harry Donahey-v.                    New York, March 3, 1928.

145720-2  Oh Gee ! Oh Joy ! - vIK                Har 611-H
145721-2  Why Do I Love You ? - vIK              Har 607-H
145722-2  Ol' Man River - vHD                    -

Manny Klein confirmed his presence on this session, but the other trumpet (or it may
be a cornet) is uncannily like Bix Beiderbecke, and Lou Raderman is quoted as
asserting it was Bix.

Probably as above.                      New York, April 4, 1928.

7898-   I'm Riding To Glory (With A Glorious     Ban 7082, Dom 4134, Imp 1969
          Girl) - v
NOTE:- Banner 7082 and Domino 4134 as PELHAM INN SOCIETY ORCHESTRA; Imperial 1969
as ERNIE GOLDEN AND HIS ORCHESTRA.

## THE RADIOLITES

Pseudonym on Columbia 2540-D (both sides) and Australian Regal G-21209 (I DON'T KNOW
WHY) for Benny Goodman and his Orchestra, q.v., and for various Ben Selvin bands
containing no known examples of interest as "hot" dance music.

## RADIO MELODY  BOYS

Pseudonym on Edison Bell Radio for Harry Hudson's Melody Men, q.v.

## RADIO RASCALS  ORCHESTRA

Pseudonym for the following items listed in this book :-

Bluebird B-5249  Down On The Farm (Gene Kardos and his Orchestra) (also Sunrise
HMV B-4921  Old Fashioned Love (Joe Haymes and his Orchestra)              )S-3332)
    B-4932  Dixie (Snooks and his Memphis Ramblers)
Victor 24007  Song Of The Fiddlers (Gene Kardos and his Orchestra)

## RADIO  RED

Pseudonym on Imperial 1777 and 1788 for Evelyn Preer, q.v., and other singers of both
sexes, but of no interest as jazz.

## RADIO RHYTHM  BOYS

Pseudonym on Edison Bell Radio for Harry Hudson's Melody Men, q.v.

At the time of making nine sides for Banner-Pathe in the spring of 1930, Karl Radlach was pianist in Bernie Cummins' Orchestra, thus it is reasonable to suggest
that the personnel was drawn from that organization. The following title is the
only one known to be of any interest as "hot" dance music.

Karl Radlach-p nominally dir. Paul Roberts-? Ernie Mathias-t/tb/Wally Smith and
another-cl-as/cl-ts/vn/Walter Cummins-bj-? v/Bill Diehl-bb/? Bernie Cummins-d.
                                          New York, May 14, 1930.

9729-2-3  Be Careful With Those Eyes - v      Or 1980, Per 15311, Cr 81422,
                                              Ang 3240, Clif 5240, Emb 9240

## IKE RAGON AND  HIS ORCHESTRA

Ike Ragon-v dir. unknown instrumentation and personnel.
                                          Hot Springs, Ark., March 14, 1937.

HS-53-   Truckin' On The Old Camp Ground - vIR  Voc 03547
HS-54-   Harlem Blues - vIR                     -
HS-55-   Slap That Bass - vIR                   Voc 03513
HS-56-   Maple Leaf Rag (Scott Joplin)          -

## RAG  PICKERS

See the Dixie Boys (Autograph).

## RAGPICKERS JAZZ BAND

Jack Raine-c/Stanley Jones-tb/Phil Goodman-as/Billy Kerdachi-vn/Harry Howard-p/
Emile Grimshaw, Jr.-bj/Dinty Moore-d. Hayes, Middlesex, February 23, 1920.

HO-5554-1-2ae  Dardanella                       HMV rejected
HO-5555-1-2-3-4ae  Bo-Bo-Beedle-Um-Bo           -

                                          Hayes, Middlesex, March 1, 1920.

HO-5566-1-2-3-4-5ae  Dardanella                 HMV rejected
HO-5567-1-2-3ae      Bo-Bo-Beedle-Um-Bo         -
HO-5568-1-2ae        I'll Sing You A Song       -
HO-5569-1-2ae        Oh ! How She Can Sing      -

## RAINBOW  DANCE ORCHESTRA

Pseudonym on Romeo 366 (ST. LOUIS BLUES) for the Broadway Broadcasters (see Sam
Lanin), and others of no known interest as jazz.

## THE RAINBOW SERENADERS

Pseudonym on Gennett 3008 for Bailey's Lucky Seven, q.v.

## MA  RAINEY

Vocal, acc. by Lovie Austin and her Blues Serenaders : Tommy Ladnier-c/Jimmy O'Bryant
cl/Lovie Austin-p.                        Chicago, December, 1923.

1596-2  Bad Luck Blues                    Pm 12081
1597-1-2  Bo-Weavil Blues                 Pm 12080, Poydras 78
1598-2  Barrel House Blues                Pm 12082, JC L-48, AF A-047
1599-1-2  Those All Night Long Blues      Pm 12081

1608-1-2  Moonshine Blues                 Pm 12083, Hg 896, JC L-66
1609-2  Last Minute Blues                 Pm 12080, Poydras 78

1612-2  Southern Blues                    Pm 12083, Hg 896, JC L-66
1613-2  Walking Blues                     Pm 12082, JC L-48, AF A-047
NOTE:- Harmograph 896 as ANNE SMITH, acc. by GOLDIE HALL AND HER BLUES SERENADERS.

Acc. by the Pruit Twins (Miles Pruit-bj/Milas Pruit-g).
                              Chicago, c. March, 1924.

1698-2  Lost Wandering Blues                Pm 12098
1699-1  Dream Blues                         -

Acc. by Lovie Austin's Blues Serenaders (Acc. by her Georgia Band on Paramount
12227 and 12257) : Tommy Ladnier-c/Jimmy O'Bryant-cl/? Charles Harris-as-ts/Lovie
Austin-p.                     Chicago, c. March, 1924.

1701-2  Honey.Where You Been So Long        Pm 12200, JC L-82
1702-2-3  Ya-Da-Do                          Pm 12257
1703-1  Those Dogs Of Mine (Famous Cornfield  Pm 12215, AM 6, JC L-78
          Blues)
1704-2  Lucky Rock Blues                    -        -        -

                              Chicago, c. April, 1924.

1741-1  South Bound Blues                   Pm 12227, JC L-107, AF A-010

                              Chicago, c. May, 1924.

1758-1-2  Lawd Send Me A Man Blues          Pm 12227, JC L-107, AF A-010
1759-2  Ma Rainey's Mystery Record          Pm 12200, JC L-82

Acc. by ? Milas Pruitt-g.     Chicago, c. August, 1924.

1824-3  Shave 'Em Dry Blues                 Pm 12222
1825-2  Farewell Daddy Blues                -

Acc. by her Georgia Band : Howard Scott-c/Charlie Green-tb/Don Redman-cl/Fletcher
Henderson-p/Charlie Dixon-bj or Kaiser Marshall-d as shown.
                              New York, c. October 15, 1924.

1922-2  Booze And Blues - d                 Pm 12242
1923-2  Toad Frog Blues - d                 -
1924-1-2  Jealous Hearted Blues - bj        Pm 12252, UHCA 86, JI 9, JC L-20,
                                            Amp R-101, AFG 6

Louis Armstrong-c replaces Scott; Buster Bailey-cl replaces Redman.
                              New York, c. October 16, 1924.

1925-1-2  See See Rider Blues - bj          Pm 12252, UHCA 85, JI 9, JC L-20,
                                            Amp R-101, AFG 6
1926-2  Jelly Bean Blues - bj               Pm 12238, 14016, UHCA 84, JI 8,
                                            JC L-10, XX 9, AF A-02
1927-2-3  Countin' The Blues - bj/d         As above, but UHCA 83 (coupled
                                            with UHCA 84)
NOTE:- XX 9 as MAMA CAN CAN AND ORPHAN WILL (WITH THE ELASTIC BAND).

Acc. by her Georgia Band : Tommy Ladnier-c/Jimmy O'Bryant-cl/Lovie Austin-p.
                              Chicago, c. November, 1924.

10001-2  Cell Bound Blues                   Pm 12257

Acc. by her Georgia Band : George "Hooks" Tilford-Cm/k-sw/? Lil Henderson-p/? Happy
Bolton-d (no d on 2139-1 and only one cymbal crash on 2138-1).
                              Chicago, May, 1925.

2136-1-2  Army Camp Harmony Blues           Pm 12284, Poydras 88
2137-1-2  Explaining The Blues              -
2138-1  Louisiana Hoo Doo Blues             Pm 12290
2139-1  Goodbye Daddy Blues - sw            -

Acc. by her Georgia Band : Probably :- Kid Henderson-c/Lucien Brown-cl-as/Lil
Henderson-p/George Williams-bj/Happy Bolton-d-chimes.
                                        Chicago, c. August, 1925.

| | | |
|---|---|---|
| 2209-1-2 | Stormy Sea Blues - cl | Pm 12295 |
| 2210-2 | Rough And Tumble Blues | Pm 12311 |
| 2211-1-2 | Night Time Blues | Pm 12303 |
| 2212-2 | Levee Camp Moan - cl | Pm 12295 |
| 2213-2 | Four Day Honory Scat | Pm 12303 |
| 2214-2 | Memphis Bound Blues | Pm 12311 |

Acc. by her Georgia Band : Joe Smith-c/Charlie Green-tb/Buster Bailey-cl/Coleman
Hawkins-bsx/Fletcher Henderson-p/Charlie Dixon-bj.
                                        Chicago, between Jan. 26 and Mar. 8, 1926.

| | | |
|---|---|---|
| 2369-2 | Slave To The Blues | Pm 12332, JC L-87 |
| 2370-1-2 | Yonder Come The Blues | Pm 12357, Sig 908, JC L-73, |
| | | Jazz 5001 |
| 2371-1-2 | Titanic Man Blues | Pm 12374 |
| 2372-2 | Chain Gang Blues | Pm 12338 |
| 2373-1-2 | Bessemer Bound Blues | Pm 12374 |
| 2374-1 | Oh My Babe Blues | Pm 12332, JC L-87 |
| 2375-2 | Wringing And Twisting Blues | Pm 12338 |
| 2376-2 | Stack O' Lee Blues | Pm 12357, Sig 908, JC L-73, |
| | | Jazz 5001 |

Acc. by her Georgia Band : Dave Nelson-c/Albert Wynn-tb/? Artie Starks or Stump
Evans-ss-as/? Lil Henderson-p/bj/? Cedric Odom-d.
                                        Chicago, c. March, 1926.

| | | |
|---|---|---|
| 2448-1-2 | Broken Hearted Blues | Pm 12364 |
| 2451-3-4 | Jealousy Blues | - |
| 2452-1-2 | Seeking Blues | Pm 12352 |

NOTE:- Matrices 2449 and 2450 are untraced.

Acc. by Jimmy Blythe-p.                  Chicago, c. March, 1926.

| | | |
|---|---|---|
| 2466-1-3 | Mountain Jack Blues | Pm 12352 |

Acc. by her Georgia Band : Kid Henderson or Homer Hobson-c/Albert Wynn-tb/William
Clinton or Tom Brown-cl-as/musical saw/Lil Hardaway, Lil Henderson or Jimmy
Flowers-p/W. J. Byrne, Rip Bassett or Silas White-bj/Fred Scott or Ben Thigpen-d.
                                        Chicago, c. August, 1926.

| | | |
|---|---|---|
| 2627-1 | Down In The Basement | Pm 12395 |
| 2628-1 | Sissy Blues | Pm 12384 |
| 2629-2 | Broken Soul Blues | - |

Acc. by Lil Henderson-p.                 Chicago, c. August, 1926.

| | | |
|---|---|---|
| 2631-1 | Trust No Man | Pm 12395 |

Acc. by (?) Leroy Pickett-vn/Blind Blake-g.
                                        Chicago, c. December, 1926.

| | | |
|---|---|---|
| 4019-2 | Little Low Mama Blues | Pm 12419, Bwy 5005 |
| 4020-1-2 | Grievin' Hearted Blues | -       - |

NOTE:- Broadway 5005 as LILA PATTERSON.

| | | |
|---|---|---|
| 4021-2 | Don't Fish In My Sea | Pm 12438, Bwy 5010, AM 5, JC L-16 |

NOTE:- Broadway 5010 as LILA PATTERSON.        JRS AA-121

Acc. by ? Jimmy Blythe-p/Blind Blake-g/Jimmy Bertrand-x.
                                        Chicago, c. February, 1927.

| | | |
|---|---|---|
| | Morning Hour Blues | Pm 12455, JC L-57, AF A-011 |

NOTE:- Paramount 12455 bears only the control number 405.

Acc. by probably :- B. T. Wingfield-c/Junie Cobb-cl/Jimmy Blythe or Tiny Parham-p.
Chicago, c. February, 1927.

-2   Weepin' Woman Blues           Pm 12455, JC L-57, AF A-011
-2   Soon This Morning             Pm 12438, Bwy 5010, AM 5, JC L-16,
                                   JRS AA-121
NOTE:- Broadway 5010 as LILA PATTERSON; Paramount 12438 as MA RAINEY AND HER
GEORGIA BAND. Only the control numbers 407 and 408 appear on Paramount 12455 and
12438 respectively, with takes as shown; from the aural and visual appearance of
both these sides, it would seem likely that they were made in the Marsh Recording
Laboratories.

Acc. by her Georgia Band : Shirley Clay-c/Kid Ory-tb/? Hop Hopson-p/bj/bb; an
unidentified male voice is heard in conversation with Ma Rainey on the side
marked **.                         Chicago, c. August, 1927.

4682-2   Big Boy Blues             Pm 12548, JD 015
4683-2   Blues Oh Blues            Pm 12566, 4, JC L-98, JRS AA-108

4690-3   Damper Down Blues         Pm 12548, JD 015
4691-2**Gone Daddy Blues          Pm 12526, 3, JC L-120
4692-1   Oh Papa Blues             Pm 12566, 4, JC L-98, JRS AA-108

Ory, Hopson and bb only, or Hopson only, where shown.
Chicago, c. August, 1927.

4707-1   Misery Blues              Pm 12508, Bwy 5018, JC L-52
4708-2   Dead Drunk Blues - pHH    -          -         -
4709-1   Slow Driving Moan - tb/p/bb   Pm 12526, 3, JC L-120
NOTE:- Broadway 5018 as LILA PATTERSON. Paramount 12508 shows the piano acc. as
by HOP HOPKINS.

Acc. by her Georgia Band (dir. by Prof. C. M. Russell, according to the label of
Paramount 12612, which has no vocal on either side by Ma Rainey; on Paramount
12590, she converses with an unidentified man, marked **, who speaks without her
where marked *. The personnel s possibly :- Shirley Clay-c/Albert Wynn-tb/?
Artie Starks-cl/p/d.               Chicago, c. December, 1927.

20228-3   Blues The World Forgot - Part 1   Pm 12647, P-1, JC L-35
20229-2  *"Ma" Rainey's Black Bottom        Pm 12590, JD 014
20230-2   Blues The World Forgot - Part 2   Pm 12647, P-1, JC L-35
20231-2   Hellish Rag                       Pm 12612
20232-1**Georgia Cake-Walk                  Pm 12590, JD 014
20233-1   New Bo-Weavil Blues               Pm 12603, P-2, JC L-42
20234-2   Moonshine Blues                   -          -        -
20235-3   Ice Bag Papa                      Pm 12612

Acc. by her Tub Jug Washboard Band : ? Tampa Red (Hudson Whitaker) (and another ?)
k/Georgia Tom Dorsey-p/bj/jug, with moaning effect by the band (m).
Chicago, c. June, 1928.

20661-1   Black Cat Hoot Owl Blues   Pm 12687
20662-3   Log Camp Blues             Pm 12804
20663-2   Hear Me Talking To You     Pm 12668, Poydras 62, Ristic 6
20664-2   Hustlin' Blues             Pm 12804
20665-2   Prove It On Me Blues       Pm 12668, Poydras 62, Ristic 6
20666-1   Victim Of The Blues        Pm 12687
20667-1-2 Traveling Blues            Pm 12706, 14011, JC L-1
20668-1-2 Deep Moaning Blues - m     -          -        -

Acc. by Georgia Tom Dorsey-p/Tampa Red (Hudson Whitaker)-g.
Chicago, September, 1928.

20878-1   Daddy Goodbye Blues        Pm 12963
20879-2   Sleep Talking Blues        Pm 12760
20880-2   Tough Luck Blues           Pm 12735
20881-1   Blame It On The Blues      Pm 12760
20882-2   Sweet Rough Man            Pm 12926
20883-3   Runaway Blues              Pm 12902

Acc. by Georgia Tom Dorsey or Eddie Miller-p.
                                    Chicago, c. September, 1928.

20885-2  Screech Owl Blues                      Pm 12735
20886-1  Black Dust Blues                       Pm 12926

Acc. by Georgia Tom Dorsey-p/Tampa Red (Hudson Whitaker)-g.
                                    Chicago, c. September, 1928.

20897-1  Leaving This Morning                   Pm 12902
20898-2  Black Eye Blues                        Pm 12963

Vocal duets with Papa Charlie Jackson, acc. by the latter-bj.
                                    Chicago, c. October, 1928.

20921-4  Ma And Pa Poorhouse Blues              Pm 12718, Poydras 11, Ristic 5,
                                                JD 013

                                    Chicago, c. December, 1928.

21044-1  Big Feeling Blues                      Pm 12718, Poydras 11, Ristic 5,
                                                JD 013

## THE RAMBLERS

Bob Hamilton-elo/Billy Kyle-p/Teddy Bunn-g-v/O'Neil Spencer-d-v.
                                    New York, April 28, 1939.

65490-A  Honey In The Bee Ball - vONS          Dec 2499, Y-5420
65491-A  'Tain't What You Do (It's The Way That Dec 2470   -
         Cha Do It) - vTB-ONS
65492-A-B Money Is Honey - vONS                  -
65493-A  Lonesome Railroad - vONS              Dec 2499

NOTE:- The Dutch dance orchestra known as THE RAMBLERS (or sometimes THE ORIGINAL
RAMBLERS) made a number of records in London and various studios in Holland during
the 1920s and 1930s, but as the personnel included no internationally famous names
(except when Coleman Hawkins and Connie Boswell recorded with them, both q.v.), it
was decided to omit them from the present volume.

## THE RAMBLING RAGADORS

Pseudonym on Pathe Actuelle 36616 and 11402 for Lou Gold and his Orchestra, q.v.

## RAMONA

Ramona Davies was one of Paul Whiteman's featured vocalists in the 1930s; she made a
number of Victor records, many of them of songs at the piano, but the following are
known to have interesting accpmaniments by other members of the Whiteman orchestra.

RAMONA AND HER GRAND PIANO : Vocal, acc. by Bunny Berigan-t/Benny Bonacio-cl/own p/
Roy Bargy-p-cel.                    New York, March 1, 1933.

75341-1  What Have We Got To Lose ?            Vic 24268, HMV EA-1218
75342-1  A Penny For Your Thoughts            Vic 24260
75343-1  My Cousin In Milwaukee                -

                                    Camden, N. J., April 20, 1933.

75671-1  Raisin' The Rent                     Vic 24316, HMV EA-1234
75672-1  Was My Face Red ?                    Vic 24310, HMV B-8046, EA-1233
75673-1  I've Got To Sing A Torch Song        Vic 24304

Bargy omitted; Herb Quigley-d added.    New York, August 16, 1933.

77498-1  You Excite Me !                      Vic 24389
77503-1  Ah ! The Moon Is Here                Vic 24408, HMV B-8090

RAMONA AND HER GRAND PIANO : Vocal, acc. by Bunny Berigan-t/Benny Bonacio-cl/Roy
   Bargy and self-p/Dick McDonough-g.      New York, October 20, 1933.

78264-1  I Found A New Way To Go To Town          Vic 24440
78265-1  I'm No Angel                             -
78266-1  Not For All The Rice In China            Vic 24445

RAMONA AND HER GANG : Vocal, acc. by Charlie Teagarden-t/Jack Teagarden-tb/Benny
   Bonacio-cl-bar/own p/Dick McDonough-g/Art Miller-sb/Larry Gomar-d.
                                           New York, September 13, 1935.

95024-1  Every Now And Then                       Vic 25138, JA-608, HMV B-8406,
                                                    EA-1589, El EG-3578
95025-2  No Strings                               Vic 25138, JA-608, HMV B-4563,
                                                    EA-1589
95026-2  I Can't Give You Anything But Love       Vic 25156
95027-1  Barrel-House Music                       -         HMV B-4563

## RAMPART STREET  WASHBOARD BAND

See the Beale Street Washboard Band.

## CLARK RANDALL  AND HIS ORCHESTRA

Clark Randall (Frank Tennille)-v dir. Charlie Spivak-Yank Lawson-t/Glenn Miller-tb-a
   /Larry Altpeter-tb/Matty Matlock-cl-as/Gil Rodin-as/Eddie Miller-cl-ts/Deane Kin-
   caide-ts-a/Gil Bowers-p-or/Nappy Lamare-g-v/Pete Peterson-sb/Ray Bauduc-d.
                                           New York, March 15, 1935.

B-17047-1  Troublesome Trumpet - vNL&ch/aDK       Br 7415, Lucky 5072
B-17048-1  When Icky Morgan Plays The Organ-vCR/aGM  -                -
 -17049-1  What's The Reason (I'm Not Pleasin'     Ban 33410, Cq 8527, Mt M-13377,
              You) - vCR                             Or 3130, Per 16107, Ro 2504,
                                                     Rex 8500
   17050-1  Restless - vCR                         As above except Cq 8527, Rex 8500

                                           New York, March 22, 1935.

B-17160-1  Jitter Bug - vNL/aDK                    Br 7466
B-17161-1  If You're Looking For Someone To Love   -
              - vCR/aDK

                                           New York, March 29, 1935.

B-17218-1  Drifting Tide - vCR                     Br 7436
B-17219-1  Here Comes Your Pappy With The Wrong    -
              Kind Of Load - vNL
   17220-1  Right About Face - vCR                 Ban 33409, Mt M-13376, Or 3129,
                                                     Per 16105, Ro 2503
   17221-1  Love's Serenade - vCR                  As above
   NOTE:- Only the Brunswicks are labelled as headed; all others appear as GIL RODIN
AND HIS ORCHESTRA.

## DUKE RANDALL AND  HIS BOYS

Pseudonym on Champion for Hightower's Night Hawks, q.v.

## SLATZ RANDALL AND  HIS ORCHESTRA

Slatz Randall-p dir. 2t/tb/cl-ss/cl-as/cl-ts/vn/Joe Roberts-bj-v/bb/d.
                                           Minneapolis, January, 1929.

MP-34-B  Bessie Couldn't Help It - vJR            Br 4331, A-8456

Later Brunswick records by this band occasionally feature short solos by Yank Lawson-
t in a conventional setting.  He is not present on the above.

MANDY RANDOLPH : Vocal, acc. by own p.    Richmond, Ind., April 30, 1923.

11427    I Got Another Lovin' Daddy            Gnt Special

                                          Richmond, Ind., May 29, 1923.

11480    Weary Way Blues                      Gnt Special (or rejected ?)
11481    If You Go, You'll Come Back By-And-By      -
11483    Two-Time Dan                               -
11484    There'll Be Some Changes Made              -
NOTE:- Matrix 11482 is by Sammie Lewis, q.v.

AMANDA RANDOLPH AND HER ORCHESTRA : Louis Garcia-t/Moe Zudecoff-tb/Al Weinstein-cl/
   Gil Bowers-p/Abe Harris-g/W. Feinbloom-sb/Arnold Klein-d/Amanda Randolph-v.
                                          New York, October 8, 1936.

02108-1  For Sentimental Reasons - vAR         BB B-6617, RZ MR-2360
02109-1  Doin' The Suzie-Q - vAR               BB B-6615, RZ MR-2460
02110-1  He May Be Your Man (But He Comes To See  BB B-6617
         Me Sometimes) - vAR
02111-1  Honey, Please Don't Turn Your Back On    BB B-6616
         Me - vAR
02112-1  Please Don't Talk About My Man - vAR  BB B-6615
02113-1  I've Got Something In My Eye - vAR    BB B-6619, RZ MR-2303

## EARL RANDOLPH'S  ORCHESTRA

Pseudonym for the following items listed in this book :-

Broadway 1128  Sorry (Fletcher Henderson and his Orchestra)
Maxsa 1545  Collegiate (Ben Selvin and his Orchestra)
      1546  Sweet Georgia Brown (Texas Ten)
Paramount 20356  Choo Choo (Joseph Samuels and his Orchestra)

## BARNEY RAPP AND  HIS ORCHESTRA

The following title from a total of only fourteen known to have been made and issued
of this dance orchestra is of some interest for the muted trumpet solo featured.

Barney Rapp-d dir. Ray Trotta-t and probably :- Fred Barman-t/Frank Henry-tb/Ed
   Stannard-Ken Albright-as/Abe Rosenberg-vn/Cliff Burwell-p/Ffloyd Campbell-bj/Hank
   Stern-bb.
                                          New York, October 17, 1923.

28753-3  Walk, Jennie, Walk !                  Vic 19182

## LEON RAPPOLO

Clarinet solos, acc. by Martin Abraham.  The latter is the real name of Chink Martin
   (tuba player of the New Orleans Rhythm Kings at the time of the recordings). Since
   it is hardly likely that a pair of clarinet solos would have been accompanied only
   by a bass, it is likely, even certain, that Abraham played piano, or possibly that
   other members of the New Orleans Rhythm Kings were also present as accompanists to
   their colleague, whose name should be spelt ROPPOLO.

                                          Richmond, Ind., July 3, 1923.

11524    Bucktown Blues                       Gnt rejected
11525    Angry                                     -

                                          Richmond, Ind., July 17, 1923.

11542    Bucktown Blues                       Gnt rejected
11543    Angry                                     -

All that is known of this negro orchestra is that the vocalists are Estelle Galloway
and Jimmy Raschel.                          Richmond, Ind., November 28, 1932.

18911     It Don't Mean A Thing (If It Ain't Got  Ch 16534
          That Swing) - vEG
18912     Nobody's Sweetheart - vJR                 Rejected

## FLOYD RAY AND HIS ORCHESTRA

Floyd Ray dir. Joe Kelley-Granville Young-Eddie Vanderveer-t/Gilbert Kelley-Clayton
Smith-tb/George Fauntleroy-Shirley Greene-as/Carroll Ridley-ts/Sol Moore-bar/Ken
Bryan-p/Gene Brown-g/Benny Booker-sb/George Ward-d/Dudley Brooks-a/Ivy Ann Glascoe
Joe Alexander-Ivy, Verne and Von-v.   New York, February 21, 1939.

65055-A  Three O'Clock In The Morning - vch     Dec 2337, Voc S-230
65056-A  Comin' On With The Blues - vIAG        -           -
65057-A  Love Is Simply Grand - vI-V-V          Dec 2500, Voc S-234
65058-A  Jammin' The Blues (Tamin' The Blues*)  Dec 2618,      -*
         - vIAG

Eddie Byrd-d replaces Ward.             New York, April 13, 1939.

65392-A  My Little Dream Girl - vJA             Dec 2923
65393-A  Side By Side - vI-V-V                  Dec 2618, Voc S-241
65394-A  Firefly Stomp                          Dec 2500
65395-A  Blues At Noon - vI-V-V                 Dec 2923, Voc S-241

## JIMMY RAY AND HIS ORCHESTRA

This was a studio group featuring its nominal leader as vocalist, and as such is of
little or no jazz interest. The following titles have no vocals and are of some
jazz value.

Leonard Joy dir. Leonard Smith-Del Staigers-Harry Shilkret-t/Alex Palocsay-tb/Sid
Stoneburn-Maurice Pierce-cl-as/Fletcher Hereford-cl-ts/Edgar Fairchild-p/Dick
McDonough-g/George Rodo-sb/Bill Dinan-d.
                                        New York, July 9, 1937.

011080-1  Caravan                           BB B-7079

                                        New York, November 19, 1937.

017088-1  Pell Street Blues                 BB B-7321
NOTE:- Bluebird B-7079 as SOUTHERN RHYTHM KINGS; B-7321 as SOUTHERN SERENADERS
ORCHESTRA.

## MARTHA RAYE

The following sides by this film comedienne are included because of their obviously
interesting accompaniments.

Vocal, acc. by Bobby Henderson-p/Lonnie Johnson-g.
                                        New York, October 6, 1932.

73783-1-2  I Heard                          Vic rejected
73784-1-2  How'm I Doin' ? (Hey-Hey)             -

## RAYMOND DANCE BAND

Pseudonym on English Regal for the following items listed in this book :-

G-8557  Clap Hands ! Here Comes Charley (The Georgians)
G-8578  Loud Speakin' Papa (The Charleston Chasers)
G-8578  I Love My Baby (The Little Ramblers)
G-8598  The Prisoner's Song (Ross Gorman's Earl Carroll Orchestra)
G-8684  The Pump Song (Earl Gresh and his Gangplank Orchestra)
G-8743  Here Comes Malinda (The Little Ramblers)
G-8744  Hard-To-Get Gertie (Francis Craig and his Orchestra)
G-8746  Scatter Your Smiles (Earl Gresh and his Gangplank Orchestra)
G-8804  Brown Sugar (Cook and his Dreamland Orchestra)
G-8849  Lonely Eyes (Al Handler and his Orchestra)
G-8904  Positively - Absolutely (Mal Hallett and his Orchestra)

Pseudonym on Broadway and Paramount for Fred Rich and his Orchestra, q.v.

## RAYNER'S DANCE ORCHESTRA

Pseudonym on English Perfect for the following items listed in this book :-

P-306  Both sides by the Six Hottentots
P-307  The Blue Room (California Ramblers)
P-308  Red Lips, Kiss My Blues Away (Sam Lanin and his Orchestra)
P-325  You Don't Like It - Not Much (Al Lynch and his Orchestra)
P-342  Dawning (Nicholas Orlando's Orchestra)

## ANDY RAZAF

This famous songwriter, a descendant of the Royal House of Madagascar, partner of
"Fats" Waller, made a few records of his own and other songs, usually to his own
piano accompaniment.  These have little or no interest as jazz, but the following
sides are obviously exceptions.

Vocal, acc. by J. C. Johnson-p, with Eddie King-or*.
                                        New York, November 4, 1927.

144956-1  Empty Arms                     Col 14265-D
144957-2  *All The World Is Lonely (For A Little    -
          Blackbird)

    Acc. by Howard Nelson-vn/David Martin-vc/Fats Waller-p.
                                        New York, January 17, 1928.

145533-1  Back In Your Own Back Yard          Col 14285-D
145534-3  Nobody Knows How Much I Love You        -
    NOTE:- This issue as JOHNNY THOMPSON.

## CASPER REARDON

CASPER REARDON, HIS HARP AND HIS ORCHESTRA : T/2-3cl/Casper Reardon-harp/sb/d and
    strings of Lud Gluskin's Orchestra.    New York, April 23, 1936.

P-19094-1  In A Sentimental Mood             LMS L-193
P-19095-1  Tormented                         -

    T/cl/bcl/o/4vn/vl/Casper Reardon-harp/sb/d/vib/Bea Giersdorf-v.
                                        New York, September 19, 1936.

P-19911-1  Summertime                        LMS L-199
P-19912-2  (If You Can't Sing It) You'll Have To   -
           Swing It - vBG

CASPER REARDON AND HIS GROUP : Tony Tortomas-t/Jimmy Lytell-Henry Wade-cl/Casper
    Reardon-harp/Mack Shopnick-sb/Herb Quigley-d-vib.
                                        New York, May 10, 1937.

P-21115-2  Washboard Blues                   LMS L-218
P-21116-1  What Is This Thing Called Love ?      -

CASPER REARDON AND HIS ORCHESTRA : Charlie Spivak-Ruby Weinstein-Russ Case-t/Andy
    Russo-Lloyd Turner-tb/Paul Ricci-cl/Arnold Brilhart-Joe Usifer-as/Rudolph Adler-cl
    ts/Harry Bluestone-Sam Korman-Benny Schmidt-Harry Hammer-vn/Dave Stirkin-vl/Casper
    Reardon-harp/Max Raderman-p/Ned Cola-g/Artie Bernstein-sb/Sammy Weiss-d/Franklyn
    Marks-a. The session was probably directed by Lou Raderman.
                                        New York, May 18, 1937.

M-476-  Ain't Misbehavin'                    Mas 133
M-477-  In A Sentimental Mood                -
M-478-  Washboard Blues                      Mas 139
M-479-  A Blues Serenade                     -

Harp solos, acc. by Angie Rattiner-t/Milt Cassell-cl-bsn/Alfie Evans-bcl/Henry Wade-
ts/Art Zazmar-Chauncey Morehouse-d/Loulie Jean-v.
                                          New York, February 5, 1940.

| | | |
|---|---|---|
| 2015 | I Can't Give You Anything But Love - vLJ | Schirmer 511 |
| 2016 | I Got Rhythm - vLJ | Schirmer 512 |
| 2017 | Easy To Love - vLJ | Schirmer 511 |
| 2018 | They Didn't Believe Me - vLJ | Schirmer 512 |

NOTE:- Casper Reardon also recorded a set of piano solos for Victor in 1933, but as
these were intended as accompaniments for tap-dancing, they have no jazz interest.

## REB'S LEGION CLUB  FORTY FIVES

See Reb Spikes.

## RECTOR'S PARAMOUNT SIX

Tommy Smith-t/Ted Heath-tb/unspecified s (according to rumour, this was Sidney
Bechet !)/George Smith-vn/Bert Romaine-p/Benny Peyton-d.
                                          Hayes, Middlesex, February 28, 1922.

| | | |
|---|---|---|
| Bb-1056-1-2 | After A While | HMV rejected |
| Bb-1057-1-2 | Everybody Step | - |

## RED AND  HIS BIG TEN

See Red Nichols.

## RED AND MIFF'S  STOMPERS

See Red Nichols.

## THE RED CAPS

See Russell Wooding.

## THE  RED DANDIES

Pseudonym on Canadian Domino for the following items listed in this book :-

21580  The Hurricane (The Red Heads)
31023  Where The Shy Little Violets Grow (The Rounders)

## THE RED DEVILS

—— Carpenter-p dir. R. E. Bennett-cl-as/Opal Cooper-banjoline/Sam Richardson-bj-as/
C. C. Thompson-d-v.                       Hayes, Middlesex, September 1, 1920.

| | | |
|---|---|---|
| HO-5829ae | The Crocodile | HMV rejected |
| HO-5830ae | My Little Bimbo | - |
| HO-5831ae | I'll Be Back There Someday | - |
| HO-5832ae | If I Forget | - |

2 combs or k/2g/d.                        New York, May 16, 1930.

| | | |
|---|---|---|
| 9740-2 | West Coast Stomp | Ban 32394,Or 8126,Per 0202,Ro 5126 |
| 9741-3 | Ballin' The Jack | -        -        -       - |
| 9742- | Parlor Social Stomp | Rejected |

Benny Nawahi-bj (and u ?) dir. comb/k/Bruce Hinkson-vn/Harry Brooks-p.
                                          New York, February 2, 1931.

| | | |
|---|---|---|
| 151260-1 | Dinah | Col 14586-D, Par R-2380 |
| 151261-1 | Tiger Rag - v | -              - |

NOTE:- The last two sessions are almost certainly by similar groups; Perfect 0202
as THE SALTY DOG FOUR (in the files as THE RED DEVILS); Parlophone R-2380 as THE
BLACK DEVILS.

Vernon Dalhart-Ed Smalle-k/John Cali or Harry Reser-bj.
                              New York, c. May 21, 1924.

    1007-D  How Come You Do Me Like You Do ?        Cam 569, Lin 2222
    NOTE:- Lincoln 2222 as THE TRAVELING MUSKETEERS.

## THE  RED HEADS

Red Nichols-t/Miff Mole-tb/Bobby Davis-Fred Morrow-cl-as/Arthur Schutt-p/Vic Berton-
    d.                            New York, c. November 13, 1925.

    106400     Fallen Arches                   PA 36384, 11456, Per 14565
                                               P X-6848, Sal 329
    106401     Nervous Charlie                 PA 36347, Per 14528
    106402     Headin' For Louisville            -  11069   -

Red Nichols-t/Miff Mole-tb/Jimmy Dorsey-t-cl-as/? Alfie Evans-cl-ts/Rube Bloom-p/Vic
    Berton-d/Arthur Fields-v.       New York, c. February 4, 1926.

    106602     Poor Papa (He's Got Nothin' At All)-vAF  PA 36387, 11134, Per 14568,
                                               Gra 9217, Sal 262
    106603     'Tain't Cold                    PA 36419, 11396, Per 14600
    106604     Hangover                          -       -        -
       NOTE:- Pathe Actuelle 11134 as RED NICHOLS AND HIS ORCHESTRA; Grafton 9217 as
    WINDSOR ORCHESTRA.

    Cl-ts omitted; Arthur Schutt-p replaces Bloom.
                              New York, c. April 7, 1926.

    106786     Wild And Foolish                PA 36492, 11206, Per 14673
    106787     Hi-Diddle-Diddle                PA 36458, 11234, Per 14639,
                                               P X-6900, Sal 382, Apex 752,
                                               Dom 21520, LS 24504, Mic 22517,
                                               St 23042
    106788     Dynamite                        PA 36458, 11456, Per 14639,
                                               P X-6903, Sal 378
       NOTE:- Some copies of Apex 752 as TEN BLACK BIRDS.

Red Nichols-Leo McConville-t/Miff Mole-tb/Jimmy Dorsey-cl-as/? Alfie Evans-cl-ts/
    Arthur Schutt-p/Dick McDonough-bj-g/Vic Berton-d.
                              New York, c. September 14, 1926.

    107094     Alabama Stomp                   PA 36527, 11236, Per 14708,
                                               P X-6946, Sal 471
    107095-A-B  The Hurricane                  PA 36536, 11331, Per 14717,
                                               Apex 26009, Dom 21580,
                                               Leo/St 23093, Sal 467
    107096     Brown Sugar                     PA 36527, 11236, Per 14708
       NOTE:- Domino 21580 as THE RED DANDIES.

Red Nichols-t/Arthur Schutt-p/Eddie Lang-g/Vic Berton-d.
                              New York, c. November 4, 1926.

    107192     Get With                        PA 11347
    107193     Get A Load Of This                -

Red Nichols-Leo McConville-t/Brad Gowans-c*/Miff Mole-tb/Jimmy Dorsey-cl-as/Arthur
    Schutt-p/Dick McDonough-bj-g/Vic Berton-d.
                              New York, c. November 11, 1926.

    107204     That's No Bargain               PA 36576, 11331, Per 14757
    107205     *Heebie Jeebies                 PA 36557, 11289, Per 14738,
                                               P X-6963, Sal 565
    107206-A-B  Black Bottom Stomp             As above, but P X-6965

Red Nichols-t/Miff Mole-tb/Jimmy Lytell-cl-as/Arthur Schutt-p/Vic Berton-d/Frank
    Gould-v.                      New York, c. January 18, 1927.

    107350-B-D  Tell Me Tonight - vFG          PA 36583, Per 14764
    107351-A-C  Here Or There - vFG              -  11376   -
    107352-A-B-C  You Should See My Tootsie - vFG  PA 36593 - Per 14774

Red Nichols-t/Wingy Manone-c*/Miff Mole-tb/Pee Wee Russell-cl/Arthur Schutt-p/Vic
    Berton-d.                              New York, c. September 16, 1927.

| 107782-1-2 | A Good Man Is Hard To Find | PA 36701, Per 14882, Cam 1260, Lin 2725, Ro 494, Sal 765, MF 101 |
| 107783 | Nothin' Does-Does Like It Used To Do-Do-Do | PA 36707, 11515, Per 14888 |
| 107784-1-2 | *Baltimore | PA 36701    -  Per 14882, Sal 764 |

NOTE:- Cameo 1260, Lin 2725, Romeo 494 as ALABAMA RED PEPPERS.  THE RED HEADS was
also a pseudonym on Melotone M-12443, M-12495, Oriole 2555, 2574 and Perfect 15648
for Red Nichols and his Five Pennies, q.v.

## RED HOT DOGS

Probably t/tb/cl-as/p/bj/d.            New York, August 1, 1927.

| 7417-2 | Blame It On The Black Bottom Craze | Ban 6057 |
| 7418- | Swanee's Calling Me | Ban 6069 |
| 7419- | I Can't Fool Around With Someone Who's Fooling Around | Rejected ? |

## RED HOT  SYNCOPATORS

Pseudonym on Bell for the Original Indiana Five, q.v., and on Australian Regal
    G-20910 for the Lazy Levee Loungers, q.v.

## THE  RED HOTTERS

Pseudonym on Silvertone 3526 and 3527 for Boyd Senter and/or the Chicago De Luxe
    Orchestra, q.v., and for the following, which is listed on a contemporary Silver-
    tone sleeve.  Neither title has yet been traced to a Paramount issue, from which
    both undoubtedly derive, but as the titles in each case are probably different from
    the originals, identification will necessarily be delayed until a copy of the disc
    is found.  The recording date is probably late 1924 or early 1925.

|  | Hot Mustard | Sil 3560 |
|  | Third Alley Breakdown | - |

See also Harry Raderman.

## DON REDMAN AND HIS ORCHESTRA

Don Redman-as-v-a dir. Leonard Davis-Bill Coleman-Henry Allen-t/Claude Jones-Fred
    Robinson-Benny Morton-tb/Edward Inge-Rupert Cole-cl-as/Robert Carroll-ts/Horace
    Henderson-p-a/Talcott Reeves-bj-g/Bob Ysaguirre-bb-sb/Manzie Johnson-d-vib/Lois
    Deppe-v.                               New York, September 24, 1931.

| E-37222-A | I Heard - vDR/aHH | Rejected |
| E-37223-A | Trouble, Why Pick On Me ? - vLD/aDR | Br 6233, 01280, A-500322 |
| E-37224- | Shakin' The African  - vDR | Br 01244, A-9250 |
| E-37225-A | Chant Of The Weed | Br 6211, 80036, 01244, A-9250, Dec BM-30360 |
| E-37225-B | Chant Of The Weed | Br A-500160, A-500765 |

NOTE:- On some issues from matrix E-37224, the title is shown as SHAKIN' THE
AFRICANN or AFRIKANN.

Langston Curl-t replaces Coleman.      New York, October 15, 1931.

| E-37291-A | Shakin' The African - vDR | Br 6211, 80036, 01244 |
| E-37291-B | Shakin' The African - vDR | Br A-500322, A-500765 |
| E-37292-A | I Heard - vDR/aHH | Br 6233, 01280, A-500160, Dec BM-30360 |

NOTE:- On some issues from matrix E-37291-A-B, the title is shown as SHAKIN' THE
AFRICANN or AFRIKANN.

Don Redman-as-v-a dir. Shirley Clay-Langston Curl-Sidney de Paris-t/Claude Jones-
  Fred Robinson-Benny Morton-tb/Edward Inge-Rupert Cole-cl-as/Robert Carroll-ts/
  Horace Henderson-p-a/Talcott Reeves-bj-g/Bob Ysaguirre-bb-sb/Manzie Johnson-d-vib/
  Harlan Lattimore-v.                        New York, February 26, 1932.

| | | |
|---|---|---|
| B-11365-A-B | Goodbye Blues | Rejected |
| B-11366-A | How'm I Doin' ? (Hey-Hey) - vDR | Br 6273, 01320 |
| B-11367-A | Try Getting A Good Night's Sleep-vDR/aHH | -        - |

New York, June 28, 1932.

| | | |
|---|---|---|
| 11979-3 | Got The South In My Soul - vHL | Mt M-12417, Pan 25317 |
| B-11994-A | If It's True - vHL | Br 6368, 01389 |
| B-11995-A | It's A Great World After All - vDR/aHH | Br 6344, 02509 |
| B-11996-A | You Gave Me Everything But Love - vHL | -    01366 |

NOTE:- Melotone M-12417 and Panachord 25317 as EARL HARLAN AND HIS ORCHESTRA.

New York, June 30, 1932.

| | | |
|---|---|---|
| B-12005-A | Tea For Two - vHL | Br 6354, 01389 |
| B-12006-A | Hot And Anxious - vDR/aHH | Br 6368, 01344, A-9903, A-500194, Par R-2955, PZ-11225, Pol 580015 |
| B-12007-A | I Got Rhythm | Br 6354, 01344, A-9903, A-500194, ARC 5-11-04, Pol 580015 |

New York, September 16, 1932.

| | | |
|---|---|---|
| B-12306-A | Pagan Paradise - vHL | Br 6412, 01400, A-9354 |
| B-12307-A | Two-Time Man - vDR | -        -        -     Par R-2955 |
| B-12307-B | Two-Time Man - vDR | Col 35689 |

New York, October 6, 1932.

| | | |
|---|---|---|
| B-12444-A | Underneath The Harlem Moon - vHL | Br 6401, 01427 |
| B-12445-A | Ain't I The Lucky One ? - vHL | -       - |
| B-12446-A | Doin' What I Please - vDR | Br 6429, 01489, Voc 4791 |
| B-12447-A | Nagasaki - vDR&ch'/aHH | - A-9560 -   ARC 5-11-04, Par R-2624,Lucky S-2,Od A-272290 |

Bill Robinson-tap dancing-v/Cab Calloway-The Mills Brothers-v.
                                 New York, December 29, 1932.

| | | |
|---|---|---|
| B-12810-A | Doin' The New Low-Down - v-tdBR | Br 6520, 01521, A-9393, A-500259 |
| B-12811-A | Doin' The New Low-Down - vCC-MB | Br 6517, 01518, A-9395, A-500256, Col DO-1143 |

Don Kirkpatrick-p-a replaces Henderson; Harry and Donald Mills-v.
                                 New York, February 2, 1933.

| | | |
|---|---|---|
| B-13006-A | How Ya Feelin' ? - vDR | Br 6528, 02076, A-9938 |
| B-13007-A | Shuffle Your Feet/Bandanna Babies-vH&DM | Br 6520, 01521, A-9393, A-500259 |
| B-13008-A | Mommy, I Don't Want To Go To Bed - vDR | Br 6528, 01989, A-9411 |
| B-13009-A | How Can I Hi-De-Hi (When I Feel So Low-De-Low) - vHL | -        -        - |
| B-13010-A | Shuffle Your Feet/Bandanna Babies | CBS OL-6770 (LP) |

New York, April 26, 1933.

| | | |
|---|---|---|
| B-13284-A | Sophisticated Lady | Br 6560, 01541, A-500270, Ban 32806, Dom 128, Mt M-12739, Per 15789, Ro 2095, Voc 15892 |
| B-13285-A | I Won't Tell - vDR | Br 6585, A-9445, A-500270 |
| B-13286-A | That Blue-Eyed Baby From Memphis - vHL | Br 6560, 01541, A-9560 |
| B-13287-A | It's All Your Fault - vHL | Br 6585, A-9445 |

NOTE:- Banner 32806, Domino 128, Melotone M-12739, Perfect 15789, Romeo 2095 as
EARL HARLAN AND HIS ORCHESTRA; Vocalion 15892 as DUKE WILLIAMS AND HIS ORCHESTRA.

Don Redman-as-v-a dir. Shirley Clay-Langston Curl-Sidney de Paris-t/Claude Jones-
Fred Robinson-Benny Morton-tb/Edgward Inge-Rupert Cole-cl-as/Robert Carroll-ts/
Don Kirkpatrick-p-a/Talcott Reeves-bj-g/Bob Ysaguirre-bb-sb/Manzie Johnson-d-vib/
Harlan Lattimore-v.            New York, August 2, 1933.

B-13694-A   Lazy Bones - vHL             Br 6622, 01589, A-9487, A-500313,
                                              Voc 4791
B-13695-A   Watching The Knife And Fork Spoon-vDR   As above, except Voc 4791

    Gene Simon-tb replaces Jones.       New York, October 19, 1933.

B-14179-A   I Found A New Way To Go To Town-vHL   Br 6684, 01638, A-9498, A-500330
B-14180-A   You Told Me But Half The Story - vHL   Br 6935, 01843
B-14181-A   Lonely Cabin - vHL                     -        -     A-500331
B-14182-A   She's Not Bad - vDR                    -

                        New York, October 20, 1933.

B-14192-A   No-One Loves Me Like That Dallas Man   Br 6684, 01638, A-9498, A-500330
            - vDR/aDK

    Henry Allen-t replaces Curl; Chick Bullock-v.
                        New York, November 14, 1933.

14298-1   Our Big Love Scene - vCB         Mt M-12840, Per 15847
14299-1   After Sundown - vCB              -          -
14315-1   Puddin' Head Jones - vCB        Mt M-12848, Per 15852
14316-1   My Old Man - vCB                 -          -
14317-1   Tired Of It All - vCB           Mt M-12867, Per 15862
14318-2   Keep On Doin' What You're Doin' - vCB    -         -
NOTE:- Melotone M-12848 and Perfect 15852 as BOB CAUSER AND HIS CORNELLIANS; all
others as EARL HARLAN AND HIS ORCHESTRA.

    Jerry Blake-cl-as-bar replaces Carroll.
                      New York, January 5, 1934.

B-14536-A   I Wanna Be Loved - vHL          Br 6745, 01744, A-9543

                      New York, January 9, 1934.

B-14559-A   Got The Jitters - vDR            Br 6745, 01744, A-9543,
                                          Par R-2624, Od A-272259

The files describe the next title as being by DON REDMAN SMALL BAND, but it was
issued as CAHN-CHAPLIN ORCHESTRA. The probable personnel is 1 or 2t/tb/1 or 2s/p/
g/sb/d from the next session.      New York, April 3, 1936.

60982-A   Christopher Columbus (A Rhythm Cocktail)Ch 40113

Don Redman-cl-ss-as-v dir. Reunald Jones-t-a/Shirley Clay-Sidney de Paris-t/Gene
Simon-Benny Morton-tb/Edward Inge-Rupert Cole-cl-as/Harvey Boone- l-as-bar/Robert
Carroll-ts/Don Kirkpatrick-p-a/Talcott Reeves-g/Bob Ysaguirre-sb/Manzie Johnson-d-
vib/Harlan Lattimore-v.           New York, May 7, 1936.

19202-1   A Little Bit Later On - vDR      ARC 6-08-02,Voc S-10,Imp 6005,18004
19203-1   Lazy Weather - vHL               ARC 6-07-09    -        -       -
19204-1   Moonrise On The Lowlands - vHL       -            Voc C-0002, Im 6026
19205-1   I Gotcha - vDR&ch               ARC 6-08-02, Voc S-18, Imp 18010

    Otis Johnson-Harold Baker-t replace Clay and de Paris; Quentin Jackson-tb added;
    Clarence Holiday-g replaces Reeves; Sidney Catlett-d replaces Johnson.
                      New York, September 30, 1936.

19979-1   Who Wants To Sing My Love Song ? - vHL   ARC 7-03-03, Voc 3359, C-0007
19980-2   Too Bad - vDR                       ARC 6-12-18, Voc/OK 3354, S-45,
                                         Br A-81104, Imp 6056, 18015
19981-1   We Don't Know From Nothin' - vDR      ARC 7-03-03, Voc 3359, C-0007,
                                         S-55, Imp 6052
19982-1   Bugle Call Rag                    ARC 6-12-18, Voc/OK 3354, S-45,
                                         Br A-81104, Imp 6002, 18015,
                                         Col DO-1676

Don Redman-cl-ss-as-v dir. Reunald Jones-t-a/Otis Johnson-Harold Baker-t/Gene Simon-
Benny Morton-Quentin Jackson-tb/Edward Inge-Rupert Cole-cl-as/Harvey Boone-cl-as-
bar/Robert Carroll-ts/Don Kirkpatrick-p-a/Bob Lessey-g/Bob Ysaguirre-sb/Sidney
Catlett-d/The Swing Choir-v.              New York, May 28, 1937.

| | | |
|---|---|---|
| M-505-2 | Stormy Weather - vSC | Vri 605, Voc/OK 3829 |
| M-506-1 | Exactly Like You - vSC | Vri 580, Voc 3823 |
| M-507-1 | The Man On The Flying Trapeze - vDR | Vri 635, Voc 3836 |
| M-508-1 | On The Sunny Side Of The Street - vSC | Vri 580, Voc 3823 |
| M-509-2 | Swingin' With The Fat Man | Realm 52539 (LP) |
| M-510-1 | Sweet Sue | - |
| M-510-2 | Sweet Sue | Vri 605, Voc/OK 3829 |
| M-511-1 | That Naughty Waltz | Vri 635, Voc 3836 |

Don Redman-cl-ss-as-v dir. Carl Warwick-Mario Bauza-t/Reunald Jones-t-a/Gene Simon-
tb/Quentin Jackson-tb-v/Eddie Barefield-Edward Inge-Pete Clarke-cl-as-bar/Joe
Garland-ts/Nicholas Rodriguez-p/Bob Lessey-g/Bob Ysaguirre-sb/Bill Beason-d/Laurel
Watson-v.                                New York, December 6, 1938.

| | | |
|---|---|---|
| 030354-1 | I Got Ya - vDR&ch | BB B-10095, HMV EA-2391 |
| 030355-1 | I'm Playing Solitaire - vQJ | BB B-10071 |
| 030356-1 | Auld Lang Syne - vch | BB B-10095, HMV EA-2391 |
| 030357-1 | Sweet Leilani - vch | BB B-10081 |
| 030358-1 | 'Deed I Do - vLW&ch | - |
| 030359-1 | Down Home Rag (Wilbur Sweatman) | BB B-10061 |
| 030360-1 | Margie - vch | - HMV EA-2616 |
| 030361-1 | Milenberg Joys | BB B-10071 - |

Don Redman-cl-ss-as-v dir. Tom Stevenson-Robert Williams-Sidney de Paris-t/Quentin
Jackson-tb-v/Gene Simon-tb/Carl Frye-Edward Inge-cl-as-bar/Eddie Williams-ts-v/
Gene Sedric-ts/Nicholas Rodriguez-p/Bob Lessey-g/Bob Ysaguirre-sb/Bill Beason-d/
Laurel Watson-The Three Little Maids-v. New York, March 23, 1939.

| | | |
|---|---|---|
| 035079-1 | Three Little Maids - vTLM | BB B-10305 |
| 035080-1 | The Flowers That Bloom In The Spring-vDR-EW - | |
| 035081-1 | Jump Session - vDR-LW | Vic 26206, El EG-6933 |
| 035082-1 | Class Will Tell - vLW | - - |

NOTE:- Bluebird B-10305 as BILLY BUNCH AND HIS SMOKY RHYTHM.
Buster Smith-Tapley Lewis-as replace Frye and Inge; Slick Jones-d replaces Beason.
                                         New York, May 18, 1939.

| | | |
|---|---|---|
| 036962-1 | Chew-Chew-Chew (Your Bubble Gum) | Vic 26258, HMV K-8390 |
| | - vRD-LW&ch | |
| 036963-1 | Igloo - vLW | - - |
| 036964-1 | Baby, Won't You Please Come Home ? -vQJ | Vic 26266 |
| 036965-2 | Ain't I Good To You ? - vDR | - |

Don Redman-cl-ss-as-v dir. Tom Stevenson-Otis Johnson-Al Killian-t/Claude Jones-Gene
Simon-tb/Scoville Brown-Tapley Lewis-Edward Inge-as/Robert Carroll-ts/Nicholas
Rodriguez-p/Bob Lessey-g/Bob Ysaguirre-sb/Manzie Johnson-d/Bootsie Garrison-v.
This personnel is from the Victor files; Mr. Johnny Simmen claims Buster Smith is
present, and plays the alto saxophone solo on the first side.
                                         New York, January 17, 1940.

| | | |
|---|---|---|
| 045946-1 or 2 | You Ain't Nowhere - vDR&ch | BB B-10615 |
| 045947-1 | About Rip Van Winkle - vDR-BG&ch | - |
| 045948-1 | Shim-Me-Sha-Wabble | BB B-10765 |
| 045949-1 | Chant Of The Weed | - |

See also Bing Crosby (April 13, 1932) and Harlan Lattimore.

## RED ONION JAZZ BABIES

Louis Armstrong-c/Aaron Thompson-tb/Buster Bailey-cl/Lil Armstrong-p/Buddy Christian-
bj.                                      New York, November 8, 1924.

| | | |
|---|---|---|
| 9177 | Of All The Wrongs You Done To Me | Gnt 5627, Sil 4029, HRS 32, JC L-36 |
| | | Tem R-21, AF A-05, XX I4, Sto KB-I04 |

Louis Armstrong-c/Aaron Thompson-tb/Buster Bailey-cl/Lil Armstrong-p/Buddy Christian
bj.                                      New York,. November 26, 1924.

  9206     Terrible Blues                      Gnt 5607, Sil 4032, HRS 32,
                                             Br 80062, JC L-62, AF A-037,
                                             Gzl 1040, Sto KB-100
  9207     Santa Claus Blues                   As above
NOTE:- AF A-037 as CLARENCE WILLIAMS' BLUE FIVE.

Charlie Irvis-tb replaces Thompson; Sidney Bechet-cl-ss replaces Bailey; Clarence
Todd-Alberta Hunter (as JOSEPHINE BEATTY)-v duet.
                                         New York, December 22, 1924.

  9248-A  Cake Walking Babies (From Home) - vCT-AH Gnt 5627, Sil 4029, UHCA 78,
NOTE:- XX 14 as CARROTS KALE AND HIS BEAT ROOTS. HJCA HC-5, JI 10, JC L-36,
See also Clesi's Areolians and Alberta Hunter.  Tem R-21, AF A-05, Gzl 1039,XX 14

### RED PEPPER SAM

Billy Costello-k-u-v-effects/Larry Adler-h/p/Frank Novak-x.
                                         New York, March 5, 1932.

  11413-1  San                           Per      , Imp 2825, Kr 21152
  11414-2  Some Of These Days                      -          -

Other records by Billy Costello are of little or no jazz interest, whether under this
name or his own, except some accompanied by Teddy Foster's band, q.v.

### THE RED ROBINS

A Belgian dance band which recorded in London in June, 1928 for the Continental
catalog.of Edison Bell Radio, but outside the scope of this work as the personnel
included no names of international status.

### RED'S DIXIE RAMBLERS

Pseudonym on Varsity 5092 for Red Perkins' Dixie Ramblers, q.v.

### SADIE REED

Pseudonym on Champion for Elizabeth Washington, q.v.

### NINA   REEVES

Vocal, acc. by Jesse Crump-p.            Richmond, Ind., July 20, 1923.

  11556-A  Indiana Avenue Blues                  Gnt Special (un-numbered)
  11557-A  An't You Comin' Back, Mary Ann, To Maryland ?-
  11559    Louisville L u (The Vampin' Lady)      -
NOTE:- Matrix 11558 is by Genevieve Stearns, q.v.

                                         Richmond, Ind., July 31, 1923.

  11562-C  Tin Roof Blues                        Gnt Special (un-numbered)
  11563-C  Farewell Blues                          -
  11564-A  Phonograph Blues                        -

### REUBEN   REEVES

REUBEN "RIVER" REEVES AND HIS TRIBUTARIES : Reuben Reeves-t/Gerald Reeves-tb/Omer
Simeon-cl-as/Jimmy Prince-p/Cecil White-bj-g/Jasper Taylor-d.
                                         Chicago, May 23, 1929.

C-3532-   River Blues                           Voc 1292

REUBEN "RIVER" REEVES AND HIS RIVER BOYS : As above.
                                         Chicago, June 10, 1929.

C-3584½-  Parson Blues                           Voc 1292

REUBEN "RIVER" REEVES AND HIS RIVER BOYS : Reuben Reeves-t/Gerald Reeves-tb/Omer
  Simeon-cl-as/Jimmy Prince-p/Cecil White-bj-g/Jasper Taylor-d.
                                        Chicago, June 19, 1929.

C-3605-    Papa Skag Stomp - v                       Voc 1297

                                        Chicago, June 25, 1929.

C-3697-    Bugle Call Blues - v2                      Voc 1297

    White omitted; Darnell Howard-cl-as/Harry Gray-bb added.
                                        Chicago, July 22, 1929.

C-3919-    Low Down Rhythm - v                        Voc 15837
C-3920-    Gotta Feelin' For You - v                  -
NOTE:- This issue as HOLLYWOOD SHUFFLERS.

                                        Chicago, July 25, 1929.

C-3943-    Blue Sweets                                Voc 1411

                                        Chicago, July 29, 1929.

C-3963-    Texas Special Blues - v                    Voc 1411

                                        Chicago, August 5, 1929.

C-3989-    Head Low - v&ch                            Voc rejected

    Blanche Calloway-v.              Chicago, August 13, 1929.

C-4029-    (What Did I Do To Be So) Black And Blue Voc 1407
                - vBC

                                        Chicago, August 15, 1929.

C-4079-    Moanin' Low - vBC                          Voc 1407

    T/vn added.                      Chicago, August 25, 1929.

C-4131-    Head Low - v&ch                            Voc 15836

    Vn omitted.                      Chicago, September 8, 1929.

C-4318-    Have You Ever Felt That Way ? - vBC    Voc 15836

                                        Chicago, September 12, 1929.

C-4403-    Do I Know What I'm Doing ? - vBC           Voc 15839
C-4404-    Shoo Shoo Boogie Boo - vBC                 -

                                        Chicago, September 19, 1929.

C-4378-    Bigger And Better Than Ever - v            Voc 15841
NOTE:- This issue as HOLLYWOOD SHUFFLERS.

                                        Chicago, September 24, 1929.

C-4525-    Bottoms Up - v                             Voc rejected

                                        Chicago, November 25, 1929.

C-4745-    Tiger Rag                                  Voc rejected
C-4746-    Shine                                      -
C-4747-    Tiger Rag                                  -

REUBEN "RIVER" REEVES AND HIS RIVER BOYS : Reuben Reeves-James Tate-Cicero Thomas-t/
Gerald Reeves-John Thomas-tb/Franz Jackson-cl-as-a/Fred Brown-cl-as/Norval Morton-
cl-ts/Eddie King-p/Elliott Washington-bj/Sudie Reynaud-sb/Richard Barnet-d.
                                        Chicago, December 14, 1933.

| C-682-1 | Yellow Five (Yellow Fire) - aFJ | Voc 2638 |
| C-683-1 | Zuddan | Voc 2723 |
| C-684-1 | Mazie | - |
| C-685-1 | Screws, Nuts And Bolts | Voc 2638 |

## REGAL   DANCE  ORCHESTRA

See Joseph Samuels, Apex/Starr 8089.

## REGAL  JAZZOLA   ORCHESTRA

Pseudonym on Regal G-7797 (MOANFUL BLUES) for Johnny Dunn's Original Jazz Hounds,q.v.

## REGAL  JAZZ  SYNCOPATORS

Pseudonym on Regal 996 for the Plantation Jazz Orchestra, q.v.

## REGAL   MILITARY BAND

Pseudonym on Regal G-6172 and G-6845 for Prince's Band, q.v.

## REGAL   NOVELTY ORCHESTRA

Pseudonym on English Regal for the following items listed in this book :-

G-7586   Venetian Moon (Kentucky Serenaders)
G-7765   Some Little Bird (Coon-Sanders' Novelty Orchestra)
G-7931   Nobody Lied (The Happy Six)
G-7991   Snakes Hips (The Georgians)
G-7993   Farewell Blues (The Georgians)
G-8004   Who Cares ? (Eddie Elkins and his Orchestra)
G-8006   Don't Bring Me Posies (Frank Westphal and his Orchestra)
G-8029   Louisville Lou (Ted Lewis and his Band)
G-8093   Runnin' Wild (Ted Lewis and his Band)
G-8095   I Love Me (California Ramblers)
G-8096   Blue Grass Blues (Chicago Blues Dance Orchestra - see Original Memphis Melody
G-8096   Blue Hoosier Blues (Ray Miller and his Orchestra)                              )Boys)
G-8097   Sobbin' Blues (Art Kahn and his Orchestra)
G-8097   Oh, Sister ! Ain't That Hot ? (Frank Westphal and his Orchestra)
G-8233   Tell All The Folks In Kentucky (California Ramblers)

## REGENT (DANCE) ORCHESTRA

Pseudonym for the following items listed in this book :-

Edison Bell Winner 3865  Open Your Arms, My Alabammy (Bailey's Lucky Seven)
                  3868/Westport 2044  No Wonder I'm Lonesome (Bailey's Lucky Seven)
                  3868/Westport 2044  Oriental (Friars Soxiety Orchestra - see
                                        New Orleans Rhythm Kings)
                  3869  Homesick (Bailey's Lucky Seven)
                  3872  Secrets (Art Landry's Call of the North Orchestra)
                  3950  Snakes Hips (Bailey's Lucky Seven)
                  3964  Dirty Hands ! Dirty Face ! (Bailey's Lucky Seven)
                  3964  When It's Night Time In Italy (Porter's Blue Devils)
                  3976/Westport 3183  No, No, Nora (Bailey's Lucky Seven)
                  4027  Oh ! You Little Sun-uv-er-gun (Bailey's Lucky Seven)
                  4071, 4072  All four sides by Bailey's Lucky Seven
                  4104  Hard-Hearted Hannah (Windy City Jazzers)
                  4121  Where Is That Old Gal Of Mine ? (The Vagabonds)
                  4127  Dreary Weather (The Vagabonds)
                  4188  Rose-Marie (The Vagabonds)
                  4197  Mandy, Make Up Your Mind (Fletcher Henderson and his Orch.)
                  4353  If You Knew Susie (Bailey's Lucky Seven)
                  4412  Don't Wake Me Up, Let Me Dream (Bailey's Lucky Seven)
Homochord C-833  Big Bad Bill Is Sweet William Now (Synco Jazz Band)

Velvet Face 1053   Pick Me Up And Lay Me Down In Dear Old Dixieland (Bailey's Lucky
                                                                              )Seven)

This pseudonym was also applied to an unidentified band from the Paramount catalog,
of some interest as jazz :-

? Phil Napoleon and another-t/tb/2as/ts/p/bj/bb/d.
                                    New York, c. November, 1924.

        When My Sugar Walks Down The Street       EBW 4306

## PHIL REGENT AND HIS ORCHESTRA

Probably a pseudonym for Jay Wilbur : 2t/tb/2as/bar/vn/p/bj/bb/d/v.
                                    London, c. March, 1930.

  293    Cryin' For The Carolines - v           Celebrity 4385, Dn C-313,Film 134
  294    Singing My Way 'Round The World - v                 -            -
NOTE:- Celebrity 4385 as CELEBRITY DANCE ORCHESTRA; Dominion C-313 as DEAUVILLE
DANCE ORCHESTRA.

## DJANGO REINHARDT

Guitar solos.                        Paris, April 27, 1937.

OLA-1739-1   Improvisation                    HMV B-8587, Vic A-1182
OLA-1740-1   Parfum                                   -

  Acc. by Louis Gaste-g/Eugene d'Hellemmes-sb.
                                    Paris, September 9, 1937.

OLA-1952-1   St. Louis Blues                   Swing 7, HMV SG-365, N-4450
OLA-1953-1   Bouncin' Around                          -         -         -

  Acc. by Louis Vola-sb or Stephane Grappelly-p as shown.
                                    Paris, December 27, 1937.

OLA-2215-1   You Rascal, You - sb              Swing 35
OLA-2220-1   Sweet Georgia Brown - p                  -
OLA-2221-1   Tea For Two                       Swing 211
   NOTE:- Matrices OLA-2216/7 are by Michel Warlop; OLA-2218/9 are by Stephane Grap-
   pelly; OLA-2222/3 are by Philippe Brun, all q.v.  They all come from this session.

  Acc. by Stephane Grappelly-vn-p.      London, February 1, 1938.

DTB-3531-1   Tornerai - p                      Dec F-6731, 23079, Y-5262
DTB-3532-1   If I Had You - p                         -      23098     -
DTB-3533-1   It Had To Be You - vn-p           Dec F-7009, 23079
DTB-3534-1   Nocturne - vn-p                          -      23098

                                    London, September 1, 1938.

DR-2903-1-2  I've Got My Love To Keep Me Warm - p  Dec F-6935
DR-2904-1    Please Be Kind - p                   Dec F-6828, Y-5266

                                    London, September 10, 1938.

DR-2907-1    Louise - p                        Dec F-6828, Y-5266
DR-2908-1    Improvisation                     Dec F-6935

  Acc. by Pierre Feret-g/Emmanuel Soudieux-sb (where marked *).
                                    Paris, June 30, 1939.

OPG-1721-1  *I'll See You In My Dreams          Swing 211
OPG-1722-1   Echoes Of Spain                    Swing 65
OPG-1725-1   Naguine                                  -
   NOTE:- Matrices OPG-1723/4 are violin solos by Stephabe Grappelly, accompanied by
   Django Reinhardt.

DJANGO'S MUSIC : OSW-118-1 - Philippe Brun-Pierre Allier-Alex Renard-Al Piguillem-t/
Guy Paquinet-Gaston Moat-Pierre Deck-tb/Alix Combelle-bsx/Charlie Kewis-p/Django
Reinhardt-Pierre Feret-g/Emmanuel Soudieux-sb; OSW-119-1 - same, plus Andre Ekyan-
as; OSW-120-1 - as for OSW-119-1, without Piguillem, Moat and Deck; OSW-121-1 -
Brun, Renard; Combelle-cl; same rhythm. Paris, March 22, 1940.

| OSW-118-1 | Tears | Swing 79 |
| OSW-119-1 | Limehouse Blues | Swing 82 |
| OSW-120-1 | Daphne | - |
| OSW-121-1 | At The Jimmy's Bar | Swing 79 |

Pierre Allier-Christian Bellest-Leverin Luino-Aime Barelli-t/Maurice Gladieu-Guy
Paquinet-tb/Hubert Rostaing-cl/Christian Wagner-Max Blanc-as/Noel Chiboust-Georges
Jacquemont-Alix Combelle-ts/Django Reinhardt-Joseph Reinhardt-g/Tony Rovira-sb/
Dierre Fouad-d.                        Paris, December 26, 1940.

| OSW-174-1 | Stockholm | Swing 95 |

Aime Barelli-Alex Caturegli-Severin Luino-t/Maurice Gladieu-Pierre Remy-tb/Hubert
Rostaing-cl-as/Maurice Cizeron-as-f/Christian Wagner-as/Noel Chiboust-ts/Paul
Collot-p/Django Reinhardt-Eugene Vees-g/Emmanuel Soudieux-sb/Andre Jourdan-d.
                                       Paris, March 31, 1942.

| 2SW-262-1 | Nympheas | Swing X-186 |
| 2SW-263-1 | Feerie | - |

Guitar solos, with own vn interludes*, acc. Ivon de Bie-p.
                                       Brussels, April 16, 1942.

| 16189 | *Vous et moi | Rythme D-5016 |
| 16190 | Distraction | - |
| 16191 | *Blues en mineur | Rythme D-5017, Olympia 5017, Sofradi 05017 |
| 16192 | Studio 24 | As above |

DJANGO REINHARDT ET SON GRAND ORCHESTRA : Maurice Gigas-Janot Morales-Luc Devroye-t/
Nic Frerar-Lou Melon-tb/Bobby Naret-Lou Logist-as/Victor Ingeveldt-Benny Pauwels-
Fud Candrix-ts/Ivon de Bie-p/Django Reihardt-Eugene Vees-g/Emmanuel Soudieux-sb/
Andre Jourdan-d.                       Brussels, April 16, 1942.

| 16194 | Place de Brouckere | Rythme D-5030 |
| 16195 | Seul ce soir | - |
| 16196 | Mixture | Rythme D-5018 |
| 16197 | Bei dir war es immer so schön | |

DJANGO REINHARDT, STAN BRENDERS ET SON GRAND ORCHESTRE : Django Reinhardt-g solo,
acc. by Stan Brenders dir. Paul d'Houdt-George Clais-Raymond Chantrain-t/Jean Damm-
Sus van Camp-Jean Douillez-tb/Jo Magis-Louis Billen-as/Jack Demany-Arthur Saguet-ts
/John Ouwerckx-p/Charles Dolne-Van der Jeught-g/Tur Peeters-sb/Jos Aerts-d, with an
8-piece string section added**.        Brussels, May 8, 1942.

| 16218 | **Divine Beguine | Rythme D-5026 |
| 16219 | **Nuages | Rythme D-5000 (12-inch) |
| 16220 | **Djangology | - |
| 16221 | Eclats de Cuivres | Rythme D-5024 |
| 16222 | Django Rag | Rythme D-5025 |
| 16223 | Dynamisme | - |
| 16224 | Tons d'Ebene | Rythme D-5024 |
| 16225 | Chez moi a six heures | Rythme D-5026 |

See also the Quintette of the Hot Club of France, and Stephane Grappelly.

## WILLIAM REINHART

Piano duets with Al Goodhart, "at the Starr Glissando Grand," acc. by the New Yorkers
(studio orchestra).                    New York, February 23, 1928.

| GEX-1102-B | Willow Tree | Gnt 6402, Spr 364 |
| GEX-1103-A | Got Myself Another Jockey Now | - - |

Piano solos.                            New York, c. December 4, 1923.

8640    Mah Jongg                          Gnt 5330, St 9494
8641-A  The Boston Trot                       -        -

                                        New York, c. April 4, 1924.

8826-A  Monkey Business                    Gnt 5439, St 9542
8827    I've Got My Fingers Crossed           -        -

## REIS AND DUNN

The following session by Les Reis and Artie Dunn is of interest for the accompanists, but the remainder of their records contains no known jazz material.

Vocal duets, acc. by Joe Venuti-vn/own p/Eddie Lang-g.
                                        New York, January 28, 1932.

152094-2; 365057-2  I Wanna Count Sheep Till The   Har 1413-H, Cl 5458-C, VT 2518-V
            Cows Come Home
152095-3; 100597-3  Starlight (Help Me Find The One I Love)-        -
            365058-3  Can't We Talk It Over ?        Har 1417-H, Cl 5463-C, VT 2523-V

## LEO REISMAN AND HIS ORCHESTRA

Although the late Leo Reisman averred that he did not like jazz, certain of his many records feature excellent "hot" solos, as follows.

Leo Reisman-vn dir. John Jacobson-Herman Brenner-t/Walter Poole-tb/Andrew Jacobson-cl ss-as/Allan Lang-ss-as/Felix Greenberg-cl-as-ts/Raymond Pugh-p/"The Count"-bj/ Joseph Tronstein-bb-sb/Harry Sigman-d-x.
                                        New York, November 29, 1925.

141324-2  A Cup Of Coffee, A Sandwich And You     Col 517-D

                                        New York, October 3, 1926.

142721-3  Alabama Stomp                            Col 776-D

Leo Reisman-vn dir. Bubber Miley-Louis Shaffrin and another-t/Ernie Gibbs-tb/Jess Smith-cl-as-f/Louis Martin-as/Burt Williams-as-bar/Bill Tronstein-cl-ss-as-ts/ Adrian Rollini-bsx/Lew Conrad-vn-v/vc/Eddie Duchin-p/bj/? Harry Atlas-bb/Harry Sigman-d.                       New York, January 20, 1930.

58183-8  What Is This Thing Called Love ? - vLC   Vic 22282, 24862, HMV K-7508
58608-3  Puttin' On The Ritz - vLC                Vic 22306, HMV B-5810, EA-719

   Rollini omitted; 1 extra vn used; ? Jack Shilkret-cel added; g/sb replace bj/bb.
                                        New York, April 9, 1930.

59744-1  Happy Feet - vLC                          Vic 22398, HMV EA-740

? Chuck Campbell-tb added; Daniel L. Haynes-v.
                                        New York, May 12, 1930.

59784-2  Rollin' Down The River - vDLH            Vic 22433, HMV EA-792

Don Howard-v.                           New York, September 13, 1930.

62370-8-9-10-11  Body And Soul - vDH              Vic rejected

Frank Luther-v.                         New York, September 19, 1930.

62370-13  Body And Soul - vFL                     Vic 22537

Frances Maddux-v; sb added.             New York, October 10, 1930.

62370-17  Body And Soul - vFM                     Vic 22537
64315-1-2  Trees - vDH                            Rejected
64315-3   Trees - vFM                                -

Leo Reisman-vn-v dir. Bubber Miley and 2 others-t/Ernie Gibbs-? Chuck Campbell-tb/
Jess Smith-cl-as-f/Burt Williams-as-bar/cl-ts/cl-ts/? bar/Lew Conrad and 2 others-
vn/Raymond Pugh-p/? Jack Shilkret-cel/g/sb/? Harry Sigman-d/Lee Wiley-v.
                                          New York, June 30, 1931.

| | | |
|---|---|---|
| 69991-1 | It's The Girl - vLR | Vic 22757, HMV EA-949 |
| 69992-1 | Without That Gal ! - vLR | Vic 22746, HMV EA-947 |
| 69993-1 | Take It From Me (I'm Taking To You)-vLW | Vic 22757, HMV EA-940 |

Miley and one s omitted; Ben Gordon-v. New York, August 20, 1931.

| | | |
|---|---|---|
| 70178-1 | Have A Heart - vBG | Vic 22794 |

Leo Reisman-vn dir. 3t/Ernie Gibbs-tb/fh/Jess Smith-cl-as/Burt Williams-as/ts/bsn/f/
o/Lew Conrad and 2 others-vn/vc/Raymond Pugh-p/? Jack Shilkret-cel/g/sb/? Harry
Sigman-d/Fred Astaire-v.                  New York, September 28, 1931.

| | | |
|---|---|---|
| 70259-1 | White Heat - vFA | Vic 22836 |

4th s/2nd p added; Fran Frey-as replaces ts (the 4th s may be ts); bb replaces sb;
Frank Luther-v.                           New York, May 4, 1932.

| | | |
|---|---|---|
| 72538-1 | If It Ain't Love - vFL | Vic 24011 |

1 t/1 vn omitted; Lee Wiley-v.       New York, June 15, 1932.

| | | |
|---|---|---|
| 73011-1 | Got The South In My Soul - vLW | Vic 24048 |

Leo Reisman-vn-v dir. Lew Sherwood and another-t/Ernie Gibbs-tb/Burt Williams-as-bar
/Jess Smith-cl-as/2ts/Lew Conrad-Sammy Schklar-vn/Raymond Pugh-p/g/sb/d/Fred
Astaire-v.                                New York, November 22, 1932.

| | | |
|---|---|---|
| 73978-1 | I've Got You On My Mind - vFA | Vic 24193, HMV B-8398, BD-5761 |

Adrian Rollini-bsx-d added*; no vn*; Harold Arlen-v.
                                          New York, May 2, 1933.

| | | |
|---|---|---|
| 76072-1 | *Happy As The Day Is Long - vHA | Vic 24315, HMV B-6378 |
| 76075-1 | The Gold Diggers' Song (We're In The | - HMV B-6376, EA-1232 |
| | Money) - vFA | |

## CHARLES REMUE AND HIS NEW STOMPERS ORCHESTRA

Charles Remue-cl-as dir. Alphonse Cox-c/Henri Leonard-tb/Gaston Frederic-cl-ts/Stan
Brenders-p/Remy Glorieux-bb/Harry Belien-d.
                                          London, June 27, 1927.

| | | |
|---|---|---|
| 10919-1 | Vladivostok | EBE 0160 |
| 10920-1 | Tampeekoe | EBE 0161 |
| 10921-2 | Sha-Wan-Da-Moo | EBE 0162 |
| 10922-2 | High Fever | EBE 0153 |
| 10923-2 | Pamplona | EBE 0163 |
| 10924-1 | Slippery Elm | EBE 0161 |
| 10925-1 | Roll Up The Carpets | EBE 0162 |

                                          London, June 28, 1927.

| | | |
|---|---|---|
| 10926-2 | Doctor Jazz | EBE 0163 |
| 10927-2 | Lucky Day | EBE 0154 |
| 10928-2 | The Faraway Bells | EBE 0164 |
| 10929-2 | Ain't She Sweet ? | EBE 0153 |
| 10930-2 | The Bridge Of Avignon | EBE 0164 |
| 10931-1-2 | Allahabad (Pearl Of The East) | EBE 0154 |
| 10932-1 | Slow Gee-Gee | EBE 0160 |

Henry "Kid" Rena-t/Jim Robinson-tb/Louis Nelson-Alphonse Picou-cl/Willie Santiago-g/
    Albert Gleny-sb/Joe Rena-d.                  New Orleans, August 21, 1940.

| 800 | *Panama | Delta 800, Cir J-1037, Esq 10-112 |
| 801 | *Gettysburg March | Delta 3 |
| 801-A | *Gettysburg March | Delta 801, Cir J-1035, Esq 10-111 |
| | | Gzl 1027 |
| 802 | Milenberg Joys | Delta 802, Cir J-1036, Esq 10-171 |
| 803 | Lowdown Blues | Delta 803, Cir J-1035, Esq 10-111 |
| | | Gzl 1027 |
| 804 | *High Society | Delta 804, Cir J-1037, Esq 10-112 |
| 805 | *Clarinet Marmalade | Delta 805, Cir J-1036, Esq 10-171 |
| 806 | *Weary Blues | Delta 806, Cir J-1038, Esq 10-181 |
| 807 | Get It Right | Delta 807      -         - |

NOTE:- The original Delta issues have no coupling numbers, but are backed in the
same way as the Esquires. The titles marked * were recorded also at a rehearsal
on the previous day, but the results were not issued.

## DUNK RENDLEMAN AND THE ALABAMIANS

Dunk Rendleman-bj dir. Bob Hamilton-t/tb/Bill Aderholt and another-cl-as/ts/Bob
    Percy-p/Worth Roberts-bb/d/Wallace Chambers-v.
                       Birmingham, Ala., c. July 26, 1927.

| GEX-752-A | Hot Heels | Gnt 6233, Universal 40103 |
| GEX-752-B | Hot Heels | Sil 5052, 25052 |

                       Birmingham, Ala., c. August 6, 1927.

| GEX-785-A | Me And My Shadow - vWC | Gnt 6233, Ch 15326, Chg 365 |
| GEX-785-B | Me And My Shadow - vWC | Sil 5052, 25052 |

NOTE:- Champion 15326 and Challenge 365 as DAVE LAWSON'S ORCHESTRA; Silvertone
5052 and 25052 as RENDLEMAN'S DANCE ORCHESTRA.

                       Birmingham, Ala., c. August 28, 1927.

| GEX-852-A | Mean Dog Blues | Gnt 6322, Ch 15399, Spr 328 |
| GEX-853 | Back Beats | Rejected |

NOTE:- Champion 15399 as DOWN HOME SERENADERS.

## LEON RENE'S ORCHESTRA

Leon Rene-p dir. 3t/tb/3cl-as-ts/bj/sb/d/Banjo Buck-Otis Rene-v.
                       Hollywood, August 19, 1932.

| 68382-1-2 | I'm Mr. African - vBB | Vic rejected |
| 68383-1-2 | That's My Home - vOR | - |

                       Hollywood, September 17, 1932.

| 68391-1-2 | I'm Gonna Pack My Grip - vOR | Vic rejected |

## HARRY RESER

The late Harry Reser was an American banjoist and guitarist who made hundreds of
    sides, solo and with many bands, for literally every recording company in New York
from 1921 to the 1950s, and he was still an active musician at the time of his
death. Despite the "commercial" character of almost all his band recordings, and
although many of them are comedy numbers given appropriate treatment, there is a
fair proportion of jazz among them; they deserve a book to themselves, and the
British banjoist-guitarist Mr. William W. Triggs, of London, is preparing such a
book. In view of this commendable, if Herculanean task, it is felt that a listing
of the names used by Harry Reser will form an adequate guide to his records, used
in conjunction with the collective personnel which varied remarkably little during
the 1920s, when his activities in the studios were at their most prolific. (It
should be noted that The Rounders, a name most usually indicating Harry Reser on
Banner and associated labels, in some instances covered other identities).

The following is a collective personnel for the Harry Reser bands listed below.

Earl Oliver-Tommy Gott-Hymie Farberman-sometimes Red Nichols (c. 1925)-t/Sam Lewis-
    tb/Larry Abbott-cl-as-comb/Norman Yorke-ts/Jimmy Johnston-bsx/Joe Venuti and/or
    Murray Kellner-vn/Bill Wirges-p/Harry Reser-bj-g/Joe Tarto-bb when used/Tom Stacks
    d-v; sometimes other vocalists, occasionally other instrumentalists.

| | |
|---|---|
| The Blue Kittens | Parlophone Syncopators |
| The Bostonians | The Plantation Players |
| The Campus Boys | The Rounders |
| The Clicquot Club Eskimos | The Seven Little Polar Bears |
| Jerome Conrad and his Orchestra | Seven Rag Pickers |
| The Four Minstrels (Oliver-Abbott-Wirges-Reser) | |
| The High Hatters (not the Victor band) | Seven Wild Men (q.v.) |
| Phil Hughes and his High Hatters (on PA/Per) | |
| The Jazz Pilots | The Six Hayseeds |
| Jimmy Johnston's Rebels | Six Jumping Jacks |
| Night Club Orchestra | Tom Stacks and his Minute Men |
| OKeh Syncopators | Victorian Syncopators |
| Earl Oliver's Jazz Babies | Bill Wirges and his Orchestra (q.v.) |

The Seven Wild Men and Bill Wirges and his Orchestra are included here as they are of
    somewhat less commercial-comedy type material.  The name of HARRY RESER'S DANCE
    ORCHESTRA on Imperial 1844 (I AIN'T GOT NOBODY) was used in error, or as a pseudo-
    nym, for the California Ramblers, q.v.

## NINA RETTE ET SON HOT TRIO

Vocal, acc. by Stephane Grappelly-vn/Emil Stern-p/Django Reinhardt-g.
                                        Paris, September 6, 1935.

| | | |
|---|---|---|
| 1968¾hpp | Points Roses | Pol F-524108 |
| 1969¾hpp | Un instant d'infini | − |
| 1970hpp | Mon coeur reste pres de toi | Pol F-524111 |

## JIMMIE REVARD'S OKLAHOMA COWBOYS

As the name suggests, this is a country-and-western band, and as such is outside the
scope of this work, although jazz collectors who like a "cowboy" flavour with their
music may be interested to know that between the vocal part on some sides, a good
cornetist and a pianist similar in style to Earl Hines can be heard.  The records
were made during the late thirties in San Antonio for Victor's Bluebird label.

## FRANKIE REYNOLDS AND HIS ORCHESTRA

Instrumentation and personnel unknown; Barbara Lane-v.
                                        Charlotte, N. C., August 4, 1937.

| | | |
|---|---|---|
| 011945-1 | Chicken On The Apple | BB B-7137 |
| 011946-1 | Paradise | − |
| 011947-1 | Lady, Be Good - vBL | BB B-7241 |

## JACK REYNOLDS AND  HIS ORCHESTRA

Pseudonym on Mayfair for Art Kahn's Orchestra, q.v.

## LYST REYNOLDS' LOGOLA ORCHESTRA

Lyst Reynolds-bj dir. Ted Grubb-t/John Reynolds-tb/Gilbert Dutton-cl-as/Kenneth Hurt-
    as/Maurice Bennett-ts/Ed Emmett-p/Orville Haynes-bb/Doc Stultz-d/Charles M. Luke-v.
                                        Richmond, Ind., August 31, 1927.

| | | |
|---|---|---|
| 13067, -A | Gotta Go Home - vCML | Rejected |
| 13068 | What Do We Do On A Dew-Dew-Dewy Day-vCB | Gnt 6235, Sil 5107, 25107, Spr 359 |
| 13069 | Barbara - vCB | Gnt 6263, Ch 15365, Spr 307 |
| 13070, -A | Logola Stomp | Rejected |

Ross Reynolds-tb dir. —— Kerns- —— Shugart-c/Benny Benson-cl-as/Joe Danksha-as/
Lee Risher-cl-ts/Harry Bason-p/Charles M. Luke-bj/Russell Barkley-bb/Jack Tilson-d.
Richmond, Ind., November 22, 1924.

| | | |
|---|---|---|
| 12087 | Creole | Gnt 5611, 3046, Buddy 8005 |
| 12088 | Pippin | — |

NOTE:- Buddy 8005 as MEMPHIS MELODY BOYS.

## DORIS RHODES

Vocal, acc. by Max Kaminsky-t/Brad Gowans-vtb/Pee Wee Russell-cl/Bud Freeman-ts/Joe
Sullivan-p/Eddie Condon-g/Billy Taylor-sb/Sidney Catlett-d.
New York, March 26, 1940.

| | | |
|---|---|---|
| 27092-1 | Let There Be Love | Col 35449 |
| 27093- | My Melancholy Baby | Col 35548 |
| 27094-1 | Sierra Sue | Col 35449 |
| 27095- | Lorelei | Col 35548 |

## THE RHYTHM ACES

Pseudonym for the following items listed in this book :-

Brunswick 4244  Jazz Battle (Jabbo Smith and his Rhythm Aces)
         7120  I Got The Stinger (Jabbo Smith and his Rhythm Aces)
Key K-610  You're Getting To Be A Habit With Me (Gene Kardos and his Orchestra)
    K-610  You've Got Me Crying Again (Adrian Rollini and his Orchestra)

## THE RHYTHMAKERS

See Billy Banks, Jack Bland and Pee Wee Russell.

## THE RHYTHM BOYS

Pseudonym on Mayfair G-2193 for Gene Kardos and his Orchestra, q.v.; for Paul Whiteman's Rhythm Boys, see Paul Whiteman.

## THE RHYTHM BREAKERS

Pseudonym on Parlophone R-3383 for Sol Wagner and his Orchestra, q.v.

## THE RHYTHM GANGSTERS

Frenchie Sartell-t/Eric Siday-vn/Jack Penn-p/Sam Gelsley-g/Don Stuteley-sb/Max
Abrams-d.
London, January 24, 1938.

| | | |
|---|---|---|
| CE-8882-1 | Blues | Par R-2505, A-6922, Od A-272138 |

## THE RHYTHMIC EIGHT

Most records issued by Zonophone under this name are of considerable interest as
jazz, or at least as "hot" dance music, but some are by the larger studio group
under the direction of Bert or John Firman, q.v., and these are practically never
within the scope of this book as they are waltzes, 6/8 one-steps etc. The following represent all the Rhythmic Eight sides in their own right, with such of the
"hybrids" as match the quality of the regular issues under this name.

Bert Firman dir. Frank Guarente-Max Goldberg-t/Perley Breed-Arthur Lally-cl-as-bar/
Bill Barton-ts/John Firman-p-a/Joe Brannelly-bj/Billy Bell-bb/d-v (not Eddie
Kollis, as was once believed; Mr. Firman says he never used him).
Hayes, Middlesex, November 29, 1927.

| | | |
|---|---|---|
| Yy-11976-2 | Polly | Zon 5046 |
| Yy-11977-2 | Is She My Girl Friend ? - v | Zon 5045 |
| Yy-11978-2 | You Don't Like It - Not Much - v | Zon 5062 |
| Yy-11979-2 | Are You Happy ? - v | Zon 5045 |
| Yy-11980-2 | Corn Fed | Zon 5046 |

Bert Firman dir. Frank Guarente-Max Goldberg-t/Perley Breed-Arthur Lally-cl-as-bar/
Bill Barton-ts/John Firman-p-a/Joe Brannelly-bj/Billy Bell-bb/d-v.
                                        Hayes, Middlesex, December 6, 1927.

Yy-12206-1  Back Beats                           Zon 5084
Yy-12207-2  Miss Annabelle Lee - v               Zon 5062, HMV AL-962

  Bert Firman plays vn; John Firman db cel.
                                        Hayes, Middlesex, December 13, 1927.

Yy-12229-2  Possibly - v                          Zon 5063, EE-97, HMV AL-963
Yy-12230-2  Under The Moon - v                    Zon 5060
Yy-12231-1  Diane (w) - v                         Zon 5063
Yy-12232-1  There's A Rickety Rackety Shack - v   Zon 5064, EE-97
Yy-12233-2  Bells Of Hawaii (w) - v              -
  NOTE:- Zonophone 5060 as BERT FIRMAN'S DANCE ORCHESTRA.

                                        Hayes, Middlesex, December 21, 1927.

Yy-12276-1  I Left My Sugar Standing In The Rain-v Zon 5084
Yy-12277-2  Did You Mean It ? - v                    Zon 5080
  NOTE:- Zonophone 5080 as BERT FIRMAN'S DANCE ORCHESTRA.

Bert Firman-vn dir. Sylvester Ahola-George Ratcliffe-t/Perley Breed-cl-as-bar/Johnny
Helfer-cl-ts/John Firman-p-a/Joe Brannelly-bj/Billy Bell-bb/Rudy Starita-d, db vib
and/or x when used.                     Hayes, Middlesex, February 6, 1928.

Yy-12657-2  Just Another Day Wasted Away         Zon 5129
Yy-12658-1-3  So Tired                           Zon 5085
Yy-12659-1-2  Momsy (w)                          Rejected
Yy-12660-2  There's A Cradle In Caroline         Zon 5085
  NOTE:- Matrix Yy-12659 was re-made at a later Bert Firman date by the larger band,
  although issued as the Rhythmic Eight on Zonophone 5083.

  Bert Firman only plays vn on Yy-12759-2; Barney Sorkin-cl-as added; Maurice Elwin-
v.                                      Hayes, Middlesex, February 23, 1928.

Yy-12758-2  I'll Be Lonely - vME                 Zon 5097
Yy-12759-2  What Do We Do On A Dew-Dew-Dewy Day-? Zon 5100
            - vME
Yy-12760-2  I Ain't Got Nobody                   Zon 5097
Yy-12761-1  Ev'ry Little While - vME             Zon 5098
Yy-12762-1  Heart-Breakin' Baby                  -
  NOTE:- Zonophone 5100 as BERT FIRMAN'S DANCE ORCHESTRA.

Bert Firman-vn dir. 2t/Perley Breed-cl-as-bar/Johnny Helfer-cl-ts/John Firman-p-cel-
a/Joe Brannelly-bj/Billy Bell-bb/? Rudy Starita-d-vib/v.
                                        Hayes, Middlesex, March 8, 1928.

Yy-13031-2  Love Baby - v                        Zon 5116
Yy-13032-2  Together, We Two - v                 Zon 5115
Yy-13033-2  Once In A Blue Moon - v              Zon 5116
Yy-13034-2  Neapolitan Nights (w)                Zon 5115, EE-106
Yy-13035-1-2  Again (w)                          Rejected

Bert Firman dir. Sylvester Ahola-Andy Richardson-t/Perley Breed-Barney Sorkin-cl-as-
bar/Johnny Helfer-cl-ts/John Firman-p-cel-a/Joe Brannelly-bj-g/Billy Bell-bb/Rudy
Starita-d-vib/Maurice Elwin-v.          Hayes, Middlesex, May 7, 1928.

Yy-13271-1  In The Evening - vME                 Zon 5130, Ar 1104
Yy-13272-1  After My Laughter Came Tears - vME   -
Yy-13273-2  Together (w) - vME                   Zon 5129
  NOTE:- Ariel 1104 as ARIEL DANCE ORCHESTRA.

                                        Small Queen's Hall, London, May 24, 1928.

Yy-12991-2  Faces At The Window                  Zon 5147
Yy-12992-2  I'm Longing For Someone              -
Yy-12993-2  Tell Me You're Sorry - vME           Zon 5148
Yy-12994-2  I Can't Give You Anything But Love - vME   -
Yy-12995-2  I'm Tired Of Waiting For You - vME   Zon 5149

Bert Firman dir. Sylvester Ahola-Andy Richardson-t/Perley Breed-Barney Sorkin-cl-as-
bar/Johnny Helfer-cl-ts/John Firman-p-cel-a/Joe Brannelly-bj-g/Billy Bell-bb/Rudy
Starita-d-vib-x/Maurice Elwin-v.          Hayes, Middlesex, June 6, 1928.

```
Yy-13432-1  Wob-a-ly Walk - vME                     Zon 5165
Yy-13433-1  We Ain't Got Nothin' To Lose               -
Yy-13434-2  Rosalie - vME                           Zon 5149
Yy-13435-1  'Way Back When                          Zon 5198
```

                                          Hayes, Middlesex, June 11, 1928.

```
Yy-13460-3  For My Baby - vME                       Zon 5166
Yy-13461-2  Can't Help Lovin' Dat Man - vME         Zon 5185
Yy-13462-2  Why Do I Love You ? - vME                  -
Yy-13463-2  Wherever You Are - vME                  Zon 5164
Yy-13464-2  Mississippi Mud                           -
```

John Firman dir. same personnel, except Bert Read-p-a replaces him, and Arthur Lally-
cl-as-bar replaces Breed.              Hayes, Middlesex, August 29, 1928.

```
Yy-14409-1  I Think Of What You Used To Think Of  Zon 5200
              Me - vME
Yy-14410-2  The Best Things In Life Are Free - vME Zon 5218, Sal FZ-964
Yy-14411-2  Saskatchewan - vME                     Zon 5199, EE-126
Yy-14412-2  I Found Sunshine In Your Smile (w) - vME  -
Yy-14413-1  Always The Same Sweet Pal (w) - vME    Zon 5198
```

    Richardson omitted.                   Hayes, Middlesex, September 20, 1928.

```
Yy-14516-2  She's A Great, Great Girl - vME         Zon 5217
Yy-14517-3  The Rag Doll                              -
Yy-14518-3  Didn't I Tell You ? - vME               Zon 5219, Sal FZ-893
Yy-14519-2  Was It A Dream ? (w) - vME                -
Yy-14520-2  Halfway To Heaven - vME                 Zon 5218
```

    Lally and Helfer also sing.        Hayes, Middlesex, October 17, 1928.

```
Yy-14598-2  Tokio - vME-AL-JH                       Zon 5235, Sal FZ-938
Yy-14599-2  Sweet Ukulele Maid - vME-AL-JH            -
Yy-14600-2  Because My Baby Don't Mean "Maybe"      Zon 5236
              Now - vME-AL-JH
Yy-14801-2  Slow Music - vME-AL-JH                  Zon 5233
Yy-14802-2  This Is The Way The Puff-Puff Goes      Zon 5236
              - vAL-JH
```

Norman Payne or Freddy Pitt-t replaces Ahola; Sorkin omitted (his presence on the
preceding session is open to doubt).    Hayes, Middlesex, November 9, 1928.

```
Yy-14914-2  Oh ! You Have No Idea - vME             Zon 5234, Sal FZ-893
Yy-14915-2  What A Wonderful Wedding That Will Be   Zon 5269
              - vME
Yy-14916-2  A Kiss Before The Dawn (w) - vME        Zon 5234
Yy-14917-3  Dusky Stevedore - vME                   Zon 5252
Yy-14918-2  Arms Of Love (w)                        Zon 5269
```

    ? Chelsea Quealey-t replaces Payne or Pitt; ? Jack Miranda-cl-as added (he may have
been present on the last date above).   Hayes, Middlesex, November 15, 1928.

```
Yy-14938-2  My Angel - vME                          Zon 5253, Sal FZ-895
Yy-14939-2  All By Yourself In The Moonlight - vME     -    EE-141
Yy-14940-1  Fascinatin' Vamp - vME                  Zon 5252
```

    Sylvester Ahola-t replaces ? Quealey.   Hayes, Middlesex, December 5, 1928.

```
Yy-15230-1  You're In My Heart - vME                Zon 5254
Yy-15231-3  In A Bamboo Garden - vME                Zon 5255
Yy-15232-1  Why Is The Bacon So Tough (w) - vME        -
Yy-15233-2  Mistakes (w) - vME                      Zon 5254, Sal FZ-938
```

John Firman dir. Sylvester Ahola-t/Arthur Lally-cl-as-bar/? Jack Miranda-cl-as/Johnny
   Helfer-cl-ts/Bert Read-p-a/Joe Brannelly-bj-g/Billy Bell-bb/Rudy Starita-d-vib-x/
   Maurice Elwin-v.                     Hayes, Middlesex, January 3, 1929.

Yy-15319-2  From Saturday Night Till Monday      Zon 5288
               Morning - vME
Yy-15320-1  Don't Be Like That - vME             Zon 5270, EE-154
Yy-15321-2  Shout Hallelujah, 'Cause I'm Home - vME    -
Yy-15322-2  For Old Time!s Sake (w) - vME        Zon 5287
Yy-15323-1  My Southern Home - vME               -

   Max Goldberg-t replaces Ahola.       Hayes, Middlesex, February 7, 1929.

Yy-15743-2  I'm Crazy Over You - vME             Zon 5304
Yy-15744-2  Avalon Town - vME                    -
Yy-15745-3  Kiddie Kapers                        Zon 5288
Yy-15746-3  Fashionette                          Zon 5305
Yy-15747-2  That's Her Now                       -

   Sylvester Ahola-t replaces Goldberg.   Hayes, Middlesex, March 7, 1929.

Yy-16107-1  A Dicky Bird Told Me So - vME        Zon 5323, Sal FZ-1010
Yy-16108-2  Umtcha, Umtcha, Da, Da, Da - vME        -      Sal FZ-1015
Yy-16109-3  Sarita                               Zon 5324
Yy-16110-2  Dancing Shadows                         -      Sal FZ-1010
Yy-16111-2  That's The Good Old Sunny South - vME   Zon 5346

                                         Hayes, Middlesex, April 8, 1929.

Yy-16200-2  Blue Moon - vME                      Zon 5325, Sal FZ-1012
Yy-16401-3  Rhythm King - vME                       -      Sal FZ-1016
Yy-16402-2  My Irish Paradise (w) - vME          Zon 5346, EE-169
Yy-16403-3  I Faw Down An' Go Boom               Zon 5348
Yy-16404-2  Hunting Medley One-Step (6/8 and f-t)    =

                                         Hayes, Middlesex, April 17, 1929.

Yy-16436-2  Sitting On The Garden Gate - vME     Zon 5363
Yy-16437-2  I Must Have That Man - vME           Zon 5347
Yy-16438-1  I'm On My Way South - vME            Zon 5363
Yy-16439-2  I Found You Out                      Zon 5382
Yy-16440-3  Is There Anything Wrong In That ?    Zon 5347

                                         Hayes, Middlesex, June 11, 1929.

Yy-16581-1  Diga Diga Doo                        Zon 5383, EE-175
Yy-16582-2  Deep Night                           -
Yy-16583-3  My Troubles Are Over                 Zon 5409
Yy-16584-2  Lady Divine (w)                      Zon 5408, Sal FZ-1036

   Danny Polo-? E. O. Pogson-cl-as replace Miranda and Lally.
                                         Hayes, Middlesex, June 18, 1929.

Yy-16595-2  Heigh Ho, Ev'rybody                  Zon 5408, Sal FZ-1036

                                         Hayes, Middlesex, June 21, 1929.

Yy-16600-1  Huggable, Kissable You               Zon 5382

   Arthur Lally-cl-as-bar replaces ? Pogson.
                                         Hayes, Middlesex, July 12, 1929.

Yy-17454-2  Haven't I ? - vME                    Zon 5410
Yy-17455-2  I'll Tell Ma - vME                   -
Yy-17456-2  You, Just You                        Zon 5409
Yy-17457-1  You're A Pain In The Heart To Me     Zon 5435
Yy-17458-2  Spring It In The Summer And She'll Fall   -

John Firman dir. Sylvester Ahola-t/Danny Polo-cl-as/Arthur Lally-cl-as-bar/Johnny
 Helfer-cl-ts/Bert Read-p-a/Joe Brannelly-bj-g/Billy Bell-bb/Rudy Starita-d-vib-x/
 Maurice Elwin-v.                        Hayes, Middlesex, August 15, 1929.

Yy-17518-1  "The Show's The Thing" Medley (Intro. Zon 5455
             Dancing Shoes/Copper Blues)
Yy-17519-2  "The Show's The Thing" Medley (Intro.    −
             Dance Away Your Blues/I'm Terribly Fond Of You)
Yy-17520-2  He's A Good Man To Have Around − vME  Zon 5434
Yy-17521-2  We Toddled Up The Hill − vME             −
Yy-17522-2  Everything I Do, I Do For You         Zon 5456

    E. O. Pogson-cl-as-f probably replaces Lally.
                                        Hayes, Middlesex, September 4, 1929.

Yy-17581-2  Kansas City Kitty                   Zon 5437, Sal FZ-1038
Yy-17582-3  Louise                                  −      −
Yy-17583-2  Come On, Baby                       Zon 5436
Yy-17584-2  I'm Just In The Mood Tonight            −
Yy-17585-2  Only For You                        Zon 5456

    Read db cel,                        Hayes, Middlesex, September 23, 1929.

Yy-17657-1-2  I'm Doing What I'm Doing For Love   Zon rejected
             − vME
Yy-17658-1-2  I'm Feathering A Nest − vME          −
Yy-17659-1-2-3  Smiling Irish Eyes                 −
Yy-17660-1-2  Wake Up, Chillun, Wake Up           −
Yy-17661-1-2  Reaching For Someone                −

                                        Hayes, Middlesex, October 4, 1929.

Yy-17657-4  I'm Doing What I'm Doing For Love-vME Zon 5457
Yy-17658-5  I'm Feathering A Nest − vME            −
Yy-17659-4  Smiling Irish Eyes                  Zon 5477
Yy-17660-4  Wake Up, Chillun, Wake Up          Zon 5476
Yy-17661-3  Reaching For Someone                  −

                                        Kingsway Hall, London, October 22, 1929.

Yy-17821-3  Welcome Home − vME                  Zon 5477, EE-190
NOTE:− The above is one title from a session by the Arcadians Dance Orchestra,
q.v., but the pipe-organ customarily used on such dates is not heard here; the
band is the Rhythmic Eight, possibly augmented by one extra trumpet.

    2nd p added for some titles (? John Firman himself).
                                        Hayes, Middlesex, November 15, 1929.

Yy-17792-1  I've Got A Feeling I'm Falling − vME  Zon 5498
Yy-17793-2  Lovable And Sweet − vME             Zon 5519, Sal FZ-1086
Yy-17794-2  My Dream Memory − vME                 −      −
Yy-17795-2  Marie (w) − vME                     Zon 5498

                                        Hayes, Middlesex, November 25, 1929.

Yy-18205-1  Painting The Clouds With Sunshine   Zon 5499, Sal FZ-1071
Yy-18206-2  Every Day Away From You             Zon 5500, EE-192
Yy-18207-1  The World's Greatest Sweetheart Is You   −      Sal FZ-1071
Yy-18208-2  S'posin'                            Zon 5518
Yy-18209-2  Tip-Toe Thru' The Tulips With Me    Zon 5499
Yy-18210-2  Fairy On The Clock                  Zon 5518, EE-209

                                        Hayes, Middlesex, January 24, 1930.

Yy-18304-1  Mickey Mouse − vME&ch               Zon 5534
Yy-18305-1  Lonesome Little Doll                Zon 5533
Yy-18306-1  Riding On A Camel                      −
Yy-18307-3  Sweethearts' Holiday − vME          Zon 5559, EE-209
Yy-18308-1  I May Be Wrong                      Zon 5534

John Firman dir. Sylvester Ahola-t/Danny Polo-? E. O. Pogson-cl-as/Johnny Helfer-cl-
ts/Bert Read-p-a/Joe Brannelly-bj-g/Billy Bell-bb/Rudy Starita-d-vib-x/Maurice
Elwin-v.                                   Hayes, Middlesex, February 7, 1930.

Yy-18327-1  Punch And Judy Show                        Zon 5559
Yy-18328-2  I'm Speaking Of Kentucky Days - vME        Zon 5535, Sal FZ-2014
Yy-18329-2  'Tain't No Sin - vME                         -            -
Yy-18330-2  Just A Lucky Moment (w) - vME              Zon 5558
Yy-18331-1  Things We Want The Most Are Hard To Get      -

    Max Goldberg-t replaces Ahola; ? Harry Hines-cl-as replaces Polo.
                                           Hayes, Middlesex, March 28, 1930.

Yy-19074-1  Moanin' For You - vME                      Zon 5579
Yy-19075-2  If I Can't Have You - vME                  Zon 5580
Yy-19076-2  Alone In The Rain                          Zon 5579
Yy-19077-2  I'll Always Be Dreaming Of Mary (w)        Zon 5601
Yy-19078-2  You Can't Believe My Eyes                  Zon 5580

                                           Hayes, Middlesex, April 7, 1930.

Yy-19110-1  Figaro                                     Zon 5601, EE-211
Yy-19111-2  Singin' In The Bath Tub                    Zon 5629
Yy-19112-2  H'lo Baby                                    -
Yy-19113-2  Gee, It Must Be Love - vME                 Zon 5602
Yy-19114-2  Silvery Moon (w)                             -

John Firman dir. Max Goldberg-t/? Chester Smith-Jack Miranda-cl-as/cl-ts/? Bert Read
p/Joe Brannelly-bj/Billy Bell-bb/Rudy Starita-d-vib-x/Maurice Elwin-v.
                                           Hayes, Middlesex, May 16, 1930.

Yy-19189-2  Happy Feet - vME                           Zon 5630
Yy-19190-2  My Blonde                                  Zon 5648
Yy-19191-2  Mysterious Mose - vME                        -
Yy-19192-1  Harlem Madness                             Zon 5630
Yy-19193-2  Wedding In The Ark                         Zon 5628

                                           Hayes, Middlesex, June 27, 1930.

Yy-19482-1  Watching My Dreams Go By - vME             Zon 5699
Yy-19483-2  On The Sunny Side Of The Street - vME      Zon 5649
Yy-19484-2  Exactly Like You                             -
Yy-19485-1  Dancing With Tears In My Eyes (w)          Zon 5702
Yy-19486-1-2  In The Still Of The Night                Rejected

                                           Hayes, Middlesex, July 22, 1930.

Yy-19486-3  In The Still Of The Night                  Zon 5699
Yy-19575-1  I Like To Do Things For You - vME          Zon 5673
Yy-19576-2  Take Along A Little Love - vME             Zon 5674
Yy-19577-2  Hangin' On The Garden Gate                   -
Yy-19578-2  Oh, What A Silly Place To Kiss A Girl      Zon 5673

                                           Hayes, Middlesex, August 15, 1930.

Yy-19585-2  Shoo The Hoodoo Away                       Zon 5701
Yy-19586-2  I Don't Wanna Go Home                      Zon 5700
Yy-19587-2  With My Guitar And You - vME               Zon 5701
Yy-19588-2  I've Got A Feeling - vME                   Zon 5700

John Firman dir. t/cl-ss-as/cl-as-bar/cl-ts/? Bert Read-p-a/Joe Brannelly-g/? Billy
Bell-bb/Rudy Starita-d-vib-x/Maurice Elwin-v.
                                           Hayes, Middlesex, September 16, 1930.

Yy-20118-2  My Heart Belongs To The Girl Who           Zon 5729
              Belongs To Somebody Else (w) - vME
Yy-20119-3  Hullabaloo - vME                           Zon 5730
Yy-20121-2  Dance Of The Wooden Shoes                    -
Yy-20122-1  After Your Kiss                            Zon 5729
    NOTE:- Matrix Yy-20120 is a waltz ballad by Maurice Elwin (acc. by the Rhythmic 8?)

John Firman dir. Max Goldberg-t/cl-ss-as/cl-as-bar/cl-ts/? Bert Read-p-a/Joe Bran-
nelly-g/? Billy Bell-bb/Rudy Starita-d-vib-x/Maurice Elwin-v.
                                    Hayes, Middlesex, October 8, 1930.

Yy-20433-2  I'd Like To Find The Guy That Wrote    Zon 5756
              The Stein Song (6/8) - vME&ch
Yy-20434-2  Oh ! Donna Clara - vME                 Zon 5757
Yy-20435-2  I Don't Mind Walking In The Rain       Zon 5756
              (When I'm Walking In The Rain With You)
Yy-20436-2  Living A Life Of Dreams                Zon 5757


                                    Hayes, Middlesex, November 14, 1930.

Yy-20499-1  O.Kay, Baby (sic)                      Zon 5784
Yy-20500-2  What Good Am I Without You ?             -
Yy-20501-1  What's The Use Of Living Without Love Zon 5785
Yy-20502-2  What A Perfect Night For Love            -


    Vocal trio including Maurice Elwin.    Hayes, Middlesex, December 12, 1930.

Yy-20559-2  Packing Up To Say "Hello" - v3         Zon 5812
Yy-20560-2  There's A Sunny Smile Waiting For Me-v3  -
Yy-20561-2  I Want A Little Girl                   Zon 5814
Yy-20562-2  My Desire                                -

The following personnel is collective, but generally the instrumentation is constant
    and as previously.

John Firman dir. Max Goldberg-t/Frank Weir-E. O. Pogson-cl-as/Sid Phillips-cl-as-bar
    /Joe Crossman-cl-as-ts/Bert Read-p/George Scott Wood-pac/Joe Brannelly-bj-g/Billy
    Bell or George Gibbs-bb/Rudy Starita or Harry Robbins-d-vib-x/Maurice Elwin-Cavan
    O'Connor-v,                    Small Queen's Hall, London, January 6, 1931.

OY-9-1   Japanese Sunshade - vME                   Zon 5838
OY-10-2  Tap Your Feet - v3                        Zon 5813
OY-11-2  Make Yourself A Happiness Pie - v3          -
OY-12-1  Love Is Like A Song                       Zon 5838


                                    Small Queen's Hall, London, Feb. 13, 1931.

OY-101-2  I'm Tickled Pink With A Blue-Eyed Baby Zon 5883
            v3
OY-102-2  Between The Devil And The Deep Blue Sea-v3  -
OY-103-1  Betty Co-ed (6/8) - v3                   Zon 5839
OY-104-3  Tears (w)                                  -


                                    Small Queen's Hall, London, March 13, 1931.

OY-140-2  Here Comes The Sun - v3                  Zon 5864
OY-153-2  Overnight                                Zon 5863
OY-162-2  If You Can't Sing, Whistle - v3          Zon 5864
OY-163-1  We All Go Oo-Ha-Ha Together - v3         Zon 5863
    NOTE:- Despite the gaps in the sequence of matrix numbers above, all four titles
    were made at this session.


                                    Small Queen's Hall, London, March 30, 1931.

OY-176-3  You'll Be Mine In Apple-Blossom Time     Zon 5922
OY-179-2  Share My Umbrella                          -
    NOTE:- Matrices OY-177/178 are two parts of a work recorded by the Rhythmic Eight
    for the Turkish market.


                                    Small Queen's Hall, London, April 10, 1931.

OY-187-3  Laughing At Life - v3                    Zon 5907
OY-188-1  Happy I Found You (Glad I'm In Love) - v3  -
OY-189-2  Reaching For The Moon (w) - vME          Zon 5906
OY-190-2  Lady Of Spain (6/8 - sic; actually paso-doble)-

John Firman dir. personnel drawn from Max Goldberg-t/Frank Weir-E. O. Pogson-cl-as/
Sid Phillips-cl-as-bar/Joe Crossman-cl-ts/Bert Read-p-a/George Scott Wood-pac/Joe
Brannelly-bj-g/Billy Bell or George Gibbs-bb/Rudy Starita or Harry Robbins-d-vib-
x/Maurice Elwin-trio usually including Maurice Elwin-v.

Small Queen's Hall, London, May 22, 1931.

| | | |
|---|---|---|
| OY-923-2 | Laughing At The Rain - vME | Zon 5923 |
| OY-924-2 | Bubbling Over With Love - v3 | - |
| OY-925-1 | Were You Sincere ? - v3 | Zon 5939 |
| OY-926-1-2 | It Looks Like Love - v3 | - |

Small Queen's Hall, London, June 4, 1931.

| | | |
|---|---|---|
| OY-965-2 | Roll On, Mississippi, Roll On | Zon 5938 |
| OY-966-2 | Tie A Little String Around Your Finger | Zon 5940 |
| | - v3 | |
| OY-967-1 | When You Were The Blossom Of Buttercup Lane - | |
| | (And I Was Your Little Boy Blue) - v3 | |
| OY-968-2 | You're Twice As Nice As The Girl In My | Zon 5938 |
| | Dreams - v3 | |

Small Queen's Hall, London, July 13, 1931.

| | | |
|---|---|---|
| OY-1269-1 | Two Heads In The Moonlight | Zon 5954 |
| OY-1270-1 | Pardon Me, Pretty Baby - v3 | - |
| OY-1271-2 | If You're Really And Truly In Love-v3 | Zon 5955 |
| OY-1272-2 | I'm A Hundred Per Cent In Love - v3 | - |

London, August 23, 1931.

| | | |
|---|---|---|
| OY-1601-2 | Maybe It's The Moon - v3 | Zon 5970 |
| OY-1602-2 | If It's Good Enough For The Birds And | - |
| | Bees - v3 | |
| OY-1603-2 | Just A Crazy Song | Zon 5990 |
| OY-1604-3 | All Change For Happiness - vME | - |

London, October 7, 1931.

| | | |
|---|---|---|
| OY-1642-2 | Whistling In The Dark - v3 | Zon 5969 |
| OY-1643-2 | Wrap Your Troubles In Dreams - v3 | - |
| OY-1644-2 | When The Circus Comes To Town | Zon 5988 |

London, October 8, 1931.

| | | |
|---|---|---|
| OY-1706-4 | It Always Starts To Rain - v3 | Zon 5989 |
| OY-1707-5 | Jolly Good Company (6/8) - v3 | - |
| OY-1708-3 | Song Of Happiness - v3 | Zon 5988 |

London, November 18, 1931.

| | | |
|---|---|---|
| OY-2235-2 | The Queen Was In The Parlour - vME | Zon 6018 |
| OY-2236-2 | Who Am I ? - vME | Zon 6019 |
| OY-2237-2 | Sing A Little Jingle - vME | Zon 6018 |
| OY-2238-1 | There Must Be A Bright Tomorrow (w)-v3 | Zon 6019 |

2nd t added for most sessions; John Thorne and an unidentified comedian (using a
number of regional accents)-v.     London, December 5, 1931.

| | | |
|---|---|---|
| OY-2488-1 | Close Your Eyes - vJT | Zon 6040 |
| OY-2492-3 | Eleven More Months And Ten More Days | Zon 6041 |
| | (6/8) - Part 1 - v | |
| OY-2493-2 | Eleven More Months And Ten More Days | - |
| | (6/8) - Part 2 - v | |
| OY-2494-2 | Rio de Janeiro (6/8) - JT | Zon 6040 |

John Firman dir. personnel drawn from Max Goldberg-t/Frank Weir-E. O. Pogson-cl-as/
Sid Phillips-cl-as-bar/Joe Crossman-cl-ts/Bert Read-p-a/George Scott Wood-pac/Joe
Brannelly-bj-g/Billy Bell or George Gibbs-bb/Rudy Starita or Harry Robbins-d-vib-x
/Cavan O'Connor-Sam Browne-v.                    London, December 28, 1931.

| OY-2530-2 | The Longer That You Linger In Virginia | Zon 6036 |
|           | - vCO'C |          |
| OY-2531-1 | Tom Thumb's Drum - vCO'C&ch | Zon 6035 |
| OY-2532-1 | Me - vCO'C | Zon 6036 |
| OY-2533-2 | Yodle Odle (6/8) - vCO'C&ch | Zon 6035 |

London, January 29, 1932.

| OY-2659-1 | My Bluebird's Back Again - vCO'C | Zon 6053 |
| OY-2660-1 | Once Aboard The Lugger - vCO'C&ch | Zon 6052 |
| OY-2661-2 | Sweetheart (In My Dreams Tonight)-vCO'C | Zon 6053 |
| OY-2662-2 | Oh ! Mo'nah - vCO'C&ch | Zon 6052 |

London, April 29, 1932.

| OY-3344-1 | One Hour With You - vSB | Zon 6127 |
| OY-3345-2 | What Would You Do ? - vSB | - |

London, late June, 1932.

| OY-2319-1 | Too Many Tears - vSB | Zon 6161 |
| OY-2320-1 | Put That Sun Back In The Sky - vSB | - |

London, September 16, 1932.

| OY-3848-2 | In A Shanty In Old Shanty Town - vSB | Zon 6207 |
| OY-3849-2 | This Is My Love Song - vSB | - |

## THE RHYTHMIC TROUBADOURS

Pseudonym on Regal for the following items listed in this book :-

| G-9414 | Hittin' The Ceiling (Paul Specht and his Orchestra) |
| G-20600 | Both sides by Fred Rich and his Orchestra |
| G-20757 | I'm In The Market For You (Ben Selvin and his Orchestra) |
| G-20770 | Dark Night (Ben Selvin and his Orchestra) |
| G-20852 | My Man Is On The Make (Ben Selvin and his Orchestra) |
| G-20890 | Dixiana (Ben Selvin and his Orchestra) |
| G-21252 | I Like A Little Girl Like That (Jack Payne and his BBC Dance Orchestra) |
| G-23945 | An Apple For The Teacher (The Six Swingers) |
| G-24262 | I Forgot The Little Things (The Six Swingers) |
| G-24316 | On The Outside Looking In (The Six Swingers) |
| MR-14 | He's So Unusual (Fred Rich and his Orchestra) |
| MR-271 | You're Lucky To Me (The Charleston Chasers) |
| MR-372 | (There Ought To Be A) Moonlight Saving Time (Guy Lombardo and his Royal Canadians) |

## THE RHYTHM KINGS

Pseudonym for the following items listed in this book :-

| Decca X-1085 | Both sides by the Casa Loma Orchestra |
| X-1192 | Bojangles Of Harlem (Bob Howard and his Orchestra) |
| X-1367 | That Southern Hospitality (Mike Riley and his Orchestra) |
| X-1430 | The Loveliness Of You (Bob Crosby and his Orchestra) |
| X-1430 | I'm Feelin' Like A Million (Casa Loma Orchestra) |
| X-1569 | You Go To My Head (Casa Loma Orchestra) |
| X-1569 | Garden Of The Moon (Jimmy Dorsey and his Orchestra) |
| X-1584 | On The Alamo (Willie Bryant and his Orchestra) |
| X-1589 | Both sides by Jimmy Dorsey and his Orchestra |
| X-1633 | Kinda Lonesome (Jimmy Dorsey and his Orchestra) |
| Regal Zonophone G-22420 | I'll Keep Warm All Winter (Ted Weems and his Orchestra) |
| G-24033 | Stompin' At The Stadium (Ozzie Nelson and his Orchestra) |
| Victor 23279 | Both sides by the Washboard Rhythm Kings (see also HMV B-4917) |

This was also a pseudonym on American Odeon for some non-jazz Sam Lanin titles.

T/tb/cl/bar or bsx/p/bj/bb/d.                    Los Angeles, October 23, 1928.

LAE-304    Wabash Blues                          Voc 15763
LAE-305    Low Down                              Rejected

## THE RHYTHM MANIACS

Pseudonym on Decca for Philip Lewis and his Orchestra, q.v., and for the following
   items also listed in this book :-

Decca F-3002  Too Many Tears (ARC-Brunswick studio band)
      F-3847  Shanghai Lil (Gene Kardos and his Orchestra)
      F-5927  I Feel Like A Feather In The Breeze (Mike Riley (q.v.)-Eddie Farley
              and their Onyx Club Boys)
Vocalion 3355 Both sides by the Musical Maniacs (one side on Vocalion S-135)

## THE RHYTHM MASTERS

The following title by this band is known to be of some interest as a "hot" dance
   record; there may be others comparable to it by the same band.

Pete Mandell dir. Arthur Williams-Sid Fearn-t/George Latimer-tb/Len Edwards-as-vn/
   George Oliver-ts/Jack Willis-p/Nat Allen-bj/Bill Davis-bb/Joe Daniels-d/v.
                                    London, c. November 15, 1929.

   5308    Everything I Do, I Do For You - v      Imp 2175

## THE RHYTHM RASCALS

This was one of the names used by Crystalate for dance bands appearing on their nine-
   inch Crown label.  The following are of considerable jazz interest, and others with
   the same artist credit may also feature short solos by the same musicians.

Jay Wilbur dir. Billy Farrell-t/Paul Fenoulhet-t-tb/Ted Heath-tb/Danny Polo-Freddy
   Gardner-cl-as-bar/? Billy Amstell-cl-ts/Cecil Norman-p/Jack Simmonds-g/Dick Ball-
   sb/Max Abrams-d/Sam Browne-v.          London, June 19, 1935.

   H-111-2  Temptation Rag (Henry Lodge)          Cr 7
   H-112-2  Tiger Rag                             -

                                    London, November 19, 1935.

   H-318    Nobody's Sweetheart - vSB             Cr 89
   H-319    Bugle Call Rag                        -

                                    London, February 27, 1936.

   H-440    Dinah - vSB                           Cr 160
   H-441    My Sweetie Went Away - vSB            -

## THE RHYTHM REVELLERS

Tommy McQuater-t/Freddy Gardner-ts/Pat Dodd-p/George Elliott-g/Billy Bell-sb/Sid
   Heiger-d/Jack Cooper-v.                London, May 1, 1939.

   DR-3527-1  Howdy, Cloudy Morning - vJC         Dec F-7081
   DR-3528-2  Could Be                           Dec F-7058, Br A-82120
   DR-3529-1  The Funny Old Hills - vJC          Dec F-7081
   DR-3530-1  (Gotta Get Some) Shut-Eye - vJC    Dec F-7058, Br A-82120

## RHYTHM WILLIE AND HIS GANG

H/p/sb/d.                              Chicago, October 10, 1940.

   C-3407-1  New Block And Tackle Blues          OK 05856
   C-3408-1  Breathtakin' Blues                  OK 05960
   C-3409-1  Bedroom Stomp                       OK 05856
   C-3410-1  Boarding House Blues                OK 05960

T/Irving Fazola-cl/as/p/stg/sb/d.          New York, September 21, 1936.

| 19916- | Sugar Blues | Voc 3341 |
| 19917- | She'll Be Comin' 'Round The Mountain | - |
| 19918-1 | Wabash Blues | Voc 3390, S-135 |
| 19919- | Alice Blue Gown | - |

Muggsy Spanier-c/cl/p/g/d/Whitey McPherson-v.
                                          Los Angeles, March 27, 1937.

| LA-1290-A | Never No Mo' Blues | Voc 3523, Br A-81214 |
| LA-1291-A | St. Louis Blues - vWM | Voc 3566 |
| LA-1292- | Blue Yodel No. 2 - vWM | - |
| LA-1293-B | Twelfth Street Rag | Voc 3523, Br A-81214 |

  Sb replaces g; Danny Stewart-v.        Los Angeles, June 9, 1937.

| LA-1346- | Red Headed Music Maker - vDS | Voc 3670 |
| LA-1347- | Blue Yodel No. 1 - vDS | Voc 3642 |
| LA-1348-A | Marie - vDS | Voc 3608, Decatur 517 |

  Pauline Byrne-v.                       Los Angeles, June 16, 1937.

| LA-1349- | Blue Yodel No. 3 | Voc 3670 |
| LA-1350- | Desert Blues | Voc 3642 |
| LA-1351-A | September In The Rain - vPB | Voc 3608, Decatur 517 |

## RIALTO DANCE ORCHESTRA

Pseudonym for the following items listed in this book :-

Domino 356  I Can't Get The One I Want (Fletcher Henderson and his Orchestra)
       369  He's A New Kind Of Man (Sam Lanin and his Orchestra)
       370  You'll Never Get To Heaven With Those Eyes (Sam Lanin and his Orchestra)
       416  Copenhagen (New Orleans Jazz Band)
       418  Southern Rose (California Ramblers)
       3439 Oh ! Mabel (California Ramblers)
Silvertone 2544  I Miss My Swiss (California Ramblers)
           2688  I'm Sitting On Top Of The World (Sam Lanin and his Orchestra)

## RIALTO VERSATILE FIVE

Tb/cl/as/p/d.                            New York, October 7, 1920.

        Tomahawk                         Vic test (un-numbered)

## FRED RICH

Although previous editions of this book have included detailed listings of the vast
output by Fred Rich's various orchestras on many labels between 1925 and 1940, an
examination of many has failed to reveal any justification for their inclusion in
toto in a jazz discography, as most of them feature only brief glimpses of the
undoubted talent within his ranks, sometimes not even that. Accordingly, those
known to have solos of some length and "hot" quality are given below; a complete
account of the known recordings will be found in THE AMERICAN DANCE BAND DISCO-
GRAPHY (Arlington House, 1975). The first personnel is collective, and represents
the musicians known or believed to have played with Fred Rich during the period
concerned.

FRED RICH AND HIS HOTEL ASTOR ORCHESTRA : Fred Rich-p dir. Hymie Farberman-Mike
  Mosiello-Leo McConville-t/Lloyd Turner-Earl Kelly-tb/Jimmy Dorsey-cl-as/Ken "Goof"
  Moyer-cl-as-mel/Rudolph Adler-ts/Jimmy Johnston-bsx/Phil Oliwitz-vn/bj/Jack Hansen
  bb/Ray Bauduc-d.                       New York, October 28, 1925.

| 141204-1 | I'm Sitting On Top Of The World | Har 64-H, Re G-8541 |
| 141205-3 | (I Wouldn't Be Where I Am) If You Hadn't Gone Away | Har 57-H |

  NOTE:- Regal G-8541 as CORONA DANCE ORCHESTRA.

FRED RICH AND HIS ORCHESTRA : (Collective) Fred Rich-p dir. Hymie Farberman-Mike
   Mosiello-Leo McConville-t/Lloyd Turner-Earl Kelly-tb/Jimmy Dorsey-cl-as/Ken "Goof"
   Moyer-cl-as-mel/Rudolph Adler-cl-ts/Jimmy Johnston-bsx/Phil Oliwitz-vn/bj/Jack
   Hansen-bb/Ray Bauduc-d.                   New York, c. December 4, 1925.

106456    A Cup Of Coffee, A Sandwich And You        PA 36360, 11062, Per 14541

FRED RICH AND HIS HOTEL ASTOR ORCHESTRA : Same.
                                           New York, December 21, 1925.

141420-1  The Monkey Doodle-Doo                      Har 84-H

                                           New York, c. January 20, 1926.

   1783-A  Flamin' Mamie                            Cam 872, Lin 2463
   1784-B  Shake That Thing                         -

Miff Mole-tb replaces previous.            New York, February 2, 1926.

141588-3  Poor Papa                                  Har 119-H, Sil 3269
141589-2-3  Bell Hoppin' Blues                       -            -

FRED RICH AND HIS ORCHESTRA : Apparently a cover name for at least some of the
   California Ramblers : Chelsea Quealey-t/Tommy Dorsey-tb/Bobby Davis-cl-as/Sam Ruby
   ts/Adrian Rollini-bsx/Irving Brodsky-p/Tommy Felline-bj/Stan King-d/Arthur Hall-v.
                                           New York, c. February 3, 1926.

106596    Chinky Butterfly - vAH                     PA 36401, Per 14582
106597    A Little Bit Bad - vAH                     PA 36394, 11297, Per 14575
106598    Drifting And Dreaming - vAH                PA 36389   -    Per 14570

FRED RICH AND HIS HOTEL ASTOR ORCHESTRA : Based on the collective personnel shown
   above for c. December 4, 1925.          New York, March 10, 1926.

141783-3  Could I ? I Certainly Could              Har 136-H, Re G-8642
NOTE:- Regal G-8642 as CORONA DANCE ORCHESTRA.

FRED RICH AND HIS ORCHESTRA : Same.        New York, April 13, 1926.

106800    Up And At 'Em                              PA 36452, Per 14633, Apex 772

FRED RICH AND HIS HOTEL ASTOR ORCHESTRA : Same, except Ray Stilwell-tb-v/Teddy Klein-
   cl-as replace Turner or Kelly/Dorsey.   New York, May 19, 1926.

142222-3  The Blue Room                              Col 660-D, 4461, 0864

                                           New York, August 23, 1926.

142562-2  Trudy - vRS                                Col 720-D, 4180
NOTE:- Columbia 4180 as THE DENZA DANCE BAND.

FRED RICH AND HIS TIMES SQUARE ORCHESTRA : Same or very similar; Leroy Montesanto-v.
                                           New York, November 4, 1926.

GEX-339-A  Don't Take That Black Bottom Away - vLM  Gnt 6001, Ch 15183, Chg 256,
NOTE: Champion 15183 as THE DANCING CHAMPIONS;   Sil 3036, Aco G-16142, Bel 1147,
   Aco G-16142 as OHIO NOVELTY BAND; Beltona 1147   Clm 1971. Gmn 2000, Sc 810
   as SOUTHERN STATES DANCE BAND; Coliseum 1971 as MARYLAND DANCE ORCHESTRA; Guardsman
   2000 as OLD SOUTHERN DANCE ORCHESTRA; Scala 810 as PAVILION ORCHESTRA.

FRED RICH AND HIS ORCHESTRA : Fred Rich-p dir. Leo McConville and another-t/Tommy
   Dorsey-t-tb/Jimmy Dorsey-cl-as-bar/cl-as/cl-ts/Al Duffy-vn/Carl Kress-bj-g/Joe
   Tarto-bb-sb/Stan King-d/Irving Kaufman-v.
                                           New York, March 29, 1929.

   8648-1-2  I Get The Blues When It Rains - vIK   Ban 6360, Bwy 1271, Chg 999,
NOTE:- Broadway 1271 and Paramount 20712 as      Cq 7333, Or 1542, Pm 20712,
(FRANK) RAYMOND'S DANCE ORCHESTRA (vocalist,     Re 8761, Apex 8944, Cr 81050
RAY WINN); Challenge 999 as JEWEL DANCE ORCHESTRA; Oriole 1542 as ORIOLE DANCE
ORCHESTRA (vocalist, CHARLES DICKSON); Crown 81050 as LLOYD HALL AND HIS ORCHESTRA.

FRED RICH AND HIS ORCHESTRA : Fred Rich-p dir. Leo McConville and another-t/Tommy
   Dorsey-t-tb/Jimmy Dorsey-Tony Parenti-cl-as/Fred Cusick-cl-as-ts/Al Duffy-vn/Carl
   Kress-g/Joe Tarto-bb-sb/Stan King-d/The Rollickers-v quartet.
                                        New York, May 10, 1929.

148502-3  Singin' In The Rain - vR               Col 1838-D, 5561, 01628
148503-3  Nobody But You - vR                       -      -      -

                                        New York, June 12, 1929.

148693-3  Wishing And Waiting For Love - vR      Col 1924-D, 5622, 01840

   Irving Kaufman-v.                    New York, mid-July, 1929.

   3978   Piccolo Pete - vIK                     Cam 9233, Lin 3260, Ro 1035
   8994   Piccolo Pete - vIK                     Ban 6508, Bwy 1327, Chg 827,
                                                 Cq 7426, Dom 4422, Je 5707,
                                                 Or 1690, Pm 20768, Re 8869,
                                                 Apex 41021, Cr 81161
108901-2-3  Piccolo Pete - vIK                   PA 37024, Per 15205
            Sweetness - vIK                      Cam 9229, Lin 3256, Ro 1031
   8895     Sweetness - vIK                      Ban 6477, Bwy 1304, Chg 828,
                                                 Dom 4388, Or 1664, Pm 20745,
                                                 Re 8834, Cr 81156, Stg 181156
108902-3  Sweetness - vIK                        PA 37022, Per 15203
   NOTE:- Broadway 1304, 1327, Paramount 20745 and 20768 as F. RAYMOND'S DANCE
   ORCHESTRA; Challenge 827, 828, Jewel 5707, Oriole 1664 and 1690 as TED WHITE'S
   COLLEGIANS; Conqueror 7426, Domino 4388, 4422, Pathe Actuelle 37022, 37024,
   Perfect 15203 and 15205 and Regal 8834, 8869 as LA PALINA BROADCASTERS; Crown
   81156 and 81161 as PIERROT SYNCOPATORS; Sterling 181156 as JIMMY POLLACK'S
   ORCHESTRA.

                                        New York, July 26, 1929.

148856-4  Tip-Toe Through The Tulips With Me - vR  Col 1924-D, 5622, A-8343, 01781
148857-3  I Don't Want Your Kisses (If I Can't     Col 1979-D, 01798
          Have Your Love) - vR

                                        New York, mid-August, 1929.

   4067   Little By Little - vIK                  Cam 9265, Lin 3292, Ro 1067
   8957   Little By Little - vIK                  Ban 6503, Bwy 1316, Chg 848,
                                                  Cq 7412, Dom 4405, Je 5702,
                                                  Or 1694, Pm 20757, Re 8849,
                                                  Apex 41027, Cr 81158
108951-3  Little By Little - vIK                  PA 37037, Per 15218
   NOTE:- Broadway 1316 and Paramount 20757 as RAYMOND'S DANCE ORCHESTRA; Challenge
   848, Jewel 5702 and Oriole 1694 as TED WHITE'S COLLEGIANS; Conqueror 7412, Domino
   4405, Pathe Actuelle 37037, Perfect 15218 and Regal 8849 as LA PALINA BROADCASTERS;
   Crown 81158 as MATTY CRAWFORD'S ORCHESTRA.

   Smith Ballew (as TED BANCROFT on most issues; as STURGIS ANDERSON on Broadway and
   Paramount, as BUDDY BLUE on Banner and Domino, anonymous on Imperial)-v.
                                        New York, late August, 1929.

9009-2  Sweetheart. We Need Each Other - vSB     Ban 0508, Bwy 1321, Cam 0108,
                                                 Dom 4408, Je 5761, Or 1760,
                                                 Pm 20762, Re 8854, Imp 2194
108972-2  Sweetheart, We Need Each Other - vSB   PA 37043, Per 15224
   NOTE:- Broadway 1321 and Paramount 20762 as RON CHADWICK'S ORCHESTRA; Jewel 5761,
   Oriole 1760 as TED WHITE'S COLLEGIANS; Domino 4408, Pathe Actuelle 37043, Perfect
   15224, Regal 8854 and Imperial 2194 as LA PALINA BROADCASTERS.

                                        New York, September 5, 1929.

148973-2  Revolutionary Rhythm - vR              Col 1965-D,5632,A-8324,Re G-20600
148974-2  When The Real Thing Comes Your Way - vR   -      -      -      -
   NOTE:- Regal G-20600 as THE RHYTHMIC TROUBADOURS.

FRED RICH AND HIS ORCHESTRA : Fred Rich dir. Bunny Berigan-Leo McConville-t/Tommy
Dorsey-t-tb/Jimmy Dorsey-cl-as-bar/Tony Parenti-cl-as/Fred Cusick-cl-ts/Al Duffy-
vn/Carl Kress or Dick McDonough-g/Joe Tarto-bb-sb/Stan King-d/The Rollickers-v
quartet/Paul Small-v.                 New York, November 15, 1929.

| | | |
|---|---|---|
| 149429-2 | He's So Unusual - vR | Col 2043-D, A-8308, Re MR-14 |
| 149430-3 | Dixie Jamboree - vR | -          - |
| 100340-1 | He's So Unusual | Har 1063-H |
| 100341-1 | Dixie Jamboree | Har 1062-H |

NOTE:- Harmony 1062-H, 1063-H and associated labels as RUDY MARLOW AND HIS
ORCHESTRA; Regal MR-14 as THE RHYTHMIC TROUBADOURS.

Unknown cl-as replaces Dorsey.      New York, January 8, 1930.

| | | |
|---|---|---|
| 149990-3 | Send For Me - vR | Col 2132-D |
| 149994-3 | Strike Up The Band ! - vR | - |
| 100367-1 | Strike Up The Band ! | Har 1143-H |

NOTE:- Harmony 1143-H as LLOYD KEATING'S MUSIC.

Bill Moore-t replaces Berigan.      New York, September 3, 1930.

150751-3   Sing Something Simple - vPS        Col 2299-D, CB-194, SO-265

FRED RICH AND HIS (LA PALINA) ORCHESTRA : Fred Rich dir. Bill Moore-Bunny Berigan-t/
Tommy Dorsey and/or Jack Lacey-tb/Tony Parenti and another-cl-as/? Fred Cusick-cl-
as-ts/p/g/bb/d/Eddie Gale-v.            New York, September 11, 1930.

10019-2   Sing Something Simple - vEG        Ban 0835, Cam 0435, Chg 898,
                                              Cq 7626, Dom 4634, Je 6087,
                                              Or 2087, Per 15356, Re 10140,
                                              Ro 1448, Cr 81453, Imp 2390

FRED RICH AND HIS ORCHESTRA : As last, plus ? Al Duffy-vn.
                                  New York, October 20, 1930.

150885-3   I Got Rhythm - vPS            Col 2328-D, CB-452, Re G-21353

Manny Klein-? Bill Moore-t/Tommy Dorsey-tb/Jimmy Dorsey-? Tony Parenti-cl-as/? ts/
Joe Venuti-vn/p/Eddie Lang-g/? Joe Tarto-sb/Stan King-d/Smith Ballew-v.  (Matrix
150909/404535 is a waltz).            New York, October 29, 1930.

| | | |
|---|---|---|
| 150907-2 | I'll Be Blue, Just Thinking Of You - vSB | Har 1233-H, Cl 5103-C, Re G-20897 |
| 404533-A | I'll Be Blue, Just Thinking Of You - vSB | OK 41466, Od ONY-36157, |
| | | Par PNY-34149, E-6391, A-3103 |
| 150908-2 | I Got Rhythm - vSB | Har 1234-H, Cl 5104-C |
| 404534-A | I Got Rhythm - vSB | OK 41465, Od ONY-36158, |
| | | Par PNY-34149 |
| 150910-1-2 | My Love For You - vSB | Har 1242-H, Re G-20938 |
| 404536-A | My Love For You - vSB | OK 41465, Od ONY-36159, |
| | | Par PNY-34151 |
| 150911-2 | A Peach Of A Pair - vSB | Har 1233-H, Cl 5180-C, Re G-20897 |
| 404537-A | A Peach Of A Pair - vSB | Od ONY-36158, Par PNY-34150, A-3127 |
| 150912-2 | Someone Sang A Sweeter Song To Mary-vSB | Har 1251-H, Cl 5177-C |
| 404538-A | Someone Sang A Sweeter Song To Mary-vSB | OK 41466, Od ONY-36157, |
| | | Par PNY-34151, A-3103 |

NOTE:- The following pseudonyms were used on issues from the above session :-

Clarion 5180-C   Frank Auburn and his Orchestra (all other Clarions, Divas and Velvet
           Tones as for the equivalents on Harmony)
Harmony 1233-H   I'll Be Blue, Just Thinking Of You (Lloyd Keating and his Music)
        1233-H   A Prach Of A Pair (Chester Leighton and his Sophomores)
        1234-H   Paul Ash and his Merry Mad Musical Gang
Odeon ONY-36157   I'll Be Blue (New York Syncopators)/Someone Sang...(Tom Rock's Orch)
      ONY-36158   I Got Rhythm (New York Syncopators)/A Peach Of A Pair (Tom Rock O.)
      ONY-36159   Tom Rock and his Orchestra
OKeh 41465   Harold Lem and his Orchestra; 41466   Bud Blue and his Orchestra (BOB BLUE
Parlophone E-6391   Merton Orchestra                            )on Par A-3108)
           PNY-34149   Both sides as The Deauville Syncopators
           PNY-34150, PNY-34151   George Wells and his Orchestra
Australian Regals and Parlophones have the same credits as their American equivalents

FRED RICH AND HIS ORCHESTRA : Fred Rich-p dir. Manny Klein-Tommy Gott-t/Tommy Dorsey
tb/Jimmy Dorsey-cl-as-t*/? Tony Parenti or Louis Martin-cl-as/? Hymie Wolfson-cl-
ts/Joe Venuti-vn/Frank Signorelli-p/Cornell Smelser-pac/Eddie Lang-g/? Joe Tarto-
sb/George Hamilton Green-d-x/Smith Ballew-v.
                                            New York, November 19, 1930.

| | | |
|---|---|---|
| 404555-B | Cheerful Little Earful - vSB | Od ONY-36165, A-221334, |
| | | Par PNY-34157, R-857 |
| 100439-1 | Cheerful Little Earful - vSB | Har 1249-H, Cl 5125-C, Re G-20967 |
| 404558-A | The Little Things In Life - vSB | Od ONY-36164, Par PNY-34157, |
| | | R-874, A-3147, Ar 4693 |
| 100437-1 | The Little Things In Life - vSB | Har 1240-H, Cl 5186-C, Re G-20955 |
| 404559-A | *I'm Tickled Pink With A Blue-Eyed Baby | Od ONY-36165, A-221334, |
| | - vSB | Par PNY-34155, R-856 |
| 100441-1 | *I'm Tickled Pink With A Blue-Eyed Baby | Har 1246-H, Cl 5179-C, Re G-20945 |

The following pseudonyms were used on issues from the above session :-

Ariel 4693  Ariel Dance Orchestra
Clarion 5179-C, Harmony 1240-H, 1249-H, Regal G-20955, G-20967  Frank Auburn and his
    Orchestra; all other Clarions - Chester Leighton's Sophomores
Harmony 1246-H, Regal G-20945  Lloyd Keating and his Music
Odeon ONY-36164  Tom Rock and his Orchestra
    ONY-36165, Parlophone PNY-34155, R-857, R-874, A-3147  New York Syncopators
Parlophone PNY-34157  Cheerful Little Earful (The Deauville Syncopators)
         PNY-34157  The Little Things In Life (George Wells and his Orchestra)
         R-856  Sam Lanin's Famous Players and Singers

Elmer Feldkamp-cl-as-v replaces Martin. New York, January 7, 1931.

| | | |
|---|---|---|
| 151190-1 | Would You Like To Take A Walk ? - vEF | Har 1269-H, Cl 5212-C |
| 404809-A | Would You Like To Take A Walk ? - vEF | Od ONY-36179, Par PNY-34172, |
| | | R-892, Ar 4743 |
| 404867-A | Would You Like To Take A Walk ? - vEF | OK 41482 |

NOTE:- Ariel 4743 as ARIEL DANCE ORCHESTRA; Clarion 5212-C, Harmony 1269-H as
FRANK AUBURN AND HIS ORCHESTRA; Odeon ONY-36179 as TOM ROCK AND HIS ORCHESTRA;
Parlophone PNY-34172 as GEORGE WELLS AND HIS ORCHESTRA; R-892 as NEW YORK SYNCO-
PATORS.

Larry Murphy-p-v present.                   New York, February 18, 1931.

| | | |
|---|---|---|
| 151329-1 | Sweet And Hot - vLM | Cl 5328-C, Har 1290-H, VT 2394-V |
| 404864-A | Sweet And Hot - vLM | Od ONY-36196, Par PNY-34186, |
| | | A-3207 |

NOTE:- All issues from matrix 151329-1 as LLOYD KEATING AND HIS MUSIC; Odeon ONY-
36196 and Parlophone A-3207 as CAROLINA CLUB ORCHESTRA; Parlophone PNY-34186 as
RICHARD HAMPTON AND HIS ORCHESTRA.

Fred Rich dir. Bob Effros and another-t/Charlie Butterfield-tb/Tony Parenti-?Louis
Martin-cl-as/? Hymie Wolfson-cl-ts/Joe Venuti-vn/Walter Gross-p/Eddie Lang-g/sb/d/
Dick Robertson (as CHESTER LEIGHTON or BOBBY DIX)-v.
                                            New York, March 18, 1931.

| | | |
|---|---|---|
| 404881-A | When I Take My Sugar To Tea - vDR | OK 41489, Od ONY-36204, |
| | | Par PNY-34197, R-944 |
| 100501-1 | When I Take My Sugar To Tea - vDR | Cl 5277-C, Har 1307-H, VT 2343-V |
| 404882-A-B | Rockin' Chair - vDR | Rejected |
| 100502-1-4 | Rockin' Chair - vDR | Cl 5273-C, Har 1306-H, VT 2339-V |

NOTE:- Clarion 5273-C, 5277-C, Harmony 1306-H and Velvet Tone 2339-V as FRANK
AUBURN AND HIS ORCHESTRA; Harmony 1307-H as CHESTER LEIGHTON AND HIS SOPHOMORES;
Odeon ONY-36204 as REX KING AND HIS SOVEREIGNS.

Bunny Berigan-t replaces Effros; rest probably as above, Tommy Dorsey-tb probably
replacing Butterfield; Scrappy Lambert-v.
                                            New York, June 15, 1931.

| | | |
|---|---|---|
| 151606-1 | Pardon Me, Pretty Baby - vSL | Col 2484-D, Re MR-403, G-21121 |

NOTE:- Regal MR-403 as THE MIDNIGHT MINSTRELS.

FREDDIE RICH AND HIS ORCHESTRA : Fred Rich dir. Nat Natoli-Red Solomon-Roy Eldridge-
t/Larry Altpeter-tb/Benny Carter-Sid Stoneburn-Sid Perlmutter-cl-as/Babe Russin-
Frank Chase-Stafford Simon-ts/Clyde Hart-p/Ken Binford-g/Hayes Alvis-sb/Johnny
Williams-d/Rosemary Calvin-v.          New York, February 14, 1940.

| | | |
|---|---|---|
| 26514-A | Till We Meet Again | Voc 5507 |
| 26515-A | A House With A Little Red Barn - vRC | Voc 5420 |
| 26516-A | I'm Forever Blowing Bubbles | Voc 5507 |
| 26517-A | How High The Moon - vRC | Voc 5420 |

### UNCLE CHARLIE RICHARDS

Pseudonym on Pathe Actuelle and Perfect for Blind Richard Yates, q.v.

### CHUCK RICHARDS

Vocal, acc. by Henry Allen-t/Benny Morton-tb/Buster Bailey-cl/Charlie Beal-p/
Lawrence Lucie-g/Billy Taylor-sb.      New York, December 19, 1934.

| | | |
|---|---|---|
| 16523-1 | Blue Interlude | Voc 2877, Br 01990, A-500546 |
| 16524-1 | A Rainbow Filled With Music | -      Br 02009 |
| 16525-1 | Devil In The Moon | Br 01990, A-86016, A-500546 |

### HERBERT RICHARDS

Pseudonym on Victory 271 for H. Peterson, q.v.

### PETE RICHARDS   AND HIS ORCHESTRA

Pseudonym on Champion for Willie Jones and his Orchestra, q.v.

### VINCENT RICHARDS AND HIS ORCHESTRA

Pseudonym on Australian Angelus 3153 for an Irving Mills band, q.v.

### BOB RICHARDSON AND HIS ORCHESTRA

Pseudonym on Mayfair G-2023 for Dick Robertson, q.v.

### DICK RICHARDSON AND HIS BAND/ORCHESTRA

Pseudonym on American Parlophone for Joe Venuti and his Orchestra, q.v.

### INEZ   RICHARDSON

Vocal, acc. by Fletcher Henderson's Orchestra : Fletcher Henderson-p dir. 2t/tb/2cl-
as-ts/vn.                              New York, c. July, 1921.

| | | |
|---|---|---|
| P-144-2 | My June Love | BS 2023 |
| P-145-2 | Love Will Find A Way | - |

### JOE RICHARDSON'S ORCHESTRA

Pseudonym on Velvet Face for the following items listed in this book :-

1048  Hortense (Bailey's Lucky Seven)
1049  Both sides by Bailey's Lucky Seven
1050  Do It Again (Bailey's Lucky Seven)

### MABEL RICHARDSON

See Mike Jackson.

### BUD RICHIE   AND HIS BOYS

Instrumentation and personnel unknown apart from Max Pugh-Richard Barry-v.
Richmond, Ind., October 10, 1930.

| | | |
|---|---|---|
| 17162 | Rockin' Chair - vMP | Ch 16109, 40010 |
| 17164-B | Slappin' The Bass - vRB | -      - |

The following records by this very famous entertainer have good jazz-styled accompaniments.

Vocal, acc. by Earl Burtnett and his Los Angeles Biltmore Hotel Orchestra : Earl
Burtnett-p dir. Fuzz Menge-t/Fran Baker-c/Lank Menge-tb/Hank Miller-Gene Miller-cl-
as/Fred Stoddard-cl-ts-a/Bill Grantham-bj/Harry Robison-sb/Jess Kirkpatrick-d.
                                    Los Angeles, January, 1930.

LAE-672-   Puttin' On The Ritz                      Br 4677, 01014

    Acc. by Bunny Berigan-t/? Slats Long-cl/as/? Forrest Crawford-ts/? Frank Signorelli
    p/? Carmen Mastren-g/? Haig Stephens-sb/Stan King-d.
                                    New York, January 26, 1936.

60391-A  Life Begins When You're In Love           Dec 700, Br 02161
60392-A  Let's Go                                   -        -
60393-A  Suzannah                                   Dec 701, Br 02162
60394-A  There'll Be No South                       -        -

## JACK  RICHMOND

Vocal, acc. by t/p/g.                  Chicago, c. March, 1928.

20409-   Weary Feet                                 Pm rejected
20412-   Chloe (Song Of The Swamp)                  -

20463-2  Chloe (Song Of The Swamp)                  Pm 12624
20464-2  Weary Feet                                 -
NOTE:- The matrix numbers of the rejected session are given on the labels of Paramount 12624, and those of the re-make in the wax.  Other titles by this artist are
of even less interest as jazz than the above.

## EARL RICKARD

The following sides by this artist, who made several for OKeh, are of interest for
their jazz-orientated accompaniments.

Vocal, acc. by the Dubs : Earl Oliver-t/Larry Abbott-cl/Jimmy Johnston-bsx/Bill
Wirges-p/Harry Reser-bj.          New York, January, 1926.

73960-A  Sweet Child (I'm Wild About You)           OK 40566, Par E-5629
73961-A  Where The Huckleberries Grow               -        -

## BOB RICKETTS' BAND

Bob Ricketts-p dir. t/tb/cl/as/bj/d.   New York, c. May 14, 1923.

8368     Mean, Mean Mama                            Gnt 5156, St 9403
8369-A   If You Want To Keep Your Daddy Home        -        -

## ETHEL RIDLEY

Vocal, acc. by Perry Bradford-p.       New York, June 9, 1923.

81067-4  Liza Johnson's Got Better Bread (Than      Col A-3941
           Old Sally Lee)
81068-3  Here's Your Opportunity Blues              -

                                       Camden, N. J., June 13, 1923.

         Here's Your Opportunity                    Vic test (un-numbered)
         That Thing Called Love                     -

    Acc. by Leroy Tibbs-p.             New York, June.23, 1923.

81096-3  Alabama Bound Blues                        Col A-3965
81097-2  I Don't Let No One Man Worry Me            -

Acc. by Bradford's Jazz Phools : Gus Aiken-c/Bud Aiken-tb/Garvin Bushell-cl-as/
? Ernest Elliott-ts/Leroy Tibbs-p/Samuel Speed-bj.
                                      New York, June 26, 1923.

28234-2  Memphis, Tennessee                    Vic 19111
28235-3  If Anybody Here Wants A Real Kind Mama      -
         (Here's Your Opportunity)

Acc. by the Choo Choo Jazzers : ? Rex Stewart-c or Bob Fuller-cl/Louis Hooper-p.
                                      New York, c. February, 1925.

31813    Get It Fixed - c                     Ajax 17126
31814-E  Low Down Daddy Blues - cl                -

Acc. by Memphis Bob (? Bob Fuller)-u or the Choo Choo Jazzers (instrumentation
unknown)*.                            New York, c. March, 1925.

31843-E *I Ain't Got Much, But What I Got, Oh My  Ajax 17131
31844-G  He Was A Good Man (But He's Dead And         -
         Gone) - uMB

## THE  RIFFERS

Eva Taylor-Lil Armstrong-v duets, acc. by Clarence Williams-p.
                                      New York, September 23, 1932.

152310-1  Say It Isn't So/Papa De Da Da        Col 14677-D
152311-2  Rhapsody In Love                          -

## HUGO RIGNOLD

Violin and viola solos, acc. by Arthur Young-p/Albert Harris-g/Don Stuteley-sb/
Ronnie Gubertini-d.                   London, November 19, 1935.

CE-7283-1  Calling All Keys                    Par R-2150, A-6364
CE-7284-1  Poor Butterfly                           -        -

## MIKE RILEY

MIKE RILEY, EDDIE FARLEY AND THEIR ONYX CLUB BOYS : Eddie Farley-t-v/Mike Riley-tb-
mel-v dir. Frank Langone-cl/Frank Froeba-p/Arthur Ens-g/George Yorke-sb/Vic Engle-
d/unknown v where shown.             New York, August 5, 1935.

39808-A  Double Trouble - v                    Ch 40042
39809-   You're All I Need - v                 Ch 40040
39810-A  In The Middle Of A Kiss - v           Ch 40041
39811-B  When I Grow Too Old To Dream (w) - v          Pan 25804
39812-A  Rhythm Is Our Business - v            Ch 40042
39813-A  I Wished On The Moon - v              Ch 40040, Pan 25804

                                      New York, September 26, 1935.

60004-A  Looking For Love                      Dec 578, Br RL-325, A-9910
60005-A-D  South                               Dec 619, Br 02135
60006-A  The Music Goes 'Round And Around-vMR-EF  Dec 578, X-1044

Conrad Lanoue-p replaces Froeba.      New York, October 23, 1935.

60102-A  You Are My Lucky Star - v             Ch 40057, Pan 25810
60103-A  I'm In The Mood For Love - v              -        -
60104-A  Santa Claus Is Comin' To Town - v     Ch 40056, Dec F-6222
60104-E  Santa Claus Is Comin' To Town - v     Dec 1031
60105-A  Jingle Bells - v                      Ch 40056, Dec F-6222
60105-E  Jingle Bells - v                      Dec 1031

MIKE RILEY, EDDIE FARLEY AND THEIR ONYX CLUB BOYS : Eddie Farley-t-v/Mike Riley-tb-
   mel-v dir. Frank Langone-cl/Conrad Lanoue-p/Arthur Ens-g/George Yorke-sb/Vic Engle-
   d,
                                          New York, October 24, 1935.

| | | |
|---|---|---|
| 60107-D | Wabash Blues | Dec 641 |
| 60108- | China Boy | Rejected |
| 60109-A | I Never Knew | Dec 619 |
| 60110-A | The Music Goes 'Round And Around-vMR-EF | Dec 578, 3364, Br RL-325, A-9910 |

Wayne Gregg-v.                            New York, November 22, 1935.

| | | |
|---|---|---|
| 60161-A | I'd Rather Listen To Your Eyes - v | Ch 40067 |
| 60162-A | I'd Love To Take Orders From You - v | - |
| 60163-A | Here's To Romance - vWG | Ch 40066, MW 5005, Pan 25828 |
| 60164-A | At Your Service, Madame - vWG | -            - |

                                          New York, November 26, 1935.

| | | |
|---|---|---|
| 60172-A | Blue Clarinet Stomp | Dec 641, Br 02135 |
| 60173-A | Twenty-Four Hours A Day - v | Ch 40065 |
| 60174-A | Don't Give Up The Ship - v | - |

                                          New York, December 10, 1935.

| | | |
|---|---|---|
| 60211-A | I Found A Dream - v | Ch 40071 |
| 60212-A | No Other One - v | -            Pan 25839 |
| 60213-A | You Took My Breath Away - v | Ch 40072, Pan 25828 |
| 60214-B | When A Great Love Comes Along - v | - |

                                          New York, December 27, 1935.

| | | |
|---|---|---|
| 60290-A | Quicker Than You Can Say "Jack Robinson" - v | Ch 40079, Pan 25838 |
| 60291-A | I Feel Like A Feather In The Breeze - v | -    Pan 25839, Dec F-5927 |

                                          New York, January 15, 1936.

| | | |
|---|---|---|
| 60344-A | Dinner For One, Please James - v | Ch 40089 |
| 60345-A | A Beautiful Lady In Blue (w) - v | -    Pan 25838 |

                                          New York, January 17, 1936.

| | | |
|---|---|---|
| 60358-A | I'm Gonna Clap My Hands - vMR | Dec 683, 3364, X-1111, Br 02171 |
| 60359-A | I Wish I Were Aladdin - vMR | Dec 684 |
| 60360- | Not Enough - vMR | Dec 683 |
| 60361-A | You're Wicky, You're Wacky, You're Wonderful - v | Dec 684, X-1111 |

Hal Burke-v.                              New York, April 14, 1936.

| | | |
|---|---|---|
| 61038-A | Melody From The Sky - vHB | Ch 40109 |
| 61039-A | Love Is Like A Cigarette - vHB | Ch 40110 |
| 61040-A | Knick-Knacks On The Mantel - vHB | - |
| 61041-A | Twilight On The Trail - vHB | Ch 40109, Dec F-5967, Pan 25857 |

                                          New York, April 16, 1936.

| | | |
|---|---|---|
| 61052- | I'm In The Mood For Love - v | Dec rejected |
| 61053- | You Are My Lucky Star - v | - |

                                          New York, April 21, 1936.

| | | |
|---|---|---|
| 61065-A | There's Something In The Wind - vMR | Ch      , Br 02324 |
| 61066-A | The Old Oaken Bucket - vMR | - |

OTE:- All Champions as TED RUSSELL AND HIS ORCHESTRA, except 40067 (as THE TOP
HATTERS); also all Panachords, and Decca F-5967; Decca F-5927 as THE RHYTHM
MANIACS.

MIKE RILEY, EDDIE FARLEY AND THEIR ONYX CLUB BOYS : Eddie Farley-t/Mike Riley-tb-mel
v/cl/p/g/sb/d.                          New York, October 27, 1936.

61353-    Trouble Don't Like Music - vMR          Dec 994
61354-    A High Hat, A Piccolo And A Cane - vMR    -
61355-A   Hey-Hey (Your Cares Away) - vMR          Dec 1041
61356-A   With Thee I Swing - vMR                   -

MIKE RILEY AND HIS ORCHESTRA : Instrumentation similar to the above; personnel may
include some of the musicians from the next session below.
                                        New York, April 27, 1937.

62154-A   I'm Hatin' This Waitin' Around - vMR     Dec 1263
62155-A   That's Southern Hospitality - vMR        Dec 1271, X-1367
NOTE:- Decca X-1367 as THE RHYTHM KINGS.

                                        New York, April 29, 1937.

62162-A   Spendin' All My Time With The Blues-vMR  Dec 1263
62163-A   Jammin' - vMR                            Dec 1271

MIKE RILEY AND HIS ROUND AND ROUND BOYS : Mike Riley-tb-v dir. Harry Prebal-John
Montelione-t/George Tookey-Llana Webster-cl-as/Joe Butaski-p/Sam de Bonis-g/Pops
Darrow-sb/Bill Flanagan-d.              New York, January 18, 1938.

63170-A   Cachita - vMR                            Dec 1662
63171-A   OoooOH Boom ! - vMR                      Dec 1655, F-6635, Br A-81551,
                                                   Pol A-61159
63172-A   You're Giving Me The Run-Around - vMR    As above
63173-A   Oh Dear, What Can The Matter Be ? - vMR  Dec 1662

### JOE RINES AND HIS ORCHESTRA

This was a popular "sweet society" orchestra that made some sides in New York between
1928 and 1938; the following is played with some feeling for jazz.

Joe Rines-v dir. 2t/2as/ts/bar/p/g/sb/d.  New York, October 3, 1932.

73737-2   Underneath The Harlem Moon - vJR-O       Vic 24151

### JUSTIN RING AND HIS OKEH ORCHESTRA

Justin Ring was Musical Director of OKeh Records in New York between 1924 and 1930,
and produced hundreds of records of all kinds during that time. The following are
of some interest as jazz, and there may well be others comparable to them.

Justin Ring dir. Mike Mosiello and another-t/tb/Andy Sannella-cl-as-stg/cl-ss-as/cl-
ts/p/bj/bb/d/Beth Challis-v.            New York, August 2, 1927.

81175-B   Miss Annabelle Lee (Who's Wonderful ?    OK 40869, Par E-4578, R-3418,
          Who's Marvelous ?) - vBC                 A-2427, Ar 4296
NOTE:- Parlophone E-4578 as THE PARLOPHONE SYNCOPATORS; R-3418 as THE TAMPA BLUE
ORCHESTRA; Ariel 4296 as ARIEL DANCE ORCHESTRA.

Justin Ring dir. 2t/Tommy Dorsey-tb/Jimmy Dorsey and another-cl-as/ts/vn/p/Eddie
Lang-g/Joe Tarto-sb/Stan King-d/Scrappy Lambert-v.
                                        New York, August 16, 1929.

402860-A  True Blue Lou - vSL                      OK 41295, Par R-463, A-2867,
                                                   Ar 4462
NOTE:- Parlophone R-463 as TAMPA BLUE ORCHESTRA; Ariel 4462 as ARIEL DANCE
ORCHESTRA.

See also Sam Lanin.

Johnny Ringer-d dir. Sammy Castin-t/Gus Fetterer-cl-as/Bill King-cl-ts/Harry Radford
  p-a/Pete Epelitto-bj/bb.                    New York, May 24, 1927.

GEX-660     Buffalo Rhythm                       Gnt 6183, Ch 15304, 40112

                               New York, June 23, 1927.

GEX-690     Rubber Heels                         Gnt 6199, Ch 15307, 40104
GEX-691     Swamp Blues                            -      Ch 15308     -

    Arthur Fields-v.             New York, September 16, 1927.

GEX-875-A  Who's That Knockin' At My Door ? - vAF Gnt 6264, Ch 15362
GEX-876-A  Moonlit Waters - vAF                    -
GEX-877-A  The Varsity Drag - vAF                 Gnt 6280, Ch 15363, Spr 309,
                                                  Voc XA-18063
GEX-878     Gold Digger                           Gnt 6280, Ch 15366, Spr 310
    NOTE:- All Champion issues as WALLY SPENCER'S GEORGIANS.

## ISSIE RINGGOLD

Vocal, acc. by c/p.                    New York, January 22, 1930.

149797-3  He's A Good Meat Cutter              Col 14509-D
149798-2  Be On Your Merry Way                    -

## RIO GRANDE DANCE ORCHESTRA

Pseudonym on Aco for the following items listed in this book :-

G-15936   Then I'll Be Happy (Bailey's Lucky Seven)
G-15955   Both sides by Bailey's Lucky Seven
G-15977   Kentucky's Way Of Saying "Good Morning" (Bailey's Lucky Seven)

## SALLY RITZ

Pseudonym on Banner, Harmograph and Regal for Rosa Henderson, q.v.

## RIVER CLUB ORCHESTRA

Pseudonym on Odeon A-221154 (I'LL NEVER ASK FOR MORE) for the Dorsey Brothers'
  Orchestra, q.v.

## RIVERSIDE DANCE BAND

Pseudonym on English Vocalion for the following items listed in this book :-

X-8726  Don't Wake Me Up (Bailey's Lucky Seven)
X-9826  Honey Bunch (Fletcher Henderson and his Orchestra)
X-9826  But I Do, You Know I Do (The Southerners)
X-9901  Cecilia (Bailey's Lucky Seven)
X-9938  Both sides by Joe Candullo's Everglades Orchestra
X-10004 I'm Looking Over A Four-Leaf Clover (Gowans' Rhapsody Makers)
X-10015 Underneath The Weeping Willow (Harry Pollock's Blue Diamonds)
X-10016 Mine (Johnny Sylvester and his Orchestra)

## RIVIERA  DANCE ORCHESTRA

Pseudonym on English Vocalion for the following item listed in this book :-

M-1140  You've Got To See Mama Ev'ry Night (Gene Fosdick s Hoosiers)

## RIVIERA PALACE ORCHESTRA

Pseudonym on Perfectaphone 3108 for the California Ramblers, q.v.

The following side by this commercial dance band is of some interest as a "hot" item featuring a good trumpet.

Vincent Rizzo dir. 2t/tb/2cl-ss-as/cl-ts/vn/p/bj/bb/d/Billy Jones-d.
New York, November 18, 1926.

80218-C  Clap Yo' Hands - vBJ            OK 40725, Par R-3376

## ROANE'S PENNSYLVANIANS

Harry Berman-Louis Martino and another-t/Terry Page-tb-a/Dyke Bittenbender-Johnny Nadlinger and another-cl-as/Joe Allard-cl-ts/Bobby Roberts-vn-v/Paul Savage-p-a/ g/bb/Herbert Lee-d/"Snowball"-v.    New York, January 28, 1932.

| | | |
|---|---|---|
| 71285-1 | When You And I Were Young, Maggie - vch | Vic 22919, BB B-5645 |
| 71286-1 | (We've Got To) Put That Sun Back In The Sky - vch | Vic 22922, HMV B-4906 |
| 71287-1 | Chinatown, My Chinatown - vBR | Vic 22919, BB B-5645 |
| 71288-2 | Between The Devil And The Deep Blue Sea - vBR-"S"-ch | Vic 22922 |

2nd tb added; one cl-as omitted; Cliff Nazarro-v.
New York, June 2, 1932.

| | | |
|---|---|---|
| 72837-2 | Is I In Love ? I Is - v"S"-CN | Vic 24036 |
| 72838-1 | Goodbye Blues - v"S"-CN-ch | - |
| 72839-2 | Why Don't You Get Lost ? - vch | Vic 24037, BB B-5108, Sr S-3191 |
| 72840-1 | Charlie Two-Step - vCN | Vic 24039, HMV B-4921 |
| 72841-1 | Cast Your Sins Away - vCN | Vic 24353 |
| 72842-1 | Sleep, Come On And Take Me - vCN | Vic 24039 |

NOTE:- Victor 24037, Bluebird B-5108 and Sunrise S-3191 as CALLOWAY'S HOT SHOTS; Victor 24039 and HMV B-4921 as WILLIAMS' COTTON CLUB ORCHESTRA; Victor 24353 as JOE HAYMES AND HIS ORCHESTRA.

## EVERETT ROBBINS

EVERETT ROBBINS AND HIS SYNCOPATING ROBBINS : Everett Robbins-pv dir. probably :- Ira Walker-t/Eddie Vincent-tb/Jimmy Dudley-Henry Johnson-cl-Cm/Benny Fields-cl-ts/Dick Larkins-bj/bb/William Hoy-d.    Chicago, c. February, 1924.

489    You Didn't Want Me When I Wanted You,    Auto (un-numbered)
         I'm Somebody Else's Now

Vocal, acc. by own p.          Chicago, c. March, 1924.

510    A Triflin' Daddy's Blues         Auto (un-numbered)

## HARRY ROBBINS AND HIS REDBREASTS

T/? Freddy Gardner-cl/p/? Joe Young-g/? Dick Ball-sb/Harry Robbins-d-x.
London, March 16, 1936.

CA-15666-1  Chicken Reel             Col FB-1555, RZ G-23018
CA-15667-1  I'm Just Wild About Harry      -      -

## JOSEPH ROBECHAUX AND HIS NEW ORLEANS RHYTHM BOYS

Joe Robechaux-p dir. Eugene Ware-t/Alfred Guishard-cl-as-v/Gene Porter-ts/? Rene Hall bj/Walter Williams-g-v/Ward Crosby-d.    New York, August 22, 1933.

| | | |
|---|---|---|
| 13851-2 | Ring Dem Bells | Voc 2575 |
| 13852-2 | St. Louis Blues | Voc 2539, Br X-2539 |
| 13853-2 | Zola - v | Voc 2646 |
| 13854-1 | Foot Scuffle | Voc 2796 |
| 13855-1 | King Kong Stomp | Voc 2539, Br X-2539 |
| 13856-1-2 | Stormy Weather | Voc 2540, Br X-2540 |
| 13857-1 | Saturday Night Fish Fry Drag | Voc 2796 |

Joseph Robechaux-p dir. Eugene Ware-t/Alfred Guishard-cl-as-v/Gene Porter-ts/? Rene
Hall-bj/Walter Williams-g-v/Ward Crosby-d.

New York, August 23, 1933.

| 13858-1 | Every Tub | Voc 2827 |
|---|---|---|
| 13859-1 | The Riff | Voc 2592 |
| 13860-2 | After Me The Sun Goes Down - v | Voc 2610 |
| 13861-1 | Jig Music - vWW | Voc 2545 |

New York, August 24, 1933.

| 13874-1 | You Keep Me Always Living In Sin - vWW | Voc 2545 |
|---|---|---|
| 13875-1 | Sleep, Come On And Take Me - vWW | Voc 2881 |
| 13876-1 | Just Like A Falling Star | - |
| 13877-1 | I Would Do Anything For You | Voc 2646 |

New York, August 25, 1933.

| 13882-1 | She Don't Love Me | Voc 2827 |
|---|---|---|
| 13883-1 | Lazy Bones - vAG | Voc 2540, Br X-2540 |
| 13884-1-2 | Forty-Second Street | Voc 2575 |
| 13885-2 | Why Should I Cry For You ? | Voc 2610 |

Chick Bullock-v.                          New York, August 26, 1933.

| 13886-1-2 | Shake It And Break It - v | Voc 2592 |
|---|---|---|
| 13887-1 | That's How Rhythm Was Born - vCB | Ban 32848, Dom 131, Or 2749, Per 15809, Ro 2122, Mt 91613 |
| 13888-1 | Swingy Little Thingy - vCB | As above, plus Rex 8051,Kr K-3517 |

NOTE:- All issues from matrices 13887-1 and 13888-1 as CHICK BULLOCK AND HIS LEVEE
LOUNGERS, except Rex 8051 and Kristall K-3517 (as BOB CAUSER AND HIS CORNELLIANS).

Unknown fourteen-piece orchestra, led by Joseph Robechaux (who probably plays piano).

New Orleans, March 20, 1936.

| 60838- | When The Sun Goes Down | Dec rejected |
|---|---|---|
| 60839- | You Were Meant For Love | - |
| 60840- | Head Stuff | - |
| 60841- | Don't Let Old Age Creep Up On You | - |

## ORLANDO ROBERSON

See Edgar Hayes.

## C. LUCKEYTH "LUCKEY" ROBERTS

Piano solos.                          New York, October 26, 1916.

| 47099-1-2 | Shoo Fly (C. Luckeyth Roberts) | Col rejected |
|---|---|---|
| 47100-1-2-3-4 | Shy And Sly (C. Luckeyth Roberts) | - |

## HELEN   ROBERTS

Pseudonym on Silvertone for Alberta Hunter, q.v.

## LEW ROBERTS AND HIS DANCE BAND

Pseudonym on Lewis L-53 for Oscar Rabin and his Romany Band, q.v.

## SALLY   ROBERTS

Pseudonym on OKeh for Sara Martin, q.v.

## DICK ROBERTSON AND HIS ORCHESTRA

Dick Robertson was a very popular light vocalist, on records and radio, during the
years from 1927 to 1942.  Of particular interest to jazz enthusiasts are most of
the large number of titles he recorded for Decca from 1935 onwards, and these are
listed here completely; a few other examples of his work that come within the
scope of this book are also shown.  See also the ARC-Brunswick studio bands.

Vocal, acc. by Red Nichols-t/Glenn Miller-tb/cl/as/ts/?vn/p/bj-g/bb/d. (The remaining records are all as by the Orchestra).  New York, April, 1929.

| E-29812- | Some Sweet Day | Br 4367, 5032 |
| E-29813- | Louise | - |

2t/Tommy Dorsey-tb/Jimmy Dorsey and another-cl-as/cl-ts/vn/p/g/bb/d/Dick Robertson-v.
New York, May 1, 1931.

| E-36678- | Ho Hum ! | Mt M-12162, Pan 25056, P-12162, Mf G-2023 |
| E-36679- | (There Ought To Be A) Moonlight Saving Time | As above, plus Emb E-136 |
| E-36680- | I Wanna Sing About You | Mt M-12163, Emb E-141 |

NOTE:- Mayfair G-2023 as BOB RICHARDSON AND HIS ORCHESTRA; Embassy E-136 as THE SOUTHERN SYNCOPATORS; E-141 as THE EMBASSY ENTERTAINERS.

Similar instrumentation, possibly including Manny Klein-t/Charlie Butterfield-tb/ Jimmy Dorsey-cl-as/Joe Venuti, Harry Hoffman and/or Al Duffy-vn/Joe Meresco-p/Carl Kress-g/Dick Cherwin-sb/Larry Gomar or Chauncey Morehouse-d-vib.
New York, June 7, 1932.

| 11908-A | Bull Fiddle Blues | Mt M-12418, Per 15632, Pan 25259 |
| 11909-A | West Bound Freight | Mt M-12417 |

NOTE:- Perfect 15632 as DUKE WILSON AND HIS TEN BLACK BERRIES.

New York, June 14, 1932.

| 11936-1 | Holding My Honey's Hand | Mt M-12408, Ro 1865 |
| 11937-1 | There's Oceans Of Love By The Beautiful Sea | - |

? Bunny Berigan (sometimes another, 2nd)-t/Al Philburn-tb/Paul Ricci and/or Forrest Crawford-cl-ts/Frank Signorelli-p/? Carmen Mastren-g/Sid Weiss-sb/Stan King-d/Dick Robertson-v.          New York, December 27, 1935.

| 60286-A | Moon Over Miami | Ch 40077, Pan 25835 |
| 60287-A | Cling To Me | -      Br SA-1002 |
| 60288-A | Lovely Lady (w) | Ch 40078, Dec F-5976, Pan 25835 |
| 60289-A | With All My Heart | -      Pan 25837 |

New York, January 27, 1936.

| 60395-A | Alone | Ch 40088, Dec F-5900, Pan 25837 |
| 60396-A | If I Should Lose You | -      -      Pan 25836 |
| 60397-A | Lights Out | Ch 40087 |
| 60398-A | A Little Rendezvous In Honolulu | -      Dec F-5927 |
| 60399-A | But Where Are You ? | Ch 40092, Dec F-5935, Pan 25843 |
| 60400- | Let's Face The Music And Dance | Ch 40093, Pan 25844 |

New York, February 5, 1936.

| 60448-A | I'm Putting All My Eggs In One Basket | Ch 40092, Dec F-5935, Pan 25843 |
| 60449-A | I'd Rather Lead A Band | Ch 40093, Pan 25844 |

New York, March 16, 1936.

| 60900-A-B | Lost | Ch 40104, Dec F-5976, Pan 25856 |
| 60901-A | Welcome Stranger | - |
| 60902-A | It's A Sin To Tell A Lie (w) | Ch 40106, Pan 25871 |
| 60903-B | The Hills Of Old Wyomin' | Ch 40105, Pan 25865 |
| 60904-A | The Touch Of Your Lips | Ch 40106, Dec F-5950, Pan 25856 |
| 60905-A | Is It True What They Say About Dixie ? | Ch 40105, Dec F-5967, Pan 25860 |

New York, April 14, 1936.

| 61042-A | Robins And Roses | Ch 40111, Pan 25862 |
| 61043-A-B | Would You ? (w) | Rejected |

Andy McKinney-t/Russ Jenner-tb/Slats Long-cl/Herbie Haymer-ts/Red Norvo-p/Pete Peterson-sb/Maurice Purtill-d/Dick Robertson-v.

New York, May 25, 1936.

| 61116- | The Glory Of Love | Ch 40116 |
| 61117- | Blazin' The Trail | - | Pan 25862 |

New York, May 26, 1936.

| 61118-A | I'll Bet You Tell That To All The Girls | Ch 40118, Dec F-5995, Pan 25871 |
| 61119- | She Shall Have Music | Ch 40117 |
| 61120-A | Would You ? (w) | Ch 40111, Pan 25861 |
| 61121- | A Waltz Was Born In Vienna (w) | Ch 40117 | - |
| 61122-A | On The Beach At Bali Bali | Ch 40118, Dec F-5965, Pan 25865 |

NOTE:- All Panachords to this date as JACK NORTH'S ORCHESTRA or JACK NORTH AND HIS BAND.

Similar instrumentation to the above, but personnel unknown; probably similar to that given for March 24, 1937.         New York, December 15, 1936.

| 61483-A | Three O'Clock In The Morning (w) | Dec 1099, X-1342 |
| 61484-A | The Waltz You Saved For Me (w) | - |

New York, January 25, 1937.

| 61546-A | Happy Days Are Here Again | Dec 1125 |
| 61547-A | While We Danced At The Mardi Gras | - |
| 61548-A | Goodnight, My Love | Dec 1131, Mt 40119 (Canadian) |
| 61549-A | When My Dream Boat Comes Home | - | - |
| 61549-B | When My Dream Boat Comes Home | - |

New York, March 1, 1937.

| 62027-A | When The Poppies Bloom Again | Dec 1181 |
| 62028-A | May I Have The Next Romance With You ? | Dec 1169, Pan 25906 |
| 62029-A | Wanted | Dec 1181 |
| 62030-A | Marie | Dec 1169 |

Bobby Hackett-c/Al Philburn-tb/Paul Ricci-cl/Frank Froeba-p-cel/Frank Victor-g/Haig Stephens-sb/Sammy Weiss-d/Dick Robertson-v.

New York, March 24, 1937.

| 62074-A | Little Old Lady | Dec 1209 |
| 62075-A | Too Marvelous For Words | - | Pan 25928 |
| 62076-A | My Little Buckaroo | Dec 1215, Pan 25919 |
| 62077-A | September In The Rain | - | Pan 25920 |

Sid Trucker-cl replaces Ricci; Frank Signorelli-p replaces Froeba; Stan King-d replaces Weiss.         New York, April 30, 1937.

| 62168-A | You'll Never Go To Heaven (if You Break My Heart) (w) | Dec 1260 |
| 62169-A | Toodle-Oo | - | Pan 25929 |
| 62170-A | It Looks Like Rain In Cherry Blossom Lane | Dec 1283 | - |
| 62171-A | On A Little Dream Ranch | - | Pan 25920 |

New York, June 17, 1937.

| 62284-A | Good Mornin' | Dec 1334 |
| 62285-A | The Miller's Daughter Marianne | Dec 1335 |
| 62286-A | The Merry-Go-Round Broke Down | Dec 1334, Pan 25928 |
| 62287-A | Gone With The Wind | Dec 1335, Pan 25942 |

Johnny McGhee-t/Buddy Morrow-tb/Paul Ricci or Don Watt-cl/Frank Signorelli-p/Frank
 Victor-g/? Haig Stephens-sb/Stan King-d/Dick Robertson-v.
                                              New York, July 21, 1937.

| | | |
|---|---|---|
| 62418-A | A Sailboat In The Moonlight | Dec 1367 |
| 62419-A | Strangers In The Dark | -          Pan 25942 |
| 62420-A | My Cabin Of Dreams | Dec 1374, Rex 9146 |
| 62421-A | Heaven Help This Heart Of Mine | - |

Johnny McGhee-Ralph Muzzillo-t/Al Philburn-tb/Sid Trucker-cl/Frank Froeba-p/Frank
 Victor-g/Haig Stephens-sb/Stan King-d/Dick Robertson-v.
                                              New York, August 24, 1937.

| | | |
|---|---|---|
| 62559-A | Ebb Tide | Dec 1407, X-1457, Pan 25960 |
| 62560-A | In A Little Carolina Town | - |
| 62561-A | You Can't Stop Me From Dreaming | Dec 1415, Pan 25950 |
| 62562-A | Blossoms On Broadway | -          Pan 25953 |
| 62563-A | Sidewalks Of New York (w) | Dec 1436 |
| 62564-A | Come, Josephine, In My Flying Machine | -          X-1895 |

Bobby Hackett-c/Johnny Carlson-t replace McGhee and Muzzillo; Don Watt-cl replaces
 Trucker; Frank Signorelli-p replaces Froeba.
                                              New York, October 7, 1937.

| | | |
|---|---|---|
| 62666-A | In My Merry Oldsmobile (w) | Dec 1511, X-1889 |
| 62667-A | Daisy Bell/Little Annie Rooney (w) | - F-6845 - |
| 62668-A | Roses In December | Dec 1487, Pan 25953 |
| 62669-A | Getting Some Fun Out Of Life | - |

Buddy Morrow-tb replaces Philburn; Frank Froeba-p replaces Signorelli.
                                              New York, October 19, 1937.

| | | |
|---|---|---|
| 62696-A | Rollin' Plains | Dec 1498, F-6876 |
| 62697-B | I Want You For Christmas | -          3365 |
| 62698-A | In A Shanty In Old Shanty Town | Dec 1512 |
| 62699-A | When It's Springtime In The Rockies | Dec 1979 |
| 62700-A | I Wonder Who's Kissing Her Now ? (w) | Dec 1512 |
| 62701-A | Sweet Rosie O'Grady (w) | Dec 1758, F-6845 |

                                              New York, October 21, 1937.

| | | |
|---|---|---|
| 62702-A | Two Little Girls In Blue (w) | Dec 1675, F-6844 |
| 62703-A | That Old Gang Of Mine | Dec 1536 |
| 62704-A | Won't You Come Over To My House ? (w) | - |

                                              New York, October 25, 1937.

| | | |
|---|---|---|
| 62705-A | That's How I Need You (w) | Dec 1952, F-6816, X-1613 |
| 62706-A | My Gal Sal | Dec 1735, F-6817 |

Bobby Hackett-c/Ralph Muzzillo-t/Al Philburn-tb/Don Watt-cl/Frank Signorelli-p/Dave
 Barbour-g/Haig Stephens-sb/Stan King-d/Dick Robertson-v.
                                              New York, November 10, 1937.

| | | |
|---|---|---|
| 62759-A-B | Somebody's Thinking Of You Tonight | Dec rejected |

                                              New York, December 6, 1937.

| | | |
|---|---|---|
| 62860-A | Ten Pretty Girls | Dec 1585 |
| 62861-A-B | In A Little White Lighthouse | -          Pan 25974 |

                                              New York, December 20, 1937.

| | | |
|---|---|---|
| 62891-A | The Rhythm Of The Snowflakes | Dec 1601 |
| 62892-A | The House On The Hill | Dec 1599 |
| 62893-A | Let's Waltz For Old Time's Sake (w) | Dec 1601, F-6817 |
| 62894-A | Three O'Clock In The Morning (w) | Dec F-6846 |
| 62895-A | Sail Along, Silv'ry Moon | Dec 1599 |

Bobby Hackett-c/Ralph Muzzillo-t/Al Philburn-tb/Don Watt-cl/Frank Signorelli-p/Dave
   Barbour-g/Haig Stephens-sb/Stan King-d/Dick Robertson-v.
                                    New York, January 14, 1938.

| | | |
|---|---|---|
| 63161-A | Bob White (Whatcha Gonna Swing Tonight?) | Dec 1620 |
| 63162-A | You're A Sweetheart | Dec 1619, Rex 9268 |
| 63163-A | You Started Something | Dec 1620 |
| 63164-A | I Wonder What's Become Of Sally ? | Dec 1675, F-6844 |
| 63165-A | Somebody's Thinking Of You Tonight | Dec 1619, Pan 25977 |

Johnny McGhee-Ralph Muzzillo-t/Jack Teagarden-tb/Tony Zimmers-cl-ts/Frank Froeba-p/
   Dave Barbour-g/Haig Stephens-sb/Sammy Weiss-d/Dick Robertson-v.
                                    New York, February 28, 1938.

| | | |
|---|---|---|
| 63353-A | Goodnight, Angel | Dec 1707, Pan 25977, Od 284389 |
| 63354-A | Let's Sail To Dreamland | -        X-1532, Pan 25984 |
| 63355-B | Drop A Nickel In The Slot | Dec 1706 |
| 63356-A | You Went To My Head | -        Pan 26003 |

   Al Philburn-tb replaces Teagarden.    New York, March 7, 1938.

| | | |
|---|---|---|
| 63374-A | Cry, Baby, Cry | Dec 1726, X-1538, Pan 25981 |
| 63375-A | Oh ! Ma-Ma ! (6/8) | - F-6692 - |
| 63376-A | Take Me Out To The Ball Game (w) | Dec 1735 |
| 63377-A | In The Good Old Summer Time (w) | Dec 1758, F-6846, X-1702 |

   Frank Signorelli-p replaces Froeba.    New York, May 10, 1938.

| | | |
|---|---|---|
| 63737-A | Teacher's Pet | Dec 1823, F-6901, X-1532 |
| 63738-A | Dust | -        F-6876, X-1693 |
| 63739-A | Chinese Laundry Blues (Mr. Wu) | Dec 1847, F-6857, X-1531 |
| 63740-A | Ferdinand The Bull (w) | -        F-6922  - |
| 63741-A | Oh ! How I Miss You Tonight (w) | Dec 1952, F-6816, X-1613 |

                                    New York, June 7, 1938.

| | | |
|---|---|---|
| 63921-A | Memories (w) | Dec 2146, X-1702 |

Johnny McGhee-t/Sid Stoneburn-cl/Nat Jaffe-p/Dave Barbour-g/Haig Stephens-sb/Sammy
   Weiss-d/Dick Robertson-v/The Men About Town (as The Alvarez Brothers on Decca
   1979) added where shown.          New York, June 30, 1938.

| | | |
|---|---|---|
| 64239-A | Rancho Grande - vMAT | Dec 1979 |
| 64240-A | Hi Yo, Silver ! - vMAT | Dec 1914, F-6857, X-1667 |
| 64241-A | When Mother Nature Sings Her Lullaby | -        Pan 26003 |

Johnny McGhee-Ralph Muzzillo-t/Al Philburn-tb/Tony Zimmers-cl-ts/Frank Froeba-p/Dave
   Barbour-g/Haig Stephens-sb/Sammy Weiss-d/Dick Robertson-v.
                                    New York, September 1, 1938.

| | | |
|---|---|---|
| 64487-A | No Wonder | Dec 2022, X-1657 |
| 64488-A | You're The Only Star (In My Blue Heaven) | Dec 2059, X-1693, Rex 9625 |
| 64489-A | You Gotta Be A Football Hero (To Get | Dec 2023, X-1656 |
| | Along With The Beautiful Girls) | |
| 64490-B | All-American Girl | -        - |
| 64491-A | Indiana Moonlight (w) | Dec 2022, X-1657 |
| 64492-A | You're The Very Last Word In Love | Dec 2146, X-1834 |

                                    New York, September 14, 1938.

| | | |
|---|---|---|
| 64672-A | Tutti-Frutti | Dec 2059, F-6922 |

                                    New York, January 12, 1939.

| | | |
|---|---|---|
| 64887-A | I Cried For You | Dec 2260, X-1723 |
| 64888-A | My Melancholy Baby | Dec 2276 |
| 64889-A | Kermit The Hermit | -        X-1758 |
| 64890-A | Gardenias | Dec 2260, X-1725 |

Johnny McGhee-Ralph Muzzillo-t/Al Philburn-tb/Tony Zimmers-cl-ts/p/Dave Barbour-g/
Haig Stephens-sb/Sammy Weiss-d/Dick Robertson-v.
                                                New York, March 8, 1939.

| | | |
|---|---|---|
| 65216-A | I Promise You | Dec 2354, Pan 26030 |
| 65217-A | Penny Serenade | — |
| 65218-A | I'm A Lucky Devil (To Find An Angel Like You) | Dec 2364 |
| 65219-A | I'm Building A Sailboat Of Dreams | —          Pan 26035 |

                                                New York, March 17, 1939.

| | | |
|---|---|---|
| 65196-A | (I'm Afraid) The Masquerade Is Over | Dec 2378, X-1775 |
| 65197-A | To Live The Life Of A Lie | —          — |

                                                New York, April 14, 1939.

| | | |
|---|---|---|
| 65396-A | Little Skipper | Dec 2419, Rex 9664 |
| 65397-A | It Makes No Difference Now | —          X-1758 |
| 65398-A | Where Do You Work-a, John ? (6/8) | Rejected |
| 65399-A | Maybe | — |

                                                New York, May 19, 1939.

| | | |
|---|---|---|
| 65602-A | Maybe | Dec 2541, X-1850, Br SA-1805 |
| 65603-A | Where Do You Work-a, John ? (6/8) | Dec 2497 |
| 65604-A | Pippinella | — |
| 65605-A | Ain't Cha Comin' Out ? (w) | Dec 2541, X-1736, Rex 9625 |
| 65606-A | Who Did You Meet Last Night ? | Dec 2807 |

Bobby Hackett-c replaces McGhee.      New York, August 30, 1939.

| | | |
|---|---|---|
| 66241-A | What Good Will It Do ? | Dec 2765, X-1781 |
| 66242-A | Baby Me | —          X-1834 |
| 66243-A | Somebody Told Me They Loved Me | Dec X-1826 |
| 66243-B | Somebody Told Me They Loved Me | Dec 2828 |
| 66244-A | I Wish I Had Died In My Cradle (Before I Grew Up To Love You) (w) | Rejected |

                                                New York, September 19, 1939.

| | | |
|---|---|---|
| 66612-A | I Only Want A Buddy - Not A Sweetheart | Dec 2807 |
| 66613-A | That's What I Want For Christmas | Dec 2782 |
| 66614-A | Don't Wait Till The Night Before Christmas | — |

Johnny McGhee-t replaces Hackett.      New York, October 27, 1939.

| | | |
|---|---|---|
| 66803-A | Lilacs In The Rain | Dec 2845, F-7393 |
| 66804-A | Are You Havin' Any Fun ? | Dec 2827 |
| 66805-A | Comes Love | — |
| 66806-A | Hello, Mister Kringle | Dec 2828, 3365 |

                                                New York, November 9, 1939.

| | | |
|---|---|---|
| 66495-A | Oh ! Johnny, Oh ! Johnny, Oh ! | Dec 2845, F-7393 |

McGhee or Muzzillo omitted.      New York, December 5, 1939.

| | | |
|---|---|---|
| 66930-A | Put Your Little Foot Right Out (w) | Dec 2926, X-1891 |
| 66931-A | She Had To Go And Lose It At The Astor | Dec 2920, X-1838 |
| 66931-B | She Had To Go And Lose It At The Astor | Nat 1 (Canadian) |
| 66932-A | As 'Round And 'Round We Go (w) | Dec 2926, X-1874 |
| 66933-A | Ma (He's Making Eyes At Me) | Dec 2920, X-1838, Rex 9804, Nat 1 |
| 66934-A | All Alone | Dec 3031 |

One t added, Philburn omitted.      New York, January 11, 1940.

| | | |
|---|---|---|
| 67038-A | Boomps-a-Daisy (w) | Dec 2973 |
| 67039-A | Playmates | —          X-1874, Rex 9804 |

From this point onwards, the personnel is difficult to determine, although probably
   largely similar to the immediately preceding.  The instrumentation is normally 2t/
   tb (on most, but not all sessions)/cl/p/g/sb/d/Dick Robertson-v.
                                                New York, February 20, 1940.

67217-A  Row, Row, Row                              Dec 3031, X-1850

                                                New York, March 8, 1940.

67275-   The Wreck Of The Old 97                    Dec 3125, X-1891

                                                New York, March 28, 1940.

67418-A  Ain't You Ashamed ?                         Dec 3124, X-1960
67419-A  Little Girl                                     -     X-1911
67420-A  If I Could Be With You One Hour Tonight     Dec 3141, X-1878
67421-A  I Want A Girl Just Like The Girl That           -     X-1903
            Married Dear Old Dad
67422-A  I Wish I Had Died In My Cradle              Dec 3125
            (Before I Gew Up To Love You) (w)
67422-B  I Wish I Had Died In My Cradle              Dec X-1903
            (Before I Grew Up To Love You) (w)

                                                New York, April 16, 1940.

67559-A  The Guy Needs A Gal                         Dec 3189, X-1881
67560-A  The Gang That Sang "Heart Of My Heart"          -       -

                                                New York, July 9, 1940.

67921-A  Ferryboat Serenade                          Dec 3305, X-1895, Br SA-1805
67922-   Goodbye, Little Darlin', Goodbye            Dec 3304
67925-A  On A Simmery Summery Day                    Dec 3305, X-1878
67926-A  I'll Never Smile Again                      Dec 3304, X-1911

The Century Quartet-v added where shown.
                                                New York, July 25, 1940.

67944-A  You're A Grand Old Flag - vCQ               Dec 3323, X-1989
67945-A  I Am An American - vCQ                      Dec   -
67946-A  When I Get You Alone Tonight                Dec 3349
67947-A  Breaking My Heart To Keep Away From You         -

                                                New York, August 27, 1940.

68013-A  Darling, How Can You Forget So Soon ?       Dec 3378
68014-A  Hello ! Little Girl Of My Dreams            Dec 3410, X-1960
68015-A  My Greatest Mistake                         Dec 3378
68016-A  It's A Mighty Pretty Night For Love         Dec 3410, X-1989
68017-A  Mickey                                      Dec 3462, X-2179
68018-   Connie's Got Connections In Connecticut         -

                                                New York, November 28, 1940.

68408-A  Oh ! How I Hate To Get Up In The Morning Dec 3558, X-2014
            (6/8)
68409-B  San Antonio Rose                            Dec 3559, X-2018, Rex 9974
68410-A  I Am A Canadian                             Dec
68411-A  Oh, They're Making Me All Over In The       Dec 3558
            Army
68412-A  I Used To Love You (But It's All Over       Dec 3559, X-2014
            Now)
NOTE:- The files show that matrix 68410-A was made for the Compo Co., Lachine,
Quebec, but it is not known if it was ever issued.

2t/tb (not present on all dates)/cl/p/g/sb/d/Dick Robertson-v.
New York, January 9, 1941.

| | | |
|---|---|---|
| 68563-A | So You're The One | Dec 3607, Rex 9974 |
| 68564-A | My Greenwich Village Sue | Dec 3632, X-2018 |
| 68565-A | Go Home, Little Girl, Go Home (w) | Dec 3607 |
| 68566-A | Many Happy Returns Of The Day (w) | Dec 3632 |

New York, February 17, 1941.

| | | |
|---|---|---|
| 68716-A | Somebody Stole My Gal | Dec 3669 |
| 68717-A | The Wise Old Owl | Dec 3659, X-1990 |
| 68718-A | Blues My Naughty Sweetie Gives To Me | Dec 3669 |
| 68719-A | The Sidewalk Serenade | Dec 3659 |

On March 4, 1941, Dick Robertson and his Orchestra made some records specially for children, which of course are of no interest as jazz.

New York, May 9, 1941.

| | | |
|---|---|---|
| 69166-A | Be Honest With Me | Dec 3791 |
| 69167-A | Just A Little Bit South Of North Carolina | Dec 3792 |
| 69168-B | G'bye Now | - |
| 69169-A | Goodbye, Dear, I'll Be Back In A Year | Dec 3791 |

The Norsemen-v group added where shown. New York, July 22, 1941.

| | | |
|---|---|---|
| 69542- | Twenty-One Dollars A Day-Once A Month-vN | Dec 3908 |
| 69543-A | Answer To You Are My Sunshine | - |
| 69544- | I'm Alone Because I Love You | Dec 3981 |
| 69545-A | What's The Good Of Moonlight (When You Haven't Got A Girl To Love ?) | Dec 3961 |

New York, July 31, 1941.

| | | |
|---|---|---|
| 69589-A | Got A Letter From My Kid Today | Dec 3961, X-2179 |

NOTE:- This number was also allocated to a side made the previous day by the Andrews Sisters.

New York, August 19, 1941.

| | | |
|---|---|---|
| 69649-A | Wedding Bells (Are Breaking Up That Old Gang Of Mine) | Dec 4031 |
| 69650- | Till We Meet Again | - |
| 69651-A | I Don't Want To Set The World On Fire | Dec 3981 |
| 69652-A | You Gotta Quit Cheatin' On Me | Dec 4330 |
| 69653-A | Uncle Eph's Got The Coon | - |

New York, October 18, 1941.

| | | |
|---|---|---|
| 69836-A | Under The Mistletoe | Dec 4060 |
| 69837-A | The Only Thing I Want For Christmas (Is Just To Keep The Things That I've Got) | - |

New York, December 9, 1941.

| | | |
|---|---|---|
| 70020-A | Walking The Floor Over You | Dec 4189 |
| 70021-A | When Your Old Wedding Ring Was New | Dec 4129 |
| 70022-A | Daddy, You've Been A Mother To Me | Dec 4167 |
| 70023-B | I Had Someone Else Before I Had You (And I'll Have Someone After You've Gone) | Dec 4129 |

The American Four-v added where shown. New York, December 16, 1941.

| | | |
|---|---|---|
| 70061- | I May Stay Away A Little Longer - vAF | Dec 4116 |
| 70062-E | We Did It Before (And We Can Do It Again) - vAF | Dec 4117 |
| 70063- | Goodbye Mama (I'm Off To Yokohama)-vAF | Dec 4116 |
| 70064-A | Everyone's A Fighting Son Of That Old Gang Of Mine - vAF | Dec 4117 |

2t/tb (not present on all dates)/cl/p/g/sb/d/Dick Robertson-v/The American Four-v
   added where shown.               New York, December 22, 1941.

70091-A  Twenty-One Years                    Dec 4233
70092-A  I Hate To Lose You                  -

                                   New York, January 9, 1942.

70138-A  Remember Pearl Harbor - vAF         Dec 4144
70139-A  One For All - All For One - vAF     Dec 4151
70140-A  You're A Sap, Mister Jap - vAF      Dec 4144
70141-A  I Paid My Imcome Tax Today - vAF    Dec 4151
70142-A  On The Street Of Regret (w)         Dec 4189

                                   New York, January 28, 1942.

70238-A  Wings Over The Navy - vAF           Dec rejected
70239-A  Eyes Of The Fleet - vAF             -

                                   New York, March 2, 1942.

70420-A  Wings Over The Navy - vAF           Dec 4308
70421-A  Eyes Of The Fleet - vAF             -
70422-A  I'm In Love With The Girl I Left Behind  Dec 4283
           Me
70423-A  She Don't Wanna                     Dec 4294
70424-A  One Dozen Roses                     -
70425-A  Keep 'Em Flying                     Dec 4283

                                   New York, March 24, 1942.

70572-   This Time                           Dec 4318
70573-   Hats Off To MacArthur (And Our Boys Down  -
           There)

The Three Larks-v added where shown.    New York, July 30, 1942.

71258-A  Under A Strawberry Moon             Dec 4373
71259-A  Ching - v3L                         Dec 4365
71260-A  Oh ! Pardon Me - v3L                Dec 4373
71261-A  Isabella Kissed A Fella - v3L       Dec 4365

See also Bunny Berigan; Eubie Blake (Varsity 5056); Joel Shaw.

                  ROBINSON'S KNIGHTS OF REST

See Bob Robinson.

                     ALEXANDER ROBINSON

Vocal, acc. by cl/? Jimmy Blythe-p/? W. E. Burton-wb.
                                   Chicago, c. February, 1928.

20377-2  My Baby                             Pm 12649

Acc. by p.                         Chicago, c. February, 1928.

20384-1  You're Not The Kind I Thought You Were   Pm 12649

                                   Chicago, March 23, 1928.

13609    My Señorita                         Ch 15489
NOTE:- This issue as BUD THURSTON.

ROBINSON'S KNIGHTS OF REST : Bob Robinson-cl/Jimmy Blythe-p/Teddy Moss or Scrapper
    Blackwell-g.                           Richmond, Ind., February 4, 1930.

    16216, -A  Rocking And Rolling                    Rejected
    16217-A  Mean Baby Blues (Hot And Bothered)       Ch 16607

ROB ROBINSON AND MEADE LUX LEWIS : Vocal duets, or Bob Robinson-v only*, acc. by
    Meade Lux Lewis-p-speech, with g where shown.
                                           Grafton, Wis., c. November, 1930.

    L-608-1 *I Got Some Of That - spMLL               Pm 13028
    L-609-1  The Preacher Must Get Me Sometime         -
    L-610-1  Don't Put That Thing                     Pm 13030
    L-611-1  Sittin' On Top Of The World - g          Rejected
    NOTE:- Some copies of Paramount 13030 use matrix L-823 (by Laura Rucker, q.v.),
    instead of L-610-1. The regular reverse of this is credited as above and titled as
    shown for L-611-1, but it is in fact by a blues group called the Harum Scarums.

                                           Grafton, Wis., c. January, 1931.

    L-738-3 *I'm Gonna Moochie - g                     Pm 13064
    L-739-2  I Don't Want It Now - g                   -
    NOTE:- Matrix L-738-3 is credited (correctly !) to ROB ROBINSON only.

BOB ROBINSON AND HIS BOB CATS : Bob Robinson-cl-v/t/? Albert Ammons-p/sb.
                                           Chicago, December 22, 1936.

    01894-1  Down In The Alley                         BB B-7898
    01895-1  Makin' A Fool Out Of Me                   BB B-6929
    01896-1  Can Use It Myself                         BB B-7898
    01897-1  She's A Mellow Thing                      BB B-6929

BOB ROBINSON TRIO : Bob Robinson-cl-v/p/sb.
                                           Chicago, January 13, 1937.

    C-1739-1  Crying For Love                          ARC 7-04-67, Voc 03453
    C-1740-1  Heart-Breaking Blues                      -              -

                              ELZADIE ROBINSON

Vocal, acc. by ? B. T. Wingfield-c/? Tiny Parham-p.
                                           Chicago, c. September, 1926.

    3019-2  Humming Blues                              Pm 12420

    Acc. by Will Ezell-p.                  Chicago, c. October, 1926.

    3053-1-2  Barrel House Man                         Pm 12417
    3054-1-2  Sawmill Blues                             -

Acc. by Shirley Clay and another-c/Preston Jackson-tb/Artie Starks-cl/Richard M.
Jones-p/Johnny St. Cyr-bj.                  Chicago, c. October, 1926.

    2751-1  Houston Bound                              Pm 12420

    Acc. by Will Ezell-p.                  Chicago, c. March, 1927.

    4253-2  Troubled With The Blues                    Pm 12469
    4254-2  Baltimore Blues                             -

                                           Chicago, c. July, 1927.

    4666-2  Back Door Blues                            Pm 12509, Bwy 5038
    4667-2  Whiskey Blues                               -           -
    NOTE:- Broadway 5038 as BERNICE DUKE.

                                           Chicago, c. October, 1927.

    20067-1  Tick Tock Blues                           Pm 12544
    20068-1  Hour Behind The Sun                        -

Acc. by Bob Call-p.                    Chicago, c. November, 1927.

20191-2  The Santa Claus Crave           Pm 12573, <u>Poydras MJC-67</u>, <u>Tem R-33</u>
20192-2  St. Louis Cyclone Blues              -                -              -

Acc. by Johnny St. Cyr-g.              Chicago, c. March, 1928.

20467-2  You Ain't The Last Man           Pm 12627
20468-3  Love Crazy Blues                     -

Acc. by Johnny Dodds-cl/Blind Blake-g (and sw*)/Jimmy Bertrand-x.
                                       Chicago, c. April, 1928.

20528-3  *Pay Day Daddy Blues             Pm 12635
20529-   Elzadie's Policy Blues           Rejected

20534-3  Elzadie's Policy Blues           Pm 12635

Bertrand omitted; Jimmy Blythe-p added.
                                       Chicago, c. May, 1928.

20583-1  Elzadie's Policy Blues           Pm 12635
20584-1-2 *Pay Day Daddy Blues                -

Acc. by ? Tiny Parham-p.               Chicago, c. June, 1928.

20642-2  Pleading Misery Blues            Pm 12676
20643-2  Mad Blues                            -

Acc. by Will Ezell-p.                  Chicago, c. July, 1928.

20782-2  Wicked Daddy                     Pm 12689
20783-2  It's Too Late Now                    -
20784-   Arkansas Mill Blues              Rejected
20785-   Gold Mansion Blues                   -

                                       Chicago, c. October, 1928.

20910-3  Arkansas Mill Blues              Pm 12701, Bwy 5088, <u>Poydras MJC-68</u>
                                          Tem R-36
20911-1  Gold Mansion Blues               <u>As above</u>
20912-2  Rowdy Man Blues                  Pm 12724, <u>Poydras MJC-15</u>, <u>Tem R-37</u>
20913-2  Going South Blues                    -                -              -
20914-2  Need My Lovin' Need My Daddy     Pm 12745
20916-1  Unsatisfied Blues                    -
NOTE:- Broadway 5088 as BERNICE DUKE.  Matrix 20915 is untraced.

                                       Chicago, c. March, 1929.

21186-2  This Is Your Last Night With Me  Pm 12768
21187-3  Cheatin' Daddy                       -
21190-2  My Pullman Porter Man            Pm 12795
21192-2  Driving Me South                 Pm 12900
21193-1  Past And Future Blues                -
21195-1-2  Ain't Got Nobody               Pm 12795
NOTE:- Matrices 21188/9, 21191 and 21194 are untraced.

## IKEY ROBINSON

IKEY ROBINSON AND HIS BAND : Jabbo Smith-c-v/Omer Simeon-cl-as/Millard Robins-bsx/
    William Barbee-p/Ikey Robinson-bj.'   Chicago, January 4, 1929.

C-2747-  Got Butter On It - vJS           Br 4963, 7057, <u>HJCA HC-79</u>
C-2748-  Roses Blues                      Rejected                    -

Walter Bishop-d added.                 Chicago, January 22, 1929.

C-2844-  Ready Hokum - v                  Br 4963, 7057, <u>HJCA HC-79</u>
C-2845-  Mammy Moon                       Rejected

"BANJO" IKEY ROBINSON : Vocal, acc. by Jimmy Flowers-p/Count Turner and self-bj/Bill
  Johnson-sb.                              Chicago, February 1, 1929.

C-2902-   Pizen Tea Blues                  Br 7052
C-2903-   Rock Pile Blues                  -

"BANJO" IKEY ROBINSON AND HIS BULL FIDDLE BAND : R. Waugh-vn/William Barbee-p*/Ikey
  Robinson-bj/Bill  Johnson-sb/Frankie "Half-Pint" Jaxon-d-wb-v.
                                           Chicago, February 9, 1929.

C-2937-   *My Four Reasons - vFJ           Br 4964, 7059
C-2939-   Rock Me Mama - vFJ               -        -
  NOTE:- Matrix C-2938 is described in the files as "Plain cut - special laboratory
  test on cold wax."

"BANJO" IKEY ROBINSON : Vocal, acc. by R. Waugh-vn/Jimmy Flowers-p/own bj/Bill
  Johnson-sb.                              Chicago, February 13, 1929.

C-2953-   You've Had Your Way              Br 7068
C-2954-   Without A Dime                   Rejected

  Johnson omitted.                         Chicago, March 1, 1929.

C-3030-   Without A Dime                   Br 7068

  Acc. by p/own g.                         Chicago, c. March 8, 1929.

C-3084-   Same Old Blues                   Br rejected

THE PODS OF PEPPER : Ralph Anderson-k-p-v/Ikey Robinson-bj-v/d.
                                           New York, February 6, 1931.

151278-1  You've Had Your Way - vIR        Col 14590-D
151279-1  Get Off Stuff - vIR             -
151280-1  Gee I Hate To Loose (sic) That Girl-vIR  Col 14664-D
151281-1  I Was A Good Loser Until I Lost You-vRA  -

BANJO IKE : Ikey Robinson-bj-v, acc. unknown.
                                           New York, August 30, 1933.

13913-    A Poor Boy                       Voc rejected
13914-    Up The River                     -

BANJO IKEY ROBINSON AND HIS WINDY CITY FIVE : Ikey Robinson-cl-bj-g-v/Willie Rendall
  cl-as/Ralph Tervalon-p/Mike McKendrick-g/Leonard Bibbs-sb/d/Tressie Mitchell-v.
                                           Chicago, July 2, 1935.

90057-A   Scrunch-Lo - clIR-WR/gMM         Ch 40011, Dec 7430
90058-A   Sunshine - clWR/bj-vIR/vTM       Ch 50073, Dec 7650
90059-A   "A" Minor Stomp - gIR            -         -
90060-A   Swing It - clIR-WR               Ch 40011, Dec 7430

## JIM ROBINSON'S JAZZ BAND

See Sam Morgan's Jazz Band.

## JOE ROBINSON

Vocal, acc. by Dot Scott's Rhythm Boys : ? Randolph Scott-t/as/Dot Scott-p/g/sb/d.
                                           Chicago, September 15, 1936.

90866-    You're Everything To Me          Dec rejected

                                           Chicago, October 13, 1936.

90922-    It's Too Late                    Dec rejected

Vocal, acc. by the Four Blackamoors : P/g/sb/vn.
                                    New York, July 23, 1941.

69549-A   You Don't Know My Mind                Dec 8580
69550-A   Somebody's Getting My Love             -
69551-    Don't Give Up Your Old Love            Dec 8568
69552-    Search Your Heart And See

Acc. by Sam Price's Blusicians : Herman Autrey-t/David Young-ts/Sam Price-p/
William Lewis-g/Vernon King-sb/O'Neil Spencer-d.
                                    New York, January 20, 1942.

70187-A   Me And My Chauffeur                    Dec 8601
70188-A   I've Got Too Many Blues                -

## NETTIE ROBINSON

Vocal, acc. by probably :- Tom Morris-c/Bob Fuller-cl/Mike Jackson-p.
                                    New York, c. December 24, 1926.

107311    I've Got The Right Man Now             PA 7523, Per 123
107312    I Never Loved But One Woman's Son      -          -

## ROB ROBINSON

See Bob Robinson.

## SAM ROBINSON

ROBINSON-MACK : Sam Robinson-Baby Mack-v duets, acc. by Clarence Williams-p.
                                    New York, c. November 13, 1925.

73762-A   Don't Lose Your Head And Put Your Hands  OK 8259
          On Me
73763-A   I Beg To Be Excused                    -

Baby Mack does not sing on the sides marked *; acc. by Richard M. Jones-p.
                                    Chicago, February 25, 1926.

9529-A   It's All The Same To Me                 OK 8298
9530-A   Make Room For Someone Else              -
9531-A   *Come Around The Corner                 OK 8321
9532-A   *Booze                                  -

## CARSON ROBISON

The late Carson Robison is best remembered as leader of a "cowboy" troupe, singing
and whistling to his own guitar accompaniment; he made countless records for most
American and many British labels between 1924 and 1955, the following being of
some jazz interest. There are others featuring short glimpses of jazz musicians
such as Mike Mosiello or Phil Napoleon-t and Andy Sannella-cl, but these hardly
warrant inclusion here.

CARSON ROBISON'S KANSAS CITY JACK-RABBITS : Earl Oliver-t/? Sam Lewis-tb/? Larry
Abbott-as/Murray Kellner-vn/? Bill Wirges-p/Carson Robison-g/Andy Sannella-stg/d.
                                    New York, July 31, 1929.

53969-2   Stuff                                  Vic V-38074, HMV R-14545
53970-3   Nonsense                               --          -

CARSON ROBISON'S MADCAPS : Instrumentation and personnel unknown, but probably very
similar to the above.               New York, October 2, 1929.

N-1168   Stuff                                   Ed 14085
N-1169   Nonsense                                -

THE CARSON ROBISON ORCHESTRA : Mike Mosiello-t/Tommy Dorsey-tb/2cl-as/cl-ts/p/Carson
Robison-g/Joe Tarto-sb/Stan King-d.   New York, November 2, 1929.

403225-B   Nothin'                               OK 41389, Od ONY-36075
403226-B   Less Than That                        -          -

Vocal, acc. by Murray Kellner-vn/p/own g/sb.
                                    New York, April 22, 1931.

53051-1  Wolf At The Door                    Vic 23556, Zon 6048

CARSON ROBISON AND HIS PIONEERS : Vocal, acc. by Max Goldberg-t/cl/p/own g.
                                    London, June 2, 1932.

GB-4541-2  Stack O' Lee Blues - Part 1       Dec F-3026
GB-4542-2  Stack O' Lee Blues - Part 2         -

## WILLARD ROBISON

The following sides from the considerable recorded repertoire of this famous American
  composer have points of interest as jazz. His vocal group the Deep River Quintette
  was featured with the Chicago Loopers, q.v., one side being issued under Willard
  Robison's name, and this is almost certainly the session Mr. Robison recalled when
  he claimed to have employed Bix Beiderbecke-c and Frank Trumbauer-Cm.

WILLARD ROBISON'S DEEP RIVER FOUR : Cl/? Bob McCracken-as/John Jarman-euphonium/
  Willard Robison-p.                 Chicago, c. September, 1924.

  604     The Rhythm Rag (Willard Robison)       Auto 600
  608     Joline                                   -

DEEP RIVER ORCHESTRA : Willard Robison-p dir. Walter Holzhaus and another-t/tb/John
  Jarman-mel (some titles)/2cl-as/Bob McCracken-cl-as-ts/? Charles Barnes-bj-g/Nick
  Fisher-bb/? Doc Ross-d/Murray John-Jack Kaufman (as WALTER NEFF)/The Deep River
  Quintette-v.                       New York, October 22, 1926.

E-2571-B-C  Mobile Mud ("American Suite No. 6")   PA 36575, 11349, Per 14756

                                    New York, November 22, 1926.

E-2599-B  Tampico ("American Suite No. 5")        OA 36574, 11349, Per 14755

                                    New York, c. April 20, 1927.

  7201     12th Street Rag (Euday L. Bowman)     Ban 6031, Dom 3998, Or 960,Re 8358
  107492-A 12th Street Rag (Euday L. Bowman)     PA 36635, 11446, Per 14816
           Peck Horn Blues                          -              -
  NOTE:- Banner 6031 and Regal 8358 as MISSOURI JAZZ BAND; Domino 3998 as IMPERIAL
  DANCE ORCHESTRA; Oriole 960 as TED WHITE'S COLLEGIANS.

                                    New York, c. May 12, 1927.

107541     Lazy Weather - vMJ                    PA 36638, 11497, Per 14825

                                    New York, c. July 29, 1927.

107689     Blue Baby - vDR5                      PA 36666, 11518, Per 14847

                                    New York, c. August 8, 1927.

107711     Frankie And Johnnie                   PA 36679, Per 14860
107712     Delirium                              PA 36690, 11519, Per 14871
  NOTE:- Pathe Actuelle 36679 and Perfect 14860 as LEVEE LOUNGERS.

Piano solos.                        New York, August 22, 1927.

E-3014     My Kind Of Blues                      PA       11516, Per
E-3015     Jubilee                                          -

WILLARD ROBISON AND HIS ORCHESTRA : Probably similar to the foregoing; Joe Wilbur-v.
                                    New York, c. November 16, 1927.

107906-3  There's A Rickety Rackety Shack - vJW  PA 36723, Per 14904, P-345
  NOTE:- Perfect P-345 as MEYER'S DANCE ORCHESTRA.

WILLARD ROBISON AND HIS ORCHESTRA : Willard Robison-p dir. probably :- Walter Holzhaus and another-t/tb/2cl-as/Bob McCracken-cl-as-ts/Charles Barnes-bj-g/Nick Fisher
   bb/? Doc Ross-d/Frank Bessinger-v.    New York, c. December 17, 1927.

       Thou Swell                        PA 36744, Per 14925, Sal 784

Jack Teagarden-tb replaces unknown.    New York, c. January 25, 1928.

   2842-A  There Must Be A Silver Lining - vFB       Cam 8136, Lin 2790, Ro 559,
                                                     Ang 3003, Elec 5026, 5057, GT 100,
                                                     Pm 2524
   108021-A  There Must Be A Silver Lining - vFB     PA 36757, 11549, Per 14938
   108022-   I Just Roll Along (Havin' My Ups And    PA 36761    -     Per 14942
             Downs) - vFB
   NOTE:- Cameo 8136, Lincoln 2790 and Romeo 559 as MIAMI ROYAL PALM ORCHESTRA; Electron 5026 and 5057 as FRANK DOYLE'S MARIGOLD ORCHESTRA; Golden Tongue 100 as BILT-
   MORE DANCE ORCHESTRA; Australian Paramount 2524 as ROY ROLLS AND HIS RED HEADS.

Unknown tb replaces Teagarden.    New York, c. April 4, 1928.

   3016-A  I'm Riding To Glory (With A Glorious      Cam 8205, Lin 2860, Ro 628
           Girl) - vFB
   108112  I'm Riding To Glory (With A Glorious      PA 36783, 11563, Per 14964
           Girl) - vFB                              (all as DEEP RIVER ORCHESTRA)

Annette Hanshaw-v.    New York, c. April 6, 1928.

   108116  There Ain't No Sweet Man That's Worth    PA 36782, 11563, Per 14963
           The Salt Of My Tears - vAH
           I Love My Old-Fashioned Man - vAH         -                -
           Speedy Boy - vAH                          PA 36785, Per 14966
           Japanese Sandman - vAH                    PA 36796, Per 14977
           Smiles - vAH                              -                -

DEEP RIVER ORCHESTRA : The following three titles are almost certainly by Willard
   Robison, though some doubt still exists in some collectors' minds. The personnel
   is probably similar to the foregoing; Scrappy Lambert-v.
                                      New York, c. July 27, 1928.

   3271    Blue Grass - vSL                          Cam 8291, Lin 2939, Ro 714,Dn A-32
                                                     Elec 5086
   108298  Blue Grass - vSL                          PA 36836, Per 15017
   NOTE:- Cameo 8291, Lincoln 2939 and Romeo 714 as THE CAROLINERS; Dominion A-32 as
   CAROLINA DANCE ORCHESTRA; Electron 5086 as PAUL CLICQUOT'S ESKIMOS.

Willis-Knight Hawks-v.    New York, c. August 27, 1928.

   3351    (I Like What She Likes-She Likes What     Cam 8321, Lin 2976, Ro 745,Dn A-54
           I Like) Ev'rything We Like We Like Alike-vWKH
   108341-1 (I Like What She Likes-She Likes What    PA 36860, Per 15041
           I Like) Ev'rything We Like We Like Alike-vWKH
   NOTE:- All issues from matrix 3351 as THE CAROLINERS, except Dominion A-54 (as
   CAROLINA DANCE ORCHESTRA).

LEVEE LOUNGERS : As above.    New York, c. September 26, 1928.

   108398-1  Easy Goin' - vWKH               PA 36883, Per 15064

Vocal, acc. by his Deep River Orchestra : ? Harry Goldfield-t/Chester Hazlett-cl/2-3
   vn/own p/? Snoozer Quinn-g/? Mike Trafficante-sb.
                                      New York, February 14, 1929.

   147845-1  We'll Have A New Home In The Morning    Har 870-H, Re G-9376
   NOTE:- Harmony 870-H as PAUL HOWE.

Mike Pingitore-bj replaces Quinn.    New York, April 19, 1929.

   48463-2  Head Low                                 Col 1818-D, Re G-9376

Piano solos, acc. by sb/d, with own v.     New York, September 27, 1940.

| | | |
|---|---|---|
| 68161- | Rocco Blues | Dec 8504 |
| 68162- | It's Wearing Me Down - vMR | Rejected |
| 68163-A | Rocco's Boogie Woogie - vMR | Dec 8523, Y-5855 |
| 68164- | Jungle Drums (Canto Karabali) | Dec 8533 |
| 68165-A | The Donkey Serenade | - |
| 68166-B | Tonky Blues - vMR | Dec 8523, Y-5855 |
| 68167-A | Rhumboogie - vMR | Dec 8504 |

Sb omitted.                  Chicago, March 11, 1941.

| | | |
|---|---|---|
| 93579-A | Tea For Two | Dec 8574 |
| 93580-A | Java Jive - vMR | Dec 8544 |
| 93581-A | The One I Love (Belongs To Somebody Else) | Dec 8574 |
| 93582-A | Hold Me Baby - vMR | Dec 8558 |
| 93583-A | How Come You Do Me Like You Do ? - vMR | - |
| 93584-A | Little Rock Getaway | Dec 8544 |

## JOHNNY ROCK AND HIS ORCHESTRA

2t/tb/2as/ts/p/g/sb/d.          Camden, N. J., October 2, 1933.

| | | |
|---|---|---|
| 77833-1 | Roses Of Picardy | Vic rejected |
| 77834-1 | My Gal Sal | - |

## TOM ROCK AND HIS ORCHESTRA

Pseudonym on American Odeon and Australian Parlophone A-3144 for Fred Rich and his Orchestra, q.v.

## ROCKAWAY RAMBLERS

Pseudonym on Perfect 14688 and 14690 for the California Ramblers, q.v.

## ROCKY MOUNTAIN TRIO

Bob Fuller-cl/Louis Hooper-p/Elmer Snowden-bj.
New York, c. September 18, 1925.

| | | |
|---|---|---|
| 9733, -A | Ketch Your Breath | Gnt rejected |
| 9734, -A-B | Old Man's Charleston | - |

New York, c. November 2, 1925.

| | | |
|---|---|---|
| 9805-A | Grand Opera Blues | Gnt 3184, Buddy 8041 |
| 9806-A | Old Man's Charleston | - |

NOTE:- Buddy 8041 as GULF COAST TRIO.

New York, March 23, 1926.

| | | | |
|---|---|---|---|
| X-47-A | Blowin' Off Steam | Gnt 3288 | |
| X-48-A | Gallopin' Dominoes | - | Buddy 8041 |

NOTE:- Buddy 8041 as GULF COAST TRIO.

## GENE RODEMICH AND HIS ORCHESTRA

This St. Louis orchestra was named by the late Frank Trumbauer as the one with which he made his first records, but nothing has so far been found to substantiate this. Similarly, the Mound City Blue Blowers are credited with appearing with the band - as they may have done on the stand, but not in the recording studio. The following records are of some interest as jazz, however.

Gene Rodemich-p dir. Charles Werner-another-t/Larry Conley-tb/cl-ss-as/cl-as/cl-ts/ Austin Wylie-2nd p/bj/bb/Paul Spoerloder-d.
New York, June 20, 1923.

| | | |
|---|---|---|
| 10893 | Oh, Sister ! Ain't That Hot ? | Br 2474* |

Gene Rodemich-p dir. Charles Werner and another-t/Larry Conley-tb/cl-ss-as/cl-as/cl-
   ts/Allister Wylie-2nd p/bj/bb/Paul Spoerloder-d.
New York, June 21, 1923.

| | | |
|---|---|---|
| 10908 | Wolverine Blues | Br 2455 |

New York, June 23, 1923.

| | | |
|---|---|---|
| 10919/23 | St. Louis Tickle (Barney - Seymore) | Br 2480 |

New York, November 12, 1923.

| | | |
|---|---|---|
| 11861/4 | Blue Grass Blues | Br rejected |

New York, November 13, 1923.

| | | |
|---|---|---|
| 11865 | Blue Grass Blues | Br 2527* |

Chicago, February 21, 1924.

| | | |
|---|---|---|
| 49-CH | Mobile Blues | Br 2599* |
| 50/52-CH | Missouri Tickler Blues | Rejected |
| 55-CH | Tenth Interval Rag | Br 2599* |

Eddie Storman-bj replaces unknown.    Chicago, September 12, 1924.

| | | |
|---|---|---|
| 141/5-CH | Worryin' Blues | Br 2731 |

Chicago, February 17, 1925.

| | | |
|---|---|---|
| 14967 | Everybody Loves My Baby | Br 2843* |

Gene Rodemich-p dir. Claude Conrad-Nick Belcastra-t/Bob Smith-tb/Ted Hunt-Bill Bailey
   cl-as/Alex Holman-ts/Freddie Wilde-vn/Tom Satterfield-p-a/Porter Brown-bj/A. Spil-
   lier-bb/Paul Spoerloder-d.    Chicago or St. Louis, February 2, 1926.

| | | |
|---|---|---|
| E-17877/9 | Hot Notes | Br rejected |

Chicago, March 10, 1926.

| | | |
|---|---|---|
| E-18362/4 | Hot Notes | Br 3073* |

GENE RODGERS

Piano solos.    London, between October 13 and 19, 1936.

| | | |
|---|---|---|
| S-128 | Was It A Lie ? | Voc 527 |
| S-129 | Three Minutes Of Blues | - |

London, October 21, 1926.

| | | |
|---|---|---|
| TB-2563-1 | Shoe-Shine Boy | Dec rejected |
| TB-2564-1 | Swing Mad | - |

IKE RODGERS AND HIS BIDDLE STREET BOYS

Ike Rodgers-tb/Henry Brown-p/Lawrence Casey-speech and (presumably) percussion. (See
   also Henry Brown).    Chicago, May 9, 1929.

| | | |
|---|---|---|
| C-3454-B | Malt Can Blues | Br 7086, Creole 12 |

JIMMIE RODGERS

The following sides by this country-singer have interesting jazz accompaniments.

Vocal, acc. by C. L. Hutchison-c/James Rikard-cl/Dean Bryan-g/John Westbrook-stg/
   George MacMillan-sb.    Atlanta, October 20, 1928.

| | | |
|---|---|---|
| 47215-1 | My Carolina Sunshine Girl | Vic V-40096, 21-0180, BB B-5556, MW M-4451, Zon 5495 |
| 47216-4 | Blue Yodel No. 4 | Vic V-40014, 21-0175, MW M-4722, Zon 5380, HMV MH-192 |

Acc. by C. L. Hutchison-c/James Rikard-cl/Dean Bryan-g/John Westbrook-stg/George
MacMillan-sb.                          Atlanta, October 22, 1928.

47223-4  Waiting For A Train                    Vic V-40014, 21-0175, BB B-5163,
                                                Eld 2060, MW M-8109, Sr S-3244,
                                                Zon 5380, HMV MH-192
47224-1-2  I'm Lonely And Blue                  Vic V-40054, MW M-4217, <u>Zon 5401</u>

Acc. by ? Tony Fougerat-c/cl/vn/p/own g/bb/d.
                                    New York, February 21, 1929.

48384-3  Desert Blues                           Vic V-40096, 21-0176, MW M-4451,
                                                Zon 5495
48385-1  Any Old Time                           Vic 22488, BB B-5664, MW M-4730,
                                                Zon 5780, EE-221

Acc. by Bob Sawyer-p dir. c/cl/own g/bj/bb.
                                    Hollywood, June 30, 1930.

54849-2  My Blue-Eyed Jane                      Vic 23549, BB B-5393, MW M-4222,
                                                HMV EA-1399, RZ G-23196,
                                                Twin FT-9114

                              Hollywood, July 10, 1930.

54861-3  Jimmie's Mean Mamma Blues              Vic 23503, MW M-4723, Zon 5859,
                                                HMV EA-1541, RZ G-23115

Acc. by Louis Armstrong-c/Lil Armstrong-p.
                                    Hollywood, July 16, 1930.

54867-2  Blue Yodel No. 9 (Standin' On The Corner)Vic 23580, MW M-4209, M-8124,
                                                RZ MR-3208, HMV MH-194, Zon EE-300
                                                Twin FT-9832, Col MZ-315

Acc. by the Louisville Jug Band : George Allen-cl/Clifford Hayes-vn/Cal Smith-bj/
Freddy Smith-g/Earl McDonald-jug.      Louisville, Ky., June 16, 1931.

69449-  My Good Gal's Gone Blues                BB B-5942, MW M-5014

## GIL RODIN AND HIS ORCHESTRA

Charlie Spivak-Tommy Thunen-t/Jack Teagarden-tb-v/Matty Matlock-cl/Gil Rodin-as/Eddie
Miller-ts/Gil Bowers-p/Nappy Lamare-g/Harry Goodman-sb/Ray Bauduc-d.
                                    New York, c. September, 1930.

1010-2  Beale Street Blues - vJT                Cr 3017
1011-2  If I Could Be With You One Hour Tonight  Cr 3016
         - vJT

Sterling Bose-t replaces Thunen; Benny Goodman-cl replaces Matlock; Eddie Gale-v.
                                    New York, c. January, 1931.

1117-1  Ninety-Nine Out Of A Hundred Wanna Be    Cr 3045
         Loved - vEG
1118-2  Hello, Beautiful ! - vEG                 Cr 3046
1118-3  Hello, Beautiful ! - vVG                    -      EBW 5287, Clif 5308,
                                                    Homestead 23126
NOTE:- Edison Bell Winner 5287 as DEAUVILLE DANCE ORCHESTRA; Clifford 5308 as BOB
GOLDEN'S ORCHESTRA.  See also Clark Randall and his Orchestra, and Irving Mills.

## CHARLES "BUDDY" ROGERS

The following records by this famous pioneer "talkie" star have good jazz accompaniments.  He later led a commercial dance band recording for Victor, but this did not
produce anything similar.

Vocal, acc. by Tommy Dorsey-t/Charlie Butterfield-tb/Jimmy Dorsey-cl/Adrian Rollini-
    bsx/? Bruce Yantis-vn/Frank Signorelli-p/Carl Kress-g/Stan King-d.
                                        New York, February 27, 1930.

150027-3  I'd Like To Be A Bee In Your Boudoir      Col 2183-D, DB-242, DO-152
150028-1-2-3  My Future Just Passed                 Rejected

   Acc. by Bob Effros-t/Tommy Dorsey-tb/? Pete Pumiglio-as/ts/? Ben Selvin-vn/? Frank
   Signorelli-p/Carl Kress-g/? Joe Tarto-sb.
                                        New York, March 4, 1930.

150028-5  My Future Just Passed                     Col 2183-D, DB-242, DO-152
150056-3  Any Time's The Time To Fall In Love       Col 2143-D, DB-162, DO-103
150057-3  Sweepin' The Clouds Away                  -        -        -

## GINGER  ROGERS

The following records by this famous film star have interesting accompaniments.

Vocal duet with Johnny Mercer, acc. by Victor Young and his Orchestra : 2t/tb/cl/ts/p
    /g/sb/d.                             Los Angeles, November 27, 1935.

LA-282-A  Eeny Meeny Miney Mo                       Dec 638, F-5838, X-1049

Vocal, acc. by Jimmy Dorsey and his Orchestra : Jimmy Dorsey-cl-as dir. George Thow-
    Toots Camarata-t/Bobby Byrne-Joe Yukl-Don Mattison-tb/Jack Stacey-as/Fud Livingston
    as-ts/Skeets Herfurt-ts/Bobby van Eps-p/Roc Hillman-g/Jim Taft-sb/Ray McKinley-d.
                                        Los Angeles, April 3, 1936.

LA-335-A  I'm Putting All My Eggs In One Basket     Dec F-5963, X-1126
LA-336-A  Let Yourself Go                           -        -

## MACK ROGERS AND HIS GUNTER HOTEL ORCHESTRA

Mack Rogers-t dir. 2t/tb/2as/ts/p/bb/d/Sibyl Hopkins-v.  Other records by this band
    are not of jazz interest as far as is known.
                                        San Antonio, August 10, 1934.

83916-1  In The Shade Of The Old Apple Tree         BB B-5603
83917-1  Casa Loma Stomp                            -

                                        San Antonio, February 2, 1935.

87865-1  Baby, Won't You Please Come Home ? - vSH BB B-5835

## MAY ROGERS

Pseudonym on Champion for Marie Grinter, q.v.

## RODNEY ROGERS' RED PEPPERS

2stg/g/sb.                               Chicago, October 14, 1927.

C-1318    Milenberg Joys                            Br 3744, A-7578
C-1320    Chile Blues                               -        -

## B. A.  ROLFE

B. A. Rolfe was a leading trumpet virtuoso in the late 1920s on American radio, whose
    band recorded copiously for Edison.  A collective personnel is given, as it appears
    that these records were made by 2-3t (including Rolfe himself)/tb/2cl-as/cl-ts/vn/p/

bj/bb/d, drawn from the following roster :- Pete Capodiferro-Vina Bono-H. Berkin-Frank Korminsky-Joe Lindwurm-Phil Napoleon-t/H. Green-Charles Harris-Dave Boyd-tb/ Andy Sannella-George Napoleon-Ross Gorman-Fred Hartman-cl-as/Lucien Smith-cl-ts-vc/ Harold van Emburgh-cl-ts/Walter Edelstein-Billy Artz-Enric Madriguera-Fritz Forsch-Harry Salter-Pete Eisenberg-vn/Milt Rettenberg-p/? Tony Colicchio-bj/Gus Helleberg-John Helleberg-Cy Harris-bb/Fred Albright-William Dorn-d; the following titles are known to be of interest as jazz.         New York, February 29, 1928.

| 18266 | Louisiana Bo Bo | Ed 52244 |

New York, June 1, 1928.

| 18557; N-284 | No Parking | Ed 52353 |

## ADRIAN ROLLINI

ADRIAN ROLLINI TRIO : Adrian Rollini-bsx-hfp/Frank Froeba-p/Teddy Bunn-g.
New York, January 31, 1930.

| | (What Did I Do To Be So) Black And Blue | Br rejected |
| | Clam House | - |
| | Round Town | - |

ADRIAN ROLLINI AND HIS ORCHESTRA : Manny Klein-t/Tommy Dorsey-tb/Jimmy Dorsey-cl-as/ Arthur Rollini-ts/Adrian Rollini-bsx-gfs-vib-x/Joe Venuti-vn/Charlie Magnante-pac/ Fulton McGrath-p/Edddie Lang-g/Art Miller-sb/Dick Robertson-v.
New York, February 14, 1933.

| 13049-1 | Have You Ever Been Lonely ? - vDR | Ban 32698, Cq 8153, Mt M-12629, Or 2651, Per 15735, Ro 2024 |
| 13050-1 | You've Got Me Cryin' Again - vDR | Ban 32699, Mt M-12630, Or 2652, Per 15736, Ro 2025, Dec F-3518, Key S-610 |
| 13051-1 | Hustlin' And Bustlin' For Baby - vDR | As above, but Imp 2846, not Key |
| 13052-1 | You Must Believe Me - vDR | Ban 32698, Cq 8108, Mt M-12629, Or 2651, Per 15735, Ro 2024 |

NOTE:- Melotone M-12629 and Perfect 15735 as OWEN FALLON AND HIS CALIFORNIANS; Imperial 2846 as THE BELL BOYS OF BROADWAY; Key S-610 as THE RHYTHM ACES.

Manny Klein-t/Tommy Dorsey-tb/Benny Goodman-cl/Jimmy Dorsey-cl-as/Arthur Rollini-ts/Adrian Rollini-bsx-vib/Fulton McGrath-p/Dick McDonough-g/Herb Weil-d-v/Irene Beasley-Howard Phillips-v.         New York, June 12, 1933.

| 265131-2 | Blue Prelude - vHP | Col 2785-D, Par R-2515 |
| 265132-2 | Mississippi Basin - vIB | - |
| 265133-2 | Charlie's Home - vHP | WRC SH-391 (LP) |
| 265134-2 | Happy As The Day Is Long - vHP | Col 2785-D |

NOTE:- Columbia 2785-D as ADRIAN AND HIS ORCHESTRA.

Bunny Berigan-t/Al Philburn-tb/Pee Wee Russell-cl/Arthur Rollini-ts/Adrian Rollini-bsx-cel-vib/Fulton McGrath-p/Dick McDonough-g/Art Miller-sb/Herb Weil-d-v/Howard Phillips-Red McKenzie-v.         New York, July 29, 1933.

| 13663-1 | Ah ! But Is It Love ? - vHP | Ban 32826, Mt M-12756, 91594, Or 2736, Per 15799, Ro 2109, Dec F-3702, Rex 8052 |
| 13664-2 | I Gotta Get Up And Go To Work - vRM | As above except Rex 8052 |
| 13675-1 | If I Had Somebody To Love - vHP | Ban 32837, Mt M 12766, 91608, Or 2743,Per 15805,Ro 2116,Rex 8035 |
| 13676-1 | Dream On - vRM | As above except Rex 8035 |

NOTE:- Rex 8035 as BOB CAUSER AND HIS CORNELLIANS; 8052 as ED LLOYD AND HIS  ORCHESTRA.

New York, September 14, 1933.

| 13999-1 | By A Waterfall - vHW | Ban 32867, Cq 8220, Dom 139, Mt M-12788, Or 2757, Per 15817, Ro 2130 |
| 14000-1 | Sittin' On A Back Yard Fence - vHW | As above, but Dec F-3827,not Cq |
| 14001-2 | I'll Be Faithful - vHW | Mt M-12790 |
| 14002-2 | Beloved - vHW | - |

ADRIAN ROLLINI AND HIS ORCHESTRA : Bunny Berigan-t/Al Philburn-tb/Benny Goodman-cl/
   Arthur Rollini-ts/Adrian Rollini-bsx-cel-vib/Fulton McGrath-p/Dick McDonough-g/Art
   Miller-sb/Herb Weil-d-v/Clay Bryson-v. New York, October 16, 1933.

| | | |
|---|---|---|
| 14147-1 | You've Got Everything - vHW | Ban 32873, Cq 8249, Mt M-12815, Or 2775, Per 15831, Ro 2148, Dec F-3796, Royal 91645 |
| 14148-1 | And So, Goodbye - vHW | As above |
| 14152-1 | Sweet Madness - vHW | Ban 32880, Mt M-12829, Or 2784, Per 15839, Ro 2157 |
| 14153-2 | Savage Serenade - vCB | As above, plus Dec F-3827 |

Pee Wee Russell-cl replaces Goodman.    New York, October 23, 1933.

| | | |
|---|---|---|
| 14001-3 | I'll Be Faithful - vHW | Ban 32863, Cq 8279, Dom 141, Mt M-12790, Or 2759, Per 15819, Ro 2132 |
| 14002-3 | Beloved - vHW | As above, plus Dec F-3848 |

NOTE:- Conqueror 8279 as ART KAHN'S ORCHESTRA.

2t/tb/cl-as/as/ts/Adrian Rollini-? bsx-vib/p/g/bb/d/Chick Bullock-v.
                                        New York, November 15, 1933.

| | | |
|---|---|---|
| 14300-1 | Did You Ever See A Dream Walking ? - vCB | Ban 32898, Cq 8277, Mt M-12849, Or 2794, Per 15848, Ro 2167, Rex 8087 |
| 14301-1 | You're Such A Comfort To Me - vCB | As above except Rex 8087 |
| 14302-1-2 | Good Morning, Glory - vCB | Ban 32899, Mt M-12850, Or 2795, Per 15849, Ro 2168, Rex 8087 |
| 14303- | Many Moons Ago - vCB | As above except Rex 8087 |

NOTE:- This session is entered in the ARC files as by ADRIAN ROLLINI AND HIS
ORCHESTRA, yet all except Rex 8087 (as ED LLOYD AND HIS BAND) were issued as GENE
KARDOS AND HIS ORCHESTRA. Adrian Rollini is readily identifiable (on vibraphone)
of course, but the use of two trumpets and a brass bass suggests that at least some
of Gene Kardos's men were present, with Adrian Rollini merely sitting in as nominal
leader.

As for October 23, 1933.        New York, November 17, 1933.

| | | |
|---|---|---|
| 13999-3 | By A Waterfall - vHW | Mt M-12788 |
| 14000-3 | Sittin' On A Back Yard Fence - vHW | - |

Benny Goodman-cl replaces Russell; Jane Vance-Howard Phillips-v.
                                        New York, November 24, 1933.

| | | |
|---|---|---|
| 14378-1 | Song Of Surrender (w) - vHP | Ban 32923, Mt M-12866, Or 2811, Per 15861, Ro 2184 |
| 14379-1 | Coffee In The Morning And Kisses In The Night - vHP | As above |
| 14380-1 | Sittin' On A Log (Pettin' My Dog) - vJV | Ban 32912, Cq 8262, Mt M-12855, Or 2803, Per 15855, Ro 2176, Dec F-3848 |
| 14381-2 | I Raised My Hat - vHW | As above, except Dec F-3848 |

New York, January 11, 1934.

| | | |
|---|---|---|
| 14565-1 | On The Wrong Side Of The Fence - vHW | Ban 32949, Mt M-12892, Or 2828, Per 15876, Ro 2201 |
| 14566-2 | Ol' Pappy - vHW | As above |
| 14567-1 | Who Walks In When I Walk Out ? - vHW | Ban 32950, Mt M-12893, Or 2829, Per 15877, Ro 2202, Rex 8107, Imp 23061, Kr 31223 |
| 14568-1 | Got The Jitters - vCB | As above, except Rex 8107 |

NOTE:- Rex 8107 and Kristall 31223 as JOE VENUTI AND HIS ORCHESTRA; Imperial 23061
as TANZ-ORCHESTER.

ADRIAN ROLLINI AND HIS ORCHESTRA : Pat Circirello-t/Jimmy Dorsey-cl/Charlie Barnet-
ts/Adrian Rollini-bsx/? Charlie Magnante-pac/Fulton McGrath-p/Carl Kress-g/Gene
Krupa-d/Chick Bullock-v.               New York, February 26, 1934.

14857-1  Keep On Doin' What You're Doin' - vCB     Br 6786, 01750
14858-1  Get Goin' - vCB                                  -        -
14859-1  A Hundred Years From Today - vCB          Voc 2675
NOTE:- Brunswick 6786 and 01750 as ADRIAN'S RAMBLERS.

Bunny Berigan-t/Al Philburn-tb/Benny Goodman-cl/Arthur Rollini-ts/Adrian Rollini-
bsx-cel-vib/Fulton McGrath-p/Dick McDonough-g/Art Miller-sb/Herb Weil-d/Joey Nash-
v.                                    New York, March 24, 1934.

14995-1  A Thousand Goodnights - vJN      Voc 2672, Dec F-3989, EBW W-125
14996-1  Butterfingers - vJN                   -    Dec F-3967, EBW W-112
14997-1-2  Waitin' At The Gate For Katy - vJN  Voc 2673, Dec F-5009, EBW W-126
14998-1  Little Did I Dream - vJN              -        -
14999-1  How Can It Be A Beautiful Day ? - vJN  Voc 2675, Dec F-3967
NOTE:- Edison Bell Winner W-112, W-125 and W-126 as SLEEPY HALL AND HIS COLLEGIANS.

ADRIAN'S RAMBLERS : Max Kaminsky-t/Milt Yaner-cl/Bud Freeman-ts/Adrian Rollini-bsx/
Roy Bargy-p/Carl Kress-g/Mel Clark-sb/Stan King-d/Chick Bullock-Ella Logan-v.
                                      New York, May 4, 1934.

B-15165-A  I've Got A Warm Spot In My Heart For    Br 6877, 01831
           You - vCB
B-15166-A  Why Don't You Practice What You Preach ?  -   01775, Col DO-1280
B-15167-A  The Better To Love You, My Dear - vCB   Br 6889, 01831
B-15168-A  I Wish I Were Twins - vEL                -   01775, 4922, Col DO-1280

ADRIAN ROLLINI AND HIS ORCHESTRA : Manny Klein-Dave Klein-t/Jack Teagarden-tb/Benny
Goodman-cl/Arthur Rollini-ts/Adrian Rollini-bsx/Howard Smith-p/George van Eps-g/
Artie Bernstein-sb/Stan King-d/Ella Logan-v.
                                      New York, October 23, 1934.

38874  It Had To Be You - vEL          Rejected
38875-A  Sugar                         Dec 265, Br 01942, A-82586,
                                       Od 284143
38876-A  Davenport Blues               Dec 359, 3862, Br 80144, 01942,
                                       Od 284143
38877-A  Somebody Loves Me             Dec 359, 3525,     -        03447
38878-A  Riverboat Shuffle             Dec 265, Br 02510, A-82586

ADRIAN AND HIS TAP ROOM GANG : Wingy Manone-t-v/Joe Marsala-cl-as/Adrian Rollini-bsx/
vib-x/Putney Dandridge-p-v/Carmen Mastren-g/Sid Weiss-sb/Sam Weiss-d/Jeanne Burns-v.
                                      New York, June 14, 1935.

92263-1  Bouncin' In Rhythm            Vic 25208, JA-658, HMV B-8660,
                                       HMV EA-1638, JF-39, JO-115
92264-1  Got A Need For You - vJB      Vic 25072, HMV B-8382, JF-43
92265-1  Weather Man - vWM-PD               -    HMV B-8660     - JO-115
92266-1  Nagasaki - vPD                Vic 25085, JA-558, HMV B-8397,
                                       EA-1546, JF-39
92267-1  Honeysuckle Rose - vPD        Vic 25208, JA-658, 25903,
                                       HMV B-8382, EA-1638, JF-39
92268-1  Jazz O' Jazz - vJB            Vic 25085, JA-558, HMV B-8397,
                                       EA-1546, JF-44

ADRIAN ROLLINI AND HIS ORCHESTRA : Irving Goodman-t/Art Drelinger-cl-ts/Adrian Rollini
bsx-vib/Jack Russin-p/Gwynn Nestor-g/George Hnida-sb/Phil Sillman-d.
                                      New York, March 17, 1936.

60906-A  Tap Room Swing                Dec 787, Col DB/MC-5006
60907-A  Swing Low                     Dec 807, Y-5114  -
60908-A  Stuff, Etc.                        -       -   Col DB/MC-5024
60909-A  Lessons In Love               Dec 787

ADRIAN ROLLINI TRIO : Adrian Rollini-vib/Frank Victor-g/Haig Stephens-sb.
                                    New York, December 4, 1936.

```
61455-A  Vibrollini                    Dec 1132, Y-5167,Br 02380, A-81379
61456-A  Driftin'                      Dec 1157, Y-5166   -         -
```

                        New York, January 11, 1937.

```
61507-A  Rebound                       Dec 1157, Y-5166, Br 02404,A-81382
61508-A  Jitters                       Dec 1132, Y-5167   -         -
```

ROLY'S TAP ROOM GANG : Jonah Jones-t/? Sid Stoneburn-cl-as/Arthur Rollini-cl-ts/
    Adrian Rollini-bsx-vib/Fulton McGrath-p/? Dick McDonough-g/? George Hnida-sb/? Al
    Sidell-d.                       New York, March 17, 1937.

```
M-270-1-2  Bugle Call Rag                  Vri rejected
M-273-1-2  Old Fashioned Love               -
NOTE:- Matrices M-271/2 are by Red McKenzie, q.v., accompanied by the same group.
```

ADRIAN ROLLINI AND HIS ORCHESTRA : Jonah Jones-t/Sid Stoneburn-cl/Fulton McGrath-p/
    Dick McDonough-g/George Hnida-sb/Al Sidell-d/Adrian Rollini-vib.
                                    New York, March 20, 1937.

```
M-286-1-2  I Don't Know If I'm Comin' Or Goin'  Mas rejected
M-287-1-2  Slap That Bass                        -
```

                        New York, March 27, 1937.

```
M-322-    Slap That Bass                   Mas 114
M-323-1-2  The Love Bug Will Bite You       Rejected
M-324-2   Let's Call The Whole Thing Off    Mas 114
M-325-1-2  I Don't Know If I'm Comin' Or Goin'  Rejected
```

    Johnny McGhee-t/Paul Ricci-cl/Adrian Rollini-bsx/Al Duffy-vn/Jack Russin-p/Frank
    Victor-g/Harry Clark-sb/Buddy Rich-d/Pat Hoke-v.
                                    New York, January 7, 1938.

```
63138-A  Bill                          Dec 1638, Voc S-191
63139-A  Singin' The Blues - vPH       Dec 1973, Y-5282 -
63140-A  The Sweetest Story Ever Told - vPH   -      -
```

ADRIAN ROLLINI QUINTET : Bobby Hackett-c/Frank Victor-g/Harry Clark-sb/Buddy Rich-d/
    Adrian Rollini-vib-x/Sonny Schuyler-v.  New York, January 18, 1938.

```
63174-A  Bei mir bist du schoen - vSS    Dec 1638
63175-A  Josephine - vSS                 Dec 1639, Y-5239
63176-A  You're A Sweetheart - vSS        - M-30120, Br 02579, A-81539
63177-A  True Confession - vSS           Dec 1654, Y-5210  -      -
63178-A  I've Hitched My Wagon To A Star - vSS   -      -
```

    The Tune Twisters-v group.          New York, June 23, 1938.

```
23147-2  (How To Make Love In) Ten Easy Lessons   Voc 4212, Col FB-2057, CQ-1493,
             - vTT                              Br A-81769
23148-1  Small Fry - vTT                     As above
23149-1  I Wish I Had You - vTT              Voc 4257, Br A-81831
23150-2  On The Bumpy Road To Love - vTT      -      -
```

ADRIAN ROLLINI TRIO : Adrian Rollini-vib/Frank Victor-g/Harry Clark-sb.
                                    Hollywood, September 28, 1939.

```
WM-1083-A  Estrellita                    Voc/OK 5435
WM-1084-A  I Can't Believe That You're In Love   Voc/OK 5621
             With Me/I Can't Give You Anything But Love
WM-1085-A  Star Dust/Solitude            Voc/OK 5376
WM-1086-A  Diga Diga Doo                   -
```

ADRIAN ROLLINI TRIO : Adrian Rollini-vib/Frank Victor-g/Harry Clark-sb.
                                    Hollywood, October 5, 1939.

| | | |
|---|---|---|
| WM-1087-A | Dark Eyes | Voc/OK 5435 |
| WM-1088-A | Dardanella | Voc/OK 5621 |
| WM-1089- | Moonglow | Voc/OK 5200 |
| WM-1090- | Pavanne | - |

New York, May 7, 1940.

| | | |
|---|---|---|
| WM-1147-1 | Honky Tonk Train Blues | OK 5582 |
| WM-1148-1 | Isle Of Capri | OK 5979 |
| WM-1149-1 | Martha | OK 5582 |
| WM-1150-1 | The Girl With The Light Blue Hair | OK 5979 |

ADRIAN ROLLINI AND HIS ORCHESTRA was the name used on Kismet K-722 for Bud Freeman
   and his Orchestra (CAN'T HELP LOVIN' DAT MAN) and Bix Beiderbecke and his Gang (OL'
   MAN RIVER), both q.v.

## ROY ROLLS AND HIS RED HEADS

Pseudonym on Australian Paramount 2524 for Willard Robison and his Orchestra, q.v.

## ROMANCE OF HARMONY ORCHESTRA

C/2cl-ss-as/cl-ts/p/bj/d.                Richmond, Ind., June 11, 1924.

| | | |
|---|---|---|
| 11919 | To-Ki-O-Ki-O | Gnt rejected |
| 11920 | Limehouse Blues | - |

   Walter H. Moehre-v.                   Richmond, Ind., June 30, 1924.

| | | |
|---|---|---|
| 11933 | Tok-okio (sic) | Rejected |
| 11934-A | Doodle Doo Doo | Gnt 20068 |
| 11935 | Blue Evening Blues | - |
| 11936 | Everybody Likes The Same Sweet Girl-vWHM | Rejected |

## PHIL ROMANO AND HIS ORCHESTRA

Willie Creager dir. Dick Landon-t/Charles Fach-tb/William Grossi-cl-ss/as/Phil Romano
   vn/Nick Goldman-p/Art Tepaldi-bj/bb/Jack Glazer-d/Billy Murray-v.
                                    New York, September 18, 1925.

| | | |
|---|---|---|
| 33393-4 | I'm Goin' Out If Lizzie Comes In - vBM | Vic 19803, HMV EA-12 |
| 33394-4 | Keep On Croonin' A Tune | -        - |

## MAMIE ROMER

Pseudonym on Oriole 325 for Nettie Potter, q.v.

## PETER ROMNEY'S DANCE BAND

Pseudonym on Peacock PS-232 for Oscar Rabin and his Romany Band, q.v.

## ROOF GARDEN ORCHESTRA

Pseudonym for the following items listed in this book :-

Odeon A-221055  That's My Mammy    (Dorsey Brothers' Orchestra)
      A-221055  Too Busy ! (Sam Lanin's Famous Players and Singers)
      A-221129  Shout Hallelujah ! 'Cause I'm Home (Ben Pollack and his Orchestra)
Parlophone R-102  Nebraska (Ronnie Munro and his Orchestra)
      R-159  Singapore Sorrows (Ronnie Munro and his Orchestra)
      R-178  Chilly-Pom-Pom-Pee (Fred Hall's Sugar Babies)
      R-300  Both sides by the Goofus Five and their Orchestra
      R-658  Both sides by Ben Selvin and his Orchestra
      R-661  Kicking A Hole In The Sky (Ipana Troubadours)
      R-743  I Love You So Much (Ben Selvin and his Orchestra)
      R-800  Dust (Ben Selvin and his Orchestra)
      R-910  I've Found What I Wanted In You (Phil Dannenberg and his Orchestra)
      R-944  If You Should Ever Need Me (Ben Selvin and his Orchestra)
      R-1175  Both sides by Spike Hughes and his Orchestra

Ronnie Munro-p dir. Frank Wilson-t/Lew Davis-tb/Buddy Featherstonhaugh-cl-as/Ben
Davis-ts-bar/Max Bacon-d/Eddie Kollis-v.
London, March 16, 1927.

4655-2  My Girl's Fine And Dandy - vEK          Imp 1727
NOTE:- Other titles issued under this name may be of equal interest.  See also the
Mimosa Dance Orchestra.

## CLARKSON  ROSE

"Clarkie" of British seaside pierrot-show fame was not himself a jazz performer, of
course, but the accompaniment to the following record is well within the scope of
this book.

Vocal, acc. by Sylvester Ahola-t/Danny Polo-cl/? Arthur Lally-as/Bert Read-p/Joe
Brannelly-bj/Billy Bell-bb.               Hayes, Middlesex, October 15, 1929.

Yy-17716-2  Don't Be So Unkind, Baby            Zon 5454

## DAVE  ROSE

HOTCHA TRIO (Bluebird B-5296, Electradisk 2167 and Sunrise S-3377); PRIMA-ROSE-GAST
(Bluebird B-5758 and Victor JR-23) : Louis Prima-t-v/Norman Gast-vn/Dave Rose-p.
Chicago, September 28, 1933.

77034-1  Chinatown, My Chinatown - vLP          BB B-5296, B-5758, Eld 2167,
                                                Sr S-3377, Vic JR-23, HMV X-4494
77035-1  Sophisticated Lady                     Rejected
77036-1  Dinah - vLP                            BB B-5296, B-5758, Eld 2167,
                                                Sr S-3377, Vic JR-25, HMV X-4494

DAVE ROSE AND HIS ORCHESTRA : Louis Prima-2 others-t/tb/2as/2ts/Norman Gast-another-
vn/Dave Rose-p/sb/d.                    Chicago, September 29, 1933.

77038-1  Shadows                                BB B-5708
77039-1  Jig-Saw Rhythm                         -
77040-1  Jamboree                               Rejected

## GEORGE ROSE  SOCIETY ORCHESTRA

Pseudonym on Australian Bon Marche 204 for Jack Pettis and his Band, q.v.

## VINCENT ROSE

This Californian bandleader and songwriter directed a number of sessions for Victor
in the 1920s and for the ARC combine in the 1930s; the following have points of
interest as jazz.

VINCENT ROSE AND HIS MONTMARTRE ORCHESTRA : Vincent Rose-p dir. Harry Owens-t/Buster
Johnson-tb/"Prof" Moore or Bobby "Buddy" Burns-cl-as-ts-v/Jackie Taylor-vn/Bob
Stowell-bj/Albert Jaeger-bb/J. M. van Cott-d.
Oakland, Calif., June 10, 1924.

PB-2-1  String Beans                            Vic 19379

Oakland, Calif., June 11, 1924.

PB-9-1  Helen Gone - vBB                        Vic 19398

Oakland, Calif., June 12, 1924.

PB-14-1  Sadie (You Are The Lady For Me) - vBB   Vic 19511

The ARC group of issues from 1930 to 1935 occasionally feature short solos of mild
interest, but hitherto no positive identification has been made.  The name of
VINCENT ROSE AND HIS ORCHESTRA was also used on Melotone M-13158,  Oriole 2989 and
Perfect 16001 for Benny Goodman and his Orchestra, q.v., and other leaders of the
same era were re-named in the same way.on the same labels.

At the turn of the 1920s and 1930s, this was considered to be one of the finest of all the bands appearing in London. Most of its Parlophone and Sterno records are of interest, the following being outstandingly so.

Arthur Rosebery-p dir. Doug Bastin-t-cl-as/Paul Fenoulhet-t-tb/Bob Wise-cl-as/Reg Pink-ts/Les Julian-vn/Jack Stephens-vn/Jim Risley-sb-bsx/Len Lee-d-v/v trio, probably comprising Bastin, Rosebery and Lee.

London, c. January 12, 1929.

| | | | | |
|---|---|---|---|---|
| E-2290-2 | My Southern Home - vLL | Par R-291, A-2739 | | |
| E-2291-2 | I'm Crazy Over You - vLL | - | Ar 4343 | |
| E-2292-1 | Blue Grass - vLL | Par R-277 | | |
| E-2293-2 | There's A Blue Ridge 'Round My Heart, Virginia - vLL | - | A-2719, Ar 4343 | |

NOTE:- Ariel 4343 as ARIEL DANCE ORCHESTRA.

London, c. February 28, 1929.

| | | | |
|---|---|---|---|
| E-2335-2 | If I Had You - v3 | Par R-302 | |
| E-2336-1 | Nobody's Fault But Your Own - vLL | - | A-2788 |
| E-2337-2 | Spread A Little Happiness - vLL | Par R-303, A-3016 | |
| E-2338-2 | I'm A One-Man Girl | - | - |

London, c. April 10, 1929.

| | | | |
|---|---|---|---|
| E-2393-1 | That's What I Call Sweet Music - vLL | Par R-349, A-2788 | |
| E-2394-2 | Mia Bella Rosa - v3 | - | |
| E-2395-2 | Looking At You - vLL | Par R-344, A-2894 | |
| E-2396-1 | What Is This Thing Called Love ? - vLL | - | - |
| E-2397-1 | Let's Do It - vLL | Par E-6150 | |

NOTE:- Parlophone E-6150 as WILL PERRY'S ORCHESTRA.

London, c. June 6, 1929.

| | | |
|---|---|---|
| E-2507-1 | Broadway Melody - v3 | Par R-383, 22521, A-2870 |
| E-2508-2 | I'll Never Ask For More | Par R-384, A-2827 |
| E-2509-2 | You Were Meant For Me - v3 | Par R-383 |
| E-2510-2 | Do Something - vLL | Par R-384, A-2831 |

London, c. June 13, 1929.

| | | | |
|---|---|---|---|
| E-2540-1 | Breakaway - v3 | Par R-390 | |
| E-2541-2 | Big City Blues | - | A-2871 |
| E-2542-2 | When Summer Is Gone - v3 | Par R-389 | - |

FLORIDA CLUB (DANCE) BAND : Same.      London, c. July, 1929.

| | | |
|---|---|---|
| S-191 | When I Met Connie In The Cornfield - v | Sterno 205 |
| S-192 | Oh ! Maggie - v | - |

London, c. August, 1929.

| | | |
|---|---|---|
| S-207 | Why Can't You ? - v | Sterno 218 |

ARTHUR ROSEBERY AND HIS DANCE BAND : Same.London, c. February 19, 1930.

| | | |
|---|---|---|
| E-3078-2 | Sitting On The Cold Wet Grass - vLL | Par R-593, Ar 4517 |

NOTE:- Ariel 4517 as ARIEL DANCE ORCHESTRA.

Arthur Rosebery-p dir. Ben Collins (and another ?)-t/? tb/Bill Rogers-cl-as/Len Lee or Lees-as-vn/Buddy Featherstonhaugh-ts/Geoff Howard-Cyril Hellier-vn/Sonny Farrar-bj/Jim Risley-sb/Lou Stevenson-d/Len Miller-v. (Note:- At the time of this session, Howard, Hellier and Farrar were members of Jack Hylton's band, yet they are always quoted as being with Arthur Rosebery. Their presence here is thus suspect).

London, September, 1930.

| | | |
|---|---|---|
| E-3600-2 | My Future Just Passed - vLM | Par R-746 |
| E-3601-1 | The Pick-Up - vLM | - |

Pseudonym for the following items listed in this book :-

Ajax 17119  Where's My Sweetie Hiding ? (Sam Lanin and his Orchestra)
Banner 1386  You'll Never Get To Heaven With Those Eyes (Sam Lanin and his Orchestra)
     6129  There's A Rickety Rackety Shack (Fletcher Henderson and his Orchestra)
     6154  Sorry (Fletcher Henderson and his Orchestra) (also Apex 8716)
Domino 3441  Araby (Fletcher Henderson and his Orchestra)
     3445  I'll See You In My Dreams (Fletcher Henderson and his Orchestra)
Imperial 1253  Aunt Haggar Blues (sic) (Lanin's Southern Serenaders)
Regal 9489  Louisville Lou (Sam Lanin and his Orchestra)

## BABY ROSE MARIE

See BABY Rose Marie.

## TIMME ROSENKRANTZ AND HIS BARRELHOUSE BARONS

Rex Stewart-c/Billy Hicks-t/Tyree Glenn-tb-vib/Rudy Williams-Russell Procope-as/Don
   Byas-ts/Billy Kyle-p/Brick Fleagle-g/Walter Page-sb/Joe Jones-d/Leo Mathiesen-a/
   Inez Cavanaugh-v.                         New York, May 27, 1938.

| | | |
|---|---|---|
| 023502-1 | A Wee Bit Of Swing | Vic 25876, HMV X-6118 |
| 023503-1 | Is This To Be My Souvenir ? - vIC | - | - |
| 023504-1 | When Day Is Done - vIC | Vic 25883, HMV X-6175 |
| 023505-1 | The Song Is Ended | - | - |

## HARRY ROSENTHAL AND HIS ORCHESTRA

Red Ballard-Jack Lacey-tb/Benny Goodman-cl/Toots Mondello-Hymie Schertzer-as/Arthur
   Rollini-Dick Clark-ts/pac/? 2vn/Fulton McGrath-p/harp/George van Eps-g/Harry Good-
   man-sb/Sammy Weiss-d/Peter Cantor-v.      New York, November 14, 1934.

| | | |
|---|---|---|
| CO-16316-1 | Say When - vPC | Col 2982-D |
| CO-16317-1 | When Love Comes Swingin' Along - vPC | - |

Probably as above; Helen Ward-v.          New York, November 20, 1934.

| | | |
|---|---|---|
| CO-16347-1 | You're The Top - vHW | Col 2986-D, RZ MR-1733, G-22612 |
| CO-16348-1 | All Through The Night - vHW | - | - | - |

NOTE:- Regal Zonophone MR-1733 as THE BROADWAY BANDITS.

## ROSE ROOM ORCHESTRA

This was a conventional New York dance band of the late 1920s under the direction of
   Tommy Gott-t, who can be heard contributing occasional short solos to the titles
   recorded for the Banner group of labels in 1928 and 1929.

## VAL ROSING AND HIS SWING STARS

P/g/stg/sb/Val Rosing-v.                    London, November 18, 1935.

| | | |
|---|---|---|
| CA-15456-1 | Avalon | Col FB-1719 |
| CA-15457-1 | Shine | Col FB-1236 |
| CA-15458-1 | My Honey's Lovin' Arms | Col FB-1719 |
| CA-15459-1 | Whispering | Col FB-1236 |

T/Tb/ts/vn/p/g/sb/Val Rosing-v.            London, January 25, 1936.

| | | |
|---|---|---|
| CAR-3889-1 | I Can't Give You Anything But Love | RZ MR-2186, Gloria GZ-3135 |
| CAR-3890-1 | I'll See You In My Dreams | - | - |

London, January 29, 1937.

| | | |
|---|---|---|
| CA-16171-1 | Gone | Col FB-1637 |
| CA-16172-1 | When Is A Kiss Not A Kiss ? | Col FB-1647 |
| CA-16173-1 | It's Still Being Done | - |
| CA-16174-2 | In Your Own Quiet Way | Col FB-1637 |

Pseudonym on Harmony and associated labels for the following items listed in this
    book :-

793-H  A Room With A View (Frank Guarente and his Orchestra)
1085-H Try Dancing (California Ramblers)

The following side was originally entered in the CBS files as by the Harmonians, a
    name usually indicating a Ben Selvin group; the next titles to it, on the same day
    and with the same vocalist, are credited to the Golden Gate Orchestra, which on
    most labels (including Harmony) is a pseudonym for the California Ramblers.  All
    have been altered to Arthur Ross's Westerners, which also covers Sam Lanin and his
    Orchestra !  This side is reported as featuring an excellent trombonist and Irving
    Kaufman (as JIM ANDREWS)-v.            New York, August 30, 1923.

146932-2  Take Your Tomorrow (And Give Me Today)    Har 723-H
              - vIK

## DOLLY ROSS

Vocal, acc. by Porter Grainger-p.         New York, c. March 21, 1927.

E-22038    He Don't Know (And I Can't Make Him       Br 7005, Voc 1166
               Understand)

    As/chimes added.                       New York, c. March 22, 1927.

E-22064    Hootin' Owl Blues                          Br 7005, Voc 1166

## LOUISE  ROSS

Vocal, acc. by Herbert Leonard-h/Dick Mitchell-p.
                                    New York, December 16, 1925.

141395-2  No Home Blues                        Col 14118-D
141396-2  Can't Fool Me Blues                      -

## OLLIE ROSS

Girl vocalist, acc. by Don Albert-t/John Henry Braggs-g/Charlie Dixon-bb.
                                    Dallas, c. October 25, 1928.

DAL-704-A  Broad Road Blues                    Br 7045
DAL-705-A-B  Ox Meat Blues                        -

## ROSS DE LUXE SYNCOPATORS

Alonzo Ross-p-v dir. Robert "Cookie" Mason-t-v/Melvin Herbert-t/Eddie Cooper-tb/
    Edmond Hall-cl-as-bar/Robert Cloud-as/Earl Evans-ts-v/Casper Tower (also spelt
    Casker Towie)-bj-v/Richard Fullbright-bb/Frank Houston-d-v/Margaret Miller-v.
                                    Savannah, August 22, 1927.

39823-2   Skad-O-Lee - vMM                     Vic 20961
39824-2   Don't You Wanna Know ? - vMM         Vic 21537
39825-1-2  Mary Bell - vCT                     Vic 20952
39825-3-4  Mary Bell                              -
39826-2   Monia - vRM                          Vic 21077
39827-2   Florida Rhythm - vFH                 Vic 20961
39828-3   Believe Me, Dear                     Vic 21537
39829-3   Lady Mine                            Vic 20952
39830-3   Baby, Stop Teasin' Me - vEE-AR       Vic 21077

## HUBERT  ROSTAING

HUBERT ROSTAING-AIME BARELLI ET LEUR ORCHESTRE : Aime Barelli-Christian Bellest-t/
    Alix Combelle-ts/Hubert Rostaing-ts-a/Raymond Wraskoff-p/Django Reinhardt-g/Francis
    Lucas-sb/Pierre Fouad-d.                Paris, October 22, 1940.

OSW-143-1  Indecision                         Swing 87
OSW-144-1  Oui, c'est ça                          -

HUBERT ROSTAING ET SON ORCHESTRE : Aime Barelli-t/Hubert Rostaing-cl-as/Noel Chiboust
   ts/Paul Collot or Robert Castella-p/Eugene Vees-g/Emmanuel Soudieux-sb/Django Rein-
   hardt-solo sb, bowed/Andre Jourdan-d.   Paris, March 31, 1942.

OSW-261-2  Seconde Idee d'Eddie                  Swing 151

Other records under the nominal direction of this well-known French reedman contain
   no  internationally famous names.

## ALMA ROTTER

See Alma Henderson.

## THE ROUNDERS

As a rule, this name indicates a Harry Reser band (q.v.), but while the following are
   apparently Reser recordings, they are probably not by his regular personnel.

2t/tb/2cl-as/ts/p/? Harry Reser-bj/bb/d/Smith Ballew-v.
                            New York, November 26, 1928.

8362-3  Where The Shy Little Violets Grow - vSB   Ban 6237, Cq 7216, Dom 4246,
NOTE:- Banner 6237 as CAMPUS BOYS; Oriole 1422   31023,Or 1422, Re 8658, Apex 8872,
as UNIVERSITY BOYS; Domino 31023 as THE RED      LS 24375, Mic 22375, St 10420
DANDIES.

                            New York, June 5, 1929.

8796-3  The Rainbow Man - vSB                    Ban 6424, Dom 4355, Or 1606,
NOTE:- Banner 6424 as CAMPUS BOYS; Oriole 1606   Re 8801, Apex 8972, Cr 81109,
as UNIVERSITY BOYS; Crown 81109 as PIERROT       Imp 2100, Arc 2022, Emb 8019,
SYNCOPATORS; Arcadia 2022 as SOUTHERN DIXIE      Sav 1028
SYNCOPATORS; Savoy 1028 as SAVOY MARIMBA BOYS ORCHESTRA (!)

## ROVERS  DANCE BAND

Pseudonym on Guardsman for the following items listed in this book :-

2081  Song Of The Wanderer (Johnny Sylvester and his Orchestra)
2110  Yes She Do - No She Don't (The Vagabonds)

## ROXY CLUB  ORCHESTRA

Pseudonym on Embassy E-149 for the Casa Loma Orchestra, q.v.

## DICK ROY AND  HIS BAND

This is probably a pseudonym for some British bandleader of the period, or simply a
made-up name for a group of sidemen from various British bands.

2t/tb/2as/ts/p/g/sb/d.                 London, c. October, 1934.

5816   Ring Dem Bells                     Emp E-187

## HARRY  ROY

The following are titles of outstanding interest as jazz or "hot" dance music made by
bands under the direction of one of Britain's most popular leaders in the 1930s.

HARRY ROY AND HIS ORCHESTRA (FROM THE CAFE ANGLAIS) : Harry Roy-cl-as-ts-v dir  Stan
   Bowsher-t-a/Bert Wilton-Tom Porter-t/Jack Collins-tb/Nat Temple-cl-as/Joe Arbiter-
   Harry Goss-cl-ts-bar/Maurice Sterndale-vn/Ivor Moreton-Dave Kaye-p/Tommy Venn-g/
   Arthur Calkin-sb/Joe Daniels-d/Bill Currie-d-v/George Scott Wood-a.
                            London, April 21, 1933.

CE-6037-1  Tiger Rag                      Par R-1505, A-3904, Od A-221586,
                                          011915, Dec 1037

HARRY ROY AND HIS ORCHESTRA (FROM THE CAFE ANGLAIS) : Harry Roy-cl-as-ts-v dir. Stan
    Bowsher-t-a/Bert Wilton-Tom Porter-t/Jack Collins-tb/Nat Temple-cl-as/Joe Arbiter-
    Harry Goss-cl-ts-bar/Maurice Sterndale-vn/Ivor Moreton-Dave Kaye-p/Tommy Venn-g/
    Arthur Calkin-sb/Joe Daniels-d/Bill Currie-d-v/George Scott Wood-a.
                                        London, May 17, 1933.

CE-6073-1  Bugle Call Rag                      Par R-1526, R-1734, A-3715,
                                               Od A-221591, 025020


HARRY ROY AND HIS ORCHESTRA FROM THE MAYFAIR HOTEL, LONDON : Same.
                                        London, November 7, 1933.

CE-6274-1  Black Panther                       Par R-1677, A-3796, B-49717,
                                               Od 011960


                                        London, July 24, 1934.

CE-6586-1  The Roy Rag (Harry Roy)             Par R-1896, A-6021, Od A-221800,
                                               025506, Dec 942


    Dick Boothroyd-tb added.            London, October 31, 1934.

CE-6696-1  When A St. Louis Woman Comes Down To  Par R-1969, A-6074, Od A-221832,
               New Orleans - vHR                 025515


                                        London, January 4, 1935.

CE-6778-1  Temptation Rag (Henry Lodge)        Par F-102, A-6398, Od A-221866,
                                               D-6948, 025393, Dec 1151, 3531


THE BUGLE CALL RAGGERS : Same.          London, March 8, 1935.

TB-1739-2  No Words - Nor Anything             Dec F-5479, Br A-81148
TB-1742-1  Temptation Rag (Henry Lodge)         -             -


HARRY ROY AND HIS ORCHESTRA FROM THE MAYFAIR HOTEL, LONDON : Same.
                                        London, May 4, 1935.

CE-6958-1  Jubilation Rag (Stan Bowsher)       Par F-158, A-6177, Od A-221936,
                                               025518, Dec 1241


                                        London, July 3, 1935.

CE-7047-1  The Dixieland Band - vHR            Par F-188, Od A-221969, A-272028


                                        London, July 11, 1935.

CE-7083-1  Red Pepper (A Spicy Rag) (Henry Lodge) Par F-302, Od 025491, OF-5040,
                                               Dec 844


                                        London, November 8, 1935.

CE-7266-1  The Man From Harlem - vHR           Par F-441, A-6488, Od 025751
CE-7267-1  Margie                              Par F-483, A-6489, Od OF-5186
CE-7268-1  Doin' The New Low-Down - vHR        Par F-441
CE-7269-1  Avalon - vHR-BC                     Par F-483, A-6489, Od 031067,
                                               OF-5186


    Stanley Black-Norman Yarlett (White)-p replace Moreton and Kaye.
                                        London, January 31, 1936.

CE-7436-1  Porcupine Rag (Charles L. Johnson)  Par F-388, A-6398, Od 031005,
                                               OF-5101, Dec 1043


HARRY ROY'S TIGER-RAGAMUFFINS : Harry Roy-cl-v-dir. Stanley Black-Norman White-p/
    Arthur Calkin-sb/Joe Daniels-d.    London, April 15, 1936.

CE-7578-1  Jazz Me Blues - vHR                 Par F-458, A-6469, Od 031056,
                                               Dec 1095
CE-7579-1  Cheerful Blues                      As above

HARRY ROY AND HIS ORCHESTRA : Harry Roy-cl-as-ts-v dir. Stan Bowsher-Bert Wilton-Tom
  Porter-t/Jack Collins-Dick Boothroyd-tb/Nat Temple-cl-as/Joe Arbiter-Harry Goss-cl-
  ts-bar/Maurice Sterndale-vn/Stanley Black-Norman White-p/Tommy Venn-g/Arthur Calkin
  sb/Joe Daniels-d.                    London, May 5, 1936.

CE-7614-1  Dill Pickles Rag (Charles L. Johnson)  Par F-460, A-6490, Od 031055,
                                                   Dec 1088

HARRY ROY'S TIGER-RAGAMUFFINS : Harry Roy-cl-v dir. Stanley Black-Norman White-p/
  Arthur Calkin-sb/Joe Daniels-d.      London, June 9, 1936.

CE-7673-1  That's A Plenty                    Par F-484, A-6516, Od 031086,
                                              OF-5187
CE-7674-1  Someday, Sweetheart - vHR          As above

                              London, July 6, 1936.

CE-7723-1  Sweet Georgia Brown - vHR          Par F-522, A-6538, Od OF-5224
CE-7724-1  Wabash Blues                        -      -      -

                              London, October 8, 1936.

CE-7874-1  I've Found A New Baby - vHR         Par F-589, A-6593, Od 031104,
                                               OF-5288, Dec 2752
CE-7875-1  I Left My Sugar Standing In The Rain  As above except Par A-6593
           - vHR

                              London, December 3, 1936.

CE-7966-1  I'm A Ding Dong Daddy - vHR         Par F-624, A-6619, Od 031126,
                                               OF-5323
CE-7967-1  Hot Lips - vHR                      As above except Par A-6619

                              London, January 13, 1937.

CE-8021-1  From Monday On - vHR                Par F-668, A-6650, Od 031141,
                                               OF-5356, Dec 1295
CE-8022-1  She's Funny That Way - vHR          As above except Par A-6650

HARRY ROY AND HIS ORCHESTRA : As for May 5, 1936 above, plus Abe Romaine-cl-ts-bar,
  but Alf Horton-t replaces Bowsher; Len Harrison-sb replaces Calkin; Ray Ellington-
  d replaces Daniels.                  London, March 9, 1937.

CE-8086-1  Limehouse Blues                     Par F-1132, A-7314, Od 031156,
                                               Dec 2339
CE-8087-1  Memphis Blues                       Par F-1110, A-6975  - Dec 2339

HARRY ROY'S TIGER-RAGAMUFFINS : Harry Roy-cl dir. Stanley Black-Norman White-p/Len
  Harrison-sb/Ray Ellington-d-v.       London, April 21, 1937.

CE-8285-1  Roy Club Rag (Harry Roy)           Par F-788, A-6696, Od 031161,
                                              OF-5425
CE-8286-1  Fate (It Was Fate When I First Met You)Par F-837, A-6756, Od 031162,
                                              OF-5466
CE-8287-1  'Way Down Yonder In New Orleans    As above
CE-8288-1  Harlem - vRE                        Par F-788, A-6696, Od 031161,
                                               OF-5425

HARRY ROY AND HIS ORCHESTRA : As for March 9, 1937.
                              London, May 11, 1937.

CE-8356-1  Clarinet Marmalade                 Par F-1133, A-7314, Od 031230,
                                              Dec 2169

                              London, May 27, 1937.

CE-8375-1  Milenberg Joys                     Par F-1109, A-6958, Od 031230,
                                              Dec 2086

HARRY ROY'S TIGER-RAGAMUFFINS : Harry Roy-cl dir. Stanley Black-Norman White-p/Len
   Harrison-sb/Ray Ellington-d-v.            London, October 12, 1937.

CE-8652-1  Sailin' On The Robert E. Lee - vRE      Par F-910, A-6800, Od 031238,
                                                   OF-5525
CE-8653-1  Ragtime Cowboy Joe                      As above
CE-8654-1  You Made Me Love You                    Par F-936, A-6826, Od 031266,
                                                   031343, OF-5546
CE-8655-1  Where Did Robinson Crusoe Go (With      Par F-936,  -           -
           Friday On Saturday Night)

HARRY ROY AND HIS ORCHESTRA : Harry Roy-cl-as-ts-v dir. Tom Porter-Alf Horton-Bert
   Wilton-t/Jack Collins-Dick Boothroyd-tb/Nat Temple-cl-as/Harry Goss-Joe Arbiter-
   Abe Romaine-cl-ts-bar/Maurice Sterndale-vn/Stanley Black-Norman White-p/Tommy Venn
   g/Len Harrison-sb/Ray Ellington-d/Sid Phillips-a.
                                        London, November 10, 1937.

CE-8728-1  Dinner Music For A Pack Of Hungry       Par F-974, A-6834, Od 031267,
           Cannibals                               OF-5565, Dec 1685
CE-8729-1  Caravan                                 Par F-974, Od 031267, OF-5565

                            London, November 25, 1937.

CE-8744-1  Comin' Thro' The Rye - aSP              Par F-974, A-6842, Od 031278,
                                                   OF-5572
CE-8745-1  There Is A Tavern In The Town - aSP     As above

HARRY ROY'S TIGER-RAGAMUFFINS : As for October 12, 1937 above.
                            London, November 28, 1937.

CE-8762-1  Ida, Sweet As Apple Cider - vHR         Par F-1002, A-6849, Od OF-5594
CE-8763-1  Sonny Boy - vHR-RE                       -           -

HARRY ROY AND HIS ORCHESTRA : As for November 10, 1937 above.
                            London, December 14, 1937.

CE-8806-1  Down Home Rag (Wilbur Sweatman)         Par F-1132, A-7323, Od 031156,
                                                   Dec 2619
CE-8807-1  Willie The Weeper                        Par F-1132, A-6975, Dec 2169
CE-8808-1  San Sue Strut                           Par F-1158, A-6982, Od OF-5734,
                                                   Dec 2501

                            London, December 16, 1937.

CE-8811-1  Maple Leaf Rag (Scott Joplin)           Par F-1133, A-6951, Dec 2240
CE-8812-1  Spanish Shawl                           Par F-1159, A-6981, - Od OF-5735
CE-8813-1  Li'l Liza Jane - vHR                     -           -        -
CE-8814-1  Sugar Foot Stomp                        Par F-1109, A-6958, Dec 2752
CE-8815-1  King Porter Stomp                       Par F-1158, A-6982, Od OF-5734,
                                                   Dec 2619

                            London, December 17, 1937.

CE-8816-1  Home Again Blues                        Par F-1007, A-7323, Od 031376,
                                                   OF-5598, Dec 2086

HARRY ROY'S TIGER-RAGAMUFFINS : As above. London, February 25, 1938.

CE-8972-1  Sarawaki - vHR                          Par F-1178, A-6991, Od OF-5750
CE-8973-1  Ragging The A.C.E.                       -           -        -

HARRY ROY AND HIS ORCHESTRA : As above.  London, April 5, 1938.

CE-9045-1  No Name Rag                             Par F-1083, A-6951, Od 031362

Subsequent records of the Orchestra and the Tiger-Ragamuffins are of little or no
   interest as jazz.

The following sides by this band are known to be of interest, and there may be some
    others comparable to them (see also the Crichton Lyricals).

Sid Roy-p dir. Stan Gosling and/or Ernest Broadhurst-t/Basil Green-tb/Harry Roy-cl-
    as/H. Lyons-as/John Swinfen-ts/Tommy Venn-bj/Eddie Kollis-d-v.
                                            London, June 1, 1928.

    4860-2  Sunny Skies - vEK                    Imp 1907
    4861-2  Stay Out Of The South - vEK          Imp 1906
    4862-2  I Can't Give You Anything But Love - vEK    -
    4863-2  How Long Has This Been Goin' On ? - vEK  Imp 1907


                                            London, July 6, 1928.

    4909-2  My Pet - vEK                          Imp 1921

## ROYAL AIR FORCE  DANCE ORCHESTRA

Although this famous unit was organized primarily as a dance band, it included in
    its ranks some of the finest jazz talent in England at the time, and this was
    given some scope on the titles listed below. Among the remainder of the numbers
    recorded there may well be other examples offering short "hot" solos.

Jimmy Miller-v dir. Tommy McQuater-Archie Craig-t/George Chisholm-Eric Breeze-tb/
    Andy McDevitt-Jimmy Durrant-cl-as/Tom Bradbury-Harry Lewis-cl-ts/Ronnie Aldrich-p-
    a/Sid Colin-g-v/Arthur Maden-sb/Jock Cummings-d, "by permission of the Air
    Council."                                London, January 10, 1941.

    DR-5234-1  All Of Me                         Dec F-7782
    DR-5235-1  Indiana                               -
    DR-5236-1  Beat Me Daddy (Eight To A Bar) - vSC    Dec F-7720
    DR-5237-1  The Nearness Of You - vJM             -


                                            London, May 20, 1941.

    DR-5766-1  Amapola - vJM                     Dec F-7880

                                            London, June 10, 1941.

    DR-5844-1  That's A Plenty                   Dec F-8127
    DR-5845-1  'Way Down Yonder In New Orleans       -

                                            London, August 2, 1941.

    DR-6087-1-2  The Darktown Strutters' Ball        Rejected
    DR-6088-1  Drummin' Man                      Dec F-7968

                                            London, September 13, 1941.

    DR-6087-3  The Darktown Strutters' Ball      Dec F-7968

                                            London, February 11, 1942.

    DR-6682-2  Ringle Dingle                     Dec F-8142

                                            London, March 13, 1942.

    DR-6733-2  I've Found A New Baby             Dec F-8180
    DR-6734-1-2  The Blue Room                   Rejected

                                            London, May 21, 1942.

    DR-6836-2  South Rampart Street Parade       Dec F-8142
    DR-6837-2  Oh, You Beautiful Doll            Dec F-8180

## ROYAL AUTOMOBILE CLUB DANCE BAND

Ebenézer Slydel dir. unknown group possibly including John Montague and Marcus
    Sanders; no other details known.     London, c. July 11, 1927.

    10965-1  St. Louis Shuffle                   EBW 4695
Other titles by this band are not known to be of interest as jazz.

Jimmy Prince-p/Billy Moore-g-v/Slam Stewart-sb-v.
                                          New York, October 23, 1939.

66465-A  In A Shanty In Old Shanty Town          Dec 2830, F-7804
66466-   Blue Skies                              Dec 7759
66467-A-B  Beat It Out, Bumpin' Boy              Dec 2830, F-7804
66468-   Peace, Brother, Peace                   Dec 7759

## MARJORIE ROYCE

Vocal, acc. by t/tb/as/vn/p/bj/bb.       New York, February 28, 1924.

72362-A  My Daddy's Growin' Old                  OK 40094

Acc. by p.                               New York, March, 1924.

72420-B  How Come You Do Me Like You Do ?        OK 40094

## LAURA RUCKER

Vocal, acc. by Cassino Simpson-p.        Grafton, Wis., c. March, 1931.

L-817-1  Little Joe                              Pm 13075, SD 103
L-818-2  St. Louis Blues                              —      SD 102

Vocal duet with George Ramsey (? Thomas A. Dorsey)-p/g.
                                          Grafton, Wis., c. March, 1931.

L-823-2  I'm The Lonesome One                    Pm 13030, Bwy 5097, Cr 3224
   NOTE:- Broadway 5097 and Crown 3224 as HARUM SCARUMS.  Paramount 13030 also exists
   using matrix L-610, by Bob (Rob) Robinson, q.v., and Meade Lux Lewis.

Vocal, acc. by Blind Blake-g.            Grafton, Wis., c. May, 1931.

L-909-1  Fancy Tricks                            Pm 13138

Acc. by her Three Bits of Rhythm : P/g/sb.
                                          Chicago, September 14, 1935.

C-1105-A-B  I'm Gonna Sit Right Down And Write   Voc rejected
            Myself A Letter
C-1106-A-B  Something's Wrong                          —

Acc. by her Swing Boys : Franz Jackson-ts/own p/Hurley Ramey-g/Bill Oldham-sb.
                                          Chicago, November 23, 1936.

90992-A  Something's Wrong                       Dec 7260
90993-A  Swing My Rhythm                              —

## CONNIE RUSSELL

Vocal, acc. by t/tb/cl-ts/p/g/sb/d-x.    London, October 14, 1936.

OEA-3874-1  Organ Grinder's Swing                HMV BD-383
OEA-3875-1  Sing Me A Swing Song                      —

## LUIS RUSSELL

RUSSELL'S HOT SIX : George Mitchell-c/Kid Ory-tb/Albert Nicholas-cl-ss-as/Barney
   Bigard-ts/Luis Russell-p/Johnny St. Cyr-bj/Richard M. Jones-speech.*
                                          Chicago, March 10, 1926.

C-2620/1  29th And Dearborn                      Voc 1010, V-1015, Or 1003,
                                                 Br A-182, A-81003, Bm 1027
C-2622/3  *Sweet Mumtaz                          As above

LUIS RUSSELL'S HEEBIE JEEBIE STOMPERS : Bob Shoffner-c/Preston Jackson-tb/Darnell
Howard-cl-as/Barney Bigard-ts/Luis Russell-p/Johnny St. Cyr-bj.
                                            Chicago, November 17, 1926.

| | | |
|---|---|---|
| 9903-A | Plantation Joys | OK 8424 |
| 9904-A | Please Don't Turn Me Down | - |
| 9905-A | Sweet Mumtaz | OK 8454 |
| 9906-A | Dolly Mine | -     HJCA HC-117 |

LUIS RUSSELL AND HIS BURNING EIGHT : Luis Russell-p dir. Louis Metcalf-t/J. C.
Higginbotham-tb/Charlie Holmes-cl-as/Teddy Hill-ts/Will Johnson-bj-g/William
"Bass" Moore-bb/Paul Barbarin-d/Walter Pichon-v.
                                            New York, January 15, 1929.

401532-A  Savoy Shout                      OK 8760, Par R-2523, Od A-272280,
                                            028245
401533-A-B  The Call Of The Freaks         OK 8656
401534-A  It's Tight Like That - vWP              -    Par R-2186

LUIS RUSSELL AND HIS ORCHESTRA : Luis Russell-p dir. Henry Allen-Bill Coleman-t/
J. C. Higginbotham-tb-v/Albert Nicholas-cl-as/Charlie Holmes-ss-as/Teddy Hill-ts/
Will Johnson-bj-g/Pops Foster-sb/Paul Barbarin-d-vib/v trio (Henry Allen-J. C.
Higginbotham-Louis Metcalf).           New York, September 6, 1929.

402938-C  The New Call Of The Freaks - v3  OK 8734, Col 35960, DO-2229,
                                            Par R-1645, Od A-286079, B-35635
402939-C  Feelin' The Spirit (Savoy Stomp*)-vJCH  OK 8766, Voc 3480*, Par R-1882,
                                            A-3992, B-27607, TT-9064,
                                            Od A-2322, HJCA HC-103
402940-B  Jersey Lightning                 OK 8734, Col 35960, DO-2229,
                                            Par R-740, Od A-286020, B-35628,
                                            028397

LOU AND HIS GINGER SNAPS : As above.    New York, September 13, 1929.

9006-1  Broadway Rhythm                     Ban 6536, Cam 9319, Je 5730,
                                            Lin 3343, Or 1728, Ro 1107,
                                            Ristic 15
9007-1-2  The Way He Loves Is Just Too Bad  Ban 6540, Cam 9320, Je 5729,
NOTE:- Jewel 5729, 5730, Oriole 1726 and 1728   Lin 3344, Or 1726, Ro 1108,
as DIXIE JAZZ BAND.                         Ristic 15 (using 9007-1)

LUIS RUSSELL AND HIS ORCHESTRA : As for September 6, 1929, but Otis Johnson-t replaces Coleman.                        New York, December 17, 1929.

403524-C  Doctor Blues                      OK 8766, Voc 3480, Par R-1273,
                                            A-3688, Od A-286066, B-35635,
                                            028245, HJCA HC-103

                                    New York, January 24, 1930.

403680-A  Saratoga Shout                    OK 8780, Par R-2225
403682-C  Song Of The Swanee                      -    Par R-1669, Od A-286080,
                                            B-35622, OR-1669
NOTE:- Matrix 403681 is by the same band, accompanied by three violins and Louis
Armstrong-t-v, under whose name it will be found in this book.

Jesse Cryor-Andy Razaf-v.               New York, May 29, 1930.

404047-A  Louisiana Swing                   OK 8811, Par R-795, Od A-2322,
                                            A-286024, B-35638
404047-C  Louisiana Swing                   OK 8811
404048-C  Poor Li'l Me - vJC                OK 8830, Par R-2212
404049-A  On Revival Day - vAR              OK 8811
404049-B  On Revival Day - vAR                    -    Par R-2186
404049-C  On Revival Day - vAR              Col KG-32338

LUIS RUSSELL AND HIS ORCHESTRA : Luis Russell-p dir. Henry Allen-Otis Johnson-t/
  J. C. Higginbotham-tb/Albert Nicholas-cl-ss-as/Charlie Holmes-ss-as/Greely Walton-
  ts/Will Johnson-bj-g/Pops Foster-sb/Paul Barbarin-d-vib/David Bee-a.
                                New York, September 5, 1930.

| | | |
|---|---|---|
| 404428-B | Muggin' Lightly | OK 8830, Par R-934, Od A-286037, 028397 |
| 404429-A | Panama | OK 8849, Par R-963, Od A-286039, B-35622, HJCA HC-117 |
| 404430-B | High Tension - aDB | OK 8849, Par R-1064, CO-148, Od A-286050 |

  Dick Robertson-v.                    New York, October 24, 1930.

| | | |
|---|---|---|
| E-34924- | You're Lucky To Me - vDR | Rejected |
| E-35025- | I Got Rhythm | Mt M-12000 |
| E-35026- | Memories Of You - vDR | Rejected |

  3rd t/Vic Dickenson-v  added.        New York, December 17, 1930.

| | | |
|---|---|---|
| E-35758-C | Saratoga Drag | Voc 1579, Br 80038,02508,A-500323 |
| E-35759-C | Case On Dawn (correct title EASE ON DOWN) | -           -  02002,A-9734 - |
| E-35760- | Honey, That Reminds Me - vVD | Br 6046, A-9365 |

NOTE:- Brunswick 6046 as THE SAVANNAH SYNCOPATORS.

Luis Russell-p dir. Henry Allen-t-v/Robert Cheek-Gus Aiken-t/Dicky Wells-tb/Albert
Nicholas-cl-as/Henry Jones-as/Greely Walton-ts/Will Johnson-g/Pops Foster-sb/Paul
Barbarin-d-vib/Chick Bullock-v.        New York, August 28, 1931.

| | | |
|---|---|---|
| 70195-1 | You Rascal You - vHA | Vic 22793, HMV B-4881 |
| 70196-1 | Goin' To Town - vCB | Vic 22789, BB B-7367, HMV B-4907, K-6439 |
| 70197-1 | Say The Word - vCB | Vic 22789, HMV K-6439 |
| 70198-1 | Freakish Blues | Vic 22815, HMV B-4897, EA-3040 |

NOTE:- Bluebird B-7367 as THE SOUTHERN SERENADERS; so is the reverse, but this is
by a totally different band of no interest as jazz.

Luis Russell-p dir. Leonard Davis-Gus Aiken-t/Rex Stewart-c/Nathaniel Story-Jimmy
Archey-tb/Henry Jones-Charlie Holmes-cl-as/Bingie Madison-Greely Walton-cl-ts/Lee
Blair-g/Pops Foster-sb/Paul Barbarin-d-vib/Sonny Woods-The Palmer Brothers-v.
                                New York, August 8, 1934.

| | | |
|---|---|---|
| 15571-1 | At The Darktown Strutters' Ball - vSW | Ban 33179, Mt M-13146, Or 2981, Per 15995, Ro 2355, Voc C-0009, Imp 6056 |
| 15572-1 | My Blue Heaven - vSW | Ban 33399, Mt M-13366, Or 3125, Per 16103, Ro 2499, Voc C-0009, Imp 6056, 18019 |
| 15573-1 | Ghost Of The Freaks - vPB | Ban 33367, Mt M-13334, Or 3104, Per 16086, Ro 2478, Voc S-2, Imp 6004, 17042, 17500 |
| 15574-1 | Hokus Pokus | As above, but Imp 6040, 17042 only |
| 15575-1 | Primitive | Ban 33399, Mt M-13366, Or 3125, Per 16103, Ro 2499, Voc S-13, Imp 6040, 18006 |
| 15576-1 | Ol' Man River - vSW | Ban 33179, Mt M-13146, Or 2981, Per 15995, Ro 2355, Voc S-13, Imp 6004, 18006 |

## PEE WEE RUSSELL'S RHYTHMAKERS

Max Kaminsky-t/Dicky Wells-tb/Pee Wee Russell-cl/Al Gold-ts/James P. Johnson-p/Freddy
Green-g/Wellman Braud-sb/Zutty Singleton-d-v; PEE WEE, ZUTTY AND JAMES P. (sic)*;
Melodisc 1144 as JAMES P. JOHNSON TRIO. New York, August 31, 1938.

| | | |
|---|---|---|
| 23391-1 | Baby, Won't You Please Come Home ? | HRS 1000, Md 1137 |
| 23391-2 | Baby, Won't You Please Come Home ? | HRS 17 |
| 23392-1 | There'll Be Some Changes Made | HRS 1001, Esq 10-051, JS 524 |
| 23393-1 | Horn Of Plenty Blues (Zutty's Hootie Blues)-vZS | -      -        - |
| 23394-1 | Dinah | HRS 1000, Md 1137 |
| 23395-1 | *I've Found A New Baby | HRS 1002, Md 1144 |
| 23396-1-2 | *Everybody Loves My Baby | -      - (dubbed 23396-2) |

Pseudonym on Superior 2719 for Henry Lange and his Orchestra, q.v.

## TED RUSSELL  AND HIS ORCHESTRA

Pseudonym on Champion and Panachord for Mike Riley (q.v.)-Eddie Farley and their
  Onyx Club Boys.

## BABE RUSSIN'S  ORCHESTRA

? Bunny Berigan-t/Babe Russin-ts, others unknown apart from Leon Lapell-v.
                                         New York, August, 1937.

| | | |
|---|---|---|
| M-586-1 | Roses In December - vLL | Mas rejected |
| M-587-1 | Red Skies | - |
| M-588- | Unknown title | - |
| M-589-1-2 | Love Or Infatuation | - |

## DAN RUSSO'S  ORIOLES

The following personnel for this band is given in ORCHESTRA WORLD for November, 1929
and may be a rough guide to that of the session below.

Dan Russo-vn dir. George Weisheipl-Ralph Pierce-t/Max Williams-tb/Fritz Holtz-Hector
  Herbert-Roy Johnson-cl-as-ts/Ralph Barnhart-p/Paul Wittenmeyer-bj/Don Hughes-bb/
  Jim Jackson-d.                          Chicago, March 17, 1932.

| | | |
|---|---|---|
| 152161-1 | Noah's Ark - v | Col 2647-D |
| 152162-2 | Old MacDonald Had A Farm - v | - |
| 152163-3 | Goofus - v | Col 2641-D, Par A-3478 |
| 152164-1 | I'm A Ding Dong Daddy - v | -         RZ MR-806 |

NOTE:- Regal Zonophone MR-806 as AL CALMAN AND HIS HOT SIZZLERS; Parlophone A-3478
as CHICAGO WASHBOARDS.

## RUSSO AND FIORITO'S ORIOLE ORCHESTRA

ORIOLE ORCHESTRA : Dan Russo-vn and Ted Fiorito-p dir. Marty Campbell-Frankie
  Quartell-t/Roy Maxon-tb/Don Mangano-cl-ss-as/Clayton Naset-cl-ss-ts/Frank Papile-
  pac/Tony Catina-bj/Eddie Storman-bj-vc/Ralph Walker-bb/Charlie Puchta-d.
                                         New York, May, 1922.

| | | |
|---|---|---|
| 8151 | Oriole Blues | Br 2300 |

                                         New York, January, 1923.

| | | |
|---|---|---|
| 9652 | Honolulu Blues | Br 2398* |

Vernon "Mutt" Hayes-cl-as replaces Mangano.
                                         New York, July 9, 1923.

| | | |
|---|---|---|
| 11063 | Shim-Me-Sha-Wabble | Br 2466 |

                                         New York, July 10, 1923.

| | | |
|---|---|---|
| 11070 | Slow Poke | Br 2473 |

Hal Matthews-tb replaces Maxon; Don Mangano-cl-as added.
                                         Chicago, January 16, 1924.

| | | |
|---|---|---|
| 1/2-CH | Sobbin' Blues | Br 2560 |

                                         Chicago, February 23, 1924.

| | | |
|---|---|---|
| 70-CH | Eccentric Rag (J. Russel Robinson) | Br 2616* |

                                         Chicago, February 26, 1924.

| | | |
|---|---|---|
| 89-CH | That Lullaby Strain | Br 2587* |

ORIOLE ORCHESTRA : Dan Russo-vn and Ted Fiorito-p dir. Marty Campbell-Frankie
Quartell-t/Hal Matthews-tb/Don Mangano-Mutt Hayes-cl-ss-as/Clayton Naset-cl-ss-
ts/Frank Papile-pac/Nick Lucas-bj-g/Eddie Storman-bj-vc/Ralph Walker-bb/Charlie
Puchta-d.                                    Los Angeles, May 28, 1924.

A-127     You'll Never Get To Heaven With Those    Br 2633*
            Eyes
A-134     I Need Some Pettin'                      Br 2637


Dan Russo-vn and Ted Fiorito-p dir. Freddy Hulme-George Jernberg-t/Hal Matthews-tb
/Don Mangano-Mutt Hayes-cl-ss-as-bar/Clayton Naset-cl-ss-ts/Frank Papile-pac/Jack
Wuerl-vn/Mark Fisher-bj-v/Ralph Walker-bb/Charlie Puchta-d.
                                             Chicago, October 16, 1924.

14008     Mandy, Make Up Your Mind                 Br 2741*

                                             Chicago, October 18, 1924.

14017     Copenhagen                               Br 2752

                                             Chicago, January 16, 1925.

14679/82  'Way Down Home                           Br 2832*

                                             Chicago, February 19, 1925.

15006     Off And Gone                             Br 2832*

RUSSO AND FIORITO'S ORIOLE ORCHESTRA.        Chicago, December 18, 1925.

34045-3   I Wanna Go Where You Go-Do What You Do-  Vic 19917
            THEN I'LL BE HAPPY

                                             Chicago, December 19, 1925.

34051-1   I Wish't I Was In Peoria - vMF&ch        Vic 19924

Carroll Martin-tb/Victor Young-vn added.
                                             Chicago, March 12, 1926.

34590-7   I Don't Believe It, But Say It Again     Vic 19989, HMV EA-63
34592-6   Let's Talk About My Sweetie - vMF          -      HMV EA-68

Other sides from the many recorded by this orchestra contain brief glimpses of the
jazz talent in its ranks, but hardly enough to warrant inclusion here.

                         GEORGE "HAMBONE" RUTHERS

Pseudonym on Champion for F. T. Thomas, q.v.

                         GERMAINE  SABLON

Vocal, acc. by Michel Warlop et son Orchestre : Probably :- Michel Warlop-vn dir.
Pierre Allier-Maurice Moufflard-Noel Chiboust-t/Marcel Dumont-Isidore Bassard-tb/
Andre Ekyan-cl-as/Amedee Charles-as/Alix Combelle-ts/Charles Lisee-as-bsx/Stephane
Grappelly-p/Django Reinhardt-g/Roger Grasset-sb/ —— McGregor-d.
                                             Paris, February 2, 1934.

OPG-1296-1  Un jour....sur la mer               HMV K-7193
OPG-1297-2  Ici l'on peche                      HMV K-7256
OPG-1298-2  Toboggan                            HMV K-7193

                                             Paris, February 26, 1934.

OPG-1362-1  Celle qui est perdue                HMV K-7238

Acc. by Michel Warlop et son Orchestre : Michel Warlop-vn dir. probably :- Maurice
Moufflard-Pierre Allier-Noel Chiboust-t/Marcel Dumont-Isidore Bassard-tb/Andre
Ekyan-cl-as/Amedee Charles-as/Alix Combelle-ts/Charles Lisee-as-bsx/Stephane
Grappelly-p/Django Reinhardt-g/Roger Grasset-sb/ —— McGregor-d.
                              Paris, March 5, 1934.

| | | |
|---|---|---|
| OPG-1362-2 | Celle qui est perdue | Rejected |
| OPG-1386-1 | La Berceuse du Marin | HMV K-7204 |
| OPG-1387-1 | La mauvaise priere | - |

                              Paris, March 16, 1934.

| | | |
|---|---|---|
| OPG-1416-1 | Je ne suis pas un ange | HMV K-7238 |
| OPG-1417-1 | La Chanson du Large | HMV K-7256 |

                              Paris, May 12, 1934.

| | | |
|---|---|---|
| OPG-1572-1 | Tendresse Waltz | HMV K-7305 |
| OPG-1573-1 | J'ai besoin de toi | HMV K-7479 |

Acc. by Michel Warlop et son Orchestre : Michel Warlop-vn dir. 2t/tb/3as/Alix
Combelle-ts/p/Django Reinhardt-g/sb/d.  Paris, November 13, 1934.

| | | |
|---|---|---|
| OLA-149-1 | Deux cigarettes dans l'ombre | HMV K-7373 |
| OLA-151-1 | Je voudrais vivre | - |

NOTE:- Matrices OLA-148 and OLA-150 are by Aime Simon-Girard, q.v. under Simon.

Vocal duets with Jean Sablon, acc. by Andre Ekyan-cl/? Alec Siniavine-p/Django Rein-
hardt-g/Louis Vola-sb-pac.           Paris, May 17, 1935.

| | | |
|---|---|---|
| OLA-520-1 | Un amour comme le notre - pac | HMV K-7517 |
| OLA-521-1 | La petite ile | - |

## JEAN  SABLON

this famous French cabaret and radio star made many records during the years covered
by this book, and after; the following have accompaniments of interest as jazz.

Vocal, acc. by Leon Ferreri-vn-p as shown/Michel Emer-p-cel as shown/Django Reinhardt
g/Max Elloy-d.                        Paris, April 3, 1933.

| | | |
|---|---|---|
| L-4257-1 | Le meme coup - pLF-ME | Col DF-1191 |
| L-4258-1 | Je suis Sex-Appeal - vnLF/celME | - |

Acc. by Andre Ekyan et son Orchestre : Eugene d'Hellemmes-tb/Andre Ekyan-as/
Stephane Grappelly-vn/Michel Emer-p/Django Reinhardt-g/Max Elloy-d and others.
                              Paris, January 15, 1934.

| | | |
|---|---|---|
| L-4661-1 | Le jour ou je te vis | Col DF-1406 |
| L-4662-1-2 | Un sou dans le poche | Rejected |
| L-4663-1 | Prenez garde au mechant loup | Col DF-1406 |
| L-4664-1 | Pas sur la bouche | Rejected |

Acc. by Andre Ekyan-cl/Alec Siniavine-p/Django Reinhardt-g.
                              Paris, April 16, 1934.

| | | | | |
|---|---|---|---|---|
| L-4807-1 | Je sais que vous etes jolie ! | Col DF-1506, | BF-404, | 4191-M |
| L-4808-1 | Par Correspondance | - | - | - |

Acc. by Garland Wilson or Alec Siniavine-p/Django Reinhardt-g* as shown.
                              Paris, January 7, 1935.

| | | | | |
|---|---|---|---|---|
| L-5176-2 | *The Continental - pGW | Col DF-1672 | | |
| L-5177-1 | Miss Otis Regrets - pGW | - | | |
| L-5178-3 | *Un Baiser - pGW | Col DF-1714, | 4178-M, | 100001 |
| L-5179-1 | *La Derniere Bergere - pAS | - | - | - |

NOTE:- Columbia 100001 is a Brazilian issue.

Acc. by Stephane Grappelly-p/Django Reinhardt-g.
                              Paris, October 18, 1935.

CL-5487-1-2  Cette chanson est pour vous          Col rejected
CL-5488-1-2  Darling, je vous aime beaucoup         -
CL-5489-1    Derniere chanson                       -

Acc. by Stephane Grappelly-vn/Django Reinhardt-Joseph Reinhardt-g/Louis Vola-sb.
                              Paris, December 7, 1935.

CL-5487-3   Cette chanson est pour vous        Col DF-1847
CL-5518-1   Rendez-vous sous la pluie            -          4222-M

Acc. by Garland Wilson-p.          Paris, March 11, 1936.

CL-5651-1  Un seul couvert, please James     Col DF-1903, DQ-2673, 4174-M
CL-5652-1  Si tu m'aimes                          - DB-1709  -      4175-M

## ST. GEORGE'S DANCE ORCHESTRA

Pseudonym on English Vocalion for the following items listed in this book :-

M-1006  My Laddie (Dabney's Band)
M-1035  Arkansas Blues (Yerkes' S. S. FLOTILLA Orchestra)

## ST. JAMES' MEISTER ORCHESTRA

Instrumentation and personnel unknown.   London, c. July, 1911.

    190    Temptation Rag (Henry Lodge)            Butterfly B-293
    196    Red Pepper Rag (Henry Lodge)                -

## ST. LOUIS AND HIS BLUES

Pseudonym on Challenge 535 (DEEP HOLLOW) for Joe Candullo and his Orchestra, q.v.

## ST. LOUIS LEVEE BAND

Jelly-Roll Morton-p dir. c/? Bill Matthews-tb/cl-ts/? Frank Pasley-bj/? Harry
   Dial-d.                          St. Louis, May 12, 1926.

  9661-A  Soap Suds                          OK 8404

## ST. LOUIS LOW DOWNS

Pseudonym on Puritan for the California Ramblers, q.v.

## ST. LOUIS NIGHTHAWKS

Pseudonym on Conqueror 7192 for Ernie Golden and his Orchestra, q.v.

## ST. LOUIS RHYTHM KINGS

Mickey Bloom-t/Pete Pellizzi-tb/Louis Maesto-cl/Nick Moleri-p/Christian Maesto-d.
                              New York, April 4, 1925.

140494-1-2  She's My Sheba, I'm Her Sheik        Col 349-D
140495-3  Papa De Da Da                             -

## ST. LOUIS SYNCOPATORS

Fletcher Henderson-p dir. ? Elmer Chambers-c/George Brashear-tb/Don Redman-cl/Cm/
   Charlie Dixon-bj.                  New York, c. May, 1923.

    583    Long-Lost Mama                    Mac-Levin/Melody/Oly 1436
           The Snakes' Hips (sic)            Oly 1437

This was also a pseudonym on Majestic 1431 for Sammy Swift's Jazz Band, q.v.

Pseudonym on Varsity for Mae Glover, Ivy Smith and Hattie Snow, all q.v., and others
    not included here.

## SALT  AND  PEPPER

These were Jack Culley and Frank Curtz, two American vocalists who played kazoos and
    banjos, doubtless in an attempt to emulate the success of the Mound City Blue
    Blowers, but they did not produce anything likely to interest a jazz collector.
    They recorded for Cameo in 1924 and 1925.

## SALTY DOG FOUR

See the Red Devils.

## THE SALVADOR  DANCE BAND

Pseudonym on Australian Grand Pree 18353 for the Lido Venice Dance Orchestra, q.v.

## SAM AND BILL

See Emmett Miller (Parlophone R-1155).

## EDGAR SAMPSON AND  HIS ORCHESTRA

2t/tb/Edgar Sampson-as/p/sb/d/The Three Swingsters-v.
                                                New York, May 25, 1939.

| WM-1023-A | Don't Try Your Jive On Me - v3S | Voc 4942 |
| WM-1024-A | Pick Your Own Lick - v3S | - |
| WM-1025-A | Sly Mongoose - v3S | Rejected |

## JOSEPH SAMUELS

The following titles from the vast number recorded under Joseph Samuels' direction
    between 1919 and 1925 are of some interest as jazz; any not listed here should be
    examined, as they may prove of comparable interest.

JOSEPH SAMUELS' JAZZ BAND : Jules Levy, Jr. and usually another (? Hymie Farberman)-
    c/Ephraim Hannaford-tb/Joseph Samuels-cl-bsx-vn/Larry Briers-p/d.
                                                New York, c. May, 1920.

| 7426-B | Slim Trombone | OK 4124 |
|  | Marriage Blues | OK 4122 |

New York, August, 1920.

| 7505-B | Dreaming Blues | OK 4167, Od 311944 |
| 7506-B | Hold Me | OK 4166 |

New York, November, 1920.

| 7608- | Zowie ! | OK 4220, Od 311954 |
| 7609-B | I'm A Lonesome Little Raindrop | OK 4213 |

New York, January, 1921.

| 7671-D | No Wonder I'm Blue | OK 4233, Od 311914 |
| 7672-B | Home Again Blues | OK 4250, Od 311903, 2495 (Swedish) |
| 7706-B | Oh, Gee ! Say, Gee ! You Ought To See | OK/Sun 4252, 16014, Od 311913 |
|  | My Gee-Gee From The Fiji Isles |  |
| 7707-B | Sweet Mama (Papa's Getting Mad) | OK 4255, Od 03190* |
|  | (Sweet Arama*) |  |
| 7708-B | Crazy Blues | OK 4250, Od 311902, 2495 (Swedish) |

NOTE:- Odeons 311902/3 are coupled.

New York, February, 1921.

| 7728-C | Spread Yo' Stuff | OK 4260, Od 311921 |
|  | Hey Paw ! | Od 20028 |

JOSEPH SAMUELS' JAZZ BAND : Jules Levy, Jr.-? Hymie Farberman-c/Ephraim Hannaford-tb/
Joseph Samuels-cl-bsx-vn/Larry Briers-p/d.
New York, March, 1921.

| | | |
|---|---|---|
| 7778-C | Tropical Blues | OK/Sun 4282, Od 311948 |
| 7782-C | Jabberwocky | OK/Sun 4282, Od 03207 |
| 7803-C | Scandinavia | OK/Apex 4302, Od 311972, Fav F-486 |
| | Ain't We Got Fun ? | Od 20051 |

New York, April, 1921.

| | | |
|---|---|---|
| 7845-B | I'm Nobody's Baby | OK/Apex 4302, Od 311973 |
| 7846-A | Oh Boy ! | OK 4370 |

NOTE:- All German (6-figure) Odeons listed hitherto as AMERICAN JAZZ BAND.

New York, June, 1921.

| | | |
|---|---|---|
| 7997-A | Pullman Porter Blues | OK 4370 |
| | Yokohama Lullaby | OK 4374 |

New York, c. July, 1921.

| | | |
|---|---|---|
| 8227-B | Dangerous Blues | Od 20087 |
| | When The Sun Goes Down | Od 20062 |
| | Apache Love | Od 20070 |

New York, August, 1921.

| | | |
|---|---|---|
| 70133- | The Village Clown | OK 4609 |
| 70134-B | Ma ! | OK/Apex 4425 |

New York, September, 1921.

| | | |
|---|---|---|
| 70203-B | Dapper Dan | OK/Apex/St 4460 |
| 70204-B | The Missing Link | OK/Apex 4453 |
| 70205-B | Mysterious Blues | - |

NOTE:- Matrix 70204-B as TAMPA BLUE JAZZ BAND.

New York, c. October 29, 1921.

| | | |
|---|---|---|
| 70283-C | Wimmin (I Gotta Have 'Em, That's All) | OK/Apex 4474 |
| 70284-B | Wabash Blues | - |
| 70285-C | I've Got My Habits On | OK 4477 |

New York, February, 1922.

| | | |
|---|---|---|
| 70503-C | 13 I'm So Unlucky 13 | OK 4573 |
| 70504- | Boo Hoo Hoo | OK 4609 |

JOSEPH SAMUELS' MASTER PLAYERS : As above, plus ? Guy Shrigley-as-ts/bj/bb.
New York, July, 1922.

| | | |
|---|---|---|
| 1124-2 | Don't Bring Me Posies | Ban 1089, Cx 40150, Pur 11148, |
| | | Re 9338, Imp 1150 |

NOTE:- Banner 1089 as BANNER DANCE ORCHESTRA; Claxtonola 40150 as EARL RANDOLPH'S
ORCHESTRA; Imperial 1150 as IMPERIAL DANCE ORCHESTRA.

JOSEPH SAMUELS' JAZZ BAND : As for March, 1921.
New York, August 10, 1922.

| | | |
|---|---|---|
| 70772-B | Houston Blues | OK 4663, Od 312904 |

NOTE:- Odeon 312904 as AMERICAN JAZZ BAND.

JOSEPH SAMUELS' JAZZ BAND : Jules Levy, Jr.-? Hymie Farberman-c/Ephraim Hannaford-tb
/Joseph Samuels-cl-bsx/Larry Briers-p/bj/d.
New York, December, 1922.

| | | |
|---|---|---|
| 1263-1 | Runnin' Wild | Pm 20190, GG 1143, Hg 772, Nat 12190, Pt/Tri 11198, Pur 11190, Rx 7012 |
| 1264-1 | Loose Feet | As above |

NOTE:- Some of the above issues are believed to have been pressed from alternative
takes.

Samuels db vn; Nathan Glantz-as/bb/? Arthur Fields or Arthur Hall-v added.
New York, January, 1923.

| | | |
|---|---|---|
| 1312-1 | Nuthin' But | Pm 20206, Pur 11206 |
| 1312-2 | Nuthin' But | Ban 1188, Bwy 11217, Re 9470, Apex 8054 |
| 1313-1 | You've Got To See Mama Ev'ry Night | Ban 1162, - GG 1153, Pm 20206, |
| | - v | Pur 11206 |

NOTE:- Banner 1162, 1188 and Apex 8054 as SIX BLACK DIAMONDS; Broadway 11217 and
Puritan 11206 as SAMUELS' JAZZ ORCHESTRA; Regal 9470 as MISSOURI JAZZ HOUNDS.

JOSEPH SAMUELS AND HIS ORCHESTRA : As for December, 1922 above.
Montreal, February 11, 1923.

| | | |
|---|---|---|
| 730 | No-One Loves You Better Than Your M-A-double-M-Y | PA 020932, Per 14144 |
| 733 | Maxie Jones (The King Of The Saxophones) | - - |

Montreal, February 12, 1923.

| | | |
|---|---|---|
| 739 | Apple Sauce | Ban 1177, Re 9458 |
| 741 | Farewell Blues | Ban 1181 - |

NOTE:- Banner 1181 and Regal 9458 as SIX BLACK DIAMONDS.

Montreal, c. February 18, 1923.

| | | |
|---|---|---|
| 815 | You Tell Her - I Stutter | Imp 1185 |

LONG BEACH SOCIETY SERENADERS : Joseph Samuels-cl-vn dir. Jules Levy, Jr.-? Hymie
Farberman-t/tb/cl-as/cl-ts/Larry Briers-p/bj/bb/d.
New York, c. February 21, 1923.

| | | |
|---|---|---|
| 70059 | Am I To Blame ? | PA 020919, Per 14103 |

JOSEPH SAMUELS AND HIS ORCHESTRA : Joseph Samuels-cl dir. Jules Levy, Jr.-? Hymie
Farberman-t/Ephraim Hannaford-tb/Larry Briers-p/bj/bb/d/Arthur Hall (as DONALD
BAKER)-v.
New York, c. May 7, 1923.

| | | |
|---|---|---|
| 5162-2 | Bugle Call Rag | Ban 1229, Re 9514, Apex 8056 |
| 5163-2-3 | That Red Head Gal/Girl* - vAH | Ban 1203, Re 9490, Apex 8039, Imp 1182* |

NOTE:- Banner 1229 as BANNER DANCE ORCHESTRA; Regal 9490 and Apex 8056 as MISSOURI
JAZZ HOUNDS; Regal 9514 as MISSOURI JAZZ BAND; Apex 8039 as LANIN AND HIS ORCH.....

New York, c. May 15, 1923.

| | | |
|---|---|---|
| 5167-1 | Slow Poke | Ban 1242, Re 9525, Imp 1235 |
| 5168- | Beale Street Mama | Ban 1218, Re 9503, Apex 8071 |

NOTE:- Banner 1242 and Imperial 1235 as HOLLYWOOD DANCE ORCHESTRA; Regal 9503 as
SIX BLACK DIAMONDS; Apex 8071 as MISSOURI JAZZ HOUNDS.

New York, c. June 1, 1923.

| | | |
|---|---|---|
| 5185-1 | Long Lost Mama (Daddy Misses You) | Ban 1217, Re 9504, Apex 8094, Imp 1162 |
| 5186- | I Ain't Never Had Nobody Crazy Over Me | Ban 1214, Re 9501 |

NOTE:- Banner 1217, Regal 9501 and Imperial 1162 as SIX BLACK DIAMONDS; Regal 9504
as MISSOURI JAZZ BAND; Apex 8094 as MISSOURI JAZZ HOUNDS.

JOSEPH SAMUELS AND HIS ORCHESTRA : Joseph Samuels-cl dir. Jules Levy, Jr.-? Hymie
  Farberman-t/Ephraim Hannaford-tb/as/ts/Larry Briers-p/bb/d/Ernest Hare (as BOB
  THOMAS)-v.                              New York, c. June 20, 1923.

  5198-4  My Sweetie Went Away - vEH            Apex/St 8089
  5198-5  My Sweetie Went Away - vEH            Ban 1227, Re 9514, Imp 1181
  NOTE:- Banner 1227 and Imperial 1181 as SIX BLACK DIAMONDS; Regal 9514 as MISSOURI
  JAZZ BAND; Apex/Starr 8089 as REGAL DANCE ORCHESTRA.

  Probably very similar.              New York, c. September 28, 1923.

  5276-2  Sittin' In A Corner                   Ban 1270, Bell P-244, Re 9557,
                                                Apex 8120, Imp 1318
  NOTE:- Ban 1270 as ROY COLLINS' ORCHESTRA; Bell P-244 as COREYPHONIC ORCHESTRA;
  Regal 9557 as JOSEPH FRANKLIN'S ORCHESTRA; Imperial 1318 as IMPERIAL DANCE ORCH-
  ESTRA.

  As for c. June 20, 1923, plus bj; the as in both sessions may be Nathan Glantz.
                                      New York, c. October 1, 1923.

  5290-1  If I Can't Get The Sweetie I Want     Ban 1268, Bell P-244, Re 9513,
                                                Apex 8117, 8128, Imp 1251
  5292-2  Sobbin' Blues                         Ban 1265, Bell P-257, Re 9553,
                                                Imp 1232, Curry's 157
  NOTE:- Banner 1265 as MISSOURI JAZZ BAND; 1268 as JOS. FRANKLIN'S ORCHESTRA; Bell
  P-244 as COREYPHONIC ORCHESTRA; P-257 as BELL SYNCOPATORS; Regal 9553 and Imperial
  1232 as SIX BLACK DIAMONDS; Apex 8117, 8128 as THE MASTER PLAYERS; Imperial 1251
  as IMPERIAL DANCE ORCHESTRA; Curry's 157 as CURRY'S JAZZ BAND.

JOSEPH SAMUELS' JAZZ BAND : Probably similar to the last above.
                                      New York, c. March, 1924.

  10098-   Jiminy Gee                           Dom 344

EARL RANDOLPH'S ORCHESTRA : Probably similar to the foregoing.
                                      New York, c. October 23, 1924.

  1936-1  Choo Choo (Gotta Hurry Home)          Pm 20358, Tri 11431
  NOTE:- Triangle 11431 as FRISCO SYNCOPATORS.

See also Husk O'Hare's Super Orchestra of Chicago; the Synco Jazz Band; and the Tampa
  Blue Jazz Band.  The name JOSEPH SAMUELS AND HIS ORCHESTRA was used on Domino 345
  for the Original Memphis Five, and on Regal 9439 for the California Ramblers, both
  q.v.

## BESSIE SANDERS

Pseudonym on Champion for Alberta Jones, q.v.

## JOE  SANDERS

Piano solos.                          New York, March 9, 1932.

  71932-1  Intangibility                        Vic 24033
  71933-2  Southology (Improvisation)           -

                                      New York, March 24, 1932.

  72206-1-2  Inhibition                         Vic rejected
  72207-1-2  Embers                             -

## RED SANDERS AND  HIS ORCHESTRA

This band made nine titles for Gennett in 1925.  The personnel is believed to have
  included Red Nichols-t, and some of the sides are of marginal interest as "hot"
  dance music.  Full details will be found in THE AMERICAN DANCE BAND DISCOGRAPHY.

Pseudonym on Gennett for the Vagabonds, q.v.

## LEILA SANDFORD

Pseudonym on Ariel 4499 for Annette Hanshaw, q.v.

## SAN FRANCISCO DANCE BAND

Pseudonym on Guardsman for the following items listed in this book :-

```
1876  I Love My Baby (Bailey's Lucky Seven)
1877  Spanish Shawl (Bob Deikman and his Orchestra)
1907  Dinah (Bailey's Lucky Seven)
1908  After I Say I'm Sorry (Bailey's Lucky Seven)
1929  Goodnight (I'll See You In The Morning) (The Southerners)
1939  Could I ? I Certainly Could (The Vagabonds)
1988  St. Louis Hop (Joe Candullo's Everglades Orchestra)
```

## LESLIE SARONY

This famous British comedian is not normally associated with jazz, but the following
  coupling is quite remarkable for its accompaniment.

Vocal, acc. by Sylvester Ahola-t/Van Phillips-cl-as/vn/Carroll Gibbons-p/Joe Brannelly-g.                          Small Queen's Hall, London, April 3, 1928.

```
Bb-12900-2  Don't Do That To The Poor Puss Cat    HMV B-2714
Bb-12901-2  Don't Be Cruel To A Vegetabuel           -
```

## GERTRUDE SAUNDERS

Vocal, acc. by Tim Brymn and his Black Devil Orchestra : Tim Brymn-p dir. ? 2c/tb/
  2as/ts/vn/bj/bb/d.                    New York, May, 1921.

```
7905-A  I'm Craving For That Kind Of Love       OK 8004
7906-A  Daddy, Won't You Please Come Home ?        -
```

Acc. by Maceo Pinkard-p.                New York, August 27, 1923.

```
28513-2  Potomac River Blues                    Vic 19159
```

Acc. by the Virginians : Ross Gorman-cl-as dir. Henry Busse-Tommy Gott-t/Sam Lewis
tb/Hale Byers-as/Ferdie Grofe-p/Mike Pingitore-bj/Jack Barsby-bb.
                                       New York, September 6, 1923.

```
28536-2  Love Me                                Vic 19159
```

Acc. by Porter Grainger-p.              New York, c. August, 1927.

```
         Don't Let Your Love Come Down          Voc 1131
         You Can't Have It Unless I Give It To You  -
```

## DOCTOR SAUSAGE AND HIS FIVE PORK CHOPS

"Dr. Sausage" Tyson-d-v dir. unknown group.
                                       New York, March 19, 1940.

```
67346-  Cuckoo Cuckoo Chicken Rhythm - vch      Dec 7776
67347-  Wham (Re-Bop-Boom-Bam) - vch            Dec 7736
67348-  Birthday Party - vch                    Dec 7776
67349-  Doctor Sausage Blues - vDST             Dec 7736
```

## HELEN SAVAGE

Vocal, acc. by the Dixie Syncopators : Omer Simeon-cl dir. Shirley Clay (and another*)
  c/William Barbee-p/Hayes Alvis-bb/Wallace Bishop-d.
                                       Chicago, August 21, 1929.

```
C-4102-  *For Just A Little Love From You       Br 4536
C-4103-   It's Bad For Your Soul                   -
```

Pseudonym for the following items listed in this book :-

Savana 1592   How Many Times ? (The Buffalodians)
        1599   Ain't She Sweet ? (Jack Pettis and his Band)
Vox Humana 48   I Like Pie, I Like Cake (Barth's Mississippians)

## SAVANNAH NIGHT HAWKS

Pseudonym on Champion for Alphonse Trent and his Orchestra, q.v.

## SAVANNAH SIX

Phil Napoleon-t/Miff Mole-tb/Jimmy Lytell-cl/Frank Signorelli-p/? John Cali-bj/Jack
   Roth-d.                              New York, October 26, 1925.

| | | |
|---|---|---|
| 141195-3 | 'Tain't Cold | Har 56-H |
| 141196-2 | Jacksonville Gal | Har 58-H |
| 141197-3 | Hot Aire | Har 56-H |

## THE SAVANNAH SYNCOPATORS

Pseudonym on Brunswick (all nationalities) for the following items listed in this
   book :-

3245   Both sides by King Oliver's Dixie Syncopators
3281   Jackass Blues (King Oliver's Dixie Syncopators)
3361   Both sudes by King Oliver's Dixie Syncopators
3373   Both sides by King Oliver's Dixie Syncopators
6046   Honey, That Reminds Me (Luis Russell and his Orchestra)
6046   Who's Blue ? (King Oliver and his Orchestra)
6176   Both sides by Connie's Inn Orchestra (see Fletcher Hwnderson)
7124   Both sides by Jimmie Noone and his Orchestra
A-500153   Both sides by Fletcher Henderson and his Orchestra

## THE SAVILE (ALL-MASTERS) DANCE ORCHESTRA

The following titles by this dance band are of some jazz interest.

Harry Savile-p dir. Jack Jackson and another-t/tb/Charles Swinnerton-as/ts/bj/bb/d.
                                        London, c. August, 1927.

| | | |
|---|---|---|
| DU-8431 | I Can't Believe That You're In Love With Me | Duo/Aerial UB-2127 |
| DU-8436 | Back Beats | Duo/Aerial UB-2130 |

## JAN SAVITT

JAN SAVITT AND HIS ORCHESTRA : Jan Savitt dir. 2t/tb/2as/ts/3vn/p/g/sb/d/Pete
   Woolery-v.                          Camden, N. J., September 20, 1934.

84509-1   You're Haunting Me - vPW            Vic rejected

JAN SAVITT AND HIS TOP HATTERS : Instrumentation as for November 17, 1937 (see page
   1357); probably similar personnel; Carlotta Dale-v.
                                        New York, February 15, 1937.

| | | |
|---|---|---|
| M-105-1 | Yonkel Doodle Goes Steppin' | Vri 585 |
| M-106- | Let's Play Geography | Vri 542 |
| M-107-1 | How Could You ? | Vri 506 |
| M-108-1 | I'll Never Tell You I Love You - vCD | — |

New York, March 15, 1937.

| | | |
|---|---|---|
| M-249- | Supposing | Vri 542 |
| M-250-1-2 | Shuffle Rhythm | Rejected |
| M-251-1 | Cross Country Hop | Vri 585 |
| M-252-1-2 | Beale Street Blues | Rejected |

JAN SAVITT AND HIS TOP HATTERS : Jan Savitt-a dir. Jack Hansen-Harold Kearns-t/Chuck
   Evans-Al Leopold-tb/James Schultz-as-a/Gabe Galinas-Harry Roberts-as/John Warring-
   ton-ts-a/Irving Leshner-p/Frank Rasmus-g/Howard Cook-sb/George White-d/Johnny
   Watson-a/Carlotta Dale-George "Bon Bon" Tunnell-Harry Roberts-The Three Toppers
   (Charlotte Kaye-Jack Carlton-Dorsey Anderson)-v.
                                        New York, November 17, 1937.

017060-1  My Heaven On Earth - vBB            BB B-7281, RZ MR-2758
017061-1  Am I In Another World ? - vBB          -              -.
017062-1  You Started Something - vBB         BB B-7283
017063-1  Gypsy In My Soul - vBB              BB B-7295, RZ MR-2683
017064-1  I Live The Life I Love - vBB           -              -
017065-1  A Kiss For Consolation - vBB        BB B-7283

                                        New York, March 18, 1938.

021185-1  Moonshine Over Kentucky - vBB       BB B-7504, RZ G-23510
021186-1  Bewildered - vCD                    BB B-7490
021187-1  Stop ! And Reconsider - vTT         BB B-7493
021188-1  Lovelight In The Starlight - vCD    BB B-7504, RZ MR-2757
021189-1  Week-End Of A Private Secretary - vCD  BB B-7493
021190-1  Something Tells Me - vBB            BB B-7490

   Charles Jensen-t added; Rasmus omitted.
                                        New York, May 13, 1938.

023220-1  My Margarita - vBB                  BB B-7593
023221-1  Why'd Ya Make Me Fall In Love ? - vTT  BB B-7595, RZ MR-2828
023222-1  Sweet And Tender - vTT              BB B-7593
023223-1  Dust - vBB                          BB B-7607, RZ MR-2847, G-23533
023224-1  I've Got A Guy - vCD                BB B-7595, RZ MR-2827
023225-1  It's The Little Things That Count - vBB  -              -

                                        New York, June 17, 1938.

023592-1  Fol Da Rol Dol - vBB                BB B-7670
023593-1  'S Good Enough For Me - vBB         BB B-7679
023594-1  We, The People - vTT                BB B-7666
023595-1  So Lovely - vBB                     BB B-7679
023596-1  Hi-Yo Silver - vBB                  BB B-7666
023597-1  When Twilight Comes - vCD           BB B-7670, RZ MR-2847

                                        New York, July 22, 1938.

024069-1  La De Doody Doo - vHR               BB B-7737
024070-1  Love Of My Life - vCD               BB B-7748
024071-1  That's A Plenty                     BB B-7733
024072-1  What Are You Doin' Tonight ? - vBB  BB B-7737
024073-1  I Haven't Changed A Thing - vBB     BB B-7748
024074-1  Futuristic Shuffle                  BB B-7733

                                        New York, August 25, 1938.

026641-1  There's No Place Like Your Arms - vBB  BB B-7797
026642-1  Sweetheart Of Sigma Chi - vBB       BB B-7786, MW M-7548
026643-1  When I Go A-Dreamin' - vBB             -              -
026644-1  Ya Got Me - vBB                     BB B-7797, RZ G-23744
026645-1  You Go To My Head - vCD             BB B-7783
026646-1  Tutti Frutti - vBB-HR                  -

                                        New York, September 13-14, 1938.
026876-1  I May Be Wrong/Get Happy/Margie/Futuristic Shuffle
                                        Thesaurus 594
026877-1  I Haven't Changed A Thing/Stumbling/Tutti Frutti/Top Hat Shuffle
                                        Thesaurus 583
026878-1  Lambeth Walk/Summer Souvenirs/Monday Morning/What Have You Got That Gets
             Me ?                       Thesaurus 584
026879-1  What Are You Doing Tonight ?/Love Doesn't Grow On Trees/When I Go
             A-Dreaming/You're Lovely, Madame    Thesaurus 578
026880-1  Could You Pass In Love ?/Put Your Heart In A Song/Prince Of A Fella/I'm In
             A Fog About You            Thesaurus 579

JAN SAVITT AND HIS TOP HATTERS : Jan Savitt-a dir. Jack Hansen-Harold Kearns-Charles
Jensen-t/Chuck Evans-Al Leopold-tb/James Schultz-as-a/Gabe Galinas-Harry Roberts-as
/John Warrington-ts-a/Irving Leshner-p/Howard Cook-sb/George White-d/Carlotta Dale-
George "Bon Bon" Tunnell-v/Johnny Watson-a.
                                        New York, October 21, 1938.

| | | |
|---|---|---|
| 028139-1 | Just A Kid Named Joe - vBB | BB B-10013 |
| 028140-1 | Sugar Foot Stomp | BB B-10005, Vic 20-2630 |
| 028141-1 | Wait Until My Heart Finds Out - vBB | BB B-10018 |
| 028142-1 | Gardenias - vBB | - |
| 028143-1 | Quaker City Jazz - aJS-JS | BB B-10005, Vic 20-2630 |
| 028144-1 | Hurry Home - vCD | BB B-10013 |

Jan Savitt-a dir. Johnny Austin-Jimmy Campbell-Jack Hansen-t/Cutty Cutshall-Fred
Ohms-Norman Sipple-tb/Ed Clausen-Frank Langone-as/Gabe Galinas-cl-ts/Sam Sachelle-
ts/Jack Pleis-p-a/Frank Rasmus-g/Maurice Rayman-sb/Bob Spangler-d/George "Bon Bon"
Tunnell-Carlotta Date-v/Johnny Watson-Eddie Durham-a.
                                        New York, January 10, 1939.

031435-1   Could Be/Kinda Lonesome/The Masquerade Is Over/Romance Runs In The Family
                                                Thesaurus 621
031436-1   On The Road To Mandalay/Love, Your Magic Spell    -
            Is Everywhere/Begin The Beguine/Have It Your Way
031437-1   Quaker City Jazz/Like A Ghost From The    Thesaurus 620
            Blue-vBB/Night Must Fall/Sha Sha

                                        New York, February 26, 1939.

| | | |
|---|---|---|
| 65071-A | There's A Hole In The Old Oaken Bucket | Dec 2331, X-1754, Br 02775 |
| | - vBB | |
| 65072-A | It's All So New To Me - vCD | - |
| 65073-A | In A Moment Of Weakness - vBB | Dec 2330, Br 02776 |
| 65074-A | I'm Happy About The Whole Thing - vBB | - X-1726 - |

Guy Smith-g replaces Rasmus.          New York, April 1, 1939.

| | | |
|---|---|---|
| 65318-A | Little Sir Echo - vBB | Dec 2391, Br 02775 |
| 65319-A | I Want My Share of Love - vCD | -    X-1826. Br 02783 |
| 65320-B | And The Angels Sing - vBB | Dec 2390    - |
| 65321-A | Snug As A Bug In A Rug - vBB | - |

                                        New York, May 1, 1939.

036579-1   Three Little Fishies (Itty Bitty Poo)/How Strange/The Chestnut Tree/You
            Grow Sweeter As The Years Go By      Thesaurus 655

Don Simes-tb replaces Sipple; Buddy Schutz-d replaces Spangler.
                                        New York, June 1, 1939.

| | | |
|---|---|---|
| 65714-A | When Buddha Smiles | Dec 2540, Br 02817 |
| 65714-B | When Buddha Smiles | - |
| 65715-A | I'll Always Be In Love With You | Dec 2583 |
| 65716-A | Get Happy | - |
| 65717-A | That's A Plenty | Dec 2540, Br 02817 |

Russ Isaacs-d replaces Schutz; Phil Brito-v.
                                        New York, July 7, 1939.

| | | |
|---|---|---|
| 65932-A | You Taught Me To Love Again - vCD | Dec 2614, Br 02879 |
| 65933-A | Running Through My Mind - vPB | -    - |
| 65934-A | Shabby Old Cabby - vPB | Dec 2600, Br 02845 |
| 65935-A | Moonlight Serenade - vCD | -    - |

                                        New York, August 29, 1939.

| | | |
|---|---|---|
| 66223-A | Twilight Interlude - vCD | Dec 2739, Br 02972 |
| 66224-A | Vol Vistu Gaily Star - vBB | -    Br 02882 |
| 66225-A | It's A Hundred To One (I'm In Love)-vBB | Dec 2738, Br 03101 |
| 66226-A | The Paper Picker - vBB | - |

JAN SAVITT AND HIS TOP HATTERS : Jan Savitt-a dir.Johnny Austin-Jimmy Campbell-Jack
  Hansen-t/Cutty Cutshall-Fred Ohms-Don Simes-tb/Ed Clausen-Frank Langone-as/Gabe
  Galinas-cl-ts/Sam Sachelle-ts/Jack Pleis-p-a/Guy Smith-g/Maurice Rayman-sb/Russ
  Isaacs-d/George "Bon Bon" Tunnell-v/Johnny Watson-Eddie Durham-a.
                                          New York, September 23, 1939.

66634-A  720 In The Books - aJS-JW                Dec 2771, Br 80108, 03101
66635-A  Stop ! It's Wonderful - vBB              Dec 2770
66636-A  The Last Two Weeks In July - vBB              -
66637-A  Alla en el Rancho Grande (My Ranch)-vBB  Dec 2771, Br 80108, 02882

                                          New York, October 4, 1939.

66707-A  If What You Say Is True - vBB            Dec 2792
66708-A  Indian Summer - vBB                      Dec 2821, X-1868, Br 02972
66709-A  Sweet Dreams, Sweetheart - vBB               -              -
66710-A  Good Morning - vBB                       Dec 2805, Br 02938
66711-A  Stranger Things Have Happened - vBB      Dec 2792
66712-A  Many Dreams Ago - vBB                    Dec 2805

JAN SAVITT AND HIS ORCHESTRA : As above, but Al Leopold-tb replaces Ohms and Simes;
  George Bohn-as replaces Langone; Frank Cudwib-Jack Ferrier-ts replace Galinas and
  Sachelle; Gene de Paul-p replaces Pleis.New York, November 5, 1939.

66821-A  It's A Wonderful World - vBB/aJS-JW      Dec 2836
66822-A  Maid Of The Mist                         Dec 2847
66823-A  After All - vBB                              -
66824-A  Honestly - vBB                           Dec 2836, Br 02938

    George Siravo-as-bar-a added.        New York, January 24, 1940.

67105-A  Make Love With A Guitar - vBB            Dec 2990, Y-5534, Br 03043
67106-A  Imagination - vBB                            -         Br 03034
67107-A  Tuxedo Junction                          Dec 2989, Br 80140, 02971
67108-A  Kansas City Moods                            -              -

                                          New York, February 4, 1940.

67147-A  Turkey In The Straw                      Dec 3041, Br 03004
67148-A  Parade Of The Wooden Soldiers                -         -
67149-A  Blues In The Groove - aED                Dec 3019, Br 03069
67150-A  Rose Of The Rio Grande - vBB                - 3945, Br 80140-
67151-A  It's Time To Jump And Shout              Dec 3185

    George Auld-ts replaces Ferrier; Allan DeWitt-v.
                                          New York, April 12, 1940.

67536-A  Secrets In The Moonlight - vBB           Dec 3153, Br 03085
67537-A  Make-Believe Island - vBB                Dec 3188, Br 03034
67538-A  Where Was I ? - vADW                     Dec 3153, Br 03085
67539-A  Ask Your Heart - vBB                     Dec 3188
67540-A  Tuxedo Junction                          Dec 2989

                                          New York, April 18, 1940.

67601-A  You're Lonely And I'm Lonely - vADW      Dec 3177
67602-A  You Can't Brush Me Off - vADW            Dec 3178

                                          New York, April 29, 1940.

67629-A    Her Name Was Rosita - vADW             Dec 3196
67630-A-B  W. P. A. - vBB                         Dec 3185
67631-A    It's A Lovely Day Tomorrow - vADW      Dec 3178
67632-A    I'm Stepping Out With A Memory Tonight Dec 3196, X-1909, Br 03043
             - vADW
67633-A    The Lord Done Fixed Up My Soul - vADW  Dec 3177

JAN SAVITT AND HIS ORCHESTRA : Jan Savitt-a dir. Jack Hansen-George Hosfeld-t/Jack
   Palmer-t-v/Al George-Al Leopold-tb/George Bohn-Ed Clausen-as/George Siravo-as-bar-
   a/Frank Cudwib-ts/Ted Duane-ts-a/Gene de Paul-Nat Jaffe-p/Guy Smith-g/Maurice
   Rayman-sb/Russ Isaacs-d/Allan DeWitt-v/Johnny Watson-Billy Moore-a.
                                        New York, January 1, 1941.

68528-A  Liebestraum (Liszt) - aTD           Dec 3876
68529-A  Nocturne in E flat major (Chopin,   Dec 3937
           Op. 9, No. 2) - aTD
68530-A  The Young Prince And The Young Princess  Dec 3640
           (Rimsky-Korsakov) - aTD
68531-A  Meditation ("Thais" - Massenet) - aTD    Dec 4124

                                        New York, January 3, 1941.

68542-A  Les Preludes (Liszt) - aTD           Dec 3671
68543-A  Green Goon Jive - aJS                -
68544-A  My Heart At Thy Sweet Voice (Saint-Saens)Dec 3640
           - aBM
68545-A  Meadowbrook Shuffle - aJS            Dec 3876

                                        New York, February 27, 1941.

68745-A  Tell Me - vADW                       Dec 3937
68746-A  April Showers - vADW                 Dec 3695
68747-A  Beloved Friend - vADW                Dec 4124
68748-A  Jolly Peter (Bummel Petrus)          Dec 3724
68749-A  By Heck                              -
68750-A  Big Beaver                           Dec 3695

JAN SAVITT AND HIS TOP HATTERS : Jan Savitt-a dir. Jack Hansen-George Hosfeld-t/Jack
   Palmer-t-v/Al George-Al Leopold-tb/Ben Pickering-tb-a/Andy Egan-cl-as/George Bohn-
   as/Joe Aglora-Sam Sachelle-ts/Ray Tucci-bar/Jack Pleis-p-a/Danny Perri-g/Howard
   Cook-sb/Russ Isaacs-d/Jane Ward-Allan DeWitt-The Toppers-v/Abe Osser-a.
                                        Chicago, April 3, 1941.

064015-1  The Things I Love - vADW            Vic 27403
064016-1  We Go Well Together - vJP-T         Vic 27382, HMV EA-3065
064017-1  Manhattan Sunrise - aJP             Vic 27403
064018-1  Horizon - aJP                       Vic 27382

   John Napton--t replaces Hansen.        Chicago, April 25, 1941.

064301-1  Where You Are - vADW                Vic 27414
064302-1  I Went Out Of My Way - vADW         Vic 27423
064303-1  Throwing Pebbles In The Millstream - vJW   -
064304-1  I Take To You - vJP-T               Vic 27414

   Gus Bivona-cl-as replaces Egan.        Chicago, May 5, 1941.

064346-1  Prelude To Carmen (Bizet) - aJP     Vic 27570
064347-1  The Sorcerer's Apprentice (Dukas) - aJS-JP   -
064348-1  It's So Peaceful In The Country - vADW   Vic 27464
064349-1  Sugar Foot Strut                    -

                                        Hollywood, May 26, 1941.

061261-1  In The Hall Of The Mountain King (Grieg) Vic 27670
           - aJP
061262-1  Jo-Jo, The Hobo - vT                Vic 27477
061263-1  La Cinquantaine (Gabriel-Marie) - aJP  Vic 27577
061264-1  Topper - aJP                        Vic 27477

                                        Hollywood, June 23, 1941.

061304-1  Keep Cool, Fool - vJP               Vic 27512
061305-3  Tattle-Tale - vADW                  -
061306-1  Love's Got Nothin' On Me - vJP      Vic 27515
061307-1  When The Sun Comes Out - vADW       -

JAN SAVITT AND HIS TOP HATTERS : Jan Savitt-a dir. Joe Weidman-George Hosfeld-Jack
  Palmer-t/Al George-Al Leopold-tb/Ben Pickering-tb-a/Gus Bivona-cl-as/George Bohn-
  as/Joe Aglora-Sam Sachelle-ts/Ray Tucci-bar/Jack Pleis-p-a/Danny Perri-g/Howard
  Cook-sb/Russ Isaacs-d/Allan DeWitt-v.  Chicago, August 4, 1941.

064661-1  Afternoon Of A Faun (Debussy)-Pt.1-aBP  Vic 27594
064662-1  Afternoon Of A Faun (Debussy)-Pt.2-aBP     -
064663-1  Little Fugue (Fugue in G minor-Bach-aJP)Vic 27670
064664-1  As We Walk Into The Sunset - vADW          Vic 27573

                              Chicago, August 6, 1941.

064675-1  I See A Million People (But All I Can  Vic 27577, HMV EA-2998
            See Is You) - vADW
064676-1  A Drop In The Bucket - vADW              Vic 27584
064677-1  Why Don't We Do This More Often ? - vADW   -
064678-1  Chattanooga Choo Choo                    Vic 27573

Ralph Harden-t replaces Palmer; Mickey Iannone-tb replaces George.
                              New York, September 25, 1941.

067928-2  Tropical Magic - vADW                    Vic 27615
067929-1  Who Calls ? - vADW                       Vic 27643
067930-1  'Tis Autumn - vADW                         -
067931-1  A Week-End In Havana - vADW              Vic 27615

Al George-tb replaces Leopold; George "Bon Bon" Tunnell-v replaces DeWitt.
                              New York, October 27, 1941.

068035-1  M-O-T-H-E-R - vBB                        Vic 27699
068036-1  Ev'ry Time - vBB                         Vic 27706
068037-1  There's A Boat Dat's Leavin' Soon For      -
            New York - vBB
068038-1  Moonlight Masquerade - vBB               Vic 27699

                              New York, November 27, 1941.

068371-1  You Don't Know What Love Is - vBB        Vic 27724
068372-1  Not A Care In The World - vBB            Vic 27720
068373-1  Now And Forever - vBB/aJS                Vic 27724
068374-1  A Nickel To My Name - vBB                Vic 27720

Bob Evans-tb replaces George; Nick Fatool-d replaces Isaacs.
                              New York, January 12, 1942.

068864-1  I Remember You - vBB                     Vic 27775
068865-1  Sing Me A Song Of The Islands - vBB      Vic 27778, HMV EA-3053
068866-1  Blue Shadows And White Gardenias - vBB     -        -
068867-1  Tica-Ti - Tica-Ta - vBB                  Vic 27775

Jan Savitt-a dir. Albert J. Davis-George Hosfeld-Ed Stress-t/Mickey Iannone-Bob
  White-Ben Pickering-tb/Gus Bivona-cl-as/Mascagni Ruffo-as/Joe Aglora-Sam Sachelle-
  ts/Ray Tucci-bar/Harry Hybda-p-cel/Danny Perri-g/Howard Cook-sb/Nick Fatool-d/Joe
  Martin-v.                   Chicago, February 19, 1942.

074091-1  Always In My Heart - vJM                 Vic 27809, HMV BD-5770
074092-1  Tomorrow's Sunrise - vJM                 Vic 27822
074093-1  Jersey Bounce                            Vic 27809, HMV BD-5770
074094-1  Me And My Melinda - vJM                  Vic 27822

JAN SAVITT AND HIS ORCHESTRA : Jan Savitt-vn-a dir. Albert J. Davis-Jack Dougherty-
  Harry Gozzard-t/Ben Pickering-Pete Lofthouse-tb/Bill Hamilton-Alan Harding-as/
  Horace Bridwell-Hugh Harding-ts/Maurice Hooven-bar/Joe Martin-vn/2vn/Victor
  Valente-p/Jess C. Bourgeois-sb/Ray Hagan-d/Gloria DeHaven-v.
                              Hollywood, July 28, 1942.

072516-1  If I Cared A Little Bit Less - vJM       BB 30-0800
072517-1  Romance a la Mode - vGDH                   -
072518-1  Manhattan Serenade - vJM                 BB B-11584
072519-1  If You Ever, Ever Loved Me (Love Me        -
            Tonight) - vGDH

Duncan Mayers dir.  Gilbert Paris-Demas Dean-t/James Reevy-tb/Carmelo Jari (Jejo)-cl-as-bar/Otto Mikell-cl-as/Ramon Hernandez-cl-ts/Leon Abbey-vn/Joe Steele-p/Freddy White-bj-g/Harry Edwards-bb/Willie Lynch-d.

New York, August 9, 1926.

| 36030-1-2-3-4-5 | Stampede | Vic rejected |
| 36031-1-2-3 | How Could I Be Blue ? | - |

Abbey omitted.                          New York, August 23, 1926.

| 36059-2 | Senegalese Stomp | Vic 20182 |
| 36060-3 | Bearcat Stomp | Vic 20307 |
| 36061-2 | Nightmare | Vic 20182 |

New York, October 11, 1926.

| 36030-7 | Stampede | Vic 20460 |
| 36031-5 | How Could I Be Blue ? | Vic 20307 |
| 36809-2 | Hot Notes | Vic 20460 |
| 36810-1-2 | Señorita Mine | Rejected |

## SAVOY DANCE BAND

Pseudonym on Savoy 1031 for Bill Haid's Cubs, q.v., and others on the same label of no outstanding jazz interest as far as is known.

## SAVOY  DANCE  ORCHESTRA

Walter Larman-as/Dick Langham-ts/Leon Daniels-vn/Claude Ivy-p/Joe Wilbur-Emil Grim-shaw-bj/Alec Williams-d.

London, February, 1920.

| 69703 | And He'd Say "Oo-La-La ! Wee-Wee" | Col 2971 |

London, March, 1920.

| 69761 | You'd Be Surprised | Col 2971 |

## SAVOY DIXIE SERENADERS

Pseudonym on Savoy 1003 for the Castle Farm Serenaders, q.v.

## SAVOY  HAVANA BAND

The following are the titles recorded by this famous London-based Anglo-American band known to be of interest as jazz; there may be others of similar quality among the many dozens recorded for Columbia, HMV and Broadcast.

Bert Ralton-cl-ss-as dir. George Eskdale-Eddie Frizzell-t/Bill Marcus-tb/Cyril Ramon Newton-vn-v/Billy Mayerl-p/Dave Wallace-bj/Jim Bellamy-bb-sx/M. L. "Whitey" Higley-d.                         London, April, 1923.

| 73353 | I Wish I Could Shimmy Like My Sister Kate | Col 3276 |

Reginald Batten-vn dir. Harry Thompson-Jimmy Wornell-t/Bernard Tipping-tb/Van Phil-lips-another-cl-as/Leslie Bates-cl-ts/Cyril Ramon Newton-vn-v/Billy Mayerl-p/Dave Thomas-bj/Jim Bellamy-bb/Ronnie Gubertini-d.

London, October 31, 1923.

| A-391-3 | My Sweetie Went Away | Col 3337 |

London, November 3, 1923.

| AX-201 | Farewell Blues | Col 953 |
| AX-202 | Blue Hoosier Blues - vRN | Col 952 |
| AX-203 | Henpecked Blues | Col 953 |
| AX-204 | Down-Hearted Blues | Col 954 |

Reginald Batten-vn dir. Harry Thompson-Jimmy Wornell-t/Bernard Tipping-tb/Van Phil-
    lips and another-cl-as/Leslie Bates-cl-ts/Cyril Ramon Newton-vn-v/Billy Mayerl-p/
    Dave Thomas-bj/Jim Bellamy-bb/Ronnie Gubertini-d.
                                           London, November 7, 1923.

AX-209    'Tain't Nobody's Business If I Do        Col 954
AX-210    Runnin' Wild                             Col 952

                                        London, c. July 1, 1924.

A-1018    That Bran' New Gal O' Mine - vCRN        Col 3476

    Rudy Vallee-cl-as replaces the unknown; Laurie Huntington-d replaces Gubertini.
                                        Hayes, Middlesex, March 12, 1925.

Bb-5879-2  Show Me The Way To Go Home - vCRN       HMV B-1997

                                        Hayes, Middlesex, April 21, 1925.

Bb-6042-2  When My Sugar Walks Down The Street     HMV B-2013, El EG-43
                - vCRN

                                        Hayes, Middlesex, May 6, 1925.

Bb-6094-2  I Like You Best Of All - vCRN           HMV B-2032

    Howard Jacobs-as replaces Vallee.      Hayes, Middlesex, November 19, 1925.

Bb-7323-2  Everybody Stomp                         HMV B-2228

Ramon Newton-vn dir. Jimmy Wornell-t/Jock Fleming-tb/Van Phillips-cl-as/Leslie Bates-
    cl-ts/Reginald Batten-vn-assistant ldr/Harry Howard-p/Dave Thomas-bj/Fred Underhaye
    bb/Laurie Huntington-d.              Small Queen's Hall, London, Sept. 23, 1926.

Bb-9245-2  Charleston, Charleston, Show Me The Way HMV B-5130

    Max Goldberg-t replaces Wornell.       Hayes, Middlesex, November 1, 1926.

Bb-9075-3-4  I Don't Want Nobody But You           HMV B-5165, El EG-336

Reginald Batten-vn dir. Max Goldberg-t/Tony Thorpe-tb/Billy Barton-cl-as/Watson Marsh
    cl-ts/Cyril Ramon Newton-vn-v/Harry Howard-p/Dave Thomas-bj/Harry Evans-bb/Laurie
    Huntington-d.                        Hayes, Middlesex, September 15, 1927.

Bb-11482-2  Miss Annabelle Lee - vCRN              HMV B-5359

    Goldberg and Howard only*.           Hayes, Middlesex, December 30, 1927.

Bb-12296-1-2 *Pretty And Blue                      HMV rejected
Bb-12297-1-2  Community Blues                         -
Bb-12298-1-2  Never Stop Raining Blues                -

## SAVOY JAZZ ORCHESTRA

Pseudonym on Australian Embassy E-135 for Benny Goodman and his Orchestra, q.v.

## SAVOY MARIMBA BOYS ORCHESTRA

Pseudonym on Australian Savoy for the Rounders, q.v.

## SAVOY ORPHEANS

The following sides by this famous Anglo-American dance band are known to contain
    points of interest as jazz, and doubtless others offer performances of similar
    standard.  It should be pointed out, however, that the titles issued on Dominion
    under this name are not only not by the Savoy Orpheans, but several of them are
    by the Grey Gull studio band, and of no known interest.

Debroy Somers dir. Vernon Ferry-Walter Lyme-t/Chick Moore-tb/Herb Finney-Al Starita-
    cl-as/Ray Starita-cl-ts/Cyril Ramon Newton-vn-v/Frank Herbin-p/Pete Mandell-bj/
    Fred Underhaye-bb/Alec Cripps-d.          London, mid-April, 1924.

  A-771      Eccentric                              Col 3432

  George Chaffin-tb replaces Moore; Billy Thorburn and/or Carroll Gibbons replace
  Herbin.                                  London, August, 1924.

  A-1155-1-2  Oh ! Eva (Ain't You Coming Out        Col 3494
              Tonight ?)

  Ronnie Gubertini-d replaces Cripps.     Hayes, Middlesex, January 9, 1925.

  Bb-5569-2  Little Old Clock On The Mantel          HMV B-1942
  Bb-5571-2  Bye-Bye, Baby                           HMV B-1955

                                           Hayes, Middlesex, January 21, 1925.

  Bb-5643-3  Hard-Hearted Hannah                     HMV B-1955
  Bb-5644-2  Copenhagen                              HMV B-1954, El EG-80

                                           Hayes, Middlesex, March 3, 1925.

  Bb-5801-3  Come On Over                            HMV B-1987

                                           Hayes, Middlesex, April 15, 1925.

  Bb-6026-2  Nobody Knows What A Red-Head Mama       HMV B-2013, El EG-43
             Can Do - vCRN

                                           Hayes, Middlesex, May 4, 1925.

  Bb-6081-2  Blue Evening Blues                      HMV B-2035

  Charlie Swinnerton-as replaces Starita.Hayes, Middlesex, July 16, 1925.

  Bb-6366-2  Oh ! That Sweet In Suite 16             HMV B-2102

  Watson Marsh-cl-ts replaces Starita; Jim Bellamy-bb replaces Underhaye.
                                           Hayes, Middlesex, October 23, 1925.

  Bb-7048-1  Stomp Off, Let's Go                     HMV B-2174

  Reginald Batten-vn replaces Somers as leader.
                                           Hayes, Middlesex, June 4, 1926.

  Bb-8502-1  Static Strut                            HMV B-5083

Cyril Ramon Newton-vn dir. Charles Rocco-Walter Lyme-t/George Chaffin-tb/Herbert
    Finney-Roy Whetstein-cl-as/Arthur Lally-cl-as-bar/Al Notorage-cl-ts/Billy Thorburn
    and/or Carroll Gibbons-p/Pete Mandell-bj/Jim Bellamy-bb/Ronnie Gubertini-d.
                                   Small Queen's Hall, London, Sept. 17, 1926.

  Bb-9217-1-2  Jig Walk                            HMV rejected

                                   Small Queen's Hall, London, Oct. 6, 1926.

  Bb-9217-4  Jig Walk - v3                          HMV B-5136, El EG-305

  Ben Evers dir. this session.          Hayes, Middlesex, December 22, 1926.

  Bb-9795-3  Pining For You                         HMV B-5194

Carroll Gibbons-p dir. Frank Guarente-t/George Chaffin-tb/Jim Cassidy-Roy Whetstein-
    cl-as/Al Notorage-cl-ts/Reg. Pursglove-Teddy Sinclair-Sidney Kyte-vn/Frank Herbin-
    2nd p/Bert Thomas-bj/Jim Bellamy-bb/Alec Ure-d.
                                           Hayes, Middlesex, January 28, 1927.

  Bb-10109-2  I'm Telling The Birds                 HMV B-5214

Carroll Gibbons-p dir. Frank Guarente-t/George Chaffin-tb/Jim Cassidy-Rov Whetstein-
cl-as/Al Notorage-cl-ts/Reg. Pürsglove-Teddy Sinclair-Sidney Kyte-vn/Frank Herbin-
2nd p/Bert Thomas-bj/Jim Bellamy-bb/Alec Ure-d.
                                        Hayes, Middlesex, February 23, 1927.

Bb-10206-1  Back Beats                          HMV B-5226


                                        Hayes, Middlesex, February 25, 1927.

Bb-10222-2  Stop It, I Love It - v2              HMV B-5228


                                        Hayes, Middlesex, March 24, 1927.

Bb-10331-2  Pretty Little Thing                  HMV B-5244

    Violins omitted.                    Hayes, Middlesex, May 4, 1927.

Bb-10674-1-2  Sax Appeal                         HMV rejected
Bb-10675-1-2-3  Snag It                             -
Bb-10676-1-2-3  Tampeekoe                            -
Bb-10677-1-2  Windy City Blues                      -
NOTE:- This session was recorded as THE SAVOY HOT HEADS, and the second take of
each was in fact approved for issue - then at the last moment this decision was
reversed on the grounds that the performances were not commercial.


                                        Hayes, Middlesex, July 15, 1927.

Bb-10674-3-4  Sax Appeal                         Rejected
Bb-11134-1  Vladivostock                         HMV B-5373
Bb-11135-1-2  Brotherly Love                     Rejected
Bb-11136-2  Ain't That Too Bad ?                 HMV B-5342
NOTE:- This session was also recorded as THE SAVOY HOT HEADS.

SAVOY HOTEL ORPHEANS : Carroll Gibbons-p dir. Lloyd "Bill" Shakespeare-Billy Higgs-t
/Paul Fenoulhet-Arthur Fenoulhet-t-tb/Sam Acres-tb/George Melachrino-cl-as/Laurie
Payne-cl-as-bar/George Smith-cl-ts/Ben Frankel-vn/Sid Bright-2nd p/Harry Sherman-g
/Jack Evetts-sb/Rudy Starita-d-vib-x.  London, February 20, 1933.

CA-13443-1-2  Tiger Rag                          Col rejected

## SAVOY PLAZA BAND

See Cecil Norman.

## SAVOY QUARTET

This unit played with great success in the ballroom of the Savoy Hotel, London, from
1915 to 1920.  In that period, it recorded a large number of sides for HMV, some
being the first British recordings of accepted jazz standards, and these are shown
below as being of some historical interest, especially as the drum work is quite
advanced for its time.

Joe Wilbur-bj-v/Emil Grimshaw-bj/Claude Ivy-p/Alec Williams-d.
                                        Hayes, Middlesex, September 28, 1918.

HO-4425ae  The Darktown Strutters' Ball (A Jazz    HMV B-991
               Melody)


                                        Hayes, Middlesex, April 11, 1919.

HO-4834ae  Tackin' 'Em Down                      HMV B-1049


                                        Hayes, Middlesex, May 29, 1919.

HO-4924ae  Ja-Da                                 HMV B-1049
HO-4928ae  After You've Gone                     HMV B-1088
HO-4934ae  Hindustan                             HMV B-1060

Joe Wilbur-bj-v/Emil Grimshaw-bj/Claude Ivy-p/Alec Williams-d.
                          Hayes, Middlesex, September 16, 1919.

HO-5231ae  Mammy O' Mine                        HMV B-1061
HO-5234ae  A Good Man Is Hard To Find              -

                          Hayes, Middlesex, June 11, 1920.

HO-5710ae  Slow And Easy                         HMV B-1121

## THE SAXOPATORS

Pseudonym on Grey Gull 1167 for the California Ramblers, q.v.

## SCALA  SOCIETY ORCHESTRA

Pseudonym on Scala 1236 (OLD MAN JAZZ) for Saxi Holtsworth's Harmony Hounds, q.v.

## THE SCANDALOUS SYNCOPATORS

According to Howard E. Penney in THE JAZZFINDER, February, 1948, p. 13, this group is
    akin to the Louisiana Five, q.v., with Alcide Nuñez-cl.
                          New York, c. April, 1921.

1251-B  St. Louis Blues                          GG 1065, Cl 3047

## BLUEY SCHAEFFER'S  ORCHESTRA

Pseudonym on Australian Embassy E-125 (SWEET JENNIE LEE) for Red Nichols and his
    Orchestra, q.v.

## ELMER SCHOEBEL AND HIS  FRIARS SOCIETY ORCHESTRA

Dick Feige-c/Jack Reid-tb/Frank Teschmacher-cl/Floyd Townes-ts/Elmer Schoebel-p/Karl
    Berger-g/John Kuhn-bb/George Wettling-d.
                          Chicago, September 20, 1929.

C-4381-A-B  Copenhagen                           Br rejected
C-4382-A-B-C  Prince Of Wails                       -

                          Chicago, October 18, 1929.

C-4559-D  Copenhagen                             Br 4652, 80065, 03309, A-8711,
                                                 A-81000, UHCA 17
C-4560-C  Prince Of Wails                        As above, but UHCA 18 (coupling 17)

## ADRIAN  SCHUBERT

Adrian Schubert was Musical Director for the Plaza group of labels (Banner, Domino,
    Regal, etc.) from 1925 to 1930;  he then transferred to Crown, and between 1922 and
    1933, he made countless records.  Of these, some are of interest as jazz, known
    examples being listed below, but as with most commercial bandleaders, there may be
    many more of equal merit.  As complete a list as possible of all Adrian Schubert's
    records will be found in THE AMERICAN DANCE BAND DISCOGRAPHY (Arlington House).

ADRIAN SCHUBERT AND HIS SALON ORCHESTRA : Adrian Schubert dir. 2t/tb/2cl-ss-as/cl-ts
    or Cm/p/bj/bb/d/Irving Kaufman-v.    New York, c. September 15, 1926.

6829-2  Sadie Green (The Vamp Of New Orleans)   Ban 1846, Bwy 1036, Dom 3814,21231,
        - vIK                                    Or 748, Re 8153, Apex 8561,St 10220
NOTE:- Banner 1846, Domino 3814, 21231, Apex 8561 and Starr 10220 as MISSOURI JAZZ
BAND; Oriole 748 as DIXIE JAZZ BAND; Regal 8153 as SIX BLACK DIAMONDS.

The only traceable issue of the following is labelled HOLLYWOOD DANCE ORCHESTRA; it
was once alleged to be by the California Ramblers, but it is almost certainly an
Adrian Schubert item, using the same instrumentation as the above, with ? Scrappy
Lambert-v, probably Andy Sannella-as.  New York, c. May 23, 1927.

7274-  Positively - Absolutely - vSL ?          Imp 1800

ADRIAN SCHUBERT AND HIS SALON ORCHESTRA : Adrian Schubert dir. Mike Mosiello-t/Tommy
Dowd-tb/Andy Sannella-cl-as/? 2nd as/Joe Dubin-ts/Russ Carlson-p/bj/bb/d/Irving
Kaufman-v.                              New York, January 17, 1929.

8470-2-3  St. Louis Blues - vIK                 Ban 6323, 6508, Chg 958, Dom 4294
                                                Je 5547, 5707, Or 1515, 1690,
                                                Re 8742, Apex 8899, Cr 81137,
                                                Stg 181137
8471-2-3  Some Of These Days - vIK              Ban 6300, 6418, Dom 4294, Je 5521
                                                Or 1481, Re 8742
8472-2  Susianna - vIK                          Ban 6298, Or 1475
NOTE:- Banner 6298, 6300 as SIX BLACK DIAMONDS; 6323, 6418 and 6508 as IRVING
KAUFMAN AND HIS BAND; Jewel 552;, 5547, Oriole 1481, 1515 and 1690 as DIXIE JAZZ
BAND.

2nd t/2vn added to some titles; bj db g; Jack Kaufman-v.
                                        New York, April 23, 1929.

8705-3  Where Has Mammy Gone ? - vJK            Ban 6383, Or 1576, Apex 8972,
                                                Cr 81092
8706-1  Why Can't It Be Me ? - vJK              Ban 6392, Apex 8998, Cr 81113,
                                                Dom/Stg 181113
8707-2  The Oliver Twist - vJK                  Apex 8964
NOTE:- Banner 6383 as SIX BLACK DIAMONDS; 6392 as IMPERIAL DANCE ORCHESTRA; Oriole
1576 as DIXIE JAZZ BAND; Apex 8964 as RUSSELL CARLSON'S DANCE ORCHESTRA; 8972 as
JOE DUBIN'S DANCE ORCHESTRA; 8998 as TOMMY DOWD'S DANCE ORCHESTRA; Crown 81113 and
Domino 181113 as MATTY CRAWFORD'S ORCHESTRA.

                           New York, May 21, 1929.

8766-  Sure Enough Blues - v              Ban 6410, Or 1598, Imp 2143
NOTE:- Banner 6410 as RUSS CARLSON'S DANCE ORCHESTRA; Oriole 1598 as BOB GREEN AND
HIS ORCHESTRA; Imperial 2143 as IMPERIAL DANCE ORCHESTRA.

                           New York, July 23, 1929.

4008   You're Gonna Regret - v            Cam 9263, Lin 3290, Ro 1065
8882-  You're Gonna Regret - v            Ban 6477, Or 1663
NOTE:- Banner 6477 as DUBIN'S DANDIES; Oriole 1663 as DIXIE JAZZ BAND; all issues
from matrix 4008 as CLIFF ROBERTS AND HIS ORCHESTRA.

Arthur Fields-v.                         New York, October 9, 1929.

4137; 9071-B  Ev'ry Once In A While - vAF       Ban 6544, Cam 9305, Lin 3332
NOTE:- Banner 6544 as HOLLYWOOD DANCE ORCHESTRA; Cameo 9305 and Lincoln 3332 as
DIXIE DAISIES.

Adrian Schubert dir. Mike Mosiello-? Manny Klein-t/Tommy Dowd or Charlie Butter-
field-tb/Tony Parenti-cl-as/? Andy Sannella-as/Joe Dubin-ts/? Jimmy Johnston-bsx/
pic/h/Russ Carlson-p/bj/bb/? Joe or George Hamilton Green-d-x/Irving Kaufman-v.
                                        New York, November 15, 1929.

9142-2  It's Not A Secret Any More - vIK        Ban 0514
NOTE:- This issue as IMPERIAL DANCE ORCHESTRA.

2vn ? or vn/vc replace bsx/pic/h; Smith Ballew-(as BUDDY BLUE when credited)-v.
                                        New York, November 26, 1929.

9187-1-4  I'm Following You - vSB              Ban 0539, Bwy 1349, Cam 0139,
NOTE:- Banner 0539, Imperial 2264 as HOLLYWOOD    Cq 7459, Dom 4469, PA 37077,
DANCE ORCHESTRA; Broadway 1349 as PALACE DANCE    Per 15258, Re 8914, Ro 1156,
ORCHESTRA; Conqueror 7459 as PARADISE CLUB BAND;  Imp 2264, Ang 3196, Clif 5196,
Domino 4469, Regal 8914 and Vocalion 565 as       Emb 8107, 9196, Voc 565
IMPERIAL DANCE ORCHESTRA; Embassy 8107 as EMBASSY DANCE BAND.

Jack Kaufman-v.                          New York, January 7, 1930.

9268-3  In Harlem's Araby - vJK                 Ban 0569, Cam 0169, Je 5824,
NOTE:- Sterling 181289 as THE TEN BLACKBIRDS;   Or 1824, Ro 1187, Stg 181289
all others as DUBIN'S DANDIES.

ADRIAN SCHUBERT AND HIS SALON ORCHESTRA : Adrian Schubert dir. Bob Effros-t/Miff Mole
tb/Tony Parenti-cl-as/? Russ Carlson-p/Charlie Magnante-pac/bj/bb/d/Scrappy Lambert
(as RALPH HAINES, or (on Paramount and Broadway) ROLAND LANCE)-v.
                                        New York, January 21, 1930.

9298-2  What Do I Care ? - vSL           Per 15274, Imp 2307
9299-1  Nobody's Sweetheart - vSL        Or 1854, Per 15273, Re 8942
9300-2-3  The Man From The South (With A Big    Ban 0590, Bwy 1353, Cam 0190,
        Cigar In His Mouth) - vSL        Chg 865, Cq 7487, Je 5845, Or 1845,
NOTE:- Broadway 1353 and Paramount 20794 as    Pm 20794, Per 15273, Re 8942,
PALACE DANCE ORCHESTRA; Conqueror 7487, Perfect Ro 1207, Cr 81304
15273 and Regal 8942 as MISSOURI JAZZ BAND; Oriole 1854 and Imperial 2307 as HOLLY-
WOOD DANCE ORCHESTRA; Perfect 15274 as IMPERIAL DANCE ORCHESTRA; Crown 81304 as
GOLDIE'S SYNCOPATORS.

Irving Kaufman-v.                        New York, January 28, 1930.

9311-   Ring Around The Moon - vIK       Ban ?
9312-3  Rainy Weather Rose - vIK         Cr 81308, Dom 181308, Stg 281308
9313-3  I've Seen My Baby (And It Won't Be Long  Ban 0596, Cam 0196, Je 5852,
        Now) - vIK                       Or 1852
NOTE:- Crown 81308 and Domino 181308 as BUD CARLTON'S ORCHESTRA; Sterling 281308 as
HEW STERLING'S ORCHESTRA; all others as MAJESTIC DANCE ORCHESTRA.

Adrian Schubert dir. probably :- Manny Klein-Mike Mosiello-t/Tommy Dowd or Charlie
Butterfield-tb/Tony Parenti-Andy Sannella-cl-as/Joe Dubin-ts/Russ Carlson-p/bj/bb/
d/Irving Kaufman-v, possibly others.  New York, March 4, 1930.

9408-1  Sing, You Sinners - vIK          Ban    , Je 5883, Or 1883,
                                         Per 15283, Imp 2309
NOTE:- Jewel 5883 as IMPERIAL DANCE ORCHESTRA; Oriole 1883 as HOLLYWOOD DANCE
ORCHESTRA; Perfect 15283 and Imperial 2309 as MISSOURI JAZZ BAND.

                                        New York, April 1, 1930.

9543-1-2  Syncopated Jamboree - vIK      Ban 0804, Cam 0404, Je 6059,
                                         Or 2059, Re 10113, Cr 81469
NOTE:- Crown 81469 as BUD CARLTON AND HIS ORCHESTRA.

The name SCHUBERT'S METROPOLITAN ORCHESTRA was a pseudonym on Carnival/Puretone/Tri-
angle 11383 and Pennington 1383 for the New Orleans Jazz Band, q.v.

## EVAN  SCHUBERT

Pseudonym on Australian Summit 134 for Roy Evans, q.v.

## BERNIE SCHULTZ AND HIS  CRESCENT ORCHESTRA

Bernie Schultz-t dir. Harry LaRue-t/Fred Hacket-tb/George Byron Webb-Eddie Anderson-
as/Omar Hoagland-ts/Vic Carlson-p/Sandy Ross-bj/Al Waffle-bb/Johnny Day-d.
                                        Chicago, c. July 19, 1927.

12926     Sweet Violets - vch            Gnt 6216, Bell 572, Ch 15324
12926-A   Sweet Violets - vch            Spr 356
12927     Sweetheart Of Sigma Chi - vch  Gnt 6216, Bell 569, Ch 15323
12927-A   Sweetheart Of Sigma Chi - vch  Chg 759
12928, -A-B  Meditation ("Thaïs" - Massenet)   Rejected
NOTE:- Bell 569 as BRUCE BRAY AND HIS ORCHESTRA; 572 as DICK BURTON AND HIS ORCH-
ESTRA; Superior 356 as RAY TAYLOR'S SINGING ORCHESTRA.

                                        Chicago, c. August 18, 1927.

13006     Show Me That Kind Of A Girl - v    Gnt 6235, Ch 15343, Sil 25107,
                                         Spr 359
13007     Hold Everything                Gnt 6234
13008     Somebody And Me                    -      Ch 15342
NOTE:- Champion 15342, 15343 as RAY TAYLOR AND HIS ORCHESTRA; Superior 359 as RAY
TAYLOR'S SINGING ORCHESTRA.

Myron Schulz-vn dir. Bill Chandler-Andy Secrest-t/Lorin Schulz-tb/Bob Hutsell-Ray
  Porter-cl-as-ts/Russell Trulock-cl-ts/Harry Bason-p/Harold Young-bj/Cyril Quinn-bb
  /Mel Miller-d/v by a group, probably Lorin and Myron Schulz and Ray Porter.
                                      Richmond, Ind., April 14, 1927.

12705, -A  Hurricane                          Gnt rejected
12706, -A  Mine - v                                 -

## ARTHUR  SCHUTT

The following records are listed in full mainly because of their illustrious personnels; it should not be assumed that because some of them are excellent examples of
"hot" dance music of the period, they are all of the same standard.

Piano solos.                          London, August 2, 1923.

A-142   Try And Play It                       Re G-8032
A-143   Pianoflage                            Re G-8046
A-144   The Ghost Of The Piano                Re G-8032
A-145   Teasin' The Ivories                   Re G-8046

                                      New York, January 11, 1928.

145503-3  Rambling In Rhythm                  Har 860-H
145504-2  Jack In The Box                           -

                                      New York, March 28, 1929.

401753-B  Lover, Come Back To Me !           OK 41243, Par R-412, A-2970
401754-B  Piano Puzzle                            -           -        -

ARTHUR SCHUTT AND HIS ORCHESTRA : Leo McConville and another-t/Tommy Dorsey-tb/Jimmy
  Dorsey-cl-as/as/Babe Russin-ts/Arthur Schutt-p/Eddie Lang-g/Joe Tarto or Hank
  Stern-bb-sb/Stan King-d/Irving Kaufman-v.
                                      New York, November 18, 1929.

403275-A  My Fate Is In Your Hands - vIK      OK 41346, Par R-587, A-2953,
                                              B-12865, Od A-189314
403276-A  Take Everything But You - vIK       OK 41345, Par R-594, A-2945,
                                              B-12865
403277-B  If I'm Dreaming (Don't Wake Me Too Soon) OK 41346   - A-2972, Od A-189314
          (w) - vIK

   Smith Ballew-v.                    New York, January 4, 1930.

403583-A  I'm Following You ! - vSB           OK 41360, Od ONY-36025, A-189317,
                                              A-221237, Par PNY-34020, R-587
403584-A  Have A Little Faith In Me - vSB     OK 41359, Od ONY-36028, A-221235,
                                              Par PNY-34025, R-619
403585-B  Cryin' For The Carolines - vSB      As above, but Par PNY-34024
490026-A  I'm Following You !                 Od ONY-36021, Par PNY-34016
   NOTE:- All Parlophone PNY- series as CYRIL MERRIVALE AND HIS ORCHESTRA or CYRIL
MERRIVALE'S ORCHESTRA.

   Scrappy Lambert-v.                 New York, March 4, 1930.

403796-A  Montana Call - vSL                  OK 41391, Od ONY-36055,
                                              Par PNY-34047, R-713, A-3025
490043-A  Montana Call                        Od ONY-36053, Par PNY-34045
   NOTE:- Parlophone PNY-34045 and PNY-34047 as CYRIL MERRIVALE AND HIS ORCHESTRA.

                                      New York, March 10, 1930.
403840-B  The Moon Is Low - vSL               OK 41391, Od ONY-36055,
                                              Par PNY-34048, R-713, A-3025
403841-B  It Must Be You - vSL                OK 41392, Od ONY-36062,
                                              Par PNY-34056, A-3030
403842-A  'Leven-Thirty Saturday Night - vSL  OK 41400, ONY-36056, A-189343,
                                              04113, Par PNY-34049, R-672,
                                              A-3022, A-4969
490047-A  The Moon Is Low                     Od ONY-36053, Par PNY-34046
490048-A  It Must Be You                      Od ONY-36060, Par PNY-34053

Probably :- Bob Effros-Manny Klein-t/Tommy Dorsey-tb/Arnold Brilhart-cl-as-f/cl-ss-
    as/Babe Russin-ts/vn/Arthur Schutt-p/Carl Kress-g/Joe Tarto-sb/Stan King-d/Smith
    Ballew-Irving Kaufman-v.                    New York, May 23, 1930.

404036-B  Lo Lo - vIK                          Od ONY-36099, Par PNY-34092,
                                                 E-6350
100404-1  Lo Lo - vIK                          Har 1182-H
404037-C  Sharing - vSB                        Od ONY-36096, Par PNY-34087
404038-B  The Song Without A Name - vSB        -             Par PNY-34089
490075-A  Sharing                              Od ONY-36100, Par PNY-34086
490076-A  The Song Without A Name              -             Par PNY-34088
    NOTE:- Parlophone E-6150 as MERTON DANCE ORCHESTRA; all other Parlophones as CYRIL
    MERRIVALE'S ORCHESTRA (including those from the last session on page 1369); Harmony
    1182-H as FRANK AUBURN AND HIS ORCHESTRA.

Piano solos.                                   New York, September 28, 1934.

16073-1-2  Limehouse Blues                     ARC rejected
16074-1-2  Bring-Up Breakdown                  -

## GEORGE SCHWEINFEST

George Schweinfest was a pioneer recording artist who played flute, piccolo and piano
    solos, and included in his repertoire a few numbers of interest as ragtime.

Piccolo solos, acc. by C. H. H. Booth-p.  New York, September 22, 1900.

225-1-2  A Rag Time Skeedaddle (George Rosey)  Vic 225, Ber 238 (Canadian)
NOTE:- Takes 3 and 4 of the above were made on March 16, 1901, and were probably
used for issue.

Acc. by ? Charles A. Prince-p.             New York, c. December, 1901.

498-4  A Rag Time Skeedaddle (George Rosey)    Col 498

Acc. by C. H. H. Booth-p.                  New York, September 11, 1902.

225-5-6  A Rag Time Skeedaddle (George Rosey)  Vic 225

Piano solo.                                New York, c. 1902.

    Coon Jim                                   Vitaphone 878

## BLUE SCOTT AND HIS BLUE BOYS

See Leonard Scott.

## CECIL SCOTT AND HIS BRIGHT BOYS/ORCHESTRA*

Bill Coleman-t/Frank Newton-t-v/Dicky Wells-tb/John Williams-Harold McFerran-as/Cecil
    Scott-cl-ts-bar/Don Frye-p/Rudolph Williams-bj/Mack Walker-bb/Lloyd Scott-d.
                                           New York, November 19, 1929.

57709-1  Lawd, Lawd - vFN&ch                   Vic V-38098, BB B-8276,HMV R-14425
57710-1  In A Corner                           -              -         -
57711-2  Bright Boy Blues                      Vic V-38117*, 1AC-0127
57712-1  Springfield Stomp                     -              -

## EFFIE  SCOTT

Vocal, acc. by ? Sam Price-p/g, with Bert Johnson-tb*.
                                           Dallas, November, 1929.

DAL-468-  *Lonesome Hut Blues                  Voc 1461
DAL-469-  Sunshine Special                     -

## GENEVIA  SCOTT

Pseudonym on Pathe Actuelle and Perfect for Hannah Sylvester, q.v.

Piano solos, acc. by J. C. Heard-d.        New York, December 11, 1940.

| | | |
|---|---|---|
| 68480-A | Valse in D flat major (Chopin, Op. 64, No. 1) | Dec 18129 |
| 68481-A | Country Gardens (Percy Grainger) | Dec 18128, Y-5828 |
| 68482-A | Ritual Fire Dance (Manuel de Falla) | Dec 18127 |
| 68483-A | Prelude in C sharp minor (Rachmaninoff) | Dec 18128, Y-5828, Br 03476 |
| 68484-A | Two-Part Invention in A minor (Bach) | Dec 18127 |
| 68485-A | Hungarian Rhapsody No. 2 (Liszt) | Dec 18129, Br 03476 |

New York, February 27, 1942.

| | | |
|---|---|---|
| 70410-A | Embraceable You | Dec 18341 |
| 70411-A | Hazel's Boogie Woogie | Dec 18340, Br 04799 |
| 70412-A | Blues in B flat | -            - |
| 70413-A | Hallelujah | Dec 18342 |
| 70414-A | Dark Eyes | - |
| 70415-A | Three Little Words | Dec 18341 |

Vocal, acc. by own p.                       New York, May 1, 1942.

70708-A   The Man I Love                     Dec rejected

## LEONARD SCOTT

BLUE SCOTT AND HIS BLUE BOYS : Leonard Scott-v, acc. by Lee Collins-t/ts/? Richard M.
Jones-p; or ? Arnett Nelson-cl/? Richard M. Jones-p/g/sb; or ? Richard M. Jones-p/g
Chicago, August 5, 1936.

| | | |
|---|---|---|
| 100677-1 | I Can Dish It - Can You Take It ?-t/ts/p | BB B-6520 |
| 100678-1 | You Can't Lose - t/ts/p | BB B-6557 |
| 100679-1 | Rubbin', Rubbin' - cl/p/g/sb | BB B-6520 |
| 100680-1 | At The Bottom - p/g | BB B-6557 |

Vocal, acc. by ? Odell Rand-cl/? J. H. Shayne-p/John Lindsay-sb.
Chicago, August 20, 1936.

| | | |
|---|---|---|
| C-1451- | She's Got Something Good | Voc 03311 |
| C-1452- | You Done Tore Your Playhouse Down | - |

## LLOYD SCOTT AND HIS ORCHESTRA

Lloyd Scott-d dir. Kenneth Roane-t-a/Gus McClung-t/Dicky Wells-tb/Fletcher Allen-John
Williams-cl-as/Cecil Scott-cl-ts-bar/Don Frye-p-a/Hubert Mann-bj/Chester Campbell-
bb.                                          New York, January 10, 1927.

| | | |
|---|---|---|
| 37529-2 | Harlem Shuffle - aKR | Vic 21491 |
| 37530-2 | Symphonic Scronch (Symphonic Screach) | Vic 20495 |
| 37531-2 | Happy Hour Blues | - |

## MAE SCOTT

Vocal, acc. by Lemuel Fowler or Lewis Thomas-p, as shown.
New York, c. July, 1923.

| | | |
|---|---|---|
| 1451-3 | Squawkin' The Blues - pLF | Pm 12048 |
| 1452-2 | I'll Get Even With You (Revengeful Blues) - pLT | - |

## RAYMOND SCOTT

RAYMOND SCOTT QUINTETTE : Raymond Scott-p dir. Dave Wade-t/Pete Pumiglio-cl/Dave
Harris-ts/Lou Shoobe-sb/Johnny Williams-d.
New York, February 20, 1937.

| | | |
|---|---|---|
| M-117-1 | Minuet In Jazz | Mas 108, Br 7992,Col 36107,DS-1674 |
| M-118-1 | Twilight In Turkey | -        -        -          - |
| M-119-1 | The Toy Trumpet | Mas 111, Br 7993, Col 36311 |
| M-120-2 | Powerhouse | -        -        - |

RAYMOND SCOTT QUINTETTE : Raymond Scott-p dir. Dave Wade-t/Pete Pumiglio-cl/Dave
  Harris-ts/Lou Shoobe-sb/Johnny Williams-d.
                                      New York, April 3, 1937.

M-351-1-2  Dead End Blues                       Mas rejected
M-352-1-2  Reckless Night On Board An Ocean Liner    -

                                      New York, April 30, 1937.

M-352-3-4  Reckless Night On Board An Ocean     Br 8000
             Liner
M-437-1-2  Dinner Music For A Pack Of Hungry    Rejected
             Cannibals
M-438-1-2  The Girl With The Light Blue Hair        -

                                      New York, May 24, 1937.

M-352-5-6  Reckless Night On Board An Ocean     Rejected
             Liner
M-437-4    Dinner Music For A Pack Of Hungry    Mas 136
             Cannibals

                                      New York, June 23, 1937.

M-352-8  Reckless Night On Board An Ocean Liner  Mas 136, Br 8000, Col 36258
M-437-5  Dinner Music For A Pack Of Hungry Cannibals -       -          -

Ted Harkins-sb replaces Shoobe.       New York, December 20, 1937.

M-702-D  War Dance For Wooden Indians           Br 8058, Col 36316
M-703-A  The Penguin                                -          -

Fred Whiting-sb replaces Harkins.     New York, April 19, 1938.

M-822-B  The Happy Farmer                       Br 8144, Col 36277

                                      New York, April 23, 1938.

M-823-B  Egyptian Barn Dance                    Br 8144, Col 36277

RAYMOND SCOTT AND HIS ORCHESTRA : Raymond Scott-p dir. unknown personnel.
                                      New York, January 18, 1939.

23950-   Moment Whimsical                       Br rejected
23951-   Siberian Sleigh-Ride                       -

RAYMOND SCOTT QUINTETTE : As for April 19, 1938 above.
                                      New York, March 27, 1939.

24275-   Boy Scout In Switzerland               Col rejected
24276-   In An 18th Century Drawing-Room            -

                                      New York, April, 1939.

RR-3131-B  Bumpy Weather Over Newark            Col 35585
RR-7031-1  Peter Tambourine                         -

                                      New York, May 8, 1939.

24486-   Siberian Sleigh-Ride                   Rejected
24487-   A Little Bit Of Rigoletto                  -
24488-B  Moment Musical                         Col 37361
24489-   The Quintette Plays Carmen             Rejected

Russ Case-t replaces Wade.            New York, June 12, 1939.

24742-B  In An 18th-Century Drawing-Room        Br 8404, Col 35347
24743-B  Boy Scout In Switzerland                   -          -
24744-A  Siberian Sleigh-Ride                   Br 8452, Col 36121

RAYMOND SCOTT QUINTETTE : Raymond Scott-p dir. Russ Case-t/Pete Pumiglio-cl/Dave
Harris-ts/Fred Whiting-sb/Johnny Williams-d.
New York, July 10, 1939.

| 24881- | Oil Gusher | Rejected |
| 24882- | Unknown title | - |
| 24883-B | The Girl At The Typewriter | Col 37359 |

Lou Shoobe-sb replaces Whiting.          New York, July 21, 1939.

| 24914-A | Manhattan Minuet | Rejected |
| 24915- | Peter Tambourine | - |
| 24916-A | New Year's Eve In A Haunted House | Col 35247 |
| 24917- | The Quintette Plays Carmen | Rejected |

New York, July 27, 1939.

| 24935-B | The Tobacco Auctioneer | Br 8452, Col 36121 |
| 24936-A | The Girl With The Light Blue Hair | Col 35247 |
| 24937-A | A Little Bit Of Rigoletto | Rejected |

New York, July 28, 1939.

| 24914-B | Manhattan Minuet | Col 37361 |
| 24937-B | A Little Bit Of Rigoletto | Col 37360 |
| 24943-B | The Quintette Plays Carmen | - |

RAYMOND SCOTT AND HIS NEW ORCHESTRA : Raymond Scott dir. Gordon Griffin-Mike Meola-
Willie Kelly-t/Irving Sonntag-Joe Vargas-tb/Pete Pumiglio-cl-as/Reggie Merrill-as
Art Drelinger-Dave Harris-cl-ts/Walter Gross-p/Vince Maffei-g/Lou Shoobe-sb/
Johnny Williams-d.                    New York, October 18, 1939.

| 26178-A | Just A Gigolo | Col 35363, Par R-2781 |
| 26179-A | Mexican Jumping Bean | Col 36211 |
| 26180-A-B | The Peanut Vendor | Rejected |
| 26181-A | Get Happy | Col 37359 |

New York, November 30, 1939.

| 26315-A | Huckleberry Duck | Rejected |
| 26316-A-B | Runnin' Wild | - |
| 26317-A-B | In A Subway Far From Ireland | Col 36211 |

New York, December 21, 1939.

| 26180-C | The Peanut Vendor | Col 35364, Par R-2781 |
| 26315-B | Huckleberry Duck | Col 35363, DO-2168, Par R-2744 |
| 26316-C-D | Runnin' Wild | Rejected |
| 26357-A | Business Men's Bounce | Col 35364, DO-2168, Par R-2744 |

New York, February 15, 1940.

| 26518-A-B | If I Had You | Col rejected |
| 26519-A-B | Whispering | - |
| 26520-A-B | Body And Soul | - |
| 26521-A-B | Time On My Hands | - |

Raymond Scott dir. Stephen Market-Lawrence Stearns-Bert LaMar-t/Wendell DeLory-
Charles McCamish-tb/Benny Lagasse-Slats Long-cl-as/Stanley Webb-Hugo Winterhalter-
ts/Bernard Lazaroff-p/Art Ryerson-g/Stewart "Chubby" Jackson-sb/Andy Picard-d,
New York, June 17, 1940.

| 26928-A | Four Beat Shuffle | Col 35565, Par R-2776 |
| 26929-A | At An Arabian House Party | Col 37362 |
| 26930-B | Birdseed Special | Col 35565, Par R-2776 |
| 26931-A | My Man (Mon Homme) | Rejected |

RAYMOND SCOTT AND HIS NEW ORCHESTRA : Raymond Scott dir. Stephen Market-Johnny Owens
Bert LaMar-t/Wendell DeLory-Charles McCamish-tb/Benny Lagasse-Slats Long-cl-as/
Stanley Webb-Hugo Winterhalter-ts/Bernard Leighton (Lazaroff)-p/Art Ryerson-g/
Stewart "Chubby" Jackson-sb/Andy Picard-d/Nan Wynn-v.
New York, July 8, 1940.

26990-A  Now I Lay Me Down To Dream - vNW        Col 35623, C-60
26991-A  And So Do I - vNW                         -        -
26992-A-B  Do You Pamper Your Husband At Night ? Rejected
           - vNW

Charles Brosen-ts replaces Winterhalter.
Chicago, August 13, 1940.

WC-3266-A  Yesterthoughts - vNW                   Col 35745, C-108
WC-3267-A  In A Moonboat - vNW                    Col 35698, C-90
WC-3268-A  A Million Dreams Ago - vNW               -        -
WC-3269-A  I Don't Want To Cry Any More - vNW     Rejected

Jimmy Maxwell-t replaces LaMar; Pete Lofthouse-tb replaces DeLory; Ray Schultz-cl-
as replaces Brosen; Clyde Burke-v.    Chicago, September 10, 1940.

WC-3285-1  I Don't Want To Cry Any More - vCB     Col 35773
WC-3286-1  Half Way Down The Street - vCB           -
WC-3287-1  Stranger-- vCB                         Col 35745, C-108
WC-3288-1  Don't Cry, My Heart - vCB              Rejected
WC-3289-1  Wellesley High Jump                      -
WC-3290-1  At An Arabian House Party                -
WC-3291-1  Pretty Little Petticoat (Theme Song)   Col 35803, 36226
WC-3292-1  A Nice Day In The Country                -

Raymond Scott dir. Jack Walker-Graham Young-Jack Hall-t/Charles McCamish-Pete
Lofthouse-tb/Benny Lagasse-Charlie Spero-Frank Gallodoro-as/Stanley Webb-ts/Don
Tiff-p/Art Ryerson-g/Mike Ruben-sb/Carl Maus-d/Clyde Burke-v.
Chicago, November 29, 1940.

CCO-3500-1  Eagle Beak                            Col 35911
CCO-3501-1  Copyright 1950                          -
CCO-3502-1-2  Happy Birthday To You - vCB         Col 35864
CCO-3503-1  All Around The Christmas Tree - vCB     -

Chicago, January 6, 1941.

CCO-3514-1  When Cootie Left The Duke             Col 35940
CCO-3515-1  Blues My Girl Friend Taught Me        Col 35980
CCO-3516-1  Petite                                Col 35940
CCO-3517-1  Evening Star                          Col 35980

Raymond Scott dir. Hy Small-Vincent Bardale-Jack Hall-t/Joe Ortolano-Sammy Levine-
tb/Benny Lagasse-Phil Olivella-as/John Albert Mosey-Stanley Webb-ts/Don Tiff-p/Zeb
Julian-g/Mike Ruben-sb/Milton Holland-d/Clyde Burke-Gloria Hart-v.
New York, April 7, 1941.

30197-  Just A Little Bit South Of North          Col 36103
          Carolina - vCB
30198-1  Keep Cool, Fool - vGH                    Col 36149
30199-1  I Understand - vCB                       Col 36083
30200-1-2  Key West                               Col 36410
30201-1  On The Jersey Side                         -
30202-1  The Things I Love - vCB                  Col 36083

Junie Mays-p replaces Tiff.          New York, April 14, 1941.

30246-1  Let's Get Away From It All - vGH         Col 36090
30247-1  In The Hush Of The Night - vCB           Col 36103
30248-1  The Band Played On (w) - vCB             Col 36090
30249-1  Beau Night In Hotchkiss Corners - vGH    Col 36288

RAYMOND SCOTT AND HIS NEW ORCHESTRA : Raymond Scott dir. Hy Small-Vincent Bardale-
  Jack Hall-t/Joe Ortolano-Sammy Levine-tb/Benny Lagasse-Phil Olivella-as/John Albert
  Mosey-Stanley Webb-ts/Junie Mays-p/Bob Dominick-g/Mike Ruben-sb/Milton Holland-d/
  Clyde Burke-Gloria Hart-v.                     New York, April 29, 1941.

| | | |
|---|---|---|
| 30341-1 | Where You Are - vCB | Col 36149 |
| 30342-1 | I Touched A Star - vCB | Col 36161 |
| 30343-1 | Do You Care ? - vCB | - |
| 30344-1 | Do You Pamper Your Husband At Night ? - vGH | Rejected |
| 30345-1 | The Merry Carrousel - vCB | Col 36288 |

RAYMOND SCOTT AND HIS ORCHESTRA : Raymond Scott dir. Buzz King-Bob Aston-Eddie Aver-
  sano-t/Bill Siegel-Mac Marlow-tb/Pete Pumiglio-cl-as/Lester Merkin-as/Stanley Webb
  ts/Charles Kiner-p/Bill Halfacre-sb/Sid Kaye-d.
                                                 New York, February 24, 1942.

| | | |
|---|---|---|
| 70385-A | Caterpillar Creep | Dec 18264, Br 03345 |
| 70386-A | Eight Letters In The Mailbox | Dec 18276, Br 03367 |
| 70387-A | Kodachrome | -    - |
| 70388-A | Symphony Under The Stars | Dec 18264, Br 03345 |

                                New York, May 4, 1942.

| | | |
|---|---|---|
| 70709-A | Carrier Pigeon | Dec 18422 |
| 70710-A | Secret Agent | Dec 18377 |
| 70711-A | Pan-American Hot-Spot | - |
| 70712-A | Careful Conversation At A Diplomatic Function | Dec 18422 |

## GEORGE  SCOTT-WOOD

See the Six Swingers.

## THE SCRANTON SIRENS  ORCHESTRA

illy Lustig-vn dir. 2t/Russ Morgan-tb/Alfie Evans-Sid Trucker-cl-as/Jim Crossan-ts/
  Itzy Riskin-p/bj/Mike Trafficante-bb/Ted Noyes-d.
                                           New Orleans, c. January 24, 1925.

| | | |
|---|---|---|
| 8909-A | Why Should I Believe In You ? | OK 40297 |
| 8910-B | Common Street Blues | OK 40329 |

## SCRAP IRON JAZZ BAND

/tb/2vn/p/bj/d.                         Paris, c. December, 1918.

| | | |
|---|---|---|
| 6503 | The Dirty Dozen | P 6461 |
| 6504 | Oh ! How I Hate To Get Up In The Morning | P 6462 |
| 6505 | Way Down In Macon, Georgia | - |
| 6506 | A.M.E.R.I.C.A. I Love You, My Yankee Land | P 6463 |
| 6507 | | |
| 6508 | The Pickaninnies' Paradise | P 6463 |
| 6509 | The Ragtime Volunteers Are Off To War | P 6461 |

ORCHESTRE SCRAP IRON JAZZERINOS : C/tb/ts/p/bj/d. (Described as FRANCAIS ORCHESTRE
  and  JAZZ BAND AMERICAN).              Paris, June 2, 1919.

| | | |
|---|---|---|
| 20532b | It's A Hundred To One You're In Love | HMV K-531 |
| 20533b | 'N Everything | - |
| 20534b | Sinbad  (Intro. I Shall Hail Cairo And Our Ancestors) | HMV K-532 |
| 20535b | Everything Is Peaches Down In Georgia | HMV K-828 |
| 20536b | How Ya Gonna Keep 'Em Down On The Farm-v | HMV K-532 |
| 20537b | Oh ! So Pretty | HMV K-732 |
| 20538b | Sweet Little Buttercup et My Mother's Eyes | - |
| 20539b | I Ain't Got Nobody | HMV K-1318, X-1484 |
| 20540b | Oui, Oui, Marie | HMV K-1317   - |
| 20541b | Everybody Shimmies Now | HMV K-828 |

Vocal, acc. by Clarence Williams-p.     New York, c. April 30, 1924.

72486-B  Everybody's Blues                OK 8142
72487-B  Why He Left Me I Don't Know        -

                                        New York, c. May 1, 1924.

72497-B  Cruel Papa But A Good Man To Have  OK 8156
            Around
72498-B  My Daddy's Calling Me              -

Acc. by King Oliver-c/Kid Ory-tb/Albert Nicholas-cl-ss/? Billy Paige-as/Luis
Russell-p/Bud Scott-bj/Paul Barbarin-d.
                                        Chicago, April 23, 1926.

C-228    Home Town Blues                  Voc 1017
C-230    Sorrow Valley Blues                -

Acc. by DeLoise Searcy-p/Lonnie Johnson-g.
                                        St. Louis, May 2, 1927.

80817-A  Lonesome Valley Blues            OK 8476
80818-A  Outsider Blues                   Rejected
80819-A  Smokey Rattler                     -
80820-A  Sorrow Valley Blues              OK 8476

DIXIE NOLAN-JOHNNY HARDGE : Irene Scruggs-Johnny Hodges (not the famous alto saxo-
phonist with Duke Ellington !)-v, acc. by ? Johnny Hodges-p/2g.
                                        Memphis, September 28, 1929.

56301-1  Worried Love - Part 1            Vic V-38556
56302-2  Worried Love - Part 2              -

CHOCOLATE BROWN : Irene Scruggs-v, acc. by Blind Blake-g.
                                        Grafton, Wis., c. May 23, 1930.

L-325-1  Stingaree Man Blues              Pm 12944
L-326-2-3  Itching Heel                     -
            How I'm Feeling               Rejected ?

                                        Grafton, Wis., May 28, 1930.

L-348-2  You Got What I Want              Pm 12978, 13121

                                        Grafton, Wis., c. May 29, 1930.

L-353-2  Cherry Hill Blues               Pm 12978

Vocal, acc. by ? J. Norman Ebron-p and/or ? Willie James-g as shown.
                                        Richmond, Ind., August 30, 1930.

16970    You've Got What I Want - p       Gnt 7296, Ch 16102, Spr 2591,
                                          Spt 9769, Var 6050, Poydras 80,
                                          Ristic 7
16973    I Want You To Give Me Some - p/g  Ch 16148, Spr 2730
16975-A  My Back To The Wall - g          Gnt 7296, Ch 16148, Spt 9769,
                                          Var 6050, Poydras 80, Ristic 7
16977    Borrowed Love - g                Ch 16102, Var 6063
16980    The Voice Of The Blues - g       Ch 16756, Spr 2591
NOTE:- Matrices 16974, 16976, 16978 and 16979 are by the Scarce Crow (see Willie
Owens); matrices 16971/2 are by Sam Tarpley, a strictly blues artist outside the
scope of this book.  Varsity 6063 as LITTLE SISTER.

Acc. by Little Brother Montgomery-p.    Grafton, Wis., c. September, 1930.

L-498-   Borrowed Love Blues             Pm 13046
L-500-   Back To The Wall                  -
            Good Meat Grinder            Pm 13023
            Must Get Mine In Front         -
            St. Louis Woman Blues        Rejected ?

Clifford King-c/Edgar Green-cl/DeLoise Searcy-p.
St. Louis, May 12, 1926.

9665-A  Kansas Avenue Blues            OK 8360
9666-A  East St. Louis Stomp           -

## JERRY SEARS SESSION WITH PEG LA CENTRA

Peg La Centra-v, acc. by Jerry Sears-p dir. Angie Rattiner-t/Jack Lacey-tb/Paul Ricci
cl-ts/Carl Kress-g/Herb Quigley-d.    New York, October 20, 1938.

028133-1  Alexander's Back In Town                BB B-10021, RZ G-23727
028134-1  Who Threw The Mush In Grandpa's Whiskers BB B-10050
028135-1  Noodlin'                                BB B-10021, RZ G-23727
028136-1  Big Mouth Minnie                        BB B-10050
028137-1  Blue Grass                              BB B-10097
028138-1  A Blind Man Could See That I Love You   -

## SEATTLE  HARMONY  KINGS

Eddie Neibaur-cl-ts dir. Earl Baker-Marvin Hamby-t/Bennie Neibaur-tb-v/Rosy McHargue-
cl-as/Joe Thomas-p/Leon "Sleepy" Kaplan-bj/Swede Knudsen-bb/Richie Miller-d.
Camden, N. J., September 2, 1925.

33195-6  If I Had A Girl Like You             Vic 19772, HMV B-5091
33196-7  Darktown Shuffle                     -

Artie Seaberg-cl-as added.            New York, July 26, 1926.

35940-1-2 Breezin' Along With The Breeze - vBN   Vic rejected

New York, August 2, 1926.

35940-6  Breezin' Along With The Breeze       Vic 20142
35950-1-2-3-4  No-One Will Know It But Me     Rejected
         (Barrel House Stomp)
35951-1-2-3  Nervous Charlie Stomp           -
35952-2  How Many Times ?                     Vic 20133

## GENE  SEDRIC

Tenor saxophone solo, unacc.          New York, May 4 or 5, 1937.

         Saxophone Doodle                 Ristic 22 (LP)
NOTE:- For other solos by Gene Sedric, made on the same occasion but accompanied by
Fats Waller-p, see Waller.

SEDRIC AND HIS HONEY BEARS : Herman Autrey-t/Jimmy Powell-Fred Skerritt-cl-as/Gene
Sedric-ts/Henry Duncan-p/Albert Casey-g/Cedric Wallace-sb/Slick Jones-d/Myra Johnson-v.                                 New York, November 23, 1938.

M-932-1  The Joint Is Jumpin' - vMJ           Voc 4576
M-933-1  Off Time - vMJ                       -
M-934-1  Choo Choo                            Voc 4552
M-935-1  The Wail Of The Scromph              -

## RAY SEELEY AND HIS ORCHESTRA

Pseudonym for the following items listed in this book :-

Odeon ONY-36106  I Love You So Much (Ben Selvin and his Orchestra)
      ONY-36107  Can  I Help It ? (Ben Selvin and his Orchestra)
      ONY-36192  I Found What I Wanted In You (Phil Dannenberg and his Orchestra)
      ONY-36203  Both sides by Ben Selvin and his Orchestra
Parlophone A-3179  I'm Crazy 'Bout My Baby (Ben Selvin and his Orchestra)
          A-3181  You'll Be Mine In Apple Blossom Time (Ben Selvin and his Orchestra)
                 (also Parlophone R-916)

CHARLIE SEGAR

Piano solos.                                      Chicago, September 10, 1934.

C-9432-B  Cuban Villa Blues                       Dec 7027
C-9433-B  Southern Hospitality                    –

                                                  Chicago, January 11, 1935.

C-9645-A  Cow Cow Blues                           Dec 7075
C-9646-A  Boogie Woogie                           –        3832

Vocal, acc. by own p/d.                           Chicago, February 23, 1940.

WC-2957-A  Key To The Highway                     Voc 05441
WC-2958-A  Stop And Fix It, Mama                  –
WC-2959-A  Lonesome Graveyard Blues               Voc 05539
WC-2960-A  Dissatisfied Blues                     –

## EMIL SEIDEL

SEIDEL'S SOUTHLAND ORCHESTRA : Emil Seidel-p dir. unknown instrumentation and
    personnel.                                    Richmond, Ind., January 2, 1925.

12114, -A  Blue-Eyed Sally                        Gnt rejected

EMIL SEIDEL AND HIS ORCHESTRA : Emil Seidel-p dir. Byron Smart-t/Hoagy Carmichael-c-
    p/Oscar Rossberg-tb/Dick Kent-as-2nd p-a/Gene Wood-as/Maurice Bennett-ts/Donn
    Kimmell-bj-g/Paul Brown-bb-vn/Cliff Williams-d-v.
                                                  Richmond, Ind., November 11, 1927.

GEX-930    The Best Things In Life Are Free - vCW  Gnt 6295, Ch 15384
GEX-930-A  The Best Things In Life Are Free - vCW  Sil 5500
GEX-930-B  The Best Things In Life Are Free - vCW  Spr 309
GEX-931    Down South - vch                       Gnt 6309, Ch 15383
GEX-931-A  Down South - vch                       Bell 576, Sil 5500, Spr 307
GEX-932-A  Together, We Two - vCW                 Gnt 6324, Ch 15400
GEX-932-B  Together, We Two - vCW                 Spr 300
GEX-933-A  The Hours I Spent With You (w) - vCW   Gnt 6309, Ch 15382
GEX-933-B  The Hours I Spent With You (w) - vCW   Bell 573, Spr 308

    Carmichael omitted; Jimmy Fisher-v.     Richmond, Ind., November 17, 1927.

GEX-959-A  Dear, On A Night Like This - vCW      Gnt 6340, Ch 15439
GEX-960, -A-B  Is She My Girl Friend ? - vch     Rejected
GEX-961-A  Did You Mean It ? - vJF               Gnt 6324, Ch 15404, Spr 303

                                                  Richmond, Ind., November 25, 1927.

GEX-975-A  For My Baby - vch                      Gnt 6327, Ch 15404
GEX-975-B  For My Baby - vch                      Spr 303
GEX-976-A  The Song Is Ended (w) - vCW           Gnt 6327, Ch 15400
GEX-976-B  The Song Is Ended (w) - vCW           Bell 572
GEX-976-C  The Song Is Ended (w) - vCW           Spr 300

                                                  Richmond, Ind., December 9, 1927.

GEX-995-C  Counting The Days - vJF               Gnt 6355, Ch 15418
GEX-996-B  One More Night - vCW                  Gnt 6340   –
GEX-997, -A  Is She My Girl Friend ? - vCW       Rejected
GEX-997-B  Is She My Girl Friend ? - vch         –

                                                  Richmond, Ind., January 9, 1928.

13340-B  Beautiful                               Gnt 6367, Ch 15422

    Benny Benson-v.                          Richmond, Ind., January 19, 1928.

13391₅ -A-B  Four Walls - vBB                    Gnt rejected
NOTE:- All Champions listed above as JACK CRAWFORD AND HIS BOYS.  It is not known
if this is simply a pseudonym, or if Jack Crawford, the mid-West bandleader, q.v.,
participated (with some of his musicians ?)  Other Seidel titles are waltzes.

The following titles by this British bandleader are of some interest as "hot" dance
music, and an examination of all his records may prove rewarding.

ALLAN SELBY AND HIS FRASCATIANS (as PICCADILLY DANCE BAND) : Allan Selby dir. probably :- Phil Lever-t/Leslie Cooper-tb/Sid Lenton-as/H. Brooks-ts/B. Davis-p/Hal
Pike-bj/R. del Perugia-bb/G. Marshall-d.
                                   London, late November, 1928.

1417-1  Heaven For Two - v                      Pic 192
1418-2  Louisiana - v                           Pic 184

ALLAN SELBY AND HIS BAND, by arrangement with Walls and Highley Theatres Ltd. : as
above, or similar; Cavan O'Connor-v.    London, November, 1929.

3188-2  The Things We Want The Most Are Hard    Met 1220, Pic 427
          To Get - v
3190-1-2  Love Me Or Leave Me - vCO'C              -     Pic 426, Oct 355
NOTE:- Metropole 1220 as THE FRASCATIANS.

                                   London, March, 1930.

3533-2  Moanin' For You - v                      Pic 526
3534-2  I May Be Wrong, But I Think You're          -
          Wonderful - v

## REGGY SELLS

Pseudonym on Parlophone PNY-34107 for Seger Ellis, q.v.

## BEN SELVIN

Beginning in 1919, Ben Selvin has recorded more titles for more companies than any
other leader, among them many of interest as jazz, known examples being  these.

SELVIN'S NOVELTY ORCHESTRA : Ben Selvin-vn dir. Harry Glantz-t/Ephraim Hannaford-tb/
Benny Krueger-as/2nd vn/Bernie Grauer-p/John Cali-bj/Milton Sands-d/Frank Clegg-x.
                                   New York, c. February, 1920.
4888-2  Yellow Dog Blues (Intro. A Good Man Is  Em 10133, Med 8164
          Hard To Find)
SELVIN'S DANCE ORCHESTRA : Ben Selvin-vn dir. Jules Levy, Jr. or Harry Gluck-Hymie
Farberman-t/Ephraim Hannaford-tb/? Loring McMurray-? Bernie Daly-ss-as/Joe Winshup
ts/Norman Spencer and another-p/John Cali-bj/Jack Helleberg-bb/Milton Sands-d.
                                   New York, c. November 16, 1921.

8253   I've Got My Habits On - v                 Voc 14277, Aco G-15043

BEN SELVIN AND HIS ORCHESTRA : Ben Selvin-vn dir. Earl Oliver and another-t/tb/Larry
Abbott-cl-as-comb/cl-as/Lou Daly-ts/Lew Cobey-p/bj/bb/Milton Sands-d.
                                   New York, July, 1924.

13393  Red Hot Mama                              Voc 14853, X-9481

                                   New York, c. July 28, 1924.

13430  San                                       Voc 14851, X-9481

                                   New York, August, 1924.

13529  Susquehanna Home                          Voc 14871, Aco G-15566, Bel 692,
                                                 Gmn 1634, Hom H-729  Mto S-1501
NOTE:- Aco G-15566 as CLEVELAND SOCIETY ORCHESTRA; Beltona 692 as SUNNY SOUTH
DANCE ORCHESTRA; Guardsman 1634 as NEW JERSEY DANCE ORCHESTRA; Homochord H-729 as
HOMOCHORD DANCE ORCHESTRA; Meloto S-1501 as SHAFTESBURY DANCE ORCHESTRA.

MOULIN ROUGE ORCHESTRA : As above.      New York, c. November 21, 1924.

5745-1  There'll Be Some Changes Made           Ban 1492, Re 9784, Apex 8302

BEN SELVIN AND HIS ORCHESTRA : Ben Selvin-vn dir. Earl Oliver and another-t/tb/Larry
Abbott-cl-as-comb/cl-as/Lou Daly-ts/Lew Cobey-p/bj/bb/Milton Sands-d.
                                        New York, April 1, 1925.

634     Suite 16                         Voc 15029, Aco G-15795, Bel 849,
                                         Duo B-5104
NOTE:- Aco G-15795 as CLEVELAND SOCIETY ORCHESTRA; Beltona 849 as THE PALM BEACH
PLAYERS; Duophone B-5104 as BURLINGTON DANCE ORCHESTRA.

                                        New York, May 13, 1925.

788     Steppin' In Society             Voc 15038, Aco G-15794, Bel 847,
                                         Clm 1789, Duo B-5095, Gmn 1764,
                                         Hom H-838
789     Charleston                       Voc 15038, X-9625, Duo B-5076
NOTE:- Aco G-15794 as CLEVELAND SOCIETY ORCHESTRA; Beltona 847 as AMERICAN DANCE
ORCHESTRA; Coliseum 1789 as MARYLAND DANCE ORCHESTRA; Duophone B-5076 as LEAS DANCE
ORCHESTRA; B-5095 as SAVILE DANCE BAND; Homochord H-838 as ROY HENDERSON'S DANCE
ORCHESTRA. The reverse of Homochord H-838 is also CHARLESTON, but this is probably
a British recording.

Arthur Hall-v.                          New York, c. June 2, 1925.

106063    Collegiate - vAH               PA 036260, 10945, Per 14441,
NOTE:- Pathe Actuelle 036260 as HOLLYWOOD    Gra 9149, Hom C-846, Max 1545,
DANCE ORCHESTRA; 10945 as SELVIN'S DANCE ORCH-   Sal 116
ESTRA; Perfect 14441 as MAYFLOWER SERENADERS; Grafton 9149 as WINDSOR ORCHESTRA;
Homochord C-846 as ELDON'S DANCE ORCHESTRA; Maxsa 1545 as EARL RANDOLPH'S ORCH.

Arthur Fields-v.                        New York, July 30, 1925.

6105-3-4  So That's The Kind Of A Girl You Are  Ban 1586, Dom 3557, 21091,NML 1127,
          - vAF                          PA 036301, Per 14482, Re 9888,
                                         Apex 8400, Mic 22031, Leo/St 10061
6106-3-4  Loud-Speakin' Papa             Ban 1586, Dom 3557, Re 9888,
                                         Apex 8394
NOTE:- NML 1127 as MANHATTAN MUSICIANS; Pathe Actuelle 036301 and Perfect 14482 as
SOUTHAMPTON SOCIETY ORCHESTRA.

                                        New York, August 12, 1925.

1138    Breezin' Along (To Georgia)      Voc 15083, Adelphi 10, Bel 881,
                                         Clm 1828, Gmn 1830
1141    Let's Wander Away                Voc 15083, Aco G-15839      -
                                         Clm 1824, Duo B-5111
NOTE:- Aco G-15839 as CLEVELAND SOCIETY ORCHESTRA; Adelphi as THE NEW MANHATTANS;
Beltona 881 as PALM BEACH PLAYERS; Coliseum 1824 and 1828 as MARYLAND DANCE ORCH-
ESTRA; Duophone B-5111 as RAY SINCLAIR AND HIS ORCHESTRA; Guardsman 1830 as OLD
SOUTHERN DANCE ORCHESTRA.

THE KNICKERBOCKERS : Same.              New York, October 15, 1925.

141140-1  You Told Me To Go              Col 482-D, 3959
NOTE:- Columbia 3959 as DENZA DANCE BAND.

BEN SELVIN AND HIS ORCHESTRA : As above; Ben Selvin-v.
                                        New York, November 23, 1925.

1799    Sleepy-Time Gal - vBS            Voc 15154, X-9759

                                        New York, December 14, 1925.

6311-4-5  Who ?                          Ban 1657, Dom 3629, 21104, Or 552,
                                         Re 9966, Apex 8433, St 10089,
                                         Imp 1637
6312-4  Spanish Shawl                    Ban 1662, Dom 3632, 21105, Re 9965,
                                         Apex 8433, Mic 22054, St 10090
6336-2  Nobody's Business - vAF          Ban 1657, Dom 3629, Re 9967,
NOTE:- Banner 1657, 1662, Domino 3629, 3632,    Apex 8469 (cont. on page 1381)
Imperial 1637 as MISSOURI JAZZ BAND; Regal 9965, 9966 as IMPERIAL DANCE ORCHESTRA;

Regal 9967 as PERRY'S HOT DOGS. The Canadian issues credit FLETCHER HENDERSON AND
HIS ORCHESTRA, q.v. in this connection; Oriole 552 as MIAMI JAZZ BAND.

BEN SELVIN AND HIS ORCHESTRA : Ben Selvin-vn-v dir. Earl Oliver and another-t/tb/
Larry Abbott-cl-as-comb/cl-as/Lou Daly-ts/Lew Cobey-p/bj/bb/Milton Sands-d/Keller
Sisters and Lynch-v.                  New York, April 15, 1926.

E-18760/2  Betty - vBS                        Br 3172*

                              New York, June 2, 1926.

E-19424/6  Hoodle-Dee-Doo-Dee-Doo-Doo - vBS   Br 3213*
E-19427/30 When The Red, Red Robin Comes       -
           Bob, Bob, Bobbin' Along - vKS&L

Instrumentation for most Columbia and associated labels is 2t/tb/2cl-ss-as/cl-ts/2nd
vn on some/p/bj-g/bb-sb/d; where a musician from the following collective personnel is known to have been present, he is identified at the heading of the session.

Manny Klein-Tommy Gott-Bob Effros-Mike Mosiello-Leo McConville-Fred Farrar-t/Tommy
Dorsey-Chuck Campbell-Sam Lewis-tb/Larry Abbott-Andy Sannella-Louis Martin-Merle
Johnston-Lucien Smith-cl-as/Hymie Wolfson-Joe Dubin-cl-ts/Sol Klein-vn/Arthur
Schutt-Larry Murphy-Rube Bloom-Irving Brodsky-p/Carl Kress-Dick McDonough-Tony
Colucci-bj-g/Jack Hansen-Joe Tarto-Hank Stern-Norman McPherson-bb-sb/Stan King-d.

Jack Palmer-v (and t ?)               New York, October 17, 1928.

147050-3  There's A Rainbow 'Round My Shoulder-vJP Col 1605-D, 5226

Irving Kaufman (as ROBERT WOOD)-v.    New York, June 5, 1929.

148658-2  I'm Feathering A Nest - vIK          Har 948-H
NOTE:- This issue as BARNEY TRIMBLE'S OKLAHOMANS.

Selvin; Klein; Charlie Butterfield-tb; Martin; Dubin; Brodsky; Tarto; King; Smith
Ballew-v.                             New York, June 13, 1929.

148691-1  Miss You - vSB                      Col 1875-D, 5704

Selvin; Effros; Gott; Dorsey; Abbott, Smith, Dubin; Brodsky; Kress or McDonough;
Hansen; King; Smith Ballew-v.         New York, July 5, 1929.

148788-3  Am I Blue ? - vSB                   Col 1900-D, 5591, 01741

Same or very similar; Irving Kaufman-v. New York, July 6, 1929.

148791-3  Ain't Misbehavin' - vIK             Har 965-H
NOTE:- This issue as JERRY MASON'S CALIFORNIANS.

THE KNICKERBOCKERS : Selvin; Dorsey-t-tb; Klein; Jimmy Dorsey-cl-as/Arnold Brilhart-
cl-as-f; Dubin; Schutt; others.      New York, August 12, 1929.

148866-3  Song Of The Blues - vSB             Col 1940-D

Irving Kaufman (as DICK BURNETT)-v.   New York, August 15, 1929.

148883-2  Bashful Baby - vIK                  Har 987-H
NOTE:- This issue as BARNEY TRIMBLE'S OKLAHOMANS.

THE KNICKERBOCKERS : Selvin; McConville; Dorsey; Martin; others; Smith Ballew-v.
                              New York, October 2, 1929.

149079-2  From Now On - vSB                   Col 2003-D

FRANK AUBURN AND HIS ORCHESTRA : Possibly as for the Irving Brodsky session (p. 177),
as it is entered under his name in the CBS files; Annette Hanshaw-v.
                              New York, November 27, 1929.

149645-2  When I'm Housekeeping For You - vAH   SR 1070-P
149646-1  I Have To Have You - vAH              Har 1075-H, SR 1069-P, 2008-P
149647-3  Ain'tcha - vAH                        -

BEN SELVIN AND HIS ORCHESTRA : Ben Selvin-vn dir. Leo McConville-Manny Klein-t/Tommy
  Dorsey-tb/Andy Sannella-cl-as/Louis Martin-as/Hymie Wolfson-cl-ts/? Irving Brodsky
  p/Tony Colucci-bj-g/? Hank Stern-bb/Stan King-d/Eva Taylor-v.
                                          New York, December 9, 1929.

```
149701-3  My Man Is On The Make - vET        Col 2067-D, CB-65, Re G-20852
149702-3  When I'm Housekeeping For You - vET  Col 2072-D, CB-33
495006-1  My Man Is On The Make             Par R-658
495007-1  When I'm Housekeeping For You     Par R-661
```
  NOTE:- Columbia 2067-D and CB-65 as THE KNICKERBOCKERS; 2072-D as KOLSTER DANCE
  ORCHESTRA; CB-33 as COASTAL DANCE ORCHESTRA; Parlophone R-658 and R-661 as ROOF
  GARDEN ORCHESTRA; Regal G-20852 as THE RHYTHMIC TROUBADOURS.

  Ben Selvin-vn dir. Bob Effros-Tommy Gott-t/Tommy Dorsey-? Charlie Butterfield-tb/
  Benny Goodman-cl/Joe Dubin-ts/vn/Irving Brodsky-p/? Tony Colucci-bj/Jack Hansen-bb
  sb/Stan King-d/Smith Ballew-v.          New York, December 11, 1929.

```
149711-3  Why Do You Suppose ? - vSB         Col 2067-D, CB-65
149712-3  Do Ya Love Me ? (Just A Tiny Bit,  Col 2072-D
            Do Ya ?) - vSB
495010-1  Why Do You Suppose ?              Par R-658
100353-1  Do Ya Love Me ? (Just A Tiny Bit,  Har 1088-D
            Do Ya ?)
495011-1  Do Ya Love Me ? (Just A Tiny Bit,  Rejected ?
            Do Ya ?)
```
  NOTE:- Columbia 2067-D and CB-65 as THE KNICKERBOCKERS; 2072-D as KOLSTER DANCE
  ORCHESTRA; Harmony 1088-H as RUDY MARLOW AND HIS ORCHESTRA; Parlophone R-658 as
  ROOF GARDEN ORCHESTRA.

  Selvin dir. but not playing (?) : Farrar, Effros; Jack Teagarden-tb; Martin, Dubin,
  ? Wolfson; Bloom; bj; McPherson or Stern; King (db k); Smith Ballew-v.
                                          New York, January 27, 1930.

```
149919-1-2  Good For You, Bad For Me - vSB   Rejected
195070-1  Good For You, Bad  For Me         Col 2129-D
149920-3  Thank Your Father - vSB            -           CB-274
100362-1  Thank Your Father                 Har 1119-H
495020-1  Thank Your Father                 Od ONY-36013, Par PNY-34012
```
  NOTE:- Columbia 2129-D, CB-274 as THE KNICKERBOCKERS; Harmony 1119-H as RUDY MARLOW
  AND HIS ORCHESTRA; Odeon ONY-36013 as EDDIE GORDON'S BAND; Parlophone PNY-34012 as
  EDDIE CURRAN'S BAND.

COLUMBIA PHOTO PLAYERS : Selvin; Klein, Effros; Dorsey; ? Martin, ? Sannella, ? Wolfson; p; bj-g; bb-sb; King; Smith Ballew-v.
                                          New York, February 14, 1930.

```
149991-3  (Up On Top Of A Rainbow)
            Sweepin' The Clouds Away - vSB   Col 2131-D, CB-99, DO-107
```

BEN SELVIN AND HIS ORCHESTRA : Selvin; Klein, Effros; Dorsey; Jimmy Dorsey-cl-as;
  Martin, Dubin; Adrian Rollini-bsx; Bloom; Kress; Stern; King; Smith Ballew-v.
                                          New York, March 3, 1930.

```
150054-1-2-3  Looking At You Across The      Rejected
            Breakfast Table - vSB
100377-1  Looking At You Across The Breakfast  Har 1145-H
            Table
495025-1  Looking At You Across The Breakfast  Par R-729
            Table
150055-1-2-3  Let Me Sing And I'm Happy - vSB  Rejected
100378-1  Let Me Sing And I'm Happy         Har 1137-H
495026-1  Let Me Sing And I'm Happy         Rejected (test exists)
```
  NOTE:- Harmony 1137-H as RUDY MARLOW AND HIS ORCHESTRA; 1145-H as LLOYD KEATING AND
  HIS MUSIC; Parlophone R-729 as ROOF GARDEN ORCHESTRA.

ED LOYD AND HIS ORCHESTRA : Selvin; McConville; Farrar or Gott; both Dorseys; Bloom;
  ? Tommy Felline-bj-g; Tarto; King.      New York, March 10, 1930.

```
403845-B  The "Free And Easy" - vSB         OK 41392, Od ONY-36061,
  (Ariel 4538 as ARIEL DANCE ORCHESTRA)    Par R-34055,R-645,A-3030,Ar 4538
490051-1  The "Free And Easy"               Od ONY-36060, Par PNY-34054
```
  NOTE:- Parlophone PNY-34054, 34055 as EARL MARLOW AND HIS ORCHESTRA.

BEN SELVIN AND HIS ORCHESTRA : Ben Selvin dir. McConville, Klein; both Dorseys;
   Martin; Wolfson; Bloom; Colucci; Stern; King; Smith Ballew-Eddie Walters-v.
                                        New York, March 13, 1930.

150054-5  Looking At You Across The Breakfast   Col 2150-D, CB-105, DO-83
             Table - vSB
150055-6  Let Me Sing And I'm Happy - vSB         -          -         -
150078-3  The "Free And Easy" - vEW             Col 2149-D, CB-93, A-8738,
                                                DF-322, DO-80
   NOTE:- All issues from matrix 150078-3 as COLUMBIA PHOTO PLAYERS.

   Lew Conrad-v (and vn ?) added.       New York, April 7, 1930.

150175-3  Leave It That Way - vLC              Col 2177-D, DO-127

   Benny Goodman-cl added; Norman McPherson-bb replaces Stern; Don Howard-v.
                                        New York, April 9, 1930.

150158-3  The Whole Darned Thing's For You - vDH  Col 2177-D, CB-103, DO-127
150192-3  I'm In The Market For You - vDH      Col 2187-D, Re G-20757
195092-1  The Whole Darned Thing's For You     Col 4094-X
195093-1  I'm In The Market For You            Col 4093-X
   NOTE:- All,the above issues as COLUMBIA PHOTO PLAYERS, except Columbia 4094-X (as
   BEN SELVIN Y SU ORQUESTA) and Regal G-20757 (as THE RHYTHMIC TROUBADOURS); Columbia
   4093-X and 4094-X have their titles in Spanish.

COLUMBIA PHOTO PLAYERS : As for March 13, 1930, but possibly only one t; The Rondoliers-v.                             New York, April 21, 1930.

150483-1-3  Dark Night - vR                    Col 2196-D, Re G-20770
150484-1-3  Dust - vR                            -          CB-103
100394-1  Dark Night                           Har 1162-H
195035-1  Dust                                 Par R-800
   NOTE:- Harmony 1162-H as RUDY MARLOW AND HIS ORCHESTRA; Parlophone R-800 as ROOF
   GARDEN ORCHESTRA; Regal G-20770 as THE RHYTHMIC TROUBADOURS.

RAY SEELEY AND HIS ORCHESTRA : Ben Selvin dir. 2t/Tommy Dorsey-tb/? Benny Goodman-cl-
   as/Louis Martin-as/Hymie Wolfson-cl-ts/? Joe Venuti-vn and another (not Selvin ?)/
   Jack Russin-p/bj/d/Scrappy Lambert (as TOM FRAWLEY on Harmony)-v.
                                        New York, June 6, 1930.

404205-B  I Love You So Much - vSL             Od ONY-36106, Par PNY-34099, R-743
404206-A  Can I Help It ? - vSL                Od ONY-36107, Par PNY-34098,E-6349
100403-1  I Love You So Much - vSL             Har 1181-H, Cl 5045-C
   NOTE:- Parlophone PNY-34098 and PNY-34099 as SAM NASH AND HIS ORCHESTRA; E-6349 as
   WILL PERRY'S ORCHESTRA; R-743 as ROOF GARDEN ORCHESTRA; Harmony 1181-H and Clarion
   5045-C as LLOYD KEATING AND HIS MUSIC.

BEN SELVIN AND HIS ORCHESTRA : Selvin; Klein, Gott; Dorsey; Goodman, Martin, Wolfson;
   2nd vn; Bloom; Stern; King; Eddie Walters-u-v.
                                        New York, July 7, 1930.

150621-1-3  Why Have You Forgotten Waikiki ?-vEW  Col 2255-D, DO-229
150622-2-3  It's Easy To Fall In Love - vEW       -          CB-225

   Jimmy Dorsey-cl-as replaces Goodman; Irving Kaufman-v.
                                        New York, August 22, 1930.

150724-3  Dixiana - vIK                        Col 2287-D, CB-180, Re G-20980
   NOTE:- Regal G-20980 as THE RHYTHMIC TROUBADOURS.

   Eva Taylor-Lew Conrad-v (Conrad probably the 2nd vn here).
                                        New York, October 24, 1930.

150900-1-3  My Man From Caroline - vET         Col 2323-D, CB-212, Re G-20902
150902-1  Still I Love Her - vLC                 -          -
   NOTE:- Regal G-20902 as DENZA DANCE BAND.

BEN SELVIN AND HIS ORCHESTRA : Selvin; Klein, Gott; Dorsey; Goodman, Martin, Wolfson;
  Cornell Smelser-pac; Bloom; Colucci; Stern; King; Helen Rowland-v.
                                      New York, December 12, 1930.

151117-1  I Miss A Little Miss (Who Misses Me     Col 2356-D, CB-226, DO-317
             In Sunny Tennessee) - v4
151118-2  Cheerful Little Earful - vHR          -      CB-225    -

  ? Charlie Magnante-pac replaces Smelser; g/sb replace Colucci and Stern; Smith
  Ballew-v.                           New York, December 26, 1930.

151177-3  Yours And Mine - vSB                    Col 2366-D, CB-235, Re G-20963

  No vn; x added; Paul Small-v.       New York, January 15, 1931.

151207-3  He's Not Worth Your Tears - vHR        Col 2381-D, Re G-21015
151217-3  Would You Like To Take A Walk ? - vHR   - CB-252  -
151218-3  Personally, I Love You - vPS           Col 2380-D, Re G-21020
  NOTE:- Columbia 2380-D and Regal G-21020 as JOHNNY WALKER AND HIS ORCHESTRA.

  Charlie Butterfield-tb may replace Dorsey; Dick McDonough-g replaces (or may be)
  the unknown g; no pac or x; 2 vn used. New York, February 6, 1931.

151285-1-2  99 Out Of A Hundred Wanna Be Loved-   Col 2400-D, CB-279, Re G-21042
             - vHR

  Sol Klein or Sam Shapiro (perhaps both) replace (or may be) the unknown 2 vn;
  Cornell Smelser-pac/x added; Irving Brodsky-p replaces Bloom; The Sunshine Boys
  (Joe and Dan Mooney)-v.             New York, February 27, 1931.

151363-2  You Said It - vHR-PS                    Col 2426-D, Re G-21108
151364-2-3  Learn To Croon - vHR-PS              -               -
151365-2  Smile, Darn Ya, Smile - vJ&DM          Col 2421-D, 38240, Re G-21040
151367-3  The One-Man Band - vJ&DM              -
151368-2  Mama Inez                              Col 2422-D, DO-392
195132-   ! Ay Mama Inez                         Col 4477-X
  NOTE:- Columbia 2422-D and DO-392 as ENRIQUE MADRIGUERA'S HAVANA CASINO ORCHESTRA;
  Columbia 4477-X as MADRIGUERA Y SUS NOTAS MAGICAS. Both have laughing effects and
  vocal chorus by members of the band.

  Charlie Magnante-pac replaces Smelser; Lew Conrad (as LOU BRADY)-v (and one of the
  vn ?)                               New York, March 16, 1931.

151423-1; 495048  If You Should Ever Need Me      Har 1308-H, Cl 5276-C, Od ONY-36202
             (You'll Always Find Me Here) - vLC   Par PNY-34194, R-944, VT 2342-V,
                                                  Ar 4729
151425-2; 495050  You'll Be Mine In Apple Blossom Har 1311-H, Cl 5286-C,Od ONY-36203,
             Time - vLC                           OK 41487, Par PNY-34196, R-916,
                                                  A-3181, VT 2352-V
151426-2  I'm Crazy 'Bout My Baby (And My Baby's  Har 1310-H, Cl 5283-C,Od ONY-36203,
             Crazy 'Bout Me) - vLC                Par PNY-34197, A-3179, VT 2349-V
  NOTE:- Harmony 1308-H, 1310-H and 1311-H as THE HARMONIANS; Clarion 5276-C, Velvet
  Tone 2342-V as CHESTER LEIGHTON AND HIS SOPHOMORES; Clarion 5283-C, 5286-C, Velvet
  Tone 2349-V and 2352-V as FRANK AUBURN AND HIS ORCHESTRA; Odeon ONY-36203, Parlo-
  phone R-916, A-3179, A-3181 as RAY SEELEY AND HIS ORCHESTRA; OKeh 41487 as ED LOYD
  AND HIS ORCHESTRA; Parlophone PNY-34194 as JACK WHITNEY AND HIS ORCHESTRA; PNY-
  34196, PNY-34197 as SAM NASH AND HIS ORCHESTRA; R-944 as ROOF GARDEN ORCHESTRA.

  Klein; Goodman; others much as above; Magnante omitted; Helen Rowland-Sid Garry-v.
                                      New York, May 7, 1931.

151547-3  Poor Kid - vSG                          Col 2463-D
151548-2  Now You're In My Arms - vHR            -

  Klein; Dorsey; Goodman; Paul Small-v.  New York, May 9, 1931.

351015-2; 404912  (There Ought To Be A)          Har 1322-H, Cl 5321-C, OK 41499,
             Moonlight Saving Time - vPS          VT 2387-V, Par R-974, A-3209
351016-2; 404913  Roll On,Mississippi,Roll On-vPS As above, but Par A-3219
351017-1; 404914  Wrap Your Troubles In Dreams    Har 1323-H, Cl 5322-C, OK 41500,
             (And Dream Your Troubles Away) - vPS VT 2388-V, Par B-27458
  (cont. on page 1385)

NOTE:- All American issues from matrices 351015-2 and 351016-2 as ROY CARROLL AND
HIS SANDS POINT ORCHESTRA; and from 351017-1 as LLOYD KEATING AND HIS MUSIC, with
the exception of OKeh 41499 (as BUDDY CAMPBELL AND HIS ORCHESTRA) and 41500 (as
GOLDEN TERRACE ORCHESTRA); Parlophone A-3209, A-3219 as TAMPA BLUE ORCHESTRA.

BEN SELVIN AND HIS ORCHESTRA : Selvin; Klein; Dorsey; Goodman; probably Martin,Wolf-
son; others similar to the foregoing; Scrappy Lambert (as ROBERT WOOD or PHIL
HUGHES as shown)-v.                         New York, May 19, 1931.

351022-2; 404945  (Yoo-Hoo-Hoo, I'll Call To You)  Har 1326-H, Cl 5334-C, OK 41505,
            Under Your Window Tonight - v"RW"      VT 2398-V, Od 193794
351023-2  Treat Me Like A Baby - v"PH"             Har 1333-H, Cl 5342-C, VT 2406-V
NOTE:- All issues from matrix 351022-2 as LLOYD KEATING AND HIS MUSIC, except OKeh
41505 (as GOLDEN TERRACE ORCHESTRA); all issues from matrix 351023-2 as PHIL
HUGHES AND HIS HIGH HATTERS.

Dick Robertson (as ROY CARROLL on the first two sides, as BOBBY DIX on the last
two)-v.                                     New York, May 21, 1931.

351024-2; 404919  Let's Get Friendly - vDR    Har 1329-H, Cl 5338-C, OK 41503,
                                              VT 2402-V
351025-2; 404918  One More Time - vDR         As above, plus Par R-995, A-3207,
                                              Od A-221374
351026-2  Love Is Like That (What Can You Do)-vDR  Har 1328-H, Cl 5337-C, VT 2401-V
351027-2  Two Little, Blue Little Eyes - vDR       -         - Par A-3218 -
NOTE:- All issues from matrices 351024-2 and 351025-2 as ROY CARROLL AND HIS SANDS
POINT ORCHESTRA (except OKeh 41503, as BUDDY CAMPBELL AND HIS ORCHESTRA, and Parlophone R-995, as GOLDEN TERRACE ORCHESTRA), and from matrices 351026-2 and
351027-2 as CHESTER LEIGHTON AND HIS SOPHOMORES; Parlophone A-3207, A-3218 as
TAMPA BLUE ORCHESTRA.
Probably Joe Venuti-vn/Eddie Lang-g added,
                                            New York, May 28, 1931.

351030-2  In The Merry Month Of Maybe - vDR   Har 1331-H, Cl 5340-C, VT 2404-V,
                                              Od 193723
351031-2  I Found A Million-Dollar Baby       As above, plus Od 238956
            (In A Five-and-Ten Cent Store)-v4
NOTE:- All American issues as FRANK AUBURN AND HIS ORCHESTRA.

Klein; Goodman; Wolfson; Brodsky; Scrappy Lambert (as JERRY FENWYCK or ROY CARROLL
as shown)-The Rondoliers (as PHIL HUGHES !)-v.
                                            New York, June 5, 1931.

351032-2  Look In The Looking Glass - vR      Har 1333-H, Cl 5342-C, VT 2406-V,
                                              Par R-994
351033-2  You Forgot Your Gloves - vSL        Har 1335-H, Cl 5344-C, VT 2408-V
351034-3  Dancing In The Dark - vSL           Har 1334-H, Cl 5343-C, VT 2407-V,
                                              Od 193722
351035-1  High And Low (I've Been Looking For You) As above
            - vSL
NOTE:- All issues from matrix 351032-2 (except Parlophone R-994, correctly labeled)
as PHIL HUGHES AND HIS HIGH HATTERS; from matrices 351033-2 as JACK WHITNEY AND HIS
ORCHESTRA; and from matrices 351034-3 and 351035-1 as ROY CARROLL AND HIS SANDS
POINT ORCHESTRA; Parlophone A-3366 as TAMPA BLUE ORCHESTRA.

Bunny Berigan-t featured on many of the remaining sessions; also on this one are
Dorsey; Goodman, Wolfson; Brodsky; Dick Robertson-Eddie Walters (the latter plays
u)-v, sharing the pseudonyms ROBERT WOOD, CHESTER LEIGHTON, JERRY FENWYCK and BOBBY
DIX interchangeably.                        New York, June 18, 1931.

351041-2  I'm Keepin' Company - vEW           Har 1339-H, Cl 5350-C, VT 2414-V
351042-2  On The Beach With You - vEW         Har 1340-H, Cl 5351-C, VT 2415-V
351043-2; 404959  Just One More Chance - vDR  Har 1342-H, Cl 5353-C, VT 2417-V,
                                              OK 41511, Par R-1015, Od A-221372
351044-2; 404973  Makin' Faces At The Man In The  Har 1342-H, Cl 5353-C, VT 2417-V,
            Moon - vDR                            OK 41517, Par R-995, Od A-221374
351045-2  404953  Without That Gal ! - vDR    Har 1340-H, Cl 5351-C, OK 41508,
                                              VT 2415-V, Par R-1036, Od 238956
351046-2  Let's Drink A Drink To The Future - vDR  Har 1343-H, Cl 5355-C, VT 2419-V
351048-1  How The Time Can Fly (Whenever I'm With  Har 1341-H, Cl 5352-C, VT 2416-V
            You) - vEW                             (cont. on page 1386)

NOTE:- All issues from matrices 351041-2 and 351046-2 as LLOYD KEATING AND HIS
MUSIC; from 351048-1 as JERRY FENWYCK AND HIS ORCHESTRA; OKeh 41511 as BUDDY CAMP-
BELL AND HIS ORCHESTRA; 41508 and 41517, Parlophone R-995 and R-1015 as GOLDEN
TERRACE ORCHESTRA; other issues from this session as CHESTER LEIGHTON AND HIS
SOPHOMORES.

BEN SELVIN AND HIS ORCHESTRA : Selvin; Klein and another; Goodman, probably Martin;
Wolfson; p; g; sb;d; Eddie Walters-The Rondoliers-v.
New York, June 22, 1931.

| 151626-3 | Sing Another Chorus, Please - vEW | Col 2491-D, Re G-21150 |
| 151627-2 | Let's Drink A Drink To The Future - vR | Col 2487-D, Re G-21126 |

Ben Selvin-vn dir. Bunny Berigan-Manny Klein-t/tb/Benny Goodman-cl-as/Louis Martin
as/Hymie Wolfson-cl-ts/? Lew Conrad-vn/Irving Brodsky-p/g/sb/d/x/Dick Robertson-
Scrappy Lambert (under the communal pseudonyms BOBBY DIX, ROY CARROLL, ROBERT WOOD
and PHIL HUGHES)-v.           New York, July 3, 1931.

| 351056-2; 404958 | My Sweet Tooth Says "I Wanna" | Har 1350-H, Cl 5362-C, OK 41511, |
| | (But My Wisdom Tooth Says No) - vDR | VT 2426-V, Par R-1015,Od A-221372 |
| 351057-2 | (With You On My Mind, I Find) | Har 1345-H, Cl 5357-C, VT 2421-V |
| | I Can't Write The Words - vSL | |
| 351059-1; 404957 | Hikin' Down The Highway - vSL | Har 1344-H, Cl 5356-C, OK 41510, |
| | | VT 2420-V, Par R-1046, Od 193767 |
| 351060-2 | It's A Long Time Between Kisses - vSL | Har 1353-H, Cl 5365-C, VT 2429-V |

NOTE:- OKeh 41510 and Parlophone R-1015 as GOLDEN TERRACE (DANCE) ORCHESTRA; OKeh
41511 as BUDDY CAMPBELL AND HIS ORCHESTRA; OKeh 41520 as CLOVERDALE COUNTRY CLUB
ORCHESTRA; all other issues labelled as follows :-
351056-2 LLOYD KEATING AND HIS MUSIC
351057-2 ROY CARROLL AND HIS SANDS POINT ORCHESTRA;
351059-1 FRANK AUBURN AND HIS ORCHESTRA;
351060-2 PHIL HUGHES AND HIS HIGH HATTERS.

Selvin; Klein; Dorsey; Goodman; Wolfson; others; Dick Robertson (as BOBBY DIX,
CHESTER LEIGHTON, JERRY FENWYCK or ROBERT WOOD)-v.
New York, July 7, 1931.

| 351065-3 | (If I Hadn't Been) So Sure Of You - vDR | Har 1354-H, Cl 5366-C, VT 2430-V |
| 351068-2; 404961 | The Kiss That You've Forgotten | Har 1351-H, Cl 5363-C, OK 41512, |
| | (Is The Kiss That I Can't Forget) - vDR | VT 2427-V |
| 351069-2 | Nobody Loves No Baby Like My Baby Loves | Har 1352-H, Cl 5364-C, VT 2428-V |
| | Me - vDR | |
| 351070-2 | Do The New York - vDR | - Od 193728 - Od 238996 - |
| 351072-1 | Take It From Me (I'm Takin' To You)-vDR | Har 1348-H, Cl 5360-C, VT 2424-V, |
| | | Par R-1046 |

NOTE:- OKeh 41512 as GOLDEN TERRACE DANCE ORCHESTRA; all issues from matrix
351065-3 as JACK WHITNEY AND HIS ORCHESTRA; 351068-2 as CHESTER LEIGHTON AND HIS
SOPHOMORES; 351069-2, 351070-2 and 351072-1 as JERRY FENWYCK AND HIS ORCHESTRA.

Selvin; Klein; Dorsey; Goodman; Venuti; others; The Pickens Sisters-The Rondoliers
v.           New York, July 14, 1931.

| 151680-3 | Do The New York - vPS-R | Col 2499-D, DO-785 |
| 151681-3 | Hikin' Down The Highway - vR | -     Re G-21150 |
| 151682-1 | My Sweet Tooth Says "I Wanna" | Col 2501-D, Re G-21162 |
| | (But My Wisdom Tooth Says No)-vPS | |
| 151683-2 | Nobody Loves No Baby Like My Baby Loves | -       - |
| | Me - vPS | |

Scrappy Lambert (as BOBBY DIX)-v.      New York, July 16, 1931.

| 351061-2 | There's A Time And Place For Everything | Har 1356-H, Cl 5368-C, VT 2442-V |
| | - vSL | |

New York, July 21, 1931.

| 351063-2; 404962 | Me ! - vDR | Har 1357-H, Cl 5369-C, VT 2433-V, |
| | | Par R-1074, Ar 4672, Od A-221394 |
| 351075-2 | There's No Depression In Love - vSL | Har 1356-H, Cl 5368-C, VT 2432-V |
| 151695-3 | Me ! - vDR (all as THE KNICKERBOCKERS) | Col 2502-D, CB-360, Re G-21162 |

NOTE:- All American issues from matrix 351063-2 as FRANK AUBURN AND HIS ORCHESTRA;
from 351075-2 as LLOYD KEATING AND HIS MUSIC; Ariel 4672 as ARIEL DANCE ORCHESTRA;

BEN SELVIN AND HIS ORCHESTRA : Ben Selvin-vn dir. Manny Klein and another-t/Tommy
   Dorsey-tb/Andy Sannella-cl-as/Louis Martin-as/Hymie Wolfson-cl-ts/vn/p/g/Gus Helle-
   berg-bb/d/Paul Small-v.                New York, August 13, 1931.

151724-1  This Is The Missus - vPS              Col 2515-D, CB-375

   Benny Goodman-cl-as replaces Sannella; Charlie Magnante-pac added; Jack Parker (as
   ROY CARROLL on all but Parlophone R-1127)-v.
                                        New York, October 2, 1931.

351107-2  Waitin' For A Call From You - vJP     Har 1379-H, Cl 5393-C, VT 2457-V,
                                                     Par R-1127
   NOTE:- All except Parlophone R-1127 as ROY CARROLL AND HIS SANDS POINT ORCHESTRA.

   No vn used; The Nitecaps-v.          New York, October 8, 1931.

351111-2; 404991  (Everyone In Town Loves)      Har 1380-H, Cl 5394-C, OK 41524,
          Little Mary Brown - v3N                     VT 2458-V
   NOTE:- OKeh 41524 as BUDDY CAMPBELL AND HIS ORCHESTRA; all others as D'ORSAY DANCE
   ORCHESTRA.

   Ben Selvin-vn dir. Manny Klein-Tommy Gott-t/Tommy Dorsey-tb/Benny Goodman-cl-as/
   Louis Martin-as/Hymie Wolfson-cl-ts/Joe Venuti-vn/Rube Bloom-p/Cornell Smelser-pac/
   Carl Kress-g/Ward Lay-sb/Gus Helleberg-d/The Rondoliers-v.
                                        New York, October 16, 1931.

151850-3  Little Mary Brown - vR                Col 2554-D, Re G-21400

   Gott omitted; Goodman db bcl; rest probably as above; Dick Robertson (as ROBERT
   WOOD)-v.                             New York, October 21, 1931.

351115-2; 405053  Lucille - vDR                 Har 1385-H,Cl 5399-C, OK 41527,
                                                     VT 2463-V
   NOTE:- OKeh 41527 as BUDDY CAMPBELL AND HIS ORCHESTRA; all others as HOTEL COMMO-
   DORE DANCE ORCHESTRA.

   Probably as last, but unknown cl-as replaces Goodman (Sannella ?); Bobby Dix Trio
   (? Dick Robertson and 2 others)-v.   New York, November 2, 1931.

351121-3; 405102  You Try Somebody Else - vBD3  Har 1388-H, Cl 5407-C, OK 41532,
                                                     VT 2467-V
   NOTE:- OKeh 41532 as BUDDY CAMPBELL AND HIS ORCHESTRA; all others as LLOYD KEATING
   AND HIS MUSIC.

   As for October 16, 1931, with unknown t replacing Gott; Irving Brodsky-p replaces
   Bloom; Dick Robertson-v.             New York, November 16, 1931.

351134-2; 405096  Potatoes Are Cheaper, Tomatoes  Har 1394-H, Cl 5415-C, OK 41537,
          Are Cheaper - Now's The Time To Fall     VT 2475-V, Od 193794
          In Love - vDR
   NOTE:- OKeh 41537 and Odeon 193794 as ED PARKER AND HIS ORCHESTRA; all others as
   JERRY FENWYCK AND HIS ORCHESTRA.

   Dick Robertson (as ROY CARROLL)-v.   New York, November 27, 1931.

351138-1  Bend Down, Sister  - vDR              Ar 4829
351138-2; 405115  Bend Down, Sister - vDR       Har 1397-H, Cl 5420-C, OK 41543,
                                                     VT 2480-V
151891-2  Bend Down, Sister - vDR               Col 2575-D, CB-406
151892-1-2  Potatoes Are Cheaper, Tomatoes Are
          Cheaper - Now's The Time To Fall In Love - vDR
   NOTE:- OKeh 41543 as BUDDY CAMPBELL AND HIS ORCHESTRA; Ariel 4829 as ARIEL DANCE
   ORCHESTRA; all others from matrix 351138-2 as ROY CARROLL AND HIS SANDS POINT
   ORCHESTRA.

   Smith Ballew (as JERRY FENWYCK)-v.   New York, December 7, 1931.

351141-2; 405114  I Wouldn't Change You For The   Har 1398-H, Cl 5421-C, OK 41543,
          World - vSB                             VT 2481-V
   NOTE:- OKeh 41543 as BUDDY CAMPBELL AND HIS ORCHESTRA; all others as JERRY FENWYCK
   AND HIS ORCHESTRA.

BEN SELVIN AND HIS ORCHESTRA : Ben Selvin-vn dir. Manny Klein and another-t/Tommy
    Dorsey-tb/cl-as/Louis Martin-as/Hymie Wolfson-cl-ts/Joe Venuti-vn/Irving Brodsky-p
    /Carl Kress-g/Ward Lay-sb/Gus Helleberg-d/"Le Dandy"-v.
                                       New York, December 18, 1931.

351144-2; 405113  I Found You - v"L"             Har 1401-H, Cl 5440-C, OK 41542,
                                                 VT 2500-V, Ar 4829
    NOTE:- OKeh 41542 as CLOVERDALE COUNTRY CLUB ORCHESTRA; Ariel 4829 as ARIEL DANCE
    ORCHESTRA; all others as D'ORSAY DANCE ORCHESTRA.

    Same instrumentation, probably similar personnel; may include Bunny Berigan-t/
    Eddie Lang-g instead of the unknown t and Kress; Dick Robertson-v.
                                       New York, January 12, 1932.

351154-3; 405121  Between The Devil And The Deep   Har 1412-H, Cl 5455-C, OK 41546,
        Blue Sea - vDR                             VT 2515-V
    NOTE:- OKeh 41546 as ED PARKER AND HIS ORCHESTRA; all others as FRANK AUBURN AND
    HIS ORCHESTRA.

                                       New York, May 12, 1932.

152193-3  Crazy People - v3                      Col 2661-D, Re G-21443
152194-3  Is I In Love ? I Is - v3                    -          -

    Helen Rowland-v.                   New York, June 9, 1932.

152209-2  Cabin In The Cotton - vHR              Col 2669-D, Re G-21473

    Muriel Sherman-Elmer Feldkamp (the latter on cl-as ?)-v.
                                       New York, December 16, 1932.

152332-2  Young And Healthy - vMS-EF             Col 2731-D, CB-578, CQ-1325,
                                                 Re G-21606

    Jack Miller-v; unknown g replaces Lang. New York, July 5, 1933.

152432-2  Morning, Noon And Night - vJM          Col 2789-D

Canadian Apex 8355 is also credited to Ben Selvin and his Orchestra; it is by the
    California Ramblers, q.v.  See also the Bar Harbor Society Orchestra.

## SEMINOLE SYNCOPATORS

Harry Cooper-t/Prince Robinson-cl/as/Graham Jackson-p/Bernard Addison-bj/H. Williams-
    d.                                 New York, April, 1924.

72484-A  Blue Grass Blues                        OK 40228, Od 03156

    Joe Garland-cl-ts added.           Atlanta, August 30, 1924.

8741-A  Sailing On Lake Pontchartrain            OK 40228, Od 03156

## LARRY  SEMON

Guitar solo, acc. by Mac McGowan-p.    Memphis, June 5, 1930.

62584-1-2  Eddie's Twister                       Vic rejected

## THE SENATORS

Pseudonym on Tremont 0506 for the Broadway Broadcasters (see Sam Lanin).

## BOYD  SENTER

Alto saxophone solos, acc. by Jack Russell-p.
                                       Chicago, c. May, 1924.

    520    Bucktown Blues                        Auto (un numbered)
    521    Ralfella                                   -

BOYD SENTER AND HIS ZO-BO-KA-ZOOS : Boyd Senter-k-bj/Russell Senter-Jack Russell-k.
Chicago, c. May, 1924.

| 522 | Omaha Blues | Auto (un-numbered) |
| 523 | You've Got Ways Blues | - |

Clarinet or alto saxophone solos, acc. by Jack Russell-p, with Russell Senter-d*.
Chicago, late June, 1924.

536    *Mobile Blues - cl                    Auto (un-numbered), Bwy 1337,
                                             Pm 20341, 12568, Pur 11341,
                                             Sil 3527, Ka K-919, Max 1504,
                                             Us 289
537    Gertie (I'm In Love With Gertie) - as  Auto (un-numbered); rev. of 536
538    Laugh - cl ?                          Auto (un-numbered)
539    Powder Rag - as ?                     -
NOTE:- Usiba 289 as LONDON PICCADILLY-JAZZ (!)

Clarinet solos, acc. by the Chicago De Luxe Orchestra, dir. by Art Larsen and Frank
De Sort : tb/as-ts/p/d (some are negroes, according to legend).
Chicago, June-July, 1924.

544    Mr. Jelly Lord                        Auto (un-numbered)
545    St. Louis Blues                       -            Pm 20341,
                                             Her 75508, Pur 11341, Sil 3526
NOTE:- Paramount 20341 as CHICAGO DE LUX ORCHESTRA; Silvertone 3526 as THE RED
HOTTERS.

Clarinet, alto saxophone and trumpet solos, all three on each side, acc. by Jack
Russell-p/Russell Senter-d.       New York, October, 1924.

1942-3  Fat Mama Blues                       Pm 20364, Ban 1633, Dom 3604,
                                             Pur 11364, Re 9937, Sil 3526,
                                             Max 1524, Us 283
1943-3  Gin Houn' Blues                      Pm 20364, Ban 1633, Dom 3604,
                                             Pur 11364, Re 9937, Sil 3527,
                                             Ka K-998, Max 1523
NOTE:- Silvertone 3526 and 3527 as THE RED HOTTERS; Usiba 283 as LONDON PICCADILLY
JAZZ. Banner, Domino and Regal issues all have false matrix numbers (6236-1 and
6235-1 respectively) in addition to the correct ones.

Acc. by Jack Russell-p/Chuck Kaley-bj. New York, c. May 1, 1925.

| 105996 | Craving | PA 36270, Per 14451 |
| 105997 | It's Time To Keep Away From You | PA 36256, Per 14437 |
| 105998 | Bucktown Blues | PA 36285, Per 14466 |
| 105999 | You've Broken My Heart | - - |
| 106000 | Slippery Elm | PA 36256, Per 14437 |
| 106001 | Gertie | PA 36270, Per 14451 |

Boyd Senter db pac and v.              Chicago, c. August, 1925.

| 874-1-2 | Milenberg Joys | PA 36320, Per 14501 |
| 875-1-2 | Sugar Babe - vBS | - - |
| 876-2 | Shake Your Dogs | PA 36336, Per 14517 |
| 878-1-2 | Wake 'Em Up - pac | - - |

Acc. by Jack Russell-p.                New York, November 10, 1925.

| 6287- | Cu-Kee-Ukee-Ute | ARC rejected |
| 6288- | Ole Crow Blues | - |

Chuck Kaley-bj added.                  New York, c. November 13, 1925.

106398-A  I'm Taking My Own Sweet Time       PA 36351, 11071, Per 14352
106399    St. Louis Blues                    PA 36397, 11122, Per 14578,
                                             Ban 0621, Ro 1240

Clarinet solos, with occasional alto saxophone and vocal choruses, acc. by Jack
Russell-p-k/Chuck Kaley-bj.            New York, c. November 19, 1925.

| | | |
|---|---|---|
| 106411 | I'm Steppin' High, Wide And Handsome | PA 36424, 11245, Per 14605 |
| 106412 | One From Eight Leaves Seven | PA 36351, 11071, Per 14532 |

New York, c. November 26, 1925.

| | | |
|---|---|---|
| 106430 | Poison | PA 36424, 11245, Per 14605 |
| 106431 | Just Dandy - vBS | PA 36397, 11122, Per 14578, |
| | | Ban 0622,Cam 0222,Ro 1248,Sal 305 |
| 106432 | The Monkey Doodle-Doo | PA 36359, 11539, Per 14540 |
| 106433 | You're The One And Only | -      11374      - |

New York, c. June 10, 1926.

| | | |
|---|---|---|
| 106915 | Hobo's Prayer | PA 36483, X-6090, Per 14664, |
| | | Ban 0620, Cam 0220, Ro 1238 |
| 106916 | Steamboat Stomp | PA 36493, 11201, Per 14674 |
| 106917 | Beef Stew | PA 36528, 11374, Per 14709, |
| | | Ban 0622, Cam 0222, Ro 1248 |
| 106918 | Lucky Break | PA 36493, 11201, Per 14674 |
| 106919 | Yes, Sir, And How ! | PA 36483, 11539, Per 14664, |
| | | Ban 0621, Cam 0221, Ro 1240 |

Eddie Lang-g replaces Kaley.          New York, January 20, 1927.

| | | |
|---|---|---|
| 80313-B | Wabash Blues | OK 40949, Cl 5195-C, VT 7120-V, |
| | | 7123-V, Voc 3075, Par R-3505, |
| | | Od 165283, A-189119, Col J-1839 |
| 80314-A | Bluin' The Blues | OK 40777, Voc 2937, Par R-3329, |
| | | A-2188 |
| 80315-B | Christine | OK 40819, Voc 3075, Par R-3351, |
| | | A-2220, Od 193010, Col J-2473 |
| 80316-A | Bad Habits | OK 40755, Diva 6034-G, VT 7060-V, |
| | | Voc 3030, Par R-3321, A-2156, |
| | | LAR A-4514,Od A-221062,Col J-1793 |
| 80317-A | Clarinet Tickle | OK 40777, Voc 2936, Par R-3329 |
| 80318-A-B | You're The One For Me | Rejected |

New York, January 21, 1927.

| | | |
|---|---|---|
| 80324-A | The New St. Louis Blues | OK 40755, Cl 5112-C, VT 7118-V, |
| | | Voc 3116, Par R-3321, F-798, |
| | | A-2156, LAR A-4514, Od 165090, |
| | | A-221062, Col J-1793 |
| 80325-A | Someday, Sweetheart | OK 40819, Voc 3014, Par R-3351, |
| | NOTE:- Parlophone F-798 as THE FOUR ACES. | A-2220, Od 193010, Col J-2473 |

New York, June 7, 1927.

| | | |
|---|---|---|
| 80985-B | Not Maybe | OK 40836, Od ONY-40836, 193041, |
| | | Voc 2937, Par R-3384, A-2251 |
| 80986-A | Hot Lips | OK 40888, VT 7121-V, Par R-3384, |
| | | A-4909, Od 165177 |
| 80987-A | Beale Street Blues (El Blues de la | OK 40836, 16246*, Cl 5181-C, |
| | Calle Bili*) | Od ONY-40836, 193041, VT 7118-V, |
| | | 7124-V, Voc 2936, Par R-107, |
| | | F-798, A-2251 |
| 80988-B | Sigh And Cry Blues | OK 40861, Voc 3031, Par R-3411, |

NOTE:- Parlophone F-798 as THE FOUR ACES.  Some  E-5386 (Jap.), Od 165147, 193076,
issues from this session credit Arthur Schutt  A-189081, A-221063, 04065
with the piano part, but Mr. Senter affirms that it is Jack Russell.

Clarinet solos, with occasional alto saxophone choruses, acc. by Jack Russell-p/
Eddie Lang-g.                              New York, June 10, 1927.

81001-B  Down-Hearted Blues              OK 41115, Diva 6044-G, VT 7070-V,
                                         Voc 3014,Par R-107,A-3642,B-27457
81002-B  The Boss Of The Stomps         OK 40949, Voc 3061, Par R-168,
                                         Od 165283, A-189119
81003-B  The Grind-Out                  OK 40888, Par R-3505, A-4909,
                                         E-5585(Jap.),Od 165177,Col J-1839
81004-B  I Ain't Got Nobody             OK 40861, Cl 5054-C, Diva 6034-G,
NOTE:- Lindström A-4528 as SAXOPHONE-SOLO MIT   VT 7060-V, Voc 3030, Par R-3411,
KLARINETTE, KLAVIER UND GUITARRE; Parlophone    E-5356 (Jap.), LAR A-4528,
A-4909 as INSTRUMENTAL TRIO WITH SAXOPHONE.     Od 04065, 165147, 193076,
                                         A-189081, A-221063

                        New York, March 20, 1928.

400153-A  'Tain't Clean                 Par R-168
400154-B  Eniale Blues                  OK 41059, Voc 3061, Par R-283,
                                         Od 193337, A-189162, Col J-1732
400155-B  Just So-So !                  OK 41018, Voc 3116, Par R-283,
                                         Od A-189174, Col J-1732

BOYD SENTER AND HIS SENTERPEDES : Mickey Bloom-t/Tommy Dorsey-tb/Boyd Senter-cl/
Jimmy Dorsey-as/Jack Russell-p/Eddie Lang-g.
                                         New York, March 23, 1928.

400168-A  I Wish I Could Shimmy Like My Sister   OK 41018, Cl 5194-C, VT 7120-V,
          Kate                           Voc 3015, Od 165335, 193162,
                                         A-189174
400169-B  Mobile Blues                  Par R-143       -            -

Clarinet solos, acc. by Jack Russell-p/Eddie Lang-g.
                                         New York, May 2, 1928.

400645-B  Prickly Heat                  Par A-3425
400645-D  Prickly Heat                  OK 41163, Col M-37, Od 165577
400646-B  No More                       Par R-501

BOYD SENTER AND HIS SENTERPEDES : As for March 23, 1928, but Charlie Butterfield-tb
replaces Dorsey.                         New York, May 3, 1928.

400647-B  Original Stack O' Lee Blues   OK 41115, Cl 5054-C, Diva 6044-G,
                                         VT 7070-V, Voc 3015, Par R-501,
                                         A-3342, B-25457, Col M-37

Tommy Dorsey-tb replaces Butterfield; Vic Berton-d added.
                                         New York, May 8, 1928.

400653-B  Original Chinese Blues        OK 41163, Par R-143, A-3342,
                                         Od 165577, 193272
400654-B  Somebody's Wrong              OK 41059, Voc 3031, Od 165577,
                                         193272, A-189162

Phil Napoleon-t/Tommy Dorsey-tb/Boyd Senter-cl/Jimmy Dorsey-as/Frank Signorelli-p/
Carl Kress-g/Stan King-d/v.              New York, January 30, 1929.

49701-2  Wabash Blues                   Vic 21864, BB B-5545, RZ MR-1316,
                                         HMV EA-1392, R-14133
49702-2  Goin' Back To Tennessee - v    Vic 21864, BB B-6203, HMV R-14133

2nd t added; Charlie Butterfield-tb replaces Dorsey.
                                         New York, February 6, 1929.

48335-3  Rich Man, Poor Man, Beggar Man, Thief   Vic 22010, El EG-1627
48336-3  I'm In The Jailhouse Now        - -      BB B-5545, RZ MR-1316,
                                         HMV EA-1392
NOTE:- Electrola EG-1627 as VICTOR ARDEN-PHIL OHMAN AND THEIR ORCHESTRA (!)

BOYD SENTER AND HIS SENTERPEDES : Mickey Bloom-t/Tommy Dorsey-tb/Boyd Senter-cl/
Jimmy Dorsey-cl-as/Frank Signorelli-p/Eddie Lang-g/Stan King-d/Paul Small-v.
New York, March 13, 1929.

| | | |
|---|---|---|
| 49780-2 | Doin' You Good - vPS | Vic 21912, HMV R-14160, X-4493, El EG-1422 |
| 49781-3 | Shine - vPS | As above |

Mickey Bloom-James Migliore-t/Herb Winfield-tb/Boyd Senter and another-cl-as/Fud
Livingston-cl-ts/Jack Russell-p/Dan Calker-bj-g-v/sb/Stan King-d-k.
New York, October 29, 1929.

| | | |
|---|---|---|
| 57031-3 | Sweetheart Blues | Vic 22464, HMV B-4913 |
| 57032-1-2-3 | Copenhagen | Rejected |
| 57033-2 | No-One - vDC | Vic 22464 |
| 57034-3 | Beale Street Blues | Vic 22303, BB B-6050, HMV X-4488 |

New York, November 25, 1929.

| | | |
|---|---|---|
| 57032-5 | Copenhagen | Vic 22303, BB B-6050, HMV X-4488, RZ G-22794 |
| 57033-4 | No-One | Vic 22464, BB B-6957, HMV B-4913 |

—— Haukenheiser-t/Ray Stilwell-tb-v/Boyd Senter-cl-as-ts/as-ts/Jack Russell-p/bj/
sb (unless marked *)/Walter Meyer-d.    Hollywood, June 19, 1930.

| | | |
|---|---|---|
| 54841-2 | Waterloo - vRS | Vic 22812, BB B-5376, Sr S-3457, HMV R-14694 |
| 54842-2 | Give It To Me Right Away - vRS | Vic 23032, BB B-5376, B-6203 - |
| 54843-1-2-3 | *'Way Down Yonder In New Orleans | Rejected |
| 54853-3 | Smiles - vRS | Vic 23032, BB B-6957 |

## THE SEPIA SERENADERS

Clarence Grimes-cl/Cliff Jackson-p/Elmer Snowden-bj/George Gray-v.
New York, December 14, 1934.

| | | |
|---|---|---|
| 86446-1 | Ridiculous Blues | BB B-5770, Vic JR-35 |
| 86447-1 | Breakin' The Ice - vGG | BB B-5782 |
| 86448-1 | Dallas Blues - vGG | BB B-5803 |
| 86449-1 | Baby Brown - vGG | BB B-5782 |
| 86450-1 | Nameless Blues | BB B-5770, Vic JR-35 |
| 86451-1 | Alligator Crawl | BB B-5803 |

## THE SERENADERS DANCE ORCHESTRA

Pseudonym on Meloto for the following items listed in this book :-

S-1757  Don't Be Angry With Me (Joe Candullo and his Everglades Orchestra)
S-1757  Lantern Of Love (Stillman Club Orchestra)

## THE SEVEN ACES

See Warner's Seven Aces.

## THE SEVEN BLACK DOTS

2c/tb/cl/p/? bb/d.                      New York, c. August 9, 1921.

| | | |
|---|---|---|
| 69330 | Shake It And Break It | PA 020634 |

New York, c. August 29, 1921.

| | | |
|---|---|---|
| 69349 | Wang-Wang Blues | PA 020634 |
| 69350 | Love Will Find A Way | PA 020655, 10232 |
| 69351 | Bandana Days | -          - |

NOTE:- Pathe Actuelle 10232 as ACTUELLE NOVELTY DANCE ORCHESTRA.

Mickey Bloom-t/Tommy Dorsey-tb/Pete Pumiglio-cl/Spencer Clark-bsx/Chauncey Gray-p/
Tommy Felline-bj/Herb Weil-d/Jack Kaufman-v.
New York, January 25, 1928.

| | | |
|---|---|---|
| 18189 | There Ought To Be A Law Against That-vJK | Ed 52209, Amb 5486 |
| 18190 | The Grass Grows Greener ('Way Down Home)-vJK- | |

Cliff Weston (Wetterau)-t replaces Bloom; Reg Harrington-tb replaces Dorsey.
New York, February 28, 1928.

| | | |
|---|---|---|
| 18263 | Tinker, Tailor, Soldier, Sailor - vJK | Ed 52298 |
| 18264 | He Ain't Never Been To College - vJK | Rejected |

Fred van Eps, Jr.-t replaces Weston; George Troup-tb replaces Harrington.
New York, April 26, 1928.

| | | |
|---|---|---|
| 18448 | What's The Color Of A "Yellow" Horse-vJK | Ed 52298 |
| 18449 | Waitin' For Katy | Rejected |

Reg Harrington-tb replaces Troup; Chick Condon-d replaces Weil.
New York, May 22, 1928.

| | | |
|---|---|---|
| 18523 | Since She Learned To Ride A Horse - vJK | Ed 52323 |
| 18524 | Mama's Grown Young - Papa's Grown Old - vJK - | Amb 5553 |

Probably very similar to the above.     New York, July 21, 1928.

| | | |
|---|---|---|
| 18624 | That's My Weakness Now - vJK | Ed 52364 |
| 18625 | Butternut - vJK | - |
| N-335-A | That's My Weakness Now - vJK | Rejected |
| N-336-A | Butternut - vJK | - |

As for May 22, 1928, without Clark.     New York, September 14, 1928.

| | | |
|---|---|---|
| 18725 | It Goes Like This (That Funny Melody) - vJK | Ed 52405   Amb 5631 |
| 18726 | Nagasaki - vJK | - |
| N-430-A-B | It Goes Like This (That Funny Melody) - vJK | Rejected |
| N-431-A-B | Nagasaki - vJK | -- |

Angie Rattiner-t/Tommy Dorsey-tb/Jimmy Dorsey-cl-as/Ch uncey Gray-p/Tommy Felline-bj/
Stan King-d/Jack Kaufman (as JACK DALTON)-v.
New York, December 19, 1928.

| | | |
|---|---|---|
| 18954 | I Love To Bumpity Bump On A Bumpy Road With You - vJK | Rejected |
| 18955 | I'm Wild About Horns On Automobiles (That Go "Ta-Ta-Ta-Ta") - vJK | Ed 52508, Amb 5648 |
| N-645 | I Love To Bumpity Bump On A Bumpy Road With You - vJK | Rejected |
| N-646 | I'm Wild About Horns On Automobiles (That Go "Ta-Ta-Ta-Ta") - vJK | - |

Angie Rattiner-t/Ted Raph-tb/Bud Wagner-cl-as/Larry Kosky- ---- McGarvey-vn/Chauncey
Gray-p/Tommy Felline-bj/Nick Pisani-bb or sb/Stan King-d.
New York, January 7, 1929.

| | | |
|---|---|---|
| 18990 | It's A Precious Little Thing Called Love | Ed rejected |
| N-681 | It's A Precious Little Thing Called Love | - |

NOTE;- For other titles from this session, see Ermine Calloway.

Miff Mole-tb replaces Raph; Carl Orech-cl-ss-as replaces Wagner; Herb Weil-d replaces King; no vn;                     New York, January 14, 1929.

| | | |
|---|---|---|
| 18954 | I Love To Bumpity Bump On A Bumpy Road With You - vJK | Ed 52508 |
| 19007 | Where Did You Get That Name ? - vJK | Ed 52516 |

Angie Rattiner-t/Miff Mole-tb/Carl Orech-cl-ss-as/Chauncey Gray-p/Tommy Felline-bj/
  Herb Weil-d/Jack Kaufman (as JACK DALTON)-v.
                                      New York, February 15, 1929.

| | | |
|---|---|---|
| 19052 | Heaven Help A Sailor On A Night Like This - vJK | Ed 52528, Amb 5718 |
| 19053 | Outside - vJK | - |
| N-743 | Heaven Help A Sailor On A Night Like This - vJK | Rejected |
| N-744 | Outside - vJK | - |

Fred van Eps, Jr.-t/ —— Walsh-tb/Pete Pumiglio-cl-as/Chauncey Gray-p/Tommy Felline-
  bj/Stan King-d/Jack Kaufman (as JACK DALTON)-v.
                                      New York, March 26, 1929.

| | | |
|---|---|---|
| 19125 | Please Don't Cut Out My Sauerkraut - vJK | Ed 52556 |
| 19126 | If I Give Up The Saxophone - vJK | - |
| N-816 | Please Don't Cut Out My Sauerkraut - vJK | Ed 14011 |
| N-817 | If I Give Up The Saxophone - vJK | Ed 14066 |

Johnny Sylvester-t replaces van Eps; Carl Loeffler-tb replaces Walsh.
                                      New York, May 7, 1929.

| | | |
|---|---|---|
| 19178 | She's A Good Girl - vJK | Ed 52583 |
| 19179 | The Whoopee Hat Brigade - vJK | - |
| N-882 | She's A Good Girl - vJK | Rejected |
| N-883 | The Whoopee Hat Brigade - vJK | Ed 14011 |

Angie Rattiner-t/Carl Loeffler-tb/Pete Pumiglio-cl-as/Chauncey Gray-p/Tommy Felline-
  bj/Chick Condon-d.                  New York, May 27, 1929.

| | | |
|---|---|---|
| 19216 | Heigh-Ho ! Ev'rybody, Heigh-Ho ! | Ed 52602, Amb 5728 |
| N-920 | Heigh-Ho ! Ev'rybody, Heigh-Ho ! | Ed 14016 |

Fred van Eps, Jr.-t replaces Rattiner; Stan King-d replaces Condon; Jack Kaufman
  (as JACK DALTON)-v.                 New York, June 20, 1929.

| | | |
|---|---|---|
| 19264 | I'm Cuckoo Again - vJK | Ed 52621 |
| 19265 | I Don't Work For A Living - vJK | - |
| N-971 | I'm Cuckoo Again - vJK | Ed 14030 |
| N-972 | I Don't Work For A Living - vJK | - |

Ward Lay-sb added.                    New York, August 6, 1929.

| | | |
|---|---|---|
| 19334 | My Wife Is On A Diet - vJK | Rejected |
| 19335 | Bessie Couldn't Help It - vJK | - |
| N-1059 | My Wife Is On A Diet - vJK | Ed 14047 |
| N-1060 | Bessie Couldn't Help It - vJK | - |

Herb Weil-d replaces King; Lay omitted. New York, September 20, 1929.

| | | |
|---|---|---|
| N-1143 | Collegiate Sam - vJK | Ed 14081 |
| N-1144 | I'm Keeping Company Now - vJK | - |

See also Ermine Calloway; Billy Murray.


## SEVEN BROWN BABIES


Pseudonym on Ajax and Apex for Fletcher Henderson and his Orchestra, q.v.


## THE  SEVEN CHAMPIONS


Pseudonym on Champion for Bailey's Lucky Seven, q.v.

Ed Allen-c/cl/Frank Robinson-bsx-h-descant recorder-v/? Willie "The Lion" Smith-p/
Clarence Williams-jug-v.              New York, December 6, 1929.

149690-1-2-3  Wipe 'Em Off - h-vFR/vCW            Rejected
149691-3  What If I Do - drFR                     Col 2087-D

                      New York, January 3, 1930.

149638-1-2-3  For My Baby                         Rejected
149639-1-2-3  What Makes Me Love You So ?         -
149690-6  Wipe 'Em Off - h-vFR/vCW               Col 2087-D, Par R-2329, PZ-11287,
                                                  Od 028077

## THE SEVEN HOT-AIR MEN

See The Hot-Air Men.

## SEVEN LITTLE CLOUDS OF JOY

See Andy Kirk.

## SEVEN LITTLE POLAR BEARS

See Harry Reser.

## SEVEN  MISSING LINKS

C/tb/cl/? Nathan Glantz-as/bsx/p/bj.     New York, c. July 21, 1925.

106159    Milenberg Joys                PA 36299, Per 14480
6136-1    Milenberg Joys                Ban 1618, Dom 3590, 21080, Or 443,
                                        Re 9920, Apex 8398
NOTE:- The above two sets of performances are identical; matrix 6136 is entered in
the ARC-CBS files under the date August 12, 1925, with a note that it was re-made
on October 15, 1925; it is not known if the re-make was issued. The band is shown
simply as HOUSE BAND, which may confirm Nathan Glantz's presence (Apex 8398 is
labeled GLANTZ AND HIS ORCHESTRA). Banner 1618, Domino 3590 and Regal 9920 appear
as PERRY'S HOT DOGS, and Oriole 443 as DIXIE JAZZ BAND.

2t/tb/cl/? Nathan Glantz-as/ts/p/bj/George Hamilton Green-x.
                                        New York, c. July 28, 1925.

106168    Angry                        PA 36299, 11026, Per 14480,
                                        Sil 2584, Hom C-942, GP 18492,
                                        Sal 164
6137-1    Angry                        Ban 1634, Dom 3605, 21085, Or 475,
NOTE:- Banner 1634, Domino 3605, 21085, Regal   Re 9940, Apex 8392, Leo/St 10051,
9940 and Imperial 1541 as MISSOURI JAZZ BAND;   Mic 22029, Imp 1541
Pathe Actuelle 36299 as IMPERIAL DANCE ORCHESTRA; 11026 as CASINO DANCE ORCHESTRA;
Oriole 475 as DIXIE JAZZ BAND; Homochord C-942 as LEW GOLD AND HIS ORCHESTRA, which
may be perfectly correct (see Lou Gold); Grand Pree 18492 as LENNOX DANCE ORCHESTRA.
See also note for previous session above.

## SEVEN  RAG PICKERS

See Harry Reser.

## THE  SEVEN NOTES

Pseudonym on Parlophone R-3336 for Jack Linx and his Birmingham Society Serenaders,
q.v.

## THE  SEVEN SYNCOPATORS

Pseudonym on Champion for Piggy Jones and his Orchestra, q.v.

# SEVEN WILD MEN

Harry Reser-bj dir. Red Nichols-t/Sam Lewis-tb/Larry Abbott-cl-as/Norman Yorke-ts/
Jimmy Johnston-bsx/Bill Wirges-p/Tom Stacks-d-v.
New York, May 24, 1926.

142239-1-3  Iyone - My Own Iyone - vTS          Har 191-H, Re G-8687
142240-1  I'm Just Wild About Animal Crackers-vTS Har 193-H
142241-2  The Lunatic's Lullaby - vTS              -
NOTE:- Regal G-8687 as CORONA DABCE ORCHESTRA.

## HATCH SEWARD

Pseudonym on Broadway 5063 for Meade Lux Lewis, q.v.

## SEXTET OF THE RHYTHM CLUB OF LONDON

Danny Polo-cl/Pete Brown-as/Hazel Scott-p-v/Albert Harris-g/Pete Barry-sb-v/Arthur
Herbert-d.                          New York, December 1, 1939.

043945-1  Calling All Bars                     BB B-10529, HMV X-7087
043946-1 or 2  Mighty Like The Blues - vHS       -           -
043947-1  You Gave Me The Go-By - vHS          BB B-10557, HMV B-9062, EA-3117
043948-1  Why Didn't William Tell ? - vPB        -           -        -

## JEANETTE SEYMOUR

Vocal, acc. by her Midnight Stompers : Instrumentation and personnel unknown.
New York, May 20, 1927.

81094-A-B  Crying For My Used-To-Be           OK rejected
81095-A-B  I Just Want One Man                  -

## SHAFTESBURY DANCE ORCHESTRA

Pseudonym on Meloto for the following items listed in this book :-

S-1501  Susquehanna Home (Ben Selvin and his Orchestra)
S-1546  Everybody Loves My Baby (Jeffries and his Rialto Orchestra)

## LLOYD SHAKESPEARE'S BAND

Lloyd "Bill" Shakespeare-t dir. Bert Bullimore-t/F. J. Cruse-tb/Jim Easton-A.Mitchell
as/W. Everitt-ts/F. Dexter-vn/W. Crawford-p/C. Cohen-bj/J. W. Mills-bb/W. Scott-d.
London, November, 1927.

E-1703-2  Kind O' Mean                        Par E-5998
E-1707-1  You Can't Have Lovin' Unless Blues     -
NOTE:- This band won a MELODY MAKER dance band contest held on October 28, 1927,
and according to a contemporaneous report, it was given a test recording session
for Parlophone within a few days. It is not known if the gap in the matrix numbers
represents a subsequent date to the test, or if a considerable number of sides was
made at one session, of which only the above were issued.

## HARRY SHALSON

Although this prolific recording artist was in no sense a jazz singer, the following
sides have interesting accompaniments in that idiom, and among the others he made
under his own and other names for many British labels between 1927 and 1931, there
may be others of comparable merit.

Vocal, acc. by Carroll Gibbons-p dir. Sylvester Ahola-t/Eric Siday-vn/Joe Brannelly-g.
Small Queen's Hall, London, May 8, 1929.

Bb-16856-1-2-3  My Sin                        Rejected
Bb-16857-2  She's Wonderful                   HMV B-3088

Acc. by Carroll Gibbons  dir. Sylvester Ahola-t/? Van Phillips-cl-as/Eric Siday-
? George Smith-vn/Leo Kahn-p/Joe Brannelly-g/sb.
Small Queen's Hall, London, June 20, 1929.

Bb-17116-2  My Ideal                          HMV B-3088

Acc. by Carroll Gibbons-p dir. Norman Payne-t/Danny Polo-cl/Laurie Payne-as-bar/g/
sb/d.                                    Small Queen's Hall, London, Sept. 25, 1930.

| | | |
|---|---|---|
| Bb-20233-2 | With My Guitar And You | HMV B-3628 |
| Bb-20234-2 | Little White Lies | - |

Acc. by t/cl/2-3vn/p/g/sb/d-x.          Small Queen's Hall, London, Oct. 10, 1930.

| | | |
|---|---|---|
| Bb-20275-2 | Just Imagine | HMV B-3647 |

## ART SHAN AND HIS NEW MUSIC

The mis-spelling on Japanese Columbia M-543 of Artie Shaw and his New Music, q.v.

## TERRY SHAND AND HIS ORCHESTRA

Terry Shand-p-v dir. 2t/tb/cl/as/ts/g/sb/d/Louanne-v.
                                         New York, May 4, 1938.

| | | |
|---|---|---|
| 22861- | Back Home - vTS | Voc 4113 |
| 22862- | When The Circus Came To Town - vTS | - |
| 22863- | Tall, Tall Corn - vTS | Voc 4131 |
| 22864- | Ferdinand The Bull - vTS | - |

New York, June 28, 1938.

| | | |
|---|---|---|
| 64235-A | Hold My Hand - vTS | Dec 1928, F-6931, X-1658 |
| 64236- | I Wish I Was The Willow - vTS | Dec 1918 |
| 64237-A | Let's Break The Good News - vTS | - F-6931 |
| 64238-B | On The Bumpy Road To Love - vTS | Dec 1928, F-6958 |

New York, December 4, 1939.

| | | |
|---|---|---|
| 66923-A | Dance With A Dolly (With A Hole In Her Stocking) - vTS&ch | Dec 2927 |
| 66924-A | Don't Make Me Laugh (With Tears In My Eyes)-vL - | X-1924 |
| 66925-A | You're Lettin' The Grass Grow (Right Under Your Feet) - vTS | Dec 2940 |
| 66926-A | Blame The Imp - vTS | - |

New York, February 3, 1940.

| | | |
|---|---|---|
| 67143-A | Knick Knack Polly Wah Jingasol - vTS | Dec 3010 |
| 67144-A | Sweet Potato Piper - vTS | - Rex 9820 |
| 67145-A | The Man Who Comes Around - vTS | Dec 2997 |
| 67146-A | Bella Bambina (w) - vTS-L | - |

New York, March 22, 1940.

| | | |
|---|---|---|
| 67372- | Scared - vTS | Dec 3250 |
| 67373-A | I Love Me (I'm Wild About Myself) - vTS | Dec 3190 |
| 67374-A | I Need Lovin' - vL | Dec 3136, X-1894 |
| 67375- | Give Me The Moonlight, Give Me The Girl - vTS | Dec 3250 |
| 67376-A | I Can't Love You Any More (Any More Than I Do) - vTS | Dec 3127 |
| 67377-A | My Extraordinary Gal - vTS | Dec 3190 |
| 67378-A | Ain't We Got Fun ? - vTS-L | Dec 3136, X-1894 |
| 67379-A | Pretty Baby - vTS | Dec 3127, X-1909 |

New York, September 10, 1940.

| | | |
|---|---|---|
| 68059-A | Practice Makes Perfect - vTS | Dec 3399 |
| 68060-A | Willie, Willie, Willie (Why Do You Cry ?)-vL | - |
| 68061-A | Southern Fried | Dec 3472, X-1970 |
| 68062-A | Li'l Boy Love - vL | Dec 3421 |
| 68063-A | Missouri Scrambler | Dec 3472, X-1970 |
| 68064-A | My Piggy Bank Is Jing-a-Ling Again-vTS | Dec 3421, X-1979 |

Terry Shand-p-v dir. 2t/tb/cl/as/ts/g/sb/d/Louanne-v.
New York, December 16, 1940.

| | | |
|---|---|---|
| 68506-A | Let's Do It - vTS | Dec 3587 |
| 68507-A | Slap-Happy Lassie - vTS | - |
| 68508-A | Talkin' Out Of Turn - vL | Dec 3641 |
| 68509-A | Pierre Of The Saskatchewan - vTS | - |

New York, March 21, 1941.

| | | |
|---|---|---|
| 68858- | K-K-K-Katy - vTS | Dec 3783 |
| 68859- | Wabash Cannon Ball - vTS | - |
| 68860-A | I've Been Working On The Railroad - vTS | Dec 3714 |
| 68861-A | Casey Jones - vTS | - |

New York, May 26, 1941.

| | | |
|---|---|---|
| 69248-A | Cindy - vTS&ch | Dec 3835 |
| 69249-A | The New River Train - vTS&ch | Dec 3836 |
| 69250-A | For Sev'n Long Years - vTS&ch | Dec 3835 |
| 69251-A | The Filipino Hombre - vTS | Dec 3836 |

New York, December 12, 1941.

| | | |
|---|---|---|
| 70049- | Pay Me No Mind - vTS | Dec 4256 |
| 70050-A | I'm Sorry That We Said Goodbye - vTS | Dec 4242 |
| 70051- | It's Been A Long, Long Time - vTS | Dec 4256 |
| 70052-A | Just One Girl - vTS | Dec 4242 |

New York, February 27, 1942.

| | | |
|---|---|---|
| 70406-A | Wait Till The Girls Get Into The Army, Boys - vTS | Dec 4320 |
| 70407- | I'll Be Back - vTS | Dec 4284 |
| 70408-A | Don't Forget To Say "No," Baby - vTS | Dec 4320 |
| 70409-A | Sh-h, It's A Military Secret - vTS | Dec 4284 |

## SHARKEY'S  NEW ORLEANS BOYS/SHARKS OF RHYTHM

See Sharkey Bonano.

## FRED SHARP'S  DIXIE PLAYERS/ROYAL CUBANS

Pseudonym on Champion for Gowans' Rhapsody Makers, q.v.

## ARTIE SHAW

ARTIE SHAW AND HIS ORCHESTRA : Artie Shaw-cl dir. Willie Kelly-t/Mark Bennett-tb/Tony
Zimmers-ts/Julie Schechter-Lou Klayman-vn/Sam Persoff-vl/Jimmy Oderich-vc/Fulton
McGrath-p/Wes Vaughan-g-v/Hank Wayland-sb/Sammy Weiss-d/Peg La Centra-v.
New York, June 11, 1936.

| | | |
|---|---|---|
| B-19434-2 | The Japanese Sandman | Br 7688, A-81034, Voc 4465, S-25, Col DO-1584 |
| B-19435-2 | A Pretty Girl Is Like A Melody | As above, plus Cq 9556 |
| B-19436-1 | I Used To Be Above Love - vWV | Br 7698, Voc 4837, Col DO-1600 |
| B-19437-4 | No Regrets - vWV | - 5058  - Cq 9096  - |

NOTE:- Matrix B-19437-4 is a dubbing of -1 or -2, re-made on June 17, 1936.

Artie Shaw-cl dir. Lee Castle-Dave Wade-t/Mike Michaels-tb/Tony Pastor-ts/Jerry Gray
Sam Rosenblum-vn/Sam Persoff-vl/Jimmy Oderich-vc/Joe Lippman-p/Gene Stultz-g/Ben
Ginsberg-sb/Sammy Weiss-d/Peg La Centra-v.
New York, August 6, 1936.

| | | |
|---|---|---|
| B-19667-1 | South Sea Island Magic - vPL | Br 7721, Voc 4637, 513, RZ G-22988 |
| B-19668-2 | It Ain't Right - vPL | -  -  - |
| B-19669-2 | Sugar Foot Stomp | Br 7735, Voc S-48, Par R-2940 |
| B-19670-3 | Thou Swell | -  Voc S-54 |

NOTE:- Regal Zonophone G-22988 as CASINO ROYAL ORCHESTRA.

ARTIE SHAW AND HIS ORCHESTRA : Artie Shaw-cl dir. Lee Castle-Zeke Zarchy-t/Mike
    Michaels-tb/Tony Pastor-ts-v/Jerry Gray-Ben Plotkin-vn/Sam Persoff-vl/Jimmy Oderich
    vc/Joe Lippman-p/Gene Stultz-g/Ben Ginsberg-sb/Sammy Weiss-d/Peg La Centra-v.
                                        New York, September 17, 1936.

B-19895-1  You're Giving Me A Song And A Dance-vPL Br 7741, Voc 518
B-19896-1  Darling, Not Without You - vPL          -           -
B-19897-1  One, Two, Button Your Shoe - vTP        Br 7750, Col DO-1634
B-19898-2  Let's Call A Heart A Heart - vPL        -           -

    Frank Siegfield-vn replaces Plotkin; Bill Schumann-vc replaces Oderich; Tony Got-
    tuso-g replaces Stultz; George Wettling-d replaces Weiss.
                                        New York, October 30, 1936.

B-20166-1  The Skeleton In The Closet            Br 7771, Voc S-48, Col DO-1625
B-20167-1  There's Something In The Air - vPL    Br 7778, 5077
B-20168-1  Take Another Guess - vPL              -       Col DO-1641
B-20169-1  There's Frost On The Moon - vPL       Br 7771, Col DO-1625

    Buddy Morrow-tb replaces Michaels.      New York, November 30, 1936.

B-20342-2  Love And Learn - vPL                 Br 7787, Voc S-79, RZ G-23031
B-20343-2  Moon Face - vPL                      -           -
B-20344-2  The Same Old Line                    Br 7794, Voc 4514, S-54, Cq 9093
B-20345-1  You Can Tell She Comes From Dixie - vPL  -     - 543, RZ G-23097 -
    NOTE:- Regal Zonophone G-23031 and G-23097 as CASINO ROYAL ORCHESTRA.

    Sides marked * as by ARTIE SHAW AND HIS STRINGS, consisting of the strings and
    rhythm shown above, with Artie Shaw-cl*.
                                        New York, December 23, 1936.

B-20448-1  Sobbin' Blues                        Br 7806, A-82102, Voc S-63,
                                                Par R-2940, Col DO-1689, DS-1510
B-20448-4  Sobbin' Blues                        Voc 4686, Cq 9193, Har 1016
B-20449-1  Copenhagen                           Br 7827, Voc 4336, S-67,
                                                Par R-2934, Col DS-1510
B-20450-1  Cream Puff                           Br 7806, A-82102, Voc S-63,
                                                Par R-2934, Col DO-1689
B-20450-4  Cream Puff                           Voc 4686, Cq 9193, Har 1016
B-20451-1-3  My Blue Heaven                     Br 7827, Voc 4336, S-79, Cq 9556,
                                                Par R-2686, Od A-2347, A-272245
B-20452-3  *Streamline                          Br 7852, A-81195, A-500712,
                                                Voc/OK 4598, Voc S-56, Par R-2984,
                                                Col DC-333, DC-553,DO-1682,DYC-132
B-20453-2  *Sweet Lorraine                      As above, except Voc/OK 4598
B-20453-3  *Sweet Lorraine                      Voc/OK 4598, Har 1014

                            New York, February 15, 1937.

B-20678-1  Love Is Good For Anything That Ails  Br 7841, 5098, Voc 548
           You - vPL
B-20679-1  No More Tears - vPL                  Br 7835
B-20680-1  Moonlight And Shadows - vPL          -       Voc/OK 4865, Voc 543,
                                                Cq 9269, RZ G-23091
B-20681-2  Was It Rain ? - vPL                  Br 7841, Voc 548
    NOTE:- Regal Zonophone G-23091 as CASINO ROYAL ORCHESTRA.

                            New York, February 19, 1937.

06230-1  Love Is Good For Anything That Ails    Thesaurus 366
           You/No More Tears-vPL/September In The Rain-vPL/The Mood That I'm In
06231-1  Trust In Me-vPL/A Message From The Man      -
           In The Moon/Was It Rain ?-vPL/Swing High, Swing Low
06232-1  Sweet Is The Word For You-vPL/Moon Face- Thesaurus 370
           vPL/Skeleton In The Closet/Sobbin' Blues
06233-1  Cream Puff/At Sundown/Copenhagen/My     Thesaurus 377, 1143/1177/1137/1177
           Blue Heaven
06234-1  When Your Lover Has Gone-vPL/All Dressed Thesaurus 385, 1134/1135/1145
           Up And No Place To Go-vPL/How Come You Do Me Like You Do ?
           The Blues                              -

ARTIE SHAW AND HIS NEW MUSIC : Artie Shaw-cl dir. John Best-Malcolm Crain-Tom di
Carlo-t/Harry Rogers-George Arus-tb/Les Robinson-Art Masters-as/Tony Pastor-ts-v/
Fred Petry-ts/Les Burness-p/Al Avola-g/Ben Ginsberg-sb/Cliff Leeman-d/Dorothy Howe
v.                                          New York, April 29, 1937.

| | | | |
|---|---|---|---|
| 07884-1 | Born To Swing | Thesaurus 395 | |
| | Milenberg Joys | - | 1137 |
| | The Bus Blues | - | |
| | Ubangi | - | |
| 07885-1 | Twilight In Turkey | Thesaurus 388, | 1140 |
| | Alibi Baby - vTP | | |
| | Night Over Shanghai | - | |
| | Study In Brown | - | |
| 07886-1 | I'll Never Tell You I Love You - vDH | - | 1145 |
| | All At Once - vDH | - | 1139 |
| | Without Your Love - vDH | - | 1178 |
| | The Love Bug Will Bite You - vTP | - | |
| 07887-1 | Johnnie One Note | Thesaurus 389, | 1139 |
| | Never In A Million Years - vDH | - | 1185 |
| | Wake Up And Live | - | - |
| | I've Got Beginner's Luck - vDH | - | 1135 |
| 07888-1 | Someday, Sweetheart | Thesaurus 402, | 1140 |
| | Symphony In Riffs | - | 1143 |
| | In The Bottom | - | |
| | Hold Your Hats | - | |
| 07889-1 | The Bus Blues (part)/Born To Swing/ | Thesaurus 389 | |
| | Someday, Sweetheart/Night And Day/Ubangi/The Bus Blues | | |

NOTE:- The titles on the last side above are different from the previous versions
on the session of the same titles, and the two versions of THE BUS BLUES differ
from each other as well as from the one on matrix 07884-1.

New York, May 13, 1937.

| | | |
|---|---|---|
| B-21134-2 | All Alone | Br 7899, Voc S-105, Par R-2661, Od A-2346, A-272258 |
| B-21135-2 | All God's Chillun Got Rhythm - vTP | Br 7895, A-81231, 5118, Voc 566 |
| B-21136-2 | It Goes To Your Feet - vTP | -          -          - |
| B-21137-2 | Because I Love You | Br 7899, Voc S-105, Par R-2686, Od A-2347, A-272245 |

Harry Freeman-as replaces Masters.    New York, May 18, 1937.

| | | |
|---|---|---|
| B-21167-1 | Night And Day | Br 7914, Voc S-111, Lucky 60353 |
| B-21168-1 | I Surrender, Dear | Br 7907, A-81280, Voc S-114, Par R-2676, Od A-2351 |
| B-21169-1 | Blue Skies | Br 7907, Voc S-111, Par R-2676, Od A-2351, Col M-139 |
| B-21170-1 | Someday, Sweetheart | Br 7914, A-81280, Voc S-114, Par R-2661, Od A-2346, A-272258, Lucky 60353 |

Peg La Centra (as BETTY LOWTHER)-v.    New York, July 13, 1937.

| | | | |
|---|---|---|---|
| 011303-1 | Whispers In The Dark | Thesaurus 419 | |
| | Don't Ever Change - vPL | - | |
| | If I Put My Heart In A Song | - | |
| | Love Is A Merry-Go-Round | - | 1172 |
| 011304-1 | Till The Clock Strikes Three | - | - |
| | The Moon Got In My Eyes-vPL/All You Want To | - | |
| | Do Is Dance-vPL/It's The Natural Thing To Do-vPL | | |
| 011305-1 | The Folks Who Live On The Hill-vPL/ | Thesaurus 426, | 1137 |
| | Can I Forget You ?-vPL/The Things I Want-vPL/Posin' | | |
| 011306-1 | If You Should Ever Leave-vPL | Thesaurus 420, | 1140 |
| | The Loveliness Of You | - | 1185 |
| | Afraid To Dream - vPL | - | - |
| | All Alone | - | |
| 011307-1 | Because I Love You | Thesaurus 433 | |
| | If I Had You | - | 1177 |
| | Together | - | 1136 |
| | Just You - Just Me | - | 1178 |

ARTIE SHAW AND HIS NEW MUSIC : Artie Shaw-cl dir. John Best-Malcolm Crain-Tom di
   Carlo-t/Harry Rogers-George Arus-tb/Les Robinson-Harry Freeman-as/Tony Pastor-ts-v/
   Fred Petry-ts/Les Burness-p/Al Avola-g/Ben Ginsberg-sb/Cliff Leeman-d/Peg La Centra
   v.                                        New York, July 22, 1937.

| | | |
|---|---|---|
| B-21423-1 | Afraid To Dream - vPL | Br 7934, A-81222 |
| B-21424-1 | If You Should Ever Leave - vPL | -       - |
| B-21425-1 | Sweet Adeline - vTP | Br 7936, A-81332, 5117, |
| | | Voc/OK 4182, Cq 9535 |
| B-21426-1 | How Dry I Am | Br 7936, A-81332, 5117, Voc 4182, |
| | | S-180 |
| B-21426-2 | How Dry I Am | OK 4182 |

   Jules Rubin-ts replaces Petry; Leo Watson-v.
                                          New York, August 4, 1937.

| | | |
|---|---|---|
| B-21458-1 | Am I In Love ? - vPL | Br 7942, A-81235 |
| B-21459-1 | Fee Fi Fo Fum - vLW | Br 7952, Voc/OK 4539, Col DO-1769 |
| B-21460-2 | Please Pardon Us, We're In Love - vPL | Br 7942, A-81235, 5118,Col DO-1641 |
| B-21461-1 | The Chant | Br 7952, Voc/OK 4539, Voc S-159, |
| | | Col DO-1769 |
| B-21462-1 | The Blues - Part 1 | Br 7947, Voc/OK 4401, Voc S-124, |
| | | Par R-2790, Col DO-1768, DS-1382, |
| | | M-343 |
| B-21462-3 | The Blues - Part 1 | Har 1057 |
| B-21463-2 | The Blues - Part 2 | As for B-21462-1 and B-21462-3 |

   NOTE:- Columbia M-343 as ART SHAN AND HIS NEW MUSIC.

   Beatrice (Bea) Wain-v.               New York, September 17, 1937.

| | | |
|---|---|---|
| B-21710-1 | It's A Long, Long Way To Tipperary | Br 7965, A-81308, Voc/OK 4306, |
| | | Voc S-120 |
| B-21711-1 | I've A Strange New Rhythm In My Heart | Br 7971, 5128, Col DO-1796 |
| | - vLW | |
| B-21712-2 | If It's The Last Thing I Do - vBW | -       -       -    Voc 4933 |
| B-21713-A | Nightmare | Br 7965, A-81308, Voc/OK 4306, |
| | | Par R-2554, Od A-2345, A-272256, |
| | | Col DS-1544 |
| B-21714-1 | Shoot The Likker To Me, John Boy - vLW | Br 7976, A-81763, Voc/OK 4198, |
| | | Voc S-120, Par R-2937, Od 275127 |
| B-21715-1 | Free Wheeling - vLW | Br 7976, A-81763, Voc/OK 4198 |

   Louise Farrell-v; Tony Pastor (as BILL RALSTON)-v.
                                          New York, October 16, 1937.

| | | | |
|---|---|---|---|
| 015507-1 | Strange Loneliness - vLF | Thesaurus 455 | |
| | Have You Met Miss Jones ? - vTP | - | 1139 |
| | I'd Rather Be Right | | 1140 |
| | Everything You Said Came True | - | |
| 015508-1 | Rosalie - vTP | - | 1135 |
| | You Have Everything | - | - |
| | Shindig | - | |
| | I've Got A Strange New Rhythm In My Heart | - | 1140 |
| 015509-1 | Sweet Varsity Sue | Thesaurus 496 | |
| | I Want A New Romance | - | |
| | Shoot The Likker To Me, John Boy - vLW ? | - | |
| | Free Wheelin' - vLW ? | - | |
| 015510-1 | S. O. S. | - | |
| | How Dry I Am | - | |
| | Black And Blue | - | |
| | Fee Fi Fo Fum - vLW ? | - | |
| 015511-1 | I'm Yours | Thesaurus 461 | |
| | Sweet Adeline - vTP | - | |
| | Old Black Joe | | |
| | It's A Long Way To Tipperary | - | 1138 |

ARTIE SHAW AND HIS NEW MUSIC : Artie Shaw-cl dir. John Best-Malcolm Crain-Tom di
    Carlo-t/Harry Rogers-George Arus-tb/Les Robinson-Harry Freeman-as/Tony Pastor-ts-v/
    Jules Rubin-ts/Les Burness-p/Al Avola-g/Ben Ginsberg-sb/Cliff Leeman-d/Dolores
    O'Neil-v.                              New York, October 18, 1937.

| | | |
|---|---|---|
| B-21895-1 | Let 'Er Go | Br 7986, A-81352, Voc 4438, S-181 |
| B-21896-1 | A Strange Loneliness - vDO'N | –    –    Par R-2554, |
| | | Od A-2345, A-272256 |
| B-21897-1 | Monsoon | Br 8019, A-81325, Voc S-140, |
| | | Col DS-1544 |
| B-21898-1 | I'm Yours | Br 8010, Cq 9269, Voc/OK 4865, |
| | | Voc S-180 |
| B-21899-1 | Just You, Just Me | Br 8010, Voc 4933, S-181 |
| B-21899-2 | Just You, Just Me | Epic EE-22023 (EP) |
| B-21900-1 | Free For All | Br 8019, A-81325, Voc S-140, |
| | | Par R-2937, Od 275127 |

Anita (Nita) Bradley-v.                   New York, December 15, 1937.

| | | | |
|---|---|---|---|
| 017807-1 | Goodnight Angel - vNB | Thesaurus 481 | |
| | One Song - vNB | – | |
| | There's A New Moon Over The Old Mill - vNB | – | |
| | Can't Teach My Old Heart New Tricks - vNB | – | 1133 |
| 017808-1 | You're Out Of This World - vTP | – | |
| | You're A Sweetheart - vNB | – | 1178 |
| | Bob White (Whatcha Gonna Swing Tonight ?)-vTP | – | 1133 |
| | Old Stamping Ground - vTP | – | |
| 017809-1 | Love For Sale | Thesaurus 487, 1133 | |
| | Big Dipper | – | |
| | The Lady Is A Tramp - vTP | – | 1139 |
| | Stalling For Time | – | |
| 017810-1 | Monsoon/Honeysuckle Rose/I'll Be With | Thesaurus 482 | |
| | You In Apple-Blossom Time-vTP/Non-Stop Flight | | |
| 017811-1 | Nightmare | Thesaurus 524 | |
| | My Bonnie Lies Over The Ocean - vTP | – | |
| | Show Me The Way To Go Home | – | 1133 |
| | Stealin' Apples | – | 1143 |

New York, December 30, 1937.

| | | |
|---|---|---|
| B-22237-2 | Whistle While You Work - vTP | Br 8050, A-81465, Voc S-147 |
| B-22238-1 | One Song - vNB | –    –    – |
| B-22239-1 | Goodnight, Angel - vNB | Br 8054, A-81481 |
| B-22239-2 | Goodnight, Angel - vNB | NBC 1004 (LP) |
| B-22240-1 | There's A New Moon Over The Old Mill | Br 8054, A-81481 |
| | - vNB | |
| B-22241-1 | Non-Stop Flight | Voc S-147, Br A-81466 |
| B-22242-2 | I'll Be With You In Apple-Blossom Time | Voc 4438, S-159 – |

New York, February 15, 1938.

| | | | |
|---|---|---|---|
| 019825-1 | Toy Trumpet | Thesaurus 501, 1133 | |
| | Hill Billy From 10th Avenue | – | 1134 |
| | Old Kentucky Home | – | |
| | Any Old Time - vNB | – | |
| 019826-1 | Power House | Thesaurus 549, 1134 | |
| | Take My Word | – | |
| | Azure | – | 1144 |
| | The Call Of The Freaks | – | 1136 |
| 019827-1 | Old Apple Tree | Thesaurus 500 | |
| | Lost In The Shuffle | – | |
| | If Dreams Come True | – | 1143 |
| | Moonlight On The Sunset Trail - vNB | – | |
| 019828-1 | More Than Ever | – | 1177 |
| | I'll Never Let You Cry | – | |
| | In The Shade Of The Old Apple Tree | | |
| | It's Wonderful - vNB | – | 1178 |
| 019829-1 | Blue Fantasy | Thesaurus 567, 1135 | |
| | Love's Old Sweet Song | – | |
| | Indian Love Call | – | 1139 |
| | Meade Lux Special | – | |

ARTIE SHAW AND HIS ORCHESTRA : Artie Shaw-cl dir. Chuck Peterson-John Best-Claude
Bowen-t/George Arus-Ted Vesley-Harry Rogers-tb/Les Robinson-Hank Freeman-as/Tony
Pastor-ts-v/Ronnie Perry-ts/Les Burness-p/Al Avola-g/Sid Weiss-sb/Cliff Leeman-d/
Billie Holiday-v,Jerry Gray-a.                    New York, July 24, 1938.

024079-1  Begin The Beguine - aJG              BB B-7746, Vic 27546, 20-1551,
                                                MW M-7525, HMV B-8906, AV-693,
                                                EA-2369, JK-2067, K-8343, TG-142,
                                                X-6461, X-7523, El EG-6883,
                                                V-Disc 13, 560
024080-1  Indian Love Call - vTP&ch            BB B-7746, MW M-7525, HMV B-8869,
                                                JK-2261, K-8296, TG-318
024081-2  Comin' On                            BB B-7772, MW M-7523, HMV B-8880,
                                                EA-2276, J0-230, K-8336
024082-1  Back Bay Shuffle                     BB B-7759, Vic 27547, MW M-7524,
                                                HMV B-8894, GW-1742, JK-2066,
                                                K-8327, TG-139, El EG-6869
024083-1  Any Old Time - vBH                   BB B-7759, HMV B-9382, V-Disc 399,
                                                Sentry/Tpl 4006
024084-1  I Can't Believe That You're In Love  BB B-7772, MW M-7523, HMV B-8948,
            With Me                            JK-2262

     Russell Brown-tb replaces Vesley; George Koenig-as replaces Robinson; Helen
     Forrest-v.                                New York, September 27, 1938.

027229-1  Nightmare                            BB B-7875, MW M-7530, HMV B-8869,
                                                EA-2790, JK-2261, K-8296, TG-318,
                                                El EG-6759, V-Disc 13
027230-1  Non-Stop Flight                      BB B-7875, MW M-7530, HMV B-8925,
                                                GW-1763, GW-1907, EA-2276, K-8391
027231-1  Yesterdays                           BB B-10001, MW M-7529, HMV B-8959,
                                                X-6505
027232-1  What Is This Thing Called Love ?     As above plus HMV JK-2262, X-6505
027233-1  You're A Sweet Little Headache - vHF BB B-7889, RZ MR-2977, G-23642
027234-1  I Have Eyes - vHF                    -            -            -
     NOTE:- Regal Zonophone G-23642 as THE MELODY MASTERS.  Some (early) pressings of
     HMV X-6505 are from original masters of matrix 027232-1.

                                               New York, November 17, 1938.

028973-1  Between A Kiss And A Sigh - vHF      BB B-10055, HMV EA-2310
028974-1  Thanks For Ev'rything - vHF          -           RZ G-23661
028975-1  Deep In A Dream - vHF                BB B-10046, RZ MR-2979,HMM EA-2369
028976-1  Day After Day - vHF                  -
028977-1  Softly As In A Morning Sunrise       BB B-10054, MW M-7950, HMV B-9396,
                                                EA-2738, J0-258, K-9208
028978-1  Copenhagen                           BB B-10054, MW M-7950, HMV B-8880,
                                                J0-230, K-8336
     NOTE:- Regal Zonophone G-23661 as THE MELODY MASTERS.
                                               New York, November 25, 1938.

          My Reverie - vHF                     Vic LPT-6000 (LP)
          Sobbin' Blues                        -

                                               New York, December 1, 1938.

          Non-Stop Flight                      Vic LPT-6000 (LP) .

                                               New York, December 6, 1938.

          Old Stamping Ground - vTP            Vic LPT-6000 (LP)

                                               New York, December 13, 1938.

          Begin The Beguine                    Vic LPT-6000 (LP)

                                               New York, December 14, 1938.

          Nightmare (Theme)                    Vic LPT-6000 (LP)

                                               New York, December 15, 1938.

          In The Mood                          Vic LPT-6000 (LP)
          The Chant                            -

ARTIE SHAW AND HIS ORCHESTRA : Artie Shaw-cl dir. Chuck Peterson-John Best-Bernie
Privin-t/George Arus-Les Jenkins-Harry Rogers-tb/Les Robinson-Hank Freeman-as/Tony
Pastor-ts-v/George Auld-ts/Bob Kitsis-p/Al Avola-g/Sid Weiss-sb/George Wettling-d/
Helen Forrest-v. (This personnel probably applies to the preceding three sessions
at least).                                New York, December 19, 1938.

| | | |
|---|---|---|
| 030731-1 | A Room With A View - vHF | BB B-10075 |
| 030732-1 | Say It With A Kiss - vHF | BB B-10079, HMV B-9355, JO-141 |
| 030733-1 | They Say - vHF | BB B-10075 |
| 030734-1 | It Took A Million Years - vHF | BB B-10079, HMV EA-2412 |
| 030735-1 | Jungle Drums | BB B-10091, HMV B-8894, EA-2529, GW-1742, JK-2016, TG-139, El EG-6869, V-Disc 362 |
| 030736-1 | It Had To Be You | BB B-10091, Vic 20-1593, HMV B-8948, JK-2068 |
| | Jeepers Creepers - vTP | Vic LPT-6000 (LP) |

New York, December 23, 1938.

| | | |
|---|---|---|
| | Together | Vic LPT-6000 (LP) |
| | Star Dust | - |

Buddy Rich-d replaces Wettling; Jerry Gray-a.
                                New York, January 17, 1939.

| | | |
|---|---|---|
| 031491-1 | Lover, Come Back To Me | BB B-10126, HMV B-8937, EA-2267 |
| 031492-1 | My Heart Stood Still | BB B-10125, Vic 20-1575, MW M-7952 HMV B-9399, EA-2267 |
| 031493-1 | Rosalie - vTP | BB B-10126, HMV B-9399 |
| 031494-1 | Supper Time - vHF | BB B-10127, HMV EA-2268 |
| 031495-1 | Vilia | BB B-10128, HMV B-8949, EA-2269, JK-2010, El EG-7831 |

New York, January 23, 1939.

| | | |
|---|---|---|
| 031823-1 | The Man I Love | BB B-10128, HMV EA-2269, JK-2010 |
| 031824-1 | The Donkey Serenade | BB B-10125, MW M-7952, HMV B-8893, El EG-6867 |
| 031825-1 | Bill - vHF | BB B-10124, HMV EA-2266, JK-2006 |
| 031826-1 | Zigeuner | BB B-10127, HMV B-8937, EA-2268, GW-1803, V-Disc 399 |
| 031827-1 | Carioca | BB B-10124, HMV B-8893, EA-2266, JK-2006, K-8327, El EG-6867 |

New York, January 31, 1939.

| | | |
|---|---|---|
| 031864-1 | Alone Together | BB B-10148 |
| 031865-1 | Rose Room | -        HMV B-8949, EA-2375 |
| 031866-1 | I Want My Share Of Love - vHF | BB B-10124, HMV EA-2627 |
| 031867-1 | It's All Yours - vHF | BB B-10141 |
| 031868-1 | This Is It - vHF | - |
| 031869-1 | Delightful Delirium - vTP | BB B-10134, HMV EA-2627 |

New York, March 12, 1939.

| | | |
|---|---|---|
| 032961-2 | Any Old Time - vHF/aJG | Vic 20-1575 |
| 032962-1 | I'm In Love With The Honorable Mr. So-and-So - vHF | BB B-10188 |
| 032963-1 | Prosschai (Goodbye, Goodbye) - vTP | -        HMV B-8925, EA-2448, GW-1763, K-8391 |
| 032964-1 | Deep Purple - vHF | BB B-10178, MW M-7957, HMV B-8906, EA-2310, JK-2067, K-8343, TG-142, X-7535, El EG-6883 |
| 032965-1 | I'm Coming, Virginia | BB B-10320, MW M-8384, HMV B-8997, EA-2654, K-8467 |
| 032966-2 | Pastel Blue (Why Begin Again ?*) | BB B-10178, MW M-7957, HMV B-8936* EA-2375*, JO-255* |

ARTIE SHAW AND HIS ORCHESTRA : Artie Shaw-cl dir. Chuck Peterson-John Best-Bernie
  Privin-t/George Arus-Les Jenkins-Harry Rogers-tb/Les Robinson-Hank Freeman-as/Tony
  Pastor-ts-v/George Auld-ts/Bob Kitsis-p/Al Avola-g/Sid Weiss-sb/Buddy Rich-d/Helen
  Forrest-v/Jerry Gray-a.                      New York, March 17, 1939.

```
032999-1  You Grow Sweeter As The Years Go By-vHF  BB B-10195
035300-1  You're So Indifferent - vHF              BB B-10215
035301-1  Snug As A Bug In A Rug - vTP             -
035302-1  If You Ever Change Your Mind - vHF       BB B-10195, HMV EA-2406
035303-1  One Night Stand                          BB B-10202, HMV B-8936, EA-2529,
                                                   JO-255, X-7523
035304-1  One Foot In The Groove                   BB B-10202
```

                                        Hollywood, June 5, 1939.

```
036237-6  Octoroon                                 BB B-10319
036238-4  I Poured My Heart Into A Song - vHF      BB B-10307, MW M-8385, HMV B-8958
036239-7  When Winter Comes - vTP                  -        -          -
036240-1  All I Remember Is You - VHF              BB B-10319
036241-3  Out Of Nowhere                           BB B-10320, MW M-8384, HMV B-8997,
                                                   K-8467
```

                                        Hollywood, June 12, 1939.

```
036264-2  I Can't Afford To Dream - vHF            BB B-10324, MW M-8383, HMV EA-2588
036265-17 Comes Love - vHF                         -        -          -
036266-11 Go Fly A Kite - vTP                      BB B-10347, MW M-8382, HMV B-8979
036267-2  A Man And His Dream - vHF                -        -          -
036268-4  Traffic Jam                              BB B-10385, MW M-8381, HMV B-9006,
                                                   EA-2970, JK-2181
036269-1-2-3-4-5-6-7  Serenade To A Savage         Rejected
```

                                        Hollywood, June 22, 1939.

```
036269-10 Serenade To A Savage                     BB B-10385, Vic 27549, MW M-8381,
                                                   HMV B-9006, JK-2181
036291-9  Easy To Say - vHF                        BB B-10345
036292-7  I'll Remember - vHF                      -        HMV EA-2428
036293-3  Moonray - vHF                            BB B-10334, HMV EA-2654
036294-5  Melancholy Mood - vHF                    -        HMV EA-2448
```

    Harry Geller-t replaces Best.            New York, August 19, 1939.

         Carioca                             Vic LPT-6000 (LP)

                                        New York, August 27, 1939.

```
042605-1  Put That Down In Writing - vTP           BB B-10406, MW M-8380, HMV EA-2550
042606-1  Day In, Day Out - vHF                    -        -
042607-1  Two Blind Loves - vHF                    BB B-10412, MW M-8379, HMV B-9017,
                                                   EA-2406, K-8483
042608-1  The Last Two Weeks In July - vHF         BB B-10412, MW M-8379
042609-1  Oh ! Lady, Be Good                       BB B-10430, Vic 20-1551, MW M-8378,
                                                   HMV B-9018, AV-693, EA-2738,
                                                   JK-2071, JO-256
042610-1  I Surrender, Dear                        BB B-10430, MW M-8378, HMV B-9018,
                                                   JK-2071, JO-256
```

                                        New York, September 28, 1939.

```
042755-1  Many Dreams Ago - vHF                    BB B-10446
042756-1  A Table In A Corner - vHF                BB B-10468
042757-1  If What You Say Is True - vTP            BB B-10446, HMV EA-2709
042758-1  Without A Dream To My Name - vHF         BB B-10468
```

                                        New York, October 20, 1939.

         Everything Is Jumpin'               Vic LPT-6000 (LP)

ARTIE SHAW AND HIS ORCHESTRA : Artie Shaw-cl dir. Chuck Peterson-Harry Geller-Bernie
   Privin-t/George Arus-Les Jenkins-Harry Rogers-tb/Les Robinson-Hank Freeman-as/Tony
   Pastor-ts-v/George Auld-ts/Bob Kitsis-p/Al Avola-g/Sid Weiss-sb/Buddy Rich-d/Helen
   Forrest-v.                              New York, October 21, 1939.

|  |  |  |  |
|---|---|---|---|
| | I'm Sorry For Myself - vTP | Vic LPT-6000 (LP) | |

New York, October 25, 1939.

| | At Sundown | Vic LPT-6000 (LP) | |
| | Maria, My Own | - | |

New York, October 26, 1939.

| | I've Got My Eyes On You - vHF | Vic LPT-6000 (LP) | |
| | Sweet Sue - Just You | - | |

| 043316-1 | Love Is Here - vHF | BB B-10482, HMV X-6584 | |
| 043317-1 | All In Fun - vHF | BB B-10492, HMV X-6539 | |
| 043318-1 | All The Things You Are - vHF | - Vic 20-1559 - | X-7535 |
| 043319-1 | You're A Lucky Guy - vTP | BB B-10482, HMV X-6584 | |

Dave Barbour-g replaces Avola.          New York, November 3, 1939.

| | El Rancho Grande (My Ranch) - vTP | Vic LPT-6000 (LP) | |

New York, November 9, 1939.

| 043367-1 | Shadows | BB B-10502, Vic 20-2865, MW M-8647, HMV X-6570 | |
| 043368-1 | I Didn't Know What Time It Was - vHF | As above except Vic 20-2865 | |
| 043369-1 | Do I Love You ? - vHF | BB B-10509, HMV X-6501 | |
| 043370-1 | When Love Beckoned - vHF | - | - |

New York, November 11, 1939.

| | My Blue Heaven | Vic LPT-6000 (LP) | |
| | Moonray - vHF | - | |
| | Diga Diga Doo | - | |

New York, November 28, 1939.

| | The Man From Mars | Vic LPT-6000 (LP) | |
| | St. Louis Blues | - | |

Artie Shaw-cl dir. Charlie Margulis-Manny Klein-George Thow-t/Randall Miller-Bill
Rank-Babe Bowman-tb/Blake Reynolds-Bud Carlton-Jack Stacey-as/Dick Clark-ts/Joe
Krechter-bcl/Jack Cave-fh/Morton Ruderman-f/Phil Nemoli-o/Mark Levant-Harry Blue-
stone-Peter Eisenberg-Robert Barene-Sid Brokaw-Dave Cracov-Alex Law-Jerry Joyce-vn
/David Sturkin-Stanley Spiegelman-Jack Gray-vl/Irving Lipschultz-Jules Tannenbaum-
vc/Stan Wrightsman-p/Bobby Sherwood-g/Jud DeNaut-sb/Carl Maus-d/Pauline Byrne-v.
                                        Hollywood, March 3, 1940.

| 042546-1 | Frenesi | Vic 26542, 27546, HMV B-9079, EA-2697, GW-2002,JK-2122,V-Disc 132 | |
| 042547-1 | Adios, Mariquita Linda | Vic 26542, HMV B-9079, EA-2697, GW-2002, JK-2122, V-Disc 148 | |
| 042548-1 | Gloomy Sunday - vPB | Vic 26563, HMV B-9116, GW-1979 | |
| 042549-1 | My Fantasy - vPB | Vic 26614 | |
| 042550-1 | A Deserted Farm | Rejected | |
| 042551-1 | Don't Fall Asleep | Vic 26563, HMV B-9116, GW-1979 | |

Artie Shaw-cl dir. Harry Geller-Manny Klein-George Thow-t/Ben Kanter-Lyle Bowen-
Jack Stacey-as/Happy Lawson-ts/Joe Krechter-bcl/Jack Cave-fh/Mischa Russell-Harry
Bluestone-Bob Morrow-Dave Cracov-B. Bower-Jerry Joyce-vn/David Sturkin-Sam Freed-
vl/Cy Bernard-vc/Lyle Henderson-p/Bobby Sherwood-g/Jud DeNaut-sb/Spencer Prinz-d/
Martha Tilton-Jack Pearle-v.            Hollywood, May 13, 1940.

| 049687-1 | Dreaming Out Loud - vMT | Vic 26642, HMV NE-506 | |
| 049688-1 | Now We Know - vMT | - | 20-1537 |
| 049689-1 | Mister Meadowlark - vJP | Vic 26614 | |
| 049690-1 | April In Paris | Vic 26654, HMV B-9105 | |
| 049691-1 | King For A Day | - | - |

ARTIE SHAW AND HIS GRAMERCY FIVE : Billy Butterfield-t/Artie Shaw-cl/Johnny Guarnieri
  harpsichord/Al Hendrickson-elg/Jud DeNaut-sb/Nick Fatool-d.
                                    Hollywood, September 3, 1940.

| | | |
|---|---|---|
| 055061-1-3 | Special Delivery Stomp | Vic 26762, HMV B-9146, EA-2909, JK-2131, V-Disc 281 |
| 055062-1 | Summit Ridge Drive | Vic 26763, HMV B-9146, EA-2974, JK-2148 |
| 055063-1 | Keepin' Myself For You | Vic 26762, HMV EA-2909, JK-2131 |
| 055064-1 | Cross Your Heart | Vic 26763, HMV EA-2974, JK-2148, X-7095, V-Disc 468 |

ARTIE SHAW AND HIS ORCHESTRA : Artie Shaw-cl dir. George Wendt-J. Cathcart-Billy
  Butterfield-t/Jack Jenney-Vernon Brown-tb/Bus Bassey-Neely Plumb-as/Les Robinson-
  Jerry Jerome-ts/E. Lamas-T. Boardman-T. Klages-Bob Morrow-B. Bower-Al Beller-vn/A.
  Harshman-K. Collins-vl/F. Goerner-vc/Johnny Guarnieri-p/Al Hendrickson-elg/Jud
  DeNaut-sb/Nick Fatool-d/Anita Boyer-v.  Hollywood, September 7, 1940.

| | | |
|---|---|---|
| 055067-1 | If It's You - vAB | Vic 26760, HMV EA-2674 |
| 055068-2 | Old, Old Castle In Scotland - vAB | -        -   JK-2191, X-7095 |
| 055069-1 | Temptation | Vic 27230, HMV N-4455, V-Disc 192 |
| 055070-1 | Chantez-les Bas | Vic 27354, HMV B-9197, EA-3025, JO-234 |

                                    Hollywood, October 7, 1940.

| | | |
|---|---|---|
| 055095-1 | Love Of My Life - vAB | Vic 26790, HMV EA-2709 |
| 055096-1 | A Handful Of Stars - vAB | -        HMV EA-2711 |
| 055097-1 | Star Dust | Vic 27230, 27547, HMV B-9288, JK-2191, N-4455, TG-140, X-7008, V-Disc 45, 560 |
| 055098-1 | Marinela | Vic 27362, HMV B-9214, AV-690 |
| 055099-1 | Danza Lucumi | Vic 27354 |

                                    Hollywood, December 3, 1940.

| | | |
|---|---|---|
| 55184-1 | This Is Romance | Vic rejected |
| 55185-1 | What Is There To Say ? | - |
| 55186-1 | Pyramid | - |
| 55187-1 | You Forgot About Me - vAB | - |
| 55188-1 | Whispers In The Night - vAB | - |

William Grant Still-a.                Hollywood, December 4, 1940.

| | | |
|---|---|---|
| 55191-3 | Blues - Part 1 - aWGS | Vic 27411, HMV B-9259, EA-3074, JK-2270 |
| 55192-3 | Blues - Part 2 - aWGS | As above |
| 55193-2 | Who's Excited ? | Vic 27385, HMV B-9341 |
| 55194-2 | Prelude in C major | Vic 27432, HMV B-9365, JK-2351 |

ARTIE SHAW AND HIS GRAMERCY FIVE : As for September 3, 1940 above.
                                    Hollywood, December 5, 1940.

| | | |
|---|---|---|
| 55195-1 | Dr. Livingstone, I Presume ? | Vic 27289, HMV B-9207, EA-3142, JK-2272, SG-39 |
| 55196-1 | When The Quail Come Back To San Quentin | As above |
| 55197-1 | My Blue Heaven | Vic 27405, HMV B-9269, AV-696, JK-2305, TG-141 |
| 55198-1 | Smoke Gets In Your Eyes | Vic 27335 |

ARTIE SHAW AND HIS ORCHESTRA : As for September 7, 1940.
                                    Hollywood, December 5, 1940.

| | | |
|---|---|---|
| 55184-2 | This Is Romance | Vic 27343, HMV B-9382 |
| 55185-2 | What Is There To Say ? | Vic 27432, HMV B-9351, EA-2882, JO-141 |
| 55186-2 | Pyramid | Vic 27343, HMV B-9197, EA-2853, JO-234 |
| 55187-2 | You Forgot About Me - vAB | Vic 27256, HMV EA-2789 |
| 55188-2 | Whispers In The Night - vAB | - |

ARTIE SHAW AND HIS ORCHESTRA : Artie Shaw-cl dir. George Wendt-J. Cathcart-Billy
Butterfield-t/Jack Jenney-Vernon Brown-Ray Conniff-tb/Bus Bassey-Neely Plumb-as/Les
Robinson-Jerry Jerome-ts/E. Lamas-T. Boardman-T. Klages-B. Bower-Bob Morrow-Al
Beller-vn/A. Harshman-K. Collins-vl/F. Goerner-vc/Johnny Guarnieri-p/Al Hendrickson-
elg/Jud DeNaut-sb/Nick Fatool-d/Anita Boyer-v.
                                            Hollywood, December 17, 1940.

| | | |
|---|---|---|
| 055224-1 | The Calypso - vAB | Vic 27315 |
| 055225-1 | Beau Night In Hotchkiss Corners - vAB | -          HMV B-9365, JK-2351 |
| 055226-1 | Concerto for Clarinet - Part 1 | Vic 36383, HMV C-3231, FKX-71 |
| 055227-1 | Concerto for Clarinet - Part 2 | -          -     - |

                                            Hollywood, January 23, 1941.

| | | |
|---|---|---|
| 055256-1 | Dancing In The Dark | Vic 27335, 27548, HMV B-9476, AV-811, HN-2655, V-Disc 132 |
| 055257-1 | I Cover The Waterfront | Vic 27362, HMV B-9214, AV-690, EA-2853, V-Disc 330 |
| 055258-1 | Moon Glow | Vic 27405, 27549, HMV B-9269, AV-696, EA-3025, JK-2305, TG-141, V-Disc 45 |
| 055259-1 | Alone Together | Vic 27385, HMV B-9341 |

    Artie Shaw-cl dir. 3t/3tb/4s/9vn-vl-vc/p/sb/d (probably very similar to the above).
                                            New York, March 20, 1941.

| | | |
|---|---|---|
| 062767-1 | If I Had You | Vic 27536, HMV B-9272 |
| 062768-1 | Georgia On My Mind | Vic 27499, HMV B-9288, EA-3674, TG-140 |
| 062769-1 | Why Shouldn't I ? | Vic 27499, HMV EA-3674 |
| 062770-1 | It Had To Be You | Vic 27536, HMV B-9348, EA-3335, V-Disc 281 |

    Artie Shaw-cl dir. Henry Allen-t/J. C. Higginbotham-tb/Benny Carter-as/12vn-vl-vc/
    Laura Newell-harp/Sonny White-p/Jimmy Shirley-sb/Billy Taylor-sb/Shep Shepherd-d/
    Lena Horne-v.                           New York, June 26, 1941.

| | | |
|---|---|---|
| 066146-1 | Confessin' | Camden CAL-584, CDN-5107 (LPs) |
| 066147-1 | Love Me A Little Little - vLH | Vic 27509, 20-2994, HMV B-9322 |
| 066148-1 | Beyond The Blue Horizon | Rejected |
| 066149-1 | Don't Take Your Love From Me - vLH | Vic 27509, 20-1593, 20-2865, HMV B-9322 |

    **Artie** Shaw-cl dir. Hot Lips Page-t-v/Lee Castle-Steve Lipkins-t/Jack Jenney-Morey
    Samuel-Ray Conniff-tb/Les Robinson-Gene Kinsey-as/George Auld-Mickey Folus-ts/15vn-
    vl-vc/Johnny Guarnieri-p/Mike Bryan-g/Eddie McKimmey-sb/Dave Tough-d/Bonnie Lake-v/
    Lennie Hayton-a.                        New York, September 2, 1941.

| | | |
|---|---|---|
| 067735-2 | This Time The Dream's On Me - vBL | Vic 27609, HMV EA-2937 |
| 067736-2 | Blues In The Night - vHLP | -          - |
| 067737-1 | Nocturne | Vic 27703 |
| 067738-1 | Rockin' Chair - aLH | Vic 27664, HMV B-9272, EA-3486, X-7008 |
| 067739-1 | Through The Years | Vic 27703 |
| 067740-1 | If I Love Again | Vic 27664, HMV B-9348 |

    Page, Lipkins, Jenney, Samuel, Kinsey and Folus omitted.
                                            New York, Sepyember 3, 1941.

| | | |
|---|---|---|
| 067747-1 | Is It Taboo (To Fall In Love With You) | Vic 27641, 20-2939, HMV B-9320 |
| 067748-2 | Beyond The Blue Horizon | -          -     - |
| 067749-1 | I Ask The Stars | Vic 27719 |

    As for September 2, 1941, plus Max Kaminsky-t/Paula Kelly-v/Fred Norman-a; Ray
    Conniff-a; Charlie di Maggio-as replaces Kinsey; 4 strings omitted.
                                            Chicago, October 30, 1941.

| | | |
|---|---|---|
| 070342-1 | Take Your Shoes Off, Baby - vHLP | Vic 27719, 20-2994 |
| 070343-2 | Make Love To Me - vPK | Vic 27705 |
| 070344-1 | Solid Sam - aFN | - HMV B-9396,EA-3486,JO-258,K-92C |
| 070345-1 | Just Kiddin' Around - aRC | Vic 27806, HMV EA-3723, JK-2350, V-Disc 303 |

ARTIE SHAW AND HIS ORCHESTRA : Artie Shaw-cl dir. Lee Castle-Max Kaminsky-Steve Lip-
kins-t/Hot Lips Page-t-v/Jack Jenney-Morey Samuel-Ray Conniff-tb/Charlie di Maggio
Les Robinson-as/George Auld-Mickey Folus-ts/15vn-vl-vc/Johnny Guarnieri-p/Mike
Bryan-g/Eddie McKimmey-sb/Dave Tough-d/Paula Kelly-v/Paul Jordan-a.
                                     New York, November 12, 1941.

| | | |
|---|---|---|
| 068194-1 | To A Broadway Rose | Vic 27838, HMV EA-3723 |
| 068195-1-2 | St. James Infirmary - Part 1 - vHLP | Vic 27895, HMV B-9307, EA-3353 |
| 068196-2 | St. James Infirmary - Part 2 | -        -        - |
| 068197-1 | Deuces Wild | Vic 27838 |

                              New York, December 23, 1941.

| | | |
|---|---|---|
| 068803-1 | Dusk - aPJ | Vic 28-0405 |
| 068804-1 | Suite No. 8 - aPJ | - |
| 068805-1 | Someone's Rocking My Dreamboat - vPK | Vic 27746 |
| 068806-1 | I Don't Want To Walk Without You - vPK | - |

Fredda Gibson (alias Georgia Gibbs)-v.  New York, January 20, 1942.

| | | |
|---|---|---|
| 071701-1 | Somebody Nobody Loves - vFG | Vic 27798, HMV EA-3313 |
| 071702-1 | Not Mine - vFG | Vic 27779, HMV NE-700 |
| 071703-1 | Absent-Minded Moon - vFG | -        - |
| 071704-1 | Hindustan | Vic 27798, HMV B-9423, EA-3291 |

                               New York, January 21, 1942.

| | | |
|---|---|---|
| 071709-1 | Carnival - aPJ | Vic 27860, HMV B-9291, EA-3534, JO-159, El EG-7749 |
| 071710-1 | Needlenose | As above |
| 071711-1 | Two In One Blues - aPJ | Vic 20-1526 |
| 071712-1 | Sometimes I Feel Like A Motherless Child | Vic 27806, HMV B-9423, EA-3291, JK-2350 |

                                JANET SHAW

Pseudonym on Parlophone PNY-34060 for Annette Hanshaw, q.v.

                         JOEL SHAW AND  HIS ORCHESTRA

Joel Shaw-p-v dir. 2t/tb/Mike Doty-cl-as/Gene Kardos-as/ts/g/bb/d/Dick Robertson (as
BOB DIXON)-v.                        New York, c. December, 1931.

| | | |
|---|---|---|
| 1566-2 | Who's Your Little Who-Zis ? - vDR | Cr 3244, Summit 164 |
| 1567-1 | One More Kiss, Then Goodnight - vDR | -    Summit 195 |

                              New York, c. January, 1932.

| | | |
|---|---|---|
| 1628-1 | Business In F - vDR | Cr 3271, Var 8035, Summit 221 |
| 1630-3 | Sweet Violets - vDR | -    Var 8034, Summit 237 |
| | Barnacle Bill (The Sailor) - vDR | Cr 3273 |
| | Stop The Sun, Stop The Moon (My Gal's Gone) - vDR | - |

                           New York, February-March, 1932.

| | | |
|---|---|---|
| 1670-1 | Some Of These Days - vDR | Cr 3285, Var 8026, Summit 224 |
| 1671-2 | Alexander's Ragtime Band - vDR | -        - |
| 1672-2 | Sing A New Song - vDR | Cr 3300, Homestead 23144 |
| 1673-1 | If It Ain't Love - vDR | Cr 3298 |

                               New York, c. March 1, 1932.

| | | |
|---|---|---|
| 1682-3 | Lawd, You Made The Night Too Long - vDR | Cr 3298, Bcst 3208, Summit 199 |
| 1683-2 | Keepin' Out Of Mischief Now - vDR | Cr 3300, Summit 237 |

NOTE:- Crown 3298 and 3300 from the above session, and Broadcast 3208 as THE HIGH
STEPPERS.

Joel Shaw-p-v dir. 2t/tb/Mike Doty-cl-as/Gene Kardos-as/ts/g/bb/d/Dick Robertson-(as
  BOB DIXON)-v.                              New York, c. March 7, 1932.

| | | |
|---|---|---|
| 1691-1 | Business in Q | Cr 3304, Var 8035, Summit 221 |
| 1692- | My Extraordinary Gal - vDR | Cr 3302 |
| 1693- | Oh ! Mo'nah -- vDR | Cr 3304 |
| 1694-1 | Goofus - vDR | Cr 3302, Var 8033, Summit 217 |

New York, c. March 10, 1932.

| | | |
|---|---|---|
| 1699-1 | Dinah - vDR | Cr 3319, Var 8029, Summit 224 |
| 1700-1 | Mouthful O' Jam - vDR | Cr 3312, Var 6012, Summit 223 |
| 1701- | Whistle And Blow Your Blues Away - vDR | Cr 3311, Var 8039, Summit 205 |
| 1702-1 | The Darktown Strutters' Ball - vDR | Cr 3319, Var 8028, Summit 225 |
| 1703-1 | Call Of The Freaks - vJS | Cr 3312, Var 6012, Summit 223 |
| | Kickin' The Gong Around - vDR | Cr 3306 |
| | Minnie The Moocher - vDR | - |

NOTE:- Varsity 6012 as HARLEM WILDCATS; all other issues on Varsity as DICK ROBERT-
SON AND HIS ORCHESTRA.

New York, June, 1932.

| | | |
|---|---|---|
| 1743-1 | How'm I Doin' ? - vDR | Cr 3333, Var 6015, Summit 222 |
| 1745-2 | The Scat Song - vDR | -      -      - |
| | Minnie The Moocher's Wedding Day - vDR | Cr 3332 |
| | When You're Getting Along With Your Gal-vDR | - |

NOTE:- Varsity 6015 as HARLEM WILDCATS.

New York, July, 1932.

| | | |
|---|---|---|
| 1776-1 | Why Don't You Get Lost ? - vDR | Cr 3349, Var 5056 |
| 1777-2 | Get Cannibal - vDR | Cr 3362, Var 6005 |
| 1778-1 | Basin Street Blues | -      Var 8028 |
| 1779-2 | You've Got Me In The Palm Of Your Hand - vDR | Cr 3349, Var 8117 |
| 1780-3 | That's A Plenty | Cr 3352, Royale 1754 |
| 1781-1 | Let's Have A Party - vDR | -      Var 6004 |

NOTE:- Royale 1754 as 52nd STREET BOYS; Varsity 6004 and 6005 as HARLEM SERENADERS;
8028 and 8117 as DICK ROBERTSON AND HIS ORCHESTRA.

New York, c. August, 1932.

| | | |
|---|---|---|
| 1849-2 | Tiger Rag | Cr 3383, Var 8029 |
| 1850-1 | Avalon - vDR | Cr 3382, Var 8025 |
| 1851-2 | Sing (It's Good For Ya) - vDR | Cr 3381, Var 6020 |
| 1852-1 | This Is The Chorus Of A Song - vDR | -      - |
| 1853-2 | Margie - vDR | Cr 3382, Var 8025 |
| 1854-3 | Clarinet Marmalade | Cr 3383, Var 8029 |

NOTE:- Varsity 6020 as HARLEM WILDCATS; 8025 and 8029 as GENE KARDOS AND HIS ORCH-
ESTRA.

New York, October, 1932.

| | | |
|---|---|---|
| 1901-1 | Reefer Man - vDR | Cr 3423, Var 8024 |
| 1902-1 | The Old Man Of The Mountain - vDR | Cr 3413    - |
| 1903-1 | Yeah Man - vDR | Cr 3414 |
| 1904-1-2 | Jazz Pie - vDR | - |
| 1905-2 | Goin' To Town - vDR | Cr 3423, Var 6013 |
| 1906-2 | White Zombie (Zombie*) | Cr 3413, Var 6014* |

NOTE:- Varsity 6014 as HARLEM WILDCATS; 8024 as DICK ROBERTSON AND HIS ORCHESTRA.

New York, c. December, 1932.

| | | |
|---|---|---|
| 1979-2 | Indiana - vDR | Cr 3451, Var 8032 |
| 1980-1-3 | Ida - vDR | Cr 3444    - |
| 1981-2 | Original Dixieland One-Step | -      Var 6005 |
| 1992-1 | Forty-Second Street - vDR | Cr 3453 |
| 1993-2 | Young And Healthy - vDR | - |
| | The Girl In The Little Green Hat - vDR | Cr 3442 |
| | The Old Kitchen Kettle - vDR | - |

NOTE:- Varsity 6005 as HARLEM SERENADERS; 8032 as DICK ROBERTSON AND HIS ORCHESTRA.

The above designation was also applied to Gene Kardos and his Orchestra, q.v., on ARC
   8-02-12 and 8-03-02.

## MILT SHAW AND HIS DETROITERS

The following titles by this commercial dance band are of some interest as jazz, as
   they feature good solo work.

Milt Shaw-vn dir. Ruby Weinstein-Johnny McGhee-t/George Troup-tb/Lyle Bowen-Aaron
   Voloshin-cl-as/Hymie Wolfson-cl-ts/Dippy d'Ippolito-p/Bill Barford-bj-g/bb/Will
   Simerall-d/Smith Ballew-v.            New York, November 26, 1928.

401392-C  Where The Shy Little Violets Grow-vSB    OK 41158, Od 165579, 193284,
                                                   A-189226, Par A-2685
   NOTE:- Odeon 193284 as SAM LANIN'S FAMOUS PLAYERS.

   Similar instrumentation, but different personnel including Ronnie Perry-ts/Scrappy
   Lambert-v.                            New York, February 13, 1931.

E-36068-   Walkin' My Baby Back Home - vSL        Mt M-12098, Pan P-12098

## THEODORE SHAW OF LAWRENCEBURG, TENN.

Piano solo.                                Richmond, Ind., April 7, 1924.

   11831-B  Hold 'Er, Newt (They're After Us)        Vaughan 825

## TED SHAWNE AND HIS ORCHESTRA

Pseudonym on Odeon ONY-41276 and American Parlophone for Louis Armstrong and his
   Orchestra, q.v.

## HARRY "FREDDIE" SHAYNE

Probably J. H. Shayne-p, with own v.       Chicago, December 19, 1935.

   90533-A  Original Mr. Freddie Blues            Ch 50061, Dec 7663
   90534-A  Lonesome Man Blues                      -          -

Piano solos.                               Chicago, October 28, 1936.

C-1630-1-2  The Pearls                            Voc rejected
C-1631-1-2  Piano Rhythm                            -

## GEORGE  SHEARING

Piano solos.                               London, January 19, 1939.

DR-3244--  Blue Boogie                            Dec rejected
DR-3245-   Nagasuckle Rose                          -

   Carlo Krahmer-d added*; piano-accordion solo, acc. by Leonard Feather-p/Carlo Krahmer-d**.                               London, March 2, 1939.

DR-3370-1  How Come You Do Me Like You Do ?       Dec F-7102
DR-3371-1  Stomp In F                               -
DR-3372-1 *Blue Boogie                            Dec F-7038
DR-3373-1**Squeezin' The Blues                      -

                                           London, February 16, 1940.

DEA-8350-1-2  Stop ! It's Wonderful               HMV rejected
DEA-8351-1-2  Corrigan Hop                           -

                                           London, March 3, 1941.

DR-5415-1  Southern Fried                         Dec F-7786
DR-5416-1  Missouri Scrambler                     Dec F-7832, X-2212
DR-5417-1  Wednesday Night Hop                    Dec F-7786
DR-5418-1  Overnight Hop                          Dec F-7832, X-2212

Piano solos.                                    London, April 23, 1941.

DR-5608-1  Delayed Action                       Dec F-7915, X-2200
DR-5609-1  Jump For Joy                         -            -
DR-5610-1  Scrub Me, Mama, With A Boogie Beat   Dec F-7857
DR-5611-1  Beat Me Daddy, Eight To The Bar      -

                                                London, August 1, 1941.

DR-6089-1  How Could You ?                      Dec F-8004
DR-6090-1  A Pretty Girl Is Like A Melody       Dec F-8181
DR-6091-1  These Foolish Things                 Dec F-8004
DR-6092-1  More Than You Know                   Dec F-8181

                                                London, December 9, 1941.

DR-6537-1  Softly As In A Morning Sunrise       Dec F-8063
DR-6538-1-2  Boogie Ride                        Rejected
DR-6539-1  You Stepped Out Of A Dream           Dec F-8063
DR-6540-1-2  Spookie Woogie                     Rejected

                                                London, January 28, 1942.

DR-6538-5  Boogie Ride                          Dec F-8148
DR-6540-4  Spookie Woogie                       -

                                                London, April 28, 1942.

DR-6798-1-2  Moonray                            Rejected
DR-6799-   Rosetta                              ACL 1161 (LP)
DR-6800-1-2  I'll Never Let A Day Pass By       Rejected
DR-6801-   Coquette                             ACL 1161 (LP)

                                                London, December 12, 1942.

DR-7136-1-2  Out Of Nowhere                     Rejected
DR-7137-   Can't We Be Friends ?                ACL 1161 (LP)
DR-7138-   (I Don't Stand) A Ghost Of A Chance  Dec F-8385
DR-7139-   Time On My Hands                     -

## JACK SHEEHAN AND HIS MUSIC

T/tb/cl-as/as-ts/bar/p/g/sb/d.                  London, c. July, 1933.

5153-2  Get Hot Foot                            Oct 1028

5194    Step By Step                            -

## BERT SHEFTER

BERT SHEFTER AND HIS RHYTHM OCTET : Bert Shefter-p dir. Dave Wade-t/Toots Mondello-cl
as/Paul Ricci-cl-ts/Vic Brenner-2nd p/Ken Binford-g/Artie Bernstein-sb/Herb Quigley
d/Adrian Rollini-vib.                           New York, June 25, 1937.

011050-1  S. O. S.                              Vic 25614, HMV BD-5273, EA-2103
011051-1  Chopin's Ghost                        Vic 25622      -          EA-2069
011052-1-2  Locomotive                          Rejected
                                                New York, June 29, 1937.

011052-3  Locomotive                            Vic 25614, HMV BD-5262, EA-2103
011060-1  Burglar's Revenge                     Vic 25632      -          EA-2069

BERT SHEFTER AND HIS ORCHESTRA : Bert Shefter-p dir. Hymie Rosenbaum-t/Al Philburn-tb
/Al Raxon-cl/Nat Brown-as/Richard von Holberg-sb/Sam Weiss-d/Phil Kraus-vib.
                                                New York, May 15, 1939.

65564-A  Monkey On A String                     Dec 2525, Br 02801
65565-A  Wig Wag                                Dec 2653
65566-A  Farmer In A Dilemma                    Dec 2584
65567-A  Trammin' At The Fair                   Dec 2525, Br 02801
65568-A  Toast To Paganini's Ghost              Dec 2653
65569-A  Deserted Desert                        Dec 2584

Vocal, acc. by p/Eddie Lang-g.                New York, May 5, 1928.

400651-A-B  Oh ! Baby                         OK rejected
400652-A-B  Forever And Ever                      -

## EZRA HOWLETT SHELTON

Piano solo.                                   Chicago, c. February, 1925.

724    Dearest Darling                        Auto (un-numbered), Ses 3

Vocal, acc. by own p.                         Chicago, December 10, 1928.

48709-1-2  Gonna Quit That Man And How !      Vic rejected
48710-1-2  Flapper Stomp                          -

## OLLIE  SHEPARD

Vocal, acc. by his Kentucky Boys : Edgar Saucier-as/own p/d.
                                              Chicago, October 28, 1937.

91305-A  It's A Low Down Dirty Shame          Dec 7384
91306-A  If It Ain't Love                         -

Lonnie Johnson-g added*.                      Chicago, November 8, 1937.

91347-A  She Walks Like A Kangaroo            Dec 7408
91348-A  Honey Bee (Let Me Be Your Honey Bee) Dec 7400
91349-A  *No One To Call You Dear (Ain't It Tough) Dec 7408
91350-A  *Sweetheart Land                     Dec 7400

Acc. by cl/ts/own p/sb/d, with Lonnie Johnson-g*.
                                              New York, March 31, 1938.

63507-A  One Woman Blues                      Dec 7435
63508-A  Brown Skin Woman                     Dec 7448
63509-A  S-B-A Blues                              -
63510-A  Good Woman                           Dec 7463
63511-A  *Pee Wee, Pee Wee                    Dec 7541
63512-A  *Drunk Again                         Dec 7435
63513-A  Biscuit Rolling Time                 Dec 7480
63514-A  What's Your Guess ?                  Dec 7463
63515-A  Hope You Haven't Forgotten Me        Dec 7480
63516-A  *At Your Mercy                       Dec 7541

Acc. by t/cl/ts/p/g/sb/d.                     New York, May 17, 1938.

63793-A  This Place Is Leaping                Dec 7493
63794-A  Solid Jack                               -
63795-A  Little Pigmeat                       Dec 7508
63796-A  Frankenstein Blues                       -

Acc. by Chu Berry-ts/? Sam Price-p/d.  New York, April 18, 1939.

65420-A  New Low Down Dirty Shame             Dec 7585
65421-A  The Numbers Blues                        -
65422-A  Sweetest Thing Born                  Dec 7629
65423-A  Shepard Blues (Pig Latin Blues)      Dec 7602
65424-A  Outdoors Blues                       Dec 7613
65425-A  Sugar Woman Blues                    Dec 7602
65426-A  Hell Is So Low Down                  Dec 7716
65427-A  My Dripping Blood Blues              Dec 7613
65428-A  Blues 'Bout My Gal                   Dec 7639

Acc. by Walter Wheeler-ts/p/Wellman Braud-sb/d.
New York, July 17, 1939.

| | | |
|---|---|---|
| 65970-A | Oh Maria | Dec 7639 |
| 65971-A | (Lovely Little Baby) Don't You Know | Dec 7651 |
| 65972-A | Jelly Roll | Dec 7629 |
| 65973-A | King Of All Evil | Dec 7665 |
| 65974-A | Li'l Liza Jane - vch | Dec 7651 |
| 65975-A | Baby It's My Time Now | Dec 7665 |

Acc. by Stafford Simon-ts/p/d/Ollie Potter-girl v.
New York, January 22, 1940.

| | | |
|---|---|---|
| 67082-A | Jitterbugs Broke It Down | Dec 7761 |
| 67083-A | Octavia Blues | Dec 7716 |
| 67084-A | I'm Stepping Out Tonight - vOP-OS | Dec 7805 |
| 67085-A | You Got Me Wondering - vOP only | - |

Acc. by Theodore McCord-cl-ts/own p/George Francis-g/Johnny Wells-d/unknown girl-v.
New York, May 2, 1939.

| | | |
|---|---|---|
| 30391-1 | Hard Times Is On Me | OK 06409 |
| 30392-1 | Cool Kind Papa - girl v. | OK 06277 |
| 30393-1 | True Love Blues | OK 06533 |
| 30394-1 | Throw This Dog A Bone | OK 06277 |
| 30395-1 | Wreckin' House Joe | Rejected |
| 30396-1 | Pay Day Blues | OK 06533 |
| 30397-1 | Army Camp Blues | OK 06409 |
| 30398-1 | I'm Nuts About My Baby | Rejected |

Acc. by Saxie Payne-ts/own p/Carl Lynch-g/Johnny Wells-d.
New York, January 6, 1942.

| | | |
|---|---|---|
| 32122- | I've Got The Blues (About My Baby) | OK rejected |
| 32123- | Navy Blues | - |
| 32124- | Young And Innocent | - |
| 32125- | Untrue Woman Blues | - |
| 32126- | You're Lucky To Me | - |
| 32127- | Gee Gee Express | - |
| 32128- | When My Gal Comes Home | - |
| 32129- | Stop That Jive | - |

## SHERIDAN ENTERTAINERS

Pseudonym on Broadway 1088 and associated labels for Al Lynch and his Orchestra, q.v.

## AL SHERMAN AND HIS COLLEGE INN ORCHESTRA

See the ARC-Brunswick studio bands (Panachord 25054 and P-12124).

## CLARENCE SHERMAN'S ORCHESTRA

Pseudonym for the following items listed in this book :-

Domino 393  Rose Marie (California Ramblers)
Microphone 22017  Save Your Sorrow For Tomorrow (Sam Lanin and his Orchestra)

## SHERMAN CLUB ORCHESTRA

Pseudonym on Challenge 715 for the Blackbirds of Paradise, q.v.

## SHERMAN'S GLOBE-TROTTERS

Pseudonym on Bell 615 for Van and his Half Moon Orchestra, q.v.

## SHERMAN SUNDODGERS

Pseudonym on Bell and Silvertone for Vic Price and his Orchestra, q.v.

Jack Shilkret, one of Nat Shilkret's brothers, recorded many sides for Victor in the
1920s and for ARC in the 1930s (on the latter he was styled JACK SHILKRET AND HIS
ORCHESTRA, and this applies also to his Bluebird sides of 1935).  Although on the
whole the earlier records have little to interest the jazz enthusiast, the later
issues were made by musicians drawn from the collective personnel shown, and often
feature excellent solos by them, and thus all the ARC sides are listed here.

Nat Shilkret dir. probably :- Earl Oliver-Tommy Gott-t/Sam Lewis-tb/Larry Abbott-cl-
as/cl-as-bar/cl-ts/Lou Raderman or Murray Kellner-vn/Jack Shilkret-p/John Cali-bj/
bb/Joe Green-d.                        New York, October 14, 1925.

33525-7  If You Hadn't Gone Away (I Wouldn't Be   Vic 19818, HMV EA-10
            Where I Am)

Jack Shilkret dir. collective personnel : 2t/tb/2cl-as/cl-ts/p/g/sb/d drawn from
Bunny Berigan-Sterling Bose-Phil Capicotta-Zeke Zarchy-t/Red Jessup-Jack Jenney-
Russ Morgan-tb/Artie Shaw-Tony Parenti-Toots Mondello-Sid Stoneburn-cl-as/Paul
Ricci-Tony Zimmers-cl-ts/Lou Raderman or Murray Kellner-vn when used/Terry Shand or
Claude Thornhill-p/Dick McDonough-g/Dick Cherwin-Artie Bernstein-sb/Sammy Weiss-
Stan King-Chauncey Morehouse-d/Chick Bullock-v, and probably others from time to
time.                                 New York, January 22, 1936.

B-18549-  Misty Islands Of The Highlands - vCB    Br 7602
B-18550-  A Little Rendez-vous In Honolulu - vCB     -
B-18551-1 Sing An Old-Fashioned Song (To A Young  Br 7603, RZ G-22854
            Sophisticated Lady) - vCB
B-18552-1 The Day I Let You Get Away - vCB          -          -


                            New York, April 2, 1936.

18914-1  A Little Robin Told Me So - vCB          ARC 6-06-02, Rex 8861
18915-   There's Always A Happy Ending - vCB        -
18916-   Robins And Roses - vCB                   ARC 6-06-03
18917-   One Hamburger For Madame - vCB             -


                            New York, June 22, 1936.

19460-   Hidden Valley - vCB                      ARC 6-09-10
19461-   Tell Me Why - vCB                          -
19462-1  There's A Small Hotel - vCB              ARC 6-09-02
19463-1  I Can't Escape From You - vCB              -
19464-1  An Old Saddle For Sale - vCB             ARC 6-09-05
19465-1  Did I Remember ? - vCB                     -          Cr 266
NOTE:- Crown 266 is a 9" British issue, edited from the American; it is labelled
BUDDY BARNETT AND HIS MUSIC.


                            New York, July 31, 1936.

19635-   Dream Awhile - vCB                       ARC 6-10-09
19636-   There Goes My Attraction - vCB           ARC 6-11-03
19637-1  Shoe Shine Boy - vCB                       -          Rex 8861, Kr 393
19638-1  San Francisco - vCB                      ARC 6-10-09, Rex 8918


                            New York, August 24, 1936.

19734-   The One Rose (That's Left In My Heart)   ARC 6-11-06
            - vCB
19735-   My Kingdom For A Kiss (Pour un baiser)-vCB  -
19736-   I'll Sing You A Thousand Love Songs-vCB  ARC 6-11-08
19737-   Coney Island - vCB                         -
NOTE:- ARC 6-11-08 as JIMMY HUNTER AND HIS ORCHESTRA.

                            New York, August 29, 1936.
19773-   The World Is Mine (Tonight) - vCB        ARC 6-11-15
19774-   So Divine - vCB                            -
19775-   Darling, Not Without You - vCB           ARC 6-11-09
19776-1  Fancy Meeting You (The Evolution Song)-vCB ARC 6-11-07
19777-1  Trouble Ends Out Where The Blue Begins-vCB  -
19778-   Here's Love In Your Eye - vCB            ARC 6-11-09
19779    Happy Birthday To You - vCB ?            Special Recording
NOTE:- ARC 6-11-09 as JIMMY HUNTER AND HIS ORCHESTRA; 6-11-07 as CHICK BULLOCK.

Jack Shilkret dir. 2t/tb/2cl-as/cl-ts/p/g/sb/d from the collective personnel shown on page 1415; Larry Stewart-Johnny Hauser-Johnny Muldooney-v.

New York, September 23, 1936.

| 19922- | I Want The Whole World To Love You - vLS | ARC 6-12-06 |
| 19923- | I Wasn't Lying When I Said "I Love You" - vLS | ARC 6-12-10 |
| 19924- | When Is A Kiss Not A Kiss ? - vJH | ARC 6-12-09 |
| 19925- | My Favorite Girl - vJH | ARC 6-12-10 |
| 19926- | Did You Mean It ? - vJH | ARC 6-12-09 |

NOTE:- ARC 6-12-09 as BOB CAUSER AND HIS CORNELLIANS; 6-12-10 as JIMMY HUNTER AND HIS ORCHESTRA.

Charlie Magnante-pac added.      New York, October 24, 1936.

| 20121- | Another Perfect Night Is Ending - vJM | ARC 7-01-05, Rex 8976 |
| 20122- | Under Your Spell - vJM | ARC 7-02-09 |
| 20123- | Never Should Have Told You - vJM | ARC 7-01-05 |

NOTE:- Other titles from this session are children's records.

Tony Parenti-Artie Shaw-cl-as present.      New York, November 21, 1936.

| 20306- | There's A Silver Moon On The Golden Gate - vCB | ARC 7-02-11 |
| 20307- | Twinkle, Twinkle, Little Star - vCB | —    Rex 9054 |

New York, December 9, 1936.

| 20374- | Hey, Babe, Hey ! - vCB | ARC 7-02-14 |
| 20375- | I Love You From Coast To Coast - vCB | — |
| 20376- | Timber - vCB | ARC 7-03-02 |
| 20377- | Gee ! But You're Swell - vCB | — |

## NAT SHILKRET

Nathaniel "Nat" Shilkret was Victor's Director of Light Music between 1915 and 1945 - an impressive service - and in addition, he conducted the studio concert and symphony orchestras in many recordings of serious works. Between 1926 and 1932, he directed many dozens of sides of dance music as NAT SHILKRET AND THE VICTOR ORCHESTRA (the English HMV equivalents omit the word "Victor" from the artist credit), for which he drew on some of the finest talent in the New York musical world. On the following - and it is quite likely that there are others of equal merit - can be heard soloists of considerable interest, in the identification of which I have had the incalculable assistance of Mr. Shilkret himself, and also of Mr. Milt Rettenberg. See also The Virginians.

NAT SHILKRET AND THE VICTOR ORCHESTRA : Nat Shilkret (sometimes playing c/cl/p/cel) dir. Del Staigers-? Earl Oliver-t/Chuck Campbell-Sam Lewis-th/Larry Abbott-Sammy Feinsmith-Andy Sannella-cl-as/Max Farley or Maurice   Pierce-cl-ts-f/Lou Raderman-Murray Kellner-vn/Jack Shilkret-Milt Rettenberg-p/Dick Maffei or John Cali-bj/Jack Pierce-bb/Joe Green-d/Franklyn Baur-Lewis James-v.

New York, March 10, 1927.

| 38153-2 | Ain't She Sweet ? - vFB | Vic 20508, HMV EA-167, El EG-506 |
| 38155-3 | Forgive Me - vLJ | Vic 20514, HMV B-5284, EA-168, El EG-588 |

Lewis and Raderman omitted; Abe Borodkin-vc added; Sannella db stg; Joe Sherman-v.

New York, May 5, 1927.

| 38374-6 | Fifty Million Frenchmen Can't Be Wrong - vJS&ch | Vic 20634, HMV B-5318, EA-187 |

Mike Mosiello-t possibly replaces Oliver; Lou Raderman and either Benny Posner or Peter Eisenberg-vn added; Johnny Marvin-u-v.

New York, May 19, 1927.

| 38814-1 | Who-oo ? You-oo, That's Who ! - u-vJM | Vic 20727, HMV B-5327, EA-211 |

NAT SHILKRET AND THE VICTOR ORCHESTRA : Nat Shilkret dir. Del Staigers-Mike Mosiello-
t/Chuck Campbell-tb/Andy Sannella-Larry Abbott-Sammy Feinsmith-cl-as/Maurice Pierce
-cl-ts/Lou Raderman-Murray Kellner-either Benny Posner or Peter Eisenberg-vn/Abe
Borodkin-vc/Jack Shilkret-Milt Rettenberg-p/John Cali-bj/Jack Pierce-bb/Joe Green-d
/Johnny Marvin-u-v.                       New York, June 9, 1927.

| 38892-3 | There's A Trick In Pickin' A | Vic 20759, HMV B-5352, EA-213 |
| | Chick-Chick-Chicken - u-vJM | |

4vn used (as above).                      New York, July 1, 1927.

| 39618-3 | What Do We Do On A Dew-Dew-Dewy Day ? | Vic 20819, HMV EA-244 |
| | - u-vJM | |

Feinsmith and one vn omitted; Harry Reser-bj replaces Cali.
                                          New York, August 11, 1927.

| 39958-2 | Where Have You Been All My Life ?-u-vJM | Vic 20902, HMV B-5535, EA-375, |
| | | K-5358 |

? Tommy Dorsey-tb replaces Campbell; Sammy Feinsmith-cl-as-bar added.
                                          New York, August 18, 1927.

| 39989-2 | Baby's Blue - vJM | Vic 20882, HMV B-5384, EA-422 |

Chuck Campbell-tb replaces ? Dorsey; all 4 vn present; Abbott db k; Feinsmith
omitted; Gene Austin-v.                   New York, September 15, 1927.

| 39181-2 | Nothin' - vGA | Vic 21080, HMV B-5429, EA-344 |

Sammy Feinsmith-cl-as-bar/William Dorn-2nd d added; Ed Smalle-v.
                                          New York, November 3, 1927.

| 40539-2 | There's A Cradle In Carolina (sic)- - | Vic 21040, HMV EA-281 |
| | - vJM-ES | |

SHILKRET'S RHYTH-MELODISTS : Lou Raderman-vn/Milt Rettenberg-p/Fats Waller-or.
                                          Camden, N. J., March 2, 1928.

| 42529-2 | Chloe (Song Of The Swamp) | Vic 21298 |

Chuck Campbell-tb/Milt Rettenberg-p/Francis J. Lapitino-harp/Fats Waller-or.
                                          Camden, N. J., March 3, 1928.

| 42532-2 | When You're With Somebody Else | Vic 21298, HMV EA-336 |

NAT SHILKRET AND THE VICTOR ORCHESTRA : Nat Shilkret dir. Del Staigers-Mike Mosiello-
t/Chuck Campbell-tb/Andy Sannella-cl-as/Sammy Feinsmith-cl-as-bar/Maurice Pierce-cl
ts/Lou Raderman-Murray Kellner-4 other vn (probably Benny Posner-Peter Eisenberg-
Yascha Zayde-Teddy Lassoff or Sam Freed)/Abe Borodkin-vc/Jack Shilkret-Milt Retten-
berg-p/John Cali-bj/Jack Pierce-bb/Al Armer-sb/Joe Green-d/Frank Marvin-u-v.
                                          New York, June 7, 1928.

| 45609-3 | That's My Weakness Now - vFM | Vic 21497, HMV EA-383, R-14001 |

All vn omitted; Wilfred Glenn-Elliott Shaw-v.
                                          New York, June 19, 1928.

| 45647-2 | Dusky Stevedore - vWG-ES | Vic 21515, HMV B-5553, EA-452 |
| 45648-1 | When Sweet Susie Goes Steppin' By | -                    - |

SHILKRET'S RHYTH-MELODISTS : Mike Mosiello-t/Chuck Campbell-tb/Andy Sannella-as-stg/
Lou Raderman-vn/Milt Rettenberg-p/Sigmund Krumgold-or/Al Armer-sb; Raderman, Rettenberg, Krumgold and Armer only*.        Camden, N. J., September 22, 1928.

| 47413-2 | I Can't Give You Anything But Love (Baby) | Vic 21688 |
| 47414-2 | I'm Sorry, Sally | - |
| 47483-1 | *Sweet Nothing (Sweet Nothings*) | Vic 21902, HMV B-3066*, EA-529 |

NAT SHILKRET AND THE VICTOR ORCHESTRA : Nat Shilkret dir. Del Staigers-Mike Mosiello-
? Harry Shilkret-t/Chuck Campbell-? Sam Lewis-tb/Andy Sannella-? Mike Ships-cl-as/
Sammy Feinsmith-cl-as-bar/Maurice Pierce-cl-ts/Lou Raderman-Murray Kellner-another-
vn/Jack Shilkret-Milt Rettenberg-p/John Cali-bj/Jack Pierce-bb/Al Armer-sb/Joe
Green-William Dorn-d/Belle Mann-v.         New York, December 13, 1928.

  49256-3  I Want A Daddy To Cuddle Me - vBM       Vic 21818, HMV B-5673, EA-515

  Nat Shilkret dir. ? Mike Mosiello-t/Chuck Campbell-tb/? Andy Sannella-cl-as/Sammy
  Feinsmith-cl-as-bar/Maurice Pierce-cl-ts/Lou Raderman-Murray Kellner-another-vn/
  Jack Shilkret-Frank Signorelli-p/Carl Kress-g/? Jack Pierce-bb/? William Dorn-d/
  Scrappy Lambert-(as BURT LORIN)-v.       New York, December 28, 1928.

  49024-1-2  Susianna - vSL                        Vic rejected

  Nat Shilkret dir. Del Staigers-Mike Mosiello-t/? Tommy Dorsey-tb/Andy Sannella-cl-
  as/Jimmy Dorsey-cl-as-bar/Max Farley-cl-ts-f/Lou Raderman-vn/Milt Rettenberg-p/Carl
  Kress-g/? Joe Tarto-bb/doe Green-d/Belle Mann-Johnny Marvin-v.
                                           New York, January 22, 1929.

  49671-2  You Wouldn't Fool Me, Would You ? - vJM  Vic 21859, HMV EA-670
  49672-2  I Want To Be Bad - vBM                      -            -

  Staigers omitted; Maurice Pierce-cl-ts replaces Farley; 2vn added, one almost
  certainly Murray Kellner.       New York, January 25, 1929.

  49024-4  Susianna - vSL                          Vic 21996, HMV B-5680, EA-562,
                                                   R-14202, El EG-1454

  Nat Shilkret dir. Del Staigers-Mike Mosiello-t/Chuck Campbell-tb/Andy Sannella-
  ? Sammy Feinsmith-cl-as/Maurice Pierce-cl-ts/Lou Raderman-Murray Kellner-vn/Milt
  Rettenberg-p/John Cali or Dick Maffei-bj/Jack Pierce-bb/Joe Green-d.
                                           New York, March 13, 1929.

  50934-2  There Is A Happy Land (Far, Far Away)    Vic 21913, HMV B-5670, EA-546

  ? Carl Kress-g replaces bj; Joe Tarto-bb replaces Pierce.
                                           New York, April 19, 1929.

  51193-3  Hittin' The Ceiling - vSL               Vic 21969, HMV B-5662, El EG-1417

  As for March 13, 1929, plus probably Hymie Farberman-t/Sam Lewis-tb/Benny Posner-vn
  /Al Armer-sb; Jack Shilkret-p replaces Rettenberg; Don Howard-v.
                                           New York, May 13, 1929.

  51995-1  Nobody But You - vDH                    Vic 21997, HMV B-5691

  As for March 13, 1929, without Kellner; Jack Shilkret-p added; ? Carl Kress-g replaces bj; Al Armer-sb/Joe Tarto-bb replace Pierce; Johnny Marvin-v.
                                           New York, July 15, 1929.

  53475-2  I'm The Medicine Man For The Blues - vJM Vic 22055, HMV B-5750

  Leonard Joy dir. Del Staigers-Mike Mosiello-? Hymie Farberman or Harry Shilkret-t/
  Chuck Campbell-tb/Andy Sannella-? Sammy Feinsmith-cl-as/Maurice Pierce-cl-ts/Milt
  Rettenberg-p/? Carl Kress-g/Jack Pierce or Joe Tarto-bb/Al Armer-sb/Joe Green-d/
  Don Howard-v.                            New York, August 30, 1929.

  55661-2  Bottoms Up - vDH                        Vic 22109, HMV B-5802

  Nat Shilkret dir. same group as for March 13, 1929, plus 3rd vn, Al Armer-sb; ?Carl
  Kress-g replaces bj; Frank Luther-v.     New York, February 6, 1930.

  58556-2  Singing A Vagabond Song - vFL           Vic 22306, HMV B-5829, EA-719

  Sam Lewis or Tommy Dorsey-tb/3rd cl-as/Abe Bonodkin-vc added; Armer omitted.
                                           New York, June 27, 1930.

  62296-2  Dixiana - vFL                           Vic 22472, HMV B-5915, EA-799

This Chicago dance orchestra made a number of titles for Vocalion in 1923, of which the following have points of interest as jazz.

Albert E. Short dir. 2t/tb/Wayne King and another-cl-ss-as/cl-ss-ts/Del Delbridge-p/ bj/bb/d.                                        New York, March, 1923.

| 11074 | Liza | Voc M-1155, X-9364 |
| 11075 | Liza | Voc 14554 |
| 11077 | Wolverine Blues | - |

New York, May, 1923.

| 11436 | Bugle Call Rag | Voc 14658 |
| 11438/9 | Sobbing Blues (sic) | Voc 14600, M-1165, X-9372 |
| 11442/4 | Long-Lost Mama | -     M-1166, X-9373 |

## SHREVEPORT SIZZLERS

Pseudonym on OKeh 8918 for Clarence Williams' Jazz Kings, q.v.

## ERIC SIDAY

Violin solos, acc. by Rudy Starita-marimba.
London, July 13, 1927.

| WA-5883-1-2 | Sweet And Black | Col rejected |
| WA-5884 1-2 | Go, Joe, Go | - |

Acc. by t/p/g/sb/d.                            London, July 10, 1936.

| CE-7761-1 | Chicago Honky-Tonk | Par rejected |

Violin duets with Reg Leopold, acc. by Sam Gelsley-g/Don Stuteley-sb/Max Abrams-d.
London, July 12, 1937.

| CE-8496-1 | Jed And Elmer | Par R-2466, A-6899, Od A-272137 |
| CE-8497-2 | Honeysuckle Rose | -     -     - |

London, January 24, 1938.

| CE-8883-1 | Tiger Rag | Par R-2505, A-6922, A-272138 |

SIDAY-SIMPSON QUARTET : Eric Siday-vn/Jack Simpson-x/Danny Perri-g/Don Stuteley-sb.
London, September 19, 1938.

| CE-9327-1 | My Blue Heaven | Par rejected |
| CE-9328-1 | Goin' Places | - |
| CE-9329-1 | Chiselin' | - |
| CE-9329-1 | Sweet Sue | - |

## AL SIEGEL

AL SIEGEL AND HIS ORCHESTRA : Al Siegel-p dir. probably :- Murphy Steinberg or Paul Mares-c/Jesse Barnes-tb/Phil Wing-cl-as/vn/bj/d.
New York, January, 1924.

| 1644-2-3 | Sooke Hey Hey | Pm 20314, Bwy/Pur 11314, Cx 40314, Pen 1314, Pt 11373 |
| 1645-1-3 | Blue Grass Blues | As above plus Ka K-1000, Max 1511 |
| 1646-1 | So Long To You And The Blues | Pm 20301, Cx 40301, Emb/Mit/Pt/Tri 11363, Pur 11301 |

NOTE:- Embassy/Mitchell/Puretone/Triangle 11363 as WADE'S MOULIN ROUGE ORCHESTRA; Puretone 11373 as BROADWAY MELODY MAKERS.

Piano acc. to BUDDY DOYLE-v.            Hayes, Middlesex, November 30, 1926.

| Yy-9705-2 | How Could Red Riding Hood ? | Zon 2850 |
| Yy-9706-2 | Could I ? - I Certainly Could | - |

AL SIEGEL (cont.)

Piano solos.                                    Hayes, Middlesex, December 22, 1926.

Yy-9791-1-2  Buzzin' Bees                          Rejected
Yy-9792-1-2  Johnny Dunn's Novelty Blues           -
Yy-9793-2  Someone Is Losin' Susan                 Zon 2862
Yy-9794-1  For Baby And Me                         -

                                                Hayes, Middlesex, February 24, 1927.

Yy-10207-2  Dusting The Keys                       Zon 5056
Yy-10208-2  Polly                                  -
Yy-10209-2  Classicanna                            Zon 2945
Yy-10210-2  Whippin' The Ivories                   -

## SIGLER'S BIRMINGHAM MERRYMAKERS

Maurice Sigler-bj dir. c/cl-as/ts/p/bb/d/N. Sol Bearman-v.
                                                Atlanta, December, 1924.

8828-A  Mama's Gone, Goodbye                       OK 40280
8829-A  Hard Hearted Hannah - vNSB                 -
8830-A  I Love Her                                 OK 40310
8831-A  Step It                                    -

## FRANK SIGNORELLI

FRANK SIGNORELLI AND HIS ORCHESTRA : Probably :- Red Nichols-t/Miff Mole or Vincent
    Grande-tb/Alfie Evans-Dick Johnson-cl-as/Fred Morrow-cl-ts/Frank Signorelli-p/Dick
    McDonough-bj/Joe Tarto-bb/Ray Bauduc-d. New York, c. August 27, 1926.

107069    St. Louis Hop                            PA 36535, Per 14716
107070    Don't Be Angry With Me                   PA 36523, Per 14704
107071    A Blues Serenade                         PA 36535, Per 14716
107072    She's Still My Baby                      PA 36518, 11359, Per 14699

Frank Signorelli-p/Matt Malneck-vn, with Mario Perry-pac*.
                                                New York, May 20, 1927.

38769-1-2  Caprice Futuristique                    Vic rejected
38770-1-2  Midnight Reflections                    -
38771-1-2  *Pretty Blue                            --
38772-1-2  *More Or Less                           -

                                                New York, June 14, 1927.

38899-1-2-3-4  *More Or Less Blues                 Vic rejected
39300-1-2-3  *Pretty Blues                         -
            Just Around The Edges                  Vic test (un-numbered)

Piano solos.                                    New York, June 22, 1927.

E-6109/11 Goose Pimples                            Br rejected
E-6112/4  A Blues Serenade                         -

                                                New York, November 5, 1928.

401294-A-B-C  Caprice Futuristic                   OK rejected

## SILENT JOE AND HIS BOYS

Pseudonym on Champion for Jack Stillman's Oriole Orchestra, q.v.

## SILVER SLIPPER ORCHESTRA

Pseudonym on Challenge 806 for the Dixieland Thumpers, q.v.  The commercial dance band
    of the same name on Columbia (1923) is of no jazz interest.

## DAN SILVER'S DANCE ORCHESTRA

Pseudonym on Variety 5054 for the Broadway Broadcasters (see Sam Lanin).

Pseudonym on Silvertone for Phil Green and his Orchestra, q.v.

## DAVID H. SILVERMAN AND HIS ORCHESTRA

David H. Silverman-p dir. Harold Ripplinger and another-c/Paul Benger-tb/Dominic
Sala-cl-as/as-f/Maurice Somers-vn/Roland Thurston-bj/Nat Shilkret-d, not the
Victor musical director, but related.    St. Louis, October 28, 1923.

| | | |
|---|---|---|
| 28850-1-2-3 | Lilac Lane | Rejected |
| 28851-3 | One Hour Of Love (w) | Vic 19200, Zon 3684 |

St. Louis, November 1, 1923.

| | | |
|---|---|---|
| 28861-3 | Mean Blues | Vic 19195, HMV B-1761, AM-190 |
| 28862-1 | Nights In The Woods | Vic 19200, Zon 3684 |
| 28863-1 | Blue Grass Blues | Vic 19237 |
| 28864-2 | Mamma Goes Where Papa Goes (Or Papa Don't Go Out Tonight) | Vic 19195, HMV B-1773 |

## JAN SIMA AND HIS ORCHESTRA

See Joe Turner.

## OMER  SIMEON

Clarinet solos, acc. by Earl Hines-p/Hayes Alvis-bb/Wallace Bishop-d.
Chicago, August 21, 1929.

| | | |
|---|---|---|
| C-4104- | Smoke-House Blues | Br 7109, HJCA 605, JSo AA-510 |
| C-4105- | Beau-Koo Jack | Rejected |

Acc. by Earl Hines-p/Claude Roberts-bj. Chicago, September 11, 1929.

| | | |
|---|---|---|
| C-4330-A | Beau-Koo Jack | Br 7109, HJCA 605, JSo AA-510 |

NOTE:- Jazz Society AA-510 as OMER SIMEON TRIO.

## LESTER SIMMONS AND HIS ORCHESTRA

Pseudonym on Champion 15475 for the Black Diamond Orchestra, q.v.

## HOWARD SIMMS

Pseudonym on Harmograph for Ollie Powers, q.v.

## AIME  SIMON-GIRARD

Vocal, acc. by Michel Warlop and his Orchestra : 2t/tb/Alix Combelle-ts/3 other as-
ts/p/Django Reinhardt-g/sb/d.        Paris, November 13, 1934.

| | | |
|---|---|---|
| OLA-148-1 | Cocktails pour deux | HMV K-7374 |
| OLA-150-1 | L'amour en fleurs | - |

NOTE:- Matrices OLA-149 and OLA-151 are by Germaine Sablon, q.v.

## JOS SIMPKINS AND HIS RUBE BAND

Pseudonym on Champion 15581 for Ezra Buzzington and his Band, q.v.

## ARTHUR SIMS AND HIS  CREOLE ROOF ORCHESTRA

Arthur Sims-as-vn dir. Bernie Young-c/William Franklin-tb/Edward Inge-Gilbert Munday
cl-as/Bert Bailey-bar/Cassino Simpson-p/Arthur Allbright-bj-v/Charles Harkness-bb/
Cliff Jones-d.                Chicago, June 21, 1926.

| | | |
|---|---|---|
| 9763-A | How Do You Like It Blues | OK 8373, Par R-3257 |
| 9764-A | As Long As I Have You - vAA | OK 40675, Par E-5711 |
| 9765-A | Soapstick Blues | OK 8373, Par R-3257 |

## JOE SIMS

See Clarence Williams.

### RAY SINCLAIR AND HIS BAND

Pseudonym on Duophone B-5111 for Ben Selvin and his Orchestra, q.v.

### THE SINGING BOYS AND THEIR NOVELTY ORCH.

Ed Kirkeby-Cyril Pitts-Tom Muir-v trio acc. by ? Pete Pumiglio-cl/Adrian Rollini-bsx/
? Al Duffy-vn/Tommy Felline-g/Stan King-d.
New York, March 5, 1929.

| | | |
|---|---|---|
| 148017-2-3 | My Kinda Love (One Way To Paradise) | Har 928-H |
| 148018-3 | You'll Recognize My Baby | Har 1087-H |

### THE SINGING TROUBADOURS

Pseudonym on Salabert 471 for the California Ramblers, q.v.

### ZUTTY SINGLETON

ZUTTY AND HIS BAND : Vernell Yorke-t-v/Horace Eubanks-cl-as-v/Henry Gordon-p/Mike
McKendrick-g/Leonard Bibbs-sb/Zutty Singleton-d.
Chicago, March 27, 1935.

| | | | |
|---|---|---|---|
| 9879-A | (I Would Do) Anything For You - vVY | Dec 432, F-42067 | |
| 9880-A-B | Look Over Yonder - vHE | Dec 431 | |
| 9881-A | Runenae Papa (I Want A Lot Of Love)-vHE | - | |
| 9882-A | Royal Garden Blues | Dec 465 | |
| 9883-A | Bugle Call Rag | - | 3685, F-42067 |
| 9884-A | Clarinet Marmalade | Dec 432 | |

ZUTTY SINGLETON AND HIS ORCHESTRA : Henry Allen-t/Benny Morton-tb/Edmond Hall-cl/Lil
Armstrong-p/Bernard Addison-g/Pops Foster-sb/Zutty Singleton-d.
New York, May 28, 1940.

| | | |
|---|---|---|
| 67841-A | King Porter Stomp | Dec 18093, M-30320, Br 03167 |
| 67842-A | Shim-Me-Sha-Wabble | -          -          - |

### SIOUX CITY SIX

Bix Beiderbecke-c/Miff Mole-tb/Frank Trumbauer-Cm/Rube Bloom-p/Min Leibrook-bb/Vic
Moore-d.
New York, October 10, 1924.

| | | |
|---|---|---|
| 9119-A | Flock O' Blues | Gnt 5569, Br 02207, Ses 7 |
| 9120-C | I'm Glad | -         -       - |

### NORMAN SISSEL AND HIS RHYTHM TWISTERS

Pseudonym on Worldecho for Cecil Norman and his Band, q.v.

### NOBLE SISSLE

Vocal, acc. unknown.
New York, c. July, 1917.

| | |
|---|---|
| Mammy's Little Choc'late Cullud Chile | P 20210 |

New York, c. November, 1917.

| | |
|---|---|
| That's The Kind Of A Baby For Me | P 20280 |
| He's Always Hanging Around | - |
| Mandy Lou | P 20295 |

Acc. by Eubie Blake-p.
New York, April 9, 1920.

| | |
|---|---|
| Goodnight, Angeline | Vic test (un-numbered) |
| Simply Full Of Jazz | - |

Acc. by Eubie Blake-p.                    New York, c. July, 1920.

41316-4-7  Broadway Blues                        Em 10296, Med 8246, Re 911
NOTE:- Regal 911 as LEONARD GRAHAM AND ROBERT BLACK.

                                          New York, December, 1920.

41564-1-2-6  Crazy Blues                         Em 10326, Med 8252, Pm 12007,
                                                      Re 911
NOTE:- Medallion 8252 as WILLIE BLACK AND RUBY BLAKE; Regal 911 as LEONARD GRAHAM
AND ROBERT BLACK; Paramount 12007 as SISSEL AND BLAKE.

Orch. acc.                                New York, c. December, 1920.

68981     Great Camp Meetin' Day               PA 020484

Acc. by Novelty Orchestra (sic).          New York, c. December, 1920-January, 1921.

69018     Crazy Blues                          PA 020484

Acc. by Eubie Blake-p.                    New York, January 11, 1921.

7734      Crazy Blues                          Ed 50754, Amb 4264

Acc. by his Sizzling Syncopators : Frank De Braithe or De Broite-t/Frank Withers-
tb/Edgar Campbell-cl/Nelson Kincaid-as/Eubie Blake-p/Steve Wright-d.
                                          New York, c. February 2, 1921.

41633-2-3-4  Royal Garden Blues                  Em 10367, 10604, Med 8286, Re 945
NOTE:- Medallion 8286 as WILLIE BROWN AND HIS SIZZLING SYNCOPATORS; Regal 945 as
LEONARD GRAHAM AND HIS JAZZ BAND.

                                          New York, c. March 2, 1921.

41671-2-3  Boll Weevil Blues                     Em 10357, 10627
41672-1-2  Loveless Love                              -     10605, Re 946
NOTE:- Regal 946 as LEONARD GRAHAM AND HIS JAZZ BAND.

                                          New York, c. March 18, 1921.

41699-2-3  Low Down Blues                        Em 10365, 10627, Re 946
41700-2  Long Gone                                    -     10574
41701-2-3  My Mammy's Tears                      Em 10367
NOTE:- Regal 946 as LEONARD GRAHAM AND HIS JAZZ BAND.

Bj added.                                 New York, c. May 3, 1921.

41783-2-3  Baltimore Buzz                        Em 10385, 10574, Re 9101
41784-1-2-3  In Honey Suckle Time (sic)               -   Med 8298, Re 9102
        (When Emaline Said She'll Be Mine)
NOTE:- Regal 9101 and 9102 as LEONARD GRAHAM AND HIS JAZZ BAND.

Acc. by Eubie Blake-p, or his Sizzling Syncopators (as last above)*.
                                          New York, c. June 9, 1921.

41848-1-2  Love Will Find A Way                  Em 10396, 10604, Re 9107,Sym 4361
41849-1-2  *Oriental Blues                            -
NOTE:- Regal 9107 as LEONARD GRAHAM AND ROBERT BLACK.

                                          New York, c. July 27, 1921.

41921-2-3  I've Got The Blues, But I'm Just Too   Em 10443
        Mean To Cry
41922-2  Arkansas Blues                               -     10605, Re 9137
NOTE:- Regal 9137 as LEONARD GRAHAM AND ROBERT BLACK.

                                          New York, c. October 10, 1921.

42011-4-5  I've Got The Red, White And Blues     Em 10484, Re 9158
42012-4  I'm A Doggone Struttin' Fool                 -       -

Acc. by Eubie Blake-p.                    New York, c. January 4, 1922.

42129-3  Boo Hoo Hoo                              Em 10512, Re 9180
42130-3-6  I'm Craving For That Kind Of Love      Em 10513, Re 9203

Acc. by Perry Bradford-p.                 New York, April 1, 1922.

    Razor Jim                             Vic test (un-numbered)

Acc. by Nat Shilkret-p.                   New York, April 25, 1922.

    Mirandy (That Gal O' Mine)            Vic test (un-numbered)

SISSEL AND BLAKE : Noble Sissle-v, acc. by Eubie Blake-p.
                                 New York, July, 1922.

1114-1-2  If You've Never Been Vamped By A       Pm 12002
      Brown Skin Gal (You've Never Been Vamped At All)
1115-3  Bandana Days                             -

NOBLE SISSLE-EUBIE BLAKE : As above.      Camden, N. J., May 25, 1923.

27975-3  Waitin' For The Evenin' Mail (Sittin'   Vic 19086
      On The Inside, Lookin' At The Outside)
27976-3  Down-Hearted Blues                       -        HMV B-1703

                         New York, August 17, 1923.

28383-1-2-3  Don't Leave Me Blues                Vic rejected
28387-1-2-3  Dear Li'l Pal                        -

                         New York, August 23, 1923.

28383-4-5-6  Don't Leave Me Blues                Vic rejected
28387-4-5-6-7  Dear Li'l Pal                      -

                         New York, January 8, 1924.

28387-8-9-10  Dear Li'l Pal                       Rejected
29188-3  Sweet Henry (The Pride Of Tennessee)    Vic 19253
29189-2  Old-Fashioned Love                       -

                        .New York, March 7, 1924.

29585-1-2-3  Manda                               Vic rejected
29586-1-2-3  Jassamine Lane                       -
29587-1-2-3  Dixie Moon                           -

Joe Smith-c added.                        New York, August 27, 1924.

30683-1-2-3  Manda                               Vic rejected
30684-1-2-3  Fate Is The Slave Of Love            -

Smith omitted.                            New York, October 22, 1924.

29587-6  Dixie Moon                              Vic 19494
30683-6  Manda                                    -

                        New York, May 27, 1925.

10407  Broken Busted Blues                       Ed rejected
10408  You Ought To Know                          -

                        New York, June 10, 1925.

10407  Broken Busted Blues                       Ed 51572, Amb 5041
10408  You Ought To Know                          -

NOBLE SISSLE-EUBIE BLAKE : Noble Sissle-v, acc. by Eubie Blake-p.
London, November, 1925.

| 9748 | Why ? | EBW 4337 |
| 9749 | Oh, Boy ! What A Girl | - |

London, December, 1925.

| 9801-1 | Ukulele Baby | EBW 4356 |
| 9802-1 | Ukulele Lullaby | - |
| 9803-1 | I Wonder Where My Sweetie Can Be ? | EBW 4371 |
| 9804-2 | There's One Lane That Has No Turning | - |

London, March, 1926.

| 9935 | Pickaninny Shoes | EBW 4402 |
| 9936 | A Jockey's Life For Mine | EBW 4417 |
| 9937 | Dinah | EBW 4402 |
| 9938 | You Ought To Know | EBW 4417 |

New York, August 17, 1926.

| 74285-B | Ukulele Lullaby | EBM 7 (LP) |

New York, February 5, 1927.

| 80394-B | 'Deed I Do | OK 40776, Par E-5796 |
| 80395-B | Ev'rything's Made For Love | -              - |
| 80396-A-B | Crazy Blues | Rejected |
| 80397-B | Pickaninny Shoes | OK 40917, Par R-186 |

New York, May 10, 1927.

| 81073-B | Slow River | OK 40824, Par R-3368 |
| 81074-A | Home, Cradle Of Happiness | -              - |

Vocal, acc. by Rube Bloom-p.          New York, July 15, 1927.

| 81171-A | Sometimes I'm Happy | OK 40859, Par R-3428, Od 193069 |
| 81172-C | Hallelujah ! | -              - A-2371   - |

New York, August 15, 1927.

| 81226-C | Broken Hearted | OK 40877, Par R-3449 |
| 81227-C | Just Once Again | -         Par R-3507 |

NOTE:- Although the label of Parlophone R-3507 states "Guitar by Andy," none is audible.

Acc. by Andy Sannella-cl-stg/Rube Bloom-p.
New York, August 17, 1927.

| 81246-A | Give Me A Night In June - clAS | OK 40882, Par R-3449 |
| 81247-B | Are You Happy ? - stgAS | -         Par R-3507 |

Acc. by Rube Bloom-p.          New York, September 6, 1927.

| 81420-B | Sweetheart Memories | OK 40917, Par R-186 |
| 81421-A | Who's That Knockin' At My Door ? | Par R-3471 |

Acc. by Murray Kellner-vn/Rube Bloom-p/Justin Ring-cel/Eddie Lang-g.
New York, September 7, 1927.

| 81422-B | Kentucky Babe | OK 40964, Par R-3471, A-2419 |
| 81423-A | Lindy Lou | -         Par R-337   - |

NOTE:- OKeh 40964 and Parlophone A-2419 as LEE WHITE.

Acc. by his own Special Orchestra : Harry Revel-p dir. t/as/vn/bj/bb/d-vib.
London, c. March 29, 1928.

| E-1812-2 | Westward Bound | Par R-101, A-2509 |
| E-1813-2 | I'm Going Back To Old Nebraska | Par R-3522, A-2705 |
| E-1814-2 | Since You Have Left Me | Par R-101, A-2509 |
| E-1815-4 | I'm Coming, Virginia | Par R-3522 |

Acc. by his own Special Orchestra : Ronnie Munro dir. as/Perley Breed-as-bar/2vn/
Harry Revel-p/? bb/d.                          London, April 29, 1928.

| | | |
|---|---|---|
| E-1897-2 | What Do We Care ? | Par R-128, A-2547 |
| E-1898-1-2 | Guiding Me Back Home (w) | Par R-129, A-2734 |
| E-1899-2 | Limehouse Rose | Par R-128 |
| E-1900-1-2 | Sunny Skies | Par R-129, A-2547 |

NOBLE SISSLE AND HIS SIZZLING SYNCOPATORS : Ronnie Munro dir. 2t/tb/2as/ts/2vn/Harry
Revel-p/bj/bb/d (probably similar to Ronnie Munro's orchestra, q.v.)/Noble Sissle-
v.                                             London, c. May 5, 1928.

| | | |
|---|---|---|
| E-1907-2 | Just Give The Southland To Me - vNS | Par R-125, A-2668 |
| E-1908-2 | Sunny Skies - vNS | - |
| E-1909-1 | Again (w) - vNS | Par R-126, A-2668 |
| E-1910-2 | Love Lies - vNS | - |

Vocal, acc. by his own Special Orchestra : Harry Revel-p dir. t/as/Perley Breed-as-
bar/2vn/bj/sb/d.                               London, c. June 11, 1928.

| | | |
|---|---|---|
| E-1955-2 | Ol' Man River | Par R-145 |
| E-1956-1 | Why Do I Love You ? | - |
| E-1957-2 | When The Clock Strikes Twelve (w) | Par R-146 |
| E-1958-2 | Just Keep Singing A Song | -      A-2671 |

                                               London, c. June 15, 1928.

| | | |
|---|---|---|
| E-1959-2 | How Can You Forget ? | Par R-164, A-2658 |
| E-1960-1 | Nothing Has Changed | Rejected |
| E-1961-2 | Broken-Hearted Doll | Par R-164, A-2634 |
| E-1962-1 | Helping Hand | Par R-337 |
| E-1963-2 | Lucky In Love | Par R-206 |
| E-1964-2 | Good News | - |

Barry Mills-p dir. same instrumentation, with 2nd as replacing Breed, and without
Revel.                                         London, c. September 24, 1928.

| | | |
|---|---|---|
| E-2146-1-2 | Get Out And Get Under The Moon | Par R-219, Ar 4308 |
| E-2147-1 | Dakota | - |
| E-2148-2 | Since You Said You Loved Me | Par R-220, Ar 4310 |
| E-2149-2 | Just Like A Melody Out Of The Sky | -      Ar 4308 |

NOTE:- Ariel 4308 and 4310 as JIM GARNETT.

Acc. by the Mississippi Chorus and Orchestra : Barry Mills-p dir. t/2as/2vn/p/bj/
bb/d.                                          London, c. November 26, 1928.

| | | |
|---|---|---|
| E-2226-3 | Great Camp Meetin' Day | Par R-251 |
| E-2227-3 | Miranda | - |

                                               London, c. December 7, 1928.

| | | |
|---|---|---|
| E-2239-2 | For Old Times Sake (w) | Par R-252 |
| E-2240-1 | All By Yourself In The Moonlight | - |
| E-2241-2 | Shout Hallelujah ! 'Cause I'm Home | Par R-259 |
| E-2242-1 | Columbo | - |

NOBLE SISSLE AND HIS ORCHESTRA : Noble Sissle-v dir. Pike Davis-Demas Dean-t/James
Reevy-tb/Buster Bailey-cl-ss-as/Rudy Jackson-cl-as/Ralph Duquesne-cl-as-ts/Ramon
Usera-cl-ts/Juice Wilson-William Rosemand-vn/Lloyd Pinckney-p/Warren Harris-bj/
Henry Edwards-bb/John Ricks-sb/Jesse Baltimore-d.
                                 Hayes, Middlesex, September 10, 1929.

| | | |
|---|---|---|
| Bb-17326-2 | Kansas City Kitty - vNS-? | HMV B-5731, El EG-1560 |
| Bb-17327-1-2-3 | On The Lazy Amazon - v | Rejected |
| Bb-17328-2 | Camp Meeting Day - vNS | HMV B-5709, R-14274 |
| Bb-17329-2 | Miranda - vNS | -        -        El EG-1560 |

                                 Hayes, Middlesex, October 10, 1929.

| | | |
|---|---|---|
| Bb-18031-1 | I'm Crooning A Tune About June - vNS | HMV B-5731, El EG-1713 |
| Bb-18032-2 | Recollections (w) - vNS | HMV B-5723 |
| Bb-18033-1-2 | You Want Lovin' And I Want Love - vNS | - |
| Bb-18034-1-2 | Yet You Forgot - vNS ? | Rejected |

NOBLE SISSLE AND HIS SIZZLING SYNCOPATORS : Noble Sissle-v dir. Arthur Briggs-Tommy
   Ladnier-t/Billy Burns-tb/Frank Goudie-Rudy Jackson-cl-ss-as/Ramon Duquesne-cl-ss-as/Ramon
   Usera-cl-ts/Lloyd Pinckney-p/Frank Ethridge-bj/Edward Coles-bb/Jack Carter-d/girl
   v.                                                 London, December 11, 1930.

WA-10968-2  Daughter Of The Latin Quarter-vNS-girl  Col CB-192
WA-10969-1  You Can't Get To Heaven That Way        Col CB-193, DF-463
            - vNS&ch
WA-10970-1  Sunny Sunflower Land - vNS              Col CB-192
WA-10971-1  Confessin' (That I Love You) - vNS      Col CB-193, DF-463

NOBLE SISSLE AND HIS ORCHESTRA : As above, but Demas Dean-t replaces Briggs; Sidney
   Bechet-cl-ss replaces Goudie.          New York, February 24, 1931.

E-36120-   Got The Bench, Got The Park - vNS        Br 6073, 01117, A-9049, Spt S-2173
E-36121-A-B  In A Cafe On The Road To Calais-vNS    Rejected
E-36122-A  Loveless Love - vNS                      Br 6073, 01117, A-9049, Mt M-12444
                                                    Per 15649, Spt S-2173
   NOTE:- Melotone M-12444 as THE GEORGIA SYNCOPATORS; Supertone S-2173 as MISSOURI
JAZZ BAND.

                                New York, April 21, 1931.

E-36644-   Basement Blues - vNS                     Br 6129, A-9149, A-500124
E-36645-   Wha'd Ya Do To Me ? - vNS                Br 6111, 01158, A-9073
E-36646-   Roll On, Mississippi, Roll On - vNS       -        -        -

NOBLE SISSLE AND HIS INTERNATIONAL ORCHESTRA : Nobl Sissle-v dir. Wendell Culley-
   Demas Dean-Clarence Brereton-t/Chester Burrill-tb/Sidney Bechet-cl-ss/Harvey Boone
   cl-as/Ramon Usera-as-vn/James Tolliver-ts/Oscar Madera-vn/Harry Brooks-p/Howard
   Hill-g/Edward Coles-sb/Jack Carter-d/Billy Banks-Lavaida Carter-v.
                                Chicago, August 15, 1934.

C-9295    Under The Creole Moon - vNS               Dec 153
C-9296-A  The Old Ark Is Moverin' - vBB&ch           -        Br 01861
C-9297-A  Loveless Love - vLC                       Dec 154   -
C-9298-A  Polka Dot Rag                              -        Br 02511

NOBLE SISSLE AND HIS ORCHESTRA : As above, but Chauncey Haughton-cl-as/Gil White-
   Jerome Pasquall-ts replace Boone, Usera and Tolliver; Jimmy Miller-g replaces Hill;
   Jimmy Jones-sb replaces Coles; Wilbert Kirk-d replaces Carter; Lena Horne-v re-
   places Lavaida Carter.                 New York, March 11, 1936.

60888-A   That's What Love Did To Me - vLH          Dec 778
60889-A   You Can't Live In Harlem - vBB             -
60890-A   I Wonder Who Made Rhythm - vBB            Dec 766, Col DB-5032
60891-B   'Tain't A Fit Night Out For Man Or Beast-vNS -    Col FB-1493
60892-A   I Take To You -vLH                        Dec 847, Col DB-5032
60893-A   Rhythm Of The Broadway Moon - vNS          -     Col FB-1493

   Erskine Butterfield-p replaces Brooks.  New York, April 14, 1937.

M-398-    Bandana Days                              Vri 552
M-399-    I'm Just Wild About Harry                  -
M-400-2   Dear Old Southland - vNS                  CBS CL-2102, BPG-62232 (LPs)
M-401-1-2 St. Louis Blues                           Rejected

NOBLE SISSLE'S SWINGSTERS : Sidney Bechet-cl-ss/Jimmy Miller-g/Jimmy Jones-sb/Wilbert
   Kirk-d/Billy Banks-v.                   New York, April 16, 1937.

M-406-1   Okey-Doke                                 Vri 648, Voc 3840
M-407-1   Characteristic Blues - vBB                 -        -       Swing 323

   Clarence Brereton-t/Gil White-ts/Harry Brooks-p-a added; O'Neil Spencer-d-v replaces Kirk.                            New York, February 10, 1938.

63263-B   Viper Mad - vO'NS                         Dec 7429, 3521, M-30397, MU-60306,
                                                    Y-5288, Br 02652, 82587
63264-A   Blackstick                                Dec 2129, 3865, M-30224, MU-60307,
                                                    Br 80132, 02702
63265-A   When The Sun Sets Down South (Southern    As above; Br 02702*
63265-B     Sunset*) - aHB                          Br 87508
63266-A   Sweet Patootie - vO'NS                    Dec 7429, M-30397, MU-60306,
                                                    Y-5288, Br 02652, 82587

NOTE:- Brunswick 02652, 02702, 80132, 82587 and 87508, and Decca 3865 as SIDNEY "POPS" BECHET WITH NOBLE SISSLE'S SWINGSTERS.

## "KENN" SISSON AND HIS ORCHESTRA

The following title by this band, issued as by PARK INN GOOD TIMERS, is of some jazz interest; there may be others similar under both names.

"Kenn" Sisson-p-a dir.  2t/tb/2cl-as/cl-Cm or ts/vn/bj/bb/d.
                                    New York, November 12, 1928.

E-28668-A  I Can't Give You Anything But Love-v    Duo D-4018

## SIX BLACK DIAMONDS

Pseudonym for the following items listed in this book :-

Ajax 17098  Hard Hearted Hannah (Fletcher Henderson and his Orchestra)
Banner 1166  Both sides by the California Ramblers
       1188  Nothin' But (Joseph Samuels' Jazz Band) (also Apex 8054)
       1217  Long-Lost Mama (Joseph Samuels and his Orchestra) (also Imperial 1162)
       1227  My Sweetie Went Away (Joseph Samuels and his Orchestra) (also Imp 1181)
       1428  Both sides by the New Orleans Jazz Band
       1656  Steppin' Fool (Perry's Hot Dogs) (also Domino 3633)
       6298  Susianna (Adrian Schubert and his Salon Orchestra)
       6300  Some Of These Days (Adrian Schubert and his Salon Orchestra)
       6383  Where Has Mammy Gone ? (Adrian Schubert and his Salon Orchestra)
Oriole 497  Melancholy Lou (New Orleans Jazz Band)
Regal 8006  Flamin' Mamie (Perry's Hot Dogs)
       8022  Say Mister Have You Met Rosie's Sister ? (Perry's Hot Dogs)
       9553  Both sides by Joseph Samuels and his Orchestra
       9695  San (Nathan Glantz and his Orchestra)
       9706  Any Way The Wind Blows (Sam Lanin and his Orchestra)
       9725  Both sides by the New Orleans Jazz Band

The following titles, issued under this name, have not been ascribed to any other band in this book :-

Harry Gluck-t/Miff Mole or Vincent Grande-tb/Ken "Goof" Moyer-cl-as-effects/cl-as/p/ bj/d.                                  New York, c. February 14, 1924.

    5425-1-2  Lots O' Mama                    Ban 1322, Re 9612
    5426-1-2  Mindin' My Business            Ban 1318    -    Apex 8167

    ? Charlie Panelli-tb replaces Mole or Grande; Ray Kitchingman or John Cali-bj may replace the previous bj.          New York, c. March 13, 1924.

    5451-2  Waitin' Around                    Ban 1336, Re 9628, Apex 8211
    5452-2  Nobody's Sweetheart              Ban 1349, Re 9646, Apex 8222

    ? Jimmy Lytell-cl replaces Moyer.      New York, c. April 3, 1924.

    5470-1-3  Josephine (Who's The Meanest Gal In    Ban 1348, Re 9643, Apex 8231,
               Town ?)                               Imp 1329
    5471-2  My Papa Doesn't Two-Time No Time         Ban 1346, Re 9646, Apex 8250

Harry Gluck-t/Charlie Panelli-tb/Jimmy Lytell-cl/cl-as/ts/p/bj/bb/d.
                                    New York, c. July 17, 1924.

    5559-2  Hinkey Dinkey Parley Voo          Apex 8226
    5560-1-2-3; 11046-3  Charleston Cabin     Ban 1385, Bwy/Cvl/Emb/Lyra/Pen/Pt,

Bubber Miley-? Louis Metcalf-c/Jake Frazier-tb/Bob Fuller-cl-as/Louis Hooper-p/Elmer Snowden-bj.                         New York, c. December 2, 1924.

    5758-1-2-3  Those Panama Mamas            Ban 1456, Dom 429, Or 374,
    NOTE:- Oriole 374 as ORIOLE DANCE ORCHESTRA;   Re 9766, Apex 8343, Imp 1490,
    Apex 8343 as ORIGINAL MEMPHIS FIVE (!)    Oly 1436 (anonymous)

Pseudonym on Domino for the following items listed in this book :-

390     Look-a What I Got Now (California Ramblers)
392     Any Way The Wind Blows (Sam Lanin and his Orchestra)
3510    Sweet Georgia Brown (Texas Ten)
21003   Eliza (California Ramblers)
21003   A New Kind Of Man (Sam Lanin and his Orchestra)
21184   How Many Times ? (The Buffalodians)
21193   Baby Face (The Buffalodians)

## THE SIX BLUE CHIPS

Pee Wee Erwin-t/Joe Marsala-cl/Frank Signorelli-p/Carmen Mastren-g/Artie Shapiro-sb/
   Stan King-d.                            New York, January 17, 1936.

60356-A   Steel Roof                      Dec 740, F-7809
60357-A   Cheatin' Cheech                   -      -

## SIX BROWN BROTHERS

The following titles by this popular vaudeville act of the years 1911-1925 are of
   considerable interest as ragtime and "near-jazz."

Tom Brown-ss-as dir. as-ts/Cm/ts/Harry Cook-bar/Harry Finkelstein (Fink)-bsx.
                              Camden, N. J., November 10, 1914.

15362-1-2  That Moaning Saxophone Rag (Harry    Vic rejected
              Cook-Tom Brown)
15363-1-2  Dill Pickles Rag (Charles L. Johnson)     -

                              Camden, N. J., November 20, 1914.

15362-3  That Moaning Saxophone Rag (Harry Cook-  Vic 17677, HMV B-526
            Tom Brown)
15363-3  Dill Pickles Rag (Charles L. Johnson)    Rejected

                              Camden, N. J., June 25, 1915.

16142-1-2-3  Down Home Rag (Wilbur Sweatman)    Vic rejected

                              Camden, N. J., July 8, 1915.

16142-5  Down Home Rag (Wilbur Sweatman)          Vic 17834

Guy Shrigley-as-ts/Sonny Clapp-ts and another (? "Slap" White) replace the unknown
   members.                     Camden, N. J., June 19, 1916.

17894-1  Pussyfoot March ("Slap" White)           Vic 18097

                              Camden, N. J., June 20, 1916.

17897-1  Bull Frog Blues (Tom Brown-Guy Shrigley) Vic 18097
17898-1-2  Walkin' The Dog (Shelton Brooks)       Rejected

                              Camden, N. J., June 21, 1916.

17898-3  Walkin' The Dog (Shelton Brooks)         Vic rejected

                              Camden, N. J., June 23, 1916.

17898-5  Walkin' The Dog (Shelton Brooks)         Vic 18140

                              Camden, N. J., May 9, 1917.

19847-2  The Darktown Strutters' Ball (S. Brooks) Vic 18376
19849-4  Smiles And Chuckles (Jazz Rag)           Vic 18385
            (F. Henri Klickmann)

Tom Brown-ss-as dir. Guy Shrigley-as-ts/James "Slap Rags" White-Cm/Sunny Clapp-ts/
   Harry Cook-bar/Harry Finkelstein (Fink)-bsx.
                                        New York, c. April, 1920.

            Jazz Band Blues                        Em 10195

                                        New York, c. May, 1920.

            12th Street Rag (Euday L. Bowman)      Em 10205

## THE SIX COLLEGIANS

Pseudonym on Canadian Domino 21055 (AH-HA !) for the California Ramblers, q.v.

## THE SIX HAYSEEDS

See Harry Reser.

## SIX HOT BABIES

Tom Morris-c/Joe Nanton-tb/Bob Fuller-cl/Nat Shilkret-p/Fats Waller-or/? Bobby Leecan
   g/d.                                 Camden, N. J., November 17, 1926.

36775-1-2-3-4  All God's Chillun Got Wings        Vic rejected

## THE SIX HOTTENTOTS

Red Nichols-t/Miff Mole-tb/Jimmy Dorsey-cl-as/Arthur Schutt-p/Joe Tarto-bb/Vic
   Berton-d/Irving Kaufman (as GEORGE CRANE on Pathe Actuelle 36643)-v.
                                        New York, c. March 23, 1927.

   7173-2  I'm In Love Again - vIK           Ban 1964, Bwy 1069, Dom 3935,
                                             21279, Or 880, Pm 20511,
                                             PA 36643, Per 14824, P-306,
                                             Re 8289, Apex 8624, Leo 10256,
                                             LS 24097, Imp 1803, BM 240,
                                             Max 1623
   7174-2-3  Sometimes I'm Happy - vIK       Ban 6008, Dom 3975, 21274,
                                             NML 1208, Or 933, Pa 36643, 11477,
                                             Per 14824, P-306, Re 8333,
                                             Apex 8614, 26050, Leo 10249,
                                             LS 24091, Mic 22165, Imp 1845
   7175-1  Rosy Cheeks - vIK                 Ban 1962, Bwy 1070, Dom 3931,
                                             21275, Or 883, Pm 20512, Re 8289,
                                             Apex 8614, Leo 10250, Max 1622
NOTE:- Oriole 880 and 883 as DIXIE JAZZ BAND; 933 as YANKEE TEN ORCHESTRA; Pathe
Actuelle 36643, 11477 as SOUTHAMPTON SOCIETY ORCHESTRA; Perfect P-306 as RAYNER'S
DANCE ORCHESTRA; Imp rial 1803 as SAM LANIN'S TROUBADOURS.

                                        New York, c. May 2, 1927.

   7241-2  The Memphis Blues                 Ban 1986, Dom 3956, Or 952,
                                             Re 8310, 8335
NOTE:- Oriole 952 as DIXIE JAZZ BAND.

                                        New York, c. May 16, 1927.

   7264-1-3  Melancholy Charlie              Ban 6009, Dom 3975, Or 931,
                                             Re 8333, MF 103
   7265-1  Hurricane                         Ban 6009, Dom 3976, 21580, Or 931,
                                             Re 8335, MF 103
NOTE:- Oriole 931 as TED WHITE'S COLLEGIANS; Domino 21580 as THE RED DANDIES.

## SIX  JELLY BEANS

Probably a Sam Lanin unit (q.v. the Imperial labelling) but not apparently composed
   entirely of regular members of the Lanin roster of the period.

Probably :- Tommy Gott-t/Miff Mole or Glenn Miller-tb/Larry Abbott-cl-as/Jimmy John-
ston-bsx/Bill Wirges-p/Vic Berton-d-vib/Irving Kaufman (as GEORGE BEAVER on most
issues)-v.                              New York, April 25, 1928.

| | | |
|---|---|---|
| 7934- | I Scream-You Scream-We All Scream For | Chg 571, Imp 1909, Kr 4205 |
| | Ice Cream - vch | |
| 7935-2-4 | Straight Back Home - vIK | Ban 7140, Or 1250 |
| 7936- | Know Nothin' Blues - vIK | Ban 7106, Je 5291  Or 1230 |

NOTE:- Banner 7106 and 7140 as MISSOURI JAZZ BAND; Jewel 5291 and Oriole 1230 as
DIXIE JAZZ BAND; Oriole 1250 as BILLY JAMES AND HIS ORCHESTRA; Imperial 1909 as
SAM LANIN AND HIS DANCE ORCHESTRA.

Scrappy Lambert-v.                      New York, May 15, 1928.

7976-3  Puttin' On The Dog - vSL                Ban 7157, Je 5331, Or 1278,
NOTE:- Banner 7157 as MISSOURI JAZZ BAND; Jewel    Apex 8823, Cr 81091, Dom 21479,
5331 and Oriole 1278 as DIXIE JAZZ BAND; Apex      LS 24351, Mic 22351, St 10381
8823 and Domino 21479 as GOLDIE'S SYNCOPATORS.

## SIX   JOLLY JESTERS

Freddy Jenkins-t-v/Joe Nanton-tb/Johnny Hodges-as/Duke Ellington-p/Fred Guy-bj/
Wellman Braud-sb/Sonny Greer-d-v.        New York, October 25, 1929.

E-31301-A  Six Or Seven Times - vFJ-SG          Voc 15843, Br 4723, Creole 15
NOTE:- Brunswick 4723 is a Canadian issue.

Cootie Williams-t/Harold Randolph-k-v/Teddy Bunn-g/Bruce Johnson-wb added.
                                        New York, October 29, 1929.

E-31371-A  Goin' Nuts - vHR                     Voc 15843, V-1041, Br 4723,
                                                Creole 15
E-31372-A  Oklahoma Stomp                       Voc 1449, V-1041, Bm 1034,
NOTE:- Brunswick 4723 is a Canadian issue.      HJCA HC-66, AF A-031

## SIX   JUMPING JACKS

See Harry Reser.

## SIX MEN AND A GIRL

Earl Thompson-t/Earl "Buddy" Miller-cl-as/Dick Wilson-ts/Mary Lou Williams-p/Floyd
Smith-elg/Booker Collins-sb/Ben Thigpen-d.
                                        New York, January 26, 1940.

| | | |
|---|---|---|
| US-1316-1 | Mary Lou Williams Blues | Var 8193 |
| US-1317-1 | Tea For Two | - |
| US-1318-1 | Scratchin' The Gravel | Var 8190 |
| US-1319-1 | Zonky | - |

## SIX SCRAMBLED EGGS

Jasper Davis-Ken Macomber dir. probably :- Louis Metcalf-c/Henry Hicks-tb/Charlie
Holmes-cl/Spencer Williams-p/Elmer Snowden-bj/Bass Moore-bb/Paul Barbarin-d.
                                        New York, April 18, 1929.

| | | |
|---|---|---|
| 51187-1-2 | Magnolia Blues | Vic rejected |
| 51188-1-2 | Soft Shoe Shuffle | - |

## THE SIX SWINGERS

George Scott Wood-p-a dir. Max Goldberg-t-mel/Lew Davis-tb/Freddy Gardner-cl-as-bar/
Albert Harris-g/Dick Ball-sb/Max Bacon-d/Sam Browne-v.
                                        London, October 29, 1934.

| | | |
|---|---|---|
| CAR-2973-1 | Your Mother's Son-in-law - vSB | RZ MR-1468 |
| CAR-2974-1 | I'm Walking The Chalk-Line - vSB | - |
| CAR-2975-1 | Hotcha Razz-ma-tazz - vSB | RZ MR-1509, OK 41588, Gl GZ-3047 |
| CAR-2976-1 | When's It Coming Round To Me ? - vSB | - - |

George Scott Wood dir. Max Goldberg-t-mel/Lew Davis-tb/Freddy Gardner-cl-as-bar/
   Arthur Young-p/Albert Harris-g/Dick Ball-sb/Max Bacon-d,
                                        London, December 18, 1934.

CAR-3122-1   Hot Pie - Part 1 (Intro.          RZ MR-1567, Gl GZ-3055
               Bugle Call Rag/Some Of These Days/After You've Gone)
CAR-3123-1   Hot Pie - Part 2 (Intro.           -          -
               St. Louis Blues/Dinah/Poor Butterfly)
CAR-3124-1   Hot Pie No. 2 - Part 1 (Intro.    RZ MR-1675, Gl GZ-3071
               Nobody's Sweetheart/Avalon/Chinatown)
CAR-3125-1   Hot Pie No. 2 - Part 2 (Intro.     -          -
               Margie/Sweet Sue/Goodbye Blues)


George Scott Wood-p-a dir. Billy Farrell-t/Tony Thorpe-tb/Freddy Gardner-cl-as-bar/
   Joe Young-bj-g/Dick Escott-sb/Max Abrams-d/Nora Williams-v.
                                        London, March 7, 1935.

CAR-3267-1   Swing, Brothers, Swing            RZ MR-1621, Col DI-4014,Gl GZ-3063
CAR-3268-1   Streamline Strut                   -          -          -
CAR-3269-1   I'm A Hundred Per Cent. For You - vNW  RZ MR-1620, Col DI-4013,Gl GZ-3062
CAR-3270-2   Dixie After Dark - vNW             -          -          -


   Marjorie Stedeford-v; Thorpe omitted*.  London, May 20, 1935.

CAR-3446-1   *The House Where I Was Born - vMS     RZ MR-1732, G-22519, Col MC-56
CAR-3447-1   What's The Reason (I'm Not Pleasin' You)-vMS -    -          -


   Brian Lawrence-v.                    London, June 27, 1935.

CAR-3494-1   Rhythm Is Our Business - vMS      RZ MR-1771, G-22551, Col MC-62
CAR-3495-1   Star Dust - vMS                    -          -      Col FB-1852
CAR-3496-1   Chicken Reel - vBL                RZ MR-1784, Col MC-64, Gl GZ-3073


   Ted Heath-tb replaces Thorpe.        London, July 1, 1935.

CAR-3506-1   Darktown Strutters' Ball - vBL    RZ MR-1784, Col MC-64, Gl GZ-3073


                                        London, September 13, 1935.

CAR-3584-1   Weather Man - vMS                 RZ MR-1841, G-22628, Col MC-75,
                                                  Gl GZ-3080, PA PA-971
CAR-3585-1   Swingin' The Lead                 As above
CAR-3588-1   Hot Pie No. 3 - Part 1 (Intro.    RZ MR-1909, Col MC-105,Gl GZ-3089
               Limehouse Blues/Miss Annabelle Lee/Everybody Loves My Baby/You Rascal,
               You/Shine)
CAR-3589-2   Hot Pie No. 3 - Part 2 (Intro.     -          -          -
               It Had To Be You/Tea For Two/Sleepy-Time Gal)


   Jock Fleming-tb replaces Heath; James Jack-d replaces Abrams.
                                        London, October 10, 1935.

CAP-21-1     Black Coffee                      RZ MR-1864
CAR-3650-1   Lulu's Back In Town                -

SCOTT WOOD AND HIS SIX SWINGERS : As last, but Jock Jacobson-d replaces Jack.
                                        London, November 13, 1935.

CAR-3722-1   I'm Livin' In A Great Big Way - vMS   RZ MR-1929, Gl GZ-3096
CAR-3723-1   Truckin' On Down - vMS             -          -


   George Scott Wood-p-a dir. Harry Owen-t/Jock Fleming-tb/Harry Hayes-cl-as/Joe Young
   g/Dick Escott-sb/Jock Jacobson-d/Sam Costa-Frank Kerslake-v.
                                        London, January 10, 1936.

CAR-3847-1   You're An Eyeful Of Heaven - vSC  RZ MR-2008, Gl GZ-3107
CAR-3848-1   I'd Love To Take Orders From You - vSC  -          -
CAR-3849-1   A Little Bit Independent - vSC    RZ MR-2009, G-22777
CAR-3850-1   Georgia Rockin' Chair - vFK        -          -

SCOTT WOOD AND HIS SIX SWINGERS : George Scott Wood-p-a dir. Harry Owen-t/JockFleming
   tb/Freddy Gardner-cl-as-bar/Joe Young-g/Dick Escott-sb/Jock Jacobson-d/Sam Costa-
   Frank Kerslake-v.                         London, March 4, 1936.

| | | |
|---|---|---|
| CAR-3966-1 | My Girl's A Rhythm Fan - vSC | RZ MR-2054, G1 GZ-3113 |
| CAR-3967-1 | Rhythm In My Nursery Rhymes - vSC | -            - |
| CAR-3968-1 | Handel In Harlem - vSC | Col FB-1405, RZ G-22894 |
| CAR-3969-1 | My Sweetie Went Away - vSC | -            - |

                                           London, June 2, 1936.

| | | |
|---|---|---|
| CA-15778-1 | Dere's Jazz In Dem Dere Horns - vSC | Col FB-1427 |
| CA-15779-1 | Meet The Boys - vSC | Col FB-1428, RZ G-22925 |
| CA-15780-1 | Sammy Saxophone - vSC | -            - |
| CA-15781-1 | Rockin' Chair - vFK | Col FB-1427 |

   Lew Davis-tb replaces Fleming.        London, July 3, 1936.

| | | | |
|---|---|---|---|
| CA-15822-1 | Is It True What They Say About Dixie ? | Col FB-1462 | |
| | - vSC | | |
| CA-15823-1 | You Gotta Know How To Dance - vSC | - | RZ G-22944 |
| CA-15841-1 | 'Way Down Yonder In New Orleans - vFK | Col FB-1472, DW-4388 | |
| CA-15842-1-2 | Nightfall | -            - | RZ G-22944 |

   Davis omitted; Max Abrams-d replaces Jacobson.
                                           London, September 1, 1936.

| | | |
|---|---|---|
| CA-15893-1 | Hot Pie - Part 1 (Intro. | Col FB-1503 |
| | Sailing On The Robert E. Lee/Alabamy Bound/California, Here I Come) | |
| CA-15894-1 | Hot Pie - Part 2 (Intro. | |
| | Japanese Sandman/I Ain't Got Nobody/The Birth Of The Blues) | |
| CA-15895-1 | Evergreens Of Jazz - Part 1 (Intro.    Col FB-1504 | |
| | Hot Time In The Old Town Tonight/In The Shade Of The Old Apple Tree/ | |
| | Dinah) - v | |
| CA-15896-1 | Evergreens Of Jazz - Part 2 (Intro.       - | |
| | Avalon/I Can't Give You Anything But Love/Nagasaki) - v | |

   Jock Fleming-tb added.               London, September 28, 1936.

| | | |
|---|---|---|
| CA-15944-1 | Basin Street Blues - v | Col FB-1520, DW-4397 |
| CA-15945-1 | Tiger Rag | -            - |

   Scott Wood db pac*; girl v (? Lavaida Carter); Gardner db. ts.
                                           London, October 22, 1936.

| | | |
|---|---|---|
| CA-15994-1 | Harlem | Col FB-1549, DW-4404, DW-4472, |
| | | RZ G-23016 |
| CA-15995-1 | Hot Pie (Second Helping) - Part 1 | Col FB-1556 |
| | (Intro. The Sheik Of Araby/Fascinating Rhythm/Bye-Bye, Blackbird) | |
| CA-15996-1 | Hot Pie (Second Helping) - Part 2 | - |
| | (Intro. If You Knew Susie/Vamping Rose/San) | |
| CA-15997-1 | *Organ Grinder's Swing - v(? LC) | Col FB-1549, DW-4404, RZ G-23016 |

                                           London, December 2, 1936.

| | | |
|---|---|---|
| CA-16080-1 | When A Lady Meets A Gentleman Down | Col FB-1578, RZ G-23062 |
| | South - v | |
| CA-16081-1 | You've Got To Blow Your Own Trumpet - v | -            - |

                                           London, January 6, 1937.

| | | |
|---|---|---|
| CA-16142-1 | Creole Lullaby - v | Col FB-1618 |
| CA-16143-1 | We're Tired Of That Tiger - v | - |

                                           London, February 25, 1937.

| | | |
|---|---|---|
| CA-16244-1 | Swing For Sale - v | Col FB-1656, DW-4454 |
| CA-16245-1 | On The Isle Of Kitchymiboko - v | - |
| CA-16248-1 | Jazz In The Rain (Jam Session) | Col FB-1684, DW-4461 |
| CA-16249-1 | Two-Gun Dan | -            - |

SCOTT WOOD AND HIS SIX SWINGERS : George Scott Wood-p-a dir. Bill Gaskin-t/Jock
  Fleming-tb/Freddy Gardner-cl-as-ts-bar/Joe Young-g/Dick Escott-sb/Sid Heiger-d.
                                     London, March 18, 1937.

| | | |
|---|---|---|
| CA-16295-1 | Chicago | Col FB-1666, DW-4468 |
| CA-16296-1 | Beale Street Blues | -       - |

  Eddie Pratt-cl-as replaces Gardner.      London, June 19, 1937.

| | | |
|---|---|---|
| CA-16428-1 | Spooky Takes A Holiday | Col FB-1731 |
| CA-16429-1 | Whoa Babe | - |
| CA-16430-1 | Slap That Bass - v | Col FB-1723, DW-4502 |
| CA-16431-1 | Beginner's Luck - v | -       - |

                             London, September 1, 1937.

| | | |
|---|---|---|
| CA-16534-1 | Twilight In Turkey | Col FB-1765, DW-4504, RZ G-23350 |
| CA-16535-1 | The Toy Trumpet | -      -      - |

  Billy Farrell-t replaces Gaskin; Dave Shand-cl-as replaces Pratt.
                        London, October 7, 1937.

| | | |
|---|---|---|
| CA-16601-1 | Just A Wee Deoch-an-Doris | Cpl FB-1792, DO-1784, DW-4515 |
| CA-16602-1 | Gettin' Thro' The Rye | -     -     - |

  The personnels are virtually impossible to determine from this point on, but they
  probably do not vary materially from the foregoing.
                           London, November 12, 1937.

| | | |
|---|---|---|
| CA-16698-1 | Hot Pie No. 3 - Part 1 (Intro. | Col FB-1832 |
| | I Got Rhythm/China Boy/Alice Blue Gown) | |
| CA-16699-1 | Hot Pie No. 3 - Part 2 (Intro. | - |
| | Hot Lips/Aunt Hagar's Blues/Am I Blue ?) | |

                             London, November 30, 1937.

| | | |
|---|---|---|
| CA-16724-1 | The Swingsome Reel | Col FB-1864 |
| CA-16725-2 | Mary O' Argyle | - |
| CA-16726-1 | I'm Getting Sentimental Over You | Col FB-1852 |

                             London, February 7, 1938.

| | | |
|---|---|---|
| CA-16840-1 | The Snake Charmer - v | Col FB-1903, DW-4577 |
| CA-16841-1 | S. O. S. | - |

                             London, April 2, 1938.

| | | |
|---|---|---|
| CA-16926-1 | Georgianna - v | Col FB-1946 |
| CA-16927-1 | Night-Time In Cairo | -       DW-4577 |

                             London, May 10, 1938.

| | | |
|---|---|---|
| CA-16967-1 | You're An Education - v | Col FB-1961 |
| CA-16968-1 | Swing And Sway | |
| CA-16971-1 | Park Lane Strut | Col FB-1975, DO-1895, DW-4591 |
| CA-16972-1 | Who Stole The Jam ? - v4 | - RZ G-23531    - |

                             London, June 7, 1938.

| | | |
|---|---|---|
| CA-16994-1 | Allah's Holiday | Col FB-1988, DW-4599 |
| CA-16995-1 | Indianola | -       - |

                             London, July 6, 1938.

| | | |
|---|---|---|
| CA-17033-1 | So You Left Me For The Leader Of A | Col FB-2000, DO-1985 |
| | Swing Band - v | |
| CA-17034-1 | The Snoop | -       DO-1895 |

SCOTT WOOD AND HIS SIX SWINGERS : George Scott Wood-p-a dir. t/tb/cl-as/g/sb/d (from
the preceding roster of musicians); Georgette-v.
                                        London, August 29, 1938.

CA-17085-2  Minuet For A Modern Miss - vG        Col FB-2036, DO-1937, DW-4616
CA-17086-1  Plastered In Paris                     -          -         -

    Harry Robbins-x-vib, next session.   London, October 7, 1938.

CA-17135-1  Time And Time Again - v              Col FB-2060
CA-17136-2  Nellie Dean - v                      Col FB-2073, DW-4631
CA-17137-1  Ida, Sweet As Apple Cider              -          -
CA-17138-1  Change In Rhythm                      Col FB-2060

                                        London, December 1, 1938.

CA-17211-1  Stop Beatin' 'Round The Mulberry     Col FB-2097, DW-4678
              Bush - v
CA-17212-1  Joseph ! Joseph ! - v-girl             -
CA-17219-1  Rhythm In The Alphabet - v           Col FB-2113, DW-4678
CA-17220-1  Georgia's Got A Moon - v               -

                                        London, January 11, 1939.

CA-17286-1  Sha-Sha - v-girl                      Col FB-2138, DW-4742
CA-17287-2  The Latin Quarter - v4                  -          -
CA-17290-1  Where Is Alexander ? - v             Col FB-2166
CA-17291-1  I'm A Savage - v                      Col FB-2179, DW-4827, GN-5034

                                        London, February 9, 1939.

CA-17344-1  Frankie And Johnnie - v              Col FB-2166
CA-17347-1  Chinatown, My Chinatown              Col FB-2179, DW-4827, GN-5034

    The Cavendish Three-v.               London, April 1, 1939.

CA-17403-1  War Dance For Wooden Indians         Col FB-2217
CA-17404-1  Hold Tight - vC3                     Col FB-2204
CA-17405-1  Swingin' The Irish Reel - v          Col FB-2217
CA-17406-1  Mutiny In The Nursery - v            Col FB-2204, DO-1985

                                        London, May 31, 1939.

CA-17473-2  Chopsticks - vC3                     Col FB-2240, DW-4856, GN-700
CA-17474-1  Three Little Fishes - v4               -          -         -
CA-17475-1  Boogy Boogy Boo - v4                 Col FB-2252, GN-929
CA-17476-1  Patty Cake, Patty Cake (Baker's Man)-vC3  -       -

    Alice Mann-v.                        London, July 24, 1939.

CA-17543-1  Wish Me Luck As You Wave Me Goodbye- Col FB-2275, DO-2014
CA-17544-1  That Sly Old Gentleman (From Featherbed   -
              Lane) - vAM
CA-17552-1  The Ghost Of Smoky Joe - v4          Col FB-2288
CA-17553-1  Floogie Walk - v4                      -

                                        London, October 30, 1939.

CA-17646-1  Swinging The Washing On The Siegfried Col FB-2314
              Line - v
CA-17647-1  Berlin Or Bust - v                   Col FB-2315, DO-2042
CA-17648-1  Oh, Ain't It Grand To Be In The Navy ? Col FB-2314, DO-2084
              - v
CA-17649-1  An Apple For The Teacher - v         Col FB-2315, RZ G-23945
    NOTE:- Regal Zonophone G-23945 as THE RHYTHMIC TROUBADOURS.

SCOTT WOOD AND HIS SIX SWINGERS : George Scott Wood-p-a dir. t/tb/cl-as-bar/g/sb/d
(from the roster shown on page 1434); Sam Browne-v.
                                        London, December 7, 1939.

CA-17712-1  It's A Hap-Hap-Happy Day - vSB       Col FB-2342, DO-2061, GN-756
CA-17713-1  Bluebirds In The Moonlight - vSB            -              -       -
CA-17714-1  On The Outside Looking In - vSB      Col FB-2343, RZ G-24316
CA-17715-1  Fare Thee Well - vSB                       -
NOTE:- Regal Zonophone G-24316 as THE RHYTHMIC TROUBADOURS.

    George Barclay-v.                   London, January 30, 1940.

CA-17811-1  My Wubba Dolly - vGB                 Col FB-2383
CA-17812-1  Stop ! It's Wonderful - vGB                -
CA-17813-1  Give Out - vGB                       Col FB-2384
CA-17814-1  'Neath The Shanty Town Moon - vGB          -            DO-2084

                                        London, February 29, 1940.

CA-17859-1  Yodel In Swing - v                   Col FB-2406
CA-17860-1  In The Mood - v                            -
CA-17861-1  Bring Out The Little Brown Jug - v   Col FB-2391
CA-17862-1  They Would Wind Him Up And He Would
              Whistle - v

                                        London, March 21, 1940.

CA-17909-1  Turn On The Old Music Box - v        Col FB-2419
CA-17910-1  I Forgot The Little Things - v             -          RZ G-24262
NOTE:- Regal Zonophone G-24262 as THE RHYTHMIC TROUBADOURS.

                                        London, March 28, 1940.

CA-17915-1  Jumpin' Jive - v                     Col FB-2431
CA-17916-1  The Jitterbug - v                          -

See also Jack Whiting.

                            THE SIZZLERS

Eddie Grosso-cl-v/Fred Hall-reed or/Al Russo-g/Joseph Mayo-d.
                                        New York, November 27, 1928.

18903     Diga Diga Doo                          Ed 52463
18904     Somebody Stole My Gal                        -
N-598     Diga Diga Doo                          Rejected
N-599     Somebody Stole My Gal                        -

Instrumentation and personnel unknown, but it is worth noting that both of these
    titles were recorded a few weeks later for Victor by Bubber Miley and his Mileage
    Makers, q.v.  Coincidence ?              New York, April 22, 1930.

9635-     I Lost My Gal From Memphis            ARC rejected
9636-     Black Maria                                 -

                    CHARLIE SKEETE AND HIS ORCHESTRA

Charlie Skeete-p dir. Leonard Davis and another-t/Jimmy Harrison-tb/Gene Johnson-cl-
    as-bsx/cl-as/Clifton Glover-cl-ts-bsx/Joe Jones-bj/Bill Brown-bb/Tommy Benford-d.
                                        New York, June 8, 1926.

11031     Tampeekoe                             Ed 51775
11032     Deep Henderson                              -

                        SKEETER  SKOOT

Pseudonym on OKeh 41549 for Howard Joyner (see Bob Howard).

Dude Skiles-t/Bobby Blair-tb/Andy Kelly-cl/Johnny Black-p/Jack Skiles-g/Leroy Holmes
  or Harlan Queish-bj/George White-sb/Al Graham-d.
                                       Hollywood, December 17, 1936.

L-0365    Blackberry Jam                       Vri 584
L-0366    My Girl                              Vri 516
L-0367    I Can't Give You Anything But Love    —
L-0368    Farewell Blues                       Vri 584
   NOTE:- The matrix numbers of the above titles are sub-numbered 9, 10, 11 and 12;
   these are obviously not takes, but the real takes are not at present known.

## SKILLET DICK AND HIS FRYING PANS

Pseudonym on Champion for Syd Valentine and his Patent Leather Kids, q.v.

## BOB SKYLES AND HIS SKYROCKETS

This was a country-and-western unit that made eighteen titles in one session in the
Blue Bonnet Hotel, San Antonio, Texas, on October 25, 1938.  The instrumentation
varied from title to title, and while some were apparently by t/tb/cl-s/p/bb or sb/
d, often with piano-accordion added, others included whistles, saws, violins and
extra piano-accordions.  The interesting-looking titles might prove rewarding from
a jazz viewpoint; the others are waltzes or ballads.

## SLIM AND HIS HOT BOYS

See Slim Lamar (Victor V-38044).


## SLIM AND SLAM

See Slim Gaillard.


## ABE SMALL

ABE SMALL AND HIS MELODY BOYS : Abe Small-c dir. tb/cl-as/bsx/p/d.
                                       New York, January, 1923.

001-1    Aunt Hagar's Blues                    Strong 10002
002-1    I Wish I Could Shimmy Like My Sister Kate    —

009-4    Georgia Cabin Door                    Strong 10003
0010-2   Love's Lament (w)                      —

1-1640, 2-1641  Tomorrow (I'll Be In My Dixie   Fed/Sil 5228, Sil 2228
           Home)
1-1647, 2-1648, 3-1649  Sister Kate                —           —

ABE SMALL'S ROSEMONT ORCHESTRA : Same.   New York, c. March, 1923.

1-1748, 2-1749  Georgia Cabin Door            Fed/Sil 5246, Sil 2246
2-1752, 3-1753  Aggravatin' Papa                 —           —

                                       New York, c. April, 1923.

1-1924   Wabash Blues                         Fed 5277, Sil 2277
2-1927   Virginia Blues                          —           —
2-1929   Ma ! He's Kissing Me                 Fed 5279, Sil 2279

NOTE:- All Silvertone issues as ABE SMALL'S ROSEMONT MELODY BOYS.

## PAUL SMALL

Vocal, with own whistling, acc. by Hymie Wolfson-ts/Joe Venuti-vn/Terry Shand-Bobby
  van Eps-p/Eddie Lang-g.          New York, December 8, 1932.

265000-2  Till Tomorrow                       Col DB-1050
265001-2  Remember Our Romance                 —
265002-1-2  Fit As A Fiddle                   Rejected
265003-2  Baby                                Col DB-1070

Acc. by Ben Selvin-vn dir. Hymie Wolfson-ts/Joe Venuti-vn/Terry Shand-Bobby van Eps
p/Eddie Lang-g.                          New York, December 27, 1932.

265019-2  Hold Me                        Col DB-1096, Re G-21791
265020-1-2  It's Winter Again            Rejected
265021-1-2  Willow, Weep For Me               -
265022-2  Just A Little Home For The Old Folks   Col DB-1070

                                         New York, February 3, 1933.

265032-1-2  I'm Playing With Fire        Rejected
265033-2  My Darling                     Col DB-1091, Re G-21791
265034-2  There's A House On The Hill         -
265035-2  The Sidewalk Waltz             Col DB-1096

Other records by Paul Small may be of mild interest for their accompaniments.

## CORNELL (SMELSER) AND HIS ORCHESTRA

Leo McConville-Joe Lindwurm-t/Jack Teagarden-tb/Jimmy Dorsey-cl-as/Fletcher Hereford-
    as/Adrian Rollini-bsx/Cornell Smelser-pac/Irving Brodsky-p/Dick McDonough-g/Tex
    Hurst-sb/Stan King-d/Artie Dunn-v.     New York, February 7, 1930.

403746-A  Collegiate Love (No vocal, despite the   OK 41386, Od ONY-36069, 194380,
            labels on some issues)               A-286023, Par PNY-34065, R-785
403747-A  Accordion Joe - vAD           OK 41386, Od ONY-36069, A-221291,
                                         Par PNY-34063, R-758
403748-C  I Was Made To Love You - vAD  OK 41395, Od ONY-36064, 194380,
    NOTE:- Parlophone PNY-34059, PNY-34063 and PNY-   Par PNY-34059
34065 as PAUL LOCH AND HIS ORCHESTRA; R-758 as CABARET DANCE ORCHESTRA.

## SMILIN' SAM'S DIXIE STRUTTERS

Nathan Glantz-as dir. 2t/tb/ts/p/bj/bb/d.  New York, c. March 30, 1923.

8306, -A  Blue Hoosier Blues            Gnt 5124, Apex 410, St 9397

## SMITH  AND  LEE

See Douglas Williams.

## ANNE SMITH

Pseudonym on Harmograph for Ma Rainey, q.v.

## BESSIE SMITH

Bessie Smith, "The Empress of the Blues," made her first records during the early
    weeks of 1921 for Emerson in New York, according to a contemporary account, but as
    far as can be ascertained, these were never issued, certainly not on Emerson.

Vocal, acc. by Bubber Miley-c/Charlie Irvis-tb/Sidney Bechet-cl-ss/Clarence Williams
    p/Buddy Christian-bj.                 New York, c. January, 1923.

        I Wish I Could Shimmy Like My Sister Kate OK rejected

Acc. by Clarence Williams-p.             New York, February 15, 1923.

80862-1-2-3-4  'Tain't Nobody's Biz-ness If I Do  Col rejected
80863-1-2-3-4  Down-Hearted Blues               -

                                         New York, February 16, 1923.

80863-5  Down-Hearted Blues            Col A-3844
80864-3  Gulf Coast Blues                    -
80865-1-2-3-4  Keeps On A-Rainin' (Papa He Can't  Rejected
    Make No Time)
NOTE:- The Dutch Columbia DCH-112 was scheduled to include TWELFTH STREET RAG by
Louis Armstrong and his Hot Seven, OKeh matrix 80864, but by an error, Bessie
Smith's GULF COAST BLUES was used to press some copies.

Acc. by her Down Home Boys*(? Ernest Elliott-cl/Clarence Williams-p/? Buddy Christian-bj) or Clarence Williams-p only.    New York, April 11, 1923.

| | | |
|---|---|---|
| 80862-5-6-7 | 'Tain't Nobody's Biz-ness If I Do | Rejected |
| 80865-5-6-7 | Keeps On A-Rainin' (Papa He Can't Make No Time) | – |
| 80949-3 | *Aggravatin' Papa | Col A-3877 |
| 80950-2 | *Beale Street Mama | – |
| 80952-3 | Baby Won't You Please Come Home Blues | Col A-3888 |
| 80953-2 | Oh Daddy Blues | – |

New York, April 26, 1923.

| | | |
|---|---|---|
| 80862-10 | 'Tain't Nobody's Biz-ness If I Do | Col A-3898 |
| 80865-10 | Keeps On A-Rainin' (Papa He Can't Make No Time) | – |

Acc. by Fletcher Henderson-p.          New York, April 28, 1923.

| | | |
|---|---|---|
| 80995-2 | Mama's Got The Blues | Col A-3900 |
| 80996-1 | Outside Of That | – |

New York, June 14, 1923.

| | | |
|---|---|---|
| 81074-1-2-3 | Sittin' On The Curbstone Blues | Rejected |
| 81075-3 | Bleeding Hearted Blues | Col A-3936 |
| 81078-3 | Lady Luck Blues | Col A-3939 |
| 81079-3 | Yodling Blues | |

New York, June 15, 1923.

| | | |
|---|---|---|
| 81080-3 | Midnight Blues | Col A-3936 |

New York, June 21, 1923.

| | | |
|---|---|---|
| 81091-1-2-3 | Play 'Em For Mama, Sing 'Em For Me | Col rejected |
| 81092-1-2 | If You Don't I Know Who Will | – |

New York, June 22, 1923.

| | | |
|---|---|---|
| 81092-4 | If You Don't I Know Who Will | Col A-3942 |
| 81095-2 | Nobody In Town Can Bake A Sweet Jelly Roll Like Mine | – |

Acc. by Irving Johns-p.                New York, September 21, 1923.

| | | |
|---|---|---|
| 81225-1-2-3 | Dot 'Em Down Blues | Rejected |
| 81226-2 | Jail-House Blues | Col A-4001 |

Jimmy Jones-p added where shown.       New York, September 24, 1923.

| | | |
|---|---|---|
| 81231-1-2 | St. Louis Gal | Rejected |
| 81231-3 | St. Louis Gal - pJJ-IJ | Col 13005-D |
| 81232-2 | Sam Jones Blues | – |

Acc. by Jimmy Jones-p.                 New York, September 26, 1923.

| | | |
|---|---|---|
| 81237-3 | Graveyard Dream Blues | Col A-4001 |
| 81238-1-2-3 | Blue Bessie (The Bluest Gal In Tennessee) | Rejected |
| 81241-3 | Cemetery Blues | Col 13001-D, DF-3073, LF-217 |

Acc. by her Down Home Trio : Probably George Baquet-cl/Jimmy Jones-p/bj.
                               New York, September 27, 1923.

| | | |
|---|---|---|
| 81244-1-2-3-4 | Whoa, Tillie, Take Your Time | Col rejected |
| 81245-1-2-3 | My Sweetie Went Away | – |

Vocal duets with Clara Smith, acc. by Fletcher Henderson-p.
                                        New York, October 4, 1923.

81261-3  Far Away Blues                    Col 13007-D
81262-2  I'm Going Back To My Used To Be        —

Vocal, acc. by George Baquet-cl/? Jimmy Jones-p.
                                        New York, October 15, 1923.

81244-7  Whoa, Tillie, Take Your Time       Col 13000-D
81245-6  My Sweetie Went Away                   —

Acc. by Fletcher Henderson-p, with Coleman Hawkins-ts*.
                                        New York, October 16, 1923.

81283-1-2 *Any Woman's Blues                Rejected
81283-3  Any Woman's Blues                  Col 13001-D, DF-3073, LF-217

Acc. by Don Redman-cl/Fletcher Henderson-p.
                                        New York, December 4, 1923.

81391-3  Chicago Bound Blues                Col 14000-D
81392-3  Mistreatin' Daddy                      —

Acc. by Jimmy Jones-p/Harry Reser-g.    New York, January 8, 1924.

81464-4  Frosty Mornin' Blues              Col 14005-D
81465-1-2-3-4  Blue Bessie (The Bluest Gal In   Rejected
         Tennessee)

Acc. by Don Redman-cl/Fletcher Henderson-p.
                                        New York, January 9, 1924.

81466-1  Haunted House Blues                Col 14010-D
81469-2  Eavesdropper's Blues                   —
NOTE:- Matrices 81467/8 are by Dolly Kay, acc. by the Georgians, the latter q.v.

Acc. by Jimmy Jones-p/Harry Reser-g, or by her Jazz Band*; the instrumentation of
the latter is not known, but presumably it includes Jones and Reser.
                                        New York, January 10, 1924.

81470-4  Easy Come, Easy Go Blues          Col 14005-D
81471-1-2-3-4 *Rampart Street Blues        Rejected
81472-1-2-3-4 *Lawdy Lawdy Blues               —

Acc. by Robert Robbins-vn/Irving Johns-p/John Griffin-g, according to notation.
                                        New York, April 4, 1924.

81664-1  Sorrowful Blues - vn/g            Col 14020-D
81665-1-2 Sorrowful Blues - vn/p           Rejected
81668-3  Pinchbacks, Take 'Em Away - p     Col 14025-D
81669-2  Rockin' Chair Blues - vn/p        Col 14020-D

                                        New York, April 5, 1924.

81670-2  Ticket Agent, Ease Your Window Down-vn/p Col 14025-D

                                        New York, April 7, 1924.

81671-3  Boweavil Blues - p                 Col 14018-D

                                        New York, April 8, 1924.

81672-2  Hateful Blues - vn/p              Col 14023-D
81675-2  Frankie Blues - vn/p                  —

                                        New York, April 9, 1924.

81676-1  Moonshine Blues - p               Col 14018-D

Acc. by Porter Grainger-p/John Mitchell-bj/Clarence Conaway-u.
                                    New York, April 23, 1924.

81720-1-2-3  Banjo Blues                        Col rejected
81721-1-2-3  Four Flushin' Papa                     -

Acc. by Don Redman-as/Fletcher Henderson-p.
                                    New York, July 22, 1924.

81881-1  Lou'siana Low Down Blues               Col 14031-D
81882-1  Mountain Top Blues                         -

Acc. by Charlie Green-tb/Fletcher Henderson-p.
                                    New York, July 23, 1924.

81883-2  Work House Blues                       Col 14032-D
81884-4  House Rent Blues                           -

                                    New York, July 31, 1924.

81893-2  Salt Water Blues                       Col 14037-D

                                    New York, August 8, 1924.

81907-1  Rainy Weather Blues                    Col 14037-D

Joe Smith-c added.                  New York, September 26, 1924.

140062-2  Weeping Willow Blues                  Col 14042-D, 3172-D, Par R-2479,
                                                B-71092, PZ-11191
140063-3  The Bye Bye Blues                     Col 14042-D

Acc. by Fred Longshaw-p.            New York, December 4, 1924.

140161-1-2-3  Follow The Deal On Down           Col rejected
140162-I-2-3  Sinful Blues                          -

Acc. by Buster Bailey-Don Redman-cl/Fred Longshaw-p.
                                    New York, December 5, 1924.

140165-1-2-3-4  Dying Gambler's Blues           Col rejected
140166-1-2-3-4  Woman's Trouble Blues               -
140167-1-2-3-4  Love Me Daddy Blues                 -

                                    New York, December 6, 1924.

140170-4  Sing Sing Prison Blues               Col 14051-D

Acc. by Fred Longshaw-p.            New York, December 11, 1924.

140161-5  Follow The Deal On Down               Col 14052-D
140162-5  Sinful Blues                              -

Acc. by Buster Bailey-Don Redman-cl/Fred Longshaw-p.
                                    New York, December 12, 1924.

140165-5-6  Dying Gambler's Blues               Rejected
140166-6  Woman's Trouble Blues                 Col 14060-D
140167-5  Love Me Daddy Blues                       -

Acc. by Charlie Green-tb/Fred Longshaw-p.
                                    New York, December 13, 1924.

140176-2  Dying Gambler's Blues                 Col 14051-D

Acc. by Louis Armstrong-c/Fred Longshaw-p or reed organ as noted.
                                    New York, January 14, 1925.

140241-1  The St. Louis Blues - or          Col 14064-D, 3171-D, DF-3074,
                                             LF-218, SE 5010-S, Par R-2344,
                                             R-2476, A-7500, B-71093, PZ-11108
                                             Od 028032, 272289
140242-1  Reckless Blues - or                Col 14056-D, 3171-D, SE 5010-S,
                                             Par R-2476, A-7500, B-71093,
                                             PZ-11108, Od 028032
140249-2  Sobbin' Hearted Blues - p          Col 14056-D
140250-2  Cold In Hand Blues - p             Col 14064-D, 35672, DF-3074,
                                             LF-218, Par R-2344, Od 272289
140251-1  You've Been A Good Old Wagon - p   Col 14079-D, 35672
  NOTE:- Matrices 140243/6 inclusive are sermons by Calvin P. Dixon; 140247/8 are by
  Ollie Powers, q.v.

   Acc. by Henderson's Hot Six : Joe Smith-c/Charlie Green-tb/Buster Bailey-cl/Coleman
   Hawkins-ts/Fletcher Henderson-p/Charlie Dixon-bj/Ralph Escudero-bb.
                                    New York, May 5, 1925.

140585-2  Cake Walkin' Babies (From Home)    Col 35673, DS-1409, DZ-342

                                    New York, May 6, 1925.

140586-1  The Yellow Dog Blues               Col 14075-D
140586-2  The Yellow Dog Blues                      - 3175-D, Par R-2480, JCl 523
  NOTE:- Columbia 3175-D as BESSIE SMITH AND HER BLUE BOYS.

   Acc. by Charlie Green-tb/Fletcher Henderson-p.
                                    New York, May 14, 1925.

140600-1-2-3  Ragtime Dance                  Rejected
140601-1  Soft Pedal Blues                   Col 14075-D
140601-2  Soft Pedal Blues                          - Par R-2482, B-71092, PZ-11248

   Buster Bailey-cl added, with train effects*.
                                    New York, May 15, 1925.

140604-1-2-3  Careless Love Blues            Rejected
140605-1-2   He's Gone Blues                        -
140606-1-2   Nashville Woman's Blues                -
140607-1 *Dixie Flyer Blues                  Col 14079-D

   Acc. by Louis Armstrong-c/Charlie Green-tb/Fletcher Henderson-p.
                                    New York, May 26, 1925.

140625-2  Nashville Woman's Blues            Col 14090-D, Bm 1010
140625-3  Nashville Woman's Blues
140626-1  Careless Love Blues                Col 14083-D, 3172-D, Par R-2479,
                                             A-7709, B-71193, PZ-11191
140626-2  Careless Love Blues                Col 14083-D

                                    New York, May 27, 1925.

140629-2  J. C. Holmes Blues                 Col 14095-D, HJCA HC-67
140630-1  I Ain't Gonna Play No Second Fiddle  Col 14090-D, Bm 1010

   Acc. by Fred Longshaw-p.         New York, June 23, 1925.

140717-3  He's Gone Blues                     Col 14083-D

   Acc. by her Band : Bob Fuller-cl-as/Isadore Myers-p/Elmer Snowden-bj.
                                    New York, August 19, 1925

140857-3  Nobody's Blues But Mine            Col 14098-D
140858-3  I Ain't Got Nobody                 Col 14095-D, HJCA HC-101

Vocal duets with Clara Smith, acc. by Stanley Miller-p, who probably plays the part
  of Charlie Grey on 140890-2.          New York, September 1, 1925.

| | | |
|---|---|---|
| 140889-1-2-3 | Down Old Georgia Way | Rejected |
| 140890-2 | My Man Blues | Col 14098-D |

Vocal, acc. by Clarence Williams-p.    New York, November 17, 1925.

| | | |
|---|---|---|
| 141275-1-2-3-4-5 | I Wish I Could Shimmy Like My Sister Kate | Rejected |
| 141276-3 | New Gulf Coast Blues | Col 14109-D |
| 141277-3 | Florida Bound Blues | - |

  Acc. by Joe Smith-c/Charlie Green-tb/Fletcher Henderson-p.
                               New York, November 18, 1925.

| | | |
|---|---|---|
| 141283-1 | At The Christmas Ball | Col 35842 |
| 141284-1-2-3 | Telephone Blues | Rejected |
| 141285-3 | I've Been Mistreated And I Don't Like It | Col 14115-D |

  Acc. by Don Redman-cl-as/Fletcher Henderson-p.
                               New York, November 20, 1925.

| | | |
|---|---|---|
| 141293-2 | Red Mountain Blues - cl | Col 14115-D |
| 141294-2 | Golden Rule Blues - as | Col 14123-D, <u>HJCA 608, Tpl 523</u> |

  Acc. by Shelton Hemphill-c/Fred Longshaw-p.
                               New York, December 9, 1925.

| | | |
|---|---|---|
| 141369-1-2-3 | At The Christmas Ball | Rejected |
| 141370-3 | Lonesome Desert Blues | Col 14123-D, <u>HJCA 608, Tpl 523</u> |
| 141373-1-2-3 | Squeeze Me | Rejected |

  Acc. by Clarence Williams-p.         New York, March 5, 1926.

| | | |
|---|---|---|
| 141767-2 | Them "Has Been" Blues | Col 14147-D, HJCA HC-105 |
| 141768-3 | Squeeze Me | Col 14133-D, <u>Bm 1095, HJCA HC-81</u> |
| 141769-2 | What's The Matter Now ? | Col 14129-D, <u>Bm 1039</u> |
| 141770-2 | I Want Ev'ry Bit Of It | -    <u>Bm 1040</u> |
| NOTE:- Some copies of HJCA HC-105 play a dubbing of NOBODY KNOWS YOU WHEN YOU'RE DOWN AND OUT 148534, q.v.) though labelled as shown above. | | |

  Acc. by Buster Bailey-cl/Fletcher Henderson-p.
                               New York, March 18, 1926.

| | | |
|---|---|---|
| 141819-2 | Jazzbo Brown From Memphis Town | Col 14133-D, Bm 1095, HJCA HC-81 |
| 141820-3 | The Gin House Blues | Col 14158-D, <u>HJCA HC-77</u> |

  Acc. by Joe Smith-c/Fletcher Henderson-p.
                               New York, May 4, 1926.

| | | |
|---|---|---|
| 142146-3 | Money Blues | Col 14137-D, 3174-D, Par R-2478 |
| 142147-2 | Baby Doll | Col 14147-D, <u>35674, DF-2264,</u> DZ-379, UHCA 6 |
| 142148-3 | Hard Driving Papa | <u>Col 14137-D</u> |
| 142149-1 | Lost Your Head Blues | Col 14158-D, <u>35674</u> |

  Acc. by Fletcher Henderson-p.        New York, October 25, 1926.

| | | |
|---|---|---|
| 142874-2 | Hard Time Blues | Col 14179-D |
| 142875-3 | Honey Man Blues | Col 14172-D |

  Acc. by her Blue Boys : Joe Smith-c/Buster Bailey-cl/Fletcher Henderson-p.
                               New York, October 26, 1926.

| | | |
|---|---|---|
| 142876-2 | One And Two Blues | Col 14172-D, <u>36281, HRS 2</u> |
| 142877-1-2-3 | It's Just That Feelin' For Home | Rejected |
| 142878-3 | Young Woman's Blues | Col 14179-D, 35673, DS-1409, <u>DZ-342, S-10002, UHCA 5</u> |

Acc. by James P. Johnson-p.                    New York, February 17, 1927.

143490-2  Preachin' The Blues                  Col 14195-D, 35842, Par R-2483,
                                                B-71094
143491-1  Back Water Blues                     Col 14195-D, 3176-D, Par R-2481,
                                                A-7588, PZ-11174, HJCA HC-105

BESSIE SMITH AND HER BAND : Vocal, acc. by Joe Smith-c/Jimmy Harrison-tb/Buster Bailey
    and/or Coleman Hawkins-cl as noted/Fletcher Henderson-p/Charlie Dixon-bj.
                                                New York, March 2, 1927.

143567-2  After You've Gone - clBB             Col 14197-D, Bm 1094, BRS 14,
                                                HJCA HC-65
143568-1  Alexander's Ragtime Band - clCH      Col 14219-D, 3173-D, Par R-2477,
                                                B-71231, DPY-1010, BRS 1012
143569-2  Muddy Water (A Mississippi Moan)-clBB-CH  Col 14197-D
143569-3  Muddy Water (A Mississippi Moan)-clBB-CH     - 3174-D, Par R-2478, B-71207
143570-2  There'll Be A Hot Time In The Old Town  Col 14219-D, 3173-D, Par R-2477,
            Tonight - clBB                      A-7709, B-71231, BRS 1012

Vocal, acc. by her Blue Boys : Joe Smith-c/Charlie Green-tb/Fletcher Henderson-p.
                                                New York, March 3, 1927.

143575-3  Trombone Cholly                      Col 14232-D, 3175-D, Par R-2480,
                                                B-71220, JC1 523
143576-2  Send Me To The 'Lectric Chair        Col 14209-D, Bm 1008
143583-2  Them's Graveyard Words                   -          -
143584-2  Hot Springs Blues                    Col 14569-D, DZ-345

Acc. by James P. Johnson-p.                    New York, April 1, 1927.

143735-3  Sweet Mistreater                     Col 14260-D
143736-3  Lock And Key                         Col 14232-D

Acc. by Porter Grainger-p/Lincoln M. Conaway-g.
                                                New York, September 27, 1927.

144796-3  Mean Old Bed Bug Blues               Col 14250-D
144797-3  A Good Man Is Hard To Find               - Bm 1094, BRS 14, HJCA HC-65

Acc. by Ernest Elliott-as/Porter Grainger-p.
                                                New York, September 28, 1927.

144800-3  Homeless Blues                       Col 14260-D
144801-3  Looking For My Man Blues             Col 14569-D, DZ-345

Acc. by Tommy Ladnier-t/Fletcher Henderson-p/June Cole-bb.
                                                New York, October 27, 1927.

144918-1  Dyin' By The Hour                    Col 14273-D, DZ/MZ-346, BRS 1002,
                                                JC1 522
144919-3  Foolish Man Blues                    As above

Acc. by Demas Dean-t/Charlie Green-tb/Fred Longshaw-p.
                                                New York, February 9, 1928.

145626-2  Thinking Blues                       Col 14292-D, Par R-2483, B-71095
145627-1-2  Pickpocket Blues                   Col 14304-D
145628-1  I Used To Be Your Sweet Mama         Col 14292-D, Par R-2482, B-71095,
                                                PZ-11248

Acc. by Ernest Elliott-Bob Fuller-cl/Porter Grainger-p.
                                                New York, February 16, 1928.

145650-2  I'd Rather Be Dead And Buried In My Grave Col 14304-D
145651-1-2  Hit Me In The Nose Blues                Rejected

Acc. by Demas Dean-t/Charlie Green-tb/Fred Longshaw-p.
New York, February 21, 1928.

| | | |
|---|---|---|
| 145670-1 | Standin' In The Rain Blues | Col 14338-D, HJCA 613 |
| 145671-1 | It Won't Be You | — |
| 145672-1-2 | I'm A Cheater | Rejected |

Acc. by Abraham Wheat-cl-ss/Bob Fuller-cl/Porter Grainger-p.
New York, March 19, 1928.

| | | |
|---|---|---|
| 145783-2 | Spider Man Blues | Col 14324-D |
| 145784-1-2-3 | Tombstone Blues | Rejected |

Acc. by Charlie Green-tb/Porter Grainger-p.
New York, March 20, 1928.

| | | |
|---|---|---|
| 145785-3 | Empty Bed Blues - Part 1 | Col 14312-D, 35675, DB-2796, BF-397, DW-5104, DZ-349, Voc 03286 |
| 145786-1 | Empty Bed Blues - Part 2 | As above |
| 145787-3 | Put It Right Here (Or Keep It Out There) | Col 14324-D |

Acc. by Bob Fuller-cl-as/Ernest Elliott-cl-as-ts/Porter Grainger-p, with Joe
Williams-tb added*. New York, August 24, 1928.

| | | |
|---|---|---|
| 146887-2 | Yes Indeed He Do | Col 14354-D |
| 146888-2 | Devil's Gonna Get You | — |
| 146889-3 | You Ought To Be Ashamed | Col 14399-D |
| 146893-2 | Washwoman's Blues | Col 14375-D |
| 146894-2 | Slow And Easy Man | Col 14384-D |
| 146895-1 | *Poor Man's Blues | Col 14399-D, HJCA 602 |

Acc. by Joe Williams-tb/Porter Grainger-p.
New York, August 25, 1928.

| | | |
|---|---|---|
| 146896-2 | Please Help Me Get Him Off My Mind | Col 14375-D, HJCA 602 |
| 146897-3 | Me And My Gin | Col 14384-D, HJCA HC-77 |

Acc. by Clarence Williams-p/Eddie Lang-g.
New York, May 8, 1929.

| | | |
|---|---|---|
| 148485-3 | I'm Wild About That Thing | Col 14427-D, DZ-378, Har 1086, Bm 1009 |
| 148486-2 | You've Got To Give Me Some | As above |
| 148487-4 | Kitchen Man | Col 14435-D, Bm 1040, HJCA 613 |

Acc. by Ed Allen-c/Garvin Bushell-as/Greely Walton-ts/Clarence Wil iams-p/Cyrus St.
Clair-bb. New York, May 15, 1929.

| | | |
|---|---|---|
| 148533-2 | I've Got What It Takes (But It Breaks My Heart To Give It Away) | Col 14435-D, Bm 1041, HJCA 613 |
| 148534-3 | Nobody Knows You When You're Down And Out | Col 14451-D, 3176-D, 37577, DF-2264, Par R-2481, A-7588, B-71076, B-71094, PZ-11174 |

Acc. by J. Rosamond Johnson and the Hall Johnson Choir (40 mixed voices) and James
P. Johnson-p dir. Joe Smith-Russell Smith-? Sidney de Paris-t/Charlie Green-tb/
Buster Bailey-cl/Happy Caldwell-ts/Charlie Dixon-bj/Harry Hull-bb/Kaiser Marshall-
d. (Soundtrack of film ST. LOUIS BLUES).New York, c. June 24, 1929.

| | | |
|---|---|---|
| NY-39 | St. Louis Blues - Part 1 | Cir J-1016 |
| NY-40 | St. Louis Blues - Part 2 | |
| NY-41 | St. Louis Blues - Part 3 | Cir J-1017 |
| NY-42 | St. Louis Blues - Part 4 | — |

Acc. by Clarence Williams-p. New York, July 25, 1929.

| | | |
|---|---|---|
| 148854-3 | Take It Right Back ('Cause I Don't Want It Here) | Col 14451-D |
| 148855-1-2-3 | What Makes Me Love You So ? | Rejected |

Acc. by James P. Johnson-p.                New York, August 20, 1929.

148901-1-2-3  My Sportin' Man                Rejected
148902-2  He's Got Me Goin'                  Col 14464-D
148903-1-2  When My Baby Comes               Rejected
148904-1  It Makes My Love Come Down         Col 14464-D, Bm 1038

                                 New York, October 1, 1929.

149074-3  Wasted Life Blues                  Col 14476-D, Bm 1038
149075-1  Dirty No-Gooder's Blues            -

                                 New York, October 11, 1929.

149134-3  Blue Spirit Blues                  Col 14527-D, Bm 1039
149135-3  Worn Out Papa Blues                -            Bm 1041
149136-2  You Don't Understand               Col 14487-D
149137-2  Don't Cry Baby                     -

Acc. by Louis Bacon-t/Charlie Green-tb/Garvin Bushell-cl-as/Clarence Williams-p.
                          New York, March 27, 1930.

150131-3  Keep It To Yourself                Col 14516-D, HJCA HC-101
150132-2  New Orleans Hop Scop Blues         -            37577

Acc. by Charlie Green-tb/Clarence Williams-p.
                          New York, April 12, 1930.

150458-3  See If I'll Care                   Col 37576
150459-3  Baby Have Pity On Me               -

Acc. by James P. Johnson-p, with the Bessemer Singers.
                          New York, June 9, 1930.

150574-4  On Revival Day (A Rhythmic Spiritual)  Col 14538-D, HJCA HC-29
150575-4  Moan, You Mourners                 -            -

Acc. by Ed Allen-c/Steve Stevens-p.        New York, July 22, 1930.

150657-1  Hustlin' Dan                       Col 14554-D, HJCA 608, Tpl 522
150658-2  Black Mountain Blues               -            -      -

Acc. by Louis Metcalf-t/William W. Christian-tb/? Clarence Williams-p/d.
                          New York, June 11, 1931.

151594-1  In The House Blues                 Col 14611-D, Par R-2329, B-71193,
                                             PZ-11285, Od 028077, HJCA 602
151595-3  Long Old Road                      Col 14663-D, HJCA HC-62
151596-1  Blue Blue                          Col 14611-D, HJCA 602
151597-3  Shipwreck Blues                    Col 14663-D, HJCA HC-62

Acc. by Clarence Williams-p.               New York, November 20, 1931.

151883-1  Need A Little Sugar In My Bowl     Col 14634-D
151884-1  Safety Mama                        -

Acc. by Buck and his Band : Frank Newton-t/Jack Teagarden-tb/Benny Goodman-cl/Chu
Berry-ts/Buck Washington-p/Bobby Johnson-g/Billy Taylor-sb.
                          New York, November 24, 1933.

152577-2  Do Your Duty                       OK 8945, Col 37575, DS-1538,
                                             UHCA 47, Par R-1793, A-7548,
                                             B-71192, Od 026927
152578-2  Gimme A Pigfoot                    OK 8949, 6893, Col 37574, DS-1601,
                                             UHCA 49, Par R-2146, B-71096
152579-2  Take Me For A Buggy Ride           As above but UHCA 50 (rev. UHCA 49)
152580-2  I'm Down In The Dumps              OK 8945, Col 37575, DS-1538,
                                             UHCA 48, (rev. UHCA 47), Par R-1793,
                                             A-7548, B-71192, Od 026927

Pseudonym on Varsity 5078 for the Original Indiana Five, q.v. The Cal Smith who made a few sides for Gennett with his American Orchestra in 1922 is not the same as the banoist-guitarist with the Dixieland Jug Blowers and Clifford Hayes' Louisville Stompers, both q.v.

## CLARA SMITH

Vocal, acc. by Fletcher Henderson-p.     New York, May 31, 1923.

| | | |
|---|---|---|
| 81059-1-2-3 | I Got Everything A Woman Needs | Col rejected |
| 81060-1-2-3 | Every Woman's Blues | - |

New York, June 28, 1923.

| | | |
|---|---|---|
| 81059-6 | I Got Everything A Woman Needs | Col A-3943 |
| 81060-5 | Every Woman's Blues | - |

New York, July 27, 1923.

| | | |
|---|---|---|
| 81150-5 | Kind Lovin' Blues | Col A-3961 |
| 81151-3 | Down South Blues | - |
| 81153-3 | All Night Blues | Col A-3966 |
| 81154-2 | Play It A Long Time Papa | - |

Elmer Chambers-c added*.     New York, August 31, 1923.

| | | |
|---|---|---|
| 81183-1 | I Want My Sweet Daddy Now | Col A-3991 |
| 81184-1 | *Irresistible Blues | - |

Acc. by Joe Smith-c/Don Redman-cl/Fletcher Henderson-p.
     New York, September 6, 1923.

| | | |
|---|---|---|
| 81198-1-2-3 | Don't Never Tell Nobody | Col rejected |
| 81199-1-2-3 | Georgia Blues | - |

Acc. by Fletcher Henderson-p.     New York, September 7, 1923.

| | | |
|---|---|---|
| 81202-2 | I Never Miss The Sunshine (I'm So Used To The Rain) | Col A-4000 |

New York, September 13, 1923.

| | | |
|---|---|---|
| 81210-3 | Awful Moanin' Blues | Col A-4000 |

Acc. by Stanley Miller-p.     New York, September 18, 1923.

| | | |
|---|---|---|
| 81221-1-2-3 | Goin' Down To The Levee | Col rejected |
| 81222-1-2-3 | Kansas City Man Blues | - |

Acc. by Fletcher Henderson-p.     New York, October 1, 1923.

| | | |
|---|---|---|
| 81198-4 | Don't Never Tell Nobody | Col 13002-D |
| 81250-2 | Waitin' For The Evenin' Mail | - |

New York, October 2, 1923.

| | | |
|---|---|---|
| 81222-6 | Kansas City Man Blues | Col 12-D |
| 81253-2 | Uncle Sam Blues | - |

NOTE:- 81222-6 credits the piano accompaniment to STANLEY MILLER.

Vocal duets with Bessie Smith, acc. by Fletcher Henderson-p.
     New York, October 4, 1923.

| | | |
|---|---|---|
| 81261-3 | Far Away Blues | Col 13007-D |
| 81262-2 | I'm Going Back To My Used To Be | - |

CLARA SMITH AND HER JAZZ BAND : Vocal, acc. by t/tb/cl/? Stanley Miller-p/bj.
                                          New York, January 11, 1924.

81476-1   It Won't Be Long Now                Col 14006-D
81477-3   Hot Papa                            -

Vocal, acc. by her Jazz Trio : Porter Grainger-k/Lincoln M. Conaway-g/Clarence Con-
   away-md.                                 New York, January 18, 1924.

81495-1   I'm Gonna Tear Your Playhouse Down   Col 14013-D
81496-1   I Don't Love Nobody (So I Don't Have Col 14016-D
             No Blues)

   Acc. by Ernest Elliott-cl-as (as noted)/Charles A. Matson-p.
                                          New York, January 29, 1924.

81508-1   Good Looking Papa Blues - cl        Col 14026-D
81509-1   You Don't Know My Mind - as         Col 14013-D

   Acc. by her Jazz Trio (Porter Grainger-k/Herbert Leonard-h/Lincoln M. Conaway-g) or
   her Jazz Band (Elmer Chambers-c/Teddy Nixon-tb/Don Redman-cl/Fletcher Henderson-p/
   Charlie Dixon-bj) as shown.            New York, January 31, 1924.

81512-2   My Doggone Lazy Man - J3            Col 14016-D
81513-2   Chicago Blues - JB                  Col 14009-D
81514-2   31st Street Blues - JB              -

   Acc. by Don Redman-cl/Fletcher Henderson-p.

                                          New York, April 10, 1924.

81683-2   War Horse Mama (Pig Meat Sweetie)   Col 14021-D
81684-1   Cold Weather Papa                   -

   Acc. by Fletcher Henderson-u/Charlie Dixon-g (despite the labels of the third and
   fourth sides, no p is audible).       New York, April 17, 1924.

81694-1-2-3  Back Woods Blues                 Rejected
81695-3   West Indies Blues                   Col 14019-D
81697-2   Mean Papa, Turn In Your Key         Col 14022-D
81698-2   The Clearing House Blues            Col 14019-D

   Acc. by Porter Grainger-p/Clarence Conaway-g or u.
                                          New York, April 23, 1924.

81722-1   Don't Advertise Your Man - u        Col 14026-D
81723-1-2-3  Mama's Gone, Goodbye - g         Rejected

   Acc. by Fletcher Henderson-u/Charlie Dixon-g.
                                          New York, April 30, 1924.

81694-4   Back Woods Blues                    Col 14022-D

   Acc. by Coleman Hawkins-ts/Fletcher Henderson-p.
                                          New York, August 19, 1924.

81931-3   Deep Blue Sea Blues                 Col 14034-D
81932-1   Texas Moaner Blues                  -

   Acc. by Ernest Elliott-cl-as as noted/Charles A. Matson-p.
                                          New York, September 20, 1924.

140052-1  Basement Blues - cl                 Col 14039-D
140053-4  Mama's Gone, Goodbye - as           -

   Acc. by her Jazz Trio (Don Redman-gfs/Cecil Scott-cl/Porter Grainger-p) or Don Red-
   man-cl/Porter Grainger-p.             New York, September 30, 1924.

140064-3  Freight Train Blues - J3            Col 14041-D
140076-3  Done Sold My Soul To The Devil (And My  -
             Heart's Done Turned To Stone) - clDR/pPG

Acc. by Cecil Scott-Don Redman-cl/Fletcher Henderson-p.
New York, October 7, 1924.

```
140090-1-2-3  Broken Busted Blues              Rejected
140091-2  San Francisco Blues                  Col 14049-D
```

Acc. by her Jazz Trio : Elmer Chambers-c/Don Redman-cl/Porter Grainger-p.
New York, October 15, 1924.

```
140108-1  Death Letter Blues                   Col 14045-D
140109-1  Prescription For The Blues           -
```

Acc. by Ernest Elliott-as/Porter Grainger-p, with percussion effects on 140181-2.
New York, December 16, 1924.

```
140181-2  Steel Drivin' Sam                    Col 14053-D
140182-1  He's Mine, All Mine                  -
```

Acc. by Cecil Scott-Don Redman-cl/Fletcher Henderson-p.
New York, December 20, 1924.

```
140090-4-5-6  Broken Busted Blues              Rejected
140200-1-2  Nobody Knows The Way I Feel Dis Mornin'   -
```

Acc. by Louis Armstrong-c/Charlie Green-tb/Fletcher Henderson-p.
New York, January 7, 1925.

```
140226-1  Nobody Knows The Way I Feel 'Dis Mornin' Col 14058-D
140227-2  Broken Busted Blues                  Col 14062-D
```

Acc. by Leon Abbey-vn/Porter Grainger-p.
New York, January 8, 1925.

```
140230-3  If You Only Knowed                   Col 14058-D
140231-2  You Better Keep The Home Fires Burning  Col 14062-D
          ('Cause Your Mama's Getting Cold)
```

Acc. by Louis Armstrong-c/Fletcher Henderson-p.
New York, January 17, 1925.

```
140266-1-2  My John Blues                      Col rejected
140267-1-2  Shipwrecked Blues                  -
```

Acc. by Herbert Leonard-h/Leonard Myers-g.
New York, March 24, 1925.

```
140459-3  My Good-For-Nuthin' Man             Col 14069-D
140460-1-2-3  Rock Pile Blues                  Rejected
```

Acc. by Lemuel Fowler-p.          New York, March 27, 1925.

```
140470-1  When I Steps Out                     Col 14069-D
140471-1  The L & N Blues                      Col 14073-D
```

Acc. by Louis Armstrong-c/Fletcher Henderson-p, with Charlie Green-tb*.
New York, April 3, 1925.

```
140491-1  Shipwrecked Blues                    Col 14077-D, HJCA HC-107
140492-1  Courthouse Blues                     Col 14073-D
140493-1  *My John Blues                       Col 14077-D, HJCA HC-107
```

Acc. by her Jazz Band : T/as/p/bj/w.   New York, July 6, 1925.

```
140751-1  Different Way Blues                  Col 14085-D
140752-1  Down Home Bound Blues                -
```

Acc. by her Band : Bob Fuller-cl-as (as noted)/Stanley Miller-p/Buddy Christian-
bj.                               New York, August 20, 1925.

```
140859-3  My Two-Timing Papa - as             Col 14097-D
140860-1  Kitchen Mechanic Blues - cl          -
```

Vocal duets with Bessie Smith, acc. by Stanley Miller-p, who probably plays the part
  of Charlie Grey on 140890-2.            New York, September ,1, 1925.

140889-1-2-3  Down Old Georgia Way              Rejected
140890-2  My Man Blues                          Col 14098-D

CLARA SMITH AND HER JAZZ BAND : Vocal, acc. by tb/cl/p/bj.
                                       New York, September 16, 1925.

140945-1-2-3  I'm Tired Of Bein' Good           Col rejected
140946-1      'Tain't Nobody's Fault But Yours  -

    Acc. by her Jazz Band (Bud Allen's Blues Trio) : Teddy Nixon-tb/Prince Robinson-cl/
    Mike Jackson-p.                     New York, September 24, 1925.

141044-1  Onery Blues                           Col 14117-D
141045-1  You Get Mad                           Col 14126-D

    Acc. by her Jazz Band : Harry Cooper-c/Bob Fuller-cl-as/Stanley Miller-p/Buddy
    Christian-bj.                       New York, September 25, 1925.

141046-2  Alley Rat Blues                       Col 14104-D
141047-1  When My Sugar Walks Down The Street
141048-1-2  You'll Never Miss Your Water        Rejected
141049-1  Disappointed Blues                    Col 14126-D

    Acc. by her Jazz Band : Tb/cl/p/bj.    New York, September 28, 1925.

140945-5  I'm Tired Of Bein' Good               Col 14117-D

    Acc. by Ernest Elliott-cl-as/Harry Stevens-cl-bsx/Porter Grainger-p.
                                       New York, November 10, 1925.

141257-3  The Market Street Blues               Col 14108-D
141258-3  It Takes The Lawd (To Tell What's On My Mind)-
141259-1-2-3  Caught You Triflin' Blues         Rejected

    Acc. by her Novelty Band : Tom Edwards-tb/Clarence Adams-cl/Stanley Miller-p/Herman
    Gibson-bj.                          New York, May 1, 1926.

142117-1  Look Where The Sun Done Gone          Col 14138-D
142118-2  Rock, Church, Rock                    -

    Gibson omitted.                    New York, May 3, 1926.

142136-1  So Long                               Rejected
142137-3  Jelly Bean Blues                      Col 14294-D

    Acc. by Lemuel Fowler-p.           New York, May 25, 1926.

142250-3  How'm I Doin'                         Col 14150-D
142251-1  Whip It To A Jelly                    -

    Acc. by Fletcher Henderson-p.      New York, May 26, 1926.

142252-1  Salty Dog                             Col 14143-D
142253-2-3  My Brand New Papa                   -

    Acc. by Clarence Parson-p.         New York, June 15, 1926.

142300-2-3  Ain't Nothin' Cookin' What You're   Col 14160-D
              Smellin'
142301-2-3  Separation Blues                    -

    Acc. by Lemuel Fowler-p, with Sisters White and Wallace-v*.
                                       New York, November 23, 1926.

143140-1  Percolatin' Blues                     Col 14202-D
143141-3  Ease It                               -
143142-2  *Livin' Humble                        Col 14183-D, 8938
143143-1  *Get On Board                         -           -

Acc. by Ernest Elliott-as/Porter Grainger-p.

                              New York, November 29, 1926.

143155-3  Cheatin' Daddy                    Col 14192-D
143156-1-2-3  Deep Down In My Soul          Rejected

    Acc. by her Jazz Babies : Joe Smith-c/ts/Stanley Miller-p/bj.
                              New York, December 30, 1926.

143230-3  You Don't Know Who's Shakin' Your Tree   Col 14192-D
143231-3  Race Track Blues                  Col 14294-D
143232-1-2-3  The Old Folks Hunch           Rejected

    Acc. by Ernest Elliott-cl-as (as noted)/Clarence Parson-p.
                              New York, April 7, 1927.

144000-2  Troublesome Blues - as            Col 14256-D
144001-3  You Can't Get It Now - cl               -

    Acc. by Bob Fuller-as/Porter Grainger-p.
                              New York, June 1, 1927.

144249-1-2  That's Why The Undertakers Are Busy   Col 14223-D
            Today
144250-1  Black Woman's Blues                     -

    Acc. by her Five Black Kittens : Gus Aiken-c/Bob Fuller-cl-as/Stanley Miller-p.
                              New York, July 30, 1927.

144527-2  Black Cat Moan                    Col 14240-D
144528-2  Strugglin' Woman's Blues                -

    Acc. by ? Porter Grainger-p/as.   New York, May 10, 1928.

146244-2  Jelly, Look What You Done Done    Col 14319-D
146245-3  It's All Coming Home To You             -

    Acc. by Lemuel Fowler-p.          New York, May 21, 1928.

146310-1-2-3-4  Down And Out Blues         Rejected
146311-2  Gin Mill Blues                    Col 14419-D

    Acc. by Freddy Jenkins-t/John Anderson-tb/Porter Grainger-p.
                              New York, May 23, 1928.

146324-3  Steamboat Man Blues               Col 14344-D
146325-1  Sobbin' Sister Blues                    -

    Acc. by Joe Smith-c/cl/Marion Cumbo-vc/Stanley Miller-p.
                              New York, July 6, 1928.

146507-1  Got My Mind On That Thing         Col 14419-D
146508-1-2-3  Ain't Got Nobody To Grind My Coffee  Rejected

    Acc. by Marion Cumbo-vc/Stanley Miller-reed or.
                              New York, July 13, 1928.

146636-1  Wanna Go Home                     Col 14368-D

    Acc. by k/cl/p/g.                 New York, August 9, 1928.

146828-3  Ain't Got Nobody To Grind My Coffee   Col 14368-D

    Acc. by ? Emerson Harper and another-cl/? Porter Grainger-p.
                              New York, January 17, 1929.

147851-3  Tell Me When                      Col 14409-D
147852-3  Empty House Blues                       -

Acc. by Charlie Green-tb/? Porter Grainger-p.
                                    New York, January 26, 1929.

147889-2  Daddy Don't Put That Thing On Me Blues   Col 14398-D
147890-3  It's Tight Like That                      -

Acc. by Ed Allen-c/tb/? James P. Johnson-p.
                                    New York, September 4, 1929.

148970-2  Papa I Don't Need You Now           Col 14462-D
148971-2  Tired Of The Way You Do             -
148972-1-2-3  Breath And Breeches             Rejected

Acc. by James P. Johnson-p.        New York, September 12, 1929.

148994-2  Oh ! Mister Mitchell                Col 14536-D
148995-3  Where Is My Man ?                   -

Acc. by Ed Allen-c/p/others unknown.   New York, December 31, 1929.

149632-3  You Can't Stay Here No More         Col 14497-D
149633-3  Let's Get Loose                     -

Acc. by Porter Grainger-p.         New York, July 21, 1930.

150649-1  Don't Fool Around On Me             Col 14553-D
150650-1  Down In The Mouf' Blues             -

Acc. by Ed Allen-c/J. C. Johnson-p.   New York, August 1, 1930.

150684-1  Why Can't You Do It Now ?           Col rejected
150685-1-2-3  Lowland Moan                    -

Acc. by c/p (not as last above).   New York, September 9, 1930.

150685-7  Low Land Moan                       Col 14580-D
150783-3  Woman To Woman

Vocal duets with Lonnie Johnson (as TOMMY JORDAN on Columbia; Clara Smith as VIOLET
  GREEN on OKeh), acc. by ? Alex Hill-p/Lonnie Johnson-g.
                                    New York, October 31, 1930.

150927-3  You're Getting Old On Your Job      Col 14568-D
150928-2  What Makes You Act Like That ?      -
404523-B  You Had Too Much                    OK 8839
404524-A  Don't Wear It Out                   -

Vocal, acc. by Porter Grainger-p.   New York, March 7, 1931.

151401-2  I Wanna Two-Fisted Double-Jointed Man   Col 14592-D
151402-2  Good Times (Come On Back Once More)     -

Acc. by Asbestos Burns-p, who also sings where shown.
                                    New York, August 4, 1931.

151706-2  Ol' Sam Tages                       Col 14619-D
151707-3  Unemployed Papa-Charity Working Mama - vAB   -

Acc. by Clarence Williams-p.       New York, September 25, 1931.

151810-1  For Sale (Hannah Johnson's Big Jackass)  Col 14633-D
151811-1  You Dirty Dog                       -

Acc. by Fred Longshaw-p.           New York, January 18, 1932.

152076-1  Street Department Papa              Col 14645-D
152077-1  Pictures On The Wall                -

                                    New York, March 25, 1932.

152159-1  I'm Tired Of Fattenin' Frogs For Snakes  Col 14653-D
152160-1  So Long Jim                         -

This is not the same artist as the subject of the previous chapter.

Vocal, acc. by Harold Lewis-c/Buster Lindsay-p.
                              St. Paul, c. June 28, 1927.

12899-A  Wandering Boy Blues              BP 8034
12900    Sand Raisin' Blues                 -

                              St. Paul, c. June 29, 1927.

12904    Clara Blues                      BP 8035
12905    After You've Gone Away             -

## CLEMENTINE SMITH

Pseudonym on Pathe Actuelle and Perfect for Helen Gross, q.v., but the following are
  by a different girl whose name may well have been Clementine Smith.

Vocal, acc. by the Kansas City Five : ? Louis Metcalf or Bubber Miley-c/Bob Fuller-
  cl/Louis Hooper-p/Elmer Snowden-bj.     New York, c. November 24, 1924.

5740-5  Everybody Loves My Baby              Re 9760
5742-1  I'm Done Done Done With You          Ban 1483, Dom 3453, Re 9782
NOTE:- Domino 3453 as CHARLOTTE EVANS; Regal 9760 and 9782 as GLADYS MURRAY.
   Matrix 5741 is by Josie Miles, q.v.

Jake Frazier-tb added; Fuller db as.     New York, c. December 2, 1924.

5759-2  Nobody Knows What A Red Head Mama Can Do Ban 1479, Re 9779
5760-2  Big Bad Bill Is Sweet William Now        Ban 1464, Dom 3456, Re 9760
NOTE:- Banner 1464 and 1479 as GLADYS MURRAY; Domino 3456 as DOLLY RANSOM.

Both c omitted.                          New York, c. January 6, 1925.

5800-1  Nobody Knows The Way I Feel This Mornin' Ban 1484, Dom 3452, Or 325,Re 9781
NOTE:- Domino 3452 as LOUELLA TAYLOR; Oriole 325 as SARA MESSON.

## ELIZABETH SMITH

Vocal, acc. by own u or Tom Morris-c/Bob Fuller-cl/Mike Jackson-p.*
                              New York, September 6, 1926.

36097-2  No Sooner Blues                  Vic 20297
36098-2  *Gwine To Have Bad Luck For Seven Years   -

Vocal duets with Sidney Easton, acc. by Phil Worde-p/Bobby Leecan-g.
                              New York, October 18, 1926.

36621-3  When My Wants Run Out            Vic 20334
36622-3  Talk 'Bout Something That's Gwine To Happen  -

Vocal, acc. by Rex Stewart-c/Ernest Elliott-Bob Fuller-cl/f/? Phil Worde-p.
                              New York, January 26, 1927.

37574-2  Police Done Tore My Playhouse Down    Vic 21539

It is suspected that the sides made in 1926 as by MANDY LEE may be by Elizabeth Smith.

## FABER SMITH

See Jimmy Yancey.

## FATS SMITH AND HIS RHYTHM KINGS

s/p/g/sb/Fats Smith-v.                  Hot Springs, Ark., March 2, 1937.

HS-11-  If I Had You In My Arms          Voc 03528
HS-12-  Music Makes Me Feel That Way       -
HS-13-  Mama, Don't Jive Me             Rejected

As/p/g/sb/Fats Smith-v.                    Hot Springs, Ark., March 4, 1937.

HS-18-   Mama, Won't You Give ?              Voc rejected
HS-19-   My Gal Stella                        -
HS-20-   Because I Love You                   -
HS-21-   I'm Crying For You                   -

## HARL SMITH AND HIS ORCHESTRA

Harl Smith-d dir. Joe Rose-c/Howard Browne-tb/Henry Nathan-cl-vn/Fred Morrow-as/Bill
   Haid-p/Evert Davidson-bj/Joe Tarto-bb.  New York, c. October 7, 1924.

105597   Bring Back Those Rock-a-Bye Baby Days   PA 036158, Per 14339
105598   Rose Marie                              - 10846, P 1862 -    GP 18503
   NOTE:- Pathe Actuelle 10846 as MAYFLOWER SERENADERS; Grand Pree 18503 as MAX  GOMEZ
AND HIS ORCHESTRA.  See also the Lido Venice Dance Orchestra.

## HAZEL  SMITH

Vocal, acc. by King Oliver-c/Clarence Williams-p.
                              New York, August 29, 1928.

401083-B  West End Blues                     OK 8620
401083-A  Get Up Off Your Knees               -

## HORACE SMITH

Vocal, acc. by Syd Valentine and his Patent Leather Kids : Syd Valentine-t/Slick
   Helms-p/Paul George-bj.          Richmond, Ind., October 2, 1929.

15709-A  Mother-in-Law Blues                 Gnt 7025, Ch 15859, Spr 2604,
                                             Spt 9683
15710-A  Love Is Dead (No Use To Hang Around*)  Gnt 7025, Ch 15382*, Spt 9683
15711, -A  The Deacon's Prayer               Rejected
15712-A  Goin' Away And Leavin' My Baby      Gnt 7056, Ch 15859, Var 6064
15713    Wrist Watch Blues                   Rejected
15714    Clickety-Clack Blues               Gnt 7056, Ch 15882
   NOTE:- Champion 15859 and 15882 as TED ROSS; Varsity 6064 as BILL BROWN.

## IKE SMITH'S CHICAGO BOYS

? Arnett Nelson-cl-as/as/Ike Smith-p-v/sb.
                              Chicago, September 9, 1935.

90311-A  Fighting Joe Louis                  Ch 50040
90312-A  Chicago State Street Blues           -

## IVY  SMITH

Vocal, acc. by Cow Cow Davenport-p, with B. T. Wingfield-c or Leroy Pickett-vn, as
   shown.                         Chicago, c. January, 1927.

4087-1  Rising Sun Blues - c                 Pm 12436
4089-1  Sad And Blue                         Pm 12447

4092-1-2  My Own Man Blues - vn              Pm 12436
4094-1  Third Alley Blues - vn               Pm 12447
   NOTE:- All the above titles as IVA SMITH.  Matrices 4088 by Cow Cow Davenport;
4090/1 are by Vance Dixon (both q.v.), and 4093 is untraced.

Davenport speaks*.                           Chicago, c. April, 1927.

4365-2  Ninety Nine Years Blues              Pm 12496
4366-1-2 *Cincinnati Southern Blues          Pm 12472
4368-1  Too Mean To Cry Blues                Pm 12496
4370-1  Barrel House Mojo                    Pm 12472
   NOTE:- Matrices 4367 and 4369 are untraced.  Both issues as IVA SMITH.

Acc. by Cow Cow Davenport-p-v.                    Richmond, Ind., April 1, 1929.

14982    Shadow Blues                            Gnt 6829, Ch 15736, Spt 9509,
                                                 Var 6040
14984-B  No Good Man Blues                       Gnt 6861, Spt 9515
14987    Gin House Blues                          - Ch 15736 -      Var 6040
14990-A  Mistreated Mama Blues - vCCD            Gnt 6875, Ch 15756, Spt 9531,
                                                 Var 6058
NOTE:- Matrices 14983, 14985 and 14986 are by Cow Cow Davenport, q.v.; 14988 and
14989 are by the Southern Blues Singers, q.v.  Gennett 6875 as IVY SMITH AND
CHARLIE DAVENPORT; Champion 15736 as RUBY RANKIN; 15756 as RUBY RANKIN AND GEORGE
HAMILTON; Varsity 6040 and 6058 as SALLY SAD.

Unknown girl-v added* (labels of all issues of these sides credit the soloist "and
her Buddies").                                   Richmond, Ind., August 27, 1929.

15495    *Doin' That Thing - vCCD               Gnt 7040, Ch 15902, Spt 9528
15496-A  *Somebody's Got To Knock A Jug - vCCD            -            -
15499    Southern High Waters Blues             Gnt 7101, Ch 16057, Spt 9533
15500-A  Cheating Only Blues                              -            -
15501-A  Wringin' And Twistin' Papa             Gnt 7024, Ch 15357, Spt 9527,
                                                 Var 6027
15502    Got Jelly On My Mind                    As above
NOTE:- Champion 15857, 15902 and 16057 as RUBY RANKIN; Supertone 9528 as MISSIS-
SIPPI TRIO.

? Walter Fennell-g added.                         Richmond, Ind., June 6, 1930.

16725-A  Gypsy Woman Blues                       Gnt 7251, Ch 16080, Var 6066
16726    Milkman Blues                                    -            -
NOTE:- Varsity 6066 as SALLY SAD; both the other issues as IVA SMITH.

                                                 Richmond, Ind., June 7, 1930.

16736, -A  She Knows How To Sell That Stuff      Rejected
16738    Alabammy Mistreated (sic)               Gnt 7231, 5006, Ch 16057, Spr 2763
16742-A  That's The Kind Of Girl I'm Looking For      --      Ch 16038
NOTE:- Gennett 7231 as COW COW DAVENPORT AND IVA SMITH (16738) or IVA SMITH AND HER
BUDDIES; Superior 2763 as DAVENPORT AND SMITH.  Gaps in the above matrix sequences
are filled by blues artists of no jazz interest.  See also Cow Cow Davenport.

## JABBO SMITH

JABBO SMITH'S RHYTHM ACES : Jabbo Smith-c-v/Omer Simeon-cl/Cassino Simpson-p/Ikey
    Robinson-bj.                                 Chicago, January 29, 1929.

C-2884-  Jazz Battle                             Br 4244, UHCA 43, AF A-042

Hayes Alvis-bb added.                            Chicago, February 22, 1929.

C-2999-A  Little Willie Blues - vJS              Br 7058, HJCA HC-111
C-3000-A  Sleepy Time Blues                               -        -

                                                 Chicago, February 23, 1929.

C-3003-  Take Your Time                          Br 7061
C-3004-  Sweet And Low Blues - vJS                        -

Simeon db as*                                    Chicago, March 1, 1929.

C-3026-  Take Me To The River - vJS              Br 7071, HJCA 616
C-3027-  Ace Of Rhythm                                    -        -
C-3028-  *Let's Get Together - vJS               Br 7065, Voc V-1031
C-3029-  *Sau Sha Stomp                                   -        -

Earl Frazier-p replaces Simpson.                 Chicago, March 30, 1929.

C-3212-  *Michigander Blues                      Br 7069

JABBO SMITH'S RHYTHM ACES : Jabbo Smith-c-v/Omer Simeon-cl-as/Earl Frazier-p/Ikey
   Robinson-bj/Hayes Alvis-bb.              Chicago, April 4, 1929.

C-3233-   Decatur Street Tutti - vJS              Br 7078, HJCA 616
C-3234-   Till Times Get Better - vJS             -          -

   Smith db tb**; Millard Robbins-bsx added.
                                    Chicago, April 17, 1929.

C-3300- **Lina Blues - vJS                        Br 7087
C-3301-   Weird Blues                             Rejected

   George James-cl-as replaces Simeon.    Chicago, June 9, 1929.

C-3576-   Croonin' The Blues                      Br 7087
C-3577-   I Got The Stinger - vJS                 Br 7120, HJCA HC-97

   Omer Simeon-ts added; Lawson Buford-bb replaces Alvis.
                                    Chicago, August 8, 1929.

C-4023-   Boston Skuffle (Boston Shuffle*)        Br 7101, UHCA 44, AF A-044*
C-4024-   Tanguay Blues                           -          HJCA HC-97

                                    Chicago, August 22, 1929.

C-4100-   Band Box Stomp                          Br 7111
C-4101-   Moanful Blues                           -

NOTE:- Some of the above Brunswicks are labelled THE RHYTHM ACES or FOUR ACES AND THE
   JOKER.

JABBO SMITH AND HIS ORCHESTRA : Jabbo Smith-t-v/Leslie Johnakins-Ben Smith-as/Sam
   Simmons-ts/James Reynolds-p/Connie Wainwright-g/Elmer James-sb/Alfred Taylor-d.
                                    New York, February 1, 1938.

63218-A   Rhythm In Spain                         Dec 1980, Voc S-219
63219-A   Absolutely - vJS                        Dec 1712, Br 02586
63220-A   More Rain, More Rest - vJS              Dec 1980, Voc S-219
63221-A   How Can Cupid Be So Stupid ? - vJS      Dec 1712, Br 02586

## JACK SMITH

Most of the original Whispering Baitone's records are either self-accompanied at the
   piano, or are accompanied by other pianists and/or small, suitably discreet light
   orchestras. The following, however, feature interesting jazz solos and ensembles.

Vocal, acc. by the Whispering Orchestra : Bert Ambrose-vn dir. Perley Breed-Jack
   Miranda-as/Joe Crossman-ts-vn/Leo Kahn-p/Joe Brannelly-g/Dick Escott-sb/Max Bacon-
   d.                              Hayes, Middlesex, January 12, 1928.

Bb-12352-3  Miss Annabelle Lee                    HMV B-2666, El EG-794

   Acc. by Carroll Gibbons-p dir. Sylvester Ahola-t/? Jack Miranda-? Laurie Payne-as/
   Leon Goossens-ts-o/? Eric Siday-? Reg Pursglove-vn/Joe Brannelly-g/? Dick Escott-
   sb/Max Bacon-d.                 Hayes, Middlesex, October 11, 1928.

Bb-14589-2  That's My Weakness Now                HMV B-2871

   Vc replaces Goossens;                Hayes, Middlesex, December 28, 1928.

Bb-15297-2  I'm Crazy Over You                    HMV B-2962

   Acc. by Leonard Joy dir. Mike Mosiello-t/Andy Sannella-? Sammy Feinsmith-as/Lou
   Raderman and 2 others-vn/Milt Rettenberg-p/Al Armer-sb/Joe Green-d.
                                    New York, May 8, 1929.

51690-2  To Be In Love (Espesh'lly With You)      Vic 21987, HMV B-3090

Acc. by Carroll Gibbons-p dir. t/2as/ts/2vn/g/sb/d.
                          Hayes, Middlesex, October 10, 1929.

Bb-17709-3  I'll Be Getting Along                HMV B-3193

## JANE SMITH

Pseudonym on Silvertone for Ida Cox, q.v.

## JIMMY SMITH AND  HIS SEPIANS

T/cl/ts/w/p/g/sb/d/Nora Lee King-v.      New York, October 15, 1941.

69817-     Boy, It's Solid Groovy - vNLK          Dec 8618
69818-A    I Ain't Got Nobody To Love             Dec 8591
69819-     Sporty Joe - vNLK                      Dec 8618
69820-A    Big Chump Blues                        Dec 8591

## JOE SMITH  AND ORCHESTRA

See Ethel Finnie.

## JOSEPH C. SMITH'S  ORCHESTRA

As this was what would later be termed a "sweet society" orchestra, it is hardly a
    matter for wonder that it produced no absolute jazz music during its career from
    1916 to 1925.  The following may be of some interest as an early example of a real
    blues - albeit one given a somewhat nightmarish treatment.

Joseph C. Smith-vn-laughing dir. Bill Hall-t-tb/Harry Raderman-tb soloist/Max Flas-
    ter-as/Harry Akst-Hugo Frey-p/d.        New York, October 1, 1919.

23282-1  Yellow Dog Blues (Intro. Hooking Cow     Vic 18618, HMV B-1089, X-702
           Blues)

## JULIA  SMITH

Pseudonym on Oriole for Mandy Lee, q.v.

## KATE SMITH

On the following sides, this famous American musical comedy, radio and cabaret star
    was accompanied by jazz musicians who were allowed solo work.  She was also accom-
    panied on one session by the Charleston Chasers, q.v.

Vocal, acc. by the Harmonians : T/tb/cl/p/g/sb.
                          New York, July 12, 1929.

148806-2  He's A Good Man To Have Around        Har 970-H
148807-3  Maybe - Who Knows ?                         -        SR 1043-P

    Tony Parenti-cl replaces the unknown; sb omitted.
                          New York, July 7, 1931.

365025-3  Makin' Faces At The Man In The Moon    Har 1347-H, Cl 5359-C, VT 2423-V

## LAURA  SMITH

Vocal, acc. by Clarence Williams' Harmonizers : Tom Morris-c/Charlie Irvis-tb/Ernest
    Elliott-cl/Clarence Williams-p/Buddy Christian-bj.
                          New York, c. August 1, 1924.

72719-B  Texas Moaner Blues                      OK 8157
72720-B  I'm Gonna Get Myself A Real Man         OK 8186
72721-B  Has Anybody Seen My Man ?               OK 8157

    Acc. by Clarence Williams-p.         New York, c. October 10, 1924.

72895-B  My Best Friend Stole My Man And Gone    OK 8186
72896-B  Two-Faced Woman Blues                   OK 8169

Acc. by Clarence Williams' Harmonizers : ? Lorenzo Tio-cl/Clarence Williams-p/Buddy
Christian-bj.                           New York, c. October 11, 1924.

72897-B  I Can Always Tell When My Man Don't Want OK 8169
           Me 'Round
72898-B  Lake Pontchartrain Bkues                 OK 8179
72899-B  Gravier Street Blues                      -

Acc. by 2vn/g.                          New York, October 1, 1925.

73663-B  Face To Face                             OK 8252
73664-B  Take Me Home, Heavenly Father, With Thee  -

Acc. by Perry Bradford's Mean Four : H/vn/vn-g/? Perry Bradford-p.
                                        New York, October 3, 1925.

73678-A  Lucy Long                                OK 8366
73679-B  Disgusted Blues                          OK 8246
73680-A  Humming Blues                             -
73681-A  Cool Can Blues                           OK 8366

                                        New York, c. April 1, 1926.

74083-A  I'll Get Even With You                   OK 8316
74084-A  If You Don't Like It                      -

Acc. by Clarence Williams-p.            New York, May 28, 1926.

80045-B  Jackass Blues                            OK 8331
80046-B  Them Has Been Blues                       -

Acc. by her Wild Cats : ? Tom Morris-c/? Bob Fuller-cl/? Mike Jackson-p.
                                        New York, c. January 15, 1927.

107313   I'm Goin' To Have Seven Years' Bad Luck  PA 7520, Per 120
107314   When A 'Gator Holler (Folks Say Sign O' Rain)-      -

Acc. by p/g.                            New York, c. January, 1927.

         If You Don't Do It Like I Want It Done  PA 7525, Per 125
           (I'll Get Somebody Else)
         I'm Gonna Kill Myself                     -        -

Acc. by k/as/p.                         New York, c. January 26, 1927.

7074-2   Gonna Put You Right In Jail              Ban 1977, Dom 3948, Re 8304

Acc. by t/p.                            New York, February 7, 1927.

80400-B  My Man Just Won't Don't                  OK 8445
80401-B  Hateful Blues                             -

Acc. by Tom Morris-c/Lukie Johnson-p.  New York, c. February 25, 1927.

7130-2   Don't You Leave Me Here                  Ban 1977, Dom 3948, Re 8304

Acc. by Perry Bradford's Mean Four : Instrumentation and personnel unknown.
                                        New York, March 9, 1927.

80510-A-B  Home (Cradle Of Happiness)             OK rejected
80511-A-B  If Anybody Here Wants A Real Kind Mama  -
             (Here's Your Opportunity)

Acc. by Clarence Jones-p.               Chicago, June 7, 1927.

38651-1  Lonesome Refugee                         Vic 20775
38652-3  The Mississippi Blues                     -
38653-2  Fightin' Blues                           Vic 20945
38654-2  Red River Blues                           -

Leroy Smith-vn dir. probably :- Frank Belt-Pike Davis-t/TeRoy Williams-tb/Emerson
Harper-cl-as-o/Harold Henson-as-vc-sb/Stan Peters-ts-bsn/Harry Brooks-p/Sam Speed-
bj/Fred Peters-bb/d.                          New York, c. June 24, 1921.

7639     Saturday                                    Voc 14218, Hom ·H-214
NOTE:- Homochord H-214 as HOMOCHORD DANCE ORCHESTRA.

                                        New York, c. July 21, 1921.

7754     Love Will Find A Way                        Voc 14218, Hom H-215
NOTE:- Homochord H-215 as HOMOCHORD DANCE ORCHESTRA.

Robert Lewis-tb replaces Williams; Edward Beeler-d replaces (or may even be) the
unknown.                                     New York, c. September, 1924.

2016-B   Indian Love Call                            Ebs 1027, Pen 1453, UTD 2016
2017-B   Harlem's Araby                              Ebs 1020, Globe/GG/Nad/Rx 1283

2020-    Dixie Dreams                                Ebs 1027, Clover 1540, Pen 1455
2021-B   June Brought The Roses (w)                  Ebs 1017, Clover 1545

         Morning (Won't You Ever Come Round ?)       B-D 1001
         Stop And Listen                             -
NOTE:- Grey Gull/Nadsco/Radiex 1283 as METROPOLITAN DANCE PLAYERS; Pennington 1453
and 1455 as MICHIGAN MELODY MAKERS.

Charlie Gaines-t replaces Davis; Wilbur de Paris-tb replaces Lewis, who plays fh;
John Long-vn replaces Smith, who directs only.
                                        Camden, N. J., February 23, 1928.

43428-2  Rhapsody In Blue                            Vic 21328
43429-2  St. Louis Blues                             -        21472, MW 1140

                                        Camden, N. J., April 2, 1928.

43432-1-2-3  I'm Riding To Glory (With A Glorious  Rejected
             Girl)
43433-2  I'm A Broken-Hearted Blackbird             Vic 21472
NOTE:- The first of the above Victor sessions was a test date, the matrix numbers
being allocated at the time of the second session.

## LLOYD SMITH'S GUT-BUCKETEERS

? Punch Miller-c/Fred Howard-as/ts/Zinky Cohn-p/bj/d.
                                        Chicago, July, 1930.

C-6028-   Wake Up, Sinners - vch                     Voc 1560
C-6029/30 Rub Me Some More - vch                     -

George Dixon-c replaces ? Miller; May Smith-Earl Roach-v.
                                        Chicago, October 27, 1930.

C-6456-   I'm Going Away Just To Wear You Off        Voc 1573
          My Mind - vER
C-6457-   That's My Stuff - vMS                      -

As for first session.                   Chicago, c..November 20, 1930.

C-6828-   That's My Stuff - v                        Voc 1617
NOTE:- Vocalion 1617 as CHOCOLATE DANDIES. The reverse, also labelled thus, is by
King Oliver and his Orchestra, q.v.

## LOUELLA SMITH

Pseudonym on Oriole 266 ('TAIN'T A DOGGONE THING BUT THE BLUES) for ? Hazel Meyers,
q.v.

Vocal, acc. by own p.                    New York, January 10, 1920.

       That Thing Called Love              Vic test (un-numbered)

Acc. by the Rega Orchestra (not so named on all editions) : ? Ed Cox-t/Dope Andrews
tb/Ernest Elliott-cl-ts/Leroy Parker-vn/Willie "The Lion" Smith-p.
                                   New York, February 14, 1920.

7275-E  That Thing Called Love              OK/Phonola 4113
7276-D  You Can't Keep A Good Man Down              -
NOTE:-  The high take letters for these two sides, and the fact that the orchestra
accompanying Mamie Smith is sometimes identified as the Rega Orchestra (a white
studio group directed by Milo Rega), suggest that there were probably two sessions
involved in recording them.  The date shown is probably correct for the second of
these; the first must have taken place between the Victor test date and this one.

Acc. by her Jazz Hounds : As above, but Addington Major or Johnny Dunn-c replaces
Cox.                                     New York, August 10, 1920.

7529-C  Crazy Blues                          OK/Phonola 4169, Od 311902
7539-B  It's Right Here For You (If You Don't Get It,       -
       'Tain't No Fault Of Mine)
NOTE:- Matrices 7530 through 7538 are by other artists of no jazz interest, or are
untraced; it is quite probable that the above coupling represents two sessions,
held perhaps as much as a week apart.

                                 New York, September 12, 1920.

7589-C  Fare Thee Honey Blues                OK/Phonola 4194
7590-B  The Road Is Rocky (But I Am Gonna Find My Way)      -

Acc. by her Jazz Hounds : Johnny Dunn-c/? Dope Andrews-tb/Garvin Bushell-cl/Leroy
Parker-vn/Porter Grainger-p/? George Howell-d.
                                 New York, November 5, 1920.

7642-B  Mem'ries Of You, Mammy                OK/Phonola 4228
7643-B  If You Don't Want Me Blues                  -

Ernest Elliott-cl may replace Bushell.  New York, November 6, 1920.

7658-E  Don't Care Blues                     OK 4253
7659-C  Lovin' Sam From Alabam                      -
NOTE:- The exact dates for the above five OKeh sessions were supplied by the late
Perry Bradford, but from what source is not known.  It is difficult to accept the
last two in particular, and here again, the fairly high takes suggest two sessions.

MAMIE SMITH'S JAZZ HOUNDS : Johnny Dunn-c/Dope Andrews-tb/Garvin Bushell-cl/? Leroy
Parker-vn or possibly a second reed/p/? Mort Perry-x.
                                 New York, January, 1921.

7724-B  Royal Garden Blues                   OK 4254, Od 311919
7725-B  Shim-Me-King's Blues                        -    Od 311915
NOTE:- Odeon 311915 and 311919 are coupled, under the name AMERICAN JAZZ BAND.

MAMIE SMITH AND HER JAZZ HOUNDS : Johnny Dunn-c/Buster Bailey-cl/Phil Worde-p/Chink
Johnson-bb/x, not Mort Perry/Mamie Smith-v (non-vocal sides as MAMIE SMITH'S JAZZ
HOUNDS).                                  New York, c. February 21, 1921.

7788-B  Jazzbo Ball - vMS                    OK 4295
7789-C  What Have I Done ? - vMS             OK 4351
7790-A  That Thing Called Love               OK 4296, Od A-312909
7791-A  Old Time Blues                              -    Od A-312908
NOTE:- Odeon A-312908 and A-312909 are coupled.

? Leroy Parker-vn added.                  New York, c. February 22, 1921.

7792-C  Baby, You Made Me Fall For You       OK 4305
7793-B  You Can't Keep A Good Man Down              -
7794-C  Frankie Blues - vMS                  OK 4856
7795-A  "U" Need Some Lovin' Blues - vMS     OK 4295

Vocal, acc. by her Jazz Band : Johnny Dunn-c/Herb Flemming-tb/Buster Bailey-cl/Phil
  Worde-p/Mort Perry-d-x.                New York, May, 1921.

7959-C  Dangerous Blues                          OK 4351

Acc. by her Jazz Band : Johnny Dunn and another-c/? Herb Flemming-tb/cl/? Leroy
  Parker-vn/p.                          New York, c. August 5, 1921.

70075-B  Daddy, Your Mama Is Lonesome For You     OK 4416
70076-A  I Want A Jazzy Kiss                      OK 4623

Acc. by her Jazz Band : T/cl/vn/p/d (according to a photograph, taken during the
  recording, and published in TALKING MACHINE WORLD, November, 1921, p. 160).
                                        New York, c. August 18, 1921.

70101-C  Sax-0-Phoney Blues                       OK 4416
70102-B  Sweet Man 0' Mine                        OK 4511

Acc. by her Jazz Band : 2c/tb/cl/vn/p, and according to some reports, bsx and d.
                                        New York, August 23, 1921.

70111-B  Mama Whip ! Mama Spank ! (If Her Daddy   OK 4427
           Don't Come Home)
70112-B  I'm Free, Single, Disengaged, Looking For   -
           Someone To Love

As added.                               New York, c. August 29, 1921.

70121-B  Weepin'                                  OK 4471
70122-B  A-Wearin' Away The Blues                 OK 4600

Acc. by c/tb/cl/vn/p/woodblocks.        New York, c. August 30, 1921.

70127-E  Down Home Blues                          OK 4446
70128-B  Get Hot                                  OK 4445

Acc. by 2c/tb/cl/vn/p/bb/others ?       New York, c. August 31, 1921.

70130-A  Oh, Joe (Please Don't Go)                OK 4542
70131-B  A Little Kind Treatment (Is Exactly      OK 4623
           What I Need)

Acc. by 2c/cl/as/vn/p/bb/d.             New York, c. September 5, 1921.

70141-A  Arkansas Blues (A Down Home Chant)       OK 4446
70142-A  The Wang-Wang Blues                      OK 4445

Tb added.                               New York, c. September 10, 1921.

70152-A  Stop ! Rest A While                      OK 4471
70153-B  Sweet Cookie                             OK 4542

MAMIE SMITH AND HER JAZZ HOUNDS : Vocal, acc. by ? Bubber Miley-c/tb/? Garvin Bushell
  cl/? Leroy Parker-vn/p.               New York, c. October 12, 1921.

70246-B  Let's Agree To Disagree                  OK 4511
70247-B  Rambling Blues                           OK 8024
70248-B  Cubanita                                 -

MAMIE SMITH'S JAZZ HOUNDS : Same instrumentation, without Mamie Smith; Everett
  Robbins may be the pianist.           New York, c. February 14, 1922.

70468-B  The Decatur Street Blues                 OK 8030
70469-B  Carolina Blues                           -

MAMIE SMITH AND HER JAZZ HOUNDS : Vocal, acc. by ? Bubber Miley-c/tb/?Garvin Bushell-
cl/? Leroy Parker-vn/? Everett Robbins-p.
                                    New York, c. February 16, 1922.

70479-C  Doo Dah Blues                              OK 4578
70480-B  There's Only One Man (That Satisfies Me)OK 4600
70481-B  Wabash Blues                               OK 4578
NOTE:- OKeh 4578 as MAMIE SMITH AND HER JAZZ BAND.

   Acc. by ? George Mullen-c/? Cecil Carpenter-tb/Bob Fuller-cl/Coleman Hawkins-ts/
   George Bell-vn/Charles Matson-p/Curtis Mosby or Cutie Perkins-d.  These four sides
   are probably the products of two sessions.
                                    New York, April-May, 1922.

70650-B  Mean Daddy Blues                           OK 4631
70651-B  Dem Knock-Out Blues                           -
70654-B  Lonesome Mama Blues                        OK 4630
70655-B  New Orleans                                   -

   Acc. by Johnny Dunn-? Bubber Miley-c/? Herb Flemming-tb/? Bob Fuller-cl/as/? Leroy
   Parker-vn/p/d.                   New York, c. June 27, 1922.

70729-C  Mamie Smith Blues                          OK 4658
70730-A  Alabama Blues                                 -

MAMIE SMITH'S JAZZ HOUNDS : Johnny Dunn-? Bubber Miley-c/? Herb Flemming-tb/? Garvin
   Bushell-cl-as/? Herschel Brassfield-as/Coleman Hawkins-ts/? Everett Robbins-p/Sam
   Speed-bj/d.                      New York, c. August 15, 1922.

70777-B  Stuttering                                 OK 8036
70778-C  Those Longing For You Blues                OK 8072

   Miley omitted; Mamie Smith-v.      New York, c. August 22, 1922.

70790-B  Got To Cool My Doggies Now - vMS           OK 4670
70791-B  You Can Have Him, I Don't Want Him,           -
         Didn't Love Him Anyhow Blues - vMS
70792-A  Strut Your Material                        OK 8036

MAMIE SMITH AND HER JAZZ HOUNDS : Vocal, acc. by t/tb/cl/as/p/d.
                                    New York, c, August 30, 1922.

70809-A  Wish That I Could But I Can't Forgive  OK 4689
         You Blues

   Bj apparently replaces d.          New York, c. September 6, 1922.

70824-B  Sighin' Around With The Blues              OK 4767
70825-B  That Da Da Strain                          OK 4689

                                    New York, c. December 6, 1922.

71079-B  I Ain't Gonna Give Nobody None O' This  OK 4752
         Jelly-Roll
71080-B  Don't Mess With Me                            -

   Acc. by possibly :- Johnny Dunn-Bubber Miley-c/tb/Ernest Elliott-cl/ts/Leroy
   Parker-vn/p/d.                    New York, c. December 8, 1922.

71085-A  Mean Man                                   OK 4856
71086-B  The Darktown Flappers' Ball                OK 4767

   Acc. by Joe Smith and another-c/? Cecil Carpenter-tb/Buster Bailey or Ernest
   Elliott-cl/Coleman Hawkins-ts/George Bell-vn/Harvey Brooks-p/Cutie Perkins-d.
                                    New York, c. December 20, 1922.

71112-B  I'm Gonna Get You                          OK 4781

MAMIE SMITH AND HER JAZZ HOUNDS : Vocal, acc. by Joe Smith and another-c/? Cecil
 Carpenter-tb/Buster Bailey or Ernest Elliott-cl/Coleman Hawkins-ts/George Bell-vn/
 Harvey Brooks-p.                         New York, c. January 9, 1923.

 71161-C  You've Got To See Mamma Ev'ry Night      OK 4781
            (Or You Can't See Mamma At All)

Vocal, acc. by p.                          New York, c. July 19, 1923.

 71675-B  You Can't Do What My Last Man Did       OK 4935

 Acc. by Clarence Williams-p.              New York, c. July 23, 1923.

 71680-B  Good Looking Papa                        OK 4935

 Acc. by the Harlem Trio : Sidney Bechet-ss/Clarence Williams-p/Buddy Christian-bj.
                                   New York, c. August 5, 1923.

 71725-B  Lady Luck Blues                          OK 4926
 71726-B  Kansas City Man Blues                    -

 Acc. by Porter Grainger-p.                New York, August 6, 1923.

 71727-A  Plain Old Blues                          OK 4960

                                           New York, c. August 15, 1923.

 71759-A  Mistreatin' Daddy Blues                  OK 4960
 71760-A  Do It, Mr. So-and-So                     OK 40019

                                           New York, c. August 16, 1923.

 71764-B  My Mammy's Blues                         OK 40019

 Acc. by the Choo Choo Jazzers : Louis Hooper-p, with Louis Metcalf-c*.
                                   New York, c. September, 1924.

 31656    My Sweet Man (Tickles The Ivories       Ajax 17068
            For Me)
 31658    *What You Need Is Me (And What I Need Is You) -

 Acc. by her Jazz Hounds : Bob Fuller-cl/Louis Hooper-p/Elmer Snowden-bj, with
 Norman Buster-d**.                        New York, c. September, 1924.

 31661    Just Like You Took My Man Away From Me  Ajax 17063
 31662   **Remorseful Blues                        -

 Acc. by her Jazz Hounds : Horace Holmes or Gene Aiken-c/Jake Frazier-tb/Ernie
 Bullock or Percy Glascoe-as/Alex Jackson-bsx/Leslie A. Hutchinson ("Hutch")-p/
 Elmer Snowden-bj/Norman Buster-d-marimba.
                                   New York, c. September, 1924.

 31669    Lost Opportunity Blues                   Ajax 17058
 31670    Good Time Ball                           -

 Acc. by Tom Morris-c/Charlie Irvis-tb/Bob Fuller-cl/Mike Jackson-p/Buddy Christian
 bj.                                       New York, August 27, 1926.

 36069-1  Goin' Crazy With The Blues               Vic LPV-534, RD-7840 (LPs)
 36069-2  Goin' Crazy With The Blues               <u>Vic 20210</u>
 36070-1-2  Sweet Virginia Blues                   Vic 20233

                                           New York, August 31, 1926.

 36081-1-2  What Have You Done To Make Me Feel     Vic 20233
              This Way ?
 36081-3  What Have You Done To Make Me Feel       Vic LPV-534, RD-7840 (LPs)
 36081-2  I Once Was Yours I'm Somebody Else's Now<u>Vic 20210</u>

Acc. by orchestra dir. by Billy —— (last name illegible).
New York, March 30, 1929.

| | | |
|---|---|---|
| 401760-A-B | Wonderful Mammy | OK rejected |
| 401761-A-B | My Sportin' Man | - |
| 401762-A-B | The Lure Of The South | - |

New York, April 1, 1929.

401763-A-B   The Show Must Go On          OK rejected

Camden, N. J., April 9, 1929.

50603-1-2-3   The Jail House Blues/You Can't Do It   Columbia Pictures soundtrack

New York, April 29, 1929.

401763-C-D   The Show Must Go On          OK rejected

Acc. by t/tb/as/ts/p/bj/sb/d.     New York, February 19, 1931.

| | | |
|---|---|---|
| 404851-A | Golfing Papa | OK 8915 |
| 404852-A | Jenny's Ball | -       Par R-1195, B-71152, DP-192, Od A-286061 |
| 404853-A | Keep A Song In Your Soul | OK 8864 |
| 404866-A | Don't You Advertise Your Man | - |

NOTE:- Matrix 404866 is a re-numbering of 404850, which is by a South American artist.

## MANDY  SMITH

Pseudonym on Jewel and Oriole for Lizzie Miles, q.v.

## SAMMY SMITH'S STOMPERS

Pseudonym on Clarion 5417-C and Velvet Tone 2477-V for King Carter and his Royal Orchestra, q.v.

## STUFF  SMITH

STUFF SMITH AND HIS ONYX CLUB BOYS : Jonah Jones-t-v/Stuff Smith-vn-v/Raymond Smith-p/Bobby Bennett-g/Mack Walker-sb/John Washington-d.
New York, January 17, 1936.

18508-   With All My Heart - vSS        Voc rejected

New York, February 11, 1936.

| | | |
|---|---|---|
| 18654-1 | I'se A Muggin' - Part 1 - vSS | Voc 3169, Br 02182, A-9986 |
| 18655-1 | I'se A Muggin' - Part 2 - vSS | -     -     - |
| 18656-1 | I Hope Gabriel Likes My Music - vSS | Voc 3170 |
| 18657-1 | I'm Putting All My Eggs In One Basket - vSS - | |

James Sherman-p replaces Smith; Cozy Cole-d replaces Washington.
New York, March 13, 1936.

| | | |
|---|---|---|
| 18817-1 | I Don't Want To Make History - vSS | Voc 3200 |
| 18818-2 | 'Tain't No Use - vSS | -    S-28 |
| 18819-1 | After You've Gone - vSS | Voc 3201, Dec J-11 |
| 18820-1 | You'se A Viper - vJJ | -    S-28 |

New York, May 12, 1936.

| | | |
|---|---|---|
| 19239-1 | Robins And Roses - vSS | Voc 3234, S-190 |
| 19240-1 | I've Got A Heavy Date - vSS&ch | -    S-154 |

STUFF SMITH AND HIS ONYX CLUB BOYS : Jonah Jones-t/Stuff Smith-vn-v/James Sherman-p/
  Bobby Bennett-p/Mack Walker-sb/Cozy Cole-d.
                                        New York, July 1, 1936.

```
19500-1  It Ain't Right - vSS                   Voc 3270, S-72
19501-1  Old Joe's Hittin' The Jug - vSS           -       -
19502-1-2  Swing Time                           Rejected
19503-2  Serenade For A Wealthy Widow            Voc 3316, S-37
```

                                        New York, August 21, 1936.

```
19731-   Knock Knock, Who's There ? - vSS&ch    Voc 3300
19732-1  Bye Bye Baby - vSS                        -       S-37
19733-1  Here Comes The Man With The Jive-vSS&ch  Voc 3316, S-154
```

  Buster Bailey-cl added; Clyde Hart-p replaces Sherman.
                                        New York, May 4, 1937.

```
62172-A  Twilight In Turkey                      Dec 1279, Br 02450, A-81273
62173-A  Where Is The Sun ? - vSS                Dec 1287    -       -
62174-A  Upstairs                                  -       M-30370, Br 02477,
                                                A-81272, A-82526
62175-A  Onyx Club Spree - vSS                   Dec 1279, Br 02477,A-81272,A-82526
62175-B  Onyx Club Stomp - vSS                   Dec X-1451
```

STUFF SMITH AND HIS ORCHESTRA : Jonah Jones-t-v/George Clark-ts/Stuff Smith-vn-v/Sam
  Allen-p/Bernard Addison-g/John Brown-sb/Herbert Cowens-d.
                                        New York, c. December, 1939.

```
US-7792-3  Sam The Vegetable Man - vSS           Var 8063
US-7793-2 ` My Thoughts                          Var 8081, Com 600
US-7794-2  My Blue Heaven - vSS&ch                 -        -
US-7795-3  When Paw Was Courtin' Ma - vSS        Var 8063
```

  Eric Henry-p replaces Allen; Luke Stewart-g replaces Addison; Stella Brooks-v.
                                        New York, c. April, 1940.

```
US-1506-1  It's Up To You - vSB                  Var 8251
US-1507-1  I've Got You Under My Skin - vSS      Var 8242
US-1508-1  Crescendo In Drums                      -
US-1509-1  Joshua - vJJ-SS&ch                    Var 8251
```

## SUSIE SMITH

Pseudonym on Ajax for Monette Moore, q.v.

## TED SMITH'S RHYTHM ACES

2t/tb/cl-as/ts/p/bj-g/bb/d/Theodore Ross-Jack Tolliver-v.  The latter may be the same
  as James Tolliver (ts-d with Noble Sissle, q.v., 1934).
                                        Richmond, Ind., August 27, 1931.

```
17965    New Moten Stomp                         Ch 16420, Spr 2737
17966    Minnie The Moocher - vTR                Ch 16321, Spr 2724
17967    Boogie Woogie                           Ch 16332, 40006 -
17968    Jig Time - vJT&ch                       Ch 16321    -      Spr 2737
  NOTE:- Superior 2724 and 2737 as MEMPHIS MELODY MEN.
```

## TRIXIE SMITH

Vocal, acc. by t/tb/cl-as/vn/p/bj/bb.    New York, c. September, 1921.

```
P-161-1-2  Desperate Blues                       BS 2039, Pm 12161
P-162-1  Trixie's Blues                            -       -
```

  Acc. by James P. Johnson's Harmony Eight : James P. Johnson-p dir. c/tb/cl/?Walter
  Watkins-ts/vn/bj.                     New York, c. November, 1921.

```
P-282-1-2  You Missed A Good Woman When You      BS 2044, Pm 12162
           Picked All Over Me
P-283-2  Long Lost Weary Blues                     -       -
```

Acc. by t/tb/cl/vn/p/bj/bb.                Long Island City, c. April, 1922.

    He May Be Your Man (But He Comes To See  BS 14114, Pm 12163
      Me Sometimes)
    Pensacola Blues                            -        -

Acc. by the Jazz Masters : T/tb/cl-(as ?)/? Fletcher Henderson-p/bb.
                                 Long Island City, c. September, 1922.

    Give Me That Old Slow Drag              BS 14127, Pm 12164
    My Man Rocks Me (With One Steady Roll)     -        -

Acc. by her Down Home Syncopators : T/tb/cl/as/p/bb.
                                 Long Island City, c. October, 1922.

    I'm Through With You (As I Can Be)      BS 14132, Pm 12165
    Take It, Daddy, It's All Yours             -        -
    Just A Little Bit More                  Rejected

Acc. by t/tb/cl/p/bj.                      Long Island City, c. Nov.-Dec., 1922.

    I'm Gonna Get You                       BS 14138, Pm 12166
    2 a.m. Blues                               -        -

Acc. by t/tb/cl/vn/p.                      Long Island City, c. March, 1923.

  528-2  Log Cabin Blues                     BS 14142, Pm 12167
  529-2  Voodoo Blues                           -        -
       Tired Of Waitin' Blues             BS 14149, Pm 12168
       Triflin' Blues                         -        -

Acc. by Fletcher Henderson's Orchestra (as HER DOWN HOME SYNCOPATORS on Paramount
12211) : ? Howard Scott-c/Teddy Nixon-tb/Don Redman-cl/Fletcher Henderson-p/
Charlie Dixon-bj.                          New York, c. May, 1924.

1766-1-2  I Don't Know And I Don't Care Blues  Pm 12208, Sil 3534, Poydras 97
1767-1-2  Freight Train Blues                  Pm 12211

1780-2  Sorrowful Blues                        Pm 12208, Sil 3534, Poydras 97
NOTE:- Silvertone 3534 as BESSIE LEE.

Acc. by vn/p.                              New York, c. June, 1924.

1807-1-2  Don't Shake It No More              Pm 12211

Acc. by her Down Home Syncopators : ? Howard Scott-c/Charlie Green-tb/Don Redman-
cl/Fletcher Henderson-p/Charlie Dixon-bj.
                               New York, September, 1924.

1886-1-2  Praying Blues                        Pm 12232, Sil 3577, Poydras 98
1887-1   Ada Jane's Blues                         -        -         -
NOTE:- Silvertone 3577 as TESSIE AMES.

Acc. by her Down Home Syncopators : Elmer Chambers-c/Charlie Green-tb/Buster
Bailey-cl/Fletcher Henderson-p/Charlie Dixon-bj.
                               New York, December, 1924.

1977-1-3  Ride Jockey Ride (Rider Blues*)      Pm 12245, Sil 3565*, Poydras 61,
                                      Ristic 1
1978-1-2-3  Choo Choo Blues                    As above
NOTE:- Silvertone 3565 as TESSIE AMES.

The following two sides are also credited to TESSIE AMES, but as neither a copy of
the record itself nor its Paramount equivalent, if any, has yet been found, it is
not possible to say if it is by Trixie Smith or not. It may be that two known
titles by this artist have undergone some re-titling.
                            ? New York, c. January, 1925.

    Can't Take My Man                       Sil 3576
    High Yellow Blues                          -

Acc. by her Down Home Syncopators : Louis Armstrong-c/Charlie Green-tb/Buster
Bailey-cl/Fletcher Henderson-p/Charlie Dixon-bj.
New York, c. February, 1925.

| | | |
|---|---|---|
| 2015-2 | You've Got To Beat Me To Keep Me | Pm 12256 |
| 2016-1-2 | Mining Camp Blues | — |

New York, March, 1925.

| | | | | |
|---|---|---|---|---|
| 2063-1 | The World's Jazz Crazy And So Am I | Pm 12262 | | |
| 2063-2 | The World's Jazz Crazy And So Am I | — | JI 7, UHCA 81, JC L-102 | |
| 2064-1 | Railroad Blues | — | | |
| 2064-2 | Railroad Blues | — | — | UHCA 82 — |

Acc. by Fletcher Henderson's Orchestra : Joe Smith-c/Charlie Green-tb/Buster
Bailey-cl/Fletcher Henderson-p/Charlie Dixon-bj/Ralph Escudero-bb.
New York, c. December, 1925.

| | | |
|---|---|---|
| 2362-1-2 | Everybody's Doing That Charleston Now | Pm 12330, MF 100 |
| 2363-1-2 | He Likes It Slow | Pm 12336, Bwy 5006, Sil 3525, Tem R-42, Poydras 20 |
| 2364-1 | Black Bottom Hop (Black Bottom Stomp*) | Pm 12336 — Tem R-42* |
| 2365-1-2 | Love Me Like You Used To Do | Pm 12330, Bwy 5006, Sil 3525, MF 100 |

NOTE:- Broadway 5006 and Silvertone 3525 as BESSIE LEE.

Acc. by Charlie Shavers-t/Sidney Bechet-cl-ss/Sam Price-p/Teddy Bunn-g/Richard
Fullbright-sb/O'Neil Spencer-d.   New York, May 26, 1938.

| | | |
|---|---|---|
| 63866-A | Freight Train Blues | Dec 7489, M-31026,Voc S-217,V-1006 |
| 63867-A | Trixie Blues | Dec 7469 — — — |
| 63868-A | My Daddy Rocks Me - Part 1* | —MB-22079 , Voc S-235*,V-1017* |
| 63869-A | My Daddy Rocks Me - Part 2* (No. 2**) | Dec 7617**- —* —* |
| 63870-A | He May Be Your Man, But He Comes To See Me Sometimes | Dec 7528, M-30344, Voc S-229 |
| 63871-A | Jack, I'm Mellow | — — — |
| 63872-A | Lady Be Good | Rejected |
| 63877-A | My Unusual Man | Dec 7489 |

NOTE:- Matrices 63873/6 inclusive are by Grant and Wilson (see Kid Wesley Wilson).
Copies exist of Vocalion S-235 that play matrix 63875-A on one side.

Acc. by ? Henry Allen-t/Barney Bigard-cl/p/g/sb/? Sidney Catlett-d.
New York, June 14, 1939.

| | | |
|---|---|---|
| 65815-A | No Good Man | Dec 7617 |

## WILLIE "THE LION" SMITH

Piano solos.                    New York, May 14, 1934.

| | | |
|---|---|---|
| 15210- | Finger Buster | ARC rejected |
| 15211- | I've Got To Have My Moments | — |

WILLIE SMITH (THE LION) AND HIS CUBS : Ed Allen-c/Cecil Scott-cl-ts/Willie "The
Lion" Smith-p/Willie Williams-wb.   New York, April 23, 1935.

| | | |
|---|---|---|
| 39489- | There's Gonna Be The Devil To Pay | Dec 7073 |
| 39490-A | Streamline Gal | Dec 7074, 1144, Br 02659 |
| 39491-A | What Can I Do With A Foolish Little Girl Like You ? | Dec 7073 |
| 39491-B | What Can I Do With A Foolish Little Girl Like You ? | Br 02388 |
| 39492-A | Harlem Joys | Dec 7074, 1144, Br 02513 |

? Willie "The Lion" Smith-v.        New York, May 22, 1935.

| | | |
|---|---|---|
| 39535-A | Echo Of Spring | Br 02388 |
| 39535-B | Echo Of Spring | Dec 7090 |
| 39536-A | Breeze (Blow My Baby Back To Me) - vWS? | Dec 7086, M-30380, Br 02791 |
| 39537-A | Swing, Brother, Swing - vWS? | Dec 7090, Br 02659 |
| 39538-A | Sittin' At The Table (Opposite You) | Dec 7086, M-30380, Br 02791 |

WILLIE SMITH (THE LION) AND HIS CUBS : Dave Nelson-t/Buster Bailey-cl/Robert Carroll
  ts/Willie "The Lion" Smith-p/Jimmy McLin-g/Ellsworth Reynolds-sb/Eric Henry-d.
                                         New York, April 13, 1937.

| 61934-B | The Swampland Is Calling Me | Dec 1291, Br 02458 |
|---|---|---|
| 61935-A | More Than That | Dec 1308, Br 02463 |
| 61936-A | I'm All Out Of Breath | -       - |
| 61937-A | I Can See You All Over The Place | Dec 1291, Br 02458 |

  Frank Newton-t/Buster Bailey-cl/Pete Brown-as/Willie "The Lion" Smith-p/Jimmy
  McLin-g/John Kirby-sb/O'Neil Spencer-d-v.
                                         New York, July 14, 1937.

| 62372-A | Get Acquainted With Yourself - vO'NS | Dec 1380, M-30190, Br 02692 |
|---|---|---|
| 62373-A | Knock Wood - vO'NS | Dec 1366   -         - |
| 62374-A | Peace, Brother, Peace - vO'NS | - |
| 62375-A | The Old Stamping-Ground - vO.'NS | Dec 1380, 4204, Br 02598 |

                                         New York, September 15, 1937.

| 62593-A | Blues, Why Don't You Let Me Alone ? | Dec 1957, X-1629, Br 02598 |
|---|---|---|
| 62594-A | I've Got To Think It Over - vO'NS | -       - Br 02636, A-505178 |
| 62595-A | Achin' Hearted Blues - vO'NS | Dec 1503, J-11 |
| 62596-A | Honeymoonin' On A Dime - vO'NS | -    Br 02636, A-505178 |

Piano solos, acc. by O'Neil Spencer-d.   New York, January 10, 1938.

| 63141-A | Passionette | Dec 2269, Br 02722, A-82659 |
|---|---|---|
| 63142-A | Morning Air | -      -      - |

  Spencer omitted.                       New York, February, 1939.

| B-531-2 | Morning Air | Com 523 |
|---|---|---|
| B-532-1 | Echoes Of Spring | Com 521 |
| B-533-2 | Concentrating | Com 524 |
| B-534-2 | Fading Star | Com 521 |
| B-535-3 | Passionette | Com 523 |
| B-536-5 | Rippling Waters | Com 522 |
| B-537-1 | Sneakaway | Com 524 |
| B-538-2 | What Is There To Say ? | Com 518 |
| B-539- | Between The Devil And The Deep Blue Sea | Com 525 |
| B-540- | The Boy In The Boat | - |
| B-541-3 | Tea For Two | Com 518 |
| B-542-4 | I'll Follow You | Com 519 |
| B-543-2 | Finger Buster | Com 522 |
| B-544-2 | Stormy Weather | Com 519 |

Piano duets with Joe Bushkin, with own cel and Jess Stacy-p*, all acc. by George
  Wettling-d.                            New York, February, 1939.

| 75961-A | *Three Keyboards | Com 520 |
|---|---|---|
| 75962-A | The Lion And The Lamb | - |

WILLIE "THE LION" SMITH AND HIS ORCHESTRA : Sidney de Paris-t/Jimmy Lane-Johnny
  Mullins-as/Perry Smith-ts/Willie "The Lion" Smith-p/Bernard Addison-g/Richard
  Fullbright-sb/Puss Johnson-d.          New York, February 17, 1940.

| R-2668 | Peace On You | Gnl 1712 |
|---|---|---|
| R-2669 | Woncha Do It To Me ? | Gnl 1713 |
| R-2670 | Rushin' | - |
| R-2671 | Noodlin' | Gnl 1712 |

### SMIZER'S  DIXIE SERENADERS

Instrumentation and personnel unknown.   Chicago, August 22, 1929.

| C-4156- | Deep River Blues | Br rejected |
|---|---|---|
| C-4157- | Weary Blues | - |

See Cliff Jackson and his Krazy Kats.

## JACK SNEED AND HIS SNEEZERS

Vocal, acc. by Charlie Shavers-t/Billy Kyle-p/John Kirby-sb/O'Neil Spencer-d. Other
sides under this name are of more strictly calypso material.

New York, September 9, 1938.

| 64608- | The Numbers Man | Dec 7522 |
|---|---|---|
| 64609- | Sly Mangoose (sic) | Rejected ? |
| 64610- | West Indian Blues (West Indies Blues) | - |
| 64611- | Big Joe Louis | Dec 7522 |

## HARRY SNODGRASS

Piano solo, announced by J. M. Witten.  Other titles by this artist are of little
interest, and even this one is more of an example of how the number should not be
played.                                    New York, June 22, 1926.

E-19646   Maple Leaf Rag (Scott Joplin)        Br 3239*

## RED SNODGRASS'S ALABAMIANS

C/tb/2cl/p/bj/d.                    Bristol, Tenn., August 4, 1927.

39769-1-2-3  Weary Blues                    Vic rejected

## SNOOKS AND HIS MEMPHIS RAMBLERS/STOMPERS

Snooks Friedman-d dir. James Migliore-t/Estes Monasco-t-v/Ken Herlin-tb-v/Walter
Ashby-Elly Bellare-cl-as-v/Al Muller-ts/Rupe Biggadike-p/Bob Cooke-bj-g/Chuck
Jordan-bb-sb/Pat McCarthy-v.       New York, January 21, 1931.

| 67407-1-2 | Wha'd Ja Do To Me ? - vKH-WA-EB-PM | Vic rejected |
|---|---|---|
| 67408-1-2 | Hello, Beautiful ! - vKH-WA-EB | - |

New York, January 27, 1931.

| 67407-3 | Wha'd Ja Do To Me ? - vKH-WA-EB-PM | Vic 23038 |
|---|---|---|
| 67408-4 | Hello, Beautiful ! - vKH-WA-EB | - |

New York, February 11, 1931.

| 64866-3 | I'm Happy When You're Happy - vKH-WA-EB | Vic 22629 |
|---|---|---|
| 64867-2 | Love Is Like That (What Can You Do ?) - vKH-WA-EB | - |

New York, March 25, 1931.

| 68822-2 | Smile, Darn Ya, Smile - vKH-WA-EB | Vic 22662, Zon EE-262 |
|---|---|---|
| 68823-2 | I'm Crazy 'Bout My Baby - vWA | - - |
| 68824-1 | Bon Soir - vWA | Vic 22684 |

Vn added.                          New York, May 11, 1931.

| 53088-2 | Some Other Time - vEB | Vic 22779 |
|---|---|---|
| 53089-2 | You Don't Need Glasses - vKH-WA-EB | Vic 22704 |
| 53090-2 | Building A Home For You - vWA | - |
| 53091-2 | I'm Blue, But Nobody Cares - vWA | Vic 22737 |

New York, May 21, 1931.

| 69634-1 | Sweet Georgia Brown - vEM | Vic 22779 |
|---|---|---|
| 69635-1-2 | Can I Rely On You ? - vKH-WA-EB | Rejected |
| 69636-2 | Dip Your Brush In The Sunshine - vWA | Vic 22720 |
| 69637-2 | Let A Little Pleasure Interfere With Business - vWA | - |

Snooks Friedman-d dir. James Migliore-t/Estes Monasco-t-v/Ken Herlin-tb-v/Walter
　Ashby-Elly Bellare-cl-as-v/Al Muller-ts/vn/Rupe Biggadike-p/Bob Cooke-bj-g/Chuck
　Jordan-bb-sb/Pat McCarthy-v.　　　　　　　New York, May 26, 1931.

| | | |
|---|---|---|
| 10676-2 | Under Your Window Tonight - v | Ban 32191, Or 2277, Per 15476, Ro 1644 |
| 10677-1 | That's My Desire - vKH-WA-EB ? | Ban 32190, Or 2279, Per 15479, Ro 1647, Cr 91152 |
| 10678-2 | One More Time - v | As above |

New York, June 10, 1931.

| | | |
|---|---|---|
| 69918-2 | Swamp Ghosts - vPM | TT C-1584 |
| 69919-2 | Some Of These Days | TT C-1583, Eld 1930 |
| 69920-2 | Roll On, Mississippi, Roll On-vKH-WA-EB | TT C-1588, Aur 36-134 |
| 69921-2 | The One-Man Band - vWA | TT C-1580 |

NOTE:- All Timely Tunes as BEN FRIEDMAN'S PARAMOUNT HOTEL ORCHESTRA; Electradisk
1930 as MEMPHIS STOMPERS.

New York, June 12, 1931.

| | | |
|---|---|---|
| E-36858- | That's My Desire - vKH-WA-EB | Mt M-12203, Polk P-9028 |
| E-36859- | Just One More Chance - vWA | Mt M-12210, Pan 25098, Mf G-2037 |
| E-36860- | That's The Time A Fellow Needs A Girl Friend-vPM - | |
| E-36861- | Makin' Faces At The Man In The Moon-vEB | Mt M-12203, Polk P-9028 |

NOTE:- Mayfair G-2037 as JACK LOCKE AND HIS ORCHESTRA.

Julia Gerity-v.　　　　　　　　　　　　New York, September 11, 1931.

| | | |
|---|---|---|
| 70225-1 | A Good Man Is Hard To Find-vKH-WA-EB-JG | Vic 22812, BB B-5038, Sr S-3136 |
| 70226-1 | The Cutest Kid In Town - vKH-WA-EB | Vic 22813 |
| 70227-1 | Japanese Sandman | Vic 22815, HMV B-6303 |
| 70228-1 | Kissable Baby - vKH-WA-EB | Vic 22813 |

New York, September 24, 1931.

| | | | |
|---|---|---|---|
| E-37171- | Goodnight, Sweetheart - vWA | Mt M-12245 | |
| E-37172- | Guilty - vWA | - | Pan 25111, Mf G-2056 |
| E-37173- | When It's Sleepy Time Down South - vPM | Mt M-12259 | - - |

2vn/p added.　　　　　　　　　　　　　New York, September 30, 1931.

| | | |
|---|---|---|
| E-37232- | Was It Wrong ? - vWA ? | Mt M-12259, Pan 25149 |

New York, December 18, 1931.

| | | |
|---|---|---|
| 70982-1 | Soliloquy | Vic 22921, BB B-5327, Sr S-3408 |
| 70983-1 | Nothin' To Do But Love - vKH-WA-EB | Vic 22895 |
| 70984-1 | Sittin' On A Rubbish Can - vKH-WA-EB-JG | Vic 22896 |
| 70985-1 | Why Did It Have To Be Me ? - vWA | Vic 22895 |

NOTE:- Victor 22812 and 22896 as JULIA GERITY AND HER PLAY BOYS; Victor 22921,
Bluebird B-5327 and Sunrise S-3408 as ELIOT EVERETT AND HIS ORCHESTRA.

One p omitted; Snooks Friedman-Oscar Grogan-v.　Ken Hurlin's absence as a vocalist
may mean he was replaced as a trombonist.
　　　　　　　　　　　　　　　　　New York, April 7, 1932.

| | | |
|---|---|---|
| 72245-1 | I Found A Peanut - vWA-EB-SF | Vic 22989, El EG-2577 |
| 72246-1 | When A Pal Bids A Pal Goodbye (w) - vOG | Vic 22988 |
| 72247-1 | Dixie - vOG | Vic 22989, BB B-5249, Sr S-3332, HMV B-4932, El EG-2577 |
| 72248-1 | 'Neath The Silvery Moon - vEB | Vic 22988 |
| 72249-1 | Sweet Birds - vWA-EB-SF | Vic 24037, BB B-5108, Sr S-3191, RZ MR-1495 |

NOTE:- All issues from matrices 72245-1 and 72247-1 as RADIO RASCALS ORCHESTRA;
all issues from matrix 72249-1 as CALLOWAY'S HOT SHOTS; some Melotones and Panachords as SNOOKS AND HIS PARAMOUNT THEATRE ORCHESTRA.　See also Memphis Stompers.

Pseudonym on Australian Bellbird 341 for Chick Bullock, q.v.

## HATTIE SNOW

Vocal, acc. by Syd Valentine and his Patent Leather Kids : Syd Valentine-t/Slick
  Helms-p/Paul George-bj.                         Richmond, Ind., October 2, 1929.

| 15715 | Two Train Blues | Gnt 7115 |
|-------|-----------------|----------|
| 15716 | Side Wheeler Blues | – |
| 15717 | Make That Gravel Fly | Gnt 7070 |
| 15718-A | Don't Say Goodbye | Gnt 7039, Ch 15881, Var 6033 |
| 15719 | Daddy, What You Going To Do ? | Gnt 7070    –      – |
| 15720-A | I Ain't Got No Man | Gnt 7039 |

NOTE:- Champion 15881 as HELEN HARRIS accompanied by SKILLET DICK AND HIS FRYING
PANS, although it is believed that neither this pseudonym for the accompanying
trio, nor its real name, appears on all issues.  Varsity 6033 as SALLY SAD.

## MARGIE SNOW

Pseudonym on Silvertone for Anna Lee Chisholm, q.v.

## Q.  ROSCOE SNOWDEN

Piano solos.                             New York, c. October 1, 1923.

| 71919-D | Deep Sea Blues | OK 8119, Od 03349 |
|---------|----------------|-------------------|
| 71920-D | Misery Blues | –       – |

## SNOWDEN'S NOVELTY ORCHESTRA

Arthur Whetsel-t/Otto Hardwick-as/Duke Ellington-p/Elmer Snowden-bj/Sonny Greer-d.
                              New York, July 26, 1923.

|  | Home | Vic test (un-numbered) |
|--|------|------------------------|

Bubber Miley-c replaces Whetsel; Charlie Irvis-tb added.
                              New York, October 18, 1923.

|  | Home | Vic test (un-numbered) |
|--|------|------------------------|
|  | M. T. Pocket Blues | – |

## BOB SNYDER AND HIS ORCHESTRA

Pseudonym on Vocalion 2660, 2661, 2707, Decca F-5010 and F-5011 for the Dorsey
  Brothers' Orchestra, q.v., and on Vocalion 4043 and 4082 for Gene Kardos and his
  Orchestra, q.v.  It sometimes covers Chick Bullock and his Levee Loungers, q.v.,
  and occasionally appears as BOBBY SNYDER AND HIS COLLEGIANS.

## CARL SNYDER AND HIS ORCHESTRA

See Joe Haymes.

## SOCIETY NIGHT CLUB ORCHESTRA

Pseudonym on Cameo 9072 and Romeo 876 for Irving Mills and his Orchestra, q.v.

## THE SOCIETY SYNCOPATORS

See Paul Specht.

## JOE SODJA

JOE SODJA AND HIS ORCHESTRA : Joe Sodja-g; remainder unknown.
                              New York, December 3, 1936.

| 20361- | Hurdy-Gurdy Man | Voc rejected |
|--------|-----------------|--------------|
| 20362- | Rhythm Lullaby | – |

JOE SODJA'S SWINGTETTE : Joe Marsala-cl/Frank Froeba-p/Joe Sodja-g/Artie Shapiro-sb/
   George Wettling-d.                          New York, June 18, 1937.

M-529-1  The Sheik Of Araby                    Rejected
M-530-1-2  Limehouse Blues                      Vri 609
M-531-1  I Never Knew                           -
M-532-1  Who's Sorry Now ?                      Rejected

## SOLEMN AND GAY

Pseudonym on Zonophone for Maurice Elwin and various partners; in the case of the
   session below, Cavan O'Connor took part.  It is the only known example of there
   being any points of interest as jazz in the accompaniment to this duo.

Vocal duet, acc. by Max Goldberg-t/Arthur Lally-bar/? Bert Read-p/Joe Brannelly-g/
   ? Billy Bell-bb.                            London, c. August 31, 1931.

OY-1616-1  Ho Hum !                             Zon 5947
OY-1617-2  Moonlight Saving Time                -

## DEBROY SOMERS BAND

From the enormous number of sides made under Debroy Somers' direction (and under his
   name), only the following is known to be of interest as jazz.

Debroy Somers dir. Jimmy Wornell-Vernon Mayall-t/Jock Fleming-tb/Charlie Swinnerton-
   J. Wright-as/Alec Avery-ts/Jean Pougnet-A. Jacobs-vn/Norman Perry-p/Nigel Newitt-
   bj/Fred Underhaye-bb/W. Barnes-d.     Wigmore Hall, London, March 30, 1927.

WA-5137-2  Brainstorm                           Col 4334

## THE SONG FELLOWS

3 male voices, singing and imitating brass instruments, acc. by cl/p/g/d.
                                    New York, September 22, 1932.

12352-1  Me Minus You                          Mt M-12504, Bcst B-112
12353-1  So Ashamed !                          Mt M-12508      -
12354-   It Don't Mean A Thing (If It Ain't Got    -
            That Swing)
12355-   Sentimental Gentleman From Georgia    Mt M-12504
NOTE:- Broadcast B-112 as THE SONGSTERS.

## JACKIE SOUDERS AND HIS ORCHESTRA

The following titles by this popular West Coast dance band of the mid- and late
   1920s are of some interest as jazz.

Jackie Souders-tb dir. Sherman Herrick-Blaine Boyden-t/George Shelton-Clarence
   Cumins-Walter Hawkins-cl-as-ts-bar/Billy Barrett-vn/Irvin Antes-p/Forrest Hart-bj-
   g/Walt Haines-bb-sb/Steve Barrett-d/Walton McKinney-v.
                                    Los Angeles, September 27, 1926.

142761-2  Every Little Thing - vWM              Col 837-D

                                    Los Angeles, February 16, 1927.

143405-3  Maybe Sometime                        Col 905-D

                                    Los Angeles, February 17, 1927.

143410-1  Gonna Get A Girl                      Col 905-D

## SOUSA'S BAND

The full strength of this famous concert band was 64 men, only a small proportion of
   which can be heard on the following records, which illustrate with commendable
   accuracy the kind of music that first introduced ragtime to Europe : John Philip
   Sousa, "The March King," toured the Continent in the spring and summer of 1900 and
   included several examples in his repertoire.  The personnel given is more or less

collective; most of the musicians appear in the contemporary Berliner and Victor catalogues as being "of Sousa's Band," so it is reasonable to assume they took part in the undermentioned sessions.

Henry Higgins-c dir. Walter B. Rogers-Rouss Millhouse-Herman Bellstedt-Herbert L. Clarke-c/Arthur Pryor-tb soloist and assistant conductor/ ——- Lyon- —— Williams tb/A. P. Stengler-Louis H. Christie-cl/Darius Lyons-John S. Cox-Marshall P. Lufsky f-pic/various ah-th-bh/Simon Mantia-eu/Herman Conrad-bb/S. O. Pryor-d.

New York, August, 1897.

| 38 | Levee Revels - An Afro-American Can-Hop | Ber 38 |
| | (O'Hara) | |
| 65 | Orange Blossoms (Arthur Pryor's new | Ber 65 |
| | negro oddity) (sic) | |

New York, c. April 7, 1898.

| 104 | Cotton Blossoms (M. H. Hall) | Ber 104 |
| 136 | At A Georgia Camp Meeting (Kerry Mills) | Ber 136 |

Arthur Pryor-cond.                         Philadelphia, April 22, 1899.

| 080 | An African Beauty (Arthur Pryor) | Ber 080 |
| 081 | Southern Hospitality Cake-Walk (Pryor) | Ber 081 |

Philadelphia, June 6, 1899.

| 0181 | Whistling Rufus (Kerry Mills) | Ber 0181 |

Philadelphia, c. June 7, 1899.

| 0197 | Cotton Blossoms (M. H. Hall) | Ber 0197 |

Philadelphia, c. June 8, 1899.

| 0214 | Levee Revels - An Afro-American Can-Hop | Ber 0214 |
| | (O'Hara) | |

Philadelphia, c. June 9, 1899.

| 0247 | At A Georgia Camp Meeting (Kerry Mills) | Ber 0247 |

Philadelphia, April 9, 1900.

| 01170 | A Coon Band Contest (Arthur Pryor) | Ber 01170 |

Philadelphia, April 13, 1900.

| 01201 | Hula Hula Cake Walk (Egbert van Alstyne) | Ber 01201 |
| 01208 | Who Dat Say Chicken In Dis Crowd | Ber 01208 |
| | (Intro. Jump Back, Honey) (Will Marion Cook) | |

Philadelphia, October 1, 1900.

| 312-1 | A Coon Band Contest (Arthur Pryor) | Vic 312 |
| 315-1-2 | At A Georgia Camp Meeting (Kerry Mills) | Vic 315 |

Philadelphia, October 2, 1900.

| 312-2 | A Coon Band Contest (Arthur Pryor) | Vic 312 |
| 316-1-2 | A Hot Time In The Old Town Tonight (Theodore Metz) | Vic 316 |

Philadelphia, October 3, 1900.

| 361-1-2 | Whistling Rufus (Kerry Mills) | Vic 361 |
| 362-1 | Who Dat Say Chicken In Dis Crowd (Will Marion Cook) | Vic 362 |

Arthur Pryor-tb dir. Walter B. Rogers-Rouss Millhouse-Herman Bellstedt-Herbert L.
Clarke-c/ —— Lyon- —— Williams-tb/A. P. Stengler-Louis H. Christie-cl/Darius
Lyons-John S. Cox-Marshall P. Lufsky-f-pic/various ah-th-bh/Simon Mantia-eu/Herman
Conrad-bb/S. O. Pryor-d.                    Philadelphia, April 2, 1901.

312-3-4  A Coon Band Contest (Arthur Pryor)      Vic 312
315-4  At A Georgia Camp Meeting (Kerry Mills)  Vic 315

                                    Philadelphia, April 5, 1901.

361-3-4  Whistling Rufus (Kerry Mills)          Vic 361

                                    Philadelphia, January 2, 1902.

1182-1-2  Creole Belles (J. Bodewalt Lampe)     Vic 1182

                                    Philadelphia, January 30, 1902.

1223-1  Trombone Sneeze - A Humoresque Cake-Walk Vic 1223
        (Arthur Pryor)

                                    Philadelphia, June 3, 1902.

1417-1-2  The Passing Of Rag Time (Arthur Pryor) Vic 1417

                                    Philadelphia, June 9, 1902.

1417-3-4-5  The Passing Of Rag Time (Pryor)      Vic 1417

                                    Philadelphia, June 16, 1902.

1223-3-4  Trombone Sneeze - A Humoresque Cake-   Vic 1223
        Walk (Arthur Pryor)

                                    Philadelphia, June 24, 1902.

1182-3-4  Creole Belles (J. Bodewalt Lampe)     Vic 1182

                                    Philadelphia, August 14, 1902.

315-5  At A Georgia Camp Meeting (Kerry Mills)  Vic 315
315-6  At A Georgia Camp Meeting (Kerry Mills)     -    G&T GC-419

                                    Philadelphia, December 17, 1902.

1417-5 (sic)-6  The Passing Of Rag Time (Pryor)  Vic 1417

                                    Philadelphia, August 13, 1903.

265-1  A Hot Time In The Old Town Tonight        Vic 316
       (Theodore Metz)

                                    Philadelphia, August 14, 1903.

267-1  Hiawatha (Neil Moret)                     Vic 2443

                                    Philadelphia, August 17, 1903.

265-2  A Hot Time In The Old Town Tonight(Metz) Vic 316

                                    Philadelphia, August 18, 1903.

311-1  The Passing Of Rag Time (Arthur Pryor)    Vic 1417

                                    Philadelphia, August 19, 1903.

265-3  A Hot Time In The Old Town Tonight (Metz)Vic 316
NOTE:- The takes shown above are all 10-inch records; alternative takes of the
same numbers on 7-inch discs were sometimes made on other dates close to these.

Herbert L. Clarke-c dir. Walter B. Rogers-Rouss Millhouse-Herman Bellstedt-c/Frank
 Holton- —— Lyon- —— Williams-tb/A. P. Stengler-Louis H. Christie-cl/Darius
 Lyons-John S. Cox-Marshall P. Lufsky-f-pic/various ah-th-bh/Simon Mantia-eu/Herman
 Conrad-bb/S. O. Pryor-d. Philadelphia, December 7, 1904.

2021-3  At A Georgia Camp Meeting (Kerry Mills)  Vic 315
2022-1-2  Whistling Rufus (Kerry Mills)  Vic 361

Philadelphia, December 14, 1904.

2054-1-2  Creole Belles (J. Bodewalt Lampe)  Vic 1182

Philadelphia, December 19, 1904.

 267-2-3  Hiawatha (Neil Moret)  Vic 2443, 31368 (10 and 12 inch)

Philadelphia, October 25, 1905.

2839-2  Silence And Fun - A Rag Time Oddity  Vic 4538
  (Mullen)

Philadelphia, October 26, 1905.

2054-3-4  Creole Belles (J. Bodewalt Lampe)  Vic 1182

Camden, N. J., April 11, 1906.

2021-2  At A Georgia Camp Meeting (Kerry Mills)  Vic 315 (8 inch)

Walter B. Rogers dir. probably much-altered personnel.
                              Camden, N. J., October 20, 1908.

2021-4-5  At A Georgia Camp Meeting (Kerry Mills)Vic rejected

Camden, N. J., October 23, 1908.

2021-6  At A Georgia Camp Meeting (Kerry Mills)  Vic 16402, HMV GC3-24, B-246

Edwin G. Clarke dir.  New York, December 20, 1910.

9730-1-2  Porcupine Rag (Charles L. Johnson)  Vic rejected

Arthur Pryor-dir.  Camden, N. J., December 13, 1912.

 267-5  Hiawatha (Neil Moret)  Vic 17252, 62443
2054-6  Creole Belles (J. Bodewalt Lampe)  -

## EDDIE SOUTH

EDDIE SOUTH AND HIS ALABAMIANS : Eddie South-vn-w-v dir. Antonia Spaulding-p/Mike
 McKendrick-g/Jerome Burke-d-v.  Chicago, December 2, 1927.

40997-2-3  La Rosita  Vic 21151
40998-2  The Voice Of The Southland - vES-JB  Vic 21155

Chicago, December 9, 1927.

41356-2-3  By The Waters Of Minnetonka  Vic 21151
41357-2  My Ohio Home - vES-JB  Vic 21155

New York, May 10, 1928.

45134-3  That's What I Call Keen - vES-JB  Vic 21605, HMV K-5554
45135-1-2-3  Tomboy Sue - vES  Rejected

 Clifford King-cl-bcl-as added; Sterling Conaway-g replaces McKendrick.
                              Paris, March 12, 1929.

BN-318-2  Doin' The Raccoon  HMV K-5628
BN-319-2  Two Guitars  -

EDDIE SOUTH AND HIS INTERNATIONAL ORCHESTRA : Eddie South-vn-v dir. ? Clifford King-
   cl/Antonia Spaulding-p/Everett Barksdale-bj-g/Jimmy Bertrand-d-bells/"Nino"-v.
                                        Chicago, September 27, 1931.

| 67556-1 | Marcheta | Vic 22847, BB B-10138 |
| 67557-1 | Hejre Kati - vES&ch | - - |
| 67558-1 | Se va la vida - v"N" | Rejected |
| 67559-1 | Mama, yo quiero un novio - v"N" | - |

EDDIE SOUTH AND HIS ORCHESTRA : As above, plus 2nd vn/Milt Hinton-sb-v; Everett
   Barksdale-v.                          Chicago, May 3, 1933.

| 75495-1 | Old Man Harlem - vMH | Vic 24324, HMV B-4984 |
| 75496-1 | No More Blues - vES | - BB B-10120 - |
| 75497-1 | Nagasaki - vEB | Vic 24383 |

   Cl and 2nd vn omitted.               Chicago, June 12, 1933.

| 75862-1 | My ! Oh My ! - vES | Vic 24343, HMV BD-193, K-7029 |
| 75863-1 | Mama Mocking-Bird | Vic 24383, BB B-10120 |
| 75864-1 | Gotta Go ! - vES-EB | Vic 24343, HMV BD-193, K-7029 |

   Probably similar.                    New York, November 23, 1934.

| 16362- | Just An Old Banjo | ARC rejected |
| 16363- | At The Ball | - |

Violin solos, acc. by Django Reinhardt-g, with Wilson Myers-sb*; TRIO DE VIOLONS
   (Eddie South-Stephane Grappelly-Michel Warlop) where marked 3V; or South and
   Grappelly (2V), all acc. by Django Reinhardt-g-a/Roger Chaput-g/Wilson Myers-sb.
                                        Paris, September 29, 1937.

| OLA-2145-1 | Eddie's Blues - g | Swing 8, HMV B-8778, Vic 26222 |
| OLA-2146-1 | *Sweet Georgia Brown - g | - - - |
| OLA-2147-1 | Lady Be Good - 3V | Swing 45 |
| OLA-2148-1 | Dinah - 2V | Swing 12 |
| OLA-2149-1 | Daphne - 2V | - |

Violin solos, acc. by Django Reinhardt-g/Stephane Grappelly-vn/Paul Cordonnier-sb as
   shown.                               Paris, November 23, 1937.

| OLA-1984-1 | Somebody Loves Me - g | Swing 31 |
| OLA-1985-1 | I Can't Believe That You're In Love With Me - | |
| | - g/sb | |
| OLA-1986-1 | Improvisation sur le premier | Swing 18 |
| | mouvement du Concerto en re mineur de Jean-Sebastien Bach-Part 1-vn/g | |

                                        Paris, November 25, 1937.

| OLA-1992-1 | Fiddle Blues - vn/g/sb | Swing 45 |
| OLA-1993-1 | Interpretation Swing du premier | Swing 18 |
| | mouvement du Concerto en re mineur de Jean-Sebastien Bach-Part 2-vn/g | |

EDDIE SOUTH AND HIS QUINTET : Eddie South-vn/David Martin-p/Isadore Langlois-g/Paul
   Cordonnier-sb/Tommy Benford-d; the side marked ** is a violin solo by Eddie South,
   acc. by David Martin-p only; the Glee Club (members of the Quintet)-v.
                                        Hilversum, March 13, 1938.

| AM-750- | Honeysuckle Rose - vGC | Br A-81504, A-81712, Pol 25855 |
| AM-751- | On The Sunny Side Of The Street - vGC | Br A-81505, Pol 25856 |
| AM-752- | **Black Gypsy | Br A-81504, Pol 25855 |
| AM-754- | Fiddleditty | Br A-81505, Pol 25856 |

   NOTE:- Matrix AM-753 has not been traced.

EDDIE SMITH AND HIS ORCHESTRA : Eddie South-vn dir. David Martin-p/Eddie Gibbs-g/
    Ernest Hill-sb/Specs Powell-d.              New York, June 10, 1940.

| 26908-A | A Pretty Girl Is Like A Melody | Col 35633 |
|---------|--------------------------------|-----------|
| 26909-A | Hejre Kati | Col 35636 |
| 26910-A | Pardon, Madame | Col 35633 |
| 26911-A | Zigeuner (w) | Col 35634 |
| 26912-A | Praeludium and Allegro (Fritz Kreisler) | Col 35636 |
| 26913-A | Melodie in A (Charles Dawes) | Col 35634 |
| 26914-A | Para vigo me voy (Say "Si Si") (c) | Col 35635 |
| 26915-A | La Cumparsita (The Masked One) (t) | - |

Charlie Shavers-t/Buster Bailey-cl/Russell Procope-as/Eddie South-vn/David Martin-
p/Eddie Gibbs-g/Doles Dickens-sb/Specs Powell-d/Ginny Simms-v (issued under her
name).                                      New York, December 17, 1940.

| 29251-1 | Sighs And Tears | OK 6087 |
|---------|-----------------|---------|
| 29252-1 | I'm Out Of Style | OK 5990 |
| 29253-1 | These Things You Left Me | - |
| 29254-1 | You Danced With Dynamite | OK 6087 |

Eddie South-vn/Stanley Facey-p/Eugene Fields-g/Doles Dickens-sb/Specs Powell-d.
                                            New York, March 12, 1941.

| 29926- | Zigeuner In Rhythm | Rejected |
|--------|--------------------|----------|
| 29927-1 | Oh Lady, Be Good | Col 36193 |
| 29928-2 | Stompin' At The Savoy | - |
| 29929- | Tea For Two | Rejected |

## SOUTHAMPTON SERENADERS

See Mayflower Serenaders.

## SOUTHAMPTON  SOCIETY ORCHESTRA

Pseudonym on Pathe Actuelle and Perfect for the following items listed in this book:-

Pathe Actuelle 036171/Perfect 14352  Everything You Do (Nathan Glantz and his Orch.)
               036252/Perfect 14433  Ah-Ha ! (California Ramblers)
               036253/Perfect 14434  Suite 16 (Nathan Glantz and his Orchestra)
               036264/Perfect 14445  If You Hadn't Gone Away (Lou Gold and his Orch.)
               036264/Perfect 14445  Flag That Train (To Alabam') (Sam Lanin's Orch.)
               036276/Perfect 14457  Both sides by the California Ramblers
               036301/Perfect 14482  Both sides by Ben Selvin and his Orchestra
                36643, 11477/Perfect 14824  Both sides by the Six Hottentots
Perfect 14395  Both sides by Fletcher Henderson and his Orchestra

## SOUTHERN ALABAMA  CHORUS

Pseudonym on Champion for Elkins' Negro Ensemble, q.v. under W. C. Elkins.

## SOUTHERN BLUES SINGERS

2 male voices, one probably being Cow Cow Davenport (p accompanist).
                                            Richmond, Ind., April 1, 1929.

| 14977 | Lighthouse Blues | Gnt 6828, Ch 15734, Spt 9441, Var 6043 |
|-------|------------------|-----------|
| 14980, -A | Harmony Blues | Rejected |
| 14981-A | Runnin' Wild | Gnt 6845, Ch 15755, Spt 9455 |
| 14988 | It's Tight Like That | Gnt 6828, Spt 9531 |
| 14989-B | Doodlin' Back | Gnt 6845, Ch 15734, Spt 9441 |

NOTE:- Matrices 14978, 14979, 14983 and 14985 are by Cow Cow Davenport, q.v.;
14982, 14984 and 14987 are by Ivy Smith, q.v.  Champion 15734 and 15755 as THE
CHARLESTON BLUES TRIO; the reverse of Varsity 6043 is also labelled SOUTHERN BLUES
SINGERS, but it is of no jazz interest.

Pseudonym on Guardsman for the following items listed in this book :-

1285   Runnin' Wild (The Southland Six)
1340   When You Walked Out (The Ambassadors)
1342   I Ain't Never Had Nobody Crazy Over Me (The Broadway Syncopators)
1343   Two Time Dan (The Broadway Syncopators)
1654   Doodle Doo Doo (Ben Bernie and his Hotel Roosevelt Orchestra)

## SOUTHERN DIXIE SYNCOPATORS

Pseudonym on Australian Arcadia for the following items listed in this book :-

2006   Ol' Man River (Castle Farms Serenaders)
2022   The Rainbow Man (The Rounders)

## THE SOUTHERNERS

Although Eddie Edwards (formerly trombonist with the Original Dixieland Jazz Band)
had a band known as Eddie Edwards and his Southerners at the Silver Slipper Club
in New York for about six months from April, 1926, it is thought that the records
listed below have more kinship with Jud Hill's Blue Devils, q.v.

C/tb/2cl-ss-as/ts/2p/bj/bb/d/Murray Wachsman ("Waxy")-v.
                                New York, c. May 1, 1925.

9506-A   Craving                       Gnt 3061
9507-A   Suite "16" (sic)               -

                              New York, c. November 16, 1925.

9842      Forever (And Ever With You)        Gnt 3212
9843, -A   Whose Who Are You ?            Rejected
9844      Clap Hands ! Here Comes Charley   Gnt 3198

                              New York, c. November 20, 1925.

9847      Someone's Stolen My Sweet Sweet Baby   Gnt 3212
9848      Rhythm Of The Day                Gnt 3199
9852-A   Roll 'em, Girls - vMW           - Ch 15054,Duo B-5136, Gmn 1880
NOTE:- Champion 15054 as DICK BEESON AND HIS ORCHESTRA; Duophone B-5136 as
MONTEREY DANCE BAND; Guardsman 1880 as DICKSON'S DANCE BAND. Matrices 9850 and
9851 are by Jud Hill's Blue Devils, q.v., but the Gennett files show neither title
nor artist for matrix 9849, merely the cryptic legend "Report to N.Y. what we
(illegible) of this crazy number." This probably refers to a recording by either
the Blue Devils or the Southerners, or both, but we shall never know now.

                              New York, c. November 26, 1925.

9866-A   That Certain Party              Gnt 3204, Ch 15055, Aco G-16010,
NOTE:- Champion 15055 as DICK BEESON AND HIS   Bel 1079, Clm 1869, Duo B-5133,
ORCHESTRA; Beltona 1079 as AMERICAN DANCE ORCH- Gmn 1878
ESTRA; Coliseum 1869 as MAYFIELD DANCE ORCHESTRA; Duophone B-5133 as LEAS DANCE
ORCHESTRA; Guardsman 1878 as CABARET DANCE ORCHESTRA.

Jack Kaufman-v.                New York, March 5, 1926.

X-26-A   My Bundle Of Love - vJK        Gnt 3265
X-27     But I Do - You Know I Do - vJK   Gnt 3266, Buddy 8007, Ch 15094,
                                      Voc X-9826
X-28-A   Goodnight (I'll See You In The Morning) Gnt 3266, Ch 15074, Aco G-16034,
NOTE:- Champion 15074 as DICK BEESON AND HIS   Bel 1017, Clm 1909, Gmn 1929
ORCHESTRA; 15094 as TRI-STATE DANCE RAMBLERS; Buddy 8007 as LONE STAR DANCE ORCH-
ESTRA; Beltona 1017 as SOUTHERN STATES DANCE ORCHESTRA; Coliseum 1909 as MARYLAND
DANCE ORCHESTRA; Guardsman 1929 as SAN FRANCISCO DANCE ORCHESTRA; Vocalion X-9826
as RIVERSIDE DANCE BAND.

## SOUTHERN FIVE

C/tb/cl/p/d.               New York, c. December, 1922.

      I Wish I Could Shimmy Like My Sister    Melody/LaB 1410
      Kate

The following title is said to feature _ good t/as/ts solos, and it is suggested it
   is a Fred Hall group, q.v.                    New York, c. April, 1928.

31315-   Oh ! You Have No Idea                    Gds 113

## SOUTHERN NIGHT HAWKS

Pseudonym on Canadian Crown for Irving Mills and his Orchestra, q.v.

## SOUTHERN RAG-A-JAZZ BAND

Robert Leroy-t/Bert Reed-tb/Harold Peterson-bcl-ss/Eddie Cressell-vn/Galen Grubb-p/
   Danville Fairchild-bj/Floyd Schultz-d.  London, September, 1921.

| 6984-2 | Do You Ever Think Of Me ? | EBW 3592 |
| 6985-1 | My Mammy | - |
| 6986-1 | Tiger Rag | EBW 3607 |

London, October, 1921.

| 7002-1 | When My Baby Smiles At Me | EBW 3607 |
| 7003-1 | Salome | Rejected |

London, November, 1921.

| 7048-2 | Coal Black Mammy | EBW 3625 |
| 7049-2 | Crooning | - |

The following was recorded under the above name, but it is by a different group.
                             London, November 7, 1923.

Someday                                    Imp test (un-numbered)

## SOUTHERN   RHYTHM KINGS

See Jimmy Ray and his Orchestra.

## THE   SOUTHERN SERENADERS

Pseudonym for the following items listed in this book :-

Bluebird B-7367  Goin' To Town (Luis Russell and his Orchestra)
Harmony 4-H  I Miss My Swiss (Fletcher Henderson and his Orchestra)
       5-H  Alone At Last (Fletcher Henderson and his Orchestra)
Silvertone 2606  Nobody Knows What A Red Head Mama Can Do (California Ramblers)
       2770  I've Found A New Baby (Dixie Washboard Band)

OH SISTER ! AIN'T THAT HOT ? (Silvertone 2320), also issued under this name, is
   reported to be of some interest, but the band responsible is not known.  If from
   Banner, as the above Silvertones are, it would be by the Original Memphis Five,
   q.v.

## SOUTHERN SERENADERS   ORCHESTRA

See Jimmy Ray and his Orchestra.

## SOUTHERN STATE   RAMBLERS

Pseudonym on Mayfair G-2014 (EV'RYTHING THAT'S NICE BELONGS TO YOU) for the ARC-
   Brunswick studio band, q.v., and others on Mayfair of no known interest as jazz.

## SOUTHERN STATES DANCE BAND/ORCHESTRA

Pseudonym on Beltona for the following items listed in this book :-

| 320 | I Ain't Never Had Nobody Crazy Over Me (The Broadway Syncopators) | | |
| 371 | Both by the Broadway Syncopators | 928 | Mother Me, Tennessee(Ben Bernie's O.) |
| 480 | Bonnie (The Broadway Syncopators) | 945 | Shanghai Honeymoon (Bob Deikman's O.) |
| 692 | Susquehanna Home (Ben Selvin & his O.) | 1014 | Mysterious Eyes (Jack Stillman's O.) |
| 757 | Both by Ben Bernie's Orchestra | 1063 | Then I'll Be Happy (Bailey's Lucky 7) |
| 825 | Panama (McKenzie's Candy Kids) | 1345 | Swing On The Gait (Harry Hudson's |
| 828 | Sweet Georgia Brown (Ben Bernie's O.) | 1377 | Make My Cot....    Melody Men) |

Pseudonym for the following items listed in this book :-

Australian Embassy E-124  I'm Happy When You're Happy (Benny Goodman and his Orch.)
                    E-134  You Didn't Have To Tell Me (Benny Goodman and his Orch.)
                    E-136  Moonlight Saving Time (Dick Robertson and his Orchestra)
Silvertone 2426  No-One Knows What It's All About (Original Memphis Five)

## SOUTHERN TRIO

See the Novelty Blue Boys.

## THE SOUTHLAND FIVE

Phil Napoleon-t/Miff Mole-tb/Jimmy Lytell-cl/Frank Signorelli-p/Jack Roth-d.
                              New York, October 23, 1922.

| | | |
|---|---|---|
| 80621-1-2-3 | I Wish I Could Shimmy Like My Sister Kate | Col rejected |
| 80622-1-2 | That Da Da Strain | - |

## THE SOUTHLAND  SIX

Probably :- Jules Levy, Jr.-c/Miff Mole-tb/Nathan Glantz or Benny Krueger-as/Larry
  Briers-p/bj or bb/d.          New York, c. May 24, 1922.

| | | |
|---|---|---|
| 69711 | Blue-Eyed Blues | PA 020805, 10360, Per 14038 |
| 69712 | Rose Of Bombay | -        -        - |

Phil Napoleon-t/Charlie Panelli-tb/Jimmy Lytell-cl/Frank Signorelli-p/Ray Kitchingman
  bj/Jack Roth-d.              New York, December 2, 1922.

| | | |
|---|---|---|
| 10393 | Runnin' Wild | Voc 14476, Aco G-15237, Bel 161, Clm 1600, Gra 9020, Gmn 1285, Hom H-415, Sc 629 |
| 10397 | Ivy (Cling To Me) | Voc 14476, Bel 306, Gmn 1379 |

NOTE:- The following pseudonyms were used :-

Aco G-15237  Ohio Novelty Band            Guardsman 1285  Southern Dance Orchestra
Beltona 161, 306  Virginia Dance Orch.    Guardsman 1379  New Jersey Dance Orchestra
Coliseum 1600  New York Casino Orchestra  Homochord H-415 Homochord Dance Orchestra
Grafton 9020  Black's Jazz Band           Scala 629  Vorzanger's Band

## SOUTHLAND  SYNCOPATORS

Pseudonym on Vocalion 15544 for Hal Kemp and his Carolina Orchestra, q.v.

## SOUTH SHORE  MELODY BOYS

Pseudonym on Champion 15036, 15037, 15638 and 15639 for Art Payne and his Orchestra,
  15062 for Bailey's Lucky Seven, and 15068 for Jack Stillman's Orioles, all q.v.

## SOUTH STREET  RAMBLERS

Pseudonym on QRS R-7019 for the Barrel House Five, q.v.

## SOUTH STREET  TRIO

Robert Cooksey-h-v/Bobby Leecan-bj/Alfred Martin-g.
                              Camden, N. J., November 22, 1926.

| | | |
|---|---|---|
| 37021-2 | Need More Blues - vRC | Vic 20402 |
| 37022-2 | Whiskey And Gin Blues - vRC | - |
| 37023-2 | Big Four | Vic V-38509 |
| 37024-1 | South Street Stomp | - |

Camden, N. J., October 27, 1927.

| | | |
|---|---|---|
| 39374-2 | Mean Old Bed Bug Blues - vRC | Vic 21135 |
| 39375-2 | Cold Mornin' Shout | Vic 21249 |
| 39376-2 | Suitcase Breakdown | - |
| 39377-2 | Dallas Blues - vRC | Vic 21135 |

C/tb/as/ts/p/bj/bb/d.                          Grafton, Wis., June, 1930.

L-359-1  Don't Lose It                              Bwy 1389
L-360-2  Good Feelin' Blues                          —

## ROY SPANGLER

Piano solos.                          ? New York, c. March, 1913.

383    Red Onion Rag (Abe Oleman) (sic)       Rex/Keenophone 5026, Rex 5342

401    Cannon Ball Rag (Northup)               Rex/Keenophone 5024

## MUGGSY SPANIER

MUGGSY SPANIER AND HIS RAGTIME BAND : Muggsy Spanier-c/George Brunies-tb-v/Rod Cless
cl/Ray McKinstry-ts/George Zack-p/Bob Casey-g/Pat Pattison-sb/Marty Greenberg-d.
                          Chicago, July 7, 1939.

040260-1  Big Butter And Egg Man - vGB        BB B-10417, MW M-8376, HMV B-9033,
                                              EA-2622, JK-2239, Bm 1036
040261-2  Someday, Sweetheart                 BB B-10384, MW M-8377, HMV B-9008,
                                              EA-2776, JK-2022, V-Disc 29, 249,
                                              Bm 1044
040262-1  Eccentric                           BB B-10417, MW M-8376, HMV B-9047,
                                              EA-2622, JK-2327, TG-165, Bm 1036
040263-2  That Da Da Strain                   BB B-10384, MW M-8377, HMV B-9008,
                                              EA-2715, JK-2022, V-Disc 211,
                                              Bm 1044

    Muggsy Spanier-c/George Brunies-tb-v/Rod Cless-cl/Bernie Billings-ts/Joe Bushkin-p/
    Bob Casey-sb/Don Carter-d.           New York, November 10, 1939.

043375-2  At The Jazz Band Ball              BB B-10518, Vic 62-0077,
                                              HMV B-9042, EA-2568, JK-2238,
                                              TG-164, V-Disc 29, 249, Bm 1043
043376-1  I Wish I Could Shimmy Like My Sister  BB B-10506, Vic 40-0139, 62-0077,
          Kate - vGB                          HMV B-9047, EA-2844, JK-2327,
                                              TG-165, V-Disc 81, 307
043377-1  Dipper Mouth Blues                  BB B-10506, Vic 62-0078,
                                              HMV B-9033, EA-2568, JK-2239,
                                              V-Disc 157, 173
043378-2  Livery Stable Blues (Barnyard Blues)  BB B-10518, Vic 62-0078,
                                              HMV B-9042, EA-2887, JK-2238,
                                              TG-164, Bm 1043

    Nick Caiazza-ts replaces Billings.    New York, November 22, 1939.

043894-2  Riverboat Shuffle                   BB B-10532, Vic 62-0075,
                                              HMV B-9145, EA-2715, JK-2226,
                                              El EG-7916, V-Disc 87, 307
043895-1  Relaxin' At The Touro               BB B-10532, Vic 40-0139, 62-0076,
                                              HMV B-9145, EA-2776, JK-2226,
                                              El EG-7916, V-Disc 157, 173
043896-1  At Sundown                          BB B-10719, Vic 29873, 68-0960,
                                              HMV B-9092, EA-3215, JK-2121,
                                              BRS 998
043897-1  Bluin' The Blues                    As above
    Al Sidell-d replaces Carter.          New York, December 12, 1939.
045745-2  Lonesome Road                       BB B-10766, Vic 68-0382,
                                              HMV B-9103, EA-2822, GW-1978,
                                              HN-2847, JK-2089, X-6908, V-Disc 211
045746-1  Dinah - vGB                         BB B-10682, Vic 62-0076,
                                              HMV B-9067, EA-2844
045747-1  (What Did I Do To Be So) Black And Blue  BB B-10682, Vic 62-0075,
                                              HMV B-9067, EA-2887
045748-2  Mandy, Make Up Your Mind            BB B-10766, Vic 68-0382,
                                              HMV B-9103, EA-2822, GW-1978,
                                              HN-2847, JK-2089, X-6908

MUGGSY SPANIER AND HIS ORCHESTRA : Muggsy Spanier-c dir. Ralph Muzillo-Frank Bruno-
Leon Schwartz-t/Vernon Brown-Bud Smith-tb/Irving Fazola-cl/Joe Herde-John Smith-
Benny Goodman II-as/Nick Caiazza-ts/Dave Bowman-p/Ken Broadhurst-g/Jack Kelleher-
sb/Don Carter-d, or MUGGSY SPANIER AND HIS RAGTIMERS* (Spanier-Brown-Fazola-
Caiazza-Bowman-Broadhurst-Kelleher-Carter only).
                                        New York, January 2, 1942.

| | | |
|---|---|---|
| 70124-A | Little David, Play On Your Harp | Dec 4271, M-30322, Y-5972, Br 03373, A-82631, Od 286012 |
| 70125-A | Can't We Be Friends ? | Dec 4168, Br 80142, 03330, Od 286345 |
| 70126-A | Chicago | Dec 4168, Br 80158, - |
| 70127-B | *Hesitating Blues | Dec 4271, 25441, M-30322, MU-60444, Y-5972, Br 03373, A-82631, Od 286012 |

Muggsy Spanier-c dir. Ruby Weinstein-Leon Scwartz-Elmer O'Brien-t/Vernon Brown-
tb/Ford Leary-tb-v/Joe Herde-Karl Kates-Joe Forchetti-Ed Caine-as/Nick Caiazza-ts/
Charlie Queener-p/Ken Broadhurst-g/Jack Kelleher-sb/Al Hammer-d/Dottie Reid-v.
                                        New York, June 1, 1942.

| | | |
|---|---|---|
| 70801-A | The Wreck Of The Old 97 - vFL | Dec 4336, Br 03530, A-82713 |
| 70802-A | American Patrol | Dec 4328, BM-1267, Br 03397, 80142, Od 286219 |
| 70803-A | Two O'Clock Jump | Dec 4336, Br 03530, A-82713, Od 286219 |
| 70804-A | More Than You Know - vDR | Dec 4328, BM-1267, Br 80158, 03397, Od 286345 |

The name SPANIER-BRUNIES DIXIELANDERS was used on BRS 1009 to cover the identity of
Ted Lewis and his Band, q.v.

### DICK SPARLING AND  HIS ORCHESTRA

Pseudonym on Canadian Aurora A-22008 (ROCKIN' CHAIR) for Duke Ellington and his
Orchestra, q.v.

### BLOSSOM SPEARS

Pseudonym on Champion for Katie Winters, q.v.

### PAUL  SPECHT

The following titles made under the direction of this famous bandleader are known to
be of interest as jazz, and among the large number he made for Columbia between
1922 and 1931, there may well be others similar.  See also The Georgians.

SPECHT'S JAZZ OUTFIT : Frank Guarente-t/Ray Stilwell-tb/Johnny O'Donnell-cl-bcl-as/
Arthur Schutt-p/Joe Tarto-bb/Chauncey Morehouse-d.
                                        New York, June 29, 1922.

| | | |
|---|---|---|
| 1100-1-2 | You Can Have Him, I Don't Want Him Blues | Ban 1090, Bwy/Pur/Tri 11148, Pm 20148, Re 9341 |
| 1101-1-2 | Hot Lips | As above plus Em 10546, Imp 1184 |

NOTE:- Banner 1090, Imperial 1184 always as SPECHT'S SOCIETY SERENADERS; Paramount
20148, Puritan/Triangle 11148 as SPECHT'S SOCIETY ORCHESTRA or SYNCOPATORS; Emerson
10546 as EMERSON DANCE ORCHESTRA; Regal 9341 as THE SOCIETY SYNCOPATORS.

PAUL SPECHT AND HIS ORCHESTRA : Paul Specht-vn dir. Frank Guarente-Donald Lindley-t/
Russ Morgan-tb/Harold Saliers-cl-bcl-as/Johnny O'Donnell-cl-as/Frank Smith-cl-ts/
Al Monquin-bsx-a/Arthur Schutt-p/Russell Deppe-bj/Joe Tarto-bb/Chauncey Morehouse-
d.                                      New York, January 13, 1923.

| | | |
|---|---|---|
| 80786-2 | When You And I Were Young Maggie Blues | Col A-3817 |
| 80787-1-2 | Some Of These Days | Rejected |

PAUL SPECHT AND HIS HOTEL ALAMAC ORCHESTRA : As above, but Elwood Boyer-t replaces
Lindley; Arch Jones-tb replaces Morgan; Dick Johnson-cl-ts replaces Smith.
                                        New York, January 4, 1924.

| | | |
|---|---|---|
| 81455-1 | I'm Goin' South | Col 60-D, 3419 |

PAUL SPECHT AND HIS HOTEL ALAMAC ORCHESTRA : Paul Specht-vn dir. Frank Guarente-
Elwood Boyer-t/Arch Jones-tb/Harold Saliers-cl-bcl-as/Henry Wade-cl-ss-ts/Dick
Johnson-cl-as-ts/Al Monquin-bsx-a/Arthur Schutt-p/Russell Deppe-bj/Joe Tarto-bb/
Chauncey Morehouse-d.                    New York, March 12, 1924.

81586-6  I'm All Broken Up Over You                Col 104-D

Charlie Butterfield-tb replaces Jones. New York, May 7, 1924.

81763-3  Forget-Me-Not                             Col 135-D, 3477
81764-3  From One Till Two                              -        -

Roy Smeck-bj-g replaces Deppe.         New York, June 5, 1924.

81806-2  I Can't Get The One I Want                Col 160-D
81807-2  Mandalay                                      -

PAUL SPECHT AND HIS ORCHESTRA : Paul Specht-vn dir. Charlie Spivak-Leo McConville-t/
Charlie Butterfield-tb/Larry Abbott-cl-ss-as/Frank Kilduff-cl-as-bar/Henry Wade-cl-
ss-ts/Arthur Schutt-p/Roy Smeck-bj/Billy Wolfe-bb/Ted Noyes-d.
                                        New York, November 28, 1924.

140154-3  Oh Peter (You're So Nice)               Col 258-D

Paul Specht-vn dir. Charlie Spivak-Sylvester Ahola-t/Al Philburn-tb/Ernie Warren-
Foster Morehouse-cl-ss-as/Jack Cressy-cl-ts/Phil Wall-p/Lou Calabrese-bj/Billy
Wolfe-bb/Johnny Morris-d-v.            New York, January 14, 1926.

141494-5  Static Strut                            Col 627-D

CONSOLIDATED CLUB ORCHESTRA : As above.  New York, January 15, 1926.

106540    Sweet Child (I'm Wild About You) - vJM  PA 36370, Per 14551
106541    Pretty Little Baby - vJM                PA 36371, Per 14552
106542    I Never Knew How Wonderful You Were     PA 36381, Per 14562
106543    Static Strut                            PA 36392, Per 14573

PAUL SPECHT AND HIS ORCHESTRA : Same.    New York, February 6, 1926.

141607-3  So Does Your Old Mandarin - vJM         Col 577-D
141608-3  Roll 'Em, Girls (Roll Your Own) - vJM       -

CONSOLIDATED CLUB ORCHESTRA : Same.      New York, February 19, 1926.

106652    Goodnight (I'll See You In The Morning) PA 36399, 11137, P 1950,
          - vJM                                   Per 14582, Gra 9216
106653    Here In My Arms (Intro. Bye And Bye)    PA 36393, Per 14574
          - vJM
  NOTE:- Pathe Actuelle 36370, 36371, 36381, 11137, Perfect 14551, 14552 and 14562
as CAROLINA CLUB ORCHESTRA; Grafton 9216 as WINDSOR ORCHESTRA.

PAUL SPECHT AND HIS ORCHESTRA : Same.    New York, April 1, 1926.

141901-2  Show That Fellow The Door - vJM         Col 627-D

Joe Lindwurm-t replaces Ahola; Thurlow Darrow-bb replaces Wolfe.
                                        New York, April 27, 1927.

144054-3  Roll Up The Carpets                     Col 1186-D
144055-4  Hot Feet - vJM                              -

                                        New York, August 23, 1927.

144550-2  St. Louis Shuffle                       Col 1307-D

                                        New York, August 24, 1927.

144558-2  Cornfed                                 Col 1307-D

PAUL SPECHT AND HIS ORCHESTRA : Paul Specht-vn dir. 2t/Larry Altpeter-tb/2cl-as/Bob
  Chester-cl-ts/p/bj-g/bb-sb/Johnny Morris-d-v.
                                    New York, May 13, 1929.

148518-3  Hittin' The Ceiling - vJM           Col 1836-D, 01629, Re G-9414
  NOTE:- Regal G-9414 as THE RHYTHMIC TROUBADOURS.

                                    New York, January 23, 1930.

149799-2  Keepin' Myself For You - vJM         Col 2106-D, CB-52, 01930
149910-2  The Harbor Of My Heart - vJM           -       -       -

  Artie Shaw-cl-as present.          New York, May 28, 1931.

151572-1  You Forgot Your Gloves - vJM         Col 2472-D, CB-360

## MIKE  SPECIALE

Mike Speciale made a considerable number of dance records for many labels in New
  York between 1924 and 1929, of which the following are of some interest as "hot"
  dance music.  Investigation of the others should prove rewarding.

MIKE SPECIALE AND HIS ORCHESTRA : Mike Speciale-vn dir. 2t/tb/Jesse Berkman-cl-ss-as/
  cl-as/ts-bsx/Sam Rose-p/Lou de Fabbia-bj/Tom Speciale-bb/Herma﹀ Berkin-d/Jimmy
  Flynn-v.                          New York, c. November 25, 1925.

106426    Mammy Chasing Blues                 PA 36345, Per 14526
106427-A  I Love My Baby (My Baby Loves Me) - vJF  PA 36355, 11055, Per 14536,
                                                     Gra 9188
106428    I "Wanna" Go Where You Go - Do What  PA 36345, 11054, Per 14526,
          You Do (Then I'll Be Happy) - vJF       Gra 9187
  NOTE:- Pathe Actuelle 36345 and 36355 as LENOX DANCE ORCHESTRA; Grafton 9187 as BAR
  HARBOUR ORCHESTRA, 9188 as WINDSOR ORCHESTRA.

CARLETON TERRACE ORCHESTRA (sic) : Same.  New York, December 8, 1925.

141360-2  A Cup Of Coffee, A Sandwich And You   Har 86-H

                                    New York, January 12, 1926.

141478-3-4  Drifting Apart                    Har 97-H, Re G-8599
  NOTE:- Regal G-8599 as CORONA DANCE ORCHESTRA.

MIKE SPECIALE AND HIS ORCHESTRA : Same; Arthur Hall (as FRANK NICHOLS)-v.
                                    New York, c. February 5, 1926.

106610-A-B  Tentin' Down In Tennessee - vAH    PA 36387, Per 14568
106611    Dinah - vAH                          PA 36388, Per 14569

MIKE SPECIALE AND HIS BAMBOO GARDENS ORCHESTRA : Probably same.
                                    New York, c. March 5, 1926.

106692    Let's Grow Old Together - vAH        PA 36417, 11114, Per 14598,
  NOTE:- Grafton 9212 as MARLBOROUGH ORCHESTRA.  Gra 9212

## SPENCER TRIO

Buster Bailey-cl/Billy Kyle-p/O'Neil Spencer-d-v.
                                    New York, May 15, 1938.

63779-A  John Henry - vO'NS                    Dec 1873, Br 02632, A-505170
63780-A  Lorna Doone Shortbread                Dec 1941, M-30167, X-1608,
                                                 Br 02657
63781-A  Afternoon In Africa                   Dec 1873, Br 02632, A-505170
63782-A  Baby, Won't You Please Come Home - vO'NS Dec 1941, M-30167, X-1608,
                                                 Br 02657

## MAMIE  SPENCER

Pseudonym on Oriole for Helen Baxter, q.v.

Pseudonym on Champion for Johnny Ringer's Rosemont Orchestra, q.v.

## SPIKES' SEVEN PODS OF PEPPER ORCHESTRA

Mutt Carey-c/Kid Ory-tb/Dink Johnson-cl/Fred Washington-p/Ed Garland-sb/Ben Borders-
    d.                       Los Angeles, June, 1922.

|  |  |
|---|---|
| Ory's Creole Trombone | Nord 3009, 5001, Sun 3003, Px 3, JC L-33, AF A-032 |
| Society Blues | As above |

NOTE:- Sunshine 3003 as ORY'S SUNSHINE (or SUNSHINNE) ORCHESTRA; the labels of this
issue are pasted over the original Nordskog labels. Paradox 3 and Nordskog 5001 as
KID ORY'S SUNSHINE ORCHESTRA.

## REB SPIKES

REB'S LEGION CLUB FORTY FIVES : Andrew Blakeney-Andrew Massingale-t/Leon White-tb/Les
    Hite-cl-as-v/William Calhoun-cl-ts-v/Reb Spikes-bsx/Gene Wright-p/Lionel Hampton-d.
                            Hollywood, c. November, 1924.

|  |  |
|---|---|
| My Mammy's Blues | Hwd (un-numbered) |
| Sheffield Blues - vLH-WC | - |

REB SPIKES MAJORS AND MINORS : Reb Spikes dir. George Morgan and another-t/William B.
    Woodman, Sr. and another-tb/ —— Slocum and another-cl-as/ts/Roland Bruce-vn/Fritz
    Weston- —— Gordon-p/2bj/bb/George Craig-d.
                        Los Angeles, October 15, 1927.

| | | |
|---|---|---|
| 144765-3 | My Mammy's Blues | Col 1193-D |
| 144766-2 | Fight That Thing | - |

## FRED SPINELLY AND HIS LIDO VENICE BAND   AT THE LIDO CLUB

Fred Spinelly-d dir.Steve Goslin-t/Tom Marshall-tb/Charles Spinelly and another-cl-as
    /ts-bsx/George Hurley-vn/Fred Aspinall-p/Jack Stephens-bj/George Shannon-bb.
                      London, October, 1927.

| | | |
|---|---|---|
| 11230-5 | I'm Coming Virginia | EBE 0188 |
| 11231-2 | Baltimore | EBE 0195 |
| 11232-1 | Just The Same | EBE 0188 |
| 11233-1 | She Don't Wanna | EBE 0195 |

## THE SPIRITS OF RHYTHM

Leo Watson-Wilbur Daniels-Douglas Daniels-tiples-v/Teddy Bunn-g/Virgil Scoggins-d-v.
                    New York, September 29, 1933.

| | | |
|---|---|---|
| 14092- | That's How Rhythm Was Born | ARC rejected |
| 14093- | I'll Be Ready When The Great Day Comes | - |
| 14094- | Nobody's Sweetheart | - |
| 14095-A-B | I Got Rhythm | - |

FIVE SPIRITS OF RHYTHM : Same.        New York, October 24, 1933.

| | | |
|---|---|---|
| B-14095-C | I Got Rhythm | Br 01715, A-9583, Par R-2662 |

New York, October 31, 1933.

| | | |
|---|---|---|
| B-14092- | That's How Rhythm Was Born | ARC rejected |
| B-14094- | Nobody's Sweetheart | - |

New York, November 20, 1933.

| | | |
|---|---|---|
| B-14358-A-B | I'll Be Ready When The Great Day Comes | Rejected |
| B-14359-A | Rhythm | Br 01715, A-9583, Par R-2662 |
| TO-1336-1 | I've Got The World On A String | CBS AL-33567 (LP) |

FIVE SPIRITS OF RHYTHM : Leo Watson-Wilbur Daniels-Douglas Daniels-tiples-v/Teddy
  Bunn-g/Virgil Scoggins-d-v.              New York, November 23, 1933.

B-14371-A-B  My Old Man                    Br rejected
B-14372-A-B  Her Majesty, My Sugar         -

  Wilson Myers-sb added.                   New York, December 6, 1933.

B-14358-C  I'll Be Ready When The Great Day Comes  Br 6728, 01698, Col DO-1200
B-14426-A  My Old Man                      -            -          -
  NOTE:- This session is entered in the ARC recording files as by THE NEPHEWS.

                                           New York, September 14, 1934.

38662-A  Junk Man                          Dec 160, Br 01944
38663-A  Dr. Watson And Mr. Holmes         -         -
38664-A  That's What I Hate About Love     Br 02058
38665-A  Shoutin' In That Amen Corner      -

THE SPIRITS OF RHYTHM : Same, but Wellman Braud-sb replaces Myers, and Leo Watson-d-v
  replaces Scoggins (only 2 tiples used). Hollywood, September 4, 1941.

H-502-  Walkin' This Town                  Rejected
H-503-  We've Got The Blues                Epic LN-24027, SN-6042,
                                           Col 33SX-1499 (microgrooves)

See also Ella Logan; Red McKenzie.

## PHILIP SPITALNY AND  HIS ORCHESTRA

The four titles comprising one of several sessions for Victor by this commercial
  dance orchestra are all of some interest as jazz, partly or wholly; others on this
  and other labels are probably not without occasional merit.

Ed Kirkeby dir. 2c/tb/2cl-ss-as/cl-ss-ts/p/bj/bb/d/Dennie Looney-v.
                                           New York, June 29, 1926.

35727-4  Hello Baby - vDL                  Vic 20115
35728-2  Jackass Blues                     Vic 20108
35729-2  Up And At 'Em                     -
35730-4  Rippin' It Off                    Vic 20475

## SWEET PEASE SPIVEY

This artist was Addie Spivey, Victoria Spivey's sister.

SWEET PEA : Vocal, acc. by Henry Allen-t/Charlie Holmes-as/Luis Russell-p/Will Johnson-g.                                   New York, November 25, 1929.

57554-1  Day Breakin' Blues                Vic 23361
57555-2  Heart-Breakin' Blues              Vic V-38565
57556-1  Leavin' You Baby                  Vic 23361
57557-1  Longing For Home                  Vic V-38565

SWEET PEASE SPIVEY AND DOT SCOTT'S RHYTHM DUKES : Vocal, acc. by ? Randolph Scott-t/
  as/? Dot Scott-p/g/sb/d.                 Chicago, July 7, 1936.

90786-A  Grievin' Me                       Dec 7204
90787-A-B  Double Dozens (You Dirty No Gooder)  Rejected
90788-A  You Weren't True (But You're Still In  Dec 7237
           In My Heart)
90791-A-B  410 Blues                       Rejected
  NOTE:- Matrices 90789 and 90790 are by Victoria Spivey, q.v.

SWEET PEASE SPIVEY AND HER RHYTHM DUKES : Vocal, acc. by ? Dot Scott-p/d (no t, in
  spite of the label of Decca 7237).      Chicago, August 12, 1936.

90787-C  Double Dozens (You Dirty No Gooder)  Dec 7204
90791-C  410 Blues                         Dec 7237

HANNAH MAY AND THE STATE STREET FOUR : Vocal, acc. by probably :- Lee Collins-t/
   Arnett Nelson-cl/J. H. Shayne-p/John Lindsay-sb.
                                  Chicago, August 20, 1936.

C-1447-1  Just A Rank Stud                    Voc 03313
C-1448-1  Kansas City Hill                      -
   NOTE:- Other records issued as by Hannah May are not by Addie Spivey, but Victoria
   Spivey confirmed that the above two titles were recorded by her late sister.

SWEET PEAS : Vocal, acc. by ? Aletha Dickerson-p/d.
                                  Aurora, Ill., October 11, 1937.

014348-1  I Got A Man In The 'Bama Mines       BB B-7224
014349-1  Cold In Hand                           -
014350-1  Ramblin' Blues                        BB B-8146
014351-1  Disgusted Blues                        -
014352-1  Blood Drippin' Blues                  BB B-8114
014353-1  Road Of Stone                          -

                         VICTORIA  SPIVEY

Vocal, acc. by own p.                   St. Louis, May 11, 1926.

   9651-A  Black Snake Blues                    OK 8338
   9652-A  Dirty Woman's Blues                  OK 8351

   Acc. by Pierce Gist-c/De Lloyd Barnes-p.
                                  St. Louis, May 13, 1926.

   9678-A  Long Gone Blues                      OK 8351
   9679-A  No More Jelly Bean Blues             OK 8338

   Acc. by John Erby-p or Erby's Fidgety Five*: T/tb/cl/John Erby-p/d.
                                  New York, August 12, 1926.

74260-A  Hoodoo Man Blues                       OK 8370
74261-A  Spider Web Blues                        -
74262-A  It's Evil Hearted Me                   OK 8410
74263-A  Santa Fe Blues                          -
74264-A  *Humored And Petted Blues             OK 8389

   Acc. by Lonnie Johnson-vn-g/? John Erby-p.
                                  New York, August 13, 1926.

74265-A  Big Houston Blues - g                  OK 8401
74266-A  Got The Blues So Bad - vn               -

   Acc. by Erby's Fidgety Five : as above.New York, August 16, 1926.

74275-B  Blue Valley Blues                      OK 8389

   Acc. by John Erby-p/Lonnie Johnson-g.  St. Louis, April 27, 1927.

80766-B  Steady Grind                           OK 8464
80767-B  Idle Hour Blues                         -
80768-B  Arkansas Road Blues                    OK 8481
80769-B  The Alligator Pond Went Dry             -
80770-B  No. 12 Let Me Roam                     OK 8494
80771-B  T. B. Blues                             -

                                  New York, October 28, 1927.

81583-C  Garter Snake Blues                     OK 8517
81584-A  Christmas Morning Blues                 -
81585-A  Dope Head Blues                        OK 8531
81586-B  Red Lantern Blues                      OK 8550

                                  New York, October 31, 1927.

81589-A  Blood Thirsty Blues                    OK 8531
81590-A  Nightmare Blues                        OK 8581

Acc. by Lonnie Johnson-g/John Erby-p.   New York, November 1, 1927.

| | | |
|---|---|---|
| 81596-B | Murder In The First Degree | OK 8581 |
| 81597-B | Jelly Look What You Done Done | OK 8550 |
| 81598-A | Your Worries Ain't Like Mine | OK 8565 |
| 81599-A | A Good Man Is Hard To Find | - |

Acc. by Clarence Williams' Blue Five : King Oliver-c/Ed Cuffee-tb/Omer Simeon-cl/
Clarence Williams-p/Eddie Lang-g.   New York, September 12, 1928.

| | | |
|---|---|---|
| 401114-B | My Handy Man | OK 8615 |
| 401115-A | Organ Grinder Blues | Spivey 2001 (LP) |
| 401115-C | Organ Grinder Blues | OK 8615 |

Vocal duets with Lonnie Johnson, acc. by his g and own p.
New York, October 13, 1928.

| | | |
|---|---|---|
| 401222-A | New Black Snake Blues - Part 1 | OK 8626 |
| 401223-A | New Black Snake Blues - Part 2 | - |

Acc. by Clarence Williams-p; Johnson does not play, but taps the back of his
guitar on 401242-B, and does not sing*. New York, October 17, 1928.

| | | |
|---|---|---|
| 401242-B | *No, Papa, No ! | OK 8634 |
| 401243-B | Toothache Blues - Part 1 | OK/Par 8744, Voc 03243 |

New York, October 18, 1928.

| | | |
|---|---|---|
| 401244-A | Furniture Man Blues - Part 1 | OK 8652, Voc 03260 |
| 401245-B | Furniture Man Blues - Part 2 | -          -        Har 1087 |
| 401246-B | *Mosquito, Fly And Flea | OK 8634 |
| 401247-A | Toothache Blues - Part 2 | OK/Par 8744, Voc 03243 |

Acc. by own p/unknown g.        New York, July 3, 1929.

| | | |
|---|---|---|
| 402491-B | You Done Lost Your Good Thing Now-Part 1 | OK 8733 |
| 402492-B | You Done Lost Your Good Thing Now-Part 2 | - |

Vocal, acc. by Louis Armstrong-t/Fred Robinson-tb/Jimmy Strong-ts/Gene Anderson-p/
Mancy Cara-bj/Zutty Singleton-d.        New York, July 10, 1929.

| | | |
|---|---|---|
| 402525-C | Funny Feathers | OK 8713, Par R-2177, JCl 568 |
| 402526-A | How Do You Do It That Way ? | -          -          - |

Acc. by Henry Allen-t/J. C. Higginbotham-tb/Charlie Holmes-ss/Luis Russell-p/Will
Johnson-g/Pops Foster-sb or bb**.       New York, October 1, 1929.

| | | |
|---|---|---|
| 56732-1 | Blood Hound Blues | Vic V-38570, BB B-8619 |
| 56733-1 | Dirty T. B. Blues | - |
| 56734-1 | Moaning The Blues | Vic V-38546, BB B-8619 |
| 56735-1** | Telephoning The Blues | - |

Acc. by Luis Russell-p/Will Johnson-g.  New York, February 4, 1930.

| | | |
|---|---|---|
| 59142-1 | New York Blues | Vic V-38584 |
| 59143-1 | Lonesome With The Blues | Vic V-38598 |
| 59144-2 | Showered With The Blues | Vic V-38584 |
| 59145-2 | Haunted By The Blues | Vic V-38598 |

Vocal duets with Porter Grainger (as HAROLD GREY), acc. by the latter-p/Teddy Bunn-g.
New York, June 26, 1930.

| | | |
|---|---|---|
| 62291-2 | You've Gotta Have What It Takes-Part 1 | Vic V-38609 |
| 62292-2 | You've Gotta Have What It Takes-Part 2 | - |
| 62293-2 | Baulin' Water Blues - Part 1 | Vic 23349 |
| 62294-2 | Baulin' Water Blues - Part 2 | - |

Vocal, acc. by ? Charles Avery or Thomas A. Dorsey-p/Hudson Whittaker (Tampa Red)-g*.
                              Chicago, March 20, 1931.

| | | |
|---|---|---|
| VO-147- | Nebraska Blues | Voc 1606 |
| VO-148- | *He Wants Too Much | - |
| VO-149- | *Low Down Man Blues | Voc 1640 |
| VO-150- | *Don't Trust Nobody Blues | - |

    Acc. by own p.                        Chicago, c. June-July, 1931.

             Telephoning The Blues           Br rejected

ORIGINAL VICTORIA SPIVEY AND HER HALLELUJAH BOYS (on Decca 7203) or VICTORIA SPIVEY
AND DOT SCOTT'S RHYTHM DUKES (on Decca 7222) : Vocal, acc. by ? Randolph Scott-t/
as/? Dot Scott-p/g/sb/d.          Chicago, July 7, 1936.

| | | |
|---|---|---|
| 90784-A | Sweet Pease | Dec 7222 |
| 90785-A | Black Snake Swing | Dec 7203 |
| 90789-A | I'll Never Fall In Love Again | - |
| 90790-A | T. B.'s Got Me Blues | Dec 7222 |

NOTE:- Matrices 90786 through 90788 are by Sweet Pease Spivey, q.v.

    Acc. by probably :- Lee Collins-t/J. H. Shayne-p/John Lindsay-sb/d.
                                 Chicago, August 20, 1936.

| | | |
|---|---|---|
| C-1449-1 | Dreaming Of You | Voc 03314 |
| C-1450-2 | I Can't Last Long | |

NOTE:- This record is labelled JANE LUCAS AND THE STATE STREET FOUR; it does not
sound very much like Victoria Spivey, but the files claim she made it. Other
records credited to Jane Lucas are by a different artist. The same remarks apply
to the next coupling.

    Acc. by Arnett Nelson-cl/J. H. Shayne-p/g/John Lindsay-sb.
                               Chicago, October 1, 1936.

| | | |
|---|---|---|
| C-1508-2 | Mr. Freddie Blues | Voc 03346 |
| C-1509-1 | Trouble In Mind | - |

VICTORIA SPIVEY AND CHICAGO FOUR : Vocal, acc. by Randolph Scott-t/ —— Collins-cl/
    Dot Scott-p/sb.                  Chicago, October 15, 1936.

| | | |
|---|---|---|
| C-1567-1 | Hollywood Stomp | Voc 03405 |
| C-1568-1 | Detroit Moan | Spivey 2001 (LP) |
| C-1568-2 | Detroit Moan | Voc 03405 |
| C-1569-2 | Any-Kind-A-Man | Voc 03366 |
| C-1570-2 | I Ain't Gonna Let You See My Santa Claus | - |

Vocal, acc. by t/cl/as/ts/p/sb.      New York, March 12, 1937.

| | | |
|---|---|---|
| 20793-1 | One Hour Mama | Voc 03505 |
| 20794-1-2 | Harlem Susie-Kue | Rejected |
| 20795-2 | Give It To Him | Spivey 2001 (LP) |
| 20796-1 | Got The Blues So Bad | Voc 03505 |

    Acc. by t/p/d.                    Chicago, July 8, 1937.

| | | |
|---|---|---|
| C-1963-1-2 | He's My Scuffler | Rejected |
| C-1964-1-2 | Down Hill Pull | - |
| C-1965-2 | From One To Twelve (The Dirty Dozens) | Voc 03639 |
| C-1966-1 | Good Cabbage | - |

    Acc. by cl/as or ts/p/d.           Chicago, July 21, 1937.

| | | |
|---|---|---|
| C-1969-1-2 | Shake Your Can | Voc rejected |
| C-1970-1-2 | Witchcraft Blues | - |
| C-1971-1-2 | Time Ain't Long | - |
| C-1972-1-2 | Don't Love No Married Man | - |

NOTE:- Jay 12, credited to Victoria Spivey, is actually by Mary Mack, q.v.

## THE SPOONEY FIVE ORCHESTRA

Vn/bj-md/g/wb-spoons.                        Atlanta, November 8, 1927.

| | | |
|---|---|---|
| 145172-1 | Chinese Rag | Col 15234-D |
| 145173-2 | My Little Girl | - |

## COMRADE P. C. V. R. SRINAVINEGAR AND HIS RED INDIANS

Pseudonym on Australian XX for Clarence Williams and his Orchestra, q.v.

## DICK STABILE AND HIS ORCHESTRA

The following records by this commercial dance orchestra are known to be of interest
as jazz; exploration of the others may produce others equally so.

Dick Stabile-cl-as dir. Bunny Berigan-Eddie Farley-t/Mike Riley-tb/Chauncey Grey-p/g
   /sb/d/Billy Wilson-v.                     New York, January 29, 1936.

| | | |
|---|---|---|
| 60412-A | Just Because - vBW | Dec 716, 25376, 28127 |
| 60413-A | Deep Elem Blues - vBW | -    -    - |
| 60414-A | If I Could Be With You One Hour Tonight | Dec 977 |
| | - vBW | |
| 60415-A | Ja Da | - |

   Probably entirely different personnel; Bert Shaw-v.
                                            New York, October 16, 1936.

| | | |
|---|---|---|
| 20083-1 | What A Dummy Love Has Made Of Me - vBS | Voc 3368 |
| 20086-2 | Riffin' At The Ritz | - |

Dick Stabile-cl-as dir. Gino Bono-Bennie Belluardo-Spencer Clark-t/Jimmy Curry-tb/
   Adrian Tei-Joe Stabile-as/Frank Gibson-ts/Harry Walton-p/Harry DuPeer-sb/Ray
   Toland-d/Paula Kelly-v.                   New York, January 10, 1938.

| | | |
|---|---|---|
| 018130-1 | In The Shade Of The New Apple Tree-vPK | BB B-7388 |
| 018133-1 | Lost In The Shuffle - vPK | - |

## TOM STACKS AND  HIS MINUTE MEN

See Harry Reser.

## JESS STACY

Piano solos, with Israel Crosby-sb/Gene Krupa-d added*.
                                            Chicago, November 16, 1935.

| | | |
|---|---|---|
| 90445-A | In The Dark/Flashes | Par R-2233, A-6561, Dec 18119, Od 286355 |
| 90446-A | *Barrelhouse | Par R-2187, A-6451, Dec 18119, Od A-2385, 286280 |
| 90447-A-B | *The World Is Waiting For The Sunrise | Par R-2233, A-6561, Dec 18110, Od A-2333, 286355 |
| 90448-A-B | Go Back Where You Stayed Last Night | Rejected |

                                            New York, April 30, 1938.

| | | |
|---|---|---|
| P-22828-2 | Ramblin' | Com 506 |
| P-22829-1 | Complainin' | Rejected |

Piano duet with Lionel Hampton.             Chicago, September 20, 1938.

|   |   |
|---|---|
| Space, Man | MGM E/X-3789, C-807, C-6078 (LPs) |

Piano solos.                                New York, January 18, 1939.

| | | |
|---|---|---|
| P-23989-1 | Candlelights | Com 517 |
| P-23990-2 | Complainin' | Com 506 |
| P-23991-1 | Ain't Goin' Nowhere (Ec-Stacy) | Com 517 |

Piano solos, with Bud Freeman-ts*.          New York, June 13, 1939.

R-2126-2 *She's Funny That Way                  Com 529
R-2127-3  You're Driving Me Crazy                 -
R-2128-2  The Sell-Out                            Com 1503
R-2129-2  Ec-Stacy                                -

JESS STACY AND HIS ORCHESTRA : Billy Butterfield-t/Les Jenkins-tb/Hank d'Amico-cl/
   Eddie Miller-ts/Jess Stacy-p/Allen Hanlon-g/Sid Weiss-sb/Don Carter-d/Carlotta Dale
   v.                                          New York, September 26, 1939.

US-1-1   What's New ? - vCD                      Var 8064, MW 10089
US-2-1   Melancholy Mood - vCD                   -          -
US-3-    Noni                                    Var 8076, Asch 350-2, MW 10088
US-4-    Jess Stay Blues                         -          -          -

   Irving Fazola-cl replaces d'Amico; Hanlon omitted.
                                                New York, November 30, 1939.

US-1110-1  Breeze (Blow My Baby Back To Me)-F. T.  Var 8121
US-1111-1  Breeze (Blow My Baby Back To Me)-Blues   -        Sig 901
US-1112-2  I Can't Believe That You're In Love    Var 8132, Com 60I, Sig 902
           With Me
US-1113-2  A Good Man Is Hard To Find             Var 8140, Sig 901
US-1114-1  Clarinet Blues                         Var 8132, Com 60I, Sig 902

JESS STACY'S ALL-STARS was a pseudonym on Polydor 580028 for Connie's Inn Orchestra
(see Fletcher Henderson).

## BILL STAFFON AND HIS ORCHESTRA

Bill Staffon-v dir. Ray Donay-Henry Madden-Leonard Michaelson-t/Albert Gibson-Max
   Smith-tb/Joe Dixon-cl-as-v/Johnny Buckner-Frank Crolena-as/Fred Pfeiffer-ts/Joe
   Lippman-p/Ray Woodman-sb/Toots Buttenck-d/The Bennett Sisters-v.
                                                New York, August 1, 1935.

92900-1  Sugar Plum - vBSis                      BB B-6115, Vic JR-44, RZ MR-1948
92901-1  Heartstrings - vJD                      BB B-6048
92902-1  Sittin' Around On Sunday - vBS          -
92903-1  Why Stars Come Out At Night - vBS       BB B-6049
92904-1  Am I Blue ? - vBS                       BB B-6175
92905-1  Baby, Won't You Please Come Home ?      -
92906-1  Lost My Rhythm, Lost My Music, Lost     BB B-6049, RZ MR-2125
         My Man - vBSis
92907-1  Love Me Or Leave Me                     Rejected

## JESSE STAFFORD

JESSE STAFFORD AND HIS ORCHESTRA : Jesse Stafford-tb dir. 2t/Gene Secrest-cl-as/as/
   ts/p/bj/Guy Wiedoeft-bb/Adolph Wiedoeft-d.
                                                Los Angeles, July, 1928.

LAE-219  Shine                                   Br 4048, A-7946

                                                Los Angeles, September 6, 1928.

LAE-266  Cinderella Blues                        Br 4048, A-7946

JESSE STAFFORD AND HIS PALACE HOTEL ORCHESTRA : Probably very similar to the above;
   Charlie Blane-v.                             Los Angeles, June 14, 1929.

LAE-529  I Don't Want Your Kisses (If I Can't    Br 4548
         Have Your Love)

   Lawrence Grey-v.                             Los Angeles, November 18, 1929.

LAE-666  I'm Sailing On A Sunbeam - vLG          Br 4630

Other titles by this band may be of marginal interest as "hot" dance music.

Vocal, acc. by her Jazz Band : Addington Major or Charlie Gaines-t/Earl Granstaff-tb
/Nelson Kincaid-Ben Whittet-cl-as/Charlie Johnson-p.
                                        New York, January 5, 1921.

79628-3   Royal Garden Blues                      Col A-3365
79629-1   Crazy Blues                             -

George Breen-vn added.                  New York, March 7, 1921.

79775-2   I'm Gonna Jazz My Way Right Straight    Col A-3390
              Thru' Paradise
79776-3   Down Where They Play The Blues          -

Acc. by her Jazz Band : C/tb/cl-as/? cl-ts/p/bb.
                                        New York, May 7, 1921.

79826-2   If You Don't Want Me Send Me To My Ma   Col A-3418
79827-2   Strut Miss Lizzie                       -

                                        New York, May 25, 1921.

79857-2   Wild Weeping Blues                      Col A-3426
79858-3   I've Lost My Heart To The Meanest Girl  -

                                        New York, June 30, 1921.

79919-1-2  "Shuffle Along" Medley (Intro.         Col rejected
              Bandana Days/Gypsy Blues/I'm Just Wild About Harry)

                                        New York, September 28, 1921.

80001-3   Arkansas Blues                          Col A-3493
80002-3   Down Home Blues                         Col A-3511
80006-2   Blind Man Blues                         Col A-3493

                                        New York, November 4, 1921.

80047-2   Monday Morning Blues                    Col A-3511

Acc. by c/tb/Buster Bailey-cl/p/bj.    New York, c. March 30, 1926.

106749    Ain't Got Nobody To Grind My Coffee     PA 7502, Per 102
              In The Morning
106750    Take Your Finger Off It                 -            -

## ARTHUR STAIGER

Pseudonym on Supertone for Seger Ellis, q.v.

## AILEEN STANLEY

Only the following title from the hundreds made by this very popular cabaret artist
in the U.S.A. and the U.K. during the 1920s and 1930s is known to be of interest as
jazz for its accompaniment.

Vocal, acc. by Max Goldberg-t/? Ted Heath-tb/cl/vn/Harry Jacobson-p/g/sb/d.
                                        London, February 12, 1934.

GB-6556-3  Who Walks In When I Walk Out ?         Br 01706

## BARRIE STANTON QUINTET

Cl/2g/sb/d-marimba.                     London, November 7, 1938.

CE-9420-1  If It Rains - Who Cares !              Par F-1280
CE-9421-1  A Garden In Granada                    -

The late Nat Star was a well-known clarinet and alto saxophone player in British band
  circles during the 1920s and 1930s, recording with studio bands on most labels, in
  particular Sterno and associated makes.  Through the courtesy of his grandson, who
  lent Nat Star's engagement books, we have a very clear picture of the personnels he
  was accustomed to using.  The following are of interest as jazz.

Nat Star-cl-as dir. Jimmy Wornell-Bert Heath-t/Ted Heath-tb/Arthur Lally-cl-as-bar/?
  George Smith-cl-ts/Claude Ivy-p/Stan Greening-bj/Jock Merritt-bb/Wag Abbey-d.
                                     Hayes, Middlesex, February 21, 1928.

HH-12746-1  I Ain't Got Nobody                     Hom D-1231

   Probably similar; Ted Heath-tb featured.
                                     London, c. April, 1931.

S-1493     Hello, Beautiful                        Sterno 695

## AL STARITA AND HIS SOCIETY ORCHESTRA

Al Starita-cl-as dir. c/tb/p/bj/bb/d/? others.
                                     New York, c. February 19, 1921.

   1178-B  Wang-Wang Blues                GG L-1055, Ct L-3049, Je L-855

For other Al Starita records, see the Gilt Edged Four, the Kit-Cat Band and the
  Piccadilly Players.

## RAY  STARITA

Ray Starita made a vast number of titles for Columbia and Sterno during his sojourn
  in London between 1925 and 1934.  Of these, the following are known to be of "hot"
  dance music interest.

RAY STARITA AND HIS AMBASSADORS BAND : Ray Starita-cl-ts dir. Sylvester Ahola and
  another-t/Ted Heath-tb/Edgar Bracewell-Chester Smith-cl-as/Ted Edbrooke-vn/Donald
  Thorne-p/Jack Hill-bj/Arthur Calkin-bb/Rudy Starita-d/Eddie Grossbart-v.
                                     London, June 13, 1928.

WA-7493-2  I Call You Sugar                        Col 4943

                                     London, June 30, 1928.

WA-7574-2  Rhapsody In Rhythm                      Col 5008
WA-7575-1  That's What I Call Keen                 -

                                     London, September 29, 1928.

WA-7905-2  I Just Roll Along (Having My Ups And    Col 5042
             Downs)
WA-7906-2  Crazy Rhythm - vEGB                     Col 5137
WA-7908-2  Where Have You Been All My Life ? - v3  -

   Ray Starita-cl-ts dir. Max Goldberg-t-mel/Bert Wilton or Nobby Knight-t/Les Carew-
   tb/Edgar Bracewell-Ernie Smith-cl-as-bar/Ted Edbrooke-vn/Donald Thorne-p/Jack Hill
   bj/Arthur Calkin-bb/Rudy Starita-d/Betty Bolton-v.
                                     London, May 4, 1929.

WA-8951-2  Wake Up, Chillun, Wake Up ! - vBB       Col 5380, 01595

RAY STARITA AND HIS BAND : Same, or very similar.
                                     London, May 23, 1930.

WA-10404-2  I'm That Way Over You                  Col CB-80

   Ray Starita-cl-ts dir. Ben Collins-D. Burgess-t/Lew Davis-tb/Chester Smith-cl-as-
   bar/Rex Owen-cl-as/George Glover-cl-ts-vn/Eugene Pini-vn/Harry Robens-p/George
   Oliver-bj-g/Arthur Calkin-sb/Rudy Starita-d-x/Maurice Elwin-v.
                                     London, December 3, 1930.

WA-10942-2  Put Your Worries Through The Mangle    Col CB-195
              - vME

RAY STARITA AND HIS AMBASSADORS : Ray Starita-cl-ts dir. Nat Gonella-t-v/t/tb/2cl-as/
   vn/p/bj/bb-sb/Rudy Starita-d.              London, January 5, 1932.

S-2107    Get Happy - v3                        Sterno 861
S-2108    Oh !  Mo'nah - v3                         -

                                           London, January 22, 1932.

S-2177    You Try Somebody Else - v               Sterno 900

                                           London, February 3, 1932.

S-2202    You Rascal You - vNG ?                  Sterno 900
                                           London, June 15, 1932.

S-2476    Do The New York - v                     Sterno 1007
                                           London, August 12, 1932.

S-2525    Sing A New Song - v3                    Sterno 1020, 4-in-1 3
S-2526    I Got Rhythm - v3                       Sterno 1023    -
   NOTE:- Sterno 1023 as TWELVE RHYTHM MONARCHS.
   Unknown girl v.                         London, September 28, 1932.

S-2598    How'm I Doin' (Hey-Hey) - vNG&girl (+?)  Sterno 1043, 4-in-1 9
   NOTE:- Both issues as TWELVE RHYTHM MONARCHS.

                              HENRY  STARR

Piano solos; self-accompanied vocals by this artist are of little or no jazz value.
                                    Los Angeles, c. March, 1928.

   1317    Mr. Froggie                           Flexo 148 (7")
   1318    Willow Tree                              -

                          STATE STREET  RAMBLERS

Natty Dominique-c/Johnny Dodds-cl/Jimmy Blythe-p/Baby Dodds-wb.
                                    Chicago, c. August 12, 1927.

   12989   There'll Come A Day                   Gnt 6249, Ch 15344, Pm 14023
   12990   The Weary Way Blues                   Gnt 6232    - GS 40103, Sil 5138,
                                                 Bm 1086, HJCA HC-40, JC L-106,
                                                 Tem R-18
   12991   Cootie Stomp                          Gnt 6232, Ch 15399, Bm 1086,
   NOTE:- Champion 15344 as BLYTHE'S BLUE BOYS;  HJCA HC-40, JC L-106, Tem R-18
   15399 as DOWN HOME SERENADERS; Paramount 14023 as JOHNNY DODDS FOUR.

   Probably the same personnel.          Chicago, March 10, 1928.

   13529, -A-B  My Baby                          Gnt rejected
   13530, -A  Pleasure Mad                          -
   13531, -A  Oriental Man                          -

Natty Dominique-c/as/Jimmy Blythe-p/W. E. Burton-wb-v.
                                    Richmond, Ind., c. April 23, 1928.

   13686   My Baby                               Gnt 6454, Ch 15528, 40115
   13686-A My Baby                               Dec 7240
   13687   Oriental Man                          Gnt 6692, Ch 15676, 40023,
                                                 JC L-137, Tem R-15
   13688-A Pleasure Mad                          Gnt 6454, Ch 15551, 40025,
                                                 Dec 7225, WS 104
   13689-A Shanghai Honeymoon - vWEB             Gnt 6485
   13690-A Some Do And Some Don't                Gnt 6552, Ch 15551, 40062
   13690-B Some Do And Some Don't                Dec 7225
   13691   Tack It Down                          Ch 40062, Dec 7224, WS 104,
                                                 JC L-137, Tem R-15
   13691-A Tack It Down                          Gnt 6485, Ch 15528
   13691-B Tack It Down                             -
   NOTE:- Champions as BLYTHE'S BLUE BOYS; Deccas as BLUE JAY BOYS.

Baldy McDonald-cl/white teenager (name not remembered)-as/W. E. Burton-k-v/Jimmy
Blythe-p/Bill Johnson-sb/Marcus H. Norman-d.
                                        Richmond, Ind., July 18, 1928.

| | | |
|---|---|---|
| 14065-A | Endurance Stomp | Ch 40025, Dec 7224 |
| 14065-B | Endurance Stomp | Gnt 6552, Ch 15615, 40025, |
| | | Dec 7224, Creole 20, Tem R-12, |
| | | Sto J-4, XX 1 |
| 14066 | Tuxedo Stomp | Gnt 6589 |
| 14067-C | Brown-Skin Mama | Gnt 6569, Ch 15676, 40023, |
| | | Dec 7240, Tem R-12, Sto J-4, XX 1 |
| 14072 | St. Louis Nightmare | Gnt 6692 |
| 14073 | Yearning And Blue | Gnt 6641 |

NOTE:- Matrices 14068 through 14071 are by Marie Grinter, q.v., acc. by the State
Street Ramblers. Decca 7224 and 7240 as BLUE JAY BOYS; all Champions as BLYTHE'S
BLUE BOYS; XX 1 as THE BACK BEACH PIRATES.

Cliff Jones-d-v replaces Norman.         Richmond, Ind., July 19, 1928.

| | | |
|---|---|---|
| 14074-A | Tell Me, Cutie | Gnt 6589, Ch 15570, 40115 |
| 14075 | Someday You'll Know | Gnt 6641, Ch 15615 |
| 14076, -A | Five O'Clock Stomp | Rejected |
| 14077, -A | Barrel House Baker | - |
| 14078, -A | Handful Of Keys | - |
| 14079, -A | Searching For A Flat | - |
| 14080 | How Would You Like To Be Me ? - vCJ | Gnt 6569, Ch 15570 |

NOTE:- Champion 15570, 15615 and 40115 as BLYTHE'S BLUE BOYS.

Alfred Bell-k-wb-v/Roy Palmer-tb/Darnell Howard-cl-as/Jimmy Blythe-p/Ed Hudson-v-?bj,
                                        Richmond, Ind., March 13, 1931.

| | | |
|---|---|---|
| 17619 | Tiger Moan (Tiger Moon*) | Ch 16247,40086*, Spr 2755, Sav 503 |
| 17620 | Barrel House Stomp | Ch 16320, 40007, JC1 515, JC L-88 |
| 17621 | Georgia Grind - vAB | Ch 16279, 40009, Spr 2648, BRS 15, |
| | | HJCA HC-71, JC L-47, XX 15 |
| 17622 | Careless Love - vEH | Ch 16464, 40086 |
| 17623-A | Kentucky Blues | Ch 16320, 40007, Spr 2670, Sav 503 |
| | | JC1 515, JC L-88 |
| 17624 | I Want To Be Your Lovin' Man | Ch 16350, Spr 2797 |
| 17625 | South African Blues | Ch 16279, 40070, Spr 2755, Sav 504 |
| | | JC1 516, JC L-83 |
| 17626 | Me And The Blues | Ch 16247, Spr 2670 |
| 17627-A | Sic 'Em, Tige' | Ch 16464, 40070, Spr 2738, |
| | | JC1 516, JC L-83 |

NOTE:- Superior 2648, 2670, 2738, 2755 and 2797 as SPEED JEFFRIES AND HIS NIGHT
OWLS; XX 15 as THE BACK BEACH PIRATES.

Palmer and Howard omitted.               Richmond, Ind., March 20, 1931.

| | | |
|---|---|---|
| 17628-A | Wild Man Stomp - vAB | Ch 16297, 40013, Spr 2648, Sav 504 |
| | | Dec 7424, Voc V-1023 |
| 17629 | Stomp Your Stuff - vAB | Ch 16297, 40013, Spr 2728, |
| | | Dec 7424, Voc V-1023, BRS 15 |
| 17631 | Richmond Stomp - vAB | Ch 16350, 40009, Spr 2797, |
| | | HJCA HC-71, JC L-47, XX 15 |

NOTE:- Matrix 17630 is a blues recording not connected with this session; Champion
16297, 40013 and Vocalion V-1023 as THE CHICAGO STOMPERS; Superior 2648, 2728 and
2797 as SPEED JEFFRIES AND HIS NIGHT OWLS; XX 15 as THE BACK BEACH PIRATES.

## STATE STREET  STOMPERS

Junie Cobb-cl-as-v/Thomas A. Dorsey-p-speech/Hudson Whittaker ("Tampa Red")-g/Jimmy
Bertrand-d.                              Chicago, December 14, 1928.

| | | |
|---|---|---|
| 48755-1-2 | Rolling Mill Stomp - vJC | Vic rejected |
| 48756-1-2 | Panama Blues - spTAD | - |

? Herb Morand-t-? speech/Arnett Nelson-cl/? Black Bob-p/g/? John Lindsay-sb/Robert
  Brown ("Washboard Sam")-wb-v.          Chicago, July 9, 1936.

C-1428-1  I Kept On Rubbing That Thing - sp      Voc 03284
C-1429-1  Chicago Rhythm - vRB                    -

   T (and g ?) omitted.              Chicago, August 28, 1936.

C-1453-2  Oh Red ! - vRB                         Voc 03319
C-1454-1  Whippin' That Jelly - vRB               -

T/Bob Robinson-? cl-v/p/? John Lindsay-sb.
                                     Chicago, October 1, 1936.

C-1506-1  You Waited Too Long - vBR             Voc 03347, Cq 8765
C-1507-1  When You Were A Girl Of Seven - vBR    -

Herb Morand or Randolph Scott-t/Arnett Nelson-cl/? Black Bob-p/sb/Robert Brown-wb-v.
                                     Chicago, October 15, 1936.

C-1563-1  Swing Cat Swing - vRB                 Voc 03364
C-1564-2  Oh Red ! No. 2 - vRB                    -

Herb Morand-t/Arnett Nelson-cl/? Myrtle Jenkins-p/? Big Bill Broonzy-g/sb/Mary Mack-
  v.                                 Chicago, November 19, 1936.

C-1686-2  Rattlesnakin' Daddy - vMM             Voc 03395
C-1687-1  You Can't Do That To Me - vMM         Voc 03572

See also Mary Mack.

## STEAMBOAT JOE AND HIS LAFFIN' CLARINET

? Percy Glascoe-cl/? Lemuel Fowler-p/bj.  New York, April 6, 1927.

GEX-575    Texas Shuffle                      Gnt 6103, BP 8020
GEX-576    Mississippi Valley Blues              -          -      Ch 15263
    NOTE:- Champion 15263 as HUNK LUNSFORD AND HIS CLARINET.

## GENEVIEVE  STEARNS

Vocal, acc. by Jesse Crump-p.          Richmond, Ind., July 20, 1923.

 11555, -A  Louisville Lou (The Vampin' Lady)    Gnt rejected (?)
 11558, -A  Farewell Blues                        -
    NOTE:- Matrices 11556 and 11557 are by Nina Reeves, q.v.

## BLUE STEELE AND  HIS ORCHESTRA

The following titles by this dance orchestra are known or thought to be of interest
   as jazz. Titles omitted are known to be of no such interest whatever (they are
   mostly waltzes).

Blue Steele-tb-mel-v dir. Frank Martinez-Frank Krisher-t/Sonny Clapp-tb/Roger Sanford
   as/Kenny Sargent-cl-as-bar-v/Pete Schmidt-ts-v/Sol Lewis-p/Ted Delmarter-bj-g-v/
   Marvin Longfellow-bb-a/Tom Summers-d.    Savannah, August 26, 1927.

 39852-3  Sugar Babe, I'm Leavin' ! - vBS-KS-PS   Vic 20971, BB B-5867, HMV B-5440

Blue Steele-tb-v dir. Sam Goble-Goof Morrison-t/Ole Hoel-eu/John Langley-cl-as/Kenny
   Sargent-cl-as-bar-v/Pete Schmidt-cl-ts/Sol Lewis-p/Ted Delmarter-bj-g-v/Marvin
   Longfellow-bb-a/Henry Cody-d/Bob Nolan-v.
                                     Atlanta, October 26, 1927.

40355-2  Betty Jean - vBS                       Vic 21183

   Pat Davis-ts replaces Schmidt.      Memphis, February 2, 1928.

41829-3  Beyond The Sunset - vKS-TD-BN          Vic 21530

Blue Steele-tb-v dir. Sam Goble-Goof Morrison-t/John Langley-cl-as/Kenny Sargent-cl-
    as-bar-v/Pat Davis-ts/Sol Lewis-p/Ted Delmarter-bj-g-v/Marvin Longfellow-bb-a/Henry
    Cody-d/Bob Nolan-v.                         Memphis, February 7, 1928.

40355-7  Betty Jean - vBS                           Vic 21183

                                            Memphis, February 8, 1928.

41865-3  Be My Baby - vKS                           Vic 21355

                                            Memphis, February 10, 1928.

41877-2  Because You Are My Dream Girl - vBN        Vic 21400

                                            Memphis, February 13, 1928.

41892-3  Washington And Lee Swing - vch            Vic 21262
41893-2  Where Has My Old Gang Gone ? - vKS-TD-BN    -

Blue Steele dir. ? Clyde Davis -and another-t/? Jesse James-tb/2cl-as/cl-ts/? Brick
    English and another-vn/p/g/bb/Moe Goodman-d/George Marks-v.
                                            Memphis, September 18, 1929.

55544-3  Coronado (Brings Memories Of You) - vGM  Vic V-40140

                                            Memphis, September 19, 1929.

55550-1-2-3  Freddy's Fog                           Vic rejected


Blue Steele dir. ? Clyde Davis and another-t/? Jesse James-tb/Frank Myers-cl-as-v/
    Jack Eacholls-cl-as/Ernie Wimburn-ts-v/? Brick English-vn/Galen Grubb-p/Red
    Rountree-bj-g/Cookie Trantham-bb/d/Kay Austin-Mabel Batson-George Marks-v.
                                            Memphis, May 14, 1930.

59922-1-2-3  Pumpernickel                           Rejected
59923-3  You Darlin' ! - vEW                        Vic 22436
59924-1-2-3  All Muggled Up - vFM                   Rejected

                                            Memphis, May 15, 1930.

59923-4  You Darlin' ! - vEW                        Rejected
59924-4  All Muggled Up - vFM                       Vic 23014, HMV B-4916, R-14562
59925-2  Shooin' Flies - vKA                        -          -         -

                                            Memphis, May 16, 1930.

59928-1-2  There's A Tear For Every Smile In        Rejected
             Hollywood - vEW
59928-3  There's A Tear For Every Smile In          Vic 22436
             Hollywood - vMB



## JOE STEELE AND HIS ORCHESTRA


Joe Steele-p dir. Ward Pinkett and Jack Wilson or Langston Curl-t/Jimmy Archey-tb/
    Charlie Holmes-cl-ss-as/E. Eugene Mikell-ts/Joe Garland-bar/Percy Richardson-bj/
    Frank Smith-bb/Gerald Hobson-d.
                                            New York, June 4, 1929.


53808-1  Coal-Yard Shuffle                          Vic V-38066, HMV R-14293
53808-2  Coal-Yard Shuffle                          Vic 741057 (LP)
53809-1  Top And Bottom                             Vic V-38066
53809-2  Top And Bottom                             Vic 741057 (LP)

Pseudonym on Australian Regal for the following items listed in this book :-

G-20243  Fascinatin' Vamp (Jan Garber and his Orchestra)
G-20272  I Want To Be Alone With Mary Brown (The Piccadilly Players)
G-20788  Here Comes Emily Brown (Jack Payne and his BBC Dance Orchestra)
G-20802  Watching My Dreams Go By (Merle Johnston and his Ceco Couriers)

## BILLY STENNETT'S CAROLINA STOMPERS

Billy Stennett-t-vn dir. Simon Carlson-t/Arthur Roehre-tb/Cecil Fransen-as-vn/Albert
    Grossberg-as/Albert Stainbeck-ts/Larry Jacques-p/Raleigh Carroll-bj-g/Leslie
    Eckert-bb/Earl Riggs-d-v.              Chicago, June, 1928.

| | | |
|---|---|---|
| 20672-3 | Somebody Sweet Is Sweet On Me - vER | Bwy 1193 |
| 20673-2 | Down Where The Sun Goes Down - vER | - |
| 20674-1 | Buffalo Rhythm | Bwy 1194 |
| 20675-1 | "Red Nichols" Five Pennies (sic) | - |

## THE STEPPERS

Pseudonym on Tremont 0529 (LUCKY KENTUCKY) for Sam Lanin and his Orchestra, q.v.

## STERLING DANCE ORCHESTRA

Pseudonym on Australian Sterling 1111 (GET OUT AND GET UNDER THE MOON) for Sam Lanin
    and his Orchestra, q.v.

## HEW STERLING'S ORCHESTRA

Pseudonym for the following items listed in this book :-

Canadian Domino 31008  My Blackbirds Are Bluebirds Now (Ernie Golden and his Orch.)
    Sterling 281308  Rainy Weather Rose (Adrian Schubert and his Orchestra)

## STERLING SYNCOPATORS

Pseudonym on Australian Grand Pree 18187 for the Synco Jazz Band, q.v.

## LEITH STEVENS AND HIS SATURDAY NIGHT  SWING CLUB ORCHESTRA

Leith Stevens dir. 3t/2tb/2-3cl-as/ts/p/g/sb/Chauncey Morehouse-d.
                                    New York, June 25, 1938.

| | | |
|---|---|---|
| 23161-2 | Love's Old Sweet Song | Voc 4350, RZ G-23686 |
| 23162-1 | Twelfth Street Rag | - - |
| 23163-1 | Memphis Blues/Royal Garden Blues | Voc 4210, Par R-2585 |
| 23164-1 | La-De-Doody-Doo | - - |

## CARLYLE STEVENSON'S EL PATIO ORCHESTRA

Carlyle Stevenson-as dir. Leslie Moe-Ralph Markey-t/Harley Luse-Doc Garrison-tb/Harry
    Vaile-Leslie Lyman-cl-as-ts/Bob Sawyer-p/Carrol McManus-bj/Oscar Martin-bb/Buddy
    Johnson-d/Walter Dupre-Carl Edwards-v.  Los Angeles, c. May, 1925.

| | | |
|---|---|---|
| | Eccentric | Hwd 1024 |

One tb only present.                Los Angeles, c. July, 1925.

| | | |
|---|---|---|
| 829 | Milenburg Joys (sic) | Sunset 1117 |
| 843 | Yes Sir ! That's My Baby - vCE | - |
| 855 | Cecilia - vCE | Sunset 1119 |
| 858 | Collegiate - v3 | Sunset 1120 |
| 859 | Summer Nights - vCE | Sunset 1119 |
| 861 | You Told Me To Go - vWD | Sunset 1120 |
| | Charleston | Sunset 1114 |
| | I Miss My Swiss | - |
| | Remember | Sunset 1134 |

NOTE:- Sunset 1114 as CARLYLE STEVENSON'S BON TON ORCHESTRA.

Piano solo, with speech.                    Chicago, December 7, 1929.

C-4921-   New Orleans Blues                          Voc 1536

## MAE  STEWART

Pseudonym on Silvertone for Priscilla Stewart, q.v.

## PRISCILLA  STEWART

Vocal, acc. by Jimmy Blythe-p.              Chicago, April, 1924.

1760-2  You Ain't Foolin' Me               Pm 12205, Sil 3520
1761-2  True Blues                                   -
NOTE:- Silvertone 3520 as MAE STEWART.

                                            Chicago, c. August, 1924.

9025-1-2  Mecca Flat Blues                  Pm 12224

Stump Evans-Cm or as added.                 Chicago, c. August, 1924.

9030 ?  Delta Bottom Blues                  Pm 12240
NOTE:- All copies of this issue so far inspected have only the control number 224
in the wax; the above matrix number is deduced from this.

Acc. by J. H. Shayne-p.                     Chicago, c. August, 1924.

9034-1-2  Mr. Freddie Blues                 Pm 12224
1832-   Mr. Freddie Blues                   Rejected ?

Acc. by Jimmy Blythe-p.                     Chicago, c. October 9, 1924.

1916-1-2  I Never Call My Man's Name        Pm 12240

Jimmy O'Bryant-cl added*.                   Chicago, c. November, 1924.

9085-1  *Tall Brown Papa Blues              Pm 12253
9086-4  The Woman Ain't Born                         -

                                            Chicago, April, 1925.

2090-1  I Was Born A Brownskin And You Can't   Pm 12286, Sil 3518
          Make Me Blue
2091-1-2  Priscilla Blues                           -
NOTE:- Silvertone 3518 as MAE STEWART.

Acc. by Clarence Johnson-p.                 Chicago, c. July, 1925.

2198-2  Switch It Miss Mitchell             Pm 12299, Sil 3541
2199-1  Going To The Nation                         -          -
NOTE:- Silvertone 3541 as MAE STEWART.

Acc. by Jimmy Blythe-p.                     Chicago, c. May, 1926.

2534-1  It Must Be Hard                     Pm 12360
2535-1  Somebody's Chewin' You Too                  -

C added.                                    Chicago, c. September, 1926.

2643-2  Biscuit Roller                      Pm 12402

C omitted.                                  Chicago, c. September, 1926.

2659-2  Jefferson County                    Pm 12402

                                            Chicago, c. March, 1927.

4251-1  Lonesome Hour Blues                 Pm 12463
4252-1  New Mr. Freddie Blues                        -

Acc. by Jimmy Blythe-p.                  Chicago, April, 1927.

| 4344-2-3 | P. D. Q. Blues | Pm 12465 |
| 4354-2 | Someday Sweetheart | - |

Acc. by Tiny Parham-p.                  Chicago, c. December, 1928.

| 21042-1 | A Little Bit Closer | Pm 12740 |
| 21043-2 | I Want To See My Baby | - |

## REX STEWART

REX STEWART'S HARLEM SERENADERS : Rex Stewart-c/probably t/tb/2-3cl-as-ts/p/bj/bb/d/
Andy Razaf-v.                    New York, April 4, 1927.

| E-4793/4 | Ten O'Clock Blues | Voc rejected |
| E-4795/7 | Oh Malinda - vAR | - |

REX STEWART AND HIS ORCHESTRA : Rex Stewart-c-v/George Stevenson-tb/Rudy Powell-cl-
as/Bingie Madison-cl-ts/Roger Ramirez-p/Billy Taylor-sb/Jack Maisel-d.
                    New York, December 12, 1934.

| 16410-1 | Stingaree | Voc 2880, Dec F-5458, Br A-500519 |
| 16411-1 | Baby, Ain't You Satisfied ? - vRS | -      -      - |

REX STEWART AND HIS FIFTY-SECOND STREET STOMPERS : Rex Stewart-c/Lawrence Brown-tb/
Johnny Hodges-ss-as/Harry Carney-cl-bar/Duke Ellington-p/? Brick Fleagle-g/Billy
Taylor-sb/Jack Maisel-d.        Hollywood, December 16, 1936.

| B-4369-A | Rexatious | Vri 517, Voc 3810, BA 226 |
| B-4370-A | Lazy Man's Shuffle | Realm M-52618 (LP) |
| B-4370-B | Lazy Man's Shuffle | Vri 517, Voc 3810, BA 226 |

Freddy Jenkins-t added; Brown omitted; Hayes Alvis-sb replaces Taylor.
                    New York, July 7, 1937.

| M-549-1 | Back Room Romp (A Contrapuntal Stomp) | Vri 618, Voc/OK 3831, Swing 313, Col MZ-333 |
| M-549-2 | Back Room Romp (A Contrapuntal Stomp) | Realm M-52618 (LP) |
| M-550-1 | Love In My Heart (Swing, Baby, Swing) | Vri 664, Voc/OK 3844, Col MZ-332, BA 232 |
| M-551-1 | Sugar Hill Shim-Sham | As above |
| M-551-2 | Sugar Hill Shim-Sham | Realm M-52628 (LP) |
| M-552-1 | Tea And Trumpets | Vri 618, Voc/OK 3831, Swing 313, Col MZ-333 |
| M-552-2 | Tea And Trumpets | Realm M-52628 (LP) |

Rex Stewart-c/Louis Bacon-t-v/Joe Nanton-tb/Barney Bigard-cl/Duke Ellington-p/
Brick Fleagle-g-a/Billy Taylor-sb/Sonny Greer-d.
                    New York, March 20, 1939.

| M-994-1 | San Juan Hill - aBF | Voc/OK 5510, BA 258 |
| M-995-1 | I'll Come Back For More - vLB | Voc/OK 5448 |
| M-996-1 | Fat Stuff Serenade | - |

NOTE:- Blue Ace 258 as DUKE ELLINGTON'S OCTET.

REX STEWART AND HIS FEETWARMERS : Rex Stewart-c/Barney Bigard-cl (and d*)/Django
Reinhardt-g/Billy Taylor-sb.      Paris, April 5, 1939.

| OSW-63-1 | Montmartre (Django's Jump) | Swing 56, HRS 1003 |
| OSW-64-1 | Low Cotton | Swing 203      - |
| OSW-65-1 | *Finesse (Night Wind*) | Swing 70, PA PG-538, PI-1062, HMV B-9154, HRS 1004* |
| OSW-66-1 | I Know That You Know | Swing 70, PA PG-538, PI-1062, HRS 1004, 1026 |
| OSW-67-1 | *Solid Old Man (Solid Rock*) | Swing 56, HRS 1004* |

NOTE:- The original HRS issues appeared as IMPROVISATIONS IN ELLINGTONIA; the
later ones, coupling the third and fifth titles under their new names on HRS 1004,
are labelled REX STEWART'S BIG FOUR.

REX STEWART'S BIG SEVEN : Rex Stewart-c/Lawrence Brown-tb/Barney Bigard-cl/Billy Kyle
    p/Brick Fleagle-g/Wellman Braud-sb/Dave Tough-d.
                                    New York, July 23, 1940.

| | | |
|---|---|---|
| 76396-B | Cherry | HRS 2004, JS 525 |
| 76397-A | Solid Rock | HRS 2005, JS 536 |
| 76398-A | Bugle Call Rag | - - |
| 76399-A | Diga Diga Doo | HRS 2004, JS 525 |

REX STEWART AND HIS ORCHESTRA : Rex Stewart-c/Lawrence Brown-tb/Ben Webster-ts/Harry
    Carney-as-bar/Duke Ellington or Billy Strayhorn*-p/Jimmy Blanton-sb/Sonny Greer-d.
                                    Chicago, November 2, 1940.

| | | |
|---|---|---|
| 053607-1 | Without A Song | BB B-10946, HMV B-9208, JK-2488 |
| 053607-2 | Without A Song | X LX-3001, EVAA-3001, Vic RA-5335, HMV 7EG-8137 (microgrooves) |
| 053608-1 | My Sunday Gal | BB B-10946, HMV EA-3144 |
| 053609-1 | Mobile Bay | BB B-11057, Vic 60-0069, HMV B-9208, EA-3144, JK-2488 |
| 053609-2 | Mobile Bay | X LX-3001, EVAA-3001, Vic RA-5335, HMV 7EG-8137 (microgrooves) |
| 053610-1 | *Linger Awhile | As above |
| 053610-2 | Linger Awhile | BB B-11057, Vic 60-0069, HMV EA-3620 |

                                    Hollywood, July 3, 1941.

| | | |
|---|---|---|
| 061342-1 | Some Saturday | BB B-11258, HMV B-9260, JK-2489 |
| 061343-1 | Subtle Slough (Just Squeeze Me) | - - - |
| 061344-1 | Menelik (The Lion Of Judah) | HMV JO-282, JK-2728 |
| 061345-1 | Poor Bubber | - - |

## SAMMY STEWART

SAMMY STEWART'S TEN KNIGHTS OF SYNCOPATION : Sammy Stewart-p dir. Fats Robins-Eugene
    Hutt-t/Mance Worley-tb/Bill Stewart-Harley Washington-Roy Butler-cl-as-ts/Millard
    Robins-bsx/Paul Jordan-vn/Lawrence W. Dixon-bj/Dave Smallwood-d.
                                    Chicago, August, 1924.

| | | |
|---|---|---|
| 1862-2 | Manda | Pm 20340, Bwy/Cvl/Lyra 11404, Pur 11340 |
| 1863-1-2 | My Man Rocks Me | As above |

NOTE:- Broadway/Lyratone 11404 as GOLDEN GATE ORCHESTRA; Carnival 11404 as BROADWAY
MELODY MAKERS.

SAMMY STEWART AND HIS ORCHESTRA : Same.  Chicago, September, 1924.

| | | |
|---|---|---|
| 1891-1-2 | Copenhagen | Pm 20359, 14003, Pur 11359 |

Sammy Stewart-p dir. George Dixon-Leon Scott-t/Kenneth Stewart-tb/Bill Stewart-
Frank Fowler-as/Paul Tyler-ts/Ed Carry-bj/Mance  Worley-sb/Dave Smallwood-d.
                                    Chicago, September 6, 1928.

| | | |
|---|---|---|
| C-2302- | 'Cause I Feel Low Down - v | Voc 15724 |
| C-2303- | 'Cause I Feel Low Down | Rejected |
| C-2304- | Ol' Man River | Voc 15724 |

    Ikey Robinson-v.              Chicago, September 20, 1928.

| | | |
|---|---|---|
| C-2328- | Wob-a-ly Walk - vIR | Voc rejected |
| C-2329- | Skadatin-Dee | - |
| C-2330- | Louder And Funnier | - |

                                    Chicago, October 3, 1928.

| | | |
|---|---|---|
| C-2390- | Crazy Rhythm | Voc 15734 |
| C-2391- | Wob-a-ly Walk | - |

                                    Chicago, November 9, 1928.

| | | |
|---|---|---|
| C-2545-A-B-C | Somebody Stole My Gal | Voc rejected |

As many of the titles recorded by this commercial dance bandleader are obviously
jazz-orientated, and those examined are of interest in this respect, all the known
output, except the waltzes, are listed, but it should not be assumed that they are
of equal merit from the point of view of a jazz enthusiast.

JACK STILLMAN'S(ORIOLE)ORCHESTRA : Jack Stillman-t dir. t/tb/Nathan Glantz-as/cl-as-
f/ts/vn on some sessions/p/bj/bb/d.    New York, November 25, 1924.

| | | |
|---|---|---|
| 9870 | Tomorrow's Another Day - v | Ed 51451 |
| 9871 | That's My Girl - v | - |

Vernon Dalhart-v.                              New York, December 17, 1924.

| | | |
|---|---|---|
| 9909 | Nobody Knows What A Red Head Mama Can Do | Ed 51471 |
| | - vVD | |
| 9910 | Let Me Be The First To Kiss You  Good | Ed 51468 |
| | Morning (And The Last To Kiss You Goodnight) | |

New York, January 12, 1925.

| | | |
|---|---|---|
| 9938 | Lucky Kentucky - v | Ed 51487 |
| 9939 | Show Me The Way - v | Ed 51486 |

Arthur Hall-v.                                 New York, February 17, 1925.

| | | |
|---|---|---|
| 10207 | Florida - vAH | Ed 51521, Amb 5004 |
| 10208 | When You Do What You Do - vVD | Ed 51509 |

New York, March 19, 1925.

| | | |
|---|---|---|
| 10264 | Let It Rain - vVD | Rejected |
| 10265 | Whistle - vVD | Ed 51531 |

New York, April 1, 1925.

| | | |
|---|---|---|
| 10264 | Let It Rain - vVD | Ed 51537 |
| 10289 | Toddle Along | - |
| 10290 | Little Peach | Ed 51538 |

New York, May, 1925.

| | | |
|---|---|---|
| | Sweet Georgia Brown | Bell 368 |
| | You're My Baby | - |

JACK STILLMAN'S ORIOLES : Same.               New York, c. August 21, 1925.

| | | |
|---|---|---|
| 106210 | Mr. Cooler Hot | PA 36304, Per 14485 |
| 106211 | Charleston Of The Evening | PA 36305, Per 14486 |
| 106212 | Feeling Blue | PA 36311, Per 14492 |
| 106213 | Give Me | PA 36307, Per 14488 |

JACK STILLMAN'S ORIOLE ORCHESTRA : Same.  New York, October 5, 1925.

| | | |
|---|---|---|
| 6207-2 | Mr. Cooler Hot | Or 499 |
| 6208-1-2 | Any Blues | Or 494 |
| 6209-2 | Give Me (Your Heart) | Or 498 |

JACK STILLMAN'S ORIOLES : Same.               New York, c. October 13, 1925.

| | | |
|---|---|---|
| 106305 ? | Go Away And Don't Come Back | PA 36329, Per 14510 |
| 106306 | 'Wish I Was A Cradle Baby | PA 36323, Per 14504 |
| 106307 | Hip ! Hip ! | PA 36327, Per 14508 |
| 106308 | Where Were You Then ? | PA 36326, Per 14507 |

JACK STILLMAN'S ORIOLE ORCHESTRA : Same.  New York, c. October 29, 1925.

| | | |
|---|---|---|
| 9791 | Cooler Hot | Gnt 3183, Ch 15051 |
| 9792 | Any Blues (Is Good Enough For Me) | -    Ch 15053 |
| 9793 | Give Me Your Heart | Gnt 3175, Ch 15052 |

NOTE:- Champion 15051, 15052 and 15053 as SILENT JOE AND HIS BOYS.

JACK STILLMAN'S ORIOLES : Jack Stillman-t dir. t/tb/Nathan Glantz-as/cl-as-f/ts/vn
on some sessions/p/bj/bb/d.          New York, c. November, 1925.

    I Wish't I Was In Peoria - v            Bell 382
    I "Wanna" Go Where You Go-Do What You      -
       Do, Then I'll Be Happy - v

 Irving Post-v.                        New York, c. November, 1925.

 2331-1  I Wonder Where My Baby Is Tonight ?-vIP  Pm 20423
 2332-2  Dream Pal - vIP                          Pm 20424, Pur 11424
 2333-1  I'm Gonna Charleston Back To Charleston  Pm 20423
            - vIP

THE STILLMAN CLUB ORCHESTRA : Same.   New York, c. December 24, 1925.

 9915-B  Go Away And Don't Come Back       Gnt 3226, Ch 15072, Chg 362
 9916    Where Were You Then ?             Gnt 3233
 9917-A  Charleston Of The Evening         Gnt 3237, Ch 15072
 NOTE:- Champion 15072 as JACK O'NEIL'S ORCHESTRA.

STILLMAN'S ORIOLES : Same.             New York, c. December 26, 1925.

 106507   A Country Girl Like You          PA 36371, Per 14552
 106508   I Found You - I Want You         PA 36368, Per 14549
 106509   If I Were You                    PA 36369, Per 14550
 106510   What A Bird - What A Girl         PA 36370, Per 14551

JACK STILLMAN'S ORIOLE ORCHESTRA : Same; Arthur Hall-v.
                                       New York, c. December, 1925.

 2356-1-2  Roll 'Em, Girls - vAH          Pm 20427, Pur 11427, Sil 3501
 2357-1    If I Had A Girl Like You - vAH  Pm 20429, Pur 11429, Sil 3503
 2358-1-2  Clap Hands, Here Comes Charley !-vAH  Pm 20427, Pur 11427, Sil 3501

JACK STILLMAN'S ORCHESTRA : Same.     New York, January 8, 1926.

 10758   Dreaming Of A Castle In The Air   Ed 51679
 10759   Love Bound                         -

                                       New York, January 25, 1926.

 10790   Song Of The Flame - v            Rejected
 10791   Looking For A Boy                Ed 51687

JACK STILLMAN'S ORIOLE ORCHESTRA : Same; Frank Bessinger-v.
                                       New York, c. January, 1926.

 2412-2  Behind The Clouds - vFB          Pm 20436

THE STILLMAN CLUB ORCHESTRA : Same.   New York, c. February 1, 1926.

 9956   Lantern Of Love - vFB            Gnt 3244, Ch 15068, Bel 1184
 9957   Mysterious Eyes                    -   3275, Bel 1014, Clm 1911
 NOTE:- Champion 15068 as SOUTH SHORE MELODY BOYS; Beltona 1014 as SOUTHERN STATES
 DANCE BAND; 1184 as SUNNY SOUTH DANCE ORCHESTRA; Coliseum 1911 as MAYFIELD DANCE
 ORCHESTRA.

JACK STILLMAN'S ORCHESTRA : Same.     New York, February 5, 1926.

 10790   Song Of The Flame                Ed 51696, Amb 5139
 10816   Blinky Moon Bay - vAH            Ed 51697, Amb 5145

                                       New York, March 2, 1926.

 10860   Wait Till Tomorrow Night         Ed 51710

STILLMAN'S ORIOLES : Jack Stillman-t dir. t/tb/Nathan Glantz-as/cl-as-f/ts/vn on some
      sessions/p/bj/bb/d.                    New York, c. March 11, 1926.

| 106707 | Rainy Day | PA 36410, Per 14591 |
| 106708 | Along The Lane In Spain | PA 36412, Per 14593 |
| 106709 | Come On And Do Your Red Hot Business | PA 36465, Per 14646 |
| 106710 | I'm Blue Because Of You | PA 36448, 11217, Per 14629 |

JACK STILLMAN'S ORCHESTRA : Same.        New York, March 29, 1926.

| 10897 | Burgundy | Ed 51726 |
| 10898 | For Heaven's Sake | - |

      Arthur Fields-v.                       New York, April 13, 1926.

| 10922 | Somebody's Lonely | Ed 51734 |
| 10923 | Roses - vAF | -        Amb 5161 |

                                           New York, April 20, 1926.

| 10935 | Lulu Belle | Ed 51738 |

STILLMAN'S ORIOLES : Same; Ernest Hare-v. New York, c. April 24, 1926.

| 106834 | Tonight's My Night With Baby - vEH | PA 36443, 11191, Per 14624 |
| 106835 | Who'd Be Blue ? - vEH | PA 36456    - Per 14637, Gra 9230 |
| 106836 | Talking To The Moon | PA 36440, 11217, P 1970, Per 14621 |
| 106837 | Blue Bonnet (You Make Me Feel Blue)-vEH | PA 36441, Per 14622 |
      NOTE:- Grafton 9230 as WINDSOR ORCHESTRA.

JACK STILLMAN'S ORCHESTRA : Same; Bud Kennedy-v.
                                           New York, May 18, 1926.

| 10987 | My Darling - vBK | Ed 51760 |
| 10988 | Valentine | Ed 51768 |

JACK STILLMAN'S ORIOLE ORCHESTRA : Same; Harry Jockin-v.
                                           New York, May, 1926.

| 2506-1 | Say It Again - vHJ | Pm 20443, Bwy 1001, Pur 11443 |
| 2507- | Oh, You Lulu Belle - vHJ | Pm 20446, Bwy 1004, Pur 11446 |
| 2508-1 | Lingering Lips - vHJ | Pm 20443, Bwy 1001, Pur 11443 |

STILLMAN'S ORIOLES : Same.               New York, c. June 25, 1926.

| 106953 | In My Heart | PA 36476, Per 14657 |
| 106954 | Thinking Of You | PA 36479, Per 14660 |
| 106955 | Nothing But Love | PA 36473, Per 14654 |
| 106956 | Twilight And You | PA 36474, Per 14655 |

JACK STILLMAN'S ORIOLE ORCHESTRA : Same; Arthur Hall-v.
                                           New York, c. June, 1926.

| 2568- | Blue Bonnet (You Make Me Feel Blue)-vAH | Pm 20455, Bwy 1013, Pur 11455 |

STILLMAN'S ORIOLES : Same.               New York, c. July 12, 1926.

| 106987-B | I Need You (You Need Me) | PA 36496, Per 14677 |
| | Alice | PA 36495, Per 14676 |

JACK STILLMAN'S ORCHESTRA : Same.        New York, October 4, 1926.

| GEX-308-A | Faustine | Gnt 3407 |

JACK STILLMAN'S ORIOLES : Same.          New York, c. October, 1926.

| | If Tears Could Bring You Back To Me - v | Em 3081, Bell 457 |
| | Gone Again Gal - v | Em 3082        - |

JACK STILLMAN'S ORIOLES : Jack Stillman-t dir. t/tb/Nathan Glantz-as/cl-as-f/ts/vn
  on some sessions/p/bj/bb/d.          New York, c. January, 1927.

```
        High, High, High Up In The Hills - v    Em 3103
        My Little Bunch Of Happiness - v        Em 3106
```

STILLMAN'S ORIOLES : Same; Les Rockwell-v.
                                        New York, c. February 22, 1927.

```
107396-A  Roses For Remembrance - vLR        PA 36608, 11357, Per 14789
107397    Hello ! Little Girl (Of My Dreams) - vLR PA 36606, Per 14787
```
NOTE:- All except Pathe Actuelle 11357 as THE ROYAL TROUBADOURS.

  Joe Sherman-v.                        New York, c. February, 1927.

```
        Coronado Nights - vJS              PA 36695, Per 14776
```

## STINKING SOCKS' SERAPHIC DUO

Pseudonym on XX 10 for Johnny Dodds, q.v., acc. by Tiny Parham.

## BERT STOCK AND HIS ORCHESTRA

Instrumentation and personnel unknown apart from Doc Mayers-Paul Dillon-v; included
  in view of the possibilities suggested by the titles.
                                        New York, November, 1929.

```
GEX-2526-B  Turn On The Heat - vDM          Gnt 7059, Ch 15886, Spt 9585
GEX-2527-B  Honeysuckle Rose - vPD          -         Ch 15932     -
GEX-2528-A  'Tain't No Sin (To Dance Around In  Gnt 7075, Ch 15886, GS 30047
            Your Bones) - vPD
```
NOTE:- Champion 15886 and 15932 as BENNY BENSON'S ORCHESTRA.

## OCIE STOCKARD AND THE WANDERERS

Ocie Stockard-bj dir. Harry Palmer-t-? cl/Robert Buchanan-John Brosky-vn/George Bell-
  p/Buster Ferguson-g/Wanna Coffman-sb.    Dallas, September 11, 1937.

```
014022-1  Ain't Nobody Truck Like You           BB B-7208
014023-1  Long Ago                              -
014024-1  What's The Matter ?                    BB B-7570
014025-1  There'll Be Some Changes Made          -
014026-1  Same Thing All The Time                BB B-7459
014027-2  One Of Us Was Wrong                    BB B-7296
014028-2  Black And Blue                         BB B-7652
014029-1  How Come (You Do Me Like You Do Do Do)  BB B-7459
014030-1  Please Sing For Me (Doodle-Lee-Doo)    BB B-8021
014031-1  Just Blues                             BB B-7716
014032-1  Why Shouldn't I ?                      BB B-7296
014033-1  (Bring It On Down) To My House         BB B-7716
014034-1  Turn Your Lights Down Low              BB B-7652
014035-1  Wabash Blues                           BB B-8021
```

## HARRY STODDARD ORCHESTRA

Of the six titles by this band issued on Emerson in 1923, the following are of some
  interest as jazz.

Harry Stoddard-p dir. t/tb/as-vn/as-ts-bar/vn/bj/bb/d.
                                        New York, c. April, 1923.

```
42376-2  I Ain't Never Had Nobody Crazy Over Me   Em 10626
42377-1  Long-Lost Mama (Daddy Misses You)        -
```

## STOKERS OF HADES

Pseudonym on Columbia and Parlophone for Fletcher Henderson and his Orchestra, q.v.

RAY STOKES

Piano solos.                                    Paris, February 19, 1940.

| OSW-100-1 | South Of The Border | Swing 76 |
| OSW-101-1 | Slidin' Thru' | Swing 219 |
| OSW-102-1 | A Pretty Girl Is Like A Melody | Swing 76 |
| OSW-103-1 | Marie | Swing 219 |

## GEORGIE STOLL AND HIS ORCHESTRA

Georgie Stoll-tb dir. 2t/cl/as/ts/p/g/sb/d.
                                    Los Angeles, July 29, 1936.

| DLA-480- | The Girl Friend | Dec 976 |
| DLA-481- | Swanee | - |

## THE STOMPIN' SIX

Sonny Clay-p dir. Ernest Coycault-t/William B. Woodman, Sr.-tb/Leonard Davidson-cl-ss
ts/Louis Dodd-bj-as/Willie McDaniels-d-k.
                                    Los Angeles, c. May, 1925.

| 673 | Jimtown Blues | Sunset 1098 |
| 676 | Roamin' Around | - |
| 678 | Down And Out Blues | Sunset 1099 |
| 679 | Creole Blues | - |

## THE STOMP SIX

Muggsy Spanier-c/Guy Carey-tb/Volly de Faut-cl/Mel Stitzel-p/Joe Gish-bb/Ben Pollack-
d.                                  Chicago, c. July, 1925.

| 828 | Why Can't It Be Poor Little Me ? (sic) | Auto 626, Ses 5, Tem R-16 |
| 829 | Everybody Loves My Baby | -     -      - |

## EDDIE STONE AND HIS ORCHESTRA

Eddie Stone-v dir. George Walters-Frank Bruno-t/Wendell DeLory-tb/Don Watt-cl/Larry
Tice-Leo White-cl-as/Tony Zimmers-cl-ts/Gil Bowers-p/Tom Moore-g/Dick Kissinger-sb/
Ray Michaels-d-vib/Earle Hagen-a.      New York, April 15, 1937.

| 20978-1 | Satan Takes A Holiday | Voc 3555, ARC 7-07-03 |
| 20979-1 | A Study In Brown | -        - |

New York, May 12, 1937.

| 21121-1 | Casey Jones - vES | Voc 3576, ARC 7-07-17 |
| 21122-1 | Caravan | -        - |
| 21123-1-2 | Dardanella | Rejected |
| 21124-1 | Rhythm On The Loose | Voc 3585, ARC 7-08-05 |
| 21125-1 | Up Popped The Devil - vES | - S-182 - |
| 21126-2 | Honeysuckle Rose | - |

New York, September 10, 1937.

| 21673-2 | Stanshaw Stomp - aEH | Voc 3703, ARC 8-01-12 |
| 21674-1 | Listen, My Children, And You Shall Hear-vES | -        - |
| 21675-2 | The Snake Charmer | Voc 3750, ARC 7-12-05 |
| 21676-1 | Midnight In A Madhouse | -        - |

New York, January 31, 1938.

| 22351- | Smuggler's Nightmare | Voc 4101 |
| 22352- | Morocco | Voc 3984 |
| 22353- | The Campbells Are Swinging | Voc 3996 |
| 22354- | Mr. Sweeney's Learned To Swing | - |
| 22355- | Burping Bassoon | Voc 3984 |
| 22356- | The Goblin Band | Voc 4101 |

Pseudonym on Vocalion 15885 for Gene Kardos and his Orchestra, q.v.

## JESSE STONE

JESSE STONE AND HIS BLUE SERENADERS : Jesse Stone-p-a dir. Albert Hinton-Slick Jack-
son-t/Druie Bess-tb/Jack Washington-as-bar/Glenn Hughes-as/Elmer Burch-ts/Silas
Cluke-bj/Pete Hassel-bb/Max Wilkinson-d.
St. Louis, April 27, 1927.

| | | |
|---|---|---|
| 80761-C | Starvation Blues | OK 8471 |
| 80762-A-B-C | In Susie's Basement | Rejected |
| 80763-A | Boot To Boot | OK 8471 |
| 80764-A-B | Shufflin' Blues | Rejected |

JESSE STONE AND HIS ORCHESTRA : Jesse Stone-pac-a dir. Bob Shoffner-George Wingfield-
Clarence Wheeler-t/David James-Alton Moore-John Anderson-tb/Bobby Holmes-cl-as/Phil
Tillar-Dorlan Coleman-as/Terry Smith-ts/Sonny White-p/Leroy Harris-g/Olin Aderhold-
sb/William McIlvaine-d.
New York, February 26, 1937.

| | | |
|---|---|---|
| M-129-2 | Wind Storm | Vri 521 |
| M-130-1-2 | Rhythm On My Mind | Rejected |
| M-131-2 | Snaky Feeling | Vri 521 |

## LEW STONE

The late Lew Stone was one one of Britain's finest dance-music arrangers, and his was
one of the most famous bands of the 1930s and the war years. The following titles
are all known to be of considerable jazz interest, and short solos of the same kind
can be heard on many others made under Lew Stone's direction.

LEWIS STONE AND HIS ORCHESTRA : Lew Stone-p-a dir. Sylvester Ahola-Max Goldberg-t/?
Tony Thorpe-tb/Arthur Lally-cl-as-bar/? Joe Crossman-cl-as/ts/Tony Hill-bj/bb/d.
Golders Green, London, September 27, 1929.

| | | |
|---|---|---|
| DF-27-1 | Breakaway | Duo F-2012 |

LEW STONE AND THE MONSEIGNEUR BAND : Lew Stone-a dir. Alfie Noakes-t/Nat Gonella-t-v/
Joe Ferrie-Lew Davis-tb/Joe Crossman-Jim Easton-Ernest Ritte-cl-as-bar/Harry Berly-
cl-ts-oc-vl/Eddie Carroll-p/Bill Herbert-g/Tiny Winters-sb-v/Bill Harty-d/Al Bowlly
v.
London, November 29, 1932.

| | | |
|---|---|---|
| GB-5261-2 | Junk Man Blues - vAB-NG&ch/aLS | Dec F-3313 |
| GB-5263-2 | My Woman - vAB/aLS | — |

Harry Sherman-g replaces Herbert.  London, August 1, 1933.

| | | |
|---|---|---|
| TB-1017-1 | Lazy Rhythm - aLS | Dec F-3644, 656 |

Con Lamprecht-a.  London, September 15, 1933.

| | | |
|---|---|---|
| TB-1068-2 | Blue Prelude - vAB/aLS-CL | Dec F-3675 |
| TB-1070-3 | Snowball - vNG | — |

London, October 24, 1933.

| | | |
|---|---|---|
| TB-1098-1 | Nagasaki - vNG/aLS-CL | Dec F-3821, 496, Pan 25709 |

Stanley Black-a.  London, November 3, 1933.

| | | | |
|---|---|---|---|
| GB-6278-1-2 | Blue Jazz - aLS-SB | Dec F-3782, 487, Pan 25743 | |
| GB-6279-1 | White Jazz - aSB | — — Pan 25690 | |

Monia Liter-p replaces Carroll; Eddie Freeman-g replaces Sherman; Paul Fenoulhet-a.
London, January 9, 1934.

| | | | |
|---|---|---|---|
| GB-6473-3 | Tiger Rag | Dec F-3839, 510 | |
| GB-6475-2 | Canadian Capers - aPF | — — Pan 25743 | |

LEW STONE AND HIS BAND at the Monseigneur Restaurant, London : Lew Stone-a dir.
  Alfie Noakes-t/Nat Gonella-t-v/Joe Ferrie-Lew Davis-tb/Joe Crossman-Ernest Ritte-cl
  as-bar/Harry Berly-cl-ts-oc-vl/Monia Liter-p/Harry Sherman-g/Tiny Winters-sb-v/Bill
  Harty-d/Stanley Black-a.                      London, March 16, 1934.

TB-1131-2  Milenberg Joys                        Dec F-3953, Pan 25690
TB-1132-1  The Call Of The Freaks - aLS          -

                                  London, March 23, 1934.

TB-1159-1  It's Psychological - vAB/aLS          Dec rejected

                                  London, April 24, 1934.

TB-1207-2  Garden Of Weed                        Dec F-5271, 361

                                  London, April 25, 1934.

TB-1213-2  That's A Plenty - aSB                 Dec F-5271, 361, Pan 25709,
  NOTE:- Super B-7034 as DANCE BAND.             Super B-7034

     Stanley Black-p-a replaces Liter; Stan Bowsher-a (SBo).
                                  London, August 1, 1934.

TB-1436-2  I Hate Myself (For Being So Mean To   Dec F-5143
             You) - vTW/aSBo
TB-1437-2  Out For No Good - vTW/aSB             -

                                  London, August 3, 1934.

TB-1434-1  As Long As I Live - vAB/aLS          Dec F-5132

LEW STONE AND HIS BAND : As last, but Don Macaffer-tb replaces Davis; Albert Harris-g
  replaces Sherman; Jock Jacobson-d replaces Harty; Gonella, Macaffer, Crossman,
  Ritte, Berly, Harris, Winters and Jacobson only*.
                                  London, December 28, 1934.

CAR-3143-1  Solitude - aLS                       RZ MR-1561
CAR-3144-1  *I Ain't Got Nobody - vTW           -

     Lew Stone-a dir. Tommy McQuater-Alfie Noakes-t/Joe Ferrie-Bill Mulraney-tb/Ernest
     Ritte-Joe Crossman-cl-as-bar/Don Barrigo-ts/Harry Berly-ts-vl/Monia Liter-p-a/
     Archie Slavin-g/Tiny Winters-sb/Barry Wicks-d/Arthur Bell-a.
                                  London, November 9, 1935.

TB-2054-1  St. Louis Blues                       Dec F-5783, X-1033
TB-2055-1  Etude - aAB                           -        -

     Lew Stone-a dir. Alfie Noakes-Chick Smith-t/Joe Ferrie-Lew Davis-tb/Joe Crossman-
     Ernest Ritte-cl-as-bar/Bill Apps-as/Don Barrigo-ts/Bob McGee-p/Archie Slavin-g/
     Tiny Winters-sb-v/Max Bacon-d.        London, November 3, 1936.

TB-2604-1  Shades Of Hades                       Dec F-6188, X-1287
TB-2605-1  Ups And Downs                         -        -
TB-2606-1  Papa Tree-Top Tall - vTW             Dec F-6208

     Eric Breeze-tb replaces Davis; Sam Gelsley-g replaces Slavin; Arthur Maden-sb re-
     places Winters; Jock Jacobson-d replaces Bacon; Eddie Carroll-a.
                                  London, April 23, 1937.

TB-3016-2  House Hop                             Dec F-6392, X-1393, Br A-81264
TB-3017-1  Ebony Shadows - aEC                   -        -        -

     Lew Stone-a dir. Bert Bullimore-Chick Smith-t/Eric Tann-Lew Davis-tb/Joe Crossman-
     Ernest Ritte-cl-as-bar/Dave Shand-as-bar/Don Barrigo-ts/Bob McGee-p/Ivor Mairants-g
     /Arthur Maden-sb/Jock Jacobson-d/Al Bowlly-v.
                                  London, August 15, 1938.

DR-2853-2  Music, Maestro, Please - vAB/aLS      Dec F-6777

LEW STONE AND HIS BAND : Lew Stone-a dir. Chick Smith-Bert Bullimore-t/Lew Davis-Eric
  Tann-tb/Jim Easton-cl-as-bar/Sid Millward-cl-as/Don Barrigo-ts/Laurie Bookin-as-ts/
  Bob McGee-p-a/Archie Slavin-g/Arthur Maden-sb/Jock Jacobson-d.
                                        London, September 26, 1938.

DR-2929-1  Plastered In Paris                  Dec F-6796, X-1610
DR-2930-1  Azure                                    -          -

LEW STONE AND HIS STONE-CRACKERS : Lew Stone dir. Dave Wilkins-Frenchie Sartell-t-v/
  Joe Crossman-cl-as/Jim Easton-as/Don Barrigo-ts/Jack Penn-p/Sidney Jacobson-g/Tommy
  Bromley-sb/Jock Jacobson-d.          London, November 15, 1940.

DR-5112-1  Basin Street Blues - vDW            Dec F-7685
DR-5113-2  Confessin' - vDW                    Dec F-7698
DR-5114-1  Loveless Love - vFS                 Dec F-7685
DR-5115-2  Farewell Blues                      Dec F-7698

  Lew Stone dir. Archie Craig-t/George Chisholm-Eric Breeze-Woolf Phillips-tb/Andy
  McDevitt-cl/Aubrey Franks-ts/Jack Penn-p/Ivor Mairants-g/Charlie Short-sb/Jock
  Jacobson-d.                          London, March 17, 1941.

DR-5477-1  Missouri Scrambler                  Dec F-7824
DR-5478-1  Wednesday Night Hop                      -
DR-5479-1  Singing In The Rain                 Dec F-7858
DR-5480-1  Ja Da                                    -

  Dave Wilkins-t replaces Craig; Dave Walters-tb replaces Phillips; Jock Cummings-d
  replaces Jacobson.                   London, May 22, 1941.

DR-5787-1  Aunt Hagar's Blues                  Dec F-7916
DR-5788-1-2  Beale Street Blues               Rejected
DR-5789-1  At The Jazz Band Ball               Dec F-7916
DR-5790-1-2  Get Happy                        Rejected

## CHARLEY STRAIGHT AND HIS ORCHESTRA

The following records by this well-known Chicago dance orchestra of the 1920s are
known or reported to be of interest as jazz.  There may be similar quality items
among the others (see THE AMERICAN DANCE BAND DISCOGRAPHY), but those examined do
not suggest a strong likelihood.

Charley Straight-p dir. Gene Caffarelli-c/? Guy Carey-tb/cl-as-vn/Wally Preissing-ts/
Leo Murphy-vn/Frank Sylvano-bj/Ike Williams-bb/Bob Conselman-d.
                                        Chicago, June, 1923.

  1445-3  Buddy's Habits                       Pm 20244, Cx 40244, Nat 12244,
                                               Pur 11244
  1446-1-2  Henpecked Blues                    As above

                                        Chicago, September, 1923.

  1505-2  Arkansas Mule                        Pm 20264, Cx 40264, Pur 11264
  1511-3  Bathing Beauty Blues                   - Bwy 11312 -            -

                                        Chicago, October, 1923.

  1542-1-3  Sweet Henry (The Pride Of Tennessee)  Pm 20271, Hg 862, Pur 11271
  1543-2-3  Easy Melody                        -          -          -

                                        Chicago, December, 1923.

  1616-2  My Sunflower Maid                    Pm 20291, Hg 889, Pur 11291
  1617-1  Forgetful Blues                      -          -          -
NOTE:- Claxtonola 40244, 40264, Puritan 11244, 11271 and 11291 as FRISCO SYNCO-
PATORS; Broadway 11312 and Puritan 11264 as MANHATTAN IMPERIAL ORCHESTRA; Harmograph 889 as HARMOGRAPH DANCE ORCHESTRA.

Charley Straight-p dir. Gene Caffarelli and another-c/Randall Miller-tb/Bob Strong-
    mel-cl-as-vn/Frank Stoddard-cl-as/Dale Skinner-cl-ts/Frank Sylvano-bj/Joe Gish or
    Gist-bb/Don Morgan-d/Hannah and Dorothea Williams-v.
                                            Chicago, March 10, 1926.

E-18371/2   What A Man ! - vHW-DW            Br 3136*, A-147
E-18374/6   Hi-Diddle-Diddle - vHW-DW        -          -

                                            Chicago, May 28, 1926.

C-325; E-19403   Deep Henderson              Br 3224*
C-328; E-19406   Hobo's Prayer               -

Charley Straight-p dir. Gene Caffarelli and another-c/tb/2cl-ss-as/cl-ts/Frank
    Sylvano-bj-v/bb/d.              Chicago, May 23, 1928.

C-1966-   Too Busy - vFS                     Br 3945, 3839, A-7792
    NOTE:- This is not the recording of TOO BUSY recalled by Mr. Rex Downing in the
    July-August, 1956 issue of RECORD RESEARCH, p.5, as being made by this orchestra,
    including himself on trombone and Bix Beiderbecke-c.  Perhaps some unissued record
    was made under Charley Straight's direction during early July, 1928, when the Paul
    Whiteman Orchestra, with Bix, was playing an engagement in Chicago.

## MARY STRAINE

Vocal, acc. by Joseph Smith's Jazz Band : Joe Smith-c/? George Brashear-tb/Clarence
    Robinson-cl/Fletcher Henderson-p.     Long Island City, c. May, 1922.

        Ain't Got Nothing Blues              BS 14115, Pm 12132

? Ralph Escudero-bb added.               Long Island City, c. August, 1922.

        I Wish I Could Shimmy (Like My       BS 14123, Pm 12149
            Sister Kate)
        The Last Go Round Blues              -          -

Acc. by Fletcher Henderson-p.            Long Island City, c. April, 1923.

        Chirpin' The Blues                   BS 14150, Maj/Oly 1522, Pm 12150
        Downhearted Blues                    -          -            -
    NOTE:- Majestic/Olympic 1522 as PEARL HARRIS.  Mary Straine also recorded in 1919
    with Bert Williams as one of the "congregation" in a comic "sermon".

## STRAND ROOF  ORCHESTRA

Pseudonym on Domino 3456 (PRINCE OF WAILS) for Fletcher Henderson and his Orchestra,
    q.v.

## ELLIS STRATAKOS AND HIS HOTEL JUNG ORCHESTRA

Ellis Stratakos-tb dir. John Hyman (Wiggs)-Howard Reed-c/John Reininger-Joe Loyacano
    as, one db bsx/Eddie Powers-ts/vn/Joe Wolf-p/Fred Loyacano-g-v/Dave Fridge-bb/Von
    Gammon-d.                        New Orleans, c. February, 1929.

NO-132-   A Precious Little Thing Called Love-vFL  Voc 15792
NO-133-   Weary River - vFL                        -

## STRAUN'S PULLMAN PORTERS

Nathan Glantz-as dir. 2t/tb/cl/ts/p/bj/bb/d/Chick Straun-v.
                                            New York, c. March 24, 1925.

9414-A   Casey Jones - vCS                   Gnt 3005

                                            New York, c. April 5, 1925.

9442   A Hot Time In The Old Town            Gnt 3005

Vocal, acc. by probably at least some of Andy Kirk's Clouds of Joy, q.v., who made
  matrices 64613 through 64615 on the same date.
                                            New York, September 9, 1938.

64612-A  The Gal That Wrecked My Life              Dec 7550, Voc S-242

  Acc. by Louis Jordan's Elks Rendezvous Band : Courtney Williams-t/Louis Jordan-as/
  Lem Johnson-ts/Clarence Johnson-p/Charlie Drayton-sb/Walter Martin-d.
                                            New York, December 20, 1938.

64823-A  Toodle-Loo On Down                        Dec 7550
64824-A  So Good                                   Dec 7579
64825-A  Away From You                             -

## FRED SUGAR AND HIS SUGAR  BABIES

See Fred "Sugar" Hall and his Sugar Babies.

## JOE SULLIVAN

Piano solos.                         New York, September 26, 1933.

265139-2  Honeysuckle Rose                 Col 2876-D, DO-1123, UHCA 32,
                                           Par R-1686, Od OR-1686
265140-2  Gin Mill Blues                   As above, but UHCA 31 (rev. of 32)
265141-2  Little Rock Getaway              Par R-2006, A-3908, UHCA 33
265142-2  Onyx Bringdown                    - Col 2925-D -    UHCA 34

                                     Los Angeles, August 8, 1935.

DLA-224-A  My Little Pride And Joy         Br 02136, A-505038
DLA-225-B  Little Rock Getaway             Dec 600, Br 02099, A-505027
DLA-226-B  Just Strolling                   -  Br 02136, A-505038
DLA-227-A  Minor Mood                      Br 02099, A-505027
DLA-227-B  Minor Mood                      JA 1 (LP)

                                     New York, September, 1939.

           Squeeze Me                       Musicraft rejected
           Unknown title                    -

JOE SULLIVAN AND HIS CAFE SOCIETY ORCHESTRA : Ed Anderson-t/Benny Morton-tb/Edmond
  Hall-cl/Danny Polo-cl-ts/Joe Sullivan-p/Freddy Green-g/Henry Turner-sb/Johnny Wells
  d/Joe Turner-v.                    New York, February 9, 1940.

26500-A  Solitude                          Voc/OK 5531, Par R-2952
26501-A  Oh, Lady Be Good                  Voc/OK 5496, Cq 9503 -
26502-A  Low Down Dirty Shame - vJT        Voc/OK 5531, Par R-2773
26503-A  I Can't Give You Anything But Love - vJT Voc/OK 5496, Cq 9503 -

  Green omitted; Billy Taylor-sb replaces Turner; Yank Porter-d replaces Wells; Helen
  Ward-v.                            New York, April 29, 1940.

26776-A  Pom Pom                           Voc 5556
26777-A  I Cover The Waterfront - vHW      -
26778-A  I've Got A Crush On You - vHW     OK 5647
26779-A  Coquette                          -

Piano solos.                         New York, March 25, 1941.

R-4053   Andy's Blues                      Com 540
R-4054-2 Del Mar Rag                       Com 538

                                     New York, c. March 28, 1941.

R-4060-1 Forevermore                       Com 538
R-4061   Summertime                        Com 540

Vocal, acc. by Frank Newton-t/Buster Bailey-cl/Pete Brown-as/Babe Russin-ts/Claude
Thornhill-p/John Kirby-sb/O'Neil Spencer-d.
New York, August 6, 1937.

| | | |
|---|---|---|
| 21472-1 | Loch Lomond | Voc/OK 3654, S-116, Col DB-1861, DB-5045, CQ-1458, DD-475, DO-2199, DS-1861, GN-5047, Par R-2901 |
| 21473-1 | I'm Coming, Virginia | Voc/OK 3654, S-116, Col 37818, DB-5045  DS-1280, Par R-2901 |
| 21474-1 | Annie Laurie | Voc/OK 3679, S-122, Col DB-5042, GN-5053, Par R-2899, B-71052 |
| 21475-2 | Blue Skies | As above |

Charlie Shavers-t replaces Newton; Russin omitted.
New York, October 22, 1937.

| | | |
|---|---|---|
| 21936-1 | Easy To Love | Voc/OK 3848, S-137 |
| 21937-1 | The Folks Who Live On The Hill | Voc/OK 3885, S-139, Col DB-5046, CQ-1454, Par R-2902, Br A-81609 |
| 21938-1 | Darling Nellie Gray | As above |
| 21939-1 | Nice Work If You Can Get It | Voc/OK 3848, S-137 |

New York, February 4, 1938.

| | | |
|---|---|---|
| 22368-1 | It's Wonderful | Voc/OK 3993, S-194 |
| 22369-1 | Dark Eyes (Black Eyes*) | Voc/OK 4015, S-144, Col DB-1861*, DB-5044, CQ-1458, DD-475, DS-1861, GN-5047, Par R-2900 |
| 22370-1-2 | A Brown Bird Singing | Voc/OK 4068, S-144, Col DB-5044, DS-1280, Pae R-2900 |
| 22371-2 | You Went To My Head | Voc/OK 3993, S-194 |

Acc. by Claude Thornhill and his Orchestra (some of the above issues are also
credited thus) : Bobby Hackett-c/Jimmy Lytell-Paul Ricci-cl-as/Bernie Kaufman-as/
Babe Russin-ts/Eddie Powell-f/Claude Thornhill-p-a/John Kirby-sb/Buddy Rich-d/male
v effects*.                              New York, March 1, 1938.

| | | |
|---|---|---|
| 021054-1 | Moments Like This | Vic 25802, HMV B-8749 |
| 021055-1 | Please Be Kind | - - |
| 021056-1 | *It Was A Lover And His Lass | Vic 25810, HMV B-8759 |
| 021057-2 | Dark Eyes (Black Eyes*) | -        -*        EA-2347 |

New York, June 29, 1938.

| | | |
|---|---|---|
| 023750-1 | Spring Is Here | Vic 25894 |
| 023751-1 | Down The Old Ox Road | - |
| 023752-1 | St. Louis Blues | Vic 25895, HMV B-8789, EA-2347, HN-2406, JO-73 |
| 023753-1 | L'amour, toujours l'amour | As above, except HMV EA-2347 |

Acc. by Bobby Hackett-c/Slats Long-Chester Hazlett-cl-as/Bud Freeman-ts/Milt
Rettenberg-p/Ken Binford-g/Ed Brader-sb/Ed Rubsam-d.
New York, December 10, 1938.

| | | |
|---|---|---|
| 030382-1 | Night And Day | Vic 26132, HMV B-8911, EA-2280, HN-1730, X-6469 |
| 030383-1 | Kinda Lonesome | Vic 26124, HMV B-8875, EA-2247, X-6469, El EG-6858 |
| 030384-1 | It Ain't Necessarily So | Vic 26132, HMV B-8911, EA-2280 |
| 030385-1 | Say It With A Kiss | Vic 26124, HMV B-8875, EA-2247, HN-1730 |

Acc. by Lloyd Reese-t/Leo Trammel-cl/Floyd Turnham-as/Ulysses Banks-ts/Eddie Beal-p
/Red Callender-sb/Oscar Bradley-d.      Hollywood, March 20, 1939.

| | | |
|---|---|---|
| 036051-3 | I Dream Of Jeanie With The Light Brown Hair | Vic 26260, HMV B-8953 |
| 036053-9 | I'm Happy About The Whole Thing | Vic 26237, HMV B-8933 |
| 036054-5 | Drink To Me Only With Thine Eyes | Vic 26260, HMV B-8953 |
| 036055-2 | Corn Pickin' | Vic 26237, HMV B-8933 |

Acc. by Reggie Merrill-Eddie Powell-cl/Carl Prager-bcl/Harold Goltzer-bsn/Mitchell
Miller-o/Walter Gross-p/Frank Carroll-sb/Cary Gillis-d.
                                    New York, August 22, 1939.

| 041596-2 | Jackie Boy | Vic 26372 |
| 041597-1 | Turtle Dove | Vic 26344, HMV X-6739 |
| 041598-1 | Sing Something Simple | Vic 26372, HMV JO-101 |
| 041599-1 | Ill Wind | Vic 26344    -          X-6739 |

Acc. by John Kirby and his Orchestra : Charlie Shavers-t/Buster Bailey-cl/Russell
Procope-as/Billy Kyle-p/John Kirby-sb/O'Neil Spencer-d.
                                    New York, May 1, 1940.

| 26788-C | St. Louis Blues | Col 36341 |
| 26789-B | The Hour Of Parting | - |

New York, June 11, 1940.

| 26916- | Mad About The Boy | Col rejected |
| 26917- | Under The Greenwood Tree | - |

New York, August 1, 1940.

| 27766-1 | If I Had A Ribbon Bow | Col 36233 |
| 27767-1 | Who Is Sylvia ? | - |
| 27768-1 | Molly Malone | Col 35710, DO-2199 |
| 27769-1 | Barbara Allen | - |

New York, June 17, 1941.

| 69364-A | Loch Lomond | Dec 3954, Br 03246 |
| 69369-A | Just Like A Gypsy | -      - |
| 69370-A-B | My Blue Heaven | Dec 4154, Br 03316 |
| 69371-A-B | St. Louis Blues | -      - |

NOTE:- Matrices 69365 through 69368 are by Sam Price, q.v.

New York, December 3, 1941.

| 69988- | When Your Lover Has Gone | Dec rejected |
| 69989- | My Ideal | - |
| 69990- | The Night We Called It A Day | - |
| 69991-A | Concerto For Two (A Love Song) | - |

New York, January 28, 1942.

| 70244-A | Kentucky Babe | Dec 18349, Br 03440 |
| 70245-A | Ma Curly-Headed Baby | -      - |
| 70246-A | When Your Lover Has Gone | Dec 18555, Br 03531 |
| 70247-A | My Ideal | -      - |

New York, March 19, 1942.

| 70541-A | Beside The River Clyde | Dec 4307, Br 03914 |
| 70542-A | How Do I Know It's Real ? | -      - |

## ANNIE SUMMERFORD

Vocal, acc. by Eddie Heywood's Black Bottom Ramblers : ? Harry Cooper-t/tb/Eddie
Heywood-p/? Bernard Addison-bj.          Atlanta, c. August 29, 1924.

| 8739-A | 'Fo Day Blues | OK 8174 |
| 8740-A | Low Down Blues | - |

## SUNKIST SERENADERS

See the New Orleans Blue Nine.

## SUNNY AND THE D'C'NS

See Sunny Greer.

Pseudonym on Beltona for the following items listed in this book :-

309 Sittin' In A Corner (The Broadway Syncopators)
978 Kentucky's Way Of Saying "Good Morning" (Bailey's Lucky Seven)
1113 St. Louis Hop (Joe Candullo and his Everglades Orchestra)
1113 On The Riviera (The Vagabonds)
1120 In A Little Garden (Joe Candullo and his Everglades Orchestra)
1133 Looking At The World Through Rose Coloured Glasses (The Vagabonds)
1184 Lantern Of Love (Jack Stillman's Orioles)
1299 Vo-Do-Do-De-O Blues (California Ramblers)

## SUNSET DANCE ORCHESTRA

Pseudonym on Champion for the following items listed in this book :-

15038 High Society (Naylor's Seven Aces)
15067 After I Say I'm Sorry (Bailey's Lucky Seven)

## THE SUNSHINE BOYS

Joe Mooney-p-cel-v/Dan Mooney-v, acc. by vn/g.
New York, March 8, 1929.

| 148050-1-2-3 | My Troubles Are Over | Col rejected |
| 148051-1-2-3 | Huggable, Kissable You | - |

New York, March 20, 1929.

| 148050-6 | My Troubles Are Over | Col 1790-D, 5448 |
| 148051-5 | Huggable, Kissable You | - - |

Acc. by Tommy Dorsey-tb/Dick McDonough-g.
New York, April 27, 1929.

| 148386-1-2 | I'm Crooning A Tune About June | Col rejected |

New York, May 6, 1929.

| 148386-3 | I'm Crooning a Tune About June | Col 1834-D, 5524 |
| 148417-3 | Do Something | - - |

Acc. by vn/g.         New York, August 29, 1929.

| 148952-4 | It's Unanimous Now | Col 1963-D, 5718 |
| 148953-2 | That's Where You Come In | - |

Acc. by vn/Carl Kress-g.     New York, December 10, 1929.

| 149703-3 | Does My Baby Love Me ? (Nobody But Me) | Col 2075-D, DB-89 |
| 149704-3 | I Have To Have You | - - |

Acc. by Manny Klein-t/Dick McDonough-g.
New York, August 25, 1930.

| 150730-3 | I Like A Little Girl Like That | Col 2303-D, DB-345 |
| 150731-5 | It Seems To Be Spring | - - |

THE MELOTONE BOYS : Joe Mooney-p-v/Dan Mooney-v, acc. by Tommy Dorsey-tb/Dick McDonough-g.            New York, February 23, 1931.

| E-36116- | Would You Like To Take A Walk ? | Mt M-12103, Spt S-2205, Pan 25018, P-12103, Mf WB-2006 |
| E-36117- | When I Take My Sugar To Tea | As above, plus Emb E-128 |

NOTE:- Supertone S-2205 as THE MANDEL SISTERS (!); Panachord P-12103 as THE PANA-
CHORD BOYS; Mayfair WB-2006 as THE HARMONY TWINS; Embassy E-128 as DESMOND DUO.

New York, April 13, 1931.

| E-36468- | Mary Jane | Mt M-12159, Pan 25038 |
| E-36469- | Boy ! Oh Boy ! Oh Boy ! I've Got It Bad | - - |

Joe Mooney-p-v/Dan Mooney-v, acc. by Hymie Wolfson-ts/Dick McDonough-g/sb.
New York, June 30, 1931.

| | | |
|---|---|---|
| 151657-1 | I'm Keeping Company | Col 2489-D  DB-609 |
| 151658-2 | Take It From Me (I'm Taking To You) | -        - |

## SUPERIOR JAZZ BAND

Ed Kirkeby dir. c/tb/cl/p/d.                    New York, April 18, 1922.

| | | |
|---|---|---|
| 20146-3 | Virginia Blues | Arto 9144, Bell P-144, Globe 7144 |
| 20147- | Georgia | Rejected |

New York, May 2, 1922.

| | | |
|---|---|---|
| 20147-5 | Georgia | Arto 9144, Bell P-144, Globe 7144 |

## SUPER  SYNCOPATORS

? Bob Pope-c/cl-as/pac/bj/? Arthur Layfield-d.
Chicago, c. March, 1925.

| | | |
|---|---|---|
| 751 | Jimtown Blues | Auto (un-numbered) |
| 754 | Oh ! That Sweet In Suite 16 | - |

Pac db p; bb added.                    Chicago, c. July, 1925.

| | | |
|---|---|---|
| 834 | South Bound | Auto 625 |
| 835-2 | When My Sugar Walks Down The Street | - |

## SUPERTONE  DANCE ORCHESTRA

Pseudonym on Supertone S-2186 and S-2191 for Red Nichols and his Orchestra, q.v., and
on Supertone S-2207 for the Casa Loma Orchestra, q.v.

## ANN  SUTER

The following title by this artist, who was a popular British radio personality in
the late 1920s and early 1930s, is of interest for its accompaniment.

Vocal, acc. by Max Goldberg-t/as/George Clarkson-ts/Norman Cole-vn/Billy Thorburn-p/
Bert Thomas or Dave Thomas-bj/Harry Evans-bb/Jack Kosky-d.
London, c. March 27, 1929.

| | | |
|---|---|---|
| 1179-3 | There Ain't No Sweet Man | Dn A-104 |

## SWANEE RIVER  STOMPERS

Instrumentation and personnel unknown.    New York, February 19, 1929.

| | | |
|---|---|---|
| E-29173- | Sunflower Blues - v | Br rejected |
| E-29174- | Windy City Wobble | - |

## SWANEE  SWINGERS

Pseudonym on Decca 1022 for Isham Jones' Juniors, q.v.

## WILBUR  SWEATMAN

WILBUR SWEATMAN AND HIS BAND : Wilbur Sweatman-cl dir. Charlie Minor-t/Dave Johnson-
tb/Laiph Mason-p/ —— Newton-bb/George Reeves-d.
Minneapolis, c. 1903-1904.

| | |
|---|---|
| Maple Leaf Rag (Scott Joplin) | Cylinder made for the Metropolitan Music Store and possibly issued by the store in limited numbers |

WILBER C. SWEATMAN (sic) : Clarinet solos, acc. by the Emerson Symphony Orchestra
(sic) : t/tb/as/p/bj.                    New York, c. December, 1916.

1200-1  My Hawaiian Sunshine              Em 5166 (6")
2375-1  My Hawaiian Sunshine              Em 7120 (7")

Acc. by M. Franklin's String Trio (or the Emerson String Trio) : Exact instrumentation and personnel unknown.              New York, c. December, 1916.

1202-1  Down Home Rag (Wilber C. Sweatman) (sic) Em 5163 (6")
2377-1  Down Home Rag (Wilber C. Sweatman) (sic) Em 7161 (7")
NOTE:- Matrix 2376 is a waltz by the so-called Emerson Symphony Orchestra, without
Sweatman.

WILBUR SWEATMAN AND HIS JASS BAND : Wilbur Sweatman-cl dir. Vess Williams-Piccolo
Jones-as/ ⸺ Minton-ts/Charlie Thorpes-bar/Frank Withers-bsx.
                                         New York, c. March, 1917.

66030   Dance And Grow Thin              P 20147
66031   I Wonder Why                     P 20145, Crescent 10058, Op 4109,
                                         World 397
66032   Boogie Rag                       P 20147, Emp 6219
66033   Joe Turner Blues                 P 20167, 1046
66037   A Bag Of Rags                    -        -
        Dancing An American Rag          P 20145
NOTE:- Operaphone 4109 and World 397 as TEXAS JASS BAND; Crescent 10058 as
SWEATMAN'S JAZZ BAND.

SWEATMAN'S ORIGINAL JAZZ BAND : Wilbur Sweatman-cl dir. Russell Smith or William
Hicks-t/Arthur Reeves or Major Jackson-tb/Dan Parish and/or Palmer Jones-p/Ogese T.
McKay or Romy Jones-bb/Henry Bowser or ⸺ Zeno-d.
                                         New York, March 29, 1918.

77740-2  Regretful Blues                 Col A-2548, 2908
77741-3  Everybody's Crazy 'Bout The Doggone Blues,  -        -
         But I'm Happy

WILBUR SWEATNAN'S JAZZ ORCHESTRA : Includes Smith, Reeves, Sweatman, Parish and Jones
from the previous personnel.              New York, May 31, 1918.

77856-3  The Darktown Strutters' Ball (Intro.   Col A-2596
         I'm Sorry I Made You Cry)
77857-3  Goodbye Alexander (Goodbye Honey Boy)    -
         (Intro. Oh ! Frenchy)

The remaining Columbia issues by this artist are variously labelled  as by WILBUR C.
SWEATMAN'S JAZZ ORCHESTRA/ORIGINAL JAZZ BAND/JAZZ BAND, sometimes omitting the
initial.  Copies are known to exist where the artist credit varies from one side to
the other, and sometimes two copies of the same record vary in this respect.

Wilbur Sweatman-cl dir. William Hicks-t/Major Jackson-tb/Dan Parish-p/Henry Bowser-d.
                                         New York, June 15, 1918.

77889-2-3  Indianola (Intro. Those Draftin' Blues)Col A-2611

                                         New York, June 25, 1918.

77924-3  Oh ! You La ! La ! (Intro. I Want Him    Col A-2611
         Back Again)

Romy Jones-bb added.                     New York, August 17, 1918.

78000-1  Rock-a-Bye Your Baby With A Dixie Melody Col A-2645
78001-1  Those Draftin' Blues (Intro. Somebody's    -
         Done Me Wrong)

                                         New York, August 22, 1918.

78016-3  Has Anybody Seen My Corinne ? (Intro.    Col A-2663
         Down On Bull Frogs' Isle/Livery Stable Blues)

WILBUR SWEATMAN'S ORIGINAL JAZZ BAND (or variants as noted on page 1516) : Wilbur
Sweatman-cl dir. William Hicks-t/Major Jackson-tb/Dan Parish-p/Romy Jones-bb/Henry
Bowser-d.                                    New York, October 7, 1918.

78096-1  Dallas Blues (Intro. At The Funny Page    Col A-2663
            Ball/Lovin' (I Can't Live Without It)

                                    New York, December 5, 1918.

78191-2  Ringtail Blues                            Col A-2682
78192-1  Bluin' The Blues                             -
         Ringtail Blues                            LW 1041 (5")
NOTE:- Little Wonder 1041 as JAZZ BAND.

Russell Smith-t replaces Hicks.      New York, January 18, 1919.

78255-2-3  Rainy Day Blues                         Col A-2707
78256-1-2-3  Ja-Da (Ja-Da, Ja-Da, Jing, Jing,Jing)Rejected

Vn added.                            New York, February 6, 1919.

78256-4  Ja-Da (Ja-Da, Ja-Da, Jing, Jing, Jing)   Col A-2707
78291-1-2-3  Lonesome Road (Intro. Salvation       Rejected
            Blues (A Camp Meetin' Croon)
78292-2  A Good Man Is Hard To Find (Intro.        Col A-2721, LaB AL-5040
            Sweet Child)
         A Good Man Is Hard To Find                LW 1091 (5")
NOTE:- LaBelle AL-5040 is anonymous; Little Wonder 1091 as JAZZ BAND.

Vn omitted.                          New York, February 10, 1919.

78294-1  That's Got 'Em                            Col A-2721, LaB AL-5040
NOTE:- LaBelle AL-5040 is anonymous.

Cm or ts added; Jones omitted.       New York, March 24, 1919.

78366-2-3  Kansas City Blues                       Col A-2768
78367-2  Slide, Kelly, Slide                       Col A-2775
         Kansas City Blues                         LW 1192 (5")
NOTE:- Little Wonder 1192 as JAZZ BAND.

Wilbur Sweatman-cl dir. Russell Smith-t/Arthur Reeves-tb/Dan Parish-p/Walter Gray-
bj-g/Arnold Ford-Arthur Shaw-Arthur Gray-banjolines/Romy Jones-bb/Henry Bowser-d.
                                    New York, March 31, 1919.

78373-2  I'll Say She Does (Intro. 'n' Everything)Col A-2752
78374-2  Lucille                                      -
         Lucille                                   LW 1169 (5")
NOTE:- Little Wonder 1169 as JAZZ BAND.

The Grays, Ford and Shaw omitted; ? as added.
                                    New York, July 22, 1919.

78588-1- -3  Hello, Hello !                        Col rejected

                                    New York, September 24, 1919.

78588-4-7  Hello, Hello !                          Col A-2818, LaB AL-5060
78692-3  I Ain't Gonna Give Nobody None O' This       -          -
            Jellyroll (sic) (Intro. Just Leave It To Me)
         Hello, Hello !                            LW 1223 or 1233 (5")
NOTE:- LaBelle AL-5060 is anonymous; Little Wonder 1223 or 1233 as JAZZ BAND.

                                    New York, June 10, 1920.

79243-1-2-3  In Gay Havana                         Rejected
79257-2  But (Intro. Tiddle-Dee-Winks)             Col A-2994

WILBUR SWEATMAN'S ORIGINAL JAZZ BAND (or variants as noted on page 1516) : Wilbur
    Sweatman-cl dir. Russell Smith-t/Arthur Reeves-tb/as/Dan Parish-p/Romy Jones-bb/
    Henry Bowser-d.                          New York, June 15, 1920.

79277-1-2-3  Think Of Me Little Daddy (Intro.      Col rejected
        I'm Going Back To My Used To Be)
79278-1-2-3  Sunbeams (Intro. Rose Of Bagdad,        —
        I Love You So)
79279-1-2  Su Ez Za                                  —

                                 New York, June 23, 1920.

79277-4  Think Of Me Little Daddy (Intro. I'm      Col A-2994
        Going Back To My Used To Be)
79297-1-2-3  Never Let No One Man Worry Your        Rejected
        Mind (Intro. I'm Gonna Jazz My Way Right Straight Thru' Paradise)
79298-1-2-3  Pee Gee Blues                          —

WILBUR SWEATMAN AND HIS ACME SYNCOPATORS : Wilbur Sweatman-cl dir. 2c/John Reeves-tb
    /Duke Ellington-p/Mike Danzi-bj/Maceo White-d.
                                 New York, c. August 12, 1924.

9017    Battleship Kate                          Gnt rejected
9018    She Loves Me                              —

                                 New York, September 20, 1924.

9083-A  Battleship Kate                          Gnt 5584
9084, -A  She Loves Me                           Rejected

WILBUR SWEATMAN'S BROWNIES : Wilbur Sweatman-cl dir. 2c/John Reeves-tb/Vess Williams
    and another-as/Dan Parish-p/bj/Ogese T. McKay-bb/Maceo White-d-v/ —— Bachlor-v
    (the latter is probably the banjoist). New York, October 10, 1924.

9781    Battleship Kate - vMW-B                  Ed 51438
9782    It Makes No Difference Now - vMW-B       Rejected

Clarinet solos, acc. by George Rickson-p/bj.
                                 New York, c. March, 1926.

3847-A-B  Get It Now                             Dandy 5156, Globe/GG/Rx/Spm 1340,
                                                 Globe 1382, 8020
3848-A-B  Poor Papa (He's Got Nothin' At All)   As above, except Globe 1382, 8020
NOTE:- Dandy 5156 as ED JOHNSON; Globe, Grey Gull and Supreme 1340 as THE DIXIE
TRIO; Radiex 1340 as C. WILBER.

John Reeves-tb replaces bj.            New York, c. March, 1929.

3296-A  Battleship Kate                          GG/Rx 7037, Rx 1701

3313-A-B  Lead Pipe Blues (Sweat Blues*)         GG/Rx 1706*, Mad 50015, VD 901,
                                                 5015
3314-B  Jimtown Blues                            GG 1702, Rx 7037
NOTE:- Madison 50015 as ATLANTA SYNCOPATORS; Grey Gull and Radiex all anonymous.

Eddie Gibbs-bj replaces Reeves.       New York, April 29, 1930.

62209-1  Sweat Blues                             Vic V-38597
62210-2  Got 'Em Blues                           Vic 23254
62211-2  Breakdown Blues                         Vic V-38597
62212-1  Battleship Kate                         Vic 23254

WILBUR SWEATMAN AND HIS ORCHESTRA : Wilbur Sweatman-cl dir. Russell Smith-t/John
    Reeves-tb/George Rickson-p/Eddie Gibbs-bj/Ogese T. McKay-bb/ —— Zeno-d/Corky
    Williams-v.                       New York, March 27, 1935.

17187-1  Whatcha Gonna Do ? - vCW                Voc 2983, Br A-86030
17188-1  The Hooking Cow Blues - vCW             —        —
17189-1  Battleship Kate - vCW                   Voc 2945
17190-1  The Florida Blues                       —

Pseudonym on Victor and Bluebird for Addie "Sweet Pease" Spivey, q.v.

## SAMMY SWIFT'S  JAZZ BAND

2t/tb/2as/Cm or ts/p/bj/bb/d, others ?      New York, c. October, 1921.

|  | Blue Danube Blues | BS 2042, Oly 15133 |
|  | Have You Forgotten ? | -      Oly 15131 |

NOTE:- Olympic 15131 as YERKES' MASTER PLAYERS; 15133 as YERKES' METROPOLITAN
DANCE PLAYERS; the connection, if any, with Harry A. Yerkes, q.v., is unknown.

New York, c. August, 1922.

|  | Away Down South | BS 2082, 10078 |
|  | The Carolina Shout | -      - |

New York, c. February, 1923.

|  | That Red-Head Gal | BS 2113, Oly 1434, Bwy 11215 |
|  | You Said Something When You Said Dixie | -      -      - |
|  | 'Way Down Yonder In New Orleans | BS 2117, Maj 1431 |
|  | You've Got To See Mama Ev'ry Night | -      - |

NOTE:- Broadway 11215 as CALIFORNIA RAMBLERS; Majestic 1431 as ST. LOUIS SYNCO-
PATORS.

## THE  SWING RHYTHM BOYS

Tommy McQuater-t/George Chisholm-tb/Freddy Gardner-cl-as-bar/Joe Crossman-as-ts/
Eddie Macauley-p/Albert Harris-g/Dick Ball-sb/Max Bacon-d/v.
London, July 9, 1936.

| H-575 | Is It True What They Say About Dixie ?-v Cr 212 (9") |
| H-576 | Let's Talk About Love - v | - |

London, August 19, 1936.

| H-600 | You Can't Pull The Wool Over My Eyes - v Cr 227 (9") |
| H-601 | Maybe - v | - |

London, September 10, 1936.

| H-622 | Somebody Stole My Gal - v | Cr 236 (9") |
| H-623 | Some Of These Days  - v | - |

## THE  SWINGTIMERS

T/cl-as/p/g/sb/d/v.                    London, October 20, 1936.

| CAR-4235-1 | 'Way Down Yonder In New Orleans | RZ MR-2514 |
| CAR-4236-1 | Pick Yourself Up - v | RZ MR-2266 |
| CAR-4237-1 | Sing, Baby, Sing - v | - |
| CAR-4238-1 | Sweet Georgia Brown - v | RZ MR-2514 |

## HANNAH SYLVESTER

Vocal, acc. by Henderson's Orchestra : ? Elmer Chambers-c/? George Brashear-tb/Don
Redman-cl/Ernest Elliott-cl-ts/Fletcher Henderson-p/Charlie Dixon-bj.
New York, c. March, 1923.

| 42374-1 | Midnight Blues | Em 10625 |
| 42375-1-2 | I Don't Let No One Man Worry Me | - |

Acc. by Fletcher Henderson's Orchestra : As above, but ? Billy Fowler-ts-bar replaces Elliott.                    New York, May, 1923.

| 1407-2-3-4 | Midnight Blues | Pm 12033 |
| 1408-1-2-3 | Farewell Blues | -   20243, Fam 3237, Pur 11243 |

Acc. by ? Elmer Chambers c/George Brashear-tb/Don Redman-cl/Fletcher Henderson-p/
Charlie Dixon-bj.                              New York, May, 1923.

1415-3  The Wicked (Dirty) Fives                Pm 12034

Acc. by Fletcher Henderson-p.         New York, c. May, 1923.

          Papa, Better Watch Your Step          Maj/Oly 1520
          Seven Or Eleven                            -          Oly 2056
          Long-Lost Mama (Daddy Misses You)    Maj/Oly 1521
          You Gotta See Mama Ev'ry Night            -

GENEVIA SCOTT : As last above.        New York, c. June 5, 1923.

70208    Gulf Coast Blues                        PA 021005, Per 12064
70209    Michigan Water Blues                        -          -

Vocal, acc. by Coleman Hawkins-ts/Fletcher Henderson-p.
                                      New York, c. September 21, 1923.

70328    Down South Blues                        PA 032007, Per 12086
70329    I Want My Sweet Daddy                       -          -

## JOHNNY SYLVESTER

JOHNNY SYLVESTER AND HIS ORCHESTRA : Johnny Sylvester-t/Pete Pellizzi-tb/Johnny
   Costello-cl/Harry Ford-p/? Tony Colucci-bj/Tom Morton-d. (The labels of the first
   issue below indicate that this was "formerly the Original Indiana Five," q.v.)
                                      New York, c. April 4, 1924.

105250   Sweet Man Joe                           PA 036086, Per 14267
105251   Clearing House Blues                        -          -

   Bsx added.                         New York, c. August 12, 1924.

105512   I Wanna Jazz Some More                  PA 036154, Per 14335
105513   Temperamental Papa                          -          -

                                      New York, c. February 3, 1925.

105825   Hot-Hot-Hottentot                       PA 036211, Per 14392
105826   King Porter Stomp                           -          -
   NOTE:- Perfect 14392 as HOLLYWOOD DANCE ORCHESTRA.

JOHN SYLVESTER AND HIS ORCHESTRA : Johnny Sylvester and another-t/tb/2cl-as/? Roy
   Madison-p/? Tony Colucci-bj/? Tom Morton-d.
                                      New York, c. October 12, 1925.

106312   I'm Goin' Out If Lizzie Comes In        PA 36331, X-6006, P 6843,Per 14512
106313   Everybody's Doin' The Charleston Now         -      X-6027    -     -Sal 233
106314   I Would Rather Be Alone In The South    PA 36354, Per 14535

On August 1, 1926, VARIETY published the following personnel for Eddie Edwards and
his Southerners.  Some, possibly all, may be on the next three sessions.

Eddie Edwards-tb dir. Johnny Sylvester-Ellie Evans-t/Carl Gauper-Wally Littlewood-
cl-ss-as/Bill King-cl-ss-ts/Bernard Pinella-vn/Larry Rosenstock-p/Lou de Fabbia-bj-
v/Earl Breckenridge-bb-sb/Frank Horsecroft-d/Arthur Hall-v.
                                      New York, c. July 15, 1926.

106996   Looking At The World Thru' Rose-Colored  PA 36502, 11274, Per 14683
            Glasses - vAH
106997   Why Do You Want To Know Why ? - vAH     PA 36491, Per 14672
106998   Cross Your Heart - vAH                  PA 36490, 11238, P 1962, Per 14671
106999   Trail Of Dreams (w) - vAH               PA 36519, Per 14700

   2s omitted; Bob Blake-v.           New York, September 21, 1926.

X-277    No-One But You (Knows How To Love) - vBB Gnt 3384, 6061, Ch 15174, GS 2010
   NOTE:- Champion 15174 as TWIN CITY BELL-HOPS.

JOHNNY SYLVESTER AND HIS PLAYMATES : Probably :- Eddie Edwards-tb dir. Johnny Syl-
vester-Ellie Evans-t/Carl Gauper-Wally Littlewood-cl-ss-as/Bill King-cl-ss-ts/
Bernard Pinella-vn/Larry Rosenstock-p/Lou de Fabbia-bj-v/Earl Breckenridge-bb-sb/
Frank Horsecroft-d/Pat Kennedy-v.      New York, October 23, 1926.

X-330    Broken-Hearted - vLdeF                    Gnt rejected
X-331, -A-B  I've Got The Girl - vPK                  -

JOHN SYLVESTER AND HIS ORCHESTRA : Johnny Sylvester-t dir. Mike Martini-tb/Andy
Sannella-Larry Abbott-cl-as/Jimmy Lytell-cl-ts/Charles Bates-p/Frank Reino-bj/Joe
Tarto-bb/Johnny Ringer-d/John Ryan-v.   New York, c. November 23, 1926.

107228    I've Got The Girl - vJR          PA 36556,11301,Per 14737,Gra 9256
107229    Idolizing - vJR                  PA 36555   -   Per 14736,Gra 9254
NOTE:- Grafton 9254 as BAR HARBOR ORCHESTRA; 9256 as WINDSOR DANCE ORCHESTRA.

JOHNNY SYLVESTER AND HIS PLAYMATES : As last above, but Henry Vanicelli-p replaces
Bates; Lou de Fabbia-bj-v replaces Reino; Ted Napoleon-d replaces Ringer.
                                        New York, January 3, 1927.

GEX-431-A  Song Of The Wanderer - vLdeF       Gnt 6027, Ch 15202, Chg 233,
                                              Bel 1256, Clm 2059, Gmn 2081
GEX-432-A  A Blues Serenade                   Gnt 6026, Ch 15203, Chg 234,
                                              Sil 5024
GEX-433-A  Indian Butterfly - vLdeF           Gnt 6056, Ch 15204, Chg 237
NOTE:- Beltona 1256 as PALM BEACH PLAYERS; Challenge 233, 234 and 237 as MEMPHIS
MELODY PLAYERS; Champion 15202, 15203 and 15204 as BOBBY JONES AND HIS ORCHESTRA;
Coliseum 2059 as COLISEUM DANCE ORCHESTRA; Guardsman 2081 as ROVERS DANCE BAND;
Silvertone 5024 as JOHNSON'S PLANTATION SERENADERS.

JOHN SYLVESTER AND HIS ORCHESTRA : Probably similar to the last above; Frank Gould-
Bob Blake-v.                           New York, c. February 18, 1927.

107373    Rio Rita - vFG                   PA 36597, Per 14778, Apex 26034,
                                           Dom 21599, LS 24555, Mic 22561,
                                           St 23109, Stg 1100, Ang 3005,
                                           Elec 5027, 5050, Mt 10001
107374-A  The Kinkajou - vFG               PA 36597, Per 14778, Apex 26034,
                                           Dom 21601, LS 24556, Mic 22561,
                                           St 23109
107375    Rosie O'Ryan (Sure I Love You) - vFG   PA 36599, Per 14780
107376    What's The Use ? - vBB                    -       -
NOTE:- Angelus 3005 as ANGELUS DANCE ORCHESTRA; Electron 5027 as HENRY HALSTEAD
AND HIS CONGRESS ORCHESTRA; Melotone 10001 as BRAYBROOK SOCIETY ORCHESTRA; Sterling 1100 as FRANK LENNON AND HIS ORCHESTRA.

JOHNNY SYLVESTER AND HIS PLAYMATES : Johnny Sylvester-t dir. t/tb/2cl-as/cl-ts/p/bj/
bb/d/Al Shayne-The Four Bachelors-v.   New York, April 7, 1927.

GEX-581-A  Mine - v4B                         Gnt 6095, Voc X-10016, XA-18001
GEX-582    Wherever You Go - Whatever You Do - vAS    -    Ch 15294
GEX-583-A  St. Louis Blues                    Gnt 6099   -    33010, GS 40110
NOTE:- Champion 15294 and 33010 as BOBBY JONES AND HIS ORCHESTRA; Vocalion X-10016
as RIVERSIDE DANCE BAND; XA-18001 as FRED GODFREY'S JAZZ KNIGHTS.

Trumpet solo, acc. by unknown instrumental group.
                                        New York, January 14, 1928.

GEX-1038, -A  Blowin' 'Em Hot                 Gnt rejected

## THE SYLVIANS

The following is the only title by this Anglo-American dance band known to be of any
interest as jazz.

Carroll Gibbons-p dir. Charles Rocco-t/George Chaffin-tb/Roy Whetstein-cl-as/Al
Notorage-cl-ts/Reg Pursglove-vn/Frank Herbin-2nd p/Bert Thomas-bj/Jim Bellamy-bb/
Alec Ure-d.                            Small Queen's Hall, London, Oct. 20, 1926.

Bb-9340-2  Where'd You Get Those Eyes ?        HMV B-5154, El EG-337

Jules Levy, Jr.-c/Ephraim Hannaford-tb/Joseph Samuels-cl-bsx/Larry Briers-p/d.
New York, January, 1919.

| | | |
|---|---|---|
| 67435 | Toreador Humoresque | P 22122, Op/Emp 31123 |
| 67436 | Slim Trombone | P 22099, 1047, Op/Emp 31107, |
| | | Arrow 503 |
| 67437 | Everybody Shimmies Now | As above, except Op/Emp 31107 |

NOTE:- Operaphone 31107 and 31123 as JAZZAZZA JAZZ BAND; Empire 31107 and 31123 as
EMPIRE JAZZ BAND; Arrow 503 as FUTURIST JAZZ BAND.

New York, March, 1919.

| | | |
|---|---|---|
| 67563 | Lassus Trombone | P 22117, Op/Emp 31115, Arrow 504 |
| 67564 | Alcoholic Blues | -           Op/Emp 31110 |
| 67565 | At The Jazz Band Ball | P 22122            -          Arrow 502 |
| | Beale Street Blues | Arrow 504 |
| | Missouri Blues | Op/Emp 31115 |
| | That's Got 'Em | Op/Emp 31117 |
| | My Desert Fantasy | Op/Emp 31120 |
| | My Lovin' Eskimo | Arrow 503 |
| | My Baby's Arms | Emp 5002 |

New York, July 23, 1919.

| | | |
|---|---|---|
| 78589-2 | Breeze (Blow My Baby Back To Me) (Intro. | Col A-2783 |
| | Dixie Is Dixie Once More) | |

New York, September, 1919.

| | | |
|---|---|---|
| 67947 | Old Joe Blues | P 22207 |
| 67948 | Hunkatin | - |

New York, October 2, 1919.

| | | |
|---|---|---|
| 78718-1-2-3 | Turko | Col rejected |
| 78719-1-2-3 | Old Joe Blues (Intro. Gimmie This | - |
| | And Gimmie That) | |
| 78720-1-2 | I Want A Beautiful Baby Like You | - |
| | (Intro. New Moon) | |

New York, c. April, 1920.

| | | |
|---|---|---|
| 809-1 | Jazzola | Arto 9003 |
| 810-1 | Bluin' The Blues | -       Arrow 502, Emp 5003 |

New York, c. September, 1920.

| | | |
|---|---|---|
| 68649 | Blacksmith Rag | PA 020461, 10126, P 1384, Op 31161 |
| 68650 | The Moan | - |

NOTE:- Operaphone 31161 as ALABAMA JAZZ BAND.

New York, c. February, 1921.

| | | |
|---|---|---|
| 69069 | Railroad Blues | PA 020499, 10126, P 1384 |
| 69070 | Sweet Mama (Papa's Getting Mad) | -                 P 1618 |

Bj added.                           New York, April, 1921.

| | | |
|---|---|---|
| 69186 | Lucky Dog Blues | PA 020558, 10156, P 1470 |
| 69187 | Satanic Blues | -         -       - |

Bj omitted.                         New York, c. October 31, 1921.

| | | |
|---|---|---|
| 69473 | Dangerous Blues | PA 020665, 10310, P 1668 |
| 69474 | Mysterious Blues | -          -      P 1648 |

Jules Levy, Jr.-c/Ephraim Hannaford-tb/Joseph Samuels-cl-bsx/Larry Briers-p/d.
                              New York, c. December 4, 1921.

69554    Carolina Blues                    PA 020699, 10281, P 1542,
                                            Per 14013, GP 18187
69555    On The 'Gin 'Gin 'Ginny Shore     As above
    NOTE:- Grand Pree 18187 as STERLING SYNCOPATORS.

    Bj added.                     New York, c. February 20, 1922.

69603    Virginia Blues                    PA 020737, Per 14003
69604    I've Got The Wonder Where He Went And   PA 020721, 10527, P 1668,
         When He's Coming Back Blues        Per 14006
69605    No Use Crying                      PA 020721, Per 14006
    NOTE:- Pathe Actuelle 020737 as JOSEPH SAMUELS AND HIS ORCHESTRA; Perfect 14003
    and 14006 as SPENCER ADAMS AND HIS ORCHESTRA.

    Bj omitted.                   New York, c. May 22, 1922.

69708    Hot Lips                          PA 020770, 10364, Per 14022,
                                           Dav 5012, Sal 100519
69709    State Street Blues                As above, except PA 10364
69710    Haunting Blues                    PA 020778, Per 14027
    NOTE:- Salabert 100519 is anonymous.

    Bj/bb added.                  New York, c. August 10, 1922.

69805    Chicago                           PA 020812, 10364, P 1648,
                                           Per 14043, I-S 7015, Sal 100518
69806    Clover Blossom Blues              PA 020812, 10391, Per 14043
69807    I Wish I Knew                     PA 020814, 10376, Per 14045
    NOTE:- Pathe Actuelle 10376 and 10391 as JOSEPH SAMUELS AND HIS ORCHESTRA; 020814
    and Perfect 14045 as SPENCER ADAMS AND HIS ORCHESTRA; Ideal Scala 7015 as ASTORIA
    ORCHESTRA.

NEW SYNCO JAZZ BAND : Apparently very similar to the foregoing; some issues are
    credited to SYNCO JAZZ BAND.       New York, c. January 5, 1923.

69989    Liza                              PA 020920, 10527, P 1716,Per 14104
69990    Aggravatin' Papa                  PA 020902, 10468, Per 14092
69991    Whoa, Tillie ! Take Your Time     PA 020893   -    Per 14087

                              New York, c. September 14, 1923.

70318    Somebody's Wrong                  PA 021075, Per 14178
70319    House Of David Blues              -           -
70320    Black Sheep Blues                 PA 021076, Per 14179

                              New York, November, 1923.

70406    Red Hot !                         PA 036061, Per 14242
70407    Land Of Cotton Blues              PA 036016, 10619, P 1807,Per 14197
70408    Do-Doodle-Oom                     -           -     - Hom C-594 -
    NOTE:- Homochord C-594 as NATHAN GLANTZ AND HIS ORCHESTRA.

T/tb/cl/ss/as/p/bj/d.              New York, c. August 5, 1924.

105503-A  West Indies Blues               PA 036134, Per 14315

                              New York, c. December 18, 1924.

105729   The Blues Have Got Me            PA 036200, Per 14381
105730   Big Bad Bill Is Sweet William Now  PA 036190, 10810, Per 14371,
                                           Hom C-833
105731   Nobody Knows What A Red Head Mama Can Do PA 036190   -       -
105732   Lovelight Lane                   PA 036191, Per 14372
    NOTE:- Perfect 14371 and 14372 as SAMUELS' JAZZ BAND; Perfect 14381 as LOU GOLD AND
    HIS CLUB WIGWAM ORCHESTRA; Homochord C-833 as REGENT DANCE ORCHESTRA.

NEW SYNCO JAZZ BAND : 2t/tb/cl-as/? Nathan Glantz-as/ts/p/bj/bb/d.
                                    New York, c. December 29, 1924.

| 105751 | Oh ! Mabel | PA 036200, Per 14381, Hom C-765, Sal 75 |
| 105752 | I Ain't Got Nobody To Love | PA 036194, Per 14375 |
| 105753 | O Katharina ! | PA 036195, Per 14376, Hg 1010, Sal 84 |

  NOTE:- Perfect 14375, 14376, 14381, Salabert 75 and 84 as LEW GOLD AND HIS CLUB
WIGWAM ORCHESTRA; Homochord C-765 as ELDON'S DANCE ORCHESTRA.

  C/tb/as/ts/p/pac/bj/d.                   New York, c. February 20, 1926.

| 106654 | Bell Hoppin' Blues | PA 36403, Per 14584 |
| 106655 | Say, Mister ! Have You Met Rosie's Sister ? | PA 36401, Per 14582 |
| 106656 | When You're Away | PA 36439, Per 14620 |

  NOTE:- Pathe Actuelle 36401, 36403 and 36439 as GREAT WESTERN SERENADERS.

## THE SYNCOPATED SIX

See Orchestre Syncopated Six.

## THE SYNCOPATING FIVE

Vernon "Mutt" Hayes-cl-as/Fritz Morris-vn/Russell Stubbs-p/Herb Hayworth-bj/Dusty
   Roads-d.                          Richmond, Ind., October 27, 1921.

| 11032-A | Maybe I'm Coming Back To You | Gnt Special (un-numbered) |
| 11033-A | Lips | - |

  NOTE:- This record was made to the order of the Wallace Music Co., Marion, Indiana.

## THE  SYNCOPATING SEVEN

Red Nichols-c/Chuck Campbell-tb/Gilbert Dutton-cl/Ray Stillson-Cm/Russell Stubbs-p/
   Herb Hayworth-bj/Dusty Roads-d.        Richmond, Ind., November 22, 1922.

| 11235-C | Chicago | Gnt Special (un-numbered) |
| 11236-C | Toot-Toot-Tootsie (Goo'bye) | - |
| 11237 | Strutting At The Strutters' Ball | - |

## THE SYNCOPATIN' SKEETERS

It has been suggested that this is the New Orleans Jazz Band; the instrumentation is
   apparently c/tb/cl/p/d.              New York, c. December, 1922.

|       | Loose Feet | Bell P-205, Globe 7205 |
|       | Telephone Blues | -          - |

## WEN  TALBERT

Piano solos, with Lethia Hill-v.       New York, October 28, 1926.

| E-4016/7 | Deep Henderson | Voc rejected |
| E-4018/9 | Milenberg Joys - vLH | - |

WEN TALBERT AND HIS FRIENDS : Wen Talbert-p dir. unknown instrumentation and personnel; Bob Blake-v.                  New York, April 8, 1927.

| GEX-584, -A | Red Hot Flo From Kokomo - vBB | Gnt rejected |
| GEX-585 | Old Folks Shuffle | - |

TAMPA BLUE ARTISTS AND THEIR SINGER : Parlophone R-560  Charles W. Hamp
TAMPA BLUE BOYS : Parlophone R-3501  Fred Hall's Sugar Babies
TAMPA BLUE ENSEMBLE AND THEIR SINGER : Parlophone R-183, R-223  Seger Ellis
TAMPA BLUE FIDDLERS : Parlophone R-3501  Larry Abbott and his Orchestra
TAMPA BLUE FIVE : Parlophone R-3461  Arnold Frank's Rogers Cafe Orchestra
TAMPA BLUE FIVE AND THEIR SINGER : Parlophone R-165  Seger Ellis

Jules Levy, Jr. and usually another-c/Ephraim Hannaford-tb/Joseph Samuels-cl-bsx-vn/
Larry Briers-p/d.                    New York, c. July 25, 1921.

70043-C  Get Hot                              OK/Apex 4397
70044-A  Dangerous Blues                         -

                                    New York, c. August 1, 1921.

70054-B-C  Mule Blues (The Hee-Haw)            OK 4405
70055-A  Bad Land Blues                          -

                                    New York, c. August 13, 1921.

70093-B  I've Got The Joys                      OK 4425

                                    New York, September, 1921.

70204-B  The Missing Link                       OK/Apex 4453

                                    New York, October, 1921.

70264-B  Brother Low Down                       OK/Apex 4461

? Nathan Glantz-as added, some sides.  New York, c. November 8, 1921.

70304-B  Sax-O-Phoney Blues                     OK 4485, Beka/LAR A-4134,
                                               Eko NS-1671
70305-B  Torrid Dora                            As above

                                    New York, c. November 14, 1921.

70313-B  Down Home Blues                        OK 4499
70314-B  Every Day                               -

Billy Jones-v.                       New York, December, 1921.

70383-B  Atta Baby - vBJ                        OK 4522
70384-B  Uncle Bud (Tennessee Blues) - vBJ       -

                                    New York, February 2, 1922.

70440-A  Hurry Back Home                        OK 4544
70441-B  Dying With The Blues                   OK 4573
70442-B  8 Rock Blues                           OK 4544

                                    New York, c. March 27, 1922.

70574-C  Ain't Got Nothin' Blues                OK 4595
70575-C  The West Texas Blues                     -

                                    New York, c. August 10, 1922.

70772-B  Houston Blues                          OK 4663, Od 312904
70773-B  Hot Lips                               Apex 4559
70773-C  Hot Lips                               OK 4663, Par E-5045, Od 312905
70774-B  Haunting Blues                         OK 4671, Od 312913
NOTE:- OKeh 4663 (HOUSTON BLUES) as JOSEPH SAMUELS' JAZZ BAND; Odeon 312904,
312905 and 312913 as AMERICAN JAZZ BAND.

                                    New York, c. January 1, 1923.

71140-B-C  Four O'Clock Blues                   OK 4773, Od 03219
71141-A  Loose Feet                              -
71142-   At The Weeping Widow's Ball            OK 4777, LAR A-4153

                                    New York, February, 1923.

71246-B  The Cootie Crawl                       OK 4791
71247-B  The Fives                               -
71248-B  Sunny Jim                              OK 4803, Od 03185

Jules Levy, Jr. and another-c/Ephraim Hannaford-tb/Joseph Samuels-cl-bsx-vn/Larry
   Briers-p/d.                              New York, March, 1923.

71324-C   Railroad Man                        OK 4816
71325-B   Keep Off My Shoes                   -
71326-C   Maxie Jones                         OK 4826, Od 03159

## TAMPA BLUE ORCHESTRA

Pseudonym on English and.Australian Parlophone for the following items listed in this
   book :-

A-3207   One More Time (Ben Selvin and his Orchestra)
A-3209   Two Little, Blue Little Eyes (Ben Selvin and his Orchestra)
A-3218   There Ought To Be A Moonlight-Saving Time (Ben Selvin and his Orchestra)
A-3219   Roll On, Mississippi, Roll On (Ben Selvin and his Orchestra)
A-3366   Both sides by Ben Selvin and his Orchestra
R-463    True Blue Lou (Justin Ring and his OKeh Orchestra)
R-3335   That's My Hap-Hap-Happiness (Irwin Abrams and his Hotel Manger Orchestra)
R-3335   The Cat (Ted Wallace and his Orchestra)
R-3380   Both sides by Ted Wallace and his Orchestra
R-3418   Miss Annabelle Lee (Justin Ring and his OKeh Orchestra)

## TAMPA  RED

This famous blues artist, whose real name is Hudson Whittaker, made hundreds of sides
   for Vocalion and Bluebird  between 1928 and 1942, of which the following have more
   ambitious and more jazz-like accompaniments, or are non-vocal guitar solos.  These
   are listed here; collectors anxious to know about "Tampa Red's" blues are strongly
   recommended to read BLUES AND GOSPEL RECORDS by W. J. Godrich and Robert M. W.
   Dixon (Storyville Publications, 1969).

TAMPA RED'S HOKUM JUG BAND : Hudson Whittaker-k-g/"Kentucky" (?)-k-jug/Thomas A.
   Dorsey-p/wb/Frankie "Half Pint" Jaxon-v.
                                           Chicago, October 31, 1928.

C-2504-   Good Gordon Gin - vFL               Voc 1254
C-2505-   Down The Alley - vFJ                -

                                           Chicago, November 9, 1928.

C-2536-   It's Tight Like That - vFJ          Voc 1228, Spt S-2230
C-2537-A  How Long How Long Blues - vFJ       -      Ban 32560, Or 8169,
                                              Per 0218, Ro 5169
C-2538-   You Can't Come In - v?              Rejected
C-2544-   You Can't Come In - vFJ             Voc 1237
   NOTE:- Supertone S-2230 as HONEY BOY SMITH'S BINGHAM BAND.

TAMPA RED, "THE GUITAR WIZARD" : Guitar solos.
                                           Chicago, January 16, 1929.

C-2807-   How Long How Long Blues             Voc 1258
C-2808-   It's Tight Like That                -

TAMPA RED'S HOKUM JUG BAND : Hudson Whittaker-k-g/? Thomas A. Dorsey-p/Bill Johnson-
   sb/jug/wb/Frankie "Half-Pint" Jaxon-v.  Chicago, c. April 15, 1929.

C-3289-   Mess, Katie, Mess - vFJ             Voc 1281
C-3290-   Sho' Is Hot - vFJ                   -

                                           Chicago, c. April 19, 1929.

C-3314-   Boot It Boy - vFJ                   Voc 1274, BRS 994, Square 2
C-3315-   My Daddy Rocks Me (With One Steady Roll)vFJ  -      -        -
   NOTE:- BRS 994 as TAMPA RED'S HOKUM JAZZ BAND.

TAMPA RED, "THE GUITAR WIZARD" : Guitar solos.
                                           Chicago, June 22, 1929.

C-3685-   Prison Bound Blues                  Voc 1404
C-3686-   You Got To Reap What You Sow        -

TAMPA RED AND HIS HOKUM JUG BAND : Hudson Whittaker-g/Thomas A. Dorsey-p/Bill Johnson
  sb*/Frankie "Half-Pint" Jaxon-v.          Chicago, July 9, 1929.

C-3805-A  I Wonder Where My Easy Rider's Gone ?     Voc 1420, JC L-58*, AF A-029
         (Easy Rider Blues*) - vFJ
C-3806-   *Come On, Mama, Do That Dance - vFJ          -

                                    Chicago, July 24, 1929.

C-3939-A  Mama Don't Allow No Easy Riders Here     Voc 1430, Ban 32560, Or 8169,
        - vFJ                                    Per 0218, Ro 5169, Spt S-2231
C-3940-   Saturday Night Scrontch - vFJ            Voc 1430            -
  NOTE:- Supertone S-2231 as HONEY BOY SMITH'S BINGHAM BAND.

TAMPA RED, "THE GUITAR WIZARD" ; Guitar solos.
                             Chicago, February 7, 1930.

C-5270-   Moanin' Heart Blues                      Voc 1484, Spt S-2230
C-5271/2  Chicago Moan Blues                            -
  NOTE:- Supertone S-2230 as HONEY BOY SMITH.

TAMPA RED AND HIS HOKUM JUG BAND : Hudson Whittaker-g/Thomas A. Dorsey-p/jug/Frankie
  "Half-Pint" Jaxon-v.               Chicago, mid-August, 1930.

C-5998-A  You Rascal You - vFJ                     Voc 1540
C-5999-   She Can Love So Good - vFJ               Rejected

                              Chicago, August-September, 1930.

C-6079-A  She Can Love So Good - vFJ               Voc 1540

Guitar solos.                       Chicago, December, 1930.

C-7135-   Dying Mercy Blues                        Voc 1572
C-7136-   Broken Love                                   -
C-7137-   Boogie Woogie Dance                      Rejected
C-7138-   Bumble Bee Blues                              -

                            Chicago, January 28, 1931.

VO-105-   Dying Mercy Blues                        Rejected
VO-106-   Broken Love                                   -
VO-107-   Boogie Woogie Dance                      Voc 1619
VO-108-   Bumble Bee Blues

TAMPA RED AND CHICAGO FIVE : Hudson Whittaker-k-g-v/cl/? Black Bob-p/2nd g/sb.
                             Chicago, April 1, 1936.

100300-1  Let's Get Drunk And Truck - vHW          BB B-6353, MW M-4832
100301-2  Maybe It's Someone Else You Love - vHW        -         -

  Arnett Nelson-cl/Willie Bee James-g replace (or may be ?) the unknowns.
                             Chicago, August 5, 1936.

100889-1  You Stole My Heart - vHW                 BB B-6620
100890-1  You Got Me Worryin' - vHW                BB B-6532, MW M-7044
100891-1  Caught My Gal Truckin' - vHW             Rejected
100892-1  All Night Long - vHW                     BB B-6532, MW M-7044
100893-1  That's The Way I Do - vHW                BB B-6578
100894-1  I Hate Myself - vHW                      BB B-6620

Vocal, acc. by ? Arnett Nelson-cl/own p/Willie Bee James-g.
                             Chicago, August 5, 1936.

100895-1  I Need You By My Side                    BB B-6681
100896-1  Blue And Evil Blues                           -

TAMPA RED AND THE CHICAGO FIVE : Hudson Whittaker-k-g-v/? Arnett Nelson-cl/Black Bob
     p/Willie Bee James-g/sb.                    Chicago, December 21, 1936.

| | | |
|---|---|---|
| 01874-1 | If It Wasn't For You - vHW | BB B-6787, MW M-7094 |
| 01875-1 | Right Or Wrong - vHW | BB B-6832, MW M-7096 |
| 01876-1 | Stop Truckin' And Suzi-Q - vHW | BB B-6755, MW M-7093 |
| 01877-1 | Cheatin' On Me - vHW | BB B-6832, MW M-7096 |
| 01878-1 | Your One And Only - vHW | BB B-6755, MW M-7093 |
| 01879-1 | My Za Zu Girl - vHW | BB B-6787, MW M-7094 |

     D added.                              Aurora, Ill., May 4  1937.

| | | |
|---|---|---|
| 07606-1 | She Said It - vHW | BB B-6990 |
| 07607-1 | It's Hard To Believe It's True - vHW | BB B-7058 |
| 07608-1 | When Love Comes In - vHW | BB B-7091 |
| 07609-1 | You've Got To Learn To Do It - vHW | BB B-6968 |
| 07610-1 | I Give My Love To You - vHW | BB B-7058 |
| 07611-1 | I See You Can't Take It - vHW | BB B-6990 |

     T/ts/? Blind John Davis-p/own g-v/d.    Aurora, Ill., October 11, 1937.

| | | |
|---|---|---|
| 014324-1 | You're More Than A Palace To Me - vHW | BB B-7225 |
| 014325-1 | Harlem Swing - vHW | - |
| 014326-1 | Oh Babe, Oh Baby - vHW | BB B-7269 |
| 014327-1 | I'm Gonna Get High - vHW | BB B-7236 |

     T/? Bill Osborn-ts/? Blind John Davis-p/own g-v/sb.
                                        Aurora, Ill., March 14, 1938.

| | | |
|---|---|---|
| 020130-1 | The Most Of Us Do - vHW | BB B-7499 |
| 020131-1 | We Gonna Get High Together - vHW | BB B-7538 |
| 020132-1 | Happily Married - vHW | BB B-7591 |
| 020133-1 | A Lie In My Heart - vHW | - |
| 020134-1 | Heck Of A How-Do-You-Do - vHW | BB B-7538 |

                                        Aurora, Ill., June 16, 1938.

| | | |
|---|---|---|
| 020800-1 | Now That You've Gone - vHW | BB B-7793 |
| 020801-1 | Rock It In Rhythm - vHW | BB B-7743 |
| 020802-1 | I Do - vHW | - |
| 020803-1 | Sweetest Gal In Town - vHW | BB B-7793 |

     Charlie Idsen-t/Bill Oldsley-ts/Blind John Davis-p/own g-v/Bill Settles-sb (these
     could well have been present on the last three sessions); Davis, Settles and self
     only (p/g/sb)*.                    Aurora, Ill., December 16, 1938.

| | | |
|---|---|---|
| 030800-1 | Mr. Rhythm Man - vHW | BB B-8011 |
| 030801-1 | Just You And I Alone - vHW | - |
| 030802-1 | Checkin' Up On You - vHW | BB B-7976 |
| 030803-1 | Oh Yes My Darling - vHW | - |
| 030804-1 | *Forgive Me Please - vHW | BB B-8046 |
| 030805-1 | Blues For My Baby - vHW | - |
| 030806-1 | Hellish Old Feeling - vHW | BB B-8086 |
| 030807-1 | She Got The Best In Town - vHW | - |

## TAMPICO DANCE BAND

Pseudonym on Australian Grand Pree 18644 for Lee Morse's Blue Grass Boys, q.v.

## FRANK TANNER'S  RHYTHM KINGS

T/tb/cl/ts/p/g/sb/d/Albert Porter-Thomas Bailey-John Cook-v (almost certainly these
     were members of the band).          San Antonio, October 24, 1936.

| | | |
|---|---|---|
| 02896-1 | Magnolias In The Moonlight - vAP | BB B-6667, RZ MR-2304 |
| 02897-1 | Wrappin' It Up | BB B-6686 |
| 02898-1 | Death In B flat - vTB | BB B-6719 |
| 02899-1 | You Don't Love Me - vJC | BB B-6667 |
| 02900-1 | Time For One More | BB B-6686 |
| 02901-1 | Sailor Man Rhythm - vTB | BB B-6690 |
| 02902-1 | Texas Teaser | BB B-6750 |

Pseudonym on German Imperial for Gene Kardos and his Orchestra (23055) and Adrian
   Rollini and his Orchestra (23061), q.v. in each case.

## TAR HEELS JAZZ ORCHESTRA

C/tb/cl/p/bj.                                    Camden, N. J., October 23, 1924.

21357-1-2  Bugle Call Rag                              Vic rejected

## CARROLL  C.  TATE

This negro comedian made several sides for Victor during the late 1920s, but owing
   to its accompaniment, this coupling warrants inclusion here.

Vocal, acc. by Bert Howell-vn/Fats Waller-or.
                                         Camden, N. J., November 14, 1927.

40078-2  Gone But Not Forgotten-Florence Mills    Vic 21061
40079-2  You Live On In Memory                         -

## ERSKINE TATE'S VENDOME ORCHESTRA

Erskine Tate-bj dir. Freddy Keppard-James Tate-c/Fayette Williams-tb/Angelo Fernan-
   dez-cl/Buster Bailey-cl-as/Norval Morton-ts/Adrian Robinson-p/Jimmy Bertrand-d.
                                         Chicago, June 23, 1923.

8399-A  Cutie Blues                              OK 4907, LAR A-4176
8400-A  Chinaman Blues                                 -       -

Erskine Tate dir. Louis Armstrong-? James Tate-t/Eddie Atkins-tb/Angelo Fernandez-cl
   /as/Stump Evans-as-bar/Norval Morton-ts/Teddy Weatherford and another-p/Frank
   Ethridge-bj/John Hare-bb/Jimmy Bertrand-d-wb.
                                         Chicago, May 28, 1926.

C-334, C-336; E-3138, E-3140  Static Strut       Voc 1027, 15372, Or 1004,
                                                 Br A-183, 80061, 03594
C-337/8; E-3141/2  Stomp Off, Let's Go           As above

## ART  TATUM

Piano solos.                             New York, March 21, 1933.

B-13162-A  Tea For Two                           Br 6553, 01554, A-9905, A-500337,
                                                 SE 5015-S, Od 286291
B-13163-A  St. Louis Blues                       Br 6543, 01506, A-9433, A-500265,
                                                 Col DO-1227
B-13163-B  St. Louis Blues                       Br 6543
B-13164-A  Tiger Rag                             As for B-13163-A
B-13165-A  Sophisticated Lady                    Br 6553, 01554, A-9905, A-500337,
                                                 SE 5015-S

                                         New York, August 22, 1934.

38387-A  Moon Glow                               Dec 155, Br 01877
38388-A  (I Would Do) Anything For You           Dec 1373, Br 02015, A-9790,
                                                 Od 284465
38389-A  When A Woman Loves A Man                Dec 741, Br 01978
38390-A  Emaline                                 Dec 155, BM-1204,M-30777,Br 01862
38391-A  Love Me                                 Dec 156, Br 02015; A-9790
38392-A  Cocktails For Two                         -      M-30777

                                         New York, August 24, 1934.

38426-A  After You've Gone                       Dec 306,BM-1204,Br 01862,A-505015
38427-C  Star Dust                                 -      BM-1203, Br 02051
38428-A-B  I Ain't Got Nobody                    Rejected
38429-A  Ill Wind (You're Blowin' Me No Good)    Br 02051, Dec BM-1203
38430-A  The Shout                               Dec 468, Br 01877, A-505015
38431-C  Beautiful Love                          Dec 306, Br 02489, A-81298
38431-D  Beautiful Love                            -
38432-A  Liza                                    Dec 1373

Piano solos.                                    New York, October 9, 1934.

| | | |
|---|---|---|
| 38388-C | (I Would Do) Anything For You | Dec 1373, Od 284030, 284465 |
| 38389-D | When A Woman Loves A Man | Dec 741, Br 01978, Od 286320 |
| 38426-C | After You've Gone | Dec 468, Br 80141 |
| 38428-C | I Ain't Got Nobody | Dec 741, Br 01978, Od 284030 |
| 38432-D | Liza | Dec 1373, Br 80131, 02489, A-81298, Od 286310 |

Hollywood, September, 1935.

| | |
|---|---|
| Tiger Rag | JP LP-15 |
| Stay As Sweet As You Are | - |
| Monday In Manhattan | - |
| I Would Do Anything For You | - |
| Theme For Piano | - |
| Take Me Back To My Boots And Saddle | - |
| After You've Gone | - |
| The Dixieland Band | - |
| The Shout | - |
| In The Middle Of A Kiss | - |
| Rosetta | - |
| I Wish I Were Twins | - |
| Devil In The Moon | - |

Chicago, December 21, 1935.

90541-    Take Me Back To My Boots And Saddle    Dec rejected

ART TATUM AND HIS SWINGSTERS : Lloyd Reese-t/Marshall Royal-cl/Art Tatum-p-cel/Bill
  Perkins-g/Joe Bailey-sb/Oscar Bradley-d.
                                    Los Angeles, February 26, 1937.

| | | |
|---|---|---|
| DLA-724-A | Body And Soul | Dec 1197, Y-5165, Br 02518,A-81278 |
| DLA-725-A | With Plenty Of Money And You | Dec 1198, M-39029, Y-5168,Br 02417 |
| DLA-726-A | What Will I Tell My Heart ? | Dec 1197    -    Y-5165    - |
| DLA-727-A | I've Got My Love To Keep Me Warm | Dec 1198, Y-5168, Br 02518,A-81278 |

Piano solos.                                    New York, November 29, 1937.

| | | |
|---|---|---|
| 62822-A | Gone With The Wind | Dec 1603, BM-1232, F-8069, Y-5206, Br 80159, 02564, A-81407, A-82455 |
| 62823-A | Stormy Weather | As above |
| 62824-A | Chloe | Dec 2052, MU-60517, Br 80160, 02591, A-81552 |
| 62825-A | The Sheik Of Araby | As above |

NOTE:- Decca F-8069 is a Swiss issue only.

Los Angeles, April 12, 1939.

| | | |
|---|---|---|
| DLA-1759-A | Tea For Two | Dec 2456, MU-60516, Br 02772, A-82196, Od 286291 |
| DLA-1760-A-B | Deep Purple | Dec 2456, MU-60516, Br 80141, 02772, A-82196, Od 286310 |

Hollywood, August, 1939.

| | |
|---|---|
| All God's Chillun Got Rhythm | JP LP-15 |
| Sweet Emaline | - |
| Indiana | - |
| Day In, Day Out | Pol 623274 (LP) |
| Fine And Dandy | - |
| I've Got The World On A String | - |
| I've Got A Right To Sing The Blues | - |
| I'm Coming, Virginia | - |

Piano solos.                          Los Angeles, February 22, 1940.

DLA-1936-A  Elegie (Massenet)          Dec 18049, 25199, Br 03162
DLA-1937-A  Humoresque (Dvorak)         -         -         -    A-82493
DLA-1938-A  Sweet Lorraine              Dec 18050, 25200, 60060, Y-5088,
                                        Br 03418
DLA-1939-A  Get Happy                   As above, except Br 03418
DLA-1940-A  Lullaby Of The Leaves       Dec 18051, 25201, Y-5562,Br 04318
DLA-1941-A  Tiger Rag                    -        -MU-60515-  Br 04319
                                        A-82493
DLA-1942-A-B  Sweet Emaline, My Gal     Rejected
DLA-1943-A  Emaline                     Dec 155, 25202
DLA-1944-A  Moon Glow                    -
DLA-1945-A  Love Me                     Dec 156
DLA-1946-A  Cocktails For Two            -        25202, M-30777,
                                        Br 80131, 233649

                                      Los Angeles, July 26, 1940.

DLA-2068-A  St. Louis Blues            Dec 8550,Br 8550,03121, Od 286291
DLA-2069-A  Begin The Beguine          Dec 8502  -       -       -
DLA-2070-A  Rosetta                      -        MU-60515, Br 80162,
                                        04319, Od 286320
DLA-2071-A  (Back Home Again In) Indiana  Dec 8550, MU-60524, MY-62831,
                                        Od 286341

ART TATUM AND HIS BAND : Joe Thomas-t/Edmond Hall-cl/Art Tatum-p/John Collins-g/
     Billy Taylor-sb/Eddie Dougherty-d/Joe Turner-v.
                                      New York, January 21, 1941.

68605-A  Wee Baby Blues - vJT          Dec 8526, 48062, F-8059, Y-5892,
                                        Od 284832
68606-A  Stompin' At The Savoy         Dec 8536
68607-A  Last Goodbye Blues - vJT        -     Od 284832
68608-A  Battery Bounce                Dec 8526, F-8059, Y-5892,Br 03430
   NOTE:- Decca F-8059 is a Swiss issue only.

   Hall omitted; Oscar Moore-g replaces Collins; Yank Porter-d replaces Dougherty.
                                      New York, June 13, 1941.

69356-B  Lucille - vJT                 Dec 8577, Br 03430, 88066
69357-A  Rock Me, Mama - vJT            -
69358-A  Corrine Corrina - vJT         Dec 8563, 29924, 48062
69359-A  Lonesome Graveyard - vJT       -     Br 03462, 88066

                          TAYLOR   BROTHERS

Banjo and mandoline duets, with kazoo.   New York, c. October 23, 1925.

106338    Isabella (Tell Your Fella)      PA        , 11145, Per
106339    Stop Flirting                    -

                          EDNA   TAYLOR

Vocal, acc. by ? Tommy Ladnier-c/? Clarence Johnson-p.
                                      Chicago, June, 1923.

   1432-3  Jelly's Blues               Pm 12057
   1433-2  Good Man Blues               -

                          EVA TAYLOR

Vocal, acc. by ? Johnny Dunn-c/? Garvin Bushell-cl/as/? Clarence Williams-p. (The
     label merely states "Piano acc." !)   New York, c. September, 1922.

        New Moon                       BS 2103

   Acc. by Ernest Elliott-cl/Clarence Williams-p and others.
                                      New York, September 5, 1922.

64171-1  I Got To Cool My Doggies Now     Rejected test (label unknown)

Acc. by Clarence Williams-p.              New York, c. November 25, 1922.

71056-B  I Wish I Could Shimmy Like My Sister    OK 4740
            Kate
71057-B  Baby, Won't You Please Come Home ?        -

IRENE GIBBONS AND JAZZ BAND : Vocal, acc. by ? Tom Morris-c/Charlie Irvis-tb/Ernest
   Elliott-cl-? as/Clarence Williams-p/Buddy Christian-bj/d. (This is Eva Taylor's
   baptismal name).                          New York, December 5, 1922.

80723-4   My Pillow And Me                      Col A-3922
80724-1-2-3  That Da Da Strain                  Rejected

Clarence Robinson-cl may replace Elliott.
                                          New York, January 6, 1923.

80724-6   That Da Da Strain                     Col A-3834

Vocal, acc. by Clarence Williams-p.       New York, c. January 10, 1923.

71152-C  Down Hearted Blues                     OK 8047, 4805
71153-B  You Missed A Good Woman When You Picked   -
            All Over Me

IRENE GIBBONS : Vocal, acc. by Clarence Williams-p.
                                          New York, February 7, 1923.

80838-3   Last Go Round Blues                   Col A-3834

Vocal, acc. by Clarence Williams-p.       New York, c. February 8, 1923.

71242-B  You Can Have My Man (If He Comes To    OK 8050
            See You Too)
71243-B  I'm Going Away Just To Wear You Off    OK 8051
            My Mind

                                          New York, c. February 14, 1923.

71260-A  12th Street Rag                        OK 4805, 8049
71261-B  My Pillow And Me                       OK 8051

Vocal duet with Sara Martin, acc. by Tom Morris-c/Clarence Williams-p.
                                          New York, c. April 24, 1923.

71465-A  Yodeling Blues                         OK 8067

Vocal, acc. by Clarence Williams' Blue Five : Tom Morris-c/? Charlie Irvis-tb/Ernest
   Elliott-cl/as/Clarence Williams-p/Buddy Christian-bj.
                                          New York, c. May 4, 1923.

71499-A  Farewell Blues                         OK 3055 (12")
71500-A  Gulf Coast Blues                        -

Acc. by Clarence Williams-p.              New York, c. May 8, 1923.

71512-B  From Now On Blues                      OK 8069
71513-B  Church Street Sobbin' Blues             -

                                          New York, c. May 15, 1923.

71533-B  You'll Never Have No Luck By Quittin' Me OK 8068
71534-A  I'm Gonna See You When Your Troubles Are  -
            Just Like Mine

Acc. by Clarence Williams' Blue Five : Tom Morris-c/? Charlie Irvis-tb/? Ernest
   Elliott-cl/as/Clarence Williams-p/Buddy Christian-bj.
                                          New York, c. May 17, 1923.

71538-B  Barefoot Blues                         OK 8073
71539-A  Do It A Long Time Papa                  -

The following re-make session fits at this point in the discography, as pointed out
by Tom Lord in his discographical masterpiece, CLARENCE WILLIAMS. Although making
four different titles at a session was exceptional at that time, the personnel for
the next two titles is undoubtedly the same as for the session listed at the foot
of page 1532, and they were either all made on the same date or on two separate,
but consecutive days.

Acc. by Clarence Williams' Blue Five : Tom Morris-c/? Charlie Irvis-tb/? Ernest
Elliott-cl/as/Clarence Williams-p/Buddy Christian-bj.
                                       New York, c. May 17-18, 1923.

71499-F  Farewell Blues                       OK 3055 (12")
71500-F  Gulf Coast Blues                         -

Vocal duets with Sara Martin, acc. by Tom Morris-c/Clarence Williams-p.
                                       New York, c. June 20, 1923.

71640-B  That Free And Easy Papa O' Mine       OK 8082
71641-B  Hesitation Blues                         -

Vocal, acc. by Clarence Williams' Blue Five : Tom Morris-c/John Mayfield-tb/Sidney
Bechet-cl/Clarence Williams-p-v/Buddy Christian-bj.
                                       New York, c. August 11, 1923.

71747-B  Oh ! Daddy Blues - vCW                OK 4927
71748-B  I've Got The Yes ! We Have No Banana Blues -

? Charlie Irvis-tb replaces Mayfield; Bechet omitted.
                                       New York, c. August 27, 1923.

71803-B  Original Charleston Strut             OK 8089
71804-A  If You Don't, I Know Who Will             -

Acc. by Clarence Williams Trio : Sidney Bechet-ss/Clarence Williams-p/Buddy
Christian-bj.                          New York, c. September 29, 1923.

71910-A  Irresistible Blues                    OK 8129
71910-C  Irresistible Blues                        -       Par E-5261
71911-B  Jazzin' Babies Blues                      -          -

Vocal duets with Lawrence Lomax, acc. by Tom Morris-c/Charlie Irvis-tb/Sidney Bechet
ss/Clarence Williams.                  New York, c. November 10, 1923.

72028-C  Old Fashioned Love                    OK 8114
72029-B  Open Your Heart                           -

Vocal, acc. by Clarence Williams' Harmonizers : Tom Morris-c/Charlie Irvis-tb/?
Lorenzo Tio-cl/Clarence Williams-p.    New York, c. May 16, 1924.

72531-B  When You're Tired Of Me (Just Let Me  OK 8145
           Know)
72532-A  Ghost Of The Blues                        -

Vocal duets with Clarence Williams, acc. by Tom Morris-c/Buddy Christian-bj.
                                       New York, c. October 17, 1924.

72912-B  Terrible Blues                        OK 8183
72913-B  Arkansaw Blues                            -

At this point, two sessions of two sides each took place, one of each pair being
issued as by Eva Taylor, the other as by Clarence Williams' Blue Five, q.v., who
accompanied Miss Taylor on both dates (January 8 and March 4, 1925).

Vocal, acc. by Clarence Williams-p/Buddy Christian-bj.
                                       New York, c. July 11, 1925.

73524-B  Far As I'm Concerned                  OK 8228
73525-B  Get Off My Money Blues                    -

Acc. by Clarence Williams-p.                    New York, c. July 1, 1926.

74206-A  Señorita Mine                          OK 40655
74207-B  Charleston Hound                        -

Acc. by Clarence Williams' Blue Five : C/Charlie Irvis-tb/cl/Clarence Williams-p/
bj.                                              New York, c. August 6, 1926.

74243-B  When The Red, Red Robin Comes Bob, Bob,  OK 40671
            Bobbin' Along
74244-B  (There's A Blue Ridge In My Heart) Virginia -

Acc. by Clarence Williams' Morocco Five : Buster Bailey-ss-as/? Arville Harris-cl-
as/Eddie South-vn/Clarence Williams-p/? Leroy Harris-bj.
                                                New York, October 5, 1926.

74388-B  Nobody But My Baby Is Getting My Love   OK 8407
74389-B  Morocco Blues                           -

Acc. by Clarence Williams' Blue Seven : Tommy Lad ier-c/Jimmy Harrison-tb/Buster
Bailey-cl/Coleman Hawkins-ts/Clarence Williams-p/Leroy Harris-bj.
                                                New York, November 16, 1926.

80214-A  Candy Lips (I'm Stuck On You)           OK 8414, 40715
80215-A  Scatter Your Smiles                     -      -

Acc. by Clarence Williams' Blue Five : Instrumentation and personnel unknown apart
from Clarence Williams-p.                        New York, December 15, 1926.

80251-A-B  I Want Somebody To Tell My Troubles To OK rejected
80252-A  If I Could Be With You One Hour Tonight  -

Acc. by Clarence Williams' Blue Five : Jabbo Smith-c/? Charlie Irvis-tb/Clarence
Williams-p/g.                                    New York, February 10, 1927.

80412-A  I Wish You Would (Love Me Like I'm      OK 8444
            Loving You)
80413-B  If I Could Be With You                   -

Acc. by Clarence Williams' Blue Five : Ed Allen-c/Buster Bailey-cl/? Howard Nelson
vn/Clarence Williams-p.                          New York, April 16, 1927.

80739-B  Smile Your Bluesies Away                OK 8463
80740-A  Red Hot Flo (From Ko-Ko-Mo)             -

Acc. by Clarence Williams' String Four : 2vn/vc/Clarence Williams-p.
                                                New York, September 29, 1927.

81491-A-B  Longing                              OK rejected
81492-A-B-C  I'm Goin' Back To Bottomland        -

                                                New York, October 13, 1927.

81492-D-E  I'm Goin' Back To Bottomland         OK rejected

Acc. by ? Marion Cumbo-vc/Clarence Williams-p.
                                                New York, November 4, 1927.

81786-B  May We Meet Again (Florence Mills)      OK 8518
81787-B  She's Gone To Join The Songbirds In Heaven -

IRENE GIBBONS : Vocal, acc. by Noel Clukies-vn/Marion Cumbo-vc/Clarence Williams-p.
                                                New York, February 17, 1928.

145652-1  Longing                               Col 14296-D
145653-2  Let Me Forget                          -

Vocal, acc. by Ed Allen-c/Buster Bailey-cl-ss or as/Albert Socarras-f/David Martin-
    vc/Clarence Williams-p.                  New York, June 2, 1928.

400738-B  Chloe                                    OK 8585
400739-A  Back In Your Own Back Yard                 -

IRENE WILLIAMS : Vocal, acc. by Clarence Williams-p.
                                          New York, July 31, 1928.

401040-C  My Different Kind Of Man                 OK 41104
401041-A  You're A Real Sweetheart                   -

IRENE GIBBONS AND CLARENCE WILLIAMS JAZZ BAND : Vocal, acc. by King Oliver-c/Omer
    Simeon-cl/Clarence Williams-p/Eddie Lang-g.
                                          New York, September 18, 1928.

147012-2  I'm Busy And You Can't Come In           Col 14362-D
147013-2  Jeannine I Dream Of Lilac Time (w)         -

Vocal, acc. by Clarence Williams' Orchestra : Ed Allen-c/Albert Socarras-cl-f/cl-as/
    Russell Procope-as/Clarence Williams-p/Cyrus St. Clair-bb.
                                          New York, December 20, 1928.

401469-A  Happy Days And Lonely Nights             OK 8665
401470-B  If You Want The Rainbow (You Must Have     -
            The Rain)

    Acc. by Clarence Williams-p.          New York, July 30, 1929.

N-1049-C  Have You Ever Felt That Way ?            Ed 14046
N-1050-A-B  West End Blues                           -
19325     Have You Ever Felt That Way ?            Ed 52646
19326     West End Blues                            -
    NOTE:- Both the above issues sub-title Miss Taylor "Queen of the Moaners."

                                          New York, October 3, 1929.

N-1173    Oh Baby ! What Makes Me Love You So ?    Ed rejected
N-1174    You Don't Understand                      -
N-1175    In Our Cottage Of Love                    -
N-1176    I'm Not Worryin'                          -

    Acc. by Ed Anderson-c/Clarence Williams-James P. Johnson-p.
                                          New York, December 16, 1929.

57782-2   What Makes Me Love You So ?              Vic V-38575
57783-1   You Don't Understand                      -

CATHERINE HENDERSON : Vocal, acc. by Ed Anderson-c/Albert Socarras-cl/? Garvin
    Bushell-as/Clarence Williams-p.       New York, February 13, 1930.

149983-2  What If We Do ?                          Diva 6050-G, VT 7076-V
149984-1  Keep It To Yourself                      Diva 6040-G, VT 7066-V

EVA TAYLOR'S SOUTHERNAIRES : Vocal, acc. by Albert Nicholas-cl/? Willie "The Lion"
    Smith-p/Jimmy McLin-g/Clarence Williams-jug-v/? Willie Williams-wb.
                                          New York, May 15, 1933.

TO-1301    I Like To Go Back In The Evening        Col test

See also Clarence Williams, inter alia, whose record of CRAZY BLUES/THE STUFF IS HERE
    AND IT'S MELLOW on Banner 33261, Melotone M-13228, Oriole 3041, Perfect 16032 and
    Romeo 2415 is labelled EVA TAYLOR AND HER BOY FRIENDS - yet the first side has a
    vocal by her husband (Clarence Williams) only, and the second no vocal at all !
    Eva Taylor alao made a ten-inch Audubon LP in Burnham, Bucks., on October 8, 1967,
    accompanied by the Anglo-American Alliance.

Freddy Taylor-t-v/Charlie Johnson-t/Chester Lanier-cl-as-bar/Fletcher Allen-cl-ts-a/
John Ferrier-p/Oscar Aleman-g/Eugene d'Hellemmes or Joe Riestra-sb/William Diemer-
d.                                              Paris, March, 1935.

| | | |
|---|---|---|
| 77285 | Blue Drag - vFT | U1 AP-1489, 11251, Or LV-105, LB-1005, Royale 1778 |
| 77286 | Viper's Dream | As above, except Royale 1778 |

Django Reinhardt-g replaces Aleman.     Paris, April, 1935.

| | |
|---|---|
| Viper's Dream | U1 rejected |
| Blue Drag - vFT | - |
| Swanee River | - |
| How Come You Do Me Like You Do ? - ?vFT | - |

## IRENE TAYLOR

Vocal, acc. by Jack Gardner's Orchestra : Jack Gardner-p dir. 2c/Stanton Crocker-tb/
cl-as/as/ts/bb/? d.                             Dallas, October, 1925.

| | | |
|---|---|---|
| 9363-A | I Did Wanta, But I Don't Wanta Now | OK 40527 |
| 9364-A | I Ain't Thinkin' 'Bout You | - |

Acc. by t/as/p/g/d.                         Chicago, June 1, 1928.

| | | |
|---|---|---|
| 42394-1-2-3 | My Castle In The Clouds | Vic rejected |
| 42395-1-2-3-4 | I Must Have That Man | - |

## JACKIE TAYLOR'S ORCHESTRA

The following titles by this commercial dance orchestra are of some interest in view
of their vocalists !

Jackie Taylor-vn dir. 2t/tb/2cl-as/cl-ts/p/bj/bb/d/The Boswell Sisters (Connie-Martha
Vet)-v.                                 Hollywood, July 20, 1930.

| | | |
|---|---|---|
| 54882-1 | We're On The Highway To Heaven - vBS | Vic 22500, HMV B-5921 |
| 54885-1-2-3 | That's What I Like About You - vBS | Rejected |

## JASPER TAYLOR

JASPER TAYLOR AND HIS STATE STREET BOYS : Freddy Keppard-c/Eddie Ellis-tb/Johnny
Dodds-cl/Tiny Parham-p/Jasper Taylor-wb.
                                        Chicago, c. January, 1927.

| | | |
|---|---|---|
| 2770-2 | Stomp Time Blues | Pm 12409,Cen 3026,JC L-13,AF A-020 |
| 2771-2 | It Must Be The Blues | -      -        -     - |

JASPER TAYLOR AND HIS ORIGINAL WASHBOARD BAND : R. Q. Dickerson-t/Johnny Dodds-cl/p/
Jasper Taylor-wb/Julia Davis-v.       Chicago, June 29, 1928.

C-2022-A or -B; E-7489  Jasper Taylor Blues - vJD  Voc 1196
C-2023-B; E-7490  Geechie River Blues - vJD         -

## LOUELLA TAYLOR

Pseudonym on Domino for Clementine Smith, q.v.

## NOEL TAYLOR

Pseudonym on Parlophone E-6187 and Ariel 4417 for Irving Kaufman, q.v., but this was
a name used for other artists on OKeh and associated labels besides Irving Kaufman.

## ROY TAYLOR AND HIS SINGING ORCHESTRA

Pseudonym on Champion for Bernie Schultz and his Crescent Orchestra, q.v.

## YACK TAYLOR

See Sam Price.

Dave Taylor dir. Lester Mitchell-t/Joe Jordan-t-v/Leslie Johnakins-as-bar/Skeets
Tolbert-as-v/Ernest Parham-ts-v/Jimmy Gunn-p/Guy Harrington-bj-v/Harry Prather-bb/
Bill Hart-d.                               Charlotte, N. C., May 23, 1931.

| | | |
|---|---|---|
| 69343-1 | Wabash Blues - vJJ-ST-GH | Vic 23277 |
| 69344-1 | Everybody Loves My Baby - vEP | - |

## JACK TEAGARDEN

JACK TEAGARDEN AND HIS ORCHESTRA : Charlie Spivak-Tommy Thunen-t/Jack Teagarden-tb-v
/Gil Rodin-Matty Matlock-cl-as/Eddie Miller-cl-ts/Gil Bowers-p/Nappy Lamare-bj-g/
Harry Goodman-bb-sb/Ray Bauduc-d/Eddie Gale-v.
                                           New York, October 1, 1930.

| | | |
|---|---|---|
| 10101-2 | Son Of The Sun - vJT | Dom 4651, Per 15363 |
| 10102-1-2-3 | You're Simply Delish - vEG | Ban 0851, Cam 0451, Cq 7635, |
| | | Dom 4649, Je 6098, Or 2098, |
| | | Per 15361, Re 10157, Ro 1465, |
| | | Ang 3266, Voc 718 |
| 10103-1 | Just A Little Dance, Mam'selle - vJT | Dom 4646, Per 15358, Voc 718 |

NOTE:- Angelus 3266 and Vocalion 718 as IMPERIAL DANCE ORCHESTRA; Perfect 15358 as
FRANK KEYES AND HIS ORCHESTRA.

Sterling Bose-t replaces Thunen; Benny Goodman-cl replaces Matlock; Eddie Miller-
Nappy Lamare-v.                            New York, c. January, 1931.

| | | |
|---|---|---|
| 1119-1 | Rockin' Chair - vEM-NL | Cr 3051 |
| 1120-1-2 | Loveless Love - vJT | - HRS 5 |

NOTE:- Other titles from this session were issued under Gil Rodin's name, q.v.

Charlie Teagarden-Sterling Bose-t/Jack Teagarden-tb-v/Pee Wee Russell-cl/Joe
Catalyne-cl-ts/Max Farley-cl-ts-a/Adrian Rollini-bsx/Fats Waller-p-v/Nappy Lamare-g
/Artie Bernstein-sb/Stan King-d.          New York, October 14, 1931.

| | | |
|---|---|---|
| 151839-1 | You Rascal, You - vJT-FW | Col 2588-D, CB-424, DO-667, |
| | | DW-4075, HJCA 611 |
| 151840-1-2 | That's What I Like About You - vJT-FW | Col 2588-D, DO-667, HJCA 611 |
| 151841-1-2 | Chances Are - vJT | Har 1403-H, Cl 5442-C, OK 41551, |
| | | VT 2502-V, Col DC-144 |
| 151842-1 | I Got The Ritz From The One I Love - vJT | RFW 4 (LP) |

NOTE:- Harmony 1403-H, Clarion 5442-C and Velvet Tone 2502-V as ROY CARROLL AND HIS
SANDS POINT ORCHESTRA; OKeh 41551 as CLOVERDALE COUNTRY CLUB ORCHESTRA (the reverse
is by a different band, though similarly labelled).

Probably :- Charlie Teagarden-Sterling Bose-t/Jack Teagarden-tb/Matty Matlock-Gil
Rodin-cl-as/Eddie Miller-cl-ts/Gil Bowers or Fats Waller-p as shown/Nappy Lamare-g/
Harry Goodman-sb/Ray Bauduc-d/Gene Austin-v (under whose name the only two sides to
be issued were labelled).                  New York, November 10, 1931.

| | | |
|---|---|---|
| 10976- | China Boy - pFW | Rejected |
| 10977-1 | Lies - pGB/vGA | Ban 32325, Or 2380, Per 15542, |
| | | Ace 351024, Dom 51024, Mt 91235 |
| 10978-3 | I'm Sorry, Dear - pGB/vGA | Ban 32325, Or 2380, Per 15542 |
| 10979- | Tiger Rag - pFW | Rejected |

Claude Whiteman-Charlie Teagarden-t/Jack Teagarden-tb-v/Tom Moore-tb/Rod Cless-cl-
as/Buddy Fisk-as/Dale Skinner-cl-ts/Bud Freeman-ts/Charlie LaVere-p/Dick McPartland
g/Eddie Gilbert-sb/Bob Conselman-d/David Rose-a.
                                           Chicago, July 29, 1933.

| | | |
|---|---|---|
| 152456-2 | I've Got "It" | Col 2913-D, DB/MC-5035 |
| 152457-2 | Plantation Moods | IAJRC LP-2 |
| 152457-3 | Plantation Moods | Col 2913-D, DB/MC-5034 |
| 152458-2 | Shake Your Hips | Col 2802-D, DO-1000, MC-3029, |
| | | Par R-1670 |
| 152459-2 | Somebody Stole Gabriel's Horn - vJT | Col 2802-D, DB/MC-5035, DO-1000 |
| 152460-1-2 | I Would If I Could But I Can't | Rejected |

NOTE:- Columbia 2802-D and DO-1000 as JACK TEAGARDEN AND HIS CHICAGOANS.

Vocal, acc. by Frank Guarente-Sterling Bose-t/own tb/Chester Hazlett-Jimmy Dorsey-cl
    as/Mutt Hayes-cl-ts/Walt Edelstein-vn/Joe Meresco-p/Perry Botkin-g/Artie Bernstein
    sb/Larry Gomar-d/Victor Young-dir.     New York, November 11, 1933.

| | | |
|---|---|---|
| B-14294-A | Love Me | Br 6741, 01703, A-500398 |
| B-14295-A | Blue River | - - - |
| B-14296-B | A Hundred Years From Today | Br 6716,01683,A-500392,Col DO-1172 |
| B-14297-A | I Just Couldn't Take It, Baby | -    -Par R-2599-  Od A-272291 |

    Joe Venuti-Lou Kosloff-vn added; Frank Worrell-g replaces Botkin; Nappy Lamare-v
    added.                              New York, March 2, 1934.

| | | |
|---|---|---|
| B-14877-A | Fare-Thee-Well To Harlem - vNL | Br 6780, 01746, A-9571, A-500427 |
| B-14878-A | Ol' Pappy - vNL | -    -    -    - |

JACK TEAGARDEN AND HIS ORCHESTRA : Charlie Teagarden-t/Jack Teagarden-tb-v/Benny
    Goodman-cl/Frankie Trumbauer-Cm/Casper Reardon-harp/Terry Shand-p/Art Miller-sb/
    Herb Quigley-d; the sides on which Jack Teagarden sings are labelled JACK TEAGAR-
    DEN, with Orchestral Accompaniment.   New York, September 18, 1934.

| | | |
|---|---|---|
| B-15938-A | Junk Man | Br 7652, 01979, A-9843, A-500512, |
| | | Par R-2599, Od A-272291, |
| | | Pol 580014, Lucky S-3 |
| B-15939-A | Stars Fell On Alabama - vJT | Br 6993, 01913, A-500482 |
| B-15940-A | Your Guess Is Just As Good As Mine-vJT | -    -    - |

    Jack Teagarden-tb-vdir. Charlie Spivak-Carl Garvin-Alec Fila-t/Jose Gutierrez-Mark
    Bennett-tb/Red Bone-tb-a/Clint Garvin-Art St. John-cl-as/John van Eps-Hub Lytle-cl
    ts/Ernie Caceres-cl-ts-bar/John Anderson-p/Allan Reuss-g/Art Miller-sb/Cubby Tea-
    garden-d/Meredith Blake-v/Hub Lytle-Fred van Eps, Jr.-Chick Reeves-a.
                                        New York, April 14, 1939.

| | | |
|---|---|---|
| B-24375-A | Persian Rug - aRB | Br 8370, A-82172, Par R-2694, |
| | | Col DO-1990 |
| B-24376-A | The Sheik Of Araby - vJT-MB | As above, plus Col M-282 |
| B-24377-A | Class Will Tell - vJT | Br 8373, A-82138  Col DO-2034 |

    Lee Castle-t replaces Fila; Charles McCamish-tb replaces Bone; Jean Arnold-v.
                                        New York, April 28, 1939.

| | | |
|---|---|---|
| B-24450-A | If It's Good (Then I Want It) - vJT | Br 8373, A-82138, RZ G-24463 |
| B-24451-B | Cinderella, Stay In My Arms - vJT | Br 8378 |
| B-24452-A | I Gotta Right To Sing The Blues-vJT | Br 8397, OK 6272, RZ G-24865 |
| B-24453-A | That's Right - I'm Wrong - vJA | Br 8378, Col DO-2034 |
| B-24454-A | Yankee Doodle - vJA/aFvE | Br 8397, RZ G-24865 |

    Linda Keene-v.                      New York, May 5, 1939.

| | | |
|---|---|---|
| B-24482-B | White Sails (Beneath A Silver Moon) | Br 8388, Col DO-2022 |
| | - vLK | |
| B-24483-A | Octoroon - vJT | -    RZ G-24941 |
| B-24484-A | Pickin' For Patsy | Br 8401, Par R-2856, DPE-56, |
| | | RZ G-24941, Col DS-1439 |
| B-24485-A | Undertow | As above, except RZ G-24941 |

                                        Chicago, June 23, 1939.

| | | |
|---|---|---|
| WC-2624-A | Especially For You - vLK | Br 8431, Par R-2721 |
| WC-2625-A | You Know Just As Well As I Know - vJT | Br 8435 |
| WC-2626-A | You're The Moment In My Life - vLK | Br 8431, Par R-2721 |
| WC-2627-A | The Little Man Who Wasn't There - vJT | Br 8435 |

                                        Chicago, July 19, 1939.

| | | |
|---|---|---|
| WC-2654-A | Puttin' And Takin' - vJT | Br 8454 |
| WC-2655-A | I Swung The Election - vJT&ch | Col 35206 |
| WC-2656-A | Blues To The Dole | Br 8454 |
| WC-2657-A | Aunt Hagar's Blues - vJT | Col 35206 |
| WC-2658-A | Rippling Waters | Col 35727 |

JACK TEAGARDEN AND HIS ORCHESTRA : Jack Teagarden-tb-v dir. Charlie Spivak-Carl
Garvin-Lee Castle-t/Jose Gutierrez-Mark Bennett-Charles McCamish-tb/Clint Garvin-
Art St. John-cl-as/John van Eps-Hub Lytle-cl-ts/Ernie Caceres-cl-ts-bar/John
Anderson-p/Allan Reuss-g/Art Miller-sb/Cubby Teagarden-d/Red Bone-a/Kitty Kallen-
v.                                  New York, August 23, 1939.

| | | |
|---|---|---|
| 26013-A | I'm Takin' My Time With You - vKK | Col 35224 |
| 26014-A | I Wanna Hat With Cherries - vKK | - |
| 26015-A | Two Blind Loves - vKK | Col 35233 |
| 26016-A | Hawaii Sang Me To Sleep - vKK | - |

New York, August 25, 1939.

| | | |
|---|---|---|
| 26021-A | It's A Hundred To One (I'm In Love)-vJT | Col 35215 |
| 26022-A | I'll Remember - vKK | - |
| 26023-A | Peg O' My Heart - aRB | Col 35727, RZ G-24463 |

Eddie Dudley-tb replaces McCamish; Jack Russin-p replaces Anderson; Dave Tough-d
replaces Teagarden.                 New York, September 25, 1939.

| | | |
|---|---|---|
| 26108-A | At Least You Could Say Hello - vKK | Col 35245 |
| 26109-A | A Table In A Corner - vKK | Col 35252 |
| 26110-A | Stop Kicking My Heart Around - vKK | Col 35245 |
| 26111-A | If What You Say Is True - vKK | Rejected |

New York, October 6, 1939.

| | | |
|---|---|---|
| 26163-A | So Many Times - vKK | Col 35252 |
| 26164-A | Muddy River Blues - vJT | Col 35297, 291295, Par R-2739, B-71164, PZ-11007, RZ G-24250 |
| 26165-A | Wolverine Blues - aRB | As above |
| 26166-A | Red Wing | Col 35450, Par R-2762 |
| 26167-A | United We Swing | OK 6272 |

Frank Ryerson-t replaces Spivak; Benny Pottle-sb replaces Miller; Fred Norman-a.
                                    New York, November 1, 1939.

| | | |
|---|---|---|
| 26243-A | Beale Street Blues - vJT | Col 35323, 291226, Par R-2735, B-71165, PZ-11005 |
| 26244-A | Somewhere A Voice Is Calling | Col 35450, Par R-2762 |
| 26245-A | Swingin' On The Teagarden Gate - aFN | Col 35323, 291226, Par R-2735, B-71165, PZ-11005 |

The following titles were recorded from a broadcast from an unknown station, late
in 1939; the personnel is probably as for the last session above.

D6-TC-6298-1  On Revival Day-vJT/Wolverine Blues  V-Disc 724

Art Miller-sb replaces Pottle.      Southland Restaurant, Boston, Jan. 23, 1940.

| | |
|---|---|
| Three Little Words | IAJRC 5 (LP) |
| New Blues - vJT | - |
| Big T Jumps | - |

Jack Teagarden-tb-v dir. John Fallstitch-Tom Gonsoulin-t/Sid Feller-t-a/Seymour
Goldfinger-Jose Gutierrez-Joe Ferrall-tb/Art St. John-as-bar/Jack Goldie-Tony
Antonelli-Joe Ferdinando-as/Larry Walsh-ts/Nat Jaffe-p/Dan Perri-g/Arnold Fishkind
sb/Ed Naquin-d.                     New York, February, 1940.

| | | |
|---|---|---|
| US-1356-1 | If I Could Be With You (One Hour Tonight) - vJT | Var 8209, Phil 83, Regent 159 |
| US-1357-1 | My Melancholy Baby - vJT | -                     - |
| US-1358-1 | Can't We Talk It Over ? - vJT | Var 8218, MW 10012 |
| US-1359-1 | The Blues | -           - Elite 5042, Phil 83 |

NOTE:- Most copies of Elite 5042 credit both sides erroneously to Jack Teagarden.

JACK TEAGARDEN AND HIS ORCHESTRA : Jack Teagarden-tb-v dir. John Fallstitch-Tom
  Gonsoulin-t/Sid Feller-t-a/Jose Gutierrez-Seymour Goldfinger-Joe Ferrall-tb/Art
  St. John-as-bar/Jack Goldie-Tony Antonelli-Joe Ferdinando-as/Larry Walsh-ts/Nat
  Jaffe-p/Dan Perri-g/Arnold Fishkind-sb/Ed Naquin-d/Irving Szathmary-a/Kitty Kallen
  v.                                        New York, February, 1940.

US-1364-1  Love For Sale - vKK/aIS              Var 8202
US-1365-1  You, You Darling - vKK               Var 8196
US-1366-1  The Moon And The Willow Tree - vKK     -
US-1367-1  Wham (Re-Bop-Boom-Bam) - vKK         Var 8202

   Benny Lagasse-as replaces Goldie; Paul Collins-d replaces Naquin; Marianne Dunne-v.
                                         New York, April, 1940.

US-1571-2  Devil May Care - vMD                 Var 8278
US-1572-1  Night On The Shalimar - vMD            -
US-1573-1  I Hear Bluebirds - vMD               Var 8273
US-1574-1  Fatima's Drummer Boy - vJT             -

   Danny Polo-cl-as replaces Lagasse; Perri omitted; David Allen-v.
                                         New York, c. late July, 1940.

US-1864-1  Now I Lay Me Down To Dream - vDA     Var 8374
US-1865-1  Wait 'Til I Catch You In My Dreams-vDA Var 8388
US-1866-2  And So Do I - vMD                      -
US-1867-1  River Home - vJT                     Var 8374

JACK TEAGARDEN'S BIG EIGHT : Rex Stewart-c/Jack Teagarden-tb-v/Barney Bigard-cl/Ben
  Webster-ts/Billy Kyle-p/Brick Fleagle-g/Billy Taylor-sb/Dave Tough-d.
                                         New York, December 15, 1940.

3414   St. James Infirmary - vJT                HRS 2006
3415   The World Is Waiting For The Sunrise     HRS 2007
3416   The Big Eight Blues                        -
3417   Shine                                    HRS 2006

JACK TEAGARDEN AND HIS ORCHESTRA : Jack Teagarden-tb-v dir. John Fallstitch-Pokey
  Carriere-t/Sid Feller-t-a/Jose Gutierrez-Seymour Goldfinger-Joe Ferrall-tb/Danny
  Polo-cl-as/Tony Antonelli-Joe Ferdinando-as/Art Moore-Art Beck-ts/Ernie Hughes-p/
  Arnold Fishkind-sb/Paul Collins-d/Lynne Clark-David Allen-v/Phil Moore-a.
                                         New York, January, 1941.

       Frenesi                               Viking 103
       Here's My Heart - vDA                    -
       Accidentally On Purpose - vLC         Viking 104
       It All Comes Back To Me Now - vDA        -

                         New York, January 31, 1941.

68636-A  Dark Eyes                           Dec 3701, M-30323, Br 03365,
                                               Od 284838
68637-A  Prelude in C sharp minor (Rachmaninoff) Dec 3642, Br 03238, Od 284838
68638-A  Chicks Is Wonderful                 Dec 3701, Od 284790
68639-A  Blues To The Lonely (Lonely Blues*)-vJT Dec 3642, Br 80112*, 03238*,
                                               Od 284790

   Truman Quigley-t replaces Feller; Perry Botkin-g added; Ruth Elsey-v; Carriere,
   Teagarden, Polo, Hughes, Botkin, Fishkind and Collins only*; Joe Glover-a. All
   these records were dubbed from the soundtrack of the film BIRTH OF THE BLUES, and
   were promotion discs for it. See also Bing Crosby.
                                         Hollywood, c. May, 1941.

PP-302  *Tiger Rag
PP-305  Cuddle Up A Little Closer - vRE
PP-306  St. Louis Blues - vRE&ch

JACK TEAGARDEN AND HIS ORCHESTRA : Jack Teagarden-tb-v dir. John Fallstitch-Pokey
 Carriere-Truman Quigley-t/Jose Gutierrez-Seymour Goldfinger-Joe Ferrall-tb/Danny
 Polo-cl-as/Tony Antonelli-Joe Ferdinando-as/Art Moore-Art Beck-ts/Ernie Hughes-p/
 Perry Botkin-g/Arnold Fishkind-sb/Paul Collins-d.
                                              Los Angeles, May 26, 1941.

DLA-2413-A  Blue River - vJT                      Dec 4071, Br 80113, 03323,
                                                  Col 299005
DLA-2414-A  St. James Infirmary - vJT             Dec 3844, BM-1198, F-8056,
                                                  Br 80111, 03264, Od 284810,
DLA-2415-A  What Did I Do To Be So Black And Blue As above
            - vJT
DLA-2416-A  A Hundred Years From Today - vJT      Dec 4317, M-30323, Br 03365
  NOTE:- Decca F-8056 is a Swiss issue only.  See also Bing Crosby.

   Art Gold-t replaces Fallstitch; Fred Keller-tb replaces Goldfinger; Botkin omitted;
   Myron Shapler-sb replaces Fishkind.     Los Angeles, July 7, 1941.

DLA-2506-A  A Rhythm Hymn - vch                   Dec 4071, Br 03323, Col 299005
DLA-2507-A  Prelude To The Blues                  Dec 4409, M-2003, Od 284906
DLA-2508-A  The Blues Have Got Me - vJT             -       - Br 80113 -
DLA-2509-A  Nobody Knows The Trouble I've Seen-vJT Dec 4317, Br 80112

Variations on Jack Teagarden's name were used as follows :-

Jack Teagarden and his All-Star Band, the Teagarden Boys and Trumbauer's Swing Band -
   see the Three T's;
Jackson Teagarden and his Trombone - see Eddie Condon (DIANE on Commodore 505).

### JOHNNIE TEMPLE

Vocal, acc. by own g, with Charlie McCoy-g*; both issues as JOHNNIE (GEECHIE) TEMPLE.
                                              Chicago, May 14, 1935.

C-983-B  *Lead Pencil Blues (It Just Won't Write)  Voc 03068
C-984-   Jacksonville Blues                        Voc 02987
C-985-A-B  Morning Prayer Blues                    Rejected
C-986-B  *Big Boat Whistle                         Voc 03068
C-987-   The Evil Devil Blues                      Voc 02987
C-988-A-B  Cypress Grove Blues

   Acc. by ? Horace Malcolm-p/Charlie McCoy or self-g. (Decca 48002 as JOHNNY TEMPLE).
                                              Chicago, November 12, 1936.

90980-A  New Vicksburg Blues                      Dec 7244
90981-A  Louise Louise Blues                        -      48002

   Sb added.                                   Chicago, May 14, 1937.

91246-A  Snapping Cat                            Dec 7416
91247-A  So Lonely And Blue                      Dec 7337
91248-A  New Louise Louise Blues                   -
91249-A  Peepin' Through The Keyhole             Dec 7316
91250-A  Pimple Blues                            Dec 7444
91251-A  East St. Louis Blues                    Dec 7316

   Acc. by the Harlem Hamfats : Odell Rand-cl/Horace Malcolm-p/Joe McCoy-g/Charlie
   McCoy-g-md/sb/Fred Flynn-d.               New York, October 6, 1937.

62653-A  Gimme Some Of That Yum Yum Yum          Dec 7385
62654-A  Hoodoo Women                             -
62655-A  Mama's Bad Luck                         Dec 7416
62656-A  Mean Baby Blues                         Dec 7444

   Acc. by ? Joshua Altheimer-p/Charlie McCoy-g/sb/T. C. Williams-d.
                                              Chicago, October 28, 1937.

C-2046-1-2  Beale Street Sheik                   Voc rejected
C-2047-1-2  My Mama's Bad Luck Child               -
C-2048-1-2  Dope Peddlin' Blues                    -
C-2049-1-2  The Hoodoo Plan                        -

Acc. by the Harlem Hamfats : Herb Morand-t*/Odell Rand-cl/Horace Malcolm-p/Joe
McCoy-g/Charlie McCoy-g-md/sb/Frank Flynn-d.
New York, April 22, 1938.

| | | |
|---|---|---|
| 63670-A | What Is That Smells Like Gravy ? | Dec 7456 |
| 63671-A | *Every Dog Must Have His Day | Dec 7495 |
| 63672-A | *Fare You Well | - |
| 63673-A | *Stavin' Chain | Dec 7532 |
| 63674-A | County Jail Blues | Dec 7456 |
| 63675-A | Gonna Ride 74 | Dec 7532 |

Acc. by Odell Rand-cl/? Joshua Altheimer-p/own g/sb. (Decca 48002 as JOHNNY TEMPLE).
Chicago, October 17, 1938.

| | | |
|---|---|---|
| 91519-A | When The Breath Bids Your Girl Friend's Body Goodbye | Dec 7564 |
| 91520-A | Big Leg Woman | Dec 7547, 48002 |
| 91521-A | What A Fool I've Been | Dec 7573 |
| 91522-A | Grinding Mill | Dec 7583 |
| 91523-A | Between Midnight And Dawn | Dec 7547 |
| 91524-A | Mississippi Woman's Blues (Walkin' Blues) | Dec 7564 |

Acc. by ? Sam Price-p/? Teddy Bunn-g/sb.
New York, March 6, 1939.

| | | |
|---|---|---|
| 65203-A | Jelly Roll Bert | Dec 7573 |
| 65204-A | Up Today And Down Tomorrow | Dec 7632 |
| 65205-A-B | Getting Old Blues | Dec 7599 |
| 65206-A | The Sun Goes Down In Blood | Dec 7632 |
| 65207-A | Better Not Let My Good Gal Catch You Here (My Regular Woman) | Dec 7583 |
| 65208-A-B | If I Could Holler | Dec 7599 |

Acc. by Odell Rand-cl/Sam Price-p/Lonnie Johnson-g/John Lindsay-sb.
Chicago, September 13, 1939.

| | | |
|---|---|---|
| 91757-A | Streamline Blues | Dec 7660 |
| 91758-A | Good Suzie | Dec 7643 |
| 91759-A | Down In Mississippi | - |
| 91760-A | Evil Bad Woman | Dec 7660 |
| 91761-A | Cherry Ball | Dec 7678 |
| 91762-A | Let's Get Together | - |

Acc. by Buster Bailey-cl/Sam Price-p/Albert Casey-g/Herb Cowans-d
New York, April 4, 1940.

| | | |
|---|---|---|
| 67489-A | Good Woman Blues | Dec 7735 |
| 67490-A | Skin And Bones Woman | Dec 7750 |
| 67491-A | I'm Cuttin' Out | Dec 7772 |
| 67492-A | Fireman Blues | Dec 7782 |
| 67493-A | Lovin' Woman Blues | Dec 7772 |
| 67494-A | Roomin' House Blues | Dec 7782 |
| 67495-A | Sugar Bowl Blues | Dec 7735 |
| 67496-A | Stick Up Woman (Let Me Make This Trip With You) | Dec 7750 |

Acc. by Henry Allen-t/Buster Bailey-cl/Lil Armstrong-p/d.
New York, September 23, 1940.

| | | |
|---|---|---|
| 68136-A | Baby Don't You Love Me No More ? | Dec 7825 |
| 68137-A | My Pony | Dec 7817 |
| 68138-A | Jive Me, Baby | Dec 7800 |
| 68139-A | Corrine Corrina | Dec 7825 |
| 68140-A | Bow Leg Woman | Dec 7817 |
| 68141-A-B | Fix It Up And Go | Dec 7800 |

Acc. by Horace Malcolm-p/own g (all as JOHNNY TEMPLE).
                                        Chicago, September 11, 1941.

| 064869-1 | Big Woman Blues        | BB B-8968 |
|----------|------------------------|-----------|
| 064870-1 | Sundown Blues          | BB B-8913 |
| 064871-1 | What Is That She Got ? | BB B-8968 |
| 064872-1 | Jinks Lee Blues        | BB B-8913 |

## THE  TEMPO  KINGS

Probably a contingent from Ross Gorman's Earl Carroll Vanities Orchestra, viz.:-
    Donald Lindley-t/Miff Mole-tb/Alfie Evans-cl-as/Barney Acquelina-bsx/Arthur Schutt-
    p/Dick McDonough-bj/David Grupp-d/Frank Bessinger-v.
                                        New York, c. January 27, 1926.

| 106580 | Flamin' Mamie - vFB  | PA 36385, Per 14566 |
|--------|----------------------|---------------------|
| 106581 | Rhythm Of The Day    | -          -        |

## TEN  BLACK BERRIES

Pseudonym on Banner, Cameo, Challenge, Conqueror, Domino, Oriole, Perfect, Regal,
    Rex and Romeo for Duke Ellington and his Orchestra, q.v., as a rule; the following
    exceptions are known, however :-

Banner 0839  St. Louis Blues (Broadway Broadcasters - see Sam Lanin) (also Oriole
    2089, Regal 10145, Romeo 1453) (and Jewel 6089 ?)
Banner 0839  Tiger Rag (The Whoopee Makers - see Irving Mills) (also as above, plus
    Jewel 6089)
Romeo 976  Sorority Stomp (The Whoopee Makers - see Irving Mills)

## THE TEN BLACKBIRDS

Pseudonym for the following items listed in this book :-

Apex 752  Hi-Diddle-Diddle (The Red Heads)
Domino 181289  In Harlem's Araby (Dubin's Dandies - see Adrian Schubert)
Domino 181289  St. James Infirmary (Duke Ellington and his Orchestra)

## TEN BLACK DIAMONDS

Pseudonym on Banner 0580, Cameo 0180 and Romeo 1125 for the Whoopee Makers (see
    Irving Mills).

## TEN FRESHMEN

Pseudonym on Pathe 37054 and Perfect 15235 for the Whoopee Makers (see Irving Mills),
    and for other bands of varying degrees of interest as "hot" dance music (e.g., Lou
    Gold and his Orchestra (MY KINDA LOVE) on Pathe Actuelle 36969 and Perfect 15150).

## TEN JACKS  OF DIAMONDS

2t/tb/2as/ts/p/bb/d-chimes/Scrappy Lambert (as RALPH HAINES on Banner, LARRY HOLTON
    on Oriole)-v.                        New York, May 15, 1928.

| 7977-3 | Bring Back My Lovin' Man - vSL | Ban 7158, Or 1308 |
|--------|--------------------------------|-------------------|
| 7978-2 | Try To Smile - vSL             | Ban 7135, Chg 638, Or 1256 |

NOTE:- The name TEN JACKS OF DIAMONDS is the one in which the above titles are
shown in the ARC files; Banner 7135 and Challenge 638 are labelled MISSOURI JAZZ
BAND, Banner 7158 as HOLLYWOOD DANCE ORCHESTRA, and both Orioles as DIXIE JAZZ
BAND.

## TENNESSEE  CHOCOLATE DROPS

Howard Armstrong-vn/Roland Martin-bj/Carl Martin-g; this allocation of instruments
    is believed to be correct, but as all three musicians could play vn and g, it may
    be that a different combination was used.
                                        Knoxville, Tennessee, March-April, 1930.

| K-8066- | Knox County Stomp | Voc 1517, 5472 |
|---------|-------------------|----------------|
| K-8067- | Vine Street Drag  | -         -    |

NOTE:- Vocalion 5472 (in the white hillbilly series !) as TENNESSEE TRIO.

Pseudonym on Harmony and associated labels for the following items listed in this
   book :-

Harmony 1375-H, 1378-H, Clarion 5389-C, 5392-C, Velvet Tone 2453-V, 2456-V  All four
   sides by the Mound City Blue Blowers (or Red McKenzie and the Celestial Beings)
Harmony 1406-H, 1422-H, Clarion 5446-C, 5469-C, Velvet Tone 2506-V, 2529-V  Loveless
   Love/No Trumps (Fred Gardner's Texas Troubadours)
Harmony 1415-H, Clarion 5461-C, Velvet Tone 2521-V  Bugle Call Rag (Eddie Lang's
   Orchestra)/Deep Harlem (Frank Trumbauer and his Orchestra)
Harmony 1420-H, Clarion 5467-C, Velvet Tone 2527-V  Choo Choo (Frank Trumbauer and
   his Orchestra)
Harmony 1422-H, Clarion 5469-C, Velvet Tone 2529-V  Baby, Won't You Please Come Home
   (Frank Trumbauer and his Orchestra)
Harmony 1427-H, Clarion 5474-C, Velvet Tone 2534-V  Shim-Me-Sha-Wabble (Miff Mole's
   Molers)/Raggin' The Scale (Joe Venuti's Blue Four)

## TENNESSEE  TEN

Phil Napoleon-Jules Levy, Jr.-t/Charlie Panelli-tb/Jimmy Lytell-cl/Rudy Wiedoeft-
   Loring McMurray-as/Frank Signorelli-p/John Cali-bj/John Helleberg-bb Jack Roth-d.
                                 New York, April 27, 1923.

27857-2  You've Got To See Mama Ev'ry Night        Vic 19073, HMV B-1677, K-2156,
                                                   Zon 3594
27858-4  Long-Lost Mama (Daddy Misses You)         Vic 19105


Levy omitted.                          New York, June 7, 1923.

28056-3  Down Hearted Blues (Intro. Chirpin'       Vic 19094
            The Blues)
28057-1  Gulf Coast Blues-Sugar Blues Medley Fox Trot -

                                       New York, June 26, 1923.

28219-4  'Tain't Nobody's Biz-ness If I Do         Vic 19109
            (Intro. Achin' Hearted Blues)
28220-2  Waitin' For The Evenin' Mail (Sittin' On    -
            The Inside, Lookin' At The Outside)

Jules Levy, Jr.-t added; Nick Lucas-bj replaces Cali.
                                 New York, July 23, 1923.

28305-1-2-3-4  Tin Roof Blues                      Rejected
28306-2  That Big Blonde Mama                      Vic 19130

Three titles on Gennett (made in 1926) under this name are of no interest as jazz.


## THE  TENNESSEE  TOOTERS

Sterling Grant-Roscoe Wickham-k/Porter Grainger-p/Sam Speed-bj.
                                 New York, May 21, 1924.

81788-3  Ground Hog Blues                          Col 144-D
81789-2  Chattanooga (Down In Tennessee)             -

## THE  TENNESSEE  TOOTERS

Red Nichols-t/? Vincent Grande-tb/Chuck Muller-as/Lucien Smith-ts/Rube Bloom-p/John
   Cali-bj/Joe Tarto-bb/Harry Lottman-d.  New York, December 23, 1924.

   152    Prince Of Wails                          Voc 14952, Gmn 1700
   155    I Ain't Got Nobody To Love                 -        Gmn 1701
   NOTE:- Guardsman 1700 and 1701 as NEW JERSEY DANCE ORCHESTRA.

Miff Mole-tb replaces ? Grande.        New York, January 23, 1925.

   256    Hot-Hot-Hottentot                        Voc 14967, Gmn 7008
   259    How Come You Do Me Like You Do ?           -          -
   NOTE:- Guardsman 7008 as THE KENTUCKY TOOTERS.

Red Nichols-t/? Vincent Grande-tb/Chuck Muller-as/Lucien Smith-ts/Rube Bloom-p/John
  Cali-bj/Joe Tarto-bb/Harry Lottman-d.   New York, February 16, 1925.

  373/5   Everybody Loves My Baby                Voc 14985
  376/7   Jacksonville Gal                          -        Gmn 7012
  NOTE:- Guardsman 7012 as THE ORIGINAL BLACK BAND.

Harry Gluck-t/? Vincent Grande-tb/Chuck Muller-as/Rube Bloom-p/John Cali-bj/Joe
  Tarto-bb/Harry Lottman-d.                New York, March 25, 1925.

599/601   Those Panama Mamas (Are Ruinin' Me)     Voc 15004
  602/5   Red Hot Henry Brown                       -        Gmn 1768
  NOTE:- Guardsman 1768 as CAROLINA DANCE BAND.

                                           New York, April 8, 1925.

  664     Jimtown Blues                           Voc 15022, Sil 3077, Duo B-5110,
                                                     Gmn 7015
  666     Kansas City Stomps                      Voc 15022    -      Gmn 7014
  NOTE:- Silvertone 3077 as GEORGIA JAZZ BAND; Duophone B-5110 as MONTEREY DANCE
  BAND; Guardsman 7014 as PETE MASSEY'S ALL-BLACK BAND.

  Unknown t replaces Gluck; Lucien Smith-ts added; unknown bj replaces Cali.
                                           New York, June 23, 1925.

  920     What-Cha-Call-'Em Blues                 Voc 15068, Gmn 7015
  922     Milenberg Joys                            -        Gmn 7017
  NOTE:- Guardsman 7015 and 7017 as PETE MASSEY'S ALL-BLACK BAND.

? Hymie Farberman or Harry Gluck-t/Miff Mole-tb/Chuck Muller-as/Lucien Smith-ts/Rube
  Bloom-p/bj/Joe Tarto-bb/Harry Lottman-d.
                                           New York, August 11, 1925.

1130/2   Charleston                               Voc 15086
1135     I Had A Sweet Mama                         -        Gmn 1833, Lev A-103
  NOTE:- Guardsman 1833 as OLD SOUTHERN DANCE ORCHESTRA; Lecaphone A-103 as DIXIE
  PLANTATION ORCHESTRA.

                                           New York, August 13, 1925.

1155     Deep Elm                                 Voc 15109, Gmn 7018
1157     Sweet Man                                  - Bel 1080 -
  NOTE:- Beltona 1080 as AMERICAN DANCE ORCHESTRA; Guardsman 7018 as PETE MASSEY'S
  ALL-BLACK BAND.

Earl Oliver and another-t/Sam Lewis-tb/Benny Krueger-as/p/Harry Reser-bj/Joe Tarto-
  bb.                                      New York, September 15, 1925.

1348     I Ain't Got Nobody                       Voc 15135, Adelphi 11, Bel 930,
                                                     Duo B-5136, Gmn 1861
1352     Everybody Stomp                          As above, except Duo B-5136
  NOTE:- Adelphi 11 as INTERNATIONAL ACES: Beltona 930 as AMERICAN DANCE ORCHESTRA;
  Duophone B-5136 as MONTEREY DANCE BAND; Guardsman 1861 as CABARET DANCE ORCHESTRA.

One t and Tarto omitted.                   New York, November 20, 1925.

1768/70   Hot Aire                                Voc 15169
1771/3    Back Home In Illinois                     -

Probably entirely different personnel.     New York, June 29, 1926.

E-3314   Minor Gaff                               Voc 15388
E-3316   Hobo's Prayer                              -

Red Nichols and another-t/Miff Mole-tb/? Alfie Evans-cl-as-ts-bar/Arnold Brilhart-cl
  as/Fred Morrow-cl-ts/Rube Bloom-p/Tony Colucci-bj/Joe Tarto-bb/? Vic Berton-d.
  (Brunswicks all as THE WOLVERINES).      New York, September 20, 1926.

E-4144; E-20206  Crazy Quilt                      Voc 15487, Br 3332*, A-221,A-81256
E-4147; E-20207  You're Burnin' Me Up (Turnin'    Voc 15488    -      -      -
           Me Down)

The above name was also used on Vocalion 15201 for the Cotton Pickers, q.v.

## TENNESSEE TRIO

See the Tennessee Chocolate Drops.

## MAX TERR AND HIS ORCHESTRA

This name was applied to the California Ramblers playing JUST A LITTLE DRINK on
Pathe Actuelle 10899 (q.v.); as far as is known, records by Max Terr and his
Orchestra correctly ascribed are of little or no interest as "hot" dance music.

## ARTHUR TERRY

Pseudonym on Parlophone E-6329 and E-6392 for Smith Ballew, q.v., and on Parlophone
E-6362 for Seger Ellis, q.v.

## BOB TERRY AND HIS ORCHESTRA

Bunny Berigan-t/Al Philburn-tb/Paul Ricci-cl/Frank Signorelli-p/Casper Reardon-harp/
Carmen Mastren-g/Sid Weiss-sb/Stan King-d/Wayne Gregg-v.
                                        New York, January 15, 1936.

| | | |
|---|---|---|
| 60337-A | Moonburn - vWG | Ch 40093, Dec F-5901 |
| 60338-A | My Heart And I - vWG | -       - |
| 60339-A | It's Been So Long - vWG | Ch 40094, Pan 25857 |
| 60340-B | Sing An Old Fashioned Song (To A Young | -       Dec F-5950 |
| | Sophisticated Lady) - vWG | |

NOTE:- Panachord 25857 as LEN HERMAN AND HIS ORCHESTRA.

## SID TERRY'S COLLEGIANS

Pseudonym on Silvertone 2682 (THEN I'LL BE HAPPY) for Fletcher Henderson and his
Orchestra, q.v.

## THELMA TERRY AND HER PLAY BOYS

Thelma Terry-sb dir. Johnny Mendel-Carl Rinker-t/Floyd O'Brien-tb/Bud Jacobson-cl/
Mike Platt-cl-as/Phil Shukin-cl-ts/Bill Otto-p/Roy Campbell-bj/Gene Krupa-d.
                                        Chicago, March 29, 1928.

| | | |
|---|---|---|
| 145852-3 | Mama's Gone, Goodbye | Col 1706-D |
| 145853-2 | Lady Of Havana | Col 01481 |
| 145853-3 | Lady Of Havana | Col 1390-D, 5015 |
| 145854-3 | The Voice Of The Southland | -       - 01481 |
| 145855-4 | Starlight And Tulips | Col 1532-D |

Thelma Terry-sb dir. Dub Fleming-c/Warren Smith-tb/Charles Dornberger-cl-as/Earl
Gray-as/Pat Davies-cl-ts/Bob Zurke-p/George Shirley-bj/Joe Davis-d-v/Wayne Smith
(? Warren Smith)-v.                     New York, September 27, 1928.

| | | |
|---|---|---|
| 146961-3 | When Sweet Susie Goes Steppin' By - vWS | Col 1588-D, 01403 |
| 146962-2 | Dusky Stevedore - vJD | -  5164    - |

## FRANK TESCHMACHER'S CHICAGOANS

Frank Teschmacher-cl-as/Rod Cless-as/Mezz Mezzrow-ts/Joe Sullivan-p/Eddie Condon-bj/
Jim Lannigan-bb/Gene Krupa-d.           Chicago, April 28, 1928.

| | | |
|---|---|---|
| C-1905-A-B | Singin' The Blues | Rejected |
| C-1906-A | Jazz Me Blues | UHCA 61 |

## THE TEXANS

Pseudonym on OKeh 40914 and 40919 for Sam Lanin and his Famous Players, q.v.

Bubber Miley-c/Arthur Ray-or.                    New York, c. October 2, 1924.

  31687    Lenox Avenue Shuffle                      Ajax 17065, AF A-016
            Down In The Mouth Blues                      -        -

                                                 New York, c. October 5, 1924.

105588     Down In The Mouth Blues                PA 036160, Per 14341
105589     Lenox Avenue Shuffle                     -         -

                                                 New York, October 7, 1924.

  13832     Lenox Avenue Shuffle                      Voc 14913
  13834     Down In The Mouth Blues                    -

## TEXAS   JASS BAND

Pseudonym on Operaphone for Wilbur Sweatman and his Jass Band, q.v.

## TEXAS  TEN

Nathan Glantz-as dir. 2t/tb/cl-as/ts/p/bj/bb/d.
                                                 New York, c. May 5, 1925.

106006     What A Smile Can Do                     PA 036251, Per 14432
106007     Sweet Georgia Brown                    PA 036247, 10901, Hg 1043,
                                                   Per 14428
  6015     Sweet Georgia Brown (I Found A Round   Ban 1540, Dom 3510, Or 424,
           About May To Hearen* (!)              Re 9835, Sil 2490, Mic 22010,
                                                   Max 1546, Us 263*
106008     Charleston                             PA 036251, 10901, X-6022, P 6823,
                                                   Per 14432, Sal 148
  6014     Charleston                             Ban 1540, Dom 3510, Or 413,
                                                   Re 9835, Sil 2493, Apex 8355,
                                                   St 10091, Imp 1477
NOTE:- Pathe Actuelle 036247 and 036251 as WESTCHESTER BILTMORE ORCHESTRA; X-6022,
Pathe 6823 and Salabert 148 as CHARLESTON RHYTHM CLOVER GARDEN (!); Perfect 14428
and 14432 as THE BLUES CHASERS; Domino 3510 as SIX BLACK DOMINOES; Silvertone 2493
as LANIN'S ROSELAND ORCHESTRA; Apex 8355 and Imperial 1477 as SIX BLACK DIAMONDS;
Maxsa 1546 as EARL RANDOLPH'S ORCHESTRA; Usiba 263 is anonymous.

## SAM THEARD

Most of this blues singer's records on Brunswick (1929-1931) and Decca (1934) are
accompanied by pianists believed to be Cow Cow Davenport or H. Benton Overstreet;
occasionally a guitar is added. Those given a jazz band accompaniment are listed
below. A complete listing will be found in BLUES AND GOSPEL RECORDS, 1902-1942.

Vocal, acc. by Banks Chesterfield's Orchestra : T/as or ts/p/sb/Louis Banks-d.
                                                 Chicago, September 17, 1934.

C-9483     That Rhythm Gal                        Dec 7025
C-9484-A   Till I Die                             Dec 7146

LOVIN' SAM AND HIS SWING RASCALS : Vocal, acc. by t/ts/p/d/v, with hand-clapping and
  bird-whistle effects*.                         Chicago, August 16, 1937.

C-1984-1-2  Let Me Jelly Your Roll                Rejected
C-1985-1-2  Shame On You                            -
C-1986-1    Spo-Dee-O-Dee                         Voc 03686
C-1987-2   *That's What I'm Talking About           -

LOVIN' SAM AND BURNS CAMPBELL ORCHESTRA : Vocal, acc. by t/2as/ts/p/g/sb/d.
                                                 Aurora, Ill., March 14, 1938.

020150-1   Walkin' Back Home                      BB B-7916
020151-1   Big Time Rose                          BB B-7629
020152-1   You Turned Your Back On Me             BB B-7514
020153-1   You're Gonna Be A Rascal 'Til You Die    -
020154-1   You're Solid With Me                   BB B-7629
020155-1   That's Chicago's South Side              -

THEM BIRMINGHAM NITE OWLS

Pseudonym on Champion for the Blackbirds of Paradise, q.v.

## HENRY THIES

Although some of Henry Thies' records have a few bars "hot" trumpet or occasionally some other instrument featured, in the main they are first-class straight dance band performances. The following may be considered exceptions to this, however.

HENRY THIES AND HIS CASTLE FARM ORCHESTRA : Henry Thies-vn dir. 2t/Tommy Dorsey-tb/ Jimmy Dorsey-cl-as/as/ts/Joe Reichman-p/? Don Dewey-bj/? Ray Fantcher-bb/d.
Cincinnati, August 31, 1925.

12335-C-E  Angry                          Gnt 3118

HENRY THIES AND HIS HOTEL SINTON ORCHESTRA : Henry Thies-vn dir. Howard Crockett-Alvin Miller-t/? Cliff Heather or George Troup-tb/Harold James-Lloyd Schaffer-cl-as/Russell Pierce-cl-ts/Henry Burgess-vn/Jack Saatkamp-p/Don Dewey-bj-v/Paul Neff bb/Fred Lower-d.                  Chicago, January 22, 1929.

48815-2  Sweet Liza - vDD                  Vic 21890

                                    Chicago, February 18, 1929.

48815-5  Sweet Liza - vDD                  Vic 21890

## THOMAS' DEVILS

Cicero Thomas-t/King Mutt-cl/p/sb/d/Dave Cross-v.
                                    Chicago, March 12, 1929.

C-3100-A-B  Sho' Is Hot - vDC              Br 7064, Spt S-2235
C-3101-A  Boot It, Boy - vDC                 -          -

## BUD THOMAS

See F. T. Thomas.

## EDDIE THOMAS' COLLEGIANS

This is almost certainly a Ben Selvin unit, although the CBS file cards do not give any definite information regarding the following title, which features a good trumpet and consists of 2t/tb/2cl-as/cl-ts/vn/p/bj/bb/d/Irving Kaufman (as FRANK HARRIS)-v.                    New York, September 27, 1927.

144798-3  Sugar - vIK                      Col 1154-D

## EMLYN THOMAS

Emlyn Thomas directing the London Band made several Vocalion records in the mid-1920s. The following serves to show the extent of his understanding of the jazz idiom and its application to a jazz standard.

THE LONDON BAND, directed by EMLYN THOMAS : Emlyn Thomas-vn dir. Jay Elms-another-t/ tb/Charles Star and another-as/Ernie Smith-ts/Leon Patey-p/bj/bb/d.
                                    London, c. September, 1924.

03683    Eccentric                         Voc X-9500

## F. T. THOMAS

The following blues record may be of some interest as jazz in view of the accompaniment.

Vocal, acc. by as/Leothus Green-p.     Richmond, Ind., July 10, 1929.

15325    Street Walkin' Blues              Gnt 6963, Ch 15795, Spt 9511
15326    Moanin' Piano Blues                 -          -          -
NOTE:- Champion 15795 as GEORGE "HAMBONE" RUTHERS; Supertone 9511 as BUD THOMAS.

Pseudonym on Champion for Henry Johnson and his Boys, q.v.

## HARRY THOMAS

This artist's real name was Reginald Thomas Broughton, and he was an Englishman.

Piano solos.                              New York, November 20, 1916.

18684-1-2-3  A Classical Spasm (Based on          Vic rejected
         Scharwenka's Polish Dance and Paderewski's Minuet) (aHT)
18685-1-2-3  Delirious Rag (William Eckstein-      -
         Harry Thomas)

                                          New York, December 4, 1916.

18684-4  A Classical Spasm (arr. as above)        Vic 18229
18685-4  Delirious Rag (William Eckstein-Harry Thomas)-

                                          New York, September 19, 1917.

77351-1-2-3-4-5  Apple Sauce (Intro. Ragging The  Col rejected
         Chimes)

                                          New York, October 18, 1917.

77351-6-7-8-9-10  Apple Sauce (Intro. Ragging     Col rejected
         The Chimes)

## HERSAL  THOMAS

Piano solos.                              Chicago, c. February 22, 1925.

  8958-A  Suitcase Blues                          OK 8227, Par R-3262

                                          Chicago, June, 1925.

  9166-A  Hersal Blues                            OK 8227, Par R-3261

THOMAS'S MUSCLE SHOALS DEVILS : C/cl/as/Hersal Thomas-p.
                                          Chicago, June, 1925.

  9169-A  Wash Woman Blues                        OK 8225
  9170-A  Morning Dove Blues                      -

## HOCIEL  THOMAS

Vocal, acc. by cl/p, with vn*.            Richmond, Ind., April 6, 1925.

12186    *I Can't Feel Frisky Without My Liquor   Gnt 3004, Buddy 8020
12188-A  Worried Down With The Blues              Gnt 3006, Buddy 8021
12189-B *I Must Have It                           -       Buddy 8020
NOTE:- Matrix 12187 is by Marie Grinter, q.v.

Acc. by Hersal Thomas-p.                  Chicago, June, 1925.

  9167-A  Worried Down With The Blues             OK 8222
  9168-A  Fish Tail Dance                         -

Acc. by Louis Armstrong and his Hot Four : Louis Armstrong-c/Johnny Dodds-cl/
Hersal Thomas-p/Johnny St. Cyr-bj.        Chicago, November 11, 1925.

  9471-A  Gambler's Dream                         OK 8289
  9472-A  Sunshine Baby                           OK 8326
  9473-A  Adam And Eve Got The Blues              OK 8258
  9474-A  Put It Where I Can Get It               -
  9475-A  Wash Woman Blues                        OK 8289
  9476-A  I've Stopped My Man                     OK 8326

Acc. by Louis Armstrong-c/Hersal Thomas-p.
Chicago, February 24, 1926.

| | | |
|---|---|---|
| 9519-A | Deep Water Blues | OK 8297 |
| 9520-A | G'wan, I Told You | OK 8346 |
| 9521-A | Listen To Ma | - |
| 9522-A | Lonesome Hours | OK 8297 |

## HOWARD THOMAS AND  HIS ORCHESTRA

The following items by this orchestra are reportedly of interest as jazz.

Howard Thomas dir. Marvin Wetzel-Les Robinson-t/Jerry King-tb/Leonard Benedict-Al
Manze-cl-as/B. Zoff-ts/Bob Lyons-p-a/Royal Epperson-bj-g-3rd t/George Dunn-bb-sb/
Bert Christian-d-vib.                          Richmond, Ind., December 11, 1931.

18251     Business in F                          Ch 16380, 40080

Richmond, Ind., January 12, 1932.

18320-A  Rose Of Washington Square               Ch 16656

Richmond, Ind., January 13, 1932.

18321-A  In The Shade Of The Old Apple Tree      Ch 16387, 40080, Spr 2801
NOTE:- Superior 2801 as HOWARD JOHNSON AND HIS ORCHESTRA.

## JOE THOMAS  DIXIELAND BAND

Charles Derbigny-t/Joe Thomas-cl-v/Frank Murray-g/Junior Wilson-d.
New Orleans, sometime in 1941.

Eh La Bas - vJT (2 takes)               MONO MNLP-12

## JOSEPHINE THOMAS

Pseudonym on Pathe Actuelle and Perfect for Rosa Henderson, q.v.

## MARIE THOMAS

Pseudonym on Royal for Dorothy Dodd, q.v.

## MILLARD G.  THOMAS

MILLARD G. THOMAS AND HIS CHICAGO NOVELTY ORCHESTRA : Millard Thomas-p dir. E. Cassa-
more-c-tb/Charles Harris-c-tb-as/C. Gordon-d.
Montreal, June 6, 1924.

1452     Page Your Puppies                       Ajax 17045

Montreal, June 10, 1924.

1460     Lazy Drag                               Ajax 17045

Montreal, July 3, 1924.

| | | |
|---|---|---|
| 1508 | More | Ajax 17052 |
| 1511 | Black Star Lines (sic) | - |

Montreal, July 10, 1924.

| | | |
|---|---|---|
| 1522 | Hard Luck Blues | Ajax 17053 |
| 1524 | Twee Twa Twa Blues | - |

Montreal, July 31, 1924.

| | | |
|---|---|---|
| 1530 | Worryin' Blues | Ajax 17056 |
| 1532 | Papa Will Be Gone | - |
| 1534 | San Francisco Blues | Rejected ? |

Piano solos.                          Montreal, August 12, 1924.

  1548   Reckless Blues                        Ajax rejected

                                      Montreal, October 28, 1924.

  1625   Blue Ivories                          Ajax 17074, Apex 678
  1628   Reckless Blues                          -              -

## SIPPIE  THOMAS

Pseudonym on Victor for Sippie Wallace, q.v.

## WASHINGTON  THOMAS

Pseudonym on Champion for W. E. "Buddy" Burton, q.v.

## EVELYN  THOMPSON

Vocal, acc. by vn/p/g.                New York, c. December 13, 1926.

E-4224/5  Someday, Sweetheart                  Voc 1075
E-4226/7  I Got A Papa Down In New Orleans,      -
            Another Papa Up In Maine

  Acc. by p/g.                        New York, c. January 31, 1927.

E-4499   After You've Gone                     Voc 1083
E-4502   Stack O'Lee Blues                       -

  Acc. by vn/vc/? Porter Grainger-p.   New York, c. February 1, 1927.

E-4542   When Tomorrow Comes                   Voc 1084, 15529

                                      New York, c. February 10, 1927.

E-4586   One More Kiss                         Voc 1084, 15529

  Acc. by c/Bob Fuller or Ernest Elliott-cl/p.
                                      New York, c. April 1, 1927.

E-4786   Looking For The Sunshine-Walking Around  Voc 15548
           In The Rain

                                      New York, c. May, 1927.

E-4941   One Sweet Letter From You             Voc 15548

## JOHNNY  THOMPSON

Pseudonym on Columbia 14285-D for Andy Razaf, q.v.

## KAY THOMPSON

KAY THOMPSON AND THE BOYS : Instrumentation (and probably personnel) similar to that
  of the next session; Kay Thompson-v.    New York, November 11, 1935.

B-18261-1  You Let Me Down                     Br 7560
B-18262-1  You Hit The Spot                      -
B-18263-1  Out Of Sight, Out Of Mind           Br 7564, RZ G-22702
B-18264-1  Don't Mention Love To Me              -

KAY THOMPSON AND HER ORCHESTRA : Jack Jenney dir. Charlie Margulis-Manny Klein-Ruby
  Weinstein-t/Chuck Campbell-Jack Lacey-tb/Toots Mondello-Alfie Evans-Eddie Powell-
  cl-as/Larry Binyon-cl-ts/Frank Signorelli-p/Dick McDonough-g/Artie Bernstein-sb/
  Johnny Williams-d/Kay Thompson-v/16-voice chorus inc. Al Rinker-Bea Wain*.
                                      New York, April 13, 1937.

  07785-1  *Carelessly                         Vic 25564
  07786-1  There's A Lull In My Life             -
  07787-1  *It Had To Be You                   Vic 25582
  07788-1  *Exactly Like You                     -

Pseudonym on Ariel for Seger Ellis, q.v.

## CLAUDE THORNHILL AND HIS ORCHESTRA

Claude Thornhill-p-vib-a dir. Manny Klein-Charlie Spivak-t/Jack Lacey-tb/Toots Mon-
dello-Jess Carneol-as/Babe Russin-ts/Eddie Powell-bar-f/Artie Bernstein-sb/Chaun-
cey Morehouse-d/Maxine Sullivan-Jimmy Farrell-v.
                                            New York, June 14, 1937.

| | | |
|---|---|---|
| 21241-2 | Whispers In The Dark - vJF | Voc 3616 |
| 21242-1 | Harbor Lights - vJF | Voc 3595, Br A-81350 |
| 21243-2 | Stop ! You're Breaking My Heart - vMS | Voc 3616, S-125 |
| 21244-1 | Gone With The Wind - vMS | Voc 3595     -     Br A-81350 |

String section added; Barry McKinley-v. New York, August 26, 1937.

| | | |
|---|---|---|
| B-21570-1 | You And I Know - vBM | Br 7951 |
| B-21571-1 | An Old Flame Never Dies - vBM | - |
| B-21572-1 | Ebb Tide - vBM | Br 7957, 5120 (It.), RZ G-23338 |
| B-21573-1 | Don't Save Your Love (For A Rainy Day)-vMS - | Voc S-175     - |

NOTE:- Regal Zonophone G-23338 as CASINO ROYAL ORCHESTRA.

Claude Thornhill-p-a dir. Joe Aguanno-Ralph Harden-Bob Sprentall-t/Tasso Harris-tb/
Bob Jenney-tb-v/Dale Brown-cl-as-a/Bill Motley-George Paulson-cl-as/John Nelson-
Hammond Russum-cl-ts/Hal Tennyson-cl-bar/Albert Harris-g/Harvey Cell-sb-a/Judy
Burke-d/Jane Essex-Dick Harding-v.        Hollywood, September 20, 1940.

| | | |
|---|---|---|
| H-15-1 | Alt Wien (Old Vienna) (w) | OK 5988 |
| H-16-1 | Love Tales | - |
| H-17-1 | Love Of My Life - vDH | OK 5901, Cq 9749 |
| H-18-1 | The Legend Of Old California - vDH | -     Col DO-2281 |
| H-19-1 | The Bad Humor Man - vBJ | OK 5838, Col DO-2231 |
| H-20-1 | I've Got A One-Track Mind - vJE | -     - |
| H-21-1 | The Doll Dance | Har 1038 |

Claude Thornhill-p-a dir. Rusty Dedrick-Conrad Gozzo-Bob Sprentall-t/Tasso Harris-tb
/Bob Jenney-tb-v/Irving Fazola-cl/Dale Brown-cl-as-a/George Paulson-cl-as/John
Nelson-Hammond Russum-cl-ts/Ted Goddard-cl-bar/Chuck Robinson-g/Harvey Cell-sb-a/
Gene Leman-d/Bill Borden-a/Dick Harding-v.
                                            New York, March 10, 1941.

| | | |
|---|---|---|
| 29904-1 | Stack Of Barley - aCT-BB | OK 6168 |
| 29905-1 | 'O sole mio (My Sunshine) - aBB | OK 6124 |
| 29906-1 | Hungarian Dance No. 5 (Brahms) - aCT | OK 6168 |
| 29907-1 | Träumerei (Schumann) - aCT | OK 6124 |

                                            New York, April 16, 1941.

| | | |
|---|---|---|
| 30261-1 | When The Lilacs Bloom Again - vDH/aBB | OK 6202 |
| 30262-1 | Do I Worry ? - vDH/aBB | OK 6178, Col 38933, Cq 9749 |
| 30263-1 | Sleepy Serenade - aBB | -     Col 39131 |
| 30264-1 | Portrait Of A Guinea Farm | OK 6234, Jay 2 |

                                            New York, May 1, 1941.

| | | |
|---|---|---|
| 30368-1 | All I Need Is You - vDH | OK 6234 |
| 30369-1 | Overnight - vDH/aBB | OK 6202 |
| 30370-1 | La Cinquantaine - aDB | Rejected |
| 30371-1 | Gomer The Goose - aCT | - |

Allen Hanlon-g replaces Robinson.        New York, May 21, 1941.

| | | |
|---|---|---|
| 30530-1 | Sing A Love Song - vDH/aBB | Col 36287 |
| 30531-1 | I'm Thrilled - vDH/aBB | - |
| 30532-1 | Snowfall - aCT (Theme Song) | Col 36268, 37271, 37540, DB-2592 |
| 30533-1 | Where Or When - aCT | - |

Claude Thornhill-p-a dir. Rusty Dedrick-Conrad Gozzo-Bob Sprentall-t/Tasso Harris-tb
/Bob Jenney-tb-v/Irving Fazola-cl/Dale Brown-cl-as-a/Jack Ferrier-cl-as/Ted
Goddard-as-ts/John Nelson-Hammond Russum-cl-ts/Allan Hanlon-g/Harvey Cell-sb-a/
Nick Fatool-d/Kay Doyle-Dick Harding-v/Bill Borden-Danny Hurd-Andy Phillips-a.
New York, July 9, 1941.

| | | |
|---|---|---|
| 30858-1 | Lovers In Glass Houses - vDH/aBB | Col 36361 |
| 30859-1 | You Were Meant For Me - vDH/aBB | Col 36298 |
| 30860-1 | Mandy Is Two - vDH/aBB | Col 36361 |
| 30861-1 | Paradise - vKD/aBB | Col 36298 |

Jimmy Abato-cl-bar/Richard Hall-Vincent Jacobs-fh added.
New York, August 25, 1941.

| | | |
|---|---|---|
| 31104-1 | Jim - vKD/aBB | Col 36371, Har 1037 |
| 31105-1 | Concerto For Two (A Love Song) - vDH | - |
| 31106-1-2 | Moonlight Masquerade - vDH/aAP | Col 36391 |
| 31107-1 | Orange Blossom Lane - vDH/aAP | - |
| 31108-1 | Miss You - vDH/aDH | Col 36413 |

Lester Merkin-cl-as replaces Goddard; Barry Galbraith-g replaces Hanlon; Lillian
Lane-v.                                 New York, October 6, 1941.

| | | |
|---|---|---|
| 31412-1 | The Bells Of San Raquel - vDH/aAP | Col 36431 |
| 31413-1 | Baby Mine - vLL/aAP | Col 36413 |
| 31414-1 | Autumn Nocturne - aCT | Col 36435, 37271 |
| 31415-1 | Where Has My Little Dog Gone ? - aBB | - V-Disc 74 |
| 31416-1 | I Found You In The Rain - vDH/aAP | Col 36431 |

Ted Goddard-cl-as-ts replaces Merkin; George Paulson-cl-ts replaces Nelson; Gil
Evans-a added; Martha Wayne-Buddy Stewart-v.
New York, November 17, 1941.

| | | |
|---|---|---|
| 31761-1 | Ev'rything I Love - vLL/aBB | Col 36456 |
| 31762-1 | I Hate You, Darling - vDH/aGE | - |
| 31763-2 | Rose O'Day - vLL-MW-DH-BS/aGE | Col 36458 |
| 31764-1 | Somebody Nobody Loves - vLL/aGE | - |

Billy Butterfield-t replaces Sprentall; Marty Berman-cl-bcl-bar replaces Abato.
New York, December 1, 1941.

| | | |
|---|---|---|
| 31837-1 | This Love Of Mine - vLL/aGE or AP | Col 36472 |
| 31838-1 | Chattanooga Choo Choo - vLL-BJ/aAP | - |
| 31839-1 | We're The Couple In The Castle - vDH/aAB | Col 36477, DO-2502 |
| 31840-1 | I Said No - vLL/aGE | - |

Rusty Dedrick-Conrad Gozzo-Louis Mucci-t/Tasso Harris-Bud Smith-tb/John Graas-
Vincent Jacobs-fh/Danny Polo-cl/Dale Brown-Jack Ferrier-cl-as/Ted Goddard-Carl
Swift-cl-ts/Marty Berman-cl-bcl-bar/Barney Galbraith-g/Marty Blitz-sb/Louis Fromm
or Dave Tough-d/Martha Wayne-Dick Harding-Buddy Stewart-Pair of Pairs-v/Gil Evans-
Andy Phillips-a.                        New York, January 22, 1942.

| | | |
|---|---|---|
| 32130-1 | Somebody Else Is Taking My Place-vPP/aGE | Col 36513, DO-2555 |
| 32131-1 | Memory Lane - vDH/aAP | Col 36527 |
| 32132-1 | Ya Lu-Blu - vDH/aAP | Col 36513 |
| 32133-2 | The Lamp Of Memory - vDH/aGE | Col 36527 |

New York, February 6, 1942.

| | | |
|---|---|---|
| 32389-1 | Smiles - vPP/aGE | Col 37055 |
| 32390-1 | America, I Love You - vPP/aGE | Col 36578 |
| 32391-1 | Something To Remember You By - vPP/aGE | - |
| 32392-1 | Night And Day - aCT | Col 37055, V-Disc 612 |

New York, February 23, 1942.

| | | |
|---|---|---|
| 32440-1 | Grieg's Piano Concerto - aCT | Col 36535 |
| 32441-1 | I'll Pray For You - vDH/aGE | - |
| 32442-1 | She'll Always Remember - vDH/aGE | Col 36560 |
| 32443-1 | Count Me In - vMW-BS/aGE | - |

Claude Thornhill-p-a dir. Randy Brooks-Conrad Gozzo-Steve Steck-t/Tasso Harris-Bud
Smith-tb/John Graas-Vincent Jacobs-fh/Danny Polo-cl/Jack Ferrier-Bob Walters-cl-as
/Ted Goddard-George Paulson-cl-ts/Buddy Dean-cl-bar/Barry Galbraith-g/Marty Blitz-
sb/Irv Cottler-d/Lillian Lane-The Snowflakes (Lillian Lane-Terry Allen-Martha
Wayne-Buddy Stewart)-Terry Allen-v/Gil Evans-a.
                                              New York, June 19, 1942.

| 32934-1 | Be Careful, It's My Heart - vLL/aGE | Col 36616 |
| 32935-1 | I'm Getting Tired So I Can Sleep-vTA/aGE | Col 36658, DO-2684 |
| 32936-1 | Buster's Last Stand - aGE | Col 36858 |
| 32937-1 | Lullaby Of The Rain - aCT | Col 36616 |
| 32937-2 | Lullaby Of The Rain - aCT | Har 1038 |

Jake Koven-t replaces Brooks; Mike Glass-fh replaces Jacobs; Conn Humphreys-cl-as
replaces Walters.                             New York, July 25, 1942.

| 33037-1 | There's A Small Hotel - vS/aGE | Col 36725, 37498, 38219 |
| 33038-1 | Rock-a-Bye Bay - vLL-S | Col 36658 |
| 33039-1 | I Don't Know Why (I Just Do) - vS/aGE | Col 36858, DO-3010 |
| 33040-1 | Moonlight Bay - vS/aGE | Col 36725 |
| 33041-1 | Stealin' Apples | V-Disc 612 |
| 33042-1 | Moments Like This - vLL-S | Col B-2056, CL-709 (microgrooves) |

## THE   THREE BARBERS

Jimmy Lytell-cl/Frank Signorelli-p/Tony Colucci-bj.
                                              New York, c. February 8, 1926.

| 106622 | Down Town Rag (Down Town Fling*) | PA 36414, 11165*, Per 14565 |
| 106623 | Buggy Blues | -        -        - |

## THREE BITS OF RHYTHM

P/g/sb/own v.                                 Chicago, March 13, 1941.

| 93592- | I'm Lonesome - v | Dec 8572 |
| 93593- | This Is The Boogie The Woogie The Boogie-v | - |
| 93594-A | The Old Blues | Dec 8553 |
| 93595-A | Bronzeville Jump | - |

## THREE BLACK DIAMONDS

See Bob Fuller.

## THREE   BLACK MINSTRELS

Pseudonym on Guardsman 7016 for the Three Jolly Miners, q.v.

## THREE   BLUE BOYS

Tony Parenti-cl/Nat Brusiloff-vn/Cornell Smelser-pac.
                                              New York, May 23, 1929.

| 53435-1-2 | Diga Diga Doo | Vic rejected |

## THREE   BLUES CHASERS

Cl/p/bj.                                      New York, June 11, 1928.

| 400777-B | Nothin' But Blues | OK 8595 |
| 400778-B | Lame Duck Blues | - |

## THE   THREE BOSWELL SISTERS

See the Boswell Sisters.

Pee Wee Russell-cl/Joe Sullivan-p/Zutty Singleton-d.
                                    New York, March 25, 1941.

| 4049   | Jig Walk                     | Com 539 |
| 4050-1 | Deuces Wild                  | Com 537 |
| 4051-2 | The Last Time I Saw Chicago  | -       |
| 4052   | About Face                   | Com 539 |

## THREE HAPPY BOYS

Male v trio, acc. by t/p/g.              London, early March, 1932.

| 14168 | Looking Up To The Sky With A Smile | Bel 1814 |
| 14169 | My Bluebird's Back Again            | -        |

## THREE HAPPY DARKIES

Pseudonym on Silvertone 3057 for the Three Jolly Miners, q.v.

## THREE HOT ESKIMOS

Bob Fuller-cl/Louis Hooper-p/Elmer Snowden-bj.
                                    New York, c. July 1, 1925.

| 106121 | Black Cat Blues | PA 036298, Per 14479 |
| 106122 | Too Bad, Jim !  | -        -           |

See also Bob Fuller (Pathe Actuelle 021141 and Perfect 11214).

## THE THREE JACKS

Rodney Rogers-stg/2nd stg/g.             Chicago, June 28, 1928.

| 400963-A | Spanish Shawl       | OK 41102 |
| 400964-B | Chile Blues         | -        |
| 400965-A-B | Twelfth Street Rag | Rejected |

## THREE JOLLY MINERS

Bob Fuller-cl/Louis Hooper-p/Elmer Snowden-bj.
                                    New York, March 9, 1925.

| 512/4 | Charleston Clarinet Blues | Voc 15009, Sil 3057 |
| 515/8 | Freakish Blues            | -        -          |

NOTE:- Silvertone 3057 as THREE HAPPY DARKIES.

                                    New York, June 22, 1925.

| 914 | Too Bad Jim     | Voc 15051, Gmn 7016 |
| 917 | Black Cat Blues | -        -          |

NOTE:- Guardsman as THE THREE BLACK MINSTRELS.

                                    New York, c. July, 1925.

| Lake George Blues | Voc 15087 |
| Louisville Blues  | -         |

                                    New York, c. August, 1925.

| Ketch Your Breath | Voc 15111 |
| Plain Old Blues   | -         |

                                    New York, September 21, 1925.

| E-1377/8 | Old Man Charleston | Voc 15141 |
| E-1379/80 | Texas Shuffle     | -         |

Bob Fuller-cl/Louis Hooper-p/Elmer Snowden-bj.
                              New York, October 29, 1925.

E-1540/2   House Party Stomp                  Voc 15164
E-1543/5   Grand Opera Blues                    -

                              New York, January 13, 1926.

E-2108     Chicago Back Step                   Voc 1004, 15271
E-2113     F Minor Blues                        -      -

                              New York, February 15, 1926.

E-2435/6   Pig Alley Stomp                     Voc 1003, 15269
E-2437/8   Ridiculous Blues                     -      -

## THE THREE KEYS

Bon-Bon (George Tunnell)-p-v/Slim Furness-g-v/Bob Pease-sb-v.
                              New York, August 18, 1932.

152270-1-2  Mood Indigo                       Col rejected
152271-1  Zonky                                 -

                              New York, August 29, 1932.

152270-3  Mood Indigo              Col 2706-D,Par R-1431,RZ G-21539
152292-2  Somebody Loses, Somebody Wins    -      Par R-1409    -

                              New York, September 8, 1932.

B-12262-A  Jig Time                     Br 6388, 01372, A-9341, Voc 2730
B-12263-A  Someone Stole Gabriel's Horn   -       -       -        -

                              New York, September 21, 1932.

B-12341-A  Basin Street Blues           Br 6423, 01381, A-9356, Voc 2744
B-12342-A  Wah-Dee-Dah                    -       -       -        -

                              New York, October 5, 1932.

B-12424-A  Nagasaki                     Br 6411, 01402, Voc 2732
B-12425-A  Fit As A Fiddle                -       -       -

                              New York, October 12, 1932.

B-12466-A  (I Would Do) Anything For You   Br 6522, 01515,A-500233,Voc 2755

                              New York, January 9, 1933.

B-12861-A  That Doggone Dog Of Mine     Br 6522, 01515, A-9389, A-500233
                                        Voc 2755

                              New York, April 6, 1933.

B-13199-A  Rasputin (That Highfalutin' Lovin' Man)  Br 6567, 01545, A-9428, Voc 2765

                              New York, April 7, 1933.

B-13204-A  Oh ! By Jingo (Oh ! By Gosh, By Gum,   Br 6567, 01545, A-9428, Voc 2765
              By Juv)
                              New York, August 16, 1933.

13809-1  Heebie Jeebies                 Voc 2523, Br 01580
13810-1  Song Of The Islands              -       -

                              New York, September 8, 1933.

13973-1  I've Found A New Baby           Voc 2569, Br 01612, A-9772
13974-1  You Can Depend On Me             -       -       -
13985-1  How Do You Do, Mr. Cupid ?     Rejected

Bob Fuller-cl/Louis Hooper-p/Elmer Snowden-bj.
                                New York, August 20, 1925.

| | | | |
|---|---|---|---|
| 140855-2 | Corn Bread Wiggle | Har 23-H | |
| 140856-2 | Cocoanut Strut | - | Re G-8539 |

                                New York, October 16, 1925.

| | | |
|---|---|---|
| 141142-3 | Uncle Remus Stomp | Har 50-H |
| 141143-1 | Montmarte Giggles (sic) | - |

## THE  THREE PEPPERS

Toy Wilson-p-v/Bob Bell-g-v/Walter Williams-sb. Some sides seem to have a third voice
   (probably Walter Williams).        New York, February 27, 1937.

| | | |
|---|---|---|
| M-138- | Get The Gold | Vri 523 |
| M-139- | The Sheik Of Araby | Rejected |
| M-140- | Alexander's Ragtime Band | Vri 523 |
| M-141-1 | Swingin' At The Cotton Club | Vri 650, Voc 3805 |

Sally Gooding the only v, plus t/cl/d.   New York, March 9, 1937.

| | | |
|---|---|---|
| M-194-1 | Yours, All Yours | Vri 554 |
| M-195-3 | The Midnight Ride Of Paul Revere | Vri 650, Voc 3805 |
| M-196-1 | It Must Be Love | Voc 4169 |
| M-197-1 | Smile Up At The Sun | Vri 554 |

NOTE:- Variety 554 and Vocalion 4169 as SALLY GOODING AND THE THREE PEPPERS.

As for February 27, 1937.          New York, May 27, 1937.

| | | |
|---|---|---|
| M-497-1 | Swing Out, Uncle Wilson | Vri 590, Voc/OK 3803 |
| M-498-1 | If I Had My Way | Vri 630 |
| M-499-2 | Serenade In The Night | - |
| M-500-1 | The Duck's Yas Yas Yas | Vri 590, Voc/OK 3803 |

                                New York, December 16, 1938.

| | | |
|---|---|---|
| 64819-A | Down By The Old Mill Stream | Dec 2239, X-1716, Br 02789 |
| 64820-A | Fuzzy Wuzzy | -      -      - |
| 64821- | The Duck's Yas Yas Yas | Rejected |
| 64822-A | Swing Out, Uncle Wilson | Dec 2557, Y-5442, Br 02846 |

                                New York, May 22, 1939.

| | | |
|---|---|---|
| 65617- | Smile Up At The Sun | Dec 2751, Y-5706, Br 03145 |
| 65618-A | Love Grows On The White Oak Tree | Dec 2557, Y-5442, Br 02846 |
| 65619- | It's A Puzzle To Me (So What !) | Dec 2609, Br 03062 |
| 65620- | Three Foot Skipper Jones | -      - |
| 65621- | Pepperism | Dec 2751, Br 03145 |

                                New York, May 2, 1940.

| | | |
|---|---|---|
| 67666- | Tom Tom Serenade | Dec 3342, Y-5862 |
| 67667- | Hot Dogs | -      - |
| 67668- | Mary Had A Little Lamb | Dec 8508 |
| 67669- | Was That All I Meant To You ? | -      Y-5680 |

## THE  THREE RIFFS

Joe ──── , Eddie ──── and Greene ──── -v, acc. by unknown orchestra (sic).
                                New York, August 30, 1939.

| | | |
|---|---|---|
| 66249- | Ace In The Hole | Dec 7634 |
| 66250- | It's A Killer, Mr. Miller | - |

Paul Ricci-cl/Jerry Sears-p/Carl Kress-g. New York, October 24, 1938.

| 027973-1 | We Want Five | BB B-10014 |
| 027974-1 | Rosetta | BB B-10051 |
| 027975-1 | That's Got 'Em | BB B-10014 |
| 027976-1 | I Would Do Anything For You | BB B-10160 |
| 027977-1 | S'posin' | BB B-10051 |
| 027978-1 | Dallas Blues | BB B-10160 |

## THE THREE SCAMPS

Vocal trio, acc. by own t/p/g.        New York, February 21, 1934.

| 81730-1 | Diga Diga Doo | Vic rejected |
| 81731-1 | Jimmy Had A Nickel | - |
| 1077-1 | Mashed Potatoes | Vic test |

New York, March 9, 1934.

| 81866-1 | Tiger Rag | Vic rejected |

New York, March 13, 1934.

| 81925-1 | Pretty Polly Perkins | Vic rejected |

## THE THREE STRIPPED GEARS

R. W. Durden-md/Cliff Vaughn-Marion Brown-g.
                              Atlanta, October 30, 1931.

| 405074-1 | Blackberry Rag | OK 45571 |
| 405075-1 | Alabama Blues | - |

Atlanta, November 2, 1931.

| 405092-1 | 1931 Depression Blues | OK 45553 |
| 405093-1 | Black Bottom Strut | - |

## THE  THREE T'S

Charlie Teagarden-t/Jack Teagarden-tb-v/Jack Cordaro-cl/Frank Trumbauer-Cm/Bud Free-
   man-ts/Roy Bargy-p/Carl Kress-g/Art Miller-sb/Bob White-d.
                              New York, March 10, 1936.

| 99447-2 | I'se A Muggin' - Part 1 - vJT&ch | Vic 25273, A-1231, JA-1307, HMV BD 5063, EA-1690 |
| 99448-1 | I'se A Muggin' - Part 2 - vJT&ch | As above |

NOTE:- Some copies of HMV BD-5063 are labelled PAUL WHITEMAN PRESENTS THE TEAGAR-
DEN BOYS & TRUMBAUER SWING BAND; Victor A-1231 as JACK TEAGARDEN AND HIS ALL-STAR
BAND; Victor JA-1307 as TEAGARDEN BOYS AND TRUMBAUER SWING BAND.

## THE THREE VIRGINIANS

Dick Reinhart-cl-v/Holly Horton and another-g.
                              Dallas, June 26, 1929.

| 402732-A | Yoo Yoo Blues | OK 45451 |
| 402733-A | June Tenth Blues - vDR | - |
| 402734-A | Hard-To-Get Papa - vDR | Rejected |
| 402735-A | Who's Sorry Now ? | - |

## THREE-FIFTEEN AND HIS  SQUARES

Dave Bluntson-v, acc. by t/ts/p/g/sb/d.   Hot Springs, Ark., March 2, 1937.

| HS-14- | Saturday Night On Texas Avenue | Voc 03515 |
| HS-15-1 | Drop My Stuff | Voc 03560 |
| HS-16-1 | Mollie Mae Blues | - |
| HS-17- | Three-Fifteen Blues | Voc 03515 |

Pseudonym on Champion for Alexander Robinson, q.v.

## LE ROY TIBBS AND HIS CONNIE'S INN ORCHESTRA

Le Roy Tibbs-p dir. Ed Allen-Gilbert Paris-c/Te Roy Williams-tb/Arville Harris-cl-as
/? Andrew Brown-as-bar/ts/Allie Ross-vn/Leroy Harris-bj/Cyrus St. Clair-bb/Hugh
Davis-d.                                    New York, February 1, 1928.

145604-2  One O'Clock Blues                       Col 14309-D, Re RS-1112
145605-2  I Got Worry (Love Is On My Mind)        -

## TOM TIMOTHY AND HIS FRIVOLITY CLUB ORCHESTRA

Tom Timothy-cl-ts dir. 2t/tb/2cl-as/? vn/p/bj/bb/d.
                                            New York, October 19, 1927.

          Missouri Squabble                     PA rejected
          Where Is My Meyer ? (Where's Himalaya ?)    -

                                            New York, c. November 24, 1927.

2707-    Ida                                Cam 1279, Lin 2744, Ro 513

## KLIEN TINDULL'S PARAMOUNT SERENADERS

Kline Tyndall-p dir. c/tb/? Vance Dixon-as/d.
                                            Chicago, June, 1926.
2600 ?  Down On The Amazon                  Pm 12377
2601-1  So Is Your Old Man (Old Man Blues*)     -        Her 92019*
NOTE:- Herwin as BIRMINGHAM BLUETETTE.

## TIN PAN PARADERS

Pseudonym on Supertone S-2185 (99 OUT OF A HUNDRED) for Benny Goodman and his Orchestra, q.v., and on Gennett for what seems to be a Fred Hall unit similar to his
Sugar Babies, q.v.

## TINSLEY'S WASHBOARD BAND

See Williams' Washboard Band.

## TIP TOP CLUB ORCHESTRA

Pseudonym on Duophone for Meyer Davis and his Orchestra, q.v.

## TITO'S SWINGTETTE

This was a novelty group directed by Tito Guidotti-pac, consisting of two other pac/
g/sb, recorded in New York on November 22, 1938 for Victor, but producing no jazz.

## T. N. T. RHYTHM BOYS

Pseudonym on Australian Parlophone for the Original Memphis Five, q.v.

## BEN TOBIER AND HIS CALIFORNIA CYCLONES

Instrumentation and personnel unknown.    New York, c. December 3, 1930.

GEX-2834  Pardon The Glove                      Rejected
GEX-2835  Hot And Heavy                         Ch 16465, Spr 2571

## TOBIN'S MIDNIGHT SERENADERS

John Tobin-bj dir. Harry Doring-c/Jac Assunto-tb/Norvelle Makofsky-ss-as/Elbridge
Westerfield-ss-ts-bar/Adrian J. Larroque-p/Benny Pottle-bb.
                                            New Orleans, c. January 22, 1925.

8893-A  I'm Afraid To Care For You              OK 40297

"The Canadian Crosby" made many records for Victor between 1938 and 1942, and on one
    session (New York, December 17, 1938) his accompanists included Bobby Hackett-c
    and Bud Freeman-ts, but no jazz resulted from this.

## MABEL TODD

Vocal, acc. by Joe Venuti's Blue Four : Joe Venuti-vn/cl-as-bar/p/? Bobby Sherwood-g.
                                        Los Angeles, July 15, 1938.

| | | |
|---|---|---|
| LA-1682- | Confidentially | ARC rejected |
| LA-1683- | The Lady On The Two-Cent Stamp | - |

## SHAKEY TODD AND HOLLAND TRIO

Clarence Todd-v and another, acc. p.      New York, April 8, 1927.

| | | |
|---|---|---|
| 80708-A-B | Home (Cradle Of Happiness) | OK rejected |
| 80709-A-B | Sweet Virginia | - |

## SKEETS TOLBERT AND HIS GENTLEMEN OF SWING

Skeets Tolbert-cl-as dir. Carl Smith-t/Otis Hicks-ts/Clarence Easter-p-v/Harry
    Prather-sb/Hubert Pettaway-d/Babe Hines-v.
                                        New York, March 1, 1939.

| | | |
|---|---|---|
| 65085-A | Skin 'Em Back - vHP | Dec 7570 |
| 65086-A | Get Up | - |
| 65087-A | Bouncing In Rhythm | Dec 7630 |
| 65088-A | I've Lost My Head Over You - vBH | Dec 7591, Voc S-245 |
| 65091-A | This Is The End - vBH | -            - |

NOTE:- Matrices 65089 and 65090 are by Milt Herth, q.v.

Skeets Tolbert-cl-as dir. Carl Smith-t/Lem Johnson-ts-v/Fred Jefferson-p/Al Hall-sb/
    Hubert Pettaway-d/Babe Wallace-v.      New York, July 5, 1939.

| | | |
|---|---|---|
| 65923-A | The Stuff's Out (It Jumped Just A | Dec 7630 |
| | Minute Ago) - vLJ | |
| 65924-A | Railroad Blues - vLJ | Dec 7653 |
| 65925-A | I'm Blowin' My Top - vBW | - |
| 65926- | Fine Piece Of Meat - vBW | Dec 7669 |
| 65927-A | Swing Out | - |

Clarence Easter-p-v replaces Jefferson. New York, January 24, 1940.

| | | |
|---|---|---|
| 67101-A | Gimme Something Like That - vCE | Dec 7751 |
| 67102-A | Hole Holy Roly-Poly - vch | Dec 7717 |
| 67103-A | Raz Ma Taz - vch | Rejected |
| 67104-A | Harlem Ain't What It Usta Be - vCE | Dec 7717 |

Skeets Tolbert-cl-as dir. Carl Smith-t/Otis Hicks-ts/Charles Richards-p-v/John
    Drummond-sb/Hubert Pettaway-d.      New York, March 12, 1940.

| | | |
|---|---|---|
| 67296-A | Papa's In Bed With His Britches On-vch | Dec 7751 |
| 67297-A | W. P. A. - vch | Dec 7722 |
| 67298-A | I Can't Go For You - vCR | - |
| 67299-A | Jumpin' Jack | Dec 7791 |

Yack Taylor-v.                          New York, October 2, 1940.

| | | |
|---|---|---|
| 68191- | Sammy's Choppin' Block - vch | Dec 8534 |
| 68192-A | Jumpin' Like Mad - vch | Dec 8528 |
| 68193-A | Sugar Boogie - vYT | Dec 8506 |
| 68194-A | I'll Make It Worth Your While - vYT | - |

Babe Wallace-v.                         New York, December 17, 1940.

| | | |
|---|---|---|
| 68514- | Those Draftin' Blues - vYT | Dec 8516 |
| 68515-A | Hit That Jive, Jack - vch | Dec 8528 |
| 68516- | Bugle Blues | Dec 8516 |
| 68517- | Four O'Clock Blues - vBW | Dec 8534 |

Skeets Tolbert-cl-as dir. Carl Smith-t/Wingy Carpenter-t-v/as/Otis Hicks-ts/Buddy
   Johnson-p/sb/Hubert Pettaway-d.      New York, May 22, 1941.

| | | |
|---|---|---|
| 69234-A | Uncle Eph's Dream | Dec 8579 |
| 69235-A | Big Fat Butterfly - vch | - |
| 69236- | The Rhumba Blues - vch | Dec 8565 |
| 69237- | Jumpin' In The Numbers - vWC | - |

   Charles Richards-p-v replaces Johnson; Jean Eldridge-v.
          New York, September 10, 1941.

| | | |
|---|---|---|
| 69730- | That's That Messy Boogie | Dec 8631 |
| 69731-A | Lazy Gal Blues - vCR | Dec 8589 |
| 69732-A | Git It ('Cause I Love To See You Wid It)-vBW - | |
| 69733- | What Is The Matter Now ? - vJE | Dec 8631 |

Skeets Tolbert-cl-as dir. Robert Hicks-t/Otis Hicks-ts/Herbert Goodwin-p-v/John
   Drummond-sb/Larry Hinton-d/Nora Lee King-Jean Eldridge-v.
          New York, January 29, 1942.

| | | |
|---|---|---|
| 70258-A | Delta Land Blues - vHG | Dec 8608 |
| 70259- | Fill Up | Dec 8617 |
| 70260-A | Ride On - vJE | Dec 8608 |
| 70261 | Because I Love My Daddy So - vNLK | Dec 8617 |

   Probably as last above.      New York, July 25, 1942.

| | | |
|---|---|---|
| 71197-A | C. O. D. - vch | Dec 8641 |
| 71198-A | Hey Man, Hey Man - vch | - |

## "T" TOLL'S SWINGTOWN FIVE

Ted Toll-d-v dir. Alfred Knapp-t-v/Rocque Dominick-cl-ts/Max Wiegand-p/Evan Moore-g.
          London, July 7, 1936.

| | | |
|---|---|---|
| CE-7718-1 | Shoe Shine Boy - vTT | Par R-2256 |
| CE-7719-1 | Robins And Roses - vAK | - |
| CE-7720-1 | Farewell Blues | Par R-2267, Od 194777 |
| CE-7721-1 | Basin Street Blues - vTT | Par R-2280 |
| CE-7722-1 | Christopher Columbus | Par R-2267, Od 194777 |

## TOM AND JERRY

Pseudonym on Champion 15507 for Jimmy Blythe, q.v., and W. E. Burton.

## PINKY TOMLIN

This well-known American songwriter made several records in the 1930s, of which the
following have jazz-orientated accompaniments.

Vocal, acc. by Joe Sullivan-p and others. Los Angeles, January 10, 1935.

| | | |
|---|---|---|
| LA-317- | A Porter's Love Song (To A Chambermaid) | Br 7377 |

          Los Angeles, January 11, 1935.

| | | |
|---|---|---|
| LA-318-A | Sittin' Bull/Shine | Br 7378 |
| LA-319- | He's A Curbstone Cutie (They Call Him Jelly Bean) | Br 7377 |
| LA-320-A | Ragtime Cowboy Joe | Br 7378 |

Acc. by Joe Haymes and his Orchestra : Joe Haymes dir. Cliff Weston-Glenn Taft or
Charlie Zimmerman-Dave Frankel-t/Cappy Krouse-tb/Hank Haupt-John Langford-as/Hawk
Kogan-Clyde Rogers-ts/Conrad Lanoue-p/Mac Cheikes-g-tb/Max Goodman-sb/Sammy Parker
d.           New York, March 9, 1937.

| | | |
|---|---|---|
| B-20770- | The Love Bug Will Bite You (If You Don't Watch Out) | Br 7849 |
| B-20771- | I'm Just A Country Boy At Heart | - |

Acc. by Manny Klein-tWAndy Secrest-c/Abe Lincoln-tb/Jack Mayhew-cl/Claude Kennedy-
p/Perry Botkin-g/Slim Jim Taft-sb/Spike Jones-d.
                                          Los Angeles, April 23, 1938.

DLA-1280-A  The Old Oaken Bucket                    Dec 1821
DLA-1281-A  Smiles                                    -        X-1620

## TOMMY "RED" TOMPKINS AND HIS ORCHESTRA

Tommy Tompkins-t dir. t/Billy Pritchard-tb-v/tb/2cl-as/cl-ts/p/g/sb/d/Sally Ann
  Harris-v.                                New York, June 24, 1936.

19472-1  Viper's Dream                              Voc 3293
19473-1  Sumpin' 'Bout Rhythm                         -
19474-   What The Heart Believes - vSAH            Voc 3271
19475-   Jes' Natch'ully Lazy (I Was Born That Way)-vSAH -

                                          New York, February 18, 1937.

M-109-1  Deep Shadows - vBP                        Vri 543
M-110-2  Oh Babe - Maybe Someday - vBP             Vri 610
M-111-2  I Never Had A Dream - vBP                   -
M-112-1  Monopoly Swing                            Vri 543

## THE  TOP HATTERS

Vocal trio, acc. by Eddie Farley-t/Mike Riley-tb/Frank Langone-cl/Conrad Lanoue-p/
  Arthur Ens-g/George Yorke-sb/Victor Engle-d.
                                          New York, February 10, 1936.

60456-A  We Saw The Sea              Dec 711,F-5917,X-1098,Br SA-1028
60457-A  Wah-Hoo !                      -        -       -        -

See also Mike Riley.

## TRACY-BROWN'S  ORCHESTRA

Clark Warren-Harry Fischer-t/Bill Anthens-tb/Al Kassel-Nelson Brown-as/Les Greissler
  ts/Manny Strand-p/Jimmy Burson-bj/Delmar Kaplan-bb/Bus Dillon-d/Sam Coslow-v.
                                          Chicago, March 20, 1928.

145817-2  Chloe (Song Of The Swamp) - vSC         Col 1344-D, 5164
145818-3  Sh-h ! Here Comes My Sugar - vSC        Col 1405-D
145819-2  Beautiful - v3                          Col 1344-D
145820-2  Joline - vSC                            Col 1541-D
145821-2  Danger ! (Look Out For That Gal)        Col 1405-D

## JEAN TRANCHANT

Vocal, acc. by Stephane Grappelly-vn/own p or cel/Django Reinhardt-g.
                                          Paris, November 12, 1936.

CPT-2931-1  Mademoiselle Adeline - cel             PA PA-1042
CPT-2932-1  Le Roi Marc - p                          -

## THE  TRAVELERS

Pseudonym on OKeh, Melotone and Australian Panachord for the Dorsey Brothers' Orchestra, q.v.

## THE TRAVELING MUSKETEERS

Pseudonym on Lincoln for the Red Flame Kazoo Travelers, q.v.

## TRAVIS CARLTON ORCHESTRA

This was apparently a real orchestra, but the name was used on Gennett 3216 (SOME-
BODY'S EYES) for Bailey's Lucky Seven, q.v.

Pseudonym on Vocalion 15556 for Duke Ellington and his Orchestra, q.v.

## PAUL TREMAINE AND HIS ORCHESTRA

Paul Tremaine-vn-v dir. J. D. Wade, Jr.-Arnold Lehner-t/Archie Newell-tb/Links
    Hussin-as-f/Cliff Harkness-cl-as/Andy Fonder-cl-ts/John Baldwin-John Triphagen-
    Robert C. Tremaine-vn/Lester Cruman-harp/Charles Bagby-p-a/Eddie Kilanoski-bj-s-a/
    Lem Lesser and another-bb/Laurie Mitchinton-d-vib.
                                            New York, October 2, 1929.

    56746-1  Aristocratic Stomp                      Vic V-40176

                                            New York, October 4, 1929.

    56753-1  Four-Four Rhythm - vPT&ch               Vic V-40176

    Probably similar.                       New York, February 14, 1930.

    149988-3  Hand Me Down My Walkin' Cane - vPT       Col 2130-D
    149989-2  She'll Be Comin' 'Round The Mountain - vPT    -

Other titles on Victor and Columbia by this band are not believed to contain any
    material likely to interest the jazz enthusiast.

## TREMENDOUS OLD JELLY

Pseudonym on XX 13 for Jelly-Roll Morton, q.v.

## GEORGE H. TREMER

Piano solos, with own h/k/v.           Birmingham, Ala., c. August 4, 1927.

GEX-778-A  Some Of These Days - h-k-v          Gnt 6242, Ch 15372
GEX-779-A  Spirit Of '49 Rag - k                  -     Ch 15436, Dec 7137

## TREMONT  DANCE ORCHESTRA

Pseudonym on Tremont 0531 (EVERYBODY LOVES MY BABY) for Lou Gold and his Orchestra,
    q.v.

## CHARLES TRENET

This famous diseur has made many records, of which the following are of interest as
    jazz in view of the accompaniment.

Vocal, acc. by Django Reinhardt and the Quintette of the Hot Club of France : Leo
    Chauliac-p/Django Reinhardt-Joseph Reinhardt-g/Tony Rovira-sb/Pierre Fouad-d.
                                            Paris, February 12, 1941.

CL-7419-   Un rien me fait chanter             Rejected
CL-7420-1  La cigale et la fourmi              Col DF-2886, DCF-62, CQ-2225

## ALPHONSE TRENT AND HIS ORCHESTRA

Alphonse Trent-p dir. Chester Clark-Irving Randolph-t/Leo "Snub" Mosley-tb-v/James
    Jeter-Charles Pillars-Lee Hilliard-as/Hayes Pillars-ts-bar/Leo "Stuff" Smith-vn/
    Eugene Crooke-bj-g/Robert "Eppie" Jackson-bb/A. G. Godley-d/John Fielsing-v.
                                            Richmond, Ind., October 11, 1928.

    14327-B  Louder And Funnier - vSM-SS-JF           Gnt 6664, Ch 15641
    14328    Gilded Kisses - vJF                        -      Ch 15656

                                            Richmond, Ind., December 5, 1928.

    14518    Black And Blue Rhapsody              Gnt 6710, Ch 15656, Spt 9487
    14519    Nightmare                             -      Ch 15641     -
    14520, -A  Adorable Dora                      Rejected
    NOTE:- Champion 15641 as SAVANNAH NIGHT HAWKS; 15656 as DEACON FOSTER AND HIS BOYS;
    Supertone 9487 as DUKE DIGGS AND HIS ORCHESTRA.

Alphonse Trent-p dir. Chester Clark-Irving Randolph-George Hudson-Peanuts Holland-t/
Leo "Snub" Mosley-tb/James Jeter-Charles Pillars-Lee Hilliard-as/Hayes Pillars-ts-
bar/Leo "Stuff" Smith-vn÷v/Eugene Crooke-bj-g/Robert "Eppie" Jackson-bb/A. G.
Godley-d.                                    Richmond, Ind., March 5, 1930.

16349-A  After You've Gone - vSS                 Gnt 7161,Ch 15956,40096,Spt 9653
16350-A  St. James Infirmary - vch               -        -             -       -
NOTE:- Supertone 9653 as DUKE DIGGS AND HIS ORCHESTRA.

Harry Edison-t replaces Randolph and Hudson; Gus Wilson-tb added; Anderson Lacy-vn
replaces Smith; unknown p replaces Trent; Peanuts Holland-v.
                                             Richmond, Ind., March 24, 1933.

19080    Clementine - vPH                         Ch 16587
19081    I've Found A New Baby - vPH              -        40096

## JO TRENT AND THE D'C'NS

Otto Hardwick-as/Duke Ellington-p/Fred Guy-bj/Sonny Greer-d/Jo Trent-v.
                                             New York, c. November, 1924.

T-2007-1  Deacon Jazz - vJT                       B-D T-1003

## TRIANGLE HARMONY BOYS

C/tb/cl-as/ts/p/bj/d.                        Birmingham, Ala., c. July 7, 1927.

GEX-704-B  Canned Heat Blues                      Gnt 6322, Bell 1182, Ch 15415
GEX-705    Sweet Patootie                         Rejected
GEX-706, -A  Smoke-House Blues                    -
GEX-707, -A  Dead Man Blues                       -
NOTE:- Bell 1182 as ALABAMA JAZZ PIRATES; Champion 15415 as THE MEMPHIS STRUTTERS.

                                             Birmingham, Ala., c. August 22, 1927.

GEX-838-A  Chicken Supper Strut                   Gnt 6275,Ch 15398,Sil 5139,Spr 372
GEX-839-A  Sweet Patootie                         -        -
NOTE:- Champion 15398 and Silvertone 5139 as ALABAMA HARMONY BOYS.

## THE TRICKY TEN

Pseudonym on Oriole 537 for Eddie Peabody and his Band, q.v.

## BARNEY TRIMBLE'S OKLAHOMANS

Pseudonym on Harmony for the following items listed in this book :-

726-H    'Round Evening (California Ramblers)
948-H    I'm Feathering A Nest (Ben Selvin and his Orchestra)
987-H    Bashful Baby (Ben Selvin and his Orchestra)
1150-H   I Never Dreamt (California Ramblers)

## TRIO DE TROMPETTES

See Dicky Wells.

## TRIO DE VIOLONS

See Eddie South.

## TRI-STATE DANCE RAMBLERS

Pseudonym on Champion for the following items listed in this book :-

15078  Gimme A Li'l Kiss, Will Ya, Huh ? (The Vagabonds)
15079  I'd Climb The Highest Mountain (The Vagabonds)
15094  But I Do - You Know I Do (The Southerners)

Helen and Josephine Trix were perhaps the first "sister" act on the American stage, certainly the first to record, but the only title they made that is likely to be of interest to the jazz enthusiast for the accompaniment is the following.

Vocal duet, acc. by the Gilt-Edged Four : Max Goldberg-t/Al Starita-as/Ray Starita-ts/vn/Sid Bright-p/Len Fillis-g/d.      London, February 6, 1929.

WA-8521-2  Pickin' Cotton                          Col 5349

## TRIXIE'S DOWN HOME SYNCOPATORS

Pseudonym on some copies of Paramount 12249 for Fletcher Henderson and his Orchestra (q.v.)

## TROMBONE RED AND  HIS BLUE SIX

This fine record has puzzled collectors for years; the following personnel has been suggested and seems feasible :-

Jabbo Smith-t/Robert Freeman-tb/Otto Hardwick-as/Duke Ellington-p/Fred Guy-bj/Sonny Greer-d.                          New York, June 18, 1931.

151615-2  Greasy Plate Stomp - v        Col 14612-D, HJCA HC-115
151616-2  B Flat Blues                        -            -

## THE  TROUBADOURS

Pseudonym on Lincoln 2652 (ST. LOUIS BLUES) for the Broadway Broadcasters (see Sam Lanin); the band recording extensively on Victor under this name between 1922 and 1940 was a studio group directed by Hugo Frey, Nat Shilkret and Leonard Joy in turn, but as far as is known, only the occasional "hot" break or four-bar solo is likely to be of the slightest interest to a jazz collector.

## CHARLIE TROUTT'S  MELODY ARTISTS

2c/tb/as/cl-ts/p/bj/bb/d/Emil Casper-v.    Atlanta, March 16, 1926.

9626-A  Running After You                    OK 40589
9627-A  Mountain City Blues                     -
9628-A  Sweet Child (I'm Wild About You) - vEC  OK 40627

                                    Atlanta, April 7, 1927.

143935-1  Transportation Blues - Part 1 : Casey    Col 1030-D, 4479, 0724
          Jones - vch
143936-2  Transportation Blues - Part 2 : Steamboat    -         -      -
          Bill - vch

                                    Atlanta, November 10, 1927.

145206-2  Transportation Blues - Part 3 : Goodbye  Col 1265-D, 01236
          My Lover, Goodbye - vch
145207-1  Transportation Blues - Part 4 : The Wreck    -          -
          Of The Southern Old 97 - vch

## THE  TROY HARMONISTS

T/tb/as/ts/p/bj/bb/d.                New York, c. March 12, 1926.

106711    Great Scott                    PA 7508, Per 108

## TRUETT AND  GEORGE

Banjo or guitar duets, or banjo and guitar duets, as shown.
                                    San Francisco, October 7, 1927.

144742-2  Wabash Blues - bj/g              Col 1182-D
144743-1-2  Slue Foot - bj/g              Rejected
144744-2  Ghost Dance - 2g                Col 1182-D

Banjo or guitar duets.            Los Angeles, April 20, 1928.

| | | |
|---|---|---|
| 145942-2 | Burning Of Rome - 2bj | Col 1419-D |
| 145943-2 | Chloe (Song Of The Swamp) - 2g | — |

## FRANKIE TRUMBAUER

Frank Trumbauer always preferred to be known thus, although his records invariably name him "Frankie Trumbauer."

FRANKIE TRUMBAUER AND HIS ORCHESTRA : Frank Trumbauer-Cm dir. Bix Beiderbecke-c/Bill Rank-tb/Jimmy Dorsey-cl-as/Doc Ryker-as unless marked */Paul Mertz-p-a/Eddie Lang-bj-g/Chauncey Morehouse-d.      New York, February 4, 1927.

| | | |
|---|---|---|
| 80391-C | *Trumbology | OK 40871, Col 36280, Par R-3419, R-2465, PZ-11245, Od 165171, A-189128 |
| 80392-A | Clarinet Marmalade | OK 40772, Col 37804, Voc 3010, 4412, Par R-3323, R-2304, A-7534, Od 165093, 194718, A-189019, A-286089 |
| 80393-B | Singin' The Blues | OK 40772, Br 7703, Col 37804, Par R-3323, R-1838, A-6235, B-27597, TT-9073, Od 165093, 295124, A-2409, A-189019,A-286085 |

NOTE:- Some of the earlier issues of the above add the credit line "with Bix" or "with Bix and Lang," without any explanation as to who these are or what they do; presumably the casual buyer in 1927 was expected to know !

Don Murray-cl-bar replaces Dorsey; Itzy Riskin-p replaces Mertz; Bill Challis-a.      New York, May 9, 1927.

| | | |
|---|---|---|
| 81071-B | Ostrich Walk | OK 40822, Col 37805, UHCA 29, Par R-3349, R-2492, A-7555, B-12501, Od 165126, 193015, 194718, A-2414, A-189048 |
| 81072-B | Riverboat Shuffle | OK 40822, Col 37805, UHCA 30, Par R-3349, R-2492, A-7555, B-12501, Od 165126, 193015, 194786, A-2409, A-189048 |

New York, May 13, 1927.

| | | |
|---|---|---|
| 81083-B | I'm Coming, Virginia | OK 40843, Br 7703, Col 36280, C-6179, M-435, Par R-3361,A-4923, Od 165134, 193050,A-2354,A-189060 |
| 81084-B | 'Way Down Yonder In New Orleans | OK 40843, Voc 3010, 4412, Col 37806, 39581, Par R-3361, R-2687, A-4923, Od 165134, 193050 194865, A-2354, A-189060 |

TRAM, BIX AND EDDIE : Bix Beiderbecke-c-p/Frank Trumbauer-Cm/Eddie Lang-g.      New York, May 13, 1927.

| | | |
|---|---|---|
| 81085-B | For No Reason At All In C | OK 40871, Col 35667, Par R-3419, R-2532, A-7459, Od 165171, A-2338 A-189128 |

NOTE:- Some issues show Arthur Schutt's name on the label, with a reference to "their four-piece orchestra" ! Columbia 35667 and Parlophone A-7459 as TRAM, BIX AND LANG.

FRANKIE TRUMBAUER AND HIS ORCHESTRA : Frank Trumbauer-Cm dir. Bix Beiderbecke-c/Bill Rank-tb/Don Murray-cl-bar/Doc Ryker-as/Adrian Rollini-bsx/Itzy Riskin-p/Eddie Lang g/Chauncey Morehouse-d/Seger Ellis-v/Bill Challis-a.      New York, August 25, 1927.

| | | |
|---|---|---|
| 81273-C | Three Blind Mice - aBC | OK 40903, Par R-105, PO-56, Od 165223,193090,A-189076,Tpl 553 |
| 81274-B | Blue River - vSE | OK 40879, Par R-3440, A-2355, A-4904, Od 165173, 193090, 04031 |
| 81275-D | There's A Cradle In Caroline - vSE | As above, but Od 193101,not 193090 |

TRAM, BIX AND LANG : Bix Beiderbecke-c-p/Frank Trumbauer-Cm/Eddie Lang-g.
New York, September 17, 1927.

81450-A  Wringin' And Twistin'                OK 40916, Col 37806, Voc 3150,
NOTE:- Some issues show Arthur Schutt's name on  Par R-3504, R-2532, Od 193104,
the label, with a reference to "their four-   A-2338
piece orchestra" !

FRANKIE TRUMBAUER AND HIS ORCHESTRA : Frank Trumbauer-Cm dir. Bix Beiderbecke-c/Bill
Rank-tb/Don Murray-cl-bar/Bobby Davis-as/Adrian Rollini-bsx/Joe Venuti-vn/Frank
Signorelli-p/Eddie Lang-g/Chauncey Morehouse-d.
New York, September 28, 1927.

81488-A  Humpty Dumpty                         OK 40926, Par R-3464, TT-9073,
                                               Od A-189075
81489-B  Krazy Kat                             OK 40903, Par R-105, PO-56,
                                               Od 165223, 193101, A-189076
81490-B  Baltimore                             OK 40926, Par R-3464, Od A-189075

FRANKIE TRUMBAUER'S AUGMENTED ORCHESTRA : As above, plus ? Wingy Manone-c; Lang
plays bj; Irving Kaufman-v.            New York, September 30, 1927.

81499-A  Just An Hour Of Love - vIK            OK 40912, Par R-3463, A-4912,
                                               Od A-189070
81500-A  I'm Wonderin' Who - vIK               As above
NOTE:- OKeh 40912 as BENNY MEROFF AND HIS ORCHESTRA.

Pee Wee Russell-cl replaces Davis; Murray db ts instead of bar; 2nd c omitted.
New York, October 25, 1927.

81570-C  Crying All Day                        OK 40966, Col 35956, Par R-2176,
                                               A-6449, Od 165291, 193217,
                                               279713, A-189125, HJCA 601
81571-B  A Good Man Is Hard To Find            OK 40966, Col 35956, Par R-3489,
                                               Od 165291, 193217, A-189125,
                                               HJCA 601

? Wingy Manone-c added; Jerry Macy-John Ryan-Les Reis-v.
New York, October 26, 1927.

81575-B  Sugar - vJM-JR                        OK 40938, Par R-3489, Od 193134,
                                               A-189092
81576-A-B-C  Did You Mean It ? - vLR           Rejected

Frank Trumbauer-Cm dir. Bix Beiderbecke-c/Bill Rank-tb/Jimmy Dorsey-cl-as/Charlie
Strickfaden-as/Min Leibrook-bsx/Matt Malneck-vn/Tom Satterfield-p-cel/Harold Mac-
Donald-d, with Charlie Margulis-t*.    New York, January 9, 1928.

400003-B  There'll Come A Time                 OK 40979, Par R-3526, R-2097,
                                               A-6311, A-7692, DP-255, Od 165330
                                               193128, A-2399, A-189143
400004-C  *Jubilee                             OK 41044, Par R-161, R-2054,
                                               Od 165539, A-189203, A-286091

Dorsey omitted; Carl Kress-g added; Bing Crosby-Frank Trumbauer-v
New York, January 20, 1928.

400033-A  *From Monday On - vBC-FT             Rejected
400034-A  *Mississippi Mud - vBC-FT            OK 40979, Par R-3526, R-2097,
NOTE:- A rumor persists that copies exist of   A-6311, A-7692, DP-255, Od 165330
Australian Parlophone A-6311, using matrix     193128, A-2399, A-189143,
400033-A when 400034-A was intended.           ND-5040-S, 031816, Bm 1029

Izzy Friedman-cl/Chester Hazlett-cl-as added; Eddie Lang-g replaces Kress; Noel
Taylor-v.                             New York, April 3, 1928.

400188-A  Our Bungalow Of Dreams - vNT         OK 41019, Par R-142, A-4543,
                                               Od 165362, 193172, A-189148,
                                               04074, Tpl 542
400189-B  Lila - vNT                           OK 41019, Par R-141, Od 165362,
                                               193172, A-189148, Tpl 542

FRANKIE TRUMBAUER AND HIS ORCHESTRA : Frank Trumbauer-Cm-as-v dir. Bix Beiderbecke-c
  Charlie Margulis-t/Bill Rank-tb/Izzy Friedman-cl/Charles Strickfaden-as/Min Lei-
  brook-bsx/Matty Malneck-vn/Lennie Hayton-p/Eddie Lang-g/Harold McDonald-d/Scrappy
  Lambert-v/Bill Challis-a.            New York, April 10, 1928.

| | | |
|---|---|---|
| 400603-B | Borneo - vSL/aBC | OK 41039, Par R-203, Od 165360, 193190, A-189159, Col 20674 |
| 400604-C | My Pet - vSL/aBC | OK 41039, Par R-141, Od 165360, 193190, A-189159 |

NOTE:- Parlophone R-203 as THE GOOFUS FIVE AND THEIR ORCHESTRA.

Strickfaden-plays bar; Roy Bargy-p may replace Hayton; George Rose-g replaces Lang;
Harry Gale-d replaces McDonald; Dee Orr-v; Margulis omitted.
                                    Chicago, July 5, 1928.

| | | |
|---|---|---|
| 400989-C | Bless You ! Sister - vFT-DO+2 | OK 41100, Par R-1882, A-3992, B-25293, B-27597, TT-9073, 22006, Od 165488, 193236, A-189190 |
| 400990-B | Dusky Stevedore - vFT-DO+2 | OK 41100, Par R-265, B-27597, 22006, Od 165488, 193236,A-189190 |

Strickfaden and Friedman db as; Roy Bargy-p definite; Eddie Lang-g replaces Rose;
Chauncey Morehouse-d replaces Gale; Scrappy Lambert-Marlin Hurt-v.
                               New York, September 20, 1928.

| | | |
|---|---|---|
| 401133-B | Take Your Tomorrow (And Give Me Today) - vFT-? SL or MH | OK 41145, Col 37807, DCH-339, Par R-265, R-2564, A-7534, Od 165526, 182473, 193297, A-189210, 031816 |
| 401134-C | Love Affairs - vSL | OK 41145, Od 165526, 182473, 193288, A-189210, Bm 1103 |
| 401135-A-B-C | Sentimental Baby - vMH | Rejected |

Leibrook omitted; Charlie Margulis-t added; unknown d replaces Morehouse; Rube
Crozier-bsr added except on the first side; Charles Gaylord-v.
                               New York, October 5, 1928.

| | | |
|---|---|---|
| 401195-B | The Love Nest - vCG | Par R-2645, Decatur 501 |
| 401196-C | The Japanese Sandman - vFT | Par R-2176, A-6449, Bm 1103 |
| 401197-A | High Up On A Hill Top - vCG | OK 41128, Par R-2644, A-2682, A-4573, Od 193254, A-189241 |
| 401198-A | Sentimental Baby - vCG | OK 41128, Par R-298, A-4573, Od 193254, A-189241, Decatur 501 |

Frank Trumbauer-Cm-as-v dir. Bix Beiderbecke-Andy Secrest-c/Bill Rank-tb/Charlie
Strickfaden-as/Izzy Friedman-cl-ts/Min Leibrook-bsx/Matty Malneck-vn/Lennie Hayton
p/Eddie Lang-g/Stan King-d.        New York, March 8, 1929.

| | | |
|---|---|---|
| 401703-B | Futuristic Rhythm - vFT | OK 41209, Par R-2625, B-27002, Od 165684, 193308 |
| 401704-D | Raisin' The Roof | As above, but Par R-2644 |

Roy Bargy-p replaces Hayton; Smith Ballew-v.
                               New York, April 17, 1929.

| | | |
|---|---|---|
| 401809-B | Louise - vSB | OK 41231, Par E-6209, A-4948, B-27029, PNY-41231, Od 165736, 182672, 193316, A-189282, A-189287 |
| 401810-C | Wait Till You See Ma Cherie - vSB | As above, but Par R-398,not E-6209 |
| 401811-C | Baby, Won't You Please Come Home ? - vFT | OK 41286, Cl 5469-C, Har 1422-H, Od ONY-41286, 165843, A-2336, A-286087, 025412, Col 37807, DCH-339, VT 2529-V, Par R-1978, 22523 |

NOTE:- Parlophone PNY-41231 as JOE CURRAN'S BAND; E-6209 as WILL PERRY'S ORCHESTRA;
Clarion 5469-C, Harmony 1422-H and Velvet Tone 2529-V as TENNESSEE MUSIC MEN.

FRANKIE TRUMBAUER AND HIS ORCHESTRA : Frank Trumbauer-Cm-as dir. Bix Beiderbecke-
Andy Secrest-c/Bill Rank-tb/Charles Strickfaden-as-o/Izzy Friedman-cl-ts/Min Lei-
brook-bsx/Matty Malneck-Kurt Dieterle-Mischa Russell-vn/Lennie Hayton-p/Eddie Lang
g/Stan King-d/Smith Ballew-v.  New York, April 30, 1929.

| | | |
|---|---|---|
| 401840-B | No-One Can Take Your Place - vSB | Par R-420, 22430, Od A-189259 |
| 401841-C | I Like That | OK 41286, Par R-714, 22523, Od ONY-41286, 165843, A-2318, A-286019 |

Charlie Margulis-t replaces Beiderbecke; Joe Venuti-vn replaces Malneck, Dieterle
and Russell; George Marsh-d replaces King; Hayton db cel.
New York, May 21, 1929.

| | | |
|---|---|---|
| 401952-C | Nobody But You - vSB | OK 41252, Par R-434, 22407, B-27028, Ar 4445, Od 238942, A-189276 |
| 401953-B | Got A Feelin' For You - vSB | OK 41252, Par R-434, 22407, B-27028, Od 182754, 238942, A-189276 |
| | NOTE:- Ariel 4445 as ARIEL DANCE ORCHESTRA. | |

New York, May 22, 1929.

| | | |
|---|---|---|
| 401961-D | Shivery Stomp | OK 41268, Par R-511, B-27061, Od 238080, A-2320, A-189272, A-189303, A-286012 |
| 401962-C | Reaching For Someone - vSB | OK 41268, Par R-420, 22430, B-27061, Od 238080, A-189259, A-286012 |

New York, September 18, 1929.

| | | |
|---|---|---|
| 402963-B-C | Love Ain't Nothin' But The Blues-vSB | OK 41301, Par PNY-41301, R-644, R-2541, A-4968, 22565, Ar 4537, Od 165912 |
| 402964-A | How Am I To Know ? - vSB | OK 41301, Par PNY-41301, R-618, 22565, Od 165912, A-2327, A-286013 |
| | NOTE:- Parlophone PNY-41301 as JOE CURRAN'S BAND; Ariel 4537 as ARIEL DANCE ORCHESTRA. | |

Hoagy Carmichael-p-cel replaces Hayton; Matty Malneck-Kurt Dieterle-vn added, but
Margulis, Rank, Friedman and Strickfaden omitted*; Joe Venuti and possibly Hoagy
Carmichael-v effects**.  New York, October 10, 1929.

| | | |
|---|---|---|
| 403050-B** | Turn On The Heat - vSB | OK 41313, Par PNY-41313, R-499, A-2916, 22628, Ar 4483, Od 165881, 193426, A-189302, A-221187 |
| 403050-C** | Turn On The Heat - vSB | Par PNY-41313 |
| 403051-C | *Manhattan Rag | OK 41330, Par R-1978, A-6235, Od 165949, 193497, A-2334, A-286087, 025412 |
| 403052-B | Sunny Side Up - vSB | OK 41313, Par PNY-41313, R-499, A-2916, 22628, B-27129, Ar 4483, Od 165881, 193246, A-189302, A-221187 |
| | NOTE:- Parlophone PNY-41313 as JOE CURRAN'S BAND. | |

Lennie Hayton-p-cel replaces Carmichael.
New York, October 15, 1929.

| | | |
|---|---|---|
| 403068-A-B-C | Great Day ! - vSB | OK rejected |

New York, October 19, 1929.

| | | |
|---|---|---|
| 403068-D-E | Great Day ! - vSB | Rejected |
| 403082-A | My Sweeter Than Sweet - vSB | OK 41326, Par R-583, R-2564, A-2915, Od 165882, 193515, A-189298 |
| 403083-B | What Wouldn't I Do For That Man ?-vSB | OK 41330, Par R-583, 22680, Od 165949, 193515 |

FRANKIE TRUMBAUER AND HIS ORCHESTRA : Frank Trumbauer-Cm-as-v (and c-cl**)dir. Andy
Secrest-c/Harry Goldfield-t/Bill Rank-tb/Charles Strickfaden-as/Izzy Friedman-cl-
ts/Min Leibrook-bsx/Joe Venuti-vn/Roy Bargy-p/Eddie Lang-g/George Marsh-d/Jeannie
Lang-Smith Ballew-v.                    New York, May 8, 1930.

| | | |
|---|---|---|
| 404007-C  Happy Feet - vSB | OK 41421, Od ONY-36091, 193495, | |
| | 238286, A-286018, Par PNY-34084, | |
| | R-701 | |
| 404008-A  I Like To Do Things For You - vJL | OK 41421, Od ONY-36091, 193495, | |
| | 238286, Par PNY-34085, R-702 | |

NOTE:- Parlophone PNY-34084 and PNY-34085 as TOM BARKER AND HIS ORCHESTRA.

New York, May 10, 1930.

| | |
|---|---|
| 404009-D**Get Happy - vFT | OK 41431, Par R-2625, Od 238121 |
| 404010-B  Deep Harlem - vFT | -      Cl 5461-C, Har 1415-H, |
| NOTE:- Clarion 5461-C, Harmony 1415-H and | VT 2521-V, Par R-1946, A-6266, |
| Velvet Tone 2521-V as TENNESSEE MUSIC MEN. | Od 238121, A-272014 |

Frank Trumbauer-Cm-as-v dir. Andy Secrest-Harry Goldfield-Nat Natoli-t/Bill Rank-
Jack Fulton-tb/Charles Strickfaden-as/Fud Livingston-cl-ts/Min Leibrook-bsx/Matt
Malneck-vn/Lennie Hayton-p-cel/Eddie Lang-g/George Marsh-d/Smith Ballew-v.
New York, July 22, 1930.

| | |
|---|---|
| 404268-D  What's The Use ? - vSB | OK 41437, Od ONY-36128, 238187, |
| | A-286045, Par PNY-34119, R-1013 |
| 404269-C  Hittin' The Bottle - vFT | OK 41437, Od ONY-36128, 238187, |
| NOTE:- Parlophone PNY-34119 and PNY-34120 as | A-2322, A-286024, Par PNY-34120, |
| TOM BARKER AND HIS ORCHESTRA. | R-795 |

Rank omitted.                    New York, September 8, 1930.

| | |
|---|---|
| 404433-B  Bye Bye Blues - vSB | OK 41450, Par R-796, 80447, |
| | Od 238228, A-2326, A-286025 |
| 404434-B  Choo Choo (El Tren*) | OK 41450, Cl 5467-C, Har 1420-H, |
| NOTE:- Clarion 5467-C, Harmony 1420-H and | VT 2527-V, Par R-821, B-27294, |
| Velvet Tone 2527-V as TENNESSEE MUSIC MEN. | TT-9010, Od 183240*, 238228, |
| | A-2323, A-286026 |

Frank Trumbauer-Cm-as dir. Nat Natoli-t/Bill Rank-tb/Rosy McHargue-cl-as/Matty
Malneck-vn/Dave Rose-p/John Tobin-bj/Dan Gaybe-sb/Bob Conselman-d/Art Uarrett-v/
v trio.                    Chicago, April 10, 1931.

| | |
|---|---|
| C-7693-  Georgia On My Mind - v3 | Rejected |
| C-7694-  Bass Drum Dan - v3 | Br 01225 |
| C-7695-  Honeysuckle Rose - v3 | Rejected |

Chicago, June 24, 1931.

| | |
|---|---|
| C-7875-A  In The Merry Month Of Maybe - vAJ&3 | Br 6146, 01261 |
| C-7876-  In The Merry Month Of Maybe | Br A-9110 |
| C-7877-A  Crazy Quilt - vAJ&3 | Br 6146, 01261 |
| C-7878-  Crazy Quilt | Br A-9110 |
| C-7879-A  Georgia On My Mind - vAJ&3 | Br 6159, 01192, A-9116 |
| C-7880-A  Honeysuckle Rose - vAJ | -      -      - |

Frank Trumbauer-Cm-as-v dir. Max Connett-Vance Rice-t/Joe Harris-tb/Gail Stant-Mac
Elstead-as/Harold Jones-ts/Leon Kaplan-vn-g/Frederick Saping-vn-g-v/Herman Crane-p
/Craig Leitch-g-v/Charles McConnell-sb/Leroy Buck-d-v/The Nitecaps-v trio/Helen
Rowland-Johnny Blake-Johnny Mercer-v.  New York, April 5, 1932.

| | |
|---|---|
| 255004-1  Sizzling One-Step Medley (Intro. Dinah-  Col 18002-D | |
|       vJM-N/My Honey's Lovin' Arms-vJM/Nobody's Sweetheart-vN) | |
| 255005-2  Medley of Isham Jones Dance Hits (Intro.     - | |
|       On The Alamo/Swinging Down The Lane-vHR/I'll See You In My Dreams-vJB) | |

FRANKIE TRUMBAUER AND HIS ORCHESTRA : Frank Trumbauer-Cm-as-v dir. Max Connett-Vance
Rice-t/Joe Harris-tb/Gail Stant-Mac Elstead-as/Harold Jones-ts/Leon Kaplan-vn-g/
Frederick Saping-vn-g-v/Herman Crane-p/Craig Leitch-g/Charles McConnell-sb/Leroy
Buck-d-v/The Nitecaps-v trio.    New York, October 17, 1932.

| | | |
|---|---|---|
| 152280-2 | Cinderella's Wedding Day - vLB | Col 2879-D, CB-542, Par A-3860 |
| 152281-2 | I Think You're A Honey - vN | Col 2710-D, DO-824, Lucky LX-17 |
| 152282-1-2 | Business In Q | - CB-542 - - |
| 152283-2 | Bass Drum Dan - vLB | Col 2879-D, CB-580, Par A-3860 |
| 152284-1-2 | The Newest St. Louis Blues (St. Louis Blues*) - vLB | Col 2729-D -* DO-867 |
| 152285-1-2 | Between The Devil And The Deep Blue Sea-vFT-LB - | DB-5007 - |

Frank Trumbauer-Cm-as dir. Nat Natoli-Charlie Teagarden-t/Jack Teagarden-tb-v/
Benny Bonacio-Charles Strickfaden-cl-as/John Cordaro-cl-ts/Roy Bargy-p/Dick
McDonough-g/Art Miller-sb/Herb Quigley-d.
New York, January 12, 1934.

| | | |
|---|---|---|
| B-14586-A | Break It Down | Br 6763, 6912, 01812, A-9555, A-500399, 4929 (It.) |
| B-14587-A | Juba Dance | Br 6763, A-9555, A-500399 |
| B-14588- | How Am I To Know ? | Rejected |

Natoli and Bonacio omitted; Mischa Russell-vn added.
New York, February 23, 1934.

| | | |
|---|---|---|
| B-14848-A | China Boy | Br 6912, 01812, A-9596, A-500423, 4929, Col DO-1253 |
| B-14849-A | Emaline - vJT | Br 6788, 01767, A-9594, A-500424, Col DO-1253 |
| B-14850-A | In A Mist | Br 6997, 01979, A-9596, A-500423 |
| B-14851-A | 'Long About Midnight - vJT | Br 6788, 01767, A-9594, A-500424 |

Frank Trumbauer-Cm-as dir. Nat Natoli-Bunny Berigan-t/Glenn Miller-tb/Artie Shaw-
cl-as/Jack Shore-as/Larry Binyon-ts/Roy Bargy-p/Lionel Hall-g/Artie Bernstein-sb/
Jack Williams-d/Dick Robertson-v.    New York, November 20, 1934.

| | | |
|---|---|---|
| 86219-1 | Blue Moon - vDR | Vic 24812, HMV BD-119, GW-1098, K-7454 |
| 86220-1 | Plantation Moods | Vic 24834, HMV BD-158, X-4454 |
| 86221-1 | Down 'T Uncle Bill's - vDR | Vic 24812, HMV BD-119, EA-1459, GW-1098 |
| 86222-1 | Troubled | Vic 24834, HMV BD-158, X-4454, Decatur 512 |

Frank Trumbauer-Cm-as-v dir. Ed Wade-Charlie Teagarden-t/Jack Teagarden-tb-v/
Johnny Mince-cl/Joe Cordaro-cl-as/Mutt Hayes-ts/Roy Bargy-p/George van Eps-g/Art
Miller-sb/Stan King-d.    New York, January 29, 1936.

| | | |
|---|---|---|
| B-18600-1 | Flight Of A Haybag | Br 7629, 02197, A-9988, A-500638, Col DO-1514 |
| B-18601-1 | Breakin' In A Pair Of Shoes | Br 7613, A-9979, A-500639, Lucky 60153, Col DO-1551 |
| B-18602-2 | Announcer's Blues | Br 7629, 02197, A-9988, A-500638, 5030, Col DO-1514 |

New York, February 5, 1936.

| | | |
|---|---|---|
| B-18630-1 | I Hope Gabriel Likes My Music - vJT-FT | Br 7613, A-9979, A-500639, Lucky 60190, Col DO-1551 |

Artie Shaw-cl replaces Mince; Carl Kress-g replaces van Eps.
New York, April 27, 1936.

| | | |
|---|---|---|
| B-19113-1 | Somebody Loves Me - vJT | Br 7665, 02232, A-81033, A-500666, Col DO-1572 |
| B-19114-1 | The Mayor Of Alabam' - vJT&ch | Br 7663, 02232, A-500665, Col DO-1571 |
| B-19115-2 | Ain't Misbehavin' - vJT | Br 7665, A-81033, A-500666, Lucky 60153, Col DO-1572 |
| B-19116-1 | 'S Wonderful | Br 7663, A-500665, Lucky 60175, Col DO-1571 |

FRANKIE TRUMBAUER AND HIS ORCHESTRA : Frank Trumbauer-Cm-as dir. Russ Case-Charlie
Teagarden-t/Jack Teagarden-tb-v/Matty Matlock-cl/John Cordaro-cl-as/Eddie Miller-
ts/Roy Bargy-p/Carl Kress-g/Art Miller-sb/Ray Bauduc-d.
                                        New York, June 15, 1936

B-19442-1  I'm An Old Cowhand - vJT          Br 7687, A-500683, Lucky 60164,
                                             Col DO-1590
B-19443-1  Diga Diga Doo                     As above

Frank Trumbauer-Cm-as-v dir. Wayne Williams-t-v/Dick Dunne-Howard Lamont-t/Del
Menton-Bernie Bahr-tb/Johnny Ross-Joe Schles-Joe Kiefer-Connie Blessing-cl-as-ts/
Rene Faure-p/John Kreyer-g/Trigger Alpert-sb/Dave Becker-d/Fredda Gibson (later
known as Georgia Gibbs)-v.             New York, March, 1940.

US-1401-1  Wearing Of The Green/Irish Washerwoman  Var 8215, Davis 22-3
US-1402-1  No Retard (China Boy)                     -              -
US-1403-1  I Don't Stand A Ghost Of A Chance - vFG Var 8256
US-1404-1  I Surrender, Dear - vFG                 Var 8239, Davis 29-5
US-1405-1  Semper Fidelis                          Var 8253, Davis 29-8
US-1406-2  Jimtown Blues                           Var 8223
US-1407-1  Not On The First Night, Baby-vWW-FT-FG  Var 8225, Juke Box 505
US-1408-1  The Laziest Gal In Town - vFG           Var 8223        -
NOTE:- Juke Box 505 as FRANKIE AND HER HOT BOYS.

                                        New York, March, 1940.

US-1415-2  Never-Never Land Fantasy              Var 8243, MW M-10055
US-1416-1  National Emblem March                   -        -          Davis 29-3
US-1417-1  Stars And Stripes Forever             Var 8253, Davis 22-4
US-1418-1  Lady Be Good                          Var 8269
US-1419-1  Sugar Foot Stomp                      Var 8256
US-1420-1  Honky Tonk Train Blues                Var 8236, Davis 29-4
US-1421-1  Walkin' The Dog - vch                 Var 8225, Davis 29-6
US-1422-1  Wrap Your Troubles In Dreams          Var 8269, Davis 29-7
US-1423-1  Little Rock Getaway                   Var 8236

## TUB JUG WASHBOARD BAND

? Tampa Red (Hudson Whittaker)-k-g-v/jug/wb/Thomas A. Dorsey-v.
                                        Chicago, c. June, 1928.

20652-3  Washboard Rag                           Pm 12682
20653-1  Lady Quit Her Husband Onexpectinly (sic)-vTAD-
20656-1  Tub-Jug Rag                             Pm 12671
NOTE:- The label of Paramount 12671 shows the matrix number as 20652 in error;
matrices 20654 and 20655 have no been traced.  Paramount 12682 as WASHBOARD TRIO.

2nd k added.                            Chicago, c. June, 1928.

20671-2  San                                     Pm 12671

## BESSIE  TUCKER

Vocal, acc. by K. D. Johnson-p.         Memphis, August 29, 1928.

45436-2  Bessie's Moan                           Vic V-38526, JCl 514
45437-1-2  The Dummy                             Vic 21708
45440-1  Fort Worth And Denver Blues               -
45440-2  Fort Worth And Denver Blues             X LVA-3016, HMV 7EG-8085 (LP/EP)
45441-2  Penitentiary                            Vic V-38526, JCl 514
45444-1  Fryin' Pan Skillet Blues                X LVA-3016, HMV 7EG-8085 (LP/EP)
45444-2  Fryin' Pan Skillet Blues                Vic V-38018
45445-1  My Man Has Quit Me                      Vic 21692
NOTE:- Matrices 45438/9 and 45442/3 are all by Ida May Mack, q.v.

                                        Memphis, August 30, 1928.

45448-1  Got Cut All To Pieces                   X LVA-3016, HMV 7EG-8085 (LP/EP)
45448-2  Got Cut All To Pieces                   Vic V-38018
45449-2  Black Name Moan                         Vic 21692

Acc. by K. D. Johnson-p/Bo Jones or Carl Davis-g, with bb*; the vocal chorus probably consists of the accompanists.      Dallas, August 10, 1929.

| | | |
|---|---|---|
| 55328-1 | *Better Boot That Thing - vch | Vic V-38542 |
| 55329-2 | *Katy Blues | - |
| 55330-1 | Mean Old Jack Stropper Blues | Vic V-38538 |
| 55331-1 | Old Black Mary | - |

Dallas, October 17, 1929.

| | | |
|---|---|---|
| 56404-2 | Key To The Bushes | Vic 23385, BB B-5218, Sr S-3208 |
| 56405-1 | Bogey Man Blues | -           -          - |
| 56406-2 | Mean Old Master | Vic 23392 |
| 56407-1-2 | Pick On Me Blues | Rejected |

Dallas, October 21, 1929.

| | | |
|---|---|---|
| 56447-1-2 | Whistling Woman Blues | Rejected |
| 56448-2 | T. B. Moan | Vic 23392 |

## GEORGE TUCKER AND HIS NOVELTY BAND

Pseudonym on Champion for Lawrence Welk and his Orchestra, q.v.

## SOPHIE TUCKER

The following sides by this world-famous cabaret artist are of jazz interest for the
accompanying artists.  She does not sing on either of the first two.

SOPHIE TUCKER'S FIVE KINGS OF SYNCOPATION : Eddie Richmond-c/Bobby Jones-as/Irving
Rothschild-vn/Julius Berken-vc/Jules Buffano-p/Danny Alvin-d/Al Beilan-v.
New York, c. March, 1921.

| | | |
|---|---|---|
| | Don't You Throw Me Down - vAB | Arto 9065 |
| | Wait Until You See My Madeline | - |

Vocal, acc. by her Five Kings of Jazz : Irving Solow-c/Al Levine-as/Irving Roths-
child-vn/George Coon-p/Danny Alvin-d.   New York, c. February 23, 1922.

| | | |
|---|---|---|
| 70499-A | Jig Walk | OK 4590 |
| 70500-B | High Brown Blues | OK 4565 |

New York, c. February 27, 1922.

| | | |
|---|---|---|
| 70505-A | Bluebird, Where Are You ? | OK 4617 |

New York, c. March 2, 1922.

| | | |
|---|---|---|
| 70514-C | She Knows It | OK 4565 |

New York, c. March 24, 1922.

| | | |
|---|---|---|
| 70564-A | Pick Me Up And Lay Me Down In Dear Old Dixieland | OK 4590 |
| 70565-A | Complainin' (It's Human Nature To Complain) | OK 4617 |

Acc. by the Arcadia Peacock Orchestra of St. Louis : Bob Pope-t/Tommy Moore-tb/
Bud Hassler-cl/Jules Schneider-ts/Ted Shapiro-p/Porter Brown-bj/Chick Harvey-bb.
St. Louis, January, 1924.

| | | |
|---|---|---|
| 8514-B | I've Got A Cross-Eyed Papa (But He Looks Straight To Me) | OK 40068, Par E-5429, E-5430 |
| 8515-B | Hula Lou | - 40129, 14083 - |

Evidently at this point, Sophie Tucker made some records in Chicago accompanied by
Muggsy Spanier-c and Volly de Faut-cl, and members of the Benson Orchestra of
Chicago.  Both musicians recalled the date independently, but nothing was ever
issued from it, apparently.  OKeh were recording extensively in Chicago just prior
to the St. Louis date above, and Muggsy Spanier and Volly de Faut recorded just a
month later with the Bucktown Five, q.v.

Acc. by Miff Mole's Molers : Red Nichols-t/Miff Mole-tb/Jimmy Dorsey-cl-as/Ted
Shapiro-p/Eddie Lang-g/Joe Tarto-bb/Vic Berton-d.
　　　　　　　　　　　　　　　　　　　　New York, April 11, 1927.

| | | |
|---|---|---|
| 80716-B | After You've Gone | OK 40837, Par R-3353, A-2588, A-4568, Od 165138, 04099 |
| 80717-C | I Ain't Got Nobody | As above, plus Par E-5483 (Jap.) |

　　　　　　　　　　　　　　　　　New York, April 15, 1927.

| | | |
|---|---|---|
| 80737-B | One Sweet Letter From You (One Sweet Letter From Home*) | OK 40813, Par R-3342*, A-2219, A-4569, Od 165137, A-189053,0410( |
| 80738-A | Fifty Million Frenchmen Can't Be Wrong | As above |

Acc. by Leonard Joy dir. Negro band : c/tb/cl/2p/bj/bb/d.
　　　　　　　　　　　　　　　　　　New York, July 10, 1929.

| | | |
|---|---|---|
| 55602-2 | Some Of These Days | Vic 22049, BB B-6835, HMV B-3720, EA-744 |

## JOSEPHINE TUMMINIA

See Jimmy Dorsey.

## TUNNEY'S FLORIDORIANS

Pseudonym on Piccadilly for Jack Harris and his Orchestra, q.v.

## AL TURK

AL TURK'S PRINCESS ORCHESTRA : Al Turk-c dir. tb/cl-as/as/ts/p/bj/bb/d.
　　　　　　　　　　　　　　　　　? New York, c. October, 1924.

| | | |
|---|---|---|
| B-1641 | Copenhagen | Oly 1461, Pen 1436 |
| | Sweet Little You | - |
| | King Porter Stomp | Oly 1463 |
| | Red Hot Mama | - |

NOTE:- Pennington 1436 as GOLDEN GATE ORCHESTRA.

AL TURK'S ORCHESTRA : As above, plus 2nd c/D. Harris-Earl Hayden-v (? members of the
band).　　　　　　　　　　　　　　Chicago, June 17, 1926.

| | | |
|---|---|---|
| 9733-A | Snag It | OK 8362, 40653, Od FF-1129 |
| 9734-A | Hi Henry Stomp | - - |
| 9735-A | Mean Man | OK 8377 |
| 9736-A | One O'Clock Blues - vDH | - |

　　　　　　　　　　　　　　　　Chicago, c. June 26, 1926.

| | | |
|---|---|---|
| 9798-A | I'm Just Wild About Animal Crackers-vEH | OK 40648 |
| 9801-A | Shanghai Honeymoon | OK 40660 |

NOTE:- Matrices 9799 and 9800 are untraced.

## BEE TURNER

Vocal, acc. by ? Oliver Cobb-c/Roosevelt Sykes-p.
　　　　　　　　　　　　　　　　Grafton, Wis., c. June 1, 1930.

| | | |
|---|---|---|
| L-445-1 | Jivin' Jelly Roll Blues | Pm 13017 |
| L-447-1 | Rough Treatin' Daddy | - |

## JOE TURNER AND HIS MEMPHIS MEN

Pseudonym on Columbia 1813-D, 5486 and 36157 for Duke Ellington and his Orchestra,
q.v. (There is no obvious connection between the pianist Joe Turner and the blues
vocalist Joe Turner and this one).

Piano solos.                          Paris, January, 1936.

77604    Liza                              Ul AP-1573
77605    Cheek To Cheek                    -

Vocal, with own piano, featured with Jan Sima's Orchestra Gramo-Klubu : Jan Sima dir.
H. Preus-A. Simburch-J. Cholinsky-t/L. Behal- —— Huttner-tb/L. Habert-J. Charvat
J. Zad-L. Ptaček-as-ts/J. Verberger-p/P. Rezek-g/J. Srbek-sb/I. Rychlik-d.
                              Prague, December 2, 1936.

40951    Joe Turner Stomp                  Ul A-11400
40952    Joe Turner Blues - vJT            -

Piano solos, acc. by Tommy Benford-d.    Paris, May 24, 1939.

OSW-82-1  The Ladder                       Swing 71
OSW-83-1  Loncy                            -

## JOE TURNER

Vocal, acc. by Pete Johnson-p.        Carnegie Hall, New York, Dec. 24, 1938.

        It's All Right, Baby                Van VRS-8524, TR 35-065,
                                            Fon TFE-5188, AURS 9015 (LPs)

                                      New York, December 30, 1938.

23891-1  Goin' Away Blues                   Voc 4607, Par R-2672, DP-265,
                                            B-71133, Od 028461, Br A-82166
23892-1  Roll 'Em, Pete                     As above, plus Col 35959, C-6151

JOE TURNER AND HIS FLY CATS : Vocal, acc. by Hot Lips Page-t/Don Byas-ts/Pete
Johnson-p/John Collins-g/Abe Bolar-sb/A. G. Godley-d.
                              New York, November 11, 1940.

68333-A  Piney Brown Blues                  Dec 18121, 29711, MU-60583

BIG JOE TURNER : Vocal, acc. by Willie "The Lion" Smith-p.
                              New York, November 26, 1940.

68394-A  Doggin' The Dog                    Dec 7824
68395-B  Careless Love                      Dec 7827
68396-A  Jumpin' Down Blues                 -
68397-A  Rainy Day Blues                    Dec 7824

Vocal, acc. by Sam Price-p/Leonard Ware-g/Billy Taylor-sb.
                              New York, July 17, 1941.

69523-A  Nobody In Mind                     Dec 7868
69524-A  Somebody's Got To Go               Dec 7856
69525-A  Ice Man                            -
69526-A  Chewed Up Grass                    Dec 7868

    Acc. by the Freddie Slack Trio : Freddie Slack-p/? Al Hendrickson-g/Jud de Naut-sb.
                              Los Angeles, September 8, 1941.

DLA-2838-A-B  Rocks In My Bed               Dec 4093
DLA-2839-A  Blues On Central Avenue         Dec 7889, Coral 65004
DLA-2840-A  Goin' To Chicago                Dec 4093
DLA-2841-A  Sun Risin' Blues                Dec 7889, Coral 65004

    Acc. by same instrumentation; probably same personnel.
                              Los Angeles, January 28, 1942.

DLA-2865-B  Blues In The Night              Dec 7885, 8606
DLA-2866-A  Cry Baby Blues                  -      -

<u>LAVINIA TURNER</u>

Vocal, acc. by her Jazz Band : Possibly :- Gus Aiken-c/Jake Frazier-tb/Garvin Bushell
    cl-as/Willie Gant-p/ ——— Spivey-bj/Joe Banks-d.
                                       New York, March, 1921.

    69168    How Many Times ?                    PA 020544, 10134, Per 12032
    69169    Can't Get Lovin' Blues                 -         -        -

                                       New York, c. May 17, 1921.

    69232    A-Wearin' Away The Blues             PA 020572, Per 12033
    69233    Sweet Man O' Mine                       -          -

Acc. by James P. Johnson's Harmony Seven : James P. Johnson-p dir. 2t/tb/cl/ts/bj.
                                       New York, c. September 2, 1921.

    69358    He Took It Away From Me              PA 020627, Per 12034
    69359    If I Were Your Daddy (And You Were A Mamma  -        -
               To Me)

                                       New York, c. September 26, 1921.

    69397    When The Rain Turns To Snow          PA 020878, Per 12039
    69398    Who'll Drive Your Cares Away            -          -

Acc. by James P. Johnson-p.        New York, c. November 21, 1921.

    69521    Watch Me Go                          PA 020705, Per 12005
    69522    You Never Miss A Good Thing Till It's Gone  -        -

Acc. by Hughie Woolford-p.         New York, late October, 1922.

    70988-B  How I Can I Be Your "Sweet Mama" When     OK 8042
               You're "Daddy" To Somebody Else ?
    70989-A  Don't Cut Off Your Nose To Spite Your Face  -

                <u>LLOYD TURNER AND HIS  VILLA VENICE ORCHESTRA</u>

The following title seems to be the only one of interest as jazz from the four made
    for OKeh by this band.

Lloyd Turner-tb dir. c/cl-ss/cl-as/cl-ts/p/bj/bb/d.
                                       Chicago, June 24, 1926.

    9783-A  My Mama's In Town                     OK 40674, Par E-5703

                        <u>TUXEDO DANCE ORCHESTRA</u>

Pseudonym on Pathe Actuelle 36990 and Perfect 15171 for Sam Lanin and his Orchestra,
    q.v.; of the many others on various labels bearing this identity, the following is
    said to be of interest as jazz or "hot" dance music.

2t/tb/2as/ts/p/bj/bb/d.            New York, c. July, 1923.

    3-2146  Somebody's Wrong                      Fed 5324, Res 75324

                            <u>TUXEDO ORCHESTRA</u>

Pseudonym on Vocalion 15556 (DELIRIUM) for Carl Fenton and his Orchestra, q.v.

                          <u>TUXEDO SYNCOPATORS</u>

Pseudonym on Globe and Madison for Cliff Jackson's Krazy Kats, q.v.

                         <u>TWELVE RHYTHM MONARCHS</u>

Pseudonym on Sterno and 4-in-1 for Ray Starita and his Ambassadors, q.v., and for
    other bands on these labels of no known jazz interest.

Pseudonym on Challenge 257 for Gowans' Rhapsody Makers, q.v.

## TWIN CITY BELL HOPS

Pseudonym on Champion for the following items listed in this book :-

15174  Ain't I Got Rosie ? (Johnny Clesi's Oriolians)
15174  No-One But You (Johnny Sylvester and his Orchestra)

## TWIN CITY DANCE ORCHESTRA

Pseudonym on Challenge 148 for the Vagabonds, q.v.

## THE TWO OF SPADES

Herbert Leonard-h/Harry Mays-bj-u.      New York, March 25, 1925.

140462-1  Meddlin' With The Blues          Col 14072-D
140463-2  Harmonica Blues                  -

## WILLIE TYSON

Piano solos.                          Dallas, December 5, 1927.

145332-1-2  Roberta Blues                Col rejected
145333-1-2  Missouri Blues               -

## CHARLES AND EFFIE TYUS

Vocal duets, acc. by Clarence Williams-p. New York, February 25-26, 1924.

72345-A  Jazz Crazy                       OK 8133
72346-A  Omaha Blues                      -

                                       New York, c. June 22, 1924.

72617-A  I Want To Go Back To The Farm    OK 8149
72618-B  You've Got To Prove It To Me     -

CHARLES TYUS : Acc. by Effie Tyus-p.     New York, c. July 14, 1924.

72666-A  You've Got To Recognize Me       OK 8330

Vocal duets, acc. by Effie Tyus-p.       New York, c. September 9, 1924.

72795-   Good Old Bygone Days             OK 8330

Acc. by Clarence Williams' Trio : ? Ernest Elliott-cl/Clarence Williams-p/? Buddy Christian-bj.              New York, c. January 18, 1925.

73113-A  I'm Funny 'Bout My Cookin', Baby  OK 8200
73114-A  Cuddle Up Close, It's Winter Time -

Acc. by t/p.                          New York, March 29, 1927.

80680-A    Alibi-ing Papa               OK 8459
80681-A-B  The Latest Fad               Rejected
80682-B    Sweet Mama Goodie            OK 8459
80683-A-B  What Am You Waitin' On ?     Rejected

TYUS AND TYUS : Vocal duets, acc. c/p.   New York, August 31, 1931.

151757-1  You Make Me Laugh              Col 14638-D
151758-1  Dad's Ole Mule                 -

See also Horace George.

See the Bay State Dance Orchestra.

## UKULELE IKE

See Cliff Edwards.

## JIMMY UNDERWOOD AND HIS ORCHESTRA

See Joe Haymes and his Orchestra.

## SUGAR UNDERWOOD

Piano solos.                          Savannah, August 23, 1927.

39835-2  Davis Street Blues              Vic 21538, Bm 1006
39836-1  Dew Drop Alley Stomp                -           -     -

## UNITED STATES MARINE BAND

The following are remarkable examples of early ragtime recording, the more so since
they are played by an organization not normally associated with syncopated music
as revolutionary as this !

Lieut. William H. Santelmann dir. conventional military band with unidentifiable
numbers of c/tb/ah/th/bh/f/pic/cl/bb/d; included are Frank Badollet-f and Jean
Moeremans-as, at least on the first four sessions.
                                  Washington, D. C., September 17, 1899.

0506    Hot Stuff - A Negro Oddity           Ber 0506

                                  Washington, D. C., September 18, 1899.

0520    You Got To Play Ragtime (Jean C. Havez - Ber 0520
          A. Baldwin Sloane)

                                  Washington, D. C., October 15, 1906.

3887-2  Maple Leaf Rag (Scott Joplin)         Vic 4911

                                  Washington, D. C., February 18, 1909.

3887-3  Maple Leaf Rag (Scott Joplin)         Vic 16792

William H. Reitz-d-x featured.      New York, March 22, 1914.

14611-1  Crazy Bone Rag (Charles L. Johnson)    Vic 35380

## UNITED STATES NAVAL RESERVE BAND

The same remarks apply here as to the previous chapter.
                              New York, July 1, 1918.

77934-1  A Slippery Place - Comic Rag (Hacker)    Col A-2627, Re G-7795

## UNIVERSAL DANCE ORCHESTRA

Red Nichols-t/? Joe Venuti-vn/p/bj/? Vic Berton-d.
                                New York, c. December, 1926.

2327-B  Pepper Blues                       Mad 1620

## UNIVERSAL SEXTET

Pseudonym on Lincoln 2417 for the Varsity Eight, q.v.

## UNIVERSITY EIGHT

The more regular pseudonym on Lincoln for the Varsity Eight, q.v.

The predecessor of Gene Fosdick's Hoosiers, q.v., but of no interest as jazz.

## UNIVERSITY ORCHESTRA

See Sam Lanin; there may be other titles under this name on Gennett containing short
  "hot" solos by various Lanin sidemen of the period (1929-1930).

## UNIVERSITY SEXTETTE

Pseudonym on Lincoln for the Varsity Eight, q.v.

## UNIVERSITY SIX

Chelsea Quealey-t/Bobby Davis-cl-ss-as/Sam Ruby-ts/Adrian Rollini-bsx-gfs/Irving
  Brodsky-p-a/Tommy Felline-bj/Stan King-d-k/Arthur Hall-v.
                                         New York, September 18, 1925.

| | | | |
|---|---|---|---|
| 140961-3 | Desdemona | Har 37-H | |
| 140962-3 | The Camel Walk | Har 36-H | |
| 140963-2 | She Was Just A Sailor's Sweetheart - vAH | - | Re G-8517 |

NOTE:- Regal G-8517 as CORONA DANCE ORCHESTRA.

                                         New York, November 24, 1925.

| | | | |
|---|---|---|---|
| 141304-2 | Fallin' Down | Har 106-H | |
| 141305-3 | Smile A Little Bit | Har 71-H | |
| 141306-1 | Then I'll Be Happy | - | Re G-8561 |

NOTE:- Regal G-8561 as CORONA DANCE ORCHESTRA.

Abe Lincoln-tb added; Ruby omitted; "incidental singing by the orchestra" (sic).
                                         New York, December 1, 1925.

| | | |
|---|---|---|
| 141339-2 | In Your Green Hat - vO | Har 73-H |
| 141340-3 | Dustin' The Donkey | Har 134-H |
| 141341-2 | I Love My Baby | Har 73-H |

Lincoln omitted; Arthur Fields-v.      New York, March 23, 1926.

| | | |
|---|---|---|
| 141838-3 | Georgianna - vAF | Har 155-H, Re G-8659 |
| 141839-3 | What A Man ! - vAF | Har 160-H, Re G-8643 |
| 141840-2 | Sittin' Around | - |

NOTE:- Regal G-8643 and G-8659 as CORONA DANCE ORCHESTRA.

Tommy Dorsey-tb added; Herb Weil-d-k replaces King.
                                         New York, May 12, 1926.

| | | |
|---|---|---|
| 142195-2-3 | Tiger Rag | Har 224-H |
| 142196-2-3 | San | - |
| 142197-2-3 | Ace In The Hole | Har 209-H |

                                         New York, August 2, 1926.

| | | |
|---|---|---|
| 142490-3 | St. Louis Hop | Har 245-H |
| 142491-3 | Oh ! If I Only Had You | Har 230-H |
| 142492-2 | I Ain't Got Nobody | - |

                                         New York, September 22, 1926.

| | | |
|---|---|---|
| 142678-3 | That's A Good Girl | Har 262-H |
| 142679-2 | Give Me A Ukulele And A Ukulele Baby | - |
| 142680-2 | Wait'll You See (My Brand New Mama) | Har 316-H |

                                         New York, November 1, 1926.

| | | |
|---|---|---|
| 142899-3 | My Baby Knows How - vAF | Har 296-H |
| 142900-2 | It Takes A Good Woman (To Keep A Good Man At Home) - vAF | Har 316-H |
| 142901-2 | Lonely Eyes | Har 296-H |

Chelsea Quealey-t/Tommy Dorsey-tb,/Bobby Davis-cl-ss-as/Adrian Rollini-bsx-gfs/Irving
  Brodsky-p-a/Tommy Felline-bj/Herb Weil-d-k/Hal White-Arthur Fields-v.
                                    New York, December 27, 1926.

143220-1-2-3  Nobody But My Baby Is Getting My      Rejected
              Love
143221-1  I Wish I Could Shimmy Like My Sister      Har 414-H
              Kate
143222-3  Beale Street Blues                        -

                                    New York, February 7, 1927.

143446-2  Nobody But (My Baby Is Getting My Love)   Har 382-H
              - vHW
143447-3  Oh Lizzie - vHW                           Har 367-H
143448-3  The Cat                                   -
143449-2  It's O.K., Katy, With Me - vHW            Har 382-H

    Dorsey omitted; Sam Ruby-ts added.    New York, April 12, 1927.

144021-2  So Long, Pal - vAF                        Har 399-H
144022-2  Rosy Cheeks - vHW                         -
144023-1  Yes She Do - No She Don't - vHW           Har 425-H

    Rollini db x*.                      New York, May 25, 1927.

144223-3  Slow River - vAF                          Har 433-H
144224-2  *She's Got "It" ! - vAF                   Har 425-H
144225-4  Lazy Weather - vAF                        Har 433-H

                                    New York, June 9, 1927.

144264-2  Bless Her Little Heart - vAF              Har 444-H
144265-2  Ain't That A Grand And Glorious Feeling ?-vAF-

                                    New York, July 20, 1927.

144472-2  *Roam On My Little Gypsy Sweetheart - v   Har 466-H
144473-1  Pastafazoola - v2                         Har 474-H
144474-1  *Swanee Shore                             Har 466-H

                                    New York, August 31, 1927.

144609-1  Who's That Knockin' At My Door ? - vAF    Har 489-H
144612-1  Oh, Doris ! Where Do You Live ? - vAF     -
144613-2  Zulu Wail                                 Har 510-H

Chelsea Quealey-t/? Frank Ferretti-tb/Pete Pumiglio-? Carl Orech or Harold Marcus-cl
  as/Sam Ruby-ts/Spencer Clark-bsx/Jack Russin-p/Tommy Felline-bj/Herb Weil-d-k/
  Arthur Fields-v.                    New York, October 17, 1927.

144877-3  Is She My Girl Friend ? (How-De-Ow-Dow)   Har 534-H
              - vAF
144878-2  The Beggar - vAF                          -
144879-2  Manhattan Mary - vAF                      Har 529-H

                                    New York, November 30, 1927.

145258-2  There's Something Spanish In Your Eyes    Har 551-H
              - vAF
145259-1  Tell Me, Little Daisy - vAF               Har 557-H
145260-2  Changes - vAF                             Har 551-H

    Frank Cush-t replaces Quealey; ? Carl Loeffler-tb replaces ? Ferretti; 2nd cl-as
    omitted.                          New York, December 31, 1927.

145454-1  When You're With Somebody Else - vAF      Har 565-H
145455-2  Mine - All Mine - vAF                     -
145456-2  Under The Clover Moon - vAF               Har 570-H

Frank Cush-t/? Carl Loeffler-tb/Pete Pumiglio-cl-as/Sam Ruby-ts/Spencer Clark-bsx/
   Jack Russin-p/Tommy Felline-bj/Herb Weil-d/Jane Gray-Dolly Kay-v.
                                            New York, January 24, 1928.

145567-1  What Do You Say ? - vJG                    Har 591-H
145568-2  You Gotta Be Good To Me - vJG                 -
145569-2  The Grass Grows Greener ('Way Down Home) Har 581-H
            - vDK
145570-3  Let A Smile Be Your Umbrella (On A Rainy      -
            Day) - vDK

Cliff Weston-t/Carl Loeffler-tb/Pete Pumiglio-cl-as/Spencer Clark-bsx/Chauncey Gray-
   p/Herb Weil-d/Arthur Fields-v.         New York, March 5, 1928.

145731-2  Stay Out Of The South - vAF                  Har 617-H
145732-2  Lila - vAF                                      -
145733-1  The Pay-Off                                  Har 651-H

     Jack Kaufman-v.                      New York, March 16, 1928.

145772-2  Speedy Boy - vJK                             Har 619-H
145773-1  She's The Sweetheart Of Six Other Guys-vJK    -
145774-1-2  Hot Time In The Old Town Tonight - vJK Rejected
145775-1-2-3  Yip-I-Addy-I-Ay ! - vJK                    -

Cliff Weston-? Fred van Eps, Jr.-t/Pete Pumiglio or Carl Orech-cl-ss-as/Spencer
   Clark-bsx/? Jack Russin-p-? cel/Herb Weil-d/Arthur Fields-v.
                                            New York, May 16, 1928.

146300-1  My Pet - vAF                                 Har 651-H
146301-3  Chilly-Pom-Pom-Pee - vAF                     Har 652-H
146302-2  C-O-N-S-T-A-N-T-I-N-O-P-L-E (6/8)-vAF        Har 653-H
   NOTE:- Both sides of Harmony 651-H as THE WESTERNERS.  The University marching
   songs, issued on Harmony and associated labels as by the University Six, are by a
   different band of no interest,  See also the Varsity Eight, and Annette Hanshaw.

## THE UP AND DOWN PRESTIDIGITATORS

Pseudonym on XX 5 for Preston Jackson's Uptown Band, q.v.

## THE  VAGABONDS

Frank Cush-Bill Moore-t/Lloyd "Ole" Olsen-tb/Bobby Davis-Arnold Brilhart-cl-ss-as/
   Freddy Cusick-ts/Adrian Rollini-bsx/Irving Brodsky-p-a/Ray Kitchingman-bj/Stan .
   King-d/Lewis James-v.                  New York, October 26, 1923.

8579-A-B  Rememb'ring - vLJ                   Gnt 5288, St 9464
8580-A-B  Sweet Butter                        Gnt 5291, St 9471
8581-A-B  Sittin' In A Corner                    -       St 9465
   NOTE:- Gennett 5288 and Starr 9464 as CALIFORNIA WANDERERS.

                                            New York, January 21, 1924.

8711    Cover Me Up With The Sunshine Of      Gnt 5362, St 9509
            Virginia
8712-A  Tripping Along (With You And Me)      St 9513
8713, -A  California, Here I Come             Gnt 5362, St 9509
   NOTE:- Starr 9513 as CALIFORNIA WANDERERS.

Vernon Dalhart-v.                           New York, May 1, 1924.

8856-A  Jealous                               Gnt 5447, St 9547
8857    From One Till Two - vVD               Gnt 5448    -
8858-A  Don't Mind The Rain                      -       St 9548
8859-A  Shine                                 Gnt 5447, Cx 40331, St 9564
   NOTE:- Claxtonola 40331 as DIXIE BOYS.

Frank Cush-Bill Moore-t/Lloyd "Ole" Olsen-tb/Bobby Davis-Arnold Brilhart-cl-ss-as/
 Freddy Cusick-ts/Adrian Rollini-bsx/Irving Brodsky-p-a/Ray Kitchingman-bj/Stan
 King-d.                                New York, June 6, 1924.

8912-A  Where Is That Old Girl Of Mine ?     Gnt 5529, St 9566, EBW 4121
8913    Where The Dreamy Wabash Flows         Gnt 5485        -
8914    Please                                       -      St 9563
NOTE:- Edison Bell Winner 4121 as REGENT ORCHESTRA.

                                       New York, July 1, 1924.

8972-A  I Wonder What's Become Of Sally ?     Gnt 5501, St 9579
8973    Nobody's Child                            -         -

                                       New York, July 9, 1924.

8996-A  You Know Me, Alabam'                  Gnt 5504, St 9582
8997, -A  Knock At The Door                   Gnt 5502, Cx 40342, St 9571
8998    Louise                                    -         -         -
8999    Put Away A Little Ray Of Golden Sunshine Gnt 5505
           (For A Rainy Day)
NOTE:- Gennett 5505 as PAUL SANDERSON AND HIS ORCHESTRA; Claxtonola 40342 as DIXIE
BOYS.

Vernon Dalhart-v.                       New York, August 21, 1924.

9049-A  Sing A Little Song - vVD             Gnt 5529, St 9594
9050    Rock-a-Bye My Baby Blues (w)         Gnt 5527, St 9593
9051-A  Kiss Me Goodnight                    Gnt     -
NOTE:- Gennett 5527 and Starr 9593 as PAUL SANDERSON AND HIS ORCHESTRA.

                                       New York, September 11, 1924.

9073-A  I Want To Be Happy                   Gnt 5539, Cx 40373, EBW 4174
9074    Dreary Weather                          -         -      EBW 4127
9075    Rose Marie                           Gnt 5540, EBW 4188
NOTE:- Claxtonola 40373 as DIXIE BOYS; Edison Bell Winner 4127 and 4188 as REGENT
ORCHESTRA; 4174 as PAVILION PLAYERS.

                                       New York, October 14, 1924.

9121    Nancy                                Gnt 5568
9122    Back Where The Daffodils Grow        Rejected
9123    I Don't Know Why                     Gnt 5568

                                       New York, October 20, 1924.

9137    Dreamer Of Dreams (w)                Rejected
9138    Lovelight                               --
9139    Southern Rose                        St 9606

Tommy Felline-bj replaces Kitchingman; the Tremaine Brothers-v.
                                       New York, November 17, 1924.

9199    On The Wings Of Love                 Gnt 5596
9200    You're Just A Flower From An Old Bouquet-vTB  -
9201-A  Back Where The Daffodils Grow        Gnt 5602, Cx 40397
NOTE:- Gennett 5596 as PAUL SANDERSON AND HIS ORCHESTRA; Claxtonola 40397 as DIXIE
BOYS.

                                       New York, December 4, 1924.

9215-A  Somebody Like You                    Gnt 5630, Cx 40412
9216    I Can't Stop Babying You                -         -
9217    Sweetheart Days - vTB                Gnt 5610
NOTE:- Gennett 5610 as PAUL SANDERSON AND HIS ORCHESTRA; Claxtonola 40412 as DIXIE
BOYS.

Chelsea Quealey-Frank Cush-t/Abe Lincoln-tb/Bobby Davis-Arnold Brilhart-cl-ss-as/Sam
Ruby-ts/Adrian Rollini-bsx/Irving Brodsky-p-a/Tommy Felline-bj/Stan King-d/Arthur
Hall-v.                                    New York, July 10, 1925.

| | | |
|---|---|---|
| 9654 | Silver Head - vAH | Gnt 3096, Ch 15009 |
| 9655 | I'm Gonna Charleston Back To Charleston | Gnt 3099, Ch 15001 |
| 9656-A | Ukulele Lady | Gnt 3100, Ch 15002 |

NOTE:- Champion 15001, 15002 and 15009 as THE DIXIE BOYS.

New York, August 18, 1925.

| | | |
|---|---|---|
| 9694 | Normandy | Gnt 3128, Ch 15012 |
| 9695 | Sweet Man | Gnt 3137, Ch 15021, Sil 4004 |
| 9696 | My Sweetie Turned Me Down | - - - |

NOTE:- Champion 15012 and 15021 as THE DIXIE BOYS.

Arthur Fields-v.                                    New York, March 19, 1926.

| | | |
|---|---|---|
| X-43-A | Gimme A Li'l Kiss, Will Ya, Huh ? - vAF | Gnt 3282, Ch 15078, Aco G-16011, Clm 1906, Gmn 1961 |
| X-44-A | Could I ? - I Certainly Could - vAF | Gnt 3282, Buddy 8008, Ch 15080, Chg 148, Clm 1906, Gmn 1939 |
| X-45 | I'd Climb The Highest Mountain | Gnt 3283, Clm 1921 |
| X-45-A | I'd Climb The Highest Mountain | Ch 15079 |

NOTE:- Buddy 8008 as BIRMINGHAM RED JACKETS; Challenge 148 as TWIN CITY DANCE
ORCHESTRA; Champion 15078 and 15079 as TRI-STATE DANCE RAMBLERS; 15080 as HICKORY
KNOLL PAVILION KINGS; Coliseum 1906 and 1921 as MARYLAND DANCE ORCHESTRA; Guards-
man 1939 as SAN FRANCISCO DANCE ORCHESTRA; 1961 as CARNIVAL DANCE BAND.

Tommy Dorsey-tb replaces Lincoln.         New York, August 13, 1926.

| | | |
|---|---|---|
| X-227 | Looking At The World Thru' Rose-Colored Glasses - vAF | Gnt 3362, Buddy 8068, Ch 15134, Chg 126, Aco G-16120, Bel 1133, Clm 1950 |
| X-228-A | On The Riviera - vAF | Buddy 8068, Chg 125 |
| X-228-B | On The Riviera - vAF | Gnt 3361, Ch 15134, Aco G-16120, Bel 1113, Clm 1950, Gmn 1984 |
| X-229 | The Birth Of The Blues | Gnt 3361 |

NOTE:- Buddy 8068 as MEMPHIS MELODY BOYS; Challenge 125 and 126 as GOLDEN GATE
SERENADERS; Champion 15134 as THE DIXIE PLAYERS; Aco G-16120 as OHIO NOVELTY BAND;
Coliseum 1950 as MAYFIELD DANCE ORCHESTRA; Guardsman 1984 as CARNIVAL DANCE BAND.

Ed Kirkeby-v.                                    New York, May 2, 1927.

| | | |
|---|---|---|
| GEX-635-B | I'm Back In Love Again | Gnt 6140, Ch 15293, GS 40108 |
| GEX-636-A | Yes She Do - No She Don't - vEK | Gnt 6172, Ch 15290, Gmn 2110, Aco GA-20014 |
| GEX-637-A | S-L-U-E Foot | Gnt 6170, Ch 15322, Aco GA-20026 |

NOTE:- Gennett 6140, 6170 and 6172 as CALIFORNIA VAGABONDS; Champion 15290, 15293
and 15322 as GORDON GRIMES AND HIS ORCHESTRA; Aco GA-20014 and GA-20026 as FRISCO
SYNCOPATORS; Guardsman 2110 as ROVERS DANCE BAND.

The remaining four sessions are by bands drawn from the following collective personnel :-

Angie Rattiner-Mickey Bloom-Fred van Eps, Jr.-Al King-Frank Cush-t/Tommy Dorsey-Ted
Raph-Frank Ferretti-tb/Pete Pumiglio-Carl Orech-Harold Marcus-cl-as/Sam Ruby-ts/
Spencer Clark-bsx/Larry Kosky-Joe LaFaro-Al Duffy-vn (when used)/Chauncey Gray-
Jack Russin-p/Tommy Felline-bj-g/Herb Weil-Stan King-Chick Condon-d/Happy Blake-
Elliott Stewart-Jud Brown-Jerry White-Al King-Joe Griffith-Al Lynch-v.
                                    New York, February 8, 1928.

| | | |
|---|---|---|
| GEX-1064-A | You Gotta Be Good To Me - vHB | Gnt 6398, Chg 334 |
| GEX-1065, -A-B | In The Sing-Song Sycamore Tree-vES | Rejected |
| GEX-1066, -A | Sunshine - vES | - |

For collective personnel for the following three sessions, see p. 1583.
                              New York, March 23, 1928.

GEX-1146-A  In The Sing-Song Sycamore Tree - vJB   Bell 595, Ch 15456
GEX-1147    Waitin' For Katy - vJB                 Gnt 6426, Bell 589, Spr 355
GEX-1148    Say "Yes" Today - vJB                       -    Bell 591, Spr 359
GEX-1149    Collegianna - vJB                      Bell 592, Spr 357
  NOTE:- Gennett 6426 as CALIFORNIA VAGABONDS; Champion 15456 as GORDON GRIMES AND
  HIS ORCHESTRA.

                              New York, May 13, 1928.

GEX-1247-A  After My Laughter Came Tears - vJW     Sil 8063, Spt 9000
GEX-1248    Dolores - vJW                               -          Ch 15496
GEX-1249-A  Oh ! Baby - vJW                        Gnt 6487, Ch 15495, Sil 8068
GEX-1250-A  Did You Mean It ? - vAK-JG             Sil 8053, Spt 9004
  NOTE:- Champion 15495 and 15496 as GORDON GRIMES AND HIS ORCHESTRA.  This session
  is entered in the Gennett files as by the Golden Gate Serenaders, to which it was
  changed from California Vagabonds and California Ramblers, and under which Gennett
  6487 was issued !

                              New York, May 22, 1928.

GEX-1322    Girl Of My Dreams (w) - vJG            Gnt 6490, Sil 8053, Spt 9004
GEX-1323-A  He's Worth His Weight In Gold - vAL    Gnt 6488, Sil 8068
  NOTE:- Gennett 6488 and 6490 as GOLDEN GATE SERENADERS.
        The name THE VAGABONDS was also used on Cameo for straight dance bands of
        little or no interest as jazz.

                                  VALAIDA

Valaida Snow-t-v acc. by Billy Mason and his Orchestra : Billy Mason-p dir. Duncan
  Whyte-t/Harry Hayes-as/Buddy Featherstonhaugh-ts/Alan Ferguson-g/Sam Molyneux-sb/
  George Elrick-d.                       London, January 18, 1935.

CE-6799-1-2  Poor Butterfly                    Rejected
CE-6800-1    I Wish I Were Twins              Par F-118, A-6116, Od 194309,
                                                A-221890, 031374

                              London, January 19, 1935.

CE-6801-1    You Ain't Livin' Right           Rejected
CE-6802-1    I Can't Dance (I Got Ants In My Pants)  Par F-118, A-6116, Od 194309,
                                                A-221890, 031374

                              London, February 20, 1935.

CE-6861-1    It Had To Be You                 Par F-140, A-6158, Od A-221911
CE-6862-2    You Bring Out The Savage In Me      -        -        -

  Dave Shand-as replaces Hayes; Bill Busby-sb replaces Molyneux.
                              London, April 26, 1935.

CE-6948-1-3  Imagination                      Par F-230, A-6305, Od A-272045
CE-6949-1-3  Sing, You Sinners                   -        -        -
CE-6952-1    Whisper Sweet                    Par F-165, Od 194433, A-221942
CE-6953-1    Singin' In The Rain                 -        -        -
  NOTE:- Odeon A-272045 spells the artist's name VALEIDA.

  Acc. by Harry Owen-t/Freddy Gardner-cl-as-ts/George Scott Wood-p/Joe Young-g/Dick
  Escott-sb/Max Bacon-d.                 London, September 6, 1936.

CE-7819-1    Until The Real Thing Comes Along  Par F-559, Od OF-5260
CE-7820-1    High Hat, Trumpet And Rhythm       - A-6755 -

  Jock Fleming-tb added; Jock Jacobson-d replaces Bacon.
                              London, September 8, 1936.

CE-7826-1    I Want A Lot Of Love             Par F-575, A-6601, Od OF-5274
CE-7827-1    Take Care Of You For Me          Par F-657, A-6649, Od OF-5348

Acc. by Harry Owen-t/Jock Fleming-tb/Freddy Gardner-cl-as-ts/George Scott Wood-p/
Joe Young-g/Dick Escott-sb/Jock Jacobson-d.
                                        London, September 18, 1936.

| | | |
|---|---|---|
| CE-7834-1 | Lovable And Sweet | Par F-657, A-6649, Od OF-5348 |
| CE-7835-1 | I Must Have That Man | Par F-575, A-6601, Od OF-5274 |
| CE-7836-1 | You're Not The Kind | Par F-631, A-6623, Od OF-5328 |
| CE-7837-1 | You Let Me Down (Intro. How Can I Face | Par F-605, Od OF-5304, Sc 330 |
| | You ?) | |

                                        London, September 25, 1936.

| | | |
|---|---|---|
| CE-7838-2 | Mean To Me | Par F-631, A-6623, Od OF-5328 |
| CE-7839-2 | Dixie Lee | Par F-605, Od OF-5304, Sc 330 |

"With Swing Accompaniment" : Johnny Claes-t/Derek Neville-as-bar/Reg Dare-ts/Gunn
Finley-p/Norman Brown-g/Louis Barreiro-sb/Ken Stewart-d.
                                        London, July 7, 1937.

| | | |
|---|---|---|
| CE-8479-1 | The Mood That I'm In | Par F-867, A-6764, Od OF-5491 |
| CE-8480-1 | Sweet Heartache | - - - |
| CE-8481-1 | Don't Know If I'm Comin' Or Goin' | Par F-868, A-6765, Od OF-5492 |
| CE-8482-1 | Where Is The Sun ? | - - - |

                                        London, July 8, 1937.

| | | |
|---|---|---|
| CE-8486-1 | Some Of These Days | Par F-952, Od OF-5558 |
| CE-8487-1 | Chloe | Par F-1048 |
| CE-8488-1 | Swing Is The Thing | Par F-891, A-6790, Od OF-5514 |
| CE-8489-1 | Nagasaki | Par F-952, Od OF-5558 |

                                        London, July 9, 1937.

| | | |
|---|---|---|
| CE-8490-1 | I Wonder Who Made Rhythm ? | Par F-891, A-6790, Od OF-5514 |
| CE-8491-1 | I Got Rhythm | Par F-1048 |

                                        London, July 14, 1937.

| | | |
|---|---|---|
| CE-8492-1 | I Can't Believe That You're In Love | Par F-923, Od OF-5537 |
| | With Me | |
| CE-8493-1-3 | Tiger Rag | - - |

Acc. by Lulle Ellboj's Orchestra : Lulle Ellboj-as dir. Engt Artander-Gunnar Green
t/Sture Green-tb/Gunnar Wallberg-as/Rudolf Eriksson-ts/Willard Ringstrand-p/Karl
Lühr-g/Roland Bengtsson-sb/Olle Sahlin-d.
                                        Stockholm, August 28, 1939.

| | | |
|---|---|---|
| 4875-SEB | Minnie The Moocher - vch | Sonora 3577, Tono M-11104 |
| 4876-SEC | Caravan | Sonora 3557, 511 |
| 4877-SEB | Swing Low, Sweet Chariot | Sonora 3577, Dec 9112, JCB-4225, |
| | | Tono M-11104 |
| 4878-SEB | My Heart Belongs To Daddy | Sonora 3557, 511 -       - |

MISS VALAIDA MED WINSTRUP OLESENS SWINGBAND : Valaida Snow-t-v/Winstrup Olesen-t
dir. Kai Moeller-cl/Leo Mathiesen-p/Helge Jacobsen-g/Christian Jensen-sb/Kai
Fischer-d.                              Copenhagen, July 26, 1940.

| | | |
|---|---|---|
| 1062-B | You're Driving Me Crazy | Tono 21165, Ekko 280 |
| 1063-B | Take It Easy | -         - |
| 1064-A-B | I Can't Give You Anything But Love | Tono 21166, Ekko 281 |
| 1065-B | St. Louis Blues | -         - |

MISS VALAIDA MED MATADORERNE : Valaida Snow-t-v/Tage Rasmussen-t/Aage Voss-cl-as-
bar/Henry Hageman-Larsen-cl-ts/Bertrand Beck-p/Willy Sorensen-sb/Eric Kragh-d-vib.
                                        Copenhagen, c. October, 1940.

| | | |
|---|---|---|
| 1140-B | Some Of These Days | Tono 21194, Ekko 309 |
| 1141-B | Carry Me Back To Old Virginny | -         - |

Syd Valentine-t/Slick Helms-p/Paul George-bj.
Richmond, Ind., October 2, 1929.

15721-A  Jelly Bean Drag (Valentine Drag) (Jelly  Gnt 7071, Ch 15996, 40085*,
          Bean Rag*)                              Creole 21
15722-A  Asphalt Walk                             Gnt 7071, Ch 15883, Spr 2692,
                                                   Spt 9686
15723    Patent Leather Stomp                     Gnt 7026     -        -
15724-A  Rock And Gravel                                -  Ch 15996, 40085, Creole 21
NOTE:- Champion 15883, 15996, 40085 and Creole 21 as SKILLET DICK AND HIS FRYING
PANS; Superior 2692 as SLIM BARTLETT AND HIS ORCHESTRA; Supertone 9686 as SID
MOSLEY'S BLUE BOYS.

## RUDY VALLEE AND HIS  CONNECTICUT YANKEES

Neither Rudy Vallee nor his band are usually associated with anything like jazz, but
the following are rather exceptional.

Rudy Vallee-cl-as-v dir. Sammy Feinsmith-another-cl-as/Joe Miller-ts/Manny Lowy-
Jules de Vorzon-vn/Cliff Burwell and another-p/Charles Peterson-g/Harry Patent-sb/
Ray Toland-d.                        New York, October 27, 1930.

64323-5  She Loves Me Just The Same - vRV          Vic 22574

Probable additions : Harry Shilkret-Del Staigers-t/Chuck Campbell-tb/Lou Raderman-
vn.                                 New York, August 7, 1931.

70157-1  This Is The Missus - vRV                  Vic 22783, HMV B-6093

## VAN'S COLLEGIANS/VAN AND HIS HALF MOON HOTEL ORCHESTRA

See Peter Van Steeden.

## FRED VAN EPS

This famous American banjoist began his recording career on wax cylinders in 1897;
sixty years later, aged nearly 80, he made an LP ! The following items from his
colossal repertoire are likely to interest the ragtime collector.

Banjo solos, acc. by orchestra.         New York, c. 1910.

        Chatterbox Rag (George Botsford)         Zon 5828

Acc. by Felix Arndt-p.                  New York, January 31, 1911.

9876-1  Rag Pickings (arr. Fred van Eps)         Vic 16934, Zon 3931
9877-1  A Rag Time Episode (Paul Eno)            Vic 16845

Acc. by Charles A. Prince dir. probably :- Vincent C. Buono or Richard McCann-c/
Leo Zimmerman-tb/Thomas Hughes or George McNeice-cl/Marshall P. Lufsky-pic/Walter
Biedermann and/or George Stell-vn/bb.   New York, November 15, 1911.

19663-3  The White Wash Man (Jean Schwartz)       Col A-1118, Phoenix 087
NOTE:- Phoenix 087 as SAM VINCENT.

Acc. by Walter B. Rogers dir. probably :- Walter Pryor or Bert Brown-c/O. Edward
Wardwell-tb/A. Levy-cl/Darius Lyons-pic/Theodore Levy-Howard Rattay-vn/Herman
Comrad-bb/William H. Reitz-d.           New York, December 19, 1911.

11387-1  Red Pepper - A Spicy Rag (Henry Lodge)   Vic 17033

                                        New York, May 1, 1912.

11952-2  Black Diamond Rag (Henry Lodge)          Vic 17168

VAN EPS TRIO : Fred van Eps-William van Eps-bj/Felix Arndt-p.
                                        New York, July 26, 1912.

12238-2  Florida Rag (Lowry)                       Vic 17308

Banjo solos, acc. by Charles A. Prince dir. probably :- Vincent C. Buono-pr Richard
  McCann-c/Leo Zimmerman-tb/Thomas Hughes or George McNeice-cl/Marshall P. Lufsky-pic
  /Walter Biedermann and/or George Stell-vn/bb.
                                        New York, February 6, 1913.

38620-2  Whipped Cream (Percy Wenrich)              Phoenix 087
38620-3  Whipped Cream (Percy Wenrich)              Col A-1294
NOTE:- Phoenix 087 as SAM VINCENT.

                                        New York, September 6, 1913.

39007-4  Junk Man Rag (Old Clo' Man Rag*)         Col A-1417, Re G-6713*
             (C. Luckeyth Roberts)

VAN EPS TRIO : Fred van Eps-bj/Felix Arndt-p/Eddie King-d.
                                        New York, March 19, 1914.

14420-3  Notoriety Rag (K. L. Widner)             Vic 17601
14587-1  Too Much Ginger (Joseph M. Daly)         Vic 17575
14588-2  The Smiler - A Joplin Rag (Percy Wenrich)     -

VAN EPS BANJO ORCHESTRA : Fred van Eps-? William van Eps-bj/? Felix Arndt-p/Howard
  Kopp-d.                                New York, July 24, 1914.

39501-2  Thanks For The Lobster (Clarence M. Jones)Col A-1593, Re G-6892

VAN EPS TRIO : Fred van Eps-bj/Felix Arndt-p/William H. Reitz-d.
                                        New York, September 4, 1914.

15093-5  Old Folks Rag (Wilbur C. Sweatman)        Vic 35400

VAN EPS BANJO ORCHESTRA : As for July 24, 1914.
                                        New York, September 25, 1914.

37042-2  Old Folks Rag (Wilbur C. Sweatman)        Col A-5618

Banjo solos, acc. by orchestra.       New York, c. 1915.

65078    Florida Rag (Lowry)                       P 29030
         The Smiler Rag (Percy Wenrich)            P 29081, 5458
         The White Wash Man (Jean Schwartz)        P 29082, 10054
         A Rag Time Episode (Paul Eno)             P 29083

    Acc. by Charles A. Prince dir. similar orchestra to that of February 6, 1913 above.
                                        New York, March 25, 1916.

46663-3  Hill And Dale (Henry Lodge)               Col A-2034

    Acc. by Rosario Bourdon dir. probably 2c/tb/cl/f/2vn/bb/William H. Reitz-d.
                                        New York, June 1, 1916.

17673-4  Ragging The Scale (Ed Claypoole)          Vic 18085, HMV B-834, X-644

VAN EPS-BANTA DANCE ORCHESTRA : Nathan Glantz-as/Frank Banta-p/Fred van Eps-bj/d.
                                        New York, c. December, 1916.

         Pretty Baby (Tony Jackson)                P 20087
         Teasin' The Cat (Charles L. Johnson)          -
         Down Home Rag (Wilbur C. Sweatman)        P 20094, 70090

VAN EPS TRIO : Fred van Eps-bj/Frank Banta-p/William H. Reitz-d.
                                        New York, December 20, 1916.

18860-2  Teasin' The Cat (Charles L. Johnson)      Vic 18226

Banjo solo, acc. by the Boudini Brothers-pac.
                                        New York, c. June, 1918.

         Key To Key Rag                            Em 957

VAN EPS TRIO : Nathan Glantz-as/Frank Banta-p/Fred van Eps-bj.
                              New York, c. May, 1920.

21541-1  Palm Beach Rag (C. Luckeyth Roberts)     Md 701 (7"), Em 10206

William van Eps-bj replaces Glantz.     New York, September 22, 1920.

24291-3  A Bunch Of Rags (Vess L. Ossman)      Vic 16667, Zon 3791
NOTE:- This recording replaced Vess Ossman's own, issued under the same number.

                              New York, September 23, 1920.

24292-2  St. Louis Tickle (Barney - Seymore)     Vic 16092
NOTE:- This recording replaced the one by the Ossman-Dudley Trio, q.v., issued on
Victor 16092.  The above is labelled PLANTATION TRIO.

Banjo solos, acc. by Frank Banta-p.     New York, September 28, 1923.

70341     Grace And Beauty (James Scott)        PA 021088, 10716, P 1138,
                                                Per 11160, Sil 1228, GP 18224
70342     The Oriole (Ragtime Oriole) (James Scott)As above
NOTE:- Grand Pree 18224 as LEO WILMOTT.

Acc. by John F. Burckhardt-p.     New York, February 6, 1924.

9365      Ragtime Oriole (James Scott)      Ed 51324
9366      Grace And Beauty (James Scott)       -

                              New York, February 25, 1925.

10222     A Ragtime Episode (Paul Eno)      Ed 51514
10223     The Smiler (Percy Wenrich)          -        Amb 5182

## PAUL VAN LOAN AND HIS ORCHESTRA

Paul van Loan, one-time trombonist and arranger with Jean Goldkette's orchestra, made
   a numner of titles with his own band for Cameo during the mid-1920s.  The following
   are of some interest as "hot" dance music; the NEW YORK CLIPPER of February 22,
   1924, gives the following personnel, which is probably the same as or very similar
   to the one used on the records :- Paul van Loan-tb-a dir. Allen McAllister-George
   Hall-t/George Vaughn-Tom Kraus-Glen Wakeman-cl-ss-as-ts/Joe Cirina-p/Whitey Camp-
   bell-bj/Ed Grier-bb/George Sterinsky-d. New York, c. September 10, 1925.

1623-C  Deep Elm (You Tell 'Em I'm Blue)      Cam 820

Red Nichols-t allegedly featured.     New York, c. November 30, 1925.

1717-B  Cross My Heart, Mother, I Love You      Cam 853, Lin 2448
1718-C  Pretty Little Baby                      Cam 848, Lin 2450
1719-B  Heading For Louisville                    -
NOTE:- The last title is labeled CAMEO DANCE ORCHESTRA; Lincoln 2448 as THE CARO-
LINERS.

## AL VANN AND HIS GANG

Al Vann-v dir. unknown instrumentation and personnel.
                              Birmingham, Ala., c. July 15, 1927.

GEX-736   What Do We Do On A Dew-Dew-Dewy Day-vAV Gnt rejected
GEX-737   Birmingham Stomp                     -

## PETER  VAN STEEDEN

The following titles made under the direction of this popular-songwriter are of some
   interest as "hot" dance music.  He made a considerable number of others for Pathe,
   Gennett and Victor between 1926 and 1932, but those auditioned tend to justify the
   leader's reputation as leader of a "sweet society" orchestra.

VAN'S COLLEGIANS : Red Nichols-t/Miff Mole-tb/Bobby Davis-as/? Rube Bloom-p/? Eddie
   Lang-bj/? Joe Tarto-bb/Vic Berton-d.    New York, c. March 5, 1926.

106690    Jig Walk                              PA 36422, 11134, Per 14603
106691    Whose Who Are You ?                   PA 36432, Per 14613
   NOTE:- Pathe Actuelle 11134 as RED NICHOLS AND HIS ORCHESTRA.

VAN AND HIS HOTEL HALF MOON ORCHESTRA : Peter van Steeden-dir. Sylvester Ahola-Red
   Rehrig-t/Lou Lentz-tb/Norman Birseck-Freddy Cusick-cl-as/Art McKay-ts-bar/Sol
   Misheloff-vn/Dick Costello-p/Jimmy Smith-bj-g/Joe Schultz-bb/Ray Gunnerman-d.
                                               New York, August 9, 1927.

107718    Cornfed                               PA 36679, 11527, Per 14860

   Unknown t replaces Ahola; possibly other changes.  Scrappy Lambert-v.
                                               New York, c. December 12, 1927.

107961-1  Without You, Sweetheart - vSL         PA 36737, Per 14918, P-359
   NOTE:- Perfect P-359 as MEYER'S DANCE ORCHESTRA.

   Jerry White-v.                              New York, May 2, 1928.

GEX-1224    Louisiana - vJW                     Gnt 6472, Bell 615, Ch 15492,
                                                 Sil 8071
   NOTE:- Bell 615 and Silvertone 8071 as SHERMAN'S GLOBE-TROTTERS; Champion 15492 as
   BLUE MOON MELODY BOYS.

                                               New York, c. June 4, 1928.

GEX-1415    My Blue Ridge Mountain Home - vJW   Gnt 6629, Ch 15542, Sil 8062,
   NOTE:- Silvertone 8062 as VAN AND HIS ORCHESTRA. Spt 9014

                             LOUISE VANT

Vocal, acc. by ? Gus Aiken-c/Bud Aiken-tb/Dan Wilson-p.
                                               New York, December 4, 1925.

73811-B  Show Me The Way To Go Home             OK 8264
73812-A  Save Your Sorrow For Tomorrow            -

   Acc. by Perry Bradford's Mean Four : C/tb/? Perry Bradford-p/bj.
                                               New York, c. January 4, 1926.

73890-A  I'm Tired Of Everything But You        OK 8275
73891-A  I Wouldn't Be Where I Am If You Hadn't   -
           Gone Away
73892-B  Do Right Blues                         OK 8293

                                               New York, c. January 15, 1926.

73924-B  Just A Little Bit Bad                  OK 8281
73925-B  I've Learned To Do Without You Now     OK 8293
73926-A  Want A Little Lovin'                   OK 8281

   Acc. by Roy Banks-p.                        New York, c. March 16, 1926.

74051-A  The Man I Love Is Oh ! So Good To Me   OK 8341
74052-A  Daddy, Don't You Try To Pull That Two-Time  -
           Thing On Me

   Acc. by Perry Bradford's Mean Four : C/tb/cl/? Perry Bradford-p.
                                               New York, c. March 18, 1926.

74055-A  Pensacola Blues                        OK 8310
74056-A  New Crazy Blues                          -

There appear to be only four musicians on this session, but the instruments heard on each title suggest quite extensive doubling. All are credited to Sanford. Vocal by the Three Bits of Rhythm.           Chicago, March 15, 1941.

| | | |
|---|---|---|
| 93600-A | Uptown Jive - vTBR (cl/vn/g/sb) | Dec 8564 |
| 93601-A | Tack Annie (T/cl/ts/p/g/sb/vib) | Dec 8549 |
| 93602-A | Harlem Fiesta (Cl/ts/vn/p/g/sb/vib) | - |
| 93603-A | The Chant (Ts/vn/g/sb) | Dec 8564 |

## VARSITY EIGHT

Bill Moore-t/Lloyd "Ole" Olsen-tb/Bobby Davis and/or Jimmy Duff-cl-ss-as/Freddy Cusick-ts/Adrian Rollini-bsx-gfs/Irving Brodsky-p-a/Ray Kitchingman-bj/Stan King-d-k/v duet.                         New York, September 6, 1923.

| | | |
|---|---|---|
| 626-A-C | Last Night On The Back Porch - v2 | Cam 400, Lin 2093, Muse 353 |
| 627-B | Oh ! Joe | Cam 420, Lin 2105 |

NOTE:- Muse 353 as TREMONT DANCE ORCHESTRA.

Arnold Brilhart-cl-as replaces Duff.     New York, October 18, 1923.

| | | |
|---|---|---|
| 684-E | Mama Loves Papa (Papa Loves Mama) | Cam 426, Lin 2116 |
| 685-D | Easy Melody | Cam 445, Lin 2130 |

New York, November 22, 1923.

| | | |
|---|---|---|
| 726-D | Take, Oh Take Those Lips Away | Cam 444, Lin 2127 |

New York, December 12, 1923.

| | | |
|---|---|---|
| 757-A | Why Should I Weep About One Sweetie ? | Cam 456, Lin 2142 |
| 758-B-C | Shake Your Feet | Cam 454      - |

New York, January 9, 1924.

| | | |
|---|---|---|
| 784-A | Mean Blues | Cam 498, Lin 2168, Muse 426 |
| 785-B | Say It With A Ukulele | Cam 480, Lin 2154 |

NOTE:- Muse 426 as MUSE NOVELTY SEXTET.

Vocal chorus by the band.        New York, February 13, 1924.

| | | |
|---|---|---|
| 838-A | Hula Lou | Cam 505, Lin 2166 |
| 839-C | I Love The Girl Who Kisses - vV8 | Cam 507, Lin 2167, Pop 1012 |

NOTE:- Popular 1012 is anonymous.

New York, March 11, 1924.

| | | |
|---|---|---|
| 881-E | Why Did I Kiss That Girl ? | Cam 516, Lin 2176 |

New York, May 14, 1924

| | | |
|---|---|---|
| 995-B | Doodle Doo Doo | Cam 559, Lin 2208 |
| 1002-D | San | Cam 556     - |

New York, May 24, 1924.

| | | |
|---|---|---|
| 1009-G | You Know Me, Alabam' | Cam 567, Lin 2219 |

New York, June 10, 1924.

| | | |
|---|---|---|
| 1026-F | I Can't Get The One I Want | Cam 567, Lin 2231 |
| 1027-D | I Can't Find A Name Sweet Enough For You | Cam 580, Lin 2241, Tre 490 |

NOTE:- Tremont 490 as THE MUSICAL COMRADES.

New York, July 9, 1924.

| | | |
|---|---|---|
| 1038-A | Maytime | Cam 571, Lin 2216 |

Bill Moore-t/Lloyd "Ole" Olsen-tb/Bobby Davis and/or Arnold Brilhart-cl-ss-as/Freddy
  Cusick-ts/Adrian Rollini-bsx-gfs/Irving Brodsky-p-a/Ray Kitchingman-bj/Stan King-d
  k.                                     New York, July 29, 1924.

1066-A  Knock At The Door                    Cam 574, Lin 2242, Tre 491
1067-A  Charleston Cabin                     Cam 577, Lin 2229
NOTE:- Tremont 491 as THE MUSICAL COMRADES.

                                    New York, August 20, 1924.

1098-C  She Loves Me                         Cam 593, Lin 2245
1099-C  Hard Hearted Hannah                  Cam 588, Lin 2238

                                    New York, September 10, 1924.

1143-C  Them Ramblin' Blues                  Cam 605, Lin 2270
1144-C  A New Kind Of Man                    Cam 602, Lin 2256

                                    New York, October 3, 1924.

1168-A  No-One Knows What It's All About     Cam 606, Lin 2270
1169-C  Talkin' To Myself                    Cam 620, Lin 2264

                                    New York, October 22, 1924.

1186-C  Copenhagen                           Cam 622, Lin 2268, Tre 0515
1187-C  I'm Satisfied Beside That Sweetie O' Cam 632, Lin 2279
          Mine
NOTE:- Tremont 0515 as THE MUSICAL COMRADES.

                                    New York, October 29, 1924.

1194-A  Those Panama Mamas (Are Ruining Me)  Cam 635, Lin 2289
1197-C  Tea For Two                          Cam 617, Lin 2264, 2386
1201-B  Beets And Turnips                    Cam 640
NOTE:- Lincoln 2289 as THE CAROLINERS; 2386 as LINCOLN DANCE ORCHESTRA.

Tommy Felline-bj replaces Kitchingman.  New York, November 19, 1924.

1215-C  How I Love That Girl                 Cam 635
1216-A  Dear One                             Cam 633, Lin 2276
NOTE:- The latter title also appeared on an Australian label, Gibsona, without a
catalogue number, as WONDER SEXTETTE.  The label was merely pasted on a Lincoln
pressing imported from the U.S.A.

                                    New York, December 10, 1924.

1255-B  Doo Wacka Doo                        Cam 641, Lin 2288
1256-A  Oh ! Mabel                           Cam 646, Lin 2290
1257-B  Happy (Watchin' All The Clouds Roll By) Cam 641, Lin 2302

                                    New York, January 16, 1925.

1330-B  Ain't My Baby Grand ?                Cam 680, Lin 2307
1331-B  I Ain't Got Nobody To Love             -   Lin 2306

Tommy Dorsey-tb replaces Olsen.      New York, February 27, 1925.

1378-A-C  I Like Pie, I Like Cake - BUT I LIKE  Cam 695, Lin 2311
            YOU BEST OF ALL - v2
1379-B  Cheatin' On Me                       Cam 725, Lin 2337, Tre 0537
1380-B  No-One                               Cam 694, Lin 2315
NOTE:- Tremont 0537 as THE MUSICAL COMRADES.

Red Nichols-t replaces Moore.        New York, April 3, 1925.

1399-C  Don't Bring Lulu                     Cam 714, Lin 2330
1400-C  Nobody Knows What A Red Head Mama Can Do  -  Lin 2328, Tre 0526
1401-C  He's The Kind Of A Man That You Like Cam 711      -
          (If You Like That Kind Of A Man)

Red Nichols-t/Tommy Dorsey-tb/Bobby Davis--Arnold Brilhart-cl-ss-as/Freddy Cusick-ts/
   Adrian Rollini-bsx-gfs/Irving Brodsky-p-a/Tommy Felline-bj/Stan King-d-k.
                                        New York, April 28, 1925.

    1435-B  Sweet Georgia Brown                 Cam 730, Lin 2340
    1436-C  Lady Of The Nile                       -    Lin 2339
    1437-B  Ah-Ha !                             Cam 732, Lin 2343

                                        New York, May 13, 1925.

    1447-A-B  If You Knew Susie Like I Know Susie  Cam 724, Lin 2352, Tre 0544
    1448-C  Charleston                          Cam 741, Lin 2355
    NOTE:- Tremont 0544 as THE MUSICAL COMRADES.

    Vocal chorus by the band.          New York, June 4, 1925.

    1488-B  Moonlight And Roses                 Cam 753
    1489-A  Yes, Sir ! That's My Baby - vV8     Cam 750, Lin 2371

Chelsea Quealey-t/Abe Lincoln-tb/Bobby Davis-Arnold Brilhart-cl-ss-as/Sam Ruby-ts/
   Adrian Rollini-bsx-gfs/Irving Brodsky-p-a/Tommy Felline-bj/Stan King-d-k.
                                        New York, July 29, 1925.

    1540-A  Row, Row, Rosie !                   Cam 774
    1541-A  Oh, Say ! Can I See You Tonight ?   Cam 772, Lin 2380
    1542-C  I Want To See A Little More Of What I Saw   -    Lin 2382
              In Arkansas

                                        New York, September 12, 1925.

    1609-B  Fallin' Down                        Cam 782
    1610-C  Tryin' To Keep Away From You        Cam 780, Lin 2387
    1615-A  Sweet Man                           Cam 797, Lin 2403

                                        New York, October 20, 1925.

    1666-C  I'm Gonna Hang Around My Sugar      Cam 824
    1668-B  Milenberg Joys                      Cam 817, Lin 2417
    NOTE:- Lincoln 2417 as UNIVERSAL SEXTET.

                                        New York, November 23, 1925.

    1698-A  Freshie                             Cam 835, Lin 2441
    1699-A  Show Me The Way To Go Home - vV8    Cam 832, Lin 2435
    1700-C  She Doesn't                         Cam 837
    NOTE:- Lincoln 2435 as UNIVERSITY SEXTETTE.

    Red Nichols-t replaces Quealey.    New York, c. January 1, 1926.

    1778-B  T. N. T.                            Cam 870
    1779-A  In My Gondola - v                      -    Lin 2463

    Chelsea Quealey-t replaces Nichols.   New York, April 2, 1926.

    1900-B  What A Man !                        Cam 925, Lin 2517

    Herb Weil-d replaces King; Tommy Dorsey-tb replaces Lincoln.
                                        New York, June 11, 1926.

    2005-A-B-C  Static Strut                    Cam rejected
    2006-A-B-C  Ya Gotta Know How To Love         --
    2007-A-B-C  I'd Give A Lot Of Love            -

                                        New York, June 25, 1926.

    2005-F  Static Strut                        Cam 975, Lin 2557
    2006-E  Ya Gotta Know How To Love              -    Lin 2543
    2007-F  I'd Give A Lot Of Love              Cam 986
    NOTE:- Lincoln 2543 as UNIVERSITY EIGHT.

Chelsea Quealey-t/Tommy Dorsey-tb/Bobby Davis-Arnold Brilhart-cl-ss-as/Sam Ruby-ts/
  Adrian Rollini-bsx-gfs/Irving Brodsky-p-a/Tommy Felline-bj/Herb Weil-d.
                                    New York, September 24, 1926.

| | | |
|---|---|---|
| 2126-B | She Knows Her Onions - v | Cam 1020, Lin 2566, Ro 266 |
| 2127-B | Lay Me Down To Sleep In Carolina | Cam 1016, Lin 2578 |
| 2128-C-D | Precious - v | Cam 1017, Ro 273 |

NOTE:- Lincoln 2566 as UNIVERSITY EIGHT; 2578 as UNIVERSITY SEXTETTE; Romeo 266
and 273 as THE RAMBLERS.

                                    New York, November 3, 1926.

| | | |
|---|---|---|
| 2169-B | Susie's Feller | Cam 1040,   Ro 288, Vri 5003 |
| 2170-B | My Baby Knows How | Cam 1049 |

NOTE:- Mr. Ed Kirkeby's files show that a third side, FOR NO GOOD REASON AT ALL,
was scheduled to be made for Cameo at this session.  It does not appear to have
been issued anywhere, and we do not know what is on matrix 2171.  Romeo 288 as
THE RAMBLERS; Variety 5003 as THE CAMPUS OCTETTE.

Ed Kirkeby-v.                       New York, December 16, 1926.

2252-D  Lonely Eyes - vEK          Cam 1077, Lin 2598

Abe Lincoln-tb replaces Dorsey.    New York, February 3, 1927.

| | | |
|---|---|---|
| 2325-C | Ain't She Sweet ? - v | Cam 1114, Lin 2626, Ro 358 |
| 2326-D-E | Crazy Words - Crazy Tune - v | Cam 1110, Lin 2606, Ro 343 |

NOTE:- Lincoln 2606 and 2626 as UNIVERSITY EIGHT; Romeo 343 as DIXIE DAISIES, 358
as LYNN COWAN AND HIS BOULEVARD THEATRE ORCHESTRA.

Brilhart omitted; Jack Russin-p replaces Brodsky.
                                    New York, June 24, 1927.

| | | |
|---|---|---|
| 2521-A | Arkansas Blues | Cam 1209, Lin 2674, Ro 437 |
| 2523-C | Vo-Do-Do-De-O Blues | Cam 1232, Lin 2697, Ro 460 |

NOTE:- Lincoln 2674 as UNIVERSITY EIGHT; Romeo 437 as THE RAMBLERS.

                                    New York, September 8, 1927.

2596-D  Clementine (From New Orleans)    Cam 1245, Lin 2710, Ro 476
NOTE:- Even Lincoln 2710 is labeled VARSITY EIGHT !

Collective personnel :- Angie Rattiner-Al King-Mickey Bloom-Fred van Eps, Jr.-Frank
  Cush-t/Ted Raph-Tommy Dorsey-Frank Ferretti-Chuck Campbell-tb/Pete Pumiglio-Carl
  Orech-Harold Marcus-cl-as/Sam Ruby-ts/Spencer Clark-bsx/Chauncey Gray or Jack
  Russin-p/Tommy Felline-bj-g/Herb Weil or Chick Condon-d/Arthur Fields-v.
                                    New York, December 1, 1927.

| | | |
|---|---|---|
| 2715-C | Is She My Girl Friend ? (How-De-Ow-Dow) | Cam 1280, Lin 2745, Ro 514, |
| | - vAF | Ang 3008, Elec 5078, Mt 10011, |
| | | Pm 2546, Stg 1114 |
| 2717-C | I Wish I Could Shimmy Like My Sister | Cam 1280, Lin 2745, Ro 514 |
| | Kate | |

NOTE:- Electron 5078 as BROADWAY BROADCASTERS; Melotone 1011 as BRAYBROOK SOCIETY
ORCHESTRA; Sterling 1114 as RAY MILLER AND HIS BAND !

                                    New York, February 3, 1928.

| | | |
|---|---|---|
| 2857-C | Chicken Reel | Cam 8141, Lin 2795, Ro 564 |
| 2858 | Steamboat Bill - v | Cam 1266, 8155, Lin 2809, Ro 578 |
| 2859-C | Farewell Blues | Cam 8141, Lin 2795, Ro 564 |

The following, all credited to the Varsity Eight, are probably not by a personnel
drawn from the above, nor do they seem to have been made under Ed Kirkeby's
direction.  Irving Kaufman-v.       New York, c. April 17, 1928.

| | | |
|---|---|---|
| 3049 | On The Vagabond Trail | Cam 8209, Lin 2864, Ro 632 |
| 3050 | Mother (Who Can Be Sweeter Than You ?) | Cam 8210, Lin 2865, Ro 633 |
| | - vIK | |

See note on the last session (foot of p. 1593).
See note on the last session (foot of p. 1593).
                                        New York, June-July, 1929.

3958    What Do We Get From Boston ? - v        Cam 9233, Lin 3260, Ro 1035

The following Varsity Eight titles were directed by Ed Kirkeby, and seem to have
  been made by a group drawn from the collective personnel shown on page 1593, but
  with Jack Hansen-bb instead of Spencer Clark-bsx.
                                        New York, October 14, 1930.

10136-3  Never Swat A Fly - vV8              Cq 7646, Dom 4658, Je 6103,
                                             Or 2103, Per 15371, Re 10160,
                                             Ro 1468, Imp 2408, Ang 3288
10137-   Sweetheart Of My Student Days - v   Ban 0854, Cam 0454, Cq 7646,
                                             Je 6102, Or 2102, Per 15369,
                                             Re 10158, Ro 1466, Bellbird 337,
                                             Voc 368
10138-   Fraternity Blues - v                Dom 4660, Je 6105, Or 2105,
                                             Per 15370, Re 10159, Ro 1467

                                        New York, November 3, 1930.

10204-   Who's Calling You Sweetheart Tonight ?-v Dom 4680, Je 6129, Or 2129,
                                             Per 15378, Re 10185, Ro 1491
10205-   Toodle-Oo (I'll Be Seeing You) - v  Dom 4679, Je 6131, Or 2131,
                                             Per 15379, Re 10186, Ro 1492
10206-   (You Can Only Wear) One Pair Of Pants  Je 6138, Or 2138, Per 15389,
          At A Time - v                      Re 10195, Ro 1501

                                        New York, November 12, 1930.

10233-1-2  You're Driving Me Crazy (What Did     Ban 32105, Dom 4679, Je 6133,
            I Do ?) - v                       Or 2133, Per 15386, Re 10193,
                                             Ro 1499, Bellbird 330, Voc 759
10234-   When Kentucky Bids The World "Good   Dom 4680, Per 15409
          Morning" - v

                                        New York, May 8, 1931.

10614-1  Mickey Mouse (You Cute Little Feller)-v  Per 15473
10615-1  Popeye (The Sailor Man) - v                 -
10616-   I Wanna Sing About You - v           Per 15472
NOTE:- Perfect 15472 as EDDIE KIRKEBY AND HIS ORCHESTRA.

Unless otherwise noted, all Lincoln issues are credited to UNIVERSITY SEXTETTE.

## THE  VARSITY MEN

Pseudonym on Broadway 1234 for Bill Haid's Cubs, q.v.

## VARSITY  SEVEN

Benny Carter-t-as/Danny Polo-cl/Coleman Hawkins-ts/Joe Sullivan-p/Ulysses Livingston-
g-v/Artie Shapiro-sb/George Wettling-d/Jeanne Burns-v.
                                        New York, December 14, 1939.

US-1158-1  It's Tight Like That - vJB        Var 8147
US-1159-1  Easy Rider - vJB-UL                  -      Elite 5032
US-1160-1  Scratch My Back                   Var 8135
US-1161-1  Save It, Pretty Mama - vJB           -

Joe Turner-v.                           New York, January 15, 1940.

US-1284-1  How Long, How Long Blues - vJT    Var 8173, Elite 5032, Sav 649, 5044
US-1285-1  Shake It And Break It - vJT       Var 8179, Com 114       -       -
US-1286-1  A Pretty Girl Is Like A Melody       -
US-1287-1  Pom Pom                           Var 8173
  NOTE:- Elite 5032 as NEW ORLEANS SEVEN; Savoy 649 and 5044 as JOE TURNER AND HIS
  BAND.

Vocal, acc. by Richard M. Jones-p.        Richmond, Ind., May 31, 1923.

| 11488-B | I'm Lonesome, Nobody Cares For Me | Gnt 5173 |
| 11489-B | Maybe Someday | Gnt 5172 |
| 11490-B | All Night Blues | - |
| 11491-B | Original Stomps | Gnt 5173 |

## EDITH   VAUGHAN

Pseudonym on Oriole for Julia Moody, q.v.

## LA VEEDA DANCE ORCHESTRA

See Tony Parenti.

## JOHN   VENTRE

Trumpet solos, acc. by Rube Bloom-p.        New York, September 3, 1927.

| 81418-B | Hot Waves | Par R-3423 |
| 81419-B | Trick Fingering | - |

## RAY   VENTURA

Ray Ventura was the French opposite number to Britain's Jack Hylton in the opinion
of connoisseurs of European dance music.  His band made many sides in Paris and
London, those featuring artists of international reputation being shown below.

RAY VENTURA ET SES COLLEGIENS : Ray Ventura dir. Gaston Lapeyronnie-Ray Binder-
Philippe Montaigut-t/Robert de Gaille-tb/Danny Polo-cl-as-bar/John Arslanian-cl-as
/Jacques Bourgas Rosselli-Pierre Simon-cl-ts/Paul Misraki-Bob Vaz-p/Henri Guesde-g
/Roger Grasset-bb/Charlie Barnes (one side)-Krikor "Coco" Arslanian (other side)-d
(it is not known which side has which drummer).
                                        Paris, c. January, 1929.

| L-1317-1 | I'm Afraid Of You | Col D-19146 |
| L-1318-1 | Sweet Ella May | - |

Alex Renard-t replaces Lapeyronnie; Edoard S. Foy-cl-as-v replaces Arslanian, who
switches to cl-ts and replaces Rosselli; Rene Barry-cl-ts replaces Simon; Barnes
omitted; Krikor Arslanian-v.        Paris, February 23, 1929.

| KI-2214-2 | Let's Do It - vESF-JA-KA | Od 165529 |
| KI-2215-1-2 | You're The Cream In My Coffee - vKA | - |

Ray Ventura-p replaces Misraki; Gaston Lapeyronnie-t replaces (probably) Renard.
                                        Paris, March 19, 1929.

| KI-2262-2 | Makin' Whoopee ! - vKA | Od 165559, Par E-6209 |
| KI-2263-1 | If I Had You - vESF-JA-KA | - |

Serge Glykson-as replaces Polo; Spencer Clark-bsx added; Al Cazentre-v.
                                        Paris, May 16, 1929.

| KI-2385-1 | I Want To Be Bad - vESF | Od 165624 | |
| KI-2386-2 | Button Up Your Overcoat - vESF-JA-KA | - | Par E-6209 |
| KI-2387-2 | Lover, Come Back To Me - vAC | Od 165625 | |
| KI-2388-2 | Louise - vKA | - | |

Philippe Brun-t replaces Lapeyronnie or Montaigut; Stephane Mougin-p replaces
Ventura; Grace Edwards-v.        Paris, September 27, 1929.

| KI-2631-2 | You'll Want Me Back Again - vGE | Od 165775 |
| KI-2632-2 | I'm Doing What I'm Doing For Love - vGE | - |
| KI-2634-1 | Some Sweet Day - v3 | Od 165776 |

                                        Paris, October 19, 1929.

| KI-2677-2 | With A Song In My Heart - vAC | Od 165803, Par E-6270 |
| KI-2678-1 | Can't We Be Friends ? - vGE | - |

RAY VENTURA AND HIS ORCHESTRA : Ray Ventura dir. Philippe Brun-Gus Deloof-Andre
    Cornille-t/Guy Paquinet-Josse Breyere-tb/Max Blanc-John Arslanian-Andre Lluis-as/
    Alix Combelle-Adrien Mareze-ts/Bob Vaz-p/Django Reinhardt-g/Louis Vola-sb/Maurice
    Chaillou-d/Coco Aslan (formerly Krikor "Coco" Arslanian)-tymps-v/Andre Dassary-v.
                                        Paris, March 4, 1938.

CPT-3836-1  Un sourire en chantant - vAD           PA PA-1476
CPT-3837-1  Siffler en travaillant - vKA            -

    Reinhardt apparently omitted.          Paris, March 29, 1938.

CM-184-1  Bugle Call Rag                            PA PA-1582, Col FB-1989, DO-1897,
                                                   GN-5033
CM-185-1  After You've Gone - vAD                   As above
                           •

## JOE VENUTI

Joe Venuti-vn/Eddie Lang-g.               New York, September 29, 1926.

142697-1-2-3  Stringing The Blues                  Rejected
142698-2  Black And Blue Bottom                    Col 914-D, 4454, DB/MC-5001,
                                                   DO-2699, DQ-1322

                                          New York, October 22, 1926.

142697-4-5-6-7  Stringing The Blues                Col rejected

                                          New York, November 8, 1926.

142697-8  Stringing The Blues                      Col 914-D, DB/MC-5001, DO-2699,
                                                   DQ-1322
142697-11 Stringing The Blues                      Col 914-D, 4454

                                          New York, January 24, 1927.

80328-A  Wild Cat                                  OK 40762, Par R-3330
80329-A  Sunshine                                   -          -        R-2493

    Arthur Schutt-p added                 New York, May 4, 1927.

81058-B  Doin' Things                              OK 40825, Par R-3352, R-2632,
                                                   Od 193014, A-189219, A-221055
81059-B  Goin' Places                              As above

JOE VENUTI'S BLUE FOUR : Joe Venuti-vn/Adrian Rollini-bsx-hfp-gfs/Arthur Schutt-p/
    Eddie Lang-g.                         New York, June 28, 1927.

81118-B  Kickin' The Cat                           OK 40853, Par R-3367, R-2551,
                                                   Od 193066, A-189141
81119-C  Beatin' The Dog                           As above

                                          New York, September 13, 1927.

81432-C  Cheese And Crackers                       OK 40897, Par R-3442, A-2342,
                                                   Od 165195
81433-C  A Mug Of Ale                              As above, plus Par R-2581,
                                                   Od A-2340, 193104

    Joe Venuti-vn/Don Murray-cl-bar/Frank Signorelli-p/Eddie Lang-g/? Justin Ring-cym.
                                        New York, November 15, 1927.

81822-B  Penn Beach Blues                          OK 40947, Par R-109, Voc 3160,
                                                   Od 193122, A-189144
81823-C  Four String Joe                           As above, plus Par R-2581,
                                                   Od A-2340

JOE VENUTI'S BLUE FOUR : Joe Venuti-vn/Don Murray-bar/Rube Bloom-p/Eddie Lang-g.
New York, March 28, 1928.

400178-A  Dinah                              OK 41025, Par R-982, Od 165359,
                                             193173, A-286041
400179-A  The Wild Dog                       OK 41025, Par R-520, A-4966,
  NOTE:- Odeon A-286004 as O. K. RHYTHM KINGS.   B-27794, TT-9081, Od 165359,
                                             193173, A-2308, A-286004,
                                             B-35626, 031750

JOE VENUTI AND HIS NEW YORKERS : Leo McConville-Fuzzy Farrar-t/Charlie Butterfield-
  tb/Arnold Brilhart-Max Farley-as-f/Don Murray-cl-bar/Herb Spencer-ts/Joe Venuti-vn
  /Arthur Schutt-p-cel/Eddie Lang-g/Hank Stern-bb/Chauncey Morehouse-d/Scrappy
  Lambert-v.                                 New York, May 25, 1928.

400706-B  I Must Be Dreaming - vSL           OK 41051, Par R-182, Od 165357,
                                             193188, A-221101
400707-A  'Tain't So, Honey, 'Tain't So - vSL   As above

  Manny Klein-t replaces Farrar; Fud Livingston-cl-ts replaces Spencer; Billy
  Hillpot-Scrappy Lambert-v.                 New York, June 8, 1928.

400767-C  Because My Baby Don't Mean "Maybe" Now  OK 41056, Par R-201, A-2527,
          - vSL-BH                           Voc 3161, Od 165491, 193208,
                                             A-189154
400768-B  Just Like A Melody Out Of The Sky-vSL-BH As above
  NOTE:- Parlophone R-182 and R-201 as JOE VENUTI AND HIS CONCERT ORCHESTRA; A-2527
  as JOE VENUTI'S LARGE BAND.

JOE VENUTI'S BLUE FOUR : Joe Venuti-vn/Don Murray-bar/Rube Bloom-p-v/Eddie Lang-g/?
  Paul Graselli-d.                           New York, June 14, 1928.

400788-C  The Man From The South - vRB       OK 41076, Par R-607, A-2545,
                                             B-27794, TT-9081, Od 165496,
                                             193218, A-2309,A-189247,A-286011
400789-B  Pretty Trix                        OK 41076, Par R-1916, A-2545,
                                             Od 165496, 193218, A-189247

Joe Venuti-vn/Eddie Lang-g, acc. by Frank Signorelli-p.
New York, June 21, 1928.

45812-1  Doin' Things                        X LVA-3036, HMV 7EG-8109 (LP/EP)
45812-2  Doin' Things                        BB B-10280
45812-3  Doin' Things                        Vic 21561
45813-1  Wild Cat                            BB B-10280
45813-2  Wild Cat                            X LVA-3036, HMV 7EG-8109 (LP/EP)
45813-3  Wild Cat                            Vic 21561

JOE VENUTI AND HIS NEW YORKERS : Leo McConville and Manny Klein or Fuzzy Farrar-t/
  Charlie Butterfield-tb/Arnold Brilhart-Jimmy Dorsey-cl-as/Fud Livingston-ts/Joe
  Venuti-vn/Frank Signorelli-p-cel/Tony Colucci-bj/Eddie Lang-g/Joe Tarto-bb/
  Chauncey Morehouse-d/Scrappy Lambert-v. New York, July 24, 1928.

400884-C  Pickin' Cotton - vSL              OK 41087, Par R-309, A-2702,
                                             Od 193234, A-189191
400885-B  I'm On The Crest Of A Wave - vSL   As above, plus Ar 4363
  NOTE:- Parlophone R-309 as JOE VENUTI AND HIS CONCERT ORCHESTRA; A-2702 as LANG'S
  DANCE ORCHESTRA; Ariel 4363 as ARIEL DANCE ORCHESTRA.

JOE VENUTI'S BLUE FOUR : Joe Venuti-vn/Jimmy Dorsey-cl-as-bar/Rube Bloom-p-v/Eddie
  Lang-g/Paul Graselli-d.                    New York, September 27, 1928.

401159-A  The Blue Room - vRB                OK 41144, Voc 3011, Par R-1916,
                                             Od 165535, 193271
401160-A  Sensation - vRB                    OK 41144, Cl 5467-C, Har 1420-H,
  NOTE:- Clarion 5467-C, Harmony 1420-H and Velvet VT 2527-V, Par R-596, Od 193271,
  Tone 2527-V as ALL-STAR RHYTHM BOYS, vocal  A-2316, A-286010
  refrain by JERRY MILLS.

JOE VENUTI AND HIS NEW YORKERS : Leo McConville and Manny Klein or Fuzzy Farrar-t/
Tommy Dorsey-tb/Jimmy Dorsey-cl-as-bar/Arnold Brilhart-cl-as/Max Farley-cl-ts-f/
Joe Venuti-vn/Frank Signorelli-p/Eddie Lang-g/Joe Tarto-bb/Chauncey Morehouse-d-v.
New York, October 4, 1928.

401193-B  Doin' Things                         OK 41133, Od 165679, 193256,
                                               A-189219, A-221110
401194-B  I Must Have That Man - vCM           As above, plus Par R-280
NOTE:- Parlophone R-280 as ED LANG'S WONDER ORCHESTRA.

JOE VENUTI'S BLUE FOUR : Joe Venuti-vn/Jimmy Dorsey-t-bar/Rube Bloom-p-v/Eddie Lang-
g/Paul Graselli-d.                   New York, December 12, 1928.

401449-A  My Honey's Lovin' Arms - vRB         OK 41251, Od 165763, 193327
401450-A  Goin' Home - vRB                       - Voc 3043 -           -

JOE VENUTI AND HIS NEW YORKERS : Leo McConville-Fuzzy Farrar-t/Tommy Dorsey-tb/Jimmy
Dorsey-cl-as/Jimmy Crossan-as/Alfie Evans-ts/Joe Venuti-vn/Arthur Schutt-p/Eddie
Lang-g/Joe Tarto-bb/Chauncey Morehouse-d/Smith Ballew-v.
New York, February 2, 1929.

401534-C  That's The Good Old Sunny South - vSB   OK 41192, Par R-340, 22305,
                                                  Od 193295, A-189244, A-221111
401585-A  Weary River - vSB                       OK 41192, Par R-341, 22304,
                                                  Ar 4563, Od 193295, A-189244
NOTE;- Parlophone R-340 and R-341 as JOE VENUTI'S CONCERT ORCHESTRA; Ariel 4563 as
ARIEL DANCE ORCHESTRA.

? Phil Napoleon-t and Joe Raymond-vn added; Stan King-d replaces Morehouse; Tarto-
a; Crossan and Evans both db cl.      New York, May 1, 1929.

401846-B  I'm In Seventh Heaven - vSB          OK 41263, Par R-427, A-2947,
                                               B-12802, Od 165813, 193374,
                                               A-189265
401847-C  Little Pal - vSB                     As above, plus Ar 4452
NOTE:- Parlophone R-427 as JOE VENUTI'S CONCERT ORCHESTRA; Ariel 4452 as ARIEL
DANCE ORCHESTRA.

Andy Secrest-Charlie Margulis-Harry Goldfield-t/Bill Rank-tb/Izzy Friedman-cl-?ts/
Charles Strickfaden-as-bar/Rube Crozier-ts-o/Joe Venuti-vn/Lennie Hayton-p-cel/
Eddie Lang-g/Joe Tarto-bb-a/Stan King-d/Smith Ballew-v.
New York, October 16, 1929.

403071-C  Chant Of The Jungle - vSB            OK 41320, Par ONY-41320, R-608,
                                               A-2922, Od 193405, A-189293
403072-C  That Wonderful Something (Is Love)-vSB  As above, plus Ar 4530
NOTE:- Parlophone PNY-41320 as EDDIE GORDON AND HIS BAND; R-608 as JOE VENUTI'S
BLUE FOUR; Ariel 4530 as ARIEL DANCE ORCHESTRA.

JOE VENUTI'S BLUE FOUR : Joe Venuti-vn/Frank Trumbauer-Cm-bsn/Lennie Hayton-p/Eddie
Lang-g.                              New York, October 18, 1929.

403078-B  Runnin' Ragged (Bamboozlin' The Bassoon) OK 41361, Par R-531, 22875,
                                               B-27793, TT-9048, Od 193424,
                                               A-2308, A-286005
403079-B  Apple Blossoms                       OK 41361, Par R-647, Od 193424,
                                               A-286015, 028324

Joe Venuti-vn/Adrian Rollini-bsx-gfs-hfp/Itzy Riskin-p/Eddie Lang-g.
New York, May 7, 1930.

404005-C  Raggin' The Scale                    OK 41432, Cl 5474-C, Har 1427-H,
                                               VT 2534-V, Voc 3043, Par R-778,
                                               DP-205, Od 238122, A-286022
404006-A-C  Put And Take                       OK 41432, Par R-973, A-3358,
                                               Od 238122, A-2362, A-189635,
                                               A-286040
NOTE:- Clarion 5474-C, Harmony 1427-H and Velvet Tone 2534-V as TENNESSEE MUSIC
MEN.

JOE VENUTI AND HIS NEW YORKERS : Ray Lodwig-Manny Klein-t/Jack Teagarden-tb/Izzy
Friedman-cl/Arnold Brilhart-as/Bernie Daly-ts/Min Leibrook-bsx/Joe Venuti-vn/
Lennie Hayton-p/Eddie Lang-g/Herb Quigley-d-vib/Smith Ballew-v.
                              New York, May 22, 1930.

404032-B-C  Promises - vSB                      OK 41427, Od ONY-36098, 238153,
                                                Par PNY-34092, R-776
404033-A-C  Dancing With Tears In My Eyes - vSB  OK 41427, Od ONY-36098, 238153,
   NOTE:- Parlophone PNY-34091 and PNY-34092 as  Par PNY-34091, R-744, A-3064,
DICK RICHARDSON'S ORCHESTRA; Ariel 4652 as       Ar 4652
ARIEL DANCE ORCHESTRA.

   Charlie Margulis-Manny Klein-t/Tommy Dorsey-tb/Jimmy Dorsey-cl-as/as/ts/? Min
   Leibrook-bsx/Joe Venuti-vn/p/Eddie Lang-g/Joe Tarto-bb/Stan King-d/Scrappy
   Lambert-v.                      New York, September 6, 1930.

404431-C  I Am Only Human After All - vSL        OK 41451, Par PNY-34130,
                                                Od ONY-36138, 238229
404432-B  Out Of Breath (And Scared To Death     As above, but Par PNY-34129
            Of You) - vSL
   NOTE:- Parlophone PNY-34129 and PNY-34130 as DICK RICHARDSON'S ORCHESTRA.

JOE VENUTI AND HIS ORCHESTRA : Manny Klein-? Charlie Margulis-t/Glenn Miller-tb/
   Jimmy Dorsey-? Pete Pumiglio-cl-as/Fud Livingston-cl-ts/Joe Venuti-vn/Rube Bloom-
   p/Eddie Lang-g/Joe Tarto-sb/d/Irene Beasley-Frank Luther-v.
                              New York, September 30, 1930.

63682-2  Wasting My Love On You - vFL            Vic 23018, HMV K-6238
63683-2  My Man From Caroline - vIB              Vic 23015, HMV B-4890
63684-2  I Like A Little Girl Like That - vFL    -

JOE VENUTI'S BLUE FOUR : Joe Venuti-vn/Pete Pumiglio-cl-bar/Frank Signorelli-p/
   Eddie Lang-g/Henry Burbig-speech.    New York, October 7, 1930.

63700-1  The Wild Dog                            Vic 23021, HMV B-4840
64301-1  Really Blue                             -        HMV B-4866, B-6290
1022-1   Dialogue on William Tell - spHB         Vic trial

   Joe Venuti-vn/Jimmy Dorsey-cl-as-bar/Frank Signorelli-p/Eddie Lang-g/Joe Tarto-sb.
                              New York, November 12, 1930.

404549-B  I've Found A New Baby                  OK 41469, Par R-924, Od A-2362,
                                                A-286036, 028324
404550-C  Sweet Sue - Just You                   OK 41469, Par R-878, A-3340,
                                                Od A-2319, A-286032

   Tarto omitted; Harold Arlen-v.      New York, June 10, 1931.

404940-B  Pardon Me, Pretty Baby - vHA           OK 41506, Cl 5358-C, Har 1346-H,
                                                VT 2422-V, Par R-993, A-3268,
                                                85052, Od A-286043
404941-B  Little Girl - vHA                       Par R-1003, A-3588, 85052,
                                                Ar 4827, Od A-286044, OR-1003
151655-1  Little Girl - vHA                       Col 2488-D, DW-4102
404942-B  Little Buttercup (I'll Never Be The Same)OK 41506, Cl 5358-C, Har 1346-H,
                                                VT 2422-V, Par R-1252, A-3588,
                                                85076, Od A-286063, 031750
404943-B  Tempo di Modernage (Tempo di Barrel*)  Par R-1063*, 85076, Od A-286049
151656-1  Tempo di Modernage                      Col 2488-D, DW-4102
   NOTE:- Clarion 5358-C, Harmony 1346-H and Velvet Tone 2422-V as ALL-STAR RHYTHM
BOYS; Ariel 4827 as ARIEL DANCE ORCHESTRA. The Columbia issues are identical to
the corresponding titles on other makes, despite the differing take symbols.

JOE VENUTI'S RHYTHM BOYS : Joe Venuti-vn/Jimmy Dorsey-cl-as-bar/Lennie Hayton-p-cel/
   Eddie Lang-g/Paul Graselli-d/Harold Arlen-v. (Parlophone R-1071, R-1115, Odeons as
   JOE VENUTI'S BLUE FOUR).       New York, September 10, 1931.

151790-1  There's No Other Girl - vHA            Col 2535-D, Par R-1287, A-3463
151791-1  Now That I Need You, You're Gone - vHA  -        -
151792-1  The Wolf Wobble                        Col 2589-D, Par R-1071, A-3292,
                                                A-286051
151793-1  To To Blues                            Par R-1115, A-3292, Od A-286054

JOE VENUTI-EDDIE LANG AND THEIR ALL-STAR ORCHESTRA : Charlie Teagarden-t/Jack Tea-
garden-tb-v/Benny Goodman-cl/Joe Venuti-vn/Frank Signorelli-p/Eddie Lang-g/Ward
Lay-sb/Neil Marshall-d.                    New York, October 22, 1931.

| | | |
|---|---|---|
| E-37269-A | Beale Street Blues - vJT | Voc 15864, Mt M-12294, Polk P-9095, UHCA 108, Br X-15864, 80078, A-9915, A-86010, A-500161, Pan 25168, Mf G-2086, Dec F-5883 |
| E-37270-A | After You've Gone - vJT | As above, but UHCA 107 (coupling 108), Br 80077 and Dec F-5884 |
| E-37271-A | Farewell Blues | Voc 15858, Mt M-12277, UHCA 106, Br X-15858, 80077, A-9916, A-86011, A-500167, Pan 25151, Mf G-2071, Dec F-5884 |
| E-37272-A | Someday, Sweetheart | As above, but UHCA 105 (coupling 106), Br 80078 and Dec F-5883 |

NOTE:- Mayfair G-2071 and G-2086 as NEW YORK STOMPERS.

JOE VENUTI-EDDIE LANG BLUE FIVE : Joe Venuti-vn/Jimmy Dorsey-t-cl-as/Adrian Rollini-
bsx-gfs-p-vib/Phil Wall-p/Eddie Lang-g. New York, February 28, 1933.

| | | |
|---|---|---|
| 265066-2 | Raggin' The Scale | Col 2765-D,CB-612,DF-1263,DO-1036 |
| 265067-2 | Hey ! Young Fella | Col CB-601,DF-1229,DO-966,DQ-1323 |
| 265068-2 | Jig Saw Puzzle Blues | Col 2782-D,CB-612,DF-1263, DO-937 |
| 265069-2 | Pink Elephants | Col CB-601,DF-1229,DO-966,DQ-1323 |

JOE VENUTI AND HIS BLUE FIVE : As above, but Dick McDonough-g replaces Lang; Venuti
db sb and unknown k added (**); 2t/tb/2as/ts added*; unknown v.
                                           New York, May 8, 1933.

| | | |
|---|---|---|
| 265116-2 | Hiawatha's Lullaby | Col CB-637, DO-979 |
| 265117-2** | Vibraphonia | Col 2782-D, DO-937, Par R-2083 |
| 265118-2 | *Isn't It Heavenly ? - v | Col 2783-D, DO-959 |
| 265119-2 | *My Gypsy Rhapsody | Col CB-637, DO-979 |

NOTE:- Columbia 2783-D and CB-637 as JOE VENUTI AND HIS ORCHESTRA; Columbia
DO-937, DO-959 and DO-979 as JOE VENUTI AND EDDIE LANG'S BLUE FIVE.

JOE VENUTI AND HIS ORCHESTRA : Max Kaminsky-2 others-t/? Red Bone-tb/Jimmy Dorsey-
? Wallace Blumberry-cl-as/ts/Joe Venuti-vn/p/Dick McDonough-g/sb/d/Don Elton-v.
                                           New York, September 25, 1933.

| | | |
|---|---|---|
| 14076-1 | You're My Past, Present And Future-vDE | Ban 32874, Cq 8250, Dom 154, Or 2776, Mt M-12815, Per 15832, Ro 2149, Dec F-3797 |
| 14077-1 | I Want To Ring Bells - vDE | Ban 32872, Dom 152, Mt M-12807, 91635, Or 2771, Per 15830, Ro 2144, Dec F-3803 |
| 14078-1 | Doin' The Uptown Lowdown - vDE | Ban 32874, Cq 8250, Dom 154, Mt M-12816, Or 2778, Per 15832, Ro 2149, Dec F-3797 |
| 14079-1 | Gather Lip Rouge While You May - vDE | Ban 32874, Dom 152, Mt M-12807, 91635, Or 2771, Per 15830, Ro 2144, Dec F-3860 |
| 14080-1 | Moon Glow | Ban 32883, 33113, Mt M-12831, M-13081, 91675, Or 2787, 2935, Per 15842, 15965, Ro 2160, 2309, Dec F-5177, Pol 1837 |
| 14081-1 | Cheese And Crackers | Ban 32883, Mt M-12831, 91675, Or 2787, 2935, Per 15842, Ro 2160, Dec F-5177, Pol 1837 |

JOE VENUTI AND HIS BLUE SIX : Benny Goodman-cl/Bud Freeman-ts/Adrian Rollini-bsx/
Joe Venuti-vn/Joe Sullivan-p/Dick McDonough-g/Neil Marshall-d.
                                           New York, October 2, 1933.

| | | |
|---|---|---|
| 265146-2 | Sweet Lorraine | Col CB-708, DO-1201, Dec 18167 |
| 265147-2 | Doin' The Uptown Lowdown | - 2934-D, DO-1036, DQ-1325 - |
| 265148-2 | The Jazz Me Blues | Col CB-686, DO-1071, Dec 18168 |
| 265149-2 | In De Ruff | -        DO-1201        - |

JOE VENUTI AND HIS ORCHESTRA : Joe Venuti-vn dir. 3t/tb/Max Farley and another-cl-as
  /? Pat Davis or Bud Freeman-and another-ts/2nd vn unless marked */p/g/sb/d/Will
  Hudson-a.                                  New York, October 13, 1933.

78187-1  Fiddlesticks - aWH                    BB B-5293, Eld 2164, Sr S-3374,
                                               Vic 24946
78188-1  *Everybody Shuffle                    BB B-5520, RZ MR-1419,HMV EA-1430
78189-1  Moon Glow (I'm Living In The Past)       -           -            -
78190-1  Phantom Rhapsody - aWH                BB B-5293, Eld 2164, Sr S-3374,
                                               Vic 24946

One t, one as omitted; 2 vn added; Dolores Read-v.
                                           New York, October 26, 1933.

14215-2  Heat Wave - vDR                       Ban 32879, Mt M-12828, 91649,
                                               Or 2783, Per 15838, Ro 2156,
                                               Dec F-5202
14216-1  Easter Parade - vDR                   As above, except Dec F-5202

Bud Freeman-ts definite; Howard Phillips-v.
                                           New York, November 3, 1933.

14253-1  Build A Little Home - vHP             Ban 32896, Mt M-12839, Or 2792,
                                               Per 15846, Ro 2165, Rex 8169
14254-1  No More Love - vHP                    As above, except Rex 8169
14255-1  My Dancing Lady - vHP                 Ban 32895, Mt M-12838, 91664,
                                               Or 2791, Per 15845, Ro 2164,
                                               Royal 91664, Dec F-3860
14256-1  Everything I Have Is Yours - vHP      Ban 32895, Cq 8264, Mt M-12838,
   NOTE:- Rex 8089 as ED LLOYD AND HIS ORCHESTRA.  91664, Or 2791, Per 15845,
                                               Ro 2164, Royal 91664, Dec F-3803,
                                               Rex 8089


                                           New York, December 22, 1933.

14483-   Personal recording for Mr. Waller - Pt.1 ARC Special
14484-   Personal recording for Mr. Waller - Pt.2     -

Slim Fortier-v.                            New York, December 29, 1933.

14488-1  One Minute To One - vSF               Ban 32939, Mt M-12882, Or 2820,
                                               Per 15869, Ro 2193
14489-1  You Have Taken My Heart (w) - vSF     As above, plus Rex 8141
14500-1  Amen Corner - vSF                     Rejected
14501-1  Cinderella's Fella - vSF              Ban 32943, Mt M-12886, Or 2822,
                                               Per 15871, Ro 2195
14502-1  Alice In Wonderland - vSF             As above, plus Cq 8264
   NOTE:- Rex 8141, included here for completeness, as ED LOYD AND HIS BAND.

Instrumentation and personnel unknown.  New York, August 17, 1934.

15663-1  Fiddlesticks                          OK 41586
15664-1-2  By The Great Horn Spoon             Rejected
15665-1-2  Intoxication                            -
15666-1  Goblin Market                         OK 41586

JOE VENUTI AND HIS BLUE FOUR : Joe Venuti-vn/Don Barrigo-ts/Arthur Young-p/Frank
  Victor-g/Doug Lees-sb, or Violin solo, acc. by Arthur Young-p**.
                                           London, September 20, 1934.

CAR-2858-1  Satan's Holiday                    RZ MR-1452, Col DO-1317,
                                               Gl GZ-3039, Tono SP-4096
CAR-2859-1  Tea Time                           RZ MR-1508, Col DO-1336,
                                               Gl GZ-3046
CAR-2860-1**Romantic Joe                       As above
CAR-2861-1  Hell's Bells And Hallelujah        RZ MR-1452, Col DO-1317,
                                               Gl GZ-3039, Tono SP-4096

JOE **VENUTI** AND HIS ORCHESTRA : Joe Venuti-vn-v dir. Louis Prima-t-v/t/Jerry Colonna-tb/2cl-as/Larry Binyon-ts/Fulton McGrath-p/Frank Victor-g/sb/Neil Marshall-d/Red Norvo-x.                New York, December 26, 1934.

| | |
|---|---|
| Wild Party | Lon HMG-5023 (LP) |
| Pardon Me, Pretty Baby | — |
| Satan's Holiday | — |
| My Monday Date (sic) - vLP | — |
| I Got Rhythm | — |
| Carmichael Medley (Intro. Rockin' Chair-vJV-LP)/ | |
|   Georgia On My Mind/Lazy River) | — |
| Rose Room | — |
| Smoke Rings | — |
| Wild Cat | — |
| I'm Confessin ' (That I Love You) - vLP | — |
| Hokus Pokus | — |
| Doin' Things | — |
| Fiddlesticks | — |
| Avalon | — |

JOE VENUTI AND HIS BLUE FOUR : Joe Venuti-vn/Arthur Rollini-cl-ts/Adrian Rollini-bsx vib/Fulton McGrath-p/Frank Victor-g/Victor Engle-d.              New York, March 20, 1935.

| | | |
|---|---|---|
| 39435-A | Mello As A 'Cello | Dec 624, BM-1071, Y-5059, Br 02018, A-9791, Pol A-61023 |
| 39436-A | Mystery | Dec 625, BM-1071, Y-5060, Br 02018, A-9791, A-82570, Od 284070, Pol A-61023 |
| 39437-A | Send Me | Dec 669, Y-5018, Br 02053, A-9828, Pol A-61024 |
| 39438-A | Vibraphonia No. 2 | As above, plus Br A-82570 |
| 39439-A | Nothing But Notes | Dec 624, Y-5059, Br 02304, A-9929, Pol A-61022 |
| 39440-A | Tap Room Blues | Dec 625, 3527, Y-5060, Br 02304, A-9929, Od 284070, Pol A-61022 |

JOE VENUTI AND RUSS MORGAN : Violin and piano duets.             New York, September 12, 1935.

| | | |
|---|---|---|
| CO-18076-1 | Red Velvet | Col 3105-D |
| CO-18077-1 | Black Satin | — |

JOE VENUTI AND HIS ORCHESTRA : Joe Venuti-vn dir. Toots Camarata-Tony Gianelli-John Owens-t/Chuck Evans-Ernie Stricker-tb/Murray Williams-Bob Romeo-as/Carl Orech-Elmer Beechler-ts/Joe White-p/Noel Kilgen-g/Buss Michaels-sb/Victor Engle-d/Ruth Lee-Tony Pasteur-v.             New York, October 28, 1935.

| | | |
|---|---|---|
| CO-18205-1 | Stop, Look And Listen - vRL | Col 3104-D, FB-1394, DW-4375 |
| CO-18206-1 | Eeny Meeny Miney Mo - vRL | Col 3103-D, FB-1319 |
| CO-18207-1 | Twenty-Four Hours A Day - vTP | — |
| CO-18208-1 | Yankee Doodle Never Went To Town - vRL | Col 3104-D, FB-1394, DW-4375 |

Joe Venuti-vn dir. Glenn Rohlfing-Bob Stockwell-t/Charlie Dahlsten-tb/Wayne Songer Charlie Spero-as/Clark Galehouse-Elmer Beechler-ts/Mel Grant-p/Frank Victor-g/ George Horvath-sb/Barrett Deems-d.      New York, January 25, 1939.

| | | |
|---|---|---|
| 64950-A | Flip | Dec 2313, BM-1050, M-30219, Br 02738, A-82043, A-82064, Pol A-61241 |
| 64951-A | Something | Dec 2312, BM-1050, M-30235, Y-5418, Br 02773, A-82043, A-82229, Pol A-61241 |
| 64952-A | Flop | Dec 2313, BM-1051, M-30219, Br 02738, A-82044, Pol A-61242 |
| 64953-A | Nothing | Dec 2312, BM-1051, M-30235, Y-5418, Br 02773, A-82044, A-82229, Pol A-61242 |

JOE VENUTI AND HIS ORCHESTRA was also used as a pseudonym (or in error) on Rex for
  Adrian Rollini and his Orchestra (WHO WALKS IN WHEN I WALK OUT ?), q.v., and for
  Todd Rollins and his Orchestra (JIMMY HAD A NICKEL) on the reverse (8107), of no
  particular interest as "hot" dance music.  See also Phil Napoleon.

## THE VERSATILE THREE/FOUR

THE VERSATILE FOUR : Gus Haston-bj-v/Tony Tuck-bj-vc/Charlie Mills-p/Charlie Johnson
  or George Archer-d.                    Hayes, Middlesex, February 3, 1916.

| | | |
|---|---|---|
| HO-1496ac | Circus Day In Dixie - vGH | HMV C-645 |
| HO-1497ac | Araby - vGH | - |
| HO-1499ac | Down Home Rag (Wilbur C. Sweatman) | HMV C-654 |
| HO-1500ac | Winter Nights - vGH | - |
| HO-2433/4ae | Oh ! You Little Bear - vGH | Rejected |
| HO-2435ae | Winter Nights - vGH | - |
| HO-2436ae | Down South | - |

  NOTE:- Matrices HO-1495ac and HO-1498ac are rejected takes of the titles on the
  numbers following.

THE VERSATILE THREE : Same, without d.    London, February, 1919.

| | | |
|---|---|---|
| 5992 | Memories - vGH | EBW 3290 |
| 5993 | I'm Sorry I Made You Cry - vGH | - |
| | I Want A Doll - vGH | EBW 3297 |
| | Smiles - vGH | - |

THE VERSATILE FOUR : Gus Haston-as-ts-bj-v/Tony Tuck-bj-vc/Charlie Mills-p/George
  Archer-d.                              London, c. September, 1919.

| | | |
|---|---|---|
| 6399 | After You've Gone - vGH | EBW 3379 |
| 6400 | What Do You Mean By Loving Somebody Else ? | - |

THE VERSATILE THREE : Same, without d.    London, c. March 11, 1920.

| | | |
|---|---|---|
| 6527 | And He'd Say "Oo-La-La ! Wee Wee" - vGH | EBW 3393 |
| 6529 | I've Got My Captain Working For Me Now-vGH | - |
| | Oh ! What A Pal Was Mary - vGH | EBW 3399 |
| | You Know What I Mean - vGH | - |

THE VERSATILE FOUR : As for c. September, 1919.
                                         London, July, 1920.

| | | |
|---|---|---|
| 6656 | Patches | EBW 3447 |
| 6657 | Mystery | - |
| 6658 | Bo-Bo-Beedle-Um-Bo | EBW 3524 |
| 6660 | Castle Of Dreams | EBW 3437 |
| 6661 | El Relicario | - |

  NOTE:- Matrix 6659 is untraced.

THE VERSATILE THREE : As for c. March 11, 1920.
                                         London, October, 1920.

| | | |
|---|---|---|
| 6790-1 | The Japanese Sandman | EBW 3524 |
| 6791-2 | Whispering | EBW 3504 |
| 6792-1 | The Love Nest | - |
| | Cuban Moon | EBW 3519 |
| | Venetian Moon | - |

  NOTE:- THE SOUND WAVE for May, 1921 refers to a recording on Edison Bell Winner by
  the Versatile Three of THE YODEL DODEL DOH, but it was never issued.

## VICKSBURG  BLOWERS

Probably :- Ernest "Mike" Michall-cl/Sterling Payne-as/vn/Troy Snapp-p/Ferman Tapp-
  bj.                                    Chicago, c. March 30, 1927.

| | | |
|---|---|---|
| 12673 | Monte Carlo Joys | Gnt 6089, BP 8010, Ch 15285 |
| 12673-A | Monte Carlo Joys | Ch 40108 |
| 12674 | Twin Blues | Ch 40111 |
| 12674-A | Twin Blues (Beans And Greens*) | Gnt 6089, BP 8010, Ch 15266, |

  NOTE:- Black Patti 8010 as DIXON'S CHICAGO          Pm 12783* (as JOE'S HOT BABIES)
  SERENADERS; Champion 15266 and 15285 as GALVESTON SERENADERS.

Pseudonym on Champion 15477 for the Berlyn Baylor Orchestra, q.v.

## VICTOR (DANCE) ORCHESTRA

The personnel shown for this orchestra is taken from a publicity sheet issued in
1905 by Victor, but it is not believed to have varied much during the following
years. The titles listed are of considerable interest as contemporary accounts of
ragtime; the first appeared simply as DANCE ORCHESTRA.

Walter B. Rogers-c dir. Emil Keneke-Walter Pryor-c/O. Edward Wardwell-tb/Louis H.
Christie-A. Levy-cl/Darius Lyons-f-pic/Arthur Trepte-o/Charles d'Almaine-Theodore
Levy-vn/Frank E. Reschke-as-vn/Herman Conrad-bb/S. O. Pryor-d.
New York, April 10, 1905.

B-2461-1-2  The Cakewalk In The Sky (Ben Harney)     Vic 4408
C-2461-1-2  The Cakewalk In The Sky (Ben Harney)     Vic 31412

New York, March 16, 1909.

B-6882-1  The Cakewalk In The Sky (Ben Harney)     Vic 16515
C-6882-2  The Cakewalk In The Sky (Ben Harney)     Vic 35088

New York, June 15, 1909.

8053-2  Black And White Rag (George Botsford)     Vic 16350

New York, January 15, 1910.

8554-2  Wild Cherries Rag (Ted Snyder)            Vic 16472

E. Frueh-vn added; William H. Reitz-bells (and probably d, replacing Pryor).
New York, February 15, 1912.

11600-1  The Gaby Glide (Louis Hirsch)          Vic 17063, HMV GC-834, B-161
NOTE:- HMV GC-834 and B-161 as BOHEMIAN ORCHESTRA (WITH BELLS).

## FRANK VICTOR

Guitar duets with Harry Volpe.          New York, June 24, 1936.

61197-A  Sweet Strings                Dec 1124, Br 02265, Od 284359
61198-A  Easy Like                    -          -           -

New York, July 20, 1936.

61206-B  Pagan Fantasy                Dec 1290, Br 02545
61207-A  Swingin' The Scale           -          -

## VICTOR LIGHT OPERA COMPANY

This body is probably the least likely candidate for inclusion in a book devoted to
jazz records, but on the following side, an outstandingly "hot" trumpet soloist is
featured, almost certainly Mike Mosiello. The other artists present are Belle
Mann-Edna Kellogg-sopranos/Lewis James-Jack Parker-tenors/Elliott Shaw-baritone/
Wilfred Glenn-bass, acc. by Nat Shilkret dir. Del Staigers-2nd t/Chuck Campbell-
Tommy Dowd-tb/Andy Sannella-cl-as-stg/Larry Abbott-Sammy Feinsmith-cl-as/Maurice
Pierce-cl-ts/Lou Raderman-Murray Kellner-Benny Posner-vn/Milt Rettenberg-Jack
Shilkret-p/John Cali or Dick Maffei-bj/Jack Pierce-bb/Al Armer-sb/William Dorn-Joe
Green-d.                               New York, June 28, 1929.

51687-5  Follow Through - Vocal Gems (Intro.     Vic 35970, HMV C-1780, EB-44
Button Up Your Overcoat/I Want To Be Bad/My Lucky Star/You Wouldn't Fool
Me, Would You ?)

## VICTOR MILITARY BAND

Despite its name, this was an organization mainly concerned with providing dance
music for Victor customers between 1911 and 1918. From its enormous output, the
following are known to be of interest for their material as ragtime - and as early
recordings of genuine blues numbers, though hardly treated as blues !

Walter B. Rogers or Theodore Levy dir. probably :- Emil Keneke-Bert Brown-c/Frank
  Schrader-tb/J. Fuchs-c-as/Otto Winkler-H. Reitzel-ah-th/Louis H. Christie-A. Levy-
  cl/Clemen Barone-f-pic/Herman Conrad-bb/William H. Reitz-d.
                              New York, September 27, 1911.

11028-2  Slippery Place Rag (Hacker)              Vic 17006, HMV GC3-5, B-240
    NOTE:- HMV GC3-5 and B-240 as PRYOR'S BAND.

                              New York, March 12, 1912.

11698-2  Stomp Dance (C. I. Stewart)             Vic 17508

                              New York, November 6, 1913.

14042-2  The Junk Man Rag (C. Luckeyth Roberts)  Vic 17489

                              New York, February 16, 1914.

14459-1  Swanee Ripples Rag (H. C. Thompson)     Vic 17585, Zon 3530

                              New York, April 14, 1914.

14704-2  Rag-a-Muffin Rag (W. T. Pierson)        Vic 17619

                              New York, July 15, 1914.

15065-3  The Memphis Blues (W. C. Handy, arr.    Vic 17619
            Cupero)

                              New York, September 25, 1914.

15221-3  Ballin' The Jack (Chris Smith)          Vic 35405

                              New York, November 29, 1914.

15427-2  Midnight Whirl Rag (Silvio Hein)        Vic 35431, HMV C-600
    NOTE:- HMV C-600 as THE METROPOLITAN BAND.

                              New York, December 3, 1914.

15455-1  Music Box Rag (C. Luckeyth Roberts)     Vic 35429, HMV C-603, S-8752
    NOTE:- HMV C-603 and S-8752 as THE METROPOLITAN BAND.

                              New York, April 8, 1915.

15835-5  Blame It On The Blues (Cooke)           Vic 17764

                              New York, February 2, 1916.

17098-1  Bugle Call Rag (Eubie Blake)            Vic 35533, HMV C-819
    NOTE:- HMV C-819 as THE METROPOLITAN BAND.  This credits the composer as Carey
  Morgan, whereas the Victor label shows no composer credit at all.

                              New York, September 15, 1916.

18339-3  Hesitation Blues (Billy Smythe)         Vic 18163
18373-1  Kansas City Blues (Euday L. Bowman)        -

                              New York, October 19, 1916.

18496-4  Brown Skin (A.J. Piron-Clarence Williams)Vic 18203

                      VICTORIAN  SYNCOPATORS

See Harry Reser.

                      VICTORY  DANCE ORCHESTRA

Pseudonym on Victory for Jay Wilbur and his Orchestra, q.v.

JOHN P. VIGAL

Vocal, acc. by Bobby Lee and his Imperial Six : Bobby Lee-p dir. t/tb/cl/as/bj/bb.
Long Island City, c. May, 1922.

Fowler Twist                                   BS 14115, Pm 12132

## VILLAGE BARN ORCHESTRA

Pseudonym on Victor 24084 for Gene Kardos and his Orchestra, q.v.

## JOHN VINCENT'S CALIFORNIANS

Pseudonym on Conqueror 7245 (DREAM TRAIN) for Devine's Wisconsin Roof Orchestra,q.v.

## SAM VINCENT

Pseudonym on Phoenix 087 for Fred van Eps, q.v.

## TED VINCENT'S ORCHESTRA

Pseudonym on Australian Worth 7048 (I'M JUST WONDERIN' WHO) for Irving Mills and his
Orchestra, q.v.

## VINNY'S DIXIE BAND

Larry Brakke-t/Vince Bastien-tb/Frank Roberts-cl-ts/Don Thompson-p/Lloyd Newton-d/
Barbara Hughes-v.                    Minneapolis, c. January, 1940.

AM-101-A  Dreams Sometimes Do Come True - vBH       Miracle 101
AM-101-B  You're Driving Me Crazy - vBH                 -

## VIRGINIA CREEPERS

Pseudonym on Pathe Actuelle for Lou Gold and his Orchestra, q.v.

## VIRGINIA DANCE ORCHESTRA

Pseudonym on Beltona for the following items listed in this book :-

161  Runnin' Wild (The Southland Six)
306  Ivy (Cling To Me) (The Southland Six)

## THE VIRGINIANS

Ross Gorman-cl-bcl-as dir. Henry Busse-c/Sam Lewis-tb/Hale Byers-as-f/Don Clark-cl-
ss-as/Ferdie Grofe-p-a/Mike Pingitore-bj/Jack Barsby-bb/Harold MacDonald-d. (The
Victor files show no drummer, but the occasional cymbal crashes and chimes may
have been played by Eddie King, the musical director for Victor at the time).
New York, March 9, 1922.

26240-3  Lonesome Mama Blues                    Vic 18895
26241-1-2-3-4-5  My Honey's Lovin' Arms         Rejected

Clark omitted.                            New York, March 22, 1922.

26241-6  My Honey's Lovin' Arms                 Vic 18881
26266-4  Memphis Blues                          Vic 18895
26267 3  Cuddle Up Blues                        Vic 18881

New York, June 2, 1922.

26606-5  Nobody Lied (When They Said That I     Vic 18913, HMV B-1421, Zon 3463
         Cried Over You)
26607-4  The Yankee Doodle Blues                   -              -

Sleepy Hall-bj replaces Pingitore.       New York, June 30, 1922.

26658-3  Send Back My Honeyman                  Vic 18920, HMV B-1555
26659-1-2-3-4-5  Why Should I Cry Over You ?    Rejected

Ross Gorman-cl-bcl-as dir. Henry Busse-c/Sam Lewis-tb/Hale Byers-as-f/Ferdie Grofe-p-
a/Mike Pingitore-bj/Jack Barsby-bb/Harold MacDonald-d.
                                        New York, July 18, 1922.

26659-9  Why Should I Cry Over You ?            Vic 18933, Zon 3466
26696-3  Blue                                        -    HMV B-1408, Zon 3495

                                        New York, August 31, 1922.

26744-1-2-3-4  My Dixie                         Rejected
26745-2  Early In The Morning Blues             Vic 18946

                                        New York, October 2, 1922.

26917-3  I Wish I Could Shimmy Like My Sister   Vic 18965, HMV B-1459, Zon 3538
         Kate
26918-1-2-3-4  Gee ! But I Hate To Go Home Alone  Rejected

                                        New York, October 5, 1922.

26918-7  Gee ! But I Hate To Go Home Alone      Vic 18965

   Tommy Gott-c added.                  New York, October 16, 1922.

26963-2  Kiss Mama - Kiss Papa                  Vic 18978, HMV B-1520, K-1767
26964-4  Rose Of The Rio Grande                 Vic 19001, HMV B-1592, Zon 3531

   George Tjordy-vn added; Isabella Patricola-v.
                                        New York, October 24, 1922.

26993-2  Choo-Choo Blues                        Vic 18978, HMV B-1555, K-1767,
                                                Zon 3496
26994-1-2-3-4  Lovin' Sam (The Sheik Of Alabam')  Rejected
         - vIP

                                        New York, October 31, 1922.

26994-6  Lovin' Sam (The Sheik Of Alabam') - vIP  Vic 18976
27107-4  Away Down East In Maine - vIP               -

   Tjordy omitted.                      New York, November 17, 1922.

27160-4  Teddy Bear Blues                       Vic 18992, HMV B-1558
27161-5  Where The Bamboo Babies Grow           Vic 18986, Zon 3502

                                        New York, December 1, 1922.

27197-4  That Da Da Strain (Intro. I've Got To  Vic 19018
         Cool My Doggies Now)
27198-3  Who Did You Fool After All ?           Vic 19001, Zon 3531

   Billy Murray-v.                      New York, December 20, 1922.

27246-3  When You And I Were Young Maggie Blues  Vic 19010
         - vIP-BM
27247-1  Bees Knees                             Vic 19000, HMV B-1592, Zon 3536

                                        New York, December 27, 1922.

27262-1  Come On Home - vIP                     Vic 19010
27263-1-3  Runnin' Wild - vIP                   Vic 19027

                                        New York, January 5, 1923.

27283-1-2-3-4-5  Aggravatin' Papa (Don't You Try  Vic rejected
         To Two-Time Me) - vIP

Ross Gorman-cl-bcl-as dir. Henry Busse-Tommy Gott-c/Sam Lewis-tb/Hale Byers-cl-ss-as
   /Ferdie Grofe-p-a/Mike Pingitore-bj/Jack Barsby-bb/Harold MacDonald-d.
                                        New York, January 23, 1923.

27424-1-2-3  He May Be Your Man                    Rejected
27425-3  Aggravatin' Papa (Don't You Try To        Vic 19021, HMV B-1638, AM-83
          Two-Time Me)

                                        New York, February 1, 1923.

27424-5  He May Be Your Man                        Vic 19018
27446-3  Aunt Hagar's Blues                        Vic 19021,HMV B-1638,AM-83,K-2135

                                        New York, February 20, 1923.

27608-1-2-3-4  You Said Something When You Said     Rejected
          Dixie
27609-2  Farewell Blues                            Vic 19032, HMV B-1648, AM-82,
                                                    Zon 3548

   Billy Murray-Ed Smalle-v.            New York, February 26, 1923.

27608-7  You Said Something When You Said Dixie    Vic 19048
27621-1  No-One Loves You Better Than Your         Vic 19039, Zon 3561
          M-A-double M-Y - vBM-ES
27622-4  Apple Sauce                               Vic 19032, HMV B-1648, AM-82,
                                                    Zon 3548

   Aileen Stanley-v.                    New York, March 2, 1923.

27635-4  Don't Think You'll Be Missed - vAS        Vic 19039
27636-4  You Know You Belong To Somebody Else      Vic 19040, HMV B-1863, Zon 3560
          (So Why Don't You Leave Me Alone)
27637-1-2-3-4-5  Maxie Jones (King Of The          Rejected
          Saxophones)
27638-4  Whoa, Tillie ! Take Your Time             Vic 19040

   Frank Siegrist-t replaces Gott; Belle Baker-v.
                                        New York, August 27, 1923.

28511-1  I've Got The Yes We Have No Bananas       Vic 19135, HMV B-1720, Zon 3611
          Blues - vBB
28512-4  Jubilee Blues - vBB                          -

                                        New York, September 6, 1923.

28535-4  The House Of David Blues                  Vic 19140, Zon 3629

   Isabella Patricola-Vernon Dalhart-v.   New York, September 11, 1923.

28549-4  Struttin' Jim - vIP                       Vic 19160
28550-2  Stavin' Change (The Meanest Man In        Vic 19189
          New Orleans) - vVD

   Roy Maxon-tb replaces Lewis.         New York, September 25, 1923.

28592-4  Down South Blues                          Vic 19175

   Pingitore omitted; Wendell Hall-v (and u ?) added.
                                        New York, October 23, 1923.

28760-3  Blue Island Blues - vWH                   Vic 19226
28761-4  Bluebird Blues - vWH                         -

                                        New York, November 7, 1923.

28913-1-2-3  Home Town Blues                       Vic rejected
28914-1-2-3-4  Melancholy                             -

Ross Gorman-cl-bcl-as dir. Henry Busse-Frank Siegrist-c/Roy Maxon-tb/Hale Byers-cl-ss-as/Ferdie Grofe-p-a/Mike Pingitore-bj/Jack Barsby-bb/Harold MacDonald-d.
New York, November 21, 1923.

28913-4-5-6-7  Home Town Blues                          Vic rejected

Jane Green-v.                              New York, December 4, 1923.

29103-2  Mama Loves Papa, Papa Loves Mama - vJG   Vic 19215
29104-2  Mama Goes Where Papa Goes                     -

Aileen Stanley-Billy Murray-v.         New York, December 13, 1923.

29126-2  You May Be Fast, But Mama's Gonna Slow   Vic 19231
           You Down - vAS-BM
29127-4  Promise Me Everything, Never Get Anything    -
           Blues - vAS-BM

Frank Crumit-v.                            New York, December 21, 1923.

29155-4  Mindin' My Business - vFC                  Vic 19259, Zon 3727

Georgie Price-Ed Smalle-v.             New York, December 28, 1923.

29164-4  I'm Goin' South - vGP                      Vic 19261, Zon 3737
29165-4  She Wouldn't Do What I Asked Her To-vBM  Vic 19241, HMV B-1850
29166-3  Happy-Go-Lucky In My Old Kentucky Home   Vic 19240, Zon 3723
           - vBM-ES

Mario Perry-pac added*.                New York, December 31, 1923.

29167-4  *Hurdy-Gurdy Blues (Hurdy-Gurdy Man*)     Vic 19241, HMV B-1794*
29168-4  Chili-Bom-Bom - vBM-ES                    Vic 19240, Zon 3723

Pingitore omitted; Wendell Hall-v (and u ?)
                                        New York, January 18, 1924.

29330-1-2-3-4  Brother, You've Got Me Wrong-vWH   Vic rejected
29331-1-2-3-4  31st Street Blues - vWH                -

Mike Pingitore-bj added.             New York, January 24, 1924.

29349-1-2-3-4  Irish Blues                          Rejected
29350-2  If You'll Come Back                         Vic 19264

                                      New York, February 2, 1924.

29379-2  Mindin' My Bus'ness                        Vic 19269
29380-4  I've Got A Cross-Eyed Papa (But He Looks    -
           Straight To Me)

George Marsh-d replaces MacDonald.   New York, March 10, 1924.

29593-3  Whose Izzy Is He ? (Is He Yours Or Is   Vic 19292, HMV B-1832
           He Mine) - vBM
29594-3-4  Scissor Grinder Joe                       -           -

Ed Stannard-cl-as replaces Byers; Al Armer or Carl Wagner-bb replaces Barsby;
Vernon Dalhart-v.                       New York, April 30, 1924.

29952-2  Bringin' Home The Bacon - vVD-ES          Vic 19334
29953-3  Shine                                       -    HMV B-1850

                                      New York, July 9, 1924.

30371-2  Superstitious Blues                        Vic 19419
30372-2  Sioux City Sue                             Vic 19439

Three years elspsed before any further records appeared under this name, and then,
for a further year only, came the following by the Victor "house" band.

Nat Shilkret dir. Mike Mosiello-Del Staigers-t/Chuck Campbell-tb/Sammy Feinsmith-
Larry Abbott-cl-as/Maurice Pierce-cl-ts/Lou Raderman-Murray Kellner-Benny Posner-
vn/Abe Borodkin-vc/Milt Rettenberg-Jack Shilkret-p/John Cali or Dick Maffei-bj/
Andy Sannella-stg/Jack Pierce-bb/Joe Green-d.
                                              New York, July 14, 1927.

39659-1  Nothing Could Be Sweeter                 Vic 20837, HMV B-5431, AM-857
NOTE:- HMV B-5431 and AM-857 as NAT SHILKRET AND HIS ORCHESTRA.

Andy Sannella-cl-as added, switching from stg; Franklyn Baur-v.
                                              New York, July 21, 1927.

39689-1  It's A Million To One You're In Love-vFB Vic 20837, HMV B-5365, AM-857,
                                                             EA-243

Max Farley-cl-as-f replaces Abbott; ? Peter Eisenberg-vn/? William Dorn-d added;
Lewis James-v.                                New York, November 25, 1927.

41107-1  Did You Mean It ? - vLJ                  Vic 21105, HMV B-5435, EA-292

? Harry Shilkret-t added; 3vn only; Harry Reser-bj replaces Cali or Maffei; Al
Armer-sb added.                               New York, December 29, 1927.

41285-3  In The Sing-Song Sycamore Tree - vLJ    Vic 21219, HMV EA-320

4vn used; S. Pasternack-vl/Charlie Magnante-pac added; Pierce-bb omitted; Scrappy
Lambert-Billy Hillpot-v.                      New York, January 5, 1928.

41520-1-2-3-4  After My Laughter Came Tears       Vic rejected
             - vSL-BH
41521-1-2-3  Away Down South In Heaven - vSL            -

G added (probably Sannella or Reser).   New York, January 26, 1928.

41520-6  After My Laughter Came Tears - vSL-BH   Vic 21219, HMV B-5460, EA-320
41521-5  Away Down South In Heaven - vSL         Vic 21228      -        EA-327

Leonard Joy dir. probably :- Mike Mosiello-Del Staigers or Harry Shilkret-Tommy Gott
t/Chuck Campbell-Tommy Dowd-tb/Andy Sannella-Sammy Feinsmith-cl-as/Maurice Pierce-
cl-ts/Milt Rettenberg-p/John Cali-bj/Jack Pierce-bb/Al Armer-sb/Joe Green-d.
                                              New York, June 8, 1928.

45572-3  Low Down                                 Vic 21680

## VIRGINIA  VARSITY  BOYS

Pseudonym on Guardsman 1087 (ROSE OF SPAIN) for Ray Miller's Black and White Melody
Boys, q.v.

## VISCONSIN ROOF ORCHESTRA

See Devine's Wisconsin Roof Orchestra.

## LILA  VIVIAN

Pseudonym on Guardsman for Edna Hicks, q.v.

## VOCAL TRIO

Pseudonym on Ariel 4637 (I DON'T MIND WALKING IN THE RAIN) for the Mariners, q.v.

## LOUIS VOLA

The bassist of the Quintette of the Hot Club of France (q.v.) was formerly a piano-
accordionist leading a quartet of violin, piano, drums and Django Reinhardt-g.
With this (styled LOUIS VOLA ET SON ORCHESTRE DU LIDO DE TOULON) he made six sides
in Toulon for HMV in May, 1931, four of them as accompaniments to a singer known

simply as Lixbot.  Despite Django Reinhardt's presence, these do not warrant in---
clusion here.

## THE  VOLUNTEER FIREMEN

Five titles appeared on Brunswick under this name.  The following is of considerable
interest as "hot" dance music.

Harry Reser-bj dir. probably :- Earl Oliver-Tommy Gott-t/Sam Lewis-tb/Larry Abbott-
cl-ss-as/Norman Yorke-cl-ts/Murray Kellner-vn/Bill Wirges-p/? Joe Tarto-bb/Tom
Stacks-d/Al Bernard-Frank Kamplain-v.  New York, January 27, 1926.

E-17694    Blinky Moon Bay - vAB-FK            Br 3077*

## DON VOORHEES

As most of the records made under Don Voorhees's direction are of interest as "hot"
dance music, his entire output with his known personnel is included here (to 1928).

DON VOORHEES AND HIS EARL CARROLL VANITIES ORCHESTRA : Don Voorhees dir. Mike
Mosiello-Leo McConville-t/Miff Mole-tb/Bill Trone-mel/Phil Gleason-Fred Morrow-cl-
ss-as/Paul Cartwright-cl-ss-ts/Joe Raymond-vn when used/p/Dick McDonough-bj-g/Jack
Hansen-bb/Vic Berton-d/Harold Yates-v.  New York, September 26, 1926.

142663-3  Climbing Up The Ladder Of Love - vHY    Col 765-D
142664-3  Hugs And Kisses - vHY                      -

  Scrappy Lammbert-v.                    New York, October 15, 1926.

11249    Just One More Kiss - vSL            Ed 51855
11250    I'd Love To Call You My Sweetheart - vSL    -        Amb 5253

  Arthur Hart (? Arthur Hall or Charles Hart)-v.
                                          New York, November 15, 1926.

11301    Just A Bird's-Eye View Of My Old          Ed rejected
           Kentucky Home (Intro. The Little White House)
11302    Because I Love You (w) - vAH              -
11303    Somebody's Eyes - vAH                     -

                                          New York, November 29, 1926.

11302    Because I Love You (w) - vAH        Ed 51887
11303    Somebody's Eyes - vAH              Ed 51888
11342    Sunday - vAH                        Ed 51890

DON VOORHEES AND HIS ORCHESTRA : As above; Herb Hobbs-v.
                                          New York, c. December 7, 1926.

107259    Some Day                          PA 36567, 11380, Per 14748
107260    Who Do You Love ? - vHH            PA 36594, Per 14775
107261    The Sphinx                         PA 36567, 11380, Per 14748
107262    Somebody's Eyes - vHH              PA 36594, Per 14775

DON VOORHEES AND HIS EARL CARROLL VANITIES ORCHESTRA : As above; Charles Kaley-The
  Shannon Quartet-v.                     New York, December 14, 1926.

143185-3  One Alone - vCK                    Col 835-D, 1824-D, 4322, 01242
143186-1  The Riff Song - vS4                  -         -       -      -

  Red Nichols-t replaces Mosiello; Cooper Lawley-v.
                                          New York, January 17, 1927.

11442    Who Do You Love ? - vHY            Ed 51919
11443    Muddy Water - vHY                  Ed 51927
11444    Blue Skies - vHY-CL                Ed 51919, Amb 5299

DON VOORHEES AND HIS EARL CARROLL VANITIES ORCHESTRA : Don Voorhees dir. Red Nichols
Leo McConville-t/Miff Mole-tb/Bill Trone-mel/Phil Gleason-Fred Morrow-cl-ss-as/
Paul Cartwright-cl-ss-ts/Joe Raymond-vn when used/p/Dick McDonough-bj-g/Jack
Hansen-bb/Vic Berton-d/Charles Kaley-Harold (Hal) Yates-v.
                                        New York, January 24, 1927.

143346-2  Who Do You Love ? - vCK              Col 881-D, 0635
143347-2  Muddy Water (A Mississippi Moan) - vCK        -         -

                                        New York, February 28, 1927.

11541     Never Without You - vHY              Ed 51963
11542     I Still Believe In You - vHY              -
11543     Pardon The Glove                     Ed 51962

                                        New York, March 9, 1927.

2378-A-B-C  Calling                            Rejected
2379-A-B-C  That's My Hap-Hap-Happiness            -
2380-C  Pardon The Glove                       Cam 1134, Ro 369
NOTE:- Romeo as ROY KING AND HIS ORCHESTRA.

                                        New York, March 21, 1927.

143696-1-2-3-4  The Same Old Moon - vCK        Rejected
143697-2  Dancing The Devil Away - vCK          Col 954-D

   William Grant Still-a.                New York, March 31, 1927.

143696-7  The Same Old Moon - vCK              Col 990-D
143730-2  Fantasy on St. Louis Blues-Pt. 1-aWGS   Col 1078-D
143731-3  Fantasy on St. Louis Blues-Pt. 2-aWGS       -

   Vaughn de Leath-J. Donald Parker-v.    New York, April 11, 1927.

11640     Dancing The Devil Away - vVdeL       Ed 51999
11641     I'll Always Remember You - vVdeL     Ed 51997
11642     The Same Old Moon - vJDP             Ed 51999

                                        New York, April 20, 1927.

2378-F  Calling                                Cam 1146
2379-F  That's My Hap-Hap-Happiness               -
2427-C  You Know I Love You                    Cam 1169
NOTE:- Cameo 1146 and 1169 as LARRY MURPHY AND HIS ORCHESTRA.

   Unknown t replaces Nichols.           New York, May 16, 1927.

11699     Room For Two - vHY                   Ed 52024
11700     Dear Eyes That Haunt Me              Rejected
11701     With Someone Like You                Ed 52024

   Arthur Fields-v.                      New York, July 6, 1927.

11780     Show Me That Kind Of A Girl          Ed 52070
11781     Oh ! Doris, Where Do You Live ? - vAF   Ed 52072
11782     Two Little Pretty Birds              Ed 52070

DON VOORHEES AND HIS ORCHESTRA : As above, but Lennie Hayton-p-cel replaces the unknown; Irving Kaufman (as VINCENT VAN TUYL)-v. (Columbia 0889 as DENZA DANCE BAND;
1131-D, 4873 as IDEAL SERENADERS).    New York, September 6, 1927.

144629-2  Soliloquy                            Col 1129-D, 4682, 0981
144630-3  Highways Are Happy Ways - vIK        Col 1124-D, 4683

   Billy Day-v.                          New York, September 7, 1927.

144634-3  Dawning - vBD                        Col 1131-D, 4873, 0889
144635-1-2-3  Say It With A Red, Red Rose - vBD   Rejected
144636-3  Rain - vBD                           Col 1126-D, 4684, CS-8
144637-3  When The Morning Glories Wake Up In The  Col 1124-D, 4683
              Morning (Then I'll Kiss Your Two Lips Goodnight) - vIK

DON VOORHEES AND HIS ORCHESTRA : Don Voorhees dir. Red Nichols-Leo McConville-t/Miff
Mole-tb/Bill Trone-mel/Phil Gleason-Fred Morrow-cl-as/Paul Cartwright-cl-ss-ts/Joe
Raymond-vn (when used)/Lennie Hayton0-p-cel/Dick McDonough-bj-g/Jack Hansen-bb/Vic
Berton-d/Norman Clark-v.　　　　　　　New York, September 8, 1927.

| | | |
|---|---|---|
| 144646-1-2-3 | Lolita - vNC | Rejected |
| 144647-2 | Worryin' (w) - vNC | Col 1225-D, 4791, 01074 |

Lewis James-v.　　　　　　　　　　　New York, September 9, 1927.

| | | |
|---|---|---|
| 144651-3 | My Blue Heaven - vLJ | Col 1129-D, 4684, 0836 |
| 144652-2 | A Shady Tree - vLJ | Col 1131-D, 0889 |

NOTE:- Columbia 1131-D as IDEAL SERENADERS; 0889 as DENZA DANCE BAND.

Irving Kaufman (as FRANK HARRIS)-v.　　New York, September 10, 1927.

| | | |
|---|---|---|
| 144641-2 | Baby's Blue - vIK | Col 1123-D, 4682, 0981, CS-8 |
| 144642-3 | Clementine (From New Orleans) - vIK | Col 1180-D |

Vaughn de Leath-Wilfred Glenn-v.　　New York, January 7, 1928.

| | | |
|---|---|---|
| 145485-3 | Can't Help Lovin' Dat Man - vVdeL | Col 1284-D, 4901, 01046 |
| 145486-3 | Ol' Man River - vWG | -　　-　　- |

## VICTOR VORZANGER AND HIS BROADWAY BAND

Among the number of sides recorded by this unit for Aco and Scala, the following are
of unusual interest, in that they must rank as the first mixed jazz band titles on
record. (The cornet, trombone and drums are played by American negroes, the others
being white Europeans). There may be other titles of equal merit as jazz, albeit
somewhat crude.

Victor Vorzanger-vn dir. "Horns-in-F" Warne-c/Ellis Jackson-tb-v/ —— Richardson-as
/Horace Ainsley-p/Mark Sheridan-bj/Al Young-d-v.
London, July, 1922.

| | | |
|---|---|---|
| CH-1107 | Yoo-Hoo - vAY | Sc 536 |
| CH-1108 | Sally | -　　Clm 1486 |

NOTE:- Coliseum 1486 as VORZANGER'S BAND.

London, August, 1922.

| | | |
|---|---|---|
| CH-1120 | Tell Her At Twilight | Sc 538 |
| CH-1121 | Roaming - vAY | Sc 541 |
| CH-1123 | Dapper Dan - vEJ-AY | Sc 539 |
| CH-1124 | Stumbling | Sc 538 |
| CH-1125 | Always Charming (w) | Sc 540 |
| CH-1126 | Cutting The Cake (A Wedding Fox Trot) | - |
| CH-1127 | You Can't Sting A Nigger In The Same Place Twice - vEJ | Sc 541 |
| CH-1128 | Vamping Rose - vAY | Sc 539 |
| CH-1129 | Buzz Mirandy | Rejected |

NOTE:- Matrix CH-1122 is untraced; the waltz is included for completeness.

THE BROADWAY BAND : As above.　　　London, September, 1922.

| | | |
|---|---|---|
| CH-1141 | Ilo | Rejected |
| CH-1142 | I'm Getting Better Every Day | Sc 558 |
| CH-1145 | I Want Some Money | - |
| CH-1146 | Goodbye, Shanghai | Sc 548 |
| CH-1148 | Ty-Tee | |

NOTE:- Scala 548 as "CAIRO" RAMBLERS (sic). Matrices CH-1143, 1144 and 1147 are
untraced. Sample pressings of matrices CH-1129 and CH-1141 exist, both bearing
the inked date September 22, 1922, which though not the recording date, gives a
clue to it; the dates given above and below are based on those of issue as shown
in THE SOUND WAVE.

THE BROADWAY BAND : Victor Vorzanger-vn dir. "Horns-in-F" Warne-c/Ellis Jackson-tb/
  Charlie Star-as/Horace Ainsley-p/Mark Sheridan-bj/Al Young-d-v.
                                    London, c. December, 1922.

C-5385    Caravan                          Aco G-15127, Bel 111, Gmn 1234
C-5386    My Sweet Hortense - vAY          Aco G-15128       -        - Sc 576
  NOTE:- Beltona 111 as AVENUE DANCE ORCHESTRA; Scala 576 as JAGGERS ELITE ORCHESTRA.

                                    London, c. February, 1923.

C-5438    Swanee Bluebird                  Aco G-15176
C-5439    Hot Lips                         Aco G-15162, Bel 133
  NOTE:- Beltona 133 as AVENUE DANCE ORCHESTRA.

THE FAMOUS BROADWAY BAND : Same.    London, c. April, 1923.

C-5568    Oogie-Oogie-Wa-Wa - vAY          Aco G-15179
C-5569    All Muddled Up                   Aco G-15176
C-5570    Oh ! Star Of Eve                 Aco G-15195
C-5571    Little Rover - vAY               Aco G-15179

The name VORZANGER'S BAND was also a pseudonym on Scala for the following items
  listed in this book :-

615  Loose Feet (Original Memphis Five)
629  Runnin' Wild (The Southland Six)

## WABASH DANCE ORCHESTRA

Red Nichols-t dir. Manny Klein-t/Miff Mole-tb/Arnold Brilhart-? Jimmy Crossan-cl-as/
  Fud Livingston-cl-ts/Kurt Dieterle-? Murray Kellner-vn/Arthur Schutt-p/Perry
  Botkin-bj-g/? Hank Stern-bb/Gene Krupa-d/Richard Roberts-Charles Small-Glenn Burt-
  v.                                New York, September 11, 1928.

E-28194-B  Get Out And Get Under The Moon - vRR   Duo D-4024
E-28195-A  That's My Weakness Now - vRR-CS         Duo D-4001
E-28199-B  My Ohio Home - vGB                      Duo D-4005
E-28200-B  My Pet - vGB                            Duo D-4012

  Carl Kress-g replaces Botkin; Chauncey Morehouse-d replaces Krupa; Phil Baker-
  Billy Potter-Tom Edwards-v.       New York, September 14, 1928.

E-28220-B  Chloe - vPB                      Duo D-4006
E-28221-B  Ready For The River - vPB        Duo D-4008
E-28222-A  Sweet Sue- Just You - vPB        Duo D-4009
E-28223-A-B  Roses Of Yesterday - vGB-BP    Rejected
E-28225-B  She's A Great, Great Girl - vTE  Duo D-4007
E-28226-B  Because My Baby Don't Mean "Maybe"  Duo D-4003
             Now - vTE
E-28227-A  Oh ! Baby - vTE                  Bwy LP-103, JA 21 (LPs)

## WABASH  TRIO

Louis Metcalf-c/J. C. Johnson-p/Bernard Addison-g.
                                    New York, March, 1929.

3382-    Hoppin' 'Round                  GG/Rx 1711, Sr 33009
3383-A-B  Lone Western Blues             GG/Rx 1714, Rx 7039, VD 77039
3384-A-B  Coal Black Blues               GG/Rx 1710    -       -       -
NOTE:- Radiex 1710 is anonymous; Sunrise 33009 as DIXIE REVELERS; Van Dyke 77039
as MISSISSIPPI TRIO.  See also NOVELTY BLUE BOYS for other sides issued as by the
Wabash Trio; still others are of no known interest as jazz.

## JIMMY WADE

WADE'S MOULIN ROUGE ORCHESTRA : Jimmy Wade-c dir. William Dover-tb/Arnett Nelson-cl-
  as/Vernon Roulette-cl-ts/Eddie South-vn/Teddy Weatherford-p/Louis "Buddy" Gross-bb
  /Edwin Jackson-d.                 Chicago, December, 1923.

1620-1-2  Someday Sweetheart             Pm 20295, Hg 893, Pur 11295
1621-1-2  Mobile Blues                      -         -        -
NOTE:- Paramount 20295 as WADE'S MOULIN ROUGH ORCHESTRA (!)

WADE'S MOULIN ROUGE ORCHESTRA : Jimmy Wade-t/William Dover-tb/Arnett Nelson-cl-as/
    Vernon Roulette-cl-ts/Eddie South-vn/Teddy Weatherford-p/Louis "Buddy" Gross-bb/
    Edwin Jackson-d.                            Chicago, February, 1924.

    1686-1  You've Got Ways I'm Crazy About         Pm 20301, Emb/Mit/Pur 11363
    NOTE:- Paramount 20301 as AL SIEGEL'S ORCHESTRA; the reverse side, also credited
    thus, really is by Al Siegel's Orchestra, q.v.

JIMMY WADE'S CLUB ALABAM ORCHESTRA : Same, but Roulette and South omitted, Antonia
    Spaulding-p replaces Weatherford; Walter Wright-bb replaces Gross; Perry Bradford
    v..                                         New York, April 5, 1927.

GEX-571    All That I Had Is Gone - vPB        Gnt 6105, BP 8019, Ch 15266
GEX-572    Original Black Bottom Dance - vPB      -        -      Ch 15263
    NOTE:- Champion 15263 and 15266 as HARVEY HOFFMAN AND HIS ORCHESTRA.

JIMMY WADE AND HIS DIXIELANDERS : Jimmy Wade-c dir. Punch Miller-c-v/Charles Lawson-
    tb/? Arnett Nelson and another-cl-as/ts/Alex Hill-p-a/Charles Jackson or Stanley
    Wilson-bj/bb/Cliff Jones-d-k.               Chicago, October 10, 1928.

C-2428-    Mississippi Wobble                  Voc 1236
C-2429-A   Gates Blues - vPM                      -       V-1029, Br 80041

### ROY WAGER AND HIS ORCHESTRA

See Joe Haymes and his Orchestra.

### CHRISTIAN WAGNER ET SON ORCHESTRE

The following records by this French band are included owing to the presence on one
    session of pianist Charlie Lewis, and guitarist Django Reinhardt on the other.

Christian Wagner-cl/Alix Combelle-as/Hubert Rostaing-ts/Django Reinhardt-g/Tony
    Rovira-sb/Pierre Fouad-d.                   Paris, December 18, 1940.

OSW-166-1  Pour Terminer                       Swing 102
OSW-167-1  Pour Commencer                         -

Alex Renard-t/Christian Wagner-cl/Roger Fisbach-as/Hubert Rostaing-Coco Kiehn-as-ts/
    Noel Chiboust-ts/Charlie Lewis-p/Louis Gaste-g/Tony Rovira-sb/Pierre Fouad-d.
                                               Paris, April 16, 1941.

OSW-210-1  Elle n'a pas tres bon caractere     Swing 114
OSW-211-1  Ne le perdez pas                       -

### LARRY WAGNER AND HIS RHYTHMASTERS

Walter Smith-t/Gene Prendergast-cl/Hub Lytell-ts/Fulton McGrath-p/Dave Barbour-g/Lou
    Shoobe-sb/Murray Gaer-d/Adrian Rollini-vib.
                                               New York, November 24, 1937.

017411-1   Autopsy On Schubert                 Vic 25723
017412-1   Two Dukes On A Pier                    -

Walter Smith-t/Art Ralston-Clarence Hutchinrider-cl-as/Pat Davis-cl-ts/Claude
    Thornhill-p/Dave Barbour-g/Stanley Dennis-sb/Milton Schlesinger-d.
                                               New York, December 14, 1937.

017709-1   Hearts Without Flowers              Vic 25772, HMV EA-2107
017710-1   Sneakin' A Sleep                       -

### SOL S. WAGNER AND HIS ORCHESTRA

Sol S. Wagner-p dir. t/tb/2as/ts/vn/bj/bb/d.
                                Richmond, Ind., between Nov. 7 and 22,1923.

11672-A   Oklahoma Indian Jazz                 Gnt 5313
11673     Havana                                  -
11674     My Sweet Gal                         Gnt 5311
11677     Teach Me                                -
11678     Dream Daddy                          Gnt 5323
11679     You Didn't Want Me When I Wanted You Rejected

Sol S. Wagner-p dir. probably :- Nate Bold-c/Hub Henning-tb/Jimmy Lord-cl-as/Milton
  Neul-cl-ts/Harry Podal-vn/Sid Pritikin-bj/Frank Wosika-bb/Harry Weinstein-d/Rus-
  sell Douglas-v.                          Chicago, May 12, 1927.

80870-C  I'm In Love Again - vRD                OK 40827, Par R-3366, A-2443,
                                                Od 193047, A-189050
80871-B  South Wind - vRD                       As above, e cept Par A-2443
  NOTE:- Parlophone R-3366 as ARCADIA PEACOCK ORCHESTRA.

The vocal trio on the next side is described on Parlophone R-3383 as BROWN SISTERS
AND GREEN, but the file card shows what looks like "Ed Camping" and something else
illegible owing to the card having been guillotined to fit the drawer in the
cabinet.  The trio sound like three girls, but so do the Keller Sisters and Lynch
(yet Lynch was a man !)                    Chicago, May 13, 1927.

80874-C  You Don't Like It - Not Much - v3      OK 40838, Par R-3383, A-2341,
                                                Od 193070, A-189043
80875-A-B-C  Zulu Wail                          Rejected
  NOTE:- Parlophone R-3383 as THE RHYTHM BREAKERS.

  Paul Small-v.                            Chicago, December 15, 1927.

80873-A-B  Beautiful - vPS                      Rejected
80874-B  Countin' The Days - vPS                OK 40973, Par E-6016, Od A-189115
80875-B  Everywhere You Go - vPS                -           -           -
  NOTE:- Parlophone E-6016 as WILL PERRY'S ORCHESTRA.

### HERMAN WALDMAN AND HIS ORCHESTRA

The following title is the only one of the total of eight made by this orchestra for
  Brunswick and Bluebird between 1929 and 1934 to be of interest as jazz.

Herman Waldman-vn dir. Rex Preis-Ken Switzer-t/Bill Clemens-tb/Bob "Baldy" Harris-
  Jimmy Segers-cl-as/Tink Nauratil-cl-ts/Tom Blake p/Vernon Mills-bj/Barney Dodd-bb/
  Reggie Kaughlin-d.                       Dallas, October, 1929.

DAL-567-  Marbles                               Br 4649, A-8649

### WALDORF-ASTORIA  ORCHESTER

Pseudonym on Beka 4101 for Ray Miller's Black and White Melody Boys, q.v.

### THE  WALDORFIANS

The following from the number of sides recorded in London in 1931 by this band are
  of some interest as "hot" dance music.

Howard Godfrey dir. Harry Thompson-t-tb/Eddie Schultz-t/Bob Kane and/or Alex Mitch-
  ell-tb/Harry Carter-as-vn/Bill Taylor-cl-bar/Charles Smith-ts/Sid Rubens or Eddie
  Grasso-vn/Alex Blackford-p/bj/Jimmy Clark-bb-sb/Harry Francis-d/Al Bowlly-v.
                                           London, c. May, 1931.

4360-2  My Canary Has Circles Under His Eyes-vAB Pic 780, Mf M-1-2019
4361-2  Miss Elizabeth Brown - vAB                  -          -

  Unknown v.                               London, August, 1931.

4426-2  Tell Me, Are You From Georgia ? - v      Pic 811, Mf G-2021
  NOTE:- Mayfair G-2021 and M-1-2019 as FIFTH AVENUE DANCE BAND.

### EDDIE WALKER AND  HIS BAND

Pseudonym on Supertone for Zach Whyte's Chocolate Beau Brummels, q.v.

### ESTHER  WALKER

Vocal, acc. by c/tb/cl-as/vn/Rube Bloom-p/bj/bb/d.
                                           New York, c. June 7, 1926.

E-19503    Ya Gotta Know How To Love           Br 3215*
E-19507    Hard-To-Get Gertie                  -
Other titles by this artist are of no known interest as jazz for their accompanists.

Pseudonym on Columbia for the following items listed in this book :-

2380-D  Personally, I Love You (Ben Selvin and his Orchestra)
2404-D  Both sides by the Charleston Chasers

## NANCY WALKER

The accompaniment to the following records by this artist is said to be of interest
as jazz, but no further details are known.
                                      New York, June 14, 1928.

| | | |
|---|---|---|
| 8033- | You're A Real Sweetheart | Ban ? |
| 8034-2 | Because My Baby Don't Mean "Maybe" Now | Ban 7146 |
| 8035-1 | Bring Back My Lovin' Man | - |

## GEO. WALLACE'S ORCHESTRA

Pseudonym on Clarite 825 for Sam Lanin and his Orchestra, q.v.

## INEZ WALLACE

Vocal, acc. by Fletcher Henderson-p.    Long Island City, c. December, 1922.

Radio Blues                           BS 14137, Pm 12145
Aggravatin' Papa (Don't You Try To Two-Time Me) -    -

Acc. by t/tb/cl/p.                    Long Island City, c. February, 1923.

520-1  Come Back Dear                 BS 14144, Pm 12155

Bj added.                            Long Island City, c. March, 1923.

560    Kissin' Daddy                  BS 14147, Pm 12146
561    Go Get It                      -           -

## SIPPIE WALLACE

Vocal, acc. by Eddie Heywood-p.        Chicago, c. October 26, 1923.

8490-A  Up The Country Blues          OK 8106
8491-A  Shorty George Blues           -

Acc. by Clarence Williams-p.          New York, c. May 26, 1924.

72567-B  Mama's Gone, Goodbye          OK 8168
72568-B  Caldonia Blues                OK 8144
72569-A  Underworld Blues              -
72570-A  Leavin' Me Daddy Is Hard To Do  OK 8168

                                      New York, c. May 27, 1924.

72579-B  Can Anybody Take Sweet Mama's Place ?   OK 8159
72580-B  Stranger's Blues              -

Acc. by Clarence Williams' Harmonizers : Tom Morris-c/Charlie Irvis-tb/? Ernest
Elliott-cl/Clarence Williams-p/Buddy Christian-bj.
                                      New York, c. June 13-14, 1924.

72606-B  Sud Bustin' Blues             OK 8177
72607-B  Wicked Monday Morning Blues   -

Acc. by Clarence Williams' Blue Five : Louis Armstrong-c/Aaron Thompson-tb/Sidney
Bechet-cl-ss/Clarence Williams-p/Buddy Christian-bj.
                                      New York, November 28, 1924.

73007-B  Baby, I Can't Use You No More  OK 8212
73008-B  Trouble Everywhere I Roam     -

Acc. by Clarence Williams-p.          New York, December 1, 1924.

73012-B  I've Stopped My Man                OK 8288
73013-B  Walkin' Talkin' Blues              OK 8206

Acc. by Sidney Bechet-cl-ss/Clarence Williams-p/Buddy Christian-bj.
                                      New York, December 2, 1924.

73014-B  I'm So Glad I'm Brownskin          OK 8197
73015-B  Off And On Blues                   -

Acc. by Clarence Williams-p/Buddy Christian-bj.
                                      New York, December 3, 1924.

73018-B  He's The Cause Of Me Being Blue    OK 8190
73019-B  Let My Man Alone Blues             -

Acc. by King Oliver-c/Hersal Thomas-p. Chicago, c. February 24, 1925.

8964-B   Morning Dove Blues                 OK 8205
8965-A   Devil Dance Blues                  OK 8206
8966-A   Every Dog Has His Day              OK 8205

Acc. by Perry Bradford's Jazz Phools : C/tb/? Buster Bailey-cl-ss/? Perry Bradford
p.                                    New York, August 19, 1925.

73555-A  Section Hand Blues                 OK 8232
73556-A  Parlor Social De Luxe              -

Acc. by Rudy Jackson-as/Hersal Thomas-p.
                                      New York, August 20, 1925.

73557-B  Being Down Don't Worry Me          OK 8276
73558-B  Advice Blues                       -

Acc. by Hersal Thomas-p.              New York, c. August 22, 1925.

73566-B  Murder's Gonna Be My Crime         OK 8243
73567-B  The Man I Love                     OK 8251

Acc. by cl/p/bj.                     New York, c. August 25, 1925.

73574-A  I'm Leaving You                    OK 8288
73575-A  I'm Sorry For It Now               OK 8251
73576-A  Suitcase Blues                     OK 8243
73577-A  I Must Have It                     OK 8381

Acc. by Louis Armstrong-c/Hersal Thomas-p.
                                      Chicago, March 1, 1926.

9546-A   A Jealous Woman Like Me            OK 8301
9547-A   Special Delivery Blues             OK 8328, HJCA HC-82, JSo AA-586
9548-A   Jack O' Diamonds Blues             -        -          -

                                      Chicago, March 3, 1926.

9559-A   The Mail Train Blues               OK 8345
9560-A   I Feel Good                        -
9561-A   A Man For Every Day In The Week    OK 8301

Acc. by c/own p.                     Chicago, November 20, 1926.

9929-A   I'm A Mighty Tight Woman           OK 8439
9930-A   Bedroom Blues                      -

Acc. by Louis Armstrong-c/Artie Starks-cl/own p, with Bud Scott-g*.
                                      Chicago, May 6, 1927.

80837-A  Dead Drunk Blues                   OK 8499
80838-B  Have You Ever Been Down ?          -
80839-B  Lazy Man Blues                     OK 8470, JSo AA-585
80840-B  *The Flood Blues                   -        -

SIPPIE THOMAS : Vocal, acc. by Hense Grundy-tb/own p/Cal Smith-g.
                                          Chicago, February 6, 1929.

48865-1-2  Go Down Sunshine Blues              Rejected
48866-2   You Gonna Need My Help               Vic V-38502

    Acc. by Natty Dominique-c/Honore Dutrey-tb/Johnny Dodds-cl/own p/Bill Johnson-sb.
                                          Chicago, February 7, 1929.

48870-2  I'm A Mighty Tight Woman              Vic V-38502
48871-1-2  Ain't Nobody Home But Me            Rejected

## TED  WALLACE

This was one of the many pseudonyms used by Wallace T. "Ed" Kirkeby, manager of the
    California Ramblers, q.v.  The OKehs listed under this name are of somewhat more
    interest generally as "hot" dance music (up to 1928) than the subsequent ARC and
    Columbia issues, which are therefore only listed selectively.


TED WALLACE AND HIS ORCHESTRA : Ed Kirkeby-v dir. Chelsea Quealey-Frank Cush-t/Tommy
    Dorsey or Abe Lincoln-tb/Bobby Davis and Johnny Rude or Arnold Brilhart-cl-ss-as/
    Sam Ruby-ts/Adrian Rollini-bsx-gfs/Al Duffy-vn when used/Jack Russin-p/Tommy
    Felline-bj/Herb Weil-d/Irving Kaufman-v.
                                          New York, January 3, 1927.

8Q275-B-C  Usen't You Used To Be My Sweetie ?-vIK OK 40751, Par E-5785, A-4900
80276-A  If All The Stars Were Pretty Babies-vIK  OK 40749      -
80277-B  When I First Met Mary - vEK                -      Par E-5907, Ar 4250
NOTE:- Ariel 4250 as ARIEL DANCE ORCHESTRA.

    Roy Johnston-t may replace Cush on either or both the next two sessions; Lincoln
    definite; Hal White-v.            New York, January 21, 1927.

80319-B  Ain't She Sweet ? - vEK              OK 40760, Par E-5787, Ar 4229,
                                              Od 193043
80320-A  There Ain't No Maybe In My Baby's Eyes  OK 40757, Par E-5769, Od 04022
         - vHW
80321-B  Crazy Words - Crazy Tune - vEK          -        - LAR A-4521 -
NOTE:- OKeh 40757 and Parlophone E-5769 as THE NEW YORK SYNCOPATORS; Ariel 4229 as
ARIEL DANCE ORCHESTRA.

    Russell Douglas (as LES REIS)-v.     New York, February 14, 1927.

80418-B  Oh ! Lizzie (A Lover's Lament) - vRD  OK 40778, Par E-5905, LAR A-4516,
                                              Od 193043, A-189023
80419-B  The Cat - vRD                        OK 40778, Par R-3335, LAR A-4516,
                                              Od A-189023
80420-B  My Regular Gal - vRD                 OK 40788, Par E-5807, A-2410,
                                              Od 193004
NOTE:- Parlophone R-3335 as TAMPA BLUE ORCHESTRA; OKeh 40788, Parlophone E-5807,
A-2410 and Odeon 193004 as ED KIRKEBY AND HIS ORCHESTRA.

    Sylvester Ahola-t replaces Johnston or Cush; Ivan Johnston-tb replaces Lincoln; no
vn.                                   New York, March 18, 1927.

80639-A  Nesting Time - vRD                   OK 40788, Par E-5807, Ar 4233,
                                              Od 193004
80640-B  For Mary And Me - vRD                OK 40816, Od 193011, 04015
NOTE:- OKeh 40788, Parlophone E-5807 and Odeon 193004 as ED KIRKEBY AND HIS ORCH-
ESTRA; Ariel 4233 as ARIEL DANCE ORCHESTRA.

    Unknown t (probably Frank Cush) replaces Ahola; Abe Lincoln-tb replaces Johnston.
                                      New York, June 27, 1927.

81110-B  Bless Her Little Heart - vRD         OK 40860, Par R-3380
81111-B  Who-oo ? You-oo, That's Who ! - vRD     -        -
81112-B  Pleading - vRD                       OK 40850, Par E-5907, A-4926,
                                              Od 193055, A-189078
81113-B  Love And Kisses - vLR                As above, but Par R-3378
 NOTE:- OKeh 40860 as THE NEW YORK SYNCOPATORS; Parlophone R-3378 as SAM LANIN'S

TED WALLACE AND HIS ORCHESTRA : Ed Kirkeby dir. Chelsea Quealey-? Frank Cush-t/Abe
    Lincoln-tb/Bobby Davis-? Arnold Brilhart-cl-ss-as/Sam Ruby-ts/Adrian Rollini-bsx-
    gfs/Jack Russin-p/Tommy Felline-bj/Herb Weil-d.
                                            New York, September 12, 1927.

81429-B  Cornfed !                          OK 40915, Par R-3444, A-4915,
                                            Od A-189065
81430-A  Buffalo Rhythm                     OK 41014, Par R-3466
81431-A  Zulu Wail                          OK 40915, Par R-3444, A-4915

Ed Kirkeby dir. Chelsea Quealey-Henry Levine-t/Al Philburn-tb/Pete Pumiglio-Harold
    Marcus-cl-ss-as/Sam Ruby-ts/Al Duffy-vn/Jack Russin-p/Tommy Felline bj/Jack Hansen
    bb/Herb Weil-d/Russell Douglas (as LES REIS)-The Decon (?) Sisters-v.
                                            New York, November 23, 1927.

81858-C  Mary (What Are You Waiting For ?) - vRD   OK 40965, Par R-106, A-2462,
                                            Od 193131
81859-C  Changes - vDS                      OK 40961, Par R-3498, Od A-189110
NOTE:- OKeh 40965, Parlophone A-2462 and Odeon 193131 as THE NEW YORK SYNCOPATORS;
Parlophone R-106 as SAM LANIN'S ARKANSAS TRAVELLERS, and R-3498 as SAM LANIN'S
FAMOUS PLAYERS.

Sammy Fain-Artie Dunn-v.                    New York, December 7, 1927.

81924-B  For My Baby - vRD                  OK 40961, Par R-3498, A-2437,
                                            Od A-189110
81925-B  There's Something Spanish In Your Eyes   OK 41091, Par R-124, A-2585,
         - vSF-AD                           B-25293, LAR A-4556, Od 193235,
                                            A-189178, 04088
81926-A  Cobble-Stones - vSF-AD             OK 40965, Par R-106, LAR A-4542,
                                            Od 193131, A-189111, 04069
NOTE:- OKeh 40965 and Odeon 193131 as THE NEW YORK SYNCOPATORS; Parlophone R-106
as SAM LANIN'S ARKANSAS TRAVELLERS; R-124 and R-3498 as SAM LANIN'S FAMOUS PLAYERS
(this probably applies to their German and Argentine equivalents).

From this point, with Quealey, Davis and Rollini, and shortly after, Russin, in
    London with Fred Elizalde, changes in personnel and musical policy took place.
    A selective list of known interesting titles follows, played by musicians drawn
    from the following collective personnel.

Tony Gianelli-Bill Moore-Mickey Bloom-Tony Russo-Cliff Weston-Fred van Eps, Jr.-Moe
    Selzer-Angie Rattiner-Frank Cush-Al King-Roy Johnston-Phil Napoleon-Tommy Gott-t/
    Tommy Dorsey-Carl Loeffler-George Troup-Reg Harrington-Miff Mole-Ted Raph-tb/Pete
    Pumiglio-Harold Marcus-Herb Dwyer-Carl Orech-Jimmy Dorsey-Bud Wagner-Rudy Ludovar-
    cl-as/Sam Ruby-cl-ts/Spencer Clark-bsx (when used)/Al Duffy-Joe LaFaro-Larry Kosky
    Sidney Harris-vn/Chauncey Gray-p/Tommy Felline-bj/Jimmy Mullen-Jack Hansen-Ward
    Lay-bb-sb/Herb Weil (early on)-Chick Condon-Stan King-d.  Vocalists are shown at
    each session heading.

Irving Kaufman-v.                           New York, November 2, 1928.

8292-1-2  There's A Rainbow 'Round My Shoulder   Ban 6203, Bwy 1225, Cq 7213,
          - vIK                             Dom 4224, 31002, Je 5441,
NOTE:- Broadway 1225 as LEW WRIGHT AND HIS  Re 8665, Apex 8850, LS 24340,
ORCHESTRA; Conqueror 7213 as CALIFORNIA     Mic 22340, St 10410, Imp 2009
COLLEGIANS.

Ed Smalle-Jerry Macy-v (as THE RADIO IMPS).
                                            New York, November 30, 1928.

8370-3  (I Got A Woman, Crazy For Me)       Ban 6231, Bwy 1233, Dom 4250,
        She's Funny That Way - vRI          Re 8691, Apex 8897, LS 24400,
NOTE:- Edison Bell Winner 4924 as THE PLAZA BAND.St 10438, EBW 4924, Imp 2065

TED WALLACE AND HIS CAMPUS BOYS : Smith Ballew-v.
                                            New York, September 10, 1929.

148988-3  Bottoms Up - vSB                  Col 1970-D, CB-36, 01847
148989-2  Bigger And Better Than Ever - vSB      -        -        -      -

ED LOYD AND HIS ORCHESTRA : 2t/tb/2as/ts/p/bj/bb/d/male voice trio-v from collective
   personnel given on page 1620, but possibly including Jack Purvis-t.
                               New York, March 18, 1930.

403859-C  Stein Song - v3                      OK 41402, Par R-672, E-6320
   NOTE:- Parlophone E-6320 as WILL PERRY'S ORCHESTRA.

TED WALLACE AND HIS CAMPUS BOYS : Ed Kirkeby dir. probably :- Jack Purvis-t/Carl
   Loeffler-tb (when used)/Pete Pumiglio-cl-as-bar/Elmer Feldkamp-cl-as-v/Tommy Bohn-
   cl-ts/Sam Hoffman-Sidney Harris-vn/Lew Cobey-p/Ed Sexton-g/Ward Lay-sb/Jack Powers
   (or Powell)-d/two other v.      New York, June 23, 1930.

150601-1  Absence Makes The Heart Grow Fonder-v3   Col 2236-D, CB-137, DO-227
150602-1  Here Comes The Sun - v3                  -          CB-182, DO-230

                          New York, July 10, 1930.

150643-3  Hittin' The Bottle - v3                  Col 2254-D, DO-223

                          New York, August 12, 1930.

150701-2  Tomorrow Is Another Day - v3             Col 2275-D, CB-184, DO-327
150702-1  Don't Tell Her (What's Happened To Me)-v3   -        DO-249

   Bobby Davis-cl-as replaces Feldkamp, and an unknown vocalist takes his place in
   the trio.                       New York, September 23, 1930.

150837-3  My Baby Just Cares For Me - v3           Col 2301-D, DO-249
150838-3  Sweet Jennie Lee - v3                    -          CB-205

TED WALLACE AND HIS SWING KINGS (....SWING MUSIC on RZ MR-2047 and MR-2080) : Gordon
   Griffin-t/Mike Michaels-tb/Lew White-cl/Freddy Fellessby-ts/Bill White-p/Brick
   Fleagle-g/Felix Giobbe-sb/Jack Maisel-d/Ted Wallace-Eddy Loyd (according to labels
   - both are Ed Kirkeby!)-v/v trio.    New York, January 17, 1936.

98648-1  I'm Gonna Sit Right Down And Write      BB B-6251, RZ MR-2047
             Myself A Letter - vEK
98649-1  Life Begins When You're In Love - vEK   BB B-6253, RZ MR-2079
98650-1  Gotta Go To Work Again - vEK            BB B-6254
98651-1  It's Been So Long - vEK                 BB B-6253, RZ MR-2104, Vic JR-55
98652-1  Sing An Old Fashioned Song (To A Young  BB B-6254
             Sophisticated Lady) - vEK
98653-1  Alone At A Table For Two - vEK          BB B-6252
98654-1  Mama Don't Allow It - vEK               BB B-6251
98655-1  Goody-Goody - v3                        BB B-6252, RZ MR-2080
   NOTE:- Regal Zonophone MR-2079 and MR-2104 as THE CALIFORNIA RAMBLERS.

TED WALLACE AND HIS ORCHESTRA was also a pseudonym on Parlophone R-3466 (BLACK
   MARIA) for Arnold Frank and his Rogers Cafe Orchestra, q.v.

## TRIXIE WALLACE

Pseudonym on Claxtonola for Kitty Irvin, q.v.

## WESLEY WALLACE

Piano solos, with own comments*.        Grafton, Wis., c. February, 1930.

L-184-2  *No. 29                         Pm 12958, JI 3
L-185-1  Fanny Lee Blues                 -

## THOMAS "FATS" WALLER

Piano solos.                            New York, c. October 21, 1922.

70948-D  Muscle Shoals Blues             OK 4757, Bm 1005, JSo AA-503
70949-D  Birmingham Blues                -         -       -
   NOTE:- As both the above are somewhat high takes, it is possible they were made at
   a re-make session about December, 1922 (cf. Sara Martin c. December 1 and 14).

Pipe-organ solos.                              Camden, N. J., November 17, 1926.

| | | |
|---|---|---|
| 36773-1 | St. Louis Blues | Vic 20357,HMV B-8501,AM-881,SG-561 |
| 36774-4 | Lenox Avenue Blues (Church Organ Blues) | -          -          -          - |

Camden, N. J., January 14, 1927.

| | | |
|---|---|---|
| 37357-1 | Soothin' Syrup Stomp | Vic RD-7599, HMV 7EG-8191 (LP/EP) |
| 37357-2 | Soothin' Syrup Stomp | Vic 20470 |
| 37357-3 | Soothin' Syrup Stomp | Vic 741052 (LP) |
| 37358-1 | Sloppy Water Blues | JA 21 (LP) |
| 37358-3 | Sloppy Water Blues | Vic 20492 |
| 37359-3 | Loveless Love | Vic 20470, 23260 |
| 37360-1-2-3 | Harlem Blues | Rejected |
| 37361-2 | Messin' Around With The Blues | JA 21 (LP) |
| 37361-3 | Messin' Around With The Blues | Vic 20655 |
| 37362-1 | Rusty Pail | Vic 741052 (LP) |
| 37362-3 | Rusty Pail | Vic 20492 |
| 37363-1 | I'd Like To Call You My Sweetheart | Trial record for Nat Shilkret |

The third and fourth titles are piano solos.

Camden, N. J., February 16, 1927.

| | | |
|---|---|---|
| 37819-1 | Stompin' The Bug (all microgrooves) | Vic RD-7599, HMV 7EG-8191, 741052 |
| 37819-2 | Stompin' The Bug | Vic 20655 |
| 37820-1 | Hog Maw Stomp | Vic 741052 (LP) |
| 37820-2 | Hog Maw Stomp | Vic 21525 |
| 37821-1-2-3 | Black Bottom Is The Latest Fad | Rejected |
| 37822-2 | Blue Black Bottom | Vic LPV-516, RD-7779 (LPs) |

Camden, N. J., May 20, 1927.

| | | |
|---|---|---|
| 38044-1 | Sugar | Vic 21525, 23331, BB B-5093, |
| | | MW M-4904, Sr S-3176 |
| 38047-1 | Beale Street Blues | Vic 20890 |
| 38049-1 | I'm Goin' To See My Ma | Rejected |

NOTE:- The same titles, in the same order, sung by Alberta Hunter (q.v.) with Fats
Waller at the organ, account for matrices 38045, 38046 and 38048.

THOMAS WALLER WITH MORRIS'S HOT BABIES : Tom Morris-c/Charlie Irvis-tb/Fats Waller-p
and or/? Eddie King-d.                         Camden, N. J., May 20, 1927.

| | | |
|---|---|---|
| 38050-2 | Fats Waller Stomp | JA 21 (LP) |
| 38050-3 | Fats Waller Stomp | Vic 20890, HMV B-10472, HE-3150 |
| 38051-1 | Savannah Blues | Vic 20776, HMV B-5417 |
| 38051-2 | Savannah Blues | Vic 741062 (LP) |
| 38052-2 | Won't You Take Me Home ? | - |
| 38052-3 | Won't You Take Me Home ? | Vic 20776, HMV B-5417 |

Pipe-organ solo.                               Camden, N. J., November 14, 1927.

| | | |
|---|---|---|
| 40081-1-2 | Memories of Florence Mills | Vic rejected |

THOMAS WALLER WITH MORRIS'S HOT BABIES : Tom Morris-c/Jimmy Archey-tb/Fats Waller-p-
or-v/Bobbie Leecan-g/? Eddie King-d, or pipe-organ solos*.
                                               Camden, N. J., December 1, 1927.

| | | |
|---|---|---|
| 40093-1 | He's Gone Away | Vic 741062, RFW 1 (LPs) |
| 40093-2 | He's Gone Away | Vic 21202, El EG-7892 |
| 40094-2 | *I Ain't Got Nobody | Vic 21127, 23331, BB B-5093, |
| | | MW M-4904, Sr S-3176 |
| 40095-1 | *The Digah's Stomp | Vic 741062 (LP) |
| 40095-2 | *The Digah's Stomp | Vic 21358, El EG-7892 |
| 40096-1 | Red Hot Dan - vFW | Vic 21127, HMV B-10472, HE-3150 |
| 40096-2 | Red Hot Dan - vFW | - |
| 40097-1 | Geechee | Vic 21358, El EG-7882 |
| 40097-2 | Geechee | - |
| 40098-1 | Please Take Me Out Of Jail | RFW 1 (LP) |
| 40098-2 | Please Take Me Out Of Jail | Vic 21202, El EG-7882 |

Piano solos*, or FATS WALLER AND HIS BUDDIES : Charlie Gaines-t/Charlie Irvis-tb/
  Arville Harris-cl-as-ts/Fats Waller-p/Eddie Condon-bj.
                        New York, March 1, 1929.

| | | |
|---|---|---|
| 49759-1 | *Handful Of Keys | Vic V-38508, 27768, HMV B-4347, B-4902, N/X-4480, SG-543, X-6292 |
| 49760-2 | The Minor Drag | Vic V-38050, 20-1583, BB B-10185, HMV EA-3265, HE-2367, JF-1, K-8196, X-6252 |
| 49761-2 | Harlem Fuss | Vic V-38050, BB B-10185, HMV EA-3713, HE-2367, K-8196, X-6252 |
| 49762-2 | *Numb Fumblin' | Vic V-38508, 25338, HMV B-4347, B-4917, HE-2381, X-6292 |

    NOTE:- THE MINOR DRAG and HARLEM FUSS are always cross-labeled; what is described
    as one plays the other.

Piano solos.                            Camden, N. J., August 2, 1929.

| | | |
|---|---|---|
| 49492-3 | Ain't Misbehavin' | Vic 22092, 22108, 20-1581, 68-0773, HMV B-3243, EA-641 |
| 49493-2 | Sweet Savannah Sue | Vic 22108, 68-0773, BB B-10264, HMV EA-641 |
| 49494-1 | I've Got A Feeling I'm Falling | Vic LPV-525 (LP) |
| 49494-2 | I've Got A Feeling I'm Falling | Vic 22092, HMV B-3243, EA-622 |
| 49495-1 | Love Me Or Leave Me | X LVA-3035, HMV DLP-1111 (LPs) |
| 49495-3 | Love Me Or Leave Me | Vic 22092, BB B-10263 |
| 49496-1 | Gladyse | Vic V-38554, HMV HE-2366, JF-4 |
| 49496-2 | Gladyse | Vic LPV-537, NL-42011 (LP) |
| 49497-1 | Valentine Stomp | X LVA-3035, HMV DLP-1111 (LPs) |
| 49497-2 | Valentine Stomp | Vic V-38554, BB B-10263, HMV HE-2366, JF-4 |

    NOTE:- Two distinct couplings exist of Victor 22092, as shown above.

Pipe-organ or piano* solos.            Camden, N. J., August 29, 1929.

| | | |
|---|---|---|
| 55375-1 | *Waiting At The End Of The Road | BB B-10264 |
| 55375-2 | *Waiting At The End Of The Road | Vic LPV-550 (LP) |
| 55376-1 | *Baby, Oh ! Where Can You Be ? | Pirate MPC-506 (LP) |
| 55376-2 | *Baby, Oh ! Where Can You Be ? | X LVA-3035, HMV DLP-1111 (LPs) |
| 56067-2 | Waiting At The End Of The Road | Vic LPV-550 (LP) |
| 56068-1 | Baby, Oh ! Where Can You Be ? | RFW 2 (LP) |
| 56068-2 | Baby, Oh ! Where Can You Be ? | RFW 1 (LP) |
| 56068-3 | Baby, Oh ! Where Can You Be ? | RFW 2 (LP) |
| 56069-1 | Tanglefoot | RFW 1 (LP) |
| 56069-2 | Tanglefoot | RFW 2 (LP) |
| 56070-2 | That's All | Vic 23260 |

Piano solos.                        New York, September 11, 1929.

| | | |
|---|---|---|
| 56125-1 | Goin' About | Pirate MPC-506 (LP) |
| 56125-2 | Goin' About | Vic LPV-516, HMV DLP-1111 (LPs) |
| 56126-1 | My Feelin's Are Hurt | Vic V-38613 |

                          New York, September 24. 1929.

| | | |
|---|---|---|
| 56710-2 | Smashing Thirds | Vic V-38613, 25338, HMV B-4902, B-8546, SG-543 |

FATS WALLER AND HIS BUDDIES : Henry Allen-t/Jack Teagarden-tb-vib/Albert Nicholas-
  Otto Hardwick-as/Larry Binyon-ts/Fats Waller-p/Eddie Condon-bj/Al Morgan-sb/Gene
  Krupa-d/The Four Wanderers (Herman Hughes-Charles Clinkscales-tenors/Maceo Johnson-
  baritone/Oliver Childs-bass)-v.       New York, September 30, 1929.

| | | |
|---|---|---|
| 56727-2 | Lookin' Good But Feelin' Bad - v4W | Vic V-38086 |
| 56728-1 | I Need Someone Like You - v4W | - |

Piano solos.                        New York, December 4, 1929.

| | | |
|---|---|---|
| 57190-4 | My Fate Is In Your Hands | Vic V-38568 |
| 57191-1 | Turn On The Heat | - |

FATS WALLER AND HIS BUDDIES : Henry Allen-Leonard Davis-t/Jack Teagarden-tb-vib/J. C.
Higginbotham-tb/Albert Nicholas-Charlie Holmes-cl-as/Larry Binyon-ts/Fats Waller-p/
Will Johnson-bj/Pops Foster-sb/Kaiser Marshall-d/Orlando Roberson-v.
New York, December 18, 1929.

| | | |
|---|---|---|
| 57926-1 | Lookin' For Another Sweetie - vOR | Vic V-38110 |
| 57927-3 | Ridin' But Walkin' | Vic V-38119, 1AC-0135, HMV B-4971 |
| | | B-6390, EA-3265, SG-431 |
| 57928-1 | Won't You Get Off It, Please ? | Vic V-38119, 1AC-0135, HMV B-4971 |
| | | B-6549, EA-3713, SG-464 |
| 57929-2 | When I'm Alone - vOR | Vic V-38110 |

Piano duets with Bennie Paine.        New York, March 21, 1930.

| | | |
|---|---|---|
| 59720-1 | St. Louis Blues | Vic 22371, 68-0830, HMV B-8496, |
| | | EA-770, GW-1341 |
| 59721-1 | After You've Gone | As above |

Piano solos, with own v.        New York, March 13, 1931.

| | | |
|---|---|---|
| 151417-3 | I'm Crazy 'Bout My Baby (And My Baby's | Col 14593-D, Voc 3016, Par R-1197 |
| | Crazy 'Bout Me) - vFW | B-71078, Od 031817, 279746 |
| 151418-2 | Draggin' My Heart Around - vFW | As above |

FATS WALLER AND HIS RHYTHM : Herman Autrey-t/Ben Whittet-cl/Fats Waller-p-cel-or-v/
Albert Casey-g/Billy Taylor-sb/Harry Dial-d-vib-speech.
New York, May 16, 1934.

| | | |
|---|---|---|
| 82526-1 | A Porter's Love Song To A Chambermaid | Vic 24648, BB B-10016, MW M-7949, |
| | - vFW/vibHD | HMV EA-2279 |
| 82527-1 | I Wish I Were Twins - vFW | Vic 24641, HMV EA-1508, JF-1, |
| | | El EG-3703 |
| 82527-2 | I Wish I Were Twins - vFW | RFW 3 (LP) |
| 82528-1 | Armful O' Sweetness - vFW | Vic 24641, BB B-10149, |
| | | HMV HE-2358, JF-7, RZ G-24194 |
| 82529-1 | Do Me A Favor - vFW | Vic 24648, HMV HE-2358, JF-7 |

Gene Sedric-cl replaces Whittet.        New York, August 17, 1934.

| | | |
|---|---|---|
| 83699-1 | Georgia May - vFW | Vic 24714, BB B-10078, HMV JF-12, |
| | | RZ G-24308 |
| 84106-1 | Then I'll Be Tired Of You - vFW | Vic 24708, HMV JF-13 |
| 84107-1 | Don't Let It Bother You - vFW/spHD | Vic 24714, HMV JF-12 |
| 84108-1 | Have A Little Dream On Me - vFW | Vic 24708, HMV JF-13 |

Floyd O'Brien-tb added; Mezz Mezzrow-cl replaces Sedric.
New York, September 28, 1934.

| | | |
|---|---|---|
| 84417-1 | Serenade For A Wealthy Widow - spFW/ | Vic 24742, BB B-10262, |
| | vibHD | HMV GW-1318, HE-2619,JF-8, K-7863 |
| 84418-1 | How Can You Face Me ? - vFW | Vic 24737, BB B-10143, HMV HN-727 |
| | | JF-14, K-7863 |
| 84419-1 | Sweetie Pie - vFW | Vic 24737, BB B-10262, |
| | | HMV GW-1318, HE-2619,JF-8, K-7861 |
| 84420-1 | Mandy - vFW | Vic 24738, HMV GY-281, JF-11, |
| | | X-4464, El EG-7790 |
| 84421-1 | Let's Pretend There's A Moon - vFW | Vic 24742, HMV EA-1510, JF-14 |
| 84422-1 | You're Not The Only Oyster In The Stew | Vic 24738, 20-2218, BB B-10261, |
| | - vFW | HMV BD-298, GY-281, HE-2344, |
| | | HN-727, JF-11, JK-2344, K-7861, |
| | | K-8526, X-4464 |

NOTE:- HMV JF-14 shows the matrix number as 84421-II. This simply indicates that
it is pressed from a dubbed master, and not that take 2 was used. There was no
take 2 of this or any other title made at this session.

FATS WALLER AND HIS RHYTHM : Bill Coleman-t/Gene Sedric-cl-ts/Fats Waller-p-cel-or-v
/Albert Casey-g/Billy Taylor-sb/Harry Dial-d-vib.
                                       New York, November 7, 1934.

| | | |
|---|---|---|
| 84921-1 | Honeysuckle Rose - vFW | Vic 24826 |
| 84922-1 | Believe It, Beloved - vFW | Vic 24808, HMV BD-134, AE-4484, EA-1509, JF-15, X-4430, X-7475, E1 EG-3703 |
| 84923-1 | Dream Man - vFW | Vic 24801, BB B-10261, HMV BD-117 EA-1457, HE-2344, JK-2344, K-7454 K-8526 |
| 84924-1 | I'm Growing Fonder Of You - vFW/vibHD | Vic 24801, HMV BD-117, EA-1510 |
| 84925-1 | If It Isn't Love - vFW | Vic 24808, HMV JF-15, X-4430 |
| 84926-1 | Breakin' The Ice - vFW | Vic 24826, HMV EA-1457 |

Piano solos.                           New York, November 16, 1934.

| | | |
|---|---|---|
| 86208-2 | African Ripples | Vic 24830, BB B-10115, HMV B-8546 EA-1458, HE-2289, JF-41 |
| 86209-1 | Clothes Line Ballet | Vic 25015, BB B-10098, HMV EA-1524, JF-35 |
| 86210-1 | Alligator Crawl | Vic 24830, A-1337, BB B-10098, HMV B-8784, EA-1458, HN-2632, IP-370, IW-89, JF-41, K-8176, X-4490, X-4507 |
| 86211-1 | Viper's Drag | Vic 25015, 27768, BB B-10133, HMV B-8784, EA-1524, HN-2632, IP-370, IW-89, JF-35, K-8176, N/X-4480 |

FATS WALLER AND HIS RHYTHM : As for November 7, 1934, but Charles Turner-sb replaces
  Taylor.                              Camden, N. J., January 5, 1935.

| | | |
|---|---|---|
| 87082-1 | I'm A Hundred Per Cent. For You - vFW | Vic 24863 |
| 87082-3 | I'm A Hundred Per Cent. For You | Vic 24867, HMV AE-4484, IW-96, JO-179, K-7508 |
| 87083-1 | Baby Brown - vFW | Vic 24846, BB B-10109 |
| 87083-3 | Baby Brown | Vic 24867, HMV GY-361, HE-2361, JF-45, K-7508, SG-464, X-4454 |
| 87084-1 | Night Wind - v-orFW | Vic 24853, JA-489, HMV EA-1482, GY-361 |
| 87085-1 | Because Of Once Upon A Time - vFW | Vic 24846, HMV BD-134 |
| 87086-1 | I Believe In Miracles - v-orFW | Vic 24853, JA-489, HMV EA-1482, JK-2796 |
| 87087-1 | You Fit Into The Picture - vFW | Vic 24863, HMV BD-5333, EA-1509, |

NOTE:- Despite the label of HMV JO-179 (87082-3),JO-179, E1 EG-6369
there is no vocal refrain by Fats Waller.

Herman Autrey-t/Rudy Powell-cl-as/Fats Waller-p-cel-v/Albert Casey-g/Charles
Turner-sb/Harry Dial-d.                New York, March 6, 1935.

| | | |
|---|---|---|
| 88776-1 | Louisiana Fairy Tale - vFW | Vic 24898, HMV HE-3083 |
| 88777-1 | I Ain't Got Nobody (And Nobody Cares For Me) - vFW | Vic 24888 |
| 88778-1 | I Ain't Got Nobody (And Nobody Cares For Me) | Vic 25026, HMV AE-4565, JF-32, E1 EG-3397 |
| 88779-1 | Whose Honey Are You ? - vFW | Vic 24892, HMV EA-1500 |
| 88780-1 | Whose Honey Are You ? - celFW | Vic 25027, HMV GY-362, HE-2361, JF-45, SG-431, E1 EG-3398 |
| 88781-1 | Rosetta - v-celFW | Vic 24892 |
| 88782-1 | Rosetta - celFW | Vic 25026, A-1241, BB B-10156, E1 EG-3397 |
| 88783-1 | Pardon My Love - vFW | Vic 24889, HMV BD-5278, GW-1103 |
| 88784-1 | What's The Reason (I'm Not Pleasin' You)-vFW-20-2643, HMV BD-156 -EA-1500 | |
| 88785-1 | What's The Reason (I'm Not Pleasin' You) - celFW | Vic 25027, HMV AE-4565, JF-32, E1 EG-3398 |
| 88786-1 | Cinders - v-celFW | Vic 24898 |
| 88787-1 | (Oh Susannah) Dust Off That Old Pianna - v-celFW | Vic 24888, HMV BD-156, EA-1508, GY-362, IW-101 |

Piano solos, with Rudy Powell-cl-as (*), and own v and/or comments as shown.  All
  titles made at this session are dubbed from 16-inch transcriptions made for
  Muzak-Associated.                              New York, March 11, 1935.

     *Baby Brown-vFW/Viper's Drag/*How Can     Vic LPT-6001, RD-7552, 430208,
       You Can Face Me ?-vFW/The Down Home Blues  HMV CLP-1035
     *Dinah-vFW/Handful Of Keys/*Solitude-vFW As above
     I'm Crazy 'Bout My Baby-vFW/Tea For Two As above; TEA FOR TWO also on
       /Believe It, Beloved - vFW           Vic LPM-1246, EPC-1246-3
     Sweet Sue-vFW/Somebody Stole My Gal-vFW As above, but Vic 430209
       /Honeysuckle Rose
     Night Wind-vFW/African Ripples/Because  RFW 4
       Of Once Upon A Time
     Where Were You On The Night Of June The Vic LPT-6001, RD-7552, 430209,
       Third ?-vFW/Clothes Line Ballet/Don't  HMV CLP-1035
       Let It Bother You - vFW
     E flat Blues/Alligator Crawl/Zonky    Vic LPT-6001, RD-7553, 430209,
                                 HMV CLP-1042
     Hallelujah/Do Me A Favor-vFW/California As above, but Vic 430208
       Here I Come
     I've Got A Feelin' I'm Fallin'/My Fate  As above
       Is In Your Hands/Ain't Misbehavin'
     How Can You Face Me ?-vFW/You're The    As above
       Top-vFW/Blue, Turning Grey Over You/Russian Fantasy

FATS WALLER AND HIS RHYTHM : Herman Autrey-t/Rudy Powell-cl-as/Fats Waller-p-v/
  Albert Casey-g/Charles Turner-sb/Harry Dial-d.
                                  New York, May 8, 1935.

89760-1  Lulu's Back In Town - vFW              Vic 25063, HMV AE-4571, EA-1563,
                                                HE-2631, JF-47
89761-1  Sweet And Slow - vFW                   As above
89762-1  You've Been Taking Lessons In Love-vFW Vic 25044, HMV B-10684, BRS 1013
89763-1  You're The Cutest One - vFW            Vic 25039, BB B-10129, HMV GW-1214
89764-1  I'm Gonna Sit Right Down And Write     Vic 25044, 42-0037, A-1241,
           Myself A Letter - vFW                HMV B-9935, BD-5031, GW-1238,
                                                HE-2362, SG-304, El EG-3602,
                                                Bm 1099, BRS 1013
89765-1  I Hate To Talk About Myself - vFW      Vic 25039, HMV GW-1214


James Smith-g replaces Casey; Arnold Boling-d replaces Dial.
                        Camden, N. J., June 24, 1935.

88989-1  Dinah - vFW                            Vic 25471, 29988, HMV BD-5040,
                                                AE-4555, EA-2083, HE-2356, JF-46,
                                                HN-2996, SG-383, X-8004, El EG-3683
88990-1  Take It Easy - vFW                     Vic 25078, HMV BD-5199, El EG-3643
88991-1  You're The Picture (I'm The Frame)-vFW Vic 25075, HMV B-10830, HE-3083,
                                                TG-224
88992-1  My Very Good Friend The Milkman - vFW  Vic 25075, HMV BD-1218, BD-5376,
                                                HN-2584
88993-1  Blue Because Of You - vFW              BB B-10322
88994-1  There's Going To Be The Devil To Pay-vFW Vic 25078
88995-1  12th Street Rag - vFW                  Vic 25087, 68-1358, A-1114,
                                                JA-585, HMV BD-262, GW-1236,
                                                GW-1900, GY-886, K-7601, SG-174,
                                                X-8004
88996-1  There'll Be Some Changes Made - vFW    BB B-10332, Vic 20-2216
88997-1  Somebody Stole My Gal - vFW            Vic 25194, JA-691, HMV EA-1630,
                                                JF-46, Bm 1099
88998-1  Sweet Sue - vFW                        Vic 25087, 68-1358, A-1114,
                                                JA-585, HMV BD-298, HMV BD-298,
                                                AE-4555

88998-2  Sweet Sue - vFW                        JA 7 (LP)
 1935-1  Somebody Stole My Gal - vFW            Test made for Raymond R. Sooy

FATS WALLER AND HIS RHYTHM : Herman Autrey-t-v/Rudy Powell-cl-as/Fats Waller-p-cel-v
/James Smith-g/Charles Turner-sb/Arnold Boling-d.
New York, August 2, 1935.

| | | |
|---|---|---|
| 92915-1 | Truckin' - vFW | Vic 25116, HMV BD-262, GW-1236, GY-886, K-7601, SG-174 |
| 92916-1 | Sugar Blues - vFW | Vic 25194, JA-691, HMV EA-1630 |
| 92917-1 | Just As Long As The World Goes 'Round And Around - vFW | HMV HE-3018, JO-291, SG-492 |
| 92918-1 | Georgia Rockin' Chair - vFW | Vic 25175, A-1261, BB B-10288, HMV AE-4606, EA-1608 |
| 92919-1 | Brother, Seek And Ye Shall Find - vFW | Vic 25175, A-1261, HMV EA-1608 |
| 92920-1 | The Girl I Left Behind Me - vFW | Vic 25116, HMV B-10439, EA-1605, TG-156 |

New York, August 20, 1935.

| | | |
|---|---|---|
| 92992-1 | You're So Darn Charming - v-celFW | Vic 25120 |
| 92993-1 | Woe ! Is Me - vFW | Vic 25140, HMV BD-5031, EA-1590, GW-1238, HE-2362, El EG-3602 |
| 92994-1 | Rhythm And Romance - vFW | Vic 25131, HMV BD-5199, EA-1587 |
| 92995-1 | Loafin' Time - vFW-HA | Vic 25140, HMV EA-1590 |
| 92996-1 | (Do You Intend To Put An End To) A Sweet Beginning Like This - v-celFW | Vic 25131, HMV EA-1587 |
| 92997-1 | Got A Bran' New Suit - vFW | Vic 25123, HMV BD-5012, HE-2896, JO-196, N-14065, El EG-3702 |
| 92998-1 | I'm On A See-Saw - vFW | Vic 25120, HMV EA-1605, HE-3018, JO-291, SG-492, El EG-3660 |
| 94100-1 | Thief In The Night - vFW | Vic 25123 |

NOTE:- Matrix 92999 was apparently not allocated.

Gene Sedric-cl-ts replaces Powell; Yank Porter-d replaces Boling. (The next two
titles are from the soundtrack of the film HOORAY FOR LOVE).
Hollywood, c. October, 1935.

| | |
|---|---|
| I've Got My Fingers Crossed - vFW | RFW 1 (LP) |
| I'm Livin' In A Great Big Way - vFW | RFW 2 (LP) |

New York, November 29, 1935.

| | | |
|---|---|---|
| 98172-1 | When Somebody Thinks You're Wonderful - vFW | Vic 25222, HMV BD-5040, HE-2356, HN-2996, SG-383, El EG-3683 |
| 98173-1 | I've Got My Fingers Crossed - vFW | Vic 25211, HMV BD-5052, EA-1637, IM-122, NE-286 |
| 98174-1 | Spreadin' Rhythm Around - vFW | Vic 25211, HMV EA-1637, NE-286, El EG-3702 |
| 98175-1 | A Little Bit Independent - v-celFW | Vic 25196, HMV BD-5012, EA-1631, El EG-3702 |
| 98176-1 | You Stayed Away Too Long - vFW | Vic 25222, 20-2216 |
| 98177-1 | Sweet Thing - vFW | Vic 25196, HMV AE-4606, EA-1631 |

Herman Autrey and another-t/Benny Morton-tb/Emmett Matthews-ss/Rudy Powell-cl-as/
Gene Sedric-Bob Carroll-ts/Fats Waller-p-vib-v/Hank Duncan-2nd p/James Smith-g/
Charles Turner-sb/Yank Porter-d/Alex Hill-Don Donaldson-a.

New York, December 4, 1935.

| | | |
|---|---|---|
| 98196-1 | Fat And Greasy - vFW&ch | RFW 1 (LP) |
| 98196-2 | Fat And Greasy - vFW&ch | RFW 2 (LP) |
| 98197-1 | Functionizin' - aAH | HMV HE-2902, SG-315 |
| 98198-1 | I Got Rhythm - vFW/aDD | - - |

FATS WALLER AND HIS RHYTHM : Herman Autrey-t/Gene Sedric-cl-ts/Fats Waller-p-cel-v/
James Smith-g/Charles Turner-sb/Yank Porter-d.
                                            New York, February 1, 1936.

| | | |
|---|---|---|
| 98894-1 | The Panic Is On - vFW | Vic 25266 |
| 98895-1 | Sugar Rose - v-celFW | -                HMV BD-5062, B-9885, GW-1282, HE-2813, HN-2763, IM/JO-133, N-14052 |
| 98896-1 | Oooh ! Look-a There, Ain't She Pretty ? - v-celFW | Vic 25255, 20-2218, HMV EA-1722 |
| 98897-1 | Moon Rose - vFW | Vic 25281, HMV EA-1704 |
| 98898-1 | West Wind - vFW | Vic 25253, HMV BD-5052, EA-1677, IM-122, El EG-3660 |
| 98899-1 | That Never-To-Be-Forgotten Night - vFW | Vic 25255, HMV BD-5062, EA-1722, GW-1282, IM-133 |
| 99035-1 | Sing An Old Fashioned Song (To A Young Sophisticated Lady) - vFW | Vic 25253, HMV BD-5135, EA-1677 |
| 99036-1 | Garbo Green - vFW | Vic 25281, HMV EA-1704 |

Albert Casey-g replaces Smith; Arnold Boling-d replaces Porter; Elizabeth Handy-v.
                                            New York, April 8, 1936.

| | | |
|---|---|---|
| 101189-1 | All My Life - vFW | Vic 25296, HMV BD-5077, EA-1726, GY-487, IM-144 |
| 101190-1 | Christopher Columbus - vFW | Vic 25295, HMV EA-1744, El EG-3682 |
| 101191-1 | Cross Patch - vFW | Vic 25315, HMV BD-5098, AX-4029, EA-1729, GW-1345, El EG-3690 |
| 101192-1 | It's No Fun - vFW | Vic 25296, HMV BD-5087, EA-1726, El EG-3718 |
| 101193-1 | Cabin In The Sky - v-celFW | Vic 25315, HMV BD-5077, EA-1729, GY-497, IM-144, El EG-3690 |
| 101194-1 | Us On A Bus - vFW | Vic 25295, HMV EA-1744, JO-123, El EG-3682 |
| 101195-1 | Stay - vFW-EH | RFW 1 (LP) |

Yank Porter-d replaces Boling.        Magic Key Show, New York, May 24, 1936.

| | |
|---|---|
| I'm Gonna Sit Right Down And Write Myself A Letter - vFW | PC 13, DJM DJB-44235, Ember CJS-839 (LPs) |
| Christopher Columbus - vFW | PC 13, Ember CJS-842 (LPs) |

Probably :- Herman Autrey-Sidney de Paris-t/Benny Morton-tb/Edward Inge-cl/Rudy
Powell-cl-as/Don Redman-cl-as-bar/Gene Sedric-Bob Carroll-cl-ts/Fats Waller-p-cel-
v/Hank Duncan-2nd p/Albert Casey-g/Charles Turner-sb/Arnold Boling-d, or piano
solo*.                                Rudy Vallee Show, New York, June 4, 1936.

| | |
|---|---|
| I've Got My Fingers Crossed - vFW | PC 13, Ember CJS-839 (LPs) |
| *Honeysuckle Rose | -        - |
| Christopher Columbus - vFW | -        - |

As for April 8, 1936.              New York, June 5, 1936.

| | | |
|---|---|---|
| 101667-1 | It's A Sin To Tell A Lie - vFW | Vic 25342, 20-1595, 42-0037, A-1230, HMV BD-5087, EA-1773, JO-205, X-7475, El EG-3718, V-Disc 359 |
| 101668-1 | The More I Know You - vFW | Vic 25348, HMV BD-5159 |
| 101669-1 | You're Not The Kind - v-celFW | Vic 25353, HMV BD-5115, AL-2307, EA-1179, El EG-3767 |
| 101670-1 | Why Do I Lie To Myself About You ?-vFW | Vic 25353, HMV BD-5150, EA-1779, GW-1390, HE-2360 |
| 101671-1 | Let's Sing Again - vFW | Vic 25348, HMV BD-5098, GW-1345 |
| 101672-1 | Big Chief De Sota - vFW | Vic 25342, A-1230, HMV EA-1773 |

FATS WALLER AND HIS RHYTHM : Herman Autrey-t/Gene Sedric-cl-ts/Fats Waller-p-cel-v/
Albert Casey-g/Charles Turner-sb/Yank Porter-d.  Fats Waller's vocal contributions
to the next six titles consist of spoken comments only.
New York, June 8, 1936.

| | | |
|---|---|---|
| 102016-1 | Black Raspberry Jam | Vic 25359, HMV BD-5376 |
| 102016-2 | Black Raspberry Jam | Vic LPV-525, FPM1-7025 (LPs) |
| 102017-1 | Bach Up To Me | Vic 25536, HMV BD-5225, GW-1597, HE-2368 |
| 102018-1 | Fractious Fingering | Vic 25652, HMV X-6014 |
| 102019-1 | Paswonky | Vic 25359, HMV BD-5354, HE-2345, JK-2345, K-8227, SG-92, El EG-6383 |
| 102020-1 | Lounging At The Waldorf | Vic 25430    -    - |
| 102021-1 | Latch On | Vic 25471 |

Slick Jones-d replaces Porter.      New York, August 1, 1936.

| | | |
|---|---|---|
| 102400-1 | I'm Crazy 'Bout My Baby - vFW | Vic 25374, HMV BD-5120, GW-1343 |
| 102401-1 | I Just Made Up With That Old Girl Of Mine - vFW | Vic 25394, HMV BD-5159 |
| 102402-1 | Until The Real Thing Comes Along - vFW | Vic 25374, 20-2640, HMV BD-5115, AL-2307, El EG-3767 |
| 102403-1 | There Goes My Attraction - vFW | Vic 25388, HMV RD-5120, GW-1343, K-7779 |
| 102404-1 | The Curse Of An Aching Heart - vFW | Vic 25394, HMV BD-5116, EA-1791 |
| 102404-2 | The Curse Of An Aching Heart - vFW | Vic FPM1-7025, JA 7 (LPs) |
| 102405-1 | Bye-Bye, Baby - vFW | Vic 25388, HMV BD-5116, EA-1791, K-7779 |

Arnold Boling-d replaces Jones.     Magic Key Show, New York, August 9, 1936.

| | | |
|---|---|---|
| | It's A Sin To Tell A Lie - vFW | PC 13, DJM DJB-44235, Ember CJS-842 (LPs) |
| | Until The Real Thing Comes Along - vFW | PC 13, Ember CJS-842 (LPs) |
| | I'm Crazy 'Bout My Baby - vFW | -          - |

Slick Jones-d replaces Boling.      New York, September 9, 1936.

| | | |
|---|---|---|
| 0339-1 | S'posin' - vFW | Vic 25415, 20-2220, BB B-10156, HMV BD-5135 |
| 0340-1 | Copper Colored Gal - vFW | Vic 25409, JA-823, HMV BD-5133 |
| 0341-1 | I'm At The Mercy Of Love | -        -        - |
| 0342-1 | Floatin' Down To Cotton Town - vFW | Vic 25415 |
| 0343-1 | La-De-De, La-De-Da - vFW | Vic 25430, HMV BD-5150, EA-1850, GW-1390, HE-2360 |

Chicago, November 29, 1936.

| | | |
|---|---|---|
| 01801-1 | Hallelujah ! Things Look Rosy Now - vFW | Vic 25478, A-1144, HMV BD-5178 |
| 01802-1 | Hallelujah ! Things Look Rosy Now | Vic 25489, HMV K-8228, X-4817, El EG-3895 |
| 01803-1 | 'Tain't Good (Like A Nickel Made Of Wood) - vFW | Vic 25478, HMV BD-5178, EA-1850, El EG-3880 |
| 01804-1 | 'Tain't Good (Like A Nickel Made Of Wood) | Vic 25489, HMV K-8228, El EG-3895 |
| 01805-1 | Swingin' Them Jingle Bells (Jingle Bells*) - vFW | Vic 25483, 20-1602, A-1144, BB B-10016, HMV BD-1229*, EA-2302, HE-2672, HN-2426, HN-2599*, JO-81, SG-65* |
| 01806-1 | Swingin' Them Jingle Bells | Vic 25490, MW M-7949, El EG-3893 |
| 01807-1 | A Thousand Dreams Of You - vFW | Vic 25483, HMV BD-5184, EA-1868, HE-2359 |
| 01808-1 | A Thousand Dreams Of You | Vic 25490, El EG-3893 |
| 01809-1 | A Rhyme For Love - vFW | Vic 25491, HMV EA-1856 |
| 01810-1 | I Adore You - vFW | -          - |

FATS WALLER AND HIS RHYTHM : Herman Autrey-t/Gene Sedric-cl-ts/Fats Waller-p-cel-v/
Albert Casey-g/Charles Turner-sb/Slick Jones-d-vib.
                                  New York, December 24, 1936.

| | | |
|---|---|---|
| 03840-1 | Havin' A Ball - vFW | Vic 25515, A-1246, BB B-10100 |
| 03841-1 | I'm Sorry I Made You Cry - vFW | - |
| 03842-1 | Who's Afraid Of Love ? - vFW | Vic 25499, HMV EA-1851,El EG-4010 |
| 03843-1 | Please Keep Me In Your Dreams - vFW | Vic 25498, JA-888, HMV BD-5184, HE-2359 |
| 03844-1 | One In A Million - vFW | Vic 25499, HMV EA-1851 |
| 03845-1 | Nero - vFW | Vic 25498, JA-888, HMV EA-1868 |

                              Magic Key Show, New York, January 3, 1937.

|  | |
|---|---|
| Hallelujah ! Things Look Rosy Now - vFW | PC 13,DJM DJB-44235,Ember CJS-842 |
| A Thousand Dreams Of You - vFW | -          -            - (LPs) |

                                  New York, February 22, 1937.

| | | |
|---|---|---|
| 04949-2 | You're Laughing At Me - v-celFW | Vic 25530, HMV BD-5215,El EG-4010 |
| 04950-1 | I Can't Break The Habit Of You - vFW | -      HMV EA-1933 |
| 04951-1 | Did Anyone Ever Tell You ? - vFW | Vic 25537 |
| 04951-2 | Did Anyone Ever Tell You ? - vFW | Vic FPM1-7048 (LP) |
| 04952-1 | When Love Is Young - vFW | Vic 25537 |
| 04953-1 | The Meanest Thing You Ever Did Was Kiss Me - vFW | Vic 25536, 20-2219, HMV BD-5431, EA-1933, El EG-6676 |

                                  New York, March 18, 1937.

| | | |
|---|---|---|
| 06413-1 | Cryin' Mood - vFW | Vic 25551, HMV BD-5278, EA-1939 |
| 06414-1 | Where Is The Sun ? - vFW | Vic 25550, A-1016, HMV BD-5212, IM-292, K-7936 |
| 06415-1 | You've Been Reading My Mail - vFW | Vic 25554, HMV B-10191, EA-1960, HE-2997, JO-274,SG-357,El EG-7719 |
| 06416-1 | To A Sweet Pretty Thing - vFW | Vic 25551, HMV EA-1939 |
| 06417-1 | Old Plantation - vFW | Vic 25550, A-1016, HMV BD-5212, IM-292, K-7936 |
| 06418-1 | Spring Cleaning - vFW | Vic 25554 |

                                  New York, April 9, 1937.

| | | |
|---|---|---|
| 07745-1 | You Showed Me The Way - vFW | Vic 25579 |
| 07746-1 | You Showed Me The Way | Vic 25565, El EG-4005 |
| 07747-1 | Boo-Hoo | Vic 25563, HMV BD-5229, EA-1938, GY-394 |
| 07748-1 | The Love Bug Will Bite You | As above, plus HMV X-4863 |
| 07749-1 | San Anton' - vFW | Vic 25579 |
| 07750-1 | San Anton' | Vic 25565, BB B-10109, HMV BD-5215, X-4918 |
| 07751-1 | I've Got A New Lease On Love - vFW | Vic 25580, HMV B-10684 |
| 07752-1 | I've Got A New Lease On Love | Vic 25571, HMV EA-1960, K-8262, SG-95, El EG-4005 |
| 07753-1 | Sweet Heartache - vFW | Vic 25580, HMV BD-5225, GW-1597, HE-2368 |
| 07754-1 | Sweet Heartache | Vic 25571,HMV K-8262,SG-95,X-4918 |
| 07755-1 | Honeysuckle Rose - vibSJ | Vic 36206, NB-6004, HMV C-2937, EB-114, FKX-121, L-1041 |

NOTE:- The last title was edited to fit a 10-inch record, issued on Victor 25779.

Piano solos, with Gene Sedric-ts*/Andy Razaf-Mrs. James P. Johnson-self-v; speech by
James P. Johnson, Eubie Blake, Willie "The Lion" Smith-self**.
                                  New York, c. April-May, 1937.

|  | |
|---|---|
| **The Gathering | Ristic 22 (LP) |
| Old Fashioned Love | - |
| I'm Crazy 'Bout My Baby - vFW | - |
| Until The Real Thing Comes Along-vMrsJPJ | - |
| I'm Comin', Virginia - vMrsJPJ | - |
| Lost Love - vAR | - |
| *Blues Is Bad | - |

FATS WALLER AND HIS RHYTHM : Herman Autrey-t/Gene Sedric-cl-ts/Fats Waller-p-cel-v/
Albert Casey-g/Charles Turner-sb/Slick Jones-d.
New York, June 9, 1937.

| | | |
|---|---|---|
| 010647-1 | (You Know It All) Smarty - vFW | Vic 25608, HMV B-10168, EA-1976, HN-3043, SG-410 |
| 010648-1 | Don't You Know Or Don't You Care ? - vFW | Vic 25604, 20-2642, HMV BD-5258, EA-2045 |
| 010649-1 | Lost Love - vFW | Vic 25604, HMV BD-5258 |
| 010650-1 | I'm Gonna Put You In Your Place (And Your Place Is In My Arms) - vFW | Vic 25608, BB B-10008, HMV BD-5493, EA-2260 |
| 010651-1 | Blue, Turning Grey Over You - vFW | Vic 36206, NB-6004, HMV C-2937, EB-114, FKX-121, L-1041 |

NOTE:- The last title was edited to fit a 10-inch record, issued on Victor 25779.

Piano solos.                    New York, June 11, 1937

| | | |
|---|---|---|
| 010652-1 | Keepin' Out Of Mischief Now | Vic 25618, 27767, 68-0499,JA-1047, BB B-10099, HMV B-8625, EA-2382, HE-2290, N/X-4479, El EG-6757 |
| 010653-1 | Star Dust | BB B-10099, Vic 20-2638, HMV AL-5020, EA-2382, HE-2290, JO-132, N-14051, El EG 6757 |
| 010654-1 | Basin Street Blues | Vic 25631, 27767, A-1263, BB B-10115, HMV B-8636, EA-1985, HE-2289, N-4479, X-4479 |
| 010655-1 | Tea For Two | Vic 25618, 27766, 68-0499, 420-0238, JA-1047, HMV B-8625, EA-3685, N-4478 |
| 010656-1 | I Ain't Got Nobody (And Nobody Cares For Me) | Vic 25631, 27766, A-1263, BB B-10133, HMV B-8636, EA-1985, N-4478 |

FATS WALLER AND HIS RHYTHM : As for June 9, 1937; Autrey does not play where marked*.
New York, September 7, 1937.

| | | |
|---|---|---|
| 013344-1 | You've Got Me Under Your Thumb - vFW | Vic 25672, HMV BD-5310, AL-2450 |
| 013345-1 | Beat It Out - vFW | - HMV BD-5377, K-8174, SG-91 El EG-6445 |
| 013346-1 | Our Love Was Meant To Be - vFW | Vic 25681, 20-2643, HMV BD-5310, EA-2033 |
| 013347-1 | I'd Rather Call You Baby - vFW | Vic 25681, HMV EA-2033 |
| 013348-1 | I'm Always In The Mood For You - vFW | Vic 25671, HMV BD-5297, AL-2450 |
| 013349-1 | *She's Tall, She's Tan, She's Terrific - vFW | - - EA-2045 |
| 013350-1 | You're My Dish - vFW | Vic 25679, HMV EA-1990 |
| 013351-1 | More Power To You - vFW | - BD-5314 - GW-1621, GW-1900 El EG-6294 |

Dorothea Driver-v.                    New York, October 7, 1937.

| | | |
|---|---|---|
| 014645-1 | How Can I ? (With You In My Heart)-vFW | Vic 25864, HMV EA-2263 |
| 014646-1 | The Joint Is Jumpin' - vFW | Vic 25689, 20-1582, HMV BD-1079, El EG-7860 |
| 014647-1 | A Hopeless Love Affair - vFW | Vic 25689, HMV BD-5314, EA-2068, GW-1621, El EG-6294 |
| 014648-1 | What Will I Do In The Morning ? - vFW | Vic 25712 |
| 014649-1 | How Ya, Baby ? - vFW | - HMV BD-5354, EA-2128, HE/JK-2345, El EG-6383 |
| 014650-1 | Jealous Of Me - vFW | Vic 25684, HMV BD-1079 |
| 014651-1 | Call Me Darling - vDD | Rejected |

Paul Campbell-t/Caughey Roberts-cl-as/Fats Waller-p-v/Ceele Burke-g-stg/Al Morgan-
sb/Lee Young-d.                    Hollywood, December 16, 1937.

| | | |
|---|---|---|
| 09884-1 | Every Day's A Holiday - vFW | Vic 25749, HMV BD-5333, EA-2068 |
| 09885-1 | Neglected - vFW | - HMV BD-5342, El EG-6369 |
| 09886-1 | My Window Faces The South - vFW | Vic 25762 |
| 09887-1 | Am I In Another World ? - vFW/stgCB | Vic 25753, HMV BD-5360 |
| 09888-1 | Why Do Hawaiians Sing Aloha ?-vFW/stgCB | Vic 25762, HMV BD-5342 |
| 09889-1 | My First Impression Of You - vFW | Vic 25753 |

FATS WALLER AND HIS RHYTHM : Herman Autrey-t/Gene Sedric-cl-ts/Fats Waller-p-cel-v/
   Albert Casey-g/Cedric Wallace-sb/Slick Jones-d.
                               New York, March 11, 1938.

| | | |
|---|---|---|
| 021150-1 | Something Tells Me - v-celFW | Vic 25817, HMV BD-5387, JO-92, N-14038, El EG-6540 |
| 021151-1 | I Love To Whistle - vFW | Vic 25806, HMV BD-5360, EA-2083, JO-273, NE-699, El EG-7727 |
| 021152-1 | You Went To My Head - vFW | Vic 25812, HMV EA-2128 |
| 021153-1 | Florida Flo - vFW | Vic 25806, HMV HE-2702, JO-110, SG-164 |
| 021154-1 | Lost And Found - vFW | Vic 25812, HMV BD-5377, El EG-6445 |
| 021155-1 | Don't Try To Cry Your Way Back To Me-vFW | Vic 25817, HMV B-10495 |
| 021156-1 | If You're A Viper - v-celFW | Rejected |

FATS WALLER, HIS RHYTHM AND HIS ORCHESTRA : Herman Autrey-John Hamilton-Nathaniel
   Williams-t/George Robinson-John Haughton-tb/William Alsop-James Powell-Fred
   Skerritt-as/Gene Sedric-Lonnie Simmons-ts/Fats Waller-p-v/Albert Casey-g/Cedric
   Wallace-sb/Slick Jones-d.          New York, April 12, 1938.

| | | |
|---|---|---|
| 022429-1 | In The Gloaming | RFW 3 (LP) |
| 022429-2 | In The Gloaming | Vic 25847, HMV EA-2167 |
| 022430-1 | You Had An Evening To Spare - vFW | Vic 25834, HMV EA-2263, JO-397 |
| 022431-1 | Let's Break The Good News - vFW | Vic 25830, HMV EA-2155, HE-2357 |
| 022432-1 | Skrontch - vFW | Vic 25834, HMV BD-5387, K-8174, SG-91, El EG-6540 |
| 022433-1 | I Simply Adore You - vFW | Vic 25830, HMV EA-2155, HE-2357 |
| 022433-2 | I Simply Adore You - vFW | Vic LPM-10118, RFW 3 (LPs) |
| 022434-1 | The Sheik Of Araby - vFW | |
| 022434-2 | The Sheik Of Araby - vFW | Vic 25847, HMV EA-2167 |
| 022435-1 | Hold My Hand - vFW | RFW 3 (LP) |
| 022435-2 | Hold My Hand - vFW | Vic 26045, HMV EA-2296, JO-89, N-14030, SG-56 |
| 022436-1 | Inside - vFW | RFW 3 (LP) |
| 022436-2 | Inside - vFW | Vic 26045 |

FATS WALLER AND HIS RHYTHM : As for March 11, 1938.
                       New York, July 1, 1938.

| | | |
|---|---|---|
| 023760-1 | There's Honey On The Moon Tonight - vFW | Vic 25891, HMV B-10297, EA-2199, HN-3079, SG-502 |
| 023761-1 | If I Were You - vFW | Vic 26002, HMV BD-5452, EA-2223, GW-1696, K-8281, SG-96 |
| 023762-1 | The Wide Open Places - vFW | Vic 26002 |
| 023763-1 | On The Bumpy Road To Love - vFW | Vic 25898,HMV BD-5431,El EG-6676 |
| 023764-1 | Fair And Square - vFW | Vic 25891, HMV B-10234, EA-2199, El EG-7836 |
| 023765-1 | We, The People - vFW | Vic 25898, HMV EA-2223 |

FATS WALLER AND HIS CONTINENTAL RHYTHM : Dave Wilkins-t (except on OEA-6703-1)/
   George Chisholm-tb (except on OEA-6384-2 and OEA-6703-1)/Alfie Kahn-cl-ts as noted
   /Ian Sheppard-ts-vn as noted/Fats Waller-p-cel-or-v/Alan Ferguson-g/Len Harrison-
   sb/Hymie Schneider-d (OEA-6383-1)/Edmundo Ros-d (all others).
                        London, August 21, 1938.

| | | |
|---|---|---|
| OEA-6383-1 | Don't Try Your Jive On Me - tsAK or IS/v-orFW | HMV BD-5415, EA-2189, IM-1020, El EG-6389, EG-7584, BB B-10100 |
| OEA-6384-1 | Ain't Misbehavin' - tsAK/v-orFW | WRC SHB-29 (LP) |
| OEA-6384-2 | Ain't Misbehavin' - tsAK/v-orFW | HMV BD-5415, EA-2189, IM-1020, El EG-6389, EG-7584, BB B-10288 |
| OEA-6701-1 | The Flat Foot Floogie - tsIS/vFW | HMV BD-5399, El EG-6557 |
| OEA-6702-1 | Pent Up In A Penthouse - vnIS/vFW | - EA-2245 - |
| OEA-6703-1 | Music, Maestro, Please-vnIS/v-celFW | HMV BD-5398 -   El EG-6556 |
| OEA-6704-1 | A-Tisket, A-Tasket - tsAK/vFW | - |

NOTE:- The reason for the break in the numerical sequence of the above session is
that the first two, with organ, were made in EMI Studio No. 1, Abbey Road, London,
and the others in Studio No. 3.

Pipe organ solos, with Adelaide Hall-v or own v and comments.
London, August 28, 1938.

| | | |
|---|---|---|
| OEA-6385-1-2 | Swing Low, Sweet Chariot - vFW | Rejected |
| OEA-6385-3 | Swing Low, Sweet Chariot | HMV B-8818, El EG-6647, Vic 27458 |
| OEA-6386-1-2 | All God's Chillun Got Wings - vFW | Rejected |
| OEA-6386-3 | All God's Chillun Got Wings | HMV B-8818, Vic 27460 |
| OEA-6387-1-2 | Go Down, Moses - vFW | Rejected |
| OEA-6387-3 | Go Down, Moses | HMV B-8816, K-8214, El EG-6647, Vic 27458 |
| OEA-6388-1-2 | Deep River - vFW | Rejected |
| OEA-6388-3 | Deep River | HMV B-8816, K-8214, Vic 27459 |
| OEA-6389-2 | Water Boy (Convict Song) | HMV B-8845, Vic 27460 |
| OEA-6390-1 | Lonesome Road | -          Vic 27459 |
| OEA-6391-1 | That Old Feeling - vAH/spFW | HMV B-8849 |
| OEA-6392-2 | I Can't Give You Anything But Love-vAH/spFW-- | |

FATS WALLER AND HIS RHYTHM : Herman Autrey-t/Gene Sedric-cl-ts/Fats Waller-p-elo-v/
Albert Casey-g/Cedric Wallace-sb/Slick Jones-d.
New York, October 13, 1938.

| | | |
|---|---|---|
| 027289-1 | Two Sleepy People - vFW | BB B-10000, Vic 20-1583, MW M-7787 HMV BD-5452, GW-1696, K-8281,SG-96 |
| 027290-1 | Shame ! Shame ! - vFW | BB B-7885, HMV EA-2261 |
| 027291-1 | I'll Never Forgive Myself (For Not Forgiving You) - v-eloFW | BB B-10000, MW M-7787, HMV EA-2302 |
| 027291-2 | I'll Never Forgive Myself (For Not Forgiving You) - v-eloFW | RFW 3 (LP) |
| 027292-1 | You Look Good To Me - vFW | BB B-10008, HMV B-10297, EA-2260, HN-3070, SG-502 |
| 027293-1 | Tell Me With Your Kisses - vFW | BB B-7885, HMV EA-2261 |
| 027293-2 | Tell Me With Your Kisses - vFW | RFW 3 (LP) |
| 027294-1 | Yacht Club Swing - eloFW | BB B-10035, HMV EA-2279 |

New York, December 7, 1938.

| | | |
|---|---|---|
| 030363-1 | Love, I'd Give My Life For You - vFW | BB B-10070, HMV B-10495,RZ G-24244 |
| 030364-1 | I Wish I Had You - vFW | BB B-10078, HMV JO-397, RZ G-24308 |
| 030365-1 | I'll Dance At Your Wedding - vFW | BB B-10070, HMV HE-2896, JO-196, N-14065, RZ G-24244 |
| 030366-1 | Imagine My Surprise - vFW | BB B-10062, HMV BD-1073,RZ G-24194 |
| 030367-1 | I Won't Believe It (Until I Hear It From You) - vFW | -       HMV B-10168, HN-3043, SG-410, RZ G-24346 |
| 030368-1 | The Spider And The Fly - vFW&ch | BB B-10205, HMV BD-5486, GY-394 |
| 030369-1 | Patty Cake, Patty Cake (Baker Man) - vFW | BB B-10149, HMV BD-5476, K-8328 |

New York, January 19, 1939.

| | | |
|---|---|---|
| 031530-1 | A Good Man Is Hard To Find - vFW | BB B-10143, HMV B-10439, ALS-5040, TG-156 |
| 031530-2 | A Good Man Is Hard To Find - vFW | RFW 3 (LP) |
| 031531-1 | You Out-Smarted Yourself - vFW | BB B-10116, RZ G-24346 |
| 031532-1 | Last Night A Miracle Happened - vFW | BB B-10136, HMV BD-5469, B-10050, GY-474, HE-2976, HN-3042, RZ G-24563 |
| 031533-1 | Good For Nothin' But Love - vFW | BB B-10129, HMV BD-5476, K-8328 |
| 031534-1 | Hold Tight (Want Some Sea Food, Mama) - vFW | BB B-10116, Vic 20-1581, HMV BD-5469, GY-474 |
| 031535-1 | Kiss Me With Your Eyes - v-eloFW | JA 7 (LP) |
| 031535-2 | Kiss Me With Your Eyes - v-eloFW | BB B-10136, HMV EA-2296 |

New York, March 9, 1939.

| | | |
|---|---|---|
| 032942-1 | You Asked For It - You Got It - vFW | BB B-10170, HMV BD-1036,RZ G-24859 |
| 032943-1 | Some Rainy Day - vFW | BB B-10192, MW M-7962 |
| 032944-1 | 'Tain't What You Do (It's The Way That Cha Do It) - vFW | -          - HMV BD-5486, GY-541 |
| 032945-1 | Got No Time - vFW | BB B-10170, HMV BD-5493,RZ G-24938 |
| 032946-1 | Step Up And Shake My Hand - vFW | BB B-10184 |
| 032947-1 | Undecided - vFW | - |
| 032948-1 | Remember Who You're Promised To - vFW | BB B-10205 |

Piano solos and vocals, acc. by Johnny Marks-d.
London, April 3, 1939.

| | | |
|---|---|---|
| You Can't Have Your Cake And Eat It-vFW | Tem A-76, Cir R-3005, JSo AA-576 | |
| Not There - Right There - vFW | —    —    — | |
| Cottage In The Rain - vFW | Ristic 8 | |
| What A Pretty Miss - vFW | Rejected | |

Marks omitted.
London, June 12, 1939.

Reminiscing Through England, No. 2-Pt. 2 Ristic 22 (LP)
NOTE:- The rest of this work, made privately in the EMI Studios, has never been
found. Fats Waller also made a recording of the LONDON SUITE in Billy Higgs'
studios on the same date as the above; Mr. Ed Kirkeby owns the original acetates,
which offer variations on the themes recorded under the same names as follows.

Max Lewin-d added, or pipe-organ solos with own v (see note on page 1632).
London, June 13, 1939.

| | | | |
|---|---|---|---|
| OEA-7878-1 | London Suite - Piccadilly | HMV B-10059, HE-2721, El EG-7630 |
| OEA-7879-1 | —    Chelsea | —    —    — |
| OEA-7880-1 | —    Soho | HMV B-10060, HE-2722, El EG-7631 |
| OEA-7881-1 | —    Bond Street | —    —    — |
| OEA-7882-1 | —    Limehouse | HMV B-10061, HE-2723, El EG-7632 |
| OEA-7883-1 | —    Whitechapel | —    —    — |
| OEA-7884-1-2 | Hallelujah | Rejected |
| OEA-7885-1-2 | Signing On At H.M.V. | — |
| OEA-7982-2 | Smoke Dreams Of You - v-orFW | HMV B-8967 |
| OEA-7983-1 | You Can't Have Your Cake And Eat It-v-orFW | — |

FATS WALLER AND HIS RHYTHM : Herman Autrey-t/Chauncey Graham-ts/Fats Waller-p-v/John
Smith-g/Cedric Wallace-sb/Larry Hinton-d.
New York, June 28, 1939.

| | | |
|---|---|---|
| 038207-1 | Honey Hush - vFW | BB B-10346, MW M-8394,<br>HMV B-10191, HE-2997, JO-274,<br>SG-357, El EG-7719, RZ G-24220 |
| 038207-2 | Honey Hush - vFW | RFW 3 (LP) |
| 038208-1 | I Used To Love You (But It's All Over<br>Now) - vFW | BB B-10369, Vic 20-2219, MW M-8393,<br>HMV BD-5533, K-8469, RZ G-24274 |
| 038209-1 | Wait And See - vFW | BB B-10405, HMV GY-552 |
| 038210-1 | You Meet The Nicest People In Your<br>Dreams - vFW | BB B-10346, MW M-8394, RZ G-24220 |
| 038211-1 | Anita - vFW | BB B-10369, MW M-8393,<br>HMV BD-5533, K-8469, RZ G-24938 |
| 038212-1 | What A Pretty Miss - vFW | BB B-10437, HMV B-10050,<br>HN-3042, NE-810 |

John Hamilton-t/Gene Sedric-cl-ts/Fats Waller-p-v/John Smith-g/Cedric Wallace-sb/
Slick Jones-d, or p only.. All tracks dubbed from private acetates, all except the
Jazz Society issues are on Vic LPT-6001; those marked ** are on Camden CAL-473,
CDN-131 and LCP-23 also.
New York, August 2, 1939.

| | | | |
|---|---|---|---|
| The Moon Is Low | Vic RD-7552, 430209, HMV CLP-1035 | | |
| **The Sheik Of Araby - vFW | —    —    — | | |
| **B Flat Blues | —    —    — | | |
| Honeysuckle Rose - vFW | —    —    — | | |
| **I'm Crazy 'Bout My Baby - vFW | Vic RD-7553    —    HMV CLP-1042 | | |
| The Spider And The Fly - vFW | —    —    — | | |
| After You've Gone - vFW | —    —    — | | |
| Poor Butterfly - pFW | —    430208    — | | |
| St. Louis Blues - pFW | —    —    — | | |
| Tea For Two - pFW | —    430209    — | | |
| Sweet Sue - vFW | JSo AA-535 | | |
| Ain't Misbehavin' - vFW | — | | |
| Nagasaki - | JSo AA-536 | | |
| Hallelujah - pFW | Ember CJS-839 (LP) | | |
| A Handful Of Keys - pFW | — | | |

FATS WALLER AND HIS RHYTHM : John Hamilton-t/Gene Sedric-cl-ts/Fats Waller-p-v/John
    Smith-g/Cedric Wallace-sb/Slick Jones-d.
                                        New York, August 10, 1939.

041528-1  Squeeze Me - vFW                      BB B-10405, Vic 20-2217,
                                                MW M-4892, HMV AL-5020, GY-552,
                                                JO-132, N-14051
041529-1  Bless You - vFW                       BB B-10393, MH-52
041530-1  It's The Tune That Counts - vFW         - HMV JO-89, N-14030, SG-56
041531-1  Abdullah - vFW                        BB B-10419, Vic 20-2639,
                                                MW M-8391, HMV NE-724, RZ G-24166
041532-1  Who'll Take My Place ? - vFW          As above, but Vic 20-2642
041533-1  Bond Street                           BB B-10437, HMV NE-810, RZ G-24274

    Una Mae Carlisle-v.                New York, November 3, 1939.

043346-1  It's You Who Taught It To Me - vFW&ch  BB B-10527, HMV HE-2731, JO-128
043347-1  Suitcase Susie - vFW                  BB B-10500, MW M-8648,
                                                HMV HN-2426, JO-81, NE-790
043348-1  Your Feet's Too Big - vFW             BB B-10500, Vic 20-1580, 40-0009,
                                                420-0235, MW M-8648, HMV B-9582,
                                                HN-2359, MH-52, NE-790, V-Disc 308
043349-1  You're Lettin' The Grass Grow Under   BB B-10527, HMV JO-273, EI EG-7727
            Your Feet - vFW
043350-1  The Darktown Strutters' Ball - vFW    BB B-10573, Vic 20-2220,
                                                HMV JO-116, N-14045, SG-388
043351-1  I Can't Give You Anything But Love     BB B-10573, Vic 20-1582, 420-0237,
            - vFW-UMC                            HMV IW-341
043351-2  I Can't Give You Anything But Love     RFW 3
            - vFW-UMC

Piano or Hammond (electric) organ solos, with own vocal, all dubbed from 16-inch
    Lang-Worth transcription discs.        New York, November 20, 1939.

043185-1  Go Down, Moses-v/Swing Low, Sweet     Riv RLP-1021, 12-109, Lon AL-3521,
            Chariot-v/Hallelujah ! I'm A Bum-v/   WRC T-336, EMI OUM-2086 (LPs)
            Hand Me Down My Walkin' Cane-v (all elo)
043186-1  Frankie And Johnny-v/She'll Be Comin'   As above
            'Round The Mountain-v/Deep River-v/The Lord Delivered Daniel-v (all elo)
043187-1  Ah ! So Pure ("Martha"-von Flotow)    PC LP-22
            Then You'll Remember Me ("The Bohemian    -      Jazz Treasury 1001
            Girl"-Balfe)/Sextet ("Lucia di Lammermoor"-Donizetti)/My Heart At Thy
            Sweet Voice ("Samson and Delilah"-Saint-Saëns) (all p)
043188-1  Intermezzo ("Cavalleria Rusticana"-   Riv RLP-1022, 12-109, Lon AL-3522*
            Mascagni)(labelled AH ! SO PURE in    WRC T-336, EMI OUM-2086 (LPs)
            error*)/When You And I Were Young, Maggie-v/Loch Lomond-v/Oh ! Susannah-
            v) (all p)
043189-1  The Old Oaken Bucket-v/Waltz ("Faust"-  As above
            Gounod)/Annie Laurie-v/Oh, Dem Golden Slippers-v (all p)

FATS WALLER AND HIS RHYTHM : As for August 10, 1939; Waller db elo, Jones vib.
                                        Chicago, January 12, 1940.

044597-1  Swinga-Dilla Street - eloFW           BB B-10858, RZ G-24504
044598-1  At Twilight - vFW                     BB B-10803, HMV JO-96, N-14033
044599-1  Oh ! Frenchy - vFW                    BB B-10658, Vic 20-1595,
                                                HMV HE/JK-2291, X-6543, V-Disc 359
044600-1  Cheatin' On Me - vFW/vibSJ            BB B-10658 -        -    RZ G-24563
044601-1  Black Maria - vFW                     BB B-10624
044602-1  Mighty Fine - vFW                     BB B-10744, HMV GY-447, IW-339
044603-1  The Moon Is Low                       BB B-10624, HMV EA-2571
044604-1  The Moon Is Low - Part 2              Rejected

The next three titles are probably from about this period, judging by the titles.

          Old Grandad - vFW                     Ember CJS-842 (LP)
          Dark Eyes - vFW                         -
          Jingle Bells - vFW                      -

FATS WALLER AND HIS RHYTHM : John Hamilton-t (unless marked **)/Gene Sedric-cl-ts/
   Fats Waller-p-cel-elo-v/John Smith-g/Cedric Wallace-sb/Slick Jones-d.
                              New York, April 11, 1940.

| | | |
|---|---|---|
| 048775-1 | Old Grand Dad - vFW | BB B-10698, HMV B-10262, GY-547, HN-3013 |
| 048776-1 | Fat And Greasy - vFW | BB B-10803, HMV JO-116, N-14045 |
| 048777-1** | Little Curly Hair In A High Chair - vFW | BB B-10698, HMV BD-1235, EA-2571, GY-547, GY-847, SG-363 |
| 048778-1 | (You're A) Square From Delaware - vFW | BB B-10730, HMV GY-553, IW-341 |
| 048779-1 | You Run Your Mouth, I'll Run My Business - vFW | BB B-10779, HMV GY-512 |
| 048780-1 | Too Tired - vFW | - HMV B-10406 - HN-3120,TG-157 |
| 048781-1 | "Send Me" Jackson - vFW | BB B-10730, HMV BD-1229, GY-553, HE-2672, HN-2599, IW-342, SG-65, El EG-7860 |
| 048782-1 | Eep, Ipe, Wanna Piece Of Pie - vFW | BB B-10744, HMV BD-906, IW-343 |

   Albert Casey-g replaces Smith.        New York, July 16, 1940.

| | | |
|---|---|---|
| 051865-1 | Stop Pretending - vFW&ch | BB B-10829, HMV B-10406, SG-515, TG-157, RZ G-24859 |
| 051866-1 | I'll Never Smile Again - vFW | BB B-10841 |
| 051867-1 | My Mommie Sent Me To The Store-vFW&ch | BB B-10892, HMV HE-2731, JO-128, RZ G-24800 |
| 051868-2 | Dry Bones - vFW | BB B-10892, HMV B-9885, HE-2813, HN-2763, JO-133, N-14052, El EG-7622, RZ G-24813 |
| 051869-1 | "Fats" Waller's Original E Flat Blues - vFW | BB B-10858, HMV BD-906, RZ G-24504 |
| 051870-1 | Stayin' At Home - vFW | BB B-10841, HMV BD-1235, SG-363 |
| 051871-1 | Hey ! Stop Kissin' My Sister - vFW | BB B-10829, HMV HE-2702, JO-110, SG-164, RZ G-24813 |

   Catherine Perry-v.                 New York, November 6, 1940.

| | | |
|---|---|---|
| 057083-1 | Everybody Loves My Baby (But My Baby Don't Love Nobody But Me) - vFW | BB B-10989, Vic 20-2217, HMV B-9935, SG-304, RZ G-25009 |
| 057084-1 | I'm Gonna Salt Away Some Sugar (For My Sugar And Me) - vFW | BB B-10943, HMV JO-92, N-14038 |
| 057085-1 | 'Tain't Nobody's Bizness If I Do - vFW | BB B-10967, HMV JO-96, N-14033, SG-388 |
| 057086-1 | Abercrombie Had A Zombie - vFW | BB B-10967 |
| 057087-1** | Blue Eyes - v-celFW | BB B-10943, HMV JO-132 |
| 057088-1 | Scram ! | BB B-10989, RZ G-25009 |
| 057089-1 | My Melancholy Baby - vCP | RFW 1 (LP) |

   From a "short" film soundtrack.     New York, November 7, 1940.

| | | |
|---|---|---|
| | Ain't Misbehavin' - vFW | RFW 1,DJM DJB-44235,Ember CJS-839 |
| | The Joint Is Jumpin'-vFW/Your Feet's Too Big-vFW/Honeysuckle Rose-vFW | RFW 2          -            - (LPs) |

Source unknown (? air-shot ?)        Chicago, December 31, 1940.

| | | |
|---|---|---|
| | Lila Lou - vFW | RFW 3,DJM DJB-44235,Ember CJS-842 |

                             Chicago, January 2, 1941.

| | | |
|---|---|---|
| 053794-1 | Mamacita - eloFW | BB B-11078 |
| 053795-1 | Liver Lip Jones - vFW | BB B-11010 |
| 053796-1 | Buckin' The Dice - vFW | BB B-11102, Vic 20-2640, RZ G-24853 |
| 053797-1 | Pantin' In The Panther Room - eloFW | BB B-11175, HMV B-10262, HN-3013, RZ G-24836 |
| 053798-1 | Come Down To Earth, My Angel - v-eloFW | BB B-11010, HMV JO-205 |
| 053799-1 | Shortnin' Bread - vFW&ch | BB B-11078, HMV BD-1218, HN-2584 |
| 059100-1 | I Repent - v-eloFW | BB B-11188 |

FATS WALLER AND HIS RHYTHM : John Hamilton-t/Gene Sedric-cl-ts/Fats Waller-p-elo-v/
    Albert Casey-g/Cedric Wallace-sb/Slick Jones-d; Waller, Casey and Jones only**.
                            New York, March 20, 1941.

| | | |
|---|---|---|
| 062761-1 | Do You Have To Go ? - vFW | BB B-11222, HMV BD-5787, NE-699 |
| 062762-1 | Pan-Pan - vFW&ch | BB B-11383, HMV BD-1011, HE-2416, MH-131 |
| 062763-1 | I Wanna Hear Swing Songs - vFW | BB B-11115, HMV BD-1028, HE-2346 |
| 062764-1 | You're Gonna Be Sorry - vFW | Vic 20-1602, HMV B-10830, TG-224 |
| 062765-1 | All That Meat And No Potatoes - vFW | BB B-11102, RZ G-24800, V-Disc 308 |
| 062766-1**Let's Get Away From It All - v-eloFW | | BB B-11115 |

    Piano solos only where marked *.       New York, May 13, 1941.

| | | |
|---|---|---|
| 063887-1 | *Georgia On My Mind | Vic 27765, HMV HE-2975, N-4477 |
| 063888-1 | *Rockin' Chair | - HMV EA-3685 -      - |
| 063889-1 | *Carolina Shout | JA 7 (LP) |
| 063889-2 | *Carolina Shout | Vic 27563, HMV AV-722 |
| 063890-1 | *Honeysuckle Rose | Vic 20-1580, 420-0235 |
| 063891-1 | *Ring Dem Bells | Vic 27563, HMV AV-722 |
| 063892-1 | Twenty-Four Robbers - vFW | BB B-11222, HMV BD-1011, JK-2651, MH-131, RZ G-24853 |
| 063893-1 | I Understand - vFW | BB B-11175 |
| 063894-1 | Sad Sap Sucker Am I - vFW | BB B-11296, HMV HE-2428,RZ G-24895 |

FATS WALLER, HIS RHYTHM AND HIS ORCHESTRA : The above Rhythm plus Herman Autrey-Bob
    Williams-t/George Wilson-Ray Hogan-tb/Jimmy Powell-Dave McRae-as/Bob Carroll-ts.
                            Hollywood, July 1, 1941.

| | | |
|---|---|---|
| 061334-1 | Chant Of The Groove | BB B-11262, Vic 20-2638,RZ G-24895 |
| 061335-1 | Come And Get It - vFW | -          Vic 20-2448 |
| 061336-1 | Rump Steak Serenade - vFW&ch | BB B-11296, HMV B-9582, HN-2369, JK-2475 |
| 061337-1 | Ain't Nothing To It | RI-Disc 2 (LP) |

    NOTE:- HMV JK-2475 as NEW ORLEANS FEETWARMERS.

FATS WALLER AND HIS RHYTHM : As for March 20, 1941; Waller plays bells on 067949-1.
                            New York, October 1, 1941.

| | | |
|---|---|---|
| 067946-1 | Oh Baby, Sweet Baby (What Are You Doing To Me ?) - vFW | BB B-11383, HMV BD-1036, HE-2416 |
| 067947-1 | Buck Jumpin' | BB B-11324, HMV HE-2446,RZ G-25055 |
| 067948-1 | That Gets It, Mr. Joe - vFW | BB B-11425, HMV BD-1028,HE-2346 - |
| 067949-1 | The Bells Of San Raquel - vFW | BB B-11324, HMV HE-2446 |
| 067950-1 | Bessie, Bessie, Bessie - vFW | Cam CAL-588 (LP) |
| 067951-1 | Clarinet Marmalade - eloFW | BB B-11469, HMV AV-750, HE-2371 |

FATS WALLER, HIS RHYTHM AND HIS ORCHESTRA : Probably similar to July 1, 1941 person-
    nel; Arthur Trappier-d replaces Jones.  Freedom's People Program, N.Y.,Dec.21,1941.

          Honeysuckle Rose - vFW            PC 13, Ember CJS-842 (LPs)

FATS WALLER AND HIS RHYTHM : Herman Autrey-t/Gene Sedric-cl-ts/Fats Waller-p-v/Albert
    Casey-g/Charles Turner-sb/Arthur Trappier-d.
                            New York, December 26, 1941.

| | | |
|---|---|---|
| 068810-1 | Winter Weather - vFW | BB B-11469, HMV B-10234, AV-750, HE-2371, El EG-7836 |
| 068811-1 | Cash For Your Trash - vFW | BB B-11425, HMV HE-2428 |
| 068812-1 | Don't Give Me That Jive - vFW | BB B-11539, HMV BD-1077,RZ G-24989 |
| 068813-1 | Your Socks Don't Match - vFW | BB 30-0814, HMV BD-1073 |

Piano solo and comments, with Hot Lips Page-t or Eddie Condon and his Band : Max
    Kaminsky-t/Pee Wee Russell-cl/Bud Freeman-ts/Eddie Condon-g/John Kirby-sb/Gene
    Krupa-d, as shown.              Carnegie Hall, N. Y., January 14, 1942.

          Blues in B flat - tHLP           PC 09 (LP)
          Honeysuckle Rose - ECB           JA 1 (LP)

FATS WALLER AND HIS RHYTHM : Probably : Herman Autrey-t/Gene Sedric-cl-ts/Fats Waller
    p-v/Albert Casey-g/Charles Turner-sb/Arthur Trappier-d.
                                          New York, February 2, 1942.

            Winter Weather - vFW                RFW 2, Ember CJS-842 (LPs)
            Cash For Your Trash - vFW            -            -

FATS WALLER, HIS RHYTHM AND HIS ORCHESTRA : Herman Autrey-John Hamilton-Joe Thomas-
    Nathaniel Williams-t/Herb Flemming-George Wilson-tb/Jackie Fields-George James-as/
    Gene Sedric-cl-ts/Bob Carroll-ts/Fats Waller-p-elo-v/Albert Casey-g/Cedric Wallace-
    sb/Arthur Trappier-d.                  New York, March 16, 1942.

073440-1  We Need A Little Love - vFW          BB B-11518
073441-1  You Must Be Losing Your Mind - vFW   BB B-11539, HMV BD-1077,RZ G-24989
073442-1  Really Fine                          Vic LPM-10118 (LP)
073443-1  The Jitterbug Waltz - eloFW          BB B-11518, Vic 20-2639,HMV HE-2976

FATS WALLER AND HIS RHYTHM : John Hamilton-t/Gene Sedric-cl-ts/Fats Waller-p-v/Albert
    Casey-g/Cedric Wallace-sb/Arthur Trappier-d/The Deep River Boys-v quartet; Hamilton
    and Sedric omitted**.                 New York, July 13, 1942.

075423-1  By The Light Of The Silvery Moon     BB B-11569, Vic 20-2448,
            - vFW-DRB                           HMV B-10748, AV-749, NE-688
075424-1  Swing Out To Victory - vFW           BB B-11569
075425-1  Up Jumped You With Love - vFW        BB 30-0814, HMV BD-1045
075426-1**Romance a la mode - vDRB             BB 30-0805     -         B-10748

Vocal, acc. by the Victor "Eirst Nighter" Orchestra.
                                          New York, July 30, 1942.

075469-1  That's What The Well Dressed Man In  Vic 27956
            Harlem Will Wear

## CHARLOTTE  WALSH

Pseudonym on Silvertone for Anna Lee Chisholm, q.v.

## JACK WALSH AND HIS ORCHESTRA

Instrumentation and personnel unknown, but probably a Bob Haring band of the period,
    q.v.                                  New York, c. May, 1927.

            Four Or Five Times                 Cam 1154, Ro 384
NOTE:- Cameo 1154 as THE WESTERN WANDERERS.  This title is listed under the name on
the subsidiary label rather than the parent label, as it is less obviously a pseudonym.  Romeo 384 bears the false number 246-A.


## EDDIE WALTERS'  DANCE BAND

Pseudonym on Plaza P-374 (RAINBOW BLUES) for Oscar Rabin and his Romany Band, q.v.,
    and for other titles on the same label by this and probably other bands, of no
    known interest as jazz.


## EDDIE  WALTERS

Vocal, acc. by p/? Andy Sannella-g/own u.
                                          New York, March 12, 1929.

148031-2  Makin' Whoopee                       Col 1763-D, 5554
148057-1  I'm Ka-razy For You                  -            -

    Acc. by ? Mike Mosiello-t/Andy Sannella-cl/? Ben Selvin-vn/? Rube Bloom-p.
                                          New York, September 6, 1929.

148982-3  Little By Little                     Col 1969-D
158983-3  Collegiate Sam                       -

Acc. by Tommy Dorsey-t/Charlie Butterfield-tb/Jimmy Dorsey-cl-as/Adrian Rollini-
bsx/Frank Signorelli-p/Carl Kress-g/own u/Stan King-d.
                                        New York, February 27, 1930.

| | | |
|---|---|---|
| 150030-3 | 'Leven-Thirty Saturday Night | Col 2137-D, DB-151 |
| 150031-3 | Me And The Girl Next Door | -        DB-169 |

Acc. by Manny Klein-t/Tommy Dorsey-tb/Benny Goodman-cl/Frank Signorelli-p/Eddie
Lang-g/own u.                           New York, May 20, 1930.

| | | |
|---|---|---|
| 150515-3 | It Must Be Love | Col 2232-D, DB-273 |

Acc. by Manny Klein-t/Frank Signorelli-p/Eddie Lang-g/own u/Joe Tarto-sb/Stan King
d.                                      New York, June 10, 1930.

| | | |
|---|---|---|
| 150581-3 | I Love You So Much | Col 2232-D, DB-273, Re G-20803 |

Acc. by ? Bob Effros or ? Manny Klein-t/? Frank Signorelli-p/Dick McDonough-g/sb.
                                        New York, September 12, 1930.

| | | |
|---|---|---|
| 150800-3 | (Since They're All Playing) Miniature Golf | Col 2290-D |
| 150801-2 | Go Home And Tell Your Mother | - |

## TOM WALTHAM ET SES "AD-LIBS" (ORCHESTRE DE L'ERMITAGE)

Tom Waltham was an Englishman who lived most of his professional life in France as a
pianist-bandleader. His orchestra is claimed by some historians to have included
Emile Christian-tb, and the following are listed here on the strength of this, but
subsequent issues that obviously do not include Christian, and "novelty" piano
solos of the Billy Mayerl-Zez Confrey type are excluded as they have no jazz value.

Tom Waltham-p-pac dir. c/? Emile Christian-tb/ ―― Mauborg-cl-as/Max Brun-cl-ts/
? Chris Waltham-bj/bb/d.                 Paris, c. October, 1925.

| | | |
|---|---|---|
| BT-10-1 | Naughty Melody | HMV K-3268 |
| BT-11-2 | Fooling | - |
| BT-12-1 | Ou, quand, comment | HMV K-3169 |
| BT-13-2 | C'est bouche a bouche | - |

Vn added*.                              Paris, c. March, 1926.

| | | |
|---|---|---|
| N-7993 | Un Bon Mouvement | PA X-6937, P 6937 |
| N-7994 | Mon Coeur | -        - |
| N-7995 | Pour Danser Le Charleston | PA X-6938, P 6938 |
| N-7996 | *La Musique Grisante | -        - |

                                        Paris, c. April, 1926.

| | | |
|---|---|---|
| N-8030 | Toujours I Love You | PA X-6953, P 6953 |
| N-8032 | Charleston Dolly | PA X-6952, P 6952 |
| N-8033 | Pour vous, mesdames | PA X-6953, P 6953 |
| N-8034 | Kiss-Ball | PA X-6952, P 6952 |

NOTE:- Matrix N-8031 is untraced.

Cl-as and bsx replace previous reeds.  Paris, c. April, 1926.

| | | |
|---|---|---|
| BD-4016-2 | Est-ce je te demande ? | HMV K-3248, K-5447 |
| BD-4017-2 | Raymond | -        - |
| BD-4018-2 | Quand on n'en a pas | HMV K-3247 |

## LORRAINE WALTON

The following blues item is of some interest as jazz in view of its accompanists.

Vocal, acc. by cl/? Blind John Davis-p/g/sb.
                                        Chicago, February 9, 1938.

| | | |
|---|---|---|
| C-2084- | If You're A Viper | Voc 03989 |
| C-2085- | Waiting Blues | - |

## THE WANDERERS

Hollis Horton-t/Dick Reinhart-cl-v/Marvin Montgomery or Fred Caceres-vn/Knocky Parker
p/Muryel Campbell ("Uncle Zeke")-g-v/Bert Dodson-sb-v.
San Antonio, January 28, 1935.

| | | |
|---|---|---|
| 87728-1 | Wanderer's Stomp | BB B-5369, Vic JR-28 |
| 87729-1 | Tiger Rag - vch | BB B-5887, HMV JF-26 |
| 87730-1 | Footwarmer | BB B-5994 |
| 87731-1 | No-One To Say Goodbye - vDR | BB B-5887 |
| 87732-1 | Sweet Uncle Zeke | Rejected |
| 87733-1 | A Good Man Is Hard To Find - vBD | BB B-5834 |
| 87734-1 | I Ain't Got Nobody - v3 | B6 B-5369, Vic JR-28 |
| 87735-1 | Nealski | BB B-5994 |
| 87736-1 | A Thousand Miles - vMC | Rejected |
| 87737-1 | It's You I Adore - vBD | BB B-5834 |

## AMY WARD

Pseudonym on Silvertone for Sodarisa Miller, q.v.

## BILLY WARD

Pseudonym on Oriole for Buster Bailey, q.v.

## FRANK E. WARD AND HIS ORCHESTRA

Frank E. Ward-ts dir. Sylvester Ahola-Eddie Brown-t/Eddie Foley-tb/Foster Morehouse-
as/Harry Baltimore-vn/Lennie Powers-p/Clayton Cunningham-bj/bb/Boogie Walker-d.
Framingham, Mass., March 25, 1924.

| | | |
|---|---|---|
| 133 | The One I Love Belongs To Somebody Else | Lin rejected |
| 134 | Lots O' Mama | - |
| 158-2 | There's Yes ! Yes ! In Your Eyes | - |

NOTE:- It is likely that the Lincoln Laboratories where the above sides were made
have no connection with the Cameo subsiduary label of the same name. Despite the
gap: in the matrix numbers, Mr. Ahola confirms all three sides were made on the
same date, his first recording session.

## JOE WARD'S SWANEE CLUB ORCHESTRA

2t/tb/3-4cl-ss-as-ts/p/g/bb/d/v trio.      New York, c. November 19, 1928.

| | | |
|---|---|---|
| 3476-C | Traffic Jam | Cam 9026, Lin 3055, Ro 830 |
| 3477-A | Scorchin' - v3 | -            -          - |

## WARD'S TRAIL BLAZER ORCHESTRA

The following title by this unknown band is said to be of interest as "hot" dance
music.

T/tb/2as/ts/vn/p/bj/bb/d.                  ? ! os Angeles, c. February, 1927.

At Sundown                                 Ward's W-110

## OZIE WARE

Vocal, acc. by Arthur Whetsel-t/Barney Bigard-cl/Duke Ellington-p/Billy Taylor-bb/
Sonny Greer-d.                             New York, October 30, 1928.

| | | |
|---|---|---|
| 48100-1 | Santa Claus, Bring My Man Back To Me | Vic 21777, Bm 1033 |
| 48101-2 | I Done Caught You Blues | - |

NOTE:- Biltmore 1033 as OZIE WARE, ACC. BY DUKE ELLINGTON'S HOT FIVE.

Acc. by the Whoopee Makers : Arthur Whetsel-t/Joe Nanton-tb/Barney Bigard-cl/Duke
Ellington-p/Fred Guy-bj/Wellman Braud-sb/Sonny Greer-d, or Duke Ellington-p only*.
New York, c. December 18, 1928.

| | | |
|---|---|---|
| 3532-B | Hit Me In The Nose Blues | Cam 9039, Lin 3068, PA 7540, Per 140, Ro 843 |
| 3533-B | *It's All Comin' Home To You | Cam 9039, Lin 3068, Ro 843 |

Acc. by Porter Grainger-p.                    New York, January 3, 1929.

407   Dese Men Don't Mean You No Good - Part 1 Vic test
408   Dese Men Don't Mean You No Good - Part 2      -

Acc. by the Whoopee Makers : Arthur Whetsel-t/Joe Nanton-tb/Barney Bigard-cl/Duke
Ellington-p/Fred Guy-bj/Wellman Braud-sb/Sonny Greer-d.
                                              New York, c. March 18, 1929.

3715-B  He Just Don't Appeal To Me            Cam 9042, Lin 3267, Ro 1042

## WARING'S PENNSYLVANIANS

The following titles by this famous dance orchestra are known to contain solo work of
some interest as jazz.

Fred Waring-v dir. Nelson Keller-t/Jim Gilliland-tb/Fred Campbell-cl-as-bar-f/Si
Sharp-as/Elton Cockerill-cl-ts/Bill Townsend-vn/Tom Waring-p-v/Fred Buck-bj/Jimmy
Mullen-bb/Poley McClintock-d.          Camden, N. J., October 16, 1923.

28665-5  Stack O' Lee Blues                   Vic 19189, HMV B-1760

? George Culley-t added.                      Camden, N. J., January 2, 1924.

29239-5  Dancin' Dan                          Vic 19257, HMV B-1810

                                              Camden, N. J., January 3, 1924.

29242-2  Oh Baby ! (Don't Say "No," Say "Maybe")  Vic 19254, HMV B-1884

                                              Camden, N. J., March 26, 1924.

29694-5  Down Home Blues                      Vic 19303

                                              Camden, N. J., June 6, 1924.

30250-2  Just Hot !                           Vic 19377

                                              Camden, N. J., December 10, 1924.

31258-1  Oh ! Mabel                           Vic 19533, HMV B-1984

3rd t/Clare Hanlon-tb-v/Frances Foster-Fred Culley-vn added; Will Morgan-cl-as-v/
Earl Gardner-as replace Sharp; Ed Radel-bb replaces Mullen.
                                              New York, March 9, 1928.

43103-7  Collegiana - vFW-TW&ch               Vic 21307, HMV B-5483

One vn omitted;                               New York, March 28, 1928.

43187-3  Farewell Blues - vFW-O               Vic 21508

4th t/3rd vn added.                           Camden, N. J., April 18, 1928.

28665-12 Stack O' Lee Blues                   Vic 21508

4th t omitted.                                Camden, N. J., October 12, 1928.

46193-6  I'm Sorry, Sally - vCH               Vic 21755, HMV B-5587

Charles Henderson and/or Frank W. Hower-p replace Tom Waring.
                                              New York, December 14, 1928.

48406-5  Glorianna - vCH                      Vic 21836, HMV B-5618

Stuart Churchill-t-as-x replaces Culley; D. Wade Schlegel-t replaces (or may even
be) the 3rd t; 2vn only.            New York, December 17, 1929.

58115-2  Hello Baby - vWM                     Vic 22266

Michel Warlop was a prominent French dance-band violinist and leader during the 1930s
    and 1940s.  Among his many records are several on which internationally-recognized
    musicians played, as shown below.  See also Coleman Hawkins.

MICHEL WARLOP ET SON ORCHESTRE : Michel Warlop-vn dir. Pierre Allier-Noel Chiboust-
    Maurice Moufflard-t/Marcel Dumont-Isidore Bassard-tb/Andre Ekyan-cl-as/Amedee
    Charles-as/Charles Lisee-as-bar/Alix Combelle-ts/Stephane Grappelly-p/Django
    Reinhardt-g/Roger Grasset-sb/ —— McGregor-d.
                                        Paris, March 16, 1934.

OPG-1415-1  Presentation Stomp                  HMV K-7314

                                        Paris, May 12, 1934.

OPG-1574-1  Blue Interlude                      HMV K-7314

    Personnel includes Alex Renard-t/Maurice Cizeron-as-f/Alix Combelle-ts/Emil Stern-
    p/Django Reinhardt-Joseph Reinhardt-g/Louis Vola-sb.
                                        Paris, April 17, 1936.

| 2422hpp | Cloud Castles | Pol F-512736 |
| 2423hpp | Magic Strings | - |
| 2424hpp | Sweet Serenade | Pol F-512737 |
| 2425hpp | Crazy Strings | - |
| 2426hpp | Novel Pets | Pol F-512738 |
| 2427½hpp | Budding Dancers | - |

    A. Pico-t*/Jean Magnien-cl/Andre Lamory-as/Charles Shaaf-ts/ —— Paquay-f* or d**/
    Pierre Zeppilli-p/Django Reinhardt-g/Louis Vola-sb.
                                        Paris, December 21, 1937.

OLA-1999-1 *Serenade For A Wealthy Widow        Swing 28
OLA-2000-1**Taj Mahal                           -

    Warlop-Reinhardt-Vola only where noted. Paris, December 27, 1937.

OLA-2214-1 *Organ Grinder's Swing               Swing 43, Col GN-5044
OLA-2216-1  Tea For Two - MW-DR-LV              Swing 15
OLA-2217-1  Christmas Swing - MW-DR-LV           -
    NOTE:- Matrix OLA-2215 is a guitar solo by Django Reinhardt, q.v.

Violin solos, acc. by Stephane Grappelly-p/Django Reinhardt-g/Louis Vola-sb.
                                        Paris, December 28, 1937.

OLA-2312-1  Sweet Sue, Just You                 Swing 43, Col GN-5044

    Acc. by Garland Wilson-p.            Paris, March 9, 1938.

OSW-18-1  You Showed Me The Way                 Swing 74

## BUD WARNER AND  HIS RED CAPS

Pseudonym on Bell 1174 for Henry Johnson's Boys, q.v.

## JOAN  WARNER

Vocal, acc. by Willie Lewis and his Orchestra : Willie Lewis-as dir. Bill Coleman-
    Bobby Martin-t/Billy Burns-tb/Joe Hayman-as-ts-bar/George Johnson-as/Frank "Big
    Boy" Goudie-cl-ts/Herman Chittison-p/John Mitchell-g/Louis Vola-sb/Ted Fields-d.
                                        Paris, c. April 21, 1936.

| CPT-2611- | Etre Parisienne | PA PA-887 |
| CPT-2612-1 | Le Coo-Coo-Coo | PA PA-888 |
| CPT-2613-1 | Magic de la Danse | - |
| CPT-2614- | Mon Proces | PA PA-887 |

Byron H. Warner-p dir. Tom Brannon-Jim O'Neal-t/Don McIlvaine-tb/C. J. Buckner-George
   McCullough-Ed Pritchett-cl-as-ts-bar/Ralph Bennett-cl-vn-v/Bob Pittman-bj-v/M. C.
   "Shucks" Park-d-v/J. L. Richmond-v.     Atlanta, June, 1923.

| | | |
|---|---|---|
| 8367-B | Wonder If She's Lonely Too ? | OK 4911, LAR A-4179 |
| 8368-A | Lonesome Lovesick Got-To-Have-My-Daddy | OK 4924 |
| | Blues | |
| 8369-A-B | Mean Eyes | - |

| | | |
|---|---|---|
| 8376-B | In A Tent | OK 4888, Par E-5174, LAR A-4168 |
| 8778-A | Eddie Steady | -    - |
| 8379-A | Dream Girl Of Pi K. A. | OK 4911, LAR A-4179 |

NOTE:- Lindström A-4168 and A-4179 as WARNER'S SEVEN AGES (!)  Matrix 8377 is
untraced.  A photograph of the band in THE TALKING MACHINE WORLD of October 15,
1923, announcing some of the above records, shows its composition as t/2as/vn/p/bj
bb/d, but the records indicate a larger group, nearer the instrumentation above.
(Years later, Ralph Bennett led a band called Ralph Bennett and his Seven Aces (All
Eleven of 'Em); as will be seen, there are eleven men listed above, without Byron
H. Warner himself).

Atlanta, c. April 9, 1924.

| | | |
|---|---|---|
| 8627-B | Ace Of Spades | OK 40080, Od 03229 |
| 8628-A | I'd Like To Be Your Sheik For Awhile | -    - |

Atlanta, August 27, 1924.

| | | |
|---|---|---|
| 8718-A | Bessie Couldn't Help It - vJLR | OK 40198 |
| 8719-A-B | Longing For You | - |

Atlanta, August 29, 1924.

| | | |
|---|---|---|
| 8733-A | Love Time | OK 40201 |

Atlanta, August 30, 1924.

| | | |
|---|---|---|
| 8743-A | Rock-a-Bye My Baby Blues (w) | OK 40201, Par E-5311 |

George MacMillan-bb added.          Atlanta, January 28, 1925.

| | | |
|---|---|---|
| 140286-2 | When My Sugar Walks Down The Street | Col 305-D, Re G-8378 |
| 140287-2 | The Blues Have Got Me | Col 336-D |

NOTE:- Regal G-8378 as CORONA DANCE ORCHESTRA.

Atlanta, January 30, 1925.

| | | |
|---|---|---|
| 140302-2 | Cheatin' On Me | Col 305-D |
| 140303-1-2 | One Stolen Kiss | Rejected |

Ralph Bennett assumes leadership; Ed Lally-p replaces Warner.
                      Atlanta, September 30, 1925.

| | | |
|---|---|---|
| 141068-2 | Go Get 'Em, Caroline | Col 491-D |

Atlanta, October 1, 1925.

| | | |
|---|---|---|
| 141069-1-2 | The Camel Walk | Rejected |
| 141070-1 | Breakin' The Leg | Col 605-D |
| 141071-1-2 | Tweedle-Dee, Tweedle-Doo | Col 491-D |

Atlanta, April 19, 1926.

| | | |
|---|---|---|
| 142046-1 | Hangin' Around | Col 752-D |
| 142047-2 | Who'd Be Blue ? | - |
| 142048-1-2 | When Spring Comes Peeping Through- | Rejected |
| 142049-1-2-3 | Betty - vRB | - |
| 142050-2 | You've Got Those "Wanna Go Back Again" | Col 656-D |
| | Blues - vRB-BP | |
| 142051-2 | So Is Your Old Lady - vMCP&ch | -    4068 |

NOTE:- Columbia 4068 as DENZA DANCE BAND.

THE SEVEN ACES : Ralph Bennett-cl-vn-v dir. Tom Brannon-J. T. Bourne-t/Russ Crump-tb/
  C. J. Buckner-George McCullough-Ed Pritchett-cl-as-ts-bar/Ed Lally-p/Bob Pittman-bj
  /George MacMillan-bb/M. C. "Shucks" Park-d-v/The Peabody Trio-v.
                                        Atlanta, November 1, 1926.

143006-3  Who'll Be The One ? - vP3              Col 863-D
143007-1  Don't Take That Black Bottom Away      Col 816-D
143008-3  Have You Forgotten ? - vP3             Col 863-D

                                        Atlanta, November 2, 1926.

143013-4  That's My Girl - vRB                   Col 816-D
143014-1-2  Sweetie Pie - vMCP                   Rejected
143015-1-2-3  Never Without You - vRB            -

                                        Atlanta, March 28, 1927.

143789-2  I Can't Believe That You're In Love    Col 1001-D
            With Me - vRB
143790-1-2-3  Sweetheart Of Sigma Chi (w) - vRB  Rejected
143791-2  That's My Hap-Hap-Happiness - vRB      Col 1046-D
143792-2  There's Everything Nice About You - vP3  Col 1001-D, 0818
  NOTE:- Columbia 0818 as DENZA DANCE BAND.

                                        Atlanta, March 29, 1927.

143793-3  When Jenny Does That Low Down Dance-vMCP  Col 1046-D
143794-1-2-3  Dream Girl Of Pi K. A. - vRB       Rejected

                        BERT   WARREN

Pseudonym on Oriole 1274 for Bob Fuller, q.v.

                  WASHBOARD RHYTHM BAND/BOYS

See Washboard Rhythm Kings.

                  WASHBOARD RHYTHM KINGS

FIVE RHYTHM KINGS : K/p/g/wb/Jake Fenderson-Dallie Foster-v.
                                        Camden, N. J., April 2, 1931.

64084-1  Minnie The Moocher - vDF                Rejected
64085-2  Please Don't Talk About Me When I'm     Vic 23269, HMV B-4866
           Gone - vJF
64086-1  Please Don't Talk About Me When I'm     Rejected
           Gone - vJF
64087-1  Minnie The Moocher - vJF                Vic 23269

WASHBOARD RHYTHM KINGS* or THE RHYTHM KINGS** : T/as/p/bj/Teddy Bunn-g/wb/Buck
  Franklin-v.                          Camden, N. J., May 8, 1931.

69021-1  One More Time - vBF                     Vic LPM-10018** (LP)
69021-2  One More Time - vBF                     Vic 23276**
69022-1  Walkin' My Baby Back Home - vBF         Vic LPM-10018** (LP)
69022-2  Walkin' My Baby Back Home - vBF         Vic 23276**
69023-1  A Porter's Love Song To A Chambermaid   Vic 22719*, BB B-5042*, Sr S-3139*
           - vBF
69024-2  Every Man For Himself - vBF             -

THE RHYTHM KINGS : Cl-as/p/bj/Teddy Bunn-g/wb/Buck Franklin-Jake Fenderson-The Melody
  Four-v.                              Camden, N. J., June 4, 1931.

68217-1  Please Tell Me - vJF                    Vic LPM-10018 (LP)
68217-2  Please Tell Me - vJF                    Vic 23283, BB 1829, B-5027,
                                                 Sr S-3116, Zon EE-283
68218-1  You Rascal You (You Salty Dog) - vJF    Vic 23279
68219-2  Crooked World Blues - vBF               Vic 23310 (as BUCK FRANKLIN)
68220-2  Call Of The Freaks - vM4                Vic 23279,BB 1848,B-5028,Sr S-3114
                                                 HMV B-4917, HE-2381, El EG-7790
68221-2  I'm Crazy 'Bout My Baby - vM4           Vic 23289 (as THE MELODY FOUR)
68222-2  Because I'm Yours Sincerely - vM4       -

Cl-as/Eddie Miles-p-v/Steve Washington-bj-md/d-wb/Jake Fenderson-v.
                              Camden, N. J., July 9, 1931.

| | | |
|---|---|---|
| 68265-2 | Star Dust - vEM | Vic 23285, Zon EE-284 |
| 68266-1 | You Can't Stop Me From Loving You - vEM | - |
| 68266-2 | You Can't Stop Me From Loving You - vJF | - |
| 68267-2 | Boola Boo - vJF | Vic 23303, HMV K-6500, R-14629 |
| 68268-1 | Boola Boo - vJF | Rejected |
| 68269-1-2 | Who Stole The Lock (From The Hen House Door) - vJF | - |
| 68270-1 | Who Stole The Lock (From The Hen House Door) - vJF | Vic 23283, Zon EE-283 |

NOTE:- Victor 23285 and Zonophone EE-284 as CHICAGO HOT FIVE.

Dave Page-t/Ben Smith-as/Carl Wade-ts/Eddie Miles-p-v/Steve Washington-bj-g/Jimmy
    Spencer-d-wb-v.                 Camden, N. J., September 23, 1931.

| | | |
|---|---|---|
| 70529-1 | Blues In My Heart - vEM | Vic 23301, BB B-6150 |
| 70530-1 | Just One More Chance - vEM | Vic 23300 |
| 70531-1 | Many Happy Returns Of The Day - vEM&ch | Vic 22814, BB B-8228 |
| 70532-1 | Shoot 'Em - vJS&ch | - BB B-5062, Sr S-3147, HMV R-14695, GW-650 |
| 70533-1 | Wake 'Em Up | Vic 23300, BB 1829, B-5027, Sr S-3116 |
| 70534-1 | Georgia On My Mind - vEM | Vic 23301, BB B-6150 |

NOTE:- Bluebird 1829, B-5027 and Sunrise S-3116 as GEORGIA WASHBOARD STOMPERS;
Victor 23300 as CHICAGO HOT FIVE.

Dave Riddick-t/Jimmy Shine-as-v (as JSh)/Carl Wade-ts/Eddie Miles-p-v/Steve Washing-
    ton-bj/Jimmy Spencer-wb-v.        Camden, N. J., March 1, 1932.

| | | |
|---|---|---|
| 70596-1 | Pepper Steak - vJSh | Vic 22958, BB B-5042, Sr S-3139, HMV B-4954, JK-2474 |
| 70597-1 | If You Don't Love Me - vEM | Vic 23323 |
| 70598-1 | You Can Depend On Me - vEM | Vic 23326 |
| 70599-1 | All This World Is Made Of Glass - vJS | Vic 23337, BB B-5127, Sr S-3210 |
| 70600-1 | Was That The Human Thing To Do ? - vJS | Vic 23323 |
| 72001-1 | Oh ! What A Thrill - vEM | Vic 23326 |

NOTE:- Victor 23326 as CHICAGO HOT FIVE.

Taft Jordan-t/Ben Smith-cl-as/Carl Wade-ts/Eddie Miles-p-v/Steve Washington-bj-v/
    Ghost Howell-sb-v/H. Smith-wb.     Camden, N. J., July 6, 1932.

| | | |
|---|---|---|
| 72691-1 | Just Another Dream Of You - vEM | Vic 23348 |
| 72692-1 | Depression Stomp - vSW | Vic 23357 |
| 72693-1 | My Silent Love - vEM | Vic 23348 |
| 72694-1 | Tiger Rag - vGH&ch | Vic 24059, BB B-6084, MW M-4892, HMV B-6289, AE-4227, JK-2011 |
| 72695-1 | Hummin' To Myself - vSW | Vic 24065 |
| 72696-1 | Holding My Honey's Hand - vSW | - HMV X-4085 |

NOTE:- Montgomery Ward M-4892 as GEORGIA WASHBOARD STOMPERS.

Valaida Snow-t replaces Jordan; Jerome Carrington-as/Bella Benson-Lavada Carter-v
added.                              New York, October 5, 1932.

| | | |
|---|---|---|
| 12426-A | Sentimental Gentleman From Georgia - vSW | Voc 1724, Br A-86014 |
| 12427-A | It Don(t Mean A Thing If It Ain't Got That Swing - vSW | - - |
| 12428-A | I Would Do Anything For You - vLS | Voc 1734 |
| 12429-A | Somebody Stole Gabriel's Horn - vLS | Voc 1725 |
| 12430-A | Spider Crawl - vBB | Voc 1734 |
| 12431-A | The Scat Song - vSW | Voc 1725 |

As for July 6, 1932; Bella Benson-v.   Camden, N. J., October 18, 1932.

| | | |
|---|---|---|
| 59030-1 | If You Were Only Mine - vSW&ch | Vic 23367 |
| 59031-1 | Ash Man Crawl - vBB | - |
| 59032-1 | The Boy In The Boat - vGH | Vic 23368 |
| 59033-1 | I'm Gonna Play Down By The Ohio-vSW&ch | Vic 23364, BB 1848, B-5028, Sr S-3114, HMV B-6362 |
| 59034-1 | Somebody Stole Gabriel's Horn - vBB&ch | Vic 23368 |
| 59035-1 | Say It Isn't So - vSW | Vic 23364 |

NOTE:- All the above six titles as WASHBOARD RHYTHM BOYS.

Frank Benton-v (and wb ?) dir. Dave Page-t-v/Ben Smith-cl-as/Jimmy Shine or Jerome
    Carrington-as/Carl Wade-ts/Eddie Miles-p/Wilbur Daniels-bj-v/Leo Watson-sb-v/wb.
                                        Camden, N. J., November 23, 1932.

| | | |
|---|---|---|
| 71790-2 | Underneath The Harlem Moon - vWD-LW | Vic 23373 |
| 71791-1 | Ikey And Mikey - vDP | Vic 23380, BB B-5063, B-6051, |
| | | Sr S-3148 |
| 71792-1 | How Deep Is The Ocean ? - vWD-LW | Vic 23373, BB B-8174 |
| 71793-1 | Sloppy Drunk Blues - vFB | Vic 23380, BB B-5389, B-8164, |
| | | HMV B-4954, JK-2194 |
| 71794-1 | A Nickel For A Pickle - vFB | Vic 23375, BB B-5063, B-8164, |
| | | Sr S-3148, HMV JK-2194 |
| 71795-1 | Fire - vDP | Vic 23375, BB B-5062, B-8174, |
| | | Sr S-3147, HMV B-6362 |

T/cl-as/as/Carl Wade-ts/p/Steve Washington-bj-v/? Ghost Howell-sb/wb.
                                        New York, December 14, 1932.

| | | |
|---|---|---|
| 12716-A | Oh ! You Sweet Thing - vSW | Voc 1730 |
| 12717-A | Something's Gotta Be Done - vSW | -         Dec F-5176 |
| 12718-A | Yes Suh ! - vSW | Voc 1731, Br 01504, A-86019 |
| 12719-A | Angeline - vSW | -           - |
| 12720-A | Old Yazoo - vSW | Voc 1733 |
| 12721-A | Gotta Be, Gonna Be Mine - vSW | Voc 1729, Dec F-3781, Br A-81318, |
| | | A-86017 |
| 12722-A | Wah-Dee-Dah - vSW | Voc 1732, Br A-86018 |
| 12723-A | Blue Drag - vSW | - Br A-81318 -      Dec F-3781 |
| 12724-A | Syncopate Your Sins Away - vSW | Voc 1729, Br 01504, A-86017 |
| 12725-A | I'm Getting Sentimental Over You - vSW | Voc 1733, Dec F-5176 |

WASHBOARD RHYTHM BAND : Taft Jordan-t-v/John Haughton-tb/Ben Smith-cl-as/? Jerome
    Carrington-as/Carl Wade-ts/? Clarence Profit-p/Steve Washington-bj-g/wb.
                                        New York, March 8, 1933.

| | | |
|---|---|---|
| 265082-2 | Midnight Rhythm - vTJ | Col CB-626 |
| 265083-2 | A Ghost Of A Chance - vTJ | - |
| 265084-2 | Hustlin' And Bustlin' For Baby - vTJ | Col CB-611, DF-1262 |
| 265085-2 | Shuffle Off To Buffalo - vTJ | - CQ-1325 -       14680-D |
| 265086-2 | Swing Gate - vTJ | Col CB-642 |
| 265087-2 | The Coming Of Hi-De-Ho - vTJ | - |
| 265088-1 | Going, Going, Gone - vTJ | Col 14680-D |
| 265089-1-2 | Trust Me For A Hamburger - vTJ | Rejected |

WASHBOARD RHYTHM KINGS : Dave Page-t-v/John Haughton-tb/Ben Smith-cl-as/? Jerome
    Carrington-as/Carl Wade-ts/? Clarence Profit-p/? Steve Washington-g/? Ghost Howell
    sb/wb/Cal Clement-v.                 Camden, N. J., June 1, 1933.

| | | |
|---|---|---|
| 76240-1 | Dinah - vDP | BB B-5127, MW M-4892, Sr S-3210 |
| 76241-1 | Sophisticated Lady | BB B-5089, Eld 2005, Sr S-3164 |
| 76242-1 | Happy As The Day Is Long - vCC&3 | BB B-5088, Eld 2004, Sr S-3163 |
| 76243-1 | Nobody's Sweetheart - vDP | BB B-5092, Sr S-3175 |
| 76244-1 | My Pretty Girl - vCC | BB B-5089, Eld 2005, Sr S-3164 |
| 76245-1 | Bug-a-Boo | BB B-5092, Sr S-3175 |
| 76248-1 | Dinah - vDP | Vic 23403 |
| 76249-1 | Sophisticated Lady | Vic 23405 |
| 76250-1 | Happy As The Day Is Long - vCC&3 | - |
| 76251-1 | Nobody's Sweetheart - vDP | Vic 23403 |
| 76252-1 | My Pretty Girl - vCC | Vic 23408, HMV B-8655 |
| 76253-1 | Bug-a-Boo | - |

NOTE:- An aura of mystery surrounds this entire block of numbers. According to the
RCA Victor files, they represent two sessions, but as many examples of duplicated
titles as could be found were checked against each other, and no differences were
apparent between the Bluebird and Victor issues. There is no obvious evidence of
one being a dubbed version of the other, and indeed, if this had been so, surely
the matrix numbers would not have differed ? Cal Clement and Dave Page do not
seem to be the same artist, as has been suggested. Only the Victor and HMV issues
bear the artist-credit WASHBOARD RHYTHM KINGS; all the others appeared as GEORGIA
WASHBOARD STOMPERS. (See Williams' Washboard Band for a further example of this
curious practice - and with a very similar unit).

WASHBOARD RHYTHM BOYS : 3t/John Haughton-tb/Ben Smith-? Jerome Carrington-as/Carl
Wade-ts/p/bj/Ghost Howell-sb-v/wb.        New York, August 19, 1933.

| | | |
|---|---|---|
| 13839-1 | St. Louis Blues - vGH | Ban 32867, Dom 145, Mt M-12794, Or 2763, Per 15823, Ro 2136, Voc 2688, Br A-86013 |
| 13840-1 | Lazybones - vGH | Ban 32854, Mt M-12781, Or 2755, Per 15815, Ro 2128 |
| 13841-1 | Some Of These Days - vGH | Ban 32867, Dom 145, Mt M-12794, Or 2763, Per 15823, Ro 2136, Voc 2688,Br 02075,A-9908,A-86013 |
| 13842-1-2 | Learn To Croon - vGH | Ban 32853, Dom 133, Mt M-12780, Or 2754, Per 15814, Ro 2127 |
| 13843-1 | Dog And Cat - vGH | Ban 32978, Dom 177, Mt M-12928, Or 2850, Per 15893, Ro 2263 |
| 13844-1-2 | I Cover The Waterfront - vGH | Ban 32853, Dom 133, Mt M-12780, Or 2754, Per 15814, Ro 2127 |
| 13845-1 | Old Man Blues | Ban 32978 Dom 177, Mt M-12928, Or 2850, Per 15893, Ro 2263 |
| 13846-1 | Mississippi Basin - vGH | Ban 32854, Mt M-12781, Or 2755, Per 15815, Ro 2128 |

NOTE:- Vocalion 2688 as ALABAMA WASHBOARD STOMPERS.

WASHBOARD RHYTHM KINGS : C. Williams-k-v (this is not Clarence Williams !)/cl/2g/sb/
wb.                                       Chicago, November 1, 1935.

| | | |
|---|---|---|
| 96258-1 | Please Come On Down To My House - vCW | BB B-6186 |
| 96259-1 | Brown-Skin Mama - kCW | BB B-6157 |
| 96260-1 | Street Walkin' Blues - vCW | BB B-6186, B-8155 |
| 96261-1 | Arlena - vCW | BB B-6157 |

## WASHBOARD SAM

Although this blues artist was occasionally accompanied by other than the usual
rhythm group, his work is strictly country blues, and does not therefore come
within the scope of this book.  See BLUES AND GOSPEL RECORDS, 1902-1942.

## WASHBOARD SERENADERS

Harold Randolph-k/Clarence Profit-p/Teddy Bunn-g/Bruce Johnson-wb-v/Gladys Bentley-v.
New York, March 24, 1930.

| | | |
|---|---|---|
| 59548-1 | Kazoo Moan - vBJ | Vic V-38127, BB B-5790, B-6633, HMV B-6289, JK-2011 |
| 59549-1 | Washboards Get Together - vBJ-GB | Vic V-38127, BB B-5790, B-6633, HMV B-6114 |

T replaces Randolph.                      New York, March 31, 1930.

| | | |
|---|---|---|
| 59568-2 | Teddy's Blues | Vic V-38610 |
| 59569-2 | Tappin' The Time Away | - HMV B-6303,E1 EG-2760,EG-6676 |

Harold Randolph-k-v/Derek Neville-cl-as-bsx/Arthur Brooks-p/Jerome Darr-g/Len
Harrison-sb/Bruce Johnson-wb-v.           London, July 19, 1935.

| | | |
|---|---|---|
| CE-7108-1 | The Sheik Of Araby - vHR-BJ | Par F-428, Od OF-5140, Grand 707 |
| CE-7109-1 | Dear Old Southland - vHR-BJ | Par F-229, A-6408, Od OF-5009 |
| CE-7110-1 | St. Louis Blues - vHR-BJ | Par F-428, Od OF-5140 |
| CE-7111-1 | Black Eyes - vHR-BJ | Par F-358, Od OF-5078 |
| CE-7112-1 | Lonesome Road - vHR-BJ | Par F-229, A-6408, Od OF-5009 |
| CE-7113-1 | Nagasaki - vHR-BJ | Par F-358, Od OF-5078, Grand 707 |

NOTE:- Grand 707 as MIAMI BEACH BAND.

## WASHBOARD TRIO

Pseudonym on Paramount 12682 for the Tub Jug Washboard Band, q.v.

## WASHBOARD WONDERS

Pseudonym on Silvertone 3548 and 3549 for Jimmy O'Bryant's Washboard Band, q.v.

Pseudonym on Superior for Mae Glover, q.v.

## BENNIE  WASHINGTON'S SIX ACES

Bennie Washington-d dir. Andrew "Big Babe" Webb-t/Harvey Lankford-tb/William "Weedy"
    Harris-cl-as/Harold Este-cl-ts/John Arnold-p/Pete Patterson-bj.
                                    St. Louis, November 4, 1925.

    9433-A  Compton Ave. Blues (sic)                    OK 8269

## FLOYD  "BUCK"  WASHINGTON

Piano solo.                              New York, March 8, 1934.

265174-1  Old Fashioned Love                    Col 2925-D, Par R-1837, A-3989,
                                                Dec 18169

See also Louis Armstrong, Buck and Bubbles, and Coleman Hawkins.

## ISABELLE  WASHINGTON

Vocal, acc. by Fletcher Henderson-p.     Long Island City, c. February, 1923.

    507-    I Want To                           BS 14141, Pm 12135
    508-    That's Why I'm Loving You                  -           -

## STEVE WASHINGTON AND HIS ORCHESTRA

Sterling Bose or Manny Klein-t/Benny Goodman-cl/ts/Joe Venuti or Harry Hoffman-vn/
    Fulton McGrath-p/Dick McDonough-g/Artie Bernstein-sb/Stan King or Chauncey More-
    house-d/Steve Washington-v.              New York, November 22, 1933.

    14363-A  We Were The Best Of Friends - vSW      Voc 2598
    14364-A  Sing A Little Low-Down Tune - vSW          -
    14365-A  Blue River - vSW                        Voc 2609
    14366-A  Love Me - vSW                              -

## THE WASHINGTONIANS

Pseudonym on Blu-Disc, Brunswick, Cameo, Diva, Harmony, Lincoln, Pathe Actuelle,
    Perfect, Romeo and Velvet Tone for Duke Ellington and his Orchestra, q.v.; it was
    also used for (apparently) Sam Lanin and his Orchestra (matrix 3613-A) and Bob
    Haring and his Orchestra (matrix 3618-A), both q.v.  Both titles are said to be of
    interest as jazz or "hot" dance music; they were probably recorded on or about
    January 28, 1929 in New York, and the instrumentation is 2t/Tommy Dorsey-tb/2as/ts
    /p/bj/bb/d/Scrappy Lambert (as HAROLD LANG)-Billy Hillpot (as WILLIAM SMITH)-v.

    3613-A  Mississippi, Here I Am - vSL        Cam 9064, Lin 3093, Ro 868
    108616  Mississippi, Here I Am - vSL        PA 36932, Per 15113

    3618-A  It's Tight Like That - vBH          Cam 9064, Lin 3093, Ro 868
    108613  It's Tight Like That - vBH          PA 36937, Per 15118
    NOTE:- Pathe Actuelle 36932 and Perfect 15113 as SAM LANIN AND HIS ORCHESTRA;
    Pathe Actuelle 36937 and Perfect 15118 as LEVEE LOUNGERS.

## ETHEL WATERS

Vocal, acc. by Albury's Blue and Jazz Seven : Wesley Johnson-t/James Reevy-tb/
    Clarence Harris and another-as/Wilson Kyer-p/Ralph Escudero-bb/Kaiser Marshall-d.
                                    New York, March 21-22, 1921.

    C-673   The New York Glide                  Cdl 2036
    C-674   At The New Jump Steady Ball             -

    Acc. by Cordy Williams' Jazz Masters : T/? Chink   Johnson-tb/Edgar Campbell-cl/
    Cordy Williams-vn/Fletcher Henderson-p/? Ralph Escudero-bb.
                                    New York, April-May, 1921.

    P-114-1-2  Oh Daddy                         BS 2010, Pm 12169
    P-115-1-2  Down Home Blues                      -           -

Acc. by her Jazz Masters : T/tb/Garvin Bushell-cl/? Charlie Jackson-vn/Fletcher
Henderson-p.                          New York, c. August, 1921.

P-146-1  One Man Nan                          BS 2021, Pm 12170
P-147-1  There'll Be Some Changes Made        -       -

? Chink Johnson-tb replaces unknown; 2nd cl/? Ralph Escudero-bb added.
                                     New York, c. August, 1921.

P-149-1  Dying With The Blues                 BS 2038, Pm 12174
P-150-1  Kiss Your Pretty Baby Nice           -       -

ETHEL WATERS' JAZZ MASTERS : Gus Aiken-c/Bud Aiken-tb/Garvin Bushell-cl/? Joe Elder-
   cl-as/bsx/Fletcher Henderson-p.     New York, c. September, 1921.

P-160-1-2  'Frisco Jazz Band Blues            BS 2037, Pm 12173
P-161-1-2  Royal Garden Blues                 BS 2035, Pm 12171
P-162-1-2  Bugle Blues (Intro. Old Miss Blues)  BS 2037, Pm 12173
NOTE:- The reverse of Black Swan 2035 and Paramount 12171, although credited to
Ethel Waters' Jazz Masters, is actually by Irving Weiss and his Ritz-Carlton
Orchestra, and of no jazz interest.  Matrices P-160, P-161 and P-162 were also
allocated to other artists (cf. Trixie Smith).

Vocal, acc. by Joe Smith's Jazz Masters : Joe Smith-c/George Brashear-tb/? Clarence
   Robinson-cl/Fletcher Henderson-p.   Long Island City, c. May, 1922.

           Jazzin' Babies Blues               BS 14117, Pm 12175
           Kind Lovin' Blues                   -       -
           Georgia Blues (two takes issued)   BS 14120, Pm 12177
           That Da Da Strain                   -       -
NOTE:- Black Swan 14120 and Paramount 12177 omit references to Joe Smith.

ETHEL WATERS' JAZZ MASTERS (on some copies as THE JAZZ MASTERS) : As last above, plus
   Raymond Green-d.                    Long Island City, June-July, 1922.

   386-2  Tiger Rag                           BS 2077, 10073
          Pacific Coast Blues                  -       -
          Struggle                            BS 2074, 10070
          Spread Yo' Stuff                     -       -

Vocal, acc. by her Jazz Masters : T/tb/cl/? Fletcher Henderson-p/bb.
                                     Long Island City, c. July, 1922.

           At The New Jump Steady Ball         BS 14128, Pm 12176
           Oh Joe, Play That Trombone          -       -

Acc. by the Jazz Masters : ? Elmer Chambers-c/George Brashear-tb/Edgar Campbell-cl/
   Fletcher Henderson-p/John Mitchell-bj.  Long Island City, c. March, 1923.

   564-   Memphis Man                         BS 14146, Pm 12179
   565-   Midnight Blues                       -       -
          Brown Baby                          BS 14145, Pm 12178
          Long-Lost Mama                      BS 14148, Pm 12180
          Lost Out Blues                      BS 14151, Pm 12181

Acc. by Fletcher Henderson-p.         Long Island City, c. March, 1923.

           Ain't Goin' Marry (Ain't Goin' Settle   BS 14145, Pm 12178
           Down)
           If You Don't Think I'll Do Sweet Pops    BS 14148, Pm 12180
           (Just Try Me)

Acc. by J. C. Johnson-p.              Long Island City, c. June, 1923.

   651-   Who'll Get It When I'm Gone ?       BS 14155, Pm 12189
   652-   All The Time                         -       -
          You Can't Do What My Last Man Did   BS 14151, Pm 12181
          Ethel Sings 'Em                     BS 14154, Pm 12182
          Sweet Man Blues                      -       -

Acc. by Joe Smith-c/Pearl Wright-p.     Chicago, c. March 25, 1924.

1737-2  Tell 'Em 'Bout Me (When You Reach          Pm 12214, Sil 3535
           Tennessee)
1740-1  You'll Need Me When I'm Long Gone          -       Sil 3537
NOTE:- Matrices 1738 and 1739 are untraced.  Silvertone 3535 and 3537 as MAMIE
JONES.  The late Lou Black distinctly recalled having made Paramount records in
Chicago as banjoist in a small band accompanying Ethel Waters, probably about this
time, but he could not remember any titles or the names of his colleagues on the
session.

Acc. by Lovie Austin's Blues Serenaders : ? Tommy Ladnier-c/? Jimmy O'Bryant-cl/as
/Lovie Austin-p.                        Chicago, late March, 1924.

1742-1-2  Craving Blues                            Pm 12313, Sil 3536
1747-2   Black Spatch Blues                        Pm 12230, Sil 3535
1749-2   I Want Somebody All My Own                -       -
NOTE:- Matrices 1743 through 1746, and 1748 are untraced.  Silvertone 3535 and
3536 as MAMIE JONES.

Acc. by p.                              New York, August 1, 1924.

13453    Pleasure Mad                              Voc 14860, Sil 3014
13455    Back-Bitin' Mamma                         -       -

Acc. by her Ebony Four : ? Joe Smith-c/ss-o/? Pearl Wright-p.
                                        New York, April 29, 1925.

140564-1-2-3  Brother, You've Got Me Wrong         Rejected
140565-2  No One Can Love Me (Like The Way You Do) Col 379-D

Acc. by her Ebony Four : ? Joe Smith-c/? Don Redman-cl-ss/bsn/? Pearl Wright or
Fletcher Henderson-p.                   New York, May 13, 1925.

140564-5  Brother, You've Got Me Wrong             Col 433-D
140597-1  Sweet Georgia Brown                      Col 379-D
140598-1-2  Too Bad Jim (bsn omitted)              Rejected

Acc. by Horace Holmes-c/Pearl Wright-p/Bill Benford-bb.
                                        New York, July 28, 1925.

140790-1  Go Back Where You Stayed Last Night      Col 14093-D
140791-1  Sympathetic Dan                          Col 433-D
140792-2  Down Home Blues                          Col 14093-D

Alex S. Jackson-bsx replaces Benford; "Slow Kid" Thompson-comments*.
                                        New York, August 25, 1925.

140863-1  Loud Speakin' Papa (You'd Better Speak   Col 472-D
           Easy To Me)
140864-1  *You Can't Do What My Last Man Did       Col 14112-D

Acc. by Pearl Wright-p/Virgil van Cleeve-u.
                                        New York, September 12, 1925.

140936-3  Pickaninny Blues                         Col 472-D

Acc. by her Plantation Orchestra : Ralph "Shrimp" Jones-vn (on 141163-2 only) dir.
Harry Tate-Horace Holmes-c/Joe King-tb/2cl-ss-as/cl-ts/Lester Armstead-p/Maceo
Jefferson-bj/Bill Benford-bb/Jesse Baltimore-d.
                                        New York, October 20, 1925.

141163-2  Sweet Man                                Col 487-D
141164-2  Dinah                                    -

Acc. by her Ebony Four : Joe Smith-c/Coleman Hawkins-bsx/Pearl Wright-p.
                                        New York, October 28, 1925.

141207-2  No Man's Mamma                           Col 14116-D
141208-1  Tell 'Em About Me                        Col 561-D
141209-3  Maybe Not At All                         Col 14112-D

Acc. by Pearl Wright-p.                    New York, December 23, 1925.

141429-1  Shake That Thing                     Col 14116-D

Acc. by Fletcher Henderson-p, with Joe Smith-c and unidentified speaker as noted.
                                           New York, January 22, 1926.

141542-1  I've Found A New Baby - cJS          Col 561-D
141543-2-3  Make Me A Pallet On The Floor - sp  Col 14125-D
141544-2  Bring Your Greenbacks                -

Acc. by Shelton Brooks, Sammy Fain, Louis Hooper, Maceo Pinkard or Nathaniel Reed-p
(as shown).                                New York, February 17, 1926.

141688-3  After All These Years - pSB          Col 14199-D
141689-1  Throw Dirt In Your Face - pSB        Col 14132-D
141690-3  I'm Saving It All For You - pLH      Col 14297-D

                                           New York, February 19, 1926.

141704-3  Refrigeratin' Papa (Mama's Gonna Warm   Col 14132-D
            You Up) - vLH
141705-1-2  If You Can't Hold The Man You Love-pSF Rejected

                                           New York, February 20, 1926.

141705-4  If You Can't Hold The Man You Love-pSF  Col 14134-D
141706-1  Satisfyin' Papa - pNR              Col 14199-D
141707-1  Sugar - pMP                        Col 14146-D
141708-3  I Wonder What's Become Of Joe ? - pMP  Col 14134-D
141709-3  You'll Want Me Back - pNR          Col 14146-D

Acc. by her Jazz Band : Thornton Brown-c/Edward Carr-tb/Lorence Faulkener-p.
                                           New York, July 29, 1926.

142476-3  Heebie Jeebies                     Col 14153-D, 8928
142477-2  Ev'rybody Mess Aroun'              -           -

Acc. by her Ebony Four (male voice quartet, unacc.) or Pearl Wright-p.
                                           New York, September 14, 1926.

142614-2-3  He Brought Joy To My Soul - E4    Col 14170-D
142615-3  Take What You Want - pPW            Col 14162-D

Acc. by Will Marion Cook's Singing Orchestra (c/vn/vc/J. C. Johnson-p) or J. C.
Johnson-p only.*                           New York, September 18, 1926.

142649-2-3  I'm Coming, Virginia             Col 14170-D
142650-3  We Don't Need Each Other Any More  Col 14162-D
142651-3  *My Special Friend Is Back In Town  Col 14182-D

Acc. by Pearl Wright-p.                    New York, September 29, 1926.

142703-1-2-3  It Takes A Good Woman To Keep   Rejected
              A Good Man At Home
142704-3  Jersey Walk                        Col 14182-D

Acc. by Joe Smith-c/Alex S. Jackson-as/Pearl Wright-p.
                                           New York, May 6, 1927.

144100-1  Weary Feet                         Col 14214-D
144101-3  Smile !                            Col 14229-D
144102-1  Home (Cradle Of Happiness)         Col 14297-D
144103-3  Take Your Black Bottom Outside     Col 14214-D

Acc. by Pearl Wright-p.         New York, June 28, 1927.

144404-1-2-3-4  Big Ben                       Rejected
144405-1-2-3    Keep An Eye On Your Man       -
144406-2  I Want My Sweet Daddy Now          Col 14229-D
144407-1-2  Clorinda                         Rejected

Acc. by William A. Tyler-vn/H. Leonard Jeter-vc/Pearl Wright-p, or Pearl Wright-p
only*.                                    New York, October 14, 1927.

144863-1-2  One Sweet Letter From You        Rejected
144864-1-2  Someday, Sweetheart              Col 14264-D
144867-1    Some Of These Days               -
144868-1-2  *It Hurts So Good                Rejected

    Acc. by James P. Johnson-p.          New York, August 21, 1928.

146871-1    Lonesome Swallow                 Col 14411-D
146872-2    Guess Who's In Town              Col 14353-D
146873-1    My Handy Man                     -            SE 5014-S
146874-2    Do What You Did Last Night       Col 14380-D  -

    Acc. by Clarence Williams-p.         New York, August 23, 1928.

146881-2    West End Blues                   Col 14365-D
146882-2    Organ Grinder Blues              -
146883-2    Get Up Off Your Knees            Col 14380-D
146884-2    My Baby Sure Knows How To Love   Col 14411-D

Acc. by ? Manny Klein-t/Tommy Dorsey-tb/Jimmy Dorsey-cl/Frank Signorelli-p/Joe
Tarto-sb.                                 New York, May 14, 1929.

148531-3    Birmingham Bertha                Col 1837-D, 5534, 01739, A-8600
148532-2    Am I Blue ?                      -       -        -        -
148532-3    Am I Blue ?                      CBS CL-2230 (LP)

    Acc. by Pearl Wright-p.              New York, June 6, 1929.

148670-2    Second-Handed Man                Col 1871-D, 5664

Acc. by Bob Effros-t/Tommy Dorsey tb/Jimmy Dorsey-cl-as/? Ben Selvin-vn/Frank
Signorelli-p/Tony Colucci-g/Joe Tarto-sb/Stan King-d.
                                          New York, June 7, 1929.

148671-4    True Blue Lou                    Col 1871-D, 5648
148672-1    Do I Know What I'm Doing ?       Col 1905-D, 5690
148673-2    Shoo Shoo Boogie Boo             -       -

    Acc. by Pearl Wright-p.              New York, July 8, 1929.

148734-1    Georgia Blues                    Col 14565-D
148735-2    I Like The Way He Does It        -

    Bob Effros-t/2vn/vc/g added*.        New York, July 11, 1929.

148798-2    *Waiting At The End Of The Road  Col 1933-D, 5664, A-8337
148799-2    *Trav'lin' All Alone             -        5648
148804-2    Long Lean Lanky Mama             Col 14458-D, 5663
148805-1    Better Keep Your Eye On Your Man -        -

Acc. by Manny Klein or Muggsy Spanier-t/? Ben Selvin-vn/Frank Signorelli-p/? Tony
Colucci-g/Joe Tarto-sb.                   New York, April 1, 1930.

150159-2    Porgy                            Col 2184-D
150160-3    What Did I Do To Be So Black And Blue ?   -

Acc. by Manny Klein-t/Tommy Dorsey-tb/Benny Goodman-cl/Adrian Rollini-bsx/? Ben
Selvin-vn/? Rube Bloom-p.                 New York, June 3, 1930.

150562-3    My Kind Of Man                   Col 2222-D
150563-4    You Brought A New Kind Of Love To Me   -

    Acc. by o/2vn/p/sb.                  New York, August 29, 1930.

150747-1    You're Lucky To Me               Col 2288-D, DB-376
150748-2    Memories Of You                  -       -

Acc. by Manny Klein-t/Tommy Dorsey-tb/Jimmy Dorsey-cl/Ben Selvin-vn/p/g.
New York, November 18, 1930.

| | | |
|---|---|---|
| 150966-2 | I Got Rhythm | Col 2346-D |
| 150967-1-2-3 | Three Little Words | Rejected |

New York, November 28, 1930.

| | | |
|---|---|---|
| 150967-5 | Three Little Words | Col 2346-D |

Acc. by Manny Klein-t/Tommy Dorsey-tb/Benny Goodman-cl/Joe Venuti-vn/Rube Bloom-p/
Eddie Lang-g.                                    New York, February 10, 1931.

| | | |
|---|---|---|
| 151298-3 | When Your Lover Has Gone | Col 2409-D |
| 151299-3 | Please Don't Talk About Me When I'm Gone | - |

Venuti omitted; Dick McDonough-g replaces Lang.
New York, June 16, 1931.

| | | |
|---|---|---|
| 151613-3 | You Can't Stop Me From Loving You | Col 2481-D, DB-579, Re G-21179 |
| 151614-2 | Without That Gal | - |

New York, August 10, 1931.

| | | |
|---|---|---|
| 151718-3 | River, Stay 'Way From My Door | Col 2511-D |
| 151719-3 | Shine On, Harvest Moon | - |

Acc. by Duke Ellington and his Orchestra : Duke Ellington-p dir. Arthur Whetsel-
Cootie Williams-Freddy Jenkins-t/Joe Nanton-Lawrence Brown-tb/Johnny Hodges-ss-as/
Harry Carney-cl-as-bar/Fred Guy-g/Wellman Braud-sb/Sonny Greer-d/unidentified male
voice on B-12783-A.                              New York, December 22, 1932.

| | | |
|---|---|---|
| B-12783-A | I Can't Give You Anything But Love | Br 6517, 6758, 01518, 01731, 05050, A-9395, A-9519, A-500256, Col DO-1143 |
| B-12784-A | Porgy | Br 6521, 6758, 01522, 01731, 05050, A-9397, A-9519, A-500260, Col C-6387, Lucky 60012 |

Acc. by the Cecil Mack Choir.                    New York, December 23, 1932.

| | | |
|---|---|---|
| B-12790-A | St. Louis Blues | Br 6521, 01522, A-9397, A-500260 |

Acc. by probably :- Sterling Bose-Bunny Berigan-t/Tommy Dorsey-tb/Jimmy Dorsey-cl-
as/Larry Binyon-cl-ts/Joe Venuti-Harry Hoffman-Walter Edelstein-Lou Kosloff-vn/
Fulton McGrath-p/Dick McDonough-g/Artie Bernstein-sb/Stan King or Chauncey Morehouse-d.                                         New York, May 3, 1933

| | | |
|---|---|---|
| B-13292-A | Stormy Weather | Br 6564, 01524, A-500266, 4842, Col 36329 |
| B-13293-A | Love Is The Thing | As above, except Br 4842 (Italian) |

New York, July 18, 1933.

| | | |
|---|---|---|
| B-13565-A | Don't Blame Me | Br 6617, 01579, 4842 (Italian) |
| B-13566-A | Shadows On The Swanee | -     - |

Acc. by Bunny Berigan and another-t/Benny Goodman-cl/ts/2vn/vl/p.
New York, October 10, 1933.

| | | |
|---|---|---|
| 152521-1-3 | Heat Wave | Col 2826-D, DB-1436 |
| 152522-2 | Harlem On My Mind | -     - |

Acc. by Benny Goodman and his Orchestra : Charlie Teagarden-Shirley Clay-t/Jack
Teagarden-tb/Benny Goodman-cl/Art Karle-ts/Joe Sullivan-p/Dick McDonough-g/Artie
Bernstein-sb/Gene Krupa-d.                        New York, November 27, 1933.

| | | | |
|---|---|---|---|
| 152566-1 | I Just Couldn't Take It, Baby | Col 2853-D | |
| 152566-2 | I Just Couldn't Take It, Baby | - | Par R-2394, A-6865 |
| 152567-1 | A Hundred Years From Today | - | |
| 152567-2 | A Hundred Years From Today | -     - | - |

Acc. by Victor Young dir. probably :- Sterling Bose or Bunny Berigan (or both)-t/
Tommy Dorsey-tb/Jimmy Dorsey-cl-as/? others-as-ts/Joe Venuti and/or Harry Hoffman-
vn/Fulton McGrath or Joe Meresco-p/Dick McDonough-g/Artie Bernstein-sb/Stan King-d.
                                        New York, March 16, 1934.

B-14956-A-B  Come Up And See Me Sometime          Br rejected
B-14957-A-B  You've Seen Harlem At Its Best            -


                                        New York, March 30, 1934.

B-14956-C  Come Up And See Me Sometime            Br 6885, 01736
B-14957-C  You've Seen Harlem At Its Best             -        -


Acc. by unidentified studio orchestra, possibly including Tommy Dorsey-tb/Jimmy
Dorsey-cl-as.                           New York, August 20, 1934.

38349-A  Miss Otis Regrets (She's Unable To       Dec 140
           Lunch Today)
38349-C  Miss Otis Regrets (She's Unable To       Br 01848
           Lunch Today)
38350-C  Dinah                                    Dec 234, Br 01975, Pol 15392
38351-C  When It's Sleepy Time Down South            - 4410 -
38352-A  Moon Glow                                Dec 140
38352-C  Moon Glow                                Br 01848, 03026


Acc. by Taft Jordan-t/Sandy Williams-tb/Edgar Sampson-as-vn/Elmer Williams-ts/vn/
vl/vc/? Joe Steele-p/John Trueheart-g/John Kirby-sb, or Sampson and the three
rhythm only*.                           New York, September 5, 1934.

38548-A  Give Me A Heart To Sing To               Dec 141, Br 01914
38549-A  I Ain't Gonna Sin No More                   -     Br 02045
38550-A  Trade Mark                                        -
38551-A  *You're Going To Leave The Old Home, Jim  Dec 234, Br 01914


Acc. by Russell Wooding and his Orchestra : Instrumentation and personnel unknown.
                                        New York, October 16, 1935.

95605-1  Hottentot Potentate                      LMS L-188
95606-1  Thief In The Night                          -


Acc. by 2t/tb/2as/ts/p/g/sb/d.         New York, January 5, 1938.

63130-B  You're A Sweetheart                      Dec 1613, X-1489, Br 02568
63131-A  How Can I Face This Wearied World Alone?  Br 03026
63131-C  How Can I Face This Wearied World Alone?  Dec 4410
63132-A  I'll Get Along Somehow                    Dec 1613, X-1489, Br 02568


Acc. by Eddie Mallory and his Orchestra : Eddie Mallory-Shirley Clay-t/Tyree Glenn-
tb-vib/Castor McCord-cl/William Steiner-as/Reg Beane-p-or/Danny Barker-g/Charles
Turner-sb; or/g/vib only**.            New York, November 9, 1938.

028387-1**You're Mine                             BB B-10038, RZ G-23696
028388-1  Frankie And Johnnie                        -        HMV BD-690
028389-1  They Say                                 BB B-10025, RZ G-23696
028390-1  Jeepers Creepers                           -        HMV BD-690


                                        New York, March 27, 1939.

035355-1  Lonesome Walls                           BB B-10222
035356-1  If You Ever Change Your Mind                -       HMV BD-740
035357-1  What Goes Up Must Come Down              BB B-10207    -
035358-1  Y' Had It Comin' To You                     -


Clay omitted; Benny Carter-as replaces Steiner; Milt Hinton-sb replaces Turner.
                                        New York, August 15, 1939.

041552-1  Bread And Gravy                          BB B-10415
041553-1  Down In My Soul                          BB B-11284
041554-2  Georgia On My Mind                       BB B-11028
041555-1  Stop Myself From Worryin' Over You       BB B-11284
041556-1  Old Man Harlem                           BB B-11028
041557-1  Push-Out                                 BB B-10415

Acc. by Eddie Mallory-t/Benny Carter-cl/Garvin Bushell-as/Reg Beane-p/Charles
Turner-sb.                              New York, September 22, 1939.

| | | |
|---|---|---|
| 042717- | Baby, What Else Can I Do ? | BB B-10517, HMV BD-820 |
| 042718- | I Just Got A Letter | - - |

Acc. by Max Meth and his Orchestra : Instrumentation and personnel unknown.
                                        New York, November 7, 1940.

| | | |
|---|---|---|
| P-29031-1 | Taking A Chance On Love | LMS L-310 |
| P-29032-1 | Honey In The Honeycomb | LMS L-311 |
| P-29033-1 | Cabin In The Sky | - |
| P-29034-1 | Love Turned The Light Out | LMS L-310 |

## KITTY WATERS

Vocal, acc. by Louis Hooper-p.          New York, c. June, 1927.

| | | |
|---|---|---|
| | Back Water Blues | PA 7531, Per 131 |
| | Rough House Blues | - - |

Acc. by p/g.                            New York, c. October 15, 1927.

| | | |
|---|---|---|
| 107835 | Mean Old Bed Bug Blues | PA 7537,  Per 137 |
| 107836 | Loud And Wrong | - - |

## WATSON'S PULLMAN PORTERS

Pseudonym on Gennett for Henry Johnson's Boys, q.v.

## EL  WATSON

Harmonica solos, acc. by Charles Johnson-g where shown.
                                        Bristol, Tenn., July 28, 1927.

| | | |
|---|---|---|
| 39732-2 | Pot Licker Blues - gCJ | Vic 20951 |
| 39733-2 | Narrow Gauge Blues | |

Acc. by unknown "bones" player, with Robert Cooksey-h or own tap-dancing as shown.
                                        New York, May 7, 1928.

| | | |
|---|---|---|
| 43952-2 | El Watson's Fox Chase - hRC | Vic 21440 |
| 43953-2 | Bay Rum Blues | Vic 21585 |
| 43954-2 | Sweet Bunch Of Daisies (w) - t-d | - |
| 43955-2 | One Sock Blues | Vic 21440 |

NOTE:- Despite the label of the last title, all the harmonica  heard on this is by
El Watson.

## GILBERT WATSON AND HIS ORCHESTRA

Curtis Little-t/tb/2as/ts/p/bj/bb/d/Charlie Hayward-v.
                                        New York, November 15, 1926.

| | | |
|---|---|---|
| E-2583-2 | Suzie's Feller (sic) | Mic 22543 |
| E-2584-1-2 | Hot As A Summer's Day | Rejected ? |
| E-2585-2 | How Could Red Riding Hood ? - vCH | Dom 21564, LS 24530 |
| E-2586-1 | St. Louis Blues | Dom 21563   -   Mic 22543 |
| E-2587-1-2 | Don't Be Angry With Me | Rejected ? |
| E-2588-1-2 | Spring Fever | - |

## LEO WATSON AND HIS ORCHESTRA

? Johnny McGhee-? Ralph Muzzillo-t/Paul Ricci-cl-as-ts/Gene de Paul-p/Frank Victor-g/
Haig Stephens-sb/O'Neil Spencer-d/Leo Watson-v.
                                        New York, August 22, 1939.

| | | |
|---|---|---|
| 66167-A | The Man With The Mandolin - vLW | Dec 2750 |
| 66168-A | Utt Da Zay (The Tailor Song) - vLW | - |
| 66169-A | Ja Da - vLW | Dec 2959 |
| 66170-A | It's The Tune That Counts - vLW | - |

Pseudonym on Ariel 4586 for Irving Kaufman, q.v.

## LU WATTERS' YERBA BUENA JAZZ BAND

Although it may be argued that Lu Watters' records belong more properly to the era
following the one covered by this book, in view of the fact they kindled the flame
that burned as the popular "trad" revival of the 1950s, nevertheless four sessions
by the band were recorded prior to the cut-off date of this work, and thus they
are included here.

Lu Watters-c dir. Bob Scobey-c/Turk Murphy-tb/Ellis Horne-cl/Wally Rose-p/Clancy
Hayes-bj-v/Russ Bennett-bj-g/Dick Lammi-bb/Bill Dart-d, or Rose-Hayes-Dart only*.
                                        San Francisco, December 19, 1941.

| MLB-106 | Muskrat Ramble | JM 3, GTJ 58, Md 1125 |
| MLB-107 | At A Georgia Camp Meeting (Kerry Mills) | JM 4, GTJ 59, Md 1123 |
| MLB-108 | Original Jelly Roll Blues | - - - |
| MLB-109 | Maple Leaf Rag (Scott Joplin) | JM 1, GTJ 56 |
| MLB-110 | Irish Black Bottom | JM 2, GTJ 57 |
| MLB-111 | *Black And White Rag (George Botsford) | JM 1, GTJ 56 |
| MLB-112 | Smokey Mokes | JM 3, GTJ 58, Md 1125 |
| MLB-113 | Memphis Blues | JM 2, GTJ 57 |

    Rose, Hayes, Bennett and Dart only.    San Francisco, March 22, 1942.

| MLB-117 | Hot House Rag (Paul Pratt) | JM 17 |
| MLB-118 | Temptation Rag (Henry Lodge) | JM 7 |
| MLB-119 | Black And White Rag (George Botsford) | JM 1 |

    As for December 19, 1941, but Squire Girsback-bb replaces Lammi.
                                        San Francisco, March 29, 1942.

| MLB-120 | Come Back  Sweet Papa | JM 6, Md 1126 |
| MLB-121 | Terrible Blues | JM 15 |
| MLB-122 | Fidgety Feet | JM 7 |
| MLB-123 | London Blues | JM 14 |
| MLB-124 | Sunset Cafe Stomp | - |
| MLB-125 | Daddy Do | JM 13, Md 1124 |
| MLB-126 | Milenberg Joys | - - |
| MLB-127 | Riverside Blues | JM 5 |
| MLB-128 | Cake Walking Babies | - |
| MLB-129 | High Society | JM 15 |
| MLB-130 | Tiger Rag | JM 6, Md 1126 |
| MLB-131 | Muskrat Ramble | JM 3 |

                              San Francisco, April, 1942.

| Fidgety Feet | JM rejected |
| South | - |
| Piano Rag | - |
| Terrible Blues | - |
| St. James Infirmary | - |
| That's A Plenty | - |
| Careless Love - vCH | - |
| Auntie Skinner's Chicken Dinner  - vCH | - |

## PHIL WATTS

Banjo solos, acc. unknown.            London, May 21, 1936.

| TB-2194-1-2 | Playing The Blues | Dec rejected |
| TB-2195-1-2 | Dere's Jazz In Dem Dere Horns | - |

                              London, May 26, 1936.

| TB-2194-3-4 | Playing The Blues | Dec rejected |
| TB-2195-3-4 | Dere's Jazz In Dem Dere Horns | - |

Piano solos.                              Paris, June 23, 1937.

OLA-1876-1  I Ain't Got Nobody                       Swing 58
OLA-1877-1-2  Tea For Two                            Swing 5
OLA-1878-1  Weather Blues                            Swing 315
OLA-1878-2  Weather Beaten Blues                     Swing 5
OLA-1879-2  Maple Leaf Rag (Scott Joplin)            Swing 315

                                          Paris, July 20, 1937.

OLA-1918-1  My Blue Heaven                           Swing 38
OLA-1919-1  Ain't Misbehavin'                          -

  Acc. by Basil Evans-sb/Trevor McCabe-d, with own v.
                                    Calcutta, c. May, 1942.

CEI-22063-1  Birth Of The Blues                  Col FB-40164
CEI-22064-1  Darktown Strutters' Ball                  -

                                    Calcutta, c. June, 1942.

CEI-22110-1  How About You ? - vTW               Col FB-40172
CEI-22111-1  Hoe Down - vTW                          -

  Acc. by George Banks-t/Willie Manuel-Harry Joseph-as Sumner Gill-ts Cedric West-g/
    Basil Evans-sb/Trevor McCabe-d.        Calcutta, c. August, 1942.

CEI-22182-1  Blues In The Night                  Col FB-40220
CEI-22183-1  Basin Street Blues - vTW            Col FB-40225
CEI-22184-1  Memphis Blues                           -
CEI-22185-1  St. Louis Blues - vTW               Col FB-40220

## FRED   WEAVER

Vocal, acc. by Leroy Tibbs-p/bj.        New York, c. November, 1924.

T-2014-2  I'll Take Her Back (If She Wants To     UTD 2018
              Come Back)
T-2015-1-2  When My Sugar Walks Down The Street       -        Ebs 1006

## RICHARD L.   WEAVER

Banjo solo.                             New York, December 14, 1899.

  0815    Ragtime Dance                          Ber 0815

## CHICK WEBB

CHICK WEBB'S HARLEM STOMPERS : Chick Webb-d dir. Bobby Stark-t/William R. Paris-
    Johnny Hodges-as/Ed Williams-ts/Don Kirkpatrick-p/Benny James-bj-g/Leon England-bb.
                                    New York, August 25, 1927.

E-6358/61  Low Levee - High Water                Voc rejected

CHICK WEBB AND HIS ORCHESTRA : Chick Webb-d dir. Shelton Hemphill-Louis Hunt-t/Louis
    Bacon-t-v/Jimmy Harrison tb/Benny Carter-cl-as-a/Hilton Jefferson-cl-as/Elmer
    Williams-cl-ts/Don Kirkpatrick-p/John Trueheart-bj-g/Elmer James-bb-sb.
                                    New York, March 30, 1931.

E-36432-  Heebie Jeebies (Heebie Jeebie*)        Voc 1607, Br 6898, 01857,
                                                 A-500324*, Pan 25047, Dec M-30361
E-36433-A  Blues In My Heart - vLB               Br 6156, 6898, 01857, A-9842,
                                                 A-82524, A-500217
E-36434-  Soft And Sweet                         Voc 1607, Br 02079, A-9941,
                                                 A-500324, Dec M-30361
  NOTE:- Some copies of Brunswick 02079 play HEEBIE JEEBIES instead of SOFT AND
SWEET, although correctly labelled according to the catalog.

CHICK WEBB'S SAVOY ORCHESTRA : Chick Webb-d dir. Mario Bauza-Reunald Jones-t/Taft
    Jordan-t-v/Sandy Williams-tb/Pete Clark-as/Edgar Sampson-as-a/Elmer Williams-ts/
    Joe Steele-p/John Trueheart-bj-g/John Kirby-sb/Chuck Richards-v.
                                        New York, December 20, 1933.

152658-1  On The Sunny Side Of The Street - vTJ    Col 2875-D, CB-741, Voc 3246
152659-2  Darktown Strutters' Ball                 CBS CL-2639 (LP)

                                        New York, January 15, 1934.

152659-4  Darktown Strutters' Ball     Col CB-754
152686-3  If Dreams Come True              -         2883-D
152687-2  Let's Get Together - aES     Col CB-741    -

                                        New York, May 9, 1934.

152733-2  I Can't Dance (I Got Ants In My Pants)    Col 2920-D, DB-5009
            - vTJ
152734-2  Imagination - vCR                          -        -
152735-1-2  Why Should I Beg For Love ? - vTJ/aES  Rejected

                                        New York, May 18, 1934.

152735-4  Why Should I Beg For Love ? - vTJ/aES    Col 2926-D, MC-3020, Par R-2117,
                                                   A-6269
152740-2  Stomping At The Savoy                    Col 2926-D, Voc 3246, Par R-2088

    Bobby Stark-t replaces Jones; Fernando Arbello-tb/Wayman Carver-ts-f added; Charles
    Linton-v.                           New York, July 6, 1934.

152769-2  Blue Minor - aES                         OK 41572, Voc 3100
152770-2  True - vCL                               OK 41571, Voc 3101
152771-2  Lonesome Moments - aES                   OK 41572    -
152772-2  If It Ain't Love - vCL                   OK 41571, Voc 3100

CHICK WEBB AND HIS ORCHESTRA : As last session above, but Claude Jones-tb replaces
    Arbello; Don Kirkpatrick-p replaces Steele.
                                        New York, September 10, 1934.

38593-A  That Rhythm Man - vTJ           Dec 173, Br 02019
38594-A  On The Sunny Side Of The Street - vTJ    Dec 172, 3318, Br 01915
38595-A  Lona - aES                      Dec 173, Br 02019
38596-A-B  Blue Minor - aES             Dec 172, Br 01915

                                        New York, November 19, 1934.

39138-A  It's Over Because We're Through - vTJ    Dec 483, Br 02029, A-9830
39140-A  Don't Be That Way                 -         -        -
39141-A  What A Shuffle - aES            Dec 1087, Br 02152,A-9969,A-505048
39142-A  Blue Lou                        Dec 1065    -        -        -
NOTE:- Matrix 39139 is untraced.

    Ella Fitzgerald-v; Wayman Carver-a.    New York, June 12, 1935.

39614-A  I'll Chase The Blues Away - vEF    Br 02602, A-81583, Dec Y-5256
39615-A  Down Home Rag (Wilbur Sweatman) - aWC    Dec 785, Br 02290, A-81065
39616-A  Are You Here To Stay ? - vCL       Dec 494
39617-A  Love And Kisses - vEF                 -

    Bill Thomas-sb replaces Kirby.      New York, October 12, 1935.

60054-A  Rhythm And Romance - vEF        Dec 588, M-39022, Br 02375
60055-A  Moonlight And Magnolias - vCL      -      Y-5256, Br 02602, A-81583
60056-A  I'll Chase The Blues Away - vEF    Dec 640    -     Br 02249, A-81030
60057-A  I May Be Wrong But I Think You're  -      Y-5159     -        -
            Wonderful - vTJ
60058-A  Facts And Figures               Dec 830, M-39024, Br 02375

CHICK WEBB AND HIS ORCHESTRA : Chick Webb-d dir. Mario Bauza-Bobby Stark-Taft Jordan-
t/Sandy Williams-Claude Jones-tb/Pete Clark-cl-as/Edgar Sampson-as-a/Elmer Williams
ts/Wayman Carver-ts-f/Don Kirkpatrick-p/John Trueheart-g/Bill Thomas-sb/Ella Fitzgerald-v.                                    New York, February, 1936.

```
        Go Harlem - aES                        Pol 236524 (LP)
        Keepin' Out Of Mischief Now            Pol 423248, IAJRC 5 (LPs)
        Nit Wit Serenade                           -
        King Porter Stomp                          -               -
        Big John's Special                         -        IAJRC 1 (LPs)
        Stompin' At The Savoy - aES                -        IAJRC 5 (LPs)
        Don't Be That Way - aES                    -
        Rhythm And Romance                                         -
```

                              New York, April 7, 1936.

```
60999-A-B  Love, You're Just A Laugh - vEF      Rejected
61000-A    Crying My Heart Out For You - vEF    Dec 785, Br 02290, A-81065
61001-A    Under The Spell Of The Blues - vEF   Dec 831, Br 02792, A-82201
61002-A    When I Get Low I Get High - vEF      Dec 1123, M-39028, Br 02405
```

Nat Story-tb replaces Jones; Ted McRae-ts replaces Williams.
                              New York, June 2, 1936.

```
61123-A  Go Harlem - aES                        Dec 995, Br 02514
61124-A  Sing Me A Swing Song (And Let Me Dance) Dec 830, 3319, Br 02264
           - vEF
61125-A  A Little Bit Later On - vEF            Dec 831   -       -
61126-A  Love, You're Just A Laugh - vEF        Dec 1114, Br 02419
61127-A  Devoting My Time To You - vEF          Dec 995, Br 02405
```

Louis Jordan-as-v replaces Sampson; Tommy Fulford-p replaces Kirkpatrick; Beverley
Peer-sb replaces Thomas.             New York, October 29, 1936.

```
61361-A  (If You Can't Sing It) You'll Have To  Dec 1032, 333397, Br 02357
           Swing It - vEF
61362-A  Swinging On The Reservation - vEF      Dec 1065, Br 02396
61363-A  I've Got The Spring Fever Blues - vEF  Dec 1087   -
61364-A  Vote For Mr. Rhythm - vEF              Dec 1032, 333397, M-39023,Br 02357
NOTE:- Decca M-39023 was issued under ELLA FITZGERALD'S name.
```

                              New York, January 14, 1937.

```
61527-A  Take Another Guess - vEF               Dec 1123, M-30117,Br 02576,A-81445
61528-A  Love Marches On - v3                   Dec 1115, Br 02381, A-81552
```

                              New York, January 15, 1937.

```
61529-A  There's Frost On The Moon - v3         Dec 1114, Br 02381, A-81552
61530-A  Gee, But You're Swell - vLJ            Dec 1115, Br 02419
```

                              New York, February 8, 1937.

```
        That's A Plenty                         JP LP-2

Charlie Dixon-a.                     New York, March 24, 1937.

62064-A  Rusty Hinge - vLJ                      Dec 1273, BM-1096,Br 02470,A-81276
62065-A  Wake Up And Live - vEF&3               Dec 1213, Br 02438
62066-A  It's Swell Of You - vLJ                   -         -
62067-A-B  You Showed Me The Way - vEF          Dec 1220
62068-A  Clap Hands ! Here Comes Charley           -
62069-A  Cryin' Mood - vEF                      Dec 1273,BM-1096, Br 02470,A-81276
62072-A  Love Is The Thing, So They Say - vEF   Dec 1356
62073-A  That Naughty Waltz - aCD                  - Br 02792, A-82201, Pol A-61278
NOTE:- Matrices 62070 and 62071 are by Louis Armstrong and his Orchestra, q.v.
```

CHICK WEBB AND HIS LITTLE CHICKS : Chauncey Haughton-cl/Wayman Carver-f/Tommy Fulford
  p/Beverley Peer-sb/Chick Webb-d.          New York, September 21, 1937.

| 62618-A | In A Little Spanish Town | Dec 1513, 3320, M-30102, Br 02546, A-81397 |
| 62619-A | I Got Rhythm | Dec 1759, Br 88067, Od 286351 |
| 62620-A | I Ain't Got Nobody | Dec 1513, M-30102,Br 02546,A-81397 |

CHICK WEBB AND HIS ORCHESTRA : Chick Webb-d dir. Mario Bauza-Bobby Stark-Taft Jordan-
  t/Sandy Williams-Nat Story-tb/Chauncey Haughton-cl-as/Louis Jordan-as/Ted McRae-ts/
  Wayman Carver-ts-f/Tommy Fulford-p/Bobby Johnson-g/Beverley Peer-sb/Ella Fitzgerald
  v/Charlie Dixon-a.                        New York, October 27, 1937.

| 62725-A | Just A Simple Melody - vEF | Dec 1521, Br 02536, A-81380 |
| 62726-A | I Got A Guy - vEF | Dec 1681, BM-1114, M-30121,M-30369, Y-5511, Br 02580, A-81499, A-505136 |
| 62727-A | Strictly Jive | Dec 1586, M-30106, Y-5215, Br 02559, A-81432 |
| 62728-A | Holiday In Harlem - vEF | Dec 1521, Y-5241, Br 02536, A-81380 |

The first title of this session is by CHICK WEBB AND HIS LITTLE CHICKS, as on
September 21, 1937 above.                   New York, November 1, 1937.

| 62737-B | Sweet Sue, Just You | Dec 1759, M-30117, Y-5239, Br 02576, A-81445, 88057 |
| 62738-A | Rock It For Me - vEF | Dec 1586, M-30106, Y-5215, Br 02559, A-81432, A-82524 |
| 62739-A | Squeeze Me | Dec 1716, Br 02793, A-82202 |
| 62740-A | Harlem Congo - aCD | Dec 1681, 3684, BM-1114, M-30121, M-30369, Br 80133, 02580, A-81499, A-505136 |

New York, November 2, 1937.

| 62743-A-B | Hallelujah ! | Dec rejected |
| 62744-A-B | I Want To Be Happy - vEF | - |

Garvin Bushell-cl-as replaces Haughton; Turk van Lake-a.
                                           New York, December 17, 1937.

| 62886-A | I Want To Be Happy - vEF/aTVL | Dec 15039, 29239, Br 0138, A-5131 |
| 62886-B | I Want To Be Happy - vEF/aTVL | Dec Z-778 |
| 62887-A | The Dipsy Doodle - vEF | Dec 1587, 3320, BM-1104, M-30113, Y-5208, Br 02569, A-81449,A-505133 |
| 62888-A | If Dreams Come True - vEF | Dec 1716, Br 02793, A-82202, Pol A-61260 |
| 62889-A | Hallelujah ! - vEF | Dec 15039, 29239, Z-778, Br 0138, A-5131 |
| 62890-A | Midnite In A Madhouse (Midnite In Harlem*) | Dec 1587, BM-1104, M-30113*, Br 02569*, A-81449*, A-505133* |
| 62890-B | Midnite In A Madhouse | Dec Y-5208 |

George Matthews-tb added.                  New York, May 2, 1938.

| 63693-A | A-Tisket, A-Tasket - vEF&ch | Dec 1840, 60730, 333298, BM-1017, M-30142, M-32723, Br 02614, A-81635, A-81723, A-82608, A-505162, Pol A-61159, A-61179 |
| 63694-A | Heart Of Mine - vEF | Dec 2721, Br 02847 |
| 63695-A | I'm Just A Jitterbug - vEF | Dec 1899,Br 02631,A-81691,A-500740 |
| 63696-C | Azure | - Br 80133 -       -        - |

NOTE:- Decca 60730 and 333298 as ELLA FITZGERALD.

Benny Carter-a.                            New York, May 3, 1938.

| 63707-A | Spinnin' The Webb | Dec 2021, M-30173, Y-5336, Br 02669, A-81796 |
| 63708-A | Liza (All The Clouds'll Roll Away)-aBC | Dec 1840, M-30142, M-32723, Br 02614, A-81635, A-505162, Od 286351 |

CHICK WEBB AND HIS ORCHESTRA : Chick Webb-d dir. Mario Bauza-Bobby Stark-t/Taft
Jordan-t-v/Sandy Williams-Nat Story-George Matthews-tb/Garvin Bushell-cl-as/Hilton
Jefferson-as/Ted McRae-ts/Wayman Carver-ts-f/Tommy Fulford-p/Bobby Johnson-g/
Beverley Peer-sb/Ella Fitzgerald-v.     New York, June 9, 1938.

| | | |
|---|---|---|
| 63934-A | Pack Up Your Sins And Go To The Devil | Dec 1894, M-30169, Y-5258, |
| | - vEF | Br 02660, A-81783, Pol A-61188 |
| 63935-A | MacPherson Is Rehearsin' (To Swing) | Dec 2080, BM-1095, M-30178, |
| | - vEF | Br 02680, A-81857, A-505189 |
| 63936-A | Everybody Step - vEF | Dec 1894, M-30169, Y-5258, |
| | | Br 02660, A-81783, Pol A-61188 |
| 63937-A | Ella - vEF-TJ | Dec 2148, BM-1035, M-30186, Y-5336, |
| | | Br 02687, A-81896, A-505190, |
| | | Pol A-61192 |

New York, August 17, 1938.

| | | |
|---|---|---|
| 64459-A | Wacky Dust - vEF | Dec 2021, M-30173, Y-5274, |
| | | Br 02669, A-81796 |
| 64460-A | Gotta Pebble In My Shoe - vEF | Dec 2231, BM-1036, M-30210, Y-5486, |
| | | Br 02723, A-81989, A-505207, |
| | | Pol A-61228 |
| 64461-A | I Can't Stop Loving You - vEF | Dec 2310, Br 02777 |

New York, August 18, 1938.

| | | |
|---|---|---|
| 64464-A | Who Ya Hunchin' ? | Dec 2231, M-30210, Br 02723, |
| | | A-81989, A-505207 |
| 64465-A | I Let A Tear Fall In The River - vEF | Dec 2080, BM-1095, M-30178, |
| | | Br 02680, A-81857, A-505189 |

Dick Vance-t replaces Bauza.     New York, October 6, 1938.

| | | |
|---|---|---|
| 64573-A | F. D. R. Jones - vEF | Dec 2105, Br 02818, A-505217 |
| 64574-A | I Love Each Move You Make - vEF | Br 02794, A-82213, Pol A-61273 |
| 64575-A | It's Foxy - vEF | Dec 2309 - - A-505225 - |
| 64576-A | I Found My Yellow Basket - vEF&ch | Dec 2148, BM-1035, M-30186, Y-5274, |
| | | Br 02687, A-91896, A-505190, |
| | | Pol A-61192 |

Recorded by RCA Victor for NBC.     New York, January 9, 1939.

| | |
|---|---|
| Tea For Two | Pol 423248 (LP) |
| How Am I To Know ? | - |
| One O'Clock Jump | - |
| The Blue Room | - |
| Crazy Rhythm | - |
| Sugar Foot Stomp | - |
| Grand Terrace Rhythm | - |
| By Heck | Pol 236524 (LP) |
| Blue Skies | Pol 423248 (LP) |
| Dinah | - |
| Who Yuh Hunchin' (sic) | Pol 236524 (LP) |
| Liza (All The Clouds'll Roll Away) | Pol 423248 (LP) |

NBC broadcast from the Blue Room of the Hotel Lincoln, New York, February 10, 1939.

| | |
|---|---|
| One O'Clock Jump | Pol 236524 (LP) |
| The Blue Room | - |

New York, February 17, 1939.

| | | |
|---|---|---|
| 65039-A | Undecided - vEF | Dec 2323, 60730, Y-5377, |
| | | Br 02743, A-82608, A-505257 |
| 65040-A | 'Tain't What You Do (It's The Way | Dec 2310, Y-5377, Br 02777 |
| | That Cha Do It) - vEF | |
| 65041-A | In The Groove At The Grove | Dec 2323, BM-1031, Y-5399, |
| | | Br 02743, A-505257, Pol A-61249 |
| 65042-A | One Side Of Me - vEF | Dec 2556, Br 02795, A-82203 |
| 65043-A | My Heart Belongs To Daddy - vEF | Dec 2309, 333298, M-30264, Y-5399, |
| NOTE:- Decca 60730, 333298 and Brunswick | | Br 02871, A-505225 |
| A-505257 as ELLA FITZGERALD. | | |

CHICK WEBB AND HIS ORCHESTRA : Chick Webb-d dir. Dick Vance-Bobby Stark-Taft Jordan-t
    /Sandy Williams-Nat Story-George Matthews-tb/Garvin Bushell-cl-as/Hilton Jefferson-
    as/Ted McRae-ts/Wayman Carver-ts-f/Tommy Fulford-p/John Trueheart-g/Beverley Peer-
    sb/Ella Fitzgerald-v.                        New York, March 2, 1939.

    65094-A  Sugar Pie - vEF                      Dec 2665, Br 02795, A-82203,
                                                  Pol A-61260
    65095-A  It's Slumbertime Along The Swanee - vEF  Dec 2389, Br 02765, A-82107
    65096-A  I'm Up A Tree - vEF                  Dec 2468, Y-5428, Br 02796,A-82204
    65097-A  Chew-Chew-Chew (Your Bubble Gum) - vEF  Dec 2389, Br 02765, A-82107

                                                  New York, April 21, 1939.

    65445-A  Have Mercy - vEF                     Dec 2468, Y-5428, Br 02796,A-82204
    65446-A  Little White Lies - vEF             Dec 2556, Br 02818, A-505217
    65447-A  Coochi-Coochi-Coo - vEF             Dec 2803, Br A-82204
    65448-A  That Was My Heart - vEF             Dec 2665, M-30264, Br 02871,
                                                  A-505225
NOTE:- Decca 2803 as ELLA FITZGERALD WITH CHICK WEBB AND HIS ORCHESTRA.

                                        Southland Cafe, Boston, May 4, 1939.

            Let's Get Together                   CC 11 (LP)
            Poor Little Rich Girl                    -
            Break 'Em Down                          -
            If I Didn't Care - vEF                  -
            The Stars And Stripes Forever          -
            My Wild Irish Rose                     -
            Chew-Chew-Chew (Your Bubble Gum) - vEF  -

                        MALCOLM WEBB AND  HIS GANG

Pseudonym on Champion for Hoagy Carmichael and his Pals, and Emil Seidel and his
    Orchestra, both q.v.

                    SPEED WEBB AND HIS HOOSIER MELODY LADS

Speed Webb-d dir. Nelson Douglas-Earl Thompson-t/Parker Berry-tb/George White-Harvey
    Scott-as/Ernest Green-ts/Leonard Gay-bar/Fritz Weston-p/Bob Robinson-bj-g/Cliff
    Levi-bb.                             Richmond, Ind., March 30, 1926.

    12494     Florida Stomp                      Gnt rejected
    12495     Shake It And Break It                  -
    12496     You Better Keep Away From Me          -
    12497,-A  It Must Be Love                       -

                    MAREK WEBER UND SEIN ORCHESTER

The following titles from the hundreds made by this famous orchestra in Germany,
    England and the U.S.A. are known to be of interest as jazz; there may be others.

Marek Weber-vn dir. Arthur Briggs-Howard McFarlane-t/F. Monetti-tb/Franz Veith-cl-as/
    C. B. Hilliam-cl-bar-bsx-a/J. Mario-cl-ts/Eugen Bermann-U. Irrlicht-vn/George
    Haentzschel-p-a/Mike Danzi-bj/Arthur Brosche-bb/Dick Stauff-d.
                                        Berlin, July 27, 1927.

BWR-1068-1  Crazy Words (sic)                    El EG-639, EG-641

    George Hurst-Max Neuf-t replace Briggs and McFarlane; Frank Goede-bj-g replaces
    Danzi.                               Berlin, September 14, 1927.

BWR-1127-2  Heebie Jeebies                       El EG-650

    Ben Pickering-tb replaces Monetti.   Berlin, December, 1928.

BLR-4838-1  Easy Goin'                           El EG-1131
BLR-4839-2  I Can't Give You Anything But Love       -

Carl Webster-bb-sb dir. Seelye Vidal-Harold Fletcher-t/Stew Pletcher-t-v/Gene Roselli
  tb/Louis Rapp (later known as vocalist Barry Wood)-cl-as/Bob Bruce-cl-as-v-a (and c
  on 170422-1)/Hank Palmer-as-a/Al Thompson-ts-v/Sidney Fine-p/Neil Waterman-g-v/Jim
  Devlin-d.                                New York, January 2, 1930.

170421-2  If I'm Without You - vSP-BB-AT-NW/aBB    Col 139-P
170422-1  Dream Child - aHP                             -

    Bob Stanley-t replaces Fletcher; Andy Wiswell-tb replaces Roselli; Dick Webster-v.
                                         New York, March 1, 1930.

403791-A  Puttin' On The Ritz - vSP/c--aBB        OK 41393, Od ONY-36054, 193470,
                                                   Par PNY-34047, R-689, A-3011
403792-B  With You - vDW/aSP                       OK 41393, Od ONY-36054, 193470,
                                                   Par PNY-34048, R-674, A-3011
490041-A  Puttin' On The Ritz                      Od ONY-36052, Par PNY-34045
490042-A  With You                                     -                -
  NOTE:- Parlophone ONY-34045 and PNY-34046 as THE OXFORD RHYTHM MAKERS.

## MARGARET WEBSTER

Vocal, acc. by Ed Anderson-c/? Albert Socarras-cl/? Garvin Bushell-as/Clarence
  Williams-p.                             New York, February 13, 1930.

149981-1  Wipe 'Em Off                            VT 7076-V
149982-3  How Can I Get It (When You Keep On       VT 7066-V, Diva 6040-G
            Snatchin' It Back)

## TED WEEMS AND HIS ORCHESTRA

Although Ted Weems' Decca records of the mid- and late 1930s are of no interest even
  as "hot" dance records, his Victors of 1923-1933 and Columbias of 1934 are mostly
  the exact opposite. They are therefore included here in full.

Ted Weems-tb dir. Art Weems-Paul Creedon-t/Norman Nugent-Walter Livingston-cl-ss-as-
  bsx/Francis Buggy-cl-ss-ts/Charles Gaylord-vn-v/Reuel Kenyon-p/Weston Vaughan-bj/
  George Barth-bb-sb/Cecil Richardson-d.  Camden, N. J., November 20, 1923.

29014-3   Covered Wagon Days                      Vic 19212, HMV B-1772, Zon 3713
29015-2   Somebody Stole My Gal                        -                -

                                         Camden, N. J., January 16, 1924.

29293-1-2-3  A Smile Will Go A Long, Long Way-vCG Rejected
29293-5   A Smile Will Go A Long, Long Way        Vic 19258, HMV B-1863, Zon 3720
29294-4   Nine O'Clock Sal                             -                -

Unknown vn replaces Gaylord.             Camden, N. J., February 6, 1924.

29442-3   Blue Rose                               Vic 19274, Zon 3757
29443-4   Don't Forget To Remember                     -         -

                                         Camden, N. J., February 22, 1924.

29497-1   I'm All Broken Up Over You              Vic 19286
29498-2   My Gal Sal                              Vic 19287, Zon 3759

Dudley Fosdick-mel added.                Camden, N. J., April 29, 1924.

30023-3   Big Boy !                               Vic 19344, Zon 3781
30029-2   Savannah (The Georgianna Blues)              -         -
30031-1-2  Dear One                               Rejected

    H. L. Wynne-cl-ss-as-bsx replaces Nugent; E. Martin Grey-cl-ss-ts replaces Buggy;
  Mark Fisher-bj-v replaces Vaughan.     Camden, N. J., June 9, 1924.

30253-3   Who Wants A Bad Little Boy ? - vMF      Vic 19424
30254-3   Red-Nose Pete                           Vic 19377, Zon 3777

Ted Weems-tb dir. Art Weems-Paul Creedon-t/H. L. Wynne-Walter Livingston-cl-ss-as-bsx
/E. Martin Grey-cl-ss-ts/Dudley Fosdick-mel/vn/Dewey Bergman-p/Weston Vaughan-bj/
Louis Terman-bb/Cecil Richardson-d.     Camden, N. J., October 14, 1924.

| | | |
|---|---|---|
| 30031-3-4-5-6 | Dear One | Vic rejected |
| 31100-1-2-3-4 | Travelin' Blues | - |

Camden, N. J., October 21, 1924.

| | | |
|---|---|---|
| 30031-10 | Dear One | Vic 19491, Zon 3847 |
| 31100-9 | Travelin' Blues | Vic 19496 |

Camden, N. J., December 11, 1924.

| | | |
|---|---|---|
| 31278-1-2-3-4 | Fascinating Rhythm | Vic rejected |
| 31279-1-2-3 | Blue-Eyed Sally | - |

Camden, N. J., December 23, 1924.

| | | |
|---|---|---|
| 31278-5-6-7 | Fascinating Rhythm | Rejected |
| 31279-6 | Blue-Eyed Sally | Vic 19547 |

Ted Weems-tb dir. Art Weems-Paul Creedon-t/Dudley Fosdick-mel/Dick Cunliffe-cl-as-bar
/Parker Gibbs-cl-ts-v/vn/Jack O'Brien-p/Weston Vaughan-bj-v/Louis Terman-bb/Dusty
Roads-d-v.       Camden, N. J., July 8, 1925.

| | | |
|---|---|---|
| 32759-1-2-3-4 | If I Ever Cry (You'll Never Know) - vWV | Rejected |
| 32759-6 | If I Ever Cry (You'll Never Know) | Vic 19722 |
| 32760-2 | Siberia | -    HMV B-2122 |
| 32761-4 | Lonesome (Gee, I'm Awf'ly Lonesome) | Vic 19804, HMV EA-13 |

Creedon-Ted Weems-Fosdick omitted*.     Camden, N. J., January 7, 1926.

| | | |
|---|---|---|
| 33658-1-2-3-4-5-6 | *Spring Fever | Rejected |
| 33659-3 | Love Bound | Vic 20033, HMV B-5089 |
| 33660-3 | Smile A Little Bit - vDR | Vic 19930 |
| 33661-4 | The Day That I Met You - vDR | Vic 19938, HMV EA-55 |

Ted Weems dir. Art Weems-Carl Agee-t/Charles Stenroos-tb/Dick Cunliffe-cl-as-bar/
Thales Taylor-cl-as/Parker Gibbs-cl-ts-v/Jack O'Brien-p/Bill Comfort-bj-v/Louis
Terman-bb/Dusty Roads-d-v.     Camden, N. J., July 19, 1926.

| | | |
|---|---|---|
| 35589-1 | Oh ! If I Only Had You - vPG-BC-DR | Vic 20133, HMV B-5145, El EG-362 |
| 35590-4 | She Belongs To Me - vPG-BC-DR | Vic 20475 |
| 35591-2 | My Cutey's Due At Two-To-Two Today-vPG | Vic 20120, HMV B-5145, EA-155, El EG-362 |
| 35592-2 | I'm Gonna Park Myself In Your Arms-vPG | Vic 20120 |

Camden, N. J., September 7, 1926.

| | | |
|---|---|---|
| 36160-1-2-3-4-5 | What's The Use Of Crying ?-vDR | Rejected |
| 36161-1-2-3-4 | Climbing Up The Ladder Of Love - vDR | - |
| 36162-3 | That's My Girl - vPG-BC-DR | Vic 20196, HMV EA-126 |

Camden, N. J., September 13, 1926.

| | | |
|---|---|---|
| 36160-10 | What's The Use Of Crying ? - vDR | Vic 20234, HMV B-5223 |
| 36161-6 | Climbing Up The Ladder Of Love - vDR | Vic 20230, HMV EA-111 |
| 36183-4 | Chick, Chick, Chick, Chick, Chicken (Lay A Little Egg For Me) - vPG-DR | Vic 20206, HMV EA-101, El EG-322 |

Carl Workman-tb replaces Stenroos; Morton Parker-bj probably replaces Comfort.
Camden, N. J., July 18, 1927.

| | | |
|---|---|---|
| 39440-1-2-3-4 | She's Got "It" - vPG | Vic rejected |
| 39441-1-2-3-4 | Miss Annabelle Lee - vPG-DR | - |
| 39442-1-2-3-4 | Shine On, Harvest Moon - vDR | - |

Ted Weems dir. Art Weems-Carl Agee-t/Carl Workman-tb/Dick Cunliffe-cl-as-bar/Thales
  Taylor-cl-as/Parker Gibbs-cl-ts-v/Jack O'Brien (and Bob Royce*)-p/Morton Parker-bj/
  Louis Terman-bb/Dusty Roads-d-v.          Camden, N. J., July 28, 1927.

39440-7  She's Got "It" - vPG                    Vic 20829, HMV B-5465, EA-222
39441-7  Miss Annabelle Lee (Who's Wonderful,    Vic 20846, HMV EA-296
           Who's Marvelous) - vPG-DR
39453-3  *Barbara - vDR                              -

  Bob Royce-p replaces O'Brien.          Camden, N. J., August 24, 1927.

39580-4  Marvelous - vPG-DR                     Vic 20901, HMV EA-247, El EG-697
39581-1  She'll Never Find A Fellow Like Me - vPG Vic 21009, HMV B-5412
39582-4  Roam On, My Little Gypsy Sweetheart-vDR  Vic 20892, HMV B-5394, EA-233

                                         Camden, N. J., September 8, 1927.

39599-1  Highways Are Happy Ways - vPG-DR        Vic 20910, HMV B-5377, EA-250,
                                                 El EG-698
40000-2  It Was Only A Sun Shower - vDR          As above

                                         Camden, N. J., September 20, 1927.

40018-3  From Saturday Night Till Monday Morning  Vic 21009, HMV B-5412
           - vPG
40019-1-2-3  Let's Make-Believe - vPG            Rejected

Ted Weems dir. Art Weems-Merrill Conner-t/Pete Beilman-tb/Dick Cunliffe and another-
  cl-as-bar/Parker Gibbs-cl-ts-v/? Bob Royce-p/Art Jarrett-bj-v/Sam Olver-bb-v/
  Ormand Downes-d.                       Camden, N. J., November 25, 1927.

40091-1  Cobble-Stones - vPG-AJ-SO              Vic 21105
40091-4  Cobble-Stones - vPG                       -    HMV B-5448
40092-2  Everybody Loves My Girl - vPG          Vic 21173, HMV B-5445, R-4979

                                         Camden, N. J., April 3, 1928.

43434-3  Dream River (w) - vPG                   Vic 21339, HMV B-5524, EA-438
43435-4  He's Tall, Dark And Handsome - vPG      Vic 21364, HMV B-5491, EA-347

                                         Camden, N. J., April 5, 1928.

43436-2  Nothin' On My Mind (But The Moonlight,  Vic 21364, HMV B-5491, EA-347
           The Starlight And You) - vPG
43437-2  Who Wouldn't Be Blue ? - vPG-AJ-SO      Vic 21511

                                         Camden, N. J., August 21, 1928.

46142-2  Flower Of Love - vAJ                    Vic 21643, HMV B-5613, EA-431,
                                                 R-14170
46143-1-2-3  I Wonder (w)                        Rejected

  2p used, next session only.          Camden, N. J., September 4, 1928.

42920-2  (You're Just A Great Big) Baby Doll-vPG  Vic 21670, HMV EA-433
42921-2  If You Want The Rainbow (You Must Have The   -          -
           Rain) - vAJ

                                         Camden, N. J., September 21, 1928.

42967-3  Come On, Baby ! - vPG                   Vic 21729
46143-4-5-6  I Wonder (w) - vAJ                  Rejected

                                         Camden, N. J., October 2, 1928.

47800-3  I Found You "Out" When I Found You "In"  Vic 21773, HMV B-5613
           Somebody Else's Arms - vAJ

Ted Weems dir. Art Weems-Merrill Conner-t/Pete Beilman-tb/Dick Cunliffe and another-
   cl-as-bar/Parker Gibbs-cl-ts-v/? Bob Royce-p/Art Jarrett-bj-v/Sam Olver-bb/Ormand
   Downes-d.                          Camden, N. J., October 19, 1928.

47851-2  You're The Cream In My Coffee - vPG      Vic 21767
47852-2  Anything Your Heart Desires - vAJ          -

   2p used, next session only.      Camden, N. J., December 7, 1928.

49169-3  Me And The Man In The Moon - vAJ      Vic 21809, HMV EA-490
49170-3  My Troubles Are Over - vPG               -      HMV B-5618

   Vn added.                         Camden, N. J., December 17, 1928.

49188-1-2-3  The Glory Of Spring (w) (Intro.      Vic rejected
      Lips That Laugh At Love) - vAJ
49189-1-2-3  No Other Love (Was Meant For Me)        -
      (Intro. I'd Like To Love Them All) - vAJ

   Vn omitted; Frank Munn-v.         Camden, N. J., January 7, 1929.

49188-4  The Glory Of Spring (w) (Intro. Lips    Vic 21840
      That Laugh At Love) - vFM
49189-4-5  No Other Love (Was Meant For Me)      Rejected
      (Intro. I'd Like To Love Them All) - vAJ
49189-7  No Other Love (Was Meant For Me) (Intro. Vic 21840
      I'd Like To Love Them All) - vFM

Ted Weems dir. Art Weems-Merrill Conner-t/Harry Turner-tb/Dudley Fosdick-mel/Dick
   Cunliffe-cl-as-bar/Don Watt-cl-as/Parker Gibbs-cl-ts-v/Jack O'Brien-p/Art Jarrett-
   bj/Country Washburn-bb-v/Ormand Downes-d.Camden, N. J., June 17, 1929.

49431-1-2-3  Sophomore Prom. - vPG-AJ-CW      Vic rejected
49432-1-2-3-4  I Don't Want Your Kisses (If I Can't  -
      Have Your Love) - vPG

                                      Camden, N. J., June 21, 1929.

49431-4  Sophomore Prom. - vPG-AJ-CW      Vic 22215, HMV B-5770, EA-661,
                                          R-14341
49432-7  I Don't Want Your Kisses (If I Can't  Vic 22138, HMV EA-654
      Have Your Love) - vPG
55061-2  Good Morning, Good Evening, Goodnight  Vic 22032, HMV B-5712, EA-615,
      - vCW                            R-14214, El EG-1740

   According to the Victor files, an eleventh man is added on bells for this session.
   (Could this be Fosdick doubling ?)      Camden, N. J., June 25, 1929.

55062-2  What A Day ! - vPG               Vic 22038, HMV B-5692, EA-606,
                                          El EG-1632
55063-2  Am I A Passing Fancy ? - vAJ     Vic 22038, HMV EA-606, El EG-1632

   The eleventh man plays celeste.    Camden, N. J., June 28, 1929.

55066-3  Here We Are - vAJ               Vic 22037, HMV EA-602, R-14226
55067-2  Piccolo Pete - vPG&ch           As above, plus Vic 20-2175,
                                          HMV B-5712, BD-1172, El EG-1629

   The files state "12 men" and mention the bell-player and Ted Weems, who perhaps was
   not present on every session ?      Camden, N. J., September 13, 1929.

56087-3  Miss Wonderful - vPG            Vic 22137, HMV B-5745, EA-678
56088-1  There's Too Many Eyes That Wanna Make  Vic 22157
      Eyes At Two Pretty Eyes I Love - vAJ
56089-3  Remarkable Girl - vCW             -      HMV B-5758
56090-1-2-3  All That I'm Asking Is Sympathy (w) Rejected
      - vAJ

Ted Weems dir. Art Weems-t-v/Merrill Conner-t/Harry Turner-tb/Dudley Fosdick-mel/
   Dick Cunliffe-cl-as-bar/Don Watt-cl-as/Parker Gibbs-cl-ts-v/Jack O'Brien-p/Art
   Jarrett-bj-v/Country Washburn-bb-v/Ormand Downes-d.  The "goofus horn" heard on
   matrix 57208-2 is probably played by Fosdick.
                                          Chicago, December 2, 1929.

56090-6  All That I'm Asking Is Sympathy (w)-vAJ  Vic 22236
57208-2  Harmonica Harry - vPG               Vic 22238, HMV EA-692, R-14339
57209-2  The Man From The South - vAJ-PG&ch        -           - B-5811  -

                                          Chicago, December 7, 1929.

57236-1-2-3  Hollywood - vAJ               Rejected
57237-3  Talk Of The Town - vPG            Vic 22304, HMV R-14401
57238-1-3  Collegiate Love - vAW-AJ&ch     Vic 22406, HMV EA-766, R-14265

                                          Chicago, April 2, 1930.

59911-1-2-3  Just Another Night With You - vAJ   Rejected
59912-2  Mysterious Mose - vPG&ch          Vic 22411, HMV B-5884, EA-751

                                          Chicago, April 3, 1930.

59913-3  Slappin' The Bass - vPG&ch        Vic 22411, HMV EA-769
59914-2  Washing Dishes With My Sweetie - vPG  Vic 22426, HMV B-5862, EA-767

                                          Camden, N. J., July 1, 1930.

62668-1  Sing (A Happy Little Thing) - vPG   Vic 22515, HMV EA-821
62669-1-2-3-4  You Never Did That Before - vAJ  Rejected

                                          Camden, N. J., July 25, 1930.

62699-2  A Girl Friend Of A Boy Friend Of Mine   Vic 22499, HMV EA-800
              - vPG
62700-2  I Still Get A Thrill (Thinking Of You)  Vic 22515, HMV EA-821
              - vAJ
64001-3  My Baby Just Cares For Me - vAJ    Vic 22499, HMV EA-800

The Keating Twins-v.                      Hollywood, October 17, 1930.

61039-1  When It's Daylight-Saving Time In     Vic Special
              Oshkosh - vPG-CW-KT

The Victor files state that the vocalist on 61046-1 is Walter Doyle, evidently a
member of the Ted Weems organization as he appears as composer on this (and on
59912-2, 67562-1 and 67564-1, sometimes with Ted Weems himself as co-composer);
his instrument, if any, is not known, but the label of 61046-1 gives the vocalist
as Country Washburn, and it sounds like him anyway !
                                          Hollywood, October 28, 1930.

61045-2  The One-Man Band - vPG            Vic 22564, HMV EA-840, R-14539
61046-1  Egyptian-Ella - vWD or CW ?       Vic 22644, HMV EA-910

Art Jarrett switches to g; Elmo Tanner-v.
                                          Chicago, February 16, 1931.

56897-2  Walkin' My Baby Back Home - vPG   Vic 22637, HMV B-6005, EA-893
56898-1  When You Were The Blossom Of Buttercup  Vic 22648, HMV B-6047, EA-896
              Lane (And I Was Your Little Boy Blue)-vET
56899-2  My Favorite Band - vPG-AJ         Vic 22656, BB B-6395

                                          Chicago, February 19, 1931.

67511-2  You Gave Me Everything But Love - vAJ  Vic 22646
67512-1  I Lost My Gal Again - vPG         Vic 22637, HMV EA-911
67513-2  Little Joe - vAJ                  Vic 22646
67514-2  Jig Time - vCW                    Vic 22644
67515-1-2  Holiday In Venice - vET&ch      Rejected

Ted Weems dir. Art Weems-Merrill Conner-t/Harry Turner-tb/Don Watt-Dick Cunliffe-cl-
as-bar/Parker Gibbs-Red Ingle-cl-ts-v/Dudley Fosdick-mel-v/Jack O'Brien-p/Weston
Vaughan-g-v/Country Washburn-bb-sb-v/Ormand Downes-d/Elmo Tanner-w-v.
                                        Chicago, September 24, 1931.

| | | |
|---|---|---|
| 67548-1 | Oh ! Mo'nah - vCW&ch | Vic 22822, HMV EA-1072, R-14695 |
| 67549-1 | Play That Hot Guitar - vPG | Vic 24053, El EG-2625 |
| 67550-1 | Hangin' Out With You - vPG | Rejected |
| 67551-1 | I Love To Hear A Military Band - vPG | Vic 22822, HMV EA-971 |

                                        Chicago, September 28, 1931.

| | | |
|---|---|---|
| 67562-1 | The Toyland Band - vET | Rejected |
| 67563-1 | Nobody's Baby Is Somebody's Baby Now-vRI | Vic 22829 |
| 67564-1 | I'll Never See My Baby Any More - vPG | Rejected |
| 67565-1 | I'm For You A Hundred Per Cent. - vPG | Vic 22838, HMV EA-982 |

                                        Chicago, October 5, 1931.

| | | |
|---|---|---|
| 70613-1 | That's What I Like About You - vPG | Vic 22838, HMV B-4894, EA-982 |
| 70614-1 | Any Corner Is A Cozy Corner - vWV | Vic 22829, HMV EA-990 |
| 70615-1 | Don't Be Mad At Me - vPG | Rejected |

                                        Chicago, December 2, 1931.

| | | |
|---|---|---|
| 70637-1 | One Of Us Was Wrong - vET | Vic 22877, HMV EA-1059 |
| 70638-1 | She's So Nice - vPG | Vic 22881, HMV EA-1061 |
| 70639-1 | Carolina's Calling Me (w) - vWV | Vic 22877, HMV EA-1059 |
| 70640-1 | This Is My Love Song - vWV | Vic 22881, HMV B-6240 |
| 70641-1 | My Piano And Me - vPG-ET | Rejected |

  Andrea Marsh-v.                       Camden, N. J., December 19, 1932.

| | | |
|---|---|---|
| 74863-1 | Look Who's Here ! - vPG | Vic 24308 |
| 74864-1 | Look Who's Here ! | Vic ("Made for theatre use") |
| 74873-1 | Hats Off, Here Comes A Lady - vPG | Vic 24308, HMV EA-1183 |
| 74874-1 | Hats Off, Here Comes A Lady | Vic ("Made for theatre use") |
| 74875-1 | So At Last It's Come To This - vAM | Rejected |
| 74876-1 | Panhandle Pete - vPG&ch | Vic 24302 |

                                        Camden, N. J., January 9, 1933.

| | | |
|---|---|---|
| 69471-2 | Lonely Park - vAM | Vic 24227, HMV EA-1195 |
| 69472-1 | Lonely Park | Vic ("Made for theatre use") |
| 69473-1 | When The Morning Rolls Around - vPG | Vic 24227, HMV EA-1195 |
| 69474-1 | When The Morning Rolls Around | Vic ("made for theatre use") |
| 69475-1 | At The Baby Parade - vDF-WV-ET | Vic 24219, HMV B-6327, El EG-2763 |
| 69476-1 | The Old Kitchen Kettle - vDF-PG-WV-ET | -     BB B-6413 |

                                        New York, March 3, 1933.

| | | |
|---|---|---|
| 75353-1 | Hy'a, Duchess - vAM-PG&ch | Vic 24265, L-16025 |
| 75354-1 | Juggling A Jigsaw - vRI | - |
| 75355-1 | I Like Mountain Music - vET | Vic 24266, HMV EA-1210 |
| 75356-1 | She Changed Her Hi-De-Hi-De (For His | - L-16025 - |
|  | Yodel-O-De-Ay) - vRI&3 | |

  Andy Secrest-t replaces Conner.      Chicago, August 4, 1933.

| | | |
|---|---|---|
| 76844-1 | If I Had Somebody To Love - vET | BB B-5148, Eld 2047, Sr S-3229 |
| 76845-1 | Hold Your Man (w) - vAM | BB B-5130, Eld 2036, Sr S-3211 |
| 76846-1 | Trouble In Paradise - vAM/wET | -      -      - |
| 76847-1 | Heartaches - wET | BB B-5131, Vic 20-2175, Eld 2037, Sr S-3212, HMV BD-1172 |
| 76848-1 | Let Me Give My Happiness To You - vET | BB B-5148, Eld 2047, Sr S-3229 |
| 76849-1 | Marching Along Together - vDF-WV-ET | BB B-5131, Eld 2037, Sr S-3212 |

Ted Weems dir. Art Weems-Andy Secrest-t/Harry Turner-tb/Dudley Fosdick-mel-v/Dick
  Cunliffe-Don Watt-cl-as-bar/Parker Gibbs-Red Ingle-cl-ts-v/Jack O'Brien-p/Weston
  Vaughn-g-v/Country Washburn-bb-sb-v/Ormand Downes-d/Elmo Tanner-v-w.
                                 Chicago, October 25, 1933.

| | | |
|---|---|---|
| 77075-1 | Doin' The Uptown Lowdown - vPG | BB B-5236, Eld 2119, Sr S-3319 |
| 77076-1 | In A One-Room Flat - vET | BB B-5235, Eld 2118, Sr S-3318 |
| 77077-1 | Buckin' The Wind - vPG | BB B-5236, Eld 2119, Sr S-3319 |
| 77078-1 | I'm A Lover Of Paree - vET | BB B-5235, Eld 2118, Sr S-3318 |
| 77079-1 | Everything I Have Is Yours - vET | Rejected |
| 77080-1 | Why Am I Happy ? - vWV | BB B-5239, Eld 2122, Sr S-3322 |

                                 Chicago, December 5, 1933.

| | | |
|---|---|---|
| 77202-1 | I Guess It Had To Be That Way - vRI | BB B-5292, Eld 2163, Sr S-3373 |
| 77203-1 | Song Of Surrender (w) - vWV | BB B-5288, Eld 2159, Sr S-3369 |
| 77204-1 | Sittin' Up Waitin' For You - vRI | BB B-5290, Eld 2161, Sr S-3371 |
| 77205-1 | The Rooftop Serenade - vDF-WV-ET | - - - |
| 77206-1 | 'Tain't So - vRI-CW-ET | BB B-5289, Eld 2168, Sr S-3370 |
| 77207-1 | The Music Man - vch | - - - |
| 77208-1 | The Boulevard Of Broken Dreams - vET | BB B-5288, Eld 2159, Sr S-3369 |

Pete Beilman-tb replaces Turner; Rosy McHargue-cl-as replaces Watt; Cliff Covert-
  g-vn replaces Vaughn.         Chicago, September 15, 1934.

| | | |
|---|---|---|
| CPCO-1122-A | Ten Yards To Go - vPG | Col 2956-D |
| CPCO-1123-A | Blue Sky Avenue - vRI | Col 2957-D, FB-1002, RZ G-22329 |
| CPCO-1124-A | Talkin' To Myself - vRI | - FB-1064 - |
| CPCO-1125-A | Out Of The Night - v-wET | Col 2956-D, RZ G-22348 |

Fred Waldman-Gene Glennan-v.        Chicago, November 11, 1934.

| | | |
|---|---|---|
| C-822-A | I'll Keep Warm All Winter (With My Sunny Summer Love) - vRI | Col 2976-D, RZ G-22420 |
| C-823-A | I'm Growing Fonder Of You - vFW | Col 2975-D, FB-1009, DW-4258, RZ G-22383 |
| C-824-A | One Little Kiss - vGG | Col 2975-D |
| C-825-A | Winter Wonderland - vPG | Col 2976-D, FB-1009 |

NOTE:- Regal Zonophone G-22420 as RHYTHM KINGS ORCHESTRA.

## LEW WEINER'S GOLD AND BLACK ACES

2t/tb/cl-as/as/cl-ts/p/bj/bb/d.         Richmond, Ind., July 28, 1928.

| | | |
|---|---|---|
| 14101-B | Louisiana Bo Bo | Gnt 6540 |
| 14102 | The Merry Widow's Got A Sweetie Now | - |

## ELIZABETH WELCH

Although Miss Welch is an outstanding actress and cabaret artist, only the following
  of her records contain anything likely to interest the jazz enthusiast.

Vocal, acc. by Benny Carter-t-as/Gene Rodgers-p/Ivor Mairants-g/Wally Morris-sb.
                                 London, October 13, 1936.

| | | |
|---|---|---|
| S-124-1 | Poor Butterfly | Voc 526 |
| S-125-1 | Drop In Next Time You're Passing | Voc 515 |
| S-126-2 | The Man I Love | - |
| S-127-1 | That's How The First Song Was Born | Voc 526, Imp 6052 |

## LAWRENCE WELK AND HIS ORCHESTRA

The following titles by this famous band, not normally one associated with jazz or
  "hot" dance music, are reportedly within the scope of this book.

Lawrence Welk dir. 2t/tb/cl-as/as/cl-ts/p/bj/bj/bb/d/Gordon Malie-v. (Champion 15639
  as GEORGE TUCKER AND HIS NOVELTY BAND). Richmond, Ind., November 16, 1928.

| | | |
|---|---|---|
| 14431 | Spiked Beer | Gnt 6712, Ch 15639 |
| 14431-B | Spiked Beer | Gnt 20341 |
| 14432 | Shanghai Honeymoon - vGM | - |

Lawrence Welk dir. 2t/tb/cl-as/as/cl-ts/p/bj/bb/d/Jim Garvey-v.
                              Richmond, Ind., November 17, 1928.

14433, -A-B  Are You Makin' A Fool Of Me ? - vJG  Rejected
14434-B  Doin' The New Low Down                   Gnt 6697, Ch 15638
NOTE:- Champion 15638 as GEORGE TUCKER AND HIS NOVELTY BAND.

Probably a different personnel; Frankie Sanders-v.
                              Grafton, Wis., c. April-May, 1931.

L-947-2  My Canary Has Circles Under His Eyes-vFS Lyric 3370, Summit Z-115
L-949-2  Thrill Me - vFS                    Bwy 1462
L-950-1  Smile, Darn Ya, Smile - vFS            -        Lyric 3370
NOTE:- Matrix L-948 is untraced.  Lyric 3370 as PAUL'S NOVELTY ORCHESTRA; Summit
Z-115 as GUS WINSON'S ORCHESTRA.

## DICKY WELLS  AND HIS ORCHESTRA

Bill Coleman-t-v, plus Bill Dillard-Shad Collins-t**/Dicky Wells-tb-a/Django Rein-
   hardt-g/Richard Fullbright-sb/Bill Beason-d/Roy Eldridge-a.
                              Paris, July 7, 1937.

OLA-1884-1**Bugle Call Rag                   Swing 6, HMV B-8799, SG-348,
                                             Vic 26220, Col GN-5038
OLA-1885-1**Between The Devil And The Deep Blue  As above
                Sea - aDW-RE
OLA-1886-1**I Got Rhythm                     Swing 27, HMV B-8826, SG-20001,
                                             Col GN-5035
OLA-1887-1  Sweet Sue                        Swing 16,200,HMV B-8763,SG-20002
OLA-1888-1  Hangin' Around Boudon - vBC         - Vic 26617 -        -
OLA-1889-1  Japanese  Sandman                Swing 27, HMV B-8826, SG-20001,
                                             Col GN-5035

Bill Dillard-Shad Collins-t as shown/Dicky Wells-tb/Howard Johnson-as/Sam Allen-p/
   Roger Chaput-g/Bill Beason-d, or Wells-Allen-Chaput-Beason only*.
                              Paris, July 12, 1937.

OLA-1894-1  I've Found A New Baby - tBD-SC   Swing 3, Vic 26617
OLA-1895-1  Dinah - tBC-SC                   Swing 39, Col GN-5043
OLA-1896-1  Nobody's Blues But My Own - tSC     -       -
OLA-1897-1  Hot Club Blues - tBD             Swing 3
OLA-1898-1 *Lady Be Good                     Swing 10, HMV SG-366
OLA-1899-1 *Dicky Wells Blues                   - Vic 27318 -    HMV EA-3740

## DICKY  WELLS

This is not the same musician as the trombonist above.

DICKEY WELLS' SHIM SHAMMERS (sic) : Heywood Jackson-Eddie Johnson-k-v/Milton Lane-k/
   Kenny Watts-p/Fred Voorhees-g/Carroll Waldron-sb/Eddie Dougherty-d/Sammy Page-w/
   "Detroit Red"-Fletch Jackson-v.    New York, June 27, 1933.

152426-3  Baby, Are You Satisfied ? - vFJ   Col 2829-D, Par R-2345, A-3806
152427-1-2  Smoke Rings - v"DR"             Rejected
152428-1-2  Angeline - vEJ                     -
152429-1-2  The Old Man Of The Mountain - vHJ-"DR"    -

DICKIE WELLS AND KENNY'S KELOWATTS (sic) : Probably as above.
                              New York, December 21, 1933.

14481-1-2  Baby, Are You Satisfied ? - vFJ  ARC rejected
14482-1-2  Red, White And Blues - vFJ          -

## GEORGE WELLS AND HIS ORCHESTRA

Pseudonym on American Parlophone for Fred Rich and his Orchestra, q.v.

Vocal, acc. by Fletcher Henderson, Jr. (sic)-p.
                                    New York, c. October 3, 1923.

70352     Baby's Got The Blues              PA 032006, Per 12085
70353     Uncle Sam Blues                      -            -

## NOLAN  WELSH

Vocal, acc. by Louis Armstrong-c/Richard M. Jones-p.
                                    Chicago, June 16, 1926.

9727-A  The Bridwell Blues         OK 8372, HJCA HC-36, AF A-041,
                                   JSo AA-502
9728-A  St. Peter Blues            As above

Acc. by Clarence Black-vn/Richard M. Jones-p.
                                    Chicago, November 18, 1926.

9916-A  Nolan Welsh's Blues        OK 8425
9918-A  Bouncing Blues               -
NOTE:- Matrix 9917 is untraced.

Other records by Nolan Welsh  (on Paramount, as BARREL HOUSE WELCH) are self-accom-
    panied at the piano, and are outside the scope of this book.

## PETE  WENDLING

Piano solos.                        New York, c. May 19, 1923.

71545-B  Papa Blues                 OK 4868

                                    New York, June 18, 1923.

71637-A  Page Paderewski            OK 4984

                                    New York, c. August 30, 1926.

2097-C  Someone Is Losin' Susan     Cam 1021, Lin 2569
2098-A  Usen't You Use To Be My Sweetie ?    -         -       Ro 310

## MAE WEST

On the following records, this great comedienne and surely the most famous of all
    Hollywood actresses is accompanied by an excellent studio group.

Vocal, acc. by Victor Young dir. Manny Klein or Sterling Bose-t/Tommy Dorsey-tb/
    Jimmy Dorsey-cl-as/? Joe Venuti or Harry Hoffman-vn/? Joe Meresco-p/? Dick
    McDonough-g/? Artie Bernstein-sb/? Stan King-or Larry Gomar-d.
                                    New York, February 7, 1933.

B-13037-A  I Like A Guy What Takes His Time    Br 6495, 01491, A-500240,
                                               Col DO-1096
B-13037-B  I Like A Guy What Takes His Time    CBS CL-2751 (LP)
B-13038-A  Easy Rider (I Wonder Where My Easy  Br 6495, 01491, A-500240,
               Rider's Gone)                   Col DO-1096

## NORA  WEST

Pseudonym on Coliseum 1846 for Peggy English, q.v.

## THEADOR WEST

Clarinet solos, acc. by ? Millard Thomas-p/k.
                                    Montreal, February 18, 1925.

1738     Back-Biters Blues           Ajax 17118
1739     Hot Jelly Blues               -

                                    Montreal, c. February 21, 1925.

1755     Nobody Knows How I Feel 'Dis Mornin'(sic)Ajax 17129
1756     Blues, Just Blues              -

Pseudonym on P$_a$the Actuelle 036245 and 036251 for the Texas Ten, q.v.

## WESTCHESTER DANCE ORCHESTRA

Pseudonym on Perfect 14387 for Hazay Natzy and his Hotel Biltmore Orchestra, q.v.

## THE WESTERNERS

Pseudonym on Harmony 651-H for the University Six, q.v., and other bands on the same
label of varying degrees of interest as "hot" dance music.

## THE WESTERN SERENADERS

Pseudonym on Australian Gr$_a$nd Pree for the following items listed in this book :-

18175  Both sides by the California Ramblers
18605  Glad Eyes (Nathan Glantz and his Orchestra)

## THE WESTERN WANDERERS

Pseudonym for the following items listed in this book :-

Cameo 1154  Four Or Five Times (Jack Walsh and his Orchestra)
Australian Paramount 2546  Get Out And Get Under The Moon (Sam Lanin and his Orch.)
                2546  Is She My Girl Friend ? (Varsity Eight)

## FRANK WESTPHAL

This pianist-bandleader made a number of sides for Columbia, solo and with bands,
between 1922 and 1924, of which the following are believed or known to be of some
interest as jazz or "hot" dance music.

FRANK WESTPHAL AND HIS RAINBO ORCHESTRA : Frank Westphal-p dir. Charles Burns and
another-t/Herb Winfield-tb/Jack Richards-Bill Richards-as/ts/bj/John Jensen-bb/d.
                                Chicago, c. August 14, 1922.

80475-2  Don't Bring Me Posies              Col A-3693, Re G-8006
80477-2  State Street Blues                 -
NOTE:- Regal G-8006 as REGAL NOVELTY ORCHESTRA.

FRANK WESTPHAL AND HIS ORCHESTRA : Same, or very similar.
                                Chicago, c. October 12, 1922.

80591-4  Choo Choo Blues                    Col A-3743
80592-2  That Barking Dog (Woof ! Woof !) (Intro.   -
         Walking The Dog)

                                Chicago, c. December 9, 1922.

80706-3  Stop Your Kidding                  Col A-3786

                                Chicago, March 29, 1923.

80915-2  Railroad Man                       Col A-3872
80916-1-2-3  Aunt Hagar's Blues             Rejected

                                Chicago, March 30, 1923.

80918-1-2-3  Beale Street Mama              Rejected
80919-1  Bugle Call Rag                     Col A-3872
80920-1  Wolverine Blues                    Col A-3911

                                Chicago, May 30, 1923.

81045-3  Off Again On Again Blues           Col A-3929
81046-1  Two-Time Dan                       -

FRANK WESTPHAL AND HIS ORCHESTRA : Frank Westphal dir. Austin Edwards-Harry Scott-t/
  Caesar Petrillo-tb/Ollie "Duke" Riehl-Hal Lage-cl-as/Howard Gratham-cl-ts/Johnny
  Winslow-p/Earle Roberts-bj/Roscoe Rubelati-bb/Ted Arnold-d.
                                        Chicago, October 16, 1923.

| | | |
|---|---|---|
| 81308-2 | Oh ! Sister, Ain't That Hot ? | Col 22-D, Re G-8097 |
| 81309-1-2-3 | Red Hot - v | Rejected |
| 81310-3 | All Wrong | Col 17-D, 3390 |

  NOTE:- Regal G-8097 as REGAL NOVELTY ORCHESTRA.
                                        Chicago, October 18, 1923.

| | | |
|---|---|---|
| 81314-3 | I've Got A Song For Sale | Col 17-D, 3379 |
| 81315-2 | Stack O'Lee Blues | Col 32-D |
| 81316-1 | Forgetful Blues | -      Re G-8098 |
| 81317-1-2-3 | Chimes Blues | Rejected |

  NOTE:- Regal G-8098 as CORONA DANCE ORCHESTRA.

## WE THREE

Red Nichols-t/Arthur Schutt-p/Vic Berton-d, with Eddie Lang-g*.
                                        New York, c. March 24, 1926.

| | | |
|---|---|---|
| 106746 | Plenty Off Center | PA 36492,11206,Per 14673,Sal 383 |
| 106747 | *Trumpet Sobs | PA 36464, Per 14645 |

## GEORGE WETTLING'S CHICAGO RHYTHM KINGS

Charlie Teagarden-t/Floyd O'Brien-tb/Danny Polo-cl/Joe Marsala-ts/Jess Stacy-p/Jack
  Bland-g/Artie Shapiro-sb/George Wettling-d.
                                        New York, January 16, 1940.

| | | |
|---|---|---|
| 67059-A | I've Found A New Baby | Dec 18045, Br 03060, Od 286128 |
| 67059-B | I've Found A New Baby | -       Y-5857 |
| 67060-A | Bugle Call Rag | Dec 18044  - Br 03059, A-82640, Od 286127 |
| 67061-A | I Wish I Could Shimmy Like My Sister Kate | Dec 18044, Y-5615 -      - Od 286127 |
| 67062-A | Darktown Strutters' Ball | - |
| 67062-B | Darktown Strutters' Ball | Dec 18045, Br 03060, Od 286128 |

## PEETIE  WHEATSTRAW

The following titles by this famous blues singer are accompanied by established jazz
musicians; others are purely country blues accompanied by the artist himself at
the piano, or guitar, and thus have no place in this book.  See BLUES AND GOSPEL
RECORDS, 1902-1942 for a complete listing in detail.

Vocal, acc. by his Blue Blowers : ? Ike Rodgers-tb/cl/Henry Brown-p/own g.
                                        Chicago, August 24, 1934.

| | | |
|---|---|---|
| C-9351- | Throw Me In The Alley | Dec 7018 |

  Acc. by Jonah Jones-t/? Lil Armstrong-p/Sid Catlett-d.
                                        New York, April 4, 1940.

| | | |
|---|---|---|
| 67481-A | Big Apple Blues | Dec 7753 |
| 67482-A | Big Money Blues | Dec 7738 |
| 67483-A | Chicago Mill Blues | Dec 7788 |
| 67484-A | Five Minutes Blues | Dec 7738 |
| 67485-A | Two Time Mama | Dec 7753 |
| 67486-A | Jaybird Blues | Dec 7798 |
| 67487-A | Suicide Blues | Dec 7788 |
| 67488-A | Pocket Knife Blues | Dec 7778 |

                                        New York, August 28, 1940.

| | | |
|---|---|---|
| 68022-A | Gangster's Blues | Dec 7815 |
| 68023-A | Cuttin' 'Em Slow | Dec 7798 |
| 68024-A | Look Out For Yourself | Dec 7815 |
| 68025-A | No 'Count Woman | Dec 7823 |
| 68026-A | What's That ? | - |

1674          PEETIE WHEATSTRAW  (cont.)

Acc. by ? Lil Armstrong--or Jack Dupree-p/sb, with ts*. (This is not Chu Berry; he
died October 30, 1941).                    Chicago, November 25, 1941.

| | | |
|---|---|---|
| 93843-A | Don't Put Yourself On The Spot | Dec 7894 |
| 93844-A | *Old Organ Blues | Dec 7901 |
| 93845-A | *Hearse Man Blues | Dec 7886 |
| 93846-A | *Bring Me Flowers While I'm Living | - |
| 93847-A | Pawn Broker Blues | Dec 7894 |
| 93848-A | Southern Girl Blues | Dec 7904 |
| 93849-A | Mister Livingood | Dec 7879 |
| 93850-A | The Good Lawd's Children | Rejected |
| 93851-A | Separation Day Blues | Dec 7901 |

### DOC WHEELER AND HIS SUNSET ORCHESTRA

Doc Wheeler-tb-v dir. Jesse Brown-Cat Anderson-Reunald Jones-t/Nat Allen-Norman Powe
tb/Julius Watson-tb-v/Cornelius King-Robert Smith-as/Sam Taylor-Shirley Green-ts/
Raymond Tunia-p/Leroy Kirkland-g/Al Lucas-sb/Joe Murphy-d/The Hardway Four-v.
                              New York, September 1, 1941.

| | | |
|---|---|---|
| 067727-1 | Foo-Gee - vJW | BB B-11314 |
| 067728-1 | How 'Bout That Mess ? | - |

New York, November 6, 1941.

| | | |
|---|---|---|
| 068152-1 | Gabby | BB B-11389 |
| 068166-1 | Big And Fat And Forty-Four - vDW-H4 | - |
| 068167-1 | Sorghum Switch | BB B-11529 |
| 068168-1 | Leave The Rest To Me | Rejected |

James Otis Lewis-v.          New York, March 30, 1942.

| | | |
|---|---|---|
| 073487-1 | Who Threw The Whisky In The Well-vDW-H4 | BB B-11559 |
| 073488-1 | Me And My Melinda - vJOL | BB B-11529 |
| 073489-1 | Tunie's Tune | Rejected |
| 073490-1 | Keep Jumpin' | BB B-11559 |

### LULU  WHIDBY

Vocal, acc. by Henderson's Novelty Orchestra : T/? Chink Johnson-tb/? Garvin Bushell
or Edgar Campbell-cl/? Cordy Williams-vn/Fletcher Henderson-p/bj/bb.
                              New York, c. April, 1921.

P-108-1-2  Home Again Blues          BS 2005, Cx 40055, Fam 3049,
                                     Pm 12127, 20055, Pur 11055
P-109-1-2  Strut Miss Lizzie         As above
NOTE:- Famous 3049 as E. WHITE AND HER ALABAMA SEVEN; some copies have the matrix
numbers transposed.

### JAY  WHIDDEN

Jay Whidden was an American violinist who directed a band of British musicians  in
the Midnight Follies cabaret in the Hotel Metropole, London, and from the autumn
of 1927 until the summer of 1930 in the Carlton Hotel there.  Both bands recorded
extensively for a variety of labels, the following sides being of considerable
interest as jazz or "hot" dance music, and there may be others similar.

JAY WHIDDEN AND HIS NEW MIDNIGHT FOLLIES BAND FROM THE HOTEL METROPOLE : Jay
Whidden-vn dir. Freddy Pitt-Tim Cave-t/Ben Oakley-tb/Douglas Foss-Alf Loader-cl-ss
as/Ernie (Chester) Smith-cl-ts-bar/Bruce Merrill-p/Cyril Gaida-bj-vn/George Gibbs-
bb/Jack Gordon-d.              London, August 12, 1926.

WA-3688-2  Up And At 'Em              Col 4087

Joe Cordell-tb replaces Oakley; Mario Lorenzi-harp added.
                              London, May 5, 1927.

WA-5393-1  Hangin' Around             Col 4448

JAY WHIDDEN AND HIS BAND (FROM THE CARLTON HOTEL, LONDON) : Jay Whidden-vn dir.
  Arthur Niblo-t/Bill Mulraney-tb/Dave Roberts-cl-as-bar/Jay Langner-cl-ts-vc/Bert
  Read-p/Al Shaw-bj-g/George Gibbs-bb/Julian Vedey-d.
                                    Small Queen's Hall, London, Nov. 8, 1927.

Bb-11784-1-2-3-4  Corn Fed                    HMV rejected

  Max Goldberg-t/Johnny Swinfen-cl-as-vn added; Jimmy Goss-cl-as-bar replaces
  Roberts; Bobby Probst-p-cel replaces Read; Eddie Cole-v.
                                    London, October 19, 1928.

  5019-1  Virginia (There's A Blue Ridge In My     Imp 1982
             Heart)


                                    London, December 12, 1928.

DC-593-1-2  All By Yourself In The Moonlight     Victory 45 (7")
NOTE:- This issue as THE MUSIC MASTERS, directed by JAY WHIDDEN.


                                    London, c. January 14, 1929.

  5086-1-3  Louisiana - vEC                   Imp 2024

Norman Payne-t replaces Goldberg.     London, early April, 1929,

  5178-2  A Dicky Bird Told Me So - vEC       Imp 2053

Unknown t replaces Payne.             London, June 12, 1929.

  5217-2  When I Met Connie In The Cornfield-vEC  Imp 2088

Jay Whidden-vn dir. probably :- Duncan Whyte-Arthur Niblo-t/tb/Eddie Pratt-cl-as/
Sid Coles-cl-as-bar/Stan Quiddington-cl-ts/George Scott Wood-p-a/Vic Andrews-bj-g/
George Gibbs-bb/Jock Jacobson-d.      London, c. November 11, 1929.

5295-1  Come On, Baby - v                     Imp 2157
5296-2  Sweet Music - v                           -

## WHISTLER AND HIS JUG BAND

Jess Ferguson-vn/Buford Threlkeld ("Whistler")-g-v-nose whistle/Willie Black-md/B.D.
  Tite-jug.                           Richmond, Ind., September 25, 1924.

| | | |
|---|---|---|
| 12025-A-B | Chicago Flip | Gnt 5554, Sil 4037 |
| 12026, -A | Jerry O' Mine | - - |
| 12027, -A | The Original Blues - vBT | Rejected |
| 12028, -A | Old Virginia Blues - vBT | - |
| 12029-A | Jail House Blues - vBT | Gnt 5614 |
| 12030, -A-B | I Wonder Where My Sweet Mama's Gone - vBT | Rejected |
| 12031, -A | The Vampire Woman | - |
| 12032, -A-B-C | National Emblem | - |
| 12033-A | I'm A Jazz Baby | Gnt 5614 |

Rudolph Thompson-jug replaces Tite.     St. Louis, April 29, 1927.

| | | |
|---|---|---|
| 80793-A | Low Down Blues - vBT | OK 8469 |
| 80794-A-B | Jim Tight Blues | Rejected |
| 80795-B | The Vamps Of "28" | OK 8469 |
| 80796-A-B | Chicken Tree | Rejected |
| 80797-A-B | The Jug Band Special | OK 8816 |

                                    St. Louis, April 30, 1927.

| | | |
|---|---|---|
| 80798-A-B | Sam Mengal Blues | Rejected |
| 80799-A-B | Pig Meat Blues | OK 8816 |
| 80800-A-B | The Little African Stomp | Rejected |
| 80801-A-B | Bye-Bye Blackbird | - |
| 80802-A-B | Hello Bluebird | - |

Luther Nichols-vn/Buford Threlkeld-g-v/Willie Black-md/Rudolph Thompson-jug-v/James
    Watts-v.                              Louisville, Ky., June 15, 1931.

69437-1  Foldin' Bed - vBT                       Vic 23305
69438-1  Hold That Tiger - vBT-RT-JW                  -

## WHITE BROTHERS' ORCHESTRA

Pseudonym on Rich-Tone 7034 (SATANIC BLUES) for Ladd's Black Aces, q.v.

## WHITE COONS ORCHESTRA

Pseudonym on Australian Embassy for the All Star Collegians, q.v.

## BOB WHITE'S DIXIE TRIO

Pseudonym on Puritan 11400 for Jimmy O'Bryant's Washboard Band, q.v.

## CLARA WHITE

Pseudonym on Oriole for Viola McCoy, q.v.

## ELLA WHITE

Pseudonym on Famous for Katie Crippen, q.v.; the same label (3049) uses E. WHIE AND
    HER ALABAMA SEVEN as a pseudonym for Lulu Whidby, q.v.

## FLORENCE WHITE

Vocal, acc. by Simeon Henry-p.            New Orleans, March 9, 1927.

37991-1  Baby Dear, I Don't Want No-One But You   Vic 20584
37992-1  Cold Rocks Was My Pillow                     -

## GEORGE WHITE

Pseudonym for Frank Marvin, whose other records are of no known interest for their
    accompaniments.

Vocal, acc. by own g/Earl Oliver-c.       New York, September 25, 1929.

402990-A  Dust Pan Blues                      OK 45482, Par R-1081
402991-A  Miss Moonshine                          -

## GEORGIA WHITE

Vocal, acc. by ? own p/g.                 Chicago, March 13, 1935.

C-9858-  Your Worries Ain't Like Mine            Dec rejected
C-9859-  You Done Lost Your Good Thing Now          -

                                          Chicago, April 10, 1935.

C-9907-A  Dupree Blues                          Dec 7100
C-9908-A  Dallas Man (Lost Lover Blues)             -
C-9909-A  Your Worries Ain't Like Mine          Dec 7072, 48001
C-9910-A  You Done Lost Your Good Thing Now         -        -

                                          Chicago, July 15, 1935.

90154-A  Honey Dripper Blues                    Dec 7122
90155-A  Freddie Blues                             -
90156-A  Easy Rider Blues                       Dec 7135
90157-A  Graveyard Blues                           -

                                          Chicago, September 7, 1935.

90309-A  Your Worries Ain't Like Mine No. 2     Dec 7143
90310-A  You Done Lost Your Good Thing Now No. 2    -

Acc. by ? own p/g.                                  New York, January 16, 1936.

60346-A  Can't Read, Can't Write                      Dec 7166
60347-A  Tell Me Baby                                 Dec 7152

  Sb added.                                         New York, January 17, 1936.

60352-C  There Ain't Gonna Be No Doggone              Dec 7174
           Afterwhile
60353-A  Someday, Sweetheart                          Dec 7166
60354-A  River Blues                                  Dec 7149

                                                    New York, January 21, 1936.

60374-A-B  If You Can't Get Five, Take Two            Dec 7149
60375-A  Rattlesnakin' Daddy                          Dec 7174

                                                    New York, January 24, 1936.

60401-B  Get 'Em From The Peanut Man (Hot Nuts)     Dec 7152

Acc. by Richard M. Jones-p/Ikey Robinson-g/John Lindsay-sb.
                                    Chicago, May 11, 1936.

90715-A  New Dupree Blues                             Dec 7209
90716-A  Daddy Let Me Lay It On You                   Dec 7323
90717-A  New Hot Nuts (Get 'Em From The Peanut        Dec 7183
           Man)
90718-A  It Must Be Love                                 —

                                                    Chicago, May 12, 1936.

90719-A  I Just Want Your Stingaree                   Dec 7199, 48006
90720-A  Black Rider                                     —
90721-A  I'll Keep Sittin' On It (If I Can't          Dec 7192
           Sell It)
90722-A  Pigmeat Blues                                Dec 7209
90723-A  Trouble In Mind                              Dec 7192

                                                    Chicago, September 4, 1936.

90854-A  Was I Drunk ?                                Dec 7216, Voc V-1038
90855-A  No Second Hand Woman                            —
NOTE:- Decca 7216 as GEORGE WHITE (!)

                                                    Chicago, September 10, 1936.

90864-A  The Boy In The Boat (B. D.'s Dream)          Rejected
90865-A  Sinking Sun Blues                            Dec 7269

                                                    Chicago, December 7, 1936.

91011-A  Little Red Wagon                             Dec 7287
91012-A  Dan The Back Door Man                        Dec 7269
91013-A  Your Hellish Ways                            Dec 7254
91014-A  Marble Stone Blues                              —

                                                    Chicago, January 28, 1937.

91102-A  You Don't Know My Mind                       Dec 7277
91103-A  When My Love Comes Down                      Dec 7323
91104-A  Walking The Street                           Dec 7277
91105-A  Grandpa And Grandma                          Dec 7287
91106-A  I'm So Glad I'm 21 Today                     Dec 7309
91107-A  Toothache Blues                                 —

                                                    Chicago, May 6, 1937.

91229-A  Mistreated Blues                             Dec 7332

Acc. by Richard M. Jones-p/Ikey Robinson-g/John Lindsay-sb.
                                Chicago, May 19, 1937.

| | | |
|---|---|---|
| 91255-A | New Trouble In Mind | Dec 7332 |
| 91256-A | Trouble In Mind Swing | Dec 7521 |
| 91257-A | Moonshine Blues | Dec 7357, Voc V-1038 |
| 91259-A | Biscuit Roller | - |

                                New York, October 5, 1937.

| | | |
|---|---|---|
| 62637-A | Georgia Man | Dec 7377 |
| 62638-A | All Night Blues | Dec 7405 |
| 62639-A | Away All The Time | Dec 7377 |
| 62640-A | The Stuff Is Here | Dec 7436 |
| 62641-A | Strewin' Your Mess | Dec 7419 |
| 62642-A | Fare Thee Honey Fare Thee Well | Dec 7405 |

Unknown d replaces Lindsay; unknown as: Chicago, November 9, 1937.

| | | | |
|---|---|---|---|
| 91351-A | *Careless Love | Dec 7419 | |
| 91352-A | *Rock Me Daddy | Dec 7436 | |
| 91353-A | *Red Cap Porter | Dec 7389 | |
| 91354-A | Alley Boogie | - | 48006 |

Acc. by ? own p/Lonnie Johnson-g/sb.    New York, April 1, 1938.

| | | |
|---|---|---|
| 63543-A | I'm Blue And Lonesome (Nobody Cares For Me) | Dec 7450 |
| 63547-A | Almost Afraid To Love | - |
| 63548-A | Too Much Trouble | Dec 7477 |
| 63549-A | Crazy Blues | Dec 7807 |
| 63550-A | 'Tain't Nobody's Business If I Do | Dec 7477 |
| 63551-A | Holding My Own | Dec 7521 |

Acc. by ? own p/Ikey Robinson-g/John Lindsay-sb.
                                Chicago, October 21, 1938.

| | | |
|---|---|---|
| 91545-A | The Blues Ain't Nothin' But | Dec 7562 |
| 91546-A | Dead Man's Blues | Dec 7534 |
| 91547-A | Love Sick Blues | - |
| 91548-A | My Worried Mind Blues | Dec 7562 |

Acc. by Sammy Price-p/Teddy Bunn-g/? John Lindsay-sb.
                                New York, May 18, 1939.

| | | |
|---|---|---|
| 65597-A | The Way I'm Feelin' | Dec 7596 |
| 65598-A | Married Woman Blues | - |
| 65599-A | How Do You Think I Feel ? | Dec 7652 |
| 65600-A | Fire In The Mountain | Dec 7608 |
| 65601-A | When The Red Sun Turns To Gray I'll Be Back) | - |

Acc. by ? Blind John Davis-p/? Teddy Bunn-g/sb.
                                New York, May 26, 1939.

| | | |
|---|---|---|
| 65652-A | Hydrant Love | Dec 7631 |
| 65653-A | Do It Again | Dec 7652 |
| 65654-A | Beggin' My Daddy | Dec 7620 |
| 65655-A | What Have You Done To Me ? | Dec 7631 |
| 65656-A | Take Me For A Buggy Ride | Dec 7620 |

Acc. by as/p/d.                 Chicago, November 3, 1939.

| | | |
|---|---|---|
| 91863-A | Furniture Man | Dec 7689 |
| 91864-A | Ain't That So ? | Rejected |
| 91865-A | I'm Doing What My Heart Says Do | Dec 7672 |
| 91866-A | You Got To Drop The Sack | Dec 7689 |
| 91867-A | 'Tain't Nobody's Fault But Yours | Dec 7672 |
| 91868-A | Worried Head Blues | Dec 7807 |

Acc. by Jonah Jones-t/Fess Williams-cl/Lil Armstrong-p/Walter Martin-d.
New York, April 18, 1940.

| | | |
|---|---|---|
| 67563-A | Jazzin' Babies Blues | Dec 7741 |
| 67564-A | Papa Pleaser | Dec 7783 |
| 67575-A | Sensation Blues | Dec 7754 |
| 67576-A | Late Hour Blues | Dec 7741 |
| 67577-B | Panama Limited Blues | Dec 7783 |
| 67578-A | You Ought To Be Ashamed Of Yourself | Dec 7754 |

NOTE:- Matrices 67565 through 67570 are by Frankie "Half Pint" Jaxon, q.v.; 67571 through 67574 are blues items by Lee Brown, and outside the scope of this book.

Acc. by ? own p/g/sb.　　　　Chicago, March 11, 1941.

| | | |
|---|---|---|
| 93573-A | Mail Plane Blues | Dec 7866 |
| 93575-A | Mama Knows What Papa Wants When Papa's Feeling Blue | Dec 7841 |
| 93576-A | Come Around To My House | - |
| 93577-A | Territory Blues | Dec 7853 |
| 93578-A | When You're Away | - |

NOTE:- Matrix 93574 is untraced, probably not allocated.

## GLADYS WHITE

Pseudonym on Oriole for Rosa Henderson, q.v.

## GRACE  WHITE

Pseudonym on Silvertone for Monette Moore, q.v.

## HAL WHITE AND HIS  ALL-STAR COLLEGIANS

See the ARC-Brunswick studio bands.

## JANE WHITE

Pseudonym on Domino 425 for Kitty Brown, q.v., and on Emerson 10874  for an unknown girl singing DON'T TRY TO CRY YOUR WAY BACK TO ME, which may be of some interest as jazz.  It was probably recorded about March, 1925.

## LEE  WHITE

Pseudonym on OKeh 40964 and Australian Parlophone A-2419 for Noble Sissle, q.v.

## SLAP RAGS LEFTON WHITE

Pseudonym on XX 8 for Jelly-Roll Morton, q.v.

## STEVE WHITE'S  DANCELAND ORCHESTRA

T/tb/cl/as/p/bj/ob/d.　　　　Hollywood, c. November, 1925.

| | | |
|---|---|---|
| | Slippery Elm | Sunset 1132, Hwd (un-numbered) |
| | Then I'll Be Happy | - |

## TED WHITE'S COLLEGIANS

Pseudonym for the following items listed in this book :-

Oriole 931　Both sides by the Six Hottentots
　　　960　12th Street Rag (Willard Robison's Deep River Orchestra)
　　1359　Both sides by Ernie Golden and his Orchestra
　　1392　Crying Blues (Willie Creager and his Orchestra) (also on Jewel 5461)
　　1392　Doin' The Raccoon (Ernie Golden and his Orchestra)
　　1398　Come On, Baby (Ernie Golden and his Orchestra)
　　1544　Both sides by Irving Mills and his Orchestra
　　1664　Sweetness (Fred Rich and his Orchestra) (also Challenge 828)
　　1694　Little By Little (Fred Rich and his Orchestra)
Several other Fred Rich titles appeared under this name on Oriole, etc., but they do not seem to be of any interest as jazz.

"The King of Jazz," the best-known bandleader in the world during the 1920s, made a
large number of records of all kinds for Victor, Columbia, Decca and Capitol from
1920 to 1945, the following being of some interest as "hot" dance music.

PAUL WHITEMAN AND HIS AMBASSADOR ORCHESTRA : Paul Whiteman dir. Henry Busse-c/Buster
Johnson-tb/Gus Mueller-cl/Ferdie Grofe-p-a/Mike Pingitore-bj/Sammy Heiss-bb/Harold
McDonald-d.                              Camden, N. J., August 9, 1920.

  24392-2  Wang-Wang Blues                        Vic 18694, HMV B-1178, Zon 3304

PAUL WHITEMAN AND HIS ORCHESTRA : Paul Whiteman-vn dir. Henry Busse-Tommy Gott-c/Sam
Lewis-tb/Ross Gorman-cl-as/Hale Byers-ss-ts/Don Clark-as/Fred Cook-vn/Ferdie Grofe
p-a/Mike Pingitore-bj/Jack Barsby-bb/Harold McDonald-d.
                                         New York, October 21, 1921.

  25664-4  Everybody Step                          Vic 18826, HMV B-1318, Zon 3343

  George Tjordy-vn replaces Cook.      New York, June 23, 1922.

  26650-2  Hot Lips (He's Got Hot Lips When He     Vic 18920, HMV B-1396, AM-86,
         Plays Jazz)(Hot Lips Blues*)          K-1723*, Zon 3464

                                         New York, February 21, 1923.

  27611-4  'Way Down Yonder In New Orleans         Vic 19030, HMV B-1649, Zon 3551

  Mario Perry-vn replaces Tjordy.      New York, March 1, 1923.

  27633-4  Nuthin' But                             Vic 19073, HMV B-1677, Zon 3595

  Perry omitted; Harry Reser-bj replaces Pingitore.
                                         Hayes, Middlesex, July 21, 1923.

Bb-3308-3  Just One More Chance                HMV B-1682

  Frank Siegrist-t replaces Gott; Roy Maxon-tb replaces Lewis; Mario Perry-vn returns; Mike Pingitore-bj replaces Reser.
                                         New York, October 29, 1923.

  28790-3  Shake Your Feet                         Vic 19185, HMV B-1741, AM-149,
                                         Zon 3682

                                         New York, January 11, 1924.

  29304-3  Learn To Do The Strut                   Vic 19252, HMV B-1813, AM-104,
                                         Zon 3726

Paul Whiteman-vn dir. Henry Busse-Frank Siegrist-t/Roy Maxon-Jim Cassidy-tb/Ross
Gorman-Ed Stannard-cl-as/Don Clark-cl-ss-as/Mario Perry-vn-pac/Ferdie Grofe-p-a/
Mike Pingitore-bj/Al Armer or Carl Wagner-bb/George Marsh-d.
                                         New York, June 9, 1924.

30172-3  San                                   Vic 19381, Zon 3768

Wilbur Hall-tb replaces Cassidy; Chester Hazlett-cl-as replaces Gorman; Harry
Perrella-p/Charles Strickfaden-as-bar/Charles Gaylord or Austin "Skin" Young-vn
added; John Sperzel-bb replaces Armer.  Camden, N. J., may 7, 1925.

32576-8  Charleston                            Vic 19671, Zon 3893

Willard Robison-p replaces Grofe (who is now arranging only); Billy Murray-v.
                                         Camden, N. J., July 7, 1925.

32756-4  Footloose - vBM                       Vic 19720, HMV B-2112, AE-1497,
                                         AM-243, El EG-24

Extra vn added.                          New York, August 20, 1925.

33331-1-2-3-4  Rhythm Rag                      Vic rejected

PAUL WHITEMAN AND HIS ORCHESTRA : Paul Whiteman (sometimes playing vn) dir. Henry
  Busse-Frank Siegrist-t/Roy Maxon-Wilbur Hall-tb/Chester Hazlett-cl-bcl-as/Hal
  McLean or Ed Stannard-cl-as/Charles Strickfaden-as-bar/E. Lyle Sharpe-cl-ts/Mario
  Perry-pac/Charles Gaylord-another (?)-vn/Harry Perrella-p/Mike Pingitore-bj/John
  Sperzel-bb/George Marsh-d.            New York, September 1, 1925.

33331-7  Rhythm Rag                        Vic 19773, HMV B-2175, AM-596,EA-2

  Ted   Bartell-t added; all 3 vn present.
                                          New York, September 16, 1925.

33385-3  Charlestonette                    Vic 19785, HMV B-5037

  Bartell omitted; Jack Fulton-tb-v replaces Maxon; Stannard omitted, McLean certain.
                                          New York, March 26, 1926.

35245-2 No More Worryin' - vJF-CG-AY       Vic 20007, HMV B-5065,AM-408,EA-60

  2vn only, rest as last above, on 35250-2; the following added for 35251-2 :- Ted
  Bartell-t/Royce Cullen-tb/Kurt Dieterle-James McKilltop-Irving Achtel-Paul Daven-vn
  /John Bowman-Julius Mindel-vl/Frank Leoncavallo-Bill Schumann-vc/Walter Bell-bsn/
  Roy Maxon-tb-bh/Ferdie Grofe-p-a; Mario Perry plays vn-pac.
                                          New York, March 29, 1926.

35250-2  Bell Hoppin' Blues                Vic 20092, HMV B-5065, AM-408
35251-2  St. Louis Blues                     -     HMV B-5162, El EG-378

  The larger orchestra used for CR-261-1 (as for 35251-2); BR-262-1 probably by a
  Dixieland quintet.  Both recorded during a performance in the Royal Albert Hall,
  London, on April 11, 1926.

CR-261-1  St. Louis Blues                  HMV rejected
BR-262-1  Tiger Rag                          -

  Paul Whiteman dir. Henry Busse-Ted Bartell-t/Vincent Grande-tb/Max Farley-cl-as-f/
  Hal McLean-cl-as/Charles Strickfaden-as-bar/Matt Malneck-vl/Harry Perrella-p/Mike
  Pingitore-bj/Wilbur Hall-g/Al Armer-sb/George Marsh-d/Bing Crosby-Al Rinker-v.
                                Orchestra Hall, Chicago, December 22, 1926.

37285-4  Wistful And Blue - vBC-AR         Vic 20418, HMV K-5131, El EG-446

  Chester Hazlett-cl-as/Kurt Dieterle-Mischa Russell-Mario Perry-vn added (on 38143-3
  only); Boyce Cullen-Jack Fulton-Wilbur Hall-tb added to this on 38144-2; Ray Turner
  p replaces Perrella, who plays cel.    New York, March 7, 1927.

38143-3  Muddy Water - vBC/aMM             Vic 20408, HMV EA-167, K-5201
38144-2  Everything's Made For Love (You Know -  Vic 20514, HMV B-5284, EA-168,
         I Know)                           X-2498

  Paul Whiteman dir. Henry Busse-Ted Bartell-Red Nichols-t/? Vincent Grande-? Wilbur
  Hall-tb/Max Farley-cl-as-a/Hal McLean-Chester Hazlett-cl-as/Charles Strickfaden-as-
  bar/Kurt Dieterle-Mischa Russell-Mario Perry-vn/Matt Malneck-vn-vl-a/Harry Perrella
  p/Mike Pingitore-bj/Gilbert Torres-g/Al Armer-sb/George Marsh-d/Bing Crosby-Al
  Rinker-Harry Barris-v.         New York, April 29, 1927.

38135-7  I'm Coming, Virginia - vBC-AR-HB/aMM   Vic LPM-2071, LVA-1000, LX-995(LP)
38135-9  I'm Coming, Virginia - vBC-AR-HB/aMM   Vic 20751, El EG-614
38378-1  Side By Side - vBC-AR-HB/aMF           Vic LPV-570 (LP)
38378-4  Side By Side - vBC-AR-HB/aMF           Vic 20627, HMV B-5318, K-5223,
                                          El EG-708, Decatur 505

  Vic d'Ippolito-t replaces Bartell (possibly on the preceding session); Jack Fulton-
  tb added; Malneck-Perry-another-vn; Ray Turner-Harry Perrella-p-cel; Al Armer or
  John Sperzel-bb; Vic Berton-d replaces Marsh; Ferdie Grofe-a.
                                          New York, May 13, 1927.

38805-2  Love And Kisses (From Baby To You)  Vic 20679, HMV B-5583, AE-2833,
                                          El EG-582

PAUL WHITEMAN AND HIS ORCHESTRA : Henry Busse-Vic d'Ippolito-Red Nichols-t/? Wilbur
    Hall-? Jack Fulton-tb/Max Farley-cl-as-a/Chester Hazlett-Hal McLean-Jimmy Dorsey-
    cl-as/Charles Strickfaden-as-bar/Kurt Dieterle-Mischa Russell-Mario Perry-vn/Matt
    Malneck-vn-vl-a/Harry Perrella-p/Mike Pingitore-bj/Al Armer-sb/Vic Berton-d/Bing
    Crosby-Al Rinker-Harry Barris-v.        New York, May 24, 1927.

38779-1   Magnolia (Mix The Lot-What Have You Got?)Vic 20679, HMV B-5317, El EG-582,
          - vBC-AR-HB/aMF                        Decatur 505

Charlie Margulis or Bob Mayhew-t replaces Nichols; Hall and Fulton, plus Tommy
    Dorsey-t-tb/Boyce Cullen-tb; Harold McDonald-d replaces Berton; Don Redman-a.
                                        Camden, N. J., August 11, 1927.

39559-1   Whiteman Stomp - aDR              Vic LPV-570 (LP)
39559-2   Whiteman Stomp - aDR              Vic 21119, HMV B-5577, X-4616,
                                            El EG-807
39560-1-2-3  Sugar Your Tea Stomp          Rejected
39561-1   Sensation Stomp - aDR            Vic 21119, HMV B-5577, K-5418,
                                            X-4616, El EG-807

Busse, d'Ippolito; Dorsey-t-tb; Hazlett-Farley-Dorsey-Strickfaden; Malneck; Per-
    rella; Pingitore; Hall-g; Armer; McDonald; Crosby-Rinker-Barris.
                                        Camden, N. J., August 16, 1927.

39569-3   Five-Step - vBC-AR-HB/aMM         Vic 20883, HMV B-5511, K-5333,
                                            El EG-700

Hall probably plays the 2nd tb (no g this side).
                                        Camden, N. J., August 20, 1927.

39577-8   It Won't Be Long Now - vBC-AR-HB    Vic 20883, HMV B-5555, El EG-700

C/tb/2s/Perrella/Pingitore/Armer/McDonald.  The matrix number of this title was
    eventually altered to 24391-3-4 to conform to Victor's normal practice of retaining
    a number for a re-make by the same artist, regardless of how long after the first
    recording this might take place.  The number 40231 was not apparently re-allocated.
                                        New York, September 22, 1927.

40231-1-2  Wang-Wang Blues                  Vic rejected

PAUL WHITEMAN AND HIS CONCERT ORCHESTRA : Paul Whiteman dir. Bix Beiderbecke-c/Tommy
    Dorsey-Boyce Cullen-tb/Jimmy Dorsey-cl-as/Chester Hazlett-bcl/Charles Strickfaden-
    bar/Kurt Dieterle-Mischa Russell-vn/Matt Malneck-vl/Hoagy Carmichael-p-v/Wilbur
    Hall-g/Steve Brown-sb/Harold McDonald-d-vib/Bill Challis-a.
                                        Chicago, November 18, 1927.

40901-1   Washboard Blues - vHC/aBCh         Vic 35877, 36186
40901-4   Washboard Blues - vHC/aBCh         Vic 741093 (LP)

PAUL WHITEMAN AND HIS ORCHESTRA : Paul Whiteman dir. Henry Busse-Charlie Margulis-t/
    Bix Beiderbecke-c/Wilbur Hall-Tommy Dorsey-tb/Chester Hazlett-Hal McLean-as/Jimmy
    Dorsey-Nye Mayhew-Charles Strickfaden-as-bar/Kurt Dieterle-Mischa Russell-Mario
    Perry-Matt Malneck-vn/Harry Perrella-p/Mike Pingitore-bj/Mike Trafficante-bb/Steve
    Brown-sb/Harold McDonald-d/Bing Crosby-Al Rinker-Harry Barris-Jack Fulton-Charles
    Gaylord-Austin Young-v/Bill Challis-a.  Chicago, November 23, 1927.

40937-2   Changes - vBC-AR-HB-JF-CG-AY/aBCh    Vic 25370
40937-3   Changes - vBC-AR-HB-JF-CG-AY/aBCh    Vic 21103, HMV B-5461, B-8913,
NOTE:- HMV K-5368 as PAUL WITHEMAN ET SON      GW-1795, JK-2809, K-5368, N-4475,
ORCHESTRE.                                     El EG-690, Bm 1032

Tommy Dorsey db t; Hall db bj; Jimmy Dorsey, McLean and Hazlett db cl; Strickfaden
    plays ts; Frank Trumbauer-Cm added.   Chicago, November 25, 1927.

40945-2  Mary (What Are You Waiting For?)-vBC/aMM Vic 21103, HMV B-5461, EA-291,
                                         K-5368. El EG-771, Bm 1032
40945-4  Mary (What Are You Waiting For?)-vBC/aMM Vic 26415, HMV EA-2764

PAUL WHITEMAN AND HIS ORCHESTRA : Paul Whiteman dir. Henry Busse-Charlie Margulis-Bob
   Mayhew-t/Bix Beiderbecke-c/Boyce Cullen-Wilbur Hall-Bill Rank-tb/Jack Fulton-tb-v/
   Chester Hazlett-Hal McLean-Frank Trumbauer-Jimmy Dorsey-Jack Mayhew-Nye Mayhew-Rube
   Crozier-Charles Strickfaden-cl-bcl-ss-as-Cm-ts-bar-bsn-f-o-ca etc./Kurt Dieterle-
   Mischa Russell-vn/Matt Malneck-John Bowman-vn-vl/Mario Perry-vn-pac/Charles Gaylord
   vn-v/Harry Perrella-p/Tom Satterfield-p-a/Mike Pingitore-bj/Mike Trafficante-bb/
   Steve Brown-sb/Harold McDonald-d/Bing Crosby-Al Rinker-Harry Barris-Austin Young-v/
   Bill Challis-Ferdie Grofe-Matt Malneck-a. This was the full personnel at the end
   of 1927. Members of the orchestra known to have taken part in each title listed
   are shown at the head of the session.

Margulis, Busse; Beiderbecke; Hall, Rank; Hazlett-cl-as-bcl; McLean-Dorsey-Crozier-
cl-as; Strickfaden-ts-bar; Dieterle; Perrella; Pingitore; Trafficante; Brown; Mc-
Donald, on 41294-1; Trumbauer-Cm replaces Crozier, Hazlett and McLean play as,
Strickfaden-ts; Russell, Malneck added, on 41295-1-3.
                                         New York, January 4, 1928.

41294-1  Smile - vAR-CG-JF/aBCh                 Vic 741093, Bwy 102 (LPs)
41295-1  Lonely Melody - aBCh                   Vic 21214, HMV B-5516, EA-371,
                                                Bm 1017
41295-3  Lonely Melody - aBCh                   Vic 25366

Margulis, Busse; Beiderbecke; Hall, Rank, Cullen, Fulton; Hazlett-cl-bcl-as; McLean
cl-as; Strickfaden-cl-ts; Dorsey-cl-bar; Trumbauer-Cm; Dieterle-Russell-Malneck-
Perry-Bowman; Perrell; Pingitore; Trafficante; Brown; McDonald.
                                         New York, January 11, 1928

41607-2  Ol' Man River - vBC/aBCh               Vic 21218, 25249, HMV B-5471,
                                                B-8929, BD-5066, IM-129, JK-28822,
                                                K-5448, R-4697, El EG-838,
                                                Sentry/Tpl 4008

Margulis; Beiderbecke; Rank; Jimmy Dorsey-c-cl; Trumbauer-Cm; Min Leibrook-bsx;
Bill Challis-p-a; Malneck  Carl Kress; McDonald.
                                         New York, January 12, 1928.

30172-6  San                                    Vic 24078, HMV B-5581, Bm 1031
30172-7  San                                    Vic 25367

The full orchestra as above (as PAUL WHITEMAN AND HIS CONCERT ORCHESTRA on Victor
35883); Hazlett-cl-bcl-as; Dorsey-cl-as; Trumbauer-Cm-as; Jack Mayhew-as; Nye
Mayhew-bar; McLean-cl-as-o; Strickfaden-cl-ts; Crozier-cl-f, on 41294-5; same for
41465-3 except that McLean and Crozier both play cl-as only, Strickfaden ts-bar; no
strings used on 41294-5.              Camden, N. J., January 24, 1928.

41294-5  Smile - vAR-JF-CG-AY/aBCh              Vic 21228, HMV B-5465, AE-2189,
                                                Bm 1017
41465-3  My Heart Stood Still-vAR-JF-CG-AY/aBCh  Vic 35883

The full orchestra as above except for Beiderbecke, Fulton, 2s and 1 vn.
                                         Camden, N. J., January 27, 1928.

41470-5  Make Believe - vBC/aFG                 Vic 21218, 25249, HMV B-5471,
                                                BD-5066, K-5448, R-4670, El EG-838
                                                Sentry/Tpl 4008

Bill Challis dir. the full orchestra, without Fulton, all three Mayhews and Bowman;
Ferdie Grofe-p replaces Perrella.      Camden, N. J., January 28, 1928.

41471-3  Back In Your Own Back Yard - aBCh      Vic 21240, HMV B-5564, K-5606,
                                                El EG-1161
41471-4  Back In Your Own Back Yard - aBCh      Vic 27689

Same, but Roy Bargy-p-a replaces Grofe; Hazlett-Dorsey-McLean-cl-as; Trumbauer-Cm;
Crozier-cl-ts; Strickfaden cl-bar.    New York, February 8, 1928.

41681-2  There Ain't No Sweet Man That's Worth  Vic 25675, HMV B-8929, JK-2822
           The Salt Of My Tears - vBC-AR-HB-JF-CG-AY/aTS
41681-3  There Ain't No Sweet Man That's Worth  Vic 21464, HMV B-5515, Bm 1031
           The Salt Of My Tears - vBC-AR-HB-JF-CG-AY/aTS

PAUL WHITEMAN AND HIS ORCHESTRA : Paul Whiteman dir. Henry Busse-Charlie Margulis-t/
    Bix Beiderbecke-c/Bill Rank-Wilbur Hall-Boyce Cullen-tb/Chester Hazlett-bcl-as/Hal
    McLean-Jimmy Dorsey-cl-as/Frank Trumbauer-Cm/Charles Strickfaden-ts-bar/Kurt
    Dieterle-Mischa Russell-Matt Malneck-vn/Roy Bargy-p/Mike Pingitore-bj/Mike Traffi-
    cante-bb/Steve Brown-sb/Harold McDonald-d/Bill Challis-a.
                                                    New York, February 9, 1928.

    41683-2   Dardanella - aBCh                     Vic 25238, A-1281, JA-677,
                                                    HMV B-8931, JK-2810


    Dorsey omitted; Trumbauer-as; Red Mayer-cl-ts added; Jack Fulton-Charles Gaylord-
    Austin Young-v.                                 New York, February 10, 1928.

    41684-2   Love Nest - vJF-CG-AY ("humming")/aBCh   Vic 24105


    Busse absent; Jimmy Dorsey-c added; sax section on this date is Chester Hazlett-
    Rube Crozier-Red Mayer-Charles Strickfaden; Harry Barris-p replaces Bargy; Matt
    Malneck-a.                                      New York, February 13, 1928.

    41689-3   From Monday On - vBC-AR-JF-CG-AY/aMM   Vic 27688, 27-0136, HMV EA-3235


    Eddie Pinder-t/Bix Beiderbecke-c/Bill Rank-tb/Izzy Friedman-cl/Chester Hazlett-
    Frank Trumbauer-as/Charles Strickfaden-ts/Roy Bargy-p/Mike Pingitore-bj/Min
    Leibrook-bb/Mike Trafficante-sb/Harold McDonald-d/Irene Taylor-v/Tom Satterfield-a.
                                                    New York, February 18, 1928.

    41696-2   Mississippi Mud-vIT-BC-AR-HB-JF-CG-AY/aTS Vic 25366, HMV EA-2764, Bm 1029
    41696-3   Mississippi Mud-vIT-BC-AR-HB-JF-CG-AY/aTS Vic 21274, HMV EA-429


    Charlie Margulis-t replaces Pinder; Red Mayer-cl-ts/Kurt Dieterle-Mischa Russell-
    vn/Matt Malneck-vn-a added; Harry Barris-p replaces Bargy; Leibrook db bsx; no sb
    (on 41689-4-6); Busse-Margulis-Pinder; Beiderbecke; Cullen-Hall-Rank-Fulton; Frank
    Trumbauer-Izzy Friedman-cl-as; Chester Hazlett-cl-bcl-as; Rube Crozier-cl-ss-as-
    bsx-bsn; Red Mayer-cl-ts; Strickfaden-ts-bar-ca; same vn plus Mario Perry; Bargy;
    Pingitore; Leibrook; Trafficante; McDonald; Bill Challis-a.(on 43118-1-2).
                                                    New York, February 28, 1928.

    41689-4   From Monday On - vBC-AR-JF-CG-AY/aMM   Vic 25368
    41689-6   From Monday On - vBC-AR-JF-CG-AY/aMM   Vic 21274, HMV B-5492, Bm 1017
    43118-1   Sugar - aBCh                           Vic 25368, HMV B-8931, JK-2810
    43118-2   Sugar - aBCh                           Vic 21464


    As for February 9, 1928, but reeds are Hazlett-Trumbauer-as; Izzy Friedman-as-ts;
    Red Mayer-ts; Strickfaden-ts-bar.               New York, February 29, 1928.

    43120-1   When You're With Somebody Else - aBCh  Vic 21365, HMV B-5497, EA-346
    43120-2   When You're With Somebody Else - aBCh  Vic 27689
PAUL WHITEMAN AND HIS CONCERT ORCHESTRA : Margulis, Pinder; Beiderbecke; Cullen,Hall;
    Trumbauer-cl-as-bsn; Crozier-cl-f; Hazlett-cl-as; Mayer-cl-ts-o;
    Strickfaden-as-f-o; Dieterle, Russell, Malneck, Perry; Bargy; Pingitore; Leibrook;
    Trafficante; McDonald; Olive Kline-Lambert Murphy-v, with chorus.
                                                    New York, March 1, 1928.

    43123-2   Selections from SHOW BOAT (Intro. Why  Vic 35912, HMV C-1505, L-657,
              Do I Love You ?-vOK/Can't Help Lovin'  El EH-225
              Dat Man-vch/You Are Love-vLM/Make Believe-vOK-LM&ch)
PAUL WHITEMAN AND HIS ORCHESTRA : As for 43118-1-2 above, without Fulton, Trumbauer
    and Perry; Hazlett bcl-as; Crozier cl-as; Strickfaden ts only, other reeds same.
                                                    New York, March 2, 1928.

    43125-1   Coquette - aBCh                        Vic 21301, HMV B-5564, K-5606,
                                                    El EG-1161
    43125-3   Coquette - aBCh                        Vic 25675

    As for March 1, 1928, without vn; Bill Rank-tb replaces Hall; Friedman-cl; Hazlett,
    Mayer-as; Trumbauer-Cm; Crozier, Strickfaden-ts.
                                                    New York, March 12, 1928.

    43138-2   When - vJF-CG-AY-AR-HB/aTS             Vic 21338, 25367, HMV B-5493
    43138-3   When - vJF-CG-AY-AR-HB/aTS             -

PAUL WHITEMAN AND HIS ORCHESTRA : Paul Whiteman dir. Henry Busse-Charlie Margulis-
Eddie Pinder-t/Bix Beiderbecke-c/Jack Fulton-tb-v/Boyce Cullen-Wilbur Hall-Bill
Rank-tb/Izzy Friedman-cl-as-ts/Rube Crozier-cl-ss-as-ts-bsn/Chester Hazlett-cl-bcl-
ss-as/Frank Trumbauer-Cm-ss/Charles Strickfaden-cl-as-ts-bar/Red Mayer-cl-ts/Kurt
Dieterle-Mischa Russell-Mario Perry-Matt Malneck-John Bowman-vn, the last two db vl
/Charles Gaylord-vn-v/Roy Bargy-Lennie Hayton-p-a/Mike Pingitore-bj/Min Leibrook-bb
bsx/Mike Trafficante-sb/Harold McDonald-d/Bill Challis-Ferdie Grofe-Tom Satterfield
a/Bing Crosby-Al Rinker-Harry Barris-Austin Young-v. On the next session, Busse,
Fulton, Rank, Trumbauer, Perry, Bowman and Gaylord are absent.
                                        New York, March 15, 1928.

43145-1  Lovable - vBC/aTS                        Vic 27685, HMV B-5509, AE-2302,
                                                  EA-3235

The full orchestra as above was used on the remaining Victor sessions.
                                        New York, April 22, 1928.

43662-1  My Pet - vBC-AR-CG-AY/aBCh               Vic 27686
43662-2  My Pet - vBC-AR-CG-AY/aBCh               Vic 21389, HMV B-5504, EA-373,
                                                  El EG-979
43662-3  My Pet - vBC-AR-CG-AY/aBCh               Bwy 102 (LP)
43663-1  It Was The Dawn Of Love-vBC-AR-CG-AY/aTS  -
43663-2  It Was The Dawn Of Love-vBC-AR-CG-AY/aTS  Vic 21453, HMV B-5522, EA-381,
                                                  R-14001, El EG-932
43663-3  It Was The Dawn Of Love-vBC-AR-CG-AY/aTS  Bwy 102 (LP)
43665-2  Forget-Me-Not - vJF/aBCh                 Vic 27686
43665-3  Forget-Me-Not - vJF/aBCh                 Vic 741093 (LP)

                                        New York, April 23, 1928.

43667-1  Louisiana - vBC-JF-CG-AY/aBCh            Vic 21438, HMV B-5522, EA-386,
                                                  GW-1759, El EG-933, Bm 1030
43667-3  Louisiana - vBC-JF-CG-AY/aBCh            Vic 25369, HMV B-8913, JK-2809,
                                                  N-4475

                                        New York, April 24, 1928.

43669-2  Do I Hear You Saying (I Love You)        Vic 21398, El EG-929
         - vBC-AR-CG/aTS

Harry Goldfield-t replaces Busse; George Marsh-d replaces McDonald.
                                        New York, April 25, 1928.

43670-1  You Took Advantage Of Me - vBC-JF-CG-AY/  Vic 21398, 25369, HMV EA-816,
         aTS                                      El EG-929, Bm 1030
NOTE:- The appearance of the figure 2 on the run-off of this title on Victor 25369
indicates a dubbing of take 1, not the use of an alternative take.


Bowman and Perry omitted.            New York, May 15, 1928.

98537-4  My Melancholy Baby - vAY/aTS             Col 50068-D, 9578, 07503

Vaughn de Leath-v.                    New York, May 16, 1928.

98538-2-4  The Man I Love - vVdeL/aFG             Col 50068-D, 07503

Pinder-Fulton-Gaylord-Bowman-Hayton out. New York, May 22, 1928.

146317-3  Is It Gonna Be Long ? - aBCh           Col 1496-D, 4956, 07004, A-8002

Pinder returns; rest as last above.   New York, May 23, 1928.

146327-2  Oh ! You Have No Idea - aBCh           Col 1491-D, 4956, 07005
Pinder-Fulton-Friedman-Strickfaden-Gaylord-Bowman-Hayton out.
                                        New York, May 25, 1928.

146334-4  Felix The Cat - aAY/aTS                Col 1478-D, 5040, 07008, A-8006,
                                                  J-541, Re 5040

PAUL WHITEMAN AND HIS ORCHESTRA : Paul Whiteman dir. Charlie Margulis-Harry Goldfield
   t/Bix Beiderbecke-c/Boyce Cullen-Wilbur Hall-Bill Rank-tb/Chester Hazlett-as-bcl/
   Rube Crozier-as-bsn/Frank Trumbauer-Cm-b&n/Izzy Friedman-cl-ts/Red Mayer-cl-ts-bar/
   Charles Strickfaden-ts-bar-ca/Matt Malneck-Mischa Russell-Kurt Dieterle-Mario Perry
   vn/Roy Bargy-p-a/Mike Pingitore-bj/Min Leibrook-bb/Mike Trafficante-sb/George Marsh
   d/Bing Crosby-v/Bill Challis-a, on 146316-9; same, plus Eddie Pinder-t/Jack Fulton-
   tb-v/Charles Gaylord-Austin Young-v; and Hazlett plays cl-as, Crozier cl-ts, Trumbauer Cm-as, Mayer as, Strickfaden ts only,on 146320-5.
                                               New York, June 10, 1928.

146316-9  'Tain't So, Honey, 'Tain't So-vBC/aBCh    Col 1444-D,4981,07003,A-8230,J-533
146320-5  I'd Rather Cry Over You-vBC-JF-CG-AY/aBCh Col 1496-D,4980,07005,A-8002,J-539

   Beiderbecke, Margulis; Cullen, Rank; Hazlett, Friedman, Trumbauer, Strickfaden; all
   four vn and five rhythm on 146542-3; same, plus Goldfield on 146543-3; Tom Satter-
   field-a.                                    New York, June 17, 1928.

146542-3  That's My Weakness Now - vBC-AR-HB/aTS    Col 1444-D,5006,07008,A-8230,J-533
146543-3  Georgie Porgie - vBC-AR-HB/aBCh           Col 1491-D,5040,07011,J-541,Re5040

   Margulis, Pinder; Beiderbecke; Hall, Rank; Hazlett, Trumbauer, Friedman, Strickfaden; Dieterle, Russell, Malneck; all five rhythm, on 146549-2; same, but Goldfield replaces Pinder, on 146550-3.    New York, June 18, 1928.

146549-2  Because My Baby Don't Mean "Maybe" Now    Col 1441-D,5007,07007,A-8010,J-532
          - vBC-JF-CG-AY/aBCh
146550-3  Out O' Town Gal - vBC-AR-HB/aBCh          Col 1505-D,5039,07011,A-8011,J-542

The next title is the most interesting, from a jazz viewpoint, of four sides recorded
   in New York by a band under Ben Selvin's direction, using scores prepared by Paul
   Whiteman arrangers Bill Challis and Ferdie Grofe. The soloists are interesting,
   but hitherto unidentifiable.          New York, July 2, 1928.

146610-4  Pickin' Cotton - v/aBCh                   Col 1464-D, 5242

At this point, over several sessions between September 5 and October 5, 1928, Paul
   Whiteman and his Orchestra recorded the complete CONCERTO IN F for Piano and Orchestra, by George Gershwin, with Roy Bargy as the soloist. Although the score pro-
   vides for other soloists, including Bix Beiderbecke on side 4 briefly, there is no
   jazz music here (perhaps not surprisingly).

   Margulis, Goldfield, Pinder, Beiderbecke: Cullen, Hall, Rank, Fulton; Hazlett-bcl;
   Friedman-cl-o; Mayer-f-bsn; Trumbauer-cl-bsn; Strickfaden-bar-o; Dieterle, Russell,
   Malneck; Perry; Bargy; Lennie Hayton-cel;Pingitore; Leibrook; Trafficante; Marsh,
                                               New York, September 18, 1928.

 98584-1  Sweet Sue - vJF/aBCh                      Col 50103-D, 35667, 9572, 07509,
                                                        A-405
NOTE:- Columbia 35667 is an edited version of the original to make a 12-inch side
   fit a 10-inch one.

   Crozier-bsn-f-o/Bowman-Gaylord added; Hazlett plays cl-bcl-as; Friedman cl-ts;
   Mayer-bsn-ca-pic; Trumbauer-cl-ss-as-Cm-bsn; Strickfaden ss-as-bar-o.
                                               New York, September 21, 1928.

 98589-3  I Can't Give You Anything But Love - vJF Col 50103-D, 9572
          /aFG

   Manny Klein-t replaces Beiderbecke; exact personnel uncertain but not materially
   different from the above.              New York, December 22, 1928.

147540-7  Makin' Whoopee - vBC/aFG                  Col 1683-D, 5556

                                               New York, January 11, 1929.

147537-9  How About Me ? - vAY/aBCh                 Col 1723-D, 5305, 07018

PAUL WHITEMAN AND HIS ORCHESTRA : Paul Whiteman dir. Charlie Margulis-Harry Goldfield
t/Bix Beiderbecke-Andy Secrest-c/Boyce Cullen-Bill Rank-Wilbur Hall-tb/Bernie Daly-
cl-ss/Frank Trumbauer-cl-as/Chester Hazlett-as/Charles Strickfaden-cl-ss-bar/Izzy
Friedman-Red Mayer-cl-ts/Kurt Dieterle-Mischa Russell-Matt Malneck-vn/Roy Bargy-p/
Mike Pingitore-bj/Min Leibrook-bb/Mike Trafficante-sb/George Marsh-d/Bing Crosby-Al
Rinker-Harry Barris-v/Bill Challis-a.      New York, April 5, 1929.

148183-3  I'm In Seventh Heaven - vBC-AR-HB/aBCh     Col 1877-D,5544,07021,A-8208,J-749

Jack Fulton-tb-v/Lennie Hayton-cel added, John Bowman-Charles Gaylord-vn replace
Malneck; Hazlett db cl; Daly, Trumbauer-as; Strickfaden-as-bar-o; Friedman, Mayer-
ts; Bargy-a, on 148407-4; same on 148408-4, without Hayton, and Trumbauer db:Cm/
Strickfaden-as only; Margulis, Beiderbecke, Secrest; Rank; Hazlett, Trumbauer, Daly-
as; Friedman-cl-ts; Strickfaden-ts; Dieterle, Russell; same rhythm, on 148409-4,
Lennie Hayton-a.                            New York, May 3, 1929.

148407-4  When My Dreams Come True - vJF/aRB      Col 1822-D, 5484, 07024, J-711
148408-4  Reaching For Someone And Not Finding Anyone  -     -     -     -
          There - vBC
148409-4  China Boy - aLH                         Col 1945-D, DC-177, 07025,
                                                  A-8278, J-1518, Tpl 529

As for 148407-4, but Daly db cl; Mayer plays as-ts-bsn; Strickfaden as-ca; Bing
Crosby-v; Bill Challis-a.                    New York, May 4, 1929.

148421-4  Oh ! Miss Hannah - vBC/aBCh            Col 1945-D, DC-176, 07025,
                                                  A-8278, J-1518, Tpl 529

As for 148407-4, but Otto Landau-Matt Malneck-vn replace Bowman, Gaylord; Eddie Lang
g added; Bing Crosby-v/Ferdie Grofe-a.     New York, September 13, 1929.

148986-8  Waiting At The End Of The Road - vBC/aFG  Col 1974-D, 5675, 07032
149005-3  When You're Counting The Stars Alone    Col 1993-D  -
          - vBC-AR-JF

Beiderbecke omitted; Joe Venuti-vn added.
                                            New York, October 9, 1929.

149123-2  Nobody's Sweetheart - aLH              Col 2098-D, 5702, A-8610
149124-3  Great Day - vBC-AR-HB-JF/aBCh          Col 2023-D, CB-116, 07034

                                            New York, October 16, 1929.

149150-4  If I Had A Talking Picture Of You-vBC/aLH Col 2010-D, 14353, 07031, A-8227

William Grant Still-a.                       New York, October 18, 1929.

149157-3  Should I ? - vJF/aLH                   Col 2047-D, 5724, 07035,Re RS-1484
149159-3  After You've Gone - vBC/aWGS           Col 2098-D, 5702, 07032,A-8610 -

                                            Los Angeles, February 10, 1930.

149810-1  Happy Feet - vBC-AR-HB/aLH             Col 2164-D, CB-86, 07037,
                                                  A-8792, CQ-217, J-918

The Brox Sisters-v.                          Los Angeles, March 22, 1930.

149825-2  A Bench In The Park - vBC-AR-HB-BS     Col 2164-D, CB-86, 07037, A-8792,
                                                  CQ-217, J-918

                                            Los Angeles, March 23, 1930.

149826-2  I Like To Do Things For You - vBC-AR-HB  Col 2170-D, CB-87, 07038, A-8793,
                                                  CQ-216

PAUL WHITEMAN AND HIS ORCHESTRA : Paul Whiteman dir. Nat Natoli-Harry Goldfield-t/
    Andy Secrest-c/Jack Fulton-tb-v/Herb Winfield-Bill Rank-tb/Chester Hazlett-cl-bcl-
    as/Charles Strickfaden-as-bar/Frank Trumbauer-Cm-as-bsn/Fud Livingstone-cl-ts/Kurt
    Dieterle-Mischa Russell-Matt Malneck-vn/Roy Bargy-p-a/Mike Pingitore-bj/Mike Traf-
    ficante-sb/George Marsh-d.              New York, July 25, 1930.

150683-1  The New Tiger Rag - aRB              Col 2277-D, CB-163, 07042

    Frank Trumbauer-a.                      New York, September 10, 1930.

150791-4  Choo Choo - aFT                      Col 2491-D

    Fritz Hummel-tb replaces Winfield; Ray McDermott-cl-ts replaces Livingston; Joh..
    Bowman-vn returns (possibly on the above also); Fritz Ciccone-g added; Pierre
    Olker-bb replaces Trafficante; Mildred Bailey-v.
                                           Chicago, November 30, 1931.

70633-1  'Leven Pounds Of Heaven - vMB          Vic 22883

PAUL WHITEMAN'S RHYTHM BOYS : Ray Kulz-t-v/George MacDonald-cl-d-v/Al Dary-p-v/Jimmy
    Noel-g-v.                               New York, August 9, 1932.

73177-1  Her Majesty (My Sugar) - pAD         Rejected
73178-1  Bahama Mama - pAD                    Vic 24095
73179-1  Jig Time - pAD                       Vic 24190, HMV B-4950
73180-1  Basin Street Blues                   Rejected
73181-1  Milenberg Joys - pAD                 -
73182-1  Lost In Your Arms - pAD              Vic 24095
NOTE:- Records made prior to the above under the name of Paul Whiteman's Rhythm
Boys are excellent examples of rhythmic singing by Bing Crosby, Al Rinker and Harry
Barris, but the accompaniment, by Harry Barris at the piano, does not seem to
warrant their inclusion here.

PAUL WHITEMAN AND HIS ORCHESTRA : As for November 30, 1931, but Art Miller-sb re-
    places Olker, and Matt Malneck dir.; Red McKenzie-The Rhythm Boys (as last above)-
    v.                                      New York, September 26, 1932.

73582-1  You're Telling Me - vRK-GM-AD-JN      Vic 24140, El EG-2689
73583-1  I'll Follow You - vRM                 Vic 24141, HMV B-6275

    Ramona Davies-p-v added.                New York, November 25, 1932.

74610-1  Rise 'n' Shine - vRD                  Vic 24197

    Norman McPherson-bb/Peggy Healy-v added. New York, April 4, 1933.

75713-1  Look What I've Got - vPH              Vic 24285, HMV B-6360

    One tb omitted.                         New York, July 20, 1933.

76673-1  Are You Makin' Any Money ? - vRD      Vic 24365

    Bunny Berigan-t replaces Secrest; Vincent Grande-tb replaces Fulton.
                                           New York, September 11, 1933.

76645-1  It's Only A Paper Moon - vPH          Vic 24400, HMV B-6427, El EG-2903
76647-1  Sittin' On A Backyard Fence-vRK-GM-AD-JN Vic 24403, HMV B-6434

PAUL WHITEMAN PRESENTS PEGGY HEALY : Vocal, acc. by Bunny Berigan-t/Benny Bonacio-cl/
    Al Dary-p-v/Roy Bargy-p/Mike Pingitore or Jimmy Noel-g.
                                           New York, October 23, 1933.

78305-1  When You Were The Girl On The Scooter   Vic 24452, HMV EA-1283
            (And I Was The Boy On The Bike) - vAD
78306-1  That's How Rhythm Was Born             -

PAUL WHITEMAN AND HIS ORCHESTRA : Paul Whiteman dir. Nat Natoli-Bunny Berigan-Harry
   Goldfield-t/Bill Rank-Vincent Grande-tb/Jack Fulton-tb-v/Bennie Bonacio-cl-bcl-as/
   John Cordaro-cl-bcl-as-bar/Charles Strickfaden-cl-as-ts-bar-o/Frank Trumbauer-cl-as
   Cm/Mischa Russell-Matt Malneck-Harry Struble-Kurt Dieterle-vn/Roy Bargy-p-a/Ramona
   Davies-p-v/Mike Pingitore-bj-g/Norman McPherson-bb/Art Miller-sb/Herb Quigley-d/
   Peggy Healy-Johnny Mercer-v.              New York, November 3, 1933.

78513-1  Something Had To Happen - vRD            Vic 24455

Charlie Teagarden-t replaces Berigan; Jack Teagarden-tb-v replaces Grande.
                                          New York, January 16, 1934.

81061-1  G Blues                                 Vic rejected

   Rank omitted.                          New York, February 16, 1934.

81714-1  True - vJF                              Vic 24566, HMV B-6481, EA-1415,
                                                 El EG-3052
81715-1  Fare-Thee-Well To Harlem - vJT-JM       Vic 24571, BB B-10969, HMV EA-3408
81716-1  Sun Spots                               Vic 24574, HMV EA-1344, RE-4382
81717-1  The Bouncing Ball                         -        - BD-187     -

   Bill Rank-tb added.                    New York, April 17, 1934.

81061-2  G Blues                                 Vic 24668, HMV EA-1407, X-4431
82319-1  Tail Spin                                 -          -          -
82320-1  Christmas Night In Harlem - vJT-JM       Vic 24615, BB B-10969,
                                                 HMV B-6549, EA-3408

   One t omitted.                         New York, June 29, 1934.

83352-1  Born To Be Kissed - vRD                 Vic 24670

   3rd t returns; no vn or bb.            New York, August 18, 1934.

84010-1  Pardon My Southern Accent - vPH-JM      Vic 24704
84012-1  Itchola                                 Vic 24885, HMV NE-255
84014-1  I Saw Stars - vPH                       Vic 24705, HMV B-6532, EA-1416

PAUL WHITEMAN AND HIS CONCERT ORCHESTRA : As for January 16, 1934, but Eddie Wade-t
   replaces Natoli; Casper Reardon-harp added; Chet Martin-Herman Fink-d replace
   Quigley.                               New York, December 14, 1934.

86459-1  Deep Forest                             Vic 24852, HMV B-8318
86460-1  Serenade For A Wealthy Widow              -          -

PAUL WHITEMAN AND HIS ORCHESTRA : As last, omitting Teagarden-tb and Reardon; Bob
   Lawrence-vn-v replaces Dieterle.       New York, December 17, 1934.

86470-1  The Night Is Young - vBL                Vic 24844, HMV BD-130

Jack Teagarden-tb-v returns; no vn used; Larry Gomar-d-vib replaces Martin and Fink;
   Durelle Alexander-v.                   New York, July 9, 1935.

92576-1  Dodging A Divorcee                      Vic 25086, HMV B-8641
92577-1  The Duke Insists                        Vic 25113
92579-1  Nobody's Sweetheart Now - bJT           Vic 25319, BB B-10957
92580-1  Ain't Misbehavin' - vJT                 Vic 25086      -        HMV EA-1560
92581-1  Sugar Plum - vDA                        Vic 25150, HMV BD-5001, EA-1594
92582-1  New O'leans - vRD                         -                   -

2vn return; Ramona Davies sings but does not play; John Hauser-v.
                                          New York, July 10, 1935.

92588-1  I'm Sittin' High On A Hill-Top - vJH    Vic 25151, HMV EA-1595, NE-248
92589-1  Thanks A Million - vJH                    - HMV BD-5001 -      -
92592-1  Garden Of Weed                          Vic 25113, HMV B-8641
92593-1  Darktown Strutters' Ball - vJT          Vic 25192, HMV B-8494, B-8548,
                                                 EA-1628, NE-316

PAUL WHITEMAN AND HIS ORCHESTRA : Paul Whiteman dir. Eddie Wade-Charlie Teagarden-
Harry Goldfield-t/Bill Rank-tb/Jack Fulton-Jack Teagarden-tb-v/Benny Bonacio-cl-bcl
as/John Cordaro-cl-bcl-as-bar/Charles Strickfaden-cl-as-ts-bar-o/Frank Trumbauer-cl
as-Cm/Kurt Dieterle-Mischa Russell-Matt Malneck-Harry Struble-vn/Roy Bargy-p/Ramona
Davies-p-v/Mike Pingitore-g/Norman McPherson-bb/Art Miller-sb/Larry Gomar-d-vib.
                                       New York, September 7, 1935.

94192-1   Farewell Blues                        Vic 25192, HMV EA-1628
94197-1   Announcer's Blues                     Vic 25404, JA-821

George Bamford-cl-ts-f added; The King's Men-v.
                                       New York, December 2, 1935.

98183-1   I'm The Echo - vKM                    Vic 25198, JA-646, HMV EA-1633,
                                                 NE-278
98184-1   I Got Love                            As above

Fulton omitted; Bob Lawrence-vn-v replaces Dieterle and Malneck; Bob White-d replaces Gomar.                          New York, February 6, 1936.

99060-1   Saddle Your Blues To A Wild Mustang   Vic 25251, HMV EA-1676
          - vBL-KM

Eddie Wade-Charlie Teagarden-Harry Goldfield-t/Bill Rank-Jack Teagarden-Hal Mat-
thews-tb/Al Gallodoro-cl-bcl-as/John Cordaro-cl-bcl-as-bar/George Bamford-cl-ts-f/
Frank Trumbauer-cl-Cm-as/Murray Cohen-o/Matt Malneck-Mischa Russell-Sam Korman-
Harry Strubel-Walt Edelstein-Robert Spokaney-Adam Fluschmn-Howard Kay-Sylvan
Kirsner-vn/Ben Pellman-Fred Glickman-vl/Abe Edison-Milton Prinz-vc/Roy Bargy-p/
Vincent Pirro-pac/Frank Victor-g/Norman McPherson-bb/Art Miller-sb/Larry Gomar-d-
vib/Allan Holt-v.                      New York, March 26, 1937.

06546-1   Shall We Dance ?                      Vic 25552, HMV BD-5221, EA-1883
06547-1   For You - vAH                         -

PAUL WHITEMAN AND HIS SWING WING : Charlie Teagarden-t/Jack Teagarden-tb-v/Sal
Franzella-cl/Al Gallodoro-as/Art Drelinger-ts/Walter Gross-p/Art Ryerson-g/Art
Miller-sb/Rollo Laylan-d/The Four Modernaires (Chuck Goldstein-Spook Dickinson-Bill
Conway-Ralph Brewster)-v.              New York, September 9, 1938.

64616-A   I'm Comin', Virginia - v4M           Dec 2145, 3943, M-30188, Y-5277,
                                                 Br 02693,A-81905,A-82544,Od 284480
64617-A   Jamboree Jones - v4M                  Dec 2074, M-30220, Y-5283,
                                                 Br 02739, A-82041
64618-A   Aunt Hagar's Blues - vJT-4M           Dec 2145, 3522, M-30188, Y-5277,
                                                 Br 02693,A-81905,A-82544,Od 284480
64619-A   I Used To Be Color-Blind - v4M        Dec 2073,BM-1043,Y-5304,Br 02674,
                                                 Pol A-369, A-61189, Od 284417
64620-A   Sing A Song Of Sixpence - v4M         Dec 2074,Y-5405,Br 02674  -
64621-A   Peelin' The Peach - v4M               Dec 2073, M-30220, Y-5304,
                                                 Br 02739, A-82041, Pol A-369

PAUL WHITEMAN AND HIS ORCHESTRA : Paul Whiteman dir. Bob Cusumano-Charlie Teagarden-
Don Moore-t/Jack Teagarden-Jose Gutierrez-tb/Sal Franzella-cl-as/Al Gallodoro-as/
Art Drelinger-ts/George Ford-Vincent Capone-Jack Bell-f/Murray Cohen-o/Roy Bargy-p/
Art Ryerson-g/Art Miller-sb/Rollo Laylan-d/The Four Modernaires (as above)-v.
                                       New York, September 20, 1938.

64673-A   There's No Place Like Your Arms - v4M  Dec 2076, BM-1045, M-30184,
                                                 Y-5305, Br 02685, Pol A-61263
64677-A   My Reverie                            Dec 3075
64678-A   Heart And Soul                        Dec 2083,Y-5345,Br 02675,Od 284472
PAUL WHITEMAN AND HIS SWING WING : Bob Cusumano-Charlie Teagarden-t/Jack Teagarden-tb
v/Sal Franzella-cl-as/Art Drelinger-ts/Frank Signorelli-p/Allan Reuss-g/Artie
Shapiro-sb/George Wettling-d/The Four Modernaires (as above)-Joan Edwards-v.
                                       New York, December 8, 1938.

64791-A   Never Felt Better, Never Had Less - v4M  Dec 2283,Br 02751,A-82094,Od 284489
64792-A   Mutiny In The Nursery - vJT-JE-4M     Dec 2222, M-30217, Y-5309,
                                                 Br 02729, A-82020, Od 284472
64793-A   Jeepers Creepers - vJT-4M             As above, but Od 284452
64794-A   I Go For That - v4M                   As for 64791-A, plus Dec Y-5345

PAUL WHITEMAN'S BOUNCING BRASS : Bob Cusumano-Bob Alexy-Charlie Teagarden-Harry
    Goldfield-t/Moe Zudecoff (Buddy Morrow)-Miff Mole-Hal Matthews-tb/Tony Gottuso-Art
    Ryerson-g/George Wettling-d.              New York, April 6, 1939.

| | | |
|---|---|---|
| 65358-A | Heat Wave | Dec 2697, Br 02861 |
| 65359-A | Home Again Blues | - - |
| 65360-A | I've Found A New Baby | Dec 2466, M-30230, Y-5401, |
| | | Br 02802, A-82209 |
| 65361-A | Rose Room | As above, except Dec Y-5401 |
| 65361-B | Rose Room | Dec 3943, Y-5401 |

PAUL WHITEMAN'S SAX SOCTETTE : Al Gallodoro-Sal Franzella-Frank Gallodoro-as/Art
    Drelinger-ts/N. M. Farquharson-Vincent Capone-Jack Bell-f/Harold Feldman-o/Art
    Ryerson-Dave Barbour-Tony Gottuso (as noted)-g/Artie Shapiro-sb/George Wettling-d.
                                             New York, April 7, 1939.

| | | |
|---|---|---|
| 65362-A | Blue Skies - gAR-DB | Dec 2698, Br 02862 |
| 65363-A | What'll I Do ? - gAR-DB | - - |
| 65364-A | I Kiss Your Hand, Madame - gAR-TG | Dec 2467, Y-5394, Br 02834 |
| 65365-A | After You've Gone - gAR-DB | - - - |

PAUL WHITEMAN AND HIS SWING WING : Bob Cusumano-Charlie Teagarden-t/Miff Mole-tb/Sal
    Franzella-cl-as/Art Drelinger-ts/Frank Signorelli-p/Allan Reuss-g/Artie Shapiro-sb/
    George Wettling-d/The Four Modernaires (Chuck Goldstein-Spook Dickinson-Bill Conway
    Ralph Brewster)-v.                       New York, April 8, 1939.

| | | |
|---|---|---|
| 65366-A | Three Little Fishies (Itty Bitty Poo) | Dec 2417, M-30234, Y-5368, |
| | - v4M | Br 02766, A-82108 |
| 65367-A | Hooray For Spinach - v4M | Dec 2418, Br 02774 |
| 65368-A | Step Up And Shake My Hand - v4M | - Y-5424 - |
| 65369-A | Now And Then - v4M | Dec 2417, M-30234, Y-5719, |
| | | Br 02766, A-82108 |
| 65370-A | Mandy - v4M | Dec 2696, Br 02860 |

                         New York, May 16, 1939.

| | | |
|---|---|---|
| 65581-A | Lazy - v4M | Dec 2696, Br 02860 |

PAUL WHITEMAN AND HIS ORCHESTRA : Paul Whiteman dir. Monty Kelly-Larry Neill-Don
    Waddilove-t/Skip Layton-Murray McEachern and another-tb/Alvy West-Dan d'Andrea-
    Lennie Hartman and another-cl-as-ts/Buddy Weed-p/Mike Pingitore-g/Artie Shapiro-sb/
    Willie Rodriguez-d/Billie Holiday ("Lady Day")-Johnny Mercer-Jack Teagarden-v/Jimmy
    Mundy-a.                                  Los Angeles, June 12, 1942.

| | | |
|---|---|---|
| CAP-30-A | Trav'lin' Light - vBH | Cap 116, CL-13845, V-Disc 286 |
| CAP-31-A | The Old Music Master - vJT-JM | Cap 137 - |

See also Ramona; The Three T's, and The Virginians. For other records by Paul
    Whiteman and his Orchestra of the period when Bix Beiderbecke was a member of it,
    but on which neither he nor anyone else contributed any jazz solos, see BIX - MAN
    AND LEGEND, by Richard Sudhalter and Philip R. Evans (Arlington House, 1974).

## WHITE STAR SYNCOPATORS

Pseudonym on Piccadilly for the following items listed in this book :-

494  In Harlem's Araby (Memphis Jazzers)
547  Puttin' On The Ritz (California Ramblers)

See also the Grey Gull studio bands.

## THE WHITE TOPS

Benny Goodman-cl/pac/John Kurzenknabe-bj/Ben Pollack-v.
                                 Chicago, September 14, 1926.

| | | |
|---|---|---|
| 36236-1-2 | Hot Stuff | Vic rejected |

Probably :- Frank Christian-c/Frank Lhotak-tb/Achille Baquet-cl-as/Jimmy Durante-p.
                              New York, c. April, 1920.

800-2  Blues My Naughty Sweetie Gives To Me     Pm 20014, Pur 11014
801-2  Tiger Rag                                  -

## WHITE WAY PLAYERS/SERENADERS

Pseudonym for the following items listed in this book :-

Goodson 205  Have A Little Faith In Me (California Ramblers)
Van Dyke 71816  Ev'rybody Dance (Memphis Jazzers)

## JACK WHITING

This popular American musical comedy star of the 1930s made several records during
   the London run of ON YOUR TOES, in which he played the leading role; the following
   are of interest as jazz for their accompaniments.

Vocal, acc. by the Six Swingers : George Scott Wood-p-a dir. probably :- Bill Gaskin
   or Harry Owen-t/Jock Fleming-tb/Eddie Pratt-cl-as/Joe Young-g/Dick Escott-sb/Sid
   Heiger-d.                                  London, May 8, 1937.

CA-16377-1  The Love Bug Will Bite You          Col FB-1695
CA-16378-1  Big Boy Blue                         -

## ESSIE  WHITMAN

Vocal, acc. by the Jazz Masters : Probably :- Gus Aiken-t/Bud Aiken-tb/Garvin Bushell
   cl/Joe Elder-cl-ts/Charlie Jackson-vn/Fletcher Henderson-p/bj.
                              New York, c. October, 1921.

P-155-1  Sweet Daddy It's You I Love          BS 2036, Pm 12172
P-156-2-3  If You Don't Believe I Love You      -         -
NOTE:- Paramount 12172 as ELSIE WHITMAN.

## MARGARET  WHITMIRE

Vocal, acc. by Charlie Alexander-p.       Chicago, October 5, 1927.

C-1194  'Tain't A Cow In Texas              Br 7024, Voc 1173
C-1197  That Thing's Done Been Put On Me     -        -

## JACK WHITNEY AND HIS ORCHESTRA

Pseudonym on Clarion 5265-C and Velvet Tone 2331-V for the California Ramblers, q.v.,
   and on other items on these labels and Harmony for Fred Rich, Ben Selvin and other
   bands of no particular interest as "hot" dance music.

## THE WHOOPEE MAKERS

See Irving Mills and his Orchestra for titles under this name on Cameo, Lincoln,
   Romeo and Vocalion, and the following others listed in this book  -

Banner 32070, BRS 1007, Jewel 6191, Oriole 2191, Pathe Actuelle 36781, 36899, 36915,
   36923, 37059, 11558, Perfect 14962, 15080, 15096, 15104, 15240, 15418, Regal 10244,
   Romeo 1556  Duke Ellington and his Orchestra
**Perfect** 15126  St. Louis Blues (The Broadway Broadcasters - see Sam Lanin)
           15376  Happy Feet (Cab Calloway and his Orchestra)

Eddie Grosso-cl-v/Fred Hall-p-reed or/Al Russo-g/Joseph Mayo-d.
                              New York, July 16, 1928.

46308-1-2-3  Two Lips (To Kiss My Cares Away)    Vic rejected
46309-1-2-3  Skadatin-Dee                         -

                              New York, September 25, 1928.

147057-4  Sister Kate                        Col 14367-D
147058-3  Somebody Stole My Gal               -

Trumpet solo, acc. by Stanley Black-p/George Chisholm-cel/Alan Ferguson-g/Doug Lees-
sb/Stanley Marshall-d.                    London, December 12, 1935.

CE-7362-1  Hummin' To Myself                      Par R-2153, A-6367
NOTE:- Parlophone A-6367 as DUNCAN WHITE.

DUNCAN WHYTE AND HIS ORCHESTRA : Duncan Whyte-t,-v/George Chisholm-tb-cel/Jock
Myddleton-as/Mickey Deans-ts/Derek Neville-bar/Jack Paines-p/Willie Davison-sb/
Len Johnson-d.                            London, march 23, 1937.

CE-8227-1  Hot And Anxious                         Par R-2338
CE-8228-1  Pennies From Heaven - vDW               -

## HAL WHYTE'S SYNCOPATORS

Pseudonym on Domino (sometimes as HAL WHITE) for the following items listed in this
book :-

371  Charleston Cabin (Six Black Diamonds)
404  Everything You Do (Southampton Society Orchestra - see Nathan Glantz)
415  Oh ! Peter (Southampton Society Orchestra - see Sam Lanin)
429  Nobody Knows What A Red Head Mama Can Do (California Ramblers)
3444 Everybody Loves My Baby (Fletcher Henderson and his Orchestra)

## ZACH WHYTE'S CHOCOLATE BEAU BRUMMELS

Zach Whyte-bj dir. Sy Oliver-Bubber Whyte-Henry Savage-t/Floyd Brady-tb/Earl Tribble-
Snake Richardson-Clarence Paige-as/Al Sears-ts-bar/Herman Chittison-p/Montgomery
Morrison-bb/William Benton-d/v by The Orchestra.
                                          Richmond, Ind., January 22, 1929.

14718-A  Mandy                                     Gnt 6781, Spt 9486

                                          Richmond, Ind., February 11, 1929.

14787, -A  Shake It And Break It                   Rejected
14788      Hum All Your Troubles Away - vO         Gnt 6781, Spt 9486
NOTE:- Supertone 9486 as EDDIE WALKER AND HIS BAND.

                                          Richmond, Ind., February 26, 1929.

14836      It's Tight Like That - vO          Gnt 6798, Ch 15714, Spt 9368
14837-A  West End Blues                           - 33010  - 40016    - Bm 1024
NOTE:- Champion 15714 as SMOKE JACKSON AND HIS RED ONIONS; 40016 as CHUCK NELSON
AND HIS BOYS; Supertone 9368 as EDDIE WALKER AND HIS BAND.

Fred Jackson-ts replaces Sears; Charlie Anderson-bj replaces Whyte, now dir-v;
Chittison db cel and Benton vib.          Richmond, Ind., December 19, 1929.

16005-A  Good Feelin' Blues (Big Blues*)           Gnt 7086, Ch 15905, Spt 9685,
                                                   Var 6029*, Poydras 22
16006    Wailin' Blues (Small Blues*)             As above
16007    When You're Smiling - vZW                 Rejected
16008, -A  Sophomore Prom.                         -

Zach Whyte-bj dir. ? Henry Savage and another-t/Vic Dickenson-tb-v/Earl Tribble-
Clarence Paige-as/ts/Herman Chittison-p/? Montgomery Morrison-bb/William Benton-d/
v trio.                                   Richmond, Ind., November 12, 1931.

18171, -A  Alabama Home                            Gnt rejected
18172, -A  Rock Me In The Cradle Of Love - vVD     -
18173, -A  Goodnight, Sweetheart - v3              -

## HERB  WIEDOEFT

The late Herb Wiedoeft, who was killed in a car accident in Medford, Oregon, on
May 12, 1928, made a number of Brunswick records between the summer of 1923 and
a few months before his death.  The following are known to be of some interest as
"hot" dance music.

HERB WIEDOEFT'S CINDERELLA ROOF ORCHESTRA : Herb Wiedoeft-t dir. Joseph Nemoli-c-vl/
    Jesse Stafford-tb-bh/Larry Abbott-Gene Siegrist-Fred Bibesheimer-cl-as-ts-o/
    Vincent Rose-p-a/Jose Sucedo-bj/Guy Wiedoeft-bb-sb/Adolph Wiedoeft-d-x.
                                            Los Angeles, August 14, 1923.

11180    Cinderella Blues                          Br 2542

Unknown p replaces Rose; Gene Secrest-cl-as-bar replaces Abbott.
                                            Los Angeles, May 8, 1924.

.A-26    Oh, Peter ! (You're So Nice)              Br 2627*

                                            Los Angeles, May 14, 1924.

A-95     Stack O'Lee Blues                         Br 2660

                                            Los Angeles, May 20, 1924.

A-109    Beale Street Blues                        Br 2795
A-115/8  Maple Leaf Rag (Scott Joplin)             Rejected

                                            New York, October 21, 1924.

14057    Hot Stuff                                 Br 2781
14060    Maple Leaf Rag (Scott Joplin)             Br 2795
14061/4  Hard Hearted Hannah                       Br 2751

Clyde Lucas-tb-v added; Dubbie Kirkpatrick now a member of the band, but it is not
known what he plays.            Los Angeles, May, 1925.

15832/4  Roamin' Around - vCL                      Br 2893

LA-36; 15855  He's Just A Horn-Tootin' Fool        Br 2916*

LA-45; 15864  Ev'rything Is Hotsy-Totsy Now-vCL    Br 2916*

                                            New York, October 14, 1925.

E-16701    Deep Elm - vCL                          Br 2982*

HERB WIEDOEFT AND HIS ORCHESTRA : As above, but Leon Lucas-v and Art Winters added,
    although their instruments are unknown. Los Angeles, c. January, 1928.

LAE-38    Sad Moments                              Br 3813, 3805

LAE-54    Maybe You'll Be The One Who'll Be The    Br 3814, 3748
          One To Care

## RUDY WIEDOEFT'S  PALACE TRIO

See the Palace Trio; other titles under the above name are of little or no known
    interest as jazz.

## WIGWAM ORCHESTRA

Pseudonym on Apex 719 (FOOTLOOSE) for the California Ramblers, q.v.

## C.  WILBER

Pseudonym on Globe and Radiex for Wilbur C. Sweatman, q.v.

## JAY WILBUR AND HIS ORCHESTRA

Jay Wilbur, whose real name was Wilbur Blanco, was Musical Director of Dominion
    Records from November, 1928 to June, 1930, at which date the firm went out of
    business and Jay Wilbur took up a similar post with Crystalate Records, first on
    Imperial, and from September, 1933 on Rex.  Of the enormous number of sides he
    recorded, the following are known to be of interest as "hot" dance music, and it
    is likely that there are others of equal or even superior merit.

Jay Wilbur dir. Max Goldberg and another-t/Ted Heath-tb/Laurie Payne or Jim Easton-as-bar/as/ts/vn/p/bj/bb/d/Les Allen-v. London, October 8, 1930.

5482-2  Happy Feet - vLA                     Imp 2339
NOTE:- An edited version was issued on 7-inch Victory as by the VICTORY DANCE
ORCHESTRA.

Billy Scott-Coomber-v.                 London, late August, 1931.

5801-2  Roll On, Mississippi, Roll On - vBSC-?   Imp 2546, Lyric 3413

Sam Browne-v.                          London, September, 1931.

5816-A  You Can't Stop Me From Lovin' You - vSB  Imp 2558

Jay Wilbur dir. Billy Farrell-Claude Findlay-t/Ted Heath-tb-a/Freddy Gardner-Harry
Hayes-cl-as/Buddy Featherstonhaugh-ts/Reg. Pursglove-vn/Cecil Norman or Harry
Rubens-p/Jack Simmonds-g/Don Stuteley-sb/Max Abrams-d/Pat O'Malley-v.  Some sides
have two trombones, the extra man being either Claude Findlay doubling, or Sam
Acres.                                 London, April, 1935.

F-1269   Lookie, Lookie, Lookie, Here Comes        Rex 8486
            Cookie - vPO'M

F-1286   Temptation Rag (Henry Lodge)              Rex 8485

Jay Wilbur's name was also used on Dominion A-29 (SAN) as a pseudonym for the
Alabama Red Peppers, q.v.

## JOE WILBUR

The vocalist and leader of the Savoy Quartet, q.v., made a few records in New York
for Pathe and OKeh after his return from London in the late 1920s. Eddie Lang is
audible on the latter, and the following has an interesting accompanying group.

Vocal, acc. by t/tb/p/bj/bb.           New York, c. August 12, 1927.

107727   Dawning                           PA      , 11537, Per

## THE  WILD WESTERNERS

Pseudonym on Panachord 25492 and 25542 for Gene Kardos and his Orchestra, q.v.

## ARNOLD WILEY

This pianist made several records accompanying his own singing, solo and with his
sister Irene Wiley, but these are of no interest as jazz.

Piano solos.                           Chicago, July 3, 1929.

C-3776-  Windy City                        Br rejected
C-3777-  Arnold Wiley Rag                   -

                                       Chicago, July 31, 1929.

C-3976-  Windy City                        Br 7113
C-3977-  Arnold Wiley Rag                   -

## LEE  WILEY

Vocal, acc. by the Dorsey Brothers' Orchestra : ? Bunny Berigan-t/Tommy Dorsey-tb/
Jimmy Dorsey-cl/Joe Venuti-2 others-vn/Fulton McGrath-p/Dick McDonough-g/Artie
Bernstein-sb/Stan King-d.              New York, March 7, 1933.

B-13122-  You've Got Me Crying Again        Epic SN-6059 (LP)
B-13123-  I Gotta Right To Sing The Blues   Epic LZN-6072, LN-24442 (LPs)

Acc. by the Dorsey Brothers' Orchestra : Probably L- Bunny Berigan-Sterling Bose-t
/Tommy Dorsey-Glenn Miller-tb/Jimmy Dorsey-? Lyle Bowen-cl-as/Larry Binyon-ts/Joe
Venuti-Harry Hoffman-Harry Bluestone-Serge Kostelarsky-vn/Fulton McGrath-p/Dick
McDonough-g/Artie Bernstein-sb/Stan King-d.
                                        New York, April 15, 1933.

B-13254-A-B  Let's Call It A Day                    Br rejected

                                        New York, May 3, 1933.

B-13254-C-D  Let's Call It A Day                    Br rejected

Acc. by t/tb/2cl-as/cl-ts/2-3vn/p/g/sb/d.
                                        New York, August 13, 1934.

38298-B  Careless Love                      Dec 132, Br 01916
38300-A-B  Motherless Child                    -           -
NOTE:- Matrix 38299 is by Justin Ring's Orchestra, which probably provided Miss
Wiley with her accompaniment.

Cel used on this session.               New York, November 26, 1934.

39100-A  Hands Across The Table             Dec 322, Br 01945
39101-   I'll Follow My Secret Heart            -      Br 02091
NOTE:- Brunswick 02091 was never issued.

Acc. by Victor Young dir. unknown orchestra.
                                        Los Angeles, August 25, 1935.

DLA-232-A-B  Mad About The Boy                  Dec rejected

                                        Los Angeles, February 10, 1937.

DLA-688-A-B  What Is Love ?                 Dec 15034
DLA-689-B  I've Got You Under My Skin            -        29216

Acc. by Max Kaminsky's Orchestra or Joe Bushkin's Orchestra, as noted : Max
Kaminsky-t/Bud Freeman-ts/Joe Bushkin-p-cel/Artie Shapiro-sb/George Wettling-d/
Brad Gowans-a.                          New York, November 13, 1939

P-26266-A  Sweet And Low Down - MKO            LMS L-284
P-26267-A  Sam And Delilah - JBO              LMS L-283
P-26268-A  My One And Only - JBO              LMS L-281
P-26269-A  'S Wonderful - JBO                LMS L-283

Pee Wee Russell-cl/Eddie Condon-g added; Fats Waller-p (and pipe or*, without the
band) replaces Bushkin.                 New York, November 15, 1939.

P-26270-A  I've Got A Crush On You - MKO        LMS L-282
P-26271-A  *Someone To Watch Over Me                -
P-26272-A  How Long Has This Been Going On ? - JBO LMS L-281
P-26273-A  But Not For Me - MKO              LMS L-284

As for November 13, 1939.               New York, February, 1940.

76246-A  Baby's Awake Now - JBO               Gala/Rabson 1
76247-A  A Little Birdie Told Me So - JBO        Gala/Rabson 3
76248-A  I've Got Five Dollars - JBO           Gala/Rabson 2
76249-A  You Took Advantage Of Me - JBO         Gala/Rabson 3

As for November 13, 1939, but Artie Bernstein-sb replaces Shapiro; Paul Weston-a.
                                        New York, February, 1940.

76264-A  A Ship Without A Sail - MKO           Gala/Rabson 4
76265-A  As Though You Were There - MKO           -
76268-A  Glad To Be Unhappy - MKO             Gala/Rabson 2
76269-A  Here In My Arms - MKO               Gala/Rabson 1
NOTE:- Matrices 76266 and 76267 are untraced.

Acc. by Bunny Berigan's Music : Bunny Berigan-t/Joe Bushkin-p/Sid Weiss-sb/George
Wettling-d.                              New York, April 10, 1940.

| | | |
|---|---|---|
| P-27150-A | Let's Fly Away | LMS L-296 |
| P-27151-1 | Let's Do It | LMS L-297 |
| P-27152-1 | Hot House Rose | - |
| P-27153-1 | Find Me A Primitive Man | LMS L-296 |

Acc. by Paul Weston's Orchestra : As last, plus Johnny Mince-cl/Hymie Schertzer-
Fred Stulce-as/Paul Mason-ts/Clark Yocum-g.
                                         New York, April 15, 1940.

| | | |
|---|---|---|
| P-27162-1 | Easy To Love | LMS L-295, V-Disc 705 |
| P-27163-1 | You Do Something To Me | LMS L-294     - |
| P-27164-1 | Looking At You | - |
| P-27165-2 | Why Shouldn't I ? | LMS L-295, V-Disc 881 |

Acc. by Muggsy Spanier-c/Jess Stacy-p.  New York, July 10, 1940.

| | | |
|---|---|---|
| R-3111 | Down To Steamboat Tennessee | Com 1507 |
| R-3112 | Sugar | - |

## WILLIAMS' COTTON CLUB  ORCHESTRA

Pseudonym on Victor for the following items listed in this book :-

24039  Both sides by Roane's Pennsylvanians (one side also thus on HMV B-4921)
24083  I Would Do Anything For You (Joe Haymes and his Orchestra)
24083  Red Blues (Alex Bartha and his Hotel Traymore Orchestra)

## WILLIAMS AND MOORE

Pseudonym on QRS R-7016 for Jimmy Blythe, q.v., and W. E. "Buddy" Burton.

## WILLIAMS' PURPLE KNIGHTS

2c/4cl-ss-as-ts/p/bj/sb/d/ —— Baldwin- —— Parry- —— Vredenburgh-v trio.
                                         New York, January 2, 1931.

| | | |
|---|---|---|
| 67752-2 | Dinah | Vic 22625 |
| 67753-2 | Living, Loving You - v3 | - |

## WILLIAMS' WASHBOARD BAND

T/John Haughton-tb/Ben Smith-Jimmy Hill-cl-as/Carl Wade-ts/Eddie Miles-p/Ted Tinsley
g-v/sb/Harry Williams-wb-v; sides marked * are by p/g/sb/wb only.
                                         Camden, N. J., September 12, 1933.

| | | |
|---|---|---|
| 77806-1 | I Want To Ring Bells - vHW | BB B-5183, Eld 2076, Sr S-3263, HMV JF-23 |
| 77807-1 | I Would If I Could But I Can't - vHW | As above |
| 77808-1 | Hard Corn - vHW | BB B-5204, Sr S-3285 |
| 77809-1 | Kelsey's - vHW | -          - |
| 77810-1 | Move Turtle | BB B-5230, Sr S-3313 |
| 77811-1 | Shoutin' In The Amen Corner - vHW | -          -          RZ MR-2138 |
| 77812-1 | I Want To Ring Bells - vTT | Vic 23415 |
| 77813-1 | I Would If I Could But I Can't - vTT | Vic 24405, BB B-6219 |
| 77814-1 | Hard Corn - vTT | Vic 23415 |
| 77815-1 | Kelsey's (Hot Nuts*) — vTT | Vic 23413, BB B-6278* |
| 77816-1 | Move Turtle | -          - |
| 77817-1 | *Mickey Mouse And The Turtle | BB B-5202, Sr S-3283 |
| 77818-1 | *I Would If I Could But I Can't | -          - |
| 77819-1 | Shoutin' In The Amen Corner - vTT | Vic 24405, BB B-6219, HMV B-8655 |

NOTE:- Victor 24405, Bluebird B-6219 and HMV B-8655 as TINSLEY'S WASHBOARD BAND;
Victor 23403, 23415 and Bluebird B-6278 as WASHBOARD RHYTHM KINGS. Although the
matrix numbers of like titles above differ, as do the vocalists, in fact the two
sets of six titles each by the full band are exactly identical. Why this is has
still to be explained satisfactorily.

Pseudonym on Domino for Kitty Brown, Rosa Henderson or Viola McCoy, all q.v.

## BILL WILLIAMS AND HIS GANG

Pseudonym on Champion for the following items listed in this book :-

15215  Make Me Know It (Jelly James and his Fewsicians)
15216  Georgia Bo Bo (Jelly James and his Fewsicians)
15226  She Looks Like Helen Brown (Ross Gorman and his Fire-Eaters)

## CLARENCE WILLIAMS

Vocal, acc. by Jules Levy, Jr.-c/? Ephraim Hannaford-tb/Joesph Samuels-cl-as/cl-ts/
   Larry Briers-p/d.                    New York, c. September 30, 1921.

70210-A-B  If You Don't Believe I Love You, Look  OK rejected
           What A Fool I've Been
70211-A-B  Roumania                              -

                                  New York, October 11, 1921.

70210-C  If You Don't Believe I Love You, Look   OK 8020
         What A Fool I've Been
70211-D  Roumania                                OK 8021
70239-B  The Dance They Call The Georgia Hunch   OK 8029
70240-B  Pullman Porter Blues                    OK 8020
NOTE:- The accompaniment on OKeh 8021 is described as JOHNNIE'S JAZZ BOYS.

   Acc. by Chappie's Hot Dogs : C/tb as/vn/p.
                                  New York, c. October, 1921.

   C-3-2  Decatur Street Blues                   C&S 5005

Vocal duet with Daisy Martin, acc. by the Tampa Blue Jazz Band : As for September 30,
   1921 above.                        New York, c. December 5, 1921.

70352-A  Brown Skin (Who You For)                OK 8027

Piano solos.                         New York, May, 1923.

71527-D  Mixing The Blues                        OK 4893
71528-D  The Weary Blues                         -

CLARENCE WILLIAMS' BLUE FIVE : Tom Morris-c/John Mayfield-tb/Sidney Bechet-cl-ss/
   Clarence Williams-p/Buddy Christian-bj. New York, July 30, 1923.

71706-B  Wild Cat Blues                          OK 4925, Bm 1096, HJCA HC-87,
                                                 JSo AA-603, Jazz Unlimited 4
71707-B  Kansas City Man Blues                   OK 4925, Bm 1096, HJCA HC-87,
                                                 JSo AA-507
NOTE:- Both these titles were scheduled for issue on HRS 30, but this never took
place.

Unknown cl replaces Bechet.         New York, c. August 27, 1923.

71797-A  Achin' Hearted Blues                    OK 4966

Sidney Bechet-ss replaces cl.       New York, c. October 3, 1923.

71928-B  'Tain't Nobody's Bus'ness If I Do       OK 4966
71929-B  New Orleans Hop Scop Blues              OK 4975, HJCA 604, Memory N-302
71930-B  Oh Daddy ! Blues (Oh Daddy ! You Won't  OK 4993, JSo AA-507
         Have No Mama At All)

                                  New York, c. November 10, 1923.

72040-B  Shreveport                              OK 40006, Memory N-302
72041-B  Old Fashioned Love                      OK 4993, JRS AA-114

CLARENCE WILLIAMS' BLUE FIVE : Tom Morris-c/John Mayfield-tb/Sidney Bechet-cl-ss/
   Clarence Williams-p/Buddy Christian-bj. New York, c. November 14, 1923.

   72059-B  House Rent Blues (The Stomp)           OK 8171
   72060-B  Mean Blues                             OK 40006, JRS AA-114, JSo AA-603

Piano solos.                               New York, July 28, 1924.

   72706-A  My Own Blues                           OK 40172
   72707-A  Gravier Street Blues                   -

CLARENCE WILLIAMS' BLUE FIVE : Louis Armstrong-c/Charlie Irvis-tb/Sidney Bechet-cl-
   ss/Clarence Williams-p/Buddy Christian-bj.
                                           New York, October 17, 1924.

   72914-B  Texas Moaner Blues                     OK 8171, HJCA HC-18, JRS AA-113

   Aaron Thompson-tb replaces Irvis; Buster Bailey-ss replaces Bechet; Eva Taylor-v.
                                           New York, November 6, 1924.

   72958-B  Of All The Wrongs You Done To Me - vET  OK 8181, HJCA HC-28, AF A-005,
                                                    JRS AA-119
   72959-B  Everybody Loves My Baby (But My Baby   As above
            Don't Love Nobody But Me) - vET

Vocal, acc. by Clarence Todd-u (and v where shown).
                                           New York, c. December, 1924.

            Temptation Blues                       OK 8204
            Just A Cotton Picker's Blues - vCT     -

CLARENCE WILLIAMS' BLUE FIVE : Louis Armstrong-c/Charlie Irvis-tb/Sidney Bechet-ss-
   sarrusophone*/Clarence Williams-p/Buddy Christian-bj/Eva Taylor-v.
                                           New York, December 17, 1924.

   73026-B  *Mandy, Make Up Your Mind - vET        OK 40260, Par E-5670, Col 35957,
                                                    DO-2727, BRS 1003, JCl 502,
                                                    JSo AA-505
   73027-B  I'm A Little Blackbird Looking For A   As above
            Bluebird - vET

                                           New York, January 8, 1925.

   73083-A  Cake-Walking Babies From Home - vET    OK 40321,HJCA HC-5,HRS 6,AF A-040
   73084-B  Pickin' On Your Baby - vET             OK 40330
   NOTE:- OKeh 40330 as EVA TAYLOR.

   Buster Bailey-ss/Don Redman-as added.  New York, March 4, 1925.

   73204-A  Cast Away (w) - vET                    OK 40330
   73205-A  Papa De-Da-Da - vET                    OK 8215, HJCA 604, HRS 29
   NOTE:- OKeh 40330 as EVA TAYLOR.  HRS 29 was never issued.

   Bechet omitted.                         New York, October 6, 1925.

   73686-B  Just Wait 'Til You See My Baby Do The  OK 8272, HJCA HC-32, JRS AA-115
            Charleston - vET
   73687-B  Livin' High Sometimes - vET            -          -          -

   Redman omitted from 73695-B.            New York, October 8, 1925.

   73694-B  Coal Cart Blues - vET                  OK 8245, HJCA HC-18, HRS 6,
                                                    JRS AA-113
   73695-B  Santa Claus Blues - vEP                OK 8245

CLARENCE WILLIAMS' TRIO : Louis Armstrong-c/Clarence Williams-p/Buddy Christian-bj/
   Eva Taylor-v.                           New York, October 16, 1925.

   73721-A  Santa Claus Blues - vEW-CW-CT          OK 8254

CLARENCE WILLIAMS' BLU  FIVE : Louis Armstrong-c/Charlie Irvis-tb/Don Redman-cl-as/
  Coleman Hawkins-ts/Clarence Williams-p/Buddy Christian-bj/Eva Taylor-bj.
                                        New York, October 26, 1925.

73738-A  Squeeze Me - vET                    OK 8254
73739-B  You Can't Shush Katie (The Gabbiest OK 8342
         Girl In Town) - vET
NOTE:- OKeh 8342 as EVA TAYLOR.

    ──── Thomas-c/Buster Bailey-cl/as/Clarence Williams-p/Buddy Christian-bj/Eva
  Taylor-v.                             New York, December 15, 1925.

73837-B  Shake That Thing - vET              OK 8267
73838-B  Get It Fixed - vET                    -

CLARENCE WILLIAMS  STOMPERS : Joe Smith-c/Charlie Irvis-tb/Don Redman-ss-as/Coleman
  Hawkins-cl-ts-bar/Clarence Williams-p/Leroy Harris (or possibly Buddy Christian)-
  bj/Cyrus St. Clair-bb.                New York, January 4, 1926.

73893-B  Spanish Shawl                       OK 40541, Od 03383
73894-B  Dinah                                  - LAR A-4337 -  Beka A-73894

CLARENCE WILLIAMS' BLUE FIVE : Bubber Miley-c/? Charlie Irvis-tb/Otto Hardwick or
  Don Redman-as/Clarence Williams-p/? Leroy Harris-bj/Cyrus St. Clair-bb/Eva Taylor
  v.                                    New York, c. January 22, 1926.

73957-A  I've Found A New Baby - vET         OK 8286
73958-B  I've Found A New Baby - vET           -
73959-B  Pile Of Logs And Stone (Called Home) - vET  -
NOTE:- Both versions of I'VE FOUND A NEW BABY, entirely different from each other
  in arrangement and tempo, were issued on OKeh 8286, the first (slower) one being
  credited to EVA TAYLOR, the second to CLARENCE WILLIAMS' BLUE FIVE.

CLARENCE WILLIAMS STOMPERS : Bubber Miley-Tom Morris-c/? Joe Nanton-tb/Don Redman-cl
  as-v/Clarence Williams-p/Leroy Harris or Buddy Christian-bj/bb.
                                        New York, April 7, 1926.

74090-B  JacKass Blues                       OK 40598, 16237
74091-B  What's The Matter Now ? - vDR         -
NOTE:- OKeh 16237 (Mexican) as CLARENCIO GUILLERMO Y SUS DIABLOS DEL JAZZ.

CLARENCE WILLIAMS' BLUE SEVEN : Instrumentation and personnel unknown, but probably
  similar to that of the next session.   New York, October 29, 1926.

80197-A  Would Ja ?                          OK rejected
80198-A-B  Senegalese Stomp                    -

  Tommy Ladnier-t/Jimmy Harrison-tb/Buster Bailey-cl-as/Coleman Hawkins-cl-ts/
  Clarence Williams-p/Leroy Harris-bj/Cyrus St. Clair-bb.
                                        New York, December 10, 1926.

74443-A  Would Ja ?                          OK 8443
74444-B  Sengalese Stomp                       -

Vocal duets with Joe Sims, acc. by Louis Metcalf or Addington Major-c/Fats Waller-p.
                                        New York, c. January, 1927.

2799-1  What Do You Know About That ?        Pm 12435
2800-2  Shut Your Mouth                        -

CLARENCE WILLIAMS' JAZZ KINGS : ? Ben Whittet- ? Benny Moten-cl/Clarence Williams-p/
  Leroy Harris-bj/Cyrus St. Clair-bb.    New York, January 25, 1927.

143348-2  Gravier Street Blues               Col 14193-D
143349-2  Candy Lips                           -

CLARENCE WILLIAMS' WASHBOARD FOUR : Ed Allen-c/Benny Moten-cl/Clarence Williams-p-v/
   Floyd Casey-wb.                        New York, January 29, 1927.

80362-C  Nobody But My Baby Is Getting My Love    OK 8440, Par R-3445, R-2531,
                                                   B-71120,PZ-11147,Od A-2339,028628
80363-B  Candy Lips - vCW                         OK 8440  Par R-3445, R-2531,
                                                   PZ-11147, Od 028628
   NOTE:- All Parlophones attributed to LOUIS ARMSTRONG'S ORIGINAL WASHBOARD BEATERS,
   with the "scat chorus" correctly attributed to Clarence Williams.

CLARENCE WILLIAMS AND HIS WASHBOARD BAND : As above, but Carmelo Jari (usually spelt
   Jejo)-cl-as replacing the cl; Clarence Lee-v.
                                          New York, March 8, 1927.

E-4728; E-21786  Cushion Foot Stomp - vCL    Br 7000, Voc 1088, Or 1012
E-4729; E-21787  Cushion Foot Stomp - vCL      -     Voc V-1034
E-4726; E-21788  P. D. Q. Blues - vCL          -     Voc 1088, Or 1012
E-4727; E-21789  P. D. Q. Blues - vCL          -     Voc V-1034

CLARENCE WILLIAMS' WASHBOARD FIVE : Probably as for the next session below.
                                          New York, March 31, 1927.

80688-A-B  Cushion Foot Stomp - vCW              OK rejected
80689-A-B-C  Take Your Black Bottom Outside - vCW   -

   Ed Allen-c/Buster Bailey-cl/Clarence Williams-p-v/Cyrus St. Clair-bb/Floyd Casey-
   wb.                                    New York, April 13, 1927.

80688-E  Cushion Foot Stomp - vCW                OK 8462, Par R-3383, R-2305,
                                                 HJCA HC-125, WS 106
80689-F  Take Your Black Bottom Outside (Yale    OK 8462, Par R-3381*, Od 07626,
         Rhythm*) - vCW                          HJCA HC-125, WS 106
   NOTE:- All Parlophones as ORIGINAL WASHBOARD BEATERS; Odeon 07626 as JAZZBAND
   ORIGINALE AMERICANO.

CLARENCE WILLIAMS' BLUE FIVE : Ed Allen-c/Charlie Irvis-tb/Ben Whittet-cl-as/Arville
   Harris-cl-as or ts/Clarence Williams-p/Leroy Harris-bj/Cyrus St. Clair-bb/Floyd
   Casey-d.                               New York, April 14, 1927.

80728-B  Black Snake Blues                       OK 8465
80729-B  Old Folks Shuffle                        -

CLARENCE WILLIAMS' BLUE FIVE ORCHESTRA : As last above, omitting Whittet and St.
   Clair; Katherine Henderson-v.          New York, April 27, 1927.

E-4861; E-23235  Baltimore - vKH           Br 3664, 7017, 3703, Voc 1130
E-4862; E-23236  Baltimore - vKH             -       -     -        -
E-4857; E-23237  Take Your Black Bottom Dance Outside-vKH   -

CLARENCE WILLIAMS AND HIS BOTTOMLAND ORCHESTRA : Henry Allen-? Ed Anderson-t/Charlie
   Irvis-tb/? Albert Socarras and another-as/Clarence Williams-p/Floyd Casey-d/Evelyn
   Preer (Peer)-v.                        New York, June 7, 1927.

E-6055; E-23500  Slow River - vEP          Br 3580, 3667, Voc 15577
E-6056; E-23501  Slow River                Br A-457
E-6057; E-23502  Zulu Wail
E-6058; E-23503  Zulu Wail - vEP           Br 3580, 3667, Voc 15577
   NOTE:- Vocalion 15577 as THE AVALONIANS. Despite the labels of Brunswick A-457,
   no vocal refrain is to be heard on either side !

CLARENCE WILLIAMS' ORCHESTRA : Ed Allen-c/Charlie Irvis-tb/? Arville Harris-cl-as/?
   Albert Socarras-cl-ss-f/Clarence Williams-p/Cyrus St. Clair-bb.
                                          New York, July, 1927.

2837-2  Shooting The Pistol               Pm 12517, Bwy 5023
2838-2-3  Bottomland                        -       -
   NOTE:- Broadway 5023 as CHARLEY HUNTER'S ORCHESTRA. It is not known which take
   was used for this.

CLARENCE WILLIAMS' JAZZ KINGS : Ed Allen-c/Charlie Irvis-tb/Albert Socarras-cl-ss-as
/Clarence Williams-p/Leroy Harris-bj/Cyrus St. Clair-bj.
                                    New York, August 18, 1927.

144546-1  I'm Goin' Back To Bottomland          Col 14244-D
144547-2  You'll Long For Me (When The Cold Winds Blow)-

Vocal, acc. by own p.                       New York, August 19, 1927.

144548-2  When I March In April With May        Col 14241-D
144549-2  Shootin' The Pistol                        -

CLARENCE WILLIAMS' BLUE SEVEN : Louis Metcalf-c/Charlie Irvis-tb/Buster Bailey- ?
Arville Harris-cl-as/Clarence Williams-p/Leroy Harris-bj/Cyrus St. Clair-bb.
                                    New York, September 23, 1927.

81472-A  Baby, Won't You Please Come Home ?     OK 8510, 16263
81473-A  Close Fit Blues                            -       -
NOTE:- OKeh 16263 (Mexican) as CLARENCIO GUILLERMO Y SUS DIABLOS DEL JAZZ (MEXICAN
ORCHESTRA) (!)  The titles on this are given in Spanish.

CLARENCE WILLIAMS' ORCHESTRA : Ed Allen-c/Ed Cuffee-tb/Buster Bailey-cl-as/Coleman
Hawkins-ts/Clarence Williams-p/Cyrus St. Clair-bb.
                                    New York, c. October, 1927.

2887-2  Shake Em Up (sic)                        Pm 12587
2888-2  Jingles                                      -

CLARENCE WILLIAMS' WASHBOARD FOUR : Ed Allen-c/Buster Bailey-cl-as/Clarence Williams
p/Floyd Casey-wb.                   New York, November 25, 1927.

81864-B  Yama Yama Blues                         OK 8525
81865-C  (Norfolk) Church Street Sobbin' Blues       -

CLARENCE WILLIAMS' JAZZ KINGS : Ed Allen-c/Ed Cuffee-tb/Buster Bailey-cl-as/Coleman
Hawkins-cl-ts/Clarence Williams-p/Leroy Harris-bj/Cyrus St. Clair-bb.
                                    New York, January 12, 1928.

145521-1  Dreaming The Hours Away                Col 14287-D
145522-2-3  Close Fit Blues                          -

Hawkins omitted; Clarence Williams-v.  New York, April 10, 1928.

145992-1  Sweet Emmalina - vCW                   Col 14314-D
145993-1  Any Time - vCW                             -

CLARENCE WILLIAMS' WASHBOARD FIVE : Ed Allen-c/Buster Bailey-cl/Clarence Williams-p/
Cyrus St. Clair-bb/Floyd Casey-wb.     New York, April 18, 1928.

400620-B-C  Sweet Emmalina                       OK 8572, 16310, Creole 17,
                                                 HJCA HC-106
400621-B  Log Cabin Blues                        As above
NOTE:- OKeh 16310 (Mexican) as CLARENCIO GUILLERMO Y SUS DIABLOS DEL JAZZ.

Ed Allen-King Oliver-c/Arville Harris-cl/Clarence Williams-p/Floyd Casey-wb.
                                    New York, May 23, 1928.

400702-B  Shake It Down                          OK 8584
400703-A  Red River Blues                            -

CLARENCE WILLIAMS' JAZZ KINGS : Ed Allen-King Oliver-c/? Ed Cuffee-tb/? Albert
Socarras-cl-as/Clarence Williams-p/Cyrus St. Clair-bb.
                                    New York, May 29, 1928.

146365-1  Red River Blues                        Col 14326-D
146366-3  I Need You                                 -

CLARENCE WILLIAMS' ORCH. (sic) : Clarence Williams-a dir. Ed Allen-King Oliver-c/Ed
   Cuffee-tb/cl-as/Arville Harris-cl-as-ts/Leroy Harris-bj/Cyrus St. Clair-bb/Floyd
   Casey-d.                                  New York, June 23, 1928.

400818-A  Lazy Mama                                OK 8592
400819-A  Mountain City Blues                        -

Piano solos.                              New York, July 2, 1928.

400844-C  Organ Grinder Blues                        OK 8604
400845-C  Wildflower Rag                             -

Vocal, acc. by James P. Johnson-p.        New York, July 20, 1928.

146761-3  My Woman Done Me Wrong (As Far As I Am    Col 14341-D
             Concerned)
146762-3  Farm Hand Papa                             -

CLARENCE WILLIAMS' JAZZ KINGS : As for June 23, 1928 above, without Casey; the cl-as
   on both may be Albert Socarras; Clarence Williams-p-v.
                                          New York, August 1, 1928.

146825-3  The Keyboard Express                       Col 14348-D
146826-3  Walk That Broad - vCW                      -

CLARENCE WILLIAMS AND HIS ORCHESTRA : As for last above, but with probably Arville
   Harris-cl/Ben Waters-cl-ts.            Long Island City, c. August, 1928.

  151     Long, Deep And Wide                        QRS R-7004, Bwy 1347, Pm 12884,
                                                     Creole 26
  152-A   Speakeasy                                  As above
  153     Squeeze Me (The Boy In A Boat*)            QRS R-7005, Bwy 1348, Pm 12885,
                                                     14008, JC L-32, XX 12*
  154-A New Down Home Blues (New Down Home Rag*) As above (Pm 14008*, XX 12*)
NOTE:- Creole 26 as KING OLIVER WITH CLARENCE WILLIAMS ORCH.; XX 12 as COMRADE
PAJANDRASAYARTHI CHUNDERNAGORE VYSHINSKY RAM SCINAVINEGAR AND HIS RED INDIANS.

CLARENCE WILLIAMS' ORCHESTRA : Ed Allen-? Ed Anderson-c/Ed Cuffee-tb/Albert Socarras
   ? Russell Procope-cl-as/Arville Harris-cl-ts/Clarence Williams-p/Leroy Harris-bj/
   Cyrus St. Clair-bb, with Floyd Casey-d on 401132-B only.
                                          New York, September 20, 1928.

401131-B  Organ Grinder Blues                        OK 8617
401132-B  I'm Busy And You Can't Come In             -

CLARENCE WILLIAMS' WASHBOARD FIVE : Ed Allen-c/Arville Harris-cl-as/Claude Hopkins-p
   /Floyd Casey-wb/Clarence Williams-v and possibly 2nd p in last chorus each side.
                                          New York, September 26, 1928.

401152-A  Walk That Broad - vCW                      OK 8629, Voc 03350, Jazz Unltd. 4
401153-A  Have You Ever Felt That Way ? - vCW        -
NOTE:- Vocalion 03350 as CLARENCE WILLIAMS AND HIS ORCHESTRA (matrix 19936-1).

CLARENCE WILLIAMS AND HIS ORCHESTRA : Ed Allen-King Oliver-c/Ed Cuffee-tb/Arville
   Harris-cl-as/Ben Waters-cl-ts/Clarence Williams-p-v/Leroy Harris-bj/Cyrus St.Clair
   bb.                                    Long Island City, November, 1928.

  267     Wildflower Rag (Wildflower*)               QRS R-7033, Pm 12839*
  267-A   Wildflower Rag                              -     MF 105, JC L-9, AF A-052
  268     Midnight Stomp                             -       -      -       -
  268-A   Midnight Stomp                             Pm 12839
  269-A   I'm Through - vCW                          QRS R-7040, Pm 14024, JC L-69

Buster Bailey-cl added; Leroy Harris omitted.
                                          Long Island City, November, 1928.

  270     Bozo                                       QRS R-7034, Creole 27, Tem R-8,
                                                     AF A-027
  271     Bimbo                                      As above
  272-A   Longshoreman's Blues                       QRS R-7040, Pm 14024, JC L-69

CLARENCE WILLIAMS AND HIS NOVELTY FOUR : King Oliver -c/Clarence Williams-p-cel-v/
   Eddie Lang-g-(and vn on 401391-A)/? Justin Ring-percussion.
                                     New York, November 23, 1928.

401390-B  In The Bottle Blues              OK 8645, Bm 1102, VJR 25,AF A-054
401391-A  What You Want Me To Do ? - vCW        -          -        -

CLARENCE WILLIAMS' JAZZ KINGS : Probably including :- Ed Allen-c/Albert Socarras-cl-
   as-f/Arville Harris-cl-as-ts/Clarence Williams-p/Leroy Harris-bj/Cyrus St. Clair-
   bb.                               New York, December 8, 1928.

147399-1-2-3  Do It, Baby                  Col rejected
147400-1-2-3  My Kitchen Man                    -

CLARENCE WILLIAMS' ORCHESTRA : Clarence Williams dir. ? Ed Anderson-c/Ed Cuffee-tb/
   ? Ben Whittet and another-cl-as/Arville Harris-cl-ts/p/? Charlie Dixon-bj/? June
   Cole-bb/? Kaiser Marshall-d.      New York, December 19, 1928.

401466-C  Watchin' The Clock              OK 8663
401467-B  Freeze Out                          -

CLARENCE WILLIAMS' JAZZ KINGS : Possibly :- Ed Allen-c/Albert Socarras-cl-as-f/
   Arville Harris-cl-ts/Clarence Williams-p-v or James P. Johnson-p/Leroy Harris-bj/
   Cyrus St. Clair-bb, perhaps others.    New York, December 21, 1928.

147399-4-5-6  Do It, Baby                  Col rejected
147400-4-5-6  My Kitchen Man                   -
147726-1-2-3  If You Like Me Like I Like You - vCW    -

CLARENCE WILLIAMS AND HIS ORCHESTRA : Ed Allen-King Oliver-c/Ed Cuffee-tb/Arville
   Harris-cl-as/Ben Waters-cl-ts (and Cm ?)/Clarence Williams-p (apparently absent
   from 308)/Leroy Harris-bj/Cyrus St. Clair-bb.
                                     Long Island City, December, 1928.

   308    Beau-Koo-Jack                  QRS R-7044, Creole 28, JC L-116,
                                         Tem R-9, AF A-015
   309-A  Sister Kate                    As above
   310-A  Pane In The Glass              Pm 12870, Bwy 5067

      Ed Allen-c/Ernest Elliott-cl/Clarence Williams-p/Laura Bryant-v (also q.v.)
                                     Long Island City, January, 1929.

   324-A  Saturday Night Jag - vLB       Pm 12870, Bwy 5067

CLARENCE WILLIAMS' JAZZ KINGS : Ed Allen-c/Albert Socarras-cl-as-f/Arville Harris-cl
   ts/James P. Johnson-p/? Leroy Harris-bj/Clarence Williams-v (and possibly 2nd p on
   147726-4).                        New York, February 5, 1929.

147726-4  If You Like Me Like I Like You - vCW    Col 1735-D
147928-3  Have You Ever Felt That Way ? - vCW        -

Piano solos.                         New York, February 12, 1929.

   48354-1  A Pane In The Glass          Vic V-38524
   48355-2  Too Low                          -

CLARENCE WILLIAMS' WASHBOARD BAND : Ed Allen-c/Arville Harris-cl-as/Clarence
   Williams-p/Floyd Casey-wb.        New York, February 14, 1929.

401611-A  Mississippi Blues (Home Town Toddle)    OK 8672
401612-B  Steamboat Days

CLARENCE WILLIAMS' JAZZ KINGS : Instrumentation and personnel possibly similar to
   that of April 6, 1929.            New York, March 19, 1929.

148104-1-2-3  Breeze (Blow My Baby Back To Me)-vCW Col rejected
148105-1-2-3  Mountain City Blues                 -

The following two titles were issued on the parent Grey Gull label (and Madison and
Radiex 1718, and Grey Gull/Radiex 1724) anonymously.

Ed Allen-c/Ed Cuffee-tb/Arville Harris-cl-as/cl-ts/Clarence Williams-p/Leroy Harris-
bj/Cyrus St. Clair-bb.                          New York, c. March, 1929.

   3394-B  Close Fit Blues                          GG/Mad 1718, Rx 1763, VD 7801,
                                             33024, 77038, JC L-59, AF A-053
   3396-B  Baby, Won't You Please Come Home ?        GG/Rx 1724
   NOTE:- Radiex 1763, Van Dyke 7801 and 33024 as MEMPHIS JAZZERS; Van Dyke 77038 as
NEW ORLEANS PEPSTERS; Jazz Collector L-59 and AFCDJ A-053 as KING OLIVER AND THE
MEMPHIS JAZZERS.  Matrix 3395 is untraced.

CLARENCE WILLIAMS' JAZZ KINGS : Ed Allen-c/Ed Cuffee-tb/Albert Socarras-Russell
Procope-cl-as/Prince Robinson-cl-ts/Clarence Williams-p-v/Leroy Harris-bj/Cyrus
St. Clair-bb.                                   New York, April 6, 1929.

148104-4  Breeze (Blow My Baby Back To Me) - vCW    Col 14422-D
148105-5  Mountain City Blues - vCW                    -

CLARENCE WILLIAMS AND HIS BAND : C/Ed Cuffee-tb/? Albert Socarras and another-cl-as/
? J. C. Johnson-p/bj/bb.                        New York, April 16, 1929.

 51230-1  I'm Not Worryin'                          Vic V-38630
 51231-1  Touch-Down                                   -
 NOTE:- A limited edition, dubbed and with white labels, was made available in 1964.

CLARENCE WILLIAMS' WASHBOARD BAND : Ed Allen-c/cl-as/Arville Harris-cl-ts/Clarence
Williams-p/Floyd Casey-wb.                      New York, May 22, 1929.

 53654-2  In Our Cottage Of Love                    Vic V-38063
 53655-1  Lazy Mama                                    -

CLARENCE WILLIAMS' JAZZ KINGS : Ed Allen-c/tb/as/Arville Harris-cl-ts/Clarence
Williams-p/Cyrus St. Clair-bb/Floyd Casey-d.
                                           New York, May 28, 1929.

148638-2  In Our Cottage Of Love                    Col 14434-D, DF-619
148639-2  Them Things Got Me                           -           -

   Probably different tb.                       New York, June 21, 1929.

148744-2  Whoop It Up - vCW                         Col 14447-D
148745-3  I'm Not Worrying - vCW                       -

CLARENCE WILLIAMS' WASHBOARD BAND : Ed Allen-c/cl-as/Clarence Williams-p/Floyd Casey
wb.                                             New York, July 2, 1929.

404289-A  High Society                              OK 8706
402489-C  High Society (High Society Rag*)             -     Col DB-3513, VJR 25*
402490-A  Whoop It Up                                  -     Par R-2243, 22875
 NOTE:- Parlophone 22875 as JERSEY LIGHTNING by LUIS RUSSELL AND HIS ORCHESTRA (!);
VJR 25 as CLARENCE WILLIAMS' ORCHESTRA.

CLARENCE WILLIAMS AND HIS BLUE MOANERS : George Temple or Kenneth Roane-t/David
"Jelly" James-tb/Felix Gregory or Perry Smith-cl/Clarence Williams or Hank Duncan-
p/Ollie Blackwell or Andy Pendleton-bj/Ralph Bedell-d-wb/Eva Taylor-v.
                                           New York, August 7, 1929.

19338; N-1063  Moanin' Low - vET                    Ed rejected
19339; N-1064  Come On Home - vET                      -

CLARENCE WILLIAMS AND HIS JAZZ KINGS : Ed Allen-Ed Anderson-c/Geechie Fields-tb/?
Russell Procope-cl-as/? Arville Harris-cl-ts/Clarence Williams-p/Leroy Harris-bj/
Cyrus St. Clair-bb.                             New York, August 26, 1929.

148940-3  A Pane In The Glass                       Col 14460-D
148941-3  Freeze Out                                   -

CLARENCE WILLIAMS AND HIS JAZZ KINGS : Ed Allen-Ed Anderson-c/Geechie Fields-tb/?
Russell Procope-cl-as/Arville Harris-cl-ts/Clarence Williams-p/Leroy Harris-bj/
Cyrus St. Clair-bb.                          New York, September 26, 1929.

149056-3  Nervous Breakdown                    Col 14468-D, OK 41561
149057-1  Railroad Rhythm                          -         OK 8918
   NOTE:- OKeh 8918 (matrix 405106-A) and 41561 (matrix 405185-A) as SHREVEPORT
   SIZZLERS.

CLARENCE WILLIAMS' WASHBOARD BAND : Charlie Gaines-t/Arville Harris-cl/Clarence
Williams-p/Floyd Casey-wb/Margaret Webster-v.
                                             New York, October 9, 1929.

403045-C  You've Got To Give Me Some - vMW       OK 8738
403046-B  I've Got What It Takes - vMW              -        Par R-2147

   Harris db as; James P. Johnson-p-cel added; Clarence Williams-v.
                                             New York, November 19, 1929.

403280-C  You Don't Understand - vCW             OK 8752, Par R-2243
403281-A  (Oh ! Baby) What Makes Me Love You So ?-vCW -   Par R-2147

CLARENCE WILLIAMS AND HIS JAZZ KINGS : Clarence Williams dir. Leonard Davis-another-
t/? Geechie Fields-tb/? Don Redman-cl-as/Arville Harris-cl-ts/James P. Johnson-p/
Leroy Harris-bj/? Richard Fullbright-sb/Eva Taylor-v.
                                             New York, December 3, 1929.

149665-4  Zonky - vET                          Col 14488-D, OK 8918
149666-3  You've Got To Be Modernistic - vET       -        OK 41561
   NOTE:- OKeh 8918 (matrix 405107-A) and 41561 (matrix 405184-A) as SHREVEPORT
   SIZZLERS.

CLARENCE WILLIAMS' ORCHESTRA : Clarence Williams dir. Charlie Gaines-t/? Geechie
Fields-tb/? Russell Procope-cl-as/Arville Harris-cl-ts/James P. Johnson-p/Leroy
Harris-bj/Cyrus St. Clair-bb.          New York, January 15, 1930.

403630-B  Left All Alone With The Blues          OK 8763, Col DB-3513
403631-A  I've Found A New Baby                     -        Par R-2225, Od 82347

Piano duets and cross-talk patter with James P. Johnson.
                                             New York, January 31, 1930.

149951-1  How Could I Be Blue ?                  Col 14502-D
149952-2  I've Found A New Baby                     -

CLARENCE WILLIAMS' WASHBOARD BAND : Charlie Gaines or Henry Allen-t/Prince Robinson-
cl-ts/Clarence Williams-p/Floyd Casey-wb.
                                             New York, April 23, 1930.

403972-A  Whip Me With Plenty Of Love            OK 8790, Od ONY-36083, Par R-2203
403972-B  Whip Me With Plenty Of Love               -
403973-A  Worn Out Blues                            -
403973-B  Worn Out Blues                            -         -           -

CLARENCE WILLIAMS' NOVELTY BAND : Cecil Scott-cl/Herman Chittison-p/Ikey Robinson-bj
/Clarence Williams-jug-v.              New York, May 22, 1930.

404034-A  He Wouldn't Stop Doin' It - vCW        OK 8798
404035-B  You're Bound To Look Like A Monkey When   -
          You Get Old - vCW

Vocal, acc. by own p.                        New York, June 18, 1930.

404219-B-C  You Rascal You                       OK 8806
404220-A-B  Michigan Water Blues                    -

CLARENCE WILLIAMS' WASHBOARD BAND : Ed Allen-c/Prince Robinson-cl-ts/Clarence
Williams-p/Floyd Casey-wb/Eva Taylor-v. New York, July 20, 1930.

404382-C  Where That Ol' Man River Flows - vET   OK 8821
404383-C  Shout, Sister, Shout ! - vET              -

CLARENCE WILLIAMS AND HIS JAZZ KINGS : Henry Allen (or possibly Charlie Gaines or
   Roy Eldridge)-t/tb/Albert Socarras-cl-as-f/cl-as/Arville Harris-cl-ts/ts/Clarence
   Williams-p/? Leroy Harris-bj/bb.         New York, July 23, 1930.

150659-2  High Society Blues                          Col 14555-D
150660-1  Lazy Levee Loungers                          -

CLARENCE WILLIAMS' JUG BAND : Ed Allen-c/? Charlie Irvis-tb/cl-ts/p/Lonnie Johnson-g
   /Clarence Williams-jug.                  New York, September 9, 1930.

404435-B  Sitting On Top Of The World                OK 8826, Creole 6
404436-B  Kansas City Man Blues                        -            -
   NOTE:- Creole 6 as KING OLIVER WITH CLARENCE WILLIAMS' JUG BAND.

CLARENCE WILLIAMS AND HIS ORCHESTRA : Bill Dillard-t/Ward Pinkett-t-v/Jimmy Archey-
   tb/Fred Skerritt-as-bar/Henry Jones-as/Bingie Madison-cl-ts/Gene Rodgers-p/Goldie
   Lucas-bj-g/Richard Fullbright-bb-sb/Bill Beason-d/Clarence Williams-Eva Taylor-
   Clarence Todd-v.                         New York, October 31, 1930.

10199-1-2  Hot Lovin' - vWP-CW-ET-CT               Ban 32063, Je 6164, Or 2164,
                                                    Per 15403, Ro 1529
10200-1-3  Papa De-Da-Da - vWP-CW-ET-CT            Ban 32021, Dom 4687, Je 6141,
                                                    Or 2141, Per 15387, Ro 1515
10201-2-3  Baby, Won't You Please Come Home ?      As above
            - vCW-ET-CT

CLARENCE WILLIAMS' WASHBOARD BAND : Ed Allen-c/Buster Bailey-cl-as/Prince Robinson-
   cl-ts/Clarence Williams-p/Floyd Casey-wb.
                                            New York, November 11, 1930.

404546-B  Kentucky                                 Par PMC-7049, Swaggie S-1237 (LP)
404547-B  Papa De-Da-Da (A New Orleans Stomp)      OK 8842
404548-B  Loving                                    -

CLARENCE WILLIAMS AND HIS ORCHESTRA : As for October 31, 1930, without Clarence
   Williams and Clarence Todd.              New York, November 24, 1930.

10276-1-3  Shout, Sister, Shout ! - vET           Ban 32063, Je 6164, Or 2164,
                                                    Per 15403, Ro 1529
10277-    Press The Button - vET                  Rejected
10278-    You're Bound To Look Like A Monkey        -
           When You Get Old - vET

CLARENCE WILLIAMS AND HIS JAZZ KINGS : As for October 31, 1930, but the vocalists
   are Fred Skerritt, Bingie Madison and Goldie Lucas as well as Clarence Williams.
                                            New York, February 19, 1931.

404854-A  Shout, Sister, Shout ! - vFS-BM-GL      Har 1368-H, Cl 5381-C, VT 2445-V
404855-A-B  Rockin' Chair - v                     Rejected
404856-A  Papa De-Da-Da - vWP-FS-BM-GL            Col 14666-D
404857-B  Baby, Won't You Please Come Home ?-vCW    -Har 1368-H,Cl 5381-C,VT 2445-V
   NOTE:- All issues except Columbia as MEMPHIS HOT SHOTS.

CLARENCE WILLIAMS' JUG BAND : Albert Nicholas-cl/? Willie "The Lion" Smith-p/Jimmy
   McLin-g/Clarence Williams-jug/wb/Eva Taylor-v.
                                            New York, June 16, 1933.

13473-    High Society                            Rejected
13474-    High Society                             -
13475-    Mississippi Basin - vET                 Voc 03350
13476-    I Like To Go Back In The Evening        Rejected
13477-    I Like To Go Back In The Evening         -
   NOTE:- Eva Taylor's Southernaires, allegedly the same group as the above, made a
   test (TO-1301) of the last title on May 15, 1933, and it has been suggested that
   this date is the correct one for these three numbers, June 16, 1933 being regarded
   as a dubbing date.  As the only issued title was itself a dubbing, in the absence
   of any original test pressings, such a theory should be regarded with some doubt.

CLARENCE WILLIAMS AND HIS ORCHESTRA : Ed Allen-c-v/cl/Clarence Williams-p/Floyd
    Casey-wb-v/bass d or tom-tom.              New York, July 14, 1933.

13544-1  Black-Eyed Susan Brown - vEA-FC          Voc 25009
13545-1  Mama Stayed Out All Night Long - vEA-FC    -
13546-1  High Society                             Voc 25010
13547-1  I Like To Go Back In The Evening (To That  -
         Old Sweetheart Of Mine)

(CLARENCE) WILLIAMS' JUG BAND : Cecil Scott-cl/Clarence Todd-k-v/Herman Chittison-
    Willie "The Lion" Smith-p/Ikey Robinson-bj-g-v/Clarence Williams-jug-v/Willie
    Williams-wb/Eva Taylor-v; sides where Eva Taylor, Clarence Williams and Clarence
    Todd all sing are credited vocally to The Lowland Singers, and Parlophone A-3805
    as CLARENCE WILLIAMS' RHYTHM RASCALS.   New York, August 7, 1933.

152463-2  Shim Sham Shimmy Dance - vCW-ET-CT      Col 2806-D, DO-1001, J-1713,
                                                  Par R-1680
152464-2  Organ Grinder Blues - vCW-ET-CT         Col 2863-D, Par A-3805
152465-2  Chizzlin' Sam - vET-CT                  Col 2829-D, Par R-1680, A-3806,
                                                  Bm 1025
152466-2  High Society - vET                      Col 2806-D
152466-3  High Society - vET                         -    DO-1001, J-1713, Bm 1025
152467-2  Mister, Will You Serenade ? - vET-CT    OK 41565
152468-2  You Ain't Too Old - vCT                 Col 2863-D, Par A-3805

CLARENCE WILLIAMS AND HIS ORCHESTRA : Ed Allen-c-v/Cecil Scott-cl/Clarence Williams-
    p-v/Floyd Casey-wb.                        New York, August 18, 1933.

13835-1  Beer Garden Blues              Voc/OK 2541, Br X-2541, Col 37680
13835-2  Beer Garden Blues              Col 30057                    -
13836-1  The Right Key But The Wrong Keyhole-vEA  Voc 2563
13837-2  Dispossessin' Me               Voc 2584
13838-1  Breeze (Blow My Baby Back To Me) - vCW   Voc/OK 2541, Br X-2541,
                                                  Col 30057, 37680
NOTE:- Although there is no vocal refrain on Vocalion 2584, some copies credit one
to Clarence Williams. Some copies of Vocalion 2541 couple 13838-1 with a title by
Bert Block.

G added*.                                  New York, September 1, 1933.

13935-2  She's Just Got A Little Bit Left - vEA   Voc 2563
13936-1  After Tonight - vCW                      Voc 2736
13937-1  *Bimbo                                   Voc 2778
13938-1  Chocolate Avenue                         Voc 2584

Ikey Robinson-bj-g/Cyrus St. Clair-bb added; Casey omitted.  The label of 14293-1
reads "Jibe by Ed Allen."            New York, November 10, 1933.

14291-2  Harlem Rhythm Dance                      Voc 2602
14292-1  'Way Down Home                           Voc 2778
14293-1  For Sale (Hannah Johnson's Big Jack Ass) Voc 2602

Ed Allen-c-v/Cecil Scott-cl-ts/Clarence Williams-James P. Johnson-p as noted/Roy
Smeck-g- or stg**/Cyrus St. Clair-bb/Floyd Casey-wb/Chick Bullock-v.
                                         New York, December 6, 1933.

14422-1  Swaller-Tail Coat - pCW/vCB              Voc 2616, EBW W-121, Br A-86051
14423-2  Looka-There, Ain't She Pretty - pJPJ/vCB   -                         -
14424-1**St. Louis Blues - pCW-JPJ                Voc 2676, Br A-86050
14425-1-2 How Can I Get It ? - pJPJ/vEA          Voc 2630
NOTE:- Vocalion 2630 credits the vocal refrain to Henry Allen.

                                         New York, January 10, 1934.

14571-1**On The Sunny Side Of The Street-2p/vCB  Voc 2630
14571-2**On The Sunny Side Of The Street-pCW-JPJ Rejected
14572-1  Won't You Come Over And Say "Hello"      Voc 2718
         - pJPJ/vCB-? CW
14573-2  Old Street Sweeper - pCW/vCB             Voc 2736
14574-2  I'm Gonna Wash My Sins Away - p-vCW      Voc 2759

CLARENCE WILLIAMS AND HIS ORCHESTRA : Ed Allen-c/Cecil Scott-cl/James P. Johnson-p/
  Roy Smeck-g-stg/Cyrus St. Clair-bb/Floyd Casey-wb/Dick Robertson-Clarence Williams
  v.                                    New York, January 17, 1934.

14611-1  Jimmy Had A Nickel - vDR            Voc 2629
14612-1  He's A Colonel From Kentucky - vDR      -       EBW W-121
14630-1  Pretty Baby, Is It Yes Or No ? - vCW  Voc 2718
14631-1  Mister, Will You Serenade ? - vCW     Voc 2676, Br A-86050

  Tb added; Casey omitted.  Clarence Williams may possibly play in the ensemble (not
  the solo) on 14806-1, which has no vocal, despite the label.
                                       New York, February 7, 1934.

14804-1  I Got Horses And Got Numbers On My Mind  Voc 2654
           - vCW
14805-1  New Orleans Hop Scop Blues - vCW         -
14806-1  Let's Have A Showdown                    Voc 2759

  Charlie Gaines-t-v/Ed Allen-c/Cecil Scott-cl-ts/Louis Jordan-as-? ts-v/as*/James P.
  Johnson-p/Cyrus St. Clair-bb/Floyd Casey-wb/Clarence Williams-Chick Bullock-v.
                                       New York, March 23, 1934.

14989-1  I Can't Dance, I Got Ants In My Pants   Voc 2689
           - vCG-LJ-CW
14990-1  Christmas Night In Harlem - vCB          -
14991-1  *Ill Wind (You're Blowing Me No Good)-vCB Voc 2674, EBW W-142
14992-1  *As Long As I Live - vCB                 -          -

                                       New York, March 30, 1934.

14989-?  I Can't Dance, I Got Ants In My Pants   Voc 2689 ?
           - vCG-LJ-CW

  C/Cecil Scott-cl-ts/as/? Lester Young-ts or unknown 2nd as/? Don Frye-p/Cyrus St.
  Clair-bb/? Floyd Casey-d/Little Buddy Farrior-v.
                                       New York, June 28, 1934.

15368-2  Tell The Truth - vLBF               Voc 2889, Br A-86004, A-86052
15369-1  Sashay, Oh Boy ! - vLBF            Voc 2838

CLARENCE WILLIAMS AND WASHBOARD BAND : Ed Allen-c/Cecil Scott-cl/Clarence Williams-p
  v/Cyrus St. Clair-bb/Floyd Casey-wb.    New York, June 28, 1934.

15370-1  I Can't Beat You Doin' What You're      Voc 2788
           Doin' Me - vCW
15371-1  Trouble                                  -

CLARENCE WILLIAMS AND HIS ORCHESTRA : Ed Allen-c/Cecil Scott-cl/James P. Johnson-p/
  Floyd Casey-wb/Eva Taylor-Clarence Williams-? Clarence Todd-v.
                                       New York, July 6, 1934.

15398-1  Jerry The Junker - vCW&ch           Voc 2854
15399-1  Organ Grinder Blues - vCW-ET-? CT   Voc 2871, Br A-86009
15400-1  I'm Getting My Bonus In Love - vCW  Voc 2889, Br A-86004, A-86052
15401-1-2  Chizzlin' Sam - vCW-ET&ch         Voc 2854
NOTE:- Clarence Williams introduces the members of the band on 15399-1, but names
the cornetist as "Red" Allen.

  Ed Allen-c-v/Cecil Scott-cl/? Clarence Williams-p, certainly v/2nd pon 15601-1/?
  Roy Smeck-g/Richard Fullbright-sb/Floyd Casey-d.  Vocalion 2838 names Clarence
  Williams as vocalist in error.         New York, August 14, 1934.

15601-1  Big Fat Mama - vEA                  Voc 2838
15602-2  Ain't Gonna Give You None Of My Jelly  Voc 2805
           Roll - vCW
NOTE:- Although a test pressing of 15602 is marked -3, the only difference between
its performance and that of the regularly-issued -2 is of timing.  It is almost
certainly a dubbing of -2, recorded at a marginally different speed.

CLARENCE WILLIAMS AND HIS ORCHESTRA (all issues from matrices 15722-2 and 15723-1 as
   EVA TAYLOR AND HER BOY FRIENDS, although Miss Taylor does not sing on either) : Ed
   Allen-c/? Dicky Wells-tb/Cecil Scott-cl/Willie "The Lion" Smith-p/Roy Smeck-g/
   Richard Fullbright-sb/Floyd Casey-d/Clarence Williams-v.
                                            New York, August 22, 1934.

| | | |
|---|---|---|
| 15721-1-2 | I Saw Stars - vCW | Voc 2899 |
| 15722-2 | Crazy Blues - vCW | Ban 33261, Mt M-13228, Or 3041, |
| | | Per 16032, Ro 2415 |
| 15723-1 | The Stuff Is Here And It's Mellow | As above |
| 15724-1-2 | Rhapsody In Love - vCW | Voc 2899 |

   Ed Allen-c/? Louis Jordan and another-as/Cecil Scott-cl-ts/bj/Richard Fullbright-
   sb/Floyd Casey-d/Chick Bullock-v.      New York, September 11, 1934.

| | | |
|---|---|---|
| 15845-1 | 'Tain't Nobody's Biz-ness If I Do - vCB | Voc 2871, Br A-86009 |
| 15846-1 | I Can't Think Of Anything But You - vCB | Voc 2958 |
| 15847-2 | Sugar Blues - vCB | Voc 2805 |
| 15848-2 | Jungle Crawl | Voc 2909 |

   Ed Allen-c/Cecil Scott-cl-ts/Clarence Williams-p-v/? Roy Smeck-g/? Cyrus St. Clair
   bb.                                    New York, February 9, 1935.

| | | |
|---|---|---|
| 16839-1 | I Can See You All Over The Place - vCW | Voc 2958 |
| 16840-1 | Savin' Up For Baby - vCW | Voc 2909 |

   Ed Allen-c/t/? Wilbur de Paris-tb except on the fourth title/Cecil Scott-cl-ts/
   Clarence Williams-p-v/? Roy Smeck-g/bb/? Bruce Johnson-wb.
                                            New York, March 7, 1935.

| | | |
|---|---|---|
| 16985-1 | Milk Cow Blues | Voc 2927 |
| 16986-1 | Black Gal | Voc 2938 |
| 16987-2 | A Foolish Little Girl Like You - vCW | – |
| 16988-1 | There's Gonna Be The Devil To Pay - vCW | Voc 2927 |

   Ed Allen-c/Cecil Scott-cl-ts/Clarence Williams-p/? Jimmy McLin-g/Cyrus St. Clair-
   bb/? Willie Williams-wb.               New York, May 14, 1935.

| | | |
|---|---|---|
| 17601-2 | This Is My Sunday Off | Voc 3195 |
| 17602-1 | Yama Yama Blues | Voc 2991 |
| 17603-1 | Let Every Day Be Mother's Day | Voc 3195 |
| 17604-2 | Lady Luck Blues | Voc 2991 |

NOTE:- Some copies of 17603-1 are labeled LET EVERY DAY BE SWEETHEART'S DAY.

CLARENCE WILLIAMS AND HIS WASHBOARD BAND : Ed Allen-c/Buster Bailey-cl/Prince Robin-
   son-ts/Clarence Williams-p/Cyrus St. Clair-bb/Floyd Casey-wb/Eva Taylor-William
   Cooley-v.                              New York, April 8, 1937.

| | | |
|---|---|---|
| 06849-1 | Cryin' Mood - vWC | BB B-6932 |
| 06850-1 | Top Of The Town - vET | BB B-6918 |
| 06851-1 | Turn Off The Moon - vWC | BB B-6919,RZ MR-2539,Twin FT-8374 |
| 06852-1 | More Than That - vET | BB B-6918 |
| 06853-1 | Jammin' - vWC | BB B-6919, Twin FT-8374 |
| 06854-1 | Wanted - vET | BB B-6932, RZ MR-2539 |

CLARENCE WILLIAMS' SWING BAND : Ed Allen-c/Buster Bailey-Russell Procope-cl-as/Cecil
   Scott-cl-ts/Clarence Williams-p/sb/? Floyd Casey-d/William Cooley-v.
                                            New York, c. April 29, 1937.

| | | | | |
|---|---|---|---|---|
| 07862-1 | Every Time I Feel De Spirit - vWC | Lang-Worth 268, JP LP-10 | | |
| | Old Time Religion - vWC | – | – | |
| | Lord Deliver Daniel - vWC | – | – | |
| | Sweet Kisses | – VJM VLP-5 | – | IAJRC 1 |
| 07863-1 | Go Down, Moses - vWC | Lang-Worth 270 | – | |
| | Do You Call That Religion ? - vWC | – | – | |
| | Jericho - vWC | – | – | |
| | Lazy Swing | – VJM VLP-5 | – | |

CLARENCE WILLIAMS' SWING BAND : Ed Allen-c/Buster Bailey-Russell Procope-cl-as/Cecil
Scott-cl-ts/? Clarence Williams-p-v-speech/Cyrus St. Clair-sb/? Floyd Casey-d/
William Cooley-v; or CLARENCE WILLIAMS' WASHBOARD FIVE (Allen-Scott-Williams-St.
Clair-Casey-Cooley; St. Clair-bb)*. New York, October, 1937.

| | | | | |
|---|---|---|---|---|
| 014994-1 | Roll, Jordan, Roll - vWC | Lang-Worth 399, | JP LP-10 | |
| | Heaven, Heaven - vWC | - | - | |
| | *There Is Love - vWC | - | VJM VEP-22 | - |
| 014995-1 | It's Me, O Lord - vCW-WC | Lang-Worth 400 | - | VJM VLP-5 |
| | Get On Board, Li'l Chillun - vWC | - | - | |
| 014996-1 | Step On It | Lang-Worth 438 | - | VJM VLP-5 |
| | Swing Low, Sweet Chariot - vWC | - | - | |

CLARENCE WILLIAMS' TRIO : Don Baker-elo/Connie Berry-p/Gozy Cole-d/Clarence Williams
Babe Matthews-v; no elo**                New York, May 24, 1938.

| | | |
|---|---|---|
| 22976-1-2 | Rattling Rhythm | Rejected |
| 22977-1-2 | Won'tcha ? - vBM | - |
| 22978-1 | Bluer Than Blue - vBM | Voc 4157, Br A-81761 |
| 22979-1 | I'm Falling For You | - - |
| 22980-1 | Liza (All The Clouds'll Roll Away) | Voc 4169 |
| 22981-1-2 | **Hop On Me Blues - vCW | Rejected |
| 22982-1-2 | **Going Home Blues - vCW | - |

CLARENCE WILLIAMS' BLUE FIVE : Clarence Williams-p-v/James P. Johnson-p/Grace Harper
Nathan Barlow-g/Wellman Braud-sb/Eva Taylor-v.
New York, October 22, 1941.

| | | |
|---|---|---|
| 071198-2 | Uncle Sammy, Here I Am - vET-CW | BB B-11368 |
| 071199-1 | Thriller Blues - vET | - |

NOTE:- AF A-037 uses the name CLARENCE WILLIAMS' BLUE FIVE for the Red Onion Jazz
Babies, q.v.

## COOTIE WILLIAMS

COOTIE WILLIAMS AND HIS RUG CUTTERS : Cootie Williams-t/Joe Nanton-tb/Johnny Hodges-
ss-as/Harry Carney-bar/Duke Ellington-p/Hayes Alvis-sb/Sonny Greer-d.
New York, March 8, 1937.

| | | |
|---|---|---|
| M-185-1 | I Can't Believe That You're In Love With Me | Vri 555, Voc 3818, Swing 359 |
| M-186-1 | Downtown Uproar | Vri 527, Voc 3814, BA 236 |
| M-187-1 | Diga Diga Doo | Vri 555, Voc 3818, Par DP-243, PZ-11283, Od D-5041 |
| M-188-2 | Blue Reverie | Vri 527, Voc 3814, Swing 359, BA 236 |
| M-189-1-2 | Tiger Rag | Rejected |

Cootie Williams-t/Juan Tizol-vtb/Otto Hardwick-as/Barney Bigard-cl-ts/Harry Carney-
bar/Duke Ellington-p/Billy Taylor-sb/Sonny Greer-d/Jerry Kruger-v.
New York, October 26, 1937.

| | | |
|---|---|---|
| M-669-2 | Jubilesta | Voc 3922 |
| M-670-1 | Watchin' - vJK | Voc 3890 |
| M-671-1 | Pigeons And Peppers | Voc 3922 |
| M-672-1 | I Can't Give You Anything But Love | Voc 3890 |

Joe Nanton-tb replaces Tizol; Johnny Hodges-ss-as replaces Hardwick; Fred Guy-g
added.                                   New York, January 19, 1938.

| | | |
|---|---|---|
| M-726-2 | Have A Heart (Lost In Meditation) | Voc/OK 3960 |
| M-729-2 | Echoes Of Harlem | - |

NOTE:- Titles on matrices M-727 and M-728 were issued as JOHNNY HODGES AND HIS
ORCHESTRA, q.v.

COOTIE WILLIAMS AND HIS RUG CUTTERS : Cootie Williams t-v/Joe Nanton-tb/Johnny
     Hodges-ss-as/Barney Bigard-cl-ts/Harry Carney-bar/Duke Ellington-p/Fred Guy-g/
     Billy Taylor-sb/Sonny Greer-d/Jerry Kruger-v.
                                              New York, April 4, 1938.

| M-801-1 | A Lesson In C - vJK | Voc 4086, Par DP-243, PZ-11283, |
| | | Od D-5041 |
| M-802-1 | Swingtime In Honolulu - vJK | Voc 4061 |
| M-803-1 | Carnival In Caroline - vJK | - |
| M-804-1 | Ol' Man River | Voc 4086 |

     Nanton and Guy omitted; Otto Hardwick-as-bsx added; Scat Powell-v.
                                              New York, August 2, 1938.

| M-876-1 | Chasin' Chippies | Voc 4425 |
| M-877-1 | Blue Is The Evening - vSP | Voc 4324 |
| M-878-2 | Sharpie - vSP | - |
| M-879-1 | Swing Pan Alley | Voc 4425 |

                                              New York, December 21, 1938.

| M-954-1 | Delta Mood | Voc 4574, <u>Swing 310</u>, <u>BA 225</u> |
| M-955-1 | The Boys From Harlem | -         -       - |
| M-956-1 | Mobile Blues | Epic LN-3237, Ph P-07075-R (LPs) |
| M-956-2 | Mobile Blues | <u>Voc 4646, BA 247</u> |
| M-957-1 | Gal-Avantin' | -         - |

     Hardwick omitted.                        New York, February 28, 1939.

| M-982-1 | Beautiful Romance | Voc 5411 |
| M-983-1 | Boudoir Benny | Voc 4726 |
| M-984-1 | Ain't The Gravy Good ? - vCW | - |
| M-985-1 | She's Gone - vCW | Voc 5411 |

     Billy Strayhorn-p replaces Ellington*.   New York, June 22, 1939.

| WM-1042-A | Night Song | Voc 4958 |
| WM-1043-A | *Blues A-Poppin' | Voc/OK 5618, Col MZ-275 |
| WM-1044-A | Top And Bottom | OK 6336, BA 253 |
| WM-1045-A | Black Beauty | Voc 4958 |

     Jimmy Blanton-sb replaces Taylor.        New York, February 15, 1940.

| WM-1143-1 | *Black Butterfly | Voc/OK 5618, Col MZ-275 |
| WM-1144-1 | Dry Long So - vCW | Voc/OK 5690 |
| WM-1145-1 | Toasted Pickles | OK 6336, BA 253 |
| WM-1146-A | Give It Up | Voc/OK 5690 |
     NOTE:- Blue Ace 253 as DUKE ELLINGTON'S SEPTET.

COOTIE WILLIAMS AND HIS ORCHESTRA : Cootie Williams-t/Lou McGarity-tb/Les Robinson-as
     /Skippy Martin-bar/Johnny Guarnieri-p/Artie Bernstein-sb/Joe Jones-d.
                                              New York, May 7, 1941.

| 30423-1 | West End Blues | OK 6370, RZ MR-3609, MR-20313, |
| | | Col DS-1407, MC-3408, 291414, |
| | | V-Disc 204 |
| 30424-1 | Ain't Misbehavin' | OK 6224, RZ MR-3596, Col DZ-363, |
| | | MZ-361 |
| 30425-1 | Blues In My Condition | As above, except Col MZ-361 |
| 30426-1 | G-Men | OK 6370, RZ MR-3609, MR-20313, |
| | | Col DS-1407, MC-3408, MZ-361, 291414 |

     Cootie Williams-Milton Fraser-Joe Guy-t/Louis Bacon-t-v/Jonas Walker-Robert Horton-
     Sandy Williams-tb/Charlie Holmes-as/Eddie "Cleanhead" Vinson-as-v/Bob Dorsey-Greely
     Walton-ts/John Williams-bar/Ken Kersey-p/Norman Keenan-sb/George Ballard-d.
                                              Chicago, April 1, 1942.

| C-4205-1 | Sleepy Valley | Rejected |
| C-4206-1 | Marcheta - vLB | - |
| C-4207-1 | When My Baby Left Me - vEV | - |
| C-4208-1 | Fly Right (Epistrophy) | CBS C3L-38 (LP) |

Clarinet solos, acc. by Elaine Elliott-p/Sam Sims-d/Thelma Lee-B. Smith-v.
                                    Memphis, January 31, 1928.

41813-2  Slow Death                              Vic 21269, BB B-6151
41814-2  Roadhouse Stomp                             -            -
41815-1  Far Away Texas Blues                    Vic 21413
41816-2  One Hour Tonight - vTL-BS                    -      V-38607, Creole 7
NOTE:- Victor 21413 as THELMA LEE-B. SMITH (41816-2 only); V-38607 as SMITH AND
LEE; Creole 7 as JOHNNY DODDS.

    Edgar Brown-p replaces Elliott.        Memphis, August 31, 1928.

45466-2  Riverside Stomp                         Vic V-38031
45467-2  Sister Ella                             Vic 23362

DOUGLAS WILLIAMS FOUR : Nathaniel Williams-c/Douglas Williams-cl/Edgar Brown-p/Sam
    Sims-d.                                Memphis, September 4, 1928.

45476-1  Kind Daddy                              Vic 21695
45477-2  Late Hours                                  -

Clarinet solos, acc. by Edgar Brown-p.     Memphis, September 10, 1928.

47005-2  Friendless Blues                        Vic V-38031
47006-1-2  Baby Jane                             Rejected

                                           Memphis, September 18, 1928.

47049-2  Buddy George                            Vic V-38518
47050-2  Neal's Blues                                -

DOUGLAS WILLIAMS AND HIS ORCHESTRA : As for September 4, 1928, plus Melvin Parker-
    g-v.                                   Memphis, September 26, 1929.

55592-1  Memphis Gal                             Vic 23362
55593-2  Clarinet Jiggles                        Vic 23337
55594-2  Undertaker Blues - vMP                  Vic V-38550
55595-2  P-Wee Strut                                 -

                                           Memphis, October 2, 1929.

56327-2  The Beale Street Sheik                  Vic 23264
56328-2  Leaving Blues - vMP                     Vic 23387
56329-2  Thrill Me - vMP                         Vic 23303, HMV AE-3914, R-14692
56330-1  Don't Treat Me Like A Dog - vMP         Vic 23387

    Parker omitted; as added.              Memphis, June 5, 1930.

62585-2  Louisiana Hop                           Vic V-38623
62586-2  Three O'Clock Blues                         -
62587-1  Darktown Jubilee                        Vic 23264
62588-1-2  Russian Blues                         Rejected

## DUKE WILLIAMS AND  HIS ORCHESTRA

Pseudonym on Vocalion 15892 for Don Redman and his Orchestra, q.v.

## ELLIS WILLIAMS

Harmonica solos, acc. by g, with spoons.* ? Greensboro, N. C., October 24, 1929.

149264-1  *Buttermilk Blues                      Col 14482-D
149265-1  Smokey Blues                              -

ProFESSor Stanley Williams dir. Fats Robins-t-o/Reuben Reeves-t/Eddie Atkins-William
  Franklin-tb/Ralph Brown-as-o/Norval Morton-ts-f/Clarence Lee-Bobby Wall-Joe Mc-
  Cutchin-vn/Lawrence W. Dixon-bj-vc/Sudie Reynaud-sb/Jasper Taylor-d.
                                        Chicago, April 3, 1928.

C-1867- ; E-7291  Dixie Stomp                      Voc 15690
C-1868- ; E-7292  Drifting And Dreaming               -

              FESS WILLIAMS AND HIS  ROYAL FLUSH ORCHESTRA

Fess Williams-cl-as-v dir. George Temple-t/David "Jelly" James-tb/Perry Smith-cl-ts-
  v/Henry Duncan-p/Ollie Blackwell-bj/Ralph Bedell-d.
                                        New York, c. October 2, 1925.

  9753    Green River Blues                         Gnt 3182

                                        New York, c. December 3, 1925.

  9873-A-B  Caroline - vFW-PS                        Gnt 3210
  9874-A  Some Other Time - vFW                         -

                                        New York, February 19, 1926.

  9983, -A  Nobody's Business                       Rejected
  9984-A  Wimmin - Aah ! - vFW                       Gnt 3259, Gmn 1918
  9985, -A  I'm Just Wild About My Sweet Gal - vFW Rejected
  NOTE:- Guardsman 1918 as NEW JERSEY DANCE ORCHESTRA.

  Unknown girl v.                       New York, c. May 6, 1926.

  74158-B  Caroline - vFW-girl                       OK 8322
  74159-B  Make Me Know It - vFW                        -
  NOTE:- This issue as FESS WILLIAMS AND HIS ROYAL FLUSH SAVOY ORCHESTRA.

                                        New York, May 24, 1926.

142244-1-2  Make Me Know It - vFW                    Har 189-H
142245-2-3  My Mama's In Town                           -

                                        New York, June 8, 1926.

  X-173    It's Breaking My Heart To Keep Away       Gnt 3336, Ch 15120, Chg 135
              From You - vFW
  X-174-A  Ya Gotta Know How To Love - vFW              -      Ch 15118, Chg 134

                                        New York, October 1, 1926.

E-3884/5; E-20398/9  Messin' Around - vFW-PS         Voc 1054, Br 3351*, A-150
E-3886/7; E-20400/1  Heebie Jeebies - vFW               -         -        -
  NOTE:- Brunswick 3351 and A-150 as BUD JACKSON'S SWANEE SERENADERS.

                                        New York, October 27, 1926.

E-4012/3  Atlanta Black Bottom                       Voc rejected
E-4014/5  High Fever                                    -

                                        New York, November 18, 1926.

E-4092    High Fever                                 Voc 1058, 15492
E-4094    Atlanta Black Bottom                          -        -

                                        New York, November 30, 1926.

  36985-1-2-3  What Did Romie-O-Juliet ? (When       Vic rejected
              He Climbed Her Balcony) - vFW             -
  36986-1-2-3  Nobody But My Baby Is Getting My Love
              - vPS

Fess Williams-cl-as-v dir. George Temple-t/Kenneth Roane-t-a/David "Jelly" James-tb/
    Otto Mikell-as/Perry Smith-cl-ts/Henry Duncan-p/Ollie Blackwell-bj/Clinton Walker-
    bb/Ralph Bedell-d.                              New York, February 2, 1927.

E-4503/5  White Ghost Shivers                      Voc 1085
E-4506/8  My Pretty Girl                           -

                                    New York, February 25, 1927.

E-4598/9  Gambler's Blues - vFW                    Voc 1087
E-4601/2  I Wasn't Scared, But I Just Thought      -
            That I Had Better Go - vFW

                                    New York, March 28, 1927.

E-4771/3; E-22361/3  Variety Stomp          Voc 15550, Br 3532, A-427,Or 1011
E-4774/6; E-22364/6  Phantom Blues             -        -        -      -

                                    New York, June 15, 1927.

E-6123/5; E-23633/5  Alligator Crawl         Voc 1117, Br 3589*
E-6126/8; E-23636/8  Ozark Blues                -       -

                                    New York, June 24, 1927.

E-23747   Number Ten                               Br 3596*
E-23750   Razor Edge                               -

    Lockwood Lewis-as replaces Mikell; Felix Gregory-cl-as-ts/Andy Pendleton-bj added;
    Emanuel Casamore-bb replaces Walker.    New York, April 17, 1929.

51234-2  Here 'Tis                                 Vic V-38056
51235-2  A Few Riffs                               Vic V-38064, HMV R-14331
51236-2  Hot Town                                  Vic V-38077, BB B-5783, B-6431

    Gregory omitted.                       New York, April 22, 1929.

51198-1  Friction                                  Vic V-38056, BB B-5783, B-6546,
                                                       HMV JF-18
51199-1  Kentucky Blues                            Vic V-38077
51900-2  Do Shuffle                                Vic V-38064, HMV JF-18, R-14331,
                                                       El EG-1525

    Ralph Brown-Felix Gregory-as replace Lewis.
                                       Camden, N. J., May 15, 1929.

50882-2  Snag Nasty                                Vic V-38128
50883-2  Big Shot                                  -

                                    Camden, N. J., May 16, 1929.

50889-2  Sell It                          Vic V-38062,HMV R-14262,El EG-1527
50890-1  Betsy Brown                         -         -           -

Fess Williams-cl-as-v dir. George Temple-t/John Brown-t-v/David "Jelly" James-tb/
    Ralph Brown-Felix Gregory-as/Perry Smith-cl-ts-v/Henry Duncan-p/Ollie Blackwell or
    Andy Pendleton-bj/Emanuel Casamore-bb/Ralph Bedell-d-v.
                                       Camden, N. J., September 20, 1929.

55928-1  Sweet Savannah Sue - vFW                  Vic V-38065
55929-3  Ain't Misbehavin' - vFW-JB-PS-RB          -
55930-3  Buttons                                   Vic V-38095
55931-2  Musical Campmeeting                       -

    Bobby Holmes-cl-as replaces Gregory or Brown.
                                       New York, December 6, 1929.

57197-1  Goin' To Getcha                           Vic V-38106
57198-1-2  Hot Mama                                Rejected
57199-1-2  Your Smilin' Face                       -
57200-2  Slide, Mr. Jelly                          Vic V-38106

Fess Williams-cl-as-v dir. George Temple-John Brown-t/David "Jelly" James-tb/Bobby
    Holmes-cl-as/Ralph Brown or Felix Gregory-as/Perry Smith-cl-ts/Henry Duncan-p/Andy
    Pendleton or Ollie Blackwell-bj/Emanuel Casamore-bb/Ralph Bedell-d/Frank Marvin-v.
                                    New York, April 18, 1930.

| | | |
|---|---|---|
| 59757-1 | She's Still Dizzy | Vic 23025, HMV B-4839, K-6263 |
| 59758-1 | Hot Mama | Vic 22864, HMV B-4898 |
| 59759-1 | 'Leven-Thirty Saturday Night - vFM | Vic V-38131 |
| 59760-2 | I'm Feelin' Devilish - vFW | - |

Emanuel Clark-t replaces Temple; Walter "Fats" Pichon-p replaces Duncan.
                                    New York, July 10, 1930.

| | | |
|---|---|---|
| 62335-1 | All For Grits And Gravy | Vic 23025, HMV B-4840, K-6263 |
| 62336-1 | Playing My Saxophone - vFW | Vic 24153, HMV B-4944 |
| 62337-2 | You Can't Go Wrong - vFW | -        HMV B-4991 |
| 62338-1-2 | Geechee Dance - vFW | Rejected |

                                    New York, July 23, 1930.

| | | |
|---|---|---|
| 63302-1-2 | Dinah - vFW | Rejected |
| 63303-1-2 | Ida, Sweet As Apple Cider - vFW&ch | Vic 23005 |
| 63304-1-2 | Just To Be With You Tonight - vFW | Rejected |
| 63305-1-2 | Everything's O.K. With Me - vFW | - |

                                    Camden, N. J., July 31, 1930.

| | | |
|---|---|---|
| 63302-4 | Dinah - vFW | Vic 23005 |
| 63304-3-4-5 | Just To Be With You Tonight - vFW | Vic 23003 |
| 63305-3 | Everything's O.K. With Me - vFW | - |

## GEORGE   WILLIAMS

Vocal duets with Bessie Brown, acc. by Fletcher Henderson-p.
                                    New York, August 2, 1923.

| | | |
|---|---|---|
| 81157-3 | Satisfied Blues | Col A-3974 |
| 81158-1 | Double-Crossin' Daddy | - |

                                    New York, October 25, 1923.

| | | |
|---|---|---|
| 81292-1 | You Need Some Lovin' | Col 14017-D |
| 81293-1-2-3-4 | Wish I Had You | Rejected |

                                    New York, November 9, 1923.

| | | |
|---|---|---|
| 81341-1-2-3 | You Can't Do What My Last Man Did | Rejected |
| 81342-3 | If Mama Quits Papa, What Will Papa Do ? | Col 13006-D |

                                    New York, November 10, 1923.

| | | |
|---|---|---|
| 81347-1-2-3-4 | He's Never Gonna Throw Me Down | Rejected |
| 81348-2 | Papa, Don't You Mean Your Mama No Good ? | Col 13006-D |

Vocal, acc. by Fletcher Henderson-p.     New York, November 14, 1923.

| | | |
|---|---|---|
| 81351-3 | A Woman Gets Tired Of One Man All Of The Time | Col 14002-D |
| 81352-3 | The Gal Ain't Born Who Can Treat Me Like You Do | - |
| 81353-1 | I'm Goin' Out Tonight And Strut My Stuff | Col 14015-D |

Vocal duets with Bessie Brown, acc. by Alexander Brown-p; or solo*.
                                    New York, February 8, 1924.

| | | |
|---|---|---|
| 81538-3 | You Ain't Quittin' Me Without Two Weeks' Notice | Col 14011-D, Diva 6027-G, VT 7053-V |
| 81539-3 | *I Won't Stand No Leavin' Now | Col 14015-D |
| 81540-4 | It Takes A Brownskin Man To Make A High Yellow Blue | Col 14011-D, Diva 6027-G, VT 7053-V |
| 81543-2 | He's Never Gonna Throw Me Down | Col 14017-D |

Vocal duets with Bessie Brown, acc. by Howard Scott-c/Fletcher Henderson-p/Charles
  Thomas-effects. New York, June 27, 1924.

81847-1  No Second-Handed Lovin' For Mine     Col 14033-D
81848-2  If You Hit My Dog I'll Kick Your Cat   -

Vocal, acc. by Don Redman-as/Fletcher Henderson-p.
                    New York, June 30, 1924.

81854-3  Hard-Headed Gal              Col 14030-D
81855-1  I'm Tired Of Begging You To Treat Me Right  -

Vocal duets with Bessie Brown, or solo*, acc. by ? Howard Scott-c/Charlie Green-tb/
  Fletcher Henderson-p (on 81887-3), ? Scott and Henderson (on 81888-1-2-3) or
  Henderson only (on 81889-3). New York, July 29, 1924.

81887-3  I Can Do What You Do        Col 14046-D
81888-1-2-3 *When I Get The Devil In Me   Rejected
81889-3 *Chain Gang Blues           Col 14049-D

Acc. by Howard Scott-c/Charlie Green-tb/Fletcher Henderson-p (on 81917-1); Green
  probably absent from 81889-4-5. New York, August 15, 1924.

81888-4-5 *When I Get The Devil In Me   Rejected
81917-1  When You Go Huntin' I'm Goin' Fishin'  Col 14046-D

Acc. by Don Redman-cl/Fletcher Henderson-p.
                    New York, February 26, 1925.

140396-1-2  Will You Love Me When I'm Gone ?   Col rejected

Acc. by Lemuel Fowler-p.      New York, February 28, 1925.

140405-1  Scat ! Mr. Sweetback        Col 14065-D
140406-2  Bald-Headed Mama Blues      -

Acc. by Charlie Green-tb/Don Redman-cl/Fletcher Henderson-p.
                    New York, March 13, 1925.

140429-2-3  She's My Sheba, I'm Her Sheik   Col 14071-D

                    New York, March 14, 1925.

140432-2  Cheatin' Blues            Col 14071-D

Vocal, acc. by Lemuel Fowler-p.    New York, March 17, 1925.

140440-2  What Makes Papa Hate Mama So ?    Col 14078-D
140441-2  Oh ! Dark Gal             -

Acc. by Harry Tate-c/Louis Hooper-p.  New York, March 31, 1926.

141897-3  Some Baby - My Gal         Col 14148-D
141898-1  Levee Blues              -

Vocal duets with Bessie Brown, acc. by Louis Hooper-p.
                    New York, April 2, 1926.

141902-2  You Can't Proposition Me      Col 14135-D
141903-3  Hit Me But Don't Quit Me     -

Vocal, acc. by Roy Banks-p.      New York, April 7, 1926.

141927-3  When I Get The Devil In Me     Col 14201-D
141928-3  West Virginia Blues       -

Vocal duets with Bessie Brown, acc. by Roy Banks-p.
                    New York, April 8, 1926.

141932-1-2-3  Bootlegging Daddy       Col rejected
141933-1-2-3  Road House Blues       -

Vocal, acc. by p.                    New York, May 20, 1930.

150445-3  It Ain't A Doggone Thing But The Blues    Col 14543-D
150446-1  Yodelin' The Blues Away                    -

## HANNAH AND DOROTHY WILLIAMS

Vocal duets, acc. by probably :- Earl Baker-c/Glenn Miller-tb/Gil Rodin-as/Wayne
    Allen-p/John Kurzenknabe-bj/Ben Pollack-d.
                                     Chicago, December 15, 1926.

37244-1-2  I've Grown So Lonesome Thinking Of You Vic rejected
37245-1-2  Sunday                                       -

## JOHN WILLIAMS

JOHN WILLIAMS' SYNCO JAZZERS : Henry McCord-t/Bradley Bullett-tb/John Williams-as-bar
    /Mary Leo Burley (Mary Lou Williams)-p/Joe Williams-bj/Robert Price-d.
                                     Chicago, February, 1927.

4187-2  Down In Gallion                Pm 12457, Poydras 5, Ristic 9
4188-1-2  Goose Grease                  - Her 92018 -          -

                                     Chicago, c. March 1, 1927.

12615, -A-B  My ! My ! My !           Gnt rejected
12616, -A  Kansas City Yellow Front      -

                                     Chicago, c. March 3, 1927.

12620, -A  Tiger Rag                  Gnt rejected
12621, -A  Someday, Sweetheart           -

                                     Chicago, c. March 7, 1927.

12626-A  Pee Wee Blues                Gnt 6124, BP 8009, Ch 15285, 40109
12627-A  Now Cut Loose                   -          -
12628    San                          Rejected
    NOTE:- Gennett 6124 as DUKE JACKSON'S SERENADERS; Champion 15285 as BUD HELMS AND
    HIS BAND; Black Patti 8009 as JOHN WILLIAMS AND HIS MEMPHIS STOMPERS.

JOHN WILLIAMS' BAND : Probably as above.  New York, May 21, 1927.

GEX-657, -A  Tiger Rag                Gnt rejected
GEX-658, -A  San                         -
GEX-659, -A-B  Someday, Sweetheart       -

JOHN WILLIAMS AND HIS MEMPHIS STOMPERS : Andy Kirk-bsx-bb dir. Gene Prince-Harry
    Lawson-t/Allen Durham-tb/John Harrington-cl-as/John Williams-as-bar/Lawrence Free-
    man-ts/Claude Williams-vn/Mary Lou Williams-p-a/William Dirvin-bj-g/Edward McNeil-
    d.                               Kansas City, c. November 9, 1929.

KC-600-  Somepin' Slow And Low        Voc 1453
KC-601-  Lotta Sax Appeal                -

## JOHNNY WILLIAMS

JOHNNY WILLIAMS AND HIS SWING SEXTETTE : Charlie Spivak-t/Jack Jenney-tb/Eddie Brown-
    cl/Babe Russin-ts/Claude Thornhill-p/Fred Whiting-sb/Johnny Williams-d.
                                     New York, June 15, 1937.

M-522-2  I'll Build A Stairway To Paradise    Vri 638, Voc 3837
M-523-1  Where's My Sweetie Hiding ?          Vri 594, Voc 3826
M-524-1  Little Old Lady                        -          -

DRUMMER MAN JOHNNY WILLIAMS AND HIS BOYS : Russ Case-t/Buddy Morrow-tb/Reggie Merrill
    cl/Hank Ross-ts/Walter Gross-p/Lou Shoobe-sb/Johnny Williams-d.
                                     New York, August 1, 1939.

24952-A  Memory Lane                  Voc 5213, Col DO-2130
24953-A  Ma Curly Headed Babby        Voc 5077
24954-A  Clarinet Marmalade           Voc 5213, Col DO-2130
24955-A  Milenberg Joys               Voc 5077, Col DO-2381

Vocal, acc. by Phil Napoleon-t/Miff Mole-tb/Johnny Costello-cl/Frank Signorelli-p/
  Jack Roth-d.                               New York, January 24, 1922.

80156-4  Cruel Daddy Blues                          Col A-3565
80157-3  Decatur Street Blues                       -

                                           New York, March 14, 1922.

80239-1-2  Achin' Hearted Blues                     Col rejected
80240-1-2-3  Struttin' Blues                        -

                                           New York, March 24, 1922.

80239-5  Achin' Hearted Blues                       Col A-3599
80240-7  Struttin' Blues                            -

  Jimmy Lytell-cl replaces Costello.       New York, May 23, 1922.

80362-1-2-3-4  It Makes No Difference Now           Col rejected
80363-1-2-3  Got To Cool My Doggies Now             -

                                           New York, June 3, 1922.

80362-5  It Makes No Difference Now                 Col A-3642
80363-6  Got To Cool My Doggies Now                 -

                                           New York, August 11, 1922.

80517-2  Sugar Blues                                Col A-3696
80518-3  The Meanest Man In The World (Milady's Blues) -

                                           New York, September 19, 1922.

80556-3  I Wish I Could Shimmy Like My Sister Kate Col A-3713
80557-1  If You Don't Believe I Love You,           -
         Look What A Fool I've Been

                                           New York, October 4, 1922.

80583-2  Uncle Bud Blues (Bugle Blues) (Intro.      Col A-3736
         Skeeter Skoot)
80584-2  Mexican Blues                              -

  Charlie Panelli-tb replaces Mole.        New York, January 11, 1923.

80777-3  I'm Goin' Away (Just To Wear You Off       Col A-3815
         My Mind)
80778-1  Bring It With You When You Come            -

                                           New York, February 5, 1923.

80834-1  That Teasin' Squeezin' Man O' Mine         Col A-3835
80835-3  If Your Man Is Like My Man                 -

## LEROY WILLIAMS

LEROY'S DALLAS BAND : Leroy Williams-c/Fred Millet-tb/Lawson Brooks or Roosevelt
  Harris-as/James Moore-p/Percy Darensbourg-bj/Octave Gaspard-bb/Percy Bagsby-d-v.
                                           Dallas, December 5, 1928.

147564-1  Tampa Shout - vPB                         Col 14402-D, Creole 22
147565-1  Going Away Blues - vPB                    -            -

Cornet solos, with own v, acc. by ? James Moore-p.
                                           Dallas, December 5, 1929.

149532-2  Lullaby Baby - vLW                        Col 14500-D
149533-2  Welcome Stranger                          -

MARGARET  WILLIAMS

Vocal, acc. by t/p.                          New York, July 10, 1928.

400857-A-B  Old Commandment Blues - Part 1          OK rejected
400858-A-B  Old Commandment Blues - Part 2          -

                          MARY LOU  WILLIAMS

Piano solos.                          Chicago, c. April 24, 1930.

C-5724-C  Night Life                          Br 7178, 80033, 01625, A-9507,
                                             A-500327, UHCA 37
C-5725-C  Drag 'Em                          Br 7178, 80033, 02507, UHCA 38

  Acc. by Booker Collins-sb/Ben Thigpen-d.
                          New York, March 7, 1936.

60877-A  Corny Rhythm                          Dec 1021, Col DB/MC-5018
60878-A  Overhand (New Froggy Bottom)          Dec 781, 3385, Col DB/MC-5013
60879-A  Isabelle                          Dec 1021          -    -

                          New York, March 11, 1936.

60894-A  Swingin' For Joy                          Dec 1155, Col DB/MC-5003,
                                                   DW-4368, MZ-490
60895-A  Clean Pickin'                          As above

  ? Ted Robinson-g added; Mary Lou Williams db cel.
                          New York, April 9, 1936.

61023-A  Mary's Special                          Dec 781, Col DB/MC-5018

  G omitted; no cel.          New York, September 14, 1938.

64662-A  The Pearls                          Dec 2796, Y-5496, Br 02836, 88060
64663-A  Mr. Freddie Blues                          Dec 2797, Y-5721          -
64664-A  Sweet (Patootie) Patunia                          -          -    Br 03009
64665-A  The Rocks                          Dec 2796, Y-5496          -          88060

Piano solos.                          New York, October 12, 1939.

25470-1  Little Joe From Chicago                          Col 37334
25471-   Margie                          Rejected

MARY LOU WILLIAMS AND HER KANSAS CITY SEVEN : Harold Baker-t/Ted Donelly-tb/Edward
  Inge-cl/Dick Wilson-ts/Mary Lou Williams-p/Booker Collins-sb/Ben Thigpen-d.
                          New York, November 18, 1940.

68365-A  Baby Dear                          Dec 18122
68366-A  Harmony Blues                          -

                          MIDGE WILLIAMS AND  HER JAZZ JESTERS

Vocal, acc. by Dave Wade-t/Pete Pumiglio-cl/Dave Harris-ts/Raymond Scott-p/g/Lou
  Shoobe-sb/Johnny Williams-d.          New York, February 26, 1937.

M-132-2  In The Shade Of The Old Apple Tree          Vri 519, Voc 3812
M-133-1  Let's Begin Again                          Vri 566, Voc 3821
M-134-2  Walkin' The Dog                          Vri 519, Voc 3812
M-135-1  I'm Getting Sentimental Over You          Vri 566, Voc 3821

  Acc. by same instrumentation (possibly the same group).
                          New York, April 1, 1937.

M-347-1-2  Old Fashioned Love                          Vri rejected
M-348-1-2  Anytime, Anyday, Anywhere                          -
M-349-1-2  Singin' The Blues                          -
M-350-1-2  Dear Old Girl                          -

Vocal, acc. by Billy Hicks-t/Fernando Arbello-tb/Edmond Hall-cl/Cyril Haynes-p/Leroy
  Jones-g/Alfred Hall-sb/Arnold Boling-d. New York, July 9, 1937.

M-553-1  I Know Now                              Vri 620, Voc 3779
M-554-1  That Old Feeling                          -              -
M-555-1  I Was Born To Swing                     Voc 3838
M-556-2  Oh ! Miss Hannah                          -

  Acc. by Frankie Newton-t/Buster Bailey-cl/Pete Brown-as/Billy Kyle-p/James McLin-g
  /John Kirby-sb/O'Neil Spencer-d.        New York, October 1, 1937.

M-661-2  The One Rose (That's Left In My Heart)  Vri 670, Voc 3801
M-662-1  The Lady Is A Tramp                     Voc 3865
M-663-2  An Old Flame Never Dies                 Vri 670, Voc 3801
M-664-1  Fortune Tellin' Man                     Voc 3865

  Charlie Shavers-t replaces Newton.     New York, November 23, 1937.

M-349-3  Singin' The Blues                       Voc 3900
M-683-1  Mama's Gone, Goodbye                      -
M-684-1  Goodnight, Angel                        Voc 3961, Cq 8993
M-685-1  The Greatest Mistake Of My Life           -

                                        New York, February 18, 1938.

M-760-1  I'm In A Happy Frame Of Mind            Voc 04026
M-761-1  Love Is Like Whiskey                      -

  Acc. by Charlie Shavers-t/Buster Bailey-cl/Russell Procope-as/Billy Kyle-p/Danny
  Barker-g/Johnny Williams-sb/O'Neil Spencer-d.
                                        New York, June 10, 1938.

23054-2  Don't Wake Up My Heart                  Voc 4192, Col DB-5052
23055-1  Where In The World                      Voc 4177
23056-1  In Any Language                           -
23057-1  Rosie The Redskin                       Voc 4192, Col DB-5052

                            NORA  WILLIAMS

Vocal, acc. by ? Max Goldberg-t/Freddy Gardner-cl-as/? George Scott Wood-p/Joe Young
  g/Don Stuteley-sb/Max Abrams-d.        London, April 12, 1935.

CAR-3365-1  Muddy Water (A Mississippi Moan)     RZ MR-1697
CAR-3366-1  Piccolo Pete                           -

Other titles by this artist on this label and from this time may have interesting
  jazz-orientated accompaniments.

                            RALPH WILLIAMS

RALPH WILLIAMS AND HIS RAINBO ORCHESTRA : Ralph Williams-bj dir. 2c/tb/2cl-as/cl-ts/
  pac/vn/Vic Lubowski-p/bb/d-k.          Chicago, November 7, 1924.

31146-1-2-3-4  You Should Have Told Me          Rejected
31147-3  Get Lucky                              Vic 19504
31148-3  Prince Of Wails                          -

                                        Chicago, November 12, 1924.

31163-1-2-3-4  Seal It With A Kiss              Rejected
31164-1-2-3-4  Wait Till You See Me With My Baby  -
          (That Little Somebody Of Mine)
31165-2  Cocaine Dance                          Vic 19775 (never issued)

                                        Chicago, November 18, 1924.

31146-7  You Should Have Told Me                Vic 19528
31164-7  Wait Till You See Me With My Baby       Vic 19573
          (That Little Somebody Of Mine)

RALPH WILLIAMS AND HIS ORCHESTRA : Ralph Williams-bj and sometimes 2nd p dir. Doc
    Lawlor and another-c/Ted Huber-tb/Ralph Boas-Ted Rickard-cl-as/Verne Rickard-cl-ts
    pac/Fred Glickman-vn/Russ Carlson-p/Dick Patterson-bb/Frank Snyder-d/Paul Small-v.
                            St. Louis, December 16, 1925.

| | | |
|---|---|---|
| 34032-1 | My Darling | Vic 19957, HMV B-5080 |
| 34033-1 | I Could Fall In Love With Someone Like | Vic 19958 |
| | You - vPS | |
| 34034-3 | You Know I Do - vPS | Vic 19957 |

## SAMMY WILLIAMS

The piano solos shown below may not be by the same Sammy Williams as the electric
    organist of the Three Naturals. His organ solos are of little or no jazz interest.

Piano solos.                          Chicago, c. November, 1923.

| | | |
|---|---|---|
| 402 | House Of David Blues | Auto (un-numbered) |
| 403 | I've Got A Song For Sale | - |

                                      Chicago, c. August, 1924.

| | | |
|---|---|---|
| 605 | Mandy, Make Up Your Mind | Auto (un-numbered) |
| 611 | Mama's Gone, Goodbye | - |

SAMMY WILLIAMS AND HIS THREE NATURALS : Johnny McGhee-t/Billy Kyle-p/Sammy Williams-
    elo/Cozy Cole-d/Mary McHugh-Chick Bullock-v.
                            New York, June 17, 1938.

| | | |
|---|---|---|
| 23119-1 | My Walking Stick - vCB | Voc 4243 |
| 23120- | Now It Can Be Told - vMM | Voc 4229 |
| 23121-2 | I'm Gonna Lock My Heart (And Throw Away | Voc 4197, Br A-81764 |
| | The Key) - vCB | |
| 23122-2 | Among My Souvenirs - vMM | Voc 4259, Cq 9083 |

                                      New York, June 18, 1938.

| | | |
|---|---|---|
| 23128-2 | Some Sweet Day - vCB | Voc 4229, Cq 9084, Br A-81851 |
| 23129-1 | Ain't She Sweet ? - vCB | Voc 4259, Cq 9083 |
| 23130-1-2 | M-O-T-H-E-R (A Word That Means The | Rejected |
| | World To Me) - vCB | |
| 23131- | All Alone - vMM | Voc 4197, Cq 9084 |

## SIDNEY  WILLIAMS

Piano solos.                          St. Paul, c. June 17, 1927.

| | | |
|---|---|---|
| 12861 | Mississippi Shivers | Gnt 6353, Ch 15372, GS 20339, |
| | | Spr 329 |

                                      Chicago, April 2, 1928.

C-1858- ; E-7285  St. Louis Blues          Voc 15691

Other Vocalion records by this artist are of "novelty" pieces of no jazz interest.

## SPEED WILLIAMS' ORCHESTRA

Pseudonym on Superior 2818 for Wingy Manone and his Orchestra, q.v.

## SUSAN WILLIAMS

Pseudonym on Lincoln for Viola McCoy, q.v.

## TE ROY WILLIAMS AND  HIS ORCHESTRA

Te Roy Williams-tb dir. Ed Allen-c/Prince Robinson-cl/cl-as/Joe Garland-cl-ts/Freddy
    Johnson and another-p/Elmer Snowden-bj/Bob Ysaguirre-bb/Walter Johnson-d.
                            New York, May 25, 1927.

| | | |
|---|---|---|
| 144214-2 | Oh Malinda | Har 439-H |
| 144215-3 | Lindbergh Hop | - |

Charley Williamson-c/Alex Hunt-tb/Albert Mathews-cl-bar/James Alston-p/Thomas
    Pinkston-bj/Booker T. Washington-d.      Memphis, February 27, 1927.

37959-1  Scandinavian Stomp                      Vic 21410
37960-2  Midnight Frolic Drag                     -

                                          Memphis, March 1, 1927.

37973-1  Memphis Scronch                          Vic 20555
37974-3  Bear Wallow Blues                        -

## VIRGINIA WILLRICH AND  HER TEXAS RANGERS

Charlie Teagarden-t/Jack Teagarden-tb/Virginia Willrich-pac/Dick McDonough-g/Jack
    Willrich-d.                        New York, November 4, 1929.

403227-B  Same Old Moon (But Not The Same Old You) OK 41328, Od A-189299
403228-C  Through (How Can You Say We're Through ?)   -          -

## BOB WILLS AND HIS TEXAS PLAYBOYS

Although this was primarily a country-and-western unit, some of the more obviously
    interesting titles may prove rewarding, but the general output is outside the
    scope of this book.

## LEO WILMOT

Pseudonym on Grand Pree for Fred van Eps, q.v.

## WILSHIRE DANCE ORCHESTRA

T/tb/cl/as/p/bj/bb/d.                    Los Angeles, c. February, 1925.

         My Best Girl                          Sunset 1059
         Charleston Charley                    Sunset 1088, Hwd 1067

## WILSON'S T. O. B. A.  BAND

Emmet Matthews or Andrew Webb-c/Sidney Costello-as/Jane Hemingway-p/Beverley Sexton-
    d/Willie Lewis (not the saxophonist-leader !)-v.
                                       Chicago, c. October, 1926.

3023-1-3  Steady Roll - vWL                      Pm 12408
3024-1  Backyard Blues                           -

## BILLIE  WILSON

Vocal duets with Eddie Green, acc. by Charles Matson-p.
                                       New York, c. June, 1924.

1786-2  I'm Leaving You                          Pm 12226, Sil 3544
1787-2  I'm Sorry For It Now                     -           -
NOTE:- Silvertone 3544 as MACK AND MITCHELL.

Vocal, acc. by t/cl/p.                   New York, c. July 11, 1928.

GEX-2002-A  Empty Bed Blues - Part 1             Ch 15549, Spt 9285
GEX-2003-A  Empty Bed Blues - Part 2
NOTE:- Both issues as LUCY COLE.


## BOB WILSON AND HIS ORCHESTRA


Pseudonym on Mayfair G-306 for Gene Kardos and his Orchestra, q.v., and other bands
    on the same label of no known interest as jazz or "hot" dance music.

Pseudonym for the following items listed in this book :-

Banner 32643  Beale Street Blues (Ben Pollack and his Orchestra)
       32733  House Of David Blues (Fletcher Henderson and his Orchestra)
Conqueror 8024  Both sides by Joe Haymes and his Orchestra
Domino 0127  House Of David Blues (Fletcher Henderson and his Orchestra)
Melotone M-12368  Both sides by Fletcher Henderson and his Orchestra
         M-12662  House Of David Blues (Fletcher Henderson and his Orchestra)
         M-12662  Red Devil (Mills Blue Rhythm Band)
         91358    Beale Street Blues (Ben Pollack and his Orchestra)
Oriole 2466  How'm I Doin' (Hey-Hey) (Fletcher Henderson and his Orchestra)
       2488  Beale Street Blues (Ben Pollack and his Orchestra)
       2677  House Of David Blues (Fletcher Henderson and his Orchestra)
       2677  Red Devil (Mills Blue Rhythm Band)
Perfect 15603  How'm I Doin' (Hey-Hey) (Fletcher Henderson and his Orchestra)
        15617  Beale Street Blues (Ben Pollack and his Orchestra)
        15632  Bull Fiddle Blues (Dick Robertson and his Orchestra)
        15662  Both sides by Joe Haymes and his Orchestra
        15697  Both sides by Andy Kirk and his Twelve Clouds of Joy
        15738  Goodbye Blues 'Fletcher Henderson and his Orchestra)
        15753  House Of David Blues (Fletcher Henderson and his Orchestra)
        15753  Red Devil (Mills Blue Rhythm Band)
Romeo 1858  Beale Street Blues (Ben Pollack and his Orchestra)

## EDITH WILSON

Vocal, acc. by Johnny Dunn's Original Jazz Hounds : Johnny Dunn-c/tb/? Garvin Bushell
   cl/vn/p.                              New York, September 12, 1921.

   79983-1-2-3-4-5  Nervous Blues                    Col rejected

                                         New York, September 15, 1921.

   79983-6  Nervous Blues                            Col A-3479
   79989-2  Vampin' Liza Jane                          -

                                         New York, September 24, 1921.

   79993-1-2-3  Old Time Blues                        Col rejected

                                         New York, September 30, 1921.

   80014-1-2-3  Frankie                               Col rejected

   Vn omitted.                           New York, October 6, 1921.

   79993-6  Old Time Blues                            Col A-3506
   80014-4  Frankie                                     -

   Acc. by her Jazz Hounds : Johnny Dunn-c/Herb Flemming-tb/Ernest Elliott-Herschel
   Brassfield-cl-as/Dan Wilson-p/John Mitchell-bj/Harry Hull-bb.
                                         New York, December 21, 1921.

   80111-2  I Don't Want Nobody Blues                 Col A-3537
   80112-2  The West Texas Blues                        -

   Earl Granstaff-tb replaces Flemming; Brassfield and Hull omitted; Leroy Tibbs may
   be the pianist.                       New York, January 21, 1922.

   80150-4  Wicked Blues                              Col A-3558
   80151-1  Birmingham Blues                            -

   Probably similar acc.                 New York, April 12, 1922.

   80304-1-2-3-4  That Thing Called Love        .     Col rejected
   80305-1-2-3-4  Stingaree Blues                       -

Acc. by her Jazz Hounds : Johnny Dunn-c/Herb Flemming-tb/Garvin Bushell-cl/Will
Tyler-vn/Dan Wilson or Leroy Tibbs-p/John Mitchell-bj.
                                    New York, May 20, 1922.

80356-3  Mammy, I'm Thinking Of You            Col A-3634
80357-3  Take It 'Cause It's All Yours            -

Tyler omitted.                      New York, June 9, 1922.

80382-4  He May Be Your Man (But He Comes To See  Col A-3653
            Me Sometimes)
80383-4  Rules And Regulations "Signed Razor Jim"    -

                                    New York, July 13, 1922.

80449-2  Lonesome Mama Blues                   Col A-3674
80450-4  What Do You Care (What I Do) ?            -

                                    New York, September 18, 1922.

80554-1-2-3  Evil Blues                       Col rejected

                                    New York, September 19, 1922.

80555-1-2-3  Pensacola Blues (Home Again Croon)   Col rejected

                                    New York, October 2. 1922.

80554-5  Evil Blues                           Col A-3746
80555-4  Pensacola Blues (Home Again Croon)         -

                                    New York, November 22, 1922.

80683-1-2-3  Dixie Blues                       Col rejected
80684-1-2-3  He Used To Be Your Man But He's My Man Now-

Acc. by her Jazz Hounds : Johnny Dunn-c/Herb Flemming-tb/Ernest Elliott-cl/George
Rickson-p/John Mitchell-bj.           New York, December 13, 1922.

80683-5  Dixie Blues                           Col A-3787
80684-6  He Used To Be Your Man But He's My Man Now   -

Acc. by Johnny Dunn's Original Jazz Hounds : Probably very similar to the above.
                                    New York, December 18, 1922.

80735-1-2-3-4  Memphis, Tennessee              Col rejected
80736-1-2-3  What Did Deacon Mose Do (When The Lights  -
            Went Out)

Acc. by her Jazz Band : Elmer Chambers-c/Teddy Nixon-tb/Don Redman-cl/Fletcher
Henderson-p/Charlie Dixon-bj.         New York, January 12, 1924.

81478-2  Daddy, Change Your Mind          Col 14008-D,Diva 6025-G,VT 7051-V
81479-3  I Don't Know And I Don't Care Blues    -          -          -

Acc. by Roy Smeck (as ALABAMA JOE)-g.   New York, June 18, 1924.

81831-4  How Come You Do Me Like You Do ?     Col 14027-D
81832-2  Muscle Shoals Blues                    -

Acc. by her Jazz Hounds : C/tb/cl-as/cl-ts/p/bj.
                                    New York, December 17, 1924.

140189-1  He's A Mean Mean Man (But He's Good To Me)Col 14054-D
140190-1  Double-Crossin' Papa (Don't Double-Cross Me)  -

Vocal duets with Doc Strain, acc. by Earres Prince-p.
                                    New York, March 6, 1925.

140415-1  It's Gonna Be A Cold, Cold Winter      Col 14066-D
140416-1  There'll Be Some Changes Made          -

Vocal, acc. by Sam Wooding and his Orchestra : Probably similar to the Sam Wooding
   Parlophones made in Barcelona in 1929 (q.v.)
                                          Berlin, 1928.

            Unknown titles                    DG/Pol rejected

   Acc. by Charlie Gaines-t/Wilbur de Paris-tb/Emerson Harper-cl/Harry Brooks-p/Sam
   Speed-bj.                            New York, c. November, 1929.

E-31585-   (What Did I Do To Be So) Black And Blue Br 4685
E-31586-   My Man Is Good For Nothing But Love       -

   Acc. by c/cl-as/cl-ts/vn/p/g/sb.     New York, October 6, 1930.

63371-3  My Handy Man Ain't Handy No More         Vic V-38624
63372-2  I'll Get Even With You                     -

   Acc. by c/p/g.                       New York, October 28, 1930.

63371-4 or 5  My Handy Man Ain't Handy No More     Vic V-38624

                           GARLAND WILSON

Piano solos, with own v where shown.     New York, May 18, 1931.

230205-1  Dear Old Southland/Limehouse Blues     Col Special (12")
230206-2  St. James Infirmary-vGW/When Your Lover    -
            Has Gone

                                   New York, September 11, 1931.

151783-1-2  Little Joe                           Col rejected
151784-1-2  The Viper Song                         -

                                   New York, February 2, 1932.

405134-A  Memories Of You              OK 41556, Par R-1862, A-3424
405135-A  Rockin' Chair                   -      Par R-1194   -Od A-286060

   Nina Mae McKinney-v.                 Paris, c. November, 1932.

5962bkp   Blues en si bemol (Blues in C flat*)  Br A-500220, 01476*, A-9501
5963bkp   Get Up, Bessie                         -          -        -
5964bkp   Minnie The Moocher's Weddin' Day - vNMM Br A-500221, 01468, Od 294189
5965bkp   Rhapsody In Love - vNMM                 -          -        -

                                   Paris, c. December, 1933.

5747bdp   Mood Indigo                  Br A-500358, 01692
5748bdp   China Boy                       -        -
5749bdp   The Way I Feel                Br A-500359, 01784
5750bdp   You Rascal You                  -        -

                                   London, September 7, 1936.

TB-2426-1  Shim Sham Drag              Br 02283, Dec F-42102
TB-2427-1  Just A Mood                 Br 03115, Dec F-42101
TB-2428-1  Just One Of Those Things       -        -
TB-2429-2  Your Heart And Mine         Br 02283, Dec F-42102

   Celeste solo*.                      Paris, March 9, 1938.

OSW-12-1  The Blues Got Me             Swing 19
OSW-13-1  You Showed Me The Way        Swing 61
OSW-14-1  The Blues I Love To Play     Swing 46
OSW-15-1  Sweet Lorraine               Swing 61
OSW-16-1  Bei mir bist du schön        Swing 19
OSW-17-1  *Blue Morning                Swing 46

George Wilson-k-g/Jimmy Hinton-h-wb or bellboard.
                              Long Island City, c. December, 1928.

```
317-A  Myrtle Avenue Stomp - gGW/wbJH        QRS R-7051
318    D. C. Rag - kGW/wbJH                  -
319-A  Chicken Wilson Blues - gGW/hJH        QRS R-7052, Pm 12843
320    House Snake Blues - gGW/hJH           -            -
321-A  Frog Eye Stomp - k-gGW/hJH            QRS R-7060
333    Station House Rag - gGW/wbJH          -
```
NOTE:- QRS R-7051 and R-7052 as CHICKEN WILSON AND SKEETER HINTON.

## HARRY WILSON AND HIS ORCHESTRA

Pseudonym on Edison Bell Winner W-67 for Gene Kardos and his Orchestra, q.v., and on
W-118 for the Dorsey Brothers' Orchestra, q.v.

## JIMMY WILSON'S PINE FOREST ORCHESTRA

Pseudonym on Embassy 8006 (OL' MAN RIVER) for the Castle Farms Serenaders, q.v.

## LENA  WILSON

Vocal, acc. by the Jazz Masters : C/tb/cl/Fletcher Henderson-p/bb.
                              Long Island City, c. September, 1922.

```
       The Wicked Fives' Blues               BS 14129, Pm 12134
       You've Got Everything A Sweet Daddy    -            -
         Needs But Me
```

Acc. by the Nubian Five : Phil Napoleon-t/Charlie Panelli-tb/Jimmy Lytell-cl/Frank
Signorelli-p/Jack Roth-d.          New York, January 31, 1923.

```
70041  He Used To Be Your Man But He's My Man  PA 020910, Per 12044
       Now
70042  Memphis, Tennessee                     -            -
```

Acc. by Johnny Dunn's Jazz Hounds : Johnny Dunn-c/Earl Granstaff, Herb Flemming or
Calvin Jones-tb/Garvin Bushell, Ernest Elliott and/or Herschel Brassfield-cl-as/
Leroy Tibbs, George Rickson or Dan Wilson-p/John Mitchell or Sam Speed-bj; others?
                              New York, February 26, 1923.

```
80875-1-2-3  I Don't Let No One Man Worry Me      Col rejected
80876-1-2-3-4  Humming Man                        -
```

Acc. by Perry Bradford's Jazz Phools : Probably similar to the last above.
                              New York, April, 1923.

```
1362-1-2  Deceitful Blues                    Pm 12029, Cx 2542, Hg 2543
1363-1-2-3  I Don't Let No One Man Worry Me   -          -         -
```

```
1378-2-3  Here's Your Opportunity            Pm 12042
1379-3  Memphis, Tennessee                   -
```

Acc. by Porter Grainger-p.          New York, May 9, 1923.

```
27894-3  'Tain't Nobody's Biz-ness If I Do       Vic 19085
27895-4  Triflin' Blues (Daddy Don't You Trifle)  -
```

Acc. by her Jazz Hounds : ? Gus Aiken-c/Herb Flemming-tb/Garvin Bushell-cl/? George
Rickson-p/John Mitchell-bj.          New York, May 12, 1923.

```
81009-1  Deceitful Blues                     Col A-3915
81010-3  Memphis, Tennessee                  -
```

Acc. by Fletcher Henderson-p.          New York, May 23, 1923.

```
11480  Your Time Now ('Twill Be Mine After      Voc 14631, Sil 3009
         A While)
```

Acc. by Fletcher Henderson-p.              New York, June 5, 1923.

11557     I Need You To Drive My Blues Away        Voc 14631, Sil 3009

Acc. by Porter Grainger-p.                 New York, June 15, 1923.

10853     Sad 'n' Lonely Blues                     Br rejected

                                           New York, June 18, 1923.

10973     Bleeding Hearted Blues                   Br 2464
10976     Chirpin' The Blues                       -

Acc. by Fletcher Henderson and his Orchestra : Fletcher Henderson-p dir. Elmer
Chambers-c/Teddy Nixon-tb/Don Redman-cl/Coleman Hawkins-ts/Charlie Dixon-bj, or by
Fletcher Henderson-p only*.                New York, August 9, 1923.

11823     Afternoon Blues                          Voc 14651, Sil 3010, Gmn 7002
11825/6  *Michigan Water Blues                     -              -
NOTE:- Guardsman 7002 as NELLY COLMAN.

Acc. by Porter Grainger-p.                 New York, August 22, 1923.

28398-1-2-3-4  'Tain't No Tellin'                  Vic rejected
28399-1-2-3    Wish I Had You                       -

Acc. by Fletcher Henderson-p.              New York, October 18, 1923.

28399-4-5-6  Wish I Had You                         Vic rejected

                                           New York, c. November 17, 1923.

70411     Mistreatin' Daddy                        PA 032015, Per 12094
70412     Love Ain't Blind No More                 -          -

                                           New York, c. November, 1923.

          Down South Blues                         Ajax 17014
          Tantalizin' Mama                         -

Acc. by Conaway's Rag-Pickers : Lincoln M. Conaway-stg/Clarence Conaway-u/?Sterling
Conaway-g.                                 New York, February 14, 1924.

12524/6  Hula Blues                                Br 2590
12527/9  Four-Flushin' Papa (You've Gotta Play     -
           Straight With Me)

Acc. by Porter Grainger-p.                 New York, c. March, 1924.

31551     He Wasn't Born In Araby, But He's A      Ajax 17025
           Sheikin' Fool
31553     If You Love Me, Act Like It              -

Acc. by p (also Porter Grainger ?)         New York, c. March, 1924.

42582-2   'Tain't No Tellin' (What The Blues Will  Em 10745
           Make You Do)
42583-2   I Don't Love Nobody (So I Don't Have No Blues)-

Acc. by Cliff Jackson-p.                    New York, February 4, 1930.

149960-2  Baby, It Upsets Me So                    Cl 5036-C, Diva 6038-G, VT 7064-V
149961-3  Chiropractor Blues                       -          Diva 6045-G, VT 7071-V

                                           New York, February 6, 1930.

149970-3  I'm A Stationary Mama (Looking For A     Diva 6038-G, VT 7064-V
           Permanent Man)
149971-3  Find Out What They Like (And How They    Diva 6045-G, VT 7071-V
           Like It)

Acc. by Cliff Jackson-p.                    New York, July 17, 1931.

151690-2  What's Your Price ?                    Col 14618-D
151691-1  My Man O' War                              -

## LEOLA B.  WILSON

Leola B. Wilson, nee Pettigrew and wife of "Kid" Wesley Wilson, recorded under both
  her maiden and her married names, and as Coot-Grant, solo and with her husband. On
  many of her records (and his), the accompaniment is purely blues and has thus no
  real place in this work, but the following are much more interesting as jazz.

COOT GRANT AND KID WESLEY WILSON : Vocal duets, acc. by Fletcher Henderson's Orchestra : Louis Armstrong-c Charlie Green-tb/Buster Bailey-cl/Fletcher Henderson-p/
  Charlie Dixon-bj/Kaiser Marshall-d.      New York, c. September, 1925.

2279-1  You Dirty Mistreater                    Pm 12324
2280-2  Come On Coot Do That Thing             Pm 12317, UHCA 80, JI 6,
                                               Amp R-104, JSo AA-506
2281-2  Have Your Chill, I'll Be Here When Your  Pm 12317
          Fever Rises
2282-1-2  Find Me At The Greasy Spoon (If You   Pm 12337
          Miss Me Here)

Kid Wesley Wilson omitted*; acc. by Joe Smith-c/Fletcher Henderson-p.
                                         New York, c. September, 1925.

2283-1  *Speak Now Or Hereafter Hold Your Peace  Pm 12324, JSo AA-506
2284-1  When Your Man Is Going To Put You Down  Pm 12337
          You Never Can Tell

GRANT AND WILSON : Vocal duets, acc. by c/tb/cl/p.
                                         Chicago, July-August, 1926.

2607-4  Scoop It                              Pm 12379

COOT GRANT : Vocal, acc. by c/tb/cl/p.     Chicago, August, 1926.

2617-1  Stevedore Man                        Pm 12379

LEOLA B. WILSON : Vocal, acc. by ? B. T. Wingfield-c/? Tiny Parham-p.
                                         Chicago, c. September-October, 1926.

3021-1  Dishrag Blues                        Pm 12403
3022-1-2  Rollin' Mill Blues                     -

GRANT AND WILSON : Vocal duets, acc. by ? Rex Stewart-c/? Charlie Green-tb/Buster
  Bailey-cl/? as/Fletcher Henderson-p; Kid Wesley Wilson omitted*.
                                         New York, November, 1928.

3489-B  Ducks                                Cam 9015, Ro 819
3490-A; 108670  Mama Didn't Do It And Papa Didn't Do It -        -  PA 7540, Per 140
3492-1  *Stevedore Blues                     Cam 9240, Lin 3267, Ro 1042
NOTE:- Matrix 3491 is by a Fletcher Henderson unit (q.v.)

Acc. by Charlie Shavers-t/Sidney Bechet-cl-ss/Sammy Price-p/Teddy Bunn-g/Wellman
  Braud-sb/O'Neil Spencer-d; Wilson omitted*.
                                         New York, May 26, 1938.

63873-A  Uncle Joe                           Dec 7500, Voc S-244
63874-A  I Am A Woman                        Rejected
63875-A  *Toot It, Brother Armstrong             -
63876-A  Blue Monday On Sugar Hill           Dec 7500, Voc S-244
NOTE:- A few copies exist of Vocalion S-235 by Trixie Smith that, although they are
correctly labelled, are pressed from matrix 63875-A, and by a strange coincidence,
this was also used in error on some copies of Decca 7500 !

Ezell Watson-cl dir. Jack Purvis-t/Sunny Clapp-tb/Tommy Christian-Pat Davis-cl-as/
Ray Watson-cl-ts/Eddie Stiles-p/Mart Britt-bj/Whitey ——— -d.
New York, November, 1930.

| | | |
|---|---|---|
| E-35056-A | Deserted Blues | Mt M-12026, Polk P-9029 |
| E-35057-A | Swamp Blues | — — |

## TEDDY WILSON

Piano solos.           New York, May 22, 1934.

| | | |
|---|---|---|
| 152751-1-2 | Somebody Loves Me | Col rejected |
| 152752-1-2 | Sweet And Simple | — |
| 152753-1-2 | Liza (All The Clouds'll Roll Away) | — |
| 152754-1-2 | Rosetta | — |

TEDDY WILSON AND HIS ORCHESTRA : Roy Eldridge-t/Benny Goodman-cl unless marked */Ben
Webster-ts/Teddy Wilson-p/John Trueheart-g/John Kirby-sb/Cozy Cole-d/Billie Holiday
v.        New York, July 2, 1935.

| | | |
|---|---|---|
| B-17766-1 | I Wished On The Moon - vBH | Br 7501, 8336, 02063, A-81010, A-86052, A-500600, Col 36205, C-6203, 291363 |
| B-17767-1 | What A Little Moonlight Can Do - vBH | Br 7498, 8336, 02066, A-9867, A-86041, A-500602, Col 36206, C-6204, 21218, 291137, S-10008 |
| B-17768-1 | Miss Brown To You - vBH | Br 7501, 8087, 02063, A-81010, A-81528, A-86052, A-500600, Col 36205, C-6203, 291363, Dec M-30371, Ph B-21177-H, RZ G-22605 |
| B-17769-1 | *A Sunbonnet Blue (And A Yellow Straw Hat) - vBH | Br 7498, 02066, A-9867, A-86041, A-500602, 603006 |

Roy Eldridge-t/Cecil Scott-cl/Hilton Jefferson-as/Ben Webster-ts/Teddy Wilson-p/
Lawrence Lucie-g/John Kirby-sb/Cozy Cole-d/Billie Holiday-v.
New York, July 31, 1935.

| | | |
|---|---|---|
| B-17913-1 | What A Night, What A Moon, What A Girl - vBH | Br 7511, 02071, A-9847, A-86043, A-500601 |
| B-17914-1 | I'm Painting The Town Red - vBH | Br 7520, 02072, A-9870, A-86042, A-500603 |
| B-17915-1 | It's Too Hot For Words - vBH | Br 7511, 02071, A-9847, A-86043, A-500601 |
| B-17916-1 | Sweet Lorraine | Br 7520, 8087, 02072, A-9870, A-81528, A-86042, A-500603, 603006, Dec M-30371, Pol 580004 |
| B-17917- | Liza (All The Clouds'll Roll Away) | Rejected |
| B-17918- | Rosetta | — |

NOTE:- There is no vocal on B-17916-1, despite the label of Brunswick 02072.

Piano solos.        New York, October 7, 1935.

| | | |
|---|---|---|
| B-18129-1 | Every Now And Then | Br 7543, 02110, A-9944, A-500617 |
| B-18130-1 | It Never Dawned On Me | — — — — |
| B-18131-1 | Liza (All The Clouds'll Roll Away) | Br 7563, A-9956, A-500618, Voc S-85, Dec M-8070 |
| B-18132-1 | Rosetta | Br 7563, 02160, A-9956, A-500618, Dec M-8070 |

TEDDY WILSON AND HIS ORCHESTRA : Roy Eldridge-t/Benny Morton-tb/Chu Berry-ts/Teddy
Wilson-p/Dave Barbour-g/John Kirby-sb/Cozy Cole-Billie Holiday-v.
New York, October 25, 1935.

| | | |
|---|---|---|
| B-18196-1 | Twenty-Four Hours A Day - vBH | Br 7550, A-9875, A-500615 |
| B-18197-1 | Yankee Doodle Never Went To Town - vBH | - 02118 - — |
| B-18199-1 | Eeny Meeny Miney Mo - vBH | Br 7554, 02141, A-500616 |
| B-18209-1 | If You Were Mine - vBH | - 02160 - Col 36206, C-6204, 291306 |

Piano solos.                          New York, November 22, 1935.

B-18295-1  I Found A Dream                     Br 7572, 02113, A-9911
B-18296-1  On Treasure Island                   -       -       -

TEDDY WILSON AND HIS ORCHESTRA : Richard Clarke-t/Tom Mace-cl/Johnny Hodges-as/Teddy
Wilson-p/Dave Barbour-g/Grachan Moncur-sb/Billie Holiday-v.
                                      New York, December 3, 1935.

B-18316-1  These 'n' That 'n' Those - vBH       Br 7577, 02118, A-500627
B-18317-1  Sugar Plum                            -       A-81076    -    Voc S-23
B-18318-1  You Let Me Down - vBH                Br 7581, A-500628, Dec J-2
B-18319-1  Spreadin' Rhythm Around - vBH        - 02141 -

Piano solos.                          New York, January 17, 1936.

B-18517-1  I Feel Like A Feather In The Breeze  Br 7599, Col DO-1531
B-18518-1  Breaking In A Pair Of Shoes          - Dec J-2 -

TEDDY WILSON AND HIS ORCHESTRA : Gordon Griffin-t/Rudy Powell-cl/Ted McRae-ts/Teddy
Wilson-p/John Trueheart-g/Grachan Moncur-sb/Cozy Cole-d/Billie Holiday-v.
                                      New York, January 30, 1936.

B-18612-1  Life Begins When You're In Love - vBH  Br 7612, A-9963, Lucky 60117
B-18613-1  (If I Had) Rhythm In My Nursery Rhymes   -       -

     Frank Newton-t/Benny Morton-tb/Jerry Blake-cl-as/Ted McRae-ts/Teddy Wilson-p/John
     Trueheart-g/Lennie Stanfield-sb/Cozy Cole-d/Ella Fitzgerald-v.
                                      New York, March 17, 1936.

B-18829-1  Christopher Columbus                 Br 7640, A-9995, A-500661,
                                                Col DO-1539, Pol 580029
B-18830-1  My Melancholy Baby - vEF             Br 7729,Col 35862,291693,Voc S-76,
                                                Par R-2868, DPE-68, PZ-11017
B-18831-1-2  I Know That You Know               Rejected
B-18832-1  All My Life - vEF                    Br 7640, 8116, A-9995, A-500661,
                                                5041, Dec J-3, Col DO-1539

     Roy Eldridge-t-v/Buster Bailey-cl/Chu Berry-ts/Teddy Wilson-p/Bob Lessey-g/Israel
     Crosby-sb/Sidney Catlett-d.           Chicago, May 14, 1936.

C-1376-1  Mary Had A Little Lamb - vRE         Br 7663, Dec J-3, Col DO-1588
C-1377-2  Too Good To Be True                   - A-81076, Voc S-23  -  Lucky S-7
C-1378-1  Warmin' Up                           Br 7684, 02256, Col 36314, C-591,
                                                DO-1589, Par R-2871, DP-212,
                                                Od A-2398, D-5044, BA 214
C-1379-1  Blues In C sharp minor               As above, plus Col M-120

     Jonah Jones-t/Johnny Hodges-as/Harry Carney-cl-bar/Teddy Wilson-p/Lawrence Lucie-g/
     John Kirby-sb/Cozy Cole-d/Billie Holiday-v.
                                      New York, June 30, 1936.

B-19495-2  It's Like Reaching For The Moon - vBH  Br 7702, Voc S-33
B-19496-2  These Foolish Things - vBH           Br 7699, Dec J-5
B-19497-2  Why Do I Lie To Myself About You ?    -       -
B-19498-2  I Cried For You - vBH                Br 7729, Col 35862, C-637,
                                                Voc S-33, Par R-2823, DPE-42
B-19499-2  Guess Who - vBH                      Br 7702, 5052, Voc S-190

     Gordon Griffin-t/Benny Goodman-cl unless marked */Vido Musso-ts/Teddy Wilson-p/
     Allen Reuss-g/Harry Goodman-sb/Gene Krupa-d/Lionel Hampton-vib/Helen Ward (as VERA
     LANE)-Red Harper-v.                  Los Angeles, August 24, 1936.

LA-1158-A  You Came To My Rescue - vHW         Br 7739, A-500679, Voc S-41,
                                                RZ G-22972
LA-1159-A  Here's Love In Your Eyes - vHW      As above, plus Br 5063 (Italian)
LA-1160-A  *You Turned The Tables On Me - vRH  Br 7736, A-81051, A-500686,
                                                Voc S-35, RZ G-22964
LA-1161-A  *Sing, Baby, Sing - vRH             As above, plus Br 5063 (Italian)

TEDDY WILSON AND HIS ORCHESTRA : Irving Randolph-t/Vido Musso-cl/Ben Webster-ts/
Teddy Wilson-p/Allan Reuss-g/Milton Hinton-sb/Gene Krupa-d/Billie Holiday-v.
                                    New York, October 21, 1936.

| | | |
|---|---|---|
| B-20105-1 | Easy To Love - vBH | Br 7762, A-81072, A-500704, |
| | | Voc S-184, RZ G-23006, Bm 1106 |
| B-20106-2 | With Thee I Swing - vBH | Br 7768, A-81089,A-500699,Voc S-53 |
| B-20107-2 | The Way You Look Tonight - vBH | Br 7762, A-81072, A-500704, |
| | NOTE:- Biltmore 1106 as BILLIE HOLIDAY. | Voc S-184, RZ G-23006, Bm 1106 |

                                    New York, October 28, 1936.

B-20142-1-3  Who Loves You ? - vBH          Br 7768, A-81089,A-500699,Voc S-53

    Jonah Jones-t/Benny Goodman (as JOHN JACKSON)-cl/Ben Webster-ts/Teddy Wilson-p/
    Allan Reuss-g/John Kirby-sb/Cozy Cole-d/Billie Holiday-v.
                                    New York, November 19, 1936.

| | | |
|---|---|---|
| B-20290-1 | Pennies From Heaven - vBH | Br 7789, A-81102,A-500695,Voc S-49 |
| B-20291-1 | That's Life I Guess - vBH | -    -    -    - |
| B-20292-2 | Sailin' | Br 7781, A-81103, A-500697, |
| | | Voc S-52, Col DO-1662, BA 262 |
| B-20293-1 | I Can't Give You Anything But Love-vBH | As above, but Br A-500696 |
| | NOTE:- Blue Ace 262 as BENNY GOODMAN WITH TEDDY WILSON'S ALL STARS. | |

    Irving Randolph-t replaces Jones; Vido Musso-cl replaces Goodman; Midge Williams-v.
                                    New York, December 16, 1936.

| | | |
|---|---|---|
| B-20410-1-2 | I'm With You (Right Or Wrong) - vMW | Br 7797, A-81112, A-500698 |
| B-20411-1 | Where The Lazy River Goes By - vMW | -    -    -    Dec J-7 |
| B-20412-2 | Tea For Two | Br 7816, A-81125,A-500696,Voc S-73 |
| B-20413-1-4 | I'll See You In My Dreams | - Col DO-1693 - A-500697,5088 - |

    Buck Clayton-t/Benny Goodman-cl/Lester Young-ts/Teddy Wilson-p/Freddy Green-g/
    Walter Page-sb/Joe Jones-d/Billie Holiday-v.
                                    New York, January 25, 1937.

| | | |
|---|---|---|
| B-20568-1 | He Ain't Got Rhythm - vBH | Br 7824,5088,Voc S-101,Col DO-1675 |
| B-20569-2 | This Year's Kisses - vBH | -    -    - |
| B-2C570-1 | Why Was I Born ? - vBH | Br 7859, A-81160, Col 36283, |
| | | C-6182, Voc S-71 |
| B-20571-1 | I Must Have That Man ! - vBH | Br 7859, A-81160, Col 36207, |
| | | C-6205, 291283, Voc S-71, |
| | | Ph B-21177-H |

    Henry Allen- /Cecil Scott-cl-as-ts/Prince Robinson-ts/Jimmy McLin-g/John Kirby-sb/
    Cozy Cole-d/Billie Holiday-v.          New York, February 18, 1937.

| | | |
|---|---|---|
| B-20698-2 | The Mood That I'm In - vBH | Br 7844, A-81159, Voc S-89, BA 263 |
| B-20699-2 | You Showed Me The Way - vBH | Br 7840, Voc S-76 |
| B-20700-2 | Sentimental And Melancholy - vBH | Br 7844, A-81159,Voc S-188,BA 263 |
| B-20701-1 | (This Is) My Last Affair - vBH | Br 7840, Dec J-4 |
| | NOTE:- Blue Ace 263 as BILLIE HOLIDAY WITH TEDDY WILSON'S ORCHESTRA. | |

    Cootie Williams-t/Johnny Hodges-as/Harry Carney-cl-bar/Teddy Wilson-p/Allan Reuss-g
    /John Kirby-sb/Cozy Cole-d/Billie Holiday-v.
                                    New York, March 31, 1937.

| | | |
|---|---|---|
| B-20911-3 | Carelessly - vBH | Br 7867, A-81174, Voc S-89, |
| | | Col DO-1693 |
| B-20912-1 | How Could You ? - vBH | Br 7867, A-81174, Dec J-8 |
| B-20913-1 | Moanin' Low - vBH | Br 7877, A-81194, Voc S-92 |
| B-20914-1 | Fine And Dandy | -    - 5098    - |

    Harry James-t replaces Williams; Buster Bailey-cl replaces Carney; Helen Ward-v.
                                    New York, April 23, 1937.

| | | |
|---|---|---|
| B-21034-1 | There's A Lull In My Life - vHW | Br 7884, Voc S-96 |
| B-21035-2 | It's Swell Of You - vHW | -    - |
| B-21036-2 | How Am I To Know ? - vHW | Br 7893, Dec J-6 |
| B-21037-1 | I'm Coming, Virginia | -    - |

TEDDY WILSON AND HIS ORCHESTRA : Buck Clayton-t/Buster Bailey-cl/Johnny Hodges-as/
    Lester Young-ts/Teddy Wilson-p/Allan Reuss-g/Artie Bernstein-sb/Cozy Cole-d/Billie
    Holiday-v.                            New York, May 11, 1937.

| | | |
|---|---|---|
| B-21117-2 | Sun Showers - vBH | Br 7917, A-81233 |
| B-21118-2 | Yours And Mine - vBH | -        -        Voc S-185 |
| B-21119-1 | I'll Get By - vBH | Br 7903,Col 35926,291283,DO-2477, |
| | | Voc S-107, Par R-2823, DPE-42 |
| B-21119-2 | I'll Get By - vBH | CBS CL-2427, BPG-62815 (LPs) |
| B-21120-1 | Mean To Me - vBH | Br 7903, Col 35926, DO-2477, |
| | | Voc S-107, Par R-2868, DPE-68, |
| | | PZ-11017 |
| B-21120-2 | Mean To Me - vBH | CBS CL-2427, BPG-62815 (LPs) |

    Buck Clayton-t/Buster Bailey-cl/Lester Young-ts/Teddy Wilson-p/Freddy Green-g/
    Walter Page-sb/Joe Jones-d/Billie Holiday-v.
                                          New York, June 1, 1937.

| | | |
|---|---|---|
| B-21217-1 | Foolin' Myself - vBH | Br 7911, Col 36207, 291306, |
| | | C-6205, Voc S-185 |
| B-21218-2 | Easy Living - vBH | Br 7911, Col 36208, 291137, |
| | | C-6206, Dec J-4 |
| B-21219-2 | I'll Never Be The Same - vBH | Br 7926, Dec J-14, Decatur 507, |
| | | BA 243 |
| B-21220-1 | I've Found A New Baby | Br 7926, Dec J-7, BA 243 |
| B-21220-3 | I've Found A New Baby | Tax 8000 (LP) |

    NOTE:- Columbia C-6205 and Decatur 507 as BILLIE HOLIDAY.

    Harry James-t/Benny Goodman-cl/Vido Musso-ts/Teddy Wilson-p/Allan Reuss-g/Harry
    Goodman-sb/Gene Krupa-d/Boots Castle-v. Los Angeles, July 30, 1937.

| | | |
|---|---|---|
| LA-1380-B | You're My Desire - vBC | Br 7940, A-81338 |
| LA-1381-A | Remember Me ? - vBC | -        -        Dec J-14 |
| LA-1382-A | The Hour Of Parting - vBC | Br 7943, A-81476, Dec J-1, |
| | | M-30390, Col DO-1771 |
| LA-1383-A | Coquette | As above, except Col DO-1771 |

    Harry James-t/Archie Rosati-cl/Vido Musso-ts/Teddy Wilson-p/Allan Reuss-g/John
    Simmons-sb/Cozy Cole-d/Frances Hunt-v; or TEDDY WILSON QUARTET (James-Wilson-
    Simmons, with Red Norvo-x)*.      Los Angeles, August 29, 1937.

| | | |
|---|---|---|
| LA-1404-A | Big Apple - vFH | Br 7954 |
| LA-1405-B | You Can't Stop Me From Dreaming | -        Voc S-186 |
| LA-1406-B | If I Had You - vFH | Br 7960 |
| LA-1407-B | You Brought A New Kind Of Love To Me-vFH | -        Voc S-150 |
| LA-1408-A-B | *Ain't Misbehavin' | Rejected |

                              Los Angeles, September 5, 1937.

| | | |
|---|---|---|
| LA-1408-C | *Ain't Misbehavin' | Br 7964, A-81362, Dec J-13, |
| | | Col DO-1771, Tpl 537, BA 228 |
| LA-1429-A | *Just A Mood (Blue Mood) - Part 1 | Br 7973, A-81363, Dec J-10, |
| | | Par R-2741, A-7575, Od D-5634, |
| | | JCl 530, Tpl 528 |
| LA-1430-A | *Just A Mood (Blue Mood) - Part 2 | As above |
| LA-1431-A | *Honeysuckle Rose | Br 7964, A-81362, Tpl 537, BA 228 |

    Buck Clayton-t/Prince Robinson-cl/Vido Musso-ts/Teddy Wilson-p/Allan Reuss-g/Walter
    Page-sb/Cozy Cole (as SWING ROO)-d/Billie Holiday-v.
                                          New York, November 1, 1937.

| | | |
|---|---|---|
| B-21982-1 | Nice Work If You Can Get It - vBH | Br 8015, Voc S-128 |
| B-21983-1 | Things Are Looking Up - vBH | -        - |
| B-21984-1 | My Man (Mon Homme*) - vBH | Br 8008,A-81516,Col 36113,DS-1414, |
| | | MZ-253*, Voc S-186, V-Disc 28, 248 |
| B-21985-1 | Can't Help Lovin' Dat Man - vBH | Br 8008, A-81516, Col 36113, |
| | | DS-1414, MZ-253, Dec J-8 |

    NOTE:- V-Discs 28 and 248 as BILLIE HOLIDAY WITH TEDDY WILSON AND HIS ORCHESTRA.

1734                              TEDDY WILSON (cont.)

Piano solos.                                    New York, November 12, 1937.

B-22025-1  Don't Blame Me                       Br 8025, A-81357, Col 36274,
                                                DO-2649, Dec J-9
B-22026-1  Between The Devil And The Deep Blue Sea  As above

TEDDY WILSON AND HIS ORCHESTRA : ? Hot Lips Page-t/Pee Wee Russell-cl/Chu Berry-ts/
   Teddy Wilson-p/Allan Reuss-g/sb/d/Sally Gooding-v.
                                                New York, December 17, 1937.

B-22192-1-2  My First Impression Of You - vSG   Br rejected
B-22193-1-2  With A Smile And A Song - vSG          —
B-22194-1-2  When You're Smiling - vSG             —
B-22195-1-2  I Can't Believe That You're In Love    —
             With Me - vSG

   Buck Clayton-t/Benny Morton-tb/Lester Young-ts/Teddy Wilson-p/Freddy Green-g/Walter
   Page-sb/Joe Jones-d/Billie Holiday-v.  New York, January 6, 1938.

B-22192-3  My First Impression Of You - vBH    CBS CL-2427, BPG-62815 (LPs)
B-22192-4  My First Impression Of You - vBH    Br 8053
B-22194-3  When You're Smiling - vBH           Br 8070, A-81506, Col 291264,
                                               C-6206, Voc S-141, V-Disc 28, 248
B-22194-4  When You're Smiling - vBH           Col 36208
B-22195-3  I Can't Believe That You're In Love  Col 36335
           With Me - vBH
B-22195-4  I Can't Believe That You're In Love  Br 8070, A-81506, Col C-6206,
           With Me - vBH                        Voc S-150
B-22255-1  If Dreams Come True - vBH           Br 8053, Voc S-141
   NOTE:- V-Disc 28 and 248 are edited so that they start at the vocal.

   Bobby Hackett-c/Pee Wee Russell-cl/Tab Smith-as/Gene Sedric-ts/Teddy Wilson-p/Allan
   Reuss-g/Al Hall-sb/Johnny Blowers-d/Nan Wynn-v.
                                                New York, March 23, 1938.

B-22610-1-2  Alone With You - vNW               Rejected
B-22611-2  Moments Like This - vNW              Br 8112, A-81592
B-22612-2  I Can't Face The Music - vNW             —    - Par R-2553, Od D-3698
B-22613-1  Don't Be That Way                    Br 8116, A-81589  - Voc S-188 -
                                                Col 36335

   Johnny Hodges (or Buster Bailey or Jerry Blake ?)-as replaces Smith; Sedric omitted
   (Wilson only where marked *).        New York, April 29, 1938.

B-22822-2  If I Were You - vNW                  Br 8150, A-81646, Par R-2569
B-22823-1  You Go To My Head - vNW              Br 8141, A-81626, A-500752
B-22824-1  I'll Dream Tonight - vNW                —      —        —
B-22825-2  Jungle Love                          Br 8150, A-81646, Par R-2569
B-22826-1-2-3 *That Old Feeling                 Rejected
B-22827-1  *My Blue Heaven                          —

Piano solos.                                    New York, May 13, 1938.

P-22826-4  That Old Feeling                     Teddy Wilson School for Pianists
P-22827-2  My Blue Heaven                           —

TEDDY WILSON AND HIS ORCHESTRA : Jonah Jones-t/Benny Carter-as/Ben Webster-ts/Teddy
   Wilson-p/John Kirby-sb/Cozy Cole-d/Nan Wynn-v.
                                                New York, July 29, 1938.

B-23305-1  Now It Can Be Told - vNW             Br 8199, A-81701, Par R-2582,
                                                Col DO-1879
B-23306-2  Laugh And Call It Love - vNW         Br 8207, A-81745, Par R-2608,
                                                Col DO-1879
B-23307-1  On The Bumpy Road To Love - vNW      As above, but Col DO-1882
B-23308-1  A-Tisket, A-Tasket - vNW             Br 8199, A-81701, Par R-2582,
                                                DO-1882

Piano solos.                                  New York, August 1, 1938.

P-23311-1  Loch Lomond                              Br rejected
P-23312-1  Tiger Rag                                -


                                              New York, August 11, 1938.

P-23311-2-3  Loch Lomond                       Teddy Wilson School for Pianists
P-23312-2-3  Tiger Rag                              -
P-23327-1  I'll See You In My Dreams                -
P-23328-1  Alice Blue Gown                          -


TEDDY WILSON AND HIS ORCHESTRA : Harry James-t/Benny Morton-tb/Edgar Sampson-Benny
  Carter-as/Lester Young-Herschel Evans-ts/Teddy Wilson-p/Albert Casey-g/Walter Page
  sb/Joe Jones-d/Billie Holiday-v.       New York, October 31, 1938.

B-23642-1  Everybody's Laughing - vBH            Br 8259, Par A-7594
B-23643-1  Here It Is Tomorrow Again - vBH        -          -


                                              New York, November 9, 1938.

B-23687-1  Say It With A Kiss - vBH             Br 8270, A-81924, A-500758,
                                                Col DO-1908
B-23688-1  April In My Heart - vBH              Br 8265, A-81959, Col DO-1909
B-23689-1  I'll Never Fail You - vBH             -         -         -
B-23690-1  They Say - vBH                       Br 8270, A-81924, A-500758,
                                                Col DO-1908, Decatur 507
B-23690-2  They Say - vBH                       CBS CL-2427, BPG-62815 (LPs)

   Bobby Hackett-c/Trummy Young-tb/Toots Mondello-Ted Buckner-as/Bud Freeman-Chu Berry
   ts/Teddy Wilson-p/Albert Casey-g/Milton Hinton-sb/Cozy Cole-d/Billie Holiday-v.
                                              New York, November 28, 1938.

B-23760-1  You're So Desirable - vBH            Br 8283, A-81934, Par A-7511
B-23761-1  You're Gonna See A Lot Of Me - vBH   Br 8281, A-81941
B-23762-1  Hello, My Darling - vBH               -         -      Col DO-1940
B-23763-2  Let's Dream In The Moonlight - vBH   Br 8283, A-81934    -


Piano solos.                                  New York, January 27, 1939.

P-24024-1-2  Coquette                          Teddy Wilson School for Pianists
P-24025-1  China Boy                                -
P-24026-1  Melody in F                              -
P-24027-1  When You And I Were Young, Maggie        -


TEDDY WILSON AND HIS ORCHESTRA : Roy Eldridge-t/Ernie Powell-cl-ts/Benny Carter-as-
  ts/Teddy Wilson-p/Danny Barker-g/Milton Hinton-sb/Cozy Cole-d/Billie Holiday-v.
                                              New York, January 30, 1939.

B-24044-1  What Shall I Say ? - vBH            Br 8314, A-82004, Col DO-1955
B-24045-1  It's Easy To Blame The Weather - vRH  -         -         -
B-24046-1  More Than You Know - vBH            Br 8319, A-82010, Col 36117,
                                                D-13194, DS-1576, MZ-250,
                                                Par R-2660, A-7511
B-24046-2  More Than You Know - vBH  (all LPs) CBS CL-2428,BPG-62816,Fon 662007TR
B-24047-1  Sugar - vBH                         Br 8319, A-82010, Col 36117,
                                                D-13194, DS-1576,MZ-250,Par R-2660


   Karl George-Harold Baker-t/Floyd Brady-tb/Pete Clark-cl-as-bar/Rudy Powell-cl-as/
   Ben Webster-George Irish-ts/Teddy Wilson-p-a/Albert Casey-g/Al Hall-sb/J. C. Heard-
   d/Thelma Carpenter-v.                      New York, May 10, 1939.

B-24497-1-2  If Anything Happened To You - vTC   Br rejected
B-24498-1-2  Why Begin Again ? (Pastel Blue) - vTC   -


                                              New York, June 28, 1939.

B-24824-B  Jumpin' For Joy                     Br 8438, Col DO-2011
B-24825-A  Booly-Ja-Ja                         Col 35220, Par R-2726, Od A-2355
B-24826-A  The Man I Love                      Br 8438, Col DO-2011
B-24827-A  Exactly Like You                    Col 35220, Par R-2726, Od A-2355,
                                                D-3719

TEDDY WILSON AND HIS ORCHESTRA : Karl George-Harold Baker-t/Floyd Brady-tb/Pete
    Clark-cl-as-bar/Rudy Powell-cl-as/Ben Webster-George Irish-ts/Teddy Wilson-p-a/
    Albert Casey-g/Al Hall-sb/J. C. Heard-d-v/Thelma Carpenter-Jean Eldridge-v/Buster
    Harding-Edgar Sampson-a.                    New York, July 26, 1939.

B-24931-A  Love Grows On The White Oak Tree - vTC  Br 8455
B-24932-A  This Is The Moment - vTC                  -
B-24933-A  Early Session Hop                        Col 35207, Par R-2732, PZ-11003,
                                                     Od A-2357
B-24934-A  Lady Of Mystery                          As above

                                        New York, September 12, 1939.

26058-A  Jumpin' On The Blacks And Whites     Col 35232
26059-A  Little Things That Mean So Much - vJE  -
26060-A  Hallelujah                           Col 35298, V-Disc 456
26061-A  Some Other Spring - vJE                -        Par PZ-11201

    Doc Cheatham-t added.           New York, December 11, 1939.

25735-1  Wham (Re-Bop-Boom-Bam) - vJCH&ch   Col 35354
25736-1  Sweet Lorraine                     Col 35711, V-Disc 456
25737-1  Moon Ray - vJE/aTW                 Col 35354
25738-1  Liza                               Col 35711

                                        New York, January 18, 1940.

26435-A  Crying My Soul Out For You - vJE   Col 35372
26436-A  In The Mood                          -        M-138
26437-A  Cocoanut Groove                    Col 35737
26438-A  71                                   -

    Bill Coleman-t/Benny Morton-tb/Jimmy Hamilton-cl/George James-bar/Teddy Wilson-p/
    Eddie Gibbs-g/Al Hall-sb/Yank Porter-d/Helen Ward-v.
                                        New York, December 9, 1940.

29233-1  I Never Knew                       Col 35905
29234-1  Embraceable You - vHW                -        38218, C-6384
29235-1  But Not For Me - vHW               Col 36084, DZ-335, Par R-2815
29236-1  Oh ! Lady, Be Good                   - 291264 -          -

Piano solos, acc. by Al Hall-sb/J. C. Heard-d where marked **.
                                        Chicago, April 7, 1941.

CCO-3653-1  Smoke Gets In Your Eyes        Col 36631, DCH-355
CCO-3654-1**Rosetta                        Col 36632
CCO-3654-2**Rosetta                          -        Par R-2981

                                        Chicago, April 11, 1941.

CCO-3686-1**I Know That You Know           Col 36633, Par R-2985, PZ-11088
CCO-3687-1**Them There Eyes                Col 36631, DCH-355 -        -
CCO-3688-2**China Boy                      Col 36634, Par R-2981
CCO-3693-1  I Surrender, Dear              Rejected
CCO-3694-1  Body And Soul                  Col 36634
CCO-3695-1  I Can't Get Started            Col 36633

TEDDY WILSON AND HIS ORCHESTRA : Emmett Berry-t/Benny Morton-tb/Jimmy Hamilton-cl/
    Teddy Wilson-p/Johnny Williams-sb/J. C. Heard-d/Lena Horne-v.
                                        New York, September 16, 1941.

31319-1  A Touch Of Boogie                 Rejected
31320-1  Out Of Nowhere - vLH              Col 36737
31321-1  Prisoner Of Love - vLH            V-Disc 317
31322-1  The Sheik Of Araby                Rejected

Piano solo.                             New York, January 21, 1942.

32282-1  These Foolish Things              Col 36632

TEDDY WILSON AND HIS ORCHESTRA : Emmett Berry-tBenny Morton-tb/Edmond Hall-cl/Teddy
 Wilson-p/Johnny Williams-sb/J. C. Heard-d/Helen Ward-v.
                                  New York, July 31, 1942.

| | | |
|---|---|---|
| 33083-1 | You're My Favorite Memory - vHW | Col 36737 |
| 33084-1 | Something To Shout About - Part 1 | Rejected |
| 33085-1 | Something To Shout About - Part 2 | - |
| 33086-1 | B Flat Swing | - |

### DALE WIMBROW (THE DEL-MAR-VA SONGSTER)  AND HIS RUBEVILLE TUNERS

The following sides by this pioneer radio artist are of interest for the musicians
 providing the accompaniments.

Sylvester Ahola-t/Phil Wall-p/Dale Wimbrow-u-v/Johnny Morris-d.
                                  New York, November 18, 1926.

| | | |
|---|---|---|
| 143121-3 | It Takes A Good Woman (To Keep A Good Man | Col 821-D |
| | At Home) | |
| 143122-2 | Country Bred And Chicken Fed | - |

                                  New York, November 22, 1926.

| | | |
|---|---|---|
| | Sleepy Time | Vic test (un-numbered) |
| | So Long North (I'm Headin' South) | - |

                                  New York, December 2, 1926.

| | | |
|---|---|---|
| 11346 | Country Bred And Chicken Fed | Ed 51894 |
| 11347 | So Long North (I'm Headin' South) | - |

### WINDSOR  ORCHESTRA

Pseudonym on Grafton for the following items listed in this book :-

| | |
|---|---|
| 9093 | An Orange Grove In California (California Ramblers) |
| 9107 | Ain't My Baby Grand ? (California Ramblers) |
| 9149 | Collegiate (Ben Selvin and his Orchestra) |
| 9188 | I Love My Baby (My Baby Loves Me) (Mike Speciale and his Orchestra) |
| 9206 | Horses (California Ramblers) |
| 9216 | Goodnight (I'll See You In The Morning) (Consolidated Club Orchestra - see |
| | Paul Specht) |
| 9217 | Poor Papa (The Red Heads) |
| 9230 | Who'd Be Blue ? (Jack Stillman's Orioles) |
| 9231 | Am I Wasting My Time On You ? (California Ramblers) |
| 9238 | Hi-Ho The Merrio ! (California Ramblers) |
| 9239 | Talking To The Moon (Jack Stillman's Orioles) |
| 9256 | I've Got The Girl (Johnny Sylvester and his Orchestra) |
| 9259 | How Could Red Riding Hood ? (Tommy Morton's Grangers) |
| 9265 | Everything's Made For Love (Joe Candullo's Everglades Orchestra) |

### WINDY CITY JAZZERS

Ed Smalle-Vernon Dalhart-k/Tom Griselle-p/Harry Reser-bj.
                                  New York, c. June 23, 1924.

| | | |
|---|---|---|
| 8954-A | Hard Hearted Hannah | Gnt 5494, Cx 40346, St 9573, EBW 4104 |
| 8955-A | Bringing Home The Bacon | As above, except EBW 4104 |

NOTE:- Claxtonola 40346 as MOBILE JAZZERS; Edison Bell Winner 4104 as REGENT
ORCHESTRA.

### WINDY CITY  TRIO

—— Kurtz-as/Sol S. Wagner-p/ —— Cottle-bj.
                                  New York, May 10, 1920.

| | | |
|---|---|---|
| | Weary Blues | Vic test (un-numbered) |

Jimmy Cobb-c/Junie Cobb-cl-ts/Ernie Smith-bsx/? Frank Melrose-p/Tommy Taylor-d.
Chicago, April, 1929.

21255-1  South African Blues                    Pm 12770, Bwy 1294, Cen 3009
21256-1  Piggly Wiggly Blues                       -           -       -

## WINEGAR'S PENN. BOYS

The following titles by this band are of some interest as jazz.

Frank Winegar-bj dir. 2t/tb/3cl-ss-as/cl-ss-ts/vn/p/bb-sb/d; one sax db pic.
New York, January 25, 1928.

18191    A Good Man Is Hard To Find              Ed 52221
18192    Since My Best Gal Turned Me Down           -
NOTE:- The Edison files show matrix 18191 for SINCE MY BEST GAL, and 18192 for
A GOOD MAN IS HARD TO FIND, contrary to the records themselves.

New York, February 10, 1928.

18192    Since My Best Gal Turned Me Down        Ed 52241

New York, May 4, 1928.

18469; N-235  My Gal Sal                         Ed 52305, Amb 5535

## ANONA WINN

This famous Australian BBC broadcaster made many records for various companies, the
following having accompaniments of interest as jazz.

Vocal, acc. by Carroll Gibbons-p dir. Sylvester Ahola-t/Van Phillips-as/? George
Hurley-vn/Joe Brannelly-g/? Dick Escott-sb.
Hayes, Middlesex, April 19, 1928.

Bb-13212-1-2  There's A Cradle In Caroline       Rejected
Bb-13214-2  I've Got A Feeling For Somebody      HMV B-2745

Johnny Helfer-as replaces Phillips.     Hayes, Middlesex, September 28, 1928.

Bb-14473-4  Sweet Ukulele Maid                   HMV B-2841

Van Phillips-as added; Helfer plays ts; Rudy Starita-d-vib added.
Hayes, Middlesex, November 5, 1928.

Bb-14884-2  Heaven For Two                       HMV B-2874

Acc. by Ray Noble dir. Norman Payne-t/? Laurie Payne-as/2vn/vc/Harry Jacobson-p/
? Tiny Stock-sb/? Rudy Starita-d.     Hayes, Middlesex, September 11, 1929.

Bb-17625-1  Am I Blue ?                          HMV B-3174

## JACK WINN/WYNN'S  DALLAS DANDIES

Pseudonym for the following items listed in this book :-

Melotone M-12008/Panachord 25008  Both sides by the Original Memphis Five
          M-12027/Polk P-9035  Both sides by Johnny Dodds' Black Bottom Stompers
          M-12051/Vocalion 15860  Both sides by Irving Mills' Hotsy Totsy Gang
          M-12064/Polk P-9034/Brunswick 02001  Melancholy (Johnny Dodds' B.B.Stompers)
          M-12064/Polk P-9034/Panachord 25035  Someday, Sweetheart (King Oliver and
          his Dixie Syncopators)

## GUS WINSON'S ORCHESTRA

Pseudonym on Australian Summit Z-115 for Lawrence Welk and his Orchestra, q.v., and
probably for other bands of less interest as jazz.

Vocal, acc. by Tom Morris-c/Charlie Irvis-tb/Bob Fuller-cl/Mike Jackson-p/Buddy
  Christian-bj.                            New York, November 23, 1926.

| | | |
|---|---|---|
| 36958-3 | I Got A Mule To Ride | Vic 20407 |
| 36959-2 | Mama's Gonna Drop Your Curtain | Vic 20424 |
| 36960-3 | Pail In My Hand | - |
| 36961-1 | Peepin' Jim | Vic 20407 |

  Fuller db as.                           New York, February 16, 1927.

| | | |
|---|---|---|
| 37786-1 | 'Way After One And My Daddy Ain't Come Home Yet | Vic 20857 |
| 37787-1 | Joogie Blues | Vic 20654 |
| 37788-1 | Ever After On | - |
| 37789-1 | Rent Man Blues | Vic 20857 |

## MARIUS B. WINTER AND HIS DANCE ORCHESTRA

The following titles by this pioneer British broadcasting band are known to be of
  interest as "hot" dance music.

Marius B. Winter dir. Arthur Williams and another-t/2 tb/Hugh Tripp and another-cl-
  as/Edgar Bracewell-cl-ts/Ted Edbrooke (and others ?)-vn/Wally Wallond-p/John
  Collins-g/Bob Lamonte-sb/Bill Airey-Smith-d.
                                         London, February-March, 1931.

| | | |
|---|---|---|
| LO-882-4 | Choo Choo | Bcst 3019 |

                                         London, March-April, 1931.

| | | |
|---|---|---|
| LO-920 | Tap Your Feet (Go Bo-De-Do-De-Doo) - v | Bcst 3036 |

## CHIC WINTERS

The following titles, issued as by CHIC WINTERS' HOTEL GRAMATIN ORCHESTRA, are known
  to be of some interest as "hot" dance music; others, as CHIC WINTER'S ORCHESTRA on
  Broadway, Carnival, Embassy, Ross and Triangle are of straight commercial performances, but on Pennington 1437, this is a pseudonym for Duke Ellington and his
  Orchestra, q.v.

Chic Winters dir. 2t/tb/2cl-as/cl-ts/p/bj/bb/d.
                                         New York, May 7, 1926.

| | | |
|---|---|---|
| X-116-A | No More Worryin' | Gnt 3320, Bel 1049 |

  NOTE:- Beltona 1049 as AMERICAN DANCE ORCHESTRA.

                                         New York, June 3, 1926.

| | | |
|---|---|---|
| X-166-A | Faded Cherry Blossom | Gnt 3340 |

## TINY WINTERS AND HIS BOGEY SEVEN

Tommy McQuater-t/Andy McDevitt-cl/Don Barrigo-ts/Ernest Ritte-bar/Monia Liter-p/
  Archie Slavin-g/Tiny Winters-sb-v/Ronny Gubertini-d.
                                         London, April 22, 1936.

| | | |
|---|---|---|
| TB-2140-1 | How Many Times ? - vTW | Dec F-6031 |
| TB-2141-1 | Frankie And Johnnie - vTW | - |

## JULIE WINTZ

The following titles by this commercial dance band are known to be of interest as
  "hot" dance music.

JULIE WINTZ AND GEORGE ZIMMER'S JERSEY COLLEGIANS : Julie Wintz-bj dir. t/tb/Bill
  Zimmer-cl-as-v/as/ts/p/bb/George Zimmer-d.
                                         New York, c. May 10, 1926.

| | | |
|---|---|---|
| 106853 | Spanish Mamma | PA 36460, Per 14641 |
| 106854 | Deep Henderson | PA 36451, Per 14632 |

JULIE WINTZ AND HIS HOFBRAU ORCHESTRA : Julie Wintz-bj dir. t/tb/Bill Zimmer-cl-as-v
   /as/ts/p/bb/George Zimmer-d.              New York, June 14, 1927.

144248-5  Magnolia - vBZ                     Har 438-H
144256-4  Vo-Do-Do-De-O Blues - vBZ         Har 436-H

JULIE WINTZ AND HIS MAYFLOWER ORCHESTRA : Julie Wintz-bj dir. Johnny ——— -t/Joe ———
   tb/Dinty Curtis-cl-as-v/Bert ——— -as/ts/Paul ——— p/bb/George Zimmer-d/Irving
   Kaufman-v.                                New York, October 15, 1929.

149140-1  I Gotta Have You - vIK            Har 1051-H

                                            New York, January 14, 1930.

149755-1  Harmonica Harry (The Harmonica King)-vDC Har 1104-H
149756-3  The Man From The South (With A Big Cigar Har 1092-H
             In His Mouth) - vDC

JULIE WINTZ AND HIS ORCHESTRA : Probably as above.
                                            New York, April 16, 1929.

150473-3  After You've Gone                 Har 1169-H

### BILL WIRGES AND HIS ORCHESTRA

The following titles by this Harry Reser band are of considerable interest as jazz.

Harry Reser-bj dir. Tommy Gott-Earl Oliver-t/Sam Lewis-tb/Larry Abbott and another-
   cl-as/Norman Yorke-cl-ts/Bill Wirges-p/Tom Stacks-d-v.
                                            New York, c. March 11, 1925.

105902    Cheatin' On Me                    PA 036223, 10963, Per 14404,
                                               Hom C-873
   NOTE:- Pathe Actuelle 10963 as HARRY RESER'S DANCE ORCHESTRA; Homochord C-873 as
ELDON'S DANCE ORCHESTRA.

Red Nichols-t replaces Oliver.             New York, c. June 2, 1925.

106061    Pango Pango Maid                  PA 036262, 10909, Per 14443,
                                               GP 18418
   NOTE:- Pathe Actuelle 10909 as HARRY RESER'S DANCE ORCHESTRA; Grand Pree 18418 as
GRAND PREE NOVELTY DANCE ORCHESTRA.

Unknown t replaces Nichols; Bob Oliver-v/?-bb added.
                                            New York, c. December 2, 1925.

106446    Shake That Thing - vBO           PA 36352, Per 14533

                                            New York, c. September 29, 1926.

107111    Meadow Lark - vTS                PA 36526, 11299, Per 14707,
                                               Gra 9271, Leo 23073
   NOTE:- Pathe Actuelle 11299 as HARRY RESER'S ORCHESTRA; Grafton 9271 as GRAFTON
ORCHESTRA.

### WISCONSIN ROOF ORCHESTRA

See Devine's Wisconsin Roof Orchestra.

### WISCONSIN U SKYROCKETS

Jesse Cohen-p dir. Bunny Berigan-t/Don Bonn-t-cl-ts/as/bj/d.
                                            Chicago, c. May, 1928.

20552-2  Slow Beef                          Pm 12641
20553-1  Dizzy Corners                      Pm 12642
20554-2  Postage Stomp                      -
20555-1  It's A Sin                         Pm 12641

Dick Voynow-p dir. Bix Beiderbecke-c/Al Gande-tb/Jimmy Hartwell-cl-as/George Johnson-ts/Bob Gillette-bj/Min Leibrook-bb/Vic Moore-d.

Richmond, Ind., February 18, 1924.

| | | |
|---|---|---|
| 11751-A | Fidgety Feet | Gnt 5408, HRS 22, Br 02204, HJCA HC-120, Tpl 546 |
| 11752, -A-B | Lazy Daddy | Rejected |
| 11753, -A | Sensation Rag | - |
| 11754-A | Jazz Me Blues | Gnt 5408, HRS 25, Br 02203, HJCA HC-120, Tpl 546 |

Gande omitted. Richmond, Ind., May 6, 1924.

| | | |
|---|---|---|
| 11852 | Oh Baby | Gnt 5453, Cx 40336, HRS 25, Br 02501, Tpl 554 |
| 11853 | Copenhagen | Gnt 5453, Cx 40336, UHCA 46, Br 02205, Tpl 554 |
| 11854-C | Riverboat Shuffle | Gnt 5454, Cx 40339, HRS 9, Tpl 536, VJR 19, Tem R-44 |
| 11855-A | Susie | As above, except VJR 19 |
| 11855-B | Susie | Gnt 5454 |
| 11856 | Royal Garden Blues | Rejected |

Richmond, Ind., June 20, 1924.

| | | |
|---|---|---|
| 11930-B | I Need Some Pettin' | Gnt 20062, Reedition Hot R-1001 |
| 11931-C | Royal Garden Blues | - HRS 26, Br 02204, Tpl 524 |
| 11932 | Tiger Rag | HRS 24, Br 02205, Pol 15387 - |

Bix Beiderbecke db p*; George Brunies-tb-k added.

New York, September 16, 1924.

| | | |
|---|---|---|
| 9079 | Sensation | Gnt 5542, Cx 40375, St 9595,9598, HRS 23, VJR 8, Poydras MJC-13, Tem R-45 |
| 9080-A | Lazy Daddy | Gnt 5542, St 9595, 9598, HRS 9 |
| 9080-B | Lazy Daddy | Cx 40375, VJR 8, Poydras MJC-13, Tem R-45 |

NOTE:- Claxtonola 40336, 40339 and 40375 as THE JAZZ HARMONISTS.

Brunies omitted. New York, October 7, 1924.

| | | |
|---|---|---|
| 9115-B | Tia Juana | Gnt 5565, HRS 26, Tpl 552 |
| 9116 | *Big Boy | - HRS 24 - Br 02203 |

Jimmy McPartland-c replaces Beiderbecke; Dave Harmon-v.

New York, December 5, 1924.

9218-B When My Sugar Walks Down The Street - vDH Gnt 5620, St 9611, Tem R-24

New York, December 12, 1924.

9231-A Prince Of Wails Gnt 5620, St 9611, Tem R-24

The name THE WOLVERINES was also used on Brunswick 3332 as a pseudonym for the Tennessee Tooters, q.v. Accordong to VARIETY, September 24, 1924, the band had made records for "a number of minor recording firms," and that Brunswick was interested in recording them. They never made any other records besides the above, however, unless perhaps for some company whose files have never been found.

## WONDER SEXTETTE

Pseudonym on Australian Gibsonia for the Varsity Eight, q.v. (The labels were pasted over Lincoln pressings imported from the U.S.A.)

Russell Wooding dir. 2t/tb/2cl-ss-as/cl-ss-ts/p/bj/bb/Percy Robinson-d/Frank Luther-
    Willie Jackson-v.                    New York, May 13, 1931.

| | | |
|---|---|---|
| 69607-2 | Nina - vWJ | Vic 23382 |
| 69608-1 | Niagara Falls - vWJ | - |
| 69609-1-2-3 | That's My Desire - vFL | Rejected |
| 69610-1 | I Can't Get Enough Of You - vFL | Vic 22718 |

NOTE:- Victor 23382 as THE RED CAPS.


? Benny Morton-tb replaces (or may be) the unknown; Albert Socarras-as-f may be
the 4th sax; one of the others db o; Dick Robertson-v.
                                     New York, May 20, 1931.

| | | |
|---|---|---|
| 69609-4 | That's My Desire - vDR | Vic 22718 |

## SAM WOODING

SAM WOODING AND HIS ORCHESTRA : Sam Wooding-p dir. Bobby Martin-Maceo Edwards-Tommy
    Ladnier-t/Herb Flemming-tb/Garvin Bushell-cl-as-o/Willie Lewis-as-bar-v/Gene Sedric
    c-ts/John Mitchell-bj/John Warren-bb/George Howe-d.
                                     Berlin, late May-early June, 1925.

Unknown titles from THE CHOCOLATE KIDDIES
NOTE:- These phantom recordings are referred to in VARIETY on June 17, 1925 as
having been made for "the German branch of Victor" (presumably Deutsche Grammophon,
as Electrola did not exist at that time, and DG used the Victor trade mark).

                          Berlin, July, 1925.

| | | |
|---|---|---|
| 2357-A | O Katharina | Vox 01882 |
| 2358-A | Shanghai Shuffle | Vox 01890 |
| 2359-A | Alabamy Bound | - |
| 2360-A | By The Waters Of Minnetonka | Vox 01882 |
| | | |
| 2755-B | O Katharina | Vox 1883 |
| 2756-B | Shanghai Shuffle | - |
| 2757-B | Alabamy Bound | Vox 1891 |
| 2758-B | By The Waters Of Minnetonka | - |

THE SAM WOODING BAND : As above, but without Ladnier; Sumner Leslie "King" Edwards-bb
    replaces Warren, and Percy Johnson-d replaces Howe.
                                     Berlin, September, 1926.

| | | |
|---|---|---|
| 53bn | Black Bottom | DG/Pol 20689 |
| 54bn | Behind The Clouds | - |
| | By The Waters Of Minnetonka | DG/Pol 20690 |
| | Dreaming Of A Castle In The Air | - |
| 603bk | Just A Cottage Small - vWL | DG/Pol 20693 |
| 604bk | Milenberg Joys | DG/Pol 20691 |
| 605bk | Lonesome And Sorry - vWL | DG/Pol 20693 |
| 606bk | Tampeekoe | DG/Pol 20691 |
| | Am I Wasting My Time On You ? | DG/Pol 20692 |
| | Dreaming Of Tomorrow | - |

MAESTRO SAM WOODING Y SUS CHOCOLATE KIDDIES : Sam Wooding dir. Bobby Martin-Doc
    Cheatham-t-v/Tommy Ladnier-t/Albert Wynn-Billy Burns-tb/Willie Lewis-cl-as-bar-v/
    Gerry Blake-cl-as-v/Gene Sedric-cl-ts/Freddy Johnson-p-v/John Mitchell-bj/Sumner
    Leslie "King" Edwards-bb/Ted Fields-d-v.
                                     Barcelona, July, 1929.

| | | |
|---|---|---|
| 76517-2 | I Can't Give You Anything But Love-vTF | Par B-25423 |
| 76518-2 | Bull Foot Stomp - vBM-FJ | Par B-25424 |
| 76519-2 | Carrie - vWL-JB-FJ-TF-DC | Par B-25420 |
| 76520-2 | Tiger Rag - vFJ | - |
| 76521-2 | Sweet Black Blues - vBM-WL-JB | Par B-25421 |
| 76522-2 | Indian Love - vTF | Par B-25424 |
| 76523-2 | Ready For The River - vJB | Par B-25422 |
| 76524-2 | Mammy's Prayer - vWL | - |
| 76525-2 | My Pal Called Sal - vWL | Par B-25421 |
| 76526-2 | Krazy Kat - vWL | Par B-25423 |

SAM WOODING AND HIS ORCHESTRA : Sam Wooding dir. Bobby Martin-Doc Cheatham-t/Albert
    Wynn-Billy Burns-tb/Willie Lewis-cl-as-bar-v/Jerry Blake-cl-as-v/Gene Sedric-cl-ts
    /Freddy Johnson-p-v/John Mitchell-bj/Sumner Leslie "King" Edwards-bb/Ted Fields-d-
    v.                      Paris, c. October 24, 1929.

```
300480-1  Smiling Irish Eyes - vWL-JB-TF          P X-8697
300481-1  Hallelujah ! - vWL-?JB-TF               P X-8696
300482-1  Downcast Blues - vWL-?JB                P X-8684, Cellodisc C-8684
300483-1-2  Weary River - vWL                       -                 -
```

    Cheatham omitted; Ralph James-cl-as replaces Blake.
                              Paris, November, 1929.

```
300501-1  Deep Night - vWL-FJ-TF                  P X-8697
300502-1  She's Funny That Wag (sic)              P X-8693
300503-1  I Lift Up My Finger And Say "Tweet-Tweet"-v-
300508-1  Button Up Your Overcoat - vWL           P X-8696
```

    Harmonium used.                  Paris, November-December, 1929.

```
300526-1  Le Pirate (Lover, Come Back To Me)-vTF  P X-96058
300527-1  The Wedding Of The Painted Doll - vTF   P X-8698
```

    June Cole-bb replaces Edwards.        Paris, December, 1929.

```
300538-1  C'est tout que j'ai (All I Have)        P X-8698
300539-1  Breakaway - vWL-?FJ-?                   P X-8707
300540-1  My Sin - vWL-?FJ-?                        -
```

SAM WOODING'S CHOCOLATE KIDDIES : As last session; Johnson db cel.
                              Paris, December, 1929.

```
2812bkp   How Am I To Know ? - vTF                DG/Pol 22994, 521597
2813½bkp  Singin' In The Rain - vWL               DG/Pol 22993, 521596
2814bkp   Can't We Be Friends ? - vTF             DG/Pol 22994, 521597
2815bkp   I've Got A Feeling I'm Falling - vTF    DG/Pol 22993, 521596
```

SAM WOODING AND HIS ORCHESTRA : Sam Wooding dir. Bobby Martin-Teddy Brook-t/Albert
    Wynn-tb/Willie Lewis-Ralph James-cl-as/Gene Sedric-cl-ts/Justo Barretto-p/John
    Mitchell-bj-g/June Cole-bb/Ted Fields-d; stg (? Mitchell) where marked *.
                          Paris, late June, 1931.

```
4385½bkp  *Love For Sale                          Br A-500097
4388½bkp  I Have Two Loves                          -
          Even If You Love Me                     Br A-500098
          I Surrender, Dear                         -
```

    Sam Wooding-p-a dir. probably :- Frank Newton-John Swan-t/Nat Story-tb/Garvin
    Bushell- ? another-cl-as/Gene Sedric-cl-ts/g/sb/d.
                         New York, January 29, 1934.

```
176355-1  My Gal Sal                              Col test
176356-1  Weary Blues                               -
```

## WOODLAND HARMONY ORCHESTRA

Pseudonym on Clarite 816 for Al Lentz and his Orchestra, q.v.

## BABE WOODS AND HIS PALS

Pseudonym on Champion 15468 for Lou Calabrese and his Hot Shots, q.v.

## EVA WOODS

Pseudonym on Silvertone for Ozie McPherson, q.v.

## HARRY WOODS AND HIS NEW JERSEY ORCHESTRA

Pseudonym on Decca for the following items listed in this book :-

F-3897  This Little Piggie Went To Market (Victor Young and his Orchestra)
F-5085  Both sides by the Dorsey Brothers' Orchestra

# JIMMY WORNELL'S HOT BLUE-BOTTLES

Jimmy Wornell-Vernon Mayall-Arthur Coborn-t/Percy Harper-Jack Creedon-tb/Gerry
  McQuillan-bsn/ ―― Mitchell-p/George Morris-bj/Tommy Blades-d-harpophone/Tommy
  Sullivan-scat v.                          London, March, 1931.

LO-909; ET-692  Stomping - vTS              Bcst 3033
LO-910; ET-693  Broadway Stomp - vTS           -

## EMMA  WRIGHT

Vocal, acc. by ? Leroy Williams-c/cl/? James Moore-p/? Octave Gaspard-bb.
                              Dallas, December 7, 1928.

147595-1-2  Police Blues                    Rejected
147596-2  Lonesome Trail Blues              Col 14413-D

## ALLISTER WYLIE AND HIS  CORONADO HOTEL ORCHESTRA

The following titles by this commercial dance orchestra are of some interest as "hot"
  dance music.

Allister Wylie-p dir. Clarence Forster-t/tb/Kenneth Albrecht-cl-as/as/ts/bsx/2vn/Bill
  Bailey-2nd p/g/Vincent Vanni-bb/d-vib-x/Rich Richards-v.
                              St. Louis, September, 1928.

STL-854-B  Come On, Baby ! - vRR            Br 4143, 3934
STL-857-  Some Of These Days - vRR             -      -

## JULIAN WYLIE JAZZ BAND

Mandolins (with rhythm acc. ?)          London, September 21, 1933.

CA-13944-1-2  Stretch Yo' Face              Col rejected
CA-13945-1-2  Unromantic Blues                 -

## ALBERT  WYNN

ALBERT WYNN'S GUT BUCKET FIVE : Dolly Jones-c/Albert Wynn-tb/Barney Bigard-ss-ts/
  Jimmy Flowers-p/Rip Bassett-bj/Lillie Delk Christian-v.
                              Chicago, June 25, 1926.

9789-A  When - vLDC                         OK 8350
9790-A  That Creole Band                       -

WYNN'S CREOLE JAZZ BAND : Punch Miller-c-v/Albert Wynn-tb/Lester Boone-cl-as-bar/
  William Barbee-p/Charlie Jackson-bj/Sidney Catlett-d.
                              Chicago, October 2, 1928.

C-2381-B  Down By The Levee - vPM           Voc 1220, V-1018, Br 80042,
                                            JSo AA-519
C-2382-B  She's Crying For Me               Voc 1252, V-1029    -  JSo AA-519

ALBERT WYNN'AND HIS GUT BUCKET FIVE : As last session above, but Alex Hill-p replaces
  Barbee, and may be the unidentified vocalist.
                              Chicago, October 9, 1928.

C-2423-  Crying My Blues Away - v           Voc 1218, Sup S-2234, Decatur 515
C-2424-B  Parkway Stomp - vPM               Voc 1220, V-1018, Br 80041

## JACK  WYNN

See Jack Winn.

## BILLY WYNNE AND HIS GREENWICH VILLAGE  INN ORCHESTRA

The following titles by this commercial dance orchestra from among the considerable
  number recorded by it for Edison, Harmony and Pathe between the autumn of 1924 and
  the spring of 1926 are reportedly of interest as "hot" performances.

Billy Wynne-d dir. Hymie Farberman-Red Nichols-t/Sam Lewis-tb/Larry Abbott and/or
  Arnold Brilhart-Alfie Evans-cl-as-bar/Jules Nassberg-cl-ts/Frank Farrell-p/Louis
  Condell-bj/Ken Snell-bb.                    New York, April 21, 1925.

10329    When My Sugar Walks Down The Street     Ed 51549
10330    Lenore                                  -

                                   New York, May 22, 1925.

10393    Pango Pango Maid                        Ed 51566
10394    Brighter Days                           -

Unknown bj/ob replace Condell and Snell.
                                   New York, July 20, 1925.

10507    Say Arabella                            Ed 51573
10508    Charleston Baby Of Mine                 Ed 51606

  Arthur Hall-v.                   New York, July 27, 1925.

10522    Cecilia - vAH                           Ed 51603
10523    Somebody's Crazy About You              Ed 51606

## THE  YACHT CLUB BOYS

The following titles by this American comedy quartet are outstanding from the viewpoint of a jazz enthusiast because of the accompaniments.

Adler-Kelly-Kern-Mann-v quartet, acc. by Benny Goodman-cl/vn/p/g/sb.
                                   New York, January 16, 1934.

152688-2  Sing-Sing Isn't Prison Any More     Col 2908-D, DB-1356, FB-1238
152689-2  The Great American Tourist          -           -          -
152690-2  We Own A Salon                      Col 2887-D, DB-1357, FB-1237
152691-1  The Super-Special Picture Of The Year  -        -          -

## YALE  COLLEGIANS

Leroy Morris and another-t/tb/Rudy Vallee-cl-as/as/ts/p/bj/bb/d/v trio, possibly including Rudy Vallee.             New York, September 26, 1927.

11912    You'll Do It Someday (So Why Not Now ?) Ed 52108
            - v3

                                   New York, December 21, 1927.

18122    Is Everybody Happy Now ?                Ed rejected
18123    (Hooray-Hooray !) It's Ray-Ray-Raining  -

Bob Bruce-cl-as-a dir. Stew Pletcher-t-v/Seelye Vidal-Bob Stanley-t/Jim Northam-tb/
  Hart Leavitt-cl-as/Bob Laidlaw-cl-as-a/Al Thompson-ts/Sidney Fine-p/Tiny Little-
  field-g/Alan Lutz-bb-sb/ ─── Pearlman-d/Spike Adriance-v.
                                   New York, November 14, 1930.

404551-B  And Then Your Lips Met Mine - vSA       OK 41474, Od ONY-36162,
                                                  Par PNY-34154
404552-B  What's The Use Of Living Without Love ? Od ONY-36162, Par PNY-34156
            - vSA/aBB
404553-A  Blue Again - vSP/aBL                    OK 41474, Od ONY-36163,
                                                  Par PNY-34155
100466-1  Blue Again - vSP/aBL                    Cl 5215-C, Har 1272-H
  NOTE:- Clarion 5215-C and Harmony 1272-H as MISSOURI COLLEGIANS; Parlophone PNY-
  34154, PNY-34155 and PNY-34156 as THE MUSICAL STUDENTS.


See also Carl Webster's Yale Collegians.

Piano solos.                                    Chicago, c. April, 1939.

| R-2417 | Jimmy's Stuff | SA 12008 | | |
| R-2418 | The Fives | - | Cir J-1051 | |
| | La Salle Street Breakdown (all LPs) | Riv RLP-1028, | 12-124, | Lon AL-3525 |
| | Two O'Clock Blues | - | - | - |
| | Janie's Joys | - | - | - |
| | Lean Bacon | - | - | - |
| | Big Bear Train | - | - | - |
| | Lucille's Lament | - | - | - |
| | Beezum Blues | - | - | |
| | Yancey Limited | - | | |

| | Rolling The Stone | Riv RLP-1061, | 12-124 (LPs) |
| | Steady Rock Blues | - | - |
| | P. L. K. Special | - | - |
| | South Side Stuff | - | - |
| | Yancey's Getaway | - | - |
| | How Long Blues | - | |
| | How Long Blues No. 2 | - | |
| | Jimmy's Stuff No. 2 | - | - |

Chicago, October 25, 1939.

| 044006-1 | Yancey Stomp | Vic 26589, HMV B-9366, HE-2347, X-7083 |
| 044007-1 | State Street Special | Vic 26589, HMV B-9381   - X-7083 |
| 044008-1 | Tell 'Em About Me | Vic 26590   - EA-2997, JK-2347 |
| 044009-1 | Five O'Clock Blues | -   HMV B-9366   - |
| 044010-1 | Slow And Easy Blues | Vic 26591, HMV B-9374, JK-2368 |
| 044011-1 | The Mellow Blues | -   -   - EA-2997 |

Faber Smith-v.                                 Chicago, February 23, 1940.

| WC-2955-A | I Received A Letter - vFS | Voc 05464, Par R-2959 |
| WC-2956-A | East St. Louis Blues - vFS | - |
| WC-2961-A | Bear Trap Blues | Voc 05490, Col 37335, C-6332 |
| WC-2962-A | Old Quaker Blues | - |

NOTE:- Matrices WC-2957 through WC-2960 are by Charlie Segar, q.v.

Jimmy Yancey-v.                                Chicago, September 6, 1940.

| 053436-1 | Cryin' In My Sleep - vJY | BB B-8630 |
| 053437-1 | Death Letter Blues - vJY | - |
| 053438-1 | Yancey's Bugle Call | Vic 27238, HMV EA-3070 |
| 053438-2 | Yancey's Bugle Call | X LX-3000, Vic 75681 (LPs) |
| 053439-1 | 35th And Dearborn | Vic 27238, HMV EA-3070 |
| 053439-2 | 35th And Dearborn | X LX-3000, Vic 75681 (LPs) |

## THE YANKEE SIX

Cal Davis-c/Bill Fitzgerald-tb/Ted Benton-cl/Jules Pillar-cl-ts/Jack McLaughlin-vn/
Dick George-p/Irving Matthews-bj/Harrison Hall-bb/Harold Tapson-d.
                                               Buffalo, March, 1925.

| 8990-A | I Never Knew How Much I Loved You | OK 40335 |
| 8991-A | Jimtown Blues | OK 40348 |
| 8992-A | No One | - |
| 8993-A | Oh ! Those Eyes | OK 40335 |

## THE YANKEE TEN (DANCE) ORCHESTRA

Pseudonym for the following items listed in this book :-

Broadway 1027/Paramount 20469/Puritan 11469  Both sides by the Buffalodians
Oriole 684  Baby Face (The Buffalodians)
       846  Ain't She Sweet ? (Jack Pettis and his Band)
       933  Sometimes I'm Happy (The Six Hottentots)
      1207  There's Something About A Rose (Devine's Wisconsin Roof Orchestra)
      1455  Makin' Whoopee (Ernie Golden and his Orchestra)

UNCLE CHARLIE RICHARDS : Vocal and kazoo, acc. by Louis Hooper-p.
                                    New York, c. March 29, 1927.

| 107448-B | Sore Bunion Blues | PA 7527, Per 127 |
| 107449-C | I'm Gonna Moan My Blues Away | -        - |
|          | Levee Blues | PA 7521, Per 121 |
|          | Wayward Roamer Blues | -        - |

Vocal and kazoo, acc. by Louis Hooper-v.   New York, April 6, 1927.

| GEX-577-A | I'm Gonna Moan My Blues Away | Gnt 6104, BP 8021, Ch 15264 |
| GEX-578-A | Sore Bunion Blues | -        -     Ch 15281 |

## HARRY A.  YERKES

Harry A. Yerkes was a pioneer recording artist on drums, handbells and xylophone in
the early years of the century, for Columbia in New York.  Between 1917 and 1924 he
directed many sessions on this and every other label, sometimes with results of
interest as jazz.  Some of these appeared as The Happy Six (q.v.); the others known
to come within this definition are listed below.

YERKES MARIMBAPHONE BAND : Joe Green-George Hamilton Green-x-marimba/bsx/p.
                                    New York, November 26, 1918.

| 49555-1 | Sensation | Col A-6116 |

YERKES JAZARIMBA ORCHESTRA : C/Tom Brown-tb/? Ed Violinsky-vn/p/Joe Green-George
   Hamilton Green-d-x.              New York, February 24, 1919.

| 78315-1-3 | Bevo Blues (Bone Dry) | Col A-2720 |

NOVELTY FIVE : C/tb/cl/p/d/Al Bernard-v.   New York, c. February, 1919.

|  | Bluin' The Blues - vAB | AV 12117 |
|  | Don't Cry, Frenchy, Don't Cry - vAB | - |
|  | Shake, Rattle And Roll - vAB | AV 12124 |
|  | Idol (Intro. In Soudan) | - |

                                    New York, c. March, 1919.

|  | I Want To Hold You In My Arms - vAB | AV 12135 |
|  | Lonesome Road Blues | - |

                                    New York, c. April, 1919.

|  | St. Louis Blues | AV 12148 |
|  | Venus Blues | - |

                                    New York, c. May, 1919.

|  | Sand Dunes | AV 12164 |
|  | Where The Lanterns Glow | - |

YERKES' NOVELTY FIVE : Alcide Nuñez-cl/Ross Gorman-as/Ted Fiorito-p/? Arthur Lange-bj
   /George Hamilton Green-Joe Green-d-x.   New York, June 2, 1919.

| 49637-2 | Easy Pickin's | Col A-6116 |

NOVELTY FIVE : Probably similar to the first session under this name, or to the last
   one above.                       New York, c. September, 1919.

|  | The Vamp | AV 12210 |
|  | You'll Be Sorry | - |
|  | Just Leave It To Me | AV 12216 |

|  | Big  Chief Blues | Lyratone 4207 |
|  | Old Joe Blues | - |

YERKE'S (sic) NOVELTY FIVE : Earl Oliver-c/Tom Brown-tb/? Ross Gorman-as/? Ted
  Fiorito-p/George Hamilton Green-d.    New York, c. November, 1919.

  12014    Missouri Blues                       Lyric 4207, Concert 1003
  12015    At The High Brown Babies' Ball (Intro.       -     Concert 1004
           There Is A Lot Of Blue-Eyed Marys Down In Maryland)
  NOTE:- Concert 1003 and 1004 as CONCERT NOVELTY FIVE.

HARRY A. YERKES DANCE ORCHESTRA : As above, plus Ed Violinsky-vn; Rudy Wiedoeft-as
  may replace ? Gorman.                 New York, c. November, 1919.

  5197    Mystery                        Voc 14024, X-9001, Hom H-172,61070
  NOTE:- Homochord H-172 as MELLOR'S DANCE ORCHESTRA; Homokord 61070 as JAZZ BAND.

  Alcide Nuñez-cl added; possibly other changes
                                        New York, c. January  1920.

  5400    Shake Your Little Shoulder (Intro.    Voc 14041, Hom H-350
          Dixieland Is Happy Land)
          Oh, By Jingo !                         -
  5405    Swanee                         Voc 14024, X-9010
  NOTE:- Homochord H-350 as HOMOCHORD DANCE ORCHESTRA.

NOVELTY FIVE : C/Tom Brown-tb/Alcide Nuñez-cl/Ross Gorman-as/Ted Fiorito-p/George
  Hamilton Green-d.                     New York, c. January, 1920.

  5420    Railroad Blues                 Voc 14047
  5423    Goodnight Boat                       -    X-9008
  NOTE:- Some copies of Vocalion 14047 are labeled YERKES NOVELTY FIVE, giving the
  title as LEFT ALL ALONE AGAIN BLUES (as do all copies of Vocalion X-9008). As this
  tune forms the major part of the performance, copies so-labeled  are obviously more
  accurate !

YERKES SOUTHERN FIVE : Tom Brown-tb/Alcide Nuñez-cl/Ted Fiorito-p/? Arthur Lange-bj/
  George Hamilton Green-d.              New York, March 5, 1920.

  79024-1-2-3  Railroad Blues                   Col A-2929, LaB AL-5088
  79025-1-2-3  Old Grey Mare Blues              Rejected
  NOTE:- LaBelle AL-5088 as JAZZ BAND.

                                        New York, March 12, 1920.

  79043-1-2-3-4  I Never Knew I Had The Blues        Col rejected

NOVELTY FIVE : C (db tb*)/Tom Brown-tb/Alcide Nuñez-cl/Ross Gorman-as/Ted Fiorito-p/
  George Hamilton Green-d.              New York, c. April, 1920.

  5703    *Laughing Hyena                Voc 14061, X-9008, Hom H-220
  5706    Barking Dog                          -               -
  NOTE:- Homochord H-220 as THE MISSISSIPPI COONS.

HARRY A. YERKES' JAZARIMBA BAND : C/Tom Brown-tb/Ross Gorman or Rudy Wiedoeft-as/bsx/
  Ted Fiorito-p/George Hamilton Green-d.  New York, c. April-May, 1920.

  5798    Syncopated Dream               Voc 14071
  5800    Dance-O-Mania                        -

YERKES SAXOPHONE SEXTET : Ss/2as/? Cm/ts/bsx.
                                        New York, c. July, 1920.

  7359    Frogs' Legs                    Gnt 9089  Gmn 1101
  7360    Squealing Pig Blues                  -        -

YERKES BLUEBIRD ORCHESTRA : Harry A. Yerkes dir. Earl Oliver-c/Tom Brown-tb/? Ross
  Gorman-as/ts/bsx/p/George Hamilton Green-d.
                                        Montreal, c. September, 1920.

         Dance-O-Mania                  HMV 216188

YERKES SAXOPHONE SEXTETTE : Ss/2as/ts/bar/bsx.
                          Montreal, c. September, 1920.

        Frogs Legs                            HMV 216190

YERKES' S. S. FLOTILLA ORCHESTRA : Unknown vn dir. Hymie Farberman-t/Tom Brown-tb/
  ? Arnold Brilhart-Bob Johnson-cl-ss-as-ts/2nd vn/? vc/p/bj/bb/d.
                          New York, November, 1921.

   8243    Arkansas Blues                     Voc 14272, M-1035, Hom H-294
   8244    Stop ! Rest Awhile                   -      Clm 1489
   NOTE:- Vocalion M-1035 as ST. GEORGE'S DANCE ORCHESTRA; Homochord H-294 as HOMO-
   CHORD DANCE ORCHESTRA; Coliseum 1489 as NEW YORK CASINO ORCHESTRA.

YERKES' NOVELTY FIVE : C/Tom Brown-tb/cl/p/d.
                          New York, April, 1922.

   578-C  On The 'Gin 'Gin 'Ginny Shore        GG 1102


                        YOUNG'S CREOLE JAZZ BAND

Bernie Young-c/Preston Jackson-tb/Philmore Holly-cl/Lil Hardaway-p/Mike McKendrick-
   bj/Eddie Temple-d.              Chicago, October, 1923.

   1535-1-2  Tin Roof Blues                    Pm 20272, 14023, Cx 40272, Hg 863,
                                               Pur 11272, Cen 3027,VJR 9, Addisco
   1536-1-2  Every Saturday Night              Pm 12060
   1537-1-2  What's The Use Of Lovin' ? - vAO    -
   1538-1-2  Jazzbo Jenkins - vOP              Pm 12059, Hg 874
   NOTE:- Paramount 12059 as OLLIE POWERS; Harmograph 874 as CLARENCE YOUNG; Paramount
   12060 (1537-1-2 only) as ANNA OLIVER AND YOUNG'S CREOLE JAZZ BAND.

Bernie Young-c/Preston Jackson-tb/Happy Caldwell-cl/Stump Evans-as/Cassino Simpson-p/
   Mike McKendrick-bj/Eddie Temple-d.    Chicago, November, 1923.

   1587-1-2  Dearborn Street Blues             Pm 12088, 14015


                        ART AND LESLIE YOUNG

Pseudonym on Guardsman 2032 for Harry Bidgood, q.v., and Sam Bogen.


                            ARTHUR YOUNG

ARTHUR YOUNG AND HIS YOUNGSTERS : Max Goldberg-t/Freddy Gardner-Ernest Ritte-cl-as/
   Harry Berly-ts-vl/Jean Pougnet-vn/Marie Goossens-harp/Arthur Young-p/Albert Harris-
   g/Don Stuteley-sb/Max Bacon-d/Helen Howard-v.
                          London, December 20, 1934.

CAR-3128-1  A Bouquet For George Gershwin-Part 1   RZ MR-1568
            (Intro. Rhapsody In Blue/Lady Be Good/Fascinating Rhythm/Do-Do-Do-vHH)
CAR-3129-1  A Bouquet For George Gershwin-Part 2    -
            (Intro. 'S Wonderful/That Certain Feeling/Looking For A Boy/I'd Rather
            Charleston-vHH)


   Unidentified male v.             London, February 7, 1935.

CAR-3219-2  A Bouquet For Cole Porter - Part 2    RZ MR-1861
            (Intro. You've Got That Thing/Let's Do It-v/Love For Sale)
CAR-3220-1  A Bouquet For Cole Porter - Part 1      -
            (Intro. What Is This Thing Called Love ?/Night And Day-v/I'm In Love
            Again)

ARTHUR YOUNG AND HIS YOUNGSTERS : Max Goldberg-t/Lew Davis-tb/Danny Polo-cl/Billy
Amstell-ts/Freddy Gardner-bar/Arthur Young-p/Albert Harris-g/Dick Ball-sb/Max
Bacon-d.                              London, August 6, 1935.

TB-1856-1  Any Old Rags - Part 2 (Intro.          Dec F-5645, Br A-9883
           Bugle Call Rag/Russian Rag/Alexander's Ragtime Band)
TB-1857-1  Any Old Rags - Part 1 (Intro.              -         -
           12th Street Rag/Temptation Rag/Tiger Rag)
TB-1858-1  Bundle Of Blues - Part 2 (Intro.       Dec F-5709, Br A-9839
           Limehouse Blues/St. Louis Blues/Dreamy Blues)
TB-1859-1  Bundle Of Blues - Part 1 (Intro.           -         -
           Wabash Blues/Jazz Me Blues/Farewell Blues)

Piano solos, acc. by Albert Harris-g/Don Stuteley-sb/Ronnie Gubertini-d.
                                      London, November 19, 1935.

CE-7285-1  Blind Man's Buff                       Par R-2153, A-6365
CE-7286-1  Ain't Misbehavin'                          -         -

ARTHUR YOUNG AND HIS BAND : 2vn/Arthur Young-p/g/sb/d.
                                      London, January 5, 1939.

CE-9535-1  Jazz Me Blues                          Par rejected

The late Arthur Young made several piano duets with Reginald Foresythe, and from 1939
he recorded for Decca on the novachord (an electronic organ device), solo and with
Hatchett's Swingtette, a group including Stephane Grappelly-vn.  The results are
more in the nature of commercial novelties, however, than of jazz.

## BILLIE YOUNG

Vocal, acc. by Jelly-Roll Morton-p.     New York, April 3, 1930.

59735-1  When They Get Lovin' They's Gone    Vic FXM1-7227 (LP)
59735-2  When They Get Lovin' They's Gone    Vic 23339
59736-1  You Done Played Out Blues           Vic FXM1-7227 (LP)
59736-2  You Done Played Out Blues           Vic 23339

## BUDDY YOUNG AND  HIS ORCHESTRA

Pseudonym on Mayfair for Gene Kardos and his Orchestra, q.v.

## CLARENCE YOUNG

Pseudonym on Harmograph 874 for Ollie Powers; see Young's Creole Jazz Band.

## LESTER YOUNG

See Glenn. Hardman and his Hammond Five, and the Kansas City Six.

## MARGARET YOUNG

The following title by this popular American vaudeville artist of the 1920s is of
some interest as jazz for its accompaniment.

Vocal, acc. by t/tb/cl/as/ts/vn/p/bj/bb/d.
                                      New York, December 5, 1925.

E-17043    Red Hot Henry Brown                   Br 2939*

## PATSY  YOUNG

Pseudonym on Harmony and associated labels for Annette Hanshaw, q.v.

## RUSSELL  YOUNG

Piano solos.                            Richmond, Ind., June 19, 1933.

19205    Thousand Finger Rag                    Ch rejected
19206    When I Get The Blues All Around Me Do'     -

Victor Young was the director of the ARC-Brunswick "house" orchestra from 1931 to
1934, and of Decca from then until his death in 1958.  The following records have
interesting solos, and there are very probably others of similar merit among the
enormous number produced under his direction.

Bunny Berigan-Bob Effros-t/Tommy Dorsey-tb/Jimmy Dorsey-and another-cl-as/ts/Joe
Venuti-vn/Arthur Schutt-p/Eddie Lang-g/? Joe Tarto-bb-sb/? Chauncey Morehouse-d-
vib/The Boswell Sisters-v.                    New York, May 25, 1931.

E-36825-   Sing A Little Jingle - vBS          Br 6128, 01193, A-9076
E-36826-   I Found A Million Dollar Baby (In A Five-   -       -       -
           And-Ten-Cent Store) - vBS

   Similar personnel; Dick McDonough-g replaces Lang; Chick Bullock-v.
                                    New York, March 31, 1933.

13190-   Two Tickets To Georgia - vCB          Ban 32731, Mt M-12660, Or 2675,
                                               Per 15751, Ro 2048, Voc 15882
13191-   You'll Never Get Up To Heaven That Way Ban 32732, Mt M-12661, Or 2676,
         - vCB                                 Per 15752, Ro 2049
13192-   Hold Me - vCB                         As above, plus Imp 2888
13193-   The Grass Is Getting Greener All The  Ban 32731, Mt M-12660, Or 2675,
         Time - vCB                            Per 15751, Ro 2048, Rex 8003
NOTE:- Melotone M-12660 and Perfect 15751 as ART KAHN'S ORCHESTRA; Melotone M-12661
and Perfect 15752 as PHIL ROMANO AND HIS DE WITT CLINTON HOTEL ORCHESTRA; Vocalion
15882 as CHICK BULLOCK AND HIS LEVEE LOUNGERS; Imperial 2888 as ED LOYD AND HIS
ORCHESTRA; Rex 8003 as BELL BOYS OF BROADWAY.

Victor Young dir. Bunny Berigan-Sterling Bose-t/Charlie Butterfield-tb/Jimmy Dorsey-
? Lyle Bowen-cl-as/? Hymie Wolfson-cl-ts/Joe Venuti-Harry Hoffman-Walter Edelstein-
Lou Kosloff-vn (2-3 of these)/Joe Meresco-p/Charlie Magnante-pac/Dick McDonough or
Carl Kress-g/Artie Bernstein-sb/Larry Gomar-d/? Red Norvo (or Gomar db)-x/Dick
Robertson-v.                                  New York, April 20, 1933.

B-13261-A  Two Tickets To Georgia - vDR        Br 6554, 01534

Victor Young dir. Frank Guarente-Sterling Bose-t/Jack Teagarden-tb/Chester Hazlett-
Jimmy Dorsey-cl-as/Mutt Hayes-ts/Joe Venuti-Walter Edelstein-Lou Kosloff-vn/Joe
Meresco-p/Perry Botkin-g/Artie Bernstein-sb/Larry Gomar-d/Harlan Lattimore-Jane
Vance-v.                                       New York, January 13, 1934.

B-14589-A  A Day Without You - vHL             Br 6747, 01749, Col DO-1173
B-14591-A  This Little Piggie Went To Market - vJV    -    Dec F-3897
NOTE:- Decca F-3897 as HARRY WOODS AND HIS NEW JERSEY ORCHESTRA.

   One vn omitted; Peg LaCentra-v replaces Jane Vance, who still receives label credit
on Brunswick 6747.                            New York, January 23, 1934.

B-14591-C  This Little Piggie Went To Market - vPL Br 6747, Col DO-1173

   Similar instrumentation, featuring Joe Dixon-cl and good p; Paul Small-v.
                                    New York, November 2, 1934.

38950-A  Mr. And Mrs. Is The Name - vPS          Dec 279, F-5504

                            THE ZA ZU GIRL

Elton Spivey Harris-v, acc. by cl-as/? Blind John Davis-p/sb, and md unless marked *.
                                    Chicago, October 19, 1937.

C-2014-1 *My Righteous Man                     ARC 8-01-66, Voc 03884
C-2015-1-2  Ocean Wide                         Rejected
C-2016-1-2  My Tweet Twaat Twaat               -
C-2017-1  He Left Me                           ARC 8-01-66, Voc 03884

Barney Zeeman dir. 2t/tb/cl-as/as/ts/p/bj bb/d/Pat Kennedy-v.
                                    New York, April 7, 1926.

| X-77 | I'd Rather Be Alone | Gnt 3299, Chg 143, Ch 15093, Clm 1927 |
| X-78-A | Horses - vPK | Gnt 3360, Ch 15090, Aco G-16035, Bel 1036, Gmn 1939, Sc 778 |
| X-79, -A-B | Am I Wasting My Time On You ? | Rejected |

NOTE:- Beltona 1036 as AMERICAN DANCE ORCHESTRA; Challenge 143 as MEMPHIS MELODY
BOYS; Champion 15090 and 15093 as JACK'S FAST-STEPPIN' BELL-HOPS; Coliseum 1927 as
MAYFIELD DANCE ORCHESTRA; Guardsman 1939 as SAN FRANCISCO DANCE ORCHESTRA; Scala
778 as PAVILION ORCHESTRA.

## ZON-O-PHONE  ORCHESTRA

The "house" orchestra of the American Zon-O-Phone label (as distinct from British
Zonophone) made a large number of records between 1903 and 1910, of which the
following is known to be an interesting ragtime performance; there may well be
others similar, but the label is rather rare, despite its being a subsidiary of
Victor.

2c/2tb/ah/th/cl/f/pic/vn/bb/d-bells.     New York, c. June, 1908.

| 8822 | Persian Lamb Rag (Winchester) | Zon 1150, 5320 |

## BOB ZURKE AND  HIS DELTA RHYTHM BAND

Bob Zurke-p dir. Nat Natoli-Sterling Bose-Chelsea Quealey-t/Vincent Grande-Billy
Pritchard-Artie Foster-tb/Sid Stoneburn-Noni Bernardi-cl-as/Larry Binyon-John
Gassoway-ts/Chuck Dale-bar/Chick Reeves-g-a/Felix Giobbe-sb/Stan King-d/Claire
Martin-v.                            New York, July 18, 1939.

| 038282-2 | Southern Exposure | Vic 26331, HMV EA-2673 |
| 038283-1 | It's Me Again - vCM | - |
| 038284-1 | Each Time You Say Goodbye - vCM | Vic 26317, HMV EA-2502 |
| 038285-2 | Hobson Street Blues | -       HMV B-9034, EA-2673 |

Pete Peterson-sb replaces Giobbe; Fud Livingston-a.
                                    New York, August 10, 1939.

| 041536-1 | Melancholy Mood - vCM | Vic 26342 |
| 041537-1 | Between The Devil And The Deep Blue Sea - vCM/aFL | Vic 26355, HMV EA-2587 |
| 041538-1 | Honky-Tonk Train Blues - aFL | Vic 26342 |
| 041539-1 | I've Found A New Baby - aFL | Vic 26355, HMV B-9034 EA-2587 |

NOTE:- HMV EA-2587 as BOB ZURKE AND HIS BAND.

                                    Chicago, September 26, 1939.

| 040451-1 | Faithful Forever - vCM | Vic 26395 |
| 040452-1 | Tom Cat On The Keys - aFL | Vic 26526, HMV X-6571 |
| 040453-2 | It's A Hap-Hap-Happy Day - vCM | Vic 26395, HMV EA-2464 |
| 040454-2 | Everybody Step - aFL | Vic 26526, HMV X-6571 |

Sterling Bose-v.                    Chicago, October 30, 1939.

| 044030-1 | Fit To Be Tied - vCM | Vic 26420 |
| 044031-2 | Peach Tree Street - vSB | - |
| 044032-1 | Cuban Boogie-Woogie | Vic 26411, HMV X-6506 |
| 044033-1 | On A Little Street In Singapore - vCM | -       - |

Bob Zurke-p dir. Jack Thompson-Chelsea Quealey-t/Sterling Bose-t-v/Ray Noonan-Seymour
Goldfinger-tb/Mike Doty-cl-as/Gus Ehrman-as-v/Ted Mack-John Gassoway-ts/Noel Kilgen
g/Pete Peterson-sb/Stan King-d/Evelyn Poe-v.  New York, December 15, 1939.

| 043995-2 | Somebody Told Me - vEP/aFL | Vic 26446 |
| 043996-1 | Between 18th And 19th On Chestnut Street - vSB | Vic 26450 |
| 043997-1 | Pinch Me - vEP | - |
| 043998-1 | Holy Smoke - vGE/aFL | Vic 26446 |
| 043999-1 | Nickel Nabber Blues - aFL | Vic 26467, HMV X-6589 |
| 046000-1 | I Want My Mama - vEP/aFL | -       - |

Bob Zurke-p dir. Wilton Hutton-Chelsea Quealey-Sterling Bose-t/Emmett Milligan-Bob
   McReynolds-tb/Gus Ehrman-James Clifford-as/John Gassoway-ts/Ernie Caceres-cl-bar/
   Noel Kilgen-g/Leonard King-sb/Al Sidell-d/Evelyn Poe-v.
                                          Chicago, January 18, 1940.

044633-1  You Hit My Heart With A Bang - vEP          Vic 26474
044634-1  Tea For Two                                 Vic 26561
044635-1 or -2  Put Your Little Foot There (w)-vEP    Vic 26474
044636-1  I Love You Much Too Much - vEP              Vic 26561

Bob Zurke-p dir. Howard Gaffney-Wayne Williams-Chelsea Quealey-t/Mac Zazmar-Hobart
   Simpson-tb/Marty Berman-Charles Spero-as/Art Wamser-John Gassoway-ts/Noel Kilgen-g/
   Harry Cohen-sb/Al Sidell-d/Evelyn Poe-v. New York, May 8, 1940.

050534-2  I'm Losing My Mind (Because Of You) - vEP Vic 26607
050535-1  Cow Cow Blues                             Vic 26646
050536-1  Rhumboogie - vEP                              -        HMV NE-506
050537-1  I Bought A Wooden Whistle - vEP           Vic 26607

## ZUTTY AND HIS BAND

See Zutty Singleton.

## compiled by MARY RUST

All names in this index are shown strictly alphabetically; thus, de Droit precedes Deems, who in turn precedes de Faut. If a name is prefixed Mac or Mc, these are shown together, provided there is a capital letter for the rest of the name,e.g. McPartland. Names such as Macaffer are shown in the normal listing of others whose first letter is M. In some cases there is doubt as to exactly how a name is spelt, and slight variations in these occur in the text, usually with such names as Clark and Clarke, in which case they are indexed thus : CLARK(E).... Where a musician is better known by a nickname than by his real one, he is shown by the former in the text, and in the index thus : ORY, Kid (r.n. Edward O.) Pages showing records that were actually issued under a musician's name are shown in the index with the page-numbers underlined.

M. E. R.

AARONSON, Abe  as  684
AARONSON, Irving  p-ldr-v  1
AARONSON, Jack  p  957-958-959
ABATO, Jimmy  cl-bar  1553
ABBEY, Ernie  t  134-1055
ABBEY, Leon  vn-ldr  1-2-1362-1449
ABBEY, Wag (r.n. Charles A.)  d-x-chimes
   134-345-639-667-784-798-799-1019-1055-
   1216-1493
ABBOTT, Larry  cl-ss-as-k-comb  2-37-89-
   127-145-319-421-532-671-813-925-926-929-
   930-932-973-998-1006-1064-1067-1068-1076
   1080-1097-1098-1163-1164-1247-1263-1288-
   1305-1323-1379-1380-1381-1396-1415-1416-
   1417-1431-1483-1521-1604-1610-1611-1694-
   1740-1745
ABEL, William  tb  398-1117
ABELARDO, Lou  v  2-537
ABERG, Sture  d  282
ABRAMO, Peter  t  417
ABRAMS, Archie  t  9
ABRAMS, Irwin  vn-ldr  2
ABRAMS, Max  d  2-3-16-140-285-801-895-
   974-1137-1225-1289-1298-1419-1432-1433-
   1695-1721
ABRIANI, Felice  bj  2
ABRIANI, John  a-dir  2
ACEHEART, Louis  t  263
ACHTEL, Irving  vn  1681
ACQUELINA, Barney  bsx  629-630-1543
ACRES, Sam  tb  16-20-1365
ADAMI, Madame  p  1161
ADAMS, Arnold  g  39-191-192-382
ADAMS, Clarence  cl  344-1450
ADAMS, Garry  g  1237
ADAMS, Jerry  ?  530-531
ADAMS, Jimmy  d-vib  328-751
ADAMS, Johnny "Bridge"  vn  274
ADAMS, Powell  d  356
ADDE, Leo  d  111-650-1065-1132
ADDISON, Bernard  bj-g  12-13-15-47-58-114
   119-282-312-526-631-686-688-691-726-727-
   730-769-828-1013-1053-1061-1104-1105-
   1388-1422-1465-1468-1513-1614
ADERHOLD, Olin  sb  650-1507
ADERHOLT, Bill  cl-as  1287
ADKINS, Rick  t  119-134-464
ADLER, Henry  d  63-321-322-323
ADLER, Larry  h-p-v  3-512-678-1280
ADLER, Oscar  vn  218

ADLER, Rudolph  cl-ts-ca-o  936-945-946-
   979-1108-1126-1273-1299-1300
ADRIANCE, Spike  v  1745
AERTS, Jos  d  1284
AGEE, Carl  t  959-1664-1665
AGLORA, Joe  ts  398-1360-1361
AGNEW, Charlie  t  919
AGUANNO, Joe  t  126-1552
AHEARN, Ollie  cl-ss-as-ts  656-657
AHLBERG, Harry  a  306
AHOLA, Sylvester  t-mel  2-4-20-21-22-31-
   236-268-302-395-500-506-507-521-524-525-
   561-562-564-565-684-784-785-788-930-949-
   950-951-952-953-971-1126-1127-1148-1155-
   1164-1165-1217-1226-1290-1291-1292-1293-
   1294-1335-1355-1396-1456-1483-1493-1507-
   1589-1619-1640-1737-1738
AIKEN, Bud  tb  164-187-645-1306-1589-1649
   1692
AIKEN, Gus  c-t  52-53-115-164-645-810-833
   940-1008-1306-1346-1451-1463-1576-1589-
   1649-1692-1727
AINSLEY, Horace  p  1613-1614
AINSWORTH, J. R. "Huppies"  ts  263
AIONA. Andrew  g-ldr  4
AIREY-SMITH, Bill  d-v-ldr  4-807-808-1739
AIREY-SMITH, Mrs.  v  808
AKST, Harry  p  1204-1457
ALABAMA JOE - see SMECK, Roy
ALABAMA MAGPIE TRIO  v  676
ALBERT, Don  t-a-ldr  7-209-533-1156-1338
ALBRECHT or ALBRIGHT, Ken(neth)  cl-as
   1271-1744
ALBRIGHT, Fred  d  1330
ALBRIGHT, Ken - see ALBRECHT, Kenneth
ALCORN, Alvin  t  7
ALCORN, Oliver  cl-ts  302
ALDRICH, Ronnie  p-a  1343
ALEMAN, Oscar  g  7-190-330-821-1238-1536
ALESS. Tony  p  1242-1243-1244
ALEXANDER, Alec  t  402-403
ALEXANDER, Alec  cl-as  833
ALEXANDER, Barney  bj  1103
ALEXANDER, Charlie  p-speech  48-49-50-414
   692
ALEXANDER, Claude  c  1209
ALEXANDER, Durelle  v  1689
ALEXANDER, Edward  as  747
ALEXANDER, Edward  vn  665
ALEXANDER, Hilda  v  7

ALEXANDER, Joe  v  1272
ALEXANDER, Van (r.n. FELDMAN, Al)  ldr-v-a
  8-9-10
ALEXANDER, Texas (r.n. Alger A.)  v  8
ALEXIS, Ricard  c  302
ALEXY, Bob  t  325-326-451-1075
ALFREDO  vn-ldr  10-11
ALIX, May  v  41-92-1152-1153
ALLARD, Joe  cl-ts  1310
ALLBRIGHT, Arthur  bj-v  1421
ALLEN, ——  bb  237
ALLEN, Betty  v  787
ALLEN, Burt  c  314-315
ALLEN, Celeste  v  154-155
ALLEN, Charlie  t  489-758-759
ALLEN, Country  tb  1108
ALLEN, David  v  1540
ALLEN, Durant  p  1195
ALLEN, Ed  c-v  5-99-118-136-146-191-411-
  412-731-802-864-1014-1395-1445-1446-1452-
  1467-1534-1535-1559-1700-1701-1702-1703-
  1704-1705-1706-1707-1708-1709-1710-1711-
  1722
ALLEN, Eddie  cl-ts  172-173
ALLEN, Edward I.  p  278-644
ALLEN, Ferdie  banjoline  315
ALLEN, Fletcher  cl-as-ts-a  1-11-283-518-
  960-1371-1536
ALLEN, George  cl-ss-as  409-519-685-1328
ALLEN, Henry  t-v  11-12-13-14-15-46-54-55-
  56-57-75-88-91-114-142-355-358-382-383-
  662-688-726-727-730-751-783-792-824-825-
  839-1073-1074-1099-1103-1107-1108-1168-
  1170-1227-1253-1276-1278-1304-1345-1346-
  1408-1422-1467-1486-1488-1542-1623-1624-
  1701-1706-1707-1732
ALLEN, Henry "Tincan"  d  177
ALLEN, Huff  tb  1047
ALLEN, J.  v  649
ALLEN, Les  as-ts-v  11-16-470-785-1126-
  1134-1202-1695
ALLEN, Lil  v  680
ALLEN, Moses  bb-preaching  310-983-984-
  985-986-987-988-989-990
ALLEN, Nat  tb  683-1674
ALLEN, Nat  bj  1298
ALLEN, Ray  p  545-546
ALLEN, Ray  v  16
ALLEN, Sam  p  550-755-756-779-1123-1124-
  1465-1670
ALLEN, Stuart  v  756
ALLEN, Terry  v  167-168-324-325-1158-1159-
  1160-1554
ALLEN, Wad  ts  274
ALLEN, Wayne  p  1201-1231-1232-1718
ALLEY, Vernon  sb  663-664
ALLIER  Pierre  t  11-16-333-465-519-689-
  776-1259-1284-1348-1349-1642
ALLOM, Maurice  ts-bar  467-1089
ALMERICO, Tony  c-v  112-173-917-918
ALONGI, Tony  vn  1095
ALPERT, Trigger (r.n. Herman A.)  sb  1572
ALSOP, William  as  1632
ALSTON, Buzz  v  623
ALSTON, James  p  1035-1091-1723
ALSTON, Ovie  t-v-ldr  18-179-773-774-775
ALSWANG, Morey  bj  919
ALTER, Lou  p  512
ALTHEIMER, Joshua  p  843-849-1541-1542
ALTIER, Charles  c  1228
ALTIER, Danny  as  18

ALTMEYER, Rollie  p  1196
ALTPETER, Larry  tb  207-562-923-1095-
  1224-1248-1276-1304-1484
ALTSCHULER, Benny  vc  905
ALVAREZ, Gerry or Jerry  ts  316
ALVERO, Phil  cl-as  416
ALVIN, Danny  d  542-1002-1003-1004-1007-
  1257-1573
ALVIS, Hayes  bb-sb-a-v  27-58-283-284-
  285-404-410-489-490-491-492-493-518-
  663-757-758-765-1071-1072-1073-1074-
  1263-1304-1355-1421-1455-1456-1500-
  1711
ALVIS, Herb  tb  251
AMARAL, Frank  t  93
AMATURO, Matthew  cl-as  119-120-919
AMBROSE, Bert  vn-ldr  20-21-22-23-24-25-
  161-1456
AMERICAN FOUR, THE  v  1318-1319
AMMONS, Albert  p  26-27-751-814-821-850-
  851-947-948-994-1135-1240-1320
AMSTELL, Billy  cl-as-ts  22-23-24-25-132-
  138-147-161-404-508-684-790-791-1224-
  1298-1750
ANDER, Rune  t  282
ANDERSON, Al  d  1029
ANDERSON, Andy  c-t-v  27-274
ANDERSON, Archie  vn  1054
ANDERSON, Bernard  t  768-1037-1038
ANDERSON, Cameron  bj  344
ANDERSON, Cat (r.n. William A.)  t  277-1674
ANDERSON, Charles  t  154-155
ANDERSON, Charlie  bj  1693
ANDERSON, Don  t  505-1150-1237
ANDERSON, Dorsey  v  1357
ANDERSON, Ed  c-t  47-285-1071-1072-1073-
  1103-1168-1169-1511-1535-1663-1701-1703-
  1704-1705-1706
ANDERSON, Eddie  as  1368
ANDERSON, Ernie  g  59
ANDERSON, Ewald  cl-ts  652
ANDERSON, Gene  p-cel  45-46-404-1488
ANDERSON, Ivie  v  27-485-486-487-488-489-
  490-491-492-493-495-496-497-498-499-500-
  631
ANDERSON, James  v  318-696
ANDERSON, Jimmy  v  763
ANDERSON, John  tb  706-1451-1507-1538
ANDERSON, John  p  1539
ANDERSON, Junie  bj  170
ANDERSON, Kenneth  p-as  337-338-824
ANDERSON, Lawrence  tb  1038
ANDERSON, Ralph  p-k-v  676-1322
ANDERSON, S.  v  316
ANDERSON, Shadrack  d  154
ANDERSON, Skippy  p-a  685-686
ANDERSON, Stewart or Stuart  ts  126-657-
  1159-1160
ANDERSON, Walter  d-ldr  28
ANDREWS, SISTERS, THE (Patti-LaVerne-
  Maxine)  v  28-29-30-363-370-430-431-
  740
ANDREWS, Dope  tb  512-513-1460
ANDREWS, Huck  v  99
ANDREWS, Jack  tb  786-787
ANDREWS, Jesse  p  1097
ANDREWS, Jim  – see KAUFMAN, IRVING
ANDREWS, Stanley  vn-as  635-788-789-801-
  809-810
ANDREWS, Vic  bj-g  1675
ANGELOTTY, Carl  bb  317

1756

ANGONOST, George bj 923
ANGST, Hartmann bb 517
ANGST, Peter g 960-961
ANSTEY, Johnny t 660
ANTES, Irvin p 1472
ANTHENS, Bill tb 1562
ANTHONY, Al as 417
ANTHONY, Ray t 417
ANTONELLI, Tony as-ts 9-364-441-1539-1540-1541
APPLE, Eddie ts 545
APPS. Bill as 1508
ARAGO, German sb 52-518
ARBELLO, Fernando tb 728-748-773-774-991-1658-1721
ARBITER, Joe cl-ts-bar 1339-1340-1341-1342
ARCHER, Bernard tb 775
ARCHER, George g-v 53-54
ARCHER, George d 1603
ARCHER, Harry vn 1066-1067
ARCHER, Ward d 1066-1067-1068
ARCHEY, Jimmy tb 12-52-53-192-283-284-528-838 1168-1169-1170-1171-1346-1497-1622-1707
ARDEN, Victor p-ldr 36-1241
ARENBURG, Bill bj 905
ARLEN, Harold p-v 194-592-736-831-1036-1143-1144-1286-1599
ARMAND, Roy p 383
ARMATO, Sammy ts 741
ARMER, Al bb-sb 17-128-129-509-869-1065-1417-1418-1456-1604-1609-1610-1680-1681-1682
ARMSTEAD, Lester p 1650
ARMSTER, Mike d 772
ARMSTRONG, Clifton v 1112
ARMSTRONG, Howard vn 1543
ARMSTRONG, Jack vn-v 1
ARMSTRONG, Lil p-v 15-39-40-41-42-43-91-213-413-415-783-794-795-824-825-1019-1129-1133-1253-1279-1280-1306-1328-1422-1542-1673-1674-1679
ARMSTRONG, Louis c-t-v-sw-ldr 39-41-42-43-44-45-46-47-48-49-50-51-52-53-54-55-56-57-58-133-165-213-251-296-314-414-503-715-716-717-718-753-794-821-845-860-965-994-1165-1166-1266-1279-1280-1328-1442-1449-1467-1488-1529-1549-1550-;617-1618-1671-1699-1700-1729
ARNDT, Felix p 59-1586-1587
ARNDT, Larry bj 1196
ARNHEIM, Gus p-ldr 59-991-992
ARNOLD, Billy p-ldr 60
ARNOLD, Harold ts 15-20-792-913-1075
ARNOLD, Henry cl-as 60
ARNOLD, Jean v 1538
ARNOLD, John p 1648
ARNOLD, Kokomo g 847-1197
ARNOLD, Phil v 1126
ARNOLD, Ted d 1673
ARODIN, Sidney cl-as-tin whistle 173-316-570-651-685-704-825-863-999-1000-1065-1129-1130-1133-1196-1248
ARONSON, Stanley as-bar 1064
ARQUESO, Nelson cl-ss-as-ts 656-657
ARSLANIAN, John cl-as 1595-1596
ARSLANIAN, Krikor "Coco" d-v 1595-1596
ARTANDER, Engt t 1585
ARTESE, Vic p 959
ARTZ, Billy vn-ldr 60-1330

ARTZBURGER, Freddy as 1160
ARUS, George tb 63-449-450-451-452-453-454-455-1400-1401-1402-1403-1404-1405-1406
ASH, Paul vn-ldr 60-61
ASHBY, Irving g 663-664
ASHBY, Walter cl-as-bar-v 563-884-1045-1469-1470
ASHCRAFT, Squirrel pac 1252-1253
ASHFORD, Bo t 76-287-648-1124-1125-1139
ASHFORD, Bob t 648-840-1064-1139
ASHLEY, Ernest g 663
ASMUSSEN, Sven vn 821
ASPINALL, Fred p 1485
ASPLIN, Charlie bb 1214-1215
ASSUNTO, Jac tb 1559
ASTAIRE, Fred v 61-62-1286
ASTON, Bob t 1375
ASTOR, Bob v 171
ASTORIA, Joe bj 552
ATHERLEY, —— tb 1019-1216
ATKINS, Boyd cl-ss-as 41
ATKINS, Ed tb 1166-1529-1714
ATKINS, Jack t 132
ATKINS, Leonard vn 454-455
ATKINS(ON), Nat tb 730-761
ATKINSON, Bill tb 1249
ATLAS, Harry bb 1285
AUBURN, Alf sb 895
AUGUST, H. sb 133
AULD, George ts-ldr 63-123-124-125-126-284-616-617-618-619-770-1359-1404-1405-1406-1408-1409
AUMEND, Joe t 566
AUSTIN, Clyde bj-g 866-867-945
AUSTIN, Cuba d-vib 311-580-1033-1034-1035
AUSTIN, Gene p-v 17-19-63-64-270-1232-1417-1537
AUSTIN, Johnny t 326-1064-1244-1358-1359
AUSTIN, Kay v 1497
AUSTIN, Lovie p 64-65-100-101-352-353-354-392-534-709-750-794-1025-1026-1037-1265-1266-1650
AUSTIN, Mildred v 65
AUTREY, Herman t-v 775-1019-1247-1323-1377-1624-1625-1626-1627-1628-1629-1630-1631-1632-1633-1634-1637-1638
AVENDORF, Fred d 489
AVERSANO, Eddie t 1375
AVERY, Alec ts 1472
AVERY, Charles p 66-842-1489
AVERY, Elijah bj-g 270
AVOLA, Al g 63-449-1400-1401-1402-1403-1404-1405-1406
AWAD, Jim c 1162
AXELROD, Jack t 19-1212
AXFORD, Dave or Ray sb 146-470
AYALLA, Amos d 866
AZEVEDO, John t 418-1120

BABCOCK, Clarence speech 41
BABY MACK v 1323
BABY ROSE MARIE v 67-726
BACHELORS, THE v 903-957-958
BACHLOR, —— v 1518
BACK-A-TOWN BOYS, THE v 7
BACKER, Les bj-g-v 28
BACON, Billy cl-ts 1009
BACON, Louis t-v 50-52-53-54-55-67-280-488-836-960-961-1446-1500-1657-1712

BACON, Max  d-v  20-21-22-23-24-25-30-147
160-161-192-302-334-393-404-467-468-508
554-568-798-949-950-951-952-953-1116-
1224-1335-1431-1432-1456-1508-1519-1584
1749-1750
BACON, Trevor  g-v  1070
BADIS, Joe  d  1038
BAGBY, Charles  p-a  1563
BAGBY, Scott  cl-ts  533
BAGSBY, Percy  d-v  1719
BAHR, Bernie  tb  1572
BAILEY, Bert  cl-as-bar  1004-1421
BAILEY, Bill  cl-as  1327
BAILEY, Bill  p  1744
BAILEY, Buster (r.n. William B.)  cl-ss-
as-ts-v  12-13-15-39-40-75-76-79-80-90-
91-131-149-165-179-273-360-382-460-466-
588-633-645-660-680-715-716-717-718-719
720-721-722-723-768-779-783-794-795-824
861-895-896-897 905-1003-1019-1028-1037
1061-1070-1123-1124-1125-1159-1166-1171
1253-1266-1267-1279-1280-1304-1426-1441
1442-1443-1444-1445-1460-1461-1462-1463
1465-1466-1467-1468-1477-1484-1492-1511
1513-1529-1534-1535-1542-1618-1699-1700
1701-1702-1703-1707-1710-1711-1721-1729
1731-1732-1733-1734
BAILEY, Cecil  cl-as  356
BAILEY, Eddie  t  185-186
BAILEY, Ilomay  v  1232
BAILEY, Joe  bb-sb  47-48-762-763-1530
BAILEY, Mildred  v  76-77-78-79-80-81-82-
290-422-593-613-614-922-1153-1157-1158-
1159-1160-1688
BAILEY, Thomas  v  1528
BAIN, Jock  tb  684
BAIRD, Joe  tb  1038

BAKER, Abbie  sb  251-252

BAKER, Al  cl-as  991-992-993

BAKER, Art  c  274
BAKER, Arthur  g  581
BAKER, Arthur  d  346-347-348
BAKER, Belle  v  82-880-1608
BAKER, Benny  t  60
BAKER, Cy  t  29-98-297-298-299-300-307-
321-431-432-433
BAKER, Don  elo  1711
BAKER, Donald  - see HALL, ARTHUR
BAKER, Earl  c-t  6-579-580-1231-1232-1377
1718
BAKER, Earl  g  251-252
BAKER, Fran  c  1305
BAKER, Harold  t  492-493-834-901-902-1278
1279-1720-1735-1736
BAKER, Jerry  v  877-880
BAKER, Kenny  t  822-1039
BAKER, Lloyd  t  218
BAKER, Phil  v  1614
BAKER, Viola  v  82
BAKER, Willie  g  892
BAKER, Winfield  tb  834
BALDWIN, ――  v  1697
BALDWIN, John  vn  1563
BALL, Balls  cl  1100
BALL, Dick  bb-sb  22-23-24-160-161-192-
387-388-393-459-508-554-684-1238-1298-
1310-1431-1432-1519-1750
BALLARD, George  d  1712

BALLARD, Red  tb  62-594-595-596-597-598-
599-600-601-602-603-604-605-606-607-608
609-610-611-612-613-614-615-616-1337
BALLEW, Smith  bj-g-v  33-34-35-83-84-245
246-247-419-420-483-508-593-627-804-931
932-933-979-1063-1077-1144-1145-1233-
1234-1301-1302-1303-1339-1367-1369-1370
1381-1382-1383-1384-1387-1411-1568-1569
1570-1598-1599-1620
BALMFORTH, Tony  t  684
BALTIMORE, Harry  vn  1640
BALTIMORE, Jesse  d  458-651-944-1230-
1426-1650
BAMBERGER, Frank  tb  314-315
BAMFORD, George  cl-ts-f  1690
BAMPTON, Claude  p-a-ldr  87
BANCROFT, Ted  - see GALE, EDDIE and
POLLACK, BEN
BAND, Tommy  t  1219
BANJO BUDDY  bj-v  1237
BANKERT, Paul  bj  1075
BANKES, Sherman  p  123
BANKS, Billy  v  87-88-89-461-1072-1427
BANKS, George  t  1657
BANKS, Joe  d  940-1576
BANKS, Louis  d  1547
BANKS, Roy  p  854-1589-1717
BANKS, Ulysses  ts  1512
BANTA, Frank  p  19-62-89-637-641-686-872-
904-1015-1016-1064-1065-1160-1587-1588
BAPTISTE, Tink  p  1095
BAQUET, Achille  cl-as  459-1194-1692
BAQUET, George  cl  359-1103-1439-1440
BARBARIN, Paul  d-vib  11-12-13-15-45-46-
52-53-54-55-358-751-1103-1167-1168-1169
1345-1346-1376-1431
BARBEE, William  p  410-1321-1355-1744
BARBER, Charles  tb  418
BARBER, Charlie  sb  82-203-392-1095
BARBER  Cliff  t  159-642
BARBER. Dudley  d  310-311-1238
BARBER. George  d  706
BARBER, Joe  ts  913
BARBERINO, Otto  vn  1193
BARBOUR, Dave  g  28-29-40-53-56-63-77-78-
81-122-382-622-623-633-704-756-780-913-
1032-1114-1115-1137-1156-1157-1231-1314-
1315-1316-1406-1615-1691-1730-1731
BARCLAY, George  v  1436
BARD, Lola  v  846-1121-1179
BARDACH, Buddy or Bunny  cl-ts  207-829
BARDALE, Vincent  t  1374-1375
BAREFIELD, Bob  as  664
BAREFIELD, Eddie  cl-as-bar  254-255-256-
257-284-527-529-660-729-770-851-1112-
1203-1204-1279
BARELLI, Aime  t  307-333-519-827-1284-
1338-1339
BARENE, Robert  vn  1406
BARETTO, Roy  p  90
BARFIELD, A. D.  t  547
BARFORD, Bill  bj-g  165-166-1228-1411
BARGY, Roy  p-cel-a-ldr  76-90-116-117-119
120-857-858-1143-1144-1269-1270-1332-
1558-1568-1569-1571-1572-1683-1684-1685-
1686-1687-1688-1689-1690
BARI, ――  p  543
BARKER  Blue Lu  v  90-91
BARKER, Danny  bj-g  13-14-15-75-90-91-131
258-259-260-261-262-662-913-967-968-1003
1075-1124-1654-1721-1735

1758

BARKER, Ozzie bj-g 89
BARKELEY, Russell bb 1289
BARKSDALE, Everett bj-g-elg-v 115-272-284-1476
BARLOW, Nathan g 1711
BARMAN, Fred t 1271
BARNARD, Frank t 1150
BARNES, Bert p-a 22-23-24-25-161-192-393 508-1224-1225
BARNES, Charles bj-g-v 930-1324-1325
BARNES, Charlie d 543-1595
BARNES, De Lloyd p 1487
BARNES, Faye v 91
BARNES, Frank ts-a 346-347-348
BARNES, George elg 848-1241
BARNES, Jesse tb 868-1056-1419
BARNES, Paul cl-ss-as 302-1103-1167-1168
BARNES, W. d 1472
BARNES, Walter ts-ldr 91-92
BARNET, Charlie cl- ss-as-ts-chimes-mara-ldr-v 92-93-94-95-96-97-98-99-134-250-482-770-1027-1048-1156-1322
BARNET MODERNAIRES, THE v 93
BARNET, Richard d 1282
BARNETT, Alfred sb 87
BARNETT, Art d 314
BARNETT, Eli d 1196
BARNETT, Irving ts 1047
BARNETT, Martin t 152
BARNETT, Stanley ts-ldr 995-996
BARNETT, Ted as 1070-1116
BARNHART, Ralph p 1347
BARO, Gerry p 778
BARONE, Clement f-pic 1256-1605
BARONE, Joe t 365-366
BARR, Ray p 8-9-80-81
BARREIRO, Louis sb 1585
BARRETT, Billy vn 1472
BARRETT, Steve d 1472
BARRETTO, Justo p 518-1743
BARRIGO, Don ts 581-582-583-584-585-1210 1508-1509-1601-1739
BARRINGER, Ambrose t 923-1029
BARRIS, Harry p-v 61-482-1681-1682-1683-1684-1685-1686-1687
BARRIS, Joe t 890
BARRITÉAU, Carl cl-as-ldr 822-841
BARRON, Sid bj-g 470
BARRON, Wally "Blue" tb 98-99-132-756
BARROW, Dick v 99
BARROW. Errol p 841
BARROW, Ray p 99
BARRY, Bill p-v 100
BARRY, James bj 682
BARRY, Pete sb-v 1396
BARRY, Rene cl-ts 1595
BARRY, Richard v 1304
BARSBY, Jack bb 732-1355-1606-1607-1608-1609-1680
BARTEL, P. vn 1260
BARTELL, Ted t 1681
BARTH, George bb-sb 1663
BARTH, Harry bb-sb 100-567-955-956-957-958
BARTHA, Alex ldr 100
BARTHOLOMEW, Billy cl-as 546-571
BARTLETT, Howard cl-ss-ts 659
BARTLETT, Owen A. as-ldr 577-870
BARTLETTE, Viola v 100-101
BARTLEY, Dallas sb 865

BARTON, Billy cl-as-ts 30-523-524- 796-797-808-809-826-1289-1290-1363-1662
BARTON, Gilbert f-pic 140-1019-1216
BASCOMB, Paul ts 108-691-693-694
BASCOMB, Wilbur t 691-692-693-694
BASIE, Count (r.n. William B.) p-ldr-v 101-102-103-104-105-106-107-108-109-110-417-607-608-615-616-617-821-1048-1112
BASKERVILLE, William Bede g 1194
BASLEY, John bj 1245
BASON, Harry p 578-579-1289-1369
BASS, Bob d 306-307
BASS, George vn 120
BASSARD, Isidore tb 1348-1349-1642
BASSART, Rene tb 172
BASSETT, Bert bj 798-799
BASSETT, Rip (r.n. Arthur B.) bj-g 41-1267-1744
BASSETT, V. cl-ss-as-ts 863
BASSEY, Bus (r.n. Clarence B.) as-ts 62-612-613-614-615-616-1407-1408
BASSMAN, George a 593-594-613
BASTIEN, Ovid "Biddy" sb 908-909-910-911 1243-1244
BASTIEN, Tony ts 457
BASTIEN, Vince tb 1606
BASTIN, Doug t-cl-as 1336
BASTOW, Francis v 894
BATES, Charles p 1521
BATES, Leslie cl-ts 156-1362-1363
BATES, Nat t 730
BATES, Walter ts 909-910-911-912
BATSON, Mabel v 1497
BATTEN, Reginald vn-ldr 1362-1363-1364
BATTLE, Dick t-fh 467-1089
BATTLE, Pudding Head (r.n. Edgar B.) t-vib-a 191-251-259-260-760-898-1250
BATEY, Harry g-v 53-54
BAUDUC, Jules bj-g 407-1122-1123-1229
BAUDUC, Ray d 16-62-122-161-162-265-266-267-269-350-363-364-365-366-367-368-369-370- 371-372-373-374-375-376-421-463-509-510-555-565-592-942-999-1000-1001-1063-1076-1077-1078-1079-1080-1081-1114-1115-1131-1144-1192-1103-1233-1234-1235-1236-1248-1270-1299-1300-1328-1420-1537-1572
BAUER, Fred J. d 2-996-1180
BAUER, Joe t 438-439-440-441-442-1242
BAUM, Al as 684
BAUM, Joe vn 119-120
BAUMGARDEN, Gene g 456
BAUR, Frabklyn v 17-133-418-648-840-870-871-1232-1416-1610
BAUZA, Mario t 259-260-261-1279-1658-1659-1660-1661
BAVE, Eddie cl-as 644
BAVITON, John cl-ts 545-546
BAXTER, Helen v 110-1128
BAXTER, Phil p-ldr 111
BAYERSDORFFER. Johnny c-ldr 111
BAYLOR, Berlyn cl-as-ldr 111
BAZELL, Evelyn t 1136
BEAL, Charlie p 51-75-1304
BEAL, Eddie p 1512
BEALE, Sis v 6
BEAN, Floyd p 370-1037
BEANE, Reg p-or 1654-1655
BEARING, Ted bb 383
BEARMAN, Sol v 1056-1174-1420

BEASLEY, Irene v 112-1330¾1599
BEASON, Bill d 80-382-527-528-529-755-
756-1105-1171-1279-1670-1707
BEATON, Colin p 141
BEATTY, Josephine - see HUNTER, ALBERTA
BEATY, Ivan cl-ss-as 194-1036
BEAU, Heinie cl-as-ts 451-452-453-454-
455-1148
BEAVER, George and Henry - see KAUFMAN,
IRVING
BECHET, Sidney cl-ss-ts-sarrusophone-p-
sb-d-v 58-113-114-115-357-509-564-650-
794-821-845-917-945-964-965-1011-1107-
1129-1223-1240-1274-1280-1427-1438-1463
1467-1533-1617-1618-1698-1699-1729
BECK, Al t 912
BECK, Art ts 364-1540-1541
BECK, Bertrand p 1585
BECK, Sigismond sb 465-632-1219
BECKER, Bill vn 919
BECKER, Dave d 1572
BECKER, Samuel tb 963
BECKER, William tb 418
BECKETT. Fred tb 664-944
BEDELL, Ralph d-wb 820-1705-1714-1715-
1716
BEE, David a 1346
BEEBE, George d 177-518-552-553-1141-
1142
BEECHLER, Elmer ts 1602
BEECRAFT, Homer as-v 314-315
BEELER, Edward d 1459
BEERS, Bob t 575
BEERS, Lewis d 89
BEHAL, L. tb 1575
BEHRENDSON, Doc c-cl 68-69-914-915-934-
935-976
BEIDERBECKE, Bix c-p 115-116-117-174-
274-275-309-576-577-578-1081-1422-1566-
1567-1568-1569-1682-1683-1684-1685-1686
1687-1741
BEIGEL, Les t 59-404
BEILAN, Al v 1573
BEILMAN, Pete tb 1123-1229-1665-1666-
1669
BEINES, Will a 988
BEITUS, Jim bar 647
BELASCO, Lionel p 117
BEL CANTO SINGERS, THE v 554-555
BELCASTRA, Nick t 1327
BELIEN, Harry d 1286
BELL, Alfred c-t k-wb-v 100-150-843-847-
848-1495
BELL, Anna v 118
BELL, Arthur a 1508
BELL, Benny t 132
BELL, Billy bb-sb 30-31-32-506-523-524-
525-1196-1289-1290-1291-1292-1293-1294-
1295-1296-1297-1298-1335-1472
BELL, Bob g-v 1557
BELL, George vn-p 1462-1463-1505
BELL, Jack f 1690-1691
BELL, James cl-as 138
BELL, Jimmy vn 337
BELL, John sb 687
BELL, Johnny v 152
BELL, Walter bsn 1681
BELLAMY, Jim bsx-bb-sb 953-1070-1362-
1363-1364-1365-1521
BELLARE, Elly cl-as-v 563-1045-1469-1470

BELLER, Al vn 162-454-1081-1131-1231-
1232-1233-1234-1235-1236-1237-1407-1408
BELLEST, Christian t 333-519-827-1284-
1338
BELLONI, ——— bb 16
BELLSTEDT, Herman c 1473-1474-1475
BELLUARDO, Benny t 1490
BELSHAW, George ldr 118
BELT, Frank t 142-1459
BEMCO, Harold vc 454-455
BENEDICT, Leonard cl-as 1550
BENEDICT, William tb 659
BENEKE, Tex ts 1048-1064
BENFORD, Bill bb 645-1061-1096-1102-
1104-1230-1650
BENFORD, Tommy d 67-190-330-465-632-
690-836-960-961-1061-1102-1104-1436-
1476-1575
BENGER, Paul tb 1421
BENGTSSON, Roland sb 1585
BENNETT, Bobby g 545-660-836-1003-1240-
1464-1465
BENNETT, Boyd sb 1179
BENNETT, Buster (r.n. Joseph B.) ss-as
751-849-1118
BENNETT, Dave cl-as 658
BENNETT, Ida v 118
BENNETT, Mark tb 366-1398-1538-1539
BENNETT, Maurice ts 274-1288-1378
BENNETT, R. E. cl-as 1274
BENNETT, Ralph cl-vn-v-ldr 1643-1644
BENNETT, Russ bj-g 1656
BENNETT, Stanley p 118
BENNETT, Walter c-t 119-633-776-778-837
854
BENNETT SISTERS, THE v 1491
BENORIC, Steve cl-as 324-325-326
BENSON, Bella v 1645
BENSON, Benny cl-as 1289-1378
BENTLEY, Gladys v 121-1647
BENTLEY, Jack tb 801
BENTON, Frank wb-v-ldr 1646
BENTON, Ted cl 1746
BENTON, Tommy p 1008
BENTON, William d 1693
BERAIDI, Frank t 398-788-1117
BERCOV, Maurie cl-as 18-1195-1206-1228
BERENDSON, Siggfried tb 120-121
BERG, George cl-ts 79-324-619-620-621-
622-788-1158-1159-1160-1242
BERG, Howard tb 89
BERGEN, Ed bb 864
BERGER, Herbert p-ldr 121
BERGER, Irving t 99
BERGER, Karl bj-g 975-976-1366
BERGER, Manny d 123
BERGER, Marty t 1005
BERGERE, Roy v 63
BERGMAN, Dewey p 576-1664
BERGMAN, Eddie vn 365-1029-1081-1143-
1144-1145-1232-1233-1234
BERIGAN, Bunny (r.n. Bernard) t-v 16-33
53-77-122-123-124-125-126-157-158-159-
161-198-199-200-201-202-203-204-205-361-
392-421-422-437-440-449-450-541-545-565-
592-596-597-756-767-780-795-821-877-878-
924-933-1009-1027-1028-1031-1032-1063-
1114-1115-1156-1269-1270-1302-1303-1305-
1312-1330-1331-1332-1347-1385-1386-1388-
1415-1490-1546-1571-1653-1654-1688-1689-
1695-1696-1697-1740-1751

1760
BERKEN, Julius vc 1573
BERKIN, H. t 1330
BERKIN, Herman d 1484
BERKIN, Leslie t 20
BERKMAN, Jeŝse cl-ŝŝ-as 1484
BERKMAN, Jules t 1263-1264
BERKSHIRE, John ts 1252
BERLY, Harry cl-ts-oc-o-vl 459-539-581-
    799-800-917-953-1070-1127-1149-1507-1508
    1749
BERMAN, Harry t 1310
BERMAN, Marty cl-bcl-bar 1244-1533-1753
BERMAN, Mike vn 572
BERMAN, Sonny t 1250
BERMANN, Eugen vn 1662
BERMON, Len d 656
BERNARD, Al v 73-127-1006-1178-1611
BERNARD, Clem p-pac 346-347-348
BERNARD, Cy vc 98-1406
BERNARD, Mike p 127
BERNARD, Peter v 10-1217
BERNARDI, Noni cl-as-a 96-161-162-249-
    250-365-366-437-438-448-505-506-609-610-
    611-612-700-701-1089-1752
BERNER, Ernest p 689
BERNHARDT, Clyde tb 695-696-752
BERNIE, Ben (r.n. WOODRUFF, Beernard A.)
    vn-ldr-v 128-129-130-131
BERNSTEIN, Artie sb 33-34-62-67-77-84-
    157-158-159-160-161-180-198-199-200-202-
    276-320-335-355-361-382-422-423-427-437-
    464-505-506-545-593-594-612-613-614-615-
    616-617-618-619-662-663-673-674-767-821-
    903-924-1016-1026-1027-1028-1031-1048-
    1082-1095-1145-1146-1156-1273-1332-1412-
    1415-1537-1538-1551-1552-1571-1648-1653-
    1654-1671-1695-1696-1712-1733-1751
BERRY, Art vn 391
BERRY, Bob d 59
BERRY, Chu (r.n. Leon B.) ts 13-39-77-
    78-91-105-131-260-261-280-281-312-382-
    466-661-662-728-729-755-756-769-792-821-
    906-1003-1156-1413-1446-1730-1731-1734-
    1735
BERRY, Connie p 1711
BERRY, Emmett t 284-728-729-730-770-1247
    1736-1737
BERRY, George v 885
BERRY, John v 6
BERRY, Leroy bj 1110-1111-1112
BERRY, Parker tb 762-763-1662
BERSON, Rudy vn 1075
BERT, Ed tb 1160
BERTON, Vic d-vib 38-74-132-174-180-304-
    319-350-351-395-462-463-502-519-532-669-
    777-804-853-868-870-871-926-927-928-934-
    977-1039-1046-1049-1064-1086-1138-1139-
    1140-1141-1145-1275-1276-1391-1430-1431-
    1545-1574-1578-1589-1611-1612-1613-1673-
    1681-1682
BERTRAM, Carl p 881
BERTRAND, Jimmy wb-bells-blocks-x-sw-
    speech 132-133-143-309-327-873-1039-
    1044-1045-1055-1228-1267-1321-1476-1495-
    1529
BESS, Druie tb 1507
BESSEMER SINGERS, THE v 1446
BESSINGER, Frsnk v 129-240-576-577-1325-
    1503-1543
BEST, Clifton g 762

BEST, John t 63-1400-1401-1402-1403-
    1404-1405
BEST, Skeeter g 692
BESTOR, Don p-a-ldr 120-121-133
BEUCHLER, George v 35
BEVARD, Sylvester tb 665-1010
BEZIMEK, Charlie cl-as 1193
BIAGINI, Henry dir 286-287-288-289
BIANCHI, Marcel g 11-16-1260
BIAS, George v 725-1035-1061-1170
BIBBS, Leonard sb 180-936-1322-1422
BIBBS, Oliver sb-ldr 133-863
BIBBS, Phil t 1196
BIBESHEIMER, Fred cl-as-ts-o 1694
BIDGOOD, Harry p-a-ldr 134-796-1055
BIEDERMAN, Walter vn 332-501-502-883-
    1250-1251-1252-1586-1587
BIERS, Bob t 972-973
BIESACKER, Carl cl-ts-a 906-907-1063-
    1064-1095-1116-1121
BIESE, Paul ts-vn-ldr 134
BIFFO, Frank t 345-667
BIGARD, Barney (r.n. Albany B.) cl-ss-
    ts 27-134-135-178-414-474-475-476-477-
    478-479-480-481-482-483-484-485-486-487
    488-489-490-491-492-493-494-495 496-497
    498-499-500-631-640-645-652-765-779-824
    1014-1075-1083-1101-1104-1167-1168-1169
    1263-1344-1345-1467-1500-1501-1540-1640
    1641-1711-1712-1744
BIGELOW, Jack tb 322-829
BIGEOU, Esther v 136
BIGGADIKE, Rupe p 563-1045-1469-1470
BIGGS, Frank d-v 856
BIGGS, Pete bb 1104
BILLEN, Louis as 1284
BILLINGS, Bernie ts 646-647-959-1481
BILLINGS, Joe pac 1030
BILLINGS, Josh d-suitcase 1113-1114-
    1119
BILLINGS, Tom - see BARNET, CHARLIE
BILLITZER, Perry as 905
BILTMORE RHYTHM BOYS, THE v 980
BILTMORE TRIO, THE v 980-981
BINDER, Ray t 1595
BINFORD, Ken bj-g 320-356-889-946-1117-
    1304-1412-1512
BINNEY, Don tb 684
BINYON, Larry cl-ts-f etc. 33-77-158-
    159-198-199-205-305-361-422-423-437-556
    592-593-853-871-932-933-1026-1027-1028-
    1029-1076-1077-1078-1079-1080-1081-1082
    1126-1141-1142-1143-1144-1145-1146-1232
    1233-1234-1551-1571-1602-1623-1624-1653
    1696-1752
BIONDI, Ray g-vn 18-518-894-906-907-908
    909-910-911-912-999-1007
BIONDI, Remo a 909
BIRCH, Tommy t 346
BIRD, Dick t 1106
BIRD, Sam E. d-v 351-1068
BIRDHEAD, Blues h 192
BIRGE, Dewey bj-g 338
BIRKBY, Arthur ts 1225
BIRSECK, Norman cl-as 1589
BISHOP, Joe flugelhorn-bb-a 163-360-390
    738-739-740-741-742-858-882
BISHOP, Neville d 535
BISHOP, Wallace d 410-758-759-862-1155-
    1169-1355-1421

BISHOP, Walter d 752-1321
BISHOP, Wendy v 183
BITTENBENDER, Dyke cl-as 1310
BITTERMAN, Nelson p-v 1006
BITTICK, Clarence d 134
BITTICK, Gerald vn 1197
BIVONA, Gus cl-as 125-126-616-617-618-
786-787-1242-1360-1361
BLACK BOB p 842-843-995-1123-1496-1527-
1528
BLACK, Clarence vn-v 138-392-862-1101-
1671
BLACK, Frank p 174-928
BLACK, Johnny p 1437
BLACK, Lou bj 1056-1131-1193
BLACK, Maurice bj-bb 320-471
BLACK, Stanley p-a 25-138-140-688-1340-
1341-1342-1507-1508-1693
BLACK, Ted p 237
BLACK, Willie md 1676
BLACKFORD, Alex p 1616
BLACKIE d 573
BLACKMAN, Teewee g 1042
BLACKSTONE, Nan v 140
BLACKWELL, Ollie bj 820-1705-1714-1715-
1716
BLACKWELL, Scrapper g 1320
BLADE, James P. p-a 188
BLADES, Tommy d-harpophone 1744
BLAINE, Andy t-v 417
BLAINE, Rex v 875
BLAIR, Bobby tb 1437
BLAIR, Bobby ts 1021
BLAIR, Jimmy v 1242
BLAIR, Lee bj-g 52-53-54-55-56-57-1096-
1102-1103-1104-1346
BLAKE, Blind (r.n. Arthur Phelps) g-v
1267-1321-1344-1376
BLAKE, BOB v 266-521-1520-1521-1524
BLAKE, Charlie d 322-323-324-325
BLAKE, Cyril t-v 141
BLAKE, Ellsworth ts 50
BLAKE, Eubie p-speech 141-142-508-793-
1422-1423-1424-1425-1630
BLAKE, Happy v 1583
BLAKE, Jerry cl-bcl-as-bar-a-v 109-260-
261-728-729-959-1099-1104-1278-1731-1734-
1742-1743
BLAKE, Jimmy t 78-79-183-447-448-449-450-
451-452-453-454-455-786-923-1158
BLAKE, Johnny v 1570
BLAKE, Meredith v 829-1538
BLAKE, Tom p 1616
BLAKEMORE, Floyd as 18
BLAKENEY, Andrew t 1485
BLAKENEY, William t 318
BLAKEY, Rubel v 663-664
BLANC, Max cl-as 188-307-333-419-652-776-
1211-1284-1596
BLANCHE, Bill bj 334-1117
BLANCHER, O. C. ? 1096
BLANCHETTE, Jack g 56-290-291-292-293-294-
295-296-297-298-299-300-858-859
BLAND, Jack bj-g 88-142-1029-1030-1112-
1113-1114-1119-1673
BLANE, Audrey v 699
BLANE, Charlie v 1491
BLANEY, Norah v 143-568
BLANK, Joe as-vc 895
BLANK, Sammy tb 772-958-959
BLANKS, Birleanna v 143

BLANTON, Jimmy sb 135-495-496-497-498-
499-767-1501-1712
BLESSING, Connie cl-as-ts 1472
BLEVINS, Harry tb-bb 652-653-654-914
BLEVINS, Lee tb 556
BLEVINS, William tb 520
BLEYER, Archie a 726
BLITZ, Marty sb 788-1553-1554
BLOCK, Sid ts 438
BLOMQUIST, Kurt as 589
BLONDELL, Fred ts 418
BLOOM, Benny c-t 68-90-915-924-925
BLOOM, Kurt ts-v 93-94-95-96-97-98-99-
250-545
BLOOM, Marty effects 1100
BLOOM, Mickey t-mel 1-62-84-98-127-239-
242-350-351-394-419-447-626-627-831-861-
887-888-889-1055-1142-1350-1391-1392-
1393-1583-1593-1620
BLOOM, Rube p-a 5-38-63-143-144-145-170-
344-350-351-378-398-473-501-502-504-509-
510-512-516-532-566-567-669-670-671-672-
673-708-777-852-853-872-882-905-922-927-
931-1055-1067-1068-1098-1142-1246-1275-
1381-1382-1383-1384-1387-1422-1425-1544-
1545-1589-1597-1598-1599-1616-1638-1652-
1653
BLOWERS, Johnny d 124-125-646-1239-1734
BLUE, Jack v 931
BLUE, William Thornton cl-as 12-46-252-
257-359-807-1084
BLUESTONE, Harry vn 34-98-149-422-1063-
1273-1406-1696
BLUMBERRY, Wallace cl-as 1600
BLUNTSON, Dave v 1558
BLYTHE, Jimmy p 100-132-133-137-149-150-
151-210-308-327-406-410-642-892-1055-
1069-1093-1161-1162-1207-1267-1268-1319-
1320-1321-1494-1495-1499-1500
BOARDMAN, T. vn 1407-1408
BOARMAN, Eddie bb-v 540
BOAS, Ralph cl-as 1722
BOBBÉ, Jean vn 1019-1216
BOBBY DIX TRIO, THE v 1387
BOB-O-LINKS, THE v 373-374
BOCAGE, Charles bj-v 136-1229-1230
BOCAGE, Peter t 136-1229-1230
BODE, Lou cl-as 979
BODGE, Merrow cl-ts 571
BOGART, Joe t 185
BOGEN, Sam p 134
BOGERT, Herman g 517
BOEHM, George sb 453
BOHAN, Joe d 1124-1125
BOHANNON, Hoyt tb 816-817-818-819-820
BÖHLER, Fred p-ldr 151-190
BOHN, George cl-as 92-98-99-125-785-786-
787-1192-1193-1244-1359-1360-1361
BOHN, Tommy as-ts 152-1621
BOLAN, Lovell p 66
BOLAR, Abe sb 18-775-850-851-1070-1203-
1204-1375
BOLD, Nate c 1616
BOLDEN, Arnold d 169
BOLDEN, Lela v 152
BOLE, Bob d 1253
BOLING, Arnold d 1626-1627-1628-1629-
1721
BOLLING, Ira d 836
BOLMAR, Red t 1249
BOLTON, Betty v 152-537-790-1493

1762

BOLTON, Happy d-chimes 1266-1267
BOLTON, Joe p 153
BOLTON, Val v 1121
BOMBURYERO, Ernestine v 66
BONACIO, Benny cl-bcl-as-bar-f 573-575
  1269-1270-1571-1688-1689-1690
BONANO, Sharkey (r.n. Joseph B.) c-t-v-
  ldr 153-188-464 704-1065-1179-1196
BOND, Frank v 829
BONE, Bud t 923
BONE, Red (r.n. E. W. B.) tb-a 439-440-
  441-1538-1539-1600
BONHAM, Ralph vn 391
BONITAS, Ray sb 153
BONN, Don t-cl-ts 1740
BONNEE, Don cl-as 1150
BONNELLY, Edward t 640-641
BONNEY, Betty v 186
BONO, Americus t 884
BONO, Gina t 1330-1490
BONSER, Jack s 589-590-591
BOOKER, Benny sb 763-1272
BOOKER, Charles as 154
BOOKER. Charles p 834
BOOKER, Elmore p 1066
BOOKIN, Laurie cl-as-ts-vn 684-687-688-
  798-995-996-1207-1509
BOONE, Chester t-v 154-832-1247
BOONE, Harvey cl-as-bar 704-705-723-724
  725-1278-1279-1427
BOONE, Lester cl-as-bar 48-49-50-404-
  757-758-770-1744
BOONE, Theodore c 320-1164
BOOTH, Charles H. H. p 154-303-939-1198
  1199-1257-1370
BOOTH, Norman tb 194-1036
BOOTHROYD, Dick tb 1341-1342
BORATI, Frank t 250
BORBEE, Ernest p 1180
BORCHARD, Henrietta vn 1075
BORCHERS, William ? 218
BORDEN, Bill a 1552-1553
BORDERS, Ben d 456-942-1485
BORDERS, Sam d 138
BORELLI, J. vn 801
BORESOME FOURSOME, THE v 300
BORGER, Bob t 1172
BORLAND, C. C. cl-as-a 418
BORODKIN, Abe vc 63-64-112-509-756-870-
  1016-1416-1417-1418-1610
BORSHARD, Jerry tb 647
BORTNER, Harry cl-as-ts 402-403
BOSE, Gene v 422
BOSE, Sterling c-t-v 32-33-67-132-161-
  198-199-200-201-202-203-204-205-209-249
  250-363-368-369-370-437-438-578-579-580
  598-647-674-700-701-795-969-1027-1031-
  1046-1063-1131-1150-1175-1234-1235-1328
  1415-1537-1538-1648-1653-1654-1671-1696
  1751-1752-1753
BOSSEN, Andy t 320
BOSTIC, Earl as 662
BOSWELL, Connie/Connee v 156-157-158-
  159-160-161-162-163-291-360-363-422-
  1145-1146-1536-1751
BOSWELL, Helvetia vc-v 161-360-1146-
  1536-1751
BOSWELL, Martha p-cel-v 156-157-158-159
  160-161-360-1146-1536-1751

BOTKIN, Perry bj-g-u-a-dir 33-62-84-159
  180-200-276-351-363-364-394-518-555-674
  871-969-1076-1125-1145-1538-1540-1541-
  1562-1614-1751
BOTNIK, Norman vl 98
BOTSFORD, Ed bj-g 1252
BOTSFORD, Walter ts 840
BOTTERELL, Charlie d 656
BOTTORFF, Al d 747
BOUCHON, Lester "Gilly" cl-ts 1123-1229
BOUDINI BROTHERS, THE pac 1587
BOULANGER, Charles vn-ldr 558-559
BOULCOTT, Victor cl-as 346
BOURDON, Rosario dir 1587
BOURGEOIS, Jess C. sb 1361
BOURJOIS, Bill bj-g 153
BOURN, Dwight p 867
BOURNE, Edward p 640-641
BOURNE, J. T. t 1644
BOWEN, Bill as 769-832-1070
BOWEN, Claude t 814-815-816-817-818-819
  820-1403
BOWEN, Lyle cl-as 83-84-422-423-756-924
  1406-1411-1696-1751
BOWEN, Wally t 841
BOWER, B. vn 1406-1407-1408
BOWERS, Ben v 1203
BOWERS, Charles d 1075
BOWERS, Freddy p 100
BOWERS, Gil p 161-365-366-829-999-1000-
  1001-1114-1131-1224-1228-1234-1235-1236
  1270-1271-1328-1506-1537
BOWERS, R. H. p 672
BOWERS, Steve d-v 563-564
BOWES, Alf t-mel 388-638-1126
BOWLES, Russell tb 983-984-985-986-987-
  988-989-990-991
BOWLING, Ray t 1100
BOWLLY, Al g-v 2-163-171-459-469-470-
  515-521-539-581-785-841-1127-1128-1136-
  1148-1149-1150-1507-1608-1616
BOWMAN, Babe tb-v 1004-1406
BOWMAN, Dave p 113-542-543-634-646-647-
  959-1007-1482
BOWMAN, Euday L. p 163
BOWMAN, John vn-vl 76-1681-1683-1685-
  1686-1687-1688
BOWMAN, Red c-v 1131
BOWSER, Henry d 1516-1517-1518
BOWSHER, Stan t-a 808-1339-1340-1341-
  1508
BOYCE, Bruce v 163
BOYCE, Harold p-v 164
BOYD, Carroll p 854
BOYD, Dave tb 1330
BOYD, Ollie cl 420
BOYD, Roger as 251-695-696
BOYD, Walter as-ts 138
BOYDEN, Blaine t 1472
BOYER, Anita v 448-1407-1408
BOYER, Elwood t 575-1482-1483
BOYLE, Earl as 1116
BRACEWELL, Edgar cl-as 347-348-1493-1739
BRACKEN, Jim - see POLLACK, BEN
BRADBURY, Tom cl-ts 1343
BRADER, Ed bb-sb 648-1512
BRADFORD, Mary H. v 164
BRADFORD, Perry p-v 138-164-165-458-562-
  645-783-794-838-859-1184-1305-1424-1458-
  1589-1615-1618-1727

BRADLEY, Anita (Nita)  v  1402
BRADLEY, Oscar  d  763-1249-1512-1530
BRADLEY, Tommy  α  328
BRADLEY, Will (r.n. Wilbur Schwichtenburg)
  tb-a-ldr  34-66-160-163-165-166-167-168-
  204-205-360-629-633-1089-1095-1145-1150
BRADSHAW, Charles  bj-v  708
BRADSHAW, Tiny  v-ldr  169
BRADT, Collis  as  866
BRADY, Floyd  tb  251-513-528-775-1070-
  1247-1693-1735-1736
BRADY, Lou  - see CONRAD, LEW
BRADY, Willard  ts  93-704
BRANDES, ——  v  236
BRAGBY, Charles  p  685-686
BRAGG, Ardelle "Shelley"  v  169
BRAGGS, John H.  bj-g  533-1156-1338
BRAKKE, Larry  t  1606
BRAMAN, Larry  bb  1252
BRANCH, Stuart  bj  1228
BRANDT, Ted  v  684-1126
BRANNELLY, Joe  bj-g  20-21-22-23-24-30-
  31-32-156-160-161-272-393-467-468-506-
  507-508-521-523-524-525-684-949-950-951
  952-953-1196-1226-1289-1290-1291-1292-
  1293-1294-1295-1296-1297-1335-1355-1396
  1456-1472-1738
BRANNON, Gus  ts  182
BRANNON, Tom  t  170-1643-1644
BRANT, Henry  a  611
BRANTLEY, Sid  tb  908-909
BRASHEAR, George  tb  170-710-793-1056-
  1089-1350-1510-1519-1520-1649
BRASSFIELD, Don  ts  912
BRASSFIELD, Frank  tb  401
BRASSFIELD, Herschel  cl-as  164-380-458-
  562-810-1462-1724-1727
BRATTON, Eddie  t  28
BRATTON, Joe  ts  552
BRAUD, Wellman  bb-sb  39-40-58-90-91-114
  115-473-474-475-476-477-478-479-460-481
  482-483-484-485-486-487-488-489-640-651
  652-783-795-824-941-970-1028-1052-1075-
  1083-1097-1107-1108-1154-1203-1253-1346
  1414-1431-1486-1501-1640-1641-1653-1711
  1829
BRAUDE, Sherman  d  517
BRAY, Lew  bj-g-v  170-316
BRECK, Joe  vn-ldr  738
BRECKENRIDGE, Earl  bb-sb  1520-1521
BRECKMAN, Wayne  as  388-389
BREED, Perley  cl-as-ts-bar-ldr  20-31-
  170-524-525-1116-1226-1289-1290-1291-
  1426-1456
BREEN, George  vn  1492
BREEZE, Alan  g-v  46-347-348
BREEZE, Eric  tb  23-24-25-87-192-279-684
  801-1343-1508-1509
BREIDIS, Vic  p-cel  591-1029-1076-1077-
  1078-1079-1080-1081-1208-1232-1233-1234
BREITENBACH, Joe  p  1068
BREITON, Joe  tb  1107
BRENDEL, Pete  as-bar  785-768-787-1116-
  1117
BRENDERS, Stan  p-dir  1284-1286
BRENNAN, Buddy  p-a  306-307
BRENNER, Herman  t  1285
BRENNER, Vic  p  1412
BRENTON, Cliff  p  316
BRERETON, Clarence  t  1124-1427

BRETHERTON, Freddy  p-a  807-808
BREWER, Burton  p  792
BREWER, Lester  t  659
BREWSTER, Ralph  v  1690-1691
BREWSTER, Tex  t  576-924
BREYERS, Josse  tb  188-1260-1596
BRIAN, Jack  g-v  1208
BRICKEY, Evelyn  v  171
BRIDGE, Cecil  v  881
BRIDGES, Henry  cl-ts  944
BRIDWELL, Horace  ts  1361
BRIERS, Larry  p  285-686-706-946-1008-
  1009-1351-1352-1353-1354-1480-1522-1523
  1525-1526-1698
BRIGGS, Arthur  t-ldr  171-172-405-689-
  827-835-836-960-1173-1259-1427
BRIGGS, James  cl-as  159-361-642
BRIGGS, John Henry  bj  209
BRIGGS, Pete  bb  41-42-45-46-404
BRIGHT, Dalbert  cl-as-ts  26-730-824
BRIGHT, Sid  p  61-143-271-521-537-563-
  568-903-982-1226-1365-1565
BRIGLIA, Nick  f  919
BRIGLIA, Tony  d  56-76-286-287-288-289-
  290-291-292-293-294-295-296-297-298-299-
  300-1068
BRIGODE, Ace  vn-ldr  172-173
BRILHART, Arnold  cl-ss-as-ts-bar-f-o-bsn
  33-37-173-223-224-225-226-227-228-229-
  230-231-275-394-395-418-419-420-421-422
  502-504-670-756-804-853-870-871-925-
  1080-1081-1088-1141-1172-1273-1370-1381
  1545-1581-1582-1583-1590-1591-1592-1593
  1597-1598-1599-1614-1619-1620-1745-1749
BRILL, Fred  t-as  82
BRING, Lou  p  969
BRISCOE, Dan  p  409-694
BRISCOE, Walter  t  1103
BRISSON, Carl  v  173
BRISTOL, Florence  v  173
BRITO, Phil  v  1358
BRITT, Mart  bj-ldr  173-1730
BRITTON, Joe  tb  208-284-695-1070
BROAD, Jim  bb  346
BROADHURST, Ernest  t  1343
BROADHURST, Ken  g  1482
BROCK, Glenn  t  685-686
BROCK, Theodore  t  835-960
BROCKMAN, Gail  t  730
BROCKMAN, Hilton  t  1148
BROCKMAN, P. C.  dir  4
BRODIE, Steve  d  532
BRODSKY, Geirge  ts  306
BRODSKY, Irving  p-cel-a  67-117-127-132-
  177-220-221-222-223-224-225-226-227-228
  229-230-231-232-274-275-320-321-421-462
  529-530-533-593-623-624-625-667-668-671
  673-870-890-928-929-930-933-966-967-977
  1064-1098-1141-1142-1172-1300-1381-
  1382-1384-1385-1386-1387-1388-1438-1579
  1580-1581-1582-1583-1590-1591-1592-1593
BROGGIOTTI, Raphael  vn  571
BROHEZ, Fred  d  172-173
BROKAW, Sid  vn  1124-1125-1406
BROMLEY, Tommy  sb  636-822-841-1039-1509
BROMMERSBURG, George  d  120
BROOCO, Joe  t  1066
BROOK, Teddy  t  1743
BROOKER, Harry  p  1046
BROOKINS, Tommy  v  1210

1764
BROOKS, Alva  as  154-155
BROOKS, Arthur  p  1647
BROOKS, Dudley  p-a  108-614-616-763-1272
BROOKS, H.  ts  1379
BROOKS, Harry  p-a  1061-1427-1726
BROOKS, Harvey  p  47-64-177-762-763-782-
  1274-1459-1462-1463
BROOKS, Jimmy  d  886-887
BROOKS, Lawson  as  1719
BROOKS, Percy  ts  660
BROOKS, Percy Mathison  speech  487
BROOKS, Randy  t  889-1554
BROOKS, Shelton  p-speech  1010-1245-1651
BROOKS, Stella  v  1465
BROONZY, Big Bill  g-v  308-843-844-847-
  848-849-995-1123-1496
BROSCHE, Arthur  bb-sb  546-1662
BROSEN, Charles  cl-ts  787-1117-1374
BROSKY, John  vn  1505
BROU, Steve  bj-g  999-1065

BROWN, ---- cl-ts  1089
BROWN, Ada  v  177-178
BROWN, Alberta  v  178
BROWN, Alexander  p  1716
BROWN, Alfred  t  142
BROWN, Andrew  cl-bcl-ts  252-253-256-257
  258-259-260-261-262-349-1084-1245-1559
BROWN, Archie  tb  730
BROWN, Bedford  cl-ts  917-918
BROWN, Ben  sb  1253
BROWN, Bernardine S.  as  1118
BROWN, Bert  c  1254-1255-1256-1586-1605
BROWN, Bert  ts  10
BROWN, Bessie  v  178-179-1717
BROWN, Bill  tb  179
BROWN, Bill  bb  1436
BROWN, Bob  - see WHARTON, DICK
BROWN, Bobby  p  310
BROWN, Boyce  as  394-936-1005-1037
BROWN, Cleo  p-v  180-396-771
BROWN, Dale  cl-as-a  1552-1553
BROWN, Dolores  v  692-693
BROWN, Eddie  t  1640
BROWN, Ed  as  986
BROWN, Eddie  cl-ts  738-1718
BROWN, Edgar  p  683-994-1713
BROWN, Forrest  bb  383
BROWN, Fred  cl-as  1282
BROWN, Gene  g  1272
BROWN, George  t  515
BROWN, Harry  t  1123-1124
BROWN, Henry  p-v  181-846-847-1009-1026-
  1029-1091-1216-1327-1673
BROWN, Herb  bj  531
BROWN, Ida G.  v  181
BROWN, Irving  cl-as  262
BROWN, Jack  t  417
BROWN, Jack  tb  866-867
BROWN, James  p  859-1040
BROWN, Jesse  t  683-1674
BROWN, Joe  t  181-1246
BROWN, Joe  v  864
BROWN, John  t-v  1715-1716
BROWN, John  as  763
BROWN, John  sb  1109-1465
BROWN, Jud  v  1583
BROWN, Judson  p  846
BROWN, Kitty  v  181-182
BROWN, L.  t  123

BROWN, Lawrence  tb-a  27-47-485-486-487
  488-489-490-491-492-493-494-495-496-
  497-498-499-500-651-652-660-662-765-
  766-767-782-1075-1500-1501-1653
BROWN, Leroy  sb'  751'
BROWN, Les  cl-as-ldr-v  182-183-184-
  185-186-1075
BROWN, Lillyn  v  187
BROWN, Lonnie  as  712-714-715
BROWN, Lucien  cl-as  1026-1267
BROWN, Ludvick  g-v  1036
BROWN, Marion  g  1558
BROWN, Nat  cl-as-ts  326-517-1412
BROWN, Nelson  as  1562
BROWN, Norman  g  55-57-1238-1585
BROWN, Ora  v  187
BROWN, Paul  vn-bb  274-1378
BROWN, Pete  t-as  75-187-518-905-1007-
  1134-1154-1396-1468-1512-1521
BROWN, Porter  bj  32-33-1327-1573
BROWN, Ralph  cl-as-o  142-856-1714-1715-
  1716
BROWN, Reggie  d  179
BROWN, Robert ("Washboard Sam")  sb-v
  1496
BROWN, Robert  announcer  391
BROWN, Russell  tb  99-814-815-1403
BROWN, Scoville  cl-as  51-832-1279
BROWN, Shirley  v  8
BROWN, Sidney  sb  1095-1096
BROWN, Skinny (r.n. Irving B.)  ts  342
BROWN, Steve  bb-sb  209-576-577-578-579-
  738-1056-1131-1193-1682-1683-1684
BROWN, Ted  as  531
BROWN, Thornton E.  c  1184-1651
BROWN, Tom  tb  111-188-675-891-1066-
  1747-1748-1749
BROWN, Tom  cl-ss-as-dir  35-1267-1429-
  1430
BROWN, Treg  bj  882-1142-1143-1144-1145
BROWN, Vernon  tb  62-335-579-606-607-
  608-609-610-611-612-613-614-615-616-
  814-1032-1047-1407-1408-1482
BROWN, Walter  cl-as-v  737
BROWN, Walter  bj-g  687
BROWN, Walter  v  1038
BROWN, Warren  tb  184-185-186
BROWN, Willard  as-ts  149-459-1092-1109

BROWNAGLE, Chester  t  188
BROWNAGLE, Ted  cl-ss-as-ts-ldr  188
BROWNE, Alta  v  188-854
BROWNE, Fats  p  66
BROWNE, Howard  tb  1454
BROWNE, Jerry  t  708
BROWNE, Sam  v  21-22-23-24-146-147-537-
  785-799-800-806-840-917-1297-1298-1431-
  1436-1695
BROWNLEE, Norman  p-ldr  188
BROWNWICK, Benny  cl  1008
BROX SISTERS, THE  v  1687
BRUCE, Bob  c-cl-as-a  1231-1663-1745
BRUCE, Carol  v  322
BRUCE, Harold  t  1038
BRUCE, Rowland  vn  1485
BRUDERER, F.  tb  151
BRUN, Max  cl-ts  1639
BRUN, Philippe  c-t-a  188-189-333-535-
  776-800-801-1238-1260-1284-1595-1596
BRUNA, ----  v  1220
BRUNIES, Albert  c-dir  650-651-1208

BRUNIES (BRUNIS), George (Georg) tb-k-v-
dir 100-153-335-336-646-764-955-956-
957-958-959-1001-1002-1004-1007-1075-
1095-1131-1132-1133-1248-1481-1741
BRUNIES, Harry tb 189
BRUNIES, Merritt c-ldr 189-190
BRUNNER, Eddie cl-ts 67-190
BRUNO, Frank t 1482-1506
BRUNTON, Al wb 538-539
BRUSILOFF, Nat vn 17-420-1079-1554
BRYAN, Dean g 1327-1328
BRYAN, Donald t 128-129-130-131-1222-
1223
BRYAN, Ken p 1272
BRYAN, Mike g 307-616-617-618-1148-1408
1409
BRYANT, Gladys v 190
BRYANT, Laura v 191-1704
BRYANT, Mutt cl-as 394
BRYANT, Nelson t 691-1070
BRYANT, Willie ldr-v 191-192
BRYMN, Tim p-dir 1355
BRYSON, Clay bj-v 130-131-1077-1078-
1079-1222-1331
BUBECK, Charlie cl-as 1124-1125
BUCH, F. vc 503
BUCHANAN, Jack v 192
BUCHANAN, Robert vn 1505
BUCHEL, Philip cl-as-tap dancing 470-
788-789-790
BUCHER, Joe bj 356
BUCHMAN, Sam d 646
BUCK, Banjo v 1287
BUCK, Clarence v 1196
BUCK, Fred bj 1641
BUCK, Leroy d-v 1570-1571
BUCKMAN, Sid t 346-539
BUCKNER, C. J. cl-as-ts-bar 1643-1644
BUCKNER, Johnny as 1491
BUCKNER, Milton g 664
BUCKNER, Ted cl-as-f 987-988-989-990-
1735
BUCKWALTER, Charles p-a 659
BUDDA, Prince vib 1252
BUFFANO, Jules p-a 134-1573
BUFORD, Lawson bb 466-1151-1167-1168-
1169-1456
BUGGY, Francis cl-ss-ts 1663
BUIE, Monk t 886-887
BULLETT, Bradley ("William Bradley") tb
91-92-820-1718
BULLIMORE, Bert t 1215-1396-1508-1509
BULLMAN, Mort tb 184-398
BULLOCK, Chick v 34-35-122-132-142-194-
195-196-197-198-199-200-201-202-203-204
205-206-207-208-255-423-484-557-678-830
874-875-876-878-879-881-1026-1027-1071-
1088-1146-1278-1311-1331-1332-1346-1415
1708-1709-1710-1722-1751
BULLOCK, Ernie cl-bcl-as 1104-1463
BULTERMAN, Jack t 282-689
BUMP, Jerry tb 544-762-882-998
BUNCH, Bob cl-ts 439
BUNCH, Carl bj 208
BUNCH, Frank p 208
BUNDOCK, Rowland sb 1063-1064
BUNN, Teddy g-v 6-113-208-357-358-390-
415-479-663-746-751-781-838-917-970-
1031-1053-1061-1135-1154-1204-1227-1240
1269-1330-1431-1467-1485-1486-1488-1542
1644-1647-1678-1729

BUONO, Nick t 457-816-817
BUONO, Vincent C. c 332-1250-1251-1252
1586-1587
BURBERRY, Mick cl-as-bar 346-347-348
BURBIG, Henry speech 1599
BURCH, Claude t 1201
BURCH, Elmer ts 1507
BURCHETT, Dave tb 346-347
BURCKHARDT, John F. p 1588
BURDICK, Bill cl 1196
BURDICK, Phil t 1196
BURGERT, Woody t 89
BURGESS, D. t 1493
BURGESS, Freddy tb 347
BURGESS, George t 346-347
BURGESS, Henry vn 1548
BURKE, Al sb 281-1083
BURKE, Ceele bj-g-stg 47-1631
BURKE, Clyde v 296-1374-1375
BURKE, Ed tb 91-92-541-766
BURKE, Hal v 1307
BURKE, Jerome d 564-1475
BURKE, Judy d 1552
BURKE, Ray cl 383-565
BURKE, Sonny ldr-v 208-209
BURKHARDT, Harry d 399
BURKISS, Dash d 999
BURLESON, —— g 842
BURLESON, Hattie v 209
BURLESON, Walter tb 788
BURLEY, Mary Lou - see WILLIAMS, MARY
LOU
BURMAN, Martin as 398
BURMAN, Maurice d 399-539-563-807-808-
822-1224
BURN, Sid cl-ts 1263
BURNESS, Les p 123-1159-1160-1263-1400
1401-1402-1403
BURNET, Bob t 94-95-96-97-98
BURNETT, Dick - see KAUFMAN, IRVING
BURNETT, Roscoe cl-as-ts 960-1175
BURNS, Asbestos p 1452
BURNS, Billy tb 827-835-836-960-961-
1427-1642-1742-1743
BURNS, Bobby cl-as-ts-v 831-1335
BURNS, Charlie t 1672
BURNS, J. vn 112-918
BURNS, Jeanne v 209-1332-1594
BURNS, Karl t 1089
BURNS, Pat d 920-921
BURNS, Robert cl-as-ts 80-81-207-946
BURR, —— v 737
BURR, Henry (r.n. Harry McClaskey) v
920
BURRILL, Chester tb 395-1427
BURRIS, Johnny t 902
BURRIS, Johnny p-ldr 209
BURROUGHS, Alvin d 661-760-761-1204
BURROWS, Jack d 345-536
BURSE, Albert bb 557
BURSE, Charlie g-md-v 1042-1043-1044
BURSON, Jimmy bj 1562
BURT, Glen v 1614
BURT, Johnny p 1150
BURT, Vera (Mrs. Saxie Hoktsworth) v
772
BURTNETT, Earl p-dir 748-1305
BURTON, Buddy (r.n. William E. B.) k-p-d
v 65-100-150-151-210-211-327-354-406-
642-852-1019-1037-1044-1045-1055-1099-
1100-1162-1319-1494-1495

BURTON, Buddy  d  943
BURWELL, Cliff  p  670-1271-1586
BURWELL, Marvin  tb  884
BUSBY, Bill  bb-sb  302-459-500-784-785-1017-1584
BUSBY, Bob  p-v  1213-1214
BUSBY, Cyril  as-bar  1048
BUSBY, Lad  tb  822-841
BUSCH, Lou  p  889
BUSH, Charlie ("Joe Horse")  d-dir  250-455-698-699-700-701-702-703-775
BUSH, Percy  t  154-155
BUSHELL, Garvin  cl-ss-as-bsn  164-187-257-258-360-459-514-527-551-645-705-810-940-978-1008-1306-1445-1446-1460-1461-1462-1531-1535-1576-1649-1655-1660-1661-1663-1692-1724-1725-1727-1742-1743
BUSHELL, Woody  sb  1116
BUSHKIN, Joe  p-cel  122-123-125-126-153-211-335-336-449-450-451-452-453-518-542-767-821-881-1007-1468-1481-1696
BUSSE, Henry  c-t  205-211-732-1355-1606-1607-1608-1609-1680-1681-1682-1683-1684-1685
BUSTER, Norman  d-marimba  1463
BUTASKI, Joe  p  1308
BUTTAFOO, Gabby  p  517
BUTIN, Roy  harp  1197-1199-1200
BUTLER, Bob  v  1208
BUTLER, Jack  c-t-v  191-632-954-960-1008
BUTLER, Roy  cl-as-ts-bar  835-836-1501
BUTLER, Teddy  as  895
BUTLER, William  as-vn  338
BUTTENCK, Toots  d  1491
BUTTERFIELD, Billy  t  82-186-363-367-368-369-370-371-372-373-618-619-620-621-1242-1407-1408-1491-1553
BUTTERFIELD, Charlie  tb  5-33-60-62-67-82-159-195-196-273-502-503-504-512-561-641-670-671-676-695-871-873-1095-1098-1303-1312-1329-1367-1368-1381-1382-1384-1391-1483-1597-1639-1751
BUTTERFIELD, Erskine  p-elo-v  214-215-216-1427
BUTTS, Jimmy  sb  764
BUZZINGTON, Ezra  pic-sw  216
BYAS, Don  ts  108-109-110-770-851-901-1046-1203-1204-1337-1575
BYERS, Bernice  v  814
BYERS, Douglas  t  154-155
BYERS, Hale "Pee Wee"  cl-ss-as-ts-f  732-1355-1606-1607-1608-1609-1680
BYLETH, Reggie  cl-as-ts  578-579
BYNG, George W.  dir  1019-1020
BYRD, Cuthbert  as  1097
BYRD, Eddie  d  1272
BYRD, John  g-v  570
BYRNE, Bobby  tb-v  53-362-427-428-429-430-431-432-433-1329
BYRNE, Pauline  v  1299-1406
BYRNE, W J.  bj  1267

CABALIERS, THE  v  261
CACERES, Emilio  vn  216
CACERES, Ernie  cl-ts-bar  113-216-646-647-959-1538-1539-1753
CACERES, Fred  vn  1640
CADMAN, Cliff  vn  1150
CAFFERELLI, Gene  c  1509-1510
CAFFREY, E. M.  tb  128
CAHN, Sammy  v  217

CAHNS, Alfred  bj  310
CAIAZZA, Nick  ts  166-1703-741-775-1244-1481-1482
CAIN, Philip ("Carfe Phillips")f  891-1223
CAINE, Ed.as  1482
CAINE, William  p  1-179
CAIRNS, Clifford  v  1177
CALABRESE, Louis  t-bj  4-217-561-562-1483
CALAMESE, Alex  c  1245
CALDWELL, Happy (r.n. Albert C.)  cl-ts  14-45-142-169-285-334-1053-1061-1096-1104-1107-1445-1749
CALHOUN, William  ts-v  1485
CALI, John  bj-g  17-19-39-69-71-72-74-75-89-90-127-137-174-176-217-349-350-463-509-510-532-557-638-641-668-676-751-752-804-882-914-916-935-1036-1188-1212-1275-1356-1379-1415-1416-1417-1418-1428-1544-1545-1604-1610
CALKER, Darrell (Dan)  bj-g-a-v  132-1392
CALKIN, Arthur  bb-sb  1339-1340-1341-1493
CALL, Bob  p  1321
CALLENDER, Howard  t  395
CALLENDER, Red (r.n. George C.)  sb  54-55-1512
CALLIES, Weiner  vn  361
CALLOWAY, Blanche  v  251-252-1281
CALLOWAY, Cab (r.n. Caleb C.)  v-ldr  252-253-254-255-256-257-258-259-260-261-262-1277
CALLOWAY, Ermine  v  262-263
CALLOWAY, William  bj-v  1241
CALVIN, Benny  md  1026
CALVIN, Rosemary  v  1304
CAMARATA, Toots (r.n. Salvador C.)  t-v-a  53-92-362-427-428-429-1095-1329-1602
CAMDEN, Ed  t  133-999
CAMERON, John  cl-as  1021
CAMERON, Ray  t  306-907
CAMPBELL, Alvin  ts  252
CAMPBELL, Art(hur)  bb'  234-840-870-871
CAMPBELL, Arthur  p  891
CAMPBELL, Bruce  t-tb  279
CAMPBELL, Chester  bb  806-807-1371
CAMPBELL, Chuck  tb  17-63-64-159-174-237-422-423-574-638-676-751-752-804-840-870-1171-1172-1224-1285-1286-1381-1416-1417-1418-1524-1551-1586-1593-1604-1610
CAMPBELL, Edgar  cl  190-360-378-379-380-512-1423-1648-1649
CAMPBELL, Floyd  bj  399-1172-1271
CAMPBELL, Floyd  d-v  263-359-807
CAMPBELL, Fred  t  391
CAMPBELL, Fred  cl-as-bar-f  1641
CAMPBELL, Harry  d  456
CAMPBELL, Howard  cl-ts  1150
CAMPBELL, Jimmy  t  433-434-435-436-1358-1359
CAMPBELL, Marty  t  1347-1348
CAMPBELL, Muryel ("Uncle Zeke")  g-v  1640
CAMPBELL, Paul  t  763-1631
CAMPBELL, Roy  bj  1546
CANDIDO, Candy (r.n. James C.)  sb  64-270
CANDOLI, Pete  t  168-457
CANDREAU, Joe  as  182
CANDRIX, Fud  ts  1284
CANDULLO, Joe  vn-v  265-266-267-268-269-270

CANNON, Gus bj-jug-v 270-271
CANNON, Jim cl-as 163-1068-1069-1150
CANOVA, Nolan v 1239
CANT, Mosey ts 730
CANTOR, Eddie v 560
CANTOR, Peter v 1337
CANVIN, Bobby v 98
CAPICOTTO, Phil t 203-981-982-1095-
1178-1415
CAPLAN, Dave bj 1134
CAPLAN, Jerry as 647
CAPLAN, Sam vn 819-820
CAPODIFERRO, Pete t 1330
CAPONE, Vincent f 1690-1691
CAPOZZI, Ernie g 756
CAPURA, Bud d 383
CARA, Mancy bj-g-v 43-44-45-46-314-
404-1488
CARAN, Byron tb 321
CARBONARO, Joe bb-sb-vn 657
CARDEW, Phil cl-as-ts 470-789-1226-
1227
CAREW, Les tb 24-25-192-801-1493
CAREW, Naomi p 1093
CAREY, Guy tb 119-120-193-857-858-1506
1509
CAREY, Mutt (r.n. Thomas C.) c 456-942
1485
CAREY, Reagan as 391
CAREY, Scoops as-a 78-263-466-728
CARHART, George bj-g-dir 1136
CARLE, Frank p 296-647-657-1028
CARLEW, Eddie d 271
CARLIN, Bill t 656-657
CARLIN, Herb t 120-121
CARLISLE, Elsie v 147-790-1791-949-950
CARLISLE, Una Mae p-v 272-273-1238-
1635
CARLSEN, Bill dir 402-403
CARLSEN, Roy p 273
CARLSON, Frank d 163-364-738-739-740-
741-742-743-744-1075
CARLSON, Johnny t 59-1314
CARLS(S)ON, Olaf/Olof t 282-652
CARLSON, Russ p 418-871-1367-1368-1722
CARLSON, Simon t 1498
CARLSON, Tony sb 417
CARLSON, Vic p 1368
CARLSTROM, Skippy - see KIRKEBY, ED
CARLTON, Bud cl-as 162-1236-1237-1406
CARLTON, Jack v 1357
CARMICHAEL, Hoagy (r.n. Hoagland C.) c-p
cel-percussion-v 46-274-275-276-296-
316-351-458-503-578-762-922-1081-1378-
1569-1682
CARNEOL, Jess cl-as-ts 756-903-1552
CARNEY, Doc d 1063-1064
CARNEY, Harry cl-bcl-ss-as-ts-bar-v 27
134-135-473-474-475-476-477-478-479-
480-481-482-483-484-485-486-487-488-
489-490-491-492-493-494-495-496-497-
498-499-500-607-631-640-651-652-662-
765-766-767-814-1075-1083-1263-1500-
1501-1653-1711-1712-1731-1732
CAROL, Lily Ann v 1250
CAROLA, William g 1015
CAROLE, Josie v 959
CAROLINERS, THE v 1077
CARON, Fern t 417
CARPENTER AND INGRAM (The Harmony Girls)
v 855

CARPENTER, —— p-dir 1274
CARPENTER, Cecil tb 1462-1463
CARPENTER, Earl cl-as 418
CARPENTER, Marie as 1075
CARPENTER, Pete 376
CARPENTER, Thelma v 690-1735-1736
CARPENTER, Vic bj 100-954-955
CARPENTER, Wingy (r.n. Theodore C.) c-t
66-278-644-1561
CARR, Dora v 278-279
CARR, Edward tb-1651
CARR, Leon a 987
CARR, Sam bj 919-920
CARR, Warren tb-a 274
CARREL, Harry as 94
CARRIERE, Pokey t 364-1540-1541
CARRIERE, Sid ss-ts 302
CARRINGTON, Jeff t 520
CARRINGTON, Jerome p-as 338-1645-1646-
1647
CARRINGTON, Louis bb 851
CARROLL, A. t 456
CARROLL, Bob t 1109
CARROLL, Bob ts 1627-1628-1637-1638
CARROLL, Bob v 97-98
CARROLL, Charlie d 326-416-417-447-923
CARROLL, Don v 880
CARROLL, Eddie p-a 279-581-656-788-789-
790-1507-1508
CARROLL, Frank sb 1513
CARROLL, Jimmy t-cl 80-81-207
CARROLL, Raleigh bj-g 1498
CARROLL, Robert ts 39-360-756-935-1276
1277-1278-1279-1468
CARROLL, Willie vn 380
CARRUTHERS, Earl cl-as-ts-bar 983-984-
985-986-987-988-989-990-991-
CARRY, Ed bj 1501
CARSELLA, Al pac-p 32-33-1068
CARSELLA, Johnny tb 18
CARSON, James cl-ts 318
CARSON, Jazz d 645
CARTER, Alice v 280
CARTER, Alice Leslie 280
CARTER, Benny t-cl-ss-as-ts-p-v-a-ldr
75-76-90-91-93-191-260-272-280-281-282-
283-284-312-445-486-518-588-594-661-662
690-723-724-727-728-752-770-779-791-792
908-911-959-1034-1035-1048-1052-1071-
1073-1263-1304-1408-1594-1654-1655-1657
1660-1669-1734-1735
CARTER, Bob v 903
CARTER, Don d 371-647-1481-1482-1491
CARTER, Francis J. p 651-652
CARTER, Harry as-ts-vn 515-1149-1616
CARTER, Jack d 1427
CARTER, Lavaida v 1427-1645
CARTWRIGHT, Paul cl-ss-ts 1611-1612-
1613
CARVER, Wayman cl-as-ts-f-a 280-281-527
631-791-792-1123-1124-1658-1659-1660-
1661-1662
CARWELL, Ed tb 1097
CARY, Dick p 1007
CASAMORE, Emanuel bb 1715-1716
CASE, Russ t 66-160-203-204-205-594-889
1027-1089-1095-1273-1372-1373-1572-1718
CASEY, Albert g 56-64-131-272-513-662-
769-770-821-839-1052-1134-1377-1542-
1624-1625-1626-1628-1629-1630-1631-1632
1633-1636-1637-1638-1735-1736

1768

CASEY, Bob g 1481
CASEY, Bob sb 821
CASEY, Floyd d-wb 5-99-411-1241-1701-
1702-1703-1704-1705-1706-1707-1708-1709
1710-1711
CASEY, Howard t 391
CASEY, Lawrence ("Papa Egg-Shell") g
181-1327
CASEY, Les g 347-348
CASH, Benny p-v 913
CASH, Clayton t 62-889
CASINO, Del v 95
CASPER, Emile v 1565
CASSAGNE, Louis bb-sb 575-1067-1068
CASSAMORE, C. tb 1550
CASSARD, Jules bb-sb 1003-1068-1069-
1257
CASSELL, Milton cl-bsn-ca-f-o-pic 936-
1274
CASSERES, Fred g 962
CASSIDY, Albert L. tb 575
CASSIDY, Jim tb 63-972-973-1680
CASSIDY, Jim cl-as 1364-1365
CASTAIN, Chet ts 203-205
CASTAING, John d 687-1250
CASTALDO, Charlie tb 622-623
CASTALDO, Lee (also known as LEE CASTLE)
t 168-204-443-444-445-446-451-676-702-
1398-1399-1408-1409-1538-1539
CASTELLA, Robert p 1339
CASTELLANO, Pete t 417
CASTELLANO, Tony cl-ts 1197
CASTELLANOS, Alcide as 827-835
CASTELUCCI, Johnny bj 571
CASTI, Nick t 237-238-626-627-826
CASTIN, Sammy t 873-874-875-1108-1309
CASTLE, Boots v 1733
CASTNER, Stan t 873-874-875
CATALYNE, Joe cl-as-ts 1146-1234-1249-
1537
CATES, Opie as 204-1236-1237
CATHCART, Jack t-as 1174-1407-1408
CATHCART, James vn 98
CATINA, Tony bj 1347
CATLETT, Sidney d-vib 51-56-57-58-113-
114-115-131-280-281-312-335-383-466-619
620-662-667-691-728-751-783-791-792-823
824-839-1019-1135-1240-1253-1278-1279-
1289-1467-1673-1731-1744
CATO, William tb 691-1103
CATON, Lauderic g 141
CATUREGLI, Alex t 519-1284
CAVALLO, Angelo tb 134
CAVALOTTI, Claude as 10-11-
CAVANAUGH, Don tb 417
CAVANAUGH, Inez v 1337
CAVE, Jack fh 1406
CAVE, Tim t 1674
CAVENDISH THREE, THE v 1435
CAWLEY, Jack g 211
CAWLEY, Joe p 975-976
CAZENTRE, Al v 1595
CECCHI, Leo tb 1244
CELESTIN, Oscar "Papa" c 301-302
CELL, Harvey sb-a 1552-1553
CENTER, Earl bb 356
CENTOBIE, Leonard cl 687
CENTURY QUARTET, THE v 1317
CEPPOS, Mac vn 203-672-943-979-980-981-
982-1121
CERBORRA, Charles t 1047

CHABAUD, Jean p 1211
CHADEL, H. P. (r.n. DELAUNAY, CHARLES) d
189-333
CHAFFIN, George tb 156-1364-1365-1521
CHAILLOUX, Maurice d-v 188-189-652-
689-1211-1596
CHALLIS, Beth v 302-626-1308
CHALLIS, Bill p-a 289-422-577-578-1566
1568-1682-1683-1684-1685-1686-1687
CHAMBERS, Dudley B. v 657
CHAMBERS, Elmer c-t 91-190-353-458-705
710-711-712-713-714-715-716-717-731-
732-733-749-750-793-1023-1051-1350-
1447-1448-1449-1466-1519-1520-1649-
1725-1728
CHAMBERS, Henderson tb 58
CHAMBERS, Wallace v 1056-1287
CHANDLER, Bill t-v 193-1369
CHANEY, Jack cl-as-ts 687-1150
CHANNEY, Alec p 412
CHANSLOR, Hal p 361-657
CHANTRAIN, Raymond t 1284
CHAPMAN, Chris x 303
CHAPMAN, Harry harp 635-636-801
CHAPMAN, Jack p 303
CHAPMAN, Paul g-v-a 342-770
CHAPPELET, Denis ts 960-961
CHAPPELLE, Juanita Stinette v 303
CHAPPELLE, Thomas E. v 303
CHAPUT, Roger g 67-333-398-465-536-556
635-776-1258-1259-1261-1476-1670
CHARIER, Elinor v 309-977
CHARIOTEERS, THE v 80-304
CHARLES, Amedee as 1348-1349-1642
CHARLES, Milton or 970
CHARON, George ts 571
CHARVAT, J. as-ts 1575
CHASE, Frank ts 1304
CHASE, Newell p 170
CHASE, Ronnie t-tb-v 185-416-702-703
CHASE, Wilder p 1003-1129-1130
CHASTAIN, Roland cl-as 1068
CHAULIAC, Leo p 1563
CHEATHAM, Doc (r.n. Adolphus C.) t-v
254-255-256-257-258-259-284-383-594-
1035-1208-1736-1742-1743
CHEATHAM, Lee tb 1009
"CHEEK" bb 6
CHEEK, Robert t 18-191-213-747-1346
CHEIKES, Mac bj-g 8-250-437-455-699-
700-701-702-703-775-1561
CHERWIN, Dick bb-sb 17-33-63-64-112-
159-160-197-332-509-751-752-805-905-
1016-1312-1415
CHESLEIGH, Jack g-v 320-321-322-323
CHESNEY, Ronald h 554
CHESTER, Bob cl-ts-a-ldr 306-307-562-
1484
CHESTER, Eddie v 267
CHESTNUT, Bob t 557
CHESTNUT, Ray cl 1174
CHIBOUST, Noel ts 189-190-307-333-519-
689-776-827-1211-1284-1339-1348-1349-
1615-1642
CHICAGOANS, THE v 936
"CHIEF" bb 1051-1052
CHILDS, F. d 1089
CHILDS, Oliver v 1623
CHILDS, Virginia v 310
CHILES, Charles v 1062
"CHIN CHIN" vn 1

CHIPPENDALE, Chips (r.n. Harold C.) bar 348-964
CHISHOLM, Anna Lee v 310
CHISHOLM, George tb-cel-a-dir 25-279-283-310-311-554-1039-1092-1224-1238-1343-1509-1519-1632-1693
CHITTISON, Herman p-cel 52-81-190-311-330-395-886-959-960-1642-1693-1706-1708
CHOLET, Nane v 312-313
CHOLINSKY, J. t 1575
CHOMER, Roger vib 1211
CHRISTENSEN, Axel p 313
CHRISTENSEN, Sigfre p 1131
CHRISTIAN, Bert d-vib 1550
CHRISTIAN, Bobby d 1206
CHRISTIAN, Buddy (r.n. Narcisse C.) bj-g 75-136-149-285-313-343-357-537-645-707-794-811-835-845-965-994-1011-1912-1013-1021-1022-1097-1128-1279-1280-1438-1439-1449-1450-1457-1458-1463-1532-1533-1577-1617-1618-1698-1699-1700-1739
CHRISTIAN, Buddy d 1159-1160
CHRISTIAN, Charlie g-elg 62-355-613-614-615-616-617-618-619-652-662-782-821-873-1046-1048
CHRISTIAN, Emile tb-v 571-1176-1177-1639
CHRISTIAN, Frank c 459-1194-1692
CHRISTIAN, Lillie Delk v 313-1744
CHRISTIAN, Frenchy (r.n. Polite C.) c 543
CHRISTIAN, Tommy ts-bar-ldr 314-552-1730
CHRISTIAN, William W. tb 1446
CHRISTIE, Hamish C. t-tb-v 532-1263
CHRISTIE, James t 1180-1181-1182
CHRISTIE, Louis H. cl 332-1254-1255-1256-1473-1474-1475-1604-1605
CHRISTMAS, Art cl-as 539
CHRISTNER, Sy ts 682
CHRISTY, Fred d 391
CHRISTY, Harlan bj 394
CHURCH, Earl t 1009
CHURCHILL, Stuart t-as-x 1641
CIBELLI, Sal vn 1
CICCONE, Anthony cl-ss-as-bar-vn 134-1047
CICCONE, Fritz g-bb 76-1047-1688
CIELO, Mickey t 416-1243
CIRCIRELLO, Pat t 1332
CIRINA, Mike vn 1066
CIZERONE, Maurice cl-as-f 571-1211-1260-1284-1642
CLAES, Johnny t 316-1092-1585
CLAIRE, Otto p 563-564
CLAIS, George as 1284
CLAPP, Sonny tb-as-ts-ldr 316-630-917-918-1028-1429-1430-1730
CLARE, Nobby vn 1128
CLARE, Pops sb 841
CLARK, Bill vm 1214
CLARK, Buddy v 594-595-1027
CLARK, Charlie p 151
CLARK, Chester t 1563-1564
CLARK, Dick cl-ts 62-363-364-534-535-594-595-596-597-598-697-698-905-1036-1037-1337-1406
CLARK, Don cl-ss-as-bar-dir 317-732-1606-1680
CLARK, Earl bj 556
CLARK, Manuel t 1716

CLARK, Garner t 306-307-1119
CLARK, Garnet p 317-752
CLARK, George ts 983-1465
CLARK, Harriet v 97
CLARK, Harry (r.n. Harry Sniffin) sb 29-756-1333-1334
CLARK, Henry tb 41-676-862
CLARK, Jimmy bb-sb 1616
CLARK, Joe as 1129-1133
CLARK, June c-t 149-280-473-645-1013
CLARK, Lynne vn 1540
CLARK, Marlon cl-as 168
CLARK, Mel sb 1332
CLARK, Norman v 1613
CLARK(E), Pete cl-as-bar 14-50-51-55-490-526-528-1279-1658-1659-1725-1736
CLARK, Sam g 860
CLARK, Spencer cl-as-bsx-v 132-235-238-239-571-626-882-981-982-1025-1393-1490-1580-1581-1583-1593-1594-1595-1620
CLARKE, Edwin G. dir 1475
CLARKE, Frank sb 832
CLARKE, George ts 310
CLARKE, Harry sb 214
CLARKE, Herbert L. c-dir 25-796-797-1473-1475
CLARKE, Kenny d-x 81-108-113-318-529-551-659-696-770-832
CLARKE, Richard t 191-281-382-1731
(shown on pp. 191-281 as CLARK in error)
CLARKSON, George ss-ts 395-1515
CLAUSEN, Ed as 1358-1359-1630
CLAUVE, Carla bj 314-315
CLAVNER, Mort bj-v 1068
CLAXTON, Rozelle p-a 520-944
CLAY, Henry t 310
CLAY, Shirley c-t 39-360-382-404-410-593-753-754-757-758-760-775-810-862-935-1014-1025-1026-1051-1235-1268-1277-1278-1320-1355-1653-1654
CLAY, Sonny p-ldr 213-318-410-1506
CLAYTON, Amos d 792
CLAYTON, Buck t-a 78-101-102-103-104-105-106-107-108-109-110-607-768-769-813-814-821-872-873-905-1263-1732-1733-1734
CLAYTON, Jenny v 1041
CLEG, Lem v 38
CLEGG, Frank x 1379
CLEMENS, Bill tb 1616
CLEMENS, Oscar d 394
CLEMENT, Cal v 1646
CLEMMONS, Bob v 1111
CLESS, Rod cl-as 764-765-1481-1537-1546
CLIFFORD, Henry jug 409
CLIFFORD, James as 1753
CLINKSCALES, Charles v 1623
CLINTON, Larry t-tb-a-ldr 123-124-293-294-320-321-322-323-324-325-326-441-1053
CLINTON, William cl-as 1267
CLITHEROW, Bob t 959
CLOSE, Paul bj 314
CLOUD, Robert as-ts 558-1263-1338
CLOUTIER, Frank p 556
CLUKE, Silas bj 1507
CLUKIES, Marion vc 1534
COATES, Freddy p 821
COBB, Alfred tb 763
COBB, Bert bb 510-1167
COBB, Gene v 1063

1770

COBB, Jimmy c 101-326-327-873-1154-1738
COBB, Junie (r.n. Eugene C.) cl-ss-ts-
    bj-g 132-327-328-1151-1152-1153-1167-
    1168-1207-1228-1268-1495-1738
COBB, Oliver c-v 328-1574
COBBS, Alfred tb 1075
COBEY, Lew/Lou p 248-249-1380-1381-1621
COBORN, Arthur t 1744
COCHRAN, Cliff ss-as 807
COCKERILL, Elton cl-ts 1641
CODY, Henry d 1496-1497
COESTIER, Marcel as 333
COFFMAN, Wanna sb 1505
COGBURN, Red p 405
COGNATA, Charles t 545
COHAN, Murray ts-o' 946-1690
COHEN, —— ts 1155
COHEN, Bernard t 361
COHEN, C. bj 1396
COHEN, Frank p 207-702-703-775-829
COHEN, Harry sb 1753
COHEN, Jack bj-g-v 112-917-918
COHEN, Jesse p-dir 1740
COHEN, Lennie as 1047
COHEN, Morris ts 829
COHEN, Paul t 307
COHEN, Ray vn 1235-1236
COHN, Harry (same as Harry Cohen ?) sb
    1121
COHN, Zinky p 404-541-780-1153-1154-
    1459
COLA, Ned g 1273
COLBY, Ross - see BALLEW, SMITH
COLE, Cozy (r.n. William C.) d 14-77-80-
    122-131-191-251-259-260-261-262-382-383
    513-518-541-545-660-661-662-767-768-769
    779-897-1003-1026-1027-1104-1134-1240-
    1464-1465-1711-1722-1730-1731-1732-1733
    1734-1735
COLE, Donald tb 1070
COLE, Eddie sb-v 328-1675
COLE, James vn 328
COLE, Johnny bb 866-867
COLE, June bb-sb-v 317-720-721-722-723-
    959-960-961-1444-1704-1743
COLE, Louis v 172-835
COLE, Martin ts 27
COLE, Nat "King" p-v 329-663
COLE, Norman vn 24-395-1210-1515
COLE, Phil cl-ss-as 1006
COLE, Roy vn 1047
COLE, Rupert cl-as-bar 55-56-57-58-179-
    360-824-825-935-1276-1277-1278-1279
COLE, Teddy p 39-78-466
COLEMAN, Bill t-v 190-207-208-284-317-
    330-333-755-770-782-886-960-1007-1008-
    1276-1345-1370-1625-1642-1670-1736
COLEMAN, Bob g 315
COLEMAN, Dorlan as 1507
COLEMAN, E. L. vn 330-803-1013
COLEMAN, Jaybird h-jug-v 137
COLEMAN, Johnson c 278
COLEMAN, Oliver d 730-759
COLEMAN, Ruth v 330-1161
COLES, Edward bb 1427
COLES, Sid cl-as-bar 1675
COLEY, Leslie bj 862
COLICCHIO, Ralph vn 575
COLICCHIO, Tony bj-g 575-629-630-1147-
    1330
COLIN, Charles t 545

COLIN, Sid g-v 1343
COLLEGIATE ROLLICKERS, THE v 236
COLLEN, Matthew t 320
COLLIER, Eddie tb 8
COLLIER, Jack sb 563
COLLIER, Ralph d 620-621-622
COLLINS, —— cl 1489
COLLINS, Ben t 1336-1493
COLLINS, Booker sb 899-900-901-902-1431
    1720
COLLINS, Jack tb 470-1339-1340-1341-
    1342
COLLINS, Jerry p 409
COLLINS, Johnny g-elg 78-81-273-466-
    729-770-851-1203-1204-1531-1575-1739
COLLINS, K. vl 1407-1408
COLLINS, Lee c-t 308-709-770-843-863-
    1100-1371-1487-1489
COLLINS, Paul d 126-364-1146-1147-1540-
    1541
COLLINS, Shad (r.n. Lester C.) t 104-
    105-106-169-257-258-259-261-262-273-281
    284-755-756-770-791-821-832-1247-1670
COLLINS, Siki (r.n. N. J. C.) cl-ss 209
    533
COLLIS, Eddie d-v 359-1226
COLLOT, Lisee p 16
COLLOT, Paul p 1284-1339
COLUMBO, Louis as 647
COLON, Joe as-ts 132
COLON, Ted t 149
COLONNA, Jerry tb 738-1027-1602
COLUCCI, Tony bj-g 2-37-38-63-71-72-75-
    139-304-395-420-502-670-671-672-777-804
    853-870-871-903-925-926 927-928-930-931
    932-933-934-036 845-946-1016-1039-1064-
    1108-1125-1138-1147-1180-1182-1183-1184
    1381-1382-1383-1384-1520-1545-1554-1597
    1652
COLUMBO, Russ vn-v 59-332
COMBELLE, Alix cl-ta-a 11-16-188-189-
    190-283-307-333-465-519-536-689-690-776
    836-1211-1238-1262-1284-1338-1348-1349-
    1421-1596-1615-1642
COMEGYS, Leon tb 763
COMER, Dave p 334-1117
COMFORT, Bill bj-v 1664
COMPTON, Glover p 794-1245
CONARD, Fred ? 218
CONAWAY, Clarence md-u 1441-1448-1728
CONAWAY, Lincoln M. g-stg 522-732-1218-
    1444-1448-1728
CONAWAY, Sterling bj-g-u 643-705-706-
    835-836-1475-1728
CONDELL, Louis bj 1745
CONDON, Chick d 240-241-243-244-648-
    1141-1393-1394-1583-160
CONDON, Eddie bj-g-v 45-88-122-123-142-
    153-309-334-335-336-382-383-541-542-543
    634-646-647-765-821-822-868-893-959-977
    1007-1030-1031-1032-1033-1087-1113-1114
    1115-1240-1289-1546-1623-1637-1696
CONDON, Jack cl-as 201-1009
CONGER, Wayne bj-g-vn 646
CONIGLIARO, Joe tb 912
CONLEY, Althea tb 1075
CONLEY, Larry tb 1326-1327
CONLEY, Norman tb 1075
CONN, Ginger d 138
CONNA, Lee bj 20
CONNELL, George t 1150

CONNELLY, Harold  ts-bar  644
CONNER, Harry  t  271
CONNER, Jack  d  747
CONNER, Merrill  t  640-641-1665-1666-1667-1688
CONNETT, Max  t  418-1068-1069-1570-1571
CONNIFF, Ray  tb-a  125-126-371-372-373-1242-1408-1409
CONNOLLY, Ray  c  274
CONNOR, Kitty  v  967
CONNORS, Leo  tb  1160
CONRAD, Claude  t  1327
CONRAD, Coonie  p  1068
CONRAD, Herman  bb  1256-1473-1474-1475-1586-1604-1605
CONRAD, Lew  vn-v  1285-1286-1383-1384-1386
CONROY, Reg  vib  635
CONSELMAN, Bob  d-vib  591-592-961-1509-1537-1570
CONSTABLE, Harry  cl-as  995-996
CONWAY, Bill  v  1690-1691
CONWAY, Sid  d  640-641
CONYERS, Walter  d  251
COOK, Fred  vn  1680
COOK, Harry  bar  1429-1430
COOK, Howard  sb  1357-1358-1360-1361
COOK, Joe  bar  457
COOK, Johnny  tb  552-553-557
COOK, John  v  1528
COOK, Will Marion  dir  1651
COOKE, Alistair  compere  821
COOKE, Bob  bj-g  563-1045-1469-1470
COOKE, Fred  p-a  345-667
COOKSEY, Robert  h-k-v  110-408-846-942-1007-1013-1023-1480-1655
COOLBERTSON, Ronnie  cl-as  346
COOLEY, William  v  1710-1711
COOMBES, Arthur  cl-as  1229
COOMBS, ——  as  275
COON, Carlton  d-v  338-339-340-341
COOPER, Al  cl-as-bar-ldr-a  342
COOPER, Casey  vn  380
COOPER, Eddie  tb  1338
COOPER, Harry  c-t  1-349-472-536-686-827-1013-1109-1388-1450-1513
COOPER, Jack  v  23-23-1224-1298
COOPER, Jerry  v  422
COOPER, L. Z.  p  47
COOPER, Leslie  tb  1379
COOPER, Les (r.n. Lester C.)  cl-as  92-416
COOPER, Opal  banjoline  1279
COOPER, Paul  p  525
COOPER, Robert  p  342
COOPER, Tracy  vn  512
COOPER TRIO, THE  v  589
COOPER, Winnie  v  855
COPE, Art  cl-ts-vn  1055
COPELAND, Andrew  v  342
COPELAND, Eddie  t  464
COPELAND, Martha  v  343-344
COPENING, Jimmy  v  6
COPESTAKE, Ray  t  656
COPSEY, Ralph  tb-v  59-1235
CORCORAN, Corky (r.n. Gene C.)  ts  457-819-820
CORDARO, Jack  cl-ts-bar  200-479-480-1558-1571-1572
CORDARO, Joe  cl-  674-1571
CORDARO, John  cl-bcl-as-bar  1689-1690

CORDELL, Joe  tb  138-1674
CORDELLA, Charlie  cl-as-ts  650-1132
CORDONNIER, Paul  sb  1476
CORLEY, George  tb  155
CORLEY, Leslie  bj  676
CORNELIUS, Corky  t  183-298-299-300-612-908-909-910
CORNELL, Dick  d  1004-1047
CORNELL, Jack  p-pac  1079-1081
CORNILLE, Andre  t  188-1260-1596
CORNWELL, Frank  vn-v  170-344-632
CORTESE, Joseph  vn  112-918
CORTESE, Nick  bj  172-173
CORTI, Bill  tb  165-166-168
COSLOW, Sam  v  1562
COSTA, Sam  v  1432-1433
COSTANZA, Edmund  as  744
COSTELLO, Billy  k-u-v-effects  1280
COSTELLO, Dick  p  1589
COSTELLO, Johnny  cl-as  68-69-139-979-1180-1520-1719
COSTELLO, Sidney  as  1723
COSTI, Al  g  207-829-1116
COTTLE, ——  bj  1737
COTTLER, Irving  d  326-1554
COTTON PICKERS, THE  v  1131
COTTRELL, Louis  d  136-1229-1230
COTTRELL, Louis, Jr., cl-ts  7
COTTRELL, Will  as-ts  1047
COTY, Bill  v  1035
COUGHLAN, Frank  tb  470
COULSON, Victor  t  1046
COUNT, THE  bj  1285
COUNTMAN, Harry  tb  565-566
COURANCE, Edgar  cl-ts  169-330
COUTARD, ——  tb  16
COVARRUBIAS, Arnold  g  612-613-614
COVERT, Cliff  bj-g-v  464-1669
COVERT, Maxwell  v  553
COVERT, Ray - see KAUFMAN, IRVING
COVETTI, Frenchy  sb  81
COVEY, Bill  cl-as-ts  59-1004-1116
COVINGTON, Ike  tb  830-1210
COWAN, Henry  t  326
COWENS, Herbert  d  748-770-1247-1465-1542
COX, Alphonse  c-t  1211-1259-1286
COX, Art  cl-ss-as  1162
COX, Baby  v  476
COX, Ed  c-t  187-1460
COX, Ida  v  352-353-354-355
COX, Jack  t  1137
COX, John S.  f-pic  1473-1474-1475
COXITO, Fred  as  1223
COYCAULT, Ernest  c-t  218-318-1506
CRACKERJACKS, THE  v  834
CRACOV, Dave  vn  1406
CRAIG, Al  d  282-518
CRAIG, Archie  t  25-87-518-554-964-1343-1509
CRAIG, Francis  p-ldr  356
CRAIG, George  d  1485
CRAIN, Malcolm  c-t  356-739-1400-1401-1402
CRANDALL, Russ  cl-as-harp  869
CRANE, Harry - see FIELDS, ARTHUR
CRANE, Herman  p  1570-1571
CRANEY, Arthur  d  646
CRANZ, Ponzi (r.n. Thurlow C.)  tb  418-881
CRAVEN, Sonny (r.n. Lutner C.)  tb  664-762-763

CRAWFORD, —— bb 395
CRAWFORD, Forrest cl-ts 122-1031-1032-1114-1115-1305-1312
CRAWFORD, Jack cl-ss-as-ldr 356
CRAWFORD, Jesse or 577
CRAWFORD, Jimmy d-vib 310-983-984-985-986-987-988-989-990-991-1053
CRAWFORD, Lillian p 357
CRAWFORD, Rosetta p-v 357
CRAWFORD, W. p 1396
CRAWLEY, Wilton cl-v 357-358
CREAGER, Willie d-dir 19-358-1212-1334
CREATH, Charlie t-ldr 359
CREEDON, Jack tb 1744
CREEDON, Paul t 1663-1664
CREGER, William cl-as 189-1122-1123
CREOLE SISTERS, THE v 1238
CRESSWELL, Eddie vn 1479
CRESSY, Jack cl-ts 1483
CRIETZ, B. sb 363
CRINER, Lucien t 172-173
CRIPPEN, Katie v 360
CRIPPS, Alec d 1364
CRISSEY, Fred as 1068
CROCKER, Davy pac 111
CROCKER, Stanton tb-v 554-555-1536
CROCKETT, David g-k-v 892
CROCKETT, Howard t 1548
CROLENA, Frank as 1491
CROMAR, Edward cl-as-bar 656
CROMWELL, Russell v 1147
CROOKE, Eugene bj-g 1563-1564
CROSBY, Bing (r.n. Harry Lillis C.) v 53-59-360-361-362-363-364-365-420-482-485-804-931-1567-1681-1682-1683-1684-1685-1686-1687
CROSBY, Bob v-ldr 62-161-162-365-366-367-368-369-370-371-372-373-374-375-376-396-423-424-425-426
CROSBY, Israel sb 26-131-652-728-729-730-905-906-936-1154-1490-1731
CROSBY, Ward d 1310-1311
CROSS, David v 376-1548
CROSS, Maurice as-v 133
CROSSAN, Jim cl-as-ts-bsn-f-o 420-422-423-1141-1375-1598-1614
CROSSIN, Morris g 829
CROSSMAN, Joe cl-as-ts-bar-vn 20-21-22-25-147-395-467-468-800-801-808-950-951-953-1196-1224-1295-1296-1297-1456-1507-1508-1509-1519
CROUSE, Cappy (Kappy) or KROUSE (r.n. Morrell C. or K.) tb 647-703-1116-1561
CROW, George v 587
CROWDER, Robert ts-a 661-760-761-762
CROWLEY, Gene v 1008
CROY, Martin tb 1147-1148
CROZIER, George tb-a 419-420-1210
CROZIER, Rube ts-bsn-o 1568-1598-1683-1684-1685-1686
CRUM, Frank ts 648-840
CRUMAN, Lester harp 1563
CRUMB, Earl d 1130-1131
CRUMBACHER, Les cl-ss-as-ts 2
CRUMBLEY, Elmer tb 985-986-987-988-989-990
CRUMBY, Alonzo d 188
CRUMIT, Frank v 1609
CRUMP, Jesse p-or 352-354-355-376-1280-1496

CRUMP, Russ tb 1644
CRUSE, F. J. tb 1396
CRUTCHER, Frank ts 547
CRYAN, Tom t 87
CRYOR, Jesse v 1345
CUDWIB, Frank ts 1359-1360
CUFFEE, Ed tb-v 108-728-729-731-1014-1034-1035-1168-1488-1702-1703-1704-1705
CUGAT, Xavier vn 973
CULBREATH, Bill p 404
CULLEN, Bruce tb 275-920-1005-1681-1682-1683-1684-1685-1686-1687
CULLEY, Fred vn 1641
CULLEY, George t 1641
CULLEY, Wendell t 252-253-1427
CULLEY, Willard fh 819-820
CULLIVER, Fred ts 1038
CUMBO, Marion vc 1451-1534
CUMINS, Clarence cl-as-ts-bar 1472
CUMMINGS, Jock d 87-684-801-1039-1343-1509
CUMMINS, Bernie d-v-ldr 376-377-1265
CUMMINS, Raby g 913
CUMMINS, Walter bj-v 376-377-378-1265
CUNLIFFE, Dick cl-as-bar 1664-1665-1666-1667-1668-1669
CUNNINGHAM, Bud d-v 540
CUNNINGHAM, Clayton bj 1640
CUNNINGHAM, Ed sb 1244
CUNY, Frank p 396
CUOMO, George g 94
CUOZZO, Alexander t 819-820
CUPERO, Joe g 704-1196
CURL, Langston t 311-360-580-935-1033-1034-1035-1276-1277-1278-1497
CURLEY, Hugh p 646
CURLY, Clarence wb 152
CURRAN, Joe t 25
CURRIE, Bill d-v 1339-1340
CURRY, Bert as 45-46-404
CURRY, James (Jimmy) tb 93-250-325-326-1490
CURTIS, Bart d 571
CURTIS, Dinty (r.n. Dennis (Denny) cl-ts f-v 920-921-1740
CURTIS, Ken v 453
CURTIS, Mert as-v 629-830
CURTIS, Tom bb 1201
CURTIS, Wally cl-as 83-84
CURTZ, Wilbur t 546-796-797
CUSH, Frank t 220-221-222-223-224-225-226-227-228-229-230-231-232-233-234-235-236-237-238-241-242-243-244-245-626-627-670-840-979-980-981-1580-1581-1582-1583-1593-1619-1620
CUSICK, Freddy cl-as-ts 220-221-222-223-224-225-226-227-228-229-230-231-232-239-966-967-1301-1302-1581-1582-1589-1590-1591-1592
CUSUMANO, Bob t 56-320-321-440-1690-1691
CUSUMANO, John t 756
CUTHBERTSON, Eric vl 656
CUTSHALL, Cutty (r.n. Robert C.) tb 616-617-618-619-620-621-622-1358-1359
CUTTING, Ernie sb 891
CYR, John d 889

DABNEY, Ford p-ldr 378-379-380-512
D'AGOSTINO, John tb 94
D'AGOSTINO, Tom t 1242-1243-1244
DAHLSTEN, Charlie tb 1602

DAILEY, Dusky  p  853
DAILEY, Pete  c-bsx  391
DALE, Carlotta  v  165-166-1356-1357-1358-
1491
DALE, Charles  cl-as  659
DALE, Chuck  bar  1752
DALE, Joe  d  94-1256
DALE, Marty  p  132
DALE, Moe  cl-as-ts  959
DALE, Peter  - see WIMBROW, DALE
DALE, Ted  p-a  992-993
DALHART, Vernon  k-u-v  37-39-89-137-230-
380-558-630-803-916-1202-1275-1502-1581-
1582-1608-1609-1737
DALL, Evelyn  v  24-25
DALLOLIO, Marino  cl-ts  207-829
D'ALMAINE, Charles  vn  332-1250-1251-
1252-1604
DALTON, Harold  cl-as  892
DALTON, Jack  - see KAUFMAN, JACK
DALY, Bernard  cl-ss-as  922-1066-1067-
1379-1599-1687
DALY, Lou  ts  1379-1380-1381
D'AMATO, Chappie  (r.n. Noel d'A.)  as-g-
v  535-636-799-800-801-809-810
DAMERON, Tadd  a  944-990-991
D'AMICO, Hank  cl-as  78-79-324-363-364-
373-374-1157-1158-1159-1491
DAMM, Jean  tb  1284
D'AMORE, Tony  p  908-909-910
D'ANDREA, Dan  cl-as-ts-vn  56-163-293-
294-295-296-297-298-299-300-455-699-
1150-1691
DANDRIDGE, Putney  p-cel-v-ldr  381-382-
1332
DANDRIDGE SISTERS, THE  v  989
DANFORD, Jack  as-bsx  383
DANFORTH, Dave  vn  1252
DANIELS, Benny  cl-as  801
DANIELS, Billy  v  691
DANIELS, Don  tb  59
DANIELS, Douglas  g-tiple-v  663-970-1031-
1485-1486
DANIELS, Joe  d-v  383-384-385-386-387-
388-389-1298-1339-1340-1341
DANIELS, Leon  vn  1362
DANIELS, Wilbur  bj-g-tiple-v  970-1031-
1485-1486-1646
DANKERS, Harold  cl-as  889
D'ANNOLFO, Frank  tb  123-443
DANKSHA, Joe  as  1289
DANT, Bud  (r.n. Charles D.)  c  274
DANTE, Frank  p  194
DANTIN, Lloyd  g  687
DANZI, Mike  bj  796-797-1518
DAPPEER, David  bb  1172
DARCY, Dan  d-v  553
D'ARCY, Jeanne  v  1047
D'ARCY, Philip  h-pic-vn-p-w  519-520-653-
654-655
DARE, Reg  ts  1039-1092-1585
DARENSBOURG, Percy  bj  543-1719
DARLING, Chuck  h  388
DARLING, Frank "Coco"  sb  318-696
DARNEDA, Frank  g  517
DARNELL, Bill  vn  545-695-1147-1148
DARR, Jerome  g  1647
DARROUGH, Louis  d  1122-1123
DARROW, Pops  sb  1308
DARROW, Thurlow  bb  1483 (same as above?)
DART, Bill  d  1656

DARY, Al  p-v  1688
DASBERG, Sam  t  283
DASH, Julian  ts  692-693-694
DASSARY, Andre  vn  1596
DATZ, Hal  a  166
DAUGHERTY, Doc  cl-as-bsx-ldr  388-389
DAVAGE, Milton  p  7
DAVEN, Paul  vn  1681
DAVENPORT, Cow Cow  (r.n. Charles D.)
p-v-speech  278-279-389-390-1454-1455-
1477
DAVENPORT, Jed  h-v  390-391
DAVEY, Arthur  as  50
DAVIDSON, Davie  cl-bj  962
DAVIDSON, Dorren  ts-v  391
DAVIDSON, Evert  bj  1163-1454
DAVIDSON, Julian  bj-g  61-508-963
DAVIDSON, Leonard  cl-as-ts  218-318-410-
1506
DAVIDSON, Milt  t  8-9
DAVI(E)S, Bernard  bb  970-971-976
DAVIES, Frankie  t  511
DAVIES, Howard  d  622-623
DAVIES, Jack  cl-as-v  391
DAVIES, Pat  cl-ts  1546
DAVIES, Ramona  p-v  1688-1689-1690
DAVIS, Al  t  619-620-621-622
DAVIS, Albert J.  t  1361 (same as above
?)
DAVIS, B.  p  1379
DAVIS, Ben  cl-as-ts-bar  1116-1335
DAVIS, Benny  v  994
DAVIS, Beryl  v  1262
DAVIS, Bill  bb  1298
DAVIS, Blind John  p  847-848-849-850-
1528-1639-1678-1751
DAVIS, Bobby  cl-ss-as-v  67-73-74-75-127-
173-223-224-225-226-227-228-229-230-231-
232-233-234-235-236-237-239-247-248-249-
462-468-469-470-529-530-533-623-624-625-
626-789-890-966-967-1264-1275- 1300-
1567-1579-1580-1581-1582-1583-1589-1590-
1591-1592-1593-1619-1620-1621
DAVIS, Bud  t  417
DAVIS, Cal  c  1746
DAVIS, Carl  c  k-sw-g-v  381-1573
DAVIS, Charlie  p-ldr  391
DAVIS, Clint  bar  818-819-820
DAVIS, Clyde  t  1497
DAVIS, Desdemona  p  1097
DAVIS, Doc  vn-v  303
DAVIS, Eddie  vn-ldr  391-1005
DAVIS, Frank  t  194-1036
DAVIS, Genevieve  v  391
DAVIS, Gilbert  p  963
DAVIS, Harry  ts  1242-1243
DAVIS, Harry  bj-g  1263
DAVIS, Henryette  v  392
DAVIS, Horace  harp-guitar  1094
DAVIS, Jack  t-f-v  881-1173
DAVIS, Jasper  dir  1431
DAVIS, Jimmy  g-v  563-564
DAVIS, Joe  cl-as  320
DAVIS, Joe  d-chimes-v  1058-1218-1546
DAVIS, Johnny  - see SMALL, PAUL
DAVIS, Johnny  t-v  34-392-396-1145-1146
DAVIS, John  as  863
DAVIS, Johnny  bj  1095-1096
DAVIS, Julia  v  1536
DAVIS, Kenny  t  126
DAVIS, Len  as  164

1774

DAVIS, Leo  cl-as  1108
DAVIS, Leonard  c-t  52-53-281-334-359-
  695-696-709-791-792-806-966-1034-1097-
  1276-1346-1436-1624-1706
DAVIS, Leora  v  520
DAVIS, Lew  tb  22-23-24-25-161-281-282-
  393-404-470-508-684-790-791-799-800-808
  IIi6-1127-1149-1224-1335-1431-1432-1433
  1493-1507-1508-1509-1750
DAVIS, Merritt  cl-ss-as-ts  640-641
DAVIS, Miles  p  28
DAVIS, Milton  p  552
DAVIS, Pat  cl-ts-f  56-76-286-287-288-
  289-290-291-292-293-294-295-206-297-298
  299-300-1496-1497-1601-1615-173∩
DAVIS, Phil  tb  391
DAVIS, Pike  t  380-472-651-944-1230-1426
  1459
DAVIS, Sammy  ts  15-283-284-1203
DAVIS, Stinky  tb  392
DAVISON, Jim  t  1150
DAVISON, Ted  cl-ts  1150
DAVISON, Walter  p-ldr  394
DAVISON, Wild Bill  c-t  314-315-394-1047
DAVISON, Willie  sb  1693
DAWSON, Claude  d  995-996
DAWSON, William  tb  338
DAY, Billy  v  1612
DAY, Doris (r.n. Doris Kappelhoff)  v  185
DAY, Fred  g  1046
DAY, Johnny  d  1368
DAY(E), Irene  v  417-906-907-908-909-910
  911
DAYDE, Josette  v  1262
DEAN, Buddy  cl-bar  1554
DEAN, Demas  t  651-706-735-944-1362-1426
  1427-1444-1445
DEAN, Wesley  d  94-95
DEANE, Laura  v  93
Dè ANGELES, James  cl-ts  314
De ANGELES, Victor  pac  314
De ANGELIS, Eddie  d  151
DEANS, Mickey  ts  1693
DEAS, Eddie  d-v-ldr  395-557
De BIE, Ivon  p  1284
De BONIS, Sam  g  1308
De BRAITHE or De BROITE, Frank  t  512-
  513-1423
DEBROW, Leon  t  450
De CAILLAUX, Pierre  p  1223
De CARLO, Frank  p  265-266-267
DECK, Pierre  tb  1211-1284
DECKER, Chet  d  274
De COCK, Omer  ts  151-689
DECON SISTERS, THE  v  1620
DEDRICK, Rusty (r.n. Lyle D.)  t  1552-
  1553
De DROIT, Johnny  c  396-397
De DROIT, Paul  b  396-397
DEEMS, Barrett  d  1602
DEEP RIVER BOYS, THE  v  1638
DEEP RIVER QUINTET  v  309-1324
De FABBIA, Lou  bj-v  1484-1520-1521
De FAUT, Volly (r.n. Voltaire D.)  cl-as
  189-193-579-580-805-1068-1100-1506
De GAILLE, Robert  tb  1595
De HAVEN, Gloria  v  1361
DEJAN, Ferdinand  g  7
De JONG, Louis  vn  1229
De JULIUS. Rudy  d  92
De KAY, ―― tb  919-920

DELANEY, Al  fh  172-173
De LANGE, Eddie  v-a-dir  785-786-787
DELLAQUILA, Alfonso  sb  1197
Dè LAURENCE, Larry  bb  656-657
DELBRIDGE, Del  p  1419
De LEATH, Vaughn  v  130-1612-1613-1685
De LEON, George  bb  179
De LEUR, Joop  p  515
DELL, Al  sb  1047
DELL, Diana  v  140-649
DELL, Herbie  t  165-166
De LOOF, Gus  t-a  188-1260-1596
De LORY, Wendell  tb  704-1373-1374-1506
DELMARTER, Ted  bj-g-v  1496-1497
DEL PERUGIA, R.  bb  1379
DELTA RHYTHM BOYS, THE  v  81
De LYS, Bobby  d  1056
De MAIO, Nick  tb  186
DEMANY, Jack  ts  1284
DEMARES, Tom  p  555
DEMPSEY, Murray  t  459-784-785
DEMRY, Wee  as  154-155
De MUREL, Jeff  dir  1173
DENAHAYE, Jack  ts  524
De NASI, Jerry  cl-as  892
De NAUT, Jud  sb  1406-1407-1408-1575
DENIZ, Frank  g  822
DENIZ, Joe  g  316-563-636-822-841-1039
DENNING, Ruth  v  1121
DENNIS, Stan  bb-sb-v  56-76-286-287-288
  289-290-291-202-293-294-295-296-297-
  298-299-300-1615
DENNISON, Mort  vn  399
DENNY, Jack  p-ldr  399
DENT, Jack  p  86-995-996-1221
DENT, LaFore(s)t  as-bar-bj  984-985-986-
  1109-1110
DENTON, Joe  cl-as-ts-bar  740-741-1197
De PAOLA, Harry  tb  19-1212
De PARIS, Sidney  t  114-284-249-360-538
  765-806-833-935-1034-1053-1107-1277-
  1278-1279-1445-1468-1628
De PARIS, Wilbur  tb  55-56-57-281-791-
  792-1061-1075-1104-1123-1124-1459-1710
  1726
De PAUL, Gene  p  1359-1360-1655
De PAUL, Joe  t  829
De PEW, Bill  cl-as  366-597-598-599-600-
  601-602-1116
DEPPE, Lois  v  401-724-1035-1276
DEPPE, Russell  bj  559-560-561-924-1482
  1483
DERBIGNY, Duke (r.n. Charles D.)  t  401
  1550
De REUVER, Annie  v  689
De REX, Billy  v  915
De ROOY, Nico  p  689
Dè ROSE, Peter  p  669-1246
De ROSE, Tom  d  684-999-1129-1130
De ROY, Nick  p  282
DER JEUGHT, Van  g  1284
DERRICK, Dorothy  v  728
DERRICK, Jesse  v  177
DERRIGOTTE, George  cl-as  1089
DESMONDE, Johnny  v  911-912
DESMONDE, Teddy  t  348
De SORT, Frank  dir  308-1389
De SOUZA, Yorke  p  283-1225
DESSINGER, George  ts  321-322-647-1179
DESVIGNES, Sidney  t  1004
DETEMPLE, Leo  p  465

DETER, Bassie  sb  183-184
"DETROIT RED"  v  1670
De VEKEY, Andre  sb  801
DEVEYDT, Albert  cl-ts-bsx  1120
De VITO, Al  d  1047
DEVLIN, Jim  d  1663
DEVOE, Joe  cl-as  1245
De VOOGDT, John  v  819
De VORZON, Jules  vn  670-1586
De VRIES, Jack  d-k  515
De VRIES, Louis  t  403-404-515-803
DEVROYE, Luc  t  1284
DEWEY, Don  bj  1548
DEWEY, Phil  v  17-18-245
De WITT, Allan  sv  448-1359-1360-1361
De WOLF, Sam  bsn  1229
DEWS, Robert  d  1203
DEXTER, F.  vn  1396
DEXTER, Ralph  bj  572
DEXTER, Roy  g-v  589-590-591
D'HELLEMMES, Eugene  sb  188-330-333-689-
  690-960-1259-1283-1349-1536
D'HOUDT, Paul  t  1284
DIAL, Harry  d-vib-speech  51-327-328-
  404-752-1350-1624-1625-1626
DIAMENT, Shanty  t  1047
DIAMOND, Harold  cl-as-ts  959
DIAMOND, Mickey  t  796-797
DIAZ, Hazel  v  1109
DIAZ, Horace  p  1-93-456-738-739-802-
  1001
DIBERT, Doc  c  737
Di CARLO, Tommy  t  168-906-907-1400-1401-
  1402
DICKENS, Doles  sb  1477
DICKENS, John  v  726
DICKENSON, Spooky  v  1115-1690-1691
DICKENSON, Vic  tb-v  107-108-115-251-252-
  283-284-775-863-1346-1693
DICKERSON, Aletha  p  642-995-1487
DICKERSON, Carroll  dir-vn-ldr  41-45-46-
  404-1170
DICKERSON, Dick  bar  316
DICKERSON, Roger Quincey  c-t  252-253-349
  -686-1084-1245-1536
DICKENSON, Dick  cl-as  59-317
DICKINSON, George  g  656
DICKSON, Dick  g-v  1-248
DICKSON, Dick  d  406
DICKSON, Dorothy  v  568
DICKSON, M.  vn  241-262
DICKSON, Ross  vn  201-1009
DIECKMANN, Ernie  vn  133
DIEHL, Bill  bb  377-1265
DIEMAN, Florence  t  1075
DIEMER, Herbert  as-bar  149
DIEMER, Horace  as  1245
DIEMER, Hurley  d  149
DIEMER, William  d  330-1536
DIEPENBROEK, Toon  sb  689
DIETERLE, Kurt  vn  76-1569-1614-1681-1682
  1683-1684-1685-1686-1687-1688-1689-1690
DIETRICH, Marlene  v  405
DILLAGENE  v  741-742
DILLARD, Bill  d-v  281-755-756-779-791-
  792-968-1171-1670-1707
DILLARD, John  t  449-450-629-704-756-1197
DILLINGHAM, Paul  cl-as  89
DILLON, Bus  d  1562
DILLON, Jim  tb  970-976
DILLON, Paul  v  1505

DI MAGGIO, Charles  as  126-1408-1409
DI MAGGIO, Joe  cl-as  788-1243
DIMMITT, Eddie  md  328
DINAN, Bill  d  1272
D'IPPOLITO, Dippy  p  1411
D'IPPOLITO, Vic  t  37-38-72-73-132-926-
  1039-1210-1681-1682
DI PRIMA, Frank  bj  1067-1068
DIRVIN, Bill  bj-g  251-898-1718
DISON, ——  bj  401
DIVEN, Ernie  as  94
DIX, Bobby - see ROBERTSON, DICK
DIX, Tommy  v  620
DIXIE DAISIES, THE  v  1077
DIXON, Bert  v  1174
DIXON, Charlie  tb-bb  209-533-1156-1338
DIXON, Charlie  bj-g-a  91-166-190-353-
  458-522-710-711-712-713-714-715-716-
  717-718-719-720-721-722-723-731-732-
  733-749-750-793-861-1023-1037-1266-
  1267-1350-1442-1444-1445-1448-1466-
  1467-1519-1520-1659-1660-1704-1725-
  1728-1729
DIXON, Clarence  d  520
DIXON, Dick  cl-as-v  418
DIXON, George  c-t-as-v  404-752-758-759
  760-1459-1501
DIXON, Joe  cl-as-v  59-123-124-125-438-
  439-440-1491-1751
DIXON, Johnny  t  826
DIXON, Lawrence  bj-g-vc  412-758-759-
  1501-1714
DIXON, Morris  cl-ts  37-38-925-926
DIXON, Otha  ts  863
DIXON, Vance  cl-as  169-401-412-413-823-
  1026-1559
DOBSON, Pompey "Guts"  d  550
DODD, Barney  bb  1616
DODD, Louis  as-bj-g  318-1506
DODD, Pat  p  281-554-636-917-953-1070-
  1083-1298
DODDS, Baby (r.n. Warren D.)  d-wb  41-42
  112-114-150-308-410-414-415-1039-1102-
  1165-1166-1494
DODDS, Johnny  cl-as  39-40-41-42-43-65-
  101-112-132-133-143-150-213-308-327-
  409-410-413-414-415-534-709-891-998-
  1039-1102-1129-1133-1164-1165-1167-1207
  1221-1321-1494-1536-1549-1619
DODSON, Bert  bj-sb-v  962-1640
DOE, Dudley  cl-as  120-121
DOENCH, Clarence  cl-ts  320
DOERR, Clyde  as-dir  60-416-572
DOGGETT, Bill  p  1070-1116
DOHERTY, ——  v  235
DOLMAN, Doug  t  684
DOLNE, Charles  g  1284
DOLSEY, Clarence  c  1203
DOMINICK, Bobby  g  306-307-1243-1375
DOMINICK, Rocque  ts  307-1561
DOMINIQUE, Natty (r.n. Anatole D.)  c  65
  150-308-410-414-415-1039-1099-1154-1494
  1619
DONAHOO, Puss  v  694
DONAHUE, Al  ts-ldr  416-417
DONAHUE, Jack  ts  416-417
DONAHUE, Norman  t  553
DONAHUE, Sam  ts-a  208-209-417-907-908-
  909
DONAHUE, Tom  p  553
DONAHY, Harry  v  266-1264

DONALDSON, Denny t 1249
DONALDSON, Don p-a 115-1627
DONALDSON, Earl dir 972
DONALDSON, Jack cl-as 467-1089
DONALDSON, Walter p 398
DONAY, Ray t 1491
DONDRON, Charles vib 419
DONIN, Bunny sb 457
DONNAY, Michel ts 16
DONNELLY, Ted tb 899-900-901-902-1720
DONOVAN, Dan bar 656
DOOF, Sal ts 282-689
DOOLEY, Phil v 697
DORAN, Jack ts 398
DORING, Harry c 1559
DORFUS, Walt as-ts 132
DORN, William d 63-64-509-1330-1417-
1418-1604-1610
DORNBERGER, Charles cl-as-ldr 90-418-
1546
DORNSIFE, Eddie cl-as 972-973
DORSEY, Bob ts-a 730-1712
DORSEY, George as 284-528-729
DORSEY, Georgia Tom - see DORSEY, THOMAS
DORSEY, Jimmy t-cl-as-bar-ldr 5-33-38-
53-67-77-84-117-134-156-157-158-159-160
161-177-194-195-196-197-198-199-200-201
202-228-231-238-242-268-274-275-276-304
305-332-351-361-362-394-418-419-420-421
422-423-424-425-426-427-428-429-430-431
432-433-434-435-436-437-462-463-464-501
502-503-504-505-508-512-514-516-519-556
576-651-659-670-671-672-673-674-789-804
805-822-852-867-871-883-922-924-931-932
933-957-977-978-1015-1016-1031-1062-
1063-1076-1077-1078-1079-1080-1081-1087
1088-1098-1114-1120-1121-1128-1131-1138
1139-1140-1141-1142-1143-1145-1146-1148
1156-1193-1275-1299-1300-1301-1302-1303
1308-1312-1329-1330-1332-1369-1381-1382
1383-1391-1392-1393-1418-1430-1438-1538
1548-1566-1567-1574-1597-1598-1599-1600
1620-1639-1652-1653-1654-1671-1682-1683
1684-1695-1696-1751
DORSEY, Mattie v 436
DORSEY, Thomas A. ("Georgia Tom") p-v
393-753-754-823-831-846-852-1268-1269-
1489-1495-1526-1527-1572
DORSEY, Tommy t-tb-a-narrator-ldr 5-16-
17-33-67-77-84-115-117-134-142-143-156-
157-158-159-160-161-194-195-196-197-198
199-200-201-202-203-230-231-238-239-250
274-275-276-305-351-361-362-394-401-418
419-420-421-422-423-424-425-426-427-436
437-438-439-440-441-442-443-444-445-446
447-448-449-450-451-452-453-454-455-456
501-502-503-504-505-508-512-516-530-556
576-591-592-659-670-671-672-673-804-805
821-822-852-853-883-922-924-928-929-931
932-933-966-967-1015-1031-1048-1062-
1063-1064-1078-1079-1080-1081-1083-1098
1120-1121-1142-1146-1193-1222-1241-1300
1301-1302-1303-1308-1312-1323-1329-1330
1369-1370-1381-1383-1384-1385-1386-1387
1388-1391-1392-1393-1417-1418-1514-1548
1579-1580-1583-1591-1592-1593-1598-1599
1619-1620-1639-1648-1652-1653-1654-1671
1682-1695-1696-1751
DOTTORE, Sal as 1160
DOTY, Clarence bj 884

DOTY, Mike cl-as-v 123-124-125-322-323-
324-326-440-441-455-697-698-704-1150-
1409-1410-1752
DOUGHERTY, Eddie d 77-80-545-769-814-
850-866-1135-1531-1670
DOUGHERTY, Jack t 1361
DOUGHTY, Raymond cl-as 1263
DOUGLAS, Beatrice v 755-756
DOUGLAS, Billy t-v 7
DOUGLAS, Boots d-ldr 154-155
DOUGLAS, Charlie t 310
DOUGLAS, Nelson t 1662
DOUGLAS, Roy ts 520
DOUGLAS, Russell - see REIS, LES
DOUILLEZ, Jean tb 1284
DOVER, Bill/William tb 165-1614-1615
DOVER, Jayne v 8-9-125-702-787
DOVIDIO, —— t 151
DOWD, Nelson cl-as 657
DOWDY Tom tb 648-1367-1368-1604-1610
DOWELL, Edgar p 182-733-1023-1090
DOWELL, Saxie (r.n. Horace D.) cl-ts-v
419-887-888-889
DOWING, Larry g 409
DOWLING, Charles sb 274
DOWNES, Ormand d 1665-1666-1667-1688-
1669
DOWNEY, Mull v 552-553
DOWNING, Rex tb 301-339-340-341
DOYLE, Buddy v 1419
DOYLE, Jack t v 348
DOYLE, John tb 93
DOYLE, Kay v 1553
DRAKE, Joe t-as-a 1218
DRAPER, Horsecollar (r.n. Barclay S. D.)
t 1103
DRAYTON, Charlie sb 187 284-864-865-
1511
DRELINGER, Art cl-ts 122-123-205-545-
829-1027-1332-1373-1690-1691
DRESLIN, Dorothy v 1026
DREWES, Bill v 632
DREWES, George tb 632
DREWES, Herman c-t 632-996-1130-1180
DREWES, William tb 996-1180
DREYER, Les cl-as 360-914
DRING, Perry bj 418
DRIVER, Dorothea v 1631
DROWN, Bunny (r.n. Elmer D.) ts 233-234
DRUCKER, Macy bj 914
DRUMMOND, Jack sb 274-1560-1561
DRUZINSKY, Meyer t 1047
DRYDEN, Bob d 581-582-583-584-585-586-
587-588-589
DUANE, Ted cl-as-ts 785-786-787-1116-
1167-1360
DUBIN, Joe cl-ts 456-932-1064-1367-1368
1381-1382
DUCHIN, Eddy p-ldr 456-1285
DUCONGE, Peter cl-as 1-52-405-827-830-
835
DUDLEY, —— md 1197-1199-1200
DUDLEY, Eddie tb 1539
DUDLEY, Jimmy cl-Cm-ts 466-1033-1310
DUEL, Dean t 919-920
DUERR, Clayton "Sunshine" g 545-1003-
1052
DUFF, Jimmy cl-ss-as 218-220-221-222-
223-1590

DUFFY, Al  vn  62-127-238-239-242-243-
244-262-394-419-457-503-626-627-641-
670-853-980-1117-1118-1300-1301-1302-
1312-1333-1422-1583-1619-1620
DUGAN, Mary  v  323-324-325
Du GASTON, Charles  bj  541
DUGAT, Ross  tb  657
DUKES, Harry  cl  1180
DUKOFF, Bob  ts  788
DULANY, Howard  v  908-909-910-911
DUMAINE. Louis  c  337-391-457
DUMONT, Jack  ts  1150
DUMONT, Marcel  tb  1348-1349-1642
DUMONT, Rene  as-ts  171-172
DUNBAR, Rudolph  cl-dir  885-1230
DUNCAN, Hank  (r.n. Henry D.)  p  113-
820-1019-1109-1170-1377-1627-1628-1705
1714-1715-1716
DUNHAM, Ralph  sb  545
DUNHAM, Sonny  t-tb-a-ldr  16-56-287-288
289-290-291-292-293-294-295-296-297-
457
DUNKEL, Sam  ts  796-797
DUNLOP, Jimmy  vn  1215
DUNN, Artie  v  239-1285-1438-1620
DUNN, George  bb-sb  1550
DUNN, Jack  p  1184
DUNN, Joe  ts  999
DUNN, Johnny  c-t  164-458-459-665-666-
1057-1058-1090-1230-1460-1461-1462-
1531-1724-1725-1727
DUNNE, Dick  t  1572
DUNNE, Marianne  v  1540
Du PEER, Harry  sb  1490
Du PONT, Roland  tb  30-214-756
Du PRE, Basil  sb  1195
DUPRE, Don  tb  566
DUPRE, Walter  v  1498
DUPREE, Jack  p  1674
DUQUESNE, Ralph  cl-ss-as-ts  1426-1427
DURAND, Wade Hampton  bj-g  118-530-531
DURANT, Ray  p  1036
DURANTE, Jimmy  p-dir  68-459-914-915-
934-935-1194-1692
DURDEN, R. W.  md  1558
DUREA, Al  d  565
DURHAM, Allen  tb  763-898-1718
DURHAM, Dave  t  409
DURHAM, Eddie  tb-g-elg-a  102-103-108-
153-191-459-761-813-872-873-944-985-936
987-988-989-1111-1112-1358-1359
DURHAM, Joe  bb  251
DURRANT, Jimmy  cl-as-bar  538-1343
DURSO, Mike  tb  37-38-61-926-963-1068-
1195
DUSSAULT, George  d  170
DUTREY, Honore  tb  41-308-414-415-1165-
1166-1619
DUTTON, Bill  v  419
DUTTON, Gilbert  cl-as-ts  561-1288-1524
DUTTON, Ken  sb  182
Du VAL, Duke  t  764
DUVIVIER, George  sb  1070
DWYER, Herb  cl-as  240-241-1620

EARL, Eugene  tb  277
EARL, Pierce  tb  321-322
EARLE, Burt  bj  460
EASSON, Bob  cl-ts-vn  1213-1214-1215
EAST, Ed  bj  391
EASTER, Clarence  p-v  680-1560

EASTON, Jim  cl-as-bar  539-581-801-808-
937-938-939-1396-1507-1509-1695
EASTON, Sidney  p-or-v  343-460-1453
EASTWOOD, Bill  bj  650-1132
EATON, Benny  vn  201-1009
EBEL, Bud  d  314-315
EBERHARD, Elliot  p  416
EBERLE, Ray  as-v  286-426-427-428-429-
430-431-432-433-434-435-436-1064
EBONY FOUR, THE  v  1651
EBRECKE, Richard  g  361
EBRON, J. Norman  p  1092-1125-1367
ECHOLLS or EACHOLLS, Jack  cl-as  685-
686-1497
ECKBERT, Leslie  bb  1498
ECKSTEIN, Billy  v  760-761-762
EDBROOKE, Ted  vn  1493-1739
EDE, Dick  bj  134
EDELSTEIN, Walter  vn  33-84-200-1330-
1538-1653-1690-1751
EDINBOROUGH, Eddie  d-wb-v  408-461-942
EDINBOROUGH, Oswald  v  461
EDISON, Abe  vc  1690
EDISON, Harry  t  103-104-105-106-107-
108-109-110-769-821-1075-1564
EDLUND, Carl  cl-as  652-653
EDWARDS, Austin  t  869-1673
EDWARDS, Ben  p-d  1089-1092
EDWARDS, Carl  v  1498
EDWARDS, Carrie  v  462
EDWARDS, Chuck  p  1116
EDWARDS, Cliff ("Ukulele Ike")  k-u-v-
jug  69-462-463-464-915-1202
EDWARDS, Eddie  tb-dir  464-573-632-1175
1176-1177-1178-1179-1520-1521
EDWARDS, Eddie  bb  341
EDWARDS, Grace  v  1595
EDWARDS, Harry/Henry "Bass"  bb  472-473
651-868-944-1362-1426
EDWARDS, Joe  v  212-213-214
EDWARDS, Len  as-vn  1298
EDWARDS, Maceo  t  564-1742
EDWARDS, S.  sb  315
EDWARDS, Sumner Leslie "King"  bb  1742-
1743
EDWARDS, Susie  v  212-213-214
EDWARDS, Tom  tb  1450
EDWARDS, Tom  v  1614
EDWARDS, W. J.  g  277
EDWARDS, Wakter  cl-ts  778
EDWARDS, Wilbur  bb-sb  919-920-921
EFFROS Bob  t  33-60-156-194-196-456-465
567-659-671-676-678-771-933-972-973-
1064-1303-1329-1368-1370-1381-1382-1639
1652-1751
EGAN, Andy  cl-as  1360
EGAN, John  t  177-871-1141-1142
EGEE, Alphonsus  g-u-v  1216
EGGERTON, or EGGERDON, Tom  bb-sb  10-515-
885
EHLERT, Eddie  t  555
EHRENKRANZ, William  vn  454-455
EHRLING, Thore  t  282-539
EHRMAN, Gus  as-v  1752-1753
EINHORN, Simon  p  1197
EISENBERG, Pete  vn  1330-1406-1416-1417
1610
EKYAN, Andre  cl-as-ts  465-536-543-632-
689-690-801-1211-1284-1348-1349-1642
ELDEN , Bob  sb  93-99-250
ELDER, Joe  cl-as-ts  1649-1692

1778
ELDRIDGE, Al  p  856-857
ELDRIDGE, Jean  v  494-766-1561-1736
ELDRIDGE, Joe  as-a  252-466-769-808-832
ELDRIDGE, Roy  t-v  78-81-131-312-382-399
  466-728-755-769-770-906-911-912-1048-
  1304-1670-1707-1730-1731-1735
ELGAR, Charlie  vn-ldr  466
ELIZALDE, Fred  p-a-ldr  467-468-469-470-
  471-509
ELIZALDE, Manuel "Lizz"  as  467-468
ELKINS, Alfred  sb  849
ELKINS, Leon  t-ldr  47
ELKINS-PAYNE JUBILEE QUARTETTE  v  794
ELLBOJ, Lulle  as-dir  1585
ELLINGTON, Duke (r.n. Edward Kennedy E.)
  p-tomtoms-a-ldr  27-134-135-173-472-473
  474-475-476-477-478-479-480-481-482-483
  484-485-486-487-488-489-490-491-492-493
  494-495-496-497-498-499-500-640-651-652
  765-766-767-854-941-1075-1083-1246-1250
  1263-1431-1471-1500-1501-1518-1564-1565
  1640-1641-1653-1711-1712
ELLINGTON, Judy  v  76-94-95
ELLINGTON, Ray  d-v  1341-1342
ELLINGTON, Ruth  v  695
ELLIOTT, Elaine  p  683-1713
ELLIOTT, E. E., Sr.  cl-as-bb  1052
ELLIOTT, Ernest  cl-ss-as-ts-bar  182-191
  343-412-458-522-537-539-545-793-835-838
  845-861-965-1012-1018-1022-1050-1058-
  1094-1096-1097-1168-1184-1224-1306-1439
  1444-1445-1448-1449-1450-1451-1453-1457
  1460-1462-1463-1519-1531-1532-1533-1551
  1577-1617-1704-1724-1725-1727
ELLIOTT, George  g  140-281-393-525-538-
  554-638-683-1137-1207-1298
ELLIS, David  ts  154-155
ELLIS, Don  cl-as-bar  1047
ELLIS, Eddie  tb  1536
ELLIS, Kinney  ss-Cm-as  1252
ELLIS, Seger  p-v  419-428-501-502-503-
  504-505-521-929-1566
ELLOY, Max  d  396-1173-1349
ELLSWORTH, Francis  cl-ts  737
ELMAN, Ziggy (r.n. Harry Finkelman)  t-tb
  62-77-100-451-452-453-454-455-505-506-
  599-600-601-602-603-604-605-606-607-608
  609-610-611-612-613-614-615-616-660-661
  662-663-814-1048-1089
ELMORE, Buster  g  211
ELMS, Jay  t  1548
ELRICK, George  d-v  281-282-656-1917-
  1584
ELSEY, Ruth  v  1540
ELSTEAD, Mac  as  1570-1571
ELTON, Don  v  1600
ELWIN, Maurice  v  31-32-132-359-403-524-
  525-917-949-950-951-952-953-1116-1290-
  1291-1292-1293-1294-1295-1296-1472-1493
EMER, Michel  p  396-1173-1349
EMERSON, Howard  d-x  919-920-1005
EMERSON, Tom  vn  652-653
EMERT, Jim  tb  165-166-168369-370
EMERY, Howard  c  388-389
EMMETT, Ed  p  1288
ENGLE, Victor  d  34-209-215-392-727-779-
  1145-1146-1147-1205-1306-1307-1562-1602
ENGLAND, Leon  bb  1657
ENGLISH, Brick  vn  1497
ENGO, Lou  p  269

ENNIS, Skinny (r.n. Bob E.)  d-v  240-419
  887-888-889
ENOCH, Tommy  t  761
ENOIS, Leonard  g  1038
ENS, Arthur  g  779-1205-1306-1307-1562
EPELITTO, Pete  bj  1309
EPPERSON, Royal  t-bj-g  1550
EPSTEIN, Jack  tb  945-946-1108
EPSTEIN, Louis  1066
ERARD, Clive  p-a-ldr-v  511-801
ERBY, John  p  1487-1488
ERDALE, Fred  v  388-389
ERIKSBERG, Folke  p  589
ERIKSSON, Rudolf  ts  1585
ERWIN, Pee Wee (r.n. George)  t  13-163-
  440-441-442-443-444-445-446-447-455-594
  595-597-598-697-698-1063-1064-1150-1241
  1249
ESCAMILLA, Bob  bb  956
ESCOTT, Dick  bb-sb  20-21-22-193-272-285
  554-583-798-952-953-974-1214-1432-1433-
  1434-1456-1584-1585-1692-1738
ESCUDERO, Ralph  bb  311-522-580-704-705-
  712-713-714-715-716-717-718-719-720-861
  1033-1056-1089-1442-1467-1510-1648-1649
ESHER, Dave  t  809-810
ESKDALE, George  t  1362
ESPOSITO, George  t  97-98-326-1242-1243-
  1244
ESSEX, Jane  v  1652
ESTE, Harold  cl-ts  1648
ESTEP, Floyd  cl-ts  339-340-341
ESTEP, Pop  bb  111-338-339
ESTERBROOK, Paul  p  511
ESTERDAHL, Lennie  bj  544-998
ESTES, Buff (r.n. Buford E.)  as  612-613
  614-615-663
ESTES, John  g  948
ESTREN, Joe  as  93-163-250-545-740-829
ESTREN, Tony  sb  126
ETHRIDGE, Frank  bj  1427-1529
ETON BOYS, THE  v  805
ETRI, Bus  g  94-95-96-97-98-786-787
ETTE, Bernard  dir  826
ETTING, Ruth  v  512
EUBANKS, Horace  cl-as-v  359-1099-1422
EVANS, Alfie  cl-ss-as-bar-vn  37-38-351-
  395-420-421-427-510-629-630-756-804-870
  871-926-927-928-934-936-945-946-1016-
  1039-1108-1126-1138-1141-1172-1192-1219
  1220-1246-1274-1275-1375-1420-1543-1545
  1551-1598-1745
EVANS, Basil  sb  1657
EVANS, Bob  tb  1361
EVANS, Chuck  tb  906-907-1357-1358-1602
EVANS, Earl  cl-as-ts-v  685-686-806-807
  1338
EVANS, Ellsworth  c-t  685-1520-1521
EVANS, George  as-ts-bar-a-v  282-538-581
  964-1039-1224
EVANS, Gil  a  1553-1554
EVANS, Harry  bb  395-1363-1515
EVANS, Herschel  cl-ts  78-101-102-103-
  104-533-661-813-814-863-1735
EVANS, J. D.  bj  1252
EVANS, Ray  as  314-315
EVANS, Red  v  513
EVANS, Roy  d-v  145-305-513-514-776-1083
  1096
EVANS, Rudy Bayfield  v  172-658

EVANS, Stump cl-ss-as-Cm 709-936-1102-
1166-1167-1245-1267-1499-1529-1749
EVANS, Warren v 832
EVERITTS, W. ts 1396
EVETTS, Jack sb 784-1127-1128-1149-1365
EWANS, Kai cl-as-ldr 282-652
EWING, John tb 760-761
EXNER, Billy d 787-788
EZELL, Will p-v 187-516-709-831-1320-
1321
FACEMYER, H. v 736
FACEY, Stanley p 1477
FACH, Charles tb 1334
FAIN, Sammy p-v 239-240-516-517-777-
1620-1651
FAIRCHILD , Darville bj 1479
FAIRCHILD, Edgar p 629-630-1272
FALLON, Bob cl-as-ts 237-238-239-626
FALLON, Owen d-ldr 517
FALLSTITCH, John t 126-364-1539-1540-1541
FALVO, Joe as 464
FANT, Edward tb 730-761
FANTCHER, Ray bb 1548
FARBERMAN, Hymie c-t 37-38-63-73-128-319-
406-509-517-804-905-924-925-926-927-928
929-934-1005-1039-1076-1097-1163-1164-
1288-1299-1300-1351-1352-1353-1354-1379
1418-1545-1745-1749
FARBERMAN, Irving d 37-38-925
FARBERMAN, Leo d 517
FARBERMAN, Willie d 905
FARLEY, Eddie t-v 672-779-781-979-980-981
982-1031-1205-1306-1307-1308-1490-1562
FARLEY, Jim as 279
FARLEY, Max cl-as-ts-f-a 17-63-237-360-
419-470-505-788-789-1139-1416-1418-1537
1597-1598-1601-1610-1681-1682
FARQUHARSON, N. M. f 1691
FARR, Tommy tb 744
FARRAR, Fuzzy (r.n. Fred F.) t-v 17-394
418-419-420-501-502-576-577-578-672-738
1381-1382-1597-1598
FARRAR, Mose p 1130-1131
FARRAR, Sonny bj-g 800-801-1336
FARRAR, Theo sb 656
FARRARA, Nick bb 265-266-267
FARRELL, Billy t 16-554-798-995-996-
1298-1432-1434-1695
FARRELL, Bob as 218
FARRELL, Charlie v 509-1064-1065-1139
FARRELL, Frank p 1745
FARRELL, Jimmy v 59-1552
FARRELL, Louise v 1401
FARRELL, Sarg bj 271
FARRIOR, Little Buddy v 1709
FARRINGTON, Robert as 457
FASO, Tony t 622-623
FASTHOFF, Jules tb 1068-1069
FASULO, Tom t 168
FATOOL, Nick d 62-506-612-613-614-615-
616-663-821-1089-1361-1407-1408-1553
FAULKENER, Lorence p 1651
FAUNTLEROY, George as 1272
FAUNTLEROY, James ts 851
FAURE, Rene p 1572
FAY, George tb 457
FAY(E), Jack sb 701-702-1147-1148
FAY, Jean v 1206
FAYE, Frances p-v 518

FAZOLA, Irving (r.n. Harry Prestopnik)
cl-as 59-153-204-363-368-369-370-371-
372-373-505-767-1063-1064-1118-1236-
1244-1482-1491-1552-1553
FAZIOLI, Billy p 1066
FEARN, Eddie t 347-348
FEARN, Sidney t 1215-1298
FEATHER, Leonard p-cel 518-1204-1411
FEATHERSTONHAUGH, Buddy ts-dir 16-132-
140-279-281-282-518-789-790-791-822-953
1017-1083-1116-1335-1336-1584-1695
FEIGE, Dick c 1228-1366
FEILER, Maurice vc 61
FEINBLOOM, W. sb 1271
FEINSMITH, Sammy cl-ss-as-bar 17-19-63-
64-1164-1212-1416-1417-1418-1456-1586-
1604-1610
FELD, Morey d 317-542-543-634
FELDKAMP, Elmer cl-as-v 34-36-201-248-
249-421-980-981-982-1009-1241-1303-1388
1621
FELDMAN, Harold o 1691
FELDSTEIN, Sid t 702-703-1116
FELLENSBY, Freddy ts 249-323-324-701-
702-703-968-1027-1621
FELLER, Sid t-a 1539-1540
FELLINE, Joe bj-g 2-33
FELLINE, Tommy bj-g 67-127-177-196-228-
229-230-231-232-233-234-235-236-237-238
239-240-241-242-243-244-245-246-247-248
262-263-529-530-533-623-624-625-626-627
670-672-673-776-882-890-966-967-979-980
981-982-1025-1088-1117-1118-1141-1142-
1306-1382-1393-1394-1422-1579-1580-1581
1582-1583-1591-1592-1593-1619-1620
FELLMAN, Walter cl-ss-as 737
FELTON, Jimmy d 186-417
FELTON, Roy v 283
FEMAN, Ben cl-as 324-325-326-912
FENDERSON, Jake k-wb-v 6-563-1644-1645
FENIMORE, Howard t 991-992
FENNELL, Eddie bj-v-a 461
FENNELL, Walter g 390-1455
FENOULHET, Arthur t-tb 1365
FENOULHET, Paul t-tb-a 459-525-535-554
800-801-1048-1224-1298-1336-1365-1507
FENT, Phil g 889
FENTON, Carl p 771
FENTON, Nick sb 273-551-1070
FERDINANDO, Joe as 364-1539-1540-1541
FER(R)ET, Pierre g 312-635-1259-1260-
1261-1262-1283-1284
FERGUSON, Alan g 2-132-272-311-346-359
427-518-789-790-791-953-1017-1164-1584
1632-1693
FERGUSON, Buster g 1505
FERGUSON, Fred t 992-993
FERGUSON, Harry ts 1038
FERGUSON, Jess vn 1675
FERNANDEZ, Angelo cl 1529
FERNANDEZ, Juan sb 405-827-835-836
FERRAL(L), Joe tb 364-1539-1540-1541
FERRANTE, Joseph t 95-99-621
FERRARO, James p 1122
FERRERI, Albert cl-ts 67
FERRERI, Leon t-tb-vn-p 396-1173-1349
FERRETTI, Andy t 249-250-365-366-437-
438-440-441-442-443-444-445-446-447-
448-699-700-701
FERRETTI, Frank tb 238-626-627-1580-
1583-1593

FERRIE, Joe  t-tb-v  346-539-581-587-1149-
1507-1508
FERRIER, Jack  cl-as-ts  369-370-739-829-
1359-1553-1554
FERRIER, John  p  330-1536
FERRY, Vernon  t  156-522-523-1364
FETTERER, Gus  cl-as  996-1003-1309
FETTERLE, Rene  as  151
FETZER, Ray  bb  314-315
FFRENCH, Clifton  t  23-24-87
FIELDS, Alfred  bb  143-568-903-1226
FIELDS, Arthur  v  5-73-74-129-187-218-
229-231-233-234-235-236-238-240-242-246-
247-265-378-379-380-519-520-530-629-631-
648-653-654-655-915-916-927-929-966-967-
1173-1219-1247-1275-1309-1353-1367-1380-
1504-1579-1580-1581-1583-1593-1611-1612
FIELDS, Benny  cl-ts  1310
FIELDS, Geechie  tb  838-1096-1102-1104-
1105-1705-1706
FIELDS, Gene (r.n. Eugene F.)  g  691-770-
839-1019-1477
FIELDS, Howard  p  1218
FIELDS, Jackie  as  153-690-691-1638
FIELDS, Kansas  d  1242
FIELDS, Len  as  805
FIELDS, Ted  d-v  330-959-960-1642-1742-
1743
FIELSING, John  v  1563
FIERSTONE, George  d  822
FILA, Alec  t  168-306-307-616-617-618-
729-1538
FILES, Ed  ts  119-120
FILLIS, Len  bj-g  61-271-468-469-470-521-
537-568-784-812-903-982-1219-1565
FINA, Jack  p  556
FINAZZO, Mario  bb  1208
FINDLAY, Bob  ts  938-939
FINDLAY, Claude  t-tb  16-1695
FINE, Sidney  p  1231-1663-1745
FINEGAN, Bill  a  447
FINGER, Ben  bb-ldr  772
FINGERS, Monroe  as  1195
FINK, Dave  vn  992
FINK, Herman  d  1689
FINK, Hy  d  203
FINK, Sam  d-vn  128-129-130-233-234-255-
572
FINKELSTEIN.(Fink), Harry  bsx  1429-1430
FINLAY, Dude  p  1008
FINLAY, Lloyd  vn-ldr  521
FINLEY, Gunn  p  1585
FINNEY, Al  d  188
FINNEY, Chick  p-dir  1194
FINNEY, Gerald  p  535
FINNEY, Herb  cl-as  522-523-524-1364
FINSTON, Nat  dir  1227-1228
FINZEL, William  t  522
FIORITO, Ted  p  675-1347-1348-1747-1748
FIORRINO, Vince  bb  919
FIRMAN, Bert  vn-dir  30-31-32-274-403-
523-524-525-1289-1290-1291
FIRMAN, John  p-cel-a  30-31-403-506-507-
523-971-1196-1289-1290-1291-1292-1293-
1294-1295-1296-1297
FIRSCH, Charlie  tb  919
FISBACH, Roger  as  1615
FISCHEL, Merwin  sb  997
FISCHER, Harry  t  1562
FISCHER, Kai  d  1585
FISH, Dave  vn  809-810

FISH, Jack  vn  809-810
FISHBERG, George  p  748
FISHEL, Bob  tb  93-94-183-184-250
FISHER, Abby  d  1002
FISHER, Dick  g  1242
FISHER, Freddy  cl  525
FISHER, Jimmy  v  1378
FISHER, Mark  bj-g-v  525-1348-1663
FISHER, Marshall  g  997
FISHER, Myron  vn  120-121
FISHER, Nick  bb  1324-1325
FISHER, Phil  t  314
FISHER, Ted  t  314
FISHKIND, Arnold  sb  123-364-006-1539-
1540-1541
FISK, Buddy  as  1537
FITCH, Dan  speech  1062
FITCH, Ernie  cl-as-vn  885
FITCH, Floyd  ?  1203
FITZGERALD, ——  bj  318
FITZGERALD, Bill  tb  1746
FITZGERALD, Ella  v  526-527-528-529-599-
1658-1659-1660-1661-1662-1731
FITZGERALD, Gerry  v  388
FITZPATRICK, James  t  889
FLANAGAN, Billy  d  93-1308
FLANNIGAN, Taylor  p  1119
FLASTER, Max  as  1457
FLATO, Ludwig  p  94
FLEAGLE, Brick (r.n. Roger F.)  g-a  494-
588-701-702-729-1337-1500-1501-1540-
1621
FLEET, Bert  g  1008
FLEISCHMAN, Ed  p  892
FLEMING, Art  d-v  59
FLEMING, Deb  c  1546
FLEMING, Frank  t-v  913
FLEMING, Jock  tb  684-789-790-953-1127-
1148-1210-1363-1432-1433-1434-1472-1584-
1585-1692
FLEMING, Lee  d  708
FLEMING, Van  bj-g-v  579-580-890
FLEMMING, Herb  tb-dir  164-187-458-459-
512-513-651-704-705-797-808-809-810-835-
836-944-1461-1462-1638-1724-1725-1727-
1742
FLETCHER, Bill  tb  685-686
FLETCHER, Chris  vn-g-v  578-697-698-1179
FLETCHER, Harold  t  1663
FLETCHER, Milton  t  759-760-863
FLETCHER, Stan  bb-sb  685-686-697-698
FLICKINGER, Marion  d  111
FLINTALL, Herman  as  550
FLOOD, Bernard  t  57-58-695-696
FLOOD, Harold  d  1092
FLOWERS, Jimmy  p  823-1267-1322-1744
FLOYD, Noble  cl-as-a  792
FLOYD, Reuben  t  792
FLOYD, Troy  cl-as-ldr  533
FLUSCHMAN, Adam  vn  1690
FLYNN, Frank  d  630-981-982-1542
FLYNN, Fred  d  678-679-680-783-824-1541
FLYNN, Jimmy  v  573-1484
FOESTE, William  bb-bsx  119-120
FOGEL, Wes  ts  517
FOGERTY, Gene  cl-ts  172-173
FOLEY, Eddie  tb  1640
FOLUS, Mickey  ts  729-742-743-744-1160-
1243-1408-1409
FONDER, Andy  cl-ts  1563
FORBES, C. Graham  p  124

FORCHETTI, Joe as 326-1482
FORD, Arnold banjoline 1517
FORD, Brylo sb 141
FORD, Chandler vc 512
FORD, Charles bb 553
FORD, George f 1690
FORD, Harry p 139-996-1108-1180-1181-
  1182-1183-1184-1520
FORD, Jack vn-dir 32-33
FOREMAN, Al sb 995-996
FOREMAN, Arthur o 1019-1216
FORKE, Heinz bb-sb 826
FORREST, Helen v 614-615-616-617-618-
  619-663-818-819-820-1404-1405-1406
FORRESTER, John tb 1173
FORSCH, Fritz vn 1330
FORSTER, Andy ts 1136
FORSTER, Clarence t 1744
FORSYTHE, Jack cl-ss-as 133
FORSYTHE, Reginald p-a-dir 534-782
FORT, Henry sb 155
FORTIER, Slim v 1601
FORYS, John as-ts 2o8-2o9-417
FOSDICK, Dudley mel-v 17-535-871-977-
  1076-1083-1087-1091-1139-1140-1663-1664
  1666-1667-1668-1669
FOSDICK, Gene cl-ss-as 391-535
FOSS, Douglas cl-ss-as 1674
FOSS, Jack bar 470
FOSTER, Abbey d-sw-v 301-302
FOSTER, Andy as- 1211
FOSTER, Art tb 29-132-161-365-366-440-
  1752
FOSTER, Dallie v 1644
FOSTER, Eddie v 563
FOSTER, Frances vn 1641
FOSTER, George d 18-39-775
FOSTER, Herman bj 541-592
FOSTER, Kay v 63
FOSTER, Pops t 512-513
FOSTER, Pops (r.n. George F.) bb-sb 11-
  12-13-15-45-46-52-53-54-55-56-57-88-113
  142-358-667-751-807-839-1052-1053-1061-
  1103-1113-1345-1346-1422-1488-1624
FOSTER, Ray t-v 59
FOSTER, Teddy t-v-ldr 22-23-345-347-348
  536
FOSTER, Wade cl 999
FOSTER, Walter d-x 12o-919
FOSTER, Willie bj-g 1004-1168
FOUAD, Pierre d 11-16-307-333-465-519-
  536-776-1262-1284-1338-1563-1615
FOUCHE, Earl as 1095-1096
FOUGERAT, Tony c 1328
FOUR BACHELORS, THE v 1521
FOUR BLACKAMOORS, THE v 1323
FOUR DUSTY TRAVELERS, THE v 957
FOUR MODERNAIRES, THE v 1690
FOURSOME, THE v 61-1143
FOUR STARS, THE v 94
FOUR WANDERERS, THE v 11-1623
FOWLER, Billy ts-bar-bsx 711-712-1519
FOWLER, Frank as 547-1501
FOWLER, Lemuel p-v 110-317-538-539-569-
  749-750-830-860-1012-1026-1371-1449-
  1450-1451-1496-1717
FOWLER, William sb 1229
FOX, Joe d 82
FOX, Roy c-t-compere 59-539-748
FOY, Edoard S. cl-as-v 1595
FOYS, Col. Ralph p 540

FRANCHINI, Tony p 632-1130
FRANCIS, David d 466
FRANCIS, Dick cl-as 1213
FRANCIS, George g 1414
FRANCIS, Harry d 1616
FRANCIS, Panama d 808-1070
FRANCIS, William g 540
FRANK, Arnold p-ldr 540
FRANK, Fred p 648
FRANK, Ivan v 826
FRANK, Joe d 856-857
FRANKE, Norman sb 192
FRANKEL, Abe p 1099
FRANKEL, Ben vn-a 469-470-656-789-1365
FRANKEL, Dave t 8-9-29-702-703-775-1561
FRANKER, Eric p 1170
FRANKHAUSER, Charles t 907
FRANKLIN, A. v 269
FRANKLIN, Buck v 1644
FRANKLIN, Chick ts 834
FRANKLIN, Dave cl 64
FRANKLIN, Ernest ts 328-1194
FRANKLIN, Tiny v 541
FRANKLIN, William tb-v 757-758-759-862-
  1169-1421-1714
FRANKS, Aubrey ts 316-822-1039-1509
FRANSEN, Cecil as-vn 1498
FRANZ, William ts 47
FRANZELLA, Sal cl-bcl-as 82-215-545-633
  1249-1690-1691
FRASER, Milton t 1712
FRASETTO, Joe vn-dir 646
FRAWLEY, Tom - see KAUFMAN, IRVING
FRAZIER, Bob sb 863
FRAZIER, Charles ts-f 191-251-362-382-
  429-430-431-432-433-434-435-436-812-838
  1123-1124-1169
FRAZIER, Earl p-cel 1061-1455-1456
FRAZIER, Jake tb 154-285-313-541-643-
  733-734-735-861-872-940-1008-1024-1057-
  1058-1090-1093-1094-1170-1184-1218-1241
  1428-1453-1463-1576
FRAZIER, John sb 39-824-1155
FRAZIER, Josiah d 302
FREDERIC, Gaston cl-ts 1286
FREDERICI, Tony sb 1242-1243
FREDERICK, Conrad p 459
FREDERICKS, Sonny ts 15-832
FREDERICO, Frank g 153-204-1216-1236-
  1249-1250
FREED, Paul p-a 571-998
FREED, Sam vn-vl 112-420-819-1406-1417
FREEDMAN, Maurice ts 276
FREEMAN, Bud (r.n. Lawrence F.) cl-ts-v
  56-117-122-200-207-274-275-302-317-335-
  421-439-440-441-442-443-444-455-541-542
  543-565-592-608-609-610-634-699-700-782
  821-822-977-999-1000-1001-1003-1030-
  1031-1032-1052-1080-1141-1143-1150-1232
  1289-1332-1491-1512-1537-1558-1600-1601
  1637-1696-1735
FREEMAN, Eddie g 518-1083-1507
FREEMAN, Hank/Harry (r.n. Henry F.) cl-
  as 63-123-1400-1401-1402-1403-1404-
  1405-1406
FREEMAN, Lawrence ts 251-898-1718
FREEMAN, Morty cl-as-ts 1-162
FREEMAN, Robert "Red" tb 214-1565
FREEMAN, Ross ts 198
FREITAG, Clarence tb 869
FRENCH, Charlie d 1242

FRERAR, Nick  tb  1284
FRESCO, Johnny  ts  818
FRESHMEN, THE  v  1150
FREY, Fran  as-v  35-1172-1286
FREY, Hugo  p  1457
FRIDGE, Dave  sb  1510
FRIEBEL, Eddie  ts-v  736
FRIED, Paul  p-ldr  544
FRIEDE, Al  vn  818
FRIEDE, Elias  vc  818-819-820
FRIEDLAND, Bernie  sb  704
FRIEDMAN, Izzy  cl-as-ts  116-117-268-269
  922-1017-1567-1568-1569-1570-1598-1599-
  1684-1685-1686-1687
FRIEDMAN, Julie  cl-as  873-874
FRIEDMAN, Maurice  p  189
FRIEDMAN, Mort  cl-ts  62-1236-1237
FRIEDMAN, Snooks (r.n. Benjamin S.)  d-
  ldr  1045-1469-1470
FRIEL, Sylvester  t  1092
FRIELS, Eugene  t-bb  1218
FRIER, Newman  p-dir  1180
FRINK, Miff  tb  999
FRISELLE, Frank  d  656-657
FRITTS, Stanley  tb-v  525
FRITZ, Anna  v  544
FRIZZELL, Eddie  t  1362
FROEBA, Frank  p-cel  28-29-30-40-122-142
  392-396-397-545-593-594-595-596-633-746
  747-779-780-781-1197-1256-1257-1306-
  1313-1314-1315-1330-1472
FROMM, Louis  d  1242-1243-1244-1553
FRUEH, E.  vn  1604
FRUITERMAN, Jerry  tb  8-517
FRY, Charlie  as-vn-ldr  545-546
FRYE, Carl  cl-as-bar  58-192-283-284-
  1279
FRYE, Don  p-a  75-905-1134-1169-1170-
  1370-1371-1709
FRYE, Menden  cl-as  566
FUCHS, J.  c-ah  1256-1605
FUCILLO, Mike  tb  1108
FUGITTE, ----  v  1220
FUHS, Julian  p-ldr  546
FULCHER, Charles  tb-cl-vn-v-a-ldr  547
FULFORD, Tommy  p  526-527-528-529-631-
  1659-1660-1661-1662
FULLBRIGHT, Richard  bb-sb  5-280-390-460
  749-755-756-779-1134-1171-1338-1467-1
  1468-1670-1706-1707-1709-1710
FULLER, Bob  cl-ss-as  153-182-285-306-
  313-343-349-531-537-547-548-564-643-733
  734-735-845-861-872-941-998-1021-1022-
  1024-1025-1051-1057-1058-1060-1090-1093
  1094-1096-1097-1121-1128-1130-1184-1218
  1240-1246-1306-1323-1326-1428-1430-1442
  1445-1449-1450-1451-1453-1458-1462-1463
  1551-1555-1556-1557-1739
FULLER, Earl  p-ldr  327-549
FULLER, Jesse  tb-bsx  795-1213-1214-1215
FULLER, Walter  t-v  661-758-759-760-1116
FULLER, Wylie  sb  1195
FULLERTON, Cyril J.  p  706
FULLERTON, Dave  d  636
FULTERMAN, Harry  d  9-1116
FULTON, Jack  tb-v  76-211-1172-1570-1681
  1682-1683-1684-1685-1686-1687-1688-1689
  1690
FUNNELL, Bon Bon (r.n. George F.)  v  153
FURNESS, Bill  p-v  529
FURNESS, Peck  sb-v  529
FURNESS, Slim  g-v  529-1556

GABRIEL, Al  vn  914
GADDY, Willie  g  683
GAER, Murray  d  1615
GAFFNEY, Howard  t  1242-1243-1753
GAGE, Irby  cl-as  91-92
GAIDA, Cyril  bj-g-vn  11-346-674
GAILLARD, Slim  g-vib-v  550-551-1134
GAINES, Charlie  t-v  50-313-835-939-1459
  1492-1623-1706-1707-1709-1726
GAISBERG, Fred  p  1197
GALBRAITH, Barry  g  1243-1553-1554
GALBRAITH, Joe  bj  578-579
GALBREATH, Frank  t  58-1116
GALE, Eddie  v  1234-1302-1328-1537
GALE, Harry  d  116-1568
GALE, Jackie  v  879
GALEHOUSE, Clark  ts  513-1263-1602
GALETTA, Nick  t  207-829
GALINAS, Gabe  cl-as-ts  1357-1358-1359
GALKIN, Lew  d  836
GALLATY, Bill  t  383
GALLODORO, Al  cl-bcl-as  1690-1691
GALLODORO, Frank  as  1374-1691
GALLOWAY, Estelle  v  1272
GALTMAN, Henry  cl-as  93-250
GAMBLE, Louis  ss-as  522
GAMET, Cliff  cl-as-ts-v  172-173-659-660
GAMMON, George  ts  418
GAMMON, Von  d  1510
GANDE, Al  tb  1741
GANT, Willie  p  940-1576
GAPPELL, Moe  tb  68-914-915-934-935
GARBER, Jan  vn-ldr  552-553
GARBER, Victor  as  829
GARCIA, Jake  bb-sb-v  159-642-991-992
GARCIA, Joe  cl  1184
GARCIA, Louis  t  132-421-422-553-1271
GARDELLE, Big Tess  v  63
GARDNER, Carroll  d  963
GARDNER, Charles  bj-g  963
GARDNER, Earl  as  1641
GARDNER, Fred  cl-ts  553
GARDNER, Freddy  cl-as-ts-bar  16-30-85-
  152-193-281-282-285-345-383-399-525-
  530-536-538-554-797-798-964-974-1137-
  1149-1298-1310-1431-1432-1433-1434-1519
  1584-1585-1695-1721-1749-1750
GARDNER, Jack  p-ldr  554-555-658-814-815
  816-999-1036-1037-1536
GARDNER, Jack  bb  553
GARDNER, Lynn  v  167-168
GARDNER, Marty  d  32-33
GAREY, Harry  tb  1243-1244
GARGANO, Tom  d  115
GARLAND, Ed  sb  456-942-1485
GARLAND, Fred  tb  337-338
GARLAND, Hattie  v  555
GARLAND, Joe  cl-ts-bar-a  13-14-57-58-
  487-695-696-1072-1073-1074-1103-1279-
  1388-1497-1722
GARLAND, Judy  v  555
GARNER, Cora  v  555
GARNETT, Blind Leroy  p  555
GARNETT, Harry  ts  520
GARRETT, Ardell  t  1063-1064
GARRISON, Bootsie  v  1279
GARRISON, Doc  tb  1498
GARRISON, Josephine  v  1112
GARRISON, Ken  bb  11
GARRISON, Ron  bb  1134
GARRY, Sid  v  241-483-556-1145-1146-1384
GARVEY, Jim  v  1670

GARVIN, Carl  t  1538-1539
GARVIN, Clint  cl-as  1538-1539
GASCALES, John  ts  363
GASKIN, Bill  t  789-1434-1692
GASPARD, Octave  bb-sb  543-569-570-1218
  1719-1744
GASSOWAY, John  ts  1752-1753
GAST, Norman  vn  556-;335
GASTE, Louis  g  188-1283-1615
GATELY, Buddy  v  438
GATES, Bob  bb  556
GATES, Stan  tb  383
GATES, Tom  ts  556
GATEWOOD, Johnny  p-v  409-556-694-891
GAUNA, Steve  bj-g  10-1214
GAUPER, Carl  cl-as  237-920-921-1520-1521
GAUTREAUX, Alvin  h  802
GAVITTE, Rex  sb  83-84
GAY, Leonard  cl-ss-as-ts-bar  863-1662
GAYBE, Dan  sb  1570
GAYLE, Paula  v  1237
GAYLOR, Ruth  v  123-124-125-785-756-1242
  1243
GAYLORD, Charles  vn-v  1568-1663-1680-
  1681-1682-1683-1684-1685-1686
GAYLORD, Chester  v  556
GEBHART, Robert  tb  1147
GEDDES, Jeanne  v  316
GEER, Gloria  v  556
GEIGER, Earl  t  887-889
GEIL, Paul  t  307
GEISER, Harold  tb  972
GELDRAY, Max  h  556-557
GELINAS, Gabe  ts  873-874
GELLER, Harry  t  63-597-1405-1406
GELLER, John  cl-as  456
GELLERS, Irving  p  1124-1125
GELPI, Rene  bj-g  1130-1131
GELSLEY, Sam  g  536-684-797-1221-1289-
  1419-1508
GEMUS, Jimmy  ts  1160
GENARDER , Ronnie  bj-g  1215
GENDERS, Harry  t  647
GENNER , Russ  tb  153-160
GENSAL, Darr  cl-as  563-564
GENTILE, Pete  v  973
GENTRY, Art  v  123-805-1027
GENTRY, Chuck  bar  619-620-621-816-817-
  818-1244
GENUSO, Sam  tb  1242
GEORGE, Al  tb  79-123-124-324-325-1158-
  1159-1360-1361
GEORGE, Dick  p  194-1036-1746
GEORGE, Harold  bb  274-578-579
GEORGE, Horace  cl-v  557
GEORGE, Karl  t  103-663-664-1735-1736
GEORGE, Paul  bj  1454-1471-1586
GEORGETTE  v  1435
GERBRECHT, Pinky (r.n. Edward G.)  c
  1122-1123-1229
GERHARDI, Tony  bj-g  955-956-957-958
GERITY, Julia  v  1470
GERLACH, Nick  vn  129-130-131-1079-1222
GERMAN, Arthur  bj  644
GEROLD, Carl  d  558-559
GERSHMAN, Manny  cl-as  306-307-452-453
GIANELLI, Tony  t  239-245-246-247-871-
  932-1602-1620
GIARDINA, Felix  tb  1126
GIARDINA, Tony  cl-as  464
GIBBONS, Bobby Joe  g  307

GIBBONS, Carroll  p-dir  156-520-564-565-
  644-784-812-1126-1127-1217-1355-1364-
  1365-1396-1397-1456-1457-1521-1738
GIBBONS, Hal  p  152
GIBBS, Arthur  p-ldr  564
GIBBS, Eddie  g  207-208-318-696-752-1477
  1518-1736
GIBBS, Ernie  tb  1285-1286
GIBBS, George  bb-sb  470-539-636-1196-
  1224-1295-1296-1297-1674-1675
GIBBS, Johnny  cl-as-ts  884
GIBBS, Parker  cl-ts-v  1664-1665-1666-
  1667-1668-1669
GIBELING, Howard  tb  325-326
GIBLIN, Tom  p  1162
GIBSON, Albert  tb  1491
GIBSON, Al(fred)  cl-ts  262-284-1116
GIBSON, Andy  a  104-105-106-107-260-261-
  815
GIBSON, Earl  p-a  1052
GIBSON, Frank  ts  1490
GIBSON, Fredda (r.n.; later known as
  Georgia Gibbs !)  v  786-1409-1572
GIBSON, George  cl-ss-as  134-1055
GIBSON, Herman  bj  1450
GIBSON, Joe  bb  346
GIBSON, Margie  a  617-618-619
GIERSDORF, Bea  v  1273
GIFELLI, Joe  t  457
GIFFORD, Gene  bj-g-a  76-209-286-287-288
  289-290-294-565
GIGAS, Maurice  t  1284
GILBERT, Blind  c  565
GILBERT, Eddie  sb  1537
GILBERT, Geoffrey  f  563
GILBERT, Les  cl-as  279-801
GILDERS, Theodore  t  154-155
GILL, Emerson  vn-ldr  565-566
GILL, Sumner  ts  1657
GILLESPIE, Dizzy (r.n. John Birks)  t-a
  187-259-260-261-662-744-756-763-1070
GILLESPIE, Joe  cl-as  1-170-344-886-887-
  888-889
GILLETTE, Bob  bj  1132-1741
GILLHAM , Art  p-v  934
GILLILAND, Jim  tb  218-1641
GILLILAND, John  cl-ts-v  540
GILLIS, Burton  cl-as  656
GILLIS, Cary  d  831-992-993-1513
GILLIS, Lee  v  879
GILLS, Charles  v  302
GILLUM, Ted  d  1089
GILMARTIN, Bill  bj  630
GILMORE, Buddy  d  512
GILMORE, Fred  cl-ts  134-1055
GILMORE, Kirk  d  1252
GILMORE, Ted  v  1257
GILMORE SISTERS, The  v  568-687
GINDER, Art  tb  317
GINSBERG, Ben  sb  204-1398-1399-1400-1401
  1402
GINSBERG, Joe  ts  1016
GINSLER, Red  tb  578-579-616
GIOBBE, Felix  sb  29-166-168-968-1095-
  1228-1242-1621-1752
GIRARD, Adele  harp  1007
GIRSBACK, Squire  bb  1656
GISH, Joseph (Joe)  bb  569-1506
GIST, Joe  cl-as  1510
GIST, Pierce  c  1487
GLADIEU, Maurice  tb  519-1284

GLANTZ, Harry t 1379
GLANTZ, Nathan as-dir 90-285-569- 861-
1353-1354-1395-1438-1480-1502-1503-1504
1505-1510-1524-1525-1547-1587-1588
GLASCOE, Ivy Ann v 1272
GLASCOE, Percy cl-ss-as 110-317-538-539
569-830-1090-1463-1496
GLASS, Henderson v 155
GLASS, Mike fh 1554
GLASSMAN, Ben cl-as-ts 959-1007
GLAZER, Jack d 1334
GLEASON, Phil cl-ss-as 560-1661-1612-
1613
GLEE CLUB, The v 186-1004-1076
GLEGHORN, Arthur f 140
GLENN, Lloyd p-a 7
GLENN, Tyree tb-vib-v 260-261-262-283-
769-1337-1654
GLENN, Wilfred v 578-1604-1613
GLENNAN, Gene v 1669
GLENY, Albert sb 1287
GLICKMAN, Fred vn 360-1690-1722
GLICKMAN, Harry vn 1125
GLOGAU, Jack p 310
GLORIEUX, Remy bb 1286
GLOVER, Cliff cl-ts-bsx 18-1436
GLOVER, George cl-as-bar-vn 347-684-
1493
GLOVER, Joe a 1540
GLUCK, Harry t 140-203-569-882-916-925-
926-1095-1128-1129-1130-1379-1428-1545
GLUCK, Henry t 71-630
GLUCKMAN, Bernie cl 29
GLYCKSON, Serge cl-as-f 571-1595
GOBALET, James sb 689
GOBLE, Sam t 82-1496-1497
GODARD, —— tb 1019-1216
GODARD, Henry c 1019-1216
GODDARD, Ted cl-as-ts-bar 1552-1553-1554
GODFREY, Howard dir 1616
GODLEY, A. G. d 851-1109-1203-1204-1563-
1564-1575
GOEBEL, Ted d 571
GOEDE, Frank bj-g 1662
GOERING, Al p 128-129-130-131-572-1077-
1078-1079-1081-1221-1222-1223
GOERNER, F. vc 1407-1408
GOFFIN, Maurice vn 177-1055-1141-1142
GOLATI, Ralph bj 1066-1067
GOLD, Al ts 1346
GOLD, Art t 1541
GOLD, Harry cl-as-ts-a 539-807-808
GOLD, Joe p 972-973
GOLD, Lou p-a-ldr 572-573
GOLD, Murray tb 8
GOLDBERG, Doc sb 166-167-168-785-786-787
1048
GOLDBERG, Max t-mel 3-22-23-25-30-31-32-
61-143-147-161-173-192-272-281-359-383-
384-387-388-395-506-508-523-524-568-684-
785-788-964-982 1116-1126-1127-1128-1149
1155-1196-1224-1225-1289-1290-1292-1294-
1295-1296-1297-1324-1363-1431-1432-1472-
1482-1493-1507-1513-1565-1675-1695-1721-
1749-1750
GOLDEN, Ernie p-v-ldr 575
GOLDEN, Lee t 806
GOLDEN, Les as-bar-v 152
GOLDENBERG, Moe timps 923
GOLDFARB, Alex bb 19-1212

GOLDFIELD, Harry t-v 76-552-875-876-
1017-1325-1570-1598-1685-1686-1687-
1688-1689-1690
GOLDFINGER, Seymour tb 364-1539-1540-
1541-1752
GOLDIE, Jack as 126-1539-1540
GOLDKETTE, Jean p-ldr 577
GOLDMAN, Nick p 1334
GOLDSTEIN, Chuck v 1690-1691
GOLDSTEIN, Len as-ts 78-79-1157-1158-
1159-1160
GOLDSTEIN, Rolf or Ralph t 283-836
GOLLAN, Bill p 1047
GOLTZER, Harold bsn 81-1513
GOMAR, Larry d-vib 37-67-84-161-198-200
360-651-674-805-1016-1031-1270-1312-1538
1671-1689-1690-1751
GOMERDINGER, Larry d 418 (as above ?)
GOMEZ, Johnny g 216
GONELLA, Bruts t-v 346-347-348-581-582-
583-584-585-586-587-588-589-791
GONELLA, Nat t-mel-v 98-138-140-147-316
346-459-539-581-582-583-584-585-586-587
588-589-590-591-808-1149-1263-1494-1507
1508
GONIER, Chet t 657
GONSOULIN, Tommy t 205-814-829-906-907-
1539-1540
GOODE, Bruce cl-as-ts 919
GOODHART, Al p 1284
GOODIE, Frank "Big Boy" - see GOUDIE,Frank
GOODING, Sally v 1557-1734
GOODLY, Clark sb 1118
GOODMAN, Benny c-cl-bcl-ss-as-bar-v-ldr
16-17-62-112-117-145-159-200-274-305-
361-378-392-515-516-519-534-556-567-591
592-593-594-595-596-597-598-599-600-601
602-603-604-605-606-607-608-609-610-611
612-613-614-615-616-617-618-619-620-621
622-623-638-670-671-673-674-804-821-853
905-906-933-957-958-977-1015-1016-1029-
1030-1040-1048-1076-1077-1078-1079-1081
1098-1140-1141-1142-1143-1144-1156-1223
1231-1232-1233-1234-1235-1242-1328-1330
1331-1332-1337-1382-1383-1384-1385-1386
1387-1446-1537-1538-1600-1639-1648-1652
1653-1691-1730-1731-1732-1733-1745
GOODMAN, Benny as 1482
GOODMAN, Freddy t 1052
GOODMAN, Harry bb-sb 274-305-505-591-
592-594-595-596-597-598-599-600-601-602
603-604-605-606-607-608-609-610-611-612
660-999-1000-1029-1076-1077-1078-1079-
1080-1081-1114-1131-1144-1223-1231-1232
1233-1234-1235-1236-1328-1337-1537-1731
1733
GOODMAN, Irving t 62-93-123-124-125-126
600-611-612-614-615-616-617-618-619-
1242-1244-1332
GOODMAN, John p 183
GOODMAN, Max sb 703-1561
GOODMAN, Moe d 1497
GOODMAN, Phil as 1265
GOODNER, Lillian v 623
GOODRICH, Bob t 374-1150-1237
GOODRICH, Fizz bar 274
GOODWIN, Bob d 1051-1052
GOODWIN, Chauncey cl-as 274
GOODWIN, Henry t-v 115-318-551-695-696-
806-807

GOODWIN, Herbert g-v 1561
GOOLD, Sam p 627
GOOSBY, Fanny Mae p-v 82-627
GOOSSENS, Leon ts-o 127-1456
GOOSSENS, Marie harp 1749
GOOSSENS, Sidonie harp 801
GORDON, —— p 1485
GORDON, Ben v 1286
GORDON, Bob ts-bsx 1051-1052
GORDON, C. d 1550
GORDON, Dexter ts 664
GORDON, Harry "Wally" d 97
GORDON, Henry p 1422
GORDON, Jack ss-as 395
GORDON, Jack d 1674
GORDON, Jimmy cl-as-bar 938-939
GORDON, Larry cl-as 207-829
GORDON-WALKER, W. E. f-pic 1216
GORHAM, Wilbur bj-g 1153
GORLING, Uno tb 282
GORLING, Zilas ts 282
GORMAN, Ross cl-bcl-as-bar-ldr 629-630-
  631-675-732-1219-1220-1330-1355-1606-
  1607-1608-1609-1680-1747-1748
GORNER, —— vn 576
GORY, Gene vn 1047
GOSLIN, Steve t 1485
GOSLING, Stan t 1210-1343
GOSS, Harry cl-ts-bar 1339-1340-1341-
  1342
GOSS, Jack g 764
GOSS, Jimmy cl-as-ts-bar 964-1675
GOIT, Tommy c-t 17-73-145-174-245-265-
  266-267-319-395-510-532-670-813-870-871
  972-1076-1080-1164-1219-1288-1303-1355-
  1381-1382-1383-1384-1387-1415-1431-1607
  1608-1610-1611-1620-1680-1740
GOTTUSO, Tony g 163-215-217-1399-1691
GOTWALLS, Dave as 93-250
GOUDEY, Russ cl-as-bar-dir 89
GOUDIE, Frank "Big Boy" t-cl-ts 330-465-
  632-827-835-960-1427-1642
GOULD, Bud tb-vn 1037-1038
GOULD, Bill t-v 404
GOULD, Frank v 1275-1521
GOVER, Emma v 632
GOWANS, Brad c-vtb cl-as 170-317-335-
  336-542-543-632-633-634-646-647-657-765
  822-959-1003-1130-1275-1289-1696
GOWANS, George d 970-971-976
GOWDY, Ruby v 633
GOZZARD, Harry t 208-209-417-1361
GOZZO, Conrad t 1552-1553-1554
GRAAS, John fh 1553-1554
GRACE, Teddy v 371-372-633-634-747
GRADY, Bill cl-as 552
GRAF, Al v 1137
GRAHAM, Al d 1437
GRAHAM, Ann v 594
GRAHAM, Bill t 214-215-216-363-370-
  437-704-756
GRAHAM, Bud tb 857
GRAHAM, Chauncey ts 154-1634
GRAHAM, Elwood c 337-338
GRAHAM, Pops bb 1009
GRAINGER, Porter p-k-p-v 178-190-343-522-
  564-623-634-643-681-682-732-735-749-750
  755-811-846-881-964-998-1011-1022-1023-
  1041-1050-1060-1061-1218-1338-1355-1441
  1444-1445-1448-1449-1450-1451-1452-1460
  1463-1488-1544-1551-1641-1727-1728

GRANADA, Jimmy cl 132
GRANCY, Harry t 748
GRANDE, Vincent tb 68-69-882-1088-1180-
  1420-1428-1544-1545-1681-1688-1689-
  1752.
GRANEER, Emery vn 1196
GRANELLO, Joe g 383
GRANSTAFF, Earl tb 458-1492-1724-1727
GRANT, Coot v 180-1729
GRANT, Freddy cl 141
GRANT, Hunt cl-bsx 405-1174
GRANT, Mel p 1602
GRANT, Sid ts 164
GRANT, Sterling k 1544
GRANTHAM, Bill bj 1305
GRANTHAM, Howard cl-ts-vn 61-1673
GRAPPELLY, Stephane vn-p 3-163-172-188-
  189-312-313-330-333-398-632-635-636-689
  690-973-1211-1219-1258-1259-1260-1261-
  1262-1283-1288-1348-1349-1350-1476-1562
  1642
GRASELLI, Paul d 1597-1598-1599
GRASSET, Roger bb-sb 3-190-1261-1348-
  1349-1595-1642
GRASSI, John tb 647-911-912-1242-1243
GRASSO, Eddie vn 1616
GRASSO, Oscar vn 1126
GRAUB, Carl v 659
GRAUER, Bernie p 1379
GRAUSO, Joe d 764
GRAVEN, Luther 47-48-318
GRAVES, Blind Roosevelt g 516
GRAVES, Henry vc 665
GRAVES, Uaroy tambourine 516
GRAVITO, Frank bj 1005
GRAY, Alfred d 684
GRAY, Arthur banjoline 1517
GRAY, Betty v 636
GRAY, Chauncey p 239-240-241-242-243-
  244-245-246-247-262-263-626-627-658-
  670-672-776-882-979-980-981-982-1117-
  1118-1124-1393-1394-1490-1581-1583-
  1593-1620
GRAY, Christina v 636
GRAY, Cora v 320
GRAY, Earl as 1546
GRAY, Geneva v 636
GRAY, George v 1392
GRAY, Glenn as-ldr 76-286-287-288-289-
  290-291-292-293-294-295-296-297-298-
  **299-300**
GRAY, Harry bb 1281
GRAY, Hunter as 520
GRAY, Ivan ts 348
GRAY, Jack vl 1406
GRAY, Jane v 1581
GRAY, Jerry vn-a 1398-1399-1403-1404-
  1405
GRAY, Ken cl-as-bar 807
GRAY, Kitty p-v 637
GRAY, Rick c 1010
GRAY, Sam p-v 964-965
GRAY, Thomas t 666
GRAY, Tick c-t 863-1167-1168
GRAY, Walter bj-g 1517
GRECO, Jimmy t 920-921
GREEN, Basil tb 1343
GREEN, Bernie a 873-874-875
GREEN, Bill ts 419
GREEN, Bill p 1252

1786

GREEN, Charlie  tb  50-165-353-354-715-716-717-718-719-720-721-722-723-794-860-861-1037-1266-1267-1441-1442-1443-1444-1445-1446-1449-1452-1466-1467-1717-1729
GREEN, Charlie  sb  185-457
GREEN, Claude  as  192
GREEN, Dick  t  752
GREEN, Eddie  d  863
GREEN, Eddie  v  1723
GREEN, Edgar  1377
GREEN, Ernest  ts  1662
GREEN, Eugene  tb  169
GREEN, Freddy  g  78-101-102-103-104-105-106-107-108-109-110-607-608-662-676-768-769-821-872-873-1048-1346-1511-1732-1733-1734
GREEN, George  sb  1-201-1009-1241
GREEN, George Hamilton  x-d-marimba-vib  26-60-62-196-410-456-503-637-641-675-676-1303-1367-1395-1747-1748
GREEN, Gordon  cl-ts  150-642
GREEN, Gunnar  t  1585
GREEN, H.  tb  1330
GREEN, Jake  tb  1-830-836
GREEN, Jane  v  638-1609
GREEN, Joe  d-x-marimba  17-26-63-64-82-196-509-637-638-641-676-751-752-853-1016-1415-1416-1417-1418-1456-1604-1610-1747
GREEN, Johnny  p-ldr  638
GREEN, Leothus  p  1548
GREEN, Marcellus  t  691-692-693-694
GREEN, Percy  cl-as  564
GREEN, Phil  p-pac-cel-harpsichord-dir  85-86-388-536-638-687-688-798-1207
GREEN, Raymond  d  1649
GREEN, Sadie  v  639
GREEN, Shirley  ts  1272-1674
GREEN, Slim  g-v  639
GREEN, Stanley  t  59-159-642
GREEN, Sture  tb  1585
GREEN, Ted  ts  19-1212
GREEN, Theron  tb  1252
GREEN, Violet - see SMITH, CLARA
GREENBAUM, Hyam  vl  953
GREENBERG, Felix  cl-as-ts  1285
GREENBERG, Harry  c  1231 1232
GREENBERG, Jack  cl-as-ts-bar  8
GREENBERG, Marty  d  1481
GREENBERG, Ruby  vn  905
GREENE, Bert  d  337-338
GREENE, Gordie  bb  28
GREENE, Homer  tb  1028
GREENE, Madeleine  v  759-761-762-1116
GREENE, Marie  v  186
GREENE, Norman  tb  58-775-1116
GREENE SISTERS, THE  v  1224-1225
GREENING, John S.  p  263
GREENING, Stan  bj-ldr  345-639-667-1493
GREENISH, Robert W.  cl-as  263
GREENOP, Norton  bj  1229
GREENWALD, Harry/Henry  t  8-123
GREENWALD, Sylvan E.  p  914
GREENWOOD, Benny  cl-ts  279
GREER, Fred  ts  683
GREER, Sonny (r.n. William G.)  d-chimes-tambourine-v  27-134-135-358-472-473-474-475-476-477-478-479-480-481-482-483-484-485-486-487-488-489-490-491-492-493-4940495 496-497-498-499-500-640-645-651-652-661-662-765 766-767 (cont. next col.)

GREER, Sonny (cont.)  1075-1083-1246-1250-1263-1431-1471-1500-1501-1564-1565-1640-1641-1653-1711-1712
GREGG, Wayne  v  217-1307-1546
GREGOR, Martin  t  682
GREGORI, Frank  pac  581-936-937-938
GREGORY, Felix  cl-as-ts  1705-1715-1716
GREISSLER, Les  ts  1562
GRESH, Earl  vn-ldr  640-641
GREY, Carolyn  v  743-744
GREY, Harry  p  382
GREY, Lawrence  v  1491
GREY, E. Martin  cl-ss-ts  1663-1664
GRIER, Art  cl-ts  159-361-642
GRIER, Jimmy  cl-ts-speech  59-159-361
GRIFFIN, Gordon  t  77-91-93-598-619-701-702-967-1088-1373-1621-1731
GRIFFIN, John  g  1440
GRIFFIN, William  ts  318
GRIFFITH, Joe  v  577-1190-1583
GRIFFITHS, Archie  p  1048
GRIFFITHS, James A.  v  1190
GRIFFITHS, Peter  t  263
GRIMES, Charlie  as-ts  392-868
GRIMES, Clarence  cl-ss-as  1119-1392
GRIMES, Jimmy  t  188
GRIMES, Johnny  v  152
GRIMSHAW, Emil Jr.  bj-g  799-800-1155-.1265-1362-1365-1366
GRINTER, Marie  v  642
GRISELLE, Tom  p-ldr-a  642-1737
GRISSOM, Dan  cl-as-v  985-986-987-988-989-990-991
GRISWOLD, Cloyd  bj  121-133
GROFE, Ferdie  p-a  732-1355-1606-1607-1608-1609-1680-1681-1683-1685-1686-1687
GROFF, Elwood  bb  659
GROGAN, Oscar  v  1470
GRONWALL, Art  p  579-1068-1069
GROSE, Slim  tb  405
GROSS, Buddy (r.n. Louis)  bb  752-1614-1615
GROSS, Helen  v  643
GROSS, Walter  p  644-1303-1373-1513-1690-1715
GROSSBART, Eddie  v  395-1226-1493
GROSSBERG, Albert  as  1498
GROSSI, Phil  t  1047
GROSSI, William  cl-ss  1334
GROSSO, Eddie  cl-as-ts-v  203-205-519-520-653-654-655-796-1436-1692
GROSSO, Elmer  t-vn  675
GROVES, Bert  bb-sb  1214-1215
GRUBB, Ebb  bb  82
GRUBB, Galen  p  1479-1497
GRUBB, Ted  t  1288
GRUBER, Bill  t  394
GRUNDY, Hense  tb  409-556-694-695-891-1619
GRUPP, David  d  629-630-962-1219-1220-1543
GUARENTE, Frank  t  33-84-200-360-403-421-422-423-424-559-560-561-644-1289-1290-1364-1365-1482-1483-1538-1751
GUARINO, Felix  d  32-1175
GUARNIERI, Johnny  p-harpsichord  62-506-614-615-1407-1408-1409-1712
GUBERTINI, Ronnie  d  281-468-469-470-780-790-791-812-917-1083-1155-1306-1362-1363-1364-1739-1750
GUDERIAN, Gus  p-v  344

GUERETTE, George  tb  1150
GUERRA, Freddy  as  417
GUESDE, Henri  g  1595
GUILFOYLE, Frank  p-a  656-657
GUIMARAES, Lionel  tb  52-518
GUION, King  ts  1236
GUISHARD, Alfred  cl-as-v  1310-1311
GUNN, Jimmy  p-ldr  646-1537
GUNNERMAN, Ray  d  1589
GUSICK, Ben  t  1052
GUSSAK, Bill  d  80-81-93-207-1028-1156-
  1197
GUSTAFERRO, Joe  t  184-416
GUTHRIE, Don  x  1196
GUTIERREZ, Jose  tb  364-1538-1539-1540-
  1541-1690
GUY, Fred  bj-g  27-134-135-472-473-474-
  475-476-477-478-479-480-481-482-483-
  484-485-486-487-488-489-490-491-492-
  493-494-495-496-497-498-499-500-640-
  651-652-765-1075-1083-1263-1431-1564-
  1565-1640-1641-1653-1711-1712
GUY, Joe  t  690-691-1712
GUY, Mickey  tb-a  646

HAAGLAND, Arthur  tb  388-389
HAAS, Dick  t  168
HAAS, Lowie  dir  89
HABBE, Arnold  bj  274
HACKET, Fred  tb  1368
HACKETT, Bobby  c-t-g  28-335-363-518-542
  545-607-633-646-647-821-959-1032-1137-
  1313-1314-1515-1316-1333-1512-1734-1735
HADALE, Gus  bb  388-389
HADEN, Evert  p  282
HADINGHAM, Tony  d  263
HADLEY, Vic  bj-g  395
HADNOTT, Bill  sb  944
HAENTZSCHEL, George  p-a  1662
HAGAN, Cass  vn-ldr  648
HAGAN, Paul  v  129-1039-1091
HAGEMANN-LARSEN, Henry  cl-ts  282-821
HAGEN, Earle  tb-a  443-444-445-1150-1237
  1506
HAGEN, Ray  d  1361
HAGER, Fred  dir  1059
HAGERTY, Bert  t  1008
HAGGART, Bob  sb-a  16-62-161-162-363-364
  365-366-367-368-369-370-371-372-373-374
  375-376-555-942-1048-1114
HAHN, Harold  d  208-209-417
HAHN, John  t  89
HAHNE, Webb  v  552
HAID, Bill  bj-g  339-340-341-649-650
HAID, Bill  p  399-463-532-962-1163-1454
HAINES, ——  c  1250
HAINES, Charles E.  d  10
HAINES, Connie  v  449-450-451-452-453-
  815
HAINES, Ralph  - see LAMBERT, SCRAPPY
HAINES, Walt  bb-sb  1472
HAISLIP, Otis L.  as  547
HALE, Chester  - see ENNIS, SKINNY
HALEY, Bill  p  417
HALFACRE, Bill  sb  1375
HALL, Adelaide  v  473-651-652-960-1073-
  1633
HALL, Al  sb  153-208-513-770-1560-1721-
  1734-1735-1736
HALL, Alfred  d  749
HALL, Archie  a  1038

HALL, Arthur  v  73-74-223-225-227-228-
  229-230-231-232-233-235-530-573-926-927
  967-1180-1220-1300-1353-1380-1484-1502-
  1503-1504-1520-1579-1583-1745
HALL, Ben  tb  94-95
HALL, Bill  t-tb  1226-1227-1457
HALL, Clarence  cl-ss-as  302
HALL, Dick  cl-as  28
HALL, Edmond  cl-as-bar  15-78-207-355-
  652-662-667-749-768-773-774-775-782-
  1134-1338-1422-1511-1531-1721-1737
HALL, Emmanuel, Quintet  v  482
HALL, Fred  p-reed or  519-520-652-653-
  654-655-1436-1692
HALL, George  t  418
HALL, H. B.  tb  310
HALL, Harrison  bb  1746
HALL, Herbert  cl-as-bar-a  7
HALL, Howard  p  56
HALL, Jack  t  1374-1375
HALL, Joe  p  76-286-287-288-289-290-291
  292-293-294-295-296-297-298-299-300
HALL, Larry  bj-g  203-205-1063-1089-1178
HALL, Lionel  g  1571
HALL, Nelson  bj-g-v  59
HALL, Philmore "Shorty"  c  138
HALL, Plunker  bj  91-92
HALL, Randy  as  1252
HALL, Rene  tb-bj-g  520-1310-1311
HALL, Richard  fh  1553
HALL, Ross  p  889
HALL, Sleepy (r.n. John Nelson)  bj  1606
HALL, Slim  bj  32-1175
HALL, Tubby  d  41-48-49-50-180-824-1154
HALL, Wally  vn  656
HALL, Wendell  u-v  1608-1609
HALL, Wilbur  tb-g  211-1680-1681-1682-
  1683-1684-1685-1686-1687
HALL, Willie  d  164-177-1109
HALL JOHNSON CHOIR, THE  v  1445
HALLDAY, Mack  d  1116
HALLER, Rod  ts  416
HALLETT, Dave  tb  457
HALLETT, Mal  cl-as-ldr  656-657
HALLIVER, Roger  d  747
HALSALL, Jack  cl-as-ts-f  346-347-656
HALSTEAD, Henry  vn-ldr  657
HALTEN, Torg  t  398-908-909-910-911-912
HAMANN, Vic  tb  742-743-744
HAMBY, Marvin  t  1377
HAMILTON, Billy  cl-as-ts  972-973-1361
HAMILTON, Billy  d  388-389
HAMILTON, Bob  t  1287
HAMILTON, Bob  elo  1269
HAMILTON, Cranston  p  359-709
HAMILTON, Chico (r.n. Forrest H.)  d  551
HAMILTON, Jack  t  52-658-808-809
HAMILTON, Jimmy  cl-ts  187-208-770-1116
  1736
HAMILTON, John  t  272-1632-1634-1635-
  1636-1637-1638
HAMILTON, Johnny  ts  59
HAMM, Fred  c-t-v-ldr  658
HAMMED, Alie  p  685
HAMMELL, Dick  d  866-867
HAMMER, Al  d  1482
HAMMER, Harry  vn  1273
HAMMERSLAG, Roy  ts  417-1243-1244
HAMMOND, Don  cl-ts  184-325-326
HAMMOND, Seldon  bb  738
HAMMOND, Tosh  one-string fiddle  213

1788

HAMP, Charles W. v 659
HAMPTON, Artie as 155
HAMPTON, Lionel p-d-vib-v 47-48-53-62-
335-355-598-599-601-602-603-604-605-606
607-608-609-610-611-612-613-614-615-616
660-661-662-663-664-782-821-1485-1490-
1731
HAMPTON, Percy d 809-810
HAMPTON RHYTHM BOYS, THE v 663
HAND, Arthur vn-dir 173-220-221-222-223
224-225-226
HANDLEY, Eric v 938
HANDY, Elizabeth v 1628
HANDY, Katherine p-v 665
HANDY, W. C. c-t-g-ldr 665-666-667-1010
HANDY, —— (Jr.) x 666
HANLON, Alan g 78-79-1158-1159-1160-
1491-1552-1553
HANLON, Clare tb-v 1641
HANN, Al t 111
HANNAFORD, Ephraim tb 285-406-686-706-
870-1008-1009-1351-1352-1353-1354-1379-
1522-1523-1525-1526-1698
HANNAS, Herbert bj 792
HANRAHAN, George sb 8-9
HANSELL, Ralph d 997
HANSEN, Carl bb 1123
HANSEN, Jack t 1244-1357-1358-1359-1360
HANSEN, Jack bb-sb 177-239-240-241-304-
419-1064-1139-1141-1142-1171-1172-1299-
1300-1381-1382-1594-1611-1612-1613-1620
HANSHAW, Annette v-p-u 573-574-667-668-
669-670-671-672-673-674-932-1192-1325-
1381
HANSON, James t 738
HANSON, Norman d 640
HAPPE, Dip t 402-403
"HAPPY JACK" v 1174
HARBERT, L. as-ts 1575
HARDAWAY, Lil p-ldr 675-676-1066-1267-
1749
HARDEE, Ashford tb 1108
HARDEE, Stanley t 461
HARDEN, Ralph t 1361-1552
HARDIN, Lil p 165-166 (see also ARM-
STRONG, LIL)
HARDING, Alan as-ts 1237-1361
HARDING, Buster p-a 108-110-260-261-618
760-761-1736
HARDING, Chet bb 402-403
HARDING, Dick v 1552-1553
HARDING, Hiram t 7
HARDING, Hugh ts 1361
HARDING, Stanley wb 538
HARDISON, Leroy tb 277
HARDMAN, Glenn elo 277
HARDMAN, Walter sb 321-322-323
HARDWAY FOUR, THE v 1674
HARDWICK, Otto cl-ss-as-bar-bsx 27-173-
472-473-474-475-477-486-487-488-489-490
491-492-493-494-495-496-497-498-499-500
640-651-652-765-854-941-1014-1075-1246-
1471-1564-1565-1623-1700-1711-1712
HARDY, Earl tb 528-690
HARDY, Leroy as 251
HARDY, Marlow cl-as-ldr 676
HARE, Ernest v 70-232-235-240-573-623-
624-625-916-1239-1354-1504
HARE, John bb 1529
HAREN, Harold cl-ts-v 418
HARGEST, Bert t 1202

HARING, Bob dir 5-401-677-678-1131
HARKINS, Ted sb 1372
HARKNESS, Charles bb 1421
HARKNESS, Cliff cl-as 1563
HARLEM HIGHLANDERS, THE v 1203
HARLEY, Harlem v-ldr 680-681-834
HARLING, Cyril vn 656-807-808
HARMAN, Dave tb-ldr 508-682-1120
HARMIN, Louis tb 2
HARMON, Dave v 1741
HARNACK, Cecil as 1051-1052
HARPER, Daryl sb 64
HARPER, Emerson cl-as-o 1451-1459-1726
HARPER, George cl-as-ts 274-544-998
HARPER, Grace g 1711
HARPER, Percy tb 1744
HARPER, Red v 1731
HARRELL, Elmer cl-ts 833
HARRELL, Elmer W. vn 1118
HARRELL, John ts 1147
HARRELL, Lynn p 866-867
HARRINGTON, Guy bj-v 1537
HARRINGTON, John cl-as-bar 251-898-899
900-901-902-1718
HARRINGTON, Reg tb 239-240-241-242-626
627-1393-1620
HARRIS, —— p 1065
HARRIS, Abe g 1271
HARRIS, Ace p-v-ldr 683
HARRIS, Al c-t 804-1029-1076-1077-1078-
1201-1231-1232-1233
HARRIS, Albert vn 919
HARRIS, Albert g 3-24-25-192-281-282-
384-554-583-683-688-938-995-996-1207-
1306-1396-1431-1432-1508-1519-1552-
1749-1750
HARRIS, Alfoncy v 683
HARRIS, Arville cl-as-ts 99-118-253-254
255-256-257-352-731-775-1014-1168-1534-
1559-1623-1701-1702-1703-1704-1705-1706
1707
HARRIS, Benny t 761
HARRIS, Bethenea v 683
HARRIS, Bob "Baldy" cl-as 1616
HARRIS, Charles tb 1179-1330
HARRIS, Charles t-cl-as-ts 353-553-665-
709-1099-1266-1550
HARRIS, Charles E. d 11
HARRIS, Clarence as 704-705-1648
HARRIS, Cy bb 1330
HARRIS, D. v 1574
HARRIS, Dave ts 205-1032-1371-1372-1373
1720
HARRIS, Elsa v 741
HARRIS, Elton Spivey v 1751
HARRIS, Frank - see KAUFMAN, IRVING
HARRIS, George a 166
HARRIS, Jack vn 629-630-684
HARRIS, James t 693
HARRIS, Jimmy t 683
HARRIS, Joe t 1047
HARRIS, Joe tb-v 365-595-596-597-598-
658-905-1036-1037-1116-1235-1236-1570-
1571
HARRIS, L. D. t 155
HARRIS, Lazy g 844
HARRIS, Leroy cl-as-bj-g-v 136-730-759-
760-761-762-939-1168-1507-1534-1559-
1700-1701-1702-1703-1704-1705-1706-1707
HARRIS, Peter v 627
HARRIS, Phil v 685-686

HARRIS, Richard  tb  693-694
HARRIS, Roosevelt  as  1719
HARRIS, Sally Ann  v  1562
HARRIS, Sam  g  543-1025
HARRIS, Sidney  vn  220-221-222-223-224-
  243-245-246-247-1620-1621
HARRIS, Slim  t  851
HARRIS, Tasso  tb  1552-1553-1554
HARRIS, Tom  cl-ss-as  87-943
HARRIS, Warren  bj  1426
HARRIS, William "Weedy"  cl-as  1648
HARRISON, Charles  v  578
HARRISON, George  as  316
HARRISON, Jimmy  tb-v  149-312-472-562-
  645-720-721-722-723-724- 806-833-1013-
  1436-1444-1534-1657-1700
HARRISON, Jules  as  1075
HARRISON, Len  sb  272-283-518-1341-1342-
  1632-1647
HARROD, Ben  bar  701-702
HARRY, Jim  cl-ts  565-566
HARSHMAN, A.  vl  1407-1408
HART, Arthur  v  1611
HART, Bill  d  1537
HART, Charles  v  231-267
HART, Clyde  p-g  14-131-153-251-252-273-
  383-466-660-661-662-767-836-1070-1240-
  1304-1465
HART, Doc  t  410
HART, Forrest  bj-g  1472
HART, Gloria  v  1374-1375
HART, Hattie  v  1042-1043
HART, Larry  cl  1180
HART, Phil  t  130-131-161-238-365-366-
  573-1077-1078
HARTMAN, Charles  tb  802-1122-1123-1208
HARTMAN, Fred  cl-as  1330
HARTMAN, George  t  687
HARTMAN, Lennie  cl-as-ts  1242-1243-1691
HARTMAN, Regis  tb  833
HARTT, Richard C.  v  657
HARTWELL, Jimmy  cl-as  1741
HARTY, Bill  d-dir  140-148-163-192-427-
  459-539-581-684-687-789-790-801-917-953
  969-1070-1127-1128-1148-1149-1150-1226-
  1507-1508
HARVEY, Aaron  s  277
HARVEY, Chick  bb-v  32-33-1573
HARVEY, King  g-v  1146-1147
HARY, Charles  ts  519
HASSEL, Pete  bb  1507
HASSLER, Bud  cl-as  32-33-1573
HASTON, Gus  as-ts-bj-v  687-1603
HATCH, Earl  p-pac  867
HATCH, Ike  bj-v  665-666-687-688
HATCH, Tom  d  29-152
HATFIELD, Boots ?  547
HATFIELD, Ernie  d  529
HATFIELD, Ted  p-v  391
HAUGHEY, Kenneth  tb  208-209
HAUGHTON, Chauncey  cl-as  252-258-259-284
  500-527-528-775-1427-1660
HAUGHTON, John  tb  191-527-695-696-1632-
  1646-1647-1697
HAUKENHEISER, ——  t  1392
HAUPRICH, Victor  cl-as  360-858-859
HAUPT, Hank  as  702-703-1561
HAUSER, Johnny  v  123-795-1416-1689
HAVLICHECK, Pete  tb  1162
HAWKES, Jason  v  930

HAWKINS, Coleman  cl-ts-bsx  12  -108-
  178-179-283-312-593-662-688-711-712-713
  714-715-716-717-718-719-720-721-722-723
  724-725-726-727-730-732-749-750-770-791
  792-801-966-1030-1034-1037-1048-1113-
  1114-1256-1263-1267-1440-1442-1444-1448
  1462-1463-1520-1534-1594-1650-1700-1702
  1728
HAWKINS, Erskine  t-a-ldr  691-692-693-
  694
HAWKINS, Ralph  d  63-814-815
HAWKINS, Walter  cl-as-ts-bar  1472
HAWLEY, Bill  v  694
HAWORSKI, Henry  vn  59
HAYDEN, Earl  v  1574
HAYES, Bob  cl-ss-as-ts  188
HAYES, Clancy  bj-v  1656
HAYES, Clifford  as-vn-speech  320-409-
  519-556-685-694-695-891-1012-1164-1328
HAYES, Curtis  bj  320-409-1164
HAYES, Ed  bb  50
HAYES, Edgar  p-ldr-a  13-14-285-318-695-
  696-1071-1072-1073-1074
HAYES, Harry  cl-as  16-279-316-383-384-
  468-469-470-518-563-964-1039-1224-1432-
  1584-1695
HAYES, Mutt (r.n. Vernon H.)  cl-as-ts
  33-61-84-200-963-1347-1348-1524-1538-
  1571-1751
HAYES, Nap  v-g-md-v  696
HAYES, Ralph  t  391
HAYES, Thamon  tb  164-177-1109-1111-1112
HAYMAN, Joe  as-ts-bar  959-960-1642
HAYMER, Herbie  ts  78-429-430-431-432-
  433-434-435-436-545-553-742-743-744-
  1075-1156-1157-1231-1313
HAYMES, Dick  v  455-622-816-817-818
HAYMES, Joe  v-a-dir  455-697-698-699-700
  701-702-703-1561
HAYNES, ——  tb  332
HAYNES, Cyril  p-a  342-749-1721
HAYNES, Daniel L.  v  1285
HAYNES, Kermit  sb  1194
HAYNES, Orville  bb  999-1288
HAYNES, Ronald  ts  913-1075
HAYTON, Lennie  p-cel-or-harmonium-timps-
  a  117-239-304-361-648-703-704-1017-
  1064-1079-1088-1139-1140-1193-1223-1408
  1568-1569-1570-1598-1599-1612-1613-1685
  1686-1687
HAYWARD, Charlie  v  1655
HAYWOOD, John  bb-vn  378-379-380
HAYWOOD, Nicholas  v  1194
HAYWORTH, Herb  bj  1524
HAZEL, Monk  c-mel-d-v  270-704-802-1196-
  1208
HAZLETT, Chester  cl-bcl-as  33-76-84-159
  200-211-1325-1512-1538-1567-1680-1681-
  1682-1683-1684-1685-1686-1687-1688-1751
HEADLINERS, THE  v  701-702
HEAGNEY, Billy  v  631
HEALY, Peggy  v  1688-1689
HEARD, ——  ts  863
HEARD, J. C.  d  114-208-284-619-691-769-
  770-1247-1371-1735-1736-1737
HEATH, Bert  t  639-798-799-1493
HEATH, Helen  v  92
HEATH, Jesse Ray  tb  788-1242
HEATH, Ted  tb-a  16-20-21-22-23-30-61-
  134-147-148-161-274-281-306-345-393-403
  507-523-524-537-554- (cont. on p. 1790)

1790

HEATH, Ted (cont.)  639-667-895-903-950-
951-952-953-964-1055-1224-1274-1298-
1432-1492-1493-1695
HEATHCOCK, `Bill  tb  1117`
HEATHER, Cliff  tb  203-320-321-923-1548
HEATHERTON, Ray  v  35
HEDEN, Gosta  d  282
HEFTI, Neal  t  98
HEGAMIN, Bill  p  704-705
HEGAMIN, Lucille  v  704-705-706-707
HEGEMAN-LARSEN, Henry  cl-ts  1585
HEGLIN, Wally  g  159-642
HEIDKE, Clarence  cl-ss-as  926-927-934-
1039
HEIGER, Sid  d  279-554-1298-1434-1692
HEILBRON, Fritz  t-v  553
HEIMAL, Otto "Coco"  g  64-270
HEIN, Wes  tb  78-79-1158-1228
HEINEMANN, Heinz  ts  151
HEINES, Fran  v  816
HEISS, Sammy  bb  1680
HEISTER, Al  t  416
HELFER, John  cl-as-ts  31-506-507-524-
525-949-950-951-952-1126-1127-1217-1290
1291-1292-1293-1294-1738
HELIAN, Jacques  ts  188
HELLEBERG, Gus  bb  90-1330-1387-1388
HELLEBERG, John  bb-sb  36-349-350-676-
1330-1379-1544
HELLER, Benny  g  449-505-506-608-609-610
611-612-816-817-818-819-820-1242
HELLIER, Cyril  vn  525-656-801-1336
HELMS, Slick  p  1454-1471-1586
HELSMORTE, Martin  c  1120
HEMINGWAY, Jane  p  1723
HEMMINGS, Will  sb  87-140-581-589-590-
591-684-964
HEMPHILL, Bob  g  163-1237
HEMPHILL, Shelton  t  54-55-56-57-58-285-
695-1071-1072-1073-1074-1443-1657
HENDERSON, Alma  v  `708
HENDERSON, Bertha  v  709
HENDERSON, Bob  p  392-1272
HENDERSON, Catherine  v  709
HENDERSON, Charles  p  1641
HENDERSON, Edmonia  v  709
HENDERSON, Fletcher  p-u-dir-a  75-91-
143-166-178-179-190-353-355-360-396-397
433-522-596-597-598-599-600-601-602-603
604-605-606-607-608-609-610-611-612-613
614-615-616-617-622-623-632-704-710-711
712-713-714-715-716-717-718-719-720-721
722-723-724-725-726-727-728-729-730-731
732-733-749-750-763-792-793-801-810-821
860-861-946-1023-1024-1037-1048-1050-
1051-1056-1057-1089-1266-1267-1304-1350
1439-1440-1441-1442-1443-1444-1447-1448
1449-1450-1466-1467-1510-1519-1520-1617
1648-1649-1650-1651-1671-1692-1716-1717
1725-1727-1728-1729
HENDERSON, Horace  p-a  12-13-92-97-98-
131-312-360-595-596-597-598-604-605-606
632-688-724-726-727-728-730-760-935-
1276-1277
HENDERSON, Jack  cl-as-ts  92-324-616-617
618
HENDERSON, Katherine  v  731-1701
HENDERSON, Kid  c  1267
HENDERSON, Leora  t  726
HENDERSON, Lil  p  1266-1267
HENDERSON, Lou  t  919

HENDERSON, Luther  t  863
HENDERSON, Lyle  p  1406
HENDERSON, Norwood  t  418
HENDERSON, Richmond  tb  944
HENDERSON, Rosa  p-v  731-732-733-734-735
HENDRICK, Clyde  t  `338
HENDRICKS, Ray  v  594
HENDRICKSON, Al  g-elg  1407-1408-1575
HENDRICKSON, Henny (r.n. Clarence H.)
cl-ss-a  736
HENDRICKSON, Norman  tb  28-1047
HENEMANN, Harry  p  919
HENKE, Mel  p  394-736
HENKEL, George  ss-as-f  1171-1172
HENLEY, John  g  1154-1210
HENNER, Stuart  bj  577
HENNING, Hub  tb  1616
HENRY, Eric  p-d  1465-1468
HENRY, Francis  bj-g  970-971-976
HENRY, Frank  tb  1271
HENRY, Fred  d  220-221-222-223
HENRY, Heywood  cl-bar  691-692-693-694
HENRY, Irish  bb  576-577
HENRY, Pat  v  880
HENRY, Reece  t  884-1120
HENRY, Simeon  p  1676
HENRY, Tal  vn-ldr  737
HENSON, Harold  as-vc-sb  1459
HENSON, Harry  bb-sb  128
HERBERT, Arthur  d-v  115-164-459-690-
1396
HERBERT, Bill  bj-g  302-459-500-784-785
800-1507
HERBERT, Elisha  t  676-862
HERBERT, Hector  cl-as-ts  1347
HERBERT, Melvin  t  806-807-1123-1124-
1338
HERBIN, Frank  p  738-1364-1365-1521
HERBUVÉAUX, Jules  dir  646
HERDE, Joe  cl-as  416-417-1482
HERDELL, Wayne  p-a  208-209-417
HEREFORD, Fletcher  cl-as-ts  207-979-
1272-1438
HEREFORD, Frances  v  738
HERFURT, Skeets (r.n. Arthur H.)  cl-as-
ts-v-a  53-320-321-322-362-424-425-426
427-428-442-443-444-445-446-447-1033-
1329
HERLIHY, Joe  p-ldr  738
HERLIHY, Walter  bj  738
HERLIN, Ken  tb-v  1045-1469-1470
HERMAN, Dave  vn  993
HERMAN, Max  t  62-183-363-364-365-371-
372-373-374-375-376-702-703
HERMAN, Oscar  p  464
HERMAN, Woody (r.n. Woodrow H.)  cl-as-
bar-v-ldr  163-360-364-738-739-740-741
742-743-744-859
HERNANDEZ, Ray (r.n. Ramon H.)  cl-ts
564-1362
HERRICK, Les  t  417
HERRICK, Sherman  t  1472
HERRIFORD, Leon  cl-as  47-177
HERSDORF, Charlie  d-k  546-796-797
HERTH, Milt  elo  745-746-747
HERZER, Glenn  vn  817-818
HESS, Julian  t  2
HESTER, Gwynn  bj  547
HEUTSCHEL, ——  t  16
HEXTER, Paul  p  89
HEYWOOD, Eddie, Jr.  p  283-795-905

HEYWOOD, Eddie  p-v  82-212-213-214-279-
343-357-358-544-627-681-682-709-736-
737-747-748-770-1013-1021-1213-1263-
1513-1617
HIBBELER, Al  v  1038
HIBBERD, Billie  v  1137
HIBBERT, Hugh  cl-as  785-786
HIBNER, John  as-bar  133
HICKS, Art  vn-v-dir  314-315
HICKS, Benbow  v  66
HICKS, Billy  t-v  50-102-141-179-749-
1337-1721
HICKS, Bud  bb  1119
HICKS, Henry  tb  47-285-392-868-1071-
1072-1073-1119-1431
HICKS, Otis  ts  646-1560-1561
HICKS, Robert  t  1561
HICKS, William  t  1516-1517
HIGGINBOTHAM, J. C.  tb-v  11-12-13-14-15
40-45-46-54-55-56-57-  75-114-281-355
534-633-662-667-688-690-725-726-751-776
837-839-854-966-1048-1053-1073-1074-
1103-1169-1240-1256-1257-1345-1346-1408
1488-1624
HIGGINS, Billy ("Jazz Casper")  v  182-
1024-1058-1094-1218
HIGGINS, George  g  665-666
HIGGINS, Henry  c-dir  1473
HIGGS, Billy  t  790-791-1365
HIGHTOWER, Willie  t  404-752
HIGLEY, M. E. "Whitey"  d  1362
HIGMAN, Fred  cl-ts  970-971-976
HILAIRE, Andrew  d-v  338-1101
HILDEGARDE  v  1211
HILDYARD, John d'Arcy  t  467-1089
HILL, Alex  p-v-a  44-191-327-335-567-752
757-767-782-1052-1073-1074-1151-1152-
1452-1615-1627-1744
HILL, Alfred  sb  1036
HILL, Art  tb  856
HILL, Benny  d  50
HILL, Bill  as  405
HILL, Billy  p  801
HILL, Bob  bb-sb  418-881
HILL, Charlie  g  1065
HILL, Cliff  sb  622-623
HILL, Elton  a  107-909-910-911-912
HILL, Ernest  hb-sb  12-191-281-312-382-
383-791-792-1008-1204-1247-1477
HILL, Eugene  d  214
HILL, George  ts  1237
HILL, Herb  bb  356
HILL, Howard  g  1104-1427
HILL, Jack  cl-as  738
HILL, Jack  bj-g  470-801-917-1226-1227-
1493
HILL, Jimmy  cl-as  1697
HILL, Leroy  t  1116
HILL, Lethia  v  1524
HILL, Milton  a  988
HILL, Ray  ts  1246
HILL, Ruth  harp  454-455
HILL, Teddy  cl-ts-bar-ldr  11-12-45-46-
208-755-756-1169-1345
HILL, Tony  bj  1507
HILLIAM, C. B.  bar-bsx-a  1662
HILLIARD, Bill  bb  541
HILLIARD, Harriet  v  1124
HILLIARD, Lee  as  1563-1564
HILLMAN, Charles  p  665-1010

HILLMAN, Roc (r.n. Roscoe H.)  g-v  53-
362-424-425-426-427-428-429-430-431-
432-433-1329
HILLPOT, Billy  v  129-130-1222-1597-
1610-1648
HINCHLIFFE, Edwin  bsn  1019-1216
HINES, Babe  v  1560
HINES, Earl  p-cel-v-speech  41-43-44-
114-314-401-414-694-695-757-758-759-
760-761-762-852-945-1151-1154-1220-
1294-1421
HINES, Harry  cl-as  22-459-789-790-791-
953-1127-1128-1148
HINES, Wes  tb  9
HINKSON, Bruce  vn  558-1274
HINRICHS, Henk  t  161-689
HINSBY, Tommy  p  1202
HINTON, Albert  t  1507
HINTON, Jimmy  h-wb  1727
HINTON, Larry  d  1561-1634
HINTON, Milton  bb-sb  131-257-258-259-
260-261-262-661-662-1210-1476-1654-
1732-1735
HIRSCH, George  d  1249
HIRSCH, Godfrey  vib  756
HIRSCH, Sol  p  772
HIRST, Lou  v  1157
HITCH, Curtis  p-ldr  762
HITCHENOR, Joseph  656
HITE, Charles  cl-as  1108
HITE, Les  cl-as-bar-v-a-ldr  47-48-614-
615-616-762-763-1108-1485
HITE, Mattie or Nellie  p-v  763
HNIDA, George  sb  1032-1332-1333
HOAGLAND, Omar  ts  1368
HOBBS, Herb - see FIELDS, ARTHUR
HOBSON, Gerald  d  1123-1124-1497
HOBSON, Hank  sb  635
HOBSON, Homer  t  45-46-404-1208-1267
HOBSON, Ray  c  1209-1210
HOCHSTEIN, Abraham  vn  820
HODES, Art  p  764-765-999
HODGES, Johnny  cl-ss-as  27-77-358-475-
476-477-478-479-480-481-482-483-484-485
486-487-488-489-490-491-492-493-494-495
496-497-498-499-500-607-631-640-645-651
652-660-661-765-766-767-1075-1083-1168-
1431-1500-1653-1657-1711-1712-1731-1732
1733-1734
HODGES, Johnny  p-v  1376
HODGES, Joy  v  642
HODGKISS, Andy  t-a  539-656
HOEL, Ole  eu  1496
HOELLERHAGEN, Ernst  cl-as  190-689-960-961
HOEY, Jerry  cl-ss-as-vn  799
HOFFMAN, Biff  bb-v  563-564
HOFFMAN, Bill  sb  416-417-923
HOFFMAN, Harry  vn  33-61-157-158-159-160
161-200-202-361-503-659-673-674-805
822-1016-1120-1145-1312-1648-1653-1654-
1671-1696-1751
HOFFMAN, Louis  bj  418
HOFFMAN, Russ  cl-as  552
HOFFMAN, Sam  vn  1621
HOFFMAN, Wilbur  sb  1243
HOGAN, Ray  tb  18-775-1247-1637
HOGE, George  bj  552-553
HOKE, Pat  v  1444
HOLDEN, Frank  bb  1203
HOLDEN, Lou  v  767

1792
HOLDER, Mike  tb-bb  884
HOLDT, Hans  bb-sb  171
HOLIDAY, Billie  v  102-593-767-768-769-
  770-1403-1691-1730-1731-1732-1733-1734-
  1735
HOLIDAY, Clarence  bj-g-v  281-312-382
  723-724-725-726-779-1278
HOLLAND, Charles  v  281-727
HOLLAND, Milton  d  1374-1375
HOLLAND, Peanuts  (r.n. Michael H.)  t-v
  99-729-1564
HOLLENBECK, Ralph  t  785-786-889
HOLLEY, Rosa  v  770
HOLLIDAY, Bert  bb  410
HOLLIDAY, Cyril  g  684
HOLLIER, Ken  ts  550
HOLLING, Gene  p  383
HOLLON, Kenneth  ts  550-769-832-864-865-
  1135
HOLLOWAY, Mike  bj  1208
HOLLY, Philmore  cl  1749
HOLM, Stig  p  282
HOLMAN, Alex  ts  1327
HOLMAN, Cliff  cl-as  32-1175
HOLMAN, Libby  v  351-676-771
HOLMES, Bobby  cl-as  47-169-1169-1170-
  1171-1507-1715-1716
HOLMES, Charlie  cl-ss-as-ts  11-12-45-46
  52-53-54-55-56-57-285-358-382-392-539-
  751-838-868-1071-1072-1119-1345-1346-
  1431-1486-1488-1497-1624-1712
HOLMES, Dick  - see KAUFMAN, IRVING
HOLMES, Horace  c  1024-1463-1650
HOLMES, Jack  t  685-686
HOLMES, Joe  cl-ts  657
HOLMES, Leroy  bj  1437
HOLST, Ernest  vn  972-973
HOLT, Allan  v  1690
HOLT, Bob  p  168
HOLT, Stanley C.  p  772
HOLT, Ted  cl-as-v  982
HOLTEN, Peck  p  1201
HOLTON, Frank  tb  1475
HOLTSWORTH, Charlie  t  772
HOLTSWORTH, Saxie  cl-ldr  772
HOLTZ, Fritz  cl-as-ts  1347
HOLZHAUS, Walter  t-v  59-361-1324-1325
HOMER, Ben  a  185-306-1242
HONEYCUTT, Red  t  547-886-887
HONORE, Gideon  p  863-1154-1155
HOOD, Harold  p  581-582-583-584-585-586-
  587-588-589-937
HOOD, Irwin  p  659
HOOKER, Jesse  cl-vc  543-1025
HOOKWAY, Warren  t  170-508-1120
HOOPER, Byron  c-t  796-797
HOOPER, Louis  p  154-306-313-343-531-541-
  547-548-566-643-733-744-745-872-1024-
  1025-1051-157-1058-1060-1090-1093-1094-
  1130-1218-1241-1257-1306-1326-1428-1453
  1463-1555-1556-1557-1651-1655-1717-1747
HOOVEN, Joe  t  579
HOOVEN, Maurice  bar  1361
HOPE, Joan  - see WRIGHT, EDYTHE
HOPE, Millicent  v  660
HOPFNER, Ray  as  98-163-739-740-741
HOPKINS, Claude  p-a-ldr  18-773-774-775-
  1010-1703
HOPKINS, Mae  v  278
HOPKINS, Sammy  p  778
HOPKINS, Sibyl  v  1329

HOPKINSON, George  f  801
HOPSON, Hop  p  1268
HORAK, Otto  t  151
HORLICK, Harry  vn  804
HORNBECK, Glenn  tb  271
HORNE, Ellis  cl  1656
HORNE, Gerry  tb  394
HORNE, Lena  v  97-98-945-1408-1427-1736
HORNSBY, Dan  v  1125
HOROWITZ, Irving  bcl-ts  81-207
HORSECROFT, Frank  d  1520-1521
HORSEY, Mabel  p  633-776-837-854
HORSLEY, Gus  bj-u-v  138-562-783-838
HORTON, Alf  t  1341-1342
HORTON, Hollis  t  962-1640
HORTON, Holly  g  1558
HORTON, Robert  tb  191-458-695-696-868-
  1712
HORVATH, Charles  d  576
HORVATH, Dick  sb  63
HORVATH, George  sb  1602
HORVATH, Jimmy  as  619-743-744
HORVATH, Lou  vn  818
HOSFELD, George  t  1360-1361
HOSKINS, Hervey  g  388
HOSKINS, James F./Jimmy  d  15-26-81-355-
  851
HOSTETTER, Joe  t-tb-v  76-93-286-287-879
HOUCK, Horace  c  577
HOUDINI, Wilmoth  v  778
HOUGHEY, Ken  tb  417
HOUGHINS, Buck  cl-ts  409
HOUSTON, Frank  d-v  1338
HOUSTON, Wyatt  vn  1093
HOWARD, Avery "Kid"  t-v  778
HOWARD, Bob  t  1068
HOWARD, Bob  (r.n. Howard Joyner)  p-v
  396-462-778-779-780-781
HOWARD, Charlie  elg  113
HOWARD, Darnell  cl-as-vn  133-466-633-
  665-752-758-759-776-837-873-1025-1044-
  1045-1101-1167-1210-1281-1345-1495
HOWARD, Don  v  17-1285-1383-1418
HOWARD, Eddie  v  782
HOWARD, Fred  cl-as  541-1459
HOWARD, Geoff  vn  801-1336
HOWARD, George  v  894
HOWARD, Harry  p  895-1265-1363
HOWARD, Helen  v  1749
HOWARD, Jack  as  748-1123
HOWARD, Jane  v  540-782
HOWARD, Joe  bb  391-457
HOWARD, Joe  v  881
HOWARD, Kenneth  t  317
HOWARD, Oscar  t  1118
HOWARD, Paul  cl-ts  177-782
HOWARD, Rosetta  v  783
HOWARD, Shirley  v  185
HOWARD, Sonny  g  59
HOWARD, Stanley  t  801
HOWARD, Thomas  tb  1092
HOWARD, Walter  jug-v  530-531
HOWARD, William "Buddy"  tb-v-dir  138
HOWE, Dorothy  v  1400
HOWE, George  d  1742
HOWE, Jack  ts  1253
HOWELL, Bert  vn-u-v  343-460-783-1529
HOWELL, Earlene  696
HOWELL, George  d  1460
HOWELL, Ghost  sb-v  563-1645-1646-1647
HOWELL, Lee  tb-v  316

HOWELL, Tom c-t-v 316-553
HOWER, Frank W. p 1641
HOWES, Bobby v 784
HOWSON, Douglas d 855
HOY, Herman bb 318
HOY, William d 1310
HUBER, Frank bj 188
HUBER, Ted tb 1722
HUCKO, Peanuts (r.n. Michael H.) cl-ts
165-166-167-168-307-829
HUDSON, Bob p-v 784-1044-1045
HUDSON, Charlie d 737
HUDSON, Ed bj-v 1495
HUDSON, Eli dir 139-1216-1217
HUDSON, George t 830-1564
HUDSON, Harry p-v-ldr 302-784-785
HUDSON, Joe d 316
HUDSON, Pres as 417
HUDSON, Will a 256-594-727-785-786-787-
788-983-988-989-1074-1601
HUFF, Bob t 356
HUFFINE, Charles t 94-95-517
HUFFMAN, Joe cl-as-ts 165-166-685-686
HUG, Armand p 153
HUGHES, Barbara v 1606
HUGHES, Bill p 1047
HUGHES, Don bb 1347
HUGHES, Ernie p 364-1003-1540-1541
HUGHES, Frank cl 1019-1216
HUGHES, Glenn as 1507
HUGHES, Herman v 1623
HUGHES, Lyle bj-g 540
HUGHES, Phil - see ROBERTSON, DICK
HUGHES, Spike (r.n. Patrick H.) sb-harm-
onium 61-132-359-427-788-789-790-791-
792-812-917-1953-1127-1148-1165
HUGHES, Thomas cl 1250-1251-1252-1586-
1587
HUISMAN, Joop cl-as 161
HULL, Harry bb-sb 164-458-459-562-838-
1184-1445-1724
HULME, Freddy t 1348
HULS, Eugene bj 133
HUMBY, Joe g 1030
HUMES, Ed t 851
HUMES, Helen v 101-103-104-105-106-107-
108-187-813-814
HUMES, Tyree tb 851
HUMMEL, Fritz tb 76-291-292-293-294-
1688
HUMPHREY, Dick bj 920-921
HUMPHREY, Earl tb 391-457
HUMPHREY, Willie cl-as 14-807
HUMPHREYS, Conn cl-as 97-98-99-1148-
1154
HUMPHREYS, Holly t 1124-1125
HUMPHRIES, John d 533
HUMPHRIES, Olly bj 887-888
HUNKLER, Joe as 1179
HUNT, Alex tb 1723
HUNT, Frances v 600-1236-1733
HUNT, George tb 101-102-761-762
HUNT, Len d 1219
HUNT, Louis t 50-1657
HUNT, Pee Wee (r.n. Walter H.) tb-v 56-
76-209-286-287-288-289-290-2 1-292-293-
294-295-296-297-298-299-300-396-579-680
HUNT, Ted cl-as 1327
HUNTER, Alberta v 792-793-794-795-809-
810-1280
HUNTER, Bud cl-ts 812

HUNTER, Harry bar 348
HUNTER, Lloyd t 792
HUNTER, Pinkey bj-v 565-566
HUNTINGTON, Laurie d 1363
HUPFER, Nick vn 738-739
HURD, Danny a 1553
HURD, Roger cl-ts 763
HURLEY, Clyde t 163-450-451-1237
HURLEY, George vn 469-470-789-1485-
1738
HURST, Geirge t 1662
HURST, Tex sb 1438
HURT, Al v 664
HURT, Kenneth as 1288
HURT, Martin v 1568
HURVITZ, Melvin v 184
HUSSIN, Links as-f 1563
HUTCHEON, Bill d 532
HUTCHINGSON, Bob t-v 316
HUTCHINRIDER, Clarence cl-as-v 56-76-
287-288-289-295-296-297-298-299-300-
1615
HUTCHINS, Clarence ts-bar 558-559
HUTCHINSON, ---- cl-as 863
HUTCHINSON, Eddie t 664
HUTCHINSON, Lavert bb 47
HUTCHINSON, Leslie A. ("Hutch") p 330-
1050-1096-1463
HUTCHINSON, Leslie "Jiver" t 822-841-
1225
HUTCHISON, C. L. c 1327-1328
HUTSELL, Bob cl-as 578-579-1369
HUTT, Eugene t 1501
HUTTNER, ---- tb 1575
HUTTON, Will (r.n. Wilton H.) t 307-
788-1753
HUXLEY, Carroll p 579-580
HYAMS, Mark p 785-786-787-788-1116-1117
HYBDA, Harry p-cel 1361
HYDE, Alex vn-v-effects-ldr 796-797
HYDE, Herman as-vn 1
HYDE, Pat pac-v 797-798
HYLAND, Bill t 78-1157
HYLTON, Jack p-ldr-v 798-799-800-801-
802
HYMAN, John (r.n. John Wiggs) c 802-
1208-1510

IANNONE, Mickey tb 417-1361
IDAHO, Bertha v 802
IDSEN, Charlie t 1528
IMBERMAN, James cl-ss-as-ts 2
IMES, Marlo tb 59
IMPEY, Norman ts 536-895
INGE, Edward cl-as-ts-a 12-360-901-902-
935-988-1035-1099-1276-1277-1278-1279-
1421-1628-1720
INGEVELDT, Victor ts 1284
INGLE, Red (r.n. Ernest I.) cl-as-ts-vn-
578-1668-1669
INGMAN, Dan d 470-515
INGRAM, Johnny as 1028
INGRAM, Roy v 831
INTLEHOUSE, Ernie t 558-559
IONA, Andy vn-stg-u-v 53-54-1108
IOOSS, Walter sb 619
IPPOLITO, Danny cl-ts 417
IRICK, Seymour t 343-538-539-704-705-
830
IRISH, Carl cl-ss-as 1120
IRISH, George ts 284-1735-1736

1794

IRISH, Mace  cl-as  979
IRRLICHT, U.  vn  1662
IRVIN, Kitty  v  805
IRVIN, Wally  d  209
IRVIN, William  t  182
IRVINE, Walt  tb-d  89
IRVING, Milton  - see MILLS, IRVING
IRVIS, Charlie  tb  136-179-313-472-794-
835-845-965-1012-1013-1014-1021-1022-
1096-1103-1280-1438-1457-1463-1471-1532
1533-1534-1617-1622-1623-1699-1700-1701
1702-1739
IRWIN, Cecil  cl-ts-a  327-404-752-757-
758-759-873-1169
IRWIN, Vic  p  805
ISAACS, Hank  d  1037
ISAACS, Russ  d  441-1358-1359-1360-1361
ISADOR, George  tb  859-1040
ISGROW, Tino  ts  1243
ISON, Earle  t  1179
IVORY, Tom  bj  138
IVY, Claude  p-chimes  2-132-359-427-507-
789-791-799-949-950-951-952-953-1164-
1154-1219-1362-1365-1366-1493


JAANG, Harald  d  1223
JACK, James  d  1432
JACKDAWS, The  v  587
JACKSON, Al ?  391
JACKSON, Alex  v-ldr  806
JACKSON, Alex S.  bsx  1463-1650-1651
JACKSON, Andy  bj-g  251-695-806-807
JACKSON, Benny  bj-g-v  312-328-834
JACKSON, Chicken (r.n. Charles)  wb  381
JACKSON, Charles  bj  1615
JACKSON, Charles E.  vn  458-1649-1692
JACKSON 'Papa' Charlie  bj-v  353-354-891
1209-1269-1744
JACKSON, Charlie  bsx-bb  1166
JACKSON, Cliff  p-cymbal  114-115-122-343
355-462-643-733-734-763-806-807-861-917
1024-1057-1119-1392-1728-1729
JACKSON, Dentist  g-v  1026
JACKSON, Dewey  c  28-359-688-807-979-1065
JACKSON, Edwin  d  165-1614-1615
JACKSON, Ellis  tb-v  346-347-348-1613-
1614
JACKSON, Fletcher  v  1670
JACKSON, Frank  ts  466
JACKSON, Franz  cl-as-ts-a  761-808-1282-
1344
JACKSON, Fred  ts  1693
JACKSON, Graham  p  1388
JACKSON, Hambone  - see ROBINSON, IKEY
JACKSON, Harrison  cl-as  1203
JACKSON, Harry  t-a  991
JACKSON, Pee Wee (r.n. Harry)  t  730-759
761-762
JACKSON, Harry  cl-as  40-808-809
JACKSON, Heyward/Heywood  k-v  1252-1670
JACKSON, Howard  p  317
JACKSON, Jack  t-v  359-468-788-789-799-
800-809-810-917-953-1070-1127-1214-1356
JACKSON, Jackie  bj  557
JACKSON, James  bb  782
JACKSON, Jim  g-v  180
JACKSON, Jim  d  1347
JACKSON, John  - see GOODMAN, BENNY
JACKSON, John  as  1038
JACKSON, King  tb  505-1004
JACKSON, Lal  bj-g  346-347

JACKSON, Major  tb  1516-1517
JACKSON, Mary  v  810
JACKSON, Mike  p-v  285-313-408-562-564-
782-795-810-835-846-941-1096-1097-1121
1128-1184-1246-1323-1450-1453-1458-
1463-1739
JACKSON, Preston  tb  48-49-50-415-753-
810-824-862-936-1025-1051-1154-1245-
1320-1345-1749
JACKSON, Quentin  tb-v  260-261-262-935-
1035-1278-1279
JACKSON, Robert "Eppie"  bb  1563-1564
JACKSON, Romayne  v  1203
JACKSON, Rudy  cl-as-ts  473-474-475-
1426-1427-1618
JACKSON, Sadie  v  811
JACKSON, Slick  t  1507
JACKSON, Chubby (r.n. Stewart)  sb  1373
1374
JACKSON, Willie  v  811-1168-1240-1742
JACKSON, Zaidee  v  812
JACOBS, A.  vn  1472
JACOBS, Dave  tb  437-445-446-447-448-
449-451-452-453-454-455-699-700-701
JACOBS, Howard  as  156-1363
JACOBS, John  d  881
JACOBS, Marty  p  747
JACOBS, Pete  d  773-774-775
JACOBS, Sid  sb  647-1003-1004
JACOBS, Sid  d  685-686-829
JACOBS, Vincent  fh  1553-1554
JACOBSON, Andrew  cl-ss-as  1285
JACOBSON, Bobby  t  943
JACOBSON, Bud  cl-ts  541-812 -1037-1546
JACOBSON, Harry  p-cel-v  521-581-1127-
1128 -1149-1492-1738
JACOBSON, Helge  g  82 -1585
JACOBSON, Jock  d  193-546-554-583-636-
1224-1432-1433-1508-1509-1585-1675
JACOBSON, John  t  1275
JACOBSON, Sidney  g  636-1508
JACOBY, Don  t  186
JACOBY, Elliott  g  2
JACQUEMONT, Georges  as-ts  171-519-1284
JACQUES, Larry  p  1498
JACQUET, Frank  tb  7
JACQUET, Illinois  ts  664
JACQUILLARD, Frank  sb  689
JACQUILLARD, Fred  sb  190
JAEGER, Albert  bb  1335
JAEGER, Harry  d  131-616-617-1148
JAFFA, Max  vn  684
JAFFE, George  t  704
JAFFE, Nat  p  29-56-94-1315-1360-1539-
1540
JAMES, Baby  c  516-834
JAMES, Benny  bj-g  285-651-944-1071-1072
1073-1657
JAMES, Billy  p-ldr  456-813
JAMES, David "Jelly"  tb  820-1507-1705-
1714-1715-1716
JAMES, Doris  v  67-890
JAMES, Elmer  bb-sb  13-14-150-75-281-
357-695-727-775-779-868-917-1053-1073-
1074-1456-1657
JAMES, George  cl-ss-as-bar-bsx  48-49-50
208-284-752 1070-1-91-1201-1456-1638-
1736
JAMES, Harold  cl-as  1548
JAMES, Harry  t-a-v  16-204-600-601-602-
603-604-605 (cont. on page 1795)
(cont. on page 1795)

JAMES, Harry (cont.) 661-813-814-815-
816-817-818-819-820-821-1048-1088-1236-
1732-1733-1735
JAMES, Ida Mae v 692-693-694-759
JAMES, Jesse tb 306-1497
JAMES, Joe t 164
JAMES, Lewis v 71-356-418-546-578-648-
1416-1581-1604-1610-1613
JAMES, Louis ts 391
JAMES, Ralph cl-as 1-179-1743
JAMES, Sadie v 821
JAMES, Willie B. g 847-1018-1376-1527-
1528
JANARRO, Mario p-cel 936-945-046
JANSON, Jean-Louis vn 556
JARI, Carmelo (alternatively spelt JAJO,
JEJO) cl-as-bar 411-651-721-722-944-
1362-1701
JARMAN, Lop (r.n. John J.) mel-eu 341-
1324
JARRETT, Art bj-g-v 822-1145-1146-1154
1570-1665-1666-1667
JARRY, Archie t 1332-1399
JARVIS, Jack sb 99-1116
JAWORSKI, Henry vn 59-159-642
JAXON, Frankie "Half-Pint" d-wb-v-ldr
327-328-822-823-824-825-831-1252-1322-
1526-1527
JAZZ CASPER - see HIGGINS, BILLY
JEAN, Loulie v 1274
JEANETTE, Joe cl-as-ts-f-a 20-21-22-23-
24-25-161-951-952-953-1224
JEAN-JEAN, Faustin t 571
JEAN-JEAN, Paul as 396-1173
JEDERBY, Thore sb 282-589
JEFFERSON, Clay d 1100
JEFFERSON, Fred p 1560
JEFFERSON, Hilton cl-as 12-13-260-261-
526-527-688-726-727-730-868-1035-1061-
1169-1170-1657-1661-1662-1730
JEFFERSON, Isaac p 1241
JEFFERSON, Kellough v 533
JEFFERSON, Maceo bj-g-v-ldr 52-172-658-
706-808-809-827-1230-1650
JEFFERSON, Viola v 730
JEFFRIES, Herb v 114-495-496-497-498-
499-500-758
JEFFRIES, Leslie vn-ldr 827-828
JEJO, Carmelo - see JARI, CARMELO
JENKINS, Al cl-as 798-799
JENKINS, Dub ? 391
JENKINS, Eddie d 126
JENKINS, Freddie t-fh-v 358-476-477-478
479-480-481-482-483-484-485-486-487-488
489-640-651-828-1075-1083-1119-1431-
1451-1500-1653
JENKINS, George d 664
JENKINS, Gordon a 858-859
JENKINS, Howard as 1146-1147
JENKINS, Jabbo t 395
JENKINS, Les tb 63-439-440-441-442-443-
444-445-450-451-452-6970698-1404-1405-
1406-1491
JENKINS, Myrtle p 1496
JENKINS, Pat t-v 342
JENKINS, Rex tb 404
JENKS, Frank tb 317
JENNER, Russ tb 92-858-859-1313
JENNEY, Bob tb-v 126-829-1552-1553
JENNEY, Brad tb 1064

JENNEY, Jack tb 82-201-204-207-360-829-
858-903-1028-1048-1063-1089-1156-1407-
1408-1409-1415-1718
JENNINGS, Al tb 111-126-840
JENNINGS, Sam v 646
JENNY, Bob - see JENNEY, BOB
JENSEN, Charles t 1357-1358
JENSEN, Christian p-sb 282-1585
JENSEN, John bb 1672
JENSSEN, Mel vn 76-286-287-288-289-290-
291-292-293-294-892
JENTES, Harry p 829
JEREMIAS, Carl t-ts 388-389
JERNBERG, George t 119-120-1348
JEROME, Jerry cl-ts 62-78-79-215-505-
506-610-611-612-613-614-615-616-622-661
662-663-1063-1064-1089-1158-1407-1408
JESSOP, Jesse p 356
JESSOP, Red tb-ldr 1-123-205-830-1415
JETER, H. Leonard vc 1652
JETER, James as 830- 1563-1564
JIMMICK, Harry tom-tom 1046
JOCKIN, Harry v 266-1504
JOHN, Murray v 1324
JOHNAKINS, Leslie as-bar-a 770-832-899-
1456-1537
JOHNS, Ed bb 923-1029
JOHNS, Harry d 884
JOHNS, Irving p 1439-1440
JOHNS, Pete ts 163-739-740
JOHNS, Russell ts 40
JOHNSON, A. J. p 154-155
JOHNSON, Albert "Budd" cl-ts-v 51-59-
615-661-663-759-760-941
JOHNSON, Ann v 180
JOHNSON, Archie t 251-252-1070
JOHNSON, Arnold ldr 831
JOHNSON, Bert tb 831-1246-1370
JOHNSON, Bill t 1247
JOHNSON, Bill cl 141
JOHNSON, Bill bj-sb-v 308-327-359-406-
414-415-642-823-831-1055-1165-1322-1495
1526-1527-1619
JOHNSON, Blanche v 831
JOHNSON, Bob t 395
JOHNSON, Bob cl-ss-as-ts 675-1749
JOHNSON, Bobby bj-g 526-806-833-866-
1099-1156-1446-1660-1661
JOHNSON, Bruce wb-v 6-358-411-1431-1647
1710
JOHNSON, Bud v 1118
JOHNSON, Buddy p-v-ldr 832-1561
JOHNSON, Buddy d 1498
JOHNSON, Buster tb 1335-1680
JOHNSON, Buster g 389
JOHNSON, Caroline v 833
JOHNSON, Charles cl-as 1209-1210
JOHNSON, Charles g 1655
JOHNSON, Charlie t 1-179-472-518-1536
JOHNSON, Charlie p-ldr 806-833-1492
JOHNSON, Charlie d 1603
JOHNSON, Chink (r.n. Douglas J.) tb 390-
792-1648-1649
JOHNSON, Chink ts 565
JOHNSON, Chink bb 1460
JOHNSON, Christopher as 310
JOHNSON, Clarence p 169-749-864-1010-
1059-1060-1069-1092-1499-1511-1531
JOHNSON, Cliff cl-ts 630
JOHNSON, Dave tb 1515

1796

JOHNSON, Dennis d 378-379-380
JOHNSON, Dick cl-as-ts-dir 37-38-72-73-
74-304-306-532-559-560-561-777-804-870-
927-928-1246-1420-1482-1483
JOHNSON, Ding cl-as-f-v 881
JOHNSON, Dink cl-d 359-456-942-1485
JOHNSON, Ed tb 1116
JOHNSON, Eddie p 834
JOHNSON, Eddie k-v 1670
JOHNSON, Edith p-v 328-834
JOHNSON, Edna v 835
JOHNSON, Edward t 944
JOHNSON, Elizabeth v 835
JOHNSON, Ella v 832
JOHNSON, Elnora v 835
JOHNSON, Elvira v 835
JOHNSON, Emmett cl-as 851
JOHNSON, Freddy p-v 67-172-283-405-689-
690-827-835-836-1722-1742-1743
JOHNSON, Gene cl-as-bsx 179-773-774-775
1134-1436
JOHNSON, George t 1179
JOHNSON, George cl-as-ts 154-317-959-
960-1642-1741
JOHNSON, Gus d 1037-1038
JOHNSON, Hall - Choir 478
JOHNSON, Harold t-v 730-856-1124-1125-
1150
JOHNSON, Harry as 60
JOHNSON, Haven v 836
JOHNSON, Henry cl-Cm 1310
JOHNSON, Henry vn-vc 836-837
JOHNSON, Howard cl-as 281-730-755-756-
775-791-792-1670
JOHNSON, Ivory bb 138-208
JOHNSON, J. C. p-dir 119-121-320-344-
392-412-458-514-811-837-1091-1240-1273-
1452-1614-1649-1651-1705
JOHNSON, J. Rosamond choir-master 1445
JOHNSON, James p-cel 836-837-1065
JOHNSON, James sb 7
JOHNSON, James P. p-cel 165-280-344-355
357-459-514-645-670-672-735-811-837-838
839-939-978-1034-1035-1053-1129-1134-
1169-1184-1346-1444-1445-1446-1452-1465
1535-1576-1630-1652-1703-1704-1706-1708
1709-1711
JOHNSON, Mrs. James P. v 1630
JOHNSON, Jerry sb 1235
JOHNSON, Jimmy sb 913
JOHNSON, Johnny p-ldr 840
JOHNSON, K. D. p 841-995-1572-1573
JOHNSON, Keg (r.n. William J.) tb 13-51-
131-257-258-259-260-261-262-281-727
JOHNSON, Ken "Snakehips" dir 841
JOHNSON, Laurie vn-bj 347-348
JOHNSON, Lem cl-ts-v 115-459-841-864-
1247-1511-1560
JOHNSON, Lennie g 392
JOHNSON, Len d 1693
JOHNSON, Leroy g 842
JOHNSON, Lil v 842-843-844
JOHNSON, Lonnie bj-g-vn-v 42-43-45-311-
359-415-458-476-477-708-753-844-845-848-
1065-1154-1272-1376-1413-1452-1487-1488-
1542-1678-1707
JOHNSON, Lukie p 1458
JOHNSON, Maceo v 1623
JOHNSON, Manzie d-vib 12-39-40-115-192-
360-917-935-1053-1099-1103-1276-1277-
1278-1279

JOHNSON, Margaret v 845-846
JOHNSON, Margaret 'Queenie' p 768
JOHNSON, Marvin as 47-48-762-763
JOHNSON, Mary v 846-847
JOHNSON, Maxine v 808
JOHNSON, Merle cl-as 804
JOHNSON, Merline v 847-848-849-850
JOHNSON, Myra v 1377
JOHNSON, Otis t 12-46-56-57-191-281-
1278-1279-1345-1346
JOHNSON, Paul p 91-92
JOHNSON, Percy d 252-806-807-1742
JOHNSON, Pete p 814-821-850-851-947-
948-1203-1204-1575
JOHNSON, Puss d 1468
JOHNSON, Ray v 1143
JOHNSON, Roy cl-as-ts 1347
JOHNSON, Roy d-ldr 851
JOHNSON, Russell d 457
JOHNSON, Ruth v 852
JOHNSON, Dr Rhythm v-ldr 834
JOHNSON, Shorty d 111
JOHNSON, Silas cl-ts 851
JOHNSON, Stella v 852
JOHNSON, Stovepipe v 852
JOHNSON, Theo d 747
JOHNSON, Tillie v 852
JOHNSON, Tom dir 1119
JOHNSON, Walter p 1108-1118
JOHNSON, Walter d 12-13-14-67-75-281-
382-688-690-723-724-725-726-727-728-
729-730-775-1722
JOHNSON, Wesley t 380-704-705-1648
JOHNSON, Will bj-g-v 11-12-46-357-751-
1103-1169-1256-1257-1345-1346-1486-
1488-1624
JOHNSON, William as-a 691-692-693-694
JOHNSTON, Frank cl-as-o 1214
JOHNSTON, George ts 126
JOHNSTON, Glen as 890
JOHNSTON, Grace v 852-853
JOHNSTON, Ivan tb 236-238-1619
JOHNSTON, Jimmy bsx 145-319-572-1098-
1288-1299-1300-1305-1367-1396-1431
JOHNSTON, Merle cl-as 925-926-928-931-
1064-1381
JOHNSTON, Roy t 231-232-233-234-235-
242-967-1067-1068-1619-1620
JOHNSTON, Stanley d 1
JOHNSTON, T. K. v 554-555
JOHNSTON, Vic p 82
JONDRO, Charlie d 1120
JONES, Alberta v 854
JONES, Anna v 855
JONES, Archie tb 560-1482-1483
JONES, Art tb 856
JONES, Bill sb 1004
JONES, Billy p 855-1177
JONES, Billy d 1310
JONES, Billy v 38-70-71-229-231-233-
349-560-624-630-804-855-925-966-973-
1188-1189-1525
JONES, Bo g 1573
JONES, Bob v 152
JONES, Bobby t 76-286-287-288-289-290-
291-292-293-835-836-1068
JONES, Bobby cl-as-ts 1147-1148-1573
JONES, Broadway v 141
JONES, C. H. t 155
JONES, Calvin tb 141-142-1230-1727
JONES, Charlie cl-ts 47-48-762-763

JONES, Clarence M.  p-ldr  855-856-1092-1093-1245-1458
JONES, Clark  bj  460
JONES, Claude  tb-v  13-58-257-258-259-311-360-580-691-723-724-725-727-730-752-935-1033-1034-1107-1108-1276-1277-1278-1279-1658-1659
JONES, Cliff  d-k-v  753-1014-1065-1421-1495-1615
JONES, Clifton  as  1195
JONES, Danny  v  681
JONES, Darwin  as-v  944
JONES, Dave  cl-as-ts  349-863-1245
JONES, Dick  p-a  112-294-437-438-439-440-918
JONES, Dolly  c  1744
JONES, Don  tb  1206
JONES, Dot  v  856
JONES, Duke  sb  1246-1247
JONES, Edmund  d  1169-1170
JONES, Gordon  as  263
JONES, Harold  ts  1570-1571
JONES, Harvey  k  863
JONES, Henry  as  52-53-1171-1346-1707
JONES, Isham  ts-ldr  360-856-857-858-859
JONES, Jab  p-jug-v  1042-1043-1044
JONES, Jack  tb-vc  885-1215
JONES, Jack  as-md-v  111
JONES, Jack  bb  1075
JONES, Jack  v  1082
JONES, Jimmy  tb  941
JONES, Jimmy  p  1439-1440
JONES, Jimmy  sb  1427
JONES, Joe  bj  1436
JONES, Jo(e)  d  78-101-102-103-104-105-106-107-108-109-110-617-619-661-676-768-769-792-813-814-821-872-873-947-1129-1263-1337-1712-1732-1733-1734-1735
JONES, Jonah  t  40-261-262-284-660-767-836-1010-1240-1333-1464-1465-1673-1679-1731-1732-1734
JONES, Leroy  g  749-1720
JONES, Linley  d  62
JONES, Marcel  baritone voice  554-555
JONES, Maud  704-705
JONES, Nimrod  vn  378-379-380
JONES, Palmer  p  1610
JONES, Piccolo  as  1516
JONES, Ralph "Shrimp"  vn  343-1086-1230-1650
JONES, Reggie  bb  47
JONES, Reunald  t  40-192-1052-1278-1279-1658-1674
JONES, Richard  t  252
JONES, Richard M.  p-v  251-308-314-393-394-415-752-753-770-862-863-936-994-1014-1025-1026-1154-1167-1241-1320-1323-1344-1371-1595-1671-1677-1678
JONES, Romy  bb  1516-1517-1518
JONES, Russell  t  775
JONES, Seth  v  315
JONES, Slick  d-vib  272-382-662-821-1019-1279-1377-1629-1630-1631-1632-1633-1634-1635-1636-1637
JONES, Spike  (r.n. Linley J.)  d  276-363-555-969-1562
JONES, Stanley  tb  1229-1265
JONES, Truett  tb  814-815-816
JONES, Wallace  t  27-382-491-492-493-494-495
JONES, Walter  bj-g  773-774-775-1169

JONES, Wardell  t  285-496-497-498-499-500-1071-1072-1073-1074
JONES, Willie  d  856-863
JORDAN, ———  tb  752
JORDAN, Al  tb  908-909-910
JORDAN, Chuck  bb-sb  517-547-1045-1469-1470
JORDAN, Emmett  vn  401
JORDAN, Genevieve  v  864
JORDAN, Joe  t-v  1537
JORDAN, Joe  p-ldr  864
JORDAN, Johnny  g  208-209-417
JORDAN, Louis  cl-as-ts-bar-v  50-526-527-864-865-868-1511-1659-1660-1709-1710
JORDAN, Paul  vn-p-a  307-1409-1501
JORDAN, Rupert  bj  318
JORDAN, Sandy  d  547
JORDAN, Steve  g-v  166-168
JORDAN, Taft  t-v  6-191-526-527-528-563-866-1645-1646-1654-1658-1659-1660-1661-1662
JORDAN, Tommy - see JOHNSON, LONNIE
JORDY, Hal  cl-as-bar  188-704-999-1065-1196-1208-1249
JOSEPH, Ferdinand  v  302
JOSEPH, Harry  as  1657
JOSEPH, Willie  cl  337-391-457
JOURDAN, Andre  d  1262-1284-1339
JOUSTRA, Wilbur  ts  126
JOY, Jack  v  938
JOY, Leonard  dir  77-112-145-509-510-751-752-1272-1418-1456-1574-1610
JOYCE, Edward  cl-as  1172
JOYCE, Jerry  vn  1406
JOYCE, Teddy  vn-ldr  867
JOYCE, Vicki  v  429
JUDGE, Dick  v  1243-1244
JULIAN, Albert  g-v  873
JULIAN, Bob  g  647
JULIAN, Eddie  d  184-185
JULIAN, Les  vn  525-1336
JULIAN, Zeb  g  1003-1004-1243-1244-1374
JULIERIE, Francis  ts  172
JUZA, Ferri  tb  2

KAHANEN, Vern  as  1150
KAHN, Alfie  cl-ts  536-1632
KAHN, Art  p-ldr  868-869
KAHN, Joe  d  394-736
KAHN, Leo  p  20-1396-1456
KAHN, Roger Wolfe  as-ts-dir  870-871
KAHN, Walter  c-t  100-549-954-955-956
KAHN-A-SIRS, THE  v  871
KAISER, Elmer  dir  871
KALEY, Charles  vn-v  869-872-928-991-992-1611-1612
KALEY, Chuck  bj  1389-1390
KALLEN, Kitty  v  1539-1540
KALLENDER, Walter  as  796-797
KAMAR, Samuel  vn  326
KAMMERN, Henrietta  or  872
KAMINSKY, Max  t-dir  204-312-335-336-445-542-543-634-821-822-1007-1052-1289-1332-1346-1408-1409-1600-1637-1696
KAMPLAIN, Frank  v  1611
KANE, Bob  tb  1616
KANE, Sol  as-ts  8-9-621-622-1064
KANTOR, Ben  cl-as  162-163-594-1236-1237-1406
KAPLAN, Alf  p  1263

1798

KAPLAN, Delmar  sb  66-163-165-166-424-
425-426-633-1063-1089-1150-1562
KAPLAN, Herman  vn  205-905-1068
KAPLAN, Leon "Sleepy"  bj-g-vn  1068-
1069-1377-1570-1571
KAPLAN, Marty  sb  913
KARDOS, Gene  as-vn-v-dir  275-873-874-
875-876-877-878-879-880-881-1409-1410
KARLE, Art  ts  593-881-1653
KARR, Harry  cl-as-ts-f  684-801-938-
939
KASHMAN, Betty  v  881
KASSEL, Al  as  1562
KASSEL, Art  cl-as-ts-a-dir  120-121-868
881-1056-1193
KATES, Karl  as-ts  457-1482
KATZ, Al  d-a-ldr  165-882
KATZ, Dick  p  822
KATZMAN, Louis  t-vn-dir  19
KAUCHEK, Joe  sb  1160
KAUFMAN, Bernie  cl-as-ts  923-1512
KAUFMAN, Irving  v  16-20-70-71-74-128-
129-141-174-177-234-235-240-242-243-
244-245-269-273-418-420-421-552-557-
562-574-575-626-627-640-644-648-678-
882-883-887-891-914-927-928-930-932-
979-1029-1078-1079-1108-1225-1264-1300
1301-1338-1366-1367-1368-1369-1370-
1381-1383-1430-1431-1548-1567-1612-
1613-1619-1620-1740
KAUFMAN, Jack  v  73-74-129-236-269-456-
557-631-675-813-883-914-1046-1078-1080
1120-1122-1173-1324-1367-1393-1394-
1478-1581
KAUFMAN, Whitey  bj-dir  883-884
KAUGLIN, Reggie  d  1616
KAUPPI, Waino  c  1028
KAVASH, Len  cl-as  128-130-131-572-1222
KAVICH, Al  cl-as  1003
KAY, Carol  v  741
KAY, Dolly  v  560-561-1581
KAY, George - see KAUFMAN, IRVING
KAY, Howard  vn  1690
KAY, Lambdin  compere  1119
KAYE, Charlotte  v  1357
KAYE, Cyril  p  885
KAYE, Dave  p  1339-1340
KAYE, Sid  d  1375
KAZEBIER, Nate  t  433-434-435-436-505-
595-596-597-598-905-907-908-1116
KEARN, Jimmy  v  631
KEARNEY, Tike  p  264
KEARNS, Harry  t  1357-1358
KEARNS, Joe  as  363-367-368-369-370-371
KEATING, Harold  cl-ts  274
KEATING, Jimmy  v  417
KEATING TWINS, THE  v  1667
KEEGAN, Edwin  ts  829
KEENAN, Norman  sb  1712
KEENE, Kahn  tb  98-99
KEENE, Linda  v  646-704-946-1538
KEEP, Gladys  v  885
KEEP SHUFFLIN' TRIO, THE  v  838
KEGLEY, Charles  d  170-1256-1257
KEITH, Earl  cl-as  1092
KEITH, Jimmy  ts  944
KELLEHER, Jack  sb  452-1007-1482
KELLEHER, Jim  cl-as-dir  345-667-885-
903
KELLER, Fred  tb  1541

KELLER, Greta  v  886
KELLER, Nelson  t  1641
KELLER SISTERS AND LYNCH  v trio  129-577
KELLEY, George  ts-v  342
KELLEY, Gilbert  tb  1272
KELLEY, Joe  t  1272
KELLIHER, Jay  tb  909-910-911-912
KELLNER, Murray  vn  2-17-63-64-202-420-
501-502-503-509-516-567-668-751-752-771
803-853-929-1016-1065-1139-1140-1141-
1288-1323-1324-1415-1416-1417-1418-1425
1604-1610-1611-1614
KELLOGG, Edna  v  1604
KELLY, Al  d  577
KELLY, Andy  cl  1437
KELLY, Earl  tb  1299-1300
KELLY, Ed  ts  1097
KELLY, Eddie  v  886
KELLY, Ernest  tb  302
KELLY, Guy  c-t-v  26-302-824-1154
KELLY, Jack "Peacock"  d  869
KELLY, Jim  d  571
KELLY, May  v  886
KELLY, Monty  t  1691
KELLY, Pat  as  640-641
KELLY, Paula  v  416  1408-1409-1490
KELLY, Willis/Willie  t  320-321-513-553-
805-1373-1393
KELLY, Willie  p  859
KEMP, Hal  cl-ts-v-dir  419-886-887-888-
889
KENDIS, Al  d  505-1089
KENDLE, Ford  cl-as  399
KENDLE, Jack  tb  399
KENEKE, Emil  c  332-1254-1255-1256-1604-
1605
KENESTRICK, Paul  p  737
KENIN, Herman  dir  890
KENNEDY, Bob  t  1160
KENNEDY, Bud  v  1504
KENNEDY, Claude  p  1562
KENNEDY, George  t  93-1147
KENNEDY, George  bb  89
KENNEDY, Howard E.  bj-v  571
KENNEDY, Joe  v-dir  890
KENNEDY, Pat  v  1521-1752
KENNY, Adrian  as-bar  461
KENNY, Battle-Axe  d  512-513
KENNY, Kay  v  788
KENNY, Ken  d  1134
KENNY, Phyllis  v  9
KENT, Betty  v  536
KENT, Bryan  g  814-815-816
KENT, Dick  as-p-a  274-1378
KENTON, Art  cl-as-a  890-1051-1052
KENTON, Stan  p-a  59
KENTUCKY  k-jug  1526
KENWORTHY, Merritt  cl  558-559
KENYON, Frank  cl-as  347-348
KENYON, Reuel  p  1663
KEPPARD, Freddy  c  337-338-359-823-891-
1529-1536
KERDACHI, Billy  vn  1265
KERNS, ——  c  1289
KERR, Charlie  d-ldr  892
KERR, Doris  v  1063
KERSEY, Kenny  p-a  15-466-617-769-808-
902-1135-1712
KERSLAKE, Frank  v  1432-1433
KESSELL, Harry  v  264

KESSLER, Lou  bj  1232
KESSLER, Ralph  t  326
KESSLER, Willie  d  972-973
KETELBEY, Albert W.  cond  334
KETTERING, Dick  bj  1162
KETTLER, Paul  d  1228
KETTLEWELL, Frank  c  1019-1216
KETTRIDGE, L. H.  as  1089
KEWIS, Charlie  p  1284
KEYES, Billy  t  237
KEYES, Joe  t  101-251-459-1112
KEYES, Zip (r.n. Horace K)cl-ts  920-991-
    992-993
KIBURZ, John  f  1254-1255-1256
KIEFER, Joe  cl-as-ts  1573
KIEHN, Coco  as-ts  959-1211-1615
KIEVMAN, Louis  vl  1125
KIHULEIN, W. C.  tb  1028
KILANOSKI, Eddie  s-bj-a  1563
KILDAIRE, Walter  p  315-1084-1085
KILDUFF, Frank  cl-as-bar  561-1483
KILFEATHER, Eddie  p-a  1171-1172
KILGEN, Noel  g  248-249-1602-1752-1753
KILLIAN, Al  t  107-108-109-110-550-1279
KIM, Jack  t  1160
KIMBALL, Ellis  t  890
KIMBALL, Henry  bb  1004
KIMBALL, Narvin  bj  302
KIMMELL, Don  bj-g  274-1378
KINCAID, Nelson  cl-as-ts  665-1230-1423-
    1492
KINCAIDE, Deane  ts-a  161-162-365-366-
    441-444-445-446-447-448-449-452-555-593-
    594-739-1235-1236-1270
KINER, Charles  p  1375
KING, Al  c-t-v  241-242-243-363-626-627-
    1047-1184-1583-1593-1620
KING, Bertie  cl-ts  272-283-518-841
KING, Bill  cl-ss-ts  1309-1520-1521
KING, Bonnie  v  373-374
KING, Buzz  t  1375
KING, Clifford  c  1377
KING, Clifford  cl-bcl-as  337-338-1475-
    1476
KING, Cornelius  as  683-1674
KING, Donald  v  1035
KING, Eddie  p-cel-d  121-156-567-1109-
    1115-1177-1273-1282-1587-1606-1622
KING, Elmer  t  1194
KING, Felix  p  1083
KING, Frances  v  892
KING, Gene  dir  377
KING, Irene  v  316
KING, Jerry  tb  1550
KING, Joe  tb  806-1650
KING, Johnny  ts  218
KING, Leonard  sb  1753
KING, Lew  v  189
KING, Marty  tb  1201
KING, Maynard  as-vn  555
KING, Miff  tb  589-590-591
KING, Nora Lee  v  187-893-1457-1561
KING, Paul  t  899-900
KING, Paul  sb  361
KING, Stan  d-vib-k  5-28-33-53-66-67-77-
    84-134-145-156-157-158-159-160-161-194-
    198-199-200-202-205-223-224-225-226-227
    228-229-230-231-232-233-241-242-243-244
    245-246-247-248-262-265-305-351-361-392
    419-420-421-422-423-427-436-437-502-503
    504-529-530-623-624-626-627-633-659-671
    672-674-676-776-780-781-804-853-(cont.)

KING, Stan (cont.)  871-883-890-893-894-
    922-924-931-966-967-979-980-981-1027-
    1031-1032-1062-1064-1083-1087-1088-1095
    1098-1115-1117-1118-1120-1137-1145-1146
    1172-1193-1248-1300-1301-1302-1305-1308
    1312-1313-1314-1315-1323-1329-1332-1369
    1370-1381-1382-1383-1384-1391-1392-1393
    1394-1415-1422-1429-1438-1537-1546-1568
    1569-1571-1579-1581-1582-1583-1590-1591
    1592-1598-1599-1620-1639-1648-1652-1653
    1654-1671-1695-1696-1752
KING, Steve  cl-as-ts  346
KING, Tempo  v  545-893-894
KING, Vernon  sb  154-830-1109-1247-1323
KING, Wayne  cl-as  919
KING'S MEN, THE  v  1690
KINSEY, Gene  as  94-95-96-97-517-619-
    1408
KINSMAN, Tommy  cl-as-ts-dir  895
KINTZLE, Pinkey (r.n. Gene K.)  bj-g-v
    888-889-1256
KIRBERRY, Ralph  v  875-895
KIRBY, John  bb-sb  12-13-14  -75-76-77-
    79-80-94-179-273-312-382-383-415-466-
    534-588-611-660-661-688-691-723-724-725
    726-727-728-730-767-768-821-866-895-896
    897-905-1000-1048-1052-1134-1159-1240-
    1468-1469-1512-1513-1637-1654-1658-1721
    1730-1731-1732-1734
KIRCHSTEIN, Harold W.  bj  171
KIRK, Andy  bsx-bb-sb-dir  251-898-899-
    900-901-902-1718
KIRK, Earl  t  183
KIRK, Mary E.  p  1097
KIRK, Wilbert  d  1246-1427
KIRKEBY, Ed  v-dir  235-236-237-238-239-
    240-241-242-243-244-245-248-249-250-262
    263-625-626-627-700-776-967-968-1422-
    1486-1515-1583-1593-1594-1619-1620-1621
KIRKLAND, Leroy  g  1674
KIRKPATRICK, Don  p-a  12-50-622-868-1099
    1277-1278-1279-1657-1658-1659
KIRKPATRICK, Dub  ?  1694
KIRKPATRICK, Jess  d  1305
KIRSNER, Sylvan  vn  1690
KISCO, Charles  p  418
KISSINGER, Byron  v  884
KISSINGER, Richard  bb-sb  360-858-859-
    1506
KITCHINGMAN, Ray  bj  218-220-221-222-223
    224-225-226-227-228-529-966-1050-1186-
    1187-1188-1428-1480-1581-1582-1590-1591
KITSIS, Bob  p  63-449-910-911-1160-1404-
    1405-1406
KITTIG, Rex  as  912
KLAGES, T.  vn  1407-1408
KLATT, Louis  p  406
KLAUBERG, Marcel  ts-vn  891-1047
KLAYMAN, Lou  vn  1398
KLEEMEYER, Ray  bb  882
KLEIN, Arnold  d  1271
KLEIN, Dave  t  100-572-954-955-956-957-
    958-1332
KLEIN, George  d  748
KLEIN, Manny (r.n. Emmanuel K.)  t  19-62
    77-84-145-156-157-158-159-160-161-174-
    196-198-199-200-202-273-275-276-398-419
    420-421-422-423-427-437-453-456-503-504
    512-514-515-516-567-592-593-598-638-651
    664-670-671-672-673-674-676-778-804-822
    853-871-903-924-932-933-957-969-997-
    1015-1016-1027-1028-(cont. on p. 1800)

1800

KLEIN, Manny (cont.) 1062-1063-1064-1076-
1080-1081-1087-1088-1098-1139-1140-1141
1142-1185-1212-1222-1241-1264-1302-1303
1312-1330-1332-1367-1368-1370-1381-1382
1383-1384-1385-1386-1387-1388-1406-1514
1551-1552-1562-1597-1598-1599-1614-1639
1648-1652-1653-1671-1686
KLEIN, Sol  vn  100-955-956-957-958-959-
1381-1384
KLEIN, Ted  cl-as  376-1146-1300
KLEINER, Charles F.  t  60
KLEINHALL, Bud  p  517
KLINE, Merrill  bb-sb  130-131-132-672-
943-980-1077-1078-1079-1222-1223
KLINE, Olive  v  1684
KLING, Jack  tb  188
KLINGER, Frank  g  93
KMEN, Hank  ts  647
KNAPP, Charlie  d  1202
KNAPP, George  c  652-653
KNAPP, Orville  cl-ts  338-339
KNASSEN, Stuart  vc  656
KNAUS, Jack  tb  1148
KNECHT, Henry  c  1208
KNEPPER, John  sb  185-186
KNIGHT, Bob  g  647
KNIGHT, Edwin  t  903
KNIGHT, Fuzzy (r.n. Forrest K.)  d-v  344-
1017
KNIGHT, Nobby  t-vn  469-470-1149-1493
KNOFF, Paul  as  682
KNOW, Paul  tb  708
KNOWLING, Ransom  sb  680-783-824-848-
1018
KNOX, Harold  t  941
KNUDSEN, Swede  bb  1377
KNUTSSON, Knut  ts  282
KOCH, George  vn  817
KOENIG, George  cl-as  168-371-372-373-
601-602-603-604-605-606-607-608-1242-
1263-1403
KOERNER, Gilbert  cl-ss-ts  575
KOGAN, Hawk (r.n. Maurice K.)  ts  79-703
1158-1159-1561
KOHN, Irving  o  420
KOKI, Sam  stg  53-54
KOLLIS, Eddie  d-v  523-524-1335-1343
KOLYER, Eddie  tb  416-785-787
KOODEN, Harold  cl-ts  869
KOPP, Howard  d-chimes  904-1250-1251-
1252-1587
KOPP, Sindel  vn  818-819
KOPPLEMAN, Lew  d  183
KORMAN, Sam  vn  1273-1690
KORMINSKY, Frank  t  1330
KORTLANDER, Max  p  640
KOSKY, Jack  d  395-1515
KOSKY, Larry (r.n. Lawrence K.)  vn  241-
242-262-626-627-1393-1583-1620
KOSLOFF, Lou  vn  33-84-1538-1653-1751
KOSLOFF, Nat  sb  518-555
KOSTELARSKY, Serge  vn  422-1696
KOTSOFTIS, Ted  sb  1063
KOUDEN, Eddie  c  882
KOUPOUKIS, Nick  pic-f  629-630
KOVEN, Jack  t  94-126-1554
KOZAK, James  t  629-630
KRAFT, Charles  t  913
KRAGH, Erik  d-vib  282-652-1585
KRAHMER, Carlo  d  316-1411
KRAMER, Don  d  182

KRAMER, Irving  as  207
KRAMER, Roy  cl-as  868-869-1056-1193
KRANENBURG, Kees  d  161-282-689
KRAUS, Phil  vib  1412
KRAUSS, Willie  p  629
KREBS, Elmer  bb  339-340-341
KRECHTER, Joe  cl-bcl-as  59-62-1406
KREITZER, Fred  p  970-971-976
KREKLOW, Joe  p  571
KREMER, Brainerd  cl-as  1253
KRENZ, Bill  p  926-927-934-1039-1068
KRESA, Helmy  a  491
KRESS, Carl  bj-g  17-33-63-64-112-134-
158-160-198-215-276-304-309-332-351-
418-419-421-427-437-503-509-515-629-
673-674-852-853-904-905-922-1027-1046-
1064-1065-1079-1082-1087-1088-1089-
1098-1139-1140-1141-1143-1144-1222-
1241-1300-1301-1302-1312-1329-1332-
1370-1377-1381-1382-1387-1388-1391-
1418-1514-1558-1567-1571-1572-1614-
1639-1751
KRESSNICH, Max  cl-as  517
KRETZMER, Steve  p  508-796-797-1120
KREUDER, Peter  p-ldr-a  405
KREYER, John  g  1572
KRIELL, Frank  bj-vc  545-546
KRISEMAN, Max  ts  208-209-417
KRITZLER, Charles  dir  271
KRIZ, Les  t  183-184
KROMPART, Henry  t  194-1036
KROUCRICK, Leo  vn  419
KROUSE, Kappy - see CROUSE, CAPPY
KROVENAS, Duke  t  566
KRUEGER, Bennie  cl-as-ts-ldr  19-68-69-
70-71-75-127-360-685-882-905-1177-1178
1230-1379-1480-1545
KRUGER, Jerry  v  905-906-1711-1712
KRUGER, Sid  tb  1038
KRUMGOLD, Sigmund  or  1417
KRUMM, George  bb  404
KRUPA, Gene  d  1-88-117-180-274-275-305-
309-334-388-534-541-592-593-594-595-596
597-598-599-600-601-602-603-604-605-606
607-608-660-829-868-905-906-907-908-909
910-911-912-977-978-999-1032-1033-1048-
1055-1063-1081-1087-1088-1113-1133-1141
1142-1143-1144-1145-1156-1332-1490-1546
1614-1623-1637-1653-1731-1732-1733
KRYL, Bohumir  c  332-1250-1251-1253
KUHLTHAN, Paul  p  1047
KUHN, John  bb  856-857-1366
KULZ, Ray  t-v  1688
KUNZ, Irwin  c  173-917-918
KUNZE, Al  sb  456-1120
KURTZ, ——  as  1737
KURTZMAN, Julian  t  545-546
KURZENKNABE, John  bj  1231-1232-1691-
1718
KUSBY, Ed (r.n. Ed Kuczborski)  tb  62-
889
KUTCH, Eugene  p  126
KYER, Peaches (r.n. Wilson)  p  705-1648
KYLE, Billy  p-a  14-15-29-75-76-79-80-81
153-273-518-588-633-661-747-781-895-896
897-913-1074-1075-1116-1159-1269-1337-
1469-1484-1501-1513-1540-1721-1722
KYSER, Kay  dir  913
KYTE, Sidney  vn  1364-1365

LAASKO, Nils c 525
LaBAHN, Kenneth cl-ts 889
LABIORECA, Harry bj 914
LaCENTRA, Peg v 1377-1398-1399-1400-
  1401-1751
LACEY, Jack tb 122-160-204-205-309-594-
  595-596-756-903-1027-1126-1224-1302-
  1337-1377-1551-1552
LACHMAN, Heinz tb 161
LACY, Anderson vn 1564
LADA, Anton d-x-dir 913-914-975-976-
  1184
LADD, Bernie oc 916
LADNIER, Tommy c-t 64-65-113-352-353-
  357-392-534-709-720-721-722-723-750-794
  917-939-1053-1092-1129-1265-1266-1427-
  1444-1531-1534-1650-1700-1742
LADSON, Ruth v 917
LaFARO, Joe vn 220-221-222-223-224-239-
  240-241-244-245-246-247-626-627-1583-
  1620
LaFELL, Leon v 765-913-1134
LaFOND, Pierre - see KAUFMAN, IRVING
LaFRENIERE, Gene t 1249
LAGASSE, Benny cl-as 1228-1373-1374-
  1375-1540
LAGE, Hal cl-as 1673
LAGESON, Walter d 360-858-859
LAIDLAW, Bob cl-as-a 1745
LAINE, Bob p 162-1236-1237
LA(I)NE, Julian tb 153-687-1249
LAKE, Bonnie v 329-1408
LAKEY, Claude as 814-815-816-817
LALLY, Arthur cl-as-ts-bar-dir 20-30-31
  32-146-274-334-403-406-407-521-523-524-
  525-917-949-950-951-952-953-1070-1116-
  1164-1289-1290-1291-1292-1293-1335-1364
  1472-1493-1507
LALLY, Ed p 1643-1644
LaMAR, Bert t 1373-1374
LAMAR, Justin v 917
LAMAR, Luther bb 704-1196
LAMAR, Slim cl-as-ldr 112-173-917-918
LAMARE, James cl-as-ts 94-95-96-97-98-
  99-1002
LAMARE, Nappy (r.n. Hilton L.) bj-g-v
  62-161-162-363-364-365-366-367-368-369-
  370-371-372-373-374-375-376-382-555-802
  942-999-1000-1001-1114-1131-1144-1234-
  1235-1236-1248-1270-1328-1537-1538
LAMAS, E. vn 1407-1408
LAMB, Merritt g 1148
LAMBE, Ivor as 345-536
LAMBERT, Donald p 918
LAMBERT, Leslie t 539-807-808
LAMBERT, Scrappy (r.n. Harold L.) v 17-
  33-34-129-130-131-240-305-351-394-419-
  420-626-627-676-805-918-930-931-932-979
  980-1078-1088-1139-1140-1141-1142-1144-
  1193-1222-1233-1234-1303-1308-1325-1368
  1369-1383-1385-1386-1411-1418-1431-1543
  1568-1589-1597-1599-1610-1611-1648
LAMMI, Dick bb 1656
LAMONT, Edward cl-as 575
LAMONT, Howard t 1572
LAMONTE, Bob sb 1739
LAMORY, Andre as 1642
LAMPE, Dell p-ldr-dir 6-919
LAMPE, J. Bodewalt dir 919
LAMPHERE, Charles as-ts 78-79-1157-1158
LAMPRECHT, Con as -ts-g-a 807-964-1215-
  1507

LANCASTER, Archie t 318
LANCASTER, Hestor v 681
LANCE, Roland - see LAMBERT, SCRAPPY and
  TEAGARDEN, JACK
LANDAU, Otto vn 1687
LANDON, Dick c-t 685-1334
LANDRUM, Neal c 405
LANDRY, Art cl-as-vn-dir 919-920-921-
  1005
LANDRY, Eddie bj 1005
LANDRY, Ed bb-sb 992-993
LANE, Al v 98-879
LANE, Barbara v 1288
LANE, Jimmy as 1468
LANE, Kathleen v 1063-1064
LANE, Lillian v 1553-1554
LANE, Milton k 1670
LANE, Muriel v 364-375-742-743
LANE, Vera - see WARD, HELEN
LANEY, Art cl-as 1075
LANG, Allan ss-as 1285
LANG, Chester p 830
LANG, Eddie (r.n. Salvatore Massaro) g-
  bj-vn 2-8-16-33-45-117-121-144-156-157
  158-160-161-194-198-199-274-275-318-357
  358-360-361-398-420-421-427-436-455-458
  463-464-501-502-503-504-508-509-510-512
  514-516-556-566-567-577-578-592-669-673
  674-708-844-845-853-869-870-871-872-882
  883-892-921-922-923-924-993-1005-1016-
  1029-1030-1062-1063-1076-1083-1087-1088
  1098-1113-1120-1121-1138-1140-1145-1221
  1222-1238-1240-1275-1285-1302-1303-1308
  1330-1369-1385-1388-1390-1391-1392-1413
  1425-1437-1438-1445-1488-1535-1566-1567
  1568-1569-1570-1574-1589-1596-1597-1598
  1599-1600-1639-1653-1673-1687-1704-1751
LANG, Harold - see LAMBERT, SCRAPPY
LANG, Jeannie v 1570
LANG, Phil a 775
LANG, Red ts 126
LANGE, Arthur bj-a 870-1747-1748
LANGE, Henry p 923-924-1029
LANGER, Jay cl-ts-vc 1675
LANGFORD, Frances v 53-428-924
LANGFORD, John - see LANGSFORD, JOHN
LANGHAM, Dick ts 1362
LANGHORN, Horace ts 806-807
LANGLEY, John cl-as 1496-1497
LANGLOIS, Isadore bj 792-1476
LANGLOIS, Norman g 632
LANGONE, Frank cl-as 1306-1307-1358-
  1359-1562
LANGSFORD, John as-bar-vn 697-698-702-
  703-1561
LANGTON, Buddy (r.n. Helge Lundström) v
  585
LANIER, Chester cl-as-bar 1536
LANIN, Joe p 924
LANIN, Sam cl-v-dir 825-914-924-925-926
  927-928-929-930-931-932-933-934-935-
  1039
LANIN, Will p 535-684-924
LANKFORD, Harvey tb 1004-1648
LANNIGAN, Jim bb-sb 309-868-977-1032-
  1037-1546
LANOUE, Conrad p 703-1001-1002-1003-
  1004-1031-1306-1307-1561-1562
LANTZ, Shorty (r.n. Roscoe L.) tb 61-963
LAPELL, Leon v 1347
LAPEYRONNIE, Gaston t 1211-1595
LAPITINO, Francis J. harp 1417

1802

LAPP(E), Edward  tb  236-237-238-648-840
LARGE, Fred  cl-as  553
LARGE, Jerry  cl-as  553
LARKINS, Dick  bj  1310
LARMAN, Walter  as  1362
LaROCCA, Nick (r.n. Dominick James L.)
  c-ldr  1175-1176-1177-1178-1179
LaROSE, Louis  t  208-209
LARROQUE, Adrian J.  p  112-917-918-1559
LARSEN, Art  dir  308-1389
LARSON, Ole  bj  919
LaRUE, Harry  t  1368
LASSOFF, Teddy  vn  112-883-1417
LATHROP, Jack  v  1063
LATHROP, Palmer  bb-sb  1253
LATIMER, George  tb  855-1298
LATTIMORE, Harlan  v  726-935-1277-1278-
  1751
LAUGHTON, Dick  ts  515
LAVAL, Paul  cl-dir  936
LaVAUGHN, Prince  v  409
LaVERE, Charlie  p-v  62-163-276-298-363-
  364-936-1237-1537
LaVIZZO, Thelma  v  936
LAW, Alex  vn  1406
LAWLEY, Cooper  v  1611
LAWLOR, Doc  c  1722
LAWMAN, Charlie  v  1071
LAWRANCE, Brian  vn-v  404-581-936-937-
  938-939-1432
LAWRENCE, Bob  vn-v  1689
LAWRENCE, Charlie  cl-as-a  782-1108
LAWRENCE, Joe  v·  636
LAWRENCE, Sara  v  939
LAWS, William  d  1103
LAWSON, Charlie  tb  359-709-1209-1228-
  1615
LAWSON, Happy  ts  1237-1406
LAWSON, Harold  cl-as  314-1197
LAWSON, Harry  t  251-898-899-900-901-902
  1718
LAWSON, Yank (r.n. John L.)  t  62-161-
  162-163-215-364-365-366-367-368-445-446
  447-448-555-821-942-1026-1114-1197-1235
  1236-1270
LAWTON, Clem  bb-sb  535-799-800-801-1226
  1227
LAY, Ward  bb-sb  59-241-242-243-244-245-
  246-247-248-305-512-626-627-776-871-979
  981-1125-1387-1388-1394-1600-1620-1621
LAYFIELD, Arthur  d-x  61-119-120-857-858
  963-1515
LAYLAN, Rollo  d  1224-1690
LAYTON, Skip  tb  1691
LAZARO, Gus  bj  573-1066
LAZAROFF, Bernard  p  1373
LEACH, Bob  p-cel  345-536
LEACH, Craig  v  304
LEACHMAN, Silas  v  939
LEADER, Harry  dir  86
LEARY, Ford  t-tb-v  97-98-123-321-322-
  323-324-1121-1482
LEATHERS, Vem  tb  890
LEATHERWOOD, Ray  sb  306-307-449
LEAVITT, Hart  cl-as  1745
LeBLANC, Dan  bb  1130-1131
LeBRUN SISTERS, THE  v  299-300
L'ECUYER, Armand  v  657
"LE DANDY"  v  1388
LE(A)DOR, Irving  sb  345-536
LEE, Baron  dir  1072

LEE, Benny  v  316
LEE, Bobby  p-dir  303-665-666-1606
LEE, Brian  g  801
LEE, Buddy  t-v  568-1035
LEE, Chauncey C.  bj  940
LEE, Chris  d  60
LEE, Clarence  vn  1714
LEE, Clarence  v  411-1701
LEE, Eddie  vn  1226
LEE, Eddie  as-v  387-1210
LEE, Eliza Christmas  v  940
LEE, George E.  ts-dir  940-941
LEE, Harriet  v  805
LEE, Herbert  d  1310
LEE, Jack  vn  819-820
LEE, Joan  v  1239
LEE, Julia  v  940-941
LEE, Len  d-v  525-1336
LEE, Mandy  v  915-916-941
LEE, Marguerite  v  941
LEE, Mary  v  942
LEE, Nappy  tb-eu  378-379-380
LEE, Peggy  v  619-620-621-622
LEE, Russell  v  942
LEE, Ruth  v  942-1602
LEE, Sonny  tb  93-124-359-360-429-430-
  431-432-433-434-435-436-593-633-858
LEE, Thelma  v  1713
LEECAN, Bobby  bj-g  110-408-461-846-942-
  1430-1453-1480-1622
LEEGARD, Cliff  cl-as  540
LEEMAN, Cliff  d  96-97-98-447-448-1400-
  1401-1402-1403
LEES, Doug  sb  279-1601-1693
LEES, Len  as-vn  469-470-1336
LeFAVE, Dick  tb  417
LEGARE, Peyton  as  1237-1249
LEGARE, Sal  cl-  687
LEHNER, Arnold  t  1563
LEIBROOK, Min (r.n. Milford L.)  bsx-bb
  116-117-275-544-998-1017-1081-1422-1567
  1568-1569-1570-1599-1684-1685-1686-1687
  1741
LEIGH, Joe  v  470
LEIGHTON, Bernie  p  616-617-1374
LEIGHTON, Chester - see ROBERTSON, DICK
LEIGHTON, Lee  v  431
LEITCH, Craig  g-v  76-1570-1571
LEITHNER, Frank  p  1150
LeMAIRE, Jack  f-g  98-889-1002-1003-1007
  1095
LEMAN, Gene  d  1552
LeMAR, Lew  effects  1102
LENORA, Sina  v  808-809
LENT, James I.  d  943
LENTON, Sid  cl-as  346-1379
LENTZ, Al  v-dir  943
LENTZ, Lou  tb  1589
LEON, ——  ts  1155
LEONARD, ——  cl  1019-1216
LEONARD, Harlan  cl-ss-as-bar-dir  944-
  1109-1110-1111-1112
LEONARD, Henri  tb  1286
LEONARD, Herbert  h  1338-1448-1449-1577
LEONARD, Jack  v  438-439-440-441-442-443
  444-445-446-447-448
LEONCAVALLO, Frank  vc  1681
LEONE, ——  bb  1254-1255-1256
LEOPOLD, Al  tb  1357-1358-1359-1360-1361
LEOPOLD, Reg  vn  784-1214-1419
LEPIN, Al  d  1126

LERNER, Al  p  816-817-818-819-820
LERNER, Rube  as-ts  132
LEROY, Robert  t  1479
LESHNER, Irving  p  1357-1358
LESLIE, Dick  cl-as-ts  884
LESLIE, Nat  a  285-725-1071-1072
LESSER, Lem  bb  1563
LESSEY, Bob  g  169-728-1279-1731
LESTER, Eddie  v  591
LESTER, Norman  p  14-179-1170
LESTER, Phil  tb  184
LEVANT, Mark  vn  1406
LEVANT, Oscar  p  129
LEVER, Phil  t  1379
LEVI, Cliff  bb  1662
LEVINE, Al  as  1573
LEVINE, Henry  t  20-132-239-467-626-648-
945-946-073-1095-1108-1172-1620
LEVINE, Jack  as  306
LEVINE, Nat  d  756-936-945-946-1108
LEVINE, Sammy  tb  1374-1375
LEVITSCH, Amo  vn  546
LEVY, A.  cl  1254-1255-1256-1586-1604-
1605
LEVY, Jack  t  914
LEVY, Jules Jr.  c-t  37-68-69-70-71-127-
263-285-406-685-686-706-882-925-946-1008
1009-1036-1351-1352-1353-1354-1379-1480-
1522-1523-1525-1526-1544-1698
LEVY, Rudolph  as  396-397
LEVY, Ted  p  803
LEVY, Theodore  c-vn  1256-1586-1604-1605
LEWIN, Max  d  85-86-388-638-687-688-798-
1634
LEWIS, Alfred  h-v  946
LEWIS, Bill  tb-bj-g  553
LEWIS, Cappy  t  364-741-742-743-744
LEWIS, Charlie  p  189-333-827-1615
LEWIS, David  d  318-410
LEWIS, Ed  c-t  101-102-103-104-105-106-
107-108-109-110-553-821-1110-1111-1112
LEWIS, Eddie  vn  974
LEWIS, Emma  p-v  946
LEWIS, Ernie  vn  20-21-22-23-24
LEWIS, George  p  682
LEWIS, Hambone  jug  1042-1043
LEWIS, Harold  c  1453
LEWIS, Harry  cl-ts  1343
LEWIS, Herne  p  387-388
LEWIS, James  v  832
LEWIS, James Otis  v  1674
LEWIS, Jimmy  g-v  203-830-1095
LEWIS, Lockwood  as-v  409-1084-1715
LEWIS, Meade Lux  p-cel-harpsichord  113-
652-751-821-947-948-1135-1240-1320
LEWIS, Mickey  cl-as-bar  470-471-796-807-
808
LEWIS, Noah  h-v  270-271-948
LEWIS, Robert  tb  1459
LEWIS, Robert  sb  520
LEWIS, Sam  tb  90-145-319-532-813-882-905
925-926-929-1006-1076-1097-1098-1128-
1163-1164-1288-1323-1355-1381-1396-1415-
1416-1418-1545-1606-1607-1608-1611-1680-
1740-1745
LEWIS, Sammie  v  953-954
LEWIS, Sammy  v  954
LEWIS, Sol  p  1496-1497
LEWIS, Steve  p  136-152-861-1229-1230
LEWIS, Sylvester  t  18-773-774-775
LEWIS, Tapley  as  1279

LEWIS, Ted  cl-as-v-dir  549-954-955-956
957-958-959
LEWIS, Teddy  v  728
LEWIS, Vic  c-g-v  959
LEWIS, Warren  t  708
LEWIS, William  g-elg  284-1247-1323
LEWIS, Willie  cl-as-bar-v-dir  959-960-
961-1642-1742-1743
LEWIS, Willie  v  1723
LEWITOW, Bernhard  dir  946
LHOTAK, Frank  tb  459-1055-1194-1692
LIGGY, Licco  vn  870
LIGHTFOOT, George  as-ts  1241
LIGHTNER, Fred  p  630
LIMBACH, Tony  sb  689
LINCOLN, Abe  tb  172-173-233-234-235-
276-362-363-364-530-555-624-625-967-
969-1124-1562-1579-1583-1592-1593-1619
1620
LINCOLN, Bud  t  172-173
LINCOLN, Chet  tb  737
LINCOLN, John  t  1116
LINDEN, Eric  ts  146
LINDLEY Donald  t  61-629-630-962-963-
1171-1172-1219-1220-1482-1543
LINDSAY, Buster  p  1453
LINDSAY, John  tb-sb-speech  48-49-50-
114-136-309-415-678-679-752-783-824-
843-1021-1101-1154-1229-1130-1371-1487
1489-1496-1542-1677-1678
LINDSAY, Tommy  t  690-691
LINDWURM, Joe  t  1330-1438-1483
LINEHAN, Tommy  p  163-364-739-740-741-
742-743-744
LINER, Sam  p  207-1126
LINGO, Gus  cl- s-as  1162
LINN, John  t  61
LINN, Ray  t  449-450-451-452-743-744
LINTON, Charles  v  1658
LINX, Jack  cl-ss-as-dir  963
LIPKINS, Steve  t  123-124-125-165-166-
168-183-323-324-439-440-785-923-1159-
1160-1408-1409
LIPOZINSKI, Xavier  cl-as-bar  826
LIPPMAN, Joe  p-a  123-124-125-126-204-
432-433-434-435-436-492-1398-1399-1491
LIPSCHULTZ, Irving  vc  1406
LIPSCOMB, Dan  p  1228
LIPSEY, Skippy (r.n. Don L.)  t  29-215-
398-517
LIPTON, Sidney  vn  20-346
LISBONA, Eddie  pac  938-939
LISEE, Charles  as-bsx  11-16-188-189-
465-1689-1211-1348-1349-1642
LISS, Joe  p  78-1157
LISTENGART, Sam  as  911-912
LISTON, Virginia  v  964-965
LITER, Monia  p-pac  383-384-404-581-582
585-586-801-965-1149-1224-1507-1508-
1739
LITTLE, Billy  bj  274
LITTLE, Curtis  t  1655
LITTLE, Eric  d  796-903
LITTLE, William, Jr.  v  1109
LITTLEFIELD, Tiny  g  1745
LITTLEWOOD, Wally  cl-ss-as  1520-1521
LIVINGOOD, Ralph  d  682
LIVINGSTON, Fud (r.n. Joseph L.)  cl-as-
ts-a  5-17-38-53-174-177-232-233-269-
304-305-362-427-428-429-470-519-591-703
977-1028-1046-1055-  (cont. on p. 1804)

1804

LIVINGSTON, Fud (cont.) 1076-1083-1086-
1087-1139-1140-1141-1142-1231-1232-1329-
1392-1570-1597-1599-1614-1688-1752
LIVINGSTON, Joel g-v 8-9
LIVINGSTON, Marty v 32
LIVINGSTON, Ulysses g 91-283-284-528-
529-770-783-851-1135-1253-1594
LIVINGSTON, Walter cl-ss-as-bsx 1663-
1664
LLEWELLYN, Frank tb 701-702
LLEWELLYN, Jack g 635-636-964-1046
L(L)OYD, Ed see KIRKEBY, ED
LLOYD , Ivor t 322-323-324-325
LLOYD, Larry as 238
LLUIS, Andre as 1596
LOADER, Alf cl-ss-as 1674
LOBAN, Maurice vn 801
LOBOVSKY, Nat tb 124-125-323-324-433-
434-435-436-959
LODICE, Don ts 126-449-450-451-452-453-
454-455-1242
LODOVAR, Rudy as 245
LODWIG, Ray c-t-v 17-117-174-275-576-577-
578-648-926-1067-1081-1599
LO(E)FFLER, Carl tb 239-241-242-243-244-
245-263-344-419-626-627-776-889-1117-
1150-1394-1580-1581-1620-1621
LOFTHOUSE, Pete tb 1361-1374
LOGAN , Bob tb 505
LOGAN, Eli as 349
LOGAN, Ella v 276-396-969-970-1332
LOGAN, Harry d 890
LOGAN, Pete as 687
LOGAN, Sumner ts-bar 189
LOGAN, William c 864
LOGIST, Lou as 1284
LOHR, Karl g 1585
LOMAX, Alan v-speech 1106-1533
LOMBARDI, Art t 250
LOMBARDO, Carmen cl-as-v 970-971-976
LOMBARDO, Guy dir 970-971
LOMBARDO, Lebert t 970-971-976
LOMBARDO, Victor bar 970-971
LONG, Benny tb 533
LONG, Dick vn-dir 972
LONG, Glyn Lea 'Red' p-v 650-651-1132
LONG, Huey g 39-863
LONG, John vn 1459
LONG, Kathleen v 93-126
LONG, Sam cl-as 359
LONG, Slats cl-as-ts 66-122-123-205-307-
321-440-545-633-704-779-781-958-1031-
1032-1095-1157-1205-1305-1313-1373-1374-
1512
LONG, Willie t 533
LONGFELLOW, Marvin bb-a 1496-1497
LONGO, Lou p 576
LONGON, Francis ? 218
LONGSHAW, Fred p-or 398-972-1441-1442-
1443-1444-1445-1452
LOONEY, Dennie v 1486
LOPEZ, Ray t 59-991-992
LOPEZ, Vincent p-ldr 972-973
LOPOSER, Avery tb-v 32-1175
LORD, Jimmy cl-as 88-1047-1616
LORD, Pierre v 973
LORENZI, Mario harp 469-470-974-1674
LoSCALZO, Mike p 544
LOTT, George t 792
LOTTMAN, Harry d 350-509-510-882-1544-
1545

LOUANNE v 1397-1398
LOUISIANA KID, THE v 648
LOURI, Joe tb 9
LOVELADY, Baby Jean v 978
LOVELESS, Leroy cl 278
LOVINGOOD, Burroughs p 359-807
LOW, Norman as 87
LOWBOROUGH, Joe sb 1008
LOWE, Francis ts 77
LOWE, Sam t-a 691-692-693-694
LOWENKRON, Paul vn 818
LOWER, Bill bb-sb 1146-1147
LOWER, Fred d 1548
LOWERY, Cliff cl-ss-as 630
LOWERY, Florence v 979
LOW(E)Y, Manny vn 670-1586
LOWN, Bert vn-dir 658-979-980-981-982
LOWRY, Ed v 982
LOWRY, Vance bj 315
LOWTH, Eddie vn 1021
LOWTHER, Betty v 1400
LOWY, Manny - see LOWEY, MANNY
LOYACANO, Arnold sb 999-1194
LOYACANO, Fred g-v 1510
LOYACANO, Joe tb-as 650-651-1510
LOYACANO, Steve bj 111
LUBE, Jack vn 9250926
LUBOVSKI, Victor p 156-1208-1721
LUCAS, Al sb 683-1674
LUCAS, Clyde tbOv 1694
LUCAS, Francis sb 307-333-1262-1338
LUCAS, Goldie bj-g-v 1171-1707
LUCAS, Joe t 647
LUCAS, John d 100-549-954-955-956-957-
958
LUCAS, Leon v 1694
LUCAS, Nick bj-g 69-70-71-72-771-982-
1348-1544
LUCE, Warren d 90
LUCIE, Lawrence g 12-13-14-58-131-281-
312-382-690-727-728-729-779-791-792-
850-1073-1074-1107-1304-1730-1731
LUCIK, Charles t 1213
LUDOVAR, Rudy cl-as 243-245-246-247-
1620
LUDWIG, Francis cl-ts 325-326
LUFSKY, Marshall P. f-pic 332-1250-1251-
1252-1473-1474-1475-1586-1587
LUINO, Severin t 333-519-1284
LUKE, Charles M. bj-v 1288-1289
LUMBERJACKS, THE v 1077
LUMPKIN, Guy g 983
LUNCEFORD, Jimmie as-f-vn-a-dir 983-
984-985-986-987-988-989-990-991-1097
LUND, Art (r.n. Art London) v 6261-622
LUNDIN, Jack bj 120-121
LUNDQUIST, Roy t 540
LUNDQVIST, Eric t-v 586
LUPER, William tb 807
LUSE, Harley tb 1498
LUSTIG, Billy vn-dir 1375
LUSTIG, Walter J. bb-sb 418
LUTHER, Bill ts 814-815-816
LUTHER, Frank v 17-18-130-389-648-751-
752-1285-1286-1599-1742
LUTZ, Alan bb-sb 1231-1745
LUVERTE, Jimmy v-dir 991
LYKINS, Lee cl-ss-as-ts-bar-vn-v 708
LYLE, William sb 327-1055
LYMAN, Abe d-ldr 991-992-993

LYMAN, Leslie  cl-as-ts  1498
LYMAN, Paul  vn  1068-1069
LYME, Walter  t  1364
LYNCH, Al  v  577-993-1583
LYNCH, Carl  g  1414
LYNCH, Frank  v  869
LYNCH, Jim  sb  505-1004-1237
LYNCH, Reuben  g  1204
LYNCH, Willie  d  47-285-1071-1072-1362
LYON, ——  tb  1473-1474-1475
LYON, Russ  cl-as-ts  34-1145
LYONS, Al  pac  1123
LYONS, Bob  p-a  1550
LYONS, Darius  f-pic  1473-1474-1475-1586
  1604
LYONS, H.  cl-as-ts  359-1343
LYTELL, Bob  cl-ts  973
LYTELL, Jimmy (r.n. James Sarrapede)  cl-as
  69-70-72-82-153-176-215-216-349-350-457
  463-532-667-668-669-670-793-825-915-916
  993-994-1015-1049-1050-1095-1125-1184-
  1185-1186-1187-1188-1189-1190-1191-1192
  1224-1273-1275-1356-1428-1480-1512-1544
  1719-1727
LYTLE, Hub  cl-ts  323-629-1538-1539-1615

McADAMS, Garry  g  162-1236-1248-1249
McAFEE, Johnny  cl-as-bar-v  622-659-660-
  819-820
McBRAYER, G. G.  p  1021
McCABE, Trevor  d  1657
McCALL, Mary Ann  v  96-97-740
McCALLAND, ——  v  269
McCAMISH, Charles  tb  906-907-1373-1374-
  1538-1539
McCANN, Richard  c  1586-1587
McCARTHY, Hank  t  505
McCARTHY, Pat  g-v-a  457-1469-1470
McCLENNON, George  cl  313-681-682-1021
McCLINTOCK, Poley  d  1641
McCLUNG, Gus  t  1371
McCLURE, Mamie  v  7
McCONNELL, Charles  sb  1570-1571
McCONNELL, Ed  tb  1116
McCONNELL, John  tb  284-528-729
McCONNELL, Maurice  t  762
McCONNEY, Edward  d  694-1203
McCONVILLE, Leo  c-t  5-265-266-267-304-
  305-395-418-419-420-421-427-561-655-659
  804-853-870-883-922-928-930-931-1062-
  1081-1083-1087-1088-1139-1140-1141-1148
  1247-1275-1299-1300-1301-1302-1369-1381
  1382-1383-1438-1483-1597-1598-1611-1612
  1613
McCOOK, Don  cl-ts  94-95-1156-1157-1231
McCORD, Castor  cl-ts  47-283-285-1071-
  1072-1654
McCORD, Henry  t  412-681-820-1718
McCORD, Ted (r.n. Theodore)  cl-as-ts  47-
  285-1034-1071-1072-1414
McCOSH, Ray  t  1146-1147
McCOY, Charlie  g-md-v  678-679-680-783-
  824-1206-1541
McCOY, Clyde  t-mel-as-dir  394-1021-1022-
  1542
McCOY, Joe  g-v  678-679-680-783-824-1206-
  1541-1542
McCOY, Memphis Minnie  g-v  1043
McCOY, Paul  t  98
McCOY, Robert  p  152
McCOY, Stan  bb-sb  394-1021

McCOY, Viola  k-v  1022-1023-1024-1025
McCOY, William  h-speech  1025
McCRACKEN, Bob  cl-as-ts  1324-1325
McCRACKEN, Mac  ts  316
McCRAE, Margaret  v  600
McCULLIN, John  as  863
McCULLOUGH, George  cl-as-ts-bar  1643-
  1644
McCULLOUGH, Mickey  cl-as  128-129
McCULLUM, George  c  302
McCUTCHIN, Joe  vn  1714
McDANIEL, Harry  t  840
McDANIELS, Hattie  v  1025
McDANIELS, Willie  d-k  218-318-1506
McDERMOTT, Ray  cl-ts  76-1688
McDERMOTT, Ray  bj-g  535-894
McDEVITT, Andy  cl-as-ts  192-281-282-316
  518-1343-1509-1739
McDONALD, Baldy  cl  642-1495
McDONALD, Earl  jug-v  320-409-519-685-
  1012-1026-1164-1328
MacDONALD, George  cl-d-v  1688
MacDONALD, Harold  d  116-317-732-994-1567
  1568-1606-1607-1608-1609-1680-1682-1683
  1684-1685
McDONALD, Helen  v  1026
MacDONALD, Richard  tb  10-11
McDONALD, Tee  v  1026
McDONOUGH, Dick  bj-g-v  5-33-66-67-77-83
  84-145-156-157-158-159-160-161-197-198-
  199-200-304-305-361-422-423-462-463-464
  519-556-565-593-629-630-651-671-673-674
  767-795-805-821-822-853-904-924-993-994
  1015-1026-1027-1028-1046-1049-1063-1081
  1086-1087-1088-1126-1128-1139-1145-1146
  1156-1222-1223-1270-1272-1275-1302-1330
  1331-1332-1333-1381-1384-1415-1420-1438
  1514-1515-1543-1551-1571-1600-1611-1612
  1613-1639-1648-1653-1654-1671-1695-1696
  1723-1751
McDOWELL, Bub (r.n. Earl M.)  d  544-762
  998
McEACHERN, Murray  tb-as  29-56-294-295-
  296-297-298-299-300-598-599-600-601-602
  603-604-605-1691
McELMURRY, Fred  v  967
McENELLY, Edwin J.  vn-ldr  1028
McFARLAND, Artie  ts  392
McFARLAND, Loretta  harp  959
MacFARLANE, Howard Ossman  t  796
McFERRAN, Harold  as  1370
McGARITY, Lou  tb  616-617-618-619-620-
  621-622-623-1048-1242-1712
McGARVEY, ——  vn  262-1393
McGARVEY, Reefe  timp  1150
McGARVIE, Red  g  78-307-1150-1157
McGEE, Erwin  v  1222
McG(H)EE, Bobby  p-cel-a  279-536-1508-
  1509
McGHEE or MAGEE, Esau  vn  996
McGHEE, George  t  1197
McGHEE, Howard  t-a  902
McGHEE, Johnny  t  29-40-56-204-205-214-
  629-756-830-1028-1314-1315-1316-1333-
  1411-1655-1722
McGILL, William  tb-cl-as-ts  572-629-
  630-1172
McGOWAN, Mac  p  1388
McGOWAN TRIO, THE  v  1028
McGRATH, Fulton  p-cel  34-53-77-124-158-
  159-198-199-200-204-  (cont. on p.1806)

1806

McGRATH, Fulton (cont.) 361-422-423-427-
437-673-674-822-924-1016-1031-1032-1046
1095-1144-1145-1146-1156-1330-1331-1332
1333-1337-1398-1602-1615-1648-1653-1654
1695-1696
McGRAW, Lether v 1028
McGREGOR, —— d 1348-1349-1642
McGREGOR, J. Chalmers p-speech 1-268-
1063-1064
McHARGUE, Rosy cl-as 1036-1037-1377-
1570-1669
McHENDRICKS, Jimmy d 676
McHENRY, Walter sb 154-155
McHUGH, Mary v 94-765-766-787-1722
McILVAINE, Don tb 1643
McILVAINE, William d 1507
MacINTOSH, Max d 218
McINTYRE, Hal cl-as-a 1063-1064
McKAY, Arthur ts-bar-v 1029-1589
McKAY, Bernie v 125
McKAY, Ernie cl-bcl-ss-as 923-1029
McKAY, Marion bj-dir 923-1029
McKAY, Ogese T. bh 1516-1518
MacKAY, Stuart as-ts 183-416-1159-1160
McKEE, Stacey g 182
McKENDRICK, Mike bj-g-speech 48-49-50-
51-63-180-864-1209-1210-1245-1322-1422-
1475-1749
McKENZIE, Red (r.n. William McK.) comb-
tincan-v 309-541-757-868-1005-1029-
1030-1031-1032-1033-1034-1035-1055-1112
1113-1114-1115-1119-1133-1141-1145-1330
1688
McKENZIE, Robert cl 1019-1216
McKEOWN, Harry t 1
McKIEVE, Norman cl 29
McKILLTOP, James vn 1681
McKIMMEY, Eddie sb 1408-1409
McKINLEY, Barry v 702-1027-1028-1088-
1089-1126-1552
McKINLEY, Ray d-v 53-165-166-167-168-
362-423-424-425-426-427-428-429-430-431
594-1033-1125-1145-1329
McKINNEY, Andy t 1313
McKINNEY, Eddie sb 647 (probably the
same as Eddie McKimmey, and a more
likely spelling)
McKINNEY, Nina Mae v 1726
McKINNEY, Ray t 439
McKINNEY, Sadie v 1035
McKINNEY, Walton v 553-1472
McKINSTRY, Ray ts 1481
McKNIGHT, Paul d 356
McLAUGHLIN, Ben v 657
McLAUGHLIN, Eddie t 863
McLAUGHLIN, Everett cl-ts 317
McLAUGHLIN, Jack vn-ldr 194-1036-1746
McLEAN, Connie cl-ss-as-v 1036
McLEAN, Hal cl-as 211-1681-1682-1683-
1684
McLEARY, Jimmy t 862-863
McLEMORE, William g 691-692-693-694
McLEWIS, Joe tb 730-759-760-761-762
McLIN, James g 75-769-905-954-1468-1535-
1707-1710-1721-1732
McMANN, Earl bj 1009
McMANUS, Carrol bj 1498
McMANUS, Jimmy v 320
McMILLAN, Dutch ts 182
MacMILLAN, George bb-sb 1327-1328-1643-
1644

McMUIR, Frank L. c-t-vn 563-564-1052
MacMURRAY, Fred cl-ts 59
McMURRAY, Loring as-ts 5-68-69-70-71-
72-176-349-825-914-934-935-1036-1185-
1379-1544
MacNAMARA, Doug bj 1253
McNEARY, Ray cl-ts 356
McNEICE, George cl 332-1586-1587
McNEIL, Ed ts 342
McNEIL, Edward d 898-1718
McNEILL, Charles bj 856-857
McPARTLAND, Dick g 1036-1037-1077-1537
McPARTLAND, Jimmy c-t 17-269-334-553-
591-804-930-1029-1032-1036-1037-1076-
1077-1078-1079-1080-1195-1232-1233-1234
1741
McPHAIL, Lindsay p 303-1037
McPHERSON, Norman bb-sb 1381-1382-1383-
1688-1689-1690
McPHERSON, Ozie v 1037
McPHERSON, Whitey v 1299
McQUATER, Tommy t 24-25-87-281-282-310-
311-384-801-1039-1224-1238-1298-1343-
1508-1519-1739
McQUILLAN, Gerry bsn 1744
McQUINNESS, Harry t 98
MacQUORDALE, Mac t 740
McRAE, Bobby g 1008
McRAE, Dave as 1637
McRAE, Ted ts-bar 14-261-382-526-527-
528-529-1099-1659-1660-1661-1662-1731
McREYNOLDS, Bob tb 1753
McREYNOLDS, Guy as 457
McSHANN, Jay p-ldr 1037-1038
McVEA, Harry bar 664
McVEIGH, Bill tb 92
McWASHINGTON, Willie d-v 1110-1111-1112

MABANE, Bob ts 1038
MACAFFER, Don tb 23-24-791-1508
MACAFFER, Jimmy t 132-279-790-791
MACAULEY, Eddie p 282-310-311-518-1238-
1519
MACE, Tom cl-as-ts 382-383-438-1002-
1731
MACFARLANE, Harry t 809
MACH, Bill t 1055
MACK, Al p 505
MACK, Cecil, Choir v 1653
MACK, Ernie d 1046
MACK, Ida May v 995
MACK, Jimmy g 1046
MACK, Mary v 1496
MACK, Ted cl-ts 919-920-1752
MACK SISTERS, THE v 832
MACKAY, Carol v 123-1236
MACKEY, Percival p-a-dir 515-799
MACKIE, Dick t 887
MACLEOD, —— v 918
MACOMBER, Ken dir 1431
MACY, Jerry v 928-1567-1620
MADDEN, Gladys v 691
MADDEN, Henry t 1491
MADDEN, Jack tb 1150
MADDILENA, Hank t 417
MADDOX, Les vn 801
MADDOX, Max t 169
MADDUX, Frances 1285
MADEN, Arthur sb 1343-1508-1509
MADERA, Oscar vn 1427

MADISON, Bingie  cl-ts-a-v  52-53-54-55-
  56-57-667-761-1171-1346-1500-1707
MADISON, George  p  792
MADISON, "Kid Shots"  c  307
MADISON, Levi  t  1194
MADISON, Roy  p  1520
MADRICK, Bernard  ts  517
MADRICK, Steve  as  183-184-185-186-829
MADRIGUERA, Enric  vn  1330
MAESTO, Christian  d  861-1350
MAESTO, Louis  cl  861-1350
MAFFEI, Dick  bj  1129-1130-1373-1416-
  1418-1604-1610
MAGEE, Sherry  cl-as  996
MAGEY, Gordon  1109
MAGINE, Frank  v  577
MAGIS, Jo  as  1284
MAGLIATTI, Joe  cl-ss-as  882
MAGNANTE, Charles  p-pac  16-62-202-203-
  410-641-670-752-805-932-1015-1016-1225-
  1330-1332-1368-1384-1387-1416-1610-1751
MAGNIEN, Jean  cl  1642
MAHONEY, Jim  bj  648
MAHR, Herman  p  1
MAINS, Dick  t  1244
MAIRANTS, Ivor  g-elg  25-316-399-539-557
  563-683-807-808-1508-1509-1669
MAIRS, Don  tb  182
MAISEL, Jack  d  588-968-1052-1500-1621
MAITLAND, John  t  919-920
MAJESTIC, Ross  t  867
MAJOR, Addington  c  1460-1492-1700
MAKOFSKY, Norvelle  ss-as  1559
MALCOLM, Horace  p  678-679-680-783-824-
  844-848-1206-1541-1542-1543
MALLORY, Eddie  t  281-676-1073-1654-1655
MALNECK, Matt  vn-vl-dir  76-77-198-673-
  674-997-1016-1077-1081-1083-1128-1223-
  1420-1567-1568-1569-1570-1681-1682-1683
  1684-1685-1686-1687-1688-1689-1690
MALONEY, Jimmy  cl-as  866-867
MALONEY, Norman  ts  279
MALTBY, Richard  a  622
MANDELL, Pete  bj  522-1298-1364
MANETTA, Manuel  p  301
MANGAN, Anthony  tb  511
MANGANO, Don  cl-ss-as-ts  134-1347-1348
MANGANO, Mickey  t  912
MANGOR, Arthur  tb  656
MANLEY, Nick  sb  417
MANN, Alice  v  554-960-1435
MANN, Belle  v  377-751-1232-1418-1604
MANN, Freddy  t  656-809-810
MANN, Hubert  bj  1371
MANN, Lewis  d  306
MANN, Marion  v  368-369-370-372-373
MANN, Peggy  v  325-326-1236-1237-1244
MANN, Sis  v  89
MANN, Zeke  bj  657-1201
MANNE, Shelly  d  1007
MANNERS, Art  cl-as  314
MANNING, Bob  d-x-vib-v  1213-1214
MANNING, Frank  bb  963
MANNING, Jack  - see KAUFMAN, IRVING
MANNING, Sam  v  998
MANNING, Ted  as  1204
MANONE, Wingy (r.n. Joseph M.)  c-t-v-dir
  32-209-302-565-592-998-999-1000-1001-
  1002-1003-1004-1133-1143-1144-1276-1332-
  1567
MANSELL, Bobby  t  126

MANSFIELD, Andy  p-v-dir  351-1068
MANSFIELD, Saxie  ts  163-360-738-739-740
  741-742-743-744-858-859
MANTIA, Simon  bb-eu  1254-1255-1256-1473
  1474-1475
MANTOVANI, Annunzio  vn  302-784-785
MANUEL, Willie  as  1657
MANZE, Al  cl-as  1550
MAPLE, Nelson  p  1017
MAPLES, Pappy  bb  867
MAPP, Eddie  h  1004
MARABLE, Fate  p-dir  1004
MARCASIE, Lou  cl-as  59
MARCOUR, Mickey  p  650
MARCUS, Bill  tb  1362
MARCUS, Billy  d  159-363-642
MARCUS, Harold  cl-ss-as  239-240-241-242
  243-244-245-626-627-1580-1583-1593-1620
MARES, Paul  t  1005-1131-1132-1419
MAREZE, Adrian  ts  1596
MARGULIS, Charlie  t  421-422-423-593-756
  903-922-1019-1028-1068-1089-1172-1224-
  1228-1406-1551-1567-1568-1569-1598-1599
  1682-1683-1684-1685-1686-1687
MARIANO, Mario  as  307
MARINEAU, Al  tb-v  920-921-1047
MARINERS, THE  v  1005
MARIO, J.  ts  1662
MARKEL, Mike  p-dir  391-1005-1006
MARKET, Stephen  t  1373-1374
MARKEY, Ralph  t  1498
MARKS, Franklyn  p-a  94098-945-1082-1089
  1273
MARKS, George  p-v  316-1497
MARKS, Johnny  d  1634
MARLAND, Albert  p-a  656
MARLOW, Mac  tb  1375
MARLOWE, Paul  t  630
MARLOWE, Sterling  g  1070
MAROWITZ, Sam  as  817-818-819-820
MARRENDINO, Angie  cl-as  100
MARRERO, Ernie  d-wb  1209-1210
MARRERO, John  bj  301-302
MARRERO, Simon  bb-sb  301-302-1123-1124
MARSALA, Joe  cl-as-ts  122-153-209-382-
  383-399-518-545-553-821-822-893-894-936
  959-1001-1002-1003-1004-1007-1027-1240-
  1332-1429-1472-1673
MARSALA, Marty  t  317-336-542-764-780-
  781-821-893-894-936-1004-1007
MARSH, Andrea  v  1668
MARSH, George  d  76-211-922-1017-1569-
  1570-1609-1680-1681-1685-1686-1687-1688
MARSH, Lloyd  d  575
MARSH, Roy  vib  636
MARSH, Watson  cl-ts  1363-1364
MARSHALL, Bert  v  398
MARSHALL, Bessie  p  392
MARSHALL, Billy  t  417
MARSHALL, Doc  tb  923-1029
MARSHALL, G.  d  1379
MARSHALL, Jack  tb  1047
MARSHALL, Kaiser  d  13-45-165-663-704-
  705-711-712-713-714-715-716-717-718-719
  720-721-722-723-791-1000-1008-1034-1266
  1445-1624-1648-1704-1729
MARSHALL, Neil  d  1600-1602
MARSHALL, Stanley  d  518-1693
MARSHALL, Tom  tb  1485
MARTEL, Benny  g  594
MARTELL, John  t  184-186-325-613-614

1808

MARTIN, Albert  d  7
MARTIN, Alfred  g-md  942-1007-1480
MARTIN, Bob  g  953-1070
MARTIN, Bobby  t-v-dir  959-960-1008-1642-
  1742-1743
MARTIN, Carroll  tb  856-857-858-1348
MARTIN, Chet  d  1689
MARTIN, Chink  bb-sb  383-650-651-1065-
  1132-1271
MARTIN, Claire  v  647-1752
MARTIN, Colin  g  1543
MARTIN, Daisy  v  1008-1009
MARTIN, David  p  333-1273-1476-1477-1535
MARTIN, Dolly  v  1009
MARTIN, Fatty  p-dir  1009
MARTIN, Freddy  cl-as-ts-dir  201-328-834-
  1009-1194-1241
MARTIN, Gordon  c  405-737
MARTIN, Howard  ts  188
MARTIN, Jackie  v  92
MARTIN, Joe  vn-v  1361
MARTIN, Louis  cl-as-bar  20-751-752-932-
  957-958-1016-1285-1303-1381-1382-1383-
  1384-1385-1386-1387-1388
MARTIN, Lovell  tb-a  449-450-451-452-743
MARTIN, Mary  v  364-740
MARTIN, Oscar  bb  1498
MARTIN, Raymond  ts  806
MARTIN, Roland  bj  1543
MARTIN, Sara  v  1010-1011-1012-1013-1014-
  1532
MARTIN, Skippy  as-bar-a  95-96-102-108-
  616-617-618-619-620-1712
MARTIN, Slim (r.n. Orlando)  tb  991-992-
  993
MARTIN, Walter  as  328-834-1194
MARTIN, Walter  d-wb  824-825-864-865-
  1511-1679
MARTINEAU ——  t  16
MARTINEZ, Frank  t  286
MARTINEZ, Ray  vn  819-820
MARTINI, Mike  tb  630-1129-1130-1521
MARTINO, Louis  t  1310
MARTIN, Quedillis  cl-ts  763
MARVIN, Bob  bj  32
MARVIN, Frank  g-v  481-484-577-930-1015-
  1034-1061-1170-1346-1417-1676-1716
MARVIN, Johnny  g-stg-u-v  17-870-1015-
  1016-1416-1417-1418
MARX, Fran  d  913
MARX, Jacques  ts  1150
MASEFIELD, Happy  bb-sb  172-173-1068
MASEK, Joe  ts  936
MASER, Elry  cl  802
MASINTER, Sherman  sb  1249-1250
MASMAN, Theo Uden  dir  282-689
MASON, Billy  p  470-790-791-1017-1584
MASON, Florence  v  961
MASON, Henry  c-t  251-565-570-737-960-
  961-1089-1215
MASON, Herb  cl-bcl-as-f  1150
MASON, Norman  cl-as  1004
MASON, Paul  cl-ts-vn  245-246-247-420-427-
  449-450-451-452-577-979-980-981-982-1697
MASON, Robert "Cookie"  t-v  1338
MASON, Sully  as-v  913
MASON, Tony  as  282
MASSA, Guido  cl-ts  151
MASSENBURG, Sam  t  342
MASSEY, Billy  v  251-898
MASSINGALE, Andrew  t  1485

MASTELER, Cliff  g  881
MASTERS, Art  as  1400
MASTERS, Frank  v  1018
MASTERSON, Frank  bj  659
MASTREN, Alex  tb  78-306-307-1002-1064-
  1148-1157-1158
MASTREN, Carmen  g-a  16-81-114-209-215-
  216-307-399-439-440-441-442-443-444-
  445-446-447-448-449-553-768-821-1001-
  1002-1004-1007-1031-1032-1063-1064-
  1115-1244-1305-1312-1332-1429-1546
MATHENSON, Sol  d  572
MATHES, Minnie  v  1018
MATHEW, Tony  v  772
MATHEWS, Albert  cl-bar  1723
MATHEWS, Gertrude  v  580
MATHEWS, Lucile  v  580
MATHIAS, Ernie  t-v  1-377-1146-1265
MATHIAS, Jack  a  815
MATHIESEN, Leo  p-a  1337-1585
MATHIEU, Carl  v  577-921
MATLOCK, Matty  cl-as-a  62-123-132-161-
  162-363-364-365-366-367-368-369-373-
  374-375-376-555-565-867-942-999-1000-
  1001-1002-1081-1234-1235-1236-1270-1
  1328-1537-1572
MATSON, Charles A.  p-dir-a  316-750-1
  1018-1448-1462-1723
MATTHEWS, Babe  v  1711
MATTHEWS, Bill  tb  1350
MATTHEWS, Bob  v  417
MATTHEWS, Dave  as-ts-a  204-429-505-542-
  608-661-814-815-816-818-1236-1243
MATTHEWS, Emmet  as-v-dir  1018-1019-
  1627-1723
MATTHEWS, George  tb  54-131-169-191-527-
  528-1660-1661-1662
MATTHEWS, George  cl-as  395
MATTHEWS, Hal  tb  1347-1348-1690
MATTHEWS, Irving  bj  1746
MATTHEWS, Johnny Mae  v  1019
MATTHEWS, Lucy Ann  v  1116
MATTHEWS, William  tb  302
MATTHEWSON, Oliver  g  739
MATTISON, Bernie  t  647
MATTISON, Don  tb-v  53-362-424-425-426-
  427-428-429-430-431-432-433-434-435-436-
  1329
MATZER, Johnny  t  152
MAJBORG, ——  cl-as  1639
MAULE or MOLL, Abe  cl-ts-vn  657-1201
MAULING, Al  cl-as-o  856-857-858
MAUPINS, Thurston  tb  940
MAUPREY, Didier  sb  543
MAURICE, Mark  bar  345-536
MAUS, Carl  d  1374-1406
MAXEY, Billy  v  113
MAXEY, Leroy  d  131-252-253-254-255-256-
  257-258-259-349-1084-1245
MAXFIELD, Harry  v  977-1068-1195
MAXON, Roy  tb  732-1347-1608-1609-1680-
  1681
MAXTED, Billy  p-v-a  168-772-1147-1148
MAXWELL, A.  v  736
MAXWELL, Clinton  d  141
MAXWELL, Dick  bj-g-v  468-469
MAXWELL, Jimmy  t  62-613-614-615-616-617-
  618-619-620-621-622-623-1374
MAY, Billy  t-v  95-96-97
MAYALL, Vernon  t  1472-1744
MAYBERRY, Tiny  v  1019

MAYER, Red cl-ts-bar 1684-1685-1686-
1687
MAYER, Roy p 513
MAYERL, Billy p 1135-1362-1363
MAYERS, Doc v 1505
MAYERS, Duncan dir 1362
MAY(E)S, Junie p 417-1374-1375
MAYFIELD, John tb 411-1011-1018-1533-
1698-1699
MAYHEW, ——— tb 1019-1216
MAYHEW, Bob t 53-274-887-888-1682-1683
MAYHEW, Gus (r.n. Wendell M.) tb 887-
888-889-1116
MAYHEW, Jack cl-as 62-276-363-364-555-
887-969-1562-1683
MAYHEW, Nye ts-v 274-419-887-888-1682-
1683
MAYO, Joseph d 519-520-652-65 -654-655-
1436-1692
MAYO, Raymond bj 1245
MAYS, Harry bj-v 1577
MAYS, John ts 168
MAYS, Maurice bj 762
MAZZA, George tb 29-324-325-756
MAZZA, Leo sb 417
MEAD, Andrew as 343
MEAD, Charles t 345-667-885
MEARS, Martha v 997
MECUM, Dudley p-v 133-189
MEDEAS, William d 361
MEENK, Eddie t 161
MEERLOO, Jack as 511
MEERSLOO, Teddy cl-ts 511
MEISEL, Ken tb-v 208-209-417
MELACHRINO, George cl-as-ts 784 785-1365
MELE, Vi v 430
MELLAND, Henry/Neville p 1038
MELLOR, Arthur t 126
MELLOR, Walt as 126
MELODY FOUR, THE v 1644
MELODY THREE, THE v 17-18
MELON, Lou tb 1284
MELROSE, Charles pac 302-1040
MELROSE, Frank p 112-302-812-1039-1040-
1738
MELROSE, Walter p 805-1039
MELTON, James cl-ss-as-v
MELTON, Porter tb 630
MELVIN, Alice v 1040
MELVIN, Lindsay bj-g 532
"MEMPHIS" comb 1099
MEMPHIS BOB u 1306
MEN ABOUT TOWN, THE V 1315
MENDELL, Johnny t 94-95-541-936-1546
MENDELLO, Toots c 1046
MENDELSOHN, Art as 62-165-166-168-364-
365-374-375
MENDELSON, Julie d 93
MENDELSSOHN, Felix g-ldr 1046
MENGE, Fuzz t 1305
MENGE, Homer tb 159-361-642
MENGE, Lank tb 1305
MENGO, Jerry d-v 330-333-465-632-1238-
1258
MENTON, Del tb 1572
MEOLA, Mike t 373
MERCER, Johnny v 35-363-422-611-612-1001
1046-1329-1570-1689-1691
MERCURIO, Walter tb 438-439-442-452-453-
704-756
MEREDITH, Jack v 1247

MERESCO, Joe p 19-33-67-84-198-200-360-
674-795-1031-1212-1312-1538-1654-1671-
1751
MERKIN, Harry cl-ss-as-ts 188
MERKIN, Lester cl-as-ts 1243-1375-1553
MEROFF, Benny as-dir 1047
MERRILL, Bob t 1038
MERRILL, Bruce p 1674
MERRILL, Reggie cl-as-ts 1-513-1373-
1513-1718
MERRIT(T), Jock bb 345-667-1493
MERRY, Elmer bj 558-559
MERRY MACS, THE v 296-364
MERSEY, Bob a 1242-1243
MERTZ, Paul p-a 115-576-577-578-1145-
1566
MESSINI (MESENE), Jimmy g-v 582-583-584
585-586-587-588-589
MESSNER, Johnny cl-as-v-dir 1047
METCALF, Louis c-t 213-343-349-392-411-
412-472-473-474-475-476-643-645-686-733
734-735-838-861-863-868-872-1013-1024-
1051-1057-1058-1060-1119-1169-1184-1241
1345-1428-1431-1446-1453-1463-1614-1700
1702
METH, Max ldr 1655
METHEHEN, Jacques (r.n. John Ellsworth)
dir 652
METZ, Benny d 1047
METZ, Fritz vc 918
MEYER, Joe t 162-429-1116-1236
MEYER, Walter d 1392
MEYERS, Anna v 1050-1185-1186
MEYERS, Billy v 1119-1193
MEYERS, Chatlotte v 522
MEYERS, Chester p 940
MEYERS, Clark s-v 303
MEYERS, Eddie t 1157
MEYERS, Hazel v 1050
MEYERS, Joe p 1085-1086
MEYERS, Vic d-ldr 1051-1052
MEZEY, John as 816-817
MEZZROW, Mezz (r.n. Milton Mesirow) cl-
ts-bells-speech 50-309-312-334-357-
660-821-868-881-917-977-1032-1033-1052-
1053-1134-1546-1624
MICHAELS, Bus sb 1602
MICHAELS, Mike tb 204-701-702-703-775-
1398-1399-1621
MICHAELS, Ray d-vib 95-320-321-913-1506
MICHAELSON, Leonard t 1491
MICHALL, Ernest "Mike" cl 1054-1603
MIDDLETON, Edward tb 520
MIDDLETON, Edwin t 520
MIDDLETON, Jack s 589-590-591
MIDGLEY, Bobby d 822
MIDGLEY Charles p 708
MIGLIORE, James c-t 1045-1392-1469-1470
MIGLIORE, Jimmy as 911-912
MIHELICH, Ed sb 911-912
MIKELL, Gene (r.n. F. Eugene M.) cl-as-ts
13-14-1072-1073-1074-1497
MIKELL, Otto cl-as 1362-1715
MILAZZO, Jimmy t 94
MILDE, Engelbert v 808-809
MILES, Eddie p-v 6-1645-1646-1647
MILES, Jack tb 970
MILES, Josie v 1056-1057-1058
MILES, Lizzie v 392-1059-1060-1061

MILEY, Bubber (r.n. James M.) c-t 154-
164-182-274-344-472-473-474-475-476-477
562-643-733-734-794-810-845-872-1013-
1014-1024-1051-1057-1058-1061-1083-1090
1093-1094-1096-1104-1170-1218-1241-1246
1285-1286-1428-1438-1453-1461-1462-1471
1547-1700
MILLAR, Harold B. t-cl-bar 532
MILLARD, Red t 111
MILLER, Alex d-v 1036
MILLER, Alvin t 1548
MILLER, Art sb 334-1031-1139-1140-1141-
1142-1143-1144-1145-1270-1330-1331-1332
1538-1539-1558-1571-1572-1688-1689-1690
MILLER, Bernard d 964
MILLER, Bill p 78-79-92-95-96-97-98-99-
565-566-701-702-1157-1158-1159-1160
MILLER, Bob v 186
MILLER, Chuck cl-as-ts 3 0-351-509¾510-
882-927-928-1544-1545
MILLER, Clarence ts 864
MILLER, David compere 316
MILLER, Donald t 307
MILLER, Earl "Buddy" cl-as 899-900-901-
902 1431
MILLER, Eddie cl-ts-v 16-62-122-161-162
363-364-365-366-367-368-369-370-371-372
373-374-375-376-555-942-999-1000-1001-
1002-1048-1063-1114-1131-1133-1144-1234
1235-1236-1248-1270-1328-1491-1537-1572
MILLER, Eddie p 847-1269
MILLER, Emmett v 1062-1063
MILLER, Frank c 383
MILLER, Gene cl-as 1305
MILLER, Gerald t 356
MILLER, Glenn tb-v-a 17-77-177-245-246-
247-269-305-351-420-421-422-423-424-425
591-592-593-5970930-977-978-1046-1055-
1063-1064-1077-1088-1113-1141-1142-1143
1144-1145-1150-1223-1231-1232-1233-1236
1270-1312-1431-1571-1599-1696-1718
MILLER, Hank cl-as 1305
MILLER, Harry cl-as 646
MILLER, Jack v 1064-1388
MILLER, Jesse t 761-762
MILLER, Jimmy g 1427
MILLER, Jimmy v-ldr 482-1064-1065-1139-
1343
MILLER, Joe cl-ts 670-1586
MILLER, Joe bj 119-120-957-858
MILLER, Johnny p 111-999-1065
MILLER, Johnny sb 661
MILLER, Len v 1336
MILLER, Lillian v 1065
MILLER, Louella v 1065-1066
MILLER, Margaret v 1338
MILLER, Max g-chimes-v 391
MILLER, Mel d 578-579-1369
MILLER, Mitch ca-o 80-81-1513
MILLER, Ned v 869
MILLER, Pop tb 547
MILLER, Punch/Kid Punch (r.n. Ernest M.)
c-t-v 133-327-328-541-823-843-892-994-
1065-1169-1201-1209-1459-1615-1744
MILLER, Randall tb 1406-1510
MILLER, Ray d-v-dir 1066-1067-1068-1069
MILLER, Richie d 1377
MILLER, Sodarisa v 1069
MILLER, Stanley p-reed or 1057-1443-1447
1448-1449-1450-1451
MILLER, Sue v 173

MILLER, Taps d 1046
MILLER, Tommy tb 1021
MILLES, Karl vn-v 1068
MILLET, Fred tb 1719
MILLHOUSE, Rouss c 1473-1474-1475
MILLIAN, Baker ts 154-155
MILLIGAN, Bruce cl-ts 889
MILLIGAN, Emmett tb 1753
MILLIGAN, Levi tb 748
MILLINDER, Lucky (r.n. Leroy M.) v-dir
1070-1073-1074-1075
MILLS, Barry p-ldr 1426
MILLS BROTHERS, THE v 284-360-361-526-
1075-1277
MILLS, Charlie p
MILLS, Debo d-v 730
MILLS, Don d 1252
MILLS, Donald tenor voice 54 55-57-1277
MILLS, Floyd tb-dir 1075
MILLS, Harry t 1213-1214
MILLS, Harry baritone voice 54-55-56-57-
899-1277
MILLS, Herbert tenor voice 54-55-557
MILLS, Irving vn-v-dir 475-476-477-480-
481-482-1076-1077-1078-1079-1080-1081-
1222
MILLS, J. W. bb 1396
MILLS, Jack d 98-99
MILLS, John, Sr. g 54-55-57
MILLS, Lincoln t 169-283-284-775
MILLS, Lloyd v 1075
MILLS, Maude v 1082
MILLS, Peck p-ldr 1082
MILLS, Reg d 87
MILLS, Vernon bj 1616
MILLWARD, Sid cl-as-o 1215-1509
MILROD, Hyman bb 1047
MILTON, Billy v 537
MIMS, Irene v 1083
MINCE, Johnny (r.n. Johnny Muenzenberger)
cl-as 203-440-441-442-443-444-445-446-
447-448-449-450-451-452-534-697-698-775
866-1063-1150-1156-1571-1697
MINDEL, Julius vl 1681
MINEO, Sam p 321-322-323-946
MINNEVITCH, Borrah h 803
MINOR, Charlie t 1515
MINOR, Dan tb 101-102-103-104-105-106-
107-108-792-821-832-1112-1129-1204
MINOR, Orville t 1037-1038
MINTON, —— ts 1516
MINTZ, Johnny - see MINCE, JOHNNY
MIRABELLA, Lennie g 457
MIRANDA, Bibi d 821
MIRANDA, Jack cl-as 20-467-468-469-470-
1083-1126-1127-1291-1292-1294-1456
MIRANTE, Hal p 565
MIRGORODSKY, Jacques g 836
MIROFF, Seymour vn 454-455
MISHELOFF, Sol vn 1589
MISRAKI, Paul p 1595
MITCHELL, —— p 1744
MITCHELL, A. as 1396
MITCHELL, Al t 166
MITCHELL, Albert tb 461
MITCHELL, Alex tb 1616
MITCHELL, Alex d 342
MITCHELL, Bernie t 208
MITCHELL, Bob t 991
MITCHELL, Charles t 786-787
MITCHELL, Dick p 1338

MITCHELL, Fred ts 284-729
MITCHELL, George c-t 178-338-410-414-
709-757-758-824-1101-1102-1129-1133-
1151-1152-1344
MITCHELL, Jack cl-as 685-686
MITCHELL, John(ny) bj-g 7-330-458-459-
645-666-836-959-960-1008-1441-1642-
1649-1724-1725-1727-1742-1743
MITCHELL, Leonard bj-g-v 27-337-391-457
MITCHELL, Lester t 1537
MITCHELL, Louis d-ldr 1085-1086
MITCHELL, Paul p 250-437-455-697-698-
699-700-701
MITCHELL, Ray v 486
MITCHELL, Sue v 123-134
MITCHELL, Tony as 185
MITCHELL, Tressie v 1322
MITCHELLE, Jimmy as-v 691-692-693-694
MITCHINTON, Laurie d-vib 1563
MITCHNER, William ts 696
MOAT, Gaston tb 1284
MOCK, Russell as 923-1029
MOE, Leslie t 1498
MOEHRE, Walter H. v 1334
MOELLER, Kai cl 1585
MOEREMANS, Jean as 1578
MOFFATT, Adelaide v 829
MOISE, Roy d 891
MOJICA, Leonard bj 317
MOLDAUR, Oscar cl-ss-as 545-546
MOLE, Miff (r.n. Irving Milfred M.) tb
5-17-19-20-37-38-70-71-72-73-74-140-242
262-304-305-306-319-349-350-351-395-462
463-509-510-519-532-566-567-620-630-667
668-777-804-805-822-825-870-871-915-916
925-927-928-934-935-962-977-979-1036-
1067-1068-1080-1081-1086-1087-1088-1117
1118-1128-1138-1139-1140-1184-1185-1188
1189-1191-1192-1193-1219-1220-1225-1246
1275-1276-1300-1356-1368-1393-1394-1420
1422-1428-1430-1431-1480-1543-1544-1545
1574-1589-1611-1612-1613-1614-1620-1691
1719
MOLERI, Nick p 861-1351
MOLINELLI, Larry ts-bar 168-1244
MOLL, Chuck cl-as 657
MOLLER, Kai cl-as 652
MOLLICK, Jack t 519-520-653-654
MOLYNEUX, Sam sb 1584
MONACO, Andy sb 398
MONASCO, Estes t-v 563-1045-1197-1469-
1470
MONCUR, Grachan sb 77-122-342-382-541-
770-1731
MONDELLO, Pete cl-as-ts 168-618-619-744
1242-1244
MONDELLO, Toots (r.n. Nuncio M.) cl-bcl-
bcl-as-v 62-123-203-205-320-455-506-
534-594-595-596-612-613-614-615-616-657
662-663-699-700-829-903-1026-1027-1028-
1048-1088-1089-1095-1224-1337-1412-1415
1551-1552-1735
MONDELLO, Vic bj 656-657
MONETTI, F. tb 1662
MONICO, Tony d 1055
MONKHOUSE, George bj-g-ldr 467-1098
MONQUIN, Al bsx-a 1482-1483
MONROE, Walter tb 944
MONTAGU(E), John p 736-1093-1343
MONTAIGUT, Philippe t 1595
MONTELEONE, Johnny t 184-1308

MONTESANTO, John bj 265-266-267
MONTESANTO, Leroy v 813-929-1300
MONTGOMERY Bob cl-ts 344
MONTGOMERY, Eugene d 1097
MONTGOMERY, J. Neal p-ldr 565-737-
1089-1215
MONTGOMERY, Little Brother (r.n. Eurreal
M.) p 644-750-1376
MONTGOMERY, Marvin vn 962-1640
MONTGOMERY, Paul t 457
MONTMARCHE, Robert d 283
MONTPELIER, Belleau cl-as 738
MOODY, Julia v 1089-1090
MOON, Henry g 836-837
MOONAN, Dennis as 636
MOONEY, Dan v 1514-1515
MOONEY, Etta v 1090
MOONEY, Hal a 457
MOONEY, Joe p-cel-v 1514-1515
MOORE, Alice v-speech 181-1091
MOORE, Alton tb 251-1507
MOORE, Arah "Baby" v 1091
MOORE, Art ts 364-1540-1541
MOORE, Bass (r.n. William M.) bb 1103-
1169-1245-1345-1431
MOORE, Bill c-t 67-128-129-130-220-221
222-223-224-225-226-227-228-229-230-233
238-239-421-529-572-623-624-890-929-966
1077-1078-1079-1081-1083-1091-1221-1222
1223-1302-1581-1582-1590-1591-1620
MOORE, Billy g-v 1253-1344
MOORE, Billy a 1360
MOORE, Billy, Jt. a 988-989-990
MOORE, Bobby t 101-102-1116-1203
MOORE, Chick tb 1364
MOORE, Clarence cl-ss-as-bar-vn-dir 708
MOORE, Cliff h 210
MOORE, Dinty d 1265
MOORE, Don t 34-670-1145-1690
MOORE, Ernest bb 392
MOORE, Estes as 691
MOORE, Eustace as 690
MOORE, Evan g 1561
MOORE, Fred d 1170
MOORE, George cl-as-ts 59-1249
MOORE, George v 649
MOORE, Gerry p 282-789-1091
MOORE, Grant cl-as-dir 1092
MOORE, Harold cl-ss-as-ts-bar-vn-v 708
MOORE, James p 1719-1744
MOORE, Jesse sb 1075
MOORE, Jimmy sb 959
MOORE, Joe s 589-590-591
MOORE, John p 508
MOORE, Melvin v 520
MOORE, Monette v 833-1092-193-1094
MOORE, Norrie p 86
MOORE, Oscar g 329-663-1531
MOORE, Phil p-a 95-375-1540
MOORE, Prof. cl-as-ts-v 1335
MOORE, Roger g 517
MOORE, Russell tb 520
MOORE, Sol bar 763-1272
MOORE, Sy d 665-666
MOORE, Tom g 99-126-1506
MOORE, Tommy tb 32-33-1537-1573
MOORE, Vic sb 1195
MOORE, Vic d 1422-1741
MOORE, Webster - see LAMBERT, SCRAPPY
MORALES, Janot t 1284
MORAN, Fatty as 891

MORAN, Leo tb 1147-1157
MORAND, Herb c-t-v 112-678-679-680-783-
824-995-1040-1206-1496-1542
MORANT, Edward tb 1070
MOREHOUSE, Chauncey d-vib-v 17-116-160-
161-163-203-204-205-309-320-394-418-419
420-559-560-576-577-578-673-674-738-871
903-924-1016-1027-1080-1081-1095-1139-
1140-1274-1312-1415-1482-1483-1498-1552-
1566-1567-1568-1597-1598-1614-1648-1653
1751
MOREHOUSE, Foster cl-ss-as 561-1483-
1640
MORELLI, Tony ts 152
MORETON, Ivor p 1339-1340
MORGAN, Al sb-v 88-131-254-255-256-257-
336-763-778-863-1004-1114-1242-1623-
1631
MORGAN, Andrew cl-ts-v 1095-1096
MORGAN, Ben tb 545-546
MORGAN, Bill sb-v 540
MORGAN, Charles "Sugar Lou" p 461
MORGAN, Dick bj-g-v 591-1029-1076-1077-
1078-1079-1080-1081-1232-1233-1234
MORGAN, Don d 1510
MORGAN, Fred bj-v-dir 1095
MORGAN, George t 1485
MORGAN, Helen v 1095
MORGAN, Ike c 1095-1096
MORGAN, Jack sb 87
MORGAN, Loumell p 550-551
MORGAN, Lyn d 87
MORGAN, Russ tb-p-vib-v-a 170-197-202-
203-205-559-560-576-727-1095-1178-1375-
1415-1482-1602
MORGAN, Sam c-v 1095-1096
MORGAN, Stan g 944
MORGAN, Tom g 93-123-124-250-619-620-
621-622-788-1242
MORGAN, Will cl-as-v 1641
MORLAND, Morris d 113
MORLEY, Alice v 1096
MORONI, Jack as-ts 1196
MORREALE, James t 1242-1243
MORRES, Don cl-as 92-93
MORRIS, Fritz vn 391-1524
MORRIS, George bj 1744
MORRIS, Ivan t-bj-v 737
MORRIS, Johnny d-v 4-561-562-973-1483-
1737
MORRIS, Leroy c-t-ss-ts 923-1029-1745
MORRIS, Lester p 905
MORRIS, Marlowe p 663
MORRIS, Maurice as 1257
MORRIS, Ralph cl-as-v 881
MORRIS, Tom c-v 285-313-408-522-531-564
627-643-732-734-782-810-845-846-941-
1011-1012-1021-1022-1058-1096-1097-1121
1128-1246-1323-1430-1453-1457-1458-1463
1532-1533-1617-1622-1698-1699-1700-1739
MORRIS, Wally sb 85-86-281-282-518-638-
1669
MORRISON, George vn-dir 1097
MORRISON, Goof t 1496-1497
MORRISON, Henry d 283
MORRISON, James d 691-692-693-694
MORRISON, Johnny t 582-583-584-585-586-
587-588-589
MORRISON, Lee bj 1097
MORRISON, Montgomery bb 1693
MORROW, Bob vn 159-642-1406-1407-1408

MORROW, Buddy (r.n. Barney Zudecoff, q.v.)
tb 62-364-365-374-375-445-446-545-
1314-1399-1718
MORROW, Fred cl-as-as-ts 38-74-456-871-
962-1049-1146-1163-1275-1420-1454-1545-
1612-1613
MORSE, Al bb 519-520-652-653-654-655
MORSE, Bill vn 840
MORSE, Lee v-k 1097-1098
MORSE, Maurice as 1068-1069
MORSE, Theodore p 1099-1200
MORTER, Al cl-as-bar 87
MORTLEDGE, Fred sb 1046
MORTON, Bea v 1204
MORTON, Benny tb 12-15-102-103-104-105-
106-207-208-281-284-360-722-723-724-725
768-770-780-782-821-935-1099-1235-1276-
1277-1278-1279-1304-1422-1511-1627-1628
1730-1731-1734-1735-1736-1737-1742
MORTON, George v 285-1071
MORTON, Jelly-Roll (r.n. Ferdinand La-
Menthe) p-or-v 358-459-709-738-1000-
1061-1099-1100-1101-1102-1103-1104-
1105-1106-1107-1108-1132-1167-1350-
1750
MORTON, Leroy v 182
MORTON, Lilian v 1080
MORTON, Norval cl-ts-f 1282-1529-1714
MORTON, Tom d-k-v-ldr 139-1108-1180-
1181-1182-1183-1184-1520
MOSBY, Curtis vn-d-ldr 847-1108-1462
MOSELEY, François d-ldr 541
MOSEY, John Albert ts 1374-1375
MOSIELLO, Mike t 5-17-37-62-63-64-82-
195-196-197-265-273-332-410-509-520-
638-641-654-655-670-676-751-752-852-
925-945-973-1015-1016-1041-1064-1065-
1299-1300-1308-1323-1367-1368-1381-1416
1417-1418-1456-1604-1610-1611-1638
MOSIER, Gladys p 1075
MOSKOWITZ, Joseph cembalom 1109
MOSLEY, Snub (r.n. Leo M.) tb-slide s-v
53-775-1109-1563-1564
MOSS, Earl t 391
MOSS, Henry vn 573
MOSS, Russell g 1047
MOSS, Teddy g 1320
MOST, Abe as-v 185-186
MOTEN, Bennie cl-as 864-1700-1701
MOTEN, Bennie p-ldr-v 164-177-1109-1110
1111-1112
MOTEN, Buster (r.n. Ira M.) p-pac 1111-
1112
MOTLEY, Bill cl-as 1552
MOTLEY, Julian p 763
MOUFFLARD, Maurice t 776-1348-1349-1642
MOUGIN, Stephane p 1595
MOUNCEY, Arthur t 279
MOXLEY, Joe cl-as 1033-1035
MOYA, Stella v 585-586-587-588-589-590-
591
MOYER, Goof (r.n. Kenneth M.) mel-cl-bcl
as-effects 265-266-267-916-925-1115-
1299-1300-1428
MOYNAHAN, Fred d 632
MOYNAHAN, Jim cl-as 632
MUCCI, Louis t 78-307-1157-1533
MUELLER, Gus cl-as 991-992-1680
MUELLER, John bb-sb 541-1228
MUERER, Ray v 578
MUIR, Tom v 240-242-627-1422

MUIRHILL, Jack  v  521
MULCAY, Gus  h  1115
MULDOONEY, Johnny  v  1416
MULHARDT, Kurt  v  808-809
MULLEN, George  c  1462
MULLEN, Jimmy  as  405
MULLEN, Jimmy  bb-sb  240-241-419-804-887-931-1620-1641
MULLENS, Eddie  t  283-1203-1246
MULLER, Al  cl-ts  1045-1469-1470
MULLER, Chuck  - see MILLER, CHUCK
MULLINS, Johnny  as  1468
MULLINS, Johnny  vn  187
MULRANEY, Bill  tb  147-193-281-282-656-790-791-1508-1675
MUMA, Dwight  vn  159-361-642
MUMMA, Tracy  cl-as  556-1174-1175
MUNDAY, Gilbert  cl-as  1421
MUNDY, Jimmy  ts-a  102-104-105-107-108-109-448-597-598-599-601-603-604-605-606-617-618-619-758-759-760-761-773-775-907-908-912-1116-1691
MUNGER, Ham  bb  405
MUNN, Billy  p  2-281-535-538-791-800-801-822-964
MUNN, Frank  v  17-580-871-1666
MUNRO, Ronnie  p-a-dir  22-506-1116-1335-1426
MUNTZ, Jack  t  907
MURPHY, Earl  sb  764-765
MURPHY, Harry  p  1124-1125
MURPHY, Joe  d  683-1674
MURPHY, Lambert  v  1684
MURPHY, Larry  p-v  697-698-1303-1381
MURPHY, Leo  vn  856-857-1509
MURPHY, Norman  t  910-911-912
MURPHY, Spud (r.n. Claude M.)  tb-a  96-97-98-505-596
MURPHY, Spud (r.n. Lyle M.)  cl-as-o-a-dir  918-1116-1117
MURPHY, Tom  t  1197
MURPHY, Turk  tb  657-1656
MURRAY, Billy  v  241-401-575-577-976-1079-1080-1117-118-1120-1171-1334-1607-1608-1609-1680
MURRAY, Charles  cl-as-v  840
MURRAY, Don  cl-cl-as-ts-bar  17-115-116-174-309-576-577-578-648-738-956-1132-1222-1566-1567-1596-1597
MURRAY, Eddie  v  267
MURRAY, Frank  g  401-778-1550
MURRAY, Fred  t  275
MURRAY, James  dir  1118
MURRAY, Joe  p  644-1118
MURRAY, Lyn  v  56
MURRAY, Matie  v  401
MUSE, Herb  as-v  182-183-184-185-840
MUSIKER, Sam  ts  907-908-909-910-911-912
MUSSO, Vido  ts  598-599-600-601-602-603-604-605-606-619-620-621-622-660-816-817-818-906-907-1048-1731-1732-1733
MUSSOLINI, Nick  tb  338-339
MUTT, King  cl-as  376-892-893-1548
MUZZILLO, Ralph  t  40-168-320-326-429-430-431-432-433-594-595-596-597-756-1095-1137-1314-1315-1316-1482-1655
MYATT, Al  cl  1257
MYDDLETON, Jock  as  1693
MYERS, Billy  v  402
MYERS, Bumps  ts  1108
MYERS, Eddie  t  92

MYERS, Ernest  sb  1240
MYERS, Evelyn  v  663-664
MYERS, Frank  cl-as-v  829-1497
MYERS, Harold  t  660
MYERS, Isadore  p  1442
MYERS, Leonard  g  1449
MYERS, Wilson  sb-v-a  7-67-113-115-284-330-333-382-383-632-770-836-886-960-1031-1476-1486
MYLES, Phyllis  v  167
MYROW, Joe  p  94

NADLINGER, Johnny  cl-as  1310
NAKCHOUNIAN, Gregoire  cl-as-dir  1120
NANCE, Ray  t-vn-v  135-497-498-499-500-730-759-761
NANTON, Joe "Tricky Sam"  tb-v  27-472-473-474-475-476-477-478-479-480-481-482-483-484-485-486-487-488-489-490-491-492-493-494-495-496-497-498-499-500-564-640-645-651-652-1075-1083-1097-1128-1430-1431-1500-1640-1653-1700-1711-1712
NAPIER, Jean  v  579-1033
NAPOLEON, George  cl-as  972-973-1330
NAPOLEON, Phil  t-bb-ldr  19-20-68-69-70-71-72-74-112-170-176-242-305-349-350-351-420-502-503-504-508-509-510-516-569-671-776-793-804-825-883-914-915-916-925-931-934-935-1036-1050-1080-1087-1088-1098-1120-1121-1128-1184-1185-1186-1187-1188-1189-1190-1191-1192-1193-1283-1330-1356-1391-1480-1544-1598-1620-1719-1727
NAPOLEON, Ted  d  1121-1128-1193-1521
NAPOLI, Ralph  bj-v  1
NAPPI, William  t-ldr  1121
NAPTON, Johnny  t  125-126-325-622-1360
NAQUIN, Ed  d  1539-1540
NARET, Bobby  as  1284
NASET, Clayton  cl-ss-as-ts  1347-1348
NASH, Joey  v  1332
NASH, Philip  ts  1253
NASH, Ted  ts  307
NASSBERG, Jules  cl-ts  1745
NATALIE, Cliff  t  123
NATHAN, Henry  t-cl-as-vn  962-1163-1454
NATHAN, Jack  c-g  539
NATHAN, Ray  d  187
NATOLI, Nat  t  76-134-361-419-566-578-579-580-1304-1570-1571-1688-1689-1752
NATZY, Hazay  dir  1122
NAUDIN, Jean  tb  171
NAURATIL, Tink  cl-ts  1616
NAWAHI, Bennie "King"  g-stg-u  558-1122-1263-1274
NAWAHI, Joe  sb  53-54
NAYLOR, Ken  cl-as  111
NAYLOR, Oliver  -p-ldr  1122-1123
NAZARRO, Cliff  v  1310
NEAGLEY, Clint  as  619-620-621-622-623-908-909-910-911
NEAL, Davey  bsx  762
NEAL, Rookie  Cm  762
NEALE, Nobby  cl  1123
NEARY, Jerry  t  163-362-424-595-596-740-1242
NEARY, Tom  cl-as  344
NEFF, Paul  bb  1548
NEFF, Walter  - see KAUFMAN, JACK
NEGUN, Bob  tb  8
NEIBAUR, Benny  tb-v  579-580-1377

1814
NEIBAUR, Eddie cl-ts-ldr 1377
NEILL, Larry t 1691
NEILSON, Jack vn 1150
NELSON, Arnett cl-as-v 165-309-823-843-
995-1123-1371-1454-1487-1489-1496-1527-
1528-1614-1615
NELSON, Bill cl-ts 1124-1125
NELSON, Dave c-t-v-a-dir 354-355-709-
838-1123-1124-1169-1170-1171-1267-1468
NELSON, Don c 1125
NELSON, Howard vn 1273-1534
NELSON, Jewell v 1124
NELSON, John cl-ts 1552-1553
NELSON, Louis cl 1287
NELSON, Ozzie v-dir 1124-1125
NELSON, Steady t-v 740-741-742-743
NEMO, Henry v 109-749
NEMOLI, Joseph c-vl 1694
NEMOLI, Phil o 1406
NESBIT, John t-a 311-580-723-1033-1034-
1035
NESTOR, Gwynn g 1332
NESTOR, Ned ? 530-531
NETTLES, Putty (r.n. Herbert N.) cl-as
61-1206
NETTO, Frank tb 1131
NEUF, Max t 1662
NEUL, Milton cl-ts-vn 1171-1172-1616
NEUMANN, Hans Ulrik g 282
NEVILLE, Derek cl-as-bar 1585-647-1693
NEWBERRY, Len ts 822
NEWCOMBE, Clyde bb-sb 152-335-542-646
NEWELL, Archie tb 1563
NEWELL, Laura harp 1125-1408
NEWITT, Nigel bj 1472
NEWMAN, Al p 992-1051-1052
NEWMAN, Cyril t 550
NEWMAN, Dick sb 702-703-775
NEWMAN, Freddy p 704-1196
NEWMAN, Joe t 664
NEWMAN, Ruby vn-ldr 1126
NEWMAN, Willie t 517
NEWTON, —— bb 1515
NEWTON, Bill bb 337-338-1151-1152-1153
NEWTON, Frank t-v 75-94-280-755-769-881
905-1052-1134-1135-1240-1370-1446-1468-
1512-1721-1731-1743
NEWTON, Lloyd d 1606
NEWTON, Ramon (Cyril) vn-v 1055-1135-
1362-1363-1364
NIBLO, Arthur t 146-459-500-676-784-789
790-1675
NICHOL, Willie (Bill) as 208-209-417
NICHOLAS, Albert cl-as-as-ts 11-12-13-
14-45-46-54-55-56-178-308-394-752-770-
828-862-967-968-1103-1104-1107-1108-1167
1344-1345-1346-1376-1535-1623-1624-1707
NICHOLS, Frank - see HALL, ARTHUR
NICHOLS, James cl-as 864
NICHOLS, Lester d-vib 328-834-954-1075
NICHOLS, Luther vn 1676
NICHOLS, Marion v 93
NICHOLS, Ray t-ldr 1137
NICHOLS, Red (r.n. Loring N.) c-t-w-a-v-
ldr 5-34-38-72-73-74-75-173-176-177-230
231-263-267-304-306-319-350-394-462-463-
510-519-530-532-561-566-567-572-573-624-
629-630-648-667-668-676-777-804-840-872-
924-926-927-928-929-946-977-978-1039-
1049-1055-1064-1086-1087-1138-1139-1140-
1141-1142-1143-1144-1145-1146- (cont.)

NICHOLS, Red (cont.) 1147-1148-1171-1192-
1246-1275-1276-1288-1312-1396-1420-1430
1524-1544-1545-1574-1578-1588-1589-1591
1592-1611-1612-1613-1614-1673-1681-1682
1740-1745
NICHOLSON, Peter t 263
NICKENS, Harry d 1118
NICKERSON, Bert cl-as-bar 100
NICKERSON, Charlie p 1042-1043
NICKERSON, George t 738
NICOLINI, John p 93-250
NIEHARDT, Fred d 545-546
NIELSEN, Kelöf sb 282
NIERMAN, Sid p 747
NIFOSI, Pietro vc 1019-1216
NILLSON, Al p 1047
NIMS, Walter tb 744
NINO v 1476
NIOSI, Joe sb 1150
NIPTON, Arthur bb 1170
NITE CAPS, THE v 1387-1570-1571
NITO, Paul vn-bj 128-129-130-572
NIXON, Teddy tb 91-113-190-711-712-713-
714-715-731-732-733-749-1023-1090-1448-
1450-1466-1725-1728
NOAKES, Alfie t 10-11-24-25-581-684-
1134-1507-1508
NOBLE, Giggs a 594-741-742-743
NOBLE, Harold cl-as-ts 399-629-630
NOBLE, James p 858-859
NOBLE, Ray cel-harpophone-a-ldr 163-
1127-1128-1148-1149-1150-1213-1738
NOEL, Jimmy g-v 1688
NOLAN, Bob v 917-918-1069-1496-1497
NOLE, Moe tb 1160
NOONAN, Ray tb 184-207-323-324-829-1752
NOONE, Jimmie cl-v-ldr 314-337-338-852-
1151-1152-1153-1154-1155-1166-1245
NOONER, Ray t III
NORBERG, Carl tb 338
NORFLEET, Bob bj 338
"NORM" p 6
NORMAN, Cecil p-a-dir 3-16-272-383-470-
523-524-525-554-583-1155-1298-1695
NORMAN, Eddie tb 826-1136
NORMAN, Fred tb-v-a 661-774-775-908-
1242-1408-1539
NORMAN, Les claas-bar 272-470-684-1155-
1219
NORMAN, Marcus H. d-wb-v 210-406-642-
892-1495
NORMAN, Patricia v 456
NORRIS THE TROUBADOUR v 762
NORRIS, Al g 983-984-985-986-987-988-
989-990-991
NORRIS, Bo g 547
NORRIS, Stanley as 1055
NORSEMEN, THE v 1318
NORSINGLE, Ben v 1156
NORTH, Dave p 541
NORTHAM, Jim tb 1745
NORTON, Freddy t 126
NORVO, Red (r.n. Kenneth N.) x-marimba-
ldr 77-78-79-80-93-276-1031-1156-1157-
1158-1159-1160-1231-1313-1602-1733-1751
NOTORAGE, Al cl-ts 1364-1365-1521
NOTTINGHAM, Gary tb-vn 563-564
NOVAK, Frank x-effects 1125-1280
NOVAK, Rudy t 787-829-909-910
NOVIS, Donald v 361
NOYES, Ted d 561-644-1375-1483

NUGENT, Norman cl-as-as-bsx 1017-1163
NUNEZ, Alcide cl 675-975-976-1747-1748
NUSSBAUM, Joe p 153
NUSSBAUM, Julius bb 1213-1214

OAKLEY, Ben tb 30-272-302-459-469-500-
507-515-524-525-784-785-917-949-953-
1070 1155-1214-1226-1674
OAKLEY, Olly (r.n. James Sharpe) bj 1161
OBENDORFER, Chappy (r.n. Eugene O.) d
171
OBER, Dillon d-x 130-131-1017-1077-1078
1079-1221-1222-1223
OBERMILLER, Eddie cl 1055
O'BRIEN, Don a 325
O'BRIEN, Elmer t 1482
O'BRIEN, Floyd tb 62-312-335-363-364-
365-373-374-375-376-392-541-685-686-907
908-909-942-1052-1546-1624-1673
O'BRIEN, Jack p 571-1136-1664-1665-1666
1667-1668-1669
O'BRIEN, James g 150
OBRIGANT, John cl 794
O'BRYANT, Jimmy cl-ss 64-65-100-352-353
354-392-709-750-794-1037-1069-1092-1161
1162-1265-1266-1499-1650
O'CALLIHAN, Joe v 1238
O'CONNELL, Helen v 431-432-433-434-435-
436
O'CONNELL, James t 785-786
O'CONNOR, Cavan v 132-147-359-507-953-
1155-1216 1295-1297-1472
O'DAY, Anita v 910-912
ODELL, George g 1197
ODERICH, Jimmy vc 1398-1399
ODOM, Cedric d-v 675-676-1267
O'DONNELL, Johnny cl-bcl-as 559-560-924-
1482
ODUN, Spencer p 661-663
OGILVIE, Ronnie p 964
OGLE, Horace tb 82
OGLE, Rod tb 908
OGLESBY, Andre tb 1218
O'HARA, Edward d 785-786-1117
O'HARA, Ted bj 890
O'HARE, Husk dir 1131-1162
OHMAN, Phil p 36-749
OHMS, Freddy tb 29-183-398-1358-1359
O'KEEFE, Jimmy p-a 630
O'KEEFE, Lester v 129-173-928
OLDE, Pete cl-ss-as 1201
OLDHAM, Bill bb-sb 51-1344
OLDHAM, George cl-as 51-661
OLDHAM, Ken ts 87
OLDSLEY, Bill ts 1528
OLESON, Winstrup t-ldr 1585
OLIVELLA, Phil cl-as 1004-1242-1243-1244
1374-1375
OLIVER, Barrie v 1164-1165
OLIVER, Bob v 1740
OLIVER, Earl c-t 19-63-71-72-90-176-637-
675-861-870-882-998-1006-1016-1066-1067-
1098-1128-1163-1219-1288-1305-1323-1379-
1380-1381-1415-1416-1545-1611-1676-1740-
1748
OLIVER, George ts 1298
OLIVER, George bj-g 1493
OLIVER, King (r.n. Joseph O.) c-t 8-212-
354-458-731-835-838-1014-1060-1061-1165-
1166-1167-1168-1169-1170-1171-1221-1376-
1454-1488-1535-1618-1702-1703-1704

OLIVER, Sy t-v-a 447-448-449-451-452-
453-454-983-984-985-986-987-988-989-990
1053-1693
OLIWITZ, Phil vn 1115-1299-1300
OLKER, Pierre bb-sb 61-76-120-121-566-
857-858-963-1688
OLSEN, George d-ldr 1171-1172
OLSEN, Ole (r.n. Lloyd O.) tb 220-221-
222-223-224-225-226-227-228-229-230-
1172-1581-1582-1590-1591
OLVER, Sam bb-v 1665-1666
O'MALLEY, Pat v 800-801-1148-1695
O'NEAL, Jim t 1643
O'NEAL, Zelma v 130
O'NEIL, Charles p 570
O'NEIL, Dolores v 1402
O'NEILL, Walker p 561-1172
ORANGE, John "Bones" tb 830
ORECH, Carl cl-ss-as-ts 241-242-243-262
626-627-943-1068-1117-1118-1121-1393-
1394-1580-1581-1583-1593-1602-1620
ORENDORFF, George t 47-48-762-763-782
ORESTE p-dir 1173-1174
ORLANDO, Joe bj-g 684
ORMANDROYD, Leslie cl-as 656
ORMANDY, Eugene cond 419
O'ROURKE, John tb 1242-1243-1244
ORR, Dee d-v 83-84-579-1568
ORTIZ, Manuel t 772
ORTOLANO, Joe tb 250-321-322-323-325-
437-438-700-701-1243-1244-1374-1375
ORTUSO, Mike bj 546
ORVIS, Frank t-cl-ts-pac 1252
ORY, Kid (r.n. Edward O.) tb 39-40-41-
42-43-65-100-101-213-308-456-942-1037-
1101-1129-1133-1167-1168-1209-1268-1344
1376-1485
OSBORN, Bill ts 1528
OSBORNE, James cl-as 665-666
OSBORNE, Stan as-pac 1215
OSBORNE, Will v-dir 36-1197
OSCAR, John p 1197
O'SHAUGHNESSY, Gilbert cl-ts 866-867
OSSER, Abe as-p-a 124-183-1360
OSSMAN, Vess L. (r.n. Sylvester Louis O.)
bj 1197-1198-1199-1200-1201
OSTERWALD, Hary t-a 151
OSWALD, Glen vn-ldr 1201
OTIS, Fred p 457
OTTO, Bill p 1546
OUGHTON, C. t 589-590-591
OUWERCKX, John p 1284
OVERSTREET, Benton p 835
OWEN, Harry t 22-23-285-798-1432-1433-
1584-1585-1692
OWEN, Larry cl-as-v 970-971-976
OWEN, Rex cl-as-ts-bar 316-468-469-470-
539-1225-1493
OWEN, Sid cl-as 790
OWEN, William bj 640-641
OWENS, Clarence ts 338
OWENS, Harry t 1335
OWENS, Jack t 1158-1159
OWENS, John t 78-95-96-97-742-743-1374-
1602
OWENS, Skid t 920-921
OWENS, Thomas g 1204
OWENS, Willie "Scarecrow" v 1201
OXLEY, Harold vn-dir 1202

1816

PACE, Sol cl-as 417-702
PACE, Tony v 268-1182
PADBURY, Jack cl-as-bar-ldr 1202
PADOVA, Al cl-as-ts 959
PADRON, Bill c 1130-1131
PAGE, Billy cl-as-ldr 1203-1221
PAGE, Dave t 563-1203-1645-1646
PAGE, Drew ts 814-815-816
PAGE, Eddie g-v 553
PAGE, Hot Lips (r.n. Orin P.) t-v 104-
131-355-769-770-821-850-851-1046-1111-
1112-1203-1204-1408-1409-1575-1637-1734
PAGE, Laurie as 87
PAGE, Sammy w 1670
PAGE, Terry tb-a 1310
PAGE, Vernon bb 1109-1110-1111-1112
PAGE, Walter bb-sb-ldr 78-101-102-103-
104-105-106-107-108-109-110-607-768-769
813-814-821-872-873-947-1112-1129-1204-
1263-1337-1732-1733-1734-1735
PAIGE, Billy cl-ss-as 1167-1376
PAIGE, Clarence as 1693
PAIGE, Jewel v 181
PAINE, Benny p-v 131-482-483-484-651-
1624
PAIR OF PAIRS v 1553
PALEY, Bill d 189-1068-1069
PALLOY, Charlie g-v-ldr 1205
PALMER BROTHERS v 261-476-759-913-1346
PALMER, Clarence v 1134
PALMER, Dick g 1116
PALMER, Francis bb-sb 162-312-1236-1237
PALMER, Gladys p-v 466-1205
PALMER, Hank as-a 1663
PALMER, Harry t 1505
PALMER, Jack t-v 79-325-814-815-816-
1158-1159-1360-1361-1381
PALMER, Kay v 580
PALMER, Len d 553
PALMER, Roy tb-v 309-355-414-754-784-
862-1044-1045-1100-1495
PALMER, Singleton sb 328-834
PALMER, Skeeter v 699-700-701-702
PALMER, Stanley as 695
PALMISANO, Angelo bj 650-651
PALOCSAY, Alex tb 320-1146-1150-1179-1272
PALSINGER, Harry d 63
PAINES, Jack p 1693
PANELLI, Charlie tb 68-69-70-71-176-349-
350-793-915-916-975-976-1050-1180-1181-
1186-1187-1188-1189-1190-1191-1480-1544-
1710-1727
PANICO, Andy bb 1206
PANICO, Charles bj-g 194-1036
PANICO, Louis t-ldr 856-857-1206
PANTON, George g 798
PAPALIA, Russ tb 396-1206-1208
PAPALIA, Tony ts 1208
"PAPA TOO SWEET" v 413
PAPILE, Frank pac 1347-1348
PAPPALARDO, Santo vc 918
PAQUAY, —— f-d 1642
PAQUE, Glyn cl-as-v 15-151-190-191-281-
1008-1123-1124-1169-1170
PAQUES, Jean (John) p 302-459-500-784-
785-1038-1120-1206
PAQUINET, Guy tb-v 188-189-133-519-689-
827-1211-1260-1284-1596
PARENTI, Tony cl-as-bar-ldr 60-204-273-
401-456-959-1079-1080-1208-1223-1301-
1302-1303-1367-1368-1415-1416-1457-1554

PARHAM, Ernest ts-v 1537
PARHAM, Fred cl-ss-as 752
PARHAM, Tiny (r.n. Hartzell Strathdean P.)
p-cel-elo-ldr 169-187-327-413-510-1026
1207-1208-1209-1210-1268-1320-1321-1500
1536-1729
PARHAM, Truck (r.n. Charles P.) 78-466-
761-762-991
PARIS, Gilbert c-t 564-1362-1559
PARIS, Joshy g 778
PARIS, William R. as 1657
PARISH, Dan p 1516-1517-1518
PARK, M. C. "Shucks" d-v 1643-1644
PARKER, Bernard "Buttercup" vn 378-379-
380
PARKER, Charlie as 1037-1038
PARKER, Don ss-as-ldr 796-1178-1210
PARKER, J. Donald v 1120-1612
PARKER, Jack d 153
PARKER, Jack v 241-242-678-973-1387-
1604
PARKER, James t-v 510
PARKER, Johnny v 17-18
PARKER, Knocky (r.n. John P.) p 962-
1640
PARKER, Leroy vn 1460-1461-1462
PARKER, Morton bj 1664-1665
PARKER, Melvin g-v 1713
PARKER, Pinkhead as 512-513
PARKER, Sammy d 703-1561
PARKS, Bob ts-v 93
PARKS, Hugh t 1075
PARQUETTE, William vn 512
PARRISH, Avery p-a 691-692-693-694
PARRISH, Dan bb-sb 1085-1086
PARRY, —— v 1697
PARRY, Harry cl-ldr 822-1039
PARSLEY, Tom cl-as-ts 923
PARSON, Clarence p 1450-1451
PARSONS, Chuck ts 307
PASCO, Mark tb 126
PASLEY, Frank bj-g 763-810-1350
PASMAN, Ben t 630
PASQUALL, Jerome (Don) cl-ts 337-338-722
723-728-1427
PASTERNACK, S. vl 1610
PASTEUR, Tony v 1602
PASTOR, Tony (r n. Tony Pestritta) ts-v
1-63-204-1398-1399-1400-1401-1402-1403-
1404-1405-1406
PATCHETT, Stan v 1207
PATE, William ts 1195
PATENT, Harry bb-sb 670-756-936-945-946-
1108-1125-1586
PATEY, Len bj-g 895
PATEY, Leon p 1548
PATRICK, Bill ts 660
PATRICOLA, Isabella v 1212-1607-1608
PATTERSON, Dick bb 1722
PATTERSON, Gus as 7
PATTERSON, Pete bj 359-708-1648
PATTERSON, Sidney cl-as 963
PATTISON, Pat bb-sb 18-1005-1481
PAUL, Ebenezer sb 1046
PAUL(L), Mitch(ell) t-v 208-209-417
PAULSON, George cl-as-ts 1552-1553-1554
PAUWELS, Benny ts 1284
PAVAGEAU, Alcide "Slow Drag" sb 996
PAVEY, Phil bj-v 1062-1212
PAVON, Arthur bb-sb 571
PAYES, Morris cl-as 870

PAYNE, Art ldr 1213
PAYNE, Benny p-cel-vib-v 253-254-255-256-257-258-259-260-261-262
PAYNE, Dolores v 1203
PAYNE, Dudley tb 457
PAYNE, Guilford "Peachtree" v 1213
PAYNE, Jack ldr-v 1213-1214-1215
PAYNE, Laurie cl-as-bar 395-812-1126-1127-1128-1148-1365-1397-1456-1695-1738
PAYNE, Norman t 395-468-469-470-554-564-784-789-790-812-917-953-1083-1127-1148-1226-1291-1397-1675-1738
PAYNE, Saxie ts 1414
PAYNE, Stanley as-ts-bar 191-283-769-836-1135
PAYNE, Sterling as 1054-1603
PAYNE, Walter cl-as-bar 133
PEABODY, Eddie vn-bj 1215
PEABODY TRIO, THE v 1644
PEACHEY, Roland stg 1046
PEACOCK, Chuck p 89
PEARL, Pinky (r.n. Jan Peerce) v 36
PEARLE, Jack v 1406
PEARLMAN, ---- d 1231-1745
PE(A)RLMUTTER, Sid cl-as 123-805-1304
PEARSON, David v 1215
PEARSON, Dick p 470
PEARSON, William p-v 555-1215-1216
PEASE, Bob sb-v 1556
PECK, Bob t 307-373-374
PECORA, Santo tb 153-1000-1005-1132-1193-1216
PECQUEUX, Louis sb 1211
PEDERSON, Kurt t 282
PEDERSON, Tommy tb 912
PEDULLA, Andy t 1055
PEEPLES, Robert v 1216
PEER, Beverley sb 526-527-528-529-1659-1660-1661-1662
PEETERS, Tur sb 1284
PELLIZZI, Pete tb 139-861-1108-1181-1182-1183-1350-1520
PELLMAN, Ben vl 1690
PELTYN, Sid t-mel 805-873-874-875
PEMBERTY, George d 1249
PEMELL, Charles t 799
PENDLETON, Andy bj-v 1168-1217-1705-1715-1716
PENEWELL, Jack g 1217
PENN, Ann v 1217
PENN, Jack p-a 684-1289-1509
PENNAK, Evelyn ts 1075
PENNSYLVANIANS, THE v 404
PEPPER, John cl-ts 188-322-829
PEPPIE, Harold t 552-804-931
PERCY, Bob p 1287
PEREGRINE, Paul cl-as-ts 402-403
PEREZ, Emmanuel c 466
PERITZ, Benny d 689
PERITZ, Hugo ts 689
PERKINS, ---- bb 1108
PERKINS, Alberta v 1218
PERKINS, Bill bj-g 47-48-762-763-1530
PERKINS, Billy - see ELLINGTON, JUDY
PERKINS, Cutie d 1462
PERKINS, Dolly v 1218
PERKINS, Gertrude v 1218
PERKINS, Ike g 26
PERKINS, Lutice d 187
PERKINS, Red (r.n. name Frank S. P.) t-v-ldr 1218

PERRELLA, Harry p 37-211-925-926-1067-1680-1681-1682-1683
PERRI, Danny g 1360-1361-1419-1539-1540
PERRIER, Jacotte v 1219
PERRIN, Johnny d 1047
PERRITT, Harry dir 1219
PERRONE, Mikr bb 134
PERRY, Bill a-dir 1123
PERRY, Ermit t 683
PERRY, Frank tb 1147
PERRY, Katherine or Catherine v 759-1220-1636
PERRY, Mario vn-pac 1204-1420-1609-1680-1681-1682-1683-1684-1685-1686
PERRY, Mort d-x 459-1460-1461
PERRY, Norman p 1472
PERRY, Ray vn 663-664
PERRY, Ron ts 63-740-741-1243-1244-1403-1411
PERSOFF, Sam vl 1398-1399
PERSON, Bob t 1243
PESKIN, Irving c 344
PET, Jack g 161-282-689
PETERS, Fred bb 1459
PETERS, Stan ts-bsn 1459
PETERS, Teddy v 1221
PETERSON, C. bb 863
PETERSON, Charles bj-g 670-1586
PETERSON, Chuck (r.n. Charles P.) t-v 63-451-452-453-454-455-744-1403-1404-1405-1406
PETERSON, H. p 1221
PETERSON, Harry bcl-ss-as 417-1479
PETERSON, Pete ts 118
PETERSON, Pete sb 53-78-79-81-92-542-543-565-634-767-780-1114-1115-1156-1157-1158-1159-1160 1231-1270-1313-1752
PETERSSON, Gosta t 282
PETIT, Dick ts 1116
PETRILLA, Paul as-bar-v 208-209-417
PETRILLO, Caesar tb 869-1673
PETRILLO, Joe bj 772
PETRONE, Johnny p 1021-1257
PETRONI, Joe g-a 184-185-186
PETRY, Fred ts 1400-1401
PETTAWAY, Hubert d 550-551-1560-1561
PETTIFER, Ern cl-dir 86-1221
PETTIS, Jack cl-Cm-ts 20-128-129-130-131-306-572-1028-1076-1077-1078-1079-1081-1131-1132-1221-1222-1223
PEVSNER, Alex vn 817-818-819
PEYTON, Benny d-ldr 1223-1274
PEYTON, Dave p 863
PFEIFFER, Fred ts 1491
PHELPS, Arthur - see BLIND BLAKE
PHENNIG, Dave cl-ss-as-ts-vn 708-1171
PHILBURN, Al tb 4-28-29-40-53-55-127-200-215-238-239-561-625-626-648-672-780 930-946-979-980-981-982-1025-1032-1114-1115 1137-1312-1313-1314-1315-1316-1330 1331-1332-1412-1483-1546-1620
PHILCOCK, Al d 635
PHILLIPS, Andy a 126-1553
PHILLIPS, Clarence bj 748
PHILLIPS, Greg tb 912
PHILLIPS, Harry t 1038
PHILLIPS, Howard v 638-1028-1330-1331-1601
PHILLIPS, Lloyd p 154-1109
PHILLIPS, Phil vn 346-347-348
PHILLIPS, Ralph bj 1038-1224

1818
PHILLIPS, Sid  cl-as-bar-a  22-23-24-25-
  161-302-393-459-500-784-785-1038-1224-
  1225-1295-1296-1297-1342
PHILLIPS, Van  cl-as-dir  61-306-521-537-
  564-565-568-1135-1355-1362-1363-1396-
  1738
PHILLIPS, Woolf  tb  279-801-822-1039-
  1225-1509
PHIPPS, James  p  153
PHRAM, —— g  1025
PHYSTER, George  sb  1047
PICARD, Andy  d  565-566-646-1373-1374
PICHON, Walter "Fats"  p-v  1169-1227-
  1263-1345-1716
PICKEL, Carl  p  314
PICKENS, Helen  v  1227-1228-1386
PICKENS, Jane  v  1227-1228-1386
PICKENS, Maria  v  1227-1228-1386
PICKERING, Ben  tb  249-250-437-438-439-
  644-1340-1361-1662
PICKETT, Leroy  vn  100-150-389-1228-
  1267-1455
PICO, A.  t  1642
PICOU, Alphonse  cl  1287
PIED PIPERS, THE  v  449-450-451-452-453-
  454-1228
PIERCE, Charles  as  1228
PIERCE, Charlie  vn  1043-1044
PIERCE, Charlie  bj  991-992
PIERCE, Harry  d  402-403
PIERCE, Hubert  sb  395
PIERCE, Jack  bb  17-63-638-1416-1417-
  1418-1604-1610
PIERCE, Kyle  p  1132-1229
PIERCE, Maurice  cl-as-ts-f  17-19-64-751-
  752-1212-1272-1416-1417-1418-1604-1610
PIERCE, Ralph  t  1347
PIERCE, Russell  cl-ts  1548
PIERCE, Vincent  p  884
PIERSON, Carl  ts  302
PIGUILLÉM, Al  t  333-1284
PIKE, Albert  ts-vl  1207
PIKE, Bill  p-dir  891
PIKE, Hal  bj  1379
PILATO, Joe  tb  182
PILCER, Murray  d-ldr  1229
PILLAR, Jules  cl-ss-ts  194-1036-1746
PILLARS, Charles  as  830  1563-1564
PILLARS, Hayes  ts-v  830-1563-1564
PINCKNEY, Lloyd  p  1426-1427
PINCKNEY or PINKEY, Wilbur  cl-as  395-557
PINDER, Éddie  t  1684-1685-1686
PINELLA, Bernard  vn  1520-1521
PINERO, Frank  p  1248-1249-1250
PINGATORE, Mike  bj  76-211-732-1325-1355-
  1606-1607-1608-1609-1680-1681-1682-1683-
  1684-1685-1686-1687-1688-1689-1690-1691
PINI, Eugene  vn  636-1149-1493
PINK, Reg  ts  525-1149-1336
PINKARD, Maceo  p  1355-1651
PINKETT, Ward  t-v  839-868-967-1061-1102-
  1104-1105-1171-1497-1707
PINKEY, Wilbur - see PINCKNEY, WILBUR
PINKSTON, Thomas  bj  1723
PIPER, Clarence  bj  189
PIPER, Gene  c  118
PIRON, Armand J.  vn-v-ldr  136-152-1229-
  1230
PIRRO, Vincent  pac  201-1009-1690
PISANI, Nick  vn-bb-sb  98-163-262-1095-
  1150-1393

PISTOCCHI, Joe  t  517
PITMAN, Booker  cl-as  251
PITT, Freddy (r.n. Alfred P.)  t  515-
  843-1226-1227-1291-1674
PITTMAN, Arthur  tb  748
PITTMAN, Bob  bj-v  1643-1644
PITTMAN, Booker  cl-as  835-836
PITTS, Cyril  v  240-242-1422
PLANT, Jack  147-1127-1128-1148
PLATT, Mike  cl-as  1546
PLEIS, Jack  p-a  1358-1359-1360-1361
PLETCHER, Stew  t-v-a-ldr  78-1156-1157-
  1231-1235-1663-1745
PLOTKIN, Ben  vn  1399
PLOTZ, Otto  tenor voice  657
PLOVEN, Mike  as-vn  577
PLUM(B), Neely  as  547-1407-1408
PLUMMER, Harold  cl-ss-as-bar  708
PLUMMER, Sid  d  1008
PLUMSTEAD, George  tb  1228
PLYLER, Coon  p  182
PODAL(SKY), Harry  vn  992-993-1616
POE, Evelyn  v  1752-1753
POGSON, E. O.  cl-ss-as-bar-f-o  281-554-
  799-800-801-809-810-1214-1292-1293-1294-
  1295-1296-1297
POHL, Harry  cl-ss  515
POINDEXTER, Rosie  v  836
POLA, Eddie  v  684
POLAND, Bob  bar  622-623
POLEN, Nat  d  457
POLIAKINE, Paul  vn  454-455
POLK, Charlie  jug-v  1041-1042
POLK, Claytie  v  1020
POLLACK, Ben  d-v-ldr  153-162-163-204-
  591-1029-1076-1131-1132-1231-1232-1233-
  1234-k235-1236-1237-1506-1691-1718
POLLACK, Eddie  cl-as-bar-v  1153-1154
POLLARD, Averil  sb  459
POLLARD, Harry  d-ldr  315-1173
POLLARD, Nat  d  786-787
POLLARD, Snub (r.n. William C. P.)  t  34-
  1146-1234
POLLARD, Tommy  p  316
POLLOCK, Harry  vn-ldr  1237-1238
POLO, Danny  cl-as-ts-bar  2-20-21-22-23-
  24-25-31-61-161-364-404-507-508-564-577-
  578-690-776-788-949-950-951-952-953-
  1136-1148-1164-1165-1238-1292-1293-1294-
  1298-1335-1396-1397-1511-1540-1541-1553-
  1554-1594-1595-1673-1750
POLZER, Mike  tb  546-796-797
PONCE, Dorothea  v  1238
PONCE, Ethel  v  1238
POND, Harry  bj  887
POOLE, Alex  cl-as  665-1100
POOLE, Walter  tb  1285
POOLEY, Harry  p  156
POPE, Bob  t-v  32-33-339-340-341-1238-
  1239-1515-1573
POPE, Bob  v-ldr  1238-
POPE, Lee  ts  730
POPPINK, Wim  cl-as-bar  161-282-689
PORETTA, Joe  cl-as  201-1009
PORPORA, Johnny  bb-sb  840
PORRET, Julian  t  571
PORT, Gil  bsx  1219
PORTER, Albert  v  1528
PORTER, Del  cl-as-v  871-1143
PORTER, Dick  p-v  1240
PORTER, Gene  ts  1310-1311

PORTER, Helen  d  142
PORTER, Jake  t  512-513
PORTER, James "King"  t  410-762-763-1108
PORTER, Ralph  t  830
PORTER, Ray  cl-as-ts-v  578-579-1369
PORTER, Tom  t  1339-1340-1341-342
PORTER, Yank  d  51-207-284-770-789-1511-1531-1627-1628-1629-1736
PORTIER, George  cl-ts  553
POSNACK, George  p  20
POSNER, Benny  vn  1015-1416-1417-1604-1610
POSNER, Leonard  vn  454-455
POST, Irving  v  1503
POSTON, Joe  as-ts-v  337-338-1151-1152-1153
POTT, Willard  cl-as  566
POTTER, Billy  v  1614
POTTER, Fred  cl-ss-as-ts  640-641
POTTER, George  bj  396-397
POTTER, Nettie  v  1241
POTTER, Ollie  v  1414
POTTLE, Benny  bb-sb  112-629-917-918-999-1000-1133-1248-1539-1559
POTTS, Cyril  v  627
POUGNET, Jean  vn  21-22-23-24-801-953-1126-1127-1472-1749
POVEROMO, Michael  g  243-244-325
POWE, Norman  tb  1674
POWELL, Bert  vn  656
POWELL, Bertha  v  188-854
POWELL, Dick  bj-g-v  391-1241
POWELL, Eddie  cl-as-ts-bar-f  80-81-923-1224-1512-1513-1551-1552
POWELL, Eleanor  tap-dancing-v  1437
POWELL, Ernie  cl-as-ts  283-284-691-770-1203-1735
POWELL, Forrest  t  763
POWELL, Herbert  vn-vl  1214-1215
POWELL, James  cl-as-ts-ldr  283-770-1203-1241-1377-1632-1637
POWELL, Johnny  d  334 1031
POWELL, Larry  t  1047
POWELL, Louis  v  1241
POWELL, Mel  p-cel-a  619-620-621-622-623-1004-1242
POWELL, Rudy  cl-as  14-318-695-696-736-806-807-901-902-1019-1093-1500-1625-1626-1627-1628-1731-1735-1736
POWELL, Scat  v  494-517-1712
POWELL, Specs (r.n. Gordon P.)  d  273-897-1477
POWELL, Teddy  bj-g-a-ldr  992-993-1242-1243-1244
POWELL, Walter  tb-ldr  1245
POWERS, Eddie  ts  1175-1206-1510
POWERS, Jack  d-v  1250-1621
POWERS, Lennie  p  1640
POWERS, Ollie  d-v-ldr  1245
PRA(E)GER, Carl  cl-bcl-as  80-81-207-1513
PRAGER, Manny  cl-as-ts  131-1027
PRAGER, Sammy  p  672-673-1235
PRATER, Matthew  vn-g-v  696
PRATHER, Harry  bb-sb  646-1103-1537-1560
PRATT, Alfred  ts  52-835-836
PRATT, Eddie  cl-as  1434-1675-1692
PRATT, Lester  baritone voice  812
PREBAL, Harry  t  1308
PREER, Andy  vn-ldr  349-1245
PREER, Evelyn (r.n. Evelyn Peer)  v  1246-1701

PREIS, Rex  c-t  866-867-1616
PREISSING, Wally  ts  1509
PRENDERGAST, Gene  cl-as-a  205-571-629-1615
PRENTISS, Bud  cl-as  1021
PRESTON, Keith  t  89
PRESTON, Walter J.  v  577
PREUS, H.  t  1575
PRICE, Abe  d  940
PRICE, Bob  t  98-740-741-742-999-1063-1064
PRICE, C. Q.  as  730
PRICE, Charles  t  518-616
PRICE, George  v  1609
PRICE, Jesse  d  528-944
PRICE, Joe  bj-g-stg  111-1236
PRICE, Robert  d  820-1718
PRICE, Sam  p-v  90-91-187-390-460-681-831-841-893-1028-1094-1246-1247-1323-1370-1413-1467-1542-1575-1678-1729
PRICE-ASPINELL, W. B. P.  sb  263
PRIEST, Billy  as-bj  1171
PRIESTLEY, Bill  c-bj-g  1252-1253
PRIMA, Leon  c  1208
PRIMA, Louis  t-v  1248-1249-1250-1335-1602
PRIME, Alberta  v  1250
PRIME, Charles  p  548
PRINCE, Charles A.  p-dir  332-346-1200-1250-1251-1252-1370-1586-1587
PRINCE, Earres  p  252-253-349-686-1013-1084-1245-1725
PRINCE, Gene  t  58-192-898-1718
PRINCE, Henry  p  47-48-138-762-763
PRINCE, Hughie  v  448
PRINCE, Jimmy  p  1280-1281-1344
PRINCE, Paul  sb  1027
PRINCE, Peppy (? W. P.)  d-v  762-763
PRINCE, Teddy  v  587
PRINCE, Wesley  sb  329-663
PRINZ, Milton  vc  1690
PRINZ, Spencer  d  1406
PRITCHARD, Billy  tb-v  517-880-1562-1752
PRITCHETT, Ed  cl-as-ts-bar  1643-1644
PRITIKIN, Arnold  ts-a  1047
PRITIKIN, Sid  bj-g  1047-1195-1616
PRIVIN, Bernie  t  63-97-98-621-622-1404-1405-1406
PROBST, Bobby  p-cel  1675
PROCOPE, Russell  cl-ss-as-v  12- 75-79-80-169-273-281-661-662-724-725-726-727-730-755-756-779-836-895-896-897-1103-1134-1159-1337-1477-1513-1535-1703-1705-1706-1710-1711-1721
PROCTOR, Helen  v  342-1253
PROFIT, Clarence  p  6-563-1253- 1646-1647
PROSPERO, Fritz  vn  163-1150
PROSPERO, Nick  t  907
PROUTING, Lionel  p  307
PRUIT, Milas  g  353-1266
PRUIT, Miles  bj  353-1266
PRYME, Charlie  p  1057
PRYOR, Arthur  tb-dir  1254-1255-1256-1473 1474
PRYOR, Martha  v  1256
PRYOR, S. O.  d  1473-1474-1475-1604
PRYOR, Walter  c  1586-1604
PTACEK, L.  as-ts  1575
PUCHTA, Charlie  d  1347-1348
PUCKETT, ——  cl-as  189
PUGH, David  v  646
PUGH, Max  v  1304

PUGH, Raymond  p  1285-1286
PUGLESE, Jimmy  bsx  234
PULLEN, Eddie  bj-g  348
PUMIGLIO, Pete  cl-as-bar  236-237-238-
   239-240-241-242-243-244-245-246-247-248
   263-626-627-776-804-831-853-882-1025-
   1032-1141-1329-1371-1372-1373-1375-1393
   1394-1422-1580-1581-1583-1593-1599-1620
   1621-1720
PURCE, Ernest  cl-as-bar  251-284-1008-
   1070
PURCELL, Bob  d-v  1048
PURNELL, Keg  (r.n. William P.)  d  283-
   284-1263
PURNELL, Theodore  as  863
PURSGLOVE, Reg  vn  16-20-21-22-23-156-
   470-521-953-1126-1127-1364-1365-1456-
   1521-1695
PURSLEY, Roosevelt  jug  328
PURTILL, Maurice  d  78-443-444-445-545-
   1157-1228-1231-1313
PURVIANCE, Don  ts  1146-1147
PURVIS, Jack  t-v  247-248-504-545-884-
   888-1256-1257-1621-1730
PUTNAM, Ray  cl-as  566-1213

QUANDER, Sis  v  1257
QUARELLA, A.  t  151
QUARTELL, Frankie  t  857-858-1232-1257-
   1347-1348
QUARTELL, Joe  tb  133-1047
QUEALEY, Chelsea  t  31-38-127-234-235-
   236-237-238-239-245-248-249-360-468-469
   470-524-530-532-533-552-624-625-626-858
   859-943-967-1025-1052-1095-1291-1300-
   1579-1580-1583-1592-1593-1619-1620-1752
   1753
QUEENER, Charlie  p  1482
QUEISH, Harlan  bj  1437
QUENZER, Artie  ts  162-1236
QUICKSELL, Howdy  (r.n. Howard Q.)  bj-v
   115-576-577-578-738
QUIDDINGTON, Stan  ts  348-1675
QUIGLEY, Herb  d-x  120-121-579-580-1269-
   1273-1377-1412-1538-1571-1599-1689
QUIGLEY, Truman  t  364-1540-1541
QUINN, Cyril  bb  1369
QUINN, Dan  v  1257
QUINN, Snoozer  (r.n. Edward McIntosh Q.)
   g  1017-1258-1325
QUINTELL, Joseph  harp  997
QUINTONES, THE  v  98-135-1263
QUINTY, George  as  126

RABIN, Oscar  bsx-vn-dir  1263
RABY, Bert  vn-g-d-x-vib  885
RACHEL, Yank  (r.n. James R.)  md  948
RADEL, Ed  bb  1641
RADCLIFFE, George (Dennis)  t  161-467-468
   524 (see also RATCLIFFE, George)
RADERMAN, Harry  tb  549-954-955-956-957-
   958-1164-1230-1263-1264-1457
RADERMAN, Harry  d  20
RADERMAN, Lou  vn-dir  17-63-64-112-332-
   509-638-751-752-756-853-1015-1016-1064-
   1065-1141-1172-1264-1273-1415-1416-1417-
   1418-1456-1586-1604-1610
RADERMAN, Max  p  1273
RADFORD, Harry  p-a  1309
RADIO IMPS, THE  v  1620
RADLACH, Karl  p  376-377-1265

RAE, Ronnie  bj  1048
RAGAS, Henry  p  1175-1176
RAGLIN, Junior  sb  499-500
RAGON, Ike  v-ldr  1265
RAGOTS, Marty  d  660
RAINE, Jack  c-t  535-799-800-801-1265
RAINER, Lloyd  g  59
RAINES, Phil  bsn  420
RAINEY, Ma  (r.n. Gertrude R.)  v  1265-
   1266-1267-1268-1269
RAINS, Gray  a  307
RAITZ, Johnny  ts  535-799-800-801
RAJULA, Matty  cl-as-bar  826
RAKSIN, Dave  cl  193
RALPH, Jesse  tb  756-1063-1064-1121
RALSTON, Art  as-bar-bsn-o  56-291-292-
   293-294-295-296-297-298-299-300-622-
   1615
RALSTON, Bill - see PASTOR, TONY
RALTON, Bert  cl-ss-as-o  1362
RAMEY, Ben  k-v  1041-1042-1043
RAMEY, Eugene  v  1222
RAMEY, Gene  sb  1037-1038
RAMEY, Hurley  g  730-761-863-1344
RAMEY, Shelton T.  c  279
RAMIREZ, Ram  (r.n. Roger R.)  p  191-382-
   527-1008-1231-1500
RAMON, Kitty  v  151
RAMONA  (r.n. Ramona Davies)  p-v  1269-
   1270
RAMSEY, George  p-v  1344
RAND, Carl  ts  184
RAND, Frank  cl-ts  418
RAND, Lionel  p  747
RAND, Odell  cl  308-678-679-680-783-824-
   1029-1197-1206-1371-1541-1542
RANDALL, Charles  tb  337-637
RANDALL, Clark - see TENNILLE, FRANK
RANDALL, Cliff  cl-as  89
RANDALL, Reavely  v  751
RANDALL, Slatz  p-ldr  886-887-1270
RANDALL, Willie  cl-as-ts  730-759
RANDO, Arthur "Doc"  as  62-363-364-365-
   373-374-375-376-1003
RANDOLPH, Harold  k-v  6-1431-1647
RANDOLPH, Irving  t  131-257-258-259-281-
   283-527-528-661-727-1563-1564-1732
RANDOLPH, Mandy  (r.n. Amanda R.)  p-v
   953-954-1271
RANDOLPH, Zilmer  t-speech-a  48-49-50-51
RANGE, Robert  tb  691-692-693-694
RANK, Bill  tb  76-116-117-174-361-576-
   577-578-738-922-1017-1139-1406-1566-1567
   1568-1569-1570-1598-1683-1684-1685-1686-
   1687-1688-1689-1690
RAPH, Ted  tb  242-243-244-262-508-626-627
   1120-1130-1393-1583-1593-1620
RAPP, Barney  d-ldr  1271
RAPP, Louis  cl-as  1231-1663
RAPPOLO, Leon - see ROPPOLO, LEON
RASCHEL, Jimmy  v  1272
RASEY, Uan  t  457
RASKIN, Milt  p  453-454-455-506-906-907-
   908-911-912-1242
RASMUS, Frank  g  1357-1358
RASMUSSEN, Alfred  sb  821
RASMUSSEN, Peter  tb  282-652
RASMUSSEN, Tage  t  1585
RASTIN, Doug  as  525
RATCLIFFE, George (incorrectly spelt thus)
   t  20-21-22-950-951-952-953-1127-1290

RATES, Sam  vn  420
RATHERT, Norman  bj  517
RATTAY, Howard  vn  1586
RATTINER, Angie (r.n. Angelo R.)  t  241-
242-243-244-245-262-626-627-936-979-
1117-1118-1224-1274-1377-1393-1394-1583
1593-1620
RAUB, Hal  bb  194-1036
RAUCH, Billy (r.n. Russel R.)  tb  56-76-
209-286-287-288-289-290-291-292-293-294
295-296-297-298-299-300
RAUSCH, Cliff  g  785-786
RAUSCH, Harry  t  785-786
RAVENSCROFT, John  v  894
RAXON, Al  cl  1412
RAY, Arthur  p-or  733-1024-1057-1058-1547
RAY, Floyd  dir  1272
RAY, Frank  sb  1148
RAY, Joey  v  1231
RAY, John  cl-as  553
RAYE, Don  v  166
RAYE, Martha  v  1272
RAYMAN, Maurice  sb  1358-1359-1360
RAYMOND, Henri  cl  396-397
RAYMOND, Irving  vn  454
RAYMOND, Joe  vn  395-870-871-1141-1598-
1611-1612-1613
RAYMOND, Ray  c  133
RAYMOND, Sid  as  1238
RAZAF, Andy (r.n. Andrea Razafinkieriefo)
v  722-1273-1345-1500-1630
READ, Bert  p-a  20-21-22-25-147-272-506-
507-656-684-1196-1291-1292-1293-1294-
1295-1296-1297-1335-1472-1675
READ, Dolores  v  1601
READ, Jack  tb  1228
REALINI, ———  ts  151
REARDON, Casper  harp  1031-1273-1274-
1538-1546-1689
REBER, Harry  v  402
REBITO, Gasparre  t  1064
REDDING, Marion  v  1147
REDLAND, Charles  cl  282
REDMAN, Don  cl-ss-as-bar-gfs-v-dir-ldr-a
44-66-91-107-110-134-165-260-311-353-360
431-472-579-580-705-706-710-711-712-713-
714-715-716-717-718-719-720-721-722-731-
732-733-749-750-770-793-794-935-966-989-
1014 1023-1033-1034-1035-1051-1266-1276-
1277-1278-1279-1350-1440-1441-1443-1447-
1448-1449-1466-1519-1520-1628-1650-1682-
1699-1700-1706-1717-1725-1728
REDMOND, Donald M  p  860
REDMOND, Paul  bj  320
REED, Bert  tb  1479
REED, D.  o  748
REED, Howard  c  1510
REED, Nathaniel  p  1651
REED, Russ  d  540
REESE, Claude  v  932-1029
REESE, Gail  v  123-124-1064
REESE, Lloyd  t-cl-as  728-1512-1530
REESE, Rostelle  t  284-761
REEVE, George  d  141
REEVE, John  tb  380
REEVES, Arthur  tb  1516-1517-1518
REEVES, Carl 'Jug'  jug-v  891-1223
REEVES, Chick  g-a  738-739-829-1224-1538-
1752
REEVES, George  d  1515
REEVES, Gerald  tb  1102-1280-1281-1282

REEVES, John  tb  1518
REEVES, Nina  v  1280
REEVES, Red  bj  III
REEVES, Reuben  t  252-253-254-843-1280-
1281-1282-1714
REEVES, Talcott  bj-g  360-935-1276-1277-
1278
REEVY, Jim (James)  tb  564-704-705-1362-
1426-1648
REGA, Milo  dir  1059
REHL, Duke  cl-as-ts  919
REHMUS, Elmer  tb  201-1009-1241
REHRIG, Red (r.n. Harold R.)  t  128-1589
REICHMAN, Joe  p  1548
REID, Dotty  v  1482
REID, Jack  tb  1366
REID, Jim  sb  1092
REID, Kit  t  913
REID, Neal  tb  163-364-738-739-740-741-
742-743-744
REIDERICH, James  t  457
REINDERS, Fritz  g  689
REINER, Lloyd  g  1118
REINER, Nat  bn  326
REINHARDT, Django  g  3-16-163-172-188-.
189-283-307-312-313-317-330-333-396-398
465-519-632-635-689-690-973-1173-1211-
1219-1221-1258-1259-1260-1261-1262-1283
1284-1288-1338-1339-1348-1349-1350-1421
1476-1500-1536-1562-1563-1596-1615-1642
1670
REINHARDT, Joseph  g  189-312-313-330-333-
398-465-519-632-635-1211-1219-1258-1259-
1260-1261-1262-1284-1350-1563-1642
REINHART, Dick  cl-v  962-1558-1640
REINHART, William  p  1284
REINHERZ, Sid  p  1285
REININGER, John  as  1510
REINO, Frank  bj-g  972-973-1521
REINWALD, Aime  t  317
REIS, Les  v  2-268-625-626-725-726-928-
1285-1567-1616-1619-1620
REISMAN, Leo  vn-ldr-v  1285-1286
REISS, Happy  d  36-905
REITZ, William H.  d-x  1256-1578-1586-
1587-1604-1605
REITZEL, H.  ah-th-bh  1256-1605
REMLEY, Frank  g  685-686
REMUE, Charles  cl-as-ldr  1286
REMY, Pierre  tb  1284
RENA, Henry "Kid"  t  1287
RENA, Joe  d  1287
RENARD, Alex  t  333-652-959-1211-1284-
1595-1615-1642
RENDALL, Willie  cl-as  1322
RENDLEMAN, Dunk  bj-ldr  1287
RENE, Leon  p-ldr  1287
RENE, Otis  v  1287
RENZULLI, Mike  t  1
REO, Tommy  tb  98-1242
REPAY, Ted  p  159-642
RESCHKE, Frank E.  as-vl  1604
RESER, Harry  bj-g-dir  89-145-319-320-
380-532-552-669-928-929-946-994-1029-
1052-1076-1098-1163-1275-1288- 1305-
1339-1395-1417-1440-1545-1610-1611-1680
1737
RETTE, Nina  v  1288
RETTENBERG, Milt  p-cel  17-63-332-509-
638-751-752-1064-1330-1416-1417-1418-
1456-1512-1604-1610

1822
REUBENS, Harry  p  459-809-810
REUSS, Allen  g  78-126-183-383-417-595-
   596-597-598-599-600-601-602-603-604-605
   606-607-608-660-661-767-905-906-1538-
   1539-1690-1691-1731-1732-1733-1734
REUTER, Spencer  v  402
REVEL, Harry  p-dir  1425-1426
REY, Alvino  g  1048
REYNAUD, Sudie (r.n. Rudolph R.)  bb-sb
   338-1282-1714
REYNOLDS, Blake  as  1406
REYNOLDS, Burt  ss-as  266-267-630
REYNOLDS, Dick  p  100-954-955-956
REYNOLDS, Ellsworth  sb  1468
REYNOLDS, George  p  810-862-863
REYNOLDS, Jimmy (James)  p  14-1203-1456
REYNOLDS, John  tb  307-1288
REYNOLDS, Lyst  bj-ldr  1288
REYNOLDS, Ross  tb-ldr  1289
REZEK, P.  g  1575
RHOADS, Phil  bb  913
RHODES, Doris  v  1289
RHODES or RHOADES, Dusty - see ROADS,
   Dusty
RHODES, Joe  bb-sb  552-553
RHODES, Todd  p-cel  311-580-1033-1034-
   1035
RHYTHM GIRLS, THE  v  663
RHYTHM SISTERS, THE  v  23
RICCI, Paul  cl-as-ts  53-122-203-204-205
   363-455-699-700-756-780-903-1032-1082-
   1088-1095-1224-1273-1312-1313-1314-1333
   1377-1412-1415-1512-1546-1558-1655
RICE, Bob  bj-g-v  1172
RICE, Buddy  cl-as-ts  552-553-1124
RICE, Floyd  t-mel-as  1171-1172
RICE, Frank  g  1134
RICE, George  as-ts  1196
RICE, Vance  t  1570-1571
RICH, Buddy  d  125-126-448-449-450-451-
   452-453-454-455-1007-1048-1333-1404-
   1405-1406-1512
RICH, Fred  p-ldr  399-1115-1299-1300-
   1301-1302-1303-1304
RICH, Harry  bb  314
RICHARDET, Louis  p  776
RICHARDS, Bill  cl-as-ts  840-1067-1068-
   1672
RICHARDS, Charles  p-v  1560-1561
RICHARDS, Chuck  v  729-1073-1075-1304-
   1658
RICHARDS, Danny  v  126
RICHARDS, Jack  as  1672
RICHARDS, Lynne  v  126-818
RICHARDS(ON), Newton  cl-ts  356-1122-1123
RICHARDS, Rick  v  1744
RICHARDSON, ---- as  1613
RICHARDSON, Andy  t  31-525 953-1070-1226
   1227-1290-1291
RICHARDSON, Ben  as-bar  18
RICHARDSON, Cecil  d  1663-1664
RICHARDSON, Dick  bar  417
RICHARDSON, Inez  v  1304
RICHARDSON, Jack  ts  457
RICHARDSON, Mabel  v  810
RICHARDSON, Noisy  tb  806-807
RICHARDSON, Oliver  p  342
RICHARDSON, Percy  bj  1497
RICHARDSON, Rudy  d  752
RICHARDSON, S.  cl-ss-as-ts  863
RICHARDSON, Sam  as-bj  1274

RICHARDSON, Snake  as  1693
RICHEL, Jerry J.  cl-as  1123
RICHMAN, Harry  v  1305
RICHMOND, Eddie  c  1573
RICHMOND, J. L.  v  1643
RICHMOND, Jack  v  286-287-1305
RICHMOND, June  v  259-429-530-901-902
RICHOLSON, Joe  t  338-339-340-341
RICHTER, Paul  d  207-325-829
RICKARD, Earl  v  624-1164-1305
RICKARD, James  cl  1327-1328
RICKARD, Ted  cl-as  1722
RICKARD, Verne  cl-ts-pac  1722
RICKENBACKER, Paul  p  320
RICKETTS, Bob  p-a-dir  136-181-190-458-
   802-846-1022-1059-1218-1305
RICKS, John  bb-sb  141-1426
RICKSON, George  p  142-458-651-944-1230-
   1518-1725-1727
RICO, Filiberto  as  827
RIDDICK, Dave  t  1645
RIDDICK, Johnny  p  32-1175
RIDGLEY, William  tb  301
RIDLEY, Carroll  ts  1272
RIDLEY, Ethel  v  1305-1306
RIEDEL, Bob  cl  647
RIEHL, Ollie "Duke"  cl-as  1673 (see
   also REHL, DUKE - correct spelling not
   certain)
RIESTRA, Joe  sb  1536
RIGGS, Earl  d-v  1498
RIGNOLD, Hugo  vn-vl-v  684-799-800-903-
   1128-1306
RIIS, Amdi  p  652
RILEY, Joe  ts  345-536
RILEY, Lee  c'  565-566
RILEY, Mike  tb-mel-v-dir  363-779-1031-
   1205-1306-1307-1308-1490-1562
RIMMER, Jack  t  1229
RINES, Joe  v-dir  1308
RING, Justin  p-cel-d-chimes-dir  420-501
   502-503-671-672-812-922-930-1059-1164-
   1308-1425-1596-1704
RINGER, Johnny  d-dir  1309-1521
RINGGOLD, Issie  v  1309
RINGSTRAND, Willard  p  1585
RINKER, Al  v trio  545
RINKER, Al  v  482-1551-1681-1682-1683-
   1684-1685-1686-1687
RINKER, Carl  c-t  406-812-1546
RIPPLINGER, Harold  c  1421
RISHER, Leo  cl-ts  1289
RISKIN, Itzy (r.n. Irving R.)  p  598
RISLEY, Jim  bsx-bb-sb  525-938-939-1336
RITTE, Ernest  cl-as-bar  459-539-581-582
   583-584-585-586-587-588-589-1149-1224-
   1507-1508-1739-1749
RITTEN, Eddie  t  571
RIVES, Georges  bj  1213-1214
RIZZO, Vincent  dir  1310
RIZZOTTO, Dalton  tb-v  815-816-817-818-
   819-820-907-908
ROACH, Earl  v  1459
ROADS, Dusty  d-vib-v  658-840-1069-1524-
   1664-1665
ROANE, Eddie  t  865
ROANE, Kenneth  t  328-650-1371-1705-1715
ROBBINS, Doris  v  1235-1236
ROBBINS, Everett  p-v-dir  1310-1461-1462
ROBBINS, Harold  bj-g  1092

ROBBINS, Harry  d-x-vib  31-32-523-524-
  799-800-801-949-953-1196-1295-1296-1297
  1310-1435
ROBBINS, Harry Snr  d  1117
ROBBINS, Lilian  sw  69
ROB(B)INS, Millard  bsx  1321-1456-1501
ROBBINS, Robert  vn  1440
ROBECHAUX, Joe  p-dir  636-863-1310-1311
ROBENS, Harry  p  1493
ROBERSON, Orlando  v  695
ROBERTS, Al  bj-g  885
ROBERTS, Bobby  vn-v  1310
ROBERTS, Lucky (r.n. C. Luckeyth)  p 1311
ROBERTS, Caughey  cl-as  101-110-1631
ROBERTS, Claude  bj-g  410-757-758-759-760
  1421
ROBERTS, Dave  cl-ss-as-ts-bar  346-1213-
  1214-1675
ROBERTS, Earl  vc-bj  869-1673
ROBERTS, Frankie  cl-as-ts  118-271-556-
  1606
ROBERTS, George  as-ts  841
ROBERTS, Gilbert  bj  149
ROBERTS, Harry  as-v  1357-1358
ROBERTS, Joe  bj-v  405-1270
ROBERTS, Keith  tb  887
ROBERTS, Paul  t  377-1265
ROBERTS, Richard  v  1614
ROBERTS, Worth  bb  1287
ROBERTSON, Bill  tb  94-95-96-97-98-99-173
ROBERTSON, Dick  v-dir  34-35-36-130-142-
  275-285-351-481-482-483-519-592-676-724-
  725-840-870-873-874-875-876-877-878-879-
  880-898-919-933-1071-1081-1142-1143-1144
  1145-1146-1193-1232-1303-1313-1314-
  1315-1316-1316-1317-1318-1319-1330-1346-
  1385-1386-1387-1388-1409-1410-1571-1709-
  1742-1751
ROBERTSON, Joe  p  27
ROBERTSON, John  t  682-1215
ROBERTSON, Orlando  v  773-774-775-1624
ROBERTSON, Zue (r.n. Calvin R.)  tb  1099
ROBESON, Paul  v  109
ROBIE, Milton  vn  1042-1043
ROBINS, Fats  t  1501-1714
ROBINS, Phyllis  v  995-996
ROBINSON, Adrian  p  1529
ROBINSON, Aletha  p  751
ROBINSON, Alexander  v  1319
ROBINSON, Anna  v  839
ROBINSON, Avery  a  761
ROBINSON, Bill  tap-dancing-v  1080-1277
ROBINSON, Bob or Rob  cl-v  1320-1496
ROBINSON, Bob  bj-g  1662
ROBINSON, Chuck  g  1552
ROBINSON, Clarence  cl  1056-1089-1510-
  1532-1649
ROBINSON, Eddie  p  566
ROBINSON, Eli  tb  108-109-110-192-252-466
  808-1070-1075
ROBINSON, Elzadie  v  1320-1321
ROBINSON, Frank  bsx-h-descant recorder-d
  704-705-1395 (believed to be the same
  artist in each case)
ROBINSON, Fred  tb  43-44-45-46-281-360-
  404-901-1019-1107-1169-1276-1277-1278-
  1488
ROBINSON, George  tb  1632
ROBI(N)SON, Harry  bb-sb  59-1305
ROBINSON, Henry  tb  1203

ROBINSON, Ikey  cl-bj-g-v  5-311-726- 1823
  752-767-823-837-862-1321-1322-1455-1456-
  1501-1677-1678-1706-1708
ROBINSON, Ivor  v  938
ROBINSON, J. Russel  p-v  127-668-706-707-
  1176-1177-1178-1179
ROBINSON, James "Geechy"  tb  7
ROBINSON, Jim  tb  1095-1096-1287
ROBINSON, Joe  v  1322
ROBINSON, Les  t  1550
ROBINSON, Les  cl-as  62-63-168-449-615-
  616-618-1400-1401-1402-1403-1404-1405-
  1406-1407-1408-1409-1712
ROBINSON, Mabel  v  864-1247-1323
ROBINSON, Milton  tb  284-902
ROBINSON, Nettie  v  1323
ROBINSON, Percy  d  1742
ROBINSON, Pete  bj  807
ROBINSON, Phil  ts  18
ROBINSON, Prince  cl-ts  39-58-149-192-
  252-311-466-472-473-645-939-1033-1035-
  1388-1450-1705-1706-1707-1710-1711-1732
  1733
ROBINSON, Robert  cl-ts  142
ROBINSON, Sam  v  1323
ROBINSON, Ted  g  899-900-901-1720
ROBINSON, Wesley  p  50
ROBISON, Carson  v  112-274-1323-1324
ROBISON, Walter  cl-ts  517
ROBISON, Willard  p  211-534-669-1324-
  1325-1680
ROBLE, Melvin  cl-as-ts  919
ROCCIOLLA, Pat  cl-ts  919
ROCCO, Charles  c-t  403-471-523-524-1067
  1068-1364-1521
ROCCO, Maurice  p-v  1326
ROCHE, Betty  v  342
ROCK, Joe  cl-as-ts  885
ROCKWELL, A. A.  bb  884
ROCKWELL, Les  v  236-505
RODDICK, Charlie  p  1146
RODDY, Reuben  ts  1204
RODEMICH, Gene  p-ldr  1326-1327
RODERICK, Stan  t  25-801
RODERMAN, Al  cl-as-ts  573
RODGERS, Dick - see ROBERTSON, DICK
RODGERS, Gene  p  282-690-691-1171-1327-
  1669-1707
RO(D)GERS, Harry  tb  63-816-817-818-819-
  820-1063-1400-1401-1402-1404-1405-1406
RODGERS, Ike  tb-vn  181-834-846-847-1009-
  1029-1091-1327-1673
RODGERS, Jimmie  v  1327-1328
RODGERS, Jim  bsx  1252
RODIN, Gil  cl-as-ts  62-161-162-363-364-
  365-366-367-368-369-370-371-372-373-374-
  375-376-555-1029-1076-1077-1078-1079-
  1080-1081-1131-1144-1231-1232-1233-1234-
  1235-1236-1328-1537-1718
RODO, George  sb  1272
RODRIGUEZ, Red (r.n. Nicholas R.)  p  281-
  791-792-1103-1279
RODRIGUEZ, Willie  d  1691
ROEHRE, Arthur  tb  1498
ROGERS, Bill  cl-as  515-1155-1336
ROGERS, Billy  t-v  743-744
ROGERS, Charles "Buddy"  v-dir  1329
ROGERS, Clovis  g  660
ROGERS, Clyde  ts-v  702-703-1116-1117-
  1561

ROGERS, Emmett  d  650-651
ROGERS, Gaby  vib  1046
ROGERS, George  dir  1169
ROGERS, Ginger  v  1329
ROGERS, Hilda  v  40
ROGERS, Mack  t-dir  1329
ROGERS, Rodney  stg  1555
ROGERS, Walter B.  c-dir  332-1473-1474-
  1475-1586-1604-1605
ROHL, Elvira  t  1075
ROHLE, Ray  d  133
ROHLFING, Glenn  t  1602
ROLAND, Johnny  d  589-590-591
ROLFE, B. A.  t-ldr  973-1329-1330
ROLLICKERS, THE  v  1174-1301-1302
ROLLINI, Adrian  bsx-gfs-hfp-p-d-x-vib
  67-116-145-220-221-222-223-224-225-226-
  227-228-229-230-231-232-233-234-235-236
  237-243-248-249-419-462-463-468-469-470
  529-530-533-553-623-624-625-626-669-672
  756-828-883-890-966-967-968-977-978-979
  980-981-1027-1031-1032-1064-1086-1088-
  1098-1138-1139-1140-1142-1143-1256-1257-
  1285-1286-1300-1329-1330-1331-1332-1333-
  1334-1382-1412-1422-1438-1537-1566-1567-
  1579-1580-1581-1582-1583-1590-1591-1592-
  1593-1596-1598-1600-1602-1615-1619-1620-
  1639-1652
ROLLINI, Arthur  ts  16-168-248-249-470-
  505-506-594-595-596-597-598-599-600-601-
  602-603-604-605-606-607-608-609-610-611-
  660-661-814-1089-1095-1330-1331-1332-
  1333-1337-1602
ROLLINS, Horace  sb  906-907
ROLLINS, William  ts  359
ROLLINSON, Fred  c-t  544-762-882
ROMAINE, Abe  cl-as-bar  801-1341-1342
ROMAINE, Bert  p  1274
ROMANO, Phil  p-ldr  358-1334
ROMANO, Raymond  p  870
ROMEO, Bob  as  1602
ROMEO, Domenic  bj  870
RONALD, Landon  p  1161-1198-1199
RONALD, Rene  p  313-973
RONDOLIERS, THE  v  1383-1385-1386-1387
RONEMOUS, Norman  cl-as  129-130
RONN, Ove  ts  589
ROOKS, Harry  d  1218
ROPPOLO, Leon  cl-as  650-1131-1132-1271
ROS, Edmundo  d  1632
ROSA, Jerry  tb  9-742-743-744
ROSATI, Archie  cl  1004-1733
ROSATI, Mike  t  398-788
ROSE, ——  tb  1254-1255-1256
ROSE, Atwell  vn  1108
ROSE, Bayless  g  390
ROSE, Clarkson  v  1335
ROSE, Dave  p-a  307-1335-1537-1570
ROSE, George  bj-g  324-325-326-579-1568
ROSE, Joe  c  535-1163-1454
ROSE, Sam  p  1484
ROSE, Vincent  p-ldr  1335-1694
ROSE, Wally  p  1656
ROSEBERY, Arthur  p-ldr  525-1336
ROSELLE, Mildred  v  1077
ROSELLI, Gene  tb  1663
ROSEMAND, William  vn  1426
ROSEN, Harry  bj  646
ROSEN, Johnny  vn  535-798-799-800-801
ROSEN, Max  bb  129-130-572-796-797
ROSEN, Sam  d  437

ROSENBAUM, Hymie  t  326-1412
ROSENBERG, Abe  vn  1271
ROSENBERG, George  g  151
ROSENBERG, Red  t  873-874-875
ROSENBLUM, Sam  vn  816-817-818-1398
ROSENSTOCK, Larry  p  1520-1521
ROSIE, Eddie  bj  632
ROSING, Val  d-v  788-789-1214-1337
ROSS, Allie  cl-as-vn  378-379-380-713-
  714-715-1559
ROSS, Alonzo  p-v-ldr  1338
ROSS, Arnold  p  829
ROSS, Bert  a  166
ROSS, Doc  d  1324-1325
ROSS, Dolly  v  1338
ROSS, Edwin  p  126
ROSS, Frank  p  956
ROSS, Hank  (r.n. Henry R.)  ts  594-805-
  1089-1718
ROSS, Henry  d  830
ROSS, James  t-v-a  944
ROSS, Johnny  cl-as-ts  1572
ROSS, Louise  v  1338
ROSS, Marty  g  1047
ROSS, Mose  d  380
ROSS, Ollie  v  1338
ROSS, Pete  as  1047
ROSS, Sam  vn  454-455
ROSS, Sandy  bj  1368
ROSS, Theodore  v  1465
ROSS, Walter  sb  394
ROSSBERG, Oscar  tb  274-1378
ROSSELLI, Jacques Bourgas  cl-ts  1595
ROSSITER, Red  t  1103
ROSTAING, Hubert  cl-as-ts-a  16-333-519-
  1262-1284-1338-1339-1615
ROTH, Jack  p-d  68-69-70-71-72-176-349-
  350-793-825-914-915-916-934-935-1050-
  1184-1185-1186-1187-1188-1189-1190-1191
  1192-1356-1480-1544-1719-1727
ROTH, James  bb  133
ROTHSCHILD, Irving  vn  1573
ROTHWELL, ——  tb  218
ROTROFF, Thurmond  ts  111
ROULETTE, Vernon  cl-ts  1614-1615
ROUNDERS, THE  v  657
ROUNDS, Clyde  as-ts  123-124-125-126-250
  437-438-440-700-701
ROUNTREE, Red  (r.n. Luke R.)  bj-g  243-
  1497
ROUSE, Morris  p  337-391-457-639
ROUSSEAU, August  tb  302
ROUSSEAU, Charlie  g  782
ROVIRA, Tony  sb  11-16-172-333-519-635-
  1262-1284-1563-1615
ROWE, George  tb  539-1224
ROWLAND, Helen  v  1009-1384-1388-1570
ROWLAND, William  p  183-184-185-186
ROY, Harry  cl-as-v-ldr  359-1339-1340-
  1341-1342-1343
ROY, Sid  p-ldr  359-1343
ROYAL, Ernest  t  664
ROYAL, Marshall  cl-as  489-663-664-762-
  763-1530
ROYCE, Bob  p  1665-1666
ROYCE, Marjorie  v  1344
RUBELATI, Roscoe  bb  1673
RUBEN, Mike  sb  1374-1375
RUBENOWITCH, Sam - see RUBINWITCH, SAM
RUBENS, Harry  p  16-1695
RUBENS, Sid  vn  1616

RUBIN, Jules  ts  1401-1402
RUBIN, Queenie Ada  p  893-894
RUBINOWICH, Sam - see RUBINWITCH, SAM
RUBINWITCH, Sam  cl-as  1-429-430-431-432-
433-434-435-436-545-742-743-744 (This
is the spelling as given in the AFM Lc
Local 802 Directory; Rubenowich and
Rubinowitch have been quoted in the
text of this book from references in
recording files)
RUBSAM, Edward P.  d-chimes  332-1250-1
1251-1252-1512
RUBY, Sam  cl-ts  234-235-236-237-238-239-
240-241-242-243-244-245-247-248-530-533-
624-625-626-627-966-967-1025-1300-1579-
1580-1581-1583-1592-1593-1619-1620
RUCKER, Laura  p-v  760-1018-1344
RUDDER, Ralph  ts  1228
RUDE, Johnny  cl-ss-as  248-249-1619
RUDERMAN, Morton  f  1406
RUDISELLI, Horace  p  552-553
RUETSCHE, Clement  sb  151
RUFFO, Mascagni  as  907-910-911-912-1242-
1361
RUGGIERIE, Peter  sb  326
RULLO, Joe  t  1047
RUNYON, Hal  tb  1196
RUPPERSBERG, Don  tb  94-95-96-97-98-166-
183
RUSCHECK, Joe  bb  399
RUSCIOLELLI, Rosie  t  1047
RUSH, James  cl-as-v  112-917-918
RUSH, Peter  cl-as-vn  22-146-917-953-1070
RUSHFORTH, E. W.  d-x-chimes  1019-1216
RUSHING, Jimmy  v  101-102-103-104-105-106-
107-108-109-110-600-1111-1112-1204
RUSHTON, Joe  cl-bsx  812
RUSSAN, Hammond  ts  647
RUSSELL, Barney  tb  962-1163
RUSSELL, Connie  v  1344
RUSSELL, Dill  g  263
RUSSELL, Elliott  vn  1197
RUSSELL, Elmer  v  1135
RUSSELL, Jack  p-k  1099-1388-1389-1390-
1391-1392
RUSSELL, Johnny  cl-ts-v  191-281-382-960-
961-1008-1052
RUSSELL, Johnny  v  973
RUSSELL, Kennedy  dir  971
RUSSELL, Lee  v  880-881
RUSSELL, Luis  p-cel-a  11-12-13-15-45-52-
53-54-55-56-57-58-178-308-358-667-751-
792-868-1167-1168-1169-1221-1344-1345-
1346-1376-1486-1488
RUSSELL, Mischa  vn  76-98-274-276-1406-
1569-1571-1681-1682-1683-1684-1685-1687-
1688-1689-1690
RUSSELL, Pee Wee (r.n. Charles Ellsworth R.
cl-ts  38-88-132-142-177-202-304-317-335-
336-519-542-543-634-646-647-648-821-822-
959-977-1031-1080-1081-1086-1113-1346-
1537-1555-1567-1637-1696-1734
RUSSELL, Robert  t  1092
RUSSELL, Sterling  v  1112
RUSSICK, Les  bj  1174-1175
RUSSIN, Babe (r.n. Irving R.)  cl-ts  34-83-
84-123-145-205-305-320-321-394-445-446-
447-448-505-606-661-768-770-780-781-804-
871-977-978-1002-1003-1026-1027-1031-
1032-1081-1082-1088-1141-1142-1143-1144-
1145-1146-1234-1304-1347-1369-1370-1512-
1552-1718

RUSSIN, Jack  p  233-234-235-236-237-238-
239-247-248-469-470-625-626-871-967-968-
977-978-1025-1114-1142-1143-1144-1145-
1146-1332-1333-1383-1539-1580-1581-1583-
1593-1619-1620
RUSSO, Al  tb  321
RUSSO, Albert  bj-g  519-520-652-53-654-
655-1436-1692
RUSSO, Andy  tb  79-125-656-657-685-871-
1095-1158-1159-1273
RUSSO, Charles  as  517
RUSSO, Charles  bj-g  941
RUSSO, Dan  vn-ldr  1347-1348
RUSSO, Tony  t  239-626-627-1620
RUSSUM, Hammond  cl-ts  1552-1553
RUTH, Van  p  1229
RUTLEDGE, Leroy  t  472-833
RYAN SISTERS, THE  v  918
RYAN, Babs  v  66
RYAN, Jack  bb-sb  429-430-431-432-433-
434--435-436-644-1248-1249
RYAN, John  d  999-1521
RYAN, Johnny  v  232-233-234-235-237-238-
242-266-268-656-657-930-1108-1172-1567
RYCHLIK, I.  d  1575
RYERSON, Arthur  g  325-1373-1374-1690-
1691
RYERSON, Frank  t  296-297-298-299-300-
1539
RYKER, Doc (r.n. Stanley R.)  cl-as-v
576-577-578-738-1566

SAATKAMP, Jack  p  314-315-1548
SABA, Johnny  v  650-651
SABLON, Germaine  v  1348-1349
SABLON, Jean  v  396-1349-1350
SACCO, Frank  t  1146
SACCO, Tony  g-v  34-249-250-594-968-1146
SACHELLE, Sam  ts  165-166-1358-1359-1360-
1361
SACHS, Coleman  c  963
SACKS, Bob  ts  999
SADDLER, Cle  as  835-836
SADOLA, John  cl-ts  320-545-633-704-756-
1121
SAFFER, Buddy  as  1179
SAGUET, Arthur  ts  1284
SAHLIN, Olle  g-d  282-1585
SAINT, Edward  tb  863
ST. CLAIR, Cyrus  bb  5-118-213-731-806-
833-939-966-1013-1014-1168-1445-1535-
1559-1700-1701-1702-1703-1704-1705-1706-
1708-1709-1710-1711
ST. CLAIR, Floyd  d  566
ST. CYR, Johnny  bj-g  39-40-41-42-43-178-
308-313-314-337-338-394-753-862-1025-
1026-1051-1101-1129-1133-1166-1320-1321-
1344-1345-1549
ST. JOHN, Art  cl-as  1538-1539-1540
ST. JOHN, Dell  v  283-1007
SAJET, Jaap  sb  822
SALA, Dominic  cl-as  1421
SALE, James  dir  1117
SALIERS, Harold  cl-bcl-as-ts-bar  1-559-
560-1482-1483
SALISBURY, Gerry  cl-as-ts  265-266-267
SALKO, Jimmy  t  1160
SALTER, Harry  vn  1330
SALTMAN, Henry  as  126
SALTO, Frank  cl-as  1197
SALVANT, Jeanette  p  302
SAMMONS, Mike  vn  895

1826

SAMONE, Robert  t  640-641
SAMPSON, Edgar  cl-as-vn-a  50-  -122-562
  597-606-608-661-725-726-767-806-833-
  1053-1240-1351-1654-1658-1659-1735-1736
SAMUEL, Morey  tb  123-553-565-1408-1409
SAMUELS, Joseph  cl-as-bsx-vn-ldr  285-
  686-706-1008-1009-1351-1352-1353-1354-
  1522-1525-1526-1698
SANDERS, Cass  v  634
SANDERS, Frankie  v  1670
SANDERS, Irene  v  210
SANDERS, Marcus  v  1343
SANDERS, Joe  p-v-ldr  338-339-340-341-
  1354
SANDERS, W. G. M. "Geck"  cl-as  263
SANDIFER, Cody  d  306
SANDIFORD, Preston  p-a  395
SANDOVAL or SANDVALL, Tom  cl-as-ts  59-
  890
SANDS, Bobby  ts  773-774-775
SANDS, Jimmy  as  307
SANDS, Milton  d  90-1379-1380-1381
SANFIELD, Mac  vn  1121
SANFORD, Herb  p  1252
SANNELLA, Andy  cl-as-f-g-stg-v  5-16-17-
  30-62-63-64-82-136-195-196-273-398-410-
  463-464-502-503-509-516-566-567-638-641
  670-673-676-708-751-752-882-928-929-930
  931-945-1015-1016-1041-1064-1065-1067-
  1068-1160-1225-1308-1323-1330-1367-1368
  1381-1382-1387-1416-1417-1418-1425-1456
  1521-1604-1610-1638
SANS, Benny  p  1055
SANSONE, Charles  p  120
SANTELMANN, Lt. William H.  dir  1578
SANTIAGO, Willie  g  1287
SAPING, Frederick  vn-g-v  1570-1571
SAPIRO, Henry  bj  1223
SARASON, Edgar  as  701-702
SARBIB, Marceau  sb  189-333
SARGEANT, Preston  p  218
SARGENT, Kenny  cl-as-bar-v  34-56-76-287
  288-289-290-291-292-293-294-295-296-297
  298-299-300-356-1496-1497
SARLO, Frank  tb  128-129-130-572
SARONY, Leslie  v  21-334-949-1116-1355
SARTELL, Frenchie  t  2-797-798-1289-1509
SASSON, Jean  g  557-822
SATTERFIELD, Jack  tb  1244
SATTERFIELD, Tom  p-cel-a  116-1067-1068-
  1327-1567-1683-1685-1686
SAUCIER, Edgar  as  1413
SAUNDARS, J. Eric  d  467
SAUNDERS, Gertrude  v  1355
SAUNDERS, Jimmy  v  819
SAUTER, Eddie  t-mel-a  77-78-81-93-612-
  613-614-615-616-617-618-619-620-621-622
  1156-1157
SAVAGE, Helen  v  1152-1355
SAVAGE, Henry  t  1693
SAVAGE, Paul  p-a  1310
SAVAGE, Turk  c-v  1162
SAVAGE, Walter  bb  646
SAVILE, Harry  p-ldr  1356
SAVILLE, James  g  1195
SAVILLE, Theodore  d  1195
SAVITT, Jan  ldr-a  1356-1357-1358-1359-
  1360-1361
SAWYER, Bob  p-dir  1328-1498
SAWYER, Chic  v  642
SAWYER, Ralph  v  695

SAX, Frank  cl-as  646
SAX, Sid  vn  684
SAXBE, Marvin  bj-g-cym  193-1005
SAXBY, Charles W.  or  31-32-971-1196
SAXE, Phil  cl-ts-vn  1-66-67
SAYLES, Emmanuel  bj  863
SBARBARO (latterly known as SPARGO), Tony
  d-k  1175-1176-1177-1178-1179
SCAGLIONI, Charlie  cl  111
SCALZA, Edward  g  98
SCALZI, Eddie  as  306-307-742-743
SCANAVINO, Mario  ts  171
SCANLAN, Walter  v  235-1079
SCARPA, Eddie  cl  1105
SCHAAP, Henri  g  556
SCHAFF or SHAAF, Eddie  d  201-508-1009-
  1120-1241
SCHAFFER, Lloyd  cl-as  1548
SCHAFFER, William  g  438-439
SCHAEFFER, Jack  t  815-816
SCHATZ, Milton  cl-as  125
SCHAUMBERGER, Howard  t  786-787
SCHECHTER, Julie  vn  1398
SCHECHTMAN, George  cl-ts  882
SCHEER, Ed  ts  185-186
SCHEIDERMAN, Bill  vn  684
SCHELLANGE, Augie  d  153-999
SCHENCK, F.  tb  151
SCHERTZER, Hymie  cl-bcl-as  16-123-444-
  445-446-447-449-450-451-452-503-534-594
  595-596-597-598-599-600-601-602-603-604
  605-606-607-608-617-618-622-623-660-661
  662-770-878-1337-1697
SCHILLING, Freddy  tb  127-905-1005
SCHILLING, Ted  t  467-657
SCHINI, Ed  cl-ss-as-ts  188
SCHKLAR, Sammy  vn  1286
SCHLEGEL, Wade  t  887-1641
SCHLES, Joe  cl-as-ts  1572
SCHLESINGER, Milt  d  207-805-1615
SCHMID, Max  vn  826
SCHMIDT, Benny  vn  1273
SCHMIDT, Bill  cl-as  32-33
SCHMIDT, George  t  1145-1147
SCHMIDT, Heinz  p  826
SCHMIDT, Herman  bb  545-546
SCHMIDT, Lucien  vc  1141
SCHMIDT, Pete  cl-ts  1496
SCHMIDT, Sylvio  vn  1211
SCHNEIDER, Hymie  d  272-518-1632
SCHNEIDER, Jules  cl-ts  32-33-1573
SCHNIER, Henry  ts  996
SCHOEBEL, ——  d  1193
SCHOEBEL, Elmer  p-a-ldr  1056-1131-1193-
  1366
SCHOEN, Gerald  vc  919
SCHOEN, Vic  t-dir  28-29-30
SCHOENBACH, Sol  bsn  534
SCHOLENBERGER, Bill  tb  9
SCHOLL, Heyo  g  961
SCHONBERGER, John  vn  991-992
SCHONFELD, Ray  s  391
SCHRADER, Frank  tb  1256-1605
SCHRIEBMAN, Ben  vn  579-580
SCHUBERT, Adrian  dir  1366-1367-1368
SCHUCHMAN, Harry  as  454-455
SCHULER, George  ts  82
SCHULTZ, Bernie  t-ldr  1368
SCHULTZ, Eddie  t  1616
SCHULTZ, Floyd  d  1479
SCHULTZ, James  as-a  1357-1358

SCHULTZ, Joe  bb  1589
SCHULTZ, Ray  cl-as  1147-1148-1374
SCHULTZE, Dave  t  906-907
SCHULZ, Lorin  tb  391-578-579-1369
SCHULZ, Myron  vn-v-ldr  578-579-1369
SCHULZA, Bill  d  1242
SCHUMACHER, Frank  cl-as  159-361-642
SCHUMANN, Bill  vn-vc  817-1063-1232-1233-
   1234-1399-1681
SCHUMANN, Harry  ts  306-307
SCHUTT, Arthur  p-harmonium-a  5-33-38-84-
   156-157-304-305-309-351-395-419-420-421-
   422-427-436-455-462-463-465-503-510-519-
   556-559-560-561-592-593-629-630-671-804-
   853-870-871-872-921-928-931-932-933-962-
   977-1016-1046-1049-1062-1063-1086-1037-
   1088-1098-1138-1139-1140-1141-1145-1219-
   1220-1275-1276-1369-1370-1381-1430-1482-
   1483-1543-1596-1597-1598-1614-1673-1751
SCHUTZ, Buddy  d  93-250-431-432-433-434-
   435-436-545-610-611-612-1358
SCHUYLER, Sonny  v  1333
SCHWARTZ, Julie  as  629-621
SCHWARTZ, Leon  t  1482
SCHWARTZ, Marty  a  306
SCHWARTZ, Wilbur  cl-as  1064
SCHWARTZMAN, Joe  sb  505
SCHWEINFEST, George  f-pic-p  332-1370
SCHWEITZER, Freddy  cl-as-ts  801
SCHWESER, Gilbert  as  1146-1147
SCOBEY, Bob  t  1656
SCOGGINS, Virgil  d-v  1031-1485-1486
SCOMA, Enrico  cl  300
SCOTT, Buck  tb  660-1003-1004-1179
SCOTT, Bud (r.n. Arthur S.)  bj-g  150-
   413-414-752-852-1102-1151-1164-1167-
   1221-1376-1618
SCOTT, Cecil  cl-ts-bar-v  5-13-14-755-
   767-779-1134-1370-1371-1448-1449-1467-
   1706-1708-1709-1710-1711-1730-1732
SCOTT, Dorothy (Dot)  p  852-917-1322-
   1486-1489
SCOTT, Effie  v  1370
SCOTT, Fred  d  1267
SCOTT, George  cl-as  1084-1245
SCOTT, Harold  t  47-48-762-763-1673
SCOTT, Harold  as  806
SCOTT, Harvey  as  1662
SCOTT, Hazel  p-v  1371-1396
SCOTT, Howard  c-t  91-190-353-522-712-
   713-714-715-716-717-733-792-1050-1051-
   1266-1466-1717
SCOTT, Jack  p  890
SCOTT, John Riley  d-v  698-1216
SCOTT, Kermit  ts  691-769
SCOTT, Lee  d  461
SCOTT, Leon  t  1501
SCOTT, Leonard  v  1371
SCOTT, Lloyd  d-ldr  1370-1371
SCOTT, Mae  v  1371
SCOTT, Randolph  t  852-917-1322-1486-
   1489-1496
SCOTT, Raymond  p-ldr  1032-1371-1372-
   1373-1374-1375-1720
SCOTT, Riley — see SCOTT, JOHN RILEY
SCOTT, Robert  tb  108-109-110-1194
SCOTT, Ulysses  as  1203
SCOTT, W.  d  1396
SCOTT, Walter  vn  512-1121
SCOTT, William  t  1070
SCOTT, William J.  ts  1037-1038

SCOTT-COOMBER, Billy  g-v  1214-1695
SCOTT-WOOD, George  p-pac-gfs-vib-a  285-
   530-532-798-974-1137-1295-1296-1297-
   1339-1340-1431-1432-1433-1434-1435-1436-
   1584-1585-1675-1692-1721
SCOVILLE, Glenn  as-ts  1132
SCRIMA, Mickey  d  815-816-817-818-819-
   820
SCRUGGS, Irene  v  1376
SEABERG, Artie  cl  1178-1377
SEABERG, George  t  743-744
SEABROOK, Thad  t  277
SEALS, Warner  ts  862
SEARCY, DeLoise  p  708-1376-1377
SEARS, Al  ts-bar  902-1693
SEARS, Jerry  p-dir  1377-1558
SEAVEY, Horace  bb  566
SECKLER, Bill  v  76
SECREST, Andy  c-t  76-274-262-263-264-
   555-578-579-922-1017-1237-1368-1562-
   1568-1569-1570-1598-1668-1669-1687-1688
SECREST, Gene  cl-as-bar  1491-1694
SEDRIC, Gene  cl-ts  752-797-839-1019-
   1279-1377-1624-1625-1627-1628-1629-1630-
   1631-1632-1633-1634-1635-1636-1637-1638-
   1734-1742-1743
SEEARCE, Sam  tb  863
SEEKATZ, Chester  cl-as  553
SEELEY, Blossom  v  561
SEGAN, Sid  d  8-9
SEGAR, Charlie  p-v  1378
SEGERS, Jimmy  cl-as  1616
SEGURE, Roger  a  989-990
SEIDEL, Emil  p-ldr  274-418-1378
SEIDMAN, Mickey  s  589-590-591
SEIGEL, —— dir  971
SELBY, Allan  dir  1379
SELDON, H.  p  863
SELINSKY, Wladimir  vn  1063-1143-1144-
   1145
SELLERS, Charles  bb  188
SELLERS, Duke (r.n. Hugh S.)  tb  566-577
SELLS, Vic  t  556-1174-1175
SELVIN, Ben  vn-v-ldr  90-176-512-567-670-
   671-672-882-883-1128-1329-1379-1380-
   1381-1382-1383-1384-1385-1386-1387-1388-
   1438-1638-1652-1653-1686
SELZER, Moe or Bromo (r.n. Morris S.)  t
   240-241-344-399-1620
SEMINOLE, Paul  p  954
SEMON, Larry  g  1388
SEND, Harold  cl-ts  1162
SENESCU, Bernie  vn  919
SENIOR, George  sb  85-383-687-688-798-
   1092-1126-1137-1207
SENIOR, Milton  cl-as  311-1033
SENTER, Boyd  cl-as-t-bj-pac-k  1099-1388-
   1389-1390-1391-1392
SENTER, Russell  d-k  1389
SETTLES, Bill  sb  848-1123-1528
SEXTON, Beverley  d  1723
SEXTON, Ed  g  1621
SEXTON, James  t  321-322-323-324-325
SEYMOUR, Jeanette  v  1396
SHAAF, Charles  ts  1642
SHADE, Will  h-g-v  1041-1042-1043-1044
SHAFFER, Howard  cl-ts  1075
SHAFFER, Sy  tb  306-307
SHAFFRIN, Louis  t  1285
SHAKESPEARE, Bill (r.n. Lloyd S.)  t  148-
   272-395-459-953-1127-1128-1149-1155-
   1365-1396

1828
"SHAKY WALTER" h 1041
SHALSON, Harry v 395-1396-1397
SHAME, Ted t 863
SHAND, Dave cl-as-bar-o 2-535-791-801-
1017-1215-1224-1434-1508
SHAND, Terry p-v-a 173-201-746-830-867-
999-1000-1009-1133-1178-1241-1397-1398-
1415-1437-1438-1538-1584
SHANKLAND, Jimmy cl-as 346-347
SHANNON, George bb 799-1485
SHANNON QUARTET, THE v 1611
SHAPLER, Myron sb 1541
SHAPIRO, Artie sb 131-153-335-336-443-
518-542-545-821-822-1001-1002-1003-1007
1032-1179-1248-1429-1472-1594-1673-1690
1691-1696
SHAPIRO, Sam t-v 445-556-592-594-853-
903-957-958-959-1027-1224
SHAPIRO, Ted p 1573-1574
SHARAF, Al t 208
SHARON, Nita v 126
SHARON, Sally v 1002
SHARP, Freddy g 1160
SHARP, Si as 1641
SHARPE, E. Lyle cl-ts 211-1681
SHARP(E), Gus cl-as-ts 19-20-68-69-70-
72-176-399-882-935
SHARPE, Jack p 913
SHARROW, Saul vn 629-630
SHATTEL, Louis tb 1257
SHAVERS, Charlie t-v-a 75-76-79-80-91-
95-115-273-415-534-633-769-783-795-895
896-897-913-1019-1028-1075-1154-1158-
1467-1469-1477-1512-1513-1721-1729
SHAW, Al bj-g 1675
SHAW, Arthur banjoline 1517
SHAW, Artie cl-as-ldr 1-34-77-122-160-
204-205-767-780-871-903-1000-1026-1027-
1156-1398-1399-1400-1401-1402-1403-1404
1405-1406-1407-1408-1409-1415-1416-1484
1571
SHAW, Bert v 1490
SHAW, Chester bb-v 737
SHAW, Elliott v 418-578-648-884-1604
SHAW, James as-sw 1085-1086
SHAW, Joel p-v 873-874-875-876-880-881-
1409-1410-1411
SHAW, Milt vn-a 456-873-874-875-1411
SHAW, Miriam v 183-184
SHAW, Theodore p 1411
SHAWKER, Bunny (r.n. Edwin S.) d 186-
704
SHAYNE, Al v 631-1028-1080-1238-1521
SHAYNE, J. H. p-v 310-843-1371-1411-
1487-1489-1499
SHEARING, George p-pac 635-636-1039-1225
1411-1412
SHEASBY, Eddie vn-a 578-926-927
SHEFFIELD, Maurice cl 855
SHEFTER, Bert p-ldr 1412
SHELBY, Bill bj 466
SHELLADY, Nelson t 63
SHELLEY, Frances v 83-1413
SHELLY, Robert bj 338
SHELTON, Ezra Howlett p-v 1413
SHELTON, Fred tenor vocal 554-555
SHELTON, George cl-as-ts-bar 1472
SHEPARD, Billy cl-ts 1147-1148
SHEPARD, Ollie v 1413-1414
SHEPHERD, Shep (r.n. Berisford S.) d
284-1408

SHEPPARD, Ian ts-vn 1632
SHEPPARD, I. V. "Bud" p-dir 1174-1175
SHERIDAN, Mark g-bj 581-936-937-1613-
1614
SHERIFF, Leslie bj 1171-1172
SHERMAN, Al tb 306-907-908-1116
SHERMAN, Frank v 829
SHERMAN, Harry g 138-939-1365-1507-1508
SHERMAN, Irving p 1115
SHERMAN, James p 39-78-382-768-1464-
1465
SHERMAN, Joe v 269-1416-1505
SHERMAN, Lynne v 109-208-209
SHERMAN, Muroel v 1388
SHERMAN, Sam cl-ss-as-ts 656-657
SHERMAN, Walter sb 208-209-417
SHEROCK, Shorty (r.n. Clarence S.) t
204-371-372-429-430-431-432-433-452-908
909-910-911-1216-1223-1236
SHERRY, Avery cl-as 1252
SHERWOOD, Bobby g 149-159-180-361-362-
1406-1560
SHERWOOD, Lew t-v 1286
SHEVAK, Bob sb 207-829
SHEVAK, Iggy (r.n. Roger S.) sb 457
SHEVILL, Len bj 134-1055
SHIELD, Leroy p-cel-dir 577-696-708-1018
SHIELDS, Harry cl-bsx 188
SHIELDS, Jack cl-as 22
SHIELDS, Joey v 790-791
SHIELDS, Johnny tb 154-155
SHIELDS, Larry cl 1175-1176-1177-1178-
1179
SHIFFMAN, Bud as 622
SHILKRET, Harry t 63-112-1272-1418-1586
1610
SHILKRET, Jack cl-as-ts-bar-p-cel 9-17-
63-64-1285-1286-1415-1416-1417-1418-
1604-1610
SHILKRET, Nat (r.n. Naftule Schildkraut)
c-cl-p-cel-dir 17-63-552-870-1416-1417
1418-1424-1430-1604-1610
SHILKRET, Nat d 1421
SHILLING, Freddy - see SCHILLING, FREDDY
SHINE, Bill as 451
SHINE, Jimmy as-v 6-1645-1646
SHIPS, Mike cl-as 64-1418
SHIRLEY, George bj 1546
SHIRLEY, Jimmy g 278-644-1253-1408
SHEARER, Jack sb 889
SHOFFNER, Bob c-t 65-209-353- 54-752-
824-1037-1161-1167-1221-1345-1507
SHOFFNER, Dub ł 286-287
SHOLDEN, Dave ts 1257
SHOOBE, Lou sb 80-81-207-829-1032-1224-
1371-1372-1373-1615-1718-1720
SHOOBE, Sam sb 805
SHOOP, Jack as 59
SHOPNICK, Mack 1126-1273
SHORE, Dinah v 945-946
SHORE, Jack as 1571
SHORES, Okey g 540
SHORT, Albert E. dir 1419
SHORT, Bill bb 37-38-925-926
SHORT, Charlie sb 316-822-1509
SHORT, Tommy bj 806
"SHORTY" bb-sb 381
SHOUP, Donald g 553
SHREVE, Philo t 100
SHRIGLEY, Guy cl-ss-as-ts 133-1352-1429
1430

"SHUFFLIN' PHIL" v 915
SHUGART, —— c 1289
SHUGART, Claude k-v 530-531
SHULMAN, Alan vc 1125
SHULMAN, Sylvan vn 1125
SHUKIN, Phil cl-ts 1546
SIACAT, Lendall sb 660
SIDAY, Eric vn 20-21-22-143-192-272-515-
520-530-538-564-565-568-798-812-953-982-
1126-1127-1214-1217-1226-1227-1289-1396-
1419-1456
SIDELL, Al d 153-542-545-633-1032-1333-
1481-1753
SIDNEY, Sid vn 1075
SIEGEL, Al p-dir 1419-1420
SIEGEL, Bill tb 1375
SIEGFIELD, Frank vn 1399
SIEGLER, George d 505
SIEGRIST, Alfred p-pac 960-961
SIEGRIST, Frank t 211-732-1608-1609-1680
1681
SIEGRIST, Gene cl-as-ts-o 1694
SIGLER, Maurice bj-v-ldr 963-1420
SIGMAN, Harry d-x 1285-1286
SIGNORELLI, Frank p 16-19-20-70-71-72-
116-134-163-176-205-305-349-350-394-419-
436-465-508-509-512-514-632-659-671-780-
793-825-883-903-915-916-922-935-993-994-
1005-1031-1032-1036-1050-1076-1081-1083-
1088-1098-1115-1120-1121-1128-1131-1178-
1179-1184-1185-1186-1187-1188-1189-1190-
1191-1192-1193-1238-1303-1305-1312-1313-
1314-1315-1329-1356-1391-1392-1418-1420-
1429-1480-1544-1551-1554-1567-1596-1597-
1598-1599-1600-1639-1652-1690-1691-1719-
1727
SILLMAN, Phil d-v 398-1332
SILLOWAY, Ward tb-v 161-162-363-365-366-
367-368-369-446-447-455-555-698-866-1001
SILVERMAN, Al d 1162
SILVERMAN, David H. p-ldr 1421
SILVERSTONE, Harry vn 1419
SILVERSTON, Phil vn 1202
SIMA, Jan dir 1575
SIMBURCH, A. t 1575
SIMEON, Omer cl-ss-as-bar-dir 404-410-
661-728-758-759-760-862-1005-1101-1102-
1116-1167-1168-1169-1280-1281-1321-1355
1421-1455-1456-1488-1535
SIMEONE, Frank as-dir 78-79-1157-1158-
1159
SIMERALL, Will d 1411
SIMES, Don tb 1358-1359
SIMMON(D)S, Jack bj-g I6-403-1298-1695
SIMMONDS, Jack vl (same as above ?) 470
SIMMONS, Bill tb 660
SIMMONS, Jesse tb-a 1218
SIMMONS, John sb 58-619-1733
SIMMONS, Kermit t 93-738-739
SIMMONS, Lee p 402-403
SIMMONS, Lonnie ts 1632
SIMMONS, Sam ts 342-527-528-1203-1456
SIMMONS, Teddy v 1154
SIMMS, Ginny v 1477
SIMOENS, Lucien sb 330-465-1259
SIMON, Gene tb 283-1278-1279
SIMON, George d. 1063
SIMON, Pierre cl-ts 1595
SIMON, Stafford cl-ts 192-284-864-865-
1070-1304-1414
SIMON-GIRARD, Aime v 1421

SIMONS, Jack bj 796
SIMONS, Nevin as-v 556
SIMONS, Seymour v 576
SIMPKINS, Georgia Boy v 728
SIMPKINS, Jesse 661-730
SIMPSON, Cassino p 393-824-852-1018-
1051-1093-1169-1245-1344-1421-1455-1749
SIMPSON, Hobart tb 1753
SIMPSON, Jack d-x-timps 22-23-24-25-536
801-1126-1215-1469
SIMPSON, James t 1204
SIMS, Arthur as-vn-ldr 1421
SIMS, Edward t-tb 691-692-693-694-760
SIMS, Joe v 1700
SIMS, Lennie ts 622-623
SIMS, Sam d 683-1713
SINACORE, Joe g 29
SINATRA, Frank v 449-450-451-452-453-
454-815
SINCLAIR, Ted sb 278
SINCLAIR, Teddy vn 22-1364-1365
SINDELAR, Andy tb 1066-1067-1068
SINES, Miff (r.n. Dominick Siniscalchi)
tb 325-326-416-417
SINGER, Harry v 85
SINGER, Henry tb 205-829
SINGER, Lou d-a 59-896-897-1118
SINGLETON, Barney d 134-1055
SINGLETON, Zutty (r.n. Arthur S.) d-v-
chimes 15-43-44-45-46-58-76-78-88-113
142-272-357-359-404-466-662-765-821-
936-959-1004-1007-1053-1104-1107-1108-
1346-1422-1488-1555
SINIAVINE, Alec p 1221-1349
SIPPLE, Norman tb 1358
SIRAVO, George as-bar-a 788-906-907-
1063-1359-1360
SIRINSKY, Koby vn 61
SISSLE, Noble vn-v 141-512-513-1422-
1423-1424-1425-1426-1427
SISSON, J. Kenn p-a-dir 128-129-130-131
1428
SKEETE, Charlie p-ldr 1436
SKERRITT, Al as 695
SKERRITT, Fred as-bar-v 1171-1377-1632-
1707
SKILES, Dude t 1437
SKILES, Jack g 1437
SKILES, Ted 1068
SKINE, Dave bj-g 508-1120-1129-1130
SKINNER, Carl d 418
SKINNER, Dale cl-ts 579-1510-1537
SKINNER, Frank p 172-173
SKINNER, Pete tb 1242
SKIPPER, Shorty t 1047
SKJOLDBORG, Anker ts 282
SKLAROFF, Jack vn 326
SKOLNICK, Sam t 97-438-439
SKOUBY, Axel t 282-652
SKYLAR, Sonny v 739
SKYLES, Jimmy tb 324-453-454-455
SLACK, Freddy p-cel-a 165-166-167-204-
429-,30-431-432-1236-1575
SLATER, Bob cl-ts 89
SLATER, George cl-ts 926-927-934-1039
"SLATS" tb 646
SLAUGHTER, Bob d 1210
SLAUGHTER, Roy d 863
SLAVIN, Archie g 279-383-1508-1509-1739
SLEVIN, Dick k-tin can 1029-1030-1112-
1113-1119

1830
SLOAN, Harry tb 664
SLOCUM, ——— cl-as 1485
SLYDELL, Ebenezer dir 1343
SMALL, Abe c-ldr 1437
SMALL, Charles v 1614
SMALL, Hy t 8-9-1374-1375
SMALL, Jack vn 1197
SMALL, Melvin p 138
SMALL, Paul v 33-305-592-879-933-1144-
1145-1302-1384-1387-1392-1437-1438-1616-
1722-1751
SMALLE, Ed p-k-v 39-89-137-380-803-1202-
1275-1417-1608-1609-1620-1737
SMALLS, Cliff p 277
SMALLS, Lonnie p 806
SMALLWOOD, Dave cl 1501
SMART, Byron t 274-1378
SMEARER, P. G. bb-sb 59
SMECK, Roy bj-g-stg-h 178-195-202-255-
310-316-350-351-561-860-1170-1483-1708-
1709-1710-1725
SMELSER, Cornell pac 60-481-1303-1384-
1387-1438-1554
SMITH, ——— c 1254-1255-1256
SMITH, Albert R. bb 2
SMITH, Alberta v 680
SMITH, B. v 1713
SMITH, Ben cl-as 6-281-563-775-902-1203-
1456-1645-1646-1647-1697
SMITH, Bessie v 1438-1439-1440-1441-1442
1443-1444-1445-1446-1447-1450
SMITH, Bill d 913
SMITH, Billy t 656-791
SMITH, Bob tb 1327
SMITH, Boyer t 699
SMITH, Bud tb 9-742-1063-1064-1482-1553-
1554
SMITH, Bud ts 1150
SMITH, Buster (r.n. Henry S.) cl-as-a
102-104-153-154-944-1203-1204-1279
SMITH, Buzz tb 93
SMITH, Cal bj-g 320-409-519-556-685-694
695-891-1026-1164-1328-1619
SMITH, Carl t 101-1560-1561
SMITH, Carl sb 248-249
SMITH, Cecil tb 1202
SMITH, Chalk v 68
SMITH, Charles c 1029-1216
SMITH, Charles ts 1616
SMITH, Charles p 164
SMITH, Chick t 790-791-801-1508-1509
SMITH, Clara v 1440-1443-1447-1448-1449
1450-1451-1452
SMITH, Clara v 1453
SMITH, Clarence t-v 251
SMITH, Clayton tb 1272
SMITH, Clementine v 1453
SMITH, Cricket c-t 378-379-380-512-1085
1086
SMITH, Curt g 1215
SMITH, Duke cl 1184
SMITH, Elizabeth u-v 1453
SMITH, Ernest sb 263
SMITH, Ernie (Chester) cl-as-bar-bsx-o
25-32-327-328-873-1226-1227-1294-1493-
1548-1674-1738
SMITH, Faber v 1746
SMITH, Fats v 1195-1453-1454
SMITH, Floyd g-elg-v 80-830-901-902-
1431
SMITH, Frank cl-ss-ts 559-560-1482

SMITH, Frank p 1154-1155
SMITH, Frank bb 142-1497
SMITH, Freddy bj-g 409-519-1685-1328
SMITH, George t 1194
SMITH, George cl-ss-as-ts 32-345-469-
470-667-903-1127-1128-1201-1226-1365-
1493
SMITH, George vn 512-1223-1230-1274-1396
SMITH, Guy g 398-433-434-435-436-1358-
1359-1360
SMITH, H. wb 1645
SMITH, Hal tb 457
SMITH, Harl d-dir 962-1163-1454
SMITH, Harold p 360
SMITH, Harry c 733
SMITH, Harry cl-as-ts 25-85-86-388-399-
536-638-684-687-688
SMITH, Hazel v 1454
SMITH, Henry as-a 459-850-1109
SMITH, Horace t 992-993-1454
SMITH, Howard p 441-442-443-444-445-446
447-448-449-858-859-1063-1332
SMITH, Howard d 183-457
SMITH, Ike p-v 1454
SMITH, Imo bb 566
SMITH, Ivy speech 389-1454-1455
SMITH, Jabbo (r.n. Cladys) c-t-v 474-
562-775-936-978-1096-1321-1455-1456-
1534-1565
SMITH, (Whispering) Jack v 1456-1457
SMITH, James g 1626-1627-1628
SMITH, Jay t 557
SMITH, Jesse cl-as-f 1285-1286
SMITH, Jimmy bj-g 756-1589
SMITH, Jimmy bb-sb 252-253-254-349-1084
1245
SMITH, Joe c-t 342-522-710-711-715-717-
718-719-720-721-722-732-750-793-861-
1034-1035-1037-1050-1056-1057-1089-1267
1424-1441-1442-1443-1444-1445-1447-1451
1462-1463-1467-1510-1649-1650-1651-1700
1729
SMITH, Joe cl-as 919-920-921
SMITH, Joe d 1109
SMITH, John g 755-756-1134-1634-1635-
1636
SMITH, Johnny cl-as-ts 660-1007-1482
SMITH, John W. v 186
SMITH, Joseph C. vn-dir 1457
SMITH, Kate v 304-1457
SMITH, Laura v 1457-1458
SMITH, Leonard t 1272
SMITH, Leonard p 512
SMITH, Leroy vn-dir 1459
SMITH, Lester ts 1130-1131
SMITH, Lucien cl-as-ts-vc 60-68-75-421-
804-927-928-1330-1381-1544-1545
SMITH, Luke t 719-720
SMITH, Lyle ts 1068-1069
SMITH, Mamie p-v 1460-1461-1462-1463-
1464
SMITH, Marshall v 1143
SMITH, Max tb 126-1491
SMITH, May v 1459
SMITH, Neil ts 126
SMITH, Norman cl-ts 867
SMITH, Perry cl-ss-ts-v 820-1468-1705-
1714-1715-1716
SMITH, Raymond p 1464
SMITH, Richard J. a 944
SMITH, Robert as-bar-a 683-851-1674

SMITH, Rollen   ts   458-705
SMITH, Ruby   v   839-1247
SMITH, Russell   t      141-261-262-281-283
   284-512-513-564-710-717-718-719-720-721
   722-723-724-725-726-727-728-729-730-
   1445-1516-1517-1518
SMITH, Stuff (r.n. Leo S.)   vn-v   1464-
   1465-1563-1564
SMITH, Tab   ss-as-a   14-15-107-108-109-
   769-913-1070-1074-1075-1135-1734
SMITH, Teddy   as   1106
SMITH, Ted   v   830
SMITH, Terry   ts   1507
SMITH, Tom   t   903-1214-1274
SMITH, Trixie   v   150-1191-1465-1466-1467
SMITH, Vernon "Geechie"   t   520
SMITH, Vic   tb   991-992
SMITH, Wally   cl-as   377-1265
SMITH, Walter   t   294-321-322-323-324-325
   326-629-1615
SMITH, Warren   tb-eu   162-363-366-367-368
   369-370-371-372-373-517-555-992-993-
   1546
SMITH, Wayne   v   1546
SMITH, William   p      278-944
SMITH, William   sb   550
SMITH, William H.   t   944
SMITH, William Oscar   sb   690
SMITH, Willie   cl-as-bar-v-a   983-984-985
   986-987-988-989-990-991
SMITH, Willie "The Lion"   p-cel-v-speech
   5-115-140-562-645-650-745-746-1052-1395
   1460-1467-1468-1535-1575-1630-1707-1708
   1710
SMITH, Wright   vn   856-1101
SMITHERS, Elmer   tb   62-363-364-365-374-
   375-445-446-447-448-449-1124-1125
SMOTHERS, Leon   t   401
SMUTS, Martin   as-vn   1207
SMUTS, Pat   ts-v   582-583-584-585-586-587
   588-589
SNAER, Albert   t   773-774-775-807
SNAPP, Troy   p   436-1054-1603
SNEAD, Archie   a   1202
SNEAD, Thomas   bb   640
SNEED, Jack   v   1469
SNELL, Ken   bb   1745
SNOW, Hattie   v   1471
SNOW, Valaida   t-v   758-1584-1585-1645
"SNOWBALL"   v   1310
SNOWDEN, Elmer   bj-g   154-306-392-541-547
   548-564-643-733-734-861-868-872-941-
   1010-1022-1023-1024-1051-1057-1058-1090
   1094-1119-1130-1218-1326-1392-1428-1431
   1442-1453-1463-1471-1555-1556-1557-1722
SNOWDEN, Q. Roscoe   p   1056-1471
SNOWFLAKES, THE   v   1554
SNURPUS, George   ts   999
SNYDER, Bob   as   616-617-907-908-909-910
SNYDER, Bruce   v   452-453-454-455
SNYDER, Carl   g   697-698
SNYDER, Dwight   v   1143
SNYDER, Frank · d   1131-1722
SNYDER, Joe   cl-ss-as   356
SNYDER, Ralph   t   168
SOBOSKI, Stan   bb   892
SOCARRAS, Albert   cl-ss-as-f   119-412-651
   731-939-944-1060-1061-1535-1663-1701-
   1702-1703-1704-1705-1707-1742
SOCCI, Charles   v   659
SODJA, Joe   g   1471-1472

SOLDEN, Anders   d   589
SOLOMON, Red (r.n. Melven S.)   t   30-80-
   81-153-207-756-829-1304
SOLOMON, Shorty (r.n. Nathan Solomson)   t
   433-434-435-436
SOLOMON, Sylvan   ts   218
SOLOMON, Will   p   518
SOLOW, Irving   c   1573
SOLOWSKY, Max   vn   360
SOMERS, Debroy   dir   1364-1472
SOMERS, Maurice   vn   1421
SOMERVILLE, Kerwin   cl-bar   923
SONGCOPATORS, THE   v   1146-1147
SONGER, Wayne   as   1602
SONIN, John   d   535
SONTAG, Irving   tb   8-1373
SORENSEN, Al   cl-as-f   919-920
SORENSEN, Willy   sb   652-1585
SORKIN, Barney   cl-ss-as-bar   525-684-
   1290-1291
SOSNIK, Harry   p-ldr   163-356-634
SOTHERN, Dixie Lee   v   1239
SOUDERS, Jackie   tb-ldr   1472
SOUDIEUX, Emmanuel   sb   465-519-536-1261-
   1262-1283-1284-1339
SOULE, Russell   g   1004
SOUTH, Eddie   vn-w-v   1475-1476-1477-1534
   1614-1615
SOUTHARD, Billy   d   265
SOUTHERN, Helen   v   325
SOUTHERN, Larry   v   165
SOWELL, Richard   h   540
SPAETH, Karl   ts   1068
SPANGLER, Bob   d   1064-1358
SPANGLER, Richard   ts   307
SPANGLER, Roy   p   1481
SPANIER, Muggsy (r.n. Francis Joseph S.)
   c-t   18-114-162-193-197-309-363-364-373
   374-421-504-672-789-822-868-956-957-958
   959-977-1033-1068-1069-1114-1133-1228-
   1236-1237-1299-1481-1482-1506-1652-1697
SPARY, Claud   tb   25
SPAULDING, Anthony or Antonia (both have
   been quoted in various sources !)   p
   165-337-1475-1476-1615
SPAVR, Paul   vn   326
SPEAR, John   v   792
SPEARS, Bill   vn-v1   818-819
SPECHT, Paul   vn-ldr   1482-1483-1484
SPECIALE, Mike   vn-ldr   1484
SPECIALE, Tom   bb   1484
"SPECKLED RED" (r.n. Willie Perryman)   p
   846
SPEED BOYS, THE   v   130
SPEED, Sam   hj   164-458-459-564-645-810-
   1018-1184-1306-1459-1462-1544-1726-
   1727
SPENCER, Herb   ts-a   77-418-419-420-421-
   1597
SPENCER, Jimmy   d-wb-v   6-1645
SPENCER, Maynard   p   999
SPENCER, Norman   p   90-1379
SPENCER, O'Neil   d-wb-v   13-14-29-40-75-
   79-80-82-91-153-215-273-415-460-633-
   745-746-747-781-783-895-896-897-901-
   913-1028-1072-1073-1074-1134-1154-1159
   1159-1247-1253-1269-1323-1427-1467-
   1468-1469-1484-1512-1513-1655-1721-1729
SPERLING, Jack   d   126
SPERO, Charlie   as   1374-1602-1753
SPERZEL, John   bb   211-1680-1681

1832

SPERZEL, Martin  v  186
SPICER, Clark  t  892
SPIEGELMAN, Stanley  vl  1406
SPIELDOCK, Al  663
SPIKES, Reb  bsx-ldr  1485
SPILLIER, A.  bb  1327
SPINELLY, Charles  cl-as  1485
SPINELLY, Fred  d-ldr  784-785-1485
SPITALNY, Herb  tb  307
SPIVAK, Charlie  t  16-320-321-362-367-368-
    424-425-445-512-561-562-671-672-1048-
    1063-1082-1095-1124-1131-1150-1234-1235-
    1236-1270-1273-1328-1483-1537-1538-1539-
    1552-1718
SPIVEY, ———  bj  940-1576
SPIVEY, Sweet Pease (r.n. Addie S.)  v
    1486-1487
SPIVEY, Victoria  v-p-g  11-792-1487-1488-
    1489
"SPO-DE-O SAM"  v  1247
SPOERLODER, Paul  d  1326-1327
SPOKANEY, Robert  vn  1690
SPRAGUE, Don  t  183-829
SPRENTALL, Bob  t  1552-1553
SPRINGER, Joe  p  912
SPROUL, Dave  bb  640-641
SPRUELL, Leon  as  214
SPRUYT, Gerard  sb  161
SPUMBERG, Sammy  ts  1160
SQUIRES, Bruce  tb  204-376-429-612-815-
    816-906-907-1236
SRBEK, J.  sb  1575
STABILE, Dick  cl-as-ldr  130-131-780-1490
STABILE, Joe  as  1490
STACEY, Jack  cl as-ts  53-362-363-364-424-
    425-426-427-428-687-1197-1329-1406
STACKS, Tom  d-v  145-319-320-1076-1098-
    1163-1288-1396-1611-1740
STACY, Jess  p  18-62-317-335-363-364-365-
    371-372-373-374-375-376-505-542-597-598-
    599-600-601-602-603-604-605-606-607-608-
    609-610-611-612-660-661-813-814-821-822-
    882-905-906-942-1005-1048-1468-1490-1491-
    1673-1697
STAFFON, Bill  v-dir  1491
STAFFORD, George  d  13-334-806-833 881-
    966-1052
STAFFORD, Harry  ts-a  546
STAFFORD, Jesse  tb-bh-ldr  1491-1694
STAFFORD, Jo  v  451-452-453-454-455
STAFFORD, Mary  v  1492
STAIGERS, Del  t  17-64-112-1272-1416-1417-
    1418-1586-1604-1610
STAINBECK, Albert  ts  1498
STAMP, Jesse  tb  798-799-1019-1216
STAMPFEL, Lucky  d  826
STAMPS, Charlie  bj  252-253-349-686-1245
STANCHFIELD, Stan  vn  817
STANFIELD, Leemie  sb  691-692-693-694-
    1731
STANLEY, ———  bb  272-1155
STANLEY, Aileen  v  1015-1492-1608-1609
STANLEY, Albert  g  656
STANLEY, Bob  t  1231-1663-1745
STANLEY, Cliff "Red"  tb-v  1
STANLEY, Ethel  v  4
STANLEY, James  v  577
STANLEY, John  tb  505
STANLEY, Walter  t  830
STANNARD, Eddie  cl-as-ts  232-233-1271-
    1609-1680-1681

STANT, Gail  as  1570-1571
STAR, Charles  cl-as  345-667-1548-1614
STAR, Nat  cl-as-dir  639-1493
STARGART, Harold  cl-ts  133
STARITA, Al  cl-as-bsx-v-ldr  143-271-522-
    537-568-982-1226-1364-1493-1565
STARITA, Ray  cl-ts-v-ldr  271-523-568-
    903-982-1226-1227-1364-1493-1494-1565
STARITA, Rudy  d-x-vib-marimba  271-525-
    537-568-949-950-951-952-953-982-1126-
    1127-1196-1226-1227-1290-1291-1292-
    1293-1294-1295-1296-1297-1365-1419-
    1493-1494-1738
STARK, Bobby  t  312-382-527-722-723-
    724-725-726-727-730-1657-1658-1659-1660-
    1661-1662
STARK, Emil  vc  420
STARK, Willie  as  47
STARKS, Artie  cl-as-ts  314-676-753-754-
    810-862-863-936-1014-1025-1026-1051-
    1267-1268-1320-1618
STARKS, Booker  s  277
STARR, Arnold  vn  632
STARR, Henry  p-g-v  1108-1494
STARR, Robert  c  1090
STARR, Tony  bj-g-v  34-422-1145
STAUFF, Dick  d  1662
STAYNER, Whitney  cl-as  317
STEAD, E.  tb  332
STEAD, William  cl-ts  892
STEARNS, Al  t  452-453-816-817-818
STEARNS, Genevieve  v  1496
STEARNS, Lawrence  t  622-623-1373
STECK, Steve  t  1554
STEDEFORD, Marjorie  v  938-974-1207-1432
STEELE, Alphonse  d  15-768
STEELE, Blue  tb-mel-v-ldr  173-1496-1497
STEELE, Fred K.  v  631
STEELE, Joe  p-ldr  1362-1497-1654-1658
STEGMEYER, Bill  cl-as  369-370-371-372-
    373
STEIL, Fred  as  404
STEIN, Cliff  sb  409
STEIN, John Hountha  d  459-464
STEIN, Manny  sb  59-180-1118-1150
STEINBACHER, Erwin  bj  1120
STEINBERG, Eddie  p  756
STEINBERG, Murphy  c-t  868-918-1056-1193-
    1233-1419
STEINER, William  as  1654
STEINFIELD, Harry  cl-as-ts-bar  8-9
STELL, George  vn  1586-1589
STENFALT, Norman  p  316-589-590-591
STENGLER, A. P.  cl  1473-1474-1475
STENNETT, Billy  t-vn-ldr  1498
STENROOS, Charles  tb  1664
STEPHENS, Bob  dir  1071
STEPHENS, Haig  sb  28-29-30-40-56-153-
    163-215-216-545-633-756-780-781-841-
    1007-1137-1305-1313-1314-1315-1316-
    1333-1655
STEPHENS, Jack  bj  525-1336-1485
STEPHENSON, David  cl-as-bar  511-1215
STEPHENSON, Louis  as  283
STERN, Edward  bb  1120
STERN, Emil  g  313-330-1288-1642
STERN, Hank  bb  33-134-161-239-360-418-
    419-420-421-508-670-671-804-853-931-
    932-1064-1271-1369-1381-1382-1383-1384-
    1597-1614

STERNDALE, Maurice  vn  1339-1340-1341-1342

STEVENS, Don  t  829-1147-1148

STEVENS, Edwin C.  p  854

STEVENS, Harry  cl-bsx  1450

STEVENS, Harry  bj  1-179

STEVENS, Leith  dir  1498

STEVENS, Phil  sb  94-95-96-97-98-453-454 455-1047

STEVENS, Steve  p  1446

STEVENS, Vol  bj-g-md-v  1041-1042-1043

STEVENSON, Carlyle  as-a-ldr  552-1498

STEVENSON, George  tb  833-1070-1203-1500

STEVENSON, Graham  d  162-444-1236-1237

STEVENSON, Lew or Lou  d  801-1336

STEVENSON, Robert  t-flugelhorn  517

STEVENSON, Tommy  t  252-691-983-984-1279

STEWART, —— one-string fiddle  460

STEWART, Bill  t  890-1051-1052

STEWART, Bill  cl-as-ts  1501

STEWART, Buddy  v  1553-1554

STEWART, Charles  tb  126

STEWART, Dan  p-speech  1499

STEWART, Danny  v  1299

STEWART, Dee  t  1112

STEWART, Elliott  v  1583

STEWART, Frohsine  v  18

STEWART, Hamilton  v  1112

STEWART, Ken  d  1585

STEWART, Larry  v  795-1027-1416

STEWART, Lucille  v  1052

STEWART, Luke  g  1465

STEWART, Priscilla  v  65-1499-1500

STEWART, Rex  c-v  27- -114-134-135-489-490-491-492-493-494-495-496-497-498-499 500-643-662-663-720-723-724-725-726-734 736-779-965-1024-1035-1058-1093-1094-1096-1203-1263-1306-1337-1346-1453-1500 1501-1540-1729

STEWART, Roy - see SHAYNE, AL

STEWART, Sammy  p-ldr  1501

STEWART, Slam (r.n. Leroy S.)  sb-v  272-550-551-1344

STILES, Eddie  p  1730

STILL, Lois  v  1236

STILL, William Grant  o-a  710-1407-1612-1687

STILLMAN, Jack  t-ldr  569-1502-1503-1504 1505

STILLSON, Ray  cl-as  659-1524

STILWELL, Ray  tb-v  265-266-267-559-640-641-1300-1392-1482

STIRKIN, Dave  vl  1273-1406

STITMAN, Harry  d  946

STITZEL, Mel  p  193-592-1132-1506

STOCCO, S. J.  t  134-1018

STOCK, Bert  p  884

STOCK, Tiny  bb-sb  146-467-468-469-470-507-521-809-810-917-949-950-951-952-953 1070-1126-1127-1738

STOCKARD, Ocie  bj-ldr  1505

STOCKWELL, Bob  t  1602

STODDARD, Frank  cl-as  1510

STODDARD, Fred  cl-ts-a  1305

STODDARD, Harold  d  556

STODDARD, Harry  p-ldr  1505

STOETZEL, Carl  d  404

STOKES, Harold  pac-v-a-dir  578-579-580-869-919

STOKES, Ray  p  11-16-172-333-1506

STOLL, —— tb  1254-1255-1256

STOLL, George  tb-dir  1143-1144-1145-1506

STOLLER, Alvin  d  622

STONE, Bill  cl-as  1124-1125

STONE, Christopher  compere  470

STONE, Eddie  vn  360-858-859

STONE, Eddie  v-dir  1506

STONE, Gene  g  204

STONE, George  as  772

STONE, Henry "Butch"  ts-bar-v  8-9-186-325-326

STONE, Jesse  p-pac-a-ldr  940-941-944-1507

STONE, Lew  p-a-dir  20-22-459-800-1507-1508-1509

STONEBURN, Sid  cl-as-bar etc.  30-33-56-204-214-215-249-250-305-320-321-437-438 592-593-700-701-756-967-968-1032-1126-1142-1143-1144-1145-1272-1304-1315-1333 1415-1752

STONER, Charles  ts  401

STORDAHL, Axel  a  442-452-453

STOREY, F. Fabian  p  233

STORM, Charlie  a  1202

STORMAN, Eddie  bj-vc  1327-1347-1348

STORME, Michael  sb  1116-1117

STORR, Alton  v  450

STORY, Lewis  cl-as-v  882

STORY, Nat  tb  527-1346-1659-1660-1661-1662-1743

STOUT, Charlie  tb  126

STOUT, Russ  bj  339-340-341

STOVALL, Don  as  40-181-832-851-1109-1203-1204-1246-1247

STOWE, Charlie  d  383

STOWELL, Bob  bj  1335

STRAIGHT, Charlie  p-ldr  1509-1510

STRAIN, Doc  v  1725

STRAINE, Mary  v  1510

STRAND, Manny  p  1146-1147-1562

STRANGE, Frank  t-v  540

STRANGE, Jimmy  t  556-891

STRATAKOS, Ellis  tb-ldr  396-397-1510

STRAUB, Bill  p  323-324-325-326

STRAUN, Chic  v  1510

STRAYHORN, Billy  p-a  135-494-495-497-498-499-500-766-767-1501-1712

STREINER, Harvey  t  1243-1244

STRESS, Ed  t  1361

STRETTON, Gordon  d-dir  1173

STRICKER, Ernie  tb  1602

STRICKFADEN, Charles  as-bar-o  76-211-503-922-1017-1567-1568-1569-1570-1571-1598-1680-1681-1682-1683-1684-1685-1686-1687-1688-1689-1690

STRICKLER, Benny  t  505

STRICKLER, Ernest  tb  307

STROHAUSER, Tom  p-a  388-389

STROM, Roy  vn-v  831-840

STRONG, Bob  cl-as-mel-vn  579-580-1510

STRONG, Jimmy  cl-ts  43-44-45-46-404-1488

STROUSE, John  d  659

STRUBLE, Harry  vn  61-1689-1690

STUART, Al  t-as-v  93-250-306

STUART, Kenneth  tb  759

STUBBS, Russell  p  1534

STUHLMAKER, Mort  sb  122-123-126-543-620-893-1026-1114-1147

1834
STULCE, Fred as-or 438-439-440-441-442-
  443-444-445-446-447-448-449-450-451-452-
  454-455-1697
STULTZ, Doc d 391-1288
STULTZ, Gene or Jean g 1170-1398-1399
STUMP, Cal sb 132
STUMP, Everett cl-ss-as-ts 640-641
STURDEVANT, John cl 318
STURGIS, Rodney v 1511
STURGIS, Ted sb 284-466-729-770-808
STURKIN, David - see STIRKIN, DAVE
STURM, George bj-a 913
STURR, Harold cl-as-ts-f 120-121-395-870-
  871
STUTELEY, Don sb 3-16-22-404-525-530-539-
  683-797-798-1207-1289-1306-1419-1695-
  1721-1749-1750
SUBLETT, John "Bubbles" v 193
SUCEDO, Jose bj 1694
SUDERMAN, Oliver t 207-829-1116
SUDLER, Joe c 466
SUGGS, Pete d-vib 729
SULKIN, Harry sb 94
SULLIVAN, Joe p 45-88-309-334-335-336-
  362-363-371-592-593-662-769-868-977-1032-
  1033-1087-1141-1143-1289-1511-1546-1555-
  1561-1594-1600-1653
SULLIVAN, Maxine v 284-897-1512-1513-
  1552
SULLIVAN, Tommy v 1744
SULSER, Bromo vn 888
SUMMERFORD, Annie v 1513
SUNSHINE BOYS, THE v 1384
SUSKIND, Milton p 629
SUSNOW, Harry t 265
SUTER, Ann v 1515
SUTHERLAND, Kitty v 587
SUTTON, Ed vn 220-221-222-223-224
SWAIN, Hal as-ts-v 1134
SWALINE, Arthur p 28
SWAN, John t 1743
SWANN, De Ford p 1253
SWARTHOUT, Eddie as 563-564-890
SWARZMAN, Joe sb 1089
SWAYZEE, Edwin c-t 253-254-255-256-257-
  868-954-1103
SWEARINGEN, Carl t 656-657
SWEATMAN, Wilbur C. cl-ldr 1515-1516-
  1517-1518
SWEET, Herbert p 457
SWENUMSEN, Swanny c 540
SWETSCHIN, ——— vn 1260
SWIFT, Carl cl-as 1147-1553
SWIFT, George t 801
SWIFT, Harry tb 466
SWINFEN, Johnny cl-as-vn 1263-1343-1675
SWING CHOIR, THE v 1279
SWINGTETTES, THE v 801
SWINNERTON, Charles as 1356-1364-1472
SWITZER, Ken t 1616
SYKES, Roosevelt p-v 834-847-1029-1574
SYLVANO, Frank v 18-118-274-658-1195-
  1231-1509-1510
SYLVESTER, Art t 594-595
SYLVESTER, Bob a 775
SYLVESTER, Charles d 27
SYLVESTER, Hannah v 1519-1520
SYLVESTER, Johnny t 1180-1394-1520-1521
SYMONDS, David ts 87
SYMONDS, Del p 646
SZATHMARY, Irving a 1540

TAFT, Glenn t 703-1561
TAFT, Harold as-bar 82
TAFT, "Slim" Jim tb-sb 53-163-276-362-427-
  428-687-890-1033-1051-1052-1237-1329-
  1562
TALBERT, Wendell P. p 731-1524
TALPHY, James t 834
TALL, Sam bj 164-177-1109-1110
TALLEY, Leonard bar 730
TAMPA BOYS, THE v 1109
TAMPA RED - see WHITTAKER, HUDSON
TANN, Eric tb 656-809-810-1224-1508-
  1509
TANNENBAUM, Jules vc 1406
TANNER, Elmo w-v 1152-1153-1667-1668-
  1669
"TAP-DANCING JOE" k-v 461
TAPLEY, Ernest bj-md 863
TAPP, Ferman bj 1603
TAPSON, Harold d 194-1036-1746
TARTO, Joe bb-sb-a 17-19-20-33-74-156-
  157-160-174-176-203-205-304-305-350-351-
  394-419-420-421-427-457-462-463-509-510-
  512-519-532-559-668-670-671-719-804-822-
  871-882-922-926-927-928-929-930-934-973-
  1015-1039-1055-1062-1063-1076-1080-1081-
  1083-1087-1120-1121-1128-1138-1141-1142-
  1163-1164-1173-1183-1193-1288-1300-1301-
  1302-1303-1308-1323-1329-1369-1370-1381-
  1382-1418-1420-1430-1454-1482-1483-1521-
  1544-1545-1574-1589-1597-1598-1599-1611-
  1639-1652-1751
TATE, Buddy (r.n. George H. T.) ts 105-
  106-107-108-109-110-821
TATE, Carroll C. v 1529
TATE, Erskine bj-dir 1529
TATE, Harry c-t 149-1650-1717
TATE, James c-t 1282-1529
TATHIM, Donald bj 179
TATUM, Art p-cel 651-1529-1530-1531
TAYLOR, Al(fred) d 284-832-1203-1456
TAYLOR, Arthur bj-g 1123-1169-1170
TAYLOR, Billy cl-ts-bar-vn 1118-1213-
  1214-1616
TAYLOR, Billy bb-sb 15-27-134-135-207-
  355-489-490-491-492-493-494-495-661-662-
  691-752-765-766-779-782-1034-1035-1099-
  1104-1105-1247-1263-1289-1304-1408-1446-
  1500-1511-1531-1540-1575-1624-1625-1640-
  1711-1712
TAYLOR, Billy d 405-835-836
TAYLOR BROTHERS bj-md-k 1531
TAYLOR, Bud ts 936
TAYLOR, Clarence ss-as-bsx 940-941
TAYLOR, Dave dir 1537
TAYLOR, E. v 403-650
TAYLOR, Edna v 1531
TAYLOR, Eva (r.n. Irene Williams) v 305-
  1011-1306-1382-1383-1531-1532-1533-1534-
  1535-1699-1700-1705-1706-1707-1708-1709-
  1710-1711
TAYLOR, Freddy t-v 1536
TAYLOR, Freddy bj-v 1021-1259
TAYLOR, Georgia v 1167
TAYLOR, Harold "Dink" as 7
TAYLOR, Herb tb 1141-1142
TAYLOR, Irene v 505-1536-1684
TAYLOR, Jackie vn-ldr 1335-1536
TAYLOR, Jackie v 156
TAYLOR, James v 1110

TAYLOR, Jasper  d-wb-woodblocks  146-150-411-665-822-864-891-1099-1161-1162-1280-1281-1536-1714
TAYLOR, Jean  d  172
TAYLOR, Jimmy  t  1
TAYLOR, Larry  v  95-96-97-99-923
TAYLOR, Louis  tb  758-759
TAYLOR, Myra  v  944
TAYLOR, Noel  v  1567
TAYLOR, Norman  tb  59
TAYLOR, Rudolph  d  761-762
TAYLOR, Sam  ts  1674
TAYLOR, Sammy  d  1236
TAYLOR, Thales  cl-as  1664-1665
TAYLOR, Tommy  d-sw-v  619-620-873-1040-1244-1737
TAYLOR, Yack  v  864-1247-1560
TAYNE, Wolffe  cl-ts  183-184-185-186-322-323-324
TEAGARDEN, Charlie  t  200-204-305-592-593-594-821-1081-1142-1143-1144-1145-1234-1270-1537-1538-1558-1571-1572-1600-1653-1673-1689-1690-1691-1723
TEAGARDEN, Cubby (r.n. Clois T.)  d  1538-1539
TEAGARDEN, Jack (r.n. Weldon Leo T.)  tb-vib-v  16-33-45-56-84-134-197-200-275-305-334-335-364-419-543-593-594-595-633-674-821-840-871-932-957-977-999-1001-1029-1031-1046-1048-1063-1076-1077-1078-1079-1080-1081-1113-1124-1131-1141-1142-1143-1144-1223-1232-1233-1234-1235-1270-1315-1325-1328-1332-1382-1438-1446-1537-1538-1539-1540-1541-1558-1571-1572-1599-1600-1623-1624-1653-1689-1690-1691-1723-1751
TEAGUE, Thurman  sb  153-204-814-815-816-817-818-819-820-1216-1236
TEELA, Dick  v  1068
TEI, Adrian  as  1490
TEMPLE, Eddie  d  1245-1749
TEMPLE, George  t  820-1705-1714-1715-1716
TEMPLE, Johnnie  g-v  1541-1542-1543
TEMPLE, Nat  cl-as  387-388-563-1339-1340-1341-1342
TEMPLETON, Alec  p  801
TEMPO TWISTERS, THE  v  647
TENNILLE, Frank  v  365-1270
TENNYSON, Hal  cl-as  1244-1552
TEPALDI, Art  bj  1334
TERMAN, Louis  bb  1664-1665
TERNENT, Billy  ts-a  799-800-801
TERR, Max  p-ldr  1097-1098
TERRELL, Pha  v  899-900-901
TERRY, Thelma  sb-ldr  1546
TERVALON, Ralph  p  1322
TESCHMACHER, Frank  cl-as-ts  134-302-309-234-419-804-868-931-956-977-999-1032-1033-1087-1228-1366-1546
TESTAERT, Julian  tb  1120
TETER, Jack  v  273
TEWKESBURY, Clayton  t  659
THALEN, Olle  as  282
THARP, Sister Rosetta  g-v  1070
THATCHER, Thomas  ts  119-120
THAYER, Buddy  bj  82
THEARD, Sam  v  390-1197-1210-1547
THIELL, Harold  cl-as  338-339-340-341
THIELL, John  cl-as  338-339-340-341
THIELMANS, Marcel  tb  161-282-698

THIES, Henry  vn-ldr  1548
THIESS, Norman-dir/Mrs. Norman  p  1005
THIGPEN, Ben  d-v  251-466-899-900-901-902-1267-1431-1720
THIGPEN, George  t  91-92
THILAND, Jean  p  543
THOM, Norman  t  646
THOMAS, ----  c  149-1013-1700
THOMAS, Al  g  801
THOMAS, Arnold  p  864-865
THOMAS, Bert  bj-g  395-683-797-949-1126-1127-1128-1149-1364-1365-1515-1521
THOMAS, Bill  as  1252
THOMAS, Bill  sb  1658-1659
THOMAS, Bob  see HARE, ERNEST
THOMAS, Bruce  ts  552-553
THOMAS, Charles  effects  1717
THOMAS, Cicero  t  91-92-376-1069-1282-1548
THOMAS, Dave  bj  395-1135-1362-1363-1515
THOMAS, Del  bb  723
THOMAS, Eddie  cl-as  517
THOMAS, Eddy  v  130-519-1143
THOMAS, Emlyn  vn-ldr  1548
THOMAS, F. T.  v  1548
THOMAS, George  tb  356
THOMAS, George  cl-as-ts-v  134-311-472-580-1033-1034-1035
THOMAS, George  g  836-837
THOMAS, George W.  p-v  378-541-1065-1069
THOMAS, Gladstone  sb-v  164
THOMAS, Herb  g  284
THOMAS, Hersal  p  1065-1549-1618
THOMAS, Hociel  v  1549-1550
THOMAS, Howard  dir  1550
THOMAS, James  bj  1090
THOMAS, Jasper  v  828
THOMAS, Jay "Bird"  d-v  553
THOMAS, Jeff  g  155
THOMAS, Joe  c-t  28-39-153-283-727-728-752-1263-1531-1638
THOMAS, Joe  cl-as-ts-bar-f-v  401-768-983-984-985-986-987-988-989-990-991-1103-1104-1550
THOMAS, Joe  p  1377
THOMAS, John  tb  41-42-414-752-1282
THOMAS, Les  vn  1214
THOMAS, Lewis  p  1371
THOMAS, Logan  p  466
THOMAS, Martin  bass voice  554-555
THOMAS, Millard G.  p-ldr  1550-1551-1671
THOMAS, Ralph  v  211
THOMAS, Red  v  920-921
THOMAS, Walter  cl-as-ts-bar-f  252-253-254-255-256-257-258-259-260-261-262-349-1004-1004-1103-1104
THOMASON, Joe  tb  555
THOMPSON, Aaron  tb  794-845-1118-1279-1280-1617  1699
THOMPSON, Al  tb  505
THOMPSON, Al  ts-v  1231-1663-1745
THOMPSON, Art  p  822
THOMPSON, Ashley  g-v  270
THOMPSON, C. C.  d-v  1274
THOMPSON, Carroll  g  1237
THOMPSON, Sir Charles  p-a  663-730
THOMPSON, Creighton  v  513
THOMPSON, Don  p  1606
THOM(P)SON, Earl  t-a  782-899-900-901-1431-1662
THOMPSON, Ed  v  1155

1836
THOMPSON, Evelyn v 720-1551
THOMPSON, Harry t-tb 156-1005-1362-1363-1616
THOMPSON, Henry t 461
THOMPSON, Hubert ts 179
THOMPSON, Jack t 647-1752
THOMPSON, Kay v 1551
THOMPSON, Leslie t-tb 52-281-282-790-791
THOMPSON, Louis bb-sb 91-92-191-881
THOMPSON, Moe v 557
THOMPSON, Phil bj 89
THOMPSON, Rudolph jug-v 1675-1676
THOMPSON, Slow Kid speech 1650
THOMPSON, Stan bj-v 540
THOMPSON, Tommy as-ts 328
THOMSON, Scoop g 93
THORBURN, Billy p 395-522-1214-1215-1364-1515
THORNE, Bob t 182-184-185
THORNE, Carroll cl-ss-as 508-1120
THORNE, Donald p 1226-1227-1493
THORNE, John (r.n. Tom Greenhalgh) v 134-784-785-827-828-1296
THORNE, Robert t 186
THORNHILL, Claude p-vib-x 163-202-203-204-295-309-541-565-594-768-1026-1027-1028-1063-1089-1095-1150-1248-1415-1512-1552-1553-1554-1615-1718
THORNTON, Norman as 775
THORPE, Bill g 428
THORPE, Tony tb 22-23-146-161-388-393-395-656-809-810-1127-1128-1149-1363-1432-1507
THORPES, Charlie bar 1516
THORSEN, Art bb-sb 708
THOW, George t 53-360-362-424-425-426-427-428-594-687-858-1033-1237-1329-1406
THRALL, Roy as 648
THREE BITS OF RHYTHM, THE v 1344
THREE ESQUIRES, THE v 439-444-445
THREE GINX, THE v 938
THREE ICKIES, THE v 1159
THREE LARKS, THE v 1319
THREE LITTLE MAIDS, THE v 1279
THREE MOAXES, THE v 97
THREE SONGIES, THE v 1147
THREE STAR SINGERS, THE v 931
THREE SWINGSTERS, THE v 1351
THREE TOPPERS, THE v 1357
THREE VARIETIES, THE v 761-762
THRELKELD, Buford Whistler g-v 1675-1676
THUNEN, Tommy t 177-977-978-1055-1078-1079-1141-1142-1328-1537
THURMAN, Glen sb 277
THURSTON, Frank cl 470
THURSTON, Roland bj 1421
THWAITE, Ray cl-ss-as 545-546
TIBBS, Leroy p-dir 164-396-397-459-645-810-1168-1217-1305-1306-1559-1657-1724-1725-1727
TICE, Larry cl-as 578-579-580-672-980-981-1506
TIETIG, Arnold vn 1252
TIFF, Don p 1374
TILFORD, Hooks (r.n. George T.) Cm 891-1223-1266
TILLAR, Phil as 1507
TILSON, Jack d 1289
TILTON, Les v 374-375
TILTON, Martha v 603-604-605-606-607-608-609-611-612-1406

TIMMS, Cliff vn 797-798-1150
TIMMS, Henry ts 1210
TIMOTHY, Tom cl-ts-ldr 1559
TINES, Oliver d 1-52-179-518-827
TINNEY, Alan "Pee Wee" p 1046
TINNEY, William as 557
TINSLEY, Ted g-v 412-681-1697
TINTEROW, Bernard vn 454-455
TIO, Lorenzo, Jr. cl-ts 136-537-1104-1229-1230-1458-1533
TIPPING, Bernard tb 156-345-790-1362-1363
TITE, B. D. jug 1675
TIZOL, Juan tb-vtb 27-134-135-479-480-481-482-483-484-485-486-487-488-489-490-491-492-493-494-495-496-497-498-499-500-651-652-1075-1263-1711
TJORDY, George vn 1607-1680
TOBIN, John bj-ldr 1559-1570
TOBIN, Louise v 166-611-612-613-829
TODD, Clarence p-k-v 5-75-146-411-794-812-1280-1560-1699-1707-1708-1709
TODD, Dick v 322-323
TODD, Mabel v 1560
TODD, Seymour bb-sb 149
TODD, Sterling p 338
TOFFEL, Billy g 689
TOLAND, Ray d 670-1490-1586
TOLBERT, Skeets cl-as-v-ldr 646-1537-1560-1561
TOLL, Ted d v-ldr 1561
TOLLIVER, Jack v 1465
TOLLIVER, James "Buster" ts-p-a 114-395-557-1427
TOMLIN, Pinky v 1561-1562
TOMLIN, William "Sleepy" t 983
TOMPKINS, Eddie t-v 768-983-984-985-986-987-988
TOMPKINS, Herb as 184-741-742
TOMPKINS, Tommy t-ldr 1562
TONISEN, Ted g 881
TONKEL, Denny d 923
TOOKEY, George cl-as 1308
TOPPERS, THE v 1360
TORRANCE, Albert cl-as 581-582-583-584-585-586-587-588-589
TORRES, Gilbert g 1681
TORRES, Jose bb 218
TORTOMAS, Tony t 139-1088-1108-1182-1183-1184-1273
TOUGH, Dave d 78-122-124-305-335-439-440-441-442-443-446-447-542-543-608-609-610-617-618-814-821-977-1114-1115-1136-1141-1142-1408-1409-1501-1539-1540-1553
TOUMEY, Willard cl-as 301
TOWBIN, Cyril vn 819-820
TOWER, Casper bj-v 1338
TOWNE, Jack cl-as-bar 648
TOWNES, Floyd cl-ts-v 881-1366
TOWNES, Wilson cl-as 665-1099
TOWNSEND, Bill vn 1641
TRABSKY, Jascha ts 836
TRAETTINO, Ricky t 320-321-322-1228
TRAFFICANTE, Mike bb-sb 503-922-1325-1375-1682-1683-1684-1685-1686-1687-1688
TRAINER, Jack t 664
TRAMMEL, Leo cl 1512
TRANCHANT, Gene p-cel 313-960-1562
TRANCHITELLI, —— cl-ts 924
TRANTHAM, Cookie bb-sb-v 1068-1497

TRAPPIER, Arthur d 1637-1638
TRASI, Sam t 188
TRAULSEN, Palmer tb 282
TRAXLER, Gene sb-v 249-250-437-438-439-
440-441-442-443-444-445-446-447-448-449
455-699-700-701-946-1007
TRAXLER, Siebert cl-ts-bar 963
TREASTER, Bob d-v 840
TREBBLE, Jack d 403
TREMAINE.BROTHERS, THE v 74-75-1563
TREMAINE, Paul vn-v-ldr 1563
TREMAINE, Robert C. vn 1563
TREMER, George H. p-h 1563
TRENET, Charles v 1563
TRENT, Alphonse p-dir 1563-1564
TRENT, Bruce sb 801
TRENT, Edward bj 851
TRENT, Jo v 1564
TRENT, Percy t 851
TREPTE, Arthur o 1604
TRESIZE, Al cl-as 172-173
TRESIZE, William as-vn 870
TREVOR, Buford tb 1146-1147
TRIAY, George d 1208
TRIBBLE, Earl as 1693
TRICE, Clarence t 900-901-902
TRIEGO, ———— tb 118
TRIMBLE BOYS, THE v 75
TRINGHAM, Bill p 146
TRIPP, Hugh cl-as-bar 539-1739
TRISKO, Ken d 525
TRITTEL, Billy tb 60
TRIX SISTERS, THE v 1565
TRIX, Phil as 1215
TROISE, Pasquale bj-g 1202
TRONE, Bill tb-mel 1141-1142-1611-1612-
1613
TRONNY, N. vn 359
TRONSTEIN, Bill cl-ss-as-ts 1285
TRONSTEIN, Joseph bb-sb 1285
TROPPER, Harry bb-sb-ldr 1055
TROTTA, Charles t-v 1-456
TROTTA, Ray t 1271
TROTTER, John Scott ldr-dir 498-887-888
889-1256
TROUP, George tb 232-234-235-239-647-
967-1393-1409-1548-1620
TROUTMAN, Jimmy t 660
TROXELL, Frank tb 314
TRUCKER, Sid cl-as-bar 53-132-203-205-
780-1095-1115-1178-1313-1314-1375
TRUEHEART, John bj-g 50-357-382-526-527
528-868-1654-1657-1658-1659-1662-1730-
1731
TRUESDALE, William dir 534
TRULOCK, Russell cl-ts 1369
TRUMBAUER, Frank as-Cm-bsn-c-cl-dir 76-
120-174-309-350-361-577-578-738-885-
1017-1067-1068-1112-1139-1422-1538-1558
1566-1567-1568-1569-1570-1571-1572-1598
1682-1683-1684-1685-1686-1687-1688-1689
1690
TRYCE, Earl bj 214
T'SAS, Eugene d 1120
"TUBI" bb 573
TUCCI, Ray bar 1360-1361
TUCK, Tony bj-vc 1603
TUCKER, Bessie v 1572-1573
TUCKER, Otto cl-ss-as-ts 2
TUCKER, Sophie v 1573-1574

TUMMINIA, Josephine v 429
TUNE TWISTERS, The v 396-1063-1333
TUNIA, Raymond p 1674
TUNNELL, Bon Bon (r.n. George T.) v
1357-1358-1359-1361-1556
TUNSILL, Johnny v 1020
TUPP, Ferman d 1054
TURK, Al c-dir 1574
TURLEY, Bobby d 917-918
TURMAN, Lew bb 391
TURNER, Bee v 1574
TURNER, Buford g 92-93
TURNER, Charlie bb-sb 676-862-1019-1625
1626-1627-1628-1629-1630-1631-1637-1638
1654-1655
TURNER, Count bj 823-1322
TURNER, Dick t 1252
TURNER, Elmer bj 1203
TURNER, Harry tb 1666-1667-166801669
TURNER, Henry bb-sb 113-773-774-775-865
1511-
TURNER, James bj-md 863
TURNER, Jim vn 665-666
TURNER, Joe p-v 47-465-632-828-1575
TURNER, Joe v 284-850-1511-1531-1575-
1594
TURNER, Lavinia v 1178-1576
TURNER, Lloyd tb 422-423-578-756-892-
1027-1273-1299-1300-1576
TURNER, Merle v 7-691-692
TURNER, Ole tb 402-403
TURNER, Raymond p 211-1681
TURNER, Toby cl-as 757-758
TURNHAM, Floyd cl-as 763-1512
TURNSTALL, Fred p 704-705
TUSCANDO, Joseph bj-vn 418
TWO FISHMONGERS, THE v 113
TYLER, Paul ts 1501
TYLER, Toby tb 740-741-907
TYLER, William A. vn 665-1652-1725
TYNDALL, Kline p 169-412-681-1026-1559
TYREE, Henry as 52
TYSON, "Dr. SAUSAGE" d-v-ldr 1355
TYSON, William p 569-785-1218-1577
TYUS, Charles v 557-1577
TYUS, Effie p-v 557-1577

UDEN MASMAN, Theo p-ldr 161
ULIN, Al p 1121
ULRICH, Carl cl-as 508
UNDERHAYE, Fred bb 1363-1364-1472
UNDERHILL, Jerry — see MACY, JERRY
UNDERWOOD, Jimmy d-v 697
UNDERWOOD, Sugar p 812-1578
UNDERWOOD, Wilson cl-as 91-92
URE, Alec d 156-1364-1365-1521
USERA, Ramon cl-ts-vn 651-944-1426-1427
USIFER, Joe as 1273
UTLEY, Chatman as 394
UTTERBACH, Sam t 940-941-1025

VAILE, Harry cl-as-ts 1498
VALENTE, Victor p 1361
VALENTI, Al g 30
VALENTINE, Gerald tb-a 761-762
VALENTINE, Jimmy v 166
VALENTINE, John t 61
VALENTINE, Syd t 1454-1471-1586
VALENTINE, Thomas bj-g 218-782-1108
VALLEE, Rudy (r.n. Herbert Prior V.) 153
670-1363-1586-1745

1838

VAN(N), Allen  p  209-533
VAN, Billy  bj  388-389
VANASEC, Artie  ss-vn  856-857-858
VAN CAMP, Sus  tb  1284
VANCE, Dick  t  527-528-728-729-1661-1662
VANCE, Jane  v  1331-1751
VAN CLEEF, Maurice  d  690
VAN CLEEVE, Virgil  u  1650
VAN COTT, J. M.  d  1335
VAN DEN BOSSCHE, Henry  tb  515
VANDERAUER, Miles  t  120
VAN DER OUDERAA, Andre  cl-ts-vn  161-282-689
VANDERVEER, Eddie  t  1272
VANDERVEER, Leroy  bj  141-142-564-710
VANDERWALLE. Carl  s  391
VAN DUSEN, Bill  tb-v  921
VANE, Alma  v  564
VANELLI, Danny  t  454-455
VAN EMBURGH, Harold  cl-ts-v  35-1330
VAN EPS, Bobby  p  53-64-83-84-201-362-424-425-426-427-428-687-997-1009-1241-1329-1437-1438
VAN EPS, Fred  bj  1160-1586-1587-1588
VAN EPS, Fred, Jr.  t-a  239-240-241-243-244-245-246-247-263-882-1393-1394-1538-1581-1583-1593-1620
VAN EPS, George  g  84-153-163-201-594-596-687-841-969-1009-1150-1156-1241-1248-1332-1337-1571
VAN EPS, John  cl-as-ts  168-250-323-437-438-700-701-889-923-1150-1538-1539
VAN EPS, William  bj  1586-1587-1588
VAN GELDER, Rudy  d  959
VAN GILS, Gide  p  171-172
VAN HELVOIRT, George  t  161-282-689
VAN HOOK, Norman  bb  189
VANICELLI, Henry  p  1178-1521
VANKIRK, Saul  p  118
VAN LAKE, Turk  g-a  1242-1243-1660
VAN LOAN, Paul  tb-a  831
VANN, Al  v-ldr  1588
VANNI, Vincent  bb  1744
VAN NORDSTRAND, C. A.  p  889
VAN OVEN, Harry  tb  283
VAN SICKLE, Andy  d  274
VAN SPALL, Lex  g  836
VAN SPEYBROECK, Omer  cl-as  884
VAN STEEDEN, Peter  dir  1589
VANT, Jeff  g  154-155
VANT, Louise  v  313-1589
VANUCCI, Joe  cl-as-a  682
VARGAS, Joe  tb  1373
VARSALONA, Bart  tb  417
VASSAR, Callie  v  1595
VASTEIN, Art  p  640-641
VAUCHANT, Leo  tb-a  571-799-800-871
VAUGHAN, Freddy  bj  1108
VAUGHAN, George  cl-as  93
VAUGHAN, Madison  tb  284
VAUGHAN, Wes(ton)  bj-g-v  117-421-921-977-978-1142-1398-1663-1664-1668-1669
VAUGHN, Cliff  p  1558
VAZ, Bob  p  1595-1596
VEDEY, Julian  d  1675
VEES, Eugene  g  3-465-519-1260-1261-1262-1284-1339
VEITH, Franz  cl-as  1662
VENN, Tommy  bj-g  359-1339-1340-1341-1342-1343
VENTRE, Frank  t-a  418

VENTRE, John  t  1595
VENTURA, Ray  p-dir  1595-1596
VENUTI, Joe  vn-sb-v  2-16-17-33-84-117-156-157-158-160-174-194-199-200-202-203-211-274-275-276-363-395-422-423-463-464-501-502-503-516-576-577-578-669-670-674-822-870-871-1016-1030-1081-1083-1095-1120-1121-1138-1140-1145-1146-1221-1222-1238-1241-1285-1288-1302-1303-1312-1330-1383-1385-1386-1387-1388-1437-1438-1538-1560-1567-1569-1570-1578-1596-1597-1598-1599-1600-1601-1602-1603-1648-1653-1654-1671-1687-1695-1696-1751
VERBERGER, J.  p  1575
VERNON, ——  v  127
VERNON, George  tb  282
VERRELL, Virginia  v  859
VERRET, Irving  tb  685-686
VESELY, Frank  d  1160
VESELY, Ted  tb  62-184-613-614-615-616-1236-1237-1403 (spelt VESLEY throughout the text in error)
VICTOR, Egbert  p  251
VICTOR, Frank (r.n. Frank Viggiani)  g  29-214-215-457-633-756-781-1000-1313-1314-1333-1334-1601-1602-1604-1655-1690
VIDACOVICH, Pinky  cl-as  1131
VIDAL, Charlie  cl-as  546
VIDAL, Jean  as  172
VIDAL, Seelye  t  1231-1663-1743
VIDE, Ted  ts-vc  470/
VIGAL, John P.  v  1606
VIGGIANO, Mike  cl  1002
VIGNEAU, Frank  p  1120-1150
VIGO, Charles  ts  683
VINCENT, Blanche  v  624
VINCENT, Eddie  tb  359-863-891-1245-1310
VINCENTO, Charlie  bj  778
VINES, Hunch  t  208
VINSON, Eddie "Cleanhead"  as-v  1712
VIOLA, Tony  as  1063-1064
VIOLINSKY, Ed  vn  675-1747-1748-
VIRGADAMO, Pat  tb  910-911
VITALE, Bill  as  742
VITALO, Nick  cl-as  1108-1180-1181-1182-1183-1184
VOLA, Louis  sb-pac  172-188-189-312-313-333-398-556-635-776-960-973-1238-1258-1259-1260-1261-1283--1349-1350-1596-1642
VOLOSHIN, Aaron  cl-as  456-1411
VOLLMER, Bob  d  274-275
VOLPE, Harry  p  1122-1604
VON HALLBERG, Richard  sb  1412
VON ZELL, Harry  v  92
VOORHEES, Don  dir  1611-1612-1613
VOORHEES, Fred  g  1670
VORIAN, Tack  417
VORZANGER, Victor  vn-dir  1613-1614
VOSS, Aage  cl-as  282-652-1585
VOYNOW, Dick  p-dir  1195-1741
VREDENBURGH, ——  v  1697
VUNK, Lyman  t  62-05-06-97-98-364-365-374-375-376

WAAK, Hank  bb  972-973
WACHSMAN, Waxy (r.n. Murray W.)  v  1478
WADDILOVE, Don  t  1691
WADE, Carl  cl-ts  6-410-563-1645-1646-1647-1697
WADE, Dave  t  1032-1371-1372-1398-1412-1720

WADE, Ed  t  160-1571-1689-1690-
WADE, Frederick L.  v  1028
WADE, Henry  cl-bcl-ss-ts  561-936-1089-
1273-1274-1483
WADE, J. D.  t-mel  83-84-1563
WADE, Jimmy  c-ldr  165-1614-1615
WAECHLE, Fritz  ts  151
WAFFLE, Al  bb  1368
WAGER, Roy  t-v  455-697-698-699
WAGNER, Al  vn  201-1009
WAGNER, Babe  tb  909-910-911-912
WAGNER, Bud  cl-as-ts  242-262-1393-1620
WAGNER, Carl  tb  1609-1680
WAGNER, Christian  cl-as  172-330-333-519-
652-1284-1615
WAGNER, Frank  cl-ts-vn  1018-1068
WAGNER, Larry  ldr-a  296-1615
WAGNER, Roy  t  685-686
WAGNER, Sol S.  p-ldr  1615-1616-1737
WAIN, Bea  v  320-321-322-323-879-880-903-
1401-1551-
WAINWRIGHT, Connie  g  1116-1203-1456
WAITE, Henry  bj  747
WAKEMAN, Glen  cl-ss-ts  943
WALD, Archie  bb  856
WALDE, Bill  bb  565
WALDE, Henry  bj  565
WALDEN, Cecil  d  511-1263
WALDER, Woody (r.n. Heran W.)  cl-as-ts-k
164-177-941-1109-1110-1111-1112
WALDMAN, Fred  v  1669
WALDMAN, Herman  vn-ldr  1616
WALDRON, Carroll  sb  545-1670
WALKER, Boogie  d  1640
WALKER, Clinton  bb  1169-1170-1715
WALKER, Edward  f  140
WALKER, Eric  p  146
WALKER, Esther  v  1616
WALKER, Ira  t  1310
WALKER, Jack  t  1374
WALKER, Joe  as-bar  41
WALKER, Jonas  tb  747-1712
WALKER, Kirby  v  328
WALKER, Mack  bb-sb  1-382-660-836-1370-
1464-1465
WALKER, Nat  p  763
WALKER, Otis  d  277
WALKER, Ralph  bb  1347-1348
WALKER, Reuben  p  171
WALKER, Sweet Papa Jonas - see WALKER,
JONAS
WALKER, T-Bone  v  763
WALKER, W. E. Gordon  f-a  1019
WALL, Bobby  vn  1714
WALL, Phil  p-a  4-60-561-669-1483-1500-
1737
WALLACE, Babe  v  1560
WALLACE, Cedric  sb  64-272-1377-1632-
1633-1634-1635-1636-1637-1638
WALLACE, Dave  bj  1362
WALLACE, Hal  tb  184
WALLACE, Inez  v  1617
WALLACE, Jack  t.v  589-590-591
WALLACE, Sippie (nee Thomas)  p-v  1617-
1618-1619
WALLACE, Ted see KIRKEBY, ED
WALLACE, Wesley  p  1216-1621
WALLBERG, Gunner  as  1585
WALLEN, Lloyd  t  1068-1069
WALLER, Fats (r.n. Thomas W. also known
as Maurice for contractual reasons)

WALLER, Fats  p-cel-or-elo-bells-v  56-63
64-88-188-303-336-459-471-634-652-720-
722-734-783-793-795-812-821-833-838-854
855-958-966-978-1010-1012-1030-1034-
1051-1082-1273-1417-1430-1529-1537-1621
1622-1623-1624-1625-1626-1627-1628-1629
1630-1631-1632-1633-1634-1635-1636-1637
1638-1696-1700 (see also foot of left-
hand column)
WALLER, Harry  vl  422-1063
WALLER, W. L.  t  1021
WALLEZ, ——  tb  16
WALLOND, Wally  p  1739
WALLS, Archie  bb-sb  665-1010
WALSH, ——  tb  1394
WALSH, Frank  p  10-11-1134
WALSH, Larry  ts  126-398-1539-1540
WALTERS, Abe  tb  995-996
WALTERS, Art  ts  913
WALTERS, Bob  cl-as  1554
WALTERS, Dave  tb  1509
WALTERS, Eddie  v-u  145-305-1383-1385-
1386-1638-1639
WALTERS, George  t  416-999-1179-1506
WALTERS, Teddy  g  912
WALTHAM, Chris  bj  1639
WALTHAM, Tom  p-pac-ldr  1639
WALTON, Blanche Smith  p  822-823
WALTON, Greely  cl-ts  12-52-53-1169-1257
1346-1445-1712
WALTON, Harry  p  1490
WALTON, John  ts  622-623
WALTON, Lorraine  v  1639
WALTZER, Phil  as  53
WALTZER, Ruby  g  756
WAMSER, Art  ts  1753
WANDELL, William  p  517
WARD, Dick  d  806
WARD, Eddie  p  32-33
WARD, Frank  tb  184
WARD, Frank E.  cl-ss-ts-ldr  508-1120-
1640
WARD, George  as-ts  1047
WARD, George  d  1272
WARD, Helen  v  371-594-595-596-597-598-
599-600-601-906-1337-1511-1731-1732-
1736-1737
WARD, Jane  v  1360
WARD, Richard  d  317-830
WARD, Tommy  tb  347-348
WARDWELL, O Edward  tb  1586-1604
WARE, Effergee  g  944
WARE, Eugene  t  1310-1311
WARE, Leonard  g-elg  113-832-1575
WARE, Ozie  v  476-477-1640-1641
WARFIELD, W.  bj  863
WARING, Fred  v-dir  1641
WARING, Tom  p-v  1641
WARLOP, Michel  vn-ldr  188-556-635-1211-
1221-1260-1348-1349-1476-1642
WARNE, "Horns-in-F"  c  1613-1614
WARNECKE, Louis  as  136-1229-1230
WARNER, ——  p  804-931
WARNER, Allen  cl-ts-o-vc  809-810
WARNER, Byron H.  p-ldr  1643-1644
WARNER, Earl  v  999
WARNER, Joan  v  1642
WARNER, Ken  ss-as  302-500-784-785
WARNER, Smokey  cl-as  383
WARNEY, Leo  d  650
WARREN, Bob  d  278-644

1840

WARREN, Charlie  v  552-629
WARREN, Clark  t  1562
WARREN, Earl  as-v  102-103-104-105-106-
107-108-109-110-769-813-814-821
WARREN, Ernie  cl-ss-as-bar  4-561-1483
WARREN, Harry  v  629
WARREN, John  bb  1-742
WARRINGTON, John  ts-a  1357-1358
WARTNER, George  g  858-859
WARWICK, Carl  t  1075-1279
WARWICK, Karl  t  126
WASHBURN, Country (r.n. Joseph W.)  bb-sb-
v  1036-1037-1666-1667-1668-1669
WASHBURN, Phil  v  435-436
WASHINGTON, Albert  cl-ts-bsx  41-48-49-
50-138-263
WASHINGTON, Benny  d-ldr  757-758-1154-
1648
WASHINGTON, Booker  c  1110-1111-1112
WASHINGTON, Booker T.  d  1723
WASHINGTON, Buck (r.n. Floyd W.)  p  47-
193-688-1446-1468
WASHINGTON, Charles  bj  803-1013
WASHINGTON, Charlie  p  1204
WASHINGTON, Elizabeth  v  409
WASHINGTON, Elliott  bj  856-1209-1282
WASHINGTON, Fred  cl-as  1203
WASHINGTON, Fred  p  456-942-1485
WASHINGTON, George  tb-a-v  13-54-55-56-
57-58-281-728-791-792-1072-1073-1074
WASHINGTON, George D.  v  863
WASHINGTON, Harley  cl-as-ts  1501
WASHINGTON, Isabelle  v  1648
WASHINGTON, Jack  cl-as-bar  101-102-103-
104-105-106-107-108-109-110-769-813-814
821-1110-1111-1112-1507
WASHINGTON, John  d  1464
WASHINGTON, Leon  ts  541-759
WASHINGTON, Steve  bj-g-v  6-563-1645-
1646-1648
WATERHOUSE, Frank  t  867
WATERMAN, Neil  g-v  1231-1663
WATERS, Benny  cl-as-Cm-ts-a  136-731-775-
806-833-991-1014-1168-1169-1203-1703-
1704
WATERS, Ethel  v  1648-1649-1650-1651-1652
1653-1654-1655
WATERS, Kitty  v  1655
WATKINS, Charles  bj-g  1218
WATKINS, Earl  t  1195
WATKINS, Press  as  890
WATKINS, W.  bj  410
WATKINS, Walter  ts  1465
WATSON, El  h-tap dancing  1655
WATSON, Ezell  cl-ldr  1730
WATSON, Fred  g  279-1207
WATSON, Johnny  a  1357-1358-1359-1360
WATSON, Julius  tb-v  683-1674
WATSON, Laurel  v  466-1279
WATSON, Leo  g-sb-d-v  518-906-907-970-
1031-1401-1485-1486-1646-1655
WATSON, Loren L.  dir  358-1169
WATSON, Milton  v  61
WATSON, Ray  cl-ts  1730
WATSON, Sandy  tb  192-1075
WATT, Don  cl-as  28-321-545-633-738-739-
1137-1314-1315-1506-1666-1667-1669
WATTERS, Lu  c-ldr  383-1656
WATTS, Archie  as  792
WATTS, Grady  t  56-287-288-289-290-291-
292-293-294-295-296-297-298-299-300

WATTS, James  v  1676
WATTS, Joe  bb-sb  401-828-838-967-968
WATTS, Kenny  p  1670
WATTS, Phil  bj  1656
WAUGH, Robert  vn  327-1322
WAUGH, William  bj  886-887
WAY, Cecil  t  892
WAYLAND, Hank  sb  123-124-125-126-153-
307-323-324-325-326-594-1046-1156-1398
WAYNE, Frances (Claire)  v  99-417
WAYNE, Martha  v  1553-1554
WEATHERFORD, Teddy  p-v  1529-1614-1615-
1657
WEATHERLEY, Fritz  t  540
WEAVER, Buck  tb  886-887-1146-1147
WEAVER, Clint  bb  940-941
WEAVER, Fred  v  1657
WEAVER, Richard L.  bj  1657
WEAVER, Sylvester  g-v  803-1012-1013-
1014
WEBB, Andrew "Big Boy"  t  1648-1723
WEBB, Chick  d-ldr  50-526-527-631-868-
1052-1116-1657-1658-1659-1660-1661-1662
WEBB, George Byron  as  1174-1175-1368
WEBB, Ray  g  283
WEBB, Speed  d-ldr  1662
WEBB, Stanley  ts  1373-1374-1375
WEBBER, Sam  d  459-500-784-785
WEBER, Al  bb-sb  241-242-245-648-979
WEBER, Bill  d  1201
WEBER, Jack  cl-ts  314-315
WEBER, Kay  v  84-365-366-396-423-424-425
426-427-429
WEBSTER, Ben  ts  191-251-257-258-281-490
491-496-497-498-499-500-662-727-729-767
779-836-1112-1501-1540-1730-1732-1734-
1735-1736
WEBSTER, Carl  bb-sb-ldr  1663
WEBSTER, Dick  vn-v  159-361-642-1663
WEBSTER, Freddy  t  759-761-865-991-1070
WEBSTER, Gilbert  d  801
WEBSTER, Llana  cl-as  1308
WEBSTER, Margaret  v  1663-1706
WEBSTER, Paul  c-t  985-986-987-988-989-
990-991-1110
WEBSTER, Tom  timps  25
WECHSLER, Jack  vn  248-249
WEED, Buddy (r.n. Harold W.)  p-a  1242
WEEMS, Art  c-t-v  1017-1663-1664-1665-
1666-1667-1668-1669
WEEMS, Ted  tb-ldr  1017-1663-1664-1665-
1666-1667-1668-1669
WEERSMA, Melle  a  801
WEGMANN, Rene  a  190
WEIDMAN, Joe  t  1361
WEIGAN, Paul  tb  130-131-1077-1078-1222
WEIL, Herb  d-v  127-233-234-235-236-237-
238-239-248-249-530-624-625-626-882-967
1025-1330-1331-1332-1393-1394-1579-1580
1581-1583-1592-1593-1619-1620
WEILER, Lovell  tb  540
WEINBERG, Meyer  cl-as  153-1216-1249-
1250
WEINSTEIN, Al  cl  1271
WEINSTEIN, Harry  d  1616
WEINSTEIN, Ruby  t  305-556-756-853-871-
903-1081-1142-1143-1144-1145-1233-1234-
1273-1411-1482-1551
WEINSTOCK, Manny  t  159-201-1082
WEIR, Frank  cl-as  85-536-554-822-1295-
1296-1297

WEIR, Tommy  v  1028
WEIRICK, Paul  t  552
WEISBARD, Al  sb  836
WEISHEIPL, George  t  1347
WEISS, Art  tb  120
WEISS, Rene  tb  1211
WEISS, Sam  d  29-40-56-204-214-215-216-
    249-250-263-437-438-594-595-629-873-874
    875-876-877-878-879-880-881-946-967-968
    1001-1002-1082-1088-1089-1248-1273-1313
    1315-1316-1332-1337-1398-1399-1412-1415
WEISS, Sid  sb  93-209-317-399-449-450-
    451-452-453-553-620-621-622-1001-1031-
    1032-1088-1115-1312-1332-1403-1404-1405
    1406-1491-1546-1697
WEISSMAN, Bernard  p  517
WELCH, Elizabeth  v  281-282-827-1076-
    1669
WELCH, Jimmy  t  440
WELCH, Ray  vn  172-173
WELDON, Will ("Casey Bill")  g-v  1041-
    1042-1123
WELK, Lawrence  dir  1669-1670
WELLBORN, Duke (r.n. Adam W.)  d-ldr  405
WELLMON, Doug  t  1068
WELLS, Clem  t  1252
WELLS, Dicky  tb-a  12-13-103-104-105-106
    107-108-109-110-280-726-727-730-755-756
    768-791-792-821-1000-1346-1370-1371-
    1670-1710
WELLS, Frank  v  301-649
WELLS, Henry  tb  774-899-900-901-902-983
    984
WELLS, Johnny  d  752-1151-1152-1153-1414-
    1511
WELLS, Tudie  v  1671
WELSH, Fred  tb  279-518-539-656-791
WELSH, Nolan  v  1671
WELTON, Jim  cl-as-t  991-992-993-1066
WENDLING, Pete  p  1671
WENDT, George  t  78-563-564-1157-1407-
    1408
WERNER, Charles  t  1326-1327
WERNER, Harry  bj-g  274
WERNICKE, Helmuth  p  2
WEST, Alvy  cl-as-ts  1691
WEST, Benny  t  417
WEST, Cedric  g  1657
WEST, George  p  149
WEST, Hal  d  273-1038-1247
WEST, Luther  as  520
WEST, Mae  v  489-1671
WEST, Ralph  bj  402-403
WEST, Theador  cl  1671
WESTBROOK, John  stg  1327-1328
WESTERFIELD, Elbridge  ss-ts-bar  1559
WESTFULL, Bill  tb  1243
WESTLUND, Oscar  dir  1005
WESTLUND, Thore  as  589
WESTON, Cliff (r.n. Cliff Wetterau)  t-v
    239-249-250-437-699-700-701-702-968-
    1028-1393-1561-1581-1620
WESTON, Fritz  p  1485-1662
WESTON, Paul (r.n. Paul Wetstein)  bb-a
    344-363-437-441-444-447-632-887-888-889
    1256-1696-1697
WESTPHAL, Frank  p-ldr  1672-1673
WETHINGTON, Crawford  as  45-46-404-695-
    1071-1072-1073-1074

WETTLING, George  d  18-30-56-78-79-123-
    124-153-302-335-336-397-518-542-821-822
    959-1002-1005-1036-1037-1158-1159-1240-
    1366-1399-1404-1472-1594-1673-1690-1691
    1696-1697
WETZEL, Marvin  t  1550
WHALEN, Tom  d  133
WHARTON, Dick  g-v  124-125-126
WHEAT, Abraham  cl-as  1445
WHEATSTRAW, Peetie (r.n. William Bunch)
    p-g-v  847-1673-1674
WHEELER, Clarence  t  538-806-1 07
WHEELER, De Priest  tb  252-253-254-255-
    256-257-258-259-349-1084-1245
WHEELER, Doc  tb-v-dir  1674
WHEELER, Walter  ts  1170-1414
WHETSEL, Arthur  c-t  475-476-477-478-479
    480-481-482-483-484-485-486-487-488-489
    514-640-651-652-1010-1075-1083-1471-
    1640-1641-1653
WHETSTEIN, Roy  cl-as  1364-1365-1521
WHIDBY, Lulu  v  1674
WHIDDEN, Jay  vn-dir  1674-1675
WHIPPLE, Clark  p  868
WHISTLER, Al  sb  320-321
WHITBY, Frances  ts  1154
WHITE, ——  sb  1122-1123
WHITE, Addison  s  277
WHITE, Al  v  235
WHITE, Amos  t  1004
WHITE, Art  v  1005
WHITE, Baxter  g-u  1216
WHITE, Benjie  cl-as-dir  1130-1131
WHITE, Beverley  v  775
WHITE, Bill  as  284
WHITE, Bill  p  968-1621
WHITE, Bill  sb  807-808
WHITE, Billy - see FIELDS, ARTHUR
WHITE, Bob  tb  1361
WHITE, Bob  d  1000-1133-1156-1558-1690
WHITE, Carl  v  100
WHITE, Cecil  bj-g  1280-1281
WHITE, Cecil  bb  359
WHITE, Dick  tb  559
WHITE, Dillon  tenor voice  554-555
WHITE, Duncan  t  2
WHITE, Ed  t  863
WHITE, Eric  as  1089
WHITE, Ernie  ts  629
WHITE, Evelyn  v  342
WHITE, Florence  v  1676
WHITE, Freddy  bj-g  726-1362
WHITE, George  as  1662
WHITE, George  sb  1437
WHITE, George  d  1357-1358
WHITE, George  v  1187
WHITE, Georgia  p-v  1153-1676-1677-1678
    1679
WHITE, Gil  ts  1427
WHITE, Hal  vn-v  631-659-1580-1619
WHITE, Harold  ts  1047
WHITE, Harry  tb-a  52-53-252-253-254-
    255-256-257-285-476-1071-1072-1203
WHITE, Hy  g  163-364
WHITE, James  c  748
WHITE, James "Slap Rags"  Cm  1429-1430
WHITE, Jerry  v  139-240-1583-1589
WHITE, Joe  p  1602
WHITE, Joe  bb-sb  138-346-347-348
WHITE, John  as  913

1842

WHITE, Leo cl-as 97-98-321-322-323-326-701-702-1506
WHITE, Leon tb 218-410-1485
WHITE, Leroy t 761
WHITE, Lew cl 968-1621
WHITE, Maceo d-x 1518
WHITE, Morris bj 252-253-254-255-256-257-258-1084-
WHITE, Norman p 1340-1341-1342
WHITE, Silas bj 1267
WHITE, Sonny p 113-192-284-769-770-1053-1048-1507
WHITE, Ted v 545
WHITE, Tony d 972
WHITE, W. tb 133
WHITE, Willie p 668
WHITEHEAD, Jim v 853
WHITELAW, Donald d 346
WHITEMAN, Claude t 1537
WHITEMAN, Henry vn 177-503-871-922-1055-1141-1142
WHITEMAN, Paul vn-ldr 1680-1681-1682-1683-1684-1685-1686-1687-1688-1689-1690-1691
WHITESIDE, Fred sb 1124-1125
"WHITEY" d 1730
WHITING, Fred sb 62-1372-1373-1718
WHITING, Jack v 1692
WHITLOCK, Elmer t 51
WHITMAN, Essie v 1692
WHITMER, Ken d 870
WHITMIRE, Margaret v 1692
WHITMORE, Bill p 650
WHITNEY, James tb 58
WHITNEY, Leonard as-a 165-166-168-429
WHITNEY, June v 879
WHITSETT, Ray c 118
WHITTAKER, Hudson ("Tampa Red") k-g-v 393-753-754-823-842-846-1268-1269-1489-1495-1526-1527-1528-1572
WHITTET, Ben cl-as 142-178-179-411-731-806-833-1492-1524-1700-1701-1704
WHYTE, Bubber t 1693
WHYTE, Duncan t 281-1017-1584-1675-1693
WHYTE, Zach bj-v-ldr 1693
WICKHAM, Roscoe k 1544
WICKS, Barry d 554-1225-1508
WICKS, Israel v 155
WIEDMAN, Joe t 165-166
WIEDOEFT, Adolph d-x 1491-1694
WIEDOEFT, Guy bb 1491-1694
WIEDOEFT, Herb t-ldr 1694
WIEDOEFT, Rudy as-ldr 349-350-544-675-803-825-1204-1544-1748
WIEGAND, Max p 1561
WIGGINS, Gerry as 763
WIGGINS, James speech 555
WIGGINS, Joe as 1040
WILBORN, Dave bj-g-v 44-311-580-1033-1034-1035
WILBUR, Jay d 395-1298-1605
WILBUR, Joe bj-v 266-1117-1324-1362-1365-1366-1695
WILBUR, Slim tb 1148
WILCOX, Edwin p-cel-a 083-984-985-986-987-988-989-990-991
WILCOX, Jesse bb 1089
WILCOX, Spiegle (r.n. Newell W.) tb 232-576-577-578
WILDE, Ernie t 25

WILDE, Freddy vn 1327
WILDE TWINS, THE v 376
WILDER, Alec dir 80
WILDER, George tb 279
WILDER, Joe t 763
WILDER, Willie tb 943
WILDERSON, Keith t 552-553
WILER, Kirk p 646
WILEY, Arnold p 1695
WILEY, Earl d 812
WILEY, Lee v 291-638-1286-1695-1696-1697
WILFONG, Lonnie a 989
WILKE, Mel d 1021
WILKINS, Bruce ts 738-739
WILKINS, Dave t-v 272-518-822-841-1039-1509-1632
WILKINS, Ole as 111
WILKINSON, Max d 1507
WILLARD, Clarence t 163-360-738-739-74-741-858-859
WILLARD, Ralph d 391
WILLETT, Chappie a 55-259-906-907-989-1075
WILLIAMS, —— tb 1473-1474-1475
WILLIAMS, —— as 310
WILLIAMS, Alec d 1362-1365-1366
WILLIAMS, Alonzo as-ts 378-379-380-1230
WILLIAMS, Arthur t 214-346-347-656-855-1298-1739
WILLIAMS, Ben cl-as-ts-bar 886-887-888-889-1075-1203
WILLIAMS, Bill "Stu" cl-as 120-826
WILLIAMS, Bobby t 284-808-1637
WILLIAMS, Bud bb 467-1089
WILLIAMS, Burt as-bar 1285-1286
WILLIAMS, Buzzy p 1208
WILLIAMS, C. k-v 1647
WILLIAMS, Clarence p-or-k-jug-v 5-8-39-99-118-136-146-178-179-191-212-213-278-330-357-411-537-555-557-627-670-672-707-731-795-802-811-812-834-835-839-845-861-864-886-939-964-965-994-1009-1010-1011-1012-1013-1014-1021-1060-1061-1083-1092-1168-1217-1306-1323-1376-1395-1438-1439-1443-1445-1446-1452-1454-1457-1458-1463-1488-1531-1532-1533-1534-1535-1577-1617-1618-1652-1663-1698-1699-1700-1701-1702-1703-1704-1705-1706-1707-1708-1709-1710-1711
WILLIAMS, Claude g-vn 101-898-899+1718
WILLIAMS, Cliff d-v 274-1378
WILLIAMS, Cootie (r.n. Charles W.) t-v 27-134-478-479-480-481-482-483-484-485-486-487-488-489-490-491-492-493-494-495-496-497-607-616-617-618-619-620-622-631-651-652-660-661-765-766-838-1048-1075-1431-1653-1771-1712-1732
WILLIAMS, Cordy vn 360-564-1648
WILLIAMS, Corky p-v 854-1518
WILLIAMS, Courtney t 832-864-865-1109-1511
WILLIAMS, Davidc as-ts 841
WILLIAMS, Dorothy v 1232-1510-1718
WILLIAMS, Douglas cl 683-1713
WILLIAMS, Eddie cl-as-v 913-1075-1107-1108-1279-1657
WILLIAMS, Ellis h 1713

WILLIAMS, Elmer cl-ts 50-528-728-729-730-866-868-1654-1657-1658-1659
WILLIAMS, Ernie v 944
WILLIAMS, Fayette tb 338-1151-1152-1524
WILLIAMS, Fess cl-as-v-ldr 1247-1679-1714-1715-1716
WILLIAMS, Fred ts 284
WILLIAMS, Freddy cl-as 656-684
WILLIAMS, Fred d 843-847-848-849
WILLIAMS, George tb 665-666
WILLIAMS, George cl-as 576
WILLIAMS, George bj-g-v 891-1223-1267
WILLIAMS, George p-a 457
WILLIAMS, George v 1716-1717-1718
WILLIAMS, Guy v 1194
WILLIAMS, Hannah v 1232-1510-1718
WILLIAMS, Harry d 401-1388
WILLIAMS, Harry wb-v 1697
WILLIAMS, Henry v 65
WILLIAMS, Ike bb 1509
WILLIAMS, Irving p 707
WILLIAMS, Jimmy cl-ts 283-588-1092
WILLIAMS, Jimmy bb-sb 436
WILLIAMS, Joe tb 1445
WILLIAMS, Joe bj 820-1718
WILLIAMS, John t 277
WILLIAMS, John "Jazz" cl 564
WILLIAMS, John cl-as-bar-bsx 251-820-898-899-900-901-1370-1371-1712-1718
WILLIAMS, John sb 14-15-58-75-80-113-690-751-769-770-814-839-913-1075-1135-1240-1721-1736-1737
WILLIAMS, John (Jack) d 207-593-1032-1304-1371-1372-1373-1551-1571-1718-1720
WILLIAMS, Johnny v 211
WILLIAMS, Johnson d 738
WILLIAMS, Joseph t 277
WILLIAMS, Lawrence bb 1092
WILLIAMS, Leo tb 730
WILLIAMS, Leona v 1719
WILLIAMS, Leroy c-v 1124-1719-1744
WILLIAMS, Les ts 1008
WILLIAMS, Lew s 277
WILLIAMS, Margaret v 1720
WILLIAMS, Mary Lou (nee Mary Leo Burley) p-a 80-185-251-602-605-608-820-898-899-900-901-902-1069-1431-1718-1720
WILLIAMS, Max tb 1347
WILLIAMS, Midge v 40-545-1088-1720-1721-1732
WILLIAMS, Murray cl-as-ts 93-99-126-738-739-906-907-1147-1602
WILLIAMS, Nathaniel t 281-1632-1638-1713
WILLIAMS, Nolan d 1095
WILLIAMS, Nora v 1432-1721
WILLIAMS, Norwood g 359
WILLIAMS, Pearlis d 678-679-680
WILLIAMS, Ralph bj-ldr 1721-1722
WILLIAMS, Robert t 192-466-1279
WILLIAMS, Rudolph bj-g 18-1370
WILLIAMS, Rudy as 342-1046-1337
WILLIAMS, Sammy p-elo 1722
WILLIAMS, Sandy tb 114-115-284-526-527-528-631-691-726-1070-1654-1658-1659-1660-1661-1662-1712
WILLIAMS, Sherman cl-as 410
WILLIAMS, Sid vn 656-1215
WILLIAMS, Sidney p 1722
WILLIAMS, Skippy as-bsx-a 760-1116-1247
WILLIAMS, Spencer p-v 835-1212-1431

WILLIAMS, Prof. Stanley dir 1714
WILLIAMS, T. C. d 1541
WILLIAMS, Te Roy tb-ldr 1459-1559-1722
WILLIAMS, Vess as 141-1516-1518
WILLIAMS, Walter t 763
WILLIAMS, Walter g-v 1310-1311
WILLIAMS, Walter sb 1557
WILLIAMS, Wayne t-v 1572-1753
WILLIAMS, Willie wb 1467-1535-1708-1710
WILLIAMS, Winston sb 1044
WILLIAMSON, Charley c-ldr 1035-1091-1723
WILLIAMSON, Doug d-v 1213
WILLIAMSON, Ernest sb 115-169
WILLIFORD, Henry t-v 391-889
WILLIGAN, James d 391-457
WILLIS, Carroll cl-ts 356
WILLIS, Eddie vn 575
WILLIS, Jack p 1296
WILLIS, Ted tb 356
WILLOWS, Dick cl-as-vn 535-801
WILLRICH, Jack d 1723
WILLRICH, Virginia pac 1723
WILLSEY, Harry p-a 394
WILMOT, Gerry compere 316
WILMOT, Jack v 545
WILSON, ——— v 269
WILSON, Bill c 41
WILSON, Billy v 1115-1490-1723
WILSON, Dan p 458-1203-1589-1724-1725-1727
WILSON, Dick ts 899-900-901-902-1431-1720
WILSON, Dick vn-v 112-917-918
WILSON, Edith v 1061-1724-1725-1726
WILSON, Ernest p 85-86-1126
WILSON, Frank t 470-656-1213-1214-1235
WILSON, Frank v 579
WILSON, Garland p-cel-v 581-1215-1349-1350-1642-1726
WILSON, George tb 1637-1638
WILSON, George k-g 1727
WILSON, Gerald t-a 988-989-990
WILSON, Gus tb 1564
WILSON, Harry sb 581-936-937
WILSON, Jack t 1497
WILSON, Jimmy d 237
WILSON, Juice vn 1426
WILSON, Junior d 1550
WILSON, Lena v 1727-1728-1729
WILSON, Lucius ts 91-122
WILSON, Quinn bb-sb-a 752-758-759-760-862-1102-1116-1154-1169-1209
WILSON, Sam p 269-270
WILSON, Shadow d 663-1116
WILSON, Socks p 461-558
WILSON, Stan t 647-1116-1117
WILSON, Stanley bj 165-337-1615
WILSON, Teddy (r.n. Theodore W.) p-a 51-77-78-81-191-207-208-280-281-312-382-383-513-594-595-596-597-598-599-600-601-602-603-604-605-606-607-608-609-610-611-767-768-769-770-779-782-821-866-1000-1052-1156-1730-1731-1732-1733-1734-1735-1736-1737
WILSON, Tom d 841
WILSON, Toy p-v 1557
WILSON, Wesley p-v-speech 180-1729
WILTON, Bert t 1339-1340-1341-1342-1493
WILTSHIRE, Basil d 799-800-801
WIMBROW, Dale v 1181-1737
WIMBURN, Ernie ts-v 1497

1844

WINCHESTER, Daisy  v  864
WINDING, Kai  tb  457
WINEGAR, Frank  bj-ldr  1738
WINESTONE, Benny  cl-ts  279-310-311
WINFIELD, George  t  142
WINFIELD, Herb  tb  232-233-558-559-926-
927-928-967-1039-1267-1392-1672-1688
WING, Phil  cl-as  61-868-963-1056-1419
WINGFIELD, B. T.  c  389-1228-1268-1320-
1455-1729
WINGFIELD, George  t  1507
WINKLER, Otto  ah-th-bh  1256-1605
WINN, Anona  v  806-1738
WINNICK, Sid  t  1244
WINSHUP, Joe  ts  1379
WINSLOW, Johnny  p  1673
WINSTEIN, Dave  ts  153
WINSTON, Billy  d  91-92
WINSTON, Edna  v  1739
WINSTON, Hank (r.n. Henry W.)  p  61-963
WINTER, Marius B.  dir  1739
WINTERHALTER, Hugo  cl-as-v  110-207-322-
323-829-1373-1374
WINTERS, Art  ?  1694
WINTERS, Chick  dir  1739
WINTERS, Tiny  sb-v  24-25-279-310-311-
383-384-536-539-557-581-688-808-938-
1149-1507-1508-1739
WINTZ, Julie  bj-ldr  1739-1740
WIRGES, Bill  p-a  2-112-145-319-532-929-
1076-1098-1163-1288-1305-1323-1396-1431
1611-1740
WISE, Bob  cl-as-ts  525-1127-1149-1336
WISE, David  vn  801
WISEMAN, ——  g  842
WISHNUFF, Sam  d  925-926
WISWELL, Andy  tb  1663
WITHAM, Bert  p  1215
WITHERS, Frank  tb-bsx  1085-1086-1423-
1516
WITHERS, Hayes B.  v  1914
WITTENMEYER, Paul  bj  1347
WOHLEBEN, Theo  t  545-546
WOLF, Joe  p  1510
WOLF, Johnny  t  869
WOLF, Sandy  g  1124-1125
WOLFE, Billy  bb  886-887-1483
WOLFE, Eddie  vn  274
WOLFSCALE, Roy  t  856
WOLFSON, Hymie  cl-ts  5-671-852-932-933-
957-958-1064-1303-1381-1382-1383-1384-
1385-1386-1387-1388-1411-1437-1438-1515
1751
WOLKOWSKY, Andrew  bj-g  511
WOOD, J. Douglas  t  1147-1148
WOOD, Robert  - see KAUFMAN, IRVING
WOOD, Tom  as  1252
WOODE, Henri  a  107-597-759
WOODFORK, Eustern  bj  65-327-328-404
WOODING, Russell  dir  1654-1742
WOODING, Sam  p-ldr  458-705-1726-1742-
1743
WOODIP, Henry (probably the same as Henri
Woode?)  a  758-792
WOODLEN, George  t  283
WOODMAN, Britt  tb  763
WOODMAN, Ray  sb  1491
WOODMAN, William B.  tb  318-1485-1506
WOODRIDGE, Cliff  t  283
WOODRUFF, Amos  t  520
WOODS, Cora  v  155

WOOD(S), Gene  as  274-391-1378
WOODS, Hosea  bj-v  270-271
WOODS, Pete  d  941
WOODS, Ray  t  162-1236
WOODS, Sonny  - see MARVIN, FRANK
WOODSON, Greta  v  579-580
WOOLERY, Pete  v  1356
WOOLFORD, Hughie  p  1576
WOOLIN, Mal  bb  1162
WOOLLEY, Frank  ts-vn  394
WORDE, Phil  p  110-343-845-846-1013-1094
1097-1453-1460-1461
WORKMAN, Carl  tb  1664-1665
WORLEY, Mance  tb-sb  1501
WORNELL, Jimmy  t  1135-1362-1363-1472-
1493-1744
WORRELL, Frank  g  80-81-1538
WORTH, Stanley  cl-as  456-973
WORTHESON, John  p  943
WOSIKA, Frank  bb  1616
WRASKOFF, Raymond  p  307-333-1338
WRIGHT, Austin  v  1194
WRIGHT, Bill  ts  328
WRIGHT, Chubby  t-v  1036
WRIGHT, Daisy  v  942
WRIGHT, Donald  cl-as  1124
WRIGHT, Earl  bj-vn  579-580-1257
WRIGHT, Edythe  v  250-437-438-439-440-
441-442-443-444-445-446-447-448
WRIGHT, Elsie  - see GAYLOR, RUTH
WRIGHT, Emma  v  1744
WRIGHT, Frank  v  129
WRIGHT, Gene  p  1485
WRIGHT, Harvey  cl  544-762
WRIGHT, J.  as  1472
WRIGHT, Lammar  c-t  164-177-252-253-254-
255-256-257-258-259-260-261-262-1084-
1109-1110-1245
WRIGHT, Pearl  p  1650-1651-1652
WRIGHT, Steve  d  1423
WRIGHT, Wallace  bb  792
WRIGHT, Walter  bb-sb  165-328-404-1615
WRIGHTSMAN, Stanley  p  505-1004-1216-
1406
WUERL, Jack  vn  1348
WULLEN, Bill  cl-ss-as  194-1036
WYATT, Malvin  ts  179
WYCHE, Leroy  p  851
WYDER, William  bb  682
WYER, Edward  vn  665-666
WYER, Paul  vn  665-666
WYLIE, Allister  p-ldr  1744
WYLIE, Austin  p  1326-1327
WYLLIE, Dan  as  467
WYNCHAM, Joe  d  1215
WYNN, Albert  tb  359-729-863-1267-1268-
1742-1743-1744
WYNN, Nan  v  401-786-1374-1734
WYNNE, Billy  d-ldr  1745
WYNNE, H. L.  cl-ss-as-bsx  1663-1664
WYSOCHANSKI, Frank  t  545-1117

YANCEY, Aubrey  t-v  1195
YANCEY, Jimmy  p-v  1746
YANER, Milt  cl-as  360-429-430-431-432-
433-434-435-436-545-608-633-756-858-859
1027-1095-1150-1332
YANTIS, Bruce  vn  83-84-245-503-1113-
1197-1329
YARLETT, Norman (White)  p  1340
YATES, Alan  ts  87

YATES, Blind Richard k-v 1747
YATES, Dan vn 973-1067-1068
YATES, Hal v 1237-1611-1612
YATES, W. g 133
YEAGLEY, Ned ts 1228
YEARWOOD, Sam f 141
YEDLA, Otto bb 218
YERKES, Harry A. d-x-bells-dir 1747-1748 1749
YOCUM, Clark g 449-450-451-452-453-454-455-1697
YODER, Buck cl-as 1171
YODER, Walter sb 163-364-738-739-740-741-742-743-744-858-859
YOLONSKY, Harry cl-as 1147
YONTZ, Ducky (r.n. Charles Y.) t 133-884
YORKE, George sb 779-780-893-894-1031-1125-1205-1306-1307-1562
YORKE, Norman cl-ts 145-319-929-1076-1163-1164-1288-1396-1611-1740
YORKE, Peter p 800
YORKE, Vernell t-v 1422
YOUNG, Al d-v 1213-1614
YOUNG, Arthur p 30-393-404-537-554-797-798-799-800-812-1148-1306-1432-1601-1749-1750
YOUNG, Austin "Skin" vn-v 1680-1682-1683 1684-1685-1686
YOUNG, Bernie c 936-1099-1245-1421-1749
YOUNG, Billie v 1750
YOUNG, Charles vn 682
YOUNG, Dave cl-as-ts 466-730-824-1070-1247-1323
YOUNG, Dutch v 170
YOUNG, Graham t 910-911-912-1374
YOUNG, Granville t 1272
YOUNG, Harold bj 1369
YOUNG, Helen v 729
YOUNG, Joe bj-g 193-285-345-383-388-530-536-683-936-974-1137-1207-1310-1432-1433 1434-1584-1585-1692-1721
YOUNG, Joe d 458-705
YOUNG, Lee d-v 329-663-664-1631
YOUNG, Lester cl-ts 101-102-103-,04-105 106-107-273-607-608-676-768¾-769-770-821 873-905-1247-1709-1732-1733-1734-1735
YOUNG, Margaret v 1750
YOUNG, Marvin - see KAUFMAN, IRVING
YOUNG, Merle p 263
YOUNG, Oscar p 558-559
YOUNG, Ralph v 186
YOUNG, Robert cl-as 665-666
YOUNG, Russell p 1750
YOUNG, Snooky (r.n. Eugene Y.) t 988-989-990
YOUNG, Sterling vn 59
YOUNG, Trummy (r.n. James Y.) tb-v 758-759-987-988-989-990-991-1116-1735
YOUNG, Victor vn-a-dir 84-365-580-822-858-1046-1231-1232-1329-1348-1538-1671-1696-1751
YSAGUIRRE, Bob bb-sb 12-136-360-806-935 1229-1230-1276-1277-1278-1279-1722
YUDER, George as 207
YUKL, Joe tb 53-162-163-362-421-425-426 427-428-687-699-700-1033-1236-1237-1329
YUMANSEN, Eddie t 321-322

ZACK, George p 1481
ZAD, J. as-ts as-ts 1575
ZAFER, Maurice cl 146

ZAHM, George cl-as-dir 89
ZAKIM, Sam t 8
ZANONI, Gene as 398-1242-1243-1244
ZARCHY, Zeke (r.n. Rubin Z.) t 78-79-162-204-363-366-367-369-370-371-372-448-449-555-599-600-701-702-1158-1399-1415
ZARDIS, Chester d 778
ZAYDE, Yascha vn 17-63-64-509-756-1417
ZAZMAR, Art d 1274
ZAZMAR, Mack tb 417-545-1753
ZBANEK, George cl-ts-v 418
ZEEMAN, Barney dir 1752
ZELBA, Billy as-ts-vn-pac 885
ZELLER, J. B. "Jelly" d 1009
ZENO, ——— d 1516-1518
ZENTNER, Si(mon) tb 185-186
ZEPPILLI, Pierre p 1642
ZIEGLER, Joe v 840
ZIEHRER, Fred vn 571
ZIMBLER, Adolf vn 1149
ZIMMER, Bill cl-as-v 1739-1740
ZIMMER, George d 1739-1740
ZIMMER, Harry p 660
ZIMMERMAN, Bill c 1051-1052
ZIMMERMAN, Charles t 98-99-703-829-1561
ZIMMERMAN, Leo tb 332-1250-1251-1252-1586-1587
ZIMMERMAN, Roy p 687
ZIMMERS, Tony cl-as-ts 29-40-320-321-322 323-449-756-1001-1095-1315-1316-1398-1415-1506
ZIR, Irving vn 756
ZITO, Jimmy t 454-455
ZOEHLER, Jerry cl-ts 324
ZOFF, B. ts 1550
ZORN, Leo vn 817-818-819-820
ZUDECOFF, Barney t 78-79-1147-1158-1159
ZUDECOFF, Moe (now known as BUDDY MORROW, q.v.) tb 153-215-456-633-1271-1691
ZULLO, Frank t 56-293-294-295-296-871
ZUMWALT, Fred tb 1184
ZURAWSKI, Walter t 120-121
ZURKE, Bob p-ldr 16-162-363-366-367-368 369-370-555-1123-1229-1546-1752-1753

compiled by BRIAN AND VICTOR RUST, PAULINE AND JOHN WADLEY.

        This index shows all the titles of songs and tunes listed in the Disco-
graphy, in close alphabetical order.  That is to say, each title is treated as if it
were one long word, disregarding apostrophes, exclamation marks, commas and inverted
commas; thus, for example, INDIANA will be found amid titles such as IN DAT MORNING
and I NEVER KNEW.  Sometimes the compositors of the original labels differed in the
manner of presenting a title; THERE WILL NEVER BE ANOTHER MARY is sometimes shown as
THERE'LL NEVER BE ANOTHER MARY, and similarly, NOBODY'S SWEETHEART occasionally gets
labelled as NOBODY'S SWEETHEART NOW.  Extra words found on some issues like this are
shown in this index in parentheses - NOBODY'S SWEETHEART (NOW), and I'M GOING AWAY
(JUST) TO WEAR YOU OFF MY MIND.

        Where there are two or more songs with the same title, these are listed
separately where possible (it has not always been possible to check exactly which
version is performed by any one artist), with the original date of publication given
in each case.  (It is quite surprising how often a title is duplicated; while a tune
can be copyright, a title cannot, and thus there are three kinds of SUGAR, two DID
YOU MEAN IT ?, and several whose titles begin with the words I NEVER KNEW, this
being the phrase by which all of them are commonly known).

        Sometimes there are variations in the spellings of otherwise identical
titles, and we find CLAP HANDS ! HERE COMES CHARLEY appearing with the last word
spelt CHARLIE (this occurs in most instances where "Charlie" or "Charley" is the
subject of a song), and Clutsam's MA CURLY HEADED BABBY is often labelled with the
"dialect" words spelt correctly.  In the case of many blues numbers, attempts were
frequently made to spell the assumed title more or less phonetically, omitting such
words as it was thought were unimportant or omitted by the artist - while other
labelling of the same number might spell it in impeccable dictionary-English. The
examples of this run into dozens : I AM GOING to do something or other can be shown
as I'M GONNA DO whatever it was, GONNA DO the same thing, or even GWINE DO so-and-so
(and the same occurs with I HAVE GOT TO do something, which of course becomes GOTTA
DO whatever it was, I GOTTA or quite often GOTTA - and the latter also serves for
I HAVE GOT A something or other).  We fully agree that dialect spelling lends color
to the scene, but standardizing the spelling would make indexing that much easier !

        Titles beginning with definite or indefinite articles, in English or any
other language, are always indexed under the next word; thus : MAN FROM THE SOUTH,
THE; LITTLE BIT INDEPENDENT, A; PALOMA, LA; SEUL COUVERT PLEASE JAMES, UN.  There
are many instances of the first word of a title being dropped from some issues while
being included on others, such as IT'S A PRECIOUS LITTLE THING CALLED LOVE appearing
as A PRECIOUS LITTLE THING CALLED LOVE.  These we have cross-referenced; and we have
applied the same procedure to such obvious variants as HOLD THAT TIGER for TIGER RAG
(although this and some other numbers appearing under totally different names, such
as WEARY WEASEL, are shown under those names, but the "up-dated" arrangements of
certain standard numbers described as THE NEW TIGER RAG, THE NEW VINE STREET BLUES
and so on are indexed under NEW as indeed they were in the contemporary literature
issued by the various companies).

                                        B. R.
                                        V. J. R.
                                        P. F. W.
December, 1977.                         J. H. J. W.

Abba Dabba (One Of The Arabian Nights) 320
Abbey Road Hop  387
Abdullah  1635
Abercrombie Had A Zombie  326-1636
About A Quarter To Nine  202-1000
About Face  1555
About My Time To Check  848
About Rip Van Winkle  1279
Absence Makes The Heart Grow Fonder  1621
Absent Minded Blues  845
Absent-Minded Moon  168-435-1409
Absinthe House Stomp  866
Absolutely  1456
Accent On Swing  281-639
Accent On Youth  490
Accidentally On Purpose  1540
Accordion Joe  481-1438
AC-DC Current  614-704
Ace In The Hole  139-204-546-640-992-1557 1579
Ace Of Rhythm  1455
Ace Of Spades  1643
Aching-Hearted Blues  303-825-1010-1468- 1544-1698-1719
Acrobat, The  805
Across The Track Blues  497
Ada Jane's Blues  1466
Adam And Eve  212
Adam And Eve Got The Blues  1549
Adams Apple (sic)  150
Add A Little Wiggle  17-571-922
Ad-De-Dey  259
Address Unknown  184-1147
Adeline  346-785
Adios, Americano  373
Adios, Mariquita Linda  1406
Adios, Muchachos  9-969
Admiration  480-481-489-647
Adorable  234
Adorable Dora  931-1563
Adoration  576
Adoree  239
Advice Blues  1618
Aekai Rag  872
Aeroplane Blues  137
Affectionate Dan  508
Afghanistan  464-972
A flat Dream  839
Afraid Of Love  259
Afraid To Dream  162-205-602-1249-1400- 1401
Afraid To Say "Hello"  98-911
Africa  1190
African Beauty, An  1473
African Echoes  1208
African 400, The (An Educated Rag)  1255
African Hunch  862
African Jive  551
African Jungle  868
African Lullaby  1073
African Ripples  1625-1626
After A Little While  134
After All  448-498-499-908-975-1359
After All I've Been To You  81-760
After All I've Done For You  1210
After All These Years  792-1245-1651
After All, You're All I'm After  1035
After Awhile  351-543-592-1274
After Dinner Speech  78-1158

Afterglow  584-1002-1027
After Hour Blues  1135
After Hours  693
After I Say I'm Sorry  39-75-166-233-449- 527-576-647-745-829-882-927-961-1039
After I've Called You Sweetheart  28
After Last Night With You  15
After Looking At You  94-322-906
After Me The Sun Goes Down  1311
After My Laughter Came Tears  469-574- 971-1584-1610
Afternoon Blues  731-946-1728
Afternoon In Africa  75-1484
Afternoon Of A Faun  1361
After School Swing Session  864
After Sundown  1278
After That  547
After The Storm  16-72-714
After The Sun Goes Down  533
After The Sun Kissed The World Goodbye 470
Afterthoughts  904
After Tonight  288-839-981-1708
After Tonight We Say Goodbye  147
After Twelve O'Clock   275
After You  429-442
After Your Kiss  1294
After You've Gone  2-46-64-146-237-304- 330-341-348-384-414-427-439-466-563-585 596-622-635-652-661-689-724-736-797-894 911-961-974-1022-1079-1080-1088-1106- 1142-1152-1237-1268-1365-1432-1444-1464 1529-1530-1551-1564-1574-1596-1600-1603 1624-1634-1687-1691-1740
After You've Gone Away  1453
Again  468-1290-1426
Aggravatin' Papa (Don't You Try To Two- Time Me)  136-559-686-706-793-856-915- 972-1059-1186-1437-1439-15231607-1608- 1617
Ah ! Ah ! Archie  32
Ah ! Ah ! Aw ! Aw ! Papa Mustn't Do That
Ah ! But Is It Love ?  1330
Ah ! But I've Learned  876
Ah-Ha !  230-658-1592
Ah ! Le Beguine  1173
Ah Now  551
Ah ! Sweet Mystery Of Life  162
Ah ! The Moon Is Here  1269
Ah-Woo ! Ah-Woo ! To You  428
Ainsi soit-il  313
Ain'tcha ?  1381
Ain'tcha Comin' Home ?  662
Ain'tcha Comin' Out ?  589-1316
Ain'tcha Glad ?  200-593-730
Ain'tcha Got Music ?  12
Ain't Givin' Nothin' Away  705
Ain't Goin' Marry (Ain't Goin' Settle Down) (sic)  1649
Ain't Goin' Nowhere (Ec-Stacy)  372-375- 1116-1490-1491
Ain't Gonna Do That  214
Ain't Gonna Pay No Toll - see TOLL
Ain't Got A Dime Blues  853
Ain't Got Nobody  1321
Ain't Got Nobody To Grind My Coffee  833- 1451-1492
Ain't Got No Gal In This Town  254
Ain't Got Nothin' Blues  1510-1525
Ain't I Good To You ? - see GEE, AIN'T I GOOD TO YOU ?

Ain't I Got Rosie ? 319
Ain't It A Cryin' Shame ? 328
Ain't It A Shame About Mame ? 1004
Ain't I The Lucky One ? 1277
Ain't It Just Too Bad ? 292
Ain't It Nice ? 752
Ain't It The Truth ? 110
Ain't Love Grand ? 802
Ain't Misbehavin' 2-31-45-56-114-155-245
305-348-385-487-503-516-538-584-647-730
774-797-836-974-1080-1106-1116-1152-
1155-1273-1381-1571-1623-1626-1632-1634
1636-1657-1689-1712-1715-1733-1750
Ain't Much Good In The Best Of Men Now
Days (sic) 179
Ain't My Baby Grand ? 228-1591
Ain't Nobody Home But Me 1619
Ain't Nobody Truck Like You 1505
Ain't No More To Be Said 834
Ain't Nothin' Cookin' What You're Smellin'
1450
Ain't Nothing To It 1637
Ain't No Use Tryin' To High-Tone Me 1213
Ain't He/She Sweet ? 126-171-236-314-467
471-668-721-937-938-942-974-988-1173-
1222-1286-1416-1593-1619-1722
Ain't That A Grand And Glorious Feeling ?
61-172-524-625-669-1015-1580
Ain't That A Shame ? 844
Ain't That Good News ? 80
Ain't That Hateful ? 1122
Ain't That So ? 1678
Ain't That The Way It Goes ? 1214
Ain't That Too Bad ? 657-1098-1365
Ain't The Gravy Good ? 1712
Ain't We Got Fun ? 1085-1352-1397
Ain't You Ashamed ? 32-560-886-1317
Ain't You, Baby ? 341-1069
Ain't You Comin' Back, Mary Ann, To Mary-
land ? 1280
Air in D flat 792
Air Mail Special 616-618-619
Air Mail Stomp 371
Alabama Barbecue 893
Alabama Blues 1462-1558
Alabama Bound Blues 1305
Alabama Home 1693
Alabama Mama 810-1202
Alabama Mistreater 279-389-1455 (as
ALABAMY MISTREATED on 1455)
Alabama Shuffle 1091
Alabama Stomp 28-383-464-720-799-872-1138
1237-1275-1285
Alabama Strut 389
Alabamy Bound 73-385-545-624-635-707-717-
797-1013-1161-1433-1742
Alabamy (Here I Come) 872
Alabamy Home 492-631
Alabamy Snow 1017
Alabamy Stay-At-Home 1130
Alabi Blues 914
A la Bridges 944
Alberta, Alberta 628
Album Of My Memories 248
Alcoholic Blues 388-975-1522
Alcoholic Ward Blues 194
Alegre Primavera 797
Alexander's Back In Town 1377
Alexander's Ragtime Band 17-54-86-159-286
287-333-347-384-563-599-601-874-938-956-
965-993-1086-1150-1409-1444-1557-1750

Alexander's Swinging 8-416
Alexander The Swoose (Half Swan, Half
Goose) 185
Alexander, Where's That Band ? 1228
Algiers Stomp 14-1074
Alias Charlie Jones Blues 737
Alibi Baby 441-522-657-1400
Alibi-ing Papa 1577
Alice 1504
Alice Blue Gown 586-789-816-1140-1177-
1236-1249-1299-1735
Alice In Wonderland 1601
All Aboard 1116
All Aboard For Dixieland 1179
All Aboard For Heaven 76
Alla en el Rancho Grande (My Ranch) 207-
448-1315-1359-1406
Allahabad (Pearl Of The East) 171-1286
Allah's Holiday 471-1140-1148-1434
All Alone 248-1094-1316-1400-1722
All Alone And Blue 569
All Alone And Lonely 434
All Alone Blues 627
All Alone Monday 235-268
All Alone On My Own 248
All-American Girl 876-1315
All Around Mama 412
All Around The Christmas Tree 1374
All At Once 1400
All By Myself 177-372-413-748
All By Yourself In The Moonlight 525-
1291-1426-1675
All Change For Happiness 1296
All Coons Look Alike To Me 1197
All Dark People Are Light On Their Feet
123
All Day Long 63
All Dressed Up And No Place To Go 1399
All Dressed Up Spic And Spanish 908
Allegheny Al 441
Allegro Blues 694
Alley Boogie 1678
Alley Man (Haul My Ashes) 639
Alley Rat 151
Alley Rat Blues 1450
All For Grits And Gravy 1716
All For Love 819
All For The Sake Of Love 140
All God's Chillun Got Rhythm 27-123-429-
492-586-729-1027-1121-1530
All God's Chillun Got Wings (Heaven,
Heaven) 854-1400-1430-1633-1711
All I Care About Is You 395
All I Do Is Dream Of You 64-201-878-1149
Alligator Blues 802
Alligator Crawl 41-183-338-517-548-894-
1392-1625-1626-1715
Alligator Hop 1166
Alligator Pond Went Dry, The 1487
All I Need 1243
All I Need Is Just A Girl Like You 544
All I Need Is You 529-622-1552
All In Favor Of Swing Say "Aye" 448-590
All In Fun 448-1406
All I Remember Is You 431-447-1405
All I Want In This World Is You 1036
All Men Blues 1009
All Muddled Up 1162-1614
All Muggled Up 1497
All My Life 182-191-217-247-382-597-1628
1731

All Night Blues 1447-1595-1678
All Night Long 1242-1527
All-Night Record Man, The 95
All Night Shags 308
All Of A Sudden 288-464
All Of Me 50-109-184-284-431-770-778-959-1262-1343
All Of No-Man's-Land Is Ours 513
All Of The Time 240-241-507-626
All On Account Of You 783
All On Account Of Your Kisses (I'm No Account Any More) 142-388
All Or Nothing At All 107-431
All Over Italy 148
All Over Nothing At All 526-894
All Right, All Right, All Right 702
All-Star Strut 1048
All That I Had Is Gone 838-1184-1615
All That I'm Asking Is Sympathy 1666-1667
All That I Need Is You 1085
All That Meat And No Potatoes 153-168-186-1637
All The Jive Is Gone 899
All The Nice Girls Love A Sailor 385
All The Things You Are 81-448-1406
All The Time 215-810-1649
All The Week Blues 570
All The World Is Lonely (For A Little Blackbird) 1273
All This And Heaven Too 96-433-450-909
All This World Is Made Of Glass 6-1645
All Those Wonderful Years 912-1244
All Through The Night (Welsh folk song) 444
All Through The Night (1934) 425-1337
All Through The Night (1941) 912-1244
All Too Soon 81-496
All Too Well 936
Alluring Lady 991
All Wrong 916-1673
All You Want To Do Is Dance 59-429-442-880-913-1400
Alma Mammy 245
Alma Mater Georgia Tech. 627
Almond Eyes 914
Almost Afraid To Love 1678
Alone 437-701-960-1312
Alone At A Table For Two 1621
Alone At Last 231-339-718
Alone In A Corner 981
Alone In The Rain 341-952-1294
Alone On The Range 1235
Alone Together 1404-1408
Alone With My Dreams 192-273
Alone With You 1734
Along Came Love 1215
Along Came Sweetness 242
Along The Lane In Spain 1504
Alphonsia Blues 354
Alreet 910
Al's Idea 333
Also Ran Blues, The 280
Altitude 663
Alt Wien (Old Vienna) 1552
Always 93-294-589-595-602-1239
Always And Always 321-367-608-1158
Always Be Careful Mama 707
Always Charming 1613
Always Got The Blues 1128
Always In My Heart 435-1361

Always Mine 917
Always The Same Sweet Pal 1291
Amapa 512
Amapola 185-208-434-618-1343
Amazon Goes A-Wooing, An 684-1224
Amen 744
Amen Corner 1601
America, I Love You 1553
A.M.E.R.I.C.A. I Love You, My Yankee Land 1375
American Jubilee 141
American Patrol 1482
American Tour 85
Am I A Passing Fancy ? 244-1666
Am I Asking Too Much ? 14
Am I Blue ? 75-149-244-272-420-505-507-564-671-1080-1091-1118-1152-1242-1381-1434-1491-1652-1738
Am I Dreaming ? 441-894
Am I Gonna Have Trouble With You ? 702
Am I In Another World ? 1357-1631
Am I In Love ? 162-1401
Am I Intruding ? 786
Am I Proud ? 448
Am I To Blame ? 222-1353
Am I Wasting My Time ? 697
Am I Wasting My Time On You ? 233-1742
Ammoniated Tincture Of Quinine 1116
Among My Souvenirs 58-171-238-283-468-501-1722
Amoresque 684-1224-1225
Amos 'n' Andy 152
Amour 911-1243
Amour comme le notre, Un 1349
Amour en fleurs, L' 1421
Amour, toujours l'amour, L' 1147-1512
Am Sonntag will mein Susser mit mir segeln geh'n 809
Anchors Aweigh 376
And Especially You ! 341
An' Furthermore 533
And He'd Say "Oo-La-La ! Wee-Wee" 1362-1603
And I Don't Mean If 734
Andiology 896
And So Do I 97-433-450-9o9-1374-1540
And So Forth 125-1203
And So, Goodbye 290-1331
And Still No Luck With You 204
And The Angels Sing 80-105-451-505-611-814-1358
And The Big Bad Wolf Was Dead 699
And Then 654
And Then I Forget 967-982
And Then Some 365
And Then They Called It Love 1028
And Then Your Lips Met Mine 592-980-1745
And They Said It Wouldn't Last 1002
Andy's Blues 1511
Anesthetic For Lovers 329
Angel (1928) 1015
Angel (1939-1940) 63-207-372-448
Angel Child 1086
Angel Eyes 928
Angel In Disguise, An 373
Angeline 254-392-1646-1670
Angels Came Thru', The 374
Angels Of Mercy 299
Angels With Dirty Faces 259-445
Angry 9-32-189-372-759-808-955-1068-1069-1132-1271-1395-1548

1850

Animal Crackers - see I'M JUST WILD ABOUT ANIMAL CRACKERS
Animule Ball, The  1105-1107
Anita  1634
Ann  760
Annabella  746
Anna In Indiana  177
Anna Mina Forty And St. Louis Shorty  100
Annie Doesn't Live Here Any More  200-455
Annie Laurie  443-987-990-1003-1224-1512-1635
Annie's Cousin Fanny  423-424
Anniversary Waltz, The  911
Announcer's Blues  1571-1690
Another Night Alone  9
Another One Of Them Things  450
Another Perfect Night Is Ending  439-1416
Another Rag (A Raggy Rag)  1251
Another Sweet Daddy  392
Answer Is Love, The  371
Answer Man  817
Answer To You Are My Sunshine  1318
Antigua  385
Anvil Chorus - see TRAVIATA, LA
Any Blues  1502
Anybody Want To Buy My Cabbage ?  842
Anybody Here Want To Try My Cabbage ?  65-860-1021 (same as foregoing ?)
Any Bonds Today ?  435
Any Corner Is A Cosy Corner  1668
Any Day The Sun Don't Shine  965
Any Ice Today, Lady ?  928
Any-Kind-A-Man  1489
Any Kind Of A Man Would Be Better Than You  1026
Any Old Time  1328-1402-1403-1404
Any Rags  781-1200
Anything  273-451-619-1121-1193
Anything Goes  425-595-1211-1224
Anything That Happens Just Pleases Me - see EVERYTHING THAT HAPPENS JUST PLEASES ME
Anything To Hold You Baby  1108
Anything To Make You Happy  239
Anything Your Heart Desires  1666
Anything You Say  871-1068
Anything You Want  1152
Anytime  154-1062-1063
Anytime, Anyday, Anywhere  199-486-703-1063-1720
Any Time At All  661-906
Any Time's The Time To Fall In Love  286-1329
Any Way The Wind Blows (My Sweetie Goes)  37-90-916-926
Anywhere Sweetie Goes (I'll Be There)  411
Any Woman's Blues  352-1440
Apache  425
Apache Love  1352
Apaloosa Blues  942
Apart From You  806
Ape Man  150
Apex Blues  1151-1152-1154
Apologies  1052
Apollo Jump  1070
Appel Indirect (also as APPEL DIRECT)  1261
Apple A Day, An  893
Apple Blossoms  1598
Apple For The Teacher, An  95-324-1435
Apple Jump, The  106
Apple Sauce  70-112-535-1175-1353-1549-1608

April In My Heart  259-1735
April In Paris  75-168-1406
April Kisses  921
April Morning  87
April Played The Fiddle  449
April Showers  218-297-1086-1360
Apurksody  907
Arab Dance - see NUTCRACKER SUITE
Arabella's Wedding Day  1230
Arabesque  792-818
Arabian Lover  479
Arabian Nightmare  629-897
Arabian Nights  512
Araby (1916)  1603
Araby (1924)  716
Arcadia Shuffle  188
Arcady  71-224
Archer Street Drag  310
Are All My Favorite Bands Playing Or Am I Dreaming ?  441
Are They Pickin' On Your Baby ? - see PICKIN' ON YOUR BABY
Are You All Reet ?  261
Are You Fer It ?  329
Are You Happy ?  172-237-669-1289-1425
Are You Havin' Any Fun ?  190-207-432-447-1316
Are You Hep To The Jive ?  260
Are You Here To Stay ?  1658
Are You In Love With Me Again ?  257
Are You In The Mood ?  1259
Are You In The Mood For Mischief ?  323
Are You Lonely ?  71
Are We Burnt Up ?  95
Are You Makin' A Fool Of Me ?  1670
Are You Makin' Any Money ?  200-1688
Are You Ready ?  1070
Are You Sorry ?  133-624
Are You Sticking ?  498
Arima Tonight - Sangre Grande Tomorrow Night  778
Aristocratic Stomp  1563
Aristocrat Of Harlem  1047
Arizona Blues  1212
Arkansas Blues (Arkansas)  80-179-192-385-468-529-625-633-704-935-940-966-1008-1030-1112-1119-1423-1461-1492-1508-1533-1593-1749
Arkansas Mill Blues  1321
Arkansas Mule, The  1115
Arkansas Road Blues  1487
Arkansas Shout  954
Arkansaw Traveler  430
Arlena  1647
Arm Breaker, The  856
Armful O' Sweetness  1624
Armour Ave. Struggle (sic)  149
Arms Of Love  1291
Army Air Corps  376
Army Camp Blues  1414
Army Camp Harmony Blues  1266
Arnold Wiley Rag  1695
Artful Artie  1255
Arthur Murray Taught Me Dancing In A Hurry  435-1160
Art's Boogie  765
As Far As I'm Concerned  530
Ash Can Blues  501
Ash Can Stomp  837
Ashes In The Tray  693
Ash Haulin' Blues  1020

Ash Man Crawl 1645
As If You Didn't Know 186-298
As I Like It 1109
Ask My Sister, Please Don't Be Like Me 1105
Asleep In My Heart 952
Asleep Or Awake 95-446
As Long As I Have You 265-1421
As Long As I Live 165-542-594-616-703-1031-1237-1508-1709
As Long As I Love You 1112
As Long As You Believe In Me 502
As Long As You Live You'll Be Dead If You Die 55-79-444-445
As Long As You Love Me 469
As Long As You're Mine 637
As Long As You're There 505
Asphalt Walk 1586
As 'Round And 'Round We Go 1316
As Though You Were There 1696
Astoria Strut 863
As We Walk Into The Sunset 186-1361
As You Desire Me 895
As You Like It 302
At A Cuban Cabaret 1082
At A Dixie Roadside Diner 97-496
At A Georgia Camp Meeting 277-332-747-765-940-971-1049-1473-1474-1475-1656
At A Little Chyrch Affair 437
At An Arabian House Party 1373-1374
At A/The Perfume Counter (On The Rue de la Paix) 321-429-881
At A Little Hot Dog Stand 370
At Dawning - see DAWNING
A-Tisket, A-Tasket 214-444-528-588-759-1632-1660-1734
Atlanta Black Bottom 1714
Atlanta Blues 570-1011
Atlanta Gal 547
Atlanta Low Down 1089
Atlanta Rag 390
At Last I'm Happy 556-957-1144
At Least You Could Say Hello 207-324-1539
At Long Last Love 296-322
A To Z Blues 212-1058
At Parson Jenkins' Ball 913
'At's In There 342
At Sundown 272-542-1056-1089-1399-1406-1481-1640
Atta Baby 1525
Atta Boy 564
At The Baby Parade 1668
At The Balalaika 704
At The Ball 1476
At The Bottom 1371
At The Cake Walk Steppers' Ball 1058
At The Christmas Ball 1443
At The Clambake Carnival 258
At The Codfish Ball 182-439
At The Cross Roads 436
At The End Of The Lonesome Trail 31-177
At The Funny Page Ball 1517
At The High Brown Babies' Ball 976-1748
At The Jazz Band Ball 116-368-543-646-764-1176-1481-1509-1522
At The Jimmy's Bar 1284
At The New Jump Steady Ball 1648-1649
At The Woodchopper's Ball 387-590-740
At The Prom. 1079
At The Rug Cutters' Ball 755

At The Swing Cats' Ball 864
At The Weeping Widow's Ball 1525
At Twilight 2-1635
At Your Beck And Call 78-430-787-1203
At Your Mercy 1413
At Your Service, Madame 365-1307
Auburn Avenue Stomp 1089
Audition Blues 521
Auld Lang Syne 1279
Aunt Caroline Dyer Blues 1043
Aunt Hagar's (Children) Blues 177-280-306-535-666-856-914-934-945-954-957-1168-1169-1186-1434-1437-1509-1538-1608-1672-1690
Auntie Skinner's Chicken Dinner 1656
Aunt Jemima (Stomp) 873-1168
Au Reet (Au Rote, Au Root) 417-434
Au revoir l'amour 425
Au revoir, pays de mes amours 827
Au Rhythme du Jazz 960
Aurora 434-590-818
Australian Stomp 318
Automobile Blues 694
Autopsy On Schubert 1615
Autumn 87
Autumn Harvest 683
Autumn Nocturne 299-1553
Avalon 85-257-291-333-347-385-601-602-607-689-789-815-913-961-1089-1139-1259-1337-1340-1410-1432-1433-1602
Avalon Town 243-1292
Avenue C Blues 390
Avenue Strut 456
A vous tout devey, a vous ? 372
Away All The Time 1678
Away Down East In Maine 1607
Away Down In The Alley Blues 844
Away Down South 1519
Away Down South In Heaven 533-1610
Away From You 1511
A-Wearin' Away The Blues 1461-1476
A-Well-A-Take-Um-A-Joe 549
Awful Lawdy Lawdy Blues 164
Awful Moanin' Blues,(An) 623-732-763-1050-1057-1447
Awful Sad 476-488
Aw, You Dawg ! (You Dog) 34-254
Ay-Ay-Ay 9-126-296-590
'Ay Now 109
Azure 124-258-492-493-1253-1402-1509-1660

Baba 650
Babalu 284
Babes In The Wood 315
Babe Takes A Bow, The 909
Babs 329-985
Babushka Hop 805
Baby 314-487-635-651-652-876-1029-1076-1132-1151-1196-1222-1437
Baby, Ain't You Satisfied ? 534-960-1500
Baby, Are You Satisfied ? 1670
Baby Be Mine 551
Baby Blue Eyes 70
Baby Blues 133
Baby Brown 1133-1392-1625-1626
Baby Dear 1109-1110-1720
Baby Dear, I Don't Want No-One But You 1676
Baby Doll 1443

1852

Baby, Don't You Cry  832
Baby, Don't You Love Me No More ?  1542
Baby, Don't You Tear My Clothes  679
Baby, Don't You Tell On Me  105-107
Baby Face  194-266-532
Baby Girl  388-389
Baby, Have Pity On Me  1446
Baby Heart Blues  1038
Baby, I Can't Use You No More  1617
Baby, If You Can't Do Better  1044
Baby, It Must Be Love  781
Baby, It's My Time Now  1414
Baby, It Upsets Me So  1728
Baby Jane  1713
Baby Knows How  1091
Baby, Look At You  850
Baby Looks Like Me, The  73
Baby Me  1316
Baby Mine ("Dumbo")  186-1553
Baby Mine  461-651
Baby O' Mine (sometimes as BABY MINE)  313-862-863-1108
Baby, Oh ! Where Can You Be ?  420-951-1623
Baby's Awake Now  1696
Baby's Back Today  112
Baby's Blue  1417-1613
Baby's Coming Back  1046
Baby's Got The Blues  864-1057-1671
Baby Stop Teasin' Me  1338
Baby, Take A Bow  92
Baby, What Else Can I Do ?  448-527-708-1655
Baby, When You Ain't There  485
Baby, Won't You Please Come Home ?  57-114-257-273-330-527-554-661-685-720-757-959-977-987-1034-1279-1329-1346-1439-1484-1491-1532-1568-1702-1705-1707
Baby, You Made Me Fall For You  1460
Baby Your Mother (Like She Babied You)  133-172
Baby, You've Got The Right Idea  1127
Bacchanal Rag, The  1217
Bachelor Blues  208
Bach Goes To Town  610-611
Bach To Boogie  326
Bach Up To Me  1629
Bacio, Il  740
Back Alley Rub  1161
Back Bay Boogie  284
Back Bay Shuffle  1403
Back Beat Boogie  815
Back Beats  143-1074-1138-1226-1287-1290-1356-1365
Back-Biters Blues  1671
Back Bitin' Mamma  1650
Backbiting Moan  66
Back Door  1206
Back Door Blues  1320
Back Door Daddy  8
Back Home  1397
Back Home Again In Indiana - see INDIANA
Back Home In Illinois  32-1545
Back Home In Tennessee  508
Back In The Alley  390
Back In The Country (Where They Ask For You)  675
Back In The Old Sunday School  1227
Back In Your Arms  786
Back In Your Own Backyard  552-728-768-930-1273-1535-1683

Back O' Town Blues  140-350-1180-1188
Back Room Romp  1500
Back Stage At The Ballet  452
Back To Back  432-447
Back To That Dear Old Farm  216
Back To The Jungle  1210
Back Water Blues  839-1024-1444-1655
Back Where The Daffodils Groww  228-1582
Back Woods Blues  733-1448
Backyard Blues  1723
Bacon's Blues  961
Bad Bad Mama  811
Bad Habits  1390
Bad Humor Man, The  433-590-1552
Bad Land Blues  187-1525
Bad Luck Blues  841-1265
Bad Luck Man  679
Bad Luck's My Buddy  948
Bad News Blues  916
Bagatelle  190
Bagdad  796
Bag O' Blues, A  1078-1222-1223
Bag Of Rags, A  1516
Bahama  868
Bahama Mama  147-1688
Baiser, Un  1349
Bajun Gal  164
Bakiff  498
Bald Headed Mama (Blues)  88-1717
Ballad In Blue  596
Ball Game Blues  1918
Ballin' The Jack  264-308-336-977-1107-1148-1274-1605
Ball Of Fire  912
Balloonacy  1074
Balloons And Kisses  1019
Bally Hoo Blues  501
Ballyhooligans Make Whoopee, The  85
Baltimore  356-468-524-722-1276-1485-1567-1701
Baltimore Blues  1320
Baltimore Buzz  141-1423
'Bama Bound Blues  352-1022
Bam Bam Bammy Shore  89
Bambino  759
Bamboo Isle  710
Bamboola (Bamboula)  74-921
Banana Peel  1196
Banana Skin Stomp  1227
Bandan(n)a Babies  477-944-1277
Bandana Days  141-837-1392-1424-1427-1492
Band Box Shuffle  1111
Band Bpx Stomp  1456
B And O Blues  850
Band Played On, The  1374
Banjo Blues  1441
Banjo Papa (Stop Pickin' On Me)  1060
Banjo Rag  940
Banjoreno  409
Bank Failure Blues  343
Banking On The Weather  35-875
Baptistown Crawl  762
Baratria  650
Bar Babble  434-457
Barbadoes Blues  733
Barbara  468-1288-1665
Barbara Allen  185-1513
Barbaric  1081
Barbary Coast Blues  385-696
Barbary Rag  1251
Barbecue Blues  837

Barb Wire Blues   1113
Barcarolle - see TALES OF HOFFMANN
Barcelona   913
Barefoot Blues   989-1532
Barefoot Boy   680
Barefoot Stomp   694
Barkin' Dog   629-1748
Barnacle Bill, The Sailor   274-591-864-
   1409
Barney Goin' Easy   135
Barney Google   560-1175
Barney's Concerto - see CLARINET LAMENT
Barnyard Blues - see LIVERY STABLE BLUES
Barrel House   1074-1490
Barrel(1) House Baker   1055-1495
Barrelhouse Bessie From Basin Street   375
   912
Barrel House Blues   733-1265
Barrelhouse Boogie   851
Barrelhouse Breakdown   851
Barrel House Flat Blues   846
Barrel House Man   516-1320
Barrel House Mojo   1454
Barrelhouse Music   80-1270
Barrel House Stomp   302-327-1495
Barrel House Woman   516
Bartender's Blues   680
Basement Blues, The   733-1427-1448
Basement Boogie   851
Bashful Baby   1233-1381
Basie Blues   109
Basie Boogie   108
Basin Street Blues   27-44-51-85-163-253-
   305-348-363-384-424-582-597-723-745-751-
   821-913-945-959-960-977-1002-1248-1410-
   1433-1509-1556-1561-1631-1657-1688
Bass Ale Blues   265-267-1191-1192
Bass Blues   216
Bass Clarinet Blues   682
Bass Drum Dan   1570-1571
Bass Goin'/Gone Crazy   27
Bassology   551
Bass On Top   948
Bateliers de la Volga, Les   961
Bathing Beauty Blues   1509
Bathtub Ran Over Again, The   699-1046
Baton Rouge Blues   387
Baton Rouge Rag   637
Battery Bounce   1531
Battle Axe   990
Battle Of Swing   494
Battleship Kate   1518
Baulin' Water Blues   1488
Bay Rum Blues   1655
B. D.'s Dream   1677
Be A Good Sport   367
Beale Street Blues   60-62-127-136-237-284-
   305-365-384-441-511-549-582-641-657-665-
   667-795-945-954-956-963-1003-1066-1102-
   1160-1171-1193-1215-1235-1328-1356-1390-
   1392-1434-1509-1522-1539-1580-1600-1622-
   1694-
Beale Street Breakdown   391
Beale Street Mama   136-190-255-564-686-
   706-710-781-915-954-1353-1439-1672
Beale Street Mess Around   1042
Beale Street Sheik, (The)   1541-1713
Beans And Greens   1603
Bearcat Blues   150
Bear Cat Crawl   947-948
Bearcat Shuffle   899

Bearcat Stomp   1362
Bear Down   900
Bear Mash Blues   352-694
Bear Trap Blues   1746
Bear Wallow Blues   1723
Beating Blues   745
Beating Me Blues   1124
Beatin' On The Washboard   386
Beatin' The Board   550
Beatin' The Dog   1596
Beat It Out   781-1631
Beat It Out, Bumpin' Boy   1344
Beat Me, Daddy, Eight To The Bar   166-
   387-590-742-1148-1343-1412
Beat O' My Heart, The   1228-1235
Beat Of The Drum, The   587
Beat The Band To The Bar   417
Beat To The Socks   335
Beat You Doin' It   834
Beau Brummel   108
Beaucoupe (sic) de Jazz   1096
Beau Koo Jack   44-91-92-757-904-1421-
   1704
Beaumont Street Blues   181
Beau Night In Hotchkiss Corners   185-
   1374-1408
Beautiful   356-792-930-1241-1378-1562-
   1616
Beautiful Dreamer   298
Beautiful Eyes   273
Beautiful Lady In Blue, A   250-382-974-
   1307
Beautiful Love   297-1529
Beautiful Ohio Blues   379
Beautiful Romance   1712
Beaver   912
Bebe   70-223-1180
Be Bo Bo   1257
Be Careful, It's My Heart   454-1244-1554
Be Careful With Those Eyes   359-1265
Because I Know You're Mine   677
Because I Love My Daddy So   1561
Because I Love You   279-568-1400-1454-
   1611
Because I'm Fond Of You   951
Because I'm Lonesome   806
Because I'm Yours Sincerely   1644
Because It's Love   534
Because My Baby Don't Mean "Maybe" Now
   144-1291-1597-1614-1617-1686
Because Of Once Upon A Time   1625-1626
Because Of You   215-325-692
Because Of You (The World Is Mine)   73
Because They All Love You   314
Because You Are My Dream Girl   1497
Because You Could Have Had Me Once   10
Because You Love Me, Baby   388-389
Because You're You   984
Because You Said "I Love You"   341
Bechet's Steady Rider   113
Bed Rock Blues   764
Bedroom Blues   216-1618
Bedroom Stomp   1298
Bed Song, The   905
Bedtime   328
Bed Time Blues   964
Beebe   427
Beedle-Um-Bo (sometimes as BO-BO-BEEDLE-
   UM-BO)   237-524-1265-1603
Beedle-Um-Bum   1033-1044
Beef Man Blues   1026

1854

Beef Stew 1390
Bee Gezindt, A 81-259
Been Some Changes Made (Since You've Been Gone) 214
Beer Barrel Polka (Roll Out The Barrel)29
Beer Garden Blues 1708
Bees Knees 69-222-505-803-1186-1607
Beethoven Bounce 416
Beethoven Riffs On 896-897
Beets And Turnips 334-1052-1117-1591
Beezum Blues 1746
Be Fair 98-186-434
Before 622
Before The Rain 887
Before We Part 836
Beg. Borrow Or Steal 533
Beggar, The 269, 1580
Begging For Love 421
Beggin' My Daddy 1678
Beginner's Luck - see I'VE GOT BEGINNER'S LUCK
Begin The Beguine 16-79-370-386-701-740-1262-1358-1403-1531
Begone 9-432
Behave Yourself 90
Behind The Clouds 74-576-1503-1742
Be Honest With Me 364-1318
Bei dir war es immer so schön 1284
Bei mir bist du schoen (Means That You're Grand) 28-295-526-606-607-745-880-1333-1726
Being Down Don't Worry Me 1618
Belgium Stomp 988-990
Believe In Someone 880
Believe It, Beloved 13-1259-1625-1626
Believe Me, Dear 1338
Believe Me, Hot Mama 872-1057
Believing 373
Bella Bambina 1397
Belleville 1262
Bell Hoppin' Blues 129-1192-1300-1524-1681
Bells Of Hawaii 1290
Bells Of San Raquel, The 1553-1637
Beloved 1330-1331
Beloved Friend 1360
Be My Baby 1497
Be My Kid Blues 835
Bench In The Park, A 21-1687
Bend Down, Sister 1387
Bein River Blues 389
Bennie The Bumble Bee Feels Bum 409
Benny Rides Again 616
Benny's Bugle 616
Benny Sent Me 609
Be Not Discouraged 744
Be On Your Merry Way 1309
Berceuse du Marin, La 1349
Berlin Or Bust 1435
Bert Williams 1106
Beside A Babbling Brook 1180
Beside A Garden Wall 921
Beside An Open Fireplace 421
Beside The River Clyde 1513
Bessemer Bound Blues 1267
Bessie Couldn't Help It 46-145-275-346-586-789-1070-1270-1394-1637-1643
Bessie's Blues 741
Bessie's Moan 1572
Best Black 568-1029
Best Cheap Car In The Market Is A Ford 737

Best Ever Did It 680
Best Friend Blues 570-846-1092
Be Still, My Heart 810-1228
Best Things Happen At Night, The 780
Best Things In Life Are Free, The 985-1291-1378
Best Wishes 486
Be Sure 615
Betcha Nickel 527
Betsy Brown 1715
Better Boot That Thing 1573
Better Get Acquainted 572
Better Get Off Your High Horse 739
Better Give Your Sweetie What She Wants 643
Better Keep Your Eye On Your Man 1652
Better Luck Next Time 900
Better Not Let My Good Gal Catch You Here 1542
Better Than Nothin' 918
Better To Love You, My Dear, The 1332
Betty 265-773-1381-1643
Betty Co-ed 1295
Betty And Dupree 633
Betty Dupre 968
Betty Jean 1496-1497
Between A Kiss And A Sigh 445-1403
Between 18th And 19th On Chestnut Street 96-363-372-1752
Between Friends 185
Between Midnight And Dawn 1542
Between Sets 913
Between Showers 392
Between The Devil And The Deep Blue Sea 33-49-106-157-254-366-456-596-686-1027-1295-1310-1388-1468-1571-1670-1734-1752
Between You And Me And The Deep Blue Sea 1108
Between You And The Devil 1109
Bevo Blues (Bone Dry) 1747
Bewildered 78-443-1357
Bewitched 618
Beyond The Blue Horizon 1408
Beyond The Moon 614-1089
Beyond The Night 820
Beyond The Sunset 1496
Be Your Natural Self 825
Be Yourself 866-1069-1208
B flat Blues 1565-1634
B flat Swing 1737
B-Happ-E 975-976
Bicycle Bounce 694
Bidin' My Time 807
Biff'ly Blues 11
Big And Fat And Forty-Four 1674
Big Apple, The 183-442-545-586-1028-1733
Big Apple Blues 1673
Big Bad Bill (Is Sweet William Now) 297-317-1062-1453-1523
Big Bass Viol 368
Big Bear Train 1746
Big Beaver 1360
Big Ben 119-1651
Big Ben Blues 281
Big Ben's Saying Goodnight 147
Big Blues 1693
Big Boat Whistle 1541
Big Boy 226-542-561-925-1190-1663-1741
Big Boy Blue 123-153-384-526-755-913-1692

Big Boy Blues   330-1268
Big Butter And Egg Man   41-999-1481
Big Chief Blues   1747
Big Chief de Sota   366-728-1150-1239-1628
Big Chief "Swing It"   586
Big Chump Blues   1457
Big City Blues   671-979-1336
Big Crash From China   368
Big Dipper, The   320-443-745-900-1402
Big Do, The   909
Big Eight Blues, The   1540
Big Fat Butterfly   1561
Big Fat Ma   976
Big Fat Ma And Skinny Pa   41
Big Fat Mama   1070-1709
Big Feeling Blues   1269
Big Feet Rag, The   558
Big Foot Ham   1099-1100
Big Foot Jump   368
Big Four   1480
Bigger And Better Than Ever   788-1281-
   1620
Big Gorilla Man   121
Big Gun Blues - see 44 BLUES
Big House Blues   482
Big Houston Blues   1487
Big Jim Blues   901
Big John('s) Special   605-607-609-691-
   727-1074-1659
Big Joe Louis   1469
Big Leg Woman   1542
Big Lip Blues   1107
Big Money Blues   1673
Big Morning   740
Big Mouth Minnie   1377
Big Noise From Winnetka   369-374-590
Big Railroad Blues   270
Big Shot   1715
Big Time Crip   902
Big Time Rose   1547
Big Time Woman   358
Big T Jumps   1539
Big Tom   374
Big Wig In The Wigwam   662-692-740-836
Big Woman Blues   1543
Bijou   307
Bill   970-;333-1404
Bill Brown Blues   179
Bill Cheatem   328
Bill Coleman Blues   330
Bill Draw   965
Billet Doux   1261
Billie's Blues   767
Bill Street Blues   330
Bill Tell   586
Bill Wilson   137
Billy (I Always Dream Of Bill)   527
Billy Boy   431
Billy Goat Stomp   1102
Bimbo   1703-1708
Bimini Bay   1085
Bingie-Bingie-Scootie   551
Bird Nest Blues   169
Bird Of Paradise   984
Birdseed Special   1373
Birds Of A Feather   451-617
Birmingham Bertha   92-580-1088-1089-1091-
   1108-1152-1155-1652
Birmingham Black Bottom   833
Birmingham Blues   137-458-1621-1724
Birmingham Bound   566

Birmingham Breakdown   38-98-311-406-472-
   953
Birmingham Papa (Your Memphis Mama's
   Coming To Town)   1164
Birmingham Special   216
Birmingham Stomp   1588
Birthday Party   1355
Birth Of Passion, The   908
Birth Of The Blues, The   267-285-364-619-
   928-1243-1246-1433-1583-1657
Biscuit Roller   1044-1499-1678
Biscuit Rolling Time   1413
Bishop's Blues   743
Bit By Bit You're Breaking My Heart   176-
   224-868
Bitter Feelin' Blues   643-1058
Bixology - see IN A MIST
Bizarre   536
Bizet Has His Day   186
Black   994
Black And Blue Blues   501
Black And Blue Bottom   1596
Black And Blue Rhapsody   241-303-1563
Black And Blue Rhythm   801
Black(And)Evil Blues   843-1091
Black And Tan Fantasy   347-394-473-474-
   478-481-485-747-801-984-1071
Black And White   1261
Black And White (Rag)   346-971-1251-1604-
   1656
Black Beauty   475-476-478-983-1712
Blackberry Jam   215-1437
Blackberry Rag   1558
Blackbirds of 1928, Gems from   1083
Black Bordered Letter Blues   709
Black Bottom   124-134-171-266-282-524-
   546-659-667-928-1116-1264-1742
Black Bottom Blues, The   66-747-748-1059
Black Bottom Hop   1467
Black Bottom Is The Latest Fad   1622
Black Bottom Stomp   546-1101-1138-1275
Black Bottom Strut   1558
Black Boy Blues   1263
Black But Sweet   778
Black But Sweet, Oh God !   994
Black Butterfly   491-1712
Black Can Call   151
Black Cat, The   1125
Black Cat Blues   547-548-1155-1555
Black Cat Bone (Blues)   408-942
Black Cat Hoot Owl Blues   1268
Black Cat Moan   1209-1451
Black Coffee   582-1000-1137-1432
Black Crepe Blues   353
Black Diamond Rag   1251-1586
Black Dog Blues   412
Black Dust Blues   1269
Black Eye Blues   1269
Black Eyed Blues   119-915
Black-Eyed Susan Brown   289-525-1708
Black Eyes - see DARK EYES
Black Gal   1710
Black Gal Blues   137-847
Black Gal, You Better Use Your Head   680
Black Ghost Blues   849
Black Girl Gets There Just The Same   278
Black Gypsy   1476
Black Gypsy Blues   849
Black Hand Blues   392-785
Black Hearse Blues   1014
Black Horse Stomp   531-719-973-1006

Blackin' Blues  554-1054
Black Jazz  281-287
Black Magic  858
Black Man (Be On Your Way) (Blues)  570-
709-763-1060-1174-
Black Maria  402-404-540-722-1061-1436-
1436-1635
Black Measles  511
Black Men Blues  846
Black Mountain Blues  1446
Black Name Moan  1572
Black Out (see also UPTOWN DOWNBEAT)  693
Black Panther (Stomp)  982-1211-1340
Blackpool Walk, The  587
Black Rag  301
Black Raspberry Jam  1629
Black Rhythm  253
Black Rider  863-1677
Black Satin  1602
Black Sheep Blues, (The)  120-143-965-
1056-1094-1523
Blacksmith Rag  1522
Black Snake Blues  343-1024-1082-1168-
1257-1487-1701
Black Snake Moan  735
Black Snake Swing  1489
Black Spatch Blues  1650
Black Spider  329
Black Star Line (A West Indies Chant)
733-1051-1550
Black Stick  1427
Black Stomp  641
Black Velvet  788
Blackville After Dark  1051
Black Woman Blues  644
Black Woman Is Like A Black Snake, A
1042
Black Woman's Blues  1451
Black Zephyr  375
Blame It On My Last Affair  79-105-814-
1116-1159
Blame It On My Youth  425
Blame It On The Black Bottom Craze  1276
Blame It On The Blues  1268-1605
Blame The Imp  1397
Blame The Weather  445
Blaze Away  127
Blazin'  340-723
Blazin' The Trail  1313
Bleeding Heart Blues  628
Bleeding Hearted Blues  706-749-793-837-
838-1022-1050-1439-1728
Bless Her Little Heart  1580-1619
Bless You  1635
Bless You, My Dear  900
Bless Your Heart  520.
Bless You, Sister  138-240-1568
Bli-Blip  499
Blind Boy Blues  181
Blind Date  325
Blind Man Could See That I Love You, A
1377
Blind Man('s) Blues  360-1011-1241-1492
Blind Man's Buff  1750
Blinky Moon Bay  1503-1611
Blitzkrieg Baby (You Can't Bomb Me)  273
Block And Tackle (Blues)  151-210-784
Blondy  83-245-951-1214
Blood Drippin' Blues  1487
Blood Hound Blues  1488
Blood Thirsty Blues  1487

Bloody Razor Blues  643
Blouey Blues  829
Blossoms On Broadway  162-205-1314
Blow, Blow, Thou Winter Wind  370-841
Blow, Gabriel, Blow  153-582
Blowin' 'Em Hot  1521
Blowin' Off Steam  153-266-267-1131-1326
Blowin' The Blues Away  557
Blowing Up A Breeze  131
Blow, Katy, Blow  1247
Blow My Blues Away  263
Blow That Horn  585
Blow The Smoke Away  298
Blow Top  107
Blue Afterglow  989-990
Blue Again  48-483-508-1144-1745
Blue And All By Myself  555
Blue (And Broken-Hearted)  81-132-220-
433-591-663-710-758-759-1036-1086-1607
Blue And Evil Blues  1527
Blue And Sentimental  103-646
Blue Baby (Why Are You Blue ?)  211-469-
626-1068-1324
Blue Bayou  1121
Blue Because Of You  760-1626
Blue Bells Of Scotland, The  969
Blueberry Hill  163-909
Blueberry Rhyme  839
Blue Bessie (The Bluest Gal In Tennessee)
1439-1440
Bluebird Blues  1608
Bluebird Boogie Woogie  1242
Bluebirds Bring Me Happiness  708
Bluebird, Sing Me A Song  565
Bluebirds In The Moonlight  613-1436
Bluebird, Where Are You ?  1573
Blue Black Bottom (Blues)  835-1622
Blue Blazes  454-987
Blue Blood Blues (1929)  458
Blue Blood Blues (1930)  1104
Blue Blowers Blues  1108
Blue Blue  1446
Blue Blues  1112
Blue Bonnet (You Make Me Feel Blue)
1504
Blue Boogie  1411
Blue Bubbles  474
Blue Champagne  434
Blue Chips  211
Blue Clarinet Stomp  414-898-1307
Blue Danube, The  429-440-1243
Blue Danube Blues  874-1519
Blue Danube Swing, The  86-279-747
Blue Dawn  741
Blue Deep Sea Blues  91
Blue Devil Blues  1012-1204
Blue Dilemma - see PASTEL BLUE
Blue Divel Jazz  184
Blue Drag  140-587-758-1195-1258-1536-
1646
Blue Echo  830
Blue Echoes  374
Blue Evening  740-1159
Blue Evening Blues  134-314-515-545-868-
997-1334-1364
Blue-Eyed Blues  1480
Blue-Eyed Sally  229-1119-1161-1378-1664
Blue Eyes  409-884-1636
Blue Fantasy  556-880-897-1402
Blue Feeling  488
Blue Feelin' Blues  330

Blue Flame  742-1071
Blue For You  547
Blue For You, Johnny  114
Blue Georgia Moon  547
Blue Goose  496
Blue Grass  394-649-1325-1336-1377
Blue Grass Blues  1189-1193-1327-1388-
1419-1420
Blue Guitars  844
Blue Guitar Stomp  694
Blue Gum Blues  1011
Blue Harlem  486
Blue Harmonica  942
Blue Harmony  694
Blue Hawaii  205-836
Blue Hoosier Blues  176-1066-1175-1362-
1438
Blue Illusion  899
Blue Ink  741
Blue Interlude  259-282-312-609-1304-1642
Blue Island Blues  1209-1608
Blue Is The Evening  1712
Blue Is The Night  979
Blue Ivories  1551
Blue Jazz  288-1507
Blue Juice  97
Blue Jump, The  417
Blue Kentucky Blues  353
Blue Kentucky Moon  287
Blue-Ku  412
Blue Lament  858
Blue Light  494
Blue Light Blues  283
Blue Little You (And Blue Little Me)  567-
1077
Blue Lou  16-123-281-528-728-1003-1658
Blue Lovebird  325
Blue Lude In C sharp minor  537
Blue Melody Blues  1209
Blue Memories  251
Blue Mirror  1658
Blue Moments  726
Blue Monday Blues  352
Blue Monday On Sugar Hill  1729
Blue Mood  486-1074-1733
Blue Moon  202-292-446-689-1292-1571
Blue Moon Blues  1210
Blue Moonlight  261-889
Blue Morning  1726
Blue Murder  1238
Blue Night  1213
Blue Nights  60-758
Blue Orchids  371-447-612
Blue Piano Stomp  414
Blue Prelude  199-289-361-741-858-990-
1330-1507
Blue Rain  80-185-297-448
Blue Ramble  486
Blue Reefer Blues  863
Blue Reverie  607-1711
Blue Rhythm  285-725-887-1071
Blue Rhythm Fantasy  755-756-908-1075
Blue Rhythm Of The Blues  386
Blue Rhythm Stomp  1246
Blue Ribbon Blues  149
Blue Ridge  179
Blue River (1927)  238-578-1566
Blue River (1933)  1538-1541-1648
Blue Romance  1224
Blue Room, The  75-154-233-422-542-607-
608-830-836-858-1112-1300-1343-1597-1661

Blue Room Blues  845
Blue Rose  71-350-1663
Bluer Than Blue  39-1711
Blues, The  16-26-27-56-122-188-495-557-
612-690-821-948-1253-1262-1289-1399-
1401-1407-1539
Blues Ain't Nothin' But, The  1678
Blues Ain't Nothin' Else But !  353
Blues A-Poppin'  1712
Blues At High Noon  1109
Blues At Midnight  520-1253
Blues At Noon  1272
Blues Be A Coward  585
Blues Before Daybreak  850
Blues 'Bout My Gal  1413
Blues de Lux  947
Blues Downstairs  740
Blue Sea  693
Blues en mineur  1284
Blue Sentimental Mood  1244
Blue September  167
Blue Serge  498-499
Blues Evermore  690
Blues Everywhere  847-848
Blues Fever  954
Blues For My Baby  1528
Blues For Roy  1155
Blues For Tommy  1240
Blues From The Everglades  1097
Blues Galore  415
Blues Got Me, The  1726
Blue Shadows  502-626-649
Blue Shadows And White Gardenias  109-
1361
Blues Have Got Me, The  1000-1523-1541-
1643
Blues I Like To Hear, The  104
Blues I Love To Play, The  1726
Blues I Love To Sing  473
Blues in A minor  149
Blues in B  618
Blues in B flat  1095-1371-1637
Blues in C flat (Blues en si bemol)  1726
Blues in C sharp minor  1731
Blues In Disguise  1053
Blues in E flat  1156
Blues in F  1113
Blues in G  844
Blues In My Condition  1712
Blues In My Flat, The  608
Blues In My Heart  76-142-253-283-285-586
726-790-791-981-1645-1657
Blues In My Mind  8
Blues In The Air  115
Blues In The Dark  103
Blues In The Groove  989-1359
Blues In The News  664
Blues In The Night  98-261-453-621-743-
819-990-1408-1575-1657
Blues In The Rain  886
Blues In Thirds  114-757 (see also
CAUTION BLUES)
Blues In Your Flat, The  608
Blues Is Bad  1630
Blues (I Still Think Of Her)  107
Blues Jumped A Rabbit  1154
Blues, Just Blues  1671
Blues, Just Blues, That's All  1164
Blue Skies  141-189-409-435-452-457-466-
596-607-695-759-896-961-974-1239-1242-
1344-1400-1512-1611-1661-1691

1858

Blues Krieg  909
Blue Sky Avenue  1669
Blue Slug  812
Blues Mixture  538
Blues My Baby Gave To Me  1134
Blues My Girl Friend Taught Me  1374
Blues My Naughty Sweetie Gives To Me  380-
    955-976-1151-1318-1692
Blues No More  455
Blues Of Avalon  155
Blues Of Bechet  114
Blues Of Israel  905
Blues Of The Vagabond  480
Blues Of Yesterday  465
Blues Oh Blues  1268
Blue Sonata  208
Blues On Central Avenue  1575
Blues On Parade  741
Blues On The Doenbeat  851
Blues Petite  896
Blue Spirit Blues  1446
Blues Please Go Away  1012
Blues Serenade, A  494-508-765-1063-1192-
    1193-1273-1420-1521
Blues Singer From Alabam', The  179-1063
Blues Stampede, The  133
Blues Stomp  181
Blues The World Forgot  1268
Blues To The Dole  1538
Blue Strings  525
Blues Sure Have Got Me  1034
Blues To The Lonely  1540
Blues Upstairs  740
Blues Upstairs And Downstairs  591
Blue Surreal  375
Blue Sweets  1281
Blues, Why Don't You Let Me Alone ?  1468
Blues With A Feelin'  477
Blues With Helen  107
Blues With Lips  104
Blues Without Words  208
Blue Tahitian Moon  591
Blue, That's All  686
Blue, Thinking Of You  1194
Blue Trombone Stomp  694
Blue Trumpet Man  536
Blue Tune  485
Blue, Turning Grey Over You  46-94-583-
    789-1626-1631
Blue Valley Blues  1487
Blue Venetian Waters  1121
Blue Washboard Stomp  414
Blue Woman's Blues  555
Blue Yodel No. 1  1299
Blue Yodel No. 2  1299
Blue Yodel No. 3  1299
Blue Yodel No. 4  1327
Blue Yodel No. 9  1328
Bluin' The Black Keys  870
Bluin' The Blues  127-855-972-996-1133-
    1176-1179-1390-1481-1522-1747
B-19  551-819
Boarding House Blues  1298
Board Meeting  151-614-763
Boar Hog Blues  752-862
Boats  342
Bobadilla  267
Bobbed Haired Bobbie (Bobbie Be Mine)  32
Bobbed Haired Woman Blues  737
Bob Lee Junior Blues  1041
Bo-Bo-Beedle-Um-Bo - see BEEDLE-UM-BO

Bob White (Whatcha Gonna Swing Tonight?)
    78-363-603-880-1315-1402
Bo De O-O-Dee O-D-O, The  681
Body And Soul  3-13-47-131-272-432-497-
    504-596-607-636-672-690-760-769-788-
    946-961-1155-1207-1253-1285-1373-1530-
    1736
Bogalousa Strut  1096
Bogey ! Bogey !  587
Bogey Man  1038
Bogey Man Blues  1573
Bogey Walk  632
Bogieman Blues (sic)  387
Bogloosa Blues (sic)  318
Bogo Joe  663
Bohunkus Blues  150
Bojangles  496-497
Bojangles Of Harlem  584-780-893-1019
Bo-La-Bo  972
Bolero (Ravel)  612-1260
Bolero At The Savoy  106-907-912
Bolero In Blue  325
Boll Weavil Blues (sometimes shown as
    BOWEAVIL BLUES)  39-192-380-803-1054-
    1265-1423-1440
Bologny  1021
Bolshevik  1098
Bombay  1209
Bond Street  1635
Bone Orchard Blues  354
Boneyard Shuffle  38-296-467-644-762-
    1131-1138
Bongo  551
Bon mouvement, Un  1639
Bonnie  176
(Bonnie) Mary Of Argyle  969-1434
Bonsoir  1469
Bon Ton One-Step  337
Boodie Bum Bum  1044
Boodle Am  409-411
Boogaboo (Blues)  936-1102
Boogie Beat'll Getcha, The  1004
Boogie de Concerto  215
Boogie Man, The  629
Boogie Rag  1516
Boogie Ride  1412
Boogie Woogie  1170
Boogie Woogie (Pinetop's)  20-27-76-101-
    104-180-183-189-259-445-588-754-851-
    865-1003-1106-1236-1378-1465
Boogie Woogie Blues  25-103-322-821
Boogie Woogie Bugle Boy  742-910
Boogie Woogie Came To Town  865
Boogie Woogie Camp Meeting  808
Boogie Woogie Cocktail  902
Boogie Woogie Conga  167
Boogie Woogie Dance  1527
Boogie Woogie Jump  851
Boogie Woogie Man  851
Boogie Woogie Maxixe  371
Boogie Woogie Moan  1247
Boogie Woogie Piano Man  298
Boogie Woogie Prayer  947-948
Boogie Woogie St. Louis Blues  215
Boogie Woogie's Mother-in-Law  832
Boogie Woogie Stomp  26
Boogie Woogie Stride  839
Boogie Woogie Sugar Blues - see SUGAR
    BLUES
Boogie Woogie Swing  795
Boogin' On The Downbeat  1242

Boog It  57-260-433-816-908
Booglie Wooglie Piggy, The  168-185-273-591
Boogy Boogy Boo  589-1435
Boo-Hoo  101-585-879-1002-1630
Boo Hoo Blues  1025
Boo Hoo Hoo  219-1162-1352-1424
Boola Boo  1645
Booly Ja-Ja (Jungle Dance)  1117-1735
Boomerang  657
Boomps-a-Daisy  589-1316
Boop-Boop-A-Doop-A-Doo Trot  788
Bootblack Blues  1005
Boot It  1111
Boot It, Boy  1526-1548
Bootlegging Daddy  1717
Boots Stomp  155
Boot-Ta-La-Za  550
Boot That Thing  327
Boot To Boot  1507
Boo-Wah Boo-Wah  260-325
Boo Woo  814
Booze  1323
Booze And Blues  1266
Booze Crazy Man Blues  354
Born And Bred In Kentucky  797
Borneo  130-1568
Born To Be Kissed  1689
Born To Love  768
Born To Swing  39-79-1400
Borrowed Love Blues  1376
Boss Of The Stomps, The  1391
Boston Skuffle  1456
Boston Tea Party, The  428-893
Boston Trot, The  1285
Bottle It Up And Go  1044
Bottomland - see I'M GOING BACK TO BOTTOM-LAND
Bottom Man On The Totem Pole, The  299
Bottoms Up  788-1281-1418-1620
Boudoir Benny  1712
Boulevard Of Broken Dreams, The  1669
Bounce  498
Bounce Me Brother, With A Solid Four  167-742
Bounce Of The Sugar Plum Fairy  896-897
Bounce The Ball (Do Da Dittle Um Day)  864
Bouncing Around  1229
Bouncin' Around  189-1283
Bouncin' 'Round  1112
Bouncing At The Beacon  663
Bouncing Ball, The  1689
Bouncing Blues  1671
Bouncing Buoyancy  495
Bouncin' In Rhythm  1332-1560
Bouncing With Bean  690
Bow Down Blues  979
Boweavil Blues - see BOLL WEAVIL BLUES
Bow-Legged Mama  398
Bow-Legged Papa  212
Bow Leg Woman  1542
Bowling Green  1194
Bow To Your Papa  151
Bow Wow  772
Bow Wow Blues  (My Mama Treats Me Like A Dog)  219-1178-1230
Box Car Blues  860
Box Of Blues  1021
Boy In Khaki, A Girl In Lace, A  454-1244
Boy In The Boat, The (The Rock)  833-1468-1645-1677 (B. D.'s Dream)

Boy, It's Solid Groovy  1457
Boy Meets Goy/Girl  615
Boy Meets Horn  494-497-612
Boy Named Lem, A  323
Boy Of Mine  315
Boy ! Oh Boy ! Oh Boy ! I've Got It Bad  1514
Boy Scout In Switzerland  747-1372
Boys From Harlem, The  1712
Boys, Take Five  829
Boy With The Wistful Eyes, The  761
Bozo  1703
Braggin'  817
Braggin' In Brass  493
Braggin' The Briggs  172
Brainstorm  338-340-1196-1472
Brand New Charleston  1161
Brand-New Mama  235
Brandy And Soda  468
Brass Boogie  375
Brazil  436
Bread And Butter  324
Bread And Gravy  1654
Bread And Jam  1083
Break A Day Schuffle (sic)  1112
Breakaway  20-420-507-1336-1507-1743
Breakdown Blues  1518
Break 'Em Down  1662
Break 'Er Down  676
Breakfast Ball  594-983
Breakfast Dance  480
Breakfast Feud  617
Breakfast In Harlem  193-536
Breakin' Down  528
Breakin' Em Down Tonight  849
Breakin' In A Pair Of Shoes  180-597-879-1239-1571-1731
Breaking My Heart To Keep Away From You  1317
Breakin' The Ice  582-779-1248-1392-1625
Breakin' The Leg  764-954-1137-1643
   (sometimes shown as BREAKIN' A LEG)
Break It Down  787-1073-1571
Break It Up  787
Break It To Me Gently  167
Break O' Day Blues  177
Breath And Breeches/Britches (Blues)  633-1452
Breathless  186
Breathtakin' Blues  1299
Breeze And I, The  96-433
Breeze (Blow My Baby Back To Me)  321-380-900-1000-1467-1491-1522-1704-1705-1708
Breeze, Ray, Breeze  1036
Breeze (That's Bringin' My Honey Back To Me), The  424-699-879-937
Breezin' Along (To Georgia)  1380
Breezin' Along With The Breeze  38-234-1377
Bric-a-Brac  923
Brick House Blues  1066
Bricktop  1260
Bridal Waltz  274
Bridwell Blues, The  1671
Bright Boy Blues  1370
Brighter Days  1745
Brighter Than The Sun  1149
Bright Eyes  1248
Bright Star Blues  1230
Bring Back My Lovin' Man  1543-1617

Bring Back The Greenback Dollar  409
Bring Back The Joys  792
Bring Back Those Rock-a-Bye Baby Days  1454
Bring 'Em Back Alive  584
Bringing Home The Bacon  561-1202-1609-
  1737
Bring It Back Daddy  854
Bring It On Down To My House  1505
Bring It On Home  278
Bring It On Home To Grandma  863-1153
Bring It With You When You Come  270-793-
  1719
Bring Me Flowers While I'm Living  1674
Bring Out The Little Brown Jug  1436
Bring-Up Breakdown  1370
Bring Your Greenbacks  1651
Brittwood Stomp, The  1134
Broadcasting Blues  354
Broad Road Blues  1338
Broadway  107-648
Broadway Baby Dolls  244-1108
Broadway Blues  1175-1423
Broadway Cinderella  427
Broadway Daddy Blues  1069
Broadway Hit Medley  512
Broadway Jump  551
Broadway Melody  809-883-949-1336
Broadway Rhythm  23-249-1345
Broadway Rose  1026-1177
Broadway's Gone Hawaii  739
Broadway Stomp (1928)  1222
Broadway Stomp (1931)  1744
Broadway Street Woman Blues  1091
Broke Again  1252
Broke Down Mama  214
Broken Busted (Can't Be Trusted) Blues
  714-1090-1424-1449
Broken Doll, A  388-938
Broken Down Horn  919
Broken Dreams Of You  1074
Broken-Hearted  469-525-648-1425-1521
  (sometimes shown as HERE AM I, BROKEN
  HEARTED)
Broken-Hearted Blues  680-843-916-1267
Broken-Hearted Doll  1426
Broken-Hearted Sue  1036
Broken Idol  245
Broken Love  1527
Broken Record, The  1001-1114
Broken Soul Blues  1267
Broken Window Pane  849
Broncho Bustin' Blues  1212
Bronzeville Jump  1554
Broomstreet  185
Brother Ben  1014
Brother, Can You Spare A Dime ?  198
Brother Low Down  914-1525
Brotherly Love  319-466-568-720-865-1120-
  1131-1365
Brother, Seek And Ye Shall Find  1627
Brother, You've Got Me Wrong  1609-1650
Brown Baby  461-1649
Brown Berries  474
Brown Bird Singing, A  325-1512
Brown Bottom Bess  308
Brown Eyes  339-377-396
Brown Eyes, Why Are You Blue ?  232-1135
Brown Gal  39
Brown Jug Blues  216
Brown Pepper - see BROWN SUGAR
Brown Skin Baby Doll  1025

Brown Skin Blues  569
Brown Skin Flapper  1035
Brown Skin Gal  212
Brown Skin Gal (In The Calico Gown)  499
Brown Skin Mama  263-1495-1647
Brown Skin Man  709
Brown Skin (Who You For ?)  1009-1605-
  1698
Brown Skin Woman  1413
Brown Suede  135
Brown Sugar  38-267-268-338-524-826-887-
  903-1182-1226-1275
Brown Sugar Mine  1074
Brush Stomp  308
BS Rules The World  834
Bubbles  841
Bubbling Over  758-759
Bubbling Over With Love  33-801-1296
Buchanan Stomp  1219
Buck Dance Rhythm  550
Bucket, The  111
Bucket Of Blood  516
Bucket's Got A Hole In It, The  556-843
Buck Fever  298
Buckin' The Dice  1636
Buckin' The Wind  92-1669
Buck Jumpin'  1637
Buckle Down, Winsocki  619-620
Bucktown Blues  764-1100-1201-1271-1388-
  1389
Bucktown Stomp  414
Budding Dancers  1642
Buddy Bolden's Blues (I Thought I Heard
  Buddy Bolden Say)  1105-1107
Buddy Burton's Jazz  150
Buddy George  1713
Buddy's Habit(s)  193-1056-1138-1166-
  1509
Buddy's Wednesday Outing  791-1073
Buds Won't Bud  449-615
Buffalo Blues (New Jersey Blues)  459-
  862
Buffalo Rag, The  1199-1200
Buffalo Rhythm  92-736-799-1226-1309-
  1498-1620
Buffalo Strut  357
Buffet Flat  494
Buffy Boy  97
Bug, The  1239
Bugaboo  1144-1646
Bugahoma Blues  138
Buggy Blues  1554
Bughouse  1156
Bugle Blues  89-102-109-258-458-1560-1649
  (sometimes shown as ORIGINAL BUGLE
  BLUES)
Bugle Breaks  499
Bugle Call Rag (1916)  1605
Bugle Call Rag (1922)  85-88-171-253-263
  270-282-293-311-313-347-380-385-474-
  485-584-594-595-598-599-601-642-647-
  780-786-791-797-801-866-913-922-955-
  962-963-991-1048-1076-1131-1138-1150-
  1223-1278-1280-1298-1333-1340-1353-
  1419-1422-1432-1501-1529-1596-1670-
  1672-1673-1750 (sometimes shown as
  BUGLE CALL BLUES)
Bugler's Dilemma  896
Bugs  863
Bugs Parade  989
Build A Little Home  1601

Building A Home For You  1469
Building A Nest For Mary  949-1141
Buji  289
Bull Blues  712-1096
Bullet Wound Blues  1093
Bull Fiddle Blues  414-1312
Bull Fiddle Rag  1055
Bull Foot Stomp  1742
Bull Frog Blues  386-1228-1429
Bull Frog Moan  844
Bull Frog Patrol, The  799
Bull Frog Serenade  657
Bull It In C  1126
Bull's Eye  1007
Bumble Bee Blues  1043-1527
Bumble Bee Stomp  610
Bump It  1154
Bumps, The  820-1154
Bumpy Weather Over Newark  1372
Bunch O' Blackberries, A  1049
Bunch Of Blues, A  665-1188
Bunch Of Rags, A  1197-1198-1200-1588
Bundle Of Blues  487
Bundle Of Love  780
Bundle Of Old Love Letters, A  246
Bungo  998
Burglar's Revenge  1412
Burgundy  265-1504
Burma Girl  782
Burmese Ballet, A  25
Burning Kisses  1203
Burning Of Rome  1566
Burnin' Sticks  1089
Burnin' The Candle At Both Ends  374
Burnin' The Iceberg  1103
Burning The Midnight Oil  417
Burnt Sugar (A Triple Rag)  565
Burping Bassoon  1506
Bury Me In The Tennessee Mountains  655
Bus Blues, The  1400
Bush To Boil Tea, De  164
Business After Midnight  1195
Business in F  557-726-874-1409-1550
Business in Q  557-874-1410-1571
Business Is Gone Away  680
Business Men's Bounce  1373
Busking Around  386
Buss Robinson Blues  850
Buster's Last Stand  1554
Busy As A Bee (I'm Buzz, Buzz, Buzzin')  96-527-614
But  1517
Butcher Shop Blues  1065
But Definitely  93-122
But I Do - You Know I Do  1478-1722
But I'll Be Back  864
But It Didn't Mean A Thing  901
But Not For Me  819-1696-1736
Butter-Finger Blues  359
Butterfingers  92-423-1332
Buttermilk Blues  1713
Butternut ('Neath The Beuatiful Butternut Tree)  654-1393
Button, Button (Who's Got The Button ?)  125
Buttons  1715
Button Up Your Overcoat  31-130-242-420-512-670-790-950-1595-1604-1743
But Where Are You ?  1312
Buy, Buy For Baby (Or Baby Will Bye-Bye You)  1232

Buy Me Some Juice  91
Buzzard, The  541
Buzz-Buzz-Buzz (Lookin' For My Honey)307
Buzzin' Around  1023
Buzzin' 'Round With The Bee  660
Buzzin' Bees  1420
Buzz Mirandy  342-1185-1613
B'wanga  23
By A Lazy Country Lane  853
By A Waterfall  200-1330-1331
Bye And Bye  57-717-1483
Bye-Bye  1175
Bye-Bye, Baby  93-209-405-702-886-1123-1364-1465-1629
Bye-Bye, Blackbird  1433-1675
Bye-Bye Blues  22-247-260-298-348-505-584-658-694-736-906-980-1570
Bye-Bye Blues, The  1093-1441
Bye-Bye Florence  783
Bye-Bye, Pretty Baby  738
Bye 'n' Bye  506
Byfield Stomp - see HERMAN AT THE SHERMAN
Bygones  219
By Heck  422-423-425-1360-1661
By My Side  980
By Special Permission Of The Copyright Owners (I Love You)  807
By The Great Horn Spoon  1601
By The Light Of The Silvery Moon  1638
By The Light Of The Stars  797
By The River Nile  554
By The River Sainte Marie  329-446-987-989
By The Sapphire Sea  220-1086
By The Shalimar  914-1143
By The Sleepy Lagoon  819
By The Sycamore Tree  422
By The Waterfall  1136
By The Watermelon Vine, Lindy Lou  284
By The Waters Of Minnetonka  468-797-895-997-1150-1475-1742
By The Waters Of Perkiomen  546
By The Way  244
By-U By-O (The Lou'siana Lullaby)  743

Cabaret Echoes  1208
Cabaret Rag  1251
Cabin In The Cotton  254-361-1072-1388
Cabin In The Sky  528-616-1628-1655
Cabin In The Skyline  182
Ça, c'est une chose  1085
Cachita  1308
Cafe Capers  466-826-1208
Cafe Society Blues  109
Cafe Society Rag  850
Cain And Abel  57
Cairo Rag  270
Caissons Go Rolling Along, The  376-912
Cake-Walking Babies From Home  794-1280-1442-1656-1699
Cake-Walk In The Sky, The  1604
Caldonia Blues  1617
Calico Rag  645-904
California  68-219
California Blues  558-991
California, Here I Come  225-335-774-1236-1433-1581-1626
California Medley  1146-1232
California Stomp  318
California Swing  782

1862

Calling  1612
Calling All Bars  26-1396
Calling All Keys  1306
Calling Corinne  824
Calling Me Home  468-668
Callin' Your Bluff  1074
Calliope Blues  739
Call It Anything, It's Love  168-374
Call It Anything (It Wasn't Love)  984
Call Me A Taxi  167-369
Call Me Darling (Call Me Sweetheart,
    Call Me Dear)  1154-1631
Call Me Happy  760-761
Call Of The Canyon, The  450
Call Of The Delta  75
Call Of The Freaks, The  772-1148-1169-
    1345-1402-1410-1508-1644
Call Of The South, The  269-511
Call Of The Wild  1203
Call The Police  329
Call To Arms, The  703
Calypso, The  1408
Camel Hop  605
Camel Walk, The  555-568-777-903-920-962-
    1130-1579-1643
Camomille  1085
Campbells Are Swingin', The  320-745-1506
Camp Meeting Blues (1919)  192-380
Camp Meeting Blues (1923)  1166
Camp Meeting Jamboree  1075
Camp Nelson Blues  154
Camptown Races  326
Campus Capers  418
Campus Crawl  1223
Campus Rush  264
Canadian Capers  85-386-442-774-1507
Canal Street Blues  15-1165
Can Anybody Take Sweet Mama's Place ?
    1617
Canary Cottage  544
Candied Sweets  919-1222
Candlelights  126-1490
C And O Whistle Blues  841
Candy Blues  841
Candy Lips (I'm Stuck On You)  1008-1534-
    1700-1701
Candy Man, The  783
Cane Break Blues  137-169
Canhanibalmo Rag  1256
Can I Be Sure ?  208
Can I Forget You ?  15-913-1400
Can I Get It Now ?  838
Can I Help It ?  324-371-708-1383
Can I Rely On You ?  1469
Can I Tell You ?  1169
Canned Heat Blues  737-1564
Cannon Ball  187
Cannon Ball Blues  570-736-1101-1184
Cannon Ball March/Rag  130-772-970-1199-
    1481 (sometimes shown as THE CANNON
    BALL)
Can't Be Bothered With No Sheik  735
Can't Be Trusted Blues  1058
Can't Do Without His Love  697
Can't Feel Jolly Blues  705
Can't Find Nobody To Do Like My Old
    Daddy Do  1013
Can't Fool Me Blues  1338
Can't Get Indiana Off My Mind  589
Can't Get Lovin' Blues  705-1576

Can't Help Lovin' Dat Man  63-124-179-273-
    469-528-541-565-897-1291-1613-1684-1733
Can This Be Love ?  421-740
Can This Be The End Of Love ?  455
Can't Make Another Day  834
Can't Read, Can't Write  843-1677
Can't Sleep Blues  1216
Can't Stop Caring For You  456
Can't Take My Man  1466
Can't Teach My Old Heart New Tricks  604-
    1402
Can't Use You Blues  627
Can't We Be Friends ?  83-367-562-595-601-
    788-896-1142-1412-1482-1595-1743
Can't We Dream A Midsummer Night's Dream ?
    250
Can't We Get Together ?  1080
Can't We Meet Again ?  982
Can't We Talk It Over ?  6-147-1030-1285-
    1539
Can't You/Yo' Hear/Heah Me Callin(g),
    Caroline ?  888-1139-1236
Can't Your Friend Find A Friend For Me ?
    903
Can't You Tell ?  614
Can't You Understand ?  246-580
Can't You Wait Till I Get You/You Get
    Home ?  822-823
Can't Use It Myself  1320
Can You Blame Me ?  580
Can You Picture That ?  1182
Can You See ?  287
Can You Take It ?  726
Can You Tell ?  1066
Canzone Amorosa (Venetian Love Song)  89
Canzonetta  388
Capinera, La  429
Capitol Blues  806
Capri Caprice  583
Caprice  837
Caprice Futuristic/Futuristique  1420
Caprice XXIV Paganini (sic)  620
Caprice Viennois  818
Captain And His Men, The  97
Caravan (1922)  1614
Caravan (1937)  3-24-124-134-279-491-492-
    497-586-603-684-695-1272-1342-1506-1585
Card Players' Rag  1106
Carefree  130
Careful Conversation At A Diplomatic
    Function  1375
Careless  448-741
Careless Blues  458
Careless/Loveless Love (Blues)  155-251-
    277-301-384-413-504-553-628-665-666-667-
    770-793-852-945-967-1123-1160-1171-1423-
    1427-1442-1495-1509-1537-1575-1622-1656-
    1678-1696
Carelessly  123-1551-1732
Careless Man Blues  1014
Caressing  226
Caressing You  242-627
Cariña  217
Carioca  1404-1405
Carmen : Prelude (Bizet)  1360
Carnegie Drag  335
Carnegie Jump  335
Carnival  1408
Carnival In Caroline  493-1712
Carnival Of Venice  325-816-817-997

Carolina 291-581
Carolina Blues 303-1461-1523
Carolina Bound 531
Carolina Home 69
Carolina In The Morning 69-739-1086-1143
Carolina Moon 445
Carolina Rolling Stone 68
Carolina's Calling Me 1668
Carolina Shout 170-837-839-1519-1637
Carolina Stomp 306-350-531-718-1229
Carolina Stompdown 4
Caroline 1714
Carpet Alley 409
Carrie 1742
Carrier Pigeon 1375
Carrier Pigeon Blues 1065
Carry It On Down 32
Carry Me Back To Green Pastures 1074
Carry Me Back To My Carolina Home 222
Carry Me Back To Old Virginny 54-208-282
   691-1585
Carry Me Back To The Lone Prairie 299-
   513
Casa Loma Stomp 286-288-289-294-726-1329
Casbah Blues 740
Cascades 333
Case Of The Blues 1109
Case On Dawn - see EASE ON DOWN
Casey Bill 1026
Casey Jones (The Brave Engineer) 236-251
   1003-1398-1506-1510-1565
Casey Jones Blues 390
Casey Jones Special 898
Cash For Your Trash 58-1637-1638
Cast Away 460-687-1699
Castle House Rag 512
Castle Of Dreams 96-297-1603
Castle's Rockin', The 795
Cat, The 1120-1580-1619
Castle Walk 512
Cast Your Sins Away 1310
Cataract Rag Blues 762
Cat Calls 683
Catchin' 'Erbs 460
Catch On 251
Catch That Tiger (probably TIGER RAG) 808
Caterpillar Creep 1375
Caterpillar Wabble 303
Caterpillar Walk, The 117
Cathedral Blues 1209
Cat's Head 999
Cat's Kittens 358
Cat's Pajamas, The 829
Cat's Whiskers, The 120 826-1175
Caught My Gal Truckin' 1527
Caught You Triflin' Blues 1450
'Cause I Feel Low Down 138-240-241-669-
   1225-1501
'Cause I'm In Love 525-1076
'Cause My Baby Says It's So 123-1134
Caution Blues 757 (see also BLUES IN
   THIRDS)
Cavalcade Of Boogie 947
Cavalerie 1260
Cavalleria Rusticana : Intermezzo
   (Mascagni) 1635
Cave Man Blues 1043
Cavernism 758-759
"C" Blues 135
C. C. Pill Blues 143
Cecilia 73-373-1498-1745
Celebratin' 974

Celery Stalks At Midnight 166-185
Celeste Blues 947
Celestial Express 652
Cell Bound Blues 1266
Celle qui est perdue 312-1348-1349
Cemetery Blues 750-1439
Central Avenue Breakdown 663
Central Limited Blues 1029
Central Tracks Blues 1025
C'est bouche a bouche 1639
C'est 'n aut' can-can, pays donc 1106
C'est Paris 1086-1173
C'est tout que j'ai 1743
Cette chanson est pour vous 1350
Chained To A Dream 75
Chain 'Em Down 555
Chain Gang 375
Chain Gang Blues 1094-1267-1717
Challenger Chop 907
Champagne Cocktail 24-1224
Champagne Lullaby 551
Champagne Waltz, The 291
Chances Are 1537
Change 1161
Changeable Daddy Of Mine 845
Change In Rhythm 1435
Change Partners 322-431
Changes 239-595-602-1580-1620-1682
Chanson Bohemienne 576
Chanson du Large, La 1349
Chansonette 469
Chant, The (1926) 268-410-720-1101-1182-
   1192-1590
Chant, The (1936) 1401-1403
Chantez-les Bas 1407
Chant In The Night 113
Chant Of Mustard Green 762
Chant Of The Groove 1637
Chant Of The Jungle 245-262-293-322-503-
   1598
Chant Of The Swamp 881
Chant Of The Tuxedos 27
Chant Of The Weed 935-1276-1279
Characteristic Blues 1427
Charleston 65-164-230-515-564-857-1260-
   1380-1498-1545-1547-1592-1680
Charleston Alley 97-434
Charleston Baby O' Mine 133-509-561-569-
   653-1745
Charleston Ball 559
Charleston Blues 642-1024
Charleston Cabin 226-227-264-772-796-884-
   886-1428-1591
Charleston, Charleston, Show Me The Way
   1363
Charleston Charlie/Charley 30-685-1723
Charleston Clarinet Blues 548-1555
Charleston Crazy 712
Charleston Dolly 1639
Charlestonette 1219-1681
Charleston Fever 1161
Charleston Geechie Dance 830
Charleston Hound 146-811-1534
Charleston Is The Best Dance After All 833
Charleston Mad 65-828-1215
Charleston Of The Evening 1502-1503
Charleston Rag 4
Charleston, South Carolina - see CHARLESTON
Charleston Stampede 1096
Charley, My Boy 226-227-558-715-890
Charlie's Home 982-1330
Charlie's Idea 782

1864

Charlie's Prelude  897
Charlie The Chiseller  874
Charlie The Chulo  135
Charlie Two-Step  158-1310
Charlie Was A Sailor  663
Charmaine  985
Charming Little Faker  163-297-449
Chasing All The Blues Away  774
Chasin' Chippies  1712
Chasing My Blues Away  775
Chasing Shadows  202-382-426-563-1248-1259
Chasing The Blues Away  1194
Chasing The Clouds Away  196
Chasin' With Chase  663
Chattanooga Blues  164
Chattanooga Choo-Choo  261-316-352-1361-
  1553
Chattanooga (Down In Tennessee)  712-713-
  1544
Chattanooga Man  707
Chattanooga Stomp  1166
Chatterbox  94-492-497
Chatterbox Rag  1586
Chauffeur's Shuffle  1241
Cheating  303
Cheatin' Cheech  1429-1717
Cheatin' Daddy  1321-1451
Cheating Only Blues  1455
Cheatin' On Me  128-215-230-231-264-317-
  541-861-987-1039-1253-1528-1591-1635-
  1643-174C
Check And Double Check  277
Checkin' Up On You  1528
Cheek To Cheek  160-382-639-701-1575
Cheerful Blues  1209-1340
Cheerful Little Earful  16-196-504-556-
  1303-1384
Cheer Up (Good Times Are Comin')  82-404
Cheer Up, Keep Smiling  982
Cheer Up, Kentucky  1118
Cheer Up, Liza  377
Cheese And Crackers  1596-1600
Chelsea Bridge  499
Cherie, I Love You  630-668
Cherokee  95-105-432-1116-1150
Cherry  57-134-369-618-692-820-1033-1501
Cherry Ball  1542
Cherry Hill Blues  1376
Cherry Picking Blues  353
Cherry Red  850
Chester's Choice  306
Chestnut Tree, The  1358
Chew-Chew-Chew (Your Bubble Gum)  1263-
  1279-1662
Chewed Up Grass  1575
Chez moi a six heures  1284
Chiapanecas, Las  743
Chica-Chica-Boom-Chic  374
Chicago  69-146-263-487-559-583-604-689-
  825-1086-1174-1185-1260-1434-1482-1523-
  1524
Chicago Back Step  1556
Chicago Blues  193-623-713-838-1066-1448
Chicago Bound Blues (Famous Migration
  Blues)  352-750-105o-1440
Chicago Breakdown  41-318
Chicago Buzz  327
Chicago Flip  1675
Chicago Gouge, The  91-1203
Chicago High Life  756
Chicago Honky-Tonk  1419

Chicago In Mind  27
Chicago Man Blues  852
Chicago Men Blues  1018
Chicago Mess Around  65
Chicago Mill Blues  1673
Chicago Moan Blues  1527
Chicago Monkey Man Blues  353-643-733
Chicago Policeman Blues  734
Chicago Rhythm  757-1075-1152-1496
Chicago Skiffle  1162
Chicago State Street Blues  1454
Chicago Stomp  149
Chicago Stomp Down  474
Chicago Tickle  1251
Chickabiddy Rag  117
Chickasaw Special  948
Chickasaw Stomp  310
Chick, Chick, Chick, Chick, Chicken (Lay
  A Little Egg For Me)  1135-1664
Chick-ee-Chick  374
Chicken Ain't Nothin' But A Bird, A  260-
  865
Chicken a la Swing  904
Chicken And Waffles  122
Chicken Chowder  1200
Chicken Gumboog(ie)  167
Chicken On The Apple  1288
Chicken Reel  384-428-938-1310-1432-1593
Chicken Rhythm  550
Chicken Supper Strut  1564
Chicken Tree  1675
Chicken Wilson Blues  1727
Chicks I Pick Are Slender And Tender And
  Tall, The  865
Chicks Is Wonderful  1540
Chico's Love Song  30-184
Chiffon Classique, Le  1221
Child Of A Disordered Brain  760
Chile/Chili Blues  301-1329-1555
Chili-Bomb-Bom  1609
Chili Con Conca  259
Chili Pepper  972
Chillen, Get Up  983-984
Chilly-Pom-Pom-Pee  653-867-1581
Chimes At The Meetin'  191
Chime(s) Blues  389-710-1007-1165-1673
Chimes In Blues  757
Chimin' The Blues  389
China Boy  64-85-114-152-154-270-384-542-
  543-554-586-597-607-635-676-745-755-821
  858-873-894-923-924-938-968-1032-1037-
  1143-1227-1228-1253-1256-1307-1434
  1537-1571-1572-1687-1726-1735-1736
China Clipper  787
China Girl  286-866
Chinaman Blues  1529
China Stomp - see CHINATOWN, MY CHINATOWN
Chinatown, My Chinatown  49-263-292-383-
  444-550-563-567-635-660-723-780-890-961
  1065-1140-1150-1248-1310-1335-1432-1435
Chinch, The  1097
Chin-Chin  315
Chinese Blues  315-719-806-1192-1391
Chinese Jumble  241
Chinese Laundry Blues  584-1315
Chinese Lullaby  469
Chinese Memories  396
Chinese Rag  1490
Ching  1319
Chinky Butterfly  1300
Chinnin' And Chattin' With May  776-1061

Chippin' Rock Blues 762
Chips' Blues 742
Chips' Boogie Woogie 742
Chiquita 950
Chiropractor Blues 1728
Chirping The Blues 793-795-1022-1510-1544
1728
Chiselin' 1419
Chitterlin' Strut 538
Chittlin' Switch Blues 550
Chizzlin' Sam 1708-1709
Chloe (Song Of The Swamp) 14-17-179-497-
501-600-601-730-742-896-1305-1562-1417-
1530-1535-1562-1566-1585-1614
Chocolate 215-990
Chocolate Avenue 1708
Chocolate Drops 648
Chocolate Shake 499
Chocolate To The Bone 823-824
Cho-King 410
Chong (He Come From Hong Kong) (sic) 1143
Choo-Choo 85-148-1070-1214-1377-1570-1688
1739
Choo Choo Blues 919-1466-1607-1672
Choo Choo (Gotta Hurry Home) 19-67-472-
623-890-1190-1354
Choo Choo Train 112
Choose Your Pal - see CRY
Chop Chop Charlie Chan 260-908
Chopinata 469
Chopin's Ghost 1412
Chopsticks 589-1435
Chris And His Gang 250-729
Christine 1175-1390
Christmas Man Blues 753
Christmas Morning Blues 1487
Christmas Night In Harlem 961-1689-1709
Christmas Swing 1642
Christopher Columbus (A Rhythm Cocktail)
366-466-553-597-601-702-728-755-899-960-
961-1278-1561-1628-1731
Chubby 155
Chuberry Jam 131
Chuck-Chuck-Chuckle Along 697
Church Bells Told, The 425
Church Mouse On A Spree 545-747-923
Church Street Sobbin' Blues 775-922-975-
1230-1532-1702
Cielito Lindo 325-969
Cigale et la fourmi, La 1563
Cigarette And A Silhouette, A 1158
Cincinnati Daddy 480
Cincinnati Southern Blues 1454
Cinderella Blues 134-1491-1694
Cinderella Brown 305-789
Cinderella's Fella 1601
Cinderella (Stay In My Arms) 1538
Cinderella's Wedding Day 1571
Cinders 1625
Cindy 1398
Cinquantaine, La 1360-1552
Circus Day In Dixie 1603
Ciribiribin 184-185-363-457-587-610-814-
815
City Called Heaven 168-186-283-299
City Night 829
C Jam Blues, The 499
Clam House 1330
Clap Hands ! Here Comes Charley/Charlie
30-96-106-232-462-561-624-719-927-1157-
1215-1478-1503-1659

Clap Yo' Hands 870-1310
Clara Blues 1453
Clarice 1209
Clarinet a la King 619
Clarinet Blues 547-1491
Clarinet Getaway 1161
Clarinet In A Haunted House 1047
Clarinetitis 592
Clarinet Jiggles 1713
Clarinet Lament 490-497
Clarinet Laughing Blues 681
Clarinet Marmalade 111-189-273-287-465-
467-468-508-513-571-605-647-720-724-
812-866-956-1007-1120-1132-1136-1146-
1176-1179-1287-1341-1410-1422-1566-
1637-1718
Clarinet Moan 629
Clarinetski 415
Clarinet Squawk 976
Clarinet Tickle 1390
Clarinet Wobble 413
Classical Spasm, A 1549
Classicanna 1420
Classic Rag 1221
Class Will Tell 95-1279-1538
Claxton Stomp 520
Clean Pickin' 1720
Clearing House Blues 733-1014-1448-1520
Clear Out Of This World 298
Clef Club March 315
Clef Club Stomp 694
Clementine (Folk-Song) 518
Clementine (From New Orleans) (1927)
238-533-578-626-1183-1564 -1593-1613
Clementine (1941) 499
Clickety-Clack Blues 1454
Climax Rag 802-1107
Climbin' And Screamin' 850
Climbing Mountain Blues 393
Climbing Up The Ladder Of Love 1611-
1664
Cling To Me 250-1312
Clipper, The 819
Clorinda 309-1651
Close Fit Blues 1083-1702-1705
Close Shave 896-897
Close To Five 901
Close To Me 439-879
Close Your Eyes 1204-1296
Closin' Hour Blues 947
Clothes Line Ballet 1625-1626
Cloud Castles 1642
Clouds 595-901-1259
Clouds Are Gwine To Roll Away, De (sic)
1058
Clouds In My Heart 134-486
Cloudy 898-899
Cloudy Skies 312
Clover Blossom Blues 1162-1523
Clownin' Around 209
Club House Swing 853
Coal Black Blues 58-1614-1699
Coal Black Mammy 170-1479
Coal Black Shine 114
Coal Oil Blues 1042
Coal River Blues 143
Coal-Yard Shuffle 1497
Cobble-Stones 238-1620-1665
Coburn Blues 665
Cocaine Dance 1721
Cocaine Habit Blues 1043

1866

Cock-a-Doodle, I'm Off My Noodle (My Baby's Back) 4-235-561-1246
Cockles And Mussels 385
Cocktails For Two 284-445-488-638-639-973-1421-1529-1531
Cocktail Swing 585
Cocoanut Grove 615-1736
Cocoanut Strut 1557
C. O. D. 1561
Co-Ed, The 32
Coffee And Cakes 417
Coffee In The Morning (Kisses In The Night) 159-1331
Coffee Pot Blues 1182
Coffin Blues 354
Cokey 594
Cold And Blue 354
Cold Black Ground Blues 353
Cold, Cold Winter 706
Cold, Cold Mamas (Burn Me Up) 72-716-797
Cold In Hand (Blues) 1442-1487
Cold Iron Walls 1091
Cold Morning Shout 1480
Cold Rocks Was My Pillow 1676
Cold Storage Papa (Mama's A Little Too Warm For You) 212
Cold Weather Papa 1051-1448
College Humor 321
College Medley 1119
College Rag, The 1161
College Rhythm 392
College Stomp 188
College Widow 786
Collegiana 1584-1641
Collegiate 73-129-231-534-1380-1498
Collegiate Fanny 913
Collegiate Love 1438-1667
Collegiate Sam 867-1394-1638
Collegiate Stomp 558
Colonel Bogey March 518
Colorado Sunset 759
Color Of Your Eyes, The 879
Columbo 1426
Comanche War Dance 96-185-1150
Come A Little Closer 1035
Come Along 799
Come And Get It 297-816-843-1637
Come And Have A Cuddle On The Common 1128
Come Around The Corner 1323
Come Around To My House 1679
Come Back Daddy And Ease My Aching Heart 1012
Come Back Dear 1617
Come Back, Sweet Papa 40-366-1656
Come Be My Love 911
Come Day, Go Day 631
Come Down To Earth, My Angel 1636
Come Easy Go Easy 783
Come Easy, Go Easy Love 316
Come From It 1123
Come Get Me Papa, Before I Faint 285
Come Home, Daddy 569
Come Home Papa Blues 1010-1092
Come, Josephine, In My Flying Machine 1314
Come On And Do Your Red Hot Business 1504
Come On And Stomp, Stomp, Stomp 414
Come On, Baby 177-575-654-723-949-1155-1293-1665-1675-1744
Come On Coot Do That Thing 1729
Come On Home 793-953-1607-1705
Come On In, Baby 1045

Come On, Mama, Do That Dance 1527
Come On Over 1364
Come On, Red 884-1067
Come On 'Round To My House, Baby 886
Come On With The Come-On 260
Come Out, Come Out, Wherever You Are 67
Come Right In 352
Comes Love 323-432-612-815-1316-1405
Come To Me 884
Come To The Fair 969
Come Up And See Me Sometime 464-1654
Comin' 'nd Going 724
Comin' Back 897
Comin' In Home 761
Coming Of Hi-De-Ho, The 1646
Comin' On 1403
Comin' On With The Come On 1053
Coming-Out Party 109
Comin' Thro' The Rye 326-444-1224-1342
Commanderism 1
Common Street Blues 1375
Community Blues 1363
Community Swing 1063
Companionate Blues 1223
Complainin' 372-1490
Complainin' (It's Human Nature To Complain) 1573
Compton Ave. Blues (sic) 1648
Concentrating 1468
Concentratin' (On You) 76-160-249-251
Concerto For Clarinet 1408
Concerto For Cootie 490-496
Concerto For Trumpet 815
Concerto For Two 151-1513-1553
Concerto No. 1 in B flat minor for Piano and Orchestra (Tchaikovsky, Op. 23) 743
Conchita 261
Coney Island 1415
Coney Island Washboard 530-993
Confessin' (That I Love You) 47-57-398-404-528-567-584-614-660-890-1249-1258-1408-1427-1509-1602
Confessin' The Blues 591-1038
Confession (Confessin') Blues 1069
Confidential Blues 352
Confidentially 1560
Conga Brava 496-497
Conga del Moaxo 98
Congaine 401
Congo 258
Congo Caravan 1074
Congo Conga, The 258
Congo Love Song 410-971
Congratulate Me 392
Congratulations 421-969-979
Congratulations Waltz 512
Conjure Man Blues 643
Connie's Got Connections In Connecticut 1317
Considerin' 31
Consider Yourself Kissed 98
Consolation 689
Consolation Blues 212-736
C.O.N.S.T.A.N.T.I.N.O.P.L.E. 653-1581
Constantly 288-686
Construction Gang 212
Contact 944
Contented 1238
Continental, The 22-879-1258-1349
Contrasts 433
Coochi-Coochi-Coo 1662

Coo-Coo-Coo, Le 1642
Coo Coo Stomp 1125
Coo, Dinny, Coo 1125
Cooking Breakfast For The One I Love 246-
 377-672-805-932
Cooks In Trinidad, The 778
Cool Can Blues 1458
Cool Kind Daddy Blues 310
Cool Kind Papa 1414
Cool Papa (You'd Better Warm Up) 1046
Coon Band Contest, A 538-549-1197-1198-
 1199-1254-1256-1473-1474
Coon Can Rag 971
Coon Jim 1370
Coon Town Capers 1049
Coon Town Caravan 387
Cootie Crawl, The 686-953-1089-1525
Cootie For Your Tootie 1090
Cootie's Concerto - see CONCERTO FOR
 COOTIE
Cootie Stomp 1039-1494
Copenhagen 23-37-121-228-293-398-416-445
 529-543-545-546-716-759-797-803-805-
 1130-1225-1348-1364-1366-1392-1399-1403
 1501-1574-1591-1741
Copper Blues 1127-1293
Copper Colored Gal 258-585-676-780-1629
Coppin' A Plea 912
Copyin' Louis 1256
Copyright 1950 1374
Coquette 58-155-330-367-419-469-501-691-
 730-896-897-960-986-1038-1147-1412-1511
 k684-1733-1735
Coral Sea 298
Corina. I'm Goin' Away 886
Co(r)rin(n)e'Cor(r)in(n)â 254-291-584-
 779-823-1003-1144-1531-1542
Corky (Stomp) 898-899
Corn And Bunion Blues 811
Corn Bread Wiggle 1557
Cornet Chop Suey 40
Cornet Omelet 565
Cornet Pleading Blues 328
Cornfed 568-722-738-1056-1138-1289-1483-
 1589-1620-1675
Cornfed Cal 874
Corn On The Cob 387
Corn Pickin' 386-1512
Corn Silk 617
Corny Rhythm 1720
Coronado (Brings Memories Of You) 1497
Coronado Nights 1173-1505
Corrigan Hop 589-787-1411
Cosi Cosa 701
Cosmics 275
Cosmoitis 1202
Cottage By The Moon 1002
Cottage For Sale, A 195
Cottage In The Rain 1634
Cotton 293-490-967-1074
Cotton Belt Blues 1060
Cotton Blossoms 538-549-1254-1473
Cotton Club Stomp 479-481-494-1021
Cotton Pickers' Ball 713-857-970-1056
Cotton Pickers' Congregation 24
Cotton Pickers' Scat 1035
Cotton Pickers' Shuffle 557
Cotton Tail 496-497
Cottonwood Corners 298
Cou-Cou 1262
Could Be 296-1298-1358

Could Be You 534
Could I ? I Certainly Could 233-967-1098
 1300-1583
Couldn't Hear Nobody Pray 188
Could You Pass In Love ? 609-1357
Count, The 619-902-1111
Count Basically, The 209
Counterpoint a la mode 923
Countin' The Blues 1266
Counting The Days (1921) 798
Counting The Days (1927) 1378-1616
Counting The Hours 796
Countless Blues 873
Count Me In 1553
Count Me Out 986
Country Boy 694
Country Boy Blues 853
Country Bred And Chicken Fed 1737
Country Farm Blues, The 570-1091
Country Gal 495
Country Gardens 1371
Country Girl Like You, A 1503
Country Spaces 995
Country Woman's Blues 861
Count's Idea, The 95
Count Steps In, The 102
County Jail Blues 1542
Courthouse Blues 1449
Courthouse Bump 1103
Courtoie, Le 312
Cousin To Chris 741
Covered Wagon Days 71-1663
Cover Me Up With Sunshine (And Feather My
 Nest With Love) 577
Cover Me Up With The Sunshine Of Virginia
 225-576-1581
Cow Bell Blues 1182
Cow Bells 221
Cowboy From Brooklyn 430-444
Cowboy In Manhattan 1047
Cowboy Serenade, The 911
Cow Cow Blues 65-278-373-389-390-1246-
 1378-1753
Crab House Blues 1168
Crab's Crawl 632
Crackerjack Stomp 1194
Cradle Of Love 243
Crap Shootin' Blues 643
Crap Shootin' Papa, Mama Done Caught Your
 Dice 941
Crashin' Through 386
Crave, The 1106-1107
Craving 797-1389-1478
Cravin' A Man Blues 570
Craving Blues 1650
Crawdad Blues 1109
Crawl, The 1182
Crawley Blues 357
Crawley Clarinet Moan 357
Crawlin' Spider Blues 516
Craze-0-Logy 541
Crazy 'Bout My Gal 1081
Crazy 'Bout My Lollipop 178
Crazy About My Rider 843
Crazy Blues 5-215-387-633-1178-1351-1423
 1425-1460-1492-1678-1710
Crazy Bone Rag 1578
Crazy Chords (Rag) 1104-1106
Crazy Feet 61-788-1127
Crazy Over Daddy 953
Crazy People 35-158-464-875-1388

1868
Crazy Pirouette 952
Crazy Quilt 134-266-267-359-412-625-928-
1545-1570
Crazy Rhythm 333-469-571-615-649-660-690-
819-871-1008-1016-1069-1087-1150-1493-
1501-1661
Crazy Strings 1642
Crazy Valves 584
Crazy Words - Crazy Tune_ 235-236-344-826-
1593-1619-1662
Creaking Old Mill On The Creek, The 207
Cream Puff 1147-1399
Creeper, The 472
Creepy Feeling 1106
Creepy Weepy 644
Creole 1289
Creole Belles 154-332-971-1049-1198-1200-
1254-1474-1475
Creole Blues 1208-1506
Creole Love Call 3-253-279-381-473-485-
747
Creole Lullaby 1433
Creole Rhapsody 484
Creole Stomp 67
Crepe Hanger Blues 1094
Crepuscule 1262
Crescendo In Blue 492
Crescendo In Drums 259-1465
Crime Don't Pay 848
Crocodile, The 1274
Crooked Notes 1206
Crooked World Blues 1644
Crooning 1479
Croonin' A Tune 1180
Croonin' The Blues 1456
Cross Country Hop 786-1356
Cross Country Jump
Cross-Eyed Kelly (From Penn-Syl-Van-Eye-
Ay) 699
Cross My Heart, Mother, I Love You 1588
Cross Patch 93-191-366-382-1249-1628
Cross Roads 241-420
Cross Street Swing 1195
Cross Tie Blues 211
Cross Word Mama (You're Puzzling Me) 1206
Cross Word Papa (You Sure Do Puzzle Me)
1058
Crossword Puzzle Blues 547
Cross Words Between My Sweetie And Me 966
Cross Your Heart 1407-1520
Crow Jane Woman 355
Cruel Back Bitin' Blues (A Heart Aching
Chant) 110-1010
Cruel Daddy Blues 1719
Cruel Mama Blues 461
Cruel Papa Blues 397
Cruel Papa, But A Good Man To Have Around
1376
Cruel Woman 762
Cry 970
Cry Baby 266
Cry Baby Blues 280-1162-1575
Cry, Baby, Cry 321-1315
Crying All Day 1089-1567
Crying And Sighing 1033
Cryin' Blues 358
Crying For Love 827-1320
Crying For My Used-To-Be 1396
Cryin' For The Carolines 21-195-395-638-
789-838-932-1153-1234-1283-1369
Cryin' For The Moon 134-664

Crying For You 837
Cryin' In My Sleep 1746
Cryin' Mood 894-1630-1659-1710
Crying My Blues Away 628-1744
Crying My Heart Out For You 1659
Crying Myself To Sleep 196-980
Crying My Soul Out For You 1736
Crying To The Moon 673
Cryin' Won't Make Me Stay 1038
Cuban Boogie Woogie 95-829-902-1752
Cubanita 1461
Cuban Moon 1603
Cuban Pete 45-384
Cuban Swing 385
Cuban Villa Blues 1378
Cucaracha, La 52
Cuckoo 1180
Cuckoo Blues 1209
Cuckoo Cuckoo Chicken Rhythm 1355
Cuckoo In The Clock 611-952-1159
Cuddles And Kisses 229
Cuddle Up 969
Cuddle Up A Little Closer 19-505-1236-
1540
Cuddle Up Blues 825-1185-1606
Cuddle Up Close, It's Winter Time 1577
Cuddle Up, Huddle Up 284
Cu-Kee-Ukee-Ute 1389
Cumparsita, La 1477
Cupid's Nightmare 260
Cup Of Coffee, A Sandwich And You, A
274-870-1285-1300-1484
Curse Of An Aching Heart, The 969-1629
Cushion Foot Stomp 411-1014-1701
Cute Little Flat 31-949
Cute Little Wigglin' Dance 544
Cutest Kid In Town, The 1470
Cutie 141-1085
Cutie Blues 1529
Cut Off My Legs And Call Me Shorty 57
Cut Throat Blues 1021
Cuttin' 'Em Slow 1673
Cuttin' The Boogie 851
Cutting The Cake (A Wedding Fox Trot)
1613
Cuttin' The Campus 896
Cuttin' Up 782 (see also LAZY BLUES)
Cut Yourself A Piece Of Cake 914
Cypress Grove Blues 1541
Cyril's Blues 141

Dad 156
Da Da Blues 213
Da-Da-Da 799-982
Da-Da-Da My Darling 1162
Dad Blame Blues 1263
D A D Blues 412
Daddy 151-818
Daddy Be Careful 755
Daddy Blues 792
Daddy, Change Your Mind 436-1725
Daddy, Come Back 735
Daddy Do 805-1656
Daddy, Don't Put That Thing On Me Blues
1452
Daddy, Don't You Try To Pull That Two-
Time Thing On Me 1589
Daddy Ease It To Me 110-750
Daddy, Ease This Pain Of Mine 1013
Daddy Goodbye Blues 1268
Daddy Let Me Lay It On You 1677

Daddy's Boy 295
Daddy, What You Going To Do ? 1471
Daddy, Won't You Please Come Home ? 671-751-1355
Daddy, You Got Everything 412
Daddy, You're A Low Down Man 412
Daddy, Your Mama Is Lonesome For You 1461
Daddy, You've Been A Mother To Me 1318
Daddy, You've Done Put That Thing On Me 343
Dad's Ole Mule 1577
Dago Hill Blues 1065
Dah's Gwineter Be Er Landslide (sic) 141
Daisy Bell 1314
Dakota 1426
Dallas Blues 46-291-548-652-704-740-858-861-898-958-1001-1392-1430-1517-1558
Dallas Doings 488
Dallas Man (Lost Lover Blues) 1676
Dallas Stomp 133
Dames 699
Damper Down Blues 1268
Damp Weather 863
Dance And Grow Thin 1516
Dance Away Your Blues 1127-1293
Dance Hall Shuffle 694
Dance Henry 805
Dance, Little Lady 469
Dance Mad 193
Dance Of The Blue Danube 566
Dance Of The Blue Devils 182-183
Dance Of The Candy Fairy - see NUTCRACKER SUITE
Dance Of The Doinks 1117
Dance Of The Flowers - see NUTCRACKER SUITE
Dance Of The Goon 766
Dance Of The Hours (Ponchielli) 321
Dance Of The Lame Duck, The 288
Dance Of The Octopus 1156
Dance Of The Reed Flutes - see NUTCRACKER SUITE
Dance Of The Wooden Shoes 1294
Dance-O-Mania 675-1748
Dance They Call The Georgia Hunch, The 1698
Dance With A Dolly (With A Hole In Her Stocking) 1250-1397
Dance Your Blues Away 1080
Dancing An American Rag 1516
Dancing And Dreaming 798
Dancing Blues 137-320
Dancin' Dan 140-560-1189-1641
Dancing Dave 12
Dancing Deacon, The 379-513
Dancing Dogs 1073
Dancing Eyes 1046
Dancing Fool 69-220-336-1086
Dancin' For A Dime 387
Dancing In The Dark 9-743-1385-1408
Dancing In The Moonlight 423-937-1235
Dancing On A Dime 325
Dancing On The Beach 550
Dancing On The Stars 766
Dancing Shadows 1292
Dancing Shoes 1127-1293
Dancing Tambourine 144-468
Dancing The Blues 1130-1218
Dancing The Devil Away 1612
Dancing Time 789
Dancing Under The Stars 59

Dancing With A Debutante 182-1116
Dancing With My Shadow 425
Dancing With Tears In My Eyes 1225-1294-1599
Danger In The Dark 95
Danger ! (Look Out For That Gal) 1562
Danger, Love At Work 545-1249
Dangerous Blues 280-413-860-1178-1352-1461-1522-1525
Daniel's Blues 553
Daniels In The Lion's Den 387
Dans la vie, faut pas s'en faire 1085
Dan The Back Door Man 1677
Danza Lucumi 1407
Danzon 904
Daphne 776-1261-1284-1476
Dapper Dan 380-781-1352-1613
Dardanella 122-132-289-386-647-747-976-1027-1076-1147-1265-1334-1506-1684
Dark Alley (Blues) 862-1021
Dark And Cloudy Blues 770
Dark Avenue 96
Dark Clouds 12
Dark Eyes (Les Yeux Noirs) 440-457-588-1253-1262-1334-1371-1512-1540-1635-1647 (often shown as BLACK EYES)
Darkies' Spring Song 1254-1255
Dark Gal Blues 872
Dark Man (You Ain't Gonna Darken My Life) 643
Darkness 758
Darkness On The Delta 199
Dark Night 1383
Dark Rapture 104
Darktown Flappers' Ball, The 190-1462
Darktown Has A Gay White Way 712
Darktown Jubilee 1713
Darktown Reveille 666-826
Darktown Shuffle 271-318-517-1377
Darktown Strutters' Ball (The) 159-169-177-341-378-386-388-430-465-469-512-526-595-604-621-686-790-701-868-938-955-1087-1114-1175-1225-1227-1249-1343-1346-1365-1410-1429-1432-1516-1635-1657-1658-1673-1689
Darling 884
Darling, How Can You Forget So Soon ? 1317
Darling, How You Lied 299
Darling, je vous aime beaucoup 1211-1350
Darling Nellie/Nelly Gray 54-184-1512
Darling, Not Without You 14-182-1399-1415
Darned Blues 285
Darn That Dream 107-214-448-614
Daughter Of The Latin Quarter 1427
Daughter Of The Old Grey Mare, The 587
Davenport Blues 115-126-304-445-994-1087-1138-1147-1332
Davis Street Blues 1578
Dawning 237-238-1196-1612-1695
Dawn Of Day Blues 846
Dawn Of Tomorrow 455
Dawn On The Desert 447-895-897
Dawn Patrol 422
Day After Day 1403
Daybreak 275-436-454-455-820
Day Break Blues (Original Bugle Blues) 164-645-1135
Daybreak Express 488

Day Breakin' Blues 1486
Day By Day 798-1230
Day-Dream 425-766
Day-Dreaming 818-912
Day-Dreaming (All Night Long) 973-1158
Day Dreams 424-699
Daydreams Come True At Night 1250
Day Dreams That Never Come True 506
Day I Let You Get Away, The 439-968-1415
Day In, Day Out 371-447-495-1405-1530
Daylight Saving Blues 645
Daylight's Breaking Blues 547
Days Of '49 841
Days Of Yesterday 565
Day That I Met You, The 1664
Day Without You, A 1751
Day You Came Along, The 688
D. C. Rag 1727
Deacon Bite-'Em-In-The-Back 213
Deacon Jazz 1564
Deacon's Prayer, The 1454
Dead Drunk Blues 846-1065-1268-1618
Dead End Blues 1372
Dead Man Blues 709-1101-1167-1564-1678
Deal Yourself Another Hand 213-214
Dear Almanzoer 302
Dearborn Street Breakdown 66-1749
Dear, Dear, What Can The Matter Be ? - see
   OH DEAR, WHAT CAN THE MATTER BE ?
Dearest Darling 1413
Dearest, Darest I ? 167
Dear Eyes That Haunt Me 1612
Dear Heart 1110
Dearie 1108
Dear Li'l Pal 1424
Dearly Beloved 623-744
Dear Old Donegal 375
Dear Old Girl 1720
Dear Old Mother Dixie 76
Dear Old Pal Of Mine 299
Dear Old Southland 7-47-64-113-295-488-
   498-595-596-606-690-691-765-837-1027-
   1048-1140-1195-1427-1647-1726
Dear, On A Night Like This 648-722-1378
Dear One 72-1591-1663-1664
Death Bell Blues 393
Death Cell Blues 846
Death House Blues 846
Death In B flat 1528
Death Letter Blues 353-355-643-1093-1449
Death Ray Boogie 851
Death Sting Me Blues 1014
Decameron Stomp 944
Decatur Street Blues (The) 280-1461-1698-
   1719
Decatur Street Drag 983
Decatur Street Tutti 1456
Decca Stomp 1156
Deceitful Blues 182-810-859-1727
Deceitful Woman Blues 847
Deck Hand Blues 1240
Dedicated To You 440-526-899
Dedication 691
Dedication (To Eddie Lang) 683
Dee Blues 312
'Deed I Do 96-126-166-268-277-443-641-943
   1109-1225-1231-1232-1279-1425
Deedle-De-Dum 528
Deedle Deedle Dum 1185
Deep Blue 61
Deep Blue Melody 7

Deep (Blue) Sea Blues 355-529-624-966-
   1448
Deep Creek 1103
Deep Down In My Soul 1451
Deep Down In The Miz 832
Deep Down South 117
Deep Elem Blues 1490
Deep Elm (You Tell 'Em I'm Blue) 211-
   534-546-967-1082-1236-1545-1588-1694
Deep Fives 947
Deep Forest 758-759-760-1689
Deep Harlem 583-1081-1570
Deep Henderson 24-194-265-339-546-928-
   1006-1167-1182-1210-1216-1436-1510-
   1524-1739
Deep Hollow 269-553-1127-1202
Deep In A Dream 163-259-369-1403
Deep In The Arms Of Love 18
Deep In The Blues 108-910
Deep In The Heart Of Texas 364
Deep In The Heart Of The South 526
**Deep Jungle 1235**
Deep Minor Rhythm 845
Deep Moaning Blues 1268
Deep Morgan Blues 181
Deep Night 243-448-506-627-741-1292-
   1743
Deep Purple 323-431-589-1404-1530
Deep River 452-1633-1635
Deep River Blues 272-402-733-884-1160-
   1227-1468
Deep Sea Blues 1471
Deep Sea Diver 893
Deep Second Street Blues 1113
Deep Shadows 1562
Deep South 155
Deep Trouble 1153
Deep Water Blues 1550
Deep Wide Ocean Blues, The 1097
Definition Of Swing 787-1245
Delayed Action 1412
Delhia 628
Delightful Delirium 1404
Delilah 268-1182
Delirious Rag 1549
Delirium 237-304-519-870-903-1138-1324
Delishious 34
Deliver Me To Tennessee 744-912
Delmar Avenue 847
Del Mar Rag 1511
Delta Bottom Blues 1499
Delta Bound 200-486-783-1031-1154
Delta Land Blues 1561
Delta Mood 1712
Delta Serenade 488-587
Demi-Tasse 134
Dem Knock-Out Blues (sic) 1462
Denison Swing 661
Dentist And The Lady, The 874
Dentist Chair Blues 191-1026
Denver Stomp 1193
Depression Stomp 1645
Derbytown 676
Dere's Jazz In Dem Dere Horns (sic) 348-
   1433-1656
Derniere Bergere, La 1349
Derniere Chanson 1350
Desdemona 73-232-998-1579
Dese Dem Dose 425-426
Dese Men Don't Mean You No Good 1641
Desert Blues 344-806-1130-1218-1299-1328

Desert Dreams  60
Deserted Blues  1730
Deserted Desert  1412
Deserted Farm, A  1406
Desert Star  684
Design For Dancing  322
Desperate Blues  1465
Destroyin' Blues  1026
Detroit Blues  1216
Detroit Moan  1489
Deuces Wild  1408-1555
Deux cigarettes dans l'ombre - see TWO
  CIGARETTES IN THE DARK
Deux pieds gauches  333
Devil Dance Blues  1618
Devil In The Moon  257-866-1304-1530
Devil In The Woodpile  948
Devil Is Afraid Of Music, The  293-790
Devilish Blues  852
Devil May Care  433-449-615-1540
Devil Sat Down And Cried, The  215-818
Devil's Gonna Get You  1445
Devil's Holiday  281-1245
Devil's Kitchen  132
Devil's Serenade  318
Devil With The Devil  323
Devotion  690
Devoting My Time To You  1659
Dew Drop Alley Stomp  1578
Dexter Blues  1038
Diane  650
Diane (I'm In Heaven When I See You Smile)
  335-468-702-1290
Dickie's Dream  106
Dicky Bird Told Me So, A  1292-1675
Dicky Wells Blues  1670
Dicty Blues  582-711
Dicty Glide, The  478
Did An Angel Kiss You (The Day You Were
  Born)  206-295
Did Anyone Ever Tell You ?  631-1630
Did I Remember ?  122-439-767-1415
Didn't I Tell You (That You'd Come Back)
  20-63-812-1226-1291
Did You Ever See A Dream Walking ?  1227-
  1331
Did You Mean It ? (1927)  533-1290-1378-
  1567-1584-1610
Did You Mean It ? (1936)  14-93-599-795-
  1179-1416
Different Way Blues  1449
Diga Diga Doo  8-369-475-477-487-528-595-
  601-764-800-949-1075-1076-1292-1333-
  1406-1436-1501-1554-1558-1572-1711
Digah's Stomp, The  1622
Dig Down Deep  454
Diggin' For Dex  108
Dig It (I Ain't Hep To That Step, But
  I'll Dig It)  62-185-944
Dig Me, Honey  325
Dill Pickles (Rag)  303-397-1341-1429
Dilly Dally  699
Diminuendo In Blue  492
Dina  706
Dinah  47-75-85-87-102-159-163-254-279-
  345-348-360-383-384-425-461-462-485-546
  576-581-589-599-636-652-662-664-687-707
  719-755-756-789-791-798-801-885-937-941
  957-965-989-1141-1150-1223-1249-1258-
  1262-1274-1298-1334-1346-1410-1425-1432
  1433-1476-1481-1484-1570-1597-1626-1646
  1650-1654-1661-1670-1697-1700-1716

Dinah Lou  13-490-1074-1146
Dinah's In A Jam  493-945
Dinette - see DINAH
Ding-Dong Blues  1110
Dinner And Dance  279-1224
Dinner For One, Please James  382-1307-
  1350
Dinner For The Duchess  1004
Dinner Music For A Pack Of Hungry
  Cannibals  1342-1372
Dipper Mouth Blues  53-322-426-1064-1065-
  1165-1481 (see also SUGAR FOOT STOMP)
Dipsy Doodle, The  443-554-587-745-1660
Dip Your Brush In The Sunshine  958-1469
Dirty Blues  1083
Dirty, Dirty, Dirty  1108
Dirty Dog  306-1079
Dirty Dozens, The  104-391-824-1105-1246-
  1375
Dirty Dozen's Cousins  1044
Dirty Ground Hog Blues  389
Dirty Guitar Blues  942
Dirty Hands ! Dirty Face !  70
Dirty Hot  575
Dirty Mistreater  462
Dirty Mistreating Blues  636
Dirty Moaner Blues  627
Dirty No Gooder's Blues  1446
Dirty Rag  188
Dirty Snake  865
Dirty T. B. Blues  1488
Dirty Woman('s) Blues  1010-1487
Disappointed Blues  1400
Disappointed In Love  759
Disaster  1021
Discarded Blues  501
Discontented Blues  1131
Discord Rag  1038
Discouraged Blues  709
Disgusted Blues  1458-1487
Dishrag Blues  1729
Dismal Dan  1256
Dispossessin' Me  1708
Dissatisfied Blues  141-1378
Dissonance  1052
Distant Moan  1040
Distraction  1284
Dites-moi quand meme  827
Divertissement  536
Divine Beguine  1284
Dixiana  1383-1418
Dixie  468-487-1470
Dixie After Dark  1432
Dixie Belles  648
Dixie Blues  458-975-1725
Dixie Dawn  419
Dixie Doorway  255
Dixie Drag  1046
Dixie Dreams  1459
Dixie Flyer Blues  1442
Dixie Flyer Sam  1129
Dixie Girl  1199-1200-1250
Dixie Is Dixie Once More  513-1522
Dixie Isn't Dixie Any More  285
Dixie Jamboree  1302
Dixie Jass Band One-Step - see ORIGINAL
  DIXIELAND ONE-STEP
Dixieland Band, The  23-365-595-1340-
  1530
Dixieland Detour  432
Dixieland Doin's  1209
Dixieland Is Happy Land  675-1748

Dixieland Shuffle  123-366
Dixieland Stomp  1039
Dixie Lee  200-290-936-1154-1585
Dixie Moon  713-1424
Dixie Stomp  530-1714
Dixie Vagabond  253
Dizzy Corners  1740
Dizzy Debutante  75
Dizzy Glide  565
Dizzy Lizzy  1208
Dizzy Lou  407
Dizzy Spells  607-608
Djangology  1259-1284
Django Rag  1284
D Natural Blues  723
Doc'oligy  376
Doctor Blues  1345
Dr. Heckle And Mr. Jibe  422-423-424-593
Doctor Jazz  739-1101-1167-1286
Dr. Livingstone, I Presume ?  1407
Doctor Rhythm  321-429-1126
Doctor Sausage Blues  1355
Dr. Watson And Mr. Holmes  1486
Do De O Do (or DOH-DE-OH-DOH)  535-586
Dodgers' Fan Dance  818
Dodging A Divorcee  23-534-889-1689
Dodgin' My Man  538
Dodgin' The Dean  322
Do Dirty Blues  753
Do-Do-Do  668-1749
Do Do Lady  210
Does My Baby Love Me ? (Nobody But Me)
   1514
Does My Sweetie Do - And How !  861
Does She Love Me ?-Positively-Absolutely -
   see POSITIVELY, ABSOLUTELY
Does Your Heart Beat For Me ?  466
Dog And Cat  1647
Dog Bottom  868
Doggin' Around  103
Doggin' Blues  1069
Doggin' Me  169
Doggin' Me Blues  569
Doggin' Me Mama Blues  143
Doggin' That Thing  1227
Doggin' The Dog  1575
Doggone Blues  735
Doggone, I've Done It !  158-936
Doggone My Good Luck Soul  785
Dog On The Piano  32
Dogtown Blues  367
Do ? (Do I-Do I Love Her ?)  120
Do I Care ? No, No  260
Do I Hear You Saying (I Love You)  1685
Do I Know What I'm Doing ?  1281-1652
Do I Love You ?  207-741-1406
Doin' That Thing  1455
Doin' The Campus Crawl  521
Doin' The Frog  474
Doing The Dooga  637
Doing The Gorgonzola  1238
Doin' The Jive  1063
Doin' The Jug Jug  1210
Doin' The New Low-Down  189-240-348-475-
   487-571-646-764-949-960-1076-1080-1083-
   1222-1277-1340-1670
Doing The Prom.  1124
Doin' The Raccoon  575-650-1117-1475
Doing The Reactionary  258-787
Doin' The Rhumba  253
Doin' The Serpentine  1249

Doin' The Shake  1072
Doin' The Suzie-Q  39-702-1271
Doin' The Uptown Lowdown  77-1600-1669
Doin' The Voom Voom  477-494
Doin' Things  789-790-1596-1597-1598-1602
Doin' What I Please  1277
Doin' You Good  1392
Doinya  820
Do I Really Deserve It From You ?  1124
Do It Again  68-132-259-432-1086-1678
Do It A Long Time, Papa  860-1532
Do It, Baby  731-1704
Do It If You Wanna  1203
Do It, Mr. So-and-So  734-1463
Do I Worry ?  316-452-1552
Do Lawd Do  354-1230
Dolimite (sic)  433-692
Dollar Blues  1007
Doll Dance, The  144-1552
Doll's House, The  952
Dolly (I Love You)  1177
Dolly Mine  1345
Dolores  208-364-452-694-817-1584
Do Me A Favor  1624-1626
Dominick Swing  759
Donegal Cradle Song  792
Done Made A Fool Out Of Me  845
Done Sold My Soul To The Devil (And My
   Heart's Done Turned To Stone)  1448
Done Throwed The Key Away  1061
Donkey Serenade, The  588-1326-1404
Donkey Want Water, De (sic)  164
Donna Maria  434
Don't Advertise Your Man  733-1448
Don't Agitate Me Blues  964
Don't Ask Any Questions  938
Don't Be A Fool, You Fool  339
Don't Be Afraid To Tell Your Mother  93-
   426
Don't Be Angry With Me  266-577-808-1017-
   1420-1655
Don't Be Blue, Little Pal, Don't Be Blue
   743
Don't Be Cruel To A Vegetabuel  1355
Don't Be Like That  241-502-579-658-670-
   1292
Don't Be Mad At Me  1668
Don't Be So Unkind, Baby  507-1335
Don't Be Surprised  907
Don't Be That Way  78-107-430-607-608-661
   1125-1658-1659-1734
Don't Blame Me  66-152-299-315-354-674-
   1653-1734
Don't Break Down  151
Don't Bring Lulu  568-966-1591
Don't Bring Me Posies (It's Shoesies I
   Need)  119-468-1352-1672
Don't Call Me Boy  373
Don't Care Blues  1460
Don't Come Cryin' On My Shoulder  865
Don't Come Over  852
Don't Count Your Kisses (Before You're
   Kissed)  182-1032
Don't Cross Your Fingers, Cross Your Heart
   588
Don't Cry, Baby  694-1446
Don't Cry, Baby (Cry-Baby, Don't Cry)  240
Don't Cry, Cherie  743-817-911
Don't Cry, Frenchy, Don't Cry  1747
Don't Cry, Honey  327
Don't Cry, My Heart  1374

Don't Cut Off Your Nose To Spite Your Face 1576
Don't Dally With The Devil (Too Long) 80
Don't Dog Me 'Round 1069
Don't Do It, Darling 300
Don't Do That To The Poor Puss Cat 1117-1355
Don't Drink It In Here 831
Don't Ever Change 441-1002-1028-1400
Don't Fail On Me, Bones 169
Don't Fall Asleep 1406
Don't Fish In My Sea 1267
Don't Fool Around With Me 1452
Don't Forget It 849
Don't Forget To Mess Around (When You Do The Charleston) 41-63-795
Don't Forget To Remember 1663
Don't Forget To Say "No," Baby 264-276-1398
Don't Forget When The Summer Rolls By 738
Don't Forget You'll Regret Day By Day 716-833-1090
Don't Get Around Much Any More 299-496 (see also NEVER NO LAMENT)
Don't Get Sentimental With Me, Baby 204
Don't Get Tired 333
Don't Give All The Lard Away 409
Don't Give It Away 404
Don't Give Me That Jive 1637
Don't Give Up The Ship 203-437-1307
Don't Give Up Your Old Love 1323
Don't Have To Sing The Blues 849
Don't Jive Me 43
Don't Keep Me In The Dark, Bright Eyes 502-506
Don't Know And Don't Care (Blues) 522-1041-1051
Don't Know If I'm Comin' Or Goin' 258-768-1585
Don't Know What I'll Do 834
Don't Know Why 540
Don't Leave Me 1253
Don't Leave Me Blues 1424
Don't Leave Me, Daddy 336-570
Don't Leave Me, Mammy 68
Don't Leave Me Now 215
Don't Let It Bother You 424-425-1624-1626
Don't Let It Get You Down 166
Don't Let It Happen Again 291
Don't Let Julia Fool Ya 168
Don't Let Old Age Creep Up On You 1311
Don't Let That Moon Get Away 94
Don't Let The Rhythm Go To Your Head 729
Don't Let Us Say Goodbye 551
Don't Let Your Love Come Down 1060-1355
Don't Let Your Love Go Wrong 12-159-581-774-878-937-1206
Don't Let Your Mouth Start Nothing Your Head Won't Stand 852
Don't Look Now 9-323-428
Don't Lose It 1481
Don't Lose Your Head And Put Your Hands On Me 1323
Don't Love Me 939
Don't Love No Married Man 1489
Don't Make A Dog Out Of Me 686
Don't Make Me Laugh (With Tears In My Eyes) 1397

Don't Make Sweet Mama Mad 1108
Don't Mean You No Good Blues 1023
Don't Mention Love To Me 1551
Don't Mess Around With Me 1076-1083
Don't Mess With Me 686-1050-1462
Don't Mind The Rain 226-377-561-1581
Don't Mistreat Your Good Boy Friend 192
Don't Name It 1038
Don't Never Figure 1013
Don't Never Tell Nobody (What Your Good Man Can Do) 860-1447
Don't Pan Me (When I'm Gone) 792-824-1185
Don't Play Me Cheap 51
Don't Pose As A Saint 953
Don't Put That Thing 1320
Don't Put Yourself On The Spot 1674
Don't Save Your Love (For A Rainy Day) 545-1552
Don't Say Goodbye 1471
Don't Shake It No More 65-1466
Don't Sit Under The Apple Tree 186-375
Don't Start No Stuff 680
Don't Start Nothin' Here Tonight 212
Don't Stop Me If You've Heard It Before 392
Don't Take 'Em Fo' Yo' Friend 180
Don't Take That Black Bottom Away 235-510-668-1300-1644
Don't Take Your Love From Me 81-818-1408
Don't Talk About Me 792
Don't Tear My Clothes No. 2 308-995
Don't Tell A Lie About Me, Dear (And I Won't Tell The Truth About You) 744
Don't Tell A Soul (We're In Love) 288
Don't Tell Her/Him What's Happened To Me 156-196-1621
Don't Tell Me Nothin' 'Bout My Man 1061
Don't Tell Your Monkey Man 192
Don't Tetch It 273
Don't Think You'll Be Missed 710-1608
Don't Treat Me Like A Dog 1713
Don't Trust Nobody 1489
Don't Try To Cry Me Back To You 409
Don't Try To Cry Your Way Back To Me 509-1632
Don't Try Your Jive On Me 272-1238-1351-1632
Don't Turn Your Back On Me 1014
Don't Wait Till The Night Before Christmas 1316
Don't You Loud-Mouth Me 390
Don't Wait Too Long 73-74-232-920
Don't Wake Me Up, Let Me Dream 73-914-924
Don't Wake Up My Heart 609-739-1064-1721
Don't Wear It Out 1452
Don't Worry 'Bout Me 105-184-370-527-1262
Don't You Advertise Your Man 1464
Don't You Care What Anyone Says ? 15-182-183-536
Don't You Worryin' About Judgment Day 182-183
Don' You Grieve 791
Don't You Know Or Don't You Care ? 739-894-1631
Don't You Leave Me Here 833-848-1107-1458
Don't You Let Your Head Hang Down 942

1874

Don't You Make Me High  90-849
Don't You Miss Your Baby ?  102
Don't You Quit Me, Daddy  522-1012
Don't You Tear My Clothes  968
Don't You Think I Love You ?  1170
Don't You Throw Me Down  1573
Don't You Try To High-Hat Me  963
Don't You Wanna Know ?  1338
Don't You Want To Ride ?  849
Doo Dah Blues  380-935-1066-1462
Doo Dee Blues  397
Doodle Bug  1216
Doodle-Doo-Doo  128-174-561-825-963-1067-
1212-1334-1590
Doodle-Um Blues, The  121
Doodlin' Back  1477
Doo Doodle Oom  711-1229-1523
Dooji Wooji  766
Doo Wacka Doo  228-558-1029-1191-1591
Dope Head Blues  1487
Dope Peddlin' Blues  1541
Dopey Joe  550
Do-Re-Mi  155-730
Do Right Blues  642-732-763-1023-1589
Do Right Papa  212
Dorsey Dervish - see WADDLIN' AT THE WAL-
DORF
Dorsey Stomp - see DUSK IN UPPER SANDUSKY
Do Shuffle  1715
Do Something  20-262-888-931-1033-1214-
1336-1514
Dot 'em Down Blues  1439
Do That Thing  628-714
Do The Black Bottom With Me  171
Do The New York  287-1386-1494
Do The Sugar Step  1226
Double Bols  690
Double Check Stomp  87-481
Double-Crossin' Daddy  1716
Double-Crossin' Papa (Don't Double-Cross
Me)  357-794-1725
Double Dozens (You Dirty No Gooder)  1486
Double Or Nothing  739
Double Talk  896
Double Trouble  66-382-701-890-1031-1306
Dough-Ray-Me  663
Doug The Jitterbug  864
Do What You Did Last Night  320-1652
Down A Carolina Lane  487
Down Among The Hee-Jee-Wee-Jees  392
Down Among The Sheltering Palms  158-758
Down Among The Sleepy Hills Of Ten-Ten-
Tennessee  70-1180
Down Among The Sugar Cane  243-677-949-
1016-1064
Down And Out Blues  350-529-534-777-1451-
1506
Down Argentina Way  373-910
Down At Cabin Inn  99
Down At Jasper's Bar-Be-Que  823
Down At The Old Village Store  844
Down At The Razor Ball  1013
Down At Uncle Bill's  425-582-1571
Down Beat  387
Down By The Levee  1744
Down By The Old Front Gate  1213
Down By The Old Mill Stream  907-987-1118-
1557
Down By The Old Sea Shore  266
Down By The Old Swimming Hole  177
Down By The River (1923)  70-350-583-711

Down By The River (1935)  1150
Down By The River Blues  1069
Down By The Riverside  1096
Down By The Winegar Woiks  530
Downcast Blues  1743
Down, Down, Down (What A Song !)  108-
619
Down For Double  109
Down Georgia Way  1256
Downhearted Blues  77-80-254-310-632-633-
666-685-706-710-711-749-792-795-1050-
1092-1362-1391-1424-1438-1510-1532-
1544
Downhearted Mama  820
Down Hill Pull  1489
Down Home  1253
Down Home Blues,(The)  215-280-633-684-
1461-1492-1525-1626-1641-1648-1650
Down Home Bound Blues  1449
Down Home Dance  178
Down Home Gal  66
Down Home In Kentucky  823
Down Home Jump  661
Down Home Rag  324-416-445-512-517-971-
971-1279-1342-1429-1516-1587-1603-1658
Down Home Special  836
Down Home Syncopated Blues  940
Down In Black Bottom  688
Down In Dixieland  342
Down In Gallion  1718
Down In Honky Tonk Town  58
Down In Jungle Town  15
Down In Mexico  590
Down In Mississippi  1542
Down In My Heart  537
Down In My Soul  1654
Down In Our Alley Blues  473
Down In Shady Lane  679
Down In The Basement  1267
Down In The Dumps  91
Down In The Alley  1065-1320
Down In The Mouf' Blues  1452
Down In The Mouth Blues  1547
Down In The Valley  171
Down My Way  1103
Down Old Georgia Way  1443-1450
Down On Biscayne Bay  316
Down On Bull Frogs' Isle  1516
Down On Pennsylvania Avenue  802
Down On The Amazon  1559
Down On The Delta  158
Down On The Farm  177-796-874
Down On The Levee Blues  357-750
Down On The Levee (Levee Lullaby)  1203
Down On The Riminent  897
Downright Disgusted (Blues)  999-1003
Down So Long Blues, The  343
Down South  747-1378-1603
Down South Blues  711-731-793-1447-1520-
1608-1728
Down South Camp Meeting  250-598-600-727
Downstream  124-899-1003
Down Sunnyside Lane  917
Down In The Alley  1526
Down The Nile (To Old Cairo)  748
Down The Old Back Road  173
Down The Old Ox Road  200-1512
Down The River Of Golden Dreams  1005
Down The Road A-Piece  166
Down The Road Bound Blues  353
Down To Steamboat Tennessee  1697

Down To The Bottom Where I Stay  1037
Down To The Bricks  1162
Down Town Rag  772-1554
Downtown Uproar  1711
Down Under  744
Down Where The Blue Bonnets Grow  111
Down Where The Rajahs Dwell  976
Down Where The South Begins  1129
Down Where The Sun Goes Down  340-394-
 1498
Down Where The Swanee River Flows  315
Down Where The Trade Winds Blow  880
Down Where They Play The Blues  1492
Down With Love  443
Down Yonder  1210
Down Yonder Blues  846
Do Ya/You Love Me (Just A Tiny Bit, Do
 Ya ?)  1382
Do Ye/You Ken John Peel ?  368-518
Do You Believe In Dreams ?  356
Do You Believe In Love At Sight ?  1035
Do You Call That A Buddy ?  58-326-461-
 865
Do You Call That Religion ?  1710
Do You Care ?  186-374-417-1375
Do You Dig My Jive ?  1247
Do You Ever Dream Of Me ?  511
Do You Ever Think Of Me ?  372-775-1146-
 1157-1479
Do You Have To Go ?  1637
Do You Intend To Put An End To A Sweet
 Beginning Like This ?  701-1627
Do You Know ?  98
Do You Know Why ?  373-451
Do You Love Me ?  972
Do You Or Don't You Love Me ?  728
Do You Pamper Your Husband At Night ?
 1374-1375
Do Yo' Dooty, Daddy  350
Do Your Duty  1028-1446
Do You Remember Last Night ?  446
Do You ?  That's All I Want To Know  804
Do You Wanna Jump, Children ?  94-104-259-
 692-907
Dracula  907
Draftin' Blues  107
Drag, The  5-391
Drag 'Em  1720
Draggin' My Heart Around  342-1624
Dream A Little Dream Of Me  421-1124
Dream Awhile  1415
Dream Blues  766-1266
Dream Boat  32
Dream Caravan  8-151
Dream Child  1663
Dream Daddy  225-1615
Dream Daddy Blues  846
Dream Dropped In, A  902
Dreamer Of Dreams  1582
Dream Girl  247
Dream Girl Of Pi K.A.  1643-1644
Dream House  240-1069
Dreaming  148
Dreaming Blues  1351
Dreaming 'Bout My Man  792
Dreaming Of A Castle In The Air  233-1503-
 1742
Dreaming Of Tomorrow  339-395-949-1742
Dreaming Of You (Blues)  1065-1489
Dreaming Out Loud  616-1406
Dreaming The Hours Away  1217-1702
Dreamland Blues  533

Dream Lover  952
Dream Lullaby  281
Dream Man (Make Me Dream Some More)  424-
 1625
Dream Mother  951
Dream Of A Doll  1147
Dream Of Life  769
Dream Of You  984
Dream On  1330
Dream Pal  73-1503
Dream River  1665
Dream Ship  465
Dreams Of Ragtime  971
Dreams Sometimes Do Come True  1606
Dream Sweetheart  461-464-1030-1227
Dream Train  243-403-627
Dream Valley  742
Dreamy Blues - see MOOD INDIGO
Dreamy Melody  919
Dreary Weary Blues  540
Dreary Weather  1582
Driftin'  1333
Drifting And Dreaming  1300-1714
Drifting Apart  274-294-295-576-1484
Drifting Tide  797-1270
Drifting With The Clouds  195
Driftwood  714-1122
Drink To Me Only With Thine Eyes  518-895-
 1512
Driving Me South  1321
Dromedary  230
Drop A Nickel In The Slot  1179-1315
Drop Down Blues  1091
Drop In The Bucket, A  1361
Drop In Next Time You're Passing  1669
Drop Me A Line  425
Drop Me Off At/In Harlem  487-1073
Drop My Stuff  1558
Dropping Shucks  41
Drop That Sack  39
Drowsy Blues  539
Drum Boogie  387-910
Drummer Boy  373-909
Drummer Goes To Town  384
Drummer Man From Dixie  385
Drummer's Delight  135
Drummin' Man  908
Drum Stomp - see CRAZY RHYTHM
Drunk Again  1413
Drunk Man's Strut  1161
Dry Bones  373-1054-1636
Dry Long So  1712
Dry Martini  1222
Duck Foot Waddle  184
Ducks  1729
Duck's Quack  16-223-350
Duck's Yas Yas Yas, The  328-834-1557
Ducky Dish, A  687
Ducky Wucky  486
Duet Stomp  863
Duke Insists, The  1689
Duke Of Ka-Ki-Ak, The  952
Duke's Idea, The  95
Duke's Mixture  817
Duke Steps Out, The  478-479
Dumbell  710
Dummy, The  1572
Dump Cart  565
Dunkin' A Doughnut  901
Dunn's Cornet Blues  459
Dupree Blues  104-739-948-1676
Dusk  496-1409

1876

Dusk In The Desert  492
Dusk In Upper Sandusky  427-430
Dusky Stevedore  51-240-269-412-514-806-
  977-1062-1076-1291-1417-1546-1568
Dust  286-1315-1357-1383
Dustin' The Donkey  230-232-1579
Dusting The Frets  381
Dustin' The Keys  151-210-1172-1420
Dust Off That Old Pianna - see OH SUSANNAH
Dust Pan Blues  1676
Dusty Bottom Blues  862
Dutch Kitchen Stomp - see BELGIUM STOMP
Dying Baby Blues  1216
Dying Blues  854
Dyin' By The Hour  1444
Dyin' Crapshooter's Blues  343-735-1025
Dying Gambler's Blues  1441
Dying Mercy Blues  1527
Dying Mother Blues  850
Dyin' With The Blues  752-1525-1649
Dynamisme  1284
Dynamite  720-882-1131-1275
Dynamite Rag  1217

Each Day  1104
Each Time You Say Goodbye  1752
Eagle Beak  1374
Eagle Rock Me Papa  1013
Earful Of Music, An  424-582-879
Earl, The  620-761
Early Bird  1239
Early Every Morn' (I Want My/Some Lovin')
  794-860-1090
Early Every Morning, Year After Year  665
Early In The Morning  550
Early In The Morning Blues  914-965-1607
Early Mornin'  135
Early Morning Blues  25-26-329
Early One Morning  518
Early Rising Blues  959
Early Session Hop  662-1736
Earthquake  959
Ease It  1450
Ease It To Me  629
Ease On Down  1346
East And West Blues  642
East Coast Florida Blues  118
East Coast Trot  327
East Commerce Stomp  155
Eastern Chimes Blues  181
Easter Parade  819-988-1211-1601
East Of The Sun (And West Of The Moon)
  203-292-365-450-652
East St. Louis Blues  945-1065-1541-1746
East St. Louis Stomp  1377
East St. Louis Toodle-Oo  472-473-474-475-
  485-491-493-495
East Side Kick  740
East Side Of Heaven  9
East Tennessee Quiver  409
East Wind  656
Easy  1046
Easy As Pie  185
Easy Come, Easy Go  133-423-638-797
Easy Come, Easy Go Blues  1440
Easy Creeping Mama  1201
Easy Does It  10-107-208-306-448
Easy Drag  456
Easy Goin'  1169-1325-1662
Easy-Goin' Mama  399-707
Easy Like  1000-1002-1604
Easy Living  781-1134-1733

Easy Melody  16-71-223-1509-1590
Easy Money  723
Easy Pickin's  379-1747
Easy Rhythm  761
Easy Rider  410-510-692-1594 (see also
  I WONDER WHERE MY EASY RIDER'S GONE ?)
Easy Rider Blues  1527-1676
Easy Rocker  788
Easy Spring Blues  886
Easy Street  499-991
Easy Swing  188
Easy To Get  542
Easy To Love  81-383-428-1274-1512-1697-
  1732
Easy To Say  1405
Easy Touring Mama  849
Easy Winner  696
Eat More Fruit  461
Eavesdropper's Blues  643-1440
Ebb Tide  124-131-205-1314-1552
Ebony Dreams  838
Ebony Rhapsody  95-107-488
Ebony Shadows  279-536-1508
Ebony Silhouette  261
Eccentric (Rag)  5-76-375-396-425-426-
  656-764-765-955-1036-1047-1131-1139-
  1187-1193-1347-1364-1481-1498-1548
Echo Blues  1209
Echoes  257
Echoes Of Harlem  94-95-490-897-1711
  (see also CONCERTO FOR COOTIE)
Echoes Of Oklahoma  1115
Echoes Of Spain  1283
Echoes Of The Jungle  485-996
Echo In The Dark  1194
Echo Of A Song, The  974
Echo(es) Of Spring  1467-1468
Eclats de cuivres  1284
Ec-Stacy - see AIN'T GOIN' NOWHERE
Eddie And Sugar Lou Stomp  461
Eddie Leonard Blues  219-935
Eddie's Blues  1476
Eddie Steady  1643
Eddie's Twister  921-1388
Edgar Steps Out  695
Edmond Hall Blues  652
Edna  1170
Edward Stomp  694
Eel, The  335-542
Een(e)y Meen(e)y Miney Mo  365-382-597-
  1114-1119-1224-1329-1602-1730
Eerie Moan  486
Effervescent Blues  895
E flat Blues  582-845-1239-1626
E flat Blues No. 2 - see MEMPHIS, TENNES-
  SEE
E flat Stride  1074
Egyptian Barn Dance  1372
Egyptian-Ella  746-958-1667
Egyptian Fantasy  114
Eh La Bas  1550
Eight Bars In Search Of A Melody  785
18th Street Strut  265-531-1109
Eight-Hour Woman  834
Eight Letters In The Mailbox  1375
8, 9 And 10  550
8 Rock Blues  1525
Eileen  72-576
Elder Eatmore's Sermon On Generosity  56
Elder Eatmore's Sermon On Throwing Stones
  56
Electrician Blues  1061

Electric Moan 211
Elegric (Massenet) 918-1531
Elegy 791
Elegy To A Jitterbug 805
Elephant Stomp 968
Elephant Swing 808
Elephant's Wobble 1109
Elevator Papa, Switchboard Mama 214
Eleven More Months And Ten More Days 1296
Eli, Eli 453-817
Eli Green's Cake Walk 1197
Elise 743
Eliza 67-228
Ella 1661
Elle a mis son smoking 10
Elle n'a pas tres bon caractere 1615
Elmer's Tune 374-619
Elm Street Blues 995
Elm Street Woman Blues 387
El Rado Scuffle 1153
El Watson's Fox Chase 1655
Elzadie's Policy Blues 1321
Emaline 92-257-593-654-1529-1531-1571
Emancipation Day In Georgia 557
Embankment Midnight 87
Embarrassment Blues 1054
Embassy Stomp 22
Embers 1354
Embraceable You 335-434-453-647-946-1143-
  1371-1736
Emperor Jones 94
Empire Party, The 21
Empty Arms 1273
Empty Ballroom Blues 765
Empty Bed Blues 679-835-1445-1723
Empty Cellar Blues 794
Empty House Blues 1451
Empty Saddles 93-122-204
Encore un tour de chevaux de bois 312
End O' Main 1009
End Of The Lonesome Trail, The - see AT
  THE END OF THE LONESOME TRAIL
End Of The Rainbow 741
End Of The World, The 942
Endurance Stomp 99-327-1045-1495
Eniale Blues 1391
Entr'acte 140
Enuff (sic) To Run You 1020
Epe, Ipe, Wanna Piece Of Pie 387-590-747-
  1636
Epler's Whiskers 971
Erwing Blues, The 511
Er sagt - I Love You 951
Escapada 279
Eskimo Song, The 547
Espagnola, La 457
Especially For You 431-1538
Essential To Me 326
Est-ce je te demande ? 1639
Estrellita 326-457-611-819-1239-1333
Ethel Sings 'Em 1649
Ethel Waters Blues 839
Ethiopian Mardi Gras, An 1197-1198-1199
Ethiopian Nightmare 762
Ethiopian Stomp 169
Etiquette 649
Etre Parisienne 1642
Etude 1508
Eucchia 232
Evangeline 562
Eve, Let That Apple Be 742

Even If You Love Me 1743
Evenin 101-107-256
Evening 288-1190
Evening Chimes Waltz 456
Evening Eyes 248
Ev'ning In Caroline, An 147-157-958
Evening Star 186-419-1374
Even Steven 743
Ev'ntide 53
Ever After On 1739
Evergreen Money Blues 1042
Everlasting Blues 754
Ever Lovin' Blues 187
Ever Since The Movies Learned To Talk
  1117-1118
Ever Since Time Began 673
Everybody And You 1253
Everybody But Me 1021
Everybody Dance 1041-1215
Everybody Does It In Hawaii 1170
Everybody Does It Now 343-794
Everybody Has The Blues Sometime 1091
Everybody Knocks 832
Everybody Likes The Same Sweet Girl 1334
Everybody Loves My Baby 153-157-345-556
  558-561-563-572-604-624-661-716-717-
  747-757-790-794-828-886-938-1053-1146-
  1172-1191-1327-1346-1432-1453-1506-
  1537-1545-1636-1699
Everybody Loves My Girl 377-929-1049-
  1665
Everybody Loves My Honey Now 1103
Everybody Loves Somebody (But Nobody
  Loves Me) 1132
Everybody Mess Aroun(d) 562-795-1651
Everybody Pile 1161
Everybody's Blues 704-1376
Ev'rybody's Charleston Crazy 559
Everybody's Crazy 'Bout The Doggone
  Blues, But I'm Happy 1516
Everybody's Doing It 388-444-1237
Everybody's Doin' That/The Charleston
  (Now) 1164-1181-1467-1520
Everybody's Got Somebody To Love Them
  1065
Everybody's Got The Blues 1012
Everybody Shimmies Now 1375-1522
Everybody Shout 12
Everybody Shuffle 281-774-1601
Everybody's Laughing 1735
Everybody's Making Money But Tchaikovsky
  186
Everybody's Man Is My Mam 1008
Everybody's Talkin' About Sadie Green
  1042
Everybody's Talking About Sammy 1095
Everybody Step 885-1085-1274-1661-1680-
  1752
Everybody Stomp 349-867-914-920-962-992
  1054-1181-1201-1363-1545
Everybody Two-Step 127-1217
Everybody Wants My Tootelum 695
Everybody Wants To See My Black Bottom
  1201
Every Day (1921) 1525
Ev'ry Day (1935) 1935
Every Day (1938) 493
Ev'ry Day Away From You 377-1127-1164-
  1293
Every Day Blues 418-732-1111
Every Day I Hear My Daddy Say "Riddle-Dum
  Bum" 134

1878

Every Day Of My Life  815
Every Day's A Holiday  258-367-1064-1631
Every Dog Has His Day  1618
Every Dog Must Have His Day  1542
Every Evening (I Miss You)  882-1151
Ev'ry Goodbye Ain't Gone  284
Every Hour  248
Every Little Bit Of Me Loves Every Little
  Bit Of You  697-875
Every Little Doggie Has His Day  1240
Every Little Moment  160-426-563-1000
Every Little Thing  1472
Ev'ry Little While  631-1290
Every Man For Himself  1644
Every Man That Wears Bell-Bottom Britches
  Ain't No Monkey Man  359
Ev'ry Minute, Ev'ry Hour Of Ev'ry Day  506
Every Minute Of The Hour  14-438
Every Night  995
Ev'ry Night About This Time  436
Ev'ry Night In The Week  240
Every Now And Then  701-809-1001-1031-1127
  1270-1730
Every Once In A While  1002-1367
Everyone Is Trying The Charleston Now  982
Everyone's A Fighting Son Of That Old Gang
  Of Mine  1318
Everyone's Wrong But Me  526-1157
Every Saturday Night  1749
Ev'ry Single Little Tingle Of My Heart
  426
Ev'ry Sunday Afternoon  96-615
Everything Depends On You  81-761
Everything Happens For The Best  769
Everything Happens To Me  452-742
Everything I Do, I Do For You  1293-1298
Everything I Have Is Yours  1601-1669
Ev'rything I Love  435-621-1553
Everything Is Hotsy Totsy Now  230-231-
  339-541-1180-1694
Everything Is Hunky Dooly  23
Everything Is Jumpin'  1405
Everything Is K.O. In K.Y.  70
Everything Is Okey-Dokey  392-701-967
Everything Is Peaches Down In Georgia  789
Everything Is Rhythm Now  152
Everything Is Still Okay  1074
Everything My Sweetie Does Pleases Me  734
Everything's Been Done Before  58-974
Everything's Gonna Be All Right  339-568-
  914
Everything's Made For Love  268-668-1425-
  1681
Everything's O.K. With Me  1716
Everything's Peaches (For Peaches And Me)
  1098
Everything Stops For Tea  974
Everything's Wrong, Ain't Nothing Right
  40
Everything That Happens Just Pleases Me
  846-1082
Ev'rything That's Nice Belongs To You  33
Everything We Like We Like Alike  654-1325
Everything You Do  569
Everything You Said Came True  1003-1401
Ev'ry Time  1361
Every Time I Feel De Spirit (sic)  1710
Every Time I Look At You  1072
Every Time I Pick A Sweetie  707
Every Tub (1927)  1167
Every Tub (1933)  1311
Every Tub (1938)  103-776

Everywhere You Go  328-1616
Every Woman('s) Blues  118-732-1447
Every Woman Needs A Man  1012
Evil And Blue  751
Evil Bad Woman  1542
Evil Blues  105-181-1725
Evil Devil Blues, The  1541
Evil Hearted Woman  1019
Evil Mama Blues  177
Evil Man('s) Blues  842-1204
Evil Minded Blues  965-1050-1136
Evil Old Nightmare  849
Evolution Blues  754
Exactly Like You  47-59-101-183-286-333-
  503-542-585-599-664-676-782-816-841-
  932-970-1250-1260-1262-1279-1294-1551-
  1735
Experience Blues  794
Explaining The Blues  1266
Exposition Swing  491
Express Train Blues  538
Extra ! (All About That Gal Of Mine)  200
Eyeful Of You, An  243-1173
Eye Opener  369
Eyes And The Ears Of The World, The  450
Eyes Of Blue  195-247
Eyes Of Blue, You're My Waterloo  1079
Eyes Of Texas, The  887
Eyes Of The Fleet  1319
Ezekiel Saw De Wheel (sic)  471
Ezell's Precious Five  516

Fable Of The Rose, The  76096-297-449-
  614
Faces At The Window  1290
Face To Face  1458
Facts And Figures  1658
Fade Away Blues  164-645
Faded Cherry Blossom  1739
Fade Out  749
Fading Star  1468
Fair And Square  1632
Fair And Warmer  937
Fairy On The Clock  951-1293
Faithful Forever  613-1752
Faithfully Yours  1145
Faithful To You  448
Fakir's Rhythm  993
Fallen Arches  129-962-963-1181-1275
Falling  401
Fallin' Down  232-351-544-867-967-1054-
  1181-1579-1592
Falling In Love Again  592-769
Falling In Love With You  52-667
Falling Leaves  433
Fall In Love With Me  1234
Family Skeleton Blues  182-736
Family Trouble Blues  1060
Fancies  710
Fancy Meeting You  108-204-1002-1415
Fancy Tricks  1344
Fanfare  791
Fan It (Boogie Woogie)  583-742-823-824-
  859-1145
Fan My Brow  781
Fanny Lee Blues  1621
Fanny May  815
Fantaisie sur une dance norvegienne  1262
Far Ago Blues  947
Far As I'm Concerned  1533
Faraway Bells, The  172-1286
Far Away Blues  1440-1447

Far Away Music  374
Far Away Texas Blues  1713
Fare Thee Honey Fare Thee Well (Blues)
  104-163-459-838-1460-1678
Fare Thee My Baby, Fare-Thee-Well  1003
Fare Thee Well  999-1436
Fare Thee Well, Annabelle  93-160-292-1000
Fare Thee Well, Annie Laurie  906
Fare Thee Well, Poor Gal  353
Fare Thee Well To Harlem  1099-1538-1689
Farewell Blues  109-237-253-264-283-304-
  310-384-402-489-490-535-559-563-582-595-
  610-625-666-710-740-764-775-797-856-914-
  946-956-992-1003-1022-1081-1115-1131-
  1168-1187-1280-1353-1362-1437-1496-1509-
  1519-1532-1533-1561-1593-1600-1608-1641-
  1690-1750
Farewell Daddy Blues  1266
Farewell, My Love  294-1032
Fare You Well  1542
Farmer In A Dilemma  1412
Farmer Takes A Wife, The  426
Farmer Took Another Load Away, The  133
Farm Hand Papa  1703
Fascinating Devil  788
Fascinating Rhythm  316-568-582-1433-1664-
  1749
Fascinatin' Vamp  552-1291
Fascination  220-839
Fascination Blonde  1038
Fashionette  270-1292
Fast And Furious  486
Fast-Fadin' Papa  214
Fast Life  628
Fast, Slow, Medium Tempo  333
Fat And Greasy  1627-1636
Fat Babes  758
Fate Introduced Me To You  33-874
Fate Is The Slave Of Love  1424
Fate (It Was Fate When I First Met You)
  222-431-1173-1341
Fat Fanny Stomp  318
Fat Frances - see FRANCES
Fat Greasy Baby  1216
Father, Dear Father  125
Father Jumps, The  761
Father's Getaway, The  760
Father's Got His Glasses On  256
Father Steps In  760
Fatima's Drummer Boy  1540
Fat Mama Blues  1389
Fat Man Blues  1209
Fat Meat And Greens  149-1101
Fats In The Fire  387
Fat Stuff Serenade  1500
Fats Waller's Original E flat Blues  1636
Fats Waller Stomp  1622
Fattening Frogs For Snakes - see I'M TIRED
  OF FATTENING FROGS FOR SNAKES
Faust : Waltz  1635
Faustine  1504
Favor Of A Fool, The  283
Fay  188
F. D. R. Jones  8-259-1661
Feather Bed  270
Feather Bed Blues  849
Feather Bed Lament  518
Feather Merchant  109
Feather Merchant's Ball  1242
Feather Your Nest  183-371
Feedin' The Bean  108

Feed Your Friend With A Long Handled
  Spoon  1042
Fee Fi Fo Fum  1401
Feelin(g) Blue  1009-1502
Feelin' Blue(s)  838
Feeling Drowsy  11
Feelin' Fancy  909
Feelin' Gay  1073
Feeling Good  723
Feelin' High And Happy  608-609-906-1203
Feeling In A Mellow Mood  897
Feelin' Kind O' Blue  510
Feeling Like A Dream  325
Feeling My Way  922
Feelin' No Pain  304-1087-1139
Feelin' The Spirit  1345
Feelin' The Way I Do  713---714
Feelin' Tip-Top  260
Feeling Tomorrow Like I Feel Today  948
Feerie  1284
Feet Draggin' Blues  815
Feist's All-Hits Medley  379
Felix Kept On Walking  1175
Felix The Cat  1685
Femme qui passe, Une  1085
Ferdinand The Bull  29-322-409-550-588-
  1315-1397
Ferryboat Serenade  497-1317
Festival Swing 1941 and 1942  519
Fetch It To Me  1246
Fetch It When You Come  994
Few Riffs, A  1715
Fickle Fay Creep  1105-1106
Fiddle Blues  1476
Fiddle-Dee-Dee  663
Fiddle Diddle  661
Fiddleditty  1476
Fiddle-obia  409
Fiddlesticks  1601-1602
Fiddlesticks Rag  1217
Fidgety  422
Fidgety Feet  32-336-367-543-721-1020-
  1176-1179-1656-1741
Fido Blues  521
Fiesta  249
Fiesta In Blue  109-618
Fievre - see MOONGLOW
Fifi's Rhapsody  896
Fifteen Cents  824
Fifteen Minute(s) Intermission  260-901
Fifth Street Blues  278
Fifty Million Frenchmen Can't Be Wrong
  269-1416-1574
50,000,000 Nickels  98
Fifty Million Sweethearts Can't Be Wrong
  453
Fifty-Second Street  899-1249
52nd Street Fever  182
57th Street Drag  306
Fifty-Seven Varieties  757
Figaro  1294
Fightin' Blues  1069-1458
Fightin' Doug McArthur  912-1070
Fighting Joe Louis  1454
Fighting Man Blues  850
Fight On  322
Fight That Thing  1485
Fille de la Madelon, La  396
Filipino Hombre, The  1398
Fill Up  1561
Finding The Long Way Home  1233

Find Me At The Greasy Spoon (If You Miss Me Here)  1729
Find Me A Primitive Man  1697
Find Out What They Like (And How They Like It)  1728
Fine And Dandy  421-740-1530-1732
Fine And Mellow  692-769-795-849-901
Fine Dinner  690
Fine Piece Of Meat  1560
Fine Romance, A  767-1002
Finesse (Night Wind)  766-1500
Finger Buster  1106-1467-1468
Fingerbustin'  434
Fingerwave  1033
Finishing Up A Date  913
Fiora Waltz  512
Fire  1646
Fire And Thunder Blues  412
Firebird  792
Firefly Stomp  1272
Firehouse Blues  1113
Fire In The Mountain  936-1678
Fireman Blues  1542
Fireworks  43-548-1136-1193
First Girl I Met Was The Last Girl I Loved The  981
First Kiss, The  506
First, Last And Always  70
First Time I Saw You, The  93-123-205-986-1239
Fisherman's Blues  886
Fish For Your Supper  342
Fish Fry  283
Fishin' In The Dark  1044
Fish Tail Blues  1100 (see also SIDEWALK BLUES)
Fish Tail Dance  1549
Fit As A Fiddle  674-871-876-1238-1437-1556
Fit To Be Tied  165-1752
Fitzwater Street  551
Five Foot Two, Eyes Of Blue  73-232-523-920-934-962
Five Guys Named Moe  865
Five Little Quints, The  1263
Five Minutes Blues  1673
Five O'Clock Blues - see THE FIVES
Five O'Clock Drag  499
Five O'Clock Stomp  406-1495
Five O'Clock Whistle  107-167-497-528-693-742
Five Pennies  304-963-1120-1138-1140-1498
Five Point Blues  368
Fives, The  104-1525-1746
Five-Step  1682
Fix It Up And Go  1542
Flag That Train (To Alabam')  73-189-658-926-934-1119
Flamin' Mamie  190-339-719-1006-1219-1300-1543
Flamingo  168-311-374-498-499-911-990
Flaming Reeds And Screaming Brass  983
Flaming Sword, The  497
Flaming Youth  477-479
Flany Doodle Swing  759
Flapperette  1206
Flapper Stomp  1413
Flapper Wife, The  230-572
Flash  815
Flashes  126-1490
Flatbush Flanagan  816
Flat Face  864

Flat Foot  1129
Flat Foot Floogie, The  55-103-550-587-609-739-746-787-1003-1261-1632
Flea On A Spree  1242
Fletcher's Stomp  11
Flight Of A Haybag  1571
Flight Of The Bumble Bee  429-816-817-997
Flight Of The Jitterbug  989
Flinging A Whing-Ding  307-387-730
Flip  1602
Flippety-Flop, The  244-341
Floatin' Down To Cotton Town  1002-1629
Floating On A Bubble  894
Flock O'Blues  1422
Flo Flo  417
Flood Blues, The  1618
Floogee Walk  259-1435
Flop  1602
Flora's Weary Blues  1057
Florence  303
Florida  797-1502
Florida Blues  379-409-538-666-1518
Florida Bound Blues  1443
Florida Flo  1632
Florida Flood Blues  633
Florida Low-Down  1182
Florida Rag  1200-1586-1587
Florida Stomp  466-719-1662
Florita  134
Flower Of Araby  222
Flower Of Love  1665
Flowers For Madame  365
Flowers That Bloom In The Spring, The  1279
Floyd's Guitar Blues  901
Flutter By, Butterfly  566
Flying Crow Blues  381
Flying Fingers  703
Flying Home  96-166-613-614-663-664
Fly Right (Epistrophy)  1712
F minor Blues  1556
'Fo' Day Blues - see 'FORE DAY BLUES
Foggy Day, A  367
Foggy Morning Blues  737
Fogyism  355
Fol Da Rol Dol  1357
Foldin' Bed  1676
Folks In New York City Ain't Like Folks Down South  845
Folks Who Live On The Hill  59-636-894-1400-1512
Following You Around  129-509
Follow The Deal On Down  1441
Follow The Swallow  189
Follow Through - Vocal Gems from  1604
Follow Thru'  641
Foo For Two  907
Foo-Gee  215-1674
Fool Am I  910
Fool And A Butterfly, A  1245
Fooled  186-744
Fooling  1639
Foolin' Me  509
Foolin' Myself  205-765-900-1733
Foolin' With The Other Woman's Man  84
Foolin' With You  258
Fool In Love, A  982
Foolish Child  71-1175
Foolish Man Blues  1444
Foolish Woman's Blues  643
Fools Fall In Love  96-433

Fools Rush In (Where Angels Fear To Tread) 81-207-373-449-815
Fool That I Am 1263
Footloose 232-1006-1164-1680
Footloose And Fancy Free 426
Foo To You 322
Foot Pedal Boogie 851
Foot Scuffle 1310
Foot Warmer 975-1640
For Baby And Me 1230-1420
Forbidden Lips 84
For Dancers Only 371-986
'Fore Day Blues ('Fo' Day Blues) 864-1184 1513
'Fore Day Creep 354-355
'Fore Day In The Morning 676
'Fore Day Rider 1038
Forever 232-241-950-1232
Forever And Ever 1413-1478
Forever More 165-403-1151
Forgetful Blues 120-1139-1509-1673
Forget It If You Can 304-768
Forget-Me-Not 800-1483-1685
Forget-Me-Not Blues 1013
Forgetting You - see THAT'S JUST MY WAY OF FORGETTING YOU
Forgive A Fool 691
Forgive Me 1250-1416
Forgive Me Please 1528
Forgive My Heart 506
For Heaven's Sake 1504
For He's A Jolly Good Fellow 518
For Just A Little Love From You 1355
Formal Night In Harlem 781-1002
For Mary And Me 1619
For Me And My Gal 207-385
For Men Only 323
For My Baby 238-239-1291-1378-1395-1620
For My Sweetheart 271-532-921-1006
For No Reason At All 591
For No Reason At All In C 1566
For Old Time's Sake 579-1292-1426
Forsaken Blues 121-715-869
For Sale (Hannah Johnson's Big Jackass) 1452-1708
For Sentimental Reasons 77-439-1271
For Sev'n Long Years 1398
For The Good Of This/Your Country 109-110
For The Last Time Call Me Sweetheart 401
For The Last Time I Cried Over You 259
For Tonight 95-740
Fortune Teller Blues 343-627-636-735-1024
Fortune Tellin' Man 1721
Fort Worth And Denver Blues 1572
Fort Worth Jail 743
Forty And Tight 112
Forty-Four Blues 570
Forty-Second Street 158-877-1311-1410
47th And State 543
47th Street Jive 902
47th Street Stomp 132-1039
Forty-Six West Fifty-Two 131
For Want Of A Star 817
For You 289-294-452-470
For You And Me 267
Found My Gal 737
Four a.m. Shout 837
Four Beat Shuffle 1373
Four Day Creep - see 'FORE DAY CREEP
Four Day Honory Scat 1267
Four-Flushin' Papa (What Kinda Man Is You) 860

Four-Flushin' Papa (You've Gotta Play Straight With Me) 623-733-1440-1728
Four Four Rhythm 1563
Four Hands Are Better Than Two 844
400 Hop 1084
400 Swing 944
Four Indian Love Lyrics 288
Four O'Clock Blues 136-316-458-685-835-850-1057-1059-1186-1525-1560
Four Or Five Times 114-311-417-522-634-662-744-764-765-816-858-985-1033-1o78-1151-1154-1168-1638-1672
Four String Joe 1596 1492 676
Fourteenth Street Blues 143
410 Blues 1486
Four-Thirty Blues 709
Fourth's Fever 1038
Fourth Street Mess Around 1043
Four Walls 840-1378
Fowler Twist 1606
Fox Trot 512
Fox Trot Classique 576-871
Foxy And Grapesy 835
Foxy Cure For The Blues, A 379
Fractious Fingering 1629
Fralich In Swing - see AND THE ANGELS SING
Frances 1103
Frankenstein Blues 1413
Frankie 1724
Frankie And Johnnie/Johnny 123-177-201-224-377-498-499-856-1004-1015-1170-1324 1435-1635-1654-1739
Frankie And Johnnie Swing 540
Frankie Blues 1051-1440-1460
Frankie's Jump 1135
Franklin Street Blues 457
Frantic 657-1247
Frasquita Serenade 896-897
Fraternity Blues 1594
Freakish 1103-1106
Freakish Blues 1555
Freakish (Light) Blues 547-548-1169-1346
Freakish Mistreater Blues 516
Freakish Papa Blues 835
Freakish Rider Blues 688
Freckle Face, You're Beautiful 201-879-1236
Freddie Blues 1676'
Freddy's Fog 1497
Freddy The Freshman 874
Fred's Jump 151
Free And Easy, The 21-1382-1383
Free For All 452-1402
Free Love 1052
Free Wheeling 1401
Freeze An(d) Melt 478-479-723-922
Freeze Out 1704-1705
Freight Train Blues 736-1057-1448-1466-1467
Freight Yard Blues 501
Frenchie's Blues 836
French Market Blues 1208
Frenesi 417-498-616-742-1406-1540
Frenzy 342
Freshie 232-640-1592
Freshman Hop 1077-1078-1222-1223
Friars' Point Shuffle 335-868-977
Friction 1715
Friday Moan Blues 946
Friday Night 274

Friendless Blues   1093-1215-1713
Friendless Gal  Blues   846
Friendly Tavern   1243
Friendship   450
'Frisco Bay   561
'Frisco Blues   1066
Frisco Flo   258
Frisco Fog   987
'Frisco Jazz Band Blues   1649
'Frisco Kitchen Stove Rag   379
'Frisco Train Blues   8
Frisky Feet   538-539
Frisky Honey   169
Fritz Blues   544
Frog, The   87
Frog Eye Stomp   1727
Froggie Moore   1100-1165
Froggy Bottom   850-898-899
Frog Hop   694
Frogs' Legs   1748-1749
Frog Tongue Stomp   65
Frogtown Blues   1210
Frolic Sam   134-141-493
From A flat To C   895
From Another World   81-96-317-324-373
From Jazz To Rhythm   470
From Maine To California   307
From Monday On   867-970-1030-1031-1226-
   1341-1567-1684
From Now On   667-1211-1234-1381
From Now On Blues   1532
From Now On (You're Gonna Be Mine)   669
From Oakland To Burbank   1150
From One Love To Another   374-619
From One Till Two (I Always Dream Of You)
   314-884-1483-1581
From One To Twelve (The Dirty Dozens)   1489
From Saturday Night Till Monday Morning
   1225-1292-1665
From Sunrise To Sunset (From Sunset Till
   Dawn)   243
From The Bottom Of My Heart   815
From The Land Of Sky Blue Water   29-78-168
From The Top Of Your Head (To The Tip Of
   Your Toes)   249-362-701-1001
From You   1211
Front And Center   896-897
Front Door Blues   849
Frosty Mornin' Blues   1440
Frozen Bill Cake-Walk   1255
Fryin' Pan Skillet Blues   1572
Fry Me Cookie, With A Can Of Lard   168
Fugitive From A Harem   696
Full Dress Hop   910
Full Moon   435-622
Fulton Street Blues   734
Functionizin'   752-1627
Funiculi', Funicula' !   186-428-457
Fun In A Boiler Factory   629
Funny Blues, The   681
Funny, Dear, What Love Can Do   83-246-789
Funny Feathers (Blues)   11-1488
Funny Feelin' Blues   547
Funny Feet   826
Funny Fumble   404
Funny Little Pedro   450
Funny Little Snowman   1159
Funny Old Hills, The   1298
Fun To Be Fooled   424
Furniture Man (Blues)   112-1488-1673
Fur Trappers' Ball   742

Fussin'   1194
Fussy Mabel   1104
Futuristic Blues   350
Futuristic Jungleism   1071
Futuristic Rhythm   788-977-1029-1077-1568
Futuristic Shuffle   1357
Fuzzy Wuzzy   208-210-1557
Fuzzy Wuzzy Rag   549-664

Gabby   1674
Gabriel Meets The Duke   692-693
Gabriel's Swing   189
Gaby Glide, The   1604
Gal Ain't Born Who Can Treat Me Like You
   Do, The   1716
Gal-Avantin'   1712
Gal From Joe's, The   94-492-495
Galion Stomp   65
Gallopin' Dominoes   1326
Gal That Wrecked My Life, The   1511
Galveston Blues   831
Gal, When I'm Through You'll Think I'm A
   Man   1105
Gambler's Blues   1715
Gambler's Dream   1549
Gamblin' George Blues   28
Gambling Jack   1105
Game Kid Blues   1105
Gangbuster's Holiday   126
Gang Of Blues   319
Gangster's Blues   1673
Gang That Sang "Heart Of My Heart", The
   1317
Garbage Man, The   679
Garbo Green   780-1628
Gardenias   1315-1358
Garden In Granada, A   1492
Garden Of Joy Blues   409
Garden Of The Moon   431-1158
Garden Of Weed   1508-1689
Garter Snake Blues   1487
Gas House Stomp   681
Gas Man Blues   570
Gate Mouth   1133
Gates Blues   1615
Gathering, The   1630
Gather Lip Rouge While You May   1600
'Gator Swing   760
'Gator Wobble   1043
Gavotte   321
Gay Caballero, A   1117-118
Gay-Catin' Daddy   735-1035
Gayest Manhattan   1197
Gay Ranchero, A   374
G Blues   1689
G'bye Now   743-1318
Gee, Ain't I Good To You ?   131-1034-
   1279
Gee, But I'd Like To Make You Happy   156
Gee, But I Hate To Go Home Alone   69-221
   303-634-1607
Gee ! But I'm Blue   567
Gee, But It's Great To Meet A Friend   124
Gee, But You're Swell   383-600-894-1416-
   1659
Geechee   1622
Geechie Dance   1716
Geechie Joe   261
Geechie River Blues   357-1536
Gee Flat   121
Gee Gee Express   1414

Gee-Goo, Gee-Goo  263
Gee, I Hate To Loose (sic) That Girl  1322
Gee, It Must Be Love  1020-1294
Gee, I Wish I Had Someone To Rock Me  508
Gee, Jane, Isn't It Wonderful ?  827
Gentleman Obviously Doesn't Believe (In
   Love), The  426-700
George Street Stomp  315
Georgette  220
Georgia  1515
Georgia Blues  37-1447-1649-1652
Georgia Bo Bo  39-820-892
Georgia Breakdown  1161
Georgia Cabin  115
Georgia Cabin Door  1437
Georgia Cake Walk  765-1268 (see also AT A
   GEORGIA CAMP MEETING)
Georgia Camp Meeting - see AT A GEORGIA
   CAMP MEETING
Georgia Gigolo  392
Georgia Grind  40-91-336-472-562-709-833-
   1044-1096-1495
Georgia Hound Blues  353
Georgia Jubilee  593-858
Georgia Home  655
Georgia Man  753-1221-1678
Georgia May  1624
Georgianna  103-586-1032-1434-1579
Georgians Blues  644
Georgia On My Mind  49-76-81-155-275-296-
   330-581-583-586-590-770-873-910-946-1114
   1207-1259-1408-1570-1637-1645-1654
Georgia Pines  562-676
Georgia Rocking Chair  4-583-1031-1432-
   1627
Georgia Rose  218
Georgia's Always On My Mind  514-645
Georgia Sam Blues  310
Georgia's Gorgeous Gal  582
Georgia's Got A Moon  1435
Georgia Skin Game, The  1106
Georgia Stockade Blues  398-1013
Georgia Stomp, The  547
Georgia Sunset  1255-1256
Georgia Swing  1102
Georgie Porgie  249-1686
Geraldine  520-641
German Blues  137
Gerry  10
Gerry Building  1092
Gertie (I'm In Love With Gertie)  1389
Get Acquainted With Yourself  780-1468
Get A Load Of This  1275
Get Away From My Window (Stay Away From My
   Door)  214
Get Cannibal  697-698-1145-1410
Get Early Blues  675
Get 'Em Again Blues  308
Get 'Em From The Peanut Man (Hot Nuts)  842
   1677
Get Going  995-1099-1332
Get Goin' (Get Ready To Love)  1112
Get Hot  584-1461
Get Happy  580-597-765-789-790-1142-1357-
   1358-1373-1494-1509-1531-1570-1721
Get Hot  1525
Get Hot Foot  1412
Get In The Groove  164
Get It Fixed (Blues)  320-719-734-872-1094
   1306-1700
Get It Now  1518
Get It Right  1287
Get It Southern Style  134
Get Low-Down Blues  1110
Get Lucky  857
Get Me On Your Mind  1038
Get Me Out Of That Crack  844
Get Off My Money Blues  1533
Get Off Stuff  1322
Get On Board, Li'l Chillun  1450-1711
Get On Out Of Here  180
Get On The Right Side  778
Get Out And Get Under The Moon  241-302-
   669-670-930-1426-1614-1672
Get Out Of Town  183
Get Rhythm In Your Feet (And Music In
   Your Soul)  13-596
Get The Bucket  1108
Get (Thee) Behind Me, Satan  168-1205
Get The Gold  209-1557
Get The "L" On Down The Road  831
Gettin' Away  637
Gettin' Away From Me  833
Gettin' Happy All The Time  217
Gettin' Hot  1121
Gettin' In The Groove  342
Gettin' Lots Of Lovin'  462
Gettin' Off A Mess  898
Getting Old Blues  705-1542
Gettin' Ready Blues  782
Gettin' Ready For Trial  137
Gettin' Sentimental  147
Getting Some Fun Out Of Life  442-443-
   768-1003-1314
Gettin' The Bird  1045
Gettin' The Blues  1182
Gettin' Thro' The Rye  1434
Gettin' Together  1053
Gettin' Told  1113
Gettin' Up Holler  666
Get Together Blues  328
Gettysburg March  1287
Get Up  1560
Get Up, Bessie  1726
Get Up Off That Jazzophone  192
Get Up Off Your Knees  1454-1652
Get With  1275
Get Your Boots Laced, Papa  741
Get Your Man  831
Get Your Mind Out Of The Gutter  628
Get Yourself A Monkey Man And Make Him
   Strut His Stuff  212-214-872-1024
Get Yourself A New Broom (And Sweep Your
   Blues Away)  487
G flat Blues  850
Ghetto  188
Ghost Dance  1565
Ghost Of A Chance, A  80-155-166-260-646
   663-901-1412-1572-1646
Ghost Of Dinah, The  583-779
Ghost Of Love  900
Ghost Of Smokey Joe, The  259-1435
Ghost Of The Black Bottom, The  318
Ghost Of The Blues  713-1230-1533
Ghost Of The Freaks  1346
Ghost Of The Piano, The  1369
Ghost Of The St. Louis Blues, The  1062
Ghost Of Yesterday  769
Ghost Walkin' Blues  643-736-1058
Giddybug Galop, The  498
Gigolette  396-1175
Gilded Kisses  1563

1884

Gill Stomp 412
Gilly - see GONE WITH WHAT DRAFT
Gimme A Li'l Kiss, Will Ya ? Huh ? 577-
 1583
Gimme All The Love You Got 795
Gimme A Pig('s) Foot (And A Bottle Of
 Beer) 825-1446
Gimme Blues 411
Gimme Some Of That Yum Yum Yum 1541
Gimme Something Like That 1560
Gimmie This And Gimmie That (sic) 1522
Gin And Jive 281-282
Gin For Christmas 662
Gin For Joan 1225
Ginger Bells 730
Gin Houn' Blues 1389
Gin House Blues 1443-1455
Gin Mill Blues 366-1451-1511
Gin Mill Special 692-693
Girl At The Typewriter, The 1373
Girl Friend, The 173-233-1506
Girl Friend Of A Boy Friend Of Mine, A
 22-1143-1667
Girl Friend Of The Whirling Dervish, The 8
Girl From Kankakee, The 771
Girl I Left Behind Me, The 1627
Girl In My Dreams Tries To Look Like You,
 The 498-499
Girl In The Little Green Hat, The 877-
 1410
Girl Of My Dreams, I Love You 295-913-
 1028-1584
Girl On The Police Gazette, The 1027
Girls Like You Were Meant For Boys Like Me
 1030
Girl Trouble 84
Girl With The Light Blue Hair, The 747-
 1334-1372
Girl With The Pigtails In Her Hair, The
 95
Git 899
Git Along 255
Git Goin' 735-1024
Git It ('Cause I Love To See You Wid It)
 (sic) 1561
Git-Wit-It 704
Give A Broken Heart A Break 180
Give A Little Whistle 741
Give Her A Kiss For Me 341
Give Her A Pint (And She'll Tell It All)
 899
Give It To Him 1489
Give It To Me Good 965
Give It To Me Right Away 1392
Give It Up 181-1712
Give Me A Break, Baby 779
Give Me A Heart To Sing To 1654
Give Me A Little Bit O' Sunshine 394
Give Me A Night In June 356-1056-1425
Give Me A Ukulele (And A Ukulele Baby) 38
Give Me Back My Heart 1148
Give Me Just A Little Bit Of (Your) Love
 510-555-1058
Give Me Just A Little Bit Of Your Time
 1013
Give Me Liberty Or Give Me Love 77-674
Give Me My Ranch - see ALLA EN EL RANCHO
 GRANDE
Give Me Some Money 91
Give Me Some More 302
Give Me Some Skin 663
Give Me That Old Slow Drag 1466

Give Me The Moonlight, Give Me The Girl
 1397
Give Me The Sunshine 871
Give Me Time 81
Give Me Today 233
Give Me (Your Heart) 1502
Give Me Your Telephone Number 751
Give Out 1224-1436
Give Us The Charleston 558
Give Your Little Baby Lots Of Lovin'
 262
Givin' It Away 137
Glad And Sorry Blues 685
Glad Eyes 569-1672
Glad Rag Doll 31-130-172-242-757-885-
 950
Glad To Be Unhappy 1696
Gladyse 1623
Glamour Girl 684
Glass Of Beer, A Hot Dog And You, A
 1014-1163
Gleeby Rhythm Is Born 1250
Gloaming 282
Gloomy Sunday 770-1406
Glorianna 242-562-804-1641
Glory 874
Glory Of Love, The 101-182-191-597-1313
Glory Of Spring 1666
Glory Shout 837
Glory To Georgia 888
G-Men 1712
Go Ahead On 850
Go Away And Don't Come Back 1502-1503
Go Back When You Stayed Last Night 100-
 530-1490-1650
Goblin Band, The 294-1506
Goblin Market 182-699-1601
Goblins In The Steeple 545-746
Go Down, Moses 460-1633-1635
Go Down Sunshine Blues 1619
God's River Blues 1062
Go Emmaline 72-121-529-623
Go Fly A Kite 432-447-1405
Go Get 'Em, Caroline 861-1643
Go Get It 1617
Go Go Blues 753
Go Harlem 839-1659
Go Home And Tell Your Mother 1639
Go Home, Little Girl, Go Home 1318
Goin' About 1623
Goin' Away And Leavin' My Baby 1454
Goin' Away Blues 1575-1719
Goin' Back To Alabama 886
Going Back To Memphis 1043
Goin' Back To Tennessee 1391
Goin' Conga 260
Goin' Crazy With The Blues 1463
Goin' Down Slow 841
Goin' Down To The Levee 1011-1093-1447
Going ! Going !! Gone !!! 199-1646
Going Harlem In Havana 1223
Goin' Haywire 786
Goin' Home 159-441-732-1598
Goin' Home Again 237
Goin' Home Blues 389-1711
Goin' Nuts 1431
Goin' Out The Back Way 767
Goin' Places 1419-1596
Going South Blues 1321
Goin' To Chicago 105
Goin' To Chicago Blues 108-1575
Goin' To Germany 270

Goin' To Getcha  1715
Goin' To Heaven On A Mule  1235
Going To Shout All Over God's Heaven  56
Going To The Nation  1499
Goin' To Town  477-479-1146-1346-1410
Go, I've Got Somebody Sweeter Than You  998
Go, Joe, Go  269-508-887-1120-1192-1226-1419
Gold Daddy Blues  1218
Gold Digger  1309
Gold Diggers Of 1933 - Medley  471
Gold Diggers' Song, The (We're In The Money)  158-878-958-1099-1241-1286
Gold Digger Stomp  738
Golden Bantam  324
Golden Brown Blues  1082
Golden Gate  648-708-1016
Golden King Shuffle, The  1263
Golden Leaf Rag  998
Golden Leaf Strut  1132
Golden Lily (Blues)  541-1209
Golden Rod  975
Golden Rule Blues  1443
Golden Wedding  742
Golden West Rag  376
Gold Mansion Blues  1321
Gold Tooth Papa Blues  393
Golfing Papa  1464
Go 'Long, Mule  67-623-715-890
Gomer The Goose  1552
Gondola Maid  1252
Gone  155-990-1337
Gone Again Gal  235-1504
Gone But Not Forgotten (Florence Mills)  373-1529
Gone Daddy Blues  1268
Gone With The Gin  1203
Gone With The Wind  1313-1530-1552
Gone With What Draft  329-617
Gone With "What" Wind  107-615
Gonna Buy Me A Telephone  187
Gonna Cut It Tonight  1044
Gonna Get A Girl  568-571-1472
Gonna Get Somebody's Daddy (Wait And See)  623
Gonna Have You-Ain't Gonna Leave You Alone  792
Gonna Make You Sorry (For Everything You Do)  213
Gonna Quit That Man And How !  1413
Gonna Ramble Blues  1014
Gonna Ride  74-1542
Gonna Start Lookin' For A Man To Treat Me Right  214
Gonna Wed That Gal O' Mine  582
Goo, The  155
Goober Dance  415
Good As I Ben To You  628
Goodbye  603-841-892-901
Goodbye Alexander (Goodbye, Honey Boy)  1516
Goodbye Blues  35-312-386-726-822-860-1012  1046-1277-1310-1432
Goodbye Daddy Blues  1266
Goodbye Dear, I'll Be Back In A Year  1318
Goodbye, Don't Cry  1155
Goodbye, Good Luck To You  644
Goodbye Jonah  442-633
Goodbye, Little Darlin', Goodbye  364-1317
Goodbye, Love  290

Goodbye Mama (I'm Off To Yokohama)  1244  1318
Goodbye Medley  85
Goodbye, My Lover, Goodbye  1565
Goodbye Rider  995
Goodbye, Shanghai  1613
Goodbye To Love  35-981
Goodbye To Summer  886
Goodbye To The World, I Know I'm Goin'  1105
Good Cabbage  1489
Good Chib Blues  834
Good Enough To Keep  618
Good Evenin'  22-504-567
Good Evenin', Good Lookin'  619
Good Evening, Pretty Lady  638
Good Feelin' Blues  873-1481-1693
Good For Nothin' (But Love)  431-611-798  812-1633
Good-For-Nothin' Joe  97
Good For You, Bad For Me  1382
Good Gal Blues  766
Good Girl  649
Good Gordon Gin  1526
Good Hearted Woman  570
Good Lawd's Children, The  1674
Good Little, Bad Little You  262-464-509  751-757
Good Little Things You Do, The  8
Good Looking Papa (Blues)  1448-1463
Good Man Blues  1531
Good Man Is Hard To Find, A  186-649-822  956-975-1002-1025-1060-1195-1241-1250-1276-1366-1379-1444-1470-1488-1491-1517-1567-1633-1640-1738
Good Man Sam  1090
Good Meat Grinder  1376
Good Mornin' (1922)  935
Good Mornin' (1937)  441-1313
Good Morning (1939)  1359
Good Morning Blues  102-591-872-873
Good Morning, Glory  1227-1228-1331
Good Morning, Good Evening, Goodnight  1666
Good News  1426
Goodnight, Angel  1315-1402-1721
Goodnight, Angeline  1422
Goodnight, Baby  258
Goodnight Boat  1748
Goodnight (I'll See You In The Morning)  1478-1483
Goodnight, My Beautiful  447
Goodnight, Lovely Little Lady  423
Goodnight, Moon  1227
Goodnight, My Lady Love  881
Goodnight, My Love  599-600-686-1313
Goodnight, My Lucky Day  15
Goodnight, My Lucky Dream  543
Goodnight, Sweet Dreams, Goodnight  443-759-1179
Goodnight, Sweetheart  1470-1693
Good Old Bosom Bread  834-1194-1203
Good Old Bygone Days  1577
Good Old Easy Street  850
Good Old New York  1107
Good Queen Bess  766
Good Sauce From The Gravy Bowl  257
Good Stuff  862-1216
Good Suzie  1542
Good Things Come To Those Who Wait  656
Good Time Ball  1463

Good Time Flat Blues   860
Good Time Mama (Blues)   343-892
Good Time Papa   1061
Good Times (Come On Back Once More)   1452
Good To Me   386
Good Woman   1413
Good Woman Blues   846-1542
Good Woman's Blues, A   278-731
Goody-Goody   365-597-1001-1621
Goofer Dust Blues - see NEW ORLEANS GOOFER
   DUST BLUES
Goofer Dust Swing   843
Goofer Feathers Blues   1045
Goofus   747-875-877-918-1146-1347-1410
Goofy Dust   1109
Goo Goo Blues   1039
Goona Goo, The   123-440-586-660-1027
Goon Drag, The (Gone Wid De Goon) (sic)
   1247
Goosby Blues   627
Goose Creek Stomp   173
Goose Grease   1718
Goose Hangs High, The   739-1249
Goose Pecked Man   737
Goose Pimples   116-722-1131-1420
Gosh Darn !   35-806
Go South, Young Man   258
Gossip   805
Got A Bran' New Suit   52-437-687-1627
Gotta Darn Good Reason Now (For Bein'
   Good)   252
Gotta Date In Louisiana   189-588
Got A/Gotta Feelin' For You   752-776-867-
   1281-1569
Gotta Great Big Date With A Little Bitta
   Girl   341
Got A Letter From My Darlin'   1043
Got A Letter From My Kid Today   911-1318
Got A Man In The 'Bama Mines   848-1487
Got A Mind To Ramble   849
Gotta Need For You   1352
Got Another Sweetie Now   312
Got A Pair Of New Shoes   703
Got A/Gotta Pebble In My Shoe   8-588-1661
Got Butter On It   1321
Got Cut All To Pieces   1572
Got 'em Blues   1518
Got Everything But You   475-708
Got Everything (Don't Want Anything But
   You)   1168
Got Gratitude   587
Got Jelly On My Mind   1455
Got Me Doin' Things   755
Got My Mind On That Thing   1451
Got Myself Another Jockey Now   1284
Got No Blues   42
Got No More Home Than A Dog   666
Got No Time (1925)   310-511-966
Got No Time (1939)   446-814-829-1633
Got To It   1123
Got The Bench, Got The Park   1427
Got The Blues For Harlem   1245
Got The Blues For My Baby   849
Got The Blues For The West End   845
Got The Blues So Bad   1487-1489
Got The Jitters   1235-1278-1331
Got The Moon In My Pocket   1244
Got The South In My Soul   157-935-1277-
   1286
Got The World In A Jug (The Stopper's In
   My Hand)   732

Gotta Be, Gonna Be Mine   1646
Got To Cool My Doggies Now   349-1185-
   1462-1531-1607-1719
Gotta Dance My Way To Heaven   939
Gotta Get Home   166-372
Gotta Get Some Shut-Eye   206-296-611-
   1298
Gotta Getta Girl   228
Gotta Get To St. Joe   744
Gotta Go !   698-1476
Gotta Go Home   1288
Gotta Go To Work Again   438-1621
Got To Have My Daddy Blues   280
Got To Leave My Home Blues   1012
Gouge Of Armour Avenue, The   91-715
Go 'Wan To Town (sic)   807
Go Wash An Elephant (If You Wanna Do
   Something Big)   269
Grabbin' Blues   172
Grab Your Partner And Swing   786
Grace And Beauty   1588
Gracias   424
Gramercy Square   1156
Grand   3
Grandfather's Clock   906
Grandma And Grandpa   847-1677
Grandma's Ball   308
Grand Opera Blues   548-1326-1556
Grandma Said "Let's Suzie-Q"   843
Grandpa's Soells   359-1099-1101
Grand Piano Blues   758
Grand Slam   615
Grand Terrace Rhythm   368-728-1661
Grand Terrace Shuffle   760
Grand Terrace Swing   728
Granny (You're My Mammy's Mammy)   219-
   1053
Grape Juice Bill   975
Grass Grows Greener ('Way Down Home),
   The   653-840-1064-1393-1581
Grasshopper Papa   570
Grass Is Always Greener (In The Other
   Fellow's Yard), The   715-1190
Grass Is Getting Greener All The Time,
   The   1751
Gravedigger's Holiday   184
Graveyard Blues   633-1676
Graveyard Bound Blues   353-1093
Graveyard Dream Blues   352-763-1011-1050-
   1057-1439
Graveyard Love   802
Gravel Pit Stomp   681
Gravier Street Blues   415-1458-1699-1700
Graysom Street Blues   846
Greasy Plate Stomp   1565
Great American Tourist, The   1745
Great Big Bunch Of You, A   147-464
Great Caesar's Ghost   728
Great Camp Meetin' Day   1423-1426
Great Day   1569-1687
Greatest Mistake Of My Life, The   1721
Great Scott   1565
Great White Way Blues   349-915-1186-1187-
   1188
Greener The Grass   534
Green Eyes   434-911
Green Fields And Bluebirds   1239
Green Gal Can't Catch On, A   1011
Green Goon Jive   1360
Green Grass   852
Green Grass Grew All Around, The   865

Green Jazz  118-876
Green River Blues  1135-1714
Grey Eyes  1048
Grieg's Piano Concerto (sic)  1553
Grievin'  495
Grieving For You  748-799
Grieving Heart Blues  849
Grievin' Hearted Blues  1267
Grievin' Mama Blues  1060
Grievin' Me  1486
Grievous Blues  627
Grinding Mill  1542
Grind-Out, The  1391
Grizzly Bear Rag  139-632-1255-1256
Groove Juice Special  551
Ground Hog Blues  121-1544
Growin' Old Blues  548
Growl, The  1072-1073
Growlin'  93
Growlin' Dan  251
Growling Dog  679
Grown-Up Baby  469
G. T. Stomp  760
Guess I'll Go Back Home (This Summer) 80-
    447-908
Guess Who ?  243-366-540
Guess Who's In Town  1652
Guiding Me Back Home  1426
Guilty  673-1470
Guitar Blues  844
Guitar In High  208
Guitar Rhythm  558
Gulf Coast Blues  5-80-136-528-633-666-685
    710-711-749-1022-1092-1438-1520-1532-
    1533-1544
Gully Low Blues (Mama, Why Do You Treat Me
    So ?)  42
Gumbo  1208
Gut Bucket Blues  40
Gut Bucket Shuffle  683
Gut Struggle  394
Guy Needs A Gal, The  1317
Guy's Got To Go  1046
Guy Wnat Takes His Time, A  510
G'wan, I Told You (sic)  1550
Gwine To Have Bad Luck For Seven Years
    (sic)  1453
Gymnastics  149
Gypsy, The  1063
Gypsy Blues  914-935-1184-1492
Gypsy Glass Blues  354
Gypsy In My Soul, The  587-1357
Gypsy Lady  70
Gypsy Love Song  162-1208
Gypsy Told Me, A  321-881
Gypsy Without A Song, A  493
Gypsy Woman Blues  1455
Gyptia  748

Haarlem Hot Club Stomp  836
Hacket Picking Blues  959
Ha ! Ha !  1095
Hairy Joe Jump  944
Haitian Blues  1059
Half A Heart  417
Half A Loaf Is Better Than None  664
Half A Moon  402
Half-Moon On The Hudson  880
Half Way Down The Street  325-1374
Halfway To Heaven  464-1291
Hallelujah !  165-171-236-402-450-453-606-
    636-648-869-1142-1371-1425-1626-(cont.)

Hallelujah ! (cont.)  1634-1660-1736-1743
Hallelujah Blues  458
Hallelujah ! I'm A Bum  1635
Hallelujah Joe Ain't Preachin' No More
    679
Hallelujah ! Things Look Rosy Now  893-
    1629-1630
Hallelujah Yeah Man  682
Hallucinations  340-977
Ham And/'n' Eggs  106-459
Ham Fatchet Blues  210
Ham Fat Swing  679
Ham Gravy  1096
Hammond Blues  1065
Hamtramck  910
Handful Of Keys  150-602-1495-1623-1626-
    1634
Handful Of Riffs, A  844
Handful Of Stars, A  433-1407
H And J  108
Handle My Heart With Care  913
Hand Me Down My Walkin' Cane  158-1563-
    1635
Hands Across The Table  424-1211-1696
Handsome Gigolo - see JUST A GIGOLO
Handsome Territorial, The  589
Handy Andy  91
Hangin' Around  190-403-559-658-1182-
    1643-1674
Hangin' Around Boudon  1670
Hangin' On The Garden Gate  246-888-1294
Hangin' On To That Man  790-791
Hanging Out With You  1668
Hangman Blues  754
Hang On To Me  804-951
Hang Out The Stars In Indiana  515
Hangover  1275
Hangover Blues  272-333
Hangover In Hong Kong  787
Hang Your Heart On A Hickory Limb  9-370
Happily Married  1528
Happiness Ahead  1228
Happy  209-917
Happy, The  155
Happy As The Day Is Long  487-698-727-
    1286-1330-1646
Happy Birthday To Love  371-441
Happy Birthday To You  1374-1415
Happy Children Blues  1030
Happy Days And Lonely Nights  31-242-506
    546-950-1535
Happy Days Are Here Again  21-246-286-
    800-877-952-1214-1313
Happy Farmer, The  1372
Happy Feet  252-346-730-785-789-800-960-
    1005-1216-1285-1294-1570-1687-1695
Happy Four  797
Happy-Go-Lucky  1197
Happy-Go-Lucky In My Old Kentucky Home
    1609
Happy-Go-Lucky You (And Broken-Hearted
    Me)  288
Happy Hour Blues  1371
Happy Humming Bird  1064
Happy I Found You (Glad I'm In Love)
    1295
Happy Mood  299
Happy Pal Stomp  851
Happy Rhythm  1119
Happy Shout  964
Happy Today, Sad Tomorrow  40
Happy Travelin'  505

Happy (Watchin' All The Clouds Roll By)
 1591
Harbor Blues  1065
Harbor Lights  1552
Harbor Of My Heart, The  1484
Hard Corn  1697
Hard Driving Papa  1443
Hardee Stomp  1108
Hard Headed Daddy  841
Hard-Headed Gal  1717
Hard-Headed Mama  343-1082
Hard-Hearted Hannah  529-707-715-733-827-
 966-1364-1420-1591-1694-1737
Hard Hearted Papa  782-1094
Hard Hustlin' Blues  891
Hard Lovin' Blues  864
Hard Luck  511-1075
Hard Luck Blues  213-643-750-1550
Hard, Oh Lawd  354
Hard Ridin' Papa  570
Hard Times  260
Hard Time(s) Blues  355-462-753-1128-1160-
 1443
Hard Times Breakdown  4
Hard Times Is On Me  1414
Hard Times Stomp  1218
Hard To Get  616
Hard-To-Get Gertie  1-233-265-356-532-644-
 719-1181-1182-1616
Hard-To-Get Papa  1558
Hare And The Hounds, The  923
Hark The Sound Of Tar Heel Voices  913
Harlem  279-536-782-964-1341-1433
Harlem After Midnight  164-1073
Harlem Ain't What It Usta Be  1560
Harlem Air-Shaft  496-497
Harlemania  478
Harlem Baby  461
Harlem Blues  941-1265-1622
Harlem Bound  835
Harlem Camp Meeting  256
Harlem Chapel Chimes  426
Harlem Confusion  307
Harlem Congo  1660
Harlem Drag  833
Harlem Fiesta  1590
Harlem Flat Blues  478
Harlem Fuss  1623
Harlem Gin Blues  1247
Harlem (Harlem's Heaven To Me)  1147
Harlem Heat  1074
Harlem Hokum Blues  584
Harlem Holiday (Harlem Holydays - sic !)
 255-403-803
Harlem Hospitality  256
Harlem Jamboree  783
Harlem Joys  1467
Harlem Lament  758
Harlem Lullaby  77
Harlem Madness  341-727-776-789-1069-1294
Harlem Nocturne  1150
Harlem On A Saturday Night  40
Harlem On My Mind  1653
Harlem On Parade  912
Harlem Rhumbain' The Blues  1204
Harlem Rhythm Dance  311-774
Harlem River Quiver  474
Harlem's Araby - see IN HARLEM'S ARABY
Harlem Shout  986
Harlem Shuffle  1371
Harlem Speaks  98-487-488-491
Harlem Stomp  57

Harlem Stomp-Down, The  945
Harlem Strut  837
Harlem Suzie-Kue  1489
Harlem Swing  188-386-1528
Harlem Symphony, A  791
Harlem Twist  474-1140
Harlem Twister, The  755
Harlem Woogie  839
Harmaniac Blues  530
Harmonica Blues  149-1577
Harmonica Harry (The Harmonica King)  655
 957-1667-1740
Harmonica Hop  322
Harmonica Rag  388
Harmonizing  468
Harmony Blues (1922)  1090-1187
Harmony Blues (1926)  810-1110-1720
Harmony Blues (1928)  1477
Harmony Blues (1930)  1104
Harmony Heaven  97-1127
Harmony In Harlem  94-492-1263
Harmony Moze  1199
Harris Blues  1065
Harrisburg Itch  4
Harry Wills, The Champion  783
Harvard Blues  109
Harvey  1081
Has Anybody Seen My Corinne ?  1516
Has Anybody Seen My Man ?  1457
Has Anyone Seen Corinne ?  27
Has Been Blues  1219
Hatchet Head Blues  1164
Hateful Blues  709-1051-1440-1458
Hateful Papa Blues  954
Hats Off, Here Comes A Lady  1668
Hats Off To MacArthur (And Our Boys
 Down There)  1319
Haunted By The Blues  1488
Haunted House Blues  643-1440
Haunted Nights  479
Haunted Town  98
Haunting Blues  263-1036-1145-1186-1523-
 1525
Haunting Me  202
Haunting Memories  155
Havana  648-1615
Have A Heart  1286 (see also LOST IN
 MEDITATION)
Have A Little Dream On Me  699-809-1624
Have A Little Faith In Me  246-421-788-
 1153-1369
Have It Ready  721
Have It Your Way  1358
Have Mercy  1160-1662
Have Mercy !  150
Have Mercy Blues  1091
Haven't Got A Dollar To Pay Your House
 Rent Man  391
Haven't I ?  1213-1292
Have To Change Keys To Play These Blues
 844
Have You Changed ?  499-911
Have You Ever Been Down ?  1618
Have You Ever Been In Heaven ?  124-1236
Have You Ever Been In Love ?  15
Have You Ever Been Lonely ?  199-1330
Have You Ever Felt That Way ?  731-757-
 1281-1535-1703-1704
Have You Forgotten ?  1519-644
Have You Forgotten So Soon ?  79-183-445
 1159                              )554-1028
Have You Got Any Castles, Baby ?  59-442-

Have You Met Miss Jones ? 294-606-1401
Have Your Chill, I'll Be Here When Your
 Fever Rises 1729
Have You Seen My Baby's Rumba ? 413
Havin' A Ball 839-913-1630
Havin' A Ball At Carnegie Hall 336
Having A Good Time-Wish You Were Here 875
Havin' Lots Of Fun 992
Having Myself A Time 768
Having Wonderful Time (Wish You Were Here)
 442-703
Hawaiian Blues 458
Hawaiian Butterfly 315
Hawaiian Capers 1122
Hawaiian Harmony Blues 836
Hawaiian Heat Wave 1223
Hawaiian Hospitality 54
Hawaiian Paradise 182
Hawaiian Rose 630
Hawaiian War Chant (Ta-Hu-Wa-Hu-Wai) 307-
 445-454-1225
Hawaii Calls 880
Hawaii Sang Me To Sleep 1539
Hayfoot, Strawfoot (1925) 718-719-867
Hayfoot, Strawfoot (1942) 500
Hayseed Blues 684
Hazel's Boogie Woogie 1371
H. C. Q. Strut 1262
Headache Blues 412
Head-Hunter's Dream, The 1209
Headin' For A Weddin' 878
Headin' For Better Times 957
Headin' For Hallelujah 816
Headin' For Harlem 187-784-994
Headin' For Louisville 523-1220-1229-1275
 1588
Headin' For The River 783
Headin' South 655
Head Low 1281-1325
Head On My Pillow 298-450
Head Over Heels In Love 24-439
Head Stuff 1311
Heah Me Talkin' 415
Heah Me Talkin' To Ya ? (sic) 44-57-1268
He Ain't Done Right By Nell 1
He Ain't Got Rhythm 14-586-600-894-986-
 1027-1732
He Ain't Never Been In/To College 242-
 1393
He Always Goes Father Than Father 883
Hear My Song, Violetta 10-433-449
Hearse Man Blues 1674
Heartaches 504-980-1668
Heart-Aching Blues 834
Heart And Soul 322-1690
Heartbreak Blues 688
Heart-Breakin' Baby 237-1290
Heart-Breaking Blues 270-1051-1320-1486
Heart-Breakin' Joe 522-1050
Heartbroken And Lonely 804-1016
Heartbroken Blues 460
Heart-Broken Rose 1054
Heart-Broken Strain 121-1257
Heart Like The Ocean, A 1075
Heart Of A Nigger, The - Suite 471
Heart Of Mine 1003-1660
Hearts And Flowers 997
Heart Sickness Blues 975
Heartstrings 1491
Hearts Without Flowers 1615
Heart You Stole From Me, The 98

Heat Wave 290-395-423-904-1601-1653-
 1691
Heat Waves 1072-1146
Heaven Can Wait 9-2o6-296-446
Heaven For Two 525-1226-1379-1738
Heaven, Heaven - see ALL GOD'S CHILLUN
 GOT WINGS
Heaven Help A Sailor On A Night Like
 This 1394
Heaven Help This Heart Of Mine 78-1314
Heaven In My Arms (Music In My Heart)
 448-613
Heavenly Hideaway 435
Heaven Will Protect The Working Girl 1263
Heavy Burden Blues 846
Heavy Stuff Blues 1029
Heavy Traffic On Canal Street 1125
He Belongs To Me 861
He Brought Joy To My Soul 1651
He Caught The B & O 90
Heckler's Hop 466
Heck Of A How-Do-You-Do 1528
He Don't Know (And I Can't Make Him
 Understand) 1338
He Don't Mean Me No Harm 278
Heebie Jeebies 40-65-156-157-625-632-
 795-1071-1182-1275-1556-1651-1657-1662
 1714
Heebie Jeebies Are Rockin' The Town 662
Heifer Dust 516
Heigh-Ho (Dwars' Marching Song, The) 124
Heigh-Ho, Everybody, Heigh-Ho 871-1292-
 1394
Hejre Kati 1476-1477
He Just Don't Appeal To Me 179-1641
He Left Me 1751
Helen 188
Helena 905
Helen Gone 1052-1085-1335
He Likes It Slow 213-1467
He'll Do You Wrong 1090
Hell In My Heart 1154
Hellish Old Feeling 1528
Hellish Rag 1268
Hell Is So Low Down 1413
Hello ! 1035
Hello, Aloha ! How Are You ? 173
Hello, Baby 979-1294-1486-1641 (some-
 times shown as H'LO BABY)
Hello, Beautiful 197-1197-1328-1469-
 1493
Hello, Bluebird 532-921-982-1675
Hello Central, Give Me No-Man's-Land 379
Hello, Cutie 929
Hello, 'Frisco 315
Hello, Hawaii, How Are You ? 315
Hello, Hello ! 1517
Hello Little Devil - see MELLOW LITTLE
 DEVIL
Hello ! Little Girl Of My Dreams 1317-
 1505
Hello, Lola 1113
Hello, Ma ! I Done It Again 528
Hello, Mister Kringle 1316
Hello ! Montreal 399-520
Hello, My Darling 1735
Hello Sandy 397
Hell's Bells 745-876-881-986
Hell's Bells And Hallelujah 1601
Help ! 640
Helping Hand 1426

1890

Helpless 1244
Help Me 696
Help Yourself To Happiness 287-593
He May Be Your Dog But He's Wearing My
 Collar 732
He May Be Your Man But He Comes To See Me
 Sometimes 349-705-706-848-1059-1185-
 1271-1466-1467-1608-1725
Henderson Stomp 616-720
Hen House Blues 1217
Henke Stomp 736
Hen Party Blues 409
Henpecked Blues 128-560-646-826-857-884-
 1187-1362-1509
Henpecked Man 629
Henry Brown Blues 181
Hep 1085
Hep And Happy 298
Hep Cat Love Song 261
Hep Cats' Ball 57
Hep-Tee-Hootie (Jook Box Jive) 433
Hereafter 186-1243
Here Am I - Broken-Hearted - see BROKEN
 HEARTED
Here Comes Emaline 194-234-265
Here Comes Emily Brown 305-800-953-1214
Here Comes Malinda 233-234-523-707-967
Here Comes Marjorie 1111
Here Comes My Baby 734
Here Comes My Ball And Chain 340-979
Here Comes The Hot Tamale Man 337-338-339
Here Comes The Man With The Jive 1465
Here Comes The Night 815
Here Comes The Show Boat 579-784
Here Comes The Sun 196-980-1295-1621
Here Comes Your Pappy (With The Wrong Kind
 Of Load) 382-1270
Here Come The British 291
Here Goes 983-1235
Here I Am 234
Here In My Arms 1483-1696
Here Is My Heart 361-424
Here It Is Monday And I've Still Got A
 Dollar 198-876
Here It Is Tomorrow Again 1735
Here Or There 668
Here Lies Love 22
Here Or There 1275
Here's A Little Package 697-698
Here's Love In Your Eye(s) 14-598-1415
Here's My Heart 1242-1540
Here's That Party Now In Person 654-1076
Here's To Romance 249-365-1307
Here's Your Change 1089
Here's Your Opportunity - see IF ANYBODY
 HERE WANTS A REAL KIND MAMA
Here 'Tis 548-1715
Here We Are 671-1666
Here You Are 186-299
Here You Come With Love 982
Her Majesty, My Sugar 1486-1688
Herman At The Sherman 741
Her Name Was Rosita 1359
Hersal Blues 27-1549
He's A Colonel From Kentucky 1709
He's A Curbstone Cutie (They Call Him
 Jelly Bean) 698-561
He's A Darned Good Man (To Have Hanging
 Around) 792
He's A Good Man To Have Around 272-351-
 890-949-1152-1293-1457
He's A Good Meat Cutter 1309

He's A Gypsy From Poughkeepsie 441-781-
 880
He's A Latin From Staten Island 97
He's Always Hanging Around 1422
He's A Mean, Mean Man (But He's Good To
 Me) 1725
He's A New Kind Of Man - see NEW KIND OF
 MAN, A
He's A Ragpicker 508
He's A Son Of The South 51-534-774-1217
He's Gone 909
He's Gone Away 1622
He's Gone Blues 1442
He's Got Me Goin' 1446
He's Had No Lovin' For A Long, Long Time
 1194
He, She And Me 659-931-1069
He's In The Jailhouse Now 874-1043
Hesitating/Hesitation Blues 127-136-177
 512-567-582-665-942-1002-1011-1252-
 1482-1532-1605
He's Just A Horn-Tootin' Fool 211-961-
 1694
He's Long Gone From Bowling Green - see
 LONG GONE FROM BOWLING GREEN
He's Mine, All Mine 783-839-1449
He's My Guy 454-529-819
He's My Man 1061
He's My Man (You'd Better Leave Him
 Alone) 192-704-735-1037
He's My Man, Your Man (Somebody Else's
 Too) 1050-1057
He's My Scuffler 1489
He's Never Gonna Throw Me Down 182-543-
 732-1012-1050-1057-1716
He's Not Worth Your Tears 592-1153-1384
He's 1-A In The Army And He's A-1 In My
 Heart 186-818
He's Pulling His Whiskers 1203
He's Red Hot To Me 1061
He's So Good 91
He's So Unusual 671-888-1302
He's Tall (And) Dark And Handsome 941-
 1665
He's The Cause Of Me Being Blue 1618
He's The Different Type Of Guy 1154
He's The Hottest Man In Town 715-797-
 997-1171
He's The Kind Of A Man That You Like (If
 You Like That Kind Of A Man) 1591
He's The Last Word 129-668-963-1221-1232
He's The Life Of The Party 697
He's The One For Me 797
He's The Sweetest Black Man In Town 337
He's Tight Like This 7
He Stole My Heart Away 591
He's Worth His Weight In Gold 1584
He Took It Away From Me 1576
He Used To Be Mine (But You Can Have Him
 Now) 1051
He Used To Be Your Man But He's My Man
 Now 1059-1725-1727
He Walked Right In 93
He Wants Too Much 1489
He Was A Good Man (But He's Dead And
 Gone) 1306
He Wasn't Born In Araby But He's A
 Sheikin' Fool 522-1728
He Went Away And Left Me Blues 1057
He Wouldn't Stop Doing It 767-1706
Hey, Babe, Hey ! 1416
Hey Barber 8

Hey ! Chief  551
Hey Doc  261-693-694-743
Hey ! Hey !  547
Hey Hey And Hee Hee (I'm Charleston Crazy)
   623-732-803
Hey-Hey-Hey ! Have You Had Your Corn Today
   698
Hey ! Hey ! Hey ! Hey !  893
Hey-Hey (Your Cares Away)  1308
Hey Huss'  1070
Hey ! I'Am Blue  695
Hey Lawdy Mama/Papa  58-104-633-902
Hey Little Hen  590
Hey Man, Hey Man !  1109-1561
Hey Paw !  1351
Hey ! Young Fella  148-289-1600
Hezekiah  323-747
Hiawatha  1199-1474-1475
Hiawatha's Lullaby  1600
Hick Stomp  24
Hidden Valley  1415
Hide And Seek  23-1117
Hi-De-Ho Miracle Man, The  258
Hi-De-Ho Romeo  258
Hi-De-Ho Serenade  260
Hi-De-Ho Swing  1244
Hi-Diddle-Diddle  719-836-955-966-1275-
   1510
Hiding All My Cares  537
Higginbotham Blues  751
High And Dry  1081
High And Low  952-1385
High Brown Babies' Ball - see AT THE HIGH
   BROWN BABIES' BALL
High Brown Blues  705-1573
High Dives  418
High-Falutin' Stomp  1036
High Fever  319-337-338-340-928-1286-1714
High Hat, A Piccolo And A Cane, A  383-439
   893-1308
High Hattin' Hattie  1046
High Hat, Trumpet And Rhythm  1584
High, High, High Up In The Hills  403-467-
   510-631-872-982-1505
High Jivin'  520
Highland Swing, The  86
High Life  477-790
High On A Windy Hill  167-434-910
High Rhythm And Low Moanin'  688
High Sheriff  4
High Society (alternatively known as HIGH
   SOCIETY BLUES or HIGH SOCIETY RAG)  51-
   118-125-145-153-371-466-563-661-704-829-
   875-876-992-1065-1100-1107-1114-1122-
   1165-1223-1251-1287-1656-1705-1707-1708
High Steppers  1263
High Tension  571-1346
High Up On A Hill Top  241-301-670-970-
   1568
High-Valued Mama, Papa's Gonna Low-Rate
   You  501
Highways Are Happy Ways  1612-1665
High, Wide And Handsome  59-695-894
High Yellow Blues  1466
Hi Henry Stomp  1574
Hi-Ho The Merrio  1-234
Hikin' Down The Highway  1386
Hi-Lee Hi-Lo  914
Hill And Dale  1587
Hill Billy From 10th Avenue  1402
Hills Of Old Wyomin', The  1312

Hilly Billy Willy  1147
Hindu Dream Man  338
Hindustan  130-370-1365-1409
Hines Rhythm  759
Hinkey Dinkey Parley Voo  1428
Hip Chick  494
Hip ! Hip !  1502
Hip-Hip-Hooray  315-902
His Old Cornet  584
Hi Spook  990
Hitch Up The Horses  555
Hitchy Koo  508
Hit Me But Don't Quit Me  1717
Hit Me In The Nose Blues  1444-1640
Hit Ta Ditty Low Down  823
Hit That Jive, Jack  329-1560
Hit That Mess  551
Hit The Ramp  329
Hittin 'Em Low  641
Hittin' On All Six  217
Hittin' The Bottle  482-677-985-1570-
   1621
Hittin' The Ceiling  21-83-677-1418-1484
Hi-Ya, Mr. Chips  788
Hi-Yo Silver  759-1315-1357
H'lo Baby - see HELLO BABY
Hobo Bill  343
Hobo Blues  737
Hoboken Bucket  296
Hoboken Prison Blues  570
Hoboken Rock  435
Hobo On Park Avenue  785
Hobo's Prayer, The  265-546-869-1167-
   1390-1510-1545
Hobo, You Can't Ride This Train  50
Hobson Street Blues  1752
Hock My Shoes  1007
Hock Shop Blues  734 735
Hocus Pocus/Hokus Pokus  727-1346-1602
Hodge Podge  766-775-816-907
Hoe Down  151-1244-1657
Hog Maw Stomp  1622
Hog Wild Blues  783
Ho-Ho-(Ho) Hogan  394-520-1117
Ho Hum !  673-678-958-1312-1472
Hoi-Polloi  889
Hokus Pokus - see Hocus Pocus
Hold 'Em, Hootie  1038
Hold 'Er, Deacon  149-811
Hold 'Er, Newt (They're After Us)  1411
Hold Everything  28-1038-1368
Hold Everything Blues  16
Hold Everything, Here Comes My Girl  649
Holding My Honey's Hand  806-1312-1645
Holding My Own  1678
Hold It Boy Blues  856
Hold It (Mean Baby)  681
Hold It Still  1045
Hold Me (1920)  1351
Hold Me (1932)  148-1438-1751
Hold Me, Baby  1326
Hold Me, Parson  1061
Hold My Hand  423-1397-1632
Hold On  81
Hold Out For Love  1116
Hold That Tiger - see TIGER RAG
Hold Tight (Want Some Sea Food, Mama)
   113-431-446-554-588-1435-1633
Hold Your Hats  1400
Hold Your Man  1668
Hole Holy Roly-Poly  1560

1892

Hole In The Wall  1014-1156
Holiday In Harlem  1660
Holiday In Venice  1667
Holler Stomp  851
Hollow Hole In The Ground  859
Hollywood  1667
Hollywood Jump  106
Hollywood Pastime  428
Hollywood Rag  270
Hollywood Revue of 1929, Sekections from
  951
Hollywood Shuffle  862
Hollywood Stomp  1489
Holy Smoke  1752
Home (1923)  71-1471
Home (1931)  50-76-249-422-470
Home Again Blues  482-1178-1230-1342-1351-
  1674-1691
Home Alone Blues  854-1021
Homebound (For Charleston, South Carolin')
  38
Home Brew Blues  762
Home Cooking  335-859
Home-Cookin' Mama (With The Fryin' Pan)
  18-746
Home, Cradle Of Happiness  1425-1458-1560-
  1651
Home Folks Blues  376
Home In Pasadena  565
Home In The Clouds  431-611
Home James  814
Homeless Blues  1444
Home Made - see REHEARSIN' FOR A NERVOUS
  BREAKDOWN
Home On The Range  162
Homesick  69
Home, Sweet Home  1238
Home Sweet Home Blues  66-547
Home Ties  425
Home Town  385
Home Town Blues  164-560-766-1376-1608-
  1609
Hoeward Bound - see FLYING HOME
Homeward Bound Blues  863
Honest And Truly  38-576-796-986
Honestly  9-1359
Honey  243-244-775-888-901-931-950-1155-
  1243
Honey Babe  991-1102
Honey Bee (Let Me Be Your Honey Bee)  1413
Honey Bunch  568-720
Honey Bunny Boo  9-1263
Honey Child/Chile  111-588
Honeycomb Harmony  1119
Honey Dear  215
Honey Do !  51-1232
Honey, Don't Go Away  845
Honey, Don't You Love Me Any More ?  51
Honey, Don't You Shake Me Down  1130
Honey Dripper Blues  834-1676
Honey Dripper Blues No. 2  834
Honey Hush  135-328-1634
Honey, I'm Bound To Go  778
Honey, I'm In Love With You  170-624
Honey In The Bee Ball  864-1269
Honey In The Honeyoomb  1655
Honey, Just For You  898
Honey, Keep Your Mind On Me  986
Honey Lu  219
Honey Man Blues  1443
Honey Mine  303

Honeymoon Blues  170
Honeymoon Hotel  200-878
Honeymoonin' On A Dime  1468
Honey, Please Don't Turn Your Back On Me
  1271
Honeysuckle Rose  2-27-56-77-101-188-279-
  311-329-382-387-424-607-614-688-690-
  700-726-730-759-760-774-821-822-864-
  1026-1034-1092-1106-1155-1156-1261-
  1332-1402-1419-1476-1505-1506-1511-
  1570-1625-1626-1628-1630-1634-1636-
  1637-1733
Honey, That Reminds Me  1346
Honey, Where You Been So Long ?  1265
Honey, You're So Good To Me  843
Hong Kong Blues  276-447
Hong Kong Dream Girl  339-511-797
Honky Tonk Blues  1105
Honky Tonk Music  1106
Honky Tonk Train Blues  369-747-947-948-
  1334-1572-1752
Honolulu  9-296-446
Honolulu Blues  1087-1145-1222-1347
Honolulu Cake-Walk, The  1197
Honolulu Lou  1008
Honolulu Moon  269
Hooch  1085
Hoochee Miss Lou  881
Hoochy Coochy Blues  538
Hoodle Dee Doo Dee Doodoo  869-1098-1381
Hoodoo Blues  178
Hoodooin' Woman  679
Hoodoo Man, The  1184
Hoodoo Man Blues  1487
Hoodoo Plan, The  1541
Hoodoo Women  1541
Hooking Cow Blues, The  665-1518
Hoola Boola Dance  164
Hoop 'Em Up Blues  972
Hooray For Love  595
Hooray For Spinach  9-1691
Hooray ! Hooray ! It's Ray-Ray-Raining
  524-1745
Hoosier Hop  752-932
Hoosier Sweetheart  578-1136
Hootie Blues  1038
Hootie's Ignorant Oil  1038
Hootin' De Hoot  1189
Hootin' Owl Blues  1338
Hopeless Blues  118-825-915
Hopeless Love Affair, A  1631
Hope You Haven't Forgotten Me  1413
Hop Head  473
Hop Head Blues  1083
Hopkins Scream  774
Hop Off  722-723
Hop On Me Blues  1711
Hoppin' 'Round  1614
Hop Skip  235
Hop, Skip And Jump  772
Hop, Skip, Jump  780
Horizon  1360
Horn Of Plenty Blues  1346
Hornpipe Swing, The  86
Horn-Tootin' Fool - see HE'S JUST A HORN
  TOOTIN' FOOL
Hors d'oeuvres  22-334-1117
Horse Feathers  806
Horses  237-561-777-855-1752
Horses And Numbers  551
Horsey, Keep Your Tail Up  314-401

Hortense (My Sweet Hortense) 68-1614
Ho-Sa-Bonnie 10
Hot Air(e) 260-555-764-1172-1219-1356-
1545
Hot And Anxious 386-724-1277
Hot And Bothered 476-481-485-1253
Hot 'n' Cold 1186
Hot And Heavy 1213-1559
Hot And Ready 862
Hot And Strong 1263
Hot As A Summer's Day 962-1655
Hot Biscuits 100
Hot Bones And Rice 833
Hot Bricks 1202-1213
Hotcha Razz-Ma-Tazz 257-1431
Hot Chestnuts 743
Hot Club Blues 1670
Hot Club Stomp 835-1053
Hot Coffee 378-531-1214
Hot Corn 1198
Hot Dawg ! 1239
Hot Dog 1045
Hot Dog, A Blanket And You, A 873
Hot Dog Joe 9
Hot Dogs 589-1557
Hot Feet 478-1483
Hot Fingers 845
Hot Foot 1158
Hot Foot'n' 523
Hot Foot Sue 460
Hot Heels 922-1080-1222-1287
Hot Henry ! 967
Hot Honey 1030
Hot-Hot-Hottentot 682-870-1161-1520-1544
Hot Hot Mama (Looking For A Fireproof Man)
881
Hot House Rag 1656
Hot House Rose 1697
(Hot) Jazz Pie 698-1410
Hot Jelly Blues 1671
Hot Licks 1174
Hot Lips 69-179-220-221-349-391-582-756-
825-923-940-1059-1147-1341-1390-1434-
1482-1523-1525-1614-1680
(Hot) Lovin' 99-1707
Hot Mallets 590-662
Hot Mamma 1715-1716
Hot Miss Molly 568
Hot Mittens 193
Hot Moments 136
Hot Mustard 720-1276
Hot Notes 1327-1362
Hot Nuts 1677-1697
Hot Nuts Swing 852
Hot Papa 1448
Hot Peanuts 413
Hot Pebble Blues 1216
Hot Peppers 404
Hot Piano 1206
Hot Piano Stomp 924
Hot Platter 692
Hot Potatoes 143
Hot Sax 154
Hotshots On Parade 386
Hot Spell 903
Hot Springs Blues 1444
Hot Springs Water Blues 1069
Hot String Beans 1007
Hot Strut 539
Hot Stuff 150-328-1691-1694
Hot Stuff - A Negro Oddity 25-1578
Hot Stuff Blues 1091

Hot Stuff Red 461
Hot Tamale Molly 624-707
Hot Tempered Blues 833
Hottentot 477
Hottentot Potentate 1654
Hotter Than 'Ell 727
Hotter Than Fire 676
Hotter Than That 43
Hottest Gal/Girl In Town, The 843-991
Hot Time In The Old Town - see THERE'LL
BE A HOT TIME IN THE OLD TOWN TONIGHT
Hot Toddy 255-281
Hot Town 1715
Hot Water 256
Hot Water Blues 1110
Hot Waves 1595
Hour Behind The Sun 1320
Hour Of Parting, The 615-981-1147-1195-
1513-1733
Hours I Spent With You, The 1378
House Hop 182-598-1071-1508
House Is Haunted (By The Echo Of Your
Last Goodbye), The 291
House Jack Built For Jill, The 362
House Of David Blues 176-640-725-1175-
1188-1193-1523-1608-1722
House Of Morgan 663
House On The Hill, The 1314
House Party Stomp 1556
House Rent Ball 712
House Rent Blues 1093-1441-1699
House Rent Lizzie 141
House Rent Party Day 1000-1248
House Rent Rag 409
House Rent Scuffle 842
House Rent Stomp 964
House Snake Blues 1727
House Where I Was Born, The 1432
House With A Little Red Barn, A 1304
Houston Blues 541-715-1352-1525
Houston Bound 1320
How About Me ? 1069-1686
How 'Bout That ? 865
How 'Bout That Mess ? 910-1070-1246-
1674
How About You ? 151-453-1244-1657
How A Little Girl Like You Can Love Me
247
How Am I To Know ? 18-316-322-447-451-
1063-1569-1571-1661-1732-1743
How Can Cupid Be So Stupid ? 1456
How Can I Be Your "Sweet Mama" When
You're "Daddy" To Somebody Else ? 1576
How Can I Ever Be Alone ? 81-325-433
How Can I Face This Wearied World Alone?
1654
How Can I Get It (When You Keep On
Snatching It Back) 178-823-1663-1708
How Can I Go On ? 850
How Can I Hi-De-Hi (When I Feel So Low-
De-Low) 1277
How Can I Miss You (When I've Got Dead
Aim) 354-1094
How Can It Be A Beautiful Day ? 1332
How Can I Thank You ? 1158
How Can I ? (With You In My Heart) 1631
How Can We Be Wrong ? 206-900
How Can You Face Me ? 292-424-1036-1624
1626
How Can You Forget ? 368-443-1158-1426
How Can You Look So Good ? 462

How Come You Do Me Like You Do ? 173-254-716-717-732-745-772-792-963-1023-1143-1144-1190-1191-1193-1275-1326-1344-1399-1411-1505-1536-1544-1725

How Could Anything So Good Be Bad ? 540

How Could I Be Blue ? 146-178-835-839-1014-1362

How Could My Good Man Turn His Back On Me Now ? 994

How Could Red Riding Hood ? 532-552-1108-1419-1655

How Could You ? 440-1088-1356-1412-1732

How Could You Be So Mean ? 392

How Could You Leave Me Now ? 1129

How Deep Is The Ocean ? 620-1205-1646

How'dja Like To Love Me ? 321-429-881

How Do ? 912

How Do I Know It's Real ? 1513

How Do I Know It's Sunday ? 423

How Do I Rate With You ? 250

How Do They/You Do It That Way ? 11-1488

How Do You Do, Mr. Cupid ? 1556

How Do You Do Without Me ? 453-1244

How Do You Expect To Get My Lovin' ? 212

How You Like It Blues 1421

How Do You Think I Feel ? 1678

How Dry I Am 1401

Howdy, Cloudy Morning 588-1298

How Happy I Would Be (If You Would Marry Me) 269

How High The Moon 324-614-816-1304

How I Love That Girl 38-128-796-1591

How I'm Feeling 1376

How I've Got Dem Twilight Blues (sic)1057

How Long Baby 1025

How Long, Baby (Will You Keep Me This Way) 783

How Long Has This Been Going On ? (1927) 334-356-469-785-930-1116-1343

How Long has This Been Going On ? (1928) 324-621-1696

How Long, How Long Blues 92-104-106-109-121-154-155-178-390-583-765-850-1003-1008-1145-1240-1526-1594-1746 (There are several variations on this title)

How Long Is That Train Been Gone ? (sic) 514

How Long Must I Wait For You ? 510

How Long, (Sweet) Daddy, How Long ? 354-792

How Many Times ? (1921) 68-1576

How Many Times ? (1926) 194-234-271-467-510-532-1377-1739

How'm I Doin' ? (Hey-Hey) 539-584-726-773 1214-1248-1272-1277-1410-1450-1494

How'm I Gonna Get 'Em (When You Keep On Holdin' 'Em Back) 733

How Much Can I Stand ? 121

How Much Do You Mean To Me ? 18-900

How's About Tomorrow Night ? 13

How She Loves Me Is Nobody's Business 462

How Strange 9-1358

How The Time Can Fly (Whenever I'm With You) 1145-1385

(How To Make Love In) Ten Easy Lessons 125-1333

How To Win Friends And Influence People 322-401

How Was I To Know ? 786

How Would You Like To Be Me ? 1495

How Ya, Baby ? 1631

How Ya Feelin' ? 1277

How Ya Gonna Keep 'Em Down On The Farm ? 379-512-1375

How You Gonna Keep Kool ? 558

Hoy-Hoy 258

Huckleberry Duck 1373

Huggable, Kissable You 243-244-378-507-1292-1514

Hugo (I'll Go Where You Go) 225-629-1122

Hugs And Kisses 921-1611

Huh ! Oh Huh ! 550

Hula Blues 522-1728

Hula Girl 4

Hula Hula Cake Walk 1473

Hula Lou 72-225-560-855-857-1129-1573-1590

Hula Mama Blues 868

Hula Shake That Thing 868

Hullabaloo 25-932-1034-1224-1294

Hum All Your Troubles Away 1693

Hum And Strum 338

Humming Blues 1320-1458

Humming Man 1727

Hummin' To Myself 697-1645

Humored And Petted Blues 1487

Humoresque (In Swing Time) (Dvořak) 216-441-896-897-997-1063-1147-1531

Humpty Dumpty 550-1567

Humpty Dumpty Heart 363-1567

103rd Street Boogie 764

Hundred To One It's You, A 392

Hundred Years From Today, A 291-1332-1538-1541-1653

Hungaria 465-1261-1262

Hungarian Dance No. 5 (Brahms) 1552

Hungarian Rag 141

Hungarian Rhapsody No. 2 (Liszt) 1371

Hungry Blues 839

Hungry For Love 1077

Hunkadola 4-595

Hunkatin 1522

Hunky Dory 332-1198

Hunting Medley 1292

Hurdy Gurdy Blues/Man 53-585-1471-1609

Hurly Burly 683

Hurricane 356-386-467-1086-1138-1275-1369-1430

Hurry Back Home 1525

Hurry Back, Old Sweetheart Of Mine 884

Hurry Back To Sorrento 742

Hurry Home 369-1358

Hurry Sundown Blues 393

Hush-a-Bye 577

Hush My Mouth (If I Ain't Goin' South) 12-464

Hustlin' And Bustlin' For Baby 51-1330-1646

Hustlin' Blues 1268

Hustlin' Dan 1446

Hut-Sut Song, The 590-970

Hy'a Duchess 1668

Hyde Park 487

Hydrant Love (Turn It On, Shut It Off) 212-1678

Hyena Stomp 1102-1106

Hylton Stomp 801

Hymn-Singing Bill 1220

Hymn To The Sun (Rimsky-Korsakov) 441

Hypnotized 250

I Adore You  14-648-1629
I Ain't 'En Got 'En No Time To Have The
Blues  975
I Ain't Gettin' Nowhere Fast  259
I Ain't Givin' Nobody None  570
I Ain't Givin' Nothin' Away  940
I Ain't Going To Sell You None  555
I Ain't Gonna Be Nobody's Fool  413
I Ain't Gonna Blame It On The Blues  681
I Ain't Gonna Do It No More  754
I Ain't Gonna Give Nobody None O' This
Jelly-Roll  115-181-336-380-757-1053-
1062-1462-1517-1709
I Ain't Gonna Grieve No More  698
I Ain't Gonna Let Nobody Break My Heart
355
I Ain't Gonna Let You See My Santa Claus
1489
I Ain't Gonna Marry, Ain't Gonna Settle
Down  1023
I Ain't Gonna Play No Second Fiddle  164-
165-1184-1442
I Ain't Gonna Sin No More  424-1654
I Ain't Gonna Study War No More  989
I Ain't Gonna Tell Nobody  1166
I Ain't Got Much, But What I Got, Oh My
1306
I Ain't Got Nobody (And Nobody Cares For
Me)  38-46-105-107-138-169-193-232-237-
239-257-283-330-340-354-364-383-384-394
468-514-533-548-649-652-653-688-736-757
780-852-929-956-961-965-1003-1025-1062-
1063-1068-1069-1106-1123-1203-1207-1290
1375-1391-1433-1442-1493-1508-1529-1530
1545-1574-1579-1622-1625-1631-1640-1657
1660
I Ain't Got Nobody To Love  230-624-869-
1457-1524-1544-1591
I Ain't Got No Gal Now  111
I Ain't Got No Man  1012-1471
I Ain't Lazy, I'm Just Dreamin'  594
I Ain't Mad With You  832
I Ain't Never Had Nobody Crazy Over Me
176-826-916-1187-1353-1505
I Ain't No Ice Man  390
I Ain't No Man's Slave  731
I Ain't Scared Of You  214
I Ain't Tellin'  1244
I Ain't That Kind Of A Baby  2-1096-1174-
1232
I Ain't Thinkin' 'Bout You  1536
I Ain't Your Hen, Mr. Fly Rooster  344
I Am A Canadian  1317
I Am Always Thinking Of Someone  884
I Am An American  909-1317
I Am A Woman  1729
I Am Calling Blues  8
I Am Going To Have It Now  7
I Am Happy In Jesus  1014
I Am Only Human After All  1599
I Apologize  421
I Ask The Stars  1408
I Beg To Be Excused  1323
I Beg Your Pardon, Mademoiselle  697-875
I Believe I Been Hoodood (sic)  628
I Believe I'll Make A Change  680
I Believe In Miracles  425-1000-1625
I Believe My Man Is Got A Rabbit's Leg
(sic)  627
Iberville And Franklin  644
I Boogied When I Should Have Woogied  167
I Bought A Wooden Whistle  433-1753

I Bring A Song  1235
I Call You Sugar  806-1493
I Came Here To Talk For Joe  299
I Came, I Saw, I Conga'd  590
I Can Always Dream  894
I Can Always Tell When A Man Is Treatin'
Me Cool  1013
I Can Always Tell When My Man Don't Want
Me 'Round  1458
I Can Beat You Plenty (That Hand You
Tried To Deal Me)  1042
I Can Dance With Anyone Except My Wife
315
I Can Deal Worry  892
I Can Dish It - Can You Take It ?  1371
I Can Do What You Do  1717
I Can Dream, Can't I ?  295-443-813-814
I Can Give You Love  661
I Can Pull A Rabbit Out Of My Hat  122-
1032
I Can Read Between The Lines  80-1159
I Can See You All Over The Place  1468-
1710
I Can't Afford To Dream  815-1405
I Can't Beat You Doin' What You're Doin'
Me (sic)  1709
I Can't Be Bothered Now  880
I Can't Believe It's True  981
I Can't Believe She's Mine  791
I Can't Believe That It's You  161-875
I Can't Believe That You're In Love With
Me  47-106-312-465-528-581-638-663-759
812-1114-1333-1356-1403-1476-1491-1585
1644-1711-1734
I Can't Be Worried Blues  1169
I Can't Be Worried Long  540
I Can't Break The Habit Of You  1088-
1630
I Can't Change My Heart  326
I Can't Dance (I Got Ants In My Pants)
201-348-424-563-581-586-637-774-779-
828-959-1584-1658-1709
I Can't Do That  213
I Can't Do Without You  218-785
I Can Tell By Looking In Your Eyes  781
I Can't Escape From You  122-362-691-986
1415
I Can't Face The Music (Without Singing
The Blues)  78-321-429-1734
I Can't Feel Frisky Without My Liquor
1549
I Can't Find A Name Sweet Enough For You
1590
I Can't Fool Around With Someone Who's
Foolin' Around  1276
I Can't Get Along Without My Baby  285-
1071
I Can't Get Enough Of You  1742
I Can't Get Mississippi Off My Mind  197
421-981
I Can't Get Over A Girl/Boy Like You
Loving A Boy/Girl Like Me  38-271
I Can't Get Started With You  98-102-122
123-124-211-587-662-768-1032-1736
I Can't Get The One I Want  72-558-714-
733-1067-1483-1590
I Can't Give You Anything But Love  45-
56-64-144-161-313-344-384-454-463-476-
487-502-564-595-603-617-626-649-652-670
780-797-894-1140-1259-1270-1274-1290-
1333-1337-1343-1417-1428-1433-1437-1511
1585-1633-1635-1653-1662-1686-1711-1732
1742

I Can't Go For You  1560
I Can't Keep From Loving That Gal  82
I Can't Keep You Out Of My Dreams  248
I Can't Last Long  1489
I Can't Lose That Longing For You  1002-1027
I Can't Love You Any More (Any More Than I Do)  615-1397
I Can't Make A Man  421-422
I Can't Make Her Happy  804-808
I Can't Pretend  204-739-767-1002
I Can't Quit That Man  355
I Can't Realize You Love Me  339-483-568
I Can't Remember To Forget  97
I Can't Resist You  10-260-433-616
I Can't Rub You Out Of My Eyes  1242
I Can't Say  1129
I Can't Say It Too Many Times  923
I Can't Sleep In The Movies Any More  520-641
I Can't Stand It  1042
I Can't Stop Babying You  1582
I Can't Stop Lovin' You  82-1169-1661
I Can't Take You Out Of My Heart  195
I Can't Tell A Lie  62
I Can't Tell Why I Love You, But I Do  207
I Can't Think Of Anything But You  1710
I Can't To Save My Life  846
I Can't Use That Thing  1036
I Can't Use You  212
I Can't Write The Words  157-197-1386
I Cash Clo'es  320
Ice Bag Papa  1268
Ice Man  1575
Ich hab' kein Auto, ich hab' ken Rittergut  809
Ich liebe dich (I Love You)  378
Ici l'on peche  1348
Icky Blues  1077
I Come From A Musical Family  53
I Concentrate On You  185-297-448
I Could Fall In Love With someone Like You  1722
I Could Make You Care  166-450
I Couldn't Believe My Eyes  426
I Couldn't Be Mad At You  1236
I Couldn't Be Mean To You  424-699-797
I Couldn't Get To It (In Time)  1196
I Couldn't If I Wanted To (I Wouldn't If I Could)  1076
I Couldn't Stand To See My Baby Lose  939
I Could Stand A Little Lovin' (From You)  510
I Could Stand A Lot Of Lovin' From You  813
I Could Use A Dream  295
I Cover The Waterfront  58-403-404-674-698-770-803-982-1408-1511-1647
I Crave You  566
I Crave Your Lovin' Every Day  7
I Cried For You  8-64-79-126-161-295-430-611-819-1032-1315-1731
Ida Cox's Lawdy Lawdy Blues  352
Idaho  622-763
Ida - I Do  555-1054
I Dance Alone  124
Ida, Sweet As Apple Cider  5-127-346-376-386-530-600-755-841-897-1083-1139-1208-1342-1410-1435-1559-1716
I'd Be A Fool Again  294
I'd Be Ever So Grateful  832
I'd Believe In You  774

I'd Be Lost Without You  663
I'd Be Telling A Lie  200
I'd Climb The Highest Mountain  233-1264-1583
Ideas  704
I'd Give A Lot Of Love  1592
I Didn't Come To Steal Nobody's Man  795
I Didn't Know  576
I Didn't Know About You  500
I Didn't Know What Time It Was  432-613-1253-1406
I Didn't Start In To Love You (Until You Stopped Lovin' Me)  1008
I Did Wanta, But I Don't Wanta Now  1536
I'd Know You Anywhere  373-451-910
I'd Leave Ten Men Like Yours To Love One Man Like Mine  1182
Idle Hour Blues  1487
Idle Hour Special  132
I'd Like To Be A Bee In Your Boudoir  1329
I'd Like To Be A Gypsy  1233
I'd Like To Be Your Sheik For Awhile  1643
I'd Like To Call You My Sweetheart  1622
I'd Love To Call You My Sweetheart  1611
I'd Like To Dunk You In My Coffee  425
I'd Like To Find The Guy That Wrote The Stein Song  1295
I'd Like To Love Them All  1666
I'd Like To See Samoa Of Samoa  566
I'd Like To See You  780
I'd Love It  1034
I'd Love To Call You My Sweetheart  268-577-908-1231
I'd Love To Live In Loveland  298
I'd Love To Love The One I Love  188
I'd Love To Play A Love Scene (Opposite You)  124
I'd Love To Take Orders From You  77-203-701-1307-1432
I'd Love You Again  743-1243
I Do  1528
I Do, Do You ? (Do You Believe In Love ?)  298
Idol  1747
Idolising  577-630-1039-1521
Idol Of My Eyes  1115
I Do Mean You  108
I Done Caught You Blues  1640
I Done Found Out  832
I Don't Believe It  542
I Don't Believe It, But Say It Again  566-882-1348-1504
I Don't Blame You  805
I Don't Care  540-887-1028
I Don't Care Any More  942
I Don't Care What You Say  683
I Don't Care Who Ain't Got Nobody  343
I Don't Care Who Gets What I Don't Want  118
I Don't Dig You, Jack  91
I Don't Know And I Don't Care Blues  714-1023-1466-1725
I Don't Know If I'm Comin' Or Goin'  1333
I Don't Know What Kind Of Blues I Got  499
I Don't Know Why  657-1202-1582
I Don't Know Why (I Just Do)  332-593-673-687-1554
I Don't Know Why I Love You So  490
I Don't Know Your Name (But You're Beautiful)  1032
I Don't Let No One Man Worry Me  182-810-946-1305-1519-1727

I Don't Like  586
I Don't Love Nobody But You  111
I Don't Love Nobody (So I Don't Have No
  Blues)  522-750-964-1448-1728
I Don't Mind  500
I Don't Mind Being All Alone  462-921
I Don't Mind Walkin' In The Rain (When I'm
  Walkin' In The Rain With You)  117-1005-
  1295-1610
I Don't Stand A Ghost Of A Chance With You
  - see GHOST OF A CHANCE, A
I Don't Wanna Go Home  1294
I Don't Want Anybody At All  99
I Don't Want It All  794
I Don't Want It Now  1320
I Don't Want Nobody Blues  1724
I Don't Want Nobody But You  462-1363
I Don't Want Nobody That Don't Want Me
  1023-1024
I Don't Want To Cry Any More  97-1374
I Don't Want To Make History (I Just Want
  To Make Love)  365-1231-1464
I Don't Want To Remember  650
I Don't Want To Set The World On Fire  153-
  499-944-1318
I Don't Want To Walk Without You (Baby)
  500-694-819-1409
I Don't Want You Blues  320
I Don't Want You (If You Don't Want Me)
  1056
I Don't Want You Loving Me  678
I Don't Want Your Kisses (If I Can't Have
  Your Love)  2-503-1301-1491-1666
I Don't Work For A Living  1394
I Dood It  744
I Double Dare You  55-190-321-554-739
I'd Rather Be Alone  1119-1181-1752
I'd Rather Be Blue  339
I'd Rather Be Blue Over You  242
I'd Rather Be Blue Than Green  1013
I'd Rather Be Dead And Buried In My Grave
  1444
I'd Rather Be Drunk  849
I'd Rather Be Right  294-1401
I'd Rather Be The Girl In Your Arms  577-
  630
I'd Rather Be With You  680-936
I'd Rather Call You Baby  1631
I'd Rather Charleston  1749
I'd Rather Cry Over You  31-506-1686
I'd Rather Dream  298
I'd Rather Drink Muddy Water No. 2  847
I'd Rather Lead A Band  122-293-1312
I'd Rather Listen To Your Eyes  77-203-249
  701-1307
I Dream A Lot About You  991
I Dream Of Jeanie With The Light Brown
  Hair  298-324-907-1512
I Dreamt I Dwelt In Harlem  215
I Dreamt I Dwelt In Marble Halls  321-356
I Drink Good Whiskey  849
I'd Trade My Air Castles For A Love Nest
  And You  737
I'd Walk A Million Miles (To Be A Little
  Bit Nearer To You)  356-567
If  937
I Fall In Love With You Every Day  321-429-
  881
If All The Stars Were Pretty Babies  1619
If All The World Was Made Of Glass - see
  ALL THIS WORLD IS MADE OF GLASS

If Anybody Here Wants A Real Kind Mama
  (Here's Your Opportunity)  810-859-1305
  1306-1458-1727
If Anything Happened To You  470-527-1735
I Faw Down An' Go 'Boom !' (sic)  520-547
  654-670-1195-1292
If Dreams Come True  606-646-839-1402-
  1658-1660
I Feel A Song Comin' On  392-974
I Feel Good  1618
I Feel Like A Feather In The Breeze  250-
  881-1307-1731
I Feel Like A Millionaire  679
I Feel Like Going To Town  679
I Feel Like Lying In Another Woman's
  Husband's Arms  91
I Fell Head Over Heels In Love With You
  930
I Fell In Love With A Dream  528
I Fell In Love With You  12
If I Can Ba-Ba-Baby You  813
If I Can't Get/Have The Sweetie I Want
  (I Pity The Sweetie I Get)  223-344-
  1354
If I Can't Have You  671-1294
If I Can't Have You  (I Want To Be Lone-
  some - I Want To Be Blue)  59-501-1006
If I Cared A Little Bit Less  1361
If I Care For Someone Else  921
If I Could Be With You One Hour Tonight
  6-47-105-114-196-504-512-590-595-597-
  786-939-941-1034-1214-1234-1250-1317-
  1328-1490-1534-1539
If I Could Holler  1542
If I Could Just Stop Dreaming  112
If I Could Only Read Your Mind  1046
If I Didn't Care  9-105-151-370-1662
If I Didn't Have You  287-651
If I Didn't Know Your Husband (And You
  Didn't Know My Wife)  235-532
If I'd Only Believed In You  668
If I Don't Find My Brown I Won't Be Back
  At All  1012
If I Don't Fit, Don't Force It  534
If I Ever Cry (You'll Never Know)  1664
If I Ever Get A Job Again  877
If I Feel This Way Tomorrow  902
If I Forget  1274
If I Forget You  433
If I Give Up The Saxophone (Will You Come
  Back To Me ?)  1394
If I Had A Girl Like You (1925)  73-926-
  927-1377-1503
If I Had A Girl Like You (1930)  195-247-
  672-736
If I Had A Million Dollars  159-699-879
If I Had A Ribbon Bow  1513
If I Had A Talking Picture Of You  503-
  562-672-952-1155-1687
If I Had My Way  64-122-296-853-1020-1557
If I Hadn't Been So Sure Of You  1386
If I Had Somebody To Love  1330-1668
If I Had You  272-279-333-366-432-469-620
  635-931-1195-1283-1336-1373-1400-1408-
  1595-1733
If I Had You And You Had Me  111
If I Had You In My Arms  1453
If I Knew Then  741
If I Let You Get Away With It Once, You'll
  Do It All Of The Time  845
If I Look Like I Feel  894

1898

If I Lose, Let Me Lose (Mama Don't Mind) 860
If I Lost You 579
If I Love Again 1408
If I'm Dreaming, Don't Wake Me Too Soon 952-1369
If I'm Without You 1663
If I Only Had Wings 589
If I Put My Heart In My Song 441-1400
If I Should Lose You 250-1312
If I Stay Away Too Long From Carolina 748 826
If It Ain't Love 35-157-697-1286-1409-1413-1658
If It Isn't Love 1625
If I Thought You Cared 135
If It Rains, Who Cares ? 322-906-1492
If It's Good Enough For The Birds And Bees 1296
If It's Good Then I Want It 57-184-662-1538
If It's Love 425
If It's The Last Thing I Do 205-442-729-1237-1401
If It's True 1277
If It's You 1407
If It Wasn't For The Moon 208
If It Wasn't For You 1528
If It Wasn't For You I Wouldn't Be Crying Now 33
If It Weren't For You 527
If I Were King 979
If I Were Sure Of You 370
If I Were You 768-1203-1503-1632-1734
If I Were Your Daddy (And You Were A Mamma To Me) 1576
If Love Is Blind 780
If Love Makes You Give Up Steak And Potatoes 191-937
If Mama Quits Papa, What Will Papa Do ? 1716
If Money Grew On Trees 215
If My Heart Could Only Talk 440-767
If My Sweetie Comes Back To Me 568
If Only I Could Read Your Mind 281
I Forgave You 1229
I Forgot The Little Things 1436
I Forgot To Buy The License 874
I Found A Dream One Day 13-365-701-1307-1731
I Found A Good Man After All 1162
I Found A Million-Dollar Baby (In A Five And Ten Cent Store) 197-619-889-933-1385-1751
I Found A New Way To Go To Town 1270-1278 1470
I Found My Sunshine In The Rain 1076
I Found My Yellow Basket 8-94-1661
I Found Out 850
I Found Sunshine In Your Smile 1291
I Found What I Wanted In You 388
I Found You 34-1030-1388
I Found You In The Rain 299-1553
I Found You - I Want You 1503
I Found You Out When I Found You In Somebody Else's Arms 564-1292-1665
If Papa Has Outside Lovin' 180
If Someone Would Only Love Me 1104
If Tears Could Bring You Back To Me 884-1504
If That's What You're Thinking 527

If That's What You Want, Here It Is 136 187
If The Man In The Moon Were A Coon 442
If The Moon Turns Green 779-866
If The Rest Of The World Don't Want You (Go Back To Your Mother And Dad) 794
If The Walls Could Talk 628
If We Never Meet Again 53-382-702-786
If What You Say Is True 1359-1405-1539
If You Are But A Dream 435-1244
If You Believed In Me 177
If You Build A Better Mousetrap 435-621
If You Can Dish It (I Can Take It) 842
If You Can't Bring It, You've Got To Send It 212
If You Can't Control Your Man 735-1060
If You Can't Get Five, Take Two 1677
If You Can't Hold The Man You Love (Don't Cry When He's Gone) 310-472-795-1246-1651
If You Can't Make It Easy, Sweet Mama 409
If You Can't Ride Slow And Easy 643
If You Can't Sing, Whistle 1295
If You Can't Tell The World She's A Good Little Girl, Just Say Nothing At All 668
If You'd Only Let Me 880
If You Don't Believe I Love You (Look What A Fool I've Been) 1692-1698-1719
If You Don't Do It Like I Want It Done (I'll Get Somebody Else) 1458
If You Don't Give Me What I Want (I'm Gonna Get It Somewhere Else) 707-731-750-843
If You Don't I Know Who Will 357-763-1439-1533
If You Don't Like It 1458
If You Don't Like It, Leave 1011
If You Don't Like (My) Potatoes 939-1094
If You Don't Love Me 399-649-1016-1645
If You Don't Love Me, Make Believe You Do 6
If You Don't Shake, Don't Get No Cake 1106
If You Don't Think I'll Do, Sweet Papa (Just Try Me) 1649
If You Don't Want Me Please Don't Dog Me 'Round 1009
If You Don't Want Me Stop Doggin' Me 'Round 10-552-1119
If You Don't Want Me (Blues) (Send Me To My Ma) 1460-1492
If You Don't Want To Be Sweethearts 289
If You Do - What You Do 560
If You Ever Change Your Mind 446-527-1405-1654
If You Ever, Ever Loved Me (Love Me Tonight) 1361
If You Go, You'll Come Back By-and-By 1271
If You Hadn't Gone Away 350-510-903-934 1225-1299-1415-1589
If You Haven't Got A Girl 592-1144
If You Hit My Dog I'll Kick Your Cat 1717
If You Just Knew 1121
If You Knew 1108
If You Knew Susie Like I Know Susie 73-129-829-992-1017-1135-1433-1592

If You Leave Me  691
If You Like Me Like I Like You  731-1704
If You'll Come Back  72-177-560-561-707-891-1609
If You Love Me  1157
If You Love Me, Act Like It  1728
If You Never Come Back  1030
If You Only Knew  434-526-744
If You Only Knowed  1449
If You Really Love Your Baby  1025
If You're A Viper  781-783-1632-1639
If You're Ever In My Arms Again  94-134-183
If You're Looking For Someone To Love  1270
If You're Old-Fashioned Your Long Underwear  566
If You're Really And Truly In Love  1296
If You're Thinking Of Me  92
If Your Good Man Quits You, Don't Wear No Black  1023
If Your Man Is Like My Man (I Sympathize With You)  916-1010-1187-1719
If You See Sally  668
If You Sheik On Your Mama, Mama's Gonna Sheba On You  709
If You Should Ever Leave  78-441-526-729-1400-1401
If You Should Ever Need Me  1384
If You Should Stop Caring  881
If You Think I'm Lovin' You, You're Wrong  886
If You've Never Been Vamped By A Brown Skin Gal (You've Never Been Vamped At All)  1424
If You Want My Heart (You Got To 'Low It, Babe)  1166
If You Want The Rainbow (You Must Have The Rain)  574-670½1565
If You Want To Be My Sugar Papa  133
If You Want To Keep Your Daddy Home  280-793-1022-1056-1305
If You Want To Live  679
If You Was Whiskey And I Was A Duck  1105
If You Were In My Place (What Would You Do ?)  78-430-492-493-765-1158
If You Were Mine  1730
If You Were Only Mine  147-198-1645
If You Were Someone Else  442
If You Were The Only Girl In The World  386-588-590-938-1238
I Get A Kick Out Of Corn  166
I Get A Kick Out Of You  324-425-1211
I Get Along Without You Very Well  94-323-431-1159
I Get The Blues When It Rains  244-511-671-1242-1300
I Get The Neck Of The Chicken  262
I Give My Love To You  1528
I Give You All My Money Blues  553
I Give You My Word  897
Igloo  1279
Igloo Stomp  1213
I Go For That  79-323-588-1159-1670
I Got A "Code" In My "Doze"  655
I Got A Feeling For You  1019
I Got A Gal  328
I Got A Guy  1660
I Got A Man In The 'Bama Mines - see GOT A MAN IN THE 'BAMA MINES
I Got A Misery  1152
I Got A Mule To Ride  1739

I Got A New Deal In Love  425-700
I Got Another Lovin' Daddy  1271
I Got A Nothin'  894
I Got A Papa Down In New Orleans (Another Papa Up In Maine)  310-1551
I Gotcha /I Got Ya  1278-1279
I Got Everything A Woman Needs  1447
I Got Good Potatoes  1044
I Got Her Off My Hands (But I Can't Get Her Off My Mind)  509
I Got Horses And Got Numbers On My Mind  1709
I Got It  989
I Got It Bad And That Ain't Good  126-186-435-499-528-620-761
I Got It, You'll Get It  915
I Got Love  1690
I Got Rhythm  3-49-56-85-87-102-147-172-216-252-290-317-384-429-539-541-557-559-601-607-614-635-651-660-730-784-821-835-836-1046-1048-1063-1143-1157-1225-1253-1274-1277-1302-1346-1434-1485-1494-1585-1602-1627-1653-1660-1670
I Got Some Of That  1320
I Gotta Get Myself Somebody To Love  668-928-1222
I Gotta Get Up And Go To Work  1330
I Gotta Go  281
I Gotta Have You (Nobody But You)  888-1055-1740
I Gotta Right To Sing The Blues  3-51-256-593-769-1530-1538-1695
I Gotta Swing  251
I Gotta Tell Someone  563
I Got The Crying Blues  1012
I Got The Potatoes-I Got The Tomatoes (But Someone Else Has Got My Girl)  875
I Got The Ritz From The One I Love  1537
I Got The Stinger  1456
I Got To Have It Daddy  849
I Got Ways Like The Devil  91
I Got What It Takes (To Bring You Back)  251-1010
I Got Worry (Love Is On My Mind)  338-867-1559
I Got Ya - see I GOTCHA
I Got Your Bath Water On  66-212
I Guess I'll Be On My Way  168-743
I Guess I'll Have To Dream The Rest  186-452-818
I Guess It Had To Be That Way  361-1669
I Had A Premonition  990
I Had A Sweet Mama  1545
I Hadn't Anyone Till You  430-444-609-692
I Had Someone Else Before I Had You (And I'll Have Someone After You've Gone)  128-623-767-1318
I Had The Craziest Dream  820
I Had To Do It  610
I Had To Live And Learn  526
I Had You, I Lost You, I Found You (Only To Lose You Again)  233
I Hate A Man Like You  1061-1106
I Hate Myself  1527
I Hate Myself (For Being So Mean To You)  159-1508
I Hate Myself (For Falling In Love With You)  84-673
I Hate Myself For Loving You  651
I Hate To Leave You Now  50
I Hate To Lose You  1319

I Hate To Talk About Myself  1626
I Hate You, Darling  1553
I Have Everything To Live For  505
I Have Eyes  183-609-1159-1403
I Haven't Changed A Thing  79-430-787-1159 1357
I Haven't Time To Be A Millionaire  297-449-589
I Haven't Told Her, She Hasn't Told Me (But We Know It Just The Same)  403
I Have To Have You  672-977-1154-1381-1514
I Have Two Loves  1743
I Hear A Rhapsody  97-434-498-617
I Hear Bluebirds  1540
I Heard  3-198-316-581-582-935-1272-1276
I Heard My Heart  990
I Heard You Cried Last Night  819
I Hear Music  325-770-910
I Hear You Knockin' (But You Can't Come In)  64
I Hear You Talkin'  369
I Hope Gabriel Likes My Music  52-906-1115 1231-1464-1571
I Hung My Head And Cried  942
I Just Can't Believe You're Gone  1249
I Just Can't Take It  849
I Just Couldn't Take It, Baby  200-661-1538-1653
I Just Got A Letter  1655
I Just Keep On Drinking  849
I Just Made Up With That Old Girl Of Mine 1002-1629
I Just Roll Along (Having My Ups And Downs) 17-669-1325-1493
I Just Wanna Be Known As "Susie's Feller" 267-1593-1655
I Just want A Daddy (I Can Call My Own) 280-860-1018-1092
I Just Want One Man  1396
I Just Want Your Stingaree  1677
I Keep Remembering  102
I Keeps My Kitchen Clean  1069
I Kept On Rubbing That Thing  1496
Ikey And Mikey  1646
I Kinda Like You  96
I Kissed The Blues Goodbye  882
I Kissed You In A Dream Last Night  322
I Kiss Your Hand, Madame  1157-1691
I Knew You When  880
I Knocks Myself Out  824
I Know A Secret  693
I Know How To Do It  1247
I Know Now  695-755-1721
I Know She Does (Because She Told Me So) 554
I Knows You  180
I Know That You Know  115-463-505-595-597-608-611-660-690-786-872-906-1007-1151-1154-1157-1500-1731-1736
I Know You (I Know What You Wanna Do)  865
I Know What It Means  530
I Know What You Do  766
I Know Why  1097
I Know Why I Think Of You  737
I Know You're Lying, But I Love It  341
I Learned About Love From Her  256
I Left My Baby  106
I Left My Heart In Your Hand  617
I Left My Sugar Standing In The Rain  187-626-1116-1290-1341
I Let A Song Go Out Of My Heart  78-94-103 430-493-609-765-1158-1203

I Let A Tear Fall In The River  18-1661
I Lift Up My Finger And Say "Tweet Tweet"  520-655-950-1743
I Like A Little Girl Like That  146-1214 1514-1599
I Like Bananas (Because They Have No Bones)  191
I Like A Guy What Takes His Time  1671
I Like Mountain Music  1668
I Like Music (With A Swing Like That) 258
I Like My Sugar Sweet  729
I Like Pie, I Like Cake (But I Like You Best Of All)  100-155-230-377-624-830-1363-1591
I Like That  1569
I Like That Face You're Wearing  879
I Like That Thing  835
I Like The Way He Does It  1652
I Like To Do Things For You  696-789-812 1231-1294-1570-1687
I Like To Go Back In The Evening  1535-1707-1708
I Like To Recognize The Tune  908
I Like To Riff  99-329
I Like What I Like Like I Like It  404
I Like What You Like  669
I Like You Because You Have Such Loving Ways  705
I Like You Best Of All - see I LIKE PIE
I Live Again  1148
I Live For Love  1178
I Live The Life I Love  1357
I'll Always Be Dreaming Of Mary  1294
I'll Always Be In Love With You  102-591 611-728-730-830-1239-1358
I'll Always Be With You  832
I'll Always Call You Sweetheart  511
I'll Always Do As You Do  467
I'll Always Remember You  1612
I'll Be A Friend "With Pleasure"  117-252
I'll Be Around  261-1150
I'll Be Back  1398
I'll Be Back There Someday  1274
I'll Be Blue Just Thinking Of You  84-512-980-1302
I'll Be Faithful  693-1330-1331
I'll Be Getting Along  1457
I'll Be Glad When You're Dead, You Rascal You - see YOU RASCAL YOU
I'll Be Good, But I'll Be Lonesome  704
I'll Be Lonely  1290
I'll Be Ready When The Great Day Comes 1485-1486
I'll Be Reminded Of You  952
I'll Be Seeing You  449
I'll Be Smiling When You're Crying  783
I'll Be True To The One I Love  375
I'll Bet You Tell That To All The Girls 14-1313
I'll Be With You In Apple Blossom Time 1402
I'll Build A Nest  982
I'll Build An Igloo For You  1252
I'll Build A Stairway To Paradise  1718
I'll Capture Your Heart  365
I'll Chase The Blues Away  1658
I'll Close My Eyes To The Rest Of The World  18
I'll Come Back For More  1500
I'll Come Back To You  373

I'll Dance At Your Wedding  1633
I'll Dream My Way To Heaven  440
I'll Dream Of You  1121
I'll Dream Tonight  444-1734
I'll Find You  436
I'll Fly To Hawaii  632
I'll Follow My Secret Heart  1696
I'll Follow You  876-1468-1588
I'll Forget  108
I'll Forgive You 'Cause I Love You  795
I'll Get Along Somehow  691-900-1654
I'll Get By (As Long As I Have You)  804-
817-829-900-1147-1195-1733
I'll Get Even With You  1371-1458-1726
I'll Get Him Yet  976
I'll Get Mine Bye And Bye  58
I'll Go Back To That Dear Old Pal O' Mine
651
I'll Go/I'm Going To My Grave With The
Blues  1092
I'll Just Go Along  236
I'll Just Keep On Dreaming  890
I'll Keep Right On Loving You  874
I'll Keep Sittin' On It (If I Can't Sell
It)  1677
I'll Keep The Lovelight Burning  375
I'll Keep Thinking Of You  374
I'll Keep Warm All Winter (With My Sunny
Summer Love)  1669
I'll Lock You In My Arms  673
I'll Make Fun For You  1034
I'll Make It Worth Your While  1560
Ill-Natured Blues  177
I'll Never Ask For More  242-398-420-1069-
1195-1336
I'll Never Be The Same  35-299-505-651-922
1599-1733
I'll Never Change  779
I'll Never Cry Over You  942
I'll Never Fail You  901-1735
I'll Never Fall In Love Again  1489
I'll Never Find A Pal Like You  951
I'll Never Forget  209-299
I'll Never Forget I Love You  250
I'll Never Forgive Myself (For Not For-
giving You)  1633
I'll Never Give In  282
I'll Never Have To Dream Again  161
I'll Never Learn  901
I'll Never Let A Day Pass By  98-452-818-
1412
I'll Never Let You Cry  633-1402
I'll Never Say "Never Again" Again  13-161
203-349-426
I'll Never See My Baby Any More  1668
I'll Never Smile Again  450-909-1317-1636
I'll Never Tell You I Love You  205-786-
1356-1400
I'll Never Tire Of You  417
I'll Pray For You  81-741-1553
I'll Putcha Pitcha In The Papers  140
I'll Put You Under The Jail  212
I'll Remember  323-1405-1539
I'll Remember April  98-743
I'll Say She Does  1517
I'll See You Go  795
I'll See You In My Dreams  38-72-206-444-
649-691-717-974-986-1089-1141-1283-1337-
1570-1732-1735
I'll See You In The Spring, When The Birds
Begin To Sing  1042
I'll Sing For You  186

I'll Sing You A Song  1265
I'll Sing You A Thousand Love Songs  14-
893-1415
I'll Stand By  182-427-702-1019
I'll Still Go On Wanting You  1153
I'll String Along With You  937
I'll Swing You A Thousand Love Songs  584
I'll Take Her Back If She Wants To Come
Back  228-718-882-1657
I'll Take Tallulah  453-454
I'll Take The Key And Lock You Up  781
I'll Take The South  180-938
I'll Take You To The Cleaners  843
I'll Tell Ma  1292
I'll Think Of You  645
I'll Try To Forget  849
Ill Wind (You're Blowing Me No Good)  284
1513-1529-1709
Il n'y en a deux comme moi  396
Ilo  1613
I Lost Another Sweetheart  92
I Lost Control Of Myself  329
I Lost Love (When I Lost You)  1247
I Lost My Baby  842
I Lost My Gal Again  1667
I Lost My Gal From Memphis  514-898-1061-
1153-1220-1436
I Lost My Man  854
I Loved You Once But You Stayed Away Too
Long  1010
I Loved You Then As I Love You Now  242
I Love Each Move You Make  1661
I Love Her  129-1420
I Love Me (I'm Wild About Myself)  222-
223-1397
I Love My Baby (My Baby Loves Me)  74-
546-927-967-1097-1484-1579
I Love My Man Better Than I Love Myself
352
I Love My Old-Fashioned Man  1325
I Love That  679
I Love That Thing  570
I Love The College Girls  235
I Love The Girl Who Isses (I Hate The
Girl Who Don't)  71-1590
I Love To Bumpity-Bump On A Bumpy Road
With You  1393
I Love To Hear A Military Band  1668
I Love To Ride The Horses (On A Merry-
Go-Round)  701
I Love To Sing-a  257-428
I Love To Sing The Words While We're
Dancing  184
I Love To Watch The Moonlight  166-433
I Love To Whistle  1632
I Love You  988
I Love You Because I Love You  758
I Love You, Believe Me, I Love You  979
I Love You Best Of All  1243
I Love You But I Don't Know Why  567
I Love You Daddy, But You Don't Mean Me
No Good  845
I Love You From Coast To Coast  1416
I Love You In Technicolor  430
I Love You Just Because  1089
I Love You More And More  248
I Love You More, More Every Day  743
I Love You Much Too Much  634-704-908-
1753
I Love Your Eyes  338
I Love You So  1097
I Love You So Much  84-247-678-1383-1639

I Love You Truly   154289-693-896-1249
I'm A Back-Bitin' Mama   861
I'm A Broken-Hearted Blackbird   338-525-1459
I'm A Cabaret Nightingale   1058
I'm A Cheater   1445
I'm A Ding Dong Daddy (From Dumas)   47-169
   595-606-607-1134-1235-1341-1347
I'm A Doggone Struttin' Fool   1423
I'm A Dreamer - Aren't We All ?   245-503-672
I'm A Fool For Loving You   728
I'm Afraid Of Myself   81
I'm Afraid Of You   506-1226-1595
I'm Afraid The Masquerade Is Over   9-323-431-1316-1358
I'm Afraid To Care For You   1559
I'm Afraid You Sing That Song To Somebody Else   659-1015
I'm A Front Door Woman With A Back Door Man   570
I'm A Gambler   427
Image Of You, The   59-123-1002-1075
Imagination (1927)   304-1087-1140
Imagination (1928)   269
Imagination (1932)   1112
Imagination (1934)   1658
Imagination (1935)   285-1584
Imagination (1940)   63-207-449-527-1359
Imagination Goes A Long Way   949
Imagine My Surprise   1633
I'm A Good Gal, But I'm A Thousand Miles From Home   521-732
I'm A Good-Hearted Mama (But I Got A Trifling Man)   845
I'm A Harmony Baby   916
I'm A Heart-Broken Mama   310-1093
I'm A Heck Of A Guy   990
I'm A Hundred Per Cent. For You   594-1432-1625
I'm A Hundred Per Cent. In Love   1296
I'm A Jazz Baby   1675
(I'm) Alabama Bound   679-864-1105-1251
I'm A Little Blackbird Looking For A Bluevird   1699
I'm A Little Prairie Flower (I'm Wild, I'm Wild)   555
I'm All Alone In A Palace Of Stone   668
I'm All Bound 'Round With The Mason-Dixon Line   1037-1229
I'm All Broken Up Over You   1483-1663
I'm All Broke Out With The Blues   65-961
I'm All Dressed Up With A Broken Heart   60-160
I'm All For You   770
I'm All Out Of Breath   1468
I'm Alone Because I Love You   1318
I'm A Lonesome Little Mama (Looking For Somebody To Love)   920
I'm A Lonesome Little Raindrop   1351
I'm Alone Without You   1000
I'm Alone With You   988
I'm A Lover Of Paree   1669
I'm A Lucky Devil (To Find An Angel Like You)   1316
I'm Always Chasing Rainbows   617-644
I'm Always In The Mood For You   258-1631
I'm A Mighty Tight Woman   1618-1619
I'm An Airman   1135
I'm An Old Cowhand   93-122-204-362-939-1572
I'm An Unemployed Sweetheart   1098

I'm A One-Man Girl   1336
I'm A Real Kinda Papa (Lookin' For A Real Kinda Girl)   1003
I'm A Real Kind Mama   861
I Married An Angel   29-322
I'm A Sales Lady   843
I'm A Savage   1435
I'm As Blue As The Blue Grass Of Kentucky   190
I'm A Stationary Mama (Looking For A Permanent Man)   1728
I'm At The Mercy Of Love   1629
I May Be Wrong, But I Think You're Wonderful   101-177-208-246-294-325-442-896-1141-1142-1154-1293-1357-1379-1658
I May Stay Away A Little Longer   1313
I'm Back In Love Again   463-1222-1583
I'm Bettin' On You   842
I'm Blowin' My Top   1560
I'm Blue And Lonesome (Nobody Cares For Me)   1678
I'm Blue Because Of You   1504
I'm Blue, But Nobody Cares   1469
I'm Bound For Tennessee   558
I'm Bringing A Red, Red Rose   21
I'm Broke, Fooling With You   731
I'm Building A Sailboat Of Dreams   206-1316
I'm Building Up To An Awful Let-Down   968-1031
I'm Busy And You Can't Come In   1535-1703
I'm Cert'ny Gonna See 'Bout That   1012
I'm Checkin' Out, Goo'm Bye   495
I'm Coming, Virginia   98-115-122-165-171-183-188-283-607-636-722-741-1183-1404-1425-1485-1512-1530-1566-1630-1651-1681-1690-1732
I'm Confessin' (That I Love You) - see CONFESSIN' (THAT I LOVE YOU)
I'm Craving For That Kind Of Love   1355-1424
I'm Crazy 'Bout My Baby   253-272-287-724-853-958-1171-1384-1469-1624-1626-1629-1630-1634-1644
I'm Crazy Over Daisy   917
I'm Crazy Over You   713-931-1126-1292-1336-1456
I'm Crooning A Tune About June   243-949-1426-1514
I'm Cryin' 'Cause I Know I'm Losing You   144-574
I'm Crying For You   1454
I'm Cuckoo Again   1394
I'm Cuttin' Out   679-1542
I'm Dancing With The Girl Of My Dreams   84
I'm Dependable (You Can Count On Me)   1236
I'm Desperately In Love With You   880
I'm Doing What I'm Doing For Love   272-949-950-1152-1293-1595
I'm Doing What My Heart Says Do   1678
I'm Done, Done, Done With You   1058-1453
I'm Down In The Dumps   1446
I'm Down Right Now, But I Won't Be Down Always   795
I'm Drifting Back To Dreamland   696-1153
I'm Drifting From You Blues   834
I Mean, It's Just Too Bad   1216
I Met Her In The Moonlight But She Keeps Me In The Dark   625
I Met My Waterloo   162-488
I Met You Then, I Know You Now   272
I'm Every Man's Mama   1051

I'm Facing The Music  426
I'm Falling For You  761-1711
I'm Feathering A Nest  950-1293-1381
I'm Feeling Devilish (Oh By Golly Oh)
723-1716
I'm Feeling Like A Million  294-586-756-
786
I'm Fer It  154
I'm Following You  672-1153-1234-1367-1369
I'm Forever Blowing Bubbles  80-591-969-
1177-1304
I'm Forever Changing Sweethearts  357
I'm Forever You A Hundred Per Cent.  1668
I'm Free  369
I'm Free, Single, Disengaged, Looking For
Someone To Love  1461
I'm Full Of The Devil  1235
I'm Funny 'Bout My Cookin', Baby  1577
I'm Getting Better Every Day  1613
I'm Gettin' Mighty Lonesome  529
I'm Getting My Bonus In Love  1709
I'm Gettin' Myself Ready For You  251
I'm Getting Nowhere With You  901
I'm Getting Sentimental Over You  422-423-
437-466-586-594-1434-1646-1720
I'm Getting Tired So I Can Sleep  436-1554
I'm Glad  1422
I'm Glad For Your Sake (I'm Sorry For
Mine)  900
I'm Glad It Was Somebody Else  917
I'm Glad There Is You  435
I'm Goin' Way (Just) To Wear You Off My
Mind  749-793-1165-1185-1459-1532-1719
I'm Goin' Back To Bottomland  1534-1701-
1702
I'm Going Back To Himazas  1055
I'm Goin' Back To My Mammy's Cabin Door
1123
I'm Going Back To My Used-To-Be  1440-1447
1518
I'm Going Back To Old Nebraska  525-1116-
1425
I'm Going Back To Old Zazoo  968
I'm Going Back Those Who Won't Go Back On
Me  1190
I'm Going Home  1155
I'm Goin' Huntin'  133
I'm Goin' Out If Lizzie Comes In  1181-
1334-1520
I'm Goin' Out Tonight And Strut My Stuff
1716
I'm Goin' Shoppin' With You  426-798
I'm Goin' South  71-796-826-891-1067-1482-
1609
I'm Goin' To Have Seven Years' Bad Luck
1458
I'm Going To See My Ma  795-1622
I'm Going To Show You My Black Bottom
1201
I'm Going To Wait On The Lord  1014
I'm Gonna Be A Lovin' Old Soul  1012
I'm Gonna Charleston Back To Charleston
231-339-546-572-624-1503-1583
I'm Gonna Clap My Hands  583-702-906-1115-
1307
I'm Gonna Cry  156
I'm Gonna Dance Wit De Guy Wot Brung Me
(sic)  822
I'm Gonna Get Acquainted In A Quaint Old-
Fashioned Town  1129
I'm Gonna Get High  1528

I'm Gonna Get Me A Man, That's All  965
I'm Gonna Get Myself A Real Man  1457
I'm Gonna Get You  1462-1466
I'm Gonna Gitcha  41
I'm Gonna Hang Around My Sugar  472-
653-934-1181-1219-1592
I'm Gonna Hoodoo You  1013
I'm Gonna Jazz My Way Right Straight
Thru' Paradise  1492-1518
I'm Gonna Kill Myself  810-1458
I'm Gonna Kiss Mysel Goodbye  123-585
I'm Gonna Leave You On The Outskirts Of
Town  865
I'm Gonna Lock My Heart And Throw Away
The Key  322-768-886-1203-1722
I'm Gonna Lose Myself Way Down In Louis-
ville  795
I'm Gonna Meet My Sweetie Now  304-578-
638-668-1238
I'm Gonna Moan My Blues Away  1747
I'm Gonna  Moochie  1320
I'm Gonna Move To The Outskirts Of Town
109-865-990
I'm Gonna Pack My Grip  1287
I'm Gonna Park Myself In Your Arms  1664
I'm Gonna Play Down By The Ohio  1645
I'm Gonna Put You In Your Place (And
Your Place Is In My Arms)  894-1631
(I'm) Gonna Put You Right In Jail  854-
1458
I'm Gonna Run You Down  863
I'm Gonna Salt Away Some Sugar (For
Sugar And Me)  1636
I'm Gonna See You (When Your Troubles
Are Just Like Mine)  397-712-1532
I'm Gonna Sit Right Down And Write My-
self A Letter  169-204-639-1001-1115-
1344-1621-1626-1628
I'm Gonna Steal You (A Million Dollars)
822-824
I'm Going To/Gonna Steal Somebody's Man
278
I'm Gonna Stomp, Mr. Henry Lee  45-334
I'm Gonna Take My Mother Out Tonight 936
I'm Gonna Tear Your Playhouse Down  1051
1220-1448
I'm Gonna Tell You In Front So You Won't
Feel Hurt Behind  390
I'm Gonna Wash My Hands Of You  582-1211
I'm Gonna Wash My Sins Away  1708
I'm Grateful To You  191-1027
I'm Grieving For You  530
I'm Growing Fonder Of You  1625-1669
I'm Happy About The Whole Thing  9-1358-
1512
I'm Happy, Darling, Dancing With You
59-123-756
I'm Happy When You're Happy  592-1469
I'm Hard To Satisfy  794
I'm Hatin' This Waitin' Around  205-1308
I'm Havin' My Fun  767
I'm Here  620
I'm Her Papa, She's My Mama  358
I'm Hummin', I'm Whistlin', I'm Singin'
201-1146
I'm In A Dancing Mood  383-439-1027-
I'm In A Fog About You  1357
I'm In A Fool's Paradise  961
I'm In A Happy Frame Of Mind  1721
I'm In A Low Down Groove  693
I'm In An Awful Mood  988

I'm In Another World  766
I'm In A Weary Mood  944
I'm In Love  292-650-903
I'm In Love Again  129-1430-1616-1749
I'm In Love All Over Again  1000
I'm In Love With The Girl I Left Behind Me  1319
I'm In Love With The Honorable Mr. So-and-So  1404
I'm In Love With You  232-809
I'm In My Glory  1237
I'm In Seventh Heaven  1598
I'm In So Much Trouble Now  680
I'm In The Jailhouse Now  1391
I'm In The Market For You  21-47-84-517-815-1383
I'm In The Mood For Love  52-203-330-365-382-652-947-1306-1307
I'm In The Mood For Swing  282-661
I'm In (The) Seventh Heaven  950-1155-1687
I Miss A Little Miss (Who Misses Me In Sunny Tennessee)  504-1035-1384
I Miss My Swiss (My Swiss Miss Misses Me)  231-713-1498
Imitations Of You  132
I'm Just A Country Boy At Heart  1561
I'm Just A Jitterbug  1660
I'm Just A Little Boy Blue  425
I'm Just A Rollin' Stone  567
I'm Just A Substitute For Love  1109
I'm Just In The Mood Tonight  800-1293
I'm Just Wearing Out My Heart For You  22
I'm Just Wild About Animal Crackers  234-472-1396-1574
I'm Just Wild About Harry  141-347-427-555-935-1017-1085-1142-1173-1310-1424-1427-1492
I'm Just Wondering Who  1o77
I'm Ka-Razy For You  658-708-1638
I'm Keepin' Company  1385-1515
I'm Keeping Company Now  1394
I'm Keeping Those Keepsakes  93
I'm Knockin' At The Cabin Door  39
I'm Laughing Up My Sleeve (Ha-Ha-Ha-Ha-Ha)  987
I'm Leaving Here Blues  354
I'm Leavin' Just To Ease My Worried Mind  398
I'm Leaving You  566-847-861-1212-1618-1723
I'm Left With A Broken Heart  181
I'm Like A Fish Out Of Water  606
I'm Like A Sailor  952
I'm Livin' In A Great Big Way  202-520-563-595-687-1205-1248-1432
I'm Living In The Past - see MOONGLOW
I'm Livin' In A Great Big Way  1627
I'm Living On Love  1136
I'm Lonely And Blue  1328
I'm Lonesome  1554
I'm Lonesome, Nobody Cares For Me  1595
I'm Lonesome, Sweetheart  1169
I'm Longing For Someone  1290
I'm Looking For A Little Bluebird  1104
I'm Looking For Someone To Love Me  540
I'm Looking For That Certain Man To Love  757
I'm Looking For The Bully Of The Town  1041
I'm Looking Over A Four Leaf Clover  577-632
I'm Losing My Mind Because Of You  990-1753
I'm Losing My Mind Over You  633

I'm Mad Because I Turned My Baby Down  812
I'm Madly In Love With You  259-692
I'm Marching Home To You  1141
Immigration Blues  472
I'm Mr. African  1287
I'm Misunderstood  168-902
I'm More Than Satisfied  2-17-309-658-970-1193-1247
I'm My Baby's Baby  832
I'm Needin' You  247-736
I'm Never Blue Where The Grass Is Green  1027
I'm No Account Any More - see ALL ON ACCOUNT OF YOUR KISSES
I'm No Angel  92-1270
I'm Nobody's Baby  81-449-589-615-1352
I'm Not Complainin'  527-617
I'm Not Much On Looks  153
I'm Not Rough  42
I'm Not Worryin'  1535-1705
I'm Not Your Fool  849
I'm Now Prepared To Tell The World It's You  254
I'm Nuts About My Baby  1414
I'm Nuts About Screwy Music  85-985
I'm Old-Fashioned  300-417-623
I'm On A Diet Of Love  932-1165
I'm On A See-Saw  382-700-701-967-1627
I'm On A Sit-Down Strike For Rhythm  39
I'm One Of God's Children (Who Hasn't Got Wings)  853-1131
I'm One Step Ahead Of My Shadow  1027-1236
I'm On My Way From You  662
I'm On My Way Home  928
I'm On My Way South  1292
I'm On The Crest Of A Wave  240-1597
I'm Out Of Style  1477
I'm Painting Pictures  981
I'm Painting The Town Red (To Hide A Heart That's Blue)  779-967-1730
I'm Perfectly Satisfied  507
I'm Playing Solitaire  1279
I'm Playing With Fire  1016-1438
I'm Prayin' Humble  94-369
Impressions  839
Impromptu  896-990
I'm Proud Of You  16-933
Improvisation  1283
Improvisation In Several Keys  644
Improvisation sur le premier mouvement du Concerto en re mineur de J. S. Bach  1476
Improvisation Swing du premier mouvement du Concerto en re mineur de J. S. Bach  1476
I'm Pulling Through  769
I'm Putting All My Eggs In One Basket  160-204-311-1312-1329 1464
I'm Ref'n' Just To Her 'n' Me  580
I'm Putting All My Eggs In One Basket 53
I'm Red-Hot From Harlem  651
I'm Rhythm Crazy Now  730
I'm Riding To Glory (With A Glorious Girl)  1264-1325-1459
I'm Sailing On A Sunbeam  1491
I'm Satisfied  488-1011
I'm Satisfidd (Beside That Sweetie Of Mine)  67-227-558-966-1591
I'm Satisfied With My Gal - see YES SHE DO, NO SHE DON'T

I'm Satisfied You Love Me  302
I'm Savin' It All For You  734-735-1024-1651
I'm Saving Myself For You  739
I'm Shooting High  52-438-960-968-1001-1114-1249
I'm Sick/Tired Of Fattening Frogs For Snakes  357-462-965-1452
I'm Sitting High On A Hill Top  365-701-1114-1178-1689
I'm Sitting On Top Of The World  630-857-870-927-1063-1299
I'm Sitting Pretty In A Pretty Little City  560-1240
I'm Slappin' Seventh Avenue (With The Sole Of My Shoe)  493
I'm So Afraid Of You  980
I'm So Alone With The Crowd  875
I'm So Blue Since My Sweetie Went Away  1037
I'm So Glad  355-679
I'm So Glad I'm Brownskin  1618
I'm So Glad I'm Twenty-One Today  1677
I'm So In Love With You  483-484-633
I'm Somebody's Somebody Now  669
I'm Sorry Blues  1013
I'm Sorry, Dear  1030
I'm Sorry For It Now  1618-1723
I'm Sorry For Myself  1406
I'm Sorry I Ain't Got It You Could Have Had It If I Had It Blues  976
I'm Sorry I Made You Blue  1072
I'm Sorry I Made You Cry  334-379-549-781-1146-1250-1516-1603-1630
I'm Sorry I Said Goodbye  82
I'm Sorry, Sally  18-470-1417-1641
I'm Sorry That We Said Goodbye  1398
I'm So Weary Of It All  446
(I'm) Speaking Of Kentucky Days  800-1294
I'm Steppin' High, Wide And Handsome  1390
I'm Stepping Out  832
I'm Stepping Out Tonight  1414
I'm Stepping Out With A Memory Tonight  1359
I'm Still Caring  634
I'm Sure Of Everything But You  674
I'm Taking My Own Sweet Time  1389
I'm Takin' My Time With You  1539
I'm Tellin' The Birds, Tellin' The Bees How I Love You  61-272-463-1364
I'm Telling You  564
I'm That Way Over You  1493
I'm The Echo  1690
I'm The Fellow Who Loves You  968
I'm The Last Of The Red Hot Mamas  459-890
I'm The Lonesome One  1344
I'm The Lonesomest Gal In Town - see LONESOMEST GAL IN TOWN, THE
I'm The Medicine Man For The Blues  264-507-952-1418
I'm The One Who Loves You  273-443
I'm Thinking Tonight Of My Blue Eyes  364
I'm Three Times Seven  534
I'm Thrilled  529-1552
I'm Through  1703
I'm Through (Shedding Tears Over You)  570
I'm Thru' With Love  197-299-506-778
I'm Through With You (As I Can Be)  136-682-1466
I'm Tickled Pink With A Blue-Eyed Baby  514-1143-1295-1303

I'm Tired Blues  795
I'm Tired Of Begging You To Treat Me Right  1218-1717
I'm Tired Of Bein' Good  1450
I'm Tired Of Everything But You  173-1589
I'm Tired Of Fattenin' Frogs For Snakes - see I'M SICK OF FATTENING FROGS FOR SNAKES
I'm Tired Of Waiting For You  108-168-1290
I'm Trusting In You  374
I'm Trying  273
I'm Up A Tree  1662
I Must Be Dreaming  17-501-677-1597
I Must Have Company  226
I Must Have It  751-1170-1549-1618
I Must Have That Man  314-477-478-487-528-610-651-652-670-800-1140-1151-1292-1536-1585-1598-1732
I Must See Annie Tonight  206-588-610
I'm Waiting For Ships That Never Come In  909
I'm Walking Around In Circles  38-921
I'm Walking Between The Raindrops  649
I'm Walking On Air  172-1174
I'm Walking The Chalk Line  1431
I'm Walkin' This Town  1154
I'm Walking Through Clover  977
I'm Walking Through Heaven With You  984-990
I'm Watching The Clock  1169-1704
I'm Wild About Horns On Automobiles (That Go "Ta-Ta-Ta-Ta")  654-1393
I'm Wild About My Patootie  7
I'm Wild About That Thing  1445
I'm Wingin' Home  1064
I'm With You, Right Or Wrong  703-1732
I'm Wonderin' Who  238-1567
I'm Writing You  808
I'm Yours  156-505-980-1401-1402
I'm Yours For The Asking  1236
I'm Yours For Tonight  981
I'm Yours To Command  637
In A Bamboo Garden  1291
In A Blue And Pensive Mood  292
In A Cafe On The Road To Calais  1427
In A Charleston Cabin - see CHARLESTON CABIN
In A Corner  1370
In A Covered Wagon  920
In A Good-For-Nothing Mood  8
In A Great Big Way  670-1029-1079-1233
In A Jam  94-491
In A Kitchenette  952
In A Little Back Alley  148
In A Little Blue Canoe With You  875
In A Little Carolina Town  1314
In A Little Garden  267
In A Little Gypsy Tea Room  365-779-1248
In A Little Hula Heaven  362-440
In A Little Red Barn (On A Farm Down In Indiana)  201
In A Little Second-Hand Store  199
In A Little Spanish Town  123-124-166-190-211-402-455-1063-1228-1660
In A Little White Lighthouse  1314
In A Mellotone  497
In A Mist (Bixology)  116-126-357-1156-1571
In A Mizz  95-495
In A Moment Of Weakness  1358

1906

In A Moonboat 1374
In An 18th-Century Drawing Room 747-889-1372
In An Old English Village 258
In An Old World Garden 1155
In A One-Room Flat 1669
In Any Language 1721
In A Persian Market 323-1242
In A Sentimental Mood 428-489-491-493-598-1027-1074-1236-1260-1273
In A Shanty In Old Shanty Town 86-875-960 1297-1314-1344
In A Subway Far From Ireland 1373
In A Tent 920-1175-1643
In Blinky Winky Chinatown 132
Inconvenience 214
In Dat Mornin' (sic) 983
Indecision - "Big Or Small Hat ?" 1085-1262-1338
In De Ruff 1600
Indiana 15-131-193-207-288-330-334-595-760-765-814-913-1113-1114-1141-1175-1176 1343-1410-1530-1531
Indiana Avenue Blues 1280
Indiana Lou 954
Indiana Moonlight 1315
Indiana Mud 139-271-1183
Indiana Shuffle 1182
Indiana Stomp 1180-1181-1191-1192
Indian Boogie Woogie 740
Indian Butterfly 1521
Indian Cradle Song 47-340-419
Indian Dawn 511-866
Indian Love 1742
Indian Love Call 796-1402-1403-1459
Indian Moon 1252
Indian Nights 38
Indianola 512-1179-1434-1516
Indian Summer 113-448-1359
Indigo Blues 379-530-1185
Indigo Echoes 489
Indigo Stomp 415
Indispensable You 952
In Dutch With The Duchess 889
I Nearly Let Love Go Slipping Through My Fingers 122-879-1178
I Nearly Lost My Mind 663
I Need A Good Man Bad 540
I Need A Man 778
I Need Lovin' 6-251-340-625-720-1154-1397
I Needs A Plenty Of Grease In My Frying Pan 941
I Need Somebody To Love 167
I Need Some Lovin' 542-1208
I Need Someone Like You 1623
I Need Some Pettin' 1348-1741
I Need You 137-731-1702
I Need You By My Side 849-1527
I Need You So 196
I Need You To Drive My Blues Away 1728
I Need You (You Need Me) 1504
In Egern On The Tegern See 289
I Never Asked To Come To This World 904
I Never Call My Man's Name 1499
I Never Care 'Bout Tomorrow 569-715-1190
I Never Did Want You 409
I Never Dreamt 761
I Never Dreamt (You'd Fall In Love With Me) 246-503-506-979
I Never Felt This Way Before 495-497
I Never Had A Chance 291-879

I Never Had A Dream 1562
I Never Had The Blues 1062
I Never Knew 58-87-95-107-149-277-288-312-386-388-393-444-530-536-586-595-608-630-635-636-698-785-786-890-913-1140-1225-1307-1472-1736
I Never Knew Heaven Could Speak 206-370 1147
I Never Knew How Much I Loved You 1746
I Never Knew How Wonderful You Were 1483
I Never Knew I Had The Blues 1748
I Never Knew Till Now 248
I Never Knew What A Gal Could Do 1132-1216
I Never Knew What The Blues Were (Until You Went Away) 964
I Never Knew What The Moonlight Could Do 463-1036
I Never Loved But One Woman's Son 1323
I Never Miss The Sunshine (I'm So Used To The Rain) 120-461-646-1187-1447
I Never Purposely Hurt You 208-816
I Never Realized 288
I Never Saw A Better Night 779
I Never See Maggie Alone 1
I Never Slept A Wink Last Night 12-291
I Never Thought (I'd Ever Care) 913
Infatuation 92-291
Informal Blues 494
In Gay Havana 1517
(In) Harlem's Araby 456-564-634-1041-1367-1459
Inhibition 1354
In Honeysuckle Time (When Emaline Said She'd Be Mine) 141-1423
Inka Dinka Doo 1154
In Love With You 850
In My Country That Means Love 292-700
In My Dreams (I'm Jealous Of You) 318-1108
In My Garden Of Memories 1069
In My Gondola 646-1592
In My Heart 1504
In My Heart, On My Mind All Day Long 68
In My Little Hope Chest 83
In My Little Red Book 881-1179
In My Meditations 441
In My Merry Oldsmobile 578-1314
In My Miz(z) 781-1252
In My Story Book Of Dreams 248
In My Wildest Dreams 900
In Other Words, We're Through 878
In Our Cottage Of Dreams 1535-1705
In Pinetop's Footsteps 1243
Insane Crazy Blues 1044
Inside 1632
In Soudan 1747 (same as SOUDAN ?)
Inspiration 759
In Spite Of All 558
Instant d'infini 1288
In Susie's Basement 1507
In Swamp Lands 761
Intangibility 1354
Intermezzo 618-742-945
International Rag, The 1237
In That Apartment Upstairs 735
In They Alley Blues 65
In The Bag 664
In The Baggage Coach Ahead 513
In The Barrel 1003
In The Blue Of The Evening 454

In The Bottle Blues  1704
In The Bottom  1400
In The Chapel In The Moonlight  14-182
In The Dark  126-1490
In The Dim, Dim Dawning  36
In The Dungeon  1208
In The Dusk  1177
In The Evening (1924)  576
In The Evening (1928)  1290
In The Evening By The Moonlight  401
In The Gloaming  58-1632
In The Good Old Summertime  1315
In The Groove  439-899-1002
In The Groove At The Grove  1661
In The House Blues  1446
In The Hush Of The Night  434-1233-1374
In The Jailhouse Now  147
In The Land Of Jazz  956
In The Land Of Yamo Yamo  1003
In The Merry Month Of Maybe  1385-1570
In The Middle Of A Dream  9-432-446-1160
In The Middle Of A Kiss  563-974-1205-1306
   1530
In The Mission By The Sea  294-442-443
In The Mood  9-590-696-1046-1224-1403-
   1436-1736
In The Moonlight  1148
In The Purple Twilight  315
In There  832
In The Shade Of The New Apple Tree  829-
   1490
In The Shade Of The Old Apple Tree  54-118
   367-383-488-774-876-1329-1402-1433-1550-
   1720
In The Shadow Of A Rose  951
In The Sing-Song Sycamore Tree  574-1583-
   1584-1610
In The Slot  1000
(In The) Soudan  1177
In The Spring  677
In The Still Of The Night  275-288-296-442
   1259-1294
In The Valley Of The Moon  148
Into My Heart  247
Intoxication  1601
In Your Green Hat  646-967-1579
In Your Own Little Way  93
In Your Own Quiet Way  1337
I Once Was Yours, I'm Somebody Else's Now
   1463
I Only Have Eyes For You  689
I Only Want A Buddy-Not A Sweetheart  1316
I Owe You  15-205
I Packed My Suitcase, Started To The Train
   1041
I Paid My Income Tax Today  1319
I Picked A Flower The Color Of Your Eyes
   438
I Poured My Heart Into A Song  431-447-
   1405
I Promised Not To Holler, But Hey ! Hey !
   458-459
I Promise You  249-296-1316
I Put A Four-Leaf Clover In Your Pocket
   529
I Raised My Hat  1331
I Received A Letter  1746
I Remember  294
I Remember You  425-763-819-1361
I Remember You From Somewhere  247
Irene  464

I Repent  1636
Irish Black Bottom  41-1656
Irish Blues  1609
Irish Washerwoman  1572
Irony Daddy Blues  357
Iroquois  1150
Irresistible  292
Irresistible, El  512
Irresistible Blues  1447-1533
Isabel  401
Isabella  133
Isabella Kissed A Fella  1319
Isabella (Tell Your Fella)  1135-1531
Isabelle  1720
I Said No  435-1553
I Saw Stars  398-699-1211-1258-1689-1710
I Scream-You Scream-We All Scream For
   ICE CREAM  524-1431
I'se A Muggin'  584-688-702-899-1052-
   1259-1464-1558
I See A Million People (But All I Can
   See Is You)  261-273-619-1243-1361
I See You Can't Take It  1528
I See Your Face Before Me  78-295
Is Everybody Happy Now ?  1745
I Shall Hail Cairo And Our Ancestors
   1375
I Shoulda Stood In Bed (sic)  80
I Should Have Known You Years Ago  167-
   742
I Should Shay Sho  883
Is I In Love ? I Is  147-697-875-1310-
   1388
I Simply Adore You  368-1632
Is It A Sin (Loving You)  902
Is It Gonna Be Long ? (Till You Belong
   To Me)  1018-1685
Is It Love Or Infatuation  15
Is It Possible ?  432-447-520-653-1056
Is It Spain ?  951
Is It Taboo (To Fall In Love With You)
   1408
Is It True What They Say About Dixie ?
   191-427-938-1001-1124-1312-1433-1519
Isle Of Capri  1000-1334
Isle Of Pines  98-434         )LOVELY DAY ?
Isn't It A Lovely Day ?-see ISN'T THIS A
Isn't It Heavenly ?  148-982-1600
Isn't It Romantic ?  827-875
Isn't It The Truth ?  509
Isn't It Time To Fall In Love ?  326
Isn't Love The Strangest Thing ?  490-
   1002
Isn't She The Sweetest Thing ?  73-230
Isn't That Everything ?  990
Isn't That Just Like Love ?  373-451-910
Isn't There A Little Love ?  999
Isn't This A Lovely Day ?  382-701
Isn't This A Night For Love ?  199
Isola Bella (That Little Swiss Isle)  97
Is She My Girl Friend ?  238-340-533-626
   799-1068-1227-1241-1289-1378-1580-1593
   1672
Is That Religion ?  77-252-346-484
Is That The Way To Treat A Sweetheart ?
   610
Is There Anything Wrong In That ?  262-
   670-1292
Is There A Place Up There For Me ?  790
Is There Somebody Else ?  527
Is This Gonna Be My Lucky Summer ?  441

1908
Is This To Be My Souvenir ? 1337
I Still Believe In You 268-1612
I Still Get A Thrill (Thinking Of You) 247-1667
I Still Have My Dreams 730
I Still Love You 31-1016
I Still Want You 1248
I Struck A Match In The Dark 109
I Surrender, Dear 6-48-312-394-610-615-647-660-900-1116-1156-1400-1405-1572-1736-1743
I Swung The Election 1538
It Ain't A Doggone Thing But The Blues - see 'TAIN'T A DOGGONE THING BUT THE BLUES
It Ain't Gonna Rain No Mo' 963-1058-1190
It Ain't Like That 273
It Ain't Necessarily So 1512
It Ain't No Fault Of Mine 655
It Ain't No Fun 182
It Ain't Right 428-1027-1398-1465
I Take To You 911-1360-1427
It All Begins And Ends With You 545-1157
It All Belongs To Me 1015-1136
It All Comes Back To Me Now 910-1242-1540
It All Depends On You 171-314-455-648-668 1222
It Always Starts To Rain 1296
It Always Will Be You 901
It Belongs To You 650
It Can Happen To You 1002-1157
Itching Heel 1376
Itchola 1689
It Couldn't Be 944
It Counts A Lot 417
It Don't Do Nothin' But Rain 566-785
It Don't Mean A Thing (If It Ain't Got That Swing) 89-151-158-384-485-635-661-801-871-1205-1272-1472
It Feels (So) Good 392-895-897-1033
It Goes Like This (That Funny Melody) 654 950-1393
It Goes To Your Feet 1400
It Had To Be You 72-188-207-226-471-610-611-635-761-990-1017-1141-1283-1332-1408 1432-1551-1584
I Thank You, Mr. Moon 157
It Happened Down In Dixieland 536-585-739 879
It Happened In Hawaii 434
It Happened In Kaloha 908
It Happens To The Best Of Friends 594
"I," The Living "I" 692
I Think Of What You Used To Think Of Me 1291
I Think Of You 82-168-453-744-912
I Think You'll Like It 671
I Think You're A Honey 1571
I Thought About You 165-371-613
I Thought I'd Do It 1026
I Thought I Heard Buddy Bolden Say - see BUDDY BOLDEN'S BLUES
I Threw A Bean Bag At The Moon 426
I Threw A Good Man Over For You 707
I Threw A Kiss In The Ocean 436-622
I Thrill When They Mention Your Name 425
It Hurts So Good 181-1652
It Isn't A Dream Any More 453
It'll Get You 920
It Looks Like Love 592-1296
It Looks Like Rain In Cherry Blossom Lane 385-1313

It Looks Like Susie 251-253
It Made You Happy When You Made Me Cry 928-1120
It Makes My Love Come Down 1446
It Makes No Difference Now 363-1023-1316-1518-1719
It Makes No Never Mind 942
It May Be My Last Night 381
It May Not Be True 86-689
It Must Be Hard 854-1499
It Must Be Jelly 762
It Must Be Love 404-566-1557-1639-1662-1677
It Must Be Religion 1002
It Must Be Swell To Be Laying Out Dead 100
It Must Be The Blues 1536
It Must Be True 900
It Must Be You 1369
It Must Have Been A Dream 762-763
It Must Have Been Two Other People 95
It Never Dawned On Me 701-1730
It Never Entered My Mind 324-615
I Told Them All About You 533
I Told You So 942
I Touched A Star 298-1375
I Travel Alone 809
I Tried 452
It's A Blue World 448-741
It's About Time 697
It's A Great Life (If You Don't Weaken) 933
It's A Great World After All 1277
It's A Hap-Hap-Happy Day 1436-1752
It's A Hundred To One (I'm In Love) 448-1358-1539
It's A Hundred To One You're In Love 1375
It's A Killer, Mr. Miller 1557
It's All Coming Home To You 1451-1640
It's All Forgotten Now 699-1031
It's All My Fault 158
It's All Over Now (I Won't Worry) 373
It's All Right, Baby 1575
It's All Right, Jack 1247
It's All So New To Me 1358
It's All The Same To Me 1164-1323
It's All Your Fault 1277
It's All Yours 431-1404
It's A Lonely Trail 323
It's A Lonesome Old Town 504-1035
It's A Long Time Between Kisses 1386
It's A Long Way To Tipperary 375-970-1401
It's A Lot Of Idle Gossip 785
It's A Lovely Day Tomorrow 207-450-1359
It's A Low Down Dirty Shame 865-1413
It's Always You 451-617
It's A Mighty Pretty Night For Love 1317
It's A Million To One You're In Love 269-784-1015-1136-1610
It's An Old Cuban Custom 386
It's An Old Spanish Custom In The Moonlight 514
It's Anybody's Moon 431
It's A Pair Of Wings For Me 589
It's A Precious Little Thing Called Love 243-670-757-950-1033-1217-1393-1510
It's A Puzzle To Me (So What ?) 1557
It's A Sin 1740
It's A Sin To Tell A Lie 382-584-632-770-1312-1628-1629

It's A Whole New Thing  372
It's A Wonderful World  96-166-190-1359
It's Bad For Your Soul  1355
It's Been A Long, Long Time  1398
It's Been So Long  122-203-597-1249-1546-
1621
It's Bologney  653
It's Breaking My Heart To Keep Away From
You  1714
It's De-Lovely  182-554
It's Easier Said Than Done  29-367
It's Easy To Blame The Weather  1116-1735
It's Easy To Fall In Love  1383
It's Easy To Remember  639-1154
It Seems I've Done Something Wrong Again
785
It Seems Like Old Times  80
It Seems To Be Spring  1514
It Sends Me  688
It's Evil-Hearted Me  1487
It's Foxy  1661
It's Funny To Everyone But Me  151-432-815
It's Funny What A Kiss Can Do  779
It's Gettin' Kinda Chilly  550
It's Glory  485
It's Gonna Be A Cold, Cold Winter (So Get
Another Place To Stay)  1250-1725
It's Gonna Be You  36-142
It's Got To Be Love  182
It's Great To Be In Love Again  366-553
It's Hard To Believe It's True  1528
It's Hard To Laugh Or Smile  1110
It's Heated  823
It's Hot - Let It Alone  150
It Should Be You  11
It's Jam Up  302
It's Just Because I'm Falling In Love With
You  668
It's Just That Feelin' For Home  1443
It's Just Like Reaching For The Moon  1731
It's Love I'm After  77-93-1157
It's Me Again  1752
It's Me, O Lord  1711
It's Murder  39
It's My Day Now  551
It's My Night To Howl  249-365
It's My Turn Now  466-526-741
It's No Fun  428-879-1001-1628
It's No-One But You  210
It's Not A Secret Any More  273-1147-1367
It's O.K., Katy, With Me  1580
It's Only A Paper Moon  464-896-1688
It's Our Business  277
It's Over Because We're Through  191-1658
It's Psychological  1508
It's Purely Coincidental  736
It's Red Hot  393
It's Right Here For You (If You Don't Get
It-'Tain't No Fault Of Mine)  192-251-
336-436-562-1178-1460
It's Sad But True  273-498-1242
It's Sand Man !  110
It's Slumber Time Along The Swanee  80-
1662
It's So Good  1079-1080
It's So Peaceful In The Country  81-818-
1360
It's Square But It Rocks  108-167
It's Still Being Done  1337
It's Sunday Down In Caroline  158-878
It's Swell Of You  205-491

It Started All Over Again  454
It's Swell Of You  1659
It's The Blues  576-858
It's The Dardnest Thing  725-1144
It's The Dreamer In Me  429-430-608-814
It's The Girl !  157-287-1098-1286
It's The Gold  832
It's The Gypsy In Me  383-1002
It's The Irish In Me  455
It's The Last Time I'll Be A Pastime For
You  1058
It's The Last Time (I'll Fall In Love)
97-816
It's The Little Things That Count  125-
729-1357
It's The Natural Thing To Do  78-205-429-
1400
It's The Rhythm In Me  584-588-1248
It's The Same Old South  108
It's The Same Old Story  770
It's The Same The Whole World Over  969
It's The Talk Of The Town  290-299-638-
674-727-1031
It's The Tune That Counts  1635-1655
It's Tight Jim  810
It's Tight Like That  91-398-574-641-950-
1033-1078-1151-1345-1452-1477-1526-1594
1648-1693
It's Time To Jump And Shout  989-1359
It's Time To Keep Away From You  1389
It's Time To Sing "Sweet Adeline" Again
199
It's Too Bad (When The Sisters Start
Truckin' Around)  309
It's Too Good To Be True  317
It's Too Hot For Words  1730
It's Too Late  1322
It's Too Late Now  237-1321
It's Torture  107
It's True  949
It's Unanimous Now  509-788-1514
It's Unbelievable  779
It's Up To You  1465
It's 'Way Past My Dreaming Time  1147
It's Wearing Me Down  728-1326
It's Winter Again  199-1438
It's Wonderful  55-367-443-526-606-1158-
1402-1512
It's Written All Over Your Face  13-159
It's Written In The Stars  437-779
It's You  157-234-1154
It's You Again  186
It's You I Adore  1640
It's You I'm Talking About  438
It's You, Only You  550
It's Your Turn  783
It's Your Yas Yas Yas  676
It's You That/Who Taught It Me  681-1635
It Takes A Brown Skin Man To Make A High
Yellow Blue  1716
It Takes A Good Woman (To Keep A Good Man
At Home)  268-531-1096-1246-1579-1651-
1737
It Takes A Long Tall Brownskin Gal  904
It Takes A Long Time To Get 'Em But You
Can Lose 'Em Overnight  1010
It Takes The Lawd (To Tell What's On My
Mind)  1450
It Took A Lot Of Blue  1080
It Took A Million Years  322-1404
It Was A Lover And His Lass  370-841-1518

It Was A Night In June  982
It Was A Sad Night In Harlem  491-691
It Was Only A Dream  374
It Was Only A Sun Shower  238-669-1665
It Was Red  679
It Was So Beautiful  35-635-673
It Was Sweet Of You  879
It Was The Dawn Of Love  1685
It Was Written In The Stars  207
It Will Never Happen Again  783
It Won't Act Right  1043
It Won't Be Long  1111
It Won't Be Long Now  712-732-1448-1682
It Won't Be You  1445
I Understand  433-590-1374-1637
I Used To Be Above Love  1398
I Used To Be Color Blind  79-1159-1690
I Used To Be Your Sweet Mama  1444
I Used To Love Her In The Moonlight (But
  She's In The Limelight Now)  1079-1141
I Used To Love You (But It's All Over Now)
  58-206-781-988-1243-1317-1654
I've A Garden In Sweden  228-796
I've A Strange New Rhythm In My Heart  1401
I've Been A Fool  919
I've Been Dispossessed By You  633
I've Been Dreaming  923
I've Been In Love Before  284
I've Been In The Storm So Long  791
I've Been Looking For A Girl Like You
  (For A Long, Long Time)  930
I've Been Mistreated And I Don't Like It
  1443
I've Been There Before  613
I've Been Waiting All Winter  132
I've Been Working On The Railroad  1398
I('ve) Found A New Baby  113-309-319-344-
  411-521-542-559-598-632-635-646-662-691-
  719-764-815-822-839-858-913-961-1033-
  1037-1134-1239-1245-1341-1343-1346-1556-
  1564-1599-1651-1670-1673-1691-1700-1706-
  1733-1752
I've Found A Sweetheart  541
I've Found The Right Girl  400
I've Found What I Wanted In You  504-724-
  980
I've Gone Off The Deep End  80
I've Gone Romantic On You  828
I've Got A Brand New Girl  918
I've Got A Cross-Eyed Papa (But He Looks
  Straight To Me)  224-560-1122-1189-1573-
  1609
I've Got A Crush On You  1511-1696
I've Got A Date With A Dream  609-768
I've Got A Do Right Daddy Now  627
I've Got A Feeling  1127-1294
I've Got A Feeling For Somebody  1738
I've Got A Feeling I'm Falling  63-131-671-
  949-1088-1155-1293-1623-1626-1743
I've Got A Feelin' You're Foolin'  203-426-
  437-959-1001
I've Got A Gal In Kalamazoo  436-622
I've Got A Guy  124-1357
I've Got A Heart Full Of Rhythm  54
I've Got A Heavy Date  182-702-1464
I've Got A Little List  323
I've Got A Mama Down In New Orleans  708
I've Got A Man Of My Own  541
I've Got A New Lease On Love  1630
I've Got An Invitation To A Dance  292-797
I've Got An Old-Fashioned Love In My Heart
  - see OLD FASHIONED LOVE

I've Got A Note  23-437-1001
I've Got Another Sweetheart  886
I've Got A One-Track Mind  373-1552
I've Got A Pocketful Of Dreams  56
I've Got A Roof Over My Head  509
I've Got A Song For Sale (That My Sweetie
  Turned Down)  224-890-916-1188-1673-
  1722
I've Got A Strange New Rhythm In My Heart
  367-1401
I've Got A Sweet Somebody  421
I've Got A Warm Spot For You  1236-1332
I've Got A Wonderful Feeling  585
I've Got A Wonderful Girl  982
I've Got Beginner's Luck  440-1027-1400-
  1434
I've Got Five Dollars  807-1098-1235-1696
I've Got Ford Movements In My Hips  565
I've Got "It"  1537
I've Got It All (If That's Any News To
  You)  856
I've Got Mine  963
I've Got My Captain Working For Me Now
  1177-1603
I've Got My Eyes On You  184-185-206-372-
  448-908-1406
I've Got My Fingers Crossed  52-968-1001-
  1114-1249-1285-1627-1628
I've Got My Habits On  68-1352-1379
I've Got My Heart Set On You  294-320-
  1003
I've Got My Love To Keep Me Warm  293-
  606-767-1157-1283-1530
I've Got No Strings  908
I've Got Nothin'-You've Got Nothin'-We
  Ain't Got Nothin' To Lose  883
I've Got Plenty To Be Thankful For  364
I've Got Rain In My Eyes  440
I've Got Sixpence  590
I've Got Somebody Now  139-735
I've Got Someone  1084
I've Got Something  391
I've Got Something In My Eye  1271
I've Got That Thing  1169
I've Got The Ain't Got Nothin' Never Had
  Nothin' Blues  646
I've Got The Blues  413
I've Got The Blues (About My Baby)  1414
I've Got The Blues But I'm Just Too Mean
  To Cry  914-1423
I've Got The Blues For Rampart Street
  352
I've Got The Blues, That's All  627
I've Got The Girl  267-577-625-1521
I've Got The Joogie Blues  1082
I've Got The Joys  935-1525
I've Got The Red, White And Blues  1423
I've Got The Right Man Now  1323
I've Got The San Francisco Blues  813
I've Got The Spring Fever Blues  1659
I've Got The Sweetest Girl In All The
  World  855
I've Got The Wonder Where He Went And
  When He's Coming Back Blues  705-1523
I've Got The World In A Jug  1023
I've Got The World On A String  51-199-
  255-361-471-486-518-774-1031-1485-1530
I've Got The Yes We Have No Bananas Blues
  71-826-1533-1608
I've Got To Be A Rug Cutter  491
I've Got To Cool My Doggies Now - see
  GOT TO COOL MY DOGGIES NOW

I've Got To Cool My Puppies Now  705
I've Got To Go And Leave My Daddy Behind 1012
I've Got To Have My Daddy Blues  914
I've Got To Have My Moments  1467
I've Got Too Many Blues  1247-1323
I've Got To Pass Your House To Get To My House  982
I've Got To Sing A Torch Song  730-1009-1241-1269
I've Got To Think It Over  1468
I've Got Two Lips  281
I've Got What It Takes (But It Breaks My Heart To Give It Away)  705-1445-1706
I've Got You On My Mind  1286
I've Got You On The Top Of My List  84
I've Got Your Number  426
I've Got You Under My Skin  428-1465-1696
I've Grown So Lonesome Thinking Of You  455-1718
I've Had My Moments  423-1259
I've Had The Blues So Long  859
I've Had Those Lonesome Blues All Day  212
I've Heard That Song Before  820
I've Hitched My Wagon To A Star  205-367-604-1333
I've Learned To Do Without You Now  1589
I've Lost My Head Over You  1560
I've Lost My Heart In Dixieland  1177
I've Lost My Heart To The Meanest Girl  1492
I've Never Been Loved (By Anyone Like You)  1077-1078
I've Nothing To Live For  374
I've Only Myself To Blame  987
I've Seen My Baby (And It Won't Be Long Now)  738-1263-1368
I've Stopped My Man  1549-1618
I've Taken A Fancy To You  633
I Vouch For My Man  995
Ivy (Cling To Me)  1186-1480-1606
I Walk Alone  829
I Walked All The Way From East St. Louis  666
I Walk With Music  317
I Wanna Be Around My Baby All The Time  287-592-853-1112
I Wanna Be In Winchell's Column  739
I Wanna Be Loved  1235-1278
I Wanna Be Loved By You  670
I Wanna Call You Sweet Mama  464
I Wanna Count Sheep (Till The Cows Come Home)  726-1285
I Wanna Get It  892
I Wanna Go Back To Harlem  689
I Wanna Go Back To Indiana  813
I Wanna Go Places And Do Things  1214
I Wanna Hat With Cherries  1539
I Wanna Hear Swing Songs  989-1637
I Wanna Hot Dog For My Roll  213
I Wanna Jazz Some More  182-643-1093-1520
I Wanna/Want To See My Tennessee  67-228-576
I Wanna Sing About You  197-287-515-736-778-981-1312-1594
I Wanna Two-Fisted Double-Jointed Man  1452
I Wanna Woo  701
I Want A Beautiful Baby Like You  1522
I Want A Daddy To Cuddle Me  1418
I Want A Doll  1603
I Want A Girl (Just Like The Girl That Married Dear Old Dad)  206-1317

I Want A Good Man And I Want Him Bad  214-672-1025
I Want A Jazzy Kiss  1461
I Want A Little Girl  6-107-459-873-1034-1295
I Want A Long Time Daddy  534
I Want A Lot Of Love  758-1584
I Want A New Romance  124-1401
I Want A Tall Skinny Papa  1070
I Want Every Bit Of It (I Don't Like It Second Hand)  1013-1443
I Want Him Back Again  1516
I Want My Lagniappe  1238
I Want My Loving  1037
I Want My Mama  63-364-590-1752
I Want My Share Of Love  323-1358-1404
I Want My Sweet Daddy  1520
I Want My Sweet Daddy Now  731-732-1057-1447-1651
I Want Plenty Grase In My Frying Pan  285
I Wants A Real Man  110
I Want Some  1020
I Want Somebody All My Own  1650
I Want Somebody To Cheer Me Up  74-462-630-719
I Want Somebody To Love  650
I Want Somebody To Tell My Troubles To  1534
I Want Some Lovin' Blues  280-413
I Want Some Money  1613
I Want Something To Live For  494-495
I Want The Waiter (With The Water)  527-528-988
I Want The Whole World To Love You  1416
I Want To  710-1648
I Want To Be Alone With Mary Brown  1226
I Want To Be A Gypsy  900
I Want To Be Bad  130 242-262-670-800-1418-1595-1604
I Want To Be Discovered  428
I Want To Be Happy  227-554-583-600-939-1142-1582-1660
I Want To Be Your Lovin' Man  1495
I Want To Dance  836
I Want To Go Back To The Farm  1577
I Want To Go Home  341
I Want To Hold You In My Arms  1747
I Want To Ring Bells  1600-1697
I Want To Rock  261-325
I Want To See A Little More Of What I Saw In Arkansas  719-1054-1592
I Want To See My Baby  1500
I Want To/Wanna Wrap You Up (And Take You Home With Me)  10-372
I Want You For Christmas  1314
I Want You, I Need You  92
I Want You Just Myself  1169
I Want You More  923
I Want Your Love  1035
I Want You To Give Me Some  1376
I Want You Tonight  113
I Want Ya To Sing  894
I Want You To Want Be To Want You  1069
I Was A Fool To Let You Go  215
I Was Born A Brownskin And You Can't Make Me Blue  1499
I Was A Good Loser Until I Lost You  1322
I Was Born To Swing  15-1721
I Was Doing All Right  321-429-526-969-1158
I Was Fooling You  866
I Was Lucky  425-595

I Was Made To Love You   481-1438
I Wasn't Lying When I Said "I Love You"
795-1416
I Wasn't Scared, But I Just Thought That I
Had Better Go   1715
I Was Saying To The Moon   893
I Was Taken By Storm   700
I Weep Over You   189
I Went Out Of My Way   1243-1360
I Whipped My Woman With A Singletree   1042
I Wished On The Moon   13-362-1306-1730
I Wish I Could Be Blue   1111
I Wish I Could Make You Cry   713
I Wish I Could Shimmy Like My Sister Kate
5-12-221-330-349-552-559-625-702-757-764
808-825-855-915-1025-1068-1129-1175-1185
1228-1362-1391-1437-1438-1443-1478-1480-
1481-1510-1532-1580-1593-1607-1673-1692-
1704-1719
I Wish I Had Died In My Cradle (Before I
Grew Up To Love You)   1316-1317
I Wish I Had Somebody   1025
I Wish I Had Wings   981
I Wish I Had You   768-1333-1633
I Wish I Knew   170-221-1523
I Wish I Was The Willow   1397
I Wish I Were Aladdin   293-362-1307
I Wish I Were Twins   12-689-699-1332-1530-
1584-1624
I Wish't I Was In Peoria   74-927-1348-1503
I Wish You Were Jealous Of Me   265
I Wish You Would (Love Me Like I'm Lovin'
You)   1534
I Woke Up Cold In Hand   359
I Woke Up Too Soon   292
I Woke Up With A Teardrop In My Eye   970
I Wonder   188-812-1665
I Wonder Blues   68-1053
I Wonder How It Feels (To Be Head Over
Heels In Love)   504-932
I Wonder How You're Spending Your Evenings
Now   813
I Wonder What My Gal Is Doin'   1079-1081
I Wonder What's Become Of Joe ?   233-266-
285-575-624-967-1651
I Wonder What's Become Of Sally ?   859-
962-1315-1582
I Wonder Where Mary Is Tonight ?   1077
I Wonder Where My Baby Is Tonight ?   73-74
573-624-969-1261-1262-1503
I Wonder Where My Brownskin Daddy's Gone ?
705
I Wonder Where My Easy Rider's Gone ?   1527
1671
I Wonder Where My Easy Rider's Riding Now ?
111
I Wonder Where My Old Gal Is Tonight ?
221-224
I Wonder Where My Sweet Daddy's Gone ?   748
I Wonder Where My Sweetie Can Be ?   1425
I Wonder Where My Sweet Mama's Gone   1675
I Wonder Who   51
I Wonder Who Made Rhythm   1427-1585
I Wonder Who's Boogiein' My Woogie (Now)
832-1197
I Wonder Who's Dancing with You To ight   72
I Wonder Who's Kissing Her Now ?   10-881-
1314
I Wonder Why   1516
I Won't Be Back 'Til You Change Your Ways
1008
I Won't Be Here Long   1203

I Won't Believe It (Until I Hear It From
You)   296-907-1633
I Won't Believe It's Raining   562
I Won't Give You None   133
I Won't Go Home 'Til You Kiss Me   10
I Won't Let You Down   795
I Won't Sell My Love   849
I Won't Stand No Leavin' Now   1716
I Won't Tell   1277
I Won't Tell A Soul (I Love You)   125-
900
I Would Do Anything For You   88-244-272-
277-299-401-595-598-698-773-774-893-
968-1106-1154-1157-1203-1311-1422-1529
1530-1556-1558 (sometimes shown as I'D
DO ANYTHING FOR YOU, I WOULD DO MOST
ANYTHING FOR YOU and ANYTHING FOR YOU)
I Would Do It For You   470
I Would If I Could, But I Can't   1537-
1697
I Wouldn't Be Crying Now   572
I Wouldn't Be Where I Am If You Hadn't
Gone Away - see IF YOU HADN'T GONE
AWAY
I Wouldn't Change You For The World
874-1387
I Wouldn't Give That For Love   94
I Wouldn't Take A Million   450-742
I Would Rather Be Alone In The South
1520
I, Yi, Yi, Yi, Yi (I Like You Very Much)
374
Iyone, My Own Iyone   234-1396

Jabberwocky   1352
Jackass Blues   65-265-720-806-1096-1167-
1182-1458-1486-1700
Jackass For Sale   848
Jack Climbed A Beanstalk   759
Jack Hits The Road   543
Jackie Boy   342-1513 Jack I'm Mellow 1467
Jack In The Box   1369
Jack O'Diamonds Blues   1618
Jackson's Blues   1065
Jacksonville Blues   812-1541
Jacksonville Gal   350-1192-1356-1545
Jack The Bear   496
Jack The Bellboy   15-663
Ja Da   18-38-373-439-512-647-917-1194-
1365-1490-1509-1517-1655
Ja Da Blues   641-1089
J'ai besoin de toi   1349
Jail House Blues, The   64-181-355-964-
1018-1439-1464-1675
Jailhouse Moan   187
Jake, What A Snake   864
Jake's Weary Blues   541
Jamaica Jam   1242
Jamaica Shout   688-1248
Jam And Jive   1004
Jambled Blues   318
Jamboree   61-429-439-879-1335
Jamboree Blues   709
Jamboree Jones   1690
James Cole Fox Trot   328
James Session   819
Jam Fever   1135
Jam Jamboree   679
Jam Man   16-875
Jammin'   686-1308-1710
Jammin' For The Jack-Pot   1075
Jammin' In Four   652

Jammin' In Georgia  681-832
Jammin' Session  387
Jammin' The Blues  1272
Jammin' The Waltz  518
Jam On Toast  906
Jam Session  599-602
Jam With Bacon  836
Janie's Joys  1746
Jangled Nerves  728
Janitor Sam  1169
Japanese Dream, A  21-478-1077
Japanese Lanterns Blues  1086
Japanese Sandman, The  172-384-554-583-
    595-759-1046-1139-1149-1261-1262-1325-
    1398-1433-1470-1568-1603-1670
Japanese Sunshade  1295
Japansy  1154
Japp-a-Jazz  555
Jasper Taylor Blues  1536
Jassamine Lane  1424
Jass Lazy Blues, The  378
Java Jive  417-1326
Javanella  796        Jaybird Blues  1673
Jazbo Dan And His Yodelin' Band  514
Jazology  549
Jazorient  549
Jazz a la Carte  134
Jazzaphobia Blues  392
Jazz Babies' Ball  891
Jazz Baby  513
Jazz Band Blues  1430
Jazz Battle  1455
Jazzbo Ball  1460
Jazzbo Brown From Memphis Town  1443
Jazzbo Jazz  549
Jazzbo Jenkins  1245-1749
Jazzbo Stomp  1043
Jazz Cocktail  281-486-996-1073
Jazz Convulsions  479
Jazz Crazy  1577
Jazz Dance, The  141
Jazz de Luxe  549
Jazzeroo  1
Jazz Holiday, A  269-591-956-992
Jazz Hot, Le  987
Jazzing Around  141-549-1099-1202
Jazzin' Babies'/Baby Blues  459-793-862-
    1165-1533-1649-1679
Jazz In The Rain  1433
Jazz It Blues - see JAZZ ME BLUES
Jazz Jamboree  388
Jazz Lips (1926)  41
Jazz Lips (1929)  480
Jazz Martini  1073
Jazz Me Blues  5-116-126-187-192-326-372-
    388-676-704-745-746-889-892-905-959-979-
    1003-1007-1033-1037-1133-1164-1178-1193-
    1228-1238-1340-1546-1600-1741-1750
Jazznocracy  959-983-989
Jazz O' Jazz  1332-1360
Jazzola  513-1522
Jazz Pie - see HOT JAZZ PIE
Jazz Potpourri  494-495
Jazz Rondo  875
Jazz Sermon, A  823
J. B. Blues  1219
J. C. Holmes Blues  1442
Jealous  132-155-583-714-808-984-1005-1581
Jealous Heartded Blues  1266
Jealous Mama Blues  860
Jealous Woman Like Me, A  1618

Jealousy Blues  1267
Jealousy Isle  86
Jean  1097
Jeannie Swings Out  756
Jeannine (I Dream Of Lilac Time)  241-649-
    922-1158-1535
Jed And Elmer  1419
Jeepers Creepers  7-56-323-554-588-821-
    907-1261-1654-1690
Jeep Is Jumpin', The  766
Jeep's Blues  342-765
Jefferson County  1499
Jeffries' Blues  817
Jelly Bean  685
Jelly Bean Blues  1266-1450
Jelly Bean (D)rag  1586
Jelly Fish, The  1124
Jelly, Jelly  215-761
Jelly, Look What You Done Done  1451-1488
Jelly-Roll  1414
Jelly-Roll Bert  1542
Jelly-Roll Blues  126-237-538-539-709-738-
    1100-1101-1105-1188-1656
Jelly-Roll Queen  213
Jelly-Roll Stomp  1040
Jelly's Blues  1011-1531
Je m' donne  1085
J'en ai marre  1085
Je ne suis pas un ange  1349
Jenny  81
Jenny's Ball  1464
Jericho  515-949-951 (see also JOSHUA FIT
    DE BATTLE OB JERICHO (sic)
Jerry O' Mine  1675
Jerry The Junker  191-536-587-1709
Jersey Bounce  435-621-761-763-1160-1250-
    1361
Jersey Joe  1103
Jersey Lightning  1345
Jersey Walk  870-1098-1651
Je sais que vous etes jolie  1349
Jes' Nach'ully Lazy (I Was Born That Way)
    257-545-585-1074-1562
Jesse  814
Jes' Shufflin'  395
Jesse James  27
Jess Stay Blues  1491
Je suis Sex-Appeal  1349
Jet Black Blues  119-458
Jet Black Snake Blues  1124
Je voudrais vivre  1349
Jewels Of My Heart  357
Jew's Harp Blues  521
Jezebel  368-443-759-1179
Jicky  748
Jig In G  216
Jig Music  1311
Jig Saw Puzzle Blues  1600
Jig Saw Rhythm  1334
Jig Time  218-539-576-582-873-1465-1556-
    1667-1688
Jig Walk  129-403-493-804-1164-1364-1555-
    1573-1589
Ji-Ji-Boo  1086-1185
Jim  434-529-770-1243-1553
Jimbo Jambo  914
Jim Crow Blues  389
Jiminy Gee  377-714-1354
Jim Jackson's Kansas City Blues  1209
Jealous Of Me 1631 Jim Jam Blues, The  285-750
Jim-Jams  90

1914

Jim Jam Stomp  1007
Jimmie Blues  149
Jimmie Meets The Count  208
Jimmie's Mean Mama Blues  1328
Jimmy Had A Nickel  993-1558-1709
Jimmy (I Love But You)  141-1085
Jimmy's Stuff  1746
Jim Nappy  209
Jim Strainer Blues  1043
Jim Tight Blues  1675
Jimtown Blues  166-264-297-350-728-858-934
   1009-1236-1506-1515-1518-1545-1572-1746
Jing-a-Ling-a-Ling  339
Jingle Bells  282-595-596-645-744-969-1306
   1629-1635
Jingle, Jangle, Jingle  591
Jingle Of The Jungle  585
Jingles  838-1702
Jinks Lee Blues  1543
Jinx Blues  187
Jitney Man, The  761
Jitter Bug, The  257-323-1270-1436
Jitterbug Blues  91
Jitterbugs Broke It Down  1414
Jitterbug's Jump  505
Jitterbug's Lullaby  151-765
Jitterbugs On Parade  1250
Jitterbug Waltz, The  1638
Jitteroo, The  923
Jitters  1333
Jitters, The  108-1135
Jive (Stomp)  486-488
Jive (Page One Of The Hepster's Dictionary)
   259
Jive At Five  105
Jive Bomber  636
Jiveformation, Please  259
Jive Is Here  783
Jive Is Jumpin', The  537
Jive Lover  534
Jive Man Blues  823
Jive Me, Baby  1542
Jivin' Jelly-Roll Blues  1574
Jivin' The Jeep  1157
Jivin' The Vibres  660
Jivin' With Jarvis  663
Jo-Anne  1213
Jockey's Life For Mine, A  1425
Jockey Stomp  1044
Joe Louis Chant  328-863
Joe Louis Stomp  330
Joe The Bomber  749
Joe Turner Blues  284-414-665-666-945-1010
   1516-1575
Joe Turner Stomp  1575
Jog Along  148
Jogo Rhythm  1209
John Hardy's Wife  498
John Henry (Blues)  540-945-1128-1160-1484
Johnnie One Note  1400
Johnny Come Lately  500
Johnny Dunn's Novelty Blues  1420
Johnny Get Your Horn And Blow It  661
Johnny's In Town  379
John's Idea  102
John Silver  430
Johnson Rag, The  165-188-324-590
Johnson "Jass" Blues  544
John, Stop Teasing Me  865
Join The Navy  1252
Joint Is Jumpin', The  1377-1631-1636

Jo-Jo, The Cannibal Kid  285
Jo-Jo, The Hobo  1360
Joke Is On Me, The  637
Joline  1324-1562
Jolly Good Company  1296
Jolly Peter  747-1360
Jolly Three Special  853
Jolly Wog  479
Joltin' Joe di Maggio  186
Jomo Man Blues  737
Jonah And The Whale  56
Jonah Joins The Cab  261
Jones Law Blues  1111
Jonestown Blues  270
Joogie Blues  1739
Jo San  664
Josephine  442-545-606-745-1333
Josephine (Who's The Meanest Gal In
   Town ?)  827-1428
Joseph ! Joseph !  25-29-429-1435
Joshua  1465
Joshua Fit De Battle Ob Jericho (sic)
   790-1710
Jour ou je te vis, Le  1349
Jour....sur la mer, Un  1348
Jovial Joe  332
Joyeux Fumee (Holy Smoke)  333
Joys, The  1161
J. P. Dooley III  819
Juanita  589-817
Juba  903
Juba Dance  1571
Jubilation Rag  1340
Jubilee  55-258-321-586-703-813-814-1324
   1567
Jubilee Blues  1180-1608
Jubilee Stomp  474-475
Jubilee Swing  527
Jubilesta  492-1711
Judgment Is Coming  447
Judy  242-275-276-292-423-661
Jug Band Blues  1012
Jug Band Quartette  1044
Jug Band Special, The  1675
Jug Band Waltz  1042
Jug Blues  391
Juggling A Jigsaw  1668
Jughead  818
Juke Box Jive  387
Juke Box Judy  374
Juke Box Jump  63
Jukin' (Ski Jump)  741
Julia  433-758-759-761
Julius Caesar  901
Jump Back, Honey  1473
Jump For Joy (1938)  1412
Jump For Joy (1941)  499
Jump For Me  105
Jumpin'  1203
Jumpin' At The Juke Box  417
Jumpin' At The Savoy  342
Jumpin' At The Woodside  103-333-612
Jumpin' Blues  740-1038
Jumpin' Down Blues  1575
Jumpin' For Joy  1735
Jumpin' In A Juleep Joint  216
Jumpin' In The Numbers  1561
Jumpin' In The Pump Room  896
Jumpin' Jack  1560
Jumpin' Jive, The (Jim-Jam-Jump)  9-30-
   184-259-432-589-662-1436

Jumpin' Like Mad 1560
Jumpin' On The Blacks And Whites 1736
Jumpin' Punkins 498-499
Jumpin' Salty 209
Jumpin' The Blues 342
Jumpin' The Boogie 1247
Jumpin' Up And Down 761
Jump, Jack, Jump 900
Jump Joe 325
Jump Jump's Here 79-94-746-1159
Jump On The Wagon 938
Jump Session 94-550-1279
Jump Steady 342
Jump Steady Blues 177
Jump The Blues Away 108
Jump Town 820
Jumpy 490
Jumpy Nerves 1003
Junction Blues 693
June 135-1077
June Brought The Roses 1459
June Days 918
June In January 775
June Night 19-128-775-886-1252
June Tenth Blues 1558
June Tenth Jamboree 864
June Time Is Love Time 981
Jungle Blues 480-591-763-956-1102-1106
Jungle Boogie 1243
Jungle Crawl 1209-1710
Jungle Drums 113-539-1326-1404
Jungle Fever 291-836-1146
Jungle Jamboree 479
Jungle Jitters 293
Jungle Jive 10
Jungle Love 1734
Jungle Madness 907-1075
Jungle Mama 868
Junior Hop 766
Junior-Senior Prom., The 1080
Junk Bucket Blues 564-1220
Junk Man 593-1486-1538
Junk Man Blues 1145-1166-1507
Junk Man Rag, The 117-1587-1605
Junk Man's Blues 583
Junk Man's Dream 1183
Junk Man's Serenade 18
Just A Bird's-Eye View Of My Old Kentucky
  Home 577-1611
Just A Blue-Eyed Blonde 287
Just About The Time 781-1245
Just A Cottage Small 914-1742
Just A Cotton Picker's Blues 1699
Just A Crazy Song (Hi-Hi-Hi) 251-583-839-
  933-1145-1296
Just A Fair-Weather Friend 292
Just A Gigolo 48-196-587-958-1373
Just A Haven (Is Heaven With You) 913
Just A Kid Named Joe 588-1358
(Just) A Little Bit Bad 32-129-1172-1300-
  1589
Just A Little Bit More 1466
Just A Little Bit South Of North Carolina
  911-1318-1374
Just A Little Closer 196-1202
Just A Little Dance 1006-1264
Just A Little Dance, Mam'selle 1005-1537
Just A Little Drink 230-658
Just A Little Home For The Old Folks 148-
  1438
Just A Little Kiss From A Little Miss 579

Just A Little Swing 7
Just A Lucky Moment 1294
Just A Memory 269-457
Just A Mood 281-959-1726 (see also BLUE
  MOOD)
Just An Echo In The Valley 199
Just An Error In The News 258-787
Just An Hour Of Love 1567
Just An Old Banjo 1476
Just Another Day Wasted Away 236-669-
  1290
Just Another Dream 135
Just Another Dream Of You 1645
Just Another Good Man Gone Wrong 975
Just Another Night With You 1667
Just Another Woman 1204
Just A Phrase 1116
Just A Quiet Evening 695
Just A Rank Stud 1487
Just Around The Corner 573-920-963
Just Around The Edges 1420
Just A-Settin' And A-Rockin' 498
Just A Shade Corn 1034
Just A Simple Melody 28-443-1660
Just As Long As The World Goes 'Round
  And Around 775-1627
Just As Though You Were Here 417-454
Just A Stone's Throw From Heaven 78
Just A Wee Deoch-an-Doris 1434
Just Because 1490
Just Because You're You (That's Why I
  Love You) 687-1036
Just Blue 379
Just Blues 640-713-724-1505
Just Blues, That's All 1096
Just Can't Stay Here 516
Just Dandy 1390
Just Forget 275
Just For Laffs 663
Just For Old Time's Sake 920
Just For The Thrill 39
Just For Tonight 567
Just For You 82-664-851
Just For You, Dear, I'm Crying 302
Just Friends 299-1030
Just Give Me The Girl 698
Just Give The Southland To Me 1426
Just Good Fun 494
Just Gone 1165
Just Goofy 1079
Just Hot 350-711-1189-1641
Just Imagine (1928) 469-579
Just Imagine (1930) 1127-1397
Justine-Agathe-Marie 171
Justin-Tyme 90
Just It 1025
Just Jivin' Around 1247
Jus' Keepin' On 951-952
Just Keep Singing A Song 1426
Just Kiddin' Around 1408
Just Leave It To Me 1517-1747
Just Let Me Alone 520
Just Let Me Look At You 443-881
Just Like A Butterfly 668
Just Like A Falling Star 1311
Just Like A Gypsy 1513
Just Like A Melody Out Of The Sky 391-
  525-1426-1597
Just Like Taking Candy From A Baby 62
Just Like You Took My Man Away From Me
  1463

Just Like You Walked In, You Can Walk Out 636

Just Met A Friend From My Home Town 165

Just Once Again 1425

Just Once Too Often 201

Just One Girl 1000-1398

Just One More Chance (1923) 1680

Just One More Chance (1931) 1385-1470-1645

Just One More Kiss 577-1611

Just One Of Those Things 1726

Just One Sorrowing Heart 1026

Just One Word Of Consolation 859

Just Plain Lonesome 744

Just Pretending 391-651

Just Riff 277

Justrite 1110

Just Say It's Me 1111

Just So-So ! 1391

Just Strolling 367-1511

Just Take One Long Last Lingering Look 964

Just The Blues 821

Just The Same 799-870-1226-1485

Just Thinkin' (Blues) 750-1011-1022

Just To Be In Caroline 545-758

Just To Be With You Tonight 1716

Just Too Bad 810

Just Too Late 954

Just Too Soon 757

Just Wait 'Til You See My Baby Do The Charleston - see WAIT TILL YOU SEE MY BABY DO THE CHARLESTON

Just Wait Until I'm Gone 941

Just We Two 249

Just Wondering 455

Just You 921-990

Just You And I 737

Just You And I Alone 1528

Just You, Honey 641

Just You, Just Me 2-83-244-503-774-840-1158-1400-1402

Kaala 4

Kaintucky 224

Kaleidoscope 683

Ka-Lu-A 218-789

Kansas Avenue Blues 1377

Kansas City Blues 165-811-1041-1045-1517-1605

Kansas City Breakdown 1110

Kansas City Farewell 851

Kansas City Hill 1487

Kansas City Kitty 341-351-513-1193-1226-1293-1426

Kansas City Man Blues 750-1057-1447-1463-1698-1707

Kansas City Moods 591-1359

Kansas City Shuffle 408-1110

Kansas City Squabble 1111

Kansas City Stomp(s) 1099-1102-1105-1545

Kansas City Yellow Front 1718

Karavan 675-978

Kater Street Rag 1109

Katinka 1120

Katy Blues 1573

Kaycee On My Mind 851

K. D. Blues 412

Kazoo Moan 1647

K. C. Moan 1042

Keep A-Knockin' 432-864

Keep An Eye On Your Man 1651

Keep A Song In Your Soul 484-724-853-933-1144-1464

Keep A Twinkle In Your Eye 193-1137

Keep Cool, Fool 185-528-693-1360-1374

Keep 'Em Flying 912-1319

Keep Goin' 525

Keepin' Myself For You 979-1407-1484

Keepin' Out Of Mischief Now 50-183-198-341-439-781-893-1409-1631-1659

Keep It Swingin' 'Round And 'Round 679

Keep It To Yourself 1446-1535

Keep It Under Your Hat 223-1187

Keep Jumpin' 1674

Keep Knockin' (But You Can't Come In) No. 2 1061

Keep Off My Shoes 1526

Keep Off The Grass (1903) 1199

Keep Off The Grass (1921) 837

Keep On Croonin' A Tune 462-884-1334

Keep On Dancing 121-377

Keep On Doin' What You're Doin' 593-937-1278-1332

Keep On Goin' 1008

Keep On Going 182-1024

Keep On Knocking 842

Keep Rockin' 944

Keep Smiling 379-897

Keep Smiling At Trouble 229-541-542-797 821 959

Keep Smilin', Keep Laughin', Be Happy 991

Keeps On A-Rainin' (Papa, He Can't Make No Time) 1010-1438-1439

Keep That Hi-De-Hi In Your Soul 257

Keep The Rhythm Going 1073

Keep Your Business To Yourself 358

Keep Your Hands Off That 998

Keep Your Last Goodnight For Me 147

Keep Your Nose Out Of Mama's Business 510

Keep Your Nose Out Of Other People's Business 628

Keep Yourself Together Sweet Papa (Mama's Got Her Eyes On You) 1060

Keep Your Skirts Down, Mary Ann 573

Keep Your Temper 149-645

Keep Your Undershirt On 1234

Keko 4

Kelsey's (Hot Nuts) 1697

Kentucky 1707

Kentucky Babe 1425-1513

Kentucky Blues 1495-1715

Kentucky Lullaby 577

Kentucky Stomp 406

Kentucky's Way Of Saying "Good Morning" 74-927

Kermit The Hermit 1315

Kerry Dancers, The 323

Ketch Your Breath 1326-1555

Keyboard Exoress, The 1703

Keyhole Blues 42

Keystone Blues 1154

Key To Key Rag 1587

Key To My Heart, The 900

Key To The Bushes 1573

Key To The Highway 1378

Key To The Mountain Blues 846

Key West 1374

Kickapoo Trail 631 (sometimes shown as KICKAPOO)

Kickin' A Hole In The Sky 805-1136

Kickin' Mule Blues  137
Kickin' My Man Around  917
Kickin' The Cat  1596
Kickin' The Conga Around  1244
Kickin' The Gong Around  34-49-254-256-584
  687-1410
Kick It  911
Kicky-Koo (You For Me-Me For You)  68-69
Kiddie Kapers  1292
Kiddin' On The Strings 149
Kid Man Blues  753-1091
Killer Diller  606
Killin' Myself  495
Killing Time  1131
Killy-Ka-Lee  430
Kinda Lonesome  431-610-1358-1512
Kind Daddy 1713
Kind Friend Blues  1040
Kind Lovin' Blues  750-1447-1649
Kind O' Mean  1396
King David Swing  277
Kingdom Of Swing  The  612
Kingfish Blues  270
King For A Day  1406
King Joe  109-1151
King Kong, The  878-1147
King Kong Stomp  1310
King Of All Evil  1414
King Of Rags, The  1254
King Of The Zulus, The (At A Chitlin'
  Rag)  41-411-1128
King Porter Stomp  121-252-260-359-375-
  595-596-602-692-717-723-726-756-774-814-
  934-1048-1099-1101-1105-1106-1107-1108-
  1167-1342-1422-152574-1659
King's Horses, The (And The King's Men)
  248
Kinkajou, The  648-1521
Kinky Kids' Parade  The  73
Kin To Kant Blues  862
Kissable Baby  1470
Kiss And Make Up  356-524-1226
Kiss-Ball  1639
Kiss Before The Dawn, A  1291
Kiss By Kiss  147-287-791
Kiss For Consolation, A  1357
Kiss For You, A  324
Kiss I Can't Forget, The  74
Kissin' Daddy  1617
Kissin' Mule Blues  782-810
Kissin' My Baby Goodnight  490
Kiss In The Moonlight, A  629
Kiss Mama-Kiss Papa  1607
Kiss Me Goodnight (1924)  1582
Kiss Me Goodnight (1938)  206
Kiss Me Sweet  181-212-1229
Kiss Me With Your Eyes  1159-1633
Kiss That You've Forgotten, The (Is The
  Kiss I Can't Forget)  1386
Kiss The Boys Goodbye  452
Kiss Your Little Baby Goodnight  668
Kiss Your Pretty Baby Nice  1649
Kitchen Blues  1065
Kitchen Man (Blues)  1014-1445
Kitchen Mechanic Blues  681-1449
Kitchen Mechanic's Day  766
Kitchen Woman Blues  118
Kitchy Coo Cake Walk  332
Kitty On Toast  730
K. K. Boogie  15
K-K-K-Katy  1229-1398

Klondyke Blues  975
Knee Drops  43
Knees Up, Mother Brown  385
K'nice And K'nifty  90
Knick Knack Polly Wah Jingasol  1397
Knick-Knacks On The Mantel  1307
Knock At The Door  1582-1591
Knockin' A Jug  45
Knockin' At The Famous Door  94
Knockin' Myself Out  1247
Knockin' On Wood  1156
Knock-Kneed Sal (On The Mourner's Bench)
  40
Knock, Knock, Who's There ?  728-960-1465
Knock Me A Kiss  694-865-912-991
Knock Wood  217-1468
Knock Ya'self Out  164
Know Nothin' Blues  1431
Knox County Stomp  1543
Kodachrome  1375
Kokey Joe  1073
Ko-Ko  496-497
Kokola Blues  393
Koo-Kee-Koo  1162
Koontown Koffee-Klatsch  1199
Krazy Kapers  312-1120
Krazy Kat  1567-1742
Krooked Blues  456-1166
Krum Elbow Blues  766
Ku-Li-A  1095
Kune Jine  913-914
KWKH Blues  461

Label Me C.O.D. Tennessee  195
Ladder, The  1595
Ladder Of Roses, The  315
La-De-De, La-De-Da  585-1629
La De Doody Doo  493-746-1357-1498
Lady, Be Good  3-101-103-105-115-128-193-
  229-321-387-550-568-584-598-736-821-830
  939-961-977-1046-1092-1155-1157-1207-
  1258-1288-1405-1467-1476-1477-1511-1572
  1670-1736-1749 (sometimes shown as OH !
  LADY, BE GOOD)
Lady Butterfly  222
Lady Divine  1292
Lady From Fifth Avenue, The  ;23-739-880
Lady From Mayfair  880
Lady From St. Paul, The  288-628
Lady In Blue  494
Lady In Red, The  563-700-1248
Lady Is A Tramp, The  442-1402-1721
Lady Love  308
Lady Luck  83-245
Lady Luck Blues  1439-1463-1710
Lady Mine  1338
Lady Of Havana  1546
Lady Of Mystery  1736
Lady Of Spain  1295
Lady Of The Evening, The  222-1175
Lady Of The Night  787
Lady Of The Nile  1592
Lady On The Two-Cent Stamp, The  1560
Lady Quit Her Husband Onexpectinly (sic)
  1572
Lady Said "Yes," The  324
Lady's In Love With You, The  370-612-907
Lady Who Couldn't Be Kissed, The  492-755
Lady Who Swings The Band, The  899
Lady With The Fan, The  256
Lafayette  1112-1203

1918

Laff It Off  522
Laff's On You, De (sic)  865
La-Haut  1173
Lake George Blues  1555
Lake Pontchartrain Blues  1458
Lake Providence Blues  678
La Lo La  1120
Lambeth Walk, The  494-554-587-746-960-1261-1357
Lame Duck Blues  1554
Lament  208
Lamentation  690
Lament For A Lost Love  95-134
Lament For Javanette  135
Lament For May  96
Lament To Love  186-818
Lamp Is Low, The  80-432-447
Lamplighter's Serenade, The  744
Lamp Of Aladdin, The  567
Lamp Of Memory, The  621-1553
Landlady's Footsteps  393
L & N Blues, The  629-1449
Land Of Cotton Blues  140-706-1523
Land Of Creole Girls  976
Land Of Dreams, The  1005
Land Of Make-Believe  329
Lane In Spain, A  578
Language Of Love, The  83-148
Lantern Of Love  1503
Lard Stomp  521
Larkin Street Blues  1021
La Salle Street Breakdown  1746
'Lasses Candy  1176-1177
Lassus Trombone  379-1522
Last Call For Love, The  375-453
Last Cent  977
Last Chance Blues  270
Last Dollar  251-456
Last Goodbye Blues  859-1531
Last Go Round Blues  1010-1050-1186-1510-1532
Last Jam Session, The  208
Last Journey Blues  643
Last Jump, The (A Jump To End All Jumps)  95
Last Kiss You Gave Me, The  284
Last Mile Blues  355
Last Minute Blues  1265
Last Night A Miracle Happened  296-1633
Last Night Blues  1090
Last Night I Dreamed You Kissed Me  314-840
Last Night I Said A Prayer  435-819
Last Night On The Back Porch  1175-1188-1590
Last Night The Nightingale Woke Me  897
Last Night's Gardenias  185-297
Last Round Up, The  905
Last Time, The  42-1013
Last Time Blues  353
Last Time I Saw Chicago, The  1555
Last Two Weeks Of July, The  324-1359-1405
Latch On  180-1629
Late Hour Blues  1679
Late Hours  1713
Late Last Night  1014
Latest Fad, The  1577
Latin Quarter, The  1435
Latins Know How  433
Latin Tune, A Manhattan Moon And You, A  298

Laugh  1389
Laugh And Call It Love  94-1734
Laughing At Life  196-695-769-872-957-1035-1295
Laughing At The Rain  1296
Laughing At You  812
Laughing Blues  975-1241
Laughing Boy Blues  739
Laughin' Cryin' Blues  190-316-686-1010-1022-1090-1187
Laughing Hyena  1748
Laughin' In Rhythm  115-550
Laughin' Louie  51
Laughing Marionette  469
Laughing My Troubles Away  195
Laughing Rag  1094
Laughing Stomp  413
Laugh Your Way Through Life  1003
La Vida Medley  1208
Lawd, Lawd  1370
Lawd Send Me A Man Blues  1266
Lawdy Lawdy Blues  352-1018-1440
Lawd, You Made The Night Too Long  50-360-461-1227-1409
Layin' On The Strings  844
Lay Me Down To Sleep In Carolina  218-235-667-1593
Lay Your Racket  113
Laziest Gal In Town, The  1572
Lazy  72-226-364-561-796-1256-1691
Lazy Afternoon  283
Lazy Blues (Cuttin' Up)  920
Lazybone Blues  1054
Lazy Bones  56-77-199-275-288-296-698-775-1278-1311-1647
Lazy Bug  95
Lazy Daddy  978-1007-1176-1741
Lazy Daddy Blues  709
Lazy Day  288
Lazy Drag  1096-1550
Lazy Duke  480
Lazy Gal Blues  1561
Lazy Levee Loungers  1707
Lazy Lou'siana Moon  195
Lazy Mama  1168-1703-1705
Lazy Man Blues  1618
Lazy Man's Shuffle  1500
Lazy Rhapsody  485-742-997
Lazy Rhythm  584-830-1215-1507
Lazy River (1924)  269
Lazy River (1930)  49-114-275-296-582-618-873-1249-1602
Lazy 'Sippi Steamer  57
Lazy Swing  1710
Lazy Waters  339
Lazy Weather  236-625-967-1095-1278-1324-1580
Lazy Woman's Blues  251
Leader's Headache Blues  959
Lead Me Daddy Straight To The Bar  1247
Lead Me To It  975
Lead Pencil Blues (It Just Won't Write)  1541
Lead Pipe Blues  1518
Leaky Roof Blues  923
Lean Bacon  1746
Leanin' On The Old Top Rail  372
Leap Frog  58
Leapin' At The Lincoln  96
Learning  173-291-338-594-879
Learn To Croon (1931)  316-1384

Learn To Croon (1933)  199-982-1647
Learn To Do The Strut  560-891-1210-1680
Least Little Thing You Do, The  786
Leave It That Way  286-1383
Leave Mine Alone  41
Leave My Baby Alone  236
Leave My Sweet Daddy Alone  1010
Leavenworth Blues  753
Leave The Rest To Me  1674
Leaving Blues  212-1713
Leaving Me  983
Leavin' Me/My Daddy Is Hard To Do  642-1617
Leaving School Blues  66
Leaving This Morning  1269
Leaving Town On Skates  111
Leaving Town To Wear You Off My Mind  954
Leavin' You Baby  1486
Left All Alone With The Blues  634-1706
Left All Alone Again Blues  60
Left My Gal In The Mountains  873
Legend Of Old California, The  1552
Lenore  1745
Lenox Avenue  455
Lenox Avenue Blues (Church Organ Blues)  1622
Lenox Avenue Shuffle  1547
Lentement, Mademoiselle  1262
Lesson In C, A  1712
Lessons In Love  1332
Less Than That  1323
Lester Leaps In  106
Let A Little Pleasure Interfere With Business  1469
Let A Smile Be Your Umbrella (On A Rainy Day)  533-871-962-1581
Let 'Em Jump  850
Let 'Er Go  123-183-294-586-729-1402
Let Every Day Be Mother's Day  1710
Let Go My Hand  998
Let Him Live  581
Let It Be Me  438
Let It Rain  1502
Let Me Be Alone With You  1077
Let Me Be The First To Kiss You Good Morning (And The Last To Kiss You Good Night)  32-1502
Let Me Call You Mine  1146
Let Me Call You Sweetheart  361-650-696-1002
Let Me Day Dream  691-1089
Let Me Dream  102-433-1148
Let Me Feel It  680
Let Me Forget  1534
Let Me Give My Happiness To You  1668
Let Me Hum A Hymn To Her Tonight  981
Let Me Introduce You To My Rosie  719
Let Me Jelly Your Roll  1547
Let Me Love You Tonight  744
Let Me Off Uptown  326-911-1070
Let Me Ride Your Train  825
Let Me Rock You Home  893
Let Me See  107
Let Me Sing - And I'm Happy  883-1136-1382-1383
Let Me Up  819
Let My Man Alone Blues  1618
Let's Agree To Disagree  1058-1461
Let's All Be Happy Together  148
Let's All Meet At My House  364
Let's All Sing Like The Birdies Sing  877

Let's All Sing Together  614
Let's Amalgamate  1164
Let's Beat Out Some Love  832
Let's Be Buddies  185
Let's Begin Again  1720
Let's Break The Good News  1003-1397-1632
Let's Call A Heart A Heart  204-428-767-1399
Let's Call It A Day  1252-1696
Let's Call It Love  39
Let's Call The Whole Thing Off  429-703-768-1147-1333
Let's Dance (At The Make-Believe Ballroom)  601-613-1008
Let's Disappear  447
Let's Do It (Let's Fall In Love)  123-376-420-562-620-770-1336-1398-1595-1697-1749
Let's Dream In The Moonlight  1735
Let's Drift Away On Dreamer's Bay  981
Let's Drink A Drink To The Future  1385-1386
Let's Face The Music And Dance  204-1312
Let's Fall In Love  200-505-674
Let's Fly Away  1697
Let's Fall In Love Again  783
Let's Get Acquainted  262
Let's Get Away From It All  452-742-911-1374-1637
Let's Get Drunk And Truck  678-843-1527
Let's Get Friendly  678-1385
Let's Get Happy  329-518
Let's Get Happy Together  40
Let's Get Hot And Truck  1239
Let's Get It  1111
Let's Get It Straight  180
Let's Get Loose  1452
Let's Get Lost  436-1244
Let's Get Together  277-520-1075-1455-1542-1658-1662
Let's Get Together And Swing  1249
Let's Give Love A Chance  621
Let's Give Love Another Chance  367
Let's Go  310-1305
Let's Go Home  729
Let's Go, Joe  262
Let's Grow Old Together  1484
Let's Have A Jubilee  489-752-1073-1248
Let's Have Another Cigarette  123
Let's Have Another One  166
Let's Have A Party  697-698-775-1410
Let's Have A Showdown  1709
Let's Have Fun  1249
Let's Just Pretend  453
Let's Knock A Jug  823
Let's Love  695
Let's Make-Believe  1665
Let's Make Hey ! While The Sun Shines  107
Let's Make It A Lifetime  295
Let's Make Memories Tonight  432
Let's Misbehave  87-145-217
Let's Not Fall In Love  780
Let's Pitch A Little Woo  739
Let's Play Geography  1356
Let's Pretend There's A Moon  1624
Let's Pretend To Be Sweethearts  357
Let's Put Our Heads Together  14-182
Let's Put Out The Lights (And Go To Sleep)  147-1205

Let's Put Some People To Work  192
Let's Sail To Dreamland  1315
Let's Say A Prayer  623
Let's Sing Again  1239-1628
Let's Sit And Talk About You  1029-1233
Let's Sit This One Out  509
Let's Sow A Wild Oat  1151
Let's Spill The Beans  1000
Let's Start Over Again  747
Let's Start The New Year Right  364
Let's Stop The Clock  431
Let's Swing It  66-1001-1031-1150-1248
Let's Take A Walk Around The Block  424
Let's Talk About Love  1519
Let's Talk About My Sweetie  61-75-734-928
  992-1348
Let's Try Again  989
Let's Waltz For Old Time's Sake  1314
Let's Wander Away  572-1380
Letter From Dixie, A  703
Let That Be A Lesson To You  55-341-587-
  604-806-1088
Let The Door Knob Hitcha  617
Let The Door Knob Hit You In The Back  213
Let The Great Big World Keep Turning  315
Let The Punishment Fit The Crime  692
Let There Be Love  433-634-1289
Let This Be A Warning To You (Baby)  125-
  692
Let Us Be Sweethearts Over Again  587
Let Your Conscience Be Your Guide  342
Let Your Linen Hang Low  783
Let Your Lips Touch My Lips  651
Let Yourself Go  122-160-293-1157-1329
Levee Blues  1218-1717-1747
Levee Camp  841
Levee Camp Moan  1267
Levee Lou  404
Levee Low Down, The  253-1071
Levee Lullaby  260
Levee Man Blues  1105
Levee Revels  1473
'Leven Pounds Of Heaven  1688
'Leven Thirty Saturday Night  21-32-736-
  785-1369-1639-1716
Lewisada Blues  956
Lewis Flat Blues  841
Liebesfreud  1262
Liebestraum (Liszt, No. 3)  440-1260-1360
Lie In My Heart, A  1528
Lies  76-1537
Life Begins At Sweet Sixteen  968
Life Begins When You're In Love  1157-1305
  1621-1731
Life Goes On And On  680
Life Goes To A Party  605-607-813
Life Is A Song  161-202-700
Life Is Fine  990
Life Is Just A Bowl Of Cherries  142
Life Spears A Jitterbug  542
Life Without You  1002
Light A Candle In The Chapel  454
Lighthouse Blues, The  738-1174-1183-1213-
  1477
Lightly And Politely  184-444-760-907
Lightnin'  486-996
Lights Out  1312
Lights Up  881
Light Up  75
Lignum Vitae (Long Life)  998
Like A Bolt From The Blue  594-1073

Like A Ghost From The Blue  1358
Like A Monkey Likes Coconuts  183
Like A Ship At Sea  987-990
Like A Ship In The Night  766
Like A Virginia Creeper  784
Like I Want To Be  948
Like Me A Little Bit Less  1154
Like The Fella Once Said  910
Lila  87-669-694-1174-1567-1581
Lilac Lane  1421
Lilacs In The Rain  95-371-1316
Lila Lou  1636
Li'l Boy Love  616-1397
Li'l Farina  472
Li'l Liza Jane  549-1342-1414
Lily  578-648
Lily Belle May June  1258
Limehouse Blues  115-131-140-226-260-288-
  291-324-385-465-485-528-554-556-563-
  588-600-620-635-698-727-759-780-791-
  800-821-956-1003-1119-1128-1129-1140-
  1195-1207-1259-1284-1334-1341-1370-
  1432-1472-1726-1750
Limehouse Rose  1426
Lina Blues  1456
Linda  592-1143
Lindbergh Hop  1042-1722
Lindy  1178
Lindy Hop  39
Lindy Hoppers' Delight  527
Lindy Lou  1425
Line-a-Jive  252
Linger A Little Longer In The Twilight
  1235
Linger Awhile  71-224-291-712-796-961-
  986-1501
Lingering Lips  1504
Lion And The Lamb, The  1468
Lion Tamers  1062
Lips  1524
Lips That Laugh At Love  1666
Lipstick  217
Listen, Listen  819
Listen, My Children, And You Shall Hear
  102-1506
Listen To Ma  1550
Listen To The German Band  147-876
Listen To The Mocking Bird  740-923-997-
  1245
Love Bug Will Bite You, The  429
Little African Stomp, The  1675
Little After Eight, A  880
Little Annie Rooney  1314
Little Birdie Told Me So, A  870-1696
Little Bit Bad, A - see JUST A LITTLE
  BIT BAD
Little Bit Closer, A  1209-1500
Little Bit Independent, A  66-365-382-
  968-1114-1432-1627
Little Bit Later On, A  122-1278-1659
Little Bit Of Heaven, A  817
Little Bit Of Jazz, A  825
Little Bit Of Rigoletto, A  1372-1373
Little Bits  132
Little Boy  184
Little Boy Blues  32
Little Brown Jug  896
Little Buttercup  1599 (see also I'LL
  NEVER BE THE SAME)
Little By Little  46-377-977-1016-1301-
  1638

Little Curly Hair In A High Chair  433-1636-
Little David, Play On Your Harp  1482
Little Devil  377
Little Did I Dream  1332
Little Did I Know  286
Little Dip  98
Little Door, A Little Lock, A Little Key, A  203-1001
Little Dutch Mill  201
Little Fugue (Fugue in G minor) (J. S. Bach)  1361
Little Gates Special  126
Little Girl  142-679-680-933-1145-1317-1599
Little Green Slippers  1044
Little Grey Sweetheart Of Mine  219-220
Little High Chairman  81
Little Joe  48-78-592-1344-1667-1726
Little Joe From Chicago  900-1003-1720
Little John Ordinary  98-609
Little John Special  1070
Little Kind Treatment, A (Is Exactly What I Need)  1461
Little Kiss At Twilight, A  759
Little Kiss Each Morning, A  952
Little Lawrence  1104
Little Love, A Little Kiss, A  568-922-1260
Little Low Mama Blues  1267
Little Man Who Wasn't There, The  80-323-371-1538
Little Man With A Candy Cigar  452-911
Little Man With The Hammer  292
Little Man You've Had A Busy Day  1221-1227
Little Mary Brown  395-1387
Little Miss  901
Little Miss Irish  185
Little Mother Of My Dreams  951
Little Nell  697-698
Little Old Clock On The Mantel, The  227-1364
Little Old Lady  296-1313-1718
Little Old Lady From Baltimore  1116
Little Orphan Annie  340
Little Pal  949-950-1598
Little Peach  1502
Little Pigmeat  1413
Little Posey  495
Little Rain Must Fall, A  774
Little Red Fox, The (N'ya, N'ya, Ya Can't Catch Me)  10-372
Little Red Wagon  1677
Little Rendezvous In Honolulu, A  438-1312-1415
Little Robin Told Me So, A  1415
Little Rock Getaway  367-1326-1511-1572
Little Rose-Covered Shack  1078
Little Rover  1614
Little Sally Water  342
Little Sandwich Wagon  309
Little Sir Echo  1358
Little Skipper  446-1316
Little Things In Life, The  196-1303
Little Things That Mean So Much  1736
Little Town Gal  256
Little White House, The  172-870-1098-1611
Little White Lies  443-457-504-672-814-1153-1397-1661
Little White Lighthouse, A  443
Little Willie Blues  1455

Live And Love Tonight  105-488-638-797
Live Or Die For You  678
Liver Lip Jones  1636
Livery Stable Blues  125-398-665-722-955-1131-1175-1176-1178-1179-1481-1576 (see also BARNYARD BLUES)
Living A Life Of Dreams  1295
Living From Day To Day  986
Livin' High Sometimes  411-1699
Livin' Humble  1450
Living In Seclusion  749
Livin' In The Sunlight, Lovin' In The Moonlight  21-131-953
Living Loving You  1697
Liza  1419-1523
Liza (All The Clouds 'll Roll Away)  7-191-576-602-603-636-727-839-988-1032-1154-1159-1529-1530-1575-1660-1661-1711-1730-1736
Liza Johnson Got Better Bread Than Sally Lee  809-1305
Liza Lee  1111
Loading Up The Mandy Lee  315
Load Of Coal  1104
Loafing Blues  164
Loafin' On A Lazy Day  417
Loafin' Time  392-1627
Lo And Behold  341
Loch Lomond  605-607-739-1003-1512-1513-L 1635-1735
Lock And Key  1444
Lock It Up  687
Lock Step Blues  118
Locomotive  1412
Log Cabin Blues  1466-1702
Log Camp Blues  1268
Logola Stomp  1288
Lois  98
Lo La Lo  219
Lolita  1613
Lo Lo  1370
Lona  1658
Lo-Nah  566-630-1181
Loncy  1575
London (Cafe) Blues  1099-1100-1132-1166-1656
London Bridge Is Falling Down  103
London Suite (Fats Waller)  1634
Lone Arranger, The  260
Lonely Acres  644
Lonely And Blue  349
Lonely Blues  178-1540
Lonely Boy Blues  1038
Lonely Cabin  1278
Lonely Co-ed, A  495
Lonely Eyes  236-268-463-1579-1593
Lonely Girl  263
Lonely Heart  1025
Lonely Lane  455
Lonely Little Bluebird  649
Lonely Little Wallflow'r  120-339
Lonely Me  377
Lonely Melody  1683
Lonely Moments  155
Lonely Park  1668
Lonely Singing Fool, A  809
Lonely Troubadour  982
Lonesome  417-649-737-754
Lonesome, All Alone And Blue  753
Lonesome And Blue  876
Lonesome And Sorry  132-313-577-644-1742

1922

Lonesome Bedroom Blues  628
Lonesome Blues  41-113-353-379
Lonesome Daddy Blues  1023
Lonesome Desert Blues  1443
Lonesome Dream Blues  1091
Lonesome For That Man Of Mine  1051
Lonesome (Gee, I'm Awf'lly Lonesome)  1664
Lonesome Ghost Blues  1060
Lonesome Graveyard Blues  1378-1531
Lonesome Hour Blues  1499
Lonesome Hours  220-1550
Lonesome Hut Blues  1370
Lonesome Journey Blues  712-1096
Lonesome Little Doll  1293
Lonesome Lover  980
Lonesome Lovesick (Blues)  251-731-914-935
Lonesome Lovesick Got To Have My Daddy Blues  1643
Lonesome Mama Blues  221-391-825-915-1005 1185-1462-1606-1725
Lonesome Man Blues  1411
Lonesome Miss Pretty  106
Lonesome Moments  1164-1658
Lonesome Monday Morning Blues  705-793-1058-1090
Lonesome Mountain Blues  636
Lonesome Nights  260-281
Lonesome Railroad  1269
Lonesome Refugee  1458
Lonesome Reverie  839
Lonesome Road Blues  1517-1747
Lonesome Road, The  49-79-159-167-447-507 957-987-1481-1633-1647
Lonesome Road Stomp  155
Lonesome Room Blues  1069
Lonesomest Gal/Girl In Town, The  317-462 528-634
Lonesome Swallow  1652
Lonesome Tag Blues  336
Lonesome Trail  314
Lonesome Trail Blues  1744
Lonesome Valley Blues  1376
Lonesome Walls  1654
Lonesome Weary Blues  753
Lonesome With The Blues  1488
Lonesome Woman Blues  357-750-1040-1091
Lonesome Yodelin' Blues  514
Lone Star Blues  850
Lone Western Blues  1614
'Long About Midnight  77-191-257-1248-1571
'Long About Three In The Morning  164
Long Ago  1505
Long Ago And Far Away  93-439
Long, Deep And Wide  1703
Long Distance Blues  353
Longer That You Linger In Virginia, The  1297
Long Gone  1423
Long Gone Blues  769-1487
Long Gone From Bowling Green  191-193
Longing  1534
Longing Blues  66
Longing For Daddy Blues  1012
Longing For Home  1486
Longing For You  1643
Longing Just For You  196
Long Lean Lanky Mama  1652
Long, Long Ago  58-259
Long Lost Daddy  813

Long Lost Mama (Daddy Misses You)  223-406-560-826-905-916-954-1022-1350-1353-1419-1505-1520-1544-1649
Long Lost Weary Blues  1465
Long May We Love  423-809
Long Night Scamper  791
Long Old Road  1446
Longshoreman's Blues  1703
Long Tall Disconnected Mama  737
Long Tall Woman Blues  853
Long Time Blues  820
Long Time Man  811
Long Time No See  370-740
Look  321
Look-a There  550
Look At 'Em Doing It (Now)  1176-1177
Look At The World And Smile  236-578
Look At You, Look At Me  374
Look-a What I Got Now  227
Look For The Silver Lining  952-973
Look Hot, Keep Cool  682
Lookie, Lookie, Lookie, Here Comes Cookie  180-252-292-755-1154-1695
Lookin' Around Corners For You  440
Lookin' At The World Through Rose-Colored Glasses  4-61-254-982-1237-1520-1583
Looking At You  1336-1697
Looking At You Across The Breakfast Table  1382-1383
Looking Down At The Stars  786
Looking For A Boy  1503-1749
Lookin' For Another Sweetie  1624
Looking For A Place To Park  137
Looking For Love  1306
Looking For My Man Blues  1444
Looking For The Blues  770-1191-1192
Looking For The Starlight  590
Looking For The Sunshine, Walking Around In The Rain  1246-1557
Looking For Yesterday  207-450-742-909
Lookin' Good But Feelin' Bad  1623
Looking Up To The Sky With A Smile  1555
Look In Her Eyes  1213
Look In The Looking Glass  1385
Look In The Mirror (And See Just Who I Love)  519-653-708
Look Me Over  1121
Look Out  550-1250
Look Out For Yourself  1673
Look Out, Mr. Jazz  1014-1163
Look Out, Papa, Don't You Bend Down  278
Look Over Yonder  1422
Look Up And Smile  1098
Look What I've Got  36-1009-1688
Look What You've Done To Me  46-245
Look Where The Sun Done Gone  1450
Look Who's Here !  231-546-652-754-774-827-876-966-1668
Looney  342
Looney Little Tooney  746
Loopin' The Loop  369
Loose Ankles  898
Loose Feet  120-349-559-1186-1353-1524-1525-1614
Loose Lid Special  452
Loose Like A Goose  1111
Lord Deliver(ed) Daniel, The  1635-1710
Lord Done Fixed Up My Soul, The  1309
Lord, I Give You My Children  1046
Lordy  261
Lorelei  1289

Lorna Doone Shortbread  1484
Losers Weepers  448
Losing My Mind Over You  537
Lost  14-960-1052-1312
Lost (A Wonderful Girl)  69-222-535
Lost And Found  430-1632
Lost Boy  948
Lost In A Fog  201-424-688
Lost In Love  818
Lost In Meditation  492-493-765-1711
Lost In My Dreams  14-702
Lost In The Shuffle  691-745-1402-1490
Lost In Two Flats  135
Lost In Your Arms  1688
Lost Letter Blues  570
Lost Love  663-1630-1631
Lost Lover Blues  1676
Lost Man Blues  354-778
Lost Motion  698-699
Lost My Baby Blues  37
Lost My Rhythm, Lost My Music, Lost My
  Man  779-1491
Lost My Sweetie Blues  1051
Lost Opportunity Blues  1463
Lost Out Blues  1649
Lost The Blackout Blues  110
Lost Wandering Blues  1266
Lost Your Head Blues  1443
Lots O' Fingers  485
Lots O' Mama  225-522-713-777-916-930-
  1056-1067-1129-1189-1428-1640
Lotta Sax Appeal  899-1718
Lou  218
Loud And Wrong  636-1655
Loud Speakin' Papa (You'd Better Speak
  Easy To Me)  304-624-718-1181-1192-1380
  1650
Louise  21-502-507-610-611-1155-1233-1283
  1293-1312-1568-1582-1595
Louise Dear  247
Louise, I Love You  737
Louise, Louise  368-1247-1541
Louise, You Tease !  339
Louisiana  107-117-394-476-506-1089-1379-
  1589-1675-1685
Lou'siana  263
Louisiana Bo Bo  557-1108-1330-1669
Louisiana Breakdown  776
Louisiana Fairy Tale  866-1625
Louisiana Glide  555
Louisiana Hayride  158
Louisiana Hoo Doo Blues  1266
Louisiana Hop  1713
Louisiana Liza  252
Lou'siana Low Down Blues  1441
Lou'siana Lullaby  199-290
Louisiana Swing  1230-1345
Louisiana, That's My Home  683
Louisiana Toddle  1184
Louisville  223
Louisville Blues  547-548-666-872-1555
Louisville Bluezees  320
Louisville, K.Y.  528
Louisville Lady  698
Louisville Lou (The Vampin' Lady)  176-
  406-564-916-925-955-1180-1256-1280-1496
Louisville Special  1026
Louisville Stomp  409
Lounging At The Waldorf  1629
Lovable (1928)  887-1685
Lovable (1932)  147-1030

Lovable And Sweet  21-59-305-576-591-671-
  932-1065-1293-1585
Lovable Eyes  1085
Love  960-1152-1153
Love Affairs  1568
Love Ain't Blind No More  1050-1728
Love Ain't Nothin' But The Blues  245-
  1569
Love And A Dime  100-292-513
Love And I  498
Love And Kisses  1001-1619-1658-1681
Love And Learn  973-1088-1399
Love Baby  1290
Love Blues  409
Love Bound  1503-1664
Love Bug Will Bite You, The  585-703-755-
  1249-1333-1400-1561-1630-1692
Love Crazy Blues  1321
Love Cries  689
Love Days  710
Love Doesn't Grow On Trees  906-1357
Loved One  1081
Love Dreams  651
Love For Sale  184-1402-1540-1743-1749
Love Found You For Me  337
Love Gave Me You  342
Love Grows On The White Oak Tree  95-297-
  1557-1736
Love, I'd ive My Life For You  1633
Love I Have For You, The  795
Love In Bloom  775
Love In My Heart  908-1500
Love In Springtime  454-765
Love In The First Degree  180-1033
Love Is A Dreamer  286
Love Is A Merry-Go-Round  93-123-1400
Love Is A Necessary Thing  80
Love Is A Song  1244
Love Is Dead (No Use To Hang Around)  1454
Love Is Flying High  94
Love Is Good For Anything That Ails You
  294-660-1399
Love Is Here  1406
Love Is Here To Stay  321-429-880-969-
  1158
Love Is In The Air Again  797
Love Is Just Around The Corner  335-361-
  424-1000-1228
Love Is Like A Cigarette  490-553-1307
Love Is Like A Song  1295
Love Is Like That (What Can You Do ?)
  1144-1385-1469-
Love Is Like Whiskey  1721
Love Is Never Out Of Season  441-880
Love Is On The Air Tonight  183-1028
Love Is Simply Grand  127
Love Is The Reason  257
Love Is The Sweetest Thing  506
Love Is The Thing  289-901-1073-1653
Love Is The Thing, So They Say  1659
Love Is Where You Find It  79-431-1159
Love Jumped Out  107
Loveless Love - see CARELESS LOVE
Love Letters In The Sand  593
Love Lies  166-325-450-909-1426
Lovelight  1582
Lovelight In The Starlight  124-1357
Lovelight Lane  572-1523
Love Like This Can't Last  499
Loveliness And Love  326-743
Loveliness Of You, The  162-205-366-1400

1924

Love Locked Out  878
Lovely Lady  293-402-438-1312
(Lovely Little Baby) Don't You Know  1414
Lovely Liza Lee  23-828-1075
Love Makes The World Go Round  701
Love Me  183-291-740-893-1152-1153-1355-
  1529-1531-1648
Love Me A Little Little  168-743-1408
Love Me And The World Is Mine (Hit Me And
  The Jail Is Yours)  213
Love Me As I Am  452-911
Love Me As I Love You  1121
Love Me Daddy Blues  436-530-1441
Love Me In Your Old-Time Way  1057
Love Me Like You Used To Do  1467
Love Me Or Leave Me  105-409-509-593-598-
  633-695-770-872-946-1147-1152-1379-1491
  1623
Love Me Tonight  77-673-75-822-875
Love Nest, The  165-371-987-1568-1603-
  1684
Love Never Went To College  432-613
Love, Nuts And Noodles  1146
Love Of My Life  62-167-742-1357-1407-
  1552
Love Or Infatuation  162-1347
Love Passes By  293
Lover, Come Back To Me  3-63-78-81-243-
  420-502-670-900-961-1369-1404-1595-1743
Lover Is Blue, A  95-448-908-1116
Lovers In Glass Houses  1553
Lover's Lament, A  1619
Lover's Lullaby  A  96-207 297-908
Love's A Necessary Thing  814
Love Sends A Little Gift Of Roses  453
Love's Got Me Down Again  283-741
Love's Got Nothin' On Me  1360
Love Shows Weakness 848
Lovesick Blues  783-1062-1678
Love's Lament  1437
Love's Last Word Is Spoken  937
Love's Old Sweet Song  1147-1402-1498
Love Song  905
Love Song Blues  461
Love Song Of A Half Wit  786
Love Song Of Long Ago, A  15
Love's Serenade  687-1073-1207-1270
Love Tales  1149-1552
Love Thief  843
Love Thy Neighbor  423
Love Turned The Light Out  1655
Love Walked In  55-272-400-554-880
Love, What Are You Doing To My Heart ?
  1027
Love Will Drive Me Away  357
Love Will Find A Way  837-1304-1392-1423
Love Will Live On  439
Love With A Capital "You"  740
Love With A Feeling  849
Lovey  525-877
Lovey Came Back  72-560-796-1067-1189
Lovey Dovey  30
Lovey Lee  1193
Love, You Are Mine Tonight  151
Love, You Funny Thing  50-147
Love, You're Just A Laugh  1659
Love, You're Not The One For Me  281-1052
Love, Your Magic Spell Is Everywhere 184-
  185-917-1358
Lovie Joe  864
Loving - see HOT LOVIN'

Loving Heart Blues  1091
Lovin' Henry Blues  1051
Lovin' (I Can't Live Without It)  1517
Lovin' Is The Thing I'm Wild About  352
Loving Is What I Crave  1014
Lovin' Johnson Rag, The - see JOHNSON RAG
Lovin' Mama Blues  850
Lovin' Man  215
Lovin' Sam (The Sheik Of Alabam')  406-
  880-1062-1173-1460-1607
Lovin's Been Here And Gone To The Mecca
  Flat  150
Loving That Man Blues  834
Lovin' Woman Blues  1542
Loving You  78
Loving You Like I Do  579
Loving You The Way I Do  305-852-980-1061
  1098
Low Cotton  1500
Low Down  1298-1610
Low Down 'Bama Blues  1057
Low Down Blues  633-1105-1287-1423-1513-
  1675
Low Down Brown  1025
Low Down Daddy Blues  734-1058-1306
Low Down Despondent Blues  736
Low Down Dirty Groundhog Blues  1028
Low Down Dirty Shame  1511
Low Down Man Blues  1489
Low Down On The Bayou  285-725-1071
Low Down Papa (Sweet Mama's Blues)  731-
  732-1050
Low Down Papa (Treat Sweet Mama Kind)
  1060
Low Down Rhythm  751-752-776-950-1281
Low Down Rhythm In A Top Hat  416
Low Down Sawed Off Blues  1183
Low Down Upon The Harlem River  199-1235
Lower Register  1007
Low Gravy  1104
Low Land Blues  753-1148
Low Land Moan  1452
Low Levee-High Water  1657
Lucia di Lammermoor : Sextette  896-897-
  918-1635
Lucille  72-227-1387 -1531
Lucille's Lament  1746
Lucky Break  1390
Lucky Day  402-1246-1286
Lucky Dog Blues  927-1522
Lucky In Love  799-1426
Lucky Kentucky  72-397-916-1002
Lucky Little Devil  1088
Lucky Me, Lovable You  170-286-952
Lucky Number Blues  854
Lucky Rock Blues  1266
Lucky Seven  694
Lucky Swing  1075
Lucky 3-6-9  1209
Lucy Long  138-164-165-1184-1458
Lullaby  323-534-688
Lullaby, The  193
Lullaby Baby  1719
Lullaby In Blue  290
Lullaby In Rhythm  94-279-608-739-814
Lullaby Of Broadway  160-202-426-1154
Lullaby Of The Leaves  161-697-875-1223-
  1531
Lullaby Of The Rain  300-1554
Lullaby Of The Volga  582
Lullaby To A Dream  284

Lullaby To A Jitterbug  29
Lullaby To A Lamp Post  94-1082
Lull At Dawn, A  135
Lulu Belle  1006-1504
Lulu's Back In Town  203-563-779-1000-
1241-1432-1626
Lunatic's Lullaby, The  1396
Lunceford Special  988-989
Lure Of The South, The  1464
Lu's Blues  91
Lyin' To Myself  53

Ma! (He's Making Eyes At Me)  141-1316-
1352-1437
Ma And Pa Poorhouse Blues  1269
Mabel  1260-1261
Mabel, Open Your Door  998
Mabel's Dream  1166
Machinalement  1085
Mack's Rhythm  1111
MacPherson Is Rehearsin' (To Swing)  1661
Macumba  98
Ma Curly-Headed Babby/Baby  1513-1718
Mad About The Boy  147-323-1513-1696
Madame Dynamite  335
Madame Will Drop Her Shawl  498
Madam Swings It, The  745-906-907
Mad ('Cause You Treat Me This Way)  1132
Mad Dog  1129
Made A Monkey Out Of Me  1193
Mademoiselle Adeline  1562
Made Up My Mind  185
Madhouse  597-603-758-1239
Madison Street Rag  270
Mad Mama's Blues  1058-1090
Mad Mean Mama, A  1046
Mad Moments  773
Maelstrom  131
Maggie ! - "Yes Ma'am ?"  1180
Magic Blues  115
Magic Carpet  459
Magic de la Danse  1642
Magic Islands  650
Magic Mountain  298
Magic Of Magnolias, The  435
Magic Strings  1642
Magnolia (Mix The Lot-What Have You Got ?)
2-236-786-826-903 1015-1582-1740
Magnolia Blues  1216-1431
Magnolias In The Moonlight  1528
Magnolia's Wedding Day  944
Mah Jongg  1285
Mah Jongg Blues  1036
Mahogany Hall Stomp  45-51-53-123-586
Maid Of The Mist  1359
Maid's Night Off, The  786-960
Maids Of Cadiz, The  740
Mail Box Blues  392
Mail Man Blues  352-1010
Mail Plane Blues  1679
Mail Train Blues, The  1618
Main Stem  500
Maja - see MAN AND HIS DRUM, A
Major And Minor Stomp  432
Make A Country Bird Fly Wild   11
Make-Believe  608-830-1683-1684
Make-Believe Ballroom  93-1126
Make-Believe Island  909-1359
Make Love To Me  529-818-1243-1408
Make Love With A Guitar  1359

Make Me A Pallet On The Floor  114-847-
965-1105-1651
Make Me Know It  251-450-820-1246-1714
Make Me Love You  755-1246
Make My Cot Where The Cot-Cot-Cotton
Grows  238-239-377-626-738-784-1139
Make Room For Someone Else  1323
Make That Gravel Fly  1471
Make Those Naughty Eyes Behave  232
Make With The Kisses  165-613
Make With The Music  184
Make Yourself A Happiness Pie  1295
Make Yourself At Home  260
Makin' A Fool Of Myself  584
Makin' A Fool Out Of Me  1320
Makin' Faces At The Man In The Moon   157
1385-1457-1470
Makin' Friends  334-1078-1079
Making Up Blues  537
Makin' Whoopee  21-130-184-575-595-1595-
1638-1686
Makin' Wicki-Wacki Down In Waikiki  346-
1127
Malady in F minor  295
Malinda's Wedding Day  725
Malt Can Blues  1327
Mama Blues  1025.
Mamacita  1636
Mama Come (On) Home  529-680
Mama Cookie  337
Mama Didn't Do It And Papa Didn't Do It
1729
Mama Don't Allow It  161-583-824-1115-
1621
Mama Don't Allow No Easy Riders (Here)
390-1527
Mama Don't Allow No Music Playing In Here
1092
Mama, Don't Jive Me  1453
Mama Don't Like Music  169
Mama Don't Want No Peas An' Rice An'
Coconut Oil  103-180
Mama Don't Want Sweet Man Any More  709
Mama Don't Want You No More  852
Mama Doo Shee (Blues)  352-633
Mama, Fold Your Hands  821
Mama Goes Where Papa Goes (Or Papa Don't
Go Out Tonight)  350-560-796-1239-1421-
1609
Mama Inez  384-1384
Mama Is Waiting For You  734-1024-1257
Mama, I Wanna Make Rhythm  124-258-554-
1236
Mama Knows What Papa Wants When Papa's
Feeling Blue  1679
Mama Like To Do It  213
Mama Long And Tall  215
Mama Loves Papa (Papa Loves Mama)  224-
560-796-857-890-1175-1239-1590-1609
Mama Mama Blues  865
Mama Mama (Don't Love Her Papa No More)
1023
Mama Mocking-Bird  1476
Mamanita  1100-1106 (sometimes shown as
MAMAMITA)
Mama ne vends pas la maison  1221
Mama, Papa Don't Wanna Come Back Home
846
Mama's Baby Boy  549
Mama's Bad Luck Child  849-1541

1926
Mama's Blues  27
Mama's Boy  1190-1216
Mama's Gone, Goodbye  155-372-970-1004-
  1023-1067-1229-1420-1448-1546-1617-1721
  1722
Mama's Gonna Drop Your Curtain  1739
Mama's Got A Baby  1108
Mama's Got The Blues  666-685-1010-1439
Mama's Grown Young, Papa's Grown Old  626
  883-1393
Mama's Little Sunny Boy  1026
Mama's Losin' A Mighty Good Chance  833
Mama Stayed Out All Night Long/The Whole
  Night Long  99-213-833-861-1708
Mama's The Boss  707
Mama's Well Has Done Gone Dry  344
Mama, That Moon Is Here Again  295-605
Mama Whip ! Mama Spank ! (If Her Daddy
  Don't Come Home)  704-1461
Mama, Why Do You Treat Me So ? - see
  GULLY LOW BLUES
Mama Will Be Gone  866
Mama ! (Won't You Come And Mama Me ?)
  501-521-861
Mama, Won't You Give ?  1454
Mama, yo quiero un novio  424-1476
Mamie  530-1119
Mamie (Desdoume)'s Blues  1106-1107
Mamie Smith Blues  1462
Mammy Chasing Blues  1484
Mammy, I'm Thinking Of You  1725
Mammy Moon  1321
Mammy O' Mine  336-1177-1366
Mammy O' Mine Blues  320
Mammy's Little Choc'late Cullud Chile
  (sic)  1422
Mammy's Prayer  1742
Man About Town  1225
Man Ain't Born Who Can Treat Me Like You
  Do, The  1050
Man And His Dream, A  432-1405
Man And His Drum, A  387-432-447-743
Man, Be On Your Way  771
Manda  228-715-1424-1501
Mandalay  1483
Mandy  699-775-988-1220-1624-1693
Mandy 'n' Me  935
Mandy Is Two  770-1553
Mandy Lee Blues  1165
Mandy Lou  1422
Mandy, Make Up Your Mind  128-314-454-664
  716-1348-1481-1699-1722
Mane du gamle van  585
Man For Every Day In The Week, A  1618
Man From Harlem, The  256-348-1340
Man From Mars, The  63-1406
Man From The South, The  145-584-785-788-
  1214-1368-1597-1667-1740
Manhattan  231-754
Manhattan Holiday  684
Manhattan Jam  258-695
Manhattan Maroomba  386
Manhattan Mary  648-1580
Manhattan Minuet  1373
Manhattan Rag  1081-1569
Manhattan Serenade  417-436-454-819-1361
Manhattan Sunrise  1360
Manhattan Transfer  908
Maniacs' Ball  287-1073
Man I Got Ain't The Man I Want, The  1061

Man I Love, The  130-179-311-469-602-607-
  616-669-769-770-1262-1371-1404-1618-
  1669-1685-1735
Man I Love Is Oh So Good (To Me), The
  861-1589
Man I Love Is Worth Talking About, The
  570
Man Never Knows When A Woman's Gonna
  Change Her Mind, A  1190
Mannone Blues  1003
Man On The Flying Trapeze, The  937-1279
Man, That's Groovy  434
Man To Man  849
Man Who Broke The Bank At Monte Carlo,
  The  386
Man Who Comes Around, The  185-590-1397
Man With A Horn Goes Berserk  75
Man With The Funny Little Horn, The  1109
Man With The Lollipop Song, The  818
Man With The Mandolin(e), The  206-1655
Many Dreams Ago  9-1359-1405
Many Happy Returns Of The Day  1318-1645
Many Moons Ago  1227-1331
Maori - A Samoan Dance  119-127-480-481-
  486
Maple Leaf Rag  36-113-145-439--645-647-
  650-753-826-1005-1021-1022-1105-1125-
  1132-1200-1265-1342-1469-1515-1578-1656
  1657-1694
Ma Rainey's Black Bottom  1268
Ma Rainey's Mystery Record  1266
Marble Halls - see I DREAMT I DWELT IN
  MARBLE HALLS
Marbles  1616
Marble Stone Blues  355-1677
Marche Slav  185
Marcheta  447-908-1476-1712
Marching Along Together  1668
Marching Along With Time  444
Marching Home  141
March Of The Bob Cats  368
March Of The Dolls  144
March Of The Hoodlums  274-480-922-1081
March Of The Mannikins  70
March Of The Toys  448-1242
March Winds And April Showers  1000
Mardi Gras Blues  383
Mardi Gras Madness  135
Margie  88-117-190-257-298-307-347-451-
  465-486-489-610-636-652-774-789-913-
  961-987-1140-1177-1279-1340-1357-1410-
  1432-1720
Marguerite  73-926-1132
Maria Elena  434-911
Maria, My Own  1406
Marianne  2-952-977
Marie  10-57-94-155-277-440-451-602-649-
  774-880-1239-1293-1299-1313-1506
Marie, Ah Marie (Maria, Mari')  457
Marinela  1407
Marines' Hymn, The  376-912
Marked Woman  91
Market Street Blues, The  359-1450
Market Street Jive  1040
Market Street Stomp  359-1084
Mark Hop, The  374
Marriage Blues  1351
Married Man Blues  1020
Married Man's A Fool, A  212
Married Woman Blues  1678

Martha : Ah ! So Pure (von Flotow)  162-
321-1003-1334-1635
Martinique, The  700
Martin On Every Block  663
Martins And The Coys, The  204
Marvelous  237-468-1015-1665
Maryana  952
Mary Ann  413
Mary Anna Cut Off  1043
Mary Bell  1338
Mary Dear  69
Mary Dear, I Miss You Most Of All  1120
Mary Had A Little Lamb  191-366-382-439-
728-1557-1731
Mary Jane  1514
Mary Johnson Blues  847
Maryland  1155
Mary Lee  1111
Mary Lou  9-132-265-625-657
Mary Lou Williams Blues  1431
Mary O' Argyle - see BONNIE MARY OF
ARGYLE
Mary's Idea  898-901
Mary's Special  1720
Mary (What Are You Waiting For ?)  573-
1620-1682
Masculine Women-Feminine Men  190-523
Mashed Potatoes  1558
Mason-Dixon Blues  143-732-763-1050
Mason Flyer  1070
Massa-Choo-Setts  688
Massachusetts  912
Master Man With A Master Mind, A  794
Match Box Blues  1247
Matilda  684
Mattie Blues  436
Matzoh Balls  550
Mauvaise Priere, La  1349
Mauve - see UNTIL TONIGHT
Maw And Paw And Me  655
Maxie Jones (The King Of The Saxophones)
982-1353-1526-1608
Maxwell And Peoria Blues  1007
Maxwell Street Stomp  892
Maybe  207-437-560-816-909-1316-1519
Maybe I'm Coming Back To You  1524
Maybe I'm To Blame  758
Maybe I'm Wrong Again  292
Maybe It's Love  980
Maybe It's Someone Else You Love  1527
Maybe It's The Moon  1296
Maybe I Will  172
Maybe Not At All  1650
Mayberry Blues  1019
Maybe (She'll Write Me, She'll 'Phone Me)
72-796-885-1139
Maybe Someday  794-942-1051-1595
Maybe Sometime  1472
Maybe This Is Love  174
Maybe - Who Knows ?  63-244-421-519-951-
956-1457
Maybe You'll Be The One Who'll Be The One
To Care  1694
Maybe You Will-Maybe You Won't  667
May I ?  423-1227
May I Have My Heart Back ?  787
May I Have The Next Romance With You ?
439-1240-1313
Mayor Of Alabam', The  584-1571
Mayotte  650
Maytime  72-796-1590

May We Meet Again  1534
May Write Blues  1092
Mazie  1282
Mazi-Pani (No Work, No Pay)  1095
M. C. Blues  642
McGhee Special  902
Me  22-917-1297-1386
Meade Lux Special  1402
Meadowbrook Shuffle  1360
Meadow Lark  271-463-1740
Meal Is Low In The Barrel, The  557
Mean Baby Blues  1320-1541
Mean Black Man Blues  846
Mean Blues  1421-1590-1699
Mean Daddy Blues  1462
Me And Brother Bill  57
Me And Columbus  760
Me And Marie  427-701
Me And My Chauffeur  1247-1323
Me And My Gin  628-1445
Me And My Melinda  126-435-912-1361-1674
Me And My Shadow  172-1287
Me And My Wonderful One  180
Mean Dog Blues  171-1138-1287
Me And The Blues  1495
Me And The Boy Friend  229-973-1067
Me And The Clock (Tick-i-ty-Tock And You)
1174
Me And The Ghost Upstairs  62
Me And The Girl Next Door  1639
Me And The Man In The Moon  241-398-650-
831-1028-1047-1069-1666
Me And The Moon  756-986
Me And You  495-496
Meanest Blues, The  1190-1191
Meanest Kind Of Blues, The  511-715-716-
973-977
Meanest Man In The World, The (Milady's
Blues)  1719
Meanest Thing You Ever Did Was Kiss Me,
The  1630
Mean Eyes  181-1643
Mean Looks  1052
Mean Low Blues  149
Mean Man  1462-1574
Mean, Mean Mama  120-1051-1180-1305
Mean Mistreatin' Daddy  847
Mean Music  873
Mean Old Bed Bug Blues  88-636-1060-1444
1480-1655
Mean Old Jack Jack Stropper Blues  1573
Mean Old Master  1573
Mean Papa Turn (In) Your Key  353-1448
Mean Tight Mama  1014
Mean To Me  31-165-272-391-420-502-564-
590-670-797-1031-1120-1585-1733
Measly Blues  267
Meat Balls  843
Meat Man Pete  413-1093
Meat On The Table  1131
Mecca Flat Blues  27-1499
Meditation  689
Meddlin' With The Blues  682-833-1577
Mediterranean Blues  402
Meet Doctor Foo  690
Meet Me At The New York Fair  881
Meet Me In The Moonlight  15-1174
Meet Me Tonight In Dreamland  335
Meet Miss Eight Beat  1148
Meet The Band  696
Meet The Beat Of My Heart  906-1237

1928

Meet The Boys  1433
Meet The Sun Halfway  297
Me For You Forever  290
Melancholy (1923)  224-1608
Melancholy (Blues) (1927)  16-28-42-414-
  415-947
Melancholy Charlie  648-703-1430
Melancholy Clown  534
Melancholy Lou  653-924-967-1130-1180
Melancholy Lullaby  283-432
Melancholy Mood  371-815-1405-1491-1752
Melancholy Weeps  467
Melinda The Mousie  528
Mello As A 'Cello (sic)  1602
Mellophone Stomp  1115
Mellow Bit Of Rhythm, A  185-759-900
Mellow Blues, The  1746
Mellow Little Devil  680
Mellow Rhythm  1061
Mellow Stuff  505-843
Melody  377-454
Melody From The Sky, A  122-1052-1307
Melody in A (Charles Dawes)  1477
Melody in F (Anton Rubinstein)  440-565-
  919-1735
Melody In Riff  279
Melody Man, The  536-985
Melody Man's Dream  922
Melody March Call  1026
Melody Moon  1252
Melody Rag  397
Meme coup, Le  1349
Me Minus You  161-1472
Memories  1315-1603
Memories of Florence Mills  1622
Memories Of France  241
Memories Of You  48-295-457-482-542-613-
  614-662-839-1155-1207-1346-1652-1726
Mem'ries Of You, Mammy  1460
Memory Lane  299-1553-1718
Mem'ry Of A Rose, The  434-617
Memphis  171
Memphis Blues (The)  23-127-136-165-192-
  282-402-512-567-666-727-745-820-856-934-
  945-954-956-960-1015-1094-1183-1193-1221
  1232-1252-1341-1430-1498-1605-1606-1656-
  1657
Memphis Bound  717-733-866-1024
Memphis Bound Blues  1267
Memphis Boy  1041
Memphis By Morning  937
Memphis Gal  1713
Memphis Glide  1187
Memphis Jug  1041
Memphis Kick-Up  918
Memphis Mamie  1210
Memphis Man  1649
Memphis Maybe Man, The  337
Memphis Rag  310-776
Memphis Scronch  1723
Memphis Shake  408-409
Memphis Shakedown  1044
Memphis Sprawler  149-1174
Memphis Stomp  696-1045-1091
Memphis, Tennessee  645-1096-1306-1725-
  1727 (also shown as E FLAT BLUES No. 2)
Memphis Wail  476
Memphis Yo Yo Blues  1042
Me, Myself And I  587-703-768-780
Men Are Like Street Cars  783
Men At Work  771

Mendel's Son's Swing Song  780-801
Me Neenyah  717
Menelik (The Lion Of Judah)  1501
Meningitis Blues  1043
Men Of Harlem  518
Men Sure Are Deceiving  7
Mental Strain At Dawn  1256
Me Queres ?  562
Mercy Blues  354
Mercy Percy  1068
Merely An Excuse  532
Merengue d'amour  650
Merritt Stomp  940
Mermaid Song, The  261
Merry Carrousel, The  1375
Merry-Go-Round  98-486-489-495-1074
Merry-Go-Round Broke Down, The  15-330-
  880-986-1313
Merry Makers' Twine  65
Merry Widow On A Spree  94-1082
Merry Widow's Got A Sweetie Now, The
  1669
Mess, The  1097
Message From Mars  25-1224
Message From The Man In The Moon, A 1399
Mess-A-Stomp  898-900
Messin' Around  150-266-337-677-891-947-
  993-1167-1714
Messin' Around With The Blues  1622
Mess Is Here, The  390
Mess, Katy, Mess  753-1526
Messy  154
Me Too  134-234
Metro Blues  1048
Mexicali Moon  1077
Mexican Blues  1717
Mexican Hat Dance  186
Mexican Jumping Bean  1373
Mexican Swing  55
Mia Bella Rosa  1336
Mia Cara  517
Mia Mia  1225
Michigander Blues  1455
Michigan Rag  1111
Michigan Stomp  863
Michigan Water Blues  703-1010-1021-1022-
  1106-1107-1520-1706-1728
Mickey  1243-1317
Mickey Mouse  809-1293
Mickey Mouse And The Turtle  1697
Mickey Mouse (You Cute Little Feller)
  1594
Midnight  284
Midnight At The Onyx  279-786
Midnight Blue  14-1027
Midnight Blues (A Wee Hour Chant)  91-280
  632-731-763-946-1022-1439-1519-1649
Midnight Call Blues  845
Midnight Dan  1090
Midnight Echoes  740
Midnight Frolic Drag  1723
Midnight Hour Blues  354
Midnight In Mayfair  24
Midnight/Midnite In The Madhouse  279-320
  517-1506-1660
Midnight Jamboree  1263
Midnight Lullaby  297
Midnight Mama  945-1110
Midnight Oil  1095
Midnight On The Trail  445
Midnight Papa  1208

Midnight Ramble  1074
Midnight Reflections  1420
Midnight Rhythm  1646
Midnight Ride Of Paul Revere, The  1557
Midnight Special  1069
Midnight Stomp  136-820-1703
Midnight Stroll  692-693-901
Midnight Strutters  1161
Midnight Susie  942
Midnight Whirl Rag  1605
Midnite In Harlem (sic) - see MIDNIGHT IN
  THE MADHOUSE
Midsummer Matinee  1244
'Mid The Pyramids  856
Mid-Week Function  95
Mighty Blue  133-861
Mighty Blues  1240
Mighty Fine  1635
Mighty Lak' A Rose  1-457-568
Mighty Like The Blues  283-494-1007-1396
Mighty River  51-198-275-288-876
Mighty Sweet  88-1072
Milenberg Joys  211-273-291-322-350-375-
  403-424-446-513-548-569-571-675-725-866-
  876-903-955-992-1033-1100-1112-1132-1162-
  1279-1287-1329-1341-1389-1395-1400-1498-
  1508-1524-1545-1592-1688-1696-1718-1742
Mile-Or-Mo Bird Rag  26
Miles Apart  124-545
Military Madcaps  321
Military Mike  568-754-1191-1192
Milk Cow Blues  137-348-1710
Milk Man Blues  849-1455
Milkman's Matinee, The  93-441
Miller's Daughter, Marianne, The  15-1313
Million Disappointments, A  880
Million Dreams, A  816-1238
Million Dreams Ago, A  742-816-1374
Milumbu  896-897
Milwaukee Walk  1080
Mindin' My Business  72-225-295-560-561-
  1067-1129-1189-1428-1609
Mine  269-467-1369-1521
Mine, All Mine  144-145-239-340-669-1580
Mine's (Just) As Good As Yours  343-708-
  1257
Mine Yesterday-His Today  592
Minglewood Blues  270
Mining Camp Blues  1467
Minka  818
Minnie  975
Minnie From Trinidad  434
Minnie The Mermaid  377
Minnie The Moocher  253-256-260-261-273-
  285-651-790-1071-1410-1465-1585-1644
Minnie The Moocher Is Dead  989
Minnie The Moocher's Wedding Day  88-158-
  601-603-730-1072-1410
Minor Blues  1218
Minor de Luxe  208
Minor Drag, The  1623
Minor Gaff  1212-1545
Minor Jive  1134
Minor Mania  774-775
Minor Mood  1511
Minor Swing  1260
Minouche  16
Mint Julep  785-1103-1245
Minuet For A Modern Miss  1435
Minuet In Blues  135
Minuet In Jazz  746-756-1371

Minute Waltz  413-895
Miracle At Midnight  787
Mirage  298
Miranda - see MIRANDY (THAT GAL O' MINE)
Mirandy (That Gal O' Mine)  513-1424-
  1426
Misery  251-357
Misery Blues  353-1268-1471
Misery Farm  470
Mishawaka Blues  350
Misirlou  743-818
Miss Annabella Brown - see MISS HALLELU-
  JAH BROWN
Miss Annabelle Lee  95-171-237-314-669-
  785-938-974-1260-1290-1308-1363-1432-
  1456-1664-1665
Miss Anna Brown  794
Miss Brown To You  1730
Miss Elizabeth Brown  1616
Miss Golden Brown  1041
Miss Hallelujah Brown  259-692
Miss Hannah  858-1034
Missing Every Note  1038
Missing Link, The  1352-1525
Missin' My Pal  112
Mission To Moscow  623
Miss Is As Good As A Mile, A  788
Mississippi Basin  51-199-982-1330-1647-
  1707
Mississippi Blues  705-964-1000-1458-
  1704
Mississippi Delta Blues  178
Mississippi Dream Boat  766
Mississippi (Dry)  479
Mississippi, Here I Am  341-757-1069-
  1648
Mississippi Melody  799
Mississippi Mildred  1103
Mississippi Moan  460-478
Mississippi Mud  2-305-394-402-976-1291-
  1567-1684
Mississippi Mud Blues  1160
Mississippi River Blues  353
Mississippi River Waltz  1042
Mississippi Shivers  1722
Mississippi Stomp  784-892-918
Mississippi Swamp Moan  946
Mississippi Town  644
Mississippi Valley Blues  1496
Mississippi Waters Blues  753
Mississippi Wobble  1615
Mississippi Woman Blues  1542
Miss Liza Johnson Got Better Bread  810
Miss Moonshine  1676
Miss Otis Regrets (She's Unable To Lunch
  Today)  257-395-809-984-1211-1349-1654
Missouri Blues  379-513-1522-1577-1748
Missouri Misery  424-840
Missouri Scrambler  324-387-1397-1411-
  1509
Missouri Squabble  269-404-654-806-994-
  1192-1559
Missouri Tickler Blues  1327
Missouri Wobble  1110
Miss Thing  105
Miss Trombone  379
Miss Wonderful  465-888-1666
Miss You  83-1351-1553
Mistakes  1291
Mr. And Mrs. Is The Name  1751
Mr. Black Man  1254-1255

Mr. Blackbird  381
Mr. Brakes Man (Let Me Ride Your Train)  343
Mr. Brown Goes To Town  153
Mr. Cooler Hot  1502
Mr. Crosby And Mr. Mercer  363
Mr. Crump Rag  376
Mr. Five By Five  820
Mr. Forty-Nine Blues  995
Mr. Freddie Blues  150-163-947-1411-1489-1499-1420
Mr. Froggie  1494
Mr. Ghost Goes To Town  440-660-739-785-1074-1249
Mr. J. B. Blues  497
Mr. Jelly Lord  945-1099-1100-1102-1105-1132-1389
Mr. Jinx Stay Away From Me  321
Mister Joe  1107
Mr. Johnson, Don't Get Gay  939
Mr. Johnson, Turn Me Loose  939-996
Mr. Livingood  865-1674
Mr. Man  353
Mr. Meadowlark  615-741-816-1406
Mr. Moore Blues  995
Mr. Music Master  276
Mr. Paganini, Swing For Minnie  259
Mr. Pickwick  1163
Mr. Polo Takes A Solo  1238
Mr. Reynard's Nightmare  684-1224
Mr. Rhythm For President  780
Mr. Rhythm Man  582-1528
Mr. Sousa's Yankee Band  379
Mr. Sweeney's Learned To Swing  786-1506
Mister, Will You Serenade ?  169-1708-1709
Mrs. Abernathy's Piano  736
Mrs. Finnigan  261
Mistreated  944
Mistreated Blues  793-1677
Mistreated Mama Blues  1011-1455
Mistreating Daddy  177-750-1023-1440
Mistreatin' Daddy (Blues)  353-1463-1728
Mistreating Man Blues  1014
Mistreatin' Woman  8
Misty Islands Of The Highlands  1157-1415
Misty Mornin'  477-479-790
Mixed Salad  1129
Mixed Up Blues, The  544-747
Mixed Up Rag  516
Mixing The Blues  1698
Mixture  1284
Mixup  987
Moan, The  1522
Moanful Blues  458-1456
Moanful Moan  8-337
Moanful Wailin' Blues  121-633
Moanin'  285-1071
Moanin' Blues  570
Moanin' For You  21-341-952-1165-1294-1379
Moanin' Groanin' Blues  352
Moanin' Heart Blues  1527
Moanin' In The Mornin'  443
Moanin' Low  305-351-671-788-790-1007-1080-1088-1281-1705-1732
Moanin' Minnie  938
Moanin' Piano Blues  1548
Moanin' Sinner Blues  1094
Moanin' The Blues  586-1488
Moan, You Moaners  725-1145-1446
Mobile Bay  1501
Mobile Blues  193-565-713-1191-1327-1389-1391-1694-1712

Mobile Flag Stop (Catching The 8.02 Local)  1047
Mobile Mud  856-1324
Mobile Stomp  1095
Modern Melody  698
Modulation  855
Moi, j'en ai deux  396
Mojo Blues, The  65-628
Mojo Hand Blues  354
Mojo Strut  1228
Mokus  28
Mo'lasses  933
Mole, The  819
Mollie Mae Blues  1588
Molly  797
Molly Malone  1513
Moment I Laid Eyes On You, The  261
Moment I Looked In Your Eyes, The  290
Moment Musical  1372
Moments In The Moonlight  373-449-908
Moments Like This  1512-1554-1734
Moment Whimsical  1372
Mommy  161
Mommy, I Don't Want To Go To Bed  582-1277
Momsy  1290
Mona  932-1165
Mon Coeur  1639
Mon Coeur a rencontre ton coeur  396
Mon Coeur reste pres de toi  1288
Monday At Minton's  131
Monday Date, A  43-57-757-1151-1602
  (also shown as MY MONDAY DATE and OUR MONDAY DATE)
Monday Evening Lullaby  87
Monday In Manhattan  1031-1530-
Monday Morning  633-1357
Monday Morning Blues  1492
Monday Struggle  27
Money Blues  718-904-1443
Money For Jam  1238
Money Is Honey  1269
Money Never Runs Out  270
Monia  1338
Monkey Business  774-871-1285
Monkey Doodle Doo  211-1300-1390
Monkeyin' Around  859
Monkey Jungle Blues  965
Monkey Man Blues  1010
Monkey On A String  1412
Monkey Parade  315
Monkeys Have No Tails In Pago Pago, The  747
Monkey Swing, The  681
Monopoly Swing  785-1562
Monotony  797
Monotony Has Got Me Down  209
Monotony In Four Flats  989
Mon Proces  1642
Monsoon  1402
Montana Call  503-1369
Monte Carlo Joys  464-1603
Montevideo  816
Montmartre  1500
Montmartre Blues  190
Montmarte (sic) Giggles  1557
Montmartre Moan  1238
Montmartre Rag, The  1085
Montmartre Rose  230-658
Montparnasse Jump  1238
Mooche, The  115-476-481-497-764
Mood At Twilight  1242

Mood Hollywood  422-703
Mood Indagroove  435
Mood Indigo  25-115-158-253-347-386-482-
   483-485-491-496-497-587-801-924-984-
   1207-1556-1726-1750
Mood In Question  1125
Mood That I'm In  585-660-1027-1399-1585-
   1732
Moody Melody  1155
Moon  147
Moon And The Willow Tree, The  1540
Moon At Sea  258
Moonburn  203-293-362-1546
Moon Country  276-291-296-581-878
Moon Dear  232-339-664
Moon Face  1399
Moon Fell In The River, The  107-166
Moonglow  257-291-313-385-404-465-489-581-
   594-598-605-635-1207-1334-1408-1529-1531
   1600-1601-1654
Moon Got In My Eyes, The  78-205-429-1400
Moon Is Cryin' For Me, The  97
Moon Is Grinning At Me, The  702-785-1074-
   1236
Moon Is Low, The  324-503-1064-1369-1634-
   1635
Moonlight And Magnolias  700-1658
Moonlight And Music  990
Moonlight And Roses  1592
Moonlight And Shadows  205-1399
Moonlight And Tears  325
Moonlight And You  339
Moonlight Bay  1063-1554
Moonlight Becomes You  819
Moonlight Blues  665-782
Moonlight Cocktail  299
Moonlight Fiesta  134-489
Moonlight Kisses  224
Moonlight March, The  245
Moonlight Masquerade  273-434-1361-1553
Moonlight Mood  299
Moonlight On The Colorado  1153
Moonlight On The Ganges  453-617-1063
Moonlight On The Prairie, Mary  894
Moonlight On The Purple Sage  443
Moonlight On The Rio Grande  248
Moonlight On The Sunset Trail  206-1402
Moonlight Reminds Me Of You, The  246
Moonlight Rhapsody  257
Moonlight Saving Time - see THERE OUGHT TO
   BE A MOONLIGHT SAVING TIME
Moonlight Serenade  106-206-908-1358
Moonlight, The Danube And You  147
Moonlit Waters  1309
Moon Looks Down And Laughs, The  768
Moon Love  80-790
Moon Mist  499-920
Moon Nocturne  109
Moon Of Japan  1120
Moon Of Manakoora, The  9-764
Moon Or No Moon  183
Moon Over Burma  298-910
Moon Over Cuba  499
Moon Over Dixie  485
Moon Over Miami  881-1312
Moon Ray  527-829-1405-1406-1412-1736
Moonrise On The Lowlands  191-428-728-1278
Moon Romance  766
Moon Rose  1032-1239-1628
Moonshine  413
Moonshine Blues  1265-1268-1440-1678

Moonshine Over Kentucky  78-94-124-1158-
   1357
Moon Song (That Wasn't Meant For Me)
   112-674
Moonstone  841
Moonstruck  982
Moon Was Yellow, The  424
Moon Won't Talk, The  615-816
Moose March  1200
Mootch Piddle  390
More  1138-1550
More I Know You, The  1628
More Or Less Blues  1420
More Power To You  1631
More Rain, More Rest  1456
More Than Ever  367-443-1158-1402
More Than Somewhat  1238
More Than That  1468-1710
More Than You Know  77-82-109-183-209-
   283-597-617-692-1412-1482-1735
More Tortilla B flat  336
More You Hurt Me, The (The More You Make
   Me Care)  981
Morning After, The  183-442-990-1157
Morning After Blues, The  1030
Morning Air  442-1468
Morning Dove Blues  642-1549-1618
Morning Feeling  776
Morning Glory  496
Morning Hour Blues  1267
Morning, Noon And Night  247-1388-
Morning Prayer Blues  1541
Morning Sun Blues  846
Morning! Won't You Ever Come 'Round ?
   916-1459
Morocco  1237-1506
Morocco Blues  864-1534
Mortgage Stomp, The  107-823
Mosquito, Fly And Flea  1488
Mosquito Song, The  1004
Most Gentlemen Don't Like Love  323
Most Of Us Do, The  1528
Most Wonderful You  506
Moten's Blues  1111
Moten's Swing  102-107-459-899-1112
Moten Stomp  729-1038-1110-1184
Mother Fuzzy  98
Mother Goose  123
Mother-in-Law Blues  1454
Motherless Blues  1156
Motherless Child - see SOMETIMES I FEEL
   LIKE A MOTHERLESS CHILD
Mother Me, Tennessee  73-74-129-998
Mother's Boy  961
Mother (Who Can Be Sweeter Than You ?)
   1593
M-O-T-H-E-R (A Word That Means The World
   To Me)  1361-1722
Mouchi, The  788
Mound Bayou  187-946
Mountain City Blues  1565-1703-1704-1705
Mountain Greenery  467
Mountain Jack Blues  1267
Mountain Music  441-830
Mountains O' Mourne, The  970
Mountain Top Blues  1441
Mournful Blues  1013-
Mournful Serenade  1102
Mournful Tho'ts/Thoughts  838
Mournin' Blues  370-1176
Mouthful O' Jam  35-1410

1932

Mouth Organ Swing No. 1  556
Move It On Out Of Here  802
Move Over  476-897
Move That Thing  1043
Move Turtle  1697
Move Your Hand  678
Moving Day  1210
Moving Day Blues  979
Movin' The Boogie  851
Mozeltov  1238
M. T. Pocket Blues  632-1471
Much More Lovely  374
Much Too Much  780
Muddy Creek Blues  846
Muddy River Blues  1539
Muddy Stream Blues  1066
Muddy Water (A Mississippi Moan)  138-171-
  467-625-872-986-1222-1444-1611-1681-1721
Muddy Water Blues  681-1093-1099
Mudhole Blues  153
Muffin Man  528
Muggin' Lightly  1346
Muggin' The Blues  863
Muggles  44
Mug Of Ale, A  1596
Mule Blues (The Hee-Haw)  1525
Mule Face Blues  1170
Mule Walk, The  839
Munson Street Breakdown  662
Murder At Peyton Hall  98
Murder Ballad, The  1105
"Murder," He Says  436-912-1214
Murder In The First Degree  843-1488
Murder In The Moonlight (It's Love In The
  First Degree)  1031
Murderistic  435
Murdy Purdy  907
Murray Walk, The  647
Muscle Shoals Blues  666-715-883-915-1059-
  1110-1621-1725
Mush Mouth  773
Mushmouth Blues  862-1241
Mushmouth Shuffle  1104
Mushy Love  731
Musical Camp Meeting  1715
Music And Moonlight  468-1136
Music At Midnight  792
Music At Sunrise  792
Music Box Blues  991
Music Box Rag  1605
Music By The Moon  741
Music For All  1224
Music For You  1224
Music From Across The Sea  290
Music Goes 'Round And Around, The  52-160-
  203-438-545-583-656-701-968-1001-1114-
  1306-1307
Music Hall Rag  386-594
Music In The Moonlight  341
Music, Maestro, Please  444-554-588-1508-
  1632
Music Makers  108-452-816
Music Makes Me Feel That Way  1453
Music Makin' Man  1121
Music Man, The  1669
Music, Music Everywhere  822-858
Music Of The Fountain, The  587
Music Puts Me In The Strangest Mood  798
Musique Grisante, La  1639
Muskrat Ramble  40-366-398-466-517-543-592
  661-945-1114-1656

Mustard And Onions  996
Must Get Mine In Front  1376
Mutiny In The Brass Section  428
Mutiny In The Nursery  386-1435-1690
Mutiny In The Parlor  906-1052
Mutiny On The Bandstand  182-183
My Angel  1291
My Angeline  1083-1193
My Baby  150-308-852-1319-1494
My Baby Came Home  1030
My Baby Doesn't Squawk  1128
My Baby Just Cares For Me  22-84-196-
  1015-1621-1667
My Baby Knows How  235-340-668-921-928-
  1182-1218-1579-1593
My Baby Left Me  847
My Baby's Arms  1177-1522
My Baby's Gone  835
My Baby's Hot  824
My Baby (Squeeze Me Again)  843
My Baby Sure Knows How To Love  1652
My Baby's Ways  637
(My) Back To The Wall  1376
My Barcelona  234-266
My Beloved Is Rugged  820
My Best Friend Stole My Man And Gone 1457
My Best Gal/Girl  339-561-926-1723
My Best Wishes  322
My Blackbirds Are Bluebirds Now  575-579-
  626-670-950
My Blonde  1294
My Blue And Gold Girl  70
My Bluebird's Back Again  1297-1555
My Bluebird's Singing The Blues  67-471-
  996
My Bluebird Was Caught In The Rain  22-
  391
My Blue Days Blew Over  142
My Blue-Eyed Jane  1328
My Blue Heaven  144-314-646-690-961-985-
  989-1195-1223-1346-1399-1406-1407-1419-
  1465-1513-1613-1657-1734
My Blue Ridge Mountain Home  1589
My Blues Is Like Whiskey  783
My Bonnie Lies Over The Ocean  295-316-
  969-1402
My Brand New Papa  1450
My Buddy  283-325-662-749-815-841-914
My Bundle Of Love  566-656-1478
My Business Ain't Right  1044
My Cabin Of Dreams  59-441-1020-1028-1314
My Canary Has Circles Under His Eyes
  1616-1670
My Carmenita  234-266
My Carolina Hideaway  1211
My Carolina Sunshine Girl  1327
My Castle In Spain Is A Shack In The Lane
  131-243-659-888-979
My Castle In The Clouds  1536
My Castle Of Love  918
My Castle Of Never-Can-Be  918
My Choc'late Soldier Sammy Boy  513
My Coo-Coo Bird (Could Sing)  261
My Cousin In Milwaukee  1269
My Cuban Dreams  1097
My Cutie/Cutey's Due At Two-To-Two Today
  319-523-967-1664
My Daddy Can't Do Nothin' Bad  344
My Daddy Rocks Me (With One Steady Roll)
  359-1152-1162-1196-1466-1467-1501-1526
My Daddy's Calling Me  1376

My Daddy's Dream Time Lullaby  338
My Daddy's Got The Mojo, But I Got The
  Say-So  213
My Daddy's Growin' Old  1344
My Daddy Was A Lovin' Man  679
My Dance  292-798-1215
My Dancing Lady  1601
My Darling (1925)  1504-1722
My Darling (1928)  1018
My Darling (1933)  1438
My Day  765
My Desert Fantasy  1522
My Desire  1295
My Devotion  436
My Different/Dif'rent Kind Of/O' Man
  1060-1061-1535
My Dixie  1607
My Dog Loves Your Dog  423
My Doggone Lazy Man  1218-1448
My Downfall  783
My Dream  944
My Dream Man  716
My Dream Memory  17-1293
My Dreams  1210
My Dripping Blood Blues  1413
My Extraordinary Gal  874-1397-1410
My Fantasy  1406
My Fate Is In Your Hands  64-141-507-952-
  1369-1623-1626
My Favorite Band  1667
My Favorite Blues  284
My Favorite Girl  795-1416
My Feelin's Are Hurt  1623
My Fightin' Gal  1204
My Fine Feathered Friend  739-1063
My First Impression Of You  429-1631-1734
My First Thrill  93
My Foolish Heart And I  743
My Four Reasons  311-1322
My Fox Trot Wedding Day  315
My Future Just Passed  156-195-247-672-
  736-1329-1336
My Future Star  517
My Gal  261-1100
My Gal Don't Love Me Any More  230
My Gal Is Good For Nothing But Love  481
My Gal Mezzanine  180
My Gal, My Pal  149
My Gal Sal  5-18-204-304-563-606-724-774-
  944-1087-1095-1105-1139-1314-1326-1663-
  1738-1743
My Gal's Been Foolin' Me  1197
My Gal Stella  1454
My Galveston Gal  12-455
My Girl  308-884-1437
My Girl's A Rhythm Fan  1433
My Girl's Fine And Dandy  1335
My Good-For-Nuthin' Man (sic)  1449
My Good Gal's Gone Blues  1328
My Good Man Sam  1169
My Good Man's Blues (Mahalia's Blues)  1011
My Greatest Mistake  325-497-816-1317
My Greenwich Village Sue  1318
My Gypsy Rhapsody  1600
My Hands Are Tied  206-907
My Handy Man  272-510-1488-1652
My Handy Man Ain't Handy No More  1726
My Hat's On The Side Of My Head  22
My Hawaiian Sunshine  1516
My Heart  40
My Heart And I  293-1546

My Heart And I Decided  529
My Heart At Thy Sweet Voice  322-1360
My Heart Beats For You  760
My Heart Belongs To Daddy  104-323-1585-
  1661
My Heart Belongs To The Girl Who Belongs
  To Somebody Else  1294
My Heart-Breakin' Gal  994
My Heart Is A Helpless Thing  990
My Heart Is An Open Book  292
My Heart Is Taking Lessons  295-880
My Heart Is Where The Mohawk Flows
  Tonight  132
My Heart Jumped Over The Moon  766
My Heart Keeps Crying  95
My Heart's Aching For My Old Gal  567
My Heart's At Ease  198
My Heart's Desire  982
My Heart's In The Right Place  700
My Heart Stood Still  238-1404-1683
My Heaven On Earth  787-1357
My Hi-De-Ho Man  39
My Home Is In A Southern Town  1108
My Honey's Lovin' Arms  220-253-361-542-
  610-631-825-856-915-946-1003-1068-1143-
  1184-1193-1337-1570-1598-1606
My Ideal  196-950-1396-1513
My Idea Of Heaven  657-668
My Imaginary Love  375
My Imaginary Sweetheart  289
My Independent Man  848
My Inspiration  369
My Inspiration Is You  502-670
My Irish Paradise  1292
My John Blues  1449
My Josephine  302
My June Love  1304
My Kid's A Crooner  798
My Kinda Love (One Way To Paradise)  92-
  420-513-723-775-918-949-1120-1202-1233-
  1422
My Kind Of Blues  1324
My Kind Of Man  1652
My Kingdom For A Kiss  366-1415
My Kitchen Man  1704
My Laddie  380
My Lady  648
My Last Affair  78-311-526-660-894-986-
  1732
My Last Goodbye  495-527
My Lips Want Kisses (My Heart Wants Love)
  35-161
My Little Bimbo  1274
My Little Brown Book  500
My Little Buckaroo  703-1313
My Little Bunch Of Happiness  1505
My Little Cousin  126-435-622-1160
My Little Dream Girl  1272
My Little Dixie Home  1104
My Little Fella And Me  1213
My Little Girl  1116-1490
My Little Grass Shack In Kealakekua,
  Hawaii  1235
My Little Home Town Down In New Orleans
  737
My Little Honey And Me  1081
My Little Isabel  415
My Little Pride And Joy  1511
My Lonely Cabin  832
My Love  290
My Love For You  184-431-504-1160-1302

1934

My Love Parade  246
My Love Is Cold  1043
My Lovey Lee  1130
My Lovin' Eskimo  1522
My Lucky Star  887-1604
My Mama's Bad Luck Child - see MAMA'S BAD
  LUCK CHILD
My Mama's In Town  955-1576-1714
My Mammy  1017-1479
My Mammy Knows  68-219
My Mammy's Blues  558-1463-1485
My Mammy's Tears  1423
My Man  289-528-1373-1733
My Man Ain't Yo' Man (sic)  643
My Man Blues  570-1012-1091-1443-1450
My Man Done Done Me Dirty  845
My Man From Caroline  1383-1599
My Man Has Quit Me  1572
My Man Is Gone  848
My Man Is Good For Nothing But Love  1726
My Man Is On The Make  678-789-1382
My Man Is Somebody Else's Too  171
My Man Jean  392
My Man Jumped Salty On Me  357
My Man Just Won't Don't  412-1458
My Man O' War  272-1729
My Man Rocks Me - see MY DADDY ROCKS ME
My Margarita  1357
My Marie  755
My Mariuccia Take A Steamboat  1003
My Mean Man Blues  353
My Melancholy Baby  3-17-79-172-202-207-
  305-311-387-419-454-466-557-598-599-609
  700-761-801-818-858-987-989-1106-1148-
  1152-1183-1261-1262-1289-1315-1539-1636
  1685-1731
My Mellow Man  1247
My Missouri Home  980
My Mom  742
My Mommie Sent Me To The Store  1636
My Monday Date - see MONDAY DATE, A
My Mother's Eyes  507-644-1375
My Mother's Rosary  315
My ! My !  10-163-190-373-449
My ! My ! My !  1718
My Name Is Jim  1247
My Name Will Always Be Chickie  566
My New York  657
My Ohio Home  578-648-930-1475-1614
My ! Oh My !  1476
My Old Daddy's Got A Brand New Way To Love
  408-795-1082
My Old Flame  109-489-619-620
My Old Girl's My New Girl Now  140-241
My Old Kentucky Home  908-1402
My Old Lady Blues  514-679
My Old Man  1278-1486
My Old Ramshackle Shack  70
My One And Only  840
My Only Passion  680-681
My Oriental Rose  710
My Own  444-467-906
My Own Blues  311-411-1182-1699
My Own Man Blues  1454
My Pal Called Sal  1742
My Pal Jerry  994
My Papa Doesn't Two-Time No Time  65-713-
  732-1129-1171-1189-1428
My Particular Man  795
My Pet  61-469-525-930-1015-1343-1568-
  1581-1614-1685

My Piano And Me  1668
My Piggy Bank Is Jing-a-Ling Again  1397
My Pillow And Me  666-1060-1532
My Pony  1542
My Pony Boy  118-876
My Pop Gave Me A Nickel  944
My Prayer  432
My Pretty Girl  547-578-724-1136-1646
My Pullman Porter Man  1321
My Ranch - see ALLA EN EL RANCHO GRANDE
My Red-Letter Day  24
My Regular Gal/Girl  2-172-1619
My Reverie  79-322-363-1403-1690
My Righteous Man  1751
My Right Hand Man  178
My Right Man  733
My River Home  198-**876**
My Rosary Of Broken Dreams  185
My Rose Marie  716
Myrtle Avenue Stomp  1727
My Sahara Rose  748
My Secret Flame  40
My Secret Love Affair  131-183
My Señorita  1319
My Serenade  1260
My Silent Love  818-875-1645
My Silent Mood  324-432
My Sin  243-244-671-949-1396-1743
My Sister And I  434-618
My Slow And Easy Man  854
My Small Town Gal  394
My Song Of Songs To You  737
My Southern Home  395-1292-1336
My Special Friend/Man Is Back In Town
  1205-1651
My Sportin' Man  1446-1464
Mysterious Blues  521-1352-1522
Mysterious Eyes  1503
Mysterious Mose  145-1294-1667
Mystery  675-**1**602-1603-1748
Mystery Pacific  1260
Mystery Song, The  485
Mystic Moan  774
My Stove's In Good Condition  843
My Success  981
My Sugar  568-652-707-903
My Sugar And Me  243
My Sunday Gal/Girl  256-268-1028-1136-
  1501
My Sunflower Maid  1509
My Sunny Tennessee  935
My Sunshine  918
My Suppressed Desire  193-243-340
My Sweet  47-1261
My Sweet Gal  867-1615
My Sweeter Than Sweet  245-804-1569
My Sweetheart  576
My Sweet Hortense - see HORTENSE
My Sweetie Turned Me Down  1583
My Sweetie Went Away  223-350-711-924-938
  1145-1224-1298-1354-1354-1362-1433-1439
  1440
My Sweet Louise  1130
My Sweet Man (Tickles The Ivories For Me)
  1463
My Sweet Tooth Says "I Wanna" (But My
  Wisdom Tooth Says "No")  725-1386
My Sweet Virginia  459-539
My Swiss Hilly Billy  545-586
My Syncopated Melody Man  1029-1030
My Thoughts  1465

My Tonia  502
My Troubles Are Over  242-627-887-949-
   1292-1514-1666
My Tweet Twaat Twaat  1751
My Twilight  797
My Two-Timing Papa  1449
My Understanding Man  681
My Unusual Man  1467
My Very Good Friend, The Milkman  66-426-
   1626
My Walking Stick  55-444-1722
My Wanderin' Man  107
My White Rose  1252
My Whole Day Is Spoiled  201
My Wife Is On A Diet  507-1394
My Wife's In Europe Today  631
My Wild Irish Rose  297-1236-1662
My Window Faces The South  1631
My Wish  273-664
My Woman !  958-1507
My Woman Done Me Wrong (As Far As I Am
   Concerned)  1703
My Wonderful One, Let's Dance  909
My Worried Mind Blues  1678
My Wubba Dolly  386-527-1436
My Yiddishe Momme  970
My Za Zu Girl  1528

Nagasaki  26-93-257-282-292-311-345-382-
   409-530-582-605-636-727-804-906-959-
   1005-1259-1277-1332-1393-1433-1476-1507
   1556-1585-1634-1647
Nagasuckle Rose  1411
Naguine  1283
Nain, Nain  261-435
Na-Jo  119
Naked Dance, The  1105-1107
Name It  563
Name It And It's Yours  9
Nameless Blues  548-1392
Nana  650-699-984
Nancy (1924)  682-1582
Nancy (1929)  918
Nancy Jane  1044
Nantucket Nan  1119
Naptown Special  456
Naptown Strut  754
Narcissus  291-292-326-386
Narrow Escape  1021
Narrow Gauge Blues  1655
Nashville Nightingale  228-306
Nashville Woman's Blues  1442
Nasty But Nice  831
Nasty Man  423-924
National Blues  409
National Emblem (March)  1572-1675
Naturally  56-1237
Naughty Man  716
Naughty Melody  1639
Naughty, Naughty (I'm Surprised At You)
   1088
Navy Blues  776-1088-1414
Nay, Dearie, Nay  1052
Neal's Blues  1713
Nealski  1640
Neapolitan Nights  1290
Nearness Of You, The  163-207-325-816-
   1343
'Neath The Shanty Town Moon  1436
'Neath The Silvery Moon  1470
'Neath The South Sea Moon  69

Nebraska - see I'M GOING BACK TO OLD
   NEBRASKA
Nebraska Blues  1489
Neck Bones And Beans  837
Need A Little Sugar In My Bowl  1446
Needlenose  1409
Need More Blues  1480
Need My Lovin', Need My Daddy  1321
Neglected  192-1631
Neglected Blues  643
Neiani  452
Ne le perdez pas  1615
Nellie  963
Nellie Dean  386-1435
Nellie, Where You Goin' ?  762
Nelson Stomp  1125-1170
Nero  894-1239-1630
Nerves And Fever  333
Nervous Blues  136-1724
Nervous Breakdown  1706
Nervous Charlie (Stomp)  266-719-1275-
   1377
Nervous Puppies  1030
Nervous Tension  1210
Nesting Time (1021)  748
Nesting Time (1927)  1619
Netcha's Dream  689
Never  60-736-981
Never Again  72-134-301-446-857
Never Brag About Your Man  91
Never Drive A Beggar From Your Door  861
Never Felt Better, Never Had Less  124-
   907-1690
Never Had  234
Never Had A Reason To Believe In You
   1113-1119-1216
Never Had No Lovin'  1000
Never In A Million Years  78-362-786-1147
   1400
Never Let No One Man Worry Your Mind 1518
Never Let Your Left Hand Know (What Your
   Right Hand Do OR ......What Your Right
   Hand's Doin')  735-842-865
Never Let Your Right Hand Know What Your
   Left Hand's Going To Do  315
Never-Never Land  945
Never-Never Land Fantasy  1572
Never No Lament  496-497
Never No Mo' Blues  1299
Never Should Have Told You  600-1416
Never Stop Raining Blues  1363
Never Swat A Fly  16-992-1035-1594
Never Tell A Woman Friend  861
Nevertheless (I'm In Love With You)  505
Never Took A Lesson In My Life  590-909
Never Too Tired To Love  180
Never Without You  631-1612-1644
'n' Everything  1375
New Birmingham Breakdown, The  491
New Black And Tan Fantasy  492
New Black Snake Blues  1488
New Block And Tackle (Blues)  211-1298
New Blues  1539
New Bo-Weavil Blues  1268
New Call Of The Freaks, The  1345
New Cow Cow Blues  389
New Crawley Blues  358
New Crazy Blues  1208-1589
New Down Home Blues  1703
New Drinking My Blues Away  848
New Dupree Blues  1677

1936

New East St. Louis Toodle-Oo, The   491
Newest St. Louis Blues   1571
New Goofy Dust Rag   1111
New Gulf Coast Blues   1443
New Hot Nuts (Get 'Em From The Peanut
    Man)   1677
New Kinda Blues   782
New Kind Of Man, A (With A New Kind Of
    Love For Me)   39-561-715-772-789-790-
    926-1171-1591
New King Porter Stomp   726
New Louise Louise Blues   1541
New Loving Blues   841
New Low Down Dirty Shame   1413
New Minglewood Blues   948
New Mr. Freddie Blues   1499
New Moon   1522-1531
New Moon And An Old Serenade, A   94-259-
    446
New Moon Is Over My Shoulder, A   161-292
New Moten Stomp   1112-1465
New Muddy Water Blues   847
New Oh ! Red   678
New O'leans   1689
New Orleans   270-276-289-956-1112-1462
New Orleans Blues   90-396-1106-1499
New Orleans Breakdown   1125
New Orleans Bump   1103
New Orleans Goofer Dust Blues   936
New Orleans Hop Scop Blues   1011-1154-
    1446-1698-1709
New Orleans Joys   1099
New Orleans Low-Down   472
New Orleans Medley   1145-1146
New Orleans Parade   1033
New Orleans Shags   862
New Orleans Shout   1170
New Orleans Shuffle   650
New Orleans Stomp   414-1166
New Orleans Twist   565-583
New Orleans Wiggle   1021-1229
New Please Mr. Johnson   832
Newport Blues   315
Newport News   1041
New River Train, The   1398
New Rubbing On The Darned Old Thing   1197
New St. Louis Blues, The   402-413-514-955
    992-993-1390
New Shade Of Blue, A   434
New Shave 'Em Dry   843
New Street Swing   282
New Tiger Rag, The   1688
New Trouble In Mind   1678
New Tulsa Blues, The   1110
New Twister, The   5-1087-1131-1195
New Vicksburg Blues   1541
New Vine Street Blues   1111
New Wang-Wang Blues   1167
New Year's Eve In A Haunted House   1373
New York Blues   959-1488
New Yorkers, The   1141-1142
New York Glide, The   1648
Niagara Falls   1742
Nice And Pretty   653
Nice Day In The Country, A   1374
Nice Work If You Can Get It   28-367-443-
    605-1512-1733
Nickel For A Pickle, A   1646
Nickel In The Slot   1000
Nickel Nabber Blues   1752
Nickel Serenade, The   186

Nickel's Worth Of Liver Blues   834
Nickel To My Name, A   1361
Night   1162
Night After Night   693
Night After Night After You   96
Night And Day   3-8-97-442-612-769-1261-
    1400-1512-1553-1749
Night And Day Blues   354
Nightfall   281-875-1433
Night Glow   95-448
Night Hawk Blues   338
Night Hop   284
Nightingale Rag Blues   762
Nightingale Sang In Berkeley Square, A
    910
Night In Harlem, A   472
Night In Manhattan   1019
Night In Sudan   447
Night Is Blue, The   828-1156
Night Is Filled With Music, The   787
Night Is Young, The   292-1689
Night Is Young And You're So Beautiful,
    The   879
Night Latch Key Blues   965
Night Life   727-1720
Nightmare, The (1926)   253-265-416-466-
    946-1131-1362-1563
Nightmare (1938)   1401-1403
Nightmare Blues   1008-1487
Night Must Fall   1358
Night Of Memories, A   188
Night Of Nights   98-744-912
Night On The Desert   1236
Night On The Shalimar   1540
Night Over Shanghai   1400
Night Owl   464
Night Ride   23-279-543-1147
Night Shades   322
Nights In The Woods   1421
Night Song   95-126-1712
Night Special   815
Nights When I'm Lonely   156
Night Time Blues   1267
Night Time In Cairo   279-1434
Night-Time In Little Italy   544-904
Night Watchman   743
Night We Called It A Day, The   453-1513
Night We Met, The   289
Night We Met In Honomu, The   326
Night When Love Was Born, The   198
Night Whispers   897
Night Will Be Filled With Music   697
Night Wind   595-866-1625-1626
Nile Of Genago   844
Nina   1742
Nine Little Miles From Ten-Ten-Tennessee
    84-483
Nine O'Clock Sal   916-1067-1663
Nine Old Men   452
1915 Rag   127
1931 Depression Blues   1558
19th Street Blues   413
Nineteen Ways Of Playing A Chorus   948
9.20 Special   108
Ninety In The Shade   388
Ninety-Nine Out Of A Hundred Wanna Be
    Loved   592-1328-1384
Ninety-Nine Years Blues   1454
Nitwit Serenade   594-1659
Nix On Those Lush Heads   91
Noah's Ark   1347

Noah's Blues  270
No Answer  902
No Blues  At All  897
Nobody  616-685
Nobody But My Baby Is Getting My Love
  179-707-1534-1580-1701-1714
Nobody But You  503-1301-1418-1569
Nobody Cares  755
Nobody Cares If I'm Blue  672
Nobody Else Will Do  709
Nobody In Mind  1575
Nobody In Town Can Bake A Sweet Jelly-
  Roll Like Mine  1011-1439
Nobody Knows And Nobody Cares Blues  1013
Nobody Knows (And Nobody Seems To Care)
  106-1142
Nobody Knows (Blues)  396-1069
Nobody Knows How I Feel  849
Nobody Knows How Much I Love You  1273
Nobody Knows The Trouble I've Seen (or
  ..DE TROUBLE I SEE)  56-81-188-316-325-
  629-818-1541
Nobody Knows The Way I Feel Dis Mornin'
  (sic) (or NOBODY KNOWS HOW I FEEL..)
  114-734-794-845-1093-1449-1453-1671
Nobody Knows What A Red-Head Mama Can Do
  229-667-882-1029-1067-1171-1191-1364-
  1453-1502-1523-1591
Nobody Knows You When You're Down And Out
  1445
Nobody Lied (When They Said That I Cried
  Over You)  69-220-675-856-1606
Nobody Loves No Baby Like My Baby Loves
  Me  1386
Nobody Rocks Me Like My Baby Do  343
Nobody Rolls Their Jelly Roll Like Mine
  1037
Nobody's Baby Is Somebody's Baby Now 1668
Nobody's Blues But Mine  845-1442
Nobody's Blues But My Own  1670
Nobody's Business  573-1380
Nobody's Business (How I Love That Man)
  99
Nobody's Child  1582
Nobody's Fault But Your Own  1213-1336
Nobody's Gonna Take You From Me  1237
Nobody's Got The Blues But Me  525
Nobody Shows What My Baby Shows  1060
Nobody's Lonesome But Me  567
Nobody's Rose  719-777-963-1192
Nobody's Sweetheart (Now)  2-7-85-142-163
  172-177-252-335-345-347-385-470-471-506
  539-581-598-609-777-780-785-792-916-925
  937-938-976-1021-1032-1033-1139-1163-
  1184-1222-1228-1272-1298-1368-1428-1432
  1485-1570-1646-1687-1689
Nobody's Using It Now  953
Nobody Worries 'Bout Me  811
No Calling Card  999
No 'Count Blues  1121
No 'Count Woman  1673
Nocturne (Chopin)  25-292-635-791-896-
  1283-1360-1408
No Easy Rider Blues  1218
Noël Blues  307
Noël Brings The Swing  636
No Foolin'  233
No Good Man (Blues)  1455-1467
No Good Town Blues  846
No Greater Love - see THERE IS NO GREATER
  LOVE

No Home Blues  1338
Noir Bleu  135
No Jug, No Jazz  505
Nola  156-441-664-859
Nolan Welsh's Blues  1671
No Lovers Allowed  1133
No, Mama, No  589
No Man's Mama  573-707-927-1181-1650
No Matter Where You Are (When Evening
  Draws Her Curtain)  1204
No More  1391
No Mo' Bench And Board  778
No More Blues  891-1476
No More Jelly Bean Blues  1487
No More Love  1601
No More Tears  311-1399
No More Worryin'  630-1681-1739
Nona  693
No Name Blues  749-750
No Name Jive  96-387-909
No Name Rag  1342
None But The Lonely Heart  453
No Need Knockin' On The Blind  824
Noni  1491
Non, non, jamais les hommes  1085
No, No, Nora  71-223-775-866
No Nothing  528
Non-Skid Tread  754
No Need Knockin' On The Blind  824
Nonsense  1323
Non-Stop Flight  1402-1403
Noodlin'  1377-1468
No-One  73-128-1392-1591-1746
No-One But Betty Brown  806
No-One But You Knows How To Love  1520
No-One Can Take Your Place  1569
No-One Can Toddle Like My Cousin Sue  623
No-One Else But You  44
No-One Is To Blame  763
No-One Knows What It's All About  115-667
  796-1191-1212-1591
No-One Loves Me Like That Dallas Man  200
  1278
No-One Loves You Better Than Your M-A-
  Double M-Y  1353-1608
No-One To Call You Dear (Ain't It Tough)
  1413
No-One To Say Goodbye  1640
No-One Will Know It But Me  1377
No Other Love (Was Meant For Me)  1666
No Other One  66-365-382-597-1307
No, Papa, No  44-1488
No Parking  351-1330
No Pay Blues  764
No Reason At All  9
No Regrets  439-518-702-767-938-939-1002-
  1398
No Retard - see CHINA BOY (p. 1572)
Norfolk Ferry  342-693
Normandy  1583
Normangee Blues  8
North Bound Blues  860
North Of The Mohawk Trail  260
North Wind Blues  570-1065
No Second-Handed Lovin' For Mine  1717
No Second-Hand Woman  1677
No Smoking  310-311
No Soap (A Jitterbug Jamboree)  692
No Sooner Blues  1453
Nostalgia  616
No Star Is Lost  8

1938

No Strings  426-701-1270
Not A Care In The World  621-1361
Not A Cloud In The Sky  858
Not Enough  1307
Not For All The Rice In China  290-1270
Not For Sale  698
Not Here – Not There  71
Nothin'  186-818-1192-1323-1416
Nothing  1602
Nothin(g)/Nuthin' But  559-914-1095-1123-
  1353-1680
Nothing But Blues  565-1554
Nothing But Love  1504
Nothing But Notes  1602
Nothin' But Rhythm  828
Nothin' But The Blues  565
Nothin' But You  317
Nothing Can Stop Me Now  545
Nothing Could Be Sweeter  1610
Nothin' Does Does Like It Used To Do-Do-Do
  238-626-1276
Nothin' Doin'  696-963
Nothing Else To Do (But Sit Around And
  Think About You)  576
Nothing Has Changed  1426
Nothing Is Sweeter Than You  157
Nothing Lives Longer Than Love  700
Nothin' On My Mind (But The Moonlight, The
  Starlight And You)  1665
Nothing's Blue But The Sky  14-879
Nothing's Too Good For You  1249
Nothin' To Do (And All Day To Do It In)
  215
Nothing To Lose  356
Nothin' To Do But Love  1470
Not Maybe  1390
Not Mine  435-621-1409
Not Now, Not Yet, But Soon  529
Not On The First Night, Baby  1572
Notoriety Rag  1587
Not So Long Ago  298-451
Not So Quiet, Please  453
Not That I Care  593
Not There – Right There  1634
Not Today, Sweet Mama  213
No Trumps  553
Not Until Then  213
No Use Crying  220-1523
No Use Squawkin'  693
No Use You Knockin'  780
Novel Pets  1642
Novelty Blues  862
Now And Forever  1361
Now And Then  748-1085-1250
Now Cut Loose  1718
Now George !  377
Nowhere  97
Now I Know  380-664
Now I Know (I Love You)  673
Now I Lay Me Down To Dream  272-901-1374-
  1540
Now I'm A Lady  700
Now It Can Be Told  79-444-1159-1722-1734
Now I Won't Be Blue  567
Now Let Me Tell You  1105
No Wonder  206-1315
No Wonder (I Love You)  73 264-566
No Wonder I'm Blue  1131-1351
No Wonder I'm Happy  1056
No Wonder I'm Lonesome  69
No Words-Nor Anything  1340

Now Or Never  1027-1236
Now's The Time To Fall In Love  805-874-
  214-1387
Now That I Need You  1112
Now That I Need You, You're Gone  1599
Now That I've Found You  1210
Now That Summer Is Gone  739-1157
Now That You're Mine  663
Now That You've Gone  1528
Now They Call It Swing  587-768-1249
Now We Know  1406
Now Will You Be Good ?  103
Now You Know  96-432
Now You're In My Arms  981-1384
Now You're Talking My Language  131
Now You've Got Him, Can You Hold Him ?
  706
Now You've Got Me Doing It  249-437-701
Nuages  1262-1284
Nuances By Norvo  1159
Number 19  760
Number Runner's Blues  628
Numbers Blues, The  1413
Numbers Man, The  1469
Numbers On The Brain  811-835-1014
Number Ten  1715
No. 12, Let Me Roam  1487
No. 29  1621
Number Two Blues  396
Numb Fumblin'  1623
Nutcracker Suite (Tchaikovsky) :
  Arab Dance; Dance of the Candy Fairies
  Dance of the Flowers  325
Nut House Stomp  892
Nutty Nursery Rhymes  295
Nympheas  1284

Object Of My Affection, The  151-159-201
  292-317-661
Ocean Motion  518
Ocean Wide  1751
Ochi Chornya  1004 (see also DARK EYES)
Octave Jump, The  306
Octavia Blues  1414
Octoroon  1405-1538
Ode To Spring  1243
O'er The Billowy Sea  978
Of All The Wrongs You Done To Me  1279-
  1699
Off Again, On Again  787
Off Again, On Again Blues  1672
Off And Gone  869-1348
Off And On  298
Off And On Blues  277-1618
Off The Record  306
Off Time  1152-1377
Off Time Blues  757
Off To Buffalo  268-720-721-1192
Of Thee I Sing  34-1250
Ogeechee River Lullaby  262
Ogoun Badagris  95
Oh, Ain't It Grand To Be In The Navy ?
  1435
Oh Ambulance Man  1043
Oh Babe, Has Your Money Come ?  680
Oh Babe ! Maybe Someday  490-493-497-
  1562
Oh Babe, Oh Baby  1528
Oh ! Baby  334-723-956-1413-1584-1614
Oh ! Baby (Don't Say "No," Say "Maybe")
  17-72-332-542-925-1022-1190-1641-1741

Oh, Baby ! Don't We Get Along ?  463-631
Oh Baby, Sweet Baby (What Are You Doing
  To Me ?)  1637
Oh Boy !  985-1352
Oh Boy ! I'm In The Groove  730-865
Oh Boy ! It's A Pleasure  883-1076
Oh Boy ! What A Girl  544-629-857-1097-
  1181-1425
Oh ! Buddy, I'm In Love  590
Oh ! By Jingo !  879-969-1556-1748
Oh Daddy (Blues)  413-632-633-749-763-
  1439-1533-1648-1698
Oh ! Daisy  1135
Oh ! Dark Gal  1717
Oh ! Darling, Do Say Yes !  828
Oh Dear ! What Can The Matter Be ?  969-
  1082-1308
Oh De Kate's Up De River, Stackerlee's In
  De Ben' (sic)  666
Oh, Dem Golden Slippers  1635
Oh, Didn't He Ramble !  1107-1257
Oh, Didn't It Rain  163
Oh Doctor  1206
Oh ! Donna Clara  1295
Oh, Doris ! Where Do You Live ?  799-1580
  1612
Oh ! Eddie  1111
Oh ! Eva (Ain't Ya/You Comin' Out Tonight)
  522-714-1364
Oh ! Faithless Maid  29
Oh ! Frenchy  1516-1635
Oh Gee, Georgie !  560
Oh ! Gee, Jenny, It's You  892
Oh Gee ! Oh Gosh !  1085
Oh Gee, Oh Gosh, Oh Golly, I'm In Love  70
Oh Gee ! Oh Joy !  1264
Oh, Gee ! Say, Gee ! You Ought To See My
  Gee-Gee From The Fiji Isle  1351
Oh ! How I Adore You  246
Oh ! How I Cried The Morning After (The
  Night Before With You)  684
Oh ! How I Hate To Get Up In The Morning
  208-444-1317-1375
Oh ! How I Love Bulgarians  16-268
Oh ! How I Love My Darling  20-67-624-640
  808-890
Oh ! How I Miss You Tonight  1315
Oh, How I've Waited For You  962
Oh ! How She Can Love  963
Oh ! How She Can Sing  1265
Oh, How She Could Yacki Hacki Wicki Wacki
  Woo  315
Oh ! I Didn't Know (You'd Get That Way)
  517
Oh ! If I Only Had You  61-1579-1664
Oh, I'm Evil  9-273
Ohio Breakaway  417
Oh ! It Looks Like Rain  146-725
Oh ! Joe  1590
Oh Joe, Play That Trombone  1649
Oh, Joe (Please Don't Go)  1461
Oh Joe, With Your Fiddle And Bow  976
Oh, Johnny ! Oh, Johnny ! Oh !  30-528-
  904-1316
Oh, Johnny ! Please Don't - Mom-Ma !  1122
Oh/ O Katharina  229-264-1524-1742
Oh ! Lady, Be Good - see LADY, BE GOOD
Oh, Lawdy  975
Oh Lawdy Mama  1246
Oh ! Leo (It's Love)  700
Oh Lizzie  413-721-1580-1619

Oh ! Look At Me Now  451-618-742
Oh Look At That Baby  659
Oh ! Lovey, Be Mine  462
Oh ! Mabel  72-229-624-1524 1591-1641
Oh ! Maggie  1336
Oh Malinda  1500-1722
Oh ! Ma-Ma !  29-587-1315
Oh Maria  1414
Oh Marie !  184
Oh Maud  1213
Oh Me ! Oh My !  963-1085-1130
Oh ! Me Oh ! My Blues  994
Oh ! Min  71
Oh Miss Hannah !  1019-1687-1721
Oh ! Miss Jaxson  99
Oh ! Mr. Johnson  1197
Oh ! Mister Mitchell  1452
Oh Mistress Mine  370
Oh Mo'nah! 581-590-687-874-1297-1410-1494
  1668
Oh ! Muki Muki Oh !  937
Oh My Babe Blues  1267
Oh ! My Goodness  879
Oh ! My Operation  533
Oh Papa Blues  1268
Oh ! Pardon Me  1319
Oh Peter (You're So Nice)  19-88-174-583-
  796-926-1145-1483-1694
Oh, Promise Me  443
Oh ! Red  678-1123-1246-1496
Oh ! Red No. 2  1496
Oh Rider  783
Oh, Say ! Can I See You Tonight ?  231-
  1592
Oh, Say ! Can You Swing ?  1002
Oh, Sing-a-Loo  1005
Oh ! Sister, Ain't That Hot ?  336-418-
  712-1151-1180-1188-1212-1326-1479-1673
Oh ! So Pretty  1375
Oh ! Star Of Eve  1614
Oh Susannah !  590-1635
Oh Susannah ! Dust Off That Old Pianna
  100-1133-1625
Oh That Nasty Man  1019
Oh ! That Sweet In Suite 16  406-418-667
  119-1364-1380-1478-1515
Oh, The Pity Of It All  299
Oh ! They're Making Me All Over In The
  Army  910-1317
Oh, They're Tough, Mighty Tough, In The
  West  586
Oh ! Those Eyes  230-1746
Oh, Wasn't It Nice ?  436
Oh ! What A Lovely Dream  10
Oh ! What A Night For Love  800
Oh ! What A Pal Was Mary  205-1603
Oh ! What A Silly Place To Kiss A Girl
  800-1294
Oh ! What A Thrill (To Hear It From You)
  34-1645
Oh Why, Oh Why  988
Oh Yeah !  213-1223
Oh Yes My Darling  1528
Oh, You Beautiful Doll  1343
Oh ! You Crazy Moon  206-371-416-447
O You Drummer (sic)  1179
Oh ! You Have No Idea  340-1016-1148-1291
  1479-1685
Oh ! You La ! La !  1516
Oh ! You Little Bear  1603
Oh ! You Little Sun-uv-er-gun  71

1940

Oh, You Lulu Belle  1504
Oh ! You Rogue (You Stole My Heart)  1240
Oh ! You Sweet Thing  89-403-699-758-1646
Oil Gusher  1373
Oil Well  1104
Oil Yo' Ankles  830
Oiseaux des Iles  1262
Okay, Baby  404-785-898-1034-1295
Okay/O.K. For Baby  284-989
Okay, Toots  424-879-1211
Okey-Doke  1427
Oklahoma Indian Jazz  1615
Oklahoma Stomp  1431
Old And New  190
Old Apple Tree, The  206-295-1402
Old Ark Is Moverin', The  1427
Old Black Joe  445-908-1401
Old Black Joe's Blues  712-714-723
Old Black Mary  1573
Old Blues, The  1554
Old Broke-Up Shoes  357
Old Chord's Stomp  694
Old Clo' Man Rag - see JUNK MAN RAG
Old Commandment Blues  1720
Ole Crow Blues (sic)  1389
Old Curiosity Shop, An  446-907
Old Doc Yak  165
Old Dog Tray  184
Oldest Swinger In Harlem, The  385
Old-Fashioned Girl  219-703
Old-Fashioned Love  19-347-560-564-611-
642-697-782-794-828-839-876-1052-1156-
1333-1424-1533-1630-1648-1720
Old-Fashioned Love Game  308 (same as
above ?)
Old-Fashioned Sara Blues  1013
Old-Fashioned Swing  153-739
Old-Fashioned Tune Is Always New, An  431
Old Flame Never Dies, An  442-1028-1552-
1721
Old Folks  79-322-363
Old Folks At Home, The  54-324
Old Folks Hunch, The  1451
Old Folks Rag  1587
Old Folks Shake  891
Old Folks Shuffle  146-864-993-1524-1701
Old Forsaken Blues  412
Old Glory Goes Marching On  379
Old Grandad  1635-1636
Old Grey Mare, The  549
Old Grey Mare Blues  1748
Old Italian Love Song, An  580
Old Joe Blade  1179
Old Joe Blues  1522-1747
Old Joe's Hittin' The Jug  1465
Old Kent Road, The  969
Old King Cole  536-695
Old King Dooji  494-495
Old King Tut  560
Old Kitchen Kettle, The  1410-1668
Old MacDonald Had A Farm  1347
Ole Mammy Ain't Gonna Sing No More  1235
Old Man Ben  1203
Old Man Blues  114-137-482-483-996-1218-
1647
Old Man('s) Charleston  1326-1555
Old Man Harlem  276-422-1476-1654
Old Man Jazz  772
Old Man Moon  880
Old Man Mose  52-583-848-1001  )1410-1670
Old Man Of The Mountain, The  255-539-698-

Old Man Rhythm  1208
Ol' Man River  15-116-169-290-300-382-469
583-658-730-817-960-961-1109-1264-1346-
1426-1501-1613-1683-1712
Old Man Sunshine (Little Boy Bluebird)
143-399-525-563-1016
Old Mill Blues  516
Ole Miss Blues  666-1649
Ole Miss (Rag)  665-1194
Old Mother Hubbard  148
Old Music Master, The  1691
Old New Orleans Blues  811
Old Oaken Bucket, The  1307-1562-1635
Old, Old Castle In Scotland  910-1407
Old Organ Blues  1674
Ol' Pappy  593-1331-1538
Old Plantation (The)  27-1630
Old Playmate  958
Old Plunk's New Coon Medley  1199
Old Quaker Blues  1746
Old Ssddle For Sale, An  1415
Old Sammies March  379
Ol' Sam Tages  1452
Old Spinning Wheel  366
Old Stamping Ground,(The)  1402-1403-1468
Old Steady Roll  863
Old Straw Hat, An  124
Old Street Sweeper  1708
Old Time Blues  1460-1724
Old Time Religion  1710
Old Town Pump, The  665
Old Virginia Blues  1675
Old White's Whiskers  1146
Old Yazoo  158-254-1072-1646
Olga  1170
Olius Brown  666
Oliver Twist, The  982-1367
Omaha Blues  1389-1577
On A Blues Kick  394
On Accounta I Love You  423
On A Cocoanut Island  53-122
On A Holiday  93
On A Little Balcony In Spain  391
On A Little Bamboo Bridge  54-440-1088
On A Little Dream Ranch  205-1313
On A Little Street In Singapore  432-815-
896-1752
On A Night Like This  73
On A Night Made For Love  248-249
On A Simmery Summery Day  1317
On A Sunday Afternoon  426
On Behalf Of The Visiting Firemen  10
Once Aboard The Lugger  1297
Once And For All  434
Once I Did  285
Once In A Blue Moon (1921)  748
Once In A Blue Moon (1927)  468-1290
Once In A Lifetime  240-840
Once In A Lovetime  166-433
Once In A While  42-54-318-442
Once Is Enough For Me  526
Once More  615
Once Or Twice  327-328-898
Once Over Lightly  1222
Once Upon A Midnight  293
Once Upon A Time  312
On Decoration Day (They'll Know Where To
Bring Your Flowers To)  343
One Alone  896-897-1611
One And Two Blues  1443
One Big Union For Two  258

On Echo Hill 436
One Cigarette For Two 704
One Dozen Roses 299-763-819-1319
One Foot In The Groove 1405
One For All-All For One 1319
One From Eight Leaves Seven 1390
One Girl, The 979
One Hamburger For Madame 1415
Our Hour 1113
One Hour For Lunch 893
One Hour Mama 355-1489
One Hour Of Love 1421
One Hour Tonight 1713
One Hour With You 248-1297
One I Love, The 443-880
One I Love Belongs To Somebody Else, The 72-225-337-450-528-787-1242-1326-1640
One I Love Just Can't Be Bothered With Me, The 21-195-672-772-979
One In A Million 123-1630
One In The World, The 671
One Kiss 244
One Last Kiss 274
One Little Kiss 937-1669
One Little Raindrop 504
One Little Word Led To Another 288-683
One Look At You 259-816
One Lost Pal 884
One Man Band, The 1384-1470-1667
One Man Nan 1649
One Minute To One 1601
One Moment More With You 502
One More Dream 906
One More Kiss 1551
One More Kiss, Then Goodnight 1409
One More Night 239-1136-1378
One More Time 59-142-515-853-958-1171-1385-1470-1644
One Morning In May 275-296
One Never Knows, Does One ? 767
One Night In Havana 274-275
One Night In June 535
One Night In Monte Carlo 365-438
One Night Stand 1405
One-Note Trumpet Player (The) 697-698
One O'Clock Baby 130-171-463-1056
One O'Clock Blues 1559-1574
One O'Clock Jump 102-103-104-107-109-113-279-589-607-608-814-1048-1661
One Of These Days 182-716-1191
One Of Us Was Wrong 287-1505-1668
One Rainy Afternoon 538
One Rose, The (That's Left In My Heart) 321-894-1415-1721
Onery Blues 1450
One Side Of Me 1661
One Sock Blues 1655
One Song 880-1402
One Step More 904
One Step To Heaven 887-1087-
One Stolen Kiss 808-1643
One Sweet Kiss 248
One Sweet Letter From You 304-418-432-613-662-668-1183-1192-1246-1551-1574-1652
One That I Love Loves Me, The 243-931
One Time Woman Blues 354
One, Two, Button Your Shoe 428-491-703-767-1399
One, Two, Three Little Hours 294
One-Two-Three-O'Lairy 108
One Umbrella For Two 437

One Week Ago 224
One Week From Now 530
One Woman Blues 1413
One Woman's Man 1038
Only A Rose 95-433-979
Only Forever 450-909
Only For You 502-1293
Only Girl I Ever Loved, The 1112
Only Mother Cares For Me 409
Only, Only One For Me, The 72-229-264
Only Thing I Want For Christmas, The (Is Just To Keep The Things I've Got) 1318
Only This Time I'll Be True 1097
Only When You're In My Arms 184-370-446
Only You And Lonely Me 266
On Patrol In No Man's Land 513
On Revival Day 145-341-781-854-1143-1153-1345-1446-1539
On Saturday Night 565
On Such A Night 225
On The Air 148
On The Alamo 192-220-333-383-452-617-699-787-1095-1140-1141-1142-1239-1570
On The Beach At Bali-Bali 14-122-162-439-938-939-986-1026-1313
On The Beach With You 736-1385
On The Beam 908
On The Bumpy Road To Love 1333-1397-1632-1734
On The 'Gin 'Gin 'Ginny Shore 68-1523-1749
On The Good Ship Lollipop 1000
On The Isle Of Kitchymiboko 585-1433
On The Isle Of May 741
On The Jersey Side 1374
On The Lazy Amazon 1426
On The Merry-Go-Round 100
On The Night Of June The Third - see WHERE WERE YOU ON THE NIGHT OF JUNE THE THIRD ?
On The Night We Did The Boom Boom By The Sea 654
On The Oregon Trail 230
On The Outside Looking In 1436
On The Parkway 841
On The Puppy's Tail 564-1220
On The Riviera 1583
On The Road Again 1042
On The Road To Mandalay 8-391-921-1358
On The Road To Samarkand 923
On The Sentimental Side 55-429-768-880
On The Shore At Le-Lei-Wi 315
On The Street Of Regret 1319
On The Streets Of Cairo 380-748
On The Sunny Side Of The Street 7-52-54-56-131-286-329-557-537-621-660-676-688-761-821-1279-1294-1476-1658-1708
On The Trail 432-433-977
On The Vagabond Trail 1593
On The Verge 788
On The Wings Of Love 1582
On The Wrong Side Of The Fence 1331
On The Z.R.3 828
On Treasure Island 13-52-203-365-437-701-1114-1731
On With Charlie 1046
On With The Dance 59-894-1233
On Your Toes 122-960-1239
Onyx Bringdown 1511
Onyx Club Spree/Stomp 1465
Onyx Hop 134

1942

Onz heures vingt  333
Ooch Ooch A Goon Attach  744
Oodles Of Noodles  427
Oogie Oogie Wa-Wa  119-1036-1614
Ooh ! Look-a There, Ain't She Pretty ?
  366-1628-1708
Ooh ! That Kiss  422
Ooh-Wee Babe  679
Ooh ! What You Said  372-1047
Oole-De-Ooo  171
OoooOH Boom !  29-608-881-1179-1308
Open House  663
Open Up The Golden Gates To Dixie  975
Open Your Arms, My Alabammy  70
Open Your Heart  1533
Operatic Medley  226
Operatic Rag  1109
Operator Special  646
Opus 5  896
Opus ½  610
Opus Local 802  614
Opus No. 1 Sans Melody  812
Opus Three-Quarters  611
Orange Blossom Lane  1553
Orange Blossom Rag  975
Orange Blossoms  1473
Orange Blossom Time  503-949-961
Orange Grove In California, An  224
Orchids For Remembrance  166-816-909
Organ Grinder Blues  764-1488-1652-1703-
  1708-1709
Organ Grinder's Swing  24-87-526-545-599-
  638-702-785-893-960-985-1344-1433-1642
Or Have I ?  167-902
Oriental  1131
Oriental Blues  1423
Oriental Illusions  918
Oriental Love Dreams  72-338
Oriental Man  150-308-410-1494
Oriental Medley  85
Oriental Moon  797
Oriental Nocturne  1095
Oriental Shuffle  1259
Oriental Strut  40
Oriental Swing  40
Original Black Bottom Dance  165-562-811-
  1615
Original Blues  1010-1675
Original Bugle Blues - see BUGLE BLUES
Original Charleston, The - see CHARLESTON
Original Charleston Strut  330-1096-1239-
  1533
Original Chinese Blues - see CHINESE BLUES
Original Dixieland One-Step  32-375-689-
  762-897-972-1036-1087-1092-1133-1140-
  1175-1179-1410
Original Haitian Music  650
Original Jelly-Roll Blues - see JELLY-ROLL
  BLUES
Original Mr. Freddie Blues - see MR.
  FREDDIE BLUES
Original Rags  1107
Original St. Louis Hop, The  921
Original Stack O'Lee Blues - see STACK
  O'LEE BLUES
Original Stomps  892-1595
Original Tuxedo Rag  301
Original Two-Time Man  349
Oriole, The  1588 (also known as RAGTIME
  ORIOLE)
Oriole Blues  1347

Or Leave Me Alone  39
Orn'ry Blues  1014
Orphan Blues  978
Ory's Creole Trombone  42-1485
Osceola Blues  154
'O sole mio  166-1147-1552
Ostrich Walk  1133-1136-1176-1177-1179-
  1566
Oui, c'est ca  1338
Oui, Oui, Marie  1375
Ou, quand, comment  1639
Our Big Love Scene  200-1278
Our Bungalow Of Dreams  1567
Our Child  995
Our Love  431-446-1147
Our Love Affair  298-450
Our Love Is Different  769
Our Love Was Meant To Be  102-441-894-
  1631
Our Monday Date - see MONDAY DATE, A
Our Penthouse On Third Avenue  441-880
Out Bound Train Blues  101
Outdoors Blues  1413
Out For No Good  937-1508
Out In The Cold Again  201-291-424
Out Of A Dream  1073-1075
Out Of Doors Blues  1025
Out Of A Million You're The Only One 796
Out Of Breath (And Scared To Death Of
  You)  1599
Out Of My Dreams  467
Out Of Nowhere  186-465-526-635-690-814-
  1405-1412-1736
Out Of Sight, Out Of Mind  701-1551
Out Of Space  291-297-558
Out Of The Dawn  31-240-269-419-502-1213
Out Of The Night  184-1669
Out O' Town Gal  1686
Out (Of) The Window  102
Outside  241-553-1394
Outside Man Blues  1069
Outside Of Paradise  124
Outside Of That (He's All Right With Me)
  136-1037-1439
Outside Of That, I Love You  1242.
Outsider Blues  1376
Out To Lunch  775
Out Where The Blues Begin  977-1077
Overhand  1720
Overheard In A Cocktail Lounge  94
Over In The Glory Land  1096
Overnight  183-286-592-1295-1552
Overnight Blues  782
Overnight Hop  1148-1411
Over The Hills To Virginia  328
Over The Rainbow  323-371
Over The Week-End  981
Over There  376
Over The Waves  373
Overture Begins At Forte  805
Overture To Love, An  435
Owls' Hoot, The  1130
Owl Strut  1194
Ox Meat Blues  1338
Ozark Blues  1715
Ozark Mountain Blues  1084


Paahana  4
Paauau  4
Pacific Coast Blues  1185-1649
Packing House Blues  570

Packing Up To Say "Hello"  1295
Pack Up Your Sins And Go To The Devil
  1661
Pack Up Your Troubles In Your Old Kit Bag
  And Smile, Smile, Smile  376
Paddle-Addle In Your Little Canoe  378
Paddlin' Madelin' Home  799-804-884-1134
Paducah  311-478
Pagan Fantasy  1604
Pagan Love Song  29-366-536-586-950-1118
Pagan Paradise  1277
Pagan Star  436
Page Paderewski  1671
Page Your Puppies  1550
Pagin' The Devil  873
Pail In My Hand  1739
Painting The Clouds With Sunshine  21-244
  516-580-641-1293
Pair Of Dimples And A Picture Hat, A  4
Palais de Danse  1224
Paleface  740
Pale Moon  314-364-453
Palesteena  368-1177
Pallet On The Floor - see MAKE ME A PALLET
  ON THE FLOOR
Palm Beach  536
Palm Beach Rag  1588
Palms Of Paradise  816
Palm Springs Jump  551
Paloma, La  817-1106
Pal O' Mine  156
Pal Of My Lonesome Hours  657
Pamplona  1286
Panama (Rag)  67-291-367-396-444-657-666-
  719-1002-1029-1037-1065-1105-1107-1131-
  1133-1139-1197-1200-1287-1346-1495
Panama Blues  245
Panama Limited Blues  136-178-753-1679
Panama Pacific Drag  1109
Pan-American Hot-Spot  1375
Panassie Stomp  104-333
Pane In The Glass, A  1704-1705
Pango Pango Maid  797-1740-1745
Panhandle Pete  1668
Panic Is On, The  161-1052-1628
Pan-Pan  865-1637
Panther Rag  757
Pantin' In The Panther Room  1636
Papa Ain't No Santa Claus (Mama Ain't No
  Christmas Tree)  214
Papa, Better Watch Your Step  645-916-
  1187-1520
Papa Blues  837-916-1187-1671
Papa De-Da-Da  75-137-178-965-1082-1171-
  1306-1350-1699-1707
Papa Dip  1133
Papa, Don't Ask Mama Where She Was  1051
Papa, Don't Hold Back On Me  213
Papa, Don't You Mean Your Mama No Good ?
  1716
Papa, I Don't Need You Now  1452
Papa, If You Can't Do Better (I'll Let A
  Better Man Move In)  343-735-1024
Papa Long Blues  1042
Papa, Mama's All Alone  845
Papa, Papa (Blues)  706-1012
Papa Pleaser  1679
Papa's Gone  553
Papa's Gone Bye-Bye Blues  275
Papa's Got The Jim-Jams  302
Papa's Got Your Bath Water On  1043

Papa's In Bed With His Britches On  260-
  272-1560
Papa Skag Stomp  1281
Papa's Mama's Blue ('Cause Mama's Papa's
  Through)  813
Papa Tree Top Tall  182-702-893-1508
Papa Will Be Gone  732-1550
Paper Picker, The  1358
Papoose  184
Parade Of The Milk Bottle Caps  428
Parade Of The Pennies, The  1147
Parade Of The Stompers  944
Parade Of The Wooden Soldiers  221-323-
  1359
Paradiddle  260
Paradiddle Joe  215
Paradise  151-471-919-1017-1288-1553
Paradise Wobble  833
Paralleles  536
Parallel Fifths  1135
Paramount Stomp  1260
Paramour  294
Parasol  377
Parceque je vous aime  396
Par correspondance  1349
Pardon, Madame  1477
Pardon Me  523
Pardon Me, Pretty Baby  283-592-638-1296-
  1303-1599-1602
Pardon Mt Love  595-779-1625
Pardon My Southern Accent  1-13-291-1689
Pardon The Glove  236-631-799-963-993-
  1559-1612
Paree  467
Parfum  1283
Park Avenue Fantasy  997
Parkin' In The Moonlight  60-421
Park Lane Strut  1434
Park No More Mama Blues  745
Parkway Stomp  1744
Parlor Social De Luxe  1250-1618
Parlor Social Stomp  472-1274
Parson Blues  1280
Parson Jones, You Ain't Livin' Right  398
Partner, It's The Parting Of The Ways  100
Paseo Strut  941
Pa's Old Hat  813
Passin' It Around  691
Passing Of Ragtime, The  1474
Passionette  442-755-1468
Passion Flower  766
Pass Out Lightly  1110
Pass The Bounce  912
Pass The Jug  1040
Pastafazoola  1580
Past And Future Blues  1321
Pastel Blue  895-1404
Pastorale  791
Pas sur la bouche  1349
Paswonky  1629
Patches  972-1603
Patent Leather Stomp  1586
Patricia Mine/My Own  961
Patrol Wagon Blues  12-848
Patty Cake, Patty Cake (Baker's Man)  126
  589-1435-1633
Pavanne  923-989-1334
Pawn Broker Blues  1674
Pawn Shop Blues, The  343
Pay Day Blues  70-1414
Pay Day Daddy Blues  1321

1944

Pay Me No Mind  1398
Pay-Off, The  239-683-1581
P. B. Flat Blues  188
P. D. Q. Blues  722-1097-1500-1701
Peace And Love For All  990
Peace, Brother !  614-741
Peace, Brother, Peace  1344-1468
Peaceful Henry  460-1199
Peaceful Valley  97-232-718-719
Peace Of Mind  951
Peace On You  1468
Peaches In The Springtime  1042
Peach Of A Pair, A  1302
Peachtree Man Blues  1213
Peach Tree Strut  741-747-1752
Peanut Cackle  738
Peanut Vendor, The  48-248-384-484-582-897
  1144-1373
Peanut Vendor Boogie, The  897
Pearls, The  1099-1101-1102-1106-1411-1720
Pebble Blues  1216
Peck-A-Doodle-Do  258
Peckin'  258-362-586-601-603-765-1124-1236
Peckin' With The Penguins  446
Peculiar  188
Peddlin' Man  180
Peekin' At The Deacon  788
Pee Gee Blues  1518
Peelin' The Peach  183-1690
Peepin' At The Risin' Sun (Blues)  847-
  1065
Peepin' Blues  65
Peepin' Jim (Blues)  782-1739
Peepin' Through The Keyhole  1541
Peer Gynt (Grieg) :
  Anitra's Dance  895-918
  In The Hall Of The Mountain King  168-
  1360
Pee Wee Blues  1718
Pee Wee, Pee Wee  1413
Peggy (1919)  972
Peggy (1929)  1034
Peggy Dear  535
Peg Leg Shuffle  904
Peg Leg Stomp  887
Peg O' My Heart  126-704-1063-1143-1539
Pelican Drag  135
Pelican Stomp  180
Pell Street Blues  1272
Penalty £5  311
Penalty Of Love, The  980-1061
Pencil Papa  415
Pencil Papa Blues  154
Penetrating Blues, The  343
Penewell Blues  1217
Penguin, The  25-1372
Penitentiary  1572
Penn Beach Blues  1596
Pennies From Heaven  53-101-428-465-536-
  585-894-1249-1693-1732
Pennsylvania Polka  417
Pennsylvania 6-5000  387-1225
Penny For Your Thoughts, A  1269
Penny Serenade  588-1316
Penny Wise And Pound Foolish  781
Pensacola  719-777-1181-1182
Pensacola Blues  1466-1589-1725
Pensacola Joe  1245
Penthouse In The Basement  864
Penthouse Serenade  370
Pent Up In A Penthouse  1632

People Say I'm Crazy  880
Pep (1926)  395
Pep (1929)  1103-1106
Pepper Blues  1578
Pepperism  1557
Pepper Pot  358
Pepper Steak  6-1645
Percolatin' Blues  539-1450
Percy, Have Mercy  1250
Perdido  499
Perdido Street Blues  58-1133
Perfect  922
Perfect Rag  1100
Perfect Song, The  979
Perfidia  433-452-618-909
Perisphere Shuffle  184
Persian Lamb Rag  1200-1752
Persian Rug  239-416-413-978-1538
Personally, I Love You  1384-1617
Peruna  320-371-1119
Pessimistic Character With The Crab-Apple
  Face, The  297
Pesticatin' Mama  60
Peter And Paul  873
Peter And The Wolf  622
Peter Gink  60
Peter Pan  796
Peter Piper  366-599-1157
Peter Stomp  16
Peter Tambourine  1372-1373
Pete's Blues (Nos. 1 and 2)  850
Pete's Mixture  851
Pete, The Dealer In Meat  413
Petite  1374
Petite Ile, La  1349
Petite Lili  16
Petit homme, c'est l'heure de faire do-
  do  - see LITTLE MAN, YOU'VE HAD A BUSY
  DAY
Petits mensonges  1262
Petter's Stomp, The  694
Pettin' In The Park  878-1241
Peu d'amour, Un - see LITTLE LOVE, A
  LITTLE KISS, A
Phantom Blues  269-524-631-1715
Phantom Fantasie  727-1095
Phantom Rhapsody  1601
Pharaoh Land  220
Philadelphia  646
Philadelphia Cut-Out  942
Philippe Brun's E flat Blues  189
Phillips Street Stomp  1125
Phil The Fluter's Ball  969
Phoebe Snow  1068
Phonograph Blues  1280
Phyllysse  97
Piano Boogie  418
Piano Breakdown  1040
Pianoflage  90-923-1004-1369
Pianology  759
Piano Man  760
Piano Man Rag  153
Piano Puzzle  1369
Piano Rag  1656
Piano Rhythm  1411
Piano Stomp - see SHINE
Pianotes  1206
Pianotrope  468
Piano Tuner Man  124
Piccadilly  1131
Piccadilly Strut, The  568

Piccolino, The  23-701
Piccolo Blues  391
Piccolo Pete  6-21-520-574-655-952-1301-
1666-1721
Pick And Slap  790
Pickaninnies' Paradise, The  1062-1063-
1375
Pickaninny Blues  1650
Pickaninny Dolls  805
Pickaninny Shoes  1425
Pick-a-Rib  208-611-612-741-761
Pickin' Cotton  649-831-1565-1597-1686
Pickin' 'Em Up And Layin' 'Em Down  121-
1085
Pickin' For Patsy  1538
Pickin' My Way  922
Pickin' On Your Baby  529-561-1699
Pickin' The Cabbage  260
Picking The Guitar  982
Pickles  70-1187
Pickles And Peppers  1255
Pick Me Up And Lay Me Down In Dear Old
Dixieland  68-1573
Pick On Me Blues  1573
Pickpocket Blues  1444
Pick-Up, The  1336
Pick Up The Groove  417
Pick Your Own Lick  1351
Pick Yourself Up  428-584-598-1519
Picnic Time  1058
Picture Me Without You  14-182-701-1157
Picture Of Me Without You, A  427
Pictures On The Wall  1452
Pidgin English Hula  583
Pied Piper, The  125-1203
Pierre Of The Saskatchewan  1398
Pig Alley Stomp  548-1556
Pig Ankle Strut  270
Pigeons And Peppers  1711
Pigeon Walk  987
Pig Foot Blues  1021
Pig Foot Shuffle  538
Pig Foot Sonata  663
Piggly Wiggly (Blues)  112-1738
Pig In A Poke  387
Pig Meat Blues  169-1675-1677
Pig Meat Mama  570
Pig Meat Papa  570
Pig Meat Stomp  6
Pigs' Feet And Slaw  1209
Pile Of Logs And Stones (Called Home)  74-
1700
Pimple Blues  1541
Pinchbacks, Take 'Em Away  1440
Pinch Me  10-371-1752
Pine Creek  851
Pineland Blues  965
Pine Top Blues  27
Pinetop Breakaway  1117
Pinetop's Boogie Woogie-see BOOGIE WOOGIE
Piney Brown Blues  1575
Pining  1257
Pining For You  1364
Pink Elephants  876-1600
Pink Slip Blues  355
Pipe Dream Blues  1051-1057
Pippin  1289
Pippinella  1316
Pip-Pip, Too-Toot, Goodbye-ee  1097
Pirate Gold  1252
Pitchin' Boogie  516

Pitter Panther Patter  497
Pixie From Dixie, A  729
Pizen Tea Blues  1322
Place de Brouckere  1284
Plain Dirt  1034
Plain Jane  25-684-1224
Plain Lenox Avenue  783
Plain Old Blues  1463-1555
Plain Old Me  203-1248
Plantation Blues  318-570
Plantation Echoes  512
Plantation Joys  1345
Plantation Moods  1537-1571
Plantation Stomp  806
Planter's Punch  75
Plastered In Paris  1095-1435-1509
Platterbrains  109
Play 'Em For Mama, Sing 'Em For Me  360-
1008-1439
Play, Gypsies, Dance, Gypsies  1036
Playhouse Party  590
Playing In The Grass  628
Playing My Saxophone  1716
Playing The Blues  1128-1656
Playing The Dozen  516
Playing With The Strings  844
Play It A Long Time, Papa  1447
Play It, Red  578-967-1183-1192
Playmates  1316
Play Me Slow  576-717-1113
Play That Hot Guitar  1668
Play That Song Of India Again  219
Play That Thing  1245
Play The Funny Blues  856
Pleading  169-269-1619
Pleading Blues  354-1012
Pleadin' For The Blues  753
Pleading Misery Blues  1321
Please (1924)  226-558-1582
Please (1932)  22-148
Please Be Careful If You Can't Be Good
154
Please Be Kind  368-608-759-1158-1179-
1283-1512
Please Believe Me  438-1001
Please Be There  744
Please Come Back To Me  848
Please Come Home Daddy Blues  1018
Please Come On Down To My House  1647
Please Come Out Of Your Dream  323
Please Don't Cut Out My Sauerkraut  1394
Please Don't Holler, Mama  519
Please Don't Break 'Em Down  1162
Please Don't Squabble  944
**Please Don't Talk About Me** When I'm Gone
142-197-563-901-980-1071-1134-1644-1653
Please Don't Talk About My Man  1271
Please Don't Tickle Me, Babe  1056-1059
Please Don't Turn Me Down  1345
Please Forgive Me  494
Please Help Me Get Him Off My Mind  1445
Please Keep Me In Your Dreams  293-767-
1630
Please Let Me Dream In Your Arms  242
Please, Mr. Johnson  832
Please Pardon Us, We're In Love  1401
Please Pity My Heart  1075
Please Say The Word  989
Please Sing For Me (Doodle-Lee-Doo)  1505
Please Take A Letter, Miss Brown  10-1242
Please Take Me Out Of Jail  1622

1946

Please Tell Me  1644
Please Tell Me The Truth  527
Pleasin' Paul  11
Pleasure Mad  19-359-509-796-884-905-942-
  1085-1494-1650
Pleasure Was All Mine, The  1047
Plenty Off Center  1673
Plenty Of Sunshine  519-573-653
Plenty Trouble On Your Hand  628
P. L. K. Special  1746
Plucked Again  495
Plucking On A Golden Harp  589
Pluckin' The Bass  259-466
Plug Ugly (The Worst Lookin' Man In Town)
  1050
Plumber's Revenge  184
Plus que lente, La  374
Plymouth Rock  283-923
Pocket Knife Blues  1673
Poem Set To Music, A  820
Points Roses  1288
Poison  404-1390
Poke Along Blues  501
Police Blues  343-735-1060-1090-1744
Police Done Tore My Playhouse Down  1453
Polka Dot-Rag  1427
Polka Dots And Moonbeams  166-207-297-449
Polka Dotty  692
Polly  1289-1420
Polly  Wolly Doodle (All The Way)  701-
  1156-1228
Polo Blues  8
Polonaise (Chopin)  897
Polo-Naise  1238
Pompanola  174
Pom Pom  284-1511-1594
Pompton Turnpike  97-865
Ponce de Leon  98
Ponchatrain (sic)  1104
Ponjola  554
Poole County Blues  886
Poor Ballerina  433
Poor Boy, A  1322
Poor Boy Blues  1026
Poor Bubber  1501
Poor Butterfly  315-595-615-646-789-798-
  807-808-900-1139-1148-1306-1432-1584-
  1634-1669
Poor Dinah  536-584
Poor Girl Blues  979
Poor House Blues  860
Poor Jab's Blues  1043
Poor Kid  1384
Poor Little Angeline  960
Poor Li'l Me  1345
Poor Little Me  68
Poor Little Rich Girl  323-1662
Poor Loulie Jean  1147
Poor Man's Blues, (The)  681-1445
Poor Me Blues  750-1012
Poor Minnie The Moocher  1071
Poor Mr. Chisholm  62
Poor Old Joe  57-275-276-726
Poor Papa (He's Got Nothin' At All)  707-
  955-1275-1300-1518
Poor Richard  1256
Poor Robinson Crusoe  543-585-1124-1240
Poor You  375-453
Popcorn Man  430-604-746-786
Popeye (The Sailor Man)  1594
Pop Goes Your Heart  959

Poplar Street Blues  377-406-717-734
Poppies  920
Poppin' 'Em Out  501
Poppy Blossoms  675
Porcupine Rag  1251-1340-1475
Porgy  487-1652-1653
Pork And Beans  839
Pork Chop Blues  178
Porter's Love Song (To A Chambermaid),
  The  6-779-839-1154-1155-1157-1203-
  1561-1624-1644
Port Of Harlem Blues  1240
Porto Rican Chaos - see MOONLIGHT FIESTA
Portrait Of A Guinea Farm  1552
Portrait Of Bert Williams  496
Portrait Of The Lion  494
Posin'  441-637-729-986-1157
Positively-Absolutely (Does She Love Me ?)
  524-552-656-1366
Possibly  1290
Postage Stomp  82-1740
Potato Head Blues  41
Potato Salad  916
Pot Licker Blues  1655
Potomac River Blues  143-712-1355
Pound Cake  106
Pounding Heart Blues  1240
Pound Ridge  619
Pour commencer  1615
Pour danser le Charleston  1639
Pouring Down Blues  211
Pourquoi n'etes-vous pas venue ?  827
Pour terminer  1615
Pour vous  172
Pour vous, medames  1639
Poutin' Papa  150
Powder Rag  1217-1389
Powerful Blues  502
Power House  25-385-889-1371-1402
Pozzo  544
Practice Makes Perfect  770-1397
Praeludium and Allegro (Fritz Kreisler)
  1477
Prairie Blues  501-503-1212
Prairie Dog Hole Blues  8
Prairieland Lullaby  167
Prater Blues  696
Pratt City Blues  753-754
Pray For The Lights To Go Out  697
Praying Blues  1466
Praying For Rain  1202
Praying The Blues  427
Preacher And The Bear, The  775
Preacher Must Get Me Sometime, The  1320
Preachin' Blues  113
Preachin' The Blues  1444
Preachin' Trumpet Blues  278
Precious  1593
Precious Little Thing Called Love - see
  IT'S A PRECIOUS LITTLE THING CALLED
  LOVE
Precious Memorym A  374
Prelude For Trumpet  897
Prèlude in C major  1407
Prelude in C sharp minor (Rachmaninoff,
  Op. 3, No. 2)  94-297-418-922-1371-1540
Prelude No. 7 (Chopin)  989
Preludes, Les (Liszt)  1360
Prelude To A Bughouse  10
Prelude To A Kiss  94-494-766
Prelude To A Stomp  906-1075

Prelude To The Blues  1541
Prenez garde au mechant loup - see WHO'S
  AFRAID OF THE BIG BAD WOLF ?
Preparedness Blues  665
Prescription For The Blues  310-754-1449
Presentation Stomp  1642
President's Birthday Ball, The  435
Press My Button (Ring My Bell)  842
Press The Button  1707
Pretending You Care  148
Pretty And Blue  644-1363
Pretty Audrey  457
Pretty Baby  978-1105-1131-1397-1587
Pretty Baby, Is It Yes Or No ?  1709
Pretty Blue(s)  1420
Pretty Cinderella  235-568
Pretty Doll  336-549
Pretty Eyes  988
Pretty Girl  710
Pretty Girl Is Like A Melody, A  465-505-
  1140-1148-1398-1412-1477-1506- 594
Pretty Girl Milking Her Cow, A  322
Pretty Lil  1103
Pretty Little Baby  1483-1588
Pretty Little Petticoat  1374
Pretty Little Thing  659-871-884-890-1365
Pretty Little You  245
Pretty Mama Blues  270
Pretty Man Blues  1065
Pretty Please  1252
Pretty Polly Perkins  1558
Pretty Puppy  1181
Pretty, So Pretty  247
Pretty Trix  1597
Pretty Ways  140
Prickly Heat  1391
Primitive  1346
Primrose Stomp  1104
Prince Charming  820
Prince Of Wails  350-543-682-716-919-966-
  1112-1257-1366-1544-1721-1741
Priscilla Blues  1499
Prison Blues  1091
Prison Bound Blues  570-1526
Prisoner Of Love  80-1743-1736
Prisoner's Blues, The  1014
Prisoner's Song, The  123-124-630-950-1002
Prison Wall Blues  270
Prize Waltz, The  1146
Procession Of The Sardar  185
Professor Hot Stuff  1112
Profoundly Blue  652
Prohibition Blues  1084
Promenade  87-923
Promise Me Everything Never Get Anything
  Blues  1609
Promises  1599
Pross-(T)chai (Goodbye-Goodbye)  29-1404
Proud Of A Baby Like You  577
Prove It On Me Blues  1268
Prowling Wolf Blues  685
P. S. - I Love You  292-779
Public Melody Number One  54-1028
Public Weakness Number One  780
Puddin' Head Jones  455-1278
Puddin' Head Serenade  899
Puddin' Papa  564
Pu-leeze ! Mister Hemingway  876
Pullman Porter Blues  1352-1698
Pumpernickel  1497
Pump Song, The  1-640

Pump Tillie  150
Punch And Judy Show  1294
Punch Drunk  841
Punchinello  207
Punishing The Piano  319
Purple Moonlight  298-299-300
Purple Rose Of Cairo  1230
Pushin' Along  186
Pushin' The Conversation Along  215
Push-Out  1654
Puss, Puss, Puss  148
Pussy  567
Pussy Cat Rag  650
Pussyfoot March  1429
Pussy In The Corner  1242
Pussy Willow  379-494-495-497
Put A Little Bait On The Hook  470
Put And Take (1921)  458
Put And Take (1930)  1598
Put Away A Little Ray Of Golden Sunshine
  (For A Rainy Day)  1582
Put 'Em Down Blues  42
Put It Away  988
Put It Right Here (Or Keep It Out There)
  1445
Put It There  1033
Put It Where I Can Get It  1549
Put Me Back In The Alley  278
Put Me In The Alley Blues  308-1093
Put On An Old Pair Of Shoes  1248
Put On Your Old Grey Bonnet  286-287-537-
  745-775-874-986-1004
Put That Down In Writing  207-740-1405
Put That Sun Back In The Sky - see WE'VE
  GOTTA PUT THAT SUN BACK IN THE SKY
Puttin' And Takin'  1538
Puttin' It On  159
Puttin' On The Dog  46-1431
Puttin' On The Ritz  61-246-331-553-812-
  1285-1305-1663
Put Your Arms Around Me, Baby  551
Put Your Heart In A Song  322-1158-1357
Put Your Little Foot Right Out  1316
Put Your Little Foot There  1753
Put Your Loving Arms Around Me  993
Put Your Mind Right On It  214-838
Put Yourself In My Place  693
Put Your Worries Through The Mangle  1493
Pyramid  493-765-1407
P-Wee Strut (sic)  1713

Quaker City Jazz  1116-1358
Quality Shout  782
Quand on n'en a pas  1639
Quatre farceurs, Les  313
Quatre tickets  333
Queen Isabella  258-695-1124
Queen Of Egypt  992
Queen Street Blues  1247
Queen Was In The Parlour, The  22-1296
Queer Notions  726-727
Quicker Than You Can Say "Jack Robinson"
  974
Quiet And Roll 'Em  907
Quiet, Please  450-453
Quintette Plays Carmen, The  1372-1373
Quintuplets' Lullaby  100
Quit Knocking On My Door  100
Quittin' My Man Today  1025

1948

Rabbit Foot Blues  317
Rabbits Jump, The  766
Race Track Blues  1451
Rackett (sic), The  945
Ra-Da-Da-Da  551
Radio Blues  1617
Radio Papa (Broadcastin' Mama)  214
Radio Rhythm  725-1071
Ragamuffin Rag  1251-1605
Ragamuffin Romeo  481
Ragamuffin Stomp  862
Rag Doll, The  1291
Raggedy Ann  225-973
Raggedy But Right  781
Ragging The A.C.E.  1342
Ragging The Chimes  1549
Ragging The Rag  85-86
Raggin' The Scale  61-85-319-986-1587-1598
  1600
Raggle Taggle, The  155
Rag Pickings  1586
Rags  23
Ragtime Cowboy Joe  9-969-1342-1561
Ragtime Dance  1442-1657
Ragtime Drummer, The  943
Ragtime Episode, A  1586-1587-1588
Ragtime Medley  1197
Ragtime Oriole - see ORIOLE, THE
Ragtime Skedaddle, A  1198-1370
Rag Time Society  1049
Ragtime Volunteers Are Off To War, The
  1375
Raid The Joint  692
Railroad Blues  390-1230-1467-1522-1560-
  1748
Railroad Man  535-837-915-1077-1081-1186-
  1526-1672
Railroad Man Blues  811
Railroad Rhythm  1706
Rain  28-540-984
Rain  1612
Rainbow Blues  1263
Rainbow Dreams  922
Rainbow Filled With Music, A  1304
Rainbow Man, The  1339
Rainbow On The River  93
Rainbow 'Round The Moon  445
Rainbows  748
Raincheck  499
Rainin'  987
Rain On The Roof  287
Rain, Rain, Go Away !  35-118-905
Rainy Day  1504
Rainy Day Blues  379-975-1517-1575
Rainy Weather  913
Rainy Weather Blues  1093-1441
Rainy Weather Rose  1368
Raisin' The Rent  487-1269
Raisin' The Roof  723-950-1568
Ralfella  1388
Ramble, The  782
Rambler's Rhythm  282
Ramblin'  1490
Rambling Blues  226-354-623-872-890-966-
  1258-1461-1487-1591 (sometimes shown as
  THEM RAMBLIN' BLUES)
Rambling In C  282
Rambling In Rhythm  1369
Ramblin' Man Blues  843
Rambling Wreck From Georgia Tech.  627-736
Ramona  183-622

Ramona Blues  751
Rampart And Gravier Blues  680
Rampart Street Blues  65-350-351-707-1440
Ramshackle Rag  1251
Rancho Pillow  818-911
Randolph Street Rag  764
Rap Tap On Wood  428
Rarin' To Go  1183
Rasputin (That Highfalutin' Lovin' Man)
  1556
Rastus On Parade  971
Ratamacue  259
Rattlesnake Bite  628
Rattlesnake Blues  847
Rattlesnake Groan  1065
Rattlesnakin' Daddy  1496-1677
Rattling Rhythm  1711
Raymond  1639
Raz Ma Taz  1560
Razor Edge  138-1715
Razor Jim  1424
Razzazza Mazzazza  1254
Razzle Dazzle  1199
Reaching For Someone (And Not Finding
  Anyone There)  21-564-1293-1569-1687
Reaching For The Cotton Moon  1073
Reaching For The Moon  265-1234-1295
Ready Eddy  135
Ready For Love  827
Ready For The River  240-340-403-566-583-
  626-669-680-723-930-1151-1614-1742
Ready Hokum  1321
Really A Pain  193
Really Blue  1599
Really Fine  1638
Really The Blues  917
Rebound  1333
Reckless Blues  1442-1551
Reckless Daddy  707
Reckless Don't Care Mama Blues  1069
Reckless Life Blues  849
Reckless Night On Board An Ocean Liner
  1372
Recollections  1426
Record Session  818
Red Bank Romp  181
Red Beans And Rice  121-854
Red Blues  100
Red Cap  54-691
Red Cap Porter (Blues)  835-1678
Red Devil  1071
Red Duster Rag  1039
Red Hair And Freckles  305-949-950
Red Head (Blues)  5-38-1128
Red Headed Baby  873
Red-Headed Music Maker  1299
Redhead, Redhead, Gingerbread Head  1147
Red Hot  239-1112-1523-1673
Red Hot Band  474
Red Hot Chicago  776
Red Hot Dan  1622
Red Hot Flo (From Kokomo)  1524-1534
Red Hot Henry Brown  211-232-304-558-718-
  867-882-1068-1130-1180-1545-1750
Red Hot Hottentot  837
Red Hot Mama  338-558-714-799-886-1054-
  1067-1190-1379-1574
Red Hot Pepper  1103
Red House Blues  993
Red Jill Rag  311
Red Lantern Blues  1487

Red Light  387

Red Lips, Kiss My Blues Away  418-708-929-1015

Red Man Blues  1230

Red Mountain Blues  1443

Red Nose  53

Red-Nose Pete  1663

Red Onion Blues  415

Red Onion Drag  457

Red Onion Rag  1481

Red Pepper (Rag)  346-1217-1251-1340-1350-1586

Red Rhythm  1074

Red River Blues  1038-1458-1702

Red River Bottom Blues  1156

Red River Valley  513

Red Robin Rag  387

Red Rose Rag  1217-1256

Red Sails In The Sunset  13-52-203-701-967 1114

Red Skies  1347

Redskin  979

Redskin Rhumba  97

Red Velvet  1602

Red Wagon  104-767-989

Red, White And Blues  1670

Red Wing  277-513-1539

Reefer Man  255-935-1072-1410

Reefer Man's Dream  211

Reese's Idea  832

Reflets  333

Refrigeratin' Papa (Mama's Gonna Warm You Up)  1651

Regretful Blues  1516

Rehearsal In Love  692

Rehearsin' For A Nervous Breakdown  895-897-1159

Reincarnation  1005

Reisenweber Rag  1176

Relaxin' At The Touro  1481

Relicario, El  1603

Remarkable Girl  659-1666

Remember - see YOU FORGOT TO REMEMBER

Remember Cherie  875

Remember I Love You  678-1029

Rememb'ring  224-1581

Remember Me ?  604-1733

Remember Me To Mary (If She Still Remembers Me)  269

Remember My Forgotten Man  1009

Remember Our Romance  1437

Remember Pearl Harbor  1319

Remember The Night  530

Remember When  786-983

Remember Who You're Promised To  1633

Reminiscing  96-246

Reminiscing At Blue Note  760

Reminiscing In Tempo  490

Reminiscing Through England  1634

Reminiscing Time  372

Remorseful Blues  1463

Rendezvous In Rio, A  911-1243

Rendez-vous sous la pluie  1350

Rendezvous Time In Paree  432-447-612

Rendezvous With A Dream  122

Rendezvous With Rhythm  765

Rent Man Blues  1739

Rent Party Blues  478-480-766

Repeal The Blues  638

Request For A Rumba  168

Restless  595-1270

Restless Blues  187

Rest Your Hips  216-394

Reunion In Harlem  1007

Reverend Is My Man, The  636

Reverie Of A Moax (Oh Claire The Goon)97

Revolutionary Blues  1053

Revolutionary Etude (Chopin)  897

Revolutionary Rhythm  1301

Rexatious  1500

Rhapsody In Blue  1459-1749

Rhapsody In Love  39-651-1306-1710-1726

Rhapsody In Rhumba  260

Rhapsody In Rhythm  239-1493

Rhapsody Junior  985

Rhinewine Rag, A  1255-1256

Rhumba Blues, The  1561

R(h)umba Jumps, The  742-908

Rhumboogie  166-306-742-910-1326-1753

Rhyme For Love, A  1629

Rhythm  511-958-1485

Rhythm And Romance  249-701-1627-1658-1659

Rhythm 'Bout Town  683

Rhythm Club Stomp  1170

Rhythm Crazy  730

Rhythm Doctor Man  342

Rhythm For Sale  193-1094

Rhythm Hymn  1541

Rhythmic Dream  580-722

Rhythmic Refrain  1252

Rhythmic Rhapsody  155

Rhythm In My Nursery Rhymes  102-438-701 968-985-1001-1115-1433-1731

Rhythm In Spain  1456

Rhythm In The Alphabet  1435

Rhythm Is My Romeo  587

Rhythm Is Our Business  67-141-582-890-959-984-1001-1306-1432

Rhythm Jam  906-1075

Rhythm King  117-130-340-1292

Rhythm Lullaby  545-687-759-1075-1471

Rhythm Mad  348-551

Rhythm Man  104-288

Rhythm Of The Broadway Moon  1427

Rhythm Of The Day  523-559-630-870-973-1478-1543

Rhythm Of The Dishes And Pans  278

Rhythm Of The River  425

Rhythm Of The Snowflakes, The  1314

Rhythm Of The Tambourine  728

Rhythm On My Mind  1507

Rhythm On The Loose  1506

Rhythm On The Radio  1249

Rhythm On The River  198-306-363-1004

Rhythm, Past And Present  470

Rhythm Rag (The)  566-646-928-1324-1680-1681

Rhythm Rhapsody  759

Rhythm, Rhythm - see I GOT RHYTHM

Rhythm Saved The World  52-122-217-438-1001

Rhythm's O.K. In Harlem, The  24-536

Rhythm Spasm  1072

Rhythm Step  467

Rhythm Sundae  759

Rice's Ragtime Opera  460-1118

Ric et Pussy  1219

Rich Man, Poor Man, Beggar Man, Thief 1391

1950

Richmond Stomp  1495
Rickety Rocking Chair  153
Ride 'Em, Cowboy  521
Ride My Blues Away  944
Ride On  110-1561
Ride On, Ride On  902
Rider Blues - see RIDE, JOCKEY, RIDE
Ride, Jockey, Ride  1466
Ride, Red, Ride  191-584-1070-1074
Rider Needs A Fast Horse  7
Ridiculous Blues  306-548-1392-1556
Ridin' Along The Moscowa  189
Ridin' And Jivin'  760
Ridin' A Riff  759
Ridin' Around In The Rain  291
Ridin' But Walkin'  1624
Ridin' High  604-1225
Ridin' In Rhythm  1073
Riding On A Blue Note  492
Riding On A Camel  1293
Riding On The Old Ferris Wheel  894
Riding The Blues  1004-1242
Ridin' Up The River Road  974
Rien me fait chanter, Un  1562
Riff, The  1161-1311
Riffin'  277-728
Riffin' At The Bar-B-Q  329
Riffin' At The Ritz  599-1490
Riff Interlude  106-107
Riffin' The Blues  40
Riffin' The Scotch  593
Riff It  824
Riff Medley  760
Riff Romp  283
Riffs  154-838
Riffs And Rhythm  827
Riff Song, The  1611
Riff Time  693
Rig(a)marole  183-191-432
Right About Face  1270
Right Idea, The  95
Right Key But The Wrong Keyhole, The - see
  YOU'VE GOT THE RIGHT KEY etc.
Right Kind Of Man, The  245-671
Right Or Wrong  78-240-567-626-1062-1063-
  1130-1528
Right Somebody To Love, The  191
Right String But The Wrong Yo-Yo, The  522
Riley's Wagon  270
Ring Around The Moon  806-1368
Ring Dem Bells  87-97-482-483-661-902-1310
  1339-1637
Ringleberg Blues  1122
Ringle Dingle  1343
Ringside Blues  640
Ringside Stomp  999
Ringside Table For Two  903
Ringtail Blues  976
Rinka Tinka Man  124
Rio de Janeiro  1296
Rio Rita  171-951-953-1521
Ripley Blues  270
Rippin' It Off  531-1486
Rippling Waters  1468-1538
Rip Saw Blues  919-920
Riptide  1228
Rip Up The Joint  115
Rise 'n' Shine  1688
Rising Sun Blues  892-1454
Rising Tide Blues  948
Rit-Dit-Ray  1111

Rite Tite  1111
Ritual Fire Dance (de Falla)  1371
River And Me, The  484-556
River Bed Blues  740
River Blues  1280-1677
Riverboat Blues  402
Riverboat Shuffle  5-111-121-276-296-349
  764-775-857-866-903-1139-1332-1481-1566
  1741
River Bottom  854
River Bottom Glide  762
River Hip Papa  843
River Home  1540
River Man  702-1002
Riverside Blues  1069-1091-1166-1656
Riverside Stomp  1713
River's Takin' Care Of Me, The  12-289
River, Stay 'Way From My Door  142-157-
  197-306-410-583-687-1154-1653
Road House Blues  642-1717
Road House Shuffle  1263
Roadhouse Stomp  1713
Road Is Rocky, The (But I Am Gonna Find
  My Way)  1460
Road Of Stone  1487
Roaming (1922)  1613
Roamin' (1930)  12
Roamin' Around  1506-1694
Roamin' Blues  397-1012
Roamin' To Wyomin'  32-71-224
Roam On, My Little Gypsy Sweetheart  469-
  1580-1665
Roberta Blues  1577
Robins And Roses  427-438-1148-1312-1415-
  1464-1561
Rocco Blues  1326
Rocco's Boogie Woogie  1326
Rock-a-Bye Basie  105-333
Rock-a-Bye Bay  300-1554
Rock-a-Bye My Baby Blues  1582-1643
Rock-a-Bye The Boogie  166
Rock-a-Bye Your Baby With A Dixie Melody
  1516
Rock And Gravel  1586
Rock And Ride  944
Rock And Roll  159-700
Rock And Rollin' Daddy  849
Rock And Rye  759
Rock Away  1035
Rock Bottom  1210
Rock, Church, Rock  1450
Rock, Daniel  1070
Rocket Ship To Mars  184
Rock Hill Special  661
Rocking And Rolling  1320
Rockin' And Swingin'  7
Rockin' Chair  6-46-56-77-78-81-196-274-
  275-296-323-325-484-568-581-582-852-911
  1124-1143-1239-1303-1304-1408-1433-1537
  1602-1637-1707-1726
Rockin' Chair Blues  643-1026-1093-1440
Rockin' In Rhythm  97-484-491-494-497-746
  995-1146
Rockin' Myself To Sleep  680
Rockin' My Troubles  1036
Rockin' Rollers Jubilee  125-692
Rockin' The Blues  108-1240
Rockin' The Town  787
Rockin' With The Rockets  944
Rock Island Flag Stop  298
Rock It For Me  78-94-633-988-1203-1660

Rock It In Rhythm  1528
Rock, Jenny, Rock  562
Rock Me  1070
Rock Me, Daddy  1678
Rock Me In My Swanee Cradle  68
Rock Me In The Cradle Of Love  1693
Rock Me Mama  1322-1531
Rock My Soul  1040
Rock Pile Blues  1322-1449
Rock, Rock, Rock-a-Bye Baby  29
Rocks, The  378-1720
Rocks In My Bed  499-1575
Rock That Thing  842
Rocky Comfort  691
Rocky Mountain Blues  482-721
Rock Your Blues Away  858
Rocky Road  1035
Roi Mare, Le  1562
Roll Along, Prairie Moon  13-365
Roll Away, Clouds  800
Roll Dem Roly-Boly Eyes  265
Roll 'Em  602-608-850
Roll 'Em Dorothy, Let 'Em Jump For Joy
  629
Roll 'Em, Girls  573-719-1478-1483-1503
Roll 'Em Pete  1575
Rolling Around In Roses  738
Rollin' Down The River  246-932-1234-1285
Rollin' Home  1146
Rolling In Love  699
Rollin' Mill Blues  1729
Rolling Mill Stomp  1495
Rollin' Plains  1314
Rolling The Stone  1746
Roll, Jordan  790-1711
Roll On, Buddy  666
Roll On, Mississippi, Roll On  1296-1384-
  1427-1470
Rolls-Royce Papa  965
Roll That Jelly  210
Roll Up The Carpet (Push Back The Chairs)
  347-996-1263
Roll Up The Carpets  140-1286-1483
Romance  286-431
Romance a la Mode  1361-1638
Romance In The Dark  321-770
Romance Runs In The Family  431-1358
Romantic Joe  1601
Romany Love  1174
Rompin'  1134
Roodles  340
Roof Garden Get Off  808
Rooftop Serenade, The  1669
Room For Two  1612
Room 1411  591
Roomin' House Blues  1542
Room Rent Blues  846-1166
Room With A View, A  431-445-469-644-658-
  871-1404
Rooster's Crowing Blues, The  270
Root Hog Or Die  680
Rootin' Tootin' Shootin' Man From Texas
  64
Ro-Ro-Rollin' Along  514
Rosalie  1249-1291-1401-1404
Rosary, The  855
Rose And A Prayer, A  434
Roseland Shuffle  101
Rose Marie  227-299-796-1454-1582
Rose O'Day (The Filla-Ga-Dusha Song)  744-
  1553

Rose Of Bagdad, I Love You So  1518
Rose Of Bombay  1480
Rose Of Mandalay  804
Rose Of Monterey  187
Rose Of Spain  1066-1610
Rose Of The Nile  534
Rose Of The Orient  664
Rose Of The Rio Grande  293-493-495-497-
  1174-1359-1607
Rose Of Touraine  975
Rose Of Washington Square  370-612-891-
  1141-1550
Rose Petals  387
Rose Rhumba  650
Rose Room (In Sunny Roseland)  115-154-
  279-330-485-553-613-728-896-897-984-
  1022-1404-1602-1691
Roses  576-1504
Roses Are Red, Violets Are Blue  875
Roses Blues  1321
Roses Brought Me You, The  74-566-576
Roses For Remembrance  171-344-1505
Roses In December  123-1314-1347
Roses Of Picardy  586-961-1140-1326
Roses Of Yesterday  130-143-1614
Roses Remind Me Of You  265
Rose-Tree Strut  646
Rosetta  13-151-310-317-465-595-600-740-
  758-760-889-1092-1134-1137-1412-1530-
  1531-1558-1625-1730-1736
Rosetta Blues  783
Rosette  579
Rosie O'Ryan (Sure I Love You)  1521
Rosie The Redskin  1721
Rosita, La  9-434-447-619-1475
Ross Tavern Boogie  764
Rosy Cheeks  129-171-657-668-1430-1580
Rosy Posy  1005
Roubin Blues  540
Rough And Tumble  1263
Rough And Tumble Blues  1267
Rough House Blues  722-735-1655
Rough Treatin' Daddy  157
Roumania  1698
Round And Round  637-1043
Rounders Blues  941
'Round Evening  240-419
'Round My Heart  341
Round The Corner  380
Round The Old Deserted Farm  79-124
Round Town  1330
Route 23  417
Rover's Blues  1156
Rowdy Man Blues  1321
Row, Row, Rosie  38-73-640-1592
Row, Row, Row  1317
Royal Family  663
Royal Flush  1048
Royal Garden Blues  109-116-120-282-286-
  293-366-438-518-595-616-633-764-896-
  958-1000-1003-1008-1053-1097-1178-1195-
  1225-1422-1423-1460-1492-1498-1649-1741
Royal Palm Blues  942
Royal Palm Special Blues  737
Roy Club Rag  1341
Roy Rag, The  1340
Rubber Ball Rhythm  387
Rubber Heels  1120-1309
Rubbin', Rubbin'  1371
Rubinesque  171
Rub Me Some More  1459

1952

Rude Interlude  488
Rufenreddy  90-923
Ruff Scufflin'  941
Rug Cutter's Function  843
Rug Cutter('s) Swing  13-727
Rukus Juice And Chittlin'  1044
Rukus Juice Shuffle  1044
Rules And Regulations "Signed Razor Jim"
   1725
Rumba da Boum, La  396
Rumba Negro  1111
Rumpel-Stilts-Kin (Oh, Could He Sew)  206
Rump Steak Serenade  1637
Rumpus In Richmond  496-497
Runaway Blues  737-1268
Runenae Papa (I Want A Lot Of Love)  1422
Run Little Rabbit  261
Run, Mary, Run  163
Running After You  510-1181-1565
Running A Temperature  986
Running Between The Raindrops  197-981
Running Down My Man  848
Runnin' Ragged (Bamboozlin' The Bassoon)
   1598
Runnin' 'Round With The Blues  1011
Running Through My Mind  184-447-1358
Runnin' Wild  60-216-328-349-384-482-582-
   600-915-936-954-985-1123-1146-1174-1186
   1225-1260-1353-1363-1373-1477-1480-1606
   1607-1614
Run, Rabbit, Run  372
Rushin'  1468
Rush Inn Blues  1077
Russian Blues  1713
Russian Fantasy  1626
Russian Love Song  1162
Russian Lullaby  7-124-306-610-1157
Russian Rag  512-1750
Russian Rose  222-1174
Russian Sailors' Dance  375
Russian Salad  563
Rustle Of Spring (Sinding)  897
Rustle Of Swing  258
Rusty Dusty Blues  11o-865
Rusty Hinge  1659
Rusty Pail  1622
Rusty Rags  1198
Rythme Futur  1262


Saboo  692
Sacred Flame, The  1040
Sacrilege In G  3
Sad, The  155
Sad And Blue  765-1454
Sad And/'n' Lonely Blues  639-749-794-
   1022-1728
Saddest Tale  489
Saddle Your Blues To A Wild Mustang  879-
   1115-1239-1690
Sad-Hearted Blues  308
Sadie Green (The Vamp Of New Orleans)  266
   530-532-625-1172-1220-1366
Sadie's Servant Room Blues  209
Sadie The Shaker  874
Sadie (You Are The Lady For Me)  1335
Sad Man Blues  1110
Sad Moments  1694
Sadness Will Be Gladness  173-999
Sad News Blues  1188
Sad Sap Sucker Am I  1637
Safely Locked Up In My Heart  40

Safety Mama  1446
Sahara  325
Sail Along, Silvery Moon  756-1032-1314
Sailboat In The Moonlight, A  93-205-765-
   768-1314
Sail Fish, The  542
Sailin'  1732
Sailing Along On A Carpet Of Clouds  938
Sailing At Midnight  445
Sailing On Lake Pontchartrain  1388
Sailing On The Robert E. Lee  147-874-
   1342-1433
Sailor Man Rhythm  1528
Sail With Me  628
St. Charles Avenue Strut  387
St. James Infirmary  44-64-145-194-246-
   252-261-480-481-519-752-763-789-790-941
   1018-1040-1081-1170-1409-1540-1541-1564
   1656-1726 (sometimes shown as ST. JOE'S
   INFIRMARY)
St. Louis Blues  3-22-27-46-51-52-79-85-
   110-112-127-136-142-145-151-160-179-210
   252-267-310-311-315-318-348-377-383-399
   404-410-424-427-465-471-485-497-503-512
   534-536-567-571-582-595-598-605-622-632
   635-666-667-702-722-731-754-759-760-765
   770-778-780-797-801-806-812-821-822-850
   866-867-872-885-897-909-918-929-934-939
   945-954-970-997-1017-1062-1079-1083-
   1115-1119-1121-1124-1150-1152-1159-1160
   1178-1183-1208-1215-1223-1225-1229-1252
   1283-1299-1310-1344-1366-1367-1389-1406
   1427-1432-1442-1445-1459-1508-1512-1513
   1521-1529-1531-1540-1585-1622-1624-1634
   1647-1653-1655-1657-1681-1708-1722-1747
   1750
St. Louis Blues, Fantasy on  1612
St. Louis Bound  873-892
St. Louis Chant, A  686
St. Louis Cyclone Blues  1321
St. Louis Fair Blues  8
St. Louis Gal  351-706-1089-1180-1188-  ?
   1193-1439
St. Louis Hop, The  266-921-1420-1579
St. Louis Man  406-642
St. Louis Nightmare  1495
St. Louis Rag  303-460-1199-1200-1254
St. Louis Shuffle  721-1221-1343-1483
St. Louis Tickle  32-971-1199-1200-1250-
   1327-1588
St. Louis Wiggle Rhythm  1074
St. Louis Woman Blues  1376
St. Peter Blues  628-1671
St. Peter Street Blues  745
St. Vitus Dance  865
Salades de l'oncle François, Les  1219
Sales Tax On It  678
Sally  1613
Sally Long Blues  964
Sally Lou  377-796-1171
Sally Of My Dreams  209-420-1233
Sally's Got A Baby  402
Sally's Got The Blues  992
Sally's Not The Same Old Sally  139
Sally Trombone  379
Sally, Won't You (Please) Come Back ?
   761-1085-1141
Salome  1479
Salt Butter  214
Salt Lake City Blues  547
Salt Water Blues  1093-1441

Salty 51
Salty Dog 154-538-891-1207-1450
Salty Mama Blues 1007
Salt Your Sugar 826
Salute To Harlem, A 155
Salvation Blues 1517
Sam And Delilah 484-1696
Same Old Blues 1322
Same Old Line, The 1399
Same Old Moon, The 1612
Same Old Moon (But Not The Same Old You) 1723
Same Old Story 897
Same Thing All The Time 1505
Same Train 478
Sam Henry Blues 1026
Sam Jones Blues (You Ain't Talkin' To Mrs. Jones) 706-1439
Sam Jones Done Snagged His Britches 864
Sam Mengal Blues 1675
Sammy Saxophone 1433
Sammy's Choppin' Block 1560
Samoa 956
Samson and Delilah : My Heart At Thy Sweet Voice (Saint-Saëns) 1635
Sam - The Hot Dog Man 843
Sam The Vegetable Man 1465
San 5-86-89-119-413-546-558-569-658-684-796-875-955-957-962-992-1037-1112-1123-1153-1162-1184-1227-1280-1379-1433-1572-1579-1590-1680-1683-1718
San Anton' 756-1630
San Antonio Rose 363-1317
San Antonio Shout 1133
San Antonio Tamales 155
Sand Dune 1117
Sand Dunes 1747
Sandman 424-425-597
Sandman Blues 1066
Sand Raisin' Blues 1453
Sandy 961
San Francisco 122-439-1415
San Francisco Blues 714-964-1449-1550
San Juan Hill 1500
Sans Culottes 1243
San Sue Strut 32-286-998
Santa Claus Blues 149-645-1280-1699
Santa Claus, Bring My Man Back To Me 1640
Santa Claus Came In The Spring 382-597-701
Santa Claus Crave 1321
Santa Claus Is Comin' To Town 249-437-744-1306
Santa Fe Blues 1487
Santana 710
Sant de Rhythmes 827
Santiago 387
Sapphire 90-143-144
Sarah, Come Over Here 379
Sarah From Sahara 141
Saratoga Drag 1346
Saratoga Shout 1345
Saratoga Swing 478-479
Sarawaki 1342
Sarita 1292
Saskatchewan 1291
Sassin' The Boss 988-1147
Satan Does The Rhumba 692
Satanic Blues 542-915-935-946-996-1176-1177-1179-1522

Satan In Satin 324
Satan's Holiday 933-1601-1602
Satan Takes A Holiday 217-441-585-695-745-1124-1434-1506
Satchel Mouth Swing 55
Satisfied 243-534-1058-1152
Satisfied Blues 110-538-749-1019-1716
Satisfyin' Papa 1651
Saturday 898-1459
Saturday Night 315
Saturday Night Blues 113
Saturday Night Fish Fry Drag 1310
Saturday Night Function 477-479-640
Saturday Night Jag 191-1704
Saturday Night On Texas Avenue 1558
Saturday Night Scrontch 1527
Saturday Night Struggle 948
Sau Sha Stomp 1455
Savage Rhythm 258-1072
Savage Serenade 290-1331
Savannah (The Georgianna Blues) 19-558-561-1163-1202-1663
Savannah Blues 1622
Savannah River Stride 4
Save It, Pretty Mama 44-57-114-663-1033-1594
Save Me, Sister 257
Save Me Some 391-1206
Save Your Man And Satisfy Your Soul 750
Save Your Sorrow For Tomorrow 297-926-1119-1589
Saving My Love For You 991
Saving Myself For You 526-609-729-1158
Savin' Up For Baby 1710
Savoy 1070
Savoyagers' Stomp 404
Savoy Blues 43-57-366
Savoy Shout 1345
Savoy Rhythm 851
Savoy Stampede 283
Savoy Strut 766
Sawmill Blues 1320
Saw Mill River Road 222
Sax Appeal 403-1365
Saxa-Woogie 865
Saxophone Blues 177
Saxophone Doodle 1377
Saxophone Sam 417
Sax-0-Phoney Blues 1461-1525
Say, Arabella (What's A Fella To Do ?) 231-572-653-1180-1745
Say "Hello" To The Folks Back Home 980
Say I Do It 737
Say It 10-291-449
Say It Again 225-901
Say It Isn't So 673-1306-1645
Say It While Dancing 221-710
Say It With A Kiss 907-1404-1512
Say It With A Red, Red Rose 1612
Say It With A Ukulele 1590
Say It With Music 148-1085-1142
Say I Wasn't Dreaming 974
Say, Mister ! Have You Met Rosie's Sister ? 133-1219-1524
Say, Persianna, Say 883
Say, Say, Sadie 1122
Say "Si Si" 185-741-908-1250-1477
Says My Heart 29-444-768-1158
Says Who ? Says You, Says I ! 261
Say That You Were Teasing Me 726
Say The Word 1346

1954

Say To Yourself "I Will Be Happy" 146-147
Say When 1337
Say ! Who Is That Baby Doll ? 462-804
Say "Yes" Today 871-1584
Say You're Mine 960
S. B. A. Blues 1413
Scagmore Green 862
Scale It Down 1172
Scandal Blues 1090-1094
Scandal In A flat 281-283
Scandinavia 1352
Scandinavian Stomp 1723
Scarecrow 618
Scare Crow Ball, The 1201
Scare Crow Blues 1201
Scared 1397
Scat ! Mr. Sweetback 1717
Scat Skunk 91
Scat Song, The 88-254-256-1072-1410-1645
Scatterbrain 9-172-190-613-747
Scatter Your Smiles 267-568-640-1534
Scattin' At The Cotton Club 491
Scattin' At The Kit-Kat 491-517
Scattin' The Skeeter Skoot 919
Scene Changes, The 1026
Schöne Frau in Mond 951
Schoolday Blues 978
School Of Rhythm 948
Scissor Grinder Joe 337-1609
Scissor Grinder's Blues 133
Scissors And Knives To Grind 184
Scoop It 1729
Scorchin' 1640
Scotch And Soda 95
Scotchin' With The Soda 329
Scottle-De-Doo 354
Scotty Blues 1084
Scouting Around 838
Scram ! 1636
Scrambles 90
Scramble Two 166
Scrapin' The Toast 321
Scrappin' Blues 1069
Scratch 149
Scratching (In) The Gravel 901-1431
Scratch My Back 1594
Screamin' The Blues 849-860
Screech Owl Blues 1269
Screenin' The Blues 181
Screws, Nuts And Bolts 1282
Scrounch 492
Scrubbin' Blues 110
Scrub Me, Mama, With A Boogie Beat 97-1
167-1412
Scrunch-Lo 1322
Scuddlin' 823
Scufflin' Blues 99
Scuffling Woman Blues 843
Sea Food Squabble 563
Seagulls 1211
Seal It With A Kiss 1721
Sea Of Dreams 1252
Searchin' For Flats 150
Search Your Heart And See 1323
Seattle Hunch 1103
Seawall Special Blues 152
2nd Avenue Clambake 805
Second Balcony Jump 342-762
Seconde Idee d'Eddie 1339
Second Hand Daddy 343-1060
Second Handed Blues 846

Second-Handed Man 1652
Secret Agent 1375
Secrets 919
Secrets In The Moonlight 166-816-1359
Section Hand Blues 1618
See If I'll Care 1449
Seeing Is Believing 700-798
Seeing Nellie Home 184
Seeing You Again Did Me No Good 153-168
Seeking Blues 1267
Seems Like A Month Of Sundays 76
Seems To Me 932
See Saw Blues 849
See See Rider (Blues) 1105-1266
See What I Mean ? 342
See What The Boys In The Back Room Will
Have 634
Selection From The Gutter, A 764
Self Portrait 948
Sellin' That Stuff 1033
Selling The Jelly 948
Sell It 1715
Sell-Out, The 1491
Selma 'Bama Blues 164
Seminola 797-1180
Seminole 1150
Semper Fidelis 325-1572
Semper Paratus 376
Send Back My Honeyman 705-1086-1606
Send For Me 1302
Sendin' The Vipers 1052
Send Me 999-1092-1602
"Send Me" Jackson 1636
Send Me To The 'Lectric Chair 1444
Senegalese Stomp 864-1362-1700
Señorita Mine 146-178-707-1362-1534
Sensational Mood 758-792
Sensation Blues 1679
Sensation (Rag) (Stomp) 38-543-582-607
721-1133-1175-1597-1682-1741-1747
Sent For You Yesterday And Here You
Come Today 103-184-591-611
Sentimental And Melancholy 205-294-686
1732
Sentimental Baby 31-1232-1568
Sentimental Blues 501-503
Sentimental Gentleman From Georgia 158
344-778-858-1072-1227-1472-1645
Sentimental Interlude 591
Sentimental Lady 500 (see also I DIDN'T
KNOW ABOUT YOU)
Separated Blues 355
Separation Blues 848-1450
Separation Day Blues 1674
Sepian Bounce 1038
Sepia Panorama 497
September In The Rain 901-1299-1313-
1399
Serenade (Schubert) 59-896-897
Serenade (Toselli) 324
Serenade d'Hiver 307
Serenade For A Wealthy Widow 534-1465-
1624-1642-1689
Serenade In Blue 436-622
Serenade In The Night 162-1557
Serenade In Thirds 211
Serenade To A Jitterbug 681
Serenade To A Maid 1244
Serenade To A Sarong 284
Serenade To A Savage 1405
Serenade To A Shylock 335

Serenade To A Sleeping Beauty  691
Serenade To A Wild Cat  398
Serenade To Nobody In Particular  427
Serenade To Sweden  494
Serenade To The Spot  452
Serenade To The Stars, A  124-1158
Serenading The Moon  1152
Serenata  144-1225
Sergeant Dunn's Bugle Call Blues  459
Sergeant Flagg And Sergeant Quirt  655
Sergeant Was Shy, The  97-495-909
Sermon, The  338
Serving Time Blues  1091
Set 'Em  754
Seul ce soir  1284
Seul couvert, please James - see DINNER
  FOR ONE, PLEASE JAMES
Se va la vida  1476
Seven Come Eleven  613-1016
Seven Day Blues  354
Seven Days' Leave  591
Seven Or Eleven  1520
720 In The Books  96-1359
71  1736
'S Good Enough For Me  322-1357
Shabby Old Cabby  1358
Shack In The Back  1033
Shack In The Back Of The Hills, A  881
Shades Of Hades  293-321-1508
Shades Of Jade  663-1089
Shades Of Twilight  325-433
Shadow Blues 1455  Shadowland Blues  533
Shadow Of The Blues  358
Shadows  297-1335-1406
Shadows In The Moonlight  798
Shadows In The Night  167
Shadows Of Love  290
Shadows On The Sand  451
Shadows On The Swanee  12-199-1653
Shadrack  55-322
Shady Lady  99-1155
Shady Lady Bird  620
Shady Lane Blues  695
Shady Tree, A  1613
Shag  113
Shaggin' At The Shore  945
Shake  233
Shake A Little Bit  854
Shake Down The Stars  63-207-372 449-528-
  615
Shake 'Em Up  1702
Shake It  1108
Shake It And Break It  114-775-914-934-
  935-996-1051-1170-1311-1392-1594-1662-
  1693
Shake It, Black Bottom  118
Shake It Daddy  570
Shake It Down  519-570-649-735-1060-1702
Shake It Up, Mooch It Up, Creole Gal  748
Shake My Tree  1201
Shake, Rattle And Roll  1747
Shake, Rattle And Roll (Afternoon Of A
  Moax)  96
Shakes  28
Shake That Jelly Roll  327
Shake That Thing  100-211-411-830-992-999
  1024-1162-1181-1300-1651-1700-1740
Shake Your Ashes  774
Shake Yo' Bones (sic)  945
Shake Your Can  415-1489
Shake Your Cans  707

Shake Your Dogs  1389
Shake Yo' Feet (sic)  1095
Shake Your Feet  560-712-1189-1590-1680
Shake Your Head (From Side To Side)  132-
  984
Shake Your Hips  1537
Shake Your Little Shoulder  675-1748
Shake Your Shimmy  892-1055
Shakin' The African  1276
Shall We Dance ?  1027-1690
Shame On You  94-737-878-1547
Shame ! Shame !  1633
Shanghai Dream Man  1173
Shanghai Honeymoon  309-397-402-537-873-
  1044-1494-1574-1669
Shanghai Lil  200-878
Shanghai Shuffle  75-121-545-716-727-
  1742
Shangri-La  184
Shanty Boat On The Mississippi  57
Shanty In Old Shanty Town, A - see IN A
  SHANTY IN OLD SHANTY TOWN
Share My Umbrella  1295
Sharing (My Love For You)  697-1370
Sharp As A Tack  817
Sharpie  1712
Sha-Sha  430-1358-1435
Shave 'Em Dry Blues  1266
Sha-Wan-Da-Moo  1286
(S)he Belongs To Me  234-266-319-735-
  1137-1664
She Brings Me Down  824
She Can Love So Good  1527
She Caught The Boat  152
She Changed Her Hi-De-Hi-De (For His
  Yodel-O-De-Ay)  1668
She'd A Hole In Her Stocking  315
She Didn't Say "Yes," She Didn't Say "
  "No" (She Only Said "Maybe")  17
She Doesn't  1592
She Done Sold It Out  1044
She Don't Love Me  1311
She Don't Wanna  359-1319-1485
Sheffield Blues  1485
She Got The Best In Town  1528
She Had To Go And Lose It At The Astor
  1316
Sheik Of Araby, The  7-114-152-169-191-
  218-307-333-385-444-445-465-486-518-
  583-590-601-615-690-740-790-816-841-
  913-1085-1125-1143-1260-1433-1472-1530
  1538-1557-1632-1634-1647-1736
She Keeps It Up All The Time  811
She Knows Her Onions  235-532-1593
She Knows How To Sell That Stuff  1455
She Knows It  1573
She'll Always Remember  744-762-1553
She'll Be Comin' 'Round The Mountain
  169-1299-1562-1635
She'll Never Find A Fellow Like Me  1665
She Looks Like Helen Brown  631
She Loves Me  37-227-1518-1591
She Loves Me Just The Same  1586
She Loves So Good  824
Sheltered By The Stars (Cradled By The
  Moon)  198-875
She Only Laughs At Me  520-654
Shepard Blues  1413
Shepherd's Serenade  1040
She Reminds Me Of You  423
Sheridan "Square", A  15

Sherman Shuffle 500
She's A Cornfed Indiana Girl (But She's Mama To Me) 656
She's A Good Girl 1394
She's A Gorgeous Thing 389
She's A Great, Great Girl 469-520-552-870-1291-1614
She Said It 1528
She's A Latin From Manhattan 202-595-1114
She's Alright With Me 327-328
She's A Mean Job 666-915
She's A Mellow Mother For You 679
She's A Mellow Thing 1320
She Saves Her Sweetest Smiles For Me 358
She's Cryin' For Me 807-1000-1004-1132-1744
She's Doin' It Now 628
She's Drivin' Me Wild 133-358-558-652
She Sends Me 824
She's Forty With Me 357
(S)he's Funny That Way 31-420-422-542-564-579-580-690-757-768-950-1062-1151-1341-1491-1620-1743
She's Gone 1712
She's Gone Again 678
She's Gone To Join The Songbirds In Heaven 941-1534
She's Got 'Em 189-658
She's Got Great Ideas 575
She's Got "It" 822-892-929-1530-1664-1665
She's Got Something Good 1371
She's Got Too Much 853
She's Got What I Need 358
She Shall Have Music 938-1148-1313
She's In The Graveyard Now 1026
She's Just Got A Little Bit Left 1708
She's Just The Baby For Me 806
(S)he's My Secret Passion 1035-1098
She's My Sheba, I'm Her Sheik 717-963-1350-1717
She's My Slip Of A Girl 676-952-1214
She's Not Bad 1278
She's Nothing But Nice 357
She's No Trouble 1110
She's Not Too Hot, Not Too Cold 530
She's One Sweet Show Girl 1232
She Squeezed My Lemon 1029
She's So Nice 805-1668
She's Still Dizzy 1716
(S)he's Still My Baby 129-194-267-402-1098-1420
She's Sweeter Than Sugar 1109
She's Tall, She's Tan, She's Terrific 258-781-1631
She Stays Out All Night Long 1042
She's The Daughter Of A Planter From Havana 54
She's The Sweetheart Of Six Other Guys 653-1581
She's Trickin' Me 679
She's Wonderful 1396
She Walked Right Up And Took My Man Away 110-330-1059-1060
She Walks Like A Kangaroo 1413
She Wants To Rattle Me All The Time 628
She Was Just A Sailor's Sweetheart 232-640-1120-1579
She Went And Did Her Dance 765
She Won't Quit But She'll Slow Down 1026

She Wouldn't Do What I Asked Her To 32-1122-1188-1609
Sh-h ! Here Comes My Sugar 351-1562
Sh-h ! It's A Military Secret 1398
Shim-Me-King's Blues 1460
Shim-Me-Sha-Wabble 26-120-138-274-543-649-956-1033-1087-1132-1143-1195-1279-1347-1422
Shim Sham Drag 1726
Shim-Shaming 886
Shim Sham Shimmy (Dance) 422-1708
Shindig 695-1401
Shine 48-67-198-226-348-360-526-603-607-639-660-796-827-894-937-946-1065-1146-1154-1190-1259-1281-1337-1392-1491-1540-1561-1581-1609
Shine On, Harvest Moon 157-198-297-443-698-887-1653-1664
Shine On Your Shoes, A 142-871
Shingled Hearth, A 1162
Ships That Pass In The Night 1252
Ship Without A Sail, A 788-1696
Shipwreck(ed) Blues 1014-1446-1449
Shipyard Ramble 693
Shirt Tail Stomp 591-1077-1078-1233
Shivers 614
Shivery Stomp 503-505-1569
Shoemaker's Holiday, The 747-936-987
Shoe-Shine Boy 52-101-362-491-584-728-938-1001-1074-1239-1327-1415-1561
Shoe-Shine Swing - see SHOE-SHINE BOY
Shoe Shiner's Drag 661-1102
Shoe String Stomp 694
Shoes We Have Left Are All Right, The 641
Sho' Is Hot (sic) 1526-1548
Sho' Nuff Blues (sic), The 810
Shoo Fly 1311
Shooin' Flies 1497
Shoo Shoo Boogie Boo 245-351-1281-1652
Shoot 'Em 1645
Shoo The Hoodoo Away 1294
Shooting The Pistol 1701-1702
Shootin' Star Blues 343-1060
Shoot The Japs For Craps 834
Shoot The Likker To Me, John Boy 589-746-1401
Shoot The Meat Balls To Me, Dominick Boy 431
Shoot The Sherbet To Me, Herbert 448
Shoot The Works 281
Short And Sweet 403-532
Short Dress Gal 1096
Shortenin' Bread 20-373-942-1636
Shorty George 104
Shorty George Blues 541-1617
Should I ? 75-194-195-503-702-1153-1687
Shout, The 1529-1530
Shout And Feel It 102
Shout 'Em, Aunt Tillie 481
Shout For Happiness 346-1127
Shout For Joy 26-27
Shout Hallelujah ! 'Cause I'm Home 500-658-1233-1292-1426
Shouting In That/The Amen Corner 77-1486-1697
Shout, Shout, Shout 259
Shout, Sister, Shout ! 156-169-1070-1706-1707
Showboat Shuffle 489-1074-1167
Showered With The Blues 1488

Show Me That Kind Of A Girl  1368-1612
Show Me The Way  339-1502
Show Me The Way To Go Home  232-233-1219-
   1250-1363-1402-1589-1592
Show Must Go On, The  1464
Show That Fellow The Door  1483
Show Your Linen, Miss Richardson  431-612
Shreveport (Blues)  570-964-1698
Shreveport (Stomp(s)  1100-1102-1120
Shuffle Boogie  850
Shufflebug Shuffle  283
Shuffle Off To Buffalo  158-877-1646
Shuffle Rhythm  1356
Shuffle Your Feet  1277
Shufflin' At The Hollywood  661
Shufflin' Blues  1507
Shufflin' Joe  730
Shufflin' Mose  350-1187-1188
Shuffling Sadie  721
Shut Your Mouth  1700
Shy And Sly  1311
Shy Anna  468
Shylock Blues  1036
Siam Blues  467
Siamese Shuffle  324
Siberia  1181-1664
Siberian Sleigh-Ride  889-1372
Sic 'Em, Tige'  1495
Sick O' Licks  391
Side By Side  463-804-912-929-1173-1272-
   1681
Sidewalk Blues  1-234-338-631-1054-1101-
   1102
Sidewalk Serenade, The  1318
Sidewalks Of New York  268-497-498-1314
Sidewalk Waltz, The  1438
Side Wheeler Blues  1471
Sidney's Blues  113
Sierra Sue  297-909-1289
Siesta  791
Siesta At The Fiesta  15-990
Siffler en travaillant - see WHISTLE
   WHILE YOU WORK
Sigh And Cry Blues  1390
Sighin' Around With The Blues  1462
Sigh No More, Ladies  370
Sighs And Tears  1477
Sigma Chi Dream Girl  70
Signing On At H.M.V.  1634
Signs Of The Highway  395
Si j'aime Suzy  396-1173
Si j'avais ete  313
Si j'avais su  1085
Silence And Fun  1475
Silent On The Southern Seas - see SIREN
   OF THE SOUTHERN SEA
Silhouette  144
Silhouetted In The Moonlight  367-604-
   1063
Sills Stomp  968
Silly Old Moon  260
Silver Head  231-1583
Silver Heels  971
Silver Moon  301
Silver Rose  1230
Silver Slipper Rag  407
Silver Threads Among The Gold  1146
Silver Wings  952
Silvery Moon  210-1294
Silv'ry Moon And Golden Sands  765
Simple And Sweet  125

Simplement  973
Simple Things In Life, The  249-974
Simply Full Of Jazz  1422
Sinbad  1375
Since I Fell In Love With Emmalina  16
Since I Found You  171-463
Since I Met Mary Jane  1226
Since I've Heard It From You  1075
Since Ma Is Playing Mah Jongg  1189
Since My Best Gal/Girl Turned Me Down
   116-551-552-906-907-984-1738
Sincere Love  259
Since She Learned To Ride A Horse  1393
Since They're All Playing Miniature Golf
   1639
Since We Fell Out Of Love  1133
Since We Parted  547
Since When  176
Since You Called Me Sweetheart  471
Since You Came Into My Dreams  809
Since You Have Left Me  1425
Since You're Gone  650
Since You Said You Loved Me  1426
Since You Went Away  476-1076
Sinful Blues  1441
Sing About The Swanee  835
Sing (A Happy Little Thing)  1202-1667
Sing A Little Ditty  1109
Sing A Little Jingle  889-1296-1751
Sing A Little Love Song  83
Sing A Little Low-Down Tune  674-1648
Sing A Little Song  227 -1582
Sing A Little Swing Song  409
Sing A Little Theme Song  246
Sing A Love Song  1552
Sing And Be Happy  781
Sing A New Song  34-146-341-1409-1494
Sing An Old-Fashioned Song (To A Young
   Sophisticated Lady)  204-1031-1415-
   1546-1621-1628
Sing Another Chorus, Please  1386
Singapore Sorrows  20-239-402-470-1089-
   1116-1232
Sing A Song Of Sixpence  1237
Sing A Song Of Sunbeams  370
Sing-A-Spell (A Musical Spelling Bee)
   1250
Sing, Baby, Sing  93-383-780-1126-1519-
   1731
Sing 'Em Blues  1086
Sing For Your Supper  104-183-610
Singing A Happy Song  425-595
Singing A Song  1263
Singing A Vagabond Song  957-1418
Singing Betweem Kisses  700
Singing Hills, The  775
Singin' In The Bathtub  562-1294
Singing In The Moonlight  917
Singin' In The Rain  21-59-421-937-950-
   1064-1301-1509-1584-1743
Singing My Way 'Round The World  395-
   1283
Singing Pretty Songs  12
Singin' River  1153
Singing Sands Of Alamosa, The  744
Singin' The Blues (1920)  583-662-724-
   725-1033-1177-1333-1546-1566-1720-1721
Singin' The Blues (1931)  1144
Sing (It's Good For You)  118-422-581-
   634-875-876-1410
Sing It 'Way Low Down  275-1248

Single Woman's Blues  861
Sing Me A Baby Song  993
Sing Me A Song Of The Islands  1361
Sing Me A Swing Song (And Let Me Dance)
  584-598-1002-1344-1659
Sing On  1095
Sing-Sing Isn't Prison Any More  1745
Sing-Sing Prison Blues  1441
Sing, Sing, Sing  122-427-536-601-607-728
  960-1036-1249
Sing Something Simple  1302-1513
Sing Song Girl (Little Yella Cinderella)
  1234
Sing Song Swing  527
Sing That Song With Feeling  65
Sing, You Sinners  18-83-305-481-729-997-
  1098-1223-1368-1584
Sinking Sun Blues  1677
Sinner Kissed An Angel, A  375-435-453-
  818
Sioux City Sue  796-1189-1609
Sioux Sue  1150
'Sippi  978
Siren Dream, A  1136
Siren Of The Southern Sea  192-328
Siren Serenade  910
Siren's Song, The  612
Sirocco  791
Sisco Harmonica Blues  285
Sissy  746-1241
Sissy Blues  1267
Sissy Man Blues  1036
Sister Ella  1713
Sister Honky Tonk  1109
Sister Kate - see I WISH I COULD SHIMMY
  LIKE MY SISTER KATE
Sittin' And Whittlin'  274
Sittin' Around  339-1182-1579
Sittin' Around And Dreamin'  900
Sittin' Around On Sunday  1491
Sittin' At The Table (Opposite You)  1467
Sittin' Bull  1561
Sittin' By The Fire With You  289-952
Sittin' In  131
Sittin' In A Corner  176-223-344-1354-
  1581
Sittin' In The Dark  51
Sittin' On A Back Yard Fence  1330-1331-
  1688
Sittin' On A Log  1331
Sittin' On A Rainbow  346
Sittin' On A Rubbish Can  1470
Sitting On The Cold Wet Grass  1336
Sittin' On The Curbstone Blues  1230-1439
Sitting On The Garden Gate  1292
Sitting On The Moon  14-702
Sittin' On The Inside, Lookin' At The
  Outside - see WAITIN' FOR THE EVENIN'
  MAIL
Sittin' On Top Of The World  1320-1707
Sittin' Up Waitin' For You  1669
Si tu m'aimes  1350
Si vous n'aimez pas ça  1086-1173
Six Appeal  616
Six Bells Stampede  281
Six Feet Of Papa  310-667
Six Flats Unfurnished  622
Six Lessons From Madame LaZonga  10-96-
  387-433-909-1225
Six Mile Stretch  417
Six Months In Jail  706

Six Or Seven Times  253-479-966-1431
1620 To 1865 (Uncle Eph's Dream)  1184
Sixth Avenue Express  851
Six-Thirty Blues  709
Sixth Street  40
627 Stomp  851
Sixty Seconds Every Minute  532
63rd And Strum  66
Six Wheel Chaser  948
Six Women (Me And Henry The Eighth)  889
Sizzling The Blues  704
Skadatin-Dee  1501-1692
Skad-O-Lee  1338
Skag-a-Lag  1209
Skaters' Waltz (In Swing Time)  369
Ske-Da-De  392
Skee  944
Skeeg-a-Lee Blues  534
Skeeter Blues  570
Skeeter Skoot  1719
Skeleton In The Closet/Cupboard, The  53
  383-536-585-1399
Skeleton Jangle  1176-1179
Skeleton Key Blues  343
Skid-Dat-De-Dat  41
Skidding  319
Skiddle-De-Scow  838
Skies Are Blue  899
Skin And Bones Woman  1542
Skin 'Em Back  1560
Skinner's Sock  977
Skip It  283
Skip, Skat, Doodle-Do  409
Skip The Gutter  43
Skirts  405
Skooter  417
Skrontch  258-517-587-1632
Skoodlum Blues  1161
Skull Duggery  1203
Skunk, The  313
Skunk Hollow Blues  766
Skunk Song, The  453
Sky Fell Down, The  449-615-741
Skylark  126-744-762-819-912
Slap Happy  404-497
Slap Hapy Lassie  1242-1398
Slap Jack  10
Slappin' The Bass  859-1304-1667
Slap That Bass  429-703-1265-1333-1434
Slats' Shuffle  646
Slave To The Blues  1267
Sleep  283-439-796
Sleep, Baby, Sleep  241-507
Sleep (Come On And Take Me)  35-158-1310
  1311
Sleeping And Dreaming Of You  1195
Sleep Talking Blues  1268
Sleepy Blues  501-531
Sleepy Gal - see SLEEPY-TIME GAL
Sleepy Head  201-797-1236
Sleepy Lagoon  436-453-454-636
Sleepy Old Town  153
Sleepy Serenade  742-1552
Sleepy Time  1737
Sleepy Time Blues  1455
Sleepy-Time Gal  129-155-168-203-295-317
  504-630-718-815-920-985-1063-1380-1432
Sleepy Town Express  248
Sleepy Town Train  216
Sleepy Valley  244-951-1712
Slide, Kelly, Slide  1517

Slide, Mr. Jelly  1715
Slide, Mr. Trombone  1070
Slidin' Around  963
Slidin' Thru'  1506
Slidus Trombonus  337
Slight Case Of Ivory, A  644
Slim Slam Boogie  551
Slim Trombone  1351-1522
Sliphorn Sam  1095
Slip Of The Lip, A  500
Slipova  90
Slippery Elm  403-920-961-1054-1286-1389-
  1679
Slippery Hank  549
Slippery Horn  486-487
Slippery Place, A/Slippery Place Rag  1578
  1605
Slippin' And Slidin'  114
Slippin' Around  1139
Slipping Through My Fingers - see I NEARLY
  LET LOVE GO SLIPPING THROUGH MY FINGERS
Sloe Jam Fizz  75
Sloppy Drunk Blues  1646
Sloppy Drunk Woman  1020
Sloppy Joe  478
Sloppy Sue  314-315
Sloppy Water Blues  1622
Slow And Easy  **976**-1145-1366
Slow And Easy Blues  1746
Slow And Easy Man  1445
Slow And Steady  1169
Slow As Molasses  868
Slow Beef  1740
Slow But Sure  592-1145
Slow Death  1713
Slow Down  329-911-1007-1184
Slow Down, Sweet Papa, Mama's Catching Up
  On You  1011
Slow Drag  390
Slow Drag Blues  379-1044
Slow Driving Moan  1268
Slow Freight  283-747
Slow Gee-Gee  1286
Slow Guitar Blues  211
Slowin' Down Blues  1123
Slow Mood  368
Slow Motion  479
Slow Motion (Blues)  318-1110
Slow Music  1291
Slow Poke  180-1180-1347-1353
Slow River  578-1425-1580
Slow Up Papa  735-1024-1060
S-L-U-E Foot  269-338-340-649-1565-**1583**
  (sometimes shown as SLUE`FOOT)
Slum Gallion Stomp  390
Slumming On Park Avenue  728-894-986-1157
Sly Mongoose  1263-1351-1469
Smack  312
Smackin' The Sax  1223
Small Black  1111
Small Blues  1693
Small Fry  79-363-588-1203-1333
Small Town Boy  865
Small Town Girl  702
Smart Alec  663
Smarty (You Know It All)  102-362-1631
Smarty Pants  495-741
Smashing Thirds  1623
Smile  179-274-469-1136-1651-1683
Smile A Little Bit  233-927-1220-1579-1664
Smile All The While  926

Smile, Darn Ya, Smile  539-889-1384-1469
  1670
Smiler (Rag), The  117-1200-1587-1588
Smiles  94-99-207-326-602-603-689-936-
  1142-1325-1392-1553-1562-1603
Smiles And Chuckles  1429
Smile Up At The Sun  1557
Smile Will Go A Long, Long Way  A  71-
  132-882-1001-1663
Smile Your Bluesies Away  1534
Smilin'  218-219
Smiling Irish Eyes  1292-1743
Smiling Joe  1230
Smiling Rose Blues  1065
Smiling Skies  193-340-1047
Smilin' The Blues Away  1104
Smoked Meat Blues  862
Smoke Dreams  585-600-1157
Smoke Dreams Of You  1634
Smoke From A Chimney  206-429-443
Smoke Gets In Your Eyes  200-442-619-
  973-1407-1736
Smoke-House Blues  1101-1421-1564
Smoke-House Rhythm  190-610
Smoke Rings  288-294-387-582-1073-1259-
  1602-1670
Smoke Shop Drag  327
Smokey Blues  1713
Smokey Rattler  1376
Smoking Reefers  3
Smok(e)y Mokes  796-1049-1197-1198-1199-
  1200-1656
Smo-o-oth One, A  261-618
Smooth Sailing  730
Smorgasbord And Schapps  494
Smuggler's Nightmare  1506
Smut  466
Snag 'Em Blues  349
Snag It  172-557-721-898-1167-1172-1365-
  1574
Snag Nasty  1715
Snake Charmer, The  321-554-587-1237-
  1434-1506
Snake Eyes  1209
Snake Hip Dance  358-479
Snake Hips  1072
Snakehips Swings  841
Snake In The Grass  844
Snake Man Blues  842
Snake Rag  1165
Snakes Hips  70-349-559-826-925-1187-
  1210-1350
Snaky Blues, The  665
Snaky Feeling  944-1507
Snapping Cat  1541
Sneakaway  1468
Sneakin' A Sleep  1615
'S Nice, Like This  263
Snitchin' Gambler Blues  1042
Snookum  650
Snoop, The  1434
Snooping Blues  1161
Snootie Little Cutie  453
Snoozer's Blues  1258
Snowball  1-51-77-275-1507
Snowfall  1552
Snowy Morning Blues  765-838-839
Snub's Blues  1109
Snug As A Bug  387
Snug As A Bug In A Rug  1358-1405
Snuggle Up A Bit  1189

1960

Soapstick Blues 1421
Soap Suds 1350
So Ashamed ! 1472
So At Last It's Come To This 1238-1668
Sobbin' Blues 120-126-183-652-868-925-
    957-1056-1132-1165-1168-1347-1354-1399-
    1403-1419
Sobbin' Hearted Blues 1013-1442
Sobbin' Sister Blues 1451
Sobbin' Tears Blues 354
Sobbin' Woman Blues 835
S. O. B. Blues 412
So Beats My Heart For You 196
So Blue 268-668
Sob Sister Sadie 1039-
Society Blues 1485
Society Steps Out 944
Sock That Thing 410
So Comfy 209
So Divine 1415
So Does Your Old Mandarin 133-1483
So Do I 428
So Far, So Good 96-166-372-496
Soft And Sweet 1657
Soft As Spring 619
Softly, As In A Morning Sunrise 1403-
    1412
Soft Pedal Blues 1442
Soft Shoe Shuffle 1431
Soft Winds 297-613-693
So Good 1511
So Help Me 79-423-759
So Is Your Old Lady 523-1182-1643
So Is Your Old Man 1559
So I Took The Fifty Thousand Dollars 1122
S. O. L. Blues 42
Sold 181
Sold American 1064
Soldier Boy Blues 1223
Soldier Dreams Of You Tonight, A 744
Sold It To The Devil 847
Soleil s'en fout, Le 960
Solid Jack 1413
Solid Mama 759
Solid Old Man (Solid Rock) 494-1500-1501
Solid Sam 1408
Soliloquy 143-144-473-1470-1612
Solitary Soul 1121
So Little Time (So Much To Do) 55-206
Solitude 3-52-386-425-488-489-491-496-498
    531-582-594-652-770-780-801-947-984-1073
    1207-1248-1260-1333-1508-1511-1626
Solo Flight 618
Solo Hop 1063
So Lonely And Blue 1541
So Lonesome 196
So Long 528-664-909-1450
So Long, Babe, I'm Gone 844
So Long, Jim 1452
So Long, Joe 1131
So Long North (I'm Headin' South) 1737
So Long, Pal 269-1580
So Long, Shorty 273-693
So Long To You And The Blues 731-1419
So Lovely 1357
So Many Times 432-448-1539
Some Baby, My Gal 530-1717
Some Blues 1012
Somebody, The 155
Somebody And Me 1368                )865
Somebody Done Changed The Lock On My Door

Somebody Done Hoodooed The Hoodoo Man
    864
Somebody Else Is Taking My Place 126-621
    1553
Somebody Else May Be Telling Her Some-
    thing She'd Love To Hear From You 567
Somebody Else's Blues 28
Somebody From Somewhere 34
Somebody I Can Call My Own 954
Somebody Like You 682-1582
Somebody Loses, Somebody Wins 1556
Somebody Loves Me 128-202-226-264-283⁴-
    453-504-599-723-745-923-924-946-1332-
    1476-1571
Somebody Loves You 958-1227
Somebody Mighty Like You 952
Somebody Nobody Knows 206
Somebody Nobody Loves 529-621-1409-1553
Somebody Said - see WHAT DO I CARE WHAT
    SOMEBODY SAID ?
Somebody's Been Lovin' My Baby 1082-
    1094
Somebody's Been Ridin' My Black Gal
    1029
Somebody's Chewin' You Too 1499
Somebody's Crazy About You 620-1745
Somebody's Doin' What You Wouldn't Do
    733
Somebody's Done Me Wrong 1516
Somebody's Eyes 74-630-1611
Somebody's Getting My Love 1323
Somebody's Gonna Get You 195
Somebody's Got To Go 1575
Somebody's Got To Knock A Jug 1455
Somebody's Lonely 129-882 1504
Somebody's Making A Fuss Over Somebody
    1184
Somebody's Thinking Of You Tonight 1244-
    1314-1315
Somebody Stole My Break 53
Somebody Stole My Gal 5-85-107-116-148-
    254-347-348-385-469-541-617-683-713-724
    780-925-938-957-1112-1118-1124-1190-
    1318-1436-1501-1519-1626-1663-1692
Somebody's Walking My Girl Out 590
Somebody Sweet Is Sweet On Me 143-1498
Somebody's Wrong 120-546-560-796-857-
    1221-1239-1391-1523-1576
Somebody Told Me (They Loved Me) 96-1316
    1752
Somebody To Love Me 580-1142
Some Cold Rainy Day 753
Some Day 797-1242-1479-1611
Someday Blues 353-851
Some Day I'll Be Gone Away 849
Someday, Someday 1019
Someday, Sweetheart 12-77-106-193-237-
    304-335-361-436-554-561-586-596-604-792
    795-821-957-1099-1101-1166-1167-1174-
    1183-1206-1241-1390-1400-1481-1500-1551
    1600-1614-1652-1677-1718
Someday We'll Meet Again 534
Someday You'll Come Back To Me 735-1024
Someday You'll Know 1495
Someday You'll Realize You're Wrong 244
Someday You'll Say "O.K." 520-653-708
Some Do And Some Don't 99-1494
Some Early Morning 706
Some Fun 1080
Somehow 761
Some Jazz Blues 1045

Some Like It Hot   95-907-1160
Some Little Bird   338
Some Little Someone   737
Some More Rhythm   470
Some Of These Days   45-140-252-282-339-348-
361-386-399-536-543-563-567-568-585-610-
625-687-689-720-780-790-797-801-826-869-
894-919-939-961-968-974-1022-1069-1123-
1130-1141-1178-1183-1259-1280-1367-1409-
1432-1470-1482-1519-1563-1574-1585-1647-
1652-1744
Some Of These Mornings   1013
Someone   500-1148
Someone Else May Be There While I'm Gone
179
Someone Else Will Yake Your Place   793
Someone I Love   170
Someone Is Losin' Susan   129-625-1036-1420-
1671
Someone Like You Around Me   178
Someone Loves You After All   796-970
Someone Outside Is Taking Your Mind Off Me
342
Someone Sang A Sweeter Song To Mary   1302
Someone's Been Lovin' My Baby   941
Someone's Falling In Love   1152
Someone's Rocking My Dreamboat   621-694-
744-1409
Someone's Stolen My Sweet (Sweet) Baby
190-462-510-573-1478
Someone's Teaching Me How To Forget   514
Someone/Somebody Stole Gabriel's Horn   142-
361-422-583-791-1537-1556-1645
Someone To Care For Me   182-738-894
Someone To Love Me   1091
Someone To Take Your Place   849
Someone To Watch Over Me   268-946-1696
Some Other Day-Some Other Girl   926
Some Other Spring   769-1736
Some Other Time   687-1469
Somepin' Slow And Low   1718
Some Rainy Day   992-1151-1633
Some Rhythm   470
Some Saturday   1501
Some Sort Of Somebody   315
Some Sunny Day   68-1085-1722
Some Sweet Day (1917)   51-1014-1033-1086
Some Sweet Day (1929)   567-658-888-1312-
1595
Some Sweet Day (1938)   824
Some Sweet Rainy Day   737
Something   1602
Somethin' Doin'   696
Somethin' Goin' On Wrong   344-824
Something Had To Happen   1689
Something Has Happened To Me   893
Something I Dreamed, No Doubt   374
Something Is Gonna Give Me Away   689
Something New   109-374-619
Something Seems Tingle-ingle-ing   315
Something's Gonna Happen To You   812
Something's Gotta Be Done   1646
Something's Wrong   1344
Something Tells Me   55-111-1357-1632
Something To Remember   203
Something To Remember You By   506-1153-1553
Something To Shout About   1737
Something's Wrong With My Mind   680
Sometimes   82-694
Sometimes I Feel Like A Motherless Child
80-401-1409-1696

Sometimes I'm Happy   15-81-172-333-505-
596-600-648-869-1142-1425-1430
Sometimes I Think I Love You   1041
Sometimes I Wonder   112
Sometime When You're Alone   1206
Somewhere   167-910
Somewhere A Voice Is Calling   453-1539-
Somewhere In Erin   234
Somewhere In Naples   885
Somewhere In The West   35-118-895
Somewhere With Somebody Else   94-125
Sonata By L. van Beethoven (sic) (part
of the "Pathetique" Sonata, Op. 13)
989
Song From A Cotton Field   179
Song I Love, The   502
Song Is Ended, The   55-669-1136-1337-
1378
Song Is You, The   447-454
Song Of Happiness   1296
Song Of India ("Sadko"-Rimsky-Korsakov)
295-440-451
Song Of Old Hawaii   742
Song Of Songs   590
Song Of Spring   293
Song Of Surrender   159-1331-1669
Song Of The Bayou   676-858
Song Of The Blues   244-245-1233-1381
Song Of The Cotton Field   472
Song Of The Fiddlers   875
Song Of The Flame   1503
Song Of The Islands   46-106-945-1236-
1556
Song Of The Plow   531-752
Song Of The Islands   1152
Song Of The Swanee   1345
Song Of The Vagabonds   754
Song Of The Vipers   52
Song Of The Volga Boatmen, The   279-430
Song Of The Wanderer   103-171-209-268-
369-668-693-764-778-814-890-921-1521
Song Without A Name, The   247-1370
So Nice Seeing You Again   203
Sonny Boy (1927)   568
Sonny Boy (1928)   144-626-1195-1342
Son Of The Sun   1537
Sonya (Yup, Alay Yup !)   231
Sooke Hey Hey   1419
Soon (There'll Just Be Two Of Us)   202-
797-809-1142-1154
Soon This Morning   1268
Soothing Lullaby   72
Soothing Syrup   859
Soothin' Syrup (Stomp)   1622
Sophisticated Jump   342
Sophisticated Lady   3-159-289-347-486-
487-491-496-583-946-984-996-1277-1335-
1528-1646 ,
Sophisticated Swing   124-696-786
Sophomore   898
Sophomore Prom.   520-655-1666
So Rare   59-603-695
Sorecerer's Apprentice, The (Dukas)   1360
Sore Bunion Blues   1093-1747
Sorghum Switch   436-1674
Sorority Stomp, The   1078
Sorrow   689
Sorrowful Blues   461-643-1440-1466
Sorrow Valley Blues   343-1376
Sorry   82-116-722-838-1068
Sorry And Blue   576

1962

S. O. S.  1401-1412-1434
So Soon This Morning Blues  352
So Sorry  514
So Sure Of You - see IF I HADN'T BEEN SO
  SURE OF YOU
So Sweet  253-1153
So's Your Old Man  138-165
So That's The Kind Of A Girl You Are  646-
  1380
So The Bluebirds And The Blackbirds Got
  Together  1089-1127
So They Say  538
So This Is Heaven  250-365
So This Is Venice  337-970
So Tired  578-1054-1290
So True  470
Soubrette  806
S(o)udan  675-748-1003 (see also IN THE
  SOUDAN)
Sou dans la poche, Un  1349
Soul And Body (He Belongs To Me)  343-708-
  1024-1257
Sounding The Lead On The Ohio River  666
Sounds From Africa  1197
So Unexpectedly  1237  Sour Grapes  139
Sourire en chantant, Un  1596
Sous les palmiers  650
South  742-1109-1110-1203-1306-1656
South African Blues  328-1495-1738
South African Stomp  328
South American Way  30
Southbound  752-930-1515
South Bound Blues  1057-1266
South Bound Rag  143
South Breeze  1081
Southern Beauties Rag  1255
Southern Belle, A  1254
Southern Blues  679-1265
Southern Casey Jones  781
Southern Echoes  664-832
Southern Exposure  832-1752
Southern Fried  97-387-417-1225-1397-1411
Southern Girl Blues  1674
Southern High Water Blues  1455
Southern Hospitality  1378-1473
Southern Rose  228-796-1582
Southern Sea Blues  859
Southern Shout  409
Southern Stomos, The  1166
Southern Sunset  1427
Southern Woman Blues  152-353
Southland  303-401
Southland Shuffle  96
South Of The Border  589-1506
Southology  1354
South Parkway Blues  750
Southpaw Serenade  167
South Rampart Street Blues  313-369-1128
South Rampart Street Parade  367-1343
South's Been A Mother To Me, The  684
South Sea Island Magic  1027-1398
South Side  761
South Side Shuffle  764
South Side Stomp  406
South Side Stuff  1746
South Street Blues  861-1007-1024-1109
South Street Stomp  1430
South Wind  269-299-394-532-573-1616
South With The Boarder  590-1004
Souvenir (Drdla)  997
Souvenir of Duke Ellington, A  487

Souvenirs (1927)-see AMONG MY SOUVENIRS
Souvenirs (1938)  1261
So What !  164-450-1161
So You Left Me For The Leader Of A Swing
  Band  1434
So You're The One  1318
So You Won't Jump  1038
So You Won't Sing  905
Space, Man  1490
Spaghetti  1131
Spain  372
Spaniard That Blighted My Life, The  970
Spanish Dream  983-1222
Spanish Dreams (Española Blues)  458
Spanish Fantasy  469
Spanish Kick  98
Spanish Mama  265-338-676-1182-1739
Spanish Shawl  397-559-561-719-862-927-
  961-1028-1068-1342-1380-1555-1700
Spanish Swat  1106
Spanish Sweetheart  148
Spanking The Baby  379
Spank It  824
Spare Ribs And Spaghetti  18
Speak Easy  373
Speakeasy (Blues)  1159-1703
Speaking Of Heaven  165
Speaking Of Kentucky Days - see I'M
  SPEAKING OF KENTUCKY DAYS
Speak Now Or Hereafter Hold Your Peace
  1729
Speak To Me Of Love  291
Special Delivery  261
Special Delivery Blues  1618
Special Delivery Stomp  1407
Specializin' In Loving You  558
Speed  471
Speedway Blues  753
Speedy Boy  130-840-1325-1581
Speevy  1260
Spellbound  291-879
Spell Of The Blues, The  420-970
Spendin' All My Time With The Blues 1308
Sphinx, The  402-631-633-1177-1242-1611
Spider And The Fly, The  588-746-1633-
  1634
Spider Crawl  88-1645
Spider Man Blues  1445
Spider's Nest Blues  1043
Spider Web Blues  1487
Spiked Beer  1669
Spinnin' The Webb  1660
Spirit Of '49 Rag  1563
Spirit's Got Me  434
Spirituelle  144
Spitfire  387-1074
Sploghm  551
Spo-De-O-Dee  537-1210-1547
Sponge Cake And Spinach  134
Spookie Woogie  1412
Spooky Takes A Holiday - see SATAN TAKES
  A HOLIDAY
Spooning  1085
Sporting House Rag  1107
Sport Model Mama  753
Sporty Joe  1457
S'posin'  83-95-503-507-562-693-901-949-
  1152-1293-1558-1629
Spread A Little Happiness  1336
Spreadin' Knowledge Around  1236
Spreadin' Rhythm Around  780-1627-1731

Spread Yo' Stuff  1204-1351-1649
Spring Cleaning  1630
Springdale Blues  270
Spreadin' Rhythm Around  1115
Spread Yo' Stuff  547-548-557-1008
Spring Cleaning (Getting Ready For Love)
  780-1027
Spring Fever  143-144-683-1655-1664
Springfield Stomp  1370
Spring Has Come  32
Spring Is Here  561-1512
Spring Is Here Again  919
Spring It In The Summer And She'll Fall
  1292
Spring Song (Mendelssohn)  440-612
Springtime  379
Springtime Is Love Time  866
Springtime Rag  1052
Squabblin'  1204
Squabblin' Blues  537-1012
Squareface  565-582-1207
Squattin' At The Grotto  687
Squaty Roo  767
Squawkin' The Blues  749-1026-1371
Squealing Pig Blues  379-976-1748
Squeeze Me  43-75-77-114-367-614-650-699-
  752-977-1008-1210-1443-1511-1635-1660-
  1700-1703
Squeeze Me Tight  848
Squeezin' The Blues  1411
Squibs  23
Stack Of Barley  1552
Stack O' Lee Blues  254-415-463-474-963-
  1267-1324-1391-1551-1641-1673-1694
Stage Fright  904
Stairway To The Stars  206-432-527
Stale Bread Blues  1128
Stalling For Time  1402
Stampede  143-267-524-578-720-728-903-
  1115-1138-1362
Stampede in G minor  108
Stamp Your Feet  1089
Stand Back And Smile (Say Ella)  832
Stand By ! For Further Announcements (And
  More Good News)  662
Standin' In The Rain Blues  1445
Standing On The Corner Blues  1037
Stanshaw Stomp  1506
Star Dust  3-49-86-131-167-183-254-274-
  275-276-296-311-317-385-401-438-439-451
  497-582-590-595-597-605-613-638-646-689
  690-696-724-782-786-829-959-984-1071-
  1076-1081-1248-1333-1404-1407-1432-1529
  1631-1645
Stardust On The Moon  442-739
Star Fell Out Of Heaven, A  93-382
Star Gazing  89-798
Starlight  287-1285
Starlight And Tulips  1546
Starlight Bay  176
Starlit Hour, The  371-448-527-704
Stars  486-594
Stars And Stripes Forever  1572-1662
Stars Fell On Alabama  201-594-809-879-
  1538
Stars In My Eyes  1026
Stars In The Making  1207
Stars Know I'm In Love With You, The 1249
Stars Remain, The  742
Start Jumpin'  788
Starvation Blues  1507

Starvin' For Love  1090
State And Madison  738-1106
State And Tioga Stomp - see BELGIUM
  STOMP
State Of Tennessee Blues  1041
State Street Blues  263-349-705-1059-
  1523-1672
State Street Jive  389
State Street Shuffle  173
State Street Special  115-1746
State Street Style  118
Static  75-1054
Static Strut  233-720-1192-1210-1364-
  1483-1529-1592
Station House Rag  1727
Stavin' Chain  843-1542
Stavin' Change (The Meanest Man In New
  Orleans)  1180-1608
Stay  1628
Stay As Sweet As You Are  1530
Stay Away From My Door  783
Stayin' At Home  215-1536
Stayin' Home  234
Stay On It  783
Stay On The Right Side Of The Road  361-
  1149
Stay Out Of Love ('Cause That's Where
  The Blues Begin)  779-959
Stay Out Of The South  340-500-785-1343-
  1581
Steady Grind  1487
Steady Grinding  847
Steady Rock Blues  1746
Steady Roll  1099-1723
Steady Roll Blues  193-356
Steady Steppin' Papa  762
Steady Teddy  1243
Steak And Potatoes - see IF LOVE MAKES
  YOU GIVE UP STEAK AND POTATOES
Steal Away  1207
Stealin' Apples  612-728-729-1092-1402-
  1554
Stealin' Blues  389
Stealing Love  1170
Stealin' Stealin'  1042
Stealing To Virginia  71
Steamboat Bill  236-1565-1593
Steamboat Days  1704
Steamboat Man Blues  1451
Steamboat Sal  552-1239
Steamboat Stomp  1101-1390
Steaming Blues  569
Steel Drivin' Sam  1449
Steel Mill Blues  750
Steel Roof  1429
Steel String Blues  803-1209
Stein Song  1621
Step By Step  1412
Step, Daddy  1193
Stephane's/Stephen's Blues  635-636
Stephane's Tune  635
Step It  1420
Step On It  1711
Step On The Blues  804
Steppin' Along  17-245-777
Steppin' Around  552
Steppin' Fool  1219
Steppin' In Society  314-1380
Steppin' It Off  1222
Steppin' Into Swing Society  492
Steppin' Old Fool  538

1964
Steppin' On The Blues  64
Steppin' On The Gas  1095-1161
Steppin' Out  71-712-891-905-973-1189
Stepping Out Of The Picture  700
Steppin' Out To Swing  387
Steppin' Pretty  899
Step Up And Shake My Hand  1633-1691
Stevedore Blues  1729
Stevedore Man  1729
Stevedore's Serenade, The  493
Stevedore Stomp  478-996
Sticks And Stones  15-184
Stick Up Woman (Let Me Make Trip With You)  1542
Still I Love Her  1383
Still The Bluebird Sings  95-324-740
Stingaree  1500 (see also STRINGAREE)
Stingaree Blues  136-436-793-1170-1724
Stingaree Man Blues  995-1376
Stinging Bee Blues  846
Stinging Snake Blues  820
Stingy Woman  1041
Stitches  342
Stockholm  1262-1284
Stockholm Stomp  546-721-994-1174-1182-1221
Stock Yards Strut  891
Stole My Man Blues  343
Stolen Heaven  321
Stolen Kisses  1021
Stomp  189-660
Stomp Along  641
Stomp Caprice  499
Stomp Dance  1605
Stomp 'Em Down  569
Stomp 'Em Down To The Bricks  181
Stomping (1931)  1744
Stompin' (1936)  540
Stompin' Around  292 (see also STOMPS, THE)
Stompin' At Decca  1261
Stompin' At The Panama  328
Stomping At The Reeny  695
Stompin' At The Savoy  309-316-428-555-595-597-599-607-614-676-745-859-879-960-1124-1477-1531-1658-1659
Stompin' At The Stadium  445-1125
Stompin' Away  1045
Stompin' 'Em Down  752
Stompin' 'Em Along Slow  844
Stompin' Fool  38-139-1183
Stompin' On Down  1209
Stompin' The Bug  1622
Stomp It, Mr. Kelly  867
Stomp It Off  447-984
Stomp It Out, Gate  783
Stomp Off, Let's Go  350-369-658-764-927-973-1130-1364-1529
Stompology  660
Stomps, The  936
Stomp That Thing  1045
Stomp Time Blues  1536
Stompy Jones  114-134-488-497
Stomp Your Blues Away  1024
Stomp Your Feet  467-468
Stomp Your Stuff  1068-1495
Stonewall Blues  1043
Stop! And Ask Somebody  168-342
Stop And Fix It, Mama  1378
Stop And Listen  849-1459
Stop ! And Reconsider  321-401-430-1357

Stop Beatin' Around The Mulberry Bush  103-183-444-588-1435
Stop Coming And Come  778
Stop Crying  1171
Stop Flirting  1531
Stop It  60
Stop It, I Love It  1365
Stop It, Joe  357-839-1023
Stop ! It's Wonderful  447-1359-1411-1436
Stop Kicking My Heart Around  448-1539
Stop Kidding  1033
Stop Laying That Stuff On Me  180
Stop, Look And Listen  94-423-427-441-1602
Stop My Barrelhouse Ways  849
Stop Myself From Worryin' Over You  1654
Stoppin' The Traffic  1084
Stop Pretending (So Hep You See)  832-1636
Stop ! Rest Awhile  1461-1749
Stop Teasin' Me  1238
Stop That Black Bottom Dance - see TAKE YOUR BLACK BOTTOM OUTSIDE
Stop That Dog (He's Goin' Mad)  1239
Stop That Jive  1414
Stop, The Red Light's On  329-911
Stop The Sun, Stop The Moon (My Gal's/Man's Gone)  34-77-157-1409
Stop The War (The Cats Are Killin' Themselves)  1004
Stop Truckin' And Suzi-Q  1528
Stop Wastin' My Time  860
Stop, You're Breaking My Heart  366-1552
Stop, You're Tickling Me  642
Stop Your Kidding  915-1185-1186-1672
Stormy Monday Blues  762
Stormy Night Blues  627
Stormy Sea Blues  1267
Stormy Weather  3-199-311-487-496-581-652-827-924-1279-1310-1468-1530-1653
Story Book Ball, The  410-665
Story Of A Starry Night, The  744
Stowaway  756
Straddle The Fence  1071
Straight Back Home  1431
Straight Eight Boogie  1243
Straight From The Shoulder (Right From The Heart)  1146
Straight To Love  761
Strange As It Seems  255-651
Strange Blues  582-999
Strange Cargo  166
Strange Enchantment  95-370
Strange Faces  700
Strange Fact, A  689
Strange Fruit  115-769
Strange Loneliness, A  124-1401-1402
Strange Lovin' Blues  1013
Strange Man  643
Stranger  1374
Stranger Blues  1061
Strangers  77-726
Stranger's Blues  1617
Strangers In The Dark  441-1314
Stranger Things Have Happened  1359
Strange Woman's Dream(s)  555-1215
Stratford Hunch  1100
Stratosphere  984
Stratton Street Strut  1238
Streamline  1399

Streamline Blues 1542
Streamlined Gretna Green 967
Streamline Gal 1467
Streamline Strut 23-277-1124-1432
Street Department Papa 1452
Street Of Dreams 454
Street Walker Blues 753
Street Walkin' Blues 1548-1647
Stretch It, Boy 1029
Stretch Yo' Face 1744
Strewin' Your Mess 1678
Strictly Cullud Affair 254
Strictly Formal 787
Strictly For The Persians 321
Strictly From Dixie 526-946
Strictly Instrumental 307-819-991
Strictly Jive 1660
Strictly Swing 692
Strike Up The Band 303-979-1142-1302
Stringaree (sic - Stingaree ?) 151
String Beans 1335
Stringin' Along On A Shoe String 12
Stringing The Blues 1596
String Of Pearls, A 622-744
Strivin' Blues 1090
Strokin' Away 1104
Struggle 1649
Struggle Buggy 1170
Strugglin' 132
Strugglin' Woman's Blues 1451
Strut Long Papa 1022
Strut Me 706
Strut Miss Lizzie 336-705-1081-1177-1204
  1225-1492-1674
Struttin' At The Strutters' Ball 1185-
  1524
Struttin' Blues 731-732-1719
Struttin' Jerry 1183
Struttin' Jim 1608
Struttin' My Stuff 841
Struttin' The Blues 320-389
Struttin' With Some Barbecue 42-55
Strut Your Material 1462
Strut Yo' Puddy 733
Strut Yo' Stuff 1208
Studio Stomp 190
Studio 24 1284
Study In Blue, A 322-692
Study In Brown, A 102-124-217-294-755-
  1400-1506
Study In Green, A 323
Study In Modernism 324
Study In Red, A 323
Study In Surrealism 324
Stuff 782-1323
Stuff, etc. 1332
Stuff Is Here And It's Mellow, The 180-
  1073-1678-1710
Stuff's Out, The (It Jumped Just A Minute
  Ago) 1560
Stumbling 9-220-367-1085-1357-1613
Stuttering 69-119-170-221-1462
Stuttering Blues 1209
Sub-Deb Blues 106
Subtle Lament 494
Subtle Slough 1501
Subway Sobs 1209
Sudan - see SOUDAN
Sud Buster's Dream 1209
Sud Bustin' Blues 713-854-1229-1617
Sue, I Don't Want You No More 212

Suey 115
Su Ez Za 1518
Sugar (1926) 133-138-179-465-468-505-608
  635-764-795-959-1032-1037-1110-1183-
  1332-1622-1651-1684-1697-1735
Sugar (1927) 524-994-1038-1139-1548-1567
Sugar (1931) 726
Sugar Babe 1162-1389
Sugar Babe, I'm Leavin' ! 1496
Sugar Baby 1120
Sugar Blues 5-109-251-284-458-527-685-
  686-749-835-915-1010-1071-1092-1119-
  1171-1299-1544-1627-1710-1719
Sugar Boogie 1560
Sugar Bowl Blues 1542
Sugar Daddy 815
Sugar Foot Stomp 189-375-403-425-543-595
  603-605-658-718-724-725-745-1165-1166-
  1228-1342-1358-1398-1572-1661 (see also
  DIPPER MOUTH BLUES)
Sugar Foot Strut 28-43-366-1360
Sugar Hill Function 12
Sugar Hill Shim-Sham 1500
Sugar House Stomp 313
Sugar Is Back In Town 20-351
Sugar Is Sweet And So Are You 1248
Sugar Pie 1662
Sugar Plum 779-1491-1689-1731
Sugar Pudding 1042
Sugar Rose 536-584-1628
Sugar Step 468
Sugar (That Sugar Baby O' Mine) 1146
  (probably the 1926 SUGAR - see above)
Sugar Woman Blues 1413
Sugar Your Tea Stomp 1682
Suicide Blues 860-1673
Suitcase Blues 27-1549-1618
Suitcase Breakdown 1480
Suitcase Susie 1635
Suite No. 8 1409
Suite 16 - see OH ! THAT SWEET IN SUITE
  16
Sultan Serenade 730
Summer Days 975
Summer Holiday 1002-1027
Summer Nights 73-133-1498
Summer Rhapsody 808
Summer Souvenirs 322-1357
Summertime 113-369-767-905-1273-1511
Summit Ridge Drive 1407
Sump'n'/Sumpin' 'Bout Rhythm 489-1562
Sunbeams 1513
Sunbonnet Blue, A (And A Yellow Straw
  Hat) 203-1730
Sunbonnet Sue 207
Sun Brimmers 1041
Sunburst 307
Sunday 186-284-324-335-462-542-577-775-
  807-808-1231-1246-1611-1718
Sunday Afternoon 1046
Sunday In The Park 787
Sunday Morning Blues 101-995
Sundays Are Reserved 913
Sunday Special 1116
Sundown Blues 666-1543
Sunflower Blues 1515
Sun Goes Down In Blood, The 1542
Sun-Kist Rose 884-914
Sunny Disposish 578-604-1136
Sunny Hawaii 632
Sunny Jim 1525

Sunny Side Of Things, The 322-1158
Sunny Side Up 952-1569
Sunny Skies 31-346-1343-1426
Sunny Sunflower Land 1427
Sunrise Serenade 296-589-590-647-889
Sun Risin' Blues 1575
Sunset 260-963
Sunset At Sea 374-1242
Sunset Blues 313
Sunset Cafe Stomp 41-1656
Sunset Lullaby 1089
Sun's Gonna Shine 112
Sunshine (1927) 1596
Sunshine (1928) 1583
Sunshine (1935) 1322
Sunshine Baby 1549
Sunshine Blues 1041
Sunshine Capers 90
Sunshine Girl 976
Sunshine Of Your Smile, The 453-1258
Sunshine Special 543-1069-1370
Sun Showers 54-703-1733
Sun's In My Heart, The 874
Sun Spots 1689
Sun Will Shine Tonight, The 661
Super Chief 107-816
Superman 617
Super-Special Picture Of The Year, The 1745
Superstitious Blues 209-1190-1609
Supper Time 1404
Suppose Nobody Cared 391
Supposing 1356
Sure Enough Blues 30-273-1367
Sur les bords de l'Alamo-see ON THE ALAMO
Surrealism 94
Susianna 961-1367-1418
Susie 542-1741
Susquehanna Home 227-1122-1379
Sutton Mutton 904-905
Susie's Feller - see I JUST WANNA BE KNOWN
    AS SUSIE'S FELLER (or as SUZIE'S FELLER)
Suva 748
Suzannah 881-1305
Swaller-Tail Coat 1708
Swamp Blues 314-721-920-967-1309-1730
Swamp Fire 183-386-432-745-1239
Swamp Ghosts 1470
Swampland 1109
Swampland Is Calling Me, The 1468
Swampy River 476-486
Swanee 138-536-977-1506-1748
Swanee Bluebird 220-1614
Swanee Butterfly 229-717
Swanee Lullaby 254-1072
Swanee Mammy 159
Swanee Rhapsody - see LAZY RHAPSODY
Swanee Ripples Rag 1605
Swanee River 123-182-451-583-691-816-907-
    985-1258-1536
Swanee River Blues 155-712
Swanee River Swing 537
Swanee's Calling Me 1276
Swanee Shore 356-708-1580
Swanee Shuffle 479-1055
Swanee Smiles 1162
Sweat Blues 1518
Sweep 'Em Clean 308
Sweepin' The Blues Away 1264
Sweeping The Clouds Away 286-341-1329-
    1382
Sweet Adeline 893-1401

Sweet And Black 1419
Sweet And High 756
Sweet And Hot 421-465-582-724-898-1144-
    1235-1303
Sweet And Lovely 197-299-673
Sweet And Low 1455
Sweet And Low-Down 573-1250-1696
Sweet 'n' Pretty Mama Blues 547
Sweet And Simple 423-1730
Sweet And Slow 89-285-1000-1626
Sweet And Tender 1357
Sweet Aneta Mine 1103
Sweet As A Song 55-295-554-880
Sweet Baby 456-976-1257
Sweet Baby Doll 541-1166
Sweet Baby, Goodbye ! 571
Sweet Beginning Like This, A - see DO
    YOU INTEND TO PUT AN END TO A SWEET
    BEGINNING LIKE THIS ?
Sweet Birds 1470
Sweet Black Blues 1742
Sweet Bunch Of Daisies 1655
Sweet Butter 1581
Sweet Chariot 483
Sweet Child 665-1517
Sweet Child (I'm Wild About You) 74-462-
    927-1305-1483-1565
Sweet Chorus 1259
Sweet Cookie 380-1461
Sweet Cookie Mine 665
Sweet Daddy (Blues) 841-1008
Sweet Daddy It's You I Love 1692
Sweet De Papa Blues 709
Sweet Dreams Of Love 481
Sweet Dreams, Sweetheart 1359
Sweet Ella May 540-757-1595
Sweet Eloise 186
Sweet Emmalina/Emmaline 994-1158-1217-
    1702
Sweet Emalina/Emaline, My Gal 781-1531
Sweetest Daddy In Town 7
Sweetest Gal In Town 1528
Sweetest Melody 1078-1223
Sweetest Of All My Dreams 874
Sweetest Story Ever Told, The 1333
Sweetest Thing Born 1413
Sweet Feet 1045
Sweet Genevieve 372-373
Sweet Georgia Brown 128-142-170-172-193-
    231-253-303-313-360-401-610-683-690-693
    758-778-814-835-857-895-910-963-1123-
    1143-1154-1180-1227-1244-1261-1341-1469
    1476-1502-1519-1547-1592-1650
Sweet Girl 155
Sweet Girl Mary 1025
Sweetheart 246-695
Sweet Heartache 1585-1630
Sweetheart Blues 1392
Sweetheart Darlin' 674
Sweetheart Days 1582
Sweetheart, Honey, Darlin', Dear 908
Sweetheart (In My Dreams Tonight) 1297
Sweetheart Land 1413
Sweetheart Memories 1425
Sweetheart Of All My Dreams 1-242-567-
    627-949-950-1069
Sweetheart O' Mine 774-1016-1101
Sweetheart Of My Dreams 211
Sweetheart Of My Student Days 1594
Sweetheart Of Sigma Chi 445-884-1357-
    1368-1644
Sweetheart Of The Dawn 918

Sweetheart Of T. K. O., The   302
Sweetheart Of Yesterday   917-1111
Sweethearts' Holiday   659-1293
Sweethearts On Parade   48-57-242-314-375-
   502-579-580-644-661-1195
Sweethearts Or Strangers   1243
Sweetheart Swing   968
Sweetheart, We Need Each Other   951-1234-
   1301
Sweet Henry (The Pride Of Tennessee)   1424
   1509
Sweet Ida May   351
Sweetie Dear   113-337
Sweetie Pie   1624-1644
Sweet Indiana Home   69-221
Sweet Is The Word For You   440-695-1399
Sweet Jazz O' Mine   481
Sweet Jennie/Jenny Lee   196-252-504-852-
   1127-1143-1196-1621
Sweet Kentucky Lou   247
Sweet Kisses   1710
Sweet Lady   141
Sweet Leilani   601-1279
Sweet Like This   1169
Sweet Like You   429
Sweet Little Buttercup   1375
Sweet Little Papa   41
Sweet Little Sis   641
Sweet Little You   595-657-808-1252-1574
Sweet Liza   31-118-1079-1548
Sweet Lizzie   328
Sweet Lorraine (1928)   67-114-274-329-608-
   1002-1032-1089-1151-1154-1155-1399-1531-
   1600-1726-1730-1736
Sweet Lorraine (1929)   415
Sweet Louisiana Louise   514
Sweet Lovable You   501
Sweet Lovin' Mama (Please Come Back To Me)
   458-863-915-1187
Sweet Lovin' Man   1132-1165
Sweet Madness   290-835-1331
Sweet Mama Goodie   1577
Sweet Mama, Papa's Getting Mad   153-474-
   480-481-705-1007-1063-1177-1351-1522
Sweet Man   89-232-313-510-624-1097-1215-
   15451583-1592-1650
Sweet Man Blues   82-1119-1649
Sweet Mandy   1218
Sweet Man Joe   1057-1520
Sweet Man O' Mine   38-1461-1576
Sweet Man Was The Cause Of It All   1011
Sweet Marie   172
Sweetmeats   1255
Sweet Misery Of Love   122
Sweet Mistreater   1444
Sweet Mumtaz   1344-1345
Sweet Music   725
Sweet Music Man   583
Sweetness   580-950-1039-1098-1301
Sweetness Rag   971
Sweet Nothing(s)   1417
Sweet Nothings Of Love   853-952
Sweet Not Sour   916
Sweet One   70
Sweet Papa   151
Sweet Papa Butterbeans And Sweet Mama
   Susie   213
Sweet Papa Joe   706-1189
Sweet Papa Low Down   143
Sweet Papa Will Be Gone   461
Sweet Papa Willie   778

Sweet Patootie   1427-1564-1720 (see also
   SWEET PATUNIA)
Sweet Patootie Blues   26
Sweet Patunia   412
Sweet Pease   1489
Sweet Peter   1103-1106
Sweet Potato Blues   892
Sweet Potato Piper   449-1397
Sweet Rhythm   255-983
Sweet Rider Blues   750
Sweet Rosie O'Grady   1314
Sweet Rosita   1144
Sweet Rough Man   1268
Sweet Safronia   550
Sweet Savannah Sue   45-1080-1623-1715
Sweet Serenade   1642
Sweet Sixteen And Never Been Kissed   147
Sweet Smellin' Mama (Poro Blues)   1059
Sweet Someone   972
Sweet Something   876
Sweet Sorrow Blues   792
Sweet Someone   205-367
Sweet Strangers   606-1064
Sweet Strings   1604
Sweet Stuff   962
Sweet Substitute   1107
Sweet Sue - Just You   20-51-63-64-85-114-
   318-383-445-501-581-599-608-636-792-821
   858-930-958-960-968-977-987-1033-1146-
   1151-1207-1213-1224-1232-1249-1258-1262
   1279-1406-1419-1432-1599-1614-1626-1633
   1642-1660-1670-1686
Sweet Summer Breeze   981
Sweet Sweet Mama   522
Sweet Talk   273
Sweet Temptation Man   707
Sweet Thing   235-720-943-1240-1627
Sweet Ukulele Maid   1291-1738
Sweet Uncle Zeke   1640
Sweet Varsity Sue   124-1401
Sweet Violets   382-873-874-1368-1409
Sweet Virginia   1560
Sweet Virginia Blues   1463
Sweet Yvette   269
Swing, The   155-396
Swinga-Dilla Street   1635
Swing Along, Honey, And Smile   112
Swing Along With Me   832
Swing And Sway   587-1434
Swinganola   24
Swing As It Comes   525
Swing Band   684
Swing, Big Ben   385
Swing, Boy, Swing   1240
Swing, Brot ers, Swing   102-769-960-1000-
   1432-1467
Swing Cat Swing   1496
Swing de Paris   1261-1262
Swing Fan   387
Swing Fever   540
Swing For Sale   182-1433
Swing 41   1262
Swing 42   1262
Swing Gate   1646
Swing Guitars   330-1259
Swing High   451
Swing High, Swing Low   293-384-686-894-
   1399
Swingin'   311
Swingin' A Dream   165-741
Swinging Along   379-568

1968
Swingin' And Jivin'  775
Swingin' And Jumpin'  730
Swinging At (The) Chez Florence  960-961
Swingin' At The Cotton Club  1557
Swingin' At Maida Vale  281
Swingin' At The Chat 'n' Chew  1195
Swinging At The Daisy Chain  101
Swingin' At The Hickory House  1001
Swingin' At The Lido  839
Swingin' At The Sugar Bowl  369-776
Swingin' Dem Cats  1084
Swingin' Down  758
Swingin' Down The Lane  168-775-925-1570
Swinging Down To Rio  94-250
Swingin' 'em Down  828
Swinging For A Swiss Miss  960
Swingin' For Joy  1720
Swingin' For Mezz  1053
Swingin' For The King  686-699-775
Swinging Guitars  217
Swingin' In A Hammock  195
Swingin' In E flat  1073
Swinging In Harlem  691
Swingin' In Paris  11
Swingin' In The Coconut Trees  864
Swingin' In The Corn  587
Swingin' In The Dell  765
Swinging In The Groove  690
Swingin' In The Key Of C  550
Swingin' In The Promised Land  696
Swingin' On C  761-989
Swingin' On Lenox Avenue  692
Swingin' On Nothin'  98-452
Swingin' On Strings  683
Swingin' On That Famous Door  399
Swingin' On The Campus  766
Swingin' On The Moon  585-780
Swinging On The Reservation  1659
Swingin' On The Strings  537
Swingin' On The Swanee Shore  153
Swingin' On The Teagarden Gate  1539
Swingin' The Apach'  828
Swingin' The Blues  16-103-281
Swinging The Elks  1108
Swingin' The Irish Reel  1435
Swingin' The Jinx Away  428-585-893
Swingin' The Lead  1432
Swingin' Them Jingle Bells  1629
Swingin' The Scale  1604
Swinging The Swing  686
Swinging The Washing On The Siegfried
  Line  1435
Swingin' To A Swing Tune  1240
Swingin' Uptown  983
Swinging With Django  1260
Swingin' With Mezz  1052
Swinging With Mose  1109
Swingin' Without Mezz  542
Swingin' With The Fat Man  1279
Swing In, Swing Out  153
Swing Is Here  906
Swing Is In The Air  24
Swing Is The Thing  388-1585
Swing It  281-285-1322
Swingitis  525
Swing It Off  151
Swing Jackson  1194
Swing Lightly  320
Swing Like A Rusty Gate  153
Swing Low  486-1332
Swing Low, Sweet Chariot  81-294-447-452-
  460-600-602-1585-1633-1635-1711

Swing Mad  1327
Swing Man Blues  991
Swing March  805
Swingmatism  1038
Swing Me A Lullaby  162-182-1249
Swing Me Sweetly  393
Swing Me With Rhythm  1248
Swing, Mister Charlie  122-553-555
Swing My Rhythm  1344
Swingology  637
Swing On The Gait  784
Swing Out  11-528-692-1235-1560
Swing Out In The Groove  1246
Swing Out Rhythm  845
Swing Out To Victory  1638
Swing Out, Uncle Wilson  1557
Swing Pan Alley  1712
Swing Parade  115
Swing Patrol  24-1121-1224
Swing Session In Siberia  1223
Swing Session's Called To Order, The
  1053
Swingsome Reel, The  1434
Swingster's Lullaby  409
Swing Street Strut  94
Swing, Swing, Swing  258-385
Swing, Swing, Swing, Daughter, Swing  585
Swing Syncopation With A Fork And Spoon
  386
Swingtette No. 1  787
Swing That Music  53-585
Swing 39  1261
Swing Time  298-960-1465
Swingtime In Honolulu  493-1712
Swingtime In The Rockies  598-657
Swing Time Up In Harlem  451
Swing Waltz, The  93
Swingy Little Rhythm, A  691
Swingy Little Thingy  1311
Swing, You Cats  57
Switch It, Miss Mitchell  1161-1499
'S Wonderful  324-610-1571-1696-1749
Sylvia  288-544-695
Sympathetic Blues  461
Sympathetic Dan  1650
Sympathizing Blues  1011
Sympathy  373
Symphonic Raps  319-404
Symphoni Scronch  1371
Symphony In Riffs  281-445-908-1400
Symphony Under The Stars  1375
Syncopated Dream  1748
Syncopated Jamboree  273-1368
Syncopated Shuffle  480
Syncopated Swing  842
Syncopated Yodelin' Man  514
Syncopate Your Sins Away  198-1646
Syncopatin' Mama  706
Syncophonic  313
Synthetic Love  281
Syrena Blues  171

Table In A/The Corner, A  324-432-1405-
  1539
Taboo  132-148-325
Tab's Blues  1135
Tack Annie  1167-1590
Tack(in') 'Em Down  359-1365
Tack Head Blues  752
Tack It Down  1494
Ta-De-Ah  329
Taggin' Along With You  545

Tailor-Made Stomp  918
Tailspin  426-1689
Tailspin Blues  1113
'Tain't A Cow In Texas  1692
'Tain't A Doggone Thing But The Blues  750
964-1050-1218-1718
'Tain't A Fit Night Out For Man Or Beast
1427
'Tain't Clean  1391
'Tain't Cold  1131-1192-1275-1356
'Tain't Nobody's Biz-ness/Business If I Do
545-793-916-1010-1018-1050-1185-1363-
1438-1439-1544-1636-1678-1698-1710-1727
'Tain't Nobody's Fault But My Own  179
'Tain't Nobody's Fault But Yours  1450-
1678
'Tain't (No) Good (Like A Nickel Made Of
Wood)  261-435-585-694-986-1244-1629
'Tain't None Of Your Business  213
'Tain't No-One But You  669
'Tain't No Sin (To Take Off Your Skin And
Dance Around In Your Bones)  177-655-777
1098-1164-1294-1505
'Tain't No Tellin' What The Blues Will
Make You Do  1022-1728
'Tain't No Use  204-427-536-599-638-1020-
1464
'Tain't So  1669
'Tain't So, Honey, 'Tain't So  300-1597-
1686
'Tain't What You Do (It's The Way That Cha
Do It)  8-528-589-814-987-1269-1633-1661
'Tain't What You Pay To Get A Thing  811
'Tain't What You Used To Have, My Friend,
It's What You're Holding Now  213
Taj Mahal  1642
Take A Good Look At Mine  521-580-1019
Take A Little Bit  180
Take A Little One-Step  225
Take Along A Little Love  1294
Take A Look At This  560
Take Another Guess  536-586-599-1399-1659
Take A Number From One To Ten  392
Take A Picture Of The Moon  726
Take A Tip From The Whippoorwill  95-432
Take Care Of You For Me  1584
Take 'Em  944
Take Everything But You  1369
Take Him Off My Mind  355
Take In The Sun, Hang Out The Moon  38-61
Take It  618
Take It And Git  902
Take It, 'Cause It's All yours  1059-1725
Take It, Daddy, It's All Yours  1466
Take It Easy  375-474-475-758-823-859-1094
1585-1626
Take It Easy Greasy  824-842
Take It Easy Greasy No. 2 (You Got A Long
Way To Slide)  843
Take It From Me (I'm Taking To You)  287-
1286-1386-1515
Take It From The Top  527
Take It Now  776
Take It On Home To Grandma  1020
Take It Prez  107
Take It Right Back ('Cause I Don't Want It
In Here)  1445
Take It Slow And Easy  88
Take Me  341-436-454-622-1123-1191
Take Me Along With You  1253
Take Me Away From The River  726

Take Me Back  154
Take Me Back Again  373
Take Me Back Baby  109
Take Me Back To My Boots And Saddle  13-
203-437-701-1530
Take Me For A Buggy Ride  1446-1678
Take Me Home, Heavenly Father, With Thee
1458
Take Me In Your Alley  680
Take Me Out To The Ball Game  970-1315
Take Me To The River  1455
Take My Heart  14-204-538-1026-1239
Take My Word  122-250-594-1402
Take Off Them Hips  825
Take, Oh Take Those Lips Away  71-1590
Takes Two To Make A Bargain  293-362-
1001
Take That Thing Away  794
Take The 'A' Train  261-498
Take This Ring  701
Take Those Blues Away  901
Take What You Want  1651
Take Your Black Bottom Outside  1014-
1651-1701
Take Your Finger Out Of Your Mouth  20-
172-1120
Take Your Finger(s) Off It  854-1044-
1492
Take Your Hands Off It  843
Take Your Love  908
Take Your Shoes Off, Baby  1408
Take Your Time  1172-1455
Take Your Tomorrow (Give Me Today)  514-
806-1062-1213-1338-1568
Taking A Chance On Love  528-616-1242-
1655
Takin' My Time  284
Taking Your Place  1042
Tales Of Hoffman : Barcarolle (Offenbach)
441-919
Talk 'Bout Somethin' That's Gwine To
Happen (sic)  1453
Talkin' Out Of Turn  1398
Talkin' To My Heart  433
Talkin' To Myself  241-879-1591-1569
Talkin' Too Much  810
Talking To The Moon  860-1504
Talking To The Wind  167-1243
Talk Of The Town  1667
Talk To Me  781-1035
Tallahassee  1074
Tall Brown Papa Blues  1499
Tall Grows The Timber  299
Tall, Tall Corn  1397
Tall Tillie's Too Tight  358
Tamiami Trail  884
Tamin' The Blues  1272
Tampa Shout  1719
Tampeekoe  719-1131-1192-1286-1365-1436-
1742
Tampico  1324
Tangerine  435-621
Tanglefoot  1623
Tanglewood 'Round My Heart  97
Tanguay Blues  1456
Tanko, The  315
Tank Town Bump  1103
Tannhauser : Pilgrims' Chorus (Wagner)
917
Tanning Dr. Jekyll's Hyde  307
Tantalizing A Cuban  760

1970

Tantalizin' Mama  1728
Tantalizing Tingles  127
Tap Dancer's Nightmare  427
Tapestry In Blue  1244
Tapioca  135
Tappin' At The Tappa  96
Tappin' Off  261
Tappin' The Barrel  593
Tappin' The Commodore Till  542
Tappin' The Time Away  1647
Tap Room Blues  1602
Tap Room Special  967
Tap Room Swing  1332
Tap-Tap, The  870
Tap Your Feet  790-1295-1739
Tarantula  24-379
Ta-Ra-Ra-Boom-Der-E  907
Tar Paper Stomp  999
Tarzan Of Harlem  259
Ta Ta Daddy  302
Tattle Tale  1360
Taxi War Dance  105
Taylor Made  1099
T. B. Blues  811-1487
T. B. Moan  1573
T-Bone Blues  **763-865**
T. B.'s Got Me Blues  1489
Tea And Trumpets  1500
Teacher (How I Love My Teacher)  865
Teacher's Pet  759-1315
Teach Me  1615
Tea Dance  527
Tea For Two  85-167-208-363-368-385-446-
530-588-600-602-822-1142-1253-1261-1262
1277-1283-1326-1431-1432-1468-1477-1529
1530-1591-1626-1631-1634-1642-1657-1661
1732-1753
Tea Leaves  748
Team Up  278
Tea On The Terrace  439-1027
Tea Pot Dome Blues  558-713
Teardrops  1127
Teardrops And Kisses  504-1144
Teardrops On My Pillow  991
Tear It Down  892-1021
Tear It Down, Bed Slats And All  1043
Tears  (1923)  1166
Tears  (1930)  1295
Tears  (1937)  1260-1284
Tears From My Inkwell  296-1147
Tears In My Heart  442-545-633-1157
Tears On My Pillow  375
Teasin'  1053
Teasing Brown Blues  1014
Teasin' Me  105
Teasin' Tessie Brown  987
Teasin' The Cat  1587
Teasing The Frets  982
Teasin' The Ivories  1369
Tea Time  469-556-1158-1601
Tech. Triumph  373
Teddy Bear Blues  222-1607
Teddy Bear Boogie  1242
Teddy's Blues  1647
Teddy's Boogie Woogie  1242
Teed Up  1247
Tee Pee Blues  119
Tee-Um, Tee-Um, Tee-I, Tahiti  259
Telephone Blues  1443-1524
Telephoning The Blues  1488-1489
Tell All The Folks In Kentucky  71-223

Tell All The World  568
Tell All Your Daydreams To Me  280
Tell 'Em About Me (1924)  1650
Tell 'Em About Me (1939)  1746
Tell Her At Twilight  220-1613
Tell Her In The Springtime  264
Telling It To The Daisies (But It Never
  Gets Back To You)  246-672
Telling You I Love You  248
Tell Me  977-1177-1360
Tell Me, Are You From Georgia ?  1616
Tell Me At Midnight  450
Tell Me Baby  1677
Tell Me, Cutie  1495
Tell Me, Dear  247
Tell Me, Dreamy Eyes  170-232-716
Tell Me, Gypsy  1059
Tell Me If You Want Somebody Else  19
Tell Me, Little Daisy  238-239-1580
Tell Me, Little Gypsy  1177
Tell Me More  769
Tell Me Tonight  235-1039-1275
Tell Me What To Do  1052
Tell Me When  1451
Tell Me Who  651-1069
Tell Me Why  753-1415
Tell Me With Your Kisses  906-1633
Tell Me Woman Blues  8
Tell Me You Love Me  540-921
Tell Me You're Sorry  1290
Tell My Mama On You  751
Tell Tales  874
Tell The Truth  1709
Tell Your Story  948
Tel Quel  333
Temper(a)mental Papa  872-1057-1520
Temple Block Swing  386
Tempo And Swing  663
Tempo de Bucket  680
Tempo de Luxe  816
Tempo di Modernage/Tempo di Barrel  1599
Temptation  298-323-416-896-897-1239-1407
Temptation Blues  1699
Temptation Rag  85-117-139-1251-1255-1298
  1340-1350-1656-1695-1750
Tempus Fugit  10-326
10 a.m. Blues  554
Ten Cents A Dance  511
Ten Day Furlough  743
Tender Is The Night  365-967
Tenderly  640
Tendresse Waltz  1349
Tenement Symphony  326
Ten Little Fingers And Ten Little Toes
  1085
Ten Little Miles From Town  130-571-931
Ten Mile Hop  324
Tennessee Blues  100
Tennessee Fish Fry  81-433
Tennessee Lazy  301-341
Tennessee Twilight  335
Ten O'Clock Blues  1500
Tenor Guitar Fiend  694
Ten Pretty Girls  586-1314
Tenth Interval Rag  1118-1327
Tentin' Down In Tennessee  568-1484
Ten Yards To Go  699-1669
Terrain a vendre  313
Terrible Blues  1280-1533-1656
Terribly Fond Of You  1127-1293
Terrific Stomp  1111

Territory Blues  1679
Terror, The  806
Tessie, Stop Teasing Me  227-529-623-657-
  797-886-966-1067
Texas And Pacific Blues  543
Texas Chatter  814
Texas Man (Blues)  861-1093
Texas Moaner (Blues)  115-794-1448-1457-
  1699
Texas Mule Stomp  313
Texas Sands  842
Texas Shout  390
Texas Shuffle  103-1496-1555
Texas Special Blues  1094-1281
Texas Tea Party  593
Texas Teaser  1528
Texas Twist  763
Thaïs : Meditation (Massenet)  1191-1360-
  1368
Thankful  53
Thanks  173-200
Thanks A Million  52-365-701-1114-1689
Thanks For Everything  163-440-446-1159-
  1403
Thanks For The Boogie Ride  912
Thanks For The Lobster  1587
Thanks For The Memory  78-206-295-606-
  1088
Thanksgiving  275-288
Thank You For The Flowers  808
Thank Your Father  286-1382
Thank Your Stars  96
That Ain't Right  329
That Barking Dog, Woof ! Woof !  1186-
  1672
That Big Blonde Mama  71-223-1544
That Black Snake Moan  343
That Blue-Eyed Baby From Memphis  1277
That Bonus Done Gone Thru'  842
That Bran' New Gal Of Mine  71-1189-1363
That Cat Is High  1244
That Certain Feeling  10-467-1749
That Certain Motion  1111
That Certain Party  624-1220-1478
That Chicago Wiggle  1090
That Creole Band  1744
That Da Da Strain  375-543-646-977-1050-
  1132-1185-1462-1480-1481-1532-1607-1649
That Dance Called Messin' Around  1013
That Did It, Marie  621
That Doggone Dog Of Mine  1556
That Don't Worry Me  991
That Drummer's Band  912
That Eccentric Rag - see ECCENTRIC
That Feeling Is Gone  94-206-430-608
That Foolish Feeling  123-383-439-879
That Free And Easy Papa O' Mine  1011-
  1533
That Fussy Rag  971
That Futuristic Rag  144
That Gets It, Mister Joe  1637
That Girl Over There  10
That Jazz Dance  665
That Kind Of Love  1209
That Lindy Hop  346-482
That Little Boy Of Mine  981
That'll Get It  390-1258
That'll Just 'Bout Knock Me Out  865
That'll Never Do  1104
That'll Never Work With Me  917
That Lovely Night In Budapest  438-1239

That Loving Baby Of Mine  1176
That Lovin' Hula  4
That Lovin' Rag  1217
That Lucky Fellow  448-613
That Lullaby Strain  120-226-1347
That Made Him Mad  91
That Man Is Here Again  258
That Moaning Saxophone Rag  1429
That Moaning Trombone  512-1229
That Naughty Waltz  1279-1659
That Never-To-Be-Forgotten Night  702-
  1239-1628
That New Love Maker Of Mine  1026
That Night In Araby  235-573
That Old Black Magic  99
That Old Feeling  162-554-652-1028-1633-
  1721-1734
That Old Gang Of Mine  185-223-647-1242-
  1245-1314
That Old Sweetheart Of Mine  649
That Peculiar Rag  127
That "Please Be Mineable" Feeling  329
That Rag  1255
That Real Romance  99
That Red-Head Gal  263-331-559-857-925-
  1187-1353-1519
That Rhythm Gal  1547
That Rhythm Man  45-346-640-761-789-1152-
  1658
That's A Bringer, That's A Hanger  550
That's A Good Girl  1579
That's All (1929)  1623
That's All (1941)  1070
That's All, Brother  527
That's All I Ask Of You  540-769-1238
That's All Right Daddy  1061
That's All There Is (There Ain't No More)
  339-462-534-828-1181
That's A Lovely Thing For You  1223
That's Alright  169
That Same Cat  683
That Same Dog  212
That's Annabelle  921
That's A Plenty  114-122-145-386-439-586-
  592-702-745-758-913-918-950-959-977-
  1068-1088-1121-1131-1132-1142-1174-1208
  1238-1251-1253-1341-1343-1357-1358-1410
  1508-1656-1659
That's A Serious Thing  334
That's Chicago's South Side  1547
That Sentimental Sandwich  370
That's For Me  97-450
That's Georgia  227-377-715-1212
That's Going To Ruin Your Beauty Spot  680
That's Got 'Em  513-1517-1522-1558
That Shanghai Melody  975
That's Her Mason-Dixon Line  167
That's Her Now  20-262-507-575-627-1292
That's How Dreams Should End  647
That's How I Feel About You (Sweetheart)
  340-627-831-950
That's How I Feel Today  966-1053
That's How I Need You  1314
That's How Rhythm Was Born  1-159-290-
  1311-1485-1688
That's How The First Song Was Born  1669
That's It  378-544
That's (Just) My Way Of Forgetting You
  188-419-579-649
That's Life, I Guess  1732
That's Like It Ought To Be  1104

1972

That's Living  243
That's Love  290-873-952
That Sly Old Gentleman (From Featherbed Lane)  80-1435
That's My Cup Blues  360
That's My Desire  1470-1742
That's My Girl  267-523-566-1067-1502-1644-1664
That's My Hap-Hap-Happiness  2-1222-1612-1644
That's My Home  50-581-590-1287
That's My Mammy  419
That's My Man  834
That's My Stuff  1459
That's My Weakness Now  31-302-463-658-785-799-883-992-1393-1417-1456-1614-1686
That's No Bargain  38-1138-1275
That's Not Cricket  437
That Soldier Of Mine  819
That Solid Old Man (Is Here Again)  186-326-453
That's Right-I'm Wrong  95-1538
That's Southern Hospitality  686-1308
That's That Messy Boogie  1561
That's The Blues, Old Man  766
That's The Good Old Sunny South  1292-1598
That's The Kind Of A Baby For Me  1422
That's The Kind Of Girl I'm Looking For  1455
That's The Kind Of Man For Me  1131
That's The Lick  763
That's The Time A Fellow Needs A Girl Friend  1470
That's The Way I Do  1527
That's The Way I Like To Hear You Talk  937
That's The Way It Goes  620-894
That's The Way She Likes It  376
That Stolen Melody  441
That Sweet Somebody O' Mine  70
That Sweet Something, Dear  687-942-1166
That's What I Call Heaven  888
That's What I Call Keen  566-1475-1493
That's What I Call Sweet Music  507-1336-1675 (sometimes shown as SWEET MUSIC)
That's What I Hate About Love  256-1486
That's What I Like About The South  686
That's What I Like About You  1536-1537-1668
That's What I'm Talking About  1111-1547
That's What I Think Of You  1232
That's What I Want For Christmas  1316
That's What Life Is Made Of  132-964
That's What Love Did To Me  1427
That's What Puts The "Sweet" in Home, Sweet Home  579
That's What The Well-Dressed Man In Harlem Will Wear  1638
That's What You Call Romance  550
That's What You Mean To Me  780-893
That's What You Think  382-687-890-912-1031-1197
That's When I'll Come Back To You  42
That's When I Want You Near  247
That's Where The South Begins  789-1143-1248
That's Where You Come In  509-1514
That's Where You're Wrong  1231
That's Why I Love You  265-667

That's Why I'm Crying For You  403
That's Why I'm Loving You  1648
That's Why The Undertakers Are Busy Today  1451
That's You, Baby  671-888-949
That's Your Last  1223
That Teasin' Rag  1175
That Teasin' Squeezin' Man O' Mine  1188-1189-1719
That Thing  466
That Thing Called Love  859-1305-1460-1724
That Thing's Done Been Put On Me  1692
That Too, Do  1111
That Twa Twa Tune  136
That Was My Heart  1662
That Wicked Stomp  641
That Wonderful Something Is Love  503-953-1598
Theme For Piano  1530
Them "Has Been" Blues  178-1458
Them Piano Blues  812
Them Ramblin' Blues - see RAMBLING BLUES
Them's Graveyard Words  1444
Them There Eyes  49-370-483-612-769-852-873-1261-1736
Them Things Got Me  1705
Then Came The Dawn  241-981-1232
Then I'll Be Happy  74-233-568-713-896-897-901-1348-1484-1503-1579-1679
Then I'll Be Tired Of You  1624
Then I Shan't Love You Any More  438
Then I Wrote The Minuet in G  997
Then My Gal's In Town  376
Then Someone's In Love  1034
Then You'll Remember Me  1635
Then You're Drunk  1155
Then You've Never Been Blue  977
Then You Went And Changed Your Mind  509
There Ain't Gonna Be No Doggone Afterwhile  781-1677
There Ain't No Flies On Auntie  1219
There Ain't No Land Like Dixieland  174
There Ain't No "Maybe" In My Baby's Eyes  1182-1237-1619
There Ain't No Nothin' Gonna Take The Place Of Love  140
There Ain't No Sweet Man That's Worth The Salt Of My Tears  771-1325-1515-1683
There Ain't No Use In Tryin'  111
There Are Rivers To Cross  744
There Are Such Things  454
There Goes My Attraction  585-1415-1629
There Goes That Song Again  743
There I Go  167-742
There Is A Happy Land (Far, Far Away)  1418
There Is A Tavern In The Town  518-1342
There Is Love.  1711
There Is No Greater Love  490-553-702-901
There Is No Moon  836
There Isn't Any Limit To My Love  879
There It Goes Again  1176
There, I've Said It Again  284
There'll Be A Great Day In The Morning  545
There'll Be A Hot Time In The Old Town Tonight  1087-1225-1433-1444-1473-1474-1510-1581
There'll Be No South  1305

There'll Be Some Changes Made  80-126-157-172-208-273-282-309-335-391-461-612-910-922-955-1030-1058-1253-1271-1346-1379-1505-1626-1649-1725
There'll Come A Day  410-1494
There'll Come A Time  954-999-1139-1567
There Must Be A Bright Tomorrow (For Each Yesterday Of Tears)  515-1296
There Must Be A Silver Lining  669-1325
There Must Be Somebody Else  111-669
There Ought To Be A Law Against That  874-1393
There Ought To Be A Moonlight Saving Time  197-512-673-971-1312-1384-1472
There's A Boat Dat's Leavin' Soon For New York  1361
There's A Boy In Harlem  368-443-1158
There's A Brand-New Picture In My Picture Frame  322
There's A Bungalow That's Waiting  1175
There's A Cabin In The Cotton  256
There's A Cabin In The Pines  51-77-148-199
There's A Cradle In Caroline  130-174-1136-1290-1417-1566-1738
There's A Faraway Look In Your Eye  430
There's A Four-Leaf Clover In My Pocket  31-654
There's A Gold-Mine In The Sky  756
There's A Hole In The Old Oaken Bucket  589-1358
There's A House In Harlem For Sale  13
There's A House On The Hill  1438
There's A Kitchen Up In Heaven  15
There's A Little White House On A Little Green Hill (Where The Red, Red Roses Grow)  171-577
There's A Lot Of Blue-Eyed Marys Down In Maryland  379-1748
There's A Lull In My Life  78-294-491-652-1551-1732
There's Always A Happy Ending  1019-1415
There's A New Moon Over My Shoulder (And A Beautiful Girl In My Arms)  878
There's A New Moon Over The Old Mill  1402
There's Another Empty Saddle  147
There's A Place In The Sun For You  403
There's A Rainbow 'Round My Shoulder  17-144-241-563-809-950-1016-1033-1195-1381-1620
There's Going To/Gonna Be The Devil To Pay  1467-1626-1710
There's A Ranch In The Sky  894
There's A Rickety Rackety Shack  532-722-1290-1324
There's A Silver Moon On The Golden Gate  1416
There's A Small Hotel  182-282-598-960-1239-1415-1554
There's A Sunny Side To Everything  259
There's A Sunny Smile Waiting For Me  1295
There's A Tear For Every Smile In Hollywood  1497
There's A Time And Place For Everything  60-1386
There's A Tiny Little Hair On Your Shoulder  148
There's A Trick In Pickin' A Chick-Chick-Chicken Today  237-639-1417
There's A Wah Wah Girl In Agua Caliente  145-247-840-858-1234

There's A Whistle In The Thistle  100
There's Been Some Changes Made  320
There's Danger In Your Eyes, Cherie  503
There's Egypt In Your Dreamy Eyes  978
There's Everything Nice About You  236-402-1015-1644
There's Frost On The Moon  182-439-1027-1399
There's Gonna Be A Wedding In The Band  699
There Shall Be No Night  497
There's Happiness Ahead  507
There's Honey On The Moon Tonight  973-1632
There's Nae Luck Aboot The Hoose  969
There's No Depression In Love  1386
There's No Gal Like My Gal  1193
There's No Green Grass Round The Old North Pole  937
There's No-One Else But You  981
There's No-One Just Like You  338
There's No Other Girl  1599
There's No Place Like Your Arms  206-445-1357-1690
There's No Substitute For You  428
There's No Two Ways About It  1134-1240
There's Oceans Of Love By The Beautiful Sea  100-697-1312
There's One Lane That Has No Turning  1425
There's One Little Girl Who Loves Me  468
There's One Thing Remains  949
There's Only One Man (That Satisfies Me)  1462
There's Plenty Of Room 'Way In The Kingdom  1014
There's Rain In My Eyes  729-1237
There's Rhythm In Harlem  1074
There's Rhythm In The River  251-1131
There's Something About An Old Love  766-787
There's Something About A Rose  402
There's Something In The Air  182-974-1399
There's Something In The Wind  1307
There's Something In Your Eyes  1030
There's Something New About The Old Moon Tonight  1077
There's Something Spanish In Your Eyes  1580-1620
There's That Look In Your Eyes Again  24
There's The One For Me  950
There's Too Many Eyes That Wanna Make Eyes At Two Pretty Eyes I Love  1666
There's Yes ! Yes ! In Your Eyes  72-1640
There Was Nothing Else To Do  503-677
There Will Never Be Another Mary  245-1040
There Will Never Be Another You  240-744-1159-1244
There Won't Be A Shortage Of Love  622-1244
These 'n' That 'n' Those  1731
These Dogs Of Mine  643
These Foolish Things (Remind Me Of You)  204-281-382-598-616-1239-1412-1731-1736
These Things You Left Me  97-617-910-. 1477

1974

They All Laughed   429-440-1147
They Brought That Gal To The Prison Gates
   1105
They Called It Dixieland   315
They Can't Take That Away From Me   81-102-
   311-429-440-768
They Cut Down The Old Pine Tree   513
They Didn't Believe Me   790-1142-1274
They Got My Number Now   1155
They Jittered All The Time   730
They Ought To Write A Book About You   372
They Played Like That   170
They Put The Big Britches On Me   824
They're Off   805
They Satisfy   980-1071
They Say   79-163-554-1159-1404-1654-1735
They Say He Ought To Dance   1137
They Still Make Love In London   417
They Were All Out Of Step But Jim   127
They Would Wind Him Up And He Would
   Whistle   1436
Thick Lip Stomp   1110
Thief In The Night   1627
Thief Of Bagdad, The   1228
Thing, The   342
Things 'Bout Comin' My Way   1247
Things Ain't What They Used To Be   99-767
Things Are Looking Up   880-937-1733
Things Done Got Too Thick   1013
Things I Love, The   434-910-1243-1360-1374
Things I Never Knew Till Now   1144
Things I Want, The   441-1400
Things Might Have Been So Different   161-
   292
Things Seem So Blue To Me   1109
Things That Were Made For Love, The   516
Things We Want The Most Are Hard To Get,
   The   244-1294-1379
Think About Me   248
Think About This Tune   913
Thinking   1247
Thinking Blues   1444
Thinking Of You   669-1217-1504
Think Of Me   120-167
Think Of Me, Little Daddy   988-1518
Think Of Me Thinking Of You   1016
Third Alley Blues   1454
Third Alley Breakdown   1276
Third Rail   92-239-351
Thirsty Mama Blues   1204
13 I'm So Unlucky 13   1352
Thirty Day Blues   979
Thirty-Eight And Plus   784
Thirty-Eight And Two (It Must Be Forty)
   1162
35th And Calumet   1052
35th And Dearborn   1746
Thirty-Fifth Street Blues   1100
31st Street Blues   712-1006-1057-1122-1189
   1448-1609
Thirty-One Blues   250
This Can't Be Love   183-610
This Changing World   165-741
This Is Heaven   950-1155
This Is It   431-446-1404
This Is Madness   94-1159
This Is My Confession To You   991
This Is My Last Affair - see MY LAST
   AFFAIR
This Is My Love Song   1297-1668
This Is My Night To Dream   1295

This Is My Song   324
This Is My Sunday Off   1710
This Is New   618
This Is No Dream   95-431-446
This Is No Laughing Matter   435
This Is Our Last Night Together   92
This Is Romance   63-290-1407
This Is The Beginning Of The End   166-
   317-373-449-
This Is The Boogie The Woogie The Boogie
   1554
This Is The Chorus Of A Song   875-1410
This Is The Day Of Days   1128
This Is The End   1560
This Is The Life   1237
This Is The Missus   145-1387-1586
This Is The Moment   1736
This Is The Way The Puff-Puff Goes   1291
This Is Your Last Night With Me   1321
This Is Worth Fighting For   436
This Little Icky Went To Town   167
This Little Piggie Went To Market   200-
   674-1751
This Love Of Mine   452-529-1553
This Never Happened Before   367
This Night (Will Be My Souvenir)   9-296-
   446
This Place Is Leaping   1413
This Side Up   329
This Time   1319
This Time It's Love   255-651-822-1031
This Time It's Real   444-526
This Time The Dream's On Me   743-911-
   1408
This Will Make You Laugh   329
This Year's Kisses   14-205-600-1732
Those All Night Long Blues   1265
Those Black Man Blues   847
Those Blues   1096
Those Broken Busted Can't Be Trusted
   Blues - see BROKEN BUSTED etc. BLUES
Those Creeping Sneaking Blues   540
Those Dogs Of Mine   1266
Those Draftin' Blues   665-1515-1560
Those Longing For You Blues   68-69-119-
   1185-1462
Those Married Man Blues   353
Those Panama Mamas (Are Ruining Me)   37-
   350-637-966-1172-1428-1545-1591
Those Things I Can't Forget   374
Thoughts   748
Thousand Dreams Of You, A   1157-1629-
   1630
Thousand Finger Rag   1750
Thousand Goodnights, A   1332
Thousand Miles, A   1640
Thousand Miles From Here, A   63
Thou Swell   9-116-840-978-1007-1325-1398
Three At A Table For Two   185-788
Three Blind Mice   309-746-1566
Three B's, The (Barrelhouse, Boogie And
   Blues)   168
Three Brass Bells   656
Three-Fifteen Blues   1558
Three Foot Skipper Jones   1557
Three J Blues   1161
Three Keyboards   1468
Three Kisses   875
Three Little Fish(i)es (Itty Bitty Poo)
   589-1159-1358-1435-1691
Three Little Maids   1279

Three Little Sisters  744
Three Little Words  196-482-483-504-505-
  528-542-595-606-684-774-905-908-951-
  1146-1147-1153-1261-1371-1539-1653
Three Minutes Of Blues  1327
Three Months Ago Blues  846
Three Moods  437
Three O'Clock Blues  1052-1713
Three O'Clock In The Morning  1272-1313-
  1314
Three O'Clock Jump  1007
Three Of A Kind  393
Three-Quarter Boogie  663
Three-Ring Ragout  167
Three's Company  393
Three's No Crowd  542
Three Swings And Out  258
3.30 Blues  858
Three Ways To Smoke A Pipe  743
Thrill Me (1929)  1713
Thrill Me (1931)  1670
Thrill Of A Lifetime, The  367
Through And Through Blues  1065
Through (How Can You Say We're Through ?)
  272-297-507-949-1152-1723
Through The Courtesy Of Love  366-893-1236
Through The Doorway Of Dreams  701
Through The Years  1408
Throw Dirt In Your Face  1651
Throw-Down Blues, The  20-1183-1191-1192
Throwing Pebbles In The Millstream  911-
  1360
Throwin' Stones At The Sun  191-700-779
Throwin' The Horns  1131
Throw It In The Creek (Don't Want Your
  Lovin' No More)  1090
Throw Me In The Alley  1673
Throw This Dog A Bone  1414
Thumpin' And Bumpin'  142
Thunder  328-985
Thunderbolt  975
Thunder In My Dreams  880-1121
Thunder In My Heart  634
Thunder Over Paradise  249-701
Thunderstorm Blues  860-1058
Thursday  9-105
Tia Juana  543-1100-1741
Tia Juana Man  178
Tica-Tee, Tica-Ta (Tica-Ti, Tica-Ta)  1250
  1361
Ticket Agent Blues  948
Ticket Agent, Ease Your Window Down  643-
  1440
Tickled To Death  1217-1251
Tickle The Ivories  300
Tickle-Toe  107
Tickling Blues  841
Tickling Julie  467
Tickling The Strings  1122
Tick Tock Blues  1320
Tidal Wave  727-1095
Tiddle-Dee-Winks  1517
Tie A Little String Around Your Finger
  389-504-1296
Tie Me To Your Apron Strings Again  74-
  203-303-869-963
Tiger Moan  1495
Tiger Rag  3-23-47-50-52-56-61-85-170-172-
  230-282-333-344-345-346-347-385-394-402-
  412-413-427-436-465-467-468-477-563-571-
  582-583-599-636-689-724-745-754-777-780-

Tiger Rag (cont.)  791-800-801-821-836-
  858-866-909-937-949-954-955-959-963-
  972-998-1046-1069-1071-1077-1078-1100-
  1105-1106-1113-1119-1120-1124-1131-
  1149-1162-1174-1175-1176-1177-1178-
  1179-1192-1215-1223-1256-1258-1274-
  1281-1298-1339-1365-1410-1419-1433-
  1479-1507-1529-1530-1531-1537-1540-
  1558-1579-1585-1640-1645-1649-1656-
  1676-1681-1692-1711-1718-1735-1741-
  1742-1750
Tiger Stomp  1108
Tight Like This  44
Till I Die  1547
Tillie's Downtown Now  541
'Til Reveille  911
Till The Clock Strikes Three  15-1400
Till T mes Get Better  1455
Till Tom Special  615-663
Till We Meet  270
Till We Meet Again  299-371-1304-1318
Timber  894-1416
Time Ain't Long  1489
Time And Time Again  206-1435
Time Changes Everything  742
Time Enough  210
Time For One More  1528
Time On My Hands (You In My Arms)  109-
  110-160-197-287-295-387-454-591-604-
  617-638-769-1030-1063-1242-1261-1373-
  1412
Time Out  102
Time Rhythm  842
Times Ain't What They Used To Be  758
Time's A Wastin'  680-767-987
Times Is Hard (So I'm Savin' For A Rainy
  Day)  214
Times Square Blues  1253
Times Square Scuttle  704
Time Was  434
Time Will Come, The  675
Tin-Ear  465-552
Ting-a-Ling, The Bells'll Ring  38
Tinker, Tailor, Soldier, Sailor  1393
Tinkle Song, The  206
Tin Pan Parade  1064
Tin Roof Blues  94-226-264-375-445-517-
  749-764-955-996-999-1055-1129-1132-
  1133-1168-1180-1188-1249-1280-1544-
  1749
Tiny Little Fingerprints  426
Tiny Old Town  324
Tiny's Stomp  1209
Tiny Town  884
Tip Easy Blues  863
Ti-Pi-Tin  29-550-587-608-881-960
Tippin' Through  694
Tip On The Numbers, A  551
Tippin' At The Terrace  759
Tip-Tip-Tippy Canoe  976
Tip-Toe Thru' The Tulips With Me  244-
  580-671-800-952-1293-1301
Ti Ralph  650
Tired  981
Tired Chicken Blues  270
Tired Of It All  290-1278
Tired Of The Way You Do  1452
Tired O' Waitin' Blues  190-1011-1022-
  1050-1082-1466
Tired Of You Driving Me  1042
Tired Socks  766

1976

'Tis Autumn  126-186-620-743-1361
Tishomingo Blues  26-138-475-1059
Titanic Blues  965
Titanic Man Blues  1267
Tit Willow  80-372
T-N-T  718-754-973-1592
To A Broadway Rose  1409
Toad Frog Blues  1266
Toadie Toddle  900-1159
Toasted Pickles  1712
Toast To Paganini's Ghost  1412
To A Sweet Pretty Thing  1630
Tobacco Auctioneer, The  1573
Tobasco Rag Waltz  971-1255
To Be In Love (Espesh'lly With You)  503-
    516-888-950-1456
To Be With You  234
Toboggan  1348
Toby  1112
To Call You My Own  700
  Today Is Today  867
Today's A Sunny Day For Me  1202
Today, Tomorrow, Forever  506
Toddle  119
Toddle Along  1502
Toddlin'  838
Toddlin' Along With You  203
Toddlin' Blues  115-1178-1179
To Do This You Gotta Know How  844
Toe To Toe  139
Together  1290-1400-1404
Together, We Two  111-840-929-1290-1378
Tokio  1291
Tokio Blues  796-1039
To-Ki-O-Ki-O  1334
To Know You Is To Love You  241-242
Toledano Street Blues  1054
Toledo Shuffle  828
To Live The Life Of A Lie  1316
Toll  697-698
To Love You  268
Tomahawk  1299
To Mary With Love  893
Tomatoes  1174
Tomato Sauce  972
Tomboy  1156
Tomboy Sue  267-1475
Tombstone Blues  1066-1445
Tom Cat (Blues)  1100-1157
Tom Cat On The Keys  1752
Tom Cat Rag  736
Tomorrow  7
Tomorrow (I'll Be In My Dixie Home Again)
    69-221-1086-1437
Tomorrow Is Another Day  1621
Tomorrow Morning  69-73-967
Tomorrow Night (After Tonight)  51-432
Tomorrow's Another Day (1924)  1502
Tomorrow's Another Day (1935)  426
Tomorrow's Sunrise  435-1361
Tomorrow's Violets  979
Tom Thumb  109
Tom Thumb's Drum  1297
Tom Tom Serenade  1557
Tom, Tom, The Piper's Son  554
To My Levee Home  646
To My Mammy  883
Ton doux sourire - see SUNSHINE OF YOUR
    SMILE
Tonight  - see PERFIDIA
Tonight's My Night With Baby  467-882-1504

Tonight Will Live  125
Tonight You Belong To Me  693
Tonky Blues  1326
Tons d'Ebene  1284
Tony's Wife  9
Too Bad  339-992-1167-1172-1182-1278
Too Bad Jim  548-1555-1650
Too Black Bad  393
Too Busy !  314-340-931-1510
Too Darn Fickle  651
Toodle-Loo On Down  1511
Toodle-Oo  586-781-830-1313
Toodle-Oo (I'll Be Seeing You)  1594
Toodle-Oo Blues  680
Toodle-Oodle-Oo  832 -1220
Toodles  228-306
Toogaloo Shout  752
Too Good To Be True  93-598-1731
Too Late  76-743-1169
Too Late Now  554
Too Late Now To Get Your Baby Back  1012
Too Lazy For Love  505
Too Long Blues  776
Too Low  1704
Too Many Dreams  693
Too Many Kisses In The Summer  235
Too Many Tears  34-147-1227-1297
Too Marvelous For Words  131-294-362-686
    1313
Too Mean To Cry Blues  1454
Too Much  944
Too Much Ginger  1587
Too Much Imagination  968
Too Much Mustard  512-632
Too Much Trouble  1678
Too Romantic  449
Too Slow Blues  1061
Too Sweet For Words  65
Toothache Blues  1488-1677
Too Tight  415-1133
Tootin' Around  25
Tootin' My Baby Back Home  506
Tootin' Through The Roof  495
Too Tired  19-227-552-1184-1636
Toot It, Brother Armstrong  1729
Toot, Toot, Toot  999
Toot-Toot-Tootsie (Goo'bye)  69-222-1086
    1524
Too Wonderful For Words  17-245
Top And Bottom  1497-1712
Top Hat Shuffle  1357
Top Hat, White Tie And Tails  160-426-
    701
Top Of The Town  1710
Topper  1360
Topsy  102-610
Topsy Turvy  760
Toreador Humoresque  1522
Tormented  14-182-584-688-702-785-859-
    938-1001-1273
Tornado Groan  1066
Tornerai  635-1283
Torrid Dora  1525
Torrid Rhythm  806
Tortilla B flat  336
To Stop The Train, Pull The Chain  310
Totem Pole  757
To To Blues  1599
Touchdown  1705
Touched In The Head  409
Touch Of Your Lips, The  14-1230-1312

Tough Breaks 1110
Tough Luck Blues 1268
Tough Truckin' 489
Toujours I Love You 1639
To-Wa-Bac-A-Wa 457
To Whom It May Concern 790-980-1035
Town Tattler 326
Town Topic Rag 976
Toy Department 805
Toyland Band, The 1668
To You 446
To You, Sweetheart, Aloha 53-1250
Toy Trumpet, The 25-586-684-746-1371-1402-1434
Tozo 721
Trade Mark 1654
Trade Winds 450
Trading Old Love For New 783
Traffic Jam (1928) 1640
Traffic Jam (1939) 528-1405
Trail Of Dreams 1520
Trail Of The Tamarind Tree, The 524
Train Imitations and The Fox Chase 1025
Trammin' At The Fair 1412
Tramp 771
Trampin' Blues 854
Transatlantic Stomp 327
Trans-Continental 1116
Transom Blues 510
Transportation Blues 1565
Traumerei (Schumann) 1552
Travelin' All Alone 160-768-1034-1153-1652
Traveling Blues 64-709-737-1201-1268-1664
Travelin' Down The Trail 786
Trav'lin' Light 1691
Travelin' That Rocky Road 898
Treasures 338
Treat By The Gang, The 338
Treated Wrong Blues 642-1093
Treated You Kind 1040
Treat 'Em Rough 1188
Treat Me Like A Baby 6-316-1385
Tree In The Park, A 557-568
Tree Of Hope 284
Trees 124-311-729-775-1106-1205-1285
Tree Top Tall Papa 355
Tres moutarde - see TOO MUCH MUSTARD
Trickeration 254-1072
Trick Fingering 1595
Triflin' Blues (Daddy, Don't You Trifle On Me) 190-749-1022-1082-1466-1727
Triflin' Daddy's Blues 1310
Triflin' Mama's Yodelin' Blues 514
Triflin' Man (Blues) 712-1060-1065
Trigger Slim Blues 629
Tripping Along (With You And Me) 32-225-1581
Trixie Blues, The/Trixie's Blues 855-1059 1465-1467
Trombone Blues 472
Trombone Cholly 1444
Trombone Man 810
Trombone Moanin' Blues 747
Trombone Slide, The 784
Trombone Sneeze 1474
Tropical 923
Tropical Blues 1352
Tropical Magic 434-912-1361
Tropical Moon 650
Tropical Nights 1253

Tropical Palms 772
Trot Along 120-710-711-855
Trouble 1709
Trouble Blues 1040-1091
Troubled 1571
Troubled Blues 1011
Trouble Don't Like Music 205-1309
Troubled Waters 489
Troubled With The Blues 1320
(Trouble Ends) Out Where The Blue Begins 14-204-1415
Trouble Everywhere I Roam 1617
Trouble In Mind (Blues) 739-753-754-863 936-1070-1110-1489-1677
Trouble In Mind Swing 1678
Trouble In Paradise 289-1668
Troublesome Blues 841-1451
Troublesome Trumpet 581-1147-1270
Trouble Trouble Blues 354
Trouble, Why Pick On Me ? 1276
Trouble With Me Is You, The 657-1032
Trovatore, Il : Anvil Chorus (Verdi) 185
Troyen Swing 832
Truckin' 13-348-392-490-583-652-700-701-775-967-1074-1092
Truckin' 1627
Truckin' On Down 1432
Truckin' On The Old Camp Ground 1265
Trudy 1300
True 1658-1689
True Blue 659
True Blue Lou 7-155-341-503-671-1152-1233-1308-1652
True Blues 1499
True Confession 55-320-605-1333
True Love 849
True Love Blues 1414
Truly 221-940
Truly (I Love You) 69-958
Truly Wonderful 766
Trumbology 1566
Trumpet Amplifications 4
Trumpet Blues 962
Trumpet Blues And Cantabile 819
Trumpet In Spades 491
Trumpet Player's Lament, The 55
Trumpet Rhapsody 817
Trumpet Sobs 1673
Trumpet's Prayer, The 1169
Trumpetuous 584
Trust In Me 78-162-1399
Trust Me For A Hamburger 1646
Trust No Man 1267
Try Again 27
Try A Little Tenderness 580
Try And Treat Her Right 519
Try And Get It 534
Try And Play It 1369
Try Dancing 245
Try Getting A Good Night's Sleep 1277
Trying 758-951
Tryin' To Keep Away From You 1592
Trying To Stop My Crying 999
Trylon Stomp 184
Trylon Swing 259
Try Me Out 1103
Try Some Of That 1197
Try To Smile 1543
T. T. On Toast 494
T-Town Blues 520
Tuba Lawdy Blues 510

1978
Tub-Jug Rag 1572
Tuck In Kentucky (And Smile) 174-267-625-
 1098
Tuck Me To Sleep 1094
Tuesday At Ten 108-619
Tu-Li-Tulip Time 430-588
Tulsa Blues 1109
Tumble In 976
Tumbling Tumbleweeds 297
Tune Town Shuffle 108
Tunie's Tune 1674
Tunin' Up 911
Turf, The 895
Turkey In The Straw 1359
Turkey Special 730
Turkish Ideals 1086
Turkish Towel 139-266
Turko 1522
Turn Left 434
Turn Off The Moon 440-1710
Turn On That Red Hot Heat 123
Turn On The Heat 11-305-676-800-952-1505-
 1569-1623
Turn On The Old Music Box 306-1436
Turn Over 825
Turn Right 434
Turn Your Lights Down Low 1505
Turque 798
Turtle Dove 1513
Turtle Twist 1104
Tutti-Frutti 386-550-906-1315-1357
Tu verras Montmartre 1173
Tuxedo Junction 214-416-589-692-693-816-
 841-909-1225-1359
Tuxedo Stomp 381-1495
Twa Twa Twa Blues 187
Tweedle-Dee, Tweedle-Doo 1219-1643
Tweed Me 897
Tweet Tweet 468
Twee Twa Twa Blues 1550
Twee-Twee-Tweet 259
Twelfth Street Blues 717-733-955-1208
Twelfth Street Rag 42-105-115-163-348-385
 484-557-662-725-745-862-902-954-992-1015
 1079-1080-1110-1207-1299-1324-1430-1498-
 1532-1555-1626-1750
Twelfth Year 1261
Twelve Bar Stampede 518
Twelve O'Clock Blues 1065
Twelve O'Clock In Jolopi 629
Twentieth Century Blues 772-1128
20th Century Closet 896-897
21st Street Blues 181
Twenty-Four Hours A Day 1307-1602-1730
Twenty-Four Hours In Georgia 699
Twenty-Four Robbers 990-1637
Twenty Grand Blues 1061
Twenty Million People 674
29th And Dearborn 415-505-862-1044
Twenty-One Dollars A Day-Once A Month 1318
Twenty-One Years 1145-1319
Twenty Swedes Ran Through The Weeds
 (Chasing One Norwegian) 248
Twiddlin' My Thumbs (Fiddlin' My Time
 Away) 566-823
Twilight 1252
Twilight And You 1504
Twilight Interlude 324-1358
Twilight In Turkey 24-441-586-602-755-
 1147-1371-1400-1434-1465
Twilight On The Trail 1307

Twilight Rose 1122
Twilight, The Stars And You 534
Twin Blues 1603
Twin City Blues 739
Twinkle Dinkle 18
Twinkle, Twinkle, Little Star 1415
Twinklin' 900
Twits And Twerps - see BOY MEETS HORN
2 a.m. Blues 682-1466
Two Blind Loves 1405-1539
Two Blue Eyes 225
Two Bouquets 429
Two-Buck Tim From Timbuctoo 148-877
Two By Four Blues 850
Two Cigarettes In The Dark 201-291-809-
 1349
Two Deuces 43
Two Dreams Got Together 295-321
Two Dreams Met 373-451-910
Two Dresden Dolls 587
Two Dukes On A Pier 1615
Two Eyes Of Blue From Kalamazoo 531
Two-Faced Man 357
Two-Faced Woman Blues 1457
Two Fools In Love 184
Two For Tonight 362
Two Guitars 1475
Two-Gun Dan 585-1433
Two Heads Against The Moon 293
Two Heads In The Moonlight 1296
Two Hearts Are Better Than One 95
Two Hearts Are Dancing 1028
Two Hearts Carved On A Lonesome Pine 437
Two Hearts That Pass In The Night 1243
Two Hundred Squabble 1084
Two In A Dream 292
Two In Love 126-375-453-911
Two In One Blues 1409
Two Left Feet 629
Two Lips (To Kiss My Cares Away) 1692
Two Little Blue Little Eyes 142-1385
Two Little Flies On A Lump Of Sugar 809
Two Little Girls In Blue 1314
Two Little Pretty Birds 1612
Two Little Slippers And Two Big Shoes
 293
Two Little Squirrels, The (Nuts To You)
 865
2.19 Blues 58
Two O'Clock Blues 1746
Two O'Clock Jump 814-1482
Two Of Everything 1010
Two Of Us, The 523
Two Old Maids In A Folding Bed 1094
Two-Part Invention in A minor (Bach) 1371
Two Red Lips 641
Two Rivers Flow Through Harlem 132-583
Twos And Fews 947
2.16 Blues 831
Two Sleepy People 206-276-588-1633
Two Tickets To Georgia 1235-1263-1751
Two-Time Dan 706-916-1180-1271-1672
Two-Time Mama 1673
Two-Time Man 1277
Two Times 1112
Two-Timin' Mama 570
Two-Timin' Man 843
Two Tiny Tots On A Teeter-Totter (Up-sy,
 Down-sy) 206
Two Tired Eyes 1180
Two Together 365

Two Tone Stomp  844
Two-Ton Tessie  646
Two Train Blues  1471
Two-Two Double-Two Timbuctoo  143
Two Weeks' Notice  1202
Tyler Texas Stomp  381
Ty-Tee  1085-1613

Ubangi  1400
Ubangi Man  936
Ugly Man Blues  7
Ukulele Baby  1425
Ukulele Benny  558
Ukulele Lady  797-992-1425-1583
Ultrafox  1258
Ultra-Modern Swing  385
Ultraphone Rhythm - see ULTRAFOX
Umbrella Man, The  163-588
Umbrellas To Mend  544
Um-Ta-Da-Da-Da  1208
Umtcha, Umtcha, Da, Da, Da  1292
Uncle Bud (Tennessee Blues)  693-1525
Uncle Bud Blues (Bugle Blues)  1719
Uncle Eph's Dream  1561 (see also 1520 TO
  1865)
Uncle Eph's Got The Coon  1318
Uncle Joe  1729
Uncle Joe's Music Store  698
Uncle Ned's Stomp  1169
Uncle Remus Stomp  1557
Uncle Sam Blues  750-1011-1447-1671
Uncle Sammy, Here I Am  1711
Undecided  151-611-895-1159-1262-1633-1661
Undecided Blues  108
Under A Beach Umbrella With You  699
Under A Blanket Of Blue  289-297
Under A Blue Jungle Moon  769
Under A Strawberry Moon  1319
Under A Texas Moon  888-979
Underneath The Arches  158
Underneath The Harlem Moon  198-394-726-
  778-876-1277-1308-1646
Underneath The Russian Moon  951
Underneath The Weeping Willow  236-269-
  1120-1238
Undertaker Blues  1713
Undertaker's Blues  643-734-860-1094
Under The Chicken Tree  1026
Under The Clover Moon  1580
Under The Creole Moon  1427
Under The Desert Moon  919
Under The Greenwood Tree  1513
Under The Mistletoe  1313
Under The Moon  468-669-1290
Under The Moon It's You  980
Under The Spell Of The Blues  1659
Under The Spell Of The Moon  951
Under The Sweetheart Tree  1214
Under The Ukulele Tree  233
Undertow  1538
Underworld Blues  1617
Under Your Spell  1416
Under Your Window Tonight  1385-1470
"U" Need Some Lovin' Blues - see YOU NEED
  SOME LOVIN'!
Unemployed Papa-Charity Working Mama  1452
Unfortunate Blues  156-857-884-916-925
United We Swing  1539
Unknown Blues, The  710
Unlucky Blues  311-902
Unlucky Woman Blues  187

Unromantic Blues  1744
Unsatisfied Blues  1321
Unsophisticated Sue  984
Until The Real Thing Comes Along  93-691
  702-770-899-938-939-1074-1584-1629-
  1630
Until The Stars Fall Down  299
Until Today  14-728
Until Tomorrow  743
Until Tonight  498
Until You Fall In Love  374
Untrue Woman Blues  1414
Up And At 'Em  129-171-234-572-1208-1300
  1486-1674
Up In The Clouds  515
Up Jumped The Devil  189-190-403-761-
  1208
Up Jumped You With Love  1638
Up On Teddy's Hill  1046
Up Popped The Devil  1506
Upright Organ Blues  676
Uproar Shout  691
Ups And Downs  1508
Upside Down  1018
Upstairs  1465
Up The Chimney Go My Dreams  372
Up The Country Blues  541-999-1617
Up The River  31-1322
Up Today And Down Tomorrow  1542
Uptown Downbeat  491
Uptown Blues  988
Uptown Daddy  1069
Uptown Jive  1590
Uptown Rhapsody  755
Uptown Shuffle  692
Used To You  950
Useless Blues  1014
Usen't You Used To Be My Sweetie ?  1619-
  1671
Us On A Bus  182-1628
Utah Mormon Blues  1212
Utt-Da-Zay (The Tailor Song)  259-1263-
  1655

Vagabond Dreams  283-908
Valencia  630-644
Valentine  1504
Valentine Drag  1586
Valentine Stomp  1623
Valetta  1247
Valparaiso  384
Valse in D flat major (Chopin, Op. 64,
  No. 1)  1371
Vamp  1135
Vamp, The  155-1747
Vamping Brown  793
Vampin' Liza Jane  1724
Vamping Lucy Long  1184
Vamping Rose  1433-1613
Vampin' Sal-The Sheba Of Georgia  458
Vampire Brown  942
Vampire Woman (The)  570-1675
Vamps Of "28", The  1675
Vamp Till Ready  471
Vaniteaser  240-241-626
Variety Is The Spice Of Life  323-907
Variety Stomp  648-721-722-1715
Varsity Drag, The  648-799-1309
Velvet Moon  820
Vendredi 13  1262
Venetian Moon  891-1603

Venus Blues  1747
Very Thought Of You, The  284-768-1146
Viaduct Blues  954
Vibraphone Blues  599-603
Vibraphonia  1600
Vibraphonia No. 2  1602
Vibrollini  1333
Victim Of The Blues  1268
Victory Ball  975
Victory March  322
Victory Walk, The  99
Vieni, Vieni  367-604-1221
Vilia/Vilja  579-756-1404
Village Clown, The  1352
Vine Street Blues  1109
Vine Street Boogie  1038
Vine Street Bustle  851
Vine Street Drag  1084-1543
Violet Ray Blues  1263
Violets  320
Violetta  217
Violets For Your Furs  453-911
Viola Lee Blues  270
Violin Blues  696
Viper Mad  1427
Viper's Drag (The)  252-1625-1626
Viper's Dream  1260-1536-1562
Viper's Moan, A  191
Viper Song, The  1726
Virginia  39-658
Virginia Blues  119-856-904-915-935-975-
  976-1059-1437-1515-1523
Virginia, Georgia And Caroline  261
Virginia Lee  1153
Virginia (There's A Blue Ridge In/'Round
  My Heart)  11-1336-1534-1675
Vladivostock  737-1286-1365
V. M. I. Spirit  373
Vo-Do-Do-De-O Blues  172-236-398-625-1593-
  1740
Voice Of Ol' Man River, The  191
Voice Of The Blues, The  1376
Voice Of The Southland, The  63-1475-1546
Volcano  106
Vol Vistu Gaily Star  448-550-815-1358
Voodoo (1923)  686
Voodoo (1929)  1209
Voodoo (1938)  25-1224
Voodoo, The  1235
Voo Doo Blues (sic)  706-1466
Voom Voom (Moaden On The Gayden)  344
Vote For Mr. Rhythm  1659
Vous et moi  1284
Vox Poppin  590
Vuelva  259
Vultee Special  375

Wabash Blues  67-87-89-119-264-304-340-
  384-533-556-582-705-721-956-1085-1092-
  1206-1225-1298-1299-1307-1341-1352-1390-
  1391-1437-1462-1505-1537-1565-1750
Wabash Cannon Ball  1398
Wabash Stomp  466
Wacky Dust  125-588-1661
Waco Blues  941
Waco Texas Blues  164
Wa-Da-Da (Ev'rybody's Doin' It Now)  116
Waddlin' At The Waldorf  428
Wade In De Water (sic)  163
Waffle Man's Call, The  111
Wagon Wheels  200

Wah-Dee-Dah  255-1556-1646
Wah-Hoo !  427-702-1115-1239-1562
Wail, The  340
Wailing Blues  302-1040-1693
Wail Of The Scromph  1377
Wail Of The Winds  1146-1147
Wait And See  1634
Waiter And The Porter And The Upstairs
  Maid, The  364
Wait For The Happy Ending  1142
Waiting  111-248-649
Waitin' Around  925-1129-1428
Waiting At The End Of The Road  17-977-
  1623-1652-1687
Waitin' At The Gate For Katy  1332
Waiting Blues  1639
Waitin' For A Call From You  249-1387
Waiting For A Train  1328
Waitin' For Benny  618
Waitin' For Katy  653-970-1232-1393-1584
Waitin' For The Evenin' Mail (Sittin' On
  The Inside, Lookin' At The Outside)
  706-911-1145-1146-1424-1447-1544
Waiting For The Moon  33-873
Waiting For The Robert E Lee  347-865
Waiting For You  641-763
Waitin' For You Blues  776
Waiting In The Garden  1074
Waitin' Thru' The Night  806
Wait'll You See (My Brand New Mama)  1579
Wait'll You See My Gal  72-558-714-1190
Wait 'Til I Catch You In My Dreams  1540
Wait 'Til It Happens To You  760
Wait Till/Until My Heart Finds Out  369-
  907-1358
Wait Till The Girls Get Into The Army,
  Boys  1398
Wait Till The Sun Shines, Nellie  364-
  591-818
Wait Till Tomorrow Night  1503
Wait 'Til You See "Ma Cherie"  1233-1568
Wait Till You See Me With My Baby (That
  Little Somebody Of Mine)  1721
Wait Till You See My Baby Do The
  Charleston  411-1699
Wait Until You See My Madeline  1573
Wake 'Em Up  1389-1645
Wake Up And Live  258-441-786-1147-1400-
  1659
Wake Up And Sing  780-879
Wake Up, Chillun, Wake Up !  83-1152-
  1293-1493
Wake Up, Sinners  1459
Wakin' Up Blues  320
Wakin' Up The Folks Downstairs  193
Walk Easy 'Cause My Papa's Here  101
Walkin' And Swingin'  185-899-907
Walking And Talking Blues  749
Walkin' Back Home  1547
Walking Blues  99-313-1265
Walkin' By The River  272-817
Walkin' Cane Stomp  891
Walking In The Sun  1214
Walkin' My Baby Back Home  48-197-305-
  673-853-1098-1411-1644-1667
Walkin' Talkin' Blues  1618
Walking Talking Dolly  314
Walkin' The Boogie  851
Walkin' The Dog  18-126-274-315-774-922-
  1007-1148-1429-1572-1672-1720
Walking The Floor Over You  365-1318

Walkin' The Street(s)  999-1677
Walkin' This Town  1486
Walking With Susie  20-888
Walk It To Me  1203
Walk, Jenny, Walk  350-597-1188-1239-1271
Walk Right In  270
Walk That Broad  1703
Walk That Thing  833
Walls Keep Talking, The  911
Wall Street Wail  480
Walnut Street Blues  1066
Waltz Clog Medley  877
Waltzing The Blues  282
Waltzing With A Dream  1211
Waltz Lives On, The  295
Waltz Was Born In Vienna, A  182-1313
Waltz You Saved For Me, The  1313
Wanderer's Stomp  1640
Wanderin' Blues  96
Wandering Boy Blues  1453
Wandering Man Blues  1007
Wandering Papa Blues  941
Wanderlust  766
Wang-Wang Blues  171-182-192-271-482-557-
    622-625-657-705-721-723-798-924-1094-
    1233-1392-1461-1493-1680-1682
Wang-Wang Harmonica Blues  285
Wanna Go Home  1451
Wanna Go South Again Blues  706
Wanna Hat With Cherries  323
Want A Little Lovin'  509-629-658-884-
    1097-1263-1589
Wanted  440-880-1032-1313-1710
Want To Woogie Some More  849
Want Your Ashes Hauled  1201
War Dance For/Of The Wooden Indians, The
    25-386-756-1372-1435
War Horse Mama  712-713-854-1051-1057-
    1448
Warmin' Up  1731
Warm Valley  497
Washboard  1161
Washboard Blues  38-79-275-276-288-296-
    444-762-764-1138-1192-1273-1682
Washnoard Cut-Out  942
Washboard Rag  1572
Washboards Get Together  1647
Washboard Stomp  538
Washboard Wiggles  1209
Washing Dishes With My Sweetie  1667
Washin' The Blue  From My Soul  247
Washington And Lee Swing  111-371-736-909-
    993-1045-1497
Washington Grays  427
Washington Squabble  774-775-1239
Washington Whirligig  99
Washington Wobble  473
Wash It Clean  153
Wash The Japs Away  834
Washwoman('s) Blues  1445-1549
Was I (Drunk) ?  843-1677
Was ist Los ?  809
Was It A Dream ?  314-419-1291
Was It A Lie ?  1327
Was I To Blame For Falling In Love With
    You ?  288
Was It Rain ?  294-1399
Was It Wrong ??  1470
Was My Face Red ?  1269
Wasn't It Nice ?  138-305-562-783-795-824
Wasn't It You ?  98-434

Wasted Life Blues  1446
Was That All I Meant To You ?  1557
Was That The Human Thing To Do ?  6-147-
    157-981-1227-1645
Wasting My Love On You  672-1098-1599
Watchin'  1711
Watching My Dreams Go By  853-1294
Watching The Clock  297
Watching The Clouds Roll By  241
Watching The Day Fade Away  151
Watching The Knife And Fork Spoon  1278
Watch Me Go  1576
Watch The Birdie  135-316-911
Watch The Clock  166
Watch Your Hornin'  274
Watch Your Step  213
Water Boy  761-1633
Waterloo  1392
Watermelon Man  493
Wa Wa Wa  1120-1167
Wa Wa Waddle Walk  60
'Way After One Amy Daddy Ain't Come Home
    Yet  1739
Way Back Blues  110
'Way Back Home  160-202-396
'Way Back When  1291
'Way Down Home  1348-1708
Way Down In Lover's Lane  359
Way Down In Macon, Georgia  1375
'Way Down South In Chicago  640
'Way Down South Where The Blues  Begin
    667
'Way Down That Lonely Road  680
'Way Down Upon The Swanee River - see
    SWANEE RIVER
'Way Down Yonder In New Orleans  2-9-70-
    330-349-375-406-467-497-535-559-584-
    690-873-939-946-1027-1031-1150-1154-
    1173-1341-1343-1392-1433-1519-1566-
    1680
Way He Loves Is Just Too Bad, The  771-
    1345
Way I Feel, The  1726
Way I Feel Today, The  672-790-1034
Way I Feel Tonight, The  199
Way I'm Feelin', The  1678
Way Low  494-495
Wayward Roamer Blues  1747
Way You Look Tonight, The  622-1019-1732
We Ain't Got Nothin' To Lose  1291
Weakness  257
We All Go "Oo-Ha-Ha" Together  1295
We All Wanna Know Why  147-459
Wear A Great Big Smile  347
Wearin' Of The Green, The  125-1572
Weary  438
Weary Blues  42-89-271-414-425-426-437-
    692-826-917-976-993-999-1052-1068-1100
    1129-1132-1208-1287-1468-1469-1698-
    1737-1743
Weary City  414
Weary Feet  1305-1651
Weary Land Blues  751
Weary Money Blues  753
Weary Of Waiting For You  566-920
Weary River  242-1510-1598-1743
Weary Stomp  1108
Weary Traveler  791-1073
Weary Way Blues, The  150-352-410-1045-
    1271-1494
Weary Weasel  649-991-992

1982

Weary Yodelin' Blues  513
Weather Beaten Blues  1657
Weather Bird (Rag)  44-1165
Weather Blues  1657
Weather Man  798-1248-1332-1432
We Better Get Together Again  198
We Can Huddle At Home  893
We Can Live On Love  592
We Can't Go On This Way  526
We Can't Use Each Other Any More  316
We'd A Surely Baked A Cake (If We'd A
  Known You Was Gonna Come) (sic)  827
We Did It Before (And We Can Do It Again)
  1318
Wedding Bells (Are Breaking Up That Old
  Hang Of Mine)  31-207-658-887-1318
Weddin' Blues  692
Wedding Glide  1217
Wedding In The Ark  1294
Wedding Of A Sophisticated Dutch Doll
  1224
Wedding Of Jack And Jill, The  1156
Wedding Of Mr. And Mrs. Swing, The  258-
  702
Wedding Of Shimmie And Jazz  380
Wedding Of The Painted Doll, The  244-809-
  949-1743
Wedding Veil Blues  954
Wednesday Night Hop  899-1411-1509
We Don't Know From Nothin'  1278
We Don't Need Each Other Any More  1651
We'd Rather Jump Than Swing  342
Wee Baby Blues  1531
Wee Bit Of Swing, A  1337
Weeds  534
Weed Smoker's Dream  679
Week-End In Havana  375-1361
Week-End Of A Private Secretary, The  430-
  1158-1357
Week-End Stomp  333
Weely  495
Weep, The  155
Weepin'  1461
Weeping Blues  776-837
Weepin' The Blues  522-857
Weeping Willow Blues  965-976-1093-1441
Weeping Willow Swing  637
Weepin' Woman Blues  1268
Weep No More, My Baby  290
Wee Wee Daddy Blues  1066
We Found Romance  758
We Gonna Get High Together  1528
We Gonna Move  1206
We Gonna Rub It  390
We Go Well Together  261-729-1360
Weird Blues  1456
We Just Couldn't Say Goodbye  147-158-198-
  673
Welcome Home  1155-1293
Welcome Stranger  182-427-1312-1719
Well, All Right ! (Tonight's The Night)
  29-447-589
Well, All Right Then !  690-988
We'll Be Married In June  806
We'll Build A Little World Of Our Own  32-
  83
Wellesley High Jump  1374
Well, Git It !  453-454
We'll Have A Honeymoon Some Day  982
We'll Have A New Home In The Morning  1325
We'll Make Hay While The Sun Shines  200

We'll Meet Again  622-744
We'll Never Know  8-611-1159
We'll Ride The Tide Together  183
Well, Well  374
We Love It  669
We Love To Swing  537
We Love Us  341-659
We Need A Little Love  1638
We Own A Salon  1745
We're Back Together Again  1068
We're Breakin' Up A Lovely Affair  258
We're Friends Again  724-1144
(We're Gonna Have) Smooth Sailing  13
We're Gonna Have To Slap The Dirty
  Little Jap  1070
We're Gonna Pitch A Boogie Woogie  679
We're On The Highway To Heaven  1536
We're The Couple In The Castle  1553
We're Tired Of That Tiger  1433
Were You Foolin' ?  392
Were You Sincere ?  981-1144-1296
We Saw The Sea  1562
West Bound Freight  1312
West Coast Rag  516
West Coast Stomp  1274
West Dallas Drag (Nos. 1 and 2)  342
West End Blues  43-57-654-731-1008-1107-
  1168-1169-1207-1454-1535-1652-1693-
  1712
West End Romp  1131
Western Melody  686
Western Swing  277
Western Union Blues  355-846-860
West Indian Stomp  498
West Indies Blues  136-732-733-812-1023-
  1229-1448-1469-1523
West Of The Weather  912
West Texas Blues (The)  154-1525-1724
West Virginia Blues  642-1717
Westward Bound  469-1425
West Wind  879-1001-1239-1628
We, The People  1357-1632
We Three  298-450-590
Wet It  824
We Toddled Up The Hill  1293
Wet Yo' Thumb  70-706-710-925
We've Come A Long Way Together  206
We've Got Rhythm  974
We've Got The Blues  1486
We've Got To Put That Sun Back In The
  Sky  147-157-303-1297-1310
We Want Five  1558
We Were Only Walking In The Moonlight
  198
We Were So Young  1211
We Were The Best Of Friends  290-1648
Whadja Do To Me ?  156-1427-1469
Whale Dip  149
Wham (Re-Bop-Boom-Bam)  81-185-901-988-
  989-1355-1540-1736
What A Bird-What A Girl  1503
What About Me ?  797
What A Day !  516-519-1017-1666
What A Difference A Day Made  284-424-
  689-779-798
What A Dream  113
What A Dummy Love Has Made Of Me  1490
What A Fool I've Been  1542
What A Funny World This Would Be  655
What A Gal ! What A Pal !  523    )1069
What A Girl ! What A Night !  193-340-

What A Life !  475-540-900
What A Life ! (Trying To Live Without You)  34-341
What A Little Moonlight Can Do  937-1730
What A Man !  233-530-777-848-869-1221-1510-1579-1592
What Am I Gonna Do For Lovin' ?  592
What Am I Here For ?  500
What Am You Waitin' On ?  1577
What A Night !  249-1079
What A Night ! What A Moon ! What A Girl!  1730
What A Perfect Combination  1149-1205
What A Perfect Night For Love  1295
What A Pretty Miss  1634
What Are You Doing Tonight ?  1237-1357
What Are Your Intentions ?  937
What Are You Thinkin' About, Baby ?  873
What A Shuffle  1658
What A Smile Can Do  1547
What A Wonderful Time  218
What A Wonderful Wedding That Will Be  521-708-1126-1291
What A Wonderful World  437
What Can A Poor Fellow Do ?  474-1183
What Can I Do ?  32
(What Can I Do With) A Foolish Little Girl Like You ?  1467-1710
What Can I Say After I Say I'm Sorry ? - see AFTER I SAY I'M SORRY
What Can You Do Without Me ?  731
What Can You Say In A Love Song ?  424
What-Cha-Call-'Em Blues  269-718-1097-1204-1545
Whatcha Gonna Do ?  1518
Whatcha Gonna Do When There Ain't No Swing ?  14-545-585
Whatcha Gotcha Trombone For ?  23
Whatcha Know, Joe ?  97-215-452-989
What-Cha-Ma-Call-It  234
What Could Be Sweeter, Dear ?  687-1118
What Could Be Sweeter Than You ?  920
What Did Deacon Mose Do (When The Lights Went Out)  1725
(What Did I Do To Be So) Black And Blue ?  45-479-584-1081-1281-1330-1401-1481-1505-1541-1652-1726
What Did I Tell Ya ?  351-892-1264
What Didja Wanna Make Me Love You For ?  262-516
What Did Romie-O-Juliet (When He Climbed Her Balcony)  531-1714
What Do I Care ?  245-672-1368
What Do I Care What Somebody Said ?  359-455-552-1030-1192-1238
What Do We Care ?  1426
What Do We Do On A Dew-Dew-Dewy Day ?  398-993-1288-1290-1417-1588
What Do We Get From Boston ?  530-1594
What Do You Bet ?  917
What Do You Care (What I Do)  1725
What Do You Do Sunday, Mary ?  224-522
What Do You Hear From The Mob In Scotland  729
What Do You Know About Love ?  446-526-692 1700
What Do You Mean By Loving Somebody Else ?  1603
What Do You Say ?  239-1064-1581
What Do You Think Of My Baby ?  520
What(Do)You Want(Poor)Me To Do ?  263-807

What Do You Want To Make Those Eyes At Me For ?  315-781
What D'Ya Hear From Your Heart ?  167-186
Whatever Happened To You ?  742
What Goes On Here In My Heart ?  609-906
What Goes Up Must Come Down (And Baby, You've Been Flying Too High)  105-184-370-1654
What Good Am I Without You ?  22-196-483-724 1144-1295
What Good Is A Sandwich (If It Hasn't Any Bread)  883
What Good Will It Do ?  1316
What Good Would It Do ?  499
What Harlem Is To Me  23-689-798
What Have I Done ?  748-1460
What Have We Got To Do Tonight (But Dance)  592
What Have We Got To Lose (Hi-Ho-Lack-a-Day)  1009-1269
What Have You Done To Make Me Feel This Way ?  1463
What Have You Done To Me ?  859-1678
What Have You Got That Gets Me ?  79-369-610-1357
What If I/We Do ?  1395-1535
What Is It ?  160
What Is Love ?  1697
What Is Sweeter (Than The Sweetness Of "I Love You")  92
What Is That She Got ?  1543
What Is That Smells Like Gravy ?  1542
What Is The Matter Now ?  1561
What Is There To Say ?  541-829-1407-1468
What Is This Going To Get Us ?  769
What Is This Thing Called Love ?  115-295 453-503-838-949-1228-1273-1285-1336-1403-1749
What Is This Thing Called Swing ?  56-987
What It Takes To Bring You Back (Mama Keeps It All The Time)  214
What It Takes To Get A Dime From Me  389
What It Takes To Keep My Wife From Running Around  389
What Kinda Love Is That ?  845
What Kinda Man Is You ?  317-922-1012-1081
What Kind O' Man Is That ?  994
What Kind Of Rhythm Is That ?  179
What'll I Do ?  11-72-351-444-643-796-1691
What'll They Think Of Next ?  614
What'll We Do For Dough ?  28
What'll You Do ?  573-784-929
What Love Will Do  168
What Makes A Bow-Legged Woman Crazy 'Bout Her Knock-Kneed Man ?  821
What Makes Me Love You So ?  1395-1445-1535-1706
What Makes My Baby Cry ?  237-531
What Makes Papa Hate Mama So ?  1717
What Makes Sammy Run ?  434
What Makes You Act Like That ?  1452
What Makes You Treat Me This A Way ?  169
What Makes You Treat Me This A Way ?  1013
What More Can A Monkey Woman Do ?  1013
What More Can I Give You ?  829
What More Do You Want ?  406
What ! No Women ?  530
What's A Poor Girl Gonna Do ?  251
What's Buzzin', Cousin ?  261

What's Buzzin', Cousin ? 261
What's Good For The Goose (Is Good For The Gander) 200-1124
What Shall I Do ? 809
What Shall I Say ? 79-1735
What's Mine Is Yours 900
What's My Baby Doin' ? 679
What's New ? 95-612-1491
What's On Your Mind ? 680
What's That ? 1673
What's That Tastes Like Gravy ? 892
What's That Thing ? 820
What's The Color Of A "Yellow" Horse ? 1393
What's The Good Of Moonlight (When You Haven't Got A Girl To Love) 326-1318
What's The Matter ? 1042-1505
What's The Matter Now ? 178-734-1013-1443 1700
What's The Matter With Me ? 527-614-775
What's The Matter With The Well ? 1044
What's The Name Of That Song ? 365-1157
What's The Reason ? 831
What's The Reason (I'm Not Pleasin' You) 330-427-639-1114-1270-1432-1625
What's The Use ? 195-216-404-504-542-655-1521-1570
What's The Use Blues 82
What's The Use Of Being Alone ? 459
What's The Use Of Crying ? 1664
What's The Use Of Cryin', Baby ? 1257
What's The Use Of Dreaming ? 576-881
What's The Use Of Getting Sober (When You Gonna Get Drunk Again) 865
What's The Use Of Getting Used To You ? 1031
What's The Use Of Living Without Love ? 411-1170-1295-1745
What's The Use Of Lovin' ? 1749
What's The Use Of Talking ? 467
What's Worth While Getting 380
What's Your Guess ? 1413
What's Your Number ? 107
What's Your Price ? 1729
What's Your Story, Morning Glory ? 900-989
What's Your Story ? (What's Your Jive ?) 729
What The Heart Believes (The Heart Will See) 786-1562
What Used To Was Used To Was (Now It Ain't) 371-506
What Was You Doing ? (sic) 680
What Will I Do ? 960
What Will I Do In The Morning ? 1631
What Will I Tell My Heart ? 362-728-879-899-1530
What Will Santa Claus Say ? 1249
What Would Happen To Me If Something Happened To You ? 36
What Would I Do Without You ? 112
What Wouldn't I Do ? 567
What Wouldn't I Do For That Man ? 305-671-788-1569
What Would People Say ? 900
What Would You Do ? 34-1297
What You Gonna Do ? 676-678
What You Need Is Me (And What I Need Is You) 1463
What You Want Me To Do ? 1169-1704
What You Was You Used To Be 1009

When (1924) 377
When (1926) 1744
When (1928) 391-1684
When (1935) 180
When A Black Man's Blue 483
When A Blonde Makes Up Her Mind To Do You Good 555-572-883
When A 'Gator Hollers, Folks Say It's A Sign Of Rain 846-1458
When A Great Love Comes Along 66-1307
When A Lady Meets A Gentleman Down South 383-536-599-1433
When A Pal Bids A Pal Goodbye 1470
When A Prince Of A Fella Meets A Cinderella 125-1357
When A St. Louis Woman Comes Down To New Orleans 1340
When Autumn Leaves Are Falling 190
When A Woman Gets The Blues 1252
When A Woman Loves A Man (1930) 21-553 672
When A Woman Loves A Man (1934) 768-797 1529-1530
When Baby Sleeps 274
When Buddha Smiles 298-320-518-597-605-690-963-1358
When Cootie Left The Duke 1374
When Day Is Done 77-183-281-690-869-1123-1337
When Did You Leave Heaven ? 14-93-122-1242
When Dreams Come True 730
When Erastus Plays His Old Kazoo 237-414-553-806-1226
When Eyes Of Blue Are Fooling You 963
When Gimble Hits The Cymbal 249
When Happiness Begins 1085
When Hearts Are Young 222-914
When He Comes Home 797
When Hollywood Goes Black And Tan 180
When I Am Housekeeping For You 672-932-1381-1382
When I Can Get It 843
When I Can't Be With You 251-316
When Icky Morgan Plays The Organ 1270
When I Come Back Crying (Will You Be Laughing At Me ?) 529
When I Dream Of Old Tennessee Blues 1056
When I First Met Mary 1231-1619
When I Get Low I Get High 1659
When I Get The Blues All Around Me Do' (sic) 1750
When I Get The Devil In Me 1717
When I Get You Alone Tonight 1004-1317
When I Go A-Dreamin' 609-1357
When I Go, Your Good Thing's Going Too 285
When I Grow Too Old To Dream 292-382-1306
When I Kissed You I Kissed The Blues Goodbye 1108
When I Look To The West 655
When I'm Alone (1929) 1624
When I'm Alone (1930) 1112
When I March In April With May 1702
When I'm Blue 650
When I Met Connie In The Cornfield 31-395-1336-1675
When I Met Sally 799
When I'm Walking With My Sweetness - see DOWN AMONG THE SUGAR CANE

When I'm With You  93-122-264-302
When I Put On My Long White Robe  697-698
When I Ring Your Front Door Bell  524
When Irish Eyes Are Smiling  297-1075
When Is A Kiss Not A Kiss ?  795-1157-1337-1416
When I Saw You  451-902
When I Steps Out  1449
When I Stopped Runnin', I Was At Home  409
When I Take My Sugar To Tea  156-197-287-678-981-993-1171-1303-1514
When I Think Of You  73-963
When It's Daylight-Saving Time In Oshkosh  1667
When It's Lamp-Lightin' Time In The Valley  148
When It's Moonlight In Brooklyn  640
When It's Night-Time In Italy  1175-1240
When It's Sleepy-Time Down South  48-58-76-87-115-197-410-505-601-602-785-1154-1470-1654
When It's Springtime In The Rockies  513-1314
When It's Too Late (You're Gonna Miss Me, Daddy)  360
When I Was The Dandy And You Were The Belle  228
When I Went Back Home  39
When I Wore My Daddy's Brown Derby (And You Wore Your Mother's Blue Gown)  249
When Jenny Does Her/That Low Down Dance  139-466-1644
When June Comes Along With A Song  70
When Kentucky Bids The World "Good Morning"  933-1144-1594
When Life Seems So Blue  1110-1111
When Lights Are Low  282-283-662
When Love Beckoned  1406
When Love Comes In  1528
When Love Comes Stealing  1028
When Love Comes Swingin' Along  1337
When Love Comes Your Way  427
When Love Has Gone  1032
When Love Is Young  1630
When Love Knocks At Your Heart  755
When Mother Nature Sings Her Lullaby  1315
When Mother Played The Organ (And Daddy Sang A Hymn)  1227
When My Baby Comes  1446
When My Baby Left Me  1712
When My Baby Smiles  380
When My Baby Smiles At Me  316-607-748-972-1239-1479
When My Baby Starts To Shake That Thing  404
When My Dream Boat Comes Home  14-102-204-365-367-1239-1313
When My Dreams Come True  950-1687
When My Gal Comes Home  1414
When My Little Pomeranian Met Your Little Pekinese  148
When My Love Comes Down  1677
When My Love Has Come Down  680
When My Man Comes Home  832
When My Man Shimmies  212
When My Ship Comes In  424-1211
When My Sugar Walks Down The Street  397-493-528-1003-1005-1029-1121-1191-1263-1283-1363-1450-1515-1643-1657-1741-1745
When My Wants Run Out  1453
When Nobody Else Is Around  874

When Paw Was Courtin' Ma  1465
When Polly Walks Through The Hollyhocks  139-644
When Ruben Swings The Cuban  53
When Shadows Fall  737
When's It Comin' 'Round To Me ?  1431
When Somebody Thinks You're Wonderful  1627
When Spring Comes Peeping Through  720-1643
When Summer Is Gone  242-579-580-1336
When Sweet Susie Goes Steppin' By  269-520-1055-1417-1546
When That Man Is Dead And Gone  81
When The Bees Make Honey  513
When The Breath Bids The Body Goodbye  1036
When The Breath Bids Your Girl Friend's Body Goodbye  1542
When The Butterflies Kiss The Buttercup  657
When The Circus Came To Town  1397
When The Circus Comes To Town  1296
When The Clock Strikes Twelve  1426
When The Dixie Stars Are Playing Peekaboo  377
When The Heather Is In Bloom  321
When The Jazz Band Starts To Play  1096
When The Lights Are Soft And Low  875
When The Lights Go On Again  186-1070
When The Lilacs Bloom Again  1552
When The Little Red Roses Get The Blues For You  206
When The Midnight Choo Choo Leaves For Alabam'  444
When The Moon Hangs High  1027
When The Moon Shines In Coral Gables  231-796
When The Morning Glories Wake Up In The Morning (Then I'll Kiss Your Two Lips Goodnight)  402-1612
When The Morning Rolls Around  1668
When The New Moon Shines  201
When The Night Comes Rolling 'Long  405
When The Organ Played "O Promise Me"  880
When The Poppies Bloom Again  162-638-1313
When The Pussy Willow Whispers To The Catnip - see WHISPER SONG, THE
When The Quail Come Back To San Quentin  1407
When The Rain Turns To Snow  1576
When The Real Thing Comes Your Way  1301
When The Red, Red Robin Comes Bob, Bob, Bobbin' Along  38-234-370-1381-1534
When The Red Sun Turns To Grey I'll Be Back  1678
When The Robin Sings His Song Again  755
When The Roses Bloom Again  435-621
When The Saints Go Marching In  55-1003
When The Spirit Moves Me  96
When The Steamboat Whistle Is Blowing  587
When The Sun Comes Out  98-434-619-1360
When The Sun Goes Down  104-848-1311-1352
When The Sun Goes Down In Harlem  680
When The Sun Sets Down South  1427
When The Swallows Come Back To Capistrano  325-909
When The Time Has Come  155

1986

When The Wind Blows North (Then I Start
Going South) 377
When The Wind Makes Connection With Your
Dry Goods 343
When The World Is At Rest 670-888
When They Changed My Name To A Number 567
When They Get Lovin' They's Gone 1750
When They Play Them Blues 824
When Things Go Wrong 962
When Tomorrow Comes 878-1551
When Twilight Comes 1357
When We Get Together In The Moonlight 262
When We're Alone 147-813
When Will I Know ? 292-914
When Will The Sun Shine For Me ? 350
When Winter Comes 1405
When Work Is Through 471
When You And I Were Pals 1208
When You And I Were Young, Maggie 168-
600-695-917-1147-1310-1635-1735
When You And I Were Young Maggie Blues
1482-1607
When You Awake 298-451-910
When You Do What You Do 717-1502
When You Get Tired Of Your New Sweetie
1060
When You Go Huntin', I'm Goin' Fishin'
1717
When You Got To Go You Got To Go 1238
When You Leave Me Alone To Pine 1166
When You Lose Your Daddy 995
When You're Alone Blues 456
When You're A Long, Long Way From Home
819
When You're Away 1524-1679
When You're Counting The Stars Alone 245-
562-1687
When You're Crazy Over Daddy 1056
When You're Feeling Blue 1257
When You're Getting Along With Your Gal
919-1410
When You're In The Arms Of The One You
Love 74
When You're Near 221
When You're Out With Me 832
When You're Smiling 46-153-257-333-387-
403-480-481-581-583-587-977-1081-1153-
1170-1693
When You're Tired Of Me (Just Let Me Know)
1533
When You're With Somebody Else 669-1417-
1580-1684
When Your Love Comes Down 211
When Your Lover Has Gone 49-142-305-592-
980-1399-1513-1653-1726
When Your Man Is Going To Put You Down
You Never Can Tell 1729
When Your Old Wedding Ring Was New 1243-
1318
When Your Troubles Are (Just) Like Mine
844-1051
When You Think Of Lovin', Baby Think Of
Me 376
When You've Lost Your Baby 650
When You Walked Out, Someone Else Walked
Right In 19-223-710-732-882-1180
When You Were A Girl Of Seven 1496
When You Were The Blossom Of Buttercup
Lane 1296-1667
When You Were The Girl On The Scooter
(And I Was The Boy On The Bike) 1688

When You Wish Upon A Star 207
When You Wore A Tulip (And I Wore A Big
Red Rose) 183-206
Where Am I ? 249-427-701
Where Are You ? 78-123-162-1439-631
Where Are You Tonight ? 289
Where Can I Find You ? 533
Where Can She Be ? 94
Where (Can That Somebody Be ?) 731-750-
1011
Where Did Robinson Crusoe Go With Friday
On Saturday Night ? 315-1342
Where Did You Get That Name ? 1393
Where Did You Stay Last Night ? 1165
Where Do I Go From You ? 741
Where Do We Go From Here ? 376
Where Do You Keep Your Heart ? 96-166-
433-450
Where Do You Work-a, John ? 1316
Where'd You Get Those Eyes ? 234-624-
955-1521
Where Has Mammy Gone ? 1367
Where Has My Little Dog Gone ? 8-1553
Where Has My Old Gang Gone ? 1497
Where Have All The Black Men Gone ? 570-
854
Where Have We Met Before ? 29-1249
Where Have You Been All My Life ? 929-
1417-1493
Where In The World ? 1721
Where Is Alexander ? 1435
Where Is My Heart ? 93-439
Where Is My Man ? 1452
Where Is My Meyer ? (Where's Himalaya ?)
1559
Where Is That Girl Who Was Stolen From
Me ? 1135
Where Is That Old Girl Of Mine ? 1582
Where Is The Sun? 755-768-1465-1585-1630
Where Love Is King 1252
Where Or When 604-621-652-1134-1552
Where's Bill Bailey ? (Won't You Come
Home ?) 147
Where Shall I Be ? 1014
Where's My Baby Gone ? 112
Where's My Sweetie Hiding ? 32-170-229-
264-926-1718
Where's That Rainbow ? 568
Where's The Waiter ? 1003
Where That Ol' Man River Flows 1171-1706
Where The Bamboo Babies Grow 69-1607
Where The Black-Eyed Susans Grow 508
Where The Blue Of The Night Meets The
Gold Of The Day 372
Where The Dreamy Wabash Flows 226-715-
1582
Where The Eagle Builds His Nest 751
Where The Four-Leaf Clovers Grow 229
Where The Golden Daffodils Grow 83
Where The Huckleberries Grow 1305
Where The Lanterns Glow 1747
Where The Lazy Daisies Grow 72-225-576
Where The Lazy River Goes By 182-204-205
466-536-585-685-974-1732
Where The Mountains Meet The Sea 809
Where There's Smoke There's Fire 292
Where There's You There's Me 728
Where The Shy Little Violets Grow 502-
650-800-809-950-970-1339-1411
Where The Sweet Forget-Me-Nots Remember
853-1065-1233

Where The Wild, Wild Flowers Grow  640-708-870
Wherever There's A Will, Baby  1034
Wherever You Are (1928)  469-1291
Wherever You Are (1932)  147
Wherever You Are (1942)  82-770
Wherever You Go-Whatever You Do  1521
Where Was I ?  96-1359
Where Were You On The Night Of June The Third ?  779-938-1626
Where Were You Then ?  1502-1503
Where Will I Be ?  1184
Where You Are  911-1360-1375
Whiffenpoof Song, The  969
While Love Lasts  983
While Miami Dreams  219
While The Music Plays On  185-433
While The Years Go Drifting By  234-546-921
While We Danced At The Mardi Gras  1313
While You're Sneakin' Out  1021
Whip It To A Jelly  539-628-1450
Whip Me With Plenty Of Love  1706
Whipped Cream  1587
Whippin' That Jelly  1496
Whippin' The Ivories  1420
Whipping The Keys  627
Whirlaway  897
Whiskey And Gin Blues  1480
Whiskey Blues  1320
Whiskey Fool  848
Whispering  7-85-203-385-403-450-539-599-611-974-1031-1140-1148-1207-1223-1337-1373-1603
Whispering Grass  433-497-692-693
Whispering Lane  547
Whispering To My Man.  834
Whispers In The Dark  162-366-603-1400-162-366-603-1400-1552
Whispers In The Night  1407
Whisper Song, The  394-463-625-921
Whisper Sweet  779-798-1584
Whisper Sweet And Whisper Low  239
Whisper That You Love Me  744
Whisper While We Dance  432-908
Whistle  1502
Whistle And Blow Your Blues Away  659-1410
Whistler And His Dog, The  746
Whistler's Mother-in-Law, The  316-364
Whistle Stop  741
Whistle While You Work  880-1402-1596
Whistlin' Blues  947-948
Whistling In The Dark  197-1296
Whistling Rufus  1161-1198-1200-1473-1474-1475
Whistling Waltz, The  974
Whistling Woman Blues  1573
White Cliffs Of Dover, The  126-435
White Ghost Shivers  641-1131-1715
White Heat  745-959-983-988-1286
White Jazz  287-737-1507
White Lightning  1072
White Lightnin' Blues  1110
Whiteman Stomp  722-1682
White Sails (Beneath A Silver Moon)  1538
White Star Of Sigma Nu  249-703
**White Wash Man (The)**  1200-1255-1586-1587
White Wash Station Blues  **1042**
White Way Blues  976
White Zombie - see ZOMBIE

Who ?  86-172-203-384-443-545-573-596-676-683-719-774-909-1134-1143-1380
Whoa Babe  188-294-585-660-1124-1239-1434
Who Am I ?  108-249-470-1296
Whoa Mule, Get Up In The Alley  270
Who Are You ?  529
Whoa, Tillie ! Take Your Time  953-1022-1186-1439-1440-1523-1608
Whoa You Heifer !  332
Who Believed In You ?  219-220
Who Beside Me (Sits Beside You)  35-118-875
Who Blew Out The Flame ?  322-1159
Who Broke The Lock Off The Henhouse Door  563
Who Calls ?  261-471-1361
Who Calls You Sweet Mama Now ?  1218
Who Can I Turn To ?  168-453
Who Can Your Regular Be Blues  32
Who Cares ?  221-1086-1141
Who Cares ? (So Long As You Care For Me)  34-62
Who Cares What You H ve Been ?  243
Who Could Be More Wonderful Than You ?  234-994
Who'd A Thunk It ?  554
Who Dat Say Chicken In Dis Crowd ?  (sic)  1049-1473
Who'd Be Blue ?  568-1006-1504-1643
Who Did You Fool After All ?  1607
Who Did You Meet Last Night ?  988-1316
Who Done It ?  679
Who Do YourLove ?  872-1611
Who Do You Think I Saw Last Night ?  321-430
Who Gives You All Your Kisses ?  567-573
Who Is She ?  472
Who Is Sylvia ?  1513
Who Is Your Who ?  1232
Who Knows ?  442
Whole Darn(ed) Thing's For You, The  84-1383
Whole World Is Dreaming Of Love, The  121
Whole World Knows I Love You, The  20
Who'll Be The One ?  523-921-1644
Who'll Be The One This Summer ?  441
Who'll Buy A Rose From Margareeta ?  591
Who'll Buy My Bublitchki ?  612
Who'll Buy My Violets ?  440-740
Who'll Chop Your Suey When I'm Gone ?  811-845
Who'll Drive My Blues Away ?  1069
Who'll Drive Your Cares Away ?  1576
Who'll Get It When I'm Gone ?  810-1649
Who'll Love You When I'm Gone ?  975
Who'll Take My Place ?  1635
Who'll Take My Place (When I'm Gone)  69
Wholly Cats  616
Who Loved You Best ?  73
Who Loves You ?  1179-1732
Who Made You Cry, Sugar Babe ?  862
Who-oo ? You-oo, That's Who !  171-524-669-1416-1619
Whoopee !  1215
Whoopee Hat Brigade, The  1394
Whoopee Stomp (The)  1029-1040-1076
Whoop 'Em Up Blues  1108
Whoop It Up  1705
Who Paid The Rent For Mrs. Rip Van Winkle ?  173

1988

Who Played Poker With Pocahontas ? 173
Who's Afraid Of Love ? 123-1630
Who's Afraid Of The Big Bad Wolf ? 1349
Who Said "It's Tight Like That" ? 478
Who's Beatin' My Time With You ? 693
Who's Blue ? 1171
Who's Calling You Sweetheart Tonight ?
1594
Who's Dis Heah Stranger ? (sic) 1096
Whose Big Baby Are You ? 780
Whose Honey Are You ? 13-1625
Whose Izzy Is He ? (Is He Yours Or Is He
Mine ?) 1609
Whose Who Are You ? 121-1478-1589
Who's Excited ? 1407
Who's Gonna Do Your Lovin' (When Your
Good Man's Gone Away) 709
Whosit 41
Who's Sorry Now ? 88-128-216-222-263-
292-367-632-691-960-1134-1137-1140-
1187-1224-1472-1558
Who's That Knockin' At My Door ? 402-
532-669-1309-1425-1580
Who's That Pretty Baby ? 356
Who Stole The Jam ? 587-1434
Who Stole The Lock (From The Hen House
Door) 6-142-413-1645
Who Stole The Tiger's Rug ? 584
Who's Yehoodi ? 260
Who's Your Little Who-Zis ? 805-1409
Who's You Tellin' ? 1216
Who Takes Care Of The Caretaker's
Daughter ? 523-884-887
Who Threw That Rug ? 1168
Who Threw The Mush In Grandpa's Whiskers
1377
Who Threw The Whiskey In The Well ? 1674
Who Told You I Cared ? 466-815
Who Walks In When I Walk Out ? 1149-1331
1492
Who Wants Love ? 768-1663
Who Wants To Sing My Love Song ? 1278
Who Will Get It ? 177
Who Wouldn't Be Blue ? 240-930-1665
Who Wouldn't Be Jealous Of You ? 242-
340-1068
Who Wouldn't Love You ? 339-500
Who Ya Hunchin' ? 1661
Who ? You ! 554
Why ? 31-1108-1425
Why Am I Happy ? 1669
Why Be Blue ? 994
Why Begin Again ? (Pastel Blue) 447-1404
1735
Why Can't I Find Somebody To Love ? 288
Why Can't It Be Me ? 1367
Why Can't This Night Go On Forever ? 289
Why Can't We Do It Again ? 900
Why Can't You ? 243-516-949-950-1336
Why Can't You Do It Now ? 1452
Why Can't You Love That Way ? 263
Why Couldn't It Be Poor Little Me ? 38-
73-128-229-593-717-1172-1191-1506
Why Couldn't It Last Last Night ? 207-
371-708
Why Cry Blues 459
Why Did I Always Depend On You ? 769
Why Did I Kiss That Girl ? 522-1590
Why Did It Have To Be Me ? 422-1470
Why Didn't William Tell ? 1396
Why Did You Do It ? 558
Why Did You Leave Me Alone ? 812

Why Did You Make Me Cry ? 650
Why Did You Pick Me Up When I Was Lone-
some, Why Didn't You Let Me Lay ? 792
Why Does My Sweetie Love ? 921
Why Doesn't Somebody Tell Me These Things
125-183
Why Do Hawaiians Sing Aloha ? 1631
Why Do I Lie To Myself About You ? 1628-
1731
Why Do I Love You ? 1264-1291-1426-1684
Why Don't I Get Wise To Myself ? 901
Why Don't We Do This More Often ? 1361
Why Don't You ? 171
Why Don't You Do Right ? 622
Why Don't You Fall In Love With Me ? 1244
Why Don't You Get Lost ? 875-1310-1410
Why Don't You Love Me Any More ? 1247
Why Don't You Practice What You Preach ?
12-159-699-1206-1332
Why Do You Jive Me, Daddy ? 917
Why Do You Make Me Lonesome ? 737
Why Do You Suppose ? 1382
Why Do You Want To Know Why ? 1520
Why Dream ? 701
Why'd Ya Make Me Fall In Love ? 609-1064
1357
Why Go On Pretending ? 901
Why Have You Forgotten ? 248
Why Have You Forgotten Waikiki ? 1383
Why He Left Me I Don't Know 1376
Why Is A Good Man So Hard To Find ? 40
Why Is The Bacon So Tough ? 525-1291
Why Little Boy Blue Was Blue 697
Why Must We Part ? 758
Why Pretend ? 787
Why Put The Blame On You ? 713
Why Should I Beg For Love ? 1658
Why Should I Believe In You ? 1375
Why Should I Care ? 367-537
Why Should I Cry For You ? 1311
Why Should I Cry Over You ? 221-1606
Why Should I Pretend ? 1249
Why Should I Say I'm Sorry ? 708
Why Should I Weep About One Sweetie ?
405-1189-1590
Why Shouldn't I ? 346-427-701-1408-1505
1697
Why Shouldn't I Care ? 1261
Why Stars Come Out At Night 701-1491
Why Talk About Love ? 28-124-739
Why Was I Born ? 382-1732
Why Worry Blues 1175
Wicked Blues 1059-1724
Wicked Daddy 1321
Wicked Devil's Blues 1216
Wicked (Dirty) Fives, The 110-749-1186-
1520
Wicked Fives' Blues, The 1727
Wicked Monday Morning Blues 1617
Widdecombe Fair 518
Wide Open Places, The 1632
Widow's Daughter, The 409
Wiggle Woogie 108
Wiggle Yo' Toes 1263
Wig Wag 1412
Wigwam Blues 1113
Wigwammin' 1158
Wild And Foolish 1275
Wild And Woolly Willie 1223
Wild Cat 1596-1597-1602
Wild Cat Blues 1698
Wild Cats' Ball 461

Wild Cats On Parade  461
Wild Cat Squall  137
Wild Cherries/Cherry (Rag)  89-139-154-
  1255-1604
Wild Dog, The  1597-1599
Wildflower Rag  1703
Wild Geese Blues  121-854
Wild Goose Chase  289-996
Wild Honey  700
Wild Indians  842
Wild Jazz  866
Wild Mab Of The Fish Pond  97
Wild Man Blues  41-114-414-415-1102
Wild Man Stomp  1044-1495
Wild Oat Joe  1087
Wild Papa  1180-1210
Wild Party  1602
Wild Ride  656
Wild Waves  1072
Wild Weeping Blues  1492
Wild, Wild Women, The  1229
Wild Women Don't Have The Blues  353
William Tell  879-893-997
William Tell, Dialogue on  1599
Willie Jackson's Blues  811
Willie The Weeper  41-338-822-1167-1342
Will I Ever Know ?  1231
Will I Ever Know It ?  438
Willie, Willie, Don't Go From Me  164
Willie, Willie, Willie (Why Do You Cry ?)
  1397
Will Love Find A Way ?  293
Willow Tree  77-978-1284-1494
Willow, Weep For Me  261-815-876-1438
Will You ?  556-703
Will You Always Love Me ?  1175
Will You Be Sorry ?  566
Will You Love Me In December As You Do In
  May ?  268
Will You Love Me When I'm Gone ?  1717
Will You Remember Me ?  314
Will You Remember Tonight Tomorrow ?  322-
  1203
Will You Still Be Mine ?  374-452
Will You, Won't You ?  274
Will You, Won't You Be My Babe/Baby ?  52-
  1033
Wimmin (I Gotta Have 'Em, That's All)  68-
  1352
Wind At My Window, The  207
Winding Daddy Come On  1018
Wind In The Willows, The  953
Window Shoppin' Blues  460
Window Show Case Shopping Blues  636
Wind Storm  1507
Windy City  1695
Windy City Blues  917-1365
Windy City Hop  551
Windy City Jive  761
Windy City Stomp  268-1087 (see also ONE
  STEP TO HEAVEN)
Windy City Wobble  1515
Wine Cellar Blues  405
Wings Over Manhattan  97
Wings Over The Navy  1319
Winin' Boy Blues  1105-1106-1107-1108
Winner Joe (The Knock-Out King)  842
Winning Fight, The  379
Winter Blues  393
Winter Nights  1603
Wintertime Dreams  738
Winter Weather  453-621-1637-1638

Winter Wonderland  202-1669
Wipe 'Em Off  1395-1663
Wipin' The Pan  773-1079
Wire Brush Stomp  906
Wise Old Owl, The  1243-1318
Wishful Thinking  528
Wish I Had You (And I'm Gonna Get You
  Blues)  713-1022-1023-1050-1716-1728
Wishing  357
Wishing And Crying For You  342
Wishing And Waiting For Love  244-950-
  1301
Wish I Was A Cradle Baby  1502
Wish Me Luck As You Wave Me Goodbye  1435
Wish That I Could, But I Can't Forgive
  You Blues  1462
Wistful And Blue  992-1038-1063-1192-1681
Witchcraft Blues  1489
With A Banjo On My Knee  536
With All My Heart  250-293-1098-1312-1464
With All My Heart And Soul  404-1156
With A Smile And A Song  1734
With A Song In My Heart  953-1595
With Every Breath I Take  639
Withered Roses  301-579
With Love In My Heart  900
With My Eyes Wide Open, I'm Dreaming  878
With My Guitar And You  1294-1397
Without A Dime  1322
Without A Dream To My Name  1405
Without A Shadow Of A Doubt  691-702-1036
Without A Song  452-789-1501
Without A Word Of Warning  203-249-293-
  362-701
Without Rhythm  254
Without That Gal !  64-251-736-1286-1385-
  1653
Without The One You Love  832
Without You  176-247-696
Without You, Emaline  1061
Without Your Love  768-1400
Without You, Sweetheart  20-525-1589
With Plenty Of Money And You  204-205-383
  1530
With Someone Like You  1612
With Summer Coming On  697
With Thee I Swing  1027-1308-1732
With The Wind And The Rain In Your Hair
  63-372
With You  672-1663
With You In My Heart  1631
With You On My Mind  79-183
Witness  790
Wizzin' The Wizz  661
Wob-a-ly Walk  402-1291-1501
Wobble It A Little Daddy  570
Woe ! Is Me  348-526-583-1224-1627
Wo ist der Mann ?  405
Woke Up With The Blues In My Fingers  844
Wolf At The Door  1324
Wolf Man  169
Wolf River Blues  270
Wolf Wobble, The  1599
Wolverine Blues  57-120-145-321-368-591-
  759-1007-1099-1100-1102-1106-1132-1327-
  1419-1539-1672
Woman Ain't Born, The  1499
Woman Gets Tired Of One Man All The Time,
  A  834-1716
Woman On My Weary Mind  366
Woman's Trouble Blues  1441
Woman To Woman  1452

1990

Woncha Do It For Me ? 1468
Wonderful Dream 862-1025-1193
Wonderful Mammy 1464
Wonder If She's Lonely Too ? 1643
Wondering 568
Wondering Where 897
Wonderland Of Dreams 1175
Wonder When My Baby's Coming Home ? 436
Won'tcha ? 1233-1711
Won't Don't Blues 359
Won't Somebody Help Me Find My Lovin'
  Man ? 1008-1057
Won't You Be My Baby ? 1111
Won't You Be My Lovin' Baby ? 650
Won't You Come Back To My Arms ? 72
Won't You Come Over And Say Hello ? 1708
Won't You Come Over To My House ? 941-
  1314
Won't You Get Off It, Please ? 1624
Won't You Stay To Tea ? 148
Won't You Take Me Home ? 1622
Wood And Ivory 24
Woodland Symphony 298
Woodman, Spare That Tree 686
Woodpecker 676
Woodpecker Song, The 908
Woodsheddin' With Woody 743
Woo Woo 27-814-1007
Wop Blues 558-840-857
Wop Stomp 174-546
Words 377-716
Words Are In My Heart, The 426
Words Can't Express The Way I Feel 1034
Workers' Train, The 260
Work House Blues 1093-1441
Working Man Blues 1166
Working On The Project 848
Workin' Woman's Blues 643
Work Out 889
World Is In My Arms, The 450-909
World Is Mad, The 107
World Is Mine Tonight, The 1415
World Is Such A Lonesome Place, The 534
World Is Waiting For The Sunrise, The
  120-298-371-622-763-829-957-1037-1134-
  1137-1242-1490-1540
World's Greatest Sweetheart Is You, The
  888-1293
World's Jazz Crazy And So Am I, The 1467
World Without You, The 788
Worn Down Daddy Blues 355
Worn Out Blues 1706
Worn Out Papa Blues 1446
Worried 72
Worried And Lonesome Blues 837
Worried Anyhow Blues 352
Worried Blues 8-121-1090
Worried 'Bout Him Blues 709
Worried Down With The Blues 393-1549
Worried Head Blues 1678
Worried Heart Blues 849
Worried In My Mind Blues 353
Worried Life Blues 902
Worried Love 1376
Worried Mama Blues 352
Worried Mind 326
Worried Mind Blues 783
Worried Over You 729-900-1157
Worries On My Mind 376
Worry Blues 1248
Worryin' 1613
Worryin' Blues 1327-1550

Worryin' Over You 1220
Wotta Life 508
Would It Make Any Difference To You ?
  1244
Wouldja ? 194-234-235-1700
Wouldja Mind ? 741
Wouldn't It Be A Wonder ? 1031
Wouldn't It Be Wonderful ? 507-952
Wouldn't Stop Doing It 555
Wouldn't You ? 870
Wouldst Could I But Kiss Thy Hand, Oh
  Babe 297
Would You ? 14-182-1312-1313
Would You Be Happy ? 1078
Would You Like To Buy A Dream ? 294-755
Would You Like To Take A Walk ? 673-1303
  1384-1514
Wow ! 891
Wow Wow Blues 641
W. P. A. 57-1359-1560
Wrappin' It Up 595-609-727-1528
Wrap Your Cares In Rhythm And Dance 1137
Wrap Your Troubles In Dreams (And Dream
  Your Troubles Away) 49-76-273-694-782-
  814-959-1020-1035-1296-1384-1572
Wreckin' House Blues 1414
Wreck Of The Old Southern 97 1317-1482-
  1565
Wringin' And Twistin' 1567
Wringing And Twisting Blues 1267
Wringin' And Twistin' Papa 1455
Wrist Watch Blues 1454
Wrong-Doin' Daddy 995
Wrong Idea, The 95
Wylie Avenue Blues 343-651

XYZ 760

Yaaka Hula Hickey Dula 61-315-1145
Yacht Club Swing 775-1633
Ya Comin' Up Tonight, Huh ? 580
Ya Da Do 1266
Ya Got Love 1112
Ya Got Me - see YOU GOT ME
Ya Gotta Know How To Love 234-523-1592-
  1616-1714
Yah De Dah 544-549
Yale Blues, The 171-419-566-867
Yalla Man 847
Yaller 252
Ya Lu Blu(e) 98-186-1553
Yam, The 322-431
Yama Yama Blues 975-1702-1710
Yancey Limited 1746
Yancey's Bugle Call 1746
Yancey's Getaway 1746
Yancey Special 368-947-948
Yancey Stomp 1746
Yankee Doodle 1538
Yankee Doodle Blues 825-915-1225-1606
Yankee Doodle Never Went To Town 66-293-
  597-1602-1730
Yankee Doodle Plays A Fugue 683
Yankee In Havana 1047
Yardbird Shuffle 743
Yard Dog Mazurka 990
Ya ! Ya ! Alma 1068
Yazoo Blues 1110
Yea Alabama 1045
Yeah Man ! 583-726-894-1410
Year From Today, A 562
Yearning (Just For You) 73-443-444-451

Yearning And Blue  372-1495
Yearning For Love  491
Yearning For Mandalay  410
Yellow Basket Blues  849
Yellow Dog Blues (The)  88-475-511-665-
  666-886-957-994-1059-1128-1160-1233-
  1379-1442-1457
Yellow Dog Gal Blues  1061
Yellow Fire  761-1195-1282
Yelping Hound Blues  177-975-976
Yelpin' (The) Blues  795
Ye Olde Time Movies  805
Yep ! 'Long About June  1068
Yes  694
Yes Baby  850
Yes Flo (The Girl Who Never Says No)  268
Yes Habit, The  697
Ye Shall Reap Just What You Sow  1011
Yes ! I'm In The Barrel  40
Yes Indeed  363-452-818-1343
Yes Indeed He Do  1445
Yes Indeedy (He Do)  673
Yes, I've Been Cheatin'  213
Yes, Mr. Brown  148
Yes, My Darling Daughter  590-617-910
Yes She Do, No She Don't  153-236-532-
  1580-1583
Yes,Sir, And How !  1390
Yes Sir, Boss  52
Yes Sir ! I Prefer Brunettes  568
Yes Sir ! That's My Baby  129-172-339-558-
  624-861-938-1013-1498-1592
Yes Suh !  58-88-582-688-1125-1646
Yesterdays  769-1403
Yesterday's Gardenias  299
Yesterthoughts  433-1374
Yes, There Ain't No Moonlight (So What)
  588-1249
Yes ! We Have No Bananas  70-223-471-595-
  796-1180-1187
Yes ! Yes !  1074
Yes Yes (My Baby Said Yes)  22-539
Yes ! Yes ! My ! My !  53
Yes ! Yes ! Yes ! Yes !  584
Yet You Forgot  1426
Yeux noirs, Les - see DARK EYES
Yiddisher Charleston  568
Yip ! I Addy I Ay  1581
Yodel Dodel Doh, The  748
Yod(e)ling Blues  1011-1439-1532
Yodelin' Jive (or Yodel In Swing)  10-185-
  363-1224-1436
Yodelin' The Blues Away  1718
Yodle Odle  1297
Yo eta cansa  260
Yokohama Lullaby  1352
Yonder Come The Blues  1267
Yonkel Doodle Goes Steppin'  1356
Yoo Hoo  1613
Yoo Yoo Blues  1558
You  14-182-193-204-217-428-438-939-1122-
  1131
You Ain't Been Livin' Right  291-425
You Ain't Foolin' Me  1499
You Ain't Gonna Feed In My Pasture Now
  861
You Ain't Got Nothin' I Want  1113
You Ain't Had No Blues  91-1061
You Ain't Livin' Right  252-1584
You Ain't No Good Blues  854-859
You Ain't Nothin' To Me  1094

You Ain't Nowhere  864-989-1279
You Ain't Quittin' Me Without Two Weeks'
  Notice  1716
You Ain't Talkin' To Me  212
You Ain't The Last Man  1321
You Ain't The One  533
You Ain't Too Old  1708
You Ain't Treatin' Me Right  136
You And I  452-499-556-1123
You And I, Babe  632
You And I Know  442-1028-1552
You And Me That Used To Be, The  102-657-
  755
You And The Night And The Music, The  1211
You And Who Else  96
You And Your Love  80-106-371-612-908
You Are Just A Vision  315-569
You Are Love  1684
You Are My Dream  9
You Are My Lucky Star  23-52-426-437-1001
  1306-1307
You Are The One  910
You Are The One In My Heart  261
You Asked For It-You Got It  1633
You Battlehead Beetlehead  308
You Been Holding Out Too Long  91
You Betcha My Life  108-452
You Better Build Love's Fire (Or Your
  Sweet Mama's Gone)  1051
You Better Change Your Tune  295
You Better Come Back  781
You Better Keep Away From Me  1662
You Better Play Ball With Me  702
You Bring Me Down  184-185-693
You Bring Out The Savage In Me  1584
You Broke My Heart, Little Darling  942
You Brought A New Kind Of Love To Me  84-
  131-195-517-1652-1733
You Brought Me Everything But Love  680
You Call It Madness (But I Call It Love)
  76-197-742-981-1249
You Came Along  590
You Came To My Rescue  1010-1731
You Can Call It Swing  162-217
You Can Call Me Baby All The Time  156
You Can Count On Me  106-495-766
You Can Depend On Me  6-49-104-455-595-
  728-760-890-1556-1645
You Can Dip Your Bread In My Gravy, But
  You Can't Have None Of My Chops  965
You Can Fool Some Of The People (Some Of
  The Time)  988
You Can Have Him, I Don't Want Him
  (Didn't Love Him Anyhow Blues)  706-915
  1185-1462-1482
You Can Have Him If You Want Him  1046
You Can Have It (I Don't Want It)  964-
  1105
You Can Have My Man (If He Comes To See
  You Too)  686-793-1532
You Can Never Tell What Your Perfectly
  Good Man Will Do  100
You Can Take Me Away From Dixie (But You
  Can't Take Dixie Away From Me)  1067
You Can Take My Man But You Can't Keep
  Him For Long  793
You Can't Believe My Eyes  1294
You Can't Be Mine And Someone Else's Too
  119-526-734-768
You Can't Bet On Love  842
You Can't Brush Me Off  1359

1992

You Can't Cheat A Cheater  436-1121
You Can't Come In  1526
You Can't Cry Over My Shoulder  1238
You Can't Do It  1464
You Can't Do That To Me  1496
You Can't Do What My Last Man Did  65-793
  837-838-855-860-1463-1649-1650-1716
You Can Tell She Comes From Dixie  600-
  635-1399
You Can't Escape From Me  692
You Can't Get It Now  1451
You Can't Get Lovin' Where There Ain't
  Any Love  976
You Can't Get To Heaven That Way  1427
You Can't Go Wrong  1716
You Can't Guess How Good It Is  540
You Can't Have Everything  366-1249
You Can't Have It All  793
You Can't Have It Unless I Give It To You
  708-735-1060-1355
You Can't Have Lovin' Unless  1396
You Can't Have My Sugar For Tea  468
You Can't Have None Of That  849
You Can't Have Your Cake And Eat It  1634
You Can't Hold A Memory In Your Arms  744
You Can't Keep A Good Man Down  1460
You Can't Live In Harlem  1427
You Can't Lose  1371
You Can't Make A Fool Out Of Me  224
You Can't Make A Woman Change Her Mind
  1213
You Can't Proposition Me  1717
You Can't Pull The Wool Over My Eyes  597
  702-938-1019-1519
You Can't Put That Monkey On My Back  824
You Can't Run Away From Love Tonight  123
  491
You Can't Shoot Your Pistol  848
You Can't Shush Katie (The Gabbiest Girl
  In Town)  509-1700
You Can't Sleep In My Bed  412
You Can't Stay Here No More  1452
You Can't Sting A Nigger In The Same
  Place Twice  1613
You Can't Stop Me  961
You Can't Stop Me From Dreaming  205-554-
  592-1314-1733
You Can't Stop Me From Falling In Love
  With You  246
You Can't Stop Me From Lovin' You  6-197-
  254-895-1645-1653-1695
You Can't Swing A Love Song  586
You Can't Take It With You  780-880
You Can't Tell  825
You Can't Throw Me Down  844
You Can't Walk Back From An Aeroplane (So
  What Are You Girls Gonna Do ?)  882
You Can't Win In Here  680
You Certainly Look Good To Me  824
You Couldn't Be Cuter  443-881
You Danced With Dynamite  910-1477
You Darlin'  1497
You Darling, You  224
You'd Be Surprised  1362
You'd Better Keep Babying Baby  560
You('d) Better Keep The Home Fires
  Burning ('Cause Your Mama's Getting
  Cold)  529-624-1449
You'd Better Leave Me Alone, Sweet Papa
  409
You Didn't Ask Me  436

You Didn't Have To Tell Me (I Knew It All
  The Time)  592-853-1234
You Didn't Know Me From Adam (And I
  Didn't Know You From Eve)  425
You Didn't Want Me When I Wanted You, I'm
  Somebody Else's Now  1310-1615
You Dirty Dog  1452
You Dirty Mistreater  214-1729
You Dog - see AW YOU DAWG
You Done Lost Your Good Thing Now  215-
  1036-1488-1676
You Done Played Out Blues  1750
You Done Tore Your Pants With Me  1206
You Done Tore Your Playhouse Down  678-
  1371
You Done Turned Salty On Me  680
You Don't Care  850
You Don't Know How Much You Can Suffer
  (Until You Fall In Love)  29-206-447
You Don't Know My Mind Blues  80-633-812-
  849-851-860-964-1023-1057-1323-1448-
  1677
You Don't Know What Love Is  529-621-761
  818-1361
You Don't Know What You're Doin'  64
You Don't Know Who's Shakin' Your Tree
  1451
You Don't Like It-Not Much  237-402-533-
  552-993-1289-1616
You Don't Love Me  7-1528
You Don't Mean Me No Good  101-730-1020
You Don't Need Glasses  1469
You Don't Understand  838-1446-1535-1706
You Don't Want Me, Honey  1013
You Don't Want Much  994-995
You Don't Worry My Mind  1213
You Do Something To Me  1697
You Do The Darndest Things, Baby  93-204-
  383
You Drink Too Much  308-679-995
You Dropped Me Like A Red Hot Penny  204
You Excite Me !  1269
You Fit Into The Picture  202-779-1625
You Forgot About Me  325-373-910-1407
You Forgot To Remember  155-597-601-629-
  841-1157-1239-1498
You Forgot Your Gloves  192-1385-1484
You, For Me, Me For You  411-795
You Gave Me Everything But Love  311-
  520-651-853-1072-1277-1667
You Gave Me The Gate (And I'm Swingin')
  493
You Gave Me The Go-By  1396
You Gave Me Your Heart  221-1162
You Get Mad  734-1450
You Gonna Need My Help  1619
You Gonna Regret  1367
You Got Another Thought Coming  279
You Got 'Em  523
You Got Everything A Sweet Mama Needs
  But Me  110-1026
You Got Me (or Ya Got Me)  94-206-445-
  609-1357
You Got Me Rollin'  1053
You Got Me Wondering  1414
You Got Me Worryin'  1527
You Got My Man  1105
You Go To My Head  94-295-321-768-1357-
  1734
You Gotta Be A Football Hero (To Get
  Along With The Beautiful Girls)  1315

You Gotta Be Good To Me  574-1581-1583
You Got To Drop The Sack  1678
You Gotta Give Credit To Love  392
You Gotta Ho-De-Ho (To Get Along With Me)  255
You Gotta Know How  32-232-1037
You Gotta Know How To Dance  1433
You Gotta Know How To Love  510-624 (see also YA GOTTA KNOW HOW TO LOVE)
You Gotta Quit Cheatin' On Me  1318
You Got The Devil To Pay  680
You Got To Be Satisfied  680
You Got To Go When The Wagon Comes  783-864
You Got To Pay  848
You Got To Play Ragtime  1578
You Got To Reap What You Sow  1526
You Got To Swing And Sway  355
You Got To Wet It  823
You('ve) Got What I Want  1376
You Go Your Way  896
You Grow Sweeter As The Years Go By  296-297-446-1358-1405
You Had An Evening To Spare  1632
Y'Had It Comin' To You  9-126-1654
You Had Too Much  1452
You Have Everything  295-1401
You Have Taken My Heart  290-798-1601
You Hi-De-Hi-ing Me  924
You Hit My Heart With A Bang  1753
You Hit The Spot  382-780-968-1115-1551
You In My Arms And Sweet Music  632
You Just Can't Have No One Man By Yourself  1011
You Just Can't Keep A Good Woman Down  1065
You, Just You  502-1292
You Keep Me Always Living In Sin  1311
You Keep Me Worried  637
You Know  754
You Know I Do - see BUT I DO, YOU KNOW I DO
You Know, I Know (That I Love You So)  675
You Know I Love You  130-1612
You Know It Ain't Right  849
You Know Jam Don't Shake  824
You Know Just As Well As I Know  1538
You Know Me, Alabam'  236-714-1190-1582-1590
You Know That Ain't Right  834
You Know What I'll Do  789
You Know What I Mean  1603
You Know Who  1253
You Know Why Your Mama Has The Blues  213
You Know You Belong To Somebody Else (So Why Don't You Leave Me Alone ?)  70-222-1608
You Know You Wasn't Raised That Way  995
You Leave Me Breathless  444-1158
You Let Me Down  203-249-427-701-988-1001-1551-1585-1731
You Lied The Last Time  844
You Lied To Me  108
You Little So-and-So  876
You Live On In Memory  1529
You'll Always Be Mine  210
You'll Always Be The Same Sweetheart To Me  673
You'll Be Left Out On A Limb  207
You'll Be Mine In Apple-Blossom Time  1295-1384

You'll Be My Lover  311
You'll Be Reminded Of Me  321-739-1237
You'll Be Sorry  375-675-1747
You'll Come Back To Me Someday  112
You'll Cry For Me, But I'll Be Gone  1084
You'll Do It Someday (So Why Not Now ?)  153-1745
You'll Find Old Dixieland In France  1194
You'll Get By (With A Twinkle In Your Eye)  36
You'll Get Them Blues  832
You'll Have To Swing It (If You Can't Sing It)  1273-1609
You'll Long For Me (When The Cold Winds Blow)  1702
You'll Need Me When I'm Long Gone  1650
You'll Never Get Up To Heaven That Way  1751
You'll Never Get To Heaven With Those Eyes  715-926-1171-1348
You'll Never Go To Heaven  765
You'll Never Go To Heaven (If You Break My Heart)  15-1313
You'll Never Have No Luck By Quittin' Me  1051-1532
You'll Never Know  326-743
You'll Never Know, Sweetheart  247
You'll Never Know The Difference (A Hundred Years From Now)  554
You'll Never Miss The Water  342
You'll Never Miss Your Jelly Till Your Jelly Roller's Gone  842
You'll Never Miss Your Water  1450
You'll Never Remember And I'll Never Forget  192
You'll Recognize My Baby  118-1422
You'll Think Of The Blues  280
You'll Want Me Back  1651
You'll Want Me Back Again  1595
You'll Want Me Back Someday  501-521
You'll Want My Love  705
You'll Wish You'd Never Been Born  50
You Look Good To Me  206-1633
You Lose  1062
You Lucky People  451-618
You Made Me Care  216
You Made Me Happy  1111
You Made Me Like It, Baby  1208
You Made Me Love You  41-205-272-435-813-1088-1237-1238-1342
You Made Me Love You-Why Did You ?  17
You Make Me Laugh  1577
You Make Me Laugh When You Cry  507
You May Be Fast, But Mama's Gonna Slow You Down  32-560-707-712-1189-1609
You May Go, But You'll Come Back Someday  860
You May Leave But This Will Bring You Back  1043
You Mean So Much To Me  39-273
You Meet The Nicest People In Your Dreams  1634
You Might Get Better, But You'll Never Get Well  12
You Might Have Belonged To Another  215-)451
You Might Pizen Me  278
You Missed A Good Woman When You Picked All Over Me  1465-1532
You Must Believe Me  1330
You Must Be Losing Your Mind  1638
You Must Have Been A Beautiful Baby  94-206-363-445-588-1159

1994

You Need Some Lovin'  459-1460-1716
You Need Someone To Love  235
You Never Did That Before  918-1667
You Never Know  296-322
You Never Looked So Beautiful  182-427-438-439-1231
You Never Miss A Good Thing Till It's Gone  1576
Young And Healthy  877-1388-1410
Young And Innocent  1414
Younger Generation, The  147-1262
Young Man's Fancy, A  748
Young Man Sings, A  166
Young Prince And The Young Princess, The  1360
Young Stuff  763
Young Woman's Blues  1440
You Only Want Me When You're Lonesome  402
You Opened My Eyes  100
You Ought To Be Ashamed  1445
You Ought To Be Ashamed Of Yourself  1679
You Oughta Be In Pictures  159-201
You Oughta Hang Your Heart In Shame  324-372
You Oughta Know  1424-1425
You Ought To Move Out Of Town  391
You Oughta See Her Now  641
You Oughta See My Gal  358-1103
You Ought To See Sally On Sunday  1149
You Out-Smarted Yourself  1633
You Please Me  358
You Rascal, You  48-58-147-197-253-347-465-539-583-725-778-898-1114-1145-1153-1283-1346-1432-1494-1527-1537-1644-1706-1726
Your Clothes Look Lonesome Hangin' On The Line  666
You're A Builder-Upper  292
You're A Darlin' Devil  374
You're A Grand Old Flag  1317
You're A Heavenly Thing  100-180-381-595-938
You're All I Need  426-1306
You're All I've Wanted  182
You're A Lucky Guy  57-432-466-769-908-1406
You're Always In My Arms  951-1234
You're Always In My Dreams  990
You're Always Messin' 'Round With My Man  749-1059
You're An Angel  209-563-1000
You're An Answer To A Maiden's Prayer  880
You're An Education  321-368-1434
You're An Eyeful Of Heaven  1432
You're A No-'Count Triflin' Man  213
You're A Pain In The Heart To Me  1292
You're A Pain In The Neck To Me  849
You're A Real Sweetheart  314-391-540-1535-1617
You're A Sap, Mister Jap  1319
You're As Pretty As A Picture  444-445-906
You're A Square From Delaware  1636
You're A Sweetheart  205-318-443-739-880-1315-1333-1402-1654
You're A Sweet Little Headache  183-609-1159-1403
You're Blase  457

You're Bound To Look Like A Monkey When You Get Old  137-373-628-767-1706-1707
You're Breaking My Heart All Over Again  451-910
You're Burnin' Me Up (Turnin' Me Down)  310-630-1545
You're Dangerous  451-617
You're Driving Me Crazy ! (What Did I Do?)  6-48-196-367-504-783-852-953-1035-1260-1491-1585-1594-1606
You're Easy To Dance With  62-622
You're Everything To Me  1322
You're Fooling With The Wrong Gal Now  1056
You're Foolin' Yourself  874
You're Getting Old On Your Job  1452
You're Getting To Be A Habit With Me  877
You're Giving Me A Song And A Dance  599-780-893-1027-1399
You're Giving Me The Runaround  1308
You're Going To Leave The Old Home (Jim)  90-1654
You're Gonna Be A Rascal Till You Die  1547
You're Gonna Be Sorry  1637
You're Gonna Go Your Way And I'm Gonna Go Mine  1247
You're Gonna Lose Your Gal  12-192-290-527
You're Gonna See A Lot Of Me  8-1735
You're Gonna Wake Up Some Morning, But Your Papa Will Be Gone  522
You're Haunting Me  1356
You're Here And I'm Here  512
You're Here, You're There, You're Everywhere  205-294-440
You're In Kentucky Sure As You're Born  71-225-781-789
You're In Love With Love  729-1088
You're In Love With Someone Else  299-819
You're In My Heart  1291
You're In Wrong With The Right Baby  530
You're Just About Right For Me  808
You're Just A Cream Puff (You Can't Take It)  843
You're Just A Dream  987
You're Just A Flower From An Old Bouquet  1582
You're Just A Great Big Baby Doll  240-1665
You're Just A Little Bit Of Everything I Love  502
You're Just A Little Dif(rent  780
You're Just A No-Account  57-769
You're Just My Type  1170
You're Just The Girl For Me  1062
You're Just Too Sweet For Words, Honey O' Mine  673
You're Laughing At Me  78-205-293-1630
You're Letting The Grass Grow (Right Under Your Feet)  1397-1635
You're Lonely And I'm Lonely  96-207-450-1359
You're Looking For Romance  93-1428
You're Lovely, Madame  369-609-1357
You're Lucky To Me  6-48-165-193-305-482-1346-1414-1652
You're Mine  1654
You're Mine, You  505-730
You're More Than A Palace To Me  1528

You're My Baby  1502
You're My Darling  942
You're My Desire  183-441-786-1733
You're My Dish  1631
You're My Everything  147
You're My Favorite Memory  1737
You're My Fever  180
You're My First Thought Every Morning  696
You're My Ideal  661
You're My Meat  864
You're My Past, Present And Future  464-1600
You're My Silver Lining Of Love  951
You're My Thrill  97-455
You're Next  40
You're Not The Kind  14-122-204-518-785-1002-1243-1585-1628-
You're Not The Kind I Thought You Were  1319
You're Not The Only Oyster In The Stew  1624
You're O.K.  426-858
You're Out Of This World  787-1032-1402
You're Precious To Me  441-781-1002
You're Simply Delish  84-980-1015-1537
You're So Darn Charming  66-426-967-1627
You're So Desirable  431-1147-1159-1735
You're So Different  1405
You're Solid With Me  1547
You're Standing On The Outside Now  637
You're Still In My Heart  288
You're Such A Comfort To Me  1227-1228-1331
You're Such A Cruel Papa To Me  1060-1
1061
You're Telling Me  876-1644-1688
You're The Cream In My Coffee  241-535-636-658-670-885-1062-1069-1087-1595-1666
You're The Cure For What Ails Me  257
You're The Cutest One  1626
You're The First Thing I Think Of In The Morning  867
You're The Greatest Discovery (Since 1492)  432-1148
You're The Limit  115
You're The Maker Of Rain In My Heart  808
You're The Moment In My Life  80-1538
You're The One  1134
You're The One And Only  1390
You're The One For Me  402-631-742-1232-1390
You're The One I Care For  196-504-673-980
You're The One In My Dreams  758
You're The One (You Beautiful Son-of-a-Gun)  35
You're The Only Star In My Blue Heaven  1316
You're The Picture (I'm The Frame)  1626
You're The Sweetest Girl This Side Of Heaven  247
You're The Top  396-425-1337-1626
You're The Very Last Word In Love  1315
You're Ticklin' Me  695
You're Too Good For Good-For-Nothing Me  819
You're Too Lovely To Last  769
You're Too Sure Of Me  702

You're Toots To Me  182-366
You're Twice As Nice As The Girl In My Dreams  1296
You're Walking In My Sleep  293
You're Wicky, You're Wacky, You're Wonderful  1307
Your Eyes Are Bigger Than Your Heart  8
Your Feet's Too Big  215-538-584-1635-1636
Your Folks  150
Your Folks Will Start Wearing Black  213
Your Going Ain't Giving Me The Blues  1013
Your Guess Is Just As Good As Mine  1538
Your Head On My Shoulder  424
Your Heart And Mine  1137-1726
Your Hellish Ways  1677
Your Ideas Are My Ideas  1179
Your Jelly-Roll Is Good  794
Your Love Has Faded  495-766
Your Mama's Gonna Slow You Down - see YOU MAY BE FAST BUT MAMA'S GONNA SLOW YOU DOWN
Your Man - My Man  706
Your Mother And Mine  421
Your Mother's Son-in-Law  593-1431
Your One And Only  1528
Yours  434-618
Yours, All Yours  296-1557
Yours And Mine  54-162-294-756-786-1143-1384-1733
Yours For A Song  1159
Yours Is My Heart Alone  297-449-615
Your Smilin' Face  1715
Your Socks Don't Match  1637
Yours Truly Is Truly Yours  879
Your Time Now ('Twill Be Mine After A While)  711-1059-1727
You Run Your Mouth, I'll Run My Business  57-864-1636
Your Words And My Music  326
Your Worries Ain't Like Mine  1060-1488-1676
You Said It  197-421-1144-1384-1519
You Said Something When You Said Dixie  1608
You Saved My Life  426
You Say The Sweetest Things, Baby  298-451
You'se A Viper  1464
You Set Me On Fire  901-987
You Shall Reap Just What You Sow  793
You Shall Reap What You Sow  40
You Should Have Told Me (You Were Only Fooling)  566-1721
You Should Live So Long  215
You Should See My Tootsie  172-921-1275
You Showed Me The Way  880-1002-1134-1630-1642-1659-1726-1732
You Started Me Dreaming  161-438-1001-1157
You Started Something  326-1315-1357
You Stayed Away Too Long  249-775-1178-1627
You Stepped Out Of A Dream  1412
You Stole My Cherry  843
You Stole My Heart  1527
You Stole My Man  355
You Talk Too Much  98
You Taught Me To Love Again  446-907-1358
You Tell Her-I Stutter  349-559-884-919-1353

1996

You Think Of Everything  450-741
You Think She Ain't  991
You Thought I Was Blind But Now I See
  964
You Told Me But Half The Story  1278
You Told Me To Go  73-1380-1498
You Took Advantage Of Me  122-151-292-301
  497-505-542-635-807-836-1087-1685-1696
You Took My Breath Away  382-1307
You Took My Love  454
You Took The Words Right Out Of My Heart
  205-295-605
You Tore Up My Heart  557
You Try Somebody Else  161-197-1387-1494
You Turned The Tables On Me  383-598-601
  893-1731
You Turned Your Back On Me  1547
You Understand  281
You Usta Be Sugar Blues  555
You've Been A Good Old Wagon  1442
You've Been Reading My Mail  1630
You've Been Taking Lessons In Love  4-
  1114-1626
You've Broken My Castle Of Dreams  737
You've Broken My Heart  1389
You've Changed  818
You've Done It Again  700
You've Gone  1232
You've Got Everything  152-1331
You've Got Everything A Sweet Daddy/Mama
  Needs But Me  749-1727
You've Got Me Crying Again  148-1330-1695
You've Got Me In The Palm Of Your Hand
  1410
You've Got Me Out On A Limb  96-297-816
You've Got Me Pickin' Petals Off O'
  Daisies  525-952
You've Got Me This Way  433-451
You've Got Me Under Your Thumb  894-1631
You've Got Me Voodoo'd  57-96
You've Got Something There  442-893
You've Got That Thing  152-246-808-957-
  1749
You've Got The Right Eye, But You're
  Peeping At The Wrong Keyhole  802
You've Got The Right Key But The Wrong
  Keyhole  965-1708
You've Got Those "Wanna-Go-Back-Again"
  Blues  472-523-1643
You've Got To Beat Me To Keep Me  1467
You've Got To Be Modernistic  346-838-
  1127-1706
You've Got To Blow Your Own Trumpet 1433
You've Got To Eat Your Soinach, Baby 122-
  439
You've Got To Get Hot  712
You've Got To Give Me Some  764-1445-1706
You've Got To Go Home On Time  904-994
You've Gotta Have What It Takes  1488
You've Got To Learn To Do It  1528
You've Got To Prove It To Me  1577
You've Got To Quit Your Low Down Ways
  994
You've Got To Recognize Me  1577
You've Got To Save That Thing  7
You've Got To See Mama Every Night  190-
  535-559-915-973-1059-1173-1187-1225-
  1353-1463-1519 1520-1544
You've Got To Sell It  873
You've Got Ways Blues  1389
You've Got Ways I'm Crazy About  1615

You've Had Your Day  705-1005
You've Had Your Last Good Time With Me
  680
You've Had Your Way  767-1322
You've Made Me Happy Today  1234
You've Never Heard The Blues  459
You've Seen Harlem At Its Best  1654
You've Simply Got Me Cuckoo  223
You Waited Too Long  1123-1496
You Walked Out Of The Picture  765
You Wanted Someone To Play With  270
You Want Lovin' And/But I Want Love 507-
  562-1426
You Went Away Too Far And Stayed Away Too
  Long  638
You Went To My Head  1315-1512-1632
You Were Meant For Love  1311
You Were Meant For Me  1336-1553
You Were Never Lovelier  744
You Weren't True (But You're Still In My
  Heart)  1486
You Were Only Passing Time With Me  84-
  567-1170
You Were There  98-911
You Will Always Be My Girl  467
You Will Always Live In Our Memory  941
You Will Come Back To Me  246
You Wonderful Thing  89
You Won't Let Me Go  832
You Wouldn't  346
You Wouldn't Fool Me, Would You ?  670-
  950-1226-1418-1604
You, You And Especially You  646
You, You And You  184
You, You Darlin'  372-496-1540
Yo Yo  1227
Yo Yo Blues  461
Yummy Yummy Yum  1226
Yump Da Da Da  893

Zaggin' With Zig  505-614
Zaz Zuh Zaz  256
Zero  1000-1130
Zigeuner  1404-1477
Zig-Zag  294-322
Zillo  647
Zing ! Went The Strings Of My Heart  555
Zola  1310
Zombie  879-958-1410
Zonky  179-455-788-1034-1153-1431-1556-
  1626-1706
Zoolithique  806
Zooming At The Zombie  896
Zoom, Zoom, Zoom  1236
Zoot Suit, A (For My Sunday Gal)  375-
  621
Zowie !  170-1037-1351
Zozoi  774
Zuddan  1282
Zulu Blues, The  136-411
Zulus Ball  1166
Zulu Wail  236-402-993-1580-1616-1620-
  1701
Zumba  67
Zutty's Hootie Blues  1346

Additions and Corrections